THE
ALL ENGLAND
LAW REPORTS

Incorporating the

**LAW TIMES
REPORTS**

**LAW JOURNAL
REPORTS**

1969
VOLUME 2

Consulting Editor for Taxation Cases

CYRIL KING, Q.C.
Bencher of the Middle Temple

Editor

PAUL H. NIEKIRK, M.A.
of Gray's Inn, Barrister-at-Law

LONDON
BUTTERWORTHS

ENGLAND:	BUTTERWORTH & CO. (PUBLISHERS) LTD. LONDON: 88 Kingsway, W.C.2
AUSTRALIA:	BUTTERWORTH & CO. (AUSTRALIA) LTD. SYDNEY: 20 Loftus Street MELBOURNE: 343 Little Collins Street BRISBANE: 240 Queen Street
CANADA:	BUTTERWORTH & CO. (CANADA) LTD. TORONTO: 14 Curity Avenue, 374
NEW ZEALAND:	BUTTERWORTH & CO. (NEW ZEALAND) LTD. WELLINGTON: 49/51 Ballance Street AUCKLAND: 35 High Street
SOUTH AFRICA:	BUTTERWORTH & CO. (SOUTH AFRICA) LTD. DURBAN: 33/35 Beach Grove

Standard Book Number: 406 85094 1

Printed in Great Britain by R. J. Acford Ltd., Industrial Estate, Chichester, Sussex.

REPORTERS

HOUSE OF LORDS

The Lord High Chancellor of Great Britain: The Rt. Hon. Lord Gardiner

Lords of Appeal in Ordinary

The Rt. Hon. Lord Reid
The Rt. Hon. Lord Morris of Borth-y-Gest
The Rt. Hon. Lord Hodson
The Rt. Hon. Lord Guest
The Rt. Hon. Lord Pearce
 (retired 2nd June 1969)

The Rt. Hon. Lord Upjohn
The Rt. Hon. Lord Donovan
The Rt. Hon. Lord Wilberforce
The Rt. Hon. Lord Pearson
The Rt. Hon. Lord Diplock
The Rt. Hon. Viscount Dilhorne
 (appointed 9th June 1969)

COURT OF APPEAL

The Lord High Chancellor of Great Britain

Lord Chief Justice of England: Lord Parker of Waddington

Master of the Rolls: Lord Denning

President of the Probate, Divorce and Admiralty Division:
Sir Jocelyn Edward Salis Simon

Lords Justices of Appeal

Sir Charles Eustace Harman
Sir Harold Otto Danckwerts
 (retired 2nd June 1969)
Sir William Arthian Davies
Sir Charles Richie Russell
Sir Cyril Barnet Salmon
Sir Charles Rodger Noel Winn
Sir Eric Sachs

Sir Herbert Edmund Davies
Sir John Passmore Widgery
Sir Fenton Atkinson
Sir Henry Josceline Phillimore
Sir Seymour Edward Karminski
Sir John Megaw
Sir Geoffrey Cross
 (appointed 3rd June 1969)

CHANCERY DIVISION

The Lord High Chancellor of Great Britain

Sir George Harold Lloyd-Jacob
Sir Geoffrey Cross
  (appointed Lord Justice of
    Appeal, 3rd June 1969)
Sir Denys Burton Buckley
Sir John Pennycuick
Sir John Anthony Plowman
Sir Arwyn Lynn Ungoed-Thomas

Sir Edward Blanshard Stamp
Sir Reginald William Goff
Sir Robert Edgar Megarry
Sir John Patrick Graham
Sir Peter Harry Batson
    Woodroffe Foster
  (appointed 3rd June 1969)

QUEEN'S BENCH DIVISION

Lord Chief Justice of England: Lord Parker of Waddington

Sir John Percy Ashworth
Sir George Raymond Hinchcliffe
Sir Gilbert James Paull
Sir Aubrey Melford Steed Stevenson
Sir Gerald Alfred Thesiger
Sir Basil Edward Nield
Sir Stephen Gerald Howard
Sir Geoffrey de Paiva Veale
Sir Federick Horace Lawton
Sir Bernard Joseph Maxwell MacKenna
Sir Alan Abraham Mocatta
Sir John Thompson
Sir Daniel James Brabin
Sir Eustace Wentworth Roskill
Sir Maurice Legat Lyell
Sir John Frederick Eustace Stephenson
Sir Helenus Patrick Joseph Milmo
Sir Joseph Donaldson Cantley
Sir Patrick Reginald Evelyn Browne

Sir George Stanley Waller
Sir Arthur Evan James
Sir Eric Herbert Blain
Sir Ralph Vincent Cusack
Sir Stephen Chapman
Sir John Ramsay Willis
Sir Graham Russell Swanwick
Sir John Francis Donaldson
Sir Geoffrey Dawson Lane
Sir Patrick McCarthy O'Connor
Sir John Robertson Dunn Crichton
Sir Samuel Burgess Ridgway Cooke
Sir Henry Arthur Pears Fisher
Sir Bernard Caulfield
Sir Nigel Cyprian Bridge
Sir Sebag Shaw
Sir Hilary Gwynne Talbot
Sir Edward Walter Eveleigh
Sir William Lloyd Mars-Jones

PROBATE, DIVORCE AND ADMIRALTY DIVISION

President: Sir Jocelyn Edward Salis Simon

Sir Geoffrey Walter Wrangham
Sir Harry Vincent Lloyd-Jones
Sir David Arnold Scott Cairns
Sir George Gillespie Baker
Sir Roger Fray Greenwood Ormrod
Sir Charles William Stanley Rees
Sir Reginald Withers Payne
Sir Neville Major Ginner Faulks
Sir Robert James Lindsay Stirling

The Hon. Sir James Roualeyn
  Hovell-Thurlow Cumming-Bruce
Sir John Brinsmead Latey
Sir Hugh Eames Park
Dame Elizabeth Kathleen Lane
Sir Alan Stewart Orr
Sir Henry Vivian Brandon
Sir Robin Horace Walford Dunn

CITATION

These reports are cited thus:

[1969] 2 All E.R.

REFERENCES

These reports contain references, which follow after the headnotes, to the following major works of legal reference described in the manner indicated below—

HALSBURY'S LAWS OF ENGLAND, SIMONDS EDITION

The reference 2 HALSBURY'S LAWS (3rd Edn.) 20, para. 48, refers to paragraph 48 on page 20 of Volume 2 of the third edition of Halsbury's Laws of England, of which Viscount Simonds is Editor-in-Chief.

HALSBURY'S STATUTES OF ENGLAND

The reference 26 HALSBURY'S STATUTES (2nd Edn.) 138, refers to page 138 of Volume 26 of the second edition, and the reference 5 HALSBURY'S STATUTES (3rd Edn.) 302, refers to page 302 of Volume 5 of the third edition, of Halsbury's Statutes.

ENGLISH AND EMPIRE DIGEST

References are to the "Blue-Band" volumes of the Digest, and to the Continuation Volumes of the "Blue-Band" or replacement volumes.

The reference 31 DIGEST (Repl.) 244, *3794*, refers to case No. 3794 on page 244 of Digest Replacement Volume 31.

The reference DIGEST (Cont. Vol. B) 287, *7540b*, refers to case No. 7540b on page 287 of Digest Continuation Volume B.

HALSBURY'S STATUTORY INSTRUMENTS

The reference 12 HALSBURY'S STATUTORY INSTRUMENTS (2nd Re-issue) 124, refers to page 124 of the second re-issue of Volume 12 of Halsbury's Statutory Instruments; references to subsequent re-issues are similar.

ENCYCLOPAEDIA OF FORMS AND PRECEDENTS

The reference 15 ENCY. FORMS & PRECEDENTS (3rd Edn.) 938, Form 231, refers to Form 231 on page 938 of Volume 15 of the third edition, and the reference 7 ENCY. FORMS & PRECEDENTS (4th Edn.) 247, Form 12, refers to Form 12 on page 247 of Volume 7 of the fourth edition, of the Encyclopaedia of Forms and Precedents.

CASES REPORTED

IN VOLUME 2

INDEX

xi

CRITICAL:

CASES NOTED

xxxiii

STATUTES, ETC., NOTED

xxxvii

COMMONWEALTH AND OTHER TERRITORIES

RULES

REGULATIONS

ORDERS

WORDS AND PHRASES

CORRIGENDA

[1969] 2 All E.R.

p. 108. Re GROFFMAN (decd.). Line A.2. Surname of second-named plaintiff: for " BLOCK " read " BLOCH ".

p. 504. ALICIA HOSIERY, LTD. v. BROWN SHIPLEY & CO., LTD. Counsel for the purchasers: read " Anthony Lincoln, Q.C., and Gerald Levy " instead of as printed.

p. 924. SIMMS v. LEIGH RUGBY FOOTBALL CLUB, LTD. Line B.1: for " Andrew Rankin " read " Andrew Rankin, Q.C."

p. 1143. GARRETT v. ARTHUR CHURCHILL (GLASS), LTD. Counsel for the respondents: for " Ashe Lincoln, Q.C." read " Anthony Lincoln, Q.C."

THE

ALL ENGLAND
LAW REPORTS

INCORPORATING THE
LAW TIMES REPORTS
AND THE
LAW JOURNAL REPORTS

OWEN v. POOK (Inspector of Taxes).

[HOUSE OF LORDS (Lord Guest, Lord Pearce, Lord Donovan, Lord Wilberforce
and Lord Pearson), February 3, 4, March 26, 1969.]

*Income Tax—Income—Emoluments—Perquisites or profits of office or employ-
ment—Travelling expenses—Medical practitioner practising at residence
and also holding part-time appointments at hospital 15 miles away as
obstetrician and anaesthetist—Emergency cases—Payment of allowance
for travel by car to hospital—Payment irrespective of the method of travel—
Whether emoluments of office—Finance Act 1956 (4 & 5 Eliz. 2 c. 54),
Sch. 2, para. 1 (1).*

*Income Tax—Deduction in computing profits—Expenses—Medical practitioner
—General medical practitioner practising at his residence and also holding
part-time appointments at hospital 15 miles away—Hospital work as
obstetrician and anaesthetist—Emergency cases—Expenses of travel by
car to and from hospital—Whether expenses deductible—Income Tax Act
1952 (15 & 16 Geo. 6 & 1 Eliz. 2 c. 10), s. 156, Sch. E, Case 1, as substituted
by Finance Act 1956 (4 & 5 Eliz. 2 c. 54), s. 10 (1), and Sch. 9, r. 7 to the
Act of 1952.*

The taxpayer was a medical practitioner and resided at Fishguard.
He held part-time appointments as obstetrician and anaesthetist at Haverfordwest, 15 miles away. Under his appointments he was on stand-by
duty for emergencies, as an obstetrician one weekend a month, as an anaesthetist one weekend a month, and on Monday and Friday nights. He had to
be accessible on the telephone at those times, and on receipt of a telephone
call telling him of an emergency he would give instructions over the telephone
to the hospital staff and then, usually, would set off immediately for the
hospital by car, although he might advise treatment on the telephone and
await a further report. His responsibility for the patient began as soon as
he received the telephone call. He was paid travelling expenses at a fixed
rate per mile for journeys between Fishguard and the hospital; but the
travelling expenses were not payable for a single journey in excess of ten
miles, and the taxpayer bore the cost of the additional five miles himself.
He was assessed to income tax under Sch. E on the amounts received
for travelling expenses as being emoluments of his office, and he claimed to
deduct from his income the expenses that he incurred in such travelling to
and from the hospital.

Held: (i) (LORD PEARSON dissenting) so far as the taxpayer's actual
travelling expenses were re-imbursed they were not emoluments as defined
in para. 1 (1) of Sch. 2 of the Finance Act 1956 and accordingly were not
chargeable (see p. 5, letter I, p. 8, letter E, and p. 9, letter H, post);

(ii) (LORD DONOVAN and LORD PEARSON dissenting) the taxpayer had, in respect of the employment in question, two places of work, and the expenses which were necessarily incurred in travelling between them in the performance of his duties properly fell within the scope of r. 7 of Sch. 9 of the Income Tax Act 1952; accordingly the expenditure was deductible (see p. 6, letter G, p. 7, letter I, and p. 12, letter G, post).

    Ricketts v. *Colquhoun* (*Inspector of Taxes*) ([1926] A.C. 1) distinguished.

    Decision of the COURT OF APPEAL (sub nom. *Pook* (*Inspector of Taxes*) v. *Owen* [1968] 1 All E.R. 261) reversed.

[As to what constitutes an emolument of an office or employment under Sch. 2 to the Finance Act 1956, see 20 HALSBURY'S LAWS (3rd Edn.) 312-314, paras. 574-576; and for cases on the subject, see 28 DIGEST (Repl.) 225-237, *971-1040.*

As to deductions in respect of travelling expenses in computing assessable emoluments, see 20 HALSBURY'S LAWS (3rd Edn.) 327, 328, para. 600; and for cases on the subject, see 28 DIGEST (Repl.) 242-247, *1059-1099.*

For the Finance Act 1956, Sch. 2, see 36 HALSBURY'S STATUTES (2nd Edn.) 448.

For the Income Tax Act 1952, s. 156, as amended, see SUPPLEMENT to 31 HALSBURY'S STATUTES (2nd Edn.), para. [158] Amended Texts; and for r. 7 of Sch. 9 to the Act of 1952, see 31 HALSBURY'S STATUTES (2nd Edn.) 524.]

Cases referred to:

    Fergusson (*Surveyor of Taxes*) v. *Noble*, 1919 S.C. 534; 7 Tax Cas. 176; 28
        Digest (Repl.) 237, *565.

    Hochstrasser (*Inspector of Taxes*) v. *Mayes*, [1958] 1 All E.R. 369; [1959]
        Ch. 22; [1958] 2 W.L.R. 982; *affd*. C.A., [1958] 3 All E.R. 285; [1959]
        Ch. 22; [1958] 3 W.L.R. 215; *affd*. H.L., [1959] 3 All E.R. 817; [1960]
        A.C. 376; [1960] 2 W.L.R. 63; 38 Tax Cas. 673; Digest (Cont. Vol. A)
        888, *987.*

    Newsom v. *Robertson*, [1952] 2 All E.R. 728; [1953] Ch. 7; 33 Tax Cas. 452;
        28 Digest (Repl.) 158, *618.*

    Nolder v. *Walters* (1930), 15 Tax Cas. 380; 28 Digest (Repl.) 244, *1074.*

    R. v. *Postmaster General* (1878), 3 Q.B.D. 428; 47 L.J.Q.B. 435; 38 L.T. 89;
        38 Digest (Repl.) 78, *539.*

    Ricketts v. *Colquhoun* (*Inspector of Taxes*), [1924] 2 K.B. 347; *affd*. C.A.,
        [1925] 1 K.B. 725; *affd*. H.L., [1926] A.C. 1; 95 L.J.K.B. 82; 134 L.T.
        106; 90 J.P. 9; 10 Tax Cas. 118; 28 Digest (Repl.) 242, *1059.*

Appeal.

This was an appeal by the taxpayer, David Norman Howell Owen from an order of the Court of Appeal (DIPLOCK and EDMUND DAVIES, L.JJ., LORD DENNING, M.R., dissenting) dated 9th November 1967, and reported [1968] 1 All E.R. 261, dismissing an appeal made by the taxpayer from an order of STAMP, J., dated 3rd March 1967, and reported [1967] 2 All E.R. 579, allowing an appeal by the Crown through John Philip Pook (Inspector of Taxes) from a determination of the Commissioners for the General Purposes of the Income Tax for Kemes in the county of Pembroke. The taxpayer had appealed against assessments made on him under Sch. E of the Income Tax Act 1952: 1962-63 (additional assessment) employment, etc., £412, plus superannuation disallowed £39, £451; 1963-64, employment, etc., £1,481, less superannuation £48, £1,433.

The following facts are taken from the Case Stated: The taxpayer was in practice as a general medical practitioner at his residence at Fishguard. He held part-time appointments with the South West Wales Hospital Management Committee as (i) obstetrician, and (ii) anaesthetist, at the Pembroke County War Memorial Hospital at Haverfordwest in the county of Pembroke which was 15 miles from Fishguard. There was a scarcity in the area of persons duly qualified to do this work. Under the terms of the appointments he was on stand-by duty at the following times: (i) as obstetrician—one weekend a month;

A (ii) as anaesthetist—on Monday and Friday nights and one weekend a month. During those periods he was required to be accessible by telephone. All his work in connection with those appointments was concerned with emergency cases at the hospital. On receipt of a telephone call from the hospital he would give instructions to the hospital staff (e.g., to prepare the patient for an operation). Usually he then set out immediately to the hospital by car. Sometimes
B he advised treatment by telephone and then awaited a further report. Not every telephone call resulted in a visit to the hospital. Sometimes the telephone call was received when he was out on his medical rounds and not thus necessarily at his house. His responsibility for a patient began as soon as he received a telephone call. Under the terms and conditions of service of hospital medical and dental staffs the hospital management committee paid to the taxpayer
C travelling expenses at a fixed rate per mile for journeys between Fishguard and the hospital at Haverfordwest. Expenses were not payable for a single journey in excess of ten miles and the taxpayer bore the cost of the additional five miles himself. In 1962-63 he made about 140 journeys to the hospital and the expenses payments for the outward and return journeys totalled £100. This sum was included in the £412 assessed for that year. In 1963-64 he made
D about 115 journeys, receiving £82, which was included in the assessment for 1963-64. At all times the taxpayer was on call for obstetric "flying squad" duties which meant that he might be called to attend an obstetric emergency in any part of Pembrokeshire. Such calls were rare.

The commissioners decided that the taxpayer's duties commenced at the moment he was first contacted by the hospital authorities; thereafter his
E travelling expenses to and from the hospital or to and from an emergency were wholly, exclusively and necessarily incurred or expended in the duties of that office.

   Hubert H. Monroe, Q.C., and *J. R. Cherryman* for the taxpayer.
   Heyworth Talbot, Q.C., *J. R. Phillips*, Q.C., and *P. W. Medd* for the Crown.

F Their Lordships took time for consideration.

   26th March. The following opinions were delivered.

   LORD GUEST: My Lords, Dr. Owen, the taxpayer, is a general medical practitioner in practice at Fishguard. He also holds two part-time appointments
G with the South Wales Hospital Management Committee as obstetrician and anaesthetist at a hospital in Haverfordwest some 15 miles from Fishguard. Under the terms and conditions of these appointments he was on "stand-by duty" as obstetrician, one weekend a month and as anaesthetist on Monday and Friday nights and one weekend a month. At such times he was required to be accessible by telephone, apart from being on call at all times for obstetric
H "flying squad" duties in any part of Pembrokeshire. He had no other duties at the hospital, all were concerned with emergency cases. The flying squad duties were very rare. On receipt of a telephone call from the hospital he gives instructions to the hospital staff. He usually sets out immediately by car to the hospital. He may advise treatment by telephone and await a further report. Sometimes the telephone call is received when he is out on his medical rounds. It is found in the Case Stated that his responsibility for a patient
I begins as soon as he receives a telephone call.

   Under the terms and conditions of service of hospital staff the management committee pay to the taxpayer travelling expenses as a part-time officer at a fixed rate per mile, said to be 8d., for single journeys between Fishguard and the hospital, limited to a single journey of ten miles. The taxpayer pays the cost of the additional five miles travel himself.

   The taxpayer in 1962-63 made about 140 journeys to the hospital and received payment of expenses amounting to £100. This sum was included in his income

assessable for that year.   In 1963-64 he made about 115 journeys receiving £82   **A**
which was also included in his assessment for 1963-64.   Before the commissioners
he sought to deduct the whole cost of travelling incurred, which for 1962-63
amounted to £150 and for 1963-64 to £123, for income tax purposes.

The General Commissioners sustained his appeal and allowed the deductions
sought under r. 7 of Sch. 9 to the Income Tax Act 1952.   STAMP, J. (1) reversed
that determination and his judgment was upheld by the Court of Appeal (2)   **B**
(DIPLOCK and EDMUND DAVIES, L.JJ., LORD DENNING, M.R., dissenting).

Two questions arise—(i) whether the travelling allowances were properly
included in the taxpayer's emoluments for income tax purposes under Sch. E,
and (ii) was the actual cost of the journeys deductible from his emoluments
under the relevant rule?

Schedule E to the Income Tax Act 1952 provides as follows: **C**

" Tax under this Schedule shall be charged in respect of any office or
employment or emoluments therefrom which fall under [Cases I, II and
III]."

Paragraph 1 (1) of Sch. 2 to the Finance Act 1956 provides inter alia:

" Tax under Case I, II or III shall, except as hereinafter mentioned, be
chargeable on the full amount of the emoluments falling under that Case,   **D**
subject to such deductions only as may be authorised by the Income Tax
Acts, and the expression ' emoluments ' shall include all salaries, fees,
wages, perquisites and profits whatsoever."

Under Sch. 9 to the Income Tax Act 1952, r. 7 applicable to Sch. E, provides
as follows:
          E
" If the holder of an office or employment of profit is necessarily obliged
to incur and defray out of the emoluments thereof the expenses of travelling
in the performance of the duties of the office or employment, or of keeping
and maintaining a horse to enable him to perform the same, or otherwise
to expend money wholly, exclusively and necessarily in the performance of
the said duties, there may be deducted from the emoluments to be assessed   **F**
the expenses so necessarily incurred and defrayed."

The first point, whether the travelling expenses paid to the taxpayer were
properly included as part of his emoluments was not taken before the general
commissioners or before STAMP, J. (1).   It was, however, raised without objection before the Court of Appeal (2) who decided it adversely to the taxpayer.
No objection was taken to the argument being raised before your Lordships.   **G**

In view of the way in which the case went before the commissioners—the
only point being whether the actual travelling expenses were properly deductible
—there is little material in the case on the point.   The taxpayer's entitlement to
these expenses is contained in condition 19 " Expenses " of the terms and conditions of service of hospital medical and dental staffs (England and Wales):

" (iv) A part-time officer, when called out in an emergency to the hospital   **H**
where his principal duties lie, shall receive expenses for such journeys."

The limitation to ten miles for a single journey is contained in condition 19 (b)
(3) (iii) and under the heading:

" Travelling Expenses, Mileage Allowances, etc.: . . .

" (iii) Where a part-time officer travels between his private consulting   **I**
room or place of residence (whichever is the nearer) and the hospital where
his principal duties lie before and/or after an official journey, expenses shall
be payable for the whole distance provided that for journeys to and from
the hospital where the officer's principal duties lie no expenses shall be
paid for any distance exceeding ten miles each way unless circumstances
warrant exceptional treatment."

---

(1) [1967] 2 All E.R. 579; [1967] 1 W.L.R. 679.
(2) [1968] 1 All E.R. 261; [1968] 2 W.L.R. 591.

A   The Court of Appeal (3), certainly Lord Denning, M.R., appear to have treated
the payments as allowances payable to the taxpayer whether he incurred the
expenses or not.   But Edmund Davies, L.J., would have decided the case the
same way whether the payments were actual re-imbursement for expenses
incurred or allowances.   From their reliance on *Fergusson (Surveyor of Taxes)*
v. *Noble* (4) I take it that the case was treated as one where the payment was
B   truly an allowance and not a re-imbursement.
        There is, in my view, a distinction between the two cases.   If the allowance
was, as in *Fergusson (Surveyor of Taxes)* v. *Noble* (4), a clothing allowance payable
whether it was expended or not, I can see the argument that it was an emolument
in the sense of a profit or gain and I do not wish to question the authority of
that case; but if the payment was merely a re-imbursement for actual expendi-
C   ture, different considerations arise.   This case is, in my view, distinguishable.
        Counsel for the Crown was prepared to take the case on the footing that it
was a re-imbursement for actual expenditure, and I so treat it.   The Crown's
contention, therefore, must be that where an officer assessed under Sch. E
receives an allowance for travelling which is, under his conditions of service,
pro tanto to re-imburse him for the expense occasioned to him on travelling, this
D   allowance is an emolument.   The fact that " emolument " as defined includes
" perquisites and profits " does not, in my view, advance the Crown's argument.
" Perquisite " is merely a casual emolument additional to regular salary or
wages.   But the allowance must, to be chargeable, accrue " in respect of any
office or employment " (Sch. E).   In *Hochstrasser (Inspector of Taxes)* v. *Mayes* (5)
Viscount Simonds quotes with approval a passage from the judgment of Upjohn,
E   J. (6), to the following effect:

        " In my judgment [he said] the authorities show this, that it is a question
    to be answered in the light of the particular facts of every case whether or
    not a particular payment is or is not a profit arising from the employment.
    Disregarding entirely contracts for full consideration in money or money's
    worth and personal presents, in my judgment not every payment made to an
F   employee is necessarily made to him as a profit arising from his employment.
    Indeed, in my judgment, the authorities show that, to be a profit arising
    from the employment, the payment must be made in reference to the service
    the employee renders by virtue of his office, and it must be something in the
    nature of a reward for services past, present or future."

G   Lord Radcliffe, who concurred with Viscount Simonds, said (7):

        "... while it is not sufficient to render a payment assessable that an
    employee would not have received it unless he had been an employee, it is
    assessable if it has been paid to him in return for acting as or being an
    employee ... The money was not paid to him as wages."

    Later in his judgment Lord Radcliffe appears to treat a claim for indemnity
H   as not assessable.   The facts in that case were widely different from the present,
but if the proper test is whether the sum is a reward for services, then, in my
view, the travelling allowances paid to the taxpayer are not emoluments.   To
say that the taxpayer is to that extent " better off " is not to the point.   The
allowances were used to fill a hole in his emoluments by his expenditure on
travel.   The allowances were made for the convenience of the taxpayer to
I   allow him to do his work at the hospital from a suitably adjacent area.   In my
view, the travelling allowances were not emoluments.
        If I am right that the allowances are not emoluments no question arises as
to deductibility of the actual sums expended on the 20-mile journey.   There

(3) [1968] 1 All E.R. 261; [1968] 2 W.L.R. 591.
(4) (1919), 7 Tax Cas. 176.
(5) [1959] 3 All E.R. 817 at p. 821; 38 Tax Cas. 673 at p. 705.
(6) [1958] 1 All E.R. 369 at p. 374; 38 Tax Cas. at p. 685.
(7) [1959] 3 All E.R. at p. 823; 38 Tax Cas. at p. 707.

A

still remains, however, the question as to the extra expense for which the tax-payer was not indemnified but had to pay himself. The basis of the Crown's argument on this aspect of the case is *Ricketts* v. *Colquhoun (Inspector of Taxes)* (8). The quotation from LORD BLANESBURGH'S speech referring to r. 7 (as it then was) is (9):

B

"But I am also struck by this, that, as it seems to me, although un-doubtedly less obtrusively, the language of the Rule points to the expenses with which it is concerned as being confined to those which each and every occupant of the particular office is necessarily obliged to incur in the per-formance of its duties, to expenses imposed upon each holder *ex necessitate* of his office and to such expenses only. It says:—' If the holder of an office ' —the words, be it observed, are not ' if any holder of an office '—' is obliged to incur expenses in the performance of the duties of the office '—the duties again are not the duties of *his* office; in other words, the terms employed are strictly, and, I cannot doubt, purposely, not personal but objective. The deductible expenses do not extend to those which the holder has to incur mainly and, it may be, only because of circumstances in relation to his office which are personal to himself or are the result of his own volition."

C

D

The recorder of Portsmouth was not allowed to deduct the expenses of travelling between London and Portsmouth. Counsel for the taxpayer did not ask your Lordships to say that *Ricketts* v. *Colquhoun* (8) was wrongly decided but he sought to distinguish it on the facts of this case. I consider that he has suffi-ciently distinguished it.

In *Ricketts* v. *Colquhoun* (8) there was only one place of employment, Ports-mouth. It was not suggested that any duties were performed in London. In the present case there is a finding of fact that the taxpayer's duties commenced at the moment he was first contacted by the hospital authorities. This is further emphasised by the finding that his responsibility for a patient began as soon as he received a telephone call and that he sometimes advised treatment by tele-phone. It is noteworthy that under condition 19 (*b*) (3) (iv) of his terms and conditions of service the hospital is referred to " where his principal duties lie ". There were thus two places where his duty is performed, the hospital and his telephone in his consulting room. If he was performing his duties at both places then it is difficult to see why, on the journey between the two places, he was not equally performing his duties. Indeed counsel for the Crown did not contend to the contrary. It follows that he had to get from his consulting room to the hospital by car to treat the emergency. The travelling expenses were, in my view, necessarily incurred in the performance of the duties of his office.

E

F

G

I would allow the appeal.

LORD PEARCE: My Lords, the taxpayer is a doctor carrying on a general practice at Fishguard, which is 15 miles from Haverfordwest. Since the medical needs of the hospital at Haverfordwest exceeded the supply of medical practi-tioners there, the hospital had to call on the part-time services of a Fishguard practitioner. Accordingly, the taxpayer was employed or appointed to act as a stand-by for emergencies, one weekend a month as an obstetrician, and one weekend a month (and also Monday and Friday nights) as an anaesthetist. He had to be available on the telephone at Fishguard. As soon as he received a telephone call his responsibility for the patient at Haverfordwest started. If he could deal with the case merely by instructions on the telephone he did so. But in the normal case he would give instructions to the hospital staff (e.g., to prepare the patient for an operation) and set out immediately in his car for the Haver-fordwest hospital. For the expense of these journeys he was re-imbursed, or partially re-imbursed, by the hospital management committee at whatever was

H

I

---

(8) (1925) 10 Tax Cas. 118; [1926] A.C. 1.
(9) (1925), 10 Tax Cas. at p. 135; [1926] A.C. at pp. 7, 8.

A the proper rate per mile under the terms and conditions of service of hospital medical and dental staffs. These conditions expressly state that:

> "Travelling, subsistence, and other expenses shall be paid to meet actual disbursements of officers engaged in the service of Boards or Committees and shall not be regarded as a source of emolument or reckoned as such for the purposes of pension."

B Nobody suggests that the re-imbursements were over-generous. The taxpayer was in fact re-imbursed only in respect of ten miles out of each 15-mile journey and had to bear the cost of five miles of the journey himself. The commissioners found, as I would expect, that "his travelling expenses ... to and from an emergency were wholly, exclusively and necessarily incurred or expended in the duties of that office".

C Yet it has been held that he must pay tax on these re-imbursements as if they were income or profit received by him. The point can be underlined by the following example. Suppose that there were some constantly recurring emergency in the most distant part of Pembroke which he was constantly expected to deal with gratuitously and without any extra pay, but he was merely re-imbursed for the railway ticket which he had taken to get there and back (or only for 2/3rds of his rail tickets so that each time he incurred an actual loss). In that case he would admittedly, if the argument of the Crown is correct, pay tax on all the re-imbursements or partial re-imbursements of his railway tickets.

D Such a situation would be obviously unjust. If it be correct, it is clear that something has gone seriously wrong with the enactments or the case law or with both. It must be disturbing to the citizen if such a situation can arise. Such an injustice is not in the interests of anyone—certainly not of the Crown since injustice causes evasion. Each year there is an adjustment of the mechanism of taxation wherever that is necessary to ensure that ingenious schemes of avoidance shall not succeed. There is a corresponding duty to adjust the mechanism where it is found to be creating a clear injustice.

E On the findings of the commissioners the expenses were incurred in the performance of his duties. In my opinion, that finding was correct and the expenses were allowable under r. 7 of Sch. 9 to the Income Tax Act 1952. It was as a doctor practising in Fishguard that the taxpayer was appointed to his stand-by duties. He was to stand-by in Fishguard. In Fishguard on the telephone he undertook his responsibilities to the patient and the hospital and no doubt he discussed the symptoms and made various arrangements as to what should be done by way of alleviation in the half-hour which must elapse before he could arrive. If he were held up on the road he would be under duty to ring through and make any resulting arrangements. If anyone asked him en route what he was doing he would probably say truthfully that he was on hospital duty. He would not, I think, be even pedantically accurate if he said: "I was on hospital duty on the telephone a quarter of an hour ago and shall be on hospital duty in a quarter of an hour's time, but at the moment I am driving on my own account". I do not find it helpful to consider whether, if he knocked down a pedestrian he would make the hospital liable or, indeed, whether he would do so if an accident happened when he had been to the hospital first and had been there directed on to an emergency case nearby. This has no decisive bearing on the point in issue. His duty to the hospital and the patient started on the telephone, and he was thereafter responsible to the hospital and the patient until he had dealt with the patient, whether he made his journey to the hospital in his own car or as passenger in a hired car. In my opinion, the finding of the commissioners was correct and should be upheld.

It is argued that the case of *Ricketts* v. *Colquhoun (Inspector of Taxes)* (10) compels us to hold otherwise. With all respect to their Lordships who decided that case, I find it, as some others have done, very unsatisfactory both in its

_____

(10) (1925), 10 Tax Cas. 118; [1926] A.C. 1.

result and in its reasoning. In order to carry out his duties as recorder, the $~~A$
taxpayer had to travel to Portsmouth, since he was a London practitioner
(and it was, no doubt, by virtue of his London practice that he was appointed
recorder). It was, therefore, unreasonable to tax him on the emoluments of
his office without allowing the travelling expenses. For that would be to tax
him on a sum larger than the true profit of the office. ROWLATT, J., described
the position as unreasonable, but felt compelled by the rules to come to an $~~B$
unreasonable conclusion. WARRINGTON, L.J., managed to give a more reasonable
meaning to the rules, but his view did not prevail. In my opinion, that case
should be considered afresh by your Lordships' House. It is contended that
Parliament by re-enacting the section in 1952 gave countenance to the case.
But the Act was a consolidation, and fresh consideration cannot, I think, have
been given to the subject since the short re-enacted section refers only to one $~~C$
express expense and that is the " keeping and maintaining a horse to enable
him to perform " the duties. This could not have resulted from a fresh consideration of a section which would be striving to do justice to modern transactions in a
modern world. Obviously difficulties are caused by the archaic artificial division
between Sch. D and Sch. E, especially if a man is taxed separately under each
when both activities are really part of the same profession. $~~D$

There is a further point raised by the taxpayer in the Court of Appeal (11).
He contends that re-imbursements such as that which is here in question do
not come within the " emoluments " of an appointment or employment under
Sch. E. They therefore never fall to be charged, and it is unnecessary to consider whether they are allowable under r. 7. In my opinion, that contention is
correct. " Emoluments " are charged. These are defined as including " all $~~E$
salaries, fees, wages, perquisites and profits whatsoever ".

The re-imbursements of actual expenses are clearly not intended by " salaries ",
" fees ", " wages " or " profits ". It is contended that they are " perquisites ".
The normal meaning of the word denotes something that benefits a man by
going " into his *own* pocket ". It would be a wholly misleading description
of an office to say that it had very large perquisites merely because the holder $~~F$
had to disburse very large sums out of his own pocket and subsequently received
a re-imbursement or partial re-imbursement of these sums. If a school teacher
takes children out for a school treat, paying for them out of his (or her) own
pocket, and is later wholly or partially re-imbursed by the school, nobody would
describe him (or her) as enjoying a perquisite. In my view, perquisite has a
known normal meaning, namely, a personal advantage, which would not apply $~~G$
to a mere re-imbursement of necessary disbursements. There is nothing in the
section to give it a different meaning. Indeed, the other words of the section
confirm the view that some element of personal profit is intended.

I would therefore allow the appeal.

LORD DONOVAN: My Lords, two questions arise in this case. First,
are the travelling expenses re-imbursed to the taxpayer by his employers' $~~H$
" emoluments " from his office or employment within the meaning of Sch. E?
Secondly, if they are, do such travelling expenses qualify as admissible deductions
under r. 7 of that schedule?

The Court of Appeal (12) answered the first question in the affirmative, LORD
DENNING, M.R., saying that the mileage allowance for travel was paid to the
taxpayer no matter how he made his way to the hospital at Haverfordwest: $~~I$
and he thought the point was covered by *Fergusson (Surveyor of Taxes)* v. *Noble*
(13). He considered that the case might be otherwise if the taxpayer was
simply re-imbursed what he had actually spent. DIPLOCK, L.J., agreed (14)
with what LORD DENNING, M.R., had said on this point, but EDMUND DAVIES,

(11) [1968] 1 All E.R. 261; [1968] 2 W.L.R. 591.
(12) [1968] 1 All E.R. 261 at p. 264; [1968] 2 W.L.R. 591 at p. 594.
(13) (1919), 7 Tax Cas. 176.
(14) [1968] 1 All E.R. at p. 265; [1968] 2 W.L.R. at p. 596.

A L.J., thought (15) that the travelling expenses paid would still be "emoluments" even though they represented recoupment of actual outgoings.

The facts regarding the taxpayer's entitlement to travelling expenses were not fully investigated before the general commissioners, the argument before them being confined to the second question under r. 7. The commissioners simply found that in the first of the two years under appeal, namely, 1962-63, the tax-
B payer made about 140 journeys to the hospital and received travelling expenses for the journey there, and back to Fishguard, of £100. For the second of the two years, namely, 1963-64 he likewise received £82 in respect of 115 such journeys: it is only in the taxpayer's contentions that it is alleged that the actual cost of these journeys was £150 for 1962-63 and £123 for 1963-64.

Since, however, the Case Stated finds that under the terms and conditions of
C service of persons like the taxpayer travelling expenses are paid at a fixed rate per mile, that they are not payable for a single journey in excess of ten miles, and that the taxpayer bears the cost himself of the additional five miles between Fishguard and Haverfordwest, it may fairly be assumed that there was no profit element in the travelling allowances he received in these two years, but that, on the contrary they left him out of pocket. Before your Lordships the case
D proceeded on that footing without demur from the Crown and on that basis I proceed to consider the first question.

Tax under Sch. E is charged " on the full amount of the emoluments " from the office or employment: and " emoluments " are defined as including " all salaries, fees, wages, perquisites, and profits whatsoever ". (The Income Tax Act 1952, s. 156, as amended by the Finance Act 1956, s. 10 (16).)
E This definition certainly gives no impetus towards the view that it covers sums paid to an employee simply in re-imbursement of expenses incurred in carrying out his duties. Nor do the dictionary definitions of the word, namely, " profit or gain, advantage, due, reward, remuneration, salary ". (MURRAY'S ENGLISH DICTIONARY: THE SHORTER OXFORD DICTIONARY.) Nor does s. 1 of the Act of 1952 which contemplates that income tax will be imposed on " profits
F or gains ".

It is also interesting to notice the decision of the Court of Appeal in R. v. Postmaster General (17). There an ex-employee of a private concern whose business had been taken over by the Postmaster General was entitled to receive from him compensation based on his past emoluments from the private employer. He used to receive from him travelling and subsistence allowances which yielded
G him a small profit. It was held that this profit was part of the ex-employee's emoluments. No one suggested that the allowances were, as a whole, part of the claimant's " emoluments ".

On the footing that the travelling expenses paid to the taxpayer simply re-imbursed what he had spent (or part of what he had spent) on travelling in performance of his duties, I do not think they should be regarded as emoluments
H of his employment within the meaning of Sch. E. I think the case is distinguishable from Fergusson v. Noble (18) where a cash allowance was paid to the employee which, although he may have been required to spend it on buying a civilian suit, yielded a benefit or advantage to him.

This does not dispose of the appeal, for the taxpayer claims the excess of such expenditure over what he received in re-imbursement as an allowable deduction
I from his salary. In this connection it is not enough to say that such excess moneys were spent in the performance of his duties. Rule 7 of Sch. E requires that they should be " necessarily " incurred and defrayed; and the decision of this House in Ricketts v. Colquhoun (Inspector of Taxes) (19) has laid down that

---

(15) [1968] 1 All E.R. at p. 267; [1968] 2 W.L.R. at p. 598.
(16) See Finance Act 1956, Sch. 2, para. 1 (1).
(17) (1878), 3 Q.B.D. 428.
(18) (1919), 7 Tax Cas. 176.
(19) (1925), 10 Tax Cas. 118; [1926] A.C. 1.

the word " necessarily " imports an objective and not a subjective test. The **A**
expenses must be such as any holder of the employment would be bound to
incur.   It is not enough that they are incurred simply because the employee
happens or chooses to live some distance from his work.

Here it is contended for the taxpayer that he really has two places of employment, one his home at Fishguard and the other the hospital at Haverfordwest;
and that the expenses of travelling between the two are deductible accordingly.   **B**
If the premises are sound the Crown would concede the conclusion.   The contention of two places of employment is rested on these considerations.   First, it is
found by the general commissioners that the taxpayer is on stand-by duty at
certain specific times, and at these times must be accessible by telephone.
Secondly, that his responsibility for a patient begins as soon as he receives a
telephone call, and that on receipt of such a call he gives any necessary pre-   **C**
liminary instructions to the hospital staff in relation to the case (which are all
emergency cases).

I do not think these facts establish the contention of two places of employment
at all.   In a very real sense almost every general medical practitioner is on
stand-by duty for emergency cases, and is in fact available on the telephone.
And almost every such practitioner will, if necessary, give preliminary instruc-   **D**
tions concerning the patient to anyone who summons him by telephone.   There
are also thousands of employees in other walks of life who have to be on stand-by
duty at their homes and are required to obey a summons to go to their factory
or their offices to cope with some emergency.   If this is to mean that they all have
two places of employment I see no reason why all of them should not be entitled
to claim travelling expenses between their homes and their places of work.   **E**

The simple truth, as I see it, is that the taxpayer has one place of employment
as an obstetrician and anaesthetist; and that is the hospital at Haverfordwest.
When he answers the telephone and gives and necessary preliminary instructions,
of course he is performing the duties of his office.   But when he then gets into
his car and drives the 15 miles to Haverfordwest he is not performing such
duties at all.   He incurs the expense of so travelling because he chooses to   **F**
live at Fishguard.   I think the case is clearly within the decision in *Ricketts* v.
Colquhoun (20) as STAMP, J. (21), and the majority of the Court of Appeal (22)
decided.   I would therefore allow the appeal so far as the assessment treats the
re-imbursement of travelling expenses as an " emolument ", but dismiss it as
regards the claim to deduct any excess expenditure under r. 7.

LORD WILBERFORCE: My Lords, the main point in this case, as the   **G**
courts below have regarded it, is whether the taxpayer is entitled to a deduction
from his emoluments as assessable to income tax, in respect of certain travelling
expenses which he had admittedly incurred.   In the alternative, he contends
that certain sums which he has received by way of partial re-imbursement of
these travelling expenses ought not to be brought into charge as part of his
taxable emoluments.   **H**

The first point is of a familiar character.   The emoluments arise under Sch. E
to the Income Tax Act 1952, and, therefore, the question is whether the deduction
is authorised by the strict and narrow r. 7 in Sch. 9.   In *Ricketts* v. *Colquhoun*
(*Inspector of Taxes*) (20) this House decided that the travelling expenses incurred
by a recorder in proceeding to Portsmouth where the duties of his office lay, could
not be brought within the rule.   On the basis of fact on which that case was   **I**
presented, this decision may have been inevitable, but it does not follow that it
governs each and every situation.   The facts must be considered and the rule
applied.

The taxpayer is a doctor whose main occupation is as general practitioner

(20) (1925), 10 Tax Cas. 118; [1926] A.C. 1.
(21) [1967] 2 All E.R. 579; [1967] 1 W.L.R. 679.
(22) [1968] 1 All E.R. 261; [1968] 2 W.L.R. 591.

A in Fishguard. As such he is taxable under Sch. D. In November 1955, he
   was offered by the South West Wales Hospital Management Committee, and
   accepted, an appointment as clinical assistant to the Obstetric Department at a
   hospital at Haverfordwest, 15 miles from Fishguard. This appointment has
   been renewed from year to year, and in the Case Stated it was found that he was
   to act as obstetrician and anaesthetist, and that he was on stand-by duty at
B specified times in respect of each activity during which period he was required
   to be accessible by telephone. All his work in connection with these appointments was concerned with emergency cases at the hospital. On receipt of a
   call from the hospital he would give instructions to the hospital staff (e.g., to
   prepare the patient for an operation). Usually he would then set out immediately
   to the hospital by car. Sometimes he advised treatment by telephone and then
C awaited a further report. Not every telephone call resulted in a visit to the
   hospital. His responsibility for a patient began as soon as he received a telephone
   call.

       This description is sufficient to show that both the nature of the taxpayer's
   appointment, and the purpose for which he incurred travelling expenses, differ
   greatly from those found or assumed to exist in the case of Mr. Ricketts (23).
D Are they sufficient to establish that he was necessarily obliged to incur and
   defray out of the emoluments the expenses of travelling in the performance of
   the duties of his office or employment?

       I agree with the Crown's contention that the mere fact of being on stand-by
   duty is not enough: if this were all the taxpayer would be in the same position
   as the airline pilot who was held (rightly in my opinion) not to come within the
E rule in Nolder v. Walters (24): this was just a case of a person having to travel
   to his place of work. Nor, in my opinion, is the mere fact sufficient that he
   might be called on, or might volunteer, to give some professional advice on the
   telephone before setting out. There are persons, who hold positions of importance, who carry their responsibility with them wherever they are: they, too,
   may be called to their offices after working hours and may give instructions or
F advice before departure. But this does not mean that they have more than
   one working place (cf., Newsom v. Robertson (25)). What is required is proof,
   to the satisfaction of the fact-finding commissioners, that the taxpayer, in a real
   sense, in respect of the office or employment in question, had two places of
   work, and that the expenses were incurred in travelling from one to the other
   in the performance of his duties.

G   In my opinion, the taxpayer satisfied this requirement. I have stated the
   basic facts; on them the commissioners found that his duties " commenced at the moment he was first contacted by the hospital authorities ",
   and that " thereafter his travelling expenses to and from the hospital . . . were
   wholly, exclusively and necessarily incurred or expended in the duties of that
   office ". I consider that this finding was fully justified. Given that the appoint-
H ment related to emergency cases, it was of the essence of his duties that he should
   give immediate, and correct, advice the moment he was contacted, and that he
   should form a decision whether to set off at once, to wait for further information,
   or to take no further action. In the event of his deciding to go at once to the
   hospital, I cannot appreciate why he was not thereafter travelling on the duty
   of his office: he was travelling not to his work but on his work. The taxpayer
I was not, it seems, in such continuous contact as the well-known Australian
   flying doctor, but the continuity of his responsibility and function is, I think,
   established by the commissioners' findings. I can find nothing fictitious or
   strained in their conclusions.

       The main argument on which these were resisted was founded on observations

   (23) (1925), 10 Tax Cas. 118; [1926] A.C. 1.
   (24) (1930), 15 Tax Cas. 380.
   (25) [1952] 2 All E.R. 728; 33 Tax Cas. 452.

in *Ricketts* v. *Colquhoun* (26), and particularly on a passage in the speech of **A**
LORD BLANESBURGH. His Lordship used these words (27):

" ' If the holder of an office '—the words, be it observed, are not ' if any
holder of an office '—' is obliged to incur expenses in the performance of the
duties of the office '—the duties again are not the duties of *his* office; in
other words, the terms employed are strictly, and, I cannot doubt, purposely,
not personal but objective. The deductible expenses do not extend to those **B**
which the holder has to incur mainly and, it may be, only because of circumstances in relation to his office which are personal to himself or are the
result of his own volition."

Then it was said that the taxpayer chose to live 15 miles from the hospital, his
case was indistinguishable from that of the recorder. Now, I would entirely
agree that r. 7 is drafted in an objective form so as to distinguish between ex- **C**
penses which arise from the nature of the office and those which arise from the
personal choice of the taxpayer. But this does not mean that no expenses can
ever be deductible unless precisely those expenses must necessarily be incurred
by each and every office holder. The objective character of the deductions
allowed relates to their nature, not to their amount: to take the often-quoted
case of the Archdeacon, it would be absurd to suppose that each holder of that **D**
office or even each Archdeacon of Plumstead Episcopi travels the same distance
or travels by the same means in a year, or that his choice of residence would
affect his entitlement. In this case the hospital management committee required
the services of doctors on a part-time basis for emergencies: it was found that
there was difficulty in obtaining suitable men. Unless a suitable retired doctor
could be appointed (and that case might be different) the committee would have **E**
to appoint a doctor with a practice of his own and also with suitable obstetric
and anaesthetic experience: he might live and practice within 15 miles or one
mile or 100 yards of the hospital: the choice in the matter, if any exists, does not lie
with the doctor, who is there in his practice, but with the committee which
decides, however near or far he works, to appoint him and to require him to discharge a part of his duty at his practice premises. **F**

A finding that expenses necessarily arise from this duality appears to me
legitimate and the undemonstrated possibility that a nearer practitioner might
have been selected to be irrelevant.

I agree, therefore, with the judgment of LORD DENNING, M.R. (28), and
would allow the appeal. I should add that, if I had not reached this conclusion,
I should have difficulty in seeing how the taxpayer could succeed, on his alterna- **G**
tive point, in establishing that re-imbursement of a non-deductible expense is
something other than an emolument.

LORD PEARSON: My Lords, I have found this case difficult. On the
one hand, the taxpayer has been unfairly dealt with, inasmuch as his necessary
professional expenses of travelling between Fishguard and Haverfordwest have **H**
not been allowed as deductions in the assessment of his net income from the
exercise of his profession. On the other hand, it seems to me that, when the
taxpayer's position is analysed, the unfairness is attributable to a defect in the
system of assessment and not to any misunderstanding or misapplication of the
rules or provisions of Sch. E, nor to any error as to the meaning of the word
" emoluments ". There is a wrong, but the remedy would have to be found in a **I**
change of the system and not in a decision in favour of the taxpayer on either
of the issues in this appeal.

The taxpayer works as a doctor treating patients in two ways: (i) as a general
practitioner in Fishguard; (ii) as an obstetrician and anaesthetist in part-time
employment at the hospital in Haverfordwest. These are two aspects of his

(26) (1925), 10 Tax Cas. 118; [1926] A.C. 1.
(27) (1925), 10 Tax Cas. at p. 135; [1926] A.C. at pp. 7, 8.
(28) [1968] 1 All E.R. at p. 263; [1968] 2 W.L.R. at p. 593.

A professional career, two professional activities. Whether he is working at his
consulting room at his home in Fishguard, or on his rounds in and from Fishguard, or at the hospital in Haverfordwest, he is working as a doctor, making
use of his professional learning, skill and experience for the benefit of his patients
and receiving remuneration for doing so. The expense of his journeys between
Fishguard and Haverfordwest is a necessary expense of his profession as he
B carries it on, because he could not engage in both activities without making
these journeys. He pays taxes on his income from both activities, and it is
unfair not to allow him to deduct expenses which he must inevitably incur so
long as he carries on both activities.

But the system apparently requires that his earnings from his general practice
have to be assessed separately under Sch. D and his earnings from his employ-
C ment at the hospital have to be assessed separately under Sch. E. The unfairness results from this separation of his two professional activities for purposes
of assessment to tax, because the expense of the journeys between Fishguard and
Haverfordwest is not an expense of either of the activities taken separately
but is an expense of combining the two.

It is clearly not necessary for his general practice at Fishguard that he should
D make these journeys to Haverfordwest and back. Under the rules or provisions
of Sch. E, as they have been authoritatively interpreted, these journeys cannot
be regarded as necessary for his employment at the hospital. For the purposes
of that employment he does not have to live at Fishguard or anywhere outside
Haverfordwest. The expense of travelling to and from Haverfordwest is not
an expense which he incurs ex necessitate of his employment. It is not an
E expense which any holder of the employment would have to incur wherever his
home might be. The employment is not an itinerant employment. These
journeys are made by him on the way to his employment and in returning
from it. They are not made in the course of his employment or in the performance of his duties therein. On this point the present case seems to me to
be indistinguishable from Ricketts v. Colquhoun (Inspector of Taxes) (29), where
F the principle was very clearly established. LORD BLANESBURGH said (30):

"... the language of the Rule points to the expenses with which it is
concerned as being confined to those which each and every occupant of the
particular office is necessarily obliged to incur in the performance of its duties,
to expenses imposed upon each holder ex necessitate of his office, and to
such expenses only ... The deductible expenses do not extend to those
G which the holder has to incur mainly and, it may be, only because of circumstances in relation to his office which are personal to himself or are the
result of his own volition ... The travelling expenses of the Appellant
from London to Portsmouth and back are, in my judgment, excluded from
the benefit of the Rule both by the application of the test I have indicated
as relevant and also for another reason quite separate. The expenses
H covered by the words ' the expenses of travelling in the performance of the
duties of the office ', are, I think, limited to those which the Master of the
Rolls has well termed ' itinerant expenses '. There are none such here ...
That the Appellant travelled from London to hold his Courts at Portsmouth
and returned to London at the close of the Sessions was, in my judgment, a
course prescribed for him by his own convenience as a practising London
I barrister and by nothing else."

Counsel for the taxpayer sought to distinguish the present case from Ricketts v.
Colquhoun (29) on the ground that in the present case the hospital employment
is at two places—the taxpayer's home, at which he receives the telephone calls
and gives advice on the telephone, and the hospital—and that he comes on
duty when he receives the telephone call and remains on duty while he makes

(29) (1925), 10 Tax Cas. 118; [1926] A.C. 1.
(30) (1925), 10 Tax Cas. at pp. 135, 136; [1926] A.C. at pp. 7, 8.

the journey to the hospital and does his work at the hospital.   But I do not think **A**
it can reasonably be said that there are two places of employment.   His only
place of employment is at the hospital.   Because for his own purposes—purposes
other than the hospital employment—he chooses to live away from Haverfordwest he has to be summoned to the hospital and has to come from a distance and
so make a car journey.   Also because he lives for his own purposes at a distance
from Haverfordwest he may have usually to give advice on the telephone as to **B**
the interim treatment of the patient until he arrives at the hospital.   If immediate advice on the telephone is required, it could be given equally well from a
home in Haverfordwest.   It is no part of the duties of his hospital employment
to live in Fishguard, and the journeys are not made in performance of his duties
in the employment.   In my view, the principle established in *Ricketts* v. *Col-*
quhoun (31)is applicable in this case anddoes not permit deduction of the travelling **C**
expenses in making the assessment under Sch. E.   There was the same unfairness in *Ricketts* v. *Colquhoun* (31) as there is in this case, and it was in that case,
as it is in this case, attributable to the artificial division of the professional
earnings between Sch. D and Sch. E.

The other question in the appeal is whether the travelling allowance which
the taxpayer receives from the hospital authorities constitutes an " emolu- **D**
ment " of his employment.   I would arrive at the answer in this way.   Suppose
that A., B. and C. are employed each at a salary of £500 per annum, and in the
first year each has to pay entirely out of his own pocket the expenses of travelling
between his home and his place of work.   Then, in the second year the employer
re-imburses to A. the cost of his season ticket or gives him an allowance of (say)
8d. per mile for coming to work and returning home by car.   A. is better off **E**
financially by the amount of the re-imbursement or allowance.   He is better off
than he himself was in the first year, and better off than B. and C. who still
have to pay entirely out of their own pockets the expenses of travelling between
their homes and their places of work. As A. has effectively a better income than
B. and C., he ought to pay more income tax than they do.   The re-imbursement
or car allowance is a benefit to A. and is a sum of money.   In my opinion, it is a **F**
perquisite, a profit, an emolument.

There is a quite different position when the employee incurs an expense in
performing the duties of his employment—e.g., making a journey from head
office to branch office and back to head office, or buying stamps and stationery
for the firm—and has it re-imbursed to him.   In such a transaction there is no
benefit—no profit or gain—to the employee. He does not receive any emolument. **G**

Although the result is unfair, I do not think it can properly be corrected
without a change in the system eliminating the artificial division of the professional income between Sch. D and Sch. E.   In my opinion, the issues raised in
this appeal should be decided in favour of the Crown, and I would dismiss the
appeal.

Appeal allowed. **H**

Solicitors: *Le Brasseur & Oakley* (for the appellant); *Solicitor of Inland
Revenue*.

[*Reported by* S. A. HATTEEA, ESQ., *Barrister-at-Law.*]

I

---

(31) (1925), 10 Tax Cas. 118; [1926] A.C. 1.

A

R. *v.* PARKER.

[COURT OF APPEAL, CRIMINAL DIVISION (Davies, L.J., Lyell and Donaldson, JJ.),
February 14, 21, 1969.]

B
Criminal Law—Indictment—Joinder—Theft charged jointly of two garments—
One accused pleaded guilty and convicted—Other accused found guilty of
independent theft of one garment—Conviction quashed.

The appellant was indicted with one Miss O. for larceny of two pairs of
tights from a supermarket; Miss O. pleaded guilty and the appellant pleaded
not guilty. The prosecution case was that both girls went into the store.
Miss O. was seen to take some tights and conceal them in her cardigan, the
C
pair of them then leaving the premises. On being requested to return,
they were taken to the manager's office where the appellant was said to
have thrown a pair of tights on the floor. The jury were directed that one
possible conclusion from the evidence was that there had been no joint
enterprise, but two separate pieces of private enterprise, and the jury
were asked, in the event of their finding the appellant guilty, to bring in a
D
special verdict stating whether they found the appellant guilty of being
jointly concerned or whether they found her guilty of independently stealing
one pair of tights. The jury returned a verdict of guilty, and, on the clerk
of the court asking whether they found the appellant guilty of stealing one
or two pairs of tights, they replied " one pair ". On the question whether
she could be convicted otherwise than as part of a joint enterprise,

E
Held: the verdict of the jury was capable of the interpretation that a
different offence was committed by the appellant from that to which Miss O.
pleaded guilty; accordingly, as only one offence was charged it was not
open to the jury to find that a second offence had been committed (see
p. 17, letter F, post); further, as the proviso* to s. 2 (1) of the Criminal
Appeal Act 1968 could not be applied for the purpose of substituting another
F
verdict, the conviction would be quashed (see p. 18, letter A, post).

R. v. Scaramanga ([1963] 2 All E.R. 852) applied.

Appeal allowed.

[As to joinder of several offences, see 10 HALSBURY'S LAWS (3rd Edn.) 391,
392, para. 708; and for cases on the subject, see 14 DIGEST (Repl.) 253, 254,
2189-2212.
G
As to permissible verdicts, see 10 HALSBURY'S LAWS (3rd Edn.) 428, para. 790;
and for cases on the subject, see 14 DIGEST (Repl.) 355, 356, *3447-3448.*]

Cases referred to:
   R. v. Scaramanga, [1963] 2 All E.R. 852; [1963] 2 Q.B. 807; [1963] 3 W.L.R.
      320; 127 J.P. 476; 47 Cr. App. Rep. 213; Digest (Cont. Vol. A) 399,
H
      6653a.
   R. v. Woods, [1968] 3 All E.R. 709; [1968] 3 W.L.R. 1192.

Appeal.
This was an appeal by Ellen Jean Parker against her conviction at Middlesex
Sessions on 9th September 1968 of stealing one pair of tights. She was sentenced
by the deputy chairman (K. BRUCE CAMPBELL, Esq., Q.C.) to undergo a period
I
of borstal training. The facts are set out in the judgment of the court. The
case noted below† was cited during the argument in addition to those referred
to in the judgment of the court.

---

   * The proviso provides: " Provided that the Court may, notwithstanding that they
are of opinion that the point raised in the appeal might be decided in favou of they
appellant, dismiss the appeal if they consider that no miscarriage of justice has ractuall
occurred ".
   †‡R. v. *Joachim* (1912), 7 Cr. App. Rep. 222.

J. H. B. *Gardner* for the appellant.

H. F. *Cassel* for the Crown.

Cur. adv. vult.

21st February. **DONALDSON, J.,** read the judgment of the court. For the reasons set out hereafter, this court on 14th February allowed the appeal of Ellen Jean Parker against her conviction at Middlesex Sessions for the theft of one pair of tights.

Eleanor Overy and the appellant, both of whom were aged 17, were indicted for larceny contrary to s. 2 of the Larceny Act 1916, the particulars being that

"Eleanor Overy and Ellen Jean Parker on the 8th day of July, 1968, in Greater London, did steal two pairs of tights, the property of Tesco Stores, Ltd."

Miss Overy pleaded "guilty" and was placed on probation for two years. The appellant pleaded "not guilty". The prosecution case was that both girls went to the nylon counter in Tesco Stores, Greenford, and Miss Overy was seen to take some tights and conceal them under her cardigan. Both girls left the shop but were brought back to the manager's office where Miss Overy produced a pair of tights. The appellant also produced a pair of tights from the waist-band of her trousers and threw them on the floor in a corner of the office. In the course of his summing-up, the learned deputy chairman said that it had occurred to him and also to counsel that a possible conclusion on the evidence was that there had been no joint enterprise, but rather "two separate pieces of private enterprise". He then directed the jury as a matter of law that if they came to that conclusion they might still find the appellant guilty of the offence. He asked them, if they found the appellant guilty, to bring in a special verdict stating whether they found her guilty of being jointly concerned or whether they found her guilty of independently stealing one pair of tights. The jury found the appellant guilty and, in response to a question by the clerk of the court "Do you find her guilty of stealing two pairs of tights or one pair of tights?" replied "One pair of tights".

Counsel for the appellant submitted that the learned deputy chairman should not have directed the jury that, on a joint indictment for stealing, the appellant could be convicted if she stole independently of her co-accused, that is to say, otherwise than as part of a joint enterprise, and he relied on *R. v. Scaramanga* (1). That case decided, to quote the passage relied on, that—

"... except where provided by statute, when two persons are jointly charged with one offence judgment cannot stand against both of them on a finding that an offence has been committed by each independently."

He also submitted that s. 6 (3) of the Criminal Law Act 1967 had no application to the facts of this case. Finally he submitted that it was not apparent whether the jury had found that: (i) the appellant stole one pair of tights independently of her co-accused; or (ii) the two girls jointly stole one pair; or (iii) two pairs were stolen in a joint enterprise, each girl stealing one pair.

Counsel for the Crown agreed that s. 6 (3) of the Criminal Law Act 1967 had no application. The subsection provides that—

"Where, on a person's trial on indictment ... the jury find him not guilty of the offence specifically charged in the indictment, but the allegations in the indictment amount to or include (expressly or by implication) an allegation of another offence falling within the jurisdiction of the court of trial, the jury may find him guilty of that other offence or of an offence of which he could be found guilty on an indictment specifically charging that other offence."

(1) [1963] 2 All E.R. 852 at p. 856; [1963] 2 Q.B. 807 at p. 814.

A   The scope of this subsection was recently considered by this court in *R.* v. *Woods* (2) and it was said that—

"No court should be encouraged to cast around to see whether somehow or other the words of the indictment can be found to contain by some arguable implication the seeds of some other offence."

B   The application of this principle to the present case does not arise because the jury failed to find the appellant not guilty of the offence charged in the indictment and the essential prerequisite for the operation of the section is therefore absent. Counsel for the Crown further submitted that *R.* v. *Scaramanga* (3) had no application because Miss Overy pleaded guilty to stealing jointly with the appellant and accordingly there was no " finding " that an offence had been committed by each independently. Any finding was limited to the fact that

C   the appellant stole independently. The scope of that decision should not, he submitted, be extended.

In our judgment the application of the principle which formed the basis of the decision in *R.* v. *Scaramanga* (3) does not depend on whether one accused pleaded guilty and there was in consequence no " finding " in relation to that accused in the sense of a verdict by a jury. The principle is wider. It is clear

D   law that if a person is accused of stealing two articles, he can be convicted if it be proved that he stole one only. It is also clear that if two persons are accused of stealing jointly one or other or both may be convicted of that joint stealing. Alternatively, either but not both could be convicted of stealing independently, or each may be convicted of stealing jointly. In each of these cases the essential

E   feature is that one offence is charged and one offence is proved. *R.* v. *Scaramanga* (3) and the other decisions therein cited all proceed on the basis that in the absence of statutory provisions, such as s. 44 (5) of the Larceny Act 1916, if only one offence is charged it is not open to the court or jury to find two offences proved. In the present case the verdict of the jury is at least capable of the interpretation that a different offence was committed by the appellant from that

F   to which Miss Overy pleaded guilty. Only one offence was charged and it was not open to the jury to find that a second offence was committed.

We have considered whether the proviso to s. 2 (1) of the Criminal Appeal Act 1968, should be applied. A similar problem arose in *R.* v. *Scaramanga* (3) where, as here, there had been a technical error and no miscarriage of justice had occurred. Lord Parker, C.J., giving the judgment of the Court of Criminal Appeal said (4):

G   " No doubt one of the objects of the proviso [to s. 4 (1) of the Criminal Appeal Act 1907] was to prevent the quashing of a conviction on a mere technicality provided, . . . that no embarrassment or prejudice to the defendant was caused thereby . . . We, however, know of no case in which the court has applied the proviso for the purpose of, in effect, substituting another verdict. The only power in this court to substitute a verdict is that contained in s. 5 (2) of the Act of 1907, which power is limited to a case

H   in which the jury could ' on the indictment ' have found the defendant guilty of some other offence."

In the context of the summing-up we consider that the clerk of the court, in asking the jury whether they found the appellant guilty of stealing two pairs of tights or one pair of tights, must be taken to have been asking whether they

I   found that she had stolen jointly or independently and that the answer indicated an independent theft. The situation is thus the same as in *R.* v. *Scaramanga* (3). The wording of the proviso to s. 2 (1) of the Act of 1968 is the same as that of s. 4 (1) of the Act of 1907 save that it refers to " no miscarriage of justice " instead of " no substantial miscarriage of justice ", an amendment first made by the Criminal Appeal Act 1966. The power to substitute a conviction of an

---

(2) [1968] 3 All E.R. 709 at p. 711; [1968] 3 W.L.R. 1192 at p. 1195.
(3) [1963] 2 All E.R. 852; [1963] 2 Q.B. 807.
(4) [1963] 2 All E.R. at p. 856; [1963] 2 Q.B. at p. 815.

alternative offence is now contained in s. 3 (1) of the Act of 1968, the wording **A**
of which differs from that of s. 5 (2) of the Act of 1907, but the power is still
limited to cases in which " the jury could on the indictment have found him
guilty of some other offence ".   In the circumstances this court felt constrained,
for the reasons and with the same reluctance as was expressed by LORD PARKER,
C.J., in *R.* v. *Scaramanga* (6) to quash the appellant's conviction.

Appeal allowed.   Conviction quashed. **B**

Solicitors: *Registrar of Criminal Appeals* (for the appellant); *Solicitor Metropolitan Police* (for the Crown).

[*Reported by* N. P. METCALFE, ESQ., *Barrister-at-Law.*]

C

BRITISH OXYGEN CO., LTD. *v.* BOARD OF TRADE.

[COURT OF APPEAL, CIVIL DIVISION (Harman, Russell and Karminski, L.JJ.),
January 20, 21, 22, 23, 24, February 14, 1969.]

*Trade—Investment grants—Machinery and plant—Gas manufacturers—Trans-
    porters and cylinders used for the sale and delivery of gas—Articulated*   **D**
    *vehicles—Hydrogen trailer, and individual gas cylinders, which were left
    with consumers for the gas to be drawn off—Whether capital expenditure on
    provision of such new equipment for distributive purposes or storage purposes
    was eligible for investment grant—Discretion of Board of Trade over approval
    of capital expenditure—Low cost of individual items not by itself a sufficient
    ground for withholding investment grant when aggregate expenditure was*   **E**
    substantial—Industrial Development Act 1966 (c. 34), *s.* 1 (1), (2) (*a*), (3)
    (*b*) (*c*), *s.* 13 (1).

A company manufactured, delivered and sold industrial and medical
gases that required special containers. The gases in liquid form had to be kept
at very low temperatures, and those in gaseous form, particularly hydrogen,
had to be kept at high pressures. To effect delivery of the gases the company   **F**
had three kinds of transporter and, in addition, the company used very
many individual cylinders in which it delivered gas to its customers who
retained the cylinders while using the gas.   One type of transporter was a
large tanker assembly, comprising a tractor and a half trailer. The tractor
was a four-wheeled vehicle and was bought by the company from suppliers.
The half trailer included an insulated tank for containing gas at low   **G**
temperature, a pump for pumping the gas into customers' storage tanks,
controls, and other incidental equipment.   When used for transport the
tractor and half trailer were always united. The second kind of transporter
equipment was the small tanker assembly, which served a similar purpose
to the large assembly. The insulated tank, pumping equipment and other
associated items on the small tanker assembly were not, however, detachable   **H**
from the chassis of the vehicle, which was not an articulated vehicle. The
third kind of equipment was a hydrogen trailer assembly, comprising a
tractor, which the company bought from outside suppliers, and a half
trailer. The half trailer had only two wheels at the rear. Nine steel cylinders
were assembled on the half trailer, capable of containing hydrogen under
pressure of about 1½ tons to the square inch. The half trailer was frequently   **I**
detached from the tractor and left detached at a customer's premises, the
customer drawing gas from the cylinders as required. The cylinders were
not usually detached from the trailer. Gas from the cylinders could, however, be delivered from the half trailer into a customer's own storage
cylinders when delivery was made. The individual gas cylinders, which
were plant for use in the company's business, were bought by the company
for about £20 each.   In the year ending September 1966, the company
expended £1,707,000 on such cylinders. It was the general policy in the

A   government department (the Board of Trade) administering investment grants not to approve for grant expenditure on items of equipment costing individually less than £25. In an action by the company against the Board of Trade the trial judge made declarations that expenditure on the provision of (i) a new large tanker assembly, or (ii) a new small tanker assembly did not qualify for investment grant under the Industrial Development Act 1966,

B   s. 1*, and that expenditure on the provision of (iii) a new hydrogen trailer assembly, or (iv) a new individual gas cylinder was eligible for such investment grant. The trial judge also made declarations: (v) that the Board of Trade was not entitled to decline to make a grant under the Act towards bulk capital expenditure on new individual gas cylinders on the sole ground that each cylinder cost less than £25; and (vi) that in any case in which

C   the Board of Trade had approved capital expenditure for the purpose of s. 1 (1) of the Act, the Board had no further discretion to refuse to make the grant. On appeal by the Board and cross-appeal by the company,

     Held: (i) the small tanker assembly, the large tanker assembly and the hydrogen trailer assembly were each a " vehicle " which carried a load of gas in addition to its machinery or plant, and so none of them were

D   " machinery or plant " as defined by s. 13 (1)† of the Act; accordingly, expenditure on the provision of these assemblies was not eligible for investment grant (see p. 23, letters F and G, p. 26, letters E to G, and p. 28, letter G, post).

     (ii) since the gas was only packed into the individual cylinders after it had been made, such cylinders were not used for a process for or incidental to

E   " the making of " the gas within the meaning of s. 1 (2) (*a*) of the Act; since

---

* Section 1 of the Industrial Development Act 1966, so far as relevant provides: " (1) Subject to the provisions of this section, the Board of Trade ... may make to any person carrying on a business in Great Britain a grant towards approved capital expenditure incurred by that person in providing new machinery or plant for use in Great Britain—(*a*) for carrying on a qualifying industrial process in the course of that

F   business; (*b*) for carrying on in the course of that business scientific research relating to a qualifying industrial process whether carried on in the course of that business or not.

     " (2) For the purposes of this section a qualifying industrial process is a process for or incidental to any of the following purposes, that is to say—(*a*) the making of any article; ..."

     " (3) For the purposes of this section—

     " (*a*) the repair or maintenance in the course of a business of an article which is used

G   in the course of that businesss for carrying on a process for or incidental to any of the purposes mentioned in subsection (2) of this section;

     " (*b*) the storage in the course of a business of anything which is to be used in the course of that business for carrying on any such process or which is to be or has been subjected to, or has resulted from, any such process carried on in the course of that business; and

     " (*c*) the packing in the course of a business of anything which is to be or has been subjected to, or has resulted from, any such process carried on in the course of that

H   business,

shall each be treated as a process incidental to that purpose, but, save as aforesaid, repair, maintenance, storage or packing shall not be treated as a process incidental to any of the purposes mentioned in subsection (2) of this section ...

     " (6) Subject to any order under section 7 of this Act, the amount of any grant under this section shall be twenty per cent. of the expenditure in respect of which it is made, except that it shall be forty per cent. of the said expenditure so far as it qualifies as

I   development area expenditure in accordance with Schedule 1 to this Act."

     † Section 13 (1) contains, inter alia, the following definitions:

     " ' approved capital expenditure ' in relation to any grant means expenditure appearing to the Board to be of a capital nature and approved by [the Board] for the purposes of the grant;

     " ' article ' means an article of any description (including any means of transport) and includes part of an article;

     " ' machinery or plant ' includes part of any machinery or plant but does not include a computer, ship or aircraft or any vehicle except—(*a*) a vehicle constructed or adapted for the conveyance of a machine incorporated in or permanently attached to it and of no other load except articles used for the purposes of the machine; ..."

these cylinders were designed for convenience of sale and delivery and for A
use by customers of the gas they had bought, they were not provided for
use in a process of storage of gas in the course of the company's business
within the meaning of s. 1 (3) (*b*); further (KARMINSKI, L.J., dissenting)
since these cylinders were plant or articles *in* which the gas was packed,
and not plant or articles *with* which the process of packing into a container
was carried out, they were not used for " the packing . . . of " the gas B
within the meaning of s. 1 (3) (*c*); accordingly expenditure on the provision
of these cylinders was not eligible for investment grant (see p. 24, letters
A, D and H, p. 26, letter H, p. 28, letter H, and p. 28, letter I, to p. 29,
letter A, post).

(iii) so long as it considered an application for grant properly the Board
of Trade could, in its discretion, decline to make a grant on the sole ground C
that each individual cylinder cost less than £25, and the trial judge's declaration to the contrary should be set aside (see p. 25, letter C, p. 27, letter E,
and p. 29, letter C, post).

(iv) declaration (vi) was wrongly made, and should be struck out, because
it dealt with a hypothetical question which did not arise in the case before
the court (see p. 24, letter I, p. 27, letter H, and p. 29, letter D, post). D

Decision of BUCKLEY, J. ([1968] 2 All E. R. 177) affirmed as to the large
and small tanker assemblies, reversed on all the other matters set out above.

[As to investment grants, see SUPPLEMENT to 38 HALSBURY'S LAWS (3rd
Edn.) para. 240A.

For the Industrial Development Act 1966, s. 1, s. 13, see 46 HALSBURY'S
STATUTES (2nd Edn.) 820, 832.] E

Cases referred to:

R. v. *Port of London Authority, Ex p. Kynoch, Ltd.*, [1919] 1 K.B. 176; 88
      L.J.K.B. 553; 120 L.T. 177; 83 J.P. 41; 16 Digest (Repl.) 327, *1056*.
Schmidt v. *Secretary of State for Home Affairs*, [1969] 1 All E.R. 904; [1969]
      2 W.L.R. 337.
F

Appeal and cross-appeal.

British Oxygen Co., Ltd. applied by originating summons, dated 7th July 1967,
for the determination of questions arising on the interpretation and effect of
Part 1 of the Industrial Development Act 1966, including the question whether
on the true construction of the Industrial Development Act 1966: (a) the tank
and pump portions of gas tankers; and (b) the hydrogen gas trailer, constituted G
" machinery or plant " or " part of any machinery or plant " within the meaning
of s. 13 (1) of the Act of 1966. The company also claimed declarations that
expenditure on the tank and pump portions of the gas tankers, the hydrogen
gas trailer and the metal cylinder was capable of being approved capital expenditure within the meaning of s. 1 (1) and s. 13 of the Act of 1966 notwithstanding
that each was a form of container or served a distributive function; that the H
Board of Trade was not entitled to decline to make a grant towards bulk capital
expenditure on the metal cylinders on the sole ground that each cylinder cost
less than £25.

On the trial of the action BUCKLEY, J., after delivering a reserved written
judgment on 10th April 1968, reported [1968] 2 All E.R. 177, made declarations,
inter alia, that: (i) both the small tanker assembly and the large tanker assembly I
were " vehicles ", and not " machinery or plant " within the meaning of Part 1
of the Industrial Development Act 1966; (ii) the hydrogen gas trailer assembly
was " machinery or plant " within that meaning; (iv) the hydrogen gas trailer
assemblies and the individual gas cylinders were each provided for carrying
on a qualifying industrial process within the meaning of s. 1 (1) of the Act;
(v) the Board of Trade was not entitled to decline to make a grant towards the
capital expenditure on new individual gas cylinders on the sole ground that
each cylinder costs less than £25; (vi) that in any case in which the Board of

A   Trade had already, in its discretion, approved capital expenditure for the purpose of an investment grant under Part 1 of the Act the Board had no further discretion to refuse to make such a grant in respect of that expenditure. The facts are set out in the judgment of RUSSELL, L.J.

The Board of Trade now appealed against declarations (ii), (iv), (v) and (vi); the company cross-apppealed against declaration (i).

B   *M. Finer, Q.C.*, and *J. P. Warner* for the Board of Trade.
J. A. Brightman, Q.C., and *P. E. Whitworth* for the company.

Cur. adv. vult.

14th February.   The following judgments were read.

RUSSELL, L.J., read the first judgment at the request of HARMAN, L.J.
C   This case raises questions of some complication on the construction of Part I of the Industrial Development Act 1966, which (in very broad terms) substitutes for a system of investment allowance against profits chargeable to tax, a system of grants in the discretion of the Board of Trade in respect of new productive machinery or plant acquired for use in the course of a business in Great Britain. The principal questions for decision are whether the Board of Trade has power
D   under the Act to approve, for the purposes of grant, expenditure by the plaintiffs, the British Oxygen Co., Ltd., on the provision for use in its business of certain machinery or plant, should the Board of Trade, in its discretion, think fit so to approve. It appears likely that even if there is such power the Board of Trade will not exercise it, but the company is anxious to establish that the Board of Trade, which considers that it has no such power under the statute, should not
E   be hampered by a view which the company says is erroneous.

Section 1 (1) refers to expenditure incurred by the company in providing new machinery or plant for use for carrying on a qualifying industrial process in the course of its business. The expenditure must be " approved capital expenditure ", which is defined as meaning expenditure appearing to the Board of Trade to be of a capital nature and approved by the Board of Trade for the
F   purposes of grant; herein lies a discretion to approve or not expenditure of such a character as the statute qualifies for approval. By s. 1 (2) " A qualifying industrial process " is (for present purposes) a process for the purpose of the making of any article or a process incidental to the purpose of the making of any article. It is convenient to state at once that the article in question is gas or different gases. By s. 1 (3) certain matters are required to be treated as a
G   process incidental to the purpose of the making of gas: one is "the storage " in the course of that business of anything which (so far as now material) has resulted from any process, carried on in the course of that business, for or incidental to the purpose of making gas; and here of course that which has resulted is the gas itself. The other matter which is required to be treated as a process incidental to the purpose of making gas is " the packing " in the course
H   of that business of anything which (so far as now material) has resulted from any process, carried out in the course of that business, for or incidental to the purpose of making gas: that is to say again the gas. I remark at this stage that under sub-s. (3) we are, therefore, concerned with new plant and machinery provided for use for carrying out in the course of the company's business the incidental process of the storage of gas or of the packing of gas. Finally, " machinery and plant " has a restrictive definition under s. 13 (1): it is defined
I   as including any part of any machinery or plant but as not including—

"... any vehicle—except (a) a vehicle constructed or adapted for the conveyance of a machine incorporated in or permanently attached to it and of no other load except articles used for the purposes of the machine ..."

the rest of the definition is not presently relevant.

We are concerned with expenditure by the company in connection with the provision for use in their business of what would ordinarily come under a description of machinery or plant under four heads:

(i) *Small tanker assemblies.* These consist of (a) lorry chassis and cab costing   **A**
£2,550, and (b) a vacuum insulated tank with pumping unit, controls, valves,
pipework, and pressure-raising coil, costing £11,300. The power source for the
alternator in the pumping unit is driven by the engine in the chassis. The whole
makes one permanent assembly—a road tanker. The tank is filled by the company
with gas made by the company in liquid (refrigerated) form and delivered by
the assembly to containers at the premises of the customers, the pumping unit   **B**
serving to overcome such pressure as may exist in those containers. These
gases include nitrogen, oxygen, argon and so on, but not hydrogen.

(ii) *Large tanker assemblies.* These are articulated assemblies. They consist
of a tractor costing £4,000: a running gear consisting of an axle and wheels
to the rear with coupling readily attached to and detachable from the tractor,
costing £1,100: and items costing £15,600 similar to those under heading (i) (b)   **C**
above, mounted on the running gear as a permanent assembly integral with the
running gear. The function of the whole assembly is the same as that of the
small tanker assembly. The only difference between the small and large tanker
assemblies is that the latter being articulated, the tractor is readily severable
from the rest which, with the aid of legs lowered at the front, can stand on its
own. In theory, discharge from the latter could take place with an alternative   **D**
source of power for the alternator, but there is no evidence that this was ever
done.

(iii) *Hydrogen trailer assemblies.* These consist of: (a) a trailer, attachable to
and detachable from a tractor, consisting of a flat with rear wheels costing £620;
(b) nine high-pressure cylinders between fore and aft bulkheads banked together
with valves and so forth, the whole permanently attached to the trailer, except   **E**
for statutory testing and maintenance, costing £6,020. The main distinction
between this and items (i) and (ii) is that this relates to hydrogen: the hydrogen
is not made in refrigerated liquid form but is delivered in these banks of cylinders
to customers in gaseous form compressed to a pressure of 224 atmospheres:
this pressure makes it unnecessary to have any pumping system (or, therefore,
dependence on the engine of the prime mover of the trailer assembly) for delivery   **F**
to the customer's container. Indeed, the hydrogen trailer assembly may be left
at the customer's premises, separate from the prime mover, to discharge the
hydrogen either into the customer's storage container or into his direct user
pipeline or a combination of both.

(iv) *Individual gas cylinders.* These are individual gas cylinders which are
filled with various gases at varying pressures higher than atmospheric pressure   **G**
and delivered in that form to customers who use the contents direct into their
pipelines and return them for exchange for fresh ones when nearly exhausted.
They remain the property of the company, who deliver and collect them as mere
lorry-loads. These cylinders are bought by the company at an average cost of
about £20 each. The company's purchases of them are very large—for example,
over £1,500,000 in the year September 1965-66.   **H**

The first question is what in respect of items (i) to (iii) inclusive, is the impact
of the definition of " machinery and plant ". I take item (i) first. It is argued
that those parts of the assembly other than the chassis and cab are plant and
machinery and not a vehicle. It is said that it is unlikely that such important
and expensive plant should be outside the contemplation of the Act just because
it is made mobile, and that its attachment to or incorporation with the chassis   **I**
and cab does not deprive it of its character or quality of plant so as to down-
grade it (so to speak) to being a part of a vehicle. Further it was argued that when
the expenditure was incurred separately on the " plant " part of the assembly,
it was not assembled with the chassis and cab and could not be described as a
vehicle. The language of s. 13 (1) para. (a) of the definition of " machinery and
plant " was relied on in this connection. It was said that in defining this exception from an exception the language selected drew a distinction in any case
covered by it of certain mobile machines between the vehicle that conveyed

A the machine which was incorporated in or permanently attached to " it ", that is to say the vehicle, and the machine which was " load " conveyed by the vehicle—see the words " no *other* load " .

For the Board of Trade it was, however, argued that there was no warrant for separating into parts what was in the ordinary use of language plainly a vehicle. The " plant " part of the assembly when separately acquired or provided was, in

B any event, not provided *at that stage* and as such for use in the business but for use by assembling it with the chassis and cab, so that the whole assembly as such might be provided for use in the business; and what of the case when the whole assembly was bought as such by a claimant? It was said that it was altogether too refined an argument to rely on the drafting of a convenient way of describing a particular type of mobile machinery—for example a mobile crane—in para. (*a*)

C in order to show that a vehicle was not a vehicle: it was not easy (it was said) to see how the draftsman could readily have described the limited type of mobile machinery embraced by para. (*a*) without using language that suggested a dichotomy between vehicle and machine. If, it was said, assemblies such as no. (i) (the small tanker) were not wholly a vehicle it would be astonishing that Parliament had left in uncertainty and for argument countless vehicles in industry that

D might or might not be considered to be mobile plant or plant or machinery conveyed by (albeit integral in assembly with) a mobile chassis. Moreover (it was said) the construction put on para. (*a*) by the company produces the improbably intended outcome that it would bring in for grant a new vehicle part to which an old crane was attached: and in the case of a totally new assembly it means that the paragraph was designed merely to bring in the vehicle part,

E assuming the machine part to be already within grant; whereas the true purpose of the paragraph was to bring into grant the whole new assembly notwithstanding that it is a vehicle.

Of these arguments I prefer those advanced by the Board of Trade and I am in agreement with the learned judge (1) in holding that no part of the no. (i) assembly is machinery or plant as defined on the ground that the whole of it is a

F vehicle. Nor can it come within the exception of para. (*a*) of the definition of machinery or plant because the whole is designed to carry also a load consisting of gas.

For the same reasons I would exclude from possibly eligible machinery or plant all parts of the trailer assembly no. (ii)—the big tanker.

The learned judge (1) was however prepared to treat the hydrogen trailer assem-

G bly differently, his ground being fundamentally that the trailer could and sometimes did fulfil its function of delivering hydrogen to the customer's container or pipeline without any association with or dependence on (once it reached the customer's intake point) the tractor that towed it. I am not able to regard this as a valid distinction. Once the point is reached when it is concluded that preponderance in make-up or cost of the " plant " aspect of an assembly designed

H to move along roads is not the solution of the question, I cannot see that the hydrogen trailer assembly is any the less a vehicle in all its parts than are items nos. (i) and (ii).

This brings me to the fourth item—the individual cylinders—about which there is plainly no problem arising from the exception of " vehicles ". These cylinders are plainly plant for use in the company's business, and it is not suggested that

I the Board of Trade would regard expenditure on their provision as other than of a capital nature. Does the expenditure on their acquisition come within s. 1 (2) (taken alone) as being expenditure on new plant for use in the company's business for carrying out a process incidental to the purpose of making gas? It is, of course, essential to a large aspect of that business that the company should buy these cylinders in order therein to deliver their gas products to their customers; and in one sense sale, transport and delivery are incidental to the making which, without

(1) [1968] 2 All E.R. 177; [1969] Ch. 57.

this, would be an academic exercise—indeed one that would soon come to an end   A
for lack of outlet. But in my judgment sub-s. (3) makes it plain that any process
incidental to the making of gas is not under sub-s. (2) alone something that
happens after the making is completed: sub-s. (3) in dealing with storage and
packing refers to matters just as incidental (in the wider sense) to the making as
is transport and delivery, and in dealing with processes following on the making
markedly stops short in point of time of transport and delivery to customers. I   B
therefore conclude that no claim can be put forward in respect of these cylinders
under s. 1 (2) taken alone.

I turn next to s. 1 (3)—" storage " or " packing ". It is claimed by the company
that expenditure in the purchase of these cylinders is expenditure in the provision
of plant for use for carrying on in the course of its business the incidental process
of the storage or the packing of the gas. In connection with storage it is to be   C
noticed that the undisputed evidence of the company is that " very large quantities of the gases produced by the company are stored under pressure " in these
cylinders. This evidence cannot, however, in my judgment, be at all conclusive
on this point. It depends on the sense in which " stored " is used in that sentence,
and the sense in which " storage " is treated as an incidental process in the statute.

These cylinders are essential containers of the gas designed for convenience of   D
sale and delivery to customers and use by them of the gas that they have bought.
It does not seem to me at all an apt application of s. 1 (3) to hold that these cylinders are provided for use in a process of the storage of gas in the company's
business. When the company wish to store the gas they produce they assuredly
do not do so in this extravagant fashion; their storage plant would be a very
different type of gasholder. That which is kept in these cylinders is ready for   E
delivery to the customer.   It would, I think, be a misuse of language to say of an
area of the factory in which these cylinders were being filled with gas that it was
an area in which the process of storage was being carried out. When a cylinder
was being filled from a gasholder the proper description of the operation or
process would not be storage of the gas but rather the taking of the gas out of
storage and into a container suitable for delivery to the customer. The fact that   F
a large stock of filled cylinders has to be stored or stacked awaiting purchase and
delivery, and no doubt disposed on racks suitable for the purpose by cranes or
other appropriate machinery, does not make the filling of the cylinders a process
of storage: though the racks and the appropriate machinery would be plant for
use in the process of storage. In my view the Board of Trade were correct in this
sense in saying that mere containers were not plant used in the process of storage.   G

Is the expenditure on the acquisition of a cylinder expenditure incurred in
providing plant for carrying on the incidental industrial process of packing?
The cylinder is undoubtedly an article in which the gas is packed: it is the container essential to the convenient delivery of the gas to the customer. But
it seems to me that the question to be asked is not whether there is plant or an article
in which the product is packed, but whether there is plant *with* which the process   H
of packing into a container is carried out. The process of packing an article when
made is the process of putting it into containers appropriate for its delivery to the
customer, and the subsection, in my view, envisages only machinery or plant
used for putting the article into its container and not the container itself—for
example, a compressor device.

In the result, therefore, declaration no. (i) in the order of BUCKLEY, J. (2),   I
stands. Declaration no. (ii) should be varied so as to state that the hydrogen gas
trailer assembly is also a vehicle and not machinery or plant. Declaration no. (iv)
should be varied by deleting the reference to the hydrogen trailer and inserting
the word " not " before the word " provided ".

Declaration no. (vi) relates and always related to a purely hypothetical question
not arising between the parties. It should not, in my judgment, have been made
in these proceedings and should be deleted. The hypothetical question is whether,

(2) [1968] 2 All E.R. 177; [1969] Ch. 57.

A in any case in which the Board of Trade has already in [its] discretion approved capital expenditure for the purpose of the grant, it has a further discretion whether to make the actual grant by force of the words " *may* make . . . a grant towards approved capital expenditure " in s. 1 (1)—that is to say, can the Board after approval change its mind. This question may arise in some case but does not arise here and there was never any ground for supposing that it might. In case **B** the deletion of declaration no. (vi) should be thought to decide the point in the opposite sense, our order should be on these lines: " This court being of the opinion that the question answered by declaration no. (vi) is not proper to be determined in these proceedings, strike out that declaration ".

Finally there is declaration no. (v), which is in the form asked for by the summons and is, in my judgment, plainly wrong in law and must be set aside. Suppose **C** an application to be made for a grant in respect of the bulk purchase of cylinders, and suppose the Board of Trade entertains and considers the application together with any material advanced by the company in support of it, and then declines to approve the expenditure for grant purposes on the sole ground that each cylinder costs less than £25, not considering that there are sufficient grounds for making an exception to the general policy about items costing under £25, quite plainly **D** this course of action is lawfully open to the Board of Trade in the exercise of the discretion conferred by the statute.   But the declaration as sought and as made says the contrary. It is suggested that really what is sought is a declaration that the Board of Trade is not entitled to refuse to *consider* an application on the sole ground of the £25 general policy: but that is not what was sought and the correspondence in no way, to my mind, shows that that was the attitude of the **E** Board of Trade or would have been the attitude had an application for grant been made. The attitude was expressly disclaimed in this court and had the declaration sought been in the other form I have no doubt that evidence would have been filed below with a similar disclaimer. In my judgment, therefore, declaration no. (v) should also be struck out.

I would allow the appeal and dismiss the cross-appeal in the manner indicated.

F   **KARMINSKI, L.J.:** The general purpose of the Industrial Development Act 1966, was to make possible grants out of public funds towards expenditure on capital assets in industry. It replaced the system of investment allowances against tax under earlier Finance Acts, and laid down provisions under which such capital expenditure could qualify for a grant. The duty of examining applications and adjudicating on them was laid on the Board of Trade, who had **G** to be satisfied first that the expenditure was of a capital nature. If so satisfied, the Board of Trade was then empowered to approve an application for the making of a grant.

Section 1 of the Act provided that the expenditure should be (inter alia) for carrying on a qualified industrial process, which was defined as a process for or incidental to a number of purposes, including the making of any article. Under **H** s. 1 (3) were set out certain processes which should be treated as a process incidental to the purpose, but laid down that save as defined in this subsection, repair, maintenance, storage or packing should not be so treated.

The applicants for an investment grant in this appeal are the British Oxygen Co., Ltd., who manufacture gases of various kinds and in very large quantities. These gases are used in many kinds of industry, and also for medical and domestic **I** purposes. Some gases so produced are left in liquid form at low temperatures, some are compressed in gaseous form in cylinders at high or very high pressures. Special kinds of tankers and machinery are required to effect delivery of the various gases. The nature of these means of conveyance and delivery is of importance in reaching a conclusion here.

By s. 13 of the Act a number of definitions are laid down. One of them deals with " machinery or plant " and excludes any vehicle except when it is constructed or adapted for the conveyance of a machine incorporated in or permanently attached to it and of no other load except articles used for the purposes

of the machine. It was accepted during argument that a mobile crane would   A
qualify as an excepted vehicle under this description.

In the present case there are three classes of gas transporters which have to be
considered. The first two are in essence tankers—one articulated, one smaller
and not articulated. Both have pumps, motors to drive the pumps, pressure-
raising coils, meters, valves and controls. In both tankers the cost of the motive
and chassis parts is a relatively small proportion of the cost of the whole unit.   B
The third class is the hydrogen trailer assembly, where the trailer containing the
hydrogen is commonly left at the customer's works by itself until its contents have
been used up.

BUCKLEY, J. (3), distinguished the hydrogen trailer from the tankers, holding
that while the tankers were vehicles within the meaning of s. 13, the trailer was
not. The company contend that none of the three classes should be treated as   C
vehicles; the Board of Trade contend that there can be no valid distinction
between them, and that all three should be treated as vehicles.

The word " vehicle " does not seem capable of any precise definition. We were
asked to consider the various meanings set out at length in the OXFORD ENGLISH
DICTIONARY, and to draw our conclusions from past and present usage of the
word. Although I gratefully acknowledge its philological interest, I found little   D
help from the OXFORD ENGLISH DICTIONARY in attributing any precise meaning
to the term " vehicle " for the purpose of construing this statute. BUCKLEY, J. (3),
after a careful analysis of the relevant facts, held that the trailer constituted a
distinct piece of equipment, describing it as a load moved by and on its own
tractor, and not capable of being appropriately described as a vehicle.

After a full consideration of BUCKLEY, J.'s (3) analysis of the facts, I am unable   E
to accept his conclusion as to the trailer. I do not myself think that there is a
real or fundamental difference between the tankers and the trailer. In neither
class can I find a real distinction between the components which would allow me
to treat them as distinct objects. In both classes the component parts, though
severable, have been built into one composite unit. It is true that the components
can in the cases of the articulated tanker and of the hydrogen trailer be separated   F
for various purposes, including repairs and parking. But using the word " vehicle "
in what I believe to be the general present-day sense, I have come to the conclusion
that both the tankers and the hydrogen trailer are vehicles within the meaning of
the Act. It follows, therefore, that in my view the Board of Trade succeed on their
first ground.

There remains the question of the small independent cylinders which are used   G
in very large quantities by the company. On the evidence, as I understand it,
various kinds of gas at the company factories are stored in large gasholders
whence it is drawn off under pressure into the smaller metal cylinders. These
cylinders, which are made by a subsidiary of the company, are sent to customers
as required for use in a wide variety of industrial and other purposes. It is difficult
to envisage any other form of container for a gas under pressure. On the whole,   H
though with some doubt, I have come to the conclusion that the small cylinders
are not a form of storage; but without any doubt I find that these cylinders
are an essential element in the process of packing. The nature of the packing
must relate to the object packed. Some delicate objects, like glass, need careful
protective packing. Beer can be packed in barrels or bottles or in metal containers.
Many raw materials, such as coal or sugar-beet, probably require no packing   I
at all to protect or conserve them. But we are dealing here with gas under
pressure. Presumably, if not packed in a suitable and strong container like a
cylinder, it will escape and disappear. In my view, the process of packing gas
cannot be limited to putting the gas into the cylinder, but must extend to the
making or acquisition of the cylinder itself.

The average cost of the cylinder is rather under £20 each, but for the year ending

_____

(3) [1968] 2 All E.R. 177; [1969] Ch. 57.

A 30th September 1966, £1,707,000 was expended on the purchase of cylinders; and for the three years ending 30th September 1968, the expenditure on cylinders will exceed £4,000,000. The Board of Trade has decided as a matter of policy that applications for grants of under £25 for single items would fail to qualify. It is not difficult to appreciate that the Board of Trade were anxious to avoid a very large number of applications for small items, since such applications by

B mere numbers might make the scheme as a whole quite unworkable.   Matters of general policy laid down in this way would no doubt also help the advisory committees set up under s. 11 of the Act. I agree with BUCKLEY, J. (4), that the question of approving a grant in whole or in part is left to the discretion of the Board of Trade. That discretion must be exercised impartially and with proper regard to the terms and policy of the Act, and the facts disclosed in the application.

C It must not be exercised capriciously or arbitrarily.

In the course of a long correspondence between the company and the Board of Trade, discussing the objects and administration of the Act, the Board of Trade made clear what their policy was. On 24th October 1967, after the present proceedings had commenced and the company had filed evidence, the Board of Trade wrote that even if the company persuaded the court on eligibility, the Board of

D Trade would exercise their discretion against a grant. At that stage no formal application had in fact been made by the company.

I agree with BUCKLEY, J. (4), that had the Board of Trade decided in advance not to consider an application in respect of the cylinders on the sole ground that they cost less than £25 each, that would have been not an exercise of discretion but an abrogation of it. In this particular case the Board of Trade would certainly

E have to consider the very large total expenditure involved in purchasing cylinders before deciding whether or not in the exercise of their discretion to adhere to the £25 policy. But that position had not been reached at the date of the issue of the summons. As a matter of law there is nothing to prevent the Board of Trade adopting or publishing such a policy, providing that it is ready to consider reasons in suitable cases for departing from that policy: see *R.* v. *Port of London Authority,*

F *Ex p. Kynoch, Ltd.* (5) and *Schmidt* v. *Secretary of State for Home Affairs* (6).

I do not think that in the present case the Board of Trade, though they may seek to adhere to their policy decision, have closed the door on reconsidering the application on its merits in the exercise of their discretion. In my view declaration no. (v) is wrong and should be set aside.

Declaration no. (vi) was criticised by counsel for the Board of Trade on the

G ground that it has no point, since the question that it seeks to deal with has not yet arisen. He conceded that it could be dealt with by the court if and when it did arise. Defending this declaration, counsel for the company explained that it was designed to meet a situation where the Board of Trade might try to reserve some residual power to withhold a grant in their discretion after using their discretion in favour of approving a grant. Counsel for the company emphasised

H that the Act confers only one discretion. I would myself prefer to consider this question if and when it arises, and not in its present abstract form. In my view declaration no. (vi) should be struck out.

HARMAN, L.J.: In this case BUCKLEY, J. (4), by his order of 5th June 1968 made six declarations turning on the true construction of the Industrial Development Act 1966. Of these, the first which dealt with two types of gas

I conveyor, was in favour of the Board of Trade and the remainder were in favour of the company. These appeals cover the whole field of the order and are thus divided technically speaking into an appeal and a cross-appeal, but it is convenient for the purposes of this judgment to deal with all the questions together and in the same order in which they were dealt with by the learned judge (4).

---

(4) [1968] 2 All E.R. 177; [1969] Ch. 57.
(5) [1919] 1 K.B. 176 at p. 184.
(6) [1969] 1 All E.R. 904; [1969] 2 W.L.R. 337.

First, then, are what are called " large tanker assemblies ". The judge decided **A**
(7) that these were articulated vehicles and so properly came within the description of " any vehicle " to be found in s. 13 and were therefore not machinery or
plant within s. 1 of the Act. Before us it was contended that it was legitimate
to separate the vehicle into its component parts and to treat the strictly mobile
part as a vehicle and the rest as " the load ". This ingenious submission was
really based on three words in s. 13, " no other load ", which were said to show **B**
that a vehicle which carried a load even if incorporated with it, that is to say the
tank, could be treated as though the vehicle were separate from the tank. I am
unable to take this view: these are, as the judge said (7), ordinary articulated
vehicles. As used on the road, all parts are one and should be treated as a vehicle
notwithstanding the fact that it is possible, and is the practice in the company's
own works, to separate the two parts for convenience of storage. I would dismiss **C**
the cross-appeal on this point.

Secondly, the small tanker assemblies. There is no articulation in this case
and the tank portion and the running portion of this machine are one. The judge
had no hesitation (7) in treating these as vehicles; nor have I. The fact that the
company for its own purposes can and does buy the trailer part and makes the
tank part seems to me to be a long way from showing that when the two are **D**
incorporated as one machine the whole is not a vehicle. I would dismiss the
cross-appeal on this point.

Thirdly, the hydrogen tankers. The learned judge thought (8) that these were
not vehicles, chiefly, I think, because the trailer portion is for the convenience
of customers frequently detached from the motor portion and left at the customer's
works to be exhausted of gas at his convenience. The point taken before us was **E**
that the bank of cylinders which compose this machine being capable of with-
standing high pressures was in truth part of the plant incidental to the making
of the article, namely hydrogen gas, under high pressure and that this was an
incidental part of its manufacture. I do not think the evidence justified such a
conclusion. True, the article to be useful to the consumer must be delivered
to him under high pressure, but I see no evidence that the pressure was not pro- **F**
duced in the company's factory before the gas was transferred to the transporter.
I am of opinion that there is no substantial difference between this articulated
vehicle and the large tanker assemblies. Both are designed for the transport of
gas from works to customer and are, as it seems to me, vehicles used in the
transport of gas and, therefore, properly classed as vehicles. I would allow the
appeal on this point. **G**

Fourthly, the small gas cylinders (9). These are of course not vehicles and are
" machines or plant ". They are also within s. 1 " for use in Great Britain for
carrying on an industrial process ". The question is whether this process is a
qualifying one as incidental to the making of gas within s. 1 (2) (a). In my opinion
the cylinders fail to pass this test because they are used after the gas has been
made and are not incidental to its making. Are they then within sub-s. (3), which **H**
enlarges the word " incidental " in three respects? The process may be treated
as incidental if, for the present purposes, the cylinders are used for storage in the
course of the business of making the gas which has resulted from that process.
In my opinion the cylinders do not pass this test either. They are not, as I see
it, used for carrying on the storage of the gas. As I understand the facts, the gas
has already been stored under pressure on the company's premises and these **I**
cylinders are used as a means of transporting the gas to the consumer. It is true
that they are an essential link between manufacturer and consumer but they are
in my view a means of transport of a specialised kind and are not plant used for
storage.

There remains para. (3) (c), which is concerned with machinery for the packing

(7) [1968] 2 All E.R. at p. 183; [1969] Ch. at p. 72.
(8) [1968] 2 All E.R. at p. 184; [1969] Ch. at p. 72.
(9) See [1968] 2 All E.R. at p. 184; [1969] Ch. at p. 73.

A in the course of a business of anything which has resulted from a qualifying industrial process. I have felt some hesitation on this point but on the whole I prefer the
view of RUSSELL, L.J., that these cylinders are not plant for the packing of
the hydrogen. They may be the plant in which the gas is packed but are not the
plant used for packing it. That expression would refer to the machinery employed
in filling the cylinders and not to the cylinders themselves, which are once again
B the specialised containers whereby the article is transferred from manufacturer
to customer. I would allow the appeal on this point.

As to the fourth declaration made in the order, having regard to what I have
said about the hydrogen trailer and the metal cylinders, it follows that, in my view,
they were not provided for the use of a qualifying industrial process and the word
" not " needs to be inserted before the word " provided " in that declaration.

C As to declaration no. (v), I agree with RUSSELL, L.J., that this is wrong. The
plaintiffs did not ask, as they might have done by their amended summons, for a
declaration that the Board of Trade was not entitled to refuse to " consider " a
grant and that for which they asked cannot be accorded to them quite apart
from the vagueness of the word " bulk ".

As to declaration no. (vi), I agree that this is a hypothetical question and
D that we ought not to answer it and that this declaration should be struck out of
the order.

*Appeal allowed. Cross-appeal dismissed. Order accordingly. Leave to appeal to
the House of Lords on declarations (i), (ii), (iii) and (iv) granted.*

Solicitors: *Solicitor, Board of Trade; Stafford Clark & Co.* (for the company).

E   [*Reported by* HENRY SUMMERFIELD, ESQ., *Barrister-at-Law.*]

F   VYE *v.* VYE.

[PROBATE, DIVORCE AND ADMIRALTY DIVISION (Sir Jocelyn Simon, P., and Baker,
J.), June 18, 19, 1968.]

Magistrates—Procedure—Submission of no case to answer—Proper time to make.
The first and only time at which a submission of no case to answer can be
G made to justices is when all the evidence for the complainant has been
heard (see p. 31, letter I, to p. 32, letter A, and p. 33, letter I, *post*).

Dicta of SCRUTTON, GREER and SANKEY, L.JJ., in *Hobbs* v. *Tinling & Co.,
Ltd.*, *Hobbs* v. *Nottingham Journal, Ltd.* ([1929] All E.R. Rep. at pp. 43, 54,
58) applied.

Observations on the position which arises when a submission of no case to
H answer is made at the proper time.

[As to submission of no case to answer in divorce suits, see 12 HALSBURY'S
LAWS (3rd Edn.) 387, para. 852, and generally as to such a submission, see 3 *ibid.*,
pp. 70, 71, para. 106; and for cases on the subject, see DIGEST (Practice) 725,
726, *3161-3167*.]

I Cases referred to:
Alexander v. *Rayson*, [1936] 1 K.B. 169; [1935] All E.R. Rep. 185; 105 L.J.K.B.
148; 154 L.T. 205; 51 Digest (Repl.) 725, *3161*.
De Freville v. *Dill*, [1927] W.N. 133; 43 T.L.R. 431; 30 Digest (Repl.) 267, *314*.
Disher v. *Disher*, [1963] 3 All E.R. 933; [1965] P. 31; [1964] 2 W.L.R. 21;
Digest (Cont. Vol. A) 828, *6826b*.
Hobbs v. *Tinling & Co., Ltd.*, *Hobbs* v. *Nottingham Journal, Ltd.*, [1929] 2 K.B.
1; [1929] All E.R. Rep. 33; 98 L.J.K.B. 421; 141 L.T. 121; 32 Digest
(Repl.) 201, *2174*.

Holzer v. *Holzer* (*Morley intervening*), [1964] 3 All E.R. 989; [1964] 1 W.L.R.   A
        1478; Digest (Cont. Vol. B) 347, *636t.*
Practice Note, [1962] 1 All E.R. 448; 33 Digest (Repl.) 227, *614.*
Ramsden v. *Ramsden*, [1954] 2 All E.R. 623; [1954] 1 W.L.R. 1105; Digest
        (Cont. Vol. A) 827, *6826a.*
Storey v. *Storey*, [1960] 3 All E.R. 279; [1961] P. 63; [1960] 3 W.L.R. 653;
        Digest (Cont. Vol. A) 772, *4921bc.*   B
Wilson v. *Wilson*, [1958] 3 All E.R. 195; [1958] 1 W.L.R. 1090; Digest (Cont.
        Vol. A) 772, *4921bd.*

Appeal.

This was an appeal by the wife from a decision of the justices for the county
borough of Hastings on 25th October 1967, dismissing her complaints that
the husband had deserted her since 10th May 1967, and had wilfully neglected   C
to provide reasonable maintenance for her. The facts are set out in the judgment of
BAKER, J.

Adrianne Uziell-Hamilton for the wife.
R. A. Headridge for the husband.

   BAKER, J.: This is an appeal from a decision of the justices for the county   D
borough of Hastings, sitting at Hastings on 25th October 1967, when they dismissed the wife's complaints that the husband had deserted her since 10th May
1967, and had wilfully neglected to provide reasonable maintenance for her.
   The parties were married on Saturday 11th February 1967 at the Hastings
register office, the husband having been married before and having a child of six
years of age. Before I deal further with the facts, it is necessary to consider an   E
important matter. It appears from the record that, at the conclusion of the
evidence of the wife, counsel for the husband submitted that there was no evidence at all of matters of a grave and weighty nature; that there was nothing
more in this marriage than happens in very many cases—the wife desired to
return to her mother and did so after five days of marriage. She returned to the
matrimonial home at the request of the husband but, at the first opportunity and   F
as a result of the slightest of tiffs, again, on 10th May 1967, returned to her mother
and has remained apart from the husband ever since. There was no evidence at
all which justified the wife leaving the husband, there was no hitting of the wife,
no cruelty by the husband at all, and money had always been provided. Counsel
for the wife, we are told, and, as is clear from the record, objected that he had
another witness to call for the wife, namely, the wife's mother, who was in court   G
and prepared to give evidence. Nevertheless, the justices ruled at that stage that
the wife had " no case in law " and, I quote from their reasons, " further we were
convinced that any evidence that the wife's mother could give could not strengthen
or assist the wife's case ". Later, they state:

   " We appreciate, however, that a case should not be dismissed at this
   stage except in very exceptional circumstances but we were quite satisfied   H
   that in this case exceptional circumstances did exist. Indeed, in our view, it
   was clear that the wife, upon the evidence, had no case in law. Our opinion
   was fortified by the fact that we had reached this conclusion prior to hearing
   the submission on behalf of the husband."

They added:
                                                                                     I
   " Upon counsel for the wife referring to the evidence which could be given
   by her mother, we stated that any such evidence could not in any way assist
   the court."

   I think that the justices went completely wrong when they directed themselves
that, in very exceptional circumstances, they could dismiss the case without
hearing all the evidence for the wife. As a matter of practice I have never heard
of such a submission being made; nor do I think that it can ever be proper for
justices to accede to such a submission, or rule that there is no case to answer,

A either as a matter of law or for any other reason before all the witnesses have been called. The duty of a tribunal is to hear the witnesses adduced by the complainant, the petitioner, the plaintiff, or whoever it may be, and to listen to their evidence. An experienced tribunal may, of course, indicate in a particular case that the evidence in its totality does not appear to be likely to be sufficient to establish a case, or a defence, and the advocate, being of the same mind, may

B decide that it is a waste of time to proceed further and throw in his hand. I think, however, that a court should take such a course only if satisfied that the advocate will agree; such occasions are rare. But an entirely different situation arises when a party wishes to call further evidence, and I do not think that it is ever possible in such circumstances for a tribunal to say, in effect, " The evidence which is to be called cannot assist us further and we will now decide against you

C without hearing it ". A good test is to ask the question " Would it be proper for a tribunal to dismiss a case on the opening? " Counsel for the husband who made the submission to the justices accepted before us that that would be improper. But what else were the justices doing? They had not heard the wife's mother's evidence although they might have heard an opening referring to it. In fact, we have been told that counsel who then appeared for the wife was not asked to

D indicate what the mother was going to say. I do not think that it would matter whether he was or was not. If he or the wife wished the mother to be heard, the court's duty was to hear her.

We can find no direct authority, probably because this is a proposition of good sense. However, the principle is, I think, to be found in the judgments in *Hobbs v. Tinling & Co., Ltd.*, *Hobbs v. Nottingham Journal, Ltd.* (1). Scrutton, L.J.,

E said (2):

> " When a jury, as sometimes happens, informs the judge, before the plaintiff's case has finished, that they desire to find for the defendant, or that they desire to find for the plaintiff, before they have heard the defendant, the judge can take two courses. (i) He may, if he thinks this premature intervention renders it impossible for the trial to proceed with justice, discharge

F the jury and order a retrial: see *De Freville v. Dill* (3). (ii) If he thinks justice can still be done, he may inquire of the party whose case has not been completed if he desires to complete it, and that party has the right to complete his case, to re-examine any witness under cross-examination, to call any other evidence he desires, and to address the jury, if he desires."

G It seems to me that this is the strongest possible authority from one of the greatest sources of English jurisprudence, Scrutton, L.J., in support of the view that the justices were wrong in dismissing the case when they did. Greer, L.J., said (4):

> " I am further of opinion that the jury ought to have been told that their intervention was premature, that they must keep an open mind until the conclusion of the plaintiff's case, that inasmuch as the defendant's counsel

H had put in documents the plaintiff's counsel would be entitled not only to re-examine, but to address the jury last."

And Sankey, L.J., said (5):

> " It is not admissible to do a great right by doing a little wrong. The inequalities of life are not so dangerous in a State whose subjects know that in a Court of law at any rate they are sure to get justice, and it is not

I sufficient to do justice by obtaining a proper result by irregular or improper means."

The first and only time at which a submission of " no case " can properly be made and at which the justices may dismiss the case is, in my view, at the close of the

---

(1) [1929] 2 K.B. 1; [1929] 2 All E.R. Rep. 33.
(2) [1929] 2 K.B. at p. 24; [1929] All E.R. Rep. at p. 43.
(3) [1927] W.N. 133.
(4) [1929] 2 K.B. at p. 46; [1929] All E.R. Rep. at p. 54.
(5) [1929] 2 K.B. at p. 53; [1929] All E.R. Rep. at p. 58.

case for the complainant, providing always that the complainant wishes to proceed   A
at that point. To attempt to dismiss the case before that time comes, however
convenient such a course may appear to the tribunal to be, is, I think, to embark
on a very slippery and dangerous slope.

This case must be sent back to another panel of the Hastings justices for
proper adjudication and the appeal allowed. I am particularly anxious not to say
anything about matters which were not fully before the justices, but I think that   B
I ought to point out that there was evidence by the wife which was in no way
demolished in cross-examination, and which seems to me clearly to require some
explanation by the husband. The wife said that on the Tuesday after she was
married—that is, Tuesday 14th February 1967—the husband told her that he
was under treatment for V.D. and attending a clinic. She immediately went back
to her mother and saw her own doctor. The husband then turned up, according   C
to the wife (this is a matter on which I would have wanted to hear the mother's
evidence), at the mother's home, and produced to the mother a certificate that
he had not been and was not suffering from V.D. The wife conceded that that
certificate must be true. But that is not the end of the matter by any means. The
relevance of this evidence is that it is prima facie an admission made two or three
days after the marriage that, within a short time before the marriage, he had been   D
with another woman. The wife said that it played on her mind. This was not a
situation of which, in my judgment, justices could fairly say " There is nothing
more in this marriage than happens in very many cases." I would have wanted to
hear the husband's version; but I say no more.

I think that it is necessary to consider briefly the position which arises when a
submission of " no case " is made at the proper time. In *Ramsden* v. *Ramsden* (6),   E
LORD MERRIMAN, P., said:

" Having heard the wife's evidence, and such evidence as her mother gave,
the justices stopped the case without calling on the husband. It is important
to ascertain exactly what that means. On the one hand, it may mean that
the justices ruled, either at their own instance, or, possibly, on a submission by
the husband, that, taking the evidence at its face value, nothing had been   F
shown which could, in law, amount to persistent cruelty. It is not suggested
that there was any such submission on the part of the husband, and, therefore, these justices could have made such a ruling only on their own initiative.
On the other hand, the decision may mean merely that they had heard the
evidence put forward by the wife in support of allegations of persistent cruelty
and did not think there was any substance in it ... It is plain, I think, on the   G
face of their statement of reasons, that they are not purporting to rule as a
matter of law that the matters complained of could not, if established, amount
to persistent cruelty. They are saying, literally and impliedly, throughout
the whole of their reasons: ' We think this case lacks substance, and we do
not want to hear any more of it.' It is said that they should not do this, that
it was their duty to hear the whole case if there were prima facie evidence in   H
support of the complaint. I think that proposition is too wide. Although I
cannot put my hand on any authority, counsel for the husband is able, from
his own experience, to support my recollection, and I am prepared to say
on my certain knowledge that this court on more than one occasion has
laid down, in similar circumstances, that justices, like a judge or a jury,
are perfectly entitled to say: ' We have had enough of this case, and we do   I
not think anything of it ', without being said to have misdirected themselves
in law. But I am confident that at the same time we have coupled with that
the advice that it is usually better to wait to hear both sides in matrimonial
cases before coming to a conclusion. I still think that advice is sound,
because, if justices do decide a case out of hand on the complainant's case, it
is argued, as in the present appeal, that they have ruled, as a matter of law,

---

(6) [1954] 2 All E.R. 623 at pp. 623, 624; [1954] 1 W.L.R. 1105 at pp. 1106, 1107.

A   that there is no case to answer. At any rate, it is liable to give rise to more difficulties than it avoids."

The justices in the present case have said that they have found " that the wife, upon the evidence, had no case in law ", and that there was no case to answer. On the other hand, it appears from their reasons that they reached that conclusion because they did not think anything of the wife's evidence. My mind is
B   confused as to which course they took or whether they were trying to steer both. If they were seeking to rule as a matter of law, they were, I think, clearly wrong, even if they had so ruled after hearing the mother.

Ramsden v. *Ramsden* (7) was referred to in *Storey* v. *Storey* (8), in the Court of Appeal, where the words of LORD MERRIMAN, P., were approved. In the course of his judgment, ORMEROD, L.J., said (9):

C   " We agree with the view expressed by the President in *Ramsden* v. *Ramsden* (7) and in other cases that it is better in matrimonial disputes for the justices to hear both sides before coming to a decision, particularly as a finding by them of desertion or persistent cruelty may form the basis for a subsequent petition for divorce. On the other hand, the practice of putting a respondent to his election appears to have been adopted in the Divorce
D   Court since *Alexander* v. *Rayson* (10) was decided. There is always a discretion remaining in the tribunal which would no doubt have the question of status well in mind in considering the exercise of that discretion."

I would refer in conclusion to the words of KARMINSKI, J., in *Wilson* v. *Wilson* (11), which I ventured to adopt in *Holzer* v. *Holzer (Morley intervening)* (12),
E   where he said:

        " There is, as counsel for the wife at once admitted, a discretion; but I am satisfied that that discretion should be sparingly exercised, and then only in quite exceptional circumstances."

The justices may have taken the words " exceptional circumstances " from this
F   judgment; unfortunately they decided prematurely that there were such circumstances.

When the matter is being re-heard, I very much hope that, if a submission of " no case " is made to the justices, and if they think that they should dismiss the complaints at the close of the wife's case, they will bear very carefully in mind and state whether they are ruling as a matter of law that the evidence does not show anything which could in law amount to desertion and to wilful
G   neglect to maintain, or whether they are ruling that they do not accept the evidence of the wife.

I think that this appeal must be allowed and the complaints re-heard by other justices.

    SIR JOCELYN SIMON, P.: I entirely agree with the judgment which
H   BAKER, J., has delivered. Since it is clear that there must be a re-hearing, I desire to say nothing whatever about the facts of the case. I merely add this. In some types of adjudication a written statement of the case to be presented to the court must be delivered to the other side before the hearing. Where that situation obtains, exceptionally the case may be stopped at that stage on the ground that the written statement establishes no case known to law. Where,
I   however, that course is not taken or is not available, the case cannot be stopped until all the evidence for the plaintiff, or the petitioner, or the complainant, has been heard. In my view, that is a fundamental principle of English judicature,

(7) [1954] 2 All E.R. 623; [1954] 1 W.L.R. 1105.
(8) [1960] 3 All E.R. 279; [1961] P. 63.
(9) [1960] 3 All E.R. at p. 282; [1961] P. at p. 69.
(10) [1936] 1 K.B. 169; [1935] All E.R. Rep. 185.
(11) [1958] 3 All E.R. 195 at p. 196; [1958] 1 W.L.R. 1090 at p. 1092.
(12) [1964] 3 All E.R. 989 at p. 990; [1964] 1 W.L.R. 1478 at p. 1480.

which accounts for the comparative lack of authority on the matter; though the **A**
passages cited by BAKER, J., from *Hobbs* v. *Tinling & Co., Ltd.*, *Hobbs* v.
Nottingham Journal, Ltd. (13), in my view, establish it beyond any question.

Sometimes, at the end of a plaintiff's, or petitioner's, or complainant's case,
but not before, the case may be stopped, either on a submission that there is no
case to answer, or on the proper motion of the court itself: see *Ramsden* v. *Rams-*
den (14), which BAKER, J., has cited. Though such action may be taken, it is   **B**
rarely satisfactory to come to a decision in a matrimonial cause without hearing
both sides: see the passage in *Ramsden* v. *Ramsden* (15) cited in *Storey* v. *Storey*
(16); and compare also the *Practice Note* (17). It is, of course, always open to a
defendant or respondent to submit that there is no case to answer. That is a right
that cannot be withheld. He can do that at the end of the complainant's case, but
not before. If it is done, it should be made perfectly plain what is the type of the   **C**
submission. I cite again from *Storey* v. *Storey* (18):

> "There are, however, two sets of circumstances under which a defendant
> may submit that he has no case to answer. In the one case there may be a
> submission that, accepting the plaintiff's evidence at its face value, no case
> has been established in law, and in the other that the evidence led for the
> plaintiff is so unsatisfactory or unreliable that the court should find that the   **D**
> burden of proof has not been discharged."

It should be made perfectly plain which of those two types of submission is being
put forward. That is not to say that they are mutually exclusive. They can, of
course, be put forward in the alternative; but the court should be perfectly clear
on what grounds it is ruling, if it does so rule, that there is no case to answer:
see, for example, *Disher* v. *Disher* (19). In the statement of reasons in the present   **E**
case there are signs of confusion as to what type of submission the justices were
responding to.

For those reasons, as well as those stated by BAKER, J., with which I entirely
agree, I concur in the order that he proposes, namely, that the appeal should be
allowed and the case remitted for re-hearing to a different panel of the bench.
There is just one matter which I think I should add. We were told, on instruc-   **F**
tions, that counsel for the wife before the justices, who was present in this court
though he did not conduct the case for the wife, asked the justices formally that
his objection to the premature ruling, as he saw it and as we have found it to be,
should be recorded. Where a formal request of that sort is made, in my view it
should be acceded to. I do not think that it is sufficiently made plain in the
documents before us.   **G**

Appeal allowed.

Solicitors: *Perring & Co.*, Hastings (for the wife); *Charles Webb & Sons*,
Brighton (for the husband).

[*Reported by* ALICE BLOOMFIELD, *Barrister-at-Law.*]   **H**

I

(13) [1929] 2 K.B. 1; [1929] All E.R. Rep. 33.
(14) [1954] 2 All E.R. 623; [1954] 1 W.L.R. 1105.
(15) [1954] 2 All E.R. at p. 624; [1954] 1 W.L.R. at p. 1107.
(16) [1960] 3 All E.R. 279 at p. 282; [1961] P. 63 at p. 69.
(17) [1962] 1 All E.R. 448.
(18) [1960] 3 All E.R. at p. 282; [1961] P. at p. 68.
(19) [1963] 3 All E.R. 933; [1965] P. 31.

A

R. *v.* McNANEY.

[COURT OF APPEAL, CRIMINAL DIVISION (Lord Parker, C.J., Widgery, L.J., and Lawton, J.), February 18, 1969.]

B *Criminal Law—Sentence—Hospital order—Restriction order—Secretary of State's powers—Administrative matters—Court of Appeal only concerned that order valid—Mental Health Act 1959 (7 & 8 Eliz. 2 c. 72), s. 65.*

The considerations which determine in which hospital a convicted person shall be detained under the Mental Health Act 1959, are matters for the Secretary of State (see p. 36, letter H, post). The primary function of the criminal division of the Court of Appeal, where an accused appeals against

C a restriction order made pursuant to s. 65 of the Act of 1959, is to consider whether the original order was properly made (see p. 36, letter I, post).

Application refused.

[As to the power of higher courts to make restriction orders under the Mental Health Act 1959, see 29 HALSBURY'S LAWS (3rd Edn.) 527, 528, para. 990.

D   For the Mental Health Act 1959, s. 60, s. 65, see 39 HALSBURY'S STATUTES (2nd Edn.) 1013, 1019.]

Application.

The applicant, Peter James McNaney, pleaded guilty at Leeds Assizes on 4th October 1967 to three counts of wounding with intent to do grievous bodily harm. He was ordered by HINCHCLIFFE, J., to be detained in Rampton Hospital

E under s. 60 of the Mental Health Act 1959, the judge also ordering under s. 65 of that Act that a restriction order should be imposed without limit of time. The applicant applied for leave to appeal against the imposition of the order. The facts are set out in the judgment of the court.

Niall MacDermot, Q.C., and *J. B. M. Milmo* for the applicant.

F   The Crown were not represented.

WIDGERY, L.J., delivered the judgment of the court: The applicant pleaded guilty at Leeds Assizes as long ago as October 1967 to three counts of wounding with intent, and he was ordered to be detained in Rampton Hospital under s. 60 of the Mental Health Act 1959, with a restriction on his dis-

G charge under s. 65 without limit of time. He now seeks leave to appeal against that order, after refusal by the single judge, and in his own grounds of appeal he describes the restriction order as being unjust, which indicates that at that stage he did not appreciate its significance, although no doubt he has now received advice from his advisers on it.

The three offences all took place on 8th or 9th July 1967 in Hull, the applicant

H being on his travels at that time, being in Hull, and attacking three individuals in each case with his walking stick. The first victim was a man of 59; he was not badly injured and did not have to go to hospital. The second was a man of 71, who was set on by the applicant with his walking stick after a conversation at a bus stop, and this man sustained a one inch laceration in his head which required stitching; then finally a widow of 72 was attacked by the

I applicant with the same weapon and again sustained a laceration which required stitching. He is 38 at the present time and has a long history of mental weakness. There were before the court below two reports, as required under the Mental Health Act 1959, by qualified medical officers, the first one, by Dr. Orr, goes in detail through the applicant's medical background. Apparently when he was nine years of age he was certified as a feeble-minded person; he then went to a hospital in Leeds called Meanwood Park Hospital, which specialised in this kind of patient. He had a number of periods on licence, but remained otherwise at Meanwood Park until he was 28 years of age. Then he was discharged, and

he had one or two sentences of imprisonment for matters which are not directly   A
relevant to this appeal, and it was at this time that he started to make threats
against his wife and said he was going to kill her. As a result he was re-admitted
to Meanwood Park Hospital as an informal patient on the same day as he was
discharged from prison, 12th November 1965. He stayed in Meanwood Park
for a while, and then was admitted to St. James's Hospital in Portsmouth,
having misbehaved himself in Portsmouth by pulling telephone handsets out of   B
kiosks, as a result of which he went back to Meanwood Park yet again on 21st
June 1966, and was discharged in the autumn of 1966. Thereafter he worked
for a time in an iron works as a labourer doing heavy work, but he had the misfortune to have an accident due to the negligence of one of his fellow workers.
That terminated his employment, and then he went on his travels, as it was put,
wandering about the country for a period, during which he committed these   C
offences in Hull.

Dr. Orr's report, having dealt with all these matters, describes how, while
under observation, the applicant had written threatening letters to his former
landlord and his former landlord's wife. Then Dr. Orr expressed this extremely
important opinion. He states:

                                                                                 D
" In my opinion his threats of violence are not the idle posturing of a person
of sub-normal intelligence and hysterical personality who is attempting to
manipulate his environment or to attract attention to himself. In my opinion
he is suffering from Subnormality within the meaning of the Mental Health
Act 1959, he is a danger to those around him, and he is in need of supervision,
treatment and training of a type that can only be provided with in Special
Hospital ".   E

The confirmatory report by Dr. Harvey goes into less details, but is broadly
speaking in step with the report of Dr. Orr.

It seems to this court that on the material facing the learned judge at Leeds
Assizes in October 1967, the only possible order was the one which he made;
it was clearly right to regard this as a case for mental treatment rather than   F
prison, and a restriction under s. 65 was absolutely necessary in a case of this
kind. Counsel for the applicant has told us today with engaging candour that
he would rather be in prison than in Rampton, and if he has to be in a special
hospital at all, would rather be in Moss Side than in Rampton. In support of
that submission, he has given us some helpful additional information about the
applicant's background, and in particular has shown us a report recently made   G
at Rampton by the consultant psychiatrist now responsible for the applicant's
treatment. This report, and I shall not read it in full, indicates that the applicant
is making progress, but it also makes it quite clear that he still requires treatment,
and there is no suggestion that he has yet reached the stage in which he can be
released and go back into circulation with the general public again.

In the view of this court it would be quite wrong for us to attempt to interfere   H
as between Rampton and Moss Side. Any considerations which determine which
hospital the applicant should be detained in are matters for the Secretary of
State, and it is not for us to interfere. So far as the suggestion that he might
serve a sentence of imprisonment is concerned, not only is there the difficulty
that the applicant still seems to require medical treatment in a hospital, but
the problem of what length of prison sentence would be appropriate would be   I
an extremely hard one to solve. It would be necessary to give him a sentence
of imprisonment which would keep him under restraint for as long as he continues
to exhibit these times of violence, and no one really could foresee what the
appropriate period would be. In any case, in the view of this court our primary
function is to consider whether the order was properly made when made, and
it is not really for us to review the applicant's progress 15 months later. That
is a process properly assigned to the Secretary of State, and one which ought

A to be carried out through administrative channels. Accordingly, in our judgment this was a correct order when made. We see no reason to vary it and the application is refused.

Application refused.

Solicitors: *Clay, Allison & Clark*, Retford (for the applicant).

B
[*Reported by* N. P. METCALFE, ESQ., *Barrister-at-Law.*]

SECRETARY OF STATE FOR EMPLOYMENT AND PRODUCTIVITY *v.* C. MAURICE & CO., LTD.

C
[HOUSE OF LORDS (Lord Guest, Lord Pearce, Lord Donovan, Lord Wilberforce and Lord Pearson), February 5, 6, March 26, 1969.]

Selective employment tax—Appeal—Tribunal's decision not to be interfered with, if it could reasonably have been reached.

Selective employment tax—Refund—Electrical industry—Laying and jointing
D *cable—Whether distribution of electricity for public supply—Standard Industrial Classification, heading 500, heading 602—Selective Employment Payments Act* 1966 (c. 32), *s.* 2 (2), (3).

Selective employment tax—Standard Industrial Classification—Construction of minimum list headings.

The respondents were engaged in work which consisted to a large extent
E of laying electricity cables, reinforcing existing cables, replacing cables and maintenance. They contracted, inter alia, to do work for electricity boards where the boards had insufficient staff available. They claimed that by reason of their activities falling within heading 602* (Electricity) of the Standard Industrial Classification they were entitled to a repayment of selective employment tax under s. 2 (2) and (3) of the Selective Employ-
F ment Payments Act 1966. The appellant contended that the respondents' activities fell within the scope of heading 500† (Construction) and thereby did not qualify for any repayment. The Industrial Tribunal found that the respondents' activities were not civil engineering work but consisted of laying and jointing cables; they held that such activities fell within heading 602. The Divisional Court reversed the decision of the tribunal which,
G however, was restored by the Court of Appeal. On appeal,

Held: the appeal would be dismissed, because—

(i) although the decision of the Industrial Tribunal on a question of industrial classification was one partly of fact and partly of law, the element of fact was prominent; accordingly, a court would be disinclined to reverse the tribunal's decision unless the decision was shown to be unreasonable;
H *Lord Advocate* v. *Reliant Tool Co.* ([1968] 1 All E.R. 162) applied.

(ii) the tribunal, having found that the respondents' work consisted of laying and jointing cables for public supply and having found that it was not civil engineering work, could not be said to have reached an unreasonable decision in holding that the work fell within heading 602.

PER LORD GUEST: this involves a legal question of the proper construction
I of the minimum list headings. Reliance was placed by the respondents on *Lord Advocate* v. *Reliant Tool Co.*‡ The speeches in that case give helpful guidance as to the proper approach to the construction of the minimum list headings. But it was a very different case from the present. In that case the question decided by the tribunal was truly a question of fact which really concluded the matter in favour of the company. In the

---

* Heading 602 is set out at p. 38, letter I, post.
† Heading 500 is set out at p. 39, letters D and E, post.
‡ [1968] 1 All E.R. 162.

A

present case, while I agree that the Standard Industrial Classification should not be construed as strictly as a legal document it is nonetheless incorporated in the Selective Employment Payments Act 1966, and subject to the qualification above mentioned must yield to the normal canons of statutory construction.

B

Per LORD PEARSON: insofar as lawyers have, by formalising and elaborating the canons of interpretation for their own special purposes of drafting and interpreting legal documents, introduced additional elements of strictness and rigidity which go beyond common-sense methods of interpreting ordinary documents, such additional elements should be eliminated from the interpretation of the headings in the Standard Industrial Classification.

Decision of the COURT OF APPEAL (sub nom. *C. Maurice & Co., Ltd.* v. *Minister of Labour** [1968] 2 All E.R. 1030) affirmed.

C

[As to Selective Employment Tax, see SUPPLEMENT to 33 HALSBURY'S LAWS (3rd Edn.), para. 479A.

For the Electricity Act 1947, s. 1, s. 9, see 8 HALSBURY'S STATUTES (2nd Edn.) 919, 932.

For the Selective Employment Payments Act 1966, s. 2, see 46 HALSBURY'S STATUTES (2nd Edn.) 171.]

D

Case referred to:

Lord Advocate v. *Reliant Tool Co.*, [1968] 1 All E.R. 162; [1968] 1 W.L.R. 205.

Appeal.

This was an appeal with leave by the Secretary of State for Employment and Productivity from the decision of the Court of Appeal (LORD DENNING, M.R., and SACHS, L.J.; DIPLOCK, L.J., dissenting) dated 21st May 1968 and reported [1968] 2 All E.R. 1030, allowing an appeal by the respondents, C. Maurice & Co., Ltd., from the decision of the Divisional Court (LORD PARKER, C.J., SALMON and WIDGERY, L.JJ.) dated 18th October 1967, and restoring an order of the Industrial Tribunal dated 16th January 1967, which ordered that the two establishments of the respondents at Bishop's Stortford and at Thundersley qualified for repayment of selective employment tax under s. 2 of the Selective Employment Payments Act 1966. The facts are set out in the opinion of LORD GUEST.

E

F

P. E. Webster, Q.C., *Gordon Slynn* and *R. E. Jack* for the appellant.
F. B. Purchas, Q.C., and *J. R. V. McAulay* for the respondents.

Their Lordships took time for consideration.

G

26th March. The following opinions were delivered.

LORD GUEST: My Lords, the short point in this appeal is whether the respondents qualify for a refund of selective employment tax under minimum list heading 602 of the Standard Industrial Classification. This classification is made the test for a refund of selective employment tax under s. 2 of the Selective Employment Payments Act 1966.

H

Minimum list heading 602 is found in Ord. XVIII of the Standard Industrial Classification under the heading: " Gas, Electricity and Water ". The activities in small type falling under heading 602 are:

" The production and distribution of electricity for public supply. Establishments producing electricity for railway, tramway and trolleybus operation and for groups of factories are included. ' District heating ' and electricity showrooms are also included."

I

The respondents are engaged in work which consists to a very large extent in the laying of electricity cable, the reinforcing of existing cables, which is really a doubling up or laying additional cables to enable a greater supply to be given

* The functions of the Minister of Labour were transferred to the Secretary of State for Employment and Productivity by S.I. 1968 No. 729.

A alongside existing cables, the replacement of cables, and in a certain amount of maintenance. In the course of its cable laying a considerable quantity of jointing the cable has to be done, and the larger part of the turnover in the company comes from the work done in jointing. It has two types of contract; it has contracts with electricity boards, which are running contracts under which it agrees to supply the labour to carry out work which these boards have not

B sufficient staff to be able to do themselves. The various boards cannot carry a sufficient labour force to meet the additional demands for supply. It also enters into specific contracts, mainly for the erection of sub-stations in conjunction with the lines which it is laying.

The respondents contend that their activities fall under heading 602 " The . . . distribution of electricity for public supply ". This contention was upheld by

C the Industrial Tribunal, rejected by the Divisional Court and restored by the Court of Appeal (1). The appellant contends that the respondents fall under minimum list heading 500 " Construction ", the activities of which are:

" Erecting and repairing buildings of all types. Constructing and repairing roads and bridges; erecting steel and reinforced concrete structures; other civil engineering work such as laying sewers and gas mains,

D erecting overhead line supports and aerial masts, opencast coal mining, etc. The building and civil engineering establishments of Defence and other Government Departments and of local authorities are included.

" Establishments specialising in demolition work or in sections of construction work such as asphalting, electrical wiring, flooring, glazing, installing heating and ventilating apparatus, painting, plastering, plumbing,

E roofing. The hiring of contractors' plant and scaffolding is included."

Had it not been for the fact that the Divisional Court unanimously rejected the respondents' claim, I should have thought it very plain that the respondents were right. The appellant complains that the Court of Appeal (1) has treated the question as one of fact on which the decision of the Industrial Tribunal should not be disturbed. I am afraid that I cannot follow the Court of Appeal (1)

F to this extent. Counsel for the appellant argued that it was a matter of construing the Standard Industrial Classification and that this was a pure question of law. The true position, in my view, is that initially this is a question of fact for the tribunal to find what were the activities of the respondents. This having been done, it is a question of law for the court to say whether there was evidence on which the tribunal could find that the respondents fell under heading 602.

G This involves a legal question of the proper construction of the minimum list headings. Reliance was placed by the respondents on *Lord Advocate* v. *Reliant Tool Co.* (2). The speeches in that case give helpful guidance as to the proper approach to the construction of the minimum list headings. But it was a very different case from the present. In that case the question decided by the tribunal was truly a question of fact which really concluded the matter in favour of the

H company. In the present case, while I agree that the Standard Industrial Classification should not be construed as strictly as a legal document it is nonetheless incorporated in the Selective Employment Payments Act 1966, and subject to the qualification above mentioned must yield to the normal canons of statutory construction.

I approach the matter in this way. Bearing in mind that the tribunal have

I found that the respondents' activities consist in laying and jointing cables for carrying electricity for public supply, I next proceed to heading 602, and on reading that heading I am left in doubt whether their work can properly be described as the " distribution of electricity ". Proceeding next to heading 500 " Construction " I find that " electrical wiring " is the only place where electricity is mentioned and this is clearly not the work the respondents do.

(1) [1968] 2 All E.R. 1030; [1968] 1 W.L.R. 1337.
(2) [1968] 1 All E.R. 162; [1968] 1 W.L.R. 205.

The tribunal have found that the respondents' work is not comprehended by **A** "civil engineering work" and therefore this is excluded. Although the heading "Construction" might cover part of the respondents' work it is noteworthy that, although the laying of sewers and gas mains is referred to, there is a notable absence of the laying of electric cables, and although erecting overhead line supports and aerial masts is mentioned, there is nothing about electric cables. I am then driven back to heading 602, and I see no reason why the "distribution **B** of electricity" should not cover effecting the means of distribution of electricity and should be limited to the actual working of the switchgear. There was material, in my view, on which the Industrial Tribunal could arrive at the decision that on a proper construction of heading 602 "distribution of electricity" covers the laying and jointing of cables to convey the electricity. The reference to s. 1 and s. 9 of the Electricity Act 1947, so far as the area boards' duties of **C** distribution of electricity are concerned support this view.

In my opinion, the Industrial Tribunal reached the correct result and I would affirm the Court of Appeal's decision (3).

I would dismiss the appeal.

LORD PEARCE: My Lords, I agree with the opinion of my noble and learned friend, LORD PEARSON. I would dismiss the appeal.   **D**

LORD DONOVAN: My Lords, I find the rival arguments in this case to be very evenly balanced. What, for me, finally tips the scales in the respondents' favour is their contention based on the language of s. 1 and s. 9 of the Electricity Act 1947. These show that when placing on the area board the duty to "plan and carry out an efficient and economical distribution" of supplies **E** of electricity, Parliament recognised that this would involve inter alia the laying of cables underground. The appellant replies that this is irrelevant, since for the purpose of the selective employment tax one would still have to look at what particular establishments belonging to the area board did in order to determine their classification. I do not think this answer disposes of the argument. It has been shown that in the Act of 1947 what Parliament meant by **F** the distribution of electricity included the provision of the means of doing so; and I feel that the same interpretation should prevail here unless there is some compelling reason to give the word "distribution" in minimum list heading 602 the narrower meaning of actual transmission of electricity. While I found the appellant's argument to have much force, I think it fell short of establishing any such reason. I accordingly agree that the appeal fails.   **G**

LORD WILBERFORCE: My Lords, in *Lord Advocate* v. *Reliant Tool Co.* (4) it was necessary to consider a single heading in the Standard Industrial Classification (332 "Metal-working Machine Tools") and to decide whether the Industrial Tribunal had correctly brought under that heading, or its penumbra, a particular activity. This House decided that the tribunal were entitled to **H** apply their knowledge and experience to the question where the process of manufacturing machine tools begins. The present case presents a different, though in some respects analogous, problem. There are two relevant headings (500 and 602) under which the respondents' activities may come—the question is, under which. This necessitates consideration and comparison of the language used in each of them and admits the argument that a question of construction, and **I** so of law, is involved, one within the province of the courts rather than that of the tribunal.

I do not think the question is as simple as this: the difference in opinion below confirms it. Both the Divisional Court and the Court of Appeal (3) have construed the headings, and it is not merely an error in an identical process of construction that has led to whichever result does not prevail. The reason

---

(3) [1968] 2 All E.R. 1030; [1968] 1 W.L.R. 1337.
(4) [1968] 1 All E.R. 162; [1968] 1 W.L.R. 205.

A for the difference is to be found in a disagreement as to how much of the tribunal's knowledge and experience in the factual field is to enter into the process of construction. The Divisional Court thought very little; the Court of Appeal (5), following the spirit of the *Reliant Tool* decision (6), thought much, and I agree with the Court of Appeal (5).

It is worthwhile to set out the main findings of the tribunal. These are:
B (i) that the [respondents are] doing what the area electricity boards would themselves have to do to ensure the distribution of electricity for public supply; the area electricity boards themselves fall under heading 602—i.e., are engaged in the production and distribution of electricity; (ii) that generally speaking, there is a distinction between civil engineering work and electrical engineering work; (iii) that the operations of the [respondents] can in no sense be classified
C as electrical wiring in the ordinary use of that phrase; (iv) that none of the [respondents'] work falls directly within any wording of heading 500. It is not the type of work which in normal parlance could be called civil engineering work: it is essentially associated with the electrical engineering industry.

The appellant said of these findings that they are not, or are not mainly, findings of primary fact and that consequently they involve questions of construction, or law, which can be reviewed. But the distinction between primary facts and secondary facts, or between primary facts and inferences from facts, though a useful tool, may be overworked. A fact finding body's decision on primary fact may be, and normally is, unassailable: but it is not a corollary of this that any finding which goes beyond one of primary fact passes into another dimension—one reserved for decisions by judges. There may well be cases
E where a tribunal, whose duties include those of finding primary facts, are also called on to carry out a process of interpretation, to apply words to those facts, or to bring those facts under words, and where the decision of the tribunal, because made by them, also acquires a strong inherent quality of strength. This is, I would think, especially the case where, as here, the language to be interpreted is admittedly imprecise, adapted (and not well adapted) from another quite
F different purpose, drafted in language not settled by a skilled revenue draftsman, but for use by statisticians and by businessmen called on to complete the statisticians' forms. When decision on the language of this classification is entrusted to the Industrial Tribunal I think that Parliament must be taken to have intended to give to their decisions on classification questions, including, as they must, consideration of the classificatory language, a strength only slightly less than
G that attracted by decisions of fact properly so called. Certainly these decisions may be reviewed; but the reviewing authority ought not, in my opinion, to attempt to construe the headings ab initio as if they were parts of an Income Tax Act or a customs regulation. It should start with the tribunal's findings, as those of a body which has the means and experience of knowing how industry works and is grouped, and see if the decision is one which reasonable men ought
H not to have come to, or if it is vitiated by some manifest misdirections. This is what the Court of Appeal (5) did.

The tribunal's decision can be simply analysed as follows. If this work (of laying and jointing cables) had been done by area boards, it would have fallen under their power and duty to distribute electricity. In respect of such activity, the boards (apart from s. 3 of the Act) would clearly fall under heading
I 602. (The Electricity Act 1947 indeed clearly confirms this view of the area boards' functions.) It seems, therefore, likely that the respondents, when they do this work for the Area Boards, the boards not having themselves sufficient manpower, fall under the same heading.

Now (the argument continues) we look at heading 500. It is one dealing mainly with civil engineering. The respondents' work is not, in common parlance, civil engineering. Certainly heading 500 is illustrative and not exhaustive and

(5) [1968] 2 All E.R. 1030; [1968] 1 W.L.R. 1337.
(6) [1968] 1 All E.R. 162; [1968] 1 W.L.R. 205.

contains the words " such as "—so we must see what else it fairly includes. **A**
We find two things: first, the only explicit reference to electricity is to electrical
wiring as part of construction work—clearly this is a different field; secondly,
there is a reference to erecting overhead line supports and aerial masts. This
does not include, indeed pointedly stops short of, installing the lines themselves,
and it seems inconceivable that this item would have been so segregated if lines
were to be included.   The obvious, perhaps the most obvious, type of overhead **B**
line is a transmission line, so that the intention seems clear to omit means of
distribution from the heading.   There are other points, very properly taken,
but this is the main argument and I find it impeccable.   It comes from a body
which has considered what civil engineering means, what area boards do, what
the respondents do; and its argument is appropriate and convinces.   In my view,
its decision is not merely maintainable but right.   **C**
     I would dismiss the appeal.

     LORD PEARSON: My Lords, the respondents have two establishments
whose main activities are laying and jointing electric cables.   Having paid
selective employment tax in respect of their employees working in or from
these establishments, they claim to be entitled under s. 2 of the Selective Employ- **D**
ment Payments Act 1966, to have the amount of the tax which they have paid
refunded to them.   They make this claim on the ground that those activities
fall under heading 602 (of which the title is " Electricity ") of the minimum
list headings in the Standard Industrial Classification, which is referred to in the
Act.   The appellant's contention is that those activities do not fall under heading
602 (" Electricity ") but do fall under heading 500 (" Construction ").   It **E**
is common ground that the activities must fall either under heading 602 or
under heading 500, and that if the activities fall under heading 602 the respondents are entitled to the refund, the other statutory conditions being fulfilled in
their case, but that if the activities fall under heading 500 the respondents are
not entitled to the refund.   Thus there is a clear and single issue in this appeal:
Do the activities fall under heading 602 or under heading 500?   **F**
     I will first refer to some general points.   The Standard Industrial Classifica-
tion is not a document drafted by lawyers to be interpreted and applied by
lawyers.   The origin and object and character of it can be ascertained from its
Introduction.   Paragraph 1 is as follows:

     " A Standard Industrial Classification was first issued in 1948 to promote
     uniformity and comparability in official statistics of the United Kingdom. **G**
     It has since been used in the published statistics of Government Departments
     and experience in using it has shown that some revisions in the Classification
     were desirable, though the main framework of the original list has been
     retained.   This new edition of the Standard Industrial Classification has
     again been prepared by an Inter-Departmental Committee on which the
     principal Departments collecting statistics have been represented.   The **H**
     Committee wishes to acknowledge the help received from trade organizations
     and individual experts familiar with different industries."

Paragraph 3 states that " the classification is based on industries and not on
occupations ", and that " The classification is also based on industries without
regard to who owns or operates them . . ."   Paragraph 6 states that " The **I**
classification has been prepared to conform with the organization and structure
of industry and trade as it exists within the United Kingdom . . ."
     As to other points which can be gathered from the Introduction to the classi-
fication and from certain provisions of the Act and may have a bearing on the
issue in this appeal, I will for convenience repeat portions of what I said in
Lord Advocate v. *Reliant Tool Co.* (7):

---

     (7) [1968] 1 All E.R. 162 at p. 175; [1968] 1 W.L.R. 205 at pp. 225, 226.

A   " It appears from para. 9 of the introduction that the adjective ' minimum ' applies to ' list ' rather than ' headings '.   There is a minimum list of headings, evidently for the guidance of statisticians compiling statistics and intended to be the shortest list of headings which will suffice for a proper industrial classification, though it might need to be enlarged by the addition of further sub-headings for the purposes of a particular statistical

B   exercise.   Paragraphs 10 and 11 of the introduction show that a heading consists of a distinguishing number, a title and a ' brief description of the main industries or services included '.   It follows from that language that the description is not necessarily exhaustive : there may be minor or subordinate industries or services included under the title and therefore in the heading, though not covered by the ' brief description of the main industries

C   or services ' . . . Section 10 (4) of the Act of 1966 shows that the title of the heading is usually ' accompanied by a description of the industries or services included therein '."

It has to be considered whether the question raised by this appeal, being one of classification under the Standard Industrial Classification as adopted and adapted by the Act, is one of fact or of law or of both. In my opinion, the question is, as

D   Lord MacDermott said in *Lord Advocate* v. *Reliant Tool Co*. (8), one of mixed fact and law.   The decision at first instance is entrusted by the Act and Regulations to the Industrial Tribunal, which is a specialist tribunal likely to have some special knowledge and experience of " the organization and structure of industry and trade as it exists within the United Kingdom ", with which the classification was prepared to conform.   The tribunal decide on the evidence, using their

E   special knowledge and experience, whether an activity or set of activities falls under this heading or that heading of the minimum list.   That is a decision partly of fact, but also partly of law, because it involves the interpretation and application of the titles and descriptions which compose the headings concerned.   But the element of fact is prominent, and a court will naturally be disinclined to reverse the decision of the Industrial Tribunal on a question of industrial classi-

F   fication unless the decision is shown to be unreasonable.

There is a question whether the canons of interpretation should be used in the interpretation of the headings in the Standard Industrial Classification.   (I am avoiding the use of the word " construction " in this context, as it is the title of heading 500.)   In my opinion, they must be so used to a large extent, because they are in essence not arbitrary rules but common-sense methods of under-

G   standing documents.   But insofar as lawyers have, by formalising and elaborating the canons of interpretation for their own special purposes of drafting and interpreting legal documents, introduced additional elements of strictness and rigidity which go beyond common-sense methods of interpreting ordinary documents, such additional elements should be eliminated from the interpretation of the headings in the Standard Industrial Classification.

H   Now the two headings concerned, and two other headings that are needed for comparison, are as follows:

" 500 *Construction*

" Erecting and repairing buildings of all types.   Constructing and repairing roads and bridges; erecting steel and reinforced concrete structures;

I   other civil engineering work such as laying sewers and gas mains, erecting overhead line supports and aerial masts, opencast coal mining, etc.   The building and civil engineering establishments of Defence and other Government Departments and of local authorities are included.

" Establishments specialising in demolition work or in sections of construction work such as asphalting, electrical wiring, flooring, glazing, installing heating and ventilating apparatus, painting, plastering, plumbing, roofing.   The hiring of contractors' plant and scaffolding is included.

(8) [1968] 1 All E.R. at p. 170;   [1968] 1 W.L.R. at p. 218.

A

601 *Gas*

"The production and distribution of gas for public supply. Showrooms are included.

602 *Electricity*

B

"The production and distribution of electricity for public supply. Establishments producing electricity for railway, tramway and trolleybus operation and for groups of factories are included. 'District heating' and electricity showrooms are also included.

603 *Water Supply*

1.   *Public authorities*
2.   *Companies*

C

"Purifying and distributing water, and the supply of hydraulic power."

I will first take heading 500. The fact that the activities of laying and jointing of electric cables are not expressly mentioned in the description is of some significance but is not conclusive to show that these activities do not fall under the heading, because: (i) the description is only "a brief description of the main industries or services included"; and (ii) the words "such as" show that the words following are only giving illustrations and not defining the types of civil engineering work which are included. More important is the absence of any express reference to electrical engineering work. The general content of the heading seems to be building work and civil engineering work. The Industrial Tribunal drew a distinction, though rather tentatively, between civil engineering work and electrical engineering work. They said—

D

E

"Generally speaking it can perhaps be said that there is a distinction between civil engineering work and electrical engineering work. Certain things obviously fall under civil engineering work, certain things obviously fall under electrical engineering work."

It has not been shown that this distinction is invalid or unreasonable, and the laying and jointing of electric cables would naturally be assigned to the category of electrical engineering rather than civil engineering.

F

Then there is the argument for the appellant that as heading 601 includes the distribution of gas for public supply and heading 602 includes the distribution of electricity for public supply, and as the description in heading 500 gives the laying of gas mains as an example of "other civil engineering work" included in the heading, it must follow that the laying of electric cable is equally included. But in my opinion this does not necessarily follow, because the laying of gas mains may be a more elaborate operation and more in the nature of constructional work than the laying of electric cables. What the tribunal said was this:

G

"In the important portion of the definition of heading No. 500 one has the words: 'other civil engineering work such as laying sewers and gas mains, erecting overhead line supports and aerial masts'. It is significant that of the three production activities for gas, electricity and water, water is not mentioned at all. The laying of water pipes, of water mains, is not mentioned; the laying of gas mains is. It may well be that water supply was regarded as so essentially a portion of civil engineering work that there was no need whatsoever to mention the laying of water mains as part of civil engineering. When it came to gas mains there may have been doubt, and so, although water mains are not mentioned, gas mains are. Then there is a further and most significant omission; when it comes to deal with electricity the words it uses are 'erecting overhead line supports'. Although the attention had been directed to the method whereby these products were brought to the public, and for gas the laying of mains is set out, when it came to deal with electricity, it was careful not to mention the line itself. It speaks only of the erection of the overhead line supports.

H

I

A   It seems to us that this careful enumeration of only the supports for the line and not of the line itself gives indication that the laying of the line itself would be part of the electrical industry. This view is reinforced by the further fact that although it was obvious that a great deal of distribution of electricity must come about not through overhead supply but through underground supply, there is no mention whatsoever of the laying of under-

B   ground cables."

This view of the tribunal, whether or not it may be debatable in some respects, has not been shown to be wrong or unreasonable, and there is no good ground for rejecting it.

Then, as the activities of laying and jointing electric cable do not fall under heading 500, and as the parties have agreed that these activities must fall either

C   under heading 500 or under heading 602, it follows that they must be taken for the purposes of this appeal to fall under heading 602. There are, however, also positive reasons for placing those activities under heading 602, because it includes distribution of electricity for public supply. As LORD DENNING, M.R., said (9): " ' Distribution ' is not confined to switching on the current. It includes all the work necessary to ensure that the electricity will get to the consumers ".

D   Distribution of electricity is a function of an area board. They have to provide a supply of electricity to the consumers in their area. They may have to lay and joint electric cables in a number of situations; existing cables may be worn out and need replacement, or may have become inadequate owing to increase of population and need to be doubled; or there may be a need for new cables to be laid in order to provide a supply of electricity to a new street or a new housing

E   estate or even a new town. In all such cases the area board as distributors of electricity will have to undertake, themselves or through contractors such as the respondents, the work of laying and jointing cables. Such work is one of their activities as distributors of electricity and is an integral part of the function of distributing electricity. This view, which seems to me to be prima facie the natural view, receives confirmation from the provisions of s. 1 (2) and s. 9 (2) of

F   the Electricity Act 1947, which treat the laying of cables as included in distribution of electricity. Having regard to the origin and character of the Standard Industrial Classification, I think the compilers of it should be assumed to have had in mind the provisions of the Electricity Act 1947, when they settled the wording of heading 602 and to have used the phrase " distribution of electricity " in the sense in which it is used in that Act.

G   The fact that the respondents perform only part of the operations necessary for bringing electricity to the consumers, so that when they have done their work no electricity has yet been transmitted, does not invalidate the conclusion that their activities come within the description " distribution of electricity ". Similarly, in *Lord Advocate* v. *Reliant Tool Co.* (10) the respondents' activity of designing machine tools was held to come within the description " manufacture

H   of machine tools ", although when they had done their work there would not yet be any machine tools.

In my opinion, the decision of the Industrial Tribunal should be upheld. I would dismiss the appeal.

Appeal dismissed.

I   Solicitors: *Solicitor, Department of Employment and Productivity*; *Barlow, Lyde & Gilbert*, agents for *H. Stanley Tee & Co.*, Bishop's Stortford (for the respondents).

[*Reported by* S. A. HATTEEA, ESQ., *Barrister-at-Law.*]

(9) [1968] 2 All E.R. 1030 at p. 1032;   [1968] 1 W.L.R. 1337 at p. 1343.
(10) [1968] 1 All E.R. 162;   [1968] 1 W.L.R. 205.

A

LANGLEY CONSTRUCTIONS (BRIXHAM), LTD. *v.* WELLS.
WELLS ESTATE (DARTFORD), LTD. *v.* WELLS.

[COURT OF APPEAL, CIVIL DIVISION (Davies and Widgery, L.JJ.), January 30, 31,
February 5, 1969.]

B

*Company—Winding-up—Stay of proceedings against company—Action by com-
pany—Counterclaim by defendant for account of moneys due from company
to defendant and declaration as to balance for which defendant entitled to
prove in winding-up—Extent to which counterclaim maintainable without
leave of Companies Court—Companies Act 1948 (11 & 12 Geo. 6 c. 38),
s. 231.*

C

If a company in liquidation brings an action, the defendant to that action
may without leave set up a cross-claim for liquidated or unliquidated
damages, but only as a set-off to reduce or extinguish the plaintiff's claim;
accordingly, the defendant cannot, without leave of the court under s. 231*
of the Companies Act 1948, counterclaim in the action for an account and a
declaration as to an amount in excess of the plaintiff's claim for which the
defendant is entitled to prove in the winding-up (see p. 51, letter H, and
p. 52, letter B, post).

D

Peat v. *Jones & Co.* ((1881), 8 Q.B.D. 147) and *Mersey Steel and Iron Co.*
v. *Naylor, Benzon & Co.* ((1882), 9 Q.B.D. 648) explained and followed.
Application dismissed.

[As to proceedings against a company in liquidation which require the leave   E
of the Companies Court, see 6 HALSBURY'S LAWS (3rd Edn.) 697, para. 1387;
and for cases on the subject, see 10 DIGEST (Repl.) 1012, 1013, *6954-6963.*
For the Companies Act 1948, s. 231, see 5 HALSBURY'S STATUTES (3rd Edn.)
299.]

Cases referred to:

F

Eastern Holdings Establishment of Vaduz v. *Singer & Friedlander, Ltd.* (*Able
Securities, Ltd., In liquidation, First Claimant; Sempah (Holdings), Ltd.,
Second Claimant*), [1967] 2 All E.R. 1192; [1967] 1 W.L.R. 1017.
International Pulp and Paper Co., Ltd., Re (1876), 3 Ch.D. 594; 45 L.J.Ch. 446;
35 L.T. 229; 10 Digest (Repl.) 1012, *6958.*
Mersey Steel and Iron Co. v. *Naylor, Benzon & Co.* (1882), 9 Q.B.D. 648;
51 L.J.Q.B. 576; 47 L.T. 369; *affd.*, H.L., (1884), 9 App. Cas. 434;   G
53 L.J.Q.B. 497; 51 L.T. 637; 10 Digest (Repl.) 990, *6813.*
Ogle v. *Earl Vane* (1868), L.R. 3 Q.B. 272; 37 L.J.Q.B. 77; 12 Digest (Repl.)
401, *3109.*
Peat v. *Jones & Co.* (1881), 8 Q.B.D. 147; 51 L.J.Q.B. 128; 4 Digest (Repl.)
434, *3854.*

H

Applications for leave to appeal.

These were applications by Leonard William Wells, the defendant in both
actions, for leave to appeal against orders of ASHWORTH, J., made in chambers on
30th October 1968, striking out the counterclaim in each action. The applications were heard together. The facts are set out in the judgment of WIDGERY,
L.J.

I

A. H. Head for the defendant.
C. S. Rawlins for the plaintiff companies.

WIDGERY, L.J., delivered the first judgment at the invitation of DAVIES,
L.J.: These are two applications, made by the defendant in each of the two
relevant actions, for leave to appeal against orders of ASHWORTH, J., in chambers

* Section 231 is set out at p. 47, letter A, post.

A whereby the learned judge ordered that the counterclaim in each case be struck out for non-compliance with s. 231 of the Companies Act 1948, which provides:

" When a winding-up order has been made or a provisional liquidator has been appointed, no action or proceeding shall be proceeded with or commenced against the company except by leave of the court and subject to such terms as the court may impose."

B

There are two actions and two applications, but since each raises precisely the same issue as the other I can deal with *Langley Constructions (Brixham), Ltd.* v. *Wells* alone.

In this case the plaintiff company is in liquidation, the winding-up order having been made in 1962, and the defendant was a director of the company. The

C plaintiff company sued for a sum of money, some £5,000, as on an account stated, the basis of the claim being that the defendant as director of the plaintiff company signed a statement of affairs that disclosed that amount as being owing by him to the plaintiff company. The defendant in his pleading denies that he is indebted to the plaintiff company. He raises questions about the acceptability of the statement of affairs as an account stated in the circumstances of this case. In para. 5 of his defence he does not admit the accuracy of the

D alleged account and goes on to say—

". . . if and in so far as the defendant is indebted to the [plaintiff company] for the sum alleged or any sum the defendant will claim to set-off against the same those sums due and owing to the defendant by the [plaintiff company] at the date of the commencement of the winding-up of the [plaintiff company]

E namely £15,086 full particulars of which exceed three folios."

There is a general denial in para. 6. Then the counterclaim starts at para. 7. In that paragraph he repeats his defence, particularly para. 5, and continues in paras. 8 and 9:

" 8. In the premises the defendant is entitled to have the said account reopened and upon the basis thereof an account by the [plaintiff company]

F of all sums received by the [plaintiff company] from or paid on their behalf by the defendant and to credit for the same after allowing for any sums which may be due from the defendant to the [plaintiff company].

" 9. The plaintiff company being in liquidation the defendant admits that he cannot during the liquidation claim payment in full of sums found due to him or the balance thereof but avers that he is entitled to a declaration

G that he is entitled to prove in the liquidation for such balance as may be found due to him."

Then the defendant counterclaims for the taking of an account and for a declaration that he is entitled to prove in the liquidation of the plaintiff company for dividend as an unsecured creditor in respect of any balance which may be found

H to be due to him.

The purpose of s. 231 is clear and has not been challenged in argument. It is to ensure that when a company goes into liquidation the assets of the company are administered in an orderly fashion for the benefit of all the creditors and that particular creditors should not be able to obtain an advantage by bringing proceedings against the company. What is contemplated is that the Com-

I panies Court shall be seized of all these matters and shall see that the affairs are wound up in a dignified and orderly way.

It is not disputed, and never has been disputed, that the defendant is entitled to use his cross-demand by way of set-off to reduce or extinguish the company's claim in the present action. The plaintiff company's argument is that that is as far as he can go and that, if and so far as he wishes to claim in respect of an amount whereby his cross-demand over-tops the claim, he must do it by proof in the liquidation in the ordinary way. The defendant's concern, as appears from his pleading, is that in these proceedings there shall be ascertained the amount (if any) whereby his cross-demand exceeds the claim and that he shall, **A** in the terms of his pleading, obtain a declaration that he is entitled to prove in the liquidation for such balance. Counsel for the defendant, in the course of the argument, has indicated that the declaration is not vital, but I am satisfied that, by one means or another, what the defendant seeks to achieve is a determination in the present proceedings of the amount due to him so that he may prove for that amount in the liquidation. It is clear from the argument that **B** underlying this dispute is some question under the Statute of Limitations which this court has not been required to go into. I say no more about it, save to indicate that there may well be some advantage under those Acts if the defendant can succeed in having his claim assessed in the present suit.

The argument of the plaintiff company can be put very briefly. Counsel for the plaintiff company points to s. 231 and recognises that there may be some **C** difference in the authorities as to whether a counterclaim is itself a separate action or merely proceedings which have to be treated for certain purposes as a separate action, yet he contends that, on any view, a counterclaim is a " proceeding ". He has drawn our attention to authority which suggests that the words in this phrase in s. 231 should be given a wide meaning. I refer to the most recent case, *Eastern Holdings Establishment of Vaduz* v. *Singer & Fried-* **D** *lander, Ltd. (Able Securities, Ltd., In liquidation, First Claimant; Sempah (Holdings) Ltd., Second Claimant)* (1). This is a judgment of BUCKLEY, J., dealing with an interpleader proceedings and the effect of s. 231 on that proceeding. He quoted (2) certain words from SIR GEORGE JESSEL, M.R., in *Re International Pulp and Paper Co., Ltd.* (3):

"The words are general—' action, suit or other proceeding'. Why **E** should I limit them? Those who say that I am to impose a limit upon those general words must show a reason for my so doing."

BUCKLEY, J., took up the same point where he said (4):

". . . the considerations which arise in this case do lead me to think that s. 231 ought to be construed widely, and sufficiently widely to embrace an **F** interpleader summons."

Accordingly, says counsel for the plaintiff company, this case is really a very simple one: the terms of the section require that leave should be obtained before this counterclaim be pleaded and since it is agreed no leave was obtained, counsel would say that is an end of the matter.

Counsel for the defendant first submits that this counterclaim is not within **G** the terms of s. 231. He will not, I hope, think I am in any sense disrespectful to his argument if I do not attempt to develop this point in any detail, because in substance that is what it amounted to. Apart from commenting on the phraseology of the section itself he has also referred us to authority which suggests that claim and counterclaim are in truth a single proceeding, and he says that if in this case claim and counterclaim are to be treated as a single **H** proceeding then it would not be right to regard that proceeding as against the company but rather as a proceeding brought by the company. Such a result, in my judgment, would be so unreal as to make the court anxious not to adopt it. I cannot find it possible to say that the words of s. 231, given their literal and ordinary meaning, have any other effect than to require leave to be obtained before this counterclaim is made. **I**

Counsel for the defendant's real argument is not on the words of s. 231 but on a very different principle. He relies on s. 31 of the Bankruptcy Act 1914, which applies to company winding-up by virtue of s. 317 of the Companies Act 1948. Section 31 of the Bankruptcy Act provides as follows:

---

(1) [1967] 2 All E.R. 1192; [1967] 1 W.L.R. 1017.
(2) [1967] 2 All E.R. at p. 1194; [1967] 1 W.L.R. at p. 1019.
(3) (1876), 3 Ch.D. 594 at p. 599.
(4) [1967] 2 All E.R. at p. 1195; [1967] 1 W.L.R. at p. 1021.

A   " Where there have been mutual credits, mutual debts or other mutual dealings, between a debtor against whom a receiving order shall be made under this Act and any other person proving or claiming to prove a debt under the receiving order, an account shall be taken of what is due from the one party to the other in respect of such mutual dealings, and the sum due from the one party shall be set off against any sum due from the other

B   party, and the balance of the account, and no more, shall be claimed or paid on either side respectively . . ."

For the purposes of company winding-up one can now read that section as though the reference were to a liquidation and not a bankruptcy.

Counsel for the defendant's argument is that s. 31 does not merely prescribe a code of procedure in the bankruptcy or winding-up, as the case may be, but

C   gives the parties concerned a right which they can enforce and which must be recognised in any court where issues of this kind arise.   Accordingly, he says that in the present proceedings he is entitled under s. 31 to have an account taken as of right and that when the account has been taken the amount shown to be due to him (if it so proves to be) is an amount which he can prove in the winding-up.   The effect of that argument, of course, could be that this court

D   would be required to recognise the equity of the statute (as it was once called) under s. 31 and since counsel for the defendant has carefully drafted his counterclaim to fit the terms of s. 31 the result, he says, is that the counterclaim must stand and insofar as s. 31 seems to be inconsistent with s. 231 of the Companies Act 1948, then s. 31 should prevail.

There is authority on this and I will refer to the two principal cases.   The

E   first one is *Peat* v. *Jones & Co.* (5).   This was a bankruptcy and not a company winding-up.   The facts were that one party to a contract had agreed to deliver iron to the other by successive monthly deliveries but became bankrupt before the instalments had all been delivered.   There was a claim by the trustee in bankruptcy for the amount due on the instalments which had been delivered and this was met by a counterclaim by the purchaser claiming damages for non-

F   delivery and a rise in the price of iron.   At the trial the jury found in favour of the defendants on the counterclaim but the Divisional Court set this aside and ordered that the plaintiff obtain judgment for £150 on the claim saying that the case was governed by *Ogle* v. *Earl Vane* (6).   The defendants then appealed and in the brief judgments in this court each of the three judges made it clear that this so-called counterclaim was available as a set-off so as to defeat wholly or

G   pro tanto the plaintiff's claim.   SIR GEORGE JESSEL, M.R., said at the beginning of his judgment (7):

" For the purpose of the questions we are about to decide, this counterclaim must be treated as a set-off."

BRETT, L.J., at the end of his judgment says of the claim (8):

H   " If cut down to a set-off, therefore, the counterclaim is maintainable."

COTTON, L.J., opens his judgment by saying (8):

" As a trustee in bankruptcy cannot be sued, a counterclaim is not maintainable against him, except so far as it is reduced to a set-off."

Finally the order made in this court (8) was that the appeal was allowed to the

I   extent of deducting damages for non-delivery from the amount recovered by the plaintiff.   That case is a clear authority (if authority were required) for the proposition that notwithstanding s. 231 or its equivalent in the Bankruptcy Act 1914 a cross-demand can be used as a set-off, namely as a shield to reduce or exclude the plaintiff's claim, but I find no word in that case to suggest that

(5) (1881), 8 Q.B.D. 147.
(6) (1868), L.R. 3 Q.B. 272.
(7) (1881), 8 Q.B.D. at p. 148.
(8) (1881), 8 Q.B.D. at p. 150.

the counterclaim can be proceeded on as a counterclaim, that is to say, so as to **A**
give the defendant some right beyond the rights of defence to the claim.

The next case is again a decision of this court following in the next year,
Mersey Steel and Iron Co. v. *Naylor, Benzon & Co.* (9). This case is an important
authority on other matters and the point with which the court is presently
concerned is a secondary issue. Here again there was a contract for the sale
and delivery of goods by instalments. Here the vendor was a company which **B**
went into liquidation before all the instalments had been completed. The company then sued for the amount of the instalments delivered and were met by a
counterclaim of greater amount for damages for failure to deliver. It is quite
clear, and counsel for the defendant rightly stresses this, that the form of pleading in this case was that the defendant was counterclaiming for a greater sum by
way of damages arising out of the contract. At an early point in the argument **C**
(10) reference was made to the difficulty of pursuing a counterclaim in those
circumstances without the leave of the court. SIR GEORGE JESSEL, M.R.,
seems to think that this is a point which is not going to trouble the court too
much, because he said (10)—

> ". . . That is a very narrow ground. I do not think we shall have much
> difficulty in dealing with that." **D**

Then in his judgment he goes on to consider matters which are fresh in this case
as compared with the matters arising in *Peat* v. *Jones & Co.* (11), to which decision
he had been a party the previous year. He said (12)—

> " Now, in reason there cannot be any question whatever that the right
> to set-off unliquidated damages against a debt is one which ought to be **E**
> supported. Irrespective of winding-up, the present defendants would
> have a right to say: ' You owe us a large sum of money for damages; you
> sold us iron at a price which, if delivered, would have left us a very handsome
> profit; we have lost that by your non-delivery of part . . .' "

Then he says (13)—

> ". . . in considering whether this can be done [namely, whether such a **F**
> set-off is possible, the court must look for] some statutory enactment upon
> which we can found our decision as to there being a right of set-off."

He goes on to consider some of the earlier Acts with which we are not concerned
and in particular he refers to s. 10 of the Supreme Court of Judicature Act 1875,
which produces a right to an account similar to that now contained in s. 31 of **G**
the Bankruptcy Act 1914. He observes (14):

> " The present case, however, is not one of proof in a winding-up, but of
> set-off in an action . . ."

Then he looks at R.S.C., Ord. 19, r. 3, which was the order dealing with set-off,
and he proceeds to deal with this matter and says (15):

> " The concluding words [of the rule] shew that the object of the rule **H**
> was to enable the Court to do that in one action which would otherwise
> require two."

He continues (16):

> " Judges had said that the assignee in bankruptcy, as he was then called,
> was not to be in a better position by bringing an action than if the claim **I**
> had been made in the Bankruptcy Court. True, the Act of Parliament

(9) (1882), 9 Q.B.D. 648.
(10) (1882), 9 Q.B.D. at p. 652.
(11) (1881), 8 Q.B.D. 147.
(12) (1882), 9 Q.B.D. at pp. 660, 661.
(13) (1882), 9 Q.B.D. at p. 661.
(14) (1882), 9 Q.B.D. at p. 663.
(15) (1882), 9 Q.B.D. at pp. 663, 664.
(16) (1882), 9 Q.B.D. at p. 664.

A   only says that when the claimant comes to prove in bankruptcy, an account is to be taken.   But the courts take the meaning of the Act to be that when one of the parties is a bankrupt an account shall be taken between the parties, and that, whether the other party brings this claim into the Court of Bankruptcy or not, there shall be no claim except for the balance.   This has been termed, I think, in one of these cases, the equity of the statute.

B   That being the law, the mode of carrying it out is an accident.   If when there are cross demands between the bankrupt and another party the assignee brings an action, we should allow the other party the same benefit as he would have obtained if he had come in to establish his claim in the Court of Bankruptcy.   According to *Peat* v. *Jones & Co.* (17), where you see that the statute enacts that in the case of winding-up there is to be a particular mode

C   of taking an account between the parties, and if the balance is one way the creditor shall prove in the winding-up, and that if it is the other way the liquidator shall be entitled only to claim the difference, the same mode of taking the account ought to apply to a different form of procedure whether in the Court of Bankruptcy or in the High Court.   Then Order XIX, rule 3 comes in, and shews how the point is to be taken, viz., by counterclaim."

D Counsel for the defendant very properly says (if I may pause there) that that passage is entirely in his favour.   It supports the view that the terms of s. 31 must be recognised in an ordinary Queen's Bench action and Sir George Jessel, M.R., in terms says that the method by which that is done is by counterclaim. Unfortunately from the defendant's point of view, one must now read on, because Sir George Jessel, M.R., concludes in these words (18):

E

" It appears to me, therefore, that if we endeavour to apply the enactments of the legislature fairly, and in a rational and beneficial manner, justice can be done by giving the defendants what they ask, viz., the right to a defence to the extent of the amount of the damages."

Sir George Jessel, M.R., is there severely limiting what he had said before.

F What the defendants in that case had asked for was a counterclaim, but all that is being recognised is a right to a defence to the extent of the amount of the damages, and if there were any doubt as to which of those two phrases was the dominant phrase in the mind of Sir George Jessel, M.R., it is solved where we find (19) the minutes of the order which are—

" Discharge the judgment.   Declare that the defendants are entitled

G to set-off against the 1,713*l.* admitted to be due to the plaintiffs such damages as they the defendants may have sustained by reason of the failure or refusal of the plaintiffs to deliver to the defendants . . .."

So it is abundantly clear that all that is being recognised in those two cases is that a cross-demand pleaded by way of counterclaim is not bad on that account, but can take effect only as a set-off.   I find no words to support counsel for

H the defendant's contention that a counterclaim as such is to be enforced beyond its effect as a defence to the claim by way of set-off.

But counsel for the defendant submits that even if the authorities go no further than that, yet we in this court should recognise his contention because he says that if full effect is given to s. 31 and the defendant is allowed to counterclaim in the fullest sense of the word, this will avoid costs and multiplicity of proceedings

I and will enable a full account to be taken between the parties in this action.   I appreciate that there may be cases in which costs might be saved by following that submission, but there may, in my judgment, be other cases where they would not be.   No doubt in many cases, even if only a set-off is pleaded, the mechanics of the matter will result in an account being taken so that an assessment of the figures is reached, and if for any special reason full account is not

(17) (1881), 8 Q.B.D. 147.
(18) (1882), 9 Q.B.D. at p. 664.
(19) (1882), 9 Q.B.D. at p. 672.

taken, because, for example, it becomes apparent early on that the cross-demand   **A**
substantially overtops the claim, then I see no particular objection on the ground
of costs in allowing the further dispute as to the totality of the cross-demand to
be settled on proof in the Companies Court in the ordinary way.   Indeed, it
seems to me it would be quite wrong for us to assume that in general there would
be a great saving of time and expense by adopting counsel for the defendant's contention, and I think that the proper course to deal with the exceptional case   **B**
where the argument may be right is by means of an application for leave to the
Companies Court under the terms of s. 231.

For all those reasons I have come to the conclusion that the learned judge's
order was right and I would refuse these applications for leave.

DAVIES, L.J.:   I entirely agree and would make but two very minor   **C**
additions to what WIDGERY, L.J., has said. The first is this. The report in the
House of Lords in *Mersey Steel and Iron Co.* v. *Naylor, Benzon & Co.* (20), gives the
result of the case after the reference which the Court of Appeal, as WIDGERY,
L.J., has just indicated, directed after the proceedings in that court.   I quote
from the statement of facts (20):

"It may be added that the referee having found that the damages due to   **D**
the defendants for non-delivery amounted to £1,723, being in excess of the
£1,713 admitted to be due to the plaintiffs for the price of the steel delivered,
the Court of Appeal by an order dated the 13th of April, 1883 gave judgment
for the defendant with costs."

That is to say, the amount of the cross-claim, whether it be counterclaim or   **E**
set-off, having exceeded the amount of the plaintiffs' claim, the defendants
were entitled to judgment on the plaintiffs' claim; but there is no suggestion
at all that the defendants were entitled to judgment for the balance of £10.
That, of course, underlines that which WIDGERY, L.J., has indicated, viz., that
any cross-claim can only be used as a set-off or as a shield (as it has often been
said) and not as a sword.

The other small matter to which I would refer is that in BUCKLEY ON THE   **F**
COMPANIES ACTS (13th Edn.) p. 500 in the notes to s. 231 of the Companies
Act 1948, there appears this:

"If a company in liquidation brings an action the defendant may without
leave counterclaim for unliquidated damages".

And as authority for that proposition there is cited *Mersey Steel and Iron Co.*   **G**
v. *Naylor, Benzon & Co.* (21). That note, in my judgment, goes very much too
far and is much too wide. It might be more accurate if the note were to say
" In such case the defendant may without leave set up a cross-claim for liquidated
or unliquidated damages, but only to the extent of a set-off for the purpose of
reducing pro tanto or extinguishing the plaintiff company's claim ".

Apart from that I do not desire to add anything to what has been said by   **H**
WIDGERY, L.J., with which, as I have already said, I entirely agree.

Leave to appeal refused in each action.

Solicitors: *Bridges, Sawtell & A. J. Adams*, agents for *Langdon & Co.*, Torquay
(for the defendant). *Sargent & Probert*, Exeter (for the plaintiff companies).

[*Reported by* HENRY SUMMERFIELD, ESQ., *Barrister-at-Law*.]   **I**

---

(20) (1884), 9 App. Cas. 434 at p. 435.
(21) (1882), 9 Q.B.D. 648.

A

COLVILLES, LTD. *v.* DEVINE.

[HOUSE OF LORDS (Lord Reid, Lord Hodson, Lord Guest, Lord Upjohn and Lord Donovan), January 23, 27, 28, March 11, 1969.]

B
Negligence—Res ipsa loquitur—Onus on defendant to disprove negligence— Evidence required to discharge onus—Plaintiff injured jumping off platform after explosion—Explanation of res not requiring positive proof—No evidence that explanation consistent with absence of negligence.

The appellants owned a steelworks in Scotland. A process for manufacturing steel by the injection of oxygen into converters containing 100 tons of molten metal had been installed 4½ months before the relevant day. The
C oxygen originated from the works of a third party approximately one mile away. It was supplied by means of a pipe, which belonged to the third party, which was connected up to the main distribution centre in the works. At the main intake there was a filter for the purpose of removing foreign bodies from the oxygen stream. From the main distribution centre the oxygen was taken by a hose, under the control of the appellants, to a
D lance by means of which it was injected into the molten metal. The respondent was employed in the steelworks by the appellants. On the relevant day, he was working on a platform some 15 feet from the ground when there was an explosion in the proximity of a converter approximately 75 yards away. Scared by this explosion, he jumped off the platform and sustained injuries, in respect of which he claimed damages from the appel-
E lants. In evidence, the probable cause of the explosion was given as a fire resulting from the ignition of particles in the oxygen stream by friction, which caused the hose to burn. The appellants had received no warning of any such dangers from the makers of the plant, nor had any comparable mishap occurred previously.

Held: (i) the plant (including the hose which caught fire) was under
F the management of the appellants and, since an explosion of such violence would not have occurred in the ordinary course of things if those who had the management had taken proper care, the maxim res ipsa loquitur applied;

(ii) it was not necessary that there should be positive proof of the existence of the particles in the oxygen stream in order to establish the appellants' explanation, but for that explanation to be available as a defence it must
G be consistent with no negligence on their part; accordingly, the appellants not having adduced evidence of any inspection of the filters in the oxygen stream, they had not discharged the onus imposed on them by the maxim.

Appeal dismissed.

[As to the application of res ipsa loquitur, see 28 HALSBURY'S LAWS (3rd Edn.) 77-80, paras. 79-83; and for cases on the subject, see 36 DIGEST (Repl.) 143-146,
H *753-778.*]

Cases referred to:
Marshall & Son v. *Russian Oil Products, Ltd.,* 1938 S.C. 773; 36 Digest (Repl.) 148, *1300.*
Scott v. *London and St. Katherine Docks Co.* (1865), 3 H. & C. 596; [1861-73]
I All E.R. Rep. 246; 34 L.J. Ex. 220; 13 L.T. 148; 159 E.R. 665; 36 Digest (Repl.) 145, *772.*
Woods v. *Duncan, Duncan* v. *Hambrook, Duncan* v. *Cammell Laird & Co., Ltd.,* [1946] 1 All E.R. 420, n.; [1946] A.C. 401; [1947] L.J.R. 120; 174 L.T. 296; 36 Digest (Repl.) 52, *286.*

Appeal.
This was an appeal by the appellants, Colvilles, Ltd., against an interlocutor of the Second Division of the Court of Session (the Lord Justice Clerk (LORD GRANT), LORD WHEATLEY and LORD MILLIGAN; LORD WALKER dissenting),

dated 8th March 1968, adhering to an interlocutor of the Lord Ordinary (LORD **A**
AVONSIDE) dated 1st December 1966 in an action for damages by the respondent,
Patrick Devine, against the appellants whereby the appellants were ordered to
pay £1,350 to the respondent in respect of loss, injury and damage arising out
of an accident that occurred on 26th June 1964.   The facts are set out in the
headnote.   In the course of his opinion in the Court of Session, the Lord Justice
Clerk (LORD GRANT) said: ". . . In deciding whether it [i.e., res ipsa loquitur] **B**
applies in this case the first question, in my opinion, is whether the hose which
ignited and its operation were at the material time under the sole management
and control of the [appellants].   To my mind they were.   It was for the [appel-
lants] (through their servants) and for them alone, to decide whether and when
to start the operation, how long it was to continue, which hose or lance was to
be used and whether and when the oxygen supply through the hose was to be **C**
turned on or cut off: and having made these decisions it was for them alone
to carry them out.   The [appellants] argue, however, that even if that be so the
occurrence of the explosion does not point to negligence on their part.   On this
matter it does not seem to me to be of consequence that this was new plant
supplied by a reputable maker or that the oxygen used was supplied by British
Oxygen Co.   Plant which is properly operated and properly maintained does **D**
not normally explode. If it does, that seems to me to afford reasonable evidence,
in the absence of explanation from those who had sole control and management
of the plant, that the occurrence arose from their want of care.   If the [appellants]
here are able to provide an explanation pointing to fault on the part of the
makers of the plant or the suppliers of the oxygen that may rebut the presumption, but it does not prevent its initial operation.   In my opinion res ipsa applies **E**
here and the real issue is whether the inference raised thereby has been rebutted
by the [appellants].
The explanation which the [appellants] give on record is that:

> ' So far as investigations have been able to reveal, it is believed that
> the said escape of oxygen may have been caused by the ignition of a rubber **F**
> hose supplying oxygen to the lance by particles in the flow of oxygen.'

In evidence three possible explanations were put forward to account for the
explosion.   As regards one of them, I need only say that it was advanced as a
mere general theoretical possibility which had in fact to be ruled out as incompatible with the particular circumstances here.   Accordingly, I need say no
more about it.   The other two were the particle explanation given on record, **G**
i.e., the ignition of the inner aspect of the hose by particles in the oxygen flow,
and ignition caused by a rupture or defect in that inner aspect.   The Lord
Ordinary has rejected both these explanations as mere speculation.   He proceeds, as I understand him, not on the basis of the credibility of Mr. Tait* and
Mr. Flanagan†, but on the content of their evidence and on the view that the
proof adduced does not establish ' conditions adequate to afford an explanation **H**
of how the accident might have happened without negligence on the part of
the [appellants] '.   (See O'Hara v. Central S.M.T. Co., Ltd.‡, per the Lord
President (LORD NORMAND).
" The passages in O'Hara‡ to which I have just referred are relied upon by the
[respondent] as authority for the proposition that, unless there be proved " conditions " existing at the relevant time in the form of either particles present in **I**
the oxygen flow or a rupture or defect in the hose lining, there are no proved
facts (' conditions ') on which the opinion evidence of Mr. Flanagan and Mr. Tait
can be based and that their evidence, for that reason, is worthless.   I do not
think that anything that LORD NORMAND said was intended to achieve such a
narrow and restrictive result.   He himself gives an example of the type of case

---

* A senior official of the appellants.
† The safety officer employed by British Oxygen Co.
‡ 1941 S.C. 363 at pp. 377-379.

A   which he had in mind—proof by the defendants in *Scott* v. *London and St. Kathe-rine Docks Co.** of a neighbouring explosion which might have disturbed the sack, but without proof that the explosion was the cause of the sack's fall.   To my mind it was with proof of ' conditions ' of this sort that he was dealing and not with the amount of factual or real evidence which, in the infinite variety of concatenating circumstances, may be required in any particular case as a mini-

B   mum foundation for opinion evidence.   To take an extreme case, if there were uncontradicted expert evidence from ex facie truthful witnesses of high standing that a particular explosion could only have occurred as a result of the combination of ' conditions ' A and B, I see no reason why the court should not be able to accept that evidence as establishing that combination as the cause or probable cause of the explosion, even although no real evidence can be found in the debris

C   that remains (or elsewhere) to show that the two ' conditions ' were in fact present at the relevant time.   It would accordingly be quite wrong, in my opinion, to discard the evidence of Mr. Flanagan and Mr. Tait, without attempting to weigh it or evaluate it, on the grounds advanced by the pursuer.

     " I now turn to that evidence. As I have indicated, the Lord Ordinary appears to accept them as credible and candid witnesses and it was the content

D   of their evidence, not their demeanour, that led him to the view which he took. A first reading of their evidence gave me the strong impression, which was con-firmed by further consideration, that the evidence was of substantially greater weight and value than the Lord Ordinary gave to it. Neither witness was present at the time of the accident and, by the very nature of things, neither of them, (and, equally, nobody else) was in a position to state whether, at the time of the

E   explosion, there were in fact, particles in the oxygen flow or a rupture or defect in the inner lining of the hose.   Both, however, were able to examine the debris, and they knew the nature of the operation which was being performed and the plant and material used to perform it. Mr. Flanagan in particular had extensive experience of the problems of piping oxygen, though mainly in small-bore pipes. It is true that neither could say what *was* the cause of the explosion.   That being

F   so, it is hardly surprising that they should have talked of ' speculating ' on the cause,—in the absence of certainty one must necessarily speculate.   We are concerned here, however, not with what *was* the cause, but, at the highest, with what was *probably* the cause.   I find Mr. Flanagan's categorical evidence that the most likely cause was the ignition of the inner lining by particles both creditworthy and convincing and it is borne out by the evidence of Mr. Tait.

G   On their evidence, the alternative theory of rupture or latent defect is possible, but less likely.   For that reason, and because it is not pleaded by the [appellants], it is not necessary to consider it further.   The third suggestion which was briefly adumbrated and rapidly rejected does not fit the facts and no other possible explanation has been suggested either in evidence or in cross-examination. There are three horses here, one which is well ahead at the finish, the second which

H   loses by a distance, and the third which, although coming under starter's orders, never in fact got past the starting gate—and it is not suggested that any other horses were eligible to run.   This is a very different case from *Moore* v. *R. Fox & Sons*† where the defendants' experts regarded the accident as inexplicable and the plaintiff's expert regarded it as consistent only with failure to maintain. It seems to me that the [appellants] here have shown that the most likely cause

I   of the explosion was the presence of particles of matter in the flow of oxygen.

     " There is, however, a final hurdle for the [appellants] and it is this which, in my opinion, they have failed to surmount.   The question is whether their innocent explanation is in fact innocent.   The oxygen was supplied by the British Oxygen Co. and it appears that the piping, at any rate until it reached the main distribu-tion centre in the works, was British Oxygen Co. piping.   There was apparently

---

* (1865), 3 H. & C. 596; [1861-73] All E.R. Rep. 246.
† [1956] 1 All E.R. 182; [1956] 1 Q.B. 596.

a filter at or about the main intake there, but we are left in the dark as to who A
owned or controlled that filter and as to the condition it was in and the maintenance it received.   It is clear that there were risks involved when foreign
bodies were present in the oxygen stream and that Mr. Tait, though not conversant
with all the details, was aware that such risks existed.   Furthermore, it seems
clear that the [appellants] had control of the flow of oxygen from at least the
main distribution centre to and through the hose in question.   B

"That being so, one asks the questions, what steps did the [appellants] take
to prevent, so far as practicable, the flow of potentially dangerous particles to
and through the hose?   And what steps would it have been reasonable and
practicable to take?   On these matters the evidence is silent and that being so
the [appellants], in my opinion, fail.   They seem to me to have given a reason
but not an excuse.   I accept their explanation of how the explosion happened, C
but I am unable to see how that explanation rebuts the presumption of negligence
raised against them.   It explains how the explosion probably occurred, but on
exculpation, even at the best for the [appellants], it is silent.   The res has the
last word as well as the first. . ."

   D. W. R. Brand, Q.C., and D. Bruce Weir (both of the Scottish Bar) for the D
appellants.
   C. E. Jauncey, Q.C., and T. G. Coutts (both of the Scottish Bar) for the respondent.

   LORD REID: My Lords, I agree with your Lordships that this appeal
should be dismissed.
                                                                                E
   LORD HODSON: My Lords, I concur.

   LORD GUEST: My Lords, the respondent was injured at the appellants'
Ravenscraig steel works when he jumped from a platform about 15 feet above
ground.   His action was the result of his having been put in a state of fear for
his own safety occasioned by a very violent explosion which occurred some F
75 yards away in proximity to a converter plant.   This plant was used for the
manufacture of steel and the explosion took place following on a fire in a flexible
hose which was used for conveying oxygen from an inlet pipe to a lance used for
injecting oxygen into the converter containing about 100 tons of molten metal.
The process by which oxygen was used for the purpose of a more rapid heating
of the metal to the desired temperature was an Austrian improvement on the G
more traditional method. The oxygen originated from the British Oxygen Co.'s
works and entered the appellants' premises by means of a pipe extending to about
one mile in length.   There is no dispute that the respondent's action in jumping
off the platform was in consequence of the violent explosion and no question,
therefore, arises as to the liability of the appellants for the accident if negligence
against them is established.   The Lord Ordinary (LORD AVONSIDE) found for H
the respondent and awarded him £1,350 damages.   The Second Division (LORD
WALKER dissenting) adhered to his interlocutor.
   The respondent accepts that his only case against the appellants is on the basis
of the maxim res ipsa loquitur.   The doctrine emanates from the well-known
passage of ERLE, C.J., in Scott v. London and St. Katherine Docks Co. which is
to the following effect (1):
                                                                                I
   "There must be reasonable evidence of negligence.   But where the
   thing is shewn to be under the management of the defendant or his servants,
   and the accident is such as in the ordinary course of things does not happen
   if those who have the management use proper care, it affords reasonable
   evidence, in the absence of explanation by the defendants, that the accident
   arose from want of care."

   (1) (1865), 3 H. & C. 596 at p. 601; [1861-73] All E.R. Rep. 246 at p. 248.

A The Lord Justice Clerk (LORD GRANT) has examined very carefully the applicability of the doctrine and has reached the conclusion that it does apply to the circumstances of this case. While I agree with the Lord Justice Clerk that the maxim is of limited ambit, I am not satisfied that any of the criticisms made by the appellants' counsel have any validity. I agree with the conclusion of the Lord Justice Clerk with which LORD WHEATLEY and LORD MILLIGAN concurred.

B LORD WALKER who dissented and did not think the maxim applicable, did so on the view that he was not satisfied on the evidence that oxygen hoses do not burst in the ordinary course of things if those who have the management of them use proper care. The res which is said to speak for itself was the explosion. I must say that without evidence to the contrary I should have thought it self-evident that an explosion of such violence that causes fear of imminent danger

C to the workers does not occur in the ordinary course of things in a steel works if those who have the management use proper care.

If the brocard does apply it becomes necessary to consider whether the appellants can escape liability. They are absolved if they can give a reasonable explanation of the accident and show this explanation was consistent with no lack of care on their part. In my view, the Lord Ordinary has imposed too heavy a

D burden on the appellants. The most probable explanation on the evidence is that the fire which caused the burning of the hose resulted from the particles in the oxygen stream being ignited by friction. The Lord Ordinary describes this explanation as " speculation ", but in my opinion it goes further than that and amounts at any rate to a " plausible explanation " (as spoken to by LORD SIMONDS in *Woods* v. *Duncan* (2)). No other more probable explanation is put forward by

E any of the witnesses. In this respect I agree with the Lord Justice Clerk. It is not necessary that there should be positive proof of the existence of the particles in the oxygen stream to establish the appellants' explanation.

But this explanation only carries the appellants half way to success. The explanation to be available as a defence must be consistent with no negligence on their part (*Woods* v. *Duncan* (3); *Marshall & Son* v. *Russian Oil Products,*

F *Ltd.* (4) per the Lord Justice Clerk (LORD AITCHISON (5))).

The appellants sought to prove a system of inspection of the hose and I agree with the Lord Ordinary that this system was not adequately established. But if the cause of the ignition was particles inside the hose, no external examination of the hose could have revealed the presence of particles and no internal examination was, in the nature of things, practicable.

G If the particles were not in the hose ab initio they must have been introduced with the stream of oxygen coming from the British Oxygen Co.'s works. Questions by the Lord Ordinary at the conclusion of Mr. Flanagan's evidence revealed that there were filters for the oxygen on the appellants' premises. No evidence was forthcoming from the appellants as to any inspection of the filters being made by them. What the inspection would have revealed I do not know. But

H if the appellants have to show that they exercised due diligence to avoid the accident, they cannot escape by saying that the oxygen came from the British Oxygen Co. They knew that particles might cause fire. A filter is presumably for the purpose of preventing the access of impurities. They led no evidence to suggest that any inspection of the filters was ever made to see if they were working properly. In those circumstances I agree with the Lord Justice Clerk

I that they have not discharged the onus on them.

I would dismiss the appeal.

LORD UPJOHN: My Lords, the question of the true ambit of the doctrine of res ipsa loquitur may one day require further elucidation from your Lordships, but in my opinion not in this case.

(2) [1946] A.C. 401 at p. 441.
(3) [1946] A.C. 401; [1946] 1 All E.R. 420, n.
(4) 1938 S.C. 773 at p. 791.
(5) (1865), 3 H. & C. 596 at p. 601; [1861-73] All E.R. Rep. 246 at p. 248.

It is common ground that the test in ascertaining whether the doctrine res **A**
ipsa loquitur applies is laid down in the well-known passage in the judgment of
ERLE, C.J., in *Scott* v. *London and St. Katherine Docks Co.* (5), and it may well be
that it should be applied within a narrow ambit, but the Lord Justice Clerk gave
cogent reasons in his judgment for thinking that on the facts of the case the
doctrine did apply, and I agree with him. He then went on to consider whether
the inference thus raised in favour of the respondent was rebutted by the **B**
evidence of the appellants.

I agree with the Lord Justice Clerk when he stated that the most likely cause
of the explosion was the presence of particles of matter in the flow of oxygen
and therefore it follows that judging the matter on the balance of probabilities
that, for the purposes of the action, was the cause of the explosion.

But then the Lord Justice Clerk went on to examine the question whether **C**
this explanation of the explosion really exonerated the appellants from liability.
Having examined that matter he concluded:

" I accept their explanation of how the explosion happened, but I am
unable to see how that explanation rebuts the presumption of negligence
raised against them. It explains how the explosion probably occurred,
but on exculpation, even at the best for the [appellants], it is silent. The **D**
res has the last word as well as the first."

I agree with that and would dismiss this appeal.

LORD DONOVAN: My Lords, the basic duty of the appellants was to
provide plant and machinery which was as safe for their servants to use as
reasonable care could make it. They did indeed buy it from reputable makers, **E**
and employed them in the installation of the plant and in the supervision of
its early operation.

They received no warning from the makers that such an accident as here
occurred was likely. Nor did they experience any such mishap during the first
$4\frac{1}{2}$ months operation of this unit nor of the other—like unit purchased and installed
at the same time. From these circumstances I think it is a fair inference that the **F**
accident was something which did not happen in the ordinary course of things if
due care were taken. The plant was obviously under the management of the
appellants.

In this state of affairs the respondent was, in my opinion, entitled in law to
say that somebody for whom the appellants were responsible could not have
exercised proper care. In other words res ipsa loquitur. That means that it **G**
was for the appellants to show that the accident was just as consistent with
their having exercised due diligence as with their having been negligent. In that
way the scales which had been tipped in the respondent's favour by the doctrine
of res ipsa loquitur would be once more in balance, and the respondent would
have to begin again and prove negligence in the usual way.

The appellants proved that the most likely cause of the accident was the **H**
presence of particles in suspension inside the hose which were driven against the
inside walls of the hose, thus causing friction and eventually a fire. This would
account for the explosion, or, if the term be preferred, the " loud bang " when the
hose burst. They also admitted that they knew of the possibility that such
particles could cause fire in this way. It also came out in evidence called by
them that there was a filter inside the oxygen supply pipe on their premises, that **I**
pipe leading back to the premises of the British Oxygen Co. In this situation,
in order to prove that the accident was equally consistent with no negligence on
their part, the appellants clearly ought to have proved that the filter was reasonably effective in keeping foreign matter out of the oxygen pipe. They never
attempted to do so. They proved no inspection of the filter from time to time,
nothing as to its condition at or about the time of the accident, and not even
that it was then still there. In these circumstances the scales remained at the end
of the day tilted by the doctrine of res ipsa loquitur in the respondent's favour.

A   This is, I think, the way the Lord Justice Clerk regarded the case, and I respectfully think it is the right approach.

The subsidiary argument for the appellants to the effect that in any event a
loud bang could not have been expected when the hose burst, such that it threw
men into some state of panic, has no persuasive force.   Here was oxygen being
forced at high pressure through a five inch hosepipe.   If it were to ignite, and

B   burst the wall of the hose, what else could be expected but a loud bang?   And
such an unusual occurrence in a steel works with molten steel in containers in the
shop is bound to cause alarm—at least among some of the less sophisticated
labourers in the vicinity.   I do not think this likelihood called for positive
proof.   It could be expected by anyone who sat down and considered the matter.

It was not argued before your Lordships that in any event it could not have

C   been foreseen that the respondent would have jumped from the staging instead
of walking down the stairway to the floor.

I would dismiss the appeal.

Appeal dismissed.

Solicitors: *Richards, Butler & Co.*, agents for *Maclay, Murray & Spens,* Glasgow,
and *Dundas & Wilson, C. S.*, Edinburgh (for the appellants); *W. H. Thompson,*

D   agents for *Teague, Leonard & Muirhead,* Hamilton, and *Courtney & Co., S. S. C.,*
Edinburgh (for the respondent).

[*Reported by* S. A. Hatteea, Esq., *Barrister-at-Law.*]

E

BUNKER *v.* CHARLES BRAND & SON, LTD.

[Queen's Bench Division (O'Connor, J.), December 19, 20, 1968.]

*Occupier—Negligence—Knowledge of danger on part of visitor—Mere knowledge
not absolving occupier from liability—" Occupier "—Occupiers' Liability*

F   *Act 1957 (5 & 6 Eliz. 2 c. 31), s. 2 (4) and (5).*
*Building—Building regulations—Safe means of access—Digging machine hired by
main contractors and used as means of access by employee of sub-contractors—
Whether main contractors owed a duty under the regulations to sub-contractors'
employee—" As affect him "—Construction (General Provisions) Regulations
1961 (S.I. 1961 No. 1580), reg. 3, reg. 7.*

G   The defendants were the main contractors responsible for the tunnel on a
new line in the London Underground.   They used a digging machine owned
by London Transport for this work. This machine required some modification
to the rams at the front and they engaged the plaintiff's employers to
undertake the modifications one weekend when no tunnelling was in progress.
Before the weekend in question the plaintiff had an opportunity of seeing the

H   machine in situ.   The machine had free running rollers on either side and
to reach the front it was necessary to cross these in some way.   No accident
had occurred before in connection with these rollers although it was found
that the plaintiff must have appreciated the danger in crossing the rollers.
At the weekend in question the defendants provided a site engineer and
labour to carry the necessary equipment.   The plaintiff, in attempting to

I   cross the rollers, fell and was injured.

Held: (i) the defendants were the occupiers of the tunnel and the machine
since, despite the employment of the plaintiff's employers as specialist
contractors, they retained control of the tunnel and the machine; accordingly,
they owed the common duty of care under s. 2 of the Occupiers' Liability
Act 1957 to the plaintiff and were not absolved by s. 2 (4) and (5) from their
liability thereunder merely by reason of the plaintiff's knowledge of the
danger (see p. 64, letter F, and p. 65, letter I, post);

(ii) although the defendants had not provided a safe means of access

A   under the terms of the Construction (General Provisions) Regulations 1961, reg. 7 (1)*, they owed no duty under that regulation to the plaintiff, because the words " as affect him " in reg. 3 (1)* referred merely to work carried out by the defendants themselves and did not extend their duty to workmen, such as the plaintiff, employed by sub-contractors (see p. 67, letter B, and p. 69, letter H, post).

B   *Upton* v. *Hipgrave Brothers* (*a firm*) ([1965] 1 All E.R. 6) not followed.

[As to the common duty of care owed by occupiers to visitors, see 28 HALS-BURY'S LAWS (3rd Edn.) 40-47, paras. 35-42.

As to the building regulations, see 17 HALSBURY'S LAWS (3rd Edn.) 125-128, para. 206.

C   For the Occupiers' Liability Act 1957, s. 1, s. 2, see 37 HALSBURY'S STATUTES (2nd Edn.) 833, 834.]

Cases referred to:
   Herbert v. *Harold Shaw, Ltd.*, [1959] 2 All E.R. 189; [1959] 2 Q.B. 138; [1959] 2 W.L.R. 681; Digest (Cont. Vol. A) 605, *356a*.
   London Graving Dock Co., Ltd. v. *Horton*, [1951] 2 All E.R. 1; [1951] A.C. 737; 36 Digest (Repl.) 54, *296*.
D   *Smith* v. *Austin Lifts, Ltd.*, [1959] 1 All E.R. 81; [1959] 1 W.L.R. 100; 34 Digest (Repl.) 249, *1811*.
   Upton v. *Hipgrave Brothers* (*a firm*), [1965] 1 All E.R. 6; [1965] 1 W.L.R. 208; Digest (Cont. Vol. B) 306, *340k*.

Action.
This was an action by William Thomas Bunker, the plaintiff, against Charles   E
Brand & Son, Ltd., for damages for personal injuries. The facts are set out in the judgment.

   P. R. Lewis for the plaintiff.
   B. W. Chedlow for the defendants.

F   **O'CONNOR, J.**: In this action the plaintiff seeks to recover damages from the defendants for injuries sustained by him on 24th July 1965. The plaintiff was a foreman welder employed by Arthur Foster Constructional Engineers, Ltd., at the material time, and the accident happened in a tunnel, part of the work being done for the new Victoria tube. The tunnel in question was being cut by a large machine which, for convenience, I will call the digger. This machine belonged to the London Transport Executive, and it was let as part of the contract   G
to the defendants who were the main contractors for doing the tunnels. It had been physically provided and assembled in the tunnel by the plaintiff's employers, Arthur Foster, Ltd. They were the experts in putting this machine into working condition, and by the time this accident occurred on this particular date it was half-a-mile or a mile into the tunnel. There were other tunnels also being excavated with which I am not concerned.
H   The machine is conveniently illustrated in the working drawing which has been put in, and basically it is of fairly simple construction. Up in front is the excavating mechanism. There are various drills. Precisely how it works, I have not been told, and it does not matter. It will be understood that as the machine digs along the tunnel, segments of steel which are going to form the wall of the tunnel have to be carried forward and placed in position as the work proceeds, and if all   I
goes well the machine can get along at about six feet an hour. If one looks at the middle drawing, which is the plan drawing, the excavating end of the machine is to the extreme right, and the place where the segments had to be put into position inevitably had to be a little way behind.
   In order to get the segments of steel up to where they are going to be placed

* S.I. 1961 No. 1580. Regulation 3 (1) and reg. 7 (1), so far as material, are set out at p. 67 letters A, C, and D, post. Regulation 7 has been revoked by the Construction (Working Places) Regulations 1966 (S.I. 1966 No. 94).

A in position, there are provided at each side of the machine, and they form part of it, a series of rollers. They start off with a run of free-running rollers, supported on angle irons, which are some ten inches wide; then they increase in size, as they run along the side of the machine, to, I think the evidence was, about 18 inches wide; and, finally, the very end of the run of rollers is considerably wider. I think perhaps it is 15 inches but the drawing is to scale, and it is 18 inches at

B the end. The layout is conveniently illustrated on the drawing.

These rollers form an integral part of the machine, and if one looks at the top drawing, where one is looking at the view in elevation, the line of rollers can be seen there about halfway up the stanchions, and the various conveyors which operate to carry away the spoil from the digging plant can also be seen. The line of rollers is illustrated in that drawing immediately above the two small trucks

C which are underneath. Above the rollers and to the left-hand side of them, if one is walking up the right-hand side of the machine, there is a girder supporting part of the mechanism which provides a convenient handhold. The position is precisely repeated on the other side of the machine.

The drawing called for there to be in position a timber walkway between the outer edge of the rollers and the wall of the tunnel, the timber walkway being

D supported on brackets, and the walkway, rollers and the whole machine all moved itself forward, the whole lot went together. As I have said, the purpose of the rollers was to take the segments of the tunnel up to where they were wanted. They were all free-running rollers and were supported on angle irons which were apparently about two inches in width on the upper surface.

Long before this accident happened the defendants had done away with this

E timber walkway. They found that as the machine advanced, for reasons with which I am not concerned, the walkways became cluttered and jammed. At all events, they had done away with them so that there was between the outer side of the rollers and the wall of the tunnel a space, not very far down because of the nature of the tunnel which is round (as can be seen from the sections) which was full of a good deal of junk and material, bits and pieces of stuff such as one can

F expect in this work. It must be remembered that we are concerned with the excavation of a tunnel, and a great deal of clobber can be expected to be lying about.

For driving the machines the crew had to be up front and so did the men who were placing the segments of the tunnel into position. Now, how was one to get up front? The walkway had gone, and the only way of getting up front was to

G negotiate the run of rollers. There was a perfectly good handhold for anybody who chose to hang on to it. Free-running rollers, everybody recognises, form a hazard if you are going to walk on them. It is quite plain that however much care one takes one may miss one's footing in so doing and fall, and, in those circumstances, quite obviously one may sustain injury.

When the machine is in operation, as I have said, those rollers are in constant

H use and must be kept free, but at the time of this accident a quite different situation had arisen. The defendants wanted a modification made to the rams at the front of the machine, the digging end, and for this purpose they engaged the services of the plaintiff's employers. Two new rams had to be fitted. They weighed about a hundredweight each. Mr. May, who is now their chief draughtsman, was in charge of the drawings for this machine and he got out the relevant drawings,

I and he did take the plaintiff down to show him what needed to be done. The work was going to be done at a weekend when no tunnelling was in progress, so that the machine was shut down.

The plaintiff told me, and I accept his evidence about this, that he went down with Mr. May a day or two before the Saturday on which he had his accident. Mr. May's recollection was not very clear about it but, as I say, I accept the plaintiff's evidence and he is supported by his mate, Mr. Fogg, that it was a day or two before the Saturday that he went down to this place for the very first time. His normal job was to work in his employers' workshop, although he had

been in the tunnel before. For one reason or another, the ordinary man who did A
this work was not available at the material time.

Mr. May and the plaintiff went down the tunnel, and when they reached the
rollers Mr. May led the way. He simply walked on the rollers hanging on to the
steel girder on his left or right, depending which side they went in. He has said
that of course there is a hazard in walking on free-running rollers but he managed
all right by holding on, and the plaintiff followed him across. Just how the B
plaintiff did it on this occasion he has not told me, but, be that as it may, he
walked across the rollers following his superior, and no one can blame him for
taking the route in that fashion at that time. They went to the front of the
machine, spent 20 minutes or so looking at what had to be done, and then came
out again in the same way.

On the Saturday morning, 24th July 1965, the plaintiff and his mate, Mr. C
Fogg, arrived at the top of the tunnel at about 7.40 a.m. and went down the
shaft, which was a considerable distance—it matters not—half-a-mile or a mile
from the face. According to the plaintiff, having gone down, he waited about
somewhere at the foot of the shaft and did not go up to the face before going out
to get some breakfast about an hour later. Mr. Fogg's recollection is that they
did go up to the face and then came back and went and got some breakfast. D
There was some sort of control being exercised by the defendants for, as will
become apparent in a moment, they were to provide the labour for carrying in the
two rams, and a site engineer turned out to be on duty. On that first point I
prefer the evidence of Mr. Fogg. I think they did go up to the face on the first
visit and went over the rollers—and I so hold—and came out again.

Then somewhere round about 10 a.m. they went down once more, and on this E
occasion the party consisted of a site engineer—not the gentleman who has given
evidence, Mr. Howes, who was a reliable and entirely honest witness. He said
quite frankly that there may have been a subordinate on duty in the tunnel on
this Saturday morning.   I accept the plaintiff's evidence and that of Mr. Fogg
that a site engineer of the defendants was present on that journey, and so were
two labourers who were to bring in the necessary material. F

On that journey the whole party went forward to the face and it involved
negotiating the rollers. According to the plaintiff, the site engineer went first
and the other man followed, and he was the rear marker. Everybody got across
safely except the plaintiff. The plaintiff's evidence about how he tackled the
journey on this occasion was that he followed the other men and that they were
walking astride the rollers, namely, on the two angle irons, with the left foot G
on the left-hand angle iron and the right foot on the right-hand angle iron. It
was while he was engaged himself in doing that and when he got about halfway
along the rollers that his right foot slipped off the angle iron on to the rollers.
They moved and he fell down, and he injured his knee.

He told me that the people in front were negotiating in the same way. I am
satisfied that he is mistaken about that in part at least, because Mr. Fogg, who, H
the plaintiff says, was in front of him, tackled the rollers in a different fashion.
According to him, he stood on the right-hand angle iron sideways on with his
back to the tunnel wall, and he went crabwise, walking sideways, on the angle
iron, with his shoulders against the tunnel wall—it will be seen that because of the
curvature it is not very far away—getting support in that fashion. That was how
he chose to negotiate the rollers, and he arrived safely at the other end. No I
one has suggested that there was not plenty of light at that stage on this part of
the work. Everybody could see exactly what they were doing.

Mr. Howes, who was not there and who is a senior engineer of the defendants,
told me that he negotiated these rollers many times and so did the defendants'
men, the driving crew and the people who put in the steel girders. The regular
drill was to walk on the rollers fair and square and to hang on to the support of
the conveyor, to which I have already referred, and I see no reason to do other
than to accept his evidence about that. I think the normal method, and I so

A find, adopted by the people who were working up front was to walk on the rollers and to hang on to the steel girder which was conveniently available for the purpose.

As far as Mr. Fogg is concerned, I accept his evidence that he went crabwise across it in this fashion; it may or may not have been a very good way of doing it. It is possible that somebody adopted the method of straddling the rollers, as **B** the plaintiff says he did, and that that is a method of going across. Again it does not in any way prevent a man if he is on the right-hand side holding on to the girder with his left hand at all material times.

At all events, there it is: the plaintiff had a fall while negotiating the rollers. His knee locked, and it took him a little while to pick himself up and to free his knee. He then continued his journey to the front of the machine and he worked **C** there until the midday break. He and Mr. Fogg came out at midday, over the rollers once more, and after the midday break went back for the afternoon, over the rollers again. The plaintiff came out at the end of the day's work. As he got up his knee locked, and he had considerable difficulty in getting home. I will deal with that aspect of the case at a later stage.

Those are the facts of this accident. The only other relevant finding is that Mr. **D** Howes told me, and I accept his evidence, that the men to whom I have referred, employed by the defendants, were making regular use of the rollers to get up front, and that he was not aware of anybody having hurt himself in so doing beforehand, or, indeed, since. All the witnesses were agreed—Mr. Fogg, the plaintiff, Mr. Howes and Mr. May (the plaintiff's employer's chief draughtsman) that negotiating the rollers was a hazardous task. Mr. May said, " I have been **E** over the rollers many times. It is a hazardous journey, but I walked on the rollers and hung on to the conveyor structure ". So too Mr. Howes: " I normally walked on the rollers themselves and hung on to the conveyor structure ". The plaintiff said, quite rightly, that moving about in tunnelling operations has its own hazards and they have to be accepted.

There was one further piece of evidence which the plaintiff gave. He said **F** that before the journey in which he had his accident, and I will not hold it against him that it was at that moment—it may have been on the first journey—he had applied his mind to the danger that existed of walking on the rollers, and that he had bethought himself of a very simple method of avoiding it at such time as the machine was shut down. It might not be practicable or reasonable during the time when the machine was working, but when it was shut down, in order **G** to provide a walkway, all that needed to be done was to lay planks on top of the rollers and to lash the planks down. The plaintiff said that indeed he had thought of that very matter. He said in cross-examination, " I did look for a plank but could not find one. I did not ask anybody for one." I am afraid I cannot accept that piece of evidence. I do not think it crossed his mind. It is quite unreal to tell me that he thought of a plank and looked for a plank when he **H** never asked anybody for one. The evidence was that there was an ample supply of materials available in various parts of the tunnel, and if that piece of evidence had any truth in it one could only expect that he would have asked the site engineer to get his labourers to get two or three planks—that was all that would be required—and to lay them down. I think that is a pure afterthought which has been thought about by the plaintiff, and it simply did not happen. He had been **I** shown by his own superior, Mr. May, had been led across the rollers and had crossed them again before the defendants' site engineer came down and was, so to speak, further lulled when the defendants' men all tackled the rollers without more ado.

On these findings of fact, the plaintiff lays his case in two ways. He says in the first place that the defendants were the occupiers of this site, including the machine, and that, as occupiers, they owed him a common duty of care as laid down by the Occupiers' Liability Act 1957. It is said that they were in breach of that because they were occupiers of the premises (it is convenient to call the whole layout

including the rollers " premises "), which, by s. 1 (3) (a) includes " any fixed or **A**
moveable structure "—and it is conceded by the defendants that this machine
apparently falls within that definition—that there was a danger here and that
they were in breach of the duty owed to the plaintiff under s. 2 of that Act. In
the alternative, the plaintiff alleges that the defendants owed him a duty under
the Construction (General Provisions) Regulations 1961 (1), and that they were
in breach of reg. 7 of those regulations requiring the defendants to provide suffic- **B**
ient safe means of access to the place at which the plaintiff had to work. They
were in breach of it because the rollers were not safe.

I will deal with the claim under the Occupiers' Liability Act 1957 first of all.
I have no doubt it is a correct finding that the rollers, at a time when the machine
was out of commission for a substantial period like a whole weekend (this job
was intended to last a whole weekend), were a hazard; they were a danger **C**
on the premises. There is no doubt that the plaintiff was the defendants' visitor
within the meaning of the Act, and it was in their express contemplation and
knowledge that he was going to use this part of the premises which was a danger.
It must be remembered that the defendants were not the plaintiff's employers.
We are concerned here with the duty under the Occupiers' Liability Act 1957.
Section 2 provides: **D**

> " (1) An occupier of premises owes the same duty, the ' common duty of
> care ', to all his visitors . . . (2) The common duty of care is a duty to take such
> care as in all the circumstances of the case is reasonable to see that the visi-
> tor will be reasonably safe in using the premises for the purposes for which
> he is invited or permitted by the occupier to be there."

E

In the first place, it was submitted by counsel for the defendants that they were
not in occupation of the machine, that having employed specialist contractors to
come and make a modification to the machine at the weekend they had abandoned
any control of the machine and this part of the working and that the occupation
had fallen to the plaintiff's employers. I reject that submission. I have no doubt
that the defendants remained occupiers of this part of the tunnel including the **F**
machine. It is quite obvious that control remained in the defendants through
their responsible officials. It is they who had control of people making use of
this part of the tunnel including the machine, and it was not the plaintiff's
employers through their foreman welder who had any such control. Whether
there was joint control at the very front end of the machine does not matter.
As far as the rollers are concerned, I have not a shadow of doubt that occupation **G**
remained in the defendants and that they were occupiers for the purposes of the
Act. Therefore, they owed a common duty of care to the plaintiff.

Were they in breach of that duty? It will be remembered that until the Act
of 1957 was passed, it had been held in the House of Lords that where a visitor
fully knew of the danger he could not recover. That was finally decided in *London
Graving Dock Co., Ltd.* v. *Horton* (2). In that case an experienced welder who had **H**
for a month been carrying out work on a ship as an employee of sub-contractors
engaged by ship-repairers in occupation of the ship, sustained injuries, without
negligence on his part, owing to the inadequacy of certain staging, constituting an
unusual danger, of which he had full knowledge and which, despite complaints,
the ship-repairers had not remedied. It was held that, the welder being an
invitee, his knowledge of the unusual risk exonerated the ship-repairers from **I**
liability for the damage sustained by him and that it was not essential to their
defence to establish that he was volens in that he was not under any feeling of
constraint in accepting the risk.

LORD PORTER had this to say about it (3):

---

(1) S.I. 1961 No. 1580.
(2) [1951] 2 All E.R. 1; [1951] A.C. 737.
(3) [1951] 2 All E.R. at p. 6; [1951] A.C. at p. 748.

A
"The difference between *sciens* and *volens* has by now been firmly established, but where the exact line is to be drawn is a matter of more difficulty. The accurate demarcation, however, in my opinion, need not be laid down in the present case, since it is enough to protect the invitor from liability if he proves that the invitee knew and fully appreciated the risk."

B
That was the position in which the law stood in 1951 and, indeed, until the Occupiers' Liability Act 1957 came into force. An example of the application of the old law was cited to me by counsel for the plaintiff—*Smith* v. *Austin Lifts, Ltd.* (4)—which merely is another example of the House of Lords saying that in order to prove knowledge one has got to prove knowledge not only of the risk but of the exact nature of it.

C
As far as this case is concerned, I do not hesitate to find that the plaintiff had full knowledge of the risk involved in walking over the rollers. It is to my mind quite unarguable to suggest that he did not appreciate what the danger was. The danger was that he might lose his footing and fall down. He is a perfectly sensible adult man, and he knew that as well as was possible. However, the law has been altered by the Act of 1957. Section 2 (4) provides:

D
"In determining whether the occupier of premises has discharged the common duty of care to a visitor, regard is to be had to all the circumstances, so that (for example)—(*a*) where damage is caused to a visitor by a danger of which he had been warned by the occupier, the warning is not to be treated without more as absolving the occupier from liability, unless in all the circumstances it was enough to enable the visitor to be reasonably
E
safe."

Section 2 (5) provides:

"The common duty of care does not impose on an occupier any obligation to a visitor in respect of risks willingly accepted as his by the visitor (the question whether a risk was so accepted to be decided on the same principles as in other cases in which one person owes a duty of care to another)."

F
I read that as meaning that in order to absolve himself the occupier must show that the visitor was volens in the proper sense to the risk. One has to return to s. 2 (2): The duty—

". . . is a duty to take such care as in all the circumstances of the case is reasonable to see that the visitor will be reasonably safe in using the
G
premises . . ."

It was submitted by counsel for the defendants that, despite the fact that the free-running rollers, mounted as these were, in the position as these were, were obviously a danger for anybody walking on them, but because of the adequate handhold which was available and because of the experience which the defendants themselves had had of safely using them, in all the circumstances of this case they
H
had taken such care as was reasonable—he did not say this but it follows as part of the argument because the place was thoroughly well lit and the danger was an obvious one—to see that the visitor would be reasonably safe in using the premises to which he had been invited. Against that, counsel for the plaintiff, has submitted that s. 2 (4) (*a*) has no application because no warning was given here and I should look solely at s. 2 (5) and, unless it is established that the plaintiff was
I
volens to the risk of falling in the true sense, the defendants are liable, subject to any contributory negligence.

I take the view that s. 2 (4) has to be read together with s. 2 (5), that the warning is a warning of the danger, and I take the view that the warning is not to be treated without more as absolving the occupier and so too that knowledge of the danger by the plaintiff is not to be treated without more as absolving the occupier from liability unless in all the circumstances it was enough to enable the visitor

(4) [1959] 1 All E.R. 81; [1959] 1 W.L.R. 100.

to be reasonably safe : note " enough to enable the visitor to be reasonably safe ".   **A**

Had I accepted the plaintiff's evidence that not only did he appreciate the danger but set about trying to find a plank and thereafter was not bothered to ask the defendants' relevant employees to find one for him, I would not have hesitated to hold that he was fully volens to the risk of going across the rollers, but, as I have said, I reject that piece of his evidence. I am, therefore, left with a skilled man doing responsible work but, nevertheless, an employee who is ordered   **B** by his own employers and with the knowledge of the defendants to go and work up front of this machine, which involved going over what was a dangerous run of rollers.

The mere fact that no accident had happened in the past does not in my judgment absolve the defendants from taking further precautions. The fact that it might be quite impossible to lay a plank on these rollers when the machine was in   **C** use again, in my judgment, does not absolve them from considering the matter when the machine was not in use. It must be remembered that the design had called for a timbered walkway alongside the rollers expressly as a means of getting a sure-footed access, inconvenient though it might be because of the curvature of the tunnel—it might require a man to bend or crouch, but it would provide him with a sure footing. That had been removed by them. They had, so to speak,   **D** created the particular danger with which I am concerned, namely, requiring anybody who was to go up front of this machine to negotiate the rollers. At a time when the machine was shut down, I take the view that in all the circumstances of the case they were required, in exercising the common duty of care, to either put down planks beside the rollers to enable a firm walkway to be provided or, alternatively, if that required too much timber, to lash planks on top of the   **E** rollers and provide a sure-footed method of getting up to the front of the machine. It is not only for a moment—it is not an interruption of work—it is a whole weekend with which we are concerned, and it must be remembered that as a part of considering this that one of the things which was to be done was that heavy pieces of equipment were to be taken up. It may be they could have been rolled up on the rollers—I do not know; I have had no evidence about that—but I   **F** am satisfied that in all the circumstances of this case for that weekend, in order to discharge the common duty of care, something more ought to have been done, that it was not enough just to leave this as it was and to rely on past practice and hanging on to the girder.

As I have said, I am satisfied that the plaintiff had no alternative but to use the path which he had been shown by his own employers' superior, and the method   **G** of tackling it had been confirmed during the journey which he was making at the time of his accident by a senior representative of the defendants. Therefore, I hold the defendants were in breach of the common duty of care owed to the plaintiff under the Occupiers' Liability Act 1957.

As far as the plaintiff is concerned, whether he adopted the method which he has told me he did, and maybe he did—I can understand somebody doing it—I am   **H** satisfied that common prudence required that he should hang on to the readily available handhold. That he did not do. He was so busy balancing himself, if he is right, on the two angle irons that he was not holding on. That is a plain example of partial fault in the case. I think he should have held on. Had he held on he might never have had this accident, and it forms a substantial element in responsibility for this case. Taking all the circumstances of the case together, it   **I** seems to me that he is equally to blame for his accident as are the defendants, and I hold him 50 per cent. to blame for this accident.

That is as far as the breach of duty and the Occupiers' Liability Act 1957 is concerned. I turn now to the claim under the Construction (General Provisions) Regulations 1961.   The regulation (5) which it was said was broken was reg. 7 (1). It provides:

---

(5) This regulation has been revoked by S.I. 1966 No. 94. See now ibid., regs. 6 and 7.

A   " Sufficient safe means of access and egress shall so far as is reasonably
practicable be provided and maintained to and from every place at which
any person has at any time to work and every such place shall so far as is
reasonably practicable be made and kept safe for any person working there."

I can say at once that if the defendants owed any duty to the plaintiff under that
regulation, they were undoubtedly in breach of it and the result would be the
B   same, because contributory negligence would still be found and under that head
too the plaintiff would be entitled to recover 50 per cent. of his damages.

The question is, does the regulation apply? The duty is laid down under
reg. 3 (1) which provides:

" It shall be the duty of every contractor, and every employer of workmen, who is undertaking any of the operations or works to which these
C   Regulations apply—(*a*) to comply with such of the requirements of the
following Regulations as affect him or any workman employed by him, that
is to say Regulations 7 [and then there are a whole string of further regulations,] Provided that the requirements of the said Regulations shall be
deemed not to affect any workman if and so long as his presence in any
place is not in the course of performing any work on behalf of his employer
D   and is not expressly or impliedly authorised or permitted by his employer;
and (*b*) to comply with such of the requirements of Regulations 12 [and there
is a further string of regulations which are different to those in para. (*a*)]
as relate to any work, act or operation performed or about to be performed
by any such contractor or employer of workmen . . ."

E   There follows the duty on contractors and employers' workmen to erect and alter
scaffolds with which I need not concern myself here.

The regulation defining the obligation is closely similar to that with which the
courts are familiar and found in the Building (Safety, Health and Welfare)
Regulations 1948 (6). In reg. 4 of the regulations of 1948, the opening words are
precisely the same as those I have just read, " (i) to comply with such of the
requirements of Regulations [they are set out] as affect any workman employed
F   by him . . ." It will be seen that the only distinction between the two is that there
has been inserted into the regulations of 1961 the additional words, " to comply
with such of the requirements of the following Regulations as affect him or any
workman employed by him ".

It was submitted by counsel for the plaintiff, that the effect of that is to make
the defendants liable under a duty to the plaintiff in the present case, and for that
G   proposition he relies on a decision of Marshall, J., in *Upton* v. *Hipgrave Brothers*
(*a firm*) (7), where the point was raised for the first time. In that case the plaintiff
was employed by sub-contractors on a building site, the main contractors having
put in a hoist. The plaintiff loaded the barrow on to the hoist; he did it carelessly
so that one of the handles protruded. As the hoist went up the handle of the barrow
H   hit some projecting part of the structure, tipped up the barrow which was full
of bricks, out came the bricks, one of which fell on the plaintiff who was standing
nearby. The question arose in that case whether the second defendants, who were
not the plaintiff's employers, were liable to him for breach of reg. 46 (1) of the
regulations of 1961, the duty to comply with which is to be found in reg. 3 (1) (*a*)
of those regulations.

I   Marshall, J., having cited the regulation had this to say (8):

" The words ' as affect him ' do not appear in reg. 4 of the Building
(Safety, Health and Welfare) Regulations, 1948. Therefore, the question of
the effect of these words has arisen in this case. There is no previous decision
on the point. The argument of counsel for the second defendants was based
on the proposition that the words were inserted to meet a lacuna in the

(6) S.I. 1948 No. 1145.
(7) [1965] 1 All E.R. 6; [1965] 1 W.L.R. 208.
(8) [1965] 1 All E.R. at p. 10; [1965] 1 W.L.R. at pp. 211, 212.

Building Regulations of 1948 under which, so the argument runs, a con-   **A**
tractor, by sub-contracting all the work and having no workman of his own
engaged on the operation, could divest himself of all responsibility under the
regulations, since liability only arose in case of injuries to his own workmen
or to the workmen of other people who were injured by the contractors'
workmen. Since the lifting operations (9) were entirely the responsibility of
the first defendants, the contention of counsel for the second defendants   **B**
was that his clients were not liable under reg. 46 (1) for the injuries to the
first defendants' workman. They, the second defendants, would only be
liable for injuries to their own workmen.

"In my view, under reg. 3 (1) of the Construction (General Provisions)
Regulations, 1961, various duties arising generally under the regulations are
allotted between the various contractors. There can be no doubt that   **C**
reg. 46 (1) places a duty on the first defendants, the plaintiff's employers.
The real problem is whether, in the circumstances, the second defendants,
the main contractors, are liable to the plaintiff under reg. 46 (1), because
its requirement 'affects' them. In this context, it must be remembered
that these regulations fix the main responsibility for safety on a building site
on the main contractors."   **D**

I pause there to say, with all respect to the learned judge, that I cannot agree
with that assertion. The whole design of the code of these regulations, and they
are repeated in the ones which are in force today, is to draw a distinction between
some regulations which are to apply insofar as they relate to any work at, or
operation performed on, the site as opposed to other regulations where the duty
is to comply with the regulations so far as they affect certain individuals. Whereas   **E**
the statement which I have read is certainly true about the regulation found, for
example, in reg. 3 (*b*), in my judgment it is not apt to describe the duties set out
in reg. 3 (*a*).

The judgment went on (10):

"The hoist tower was provided by them. It was used by their own work-   **F**
men, and the sub-contractors' workmen only used it with their leave and
licence. [Counsel for the plaintiff says that that is very close to the present
case.] The hoists were in constant use to advance the main contracting work
in all its aspects. A workman of the main contractors could just as easily
have been injured; it was a place where workmen habitually worked, and a
place where the possibility of material falling had to be borne in mind. I
have come to the conclusion that reg. 46 (1) of the Construction (General   **G**
Provisions) Regulations, 1961, was intended to, and did, 'affect' the main
contractors. It laid on them a duty, when constructing the hoist for use by
their own workmen and sub-contractors alike, to take steps 'to prevent any
person who is working in that place from being struck by any falling material
or article'. This they failed to do, and I hold that the second defendants,
as well as the plaintiff's own employers, the first defendants, have committed   **H**
breaches of reg. 46 (1)."

As I have said, it is with regret that I find myself unable to agree with the reasoning of MARSHALL, J., in *Upton* v. *Hipgrave Brothers* (*a firm*) (11). The whole code of
these regulations, as I have said, started by drawing a sharp distinction between
the duty which was owed under some regulations to the workmen of the contrac-   **I**
tor undertaking any of the operations, and a duty owed by such person to all and
sundry who might come on the site insofar as they relate to any work, act or
operation performed. Then, if more was wanted, a third part of the regulations
expressly provided for those who construct or alter scaffolds.

If the reasoning behind the decision in *Upton* v. *Hipgrave Brothers* (*a firm*) (11) is

(9) The Construction (Lifting Operations) Regulations 1961 (S.I. 1961 No. 1581).
(10) [1965] 1 All E.R. at p. 10; [1965] 1 W.L.R. at p. 212.
(11) [1965] 1 All E.R. 6; [1965] 1 W.L.R. 208.

A correct, it follows that reg. 3 (*b*) becomes unnecessary, because if " affect " was to be given so wide a meaning, as I apprehend it was given in *Upton* v. *Hipgrave Brothers* (*a firm*) (12), being used as merely being in some way connected with the work which the main contractor had undertaken to carry out, then I can see no reason for dividing the duties as they are in fact divided and have been for a very long time.

B   Is there another meaning which it is reasonable to give to the words " as affect him " now inserted in the new code of regulations? In my judgment there is, and a very straightforward one. In *Herbert* v. *Harold Shaw, Ltd.* (13), the plaintiff was an independent roofing contractor who was working on his own. He was engaged in roofing work on a shed which the defendants were building as building contractors, and he had an accident while so engaged. He brought an action **C** against the defendants saying that he was entitled to the benefit of duties imposed by reg. 4 and reg. 31 of the Building Regulations 1948. Remember that reg. 4 (1) of the Building Regulations 1948, did not contain the words " as affect him " but only " as affect any workman employed by him ".   The Court of Appeal held, upholding the learned trial judge, that no duty was owed by the defendants to the plaintiff because he was not a " workman employed by him ". Regulation 31 **D** fell within reg. 4 (1) of the regulations of 1948 just as reg. 7 of the Construction (General Provisions) Regulations 1961 falls within reg. 3 (1) of those regulations.

The result of that decision was that the plaintiff in that case was not in breach of reg. 31 and thus he could not be prosecuted. It must be remembered that the purpose of the code of regulations, of which the Construction (General Provisions) Regulations 1961 form part, is that they are not for the prime purpose of giving **E** a civil remedy to persons who are injured but of promoting safety in the relevant operations and of providing a criminal sanction if the regulations are not obeyed. The loophole which, in my judgment, " as affect him " filled is that to be found in *Herbert* v. *Harold Shaw, Ltd.* (13), and to make it quite clear where a single man is carrying on what is itself an operation to which the regulations ought to apply, he is under a duty, be it said a duty to himself but a duty, with the sanction **F** of a penal section on it, to take the necessary precautions required by those regulations.

It seems to me that that is the purpose of putting in the words " as affect him " within the present-day code, and that it cannot be right to construe those words as making the wide change in the law which follows from giving those words the interpretation given to them by MARSHALL, J., in *Upton* v. *Hip-* **G** *grave Brothers* (*a firm*) (12). As I say, reluctant as I am to disagree with a judgment from that learned judge on a topic of this sort, I have no doubt in my mind that the construction given to those words by him was wrong.

In the result, so far as the present case is concerned, I hold that the defendants were under no duty to the plaintiff to comply with the requirements of reg. 7 of the Construction (General Provisions) Regulations 1961, and on that ground **H** his claim would fail.

However, as I have said, he is entitled to recover damages to be set in such sum as I award him. [HIS LORDSHIP considered the injuries and continued:] I do assess the general damages at £1,250, and in the result there is a total of £1,463 9s. 1d. to be divided in half. I think we had better forget the penny.

Judgment for the plaintiff for £731 14s. 6d.

I
Solicitors: *Shaen, Roscoe & Bracewell* (for the plaintiff); *Barlow, Lyde & Gilbert* (for the defendants).

[*Reported by* MARY COLTON, *Barrister-at-Law.*]

---

(12) [1965] 1 All E.R. 6; [1965] 1 W.L.R. 208.
(13) [1959] 2 All E.R. 189; [1959] 2 Q.B. 138.

HEATON (Inspector of Taxes) v. BELL.

[HOUSE OF LORDS (Lord Reid, Lord Morris of Borth-y-Gest, Lord Hodson, Lord Upjohn and Lord Diplock) February, 3, 4, 5, March 12, 1969.]

Income Tax—Income—Perquisites or profits of office or employment—Car loan scheme for employees—Adjustment of employee's wage to meet cost—Scheme terminable by 14 days' notice—Whether car loan a taxable perquisite of employment—Income Tax Act 1952 (15 & 16 Geo. 6 & 1 Eliz. 2 c. 10), s. 156 (Sch. E), as amended—Finance Act 1956 (4 & 5 Eliz. 2 c. 54), s. 10, Sch. 2, para. 1.

Income Tax—Wages—Car loan scheme—Employees participating in scheme receiving lower wages—Whether gross wages affected by acceptance of lower wages and use of car.

The taxpayer's employers introduced a car loan scheme under which certain of their employees were able, in consideration of accepting an amended wage basis, to obtain the use of a motor car. The scheme was described by the managing director in a letter to each employee. The scheme was described as one evolved " whereby a craftsman may run a car, if he so desires, at most reasonable terms "; the employers loaned, to a participating employee, a new car of certain stated makes and they paid comprehensive insurance and road tax; the employee accepted the amended wage basis which applied even if the vehicle was under repair. The taxpayer applied to join the scheme in 1961; he selected the car he wanted and signed the agreement presented to him. This agreement provided that during his service with the employers he was to make use of a specified car for the " more efficient discharge of his duties "; he was not to permit anyone else to drive or use the car except in an emergency and was himself responsible for running and maintenance costs; the agreement concluded " Either of us may cancel my obligation and authority to use the car on 14 days' notice ". On joining the scheme the taxpayer was required to forego part of his wages (i.e., accept the " amended wage basis "). On his weekly pay-slip, however, the only difference was that the adjustment in respect of the car loan scheme was deducted before his taxable gross earnings were totalled. Early in 1962, the employers informed those employees participating in the scheme that a rise in costs " makes it imperative for a heavy increase of 8s. to 10s. per week ". On the question whether the car loan scheme adjustments were correctly included in computing the taxpayer's emoluments from his employment under Sch. E* to the Income Tax Act 1952, as amended by the Finance Act 1956, s. 10, Sch. 2, para. 1,

Held: (i) (LORD REID dissenting) the true agreement between the taxpayer and his employers was that, under the scheme, the taxpayer's wages were to remain unchanged but the employers were entitled to deduct from his wages each week a sum in respect of the use of a car under the scheme; accordingly the car loan scheme adjustments were properly included under Sch. E, in computing the amount of the gross wages of the taxpayer from his employment (see p. 80, letter I, to p. 81, letter A, p. 84, letter F, p. 88, letter H, p. 89, letter H, p. 90, letter I, to p. 91, letter A, p. 92, letter F, and p. 93, letter G, post); alternatively,

(ii) (LORD HODSON and LORD UPJOHN dissenting) assuming that the taxpayer had contracted, under the scheme to receive a lower gross wage and to have the use of a car, the use of a car was a perquisite which, since by its surrender the taxpayer would become entitled to a higher monetary

---

* Tax under Sch. E., para. 1 (s. 10 of the Finance Act 1956) is charged on the " emoluments " of the employment " for the year of assessment ". " Emoluments " are defined in para. 1 (1) of Sch. 2 to the Act of 1956 as including " all salaries, fees, wages, perquisites and profits whatsoever ".

A   wage, was itself taxable (see p. 79, letter G, p. 87, letter E, and p. 96, letter
     C, post).
         Tennant v. *Smith* ([1892] A.C. 150) and *Abbott* v. *Philbin* (*Inspector of Taxes*)
     ([1960] 2 All E.R. 763) applied.
         Wilkins (*Inspector of Taxes*) v. *Rogerson* ([1961] 1 All E.R. 358) approved.
         Per LORD DIPLOCK: it must not be supposed that I assent to the proposi-
B   tion that a benefit in kind can escape all charge to tax as a perquisite by
     limitations on the employee's right to deal with it imposed by a contract
     collateral to his contract of employment into which he enters by his own
     volition (see p. 95, letter F, post).
         QUAERE: whether, if the use of a car were deemed taxable as a per-
     quisite (i.e., as in holding (ii) supra), the taxpayer would have been assess-
C   able in respect of the full annual amount of the benefit or whether from such
     full annual amount there should be deducted an amount representing the
     period of notice requisite to convert the perquisite into higher wages (see p.
     79, letter H, to p. 80, letter A, and p. 96, letters D to I, post).
         Decision of the COURT OF APPEAL ([1968] 2 All E.R. 1156) reversed.

D   [As to the character of emoluments chargeable to income tax under Sch. E,
     see 20 HALSBURY'S LAWS (3rd Edn.) 312, 313, para. 574, and as to deductions
     from such emoluments, see ibid., p. 326, para. 598; for cases on taxation of
     salaries, perquisites and profits of employment, see 28 DIGEST (Repl.) 225-237,
     971-1040, and on deductions for the purposes of Sch. E, see ibid., 242-247, *1059-
     1099.*

E   For Sch. E as amended, see 36 HALSBURY'S STATUTES (2nd Edn.) 408, 409,
     448, 449, and 31 ibid., 149, 156.]

     Cases referred to:
         Abbott v. *Philbin* (*Inspector of Taxes*), [1960] 2 All E.R. 763; [1961] A.C. 352;
             [1960] 3 W.L.R. 255; 39 Tax. Cas. 82; Digest (Cont. Vol. A) 890,
             1058a.
F   *Bell* v. *Gribble, Hudson* v. *Gribble,* [1903] 1 K.B. 517; 72 L.J.K.B. 242; 88
             L.T. 186; 67 J.P. 85; 4 Tax Cas. 522; 28 Digest (Repl.) 246, *1088.*
         Inland Revenue Comrs. v. *Westminster* (*Duke*), [1936] A.C. 1; [1935] All E.R.
             Rep. 259; 104 L.J.K.B. 383; 153 L.T. 223; sub nom. *Westminster*
             (*Duke*) v. *Inland Revenue Comrs.*, 19 Tax Cas. 490, 28 Digest (Repl.)
             339, *1505.*
G   *Machon* v. *McLoughlin* (1926), 11 Tax Cas. 83; 28 Digest (Repl.) 234, *1025.*
         Tennant v. *Smith,* [1892] A.C. 150; 61 L.J.P.C. 11; 66 L.T. 327; 56 J.P. 596;
             3 Tax Cas. 158; 28 Digest (Repl.) 216, *916.*
         Wilkins (*Inspector of Taxes*) v. *Rogerson,* [1960] 1 All E.R. 650; [1960] Ch. 437;
             [1960] 2 W.L.R. 515; *affd.,* C.A.; [1961] 1 All E.R. 358; [1961] Ch.
             133; [1961] 2 W.L.R. 102; 39 Tax Cas. 344; Digest (Cont. Vol. A)
H   890, *1048a.*

     Appeal.
         This was an appeal by the Crown from an order of the Court of Appeal
     (DANCKWERTS, SALMON and FENTON ATKINSON, L.JJ.) dated 9th May 1968 and
     reported [1968] 2 All E.R. 1156, allowing an appeal by the taxpayer Ralph Garland
I   Bell from an order of UNGOED-THOMAS, J., dated 11th July 1967 and reported
     [1968] 1 All E.R. 857, who allowed an appeal by the Crown by way of Case Stated
     from a determination of the Commissioners for the Special Purposes of the
     Income Tax Acts dated 1st March 1966.
         The following facts are taken from the Case Stated. The taxpayer was at all
     material times employed by John Waddington, Ltd. (" the employers "), as a
     machine minder in the lithographic department. In 1954 the employers decided to
     introduce a voluntary car loan scheme for the benefit of certain employees who
     earned less than £2,000 a year and who were not directors of the company. The

managing director wrote to each employee who was eligible to join in the **A**
scheme as follows:

" Dear Mr.

In view of the keen competition which is developing both at home and
overseas I am most anxious to obtain the highest production possible through
the simple economies of: (a) Running the machines to the maximum amount
of time and speed. (b) Prevention of wastage. (c) Concentration on the job **B**
in hand, and all the other efforts which can be made to greater efficiency.

I believe that a motor car is of great assistance when people live at some
distance from their work and occasionally have to work unusual hours, also
a motor car enables a man to have more recreation. Therefore, I have
evolved a scheme whereby a craftsman may run a car, if he so desires, at most
reasonable terms. Motoring is not enjoyable unless it is trouble-free and **C**
safe. Only new cars (up to two years old) can give this assurance and safety.
So my scheme concerns new cars only. At the end of two years the [employers]
will trade the car (or cars) for new ones. This scheme will enable the craftsman
to travel to and from his work with speed and comfort and will also enable
him, with his family, to make the most of his leisure hours.

The literature enclosed is Private and Confidential and the Agreement **D**
which will be necessary for you to sign is made as simple as possible. From
the original four-page document of here-to-fores, etc., I have whittled it down
to a short paragraph which both of us can understand. In starting this scheme
(which I hope will shortly include not only craftsmen, but others) I am laying
myself open to all manner of criticism from all manner of quarters. All kinds
of objections have already been raised but steadily, one by one, I have over- **E**
come them. It has been suggested that this scheme will create jealousies.
A man with no family may be able to afford to come into the scheme
where perhaps a man with four children could not. My reply to that was that
the man with four children was indeed fortunate. I would sooner have four
kiddies than forty cars. But children grow up rapidly, all too rapidly, and
the scheme will still be available when the pocket permits. **F**

An application form is enclosed and subject to all things being satisfactory
the application will be accepted. Afterward, the delivery of the car should
take a matter of a few weeks only.

In conclusion, I hope this scheme will be a success and will prove of
advantage to you, your family and the [employers].

Yours sincerely,

Managing Director."

G

The following documents were enclosed with the letter:

(a)   " *Private and Confidential.*

WADDINGTONS CRAFTSMEN'S CAR LOAN SERVICE.

H

CONDITIONS.

1. [The employers] will loan a new car (Ford Popular—Austin A30—
Ford Anglia or Morris 8.) selected by the proposed user.

2. [The employers] will pay full comprehensive Insurance for each year
of the service. (£15 per annum).

3. [The employers] will pay the Road Tax for each year of the service. **I**
(£12. 10. 0d. per annum).

4. [The employers] will arrange for the decarbonizing of the car during
the second year.

5. The user will sign a simple agreement.

6. An amended wage basis will come into operation if the application
is accepted.

7. The user will provide his own petrol, oil, grease and other incidentals.

8. The user will provide for cleaning and running maintenance.

A   9. If the car is under repair for maintenance or following an accident the amended wage basis will still apply.

10. Completion of application form does not mean acceptance by the [employers]. They reserve full discretion on each application.

B   John Waddington Limited."

(b) A Memorandum of Terms of Service to be signed by an employee who wished to join the scheme. (See p. 81, letters H and I, post.)

(c) An Application Form to be filled in and signed by an employee who wished to join the scheme.

When in 1954 the scheme was finally settled, a meeting was arranged for all the

C employers' employees concerned to hear the details of how the scheme would operate.

The taxpayer attended the meeting of employees in 1954 when the scheme was introduced but did not join the scheme until 1961. In the meantime the taxpayer did not attend any further meetings in connection with the scheme but all relevant information was circulated to the employees and detailed information

D could be obtained if desired. On 10th February 1961, the taxpayer signed an application form to join the scheme. The taxpayer selected an Austin A40 De Luxe car and on 3rd March 1961 signed a " Memorandum of Terms of Service ".

On 30th May 1961, Mr. H. D. Brearley, the officer of the employers in charge of the scheme wrote to Mr. Stephens, the secretary of the employers as follows:

" Craftsmen's Car Service.

E   The Austin A40 Deluxe car Reg. No. 3248 RO recently delivered has been allocated to [the taxpayer] of the Litho Department.

[The taxpayer] is a newcomer on the scheme and I am sending with this letter his signed agreement form and his completed application form fully approved.

He would like to take the car away today at 5.15 p.m. and if you will let

F me have the usual note saying that the car is insured, I will see that it is handed over to him."

On the same day, 30th May 1961, Mr. Stephens wrote to Mrs. Nicholson of the employers' wages office, as follows:

" Dear Mrs. Nicholson,

A new car has been made available to the following person(s). Will you

G please arrange the necessary weekly wage reduction.

Craftsmen:—. . . [the taxpayer], Litho Dept., Leeds, Clock No.

On and from:—Pay day Friday, 2nd June, 1961.

Yours sincerely,   ."

The " necessary weekly wage reduction " made in respect of the taxpayer's Austin A40 car, Registered No. 3248 RO was £2 9s., first applied on pay day

H Friday, 2nd June 1961.

The Austin car was handed over to the taxpayer on 30th May 1961. The employers made a summary giving details of each of the cars supplied and the weekly wage reductions of some of their employees under the Craftsmen's Car Scheme. The employers also kept a register of the cars supplied to craftsmen,

On 26th February 1962, Mr. Brearley wrote to all the employees in the scheme

I as follows:

" JOHN WADDINGTON LIMITED

LEEDS TO......................

26th February, 1962.

Dear

Craftsmen's Car Service

Since writing my letter of the 15th January, I have very carefully surveyed the costs relating to cars.

A

The present wage adjustments have remained the same since the beginning of the scheme and since that time costs have risen in many different ways —the cost of the car, the cost of insurance and now the tax. The very fact that the tax has risen from £12. 10s. to £15. per year means 1s. per week on every car, but this is trifling compared with other increases.

B

The higher costs coupled with the greater difficulty of obtaining the right price when we sell returned cars as second-hand cars makes it imperative for a heavy increase of 8s. to 10s. per week.

This is a very steep rise, but the car you are already running will be at a slightly less rate because of the cheaper purchase price of the car. Unfortunately a new car will have to stand the full increase and you must bear this in mind when you are thinking of changing.

C

There are two Schedules attached, the first one which you will refer to now and the second which you will have to refer to if and when you are wanting a new car.

As promised I am giving you one month's notice and the change will take place as from 1st April, 1962 when cars already on the road by Monday, 26th February will be according to Schedule No. 1 and any cars delivered and handed over after this date will be as Schedule No. 2.

D

Yours sincerely,

H. D. Brearley."

The effect of this alteration in the rate on the taxpayer's weekly wage reduction was to increase the amount to £2 14s. 6d. from 1st April 1962. On 1st June 1962, the Austin car being one year old the taxpayer's wage reduction was amended to £2 10s. The memorandum from the secretarial department to the wages office effecting this change read as follows:

E

" Adjustment to Craftsman's wages.

Name:	[the taxpayer]	Clock No.
Department:	Litho	Whether in scheme already: Yes
Adjustment required:	£2. 10. 0d.	
with effect from pay		
week ended:	1st June 1962 "	

F

At the end of May 1963, the Austin being two years old, the taxpayer arranged with Mr. Brearley to exchange it for a Morris 1100 De Luxe, Reg. No. 330 RAR. The taxpayer signed an amendment to his Memorandum of Terms of Service to cover the Morris car. The taxpayer's wage reduction was amended to £2 18s.

G

Each employee received a weekly pay-slip showing the wages to which he was entitled. The taxpayer's pay-slip for the week ending 5th June 1964, was taken as an example of the manner in which the employers calculated the wages of their employees. The figures for that week were set out thereon as follows:

" 1.	Flat Rate	43¼ hours	£22.	6. 7.
2.	Overtime premium	2·0625 hours	£1.	5. 7.
3.	Cost of Living Bonus			11. 8.
4.	Shift Premium		£4.	9. 4.
5.	Bonus		£4.	12. 8.
6.	Spray or Hair Money			3. 4.
7.	Holiday Pay			
8.			£2.	13. 6.

H

Taxable Gross Wage			£30.	15. 8.
Standard Deductions	£1.	17. 0.		
Graduated Pension Contribution		7. 8.		
P.A.Y.E.	£2.	3. 0.	£4.	7. 8.
Net Wage			£26.	8. 0."

I

A   The taxpayer's weekly wage reduction under the scheme was shown in the pay-slip as £2 13s. 6d., item number 8, which was the only deduction in arriving at the taxable gross wage, items 2 to 6 being additions to the flat rate of £22 6s. 7d. for 43¼ hours work. The wage reduction had been amended to this figure on the car becoming one year old in a manner as described above. The taxpayer was paid the flat rate per hour which was standard for his classification. The overtime

B   premium was calculated at 1¼ times the flat rate. The cost of living bonus was fixed each January. The shift premium was paid for shift work and was calcu-lated on the basis of the flat rate. The bonus figure was calculated on production figures but came in one week later than the flat rate of wages.

Whenever an employee was absent through sickness and received no wage, no deduction was made for the use of the car because the agreement between the

C   employers and the employee under the scheme was that the employee should accept a reduced wage. If there was no wage it could not be reduced and no adjustment of any kind was made under the scheme. The taxpayer's pay-slip for the week ending 13th December 1963, when the taxpayer was absent through sickness was in the usual form but with an entry only for one item (number 5) being a bonus of £2 8s. 10d. which related to the previous week. No wage re-

D   duction was made under the scheme and the taxable gross wage was shown as £2 8s. 10d. The payslip for the week ending 8th November 1963 showed similarly no reduction where there was no wage.

In his evidence before the commissioners the taxpayer stated that if he had ever been asked whether the employers supplied him with a car at a rent deducted from his wage he would have said that he had accepted instead a lower wage and

E   a car free. He admitted that he had probably made a rough estimate of what it would cost to obtain the use of a car but added that his main concern had been to see whether he could afford to run a car. The taxpayer did not agree that in order to check his wages he would have to calculate the wage he would have received if he had not joined the scheme and then make a deduction for the car. As the figures were all set out on the pay-slip all that he had to do was to check the

F   arithmetic.

The taxpayer understood the last two lines of the Memorandum of Terms of Service to mean that the agreement could be cancelled by either party giving 14 days' notice and, that if it were cancelled, he would receive his former wage without any deduction.

Desmond C. Miller, Q.C., and *J. R. Phillips, Q.C.,* for the Crown.

G   *G. B. Graham, Q.C.,* and *T. H. Walton* for the taxpayer.

Their Lordships took time for consideration.

12th March. The following opinions were delivered.

LORD REID: My Lords, the question of general importance in this case relates to the proper method of taxing perquisites. The taxpayer is a craftsman.

H   His employers introduced a scheme under which they provided private cars for certain classes of their employees at moderate cost to them. A man who took advantage of the scheme, which was optional, could use the car to travel to and from his work but he was under no obligation to do so; and he could use the car otherwise in any way he chose provided that he drove it himself. We are not concerned with the effect of this scheme on the tax position of the employers.

I   The taxpayer is assessed to income tax under Sch. E and the question which the Special Commissioners had to determine was whether sums of £2 10s. per week and later of £2 18s. per week " being the amount of Car Loan Scheme adjustments " were correctly included in computing the amount of his emolu-ments. The commissioners held that " the use of the car is not in our view money's worth " and that therefore these sums were not part of the taxpayer's emoluments. Their decision was reversed by UNGOED-THOMAS, J. (1), but restored by the Court of Appeal (2).

(1) [1968] 1 All E.R. 857; [1968] 1 W.L.R. 263.
(2) [1968] 2 All E.R. 1156; [1968] 1 W.L.R. 1385.

The first question to be decided is the true construction of the agreement made **A** between the taxpayer and his employers when he came into the scheme. This agreement is not embodied in any document and its terms must be inferred from what the parties said and did. The Crown say that there was no variation of the existing wage and that the taxpayer merely authorised his employers to deduct from that wage the weekly sum which he had to pay to them for the use of the car which they provided. If that is right then no question as to perquisites arises. **B** It is well settled that a taxpayer's liability to tax on his emoluments is not diminished by the fact that he has authorised his employer to make a deduction from his wages or salary before paying it to him and to apply the part deducted in an agreed manner. What he chooses to do with the wage or salary to which he is entitled is of no moment.

But the taxpayer says that that is not what the parties agreed. He says that **C** he agreed to accept a reduced wage and that as a counterpart his employers agreed to give him the use of a car. If that is right then he became entitled to two things—first the reduced wage and secondly the use of the car. Then the question arises whether the use of the car was a perquisite within the meaning of the Income Tax Acts so that he had to pay tax in respect of it. All the learned judges in the courts below have held that this was what was agreed. But they differed as **D** to whether the right to use the car was a taxable perquisite; UNGOED-THOMAS, J. (3), held that it was but the Court of Appeal (4) held that it was not.

The only documents we have which were made before the agreement are a letter from the managing director setting out the conditions of the scheme, an application by the taxpayer to join the scheme dated 10th February 1961, and a so-called " Memorandum of Terms of Service " signed by the taxpayer on **E** 3rd March 1961. On or about that date the taxpayer selected an Austin A40 De Luxe car and it was handed over to him on 30th May 1961. The employers' cashier was then told to make " the necessary weekly wage reduction " and when the taxpayer received his next weekly wage on 2nd June this was incorporated in the pay-slip which he then signed. We do not have that pay-slip but another of 5th June 1964 is admittedly in the same form and in my view that clearly shows that **F** both parties were proceeding on the assumption that their agreement was in the form for which the taxpayer now contends. His former wage had been made up of a number of elements including flat rate, overtime and bonuses. That was his taxable wage and in order to reach the net wage which he received in cash, it was necessary to deduct various items including P.A.Y.E. tax. If the Crown are right the taxable wage remained the same after the taxpayer came into the **G** scheme and the payment for the use of the car should have appeared as one of the deductions made from it. But if the taxpayer is right and he agreed to forego a part of his old wage and accept a smaller wage, then the sum which he agreed to forego was an element in calculating the new wage and must be taken into account in calculating what was now his gross or taxable wage. The pay-slip shows that this is what was done. For the week in question the amount which he **H** had agreed to forego in respect of his right to use the car was taken into account before reaching the taxable gross wage. If the parties had thought that the agreement meant what the Crown now say it means the taxable gross wage would have been larger and the deduction for P.A.Y.E. would therefore also have been larger. And all the other evidence corroborates the fact that throughout the parties acted on the assumption that the agreement regarding the use of the car was in **I** the form for which the taxpayer now contends.

One might think that, where an agreement is not in writing but has to be spelled out of facts and circumstances, it ought to be relevant to take into account the actions of the parties after the date of the agreement. But I shall accept the view that as yet that is not the law, for in this case a consideration of what occurred before the date of the agreement leads me to the same conclusion.

---

(3) [1968] 1 All E.R. 857; [1968] 1 W.L.R. 263.
(4) [1968] 2 All E.R. 1156; [1968] 1 W.L.R. 1385.

A The most important indication of what was intended was condition 6 appended to the managing director's offer: " An amended wage basis will come into operation if the application is accepted ". I do not see how this can be reconciled with the Crown's contention that under the agreement made by the acceptance of the taxpayer's application the wage was to remain exactly the same. If the agreement was that there should be an " amended wage basis " then it seems to me that an

B amendment of the wage basis must result in a different wage, for the " wage basis " must mean the basis on which the amount of the wage was calculated. The only other documents are the application form which throws no light on the matter, and the " Memorandum of Terms of Service ". It is true that the contents of this document do not assist, but, if the Crown are right and the agreement as to the use of the car had nothing to do with the terms of service, I find it difficult

C to account for this heading. It seems to me to be an indication that before the agreement was made the parties thought that it would affect the terms of service. And there is one other matter to be considered. Normally, if the employee agrees that the employer is to deduct part of his wage and apply it in an agreed way, that means that the employer will pay the part deducted to some third person or into some fund. But here, if this was an agreement to deduct part of the

D taxpayer's wage the employers simply put the part deducted back into their own pockets. It seems to me a very artificial conception that the employers first put the wage on the table and then simply take part of it back again. It is a much more natural interpretation to say that the parties agreed that the employers should pay a smaller wage. I am therefore of opinion that in this matter the Court of Appeal (5) were right.

E If that is right then after the agreement was made the taxpayer was entitled to two things, the reduced wage and the right to use the car. It is then necessary to consider whether that right was taxable. If it was, it could only be because it was a " perquisite " within the meaning of the Income Tax Acts. Perquisites have been taxable at least since the Income Tax Act 1842, and it is necessary to examine the legislation to see what is meant by a " perquisite ". I shall examine

F the Income Tax Act 1918, where the relevant provisions were in substantially the same form as in the Act of 1842, because since 1918 there have been two alterations neither of which can possibly have been intended to introduce a fundamental change of the meaning of " perquisite ". One was a repeal in 1922 consequent on the abolition of the three years average, and the other was an alteration of phraseology made in the 1952 consolidation.

G Schedule E of the Act of 1918 provided that tax should be charged in certain matters " for every twenty shillings of the annual amount thereof ", and one goes to the rules applicable to Sch. E for particulars. Rule 1 provides for tax under this schedule " in respect of all salaries, fees, wages, perquisites or profits ...". " Perquisites " is not defined, but rule 4 provides—

H " (1) Perquisites may be estimated either on the profits of the preceding year, or on the average for one year of the amount of the profits thereof in the three preceding years ... (3) Perquisites shall be deemed to be such profits as arise in the course of exercising an office or employment from fees or other emoluments."

Income tax is a tax on income and income means money income. The words profits and gains are used throughout the legislation in reference to sums of money.

I And the passage which I have quoted appears to me to indicate that perquisites here must mean money perquisites, if profits means money profits. There is no provision for the valuation in money of other kinds of advantages which one might call perquisites. In 1842 income tax was at the rate of a few pence in the pound, " fringe benefits " were unknown for there was no incentive to create them, and it appears to me to be clear that there was no intention to saddle the commissioners with the difficult and at that time unprofitable task of putting

_____

(5) [1968] 2 All E.R. 1156; [1968] 1 W.L.R. 1385.

a money value on advantages arising out of the employment which did not **A**
sound in money. But the division between money and that which can readily
be used to produce money is thin. A cheque is not money but it would be absurd
to suppose that payment by cheque instead of in legal tender could make any
difference. And it would be almost equally absurd to suppose that a transfer
of shares which can immediately be sold to produce money should not be
regarded as a money perquisite.   **B**

This was recognised in the leading case of *Tennant* v. *Smith* (6). LORD HALSBURY,
L.C., having said that the Act refers to money payments, used the phrase (7)
" capable of being turned into money ". LORD WATSON referred to things a
person (8) " can dispose of to his advantage " and farther referred to (8) " money
—or that which can be turned to pecuniary account ". LORD MACNAGHTEN
referred to (9) " money payments or payments covertible into money "; and he **C**
pointed out that the tax is (10) " on what ' comes in '—on actual receipts . . . not
on what saves his pocket, but on what goes into his pocket ". The Crown say
all this was obiter and possibly it was. But its authority has been recognised for
three quarters of a century; it was recognised by this House in *Abbott* v. *Philbin*
(*Inspector of Taxes*) (11); and even if I had doubts about it, which I have not,
I would think it must stand.   **D**

The Crown argue that " perquisites " has a meaning wider than money
perquisites, and that tax is assessable on the value of the perquisite and not
merely on the money which the recipient could get by dealing with it. " Value "
is an elusive word: it may mean market value, it may mean value in money to
the owner, or it may have other meanings like the value of the work necessary
to produce it or even sentimental value. No one suggests that here it means **E**
sentimental value and I do not think that the Crown argued that it means cost
of production—for that may have no relation to the present value of the thing
or right to anybody. And the Crown rightly declined to argue that it means value
to the owner, for that was expressly disapproved in *Tennant's* case (6) and would
often be almost impossible to assess. I think that in the end counsel argued for
market value. If the recipient of the perquisite could immediately sell or assign **F**
it that is the same thing as the money equivalent approved in *Tennant's* case (6).
But what if he could not? A good example is to be found in *Wilkins* (*Inspector
of Taxes*) v. *Rogerson* (12). There the perquisite was the right to get a suit of
clothes without payment from a particular tailor—or it may have been the suit
of clothes itself. The recipient could not sell or assign the right to get the suit;
if he had been entitled to do that the money equivalent would have been almost **G**
as much as the tailor's price. But he could sell the suit once he got it; but then
it would only have a secondhand value, in that case about a third of the tailor's
price. The Court of Appeal (12) held that he could not be assessed to tax on the
tailor's price or on the value of the suit to him but only on the secondhand value.
The Crown argued that that case was wrongly decided. In my opinion the decision
was right.   **H**

As I understood it, the argument with regard to the present case was that
we should value the right to use the car on the untrue assumption that the taxpayer could assign his right to use the car to the highest bidder, and that if he
did so the employers would not exercise their right to terminate this right on
14 days' notice; but as there was no evidence as to what anyone else would pay
for the right we should take the weekly sum which the taxpayer was willing to **I**
forego in wages as the best evidence of market value. I have no hesitation in
rejecting that argument. Not only is it inconsistent with what I hold to be the true

(6) [1892] A.C. 150; 3 Tax Cas. 158.
(7) [1892] A.C. at p. 156; 3 Tax Cas. at p. 164.
(8) [1892] A.C. at p. 159; 3 Tax Cas. at p. 167.
(9) [1892] A.C. at p. 163; 3 Tax Cas. at p. 170.
(10) [1892] A.C. at p. 164; 3 Tax Cas. at p. 171.
(11) [1960] 2 All E.R. 763; 39 Tax Cas. 82.
(12) [1961] 1 All E.R. 358; 39 Tax Cas. 344.

A meaning of the Act and with the whole course of authority, but it could lead to most unfair results. Any right or property has different values for different people; if put up to auction many people bid at first but one by one they drop out when the bids of others go beyond its value to them, and the highest bid, the market value, is the value to one alone of all the bidders. Why should a man who finds it only just worth-while to accept an unassignable perquisite on favourable terms

B be taxed on something far above its value to him or what he would have been willing to pay for it? Parliament may see fit to make such an enactment in special cases, as it did in Part 4 of the Income Tax Act 1952, but I am satisfied that that is not the meaning of the general provisions with regard to perquisites.

I am not sure whether in the end counsel supported the argument that the fact that the taxpayer was willing to forego a part of his wages to get the perquisite

C got rid of any difficulty in determining its value to him and that therefore in this case he could be assessed on the value of the perquisite to him. But if the general rule is that the value of a perquisite to the particular recipient is not a basis of assessment consonant with the provisions of the Act, it cannot in my view be right to make exceptions in cases where it is easy to prove that value. Just how easy must that proof be in order to take the case out of the general rule? In my

D judgment the recipient of a perquisite other than a sum of money can be assessed, and can only be assessed, on the amount of money which he could have obtained by some lawful means by the use or in place of the perquisite. I say by lawful means because I can see no ground for the Crown being entitled to disregard a genuine condition restricting the recipient's right to use or dispose of the perquisite. But of course if any restrictive condition is a sham or inserted simply to defeat the

E claims of the Crown it can be disregarded.

So the question is—what could the taxpayer have done to turn his right to use the car to pecuniary account? Admittedly he could not assign it and he could not get money so long as he kept the right. But he could have surrendered the right and if he had done so the agreement provided that his wage would be increased. So why should he not be taxed on the amount of increased wages

F which he had it in his power to get by making that surrender?

The taxpayer argues that there is a fundamental difference between assigning a right on the one hand and surrendering it on the other, because in the one case the right continues to exist, whereas in the other it does not. I cannot see that this makes any difference. In both cases the result of the operation is that he no longer has the right but he has money instead. That seems to me to be well

G within the principle recognised in *Tennant's* case (13), and indeed within the words used in this House. By surrendering the right he has disposed of it to his advantage, he has turned it to pecuniary account, and as a result of the surrender money comes in and goes into his pocket.

So it appears to me that we must ask what money would have come in and gone into his pocket if he had surrendered his right to use the car? Under

H the agreement he had to give 14 days' notice if he wished to surrender his right to use the car. So when are we to suppose him to have given this notice? Each year of assessment stands by itself. In the present case the assessment is for the year 1963-64. If we suppose him to have given notice on the first day of that year of assessment then he was only entitled to the increased wage for 50 weeks of that year of assessment. But if we suppose him to have given notice

I at an earlier date he would have been entitled to the increased wage for the whole year. Unfortunately counsel for the Crown were extremely reluctant to argue the case on the basis that what is assessable is the money which he could have got by surrendering the perquisite, and no argument was submitted on this question. So I think that the only course open is to leave that point undecided and open to argument in future cases and to restore the judgment of UNGOED-THOMAS, J. (14), who held that the proper basis of assessment was the increase

(13) [1892] A.C. 150; 3 Tax. Cas. 158.
(14) [1968] 1 All E.R. 857; [1968] 1 W.L.R. 263.

of wages to which the taxpayer would have been entitled during the year of A assessment if he had chosen to surrender his right to have the car on the first day of that year. I would allow this appeal and restore the order of UNGOED-THOMAS, J. (15).

LORD MORRIS OF BORTH-Y-GEST: My Lords, the taxpayer, who was employed by a company as a machine minder in their lithographic department, appealed against an assessment made on him under Sch. E for the B year 1963-64. He had been employed by the company for many years. In 1954 the employers introduced a scheme under which they loaned motor cars to certain of their employees. Having known of the scheme since that year the taxpayer decided to join it in the year 1961. It is beyond question that financial consequences were to result for those employees who hired cars. In one way or another their financial position was to be affected. C

The taxpayer claimed that the assessment made on him should be reduced by an amount which was the amount in fact referable to the hiring by him of his car. Thus if it be assumed that by his work and labour and as the result of the application of agreed rates and terms he became entitled to receive in a week the sum of £33 9s. 2d. and if in that week the amount referable to the hire by him or loan to him of his car was £2 13s. 6d. he claimed that he was only D liable to pay tax on £30 15s. 8d. (being £33 9s. 2d. less £2 13s. 6d.). He claimed that his taxable gross wage for the week would be £30 15s. 8d. He so claimed because he contended that as from the date when he decided to join the scheme he had agreed to take a reduced wage. The assessment made on him was on the basis that (assuming the above figures) the £2 13s. 6d. was to be included in computing the amount of his emoluments from his employment within the E meaning of para. 1 of Sch. E of the Income Tax Act 1952.

For the year which is in question the actual sums referable to the loan of the car were, up to 31st May 1963, £2 10s. per week, and £2 18s. per week thereafter. In the assessment made on the taxpayer those weekly amounts were included in computing his emoluments.

It is necessary, in the first place, to decide as to the true interpretation of F the agreement subsisting at the relevant time between the taxpayer and his employers. When he joined the car loan scheme did he vary his terms of employment by agreeing to accept a reduced wage or did he agree that from his wage there would be deducted such sum as represented the sum payable to him in respect of his hiring of a car? That there would be less money to take home week by week would follow in either event. But there would be rather more G to take home week by week if the amounts referable to the car are excluded from the taxable income. I use the phrase " amounts referable to the car " so as not to prejudge the issue. There was, however, no suggestion that the car loan scheme was a benevolent scheme of the employers which was not to have any financial consequences for those employees who joined it. If there was a wage reduction the reduction was of an amount decided on because there was H the hiring of the car. If there was a deduction from wages the deduction was of the same amount. The only practical difference resulting from the view, on the one hand, that there was an agreement for a wage reduction and the view, on the other hand, that there was an agreement for a deduction from wages lies in the tax implications and consequences.

I turn, therefore, to consider on the facts as found what the true position was I as between the taxpayer and his employers. The quest must be to find the realities of the arrangements that were agreed. If (taking these figures merely to state the point) the taxpayer, before he joined the scheme, had been entitled to receive in a week the gross wage of £33 9s. 2d. and if, when he hired a car, his employers wished to receive £2 13s. 6d. a week because the car was loaned to him, was the position thereafter that, for the same labour as before, rendered on

(15) [1968] 1 All E.R. 857; [1968] 1 W.L.R. 263.

A the same terms as before, the taxpayer was still entitled to receive a gross wage of £33 9s. 2d. and that from his gross pay or from his take home pay there was to be deducted the amount of £2 13s. 6d., or was the position thereafter that he agreed that his gross wage was to be £30 15s. 8d. and that he was to have the free use of a car? My Lords, I consider that the former position was the true one. To describe the use of the car as being free seems to me to be trifling with words.

B There was nothing free about it. The letter written in 1954 by the managing director to each employee (a letter fully set out in the Case Stated) mentioned that a man with no family might be able to " afford " to come into the scheme where perhaps a man with four children could not. But most people can afford that which is free. So also the letter explained how the scheme would be available " when the pocket permits ". The pocket readily permits that which makes

C no demands on it. It is true that the Case Stated records that the taxpayer in his evidence said that if he had ever been asked whether the company supplied him with a car at a rent deducted from his wage he would have said that he had accepted instead a lower wage and a car free. But whether he would have said that or not and whether or not he derived some personal happiness in a belief that he was having a car free the incidence of tax must depend on what the state of

D affairs really is rather than on what someone can think it to be or can somehow state it to be.

In the letter which the managing director wrote to each employee the scheme was described as one evolved " whereby a craftsman may run a car, if he so desires, at most reasonable terms ". It is difficult to understand how anyone could have thought that such language denoted the free loan of a car. To have

E the free use of a car would be to have it on terms that would be more than most reasonable. The scheme was a " Craftsmen's Car Loan Service ". The employers were to loan a new car of certain stated makes and they were to pay full comprehensive insurance and the road tax on the car. Certain of the conditions are to be noted. Condition 5 was " The user will sign a simple agreement ". Condition 6 was " An amended wage basis will come into operation if the application is

F accepted ". Condition 9 was " If the car is under repair for maintenance or following an accident the amended wage basis will still apply ".

When the taxpayer decided to join the scheme he signed an application form (dated 10th February 1961). On that form he merely stated that he wished to join the scheme and he gave certain information. Nothing was set out as to his wages or as to payments. The taxpayer selected the make of car that he

G wished to have and then signed the " simple agreement ". It was a printed form of agreement presented to him by his employers. It was rather a remarkable document. It was in the following terms:

"TO: John Waddington, Limited, Leeds.

MEMORANDUM OF TERMS OF SERVICE

H During my service with you as LITHOGRAPHER and the carrying out of the various duties you properly assign to me, I am to make use of Motor Car No. 3248 RO for the more efficient discharge of my duties. I am not to permit anyone other than myself to drive or use the car except in an emergency. I am to pay for maintenance and running. I agree to keep the car clean and in good condition and to hold it ready for inspection at any

I time. You have generously agreed to licence and insure the car and to pay for decarbonisation when necessary. Either of us may cancel my obligation and authority to use the car on 14 days' notice. Dated 3rd March 1961. Signature Ralph G. Bell."

Though headed " Memorandum of Terms of Service " it will be seen that it contains nothing about the terms of his employment. It does not mention his wage rate or the money entitlements which were to result from his work. The mention of service is in the opening sentence in which were the words

" During my service with you as LITHOGRAPHER and the carrying out of

the various duties you properly assign to me, I am to make use of Motor Car **A**
No ..."

It is admitted, however, that it was wholly erroneous that the taxpayer was to be
under any obligation to use the car. The words " I am to make use " were not
correct. The taxpayer was under no duty to use and did not need to use the
car during " the carrying out of the various duties " which his employers might
assign to him. By the use of a car an employee might be aided in his travel **B**
to and from his work and might be enabled " with his family, to make the most
of his leisure hours "; but he owed no duty to use the car in any particular way.
It was quite wrong, therefore, to state that either party could on 14 days' notice
cancel the " obligation " of the taxpayer to use the car.

By signing the memorandum the taxpayer was required to assent to the
statement that his employers had " generously " agreed to license and insure **C**
the car. By a letter of 26th February 1962 (set out in the Case Stated) the
officer of the company in charge of the scheme informed all the employees in
the scheme that he had " carefully surveyed the costs relating to cars ". The
letter contained the following paragraphs:

> " The present wage adjustments have remained the same since the **D**
> beginning of the scheme and since that time costs have risen in many
> different ways—the cost of the car, the cost of insurance and now the tax.
> The very fact that the tax has risen from £12 10s. to £15 per year means
> 1s. per week on every car, but this is trifling compared with other increases.
> " The higher costs coupled with the greater difficulty of obtaining the
> right price when we sell returned cars as second-hand cars makes it impera-
> tive for a heavy increase of 8s. to 10s. per week." **E**

Not surprisingly that was described as a " very steep rise ". Again, it is difficult
to understand how anyone could possibly think that such language was used in
reference to the free loan of a car. What was it that was being subject to the
heavy increase of 8s. to 10s. per week? What was it that was subject to a
" very steep rise "? In my view, it is impossible to resist the view that the **F**
increase was in the payment that was to be made for the hire of the car.

On behalf of the taxpayer reference has been made to certain office documents
of the company. They are purely internal documents. They show that when the
taxpayer joined the scheme and received a car on loan the wages office were asked
to arrange "the necessary weekly wage reduction". They show that the " heavy
increase " imposed after the letter of 26th February 1962, was noted as involving **G**
the increase of the reduction. My Lords, I cannot think that the adoption of
this phraseology can in any way mask the realities in regard to what was actually
arranged. Nor do I think that realities could be cloaked merely by some future
adroit change of selected words.

In my view, there can be no doubt that the taxpayer obtained from his
employers the right to use a car on terms which involved that he should pay to **H**
them whatever was from time to time an appropriate hire charge. As a matter
of convenience he agreed that his payment was to be set-off or deducted week
by week from the amount which by his labour he had earned and which his
employers therefore owed him. To dress that up as a wage reduction seems to
me to be fanciful. The terms and conditions relating to the method of computing
the taxpayer's earnings were in no way changed. If two craftsmen worked under **I**
precisely the same conditions so that they earned precisely the same amount and
if one joined the car loan scheme while the other did not it would, in my view,
be a mere delusion to treat the former as having agreed to a wage reduction
(being a wage reduction which was to vary from time to time according as to
how the cost of hiring the car varied). In truth there would have been an
arranged and agreed deduction from wages. A deduction by any other name
would be a payment just the same. To speak of a wage reduction increase
brought about by new charges affecting a car the loan of which is free involves

A   a measure of verbal distortion which suggests tax adjustments rather than " wage adjustments ".

Reliance was placed on two matters in support of the contention that there had been a wage " reduction " having the result that tax was only payable on an agreed reduced wage. The first of these involved consideration of condition 6 which I have quoted above. The second involved consideration of the form and **B** contents of the weekly pay slips which the taxpayer saw and signed. The two matters are considerably interrelated.

Under condition 6 an amended wage basis was to come into operation if a craftsman hired a car under the scheme. The words " wage basis " are somewhat ambiguous. They might denote the rate of pay which someone is to earn by his work. They might denote the way in which his pay is dealt with or **C** adjusted before the amount is arrived at which the employed person is to receive to take away. One thing is quite clear. Rates of pay and terms affecting what was to be the financial reward for work done were in no way altered if a craftsman joined the scheme. They were the same, other circumstances being equal, for those within and for those without the scheme. The " simple agreement " which was signed did not even purport to alter the terms **D** of employment relating to the wage which one who signed was to receive. It made no mention whatsoever of payment or of wages. So there was no agreement made which produced an " amended wage basis " in any sense which meant that gross earnings were to be less. Work done after joining the scheme was to earn the same reward as would have been earned by similar work done before joining the scheme. No different conclusion follows from a study of the form of **E** the weekly pay slips referable to those who joined the scheme. It appears that if someone became ill he received no wage. The Case Stated contains the statement that—

> " Whenever an employee was absent through sickness and received no wage, no deduction was made for the use of the car because the agreement between the employers and the employee under the scheme was that the
> **F** employee should accept a reduced wage."

But the question whether there was an agreement for the acceptance of a reduced wage is the very question to be decided. If there was such an agreement for a reduced wage then there could be no thought of a " deduction ". If, however, the terms of employment of someone who joined the scheme were, as a result of joining it, in no way affected but if payment for the hire of a car was to be **G** made by deduction from wages earned and if the employers were not going to pay wages to anyone absent through sickness it would follow that there was no sum from which a deduction could be made. It appears to have been the position, however, that no charge for the hire of a car was carried forward; but this proves no more than that the employers decided that as they paid no wage to someone who because of illness could not work they would not during such **H** period of illness exact payment from him in respect of his hire of a car.

The entries made on a weekly pay-slip were somewhat revealing. The taxpayer's pay-slip for a particular week (actually the week ending 5th June 1964) was taken merely as an example of the manner in which the employers calculated the wages of their employees. The figures for that week were set out as follows:

I 1. Flat Rate	$43\frac{1}{4}$ hours	£22.	6.	7.
2. Overtime premium	2·0625 hours ..	£1.	5.	7.
3. Cost of Living Bonus			11.	8.
4. Shift Premium		£4.	9.	4.
5. Bonus		£4.	12.	8.
6. Spray or Hair Money			3.	4.
7. Holiday Pay				
8.		£2.	13.	6.
9.				
TAXABLE GROSS WAGE		£30.	15.	8.

Standard Deductions	..	..	..	£1. 17. 0.	**A**
Graduated Pension Contribution		..		7. 8.	
P.A.Y.E.	..	..	..	£2. 3. 0.	£4 7. 8.

NET WAGE	..	..	..	..	..	£26. 8. 0.

It will be seen that items 1 to 6 all represent sums earned by work. A side- **B** note shows that of the 43¼ hours worked 39 were to be paid at the ordinary rate, ¼ hour at a rate of 1¼, and four hours at a rate of 1½ the ordinary rate. All this would be just the same whether the person concerned was or was not within the car loan scheme. So also in regard to the other named premium and bonus items. Anyone looking at the pay-slip would be pardoned if he thought that just as the first six items must be added together so also should be added **C** the unnamed and undescribed item of £2 13s. 6d. But the first six items when added together come to £33 9s. 2d. The sum of £2 13s. 6d was in fact a sub-traction or deduction. It is beyond all question that it was in fact the amount then currently referable to the car which at the time the taxpayer was using and hiring. Conforming to the pattern of the employers' internal records the amount was duly recorded in one document as a " reduction ": in another was the **D** entry: " Wage reduction changed to 53s. 6d. per week on Friday 5th June 1964 ". It may well be that one of the reasons why what at first glance would have seemed to be an item of addition of £2 13s. 6d. in arriving at the taxable gross wage was given no label and no description was that it would have been difficult to devise words which would not reveal it to be what it really was. In my view, the reality was that the £2 13s. 6d. (or such sum as related to any **E** period in question) was an agreed deduction from the taxpayer's wage and was the sum payable by him in respect of his participation in the car loan scheme.

The only " amended wage basis " that resulted and that the documents reveal was that a sum referable to the hiring of a car was retained by the employers as a deduction from the sums which were owing to the taxpayer as his earnings for work that he had done. In my view, therefore, the question raised in the Case **F** Stated, i.e., whether sums of £2 10s. per week up to 31st May 1963, and £2 18s. thereafter, being the amount of car loan scheme adjustments, were correctly included in computing the amount of the emoluments of the taxpayer from his employment should be answered in the affirmative.

For the reasons that I have set out I consider that on a true interpretation of the contractual arrangements the position was that the monetary wage to **G** which the taxpayer was entitled remained unaltered. When the taxpayer joined the scheme he agreed that some part of the earnings to which, by his work, he had become entitled might be retained by his employers as the money consideration of his hire of a car. The assessment that was made on him was therefore, in my view, correct. Had I been of the alternative view, that the taxpayer agreed to take a reduced monetary wage during such time as he had **H** the free hire of a car I would still have been of the view that the assessment made on him was correct. On that basis the entitlement to use the car would, in my view, have been a perquisite to be included in the full amount of the taxpayer's emoluments chargeable to tax.

In considering this alternative basis it is relevant to note what its features would be. The taxpayer would voluntarily have agreed to forego an amount **I** in money and in exchange would have the free use of a car. He would have agreed to take a reduced wage. He would be under no obligation to use the car though he would be under the restriction that (except in an emergency) he was not to permit anyone other than himself to drive or use it. He would not be using the car in the performance of his duties. But the new agreement would be subject to unilateral alteration by either party to it. The employers might decide (because of increased costs referable to the car) to reduce the taxpayer's wage to a lower figure than that which he had previously agreed; or (if costs

A   decreased or if a car was in its second year of hiring), the taxpayer's wage might rise. Furthermore, the taxpayer could at any time decide to cease to hire a car and by giving two weeks' notice to this effect he could produce an increase of his wage. So also his employers, whether he liked it or not, could end the hiring on two weeks' notice and then his wage would automatically increase.

The question that arises is whether his participation in the car loan scheme
B   would form part of his emoluments so as to come within the wording of the taxing statute. Tax is chargeable on the " full amount " of the taxpayer's emoluments. The expression " emoluments " includes all salaries, fees, wages, perquisites and profits. The tax being a tax on income or (as LORD MACNAGHTEN said in *Tennant* v. *Smith* (16)) on what " comes in ", the word " amount " denotes that in order to be taxable a perquisite must either be a cash or money payment
C   or must be money's worth or of money value in the sense that it can be turned to pecuniary account. This conception in regard to the nature of a taxable perquisite was, in my view, revealed in earlier Acts. Thus, under the Income Tax Act 1918, in reference to the sums to be charged to tax under Sch. E are the words " the annual amount thereof ". In the Income Tax Act 1842, in reference to perquisites to be assessed there occurs the word " payable ". This denotes
D   that the mere fact that a benefit in kind accrues does not mean that there is a perquisite which is taxable. In his speech in *Abbott* v. *Philbin* (*Inspector of Taxes* (17)), LORD RADCLIFFE said (18) that it had been generally assumed that the decision in *Tennant* v. *Smith* (19) does impose a limitation on the taxability of benefits in kind which are of a personal nature: it is not enough to say that they have a value to which there can be assigned a monetary equivalent. LORD
E   RADCLIFFE added (20):

"   " If they are by their nature incapable of being turned into money by the recipient they are not taxable, even though they are, in any ordinary sense of the word, of value to him."

The " attendant uncertainties " which, as was pointed out, the conception
F   raises need not in the present case be resolved.

It was clearly the view of the House in *Tennant* v. *Smith* (19) that, in order that they should be taxable, perquisites need not necessarily take the form of money payments. LORD HALSBURY, L.C., in coming to the conclusion that the then applicable taxing Act referred to money payments made to the person who received them, added (21)—

G   ". . .though, of course, I do not deny that if substantial things of money value were capable of being turned into money they might for that purpose represent money's worth and be therefore taxable."

He adopted (22) the words of LORD YOUNG " that the thing sought to be taxed is not income unless it can be turned into money ". In regard to the word " profits " LORD WATSON considered that in its ordinary acceptation it appeared
H   to denote (23):

"   ". . . something acquired which the acquirer becomes possessed of and can dispose of to his advantage—in other words, money—or that which can be turned to pecuniary account."

In reference to Sch. E, LORD MACNAGHTEN said that it extended (24) " only to
I

---

(16) [1892] A.C. 150 at p. 164: 3 Tax Cas. 158 at p. 171.
(17) [1960] 2 All E.R. 763; 39 Tax Cas. 82.
(18) [1960] 2 All E.R. at p. 774; 39 Tax Cas. at pp. 124, 125.
(19) [1892] A.C. 150; 3 Tax Cas. 158.
(20) [1960] 2 All E.R. at p. 774; 39 Tax Cas. at p. 125.
(21) [1892] A.C. at p. 156; 3 Tax Cas. at p. 164.
(22) [1892] A.C. at p. 157; 3 Tax Cas. at p. 165.
(23) [1892] A.C. at p. 159; 3 Tax Cas. at p. 167.
(24) [1892] A.C. at p. 163; 3 Tax Cas. at p. 170.

money payments or payments convertible into money ". LORD FIELD con- **A** sidered that the residence of the appellant on bank premises, though rent free (25), " could not in any way be converted by him into money or money's worth (26) ". LORD HANNEN considered that different considerations would apply to the case of an agent who as part of his remuneration had a residence provided for him which he could let (26): " That which could be converted into money might reasonably be regarded as money . . ." **B**

My Lords, the principles enunciated in the passages to which I have referred were recognised in 1961 in the speeches in *Abbott* v.*Philbin* (*Inspector of Taxes*) (27). That the principles can apply not only in respect of objects or chattels or things of value received but also in respect of certain rights received was, I think, recognised in both cases. In *Abbott* v. *Philbin* (27) what was in question was an option or right to acquire shares at a fixed price. The majority considered **C** that the grant of an option in the year 1954-55 was a profit or perquisite (arising from the appellant's employment) of that year and that tax was exigible on its monetary value, if any. The option was something which could " assuredly be turned to pecuniary account ". (See the speech of VISCOUNT SIMONDS (28).) That was so, even though the option itself was not transferable. The option could be exercised and the acquired shares transferred. The test, said LORD **D** SIMONDS (29), was whether it was something which was by its nature capable of being turned into money. In that case a sum of £20 was paid for the option. It was said that the Revenue authorities could easily have ascertained whether the option had any and what value.

" If [said LORD SIMONDS (29)] it had no ascertainable value, then it **E** was a perquisite of no value—a conclusion difficult to reach since £20 was paid for it."

LORD REID pointed out (30) that the parties agreed that the option was some- thing which was within the words " perquisites or profits whatsoever ". He said (30):

" I agree that the question is whether this option was a right of a kind **F** which could be turned to pecuniary account. I do not use these words as a definition, but it is undesirable to invent a new phrase if an old one of high authority fits this case, and the parties agree that it does "

and (31) " It appears to me that, if a right can be turned to pecuniary account, that in itself is enough to make it a perquisite ". In reference to the option, **G** LORD RADCLIFFE said (32):

" I think that the conferring of a right of this kind as an incident of service is a profit or perquisite which is taxable as such in the year of receipt, so long as the right itself can fairly be given a monetary value . . ."

The principles laid down and recognised in the two cases in this House were, I think, correctly applied in *Wilkins* (*Inspector of Taxes*) v. *Rogerson* (33). The **H** opportunity to acquire the suit of clothes (or overcoat or raincoat) could not be assigned or sold but the suit when received could be sold. In that way the perquisite could be turned to pecuniary account, i.e., it could be turned into money.

How, then, should the well-established principles be applied if it be assumed that since 1961 the taxpayer was employed on the terms that his wage was a **I**

---

(25) [1892] A.C. at p. 164; 3 Tax Cas. at p. 171.
(26) [1892] A.C. at p. 165; 3 Tax Cas. at p. 172.
(27) [1960] 2 All E.R. 763; 39 Tax Cas. 82.
(28) [1960] 2 All E.R. at p. 766; 39 Tax Cas. at p. 117.
(29) [1960] 2 All E.R. at p. 767; 39 Tax Cas. at p. 117.
(30) [1960] 2 All E.R. at pp. 769, 770; 39 Tax Cas. at p. 120.
(31) [1960] 2 All E.R. at p. 770; 39 Tax Cas. at p. 121.
(32) [1960] 2 All E.R. at p. 774; 39 Tax Cas. at p. 125.
(33) [1961] 1 All E.R. 358; 39 Tax Cas. 344.

A reduced one but that he was to have the free use of a car?   In my view, his free use of a car was a perquisite which represented money's worth and was taxable. It is true that his right to use the car could not be assigned (just as the option in *Abbott* v. *Philbin* (34) could not be transferred) but the right could be converted into money.   The option in *Abbott* v. *Philbin* (34) could be exercised and the shares acquired by its exercise could then be sold.   It was recognised that by such pro-

B cess the option was by its nature capable of being turned into money.   In the present case the taxpayer's right to use the car could be converted into money or was capable of being turned into money by a much simpler process.   The taxpayer could at any time (subject only to giving two weeks' notice) and without making any new contract say to his employers that he relinquished in their favour his right to use the car and in exchange could require that an ascertained

C sum of money should be paid to him.   His employers would be bound to accept the use of the car—which was all that the taxpayer had a right to.   They would then be bound to pay him a sum which (on the basis now being considered) was equal to the amount by which he had agreed that his wage was to be reduced. His employers, for their part, could at any time (subject only to giving two weeks, notice) require him to give up his right to use the car and require him to accept

D a sum of money in exchange.   At all times and at any time since 1954 the taxpayer was in a position to decide whether he would choose to have from his employers a particular and ascertained sum of money and no car or whether he would choose not to have that particular and ascertained sum of money but to have a car.   The fact that two weeks' notice of change of will was needed does not, in my view, alter the fact that the perquisite represented money's worth.

E At any time since 1961 the taxpayer, after giving notice, could have had money rather than the use of a car.   Accordingly, throughout the year of assessment the taxpayer could, had he so wished, have had the money equivalent into which his perquisite was convertible.   The right to use the car, on the one hand, was alternative to and interchangeable with the right to the receipt of a definite sum of money on the other.   For administrative convenience a period of two weeks was

F agreed to as being requisite for effecting the exchange of the one for the other; that did not, in my view, affect the circumstance that the perquisite represented money's worth of known amount.

For these reasons I am of the opinion that the assessment made on the taxpayer was correct and, accordingly, I would allow the appeal.

G **LORD HODSON:** My Lords, the taxpayer, Mr. Bell, is a machine minder who has been employed by a company called John Waddington, Ltd., since about the year 1948.   In 1954 the employers introduced a voluntary car loan scheme for the benefit of employees who earned less than £2,000 a year and were not directors of the company.   The taxpayer received an invitation to join the scheme and attended a meeting at which the scheme was discussed but did not

H join it until 1961.   Enclosed with the invitation was a list of conditions relating to the car loan service.   These provided that the employers would loan, insure and tax a car for each year of the service, that the user would sign a simple agreement and provide his own petrol, oil and running maintenance.   Condition 6 reads: " An amended wage basis will come into operation if the application is accepted." Condition 9 reads: " If the car is under repair for maintenance or following an

I accident the amended wage basis will still apply."

On 10th February 1961, the taxpayer applied to join the scheme and, on 3rd March 1961, signed a form which reads as follows:

" To: John Waddington, Limited, Leeds

MEMORANDUM OF TERMS OF SERVICE

During my service with you as LITHOGRAPHER, and the carrying out of the

---

(34) [1960] 2 All E.R. 763; 39 Tax Cas. 82.

various duties you properly assign to me, I am to make use of Motor Car   **A**
No. 3248 RO for the more efficient discharge of my duties. I am not to permit
anyone other than myself to drive or use the car except in an emergency.
I am to pay for maintenance and running. I agree to keep the car clean and in
good condition and to hold it ready for inspection at any time. You have
generously agreed to licence and insure the car and to pay for decarbonisation when necessary. Either of us may cancel my obligation and authority   **B**
to use the car on 14 days' notice. Dated 3rd March 1961.

Signature Ralph G. Bell "

There is no other evidence of the terms of the arrangement which the taxpayer
made with the employers for the loan of the car, although there are internal office
communications showing that, as from 2nd June 1961, when he received the car,   **C**
sums described as " wage reductions " were subtracted from his wages each week.
These items were fixed first at the rate of 49s. a week, increased to 54s. 6d. on
6th April 1962, changed to 50s. on 1st June 1962, to 58s. on 7th June 1963, and
to 53s. 6d. on 5th June 1964.

The taxpayer was assessed for income tax under Sch. E, Income Tax Act
1952, for the year 1963-64, and the question is whether the sums of £2 10s. a   **D**
week up to 31st May 1963, and £2 18s. a week subsequently were correctly included
in computing the amount of his emoluments within the meaning of para. 1 of
Sch. E; emoluments by definition including all salaries, fees, wages, perquisites
and profits whatsoever.

His wages were shown each week on a pay-slip and his pay-slip for the week
ending 5th June 1964, was taken as an example of the way in which the employers   **E**
calculated the wages of their employees. The pay-slip shows that the wage is calculated in order to arrive at what is described as the taxable gross wage (which
would be the figure on which P.A.Y.E. was calculated) by adding together items
into which the weekly wage was split. This produces a total of £30 15s. 8d. and
excludes from the addition the £2 13s. 6d. attributable to the car loan scheme
payments. If the sum of £2 13s. 6d. had not been excluded the total would have   **F**
been £33 9s. 2d., the total wage to which the taxpayer was entitled had he not
agreed to the application of the sum of £2 13s. 6d. under the car loan service
scheme.

It is argued that the use of the phrase " an amended wage basis " in the conditions which the employers put forward points to a reduction in wages during
the operation of the scheme in the case of each individual rather than a deduction   **G**
from his wages applied at his request in a particular manner.

In my opinion, there was no change in the terms of the employment of the
taxpayer in any real sense at any time. During the operation of the scheme there
was an allocation for the purposes of the scheme of wages already earned and not,
in my opinion, a fresh contract of employment at a reduced wage. This is no
less true although the alteration is made through the employers by returning the   **H**
money to them. The allocation is for the specific purpose of the scheme made at the
request of the employee and is to be treated as a deduction from his gross wage.
I do not think any other conclusion is to be drawn from the ambiguous phrase
" amended wage basis ". The basis was not amended. It remained the same
throughout. The variation which took place during the operation of the scheme
was in the amount applied by the employee out of his wages.

I have referred to what I regard as the real facts of the case, for it appears that   **I**
the learned judge (35) may have attached undue importance to the words " an
amended wage basis will come into operation if the application is accepted ", as
indicating that a different calculation of the gross wage itself would occur.
In reaching his conclusion he cited a passage from a judgment of ROWLATT, J.,
in *Machon* v. *McLoughlin* (36), in which he said (37):

(35) [1968] 1 All E.R. 857; [1968] 1 W.L.R. 263.   (36) (1926), 11 Tax Cas. 83.
(37) (1926), 11 Tax Cas. at p. 90.

A   " But what has been done? I have to find out whether the true way of looking at it is that he is paid a gross wage and has to pay something back or that he is only paid a net wage. That was VAUGHAN WILLIAMS, L.J.'s test in *Bell* v. *Gribble* (38), and that is the test I have to apply. As I pointed out before, it may be a question of words. I do not think there is very much to show that it is not a question of words."

B   ROWLATT, J., made, as we all know, a great contribution to the law at a time when Revenue cases began to be numerous under the weight of increased taxation following on war necessities. I cannot think that he could have meant to say anything to suggest that words could be used legitimately to obscure or to distort the facts. Indeed, here the words used by the parties are not of assistance to the taxpayer. I have quoted in full the so-called Memorandum of Terms of Service
C   which he signed. It is not very helpful and is to a large extent meaningless. There are no terms of employment mentioned in the memorandum. He was not bound to make use of the car for the more efficient discharge of his duties or under any obligation to use the car at all. There are no documents and no other facts which, to my mind, lend support to the case put forward by the taxpayer that the wages to be assessed were other than his gross wages before deduction in respect of his
D   participation in the car loan scheme.

        This disposes of the matter, but I will add my opinion on the second point in the case, which depends on whether the benefit which the taxpayer received in the form of the use of the car was a " perquisite ". It would at first impression appear to me to be an obvious perquisite. I have, however, been persuaded that the answer is not as simple as it seems. I am satisfied on consideration of the
E   judgment in *Tennant* v. *Smith* (39), and the whole tenor of the relevant legislation, that the teaching of that case, confirmed as it was by your Lordships' House as recently as 1961 in the case of *Abbott* v. *Philbin* (*Inspector of Taxes*) (40), compels me to the same conclusion as that reached by the Court of Appeal (41). Income tax being a tax on income, it follows that a perquisite is not taxable as income unless it is capable of being turned into money. It is this question which must be
F   answered and I cannot escape from the conclusion that the use of the motor car is not convertible into money for it cannot be so converted in the ordinary sense of the word by sale or assignment to another (cf., *Wilkins* (*Inspector of Taxes*) v. *Rogerson* (42) where the suit of clothes was capable of being so converted and was, I think correctly, regarded as a perquisite). True that no further deduction would be made from the taxpayer's wages after he had, by giving notice, termin-
G   ated his agreement for the use of the car. I cannot, however, for that reason agree that, in any true sense, he could convert the use of the car into money. He could give it up but that appears to me to be a different thing. I am in agreement with the unanimous judgment of the Court of Appeal (41) on this point, but for the reasons I have given I would allow the appeal on the first ground put forward by the Crown, namely, that the emoluments of the taxpayer, taxable under Sch. E,
H   were his gross wage before deduction of any sum in respect of his right to participate in the car loan scheme.

        LORD UPJOHN: My Lords, the taxpayer was at all material times employed by John Waddington Ltd., as a machine minder at wages of over £30 a week and he had no need for the use of a motor car in the course of his employment.
I   But his employers had an excellent scheme called Waddingtons Craftsmen's Car Loan Service whereby (and I am now using neutral language) an employee could, if he so wished, and it was entirely at his option, forego part of his weekly wages in cash and have for his own private use a brand new motor car licensed and

---

(38) [1903] 1 K.B. 517; 4 Tax. Cas. 522.
(39) [1892] A.C. 150; 3 Tax Cas. 158.
(40) [1960] 2 All E.R. 763; 39 Tax Cas. 82.
(41) [1968] 2 All E.R. 1156; [1968] 1 W.L.R. 1385.
(42) [1961] 1 All E.R. 358; 39 Tax Cas. 344.

insured by his employers at their expense but on the terms that he alone drove it, **A**
except in an emergency, and he had to continue to suffer the diminution in his
cash wages when it was off the road for repairs or after an accident. It is quite
clear he had no right nor title to the car, so could not sell, mortgage, nor hire it
out to others. This arrangement was determinable by employers or employee on
giving 14 days' notice, when of course the employee would revert to his full wages
in cash. The scheme was introduced in 1954.   **B**

The questions that arise on this appeal are whether: (i) on the true interpretation of the contractual arrangements made in 1961 between the taxpayer and
his employers, the monetary wage which the taxpayer was entitled to remained
unaltered, the taxpayer agreeing that some part of it might be retained by his
employer in consideration of his being entitled on certain defined terms to use a
car provided by his employers; in which case admittedly the taxpayer is taxable **C**
on his gross wage and no further question arises: or whether (ii) the monetary
wage to which the taxpayer would otherwise have been entitled was to be reduced
during such time as he was entitled to use such car and, if so, such entitlement
constituted a perquisite or profit effectively charged to income tax under Sch. E.

The first question on which the taxpayer has unanimous findings in his
favour in the courts below depends on an examination of the scanty documents **D**
which, however, are set out in full in the report of UNGOED-THOMAS, J. (43).

The offer contained in this car loan service contained among other conditions:
"6. An amended wage basis will come into operation if the application is accepted."
In February 1961, the taxpayer applied to enter the scheme and he was in due
course accepted, and he drove away the car provided for him on 30th May 1961.
On the same day an interdepartmental note went to the employers' wages office **E**
to make the necessary wage reduction, and on the next wage day, 2nd June
1961, his wages were reduced by £2 9s.

The wages slip that he was accustomed to receive was quite a complex document but all the argument was based on a much later slip, for the weekend of
5th June 1964 (44), which was accepted by all parties as exemplary of the taxpayer's wages slip. It is quite clear that the exercise of this option to have the **F**
use of a motor car in lieu of full wages had no effect on the employment of the
taxpayer in the sense that whether he had full wages or the use of a motor car
he performed precisely the same duties during precisely the same hours for a
recompense at precisely the same rates as before and that his gross wages,
taking this example with all its complex features, amounted to £33 9s. 2d. From
this, though for a reason unspecified in the slip, the amount of £2 13s. 6d. due in **G**
respect of the operation of the car loan service was deducted. From this the
usual tax deductions were made. This slip (I treat it as though delivered on
2nd June 1961) was no part of the contract between the employers and the
taxpayer; that had been concluded when the taxpayer drove away his car three
days earlier: it was merely the way in which the wages office regarded it and that
by itself is irrelevant. What does appear quite clearly is that it was a deduc- **H**
tion from or reduction of (for there cannot be any real difference between
the two phrases) the monetary wages which had already been plainly earned
by the taxpayer. The phrase in condition 6 " amended wage basis " taken
by itself may be ambiguous; but in this case I can have no doubt that it
meant no more to the parties than that the monetary wage would have to be
adjusted and each knew by how much, namely, (taking the example) £2 13s. 6d. **I**

In my opinion, and with all respect to the judgments in the courts below (45),
I think it is clear that the legal result of the transaction between the parties was
that the taxpayer was agreeing to a retention or deduction or, if you like, reduction
from the wages earned by him and clearly due to him in cash for the pleasure

(43) [1968] 1 All E.R. 857 at pp. 858, 859; [1968] 1 W.L.R. 263 at pp. 264-269.
(44) See p. 74, letters H and I, ante.
(45) [1968] 1 All E.R. 857; [1968] 1 W.L.R. 263; [1968] 2 All E.R. 1156; [1968]
1 W.L.R. 1385.

A having a motor car supplied to him for his personal use on very advantageous terms.

It was suggested that a decision on these grounds could easily be circumvented by clever draftsmanship to make it clear that in fact the wage of the employee was reduced by £2 13s. 6d. and that in lieu he received a perquisite. I am not quite sure what ROWLATT, J., meant in *Machon* v. *McLoughlin,* when he said

B (46) " In every case you have to see whether it is a question of words ". Like UNGOED-THOMAS, J. (47), I find them confusing though I think the learned judge misapplied them. Of course one has to look at the real nature of the transaction and not merely at its substance. That was decided in your Lordships' House in *Inland Revenue Comrs.* v. *Duke of Westminster* (48). But having ascertained the real nature of the transaction one cannot, in my opinion, disguise

C it by using camouflaged clothing. Here the whole essence of the employment of the taxpayer was as a machine minder at a weekly wage. If he so wished he could have part of his wages applied in providing for his own personal use, quite unconnected with the affairs of the employers, a motor car, and that use was terminable by employers or taxpayer on short notice. Dress that up how you will, I hope a court would not be deceived by the disguise.

D For these reasons, I would allow this appeal on the ground that the emoluments of the taxpayer for the purposes of taxation under Sch. E were his gross wages before any deduction for his participation in the car loan service.

So, in my opinion, the second question does not arise, but as it has been the subject of some judicial conflict of opinion in the courts below (49), I propose to make some observations on it. Did the privilege of having this use of the car at

E clearly advantageous rates amount to a perquisite within the meaning of the word " perquisite " in the Income Tax Acts as part of the taxpayer's taxable emoluments?

My Lords, I think the officious bystander uninstructed in the law would say that for an employee to have the use of a brand new car licensed and insured for himself and his family and not at all for the purposes of the employer at a rate

F in the neighbourhood of £2 to £3 a week, would be a valuable perquisite if the employee liked to avail himself of it. But that is not the test; the word " emolument " (of which the word " perquisite " is only an example) in the Income Tax Acts means an incoming in the sense of a money incoming; a benefit such as the right or indeed obligation (for in the case I am about to mention no difference was made between the two) to live in a house free was not an incoming

G merely because it relieved the taxpayer from the obligation he would in common sense otherwise be under of providing a roof over his head. All this was decided in your Lordships' House in *Tennant* v. *Smith* (50) where it was pointed out, however, that profits or perquisites in kind readily convertible into money might be taxable as though they had been money received.

This principle has been repeatedly approved and quite recently in your

H Lordships' House in *Abbott* v. *Philbin (Inspector of Taxes)* (51). LORD RADCLIFFE very conveniently collected together and approved the statements of their Lordships on this point, so I will repeat these observations (52):

" The basis of the Revenue's claim in *Tennant* v. *Smith* (50) was really to tax the bank manager on expenditure which he was saved, not on any money that he got or could get, while tax on the full annual value of the

I premises was taken from the bank itself. It was not, however, the view of

---

(46) (1926), 11 Tax Cas. 83 at p. 90;
(47) [1968] 1 All E.R. at p. 861; [1968] 1 W.L.R. at p. 272.
(48) [1935] All E.R. Rep. 259; 19 Tax Cas. 490.
(49) [1968] 1 All E.R. 857; [1968] 1 W.L.R. 263; [1968] 2 All E.R. 1156; [1968] 1 W.L.R. 1385.
(50) [1892] A.C. 150; 3 Tax Cas. 158.
(51) [1960] 2 All E.R. 763; 39 Tax Cas. 82.
(52) [1960] 2 All E.R. at pp. 773, 774; 39 Tax Cas. at pp. 124, 125.

the House that profits or perquisites, to be taxable, could consist only of money paid. It was accepted that they could include objects or things of value received, payments in kind, so long as they were [as was said by several law Lords] ' capable of being turned into money ' (LORD HALSBURY, L.C. (53)) 'money, or that which can be turned to pecuniary account ' (LORD WATSON (54)), ' money payment or payments convertible into money ' (LORD MACNAGHTEN (55)) ' that which could be converted into money ' (LORD HANNEN (56)).

" I think that it has been generally assumed that this decision does impose a limitation on the taxability of benefits in kind which are of a personal nature, in that it is not enough to say that they have a value to which there can be assigned a monetary equivalent. If they are by their nature incapable of being turned into money by the recipient they are not taxable, even though they are, in any ordinary sense of the word, of value to him."

LORD RADCLIFFE went on to discuss some of the uncertainties which this decision raised but in reference to circumstances so different from those before your Lordships that I do not think they are of assistance.

So is this perquisite a taxable perquisite? Of course one can sensibly value it at £2 13s. 6d. per week but that plainly is not the test; one must be able (and I care not what expression is used, for we are not now construing an Act of Parliament) to turn it into money. UNGOED-THOMAS, J., was of opinion (57) that as the taxpayer could terminate the car loan scheme so far as he was concerned by giving 14 days' notice he could convert the perquisite into money by receiving higher wages thereafter.

My Lords, powerful reasons were advanced by the judges of the Court of Appeal (58) for disagreeing with and overruling that reasoning. I agree with them. The taxpayer could not turn the perquisite, which was no more than the personal use of the car, into money or anything which could be equated to money; all he could do would be to give up his perquisite and obtain higher wages. In my opinion, this personal unassignable right for use of the car was not equivalent to money while it continued and that, surely, must be the test.

So on the second question I would have dismissed the appeal, but for the reasons I have given earlier I would allow the appeal on the footing that the taxpayer is properly assessable under Sch. E in respect of his gross wages before any deduction for the car hire.

LORD DIPLOCK: My Lords, by the ingenious " Car Loan Service " which gives rise to this appeal the taxpayer's employers, whom I will call " the company ", were able to provide their employees with motor cars for their personal and private use at a very advantageous weekly rate of hire the amount of which was debited to the employee's weekly wages. This they were able to do partly at the expense of the general body of taxpayers by deducting in the computation of their own profits for tax purposes the initial and annual allowances for depreciation of cars so hired out to their employees. The propriety of such deductions is not, however, in issue in the present appeal. What is in issue is whether the taxpayer, an employee who availed himself of the " Car Loan Service ", is entitled to exclude from his income assessable to income tax under Sch. E the weekly sum debited to his wages by the company for the use of the car supplied to him under the scheme.

The Crown claim that this sum is chargeable to income tax because it is included in " the full amount of the emoluments " from his employment (see Income Tax

---

(53) [1892] A.C. at p. 156; 3 Tax Cas. at p. 164.
(54) [1892] A.C. at p. 159; 3 Tax at p. 167.
(55) [1892] A.C. at p. 163; 3 Tax Cas. at p. 170.
(56) [1892] A.C. at p. 165; 3 Tax Cas. at p. 172.
(57) [1968] 1 All E.R. at p. 867; [1968] 1 W.L.R. at pp. 280, 281.
(58) [1968] 2 All E.R. 1156; [1968] 1 W.L.R. 1385.

A   Act 1952, s. 156, Sch. E, para. 1, and Finance Act 1956, Sch. 2, para. 1). The expression " emoluments " is so defined in the Finance Act 1956, as to include " all
salaries, fees, wages, perquisites and profits whatsoever " and the Crown advance
as alternative contentions: either that the sums debited to his weekly wages in
respect of his use of the car were a part of his " wages " which were allocated to the
discharge of a debt due by him to the company under a contract of car hire

B   collateral to his contract of employment, or that the use of the car was a " perquisite " or " profit " from his employment in respect of which those sums are
the amount on which he is assessable to tax.

I agree with those of your Lordships who are of opinion that the only proper
inference to be drawn from the facts and documents relating to the taxpayer's
participation in the " Car Loan Service " which are disclosed in the Special

C   Case, is that the agreement which he made with the company collateral to his
contract of employment with them, was that he should pay to the company
a weekly sum for hire of the car and that the company should deduct and retain
that sum out of his weekly wages so long as he continued to hire the car from them.
The only reference to the hire charge which is to be found in the formal documents
relating to the " Car Loan Service " is a provision in the conditions forwarded to

D   him with an application form which reads " An amended wage basis will come
into operation if the application is accepted ". This is an ambiguous expression
and the word " basis " is otiose if all it means is that the applicant's contract of
employment will be varied by the substitution of a different wage from that
which previously constituted the consideration for his services. The written
documents issued by the company and executed by them and the taxpayer,

E   which included, in addition to the conditions and the application form, a so-called
" Memorandum of Terms of Service " incorporating what are conceded to be, in
part at any rate, sham provisions, do not contain the full terms of the agreement
between them and in particular do not provide what the " amended wage basis "
was to be. What they in fact agreed on this essential term can only be inferred
from what they did in the performance of the agreement. The weekly pay-slips

F   issued by the company to the taxpayer thereafter and receipted by him, disclose
that he continued to be credited with flat rate wages, overtime and shift premiums
and bonuses for the hours he worked at precisely the same rates as previously.
These were, no doubt, those applicable to craftsmen of his grade under national
or shop agreements. But he was debited with a weekly sum for the hire of the
car, though no description of what it was appeared on the pay-slip. When he was

G   absent sick no deduction was made.

In my view, the overwhelming inference is that the true agreement between
him and the company was that the wages constituting the consideration for his
services under his contract of employment should remain unchanged but that the
company should be entitled each week to recoup themselves out of his wages, but
not from any other source, the amount of his liability to them under his collateral

H   agreement for the hire of the car. The inference is not, in my view, weakened by
the fact that this debit against the wages credited to him was made before arriving at a figure described as " taxable gross wage " and that the amount subsequently deducted for P.A.Y.E. is calculated on this latter figure. Whether or not
both parties thought that the taxpayer could escape liability for income tax on
the amount debited against his wages is nihil ad rem aut regem. What this appeal

I   is about is whether they were right in so thinking. In my view, they were not.

But I should not wish to decide the present appeal on this narrow ground of
construction only. The alternative contention of the Crown, that the use of the
car was a " perquisite " or " profit " from the taxpayer's employment and as such
assessable to tax, attacks the substance of the transaction rather than its form
and in these days of multifarious " fringe benefits " in contracts of employment
it is this contention which is the important one in this appeal.

For the purpose of this part of my judgment I will therefore assume that
the construction placed by my noble and learned friend, LORD REID, on the

agreement between the company and the taxpayer relating to the use of the car
is right and that, contrary to the view which I have so far expressed, the taxpayer
on entering into the scheme agreed to serve the company for such period as they
would afford him the free use of a car, at a wage less than his former wage by an
agreed amount.

For my part, if it were permissible to confine myself to a consideration of the
relevant words in the current statutes (viz., the Income Tax Act 1952, and the
Finance Act 1956), by which income tax under Sch. E is currently charged, I
should have little hesitation in deciding that the free use of a car for his own
purposes provided to an employee by an employer by reason of his employment
was a perquisite from that employment and that the full amount of that perquisite on which tax is chargeable was the amount of money which the employee
would have had to pay on the open market for a right to use a car on similar terms
as to its user. I have no doubt that the man in the street would call the benefit
of the use of the car, if not a " perquisite " at any rate a " perk ".

But it is I fear too late to read the relevant words of the current legislation in
what I should regard as being their current acceptation. In *Tennant* v. *Smith*
(59) the House of Lords placed a judicial gloss on the word " perquisite " appearing
in the corresponding section of the Income Tax Act 1842, by confining it to actual
money payments and to benefits in kind variously described by LORD HALSBURY,
L.C. (60), as " capable of being turned into money ", by LORD WATSON (61) as
" that which can be turned to pecuniary account ", by LORD MACNAGHTEN
(62) as " payments convertible into money " and by LORD HANNEN (63) as
" that which could be converted into money ". LORD HALSBURY and LORD
WATSON expressly founded their conclusion on the presence in the definition of
" perquisite " in the statute they were construing of the adjective " payable "
qualifying the " perquisites " to be assessed under that Act. But LORD MAC-
NAGHTEN and LORD HANNEN did not base their gloss on the meaning of " perquisite " on this narrow ground. In the Income Tax Act 1918, the relevant sections
were redrafted and in the process the word " payable " disappeared, but this
professed to be a consolidation Act and the presumption is that the change
in wording was not intended to give to the new enactment a meaning different
from that of the enactment which it replaced. Further changes in drafting and
arrangement which were made by subsequent legislation, including the Income
Tax Act 1952, and the Finance Act 1956, which are applicable to the present
appeal, have not, in my view, affected the meaning which the word " perquisite "
bore in the Income Tax Act 1918. I think that it must be accepted that " perquisite " in each of these subsequent statutes still means what it meant in the
Income Tax Act 1842.

The benefit in kind which it was contended in *Tennant* v. *Smith* (59) was a
" perquisite " arising in the course of the taxpayer's employment was the residence by a bank manager in a house on the bank's premises in respect of which it
was conceded that his employers were liable to income tax under Sch. A, and in
which he was required to reside by the terms of his contract of employment.
His residence there thus formed part of the services which he undertook to render
to his employers under his contract of employment and not a benefit granted to
him by them as a consideration for his services. On its facts *Tennant* v. *Smith* (59)
is thus clearly distinguishable from the present case. The taxpayer was under
no duty to the company to use the car provided for him under the car loan scheme.
His use of it formed no part of the services rendered to the company under his
contract of employment. His right to use it was a benefit granted to him by
them as a consideration for his services. Nevertheless *Tennant* v. *Smith* (59)
was not decided, as in my view it might have been, on this obvious ground which
distinguishes it from the present case but on the ground that the benefit

(59) [1892] A.C. 150; 3 Tax Cas. 158.   (60) [1892] A.C. at p. 156; 3 Tax Cas. at p. 164.
(61) [1892] A.C. at p. 159; 3 Tax Cas. at p. 167.
(62) [1892] A.C. at p. 163; 3 Tax Cas. at p. 170.
(63) [1892] A.C. at p. 165; 3 Tax Cas. at p. 172.

A of residence in the bank house was not a "perquisite" because of its inconvertibility into money—a concept which each of their Lordships expressed in the
slightly different words to which I have already referred.

The judicial gloss placed on the expression "perquisite" in *Tennant* v.
Smith (64) has been consistently accepted by the courts in subsequent cases and
in particular by your Lordship's House in *Abbott* v. *Philbin* (*Inspector of Taxes*)
B (65). It would not, in my view, be right after this lapse of time to challenge its
correctness, but it is at least permissible to enquire: what exactly does it mean?

In any such enquiry one must strive to avoid the all too tempting error of
construing the actual words used in the speeches of the individual Lords of Appeal
to express the concept which they had in mind as if those words formed part of
the statute itself. What one is seeking are the characteristics of the taxable
C benefit in kind which are alluded to by those words. The underlying reason, as I
think, for ascribing to the word "perquisite" in the Income Tax Acts a more
restricted meaning than in ordinary speech is the simple notion that since income
is payable in money Parliament cannot have intended to exact it from employees
in respect of benefits in kind from which the employee cannot himself by dealing
with, foregoing or disposing of the benefit raise money to pay the tax.

D It was conceded on behalf of the taxpayer that if he had been able to permit
another person to use the car he might have raised money by hiring it out and
the benefit would in that case possess the characteristics of a taxable perquisite.
But it was contended that since he had contracted with the company "not to
permit anyone other than myself to drive or use the car except in an emergency"
this means of raising money by dealing with the benefit was not open to him.

E This contention raises one of the questions which in his speech in *Abbott* v. *Philbin*
Lord Radcliffe (66) specifically mentioned as left open by the decision in
Tennant v. *Smith* (64): "Must the inconvertibility arise from the nature of the
thing itself, or can it be imposed merely by contractual stipulation?" It is not, I
think, necessary to answer that question in the present appeal, which I am
content to dispose of on simpler grounds, but it must not be supposed that I
F assent to the proposition that a benefit in kind can escape all charge to tax as a
perquisite by limitations on the employee's right to deal with it imposed by a
contract collateral to his contract of employment into which he enters of his own
volition.

By the terms of his agreement with the company under which he received the
benefit in kind which the Crown seek to tax, viz., the free use of a car, the tax-
G payer on giving two weeks' notice could surrender it and on doing so would become
entitled to be paid by the company a new weekly wage greater than the agreed
amount by which his former weekly wage had been reduced when he joined the
car loan scheme. In this way, say the Crown, the benefit could be converted into
money or turned to pecuniary account during the year of assessment—and this
sounds remarkably like common sense. As such it commended itself to Ungoed-
H Thomas, J. (67) On the contrary, says the taxpayer, when the notice expires the
benefit vanishes. There is nothing left to be converted into money. It is an irrelevant coincidence that on the disappearance of the benefit I become entitled to
resume my employment at a higher money wage.

This argument, although accepted as valid by the Court of Appeal (68), is
altogether too subtle for me. It is really no more than a linguistic one about
I what "convertible into money" means; and had these words been used in the
taxing statute, we might have been driven to embark on this sterile exercise. But
they do not appear in any statute. They are to be found in a lengthy speech of
Lord Macnaghten in *Tennant* v. *Smith* (64) from which they have been often
borrowed by judges in later cases as a convenient way of alluding to one characteristic of a benefit in kind enjoyed by an employee by reason of his employment

(64) [1892] A.C. 150; 3 Tax Cas. 158.   (65) [1960] 2 All E.R. 763; 39 Tax Cas. 82.
(66) [1960] 2 All E.R. at p. 774; 39 Tax Cas. at p. 135.
(67) [1968] 1 All E.R. 857; [1968] 1 W.L.R. 263.
(68) [1968] 2 All E.R. 1156; [1968] 1 W.L.R. 1385,

which was absent in the benefit under discussion in *Tennant's* case (69), but is $\quad$ **A**
requisite to render the benefit taxable.

Their Lordships in *Tennant* v. *Smith* (69) were not directing their minds to
benefits in kind which an employee at his option could surrender or reject in
favour of a money payment. I find nothing in their speeches to indicate that, if
Mr. Tennant had had an option instead of living in the bank house to live elsewhere and receive a higher salary, they would not have held that the benefit $\quad$ **B**
of free residence was chargeable to tax; and insofar as their decision was based
on considerations of the general policy of the Income Tax Act 1842, I find nothing
to suggest that they intended to exclude from " perquisites " chargeable to tax
benefits in kind which enable the employee to put money into his pocket by foregoing them even though he cannot otherwise deal with or dispose of them.

I accept, therefore, the contention of the Crown that the free use of a car for $\quad$ **C**
his own purposes under the company's car loan scheme was a " perquisite " from
his employment in respect of which the taxpayer was chargeable to income
tax under Sch. E, because if he had chosen to forego it he could have received a
higher money wage in its stead.

The remaining question is: What is the full amount of the perquisite on which
he should be assessed? The Crown do not seek to assess it at a higher figure than $\quad$ **D**
that of the reduction in the weekly wage which he agreed to accept so long as he
retained the use of the car. Accordingly, there is no evidence of any higher
weekly sum which the taxpayer would have to pay on the open market for a right
to use a car on similar terms. This makes it unnecessary to consider whether
Wilkins (Inspector of Taxes) v. *Rogerson* (70) was rightly decided. The full
amount of the perquisite was at least that sum of money which the taxpayer could $\quad$ **E**
have received had he chosen to forego the use of the car.

UNGOED-THOMAS, J., reduced the assessment by excluding the amount of the
reduction in the taxpayer's weekly wage for the two weeks which would have
elapsed between his giving notice terminating the agreement for use of the car,
and his receiving the higher weekly wage. The ground on which he did this is not
wholly clear, but the exclusion of a sum representing the reduction in wages for $\quad$ **F**
these two weeks has been justified before your Lordships' House on the ground
that the taxpayer having entered into the agreement could not have entitled
himself to receive a higher wage in lieu of the use of the car during this two week
period. For my part, I cannot accept this argument. From 1954 onwards when the
car loan service was first introduced, the taxpayer had the option either to forego
the benefit and accept a higher money wage instead or to accept the benefit and $\quad$ **G**
forego the higher money wage. Until 1961 he chose to forego the benefit and accept
the higher money wage. He could have continued to do so. If he had, he could
have received a higher money wage throughout the whole period of the agreement.
When an employee has chosen to accept a benefit in kind from his employer
instead of money it does not lose its characteristic as a " perquisite " during the
minimum period in any year of assessment for which by his previous choice he $\quad$ **H**
has committed himself to accept it.

I would, therefore, assess the full annual amount of the benefit at the total
amount of the higher wage which he would have received during the year if he had
not entered into the car loan scheme.

I would allow the appeal and restore the judgment of UNGOED-THOMAS, J. (71),
with the variation that the value of the perquisite to be included in the assessment $\quad$ **I**
should be the full amount debited to the taxpayer's wages in respect of the use of
the car during the respective years of assessment. $\qquad$ *Appeal allowed.*

Solicitors: *Solicitor of Inland Revenue*; *Biddle & Co.*, agents for *Hepworth &
Chadwick*, Leeds (for the taxpayer).

[*Reported by* S. A. HATTEEA, ESQ., *Barrister-at-Law.*]

---

(69) [1892] A.C. 150; 3 Tax Cas. 158.   (70) [1961] 1 All E.R. 358; 39 Tax Cas. 344.
     (71) [1968] 1 All E.R. 857; [1968] 1 W.L.R. 263.

A

DEVOTWILL INVESTMENTS, LTD. *v.* MARGATE CORPORATION.

[COURT OF APPEAL, CIVIL DIVISION (Lord Denning, M.R., Russell and Winn, L.JJ.), November 15, 18, 20, December 11, 1968.]

B *Compulsory Purchase—Compensation—Purchase notice—Assumptions on valuation—Planning permission reasonably to be expected—Assumption that no part of reference land to be acquired—Proposed by-pass to relieve congestion inapplicable—Assumption of alternative line—Resulting relief of congestion—Justification for immediate full development of land—Assumption of permission therefore—Validity of assumptions—No scheme giving rise to*

C *acquisition—Land Compensation Act 1961 (9 & 10 Eliz. 2 c. 33), s. 16 (2), (7).*

The owners of 1·35 acres of land fronting on to Canterbury Road, Birchington-on-Sea, Margate, which was allocated on the town map as primarily for residential use, applied to the local planning authority for outline planning permission for its residential development. They were

D refused permission on the ground that part of the site would be required for road improvement works designed to by-pass Birchington Square to the north and that residential development of the land would be premature until it had been possible to finalise details of the road improvement scheme. The scheme was expected to be implemented in 1970 and there was no evidence of any acquisitions of land on the by-pass route or of any resolution passed or

E compulsory purchase order made for such acquisition. The owners served a purchase notice in respect of the land which the local authority accepted in February 1966. The compensation payable under the notice was required by s. 16 (2) and (7) of the Land Compensation Act 1961 to be assessed on the assumption that, at the time of the deemed notice to treat on that date, planning permission would have been granted for residential development so

F far as then reasonably to be expected but that neither the local authority nor any other authority possessing compulsory purchase powers would acquire the land. The owners claimed that compensation should be assessed on the basis of planning permission for full development with 20 houses immediately, with access to Canterbury Road, giving a value of £16,000. The local authority contended that planning permission should be assumed for develop-

G ment with nine houses only immediately and with 11 houses deferred until suitable access became available because the extreme traffic congestion in Canterbury Road had to be assumed not to be relieved by the scheme; that gave a value of £8,200. The Lands Tribunal determined the compensation at £13,500 on the assumption that, while no part of the land could be taken for the actual by-pass, a by-pass would be provided on some other line taking

H through traffic away from Canterbury Road (which was found to be a practical possibility), the easing of traffic consequent on which would allow planning permission to be given for development with the full 20 houses immediately, with access to Canterbury Road.

Held (LORD DENNING, M.R., dissenting): the Lands Tribunal's determination of compensation at £13,500 must be confirmed on the following grounds—

I (i) (per RUSSELL, L.J.): (a) the provision in s. 16 (7) of the Land Compensation Act 1961 that the possibility should be ignored of the land being acquired by an authority possessing compulsory powers for a purpose inconsistent with full development for residential purposes had the artificial strictly limited purpose and effect of preventing the local authority from asserting that permission for a particular development could not be reasonably expected because the land was or was likely to be required for some other purpose inconsistent with that development, and (b) on that basis the Lands Tribunal was entitled to reject the postponement of 11 houses based on the

B

assumption of no relief to the traffic situation in Canterbury Road even   **A**
without looking for an alternative site for a by-pass, but (c) even if the
suggested construction of s. 16 (7) was wrong, it was right to assume that
the urgent traffic problem would lead to a by-pass which would pass to the
south of the reference land (see p. 103, letters E, F and I, and p. 104, letter A,
post).

(ii) (per WINN, L.J.) (a) s. 16 (7) of the Land Compensation Act 1961   **B**
simply protected the land owner against any diminution of the value of his
land being secured by a contention that planning permission would have been
refused on the ground that his land was likely to be compulsorily acquired,
and its effect was the planning permission " which might reasonably have
been expected " had to be assumed to be the same as if there had been no
actual or anticipated acquisition of the land; and (b) in that highly artificial   **C**
notional and unreal situation in which the Lands Tribunal member was
bound to visualise the application for planning permission the assumptions
and corollaries on which he built the foundations of his valuation did not
reveal any error of law (see p. 106, letter H, and p. 107, letters F and G, post);

(iii) (per RUSSELL and WINN, L.JJ.):   the principle excluding any advantage due to the carrying out of the scheme for which the property is   **D**
compulsorily acquired did not apply, because—

(a) the facts were all too slight to enable the court to find that there was
anything which could be dignified by the title of scheme, the particular compulsory acquisition falling far short of establishing the existence of an
adopted and existing scheme as distinct from an intention or contemplation
in the minds of some members of the council (see p. 104, letter D, and p.105,   **E**
letter D, post).

(b) (per RUSSELL, L.J.): the principle had no application to the ascertainment of what residential development permission might reasonably have
been expected as distinct from the valuation of the interest (see p. 104,
letter E, post); and

(c) (per WINN, L.J.):   there was no suggestion that any use of adjoining   **F**
lands to the north-east of the reference land could increase the value of the
reference land when itself used as a road (see p. 106, letter C, post).

Pointe Gourde Quarrying and Transport Co., Ltd. v. *Sub-Intendent of Crown
Lands* ([1947] A.C. 565) distinguished.

Per WINN, L.J.: as at present advised I incline to the view that the provisions as to what is to be regarded in assessing compensation, under s. 6   **G**
of the Land Compensation Act 1961, must so prevail as to leave no room for
the application of any wider common law doctrine such as that laid down in
Pointe Gourde Quarrying and Transport Co., Ltd. v. *Sub-Intendent of Crown
Lands* ([1947] A.C. 565), and that that principle cannot apply to any case
where the value of the relevant land is said to be affected by development
on other land unless that other land forms, together with the relevant land,   **H**
part of an aggregate authorised to be acquired by the same compulsory
purchase order or special enactment (see p. 106, letters E and F, post).

Appeal dismissed.

[As to the assumption of planning permission in the assessment of compensation
on compulsory purchase (and on a purchase notice), see 10 HALSBURY'S LAWS
(3rd Edn.) 107-109, paras. 181, 182 and SUPPLEMENT.   **I**

For the Land Compensation Act 1961, s. 16, see 41 HALSBURY'S STATUTES
(2nd Edn.) 60.]

Cases referred to:
   Camrose (Viscount) v. *Basingstoke Corpn.*, [1966] 3 All E.R. 161;   [1966]
      1 W.L.R. 1100; Digest (Cont. Vol. B) 698, *176b*.
   East End Dwellings Co., Ltd. v. *Finsbury Borough Council*, [1951] 2 All E.R.
      587; [1952] A.C. 109; 115 J.P. 477; 45 Digest (Repl.) 369, *169*.

A   *Fraser* v. *Fraserville City*, [1917] A.C. 187; 86 L.J.P.C. 91; 11 Digest (Repl.)
      128, *83.
      Pointe Gourde Quarrying and Transport Co., Ltd. v. *Sub-Intendent of Crown
            Lands*, [1947] A.C. 565; 11 Digest (Repl.) 131, *149.
      *South Eastern Ry. Co. and London County Council's Contract, Re, South Eastern
            Ry. Co.* v. *London County Council*, [1915] 2 Ch. 252; 84 L.J.Ch. 756;
B   113 L.T. 392; 79 J.P. 545; 11 Digest (Repl.) 126, *164.*

Case Stated.

The compensating authority appealed by way of Case Stated against a decision
of the Lands Tribunal (J. S. DANIEL, ESQ., Q.C.) given on 2nd October 1967,
awarding the claimants compensation in the sum of £13,500 in respect of the
acquisition of 1·35 acres of land owned by them fronting on to Canterbury Road,
C Birchington-on-Sea, Margate. Their contentions on the appeal were as follows:
(i) the Lands Tribunal in arriving at a valuation of the claimants' interest failed
to take account in determining whether planning permission was likely to be
granted or failed to take proper account of the provisions of s. 16 of the Land
Compensation Act 1961 and in particular of s. 16 (7); (ii) in construing and applying s. 16 (7) the Lands Tribunal erred in finding that on the true construction of
D the provision the actual facts and circumstances relating to adjoining land, not
being the subject land, had to be or could be assumed to be altered for the purposes
of ascertaining whether planning permission could reasonably be expected to be
granted; (iii) in making such an assumption the Lands Tribunal erred in valuing
the claimants' interest in that such assumption, unless authorised by the provisions of the Land Compensation Act 1961, was inconsistent with the principle
E that the interest must be valued rebus sic stantibus as at the proper date for
valuation, and such assumption was not so authorised; (iv) in the alternative,
whether or not under the provisions of s. 16 of the Land Compensation Act 1961
the Lands Tribunal might assume that the existing facts and circumstances were
altered otherwise that as authorised by s. 16 (7) in the circumstances of the
decision, such assumption would conflict with the rule that no increase in com-
F pensation might be awarded which resulted from the scheme in relation to which
the acquisition was made; (v) in the further alternative there was no evidence on
which the Lands Tribunal could find that an alternative by-pass was inevitable,
having regard to the true meaning and construction of the expression
"inevitable"; (vi) insofar as the Lands Tribunal arrived at the value of £13,500
for the claimants' interest by taking into account the possibility of an alternative
G by-pass removing the traffic from the vicinity of the subject land, the Lands
Tribunal erred in law in making its comparisons and in arriving at the value to be
awarded for the reasons advanced in grounds (i) to (v).

R. W. Bell for the compensating authority.
Douglas Frank, Q.C., and *B. A. Marder* for the claimants.

H   **LORD DENNING, M.R.:**   At Birchington in the borough of Margate
there is a very busy square called Birchington Square. Through it passes all the
traffic of Canterbury Road. The congestion is so bad that the authorities have
for years been trying to ease the burden. At first they thought it was best to
widen and improve Canterbury Road. Now they think it best to make a by-pass
to carry the traffic round the square. The scheme is still on paper and is in its
I early stages. There is much to do. Inquiries will have to be held. Lands acquired.
And the by-pass made.

The claimants, Devotwill Investments, Ltd., own a small piece of land which
fronts on to Canterbury Road. It is only 1·35 acres. It is in part an old builder's
yard and in part waste land. Years ago a town map was prepared in which this
1·35 acres was shown as allocated primarily for " residential use ". The map was
approved in 1958 and this land was shown as suitable for development for
" residential use " in from six to 20 years. At that time the planners looked into
the future as best they could. No doubt they thought that Canterbury Road

could take the traffic from such a development. They did not foresee the great **A**
increase in through traffic. They did not envisage a by-pass. At any rate, there
is no sign of it in the town map.

On 2nd September 1965 the claimants, the owners of the 1·35 acres, applied to
the planning authorities for outline permission to develop it for residential use.
On 1st October 1965 the planning authorities refused permission on these grounds:

" (a) Part of the site, the subject of this application, will be required for   **B**
road-improvement works to Canterbury Road, designed to by-pass Birchington Square.

" (b) Residential development of the land would be premature until it
has been possible to finalise details of the road-improvement scheme referred
to in ground (a) above."

Two things can be inferred from those grounds. The *first* is that there was a   **C**
scheme to make a road to by-pass Birchington Square, but the details of the
scheme had not been finalised. The *second* is that part of this 1·35 acres would
be required for the by-pass road and part would not.

On receiving that refusal, the claimants, on 26th November 1965 called on
the compensating authority to buy these 1·35 acres. (Owners of land, who
are refused permission to develop, are entitled to require the council to purchase   **D**
the land: see s. 129 of the Town and Country Planning Act 1962.)   On 24th
February 1966 the compensating authority replied, saying:

" After consultation with the Ministry of Transport, the [compensating
authority] are agreeable to purchase the land, and the district valuer has
been asked to negotiate the terms of the acquisition."
                                                                                     E
It is worth noting that the compensating authority consulted with the Ministry
of Transport. That shows that the scheme for the by-pass was well in hand.

The parties did not agree on a price. So the matter was referred to the Lands
Tribunal. The claimants claimed £16,000 for these 1·35 acres, plus surveyors'
fees and legal charges. The compensating authority suggested £8,200 was the
proper figure. The tribunal awarded £13,500. The compensating authority   **F**
appeal to this court. The Lands Tribunal gave its decision in writing, from which
this point of law emerges: The claimants submitted that the 1·35 acres should
be valued on the footing that no part of it was to be used for the by-pass; that
it should be assumed that there would be a by-pass on some other line which
would take the through traffic away from Canterbury Road; that the by-pass
would be made *immediately*; and that the easing of traffic would be so great   **G**
that permission would be given for it to be built on to full capacity, that is, for
20 houses (which is all it could physically contain), all of which would gain
access by Canterbury Road.

The compensating authority submitted that it would be wrong to assume a
by-pass on another line; and that the situation should be considered as it was
at the time of the agreement to purchase on 24th February 1966. At that time   **H**
nine houses might be permitted immediately on the front land, but another
11 houses might be allowed on the back land in later years when suitable access
became available. The tribunal accepted the submission of the owners, stating:

" I accept [counsel for the claimants'] submission that, at the date of the
demand notice to treat, planning permission might reasonably have been
expected for *immediate* residential development on the whole of the land."   **I**

The question comes to this: Was the tribunal right in assuming that a by-pass
would be made on some other line, leaving these 1·35 acres available for *immediate*
development for 20 houses? The statutory provisions may be summarised as
follows: As soon as the compensating authority agreed to purchase the 1·35
acres, they were deemed to acquire that land compulsorily, just as if they had
acquired it for any purpose for which they had compulsory powers: see s. 130
of the Act of 1962. The valuation had, therefore, to proceed in accordance with

A the assumptions contained in s. 14 to s. 16 of the Land Compensation Act 1961. It was, therefore, to be assumed: (a) that planning permission would be granted for the use of the land for residential purposes: see s. 16 (2) (*a*); (b) that no part of the land would be acquired by the compensating authority or by any other authority possessing compulsory purchase powers: see s. 16 (2) (*b*) and (7).

B Those are the only two assumptions which the Act requires the tribunal to make; and I see no reason why the tribunal should make any further assumptions. In particular, I see no reason why the tribunal should assume that a by-pass would be made on this present line or on any other line.   Clearly the tribunal cannot assume that a by-pass would be made on *this present line*.   Section 16 (7) excludes that assumption.   And the tribunal should not assume a by-pass on *some other line*; because that is contrary to all probabilities.   If any scheme is

C adopted for a by-pass, it will very likely be the present scheme and none other.

Moreover, if one assumes that a by-pass along *some other line*—and *immediately* made, so as to be at once in use—then these 1·35 acres will gather considerable betterment from the assumed scheme.   Canterbury Road will be deemed a quiet town street.   The 1·35 acres will be deemed to be an attractive housing estate for 20 houses next to it.   It will be considerably increased in value.   The

D tribunal recognised this.   It stated:

" The assumed corollary of a by-pass on another line might be said to be letting in some increment in the nature of betterment."

It follows that, by assuming a by-pass on another line to be *immediately* carried out, the claimants would be getting an increase in value which was due, not to the intrinsic advantages or potentialities of their own land, but to an assumed

E scheme of compulsory acquisition which in all probability will never be carried out.   It would, I think, be contrary to the intentions of Parliament that they should be given an increment on that account.   It is a general principle that

". . . compensation for the compulsory acquisition of land cannot include an increase in value which is entirely due to the scheme underlying the

F acquisition "

see *Pointe Gourde Quarrying and Transport Co., Ltd.* v. *Sub-Intendent of Crown Lands* (1) and *Viscount Camrose* v. *Basingstoke Corpn.* (2).   So also compensation cannot include an increase in value which is entirely due to an assumed scheme of compulsory acquisition which is never likely to be carried out.

The claimants, the owners of the 1·35 acres, drew attention to the fact that

G in 1958, when the town map was prepared, there was another empty piece of land which was shown as allocated primarily for residential use.   It was the other side of Birchington Square.   In 1961 the owners of that piece were given outline permission for a housing estate.   In 1962 they obtained approval for the details.   In 1963 they built the houses and called it the Yew Tree Estate.   So they did well out of their " residential " allocation.   The owners of the 1·35

H acres claim that they should be entitled to do the same.   I do not think so. Some years have passed.   The congestion is worse now than it was in 1961. Permission would not in 1966 be given for such extensive development on to Canterbury Road.   And it was at 1966 that the compensation has to be decided.

Viewing the matter quite broadly, it seems to me that the claimants, the owners of this little piece of waste land (1·35 acres), are doing quite well out of the

I fact that it was allocated in the town map for " residential development ".   It means that, apart altogether from the by-pass scheme, they will get at least £8,200 for it—a sum which shows them, no doubt, a handsome profit without doing a hand's turn to develop it.   I see no reason why they should get an extra £5,000 by assuming in their favour a by-pass scheme on another line.   It would give them, contrary to all principle, an added profit which was entirely due to the scheme for a by-pass.

(1) [1947] A.C. 565 at p. 572.
(2) [1966] 3 All E.R. 161; [1966] 1 W.L.R. 1100.

The Lands Tribunal stated that

> " there was much evidence and argument addressed to the question of whether, assuming no permanent access to Canterbury Road in the position supposed by the claimants, the back land would be expected to be developed in due course in co-operation with the adjoining owners."

But it did not make any alternative award on that basis.   In the circumstances I think the case should go back to it for reconsideration, for I think it was the right basis.   I would allow the appeal and remit the case to the tribunal for him to reconsider his award, having regard to this judgment.

RUSSELL, L.J.: Application was made for planning permission for residential development of the site adjacent to Canterbury Road, Birchington. The land was allocated in the town map for such development and programmed for such development in a period that includes the relevant date for assessment of compensation.   The compensating authority refused such permission on the grounds that—

> " part of the site will be required for road improvement works to Canterbury Road, designed to by-pass Birchington Square [and] residential development of the land would be premature until it has been possible to finalise details of the road improvement scheme."

The claimants as owners served a purchase notice under s. 129 of the Town and Country Planning Act 1962, claiming that the land had been rendered incapable of reasonable beneficial use in its existing state: the compensating authority served notice that they were willing to comply with the purchase notice on 24th February 1966.   On that date, accordingly, the compensating authority were deemed to be authorised to acquire the land compulsorily in accordance with Part 5 of the Act of 1962 and to have served notice to treat.   As a result compensation has to be assessed and the question in this appeal is whether the Lands Tribunal has erred in assessing that compensation.   Compensation was to be assessed under the Land Compensation Act 1961.   The main feature of s. 5 for present purposes is that the value of land shall be taken to be the amount which that land if sold in the open market by a willing seller might be expected to realise.   Section 14 to s. 16 contain assumptions as to planning permission that are to be made in the course of assessing compensation.   Section 16, so far as concerns the present case, requires it to be assumed that planning permission would be granted for any development for residential use which might (if no part of the land were proposed to be acquired by an authority having compulsory powers) reasonably have been expected to be permitted, and subject to such conditions, if any, as might reasonably be expected to be imposed. (It is not material in the present case, but I am inclined to disagree with the view expressed by the Lands Tribunal on the construction of the section that it is possible to find that no such development might reasonably have been expected to have been permitted: I would prefer the view that the function of s. 16 (2) (b) is to restrict the carte blanche of the rest of the subsection but never to extinguish its operation.)   The Lands Tribunal as a first step in assessing compensation was therefore required to apply to the case the above assumptions, in order to determine the quality or character—in the sense of development potential—of the property which the hypothetical purchaser must evaluate.

The case has two main factors.   One is that Canterbury Road carries heavy traffic, which introduces problems in access thereto from the relevant land if developed residentially, with associated sight line difficulties: though it will have been seen that this was not in terms the ground for refusal of planning permission.   The other is that the compensating authority consider it urgently necessary to relieve the congestion in the relevant stretch of Canterbury Road, and the present idea is to do so by a by-pass, part of the route of which, according

A to some current plan, passes through and occupies a large part of the relevant land.

The development for which permission could reasonably have been expected at the relevant date, put forward by the claimants, consisted of four blocks of five, four, five and six houses with appropriate garage or parking space, and access to Canterbury Road. The compensating authority put forward, some-
B what unwillingly, a development, consisting of two blocks of four and five houses respectively with temporary access to Canterbury Road, as being that for which permission could reasonably have been expected at the relevant date, together with a possible full development of the relevant land when the other land behind it became developed and road access to the relevant land would not be from Canterbury Road at all.

C In both cases the proposals of what residential development might reasonably be expected to be permitted ignored the possibility that any part of the relevant land might be acquired by an authority having compulsory powers for a purpose inconsistent with full development of the land for residential purposes, whether for a burial ground or a by-pass. This was in accordance with s. 16 (7) of the Land Compensation Act 1961. The compensating authority's proposals,
D however, were put forward on the assumption that the traffic situation in Canterbury Road would not be relieved in any way. This was on the footing that s. 16 (7) required that the only current plan for relieving that traffic situation, the construction of a by-pass through the relevant land, must be ignored, and no other idea for such relief was in mind.

In my judgment that is the wrong approach. In my view, s. 16 (7) has the
E artificial strictly limited purpose and effect of preventing the compensating authority from asserting that permission for a particular development could not be reasonably expected because the land was or was likely to be required for some other purpose which if achieved was inconsistent with that development: which was indeed the ground on which planning permission was in fact refused in this case. Having had that effect the subsection is in my view spent. This
F leaves at large the question whether the only stumbling block in the way of a reasonable expectation of permission for full development—viz., the traffic congestion in Canterbury Road—is likely to remain indefinitely. Here it seems to me that we move from the field of the artificial to the field of fact, where s. 16 (7) has no part.

The Lands Tribunal took the view that in the field of fact it was bound to
G assume that traffic in Canterbury Road would not be relieved by the by-pass as at present envisaged, but that in the light of the urgent need to reduce the traffic in Canterbury Road it must be assumed as an artificial corollary that the reduction would be achieved by a by-pass in a situation that would incorporate no part of the relevant land: and that other situation could on the ground only be such as to relieve congestion in the part of Canterbury Road in which access to the
H development was proposed, thus removing the only obstacle put forward by the compensating authority to a reasonable expectation of permission for full development. The Lands Tribunal relied in part for this approach on the dictum of LORD ASQUITH OF BISHOPSTONE in *East End Dwellings Co., Ltd.* v. *Finsbury Borough Council* (3) though I observe that that dictum related to an inevitable corollary *in law* of an imaginary state of affairs.

I For my part I do not think that it was necessary for the Lands Tribunal to look for and find an alternative site for a by-pass, taking as I do a strictly limited view of the function and effect of s. 16 (7). Thus far I consider that the Lands Tribunal was well entitled, when faced with the simple alternative between a development of 20 houses, and a development of nine houses with further development postponed, to reject the postponement of 11 houses, which postponement was based on an assumption of no relief to the traffic situation in

___

(3) [1951] 2 All E.R. 587 at pp. 598, 599; [1952] A.C. 109 at p. 132.

Canterbury Road.   If I were wrong in my strictly limited view of the function **A**
and effect of s. 16 (7), I would however agree with the view of the Lands Tribunal
that the state of affairs to be assumed by that subsection should lead to the
further assumption that the urgent traffic problem will lead to a by-pass which
will pass to the south of the relevant land.

That concludes the exercise in the first stage of assessing compensation:
that which I have described as the determination of the quality or character— **B**
in the sense of development potential—of the property which the hypothetical
purchaser must evaluate.   The second stage is a pure exercise in valuation of
the property of that quality or character, on which I have nothing to say.

Somewhat late in the hearing, counsel for the compensating authority raised
the argument that the decision infringed the principle of *Pointe Gourde Quarrying
and Transport Co., Ltd.* v. *Sub-Intendent of Crown Lands* (4), which can scarcely **C**
have been raised below since no mention is made of that case.   As I understand
the argument it is said that the land is being acquired as part of a scheme
for the construction of a by-pass, that the decision of the Lands Tribunal involves
including in the assessment of compensation an increase in value of the relevant
land attributable to the scheme, and that such inclusion is contrary to well-
established principle.   With all respect to the contrary view I am unable to **D**
accept that proposition.   In the first place I think that the facts as set out in
the Case Stated are all too slight to enable this court to find that there was
anything that could at the date of the assumed notice to treat be dignified by the
title of scheme.   Maybe this is because this case was not put forward by the
compensating authority before the Lands Tribunal.   In the second place in my
view the principle has no application to the first operation to be performed, viz., **E**
under s. 16, the ascertainment of what residential development permission
might reasonably have been expected.   If there had been a recognisable scheme,
and had at the pure valuation stage evidence been led to show that the purchasers
of the houses when built would be probably prepared to pay £100 more per
house for fronting on or access to a relieved rather than a traffic-congested road,
the point might well have been of substance.   This may I think be the explana- **F**
tion of the reference in the decision of the Lands Tribunal to " some increment
in the nature of betterment ".   But that is not the proposition argued before us.
For these reasons I would dismiss the appeal.

WINN, L.J.:   The main contention raised by the compensating authority is
that in valuing land taken by them from the claimants the Lands Tribunal
erred in law by failing to take proper account of the provisions of s. 16 (7) of the **G**
Land Compensation Act 1961.   The land in question consisted of a small area
of 1·35 acres fronting Canterbury Road, Birchington.   This county road A.28
carries heavy traffic, including some from London bound for Margate: it runs
south-west to north-east through Birchington Square near the centre of the town
and through the busiest shopping area.

The borough engineer gave evidence before the tribunal that improvement **H**
of the traffic flow had long been under consideration and that it was now hoped
to construct a by-pass in 1970; a line for the road had been decided, departing
from Canterbury Road where the relevant land adjoined it and running across
that land, although not absorbing all of it.   This proposed road has not yet been
approved by the Minister of Transport nor was there any indication of it on the
Thanet town map of 1958, which had not been amended.   On that map the **I**
relevant land was allocated primarily for residential use: the programme map
indicated that development of it was contemplated in the period six to 20 years
after 1958.

In September 1965 the claimants applied for permission for such development;
this was refused by notice dated 1st October 1965 on the ground, inter alia, that—

---

(4) [1947] A.C. 565.

A   " part of the site will be required for road improvement works to Canterbury Road, designed to by-pass Birchington Square."

They thereupon served a purchase notice which the compensating authority
accepted; there was therefore a deemed notice to treat of date 24th February
1966.   Earlier refusals dated respectively 21st January 1963, 30th April 1963
and 13th August 1965 referred somewhat vaguely to a " scheme to widen and
B   improve this part of Canterbury Road " and to " road improvement works to
Canterbury Road, namely the by-pass of Birchington Square ".

There was no evidence that any other land had been acquired on the proposed
route of the contemplated by-pass or that any compulsory purchase order had
been made or any resolution passed or proposed to lead to any such acquisition.
It is of course clear that the relevant land is to be regarded as having been
C   compulsorily acquired and the motive, and, it is probably right to say, the purpose
of the compensating authority in accepting the claimants' notice to purchase
is indicated with adequate certainty by the terms of the refusal of permisision
dated 1st October 1965.   This acquisition, in isolation, falls far short of establishing the existence of an adopted and existing scheme, as distinct from an
intention or contemplation in the minds of some, but not necessarily all the
D   members of the compensating authority and their advisers: what was shown by
the evidence was that, so soon as the necessary approvals and financial resources
had been obtained, the compensating authority would in all probability proceed
in 1970 or thereafter to initiate compulsory purchase procedure to enable a by-
pass to be built over lands to the north-east of the relevant land and across that
land.

E   This situation bore only remote resemblance to that which fell to be considered
by the Privy Council in the well-known case of *Pointe Gourde Quarrying and
Transport Co., Ltd.* v. *Sub-Intendent of Crown Lands* (5).   There the Crown had
compulsorily acquired lands in Trinidad required by the United States of America
in connection with the establishment of a naval base in the island.   The construction of the base would create additional demand for the limestone which
F   the claimants had quarried in part of the land acquired.   One of the grounds
on which it was held that no head of claim related to this extra demand could in
law be upheld was that compensation cannot include any increase in value which
is entirely due to the scheme underlying the acquisition.   Approval was given
to a passage in the judgment of Eve, J., in *Re South Eastern Ry. Co. and London
County Council's Contract, South Eastern Ry. Co.* v. *London County Council* (6), in
G   which he said:

".. . increase in value consequent on the execution of the undertaking for
or in connection with which the purchase is made must be disregarded."

However, the facts of the case in and for the purposes of which Eve, J., stated
that proposition were very special inasmuch as the owner of the land taken,
H   which abutted on the West Strand, in London, was also owner of contiguous land,
not acquired, fronting on Craven Street; it was unsuccessfully argued for London
County Council that regard should be had to the fact that the contemplated
widening of the Strand would increase the value of the Craven Street plot.
Accordingly the dictum of Eve, J., had no relevance.   In the Court of Appeal
it was emphasised that the relevant Act contained no provision for off-setting
I   betterment.

There is further authority, were it needed, in *Fraser* v. *Fraserville City* (7)
for the general proposition, which I would regard as a common law principle,
stated in that case in the words (8):

".. . the value to be ascertained is the value to the seller of the property
in its actual condition at the time of expropriation with all its existing

---

(5) [1947] A.C. 565.   (6) [1915] 2 Ch. 252 at p. 258.
(7) [1917] A.C. 187.   (8) [1917] A.C. at p. 194.

advantages and with all its possibilities, excluding any advantage due to   A
the carrying out of the scheme for which the property is compulsorily
acquired, the question of what is the scheme being a question of fact for the
arbitrator in each case.''

I pause to comment that those last words seem important in the present case:
in the *Fraser* case (9) it was manifest that the scheme was to acquire land to
construct reservoirs in order to supply a hydro-electric power station and the   B
arbitrator had erred by including the value of the power which would thus be
generated.   There was an equally definite scheme in *Viscount Camrose* v.
Basingstoke Corpn. (10).

It must be borne in mind that as a matter of logic there is no room in the
circumstances of the instant case for any application of the *Pointe Gourde* (11)
principle because there has been no suggestion, or if there has been it has escaped   C
me, of any respect in which any use of adjoining lands to the north-east of the
relevant land could increase the value of the relevant land when itself used as a
road.   The issue is, on a proper analysis, not one of value, but, treating it for the
moment and for convenience of the argument as though it had been, it is a
manifest absurdity to suppose that by turning the whole or the greater part of
1⅓ acres allocated for residential user into a road a scheme so to use it and adjoin-   D
ing lands in different ownership could give any increased value to the relevant
land.

To what extent, if at all, the *Pointe Gourde* (11) principle co-exists with the
express statutory provisions found in s. 6 of the Land Compensation Act 1961 it
is accordingly unnecessary to decide.   As at present advised I incline to the view
that these provisions must so prevail as to leave no room for the application   E
of any wider doctrine.   Without attempting to emulate the gallantry with
which counsel for the compensating authority strove to interpret the lamentable
language of this section before finally abandoning any reliance on it, I am content
to hazard the view that it cannot apply to any case where the value of the relevant
land is said to be affected by development on other land unless that other land
forms, together with the relevant land, part of an aggregate authorised to be   F
acquired by the same compulsory purchase order or special enactment.   Such
is not the present case: ground 4 of the appeal is not made good.

As already recognised, the issue to which consideration of the prospects of
the future construction of any by-pass across the relevant land, or elsewhere,
is relevant is not one of value but of probability with respect to the obtaining of
planning permission for residential development of the relevant land.   The Act   G
of 1961 requires certain assumptions to be made by any tribunal concerned to
assess that probability, but ultimately the issue is one of fact to be determined
by the application of expert knowledge and experience aided normally, as in this
case, by a personal inspection of the relevant site and neighbourhood.

Section 16 (7) of the Act of 1961, which the compensating authority maintained, for reasons which were neither wholly clear nor convincing, had not been   H
properly applied by the Lands Tribunal, is a provision wholly favourable to the
landowner: it simply protects him against any diminution of the value of his
land being secured by a contention that planning permission would have been
refused on the ground that his land was likely to be compulsorily acquired.

For the purposes of the instant case the important statutory assumptions are
those enacted in s. 16 (2) (*a*) and (*b*), and (6) (*a*).   The last provision reduces,   I
of course, the strength of the favourable wind with which s. 16 (2) (*a*) and (*b*)
fill the sails of a claimant.   Taking all these provisions, including s. 16 (7),
together, they constitute the terms of reference or instructions for the Lands
Tribunal member, or other arbitrator: he is to use his skill and knowledge, the
evidence and his own eyes, to assess with the aid of the sections what residential,

(9) [1917] A.C. 187.
(10) [1966] 3 All E.R. 161; [1966] 1 W.L.R. 1100.
(11) [1947] A.C. 565.

A or mutatis mutandis other, development would have been permitted on the relevant land by a permission issued on 24th February 1966, directing himself to assume that some such development would have been so permitted.

It is manifest from the Case Stated that this is precisely the exercise performed by J. S. DANIEL, Esq., Q.C., the member of the Lands Tribunal. Whether or not his conclusion and the consequential valuation represented a correct exercise
B of expertise is not a matter for this court, provided, as I think is the case, that no error of law is shown to have vitiated his reasoning. Without purporting to review the whole of his reasoning I think it is clear that the tribunal member properly had regard to the established need for residential development in Thanet and may well have taken into account the pressure which any such development would exert on available financial and other resources of the compensating
C authority. He had evidence that an estate, called Yew Tree Estate, of some 60 dwellings had been granted in 1961 detailed approval including access to Canterbury Road. It was amply proved that already in 1966 traffic conditions would necessitate the provision of a by-pass within the foreseeable future: the layout of Birchington would preclude any junction of this future road and Canterbury Road at any point north of the relevant land: a by-pass from any
D point south of the relevant land would greatly lessen the traffic passing that land.

There was no contemplation of any other line for such a by-pass than one leaving Canterbury Road across the relevant land, but it would not be impossible to construct one from a more southerly point. In fact, therefore, the probabilities were that the compensating authority would decide to make a road
E across the relevant land, if they could, rather than elsewhere, but this they could do only by somehow acquiring it. The compensating authority as the county roads authority possessed compulsory purchase powers (cf., the Highways Act 1959, s. 214 (2)) and, of course, had such powers for other purposes such as the provision of schools or cemeteries; they were in reality acquiring the relevant land yet the tribunal was required when assessing the probable permission to
F ignore this fact, and to treat it as non-existent, by force of s. 16 (7) of the Act of 1961. The effect of this subsection was that the planning permission " which . . . might reasonably have been expected to be granted " had to be assumed to be the same as that reasonably to have been expected had there been no actual or anticipated acquisition of the relevant land by the compensating authority (or any other " authority possessing compulsory purchase powers ").

G This being the highly artificial, notional and unreal situation in which the tribunal member was bound to visualise an application for planning permission, as it were to develop an estate in cloud cuckoo land, the assumption and corollaries on which he built the foundations of his valuation do not reveal any error of law. I would dismiss the appeal.

Appeal dismissed. Leave to appeal to the House of Lords granted conditional
H *on orders for costs in favour of the claimants in the Court of Appeal and below not being disturbed.*

Solicitors: *Sharpe, Pritchard & Co.*, agents for *T. F. Sidnell*, Town Clerk, Margate (for the compensating authority); *Girling, Wilson & Harvie*, Margate (for the claimants).

[*Reported by* F. A. AMIES, ESQ., *Barrister-at-Law.*]

A

Re GROFFMAN (*deceased*).
GROFFMAN AND BLOCK *v.* GROFFMAN.

[PROBATE, DIVORCE AND ADMIRALTY DIVISION (Sir Jocelyn Simon, P.), December 16, 17, 1968.]

Will—Attestation—Acknowledgment of signature—Testator's signature on will B
before asking attesting witnesses to act—Attesting witnesses signing in
testator's presence but not in each other's presence—Wills Act 1837 (7 Will. 4
& 1 Vict. c. 26), s. 9.

The deceased, having at some previous time signed his will, asked two friends to witness it. There being no convenient space in the room in which they were, one of the witnesses took the deceased into an adjacent room, where C
the deceased took the will from his pocket, unfolded it and asked the witness to sign giving his occupation and address. The witness noticed the deceased's signature on the will and signed his name. He then returned to the other room and asked the other witness to go and sign, which he did in the presence of the deceased, the first witness not going with him. On the question whether the deceased acknowledged his signature in the presence of both the witnesses D
in accordance with s. 9* of the Wills Act 1837,

Held: there was no acknowledgment by the deceased in the presence of two or more witnesses present at the same time (see p. 113, letter G, post).

In the Goods of Gunstan (or Gunston), Blake v. Blake ([1881-85] All E.R. Rep. 870) and *Daintree v. Butcher & Fasulo* ((1888), 13 P.D. 102) followed.

[As to attestation of wills, see 39 HALSBURY'S LAWS 880, para. 1333; and for E
cases on the subject, see 48 DIGEST (Repl.) 114-116, *910-930.*

For the Wills Act 1837, s. 9, see 26 HALSBURY'S STATUTES (2nd Edn.) 1332.]

Cases referred to:

Daintree v. Butcher & Fasulo (1888), 13 P.D. 102; 57 L.J.P. 76; 58 L.T. 661; 48 Digest (Repl.) 121, *993.*

Gunstan (or Gunston), In the Goods of, Blake v. Blake (1882), 7 P.D. 102; [1881- F
85] All E.R. Rep. 870; 51 L.J.P. 36; 51 L.J.Ch. 377; 46 L.T. 641; 48 Digest (Repl.) 120, *976.*

Hudson v. Parker (1844), 1 Rob. Eccl. 14; 163 E.R. 948; 48 Digest (Repl.) 114, *910.*

Ilott v. Genge (1842), 3 Curt. 160; 163 E.R. 689; *affd.* (1844), 4 Moo. P.C.C. 265; 48 Digest (Repl.) 115, *922.*
  G

Probate Action.

This was an action by Sidney Groffman and Arthur Henry Block, executors of the will of Charles Groffman, deceased, claiming that the court should pronounce for the will in solemn form of law, the defendant, Millie Groffman, having entered a caveat and appeared to the warning thereto as widow of the deceased H
and the person entitled to the estate of the deceased in case of an intestacy. The facts are set out in the judgment.

S. I. R. Craig for the plaintiffs.
J. E. Williams for the defendant.

SIR JOCELYN SIMON, P.: In this case the executors of a will dated I
1st September 1964, propound it in solemn form of law. The will is of the late Mr. Charles Groffman, who died on 11th April 1967. The first plaintiff, being the first executor named, is the son of the deceased testator. The second plaintiff, Mr. Block, is the second executor named and is the solicitor who prepared the will. The defendant, who claims that the will was not properly executed, is the widow of the deceased; and in the circumstances, the estate being of the region

---

* Section 9 is set out at p. 111, letter H, post.

A of £8,000 or £9,000 in total, she takes the whole of it in the event of an intestacy. The estate consists partly of what was the matrimonial home (as to just over half the total estate). That house belonged to the deceased. There was also a building society account held by the deceased; the defendant claims that that was held jointly with her, or that at least she has some interest in it. The defendant was the second wife of the deceased. They married in about 1948, the deceased being

B a widower and the defendant a widow. The marriage was childless; but the deceased had two children, the first plaintiff and a daughter who is in America. The defendant has a daughter by her first marriage, a Miss Berenson.

Most of the relevant events took place in 1964, and I do not think any witness can really be expected to remember the details, even the second plaintiff, the solicitor who prepared the will. Indeed, I think that many of the witnesses now

C think that they can remember more than they actually can. But the rough outline of events was this. Some time in the summer of 1964 the deceased went to the second plaintiff, the solicitor. He was senior partner in the firm of Maxwell & Lawson. The deceased was not a regular client of his, but had been recommended to him by another client. The deceased gave instructions for a will and the instructions were put into a draft, which is exhibited to the plaintiffs' affidavit of scripts.

D That appointed the executors and trustees; it devised the house to the trustees on trust to allow the defendant to have the use and enjoyment of this during her lifetime. It also bequeathed all chattels to her for use during her life. Then the residue—what was not disposed by the dispositions I have referred to—was disposed of in this way. It was to be divided between the first plaintiff, the daughter in America and the stepdaughter, Miss Berenson. There was in that

E draft a clause dealing with the advancement of the residuary estate in the interest of the defendant, which subsequently disappeared. That draft was handed by the second plaintiff to the deceased, who took it away to discuss it with his son, the first plaintiff. As a result of that discussion, in which the first plaintiff made no comment as to the dispositions, the draft was brought back to the second plaintiff; some nine corrections were made and the advancement clause to which I have

F referred was cancelled. The document as amended was then typed out, engrossed ready for execution. The second plaintiff told the deceased very generally what was the right method of execution; but, realising that the deceased was an intelligent man, he relied in the main on the attestation clause to be a guide to the deceased. That was in the usual form, and it seems to me to have been a perfectly reasonable course for the second plaintiff to have taken.

G The deceased and his wife were close family friends of a Mr. and Mrs. David Block and a Mr. and Mrs. Julius Leigh. They spent at least the summer holidays of 1964 together, and it was their custom to meet alternately at their respective houses, generally on a Tuesday night. This was because Mr. Leigh was a taxi driver and the Tuesday was his free evening. On a number of occasions after the engrossed document was handed to the deceased, he mentioned the matter to

H Mr. David Block, saying that he would like Mr. David Block and Mr. Leigh to be witnesses to his will. Mr. David Block, in a very usual reaction, said, " There's no hurry about that; there's plenty of time to be thinking about that sort of thing "—or words to that effect. The parties met on a Tuesday evening in September 1964. That may have been 1st September, which is the date that the will bears. They met at the house of Mr. and Mrs. David Block, and the will

I purports to have been executed that evening in circumstances to which I shall have to refer. It is sufficient to say that, as I have already indicated, the attestation clause is the normal one, and Mr. David Block and Mr. Leigh purported to sign as attesting witnesses. The document also bears what is admittedly the signature of the deceased, and a date 1st September 1964. I am perfectly satisfied that that document was intended by the deceased to be executed as his will and that its contents represent his testamentary intentions. After he had obtained the signatures of his friends, he took the will and handed it to his son, the first plaintiff. He appears to have referred to it to the second plaintiff on a number of occasions thereafter; but nothing turns on that, since the only question that arises in this suit is as to the execution of the document.

The deceased died, as I have said, on 11th April 1967. The funeral was on 13th April, and thereafter the widow and the first plaintiff observed a period of ritual mourning, during which there was no discussion of any testamentary instrument or disposition. At the end of that period, within a matter of a few days, the first plaintiff handed the document to the second plaintiff. At some time towards the end of April, and again within a month or two, there were meetings between the plaintiffs and the defendant, and I think that at least on one of the occasions, if not more, the defendant's daughter was present. I do not think that any of the persons present on those occasions can really remember very precisely what occurred. There was some discrepancy of recollection. It is, in my view, quite immaterial; but, if I had to choose between them, I would prefer the recollection of the second plaintiff. Suffice it to say that I think that the dispositions in the will must have been discussed on the first occasion in outline at least, even if the will was not read on that occasion. Certainly at the end of April, I think 28th April, Miss Berenson, at the request of the defendant, wrote to the second plaintiff asking for a photocopy of the will, which was sent on 17th May.

Some time shortly thereafter there was another meeting, as I have indicated, and the defendant showed considerable dissatisfaction with the dispositions in the purported will. She used the words, " My Charlie wouldn't have done that to me ". She consulted first a nephew of hers who was an accountant.   There was at that stage no question of disputing the validity of the will. The only question was about such matters as to who had rights, and to what extent, in the building society fund that I have described. However, it appears that at some time at the beginning of July the defendant made an appointment to see her present solicitors, whom she saw about the middle of July. The first claim from them only related to the building society account. But on 25th July they entered a caveat. That was the first indication that the will was disputed. Thereafter in due course the caveat was warned; there was an appearance to the warning and the writ was issued on 3rd January 1968.

As I have said, the only question that arises for the determination of the court is whether this will was duly executed. That takes me back to the occasion in September 1964, which may have been 1st September—the episode at the house of Mr. and Mrs. David Block. Mr. Leigh, the second purported attesting witness, has suffered a disabling ailment; and his evidence has been placed before me only in the form of a statement, dated 22nd August 1967, which was obviously taken for the purposes of litigation. It has, therefore, not been cross-examined to. Since I am satisfied that the document propounded represents the deceased's testamentary intentions and since the document is in regular form, a very strong presumption arises in its favour. If I merely had the statement of Mr. Leigh and the other witnesses, except for Mr. David Block and his son Stewart, I should pronounce for the validity of this will. But that is not all that I have. Mr. David Block and his son Stewart seem to me to be credible and reliable witnesses. I have it in mind that the evidence which they have given contradicts the statement in the attestation clause. I have it in mind that they are friends of the defendant and desire her to succeed in this action. I have it in mind that there is some discrepancy between the evidence that they respectively gave, though no more than I should expect in perfectly honest witnesses trying to recollect what happened over four years ago.   I accept the evidence of Mr. David Block, borne out as it is by Stewart, and, indeed, by what Mr. Leigh says in his proffered statement.

I think that what happened on the evening in question was this. I have already said that the deceased had previously indicated to Mr. David Block that he would like him and Mr. Leigh to witness his will. On the evening in question, which was in all probability a Tuesday and possibly 1st September 1964, the deceased and the defendant, Mr. and Mrs. David Block and Mr. and Mrs. Julius

A Leigh were all together in the lounge of the Blocks' house. Mr. David Block's son Stewart was also in the house, though not in the lounge at the commencement of the transaction to which I refer. During the course of the evening, when the coffee table, the only available table, was laden with coffee cups and cakes, the deceased said words to this effect, which he addressed to Mr. David Block and Mr. Julius Leigh: " I should like you now to witness my will ". I think that he

B may well have gestured towards his coat. The will in question as engrossed was of the usual double foolscap, folded in two, and then in four, so as to be a convenient size for putting in an inside pocket of a coat. That is where it was on this occasion. However, it was not taken out by the deceased in the lounge. At the most, he gestured towards the pocket where it was. There seems to me to be an overwhelming inference that his signature was on the document at that time. There being no

C convenient space for the execution in the lounge, Mr. David Block led the deceased into the adjacent dining room. That was just across a small hall. There the deceased took the document from his pocket, unfolded it, and asked Mr. David Block to sign giving his occupation and address. The deceased's signature, as I have already said, was on the document at the time and was visible to Mr. David Block at the time; indeed, he noted it. Mr. Leigh, who seems to have been some-

D what cumbrous in his movements, was left behind. He was not there when Mr. David Block signed his name. Mr. David Block then returned to the lounge, leaving the deceased in the dining room. He said to Mr. Leigh words to this effect: " It is your turn now, don't keep him waiting, it's cold in there." Mr. Leigh then went into the dining room and, according to his statement, and as is indeed borne out by the form of the document that we now have, signed his name beneath that

E of Mr. David Block. In the meantime, Mr. David Block had remained in the lounge.

   In other words, we are left with this situation—that the signature of the deceased was on the document before he asked either Mr. David Block or Mr. Leigh to act as his witnesses; that Mr. David Block signed his name in the presence of the deceased but not in the presence of Mr. Leigh; and that Mr.

F Leigh signed his name in the presence of the deceased but not in the presence of Mr. David Block. The deceased did not sign in the presence of either of them; and the question is whether he acknowledged his signature in the presence of both of them. As must appear from the fact that I have been satisfied that the document does represent the testamentary intentions of the deceased, I would very gladly find in its favour; but I am bound to apply the Act, which has

G been enacted by Parliament for good reason. The provision with which I am concerned is s. 9 of the Wills Act 1837. That provides:

   ". . . no will shall be valid unless it shall be in writing, and executed in manner herein-after mentioned; (that is to say), it shall be signed at the foot or end thereof by the testator, or by some other person in his presence and by his direction; and such signature shall be made or acknowledged by

H the testator in the presence of two or more witnesses present at the same time, and such witnesses shall attest and shall subscribe the will in the presence of the testator, but no form of attestation shall be necessary."

   The question, as I have indicated, is whether the testator acknowledged his signature in the presence of Mr. David Block and Mr. Leigh, those two witnesses being present at the same time. The matter has been considered by a number of

I eminent judges, starting with DR. LUSHINGTON, and followed by the members of the Court of Appeal in *In the Goods of Gunstan (or Gunston), Blake v. Blake* (1), and *Daintree v. Butcher & Fasulo* (2). It seems presumptious to say that I agree with their construction of the Act; but it appears to me to be clear. In any event, I am bound by what was decided by the Court of Appeal, even if I were to disagree with it, which I do not. It seems to me that the authorities

(1) (1882), 7 P.D. 102; [1881-85] All E.R. Rep. 870.
(2) (1888), 13 P.D. 102.

establish that the signature of the testator must be on the document at the time A
of acknowledgment (which, I think, it was), and that the witnesses saw, or had
an opportunity of seeing, the signature at that time—in other words, at the time
of acknowledgment.

In *In the Goods of Gunstan* (3), SIR GEORGE JESSEL, M.R., gave a judgment in
which he said: " The question, then, arises whether the testatrix had acknowledged her signature before the witnesses." That was a case where the testatrix B
had signed and had asked two attesting witnesses to add their signatures, but had
covered her own signature with blotting paper so that they could not see it. SIR
GEORGE JESSEL, M.R., in those circumstances posed the question (4):

" **What is in** law a sufficient acknowledgment under the statute? What
I take to be the law is correctly laid down in JARMAN ON WILLS, 4th
Edn., p. 108, in the following terms: ' There is no sufficient acknowledgment C
unless the witnesses either saw or might have seen the signature, not even
though the testator should expressly declare that the paper to be attested
by them is his will '."

He quoted (5) DR. LUSHINGTON in *Hudson* v. *Parker* (6):

" What do the words import but this? ' Here is my name written, I D
acknowledge that name so written to have been written by me; bear
witness '."

And then SIR GEORGE JESSEL, M.R., said (7):

". . . if . . . the witnesses would not be able to see his signature, that is not
a sufficient acknowledgment."

And then, discussing *Hudson* v. *Parker* (8) again, he said (9):   E

" The witnesses were taken to have seen the signature and the testator
having then asked them to witness his will, he was held to have acknowledged
his signature."

BRETT, L.J. (10), is even more strongly to the same effect; and, although he
differed in one respect from SIR GEORGE JESSEL, M.R., he, like HOLKER, L.J. (11), F
the third member of the court, agreed that the witnesses at the moment of
acknowledgment must either see, or have the opportunity of seeing, that the
signature is on the will.

Counsel who has argued this case vigorously for the plaintiffs has propounded
that the decision in *Daintree* v. *Butcher & Fasulo* (12) in the Court of Appeal is
in his favour. I cannot read it as such. While COTTON, L.J., with whom FRY G
and LOPES, L.JJ., concurred, was dealing with what amounts to acknowledgment,
he adverted to *Ilott* v. *Genge* (13), and said (14): " The paper there was so folded
that the witnesses could not see the signature ". That was, therefore, held to
be insufficient acknowledgment. Then COTTON, L.J., said (15):

" No doubt, if they cannot see the signature, the mere calling on them H
to sign as witnesses is not enough. But here there was a signature on the
paper which they could have seen, and which the testator would suppose
that they did see."

At the end of the judgment he gave his view as to what was decided in *In the
Goods of Gunstan* (16), saying (17): ". . . the Court only affirmed the proposition

(3) (1882), 7 P.D. at p. 107; [1881-85] All E.R. Rep. at p. 872.   I
(4) (1882), 7 P.D. at pp. 107, 108; [1881-85] All E.R. Rep. at p. 872.
(5) (1882), 7 P.D. at p. 108; [1881-85] All E.R. Rep. at p. 872.
(6) (1844), 1 Rob. Eccl. 14 at p. 25.
(8) (1844), 1 Rob. Eccl. 14.   (7) (1882), 7 P.D. at p. 109.
                                                (9) (1882), 7 P.D. at p. 110.
(10) (1882), 7 P.D. at pp. 114, 115; [1881-85] All E.R. Rep. at p. 874.
(11) (1882), 7 P.D. at p. 116; [1881-85] All E.R. Rep. at pp. 874, 875.
(12) (1888), 13 P.D. 102.   (13) (1844), 4 Moo. P.C.C. 265.
(14) (1888), 13 P.D. at p. 103.   (15) (1888), 13 P.D. at pp. 103, 104.
(16) (1882), 7 P.D. 102; [1881-85] All E.R. Rep. 870. (17) (1888), 13 P.D. at p. 104.

A laid down in JARMAN ON WILLS . . ." [which I read when citing from *In the Goods of Gunstan* (18)]. In my view, *Daintree* v. *Butcher & Fasulo* (19) bears out what I have descried from *In the Goods of Gunstan* (18), namely, that, if there were to be an acknowledgment within the Act, the attesting witnesses must either see or be capable of seeing the signature of the testator. In the present case, neither of those conditions was satisfied at any time when the witnesses were together.

B   In deference, however, to the interest and vigour of counsel for the plaintiffs' argument, I must deal with various alternative ways in which he puts his case. He says, first, that *In the Goods of Gunstan* (18) is to be distinguished in that there was a deliberate concealment by the testatrix of her signature, which, he says, is the very negation of acknowledgment. But there is nothing at all in the judgments of *In the Goods of Gunstan* (18) to indicate that that was the ratio decidendi,

C which was indeed afterwards explained in *Daintree* v. *Butcher & Fasulo* (19). Secondly, he says there is sufficient acknowledgment if the attesting witnesses had an opportunity to see the signature if they had wished to. Opportunity to see, says counsel, does not mean physical opportunity: it means that they could have seen if they expressed the desire to see. If that were so, it seems to me that *In the Goods of Gunstan* (18) could not have been decided in the way

D it was. The attesting witnesses could have asked the testatrix to remove the blotting paper, just as in the present case Mr. David Block or Mr. Leigh could have asked the deceased to remove the paper from his pocket and show them his signature.

     There is, however, one final argument. Having submitted originally that there was a sufficient acknowledgment to satisfy the Act in what happened in the

E lounge, when admittedly both attesting witnesses were present, counsel for the plaintiffs puts his argument alternatively in this way. He says that what happened was all part of one res gestae—there was no break in the continuity of the transaction. Both attesting witnesses had an opportunity of seeing the signature at the time they signed the will, which was within a matter of seconds of each other and within a matter of seconds of being asked to witness it. On that argument the

F acknowledgment started in the lounge but ended in the dining room. It seems to me that there is one fatal flaw in that argument; namely, that if the acknowledgment was not completed until the dining room, then there was no completed acknowledgment in the presence of both attesting witnesses being present at the same time.

     In the end, therefore, although I would gladly accede to the arguments for the

G plaintiffs if I could consistently with my judicial duty, in my view there was no acknowledgment or signature by the testator in the presence of two or more witnesses present at the same time; and I am bound to pronounce against this will.

Order accordingly.

H   Solicitors: *Maxwell & Lawson* (for the plaintiffs); *Maltz, Mitchell & Co.* (for the defendant).

[*Reported by* ALICE BLOOMFIELD, *Barrister-at-Law.*]

I

---

(18) (1882), 7 P.D. 102; [1881-85] All E.R. Rep. 870.
(19) (1888), 13 P.D. 102.

A

GREENHALGH *v.* BRITISH RAILWAYS BOARD.

[COURT OF APPEAL, CIVIL DIVISION (Lord Denning, M.R., Davies and Widgery,
L.JJ.), January 24, 1969.]

*Railway—Accommodation bridge—Pedestrian injured by tripping over pot-hole
on bridge—British Railways Board not responsible—Duty of local authority
to maintain and repair bridge—Railways Clauses Consolidation Act* 1845
(8 & 9 *Vict. c.* 20), *s.* 68—*Occupiers' Liability Act* 1957 (5 & 6 *Eliz.* 2 *c.* 31),
s. 1 (2), (4) *and s.* 2 (6).

B

In December 1963, Mrs. G. was walking over an old railway bridge on
which there were pot-holes. She tripped and fell and was injured. She
sued the British Railways Board claiming that they were responsible and
was awarded £462 10s. The bridge was built in about 1870 as an accommodation bridge under s. 68* of the Railways Clauses Consolidation Act 1845,
i.e., it was " for the accommodation of the owners and occupiers of lands
adjoining the railway ". People began to use the bridge as a footpath.
The public right was confirmed by the definitive map prepared in 1953
under the National Parks and Access to the Countryside Act 1949. During
the last ten or 15 years the local authority had built housing estates on
either side of the railway and built excellent approach roads up to the
bridge on both sides and left the bridge out of repair. Mrs. G. did not
live on the land adjoining the railway. The board was held liable and
appealed.

C

D

Held: the appeal would be allowed, because—

(i) the board owed no duty to Mrs. G. under s. 68 of the Railways Clauses
Consolidation Act 1845, as she was not an owner or occupier of adjoining
land (see p. 116, letter I, and p. 118, letter C, post).

E

Dictum of BRAMWELL, B., in *Dawson* v. *Midland Ry. Co.* ((1872), L.R. 8
Exch. at p. 9) distinguished. *Manchester, Sheffield & Lincolnshire Ry. Co.*
v. *Wallis* ((1854), 14 C.B. at p. 213) as applied in *Midland Ry. Co.* v. *Daykin*
((1855), 17 C.B. 126) distinguished.

F

(ii) Mrs. G. was not a visitor of the board under the Occupiers' Liability
Act 1957, s. 1 (2)†, (4) or s. 2 (6)‡ for a " visitor " did not include a person
who used the land in pursuance of a public or private right of way; accordingly the board owed no duty to Mrs. G (see p. 117, letter H, and p. 118,
letters C and I, post).

Per CURIAM: The duty of the Railways Board is laid down by the Railways
Clauses Consolidation Act 1845, and is not to be increased by the adventitious acts of strangers; it is the responsibility of the local authority who
made the approach roads to the bridge, to maintain and repair the bridge
in a state fit to take traffic (see p. 117, letter I, and p. 118, letter C, post).

G

Appeal allowed.

H

[As to maintenance of accommodation bridge over railway, see 31 HALSBURY'S
LAWS (3rd Edn.) 589, para. 897; and for cases on the subject, see 38 DIGEST
(Repl.) 326-335, *238-273.*

For the Railways Clauses Consolidation Act 1845, s. 68, see 19 HALSBURY'S
STATUTES (2nd Edn.) 628.

For the National Parks and Access to the Countryside Act 1949, s. 32, see
28 HALSBURY'S STATUTES (2nd Edn.) 575.

I

For the Occupiers' Liability Act 1957, s. 1, s. 2, see 37 HALSBURY'S STATUTES
(2nd Edn.) 833, 834.]

---

* Section 68, so far as material, is set out at p. 115, letter H, post.
† Section 1 (2), so far as material, is set out at p. 118, letter G, post.
‡ Section 2 (6) is set out at p. 117, letter E, post.

A Cases referred to:

Dawson v. *Midland Ry. Co.* (1872), L.R. 8 Exch. 8; 42 L.J.Ex. 49; 38 Digest (Repl.) 332, *260.*

Gautret v. *Egerton* (1867), L.R. 2 C.P. 371; 36 L.J.C.P. 191; sub nom. *Gantret* v. *Egerton,* 16 L.T. 17; 38 Digest (Repl.) 443, *946.*

Manchester, Sheffield & Lincolnshire Ry. Co. v. *Wallis* (1854), 14 C.B. 213;
B 23 L.J.C.P. 85; 18 J.P. 138; 139 E.R. 88; sub nom. *Wallis* v. *Manchester, Sheffield & Lincolnshire Ry. Co.,* 22 L.T.O.S. 286; 38 Digest (Repl.) 330, *251.*

Midland Ry. Co. v. *Daykin* (1855), 17 C.B. 126; 25 L.J.C.P. 73; 26 L.T.O.S. 78; 20 J.P. 23; 139 E.R. 1016; 38 Digest (Repl.) 332, *258.*

Taff Vale Ry. Co. v. *Gordon Canning,* [1909] 2 Ch. 48; 78 L.J.Ch. 492; 100
C L.T. 845; 19 Digest (Repl.) 125, *785.*

Appeal.

This was an appeal by British Railways Board, the defendants to an action in which LLOYD-JONES, J., on 10th May 1968 adjudged that the plaintiff, Gladys Greenhalgh, should have judgment against them for £462 10s. and costs. The board asked that the judgment be reversed and that judgment might be entered
D in the action for them. The facts are set out in the judgment of LORD DENNING, M.R.

H. E. Francis, Q.C., and *I. D. L. Glidewell* for the defendants.
D. B. McNeill, Q.C., and *H. Gore* for the plaintiff.

LORD DENNING, M.R.: In December 1963, the plaintiff, Mrs. Green-
E halgh, was walking over an old railway bridge in Lancashire, near Little Hulton. There were pot-holes on the bridge. She tripped and fell and hurt her elbow. Fortunately her injuries were not serious. Now she sues the defendants, British Railways Board, claiming that they are responsible. The judge has found in her favour and awarded her £462 10s. The defendants appeal to this court.

About 1873 a single-line railway was built near Little Hulton to carry coal.
F It was built in pursuance of statutory powers. The company made a cutting which severed the lands of the owners. So the company came under the obligations imposed by s. 68 of the Railways Clauses Consolidation Act 1845. The company had to make an accommodation bridge over the railway. There was no public highway there previously. So it was not a public bridge within s. 46 of the Act of 1845. It was simply an accommodation bridge under s. 68 which
G provides that:

"The company shall make and at all times thereafter maintain the following works for the accommodation of the owners and occupiers of lands adjoining the railway; (that is to say,) Such and so many convenient gates, bridges, arches, culverts, and passages, over, under, or by the sides of or leading to or from the railway, as shall be necessary for the purpose
H of making good any interruptions caused by the railway to the use of the lands through which the railway shall be made . . ."

So the bridge was built nearly 100 years ago. It was used, no doubt, for many years, only by the owners of the adjoining farmlands. They used to take their carts and wagons over it. But the district developed. The population increased.
I People began to use the bridge as a footpath. So much so that in time the public acquired a right of footway across the bridge. And this public right was confirmed by the definitive map which was prepared in 1953 under the National Parks and Access to the Countryside Act 1949. The definitive map and the accompanying statement showed a public footpath across this old bridge. It is conclusive evidence that there was a public footpath and a public right of way on foot across the bridge, see s. 32 (4) of the Act of 1949.

During the last ten or 15 years the local authority, the Worsley Urban District Council, have built large housing estates on the land on either side of the old

mineral railway. On one side of it they have put up 1,236 dwellings; and on **A**
the other side 391 dwellings. During the construction of these housing estates
the local authority, or their contractors, used this accommodation bridge a great
deal for their heavy lorries, and so forth. After the housing estates were built
it has been used by all kinds of traffic to and from the houses. The people
who live there use it on foot as well. It is clear that this greatly increased the
burden on the bridge. It was so heavy that I have no doubt that the railway **B**
company or their successors could have objected to it and obtained an injunction
to stop it. That is shown by *Taff Vale Ry. Co.* v. *Gordon Canning* (1). But
the company did not take objection. They just submitted to it. There was
some desultory correspondence with the local council about the maintenance
of the bridge, but it came to nothing.

There was a further important matter. The local authority made excellent **C**
approach roads right up to the accommodation bridge on both sides; but left
the bridge itself out of repair. So that motor traffic, and people on foot, had
good approaches on either side, but then a very bad surface over the bridge
itself. The local authority did nothing to repair it. Nor did the defendants.
It was full of pot-holes. So it was when in December 1963 the plaintiff walked
over the bridge and fell. She lived in one of the houses on the new housing **D**
estate of Spa Crescent. It was quite a long way from the bridge.

Such being the facts, I turn to the arguments put on behalf of the plaintiff.
In the first place, it was said that the defendants owed a duty to the plaintiff
under s. 68 of the Railways Clauses Consolidation Act 1845, which I have read.
Under s. 68 the defendants owed a duty to the " owners and occupiers of lands
adjoining the railway ", but to no others. The plaintiff's house in Spa Crescent **E**
did not bring her into that category. It was too far away from the bridge to
be considered to be " adjoining lands ". That is conceded. But it is said on her
behalf that her user of the approach roads brought her within that category.
The approach roads were " adjoining lands "; and it is said that, as she was
lawfully using them, the defendants owed a duty to her. In support of this
contention, reliance was placed on an observation of BRAMWELL, B., in *Dawson* **F**
v. *Midland Ry. Co.* (2):

  " The statute appears to me to be for the benefit of all persons who are
  lawfully using adjoining land."

Those words were used in a case where the railway company had failed to maintain a fence alongside the railway. A man had lawfully put his horse out to **G**
graze in a field next to the railway. It strayed through a defective fence on to
the line and was killed. Further support was sought from other cases where
animals were being driven lawfully along a highway which ran alongside the
railway. They escaped through a defective fence and were run over by a train.
The company was held liable, see *Manchester, Sheffield & Lincolnshire Ry. Co.*
v. *Wallis* (3), as applied in *Midland Ry. Co.* v. *Daykin* (4). But those fencing **H**
cases seem to me to be entirely different. The very object of a fence is to keep
cattle from straying on the line; and naturally enough, the courts held that the
company were under a duty to all cattle lawfully on adjoining land, no matter
whether it was a highway or a field. But it is different with an accommodation
bridge. The object of a bridge is so that the owners and occupiers of adjoining
lands, and those authorised by them, can use it. There is a duty to them; **I**
but not to any other person who may happen to use the bridge. There was
certainly no duty to such a person in the days before there was a public footpath
across the bridge. And the duty of the defendants is not to be increased simply
because the public choose to use it as a public way and acquire in time a public
right to do so. I hold, therefore, that the defendants owed no duty to the
plaintiff under s. 68.

(1) [1909] 2 Ch. 48.   (2) (1872), L.R. 8 Exch. 8 at p. 9.
(3) (1854), 14 C.B. 213.   (4) (1855), 17 C.B. 126,

A   In the second place, it was said that the defendants owed a duty to the plaintiff under the Occupiers' Liability Act 1957. It was said that she was a " visitor ". But I do not think she was. Section 1 (2) shows that, in order to determine whether a person is a " visitor ", we must go back to the common law. A person is a " visitor " if at common law he would be regarded as an invitee or licensee; or be treated as such, as for instance, a person lawfully using premises provided

B   for the use of the public (e.g., a public park) or a person entering by lawful authority (e.g., a policeman with a search warrant). But a " visitor " does not include a person who crosses land in pursuance of a public or private right of way. Such a person was never regarded as an invitee or licensee, or treated as such. As WILLES, J., said in *Gautret* v. *Egerton* (5):

C   " But, what duty does the law impose upon these defendants to keep their bridges in repair? If I dedicate a way to the public which is full of ruts and holes, the public must take it as it is."

The judge seems to have thought that s. 1 (4) threw some light on the question. But I do not think it does. It has nothing to do with public or private rights of way. It deals only with persons who wander across open country in pursuance of an access agreement or access order under Part 5 of the National Parks and

D   Access to the Countryside Act 1949. Such persons might have been treated at common law as invitees or licensees, but s. 1 (4) expressly excludes them from being regarded as " visitors ".

Some mention was also made of s. 2 (6) of the Act of 1957 which provides that:

E   " For the purposes of this section, persons who enter premises for any purpose in the exercise of a right conferred by law are to be treated as permitted by the occupier to be there for that purpose, whether they in fact have his permission or not."

The important words to notice are the opening words: " For the purposes of this section ", i.e., for the purposes of s. 2, which defines only the *extent* of the occupier's duty to acknowledged visitors. It does not expand the range of

F   persons who are to be treated as visitors. Section 2 (6) applies, for instance, to persons who enter a public park, or a policeman who enters on a search warrant, for they enter in the exercise of a right conferred by law and are treated as if they were invitees or licensees. They are acknowledged " visitors ". Section 2 (6) shows that the occupier owes to such persons a duty of care when they are using the place for the authorised purpose, but not when they are abusing it.

G   But s. 2 (6) does not apply to persons crossing land by virtue of a public or private way; because they are never " visitors " at all. This view is confirmed by all the textbooks such as CLERK AND LINSELL'S TORTS (12th Edn.), para. 846; SALMOND'S LAW OF TORTS (14th Edn.), p. 399; WINFIELD'S TEXTBOOK ON THE LAW OF TORT, p. 179.

Applying these considerations, it is apparent that the plaintiff was not a

H   " visitor " of the defendants. She was a person who was exercising a public right of way and to her the defendants owed no duty under the Occupiers' Liability Act 1957.

So the claim fails on both heads. I would only add this. This case is of importance, because it is an attempt to put the defendants under a higher duty in respect of accommodation bridges than properly belongs to them. The

I   duty of the defendants is that laid down by the Railways Clauses Consolidation Act 1845. It is not to be increased by the adventitious acts of strangers. It is the local authorities who built the great housing estates in the vicinity. It is they who made approach roads right up to the bridge on both sides. It is they who invited the public to use it by vehicles and on foot. It is their responsibility, therefore, to maintain and repair the bridge in a state fit to take the traffic. The burden on the defendants is not to be increased by saying that they submitted to the increased user.

---

(5) (1867), L.R. 2 C.P. 371 at p. 373.

I would, therefore, allow this appeal and enter judgment for the defendants.   **A**

DAVIES, L.J.: Though one naturally has considerable sympathy for the plaintiff who suffered this unfortunate though not too serious injury through no fault of her own, I agree and feel that in the circumstances, LORD DENNING, M.R., having dealt with the matter so thoroughly, there is nothing that I can usefully add save this. So far as concerns the Railways Clauses Consolidation **B** Act 1845, reliance was placed in the statement of claim on s. 46, which admittedly has nothing to do with this case at all. But one finds in the statement of claim no reference at all to s. 68 of that Act, on which, of course, the plaintiff's case was partly based. Apart from that, I agree entirely with everything that LORD DENNING, M.R., has said and that this appeal must be allowed.

C

WIDGERY, L.J.: I also am in entire agreement but would add a few words on the Occupiers' Liability Act 1957 argument, as we are differing from the learned judge below. Before considering the plaintiff's position under the Occupiers' Liability Act 1957, it is important to see what her position would have been at common law apart from that Act; and I cannot put the position more clearly than it is put in SALMOND'S LAW OF TORTS (14th Edn.) at p. 398, **D** dealing with the responsibility of the owner of the soil towards persons who pass over the land by virtue of a public right of way. The learned author's words are these:

" It is well established that such an occupier is under no responsibility as such towards users of the highway for its safety and is not liable for **E** dangers thereon whether they exist at the time of dedication or come into existence later."

That position has prevailed from time immemorial and undoubtedly would provide a complete answer apart from the Act of 1957 to any owner of land who was sued by a passer-by exercising a public right of way over that land. **F**

The question is, has the Act of 1957 made any difference? I am confident that it has not. If one looks at s. 1, it is to be observed at once that the rules laid down by the Act are to take the place of the common law rules in respect of the liability of an occupier in certain circumstances. By s. 1 (2):

" The rules so enacted shall regulate the nature of the duty imposed by **G** law in consequence of a person's occupation or control of premises and of any invitation or permission he gives (or is to be treated as giving) to another to enter or use the premises, but they shall not alter the rules of the common law as to the persons on whom a duty is so imposed or to whom it is owed . . ."

As I endeavoured to show, there was at common law no duty on an occupier of land over which there is a public highway towards persons using the highway **H** and arising out of his occupation or control of the premises. His liability was limited to acts of positive misfeasance and nothing else. It seems to me there is nothing in the Act of 1957 which creates the far-reaching obligation for which counsel for the plaintiff argues in this case. The situation of this particular bridge is one of some complexity, because although it is clear that there is a public right on foot across the bridge, the existence or non-existence of a public **I** right for vehicles is obscure. I am satisfied that in this case, as the plaintiff entered as a pedestrian, we must assume that she was exercising her right as a member of the public to use the public footpath. The extent of the defendants' obligation to drivers of vehicles if the position be that there is no public right for vehicles may, of course, be different. So far as the plaintiff is concerned, she was exercising a public right, and in those circumstances the obligation of the occupiers towards her in regard to repair was non-existent. Accordingly, the

A learned judge in my opinion came to the wrong conclusion and I would allow this appeal.

Appeal allowed.

Solicitors: *M. H. B. Gilmour* (for the defendants); *Leslie M. Lever & Co.,* Manchester (for the plaintiff).

[*Reported by* JENIFER SANDELL, *Barrister-at-Law.*]

B

DOYLE *v.* OLBY (IRONMONGERS) LTD. AND OTHERS.

[COURT OF APPEAL, CIVIL DIVISION (Lord Denning, M.R., Winn and Sachs, L.JJ.),
C   January 30, 31, 1969.]

Damages—Measure of damages—Fraud.

The object of damages in fraud, unlike contract, is that the damages should compensate the plaintiff for all the loss he has suffered, i.e., for all the actual damage directly flowing from the fraudulent inducement (see
D p. 122, letter F, p. 123, letter I, to p. 124, letter A, and p. 126, letter C, post).
Appeal allowed.

[As to the measure of damages in tort, see 11 HALSBURY'S LAWS (3rd Edn.) 251-253, paras. 423, 424; and for cases on the subject, see 17 DIGEST (Repl.) 101, 102, *155-173.*]

Cases referred to:

E *Clark* v. *Urquhart, Stracey* v. *Urquhart,* [1930] A.C. 28; 99 L.J.P.C. 1; 141
          L.T. 641; 17 Digest (Repl.) 75, *2.*
  Firbank's Executors v. *Humphreys* (1886), 18 Q.B.D. 54; 56 L.J.Q.B. 37;
          56 L.T. 36; 1 Digest (Repl.) 758, *2960.*
  Hadley v. *Baxendale* (1854), 9 Exch. 341; [1843-60] All E.R. Rep. 461; 23
          L.J.Ex. 179; 23 L.T.O.S. 69; 156 E.R. 145; 17 Digest (Repl.) 91, *99.*
F *McConnel* v. *Wright,* [1903] 1 Ch. 546; 72 L.J.Ch. 347; 88 L.T. 431; 35 Digest
          (Repl.) 46, *402.*

Appeal.

This was an appeal by the plaintiff, Herbert Leonard Doyle, from a judgment of SWANWICK, J., dated 24th July 1967, awarding him £1,500 damages for fraudulent misrepresentations by the defendants, Olby (Ironmongers), Ltd.,
G Cecil Augustus Olby, Leslie Morton Olby and A. Olby & Son, Ltd. The grounds of appeal were, inter alia, that the judge applied the wrong measure of damages. The facts are set out in the judgment of LORD DENNING, M.R.

The plaintiff appeared in person.
D. A. L. Smout for the defendants.

H   **LORD DENNING, M.R.:** The plaintiff in 1963 was minded to buy a business. He saw an advertisement in Dalton's Weekly. He got particulars. The business was said to belong to the first defendant, at 12, Upper High Street, Epsom, Surrey, and the turnover £27,000.   The price asked for the lease, the business and goodwill was £4,500.   The stock was to be taken at valuation. The plaintiff made further enquiries about it. On 6th November 1963, the
I third defendant, Mr. Leslie Olby, a director of the company, produced accounts to him. They were for the three years ending 31st December 1962. In a covering letter the third defendant wrote:

  " Dear Mr. Doyle, As requested we are enclosing accountant's figures covering [the first defendant], 12 Upper High Street, Epsom, Surrey."

Those figures showed that for those three years there had been considerable profits: £1,921 net profits in 1960; £1,749 in 1961; and £1,361 in 1962.   The plaintiff also saw the second defendant, Mr. Cecil Olby, who worked on the

premises.   The plaintiff asked the second defendant what staff were employed.   **A**
The second defendant said: " One manager, two assistants, one van-driver, and
a part-time clerical assistant; with a wage bill of £42 a week ".   He added that
one of the staff was a very old man.   The plaintiff also asked the second defendant
how the trade was geared as between the retail trade and the wholesale trade.
The second defendant said: " Two-thirds retail; one-third wholesale—all over
the counter."   In other words, it was trade which was done from the shop   **B**
itself and would not need a traveller to go round and canvass for orders.   On
those representations, the plaintiff agreed to buy this business.   The agreement
was entered into in January 1964.   The plaintiff agreed to pay £4,500 down in
cash, which covered the goodwill, fixtures and fittings, and the remainder of the
lease (which had about four years to run).   The stock was to be bought on
valuation.   In addition, there was a restrictive covenant on the first defendants   **C**
in which it covenanted that it would not for five years engage in any ironmongers'
business within a radius of ten miles from 12, Upper High Street, Epsom.

The plaintiff paid the £4,500.   He took over stock at a valuation of £5,000
which he paid.   He needed a longer lease, so he surrendered the existing lease
and took a longer lease at a greatly increased rent.   The freeholder who benefited
was the second defendant.   In order to pay all the money, the plaintiff put up   **D**
all the cash he had—£7,000; and he raised £3,000 on mortgage from Askinex,
Ltd.

So he went into occupation.   But I am afraid that things were very different
from what he was led to believe.   The turnover was far less than he had been
told.   The trade was not all over the counter.   Half of the trade was wholesale
business which could only be obtained by employing a traveller to go round   **E**
to the customers.   The plaintiff could not afford to employ a traveller.   So
all that trade was lost.   The whole transaction was a disaster for him.   To add
to his troubles, in February 1964, soon after he went into occupation, the fourth
defendant, a company called A. Olby & Son, Ltd., of Penge (which was closely
associated with the vendor company, the first defendant) canvassed and sent
travellers round to customers who had been previously customers of the Epsom   **F**
business.   The judge held that this was not a breach of the restrictive covenant,
though I am not so sure about it.

The plaintiff was most dissatisfied, and in May 1964 he brought an action for
damages for fraud and conspiracy against the company which sold him the
Epsom business, i.e., the first defendant, Olby (Ironmongers), Ltd.; the second
defendant, Mr. Cecil Olby, who was the man who worked in that business; the   **G**
third defendant, Mr. Leslie Olby, his brother, who was a director; and the fourth
defendant, A. Olby & Son, Ltd., which was the company at Penge, of which
the third defendant was managing director.

Although the plaintiff had started the action, he had to remain in occupation.
He had burnt his boats and had to carry on with the business as best he could.
He tried to sell it, but there were difficulties.   One was that the landlord, the   **H**
second defendant, would not give him a licence to assign, and so forth.   After
three years he did manage to sell it for a sum of some £3,700.   This cleared off
the mortgage to Askinex, Ltd., but he was left with many outstanding debts to
the bank, to suppliers, and the like.   His debts came to £4,000, and he has been
sued in the county court by many of his creditors.

The case came for trial before SWANWICK, J., in July 1967.   It took many   **I**
days, but in the end SWANWICK, J., found that the defendants had been guilty
of fraud and conspiracy.   The accounts which were produced in November 1963
to the plaintiff contained " a blatantly wrong figure " for wages and management
remuneration.   The representation by the second defendant that the sales were
" all over the counter " was completely untrue, and must have been known to
the second defendant to be untrue.   He was a traveller himself and went round
to customers on two days a week at least.   His wages amounted in the year

A 1962 to £555. That figure was not brought into the accounts which were produced to the plaintiff, and made them completely false. It turned out that the second defendant had had a breakdown and was not really capable of doing much business. But the plaintiff was not to know that. The judge found that the representations were false to the knowledge of the second defendant, and that this knowledge must be imputed to the other defendants because he was
B acting on their behalf. Furthermore, there was a conspiracy between them to defraud the plaintiff.

The defendants put in a notice of appeal against the finding of fraud and conspiracy. It was in the list in this court when the case was called on for hearing yesterday, but it was not persisted in. Counsel for the defendants abandoned it. So we approach the case on the accepted footing that the plaintiff
C was induced by the fraud and conspiracy of the defendants to buy this business.

The judge awarded the plaintiff £1,500 damages. The plaintiff appeals against that award. He says it is far too small. The judge arrived at the figure of £1,500 by accepting the submissions of counsel then appearing for the plaintiff. The judge said as to damages:

D " My task is simplified . . . by the submission of [the plaintiff's counsel] which I accept, that there are two alternative bases for damages, each of which arrives at virtually the same round figure . . . The first is that, to preserve the trade custom it would have been necessary to employ a part-time traveller at about £600 a year and I think there is a reasonable prospect that such a person could have been obtained. If 2½ times that figure is taken, that being the normal basis for valuing goodwill, it actually represents,
E as I have said, a reduction in the value of the goodwill equivalent to the cost of making good the representation; that is, about £1,500. Second and alternatively, if the trade custom was 50 per cent. of the turnover its loss would result in a reduction in the value of the goodwill of 35 per cent. to 40 per cent. which, applied to [the accountant's] figure of £4,000, again would approximate to a round figure of £1,500. Therefore, I think it is at
F this figure that I can best quantify the loss."

It appears, therefore, that counsel for the plaintiff submitted, and the judge accepted, that the proper measure of damages was the " cost of making good the representation ", or what came to the same thing, " the reduction in value of the goodwill " due to the misrepresentation. In so doing, he treated the representation as if it were a contractual promise, that is, as if there were a
G contractual term to the effect " The trade is all over the counter. There is no need to employ a traveller ". I think it was the wrong measure. Damages for fraud and conspiracy are assessed differently from damages for breach of contract.

It was submitted by counsel for the defendants that we could not, or, at any rate, ought not, to correct this error. I do not agree. We never allow a client
H to suffer for the mistake of his counsel if we can possibly help it. We will always seek to rectify it as far as we can. We will correct it whenever we are able to do so without injustice to the other side. Sometimes the error has seriously affected the course of the evidence, in which case we can at best order a new trial. But there is nothing of that kind here. The error was made at the end of the case. All the evidence had been taken on the footing that the damages were at large.
I It was only in the final submission that the error was made. Such an error we can, and will, correct.

The second question is what is the proper measure of damages for fraud, as distinct from damages for breach of contract. It was discussed during the argument in *Hadley* v. *Baxendale* (1), and finds a place in the notes to Smith's Leading Cases (13th Edn.) p. 563, where it is suggested there is no difference. But in *McConnel* v. *Wright* (2) Sir Richard Henn Collins, M.R.,

---

(1) (1854), 9 Exch. 341; [1843-60] All E.R. Rep. 461.   (2) [1903] 1 Ch. 546 at p. 554.

pointed out the difference.   It was an action for fraudulent statements in a   A
prospectus whereby a man was induced to take up shares.   He said of the action
for fraud:

" It is not an action for breach of contract, and, therefore, no damages in
respect of prospective gains which the person contracting was entitled by
his contract to expect come in, but it is an action of tort—it is an action
for a wrong done whereby the plaintiff was tricked out of certain money in   B
his pocket; and therefore, prima facie, the highest limit of his damages is
the whole extent of his loss, and that loss is measured by the money which
was in his pocket and is now in the pocket of the company."

But that statement was the subject of comment by LORD ATKIN in *Clark* v.
Urquhart, Stracey v. *Urquhart* (3).   He said:
                                                                          C
" I find it difficult to suppose that there is any difference in the measure
of damages in an action of deceit depending upon the nature of the transaction into which the plaintiff is fraudulently induced to enter.   Whether
he buys shares or buys sugar, whether he subscribes for shares, or agrees to
enter into a partnership, or in any other way alters his position to his detriment, in principle, the measure of damages should be the same, and whether   D
estimated by a jury or a judge.   I should have thought it would be based
on the actual damage directly flowing from the fraudulent inducement.
The formula in *McConnel* v. *Wright* (4) may be correct or it may be expressed
in too rigid terms."

I think that SIR RICHARD HENN COLLINS, M.R., did express himself in too rigid
terms.   He seems to have overlooked consequential damages.   On principle the   E
distinction seems to be this: in contract, the defendant has made a promise
and broken it.   The object of damages is to put the plaintiff in as good a position,
as far as money can do it, as if the promise had been performed.   In fraud, the
defendant has been guilty of a deliberate wrong by inducing the plaintiff to act
to his detriment.   The object of damages is to compensate the plaintiff for all
the loss he has suffered, so far, again, as money can do it.   In contract, the damages   F
are limited to what may reasonably be supposed to have been in the contemplation of the parties.   In fraud, they are not so limited.   The defendant is
bound to make reparation for all the actual damage directly flowing from the
fraudulent inducement.   The person who has been defrauded is entitled to say:
" I would not have entered into this bargain at all but for your representation.
Owing to your fraud, I have not only lost all the money I paid you, but, what is   G
more, I have been put to a large amount of extra expense as well and suffered
this or that extra damages. "   All such damages can be recovered: and it does
not lie in the mouth of the fraudulent person to say that they could not reasonably
have been foreseen.   For instance, in this very case the plaintiff has not only
lost the money which he paid for the business, which he would never have done
if there had been no fraud: he put all that money in and lost it; but also he has   H
been put to expense and loss in trying to run a business which has turned out to
be a disaster for him.   He is entitled to damages for all his loss, subject, of course,
to giving credit for any benefit that he has received.   There is nothing to be
taken off in mitigation: for there is nothing more that he could have done to
reduce his loss.   He did all that he could reasonably be expected to do.

This brings us to the third question: must we send the case back for a new   I
trial for damages; or can we assess them ourselves?   The difficulty is that
we have not got a transcript of all the evidence.   The plaintiff is a poor man.   He
comes here without legal aid.   He was unable to afford a transcript.   The
defendants, I presume, could afford it, but they have not thought fit to get one.
There was a finding of fraud and conspiracy against them.   They gave notice
of appeal against that finding.   Yet they did not get a transcript of the evidence.

(3) [1930] A.C. 28 at pp. 67, 68.
(4) [1903] 1 Ch. 546.

A   It was they who ought to have done so.   In these circumstances I do not think
it would be right to put either party to the expense of getting a full transcript
of eight or nine days' evidence with all the delay that would entail.   The court
must do the best it can to put right the error which has taken place.   I will not
go into the details myself ,as to the figures. It is a case for assessing damages at
large much as a jury would do.   WINN, L.J., has considered the matter carefully
B   and he will deal with it; but I say in advance that I agree with the figure which
he is going to propose, that the damages should be in the sum of £5,500.

WINN, L.J.: I agree respectfully and entirely with the judgment delivered
by LORD DENNING, M.R., and desire only to echo and then add a little to what he
has said about the proper measure of damages for deceit.   It is a most remark-
C   able fact, as LORD DENNING, M.R., has remarked, that there is a complete dearth
of authority on the topic of the proper measure of damages in such a case.   I
would pay tribute to the passage in chapter 41 in MAYNE & MCGREGOR ON
DAMAGES (12th Edn.) where, in para. 955 and some following paragraphs, the
learned authors have in effect proposed, in the absence of authority—since the
cases to which they refer really lend no support for their proposition—that
D   there should be a clear distinction drawn between the measure of damages
which can be recovered for such a breach of contract as a breach of warranty
as to the quality or value or condition of goods or premises sold, and the measure
of damages for deceit—tortious fraudulent deceit.   They make that proposition,
and perhaps, if the judgment of this court were to stand, they will in their next
book have support for what they themselves were thinking.   They refer to
E   *McConnel* v. *Wright* (5), the case which LORD DENNING has mentioned, and *Clark*
v. *Urquhart, Stracey* v. *Urquhart* (6) where a passage from LORD ATKIN may be
found which has been read by LORD DENNING.   It is right to observe that that
passage of LORD ATKIN's speech was entirely obiter, since the subject-matter of
the case then before their Lordships' House was nothing more than the proper
form of order which should be made in the particular case, where there had been a
payment into court with a denial of liability and a number of complicated events.
F   When one finds a great lawyer of LORD ATKIN's standing saying that which LORD
DENNING has quoted, for my part I think there is ample authority for the propositions in the edition of MAYNE to which I have referred and the ruling which
this court is now giving.   It is of interest, though of no direct support to that
ruling, to note that a very similar distinction is found in decided authorities
between damages for breach of contract and damages for breach of warranty
G   of authority to contract on a principal's behalf.   In *Firbank's Executors* v.
Humphreys (7) LORD ESHER, M.R., said:

"The damages, under the general rule, are arrived at by considering the
difference in the position he would have been in had the representation
been true, and the position he is actually in, in consequence of its being
H   untrue."

It appears to me that in a case where there has been a breach of warranty of
authority, and still more clearly where there has been a tortious wrong consisting
of a fraudulent inducement, the proper starting point for any court called on to
consider what damages are recoverable by the defrauded person is to compare
his position before the representation was made to him with his position after it,
I   brought about by that representation, always bearing in mind that no element
in the consequential position can be regarded as attributable loss and damage if
it be too remote a consequence: it will be too remote not necessarily because it
was not contemplated by the representor but in any case where the person
deceived has not himself behaved with reasonable prudence, reasonable common
sense or can in any true sense be said to have been the author of his own misfortune.   The damage that he seeks to recover must have flowed directly from

---

(5) [1903] 1 Ch. 546.   (6) [1930] A.C. 28 at pp. 67, 68.
(7) (1886), 18 Q.B.D. 54 at p. 60.

the fraud perpetrated on him.   I gave myself during the argument in this court   A
an illustration—hypothetical, of course—which I understood counsel for the
defendants was prepared to accept as theoretically a sound illustration of the
principle which these judgments are enunciating, for the first time, it may be,
always assuming, of course, that that principle was itself to be accepted.   If a
man in this country is made the victim of a fraudulent misrepresentation that a
business in Bangkok, Hong Kong, Manila or the Fiji Islands has certain equip-   B
ment, certain assets, certain goodwill, certain trade contracts and profits, and
is thereby induced to pay for that business, it being, of course, understood by
both parties to the transaction of sale for the procurement of which a fraudulent
misrepresentation is made, that he will set out to that remote place with his
family and, it may be, his household goods, at very considerable expense, and
on arrival will acquire living accommodation and perhaps have to buy additional   C
furniture and engage staff or servants, and he acts on the representations and
incurs all such expenses, and the business is found to be very different from that
which it was fraudulently represented to be, so that he cannot survive out in the
remote place to which he has gone and is bound to come back again, then I,
speaking for myself, would not hesitate to give him all the outgoings from his
pocket of the kinds which I have indicated up to such time as he should sensibly   D
have come home again and had the money to come back again, less, of course,
by way of set-off, any benefit which he has derived from the exploitation of such
assets as he found there upon his arrival.

   Having said that much, one turns to the instant case.   It is, as LORD DENNING,
M.R., has said and I respectfully agree, essentially a matter for a jury.   I think
myself with confidence that there is already sufficient evidentiary material   E
available to enable this court to make a jury assessment in round figures.   It
would be wrong and indeed an intolerable expenditure of judicial time and
money of the parties to embark on any detailed consideration of isolated items
in the account on which a balance must be struck.   I have looked at it myself
in this way, and have arrived, let me say at once, at the same figure that LORD
DENNING, M.R., has already mentioned.   The starting point is a simple one: F
£4,500 was paid away out of his pocket by the plaintiff to acquire this business;
and a further £5,000, in round figures, to take over stock at valuation.   That was
£9,500.   When he came ultimately to leave the business, I say quite confidently
that he is not revealed by the evidence now before this court, nor do I think it
could have been shown by any evidence, having regard to the general circumstances of the case, to have hung on too long or to have behaved otherwise than   G
as a sensible business man or to have brought misfortune on himself.   When he
gave up the business after three years, he got out of it at that time £3,500 from
the purchaser to whom he sold it, and he had, at a knock down price, which I
think was forced on him, £800 for the sale of such stock as he then had.   During
the time that he was running or trying to run and revive this moribund, if not
dead business, he drew £10 a week to live on out of the till, if one may use that   H
expression, and he lived with his wife in part of the premises, for the totality of
which he was paying a rental of £800 a year, plus, of course, rates.   I think he
should be debited with the £10 a week for the period and debited with £300 a
year, making £900, for such living accommodation benefit as he then and his
wife received from these premises.   I would take those two items at a round
figure together of £2,500.   Adding up the benefits which I have mentioned, I   I
arrive at a figure of £6,700 and call it £7,000.   At that point, comparing outgoings with such benefits as ought to be set-off, there is a gap or balance of losses
of £2,500.   Then one considers other consequences in terms of finance, because
no damages are being awarded, at any rate, in this case today, by the court for
worry, strain, anxiety and unhappiness; it may be that in some cases such
considerations might well be appropriate.   He lost during the time he was
trying to run this business additionally £700 that he borrowed from his mother
and another relative.   He incurred an overdraft of £1,400 with his bankers.

A At the time when he came out of occupation he was owing £480 odd for rates. He also owed some items, the items which he could actually recall in court, totalling about £100, for goods supplied. He had been paying £22 odd a month interest on the loan of £4,000 which he had to raise in order to enable him to meet the purchase price of the business and the stock, which I have already mentioned. I do not propose to say more about details. If it were appropriate to go into

B those item by item, then I would think that three or four days would be set aside before some tribunal to investigate with more complete discovery; I venture to hope the result would not differ very much from that which I, as a common juror, have arrived at. As I say, one brings in those items. I have taken them at £6,800 which I have called £7,000 for the benefits, a gap of £2,500; and, having regard to the plaintiff's evidence—when I say " evidence " I mean

C evidence before the trial judge—and his answers to questions in this court which I accept from him as an honest man, I think that a further round figure of £3,000 (for an estimated £3,380) should be added, and that his total loss should be £2,500 plus £3,000—£5,500 as an award of damages. That means that this appeal should be allowed, in my view, to that extent.

D SACHS, L.J.: I agree with all that has fallen from my Lords and with the award they propose. I would first like to add a few words on the question whether anything that happened at trial should debar the plaintiff from recovering the amount of damages to which he is in law entitled. It has been submitted on behalf of the defendants that because in his closing address counsel for the plaintiff adopted at first instance an approach which led to the judge making an assessment of damages on the wrong basis, this court cannot now award the

E plaintiff the sum to which in law he is entitled. Where an argument presented to this court is different from that put before the trial judge, this court must approach with a degree of caution the question of whether to consider the new argument: but, after such examination it should be slow to impose a bar which would drive from the judgment seat any man with a just claim merely because

F it was not at trial presented in the best way. Unless the defendants can, at any rate, show that they have been prejudiced by the course taken at first instance to such an extent that departure from it would be unjust to them, there should be no bar. The books are full of instances where an appellant has succeeded on a different point from that taken at the trial. If and insofar as an erroneous approach at trial merely results in additional costs to the defendants, that can, of course, in appropriate cases, be a matter to be dealt with by the appellate

G court.

In the present case one has the position that the plaintiff has been the victim of a deplorable fraud—deplorable as regards the complete disregard of the defendants for commercial honesty; he has been awarded a sum that goes nowhere near the proper compensation, and to my mind, for the reasons given

H by LORD DENNING, M.R., there is no good reason why this court should not order a proper compensatory award.

Turning now to the issue as to how much shall be awarded, it is the fact that the law as to the measure of damages recoverable in actions for deceit is one in which there is a dearth of direct authority except in cases relating to the purchase of shares, of goods, and of land, all of which have certain factors in common. The resulting problem is one which for my part I first came across

I some 35 years ago, and it is a problem that has in various forms recurred not infrequently in cases with which it has been my lot to be concerned. I take some comfort in the fact that over all that period it has seemed to me that practitioners have in general taken the same clear course as this court is today adopting—based on that passage in *Clark* v. *Urquhart, Stracey* v. *Urquhart* (8) which is worth again recalling. There LORD ATKIN said in a concise manner:

(8) [1930] A.C. 28 at p. 68.

" I should have thought it [the measure of damages] would be based   A
on the actual damage directly flowing from the fraudulent inducement."

In cases such as the present the wrong done is tricking a plaintiff into a contract,
and the plaintiff is entitled by way of damages to whatever sum he has lost by
being thus tricked.   The question as to what a purchaser has lost must naturally
depend on the subject-matter of the contract.   If the contract is simply one
such as the purchase of shares, normally the maximum loss will be the money   B
out of which the purchaser has been tricked, a sum which, however, may well
include brokerage or stamp duty: the value of benefits received will be taken
into account.   If the purchase is one of a business which the plaintiff but for
the fraud would not have acquired at all, the objective of the court is to put the
plaintiff, insofar as it is possible, into the same position financially as if he had
not entered into the contract at all; in other words, one must look at the end result   C
of his having entered into the transaction and find out what was his loss over all.
In this behalf I entirely agree with what has fallen from my Lords.   The acquiring
of a business normally entails the expenses of moving into fresh premises, keeping the business going, and at any rate continuing to keep it going until such
time as it can be disposed of; and then one looks also at the expenses of selling.
The computation of the loss may in many cases not be easy.   Thus the court   D
must obviously take care not to include sums for consequences which may be
due to the plaintiff's own unreasonable actions, and also not to include results
which are too remote —matters which often involve difficult questions of fact and
degree.   But such difficulties do not alter the duty of the court which should
approach the matter on a broad basis.

In this case the central fact is that the plaintiff was tricked into buying a   E
business which he would not otherwise have bought at all.   It was one which,
even with suitable protective covenants from the fourth defendant—and none
were acquired—would any way have been singularly unattractive to anyone
who had honestly been told all the relevant facts.   It was a business on which
such goodwill as there was depended greatly on whatever course might be adopted
by the fourth defendant in the future; and I for my part doubt whether a suitable   F
protective covenant which would have worked from a practical point of view
could have been devised.   Any value attached to the business itself as being a
going concern on an independent basis was very small indeed; and it would
seem to me that when once the facts were fully known to a purchaser, any sizeable
payment for goodwill would have been very unlikely.

In fact as matters turned out, the fourth defendant, A. Olby & Son, Ltd., part   G
of what was called " the Olby empire ", did within weeks of the sale of the
relevant business (which was being carried on as A. Olby & Sons), for reasons
which it was in law entitled to adopt, did take a course which in practice saw
to it that any goodwill, of the business that was sold, was recovered for the
empire, and got back into the hands of the fourth defendant.   For when the
plaintiff raised the question of whether he had not been tricked by the first   H
defendant, the fourth defendant cut off his supplies and set about canvassing
the customers of the business sold.   We have had the benefit of having seen a
letter signed by a director of the fourth defendant which contains, amongst
other things, two lists, " B " and " C " and refers to them as follows:

" The list marked ' B ' contains accounts which dealt with Epsom—[the
business sold]—and Mr. Coombe was instructed on the 20th February 1964   I
to call on those customers on behalf of Penge."

As regards list " C ", also containing Epsom accounts, another gentleman
was asked " to call on behalf of Penge " (i.e., the fourth defendants) as from the
same date.

I mention those facts because, whilst that defendant was in law entitled to
take that course, it does demonstrate the risks which a purchaser of the business
sold would take and would thus have a bearing on what is the proper measure

A of damages if one had in this instance to make a separate assessment of the value of the business sold, as counsel for the defendants submitted. In practice, however, any value it had is taken into account in the balance worked out by Winn, L.J.

Now turning from the general picture to figures, for my part I do not wish to add anything to what has been said on detail by Winn, L.J. I would only add

B this, that, making my calculations, at times by a slightly different route, from that taken in the course of his judgment, I came to a figure within a very small margin indeed of £5,500, before I had heard any of the questions put to or answers given by the plaintiff to certain matters in this court. That figure of £5,500 seems the right figure, purely on the basis of those facts which were, we have been told, in evidence before the trial judge: it has been reached on a broad

C basis and it is one with which I find myself in full agreement.

Appeal allowed. Judgment for the plaintiff for £5,500.

Solicitors: *George & George* (for the defendants).

[*Reported by* F. Guttman, Esq., *Barrister-at-Law.*]

D _____

EDMEADES *v.* THAMES BOARD MILLS, LTD.

[Court of Appeal, civil division (Lord Denning, M.R., Davies and Widgery,
E   L.JJ.), January 17, 20, 1969.]

Practice—Stay of proceedings—Jurisdiction—Just and reasonable—Unreasonable refusal by plaintiff to submit to medical examination.

The plaintiff brought an action for injuries received at his work. There was no contest as to liability. The only question was damages. The statement of claim described his injuries but made no suggestion of osteoarthritis. The

F order giving directions said there should be one medical witness on each side and the plaintiff was accordingly examined. Medical reports were exchanged. The defendants noticed that the plaintiff's doctor raised a new complaint, viz., that he suffered from osteoarthritis caused or aggravated by the accident. The defendants' solicitors realised that the plaintiff's solicitors would apply to amend the statement of claim accordingly. The defendants'

G solicitors wished to have the plaintiff examined on their own behalf and they wrote suggesting six possible doctors. The plaintiff's solicitors replied that they would allow examination by the original doctor but not by any of the six suggested. The defendants applied to the master for the action to be stayed unless the plaintiff submitted to examination by one of the six doctors. The master refused the application. The defendants appealed to

H Milmo, J., who also refused to stay the proceedings.

Held: the appeal would be allowed because the court had jurisdiction to grant a stay whenever it was just and reasonable to do so, as where the conduct of the plaintiff in refusing a reasonable request to have a medical examination was such as to prevent the just determination of the cause (see p. 129, letter E, and p. 130, letters B and G, post).

I *Pickett* v. *Bristol Aeroplane Co., Ltd.* (16th March 1961), unreported, not followed.

Appeal allowed.

[As to circumstances in which action may be stayed, see 30 Halsbury's Laws (3rd Edn.) 407, 409, para. 768; and for cases on the subject, see 51 Digest (Repl.) 1003-1008, *5374-5404*.]

Case referred to:
Pickett v. *Bristol Aeroplane Co., Ltd.* (16th March 1961), unreported.

Interlocutory appeal.

This was an appeal by the defendants, Thames Board Mills, Ltd., from an order of MILMO, J., made on 28th November 1968, dismissing their appeal from the decision of Master BICKFORD-SMITH made on 23rd September 1968 when the master refused to order that all proceedings in the action be stayed until not less than 21 days after the plaintiff, Elvey Charles Edmeades, should have submitted himself to a medical examination by any one of six doctors named, on behalf of the defendants, in a letter to the plaintiff's solicitors dated 29th May 1968. The grounds of appeal were that the judge misdirected himself in holding that the plaintiff's refusal to submit to a medical examination was not a proper case in which to grant a stay of the action, and was not an abuse of the process of the court, and that the judge ought to have stayed the action on the terms sought. The facts are set out in the judgment of LORD DENNING, M.R.

Marven Everett, Q.C., and *Hugh Carlisle* for the defendants.
R. M. O. Havers, Q.C., and *J. D. W. Hayman* for the plaintiff.

LORD DENNING, M.R.: The plaintiff, Mr. Edmeades, brings an action against the defendants, Thames Board Mills, Ltd., for injuries received at his work. There is no contest on liability. The only question is damages. This depends on the extent of the injuries which the plaintiff sustained. The statement of claim said that his injuries were:

"Abrasions of the left shin; swelling of the left foot, ankle and thigh; partial rupture of the quadriceps muscle."

It is to be noted in those particulars there is no suggestion of osteoarthritis.

The order giving directions said there should be one medical witness on each side. The plaintiff was examined on his own behalf by a Mr. Bingold. He was examined on behalf of the defendants by a Dr. Abrahamson. The medical reports were exchanged. The defendants then noticed that the plaintiff's doctor, Mr. Bingold, in his report raised a new complaint altogether. He said that the plaintiff suffered from osteoarthritis caused or aggravated by the accident. That complaint had not been mentioned in the statement of claim at all, and so the defendants' doctor, Dr. Abrahamson, had not made any investigations about it.

It was apparent to the defendants' solicitor that, at the trial, if not before, the plaintiff's advisers would apply to amend the statement of claim so as to allege that the plaintiff suffered from osteoarthritis as a result of the accident. Such an amendment would certainly be granted. So the defendants desired to have the plaintiff examined on their own behalf by a specialist who could deal with the osteoarthritis. Accordingly, on 29th May 1968, the defendants' solicitors wrote to the plaintiff's solicitors:

"We would like to have [the plaintiff] medically examined by Mr. R. H. Sewell. We shall be pleased to receive confirmation that you do not object. If for any reason [the plaintiff] does not wish to be examined by Mr. Sewell then we would like him to be examined by one of the following: . . . ."

Then there were five further names of surgeons or doctors added, making six altogether. The plaintiff's solicitors replied that they had no objection to his being examined by the original doctor for the defendants, Dr. Abrahamson, but they were not agreeable to any examination by any of the six new names. A rather acrimonious correspondence passed. Each solicitor maintained his point of view. The defendants then applied to the master for the action to be stayed unless the plaintiff submitted to a medical examination by one of those six doctors. The master refused the application for a stay and made a compromise order under which the plaintiff was not to give evidence of the osteoarthritis unless the statement of claim was amended. The defendants appealed to MILMO, J. He was

A impressed by an unreported decision of this court on 16th March 1961—*Pickett v. Bristol Aeroplane Co., Ltd.* (1). He refused to stay the proceedings. He held that the action should go on as it was. The court, he thought, had no jurisdiction to order the plaintiff to be medically examined on behalf of the defendants, and it could not do so indirectly by means of a stay. He said that it would be almost "writing into the White Book a rule that does not exist" if a stay were to be

B ordered in order to compel the plaintiff to submit to a medical examination.

In 1949 the Evershed Committee in their Report (para. 342) considered whether the plaintiff should be ordered to submit to a medical examination, and said they thought it was unnecessary. They said it might raise important questions of principle in relation to the liberty of the subject. But a great deal of water has gone underneath the bridges since that time. In the recent Report, Winn, L.J.'s

C Committee on Personal Injuries Litigation, state in para. 312:

"We have carefully considered all the objections made to us, including that received from the National Council of Civil Liberties, but we entertain no doubt that every claimant of damages for personal injuries must be bound to submit himself or herself to medical examination of a reasonable character which is reasonably required, subject, of course, to proper safeguards and to

D the claimant's right to object to any particular doctor. In case of need, we consider that the Court must have a power if necessary by legislation to stay the action pending the plaintiff submitting to such an examination."

I do not think legislation is necessary. This court has ample jurisdiction to grant a stay whenever it is just and reasonable so to do. It can, therefore, order a stay if the conduct of the plaintiff in refusing a reasonable request is such as to prevent

E the just determination of the cause. The question in this case is simply whether the request was reasonable or not.

I think that the request of the defendants was perfectly reasonable. They were faced with a new allegation which had not been made in the statement of claim, an allegation of osteoarthritis. The defendants ought in all reason to have an opportunity of considering it and being advised on it. They would need it in order

F to assess the amount to pay into court so as to dispose of the whole matter without it coming to trial. It might be different if the defendants had suggested one particular name to which the plaintiff could reasonably object. That seems to be the explanation now of *Pickett's* case (1). But when six names are suggested and no reasonable objection is taken to them, I have no doubt that the defendants ought to have the opportunity of having the plaintiff medically examined so that evi-

G dence can be given by one of those doctors. The court can ensure this result by granting a stay unless and until the plaintiff submits himself to such a medical examination.

I would allow the appeal and grant a stay accordingly.

DAVIES, L.J.: I agree. As has been pointed out by Lord Denning, M.R.,

H the particulars of injury in the statement of claim are very short and are in these terms:

"Abrasions of the left shin; swelling of the left foot, ankle and thigh; partial rupture of the quadriceps muscle."

That statement of claim was served on 14th July 1967, and the second examina-

I tion on behalf of the defendants by Dr. Abrahamson, who is a consultant physician, took place after the service of that statement of claim, namely, on 6th September 1967.

But the second of Mr. Bingold's reports states that there is "a small marginal fracture of the patella". It continues:

"He did not tell me that he had previously injured his left knee and unless such a history is obtained the present clinical picture must be attributed to

(1) (16th March 1961), unreported.

A

the accident under discussion. If this is so there has been a substantial aggravation of the long-standing osteoarthritis of the left knee.''

Obviously that is a very different picture from the one which we would gather from the particulars in the statement of claim, the one to which Dr. Abrahamson, though no doubt making a general examination, would primarily devote his attention.

B

I entirely agree that in the circumstances of this case it is quite unreasonable that the plaintiff should refuse to be examined by one of the six other surgeons or doctors who have been suggested on behalf of the defendants. One can well understand that a particular firm of solicitors might from previous experience of a particular doctor or surgeon object to having an examination by that gentleman, or indeed that a plaintiff himself or herself might object to a particular doctor. And it is to be remembered that in *Pickett* v. *Bristol Aeroplane Co., Ltd.* (2) there was only one particular doctor under discussion. But I entirely agree with LORD DENNING, M.R., that in the circumstances of the present case it is quite unreasonable for the plaintiff or his solicitors to refuse to allow the plaintiff to be examined by one of these gentlemen in order that, in effect, the defendants may have a second opinion in the light of the aggravated injuries which it is now alleged were suffered by the plaintiff. I too would allow the appeal and make the order for a stay.

C

D

WIDGERY, L.J.: I agree. I can see the objections that would be raised if it were sought to give the court power to make a direct order for medical examination with, presumably, power to commit the plaintiff for contempt if he refused. But none of those objections to my mind arise where it is sought to give the plaintiff a right to elect between not going on with his action, or submitting himself to medical examination, especially where his refusal to be examined is based on no reason and will result in the defendants being unable to prepare their defence and will thus result in the court being unable to do justice towards the defendants. In *Pickett* v. *Bristol Aeroplane Co., Ltd.* (2), as has been shown, both the learned Lords Justices considered that there would be other sanctions or other ways of protecting the defendants; but I confess I find it difficult to know what those sanctions or safeguards would be. If, in fact, the defendants are deprived of medical advice on some aspect of the case and the only evidence on that aspect is that given by the plaintiff's doctors, I see no way by which the balance can be adjusted. If the trial judge thinks that the plaintiff's doctors are credible, it seems to me that he would then have to follow their evidence and a great injustice to the defendants might arise. The test, I agree, is whether in the circumstances of the particular case it is reasonable that a stay should be ordered so that justice shall be done between the parties. In this case the fact that the pleadings at present do not raise issues relating to osteoarthritis is to my mind irrelevant, because counsel for the plaintiff fairly accepts that an amendment made to introduce that issue would readily be made at the trial.

E

F

G

H

I would allow the appeal and order the stay requested.

Appeal allowed. Leave to appeal to the House of Lords refused.

Solicitors: *J. F. Coules & Co.* (for the defendants); *W. H. Thompson* (for the plaintiff).

[*Reported by* JENIFER SANDELL, *Barrister-at-Law.*]

I

---

(2) (16th March 1961), unreported.

A

INSTRUMATIC, LTD. *v.* SUPABRASE, LTD.

[COURT OF APPEAL, CIVIL DIVISION (Lord Denning, M.R., Edmund Davies and Phillimore, L.JJ.), February 3, 1969.]

Practice—Want of prosecution—Dismissal of action—Delay—Inordinate delay without excuse—Plaintiffs' claim virtually undisputed—Counterclaim not proceeded with—Limitation period not expired—Action not dismissed.

B

Court of Appeal—Discretion of official referee—Review—Dismissal of action for want of prosecution—Exercise of discretion—Error in law—Appeal to Court of Appeal.

The plaintiffs sold and delivered quantities of precision instruments to the defendants. The total value was £18,461 19s. 8d. The defendants made several payments on account. Eventually the plaintiffs said there was a balance of £8,782 0s. 11d. owing to them. On 4th January 1966 they issued a writ for the amount owing. The plaintiffs took out a summons under R.S.C., Ord. 14. The defendants put in an affidavit of defence in which they admitted that nearly £8,000 was due and counterclaimed £2,205 3s. 10d. as the cost of repairs to goods that did not come up to standard and, in addition, £20,000 for loss of profits. When the matter came before the master he disregarded the counterclaim for loss of profits and ordered that £2,250 be paid to the plaintiffs' solicitor. He gave the defendants leave to defend as to the balance and referred the case to the official referee. The pleadings were closed on 5th June 1966. In October 1968 the plaintiffs set about preparing their list of documents and gave a month's notice of intention to proceed. They duly delivered their list of documents and took out a summons for further and better particulars of the defence and counterclaim. On 13th December 1968 the defendants took out a summons to strike out the claim for want of prosecution. On 20th December 1968 the official referee struck out the claim for want of prosecution and ordered that the sum of £2,250 which the defendants had paid over, should be repaid to them. He struck out the counterclaim as it could not proceed by itself. On appeal,

C

D

E

F

Held: the appeal would be allowed and the summons for want of prosecution dismissed, because—

(i) if a tribunal exercised its discretion in a way which was plainly wrong, it erred in law and its decision could be reviewed by the courts; accordingly, the court could review the official referee's exercise of his discretion (see p. 132, letter G, p. 133, letter H, and p. 134, letter H, post).

G

Edwards (Inspector of Taxes) v. *Bairstow* ([1955] 3 All E.R. 48) and *Ward* v. *James* ([1965] 1 All E.R. 563) applied.

Theo. Conway, Ltd. v. *Henwood* ((1934), 50 T.L.R. 474) explained.

(ii) since the claim was virtually undisputed and £2,250 had been paid to the plaintiffs' solicitors, the defendants had been equally guilty of delay (i.e., in respect of their counterclaim) and the plaintiffs would be able to institute fresh proceedings at once (the limitation period not having expired), the official referee was wrong in the way in which he exercised his discretion (see p. 133, letters E and F, p. 134, letter G, and p. 135, letter I, post).

H

Appeal allowed.

[As to dismissal of actions for want of prosecution, see 30 HALSBURY'S LAWS (3rd Edn.) 410, 411, para. 771.

I

As to appeals from the exercise of a judge's discretion, see 30 HALSBURY'S LAWS (3rd Edn.) 452, para. 856.]

Cases referred to:

Edwards (Inspector of Taxes) v. *Bairstow*, [1955] 3 All E.R. 48; [1956] A.C. 14; [1955] 3 W.L.R. 410; 28 Digest (Repl.) 397, *1753*.

Conway (Theo.), Ltd. v. *Henwood* (1934), 50 T.L.R. 474.

Gardner v. *Jay* (1855), 29 Ch.D. 50; 54 L.J.Ch. 762; 52 L.T. 395; 51 Digest **A**
    (Repl.) 651, *2588*.

Osenton (Charles) & Co. v. *Johnston*, [1941] 2 All E.R. 245; [1942] A.C. 130;
    110 L.J.K.B. 420; 165 L.T. 235; 51 Digest (Repl.) 681, *2840*.

Ward v. *James*, [1965] 1 All E.R. 563; [1966] 1 Q.B. 273; [1965] 2 W.L.R. 455;
    51 Digest (Repl.) 656, *2637*.

Zimmer Orthopaedic, Ltd. v. *Zimmer Manufacturing Co.*, [1968] 3 All E.R. 449; **B**
    [1968] 1 W.L.R. 1349.

Interlocutory appeal.

This was an appeal by the plaintiffs, Instrumatic, Ltd., from an order of His
Honour PERCY LAMB, Q.C., made on 20th December 1968, dismissing the claim
and counterclaim for want of prosecution and ordering that the sum of £2,250
deposited with the Guardian Building Society be paid out to the defendants' **C**
solicitors and that the defendants, Supabrase, Ltd., have their costs of the action
taxed. The appeal was for the order to be set aside and for the plaintiffs to
have leave to proceed with the trial of the action. The facts are set out in the
judgment of LORD DENNING, M.R.

J. F. A. Archer for the plaintiffs.
D. G. Wright for the defendants. **D**

    LORD DENNING, M.R.: The official referee made an order dismissing
this action for want of prosecution. The plaintiffs seek to appeal to this court.
The defendants take a preliminary point. They say that an appeal to this
court lies only on a point of law; and that there is no point of law here. The
official referee, they say, exercised his discretion; and the manner of its exercise **E**
is not a point of law.

    There are many tribunals from which an appeal lies only on a " point of law ";
and we always interpret the provision widely and liberally. In most of the
cases the tribunal finds the primary facts (which cannot be challenged on appeal);
and the question at issue is what is the proper inference from those facts. In
such cases, if a tribunal draws an inference which cannot reasonably be drawn, **F**
it errs in point of law, and its decision can be reviewed by the courts. That was
settled, once and for all, in *Edwards (Inspector of Taxes)* v. *Bairstow* (1). In
other cases the question is whether, given the primary facts, the tribunal rightly
exercised its discretion. In such cases, if the tribunal exercises its discretion in
a way which is plainly wrong, it errs in point of law, and its decision can be
reviewed by the courts. The courts can review the discretion of a tribunal, **G**
just as they can review the discretion of a judge in chambers, and on like grounds.
The principles stated in *Ward* v. *James* (2), apply as much to the discretion of
a tribunal as to the discretion of a judge. There was one case cited to us which
appeared at first sight to be to the contrary. It was *Theo. Conway, Ltd.* v.
Henwood (3), where it was held that an appeal did not lie to this court from an
order of the official referee dismissing the action for want of prosecution. But **H**
on examining the case, it will be seen that counsel did not raise any point about
the wrong exercise of discretion. So it is no decision on the point. Moreover,
it was an interlocutory decision of two Lords Justices which is not binding on a
court of three.

    So the preliminary objection fails and I turn to consider whether the official
referee exercised his discretion rightly or not. The plaintiffs sold and delivered **I**
quantities of precision instruments to the defendants. The total value was
£18,461 19s. 8d. The defendants made several payments on account. Eventually the plaintiffs said there was a balance of £8,782 0s. 11d. owing to them.
On 4th January 1966, they issued a writ for the amount owing. The plaintiffs
took out a summons under R.S.C., Ord. 14. The defendants put in an affidavit of

(1) [1955] 3 All E.R. 48; [1956] A.C. 14.
(2) [1965] 1 All E.R. 563 at p. 570; [1966] 1 Q.B. 273 at p. 293.
(3) (1934), 50 T.L.R. 474.

A defence in which they admitted that £7,978 19s. 5d. was due. But they said they had a counterclaim because there was bad workmanship and the goods did not come up to standard. They counterclaimed £2,205 3s. 10d. as the cost of repairs, and, in addition, £20,000 for loss of profit on all the other machines they might have sold. The master did not think much of the counterclaim for loss of profits. He thought that £2,250 was clearly owing and made an order
B for that sum to be paid to the plaintiffs' solicitor. He gave the defendants leave to defend as to the balance, and referred the case to an official referee.

The pleadings were closed on 5th June 1966. Both sides ought then to have prepared a list of documents. Neither did so. There were some negotiations up to August 1967. But then the matter went to sleep for 14 months. Then, in October 1968, the plaintiffs set about to prepare their list of documents and
C gave one month's notice of intention to proceed. After the month was up, the plaintiffs duly delivered their list of documents. And they took out a summons for further and better particulars of the defence and counterclaim. It was not till then that the defendants, on 13th December 1968, took out a summons to strike out the claim for want of prosecution.

On 20th December 1968, the official referee acceded to the application. He
D struck out the claim for want of prosecution. He ordered that the sum of £2,250 (which the defendants had paid over) should be repaid to them. He struck out the counterclaim, too, for he could not allow that to go in by itself, see Zimmer Orthopaedic, Ltd. v. Zimmer Manufacturing Co. (4).

I cannot agree with the order made by the official referee. The basic fact is that the claim was virtually undisputed and £2,250 had already been paid. It
E is very, very rare for the court to strike out an admitted claim. It has been done once, but that was a most exceptional case. But there is this further fact. The defendants had a counterclaim. If they had any faith in it, they should have pressed on with it. They cannot justly complain of delay of the plaintiffs on the claim, when they were equally guilty of delay on the counterclaim. It was as much their own fault as the plaintiffs. There is another point
F too. The period of limitation is six years. It has not run. If this action were dismissed, the plaintiffs could start another action tomorrow. So what good is it to dismiss the claim for want of prosecution? Having regard to all these points, I think that the official referee was wrong in the way he exercised his discretion.

There was one further matter which I should mention. There was a change
G of solicitors, but the notice of change was not filed, as it should have been. That was a mere irregularity which should be ignored. It does not affect the decision in this case.

I would allow the appeal and dismiss the summons for want of prosecution.

EDMUND DAVIES, L.J.: I agree. Whether there was material justifying the court in exercising its discretion by way of dismissing an action for want of
H prosecution is, in my judgment, clearly a matter of law. There is nothing in the decision in Theo. Conway, Ltd. v. Henwood (5) to the contrary. The central point of the present appeal was never canvassed there at all. That being so, it follows that under R.S.C., Ord. 58, r. 5, an appeal does lie to this court against the official referee's decision that the plaintiffs' claim, like that of the defendants' counterclaim, be dismissed.

I The only question, accordingly, is on what ground the official referee should have proceeded. The proper approach in such a case was considered at length in Ward v. James (6), and the principal authorities were collected by LORD DENNING, M.R. Perhaps I may be permitted a brief extract from one of the cases there cited, viz., Charles Osenton & Co. v. Johnston (7) where VISCOUNT SIMON, L.C., said:

(4) [1968] 3 All E.R. 449; [1968] 1 W.L.R. 1349.   (5) (1934), 50 T.L.R. 474.
(6) [1965] 1 All E.R. 563 at p. 570; [1966] 1 Q.B. 273 at p. 293.
(7) [1941] 2 All E.R. 245 at p. 250; [1942] A.C. 130 at p. 138.

A

" The law as to the reversal by a Court of Appeal of an order made by the judge below in the exercise of his discretion is well-established, and any difficulty which arises is due only to the application of well-settled principles in an individual case. The appellate tribunal is not at liberty merely to substitute its own exercise of discretion for the discretion already exercised by the judge. In other words, appellate authorities ought not to reverse the order merely because they would themselves have exercised the original discretion, had it attached to them, in a different way. If, however, the appellate tribunal reaches the clear conclusion that there has been a wrongful exercise of discretion, in that no weight, [and I particularly stress the following words] or no sufficient weight, has been given to relevant considerations such as those urged before us by the appellant, then the reversal of the order on appeal may be justified."

B

C

The touchstone on this topic is, in my judgment, to be found in one sentence of BOWEN, L.J., in *Gardner* v. *Jay* (8). Discussing the discretion of a judge in regard to the mode of trial, he said:

"That discretion, like other judicial discretions, must be exercised *according to common sense and according to justice*, and if there is a miscarriage in the exercise of it it will be reviewed . . ."

D

I ask myself, What did the justice of the present case demand should be done in relation to the application to dismiss? As LORD DENNING, M.R., has already said, the claim for £8,782 0s. 11d. was very largely admitted. Indeed it was *entirely* admitted with the exception of some £804, the defendants confessing their liability to the plaintiffs in the sum of £7,978 19s. 8d., subject only to their establishing their counterclaim, at least to an extent sufficient to extinguish the plaintiffs' claim. But the matter does not stop there. On 17th February 1966, the plaintiffs virtually recovered judgment for £2,250. That judgment has never been appealed from, and if the decision of the official referee stands, the plaintiffs have lost every penny of that £2,250 and stand condemned to pay the defendants' costs of the proceedings, notwithstanding that the establishment of the counterclaim was essential to the defence advanced. The defendants themselves did nothing to pursue that counterclaim. A request for further and better particulars thereof was made as long ago as 20th May 1966, and it has never been answered. It is further to be observed that the plaintiffs are, despite their extreme dilatoriness, not in point of fact or law in breach of any of the rules; and, finally, they are still in time to issue a fresh writ. When one considers all those matters collectively, to my way of thinking the question, What does justice demand in the present case?, is easily answered. The answer I would give is that the order dismissing the plaintiffs' claim cannot be allowed to stand. I would accordingly concur with LORD DENNING, M.R., in holding that this appeal must be allowed.

E

F

G

PHILLIMORE, L.J.: I agree. The question of whether the learned official referee exercised his discretion correctly in this case is a pure question of law. There was absolutely no dispute as to the facts on which he had to exercise his discretion. In the first place, the plaintiffs had cured their position; they had given a month's notice to continue and had thereafter taken a further step before the defendants took out their summons to dismiss. There is, so far as I am aware, no precedent for striking out a claim in such circumstances. Indeed it is contrary to the practice, and that alone is a clear point of law. In addition, there are the facts which have been fully described in the judgments of my Lords. This claim was very largely admitted. The plaintiffs had in effect recovered judgment for £2,250. They were in a position to start a fresh action, for the statutory period had not elapsed, and the only difficulty they faced was this counterclaim— a counterclaim for £20,000 which the defendants had been content to allow to go to sleep and which they are quite content to have

H

I

(8) (1855), 29 Ch.D. 50 at p. 58.

A had dismissed, because the learned official referee dismissed both claim and counterclaim, which is some indication of the confidence they had in it. In such circumstances the decision reached was clearly an unjust decision. It was a decision on a point of law and accordingly this appeal should be allowed.

Appeal allowed.

B   Solicitors: *Dale & Newbery* (for the plaintiffs); *Allibones* (for the defendants).

[*Reported by* JENIFER SANDELL, *Barrister-at-Law.*]

OGDEN *v.* OGDEN.

C   [PROBATE, DIVORCE AND ADMIRALTY DIVISION (Sir Jocelyn Simon, P., and Baker, J.), June 26, 27 and 28, 1968.]

Divorce—Desertion—Constructive desertion—Dismissal of charge of persistent cruelty—Whether charge of constructive desertion compatible.

It is open to justices, in spite of finding that the conduct of one spouse could not be described as cruel in the ordinary acceptation of that word, nevertheless to find that it was sufficiently grave and weighty to warrant **D** the other spouse leaving the former (see p. 140, letter G, p. 141, letter A, and p. 144, letter B, post).

Pike v. *Pike* ([1953] 1 All E.R. 232) distinguished.

Appeal dismissed.

[As to what constitutes cruelty, see 12 HALSBURY'S LAWS (3rd Edn.) 269-271, **E** paras. 514-516; and for cases on the subject, see 27 DIGEST (Repl.) 294-296, *2393-2422.*

As to constructive desertion, see 12 HALSBURY'S LAWS (3rd Edn.) 246, para. 459; and for cases on the subject, see 27 DIGEST (Repl.) 350-352, *2897-2913.*

As to the relationship between constructive desertion and cruelty, see 12 HALSBURY'S LAWS (3rd Edn.) 249-251, para. 464.]

F Cases referred to:

Buchler v. *Buchler*, [1947] 1 All E.R. 319; [1947] P. 25; [1947] L.J.R. 820; 176 L.T. 341; 111 J.P. 179; 27 Digest (Repl.) 350, *2899.*

Clarke v. *Edinburgh and District Tramways Co.*, 1919 S.C. (H.L.) 35; [1919] 1 S.L.T. 247.

Edwards v. *Edwards*, [1948] 1 All E.R. 157; [1948] P. 268; [1948] L.J.R. 670; **G** 112 J.P. 109; 27 Digest (Repl.) 351, *2911.*

Foster v. *Foster*, [1953] 2 All E.R. 518; [1954] P. 67; [1953] 3 W.L.R. 623; 117 J.P. 377; Digest (Cont. Vol. A) 826, *6803a.*

Frampton v. *Frampton*, [1951] W.N. 250; 27 Digest (Repl.) 717, *6843.*

Gollins v. *Gollins*, [1963] 2 All E.R. 966; [1964] A.C. 644; [1963] 3 W.L.R. 176; Digest (Cont. Vol. A) 705, *2416a.*

H *Hall* v. *Hall*, [1962] 3 All E.R. 518; [1962] 1 W.L.R. 1246; Digest (Cont. Vol. A) 725, *2913a.*

Hutchinson v. *Hutchinson*, [1963] 1 All E.R. 1; [1963] 1 W.L.R. 280; Digest (Cont. Vol. A) 721, *2802a.*

Jones v. *Jones*, [1954] 3 All E.R. 476, n.; [1954] 1 W.L.R. 1474; 118 J.P. 563; Digest (Cont. Vol. A) 827, *6807b.*

I *Lang* v. *Lang*, [1954] 3 All E.R. 571; [1955] A.C. 402; [1954] 3 W.L.R. 762; 119 J.P. 368; Digest (Cont. Vol. A) 724, *2899a.*

Le Brocq v. *Le Brocq*, [1964] 3 All E.R. 464; [1964] 1 W.L.R. 1085; Digest (Cont. Vol. B) 351, *2395d.*

Marsden v. *Marsden*, [1967] 1 All E.R. 967; [1967] 3 W.L.R. 230; Digest (Repl.) Supp.

Mulhouse (formerly Mulhausen) v. *Mulhouse (formerly Mulhausen)*, [1964] 2 All E.R. 50; [1966] P. 39; [1964] 2 W.L.R. 808; Digest (Cont. Vol. B) 351, *2395c.*

Pike v. *Pike*, [1953] 1 All E.R. 232; [1954] P. 81, n.; [1953] 3 W.L.R. 634, n.; **A**
    Digest (Cont. Vol. A) 730, *3022a*.
Powell v. *Streatham Manor Nursing Home*, [1935] All E.R. Rep. 58; [1935]
    A.C. 243; 104 L.J.K.B. 304; 152 L.T. 563; 51 Digest (Repl.) 816,
    3720.
Price v. *Price*, [1951] 2 All E.R. 580, n.; [1951] P. 413; 115 J.P. 468, n.;
    27 Digest (Repl.) 85, *636*.   **B**
Saunders v. *Saunders*, [1965] 1 All E.R. 838; [1965] P. 499; [1965] 2 W.L.R.
    32; Digest (Cont. Vol. B) 351, *2395e*.
Timmins v. *Timmins*, [1953] 2 All E.R. 187; [1953] 1 W.L.R. 757; Digest
    (Cont. Vol. A) 703, *2350a*.
Watt (or Thomas) v. *Thomas*, [1947] 1 All E.R. 582; [1947] A.C. 484; [1947]
    L.J.R. 515; 176 L.T. 498; 51 Digest (Repl.) 815, *3713*.   **C**
Young v. *Young*, [1962] 3 All E.R. 120; [1964] P. 152; [1962] 3 W.L.R. 946;
    126 J.P. 406; Digest (Cont. Vol. A) 730, *3037b*.

Appeal.

This was an appeal by the husband against a finding of the Bath justices on
8th January 1968. The facts are set out in the judgment of SIR JOCELYN SIMON, P.

    D

M. D. Kennedy for the husband.
A. R. Tyrrell for the wife.

    SIR JOCELYN SIMON, P.: This is an appeal by the husband against a
finding of the Bath justices on 8th January 1968. The justices had before them on
that date five charges: persistent cruelty to the wife; persistent cruelty to the
children of the marriage; constructive desertion of the wife; and wilful neglect **E**
to maintain the wife and the children. The justices dismissed the two complaints
of persistent cruelty. They found constructive desertion and wilful neglect
proved. A separate issue could conceivably arise on wilful neglect: it has not,
however, been argued; and on the conclusion to which I have come on the main
issue of contention on this appeal it is not necessary to say anything about the
complaints of wilful neglect to maintain.   **F**
    The appeal has raised some quite important aspects of the matrimonial law
which have been helpfully argued, but in the end, in my view, the appeal turns
on the proper attitude of an appellate tribunal towards the findings of the instance
tribunal which saw and heard the parties.
    The parties were married in December 1946. The husband is an Englishman,
the wife an Italian woman. The husband was, I think, at that time serving in **G**
Italy. They returned to spend their matrimonial life in this country, at first
in Rochdale and latterly in the west country. The husband is a clerk in local
government service. There are three children of the marriage, two of whom
gave evidence. The eldest child, Linda, was about eighteen or nineteen at the
time. The middle child, Sandra, was somewhat younger. She was, I think
wisely, not subjected to cross-examination; and the justices, again I think **H**
with wisdom, do not seem to have attached significance to her evidence. The
youngest child of the marriage was born in October 1962. That pregnancy
was a shock to both parents and the wife suffered acute depression. Previous to
that, she alleged, and the husband to some extent conceded, the husband
had complained of her association with other men—on more than one occasion
and with more than one man. The matter was not explored in detail; but, **I**
certainly as the evidence stands, I can see nothing to justify any suggestion of
impropriety on the part of the wife. Two of the associates were Italians. Rows
about one of the associations (the parties differed as to which) resulted in the
only act of violence that was charged against the husband. It was corroborated
by Linda and admitted by the husband. The justices seem to have attached no
specific importance to it. It occurred some eight years before the break-up
of the marriage. On the other hand, it seems to me that with persons in this
class of society it would be wrong to close one's eyes to it entirely: once a husband

A has used violence to his wife, manifestations of temper and jealousy are apt to assume a different significance.

As I have said, in 1962 the wife became pregnant and was acutely—indeed dangerously—depressed. She received treatment, including shock treatment. This was unquestionably a difficult time for both parties. She happily recovered and the marriage continued. As I read the evidence, it did not cease to be free

B from turmoil. The wife alleged, and Linda corroborated, that the husband frequently cast painful and wounding aspersions both on her national origin and the character of Italians, and also on her religious faith—she being a Roman Catholic and he not. That was done in the presence of the children, who were brought up as Roman Catholics. The wife also alleged that he used obscene and blasphemous language to her—again, on an occasion, in the presence of

C the children.

Early in 1967 the wife took up employment at a café. The proprietor was an Italian, a Mr. Franco. The husband at that time raised no objection. Previously when he had manifested his jealousy—in the years before 1962—the wife, to keep the peace, had given up employment. On this occasion, as I have said, the husband initially offered no objections. Money was understandably scarce;

D and the wife, quite apart from her employment in the café, supplemented the family income by work as a seamstress. In the middle of August 1967, the wife accompanied Mr. Franco on a trip to London to act as an interpreter for him. The husband initially agreed, but later—whether or not he clearly expressed his change remains uncertain—certainly he did change his mind about it and felt the wife should not go. For some reason he regarded it as a very serious matter

E that on the actual day of this trip the wife did not bring Mr. Franco into the house before their departure early in the morning. At any rate that day-trip deeply disturbed the husband and he asked the wife to break off the association and to give up her employment. Shortly after that she determined to leave him. The husband admitted that he had accused her of adultery. She gave her reasons for determining to leave in a letter she wrote later, on 20th November 1967.

F The husband himself left for a short time in September for a "cooling-off period". I do not think anything turns on that. I think it was before that, although the date was not ascertained with precision that I can see, that there was a furious row between the parties about some contraceptive tablets. The wife had been given them by a friend, Mrs. Capetti, earlier in the year. She had very unwisely kept them in her handbag and the husband had apparently found them there.

G I do not doubt that that exacerbated his suspicions. The wife finally left on 2nd October; and on 17th November she issued her summons making the five complaints that I have rehearsed. On 19th November, the husband wrote a letter seeking a reconciliation. It seems to me to be a good letter. The wife replied on 20th November, refusing the reconciliation.

The justices heard the complaints on 18th December, 1st January and 8th

H January. It was obviously a most careful investigation. The wife called a Dr. Dougall. He established that her health had indeed been impaired in 1962; but his evidence established that so far as he knew the cause—whether it was the exclusive cause I do not know—but obviously from the general tenor of his evidence the main cause was depression due to the unwanted pregnancy. Dr. Dougall also established that he had been called in in the autumn of 1967 on occasions when

I the wife had been in distress. It was plain from the rest of the evidence, including an admission made by the husband, that on one occasion—I think it was 19th or 20th September—the husband had stormed into the place where the wife was living, accused Linda of improper behaviour and said that she was just like her mother, or words to that effect; so disturbing and alarming the wife that she had actually fainted.

The wife, of course, gave evidence herself. Her complaints are summarised in the justices' reasons. I propose to summarise them further. They were the abuse of her religious faith and its clergy, of Italians and of the Italian character;

accusations of " carrying on ", which she understood—and obviously rightly **A**
understood in view of the husband's admission—as an accusation of adultery;
rows and arguments; swearing and blasphemy, on occasions in front of the
children; and accusations that she was mad.   It was part of her case that her
nervous breakdown in 1962 was due to her husband's ill-treatment.   There is
one final allegation which I mention only to dismiss it as irrelevant—namely,
that the husband, having learned that she was going to leave, told her to get out, **B**
or words to that effect.   He admitted he said that; but she had determined to
leave already.   It was something said in rage.   He subsequently made offers
to get her to return; and, although some argument had been advanced to the
contrary, it seems to me that the one thing that this separation cannot have
been was a consensual one.

The wife called Mrs. Capetti, whom I have referred to, who was present on some **C**
of the occasions in the autumn of 1967 when the wife was distressed after quarrels;
and Mrs. Capetti also spoke to the circumstances in which the wife came by the
contraceptive tablets and how many there were, as to which there might have
been some question.

The justices also heard, as I have said, the evidence of the two elder daughters.
They attached importance to Linda's evidence, as they were entitled to.   Among **D**
other things she said, " My father's temper got out of control many times ".
She spoke of his ill-treatment of Sandra; but I need not go into that because the
justices dismissed the charge of cruelty to the children and that finding has not
been questioned on this appeal.   However, Linda also said:

" I have heard my father say that Italians are backward people; and they
are thieves and liars and cheats, and he said that in the presence of my **E**
mother and that has affected my mother.   Sometimes it gets too much and
she breaks down, and sometimes she answers back.   I have heard my
father say things about the Catholics and the Catholic Church, priests are
no good and out for what they can get.   I am a Catholic and he has said
those things in my presence and the presence of my mother.   They used to
upset me but not any more." **F**

Those last words are important because when the husband came to give evidence
he plainly made an admission that he had said such things but not, he said—
and that was the first time that was suggested—after 1962.   That seems to me
to be incompatible with the tenor of Linda's evidence.

So far as the husband was concerned, he gave evidence alone on his side.
In addition to the admission that I have referred to, he said, " I have accused my **G**
wife of carrying on with another man.   I have said Italians are peasants in the
presence of my wife.   I did not say all were peasants ".   He said that he wanted
his wife to return.   However, his wife was adamant that she would not do so.
He spoke of the fact that what upset him initially was the trip to London and
said, " After a few days I told her it was getting on my mind and I told her the
best thing to do was to leave the job ". **H**

On that evidence the justices made the findings that I have described.   I must
read the reason that they give for dismissing the charges of cruelty.   They said:

" The conduct of the husband during the subsistence of this marriage
could not be said to be cruel within the ordinary and decided meaning of this
term, either to his wife or to his children: and whilst we did not regard
the husband's treatment of his children as amounting to cruelty, he never- **I**
theless adopted an attitude towards them which he must have known would
cause distress and particularly to his wife."

I have said that in my view this case turns on the proper attitude of an appellate
tribunal to a finding of fact.   The finding of fact in question is contained in
para. 10 and para. 11 of the justices' reasons:

" The husband having been so warned and persisting in his conduct
thereafter must have foreseen the probable consequences of his continued

A   conduct. The conduct of the husband was sufficiently grave and weighty to warrant the wife leaving him."

The attitude of an appellate court in these circumstances was dealt with in the judgment of the Divisional Court in *Marsden* v. *Marsden* (1), and I do not propose to add to what was said there. I do, however, wish to quote, or rather mainly refer to (since the passage is so well known), what LORD THANKERTON said in B *Watt (or Thomas)* v. *Thomas* (2). What he said was specifically advertent to matrimonial cases and to cases of alleged cruelty in particular (3):

"Normally, the cruelty is alleged to have occurred within the family establishment, and the physique, temperament, standard of culture, habits of verbal expression and of action, and the interaction between the spouses in their daily life, cannot be adequately judged except by seeing and hearing C them in the witness box. The law has no footrule by which to measure the personalities of the spouses. In cases such as the present it will be almost invariably found that a divided household promotes partisanship, and it is difficult to get unbiased evidence."

Those observations apply equally to constructive desertion. There is one other D passage which was cited in that speech to which I would advert. It is a passage from a speech of LORD SHAW OF DUNFERMLINE in *Clarke* v. *Edinburgh and District Tramways Co.* (4). It had in turn been cited by LORD SANKEY, L.C., in *Powell* v. *Streatham Manor Nursing Home* (5), before LORD THANKERTON himself quoted it in *Watt (or Thomas)* v. *Thomas* (6). It runs:

"... witnesses without any conscious bias towards a conclusion may have E in their demeanour, in their manner, in their hesitation, in the nuance of their expressions, in even the turns of the eyelid, left an impression upon the man who saw and heard them which can never be reproduced on the printed page."

In the present type of case, moreover, we do not, other than exceptionally (and this is no exception), have the evidence by way of question and answer but only F a summary of the two; it is, furthermore, the evidence which the notetaker considers of significance and might not represent exhaustively what the court considers of significance: see *Hall* v. *Hall* (7).

It is against that background that I consider the contentions that have been raised in this case. Counsel for the husband seeks to circumvent the line of authorities I have cited in two ways, although he is prepared to face them as G well. He says, first, that the findings of no persistent cruelty and yet constructive desertion are mutually incompatible, and that the finding of constructive desertion once cruelty had been negated was perverse. He says, secondly, that the justices have shown that they did not make proper use of the advantage they had of seeing and hearing the witnesses: that they misdirected themselves as to corroboration and they believed the wrong party. He says, however, in any H event that the finding of constructive desertion was plainly wrong, even if it was one open to the court properly directing itself. He finally says that even if the husband was in constructive desertion that was terminated by a bona fide offer on his part to return to cohabitation which the wife ought to have accepted: she refused it and therefore was herself the deserting party.

I turn to consider the first line of argument. That is based on the decision I of the Court of Appeal in *Pike* v. *Pike* (8), as explained in *Young* v. *Young* (9) in this court. The argument runs in this way. *Pike* v. *Pike* (8) shows that one

(1) [1967] 1 All E.R. 967.
(2) [1947] 1 All E.R. 582 at pp. 586, 587; [1947] A.C. 484 at pp. 487, 488.
(3) [1947] 1 All E.R. at p. 587; [1947] A.C. at p. 488.
(4) 1919 S.C. (H.L.) 35 at pp. 36, 37.
(5) [1935] All E.R. Rep. 58 at p. 61; [1935] A.C. 243 at p. 250.
(6) [1947] 1 All E.R. at p. 587; [1947] A.C. at p. 489.
(7) [1962] 3 All E.R. 518.   (8) [1953] 1 All E.R. 232; [1954] P. 81, n.
(9) [1962] 3 All E.R. 120 at p. 124; [1964] P. 152 at p. 158.

cannot " dress up " a failed case of cruelty or persistent cruelty as a successful **A**
case of constructive desertion unless the case of cruelty has failed on some matter
which is irrelevant to constructive desertion, such as injury to health, persistence,
no act of cruelty within the six months' period before the summons, and so on;
but where such matters are not in question, in both persistent cruelty and in
constructive desertion the standard of conduct which must be proved to have
occurred is the same—in other words such grave and weighty misconduct as **B**
renders cohabitation virtually impossible. Where, therefore, the conduct is
found not to amount to persistent cruelty it cannot amount to constructive
desertion. Here the justices have found cruelty not proved. They should
therefore have found constructive desertion not proved. It was implicit in
their rejection of persistent cruelty that they found the husband's conduct not
sufficiently " grave and weighty ". If they so found they were not entitled to **C**
find constructive desertion.

In my view that argument ought not to succeed for the following reasons.
First, what was said before the decisions in *Gollins* v. *Gollins* (10) and *Le Brocq*
v. *Le Brocq* (11), what was said in *Pike* (12) and *Young* (13), might require review
in the light of the later cases. Secondly, the justices did not reject persistent
cruelty (explicitly, at any rate) on the ground that the conduct was not of **D**
sufficient weight and gravity; but, applying the test laid down in *Mulhouse*
(*formerly Mulhausen*) v. *Mulhouse* (*formerly Mulhausen*) (14) and *Le Brocq* v.
Le Brocq (11), they held that it could not be described as cruel in the accepted
and decided meaning of that term. Thirdly, the justices may well have refused
to find persistent cruelty because the doctor did not substantiate the allegation
of the wife that the main cause of her breakdown in 1962 was the husband's **E**
ill-treatment: though in my view the fact that it was primarily due to depression
caused by an unwanted pregnancy does not exclude the possibility that there
were other causes as well, and certainly does not mean (as has been argued) that
the wife should not have been accepted as a generally truthful witness. Fourthly,
Pike v. *Pike* (12) and *Young* v. *Young* (13) are not in my view to be taken as an
exhaustive statement of the law. I think that appears from HODSON, L.J.'s **F**
judgment itself in *Pike* v. *Pike* (15). See also *Foster* v. *Foster* (16). So to treat
them tends to reduce the law to a formulary—something which authorities have
always discouraged in this branch of jurisprudence. I am far from saying that
Pike v. *Pike* (12) and *Young* v. *Young* (13) have ceased to be a useful general test.
In the overwhelming number of cases where persistent cruelty fails, a case
of constructive desertion based on the same facts should be approached with **G**
considerable reserve: but I do not believe it to be the law that a negation of
persistent cruelty or cruelty necessarily and in all circumstances precludes a
finding of constructive desertion, even subject to the conceded limitations.
Lastly, there seems to me to be a cogent social reason for accepting that as the
state of the law: it is that which is most conducive to reconciliation. A finding
of cruelty or persistent cruelty is apt to set up a state of affairs where the party **H**
who has won the finding is entitled on the face of it to say, " I have in my
favour a finding of a matrimonial offence which I am not bound to condone ";
whereas the aggrieved party is bound in certain circumstances to forgive conduct
which amounts to constructive desertion: see *Edwards* v. *Edwards* (17). I would
add that if counsel for the husband's argument is valid, it would be perfectly
possible to start with the finding of constructive desertion and, retracing its **I**
steps, arrive at the conclusion that the complaint of persistent cruelty was

(10) [1963] 2 All E.R. 966; [1964] A.C. 644.
(11) [1964] 3 All E.R. 464.
(12) [1953] 1 All E.R. 232; [1954] P. 81, n.
(13) [1962] 3 All E.R. 120; [1964] P. 152.
(14) [1964] 2 All E.R. 50 at pp. 56, 57; [1966] P. 39 at p. 50.
(15) [1953] 1 All E.R. at p. 235; [1954] P. at p. 87.
(16) [1953] 2 All E.R. 518; [1954] P. 67.
(17) [1948] 1 All E.R. 157 at p. 160; [1948] P. 268 at p. 272.

A wrongly dismissed. For all those reasons I am unable to accede to counsel's persuasiveness on this part of the case. I think that it was open to the justices, in spite of finding that the conduct of the husband could not be described as cruel in the ordinary acceptation of that term, nevertheless to find that it was sufficiently grave and weighty to warrant the wife leaving her husband.

I turn then to the second main attack, namely that the justices have mis-

B directed themselves and in the end believed the wrong party. Counsel for the husband says that the justices purport to have found corroboration in evidence which, properly analysed, does not corroborate—in particular, the evidence of Mrs. Capetti and Dr. Dougall. Indeed, in the case of the latter, claims counsel, the evidence contradicts that of the wife and indicates that she ought to have been disbelieved generally. I have already dealt with that argument. I have

C also dealt with the extent to which Mrs. Capetti was able to bear out the wife's case. I would only add that the justices did not go further than to say they found some corroboration of the complainant's evidence. They obviously placed great reliance on Linda's evidence, which very strongly supported the wife's case. They say of Linda: " She impressed us by the factual and unemotional manner in which she gave her evidence under such unhappy circumstances."

D Although they do not explicitly say so, I think they generally believed the evidence of the wife. In my view they were entitled to do so: and I find myself quite unable, merely from a scrutiny of the notes of evidence, to come to the conclusion that the justices have believed the wrong evidence or even that it is probable that they have done so.

However, counsel for the husband also attacks the justices on a further matter,

E which amounts, he says, to misdirection. That is this. The wife said, and the husband admitted, that the husband had accused the wife of committing adultery. The justices said:

" The wife had no particular attachment to any other man, Italian or otherwise. Such contacts with Italians as she may have had were nothing more than the natural and understandable affinity for others of the same

F race when working together in a foreign land."

Counsel says that even accepting that, the justices have missed the point, which was this: was this husband unreasonable in voicing his suspicions? Did the wife give him grounds on which he could reasonably suspect her of improper conduct? In my view, the justices are not to be criticised on that ground. If that were the husband's case it should have been made plain to the justices;

G and the proper way of making it plain was by notice to the other side that such was his case, communicated to the court: see *Frampton* v. *Frampton* (18) and *Jones* v. *Jones* (19). The truth is that this husband was willing enough to wound, but he was not willing to serve notice or state explicitly at any stage that he had reasonable grounds for suspicion. That being so it seems to me that the point is not open before this court. The justices are not to be criticised for refusing

H to consider it or state explicitly in their reasons what conclusion they would have come to on the matter, and I express no view myself.

I come finally then, on this part of the case, namely whether the husband was ever in constructive desertion, to counsel for the husband's last point—that even accepting the limitations of an appellate court, even accepting the advantages of the justices, this was a perverse verdict. I am quite unable to come to

I that decision. In my view there was material here which entitled the justices properly directing themselves to find that the husband was in constructive desertion. Although once again I do not propound this as an exhaustive test, it was said in *Saunders* v. *Saunders* (20):

" The generally accepted test of what conduct amounts to constructive desertion is this: has the defendant been guilty of such grave and weighty

---

(18) [1951] W.N. 250.   (19) [1954] 3 All E.R. 476, n.
      (20) [1965] 1 All E.R. 838 at p. 841; [1965] P. 499 at p. 504.

A

misconduct that the only sensible inference is that he knew that the complainant would in all probability withdraw permanently from cohabitation with him, if she acted like any reasonable person in her position? "

I think that that is in effect the test that the justices applied. In any event, as was said in the same case (21):

B

" They [that is the justices in *Saunders'* case (22)] did not expressly direct themselves at all as to what the test was. I think that justices would be well advised, when proceeding to adjudication, to direct themselves both as to the test to be applied and as to the onus and standard of proof; but merely because they do not set out the test they are certainly not to be taken as having failed to appreciate it: . . ."

C

On this part of the case I think it is useful to test the matter by seeing what is involved if the husband's case here is correct. I have said that there is not one shred of evidence that this was a consensual parting. It follows, in my view, that if the husband was not in constructive desertion, the wife was in desertion herself and that she is bound to return to cohabitation and continue to endure conduct which, ex hypothesi, did not justify her in leaving: see what HODSON, L.J., said in *Price* v. *Price* (23). Is it really suggested, I ask myself, that the wife should have to return to cohabitation and have her chastity unjustly impugned, her religious faith vilified, and her national origin aspersed? I cannot believe that the law would say any such thing. In my view, therefore, the justices were fully entitled to come to the conclusion that they did on constructive desertion.

D

As to whether the husband terminated that desertion, I have said that I think his letter of 19th November reads well. The justices, however, found that he was not genuine. It may be—I think it is—that in that finding they telescoped together two concepts: one, was he prepared to implement his offer if it was accepted; the other, did he give the wife reasonable assurances that, if she did accept the offer, cohabitation would not once again be disrupted by grave and weighty misconduct? I would myself unhesitatingly draw the inference that he did want cohabitation to be resumed; but that is not enough to negative or to terminate constructive desertion: see *Lang* v. *Lang* (24). As for the second concept, I think that that is what the justices really found to be determined in the negative; I would myself, applying r. 73 (7) of the Matrimonial Causes Rules 1957 (25). It is clear from the way the husband's case was conducted that the poison of suspicion was still running in his veins. If the wife had returned to cohabitation I cannot believe that the deplorable situation which had led to her departure would not have been resumed. I do not think that the husband has at any time as yet—and I emphasise those words—given the wife the assurances to which she is entitled, that if she does resume cohabitation it will be in reasonable felicity.

E

F

G

That brings me to the last thing that I wish to say in this case. It was suggested in argument on behalf of the husband that if the wife is left with her order she will, so to speak, be entitled to sit on it and to continue her rejection of any overture from the husband. I entirely disagree with that. As BAKER, J., pointed out in argument, the decision of the justices creates a completely new situation in this regard. On the one hand, the husband is not entitled to continue to voice any suspicion or hint of immoral conduct against the wife or to insist that she breaks off what the justices find to be a natural and understandable relation with others of the same race. He is not entitled to resume what the justices have found to be grave and weighty misconduct in other ways: the insults, the improper language, and so on. The wife is entitled to look for assurances in all those respects. On

H

I

(21) [1965] 1 All E.R. at p. 843; [1965] P. 507.
(22) [1965] 1 All E.R. 838; [1965] P. 499.
(23) [1951] P. 413 at p. 421; [1951] 2 All E.R. 580, n., at p. 581.
(24) [1954] 3 All E.R. 571; [1955] A.C. 402.
(25) S.I. 1957 No. 619.

A the other hand, the wife is not entitled, on the finding of the justices, to treat the husband's behaviour as unforgivable. That is clearly not the view of the justices: they say that she was under no obligation in law at this stage to resume cohabitation with him, thereby envisaging the situation whereby at some stage she might be under such obligation. If the husband does make the proper overtures, give the proper assurances, the wife is, in my view, bound to give them consideration;

B and unless she accepts proper assurances she is in danger of putting herself in desertion. However, that situation has not yet arisen and I would dismiss the appeal.

    BAKER, J.: With considerable hesitation and doubt I have come to the conclusion that I cannot dissent from the view expressed by SIR JOCELYN

C SIMON, P., that there was material here, albeit I think slight material, but in particular the evidence of Linda, on which the justices could reach the conclusion, properly directing themselves, that there was constructive desertion. I, for my part, could not find on the material before this court that there was grave and weighty misconduct by the husband which drove the wife from the house. Of the numerous reasons advanced by counsel for the husband for that conclusion, it

D seems to me in particular, though not exhaustively, that the wife's association with Mr. Franco, albeit an innocent association and so found, was potentially disruptive, and she knew it. Secondly, the justices accepted the evidence of the doctor as being corroboration, and this, in my view, was a misapprehension of the doctor's evidence. Thirdly, the justices did not, and did not pretend to have, directed their minds to the relevant date, which was the date at which the wife

E formed the intention of leaving the matrimonial home, which was somewhere about 8th September 1967, and not 2nd October, by which time many further events had happened and in particular the incident relating to the contraceptives. The view that I would form is not, however, the test: see the passage which SIR JOCELYN SIMON, P., has already cited from the speech of LORD THANKERTON (26), and SIR JOCELYN SIMON's own words in *Marsden* v. *Marsden* (27), where he said:

F " Where the point of issue lies in such a ' no-man's land ', we are very reluctant indeed to interfere with the decision. It inevitably follows that, in spite of r. 73 (7), there may be occasions when this court, although inclined to feel that it might itself have come to a different decision from that at which the justices have arrived, must leave it undisturbed."

    I want to add a very short word about the problem whether a failed cruelty

G charge can or cannot be dressed up as a constructive desertion finding: see *Pike* v. *Pike* (28) and *Young* v. *Young* (29). It is I think inaccurate to say as a general proposition that there cannot be such a finding for it is accepted that there are cases in which constructive desertion can be found but cruelty cannot: for example, when the element of injury to health is missing: see *Timmins* v. *Timmins* (30); where there is no persistence in the cruelty charged before

H the magistrates; where the charge is not made in time within the relevant six months; or where there is a refusal of sexual intercourse: see *Hutchinson* v. *Hutchinson* (31). I think also there is an undefined and probably indefinable category where the conduct though properly described as grave and weighty is not of the nature and quality of the matrimonial offence of cruelty: see the judgment of ASQUITH, L.J., in *Buchler* v. *Buchler* (32) and of LORD GREENE, M.R.,

I in the same case. The conduct must be cruel: see *Le Brocq* v. *Le Brocq* (33). I think a useful test may be whether the conduct is " forgivable ". If the

(26) In *Watt (or Thomas)* v. *Thomas*, [1947] 1 All E.R. at p. 587; [1947] A.C. at p. 488.
(27) [1967] 1 All E.R. at p. 968.
(28) [1953] 1 All E.R. 232; [1954] P. 81, n.
(29) [1962] 3 All E.R. 120; [1964] P. 152.
(30) [1953] 2 All E.R. 187.
(31) [1963] 1 All E.R. 1.
(32) [1947] 1 All E.R. 319; [1947] P. 25.
(33) [1964] 3 All E.R. 464.

conduct is grave and weighty but in all the circumstances is considered to be   A
forgivable the court may find constructive desertion although dismissing the
cruelty charge.   Magistrates almost invariably insert a non-cohabitation clause
in their order on such a finding of cruelty.   Such a clause was asked for by the
wife in this case but was not granted on the finding of constructive desertion,
and that, I think, is the usual practice of magistrates.   They have, I infer from
their findings, said to themselves " Is this forgivable conduct? " and they have   B
answered " Yes ".   To the question " Was it grave and weighty misconduct? "
they have also answered " Yes ", and therefore they have said " This is constructive desertion although it is not cruelty ".   From that decision I cannot
dissent as there was some evidence to support it.

Finally the wife has said and the justices have recorded there were no circumstances in which she would return to her husband to live with him.   That, in   C
my view, is nonsense, and I want to add all the weight I can to what SIR JOCELYN
SIMON, P., has already said about the possibility of reconciliation in this case.

Appeal dismissed.

Solicitors: *A. F. & R. W. Tweedie*, agents for *Titley, Long & Co.*, Bath (for the
husband); *Peake & Co.*, agents for *W. A. Sparrow & Son*, Bath (for the wife).   D

[*Reported by* ALICE BLOOMFIELD, *Barrister-at-Law.*]

TRADAX S.A. *v.* VOLKSWAGENWERK A.G.   E

[QUEEN'S BENCH DIVISION (Megaw, J.), January 17, 20, 27, 1969.]

*Shipping—Charterparty—Construction—Incorporation of amended Centrocon
arbitration clause—Whether applicable between owners and charterers.*

*Arbitration—Appointment of arbitrator—Appointment within three months of
final discharge—Centrocon arbitration clause—Appointment meant effective   F
appointment—Communication of nomination not sufficient.*

On 6th September 1963 the parties entered into a charterparty, known as
Approved Baltimore Berth Grain Charter Party—Steamer, which provided
for the carriage of a cargo of grain from Toledo, Ohio, to London or Hull.
As a result of a dispute between the parties the defendants, the time chartered
owners, exercised their lien in respect of a part of the cargo which was to have   G
been delivered to buyers in Hull.   Unloading was completed on 15th December
1963.   The plaintiffs, the charterers, on or about 27th January 1964 paid the
defendants, under protest, the sum in respect of which the lien had been
exercised.   The charterparty incorporated, " as far as applicable " bills of
lading clauses, including cl. 10, which contained the Centrocon arbitration
clause (together with a deleted New York arbitration clause) providing,   H
inter alia, that any claim must be made in writing and the claimant's
arbitrator be appointed within three months of final discharge failing
which the claim was deemed waived and barred.   On 27th January 1964
the plaintiffs notified the defendants that they nominated C. as their
arbitrator.   However, they only notified him of the dispute and that they
wished him to act on their behalf on 24th July 1964.   On the question   I
whether the Centrocon clause applied and whether the plaintiffs had
appointed their arbitrator within three months of final discharge,

Held: (i) where the amended Centrocon arbitration clause was incorporated in a charterparty it applied, not only to arbitration between the
owners and the bills of lading holders but also, to arbitration between the
owners and charterers notwithstanding the fact that another arbitration
clause, albeit deleted, had been included in the charterparty (see p. 148,
letters C and E, post).

A   *N.V. Reederij Amsterdam* v. *President of India* ([1960] 2 Lloyd's Rep. 82) followed.

(ii) in the context of the Centrocon arbitration clause the word " appointed " meant " effectively appointed "; communication of a mere nomination to the other side, unknown to the appointee, did not constitute an " appointment " of him; accordingly C. had not been appointed within **B**   three months of final discharge even though he would at all times have been willing to act as arbitrator had he been asked to do so by the plaintiffs (see p. 149, letters A and D, post).

[As to the construction of charterparties, see 35 HALSBURY'S LAWS (3rd Edn.) 255-261, paras. 391-401; and for cases on the subject, see 41 DIGEST (Repl.) 169, 170, *127-137.* **C**   As to arbitration clause, see 2 HALSBURY'S LAWS (3rd Edn). 19, 20, para. 47; and for cases on the subject, see 41 DIGEST (Repl.) 209, 210, *380-382.*]

Cases referred to:

Cox v. *Johnson* (1914), 14 S.R.N.S.W. 240; 2 Digest (Repl.) 524, **499.*
N.V. Reederij Amsterdam v. *President of India*, [1960] 2 Lloyd's Rep. 82;   *affd.* C.A., [1961] 2 Lloyd's Rep. 1; 41 Digest (Repl.) 473, *2485.*
D   *Ringland* v. *Lowndes*, (1863) 9 L.T. 479; 15 C.B.N.S. 173; 143 E.R. 749;   11 Digest (Repl.) 305, *2102.*

Summons.

This was an originating summons taken out by Tradax Export S.A., the plaintiffs, against Volkswagenwerk A.G., the defendants, asking for the determina-**E**   tion of four questions with regard to the construction of a charterparty, entered into on 6th September 1963, between the plaintiffs as charterers and the defendants as time chartered owners. The facts are set out in the judgment.

R. L. A. Goff, Q.C., and *Brian Davenport* for the plaintiffs.
A. E. J. Diamond for the defendants.

                                              Cur. adv. vult.

F   27th January. **MEGAW, J.,** read the following judgment: This is an originating summons asking for the determination of four questions. Only two of those questions are now in dispute. They are questions of construction of a charterparty entered into, on 6th September 1963, between the plaintiffs, Tradax Export S.A., as charterers, and the defendants, Volkswagenwerk A.G., as time chartered owners. The charterparty is in the form known as " Approved Balti-**G**   more Berth Grain Charter Party—Steamer ". It provided for the carriage by the motor vessel La Loma of a cargo of grain from Toledo, Ohio, to London or Hull.

Before and after completion of loading the defendants made a claim against the plaintiffs on the grounds that the plaintiffs were in breach of a clause of the charterparty whereby the plaintiffs gave a guarantee as to the freshwater **H**   draft available at the port of loading. The plaintiffs rejected the claim as unfounded. By reason of that claim, when the vessel discharged at Hull, discharge being completed on 15th December 1963, the defendants exercised their lien in respect of a parcel of 125 tons of the cargo which was to have been delivered to buyers in Hull. In consequence the plaintiffs on or about 27th January 1964, paid the defendants the sum in respect of which the lien had been exercised, **I**   namely £1,103 13s.

In a telex of 27th January 1964, the plaintiffs said:

" this payment is under reserves and we will get into arbitration to settle this question. Please note that we nominate Mr. J. Chesterman, 3 Lloyds Avenue, London, E.C.3. Please let us know the name of your arbitrator. We request you to cancel immediately the lien on the cargo."

This was confirmed by letter dated 30th January 1964, the fourth paragraph of which is as follows:

" For good order's sake, may we remind you that this payment was made

under reserves and we will proceed with arbitration to settle this dispute **A**
accordingly. The amount involved will be the deadfreight of £1,103 13s.,
plus docks board stowage charges incurred at Hull. In this respect, we have
nominated Mr. John Chesterman, 3, Lloyds Avenue, London, E.C.3., who
will act as our arbitrator."

The plaintiffs did not at that time inform Mr. Chesterman of this dispute or of
the fact that they wished him to act as their arbitrator with regard thereto. **B**
They did not even send him a copy of their letter of 30th January. It was not
until 24th July 1964, that Mr. Chesterman was informed by the plaintiffs of
their desire or intention that he should act as their arbitrator in this matter.
Meanwhile, on 17th February the defendants wrote to the plaintiffs as follows:

"Dear Sirs, ' La Loma '—Arbitration. We herewith nominate as arbitrator
acting on our behalf Mr. R. A. H. Clyde, Forum House, 15/18, Lime Street, **C**
London, E.C.3. We think your and our arbitrator will first appoint an umpire.
Then we will wait for your written claim."

On 9th March Mr. Clyde wrote to Mr. Chesterman as follows:

" Dear Mr. Chesterman, ' La Loma '. You are representing the Charterers,
Messrs. Tradax, I the disponent owners of the ship, Messrs. Volkswagenwerk. **D**
I have got my file. I think it is complete, or nearly complete. Let me know
what is the situation at your end."

Mr. Chesterman thereupon informed Mr. Clyde, orally, that he had no knowledge
of the matter and that he could not trace having been nominated. Mr. Clyde
reported this to the defendants, who did nothing to raise the question with the
plaintiffs. They awaited events. Nothing further happened until 24th July 1964, **E**
when the plaintiffs wrote to Mr. Chesterman as follows:

" Dear Mr. Chesterman, Re: s.s./' La Loma '—from Toledo to Hull—
Charterparty dated New York September 6th, 1963. A dispute has arisen
between the owners of the s.s./' La Loma ', Messrs. Volkswagenwerk A.G.,
Wolfsburg, and ourselves, as to the payment of the deadfreight. We have **F**
taken the liberty of appointing you as our arbitrator; vessel owners have
nominated Mr. R. A. H. Clyde to act as their arbitrator."

On 14th August 1964, Mr. Chesterman wrote to the plaintiffs. He said:

" Dear Sirs, ' La Loma ' C/P 6.9.1963. I thank you for your letter of the
24th July, and am pleased to accept appointment as your arbitrator in this **G**
dispute. I am in touch with my co-arbitrator in an endeavour to get information from the Great Lakes Towing Company."

On the same day Mr. Chesterman wrote to Mr. Clyde enclosing a copy of the
plaintiffs' letter of 24th July. On 17th August, Mr. Clyde replied as follows:

" Dear Mr. Chesterman, ' La Loma ' C/P 6.9.63. Thank you for your letter **H**
of the 14th August enclosing a copy of [the plaintiffs'] letter to you of the
24th July. This is the same case as that in which in March of this year I
approached you and you told me you had not been appointed arbitrator.
I reported that to my people [the defendants] on the 13th March: and my
people decided to wait to see if [the plaintiffs] did appoint you within the
three months' time limit under the Centrocon Arbitration Clause. My **I**
people and I both concluded in July that [the plaintiffs] were not pursuing
the arbitration: and I have sent my papers back to [the defendants]. So far
as I could see that was the end of the arbitration, but you will let me hear
from you."

So deadlock was reached. The defendants contended that the Centrocon arbitration clause was incorporated as a term of the charterparty; that under that
clause claims were deemed to be waived and absolutely barred unless the claimants
(the plaintiffs) inter alia appointed their arbitrator within three months of final

A discharge. The final discharge had taken place on 15th December 1963, and that therefore the arbitrator had to be appointed before 15th March 1964; that the plaintiffs had not appointed their arbitrator before that date and that the plaintiffs' claim was thus barred. The plaintiffs accepted that final discharge took place on the 15th December 1963, but they disputed the defendants' other two contentions, namely; (i) that the Centrocon arbitration clause was applicable,

B and (ii) if it was applicable, that the plaintiffs' arbitrator had not been appointed before 15th March 1964. The plaintiffs contended that Mr. Chesterman, though he knew nothing about his supposed appointment in respect of this particular dispute until July 1964, had been appointed on 27th January, when the plaintiffs sent to the defendants the telex message which I have read, stating that they nominated Mr. Chesterman.

C   These are the two effective questions of construction raised by the originating summons, being questions (ii) and (iii) in that document. Although the dispute giving rise to it crystallised in the summer or autumn of 1964, the originating summons was not issued until 31st October 1967. If the plaintiffs, the charterers, succeed, the result will be that the arbitration, claimed in January 1964, and relating to events in September 1963, will proceed in the year 1969.

D   Although the question whether the Centrocon arbitration clause is applicable was not put forward by counsel for the plaintiffs as his primary contention, logically it comes first. What the plaintiffs say is that, as a matter of construction, the Centrocon arbitration clause applies to disputes arising under a bill of lading issued under the charterparty, but that it does not apply to this dispute, which (as is accepted by both sides) is a dispute arising under the charterparty. Hence,

E it is contended, the arbitration which was invoked, and the appointment of arbitrators, were in no way concerned with, or restricted by, any limitations or special requirements contained in the Centrocon arbitration clause. In particular the time limit for appointment of the plaintiffs' arbitrator did not apply. Hence, even if the appointment of Mr. Chesterman was outside the three months' period, that in no way bars or invalidates the claim. The arbitration should now proceed.

F   To understand the plaintiffs' contention, it is necessary to set out an extract from the charterparty terms. I shall keep the extract to the minimum.

The charterparty provides:

" Bills of lading. It is also mutually agreed that this contract shall be completed and be superseded by the signing of bills of lading on the same form as in use by regular line steamers from loading port to port of destina-

G tion; or, if port of destination be one to which there is no regular line of steamers from loading port, this contract shall be superseded by the signing of bills of lading in the form customary for such voyages for grain cargoes, which bills of lading shall however contain the following clauses."

Then follow clauses numbered 1 to 14 dealing with a miscellany of topics. The

H only one of these clauses which I need set out is cl. 10. That reads as follows:

" ' Centrocon ' Arbitration Clause. ' All disputes from time to time arising out of this contract shall, unless the parties agree forthwith on a single Arbitrator, be referred to the final arbitrament of two Arbitrators carrying on business in London who shall be members of the Baltic and engaged in the Shipping and/or Grain Trades, one to be appointed by each

I of the parties, with power to such Arbitrators to appoint an Umpire. Any claim must be made in writing and Claimant's Arbitrator appointed within three months of final discharge and where this provision is not complied with the claim shall be deemed to be waived and absolutely barred. No award shall be questioned or invalidated on the ground that any of the Arbitrators is not qualified as above, unless objection to his acting be taken before the award is made '."

Thereafter four lines of print are struck out. If I am allowed to look at them, I see that they consist of another arbitration clause.

At the end of cl. 14 there appear these words outside the inverted commas **A**
which have surrounded all (or almost all) of cl. 1 to cl. 14: "It is understood that
Clauses Nos. 1 to 22 above and below are incorporated in this Charter Party as
far as applicable". Then follow, though no longer in inverted commas, cl. 15 to
cl. 22.

The plaintiffs submit that cl. 1 to cl. 14, and therefore cl. 10, the Centrocon
arbitration clause, are primarily clauses of bill of lading contracts. They become **B**
terms of the charterparty contract only insofar as this is brought about by the
words which I have just quoted, "It is understood ...". But those words
incorporate them in the charterparty contract only "as far as applicable".
The Centrocon arbitration clause is not applicable, because it refers to "disputes
arising out of this contract". "This contract", it is said, can mean only the
bills of lading contract. It has no application, therefore, to disputes under the **C**
charterparty contract.

I do not accept that argument. I respectfully adopt and follow the decision
and reasoning of PEARSON, J., as he then was, in *N.V. Reederij Amsterdam* v.
President of India (1). There were verbal differences in the charterparty which
PEARSON, J., had to construe; but none of the differences in my opinion begin to
invalidate the application of the judgment in that case to the present case. **D**
It will be sufficient to quote a few lines from the judgment (2):

> "Finally, there is cl. 11, incorporating several clauses. One of the
> incorporated clauses is the amended Centrocon arbitration clause. It is the
> only arbitration clause in this charterparty. There is no reason for supposing
> that there is to be arbitration between the owners and the bills of lading
> holders, but not between the owners and the charterers". **E**

I do not accept the submission of counsel for the plaintiffs that there is a valid
distinction because in the present charterparty cl. 10 included not only the Centrocon arbitration clause but also, though struck out in the print, another arbitration
clause. I doubt whether I am entitled to look at a clause which has been deleted
by the parties or to draw inferences from the deletion. Even if it be permissible, **F**
no inference appears to me to arise which would affect my conclusion.

The charterparty in PEARSON, J.'s case did not include the words corresponding
to those which I have cited from the present charterparty: "It is understood
that Clauses 1 to 22 above and below are incorporated in this charterparty as
far as applicable". Counsel for the plaintiffs submits that those words enable
him to draw a distinction in favour of the plaintiffs. In my judgment, their effect **G**
is the contrary. How can it be suggested, having regard to the passage which I
have quoted from the judgment of PEARSON, J., that he would have taken the
view that the provisions of the Centrocon arbitration clause were not applicable,
or were less than fully applicable, to arbitration between the defendants and the
plaintiffs?

I pass to the other question. Was Mr. Chesterman "appointed" by the **H**
plaintiffs as their arbitrator for the purpose of this dispute with the defendants
before 15th March 1964? The answer depends on the meaning of the word
"appointed" in the context of this clause. If it is sufficient, as the plaintiffs
contend, to constitute the appointment of an arbitrator by a party to a dispute
that that party should have notified the other party to the dispute that he
has nominated Mr. X to act as arbitrator, then the plaintiffs duly fulfilled the
requirements of the clause. The defendants contend that that is not sufficient. **I**
In order that an arbitrator may have been "appointed" for the purposes of this
clause, it is neccessary, they say, that at least there should have been a communication by the appointor to the intended appointee authorising him to act
in respect of the particular dispute: and that there should have been an
acceptance, or agreement to act, on the part of the intended appointee.

(1) [1960] 2 Lloyd's Rep. 82.
(2) [1960] 2 Lloyd's Rep. at p. 88.

A   The word "appoint" has many different meanings in different contexts. In the context of this Centrocon arbitration clause, I am satisfied that "appointed" connotes "effectively appointed". A mere nomination, unknown to the appointee, is not an "appointment" of him. It does not become an "appointment" merely by being communicated to the other side. It becomes an "appointment" of him as arbitrator only when he is effectively in the position

B   of an arbitrator, clothed with the duties and authority of such. That stage of effective appointment is not reached before he has been told that it is desired to appoint him in a particular matter and he has indicated his willingness to act in that matter.

I agree with the view expressed on this point by the learned editor of RUSSELL ON ARBITRATION (17th Edn.) p. 160. That view is supported by a passage in

C   the judgment of BYLES, J., in *Ringland* v. *Lowndes* (3). So far as the judgments in the New South Wales case, *Cox* v. *Johnson* (4), are inconsistent with this view, I very respectfully differ from them.

I should add that I do not think that there is anything in the affidavit evidence before me, as to general or individual practice in the appointment of arbitrators, which really assists on this question of construction: nor does it help that Mr.

D   Chesterman would at all times have been willing to act as arbitrator in this matter if he had been asked by the plaintiffs so to do.

For reasons which I need not elaborate, I am satisfied that the balance of commercial convenience weighs heavily on the side of a construction which helps to ensure that, when one party to a dispute informs the other party that he has appointed Mr. X as his arbitrator, the other party can be confident that Mr. X

E   has been effectively appointed; that Mr. X knows that he has been appointed, and that he is ready and willing to embark on his duties as arbitrator. Section 27 of the Arbitration Act 1950 is available, in proper cases, to mitigate hardship which would otherwise be caused by reason of the existence of a time limit such as is imposed by this clause.

I must deal formally with the four questions raised by the originating summons,

F   though only nos. (ii) and (iii) have been the subject of dispute.

Question (i) is, in effect, whether there is an arbitration agreement relating to the dispute in question about the £1,103 13s. The answer, by consent, is "yes". Question (ii) reads: "If the answer to question (i) is ' yes ', whether such arbitration agreement is contained in or is otherwise subject to the terms of the Centrocon arbitration clause set out in the said charterparty". The answer is "yes".

G   Question (iii) reads: "If the answer to question (ii) is ' yes ', whether the plaintiffs appointed their arbitrator in respect of the said dispute within three months of final discharge of the La Loma on her voyage under the said charterparty, as required by the said Centrocon arbitration clause". The answer is "no". Question (iv) reads: "If the answer to question (ii) is ' yes ', and the answer to question (iii) is ' no ', whether the plaintiffs' claim to repayment of the

H   said sum of £1,103 13s. is to be deemed to be waived and absolutely barred". It is conceded by counsel for the plaintiffs that, if questions (ii) and (iii) are answered as I have answered them, the answer is "yes".

Judgment accordingly.

Solicitors: *Richards, Butler & Co.* (for the plaintiffs); *Holman, Fenwick & Willan* (for the defendants).

I
[*Reported by* K. DIANA PHILLIPS, *Barrister-at-Law.*]

(3) (1863), 15 C.B.N.S. 173 at p. 196.
(4) (1914), 14 S.R.N.S.W. 240.

FIELDING AND PLATT, LTD. *v.* NAJJAR.

[COURT OF APPEAL, CIVIL DIVISION (Lord Denning, M.R., Davies and Widgery, L.JJ.), January 16, 17, 1969.]

Bill of Exchange—Promissory note—Failure of consideration—Promissory notes payable over ten months—Failure to pay first promissory note when due—Suspension of work under contract—Claim for payment of first two promissory notes—No defence in action on first promissory note.

Contract—Illegality—False invoice—Request to describe goods misleadingly on invoice—Request not term of contract—Had request amounted to term, term severable.

Contract—Illegality—Defence to claim—Knowledge of illegality and active participation essential to defence.

The plaintiffs were negotiating the sale of an aluminium extrusion press, to a Lebanese company, of which the defendant was managing director, at a price of £235,000. Payment was to be by promissory notes. The press was to be manufactured by the plaintiffs and to be delivered in 10½ months. On 16th June 1965 the plaintiffs stated that they were agreeable to the proposed contract subject to evidence of satisfactory importing licensing arrangements. The Lebanese company replied by telex on 18th June confirming that they had an import licence for an aluminium plant and asking for the material to be invoiced as " parts for rolling mill " so as to mislead the Lebanese authorities regarding the true nature of the goods. The chief contractual document was a formal and lengthy quotation, which the Lebanese company accepted on 13th July, by letter stating " please consider this letter as an official order based on your quotation of July 5, 1965 and our different telexes to which you have given your agreement ". The first promissory note for £23,500 was payable on 4th October 1965, the second one for £47,000 on 4th December 1965. When the first payment became due the defendant twice asked for and was granted further time in which to pay. On 27th October, the plaintiffs cabled the defendant that they were suspending all work on the contract. The defendant never paid the note or any of the others and work on the contract remained suspended. The plaintiffs sued on the first two promissory notes and obtained judgment under R.S.C., Ord. 14. On appeal,

Held: (i) since at the date when the first promissory note became due the plaintiffs had performed their contractual obligations there was no failure of consideration and they were entitled to payment of the first note (see p. 152, letter C, p. 153, letter H, and p. 154, letter I, post); however, after the suspension of work, the plaintiffs could not sue on the second promissory note, because they were only entitled to damages for breach of contract, if any; accordingly, the defendant ought to have leave to defend the action on the second promissory note (see p. 152, letter D, p. 153, letter H, and p. 154, letter I, post);

(ii) the request for the plaintiffs to invoice the goods as part of a rolling mill did not amount to a term in the contract; although, had there been such a term, it would have been illegal, nevertheless, it would also in all the circumstances, have been severable leaving the contract enforceable (see p. 152, letter H, p. 153, letters F and H, and p. 154, letter D, post);

(iii) in order to succeed on the defence of illegality the defendant had to show that the plaintiffs were aware of the illegal purpose of the falsification of the invoice and that they agreed actively to participate in that purpose so that goods could be illegally imported which would not otherwise be allowed to enter and there was no such evidence in this case (see p. 152, letter I, and p. 153, letters H and I, post).

Appeal allowed in part.

A   [As to illegality of contract under foreign law, see 8 Halsbury's Laws (3rd Edn.) 184, 185 para. 319.

As to failure of consideration on promissory notes see 3 Halsbury's Laws (3rd Edn.) 177, para. 293.]

Case referred to:

B   *Foster* v. *Driscoll, Lindsay* v. *Attfield, Lindsay* v. *Driscoll,* [1929] 1 K.B. 470; [1928] All E.R. Rep. 130; 98 L.J.K.B. 282; 140 L.T. 479; 6 Digest (Repl.) 65, *588.*

Appeal.

This was an appeal by the defendant, Selim Najjar, from an order of Roskill, J., dated 5th November 1968, dismissing the appeal of the defendant from an order of Master Diamond on the hearing of the summons under R.S.C., Ord. 14,

C   on 24th October 1968, that the defendant pay to the plaintiffs, Fielding and Platt, Ltd., the sum of £80,878 11s. 9d. The facts are set out in the judgment of Lord Denning, M.R.

The authority and the cases noted below* were cited during the argument in addition to the case referred to in the judgment of Lord Denning, M.R.

D   *John Wilmers, Q.C.,* and *P. C. R. Rountree* for the defendant.
C. H. L. Bathurst for the plaintiffs.

LORD DENNING, M.R.: The plaintiffs, Fielding and Platt, Ltd., are manufacturers of machinery. Their business is in Gloucester. In the middle of 1965 they entered into a contract with a Lebanese company called S.C.I.A.L.E., Aluminium of Lebanon. They agreed to make and sell to the Lebanese company

E   an aluminium extrusion press for a total sum of £235,000. The plant and equipment was to be delivered free on board at a British port. The time for delivery was 10½ months from 19th June 1965. Payment was to be made by six promissory notes given by the defendant, the managing director of the Lebanese company, Mr. Selim Najjar, personally; and he deposited shares, of his own, as security for the due payment of the promissory notes. The promissory notes were payable

F   at intervals during the progress of the work. The first four were payable whilst the plaintiffs were making the machinery in England. Thus the first note was payable on 4th October 1965, for £23,500; the second on 4th December 1965, for £47,000; the third on 4th February 1966, for £47,000; and the fourth on 4th April 1966, for another £47,000. The fifth note was payable on 4th June 1966, for £47,000, which was just about the time when the machinery was to be

G   delivered to the port. The sixth note, the final one, for £23,500, was payable on 4th August 1966.

On 4th October 1965, the first promissory note, for £23,500, fell due. It was not paid. The defendant apologised for not paying it. He asked for a few days' grace. He said that had been agreed. So be it. He was given a few days—indeed more than a few days. Still he did not pay. When the note was a fortnight

H   overdue he wrote on 18th October 1965: " It is my estimate that by the middle of next month all will be arranged and I will be able to proceed with the payments." He realised that his non-payment might result in delays on the English side, for he added: " Please remember that any delays on your part due to delayed payments will be acceptable." When the note was more than three weeks overdue, the plaintiffs decided to suspend work on the contract. On

I   27th October 1965, they cabled to the Lebanese company:

" We have today suspended all work on your contract with us and this includes notification to all our material suppliers that they must do no further work on this contract. We have been forced to take this action to comply with the requirements of our authorities. Our current financial commitment to material and equipment suppliers plus design and stock

*Byles on Bills of Exchange (22nd Edn.) p. 218; *Scott* v. *Gillmore* (1810), 3 Taunt. 226; *Regazzoni* v. *K. C. Sethia* (1944), *Ltd.* [1956] 2 All E.R. 487. [1956] 2 Q.B., 498.

material and labour charges, is extremely heavy. We trust you appreciate
that this is your liability. As a result of suspending all work you will appreciate that our delivery date will be considerably extended and the amount of
the delay will depend on the time taken for you to resolve your difficulties."

The defendant never paid the first promissory note or any of the others. He
never paid anything. In consequence, the plaintiffs suspended work on the contract, and it remained suspended. No further work was done on it. There were
negotiations for a revival of the contract, but they came to nothing.

Stopping there, it is quite plain to me that the defendant was liable to pay the
first of the promissory notes. We have repeatedly said in this court that a bill
of exchange or a promissory note is to be treated as cash. It is to be honoured
unless there is some good reason to the contrary. It is suggested that, on the
first note, there was a failure of consideration. That suggestion is quite unfounded.
The plaintiffs were getting on with their part of the contract. They were, they
say, ordering goods from their suppliers and getting on with the work. At any
rate, there is no evidence to the contrary; and, unless they were themselves in
default, they were clearly entitled to payment of the first note. The position as
to the second note is different. Before it fell due, the defendant said: " I cannot
pay "; and the plaintiffs replied: " We, therefore, suspend work." Seeing that
the plaintiffs had suspended work, they could not claim payment in full, but
at most damages. They could not sue on each note as it fell due—each of the
six—when they had suspended all work on the contract. So there is an available
defence on the second note. But not on the first note.

This brings me to the second point. In answer to the claim in both notes,
the defendant raises a defence of illegality. He says that it was his intention
to break the laws of the Lebanon and that the plaintiffs were parties to it. In
order to import the extrusion press into the Lebanon, he had to get an import
licence from the Lebanon authorities. He had already got a licence to import a
two million pound rolling mill, but he had not got a licence to bring in an extrusion press. His intention was to import it without a licence, and he says that
the plaintiffs agreed to help him to do so. The plaintiffs agreed, he says, to put
in a false invoice. He says: " I asked you to invoice the press as part of a rolling
mill, and you agreed to it, and, therefore, you cannot recover anything." That
defence does not commend itself to me. Here is a man who prays in aid his own
illegality—he admits he was trying to evade the laws of his own country—and
he seeks to implicate the plaintiffs in it.

In order for this to be any kind of defence, he must show first of all that the
contract contained a term that the plaintiffs were to give a false invoice; so that
it could not lawfully be performed. For if it would be lawfully performed (by
giving a correct invoice) the plaintiffs can certainly sue on it. I do not think
there was any such term. During the negotiations the Lebanese company did
ask the plaintiffs to invoice the press as " parts for rolling mill ". But this
request did not, as I read the correspondence, become a term of the contract.
The contract was concluded on 13th July 1965. And the only subsequent reference was contained later in the confirmation which the plaintiffs sent to the
Lebanese company. There was a long detailed description of the goods covering
many pages and then, in brackets, were the words (" to be invoiced as ' parts
for rolling mill ' "). That was a mere notification by the Lebanese company of
the way they wanted an invoice made out. It was not a term of the contract
itself. The plaintiffs would therefore quite justifiably refuse to give such invoice,
and insist on the contract being lawfully performed.

In the second place, even if it were a term, the defendant would have to show
that the plaintiffs were implicated in this illegality, that is that they had knowledge of it and were actively participating in it, see *Foster* v. *Driscoll, Lindsay* v.
Attfield, Lindsay v. *Driscoll* (1) per SANKEY, L.J. I can see no evidence worthy

(1) [1929] 1 K.B. 470 at p. 518; [1928] All E.R. Rep. 130 at pp. 146, 147.

A of the name to suggest that the plaintiffs knew of this illegality. The only evidence is contained in a cable about the import licence. On 16th June 1965, the plaintiffs stated that they were agreeable to the proposed contract " subject to evidence of satisfactory importing licence arrangements ". The Lebanese company replied:

B " Concerning our import licence, we have a regular import licence for a total amount of two million sterling, for a complete aluminium plant. This licence is more than what we require for an extrusion press, and since we don't want to lose our right for the remaining amount, we want the material to be invoiced as ' parts for rolling mill '. This of course is for local consumption. We discussed these details with your representative here, and will make sure that you do the correct thing when the time comes. Please bear in mind that few items (just any thing) of the total order should be in Beirut

C the first week of October the latest, because our licence is valid until October 24, 1965, and before that date something should have arrived."

I do not think that cable was enough to give the plaintiffs knowledge of the illegality. It only shows that the Lebanese company thought it convenient, for local consumption, to have the machines invoiced as parts for a rolling mill, instead of the more accurate description of an aluminium extrusion press.

D I cannot help remarking that the defendant seems to have a special fondness for false invoices. At a later stage he suggested that the plaintiffs should give an invoice for only half the cost, instead of the whole; so as to save customs duties. He also suggested that the plaintiffs should write a false letter (which he drafted) to show the Lebanese customs authorities. The plaintiffs very properly

E did not agree to those suggestions. And when the matter finally came to a head, the plaintiffs firmly said: " We must invoice the goods correctly." I know there is a suggestion in the affidavit of the defendant that the plaintiffs were implicated, but, in the face of the documents, I see no substance in this suggestion.

There is another point: even if there was a term that these goods should be

F invoiced falsely in order to deceive the Lebanese authorities, I do not think it would render the whole contract void. That term would be void for illegality. But it can clearly be severed from the rest of the contract. It can be rejected, leaving the rest of the contract good and enforceable. The plaintiffs would be entitled, despite the illegal term, to deliver the goods f.o.b. English port, and send a true and accurate invoice to the Lebanese buyer. The Lebanese buyer could

G not refuse the goods by saying " I stipulated for a false invoice ". He could not rely on his own iniquity so as to refuse payment.

In my opinion, therefore, the defence of illegality is clearly bad. I would allow judgment to be entered on the first note and for the interest thereon; and give leave to defend as to the second.

DAVIES, L.J.: I agree with the result reached by Lord Denning, M.R.,
H and I do not propose to add anything.

WIDGERY, L.J.: I also agree. I find each of the main issues in this case one of some difficulty and I am much indebted to counsel for the defendant for his argument; but in the end I have concluded that they are sufficiently determined to justify judgment under R.S.C., Ord. 14 in respect of the amount of

I the earlier promissory note. So far as the allegation of illegality is concerned, there are I think two independent and sufficient answers to it. First, in order to succeed on this question, the defendant must show that the plaintiffs were aware of the illegal purpose in the falsification of the invoice and that they agreed actively to participate in that purpose so that goods could be illegally imported into the Lebanon which would not otherwise be allowed to enter. The only basis on which it is said that the plaintiffs at any material time had knowledge of that illegal purpose is the telex message of 18th June from the Lebanese company, to which Lord Denning, M.R., has referred. If I may just repeat again

the essential words, they were replying to an enquiry from the plaintiffs as to their   **A**
import licence, and they stated:

> " We have a regular import licence for a total amount of two million
> sterling, and for a complete aluminium plant.   This licence is more than
> what we require for an extrusion press and since we don't want to lose our
> right for the remaining amount, we want the material to be invoiced as ' parts
> for rolling mill '.   This, of course, is for local consumption . . ."   **B**

When that was first read to us, for my part I found it quite incomprehensible,
and it is not until one gets further in the correspondence that the real point of
it becomes clear. The plaintiffs, of course, had to judge the legality or illegality
of what was proposed, without the benefit of the correspondence which developed
months later as to the terms of that telex message. I can see no reason what-   **C**
ever to suppose that the plaintiffs should see more in that message than that the
invoice was to indicate that the goods were part of a larger matter, which in
itself would not involve any illegality that I can see. It is only later that one
appreciates that the character of the goods may be of some relevance, and if
the plaintiffs did agree to invoice the goods as part of a larger whole, I cannot
for my part see that that would involve them in any illegality sufficient to   **D**
excuse the defendant from liability in this case. Alternatively, as LORD DENNING,
M.R., has said, I am of the opinion that there was no term in this contract
requiring the plaintiffs to invoice the goods as part of a rolling mill. The chief
contractual document is a formal and lengthy quotation which the plaintiffs
submitted to the defendant setting out details of the machine to be supplied;   **E**
and on 13th July the Lebanese company accepted that quotation in these words:

> " please consider this letter as an official order based on your quotation
> of July 5, 1965 and our different telexes to which you have given your agree-
> ment."

At that point there was nothing in the contractual documents to imply an   **F**
obligation on the plaintiffs to invoice the goods as part of a rolling mill. Counsel
for the defendant has referred to the telexes mentioned in that letter, but there
was no agreement by the plaintiffs to any telex involving a special form of
invoicing. When the plaintiffs received that acceptance of their offer, they sent
a formal and detailed confirmation; and it is to be observed that under the
terms of their agreement no contract was to be binding on them until that   **G**
confirmation had been given. In my judgment, that was no more than a confirmation of that which was already agreed, and it would be quite unreal to regard
it as a counter-offer containing a new term whereby the goods were to be invoiced
as part of a rolling mill.

On the second issue, namely, the failure of consideration, for which the notes   **H**
were given, my opinion is that these notes were given by the defendant in consideration of the plaintiffs entering into the agreement with the Lebanese company
and carrying out that agreement. It is arguable that if counsel for the defendant
can sustain his contention that the plaintiffs repudiated the contract in November
and that that repudiation was accepted by the Lebanese company, then perhaps
it can be shown that liability on bills maturing after the date of the repudiation   **I**
had itself been determined; but, like LORD DENNING, M.R., I can see no possible
ground on which it can be said that the consideration for the first bill, which
would mature in October 1965, at a time when the plaintiffs were in no way
in default, can have been rendered wholly ineffective by virtue of that which
followed.

I also would accordingly allow the appeal to the extent that judgment should
be entered only in respect of the amount of the first bill and interest thereon.

A   *Appeal allowed in part; judgment to be for the first promissory note and interest
thereon, at the agreed sum of £27,138 10s. 5d. only. Leave to defend with regard to
the balance of the claim. Leave to appeal to the House of Lords refused.*

Solicitors: *Fox & Gibbons* (for the defendant); *Ashurst, Morris Crisp & Co.*
(for the plaintiffs).

[*Reported by* F. GUTTMAN, ESQ., *Barrister-at-Law.*]

B

THE TOJO MARU.

N. V. WIJSMULLER *v.* OWNERS OF MOTOR TANKER TOJO MARU

C   (HER CARGO AND FREIGHT).

[PROBATE, DIVORCE AND ADMIRALTY DIVISION (Willmer, L. J., sitting as
an additional judge), December 12, 13, 16, 17, 18, 1968, January 13, 1969.]

*Shipping—Salvage—Award—Amount—Counterclaim by shipowner—Credit in
counterclaim for reduction in salvage award by reason of negligence giving rise
D   to counterclaim.*

*Shipping—Limitation of liability—Salvage work—Damage to salved ship caused
by diver from salvors' tug—Whether Merchant Shipping Act 1894 (57 & 58
Vict. c. 60), s. 503 (1) (d), as amended by Merchant Shipping (Liability of
Shipowners and Others) Act 1958 (6 & 7 Eliz. 2 c. 62), applied.*

*Set-off—Cross-claim—Equitable right of set-off—Counterclaim by owners of
E   salved vessel for damage done by salvors' diver—Right of limitation restricting
amount of counterclaim.*

The Tojo Maru was damaged in a collision with another ship. Salvage
services were rendered by the contractors under the Lloyd's standard form
of salvage agreement. In the course of repairs V., a diver, operating from
the contractors' tug, entered the water intending with his Cox bolt gun to
F   fix a patch which had been prepared to cover and make watertight a hole in
the side of The Tojo Maru; he fired a bolt through shell plating into one of
the cargo tanks, which had not, as intended, been ballasted down so as to
make it gas-free. As a result there was a violent explosion, followed by other
explosions and a fire which caused substantial additional damage to the
ship. In the subsequent arbitration proceedings the arbitrator held that the
G   owners were entitled to counterclaim against the contractors in respect of
the damage caused to The Tojo Maru. The contractors sought to limit
their liability under s. 503* of the Merchant Shipping Act 1894, as amended
by s. 2 (1) of the Merchant Shipping (Liability of Shipowners and Others)
Act 1958, on the basis of the tonnage of their tug from which V. had been
working.

H   **Held:** (i) the arbitrator properly left the damage done to The Tojo Maru
by V. to be dealt with by way of counterclaim (see p. 167, letter E, post);
nevertheless, some credit ought to have been given against the owners'
claim in respect of the amount by which the contractors' proper remuneration was found to be less than it would otherwise have been because of the
reduction in the salved value (see p. 167, letter F, post);

I   Dictum of SCOTT, L.J., in *Anglo-Saxon Petroleum Co., Ltd.* v. *Damant*
([1947] 2 All E.R. at p. 468) applied.

(ii) the contractors could not bring themselves within the scope of
s. 503 (1) (d) of the Merchant Shipping Act 1894, as amended, since the act
of V. was not the act of a person on board the contractors' tug, nor when
he fired the Cox bolt gun into the side of The Tojo Maru, was he performing
an act in the management of the contractors' tug (see p. 168, letter G, and

* Section 503 (as amended by s. 2 (1) of the Act of 1958), so far as material, is set out
at p. 167, letter I, to p. 168, letter A, post.

p. 170, letter D, post); accordingly, the contractors were liable in full for **A**
the damage caused by V. to The Tojo Maru (see p. 170, letter E, post).

Dictum of ASHWORTH, J., in *Moore* v. *Metcalf Motor Coasters, Ltd.* ([1958]
2 Lloyd's Rep. at p. 189) applied.

Dictum of PILCHER, J., in *The Athelvictor* ([1946] P. at p. 51) disapproved.
(iii) assuming (contrary to holding (ii) supra) that the contractors had been
entitled to limit their liability under s. 503 (1), the owners had an equitable **B**
right to set-off their claim against the contractors' claim (see p. 172, letter
A, post); the amount to be set-off, however, would have been the amount
of the limited sum (see p. 172, letter C, post).

Dictum of MORRIS, L.J., in *Hanak* v. *Green* ([1958] 2 All E.R. at p. 150)
applied.

Stoomvaart Maatschappij Nederland v. *Peninsular and Oriental Steam* **C**
Navigation Co. ([1881–85] All E.R. Rep. 342) distinguished.

Per WILLMER, L.J.: the phrase " on board the ship " occurs in s. 503 (1) (*b*)
of the Merchant Shipping Act 1894 where its meaning is plainly restricted to
goods, etc., physically on board the ship, other goods situated elsewhere being
subject to para. (*d*), where the words are " act or omission of any other person
(whether on board the ship or not)". Here again the phrase can only refer **D**
to a person physically on board. When the same phrase is again used at
the end of para. (*d*) in relation to " any other act or omission ", it must as a
matter of construction bear the same meaning as in the previous passages
(see p. 168, letter H, post).

Per WILLMER, L.J.: the word " management " in s. 503 (1) (*d*) of the
Merchant Shipping Act 1894, as amended, must be read in conjunction with **E**
" navigation ", which can only refer to navigation of the ship as a whole.
Similarly, management must refer to management of the ship as a whole, or
at least management of some integral part of the ship (see p. 169, letter E,
post).

[As to general principles of salvage awards, see 35 HALSBURY'S LAWS (3rd **F**
Edn.) 749, para. 1138; as to misconduct and negligence of salvors, see ibid.,
751, paras. 1144, 1145; and for cases on the subject, see 42 DIGEST (Repl.)
1018, 1019, *8214-8220, 8223-8228*, 1021, 1022, *8262-8267, 8277*, 1024, *8295-8299*.

As to limitation of liability in shipping cases, see 35 HALSBURY'S LAWS (3rd
Edn.) 771-775, paras. 1185, 1186, 1190; and for cases on the subject, see 42
DIGEST (Repl.) 1070, *8854*, 1072, *8876*, 1079, *8920*. **G**

As to set-off generally, see 34 HALSBURY'S LAWS (3rd Edn.) 396-398, paras.
673, 674; as to counterclaims, see ibid, 410-413, paras, 719 to 724; and for
cases on the subject, see 40 DIGEST (Repl.) 406, *2, 3*, 443, 444, *304-316*.

For the Merchant Shipping Act 1894, s. 503, see 23 HALSBURY'S STATUTES
(2nd Edn.) 656.

For the Merchant Shipping (Liability of Shipowners and Others) Act 1958, **H**
s. 2, see 38 HALSBURY'S STATUTES (2nd Edn.) 1093.]

Cases referred to:
Alenquer, The, The Rene, [1955] 1 W.L.R. 263; [1955] 1 Lloyd's Rep. 101, 42
    Digest (Repl.) 1022, *8277*.
Anglo-Saxon Petroleum Co., Ltd. v. *Damant, Anglo-Saxon Petroleum Co., Ltd.* **I**
    v. *Regem*, [1947] 2 All E.R. 465; [1947] K.B. 794; [1948] L.J.R. 153;
    80 Lloyd, L.R. 459; 16 Digest (Repl.) 269, *371*.
Athelvictor, The, [1946] P. 42; 115 L.J.P. 17; 175 L.T. 256; 78 Lloyd, L.R.
    529; 42 Digest (Repl.) 1070, *8854*.
Atlas, The (1862), Lush. 518; 31 L.J.P.M. & A. 210; 6 L.T. 737; 42 Digest
    (Repl.) 972, *7609*.
Basten v. *Butter* (1806), 7 East, 479; 103 E.R. 185; Digest (Cont. Vol. B)
    35, *289t*.

A   *C. S. Butler, The, The Baltic,* (1874), L.R. 4 A. & E. 178; 43 L.J. Adm. 17; 30 L.T. 475; 2 Asp. M.L.C. 237; 42 Digest (Repl.) 1022, *8276.*

Cape Packet, The (1848), 3 Wm. Rob. 122; 8 L.T. 582; 42 Digest (Repl.) 1019, *8228.*

Charles Adolphe, The (1856), Sw. 153; 166 E.R. 1069; 42 Digest (Repl.) 976, *7654.*

B   *Chieftain, The* (1863), Brown. & Lush. 104; 32 L.J.P. M. & A. 106; 8 L.T. 120; 167 E.R. 316; 42 Digest (Repl.) 1090, *9031.*

Dwina, The, [1892] P. 58; 61 L.J.P. 71; 66 L.T. 862; 7 Asp. M.L.C. 173; 42 Digest (Repl.) 1018, *8220.*

Everard (F. T.) & Sons, Ltd., v. *London and Thames Haven Oil Wharves, Ltd., The Anonity,* [1961] 1 Lloyd's Rep. 203; *on appeal* [1961] 2 Lloyd's

C   Rep. 117; 42 Digest (Repl.) 1072, *8875.*

Glengyle, The [1898] P. 97; 67 L.J.P. 12; 78 L.T. 139; 8 Asp. M.L.C. 341; *on appeal,* H. L. Sub nom. *Glengyle (Owners), Cargo and Freight* v. *Neptune Salvage Co., Ltd.; The Glengyle,* [1898] A.C. 519; 67 L.J.P. 87; 78 L.T. 801; 8 Asp. M.L.C. 436; 42 Digest (Repl.) 1016, *8188.*

Goulandris Brothers, Ltd. v. *B. Goldman & Sons, Ltd.,* [1957] 3 All E.R. 100;

D   [1958] 1 Q.B. 74; [1957] 2 W.L.R. 596; [1957] 2 Lloyd's Rep. 207; 41 Digest (Repl.) 520, *2946.*

Hanak v. *Green,* [1958] 2 All E.R. 141; [1958] 2 Q.B. 9; [1958] 2 W.L.R. 755; Digest (Cont. Vol. A.) 1318, *117a.*

Mondel v. *Steel* (1841), 8 M. & W. 858; [1835-42] All E.R. Rep. 511; 10 L.J. Ex. 426; 151 E.R. 1288; 39 Digest (Repl.) 583, *1054.*

E   *Moore* v. *Metcalf Motor Coasters, Ltd.,* [1958] 2 Lloyd's Rep. 179; *on appeal* [1959] 1 Lloyd's Rep. 264.

Perla, The (1857), Sw. 230; 8 L.T. 612; 166 E.R. 1111; 42 Digest (Repl.) 1018, *8217.*

Prehn v. *Bailey, The Ettrick,* (1881), 6 P.D. 127; 45 L.T. 399; 4 Asp. M.L.C. 465; 42 Digest (Repl.) 1044, *8633.*

F   *R.* v. *Lynch and Jones,* [1898] 1 Q.B. 61; 67 L.J.Q.B. 59; 77 L.T. 568; 8 Asp. M.L.C. 363; 42 Digest (Repl.) 721, *4730.*

Stoomvaart Maatschappij Nederland v. *Peninsular and Oriental Steam Navigation Co.,* (1882), 7 App. Cas. 795; [1881-85] All E.R. Rep. 342; 52 L.J.P. 1; 47 L.T. 198; 4 Asp. M.L.C. 567; 42 Digest (Repl.) 1079, *8920.*

Sydney, The, [1916] P. 300; 86 L.J.P. 24; 115 L.T. 638; 13 Asp. M.L.C. 521;

G   37 Digest (Repl.) 572, *1513.*

Teal, The (1949), 82 Lloyd L.R. 414; 42 Digest (Repl.) 1072, *8876.*

Special Case Stated.

This was a Special Case stated by JOHN NAISBY, ESQ., Q.C., in an arbitration held in pursuance of a contract on Lloyd's standard form of salvage agreement dated 2nd May 1968. By an agreement dated 28th February 1965 made on the

H standard form of salvage agreement approved and published by the Committee of Lloyd's and known as "No Cure—No Pay" it was agreed amongst other things between Captain Tsurumi Higo for and on behalf of the owners of the motor tanker The Tojo Maru her cargo and freight and Captain T. P. Hoek for and on behalf of N.V. Bureau Wijsmuller ("the contractors") that the latter should use their best endeavours to salve The Tojo Maru and her cargo and take

I them into a safe port or other place to be thereafter agreed with the master. The contractors salved The Tojo Maru and the majority of her cargo and during the course of the salvage services explosions occurred in the vessel causing damage thereto. The agreement provided that the remuneration for the salvage services should be decided by arbitration in the manner therein set out and prescribed, and in it was provided that any other difference arising out of the agreement or the operations thereunder should be referred to arbitration in the same way. The owners of The Tojo Maru counterclaimed for damages sustained by them as a result of the explosions, and under the provisions of the agreement

the Committee of Lloyd's appointed JOHN NAISBY, ESQ, Q.C. as sole arbitrator, **A**
who made the following award in the form of a Special Case.

The following facts were found: 1. The Tojo Maru was a motor tanker of
25,104 tons gross 692 feet in length and 95 feet in beam built in 1962. When
the salvage services began she was laden with 267,639 barrels of crude oil.
2. The salved value of the vessel was £1,280,627, that of the freight at risk
£49,248, and that of her cargo £142,348. 3. When the arbitration began the **B**
parties represented before the arbitration were: (i) the contractors; (ii) the
owners of the ship and freight; and (iii) the owners of the cargo. On the 6th day of
the arbitration he was informed that the contractor's claim against the owners of
the cargo had been settled. The value on which he had to make his award was
therefore £1,329,875 though he had to bear in mind that the contractors were
entitled to receive remuneration in respect of their salvage of cargo of a value **C**
of £142,348. 4. The contractors employed two of their vessels: the motor tug
Groningen which was on salvage station in the Persian Gulf some 180 miles
distant from the casualty. She was a tug of 598 tons gross 158 feet in length
and 34 feet in beam fitted with engines of 2950 H.P.I. and of the value of £400,000.
The motor tug Jacob Van Heemskerck of 658 tons gross 172 feet in length and
35 feet in beam fitted with engines of 5375 H.P.I. and of the value of £500,000. **D**
Both tugs carried a considerable amount of salvage equipment. 5. On 25th
February 1965 The Tojo Maru shortly after loading her cargo at Mena al Ahmadi
was in collision with a vessel named Fina Italia. As a result of the collision
The Tojo Maru sustained extensive damage to her port side in the way of no. 3 fuel
tank which was open to the sea. The engines of The Tojo Maru were aft and at
the forward end of the engine-room was no. 3 fuel oil tank, forward of that was a **E**
cofferdam and forward of the cofferdam the no. 11 cargo tanks divided port,
centre and starboard. The engine-room was flooded and there was leakage into
the cofferdam and no. 11 port tank. 6. On 26th February The Groningen arrived
at The Tojo Maru but her services were not accepted until the 28th February
whereupon a party of eight including two salvage inspectors and a chief diver
named Vis with a quantity of gear were sent by air from Holland arriving at **F**
The Tojo Maru on 2nd March. 7. The main items in the salvage plan were:
(i) Stop the leaks from no. 3 fuel oil tank into the engine-room. (ii) Pump the
water out of the engine-room by stages taking preservative measures to minimise
damage to the engine parts as they came above water. (iii) Construct a steel
patch and place it over the wound in the side of the vessel and make it watertight. (iv) Thereafter to tow the vessel to a repair port for which purpose it **G**
was decided to discharge the cargo where the vessel was. 8. By 20th March the
cargo had been discharged. On 4th April The Jacob Van Heemskerck arrived
and relieved The Groningen which left. By 10th April the salvage plan had
progressed to the stage when the patch was in position hanging down the side of
the ship but not yet fixed. It was to be secured by chains from the patch athwart-
ships across the fuel oil tank and bolted to the shell plating. The Tojo Maru was **H**
not gas-free and the plan was to haul the patch as close as possible to the ship,
ballast down the no. 3 fuel oil tank, the cofferdam and no. 11 port tank and then
bolt the patch firmly into place. 9. On the morning of 11th April the patch
was still being hauled as close as possible to the ship by men in the no. 3 fuel
oil tank and neither that tank, the cofferdam nor no. 11 port tank had been
ballasted down. The contractors' chief diver, Mr. Vis, contrary to the orders he had **I**
received proceeded to bolt the patch into place by firing a bolt from a Cox bolt
gun through the shell plating of The Tojo Maru into no. 11 port tank. The
result was an explosion inside the vessel followed by other explosions causing
very substantial damage in several of the tanks, and rupturing the deck on the
port side aft over a considerable distance. 10. The action of Mr. Vis was a breach
of the duty owed by the contractors to the owners of the vessel and was negligent
and was the sole cause of the explosions. The ensuing damage was foreseeable.
11. The absence of fault or privity on the part of the contractors was established.

A 12. As a result of the explosions fire broke out on The Tojo Maru and salvage assistance had to be taken for its extinction. 13. For nearly two days after the explosions the salvage by the contractors was interrupted. Further work was required to make The Tojo Maru fit for towage to a repair port and the owners had to decide what that port was to be. They finally decided on Kobe. It was agreed that when the vessel was ready for towage she should be towed as far as **B** Singapore by the contractors and that on safe arrival at Singapore the services should be deemed to have ended when the towage to that port began the contractors being paid an agreed lump price of £24,000 for the towage. 14. By 18.00 hours on 24th April The Tojo Maru was ready for towage to Singapore but as some experts were coming out to Kuwait from the repair yard in Japan in order to survey the damage and enable preparations for its repair to be made during **C** the towage it was agreed to delay the towage until after their survey. 15. About midday on 27th April the towage began and was successfully accomplished. The contractors' salvage services were therefore deemed to have terminated on 27th April having lasted about 59 days; apart from the incident on the morning of 11th April they were well and skilfully rendered. 16. The damages suffered by the owners of The Tojo Maru as a result of the said explosions amounted to **D** £331,767 as converted into sterling at the time they were incurred that is before devaluation of the pound sterling in November 1967. Of this sum £202,514 was in respect of the repairs rendered necessary by the explosions. 17. The contractors' actual out-of-pocket expenses but not including anything for the costs of running the tugs or over-head costs were £44,600 as converted into sterling before the devaluation of sterling but at $\frac{1}{6}$th more if calculated at the **E** present rate. 18. The amount of the limitation fund of The Jacob Van Heemskerck was agreed at £10,725 11s. but it was in dispute whether the contractors were entitled to limit their liability. 19. The proper remuneration for the services of the contractors to ship and freight was £125,000. 20. When diver Vis fired the Cox bolt gun he was under water having descended from the tug. The gun was not part of the regular equipment of the tug but was an **F** appliance provided by the contractors for use in the salvage services. Some salvage tugs do carry such a gun as part of their regular equipment. The log of The Jacob Van Heemskerck contained an entry on 4th April, the day of the tug's arrival, that certain persons including the two salvage inspectors and Mr. Vis were signed on as additional crew. The arbitrator found that Mr. Vis was a temporary member of the crew of the tug and was operating from the tug with **G** an appliance which temporarily formed part of the tug's equipment. 21. The arbitrator was requested by both parties to state a Case for the opinion of the court on a number of points of law. Some of these seemed to him to involve the same point of law but efforts on his part to get an agreed wording on some of the points proved unsuccessful. He, therefore, stated the questions for the court as requested by the respective parties. The answers to these questions raised a **H** number of possible alterations to the amount of the award. He, therefore, felt compelled to make one award only but if the court was of opinion that his findings on one or more of these questions were wrong the court might desire to remit the award for reconsideration under s. 22 of the Arbitration Act 1950. 22. The questions for the court and the arbitrator's holdings thereon were:

At the request of the contractors. Whether on the facts found and on the true **I** construction of the contract:

A. The contractors were in breach of their contract.—The arbitrator held that they were.

B. The owners of The Tojo Maru were entitled by any term of the submission to counterclaim for damages caused by the breach of contract.—The arbitrator held that they were.

C. (i) The breach of contract and damage caused thereby and/or (ii) that part of the counterclaim which affected the salved value of the vessel should be taken into account in assessing the salvage remuneration.—Insofar as the breach of

contract and the damage caused thereby reduced the salved value of the vessel A
and as the salved value of the vessel was one of the factors to be taken into
account in assessing the salvage remuneration the arbitrator held that to that
extent it was right that they should be taken into account when assessing the
proper remuneration for the salvage services and he had done so.

D. The counterclaim should be reduced: (i) arithmetically namely by the
amount, if any, by which the award was reduced as aforesaid; or (ii) by B
such greater amount as the arbitrator might determine.—There was no
settled practice how claim and counterclaim should be dealt with in cases of this
kind. The two alternative methods which seemed to be most applicable to this
case were: (i) make one award on the claim and one award on the counterclaim;
(ii) make one award on the counterclaim having reduced the amount thereof by
the amount that would have been awarded on the claim. The arbitrator held C
insofar as it was a matter of law that the latter was the proper method to use in
this case. This produced a balance in favour of the owners of £206,767.

E. The defence of equitable set-off could operate to counteract the statutory
right of the contractors to limit their liability in damages.—The arbitrator held
that it could not, but the real questions were whether the right to limit liability
arose on the original claim for damages or on the balance after the counterclaim had D
been taken into account and whether the right to an equitable set-off had been
established. He held also that where the right to an equitable set-off had been
established the right to limit liability was in respect of the balance after such
set-off had been taken into account and that in this case the right to an equitable
set-off had been established.

F. The counterclaim should be reduced so as to allow for the contingency E
existing at the date of the explosion that the salvage services would not prove
successful.—The arbitrator held that no such reduction should be made.

At the request of the owners of The Tojo Maru.

(I) Whether it was right in law to enhance the award beyond what he would
have awarded if there had been no alteration in the rate of exchange since the
date when the services terminated in order to take account of the devaluation F
of the pound sterling which had occurred since that date.—The arbitrator held
that devaluation could be a proper factor to be taken into account in assessing a
salvage award just as the cost of living and the variation in the cost of maintaining and running salvage tugs could be taken into account. He further held
that if taken into account the result was not necessarily to increase the award
by the difference between the two rates of exchange. He further held that in G
all the circumstances of this case it would be inequitable to take the devaluation
of sterling into account and he had not done so.

(II) Whether on the true construction of the contract the contractors owed
the owners a duty of care in carrying out salvage operations on The Tojo Maru
under the provisions of the contract.—The arbitrator held that they did. H

(III) (a) Whether on the facts found and on the true construction of s. 503
of the Merchant Shipping Act 1894, as amended, the contractors had shown that
their liability to the owners was a liability in damages arising from an occurrence
specified in the section.—The arbitrator held that they had.

(b) If not whether on the facts found the contractors had shown that they
were entitled to limit their liability to the owners under any other provisions of I
the Merchant Shipping Acts 1894 to 1958 relating to limitation of liability.—Did
not arise.

(IV) (a) Whether on the facts found and on the proper holdings of law relating
to liability and limitation of liability the owners were entitled to any or all of the
following relief: (i) Forfeiture or diminution of the amount of salvage which
would otherwise have been awarded to the contractors: (ii) Set-off, equitable
set-off or other equitable defence: (iii) Damages.—The arbitrator held that the
owners were entitled to set-off against their claim for damages the amount of

A salvage which would otherwise have been awarded and that their damages should be reduced accordingly, namely to £206,767.

(b) Whether if the owners were entitled to damages in addition to one or both other kinds of relief set out in (a) above, the damages should be reduced to the extent of the saving resulting to the owners from the application of such other kind or kinds of relief.—The arbitrator held that they should be so reduced as in **B** (a) above.

The arbitrator concluded that he awarded and adjudged that the contractors should pay to the owners of The Tojo Maru the sum of £10,725 11s. with interest thereon at 5½ per cent. per annum from 6th June 1965 until payment to the Committee of Lloyd's. He further awarded and directed that the contractors should bear their own costs of the arbitration up to and including 25th January **C** 1968 and that the owners of The Tojo Maru should bear their own costs of the arbitration and should pay to the contractors one-half of the costs incurred by the contractors subsequent to 25th January 1968 and that the contractors and the owners of The Tojo Maru each pay one-half of the costs and/or fees charged by the Committee of Lloyd's for their services and of this his award amounting to £3,209 1s. and he further directed that unless the Special Case was set down for **D** hearing before the court within six weeks of the publication of his award, the award should stand.

The authorities and the cases noted below* were cited during the argument in addition to those referred to in the judgment.

E *R. A. MacCrindle, Q.C., Gerald Darling, Q.C.* and *Anthony Evans* for the contractors.
Michael Kerr, Q.C., J. Franklin Willmer, Q.C., and *N. A. Phillips* for the owners.

Cur. adv. vult.

13th January. **WILLMER, L.J.,** read the following judgment. This case comes before me on an award in the form of a Special Case stated by John Naisby, Esq. Q.C., in an arbitration held in pursuance of a contract on Lloyd's **F** standard form of salvage agreement made between N. V. Bureau Wijsmuller (to whom I will refer hereafter as the " contractors ") and the owners of The Tojo Maru, her cargo and freight. We are now only concerned with the owners of the ship and freight (to whom I will refer hereafter as the " owners "), the contractors having reached an amicable settlement of their claim against the cargo-owners.

G

---

* 14 Halsbury's Laws (3rd Edn.) 634, 636; The Supreme Court Practice, 1967, Vol. 2, pp. 268, 269, 844, 845; Maxwell's Interpretation of Statutes (11th Edn.), pp. 275, 285; Kennedy on Civil Salvage (4th Edn.), pp. 140, 184, 187, 200; Roscoe's Admiralty Practice (5th Edn.), pp. 156, 158, 232; Russell on Arbitration (17th Edn.), p. 386; 2 British Shipping Laws (11th Edn.), para. 207; 4 British Shipping Laws (11th Edn.), paras. 155, 1286; 11 British Shipping Laws (6th Edn.), paras. 800, **H** 1752 to 1755; *Green v. Farmer* (1768), 4 Burr. 2214; *Piggott v. Williams* (1821), 6 Madd. 95; *Gale v. Laurie* (1826), 5. B & C. 156; *The Duke of Manchester* (1847), 6 Moo. P.C.C. 90; *The Magdalen* (1861), 31 L.J.P.M. & A. 22; *Wahlberg v. Young* (1876), 45 L.J.Q.B. 783; *Young v. Kitchen* (1878), 3 Ex.D. 127; *The Yan Yuen* (1883), 8 P.D. 147; *The Cheerful* (1885), 11 P.D. 3; *The Bernina* (1886), 12 P.D. 36; *Wilson, Sons & Co.* v, *Xantho (Cargo Owners)*, (1887), 12 App. Cas. 503; [1886-90] All E.R. Rep. 212; *Newfoundland Govt.* v. *Newfoundland Ry. Co.* (1888), 13 App. Cas. 199; *Bankes v. Jarvis,* **I** [1903] 1 K.B. 549; [1900-03] All E.R. Rep. 656; *The Vigilant,* [1921] P. 312; *Ruapehu (Owners)* v. *R. and H. Green and Silley Weir, Ltd., The Ruapehu,* [1927] A.C. 523; [1927] All E.R. Rep. 564; *Gosse Millerd, Ltd.* v. *Canadian Govt. Merchant Marine, Ltd., The Canadian Highlander,* [1928] 1 K.B. 717; [1929] A.C. 223; [1928] All E.R. Rep. 97; *Young v. Merchants' Marine Insurance Co., Ltd.,* [1932] 2 K.B. 705; [1932] All E.R. Rep. 928; *The Kafiristan,* [1937] 3 All E.R. 747; sub nom. *The Beaverford (Owners)* v. *The Kafiristan (Owners),* [1938] A.C. 136; *The Delphinula* (1946), 79 Lloyd L.R. 611; *Morgan & Son, Ltd.* v. *S. Martin Johnson & Co., Ltd.,* [1948] 2 All E.R. 196; [1949] 1 K.B. 107; *Susan V. Luckenbach (Owners)* v. *Admiralty Comrs.,* [1951] 1 All E.R. 753; [1951] P. 197; *Hale v. Victoria Plumming Co., Ltd. and En-Tout-Cas Co., Ltd.,* [1966] 2 All E.R. 672; [1966] 2 Q.B. 746.

The salvage services the subject of the contract were rendered in the Persian **A**
Gulf in the months of February to April 1965. On 25th February, The Tojo Maru,
a motor tanker of 25,104 tons gross, had just loaded a cargo of crude oil at
Mena al Ahmadi when she was involved in a serious collision with a vessel
called The Fina Italia. In consequence of the collision The Tojo Maru received
extensive damage to her port side in the way of no. 3 fuel tank, which became
open to the sea. This tank is immediately forward of the engine-room, which **B**
was also flooded because of damage to the bulkhead. Forward of no. 3 fuel tank
is a cofferdam, beyond which is no. 11 cargo tank. There was leakage both into
the cofferdam and into no. 11 cargo tank. The contractors' tug The Groningen
arrived on the scene on the next day, and on 28th February the salvage agreement was signed by the master of The Tojo Maru on behalf of the owners and
by the master of The Groningen on behalf of the contractors. By the terms **C**
of the contract, which was in the usual form, the contractors agreed to use their
best endeavours to salve The Tojo Maru.

The work that had to be done in pursuance of the contract may be summarised
under the following headings: (a) Stopping the leaks from no. 3 fuel tank into
the engine-room; (b) Pumping out the engine-room and taking steps to minimise
the damage to the engines: (c) Discharging the cargo: (d) Constructing and **D**
fitting a patch over the wound in the side of the vessel so as to make her watertight: (e) Preparing the vessel for towage to Singapore—which in the event was
done under a separate contract and separately paid for.

On 2nd March a team of salvage experts sent out from Holland by the contractors arrived on the scene, and this team included two salvage inspectors and
a chief diver called Vis, together with a certain amount of salvage equipment. **E**
By 20th March the cargo had been discharged and removed to a place of safety.
On 4th April, The Groningen was replaced by another tug belonging to the
contractors called The Jacob Van Heemskerck. By 10th April the patch had
been constructed, towed out to the ship and secured by chains to the side of the
ship ready to be fixed. On 11th April the diver, Mr. Vis, descended into the water
armed with a Cox bolt gun for the purpose of fixing the patch in position. He **F**
proceeded to fire a bolt through the shell plating into no. 11 cargo tank.   Unhappily that tank had not, as intended, been ballasted down so as to render it
gas-free. The result was a violent explosion, followed by further explosions and
a fire, which caused very substantial additional damage to the ship.   This
involved the necessity for carrying out additional repair work before the vessel
could be made ready for the towage, and resulted in delay.   The towage to **G**
Singapore did not in consequence start until 27th April; but the voyage was
thereafter successfully accomplished.

The learned arbitrator held that under the contract the contractors owed the
owners a duty of care in carrying out the salvage operations. He held that the
act of Mr. Vis in firing the bolt when he did constituted a breach of that duty.
He found that the act of Mr. Vis was the sole cause of the explosions and fire, **H**
and that the resulting damage was foreseeable. He found that apart from the
incident of 11th April the services of the contractors were well and skilfully
rendered. There is no longer any issue as to any of these matters. The learned
arbitrator further held that, insofar as the damage resulting from the act of
Mr. Vis reduced the salved value of The Tojo Maru, it was a factor to be taken
into account in assessing the proper amount of salvage remuneration due to the **I**
contractors. He stated that he had in fact taken this factor into account, though
he did not state by what amount (if any) he reduced his assessment of the proper
remuneration for the services. He found the salved value of The Tojo Maru
and her freight to be £1,329,875. On that value, after finding that the contractors incurred out of pocket expenses amounting to £44,600, he assessed the
proper remuneration for the services of the contractors to ship and freight at
£125,000. He held that in the circumstances the owners were entitled to counterclaim in the arbitration in respect of the damage sustained by The Tojo Maru

A in consequence of the explosions and fire, and he assessed the amount of such damage at £331,767. No issue has been raised before me as to any of these figures as figures.

The problems which have given rise to the statement of the Special Case and the consequent argument before me result in the main from the claim of the contractors to limit their liability in respect of the damage caused to The Tojo

B Maru to a figure based on the tonnage of their tug The Jacob Van Heemskerck. As to this, the learned arbitrator found that, in the event of the right to limitation of liability being established, the limitation fund would be £10,725 11s., which is again an agreed figure. In para. 21 of the Special Case the learned arbitrator stated:

C "I was requested by both parties to state a Case for the opinion of the Court upon a number of points of law. Some of these seemed to me to involve the same point of law but efforts on my part to get an agreed wording upon some of the points proved unsuccessful. I have therefore stated the questions for the Court as requested by the respective parties. The answers to these questions raised a number of possible alterations to the amount of the Award.

D I have therefore felt compelled to make one Award only but if the Court is of opinion that my findings upon one or more of these questions is wrong the Court may desire to remit the Award for reconsideration under Section 22 of the Arbitration Act, 1950."

I can omit reference to a number of the questions raised by either side, which no longer constitute live issues. I should, nevertheless, read some of the questions submitted by either side, and the arbitrator's determination of those questions,

E notwithstanding that there is some degree of overlap between them. Questions submitted on behalf of the contractors:

"Whether on the facts found and on the true construction of the contract: ... C (i) The breach of contract and damage caused thereby and/or (ii) that part of the Counterclaim which affects the salved value of the vessel should

F be taken into account in assessing the salvage remuneration."

The learned arbitrator's reply to that question was:

"Insofar as the breach of contract and the damage caused thereby reduced the salved value of the vessel and as the salved value of the vessel is one of the factors to be taken into account in assessing the salvage remuneration

G I hold that to that extent it is right that they should be taken into account when assessing the proper remuneration for the salvage services and I have done so."

Question D: whether—

"The counterclaim should be reduced (i) arithmetically, namely by the amount, if any, by which the award is reduced as aforesaid or (ii) by

H such greater amount as the arbitrator may determine."

The learned arbitrator answered that as follows:

"There is no settled practice as to how claim and counterclaim should be dealt with in cases of this kind. The two alternative methods which seem to be most applicable to this case are (i) make one award on the claim

I and one award on the counterclaim (ii) make one award on the counterclaim having reduced the amount thereof by the amount that would have been awarded on the claim. I hold insofar as it is a matter of law that the latter is the proper method to use in this case. This produces a balance in favour of the Owners of £206,767".

Question E: whether—

"The defence of equitable set-off can operate to counteract the statutory right of the Contractors to limit their liability in damages".

The learned arbitrator answered that:

"I hold that it cannot but the real questions are whether the right to limit liability arises on the original claim for damages or on the balance after the Counterclaim has been taken into account and whether the right to an equitable set-off has been established. I hold that where the right to an equitable set-off has been established the right to limit liability is in respect of the balance after such set-off has been taken into account and that in this case the right to an equitable set-off has been established".

Questions submitted on behalf of the owners: Question III (a):

"Whether on the facts found and on the true construction of Section 503 of the Merchant Shipping Act, 1894, as amended, the Contractors have shown that their liability to the Owners is a liability in damages arising from an occurrence specified in the said Section".

The learned arbitrator of that said: "I hold that they have".
Question IV (a):

"Whether on the facts found and on the proper holdings of law relating to liability and limitation of liability the Owners are entitled to any or all of the following relief: (i) Forfeiture or diminution of the amount of salvage which would otherwise have been awarded to the Contractors; (ii) Set-off, equitable set-off or other equitable defence; (iii) Damages".

The learned arbitrator answered that:

"I hold that the Owners are entitled to set-off against their claim for damages the amount of salvage which would otherwise have been awarded and that their damages should be reduced accordingly, namely, to £206,767".

Question IV (b):

"Whether if the Owners are entitled to damages in addition to one or both other kinds of relief set out in (a) above the damages should be reduced to extent of the saving resulting to the Owners from the application of such other kind or kinds of relief".

The learned arbitrator's answer was: "I hold that they should be so reduced as in (a) above". In the result, having applied the owners' counterclaim so as to extinguish the contractors' claim for salvage, the learned arbitrator awarded to the owners the limitation sum of £10,725 11s. in discharge of the balance of their counterclaim.

It seems to me that the points which arise for decision can be re-stated in the following way, putting them in their logical sequence: (i) What is the proper way to deal with the owners' complaint as to the damage resulting from the negligent act of Mr. Vis? In particular, in the circumstances of this case, is it permissible to entertain the owners' counterclaim for damages, or should the negligence of Mr. Vis be allowed for by merely reducing the contractors' award of salvage? (ii) Assuming that it is open to the owners to counterclaim for the actual loss sustained by them, can the contractors limit their liability? (iii) Assuming that the contractors are entitled to limit their liability, is there a right of set-off as between the contractors' claim for salvage and the owners' counterclaim for damages? If so, is it right first to set-off so much of the owners' counterclaim as will extinguish the contractors' claim, so as to apply the right to limitation of liability only to the balance of the counterclaim? Or is the sum to be set-off only the limited amount of the contractors' liability, so as to leave them with all but £10,725 of the " proper remuneration " of £125,000?

I begin, therefore, by considering the owners' complaint as to the damage received by their vessel. Counsel for the contractors started by reminding me of the basic principles on which salvage is awarded. He reminded me that it has always been the policy of the court to encourage salvors. I would add that this applies particularly to professional salvors, such as the contractors in this

A   case, who maintain tugs and salvage equipment in constant readiness to go to
the assistance of vessels in distress—see *The Glengyle,* (1).   Remuneration for
salvage services is based on the value of the salved property, the degree of
danger from which it has been saved, and the merit of the services rendered.   In
the present case £1,300,000 odd was saved from danger, and it has been found
that, apart from one incident, the services rendered by the contractors were
B   successful and meritorious.   There is no finding as to the degree of danger from
which The Tojo Maru was saved.   But it has been argued that the assessment
of £125,000 as the " proper remuneration " implies that the danger must have
been substantial, and that the money value of the benefit conferred by the
contractors' services must have been something substantially greater.   It is well
established that the court, recognising the need to encourage salvors, should
C   take a lenient view where negligence or lack of skill is alleged against salvors.
But, assuming negligence to be established, as in the present case, it was said that
normally the result should be merely to diminish the award that would otherwise
be made in favour of the salvors.   Such diminution, however, is not normally to
be assessed pound for pound on the basis of the damage caused to the salved
property, but rather in proportion to the degree of negligence or lack of skill
D   shown in the performance of the services.

In support of these propositions I was referred to several of the old cases
from the middle of the last century which are collected in KENNEDY ON CIVIL
SALVAGE, (4th Edn.) p. 184 and on the following pages.   From these it appeared
that the general rule then followed was as stated.   But it was recognised even
then that there might be some cases, for instance, where the misconduct of the
E   salvors was wilful, or where their negligence was so gross, as to result in the
total forfeiture of any award.   In *The Cape Packet* (2), DR. LUSHINGTON referred
to such cases, but he went on to say (3):

" There is also another kind of negligence, the effect of which is to diminish
the amount of salvage reward, not to take it entirely away.   The extent of
this diminution, I may further state, is not measured by the amount of loss
F   or injury sustained, but is framed upon the principle of proportioning
the diminution to the degree of negligence, not to the consequences ".

A similar statement of principle is to be found in *The Perla* (4).   Again in *The
Charles Adolphe* (5), DR. LUSHINGTON referred to the possibility of total forfeiture, but said that the evidence to establish this must be " conclusive ", which
the Privy Council in the later case of *The Atlas* (6) interpreted as meaning proved
G   beyond reasonable doubt.   Founding himself on this line of authority counsel
for the contractors argued that the proper way to deal with the damage resulting
from the negligent act of Mr. Vis in the present case would be to make a suitable
reduction in the salvors' award, thus leaving the salvors (who on the arbitrator's
findings had rendered a beneficial service) still with some award in their favour,
rather than under a liability to the owners, as is the effect of the actual award.
H   He submitted that the fact of the arbitrator having assessed the " proper
remuneration " at £125,000 showed that in his view the overall result of the
contractors' efforts was to confer a substantial benefit on the salved property,
entitling them at least to a positive or " plus " award after making such deduction as might be proper to penalise them for the negligence of Mr. Vis.

I   There was some discussion before me as to what exactly is meant by the learned
arbitrator's answer to question C, as to which it was suggested that there might
be some ambiguity.   The assessment of the " proper remuneration " at £125,000
either does or does not already reflect some diminution of what would otherwise
have been the proper remuneration so as to allow for the negligence of Mr. Vis.
It was said that if it does, then that is the end of the case, and the arbitrator

(1) [1898] A.C. 519.   (2) (1848), 3 Wm. Rob. 122.
(3) (1848), 3 Wm. Rob. at p. 125.   (4) (1857), Sw. 230.
(5) (1856), Sw. 153.   (6) (1862), Lush. 518.

ought simply to have made an award of £125,000 in the contractors' favour; **A**
if it does not, it ought to have done so. In either event the award should be
remitted to the learned arbitrator for him to make some award in the contractors' favour—either £125,000 or such lesser sum as he might think appropriate in all the circumstances, but still a " plus " award. For my part I have
no doubt as to the meaning of the learned arbitrator's answer to question C—
that is to say that in assessing the " proper remuneration " he took into account **B**
the negligence of Mr. Vis insofar as its effect was to reduce the salved value of
The Tojo Maru, but not otherwise.

I find myself unable to accept the argument for the contractors, for two main
reasons. In the first place, it seems to me to rest on a fallacious view as to what
is meant by the benefit conferred by a salvage service. The benefit conferred is
the saving of the property from the risks to which it was exposed, whatever **C**
those risks may have been. It is that benefit which has to be measured by the
arbitrator, and I would regard his assessment of the " proper remuneration "
as his estimate of the measure of benefit conferred that is to say the value of
the services. If that is right, and if it be the fact that in conferring that benefit
the contractor has negligently caused damage to a greater amount, it simply
means that in the end he has done more harm than good. If so, there is no good **D**
reason why he should be left with a " plus " award.   Nor is there any reason
why he should not be made to compensate the owners for the balance whereby
the damage which he has done exceeds the benefit conferred.

Secondly, all the old cases on which the contractors' argument was founded
were prior to the Supreme Court of Judicature Act 1873, before which date
it would not have been competent for the Court of Admiralty to entertain a **E**
counterclaim. Since that date there have in fact been a number of cases—to
some of which I was referred—in which the court has thought it proper in dealing
with salvage claims to entertain and give effect to a counterclaim for damages.
The earliest brought to my attention was *The C. S. Butler, The Baltic* (7). In
that case there were cross-actions heard together, in which the salvors were
claiming an agreed sum of £100 for salvage services rendered, while the owners **F**
were claiming damages in respect of a collision between their vessel and the
salving vessel due to the alleged negligence of the latter. SIR ROBERT PHILLIMORE
awarded the salvors the agreed sum of £100, but in the cross-action gave judgment
in favour of the owners for damages to be assessed by the registrar and merchants.
In *The Dwina* (8), there was a counterclaim by the owners for damage caused by
the salvors in the course of rendering the salvage services, and the court thought **G**
it right to make a straight deduction of the amount of the damage from the
salvage award that would otherwise have been made. In the more recent case
of *The Alenquer, The Rene* (9), there were again cross-actions. The services in
respect of which salvage was claimed were stand-by services which in fact conferred no benefit, but in respect of which in the ordinary way a small salvage
award could have been made on the basis of " engaged services ", the vessel **H**
at risk having been ultimately salved by other salvors. But in the course of
standing-by and endeavouring to take the salved vessel in tow the salving
vessel collided with her and caused very substantial damage. The salving vessel
having been found alone to blame for the collision, the court thought it right
to decree a total forfeiture of any salvage award, and give judgment in favour
of the salved vessel for the full amount of the collision damage. **I**

These cases reflect the modern approach to the problem that arises when in
the course of rendering salvage services damage is caused to the salved property
through negligence on the part of the salvors. But in addition to these cases I
have derived considerable assistance from the decision of the Court of Appeal in
Anglo-Saxon Petroleum Co., Ltd. v. *Damant, Anglo-Saxon Petroleum Co., Ltd.* v.
Regem (10). Let it be said at once that that case did not arise out of a claim for

(7) (1874), L.R. 4 A. & E. 178.   (8) [1892] P. 58.
(9) [1955] 1 W.L.R. 263; [1955] 1 Lloyd's Rep. 101.
(10) [1947] 2 All E.R. 465; [1947] K.B. 794.

A   salvage. In the course of salvage services being rendered to her the ship in question was totally lost owing to the alleged negligence of the salvors. The claim was by the owners of the ship against the Crown as salvors for the value of the ship lost. But in the course of assessing the value of the ship it was necessary to consider what award of salvage should have been made had the services been successful, since credit would have to be given for that in assessing the notional

B   salved value of the ship, that is, the amount of the owners' true loss. In the course of the argument the very same point was taken on behalf of the salvors as has now been argued on behalf of the contractors, but was decisively rejected by SCOTT, L.J., in delivering the judgment of the Court of Appeal (11). The proper way to deal with a complaint of misconduct on the part of a salvor was set out in the report, where, after referring to s. 1 (1) of the Merchant Shipping

C   (Salvage) Act 1940 (whereby it was provided that His Majesty was entitled to claim salvage in the same way as " any other salvor "), SCOTT, L.J., said (12):

> " It is clear that, if persons in the employ of any ' other salvor ' were guilty of misconduct the reduction in value of the salved property thereby caused would be taken into consideration in the decision on the amount of the salvage award, and also, if we are right in the preceding judgment, that
> **D**   a claim would lie on counterclaim or by cross-action or even independent action for damages ".

It seems to me that this is precisely what the learned arbitrator has done in the present case—see his answer to question C submitted by the contractors—and he has rightly left the damage inflicted on The Tojo Maru to be dealt with by way

E   of counterclaim. My only criticism is that, in answer to question D he has stated the balance in favour of the owners to be £206,767, that is, the straight difference between the total damages of £331,767 and the " proper remuneration " for the contractors of £125,000. It seems to me that some credit ought to have been given against the owners' claim for damages in respect of the amount by which the contractors' " proper remuneration " was found to be less than it otherwise

F   would have been because of the reduction in the salved value. Otherwise the contractors are to that extent penalised twice. The learned arbitrator has not said by how much his assessment of the " proper renumeration " would have been greater but for the negligence of the contractors. But since, for reasons which will later appear, the award will in any event have to be remitted to the arbitrator, this is a point that he can then consider, so as to make whatever

G   adjustment seems to him appropriate in the total of the owners' claim for damages. Subject to that point I hold that the argument on behalf of the contractors on this aspect of the case fails.

I turn next to consider the contractors' claim to limit their liability. The relevant statutory provision is s. 503 of the Merchant Shipping Act 1894, as amended (13) in 1958 to give effect to the Brussels Convention of 1957. The

H   relevant part of s. 503 provides:

> " (1) The owners of a ship, British or foreign, shall not, where all or any of the following occurrences take place without their actual fault or privity; (that is to say,) . . .
>   (b) Where any damage or loss is caused to any goods, merchandise, or other things whatsoever on board the ship; . . .
> **I**   (d) Where any loss or damage is caused to any property (other than any property mentioned in paragraph (b) of this subsection) or any rights are infringed through the act or omission of any person (whether on board the ship or not) in the navigation or management of the ship,

---

(11) [1947] 2 All E.R. at p. 467; [1947] K.B. at p. 801.
(12) [1947] 2 All E.R. at p. 468; [1947] K.B. at p. 801.
(13) I.e., by s. 2 of the Merchant Shipping (Liability of Shipowners and Others) Act 1958.

or in the loading, carriage or discharge of its cargo or in the embarkation,   A
carriage or disembarkation of its passengers, or through any other act
or omission of any person on board the ship;
be liable to damages beyond [the limited amount] . . ."

The contractors sought to limit their liability by reference to the tonnage of
their tug Jacob Van Heemskerck. The following facts relevant to this question
were found or admitted. The diver, Mr. Vis, had become a temporary member of   B
the crew of the tug Jacob Van Heemskerck. He descended into the water from
the tug for the purpose of working on The Tojo Maru, carrying with him the
Cox bolt gun. This was not part of the tug's regular equipment; it had been
provided by the contractors specially for this service, and had become a temporary part of the tug's equipment. In carrying out his work Mr. Vis was acting
under the orders, not of the tugmaster, but of the salvage inspectors. It was   C
not suggested that there was any fault or privity on the part of the contractors
themselves. The learned arbitrator held that the contractors were entitled to
limit their liability—see his answer to question III (a). He gave no reasons for
his conclusion. I do not criticise him for that, since his duty was limited to finding
the facts and stating his conclusions thereon; it was no part of his duty to give
a reasoned judgment.   D
The contractors' claim to limit their liability was based on two alternative
grounds, that is to say: (a) The act of Mr. Vis which caused the damage was
the act of a " person on board " the tug; (b) alternatively, it was an act " in
the management " of the tug. Before considering whether either of these claims
can be substantiated, I remind myself of the correct approach to a claim for
limitation of liability. The section of the Act takes away what would otherwise   E
be the common law right of the injured party to recover compensation in full;
its provisions must therefore be strictly construed. Moreover, the burden is on
the wrongdoer seeking to claim the benefit of the section to bring himself within
its terms. On the face of it the section appears to provide for two categories of
activity in respect of which the right to limitation of liability is conferred.
These are: (a) certain defined activities, of which the only relevant one is an   F
act in the management of the ship (in this case the tug); and (b) any other act,
if it is that of a person on board. I do not think that there is any room for
ambiguity in the terms of the section with regard to this; but if there is, any
such ambiguity is removed by the wording of art. 1 (1) (b) of the Convention
itself, at which I was invited to look.
Was the act of Mr. Vis the act of a person on board the tug? If it is permissible   G
to apply any measure of common sense, plainly it was not. Mr. Vis was not on
board the tug; he was operating from the water, and had no connection with
the tug apart from his temporary membership of the crew. But if there is no
room for the exercise of common sense, and the question depends solely on a
pedantic construction of the actual words of the section, I think the same result
follows. The phrase " on board the ship " occurs in para. (b), where its meaning   H
is plainly restricted to goods, etc., physically on board the ship, other goods
situated elsewhere being subject to para. (d). The phrase occurs again in the
earlier part of para. (d), where the words are " act or omission of any person
(whether on board the ship or not)". Here again the phrase can only refer to
a person physically on board. When the same phrase is again used at the end
of para (d) in relation to " any other act or omission ", it must as a matter of   I
construction bear the same meaning as in the previous passages. I was, however,
referred on behalf of the contractors to three cases where the words " on board "
have been differently construed in different contexts. In *The Sydney*, (14) in
which the question at issue was as to the distribution of prize bounty, it was held
that those " on board " an enemy vessel (The Emden) could include members
of the crew temporarily on shore or employed as a prize crew of a captured

_____

(14) [1916] P. 300.

A vessel. In *The Chieftain* (15) it was held that the words " wages earned on board the ship " within the meaning of s. 10 of the Admiralty Court Act 1861, were wide enough to cover wages earned by a ship's master although he was not actually living on board while his ship was in port. Lastly, in *R.* v. *Lynch and Jones* (16), it was held that a seaman may be " employed . . . on board " a ship, for the purposes of the definition of " seaman " within s. 742 of the Merchant **B** Shipping Act 1894, notwithstanding that he might be sent ashore to perform duties connected with the ship.

I have not found any of these cases, depending as they did on the construction of different enactments, of any help in the construction of s. 503, where I think the meaning of the words " on board the ship " is perfectly plain. I prefer the view expressed by ASHWORTH, J., in *Moore* v. *Metcalf Motor Coasters, Ltd.* (17), **C** when he held (it is true, only obiter) that the words in para. (*a*) of s. 503 (1) " carried in the ship " are referable to the status of the person concerned, and are to be contrasted with the words " on board the ship " in para. (*d*), which he thought meant exactly what they say, that is to say, physically on board the ship. For these reasons I am not prepared to hold that the negligent act of Mr. Vis was the act of a person on board the contractors' tug.

D Then can it be said that, although Mr. Vis was not on board the tug, his act was an act in the management of the tug? Once more common sense revolts against any such idea. Mr. Vis was operating away from the tug, being engaged on the repair of The Tojo Maru. His only connection with the tug was that he had descended into the water from the tug and carried with him a tool which formed part of the temporary equipment of the tug—it might just as well, for **E** the purposes of the argument, have been a mere screwdriver or spanner.

As a matter of construction the word " management " must be read in conjunction with " navigation ", which can only refer to navigation of the ship as a whole. Similarly, management must refer to management of the ship as a whole, or at least to the management of some integral part of the ship, the " ship " in this case being of course the tug Jacob Van Heemskerck. I do not **F** find anything in the authorities cited to lead me to a different construction of the word " management " in the context of s. 503. The authorities principally relied on on behalf of the contractors were the decisions of PILCHER, J. in *The Athelvictor* (18) and *The Teal* (19). In the former case certain sea valves on board a tanker were negligently left open, thereby allowing petrol to escape into the sea, where it became ignited and caused a disastrous fire. In the latter **G** case a dangerous cargo was loaded into a barge, where it caught fire and caused considerable damage. In both cases PILCHER, J. held that the act complained of was an act in the management of the ship within s. 503. In both cases he held that the narrower construction of the words " management of the ship " which has been applied in relation to the Carriage of Goods by Sea Act 1924 and other similar contractual or statutory exceptions clauses, did not apply in the context **H** of s. 503. Before me it was not sought to argue that in drawing this distinction, PILCHER, J., was wrong, but counsel for the owners reserved the right to challenge these decisions in a higher court.

For my part I am happy to accept both these decisions as correct on the facts of the respective cases. The only part of the judgment in *The Athelvictor* (20) which I would venture to question is PILCHER, J.'s statement that:

I

" The business of a shipowner is to carry cargo and passengers and in the very broadest sense the management of a ship must include the management of the cargo or passenger-carrying adventure ".

This view was substantially repeated in *The Teal* (19), but in neither case was

---

(15) (1863), Brown & Lush 104.   (16) [1898] 1 Q.B. 61.
(17) [1958] 2 Lloyd's Rep. 179 at p. 189.   (18) [1946] P. 42.
(19) (1949), 82 Lloyd L.R. 414.   (20) [1946] P. at p. 51.

it in any way necessary for the decision. In my judgment PILCHER, J., was **A** going too far in this expression of view.

Assuming, however, the correctness of the actual decision in these two cases, I do not find them of much assistance in relation to the facts of the present case. In *The Athelvictor* (21) the opening of the sea valves was, in the ordinary sense of the words, clearly an " act in the management " of an integral part of the ship, in a way that could not possibly be said of the act of Mr. Vis in relation **B** to the tug when he was manipulating the Cox bolt gun. In *The Teal* (22) the barge herself was being used as a receptacle for a dangerous cargo; and I see nothing remarkable, or in any way helpful to the present case, in holding that to be an act in the management of the barge. Nor do I derive much assistance from the decision of HEWSON, J., in *The Anonity* (23), where the misuse of a ship's galley stove in such a way as to cause sparks to fly and start a disastrous fire **C** was held to be an act in the management of the ship. Here again it was an act of management of an integral part of the ship. It seems to me that the facts in all three of these cases are quite remote from the circumstances of the present case.

I can find nothing in the strict construction in their context of the actual words of the section, or in the authorities which have been cited to me, which compels me to hold that Mr. Vis, when he fired his Cox bolt gun into the side **D** of The Tojo Maru, was performing an act in the management of the contractors' tug. I see no reason why common sense should not prevail. In the result I find myself unable to agree with the learned arbitrator's answer to question III (a), or to hold that the contractors have brought themselves within s. 503 of the Act. It follows that in my judgment the award must be remitted to the learned arbitrator for reconsideration on the basis that the contractors are liable **E** in full for the damage caused to The Tojo Maru.

If my conclusion on this point is correct it is really decisive of the case, subject only to a possible adjustment in the amount of the owners' counterclaim having regard to the fact that they will have the benefit of such reduction, if any, in the contractors' proper remuneration as the arbitrator may hold to have resulted from the diminution in the salved value of The Tojo Maru. The contractors will **F** have their claim for salvage, and the owners will have their counterclaim for the damage sustained. Any question of set-off is for practical purposes irrelevant, and the owners will be entitled to recover the sum by which their damages, as adjusted, exceed the contractors' proper salvage remuneration.

But in case I am wrong, and since the question of set-off has been fully argued before me, I think that I should as briefly as possible state my conclusions thereon. **G** For this purpose I assume, contrary to what I have held, that the contractors are entitled to limit their liability. The questions which then arise are: (i) whether the circumstances are such as to give rise to a set-off; and (ii) if so, at what stage should the contractors' right to limit their liability be applied. As to the latter question, the contention for the owners is that they are entitled to have their full counterclaim applied as a set-off to extinguish the contractors' claim **H** for salvage, and that the contractors' right to limit their liability only applies to the remaining balance of the counterclaim. In other words they contend that they are entitled to use their counterclaim as a shield against the contractors' claim for salvage before any question of limitation arises. This is the view to which the learned arbitrator gave effect, and the result is to extinguish the contractors' claim for salvage and leave a balance of £10,725 odd—that is the tug's limit of **I** liability—in favour of the owners. The contractors on the other hand contend that, assuming a right of set-off, all that can be set-off is their liability in damages, which in this case is limited to £10,725. The result of that would be to diminish the contractors' proper salvage remuneration by £10,725, but to leave them with a substantial balance in their favour. The questions to be decided are by no means easy, but for reasons which I will attempt briefly to explain I have come

(21) [1946] P. 42.   (22) (1949), 82 Lloyd L.R. 414.
(23) [1961] 1 Lloyd's Rep. 203.

A to the conclusion that on this part of the case the contention on behalf of the contractors is right.

As to the question whether there is a right of set-off, I am relieved from the necessity of referring in detail to the numerous older authorities by the fact that the whole subject was recently reviewed by the Court of Appeal in *Hanak* v. *Green* (24). From the decision in that case it emerges that there are three **B** classes of case in which a right of set-off may arise. Morris, L.J., who delivered the leading judgment, said (25):

> "The position is, therefore, that since the Judicature Acts there may be
> (i) a set-off of mutual debts,   (ii) in certain cases a setting up of matters
> of complaint which if established reduce or even extinguish the claim and
> (iii) reliance on equitable set-off and reliance as a matter of defence on
> **C** matters of equity which formerly might have called for injunction or
> prohibition ".

It has not been suggested that the present case falls within class (i), but it has been contended on behalf of the owners that it comes within both class (ii) and class (iii). On behalf of the contractors it has been argued that any right of set-off in the present case could only be within class (iii). Class (ii) set-off, as pointed **D** out by Morris, L.J., stems from the decision of Parke, B., in *Mondel* v. *Steel* (26). The principle enunciated by Parke, B., in that case related to cases where goods were sold with a warranty, or work was to be done according to a contract, at a fixed price, in which case it was competent for the defendant when sued for the stipulated price to set up a breach of warranty or breach of contract as going to diminish or even extinguish the plaintiff's claim, on the basis that the goods **E** supplied or the work done were worth so much less than the stipulated price. Notwithstanding the submission to the contrary by counsel for the contractors, I think it is clear from *Basten* v. *Butter* (27), that the principle may equally apply to goods supplied or work done on a quantum meruit basis. But I do not think that this makes any difference. The principle was stated by Parke, B., in *Mondel* v. *Steel* (26), in the following terms (28):
F

> "It must however be considered, that in all these cases of goods sold
> and delivered with a warranty, and work and labour, as well as the case
> of goods agreed to be supplied according to a contract, the rule which has
> been found so convenient is established; and that it is competent for the
> defendant, in all of those, not to set off, by a proceeding in the nature
> **G** of a cross-action, the amount of damages which he has sustained by breach
> of the contract, but simply to defend himself by shewing how much less
> the subject-matter of the action was worth, by reason of the breach of
> contract. . . .".

I do not find this principle easy to apply to a case such as the present where there is a claim for salvage on one side (a claim which of its very nature is **H** peculiarly at large) and a cross-claim for damages on the other side. I have no doubt, however, that the present case would fall within class (iii), which was explained by Morris, L.J., in *Hanak* v. *Green*, as follows (29):

> "The cases within group (iii) are those in which a court of equity would
> have regarded the cross-claims as entitling the defendant to be protected
> in one way or another against the plaintiff's claim. Reliance may be placed
> **I** in a court of law on any equitable defence or equitable ground for relief;
> so also any matter of equity on which an injunction against the prosecu-
> tion of a claim might formerly have been obtained may be relied on as a
> defence ".

(24) [1958] 2 All E.R. 141; [1958] 2 Q.B. 9.
(25) [1958] 2 All E.R. at p. 149; [1958] 2 Q.B. at p. 23.
(26) (1841), 8 M. & W. 858; [1835-42] All E.R. Rep. 511.   (27) (1806), 7 East. 479.
(28) (1841), 8 M. & W. at pp. 871, 872; [1835-42] All E.R. Rep. at pp. 515, 517.
(29) [1958] 2 All E.R. at p. 150; [1958] 2 Q.B. at pp. 23, 24.

It seems to me that the present is eminently a case in which a court of equity **A**
would have restrained the contractors from proceeding with their claim for
salvage without having the owners' cross-claim taken into account. Assuming,
therefore, as I think, that there is in this case a right of set-off within MORRIS,
L.J.'s class (iii), the question arises what it is that the owners are entitled to
set-off. As to that, counsel for the contractors was in my judgment well founded
in submitting that all that can be set off is a liability for damages accrued due. **B**
Thus if the cross-claim for damages is statute-barred under the Limitation Acts,
there would be nothing to set-off. Similarly if there were an exceptions clause
exempting the contractors from any liability in damages, there would be no
cross-claim capable of being set-off. Equally, I apprehend, there would be
nothing to set-off if the contractors were entitled under s. 502 of the Act to be
wholly relieved from liability. It seems to me that the same principle must **C**
apply where s. 503 is invoked to limit the liability; all that remains to be
set-off is the limited sum.

In reaching this conclusion I have not overlooked the decision of the House
of Lords in *Stoomvaart Maatschappij Nederland* v. *Peninsular and Oriental Steam
Navigation Co.* (30). In that case two ships had been involved in a collision
for which both were held to blame, which at that date meant that the loss had **D**
to be divided equally. The owners of the ship which had sustained the smaller
amount of damage took proceedings to limit their liability, and paid the amount
of their statutory liability into court. The owners of the other ship were held
entitled to prove against the fund in court for a sum arrived at by taking half
their loss less a moiety of the loss of the ship whose liability was limited. The
question which was debated by the House of Lords in that case is thus analysed **E**
in MARSDEN ON COLLISIONS AT SEA (11th Edn.) para. 156:

" The question to be decided was whether in such cases there are two
liabilities in damages, one on the part of each shipowner to the other shipowner for half the loss of the latter, or only one liability, namely, a
liability on the part of the owner of the ship that had done the greater
damage, for the difference between half the loss of the one and half the **F**
loss of the other—in the words of LORD SELBORNE, (31), ' a moiety of the
excess of the aggregate loss beyond the point of equality .. ' ".

The reason for the decision was that according to the rules of the old Court of
Admiralty there was but one action and one final judgment, that judgment
being for the balance between a moiety of the loss of the one ship and a moiety **G**
of the loss of the other. The only liability for damages was thus a liability for
that balance, and accordingly it was to that balance that the right of limitation
applied. It will be seen, therefore, that *Stoomvaart Maatschappij Nederland* v.
Peninsular and Oriental Steam Navigation Co. (30) was not a case of true set-off
at all, as was made abundantly clear in the speech of EARL OF SELBORNE, L.C.
It has been submitted, however, that the same approach ought by analogy to be **H**
followed in the present case, the contractors' limit of liability being applied only
after their claim for salvage has been deducted from the owners' larger counterclaim for damages. But having regard to the special reasons for the decision of the
House of Lords in *Stoomvaart Maatschappij Nederland* v. *Peninsular and Oriental
Steam Navigation Co.* (30), I cannot find that there is any true analogy between
that case and the present, where there is a claim for salvage on the one hand **I**
and a wholly independent claim for damage on the other.

Nor do I think that any help is to be derived from *The Ettrick* (32), or from
Goulandris Brothers, Ltd. v. *B. Goldman & Sons, Ltd.* (33), both of which were
relied on by way of analogy on behalf of the owners. In both cases shipowners were

(30) (1882), 7 App. Cas. 795; [1881-85] All E.R. Rep. 342.
(31) (1882), 7 App. Cas. at p. 803; [1881-85] All E.R. Rep. at p. 346.
(32) (1881), 6 P.D. 127.
(33) [1957] 3 All E.R. 100; [1958] 1 Q.B. 74.

A   claiming a general average contribution from cargo in respect of casualties brought about by their own negligence. In the former case the shipowners had paid into court the amount of their statutory liability, and contended that thereafter they were entitled to be treated as innocent parties, so that the cargo owners could have no defence to their claim for a general average contribution. In the latter case the shipowners contended that any claim against them by

B   the cargo owners was time-barred under the Hague Rules, so that the cargo owners were deprived of the defence which they would otherwise have had against the claim for a general average contribution. But in both cases it was held that the cargo owners were entitled to rely on the shipowners' fault by way of defence, although not for the purpose of asserting a claim. Neither case, however, involved any question of set-off, and both were in effect decided against

C   the shipowners on the basis that they were not entitled to take advantage of their own wrongdoing for the purpose of asserting a claim. With all respect to the argument on behalf of the owners I do not think that either of these authorities is of assistance in relation to the question in the present case.

    In these circumstances, if I had thought that the contractors were entitled to limit their liability in the present case, I should not have felt able to agree with

D   the arbitrator's conclusion that the owners were entitled to use their claim for damages unlimited for the purpose of extinguishing the contractors' claim, leaving the latter to limit their liability only in respect of the outstanding balance of the owners' counterclaim. This, however, does not in any way affect the conclusion at which I have arrived on the case as a whole, namely, that the award must be remitted to the arbitrator for reconsideration in the light of the

E   opinions which I have expressed.

Case remitted.

    [*After hearing submissions* HIS LORDSHIP *made the following order:* " *So far as the question of costs is concerned I propose to make no order for costs on the motions, but in relation to the Special Case, doing rough justice to the best of my*

F   *ability, I direct that the owners shall recover 70 per cent. of their costs; the contractors will have no order for costs. So far as the other matters are concerned I think that the terms of the order have been sufficiently adumbrated in the course of exchanges by counsel. The case will be remitted to the arbitrator under s. 22. I will direct a stay for 14 days and if within that time notice of appeal is given stay on appeal to continue until the matter is dealt with by the Court of Appeal. If leave to appeal is necessary it is granted and although it does not marry very*

G   *well with the order for the stay of 14 days I am prepared to say that the appeal can be brought within six weeks, but it had better be 14 days if application for a further stay is to be avoided and then I will leave it, if I may, to learned counsel on both sides to agree a form of words answering specific questions by the arbitrator in the light of the opinions I have expressed and that can be embodied in the order.*]

H   Solicitors: *Richards, Butler & Co.* (for the contractors); *Whitehouse-Vaux & Elborne* (for the owners).

[Reported by N. P. METCALFE. ESQ., Barrister-at-Law.]

NOTE.

R. *v.* GREGORY AND MILLS.

[COURT OF APPEAL, CRIMINAL DIVISION (Davies, L.J., Lyell and Donaldson, JJ.),
February 21, 1969.]

*Criminal Law—Sentence—Consecutive sentences—Undesirability of proportion
of sentence on one indictment being made to run consecutively to sentence
imposed on second indictment.*

[As to concurrent and consecutive sentences, see 10 HALSBURY'S LAWS
(3rd Edn.) 492, 493, para. 898].

Appeals.

These were appeals by Colin Gregory and Michael James Mills against sentences of 21 months' imprisonment imposed by MACKENNA, J., at Leeds Assizes
on 25th June 1968, when they both pleaded guilty to an indictment charging
them with storebreaking and larceny and to a second indictment charging
them with storebreaking with intent.

S. Levine for the appellants.
J. S. Snowden for the Crown.

DAVIES, L.J., delivered the judgment of the court: The appellants, who
were given leave to appeal against sentence by the full court on 16th January
1969, came up before MACKENNA, J., at Leeds Assizes on 25th June 1968, when
they, with other accused, pleaded guilty to an indictment charging them with
storebreaking and larceny and to a second indictment charging them with
storebreaking with intent. On the first indictment all the accused were sentenced to 18 months' imprisonment. On the two appellants the judge passed
a sentence of 18 months on the second indictment and directed that three months
of that sentence should be consecutive to the sentence on the first indictment.
It is on that point, the form of sentence, that the full court gave leave to appeal
against sentence. Counsel have not been able to find any authority for the
proposition that a second sentence can be made partly consecutive to a first
sentence. It is quite obvious that administrative difficulties might, in some
cases, as has been pointed out by counsel for the appellants, arise out of the
imposition of a sentence in that form. It probably would not do so in the present
case, since the court has been informed by the prison governor that the sentence
is being treated as one of 21 months.

The court has come to the conclusion that to impose a sentence in this form
is undesirable and wrong and that such a practice should not be followed. If
the judge considered that a sentence of 21 months was appropriate, he could
achieve that end in a number of different ways, for example, by giving concurrent
sentences of 21 months or consecutive sentences of 12 and 9 months as to which
there could be no complaint. In the opinion of this court, the desired end should
be attained in one of these two ways or possibly by other means. We pass now
to consider the overall length of the sentences. [HIS LORDSHIP stated the facts,
and said that, in the case of the appellant Gregory, concurrent sentences of 18
months' imprisonment on each indictment would be imposed, and in the case
of the appellant Mills concurrent sentences of 12 months on each indictment
would be imposed.]

Appeals allowed in part. Sentences varied.

Solicitors: *Registrar of Criminal Appeals* (for the appellants); *M. D. Shaffner,*
Wakefield (for the Crown).

[*Reported by* N. P. METCALFE, ESQ., *Barrister-at-Law.*]

A

NOTE.

MAIN *v.* MAIN.

[Probate, Divorce and Admiralty Division (Wrangham, J.), February 10,
11, 12, 13, 1969.]

B

*Divorce—Collusion—Disclosure—Negotiations which may affect conduct of suit—
No agreement—Whether duty to disclose to court—Matrimonial Causes Act
1965 (c. 72), s. 5 (2).*

[As to collusion and the effect of monetary and other arrangements, see
12 Halsbury's Laws (3rd Edn.) 301, 302, paras. 595, 597; and for cases on the
C subject, see 13 Digest (Repl.) 388-393, *3206-3236.*

For the Matrimonial Causes Act 1965, s. 5, see 45 Halsbury's Statutes
(2nd Edn.) 451.]

Case referred to:
  Pratt v. *Pratt*, [1966] 3 All E.R. 272; [1966] 1 W.L.R. 1568; Digest (Cont.
    Vol. B) 359, *3219aa.*

D
  Petition.
  This was a petition by the wife for dissolution of her marriage on the ground
of the husband's cruelty.   By his answer, as amended, the husband denied
cruelty and alleged adultery by the wife.   By a new petition, presented by leave
in the course of the proceedings and consolidated with them, the husband prayed
for dissolution on the ground of the wife's desertion.   By her answer the wife
E denied desertion and alleged constructive desertion.   During the hearing of the
wife's evidence, it appeared that there had been considerable negotiations between
the parties and the question arose whether such negotiations ought to have
been disclosed to the court for consideration under s. 5 (2) of the Matrimonial
Causes Act 1965.   The report deals only with that question.

F *M. E. Ward* for the wife.
  C. Sleeman for the husband.

  WRANGHAM, J., in the course of his judgment, said: I propose to deal
with a separate matter which arose in the course of these proceedings.   It arose
in this way: from a chance piece of evidence from the wife, it appeared that
there had been, in the course of the proceedings, considerable negotiations which
G only did not result in an agreement because the final offer was rejected.   The
agreement which was proposed, but rejected, was one which would have had
to be submitted to the court as a possibly collusive agreement under the section (1)
which provides for that procedure.   The negotiations had not been disclosed to
the court.   I hasten to add that nothing in what I say from now onwards is
meant to hint at the smallest criticism of anybody for not disclosing it.   The
H question whether it ought to have been disclosed or not is a difficult one, or so
I have found it, and one in which certainly no criticism can be made of anybody
who took the opposite view.
  The existence of these negotiations having been revealed, it became clear
that counsel for the wife was not anxious to disclose what the negotiations
were, and that for an entirely honourable reason, which became obvious in the
I end.   The reason was that, if they were disclosed, the disclosure might prejudice,
in a way that could be regarded as unfair, the case of the husband.   But the question whether these negotiations ought to be disclosed or not having been raised in
this way, I was invited by counsel to give such assistance as I could on the
question whether negotiations of this kind ought, in every case, to be disclosed,
and, if not in every case, where the line should be drawn.   Both counsel in this
case had clearly taken the view (I do not think that I do them an injustice)

(1) Section 5 (2) of the Matrimonial Causes Act 1965.

that mere negotiations which did not result in a concluded agreement need **A** not be disclosed at all. That view (and again I say this, I hope, without any hint of criticism) was not, I think, a correct view.

This matter was fully considered by a Divisional Court consisting of KARMINSKI and PARK, JJ., in *Pratt* v. *Pratt* (2). That was a case in which a husband moved for a rehearing of a divorce suit on the ground that he had been misled by negotiations which had taken place between his solicitors and the **B** wife's solicitors, thereby causing him not to appear in the proceedings and not to put his defence before the court. It became necessary in those circumstances for the Divisional Court to consider what steps ought to have been taken by the legal advisers of the parties in relation to the negotiations which had taken place between them. For that purpose they invited the assistance of the Queen's Proctor. Accordingly, that case was one in which the very problem which has **C** come before me came to be fully considered by the two learned judges of that court, with the assistance of counsel for the Queen's Proctor, as well, of course, as the assistance of counsel for the parties. KARMINSKI, J., pointed out that the correspondence in which the negotiations in that case were contained had not been disclosed to the court at all (3). He said:

"From the letters which I have already read it is quite clear that the **D** question of providing evidence was not discussed, or at least mentioned, as the reason on behalf of the husband for agreeing to a nominal order,"

the nature of the agreement proposed in that case being this, that the wife should agree to a nominal order for maintenance, and the husband should agree not merely not to oppose her petition but to provide evidence of his own adultery in support of it. I continue with the judgment of KARMINSKI, J. (4): **E**

"On this point we called on counsel for the Queen's Proctor again and in the course of discussion he put forward a formula with which I desire to say I entirely agree. What he submitted was that any negotiations which might affect the conduct of the suit should be disclosed. Such a course would enable the court to commence to discharge its duty of deciding **F** whether or not there was any agreement or arrangement."

PARK, J., said (5):

"I agree too with KARMINSKI, J., that negotiations which might affect the conduct of the suit should be disclosed to the court to enable the judge to discharge his duty of enquiring into whether or not there had been collusion." **G**

It is, therefore, plain that the test of the necessity of disclosure is not the question whether the negotiations have fructified into an agreement. The test is whether they are negotiations which might affect the conduct of the suit.

It is plain that the disclosure of negotiations may well create great diffi- culties for the parties. Negotiations between parties in the Queen's Bench **H** Division commonly take place without prejudice, under a shield which is especially devised to prevent the judge from knowing what negotiations have taken place in order that parties may be free to negotiate without putting themselves in a position in which a judge might draw an adverse inference from their willingness to resile, wholly or partly, from their pleaded contentions. It is, of course, obviously a matter which may cause great difficulty to parties **I** in this division if they are not merely not allowed to conduct their negotiations without prejudice but are compelled always to disclose those negotiations to the court of trial. This case afforded an example. Counsel decided, after considera- tion of *Pratt* v. *Pratt* (2), that it would be right that the negotiations which

(2) [1966] 3 All E.R. 272; [1966] 1 W.L.R. 1568.
(3) [1966] 3 All E.R. at pp. 275, 276; [1966] 1 W.L.R. at p. 1573.
(4) [1966] 3 All E.R. at p. 276; [1966] 1 W.L.R. at pp. 1573, 1574.
(5) [1966] 3 All E.R. at p. 276; [1966] 1 W.L.R. at p. 1574.

A had taken place in this case should be disclosed to me, and it then appeared that the negotiations, which only failed on the question of finance, provided for the husband abandoning his defence to the cruelty petition. Of course, no one has suggested, naturally, that his answer to the cruelty petition should not now be taken seriously because at one time he was prepared, apparently, to abandon it. But it must, inevitably, be a matter of embarrassment that offers

B of that kind should have to be disclosed to the court of trial.

One has, I think, to consider the various ways in which negotiations which do not result in an agreement may have failed to do so. One way in which negotiations may fail to result in an agreement is demonstrated by the facts in *Pratt* v. *Pratt* (6), where the negotiations seem simply to have petered out, leaving one side under the impression that an arrangement had been made

C and the other side under the impression that it had not been made, with the result that, as the Divisional Court found on the facts, the parties were never of the same mind, and, therefore, no agreement was concluded. Another way in which negotiations may fail to result in an agreement is exemplified by the facts in this case, where a perfectly plain offer was made, and was refused in terms, leaving nobody under any doubt whether an arrangement had been made or not.

D It seems to me that, in the first class of case, the case where negotiations are never clearly ended by a flat refusal of the offer made by the other side, it must nearly always be desirable to disclose them on the ground that they may affect the conduct of the suit. (I am speaking, of course, only of negotiations which could conceivably affect the conduct of the suit if they resulted in an agreement, not of negotiations about some wholly neutral matter.) On the other hand,

E negotiations which end in a perfectly flat refusal of a definite offer may, and usually will, have no effect whatever on the conduct of the proceedings. In the view that I have formed, the proper course in such cases is for the parties, through their representatives no doubt, to inform the court that negotiations have taken place and have fallen through completely, and to indicate to the court that, if necessary, those negotiations can be disclosed, but that, in the

F view of the parties, or their counsel, the negotiations have in fact, because they have failed, had no possible effect on the conduct of the proceedings. Obviously the judge is not bound by that expression of opinion on the part of counsel and may call for complete disclosure. On the other hand, he may take the view that his inquisitorial duty under the Matrimonial Causes Act 1965 is adequately discharged by accepting the assurance of counsel. A more extreme case still,

G of course, may be considered. That is the case when an overture is made by the one party to the other, and it is rejected at once before any really detailed or defined offer has been made. In such a case I would think that counsel in charge of the case might reasonably take the view that such negotiations could not affect the conduct of the suit, and therefore do not come within the category which, according to the rule in *Pratt* v. *Pratt* (6), ought to be disclosed

H to the court.

I have dealt with this matter at some length because I was invited to do so. It had, in fact, not the slightest effect whatsoever on the proceedings in this case.

Solicitors: *A. J. Dalton*, Southend-on-Sea (for the wife); *Bates, Son & Braby*, Southend-on-Sea (for the husband).

I

[*Reported by* ALICE BLOOMFIELD, *Barrister-at-Law.*]

---

(6) [1966] 3 All E.R. 272; [1966] 1 W.L.R. 1568.

A

MALLETT v. McMONAGLE.

[HOUSE OF LORDS (Lord Reid, Lord Morris of Borth-y-Gest, Lord Pearce, Lord Wilberforce and Lord Diplock), December 16, 1968, February 11, 1969.]

Fatal Accident—Damages—Assessment—Measure of damages—Excessive damages —Sum awarded sufficient to produce income exceeding double the rate of the dependency at the time of death without resort to the capital—Deceased a machine operator aged 25 earning £12 a week—Effect of inflation— Arithmetical calculation of damages—Fatal Accidents Act 1846 (9 & 10 Vict. c. 93), s. 2.

B

The appellant's husband died on 21st November 1964 in a motor accident caused by the respondents' negligence. At the date of his death the deceased was aged 25½ and the appellant was aged 24. They had three infant children. Prior to his death the deceased was employed in Londonderry as a machine operator at a weekly wage of over £12; and for six weeks before his death he had supplemented his earnings by singing in a dance band on three nights a week for which he earned £6 to £10 a week. Out of his weekly wage the deceased had given the appellant £9 10s. to £10 10s. a week for housekeeping, and it was established that her dependency at the date of death was about £10 a week. After the deceased's death his employers had ceased to carry on business but there was evidence that if he had then been alive he would have been offered employment in Londonderry as an asphalter at an average weekly wage of £22 10s. Although this work would have involved much travelling and long hours it was submitted that he would still have been able to supplement his wages by singing in a dance band and that in these changed circumstances he could and would have given the appellant a much higher sum for housekeeping than at the date of his death. In the appellant's action in Northern Ireland, as the widow and administratrix of the deceased, claiming damages under the Law Reform (Miscellaneous Provisions) Act (Northern Ireland) 1937 for herself, and damages for herself and the three children as dependants under the Fatal Accidents Acts (Northern Ireland) 1846-1959, the jury awarded total damages of £22,000 against the respondents. Of this sum £500 was by consent appropriated as the damages under the Act of 1937 leaving £21,500 as the amount of the damages awarded under the Fatal Accidents Acts. The amount of the award if reasonably invested in long-term securities would, without resort to capital, have produced an income exceeding double the rate of the dependency at the time of the deceased's death. The Northern Ireland Court of Appeal set aside the award, and ordered a new trial limited to the issue of damages under the Fatal Accidents Acts, on the ground that the award was excessive and an amount that no reasonable jury could properly award. On appeal,

C

D

E

F

G

Held: the appeal would be dismissed because, although it was inevitable in assessing damages under the Fatal Accidents Acts that there must be elements of estimate and conjecture, when applying the proper test for an appellate court, whether the award was out of all proportion to the circumstances of the case so that it exceeded any sum that a reasonable jury could have given, the award under the Fatal Accidents Acts should be set aside (see p. 187, letter D, p. 188, letters G and H, p. 189, letters C to E, and p. 192, letter H, post).

H

I

Per LORD DIPLOCK: (i) the purpose of an award of damages under the Fatal Accidents Acts is to provide the widow and dependants with a capital sum which with prudent management would be sufficient to supply them with material benefits of the same standard and duration as would have been provided for them out of the earnings of the deceased had he not been killed by the tortious act of the respondent (see p. 189, letter F, post).

(ii) in estimating the amount of the annual dependency in the future,

A had the deceased not been killed, money should be treated as retaining its value at the date of the judgment, and in calculating the present value of annual payments which would have been received in future years, interest rates appropriate to times of stable currency such as 4 per cent. to 5 per cent. should be adopted (see p. 190, letter I, post).

B Observations by LORD DIPLOCK on the calculation of the number of years that a dependency would have endured and of the amount of a dependency (see p. 191, letter B, to p. 192, letter B, post).

Appeal dismissed.

[As to the assessment of damages under the Fatal Accidents Acts, see 28 HALSBURY'S LAWS (3rd Edn.) 100, 101, para. 110; and for cases on the subject **C** see 36 DIGEST (Repl.) 221-224, *1176-1194.*

For the Fatal Accidents Act 1846, s. 2, see 17 HALSBURY'S STATUTES (2nd Edn.) 5.]

Cases referred to:

Davies v. *Powell Duffryn Associated Collieries, Ltd.,* [1942] 1 All E.R. 657; [1942] A.C. 601; 111 L.J.K.B. 418; 167 L.T. 74; 36 Digest (Repl.) **D** 231, *1229.*

Nance v. *British Columbia Electric Ry. Co., Ltd.,* [1951] 2 All E.R. 448; [1951] A.C. 601; 36 Digest (Repl.) 172, *922.*

Appeal.

This was an appeal by Elizabeth Ann Mallett, from an order of the Court of Appeal in Northern Ireland (LORD MacDERMOTT, C.J., and McVEIGH, L.J.; **E** CURRAN, L.J., dissenting), dated 12th January 1968, whereby the court by a majority allowed the appeal of Hugh Joseph McMonagle, a minor, and Seamus McMonagle, the respondents, against the judgment in favour of the appellant against them on 23rd May 1967, in an action tried by SHEIL, J., and a jury in the Queen's Bench Division of the Northern Ireland High Court of Justice. The appellant had sued the respondents under the Law Reform (Miscellaneous **F** Provisions) Act (Northern Ireland) 1937, and the Fatal Accidents Acts (Northern Ireland), 1846-1959, for loss and damage sustained by her and her three infant children from the death of her husband, William John Mallett, in a motor accident on 21st November 1964, when he was a passenger in a car driven by the respondent, Hugh Joseph McMonagle, and owned by the respondent, Seamus McMonagle. The action resulted in a verdict for the appellant for damages of **G** £22,000. It was agreed that £500 of this sum should be appropriated as the damages under the Act of 1937. This left the damages awarded under the Fatal Accidents Acts at £21,500. The respondents' grounds of appeal to the Northern Ireland Court of Appeal were that the damages of £21,500 awarded under the Fatal Accidents Acts were so excessive as to be out of all proportion to the circumstances of the case and they sought a new trial. The Court of Appeal **H** held that the damages were excessive and ordered a new trial limited to the issue of the amount of damages under the Fatal Accidents Acts.

The judgments of the Northern Ireland Court of Appeal were delivered on 12th January 1968.

LORD MacDERMOTT, C.J., having referred to the nature of the appeal, **I** continued: In view of the conclusion I have reached I do not propose to go into the facts at length or to refer to all the points that were discussed before us; but the following summary of the salient features of the case may help to indicate the general nature of the issue.

The deceased was married on 14th November 1959. He was 25 years of age at his death. He had enjoyed good health and was constantly employed from the time of his marriage, his last employment being in Londonderry with two companies referred to at the hearing as Monarch Electric, Ltd., and B.S.R. His average net wage in this employment over the last three months was £12 16s. 7d. He

was also, in his spare time, a member of a dance band. He had been working A
with this band as a vocalist for six weeks before his death and his average weekly
remuneration from this source was in the region of from £6 to £10. [The appellant]
spent £3 10s. a week at most on his food. He bought his own clothes. He gave
[the appellant] each week out of his wages from £9 10s. to £10 10s. and while he
was with the band a further £3 10s. At the deceased's death the dependency
was therefore round or about £10 per week. It appeared that since the deceased's B
death his employers had closed down. But from the evidence of Noel Vincent
Murphy, an asphalt contractor, the jury could well have come to the conclusion
that if the deceased had been alive when his employers ceased business he would
have got steady employment as an asphalter with Mr. Murphy at a wage which,
taken over the year would have been about £22 10s. a week. This employment
would have meant travelling round the north-west, but his travelling expenses C
would have been paid for him.

The [appellant] was 24 when this tragic accident made her a widow, and her
three children were then aged four, two and one respectively. Her financial
loss was what the jury had to assess and, on any view, it was substantial. In
cases like the present the task which the jury have to discharge is onerous and
difficult. They have not only to measure the dependency as it exists; they must D
regard the future as well—what LORD WRIGHT, referred to in *Davies* v. *Powell
Duffryn Associated Collieries, Ltd.**, as " reasonable future probabilities " the
family's prospects, the many uncertainties of life and any evidence which may
bear on relevant economic trends. I think this jury discharged this task in a
very open-handed manner indeed. Coming to the best conclusion I can without
seeing the witnesses I would have awarded a much smaller sum. E

That, however, is not the test. The question is whether a reasonable jury
might, on the evidence before them and taking the case at its height in favour
of the [appellant], have awarded this sum of £21,500. Applying that test, my
opinion is that this award should not stand and that there ought to be a new
trial. I do not think damages under the Fatal Accidents Acts (Northern Ireland)
1846-1959 have to be calculated on a strictly actuarial basis, or in a manner F
that is businesslike to the point of meanness, or that refuses to face the future
and the changes it may bring to those whose breadwinner has gone. On the
other hand, it is, I believe, equally clear that those who have to pay the damages
are entitled to say that the extent of their obligation should not be founded on
mere guesswork and conjecture.

In the present case the amount of the verdict, if wisely invested in long-term G
securities, could, without resort to capital, produce an income exceeding double
the rate of dependency at the time of death. That seems to me far more than
ample to discount the risk of rising costs and weaker money. I can find nothing
in the evidence to justify it and I hope I will not be thought lacking in sympathy
for this sorely bereaved family if I say that to my mind no reasonable jury,
which avoided acting on the merest guesswork and conjecture, could have H
awarded this sum. For these reasons I would set aside the judgment as entered
and order a new trial on the sole issue of damages under the Fatal Accidents Acts.

CURRAN, L.J., referred to the facts and continued: There are two elements
in the award of £22,000 damages: (a) pecuniary loss from the date of the accident,
21st November 1964, up to the date of trial, which commenced on the 22nd
May 1967, a period of 2½ years. At £10 10s. per week this loss would be £1,365. I
But from 17th January 1967 up to the date of trial, there was a period of about
18 weeks, during which the jury might have formed the view that the deceased
would have been employed by Noel Vincent Murphy at an average weekly wage
of £22 10s., and would probably have increased the weekly amount he gave
the [appellant]. I take a round figure of £1,500 to represent total pecuniary loss
up to date of trial; (b) future pecuniary loss from date of trial. To ascertain

---

* [1942] 1 All E.R. 657 at p. 665.

A what amount the jury may be taken to have awarded in respect of such loss, I deduct the £1,500 allowed for loss to date of trial from the total damages of £22,000. This gives a figure of £20,500, which would represent 16 years' purchase of between £24 and £25 per week.

The jury were entitled to foresee probable future increases in the deceased's earnings, had he lived. In my view they were also entitled to find that, being a
B good worker, a good husband and a good father, [the appellant and the] family would have enjoyed greater benefits from those increased earnings. But as the extent of those benefits would have been entirely within the discretion of the deceased, the members of the jury would have to rely on their own experience and common sense in determining what proportion of future earnings should be credited to the [appellant] and the family. It would appear, from what Lord
C Wright said in *Davies* v. *Powell Duffryn Associated Collieries, Ltd.**, that the jury could resolve this difficulty by estimating the deceased's probable earnings, subtracting from that sum what they estimated would be required for his own personal or living expenses, and taking the balance as the amount the deceased would probably have contributed to [the appellant] and the family.

If the jury on the balance of probabilities found, as in my view it was open
D to them to do, though I personally would have some doubt about it, that the deceased could have worked as an asphalter and also earned money as a vocalist, they could reasonably find that his earnings from 17th January 1967, would probably have been about £30 per week. Out of his earnings of about £20 per week, when he was alive, the deceased had been content to retain about £6 per week for his own personal or living expenses, apart from the £3 10s. it took to
E feed him at home, leaving the [appellant] and the family about £10 10s., or about one-half of his earnings. I think a reasonable jury might estimate that out of increased earnings of £30 per week a larger proportion of the earnings should be credited to the [appellant] and the family. The deceased as a good husband and father could be reasonably expected to have restrained his personal spending to provide for the growing expenses of a growing family.
F Even with earnings of £30 per week a reasonable jury might get within striking distance of, and might even reach, £20 per week as a basic figure for damages. The jury were entitled, however, to foresee probable increases in earnings, and increased contributions to the [appellant] and the family out of those earnings. When this is taken into account I am not prepared to hold that 16 years' purchase of a basic figure of £24-£25 is out of all proportion to the loss sustained.
G At the date of the trial the deceased, had he lived, would have been 28 years of age, with a working life before him of 32-37 years. His career as a vocalist with a band would have been, of course, very much shorter. In taking 16 years' purchase in order to test whether there is a reasonable proportion between the amount of damages awarded by the jury and the circumstances of the case, I consider that all foreseeable eventualities are reasonably provided for. The
H basis of this appeal is that the members of the jury were so unreasonable that they gave an award of damages out of all proportion to the loss sustained. I have ascertained from the jury panel that the jury consisted of one director, two engineers, one surveyor, one salesman, one shop fitter and one clerk.

I would dismiss the appeal.

I **McVEIGH, L.J.:** This case comes before us by way of appeal from the verdict of the jury whereby the [appellant] was awarded the sum of £22,000. The grounds of appeal were that the award of damages was so excessive as to be out of all proportion to the circumstances of the case and that the trial judge had failed to direct the jury adequately or properly on the issue of damages.

The [appellant] in this case was the administratrix of her husband, William John Mallett, who was killed in a collision between two motor vehicles on 21st November 1964. This court is not concerned with any question of liability, but

* [1942] 1 All E.R. 657 at p. 665.

merely with the amount of damages. There is no doubt that the [appellant] and **A**
her three children were dependent on the deceased. They were all in good health
as had been the deceased. The [appellant] at the date of the accident was aged 24.
Her daughter Sarah was then aged about 3½, Geraldine was then aged about 2½
and William aged about 13 months. The deceased was at that time aged 25½
and he was employed with Monarch Electric, Ltd., at an average wage of £12
16s. 7d.; out of this he gave his wife " £9 10s. up to £10 10s."   **B**

In addition to this he was the vocalist with a dance band and was described
by the owner of the band as a "good vocalist " and as one who " could get a
job with any band ". There were four Malletts (brothers) working with this
band, some of them had been there longer than the others. The deceased had
been with the band for some six weeks before the accident and was being paid
on an average £6 to £10 per week for an average of three nights per week. Thus **C**
his total earnings at this time from both sources were between £18 16s. to £22 16s.
Out of the band earnings he gave [the appellant] £3 10s. per week. She estimated
that she spent " at the very most " £3 10s. on his food. Accordingly, the net
dependency at this stage appears to be in the region of £10 10s. per week which
figure the jury may have accepted. This left the deceased with a balance from
his earnings of some £7 10s. to £10 which he kept to himself and out of which **D**
he bought his own clothes. In other words, the amount of the dependency after
deducting his own keep was in or about half his total remuneration.

At the time when the case came to trial it was known that Monarch Electric,
Ltd., had closed down on 17th January 1967, and it was also known that the
basic wages from the date of death of the deceased had increased from £10 10s. 7d.
at the date of death, to £10 19s. on 16th August 1965 and to £11 7s. 9d., on 15th **E**
August 1966. The average net wage (with overtime) in 1963 was £11 and in 1964
was £12 16s. 7d. Also, we were informed that at the date of death the working
week was 42 hours and that it was reduced to a 40-hour week in August 1966.
The court however has no information as to what employees in the deceased's
level of employment were in fact earning as an average wage in the years 1965
and 1966. We do not know how much, if any, overtime was being worked. **F**
It may well be that the deceased, as his average wage increased, would have
given a larger share to [the appellant]. So far as I can make an estimate, the
percentage differential shown between the basic wage for 1964 and the average
net wage for that year was in the region of 20 per cent. If one applies this percentage to the basic wage for the year 1966 it would seem that the average net
wage for that year would have been about £13 13s. Whether his remuneration **G**
as a vocalist would have then increased one does not know. In the case of [the
respondent], Mr. McMonagle, the owner of the band, he gave up his job as a
postman because of the difficulty of doing that and also playing in the band.
He only kept on the two jobs for a year. The band " keeps you up to the early
hours of the morning ", he said, and it is relevant to notice that on the night
of the accident they were playing at Cloughmills which they did not leave until **H**
shortly after 2.00 a.m. and Cloughmills is some 35 or more miles from Londonderry. It also seems that people kept dropping out of the band, and there were
three changes of vocalists since 1960. Mr. McMonagle said—" It was impossible
to say how long the deceased would have stayed with the band." It is also
relevant, I think, to have in mind that the deceased has a wife and three young
children. None of the Malletts had been with the band for very long. All this **I**
seems to make any assessment of his future with the band very speculative
especially if he was at the same time trying to hold down another job.

So far as the evidence goes the most probable thing was that the deceased
would have remained in his employment in Monarch Electric until it closed
down, there being no suggestion that Mr. Murphy (who said he was prepared
to employ the deceased) or anyone else had offered him a job nor was there any
indication that he was considering leaving his employment with Monarch Electric.
So far as one can infer from the evidence the deceased had been working with the

A North-West Asphalt Co. at the same time as Mr. Murphy and his employment
   there had ceased for whatever reason. When this was we don't know, but we
   do know that Mr. Murphy began in business on his own as an asphalter some three
   years before the date of the trial. He said in evidence that the deceased, when
   working with the North-West Asphalt Co., was an " extremely good worker "
   and that he would have employed him. Asphalters, he said, were in short supply
B in Derry. Taking the year as a whole, he said, the wages would be " about
   £22 10s." According to Mr. Murphy he started in business with three men and
   at the date of trial he was employing 11 men. When asked had he made any
   approach to the deceased to join him when he set up in business on his own he
   replied—" Not at the time, because I knew he was otherwise engaged "; and
   when further asked if he had ever approached the deceased to join him, he replied,
C " No ". In this job according to Mr. Murphy the deceased would have had to
   work a lot more than 44 hours per week and would have had " a terrible lot of
   travelling ". He would have had to work " all round the North-West and in
   Donegal as well ". It is difficult to see how the deceased could have carried on
   both as a vocalist and an asphalter. Mr. Murphy's evidence was however
   admissible. It was for the jury to assess the weight they would give this piece
D of evidence as left to them by the trial judge. They had also to direct their
   minds to finding some reasonable figure for his prospects in the years that lay
   ahead of him. This was a particularly difficult matter in the case of one who
   had not long begun his working life. Furthermore, the jury had not only to
   try to prognosticate his future earnings, but also what would be the contribution
   that the deceased would have made to [the appellant] and the family. They were
E entitled to consider that as his prosperity increased he might increase his contribution to [the appellant]. They were also entitled to take into account that
   the children would probably begin to work and would no longer be dependent
   to the same extent and were entitled to come to some decision as to whether when
   the children began to earn the deceased would have continued his own contribution to his wife at the same level. He might have increased it or reduced it
F or left it as it was. These were, of course, all matters entirely for the jury. They
   had, of course, a lot of other matters to assess as appears from the summing-up
   —prospects of remarriage, the erosion of the value of money, the fact that the
   [appellant] will receive a lump sum, the possibility that the [appellant] might
   have died before the deceased and the particular deceased's probable expectancy
   of working life having regard to his health and prospects. There can be no doubt,
G in my view, that the possibility of remarriage of the [appellant] in circumstances
   which would improve her financial position is a factor which must be taken
   into account. But, as VISCOUNT SIMON said in Nance v. British Columbia Electric
   Ry. Co., Ltd.*, this contingency is " in most cases . . . incapable of evaluation ".
       LORD WRIGHT in Davies v. Powell Duffryn Associated Collieries, Ltd.† refers
   briefly to these matters as follows:

H   " It is a hard matter of pounds, shillings and pence, subject to the element
      of reasonable future probabilities. The starting point is the amount of wages
      which the deceased was earning, the ascertainment of which to some extent
      may depend on the regularity of his employment. Then there is an estimate
      of how much was required or expended for his own personal and living
      expenses. The balance will give a datum or basic figure which will generally
I   be turned into a lump sum by taking a certain number of years' purchase.
      That sum, however, has to be taxed down by having due regard to uncer-
      tainties, for instance, that the widow might have again married and thus
      ceased to be dependent, and other like matters of speculation and doubt."

   On the question of the remarriage factor the Court of Appeal in England have
   recently expressed themselves in Goodburn v. Thomas Cotton, Ltd.‡. They

---

* [1951] A.C. 601 at p. 615.   † [1942] 1 All E.R. 657 at p. 665.
                        ‡ [1968] 1 All E.R. 518.

have made it clear that the prospect of remarriage, like any other contingency, **A**
has to be taken into account, but that the jury are under no obligation to make
deductions for those contingencies.

The method whereby the jury arrived at their verdict in this case under the
guidance of the judge was one method and indeed, so far as I am aware, the
usual, I might say the only, method used in our courts in Northern Ireland. It
is described by BLACK, L.J., in his judgment in *Brennan* v. *Gale**. He begins **B**
by quoting the passage I have already set out from LORD WRIGHT'S speech in
Davies' case† and then he goes on:

> " This is a method which can be readily followed in the case of a weekly
> wage earner who leaves a widow and a family of young children, but it is
> obviously not capable of providing a simple and complete solution in a com-
> plicated case such as the present one. And even in cases where the method is **C**
> appropriate difficulties arise in its application. The first difficulty is to deter-
> mine what LORD WRIGHT calls the datum or basic figure. This has to be
> arrived at as best one can on the evidence. The next difficulty, and a much
> more serious one, is to settle the number of years' purchase by which this
> annual figure is to be converted into a lump sum. LORD WRIGHT speaks as if
> the annual figure is converted into a lump sum by taking a number of years' **D**
> purchase, and this lump sum is subsequently reduced to allow for all the
> various uncertainties and matters of speculation and doubt. In practice,
> however, I think it is much more usual after settling on the basic annual
> figure to apply to it as a multiplier such a number of years' purchase as will
> be thought to take into account all the doubts and uncertainties which point
> to a reduction in the sum to be awarded. What this appropriate multiplier **E**
> may be in any individual case must depend on the particular circumstances
> of that case. But there is no real yardstick by which the number of years'
> purchase can be measured. One has to take into account the probable
> duration of the earning life of the deceased and also the probable duration
> of life of the widow, the possibilities of increased earnings on the one hand
> and of disablement or unemployment on the other, and all the other **F**
> probabilities and chances which should be taken into consideration in endeav-
> ouring to fix a fair compensation for the pecuniary loss."

He then pointed out that the number of years' purchase varied greatly from case
to case, and then added‡ that he thought the figure of 16 years' purchase
fixed by the Court of Appeal in *Johnson* v. *Hill*§, " will approach the upper **G**
limit of any calculation of damages which has received the sanction of an
appellate court ". The case he was dealing with was that of a man of 51 and the
case was by no means a simple one apart altogether from the question of an
appropriate multiplier.

Thus, the usual method in our courts to arrive at Fatal Accidents Act damages
is to settle on the basic annual figure of dependency and then apply a multiplier **H**
which affects to take care of the uncertainties and vicissitudes of life, also the
fact that the widow is getting an immediate lump sum which can be invested.

In *Woods* v. *Hartley*‖ to the transcript of which we were referred, BRABIN, J.,
stated that there was more than one way of calculating the damage. Then
later in his judgment he said:

> " I have not calculated the damages by the formula set out in *Nance's* **I**
> case¶; that is to say, taking the deceased's expectation of life, allowing
> for the contingency of possible earlier death and ill-health to produce *x* years
> which multiplied by £*y*, the amount of estimated dependency, produces
> a lump sum to be discontinued to its equivalent in the form of a lump sum

---

* [1949] N.I. 178 at p. 184.   † [1942] 1 All E.R. 657 at p. 665.
‡ [1949] N.I. at p. 185.   § [1945] 2 All E.R. 272.
‖ (9th June 1967), unreported.   ¶ [1951] 2 All E.R. 448.

A payable at death and further discounted for such contingencies as the premature death or remarriage of the widow."

He goes on:

"I prefer to use the alternative method which, in my experience is nowadays the one more frequently involved, of fixing an estimated sum B for annual dependency and using an appropriate multiplier."

He then went on to consider certain figures and continued:

"In fixing the figures for dependency and the multiplier I have as best I can taken into account the various contingencies and deductions which must be borne in mind in the calculation."

C He concluded that the risk of premature death called for a small deduction only, and earlier he had indicated, for reasons stated, that nothing should be deducted for that contingency.

He then fixed on a multiplier of 16½ which was applied to a basic dependency figure of £1,600 giving a lump sum of £26,400. This was in respect of a deceased man who was 31 at the date of death. The judge appears to have settled on an D expectancy of some 36 years and it appears from his observations that he was referring to or had been referred to the tables of present value of immediate annuities; he appears to have used these as a guide finally to determine on a multiplier of 16½. It seems to me that in making these kind of assessments it is of some importance to have knowledge of the cost of an immediate annuity of the amount of the basic dependency figure. And indeed it has to be present to E the mind of the court and jury that it is not permissible to award a figure which allows the dependants to live off the income at about the dependency rate leaving the capital untouched. This is a matter which can be done actuarially from the tables of expectancy of life compiled by the registrar general used in conjunction with actuarial tables which provide multiplying factors. These multiplying factors when applied to the net average dependency figure give the present value F of an immediate annuity of the amount of the dependency. In using this method, of course, allowances will have to be made for all the contingencies which have to be taken into account in respect of the particular individual deceased with whom one is dealing, and also the contingencies concerning the widow. This was the method used as a guide by BRABIN, J., and also was used in the case of *Daniels* v. *Jones**—it is a guide which enables one to check on the appropriate- G ness of the lump sum. The multiplying factors take into account net tax figures. In a case such as the present the calculation is not one of any difficulty, but it seems to me that as the necessary tables were not made evidence as in *Daniels* v. *Jones** and other cases it is not open to this court to use them as a guide in the case now before us.

When the jury began their consideration of this case they had the knowledge H that the deceased was a healthy man, a good worker according to Mr. Murphy and a person who had been able to supplement his income by working as a vocalist. The court had no information as to his educational attainments or whether he had any special skills and as the onus was on the plaintiff to prove such facts, if they were to be relied on, one can make no assumption in his favour about such matters. All that is known about his daily employment is that he I was a machine operator employed by Monarch Electric and that fact I have gathered from the statement of claim and not from the evidence given in the case. The jury had no information whether there was any demand for machine operators in Londonderry, apart from Monarch Electric Ltd., and Monarch Electric had closed down. One has no information as to the availability of such employment elsewhere. He could, no doubt, have undergone some retraining, but apart from his opportunities as a vocalist, he was a wage earner who had been earning in or about £12 16s. 7d. and would have been out of employment

* [1961] 3 All E.R. 24.

on 1st January 1967, in an area where employment is not all that easy to find. **A**
He could, of course, have gone to England to look for work.

No evidence was given in this case that the deceased had the prospect of a
settled and secure job which would provide constant and continuing employment
for him in the years ahead with chances of promotion attached. And so the
jury were very much on their own in trying to assess what would be the reasonable probabilities for the future of the deceased and what he might reasonably **B**
have been expected to contribute to [the appellant] in the future. It is not
possible to know in what way the jury went about their difficult problem but one
can attempt to deduce the average yearly amount of dependency from the
capital figure arrived at by dividing that figure by supposedly acceptable multi-
pliers which might have been used in computing the capital figure. One can show
this by an actual example. The capital sum under consideration is £22,000 and **C**
if one adopts a multiplier of 20 then the yearly dependency figure would appear
to be in or about £1,100. The average weekly dependency on this calculation
would be in or about £21. This would have had to be paid out of taxable income.
If the jury had considered that the deceased would have continued to pay [the
appellant] one-half (approximately) of his net wages then it would appear that
they assessed that his average net wages from the date of death would have been **D**
in or about £42 per week. Alternatively, the jury might have thought that he
would have increased his contribution to [the appellant] by giving her, say,
two-thirds of his wages in which event they might have assessed his average
net wages at about £33 per week. Having regard to the paucity of evidence
£1,100 seems to me to be a very high figure for average dependency.

I imagine that the jury began by assessing an average figure for dependency **E**
which they applied from the date of death which is the usual way to compute
the matter, and this seems to be in accordance with the judge's summing-up.
If, however, they assessed first of all the loss from the date of death until the
date of trial this would amount to a figure of roughly some £1,500 arrived at by
taking two years and five weeks' loss at £10 10s. per week from the date of death,
21st November 1964, until 1st January 1967, when Monarch Electric Ltd., **F**
closed down. Then adding further loss from 1st January 1967 until date of trial
23rd May 1967 (say 20 weeks), at the rate of £20 per week based on asphalters'
wage amounting to about £400.

The balance of the £22,000 (less £1,500) being £20,500 would be then made up
of estimated loss of dependency from 23rd May 1967 (the deceased being then 28).
This method involves allowing 2½ years of dependency at a figure of some £600 **G**
per annum and some further multiplier for the balance. I don't think this
method provides much help in solving the problem we are faced with.

Next one has to consider whether a multiplier of 20 which results in a capital
sum of £22,000 is a realistic and rational one. There is no doubt that a jury ought
to take into account and consider that a capital sum earns interest when invested
and that the [appellant] is having the benefit of this income which she would **H**
not otherwise have had. The income on £22,000 at say 5 per cent. (not a high
figure) is £1,200 which is in fact more than the dependency figure arrived at by a
multiplier of 20. This is, of course, subject to tax on unearned income and in the
case of a widow and three children under four years of age one could assume
that it was in or about £177. The figure of 5 per cent. could be improved on if one
invested in a fixed interest long dated stock, but if one allows for some growth as **I**
a hedge against inflation one must generally accept a lower income and I have
taken 5 per cent. But even so, and accepting a dependency figure of £1,100
which, as I have said, seems high, the [appellant] will be in possession of a lump
sum which will yield her an income virtually equal to the dependency and leave
capital intact.

This leads to the conclusion that the jury have failed to make any proper
allowance for the immediate receipt of the capital sum. Obviously a considerable
deduction requires to be made and this shows in my view that the award is

A inordinately large and that the jury have failed to discount the effect of the immediate receipt of a large capital sum. In fact it is difficult to discern what significant weight was given to the various contingencies which had to be taken into account by the jury. Having given the matter careful and I hope sympathetic consideration I have come to the conclusion that no reasonable proportion exists between the verdict and the circumstances of this case.

B   I would therefore set aside the judgment and order a new trial on the issue of damages under the Fatal Accidents Acts.

The Attorney-General for Northern Ireland (E. W. Jones, Q.C.), B. Kelly, Q.C., J. P. Higgins, Q.C., and J. M. A. Nicholson (all of the Northern Ireland Bar) for the appellant.

C   *J. C. MacDermott, Q.C., and J. F. B. Russell, Q.C.* (both of the Northern Ireland Bar) for the respondents.

Their Lordships took time for consideration.

11th February. The following opinions were delivered.

LORD REID: My Lords, I agree with my noble and learned friend, LORD MORRIS OF BORTH-Y-GEST, that this appeal should be dismissed.

D

LORD MORRIS OF BORTH-Y-GEST: My Lords, this is an appeal from the judgment of the Court of Appeal in Northern Ireland whereby the court by a majority (LORD MACDERMOTT, C.J., and McVEIGH, L.J.; CURRAN, L.J., dissenting) set aside the verdict and judgment which had been entered for the appellant and directed that there should be a new trial on the issue of damages under the Fatal Accidents Acts. The appellant is the administratrix of her late

E husband, William John Mallett, who died as the result of a motor accident on 21st November 1964. He was a passenger in a motor vehicle driven by the first respondent and owned by the second-named respondent. There was a collision between that vehicle and a lorry. In the action brought by the appellant only the respondents were held to be to blame for the accident. The appellant was

F awarded damages under the Law Reform (Miscellaneous Provisions) Act (Northern Ireland) 1937, and also for herself and for the three young children of the marriage under the Fatal Accidents Acts (Northern Ireland) 1846-1959. The judgment was set aside on the ground that the damages awarded by the jury were excessive and were of an amount that no reasonable jury could properly award.

G   The trial of the action took place on 22nd and 23rd May 1967. The appellant was 24 years of age at the time of her husband's death; he was then $25\frac{1}{2}$; they had married in 1959. At the date of the trial the three children were aged six, four and two. Prior to his death the deceased had been employed in London-derry as a machine operator by a company called Monarch Electric, Ltd. His net wage was over £12 a week. He had supplemented his earnings by singing

H in a dance band in his spare time in the evenings. He had done that for about six weeks before his death. He had done so on an average of three nights a week. By so doing he had earned from £6 to £10 per week. Out of his weekly wage he had been in the habit of giving £9 10s. to £10 10s. to the appellant for the house-keeping; he gave her a further sum of £3 10s. per week out of his dance band earnings. She spent about that amount per week on his food. It was established

I therefore that the dependency of the appellant was about £10 per week.

Before the date of the trial the company (Monarch Electric, Ltd.) that had employed the deceased had ceased to carry on business; they had closed down on 17th January 1967. Evidence was given that if the deceased had then been alive he would have been offered employment also in Londonderry as an asphalter. If he had become an asphalter his average weekly wage taking the year as a whole would have been £22 10s. In reaching this average he would in the summer months have worked from 9.00 a.m. to 9.00 p.m. or 10.00 p.m., during which period the weekly earnings would have been about £40. The potential employer

said that a considerable amount of travelling would have been entailed in the   A
work as an asphalter. Notwithstanding this it was contended at the trial that
if the deceased had been employed as an asphalter he could still have supplemented his earnings by singing in a dance band in the evenings. In the changed
circumstances it was further contended at the trial that the amount that he
could and would have given to the appellant would have been very much higher
than it was at the time of his death.   B

On the evidence which I have summarised the jury made an award of £22,000.
By agreement, £500 out of that sum was appropriated as damages under the
Law Reform (Miscellaneous Provisions) Act (Northern Ireland) 1937. The jury
made apportionments as between the appellant and the three children.

On appeal by the respondents to the Court of Appeal, the substantial contention was that the damages awarded were excessive. There was no appeal in   C
regard to the finding of the jury that the respondents had been guilty of the
negligence that caused the accident. No complaint of misdirection was urged.
What was said was that having regard to the evidence and to such facts as were
not in dispute the jury had awarded an amount of damages which was so excessive
as to be out of all proportion to the circumstances of the case. It was pointed
out that not only would there be the immediate receipt of the capital sum of   D
£21,500 but that such sum, if reasonably invested, would without any resort to
capital, produce an income exceeding double the rate of dependency at the
time of death. Accepting these contentions the majority in the Court of Appeal
held that the amount awarded exceeded what any reasonable jury could properly
award.   Accordingly a new trial was ordered but limited to the issue of the
amount of damages under the Fatal Accidents Acts.   E

My Lords, it is well established that in considering questions as to the quantum
of damages which have been awarded the approach of an appellate court must
differ according to whether the assessment has been by a judge or by a jury.
It seems manifest that had the award now being considered been that of a
judge alone the Court of Appeal would have decided that it represented a wholly
erroneous estimate. But it is clear that the Court of Appeal had it firmly in mind   F
that as the award was that of a jury a very different test must be applied. My
Lords, I do not think that any useful purpose would be served by seeking to
summarise or to re-iterate the principles which have often been stated. Guidance
is to be found in *Davies* v. *Powell Duffryn Associated Collieries, Ltd.* (1), and in
Nance v. *British Columbia Electric Ry. Co., Ltd.* (2).

In cases such as that now being considered it is inevitable that in assessing   G
damages there must be elements of estimate and to some extent of conjecture.
All the chances and the changes of the future must be assessed. They must
be weighed not only with sympathy but with fairness for the interests of all
concerned and at all times with a sense of proportion.

My Lords, in reviewing the evidence that was given in this case and in
endeavouring to decide what the future would have been and will be for the   H
persons concerned the jury had to have many considerations in mind. Their
conclusions must not be disturbed unless the appellate court is satisfied that
for some reason or another the result reached was out of all proportion to the
circumstances of the case so that the award of damages exceeded any sum
that a reasonable jury could have given. The majority in the Court of Appeal
were so satisfied. I see no reason to disturb their conclusion and, accordingly,   I
I would dismiss the appeal.

LORD PEARCE: My Lords, I agree with the judgments of the majority
of the Court of Appeal in Northern Ireland. LORD MACDERMOTT, C.J., observed
that " the amount of the verdict, if wisely invested in long-term securities, could,
without resort to capital, produce an income exceeding double the rate of depen-

(1) [1942] 1 All E.R. 657 at p. 664; [1942] A.C. 601 at p. 616.
(2) [1951] 2 All E.R. 448; [1951] A.C. 601 at p. 614.

A dency at the time of death." In a certain class of case, this would not necessarily show that a verdict was too high. If, for instance, a young man with clear prospects of rising high on the ladder of financial prosperity were killed, the amount of dependency at the date of death might be far less than it would have been in the future. But this was not such a case. There was no evidence that the deceased was likely to rise high on any ladder of success. It was likely that he would, on

B closure of the factory where he had worked, have got employment from a friend in the work of an asphalter, which would have brought a substantially higher wage, but also might, either on a short-term or long-term view, have entailed his giving up his work as a singer with a band which brought him in an extra £6 to £10 per week of which the appellant, his wife, got nearly half the benefit.

The various matters of evidence to be considered and the various arithmetical

C calculations which may help in arriving at a verdict are clearly set out in the conflicting judgments of CURRAN and McVEIGH, L.JJ. Any assessment must contain elements of reasonable prophecy and arithmetic. In assessing the proper figure, the jury have to take into account both the possibilities for good and for bad, striking a fair balance as they see it, on such evidence of the future probabilities as is given to them. To assume for certainty all the most advantageous

D possibilities and take no account of the disadvantageous is not to strike a fair balance. And in this case the verdict is larger than even the most advantageous assumptions would seem to justify. One is naturally loth to disturb the verdict and one can only do so if it be unreasonable. But LORD MACDERMOTT, C.J., and McVEIGH, L.J., applied the right test to the matter and decided that the verdict could not stand.

E In spite of the able and attractive arguments of counsel who supported the verdict for the appellant, I find myself in agreement with the majority of the Court of Appeal. I would therefore dismiss the appeal.

LORD WILBERFORCE: My Lords, I concur.

LORD DIPLOCK: My Lords, the purpose of an award of damages under

F the Fatal Accidents Acts is to provide the widow and other dependants of the deceased with a capital sum which with prudent management will be sufficient to supply them with material benefits of the same standard and duration as would have been provided for them out of the earnings of the deceased had he not been killed by the tortious act of the respondents, credit being given for the value of any material benefits which will accrue to them (otherwise than as the fruits of

G insurance) as a result of his death.

To assess the damages it is necessary to form a view on three matters each of which is in greater or less degree one of speculation: (i) the value of the material benefits for his dependants which the deceased would have provided out of his earnings for each year in the future during which he would have provided them had he not been killed; (ii) the value of any material benefits which the dependants

H will be able to obtain in each such year from sources (other than insurance) which would not have been available to them had the deceased lived but which will become available to them as a result of his death; (iii) the amount of the capital sum which with prudent management will produce annual amounts equal to the difference between (i) and (ii) (i.e., " the dependency ") for each of the years during which the deceased would have provided material benefits for the depend-

I ants had he not been killed.

Since the essential arithmetical character of this assessment is the calculation of the present value of an annuity it has become usual both in England and in Northern Ireland to arrive at the total award by multiplying a figure assessed as the amount of the annual " dependency " by a number of " years' purchase ". If the figure for the annual " dependency " remained constant and could be assessed with certainty and if the number of years for which it would have continued were also ascertainable with certainty it would be possible in times of stable currency, interest rates and taxation to calculate with certainty the number of years' purchase of the dependency which would provide a capital sum sufficient **A** to produce an annuity equal in amount to the dependency for the number of years for which it would have continued. If the estimated " dependency " did not remain constant but altered at intervals during the period of its enjoyment an accurate assessment of the appropriate award would involve calculating the present value of a series of annuities for fixed periods progressively deferred. For reasons to which I shall advert this is seldom if ever done. Anticipated future **B** variations in " dependency " are normally dealt with by an adjustment in the multiplicand to be multiplied by the single multiplier—the number of years' purchase.

During the last 20 years, however, sterling has been subject to continuous inflation. Its purchasing power has fallen at an average rate of 3 per cent. to $3\frac{1}{2}$ per cent. per annum and the increase in wage rates has more than kept pace **C** with the fall in the value of money. It has been strongly contended on behalf of the appellant that inflation and increased wage rates are irreversible phenomena in the modern world and that in assessing damages under the Fatal Accidents Acts, the " dependency " should be calculated as a continuously increasing amount to allow for the increasing cost in a depreciating currency of equivalent material benefits which the deceased would have provided for his dependants out **D** of his rising wages. But this is to isolate but one of many interrelated factors. The damages will be paid in currency which has the value of sterling at the date of the judgment. Experience of the 20 years of inflation has shown that its effects can be offset to some extent at any rate by prudent, investment in buying a home, in growth stocks, or in the short-term high-interest bearing securities.

A simple example will illustrate the effect of high interest rates: the sum **E** which represents the capital value of an annuity of £100 per annum for five years at compound interest rates of $4\frac{1}{2}$ per cent. per annum would purchase an annuity for the same period of about £110 per annum at current short-term interest rates of 8 per cent. per annum. During the same five years at a rate of inflation of $3\frac{1}{2}$ per cent. per annum compound the purchasing power of the pound would fall progressively until at the end of the five-year period about £119 would be needed **F** to buy the equivalent of £100 at the beginning of the period. During the first part of the five-year period an annuity of £110 would more than compensate for inflation and the excess, invested at 8 per cent., would largely compensate for the shortfall at the end of the period.

Fiscal policy, too, may have a considerable effect on the annual amounts which can be produced by a given capital sum. The changes in income tax and **G** the introduction of capital gains tax during the last 20 years would themselves have been sufficient to falsify actuarial calculations of the capital value of an annuity made before those changes were introduced; and it would be unwise to assume that fiscal policy will not alter further in the coming years.

In my view, the only practicable course for courts to adopt in assessing damages awarded under the Fatal Accidents Acts is to leave out of account the risk of **H** further inflation on the one hand and the high interest rates which reflect the fear of it and capital appreciation of property and equities which are the consequence of it on the other hand. In estimating the amount of the annual dependency in the future, had the deceased not been killed, money should be treated as retaining its value at the date of the judgment, and in calculating the present value of annual payments which would have been received in future years, interest rates **I** appropriate to times of stable currency such as 4 per cent. to 5 per cent. should be adopted.

But this still leaves the court with the task with which it has been confronted since the first Fatal Accidents Act was passed of estimating how long the dependants would have continued to benefit from the dependency had the deceased not been killed and what the amount of the dependency would have been in each year of that period.

The role of the court in making an assessment of damages which depends on its

A   view as to what will be and what would have been is to be contrasted with its
ordinary function in civil actions of determining what was. In determining what
did happen in the past a court decides on the balance of probabilities. Anything
that is more probable than not it treats as certain. But in assessing damages which
depend on its view as to what will happen in the future or would have happened
in the future if something had not happened in the past, the court must make an
B   estimate as to what are the chances that a particular thing will or would have
happened and reflect those chances, whether they are more or less than even, in
the amount of damages which it awards.

The starting point in any estimate of the number of years that a dependency
would have endured is the number of years between the date of the deceased's
death and that at which he would have reached normal retiring age. That falls
C   to be reduced to take account of the chance not only that he might not have lived
until retiring age but also the chance that by illness or injury he might have been
disabled from gainful occupation. The former risk can be calculated from available actuarial tables. The latter cannot. There is also the chance that the widow
may die before the deceased would have reached the normal retiring age (which
can be calculated from actuarial tables) or that she may remarry and thus
D   replace her dependency from some other source which would not have been
available to her had her husband lived. The prospects of remarriage may be
affected by the amount of the award of damages. But insofar as the chances
that death or incapacitating illness or injury would bring the dependency to an
end increase in later years when, from the nature of the arithmetical calculation
their effect on the present capital value of the annual dependency diminishes, a
E   small allowance for them may be sufficient where the deceased and his widow were
young and in good health at the date of his death. Similarly even in the case of a
young widow the prospect of remarriage may be thought to be reduced by the
existence of several young children to a point at which little account need be
taken of this factor. In cases such as the present where the deceased was aged 25
and the appellant, his widow, about the same age, courts have not infrequently
F   awarded 16 years' purchase of the dependency. It is seldom that this number of
years' purchase is exceeded. It represents the capital value of an annuity certain
for a period of 26 years at interest rates of 4 per cent., 29 years at interest rates of
4½ per cent. or 33 years at interest rates of 5 per cent. Having regard to the uncertainties to be taken into account 16 years would appear to represent a reasonable maximum number of years' purchase where the deceased died in his twenties.
G   Even if the period were extended to 40 years, i.e., when the deceased would
have attained the age of 65, the additional number of years' purchase at interest
rates of 4 per cent. would be less than four years, at 4½ per cent. would be less
than 2½ years, and at 5 per cent. would be little more than one year.

The starting point in any estimate of the amount of the " dependency " is the
annual value of the material benefits provided for the dependants out of the
H   earnings of the deceased at the date of his death. But quite apart from inflation
with which I have already dealt there are many factors which might have led to
variations up or down in the future. His earnings might have increased and with
them the amount provided by him for his dependants. They might have diminished with a recession in trade or he might have had spells of unemployment. As
his children grew up and became independent the proportion of his earnings spent
I   on his dependants would have been likely to fall. But in considering the effect
to be given in the award of damages to possible variations in the dependency there
are two factors to be borne in mind. The first is that the more remote in the future
is the anticipated change the less confidence there can be in the chances of its
occurring and the smaller the allowance to be made for it in the assessment. The
second is that as a matter of the arithmetic of the calculation of present value, the
later the change takes place the less will be its effect on the total award of damages.
Thus at interest rates of 4½ per cent. the present value of an annuity for 20 years
of which the first ten years are at £100 per annum and the second ten years at

£200 per annum is about 12 years' purchase of the arithmetical average annuity   A
of £150 per annum, whereas if the first ten years are at £200 per annum and the
second ten years at £100 per annum the present value is about 14 years' purchase
of the arithmetical mean of £150 per annum. If therefore the chances of variations
in the " dependency " are to be reflected in the multiplicand of which the years'
purchase is the multiplier variations in the dependency which are not expected
to take place until after ten years should have only a relatively small effect in   B
increasing or diminishing the " dependency " used for the purpose of assessing
the damages.

At the date of his death on 21st November 1964, the deceased, Mr. William
John Mallett, then aged 25, was employed in his home town of Londonderry
as a machine operative by Monarch Electric, Ltd., at an average weekly wage
of £12 16s. 7d. From these wages his average weekly contribution to the main-   C
tenance of the appellant, his wife, then aged 24, and his three infant children was
£9 10s. a week. But for six weeks before his death he was receiving an additional
£6 to £10 per week for spare-time work as a vocalist in a dance band and from these
(untaxed) receipts he gave the appellant for household expenses another £3 10s.
on the average. Thus up to six weeks before his death the total " dependency "
of the appellant and the children had been £338 per annum but for the last six   D
weeks had risen to £520 per annum.

Between the date of his death and the date of the trial of the appellant's action
for damages under the Fatal Accidents Acts (Northern Ireland) 1846-1959 on
18th September 1967, two things happened. Up to January 1967, the average weekly wages of operatives of the grade of the deceased had risen by 17s., but the company by which he was employed had closed down in that month. Londonderry   E
is an area of high unemployment but there was evidence of a witness who said
that if the deceased had lived and been out of a job he would have employed
him as an asphalter at an average weekly wage of £22 10s. though he would have
had to work very long hours at times in order to earn this average wage. These
hours would seem to be incompatible with spare-time work with the band, but his
average weekly earnings would have been about £2 per week more than during the   F
last six weeks of his life when the " dependency " was £520 per annum.

The jury awarded a total of £22,000 damages. By a majority (LORD MAC-
DERMOTT, C.J., and McVEIGH, L.J.;   CURRAN, L.J., dissenting) the Court of
Appeal of Northern Ireland set aside this verdict and ordered a new trial. Both
CURRAN, L.J. (in his dissenting judgment), and McVEIGH, L.J., considered that
the loss of dependency during the two years and ten months up to the date of the   G
trial might be reasonably assessed at £1,500. This leaves £20,500 for future loss.
Accepting, as would be appropriate for a deceased who would have been 27 years
old at the date of the assessment, 16 years' purchase as the multiplier this means
that the multiplicand was a " dependency " of £1,281 per annum or almost two
and a half times the actual dependency at the date of the death.

I can see no possible justification for an award of this magnitude. I would   H
dismiss the appeal.

Appeal dismissed.

Solicitors: *Asher Fishman & Co.*, agents for *Roderick B. Campbell*, Londonderry
(for the appellant); *Wm. Easton & Sons*, agents for *McKinty & Wright*, Belfast
(for the respondents).
                                                                                      I
[*Reported by* WENDY SHOCKETT, *Barrister-at-Law.*]

A

LONDON ARTISTS, LTD. *v.* LITTLER.

[AND ASSOCIATED ACTIONS].

[COURT OF APPEAL, CIVIL DIVISION (Lord Denning, M.R., Edmund Davies and
Widgery, L.JJ.), December 4, 5, 6, 9, 10, 1968.]

B

*Libel—Fair comment—Public interest—Communication to press—Letter deploring
simultaneous termination of engagements privately by four artistes in a
play running at London theatre—Simultaneous giving of notices a matter
of public interest—Whether statements in letter comment or fact—One fact
not proved—Defence of fair comment—Necessity to distinguish between fact
and comment—Whether question whether comment or fact could have been
left to jury.*

C

On 22nd June 1965, four theatrical artistes, through their agents, the
first plaintiffs, wrote to the defendant determining with one month's notice
their engagements in a play being staged by the defendant at Her Majesty's
Theatre, London (the notices were in accordance with their contracts). For
all the top performers in a play to move at once was almost unprecedented

D

in the theatre world and was likely to bring the play to an end.   Around
the same time the management of the theatre was trying to transfer the
play to another theatre.   The defendant, who was convinced there was a
plot to stop the play, wrote a letter* to each artiste concerned and held
a press conference where he distributed the letter to the press, in which
he suggested that the plaintiffs, all of whom were connected with the enter-

E

tainment industry, had taken part in what appeared to be a plot to force
the end of a successful play.   In actions against the defendant for libel
the defendant pleaded justification, fair comment on a matter of public
interest (i.e., the fate of the play) and publication on an occasion of qualified
privilege.   At the close of the plaintiffs' evidence the defence of justification
was withdrawn (i.e., the existence in fact of a conspiracy).   The judge

F

held, inter alia, that the plea of privilege failed and the plea of fair comment
failed because the matter was not one of public interest.   The only issue left to
the jury was that of damages.   The defendant appealed on the ground that
the judge had erred in law when he ruled that the defence of fair comment
could not be left to the jury.

G

Held: the plea of fair comment failed because, although the comment
was on a matter of public interest in which people at large were legitimately
interested, the allegation of a plot was a statement of fact in itself defamatory of the plaintiffs which was not reasonably capable of being considered
as comment and which the defendant had failed to prove as true (see p. 198,
letter D, p. 199, letters B, C and E, p. 200, letter F, p. 203, letter D, and

H

p. 204, letters E, F and I, post).

South Hetton Coal Co., Ltd. v. *North-Eastern News Association* ([1894] 1 Q.B.
133); *Jones* v. *Skelton* ([1963] 3 All E.R. 952); *Kemsley* v. *Foot* ([1952]
1 All E.R. 501); and dicta of FLETCHER MOULTON, L.J., in *Hunt* v. *Star
Newspaper, Co., Ltd.* ([1908-10] All E.R. Rep. at p. 517) applied.

Per LORD DENNING, M.R.: In order for the defence of fair comment to

I

be left to the jury there must at least be a sufficient basis of fact to warrant
the comment (see p. 199, letter F, post).

Decision of CANTLEY, J. ([1968] 1 All E.R. 1075) affirmed, but on different
grounds.

[As to the defence of fair comment, see 24 HALSBURY'S LAWS (3rd Edn.)
70, 71, paras. 123, 124; and for cases on the subject, see 32 DIGEST (Repl.)
169, 170, *1835-1843*; and as to what matters rank as matters of public interest,

---

* The letter to Miss Coral Browne is printed at p. 195, letter I, to p. 196, letter F, post.

H

see 24 HALSBURY'S LAWS (3rd Edn.) 72-74, para. 126; and for cases on the subject, **A**
see 32 DIGEST (Repl.) 172-176, *1859-1895*.]

Cases referred to:

Aga Khan v. *Times Publishing Co., Ltd.*, [1924] 1 K.B. 675; 93 L.J.K.B. 361;
   130 L.T. 746; 32 Digest (Repl.) 182, *1958*.

Andrews v. *Chapman* (1853), 3 Car. & Kir. 286; 21 L.T.O.S. 108; 32 Digest
   (Repl.) 166, *1808*.   **B**

Broadway Approvals, Ltd. v. *Odhams Press, Ltd.*, [1965] 2 All E.R. 523;
   [1965] 1 W.L.R. 805; Digest (Cont. Vol. B) 493, *1910a*.

Burton v. *Board*, [1929] 1 K.B. 301; [1928] All E.R. Rep. 659; 98 L.J.K.B.
   165; 140 L.T. 289; 32 Digest (Repl.) 183, *1963*.

Cunningham-Howie v. *F. W. Dimbleby & Sons, Ltd.*, [1950] 2 All E.R. 882;
   [1951] 1 K.B. 360; 32 Digest (Repl.) 183, *1964*.   **C**

Grech v. *Odhams Press, Ltd., Addis* v. *Odhams Press, Ltd.*, [1958] 2 All E.R. 462;
   [1958] 2 Q.B. 275; [1958] 3 W.L.R. 16; 32 Digest (Repl.) 179, *1922*.

Hunt v. *Star Newspaper Co., Ltd.*, [1908] 2 K.B. 309; [1908-10] All E.R. Rep.
   513; 77 L.J.K.B. 732; 98 L.T. 629; 32 Digest (Repl.) 165, *1803*.

Jones v. *Skelton*, [1963] 3 All E.R. 952; [1963] 1 W.L.R. 1362; Digest (Cont.
   Vol. A) 1115, *917a*.   **D**

Kemsley v. *Foot*, [1952] 1 All E.R. 501; [1952] A.C. 345; 32 Digest (Repl.)
   176, *1887*.

Lefroy v. *Burnside* (*No. 2*) (1879), 4 L.R.Ir. 556.

Mangena v. *Wright*, [1909] 2 K.B. 958; 78 L.J.K.B. 879; 100 L.T. 960;
   32 Digest (Repl.) 167, *1823*.

South Hetton Coal Co., Ltd. v. *North-Eastern News Association, Ltd.*, [1894]   **E**
   1 Q.B. 133; 63 L.J.Q.B. 293; 69 L.T. 844; 58 J.P. 196; 32 Digest
   (Repl.) 177, *1903*.

Stopes v. *Sutherland* (1923), 39 T.L.R. 677; *rvsd.* H.L., sub nom. *Sutherland*
   v. *Stopes*, [1925] A.C. 47; [1924] All E.R. Rep. 19; 94 L.J.K.B. 166; 132
   L.T. 550; 32 Digest (Repl.) 170, *1845*.

Thomas v. *Bradbury, Agnew & Co., Ltd.*, [1906] 2 K.B. 627; [1904-07] All   **F**
   E.R. Rep. 220; 75 L.J.K.B. 726; 95 L.T. 23; 32 Digest (Repl.) 194,
   2081.

Truth (*N.Z.*), *Ltd.* v. *Avery*, [1959] N.Z.L.R. 274.

Turner (*otherwise Robertson*) v. *Metro-Goldwyn-Mayer Pictures, Ltd.*, [1950]
   1 All E.R. 449; 32 Digest (Repl.) 31, *186*.

Walker (*Peter*) *& Son, Ltd.* v. *Hodgson*, [1909] 1 K.B. 239; 78 L.J.K.B. 193;   **G**
   99 L.T. 902; 32 Digest (Repl.) 171, *1848*.

Appeal.

This was an appeal by the defendant, Emile Littler, from the judgment of
CANTLEY, J., dated 5th March 1968 and reported [1968] 1 All E.R. 1075, in
the associated actions whereby on the verdict of a jury it was ordered that the   **H**
defendant pay the sum of £250 to the first plaintiffs, London Artists, Ltd., the
sum of £500 to the second plaintiffs, the Grade Organisation, Ltd., the sum of
£500 to the third plaintiffs, Associated Television, Ltd., and £1,000 to the fourth
plaintiff, Lew Grade, as damages for libel. The defendant appealed on the
ground that the judge had erred in law in ruling that the defence of fair
comment could not be left to the jury and asked that judgment be set aside in
each action and a new trial ordered. The facts are set out in the judgment of   **I**
LORD DENNING, M.R.

Colin Duncan, Q.C., Peter Bristow, Q.C., and *Michael Kempster* for the
defendant.

Desmond Ackner, Q.C., A. L. J. Lincoln, Q.C., for the first plaintiffs, London
Artists, Ltd.

G. R. F. Morris, Q.C., and *A. T. Hoolahan* for the second plaintiffs, the Grade
Organisation, Ltd.

A   *C. L. Hawser, Q.C.*, and *Brian T. Neill, Q.C.*, for the third and fourth plaintiffs, Associated Television, Ltd., and Lew Grade.

LORD DENNING, M.R.: In May 1964 there opened in London a play called " The Right Honourable Gentleman ". It was staged by the defendant, Mr. Emile Littler, at Her Majesty's Theatre in Haymarket. The three principal
B   actors were Mr. Anthony Quayle, Miss Coral Browne and Miss Anna Massey. Another actor of a well-known family was Mr. Corin Redgrave. The theatre was owned by a subsidiary of the third plaintiffs, Associated Television, Ltd., of which the managing director was Mr. Prince Littler, a brother of the defendant. The defendant rented the theatre on the terms that the owners could determine his tenancy if the takings fell below £3,500 a week for two weeks in succession.
C   That is called the " get-out " figure.

Some months later, in September 1964, there opened in London another play called " Robert and Elizabeth ". It was staged at the Lyric Theatre in Shaftesbury Avenue. The management of " Robert and Elizabeth " were very keen to move the play from the Lyric to Her Majesty's Theatre. The Lyric Theatre was controlled by another subsidiary of Associated Television, Ltd., of which,
D   as I have said, Mr. Prince Littler was managing director. So Mr. Prince Littler had a considerable voice in the ownership of both theatres.

On 18th June 1965 Mr. Prince Littler wrote to the defendant as follows:

E   ". . . I have had instructions from my Board at our meeting yesterday to give you notice as soon as you fall below the get-out figure in order to move ' Robert and Elizabeth ' which is playing to capacity at the Lyric Theatre to Her Majesty's Theatre . . . there is an alternative which is— would you be willing to transfer to the Lyric Theatre to enable us to move ' Robert and Elizabeth ' in to Her Majesty's."

The defendant replied the same day saying that " ' The Right Honourable Gentleman ' is playing to about the biggest business of any play in London at
F   the present time ", and went on to say that he was not prepared to move unless it was made very much worth his while.

A day or two later, on 22nd June 1965, the defendant received what to him was a stunning blow. The three top stars in " The Right Honourable Gentleman " and the satellite all gave four weeks' formal notice in writing to terminate their engagement. Each said that he or she would finish in the play after the
G   evening performance of 24th July. The letters were all in the same wording and were all sent by the actors' agents, the first plaintiffs, London Artists, Ltd. There had clearly been close collaboration in the sending of them. Such a thing—for all the top performers to remove at once—was almost unprecedented in the theatre world. It was likely to bring " The Right Honourable Gentleman " to a full stop. The defendant drew the conclusion that it was all a plot to get his play out of Her Majesty's Theatre, so as to get " Robert and Elizabeth "
H   in. He thought that the owners had got hold of the artistes and induced them to give the notices; and that the intermediary between them was the fourth plaintiff, Mr. Lew Grade, and the second plaintiffs, the Grade Organisation, Ltd. So firm was his belief in this plot that the next day, 23rd June 1965, he wrote a letter to each of the four artistes; and he held a press conference at which he distributed the letter to the press. It was published in the papers the next
I   day. It was in these words. I will read the one to Miss Coral Browne.

" My dear Coral, We have been friends for years and I am hurt that you did not see me before being a party to what, on the face of it, appears to be a plan to close the run of ' The Right Honourable Gentleman ' by joining in and sending me a month's formal notice from your agent.

" ' The Right Honourable Gentleman ' has been one of your greatest hits in London and is still doing better than any play in the West End. In spite of this Her Majesty's Theatre's new directorate are trying to get

our play out of the theatre.   Fighting for you all, play, Artistes, staff and   A
author, I have not acceded to their request to move because we have a
valid contract and are paying top rent and faithfully fulfilling all obligations.
Until Box Office takings drop below £3,500 for two consecutive weeks we
can contractually continue at Her Majesty's Theatre.

" Her Majesty's Theatre, and a great many other theatres in London,
are now controlled by Associated Television of which Mr. Lew Grade is   B
the Managing Director.   Mr. Grade's contract for service with Associated
Television Ltd. is with the Grade Organisation Ltd.   The Grade Organisation Ltd. owns ' London Artists Ltd.' (and other theatrical agencies) and
they manage our stars:—Anthony Quayle, Coral Browne, Anna Massey and
Corin Redgrave.   London Artists Ltd., on the 22nd June, by identical
letters, gave notice to me by hand for each Artiste to terminate their services   C
with the play on the same identical date of July 24th.

" In other words because I do not wish to disturb over a year's established
success at Her Majesty's Theatre, I am being put into a position by my
landlords, Associated Television Ltd., whereby, by withdrawing all Grade
Star Labour, the play must close down on the date on which these notices   D
expire.

" A great part of the success of ' The Right Honourable Gentleman '
has been the casting of this show and the combined effort of withdrawing
suddenly the three Grade Stars and another Grade Artiste on a given date
must finish our play for everybody at Her Majesty's and give Associated
Television Ltd. possession of the theatre.   You must all realise this and
know that there has never been such a situation in the History of the Theatre.   E
I feel this is such a serious matter, affecting all branches of the Industry,
that I must make this correspondence available to Equity, the Society of
West End Theatre Managers and the National Press.   Sincerely yours,
Emile."

That letter brought a quick retort.   On the very next day four writs for libel
were issued against the defendant.   The plaintiffs were those who were accused   F
of taking part in a plot: London Artists, who looked after the artistes; Associated
Television, who controlled the theatres; and Mr. Lew Grade, and the Grade
Organisation who were in between.

The defendant in his defence pleaded justification, privilege and fair comment.
The original pleading appeared to be defective, because there was nothing on the
face of the particulars to suggest a plot.   The master ordered the defence to   G
be struck out unless it was amended.   So the defendant did amend his particulars
as to allege a plot.   He did it in a paragraph of the particulars numbered 20A,
in which he alleged that the plaintiffs:

"... combined and planned ... by themselves their servants or agents
to procure the termination of the run of ' The Right Honourable Gentleman '
at Her Majesty's Theatre."   H

The defendant went to the court hoping to prove the plot.   He had no direct
evidence of a plot; but hoped to get something in cross-examination out of the
mouths of the plaintiffs.

He failed utterly.   The stars all gave evidence from which it became apparent
that there was no combination between them and the owners at all.   Miss Coral   I
Browne, earlier in the year had not been in good health.   Her husband had
recently died.   She wished to make arrangements to go to the United States,
but, when her agent indicated this to the defendant, he made such a fuss that
she decided to wait and give formal notice when the time came.   Mr. Anthony
Quayle decided to leave because he wanted to write a film script and needed a
holiday first.   When Miss Anna Massey heard that Mr. Anthony Quayle was
leaving, she decided to go too.   Mr. Corin Redgrave was a young man who wanted
to get more experience.

A   Seeing that there was no evidence of the suggested plot, the defendant on the eighth day of the trial withdrew the plea of justification; and with it para. 20A of the particulars which alleged the plot.   Then the plaintiffs submitted to the judge that there was nothing left in the defence save damages.   The judge upheld the submission.   He held that the plea of privilege failed because the publication to the press was not privileged.   He held that the plea of fair

B   comment failed because the matter was not one of public interest, and in addition there was no basis of fact to support the plea.   His rulings are reported (1).   The action then proceeded on the issue of damages.   The plaintiffs asked for substantial damages, because they said that the defendant had no honest belief in what he said.   They also asked for punitive damages because he was seeking to make money by giving additional publicity to " The Right Honourable

C   Gentleman ".   The defendant went into the witness box and refuted these suggestions. He asserted his honest belief that there was a plot to get " The Right Honourable Gentleman " out of Her Majesty's Theatre.   He was cross-examined. At one point he was asked—

D   " The whole core and sinew of the story was the conspiracy between Grade Organisation manipulating stars to get the play out of the theatre; that was the twist of the story, was it not? "   A.—" That is what I firmly believed at the time."

The judge asked him : " You were really saying, were you not, that there had been a dirty trick and Lew Grade had been taking part? "   He answered " Yes ".

E   After he had given his evidence the judge summed up.   The jury rejected the claim to punitive damages.   They awarded very modest sums.   They gave the first plaintiffs, London Artists, £250; the second plaintiffs, the Grade Organisation, £500; the third plaintiffs, Associated Television, £500; and the fourth plaintiff, Mr. Lew Grade, £1,000.   On hearing these figures, the defendant felt that he might have got clear away if the defence of fair comment had been left to the jury.   So he appeals to this court on the ground that the judge was

F   wrong in shutting out the defence of fair comment.   He does not appeal against the judge's ruling on privilege.   He appeals only on fair comment and asks that there should be a new trial.

The plea of fair comment was in these words :

G   " Further or in the alternative, the said words were fair comment made in good faith and without malice upon a matter of public interest, namely the fate of the play ' The Right Honourable Gentleman ' which was at all material times enjoying a successful run on the public stage at Her Majesty's Theatre, London.   The Defendant will rely if necessary on s. 6 of the Defamation Act, 1952."

That plea has been criticised and I think rightly.   It refers to " the said words " as if they consisted only of comment.   But " the said words " also contain state-

H   ments of fact.   And the plea leaves those statements of fact untouched.   In my days at the Bar we used to meet the difficulty by the " rolled-up " plea which had the great advantage that the defendant was not bound to distinguish between fact and comment : see *Aga Khan* v. *Times Publishing Co., Ltd.* (2).   But that plea fell into disfavour after 1949, when R.S.C., Ord. 82, r. 3 (2), compelled the defendant to distinguish between fact and comment.   Instead of the " rolled-up "

I   plea, the defendant now pleads simply " the said words were fair comment "— a plea which is obviously incomplete when the said words contain facts as well as comment.   But the plea carries with it an implication that the facts are true on which the comment is based; and the defendant can be ordered to give particulars of those facts: seee *Cunningham-Howie* v. *F. W. Dimbleby & Sons, Ltd.* (3). So long as that implication is read into the plea, it is unobjectionable.

(1) See [1968] 1 All E.R. 1075 at p. 1088;   [1968] 1 W.L.R. 607 at pp. 623, 624.
(2) [1924] 1 K.B. 675.
(3) [1950] 2 All E.R. 882 at p. 883;   [1951] 1 K.B. 360 at p. 364.

Three points arise on the defence of fair comment. First, was the comment
made on a matter of public interest? The judge ruled that it was not (4). I
cannot agree with him. There is no definition in the books as to what is a
matter of public interest. All we are given is a list of examples, coupled with
the statement that it is for the judge and not for the jury. I would not myself
confine it within narrow limits. Whenever a matter is such as to affect people
at large, so that they may be legitimately interested in, or concerned at, what
is going on; or what may happen to them or to others; then it is a matter of
public interest on which everyone is entitled to make fair comment. A good
example is *South Hetton Coal Co., Ltd.* v. *North-Eastern News Association, Ltd.* (5).
A colliery company owned most of the cottages in the village. It was held that
the sanitary conditions of those cottages—or rather their insanitary condition—
was a matter of public interest. LORD ESHER, M.R., said (6) that it was " a
matter of public interest that the conduct of the employers should be criticised ".
There the public were legitimately *concerned*. Here the public are legitimately
interested. Many people are interested in what happens in the theatre. The
stars welcome publicity. They want to be put at the top of the bill. Producers
wish it too. They like the house to be full. The comings and goings of the
performers are noticed everywhere. When three top stars and a satellite all
give notice to leave at the same time—thus putting a successful play in peril—
it is to my mind a matter of public interest on which everyone, press and all,
are entitled to comment freely.

The second point is whether the allegation of a " plot " was a fact which the
defendant had to prove to be true, or was it only comment? In order to be fair,
the commentator must get his basic facts right. The basic facts are those which
go to the pith and substance of the matter, see *Cunningham-Howie* v. *F. W.
Dimbleby & Sons, Ltd.* (7). They are the facts on which the comments are based
or from which the inferences are drawn—as distinct from the comments or
inferences themselves. The commentator need not set out in his original article
all the basic facts, see *Kemsley* v. *Foot* (8); but he must get them right and be
ready to prove them to be true. He must indeed afterwards in legal proceedings, when asked, give particulars of the basic facts, see *Burton* v. *Board* (9);
but he need not give particulars of the comments or the inferences to be drawn
from those facts. If in his original article he sets out basic facts which are
themselves defamatory of the plaintiff, then he must prove them to be true:
and this is the case just as much after s. 6 of the Defamation Act 1952, as it was
before. It was so held by the New Zealand Court of Appeal in *Truth (N.Z.), Ltd.*
v. *Avery* (10), which was accepted by this court in *Broadway Approvals, Ltd.* v.
Odhams Press, Ltd. (11). It is indeed the whole difference between a plea of fair
comment and a plea of justification. In fair comment he need only prove the
basic facts to be true. In justification he must prove also that the comments
and inferences are true also.

So I turn to ask what were the basic facts in this case? In the particulars
(as amended by including para. 20A) the defendant set out very many facts
which conveyed no clear picture. But, putting them together, it appears that
he was relying on three basic facts. First, that the owners wanted to get " The
Right Honourable Gentleman " out of Her Majesty's Theatre. Second, that
the stars and satellite all gave notice by the same agents at the same time in
the same form. Third, that there was a plot between the owners and the stars
(through the second plaintiffs, the Grade Organisation, Ltd.) to bring to an end

(4) [1968] 1 All E.R. at p. 1088; [1968] 1 W.L.R. at p. 623.
(5) [1894] 1 Q.B. 133.
(6) [1894] 1 Q.B. at p. 140.
(7) [1950] 2 All E.R. at p. 883; [1951] 1 K.B. at p. 364.
(8) [1952] 1 All E.R. 501; [1952] A.C. 345.
(9) [1929] 1 K.B. 301; [1928] All E.R. Rep. 659.
(10) [1959] N.Z.L.R. 274.
(11) [1965] 2 All E.R. 523; [1965] 1 W.L.R. 805.

A the run of " The Right Honourable Gentleman ".   The defendant proved the first two basic facts, but did not prove the third.   He failed to prove a plot and had to withdraw the allegation.   That put him in a quandary on fair comment. He could not prove one of the basic facts.   So he turned right about.   He then submitted that the allegation of a " plot " was not a fact at all but only a comment.   In my view that submission cannot be sustained, and for these reasons:

B In the first place, the defendant in his pleadings, treated the " plot " as a statement of fact, and I do not think we should look with favour on such a complete turnabout in the middle of the case.   In the second place, the defendant in his evidence said it was a statement of fact.   He was asked:

" What was said in the letters was deliberately intended by you to be said. That is right, is it not? A.—It was a statement of fact. Q.—What you believed
C to be a fact?   A.—Yes."

In the third place, on a fair reading of the whole letter, I think the allegation of a plot was a statement of fact.   The first paragraph runs in guarded language, " it appears "; and the fourth paragraph says " In other words "; but the last paragraph speaks of " the combined effort ".   Reading the letter as a whole, I have no doubt that it stated *as a fact* that there was a plot between the plaintiffs
D to bring down a chopper on the head of " The Right Honourable Gentleman ".

Counsel for the defendant submitted, however, that the question whether the statement was a statement of fact or comment should have been left to the jury. He would be right if it was reasonably capable of being considered as comment. That is clear from many of the cases, finishing with the judgment of the Privy Council in *Jones* v. *Skelton* (12).   But for the three reasons which I have given, I do
E not think the statement of a " plot " was reasonably capable of being considered as comment.   It was a statement of fact which was itself defamatory of the plaintiffs.   The defendant, in order to succeed, had to prove it to be true.   He failed to do so, and along with it went the defence of fair comment.

In case, however, I am wrong about this and it could be regarded as comment, then I turn to the third point, which is this: Were there any facts on which a
F fair-minded man might honestly make such a comment?   I take it to be settled law that, in order for the defence of fair comment to be left to the jury, there must at least be a sufficient basis of fact to warrant the comment, in this sense, that a fair-minded man might on those facts honestly hold that opinion.   There is no need for the defendant to prove that his opinion was correct or one with which the jury agree. He is entitled to the defence of fair comment unless it
G can be said: " No fair-minded man could honestly hold that opinion."   See what Buckley, L.J., said in *Peter Walker & Son, Ltd.* v. *Hodgson* (13).

In this case I am sure that the defendant acted honestly and in good faith. He honestly thought that there was a plot to bring to a stop the run of " The Right Honourable Gentleman ".   He was himself so convinced of it that he took the extreme step of telling it to the world.   But I fear that he went beyond
H the bounds of a fair-minded man.   He jumped too hastily to his conclusion. He ought not to have been so precipitate.   He ought to have made enquiries of the artistes.   He ought to have made enquiries of his brother, or wait till he had a letter from him.   We know that the brother had on 23rd June, that very day, written saying " We shall have to continue on the same basis as now ". By jumping so quickly to a conclusion the defendant came at odds with the law.
I He made a public condemnation not only of the artistes themselves but of the plaintiffs, Associated Television, and the agents, London Artists, Mr. Lew Grade and the Grade Organisation.   The judge held (14) that in alleging that all those were parties to a plot he was making an imputation without any basis of fact to support it.   I think the judge was quite right in so holding and in not leaving it to the jury.

_____

(12) [1963] 3 All E.R. 952; [1963] 1 W.L.R. 1362.
(13) [1909] 1 K.B. 239 at p. 253.
(14) [1968] 1 All E.R. at p. 1088; [1968] 1 W.L.R. at p. 624.

In the upshot it comes to this: the fate of " The Right Honourable Gentle- **A**
man " was a matter of public interest. The defendant was fully entitled to
comment on it as long as his comment was fair and honest. He was entitled
to give his views to the public through the press. But I think he went beyond
the bounds of fair comment. He was carried away by his feelings at the moment.
He did not wait long enough to check the facts and to get them right. He had
no defence except as to damages; and on that he did well. I would dismiss this **B**
appeal.

   EDMUND DAVIES, L.J.: I agree that this appeal should be dismissed,
but I have arrived at that conclusion by a route quite different from that which
led the learned trial judge (15) to reject as he did the plea of fair comment.

   The first question he posed was whether any matter of public interest had
arisen for comment. The burden of establishing to the satisfaction of the judge **C**
that this was so lay on the defendant—see *Peter Walker & Son, Ltd.* v. *Hodgson*
(16); and he asserted that " the fate of the play ' The Right Honourable Gentleman ', which was at all material times enjoying a successful run at Her Majesty's
Theatre, London ", was in truth a matter of public interest. The learned
judge ruled otherwise, but added that he found it (17) " something of a borderline
case ".   He held that, since all four actors did no more than they were entitled **D**
to do, and did it privily, no matter of public interest arose even though it was
established that the probable result of their synchronising their notices would
be the abrupt termination of public presentation of the play. I find that ruling
somewhat difficult to follow, especially in view of the judge's acceptance of the
proposition that a strike of actors appearing in a particular production could
well be a matter of public interest and give rise to the plea of fair comment, for **E**
such a strike might equally be brought about by each actor individually and
lawfully terminating his engagement.

   In my respectful view, the judge misdirected himself on this first point. Just
as the presentation of a new play is of public interest, so also, in my judgment,
is the sudden and surprising closure of a play enjoying a highly successful run.
It was not, for example, as though Miss Coral Browne had changed her accountant, **F**
or Mr. Anthony Quayle had turned Buddhist, or Miss Massey had taken some
other step equally unconnected with her public career. On the contrary, not
only did they act collectively, but their collective action was immediately and
dramatically connected with their careers as public entertainers.

   It is not difficult to think up examples of the sort of public comment which
such an unusual event might legitimately provoke. For example, it might well **G**
lead to a discussion of whether the paucity of West End theatres is such that
even highly successful plays have to be taken off to make way for new ones
awaiting production, or to an examination of theatre finances, or to an assessment
of the virtues and vices of the starring system, all such comment springing from
and primarily illustrated by the abrupt taking-off of one highly praised and
successful production. If one of our theatre critics had written a piece on the **H**
lines I have indicated, could it be doubted that his comments on, inspired by, and
expressly referring to such an event related to a matter of public interest? In
my judgment, it could not. Similarly, while the defendant possessed no special
right simply because of his financial and other particular interest in the continual
success of " The Right Honourable Gentleman ", he was as much entitled as
anyone else to make proper comment on such a striking and unusual event in **I**
the theatrical world as its withdrawal during a triumphant run. For these
reasons, I differ from the trial judge on this point. This defendant went wrong
not for lack of a topic of public interest, but because of his maltreatment of the
one which suddenly confronted him.

   I differ from the judge, too, in relation to the second question he posed, namely,

(15) [1968] 1 All E.R. at p. 1088; [1968] 1 W.L.R. at p. 624.
(16) [1909] 1 K.B. 239 at p. 249.
(17) [1968] 1 All E.R. at p. 1087; [1968] 1 W.L.R. at p. 623.

A   as to (18) " whether the part of the letter relied on as comment is capable of being so understood ".   He expressed himself as unable to hold that the words complained of were not reasonably capable of being construed as comment and accordingly said that, had he decided the first question in the defendant's favour, he would have left this issue to the jury.   While in my judgment he fell into error in applying it, that was the correct test, for, as Lord Porter said in *Turner*

B   *(otherwise Robertson)* v. *Metro-Goldwyn-Mayer Pictures, Ltd.* (19):

> ". . . it is for the jury in a proper case to determine what is comment and what is fact, but a pre-requisite to this right is that the words are capable of being a statement of a fact or facts.   It is for the judge alone to decide whether they are so capable . . ."

C   It follows that the question whether the words complained of were reasonably capable of being regarded as mere *comment* is likewise essentially a matter for the judge, it being incumbent on the defendant to establish that they were so capable—see *Jones* v. *Skelton* (20).   If the judge takes the view that they amount clearly to assertions of fact alone, no question of fair comment arises and that plea must accordingly not be left to the jury.

D   It may be difficult in a particular case to distinguish between assertions of fact, on the one hand, and comment in the form of expressions of opinion, on the other.   Yet the problem must be solved, be it by judge alone or by jury, and this for at least two reasons: *First,* if the words complained of are comment, it is not necessary to prove their truth, but merely that they express a view such as an honest (though possibly prejudiced) man might form.   *Secondly,* comment

E   must be disentangled from fact, for fair comment is available as a defence only in relation to facts which are either (a) true, or (b) if untrue, were published on a privileged occasion—see *Mangena* v. *Wright* (21) and *Grech* v. *Odhams Press, Ltd.* (22).   Leaving aside privilege, which does not now arise for consideration, if the alleged facts relied on as the basis for comment turn out to be untrue, a plea of fair comment avails the defendant nothing, even though they expressed

F   his honest view.   As was pointed out in *Lefroy* v. *Burnside* (23) the very nature of the plea

> ". . . *assumes* the matters of fact relied upon to be somehow or other ascertained.   It does not mean that a man may invent facts and then comment on the facts so invented in what would be a *bona fide* manner on the supposition that the facts were true."

G   A man may be led to invent quite honestly and without realising that he is doing so, by mistake, through ignorance or prejudice, or (as probably occurred in the present case) under the stress of emotion.   But, whatever the source of error, the defence " does not extend to cover misstatements of fact, however bona fide "—see *Thomas* v. *Bradbury, Agnew & Co., Ltd.* (24).

It behoves a writer to indicate clearly what portions of his work are fact and

H   what are comment, for, in the words of Fletcher Moulton, L.J., in *Hunt* v. *Star Newspaper Co., Ltd.* (25)—

> ". . . comment, in order to be justifiable as fair comment, must appear as comment and must not be so mixed up with the facts that the reader cannot distinguish between what is report and what is comment: see *Andrews* v. *Chapman* (26)."

I

---

(18) [1968] 1 All E.R. at p. 1087; [1968] 1 W.L.R. at p. 623.
(19) [1950] 1 All E.R. 449 at p. 461.
(20) [1963] 3 All E.R. 952 at p. 964; [1963] 1 W.L.R. 1362 at p. 1379.
(21) [1909] 2 K.B. 958.
(22) [1958] 2 All E.R. 462; [1958] 2 Q.B. 275.
(23) (1879), 4 L.R.Ir. 556 at p. 565.
(24) [1906] 2 K.B. 627 at p. 638; [1904-07] All E.R. Rep. 220 at p. 223.
(25) [1908] 2 K.B. 309 at p. 319; [1908-10] All E.R. Rep. 513 at p. 517.
(26) (1853), 3 Car. & Kir. 286.

Failure to exhibit clarity in this respect carries its own risks, for, as FLETCHER A
MOULTON, L.J., went on to say (27)—

> " Any matter . . . which does not indicate with a reasonable clearness
> that it purports to be comment, and not statement of fact, cannot be
> protected by the plea of fair comment."

This desirability is further borne out by the following passage from ODGERS ON B
LIBEL AND SLANDER (6th Edn., 1929), p. 166, quoted with approval by LORD
PORTER in *Kemsley* v. *Foot* (28)—

> " . . . if [a defendant] sets out the facts correctly, and then gives his
> inference, stating it as his inference from those facts, such inference will as
> a rule, be deemed a comment.   But even in that case, the writer must be
> careful to state the inference as an inference, and not to assert it as a new C
> and independent fact; otherwise the inference will become something more
> than a comment, and he may be driven to justify it as an allegation of
> fact."

Care is therefore called for, notwithstanding the many cases (among which are
Stopes v. *Sutherland* (29) and *Aga Khan* v. *Times Publishing Co., Ltd.* (30)) holding
that in doubtful cases the question of whether the words are comment *must* be D
left to the jury.

Such considerations having an obvious importance, the plaintiffs requested
further and better particulars, not only of the defence of justification, but also
of the plea of fair comment, seeking " Particulars of the facts and matters on
which the alleged comment is made ".   Those originally delivered in no way
connected any act of the four plaintiffs with the event which was said to threaten E
the fate of the play, namely the simultaneous giving of notice by four members
of the cast.   The plaintiffs accordingly applied to strike out both pleas.   The
master agreed to do this unless the defendant amended, holding that as they
stood the particulars delivered disclosed no reasonable defence and were calculated
to prejudice and embarrass the fair trial of the action.   From that order the
defendant never appealed.   Instead, doubtless recognising the force of the F
plaintiffs' criticism and in order to salvage his pleading, he amended his particulars in the important respects already indicated by LORD DENNING, M.R.   The
essential allegation expressly advanced for the first time in the new para. 20A
was that the four plaintiffs had combined together to procure the termination of
(a) the run of the play, and (b) the contracts entered into by the leading members
of the cast as a means to that end. G

While that paragraph remained, it provided the needed link between the
plaintiffs and the combined action of the four actors.   Nevertheless, counsel
for the defendant has strenuously submitted that, despite the contrary intimation
made to the plaintiffs, para. 20A ought not to be read as supplying any factual
basis for the alleged comment.   I regret that I am quite unable to follow that
submission.   On the contrary, I think that the defendant should be held to what H
he himself indicated was the role of para. 20A, in common with the rest of his
particulars of the plea of fair comment.

The stage was reached during the trial when the overwhelming weight of
evidence compelled the defendant to withdraw para. 20A in toto (together with
certain other important allegations to which LORD DENNING, M.R., has already
referred), for there was simply no evidence that any of the plaintiffs had taken I
any step (acting either singly or collectively) to procure the termination of the
play.   Even so, it has been submitted that the particulars, emasculated though
they had become, still retained sufficient virility to play their designated role of
stating the facts on which the alleged comment could honestly (even though

---

(27) [1908] 2 K.B. at p. 320; [1908-10] All E.R. Rep. at p. 517.
(28) [1952] A.C. 345 at p. 356; [1952] 1 All E.R. 501 at p. 505.
(29) (1923), 39 T.L.R. 677 at p. 679.
(30) [1924] 1 K.B. 675 at p. 680.

A mistakenly) be based. I disagree. Without the now excised amendments to the particulars of the plea of fair comment, what remained consisted simply of the itemisation of a series of assertions of fact which, even assuming all were true, could not, and did not (as the defendant himself clearly recognised during the interlocutory stage) provide the basis of an assertion that any of the plaintiffs had conspired together to get the play stopped. The situation which thus arose

B was such as was envisaged by Lord Tucker in *Kemsley* v. *Foot* (31) in saying that:

"... where the facts relied on to justify the comment are contained only in the particulars, it is not incumbent on the defendant to prove the truth of every fact so stated in order to establish his plea of fair comment, *but* he must establish sufficient facts to support the comment to the

C satisfaction of the jury."

It follows that, if *none* of the facts so relied on exist, the plea has no foundation and must therefore be withdrawn from the jury—see *Lefroy* v. *Burnside* (32). Again, if (as I think is the case) para. 20A has to be regarded as setting out a vitally important part of the alleged facts on which the defendant purported to

D comment, it is impossible to regard such comment as reasonably capable of being fair, focussed as it very largely was on that paragraph, once its complete falsity was established and, indeed, conceded.

That is sufficient to dispose of this matter. Even so, one has perhaps not said all that needs to be said, for, even if the amended particulars had subsisted in their entirety, it remains to be considered whether the defamatory letter consisted

E of comment or fact or partly of fact and partly of comment. It is here to be observed that, although counsel for the defendant sought valiantly to establish that the libel complained of was a mélange of fact and of inference, the defence pleaded without qualification and in relation to the letter *as a whole* that "the said words were fair comment ..." Having thus abjured the "rolled-up" plea, the defendant, through his counsel, nevertheless proceeded to dissect the letter,

F submitting that the opening words expressed a mere inference, that the next two paragraphs contained facts alone, and that the entire paragraph beginning, "In other words ..." was mere comment. But it seems to have been clearly conceded at the trial that the important reference in the final paragraph to "... the combined effort of withdrawing suddenly the three Grade Stars and another Grade Artiste on a given date" amounted to an assertion of fact. Its falsity

G became demonstrated, and that it was highly defamatory of all four plaintiffs is not challenged. Accordingly, no plea of fair comment could protect the defendant in respect of it. Nor, in my judgment, did such a plea avail him in relation to the reference in the opening paragraph to the alleged "plan to close the run of [the play]". Notwithstanding the prefatory words, "... what, on the face of it, appears to be a plan", that was as much an assertion of fact that a plan existed as was the claim made in para. 20A of the particulars that the

H plaintiffs "combined and planned" with each other for the purposes therein indicated. As counsel for the first plaintiffs neatly put it, the defendant was in effect pleading, "I commented *on a plot*" and not "*My comment* was that a plot existed". Indeed, I would have thought that this was beyond argument had counsel for the defendant not forcefully demonstrated the contrary before us.

I It is not presently necessary to decide whether a defendant who chooses not to adopt the "rolled-up" plea (which presents him with the necessity of distinguishing between fact and comment—now see R.S.C., Ord. 82, r. 3 (2)—a task which, as counsel for the defendant himself indicated, may prove difficult) and instead pleads, as here, simply that the words complained of were comment, may nevertheless at the trial pick and choose, then for the first time describing parts as comment and the rest as facts; but I certainly must not be taken as necessarily

(31) [1952] 1 All E.R. at p. 508; [1952] A.C. at p. 362.
(32) (1879), 4 L.R.Ir. at p. 565.

agreeing that he is free to do this. Be that as it may, however, the effect of A counsel for the defendant's detailed analysis of the offending letter was to invite this court to bring to its interpretation a subtlety and perspicacity well beyond that reasonably to be expected of the ordinary reader whom the defendant was clearly aiming at by holding his press conference, and to ignore the obviously fair and common-sense test propounded by FLETCHER MOULTON, L.J., in *Hunt* v. *Star Newspaper Co., Ltd.* (33). And whatever degree of subtlety be applied in B its interpretation, in my judgment the words complained of were clear assertions of facts and the judge should have so ruled, and for this additional reason should have withdrawn the plea from the jury. As it was, he was led to adopt that course by holding that no matter of public interest was involved.

Regarding the third point which he canvassed, I agree with the learned judge in rejecting the defence submission that (34):
C

"... it does not matter that the comment defames persons who were not actually involved in the conduct commented on, provided the conduct commented on was a matter of public interest."

Were this indeed the law it could work most oppressively, for, the issue of whether the comment was fair being for the jury and counsel for the defendant doubting (if not actually denying) the right of a judge to rule that the comment D complained of was not reasonably capable of being regarded as fair, it would follow that, however widely he had defamed in commenting on a matter of public interest, the issue of fair comment would *have* to be left to the jury. No authority was cited for this startling proposition and its absence causes me no surprise.
E
In the result, although I hold that a matter of public interest existed (whereas the judge held (35) that there was none) and although I also hold that the words complained of were not reasonably capable of being regarded as comment (whereas the judge held that they were), I agree with his ruling (34) that the only issue which should be left to the jury was that of quantum of damages. I accordingly concur in dismissing this appeal.
F

WIDGERY, L.J.: I agree that this appeal must be dismissed, and since my reasons are identical with those which have been indicated in the judgments of my Lords, I do not propose to deal with them in great detail. In particular, I agree that the learned judge erred in ruling (35) that the defendant's letter of 23rd June 1965 was not written on a matter of public interest, Here was a successful play receiving considerable public support which many members of G the public no doubt still wished to see. Any event which prematurely curtailed the run of the play and deprived the public of this entertainment was in my judgment a matter of public concern. I think the situation is aptly described in the defendant's pleading where he says that the relevant matter of public interest was "the fate of the play". Counsel for the first plaintiffs seeks to answer this argument by saying that when an actor gives notice to determine H his contract, the giving of that notice, and the motives which prompted it, are part of the private sector of the actor's life and are not a matter of public comment; but although this will often be true, I think this is not necessarily so. The fact that the fate of the play is a matter of public interest does not give a licence to comment at large on the actor's private life, but his conduct in relation to the termination of the run is within the sphere of public interest for this I purpose.

This conclusion does not in the end profit the defendant since in the remainder of this appeal there are in my judgment overwhelming grounds for saying that the defence of fair comment was not open to him. I agree with my Lords that the words complained of were not comment but were a statement of fact. I

(33) [1908] 2 K.B. at pp. 319, 320; [1908-10] All E.R. Rep. at p. 517.
(34) [1968] 1 All E.R. at p. 1088; [1968] 1 W.L.R. at p. 624.
(35) [1968] 1 All E.R. at p. 1088; [1968] 1 W.L.R. at p. 623.

A   confess readily that at one stage during counsel for the defendant's argument I had considerable doubt as to this issue, but in the end I am satisfied that the conclusion already stated is the right one, and that this would be enough of itself to dispose of the matter.   But for myself I find that the third point referred to by Lord Denning, M.R., is perhaps the dominant one, because even if one assumes the view contrary to that which we have all formed, that these words

B   were comment, it seems to me abundantly clear that there was no sufficient factual foundation to support that comment.   Of course, if the defendant had succeeded in proving that the third plaintiffs, Associated Television, had a financial stake in the play " Robert and Elizabeth ", and if he had further proved that the fourth plaintiff, Mr. Lew Grade, had a controlling interest in the second plaintiffs, the Grade Organisation, it is possible that the result would have been

C   different; but it is idle, I think, to speculate on this, because those facts were not proved and indeed it is recognised that they were not correct.   At the end of the day the only relevant facts on which the comment could have been based were I think five: First, that the third plaintiffs, Associated Television, through their subsidiaries was the lessee of Her Majesty's Theatre.   Secondly, that the fourth plaintiff, Mr. Lew Grade, was the managing director of the third plaintiffs,

D   Associated Television.   Thirdly, that Mr. Lew Grade was a shareholder with a minority holding in the second plaintiffs, the Grade Organisation.   Fourthly, that the first plaintiffs, London Artists, were a wholly-owned subsidiary of the Grade Organisation.   And fifthly, the first plaintiffs, London Artists, had given the notices in question on behalf of the four members of the cast.   These facts no doubt showed a connection, in the person of the fourth plaintiff, Mr. Lew

E   Grade, between the lessees of the theatre who would have obtained possession of the theatre if the play had been taken off, and the first plaintiffs, London Artists, who gave the notices, and in the absence of any other material I suppose a particularly suspicious mind or a mind whose judgment was upset by emotion might have conjured up a plot, with the fourth plaintiff, Mr. Lew Grade, as the moving spirit.   But when the fourth plaintiff gave evidence he flatly denied

F   this and the defendant eventually properly conceded that the jury could not be invited to draw the conclusion that the fourth plaintiff had taken any personal part in the alleged plot.   From that moment, as it seems to me, counsel for the defendant was producing Hamlet without the prince; and indeed the defendant was quite unable to identify any plotter among the numerous influential witnesses called by the plaintiffs.   In my judgment, no reasonably-minded man

G   could have drawn the inference from such material that any of the plaintiffs were a party to the alleged plot; and I think the judge was entirely right (36) in announcing that he would withdraw this issue from the jury and in consequentially ruling that the defence of fair comment was not open.   Accordingly I concur in the order proposed.

Appeal dismissed.   Leave to appeal to the House of Lords refused.

H
   Solicitors: *M. A. Jacobs & Sons* (for the defendant); *Oswald Hickson, Collier & Co.* (for the first plaintiffs); *Allen & Overy* (for the second plaintiffs); *Nicholson, Graham & Jones* (for the third and fourth plaintiffs).

[Reported by Rosalie Long, *Barrister-at-Law.]*

I

---

(36) [1968] 1 All E.R. at p. 1088; [1968] 1 W.L.R. at p. 624.

A

ANDERSON v. GRADIDGE.

[QUEEN'S BENCH DIVISION (Lord Parker, C.J., Blain and Donaldson, JJ.), March 4, 1969.]

Betting—Licensed betting office—Conduct—User outside closing hours—Offence to use premises at any time for purpose other than betting transactions— Private meeting held on premises after closing hours—Betting, Gaming and Lotteries Act 1963 (c. 2), s. 10 (1), Sch. 4, para. 1.

B

The words in para. 1 of Sch. 4 to the Betting, Gaming and Lotteries Act 1963, that licensed premises " shall not be used for any purpose other than the effecting of betting transactions " mean that at no time must the premises be used for any purpose other than the effecting of betting transactions and are not confined to times when the betting office is licensed to be open. Accordingly, where the licensee of a betting office used the office after closing hours for a private meeting of the local bookmakers' association he committed an offence under s. 10 (1)* of the Betting, Gaming and Lotteries Act 1963.

C

[For the Betting, Gaming and Lotteries Act 1963, s. 10, Sch. 4, see 43 HALSBURY'S STATUTES (2nd Edn.) 323, 401.]

D

Case Stated.

This was a Case Stated by justices for Hampshire in respect of their adjudication as a magistrates' court sitting at Aldershot on 29th July 1968, when, on an information preferred by the respondent, Frederick Philip Gradidge, against the appellant, William Hugh Anderson, that the appellant being the holder of a betting office licence had used the licensed premises for purposes other than for betting transactions, namely for the purpose of holding a meeting, contrary to s. 10 of the Betting, Gaming and Lotteries Act 1963 and para. I of Sch. 4 to the Act, the magistrates held that such user of the premises was an infringement of the Act even though the meeting was held at a time when the betting office was closed in pursuance of r. 1 of the Rules for Licensed Betting Offices. The facts are set out in the judgment of LORD PARKER, C.J.

E

F

I. S. Hill for the appellant.
M. T. Underhill for the respondent.

PARKER, C.J.: This is an appeal by way of Case Stated from a decision of justices for the county of Hampshire sitting at Aldershot who convicted the appellant of an offence against the Betting, Gaming and Lotteries Act 1963, the allegation being that he at nos. 11 to 13, Cove Road, being the holder of a betting office licence, did use such premises for purposes other than betting transactions, the placing of bets and collection of winnings, namely for the purpose of holding a meeting.

G

The short facts were that soon after 10.0 p.m. on an evening in March a police constable passed these premises and noticed that there were lights on, and indeed he saw a lady open the door and go in. He then entered the premises, as he was entitled to do, which were not locked, though they had a closed sign up. Inside the betting shop there were a number of men sitting in chairs; there were bottles and glasses on the counter and most of them were drinking, He was told it was a private meeting, as indeed it was, being a meeting of the Aldershot and District Bookmakers' Association, of which the appellant was a member; and the lady who had gone in was his wife.

H

I

The sole point here is whether the Act of 1963 makes it an offence to use the premises for some other purpose at any time, or whether it is confined, as the appellant suggests, to such times as the betting office is licensed to be open. Section 10 (1) of the Betting, Gaming and Lotteries Act 1963, provides:

---

* Section 10 (1), so far as material, and Sch. 4, para. 1 are set out at p. 207, letters A and B, post.

A
" A licensed betting office shall be managed in accordance with the rules set out in Schedule 4 to this Act . . . "

and provides that any contravention shall be an offence. Then one goes to Sch. 4, para. 1, which is in these terms:

B
" The licensed premises shall be closed throughout Good Friday, Christmas Day and every Sunday, and at such other times, if any, as may be prescribed, and shall not be used for any purpose other than the effecting of betting transactions ".

It is a short point; it seems to me that those words mean what they say, that at no time must the premises be used for any purpose other than the effecting of betting transactions, and to give it the meaning suggested by the appellant would mean reading in words, and accordingly I come to the conclusion the justices

C
were perfectly right; I would dismiss this appeal.

BLAIN, J.: I agree. I add only that there is no reason to think that this was anything but a reputable meeting or gathering which happened to take place on premises where it was unlawful that any use other than the statutory one should be made.

D
DONALDSON, J.: I agree.

Appeal dismissed.

Solicitors: *Batchelor, Fry, Coulson & Burder*, agents for *Foster, Wells & Coggins*, Aldershot (for the appellant); *P. K. L. Danks*, Winchester (for the respondent).

[*Reported by* Wendy Shockett, *Barrister-at-Law.*]

E

CURTIS *v.* CURTIS.

[Court of Appeal, civil division (Danckwerts, Winn and Edmund Davies, L.JJ.), December 16, 1968.]

F
Divorce—Maintenance of wife—Lump sum payment—Alternative or additional to annual sum—Factors to be regarded—Securing payment—Husband in defiance of orders of court—Danger of evading annual payment—Capital sum enforceable as bankruptcy debt—Matrimonial Causes Act 1965 (c. 72), s. 16 (1).

The husband left the wife in October 1966 and in December 1967 she was granted a decree nisi of divorce on the ground of his adultery. He was a

G
man of very considerable means (apparently of £250,000) and was in calculated defiance of the orders of the court. In determining the amount of maintenance to be awarded to the wife, the judge held that he was not entitled to take into account the conduct of the husband, but he decided that, if he simply awarded maintenance, in the light of that conduct the husband might defy the order of the court, go abroad or transfer some of his assets out of the country so as to make it as difficult as possible for the wife

H
to obtain her proper due. He therefore awarded a capital sum of £33,600 which would be enforceable as a bankruptcy debt, and maintenance of £810 per annum.

Held: the judge's order must be upheld because he had directed himself properly in holding that he was not entitled to take the husband's conduct into consideration in determining the amount of the maintenance, but he was

I
entitled to take into account the character and conduct of the husband in securing payment of the sums awarded, particularly in giving a capital sum because it would be enforceable as a bankruptcy debt (see p. 208, letter H, and p. 209, letters C, E and F, post).

Appeal dismissed.

[As to the form of maintenance on divorce see 12 Halsbury's Laws (3rd Edn.) 431, para. 968; and for cases on the subject, see 27 Digest (Repl.) 626, 627, *5868-5880.*

For the Matrimonial Causes Act 1965, s. 16, see 45 HALSBURY'S STATUTES A (2nd Edn.) 468.]

Case referred to:

Davis v. *Davis* [1967] 1 All E.R. 123; [1967] P. 185; [1966] 3 W.L.R. 1157; Digest (Repl.) Supp.

Appeal.

This was an appeal by the husband against an order of FAULKS, J., made on B 21st November 1968, varying an order of Mr. Registrar COMPTON MILLER made on 24th October 1968, by ordering that the husband pay to the wife a lump sum of £33,600 within 28 days and, also as from 21st October 1968, maintenance at the rate of £810 per annum less tax payable monthly for herself during their joint lives. The grounds of appeal were that the terms of the judge's order were unreasonable and excessive and that he did not give due weight to the registrar's C decision in the exercise of his discretion.

A. R. Campbell, Q.C., and *F. Lowe* for the husband.
M. Graham for the wife.

DANCKWERTS, L.J.: This is an appeal against a judgment of FAULKS, J., given on 21st November 1968. The history of the matter is sufficiently set out D in the second paragraph of the learned judge's judgment where he says:

" The husband is 45 years of age and the wife 40; there are two children, a boy of 14 and a girl of 12. They were married on 6th August 1950, and on 1st December 1967 the wife was granted a decree nisi on the ground of her husband's adultery. He had in fact left her in October 1966, at which time E the wife was unaware of the existence of a mistress. The husband said that if she wanted maintenance she would have to sign a separation agreement, and she did that. As a result he paid her £27 a week and £871 a year for household expenses and outgoings respectively; those two sums gross up to some £2,400 a year ".

FAULKS, J., was hearing an appeal against the decision of Mr. Registrar COMPTON F MILLER dated 24th October 1968, whereby he ordered the husband to pay a lump sum of £3,000 and alimony at £3,000 per year, of which I understand £1,000 was secured on the security of the matrimonial home. The decree was made absolute on that very day. The learned judge then goes on to say:

" This is the case of a husband with very considerable means, [apparently of £250,000] who is in calculated defiance of the orders of the court, and who G indeed wrote to Mr. Registrar COMPTON MILLER stating: ' I realise that I have not obeyed the orders of the court, and further I am aware that I shall have no rights while I remain in contempt of court ' ".

The learned judge heard him, and the judge very properly said that he was not entitled to take into consideration the conduct of the husband in regard to the amount of maintenance (whatever it might be) which was to be awarded. But H on the other hand, in my opinion the learned judge was well entitled to take into account the character of the husband and his conduct when it came to securing payment of the sums which were awarded by the learned judge in the ways he mentioned in his judgment.

The sum awarded by the judge was a capital sum; there is an error in the print of the judgment which was corrected, I think, in the order of the court. I The error appears in the transcript of the judgment where the sum was expressed as being a sum of £33,600, which was to be secured, and maintenance in the sum of £810 per annum. The word " secured " should not go in; it was in fact an order for payment of the sum of £33,600 and payment of the small sum for maintenance.

The matter was pre-eminently one for the discretion of the learned judge. He takes into account the fact that the husband is a rich man, and he felt, from the conduct of the husband in the past, that if he simply awarded maintenance, or

A something of that sort, the husband might defy the order of the court; he might have gone abroad and it may be that he would transfer some of his assets from this country so as to make it as difficult as possible for the wife to obtain her proper due.

In those circumstances, in my view, because the law of bankruptcy suggested a method of sanctions over the husband's behaviour, the learned judge was well

B entitled to make the order which he did. £33,600 is a large sum; it was indeed, I think, capitalising the sum of £2,400. It may be that the judge's figures did not come out quite right, but I think that we should accept the figure which he mentioned, and not attempt to correct it, or his arithmetic, or anything of that sort. I think that the learned judge was entirely correct in giving a capital sum because it would be enforceable as a bankruptcy debt, and I therefore see no

C reason for interfering with the order appealed from. I would dismiss the appeal.

There is one other point I should mention. The wife is in occupation of the matrimonial home, which is in the name of the husband. It is said to be worth £17,000 and it has a mortgage on it of £5,000. If the wife decided that she would be prepared to accept a conveyance of the house to her and payment off of the mortgage on it so that the house would be free of encumbrances, in part satis-

D faction of the sum which was awarded by the court, in my view she will be well justified in doing that; and, if the husband is prepared to agree, then the house representing that sum of £17,000 clear might be accepted in part payment of the sum of £33,600. But that is not part of the order of this court; that will be for the decision of the wife if she so chooses.

E WINN, L.J.: I entirely agree and desire to add only one very short point: In my opinion the glossary and literature, which no doubt will in course of time become voluminous, relating to the proper construction of s. 16 (1) of the Matrimonial Causes Act 1965, so far as it yet exists, does not reveal any clear indication that any proportion should be maintained by the court between the total fortune of the husband, and the amount awarded as a lump sum to the wife. I agree

F that the appeal should be dismissed.

EDMUND DAVIES, L.J.: I also agree. Counsel for the husband has submitted that in assessing the figure of £33,600 as a lump sum, the learned judge was gravely in error and that he should have awarded in its place a figure in the region of £10,000. His position is an unhappy one as counsel, lacking as he does proper instructions from his fugitive client, and in the result he has

G advanced no ground why that or any reduction should be effected. He has valiantly sought to extract from one solitary decision of this court, Davis v. Davis (1) a so-called principle that in assessing the lump sum (if any) to be awarded under s. 16 (1) (c) of the Matrimonial Causes Act 1965, there must always be taken into consideration (and apparently as a dominant feature in the calculation) the position in relation to the matrimonial home. Of course, the position in

H relation to the matrimonial home has its place in consideration by the learned judge of what lump sum (if any) the court thinks reasonable. But these are far too early days to say that any principle or tariff has been established in such cases as the present. Indeed, at this stage I take leave to doubt the desirability of a tariff ever being established and so tying the hands of this court, or the trial judge, in arriving at a proper assessment by adverting to all the circumstances

I of the particular case.

I entirely agree with my Lords that this appeal must be dismissed.

Appeal dismissed.

Solicitors: *Howard, Kennedy & Co.* (for the husband); *Tringhams* (for the wife).

[*Reported by* F. A. AMIES, ESQ., *Barrister-at-Law.*]

(1) [1967] 1 All E.R. 123; [1967] P. 185.

WHITWORTH STREET ESTATES (MANCHESTER), LTD. *v.* JAMES MILLER AND PARTNERS, LTD., AND ANOTHER.

[COURT OF APPEAL, CIVIL DIVISION (Lord Denning, M.R., Davies and Widgery, L.JJ.), January 28, 29, 1969.]

Conflict of Laws—Contract—Proper law of contract—Building contract in R.I.B.A. form—Building site in Scotland—English owners—Scottish contractors—Contract governed by English law.

Arbitration—Special Case—Scottish arbitrator—Arbitration and contract governed by English law—Arbitrator directed to state case—Arbitration Act 1950 (14 Geo. 6 c. 27), s. 21.

The building owners, an English company, wished to convert some factory premises in Scotland which they owned. They approached the contractors, a Scottish company, with a view to their carrying out the conversion. The contract negotiations were held in London and the contractors expected an R.I.B.A. standard form of contract. This was prepared and the contract was finally concluded in Scotland. The R.I.B.A. contract, which contained many obvious connections with English law, included an arbitration clause but made no reference as to the law to govern the contract. A London architect was appointed to superintend the performance of the contract. Later, disputes arose between the parties and work under the contract was suspended. The contractors issued a writ in the High Court for £40,000 but the action was stayed pursuant to s. 4 of the Arbitration Act 1950. Thereupon, at the contractors' request, the President of R.I.B.A. (in accordance with the arbitration clause in the contract) nominated U., a Scottish architect, as arbitrator. The arbitration was held in Glasgow in accordance with Scottish procedure. The building owners asked the arbitrator to state his award in the form of a Special Case for the opinion of the court. This he refused to do, since he was not required by Scottish law to accede to such a request. The building owners applied for an order that the arbitrator should state a Special Case.

Held: (i) there being nothing to the contrary in the contract, the arbitration proceedings were governed by the same law as the contract;

(ii) English law was the proper law of the contract and the arbitration should therefore be governed by English law because (per LORD DENNING, M.R., and DAVIES, L.J.) the system of law with which the transaction had the closest connection was English law, or (per WIDGERY, L.J.) the proper inference from the conduct of the parties was that they had adopted English law as the proper law.;

Dictum of LORD DENNING, in *Re United Railways of Havana and Regla Warehouses, Ltd.* ([1960] 2 All E.R. at p. 355) explained.

(iii) even though an arbitrator who has made an award was functus officio under Scottish law, he was not functus officio under English law and his award would be set aside by the court and he would be directed to make it again in the form of a Special Case.

Appeal allowed.

[As to application to compel an arbitrator to state a case, see 2 HALSBURY'S LAWS (3rd Edn.) 40, 41, para. 91; and for cases on the subject, see 2 DIGEST (Repl.) 680, *1948-1950* and 696, *2098.*

As to the proper law of contracts, see 7 HALSBURY'S LAWS (3rd Edn.) 72, 73, para. 137; and for cases on the subject, see 11 DIGEST (Repl.) 420-429, *715-750.*

For the Arbitration Act 1950, s. 21, see 2 HALSBURY'S STATUTES (2nd Edn.) 450.]

A Case referred to:

    United Railways of Havana and Regla Warehouses, Ltd., Re, [1960] 2 All E.R.
        332; [1961] A.C. 1007; [1960] 2 W.L.R. 969; Digest (Cont. Vol. A),
        231, *862a.*

Interlocutory appeal.

B   This was an appeal by Whitworth Street Estates (Manchester), Ltd., the
building owners, from an order of EVELEIGH, J., dated 31st October 1968, allowing
an appeal of James Miller and Partners, Ltd., the contractors, from Master ELTON
of 22nd July 1968 who ordered Walter Underwood, the arbitrator, to state
a Special Case. EVELEIGH, J., dismissed the application and granted leave to
appeal. The facts are set out in the judgment of LORD DENNING, M.R.

C   *M. Finer, Q.C.,* and *M. E. I. Kempster* for the building owners.
    J. R. Phillips, Q.C., A. J. Butcher and *J. A. Tackerberry* for the contractors.

    LORD DENNING, M.R.: In May 1965 an English company called
Whitworth Street Estates (Manchester), Ltd. (whose registered office is in
Albemarle Street in London), owned factory premises in Dumbarton in Scotland.
D They wished to convert it into a whisky bonded warehouse. They employed
a Scottish company, James Miller and Partners, Ltd., big contractors of Glasgow,
to do the conversion work. The agreement was made and signed on 10th May
1965. It was on the usual R.I.B.A. form with the usual arbitration clause.
Work went forward for a time. The building owners paid sums amounting to
some £200,000 to the contractors. But then differences arose. The work was
E suspended. Claims were made on each side. The contractors claimed that
further moneys were due to them. The building owners said that the work
had been wrongly broken off and counterclaimed damages. The President of
the R.I.B.A. was asked to appoint an arbitrator. He appointed Mr. Underwood,
an architect of Glasgow. He heard the arbitration in Glasgow in June and
July 1968. It was held in accordance with the Scottish procedure. It went
F on for several days. Two or three points of law emerged in the course of the
arbitration. They were of much importance in the determination of the case.
So the building owners asked the arbitrator to state his award in the form of a
Special Case for the opinion of the court. (That is a very familiar procedure
under the English Arbitration Act 1950, whereby the opinion of the court can
be given on points of law that arise in the course of the arbitration.) The
G arbitrator declined the request. He said that by Scottish law an arbitrator is
not bound to give his award in the form of a Special Case. So he gave a final
award there and then in favour of the contractors against the building owners
for some £120,000.

    The building owners claim that the arbitrator was in error: that he ought to
have acceded to their request for the award in the form of a Special Case.

H   There is a great difference between the English law of arbitration and the
Scottish law. The English law is codified and set out in the Arbitration Act
1950, whereas, the Scottish law is still based on textbooks. The Scottish courts
do not seem to exercise so great a control over arbitrators as do the English
courts. The award of an arbitrator can rarely be impeached. In particular,
it is common ground that in Scottish law there is no power in the courts to compel
I an arbitrator to state his award in the form of a Special Case.

    The root question, therefore, is: By what law are the arbitration proceedings
to be governed? There is nothing expressed in the contract about it. The
arbitration clause states simply that in case of any dispute or difference

    " it is to be referred to the decision of a person to be agreed, or failing
    agreement, by a person to be appointed at the request of either party by the
    President or Vice-President for the time being of the Royal Institute of British
    Architects."

There being nothing in the contract, the arbitration proceedings are to be governed by the same law as the contract itself. So we have to enquire: What is the proper law of the contract? The test is to ask: What is the system of law with which the transaction has the closest and most real connection? I made a slip in the case of *Re United Railways of Havana and Regla Warehouses, Ltd.* (1) when I said " what is the country, etc? " I should have said " What is the *system of law* with which the transaction has the closest and most real connection "?

In my opinion the outstanding factor here is that the contract was on the standard form issued by the Royal Institute of British Architects. The clauses of that form are redolent of English law. They contain references to the " common law " in terms which show it is the common law of England. They contain references to liens, to receiverships under floating charges, and such like concepts which are well known to English law and unknown to Scottish law. The clauses contain also references to practical matters, such as rates, and measurements which are taken by English standards and not by Scottish standards.

In addition to that factor, there is the fact that the architect, who was appointed to superintend the contract, was a London architect, Mr. Seymour, of Elliott, Son and Boyton, Wimpole Street, London. He was no doubt familiar with the R.I.B.A. form and its interpretation by English law, and not by Scottish law. Also, there is striking evidence that the contractors appreciated the significance of the R.I.B.A. contract and were content to accept it. I would refer to the evidence of Mr. Hayworth of the contractors. He came down to London and negotiated the contract with the London people. He was asked:

" Q.—When did you yourself appreciate that there was liable to be a R.I.B.A. contract? A.—When we went down to London to meet Mr. Seymour and Mr. Forrest. The matter was brought up at that meeting. Q.—Up until that time is it your evidence that [the contractors] didn't know there was going to be an R.I.B.A. contract and you thought that you were just going to go ahead on acceptance of the tender; is that right? A.—No, we knew there would have to be some sort of agreement, and the surveyors, being a London-based firm, we thought it probably would be an R.I.B.A. contract."

I can well see, of course, the factors which tend to favour Scottish law as the proper law of contract. The contract was finally concluded in Scotland. It concerned land in Scotland. One party to the contract was a Scottish contractor. The other party was an English company but it was the owner of Scottish land and it was in that capacity that it entered into this contract. If the question were: What is the *country* with which the transaction has the closest connection? I would say Scotland. But the question is: What is the *system of law* with which the transaction has the closest connection? To that question, I answer English law. And I say so because the parties deliberately used the R.I.B.A. form which has so many connections with English law.

I am confirmed in this view by the subsequent conduct of the parties. This is always available to aid the interpretation of a contract and to find out its closest connections. On two occasions the parties seem to have assumed that the transaction was governed by English law. In the first place, after the dispute arose the contractors issued a writ in the English courts for an instalment of some £40,000. The building owners applied to stay the action on the ground that there was an arbitration clause. The master made an order staying the action, " pursuant to s. 4 of the Arbitration Act 1950 ". That shows that the parties were acting on the basis that English law applied.

In the second place, when it came to the appointment of an arbitrator, the contractors themselves applied to the President of the Royal Institute of British Architects for the appointment of an arbitrator. In their request they stated

---

(1) [1960] 2 All E.R. 332 at p. 355; [1961] A.C. 1007 at p. 1068.

A specifically that there was " a submission to arbitration within the meaning of the Arbitration Act 1950 ". It was in pursuance of that request—mentioning the English Act—that the President of the R.I.B.A., Lord Esher, appointed Mr. Underwood to be arbitrator.

In all the circumstances, I am prepared to hold the proper law of the contract was English law. It follows, I think, that the arbitration is governed by English

B law. For if the contract is governed by English law, it means that any differences between the parties are to be determined by English law: and so the arbitration on those differences should also be governed by English law. I know that the arbitrator was a Scot who lived in Glasgow; and that he held the arbitration in Glasgow; and he went by the Scottish forms and procedures. Nevertheless it remained an English arbitration subject to English law and subject to control

C by the English courts; so s. 21 of the Arbitration Act 1950 applies. It enables the High Court to direct the arbitrator to state his award in the form of a Special Case for the decision of the court.

Once this conclusion is reached, it is agreed on all hands that this is a very proper case for a Special Case. Important questions of law have arisen as to what are the contract documents; what was the nature of the breach or the

D repudiation; and such like. Large sums depend on the answer. Such matters should, in all fairness, be determined in a court of law if either of the parties so desire.

It is interesting to note that a few months after this contract was signed, there was brought into use in Scotland, in the autumn of 1965, a form of building contract based on the form of the Royal Institute of British Architects with a

E few modifications by way of a Scottish supplement. The Scottish supplement provides that the law of Scotland shall apply to all arbitrations; but it goes on significantly to state that:

" at any stage of arbitration the Arbiter may, and if so requested by either of the parties, shall prepare a statement of facts in a Special Case for the opinion and judgment of the Court of Session on any question or questions

F of law arising in the arbitration."

So we see that in Scotland itself parties have taken on themselves by agreement to give the Court of Session a power similar to that conferred on the High Court of England by s. 21 of the Arbitration Act 1950. That is a pointer to the desirability of a review by the court, but does not otherwise affect this case.

There is one point more. Counsel for contractors urged us in our discretion

G not to make an order for a Special Case. It might lead, he said, to a conflict between the courts of England and of Scotland. He said that in Scottish law the arbiter's award is final; and it cannot be re-opened. He is functus officio. He should not be ordered by the English courts to do a thing inconsistent with Scottish law. I do not think we should anticipate any such conflict. If we are right in thinking that the contract and the arbitration are governed by English

H law, we may fairly expect the arbitrator to go by our ruling. His award in our eyes is not final. He is not functus officio. We can order his award to be set aside and direct him to make it again in the form of a Special Case for the decision of the court. I do not think we should be deterred from making the order which we think right by any supposed difficulties on that score.

For these reasons I would allow the appeal and make the order asked for.

I
DAVIES, L.J.: I agree and wish to add but little. As Lord Denning, M.R., has said, it is plain that when the contractors came to London to negotiate this contract they expected that the contract would be in the R.I.B.A. form. That was expressly stated by Mr. Hayworth during the arbitration. And for that there was the excellent reason that the architect and surveyor was Mr. Seymour, a London architect. The contractors, we understand, are a very large and very experienced company with contracts all over the place; and, if it were to be a contract governed by Scottish law, it would have been perfectly simple

for them to object to signing the unmodified and unamended R.I.B.A. contract A
and to insist on some clause bringing in Scottish law. They did not do so.

In that connection it is not uninteresting to observe that the standard form of
contract in Scotland at the date when this contract was entered into was the
Regulations and General Conditions of Contract for Building Works in Scotland
dated 1st September 1954; and though there is no provision in that contract as
to the law by which it is to be governed, there is in cl. 38—that is the arbitration B
clause—an express provision that " The Law of Scotland shall apply to all
arbitrations under these conditions "; and it is to be observed that in default of
agreement, the arbitrator—or, to be more accurate, in the Scottish term, the
" arbiter "—is to be appointed by the sheriff of the county. Similar provison
is made in the Scottish addendum to and modification of the present R.I.B.A.
contract of 1963. In that there is an express provision that the law of Scotland C
shall apply to arbitrations under the contract and that the appointment of the
arbiter shall be made by the sheriff; there is also the additional and new provision
providing for an award to be stated as a Special Case. In the present instance we
find none of those factors but the straight R.I.B.A. contract.

The arbitrator was, of course, a Scot and the arbitration was held in Scotland.
But that, as I think, was merely accidental. The gentleman was nominated and D
held his arbitration where he did for the sole and simple reason that it would be
more convenient to everybody concerned to have somebody familiar with Scottish
affairs and Scottish builders rather than to have a stranger who might wish to sit
elsewhere. It seems to me that those factors should not really militate against
the conclusion to which I have clearly arrived that this contract was from its
inception one to be governed by English law.   E

I would mention one point which counsel for the contractors took towards
the end of his address to the court. He submitted that even if the view which
LORD DENNING, M.R., and I have stated be correct and the contract was governed
by English law, nevertheless, as the arbitration was held in Scotland, the arbitrator and the conduct of the arbitration should be subject to the jurisdiction of
the Scots courts. For that purpose he referred us to a passage in DICEY AND F
MORRIS, THE CONFLICT OF LAWS (8th Edn. 1967), at p. 1048, where the learned
editors of that work express an opinion to the effect that—

> " if parties agreed on an arbitration clause expressed to be governed by
> English law but providing for arbitration in Switzerland, it may be held that,
> whereas English law governs the validity, interpretation and effect of the
> arbitration clause as such (including the scope of the arbitrators' jurisdiction), G
> the proceedings are governed by Swiss law."

That may very well be so, though no authority is cited for the proposition. But
this is an entirely different case. Here there was no agreement that the arbitration should be held in Scotland; as I have said, it was mere accident due to the
view that the President of the Royal Institute of British Architects took of the H
convenient course for all parties.

A final matter on which one would touch is the argument that this court ought
not to interfere because the arbitrator was functus officio once he made his
award. As LORD DENNING, M.R., has said, there is always power under the
Arbitration Act 1950 to direct an arbitrator to state his award in the form of a
Special Case, or, under s. 22, to remit the award to the arbitrator. Speaking for I
myself, I should be sorry indeed if it had been shown that though the building
owners were otherwise right in their appeal to this court, that they nevertheless
should be baulked of their remedy, merely because the arbitrator had chosen,
after having received notice of the appeal from the judge in chambers to this court,
to bar the door to this court by publishing his award.

Apart from those few observations, I do not desire to add anything to what
LORD DENNING, M.R., has said, with all of which I agree.

A   **WIDGERY, L.J.:** I also agree that this appeal should be allowed. The proper law of the contract is the law which the parties intend should govern its operation. To solve a problem such as arises in this case one looks first at the express terms of the contract to see whether that intention is there to be found. If it is not, then in my judgment the next step is to consider the conduct of the parties to see whether that conduct shows that a decision in regard to the proper law of the

B   contract can be inferred from it. If the parties' conduct shows that they have adopted a particular view with regard to the proper law, then it may be inferred that they have agreed that that law shall govern the contract accordingly. Finally if one fails in this enquiry also and is driven to the conclusion that the parties never applied their minds to the question at all, then one has to go to the third stage and see what is the proper law of the contract by considering what

C   system of law is the one with which the transaction has its closest and most real connection. It is at this stage that what counsel for the contractors referred to as the traditional tests, such as, considering the place where the contract is made, the place where it is to be carried out, etc., are of the utmost importance. In the present case, in my judgment it is clear that the parties had not expressly decided what was the proper law of their contract; but I am satisfied, for the reasons that

D   LORD DENNING, M.R., has given, that one can properly here infer from their conduct that they were adopting English law as the proper law. I am driven to that conclusion partly by the conduct of the contractors to which reference has been made, namely, their attitude when a stay was applied for in the earlier English proceedings and also the terms in which they applied to the President of the Royal Institute of British Architects for him to appoint an arbitrator. But

E   above all I am influenced in this view by the fact that these experienced people, advised by experienced advisers, chose to adopt the R.I.B.A. form of contract. Now, this is not just an English contract on a printed form; it is a form of contract which has a long and, perhaps one may say, distinguished history, and a form of contract which is intimately known in the building trade. Its purpose is to provide a code governing all kinds of problem which arise in a building tran-

F   saction, but anyone with the slightest knowledge of these matters appreciates that the code is incomplete unless the contract is set in the frame for which it is intended, namely, English law. It is clear that the provisions in regard to arbitra-tion are inadequate except on the footing that they are re-inforced by the pro-visions of English law. I am not going so far as to say that everybody who signs an R.I.B.A. form of contract must necessarily accept that English law is the proper

G   law, but I am quite satisfied that this is so in this case, having regard to the experience of the parties concerned and having regard to the fact that the adop-tion of this form of contract was the deliberate act of both, the matter having been considered and decided in that way. Accordingly it seems to me that the proper inference from the conduct of the parties here is that they had adopted English law as the proper law of the contract. As has been already demonstrated,

H   that is decisive of the issues in this case. I would, therefore, allow this appeal.

Appeal allowed. Arbitrator ordered to state his award in the form of a Special Case for the opinion of the court. Leave to appeal to the House of Lords granted.

Solicitors: *A. Kramer & Co.* (for the building owners); *Beddington, Hughes & Hobart,* agents for *A. & W. Urquhart,* Edinburgh (for the contractors).

[*Reported by* F. GUTTMAN, ESQ., *Barrister-at-Law.*]

A

PEPPER *v.* WEBB.

[COURT OF APPEAL, CIVIL DIVISION (Harman, Russell and Karminski, L.JJ.),
February 20, 1969.]

*Master and Servant—Wrongful dismissal—Summary dismissal—Disobedience
of orders—Insolence—Gardener.*

B

The wife of a house owner with a five to six acre garden engaged a head
gardener for her husband in January 1967. His hours of work on Saturday
were 8 a.m. to 12 noon, he was paid weekly, and provided with a rent-free
cottage. The employer and his wife went away until the end of March, and
on their return were very pleased with the employee's work, but thereafter
he did not give satisfaction and did not get on with the employer and his
wife. On Saturday 10th June 1967, between 9.0 a.m. and 10.0 a.m. the
employer's wife told the employee to put some plants in at once or they would
die. He replied " I am leaving at 12 o'clock; you can do what you like
about them. If you don't like it you can give me notice ". When it was
nearly 12 noon the employer came out into the garden, said the job would
only take a half hour, and asked the employee why he was making so much
trouble and fuss about it. He replied " I couldn't care less about your
bloody greenhouse and your sodding garden ", and walked away. The
employer then dismissed the employee forthwith, without notice or wages
in lieu. In an action by the employee for damages for wrongful dismissal,

Held: the action failed, and the summary dismissal was justified, because
the employee had repudiated his contract of service by—

(i) (per HARMAN and RUSSELL, L.JJ.) his refusal to obey the lawful and
reasonable order to put plants in, his statement that he did not care about
the grounds and greenhouse, and his insolence to the employer (see p. 218,
letters B, D and H, post); and

(ii) (per KARMINSKI, L.J.) his wilful disobedience of this lawful and
reasonable order (see p. 218, letter I, to p. 219, letter A, post).

Appeal allowed.

[As to summary dismissal of servant for disobedience of orders, see 25
HALSBURY'S LAWS (3rd Edn.) 485, para. 933.]

C

D

E

F

Appeal.

This was an appeal by the defendant employer, Major G. L. Webb, against
so much of the judgment of His Honour DEPUTY JUDGE BLACKETT-ORD at
Dorking County Court on 8th May 1968 as awarded the plaintiff employee,
Sidney Pepper, damages for wrongful dismissal, and as rejected the employer's
counterclaim for £49 10s. mesne profits. He also appealed against certain other
orders by the trial judge, but this case is reported only on these two points. The
facts are set out in the judgment of HARMAN, L.J.

G

B. H. Pryor for the employer.
B. Leech for the employee.

H

HARMAN, L.J.: This is an appeal from the Dorking County Court in an
action for wrongful dismissal. The deputy county court judge concluded his
judgment on the case:

I

" But considering the matter as carefully as I can I am not satisfied
that misconduct of Pepper [that is the plaintiff employee] justified summary
dismissal. Even taking all together don't think add up to justify course
taken up by Webb [that is the defendant employer]. Think getting on
that way [which apparently means that it was a pretty near thing, in the
judge's view]. Perhaps if [the employer] ever had given [the employee] a
good dressing down position would be different. [The employer] not
justified in dismissing [the employee] summarily without notice or wages."

A   So that the learned deputy county court judge came to the conclusion, with some doubt, that the employee's conduct did not merit summary dismissal without notice but it came somewhere near it, and if the employee had had a warning that something like that would happen if he went on as he did then the position might have been different. I myself do not accept that view.

     The facts are within a small compass. The employer, Major Webb, is a man

B   with a large house near Dorking called Woodlands Park, which has a garden of five or six acres, mostly decorative though with some kitchen garden. Like all people with places of that sort, he finds it very difficult to keep up. Both he and his wife are keen gardeners. He is also a busy man, having business interests in Kingston, and is away all day, and his wife does the day-to-day running of the place. She engaged the employee in January 1967 as head

C   gardener and entered into a written contract, which is before us, from which it appears that the remuneration was £14 a week, there was free occupation of a cottage, part of it in consideration of the employee's wife's services, and some electric light allowance; the first clause ended—

D   " You will be responsible for maintaining your garden in a responsible manner [that was the cottage garden and had nothing to do with the main garden]. Hours of work: subject to the usual responsibilities of a head gardener. Your normal hours are 8 a.m. to 5 p.m. on Monday to Friday with a lunch break of one hour, and 8 a.m. to 12 noon on Saturday."

     Then there is something about holidays. Then there is " Sickness or injury " and so on. Clause 6 is:

E   " Notice. (a) Period of notice by the employer: three months. (b) Period of notice by the employee: three months."

     The employee entered on that employment. About the time he did so the employer and his wife went away to the West Indies and were away January, February and March. During that time the employee apparently worked very well. He was his own master; he had no employers to irritate him. When

F   they came back at the end of March the employer went round the garden with the employee and, being very pleased, increased his salary by £1 a week; but shortly thereafter trouble began. The employer described himself as " a perfectionist ". I dare say he was an irritating employer. The employer's wife was an expert and she may have been rather exacting; I do not know. Anyhow the employee began (as they said) to lose interest; he did not give satisfaction.

G   There were complaints of inefficiency and an insolent manner—what the judge described as " dumb insolence "—at times. Things went on very uncomfortably during April, May and June. During part of that time he was very short of help; the promised second gardener did not turn up until May, though there was a third—jobbing—gardener from Monday to Friday.

     The matter came to a head on Saturday 10th June, when the employer's wife

H   went out between 9.0 a.m. and 10.0 a.m. and found that there were some fuchsia plants and geranium plants that had not yet been planted. She told the employee to put them in at once or they would die. There had been a good many plants —sweet peas in particular, and dahlias—that had died, according to her, from neglect previously, though it is fair to say that the employee denies it. Anyway on the morning of 10th June she said " Put in these plants ". There were fuchsias,

I   geraniums and some heath plants. The employee said:

     " I am leaving at 12 o'clock; you can do what you like about them. If you don't like it you can give me notice ";

and he walked off. The employer's wife was upset and went in and complained to the employer. He says that he went out to speak to the employee. The employee says he was ordered into the house but that is not accepted by the judge. I think that probably the critical interview occurred in the garden. Anyhow according to the employer, he went out, not with the idea of sacking the employee

—because he could ill afford to do that in June—but in order to remonstrate A
with him, and he apparently said " This job will only take you half an hour: why
make all this trouble and fuss about it? "   It was then fairly near 12 noon,
which was shutting-up time for the employee. The employee, I think, must
have lost his temper, for he said: " I couldn't care less about your bloody greenhouse and your sodding garden "; and he walked off. The employer felt that he
could not abide that degree of insolence and he gave him notice forthwith; and B
this action is for seven weeks' wages on the footing that that dismissal was not
justified.

Now what will justify an instant dismissal?—something done by the employee
which impliedly or expressly is a repudiation of the fundamental terms of the
contract; and in my judgment if ever there was such a repudiation this is it.
What is the gardener to do? He is to look after the garden and he is to look C
after the greenhouse.   If he does not care a jot about either then he is repudi-
ating his contract. That is what it seems to me the employee did, and I do not
see, having done that, that he can complain if he is summarily dismissed. It is
said on his behalf that one act of temper, one insolent outburst, does not merit
so condign a punishment; but this, according to his employer, and I think
rightly on the evidence, was the last straw. The employee had been acting in a D
very unsatisfactory way ever since April. He had that morning refused to
obey the employer's wife's quite reasonable instructions, and when he in addition
behaved in this way to the remonstrances of his employer I think he brought
his dismissal upon himself and cannot complain of it. In my judgment, therefore, the appeal should be allowed and the claim dismissed.

There is a counterclaim. The counterclaim is an odd document which has E
what is called a " summary " at the end. Under para. 1: £45. That has
been abandoned, because the learned deputy county court judge found as a fact
that there was no foundation for it and there is no appeal. Under para. 2:
£49 10s. for mesne profits. On the footing that the dismissal was justified that
was to be allowed, and there ought to be judgment for that sum. [HIS LORDSHIP
then considered other claims not dealt with in this report and concluded:] F
On the counterclaim, therefore, the employer succeeds in this court on the
amount of the mesne profits of the cottage and on the damage done by having to
have a new key, but not otherwise.

RUSSELL, L.J.: I agree. I do not myself think that the employee really
should be taken necessarily as having said what he said—which seems to me
something quite repudiatory of the contract—" in a temper ".   The evidence G
from the employer was that *after* the summary dismissal he, the employer, cut
short the interview and walked away because the employee was " about to
lose his temper ".   In other respects I entirely agree that, against the background of what counsel for the employee must admit the deputy county court
judge found or assumed to be quite a number of disobediences and a certain
amount of insolence, it must be taken as conduct repudiatory justifying summary H
dismissal. On the other two points I agree that the claim for mesne profits
follows that finding. [HIS LORDSHIP then considered the other points which
are not dealt with in this report.]

KARMINSKI, L.J.: I agree that this appeal must be allowed. In my
view the essential question here is whether the employer was justified in his I
summary dismissal of the employee on the ground of wilful disobedience of a
lawful and reasonable order. HARMAN, L.J., has set out the facts and I do not
propose to add anything to what he has said. It has long been a part of our
law that a servant repudiates the contract of service if he wilfully disobeys the
lawful and reasonable orders of his master. There is no suggestion here that the
order initiated by the employer's wife, and repeated by the employer a couple of
hours later, was other than lawful. I see nothing on the facts before the learned
deputy county court judge to suggest that that order was unreasonable; and

A there is ample evidence to show that the refusal by the employee was wilful. That being so, I have come to the conclusion that the employer was fully justified in dismissing the employee summarily.

Appeal allowed. Judgment on claim set aside and judgment entered for employer. Judgment for employer on issue under para. 2 of counterclaim for £49 10s.

B Solicitors: *Frere, Cholmeley & Co.* (for the employer); *Rodgers, Horsley & Burton* (for the employee).

[*Reported by* HENRY SUMMERFIELD, ESQ., *Barrister-at-Law.*]

C # MAYFIELD *v.* MAYFIELD.

[PROBATE, DIVORCE AND ADMIRALTY DIVISION (Sir Jocelyn Simon, P.), December 18, 1968.]

Divorce—Foreign decree—Recognition by English court—Basis of recognition— Respondent's nationality and residence.

D The husband was of British nationality, and was domiciled and permanently resident in England. His wife, who was German, acquired dual nationality by marriage. The parties separated. The wife was permanently resident in Germany and the husband was granted a decree of divorce by a German court. On an application for a declaration that the decree of the German court was valid and would be recognised, expert evidence established

E that the German court had jurisdiction under municipal law to grant the decree and that the decree would be recognised in German law as finally dissolving the marriage.

Held: although the German proceedings were instituted by the husband, his lack of real or substantial connections with Germany was not material and the decree which operated on the status of the wife should be recognised

F as also operating on the status of the husband; accordingly, the declaration would be granted (see p. 220, letters F and G, post).

Indyka v. *Indyka* ([1967] 2 All E.R. 689) and dictum of SIR JOCELYN SIMON, P., in *Lepre* v. *Lepre* ([1963] 2 All E.R. at pp. 55–57) applied.

[As to recognition by the English courts of foreign decrees of divorce, see

G 7 HALSBURY'S LAWS (3rd Edn.) 112, 113, para. 200; and for cases on the subject, see 11 DIGEST (Repl.) 481–483, *1079–1097.*]

Cases referred to:

Indyka v. *Indyka,* [1967] 2 All E.R. 689; [1969] 1 A.C. 33; [1967] 3 W.L.R. 310; Digest (Repl.) Supp.
Lepre v. *Lepre,* [1963] 2 All E.R. 49; [1965] P. 52; [1963] 2 W.L.R. 735; Digest

H (Cont. Vol. A.) 248, *1101c.*

Petition.

This was a petition by J. M. Mayfield, the husband, asking for a declaration that a decree of divorce granted to him by a German court was valid and should be recognised in English law or, in the alternative, he should be granted a decree of divorce on the ground of the wife's desertion. The facts are set out in the judg-

I ment.

P. T. H. Morgan for the husband.
The wife did not appear and was not represented.

SIR JOCELYN SIMON, P.: These proceedings started with the husband's petition for divorce on the ground of the wife's desertion, he asking for relief in the discretion of the court. That case came on for hearing in the undefended list before His Honour JUDGE MCKEE, when he was told by counsel that on 11th July 1966 a German court had purported to dissolve this marriage at the

suit of the husband.   Under those circumstances the learned judge declined to   A
proceed with the matter, since he was not satisfied, and required to be satisfied,
that there was a subsisting marriage for him to dissolve.   In consequence,
the petition was amended to ask in the alternative for a declaration that the
decree of divorce by the German court was valid and should be recognised in
English law.

The matter was not restored before His Honour JUDGE McKEE; and in case   B
it should have been, and so that there should be no further delay, which is
particularly undesirable in this case, I made an immediate order under R.S.C.,
Ord. 4, r. 8 (2), nominating myself to exercise further jurisdiction in the case.
I would have liked to have adjourned it for argument on behalf of the Queen's
Proctor; but I felt that the urgency to which I have referred precluded this
course.   C

The German court assumed jurisdiction on the ground that the wife was a
German national, having dual nationality after her marriage to the husband, and
also on the ground that she was permanently resident within the jurisdiction
of the court.   I have been satisfied by expert evidence that the German court
had jurisdiction in the matter by its municipal law, and that the decree would
be recognised in German law as finally dissolving the marriage.   The wife had,   D
to use expressions that were employed in *Indyka* v. *Indyka* (1), real, close and
substantial connection with the territorial area over which the German
court exercised its jurisdiction.   The husband, on the other hand, had no such
connection.   He is of British nationality, a citizen of the United Kingdom and
Colonies, and domiciled and permanently resident in England.   He was the
person who brought the proceedings in Germany and in whose favour the decree   E
was granted.   So far as I can gather from the notarial translation, the decree
was for denial of conjugal rights and desertion; though I do not think that the
grounds on which the decree was granted are material.

If the wife had brought the proceedings and had secured a decree, there can
be no question in my view that the case would be covered by *Indyka* v. *Indyka* (1)
and that we should recognise the German decree as valid to dissolve the marriage.   F
Is it, then, a material distinction that the proceedings were brought by the
husband, who had no close or real or substantial connection with Germany, and
not by the wife?   In my view, the difference is not material.   What is the material
fact is that the German decree operated on the status of the wife, who had such
close, substantial and real connection.   If it operated on the status of the wife and
should be recognised as such, for the reasons which I ventured to give in *Lepre* v.   G
Lepre (2) we should recognise the decree as also operating on the status of the
husband.   It follows that there is no subsisting marriage to be dissolved by this
court.   I have jurisdiction so to declare because the husband, who seeks such a
declaration, is domiciled in England.

I only add this—that if there were a subsisting marriage, I have been satisfied
on the plainest evidence that the husband has proved the contents of his petition   H
so far as his case of desertion is concerned, and I would have exercised discretion
in his favour.   However, since in my view we should recognise the German
decree of 11th July 1966 as terminating the marriage, that question does not
arise; and all that I have to do is to make a declaration that the German decree
did terminate this marriage.

Declaration accordingly.   I

Solicitors: *Barlow, Lyde & Gilbert*, agents for *John Anthony Crowley & Co.*,
Cardiff (for the husband).

[*Reported by* ALICE BLOOMFIELD, *Barrister-at-Law.*]

---

(1) [1967] 2 All E.R. 689; [1969] 1 A.C. 33
(2) [1963] 2 All E.R. 49 at pp. 55-57; [1965] P. 52 at pp. 61-63.

A

PETT v. GREYHOUND RACING ASSOCIATION, LTD. (No. 2).

[QUEEN'S BENCH DIVISION (Lyell, J.), January 20, 21, 22, 23, 24, February 12, 1969.]

B
Tribunal—Procedure—Legal representation—Inquiry into matter affecting licence-holder's reputation and livelihood—National club rules silent as to procedure —Stewards of dog-racing track inquiring into drugging of dog and requiring trainer's presence at inquiry—Whether trainer entitled to be represented by counsel and solicitor—Duties of domestic tribunal exercising quasi-judicial powers—Whether requirements of natural justice included legal representation.

C
The local stewards of a greyhound racecourse owned by the defendants and licensed by the National Greyhound Racing Club (the club), proposed to hold an inquiry into the withdrawal of a dog from a race for which it had been entered by its trainer, the plaintiff. The inquiry involved the question whether drugs had been administered to the dog. The plaintiff held a licence from the club which entitled him to train dogs for racing on the

D
large number of tracks licensed by them, and under the terms of which he agreed to abide by the rules of the club. Under these rules the local stewards who were employed by the defendants and licensed by the club, were required to control, take cognisance of and adjudicate on the conduct of all owners, trainers, kennelhands and persons attendant on the greyhounds; they also had disciplinary powers, including the power of suspension, and

E
were required to report their findings to the club stewards, who could, at their discretion, hold a further inquiry and make such order, including the withdrawal of a trainer's licence, as they thought fit. The club's rules did not prescribe the procedure to be followed by local stewards at their inquiries, and did not exclude legal representation. The procedure in fact followed at such an inquiry allowed the trainer to be present with his kennelhand,

F
to hear the evidence, to have an opportunity to question witnesses and to give evidence himself in the course of which the stewards could ask him questions. The plaintiff sought to be represented by counsel and solicitor at the proposed inquiry, but after consideration the local stewards decided not to allow him legal representation. In an action for, inter alia, a declaration that the defendants were acting ultra vires in refusing to allow the

G
plaintiff legal representation at the proposed inquiry, the defendants contended that at common law the only duty imposed on the local stewards as persons empowered to make quasi-judicial decisions was to observe the rules of natural justice.

Held: the plaintiff did not have a right to be legally represented because in the absence of express requirements in the instrument conferring quasi-

H
judicial powers on a domestic tribunal, the tribunal was required only to comply with those elementary and essential principles of " fairness " which must as a matter of necessary implication be treated as applicable in the exercise of those powers, that is, the principles of natural justice, and, in the present case, legal representation before the local stewards was not essential to a fair dispensation of justice.

I
University of Ceylon v. *Fernando* ([1960] 1 All E.R. 631) followed.

[As to the right to appear by counsel before tribunals and inquiries, see 3 HALSBURY'S LAWS (3rd Edn.) 19, 20, para. 24, 22-26, paras. 30-33; for cases on counsel's right of audience, see 3 DIGEST (Repl.) 357, *58-70.*

As to the basis of jurisdiction of domestic tribunals, see 9 HALSBURY'S LAWS (3rd Edn.) 577, para. 1349.

As to the rules of natural justice, see 11 HALSBURY'S LAWS (3rd Edn.) 64-66, para. 122, and 30 HALSBURY'S LAWS (3rd Edn.) 718, 719, para. 1368.]

Cases referred to: A

Board of Education v. *Rice*, [1911] A.C. 179; [1911-13] All E.R. Rep. 36;
    80 L.J.K.B. 796; 104 L.T. 689; 75 J.P. 393; 19 Digest (Repl.) 630, *206*.

Byrne v. *Kinematograph Renters Society, Ltd.*, [1958] 2 All E.R. 579; [1958]
    1 W.L.R. 762; 45 Digest (Repl.) 401, *147*.

De Verteuil v. *Knaggs*, [1918] A.C. 557; 87 L.J.P.C. 128; 8 Digest (Repl.)
    691, *38*.   B

General Medical Council v. *Spackman*, [1943] 2 All E.R. 337; [1943] A.C. 627;
    112 L.J.K.B. 529; 169 L.T. 226; 33 Digest (Repl.) 520, *27*.

Jackson & Co. v. *Napper, Re Schmidt's Trade Mark* (1886), 35 Ch.D. 162;
    56 L.J.Ch. 406; 55 L.T. 836; 46 Digest (Repl.) 83, *460*.

Local Government Board v. *Arlidge*, [1915] A.C. 120; [1914-15] All E.R. Rep.
    1; 84 L.J.K.B. 72; 111 L.T. 905; 793 J.P. 97; 18 Digest (Repl.)   C
    142, *1281*.

Maclean v. *Workers Union*, [1929] 1 Ch. 602; [1929] All E.R. Rep. 468;
    98 L.J.Ch. 293; 141 L.T. 83; 45 Digest (Repl.) 541, *1222*.

Macqueen and Nottingham Caledonian Society, Re, (1861), 9 C.B.N.S. 793;
    142 E.R. 312; 2 Digest (Repl.) 564, *983*.

Pett v. *Greyhound Racing Association, Ltd.*, [1968] 2 All E.R. 545; [1968]   D
    2 W.L.R. 1471.

R. v. *St. Mary Abbotts, Kensington Assessment Committee*, [1891] 1 Q.B. 378;
    60 L.J.M.C. 52; 64 L.T. 240; 55 J.P. 502; 38 Digest (Repl.) 697, *1362*.

Russell v. *Norfolk (Duke)*, [1949] 1 All E.R. 109; *affg.* [1948] 1 All E.R. 488;
    12 Digest (Repl.) 693, *5321*.

University of Ceylon v. *Fernando*, [1960] 1 All E.R. 631; [1960] 1 W.L.R. 223;   E
    19 Digest (Repl.) 655, *362*.

Action.

By writ issued on 3rd November 1967, the plaintiff, David Pett, sued the
defendants, Greyhound Racing Association, Ltd., for a declaration that they
were acting ultra vires in refusing to allow him to appear and be heard by
counsel at an inquiry which they proposed to hold into the alleged drugging   F
on 9th September 1967 of a greyhound, Dogstown Star, owned and trained by
the plaintiff and entered for the 700 yards open race at White City Stadium on
that date; the plaintiff further sought an injunction to restrain the defendants
and their servants or agents from holding an inquiry into the alleged drugging
unless he were allowed to appear and to be represented by counsel at any such
inquiry, and he asked for further relief not material to this report.   The plaintiff   G
at the same time applied by summons for an interlocutory injunction to restrain
the holding of the proposed inquiry unless he were allowed to appear with counsel
to represent him, and on 22nd February 1968 CUSACK, J., granted the injunction
asked for.   The defendants appealed against the judge's order, and on 5th April
1968 their appeal was dismissed by the Court of Appeal.*   The facts are stated
in the judgment reported below.   H

The statute and cases noted below† were cited during the argument in addition
to those referred to in the judgment.

Gabriel Cohen for the plaintiff.
Raymond Kidwell, Q.C., and *Robert Johnson* for the defendants.

                                                Cur. adv. vult.   I

    12th February.   **LYELL, J.,** read the following judgment: The facts in
this case were not substantially in dispute.   The plaintiff was, in 1967, a trainer

---

*See [1968] 2 All E.R. 545; [1968] 2 W.L.R. 1471.

† Tribunals of Inquiry (Evidence) Act 1921; *Ipswich Tailors Case*, 11 Co. Rep. 53a;
Hewlett v. *Laycock* (1827), 2 C. & P. 574; *Collier* v. *Hicks* (1831), 2 B. & Ad. 663; *Ex p
Evans* (1846), 9 Q.B. 279; *Tillam* v. *Copp* (1847), 5 C.B. 211; *Weinberger* v. *Inglis*,
[1919] A.C. 606; *Faramus* v. *Film Artistes' Assocn.*, [1964] 1 All E.R. 25; [1964] A.C.
925; *Nagle* v. *Feilden*, [1966] 1 All E.R. 689; [1966] 2 Q.B. 633.

A of greyhounds and held a licence from the National Greyhound Racing Club to train greyhounds for racing on all tracks which are licensed by the club.   The defendants are the owners of the White City Stadium where there is a greyhound race track.   This track, in common with a very large proportion of the tracks in the United Kingdom where greyhound racing is carried on, is licensed by the club.   The club also issues licences to stewards to act as local stewards for the

B control of the racing at the various tracks licensed by the club.   Local stewards were duly licensed by the club to act in relation to race meetings held at the White City Stadium.

When a licence is issued to a trainer he is required to sign and return a tear-off counterfoil attached to the licence acknowledging its receipt and stating that he agrees to abide, inter alia, by conditions 1, 2 and 4 set out on the licence:

C " 1.   The applicant to be licensed agrees to be subject to the Rules of Racing of the National Greyhound Racing Club in force for the time being and it is the duty of the holder of this licence to read such rules and in particular those which relate to his or her appointment.   2.   The holder of this licence is responsible for the condition, fitness and security of all

D greyhounds in his/her charge . . .   4.   This licence may be withdrawn or suspended by the Stewards of the National Greyhound Racing Club in their absolute discretion, and such withdrawal or suspension may be published in the National Greyhound Racing Calendar for any reason which may seem proper to them and they shall not be bound to state their reasons."

Without such a licence the plaintiff could not effectively remain in business

E as a greyhound trainer and the loss of his licence might materially affect his livelihood.

On 9th September 1967, the plaintiff entered a dog called Dogstown Star to run in an open race at the White City Stadium timed to start at 7.45 p.m.   He sent the dog with a kennelhand to the stadium.   In accordance with the rules of the meeting the dog arrived at 5 p.m. and on or shortly after arrival gave a

F sample of urine which was then handed to a security officer who sent it for examination.   At 7.30 p.m. a report of the test was received which showed positive for a barbiturate drug.   In consequence of this report, the stewards withdrew the dog from the race and a further sample of urine was taken in the presence of the kennelhand.   He asked for part of this sample but that request was refused.   On 11th September, parts of the samples were sent to

G Glasgow University for analysis, and, on 13th September, a report was received by the defendants that the samples showed the presence in the urine of the barbiturate phenobarbitone.   The next day the defendants' racing manager telephoned to the plaintiff saying that an inquiry into the drugging of the dog would be held on 19th September.   This was confirmed by a letter of 16th September, which also required the presence at the inquiry of the plaintiff and

H his kennelhand. This letter was received by the plaintiff on 18th September. He forthwith consulted his solicitor, who replied on his behalf that the notice was too short for the plaintiff to give instructions for him to be represented and asking for the inquiry to be adjourned for 14 days.   It was clear from this letter that the plaintiff desired to be legally represented at the inquiry.   The general manager replied in the following terms:

I " . . . we are agreeable to postpone the date of the Inquiry to Tuesday, 3rd October.   Please advise [the plaintiff] that he is required to attend the inquiry at White City Stadium at 11 a.m. on 3rd October, 1967, together with his kennelman . . ."

On that day the plaintiff and his kennelman, together with his solicitor and counsel, went to the stadium.   The stewards were surprised at the presence of the solicitor and counsel and were unwilling to admit them to attend the inquiry but decided to adjourn the inquiry till 31st October so that they might consider

the matter.   On 30th October the general manager telephoned the plaintiff's   A
solicitor and informed him that the plaintiff would not be allowed to be legally
represented at the inquiry.   No inquiry was in fact held on 31st October, and
on 3rd November 1967 the writ in this action was issued, claiming, inter alia, a
declaration that the defendants were acting ultra vires in refusing to allow the
plaintiff to appear and be heard by counsel at an inquiry to be held into the
alleged drugging on 9th September 1967 of a greyhound, Dogstown Star " trained   B
by the Plaintiff, and entered for the 700 yards Open Race at White City Stadium
on 9th September 1967 ".   Other relief was also claimed, but in the course of
the hearing before me it was agreed by counsel that it was unnecessary for me
to decide whether the plaintiff was entitled to any of such further relief and that the
sole question for my determination was whether, at the intended inquiry, the
plaintiff had the right to be represented by counsel.   C
    Shortly after the issue of the writ the plaintiff moved for an injunction to
restrain the defendants from holding the intended inquiry unless the plaintiff
was allowed to be represented by counsel.   CUSACK, J., granted this injunction
and the defendants appealed against his order.   The appeal was heard on 4th
and 5th April 1968 and was dismissed (1).   The Court of Appeal held that a
sufficient prima facie case had been made out in support of the claim and that   D
the balance of convenience was in favour of the granting of the injunction.
While leaving the plaintiff's claim to be decided at the hearing of the action and
any appeal thereon, all the members of the court expressed views favourable to
the plaintiff's claim to be entitled to be represented by counsel, to which I shall
refer in detail when I come to consider the authorities cited to me.
    The disciplinary powers of the club are contained in the Rules of Racing by   E
which the plaintiff in accepting his licence had agreed to be bound.   The relevant
rules are r. 27, r. 48 and r. 49:

> " 27: The Stewards of the National Greyhound Racing Club may in their
> absolute discretion warn off any person from all Racecourses where these
> Rules are in force without necessarily assigning any reason for so doing,
> and may at their discretion report such person to The National Coursing   F
> Club, The Jockey Club, Irish Coursing Club and The Kennel Club.   They
> are hereby authorised to publish any decision or order given or made by them
> relating to any person, greyhound or Racecourse in the Calendar and/or in
> any other manner, which in their absolute discretion they may think fit.
>   " 48: The Stewards (2) shall regulate, control, take cognisance of, and
> adjudicate upon, the conduct of all Officials and of all Owners, Trainers,   G
> Kennelhands, and persons attendant on the greyhounds.
>   " 49: The Stewards shall have power to punish at their discretion any
> person, subject to their control, with a fine not exceeding £20 (Twenty
> Pounds), and with suspension, and shall report all such facts and remit the
> amount of the fine to the Stewards of the National Greyhound Racing Club,
> who may at their discretion themselves hold a further inquiry into the matter   H
> and make such order as they think fit.   A right of appeal against the decision
> of the Stewards of the Meeting will lie if leave to appeal is given by the
> Stewards of the National Greyhound Racing Club.   Such an appeal must
> be forwarded by the appellant in writing to the Secretary of the National
> Greyhound Racing Club within 48 hours of the decision of the Stewards
> being communicated to him/her, and be accompanied by a deposit of £10   I
> (Ten Pounds), Kennelhands £2 (Two Pounds), and the Stewards of the
> National Greyhound Racing Club may, after hearing the appeal, make such
> order as to the deposit as they think fit, and shall decide by whom the
> expenses of the appeal shall be defrayed."

(1) See *Pett* v. *Greyhound Racing Association, Ltd.*, [1968] 2 All E.R. 545; [1968]
2 W.L.R. 1471.
(2) I.e., the stewards of the meeting.

A   From these rules, and from the definition of the term " Stewards " contained
in r. 2, it will be seen that there are two classes of stewards provided for, stewards
of the meeting (hereinafter referred to as " local stewards "), that is to say
stewards appointed to supervise the conduct of a particular race meeting, and
stewards of the club (hereinafter referred to as " club stewards ") who exercise
the general control over all race meetings on behalf of the club and have, in
B   addition to their wide powers under r. 27, the power under r. 29:

> ". . . at their discretion to grant, suspend and to withdraw licences to or
> from the proprietors of racecourses, Racecourse Officials, Trainers, Private
> Trainers and Kennelhands without assigning any reason . . . to make
> inquiry into and deal with any matters relating to Greyhound Racing . . ."

C   At the hearing before me no oral evidence was given on behalf of the plaintiff
but counsel for the plaintiff read and accepted as accurate the matters of fact
deposed to in the affidavit of Major Higson, the general manager of the defendants
and a steward of the White City Stadium. In para. 8 of that affidavit, which
reads as follows, Major Higson described the procedure adopted at an inquiry
by local stewards:

D   > " 8.   As a Steward of the Defendants' Stadium, I have been present at
> numerous Stewards' Inquiries and am conversant with the procedure
> involved.   The trainer, whose greyhound is the subject of the Inquiry, is
> informed of the date, time and place of the Inquiry and is told that he and
> his Kennelhand may attend to give evidence.   If the Inquiry is as a result of
> a positive urine test, the Stewards receive written statements from the
E   > Security Officer, the Chromatography Analyst, the Veterinary Surgeon and
> the Racing Manager, and they consider the analyst's report from Glasgow.
> The Trainer is present to hear all the evidence given by witnesses and is
> given the opportunity to question the witnesses.   There is now produced
> to me marked G.R.A. 7, a bundle containing copies of statements that were
> made for the purposes of the Inquiry in relation to the Plaintiff's greyhound
F   > ' Dogstown Star '.   The Stewards then receive evidence from the trainer,
> and usually ask the trainer a number of questions.   They may also ask the
> Security Officer or the veterinary surgeon questions.   On this information
> the Stewards then prepare an opinion, which is submitted to the Club with
> the Stewards' recommendations."

G   On behalf of the defendants, Colonel Forsdike, the secretary of the club, also
gave evidence.   He confirmed the evidence in an affidavit sworn by him in the
interlocutory proceedings and also gave evidence that so far as he knew no
written evidence was received except that of an analyst, and that the contents
of his report would always be disclosed to the person whose conduct was the
subject of inquiry.   He knew of no case in which a request had been made that
H   an analyst should attend so that he could be questioned but expressed the view
that if such a request were made it would be granted.   He was also asked about
confidential information received but not disclosed to the person whose conduct
was being investigated.   This information he said was what he described as a
" tip off ", that is to say a warning to the stewards that someone was intending
to commit some malpractice.   He expressed the view that while the stewards
I   had this in their minds they did not adjudicate at the inquiry except on the
information produced to them at the inquiry.   I see no reason to think that the
stewards who would be chosen as persons of experience and integrity would not
be capable of shutting out such information from their minds when called on to
adjudicate in an inquiry and of treating it as no more than an alert which might
or might not be well founded.   It has to be borne in mind that stewards are
appointed to be watchful against malpractices and to act if their suspicions are
aroused either by their own observations or by hints received from other sources,
and that disclosure of information from outside sources or the name of the

I

informant might well make it more difficult to perform their essential duty to **A**
assure, so far as they can, that the racing is conducted fairly.

Subject only to the disputed question whether a right to be represented by
counsel is an essential to a fair hearing at an inquiry by stewards of either class,
I am satisfied that the procedure adopted by the stewards would provide a fair
hearing at the inquiry into the plaintiff's conduct.

The claim is an unusual one in that, unlike other cases in which the conduct **B**
of an inquiry by a domestic tribunal has been considered by the courts, the claim
is in respect of the conduct of an inquiry which has not yet been held; a claim
that such inquiry cannot fairly be held unless the plaintiff is allowed to be represented by counsel. The case put by the plaintiff in support of it rested first,
on the reasoning contained in the interlocutory judgments of the Court of Appeal
(3); and secondly, on the ground that the defendants, having granted an adjourn- **C**
ment with the knowledge that the plaintiff desired to be represented, are estopped
from refusing to allow the plaintiff to present his case by counsel.

The plaintiff's argument based on estoppel I am unable to accept. It is
founded on the assumption that the defendants were entitled to refuse to allow
the plaintiff to be represented by counsel but by granting the adjournment were
implicitly stating that they would not exercise that right. The defendants' **D**
letter of 20th September 1967 agreeing to adjourn the hearing of the inquiry
makes no reference to representation and is, in my judgment, as consistent
with an intention to do what the local stewards in fact did—hear the plaintiff's
request to be represented by counsel and consider it. I am unable to read into
the letter an implied statement of intention to allow representation by counsel
which would be necessary to found the equitable estoppel on which the plaintiff **E**
seeks to rely.

As to the first ground on which the plaintiff's case was put, the reasoning of
the Court of Appeal (3) may be summarised as follows: (i) that by implication
from the reference in r. 49 to a further inquiry, the local stewards, in order to
adjudicate in respect of the plaintiff's conduct, were bound to hold an inquiry;
(ii) that such an inquiry should be conducted in accordance with the rules of **F**
natural justice; (iii) that at common law the plaintiff had a right to be heard
at such inquiry in accordance with the rules of natural justice; (iv) that the
plaintiff had a common law right to do by an agent of his choice that which he
had a right to do in person and that unless prevented by the terms of the licence
he could employ a lawyer to present his case; and (v) that natural justice required,
either because of the common law right to representation or independently of **G**
it, that he should be entitled to be represented by counsel.

All these propositions were challenged by the defendants, save that they
accepted that if an inquiry had to be held, then it must be conducted according
to the rules of natural justice and that the plaintiff was entitled in accordance
with natural justice to attend the inquiry and present his case (the second and
third propositions). **H**

As to the first of these propositions, it was contended on behalf of the defendants
that as the club stewards had the right in their absolute discretion under r. 29
to withdraw the plaintiff's licence (4), no inquiry was required before taking this
or any lesser action against him, and they relied on the decision of the Court
of Appeal in the case of *Russell* v. *Duke of Norfolk* (5). This contention of the
defendants I am unable to accept. Whatever may be the powers of the club **I**
stewards to act without inquiry, I am satisfied that the clear implication of the
use of the words " further inquiry " in r. 49 is that before the local stewards
could exercise their powers under r. 49 they must hold an inquiry. I am fortified
in this view by the evidence that the local stewards never in fact acted under

(3) [1968] 2 All E.R. 545; [1968] 2 W.L.R. 1471.
(4) The material part of r. 29 is set out at p. 225, letter B, ante; see also condition 4
of licence, set out at p. 223, letter D, ante.
(5) [1949] 1 All E.R. 109.

A r. 49 without holding an inquiry at which the person whose conduct was to be considered was invited to attend.

As to the fourth proposition enunciated by the Court of Appeal, the plaintiff's contentions are set out in the following passage from the judgment of LORD DENNING, M.R., on the interlocutory appeal which was adopted by counsel for the plaintiff before me (6):

B "The plaintiff is here facing a serious charge. He is charged either with giving the dog drugs or with not exercising proper control over the dog so that someone else drugged it. If he is found guilty, he may be suspended or his licence may not be renewed. The charge concerns his reputation and his livelihood. On such an inquiry, I think that he is entitled not only to appear by himself but also to appoint an agent to act for him . . . The

C general principle was stated by STIRLING, J., in *Jackson & Co.* v. *Napper, Re Schmidt's Trade Marks* (7): '. . . that, subject to certain well-known exceptions, every person who is sui juris has a right to appoint an agent for any purpose whatever, and that he can do so when he is exercising a statutory right no less than when he is exercising any other right'. This was applied to a hearing before an assessment committee in the case of

D *R.* v. *St. Mary Abbotts, Kensington Assessment Committee* (8). It was held that a ratepayer had a right to have a surveyor to appear for him. Once it is seen that a man has a right to appear by an agent, then I see no reason why that agent should not be a lawyer. It is not every man who has the ability to defend himself on his own. He cannot bring out the points in his own favour or the weaknesses in the other side. He may be tongue-

E tied or nervous, confused or wanting in intelligence. He cannot examine or cross-examine witnesses. We see it every day. A magistrate says to a man: 'You can ask any questions you like'; whereupon the man immediately starts to make a speech. If justice is to be done, he ought to have the help of someone to speak for him; and who better than a lawyer who has been trained for the task? I should have thought, therefore, that when

F a man's reputation or livelihood is at stake, he not only has a right to speak by his own mouth. He has also a right to speak by counsel or solicitor.

"I am aware that MAUGHAM, J., once expressed a different view. In *Maclean* v. *Workers Union* (9), speaking of domestic tribunals, he said: 'Before such a tribunal counsel have no right of audience and there are no effective means of testing by cross-examination the truth of the statements

G which may be made'. All I would say is that much water has passed under the bridges since 1929. The dictum may be correct when confined to tribunals dealing with minor matters where the rules may properly exclude legal representation. (*Re Macqueen and Nottingham Caledonian Society* (10), seems to have been such a case.) The dictum does not apply, however, to tribunals dealing with matters which affect a man's reputation or livelihood

H or any matters of serious import. Natural justice then requires that he can be defended, if he wishes, by counsel or solicitor."

In this case I am in the unusual and invidious position that it is my duty to consider whether, in my judgment, the views already expressed by the Court of Appeal, albeit obiter, on the same facts and law which I have to consider are well founded. In the result, after giving them the most anxious consideration,

I I have the misfortune to be unable to agree with them. That the common law right to appoint an agent for any purpose is qualified by exceptions is stated in the passage from the judgment of STIRLING, J. (11), quoted by LORD DENNING,

(6) [1968] 2 All E.R. at p. 549; [1968] 2 W.L.R. at pp. 1475, 1476.
(7) (1886), 35 Ch.D. 162 at p. 172.
(8) [1891] 1 Q.B. 378.
(9) [1929] 1 Ch. 602 at p. 621; [1929] All E.R. Rep. 468 at p. 471.
(10) (1861), 9 C.B.N.S. 793.
(11) In *Jackson & Co.* v. *Napper, Re Schmidt's Trade Marks* (1886), 35 Ch.D. at p. 172.

M.R. It seems to me that that right must be ousted when it is sought to be   A
exercised in circumstances in which another rule of the common law does not
permit it.

Rule 49 of the rules of the club (12) is entirely silent as to how an inquiry by
the local stewards is to be conducted, and the defendants contend that at common
law the only duty imposed on the local stewards as persons empowered to make
quasi-judicial decisions is to observe the rules of natural justice. The Court of   B
Appeal did not accept this contention and appears to have accepted that *R.* v.
St. Mary Abbotts, Kensington Assessment Committee (13) was authority to the
contrary. By s. 19 of the Union Assessment Committee Act 1862 the assessment
committee of a parish was required to " hold such meetings as they may think
necessary for hearing objections to the valuation lists " made for the purpose
of rating valuations. The assessment committee of St. Mary Abbotts refused   C
to hear an agent of a ratepayer present the objection, and on an application by
the objector for a mandamus the Divisional Court held, and the Court of Appeal
confirmed the decision, that the assessment committee were not entitled to
refuse to hear the agent. The judgments in the Divisional Court appear to
decide that the question for the court was simply one of construction of the
statute and to have accepted the contention of the ratepayer that the assessment   D
committee were not a judicial tribunal. That contention was also accepted by
LORD ESHER, M.R., who said (14)

> " The assessment committee have been called a court or tribunal, and
> spoken of as exercising judicial functions. They are a certain number of
> persons, in this case selected vestrymen, to whom power has been given by
> statute to hear objections which have been made to the valuation list, and to   E
> decide whether such objections are well founded. I do not think that they
> are a court or a tribunal exercising judicial functions in the legal acceptation
> of the terms. The question here is whether, being such as they are, they have
> a right to say that a person may not appoint any agent he pleases to appear
> in support of an objection made by him to the list."

It appears to me that the Court of Appeal in that case regarded the overseers   F
as performing an administrative act in preparing the valuation lists, in the same
way as under the Local Government Act 1948 the draft valuation lists are made
and revised by the valuation officer to whom objections to the draft valuation
list may be made under s. 36 of that Act. It has, so far as I am aware, never
been suggested that the valuation officer in considering such objections is acting
otherwise than in an administrative capacity.   G

In view of the many authorities that domestic tribunals are subject only to the
duty of observing what are called the rules of natural justice and any procedure
which is laid down or necessarily to be implied from the instrument that confers
their power, I am unable to follow the views expressed in the present case by the
Court of Appeal (15), that the plaintiff is entitled to appear by an agent unless
such right was expressly negatived by the rules of the club. The only authority   H
cited to the Court of Appeal was the dictum of MAUGHAM, J., in *Maclean* v.
Workers Union (16), which LORD DENNING, M.R., distinguished on the ground
that it should apply only where the matter in issue was a minor one, not affecting
(17) " a man's reputation or livelihood or any matters of serious import ".
Clearly in the present case the subject-matter of the inquiry to be held by the
local stewards falls within these categories.   I

Unfortunately the much more recent decision of the Privy Council in *University
of Ceylon* v. *Fernando* (18) was not cited to the Court of Appeal. The issue to

---

(12) Rule 49 is set out at p. 224, letters H and I, ante.
(13) [1891] 1 Q.B. 378.   (14) [1891] 1 Q.B. at p. 382.
(15) [1968] 2 All E.R. 545; [1968] 2 W.L.R. 1471.
(16) [1929] 1 Ch. at p. 621; [1929] All E.R. Rep. at p. 471.
(17) [1968] 2 All E.R. at p. 549; [1968] 2 W.L.R. at p. 1476.
(18) [1960] 1 All E.R. 631; [1960] 1 W.L.R. 223.

A be decided by the vice-chancellor of the University of Ceylon as a domestic tribunal clearly fell within the class of cases stated by LORD DENNING, M.R. The allegation investigated by the vice-chancellor of the university and two other members of the court of inquiry which he set up, was a serious allegation that the respondent student had cheated in an examination, and the adverse decision of the court of inquiry resulted in the finding that the allegation was

B proved and in the indefinite suspension of the respondent from taking any university examinations. It would be hard to find a more serious allegation against a young man which would fall within the competence of university authorities to decide.

The question whether the respondent was entitled to representation was not raised but one of the main grounds of objection to the decision of the court of

C inquiry was that the respondent was not given an opportunity to question the "essential witness" against him. The Board rejected the contention that the failure to give such opportunity was a breach of the rules of natural justice. If a right to question the witnesses brought against a man is not required by natural justice, then much of the force of the fact that many people are not good at formulating questions, that when invited to do so, they make speeches

D instead and, therefore, should have the assistance of an advocate, is destroyed. The respondent student was not represented before the Board but, as was to be expected, a very full citation of the relevant authorities favourable or unfavourable to his case was given by counsel for the university, and the Board advised that the court of inquiry had not fallen short of the requirements of natural justice. In the course of their advice the Board reviewed the authorities

E at length in the following passage of the report which I venture to quote in full (19):

F   "Accordingly (apart from a subsidiary question as to the jurisdiction of the courts in Ceylon to grant declaratory relief in such a case), the present appeal resolves itself into the question whether this inquiry was conducted with due regard to the rights accorded by the principles of natural justice to the plaintiff as the person against whom it was directed.

"These rights have been defined in varying language in a large number of cases covering a wide field. Their Lordships do not propose to review these authorities at length, but would observe that the question whether the requirements of natural justice have been met by the procedure adopted

G in any given case must depend to a great extent on the facts and the circumstances of the case in point. As TUCKER, L.J., said in *Russell* v. *Duke of Norfolk* (20): ' There are, in my view, no words which are of universal application to every kind of inquiry and every kind of domestic tribunal. The requirements of natural justice must depend on the circumstances of the case, the nature of the inquiry, the rules under which the tribunal is acting, the subject-matter that is being dealt with, and so forth'. In

H the earlier case of *General Medical Council* v. *Spackman* (21) LORD ATKIN expressed a similar view in these words: ' Some analogy exists no doubt between the various procedures of this and other not strictly judicial bodies; but I cannot think that the procedure which may be very just in deciding whether to close a school or an insanitary house is necessarily right in deciding a charge of infamous conduct against a professional man. I would,

I therefore, demur to any suggestion that the words of LORD LOREBURN, L.C., in *Board of Education* v. *Rice* (22) afford a complete guide to the General Medical Council in the exercise of their duties.'

"With these reservations as to the utility of general definitions in this

---

(19) [1960] 1 All E.R. at pp. 637-639; [1960] 1 W.L.R. at pp. 231-233.
(20) [1949] 1 All E.R. at p. 118.
(21) [1943] 2 All E.R. 337 at p. 341; [1943] A.C. 627 at p. 638.
(22) [1911] A.C. 179 at p. 182; [1911-13] All E.R. Rep. 36 at p. 38.

branch of the law, it appears to their Lordships that LORD LOREBURN's   A
much quoted statement in *Board of Education* v. *Rice* (23) still affords as good
a general definition as any of the nature of and limits on the requirements of
natural justice in this kind of case. Its effect is conveniently stated in this
passage from the speech of VISCOUNT HALDANE, L.C., in *Local Government
Board* v. *Arlidge* (24), where he cites it with approval in the following words:
' I agree with the view expressed in an analogous case by my noble and   B
learned friend LORD LOREBURN. In *Board of Education* v. *Rice* (23) he
laid down that, in disposing of a question which was the subject of an appeal
to it, the Board of Education was under a duty to act in good faith, and to
listen fairly to both sides, inasmuch as that was a duty which lay on every
one who decided anything. But he went on to say that he did not think it
was bound to treat such a question as though it were a trial. The board had   C
no power to administer an oath, and need not examine witnesses. It could,
he thought, obtain information in any way it thought best, always giving a
fair opportunity to those who were parties in the controversy to correct or
contradict any relevant statement prejudicial to their view.'
    " From the many other citations which might be made, their Lordships
would select the following succinct statement from the judgment of this   D
Board in *De Verteuil* v. *Knaggs* (25): ' Their Lordships are of opinion that
in making such an inquiry there is, apart from special circumstances, a duty
of giving to any person against whom the complaint is made a fair opportunity to make any relevant statement which he may desire to bring forward
and a fair opportunity to correct or controvert any relevant statement
brought forward to his prejudice.'   E
    " The last general statement as to the requirements of natural justice to
which their Lordships would refer is that of HARMAN, J., in *Byrne* v. *Kinematograph Renters Society, Ltd.* (26), of which their Lordships would express
their approval. The learned judge said this: ' What, then, are the requirements of natural justice in a case of this kind? First, I think that the
person accused should know the nature of the accusation made; secondly,   F
that he should be given an opportunity to state his case; and, thirdly, of
course, that the tribunal should act in good faith. I do not think that
there really is anything more.'
    " Turning now to the actual terms in which the vice-chancellor is invested
with the quasi-judicial function here in question, it is to be observed that all
that cl. 8 provides is that where the vice-chancellor is satisfied that any   G
candidate has acquired knowledge of the nature or substance of any question
or the content of any paper before the date and time of the examination
' the vice-chancellor . . . shall report the matter to the Board of Residence
and Discipline . . .' The clause is silent as to the procedure to be followed
by the vice-chancellor in satisfying himself of the truth or falsity of a given
allegation. If the clause contained any special directions in regard to the   H
steps to be taken by the vice-chancellor in the process of satisfying himself
he would, of course, be bound to follow those directions. But as no special
form of procedure is prescribed, it is for him to determine the procedure to
be followed as he thinks best, but, to adapt to the present case the language
of the judgment of this Board in *De Verteuil* v. *Knaggs* (27), subject to the
obvious implication that some form of inquiry must be made, such as will   I
enable him fairly to determine whether he should hold himself satisfied that
the charge in question has been made out.

(23) [1911] A.C. at p. 182; [1911-13] All E.R. Rep. at p. 38.
(24) [1915] A.C. 120 at p. 132; [1914-15] All E.R. Rep. 1 at p. 7.
(25) [1918] A.C. 557 at p. 560.
(26) [1958] 2 All E.R. 579 at p. 599; [1958] 1 W.L.R. 762 at p. 784.
(27) [1918] A.C. at p. 560.

A   "As was said by LORD SHAW OF DUNFERMLINE in *Local Government Board* v. *Arlidge* (28), of the authority there concerned it '... must do its best to act justly, and to reach just ends by just means. If a statute prescribes the means it must employ them. If it is left without express guidance it must still act honestly and by honest means.'

"In the present case no shadow of doubt is cast upon the honest and bona
B   fides of the vice-chancellor or of those who sat with him in the commission of inquiry. So far as the plaintiff is concerned, it appears to their Lordships that he must be taken to have agreed, when he became a member of the university, to be bound by the statutes of the university, including cl. 8, and in the event of cl. 8 being put in operation against him, could not insist on the adoption by the vice-chancellor of any particular procedure beyond
C   what the clause expressly or by necessary implication requires. In the absence of any express requirement, he is thrown back on the necessary implication that the vice-chancellor's procedure will be such as to satisfy the requirements indicated in the passages from *De Verteuil* v. *Knaggs* (29), *Local Government Board* v. *Arlidge* (30), and *Byrne* v. *Kinematograph Renters Society, Ltd.* (31), to which their Lordships have just referred, and thus to
D   comply with those elementary and essential principles of ' fairness ' which must, as a matter of necessary implication, be treated as applicable in the discharge of the vice-chancellor's admittedly quasi-judicial functions under cl. 8, or, in other words, with the principles of natural justice."

That authority, like the dicta of the Court of Appeal in the present case, is not binding on me.   The two are irreconcilable and I have no alternative but to
E   choose between them. I have given this difficult decision long and anxious consideration but in the result I have come to the conclusion that the view of the Privy Council is to be preferred. In coming to that conclusion I have had particularly in mind the phrase used by the Board in the last sentence of the passage cited (32)—

F   "... those elementary and essential principles of ' fairness ' which must as a matter of necessary implication be treated as applicable in the discharge of the vice-chancellor's admittedly quasi-judicial functions ... ,"

which the Board equated with the other phrase " the principles of natural justice ".

I find it difficult to say that legal representation before a tribunal is an elemen-
G   tary feature of the fair dispensation of justice. It seems to me that it arises only in a society which has reached some degree of sophistication in its affairs.

For these reasons the plaintiff is not, in my judgment, entitled to the declaration which he seeks and the action must be dismissed.

Order accordingly.

Solicitors: *Shindler & Co.* (for the plaintiff);   *Herbert Smith & Co.* (for the
H   defendants).

[*Reported by* K. DIANA PHILLIPS, *Barrister-at-Law.*]

I

---

(28) [1915] A.C. at p. 138; [1914-15] All E.R. Rep. at p. 9.
(29) [1918] A.C. 557.
(30) [1915] A.C. 120; [1914-15] All E.R. Rep. 1.
(31) [1958] 2 All E.R. 579; [1958] 1 W.L.R. 762.
(32) [1960] 1 All E.R. at p. 639; [1960] 1 W.L.R. at p. 233.

A

Re FLAVEL'S WILL TRUSTS.
COLEMAN AND ANOTHER v. FLAVEL AND OTHERS.

[CHANCERY DIVISION (Stamp, J.), February 17, 18, 1969.]

Charity—Uncertainty—Uncertainty in description of persons to benefit—Super-
annuation fund—Uncertainty as to persons to benefit fatal to gift.

B

Charity—Validation by Charitable Trusts (Validation) Act 1954—Imperfect
trust provision—Scheme for administration of fund for benefit of employees
of company—Rule against perpetuities—Whether trusts validated.

Perpetuities—Rule against perpetuities—Remoteness—Scheme for administration
of fund for benefit of employees of company—Uncertainty in description
of persons to benefit—Whether validated by Superannuation and Other   C
Trust Funds (Validation) Act 1927 (17 & 18 Geo. 5 c. 41), s. 1 and s. 2.

The testator, who died in 1939, provided by cl. 10* of his will that on his
widow's death (which occurred in 1966), 2/6ths of his residuary estate was to
be held by trustees and used by them " for formation of a superannuation
and bonus fund for the employees of Sidney Flavel & Co., Limited such fund
to be established and constituted in such manner as my Trustees shall in their   D
absolute discretion think fit ". The question arose, inter alia, whether the
direction cl. 10 was void under the rule against perpetuities, and failed for
uncertainty.

Held: the bequest did not constitute a valid charitable trust and hence was
not validated by the Charitable Trusts (Validation) Act 1954, because—

(i) the direction was void for perpetuity because the cestui que trusts were   E
not confined to those employees who were employees at the determination
of the prior interest but extended to those as yet unborn who might become
employees (see p. 234, letters B and E, post);

(ii) that the doctrine of executory trusts did not apply because although
the trust did not fail for want of a cestui que trust, it was not ascertainable
(even in general terms) from the language of the will the trusts on which the   F
property was to be settled; further the trust could not be executed in such a
way so as to prevent it being void for remoteness because it was impossible
to extract the necessary intention from the will that the trustees were to
benefit only employees superannuated during the perpetuity period (see
p. 234, letter G, and p. 234, letter I, to p. 235, letter A, and p. 235, letter I,
to p. 236, letter A, post).

G

Miles v. *Harford* ((1879), 12 Ch.D. 691) distinguished.

(iii) the Superannuation and Other Trust Funds (Validation) Act 1927,
s. 1 and s. 2†, did not validate the direction because what was contemplated
by the Act was a fund established in connection with the undertaking and
not a fund established by a third person for the benefit of the employees
of a company (see p. 236, letters E and H, post).

H

[As to executory trusts, see 38 HALSBURY'S LAWS (3rd Edn.) 842, 843, paras.
1413-1415; and for cases on the subject, see 47 DIGEST (Repl.) 78-82, *555-581.*

As to superannuation trusts, see 38 HALSBURY'S LAWS (3rd Edn.) 851-855,
paras. 1430-1439.

For the Superannuation and Other Trust Funds (Validation) Act 1927, s. 1,
s. 2, Schedule, see 26 HALSBURY'S STATUTES (2nd Edn.) 160, 166.]

I

Cases referred to:

Houston v. *Burns,* [1918] A.C. 337; [1918-19] All E.R. Rep. 817; 87 L.J.P.C.
          99; 118 L.T. 462; 48 Digest (Repl.) 403, *3512.*
Miles v. *Harford* (1879), 12 Ch.D. 691; 41 L.T. 378; 47 Digest (Repl.) 82, *583.*

---

* Clause 10 is set out at p. 233, letter G, post.
† The provisions of the Act, so far as material, are set out at p. 236, letters C and D,
post.

A   *Morice* v. *Durham* (*Bishop*) (1805), 10 Ves. 522; [1803-13] All E.R. Rep. 451;
     32 E.R. 947; 47 Digest (Repl.) 47, *308*.

Adjourned Summons.

This was an application by originating summons dated 5th June 1967 by the
plaintiffs Thomas Herbert Gaitskell Coleman and Edward Denyer Cox, the
trustees of the will dated 31st August 1933 of Percival William Flavel, deceased,
B   who died on 28th February 1939 for the determination by the court of the following questions: whether on the true construction of cl. 10 of the will the equal
sixth part shares to be retained by the trustees and used by them for a superannuation and bonus fund for the employees of Sidney Flavel & Co., Ltd. (a) failed
for perpetuity and uncertainty or otherwise, or (b) were validated under the
Charitable Trusts (Validation) Act 1954, or (c) constituted a valid charitable
C   bequest without the assistance of the Act, or (d) constituted a valid non-charitable
bequest. The defendants to the originating summons were (i) Sidney William
Basil Flavel, (ii) Gilbert Henry Flavel (deceased) represented by Midland Bank
Executor and Trustee Co., Ltd., (iii) William Edward Cox, (iv) Evan Augustus
Norton (deceased) (the personal representatives of the testator's widow who all
claimed to be interested in an intestacy), (v) Alfred Adderley, who represented
D   the employees of the company, and (vi) Her Majesty's Attorney-General. The
facts are set out in the judgment.

The cases noted below* were cited during the argument in addition to those
referred to in the judgment.

H. Hillaby for the plaintiffs.
E   *E. W. H. Christie* for the first, second, third and fourth defendants.
P. J. Millett for the fifth defendant.
N. C. H. Browne-Wilkinson for the sixth defendant.

STAMP, J.: The testator, Percival William Flavel, died on 28th February
1939 without issue leaving a widow to whom he gave the income of his residuary
estate, in the will called " the trust fund ", as to half during widowhood and as to
F   the other half during her life. She died without having remarried on 14th November 1966.

What is now in question is the destination of the 2/6ths of the trust fund of the
value of some £33,000 as to which the testator directed by cl. 10 of his will as
follows:

G   " And as to the remaining two equal sixth parts of shares of the trust
fund I Declare that the same shall be retained by my Trustees and be
used by them for formation of a superannuation and bonus fund for the
employees of Sidney Flavel & Co. Limited such fund to be established and
constituted in such manner as my Trustees shall in their absolute discretion
think fit."

H   I ought perhaps to have mentioned that it appears from the probate of the
testator's will that at the date of his death the net value of his estate amounted to
rather less than £11,000.

At the date of the will the company was a private company owned by members
of the testator's family. In the year 1944 the company was sold to the Whitehead
Industrial Trust and was subsequently floated as a public company. This no
I   doubt accounts for the phenomenal rise in the value of the residuary estate.
The company now employs about 1,000 persons and there is, and has for some time
been, in force a pension scheme for the benefit of the employees of the company

* *Marchioness of Blandford* v. *Dowager Duchess of Marlborough* (1743), 2 Atk. 542;
Re Parrott (1886), 33 Ch.D. 274; *Re Drummond*, [1914] 2 Ch. 90; [1914-15] All E.R.
Rep. 223; *A.-G.* v. *National Provincial and Union Bank of England*, [1924] A.C. 262;
Re Ogden, [1933] Ch. 678; [1933] All E.R. Rep. 720; *Re Taylor*, [1940] 2 All E.R. 637;
[1940] Ch. 481; *Re Wood* (*decd.*), [1949] 1 All E.R. 1100; [1949] Ch. 498; *Re Meyers*,
[1951] 1 All E.R. 538; [1951] Ch. 534; *Re Eden* (*decd.*), [1957] 2 All E.R. 430; [1957]
1 W.L.R. 788.

and a supplementary pension fund which has been set aside out of profits for A implementing the scheme which is effected by the usual type of group policy with an insurance company.

Before I can attempt to answer the questions raised in the originating summons as to the validity of the trust which I have read, I must construe cl. 10. First, it is to be noted that the fund in question does not fall to be distributed among the employees of the company on the determination of the widow's interest therein. B It is to be retained by the trustees and I cannot escape the conclusion that the cestui que trusts are not confined to those employees who are employees at the determination of the prior interest but extend to those as yet unborn who may become employees and are in due course superannuated by the company. What is contemplated is the establishment and constitution of a trust fund which is to be held for an unspecified period and the income, and perhaps the capital of which, C is to be applicable to provide benefits for the employees of the company. Subject to the significance, if any, which ought to be attached to the expression " bonus ", it is clear that the benefits to be provided are to be retirement benefits.

It is also to be noted that an imperative duty is cast on the trustees to form, establish and constitute the fund. They are not merely given power to do so. Nor in the terms of the provision are the trustees given power to determine which D of the employees of the company are to be benefited.

What is contemplated, again ignoring the word " bonus " in the description of the fund, is the provision of superannuation benefits for the employees. I underline the definite article. This, prima facie, includes all those employees who are in due course to be superannuated.

In my judgment the direction is void in the first place on the ground that what E is contemplated is a trust void for remoteness. A trust for the employees for the time being of a company not confined within the limits allowed by the rule against perpetuities is in accordance with well-known principles void, and similarly in my judgment, subject to the argument advanced by counsel for the fifth defendant, the representative of the employees, to which I will refer in a moment, a direction to set up a trust having that same characteristic must likewise be void. F

There is a further difficulty in giving effect to the direction. Counsel for the fifth defendant is no doubt right that here we have an executory trust and that since the beneficiaries consist of a class of persons, namely the employees for the time being of the company, the trust does not fail for want of cestui que trust; see cases such as *Morice* v. *Bishop of Durham* (1) and *Houston* v. *Burns* (2). Nevertheless, it appears to me that the testator has offended the axiom that a G testator cannot leave it to trustees to make a will for him. Although the beneficiaries are specified and although they are to take benefits on superannuation, the rest is left in obscurity.

By what yardstick are the superannuation benefits to be calculated or measured? To what extent is the capital of the fund to be resorted to to augment those benefits? Above all, to whom and on what basis are bonuses to be awarded? H No doubt it would, as counsel for the fifth defendant submits, be well within the capacity of any of those counsel whom I see before me to draw a deed which could appropriately be called a superannuation and bonus fund, but having done so, how could you say that that deed so drawn gave effect to the testator's intention unless that intention simply was to leave it to his trustees to determine on what trust for the benefit of the superannuated employees the fund should be I held?

Of course, where a testator has directed that a settlement be made on a named person and his children, the court can execute the trust, but it appears to me that a direction to settle property for the benefit of a class of employees such as is here contemplated is beyond the limits of the doctrine of executory trust. Before that doctrine can be applied, one must, in my judgment, be able to

(1) (1805), 10 Ves. 522; [1803-13] All E.R. Rep. 451.
(2) [1918] A.C. 337; [1918-19] All E.R. Rep. 817.

A   ascertain from the language of the will directing the setting-up of the trust, at least in general terms, the trusts which one is to impose on the property to be settled.

Counsel for the fifth defendant urged in argument which was as forceful as it was almost convincing that, in framing the limitations or trusts to be inserted pursuant to the executory trust, appropriate provisions ought to be inserted to

B   prevent the trusts being void for remoteness and he relied particularly on *Miles* v. *Harford* (3) for that purpose. The facts in *Miles* v. *Harford* (3) can, I think, best be taken from the headnote which reads as follows (4):

"A testator devised his freehold estates in *Worcestershire* to his third son and his issue male, with remainder to his fourth son and his issue male, in strict settlement; and he devised his freehold estates in *Cardiganshire*

C   to his fourth son and his issue male, with remainder to his fifth son and his issue male, in strict settlement. By a shifting clause it was provided that if his fourth son, or any issue male of his fourth son, should become actually entitled to the possession of his *Worcestershire* estates, and if his fifth son or any of his issue male should be then living, the limitations of his *Cardiganshire* estates in favour of his fourth son, or his issue male, should absolutely

D   cease. He bequeathed his leasehold estates in *Cardiganshire* to trustees upon such trusts as, regard being had to the difference in the tenure of the premises respectively, would best or most nearly correspond with the uses declared of the *Cardiganshire* freeholds."

So far as is relevant for present purposes, it was held (4):

E   "that the fifth son was entitled to the rents and profits of the *Cardiganshire* leaseholds, because they were given upon an executory trust; and, assuming the shifting clause, if applied verbatim to the leaseholds, to be bad for remoteness, it ought to be so modified as to render it free from that objection."

That appears to me to be a very different case from the present case. Here

F   the draftsman of the settlement contemplated by the testator, in order to take the case outside the rule against perpetuities, would have to limit the objects of the trust to those employees who were superannuated before the expiration of 21 years from the death of some person living at the date when the testator died, on 28th February 1939. So to limit the class of persons to take under the trust would be to exclude a class of employees whom the testator intended to

G   benefit and so not implement but defeat the testator's intention.

In *Miles* v. *Harford* (3) it was possible to treat the testator as intending the executory trusts to take effect so far as they could effectively do so and not further. Sir George Jessel, M.R., remarked (5):

"In that way it is executory, that if he has not put into words the precise nature of the limitations, he has said in effect: 'Now these are my inten-

H   tions; do your best to carry them out'..."

Later in the report, having called attention to the fact that if one repeated the shifting clause for the leaseholds it would fail to a great extent for remoteness, Sir George Jessel, M.R., said (6):

"If we imported them into the leaseholds they would fail altogether after the gift to the first. Then when you have to write it out you are

I   to have regard to the difference of the tenure. What does that mean? When according to the tenure it will not take effect you cannot put it in; that is all. It will be absurd to suppose that you have regard to the difference of the tenure to make them best correspond when you simply made them null and void."

In the present case it is quite impossible in my judgment to extract from this

---

(3) (1879), 12 Ch.D. 691.   (4) (1879), 12 Ch.D. at p. 691.
(5) (1879), 12 Ch.D. at p. 699.   (6) (1879), 12 Ch.D. at pp. 700, 701.

testator's will an intention that one is to do the best one can to benefit the **A** employees for the time being of the company. Here there is an intention to benefit a class which cannot effectively be done because of the rule against perpetuities.

I must, however, notice a further argument advanced by counsel for the fifth defendant and based on the Superannuation and Other Trust Funds (Validation) Act 1927. Counsel contends that if a deed be executed which does in fact **B** embrace all the employees for the time being of the company in perpetuity within its ambit, that deed could be registered under the Act. Section 1 of the Act provides that—

" The rule of law relating to perpetuities shall not apply and shall be deemed never to have applied to the trusts of any fund registered under this Act (in this Act referred to as a ' registered fund ')." **C**

Section 2 provides:

" Subject to the provisions of this Act, any fund established under trusts subject to the laws of Great Britain, in connection with an undertaking or combination of undertakings carried on wholly or partly in Great Britain, being a fund of which the main purpose is either—(a) [and para. (a) is the **D** paragraph on which counsel relies], the provision of superannuation allowances on retirement to persons employed in the undertaking or combination of undertakings in connection with which the fund is established . . . shall be qualified for registration under this Act if the rules of the fund comply with the requirements set out in the Schedule to this Act."

I venture to doubt at this point whether a fund set up by an individual settlor **E** or by the direction of a testator can properly be said to be established in connection with an undertaking, and that such a fund is not within the contemplation of the Act is, I think, made clear by the nature of the requirements set out in the Schedule to the Act.

When one looks at these one finds that one at least of the 11 requirements cannot be satisfied in the case of a trust such as that with which I am concerned. What **F** the Schedule provides is this:

" The rules of a fund qualified for registration under this Act must make provision for the following matters, that is to say:— . . . 5. The making of contributions to the fund by the employers of persons employed in the undertaking or combination of undertakings in connection with which the fund is established; 6. The contributions payable to the fund, and the rates **G** of benefit payable thereout or the method of calculating the benefits so payable: . . . ."

In my judgment what is contemplated by that Act is a fund established in one way or another in connection with the undertaking and not a fund established by a third person for the benefit of the employees of a company. **H**

It being conceded, as I think rightly, that on the view I have formed as to the true construction of the gift, it is not arguable that it is validated by the Charitable Trusts (Validation) Act 1954, I will declare for the reasons I have given that it does not constitute a valid charitable bequest and that it is not validated under the Charitable Trusts (Validation) Act 1954.

Order accordingly. **I**

Solicitors: *Devonshire & Co.*, agents for *Wright, Hassall & Co.*, Leamington Spa (for the plaintiffs and the first, second, third, fourth and fifth defendants); *Treasury Solicitor*.

[*Reported by* ROSALIE LONG, *Barrister-at-Law.*]

A   # R. v. O'SULLIVAN.

[COURT OF APPEAL, CRIMINAL DIVISION (Winn and Widgery, L.JJ., and Lawton, J.), February 13, 1969.]

Criminal Law—Evidence—Handwriting—Signature disputed—No expert evidence —Jury warned that it would be dangerous to make comparisons of signatures
B   *without expert guidance—Whether conviction should stand.*

The appellant was the servant of a company whose custom it was to make overnight deposits in the night safe of their bank in a wallet or wallets. He was charged with the larceny as a servant of £400 odd, the contents of one of the wallets. The evidence was that a man had asked the bank official for the firm's wallet by number and signed for it in the register.
C   The official recognised the appellant as that man; she had seen him several times before and she later picked him out on an identification parade; only four other persons knew of the wallet's number. Photographic copies of the register on which appeared the signature of the man who had taken the wallet and the genuine signature of the appellant were given to the jury. The defence disputed that the signature of the man who had taken the
D   wallet was that of the appellant, but no expert evidence of handwriting was given. The jury had the two specimens of handwriting before them but were warned more than once carefully and stringently that it would be dangerous without expert guidance to make comparisons. On appeal against conviction,

Held: the appeal would be dismissed because the deputy chairman did
E   not himself purport to make any comments of any kind about similarities or dissimilarities between the signatures and, in the circumstances, the jury could not be said to have been left to decide questions of disputed handwriting on their own, and there was ample evidence to support the conviction (see p. 242, letters B and C, and p. 242, letter I, to p. 243, letter A, post).

F   Dictum of BLACKBURN, J., in *R.* v. *Harvey* ((1869), 11 Cox C.C. at p. 548) approved;

R. v. *Tilley* ([1961] 3 All E.R. 406) explained and dictum of WINN, J., in *R.* v. *Stannard* ((1962), 48 Cr. App. Rep. at p. 95) criticised.

Per CURIAM: there is a very real danger where the jury make comparisons of handwriting, but as a matter of practical reality all that can be done is
G   to ask them not to make such comparisons themselves and to have vividly in mind the fact that they are not qualified to make comparisons (see p. 242, letter G, post).

Appeal dismissed.

[As to evidence of handwriting, see 10 HALSBURY'S LAWS (3rd Edn.) 872, 873, para. 1691, note (*p*); and 15 HALSBURY'S LAWS (3rd Edn.) 324, 325, para.
H   591; and for cases on the subject, see 14 DIGEST (Repl.) 298, *2782*; 22 Digest (Repl.) 194, *1811*, 195, *1825*, 196, *1831*, *1832*.]

Cases referred to:
   R. v. *Harvey* (1869), 11 Cox, C.C. 546; 22 Digest (Repl.) 195, *1829*.
   R. v. *Rickard* (1918), 88 L.J.K.B. 720; 119 L.T. 192; 82 J.P. 256; 13 Cr. App. Rep. 140; 22 Digest (Repl.) 196, *1831*.
I   *R.* v. *Stannard* (1962), [1964] 1 All E.R. 34; [1965] 2 Q.B. 1; [1964] 2 W.L.R. 461; 128 J.P. 224; 48 Cr. App. Rep. 81; Digest (Cont. Vol. B) 177, *5018e*.
   R. v. *Tilley*, *R.* v. *Tilley*, [1961] 3 All E.R. 406; [1961] 1 W.L.R. 1309; 125 J.P. 611; 45 Cr. App. Rep. 360; Digest (Cont. Vol. A) 530, *1831a*.

Appeal.

This was an appeal by John David O'Sullivan against his conviction on 23rd May 1968 at Inner London Quarter Sessions before the deputy chairman (His

Honour JUDGE MOYLAN) and a jury of larceny as a servant. He also appealed A
against his sentence of 12 months' imprisonment. The facts are set out in the
judgment of the court.

The authority and cases noted below* were cited during the argument in
addition to the cases referred to in the judgment.

C. V. Nicholls for the appellant.
M. Gale for the Crown.   B

WINN, L.J., delivered the judgment of the court: This is an interesting
and indeed an important case which has been extremely well argued both by
counsel for the appellant and also by counsel for the Crown. It involves—
though it is convenient first to state the general narrative and background—
a question of handwriting and the way in which a court should deal with ques- C
tions of similarity of handwriting if and when any question of that kind arises
in the course of trial.

It appears that the appellant, who was convicted of larceny as a servant of
some £400 odd on 23rd May 1968 at Inner London Sessions, and sentenced to
12 months' imprisonment (having subsequently obtained bail in September),
was employed for about seven years as a salesman and to some extent a porter D
by a firm called British and Colonial Furnishing Co., Ltd. For about two years
before the relevant events he had been working in London Road at their shop
there which traded under the name of Smarts and banked with Westminster
Bank, Ltd., at Newington Causeway branch. This particular firm had a system
of obtaining security for cash and other valuables for short periods of time by
depositing such things in this branch of the bank, their bankers, in one or other E
(sometimes in both) of two leather wallets which bore numbers, respectively,
1777 and 1778, overnight or over a weekend, as the case might be. There was
a well established and proved system whereby the cashier usually went to the
bank with such wallets but always with the protection of at least one and usually
two male representatives of the firm. In the course of that practice, on Saturday
night 18th February, or it may be 17th February, and it may possibly be also on F
the following day, the Sunday, but at any rate before or during the weekend, both
these wallets whose numbers have been mentioned were deposited in the night
safe of the bank. On the morning of Tuesday, 20th, the cashier went to the
bank with the appellant and another man, both wallets being then there; she
was asked to speak to the senior cashier who spoke a cautionary word about the
desirability of having straps on such wallets; then one of the wallets was opened G
by the cashier, having been handed to her by the bank representative, and the
money in it was paid into the bank account of the firm. The other wallet was
left in the bank, no. 1777. The empty one, no. 1778, was taken away, as it
happened under the jacket of the appellant.

The next event, which was the vital one, happened shortly after midday the
same day—within therefore quite a brief period of time; it is necessary to H
emphasise that when this earlier call which has been described took place a
certain Miss Clements, a bank official, saw those who came that day, Miss
Rivett, the appellant and another man, and she had seen during the period of
some 2½ weeks during which she had been on duty at this bank, on relief duty,
several times during that period this same man, the appellant, coming and going
in the course of such transactions as have been referred to. When 12 noon or I
shortly after that came she was alone on duty in the bank though no doubt
there was in some inner room a senior official of the bank; she was alone at the
counter. According to the evidence which she gave at the trial, a man came in
shortly after 12 noon, very shortly after, and asked for no. 1777 wallet in the

* ARCHBOLD'S CRIMINAL PLEADING, EVIDENCE AND PRACTICE (36th Edn.), paras.
1261, 1262; R. v. Crouch (1850), 4 Cox, C.C. 163; R. v. Smith (1909), 3 Cr. App. Rep. 87;
R. v. Harden, [1962] 1 All E.R. 286; [1963] 1 Q.B. 8; R. v. Moet, 23rd May 1966, unreported; R. v. Davies (4th December 1967), unreported.

A name of Smarts, saying he wanted Smarts' wallet, giving that number. According to her evidence, she recognised him without any doubt at all as being the man that she had seen there earlier that morning, namely the appellant. She called on the man who asked for the wallet, and to whom she gave the wallet, to sign for it, and, according to her, in her presence that man did sign; the register was available at the trial. The court now has, as the jury had at the trial, photo-

B stats of the register. On the fifth line an entry appears of the withdrawal on 20th February of no. 1778 and on the top line there purports to be an entry of the withdrawal of no. 1777. Against each of those is a word or name, somewhat resembling the name Sullivan or O'Sullivan, and the two of them somewhat resemble one another. The entry on the fifth line was admittedly made without any doubt at all by the appellant during the earlier morning visit. There was

C evidence that Miss Clements made that identification in her own mind at the time and that she had seen the signature being placed on the register. An identification parade was held two days later on 22nd February, the Thursday, and Miss Clements picked out the appellant as being the man to whom she had delivered the wallet. A perfectly proper cross-examination was carried out on behalf of the appellant at the trial to see whether it could be effectively suggested

D against her, so that the jury might lose confidence in her evidence, that she had what is sometimes called her own axe to grind in that she had admittedly given this wallet to one purported representative of Smarts, whereas the banking procedure and instructions to her were that she should only deliver a wallet to two representatives, and it was suggested that she was covering up for her own error. A witness called Parker, who was the other salesman who came and

E went on such errands to the bank and had been there earlier in the morning, gave evidence that the appellant left the shop at about midday for his customary lunch break and returned at about 1.25 p.m. A very important feature of this case was established by the evidence of Mr. Kohler, the shop manager, that there were only four people beside himself who knew these wallet numbers, and they were the head clerk, a certain Mrs. Wylie, the cashier already mentioned,

F Miss Rivett, Mr. Parker, already mentioned, and the appellant. There was therefore a narrow circle circumscribed by those facts within which, it was contended, was to be found the perpetrator of this theft of the wallet. Of course, it need hardly be added that the wallet was not seen again. On the next day, 21st, the Wednesday, detective constable Cox, according to his evidence, saw the appellant and told him what the trouble was, and the appellant said,

G " Well, it was not me " and, asked about time, said he went straight home to lunch, using the firm's van, and that his wife was at home, being sick and not able to go to work; he did not fancy his dinner so he ate nothing but stopped at a pub on the way back and had a couple of gins. It is to be observed that the appellant and his wife did not precisely agree about the time at which he arrived home for this luncheon break. She thought it might have been as late as 35

H minutes after midday, i.e., 25 minutes short of 1.0 p.m., and that would, according to police evidence and a check made, have given him time to carry out this theft before going on to his home. The defence always was that it was a mistake, a misidentification, and that he knew nothing about it, and that he was perfectly innocent.

It is a serious case because he is a man of 27, married, earning £25 or £30 a

I week, with a wife working as a conductress, and apart from one fairly trivial previous conviction at the age of 18, some considerable time ago, he had a perfectly clean character. It was a very stupid thing for a man to do since the finger of suspicion would be pointed, as he ought to have realised if he had any sense, so directly at him.

The real point of this appeal is that notwithstanding the great strength, as it seems to this court, of that identification which was an identification by Miss Clements who had seen the man quite often in the course of the previous three weeks, the corroboration of her identification—not of course any corroboration required as a matter of law—was very largely to be found, if properly to be found, in the fact that his signature appeared on the register. When the matter was first referred to by the learned chairman he said:

> " Members of the jury, of course you will all want to look at this document, and I have something more to say about the question of the signature. Look at the signature on the top right sheet, and consider whether you think that that, in fact, was [the appellant's] signature, or whether or not at least, it indicates that whoever made that signature, if it was not [the appellant] was having a shot at making a signature which looked something like [the appellant's] signature."

That passage which could, the court recognises, be construed as some sort of invitation to the jury to look at the signature and consider what its effect was in their minds, occurred in a context which controls that remark or invitation in as much as the learned chairman had been fairly, lucidly and without bias tabulating the coincidences or special factors which had to be assumed as a matter of logic if the view were to be taken that some person other than the appellant had taken this wallet. He said, for example, it must have been somebody who knew of the procedure for getting the wallet from the bank; it must have been somebody who either knew that one of the firm's wallets was in the bank or there was a fair chance of it being there, and must have known the number of this particular wallet left in the bank when the other was taken away. Somebody also—and this is where the matter is particularly relevant— he rightly said who knew the appellant's name and his initials, and that he was one of the people entitled to draw wallets of the firm from the bank.

The trial of this case was made very much more difficult and the approach of the learned chairman to this problem of handwriting was made awkward, and indeed intractable, by the policy adopted at the beginning of the trial and for some considerable time pursued by the defence of asking that the jury should have the opportunity of checking the register and alleged register signature against other genuine signatures of the appellant, and that made the case much more difficult also for counsel for the Crown. It made it much more difficult for everybody since, until it was first raised by the defence that there was going to be a challenge, there was no reason whatever for the prosecution to foresee that this entry in the register would be challenged as a bogus, forged entry.

In the circumstances, the learned deputy chairman set out to navigate amongst the reefs knowing very well the decision in *R.* v. *Tilley, R.* v. *Tilley* (1) to which reference would have to be made, and he set himself strenuously to warn the jury against the dangers implicit in their making comparisons of writing without being expert, as of course they were not, and without the assistance of any witness who was expert about handwriting. He reminded them that it had not been the final policy of the defence to allow or request that the jury be allowed to compare the signatures. He reminded them, without mentioning, I think, the name of the case, that higher courts had several times said that it was extremely difficult and dangerous for juries to make comparisons, and he said:

> ". . . it is very dangerous for you or me—we are not experts at this sort of thing—to start looking at signatures and comparing them, and saying yes, they are the same, or no, they are not."

And he said:

> ". . . my advice to you is to be very very careful indeed about just looking at those two signatures."

Then he said:

> ". . . you may well think, looking at these two signatures, that all one can say at the end was, well there is some similarity . . . my advice to

(1) [1961] 3 All E.R. 406; [1961] 1 W.L.R. 1309.

A   you would be, be very very cautious about going into any details in comparing these two."

The point is one of importance and indeed from time to time the courts have had to consider it. It seems to this court that possibly there has been a misunderstanding from a very early date of what was said by BLACKBURN, J., in *R.* v. *Harvey* (2). That was a case where there had been an objection taken by

B   the defence to certain evidence found in the house of the prisoner, certain copy books said to contain his handwriting, on the ground that police officers are not competent to give evidence as experts as to handwriting. The learned judge said—and he has been accepted as one of the greatest judges this country has ever had the fortune to possess (3):

C   "But the jury can inspect them and compare them with the forged document. [He went on to say] But still they are only copy books, which go no further than to show that the prisoner was taught writing. I think the evidence is very weak, and I do not think the jury ought to act on it without the assistance of an expert. The policeman is certainly not a skilled witness ... [and in three lines he gave his ruling:] But here we have no

D   expert and I do not think it would be right to let the jury compare the handwriting without some such assistance. The evidence is very slight."

It seems to this court today that that was a ruling of a very narrow character indeed. The learned judge was saying: "in this particular case: (a) we have no expert; (b) the evidence is of very poor evidentiary value; therefore I am going to exercise my discretion in not allowing it to go to the jury".

E   Now there has been a long sequence of authority and really it does not merit the time that otherwise would be taken that this court should go right through all those cases. *R.* v. *Tilley* (4) is undoubtedly the most important, most prominent, of the decisions and was a case where ASHWORTH, J., giving the judgment of the Court of Criminal Appeal, of which it happened that I was myself the junior member, used this expression which this court today, no longer

F   the Court of Criminal Appeal but the Court of Appeal, Criminal Division, thinks has been not only misinterpreted to some extent but has been more widely applied and held to be of stricter restrictive effect than really is justified by the words of the court. This was said (5):

G   "In the present case there was no evidence, not even questions directed to alleged similarities, and the matter only arose in the course of the summing-up."

That point stresses the importance of what counsel for the Crown said to the court today in his submission, that it may very well be the proper practice where the prosecution does or should anticipate that there will be an issue as to the genuineness of some signature, that the prosecution should tender a witness who is properly expert to give evidence on that matter; in *R.* v. *Tilley* (4), as

H   in the instant case, the matter only arose long after the trial had begun, at a time when even if the matter were dealt with by rebuttal, almost certainly there would have to be a second trial rather than such a long adjournment as would be required to obtain the expert advice. There was no evidence in *R.* v. *Tilley* (4), said the judge, and the matter only arose in the course of the summing-up. He went on (5):

I   "This court indorses and re-affirms the statement of principle to be found in the judgment of SALTER, J., on behalf of this court in *R.* v. *Rickard* (6). A jury should not be left unassisted to decide questions of disputed handwriting on their own."

(2) (1869), 11 Cox, C.C. 546.   (3) (1869), 11 Cox, C.C. at p. 548.
(4) [1961] 3 All E.R. 406; [1961] 1 W.L.R. 1309.
(5) [1961] 3 All E.R. at p. 408; [1961] 1 W.L.R. at p. 1312.
(6) (1918), 13 Cr. App. Rep. 140 at pp. 142, 143.

The question arises whether within the proper understanding of those words A
in the instant case the jury was " left unassisted to decide questions of disputed
handwriting ".   The document had to go before the jury in the instant case
since it formed part of the probative material establishing the visit by the man
who took away the wallet and the fact that he had entered somebody's name
in the register of the bank.   The jury was not in the instant case invited to
make any comparisons, as the jury had been in *R.* v. *Tilley* (7).   The learned B
deputy chairman in the instant case did not himself purport to make any
comments of any kind about similarities or dissimilarities as had been done by
the learned deputy chairman in *R.* v. *Tilley* (7).   The jury were warned very,
very carefully and stringently not to make these comparisons.   In the circumstances, it does not seem to this court that the jury in the instant case can be
said to have been left to decide questions of disputed handwriting on their C
own.   It is true they were not effectively prevented from doing it.   What could
possibly have been done effectively to prevent them from making the comparison
passes the comprehension of this court.   It can hardly be right to suppose that
the documents already before them for a legitimate, proper and necessary
purpose should have been snatched away from them since that could only have
aroused dissatisfaction and grave doubt in their minds as to the fairness of the D
proceedings which were being conducted before them.

There have been subsequent references; it is right I should say that one of
them was a part of a judgment of mine in *R.* v. *Stannard* (8) which was quite a
complicated and heavy appeal.   A very subsidiary issue on the appeal was
whether or not there had been any impropriety in the manner in which the jury
were allowed to look at certain signatures.   I attempted then (9) to give what, E
on looking at it again, I feel was not a very satisfactory paraphrase of the
earlier case of *R.* v. *Tilley* (7).   I referred to the undoubtedly correct statement
(10) that the " court does not decide that expert evidence in such cases is
necessary " and the observations of BLACKBURN, J., in *R.* v. *Harvey* (11) do
not so decide.

I referred to the danger involved.   Then I said (9):   F

" The situation here was quite the obverse of the medal because what
defending counsel desired to have from the learned judge was a direction
that they should make this comparison . . ."

It seems to the court that in the instant case the matter was properly dealt with.
The fact remains that there is a very real danger where the jury make such G
comparisons, but as a matter of practical reality all that can be done is to ask
them not to make the comparisons themselves and to have vividly in mind
the fact that they are not qualified to make comparisons.   It is terribly risky
for jurors to attempt comparisons of writing unless they have very special
training in this particular science.   All possible was done, this court thinks,
with great care and very fairly by the court in the instant case.   It may well be H
that, despite it, the jury did try to make comparisons.   That is really unavoid-
able and it should be accepted these days that *R.* v. *Tilley* (7) cannot always be
in its literal meaning exactly applied; nevertheless every possible step and
regard should be had to what was said by the court in that case, in as much as
never should it be deliberately a matter of invitation or exhortation to a jury
to look at disputed handwriting.   There should be a warning of the dangers; I
further than that, as a matter of practical reality, it cannot be expected that the
court will go.   That being the whole burden of this case and there being ample
evidence to support this conviction, this court dismisses the appeal against

---

(7) [1961] 3 All E.R. 406;   [1961] 1 W.L.R. 1309.
(8) (1962), [1964] 1 All E.R. 34;   [1965] 2 Q.B. 1.
(9) (1962), 48 Cr. App. Rep. 81 at p. 95.
(10) Per SALTER, J., in *R.* v. *Rickard* (1918), 13 Cr. App. Rep. at p. 143.
(11) (1869), 11 Cox, C.C. at p. 548.

A   conviction and then turns to sentence, saying about it no more than that it was really a lenient sentence for a carefully contrived and planned crime of this kind, notwithstanding the virtually clean record of this man. He has surrendered to his bail and the appeal is dismissed.

Appeal dismissed.

B   Solicitors: *E. D. H. MacGreevy* (for the appellant); *Solicitor, Metropolitan Police* (for the Crown).

[*Reported by* N. P. Metcalfe, Esq., *Barrister-at-Law.*]

C

M. (D.) *v.* M. (S.) AND G. (M. (D.A.) intervening).

[Court of Appeal, civil division (Lord Denning, M.R., Davies and Widgery, L.JJ.), October 15, 1968.]

D

Divorce—Infant—Jurisdiction—Paternity of child in issue—Blood test—Inconclusiveness of result—Allegation of adultery—Child ten years old—Purpose of test, provision of evidence of adultery—Whether court would order test.

E   The parties were married in July 1955, and separated in May 1957 there being one child of the marriage. In September 1957 the wife obtained an order for maintenance against the husband on the ground that he had deserted her on 1st May 1957. The wife gave birth to an infant in July 1958. She applied to the magistrates under the Guardianship of Infants Act 1925 alleging that the husband was the child's father. He denied paternity and asked for a blood test, which however the wife would not allow. She was

F   allowed 2s. 6d. a week for the boy. Five years later the wife met another man (whom she had not known previously) with whom she lived as his wife and had children by him. In October 1966, the husband brought divorce proceedings alleging desertion from May 1957, and adultery with the man with whom the wife was living. In January 1967, the husband amended his grounds by alleging that in October 1957 the wife committed adultery with

G   a man unknown, and as a result of that adultery, gave birth to the infant. The husband asked for the infant to have a blood test, and the wife did not oppose this. The application was heard in June 1968. The official solicitor, as the infant's guardian ad litem, objected on the ground that it was not for the benefit of the infant and the commissioner refused to order a blood test. On appeal,

H   **Held:** although the cardinal principle was that the court could order a blood test on an infant whenever it was in the best interests of the infant, it would not order a test where the sole purpose was to prove the wife's past adultery and where the result of such a test would be inconclusive with possible harmful and disturbing effects on the infant (see p. 244, letters H and I, and p. 245, letters B, D, F, H. and I, post).

I   Appeal dismissed.

[As to jurisdiction of the court to order blood tests in matrimonial proceedings see Supplement to 21 Halsbury's Laws (3rd Edn.) para. 428.]

Interlocutory appeal.

This was an appeal by the husband from a decision of His Honour Judge Jellinek, given on 17th June 1968 sitting as a special commissioner in divorce dismissing an application for a blood test to be carried out on the infant, D. A., to ascertain the infant's paternity.

L. A. F. Borrett for the husband.   A

E. J. Prince for the wife.

D. J. Hyamson for the official solicitor as guardian ad litem of the infant intervener.

LORD DENNING, M.R.: In this case a young couple married in July 1955. The husband was 18 and the wife 19. She was pregnant by him. A month   B later, on 1st August 1955, the wife had a baby girl. They lived together for less than two years. Then in May 1957 they separated. In September 1957 the wife obtained an order for maintenance against the husband on the ground that he had deserted her on 15th May 1957. She was awarded maintenance of £1 10s. a week for herself and £3 10s. a week for the child.

A month later, in October 1957, the wife conceived another child, and on   C 30th July 1958 she gave birth to a boy, D. A. She applied to the magistrates under the Guardianship of Infants Act 1925, alleging that the husband was the father. He denied that he was the father. He said that he had never had access to the wife after their separation. She said that, after he deserted her, he came back and visited her occasionally and had intercourse with her, even after the magistrates' order. The husband asked that there should be a blood test. But   D the wife did not agree to it. So no blood test was held. The magistrates do not seem to have been very impressed with the wife. They were entitled to doubt her story, especially when she refused to have a blood test. They gave her the custody of the boy, but they only ordered the husband to pay 2s. 6d. a week for the boy. That sum was so small as to speak for itself.

That was ten years ago. Since that time each party has set up an establish-   E ment with another. Five years ago the wife met with another man (whom she had not known before). She has been living with him as his wife and has children by him. The husband has for seven or eight years been living with another woman and has children by her. In October 1966, the husband brought divorce proceedings against the wife, alleging desertion from May 1957, and adultery with the man with whom she has been living for the last five years. The wife   F put in an answer denying the desertion and alleging that the husband has committed adultery with the woman with whom he has been living for years, and also alleging cruelty. Then on 5th January 1967 (a year after he launched his petition) the husband amended his grounds by alleging that ten years before, in October 1957, the wife committed adultery with a man unknown, and, as a result of that adultery, gave birth to the boy, D. A.   G

On the issue raised by the amendment, the husband asked for the child to be blood-tested. The legal advisers on each side, very properly, thought the child ought to be separately represented. The official solicitor has been appointed as guardian ad litem on behalf of the infant. On 17th June 1968 the application for a blood test was heard by His Honour JUDGE JELLINEK, sitting as a commissioner. The wife did not oppose. But the official solicitor objected on the ground   H that it was not for the benefit of the child. The commissioner refused to order a blood test. The husband appeals to this court. The cardinal principle, as I understand it, is that the court can order a blood test on an infant, whenever it is in the best interests of the infant to do so. But in the present case I cannot see that there is any benefit to the infant in having a blood test. He is now ten years of age. He has been brought up from his birth by the wife, for the first five   I years by her alone, and for the last five years by the wife and the man with whom she is now living, as one of their family. There is no doubt that he will continue to be brought up by them. The wife will have the custody, and the man will support the boy as one of the family. On the other hand, the husband has always denied that he is the father. He has never taken any interest in the boy. He does not want custody or access to anything to do with him.

If it were possible, by means of the blood test, to show that the husband was the father, it might be to the child's benefit. But it cannot show that. This

A is not a case where one of two known men is the father. The only known man is the husband. There is a 70 per cent. chance that it may show that the husband was *not* the father. But, if that is shown, what good is it to the boy? It would only show that he is illegitimate and that the wife was telling lies when she said that the husband was the father. That does the boy no good. On the other hand, if the blood test should show that the husband *could* be the father, that will

B not do the boy any good either. Hundreds of other men also *could be* the father. This husband will not recognise the child as his. He has always denied paternity and will doubtless continue to do so.

In this situation, I cannot help thinking that the sole reason why the husband wants a blood test is to prove that the wife was guilty of adultery over ten years ago. Now in most cases it is best to know the truth: and I think the courts

C should help in the ascertainment of it, by ordering a blood test, if it is of any possible benefit to the infant. But I do not think the infant should be made a pawn in a contest between husband and wife—not, at any rate, in the case of an infant of ten who can understand what is happening. The wife has probably already told the boy her side of the story. She will have told him that the husband was the father. He may ask: " Why am I to have a blood test? " If he does,

D what is to be the answer? Perhaps he will be told: " To find out who is your father "; or, " To see if your mother is right about who is your father "; or, it may be some evasive answer. It seems to me that the answer may well be disturbing to the infant. It may shake his confidence in the wife. He may feel insecure. So far from being in his interest, the blood test may be harmful to him.

In all the circumstances, I think these adults should fight out their own battle

E without bringing the infant into it. The divorce proceedings should go for trial, as they are, without the child having a blood test. I think the commissioner was quite right to refuse a blood test. I would dismiss the appeal.

DAVIES, L.J.: I agree. If this test were to take place and were to prove to be negative in the sense that it showed that the husband could not be the

F father, it could be of no possible advantage to this boy to find himself in the position of having no identifiable father. And, of course, it might well be disastrous to the wife, insofar as that is relevant, since it would show that she had been telling a pack of lies. If, on the other hand, the test were not to prove negative, it would be entirely inconclusive and would be of little help to the wife or to the child. The issue would then depend on the evidence of the parties,

G the husband and the wife, about this alleged access during the period of separation, coupled, of course, with the presumption of legitimacy. The only possible benefit that the test might confer would be that it would be consistent with the wife's story, and she might be able to satisfy the judge as to the paternity of this child; and that would, I suppose, give her the right to maintenance for the child until he reached the age of 16, and would give the boy a father. But the

H inconclusiveness of such a test even in that event seems to me to make it quite clear that it would be completely undesirable to make the order prayed for in this case. I agree, therefore, with LORD DENNING, M.R., and the learned judge. The order should not be made and the appeal should be dismissed.

WIDGERY, L.J.: I agree with both judgments and would dismiss the appeal accordingly.

I
Appeal dismissed.

Solicitors: *Mileham, Scatliff & Allen,* Brighton (for the husband); *F. H. Carpenter & Oldham,* Brighton (for the wife); *Official Solicitor.*

[*Reported by* F. GUTTMAN, ESQ., *Barrister-at-Law.*]

DAWKINS (Valuation Officer) *v.* ASH BROTHERS & HEATON, LTD.

[HOUSE OF LORDS (Lord Guest, Lord Pearce, Lord Donovan, Lord Wilberforce and Lord Pearson), February 10, 11, March 26, 1969.]

Rates—Valuation—Hypothetical tenancy—Impending redevelopment—Part of factory required for road widening—Expectation of demolition in a year— Effect on value taken into account—Rating and Valuation Act 1925 (15 & 16 Geo. 5 c. 90), s. 22 (1) (b).

Under a compulsory purchase order made by a local authority in 1946 and duly confirmed, part of a factory included in the order was shown in the town plan annexed to it as due for development in 1965 in connection with a road-widening scheme.   After the purchase the local authority in 1949 re-let the part to the owner-occupiers of the rest of the factory on a yearly tenancy.   In 1963, the owner-occupiers made a proposal for the reduction of the assessment of the factory in the valuation list.   At that date the probability was that the part of the factory would be demolished under the road-widening scheme within about a year.   It was agreed that, if the probability of demolition should properly be taken into account when estimating the notional rent under s. 22 (1) (b)* of the Rating and Valuation Act 1925, the rateable value of the hereditament should be £3,050 but otherwise it should be £3,400.

Held (LORD GUEST and LORD DONOVAN, dissenting): the demolition order, by being a fact which was essential to and not accidental to the hereditament itself, prima facie could not be excluded as irrelevant and therefore had to be taken into consideration in calculating the rateable value (see p. 252, letter I, p. 257, letter H, and p. 260, letter B, post).

Dictum of LORD COCKBURN, C.J., in *Great Eastern Ry. Co.* v. *Haughley* ((1866), L.R. 1 Q.B. at p. 679) applied.

Poplar Metropolitan Borough Assessment Committee v. *Roberts* ([1922] All E.R. Rep. 191), and dictum of LORD ESHER, M.R., in *R.* v. *South Staffordshire Waterworks Co.* ((1885), 16 Q.B.D. at p. 370), approved.

Robinson Brothers (Brewers), Ltd. v. *Houghton and Chester-le-Street Assessment Committee* ([1937] 2 All E.R. 298) considered.

Per LORD PEARSON: there is in the law of valuation for rating a principle that the statutory machinery is adaptable and should, whenever this is possible, be so operated as to produce a just and true result, attributing to the hereditament its actual annual value—the real value of the beneficial occupation to the occupier—rather than some artificial and fictitious value (see p. 258, letter G, post).

Decision of the COURT OF APPEAL (sub nom. *Almond (Valuation Officer)* v. *Ash Bros. & Heaton, Ltd.*, [1967] 3 All E.R. 952) affirmed.

[**Editorial Note.** The definition of net annual value for rating purpose in s. 22 (1) of the Rating and Valuation Act 1925, has been repealed and re-enacted in s. 19 (3) of the General Rate Act 1967.

As to assumptions of the hypothetical tenancy and rebus sic stantibus, see 32 HALSBURY'S LAWS (3rd Edn.) 67, 68, paras. 94, 95; and for cases on the subject, see 38 DIGEST (Repl.) 614-619, *848-878.*

For the Rating and Valuation Act 1925, s. 22 (1), see 20 HALSBURY'S STATUTES (2nd Edn.) 127.]

Cases referred to:

Burley (Valuation Officer) v. *A. & W. Birch, Ltd.* (1959), 5 R.R.C. 147.
Consett Iron Co., Ltd. v. *Durham (North-Western Area) Assessment Committee,*
      [1931] A.C. 396; [1931] All E.R. Rep. 62; 100 L.J.K.B. 242; 144
      L.T. 649; 95 J.P. 98; 38 Digest (Repl.) 674, *1248.*

---

* Section 22 (1) (b), so far as material, is set out at p. 248, letter F, post.

A   *Great Eastern Ry. Co.* v. *Haughley* (1866), L.R. 1 Q.B. 666; 35 L.J.M.C. 229;
        14 L.T. 548; 30 J.P. 438; 38 Digest (Repl.) 615, *854.*
    Langlands v. *Midlothian Assessor,* [1963] R.V.R. 443; 1962 S.C. 341.
    London County Council v. *Erith Churchwardens,* [1893] A.C. 562; [1891-94]
        All E.R. Rep. 577; 63 L.J.M.C. 9; 69 L.T. 725; 57 J.P. 821; 38
        Digest (Repl.) 481, *47.*
B   *Poplar Metropolitan Borough Assessment Committee* v. *Roberts,* [1922] 2 A.C.
        93; [1922] All E.R. Rep. 191; 91 L.J.K.B. 449; 127 L.T. 99; 86
        J.P. 137; 38 Digest (Repl.) 612, *847.*
    R. v. *Adames* (1832), 4 B. & Ad. 61; 2 L.J.M.C. 90; 110 E.R. 378; 38 Digest
        (Repl.) 621, *888.*
    R. v. *Hull Dock Co.* (1816), 5 M. & S. 394; 105 E.R. 1095; 38 Digest (Repl.)
C   666, *1173.*
    R. v. *London School Board* (1886), 17 Q.B.D. 738; [1886-90] All E.R. Rep. 379;
        55 L.J.M.C. 169; 55 L.T. 384; 50 J.P. 419; 38 Digest (Repl.) 616, *862.*
    R. v. *Mirfield (Inhabitants)* (1808), 10 East. 219; 103 E.R. 758; 38 Digest
        (Repl.) 678, *1273.*
    R. v. *South Staffordshire Waterworks Co.* (1885), 16 Q.B.D. 359; 55 L.J.M.C.
D   88; 54 L.T. 782; 50 J.P. 20; 38 Digest (Repl.) 656, *1104.*
    Railway Assessment Authority v. *Southern Ry. Co.,* [1936] 1 All E.R. 26; [1936]
        A.C. 266; 105 L.J.K.B. 115; 154 L.T. 314; 100 J.P. 123; 38 Digest
        (Repl.) 633, *966.*
    Robinson Brothers (Brewers), Ltd. v. *Houghton and Chester-le-Street Assessment
        Committee,* [1937] 2 All E.R. 298; [1937] 2 K.B. 445; 106 L.J.K.B.
E   835; 157 L.T. 147; 101 J.P. 321; *affd.* H.L., [1938] 2 All E.R. 79;
        107 L.J.K.B. 369; *sub nom. Robinson Brothers (Brewers), Ltd.* v.
        Durham County Assessment Committee (Area No. 7), [1938] A.C. 321;
        158 L.T. 498; 102 J.P. 313; 38 Digest (Repl.) 674, *1244.*
    Smith v. *Birmingham (Churchwardens)* (1888), 22 Q.B.D. 211; *on appeal*
        (1889), 22 Q.B.D. 703; 58 L.J.M.C. 161; 53 J.P. 787; 38 Digest
F   (Repl.) 617, *868.*

Appeal.

   This was an appeal by the valuation officer, William John Dawkins, from an
order of the Court of Appeal (WILLMER, DANCKWERTS and RUSSELL, L.JJ.)
dated 28th July 1967 and reported [1967] 3 All E.R. 952, dismissing an appeal
from a decision of the Lands Tribunal dated 26th July 1966, which dismissed an
G appeal from a decision of the Birmingham local valuation court dated 27th April
1965. By its decision the local valuation court had reduced the assessment of the
hereditament at 69/71, Dartmouth Street, Birmingham 5, to the ratepayers,
Ash Brothers & Heaton, Ltd., from rateable value of £3,500 to £3,050. By an
order dated 17th May 1968 the name of William John Dawkins was substituted
for that of K. R. Almond who died on 22nd April 1968 and the title of the appeal
H was amended accordingly.

   The facts are set out in the opinion of LORD GUEST.

   Douglas Frank, Q.C., and *W. J. Glover* for the valuation officer.
   S. Brown, Q.C., and *M. K. Harrison-Hall* for the ratepayers.

   Their Lordships took time for consideration.

I   26th March.   The following opinions were delivered.

   LORD GUEST: My Lords, this appeal raises an important and far-
reaching question on the law relating to rating. It is, shortly stated, whether
the prospect of an early demolition of premises by a local authority is a relevant
factor to be taken into consideration in assessing the rateable value of the
property.

   The ratepayers were originally owners of the whole property consisting of
works and premises at Dartmouth Street, Birmingham.   Early in 1946 the

Birmingham Corporation, as the local planning authority, made an order for   A
the compulsory purchase of part of the ratepayers' property. This order having
been confirmed by the Minister, the corporation acquired the ratepayers' interest
in that portion, which they thereupon let to the ratepayers on a yearly tenancy
at a rent of £300 per annum exclusive of rates. The part of the hereditament
compulsorily acquired was shown on a plan as due for redevelopment in 1965
in connection with a road widening scheme. It was reasonably anticipated that   B
the part in question would be demolished for these purposes within about a year.

The local valuation court on 27th April 1965, on a proposal by the ratepayers
reduced the assessment from £3,500 to £3,050 rateable value. An appeal by
the valuation officer suggesting a figure of £3,400 as the rateable value was dismissed by the Lands Tribunal (1) who upheld the decision of the local valuation
court. The Lands Tribunal stated a case for the opinion of the court and the   C
Court of Appeal (2) unanimously dismissed the appeal.

It was agreed between the parties:

" Any actual tenant of the hereditament taking a tenancy thereof on the
date of the [ratepayers'] proposal would have paid less rent in each year
for the said hereditament if it was known or reasonably anticipated that the
part [of it in question] would be demolished for road widening purposes   D
within about a year. At the date of the said proposal it could have been
reasonably anticipated that [that part] would be required for road widening
purposes within about a year."

The parties were not agreed as to the type of tenancy or the term thereof on
which a tenant would have taken an actual tenancy of the hereditament in the
circumstances at the date of the proposal. It was agreed that, if the probability   E
of demolition should properly be taken into account, the rateable value of the
hereditament should be £3,050 but that otherwise it should be £3,400.

Section 22 (1) (b) of the Rating and Valuation Act 1925, provides as follows:

". . . there shall be estimated the rent at which the hereditament might
reasonably be expected to let from year to year if the tenant undertook to pay   F
all usual tenant's rates and taxes . . . and to bear the cost of the repairs and
insurance and the other expenses, if any, necessary to maintain the hereditament in a state to command that rent, and the annual rent as so
estimated shall, for the purposes of this Part of this Act, be taken to be the
net annual value of the hereditament."

There is a long series of cases in which the test for assessing the rateable value   G
of hereditaments has been considered. In *Great Eastern Ry. Co.* v. *Haughley*
SIR ALEXANDER COCKBURN, C.J., said (3):

" But I think it is one thing to start with the assumption that you are
dealing with a tenancy from year to year, and another thing to say that
the hypothetical tenant, in calculating what he can reasonably pay as rent   H
for the premises, is necessarily to assume that his tenancy would not last
beyond a year. I think the possibility of its longer duration is one of the
surrounding circumstances which the tenant from year to year would
take into account."

This was followed by *R.* v. *South Staffordshire Waterworks Co.* (4), where LORD
ESHER, M.R., said (5):   I

" A tenant from year to year is not a tenant for one, two, three or four
years, but he is to be considered as a tenant capable of enjoying the property
for an indefinite time, having a tenancy which it is expected will continue
for more than a year, but which is liable to be put an end to by notice."

---

(1) (1966), 12 R.R.C. 268.   (2) [1967] 3 All E.R. 952; [1968] 1 W.L.R. 133.
(3) (1866), L.R. 1 Q.B. 666 at p. 679.   (4) (1885), 16 Q.B.D. 359.
                    (5) (1885), 16 Q.B.D. at p. 370.

A In *Smith* v. *Birmingham* (*Churchwardens*) WILLS, J. said (6):

" It is to no purpose to say that such property cannot in practice be let by the year: no more can railways, canals, docks, or gasworks. The Act of Parliament requires the assumption of a tenancy from year to year to be made, and you can no more impugn the hypothesis of such a tenancy in rating matters than in logic you are permitted to deny your opponent's hypothetical premiss."

B
Later he said (7):

" It seems to me to follow that, if you are compelled to assess the occupier, whatever his actual period of past or prospective occupation, upon the assumption that there is a tenancy for a year, it is idle to talk of his being C assessed at a less sum than he otherwise would be assessed at because he may in fact occupy for a week only. The hypothetical tenant and the actual tenant are two separate and distinct entities. The hypothetical tenant will give neither more nor less for his year's occupation because the actual tenant only wants to occupy for a week or a fortnight. The tenant who, ex hypothesi, is to occupy for a year cannot be put as a person who ought D to pay a rent less than the fair rent for a year on the ground that there will be a week or a fortnight out of the year when the occupation will cease. That would be to contradict the hypothesis which you are bound to assume."

His decision was affirmed by the Court of Appeal (8), where LORD COLERIDGE, C.J., said (9):

E " In this case we have to do what Courts have from time to time in such cases complained of having to do, viz., to apply the terms of the Parochial Assessment Act (10) to a subject-matter to which they are not really applicable. It has been pointed out in the court below that the terms of the Act are really not applicable to a number of very valuable rateable properties, which have come into existence since the Act was passed, and which therefore F were not in the contemplation of the legislature in passing it, such as railways and gasworks. In such cases the hypothesis of a tenancy from year to year is really inapplicable. How can it be supposed that anyone would become tenant from year to year of an isolated portion of a railway? What is true of great properties, such as railways, may also be true of smaller matters; and it is found that this tenement of the value of five shillings a G week is not capable of being let on a tenancy from year to year, but can only be let on a tenancy from week to week at a weekly rent. Therefore here, too, we have to apply to what is undoubtedly a rateable subject-matter a test which is in reality inapplicable. By the terms of the statute the matter to be ascertained is at what rent this tenement might reasonably be expected to let from year to year upon the hypothesis that it could be so let, a some-H what difficult problem when such hypothesis is in fact found to be an impossible one. Under these circumstances one must get at the amount of such rent in the best way one can, applying the principles of the law of rating as far as they can be made applicable."

In *Railway Assessment Authority* v. *Southern Ry. Co.* LORD HAILSHAM, L.C. said (11):

I " The definition requires an estimate of the sum which a hypothetical tenant might be expected to pay to a hypothetical landlord. It was well settled before the Act that it was necessary in estimating such a rent to take

---

(6) (1888), 22 Q.B.D. 211 at p. 219.
(7) (1888), 22 Q.B.D. at pp. 220, 221.
(8) (1889), 22 Q.B.D. 703.
(9) (1889), 22 Q.B.D. at pp. 705, 706.
(10) I.e., the Parochial Assessment Act 1836.
(11) [1936] 1 All E.R. 26 at p. 37; [1936] A.C. 266 at p. 284.

into account the owner of the hereditaments as a possible tenant (*R.* v. **A**
London School Board (12); *London County Council* v. *Erith Churchwardens*
(13)); and, further, that the hypothetical tenant, though only a tenant
from year to year, is supposed to have a reasonable prospect of continuing
to be a tenant (*R.* v. *South Staffordshire Waterworks Co.* (14))."

This series of cases establishes that the hypothetical tenancy from year to year
envisaged by the relevant section of the Rating and Valuation Act 1925 is for **B**
an indefinite time with an expectation that it will continue for more than a
year. Such a tenancy must be assumed even though it is improbable or even
impossible in fact.

I pause to mention LORD SORN's observations in *Langlands* v. *Midlothian
Assessor* (15), where he said that the world of rating is a hypothetical realm in
which there is no place for demolition orders. No doubt the point in the case **C**
was different, but the dictum in my view expresses the proper approach to the
present problem.

Such being the construction of the statutory formula for the assessment
of value I proceed to consider the decision of the Lands Tribunal (16). At
the conclusion of their findings the member states (17):
D
" In the present case it is admitted that as a result of statutory proceedings
a tenant would reasonably have anticipated the termination of his tenancy
of the hereditament as it exists within about a year. It follows therefore
that ' the possibility of its longer duration ' is extremely remote and taking
that fact into consideration a lower rent might reasonably be anticipated
to be offered. The amount of that lower offer is agreed to be the figure of **E**
£3,050 determined by the Local Valuation Court."

The Lands Tribunal (16) have, therefore, in my view contrary to the statutory
formula, valued the hereditament on the basis of a tenancy for a term of years
certain or at any rate on the basis that a tenancy for more than a year was
improbable or impossible. Some difficulty may have been caused by undue
emphasis on the expression " year to year " as if this was limited to a yearly **F**
tenancy. The expression " taking one year with another " which appears in the
Valuation Metropolis Act 1869, quoted in *Poplar Metropolitan Borough Assessment Committee* v. *Roberts* (18) and treated as having the same effect as a tenancy
" from year to year ", makes it clear that, although as a matter of valuation a
yearly tenancy is to be assumed, the hypothesis is that it will be of indefinite
duration. Such a construction is, in my view, implied in the statutory formula. **G**

The Lands Tribunal (16) and the Court of Appeal (19) have placed great
reliance on certain dicta in a number of rating cases as justifying the conclusion
that the prospect of an early termination of the tenancy was a relevant factor
in the assessment of the rateable value. At the outset of a discussion of these
cases it is, I think, important to stress the distinction between the actual hereditament itself and the hypothetical method of valuation enjoined by the statute. **H**
As counsel for the valuation officer succinctly expressed it: " The beneficial
occupation is factual. The tenancy is hypothetical."

WILLMER, L.J., prefaces his consideration of these cases with these words (20):
" While it is no doubt true that the world of rating is a hypothetical
realm so far as concerns the presumed landlord and tenant, I do not think
that this represents the whole picture. For the hereditament which has to **I**

(12) (1886), 17 Q.B.D. 738; [1886-90] All E.R. Rep. 379.
(13) [1893] A.C. 562; [1891-94] All E.R. Rep. 577.
(14) (1885), 16 Q.B.D. 359.
(15) [1963] R.V.R. 443 at p. 445; 1962 S.C. 341 at p. 349.
(16) (1966), 12 R.R.C. 268.
(17) (1966), 12 R.R.C. at p. 274.
(18) [1922] 2 A.C. 93; [1922] All E.R. Rep. 191.
(19) [1967] 3 All E.R. 952; [1968] 1 W.L.R. 133.
(20) [1967] 3 All E.R. at p. 956; [1968] 1 W.L.R. at p. 141.

A   be valued is a real and actual hereditament, the circumstances of which
have to be evaluated in estimating what the hypothetical tenant from
year to year would be prepared to pay for it."

In this he has, in my view, confused the actual hereditament with the method
of valuation which is on a hypothetical basis.

In *Poplar Metropolitan Borough Assessment Committee* v. *Roberts* (21) LORD
B   PARMOOR said:

"In ascertaining this annual value, all that can reasonably influence
the judgment of an intending occupier ought to be taken into consideration,
including not only the natural conditions, but any statutory provisions
which may tend either to enhance or diminish the value of the beneficial
C   occupation of the property or its profit-earning capacity."

In *Robinson Brothers (Brewers), Ltd.* v. *Houghton and Chester-le-Street
Assessment Committee* (22) SCOTT, L.J., said:

" . . . it is the duty of the valuer to take into consideration every intrinsic
quality and every intrinsic circumstance which tends to push the rental
value either up or down, just because it is relevant to the valuation, and
D   ought therefore to be cast into the scales of the balance . . ."

and later he said (23):

" Whilst the tenant is hypothetical, and the landlord who is to let to the
tenant is necessarily also hypothetical, the hereditament is actual . . . All
the intrinsic advantages and disadvantages must be considered and weighed.
E   It is just that particular hereditament . . . with all its attractions for would-
be tenants . . . and also with all its imperfections and drawbacks which
may deter or reduce competition for it."

None of these cases in any way detracts from the principles previously expressed.
The basic law of valuation for rating purposes is that the ratepayer is assessed
in respect of the beneficial occupation of the hereditament rebus sic standibus.
F   To envisage that the hereditament will not support that beneficial occupation
is to envisage a different hereditament. The actual circumstances are relevant
so far as they affect the value of the beneficial occupation but they are inadmissible, in my view, in determining the length of time for which that beneficial
occupation will continue.

The error into which the Court of Appeal (24) fell was in considering the
G   intention of the actual landlord to terminate the tenancy within a definite
period as affecting the rateable value of the premises.

It remains only to mention the case of *Burley (Valuation Officer)* v. *A. & W.
Birch, Ltd.* (25), decided by the same member of the Lands Tribunal who decided
the present case. In that case the expressed intention of a private landlord to
demolish the hereditament was held not to be a factor which could be taken
H   into account in valuing the hereditament. This decision appears quite inconsistent
with the decision of the Lands Tribunal (26) in the present case. If the decision
was right in the present case, it follows that it must have been wrong in *Burley*
v. *Birch* (25). I am unable to see the distinction sought to be drawn between
Burley's case (25) where the intention to demolish was " at the whim " of a
private landlord who might change his mind, and the present case where there
I   was the practical certainty of demolition by a local authority. In my view,
the decision in *Burley* v. *Birch* (25) was right.

With most of the judgment of RUSSELL, L.J., I find myself in agreement,

---

(21) [1922] 2 A.C. at pp. 120, 121; [1922] All E.R. Rep. at p. 203.
(22) [1937] 2 All E.R. 298 at p. 307; [1937] 2 K.B. 445 at p. 469.
(23) [1937] 2 All E.R. at p. 311; [1937] 2 K.B. at p. 474.
(24) [1967] 3 All E.R. 952; [1968] 1 W.L.R. 133.
(25) (1959), 5 R.R.C. 147.
(26) (1966), 12 R.R.C. 268.

in particular with his statement of the question affecting the hypothetical   **A**
tenant as being (27) " Will my yearly tenancy be cut short very soon? " But
it is when he says that he finds nothing in principle or authority which excludes
the view of the law found by the Lands Tribunal (28) that I part company.

I would allow the appeal and remit to the local valuation court to fix the
valuation at £3,400.

    LORD PEARCE: My Lords, the question here is whether reduction in   **B**
value due to an impending demolition order comes within that area of rating
where realities are acknowledged or within that where necessarily fiction prevails
over fact. It is near the border-line which separates those areas. One has a natural
inclination to prefer reality to fiction if and where this is compatible with the
basis of rating, with the statute, and with the cases.

    Rating seeks a standard by which every hereditament in this country can   **C**
be measured in relation to every other hereditament. It is not seeking to establish
the true value of any particular hereditament, but rather its value in comparison
with the respective values of the rest. Out of various possible standards of comparison it has chosen the annual letting value. This is appropriate since the
tax is charged annually. One therefore has to estimate " the rent at which
the hereditament might reasonably be expected to let from year to year ", the   **D**
tenant paying rates, repairs, etc. This standard must be universal even though
in many cases it demands various hypotheses. In practice, sewage works, portions
of railway-lines, shops and factories where heavy and valuable machinery is
installed are not let from year to year. So one must assume a hypothetical
letting (which in many cases would never in fact occur) in order to do the best
one can to form some estimate of what value should be attributed to a heredita-   **E**
ment on the universal standard, namely a letting " from year to year ". But
one only excludes the human realities to a limited and necessary extent, since
it is only the human realities that give any value at all to hereditaments. They
are excluded insofar as they are accidental to the letting of a hereditament.
They are acknowledged insofar as they are essential to the hereditament itself.
It is, for instance, essential to the hereditament itself that it is close to the sea   **F**
and that humans will pay more highly for a house close to the sea. One can
therefore take that into account in the hypothetical letting. It is, however,
accidental to the house that its owner was shrewd or that the rich man happened
to want it and that therefore the rent being paid is extremely high. In the same
way I think it would be accidental to the hereditament that its owner intended
to pull it down in the near future. For the hereditament might have had a   **G**
different owner who would not pull it down. So the actual owner's intentions are
thus immaterial since it is the hypothetical owner who is being considered. But
when a demolition order is made by a superior power on a hereditament within
its jurisdiction different considerations apply. The order becomes an essential
characteristic of the hereditament, regardless of who may be its owner or what
its owner might intend. That particular hereditament has had branded on its   **H**
walls the words " doomed to demolition whatever hypothetical landlord may
own it ".

    Thus the demolition order, by being a fact which is essential to and not
accidental to the hereditament itself, prima facie cannot be excluded as irrelevant
or shrouded by any necessary cloud of fiction. On this point I cannot accept
LORD SORN's dictum to the contrary in *Langlands* v. *Midlothian Assessor* (29).   **I**
Since, however, the fact of a demolition order relates to length of tenure, is it on
that ground excluded by the express fiction imposed by Parliament in the
words " let from year to year "?

    SIR ALEXANDER COCKBURN, C.J., said in *Great Eastern Ry. Co.* v. *Haughley* (30):

(27) [1967] 3 All E.R. at p. 960; [1968] 1 W.L.R. at p. 147.
(28) (1966), 12 R.R.C. 268.
(29) [1963] R.V.R. 443 at p. 445; 1962 S.C. 341 at p. 349.
(30) (1866), L.R. 1 Q.B. 666 at p. 679.

A   " But I think it is one thing to start with the assumption that you are dealing with the tenancy from year to year, and another thing to say that the hypothetical tenant, in calculating what he can reasonably pay as rent for the premises is necessarily to assume that his tenancy would not last beyond the year. I think the possibility of its longer duration is one of the surrounding circumstances which the tenant from year to year would
B   take into account. It may be that the circumstances are such, that it is worth his while to deal with the stock as though he were certain that his tenancy would not be put an end to at the expiration of the year. He is to calculate for himself how much his stock will be depreciated and what it is worth his while to give, having taken that matter sufficiently into consideration. Now that seems to me to be a question of fact . . ."

C   And in *Poplar Metropolitan Borough Assessment Committee* v. *Roberts* (31) LORD PARMOOR said:

    " In ascertaining this annual value, all that can reasonably influence the judgment of an intending occupier ought to be taken into consideration, including not only the natural conditions, but any statutory provisions which may tend either to enhance or diminish the value of the beneficial
D   occupation of the property or its profit-earning capacity."

The Lands Tribunal relying on these two passages said (32):

    " If the hypothetical tenant can ' consider the possibility of its longer duration ' as ' one of the surrounding circumstances ' which he can take into account in making his bid, it seems to me that it necessarily follows that a
E   practical certainty that the lease will have no longer duration consequent upon the provisions of a statutory scheme is also a circumstance which can and should be taken into account, within the passage from LORD PARMOOR'S speech . . ."

In no case has this exact point been decided. The words " let from year to year " raise the obvious question: " Is one in general thinking of a tenant who will
F   be turned out at the end of a year, or a person who can enjoy an anticipation of staying on for a reasonable time? " For this must make a difference in the rent. LORD ESHER, M.R., answered that question in *R.* v. *South Staffordshire Waterworks Co.* (33):

    " A tenant from year to year is not a tenant for one, two, three or four
G   years, but he is to be considered as a tenant capable of enjoying the property for an indefinite time, having a tenancy which it is expected will continue for more than a year, but which is liable to be put an end to by notice."

This general principle has been accepted and followed in many cases (e.g., *Railway Assessment Authority* v. *Southern Ry. Co.* (34). Moreover, it is clearly right, I respectfully think, as a general principle. But should one append to the
H   principle a gloss that, in particular circumstances where it is essential to the hereditament (and not due to any accident of ownership) that it cannot survive for more than a year, one may take that fact into account? This is what the Lands Tribunal (35) and the Court of Appeal (36) have done. Such a gloss is not inconsistent with any decided case. Nor would it offend against the spirit of the general rule laid down by LORD ESHER, M.R., and others. They did not
I   have their attention directed to such a situation. I find nothing in the judgments to show whether, if attention had been directed to it, such a gloss would or would not have been acceptable. *Smith* v. *Birmingham (Churchwardens)* (37) does not, in my opinion, help on this point.

It is conceded, as I think it must be, that if the state or construction of some

---

(31) [1922] 2 A.C. 93 at pp. 120, 121; [1922] All E.R. Rep. 191 at p. 203.
(32) (1966), 12 R.R.C. at p. 273.   (33) (1885), 16 Q.B.D. 359 at p. 370.
(34) [1936] 1 All E.R. 26; [1936] A.C. 266.   (35) (1966), 12 R.R.C. 268.
(36) [1967] 3 All E.R. 952; [1968] 1 W.L.R. 133.   (37) (1889), 22 Q.B.D. 703.

hereditament was such that it must predictably collapse in a year, its imper-   **A**
manence would be a relevant fact in estimating the rent, i.e., there could not
be imputed to a hypothetical tenant the advantage of contemplating an
indefinite continuance of tenancy. If this be right, I find it difficult to see why
there should be a difference in principle between demolition by force of gravity
(and the elements) and demolition by force of government. Both are superior
forces which bear alike on a hereditament. Either may turn out to bear less   **B**
hardly than was anticipated; but this is no more than saying that any prediction
may be falsified by events. On principle, therefore, I think that the Lands
Tribunal (38) and the Court of Appeal (39) were right.

I do not accept the argument that the hereditament that will either demolish
itself by force of gravity or be demolished by force of government in *less* than
a year (say eight months) proves that this view cannot be right. Under the   **C**
Rating and Valuation Act 1925 one has to give the hypothetical tenant a tenancy
from year to year and see what he will pay for it. In the normal case one tells
him that he will have an indefinite prospect of continuance although the tenancy
can be determined at the end of one year. In the suggested particular case one
has to tell him that although he is being given a tenancy " from year to year "
his actual occupation will almost certainly end in eight months. How much   **D**
he would pay depends on what his view of the circumstances is (see the words
of SIR ALEXANDER COCKBURN, C.J. (40)).

I appreciate that this view of the matter may cause some additional consideration and work, but I think with respect that undue alarm has been raised in
argument. There is no trace of this alarm in the judgment at first instance
which comes from a very practical tribunal. Inevitably more difficulties are   **E**
caused when one tries to ascribe true values to hereditaments than when one
excludes some element that does in real life cause variations of value and substitutes for it a hypothetical rule of thumb. But, in my view, the judgment
of SIR ALEXANDER COCKBURN, C.J. (41), shows that though much hypothesis is
necessary, it should not be extended so as unnecessarily to exclude realities.

I would therefore dismiss the appeal.   **F**

LORD DONOVAN: My Lords, the common-sense approach to this problem
is, of course, to say that a tenant of premises soon to be demolished would pay
less rent for them than he would otherwise offer; and that the rating assessment
should give effect to this truth. If, however, Parliament by statute prescribes a
formula by which the annual value of premises for rating purposes is to be
measured, then the formula must be applied, whether the resultant valuation   **G**
yields a figure either more or less than the figure obtainable in real life. Rating
statutes are not unique in this respect. Under other taxing statutes a man may
have no income at all in the year of assessment and yet be deemed to have a
large one, simply because he had a large one the year before; and sometimes
even if he had not.

Section 22 (1) (*b*) of the Rating and Valuation Act 1925, lays down the formula   **H**
to be applied here. It is to be the rent reasonably to be expected if the hereditament were let from year to year, etc.; the section going on to say that the rent
so estimated " shall . . . be taken *to be* the net annual value of the hereditament ".

What has happened here is that in flat contradiction of the Act a lower rent
than the formula would yield has been taken " to be " the net annual value;
and the justification tendered for this is that the premises could not in fact be   **I**
let from year to year because of the demolition order. This confers no right on
anybody to ignore the statutory command that such a letting is to be assumed
and to substitute a different formula altogether. If, for example, a preservation
order had been made instead of a demolition order, thus increasing the security
of tenure available, would an increase in the valuation have been permissible?

---

(38) (1966), 12 R.R.C. 268.   (39) [1967] 3 All E.R. 952; [1968] 1 W.L.R. 133.
(40) (1866), L.R. 1 Q.B. at p. 679.   (41) (1866), L.R. 1 Q.B. at p. 677.

A   Or in the case of a long lease? And how, on the basis of the existing decision, is a tenancy for eight months to be valued?

I share the views of everybody that it is unreal to ignore the fact of the demolition order; but if the statute requires the application of a formula which involves doing so, it is not for me to be astute in applying another.

I have read the opinion of my noble and learned friend, Lord Guest. I entirely
B   agree with it, and like him would allow the appeal.

LORD WILBERFORCE: My Lords, it is agreed by both sides first, that a part of the hereditament whose rateable value is in dispute was reasonably likely to be demolished within about a year, and second, that a prospective tenant having regard to this probability, would be willing to pay £350 per annum less rent than one who did not. Can this reasonable probability of demolition and the
C   impact it would have on an intelligent occupier be taken into account in assessing the hereditament's annual value for rating purposes? Common sense would seem to suggest that it should; the accepted structure of the law of rating that it should not; which is it to be? A natural inclination towards the common-sense solution is not enough to determine this type of issue, since a decision in favour of one ratepayer necessarily affects others, and it is important that the law of
D   rating should be both uniform in its application and rational in principle. Moreover, any particular case must be decided against the wording of the statute and the background of authority.

It is convenient first to refer to statute, for it is on the statutory wording that the valuation officer's claim principally rests. The relevant words are those contained in s. 22 (1) (*b*) of the Rating and Valuation Act 1925 "... there shall
E   be estimated the rent at which the hereditament might reasonably be expected to let from year to year. . . ." The interpretation of these words has come over the years to be invested with a good deal of learning, and even of mystery, but up to a point there is nothing very difficult about them. It is on the delimitation of the " actual ", on the one hand, and the " hypothetical ", on the other, that the argument in the present case takes its shape.

F   Let us start from the actual. The principle that the property must be valued as it exists at the relevant date is an old one, certainly older than the Parochial Assessments Act 1836. It has been spelt out in modern terminology in *Poplar Metropolitan Borough Assessment Committee* v. *Roberts* (42) and in *Robinson Brothers (Brewers), Ltd.* v. *Houghton and Chester-le-Street Assessment Committee* (43) in passages which have been cited. The principle was mainly devised to meet, and
G   it does deal with, an obvious type of case where the character or condition of the property either has undergone a change or is about to do so; thus, a house in course of construction cannot be rated; not can a building be rated by reference to changes which might be made in it either as to its structure or its use.

But it would surely be unreasonable to suppose that the hypothetical tenant is so inescapably imprisoned in the present that no anticipation is permitted of
H   what is to come. Whether the test is what would influence his judgment, or what intrinsic qualities the hereditament possesses, any occupier in real life has to ascertain and to consider whatever may make his tenancy more or less advantageous over the period for which he takes it. I appreciate that the statutory hypothesis as to the length of the tenancy may have a bearing on what the tenant may take into account, and I shall shortly consider this critical point but, apart
I   from this, it would seem clear that any occupier would take into account, not only any immediately actual defects or disadvantages (such as planning restrictions), but disadvantages, or advantages, which he can see coming. If the actual presence of a motorway close to the property depreciates it, or adds to its value, surely he must take account of a motorway whose irresistible progress will bring it alongside in six months—there is no presumption that juggernauts are immobile; and similarly of an airport, an open prison, or an open space. How

---

(42) [1922] 2 A.C. 93 at pp. 120, 121; [1922] All E.R. Rep. 191 at p. 203.
(43) [1937] 2 All E.R. 298 at p. 307; [1937] 2 K.B. 445 at p. 469.

much allowance ought to be made for the uncertainty, the speed of arrival, or   A
the impact of such events, is no doubt a matter of estimation, but this is well within the expert field of the surveyor or land agent whose evidence he will supply.
These persons are well aware that programmes jerk in their progress and can
make suitable allowances for the movements in county halls.

But now we must consider the tenancy's period, and we have the words,
claimed to be decisive, " to let from year to year ". It is said that these limit,   B
and in this case totally exclude, the common-sense approach; that they require
us to assume a tenancy of a particular kind known to the law, of indefinite
duration though determinable by notice, which assumption is inconsistent with,
and so excludes, the possibility or probability of impending demolition.

My Lords, I have no desire to derogate from the elegant technicality of the
law of rating, which in some respects is commendable and useful. Where so   C
many separate operations have to be carried out every year, firm and logical
rules are very necessary. But I do not think that the history of this expression
supports a technical interpretation, at least so technical as it bears in the law of
real property. The Poor Law Relief Act 1601 (43 Eliz. 1, c. 2) contained no reference to any tenancy period; and it was left to the judges to determine, as they
did over a series of decisions, on what principles the annual value was to be   D
arrived at.   One case, shortly before the Parochial Assessments Act 1836,
illustrates the process: *R.* v. *Adames* (44), where the question was whether an
occasional sewers' rate should be taken into account in fixing the annual value.
PARKE, J., said (45):

" It is obvious that the average annual net profit of one description of land
is not the same as that of the other; and, both upon principle and authority,   E
we think the rate ought to be made in proportion to that profit ...   Now
it is quite clear it ought not to be made according to the profit derived by
the occupier himself; for if that were so, the rate must vary according
to the nature of the occupier's interest. An occupier who is tenant at will
at rack-rent, and therefore receives a less share of the annual profit of the
land than one who is tenant for years at a small rent, and still less than one   F
who is a tenant in fee simple, and pays none at all, would be rateable at a
less sum; a proposition which was never yet contended for ... This being
so, it follows that, in order to make an equal rate, the nature of the occupier's
interest must be disregarded, and the rate imposed according to some value
of the subject of occupation. Usage and convenience have established this
value to be not that of the estate or property itself, but that of the profit which   G
is or might be made from the estate or property; and as it would be
very difficult and extremely troublesome to ascertain the precise value of
that profit during the time for which each rate is made, and in case of
occasional profit both troublesome and unjust (*R.* v. *Mirfield* (*Inhabitants*)
(46), *R.* v. *Hull Dock Co.* (47)), to make a rate for a large sum at one time
and a small one or none at another, upon the same land, the rule has been   H
to assess according to the annual profit of the land; or, where the produce
is not matured in one year, then upon an average of years, from which profit
deductions are allowed for all the expenses necessary to its production. It
is not material whether the whole or a certain aliquot part of that net profit
be rated, provided all lands of the same description are rated equally upon
that aliquot proportion of the profit; and in practice it is usual, and it is most   I
convenient, to rate lands at the rack-rent which they would pay to a landlord,
or some certain portion of it, the tenant paying all rates, charges and outgoings; which is in effect rating according to a part of the net profit only; but
provided it be the same aliquot part in all cases, it makes no difference."

(44) (1832), 4 B. & Ad. 61.
(45) (1832), 4 B. & Ad. at pp. 66, 67.
(46) (1808), 10 East. 219.
(47) (1816), 5 M. & S. 394.

A This passage, and it is typical, illustrates very well the practical approach of the judges, and I would assume that when the Parochial Assessments Act 1836 provided a—statutory definition of " net annual value " as—" the rent at which the [hereditament] might reasonably be expected to be let from year to year, free of all usual tenant's rates and taxes . . ." it was endorsing this approach.

It is interesting to note that as regards the metropolis the Valuation Metro-

B polis Act 1869, adopted a different verbal formula—that of the annual rent which a tenant might reasonably be expected, taking one year with another, to pay; but this has always been regarded as supplying an identical test. The leading case of *Poplar* (48) to which I have referred was decided under it.

So we should regard the words " from year to year " as meaning no more than that the tenancy is not a fixed or definite one, it is one of indefinite duration,

C determinable by notice, but not, I would think, according to the technicalities governing the giving of notice in tenancies of this kind. What, then, are we to say of the tenant's expectations and of the rent he is consequently willing to pay? I see no reason why, if there is evidence to prove it, a greater and more reliable expectation of continuance should not be allowed to affect his calculation. In this I am content, as this House did in *Consett Iron Co., Ltd.* v. *Durham* (*North-*

D *Western Area*) *Assessment Committee* (49) to follow SIR ALEXANDER COCKBURN, C.J., in *Great Eastern Ry. Co.* v. *Haughley* (50):

" I think the possibility of its longer duration is one of the surrounding circumstances which the tenant from year to year would take into account."

Then if " longer ", why not " shorter ", if that is material to the tenant's calcu-

E lations? The present case provides a good test either way. So long ago as 1946 the Birmingham City Council made an order for the compulsory purchase of some 200 acres including a part (the " red portion ") of the relevant lot—this order was confirmed in 1947. The plan annexed to the compulsory purchase order showed the " red portion " as due for redevelopment in 1965 in connection with a road widening scheme. The red portion was acquired by the corporation in

F 1949 and let to the ratepayers on an annual tenancy. We do not know on what basis the annual value was assessed during the period from 1949-63—probably the matter was never attended to with any accuracy, but it would not have been wrong, in this period, to assume a probable continuance of the annual tenancy for a considerable time. At any rate a new proposal, that we are now considering was made on 27th September 1963. The agreed facts include that any actual tenant taking a tenancy at this date would have paid less rent (viz., £350 per annum

G less) in each year if it was known or reasonably anticipated that the red portion would be demolished within about a year; and that at the proposal date it could have been reasonably anticipated that the red portion would be required for road widening within about a year.

In my opinion, these agreed facts provide amply sufficient basis on which to fix (as the Lands Tribunal (51) did fix) the lower basis of annual value. The

H circumstances were actual and intrinsic and such as would affect a prospective tenant's mind; there is nothing in them which requires any contrary assumption to that of a tenancy from year to year—they are consistent with such a tenancy with severely reduced expectation of renewal.

The arguments for the valuation officer are four. First, it is said that the Lands

I Tribunal (51) proceeded on the assumption that the ratepayers were taking a tenancy for a year certain, which assumption is not permissible under the statutory formula. But I do not accept this. The tribunal had before them the dates as I have stated them above, which lead to an anticipation of demolition in " about a year ", on the dates rather more than a year. This anticipation may

(48) [1922] 2 A.C. 93; [1922] All E.R. Rep. 191.
(49) [1931] A.C. 396; [1931] All E.R. Rep. 62.
(50) (1866), L.R. 1 Q.B. 666 at p. 679.
(51) (1966), 12 R.R.C. 268.

K

well have been too confident and too definite, the consequent deduction may
have been too great—I endorse neither—but it was agreed by both sides; it
fits perfectly well into the conception of a tenancy from year to year whose
duration is likely to be curtailed.

Secondly, it was claimed that to allow a prospect of this kind to enter into the
estimation of rent would necessitate yearly, or more frequent, revisions of rateable
values, on a kind of sliding scale as the critical event approaches. I think that
these are exaggerated fears. Annual values may indeed diminish (or increase)
together with the progress of matters that affect them but, as this case shows,
the curve of change is not an even one, it is more likely to move in quanta jumps
and, when one such occurs, it would be unjust not to allow it to take its effect.

Thirdly, the logical difficulty was put that if it is permissible to suppose a
yearly tenancy with diminished prospect of renewal, the consequence would
follow that an anticipated demolition (or similar events) within a year (e.g.,
in six months) must also be taken into account, yet this would be flagrantly
contrary to the statutory hypothesis. The case may be debatable, but it is not
before us and it is further complicated by statutory provisions—see the Local
Government Act 1948, s. 42, and the General Rate Act 1967, s. 79. I do not think
that it is comparable with or should affect those where the anticipated event is
outside the hypothetical year.

Lastly, it was suggested that to allow this reduction would destroy the necessary
basis of uniformity between one lot and another. This would be a serious objection if the fact were so, but it is not. The essence of the ratepayers' claim is
that their hereditament differs from others in the locality. It is as if on the red
portion, but nowhere else, there were fixed a board inscribed " Due for demolition in 1965 ". There is nothing, happily, in rating law which prevents a property
with such a mark of death from being assessed differently from its unmarked
neighbours.

In my opinion the Lands Tribunal (52) reached a correct decision and I would
dismiss the appeal.

LORD PEARSON: My Lords, in my opinion, there is in the law of valuation
for rating a principle that the statutory " machinery ", which at the material
time was contained in s. 22 (1) (b) of the Rating and Valuation Act 1925, is adaptable and should, whenever this is possible, be so operated as to produce a just
and true result, attributing to the hereditament its actual annual value—the real
value of the beneficial occupation to the occupier—rather than some artificial
and fictitious value. The words of s. 22 (1) (b) which are material for the present
purpose are these:

" . . . there shall be estimated the rent at which the hereditament might
reasonably be expected to let from year to year . . . and the annual rent as
so estimated shall, for the purposes of this Part of this Act, be taken to be the
net annual value of the hereditament."

The principle was strikingly illustrated by the decision and reasoning of this
House in the case of *Poplar Metropolitan Borough Assessment Committee* v. *Roberts*
(53). In that case the hereditament was subject to the Increase of Rent and
Mortgage Interest (Restrictions) Act 1920, which restricted the rent which a
tenant could be required to pay to his landlord. The restricted rent for the
hereditament was less than the true value of the occupation. In order to produce
the right result—coincidence of the annual value for rating purposes with the true
value—it was held that the rent was as hypothetical as the landlord and the tenant, and that the hypothetical tenant might reasonably be expected to pay to
the hypothetical landlord a hypothetical rent greater than the restricted rent,

---

(52) (1966), 12 R.R.C. 268.
(53) [1922] 2 A.C. 93; [1922] All E.R. Rep. 191.

A though no actual tenant would pay more than the restricted rent. LORD BUCKMASTER said (54):

" So far as the occupier is concerned, the provisions of the Rent Restriction Act have not in any way made his occupation less beneficial . . . If . . . the rent which has to be ascertained under the section is the real rent, then the fact that that cannot be increased will have a material effect upon the B valuation. I agree, however, with what was said by counsel for the appellants that so to interpret the statute would be to deal with something which was nothing but a measure of value in such a manner as completely to destroy the very object for which that measure was set up. Just as the tenant is hypothetical, so also is the rent; it is only used as a standard which must be examined without regard to the actual limitation of the rent paid by virtue C of covenant as between landlord and tenant, and also, as I regard it, to statutory restrictions that may be imposed upon its receipt. From the earliest time it is the inhabitant who has to be taxed. It is in respect of his occupation that the rate is levied, and the standard in the Act is nothing but a means of finding out what the value of that occupation is for the purposes of assessment."

D In *Robinson Brothers (Brewers), Ltd.* v. *Houghton and Chester-le-Street Assessment Committee* (55) (affirmed in the House of Lords (56)) SCOTT, L.J., said (57):

" The objective being the real value of the actual hereditament, the inquiry is primarily economic, and not legal; it is legal only in so far as logical relevance is the measure of legal admissibility. That the value is to be expressed E in the terms of the statutory definition of gross value is ' nothing to the matter ', as LORD HOLT would have said. That definition does not prevent the objective being the real value; it merely states certain data in regard to the terms of the hypothetical tenancy which are to be assumed in order to get a fixed instead of a variable figure. Some terms must be assumed by every valuer in any calculation: the statute merely chooses the terms, in order that F all resultant figures may be strictly comparable; but the statutory definition contains no provision which prevents real value being the one and only objective of the inquiry."

The material facts of this case were agreed between the parties and set out in the decision of the Lands Tribunal (58) and incorporated into the Case Stated. The hereditament as shown on the plan consisted of a major part coloured blue G (" the blue area "), having a frontage of 340 feet on Adams Street, and a minor part coloured red (" the red area ") which jutted out from the back of the blue area and extended to a frontage of 53 feet on Dartmouth Street. The ratepayers were at one time the owners as well as the occupiers of the entire hereditament. But in 1946 the Birmingham Corporation made a compulsory purchase order in respect of a larger area which included the red area. In 1947 the order H was confirmed by the Minister, and in 1949 the Birmingham Corporation acquired the ratepayers' interest in the red area and thereupon let the red area to the ratepayers on an annual tenancy. But the hereditament was still treated as one hereditament comprising both the blue area and the red area. The ratepayers as occupiers of the hereditament on 27th October 1963, made a proposal for reduction of the assessment.

I It was agreed that any actual tenant of the hereditament taking a tenancy thereof on the date of the ratepayers' proposal would have paid less rent in each year for the hereditament if it was known or reasonably anticipated that the red area would be taken over and the buildings demolished for road widening purposes

(54) [1922] 2 A.C. at pp. 103, 104; [1922] All E.R. Rep. at pp. 194, 195.
(55) [1937] 2 All E.R. 298; [1937] 2 K.B. 445.
(56) [1938] 2 All E.R. 79; [1938] A.C. 321.
(57) [1937] 2 All E.R. at pp. 308, 309; [1937] 2 K.B. at pp. 470, 471.
(58) (1966), 12 R.R.C. 268.

within about a year. It was also agreed that at the date of the proposal it could
have been reasonably anticipated that the red area would be required for road-
widening purposes within about a year. It was further agreed that, if the proposed
demolition on road widening of a portion of the hereditament could be taken
into account in assessing the rateable value, the rateable value had been correctly
assessed by the local valuation court at £3,050, while if such proposed demolition
could not be taken into account the rateable value should be £3,400.

Thus, the probability of a demolition of a portion of the hereditament within
about a year by action of the Birmingham Corporation did in fact reduce the
annual value of the hereditament, and the lower figure of £3,050 was the actual
annual value. Prima facie that is the figure at which the rateable value should
be assessed. But can the statutory " machinery " be so operated as to produce
that result? I think it can.

First, it is conceded on behalf of the valuation officer that the special features
of this case, that at the material time the Birmingham Corporation had acquired
the ownership of the red area and had let it to the ratepayers, can be disregarded
for the purposes of this appeal. The concession was made because it is not desired
to have the case decided on a narrow ground which would not be generally
applicable. But I think that, even without any such concession, these special
features would have to be disregarded, because the Birmingham Corporation,
being in that position, could not be the hypothetical landlord. The hypothetical
landlord, Mr. X, must be the owner of (or at any rate in a position to let) the entire
hereditament and must not have let any portion of it already. The Birmingham
Corporation did not have these qualifications.

Secondly, at the material time, the hypothetical landlord is assumed to have
granted, and the hypothetical tenant to have taken, a tenancy from year to year
of the entire hereditament, comprising both the blue area and the red area.
The assumed tenancy is a normal tenancy from year to year, running on indefinitely until terminated by notice. There has not been in this appeal any
argument or discussion as to the required length of the notice or when it must
expire, and I am not expressing a concluded opinion, but I think it is usually
taken to be a six months' notice expiring at the end of the first or any later year
of the tenancy. Therefore, the tenancy may be terminated by notice at the end
of the first year or it may have a longer duration. The nature and the terms of the
hypothetical tenancy could be the same in this case as in any other case.

Thirdly, as the Birmingham Corporation could not be the hypothetical landlords, their demolition action, if and when it came, must be considered to involve
an exercise of statutory powers. They would enter into possession of the red area,
ousting the hypothetical landlord from his ownership and the hypothetical
tenant from his occupation, and they would demolish the buildings and convert
the site to form part of the widened roadway. I do not know exactly what is
then supposed to happen to the hypothetical tenancy of the entire hereditament.
Perhaps the hypothetical parties arranged in advance that, if and when the
Birmingham Corporation carried out their demolition action, the tenancy would
continue at a reduced rent for the reduced hereditament. Or perhaps that hypothetical tenancy could come to an end and the hypothetical parties would have
to negotiate a new one in respect of the new hereditament consisting only of the
blue area. I do not think a final answer to this question has to be given in this
appeal, but I shall assume in considering the valuation officer's argument that
the demolition of a portion of the hereditament would bring to an end the
hypothetical tenancy of the entire hereditament.

Fourthly, although the demolition was expected to happen within about a
year, there was no certainty that it would happen so soon or even that it would
happen at all. The policy might be reversed, or the implementation of it might
be postponed, owing to developments in the financial, economic, administrative
or political situation, whether national or local. The phrase " practical certainty "

A was used by the Lands Tribunal (59) in a passage near the end of the decision, but in my opinion it was not warranted by the agreed facts set out in the earlier passage of the decision. There was a reasonable expectation, a probability, that the demolition would take place in about a year. It was a sufficient probability to affect the mind of the hypothetical tenant and so to reduce the rent that he would be willing to pay.

B   That is how I envisage the operation of the statutory " machinery " in relation to the facts of this case. There would be a normal hypothetical tenancy from year to year subject to the external risk that within about a year the local authority (not a party to the hypothetical tenancy) would in the exercise of statutory powers step in and demolish a portion of the hereditament. Because of that risk, which was regarded as a probability, the hypothetical tenant would be willing

C to pay only a reduced rent. That is the result produced by operating the statutory "machinery" , and it accords with the real fact that the actual annual value of the hereditament was reduced. The lower figure of £3,050, giving effect to the reduction in value, should be entered in the valuation list as the rateable value of the hereditament.

   I think the main argument for the valuation officer, which has been clearly

D and cogently presented, is that one cannot bring into account the probability of a portion of the hereditament being demolished in about a year without destroying the hypothesis, required by statute, of a tenancy from year to year. Put at its highest the argument was that the ratepayer's contention and the Lands Tribunal's decision (59) necessarily assumed that the tenancy would come to an end in a year, and therefore it would be in effect a tenancy for one year only, which

E would not comply with the statutory requirement. To the valuation officer's argument so presented there is the simple answer that on the agreed facts it could not be assumed that the hereditament *would* come to an end in a year; it might go on for several years. But the argument for the valuation officer can also be presented in this form: that, although the statute is silent on this point, authoritative dicta (especially in *R.* v. *South Staffordshire Waterworks Co.* (60) and

F *Railway Assessment Authority* v. *Southern Ry. Co.* (61)), have put a gloss on the statute, requiring a reasonable expectation of continuance of the hypothetical tenancy; and a reasonable expectation of continuance cannot be reconciled with a reasonable expectation of termination within about a year; and therefore the reasonable expectation of termination within about a year must be disregarded in order to permit the application of the statutory measure of value as

G authoritatively interpreted. In my opinion, however, the authoritative dicta should not be understood as putting a gloss on the statute. The statute requires quite simply a tenancy from year to year, and that is a tenancy which may be determined at the end of the first year or may run on for several years or many years. The circumstances of a particular case may show that the hypothetical tenancy from year to year is likely to be long (e.g., where the subject-matter is

H or forms part of a waterworks undertaking or a railway undertaking) or that it is likely to be short (as in this case). That seems to me to be the right inference from the passage in the judgment of SIR ALEXANDER COCKBURN, C.J., in *Great Eastern Ry. Co.* v. *Haughley* (62) which was cited by LORD SANKEY, L.C., in *Consett Iron Co., Ltd.* v. *Durham (North-Western Area) Assessment Committee* (63) as stating the true principle to be applied. SIR ALEXANDER COCKBURN, C.J.

I said (62):

   " . . . it is one thing to start with the assumption that you are dealing with a tenancy from year to year, and another thing to say that the hypothetical tenant, in calculating what he can reasonably pay as rent for the premises, is necessarily to assume that his tenancy would not last beyond a year. I think the possibility of its longer duration is one of the surrounding

---

(59) (1966), 12 R.R.C. 268.   (60) (1885), 16 Q.B.D. 359 at p. 370.
(61) [1936] 1 All E.R. 26; [1936] A.C. 266.
(62) (1866), L.R. 1 Q.B. 666 at pp. 679, 680.
(63) [1931] A.C. 396 at pp. 409, 410; [1931] All E.R. Rep. 62 at p. 68.

A

circumstances which the tenant from year to year would take into account. It may be that the circumstances are such, that it is worth his while to deal with the stock as though he were certain that his tenancy would not be put an end to at the expiration of the year. He is to calculate for himself how much his stock will be depreciated and what it is worth his while to give, having taken that matter sufficiently into consideration. Now that seems to me to be a question of fact for the sessions . . ."

B

It was also said on behalf of the valuation officer that equality of rating requires that each hereditament should be valued as it now is—rebus sic stantibus—and the prospect of a future partial destruction of it must be disregarded. But it seems to me that this point can be turned against the valuation officer. In the expression rebus sic stantibus which are the res? In other words, which are the factors to be taken into account in order to produce equality of rating? There is, in this case, a present probability of a future happening, and the present probability affects the present value of the hereditament. There is inequality of actual values if of two otherwise identical hereditaments one is likely to have part of it demolished within about a year and the other is likely to remain intact. If they had to be deemed to be of the same value, although in fact one is worth less than the other, there would be artificiality and fiction and unfairness in the valuations.

C

D

LORD PARMOOR said in *Poplar Metropolitan Borough Assessment Committee* v. *Roberts* (64):

" In ascertaining this annual value, all that can reasonably influence the judgment of an intending occupier ought to be taken into consideration, including not only the natural conditions, but any statutory provisions which may tend either to enhance or diminish the value of the beneficial occupation of the property or its profit-earning capacity."

E

The mind of the hypothetical tenant would be affected by the prospect that within about a year he would probably lose a portion of his premises, whether the loss was expected to arise from some physical cause such as a building being brought down by subsidence or sliding over clay into the sea or from some governmental action such as requisition by a Minister or dispossession and demolition by a local authority.

F

Also it was said on behalf of the valuation officer that, if the prospect of future dispossession and demolition is to be taken into account, the valuation in such a case will have to be changed progressively as the expected date of demolition approaches. That is, in my opinion, a valid argument ab inconvenienti so far as it goes. On the other side, it was pointed out that the same problem is presented in any case of a progressive change in relevant circumstances, e.g., progressive deterioration of a district or progressive redevelopment of an adjoining district affecting the value of a shop. Also, as was pointed out by the Court of Appeal (65), a tenancy from year to year is of indefinite duration and may be terminated even at the end of one year, and the value of such a tenancy is not materially affected by the prospect of an event which is not likely to take place within a relatively short period of time. Moreover, valuers may reasonably be inclined to take a sceptical view of forecasts as to the exact time at which governmental action will be taken. The present case affords a warning: I understand that the dispossession and demolition, which were expected to take place within about a year, did not in fact take place for several years.

G

H

I would dismiss the appeal.

I

Appeal dismissed.

Solicitors: *Solicitor of Inland Revenue; Sherwood & Co.*, agents for *Johnson & Co.*, Birmingham (for the ratepayers).

[*Reported by* S. A. HATTEEA, ESQ., *Barrister-at-Law.*]

(64) [1922] 2 A.C. at pp. 120, 121; [1922] All E.R. Rep. at p. 203.
(65) [1967] 3 All E.R. 952; [1968] 1 W.L.R. 133.

A

ATTORNEY-GENERAL v. BEYNON.

[CHANCERY DIVISION (Goff, J.), January 13, 14, 15, 16, 17, 20, 30, February 26, 1969.]

B
Highway—Boundary of highway—Road running between fences—Presumption—Rebuttable.

The mere fact that a road runs between fences, which includes hedges, does not per se give rise to any presumption that the right of way extends to the whole space between the fences. It is necessary to decide the preliminary question whether those fences were put up by reference to the highway that is to separate the adjoining closes from the highway or for
C
some other reason, and that question is to be decided in the sense that the fences do mark the limit of the highway unless there is something in the condition of the road or the circumstances to the contrary. When that has been decided, then a rebuttable presumption of law arises, supplying any lack of evidence of dedication in fact, or inferred from user that the public
D
right of passage, and, therefore, the highway, extends to the whole space between the fences and is not confined to such part as may have been made up (see p. 267, letter I, to p. 268, letter B, post).

Dictum of WARRINGTON, J., in *Offin* v. *Rochford Rural District Council* ([1906] 1 Ch. at p. 354) adopted.

Countess of Belmore v. *Kent County Council* ([1901] 1 Ch. 873) and *Neeld*
E
v. *Hendon Urban District Council* ((1899), 81 L.T. 405) distinguished.

[As to extent of space subject to public right of passage where fences exist, see 19 HALSBURY'S LAWS (3rd Edn.) 75, 76 para. 112; and for cases on the subject, see 26 DIGEST (Repl.) 329-332, *477-497.*]

Cases referred to:
F
Belmore (Countess) v. *Kent County Council,* [1901] 1 Ch. 873; 70 L.J.Ch. 501; 84 L.T. 523; 65 J.P. 456; 26 Digest (Repl.) 331, *492.*

Copestake v. *West Sussex County Council,* [1911] 2 Ch. 331; 80 L.J.Ch. 673; 105 L.T. 298; 75 J.P. 465; 26 Digest (Repl.) 317, *349.*

Evelyn v. *Mirrielees* (1900), 17 T.L.R. 152; 26 Digest (Repl.) 332, *497.*

Hanscombe v. *Bedfordshire County Council,* [1938] 3 All E.R. 647; [1938]
G
Ch. 944; 159 L.T. 357; 102 J.P. 443; 26 Digest (Repl.) 465, *1556.*

Hinds and Diplock v. *Breconshire County Council* [1938] 4 All E.R. 24; 26 Digest (Repl.) 331, *495.*

Locke-King v. *Woking Urban District Council* (1897), 77 L.T. 790; 62 J.P. 167; 26 Digest (Repl.) 330, *485.*

Neeld v. *Hendon Urban District Council* (1899), 81 L.T. 405; 63 J.P. 724; 26
H
Digest (Repl.) 331, *487.*

Offin v. *Rochford Rural District Council,* [1906] 1 Ch. 342; 75 L.J.Ch. 348; 94 L.T. 669; 70 J.P. 97; 26 Digest (Repl.) 330, *481.*

R. v. *Ramsden* (1858), E.B. & E. 949; 27 L.J.M.C. 296; 31 L.T.O.S. 327; 23 J.P. 196; 120 E.R. 763; 26 Digest (Repl.) 406, *1123.*

R. v. *United Kingdom Electric Telegraph Co., Ltd.* (1862), 2 B. & S. 647, n;
I
31 L.J.M.C. 166; 6 L.T. 378; 26 J.P. 390; 121 E.R. 1212.; 26 Digest (Repl.) 330, *478.*

Action.

This was an action by the Attorney-General on the relation of Leicester County Council, the highway authority, against the defendant, Joseph Gwynfor Beynon, the owner of a house in Leicester Lane, a road leading from Desford to Enderby, claiming a declaration that a roadside strip of greensward approximately 40 feet wide opposite his house on the other side of the roadway was part of the highway. The facts are set out in the judgment. The cases noted below* A were cited during the argument in addition to those referred to in the judgment.

Douglas Frank, Q.C., and *K. H. T. Schiemann* for the Attorney-General.
Jeremiah Harman, Q.C., and *O. R. W. W. Lodge* for the defendant.

Cur. adv. vult.

26th February. **GOFF, J.,** read the following judgment: In this case, B Her Majesty's Attorney-General sues on the relation of the Leicester County Council, who are the highway authority and as such have vested in them the road called Leicester Lane leading from Desford to Enderby. It is an ancient coal road and the metalled portion in the material stretch is about 20 feet wide. The defendant is the owner of a property called Acacia Lodge, which he bought on 21st April 1938, and which lies on the north side of the road. C

The action concerns a roadside strip of greensward, which I will call " the verge ", on the south side of the road beginning approximately opposite the defendant's property and running westwards for a little under 200 feet, part of a larger strip which I will call " the strip " and which is in all some 570 feet as I scale the measurements from the plan. The council claim that the verge is part of the highway. The strip is of a fairly uniform depth of approximately D 40 feet, and is bounded at the rear or southern boundary by an ancient hedge with a ditch in front of it, that is to say on the roadward side. The verge does not belong to the adjoining owner to the south and no evidence was adduced to show a paper title of any kind, although it is possible that the defendant may have acquired a statutory title. This hedge stands on a small bank. One of the witnesses, a Mr. Deacon who lives at a house called Far Forest just to E the west of the strip, gave this bank as being some two or three feet high, but the defendant said that there was not much of a bank and along the western end of the verge he said that there was little or no bank. This evidence does not seem to me to suggest a prominent natural feature which might account for the hedge being on that line. More probably, the bank was made by digging out the ditch. The strip is clearly level with the road. F

The ditch serves to drain the land lying to the south of the road where there is a pond. It was established by the evidence of Mr. Deacon that the overflow drains from this pond down the side of his property to the ditch and then along the front of the strip to a place where it meets a ditch coming from the opposite direction, that is to say the east end and then the combined flow turns northwards across the road into the defendant's property. In former days this part G was an open ditch or water course which he called " the brook " and it was very boggy in the hollow where the brook ran. Cows used to drink there. In Mr. Deacon's early days, until he was about 13, there were cattle which he tended there for his father when they lived at Caldecott Croft, a property on the north side of the road next to the defendant's house, and apparently for one other farmer, though it did not appear where his farm was. Mr. Deacon H further said that the defendant, in common with other farmers, let his cattle on to the road and they went to drink at the brook.

I think that this brook or stream, or whatever it was at one time, flowed over the road but that it was culverted under the road sometime, I think, after Mr. Deacon first knew the property. This culvert, however, began in the strip very near the roadside and cattle could still drink there. The defendant says I that, when he bought his property in 1938, he was told by his vendor, who owned the land on the south, that he, the defendant, could water his cattle at the brook in dry weather. It was not shown, however, that the vendor owned

---

* *Steel* v. *Prickett* (1819), 2 Stark. 463; [1814-23] All E.R. Rep. 537; *Arnold* v. *Holbrook* (1873), L.R. 8 Q.B. 96; *Coverdale* v. *Charlton* (1878), 4 Q.B.D. 104; *Curtis* v. *Kesteven C.C.* (1890), 45 Ch.D. 504; *Harvey* v. *Truro R.D.C.*, [1903] 2 Ch. 638; *A.-G.* v. *Meyrick and Jones* (1915), 79 J.P. 515; *Stoney* v. *Eastbourne R.C.*, [1927] 1 Ch. 367; *A.-G.* v. *Stokesley R.D.C.* (1928), 26 L.G.R. 440; *Webb* v. *Eastleigh B.C.* (1958), 56 L.G.R. 127.

A the strip or verge or had any rights over them. The defendant extended this culvert further into his own land because the outlet was too boggy, but nothing turns on that. Then, in 1950, when the council were making up a footpath they extended the culvert nearly right across the strip to make it safe for pedestrians to walk there. Also, there were and are two drainage grips cut from the road into the strip between the western end and the culvert. These do not reach the ditch

B but serve to drain the road into it by percolation. Further east opposite Caldecott Croft there are and have been for as long as the defendant can remember one or two grips reaching to the ditch in that place.

The hedges beyond the western end of the strip and the eastern end of the verge are much nearer the metalled road at distances of as little as six feet to ten feet. At each of these ends the rear hedge comes forward to meet this more

C advanced frontage line. At the south-east corner of the rear hedge there is a large oak tree. The strip is crossed by an access way at the west end of the verge to a property on the south side called Forest Field. This is a modern way and was made after the defendant acquired his property in 1938. A little to the east of this way there is a smaller tree. At the extreme western end of the strip there is another access way, and this has existed for as long as any of the

D witnesses could remember. This was clearly the original way into the whole of what was a large field lying immediately to the south of the strip and the new way was made when a house called Forest Field was built.

The land immediately behind the verge has no convenient front access. It is possible to get there through the adjoining property called Laburnum Grove and thence to a path at the rear, but that is really a footpath and it is difficult

E to manoeuvre thence into the field. However, the evidence shows that access was originally gained from the way in at the western end of the strip as the field behind the verge was not separated from the whole large field until 1941. Then, or soon afterwards, a front gate was made leading on to the verge but no access way across it. The property called Laburnum Grove immediately to the east of the verge has a second hedge behind the more forward one to which

F I have referred and a little nearer the road than the hedge at the rear of the verge, but it is clear that this was planted some time between 1886 and 1903 as it is not shown on the ordnance survey map for the former year but is on that for the latter and nothing turns on this second hedge.

Considerably further along the road to the west, the frontage reverts to approximately the line of the rear hedge of the strip; and it is clear from the tithe

G map of 1847 that there had been at some time before that date a roadside margin beginning at a point a little to the east of Laburnum Grove and widening on a diagonal line to the depth of the strip and then continuing in a more or less straight line past Laburnum Grove and the rear of the strip and on for a considerable distance to a point where the road turns sharply north east. That tithe map itself shows two plots numbered respectively 121 and 128 and des-

H cribed in the tithe award as intakes having the modern frontage to the road and as their rear boundary the rear line of the margin I have just described, but how the rear of those two intakes was then fenced off does not appear. It is clear, therefore, that the hedge at the rear of the strip was an ancient boundary of some kind and that it had been advanced on either side.

Two closes beyond the point where the road turns north east there is a peculiar

I shape referred to at the trial as a rhomboid which is coloured in the same way as the rest of the untitheable land representing road margins. This suggests that the wide margin may have continued past those two closes to the rhomboid, but that is little more than conjecture. The rhomboid itself was enclosed before the ordnance survey of 1886. To the west of intake 121 the tithe map appears to show a wide verge on the north side of the road also and it shows a number of intakes on that side of the road as well, all of which would suggest that originally there was a wide margin on the north as well as on the south from about the same point as it commences on the south side right up to the point where the

road turns to the north east, but it has now largely disappeared and opposite **A**
the strip it is of the order of six or seven feet and no more.

The turnpike map of 1788 was also given in evidence. This appeared to be
drawn to scale laterally along the length of the road. If that scale be applied
to measure the width of the road, it would produce the absurd result of 70 feet
for the road alone with margins either side of 70 feet. I cannot regard the width
of the road and margins as being true to scale, but it does support the indications **B**
from the tithe map of a road with a wide margin on either side. Also, it is to be
observed in passing that, by s. 26 of the Turnpike Act 1788, the trustees were
authorised but not required to widen the road to 40 feet which clearly was not
done along any material part. It was also provided by that section that the
trustees might alter the route and the adjoining owners might purchase the
old site, but that, if they did not, then by s. 29 they were to fence off their land **C**
from the site of the old road. There have been further intakes since 1847, and
comparison of the tithe map and the latest ordnance survey of 1961 shows that,
from and including the rhomboid past the strip to the White Horse Inn which
lies south of Laburnum Grove a distance of just under one mile, the later enclosures amount in all to 0·6 acres plus very small pieces which were not such
as could be calculated.   **D**

The council tried to establish as an act of ownership that they had regularly
mowed the grass on the verge right back to the ditch, but I am satisfied that
they did no more than keep the edge tidy and cut the near side. At first a road-
man cut the edge with his spade and turned it back on to the grass of the verge.
Later, the council cut a swaythe about four feet wide and still later a second
swaythe of similar width from the footpath. All the rest was originally left **E**
uncut, dying down each year, and afterwards was cut in part by a man who had
poultry houses in the southern field and in part by the defendant himself. It
was established on behalf of the defendant that, between the wars, Mr. Basford,
the previous owner of the defendant's property, kept an obsolete furniture van on
the verge for about three years and also a quantity of farming equipment. I do
not think that this can have been very considerable for most of the time as the **F**
witness Mr. Deacon said that it was kept under the oak tree being, as I find,
the large one in the corner. There is evidence, however, from the defendant that
he went to look at Acacia Lodge twice before purchasing it and that he saw on
the strip or verge horse-drawn farm vehicles which he identified as a hay rack,
a turner and a four-wheel dray. In addition, Mr. Deacon said that a contractor
who owned threshing equipment would work in the neighbourhood for about a **G**
month and that he was accustomed to leave his machine on the strip overnight.
That, however, is common in country districts. If Mr. Basford was owner or
tenant of the southern field his title was not proved, but there was evidence that
he used it for his trotting horses, I suppose for grazing. When the defendant
acquired his property, there was a large clamp of manure under the oak tree and
the remains of some kind of farm implement in front which he had to remove **H**
to get at the manure which he carted away.

The defendant had a large trailer horse box which he used for taking his cattle
to market, and this he at once began to keep on the verge together with his own
private car. He soon commenced buying and selling cars, at first in a small way
as a hobby, and these, too, he kept on the verge. There were Austin Cambridge
cars and he says that there were only one or two, which is confirmed by the **I**
witness, Mr. Stableford, who says there were only one or two cars or farming
implements as late as 1953. During the war the defendant dealt in farm vehicles,
and he kept these also and others of his own farm vehicles on the verge. In later
years, which I place as after 1953, the defendant developed his car dealing business
and since then he has regularly parked on the verge a number of cars and farm
vehicles which he has for sale. The photographs show some five cars, three hay
bailers and two lorries.

The council complain that, in this way the defendant is and has been obstruct-

A ing the highway, and it is conceded that they are right in that if the verge is part of the highway, which is denied save a width of some ten feet immediately adjoining the metalled way where no cars or vehicles have been or are kept. The parking is confined to the verge and does not extend to the rest of the strip.

When the defendant purchased Acacia Lodge, a portion of the verge was already covered with some kind of grit or stone which may have been the residue

B of dumps placed there by the council when making up the road. There was at all events no evidence how they came to be there. Afterwards the defendant put down gravel in this area. Apart from this and apart from the fact that parts are more rough than others, the whole strip is similar in appearance. There is a large clump of willow and other smaller growths but no appreciable obstruction to public user. It is particularly significant that there is no natural or other division

C between the metalled track and the ditch, and nothing to distinguish the ten feet or so of the verge which the defendant admits to be highway from the rest. This counsel for the defendant distinguishes by a notional line drawn between the two advanced hedges on either side of the strip.

There was no evidence of any use of the strip by the public for passage before 1930 as the traffic on the road was light and the people walked in the road itself,

D but thereafter they began to walk on the verge near the edge. In 1945, the council widened the road by some four or five feet, and this I find as a fact was carried out on the southern side. In 1950, they made up a footpath from the White Horse Inn which lies as I have said east of the strip to Stud Farm to the west. It seems they did not make it up where the gravel was because it was unnecessary, but subject to this they carried it right across the strip but wholly in front of the

E notional line which I have mentioned. There was a dispute on the evidence as to its width. According to the council's directions it should have been four feet six inches, but I doubt whether it was ever much more than three feet six inches wide if that. This path quickly gets overgrown and, when required, the council have sided it out. The council have also cut the willows on complaint made by the parish council.

F No other acts of ownership were proved on either side, and it was clear that the council did not clean out the ditch. However, the presumption would be that the ditch was not part of the highway (see *Hanscombe* v. *Bedfordshire County Council* (1)) and this would not prevent the fence to fence presumption from applying up to the ditch. The council rely on what may be called the fence to fence presumption which to quote the hypothetical direction given by MARTIN, B.,

G in *R.* v. *United Kingdom Electric Telegraph Co., Ltd.* (2), may be stated in these terms:

" In the case of an ordinary highway, although it may be of a varying and unequal width, running between fences, one on each side, the right of passage or way, *prima facie*, and unless there be evidence to the contrary, extends to the whole space between the fences; and the public are entitled

H to the use of the entire of it, as the highway, and are not confined to the path which may be metalled or kept in order for the more convenient use of carriages and foot passengers ".

There was, however, before me a long argument as to the precise nature and effect of this presumption and the many cases on the subject were exhaustively

I canvassed.

It is clear that the mere fact that a road runs between fences, which of course includes hedges, does not per se give rise to any presumption. It is necessary to decide the preliminary question whether those fences were put up by reference to the highway that is to separate the adjoining closes from the highway or for some other reason. When that has been decided, then a rebuttable presumption of

(1) [1938] 3 All E.R. 647; [1938] Ch. 944.
(2) (1862), 31 L.J.M.C. 166 at p. 167.

A law arises, supplying any lack of evidence of dedication in fact, or inferred from user that the public right of passage, and, therefore, the highway, extends to the whole space between the fences and is not confined to such part as may have been made up.

It seems clear to me, however, as the principle has developed that one is to decide that preliminary question in the sense that the fences do mark the limit of the highway unless there is something in the condition of the road or the B circumstances to the contrary. This was the basis of the decision of WARRINGTON, J., in *Offin* v. *Rochford Rural District Council* (3), where he said:

" It seems to me that the result both of that case [that was *Neeld* v. *Hendon Urban District Council* (4)] and of *R.* v. *United Kingdom Electric Telegraph Co., Ltd.* (5) is this—that the mere existence of fences on either side of a high-way is not enough to raise the presumption. You have to find whether those C fences are prima facie to be taken to have been made in reference to the high-way, and, therefore, to be the boundaries of the highway, and, further, I think that, having regard to the judgment of VAUGHAN WILLIAMS, L.J., if you find a fence by the side of the highway, then prima facie that fence is the boundary of the highway, unless you can find some reason for supposing that it was put up for a different purpose ". D

This passage I confess puzzled me at first and appeared indeed to be self-contra-dictory, but, carefully analysed, I think that its meaning is succinct and clear. WARRINGTON, J., said " You have to find whether those fences are prima facie to be taken to have been made in reference to the highway ", because that preliminary finding may be rebutted by evidence of acts of ownership inconsistent with that conclusion, but then he says further " prima facie that fence is the E boundary of the highway, unless you can find some reason for supposing that it was put up for a different purpose." This was accepted by SINGLETON, J., as a concise summary of the law in *Hinds and Diplock* v. *Breconshire County Council* (6), and I, too, respectfully adopt it. *Countess of Belmore* v. *Kent County Council* (7), on which the defendant placed great reliance, is distinguishable F because in that case there were clear acts of ownership inconsistent with the public right to rebut the presumption, notably making access ways raised some three or four feet above the level of the ground. *Neeld* v. *Hendon Urban District Council* (4) is also distinguishable. I doubt whether the fact that it dealt with a highway over manorial waste would be sufficient (see *Evelyn* v. *Mirrielees* (8)), but again there were adverse acts of ownership and the local authority surveyor G had actually assisted the private owner in the erection of his fence.

I have now to apply these principles to the facts of the present case, and I start with this that, in my judgment, there is nothing in the terrain to show the contrary of the prima facie rule, unless it be in the width of the verge or in the intakes. I do not consider the clump of willows or the brook as sufficient for this purpose. So far as concerns the bank, as I have said I do not regard this H as a natural feature explaining the rear hedge being sited there, and I would refer to these words in the judgment of KEKEWICH, J., in *Locke-King* v. *Woking Urban District Council* (9):

" No one can tell by whom, when, and under what circumstances they were made; but they have been made, and made according to the ordinary rule, that the incloser goes to the extremity of his land, or, as one may say in this I case, the extremity of that which he determines to keep for himself, and digs a ditch and throws the soil from the ditch backwards on to his own land, that is to say, on to the land he intends to keep for himself, so as to form the hedge."

---

(3) [1906] 1 Ch. 342 at p. 354.   (4) (1899), 81 L.T. 405.
(5) (1862), 31 L.J.M.C. 166.   (6) [1938] 4 All E.R. 24 at p. 30.
(7) [1901] 1 Ch. 873.   (8) (1900), 17 T.L.R. 152.
(9) (1897), 77 L.T. 790 at p. 791.

A The depth of the verge is, however, considerable, being of an order equal to the full width to which the turnpike trustees were authorised to make up the road, but I cannot consider it so extravagant as to exclude the prima facie rule, and in *Offin's* case (10) itself the area was very large, being 900 square yards and being triangular in shape its depth at the apex was 90 feet.

B The intakes do not, in my view, exclude the rule merely because they produce irregularity (see *Locke-King's* case (11)), but do they suggest, and, if so, sufficiently, that the rear line of hedge was not put up with reference to the highway? If the council are right, of course the intakes were unlawful encroachments on the highway, but such things are by no means unknown, particularly where they have occurred in earlier times when the public right was not so vigilantly guarded. Here, of course, there have been more modern intakes, but not to a dramatic extent.

C Counsel for the defendant argues, however, that, rather than reach that conclusion, I should infer that these intakes were into manorial waste. As I have said, having regard to *Evelyn's* case (12), I am not sure that this would place him in any better plight. Apart from this, the intakes would still be unlawful in the absence of an ancient custom authorising enclosure with or without the consent of the lord of the manor, and none was shown. There seems to me,

D however, to be a very serious difficulty in the way of this theory. In support of it, counsel for the defendant says that this area was all part of the Forest of Leicester, as indeed it was, and within the Honour of Leicester and manor of Desford. Reference to the map at the back of Fox AND RUSSELL ON LEICESTER FOREST shows that this may well be right. However, it is clear from the

E order of the Court of Exchequer in 1628 confirming the agreement for de-afforestation and allotment that the rights of the commoners in the Manor of Desford were bought out by allotting them parcels of the land in severalty. Moreover, great landowners interested in the forest gave up to the Crown substantial parts of their holdings to rid themselves from His Majesty's right of deer in the rest. It seems highly improbable, therefore, that the agreement would have provided for strips along the highway to remain unallotted waste of the

F manor.

That leaves the possibility that this wide margin was left in order to avoid liability ratione clausurae. It is clear that such liability would not in fact have arisen unless the public were actually using the right of deviation (see *R.* v. *Ramsden* (13)), and there appears to be some conflict of judicial opinion whether

G leaving a space as a mere precaution would not in itself amount to dedication of that space. CHANNELL, J., clearly thought it would (see *Neeld's* case (14)), but LORD RUSSELL, C.J., doubted (15) that. However, for all I know there may have been an ancient right actually exercised in 1628 and in any case I do not think that I could exclude the prima facie rule that the back hedge was made with reference to the highway on what is only a supposed explanation.

H I am left with no satisfactory explanation why the hedge was placed where it was, and, therefore, must, as it seems to me, adopt the prima facie view.

I turn, then, to the alleged acts of ownership. The dumping of an obsolete furniture van, the heap of manure and the overnight parking of the threshing equipment I dismiss as inadequate: see *Offin's* case (16). I also regard the user of the strip as a means of access to the highway as not really of material assistance

I either way. A more serious question arises from the evidence that Mr. Basford kept farming equipment on the strip or verge more or less regularly perhaps, though the evidence was not very specific, and from the continued user by the defendant, although the evidence was that he did not do much till 1953 and the council first began to challenge his right in 1960 or 1961. However, it was not

---

(10) [1906] 1 Ch. 342.
(12) (1900), 17 T.L.R. 152.
(14) (1899), 81 L.T. at pp. 406, 407.

(11) (1897), 77 L.T. 790 at p. 791.
(13) (1858), E.B. & E. 949.
(15) (1899), 81 L.T. at p. 409.

(16) [1906] 1 Ch. at p. 345.

shown that Mr. Basford was the owner or tenant of the strip or verge or even A
of the fields to the south, and the defendant certainly never has been. This seems
to me greatly to detract from the value of these acts. These were not acts of
ownership by a person claiming title to the verge, but the conduct of strangers
taking advantage of this convenient strip of land. The same objection of course
applies to the defendant's evidence that he used to cut the grass and use it
for his bull.

Against this, although the council have failed to prove any acts of public
right over the strip other than its edge, they have clearly shown that part of the
verge was included in the highway since they widened the road on that side
without paying compensation, and afterwards made up a footpath. The defendant
was forced to concede that some part of the verge was public highway, and he
could show no differentiation or boundary between that which was and that C
which was not highway other than a notional line. To draw this line is an attractive temptation but not in my view justified. In *Copestake* v. *West Sussex
County Council* (17), PARKER, J., divided the margin in question into three
sections and considered each on its own merits. In the centre section he held
that there was sufficient evidence of user over the whole depth but he intimated
(18) that he would probably have applied the presumption notwithstanding the D
fences on either side had been advanced. True in that case the margin was
narrow, but that is another point. The significant feature is the division of the
problem into three sections. This also bears on another point much argued for
the defendant that, if the council be right, they will be able to throw down the
forward hedges and recover the intakes without compensation. I am not at
all satisfied that that is so. This judgment will not be directly binding on the E
owners of the intakes because they are not parties to the action, and *Copestake's*
case (17) shows that the presumption has to be applied according to the facts
as they are at the time of the action, and in the northern and southern sections
PARKER, J., would not go behind the comparatively modern fences. A fortiori
where the point arises in separate actions against different parties.

Finally, the defendant relied on the fact that, since 1960 or even before, he F
had been rated in respect of his occupation of the verge. This, however, appears
to me to be irrelevant, both because the highway authority is not the rating
authority, and because the latter is concerned only with occupation and not
whether it is lawful.

As I have said, it is conceded that what the defendant is doing is an actionable
obstruction of the highway if such the verge be, and for the reasons given I G
find that it is. Accordingly, the action succeeds and the council are entitled to
the relief claimed.

Declaration accordingly.

Solicitors: *Kingsford, Dorman & Co.*, agents for *John A. Chatterton*, Leicester
(for the Attorney-General); *James & Charles Dodd* agents for *Josiah Hincks,
Son & Bullough*, Leicester (for the defendant).   H

[*Reported by* R. W. FARRIN, ESQ., *Barrister-at-Law.*]

I

---

(17) [1911] 2 Ch. 331.
(18) [1911] 2 Ch. at p. 340.

A

ALDERSON v. BOOTH.

[QUEEN'S BENCH DIVISION (Lord Parker, C.J., Blain and Donaldson, JJ.),
February 26, 1969.]

Arrest—Arrest without warrant—Conduct of arrest—Form of words to be used.

B
An arrest is constituted where any form of words is used which, in the
circumstances of the case, were calculated to bring to the accused's notice,
and did bring to the accused's notice, that he was under compulsion and
thereafter he submitted to that compulsion (see p. 273, letters E, H,
and I, post).

Per LORD PARKER, C.J.: it is advisable that police officers should use
some very clear words to bring home to a person that he is under compul-
C
sion . . . by far and away the simplest thing is for the police officer to say
" I arrest you " (see p. 273, letter G, post).

Per DONALDSON, J.: it is particularly desirable that clear words should be
used in circumstances in which, as a result of the effect of drink or drugs,
a person's understanding may be dulled (see p. 274, letter A, post).

D
Appeal dismissed.

[As to the meaning of arrest, see 10 HALSBURY'S LAWS (3rd Edn.) 342,
para. 631; and for cases on the subject, see 14 DIGEST (Repl.) 189, 190, *1541-1545.*
As to power to arrest under the Road Safety Act 1967, see SUPPLEMENT to
33 HALSBURY'S LAWS (3rd Edn.) 1061A, 2.

For the Road Safety Act 1967, s. 2, see 47 HALSBURY'S STATUTES (2nd Edn.)
E
1556.]

Case Stated.

This was a Case Stated by the justices of the peace for the West Riding of the
county of York acting in and for the petty sessional division of Saddleworth in
respect of their adjudication as a magistrates' court sitting at Uppermill on
26th June 1968.

F
On 23rd May 1968 an information was preferred by the appellant, Jack
Alderson, against the respondent, Geoffrey Booth, charging that he on 26th April
1968 in Chew Valley Road, Greenfield, at the junction with Ladhill Lane did
drive a motor car on a road having consumed alcohol in such a quantity that the
proportion thereof in his blood, as ascertained from a laboratory test, exceeded
the prescribed limit at the time he provided the specimen, contrary to s. 1 (1)
G
of the Road Safety Act 1967.

The following facts were found. On 26th April 1968, the respondent was the
driver of a motor car in Chew Valley Road, Greenfield, when he was involved in
a road accident with another vehicle; shortly after the accident had occurred,
a police constable in uniform visited the scene and there saw and spoke
to the respondent; the constable had reasonable cause to believe that the
H
respondent was the driver of a motor vehicle involved in an accident and also
had reasonable cause to suspect him of having alcohol in his body; acting under
the authority of s. 2 (1) and s. 2 (2) of the Road Safety Act 1967 the constable
required the respondent to provide a specimen of breath for a breath test;
making use of a device of a type approved for the purpose of such a test by the
Secretary of State, the respondent duly provided a specimen of breath and the
I
result of the test was positive, indicating that the proportion of alcohol in the
blood exceeded the prescribed limit; the constable informed the respondent of
the result of the test and said, " I shall have to ask you to come to the police
station for further tests "; the respondent accompanied the constable to a
police station where the respondent was given an opportunity to provide a
specimen of breath for a breath test there; making use of the approved device
referred to, the respondent provided a specimen of breath and the result was
again positive, indicating that the proportion of alcohol in the blood exceeded
the prescribed limit; the constable then required the respondent to provide a

specimen for a laboratory test in accordance with the provisions of s. 3 (1) of **A**
the Road Safety Act 1967; the respondent agreed to give a sample of blood
which was duly taken by a doctor; the respondent was then admitted to bail
by a police inspector pursuant to s. 38 (2) of the Magistrates' Courts Act 1952
to appear at Uppermill police station on 24th May 1968 and the respondent was
then taken to his home by the constable; on analysis, the sample of blood
provided by the respondent was found to contain not less than 203 milligrammes **B**
of alcohol in 100 millilitres of blood, which exceeded the prescribed limit as
defined in s. 7 (1) of the Road Safety Act 1967.

On behalf of the respondent it was contended that he had not been " arrested "
pursuant to the power contained in s. 2 (4) of the Road Safety Act 1967 and that
the respondent had voluntarily accompanied the constable to a police station
for further tests and, in these circumstances, the court could not act on the **C**
subsequent evidence as to the breath tests and the analysis of the blood sample.
On behalf of the appellant it was contended that the respondent had been duly
arrested and that the offence under s. 1 (1) of the Road Safety Act 1967, as
set out in the said information, was made out.

The justices were of opinion that when the respondent accompanied the
constable to the police station it was not made clear to him either physically or **D**
by word of mouth that he was under compulsion. They considered that compulsion was a necessary element of arrest and they, therefore, did not regard the
respondent as a person who had been arrested. As a consequence they did not
consider that the blood sample had been provided under s. 3 of the Road Safety
Act 1967, and they accordingly dismissed the information.

The prosecutor now appealed. The authorities and cases noted below* were **E**
cited during the argument.

R. A. R. Stroyan for the appellant.
Quintin Hogg, Q.C. and *H. K. Goddard* for the respondent.

LORD PARKER, C.J.: This is an appeal by way of Case Stated from a
decision of justices of the peace for the West Riding of the county of York **F**
sitting at Uppermill, who dismissed an information preferred by the appellant
against the respondent for an offence against s. 1 (1) of the Road Safety Act
1967. The only relevant facts so far as this case is concerned are that a police
officer came on a road accident involving the driver of a motor car who was the
respondent; he asked, as he was entitled to under s. 2 (1) of the Road Safety
Act 1967, for the respondent to provide a specimen of breath for a breath test.
The respondent did, and it proved positive. Thereupon the finding is that the **G**
constable informed the respondent of the result of the test and said " I shall
have to ask you to come to the police station for further tests ". The respondent
accompanied the constable to a police station, where the respondent was given
an opportunity to provide a specimen of breath for a breath test there, but that
in turn proved positive; he was then asked for a sample of blood which from
analysis showed that his blood contained no less than 203 milligrammes of **H**
alcohol in 100 millilitres of blood, against the prescribed limit of 80 milligrammes.

It is quite clear, and the justices recognise the fact, that in order to prove
this offence it is necessary to prove that a specimen of blood has been taken in
accordance with s. 3, and when one looks at s. 3 one finds that a specimen of
blood can only be taken if, amongst other things, a man has been lawfully
arrested. The question arises at once: had this man been arrested after the **I**
first breath test under s. 2 (4), which provides that:

---

* 10 HALSBURY'S LAWS (3rd Edn.) 342, para. 631; MORIARTY'S POLICE LAW (1968,
19th Edn.) p. 15; [1966] Crim. L.R. at p. 667; *Horner* v. *Battyn* (1739), Bull. N.P. 61;
Arrowsmith v. *Le Mesurier* (1806), 2 Bos. & P.N.R. 211; *Wood* v. *Lane* (1834), 6 C. &
P. 774; *Grainger* v. *Hill* (1838), 4 Bing. N.C. 212; *Christie* v. *Leachinsky*, [1947] 1 All
E.R. 567; [1947] A.C. 573; *R.* v. *Jones, Ex p. Moore*, [1965] Crim. L.R. 221; *Scott* v.
Baker, [1968] 2 All E.R. 993; [1968] 3 W.L.R. 796; *Campbell* v. *Tormey*, [1969] 1 All E.R.
961; [1969] 1 W.L.R. 189; *R.* v. *Wall* [1969] 1 All E.R. 968; [1969] 1 W.L.R. 400.

A   " If it appears to a constable in consequence of a breath test carried out by him on any person under subsection (1) or (2) of this section that the device by means of which the test is carried out indicates that the proportion of alcohol in that person's blood exceeds the prescribed limit, the constable may arrest that person without warrant except while that person is at a hospital as a patient."

B   Accordingly, the narrow point here was whether the justices were right in holding, as they did, that there never had been an arrest. In their opinion, which is clearly partly opinion and partly of finding of fact, they say this:

C   " We were of opinion that when the respondent accompanied the constable to the police station it was not made clear to him either physically or by word of mouth that he was under compulsion. We consider that compulsion is a necessary element of arrest and we therefore did not regard the respondent as a person who had been arrested."

There are a number of cases, both ancient and modern, as to what constitutes an arrest, and whereas there was a time when it was held that there could be no lawful arrest unless there was an actual seizing or touching, it is quite clear that
D   that is no longer the law. There may be an arrest by mere words, by saying " I arrest you " without any touching, provided of course that the accused submits and goes with the police officer. Equally it is clear, as it seems to me, that an arrest is constituted when any form of words is used which, in the circumstances of the case, were calculated to bring to the accused's notice, and did bring to the accused's notice, that he was under compulsion and thereafter
E   he submitted to that compulsion.

Looked at in that way, I for my part have little doubt that just looking at the words used here " I shall have to ask you to come to the police station for further tests " they were in their context words of command which one would think would bring home to an accused that he was under compulsion. But the justices here had the evidence not only of the police officer but of the respondent,
F   and they were not satisfied, having heard him, that it had been brought home unequivocally to him that he was under compulsion. I confess it surprised me he was believed, but believed he was when he said or conveyed that he was not going to the police station because he thought he was under compulsion, but was going purely voluntarily. It seems to me that this is so much a question of fact for the justices that, surprising as this decision is, I feel that this court
G   cannot interfere.

I would only say this, that if what I have said is correct in law, it is advisable that police officers should use some very clear words to bring home to a person that he is under compulsion. It certainly must not be left in the state that an accused can go into the witness box and merely say " I did not think I was under compulsion ". If difficulties for the future are to be avoided, it seems to me that
H   by far and away the simplest thing is for a police officer to say " I arrest you ". If then the accused goes to the police station after hearing those words, it seems to me that he simply could not be believed if he thereafter said " I did not think there was any compulsion, I was only going voluntarily ". Accordingly, I would dismiss this appeal.

BLAIN, J.: I agree. I would add that I have considerable sympathy
I   with any police officer who believes that he has arrested a person with good reason, and finds that he has failed to do so through using words selected with a laudible desire to perform his duties with the maximum of courtesy. That, however, is of far less importance than the vital right of the subject to know when he is compellable and when he is free. I agree that this court cannot interfere.

DONALDSON, J.: I, too, agree. I agree in particular that courtesy is to be encouraged and that police officers in these circumstances are faced with a

A

difficult decision to make. But it is particularly desirable that clear words should be used in circumstances in which, as a result of the effect of drink or drugs, a person's understanding may be dulled.

Appeal dismissed.

Solicitors: *Cummings, Marchant & Ashton*, agents for *M. D. Shaffner*, Wakefield (for the appellant); *Philip Ross, Elliston & Co.*, agents for *Elliott & Buckley*, Manchester (for the respondent).

B

[*Reported by* N. P. METCALFE, ESQ., *Barrister-at-Law.*]

C

JOHN v. REES AND OTHERS.
MARTIN AND ANOTHER v. DAVIS AND OTHERS.
REES AND ANOTHER v. JOHN.

[CHANCERY DIVISION (Megarry, J.), July 10, 11, 12, 15, 16, 17, 18, 22, 23, 24, 25, 29, October 17, 18, 1968.]

D

Practice—Representative action—Unincorporated body—Proceedings to determine who were its lawfully elected officers—Writ issued by purported president claiming to represent all members—Division of opinion between plaintiff and the members—Community of interest in determination of issue—Whether representative action appropriate—R.S.C., Ord. 15, r. 12.

E

Unincorporated body—Meeting—Constituency Labour Party—Disorder—Powers of chairman to adjourn—Grounds for and length of adjournment.

Natural justice—Domestic tribunal—National Executive Committee of Labour Party—Resolution to " suspend activities " of constituency party—No charges made and no opportunity of being heard—Whether contrary to principles of natural justice.

F

The annual meeting of the Pembrokeshire Divisional Labour Party (P.D.L.P.), was held on 6th April 1968, a properly constituted meeting at which the plaintiff as president of the P.D.L.P. took the chair. On 27th March D., the member of Parliament for the constituency had been expelled from the National Labour Party and at this meeting a profound conflict of views arose between those supporting D.'s views and those who opposed them. There was evidence of a good deal of noise, disorder and some minor violence and after warnings from the plaintiff that it would be impossible for the meeting to continue if the disorder persisted, he announced that he adjourned the meeting sine die and walked out followed by about 20 others. The meeting which, however, continued after he had left elected the second defendant as president of the P.D.L.P. in place of the plaintiff, the third defendant was elected treasurer and the first defendant remained secretary. Further, after the plaintiff had left, the meeting passed a resolution to disaffiliate from the National Labour Party but no notice of such a resolution appeared in the agenda. The plaintiff issued a writ in which he claimed " as representing all members of the P.D.L.P. except the defendants and personally ", and by notice of motion now sought an injunction restraining the defendants from handling the property of the P.D.L.P. until trial of the action. The defendants by their notice of motion asked that the writ be set aside or that so much of the plaintiff's claim as sought relief for parties other than the plaintiff should be struck out.

G

H

I

Held: (i) although there was a division of opinion between the plaintiff and those he claimed to represent, so long as there was an interest common to them all as members of the P.D.L.P. in having the issue determined and so

A long as both sides were fairly argued out, a representative action of this kind was appropriate and within the provision of R.S.C., Ord. 15, r. 12.*

Smith v. *Cardiff Corpn.* ([1953] 2 All E.R. 133) distinguished.

(ii) the chairman of a meeting had an inherent power to adjourn it in the event of disorder if he acted bona fide with the purpose of forwarding and facilitating the meeting and if the adjournment were for no longer than

B necessary for the restoration of order, but since in this case the grounds for adjournment fell far short of what the law required, the purported adjournment by the plaintiff was bad and the meeting remained in being and competent to transact business; accordingly the elections of the defendants to office were valid.

(iii) the resolution to disaffiliate from the National Labour Party was

C invalid: (a) because no notice of such a proposal appeared on the agenda for the meeting, contrary to the standing orders of the P.D.L.P.; and (b) because such a resolution was in breach of the rules governing the P.D.L.P. and through those rules, the constitution of the Labour Party; however, an injunction restraining the defendants who were the lawfully elected officers of the P.D.L.P., from handling the property of the P.D.L.P. would not be

D granted since there was no evidence that they would act unlawfully in relation to it.

E By cl. 8 (2) (*b*) of the constitution of the Labour Party it was provided that the National Executive Committee (the N.E.C.) should have powers to enforce the constitution and rules of the party and to take any action it deemed necessary for that purpose " whether by way of disaffiliation of an organisation or expulsion of an individual or otherwise ". On 24th April 1968, the N.E.C. passed resolutions: first, that action be taken under cl. 8 (2) (*b*) to suspend the activities of the P.D.L.P. and that its officers should

F have no rights to handle party funds; and second, that the P.D.L.P. be " re-organised ", the national agent to have authority to take the steps necessary for re-organisation. The national agent, in pursuance of her decision to convene a meeting of the Haverfordwest Local Labour Party, first sent letters to all the supporters of D., who included the present plaintiffs, informing them of the intended re-organisation and requesting

G them, in effect, to declare their loyalty to the Labour Party, its rule and policies, etc. Notice of the meeting was not sent to the plaintiffs and others who had been immediately before the dispute, members of the local party, on the ground that because they had failed to give the undertaking requested, they were disqualified from membership. At the meeting which the national agent convened and which took place

H on 20th May 1968, all members attending produced the signed declaration of loyalty, and the five defendants were elected officers of the local Labour Party. The plaintiffs now moved for an injunction restraining the defendants from handling the property and moneys of the local Labour Party and from acting as delegates on behalf of the local Labour Party. On the question whether the N.E.C. resolutions authorised the actions of the national agent,

I the court assumed that cl. 8 (2) (*b*) of the constitution applied to the local Labour Party.

Held: (i) a club or other body when exercising the powers conferred by its rules must act in accordance with the principles of natural justice unless they were expressly excluded by the rules themselves and here neither cl. 8 (2) (*b*) nor the resolutions did so; accordingly, the resolution purporting to suspend the P.D.L.P.'s activities and to deprive its officers of their right to handle

---

* R.S.C., Ord. 15, r. 12, so far as material, is set out at p. 283, letter D, post.

funds was contrary to natural justice because no notice of the charges against   **A**
them was given affording them the right to be heard; the first resolution
was, therefore, a nullity.

(ii) the second resolution of the N.E.C. to " re-organise " the P.D.L.P.
did not include a process which excluded from the benefits of membership,
without making a charge or affording a hearing, anyone who failed to sign
and return the declaration of loyalty; accordingly, as no notice of the   **B**
meeting of 20th May 1968 was given to such persons the meeting was not
properly constituted and its proceedings were a nullity: an injunction would
be granted in the terms of the notice of motion because it followed that the
defendants were not the lawfully elected officers of the local Labour Party.

[As to representative proceedings in general, see 30 HALSBURY's LAWS (3rd
Edn.) 315-318, paras. 575-579; and for cases on the subject, see 50 DIGEST   **C**
(Repl.) 465-472, *1603-1654*.

As to powers of a chairman to adjourn a meeting, see 6 HALSBURY's LAWS
(3rd Edn.) 338, para. 663; and for a case on the subject, see 9 DIGEST (Repl.) 607,
4022.

As to expulsion of members under rules of unincorporated bodies, see 5 HALS-
BURY's LAWS (3rd Edn.) 262-265, paras. 616-621, and for cases on the subject, see   **D**
8 DIGEST (Repl.) 655-658, *30-44*.]

Cases referred to:

Adair v. *New River Co.* (1805), 11 Ves. 429; 32 E.R. 1153; 30 Digest (Repl.)
    341, *32*.

Bedford (Duke) v. *Ellis*, [1901] A.C. 1; [1900-03] All E.R. Rep. 694; 70 L.J.Ch.   **E**
    102; 83 L.T. 686; *affg.* sub nom. *Ellis* v. *Bedford (Duke)*, [1899] 1 Ch.
    494; 50 Digest (Repl.) 466, *1605*.

Bromley v. *Smith* (1826), 1 Sim. 8; 5 L.J.O.S. Ch. 53; 57 E.R. 482; 11 Digest
    (Repl.) 47, *670*.

Burn v. *National Amalgamated Labourers' Union of Great Britain and Ireland*,
    [1920] 2 Ch. 364; 89 L.J.Ch. 370; 123 L.T. 411; 45 Digest (Repl.) 547,   **F**
    1249.

Cabell v. *Markham* (1945), 148 F. (2d) 737.

Calder v. *Bull* (1798), 3 U.S. 386.

Catesby v. *Burnett*, [1916] 2 Ch. 325; 85 L.J.Ch. 745; 114 L.T. 1022; 9 Digest
    (Repl.) 620, *4133*.

Cockburn v. *Thompson* (1809), 16 Ves. 321; 33 E.R. 1005; 24 Digest (Repl.)   **G**
    818, *8086*.

Finch v. *Oake*, [1896] 1 Ch. 409; 65 L.J.Ch. 324; 73 L.T. 716; 8 Digest (Repl.)
    654, *29*.

Fisher v. *Keane* (1878), 11 Ch.D. 353; 49 L.J.Ch. 11; 41 L.T. 335; 8 Digest
    (Repl.) 656, *36*.

Fountaine v. *Chesterton* (1968), 112 Sol. Jo. 690; The Times, 20th August.   **H**

Fraser v. *Cooper, Hall & Co.* (1882), 21 Ch.D. 718; 51 L.J.Ch. 575; 46 L.T.
    371; 50 Digest (Repl.) 468, *1624*.

Free Church of Scotland (General Assembly) v. *Overtoun (Lord)*, *Macalister* v.
    Young, [1904] A.C. 515; 91 L.T. 394; 19 Digest (Repl.) 240, *1*.

General Billposting Co., Ltd. v. *Atkinson*, [1909] A.C. 118; [1908-10] All E.R.
    Rep. 619; 78 L.J.Ch. 77; 99 L.T. 943; 28 Digest (Repl.) 811, *586*.   **I**

Harrington v. *Sendall*, [1903] 1 Ch. 921; 72 L.J.Ch. 396; 88 L.T. 323; 51
    W.R. 463; 19 T.L.R. 302; 8 Digest (Repl.) 652, *20*.

Harrison v. *Marquis of Abergavenny* (1887), 3 T.L.R. 324; 57 L.T. 360;
    50 Digest (Repl.) 185, *1567*.

Henderson v. *Bank of Australasia* (1890), 45 Ch.D. 330; 59 L.J.Ch. 794; 63
    L.T. 597; 9 Digest (Repl.) 607, *4025*.

Indian Zoedone Co., Re (1884), 26 Ch.D. 70; 53 L.J.Ch. 468; 50 L.T. 547;
    9 Digest (Repl.) 621, *4139*.

A   *Labouchere* v. *Wharncliffe (Earl)* (1879), 13 Ch.D. 346; 41 L.T. 638; 8 Digest (Repl.) 655, *30*.

Lee v. *Showmen's Guild of Great Britain*, [1952] 1 All E.R. 1175; [1952] 2 Q.B. 329; 45 Digest (Repl.) 541, *1221*.

London Graving Dock Co., Ltd. v. *Horton*, [1951] 2 All E.R. 1; [1951] A.C. 737; 36 Digest (Repl.) 54, *296*.

B   *MacDougall* v. *Gardiner* (1875), 1 Ch.D. 13; 45 L.J.Ch. 27; 33 L.T. 521; 9 Digest (Repl.) 619, *4130*.

Maclean v. *Workers' Union*, [1929] 1 Ch. 602; [1929] All E.R. Rep. 468; 98 L.J.Ch. 293; 141 L.T. 83; 45 Digest (Repl.) 541, *1222*.

Markt & Co., Ltd. v. *Knight Steamship Co., Ltd., Sale & Frazar* v. *Knight Steamship Co., Ltd.*, [1910] 2 K.B. 1021; 79 L.J.K.B. 939; 103 L.T. 369;
C   50 Digest (Repl.) 465, *1603*.

Morris v. *Kanssen*, [1946] 1 All E.R. 586; [1946] A.C. 459; 115 L.J.Ch. 177; 174 L.T. 353; *affg.* sub nom. *Kanssen* v. *Rialto (West End), Ltd.*, [1944] Ch. 346; 9 Digest (Repl.) 460, *3012*.

National Dwellings Society v. *Sykes*, [1894] 3 Ch. 159; 63 L.J.Ch. 906; 9 Digest (Repl.) 607, *4022*.

D   *Pet Library (London), Ltd., The* v. *Walter Ellson & Son, Ltd.*, [1968] F.S.R. 359.

R. v. *Chester (Archdeacon)* (1834), 1 Ad. & El. 342; 3 L.J.M.C. 95; 110 E.R. 1236; 19 Digest (Repl.) 289, *556*.

R. v. *D'Oyly, R.* v. *Hedger* (1840), 12 Ad. & El. 139; 4 J.P. 523; 113 E.R. 763; 19 Digest (Repl.) 285, *512*.

R. v. *Gaborian* (1809), 11 East 77; 103 E.R. 933; 13 Digest (Repl.) 256, *828*.

E   *R.* v. *St. Mary, Lambeth (Churchwardens)* (1832), 1 Ad. & El. 346, n.; 110 E.R. 1238.

R. v. *University of Cambridge* (1723), 1 Stra. 557; 93 E.R. 698; 8 Digest (Repl.) 506, *2281*.

Raggett v. *Musgrave* (1827), 2 C. & P. 556; 172 E.R. 252; 8 Digest (Repl.) 652, *19*.

F   *Ridge* v. *Baldwin*, [1963] 2 All E.R. 66; [1964] A.C. 40; [1963] 2 W.L.R. 935; 127 J.P. 295; 37 Digest (Repl.) 195, *32*.

Royal British Bank v. *Turquand* (1856), 6 E. & B. 327; [1843-60] All E.R. Rep. 435; 25 L.J.Q.B. 317; 119 E.R. 886; 9 Digest (Repl.) 660, *4374*.

Salisbury Gold Mining Co., Ltd. v. *Hathorn*, [1897] A.C. 268; 66 L.J.P.C. 62; 76 L.T. 212; 9 Digest (Repl.) 619, *4129*.

G   *Satanita, The*, [1895] P. 248; *affd.* H.L. [1897] A.C. 59; 12 Digest (Repl.) 74, *413*.

Second Consolidated Trust, Ltd. v. *Ceylon Amalgamated Tea & Rubber Estates, Ltd.*, [1943] 2 All E.R. 567; 169 L.T. 324; 9 Digest (Repl.) 611, *4057*.

Shaw v. *Thompson* (1876), 3 Ch.D. 233; 45 L.J.Ch. 827; 34 L.T. 721; 19 Digest (Repl.) 290, *565*.

H   *Smith* v. *Cardiff Corpn.*, [1953] 2 All E.R. 1373; [1954] 1 Q.B. 210; [1953] 3 W.L.R. 994; 50 Digest (Repl.) 469, *1635*.

Smith v. *Cardiff Corpn. (No. 2)*, [1955] 1 All E.R. 113; [1955] Ch. 159; [1955] 2 W.L.R. 126; 119 J.P. 128; 26 Digest (Repl.) 704, *139*.

Smyth v. *Darley* (1849), 2 H.L. Cas. 789; 9 E.R. 1293; 13 Digest (Repl.) 252, *789*.

I   *Sneyd* v. *Stewart* (1858), 10 Ir. Jur. 105; 22 Digest (Repl.) 174, **897*.

Stoughton v. *Reynolds* (1736), Fortes. Rep. 168; 2 Stra. 1045; 92 E.R. 804; 19 Digest (Repl.) 289, *555*.

Wall v. *London & Northern Assets Corpn.*, [1898] 2 Ch. 469; 67 L.J.Ch. 596; 79 L.T. 249; 9 Digest (Repl.) 605, *4012*.

Wandsworth & Putney Gas-Light and Coke Co. v. *Wright* (1870), 22 L.T. 404; 9 Digest (Repl.) 458, *3002*.

Watson v. *Cave (No. 1)* (1881), 17 Ch.D. 19; 44 L.T. 40; 50 Digest (Repl.) 467, *1617*.

Wilson v. *Church* (1878), 9 Ch.D. 552; 39 L.T. 413; 50 Digest (Repl.) 468, *1622*. A
Wood v. *McCarthy*, [1893] 1 Q.B. 775; [1891-94] All E.R. Rep. 224; 62 L.J.Q.B.
    373; 69 L.T. 431; 50 Digest (Repl.) 471, *1642*.
Wyld v. *Silver*, [1962] 3 All E.R. 309; [1963] Ch. 243; [1962] 3 W.L.R. 841;
    33 Digest (Repl.) 487, *416*.
Young v. *Ladies' Imperial Club, Ltd.*, [1920] 2 K.B. 523; [1920] All E.R. Rep.
    223; 89 L.J.K.B. 563; 123 L.T. 191; 8 Digest (Repl.) 655, *31*.   B

Motions.

These were four motions arising out of three writs concerning the control of
the Pembrokeshire Divisional Labour Party and its assets. By writ dated 6th
May 1968, the plaintiff, James Cecil Gough John, claimed as representing all
members of the Pembrokeshire Divisional Labour Party except the defendants
and personally the following relief: (i) a declaration that all purported proceed- C
ings of the meeting on 6th April 1968 of the General Committee of the Pembrokeshire Divisional Labour Party subsequent to the adjournment of such meeting
by the chairman were invalid and of no effect; (ii) a declaration that the purported appointment on 6th April 1968 of the defendants as officers of the said
party was invalid and of no effect; (iii) an injunction to restrain the defendants
and each of them from collecting expending remitting transferring or otherwise D
dealing with any moneys or other property belonging to or held for the purposes
of the Pembrokeshire Divisional Labour Party. The defendants were Glyn Rees,
Bartholomew Cleare and Haydn J. Lewis.

By notice of motion on the same date the plaintiff moved for an injunction
to restrain the defendants and each of them until judgment in the action or
further order from doing or purporting to do or being a party to (whether by E
themselves their servants or agents or otherwise howsoever) any of the following
things namely collecting expending remitting transferring or otherwise dealing
with any moneys or other property belonging to or held for the purposes of the
Pembrokeshire Divisional Labour Party.

By notice of motion dated 14th May 1968 the defendants claimed that the
writ in the action be set aside or, in the alternative, that so much of the claim F
endorsed on the writ as sought relief for parties other than the plaintiff named in
the writ should be struck out.

A second action was commenced by writ dated 12th June 1968 in which the
plaintiffs, Thomas Henry Martin and Brian Lloyd Davies claimed a declaration
and two injunctions against Leonard Davis, W. Webb, R. C. Davies, J. B. W.
James and A. James. On the same day the plaintiffs gave notice of motion for G
the following relief: (i) an injunction to restrain the defendants and each of them
in their capacities as officers of the unincorporated association which purported
to call itself the Haverfordwest Local Labour Party being an association purported
to have been constituted at a meeting convened and held by order of the National
Executive of the Labour Party at the Gold Room, Market Hall, Haverfordwest,
on Monday 20th May 1968, until judgment in the action or further order (whether H
by themselves their servants or agents or otherwise howsoever) from doing or
purporting to do or being a party to any of the following things namely collecting
expending remitting transferring or otherwise dealing with any moneys or other
property belonging to or held for the purposes of the Haverfordwest Local
Labour Party as constituted prior to the said meeting; (ii) an injunction to restrain
the defendants and each of them until judgment in the action or further order I
from purporting to act as general committee delegates on behalf of the Haverfordwest Local Labour Party as constituted prior to 20th May 1968 at any meetings
whatsoever whether at constituency level or otherwise.

By a third writ dated 5th July 1968 the plaintiffs, Glyn Rees and Bartholomew
Cleare, who were two of the three defendants in the first action, claimed against
James Cecil Gough John, the defendant who was the plaintiff in the first action,
a declaration and injunction. By notice of motion on the same day the plaintiffs
claimed " an injunction to restrain the defendant in his purported capacity as an

A officer of the Pembrokeshire Constituency, . . . until judgment in the action or
further order (whether by himself his servants or agents or otherwise howsoever)
from doing or purporting to do or being a party to any of the following things
namely collecting expending remitting or otherwise dealing with any moneys or
other property belonging to or held for the purpose of the Pembrokeshire
Constituency Local Labour Party ". The facts are set out in the judgment.

B   The cases noted below* were cited during the argument in addition to those
referred to in the judgment.

Charles Sparrow, Q.C., and *Gavin Lightman* for the plaintiff in the first action
and for the defendants in the second and third actions.
David Hirst, Q.C., and *C. Drake* for the defendants in the first action and for
the plaintiffs in the second and third actions.
C
                                                                    Cur. adv. vult.

      17th October. **MEGARRY, J.,** read the following judgment: I have before
me four motions in three actions, all arising out of the same series of events. All,
by consent, have been brought on together, and all have been argued by the same
counsel. The principal bone of contention is the control of an unincorporated
D body and its substantial assets. That body is described sometimes as " The
Pembrokeshire Constituency Labour Party " (occasionally, and I think inaccur-
ately, with " Local " inserted before " Labour "), and sometimes as the " Pembrokeshire Divisional Labour Party ". For brevity I shall throughout refer to it
as " P.D.L.P."
      The argument before me concluded on 29th July 1968. I was confronted with
E some 60 or 70 authorities, about 75 affidavits, with many exhibits, and the fruits
of much closely reasoned argument spread over 12 days; I therefore reserved my
judgment. In order to avoid delay I had hoped to deliver judgment during the
Long Vacation, the parties consenting. But I was vacation judge in August, and
such was the daily press of work, sometimes taking me into court at 9.30 a.m.
and sometimes keeping me there until after 6 p.m., that I was able to give virtually
F no time to the consideration of the wealth of material in this case; and so I deliver
judgment today.
      This is a tale of three meetings. The first was the annual meeting of P.D.L.P.
or, as it is more properly called, of the general committee of P.D.L.P.: for it was
primarily a delegate meeting. It was held on 6th April 1968, and was attended by
about 100 people. I shall call this the " first meeting ". It is common ground that
G it began as a properly constituted meeting; what is challenged is whether, after
a purported adjournment, it continued thereafter as a valid meeting. It is this
meeting which is put in issue in action no. 1, *John v. Rees and Others* (1968 J. No.
2692), in which the writ was issued on 6th May 1968.
      Out of this meeting a profound conflict of views emerged. On one side lie those
who say that as a result of the meeting P.D.L.P. has disaffiliated itself from the
H Labour Party, and that a new set of officers, who supported the disaffiliation,

    * *Bagg's Case* (1615), 11 Co. Rep. 93 b; *Mozley* v. *Alston* (1847), 1 Ph. 790; *Cooper*
v. *Wandsworth Board of Works* (1863), 14 C.B.N.S. 180; *Bromley* v. *Williams* (1863),
32 Beav. 177; *Osgood* v. *Nelson* (1872), L.R. 5 H.L. 636; *R.* v. *Langton* (1876), 2 Q.B.D.
296; *Brogden* v. *Metropolitan Ry. Co.* (1877), 2 App. Cas. 666; *Dawkins* v. *Antrobus*
(1879), 17 Ch.D. 615; [1881-85] All E.R. Rep. 126; *Thellusson* v. *Viscount Valentia,*
I [1907] 2 Ch. 1; *Blythe* v. *Birtley,* [1910] 1 Ch. 228; *Mercantile Marine Service Association*
v. *Toms,* [1916] 2 K.B. 243; [1914-15] All E.R. Rep. 1147; *Hardie and Lane, Ltd.* v.
Chiltern, [1928] 1 K.B. 663; [1928] All E.R. Rep. 36; *Barker* v. *Allanson,* [1937] 1 All
E.R. 75; [1937] 1 K.B. 463; *Carltona, Ltd.* v. *Commissioners of Works,* [1943] 2 All
E.R. 560; *A.-G.* v. *Smith,* [1947] I.R. 332; *Russell* v. *Duke of Norfolk,* [1948] 1 All
E.R. 488; *Lewisham Borough Council* v. *Roberts,* [1949] 1 All E.R. 815; [1949] 2 K.B.
609; *Sherriff* v. *McMullen,* [1952] I.R. 236; *Dale* v. *Inland Revenue Comrs.,* [1953] 2
All E.R. 671; [1954] A.C. 11; *Hughes* v. *Architects' Registration Council of the United
Kingdom,* [1957] 2 All E.R. 436; [1957] 2 Q.B. 550; *Re Webb (decd.),* [1964] 2 All E.R.
91; [1964] 1 W.L.R. 509; *Foss* v. *Harbottle* (1843), 2 Hare 461; *Re N. (Infants),* [1967]
1 All E.R. 161; [1967] Ch. 512.

were validly elected to office in P.D.L.P. This is the side that espouses the cause **A**
of Mr. Desmond Donnelly, the member of Parliament for Pembrokeshire; and
it was his expulsion from the Labour Party on 27th March 1968, a mere ten days
before the first meeting, which formed an important part of the background to that
meeting. For brevity, I shall call those who supported disaffiliation and Mr.
Donnelly the " disaffiliates ". On the other side, there are those who opposed
Mr. Donnelly's views, and contend that the disaffiliation and the elections **B**
at the first meeting were nullities. These I shall call the " affiliates ":
" unionists ", though apposite in one sense, would not be in another. All three
actions are between affiliates and disaffiliates; an affiliate as plaintiff attacks
the first meeting in the first action, and disaffiliates as plaintiffs attack the second
and third meetings in the second and third actions respectively.

The second meeting (which I shall refer to as such) was held on 20th May 1968. **C**
It purported to be a meeting of the Haverfordwest Local Labour Party, and was
convened by the National Executive Committee of the Labour Party (which
I shall call the " N.E.C.") as a result of what occurred at the first meeting. The
validity of the whole of this meeting is in issue. It may be conducive to clarity
if I say at once that, without in any way defining their functions or their relation
to each other, the bodies with which I am concerned in this case are at three levels. **D**
First, at the top there is the Labour Party, which of course is a national body.
Second, there are the constituency labour parties, of which P.D.L.P. is one.
Third, there are a number of local Labour Parties in the area of each constituency
Labour Party. There are some other bodies in the organisation, but I do not need
to refer to them here. The first meeting was thus a meeting of one of the bodies
at the intermediate level, and the second meeting was a meeting of one of the **E**
bodies at the lowest level. It is the second meeting which is in issue in the second
action, *Martin and Davies* v. *Davis and Others* (1968 M. No. 2390), in which the
writ was issued on 12th June 1968.

The third meeting (which I shall refer to as such) was held on 22nd June 1968.
This, like the first meeting, was a meeting of P.D.L.P.; and the validity of the
whole of the meeting is in issue. The meeting is the subject of the third action, **F**
Rees and Cleare v. *John* (1968 R. No. 2276), in which the writ was issued on 5th
July 1968. The two plaintiffs in this action are defendants in the first action,
and the defendant in this action is the plaintiff in the first action. There is thus
a certain symmetry in the actions: for each meeting was unfailingly followed by a
writ within the month, and in substance the parties to the first and third actions
are the reverse of each other. Procedurally, what is before me is not the three **G**
substantive actions themselves, but, as I have indicated, four motions in the three
actions. Action no. 1 has engendered two motions, one by the plaintiff and one
by the defendants. In action no. 2 there is a motion by the plaintiffs, and similarly
in action no. 3 there is a motion by the plaintiffs.

I pause at this point for three reasons. First, it may be convenient if I indicate,
in the broadest of outlines, how the three meetings are related to each other. The **H**
constitution of the Labour Party confers on the N.E.C. power to enforce the
constitution, standing orders and rules of the party, and to take any action it
deems necessary for that purpose. After the first meeting, the N.E.C. passed
a resolution that action be taken to suspend the activities of P.D.L.P. and the
right of its officers to handle its funds, that P.D.L.P. be re-organised, and that the
national agent of the Labour Party be given authority to take such steps as were **I**
necessary to complete the re-organisation. Pursuant to this resolution, the national
agent convened the second meeting; and this meeting elected officers, and also
delegates to attend the general committee of P.D.L.P. The national agent also
convened similar meetings of other local Labour Parties in the constituency;
and there were similar results. The national agent then convened the third
meeting, a general committee of P.D.L.P., composed in the main of delegates
elected by the local Labour Parties under the re-organisation. Those who refused
or failed to sign declarations of loyalty to the Labour Party were excluded from

A the second and third meetings; and the disaffiliates attack these meetings on this score.

Second, I must make explicit what all lawyers will recognise as implicit, but which those who are not lawyers may not fully appreciate. I am not in the least concerned in this case with the rightness or the wrongness or the desirability or undesirability of any political views or policies that there may be. This is so
B whether the views or policies are political in the ordinary external sense, in relation to other political parties or otherwise, or whether they are internal politics within the confines of any political or other unit. My concern is merely to see that those concerned in these proceedings obtain justice according to law, irrespective of politics.

Third, all the proceedings before me are on motion, and all the evidence is in
C the form of affidavits and exhibits. The affidavits are not only numerous (there are over 60 in action no. 1), but also far from harmonious; and without any oral evidence, and in particular without the aid of cross-examination, it is impossible to resolve such conflicts. On the main issues I am merely called on to grant (or refuse) injunctions which will continue until the trial of the action, unless sooner determined. I have thus to do the best I can until the actions are tried. This, too,
D I say for the benefit of those who are more interested in politics than law; this is not the final determination of the case, but merely an interim decision.

I return, then, to the first meeting. Immediately prior to that meeting the plaintiff in the first action was president of P.D.L.P.: and he accordingly took the chair at that meeting, at all events at the outset. He claims that he is still president of P.D.L.P.: the defendants dispute this. The second defendant claims
E that he and not the plaintiff is now president of P.D.L.P. It is common ground that prior to the meeting he was the senior vice-president; and on the agenda for the meeting he was the sole nominee for election as president. What is in dispute is whether he was ever validly elected president as a result of the later and disputed stages of the meeting, after the plaintiff had purported to adjourn it. The third defendant had for some years been treasurer of P.D.L.P., and on the
F agenda for the first meeting he was the sole nominee for that office. On any footing he was thus still treasurer at the end of the meeting. Similarly the first defendant was secretary of P.D.L.P. before the meeting and remained so at the end of it.

By the writ, the plaintiff claims " as representing all members of the Pembrokeshire Divisional Labour Party except the defendants and personally the following
G relief, namely:

" 1. A declaration that all purported proceedings of the meeting on the 6th April 1968 of the General Committee of the Pembrokeshire Divisional Labour Party subsequent to the adjournment of such meeting by the Chairman were invalid and of no effect.

" 2. A declaration that the purported appointment on the 6th April 1968
H of the defendants as officers of the said Party was invalid and of no effect.

" 3. An injunction to restrain the defendants and each of them from collecting expending remitting transferring or otherwise dealing with any moneys or other property belonging to or held for the purposes of the Pembrokeshire Divisional Labour Party."

In this action the plaintiff moves under a notice of motion dated 6th May 1968
I for:

" An injunction to restrain the defendants and each of them until judgment in this action or further order from doing or purporting to do or being a party to (whether by themselves their servants or agents or otherwise howsoever) any of the following things namely collecting expending remitting transferring or otherwise dealing with any moneys or other property belonging to or held for the purpose of the Pembrokeshire Divisional Labour Party."

This notice of motion also seeks the appointment of a receiver; but counsel for

the plaintiff has left this claim in abeyance. The other motion in this action is by A
the defendants. This notice of motion, dated 14th May 1968, claims:

" 1. That the writ in this action be set aside or, in the alternative 2. That
so much of the claim endorsed on the writ in this action as seeks relief for
parties other than the plaintiff named in the writ should be struck out . . ."

Putting matters broadly, the disaffiliates say that they are in the saddle of B
P.D.L.P. and that that body has disaffiliated itself from the Labour Party.
The affiliates deny this, and seek to enjoin the disaffiliates from dealing with
the property of P.D.L.P. Instead, they say that the disaffiliates never got into
the saddle, or, if they did, that the N.E.C. has duly exercised the wide powers
that it has to suspend their activities. The disaffiliates deny this, and seek to
enjoin the affiliates from dealing with the property of P.D.L.P. There is also the C
procedural point of some technicality raised by the disaffiliates in the defendants'
motion. This concerns the plaintiff's claim in writ no. 1 to sue on behalf of himself
and all members of P.D.L.P. except the defendants; and I think that I should
deal with this last point first.

Over 20 affidavits by disaffiliates have been filed in support of the defendants'
motion in action no. 1. These are all by members of P.D.L.P., stating in common D
form that the affiant does not wish to be represented by the plaintiff in the action.
On this foundation counsel for the defendants has erected an argument in support
of his motion in action no. 1 that as the plaintiff purports to sue " as representing
all members of the Pembrokeshire Divisional Labour Party except the defendants ", as well as personally, either the writ should be set aside, or alternatively
the words of representation on the writ should be struck out. For, he says, the E
words of representation simply are not true: the plaintiff may represent some
members of P.D.L.P. (a minority, he says), but he assuredly does not represent
all members except the three defendants.

Such a contention indeed wears an engaging air of simplicity and reason:
but having listened to much argument and many authorities, spread over a number of days, I cannot at the end say that this simplicity is more than skin deep.
The rule as to representative actions is an old Chancery rule which the Rules of F
the Supreme Court later made statutory. The present provision is R.S.C.,
Ord. 15, r. 12. The classic statement is that made by LORD MACNAGHTEN in
Duke of Bedford v. *Ellis* (1). He said there:

" The old rule in the Court of Chancery was very simple and perfectly well
understood. Under the old practice the Court required the presence of all G
parties interested in the matter in suit, in order that a final end might be
made of the controversy. But when the parties were so numerous that you
never could ' come at justice,' to use an expression in one of the older cases,
if everybody interested was made a party, the rule was not allowed to stand
in the way. It was originally a rule of convenience: for the sake of convenience it was relaxed. Given a common interest and a common grievance, H
a representative suit was in order if the relief sought was in its nature
beneficial to all whom the plaintiff proposed to represent."

From the time the rule as to representative suits was first established, he said (2)

". . . it has been recognised as a simple rule resting merely upon convenience. It is impossible, I think, to read such judgments as those delivered
by LORD ELDON in *Adair* v. *New River Co.* (3), in 1805, and in *Cockburn* v. I
Thompson (4) in 1809, without seeing that LORD ELDON took as broad and
liberal a view on this subject as anybody could desire. ' The strict rule,' he
said, ' was that all persons materially interested in the subject of the suit,
however numerous, ought to be parties . . . but that being a general rule

(1) [1901] A.C. 1 at p. 8.
(2) [1901] A.C. at pp. 10, 11.
(3) (1805), 11 Ves. 429.
(4) (1809), 16 Ves. 321 at pp. 325, 329.

A established for the convenient administration of justice must not be adhered to in cases to which consistently with practical convenience it is incapable of application.' ' It was better,' he added, ' to go as far as possible towards justice than to deny it altogether.' He laid out of consideration the case of persons suing on behalf of themselves and all others, ' for in a sense,' he said, ' they are before the Court.' As regards defendants, if you cannot make

B everybody interested a party, you must bring so many that it can be said they will fairly and honestly try the right. I do not think, my Lords, that we have advanced much beyond that in the last hundred years, and I do not think that it is necessary to go further, at any rate for the purposes of this suit '.''

This seems to me to make it plain that the rule is to be treated as being not a rigid matter of principle but a flexible tool of convenience in the administration

C of justice. Such an approach is, I think, at least consistent with cases such as *Bromley* v. *Smith* (5), *Wood* v. *McCarthy* (6), and *Wyld* v. *Silver* (7); and in *Harrison* v. *Marquis of Abergavenny* (8), KAY, J., described the rule as being " a rule of convenience only ". The approach also seems to be consistent with the language of R.S.C., Ord. 15, r. 12 (1). This provides that

D   " Where numerous persons have the same interest in any proceedings . . . the proceedings may be begun, and, unless the Court otherwise orders, continued, by or against any one or more of them as representing all or as representing all except one or more of them."

By r. 12 (3)-(6), ample provision is made for protecting those who, being bound by a judgment against a person sued on their behalf, nevertheless wish to dispute

E personal liability. The language is thus wide and permissive in its scope; yet it provides adequate safeguards for the substance. I would therefore be slow to apply the rule in any strict or rigorous sense: and I find nothing in the various passages cited to me from DANIELL'S CHANCERY PRACTICE (8th Edn., 1914) which makes me modify this view.

What I am concerned with in action no. 1 is the validity of proceedings at a

F meeting which had as part of its business the election of the officers of P.D.L.P. All members of P.D.L.P. have a common interest in P.D.L.P., its officers and its assets: and it is plainly desirable that all should know and recognise who its officers are and are not. If there were to be two different actions brought, one between A and B and the other between X and Y, it might be that, on the different evidence adduced in the two actions, the court would reach a different

G conclusion in each action, holding in A v. B that the officers were one set of persons, and in X v. Y that another set were the officers. Other members might then institute other proceedings and, not being bound by the two actions already brought, contend for yet other persons as officers. Accordingly, it seems at least desirable that any proceedings should be so constituted that they will bind all members. This can be achieved only if all are parties to the proceedings, either

H directly or as being represented by one of the parties.

Although there is thus a clear common interest between all the members in having the issue determined, they may be far from united in the way in which they wish it to be resolved. Some may support one faction, some another. But if the named parties to the action together put forward every view that is seriously advanced, I cannot see that any real harm is done to a person whose part in the

I action is merely that he is represented by the plaintiff, even if the plaintiff is supporting a different cause, provided that there is a defendant who does stand for the cause espoused by the person being represented: actions are decided by reference to justice according to law, and not by counting heads. The remedy for someone who is not consoled by this thought is, as SIR GEORGE JESSEL, M.R.,

(5) (1826), 1 Sim. 8.
(6) [1893] 1 Q.B. 775; [1891-94] All E.R. Rep. 224.
(7) [1962] 3 All E.R. 309; [1963] Ch. 243.
(8) (1887), 3 T.L.R. 324 at p. 325.

held in *Wilson* v. *Church* (9), and as JAMES, L.J., pointed out in *Watson* v. *Cave* A
(*No. 1*) (10), for him to apply to be joined as a defendant. Alternatively, he may
be able to procure an order, made under R.S.C., Ord. 15, r. 12, whereby he will be
represented by a defendant: see *Fraser* v. *Cooper, Hall & Co.* (11). In *Wilson*
v. *Church* (12), the dissentient not only sought to be made a defendant but also
applied to represent all other dissentients. The latter part of his application
failed because there was no evidence that there were any other dissentients; and, B
said SIR GEORGE JESSEL, M.R. (13), " he cannot be a representative without a
constituency ". If there had been constituents a-plenty, the judgment suggests
that he would have succeeded on this too.

It seems to me that the important thing is to have before the court, either in
person or by representation, all who will be affected: and provided that the issue
will be fairly argued out, a mathematical precision in securing that each side is C
shown as representing the right number of supporters is of little moment. As
COTTON, L.J., said in *Watson* v. *Cave* (*No. 1*) (14):

"... the plaintiff sues on behalf of himself and all others who have the same
interest as himself, that is, not all those who take the same view of what is
for their benefit, but all those who, being interested jointly with him in some
property, have not taken any steps to assert their rights adversely to those D
which the Plaintiff chooses to assert."

The artificial nature of the process is shown by the fact that, as FLETCHER MOUL-
TON, L.J., pointed out in *Markt & Co., Ltd.* v. *Knight Steamship Co., Ltd.* (15),
a plaintiff suing in a representative capacity does not have to obtain the consent
of those whom he purports to represent, and they are not liable for costs, though by
estoppel or res judicata they will be bound by the result of the case. E

Counsel for the defendants relied strongly on the *Markt* case (16) and on *Smith*
v. *Cardiff Corpn.* (17). In the *Markt* (16) case a ship owned by the defendants
had been sunk by a Russian cruiser during the Russo-Japanese war on the
ground that it was carrying contraband of war. Goods had been shipped on the
vessel as a general ship. One of the shippers sued the defendants for damages
for breach of contract and duty, suing on behalf of himself and other owners F
of cargo on the ship. A letter written by the plaintiff's solicitors when the writ
was issued identified 44 other shippers as being thus represented. The Court of
Appeal unanimously held that the representative action would not lie, as the
plaintiff and other shippers lacked the " same interest in one cause or matter "
within R.S.C., Ord. 16, r. 9: the corresponding provision in the present Rules of
the Supreme Court is R.S.C., Ord. 15, r. 12 (1), which uses the phrase " the same G
interest in any proceedings."

BUCKLEY, L.J., took the view that the writ should be amended by limiting
the representation to those who had not shipped contraband, and by praying a
declaration of liability, leaving the individual claims for damages to subsequent
proceedings. But VAUGHAN WILLIAMS and FLETCHER MOULTON, L.JJ., held that
the writs were incapable of amendment so as to maintain any representative H
action: and FLETCHER MOULTON, L.J., held that no representative action could
be brought where the sole relief sought was damages. As VAUGHAN WILLIAMS,
L.J., observed (18), " All sorts of facts and all sorts of exceptions may defeat
the right of individual shippers." FLETCHER MOULTON, L.J., said (19):

"... I can conceive no excuse for allowing any one shipper to conduct
litigation on behalf of another without his leave, and yet so as to bind I
him. The proper domain of a representative action is where there are like
rights against a common fund, or where a class of people have a community

(9) (1878), 9 Ch.D. 552 at p. 559.   (10) (1881), 17 Ch.D. 19 at p. 21.
(11) (1882), 21 Ch.D. 718.   (12) (1878), 9 Ch.D. 552.
(13) (1887), 3 T.L.R. 324 at p. 325.
(14) (1881), 17 Ch.D. at p. 22.   (15) [1910] 2 K.B. 1021 at p. 1039.
(16) [1910] 2 K.B. 1021.   (17) [1953] 2 All E.R. 1373; [1954] 1 Q.B. 210.
(18) [1910] 2 K.B. at p. 1030.   (19) [1910] 2 K.B. at p. 1040.

A   of interest in some subject-matter. Here there is nothing of the kind. The defendants have made separate contracts which may or may not be identical in form with different persons. And that is all."

It has been contended that the actual result of the case was that the writ was set aside: but I think that it is reasonably plain (20) that the plaintiff was held to be entitled to continue with the action as a personal action, and that all that was
B   struck out was the representative capacity.

A similar result was reached in *Smith* v. *Cardiff Corpn.* (21). This is a case which has, I think, the odd distinction of being a Chancery action reposing uneasily in the Queen's Bench series of reports: the confusion seems to have arisen from the case having been heard originally in the Vacation Court, as may be per-
C   ceived from the report of a later stage of the same case, *Smith* v. *Cardiff Corpn.* (*No. 2*) (22). Four plaintiffs sued Cardiff Corporation on behalf of themselves and all other tenants of Corporation houses provided under Part 5 of the Housing Act 1936, seeking a declaration that the corporation's scheme for increasing rents was ultra vires, and claiming an injunction to restrain the corporation from putting the scheme into operation. The scheme was one of the type commonly
D   described as providing for differential rents, thus taking into consideration the financial circumstances of each tenant. Of some 13,000 tenants, some 8,000 would have their rents increased, and the other 5,000 would not. The Court of Appeal reversed the order of GLYN-JONES, J., striking out the writ, and held that the action should proceed as a personal action by the four plaintiffs and not as a representative action. SIR RAYMOND EVERSHED, M.R., stated the established
E   requirements for a representative action succinctly: it must be shown (23)

"... that all the members of the alleged class have a common interest, that all have a common grievance, and that the relief is in its nature beneficial to them all."

Even if there were a common interest, there was no common grievance, and the relief was not in its nature beneficial to them all. Those whose rents were to
F   be increased would in effect subsidise those whose rents remained unchanged, so that there were two classes of tenants whose interests were in conflict.

Counsel for the defendant's primary contention is that the writ should be struck out. The plaintiff, he said, knew from the outset that he did not represent all save three members of P.D.L.P., and in this respect the writ was " utterly bogus ". I can say at once that I see no justification whatever for taking so drastic
G   a step. The plaintiff sues on behalf of himself, and I can see no reason why, even if the words of representation are bad, they should infect the claim by the plaintiff himself. In a sphere dominated by convenience in the administration of justice, I reject the concept of contagious invalidity on which such a claim appears to rest. I know of no authority to support it, except insofar as the decision at first instance in the *Cardiff* case may be relied on: but no reasons for that decision are
H   reported, and in any case it was reversed by the Court of Appeal (21). Accordingly, I refuse to set aside the writ as prayed in para. 1 of the defendants' notice of motion.

Counsel for the defendant's alternative contention is that the words of representation should be struck out. He stresses the divided state of the views of the members of P.D.L.P., and urges that this division resembles the division between
I   the two categories of tenants in the *Cardiff* case (21). Just as a representative action was bad both there and in the *Markt* case (24), so it must be bad here: there was no common interest and no common grievance, and the relief was not beneficial to all. It seems to me, however, that there is an essential distinction

(20) [1910] 2 K.B. at pp. 1032, 1042.
(21) [1953] 2 All E.R. 1373; [1954] 1 Q.B. 210.
(22) [1955] Ch. 159 at p. 160; [1955] 1 All E.R. 113.
(23) [1953] 2 All E.R. at p. 1377; [1954] 1 Q.B. at p. 221.
(24) [1910] 2 K.B. 1021.

between those cases and this. In the case before me, I have a simple division of A
opinion between numerous members of a single body. The plaintiff is on one side,
the defendants on the other, and in essence the only vice suggested in the plaintiff's
claim to represent all members of P.D.L.P. except the defendants is that some of
these members in fact support the defendants and do not wish to be represented
by the plaintiff. Any misrepresentation may thus be cured with comparative
simplicity. Those who do not support the plaintiff and wish to appear on the B
other side, either individually or by representation, may, if they wish, take
the appropriate steps to achieve this; and counsel for the plaintiff has made
it plain that the plaintiff will co-operate in achieving this result. Subject to that,
the plaintiff and those he represents all have a common interest and a common
grievance, and seek relief beneficial to all. All members of P.D.L.P. are bound to
each other by contract, linked by a common membership and a common interest C
in the assets. In such a case I would respectfully echo the words of LORD ELDON
which LORD MACNAGHTEN quoted in a passage that I have already read: " all
persons materially interested in the subject of the suit, however numerous,
ought to be parties ". I would add only that " ought " does not by any means
necessarily mean " must, on peril of the action being struck out ". What is
desirable is by no means always essential: and I was referred to a number of D
examples of cases where there might have been, but apparently were not, representative actions.

In the *Cardiff* case (25), no solution by transferring those represented from one
side of the action to another was possible. The action was constituted as an
action by 13,000 tenants against the corporation, their landlord: 5,000 of those
had interests in conflict with the other 8,000. The transfer of the 5,000 from the E
plaintiffs' side to the corporation side was a question which neither arose nor could
very well arise: for the declaration and injunction sought against the corporation
were patently inappropriate remedies to seek against the 5,000 tenants. The case
was one where the issue lay between some of those linked together by a common
interest and an extraneous body, the corporation. In the case before me there is no
extraneous body as a party to the lis: the issue lies solely between persons linked F
by the common interest of membership.

From what I have said, it will be seen that the second motion fails. The first
prayer is to set the writ aside, and the second is to strike out the endorsement so
far as it relates to relief for parties other than the plaintiff. I dismiss both claims.

I turn, then, to the plaintiff's motion in the first action. If the second defendant
is not president of P.D.L.P., he lacks authority to take part as such in any dealing G
with the property of P.D.L.P. Whether or not he was elected depends on whether
the meeting of the general committee of P.D.L.P. on 6th April 1968 was still in
existence when his election took place. That in turn depends on whether the
plaintiff's purported adjournment of that meeting a short while earlier was valid;
and that in turn depends on a complex of issues of law and fact as to the powers
of adjournment of the chairman of a meeting, and whether in fact the plaintiff H
exercised any power of adjournment that he had. If the defendants succeed on
these issues, there still remains a claim by the plaintiff that subsequent action
taken by the N.E.C. has deprived the defendants of their authority. In order to
resolve these and other issues, I must summarise the facts.

The plaintiff has exhibited a 20-page document containing a notice of the
meeting of 6th April, together with the agenda and proposed resolution. In fact, I
it contains rather more than that. The date on the agenda is 29th March 1968,
two days after Mr. Donnelly's expulsion from the Labour Party; and at the head
of the agenda the defendant gave notice of the annual meeting of P.D.L.P. on
6th April. In addition to the agenda, the document contains the minutes of a
previous meeting of the general management committee of P.D.L.P., and a report
by the first defendant (who was of course the secretary and agent) dated 1st

(25) [1953] 2 All E.R. 1373; [1954] 1 Q.B. 210.

A April. In this he strongly supported Mr. Donnelly and urged temporary disaffiliation from the Labour Party.

> " *Why* [he said] *cannot we as a Constituency Labour Party disaffiliate from the Party nationally temporarily until such time that matters can be put right again,* which could well be by the time the next election takes place. It is nothing new for a member to be expelled and eventually end up as a
B Cabinet Minister."

His view was that to face an election in Pembrokeshire without Mr. Donnelly " would be disastrous—like giving the seat to the Tories on a silver plate ". His loyalties, he said, were " with the basic aims of socialism "; and, he added, " today the Labour Party is its own worst enemy ". He referred to Mr. Donnelly's
C memorandum to the N.E.C. dated 20th March, which appeared as the next three pages in the document, and said that his criticisms " are about the party's policies of today and not against the Labour Party's principles."

Mr. Donnelly's memorandum asserted that his criticisms " have been of the Prime Minister and government, never of the basic aims of the party ". He set out four promises in the 1964 Labour manifesto and said that " not one of these
D 1964 promises has been kept. The aggregate is a deplorable national story. It is a disgrace to the Labour party ". He ended by saying:

> " I am not prepared to re-apply for the Labour whip so long as the present Prime Minister is leader of the party and his policy prevails. I have not resigned the whip in protest against the party, but in protest against the leadership."

E The document containing the agenda for the meeting then set out certain financial statements and nominations for offices and committees, and ended with nine resolutions to be submitted to the meeting. Four of these were direct resolutions in support of Mr. Donnelly, submitted by three local labour parties and a trade union branch, while two trade union branches submitted resolutions which, by proposing to find a suitable candidate for the next election, seem to have been
F anti-Donnelly.

I have referred to this document at some length for two reasons. First, nobody who read the document could be in any doubt that fundamental cleavages of opinion on important issues would be canvassed at the meeting. Second, the document illustrates the view that counsel for the defendants so forcefully urged on me for the disaffiliates, namely, that whatever anyone else may think, they
G regard themselves as being faithful to Labour policy: it is the others, and not least the government in general and the Prime Minister in particular, who have, they say, departed from the pure light of true Labour principles. In the eyes of the disaffiliates, they are the faithful; it is the affiliates who are the deviants. Nothing in this case requires me to resolve this issue, and I say no more about it. I mention it only to make intelligible some of the things said and done, and also, as any
H lawyer would expect, because I was referred more than once to the great " *Wee Free* " case (*General Assembly of Free Church of Scotland* v. *Lord Overtoun* (26)), which can be said to provide something of an ecclesiastical analogue on this point. I hasten to add that any analogy must be contained within due limits: for the practical result of the " *Wee Free* " case was promptly reversed by statute (the Churches (Scotland) Act 1905), whereas I intend no prophecies about this
I case.

Nobody has suggested that the meeting was not duly convened, or that there were material defects in the agenda: and I can come forward to Saturday, 6th April. From this point onwards there is much conflicting evidence. At about 1.30 or 1.45 p.m. certain officers of P.D.L.P. arrived in order to meet two officials of the Labour Party, Mr. Underhill (assistant national agent of the Labour Party) and Mr. Jones, who were going to present themselves at the annual meeting.

---

(26) [1904] A.C. 515.

It is not clear whether the two officials had wanted to meet the officers or merely A
the plaintiff. The standing orders of P.D.L.P. provide by standing order 1 (a) (ii)
for the election of a standing orders committee of six members, without particu-
larising the functions of the committee: but the committee seems to be treated
as having duties to perform in relation (inter alia) to the conduct of meetings.
Standing order 5 (a) provides that the business transacted at the annual meeting
is to—   B

  " consist of the following items in order: (i) President's welcome to
  delegates and apologies for absence. (ii) Report of Standing Orders Committee."

There then follow other items, including the election of officers and members of
committees, among them the standing orders committee which, this time, is to C
have seven members. The last item is " To consider resolutions ". In its essentials,
this order was followed in the agenda for this particular meeting. In neither is any
place given to " Any other business ". As matters stood, the report of the
standing orders committee would come immediately after the president's welcome
and apologies for absence, and the controversial pro-Donnelly and anti-Donnelly
resolutions would be left until the end. The first defendant's suggestion of D
disaffiliation does not appear anywhere among the list of resolutions for consideration by the meeting.

  A Mr. Moores took the chair at the standing orders committee meeting, with
the plaintiff present. The plaintiff said that he wanted the visiting officials to
address the meeting before starting with the agenda. After discussion, it was in
the end unanimously agreed that this address should be made after the report of E
the standing orders committee. The plaintiff also wanted a resolution to be put
to the meeting after the address, but either unanimously or by a majority it was
decided that this could not be done then, though it could be done after the
resolutions on the agenda had been considered. The discussion did not run
smoothly, and once or twice the plaintiff left the meeting and returned. He says
that he did not know of the decision of the standing orders committee when he F
went into the main meeting: but the inevitable comment is that if that was so,
he, as chairman, ought to have found out what that decision was before he
presided over the meeting to which it related.

  At the main meeting the plaintiff welcomed the delegates. He then explained
that Mr. Underhill was present, and called on him to address the meeting. Mr.
Underhill did so, reminding members of their obligations and referring to Mr. G
Donnelly's expulsion. He ended by suggesting that the meeting should pass a
resolution whereby P.D.L.P. undertook to continue to act in strict conformity
with its constitution and rules and the constitution of the Labour Party. A
delegate then attempted to move such a resolution, and at that point the meeting
became less than sedate. There had been some noise during Mr. Underhill's
address, and now there were many attempts to raise points of order, including H
attempts by Mr. Moores, the chairman of the standing orders committee. The
resolution was seconded, said the plaintiff, and " I tried to put this resolution to
the vote."

  Much has been said about the duties of a chairman of a meeting, a subject to
which I must return later. What the plaintiff did at this meeting was to insert
into the proceedings, as the second item, an item which did not appear on the I
agenda at all, namely, Mr. Underhill's address. He then accepted and tried to
put to the vote a resolution to the effect suggested by Mr. Underhill; and this in
effect was the third item in the proceedings. In taking these steps the plaintiff
was, in my judgment, acting in contravention of the standing orders of P.D.L.P.,
in contravention of the agenda for the meeting, and in contravention of the
decision of the standing orders committee. I have heard no suggestion that he
ever sought or obtained the sanction of the meeting to his actions. However

A worthy his motives, and however politically desirable it was, I can see no justification for what he did.

It is one of the main duties of the chairman of a meeting of a club or association to secure its orderly conduct according to its rules. He has wide powers, but he has also the duty of using those powers for proper and not improper purposes. Above all, his duty is to act not as a dictator but as a servant of the members of the body, according to law. On the uncontradicted evidence it seems clear to me that the plaintiff was guilty of a determined and substantial breach of his duty, and that the responsibility for much of the disturbance that took place must be laid to his charge. It is not without a touch of irony that those attending the meeting should have been required to listen to an address reminding them of the rules and obligations that bound them, and to consider a resolution to act in strict conformity with those rules, when the chairman himself was, by so doing, in open breach of the rules himself. Indeed, according to the plaintiff, Mr. Underhill " asked the meeting to declare that they still observed their own standing orders and this seemed to me to be a wholesome and unobjectionable thing to do ". In these circumstances, I am not in the least surprised that the plaintiff's actions caused disturbances. Quis custodiet ipsos custodes?

D Counsel for the plaintiff has vigorously contended that the plaintiff had an inherent right as chairman to put to the meeting a " loyalty resolution " (to use counsel's convenient and compendious term) at any stage he thought fit. Not surprisingly, no authority was adduced in support of this contention; and this judgment will not provide one. Depending on the circumstances, to put such a resolution may be regarded by some or all present as an insult, an incitement, a time-waster, an irritant, or many other things. It may be a nuisance, or worse; but in any case I think that those who attend a meeting are entitled (subject to the rules) to have the business taken in the order prescribed by the agenda, unless a majority at the meeting otherwise resolves. Despite the persuasions of counsel for the plaintiff I can see no basis of need or common sense, or, for that matter, law or equity, on which such a right could be implied: and I reject it.

F I do not propose to attempt any analysis of the disturbances at the meeting: the evidence is in a state of marked conflict. On any footing there was a good deal of noise. There was also some degree of minor violence. There was a delegate who was, perhaps, pulled back into his chair when he tried to speak. The plaintiff perhaps prodded Mr. Donnelly in the back with his gavel. Mr. Donnelly pushed the plaintiff, perhaps mightily so that he fell against the wall, perhaps merely firmly so that he sat down in his chair. Mrs. Donnelly pulled out a chair for Mr. Moores to stand on and address the meeting; but he fell off it. During the argument I ventured to describe it as a good robust Welsh political meeting; but out of these four adjectives it was to the word " political " that counsel for the plaintiff demurred. It was, he said, a domestic meeting; and I abstained from pursuing the point further. Unto each his own form of domesticity. At all events, there is evidence that the plaintiff uttered warnings (which some did not hear) that it would be impossible to continue the meeting: and when the disorder still continued he says that he " announced in a loud voice, ' I now adjourn this meeting sine die ' ", and then walked out.

This is perhaps the most controversial incident of all. It features in some 20 affidavits filed by the plaintiff, half of these sworn by those who were sitting at the back of the hall. The plaintiff's voice is variously described as being " loud, penetrating and clear ", " loud and booming ", " stentorian and loud ", " loud and firm ", " loud and strong " and " the voice of a good schoolmaster ". All save one of those seated at the back heard the words of adjournment. On the other hand, the defendants have filed some ten affidavits by those who were close to the plaintiff but say that they heard no such words. Any suspicion that the hall may have peculiar acoustic properties which make inaudible at the front what is loud and clear at the back cannot survive the evidence of

those of the plaintiff's witnesses who sat at the front and heard the words; A
and this includes a man of 73 who says that he is " a little hard of hearing ".
There is also evidence that some of those present heard Mr. Underhill say that the
plaintiff had adjourned the meeting, and there is other evidence that no such
statement was heard by those close to Mr. Underhill.

This issue of fact is accordingly one that it is impossible to resolve on motion:
and not surprisingly a number of submissions have been advanced by counsel B
for the defendants to support his contention that even if the words were uttered,
they were ineffective to adjourn the meeting. The point of this is that after the
plaintiff and a number of others had left the meeting, those who remained
continued with the agenda; and it is the decisions thus made which are in issue.

Although there can plainly be no final resolution of the question of fact on
this motion, I think it right to say that for the purposes of the motion the pro- C
bability seems to me to lie with the words of adjournment having been uttered
by the plaintiff. The positive evidence of those who say that they heard seems
to me to outweigh the negative evidence of those who say that they did not
hear, and therefore that the words were not uttered. There may, of course, be
positive evidence of a negative which is as cogent as any positive evidence of an
affirmative. But in a noisy meeting, with the attention of many of those present D
being given to what other people were doing and saying, it may well be that
even those close to the plaintiff may have failed to notice or remember the
few words of adjournment; they can have taken only a second or two to utter,
and they were spoken by a chairman who had for some while been calling in
vain for order.

On the footing that the plaintiff did purport to adjourn the meeting for E
disorder, I have to consider the question of law whether the chairman of a
meeting has an inherent power to adjourn it for disorder. Counsel for the plaintiff
contends that there is such a power, though he accepts that if it is improperly
exercised, the adjournment is ineffective. Counsel for the defendants primarily
contends that the chairman has no such inherent power. However, if that
submission is wrong, he has a battery of alternative submissions. First, the F
chairman cannot use this power if, by his own improper conduct of the meeting,
he has provoked the disorder. He may, however, restore his power if he first
purges his impropriety (in the present case by returning to the correct order of
business), and he may avail himself of any provision for the suspension of standing
orders, here by a two-thirds majority under standing order 22. Second, the
chairman cannot use his power to frustrate the will of the majority at the meeting. G
Third, the chairman cannot use his power without first trying to comply with
standing orders, in this case by securing or attempting to secure a vote on the
motion for adjournment under standing orders 11 or 19. Fourth, such a power
is exercisable only for the minimum period reasonably necessary for the restoration
of order, so as to enable the business of the meeting to be carried on: an adjournment sine die would not be a proper exercise of this power, and would be void. H
Those are the contentions.

The cases put before me on this branch of the case begin with *Stoughton* v.
Reynolds (27). They include *R.* v. *Gaborian* (28); *R.* v. *Archdeacon of Chester* (29);
R. v. *D'Oyly, R.* v. *Hedger* (30); *Wandsworth & Putney Gas-Light and Coke Co.*
v. *Wright* (31); *MacDougall* v. *Gardiner* (32); *Shaw* v. *Thompson* (33); *Re
Indian Zoedone Co.* (34); *Henderson* v. *Bank of Australasia* (35); *National Dwellings* I
Society v. *Sykes* (36); *Salisbury Gold Mining Co., Ltd.* v. *Hathorn* (37); *Wall* v.
London & Northern Assets Corpn. (38); *Catesby* v. *Burnett* (39); *Second*

---

(27) (1736), 2 Stra. 1045; more fully reported Fortes. Rep. 168.
(28) (1809), 11 East 77.   (29) (1834), 1 Ad. & El. 342.
(30) (1840), 12 Ad. & El. 139.   (31) (1870), 22 L.T. 404.
(32) (1875), 1 Ch.D. 13.   (33) (1876), 3 Ch.D. 233.
(34) (1884), 26 Ch.D. 70.   (35) (1890), 45 Ch.D. 330.
(36) [1894] 3 Ch. 159.   (37) [1897] A.C. 268.
(38) [1898] 2 Ch. 469.   (39) [1916] 2 Ch. 325.

A   *Consolidated Trust, Ltd.* v. *Ceylon Amalgamated Tea & Rubber Estates, Ltd.* (40); and *Ridge* v. *Baldwin* (41). I was also referred to certain textbooks. Neither individually nor collectively are the cases decisive of the points before me. The power of a meeting to adjourn by passing a resolution to that effect is not in issue. The existence of such a power neither supports nor precludes the existence of a further power in the chairman. Nor, I think, does the denial of any power for the

B   chairman to disrupt a meeting while it is in orderly progress (as in *Stoughton* v. *Reynolds* (42)) preclude the existence of a power for the chairman to adjourn for disorder.

Counsel for the plaintiff placed much weight on *R.* v. *D'Oyly* (43), where LORD DENMAN, C.J., in considering the power of a rector to adjourn a parish meeting, said:

C   " Setting aside the inconvenience that might arise if a majority of the parishioners could determine the point of adjournment, we think that the person who presides at the meeting is the proper individual to decide this. It is on him that it devolves, both to preserve order in the meeting, and to regulate the proceedings so as to give all persons entitled a reasonable opportunity of voting. He is to do the acts necessary for those purposes

D   on his own responsibility, and subject to the being called upon to answer for his conduct if he has done anything improperly."

However, as counsel for the defendants pointed out, that was a case not of adjournment for disorder, but an adjournment for the purpose of taking a poll; and LORD DENMAN's words must be read in that context.

E   *National Dwellings Society* v. *Sykes* (44), is valuable in that it contains a concise summary by CHITTY, J. He said:

       " Unquestionably it is the duty of the chairman, and his function, to preserve order, and to take care that the proceedings are conducted in a proper manner, and that the sense of the meeting is properly ascertained with regard to any question which is properly before the meeting. But, in

F   my opinion, the power which has been contended for is not within the scope of the authority of the chairman—namely, to stop the meeting at his own will and pleasure."

But there again the question was not one of a disorderly meeting.

There are, however, two cases of disorderly meetings that I should refer to: both are disappointing. One is *Shaw* v. *Thompson* (45), where it is said that

G   " a great disturbance and uproar arose " at a parish meeting when the chairman had announced the arrangements for taking a poll. A parishioner came forward to move an amendment, but " the chairman, without hearing him, rose and quitted the chair, declaring the meeting to be at an end ". However, in considering this event SIR JAMES BACON, V.-C. referred (46) to the chairman's evidence that he rose from the chair because he thought the parishioner "was out of order ";

H   not, it will be observed, because of the disorder in the meeting. SIR JAMES BACON, V.-C., then said:

       " What right had the chairman, by leaving the chair, to put an end to a meeting duly convened? Leaving the chair did not put an end to the meeting. It is said that there was a vote of thanks then moved and seconded, but

I   whether anybody, in the uproar that took place, heard the motion made and seconded, is a matter which is left in considerable doubt. The minute announces that ' a vote of thanks having been passed to Mr. Culver for

(40) [1943] 2 All E.R. 567.
(41) [1963] 2 All E.R. 66; [1964] A.C. 40.
(42) (1736), 2 Stra. 1045; more fully reported Fortes. Rep. 168.
(43) (1840), 12 Ad. & El. at p. 159.
(44) [1894] 3 Ch. at p. 162.
(45) (1876), 3 Ch.D. at p. 236.
(46) (1876), 3 Ch.D. at p. 249.

his services in the chair, the meeting adjourned '. How could the meeting   **A**
adjourn except upon a resolution? Who moved that the meeting should
be adjourned? The meeting did not adjourn, and the entry in the minute
book is wholly erroneous."

Various interpretations can be put on that case, but what does seem plain is
that SIR JAMES BACON, V.-C., is not deciding anything about a chairman's
power to adjourn for disorder.   **B**

The other case is one that I mentioned to counsel, *R.* v. *Churchwardens of
St. Mary, Lambeth* (47). There, the rector was presiding over a meeting to elect
churchwardens. On his own authority and without notice, he adjourned the
meeting from the schoolhouse to the church so that a poll could be held on the
same day; and there was evidence that the poll could not have been " properly,
if at all, taken in the schoolhouse, from the nature of the place, and the numbers   **C**
and tumultuous state of the meeting ". After the churchwardens had been
elected, a mandamus to elect churchwardens was sought on the ground that the
election held after the adjournment was invalid: and this was opposed " on
other grounds, independent of the discretionary power of the chairman to
adjourn ". *Stoughton* v. *Reynolds* (48) was duly cited, but the Court of King's
Bench, consisting of LORD TENTERDEN, C.J., and LITTLEDALE, PARKE and   **D**
TAUNTON, JJ., refused to grant mandamus. Unfortunately they seem to have
given no reasons, and in any case the report is no more than a note to *R.* v.
Archdeacon of Chester (49), in which the court adverted to it during argument.
So far as it goes, the case is not inconsistent with a chairman having an inherent
power to adjourn a meeting for disorder: but counsel attached little importance
to the case, and I think that in this they are right. I may add that I do not think   **E**
that there is any importance in the fact that many of the cases are decisions
on parish meetings, whereas I am concerned with a meeting of a different type;
certainly counsel took no such point. If today much of the excitement to be found
in the last century at parish meetings has now transferred itself to political
meetings (using " political " in the widest sense), I see no reason why the law
governing each type of meeting should not in its essentials be the same; a   **F**
meeting is a meeting.

Although the *Lambeth* case (47) is of no great assistance in this case, it did, by
devious means, ultimately lead me to what I think is a useful passage in a book
published in 1840, A PRACTICAL ARRANGEMENT OF ECCLESIASTICAL LAW, by F. N.
ROGERS, Q.C. In discussing vestry meetings at p. 874, the author considers
Stoughton v. *Reynolds* (48), and then says that this decision—   **G**

    " by no means interferes with the right which every chairman has to
    make a bona fide adjournment, whilst a poll or other business is proceeding,
    if circumstances of violent interruption make it unsafe, or seriously difficult
    for the voters to tender their votes; nor of adjourning the place of polling,
    if the ordinary place used for that purpose be insufficient, or greatly incon-
    venient. In most of such cases, the question will turn upon the intention and   **H**
    effect of the adjournment, if the intention and effect were to interrupt and
    procrastinate the business, such an adjournment would be illegal; if, on
    the contrary, the intention and effect were to forward or facilitate it, and no
    injurious effect were produced, such an adjournment would, it is conceived,
    be generally supported."

This seems to me sound sense. It does not appear to be inconsistent with any   **I**
of the authorities, and in its essentials I adopt it for the purposes of this judgment.
I do not think it can be right to say that the chairman of a meeting has no inherent
power to adjourn the meeting for disorder. It seems generally accepted that
one of his functions is to preserve order: if despite his efforts serious disorder

(47) (1832), 1 Ad. & El. 346, n.
(48) (1736), 2 Stra. 1045.
(49) (1834), 1 Ad. & El. 342.

A persists, and he is denied any power of adjournment, what is he to do? The disorder will almost by necessity make it impossible for the meeting to pass a resolution for adjournment. One must remember that serious disorder may put in a dilemma many of those who are peacefully attending the meeting. If they retire from it, they may afterwards find that the disorder soon subsided, and that the meeting then transacted its business without their voice and vote,

B and in a sense contrary to their wishes. If they remain, their personal safety may be in peril. The frail and timorous are as much entitled as the robust and bold to a meeting to which they can give their attention, and at which they may make their voices heard without fear of violence; and they need it more.

The first duty of the chairman of a meeting is to keep order if he can. If there is disorder, his duty, I think, is to make earnest and sustained efforts to restore

C order, and for this purpose to summon to his aid any officers or others whose assistance is available. If all his efforts are in vain, he should endeavour to put into operation whatever provisions for adjournment there are in the rules, as by obtaining a resolution to adjourn. If this proves impossible, he should exercise his inherent power to adjourn the meeting for a short while, such as 15 minutes, taking due steps to ensure so far as possible that all present know of this adjourn-

D ment. If instead of mere disorder there is violence, I think that he should take similar steps, save that the greater the violence the less prolonged should be his efforts to restore order before adjourning. In my judgment, he has not merely a power but a duty to adjourn in this way, in the interests of those who fear for their safety. I am not suggesting that there is a power and a duty to adjourn if the violence consists of no more than a few technical assaults and batteries. Mere

E pushing and jostling is one thing; it is another when people are put in fear, where there is heavy punching, or the knives are out, so that blood may flow, and there are prospects, or more, of grievous bodily harm. In the latter case, the sooner the chairman adjourns the meeting the better. At meetings, as elsewhere, the Queen's Peace must be kept.

If, then, the chairman has this inherent power and duty, what limitations, if

F any, are there on its exercise? First, I think that the power and duty must be exercised bona fide for the purpose of forwarding and facilitating the meeting, and not for the purpose of interruption or procrastination. Second, I think that the adjournment must be for no longer than the necessities appear to dictate. If the adjournment is merely for such period as the chairman considers to be reasonably necessary for the restoration of order, it would be within his power

G and his duty; a longer adjournment would not. One must remember that to attend a meeting may for some mean travelling far and giving up much leisure. An adjournment to another day when a mere 15 minutes might suffice to restore order may well impose an unjustifiable burden on many; for they must either once more travel far and give up their leisure, or else remain away and lose their chance to speak and vote at the meeting.

H As I have already mentioned, counsel for the defendants has contended that if the chairman's own improper conduct of the meeting has provoked the disorder, he loses his inherent power of adjournment and can recover it only by returning to the paths of propriety. I very much doubt this. The mischief to the innocent members of the meeting is as great whether it is the chairman or anyone else who provoked the disorder: unless the adjournment is valid their departure

I may disfranchise them for that meeting. Disorder is disorder, and if the adjournment is made bona fide for the purpose of restoring order and for a reasonable period, I think there would be less injustice in holding that the adjournment is valid than in making its validity depend on the outcome of the often difficult question whether the disorder was due to the chairman's misconduct. Causation is seldom pure.

I am conscious that for much of what I have said there is little or no authority. Furthermore, not all of what I have said arises for decision in this case, at any rate directly. But the matter has been much debated before me, and it has

seemed better to attempt a reasonably comprehensive and intelligible statement A
of this corner of a chairman's powers and duty than to confine myself to those
segments of it which directly arise for decision. On the other hand, let me add
that I have not attempted to be exhaustive. In particular, there may well be
limitations on the chairman's inherent power of adjournment other than those that
I have mentioned. I should also add that I do not think that in this case the
chairman's inherent power of adjournment for disorder is affected by the standing B
orders of P.D.L.P. Standing order 11 (c) provides for the adjournment to be
moved without notice, and standing order 19 provides for such a motion to be
put to the vote without discussion. But if there is serious disorder it is improbable
that it would be practicable to follow this procedure: and I cannot perceive
any intention to oust or curtail the chairman's inherent power of adjournment
for disorder.   C
    I turn, then, to the adjournment in the present case. In my judgment the
grounds for the adjournment fell far short of what the law required. Even if
one accepts to the full the most pungent portions of the evidence, I do not
think that this was a meeting where people were put in fear. Certainly there
was noise, disorder, and, in a few cases, bodily contact; but whatever affronts
to dignity there may have been, there was nothing that could really be called D
violence. The plaintiff made no attempt to apply the provisions of the standing
orders relating to adjournment. There is nothing to suggest that he attempted
to restore order by any means other than calling out to the meeting. He purported to adjourn the meeting not for a reasonable period so that order might
be restored, but sine die; and he then left the place of meeting.
    Now the plaintiff did not, of course, have the advantage of hearing in peace, E
and at length, either the arguments on his powers that have been addressed to
me, or this judgment. He was subject to all the disadvantages of having to decide
at short notice what to do when presiding over a disorderly meeting. In other
spheres, due credit is given to a man who is put into a dilemma and has to make
a decision in what is called " the agony of the moment ". Here I think it right
to make full allowance for that, subject to one point. I have already rejected F
counsel for the defendant's contention that a chairman's improper conduct of
a meeting deprives him of his inherent power of adjournment. But where there
is such impropriety, I think that it may have a different effect. For if in any
real degree that impropriety has caused or contributed to the disorder of the
meeting, and has thus played a real part in creating the dilemma, I do not
think that it then lies in the mouth of the chairman to excuse his conduct by G
relying on that dilemma. A self-imposed dilemma offers but a slender claim to
justification. In this case the fact remains that the chairman did go wrong,
and that those who complain of his conduct are entitled to do so. Whether
or not his sole motive for adjournment was the disorder is a matter which must
be left until the trial. He will then, as now, start with the disadvantage of
being a chairman who in my judgment had been conducting the meeting in dis- H
regard of the standing orders, the agenda, and the resolution of the standing
orders committee. On this motion I need do no more than say that in my judgment, on the undisputed evidence, the purported adjournment was bad, and
failed to produce any effective adjournment of the meeting. Those who departed
from the meeting with the plaintiff, said to be some 20 in number, may wish to
complain that they thereby lost their opportunity of opposing what happened I
later in the meeting; if so, they must lay their complaints to the charge of the
plaintiff.
    On the footing that there was no valid adjournment, it follows that, as the
cases establish (see, for example, *National Dwellings Society* v. *Sykes* (50)) and as
counsel for the plaintiff concedes, the meeting remained in being and competent
to transact business. The elections conducted after the departure of the plaintiff

(50) [1894] 3 Ch. 159.

A were accordingly valid; for no other contention that they were bad has been
put forward. It has not been suggested that the minutes of the meeting prepared
by the first defendant do not correctly record what happened at the meeting
after the plaintiff's departure. Accordingly, as a result of the meeting the second
defendant was elected president of P.D.L.P. in place of the plaintiff, and the
third defendant was elected treasurer. The first defendant remained the secretary;
B he was not up for election.

   In addition to the election of officers and delegates, the business transacted
at the meeting after the plaintiff had departed included a resolution to disaffiliate
from the Labour Party; and I must now consider the validity of this. In order
to do so, it is necessary to resolve what rules governed P.D.L.P.: and on this point
there has been strenuous debate over the rules known as " set B ". For the
C affiliates, counsel for the plaintiff has contended that these apply and govern
P.D.L.P., whereas counsel for the defendants has argued the contrary. I must
therefore first consider set B.

   The Labour Party publishes a booklet (which I shall call " the White Booklet ")
which contains a memorandum, and two sets of model rules, set B and set C.
The copies of the White Booklet before me appear to have been printed in
D January 1968, but no point has been taken on that, and probably the booklet
is merely a reprint of rules that have been in existence for some while. Set B is
stated to be " For Constituency Labour Parties in County Constituencies ",
whereas set C is " For Local Labour Parties in County Constituencies ". Clause
3 (2) of the Labour Party constitution (the format of which leads me to call it
" the Yellow Booklet ") provides that " Each Constituency Labour Party . . .
E must . . . adopt the Rules laid down by the Party Conference ": and the
memorandum in the White Booklet states (inter alia) that sets B and C are the
appropriate rules for this purpose. The question is whether set B was ever
adopted by P.D.L.P.

   The plaintiff says that they were. He exhibits a sheet of paper setting out
certain adjustments and insertions which he says were made to set B, inserting
F the name " Pembrokeshire " in the blanks and so on. He also exhibits a five-
page document setting out the standing orders of P.D.L.P., to which I have
already referred. These state in order 1 (a) (i) that the general management
committee is at its annual meeting to elect " An Executive Committee in accordance with Constitution and Rules Set B ": and cl. 9 (3) of set B, when read with
the adjustments and insertions that I have just mentioned, duly provides for
G the constitution of an executive committee. The first defendant, who has been
secretary of P.D.L.P. since 1955, points out that it is not said when set B was
adopted, and that the minutes contain no record of the adoption of set B, although
he has not been able to trace any minute books prior to 1955. The plaintiff,
who has been a member of P.D.L.P. for 24 years, replies by saying that he has
been present at meetings of P.D.L.P. when the adoption of set B was discussed,
H and that he has always believed and understood that set B was duly adopted.
Mr. Lewis, on the other hand, who was a member of the Executive Committee of
P.D.L.P. in 1947, and attended regularly, had no recollection of any discussion
or adoption of set B. The plaintiff and Mr. Underhill also exhibit correspondence
in 1947 and 1954 which refers to the rules and constitution of P.D.L.P., and
the approval of the rules by the N.E.C. on 3rd December 1947. The 1947 corres-
I pondence was between the Welsh regional office of the Labour Party and the
national agent's department, while in the 1954 correspondence the then secretary
of P.D.L.P. joined in as well.

   The correspondence certainly suggests that the rules were set B, as amended;
and Mr. Prothero, who was Welsh regional officer in 1947 and 1954, confirms this.
In addition, counsel for the plaintiff relies strongly on the presumption of regularity, or omnia praesumuntur rite esse acta, to carry him over the undoubted
absence of any cogent direct evidence of the adoption of the rules by P.D.L.P.:
and for this he cited a number of authorities where the facts were rather different.

He further contends that, irrespective of any evidence of the formal adoption of A set B, those who join a club or association bind themselves by whatever the rules are, even if they have become established merely by usage among the members.

To these contentions, counsel for the defendants replied by emphasising that the issue was whether or not the members of P.D.L.P. were bound to each other by a contract which incorporated set B. He said that there was no evidence of B the adoption of set B, or of the members knowing of set B or agreeing to accept set B. Furthermore, he said, the presumption of regularity cannot apply to establish the terms of a contract. In any case, he added, *Morris* v. *Kanssen* (51) established that the maxim omnia praesumuntur rite esse acta cannot apply in favour of someone who, like the plaintiff, is a member of P.D.L.P., for it can apply only in favour of outsiders, or non-members.   C

This last point was vigorously debated: and I will deal with it first. The point came up in *Morris* v. *Kanssen* (51) as something of an afterthought, and was argued only by the indulgence of the House of Lords: for the appellant had not raised the point in his formal case. What was in issue was the validity of an allotment of shares made at a meeting of the directors of a company at which one director, M., had been appointed immediately before the allotment. D In fact, both the appointment and the allotment were ineffective because the other two persons present, although formerly directors of the company, had by virtue of the articles of the company ceased to be directors some while before the meeting; for the company had held no general meeting for a year. In those circumstances, M. claimed that despite the defects in the allotment produced by the operation of the articles, the rule in *Royal British Bank* v. *Turquand* (52) E made good his title to the shares allotted: acting in good faith, he was not concerned to inquire into the regularity of acts of internal management.

This contention failed. Only LORD SIMONDS delivered a reasoned speech: the other members of the House merely concurred. LORD SIMONDS discussed the rule in *Turquand's* case (52), and in doing this he referred (53) to the maxim omnia praesumuntur as " one of the fundamental maxims of the law ". He gave F some illustrations of it, and then uttered a sentence on which counsel for the defendants placed great emphasis (53):

" It is a rule designed for the protection of those who are entitled to assume, just because they cannot know, that the person with whom they deal has the authority which he claims."

This, said counsel for the defendants, referred to the maxim omnia praesumuntur, G and not the rule in *Turquand's* case (52). Therefore in the present case the plaintiff could not rely on the maxim: for he is a member of P.D.L.P., and so cannot claim to be one of those " who are entitled to assume, just because they cannot know, " whether set B was ever formally adopted.

As a mere matter of grammar, it certainly seems that LORD SIMONDS was speaking (53) of the maxim rather than the rule. He set out the maxim, said H that it had many applications, and gave illustrations. He then said (53) " But the maxim has its proper limits ": and still he was speaking of the maxim. He then gave two illustrations, and said (53) " Nor is this the only limit to its application ": and grammatically the word " its " must refer back to the maxim. He then proceeded with the sentence to which counsel for the defendants has attached so much importance, beginning " It is a rule . . .": and still the I " It " grammatically refers back to the maxim. Accordingly, if grammar were the only criterion, there would here be a declaration by a unanimous House of Lords that the maxim " omnia praesumuntur rite esse acta " is confined in its operation to protecting those who are entitled to assume, because they cannot

---

(51) [1946] 1 All E.R. 586; [1946] A.C. 459.
(52) (1856), 6 E. & B. 327; [1843-60] All E.R. Rep. 435.
(53) [1946] 1 All E.R. at p. 592; [1946] A.C. at p. 475.

A know, that the person they deal with has the authority which he claims. On this foundation counsel for the defendants has built his elaborate claim that the maxim applies only for the protection of outsiders, or non-members of P.D.L.P., and so cannot avail a member.

In ascertaining what a case decided, grammar is, no doubt, a good servant. But it may be a bad master; and if it is treated as the sole master, it may become

B a tyrant. As LORD REID once said of a famous passage in a famous judgment of WILLES, J. (54):

> " In dealing with a situation different from anything contemplated in that judgment, I do not think that it is very helpful to analyse that passage as if it were a section in an Act of Parliament "

C (*London Graving Dock Co., Ltd.* v. *Horton* (55)); and the other members of their Lordships' House (56) evidently shared that view. I remember, too, the classic warning of LEARNED HAND, J., in *Cabell* v. *Markham* (57): one ought " not to make a fortress out of the dictionary ", or, I may add, out of a textbook of grammar either. In applying even the most authoritative language in a decided case, it is in my judgment essential to bring to the task a lively sense of the

D subject-matter arising for decision. The facts of *Morris* v. *Kanssen* (58) were far removed from those in this case. There, the question was whether a person who was not a director of a company but was acting as such could pray in aid the rule in *Turquand's* case (59) so as to validate an allotment of shares to himself which he and two others of like status had made. No authority for the invocation of that rule by actual or de facto directors could be produced, and their Lordships

E refused to hold that an invalid allotment of a company's shares could be validated by the application of the rule. What was argued (60) and what was decided was the scope of that rule. In the process of decision, the maxim was considered as part of the process. So far as the maxim relates to companies, it deals with the acts which bind or do not bind the company.

The case I am concerned with, on the other hand, concerns not a company

F but an unincorporated club or association. No question arises whether or not any artificial or juristic person is bound, for there is no such person. Instead, the question is that of the terms of the rules of that association, as constituting the contract which bind the members to each other. There is no direct evidence that any meeting of P.D.L.P. ever adopted set B, but on the other hand there is some evidence that for many years at least some of the officers have treated

G set B as being the rules of P.D.L.P. Where those concerned have acted for many years on the assumption of a particular state of affairs, the court is slow to hold that a different state of affairs exists: see, for example, *Sneyd* v. *Stewart* (61), per CUSACK SMITH, M.R., in a case concerning the size of various beneficiaries' shares in a fund. Further, in the standing orders of P.D.L.P. (which nobody challenges) there are significant words in cl. 1 (a) (i), providing for the election of " An Executive Committee in accordance with Constitution

H and Rules Set B ".

On the facts of this case, therefore, I have to consider whether in those circumstances there is anything in *Morris* v. *Kanssen* (58) which prevents me from applying the maxim omnia praesumuntur rite esse acta and holding that set B was, at some time unknown, adopted by P.D.L.P. as the rules of the party.

I I do not think that there is. The House of Lords was dealing with an entirely

---

(54) In *Indermaur* v. *Dames* (1886), L.R. 1 C.P. 274 at p. 288; [1861-73] All E.R. Rep. 15 at p. 21.
 (55) [1951] 2 All E.R. 1 at p. 25; [1951] A.C. 737 at p. 779.
 (56) [1951] 2 All E.R. at pp. 4, 8, 14; [1951] A.C. at pp. 745, 751, 761.
 (57) (1945), 148 F.(2d) 737 at p. 739.
 (58) [1946] 1 All E.R. 586; [1946] A.C. 459.
 (59) (1856), 6 E. & B. 327; [1843-60] All E.R. Rep. 435.
 (60) [1946] A.C. at p. 466.
 (61) (1858), 10 Ir. Jur. 105 at p. 107.

different situation, and I cannot believe that, in referring to the maxim when   A
considering the ambit of the rule in *Turquand's* case (62) (which doubtless is or
contains one manifestation of the operation of the maxim), there was any
intention to limit the operation of the maxim in other spheres. As is shown by
even a cursory examination of Broom's Legal Maxims (10th Edn., 1939) pp. 640-
648, the maxim operates in a wide diversity of circumstances; and if it were
confined in its operation, as counsel for the defendants contends, to cases where   B
it is invoked by outsiders, I can foresee much difficulty in applying some of the
long-established authorities. Lastly, of course, this is merely a motion : the final
elucidation of this point must await the trial, and such further evidence as may
be adduced.

That is not all. For I do not think that I am required to apply the presumption
of regularity in a vacuum, ignoring the evidence which supports the view that   C
set B was adopted. Certainly I do not think it is necessary to bring home to
every member when he joins exactly what the rules of the association are. I do
not see why someone who joins a club should not do so on the basis that he will
be bound by the rules of the club, whatever they may be : see, for example,
Raggett v. *Musgrave* (63), where the rules, though accessible, were neither posted
up nor sent to members. *The Satanita* (64) does not seem to me to bear on the   D
point, as it concerned not membership of a club but the terms of a contract
between those who entered for a race. In the case of a club, if nobody can
produce any evidence of a formal resolution to adopt a particular set of rules,
but on enquiry the officers would produce that set as being the rules on which
it is habitual for the club to act, then I do not think the member would be free
to reject those rules merely because no resolution could be proved.   E

Accordingly, in my judgment I must deal with the motion on the footing
that P.D.L.P. has at all material times been governed by set B, subject to the
provisions of the document which sets out the minor adjustments and insertions
to be made, and subject also to the deletion of the office of financial secretary
from cl. 9 (2) which some correspondence of 1954 records. In addition, there
is no dispute that P.D.L.P. has at all material times been subject to the standing   F
orders which have been put in evidence.

On the footing that set B applies, counsel for the plaintiff says that the result
is to show that P.D.L.P. is a mere branch of the national Labour Party, and
that the members of it are bound by contract to be loyal to the Labour Party.
This he deduces from, in the main, cll. 4 (1), (2) (a), 6 (2), 7 (1), 8 (2) (d), and
(3), of set B. So far as the " mere branch " argument is concerned, I feel some   G
doubts. By cl. 2 (1) of the Labour Party constitution, there are two classes of
members, namely, affiliated members (or organisations: see cl. 3 (1)), and
individual members : and I do not consider that an organisation which affiliates
itself to the Labour Party thereby becomes a " mere branch " of that party,
whatever that may mean, any more than an individual member does. Such an
organisation remains, I think, a separate entity, though bound by certain   H
obligations. On the other hand, the rules do seem to me to require acceptance
of the constitution, programme, principles and policy of the Labour Party,
both by P.D.L.P. and by its members; see cll. 4 (1) (a), (2) (a). On this foundation, counsel for the plaintiff has sought to erect a structure which would support
the plaintiff's act in inserting into the meeting Mr. Underhill's address and the
loyalty resolution. He fortified his position by reference to standing orders 6,   I
7 and 20. Standing order 6 provides that " Party business shall have precedence
on the Agenda ". Standing order 7 deals with notice of motions, and standing
order 20 provides that " The Chairman's Ruling to any point of order arising
from these standing orders or any point arising not provided for by these
Standing Orders shall be final," with a provision for a challenge and a vote.

(62) (1856), 6 E. & B. 327; [1843-60] All E.R. Rep. 435.
(63) (1827), 2 C. & P. 556.
(64) [1895] P. 248; *on appeal*, [1897] A.C. 59.

A   I do not think that these provisions, either individually or collectively, suffice to support the plaintiff's actions.

I can now turn to the question of disaffiliation. The motion before me does not in terms seek a decision on the validity of the resolution to disaffiliate; but I do not think I can avoid considering it, and it is at least relevant to the claim to an injunction against the disaffiliate defendants. The injunction cannot be

B granted on the basis that the defendants were not officers of P.D.L.P. after the first meeting; for they all were. But that does not dispose of the matter. Even if all were still officers of P.D.L.P., counsel for the plaintiff contends that they should all be enjoined in terms of the notice of motion because they have manifested an intention to deal with the property of P.D.L.P. otherwise than in accordance with its constitution and rules. In particular, there was the resolution

C to disaffiliate. This was moved by the third defendant and passed by 69 votes to one at the meeting after the plaintiff had left. The motion was that P.D.L.P. should " dis-affiliate from the National Labour Party in order that Mr. Desmond Donnelly could continue as a Labour Member for Pembrokeshire ". The validity of this resolution is impugned under two heads.

First, no notice of any intention to propose such a resolution appeared in the

D formal agenda for the meeting. True, in the first defendant's duplicated report for the meeting which accompanied the agenda he asked why P.D.L.P. could not disaffiliate temporarily: but nothing on this point appeared in the agenda proper. On this ground alone it seems to me clear that the resolution was invalid. The standing orders (which nobody challenges) require ten days written notice of motion " unless on matters of urgency accepted by the majority as such "

E (standing order 7): and the minutes record no such acceptance of urgency. In any case, standing order 7 continues by saying that:

> " where such urgency is known or anticipated before the meeting, notice in writing of the urgent business or motion shall be transmitted to the Secretary as early as may be practicable before the meeting ":

F and there is no suggestion that this was done. Further, a motion to disaffiliate is not amongst those motions for which, by standing order 11, no notice is required. Where a motion deals with such important and fundamental matters as this, it seems to me particularly important that there should be a full and substantial compliance with all the requirements as to notice and otherwise.

Second, quite apart from procedural defects (which might be cured if another

G meeting were held), there is the substantial question whether as matters stand P.D.L.P. is able to disaffiliate or sever itself from the Labour Party, whatever the procedure adopted. Counsel for the defendants very properly accepts that P.D.L.P. cannot do so in breach of its own rules, and so if, as I have held, P.D.L.P. is governed by set B, the question is whether set B (or any other relevant rules) prevents severance or disaffiliation. It seems to me clear that P.D.L.P.

H is bound to the Labour Party by set B and, through set B, by the constitution of the Labour Party. In counsel for the plaintiff's phrase, P.D.L.P. and the Labour Party are so clamped together by these provisions that they cannot be separated without first altering those provisions. Not surprisingly, set B, set C and the Labour Party constitution all dovetail in with each other.

In one sense counsel for the defendants was right when he said that there

I is nothing in set B to say that P.D.L.P. cannot disaffiliate from the Labour Party: there is indeed nothing which says this in terms. But it seems to me that when the provisions of set B are read as a whole, the inescapable conclusion is that while they stand unaltered P.D.L.P. cannot separate itself from the Labour Party: and I do not think it matters much whether the process is called disaffiliation or severance. In my view, it is unnecessary to refer in detail to the rules in set B which produce this result. It seems sufficient to say that, on making the assumption that P.D.L.P. has severed itself from the Labour Party, I find it impossible to read through the rules of set B and make them work sensibly. Thus if there were a severance, cl. 8 (as to affiliation fees payable to **A** the Labour Party) and cl. 13 (applying the general provisions of the constitution and standing orders of the Labour Party) would both require substantial revision. By cl. 4 the two classes of members of P.D.L.P., namely, affiliated organisations and individual members, would have to accept and conform or agree to conform to the constitution, programme, principles and policy of the Labour Party, while (on this hypothesis) P.D.L.P. would have separated itself from the **B** Labour Party. By cl. 6 (2), the rules of set B may, subject to important limitations, be altered, amended or deleted, but only with the approval in writing of the N.E.C.; and in such circumstances no such approval is likely to be given, even if it were to be sought. In any case, a proviso precludes any changes of the rules which " effect a change in the relationship of . . . Constituency Labour Parties with the Labour Party ": and although I agree that this does not eo **C** nomine preclude disaffiliation, I think it is plain that in substance and effect it does so.

If a severance between P.D.L.P. and the Labour Party cannot be effected without a change of rules (as I hold to be the case), and if no change of rules is permitted which will effect a change in the relationship of P.D.L.P. with the Labour Party, then I do not see how any severance can lawfully be made. I **D** need hardly say that I am not for one moment asserting that any members of P.D.L.P. are unable to form some new political organisation or group: what I do say is that the existing P.D.L.P., with its property, has not effectually been severed or disaffiliated from the Labour Party.

Counsel for the defendants pressed me with authorities such as *Finch* v. *Oake* (65) on the right of a member of a club or society to resign or retire at any **E** time, without any concurrence or acceptance by the club or society. I do not find the analogy persuasive. An individual who resigns severs the link between himself and his fellow members: he does not affect their rights in other ways. They remain bound inter se by the existing rules. The majority of a club which resolves on disaffiliation, however, would alter the rights not only of themselves but also of all other members, effecting a change of the rules which would continue **F** to bind all members. Such a change must, I think, be made in accordance with whatever procedure there is for changing the rules: and if none is applicable, the change cannot be made. Those who do not like the situation may, as individuals, resign: but I do not think they can collectively secure a disaffiliation except in accordance with the rules which bind them all.

The matter may be put in this way. If an individual resigns from a club, no **G** question arises of the validity of his own act quoad himself. He can make up his own mind, and act for himself. On the other hand, where the question is one of a club disaffiliating itself from some other organisation, there is a preliminary question to be resolved, namely, whether the act of disaffiliation was validly done according to the rules of the club and the general law so as to be the act of the members of the club as a body. The question " Has there been a valid **H** decision to resign or disaffiliate? " arises in the case of the club but not in the case of the individual. The analogy between the two categories thus breaks down. In the present case, the principal question is that of the effectiveness of the resolution to disaffiliate, and this is just the question which does not arise when an individual resigns from a club. Accordingly, I derive little help from the analogy. **I**

The position is thus that the three defendants were, immediately after the meeting, officers of P.D.L.P. who were wrongly asserting that P.D.L.P. had disaffiliated itself from the Labour Party. They also supported the candidature of Mr. Donnelly, who had been expelled from the Labour Party. Indeed, after the plaintiff had left the meeting, a resolution of support for Mr. Donnelly was passed unanimously. If, despite subsequent events, they are still in office,

---

(65) [1896] 1 Ch. 409.

A there is the question whether they should be enjoined from dealing with the property of P.D.L.P. There is no evidence before me of any improper use of the funds, nor of any threat to flout the law. There has been a strenuous disagreement whether or not there has been an effective disaffiliation; but there is nothing to suggest that the defendants are lawless men who will act in breach of the law once they know it. Accordingly, I do not think it would be right to

B grant an injunction in the terms of the notice of motion which would restrain the lawfully elected officers of P.D.L.P. from any dealing with the property entrusted to them when there is no subsisting threat that they will deal with it otherwise than lawfully. If there should hereafter be any such threat, then no doubt such an injunction may be sought anew: but I do not think that there is any sufficient reason for granting an injunction now.

C   When I put to counsel for the plaintiff the possibility of an injunction being granted in more limited terms, restraining not all dealings with the property but any dealings contrary to the rules of P.D.L.P., he said that the injunction must be all or nothing, and not merely an injunction against the unconstitutional use of the funds. In those circumstances, and as in any event I feel some doubt whether it would be right to grant a limited injunction, I do not think that I

D need consider the point further; and I am clear that the injunction sought by the notice of motion must be refused. I accordingly dismiss the first motion.

I now turn to action no. 2. As I have said, this action relates to the second meeting, and this was part of the process whereby the N.E.C. sought to re-organise P.D.L.P. The writ claims a declaration and two injunctions, which I do not think I need read. On the day the writ was issued, 12th June 1968, the

E plaintiffs gave notice of motion claiming two injunctions in the following terms:

" 1. An injunction to restrain the defendants and each of them in their capacities as officers of the unincorporated association which purports to call itself the Haverfordwest Local Labour Party being an association purported to have been constituted at a meeting convened and held by order of the National Executive of The Labour Party at The Gold Room, Market

F Hall, Haverfordwest, on Monday the 20th day of May, 1968, until judgment in this action or further order (whether by themselves their servants or agents or otherwise howsoever) from doing or purporting to do or being party to any of the following things namely collecting expending remitting transferring or otherwise dealing with any moneys or other property belonging to or held for the purpose of the Haverfordwest Local Labour Party as

G constituted prior to the said meeting. 2. An injunction to restrain the defendants and each of them until judgment in this action or further order from purporting to act as General Committee delegates on behalf of the Haverfordwest Local Labour Party as constituted prior to the 20th May 1968 at any meetings whatsoever whether at constituency level or otherwise."

The main issue is the efficacy of the steps taken by the N.E.C. to re-organise

H P.D.L.P.

The starting point, I think, is in the Labour Party constitution, as set out in the Yellow Booklet. By cl. 8 (2), it is provided that:

" The duties and powers of the National Executive Committee shall include the following:—. . . (b) To enforce the Constitution, Standing Orders, and Rules of the Party and to take any action it deems necessary

I for such purpose, whether by way of disaffiliation of an organisation or expulsion of an individual, or otherwise. Any such action shall be reported to the next Annual Conference of the Party."

By cl. 13 (1) of set B, " the general provisions of the Constitution and Standing Orders of the Labour Party shall apply to the organisation." On 24th April 1968, after the first meeting, the N.E.C. passed two resolutions. They read as follows:

" (i) That action be taken under Clause VIII Section 2 (b) of the Party

Constitution to suspend the activities of the Pembroke Constituency Labour
Party and that the officers should have no rights for the time being to handle
the funds of the Party; (ii) that the Pembroke Constituency Labour Party
be reorganised and that the National Agent be given authority to take such
steps as are necessary to complete the reorganisation."

What followed may be described in the language of Mr. Underhill, assistant
national agent of the Labour Party, in his affidavit sworn 9th July 1968. In
this, I think " prescribed " is a slip for " proscribed ", and " prescribed re-
organisation " should be " proscribed organisation ". He states that—

"In pursuance of these resolutions the National Agent for the Labour
Party resolved to convene a meeting of the Haverfordwest Local Labour
Party. However, before doing so, in accordance with the usual procedure
followed by the National Executive Committee of the Labour Party in the
case of the re-organisation of Constituency Parties, the National Agent first
sent a letter by registered post to the leading members of the dissident
faction who supported Mr. Donnelly informing them of the proposed re-
organisation and requesting from them an undertaking that they accepted
and would conform to the constitution programme principles and policy of
the Labour Party and that they did not belong to nor were actively
associated with any prescribed organisation and that they would co-operate
with the National Executive Committee in re-establishing the Constituency
Labour Party in accordance with the provisions of the Party Constitution
and Rules. A true copy of the letter sent to the First Plaintiff is now
produced and shown to me marked ' U.1 '. A letter in the same terms was
sent to each of the other leaders."

The letter exhibited in U.1. is addressed to the person concerned, and reads as
follows:

"I have been charged by the National Executive Committee with the
responsibility of re-organising the Pembrokeshire Constituency Labour
Party. Before making any recommendation to the National Executive
Committee about your continued membership of the Party, I shall be
grateful if you will let me have, in writing, an undertaking that you accept
and conform to, the Constitution, Programme, Principles and Policy of the
Labour Party that you do not belong to, or are actively associated with, any
prescribed organisation, and that you will co-operate with the National
Executive Committee in re-establishing the Constituency Labour Party in
accordance with the provisions of the Party Constitution and Rules. I am
enclosing a stamped addressed envelope for your reply."

It is then signed in the name of the " National Agent and Acting General
Secretary ".

Mr. Underhill, in his affidavit, continues as follows:

"Four persons to whom such a letter was sent namely, the first and
second plaintiffs, Mr. Fulton and Mr. H. McEntee did not reply to this
letter. Four others namely, Mr. T. R. Merriman, Mr. J. Phillips, Mr. A.
Glyn Rees and Miss M. L. Jones all replied in similar terms to the effect
that they were members of the Pembroke Labour Party, that they did not
understand the National Agent's reference to the prescribed re-organisation
and that they did not accept the right of the National Executive Committee
to interfere in any way. The National Agent replied to all these letters
(except for the letter of Mr. A. Glyn Rees) pointing out that every member
of the Labour Party was bound by its constitution and rules and that it was
not open to any member to break this contract and remain a member of the
Labour Party. The National Agent in the last paragraph of her letter asked
the persons to whom she was writing to give the undertaking which she had

A requested in her first letter. No replies were received from any of them. The National Agent did not reply to the letter of Mr. Glyn Rees because he is a defendant in a separate action . . .; [and then there is a reference to action no. 1.] Clause 4 (2) (a) of model rules Set C, the model constitution for Local Labour Parties in County Constituencies provides that each individual member must accept and conform to the constitution programme B principles and policy of the Labour Party and the Rules of the Local Parties. By reason of the refusal of the eight dissident members to give the undertakings requested by the National Agent, the National Agent considered that they were disqualified from membership of the Haverfordwest Local Labour Party."

C These last words point to the view that the failure to give the undertakings had in some way automatically terminated the membership of those concerned. On Day 2, counsel for the defendants told me that the dissidents were still members of the local Labour Party until they were expelled; but on Day 12 he expressly withdrew this statement, and replaced it with some far-reaching propositions. He said that the dissidents were now no longer members of the local Labour Party. They had, he said, destroyed their own membership either by D stating that they would not give the undertaking, or by failing to reply to the letter within a reasonable time. It might be, he added, that they ceased to be members when they inwardly harboured disloyal notions in their bosoms, a concept which seems to me to give rise to many interesting speculations. He also contended that by their acts they had resigned their membership: and this, he added significantly, " got round all problems relating to expulsion ". An alterna-E tive formulation of his point was that by their unconstitutional action and demonstration of disloyalty they had repudiated their membership. It might even be, he said, that a deliberate breach of any rule would bring about an ipso facto determination of their membership. Apart from some reference to authorities on the general law of contract as to discharge by repudiation, these submissions were put forward without the support of authority.

F Before I turn to consider these submissions, I must conclude the statement of facts. In his affidavit Mr. Underhill continues as follows:

" By letters dated the 11th May 1968 the National Agent gave notice of a meeting of the Haverfordwest Local Labour Party on the 20th May 1968 to all members whose names appeared on the list of members supplied by Mr. Ronald Clifford Davis the Secretary of the Haverfordwest Local Labour G Party and compiled by him from the records of the Party or of a list of members supplied by Mr. Glyn Rees Secretary/Agent of the Pembroke Constituency Labour Party except for the eight dissident members above referred to. The letters were in the terms of the letters exhibited to the affidavits herein of Alice Damant and Marjory Phillips.

H " The meeting was duly held on the 20th May 1968. All members attending the meeting were asked to complete a declaration which was attached to the notice convening the meeting. Everyone who attended the meeting did in fact produce and sign a declaration."

He then exhibits a copy of the minutes of the meeting which he prepared two days after the meeting from notes that he took. These minutes record the I proceedings, the persons elected to various offices and positions, and so on.

On behalf of the plaintiffs there is evidence that no notice of the meeting was received by the two plaintiffs, who at all events before these disputes arose were respectively the treasurer and a member of the local Labour Party. The annual general meeting of the local Labour Party (about which there is no dispute) had been held on 6th March 1968, less than three months before the meeting convened by the national agent on 20th May. At that meeting the first plaintiff had been elected treasurer (an office which he had held for some while), and the second plaintiff was elected a delegate.

Other members of the local Labour Party received a notice of the meeting. **A**
The notice began with the words:

"Arising from unconstitutional actions which have taken place in the
Pembrokeshire Constituency Labour Party, the National Executive
Committee of the Labour Party at its meeting on 24th April, 1968, decided
to suspend the activities of the Pembrokeshire Constituency Labour Party
and to re-organise it."   **B**

It then referred to the business to be done at the meeting, and gave the time and
the place of the meeting. It ended with the words, "If you are able to attend,
please complete the attached declaration and hand it to the steward at the
meeting." There is then a provision at the bottom of the speech for a tear-off
slip in which the person signing it declares that he accepts and conforms to   **C**
the constitution, programme, principles, and policy of the Labour Party, says
that he is not a member of various other organisations, and then says:

"I accept the decision of the National Executive Committee to re-
organise the Pembrokeshire Constituency Labour Party and I am willing to
co-operate by re-establishing the Local Labour Party."
                                                                                 D
Two of the members who received these notices say that they attempted to
attend the meeting but were refused admittance; but this is denied by the
defendants, and I shall not attempt to resolve this point on motion. What is
common ground is that notice of the meeting was not sent to all of those who,
immediately before the dispute, were members of the local Labour Party (as
mentioned in the affidavit, there were eight in this excepted category), and   **E**
that this was no accident, but was based on the contention that those concerned
had ceased to be members. The question is the effect of this.

There are, I may say, many other questions, some of which I must mention.
One is whether or not set C of the Labour Party's model rules, intended for
local Labour Parties in county constituencies, in fact apply to this local Labour
Party. Another is the application of the maxim delegatus non potest delegare   **F**
to the acts of the representative of the national agent. Another is whether a
local Labour Party is a separate body or is merely a group within the constituency
Labour Party. I do not think it right to examine in any detail more than is
necessary to decide what is, after all, merely a motion. Needless to say, these
other points remain open to either side in any further proceedings: and I return
to the main question.
                                                                                 G
Clause 8 (2) of the Labour Party constitution empowers the N.E.C. to do
certain acts. Let me assume that either because set C applies or otherwise, this
clause applies to the Haverfordwest Local Labour Party. What it does is to put
into the hands of the N.E.C. power for it to take "any action it deems necessary"
for the purpose of enforcing the constitution, standing orders and rules of the
Labour Party: and the "disaffiliation of an organisation" and "the expulsion **H**
of an individual" are expressly stated as being within the competence of the
N.E.C. The two resolutions of the N.E.C. on 24th April deal respectively with
suspension and re-organisation. The suspension resolution falls into two parts:
first, that action be taken under cl. 8 (2) "to suspend the activities of the
Pembroke Constituency Labour Party", and second "that the officers should
have no rights for the time being to handle the funds of the Party." The re-
organisation resolution also, in a sense, falls into two parts. First, there is the   **I**
resolution in principle that "the Pembroke Constituency Labour Party be
re-organised", and second there is the machinery, namely, that "the National
Agent be given authority to take such steps as are necessary to complete the
re-organisation."

Assuming that cl. 8 (2) and the resolution apply to the local Labour Party,
do they authorise what was done? Counsel for the plaintiffs answers "No",
for a variety of reasons: but in the forefront of his argument was the concept of

A natural justice. The rules of natural justice, he said, apply not only to expulsion
or dismissal, but also to suspension from office: and he cited a number of
authorities including *Fisher* v. *Keane* (66), *Labouchere* v. *Earl of Wharncliffe* (67),
Burn v. *National Amalgamated Labourers' Union of Great Britain and Ireland* (68)
and *Ridge* v. *Baldwin* (69).

   Burn's case (68) concerned a trade union. A rule required the executive
B committee of the union to " take every means to secure the observance of the
Union's rules," and authorised it to " suspend, expel and prosecute members "
and to " remove any incompetent or insubordinate officer." The committee
passed a resolution removing the plaintiff from any office held by him, and
preventing him from holding any delegation on behalf of the union for five years.
The plaintiff had been treasurer of his branch, and was chairman of it at the
C date of the resolution. The complaint against him related solely to his conduct
as treasurer; and the resolution was passed without hearing the plaintiff or
giving him any opportunity of explaining. P. O. LAWRENCE, J., construed the
rules strictly, and held that the language of the rule did not authorise the resolution that was passed. He went on to consider the position if he were wrong in
thus construing the rules, and said (70):

D   " I have no hesitation in holding that the power to suspend or expel a
      member for acting contrary to the rules is one of a quasi-judicial nature. "

   He accordingly held the resolution bad because the plaintiff had not been
given an opportunity of being heard in his defence. In relation to the rules of
natural justice, P. O. LAWRENCE, J., thus made no distinction between suspension
E and expulsion. I would respectfully concur: in essence suspension is merely
expulsion pro tanto. Each is penal, and each deprives the member concerned
of the enjoyment of his rights of membership or office. Accordingly, in my
judgment the rules of natural justice prima facie apply to any process of
suspension in the same way that they apply to expulsion.

   In the present case, there has not in terms been any process of expulsion.
F Instead, there has been the process which, on the argument of counsel for the
defendants, resulted in what for brevity may be described as an ipso facto
cessation of membership which, he contended, " got round all problems relating
to expulsion ". Viewed from the point of view of the members, however, the
practical result is indistinguishable from expulsion. Before, they were members;
after, they had been deprived of their membership against their will. The precise
G legal description of the process by which this occurred, whether by destruction
of their own membership, or acts constituting resignation, or repudiation of
membership, may well be a matter of indifference to them: they have been
unwillingly evicted.

   I cannot believe that the principles of natural justice can be ousted by the
simple process of describing expulsion by another name, or resting it on an
H alternative theoretical basis. Membership of a club or association is doubtless
founded on a basis of contract: but in many cases it is not merely a contract.
Membership often gives the member valuable proprietary and social rights, and
these, as well as the contract, would be terminated by expulsion. There is thus
involved in expulsion not merely the termination of the contract but also the
forfeiture of these other rights; and however ready the law may be to recognise
I the discharge of a contract by repudiation, it is far less ready to accept that
there has been a forfeiture of these other rights, whether the process is described
as " ipso facto determination " or otherwise.

   At one stage counsel for the plaintiffs submitted that if there were a doctrine

(66) (1878), 11 Ch.D. 353.
(67) (1879), 13 Ch.D. 346.
(68) [1920] 2 Ch. 364.
(69) [1963] 2 All E.R. 66; [1964] A.C. 40.
(70) [1920] 2 Ch. at p. 374.

of ipso facto determination, every member of the government and the Labour A
Party would have ceased to be members of that party, and all its assets would
pass to the Crown as bona vacantia. I am happy to think that it is unnecessary
for me to decide that; and I abstain from any comment on his interesting
submission. I may, however, observe that if there were a doctrine of ipso facto
determination the terms of the letter sent by the national agent to the dissident
members would be singularly misleading in its reference to "making any B
recommendation to the National Executive Committee about your continued
membership of the Party ": for that plainly suggests that the membership was
still continuing but that the N.E.C. would, at some unspecified stage, make a
decision about it.

However that may be, what matters here is, in my judgment, not the terminology but the substance and the reality: and looking at that it seems plain that C
the principles of natural justice prima facie apply. Counsel for the defendants
sought to avoid this conclusion by urging that what was done bore generally on
P.D.L.P. and was not directed against individuals. He further contended that
the principles of natural justice did not apply because the acts were administrative, because there had been no dismissal of any disaffiliates, and because these
principles did not apply to unpaid offices. D

I do not find any of these contentions persuasive. A " party " or a " club ",
if unincorporated, is not an entity separate from its members; and action
against the collective unit takes direct effect against the individuals comprising
that unit. This seems to me to be quite different from the indirect effect that a
proposal for a new road may have on the individual landowners, to which LORD
REID referred in *Ridge* v. *Baldwin* (71). On these submissions, as throughout, E
I look to the realities and not to the labels. Further, without authority to
support it, I can see no warrant for the view that the application of the principles
of natural justice to dismissal or suspension should be withheld from honorary
office and yet accorded to ordinary membership. My reference to the office of
Treasurer of an Inn of Court was later to move counsel for the defendants to
protest on the ground that the Inns were peculiar bodies. Indeed, they may be; F
but there are many other offices, both honourable and honorary, in other bodies,
and unless constrained by authority (and none has been cited) I refuse to hold
that the right to natural justice depends on the right to a few pieces of silver.

Accordingly, I must consider what are the principles of natural justice which
prima facie are applicable, and whether or not there is anything to oust their
application. In doing this, it is convenient to refer to a case concerning an G
avowed expulsion from a political party which came before me some three weeks
after the conclusion of the argument in this case, namely, *Fountaine* v.
Chesterton (72). It may be that there is other authority on the point that I have
in mind: but none was cited to me in that case or in this. As it seems unlikely
that the case will be fully reported it may be convenient if I set out as best I
can from my notes the passages in that judgment which I have in mind. H
In that case I said:

"The expression ' the principles of natural justice ' is, I think, now a
technical term. As MAUGHAM, J., pointed out in *Maclean* v. *Workers'*
Union (73), among most savages there is no such thing as justice in the
modern sense. In a state of nature, self-interest prevails over any type of
justice known to civilisation; the law of the jungle is power, not justice. I
Nor am I clear what the word ' natural ' adds to the word ' justice '. It
cannot be intended to indicate the antithesis of ' unnatural justice ', which
would indeed be an odd concept; I imagine that it is intended to suggest
justice that is simple or elementary, as distinct from justice that is complex,
sophisticated and technical.

(71) [1963] 2 All E.R. at p. 76; [1964] A.C. at p. 72.
(72) (1968), 112 Sol. Jo. 690; The Times, 20th August.
(73) [1929] 1 Ch. 602 at p. 624; [1929] All E.R. Rep. 468 at p. 472.

A   " The term ' natural justice ' has often been used by eminent judges, and
although MAUGHAM, J., said (74) that it ' is, of course, used only in a popular
sense ', I would prefer to regard it as having become something of a term
of art.   To extract the quintessence of the process of justice is, indeed,
notoriously difficult.   ' The ideas of natural justice ', said IREDELL, J.,
' are regulated by no fixed standard; the ablest and the purest men have
B   differed on the subject ': *Calder* v. *Bull* (75).   In *Ridge* v. *Baldwin* (76) LORD
HODSON referred to a ' certain vagueness ' in the term, but rejected the view
that because the requirements of natural justice depended on the circumstances of the case, this made natural justice so vague as to be inapplicable.
He added: ' No one, I think, disputes that three features of natural justice
stand out—(1) the right to be heard by an unbiassed tribunal; (2) the right
C   to have notice of charges of misconduct; (3) the right to be heard in answer
to those charges '.   I do not think that I shall go far wrong if I regard these
three features as constituting in all ordinary circumstances an irreducible
minimum of the requirements of natural justice.   I need only add that all
these requirements are essentially procedural in nature; I regard natural
justice as a distillate of due process of law."

D   I then turned to consider a submission based on the judgment of DENNING,
L.J., in *Lee* v. *Showmen's Guild of Great Britain* (77), to the effect that public
policy would invalidate any stipulation excluding the application of the rules of
natural justice to a domestic tribunal, and said that although I respectfully
inclined to the same view, it seemed to have been expressed obiter and was not
mentioned by the other members of the court, so that I would hesitate to decide
E   the case on that ground.   I went on to refer to the rule which was said to justify
the expulsion, and then said this:

" It is trite law that the rules of an unincorporated association form a
contract between all the members of that association.   It is, indeed, a somewhat special form of contract; but subject to that, what I am required to
do is to construe the terms of a contract.   Where the terms in issue deal with
F   the exercise of a power of peremptory suspension or termination of the rights
of one of the parties to such a contract, then I think that the common
expectation of mankind would be that the power would be exercised only in
accordance with the principles of natural justice unless the contrary is made
plain.   This expectation rests upon high and ancient authority.   When a
member of a university was deprived of his degrees without being given
G   an opportunity to defend himself, FORTESCUE, J., said: ' The laws of God
and man both give the party an opportunity to make his defence, if he has
any.   I remember to have heard it observed by a very learned man upon
such an occasion, that even God himself did not pass sentence upon Adam,
before he was called upon to make his defence.   Adam (says God) where
art thou?   Hast thou not eaten of the tree, whereof I commanded thee that
H   thou shouldst not eat?   And the same question was put to Eve also ': *R.* v.
University of Cambridge (78).   Even if the law permits the principles of
natural justice to be effectually excluded by suitable drafting, I would not
readily construe the rules as having achieved this result unless they left me
in no doubt that this was the plain and manifest intention.   Put a little
differently, I would say that if there is any doubt the applicability of the
I   principles of natural justice will be given the benefit of that doubt.   The
cry ' That isn't fair ' is to be found from earliest days, in nursery, street and
school alike;   and those who wish to confer on the committee or other
governing body of a club or association a power to act unfairly or arbitrarily

(74) [1929] 1 Ch. 602 at p. 624; [1929] All E.R. Rep. 468 at p. 472.
(75) (1798), 3 U.S. 386 at p. 399.
(76) [1963] 2 All E.R. at p. 114; [1964] A.C. at p. 132.
(77) [1952] 1 All E.R. 1175 at p. 1180; [1952] 2 Q.B. 329 at p. 342.
(78) (1723), 1 Stra. 557 at p. 567.

in derogation of a common and universal expectation must make it plain A
beyond a peradventure that this has been done. This view is, I think, at
least consistent with the approach of ROMER, L.J., in *Lee* v. *Showmen's
Guild of Great Britain* (79), on a not dissimilar point, where he said that it
would require ' the use of clear language ' before he was satisfied that the
members of any body such as the trade union in question had agreed to leave
the construction of the trade union's rules to the committee, to the exclusion B
of the courts."

Having now had the opportunity of reconsidering the language that I used in
that case, I must say that I can see no reason for resiling from it. Before resorting
to public policy, let the rules of the club or other body be construed: and in
the process of construction, the court will be slow to conclude that natural
justice has been excluded. Only if the rules make it plain that natural justice C
was intended to be disregarded will it be necessary for the courts to resolve the
issue of public policy. In this case, accordingly, I approach both cl. 8 (2) of the
Labour Party constitution and the resolution of the N.E.C. dated 24th April
1968 as provisions requiring to be construed strictly, and as not excluding the
processes of natural justice except insofar as this is made plain. Nothing that
I can see in cl. 8 (2) even begins to exclude the process of natural justice. The D
phrase " to take any action it deems necessary " cannot, in my judgment, be
read as if it continued " however contrary to natural justice it may be "; nor,
in my judgment, are the words " disaffiliation ", " expulsion " or even " or
otherwise " to be qualified in any such way. These things may be done but
they must be done fairly and justly and not unfairly or unjustly. Accordingly,
the first resolution, suspending the activities of the Pembroke Constituency E
Labour Party and depriving the officers of the right for the time being to handle
the funds of the party, falls to be tested by the standard of whether it was made
in accordance with the rules of natural justice. Whatever may be said about
the right to an unbiassed tribunal, the process of giving notice of the charges
and giving those concerned the right to be heard in answer to the charges was
plainly not followed. Accordingly, in my judgment the resolution was a nullity. F
It was effective neither to suspend the activities of the Pembroke Constituency
Labour Party nor to deprive the officers of that party of their right to handle
the funds.

The two limbs of the second resolution, though directed to the same end, are
markedly different in function. The first is an operative decision that the
Pembroke Constituency Labour Party be " re-organised ". The second provides G
that the national agent be " given authority " to take such steps as are necessary
to " complete the re-organisation ", and so confers authority on another to take
certain steps. Both are very wide and indefinite in their terms, depending on
the protean word " re-organise ". Plainly there is considerable scope for argument
about what that word means. But whatever it means, I do not think it can be
said to include a process which excludes from the benefits of membership, without H
making a charge and without affording a hearing, anyone who fails to sign and
return within a reasonable time the form put forward in this case.

Counsel for the defendants did contend that sending out the form amounted
to affording the members an opportunity of being heard: but not even his
considerable powers of advocacy sufficed to give any life to as barren a contention
as I have heard. I cannot believe that the concept of " Write a letter in the I
form I dictate, or you are out " would seriously be regarded by any of the great
judges who have spoken on the subject as making even an approach to conformity with the requirements of natural justice: and the prospects of this are
not increased by the words " or you are out " not being there but being represented only by the hint to be derived from the reference to " making any
recommendation to the National Executive Committee about your continued
membership of the Party ".

(79) [1952] 1 All E.R. 1175 at p. 1185; [1952] 2 Q.B. 329 at p. 349.

A　　These are not days of linguistic accuracy. Euphemisms abound; and as I said on a completely different subject in *The Pet Library (London), Ltd.* v. *Walter Ellson & Son, Ltd.* (80), today—

　　" many words of precision are being weakened by misapplication, sometimes for convenience but more often by ignorance: words such as ' alibi ' and ' disinterested ' spring readily to mind. There are also words which are
B　persistently misused; thus even in circles of high respectability (and I look with sorrow at 29 HALSBURY'S LAWS OF ENGLAND (3rd Edn. 1960) p. 646) the word ' escapees ' is sometimes applied to the fugitive prisoners rather than the governor and prison officers that they left behind them."

　　Nevertheless, after making all due allowance for an age of semantic laxity, I do not think the word "re-organise" can be held to comprehend a process
C　which in substance amounts to expulsion without a charge and without an opportunity to meet it. The more indefinite the language, the less apt it is to exclude the members' reasonable expectation of being accorded natural justice.

　　I also bear in mind the rule that, in general, a failure to give due notice of a meeting to even one member of a body who is entitled to attend invalidates the decisions of that body: see, e.g., *Smyth* v. *Darley* (81), concerning the election of
D　an officer, and *Young* v. *Ladies' Imperial Club, Ltd.* (82), where an expulsion was in issue. Here, no notice of the second meeting was given to a number of the members of the local Labour Party; and it is clear that this was due not to inadvertence or accident but to deliberation. It follows that the meeting was not validly constituted, and so its proceedings were void. In the words of LORD CAMPBELL, L.C., in *Smyth* v. *Darley* (83), " even a unanimous election by those
E　who did attend would be void ".

　　It may be that there are some who would decry the importance which the courts attach to the observance of the rules of natural justice. " When something is obvious," they may say, " why force everybody to go through the tiresome waste of time involved in framing charges and giving an opportunity to
F　be heard? The result is obvious from the start." Those who take this view do not, I think, do themselves justice. As everybody who has anything to do with the law well knows, the path of the law is strewn with examples of open and shut cases which, somehow, were not; of unanswerable charges which, in the event, were completely answered; of inexplicable conduct which was fully explained; of fixed and unalterable determinations that, by discussion, suffered a change. Nor are those with any knowledge of human nature who pause to think for a
G　moment likely to underestimate the feelings of resentment of those who find that a decision against them has been made without their being afforded any opportunity to influence the course of events.

　　Let me add this. What was done was, in my judgment, wrong; but there is nothing before me to suggest that it was consciously wrong. I do not for one moment say that the N.E.C. deliberately or knowingly resolved to ignore the
H　rules of natural justice. There is no evidence before me on the point, but it may very well be that the thought never entered the minds of the members of that committee. I am content to assume that the process of " getting round all problems relating to expulsion " was not the object of the committee, but merely the contention of the advocate seeking, quite properly, to make the best that he could of what had been done. Nevertheless, however innocent the committee,
I　what was done was wrong. It follows that, subject to any argument that there may be about the precise terms of the order, the plaintiffs are entitled to the injunction sought by the notice of motion.

　　Before I turn to action no. 3, I ought to mention certain technical objections taken by counsel for the defendants in action no. 2. He contended that on the writ and notice of motion as drafted it was not competent for the plaintiffs,

---

(80) [1968] F.S.R. 359 at p. 361.　　　　　　(81) (1849), 2 H.L. Cas. 789.
(82) [1920] 2 K.B. 523; [1920] All E.R. Rep. 223.
(83) (1849), 2 H.L. Cas. at p. 803.

being merely two of the members of the local Labour Party, to sue or move by A
themselves without joining all the members of the party on one side or the
other. In view of what I have said earlier in this judgment, I do not think that
is right: and counsel for the defendants cited no authority to carry the point.
No doubt, as in *Harrison* v. *Marquis of Abergavenny* (84), it is possible for such
an action to be brought in this way: and there are manifest advantages in
proceedings which are so constituted that they will bind all concerned. But B
that does not mean that an action cannot be brought in the other way. Counsel
for the defendants said that *Harrington* v. *Sendall* (85) ought to have been a
representative action, and that it was not clear whether or not it had been.
I have now looked at the reports of the case in the other series of reports (72
L.J. Ch. 396; 88 L.T. 323; 51 W.R. 463; and 19 T.L.R. 302), and I have found
nothing to suggest that it was a representative action. Indeed, such indications C
as there are point to it not being such an action. What sufficed for JOYCE, J.,
and the distinguished counsel engaged in that case suffices for me. I hold the
action and the motion to be perfectly competent.

Counsel for the defendants also contended that as the plaintiffs had set up no
constitution of the local Labour Party, and the proceedings concerned the
constitution, the action failed: and if the local Labour Party lacked any known D
rules, the local Labour Party should be wound up, a receiver appointed, and the
funds distributed as bona vacantia. I will say no more than that I reject these
contentions, so far as they arise for decision on this motion. Furthermore, basing
himself on *General Billposting Co., Ltd.* v. *Atkinson* (86), counsel for the defendants
also contended that the plaintiffs had disentitled themselves to an injunction
by acting in breach of their contract and seeking to defy the Labour Party. E
If this principle were to apply to cases of expulsion and suspension, it would
mean that the very breach which gave rise to the expulsion or suspension might
disable the member concerned from complaining of any lack of natural justice
in the process: and that cannot be right. In any case, I do not think the mere
failure to answer the national agent's letter can invoke the principle.

Finally, there is action no. 3. This may briefly be described, in broad terms, F
as action no. 1 in reverse, and up-to-date. As I have already mentioned, the
writ was issued on 5th July 1968, by which time all three meetings had taken
place. The third meeting purported to be a meeting of P.D.L.P., attended by
delegates from the Haverfordwest Local Labour Party elected at the second
meeting, and by delegates from other local Labour Parties elected at meetings
convened by the N.E.C. and elected in a similar manner. The plaintiffs are two G
of the three defendants in action no. 1: and the defendant, Mr. John, is the
plaintiff in action no. 1. The writ claims a declaration and an injunction which
I need not read: and the notice of motion, given on the day the writ was issued,
claims an injunction—

" to restrain the defendant in his purported capacity as an officer of the
Pembrokeshire Constituency, until judgment in this action or further order H
(whether by himself his servants or agents or otherwise howsoever) from
doing or purporting to do or being party to any of the following things
namely collecting expending remitting transferring or otherwise dealing
with any moneys or other property belonging to or held for the purpose of
the Pembrokeshire Constituency Local Labour Party."

The omission of " Labour Party " after the first mention of " Constituency ", and I
the use of the word " Local ", are, I think, mere slips.

Counsel for the defendants frankly accepted that the third meeting was bad if
(as I have already held) the second meeting was bad: and it follows that the
acts of the third meeting were ineffective to elect officers of P.D.L.P. Those
attending the third meeting purported to elect Mr. John president of P.D.L.P.;
and it follows from the invalidity of that meeting that the election was void. I

(84) (1887), 3 T.L.R. 324; 57 L.T. 360.   (85) [1903] 1 Ch. 921.
    (86) [1909] A.C. 118 at p. 122; [1908-10] All E.R. Rep. 619 at p. 624.

A   have already held that as a result of the first meeting, Mr. Cleare, who is the second defendant in the first action and the second plaintiff in the third, had become president of P.D.L.P. in place of Mr. John; and as it is not alleged that Mr. John holds any other office in P.D.L.P., it seems plain that Mr. John holds no office which would entitle him to deal with the property of P.D.L.P. Accordingly, subject to what I am about to say, the injunctions

B   sought by the notice of motion in the third action, restraining him " in his purported capacity as an officer " of P.D.L.P. from dealing with that property, ought to be granted. I should add that counsel for the defendants' contentions on procedural and other points meet the same fate here as in action no. 2.

Whether an injunction should in fact be granted is a matter for consideration. There is no suggestion of any wilful wrongdoing by the defendant. I am in the

C   sphere of honest disagreement on matters which I readily confess I have not found altogether easy. I think, however, that there is an important difference between this case and the plaintiff's motion in action no. 1, where, it may be remembered, I refused to grant an injunction. There, I held that the defendants were validly in office, and I refused the injunction because I would not assume that in exercising their offices they would act in disregard of this judgment.

D   Here, the defendant is not in office at all, and so has no title to the property of P.D.L.P. But if the defendant, who is a man of some standing in his community, offered an undertaking to the court in the terms of para. 1 of the notice of motion, then subject to anything that counsel have to say and to details of drafting, I would be disposed to accept it in lieu of any injunction.

That, I think, disposes of the motions, subject to the point that I have just

E   mentioned. But I cannot part from the case without expressing my indebtedness to counsel for their careful and thorough submissions, and particularly for the way in which they performed the feat of segregating the issues and their submissions in what for all has been a prolonged embarras de richesse. Any clarity in this judgment is largely due to their efforts; and, let me add, if it is found to be prolix or obscure, most assuredly the fault is not theirs.

F   *Orders accordingly.*

Solicitors: *Goodman, Derrick & Co.* (for the plaintiff in the first action and the defendants in the second and third actions); *Theodore Goddard & Co.* (for the defendants in the first action and for the plaintiffs in the second and third actions).

[*Reported by* R. W. FARRIN, ESQ., *Barrister-at-Law.*]

G
                   ———————

Re 33, BYRNE ROAD, BALHAM.
BYRNLEA PROPERTY INVESTMENTS, LTD. v. RAMSAY.

[COURT OF APPEAL, CIVIL DIVISION (Lord Denning, M.R., Edmund Davies and Phillimore, L.JJ.), February 17, 18, 19, 26, 1969.]

H   *Landlord and Tenant—Leasehold enfranchisement—Tenant's notice—Prescribed notice—Notice of desire to have " the freehold or an extended lease "—Failure to delete alternative—Validity of notice—Transitional provisions—Leasehold Reform Act* 1967 (c. 88), *s.* 5 (1), *s.* 34.

In 1958 R. purchased a leasehold dwelling-house with seven years to run. On the expiry of the term, on 30th June 1965, the tenancy continued under

I   the provisions of Part I of the Landlord and Tenant Act 1954. This continuation of the tenancy was determined by a surrender and grant of a new tenancy from year to year. The grant was by way of continuation of the original long tenancy and fell to be treated, under the transitional provisions of the Leasehold Reform Act 1967, as a long tenancy at a low rent for the purposes of s. 34 (1) (a) of that Act. Under s. 34 of the Act, R., having occupied the house as his residence for more than five years, was entitled to acquire the freehold or an extended lease provided that he gave the prescribed notice. Within the prescribed time (i.e., before 28th January

1968) R. gave the landlord notice of his desire to acquire the freehold but   A
these notices failed to contain particulars of the tenancy required by Sch. 3
to the Act and did not, therefore, satisfy the requirements of s. 34 (4) (*a*).
Schedule 3, para. 6 (1) provided that a tenant's notice given after 1st
January 1968 had to be in "the prescribed form" this being a printed form
in the following terms: "Take notice that I as tenant of the house and
premises described in the Schedule hereto, desire to have* (the freehold   B
or an extended lease) of the said house and premises. I am making my
claim in exercise of my rights under the Leasehold Reform Act 1967. The
particulars on which I rely are set out in the Schedule to this notice".
In small print in the margin under an asterisk were the words "Delete
whichever is inapplicable". R.'s notice in this form and dated 3rd January
1968 contained all requisite particulars in the schedule, but he failed to   C
delete either alternative of "the freehold *or* an extended lease". After
the material date, 28th Janaury 1968, had lapsed the landlord put in a
notice of objection that R. had not specified which alternative he required
and subsequently applied to the county court to determine whether he
was entitled to the freehold. On appeal from a decision that R.'s notice
of 3rd January was invalid,   D

Held: a notice in the alternative was invalid; a tenant must claim
either the freehold or the extended lease because on service of the notice,
by virtue of s. 5 (1)† of the Act, there came into being a statutory contract
binding on both landlord and tenant; accordingly R.'s notice was invalid
for uncertainty and the appeal would be dismissed.

Per CURIAM: The prescribed form of notice required by Sch. 3, para. 6 (1)   E
should be amended. At present it was misleading, for on reading the note
in the margin "delete whichever is inapplicable" an applicant who desired
either alternative might think that either was applicable and so make no
deletion.

Appeal dismissed.

[As to a tenant's notice of claim to enfranchisement, see SUPPLEMENT to   F
23 HALSBURY'S LAWS (3rd Edn.) para. 1755.

As to transitional provisions relating to leasehold enfranchisement, see ibid.,
new para. 1771.

For the Leasehold Reform Act 1967, s. 5, s. 34, Sch. 3, Pt. 2, see 47 HALSBURY'S
STATUTES (2nd Edn.) 887, 932, 956.]
  G
Cases referred to:

Barclays Bank, Ltd. v. Ascott, [1961] 1 All E.R. 782; [1961] 1 W.L.R. 717;
    Digest (Cont. Vol. A) 1047, *7417kac.*

Mountford v. Hodkinson, [1956] 2 All E.R. 17; [1956] 1 W.L.R. 422; 2 Digest
    (Repl.) 14, *62.*

Scammell v. Ouston, [1941] 1 All E.R. 14; [1941] A.C. 251; 110 L.J.K.B. 197;   H
    164 L.T. 379; 39 Digest (Repl.) 448, *31.*

Sunrose, Ltd. v. Gould, [1961] 3 All E.R. 1142; [1962] 1 W.L.R. 20; Digest
    (Cont. Vol. A) 1047, *7417kad.*

Appeal.

This was an appeal by Risckbil Ramsay, from a judgment of His Honour
JUDGE IFOR LLOYD, Q.C., given on 30th May 1968 in the Wandsworth County   I
Court, whereby it was adjudged that Ramsay, as tenant, was not entitled to have
the freehold of 33, Byrne Road, Balham, London, S.W.12, by reason of the
invalidity of a notice given on 3rd January 1968. The appeal was for an order
that that judgment might be set aside and judgment entered for the tenant,
that he be entitled to the freehold. The facts are set out in the judgment of
LORD DENNING, M.R.

---

† Section 5 (1), so far as material, is set out at p. 314, letter H, post.

A   F. R. C. *Such* for the tenant.
     J. S. *Colyer* for the landlords.

     Cur. adv. vult.

     26th February.   The following judgments were read.

     LORD DENNING, M.R.: We are here called on to consider the provisions
B   of the Leasehold Reform Act 1967. This Act confers on sitting tenants of long
     leaseholds a right to buy the freehold at a fair price, or, alternatively, to get an
     extra 50 years' lease at a fair rent. But this case concerns a long leasehold which
     had expired two years before the Act was passed. It comes under the transitional
     provisions of the Act, which impose a stringent time limit.

     The house is No. 33 Byrne Road, Balham. The lease was for 99 years, expiring
C   on 30th June 1965. The ground rent was £7 10s. a year. The tenant, Mr. Ramsay,
     who comes from Guyana, bought the leasehold in 1958 for £850. It had seven
     years then to run. He lived there with relatives, also from Guyana. On 30th
     June 1965, the lease came to an end, but he stayed on under the provisions of
     Part I of the Landlord and Tenant Act 1954. His tenancy was thus continued
     by statute. This continuation of the tenancy was determined, so the judge
     found, by a surrender and grant of a new tenancy from year to year at £8 8s. a
D   a week (£436 16s. a year). This was granted by way of continuation of the
     former long tenancy. It was to be treated, therefore, under the transitional
     provisions, as a long tenancy at a low rent for the purpose of the Leasehold
     Reform Act 1967, see s. 34 (1) (*a*). He had occupied the house as his residence
     for more than five years. So he was entitled to acquire the freehold or an extended
E   lease; provided that he gave the prescribed notice within the prescribed time.
     I say " within the prescribed time " because, in these transitional cases, where
     the term of the lease had expired before the Act was passed, s. 34 sets a time limit.
     The prescribed notice must be given before 28th January 1968. It cannot be
     given afterwards. This is clear from s. 34 (2) which provides:

     " A notice of a person's desire to have the freehold or an extended
F   lease of a house and premises, if given by virtue of subsection (1) above
     [which allows it when a long tenancy has been continued after its expiry
     date as here] may be given before the appointed day [1st January 1968]
     but shall be of no effect if given more than three months after the day
     this Act is passed [27th October 1967]."

     The tenant followed keenly the passing of the bill through Parliament. Two
G   days after the Act was passed, on 29th October 1967, he gave this notice to the
     landlords:

     " Sir, now that the Leasehold Bill becomes law, I hereby serve notice on
     Byrnlea Property Investments Limited, that I wish the enfranchisement
     of 33 Byrne Road, Balham, S.W.12."

H   A month later, on 29th November 1967, he gave another notice to the landlords:

     " Sir, I was hoping to receive a reply to my letter dated 29/10/1967.
     Anyhow I am sending a reminder. Now that the Leasehold Bill becomes
     law, I hereby serve notice on Byrnlea Property Investments Limited, that
     I wish the freehold of 33 Byrne Road, Balham, S.W.12."

     Those two notices would seem at first sight to be good enough: but they did
I   not contain the particulars required by Sch. 3 of the Act of 1967 (i.e., particulars
     of the tenancy, etc.). They were, therefore, not sufficient to satisfy the Act,
     see s. 34 (4) (*a*). That is accepted by counsel for the tenant.

     After the appointed day, 1st January 1968, the tenant's notice had to be
     " in the prescribed form ", see Sch. 3, para. 6 (1). So on 3rd January 1968,
     the tenant obtained a printed form and served it on the landlords. It read:

     " *Delete whichever is inapplicable. Take notice that I as tenant of
     the house and premises described in the Schedule hereto, desire to have*

A

(the freehold *or* an extended lease) of the said house and premises. I am making my claim in exercise of my rights under the Leasehold Reform Act, 1967. The particulars on which I rely are set out in the Schedule to this notice."

The tenant set out all the required particulars in the schedule. There were some errors in his particulars but these could be overlooked, see para. 6 (3) of Sch. 3. But, in addition, he made a serious mistake in the body of the notice. He left the phrase intact: " The freehold or an extended lease ". He did not follow the advice in small print in the margin: " Delete whichever is inapplicable ". He did not delete either of them.

B

The landlords must have noticed that he made a mistake. But they did not tell him about it. They waited until after 28th January 1968, so that it was too late for him to correct it. Then on 30th January 1968, they put in a notice of objection, stating: " You do not specify in your notice whether you require the freehold or whether you require an extended lease ". They knew, of course, perfectly well from his earlier letters that he wanted the freehold and not an extended lease. The judge so found. And it is apparent that they knew, because on the same day, 30th January 1968, they wrote a letter stating: " We are applying to the Wandsworth County Court for a declaration that you are not entitled to the freehold," and they actually took out an application to determine " whether the [tenant] is entitled to have the freehold ". In reply, the tenant, on 31st January 1968, made it quite clear that he wanted the freehold. He wrote: " We know that we are entitled to the Freehold as defined in Section 1 of the Leasehold Reform Act, 1967 ".

C

D

Nevertheless, although the landlords were not in the least misled—they knew he wanted the freehold—they contend that his notice was invalid because he did not delete on the form one or other—" the freehold or extended lease "—but left the phrase intact. The judge upheld this contention. He said that—

E

" the notice sent to the landlords by [the tenant] on 3rd January 1968, was bad for ambiguity and for non-compliance with the form prescribed by the Act and Regulations."

F

This raises an important point. I think that a notice, to be good, must be in writing; and it must make it clear whether the tenant is claiming the freehold or whether he is claiming an extended lease. He cannot claim both. He cannot claim one or other. He must claim one only. The reason is because, on the giving of a notice, the parties are bound as effectually as by a concluded contract. Section 5 (1) provides in terms that:

G

" Where . . . a tenant of a house has the right to acquire the freehold or an extended lease and gives notice of his desire to have it, the rights and obligations of the landlord and the tenant arising from the notice shall inure for the benefit of and be enforceable against them, their executors, administrators and assigns to the like extent (but no further) as rights and obligations arising under a contract for a sale or lease freely entered into between the landlord and tenant . . ."

H

There is, therefore, as soon as the notice is given, a statutory contract binding on the landlord and tenant. And the Act makes provision for all the terms of this contract. If the tenant gives notice of his desire to have the freehold, the landlord is bound to grant him an estate in fee simple on the terms and conditions set out in the Act (s. 8 to s. 13) and in the regulations (Pt. 1 of Sch. 3). If the tenant gives notice of his desire to have an extended lease, the landlord is bound to grant him a new tenancy on the terms and conditions set out in the Act (s. 14 to s. 16) and in the regulations (Pt. 2 of Sch. 3).

I

Once the notice is given, both parties are bound just as they are by an ordinary contract. Neither can get out of it except in circumstances provided in the Act. Thus if the tenant gives notice for the freehold and afterwards finds that the

A price is more than he is able or willing to pay, he can withdraw his notice on paying compensation to the landlord (s. 9 (3)). *Or* if the tenant gives notice for an extended lease and afterwards changes his mind, he can acquire the freehold by giving notice of his desire to have it (s. 5 (8)).

Seeing, therefore, that as soon as the written notice is given, there is a binding contract, I cannot see any room for a notice in the alternative. If a tenant
B gives a notice that he desires " the freehold or an extended lease ", without saying which, there can be no binding contract. The Act simply cannot begin to operate. If I may put it into the form of offer and acceptance, it stands in this way: the landlord, under the compulsion of the Act, whether he likes it or not, makes an *offer* to the tenant to let him *either* buy the freehold at a fair price *or* to take an extended lease of 50 years at a fair rent. In order to accept
C that offer, so as to make a binding contract, the tenant must accept *one* of these alternatives. If he replies: " I desire to have *either* the freehold *or* an extended lease ", then there is no contract, because no one knows which it is. It is too uncertain to be a contract. It is just as if I say: " I offer to sell you my horse for £100 *or* my cow for £50 " and you reply: " I accept your offer ". There is no contract for the simple reason stated by Lord Wright: When the words—
D   " . . . fail to evince any definite meaning on which the court can safely act, the court has no choice but to say that there is no contract."

(see *Scammell* v. *Ouston* (1)).

So also if a tenant sends in two notices, one for the freehold, the other for an extended lease, in the same envelope, both would be bad: for it would again be
E quite uncertain which of them he desired. There would be no contract. He must make up his mind which he wants and give a certain notice for that one. In this situation I venture to suggest that the prescribed form should be amended. At present it may mislead some people. The form runs: " I desire to have the freehold or an extended lease ", and than a note in the margin: " Delete whichever is inapplicable ". I can imagine an applicant might think to himself: " I
F desire either of them, whichever I can get "; and so either is applicable, neither is inapplicable. So he would not delete either of them; whereas, for his notice to be valid, he *must* delete one or other.

The tenant fell into this very mistake and, by reason of it, his notice of 3rd January 1968, was bad. As soon as his error was pointed out to him, he corrected it, or as good as corrected it, by his letter of 31st January 1968, when he wrote
G that he wanted the freehold. At that date, 31st January, the form and the letter together constituted a good notice. But by then it was too late. His was a transitional case. And s. 34 (2) provides that a notice " shall be of no effect if given " after 28th January 1968. If it had not been a transitional case, he could have corrected his mistake at any time. He could have served a fresh notice for the freehold only. But, being a transitional case, he is barred by the time limit.

H I am sorry to have to come to this conclusion, because the landlords knew perfectly well that he wanted the freehold. They must have known that he had made a mistake in filling in the form. And yet they did nothing to correct it. But I do not think we can help the tenant on this account. We are dealing here with a contract, a statutory contract, no doubt, but still a contract; and, what is more, a contract which has to be in writing. To it, we must apply the rules
I which regulate the formation of a written contract, else we should lose the certainty which is so important in this field of law. On the face of the written documents here there was no contract before 28th January 1968; and we cannot construct a contract out of the mistake made by the tenant. A mistake made by one party to the knowledge of the other is a ground for avoiding a contract, but not for making one.

My regret is tempered, however, by the fact that the tenant's long lease expired as long ago as 24th June 1965—long before the Leasehold Reform Act 1967,

was thought of by Parliament. The lease has been continued by statute and he is   A
still protected by the Rent Acts. So he is able to stay in the house and let off
rooms and make a profit for some time to come. All he has missed is the opportunity to buy the freehold.

I would, therefore, dismiss the appeal.

EDMUND DAVIES, L.J.: As I view this case, the tenant lacks one
powerful ally. He has merits in abundance, but in my judgment the law is   B
unhappily not on his side. Bereft of that essential support, I have with confessed
reluctance concluded that he should lose this appeal.

As to the merits, not only were the tenant's letters of 29th October and 29th
November 1967 (to which LORD DENNING, M.R., has referred) completely clear
that what he sought to acquire was none other than the freehold, but the landlords have themselves provided convincing proof of that fact. Before the tenant   C
took the step of sending his letter of 31st January 1968, the landlords demonstrated
that no misunderstanding existed, for on 30th January they made their application to the court for a declaration that the tenant was, by reason of his flawed
notice, not entitled to the *freehold*. They knew, beyond all doubt, what the tenant
wanted. I am equally convinced that the landlords bided their time until the
crucial day, 27th January 1968, had passed in order to ensure that the tenant   D
would have lost his opportunity of rectifying the purely clerical error into which
he had unwittingly fallen.

In these circumstances, counsel for the landlords has understandably relied
not so much on ambiguity in the tenant's notice as on its failure to conform to
Sch. 3, Pt. 2, para. 6 (1) to the Leasehold Reform Act 1967, which requires that—   E

" A tenant's notice under Part I of this Act of his desire to have the freehold or an extended lease of a house and premises *shall* be in the prescribed
form, and shall contain the following particulars . . ."

Doubt as to what the tenant had in mind being eliminated (despite his failure
to delete the words ". . . or an extended lease " from the Form I notice which
he served on the landlords), I have reflected on whether it might be open to the   F
court properly to hold his notice nevertheless valid, on the ground that what
the tenant was in effect saying was that, if he could not have the one, then he
would like the other. But this will not do, for either was his for the asking.
This tenant was as much entitled to the freehold as he was to an extended term,
while the landlords (on the other hand) had *no* choice as to which they would
grant. That being so, the landlords were entitled to be told expressly which   G
of the two the tenant was claiming, and the Act requires that their entitlement in
this respect must be reflected by the notice served by their tenant.

I have also entertained the suggestion (and, indeed, threw it out in the course
of argument) that it might be possible to argue that (even conceding its formal
duplicity) the document was nevertheless capable of being strictly regarded as
in simple truth " a notice of a person's desire to have the freehold or an extended   H
term " and that it was, therefore, both formally valid within para. 6 (1) and
timeously served within s. 34 (2). But, as I shall later indicate, I do not consider
that the problem presented by this appeal can be so solved.

It remains to consider the submission by counsel for the tenant that, there
being no doubt in the landlords' minds what the tenant was seeking, this court
is free to apply the liberal principles of construction applicable to common law   I
notices to quit and can thereby uphold the present application. But *Mountford*
v. *Hodkinson* (2), cited in support of this submission, had nothing to do with
failure to give notice in accordance with a prescribed form. The other decision
relied on by the tenant was *Sunrose, Ltd.* v. *Gould* (3), and that, it is true, did
deal with non-compliance with the requirement of the Landlord and Tenant
Act 1954, s. 25 (1) that:

(2) [1956] 2 All E.R. 17; [1956] 1 W.L.R. 422
(3) [1961] 3 All E.R. 1142; [1962] 1 W.L.R. 20.

A   " The landlord may terminate a tenancy . . . by a notice given to the tenant in the prescribed form specifying the date at which the tenancy is to come to an end . . ."

What happened there was that the landlord used the form prescribed by the Act, filling in the blanks. He inserted his name and address, and there followed the printed words,

B

  " . . . . landlord (*Note* 7) of the above-mentioned premises, hereby give you notice terminating your tenancy on the . . . blank . . . [into which was typed " 15th "] day of . . . blank . . . [into which was typed " July "], 196 . . . blank . . . (*Note* 1)."

On the back of the form were the various notes inserted pursuant to s. 25 (2) of

C the Landlord and Tenant Act 1954, and from Note I it was clear that the date intended *must* have been 15th July 1961. Holding that the notice was valid, Holroyd Pearce, L.J., cited (4) with approval the test propounded by Barry, J., in *Barclays Bank, Ltd.* v. *Ascott* (5) that:

  " . . . provided that [the notice] does give the real substance of the information required, then the mere omission of certain details, or the failure

D   to embody in the notice the full provisions of the section of the Act referred to, will not in fact invalidate the notice."

But does the notice in the present case measure up to that test? I do not think it does. In *Sunrose, Ltd.* v. *Gould* (6) the document contained within its four corners all the information necessary to clear up all ambiguity, but it is quite

E otherwise in the present case. There can be no doubt, in my judgment, that the tenant's notice was in itself ambivalent and that one has to look outside it—to other documents to which it makes no reference and which, in turn, make no reference to it—in order to remove the obscurity. May this be done? I have earnestly considered that question, for its implications are possibly far wider than the particular events of the present case, which speak strongly in favour of

F the tenant.

  The conclusion I have come to is that the formal validity of a tenant's notice under the Act of 1967 must be decided solely by reference to the document itself and that (apart from accompanying documents, such as a covering letter) it cannot be supplemented or clarified by extrinsic evidence. The notice served in this case was, therefore, in law a nullity.

G

  The reason impelling me to this conclusion became clearer the more we were skilfully taken through the Act by learned counsel. The giving of a tenant's notice has the automatic effect under s. 5 (1) of creating what I have ventured to call a " statutory contract ". The terms of the contract thereby created and the obligations arising thereunder vary in important respects according to whether what the tenant seeks is the freehold or an extended term. The land-

H lord *must*, therefore, know to which of the two types of contract he is committed. The fact that s. 5 (8) makes provision whereby the tenant may give notice of his desire to have an extended lease and thereafter may give another notice of his desire to have the freehold (thereby in effect withdrawing his first notice) does not affect the landlord's right to know where he stands.

  Section 8 to s. 13 of the Act deal with enfranchisement, s. 14 to s. 16 with

I extension of leases, and these two fasciculi of sections have important differences. In the light of s. 5 (1), were the tenant's notice served in the present case to be held valid, the remarkable result would be that there would instantly spring into being at the moment of its service *two* statutory contracts, both binding on the parties and each differing in important respects from the other. That such a hydra-headed result should flow from the one notice seems unthinkable. The

---

(4) [1961] 3 All E.R. at p. 1145; [1962] 1 W.L.R. at p. 24.
(5) [1961] 1 All E.R. 782 at p. 786; [1961] 1 W.L.R. 717 at p. 722.
(6) [1961] 3 All E.R. 1142; [1962] 1 W.L.R. 20.

possible complications or confusions are endless. PHILLIMORE, L.J., instanced A
one of these in the course of argument by speculating how the provisions of
s. 5 (5) that—

> ". . . any such notice shall be registrable under the Land Charges Act
> 1925 or may be the subject of a notice or caution under the Land Registra-
> tion Act 1925, as if it were an estate contract."

would operate were the notice permitted to embrace both enfranchisement and B
extension, even though separated by a disjunctive.

Finally, in my judgment, it is not without significance that Sch. 3, para. 6 (3)
provides that:

> " The notice shall not be invalidated by any inaccuracy in the particulars
> . . . or any misdescription of the property to which the claim extends . . .", C

whereas no such indulgence relaxes the insistence under para. 6 (1) that the
tenant's notice " shall be in the prescribed form ".

We were told by counsel that a number of cases await the decision of this court
in the present appeal. We know nothing of the facts of those other cases and I
naturally say nothing about them. Nevertheless, it is clear that, in circumstances
other than those here existing, a notice in the defective form adopted in the D
present case could give rise to genuine doubt on the part of the landlord. Were
that so, I think it would be impossible to hold that either the Act or the common
law cast on the landlord any duty to enquire of his tenant before 27th January
1968, which form of relief was being sought and so give the tenant an opportunity
of putting the matter right within time. That being the case, I can see no reason
in strict law why the position should be any different if, as here, the landlords E
were in no doubt what the tenant had in mind despite the duplicity of his notice.

For these reasons, I am driven to hold that the excellent judgment of the
learned county court judge was right and should not be disturbed. I would,
therefore, dismiss this appeal.

PHILLIMORE, L.J.: This is, so we were told, the first case on the inter- F
pretation of this particular Act—the Leasehold Reform Act 1967. I confess that
I find myself in entire agreement with the admirable judgment of the county
court judge—His Honour JUDGE IFOR LLOYD.

It seems to me that one has only to read s. 5 (1) of the Act to realise that the
moment the tenant serves the landlord with his notice of application a statutory
contract is imposed on both the landlord and the tenant. The contract requires G
the landlord either to sell the freehold or to grant an extended lease dependent
on the terms of the notice. Obviously one cannot have two conflicting contracts
imposed simultaneously and so the contract must be either: (A) a contract to
grant an extended lease; or (B) a contract to sell the freehold. As one reads on
through the provisions of the Act it becomes clearer and clearer that one must
if one is a tenant make up one's mind before one serves the notice *whether* one H
wants to buy the freehold or whether one wants an extended lease. It becomes
equally clear of course that one *cannot* fill up the form so that it reads " I desire
to have the freehold *or* an extended lease ". One has got to opt.

Without embarking on a great deal of detail I would refer particularly to
s. 5 (5) and (8) and s. 8 (1) and s. 14 (1) as demonstrating the chaos which would
result from any other construction of the Act. I

The hardship in the present case has arisen because the tenant's contractual
tenancy having terminated in 1965, he had until 27th January 1968 to serve
the landlords with notice of his desire to have either the freehold or an extended
lease. See s. 34 (2). He had to comply with Sch. 3, Pt. 2 in giving his notice,
and accordingly under para. 6 (1) of that schedule he had to use the prescribed
form and to give certain particulars which were listed in the subsection and in
the schedule which forms part of the form. Under para. 6 (3) it is provided,
inter alia, that—

A   " The notice shall not be invalidated by any inaccuracy in the particulars required by this paragraph . . ."

The clear inference is that some other error may invalidate the form.

The prescribed form is to be found in the Appendix to the Leasehold Reform (Notices) Regulations 1967 (7), and its use is prescribed by reg. 4 (i) where it is stated—

B   " a tenant's notice of his desire to have the freehold or an extended lease of a house and premises given under Part 1 of the Act shall be in Form 1."

Nothing in the regulations warns the tenant that he cannot follow the phrase used throughout the Act and apply in the alternative, that is " to have the freehold *or* an extended lease ".

C   Paragraph 1 of the Form 1 provides:

" Take notice that I, as tenant of the house and premises described in the Schedule hereto, desire to have* [at this point there is an asterisk followed by brackets which include the words] [the freehold *or* an extended lease . . ."]

The asterisk refers to another in the margin opposite and against which are the words " Delete whichever is inapplicable ". Similar wording is to be found D in para. 2 which informs the landlord what action he must take on being served with the form or notice.

Now the tenant was well aware of his rights. He wrote to the landlords in October and again in November 1967 informing them of his desire to have the freehold. Counsel concedes that neither of these letters can constitute a notice of application. The regulations of 1967 containing the form came into force on E 1st January 1968, and the tenant procured a copy, completed and posted it on 3rd January. Now he wanted the freehold, but if he could not have the freehold he wanted an extended lease, so he made no deletion. What he did was quite logical, but unfortunately was in direct conflict with the whole scheme of the Act. The landlords knew perfectly well what he wanted, but they did nothing until after 27th January, when it was too late for the tenant to correct his F mistake. They then instituted proceedings as a result of which the county court judge found himself compelled to hold that the form as completed by the tenant was a nullity. He was clearly right. Counsel has tried to argue that since he wanted the freehold or if he could not get that at any rate an extended lease none of the words were inapplicable. Accordingly, so it is said, the form was properly completed within the provisions of s. 34 (2) and the tenant was then free G to declare his option within a reasonable time. I cannot think this argument is right. The whole matter is statutory and the Act does not say anything of the sort.

It is tempting to criticise the landlords, but the Act took away their common law rights and disrupted plans under which they had commenced in 1960 to buy a series of blocks of property in this area. The temptation to stand on their H strict rights was very great. The real blame rests with those responsible for this legislation and in particular for the regulations governing the form and the form itself. We were told that many tenants had made this same mistake. Surely it should have been realised that there ought to have been a clear warning both in the regulations and on the form itself so as to stop the tenant applying in the alternative. It might even have been safer to have *one* form if one wanted the I freehold and another if one wanted an extended lease and a warning that one could not serve both. In my judgment this appeal must be dismissed.

Appeal dismissed.

Solicitors: *W. Timothy Donovan* (for the tenant); *Gilbert Samuel & Co.* (for the landlords).

[*Reported by* Jenifer Sandell, *Barrister-at-Law.*]

---

(7) S.I. 1967 No. 1768.

A

PRACTICE DIRECTION.

SUPREME COURT TAXING OFFICE.

B

*Costs—Taxation—Procedure—Postal facilities—References balloted—Sitting
Master cases—Documents to be sent—Receipts.*

In order to save personal attendance and in certain cases to expedite taxation,
the following postal facilities are available to solicitors. Business will continue to
be conducted by personal attendance where this is preferred.

1. References will be balloted in the normal way providing the judgment C
order, etc., and a certified copy and statement of parties are enclosed, and in
the case of a notice of acceptance the notice of payment into court. Where a
reference to a master for taxation has been taken in the same or related matter or
action within the preceding seven years the name of that master must be supplied,
and if a related matter or action, its title. The original document will be returned
by post by the chambers of the master to whom it has been referred with the D
name of that master endorsed thereon. All further communications should be
addressed to the chambers of the master.

2. Sitting Master cases (R.S.C., Ord. 62, r. 24). The same procedure as in para. 1
above, with the addition of the bill of costs and papers. The notice of the appointment will be endorsed on the original document and returned to the solicitors
who should give notice to the other side. E

3. Bills and papers relating to the taxation may be lodged by post. A receipt
will be despatched by the chambers in which the taxation is proceeding.

PAUL ADAMS,
Chief Master
Supreme Court Taxing Office. F

22nd April 1969.

A

R. *v.* CHAPMAN.

[COURT OF APPEAL, CRIMINAL DIVISION (Fenton Atkinson and Phillimore, L.JJ., and Caulfield, J.), March 3, 1969.]

B
Road Traffic—Driving with blood-alcohol proportion above prescribed limit—Evidence—Provision of specimen—Breath test—Hospital patient—Evidence of no objection by medical practitioner—Road Safety Act 1967 (c. 30), s. 2 (2), s. 3 (2) (a), (b).

The appellant, who had been out drinking, was taken to hospital following an accident involving the car which he had been driving. A breath test was administered and since this proved positive, a specimen of blood was taken.
C The specimen of blood, on analysis, indicated alcohol in excess of the prescribed limit. The appellant was charged with an offence under s. 1* of the Road Safety Act 1967. At his trial the police gave evidence that before the appellant took a breath test the medical practitioner, in whose care the appellant was, was notified (under s. 2 (2)† of the Road Safety Act 1967) and did not object: the appellant took the breath test and inflated the bag on D the breathalyser with one breath. The medical practitioner was not called. The appellant in evidence maintained that when he took the breath test he had to take three or four blows before he could inflate the bag (in the instructions accompanying the breathalyser it is stated that the bag must be inflated by a single breath). The recorder, in his summing-up to the jury, said that if the jury believed the evidence that the bag had been E inflated in a single breath the condition precedent to the request to provide a specimen for a laboratory test had been satisfied under s. 3 (2) (a)‡ of the Act of 1967; if the jury believed the evidence that the bag had been inflated only after three or four blows the condition precedent under s. 3 (2) (b)‡ had been satisfied. On appeal against conviction,—

Held: the appeal would be dismissed, because—
F (i) it was perfectly proper for the police to give evidence of the fact that the medical practitioner did not object to the appellant's providing a specimen of breath (see p. 323, letter E, post);

(ii) in his summing-up the recorder gave a correct direction to the jury as to the application of s. 3 (2) (see p. 324, letter A, post).

Appeal dismissed.

G [As to driving with excess alcohol in blood, see SUPPLEMENT to 33 HALSBURY'S LAWS (3rd Edn.) para 1061A; as to breath tests see ibid; para. 1061A, 2.

For the Road Safety Act 1967, s. 2, s. 3, see 47 HALSBURY'S STATUTES (2nd Edn.) 1556, 1558.]

Appeal.
This was an appeal by David Chapman against his conviction at Teesside
H Quarter Sessions before the recorder (D. S. FORRESTER-PATON, ESQ., Q.C.) and

---

* Section 1 (1), so far as material, provides: " If a person drives . . . a motor vehicle on a road . . . having consumed alcohol in such a quantity that the proportion thereof in his blood, as ascertained from a laboratory test for which he subsequently provides a specimen under section 3 of this Act, exceeds the prescribed limit at the time he provides the specimen, he shall be liable—(a) on summary conviction, to a fine . . ."
I † Section 2 (2), so far as material is set out at p. 322, letter I, post.
‡ Section 3 (2) provides: " A person while at a hospital as a patient may be required by a constable to provide at the hospital a specimen for a laboratory test—(a) if it appears to a constable in consequence of a breath test carried out on that person under section 2 (2) of this Act that the device by means of which the test is carried out indicates that the proportion of alcohol in his blood exceeds the prescribed limit; or (b) if that person has been required, whether at a hospital or elsewhere to provide a specimen of breath for a breath test, but fails to do so and a constable has reasonable cause to suspect him of having alcohol in his body; but a person shall not be required to provide a specimen for a laboratory test under this subsection if the medical practitioner in immediate charge of his case . . . objects to the provision of a specimen . . ."

M

a jury of driving a motor vehicle with his blood-alcohol concentration above the   A
prescribed limit contrary to s. 1 (1) of the Road Safety Act 1967. In the recorder's
summing-up he directed the jury: (a) that the appellant ought not to be convicted
unless the requirement that he should provide a specimen for a laboratory test
was made lawfully, in accordance with the conditions laid down in s. 2 and s. 3
of the Road Safety Act 1967; (b) that they ought not to find that the conditions
contained in s. 3 (2) (a) of the Act were fulfilled unless they were satisfied, inter   B
alia, that a breath test was carried out in the manner described by the police
officers and that the result of the test was positive; (c) that if they were satisfied
that the appellant used the breath test device in the manner which he described,
and that he did so because he was incapable of filling the bag with a single
breath and not because of any failure by the police officers to give him proper
instructions, then he had failed to provide a specimen of breath for a breath test   C
within the meaning of s. 3 (2) (b) of the Act. The facts are set out in the
judgment of the court.

The cases noted below* were cited during the argument.

R. A. R. Stroyan for the appellant.
F. J. Müller for the Crown.

                                                                       D

    FENTON ATKINSON, L.J. delivered the judgment of the court: On 5th
August 1968 at Teesside Quarter Sessions before the learned recorder the appellant
was convicted of driving a motor vehicle with a blood-alcohol concentration
above the prescribed limit contrary to s. 1 of the Road Safety Act 1967, and he
was fined £15 and disqualified for a modified period (the recorder finding certain
special reasons (1)). He now appeals against conviction on a certificate by the   E
recorder with particular reference to the direction given to the jury on the
meaning of the word " fails " in s. 3 (2) (b) of the Act.

    The facts were very straightforward. In the early hours of the morning of
24th February 1968 the appellant, when driving his motor car, crashed into a
tree on the offside of the road. He had admittedly been out drinking with his
friends that night. He was apparently the one supposed to keep sufficiently   F
sober to drive the others home. At 3.30 a.m. he dropped his last passenger, and
thereafter, within about 20 yards, the accident happened when, according to
him, possibly through a burst tyre, his car veered across the road and collided
with a tree. He was found at about 6.45 a.m. by P.c. Dodd, who noticed his
speech was indistinct and his breath smelt strongly of alcohol, and undoubtedly
there was reasonable cause for the policeman to suspect him of having alcohol   G
in his body. He was taken to hospital to the casualty ward, and the duty casualty
officer was a Dr. Din. A point was rather faintly taken at the trial that there
was no evidence that Dr. Din was the medical practitioner in the immediate
charge of his case, and our view is that there is absolutely nothing in that. He
had been taken to the casualty ward, Dr. Din was obviously the casualty officer
and plainly was the medical practitioner in the immediate charge of his case.   H
At this stage Dr. Din was joined by a Sergeant Watson, and the unchallenged
evidence was that Sergeant Watson notified Dr. Din that he proposed to require
the appellant to provide a specimen of breath, and his evidence was that Dr. Din
made no objection. The first point that arises is under s. 2 (2) of the Act where
it is provided that in a case like this at hospital—

    " . . . a person shall not be required to provide such a specimen [that is a   I
    breath specimen] while at a hospital as a patient if the medical practitioner
    in immediate charge of his case is not first notified of the proposal to make
    the requirement . . .".

---

    * *Subramaniam* v. *Public Prosecutor*, [1956] 1 W.L.R. 965; *Glinski* v. *McIver*, [1962]
1 All E.R. 696; [1962] A.C. 726; *Scott* v. *Baker*, [1968] 2 All E.R. 993; [1968] 3 W.L.R.
796.

    (1) The appellant was disqualified until 30th April 1969 and for a further period until
he thereafter passed a driving test.

A Pausing there, there was clear evidence that Dr. Din was notified by the police of the proposal to make the requirement, and further evidence from them that when the requirement was made, Dr. Din examined the patient. The section then goes on—

    " . . . objects to the provision of a specimen on the ground that its provision or the requirement to provide it would be prejudicial to the proper care or
B   treatment of the patient ".

  Counsel for the appellant's first point, and this point was taken in the court below, was this, that it was not open to the police to say " We notified Dr. Din, he made an examination and raised no objection to the provision of the specimen." It is said that that is hearsay, and it is necessary in such circumstances for the
C prosecution to call the doctor to prove affirmatively that he had no objection. In the view of this court that is a bad point. It was dealt with summarily when first raised, and in our view absolutely rightly by the recorder who said that either Dr. Din objected which is a fact or he did not object. We would adopt a passage from Professor Cross' work Cross on Evidence (3rd Edn.) at p. 380 which seems to put the position exactly (2):

D   " Evidence of a statement made to a witness by a person who is not himself called as a witness may or may not be hearsay. It is hearsay and inadmissible when the object of the evidence is to establish the truth of what is contained in the statement. It is not hearsay and is admissible when it is proposed to establish by the evidence, not the truth of the statement, but the fact that it was made ".

E What was to be established here was the fact that Dr. Din made no objection, and in our view it was perfectly proper for the police to give that evidence without Dr. Din being called. That is the first of the two points counsel for the appellant raises, and the court is against him on that. Then the matter went on and this breath test was taken. Sergeant Watson said that he told the appellant that he had reason to believe he had been involved in an accident and
F had alcohol in his body, and that he required a specimen of breath. The appellant said " Yes ", and the test was taken with an Alcotest device of the type approved by the Secretary of State, and his approval no doubt embraced the instructions of how the test is to be taken. Those instructions require a bag to be blown up in one breath by the person taking the test (3). The police evidence was that he did take the test, that with a proper Alcotest device he inflated it in one breath,
G taking a little over ten seconds, and the test was positive. The appellant's evidence, on the other hand, was to the effect that he tried to take the test, had three or four blows and finally inflated the bag, but for some reason had been unable to do it as the device required with one breath. That having been done, the police said they wished to take a sample of blood or urine. They again notified Dr. Din, and their evidence was he made no objection. The specimen of blood
H was taken with the consent of the appellant, and that showed a concentration of 86 milligrammes of alcohol against the permitted 80.

  The next point made by counsel for the appellant is that the condition preceding the taking of a laboratory specimen under s. 3 (2) of the Act is that a proper breath test has been taken first. Complaint is made of the summing-up of the learned recorder, who put it to the jury in effect in this way, " Well, if
I the police evidence is right, he took the test perfectly properly, he blew the bag up in one blow and it was positive ", and that would clearly satisfy s. 3 (2) (*a*) of the Act. But, alternatively, said the recorder, " if you have any doubt about that, and it may be right [the appellant] took three or four blows before he could inflate the bag, then that would be a failure to take the test properly ". The

---

  (2) Quoting *Subramaniam* v. *Public Prosecutor*, [1956] 1 W.L.R. at p. 970.
  (3) The test device called Alcotest ® 80. The instructions on this device state that the measuring bag must be fully inflated by one single breath in not less than ten and not more than 20 seconds.

appellant would then be caught by s. 3 (2) (b), and in our view that was a perfectly **A**
proper direction, because if the police evidence is right, there was no doubt about
it; the test was properly taken and the test was positive. But even if it was
right that the appellant was unable to blow it up in one, and took three or
four blows, then in our view it was perfectly right and proper to say he had
failed to take the test in the manner prescribed, which requires it to be done
in one blow. It was a clear case of guilt if the necessary preliminaries had been **B**
correctly gone through by the police officers. In our view, the evidence amply
justified the conviction, the summing-up cannot be faulted and there is really
nothing in this appeal, and the appeal will be dismissed.

Appeal dismissed. Leave to appeal to House of Lords refused.

Solicitors: *Registrar of Criminal Appeals* (for the appellant); *P. S. Ross,* **C**
Middlesborough (for the Crown).

[*Reported by* N. P. METCALFE, ESQ., *Barrister-at-Law.*]

Re WINDEATT'S WILL TRUSTS.   D

[CHANCERY DIVISION (Pennycuick, J.), March 7, 1969.]

*Trust and Trustee—Variation of trusts by the court—Jurisdiction—Discretion
—English trusts to be replaced by trusts established in Jersey—New trustees
to be appointed in Jersey—Beneficial trusts not varied—Beneficiaries
resident and domiciled in Jersey for* 19 *years—Whether court should approve* **E**
variation—Variation of Trusts Act 1958 (6 & 7 *Eliz.* 2 *c.* 53), *s.* 1.

The testator, who was resident and domiciled in England, by his will
constituted a residuary estate and directed, inter alia, that the trustees
(the testator's wife and the third defendant) pay the income to the testator's
wife for life and after her death to the plaintiff, the testator's daughter,
and on her death to hold the residuary estate as to capital and income in trust **F**
for such of her children or remoter issue as she should by deed or will appoint.
The testator died in 1959 and his wife in 1965. The plaintiff married and
had two children, the first and second defendants; the plaintiff's family
had lived in Jersey for 19 years, her children had been born there and
they believed themselves domiciled there. An application was made to
the court under s. 1* of the Variation of Trusts Act 1958 for the approval **G**
of an arrangement whereby two persons resident in Jersey should be
appointed trustees in place of the third defendant (the sole surviving trustee)
and the trust fund transferred to the new trustees in Jersey to be held by
them on the trusts of a new declaration of trusts to be made by them in
Jersey, the trusts corresponding in all respects with the trusts in the will.

Held: the court had jurisdiction to make an order having the effect of **H**
transferring the trust to Jersey because the plaintiff and her family had
been resident there for 19 years and Jersey was their genuine and permanent
home (see p. 327, letter F, post).

Re Seale's Marriage Settlement ([1961] 3 All E.R. 136) applied.
Re Weston's Settlements ([1968] 3 All E.R. 338) distinguished.

[As to the appointment of a person resident outside the jurisdiction as trustee, **I**
see 38 HALSBURY'S LAWS (3rd Edn.) 930, para. 1596; and for cases on the
subject, see 47 DIGEST (Repl.) 161, *1229-1235.*

As to the variation of trusts by the court, see 38 HALSBURY'S LAWS (3rd Edn.)
1029-1031, para. 1772; and for cases on the subject, see 47 DIGEST (Repl.)
332-338, *2993-3018.*

---

* Section 1, so far as material, provides: " (1) Where property . . . is held on trusts
arising . . . under any . . . settlement . . . the court may if it thinks fit by order approve
. . . any arrangement . . . varying or revoking all or any of the trusts . . ."

A   For the Variation of Trusts Act 1958, s. 1, see 38 Halsbury's Statutes (2nd Edn.) 1130.]

Cases referred to:

Seale's Marriage Settlement, Re [1961] 3 All E.R. 136; [1961] Ch. 574; [1961] 3 W.L.R. 262; 47 Digest (Repl.) 333, 2995.

B   *Weston's Settlements, Re,* [1968] 1 All E.R. 720; [1969] Ch. 223; [1968] 2 W.L.R. 1154; *affd.* C.A., [1968] 3 All E.R. 338; [1969] Ch. 223; [1968] 3 W.L.R. 786.

Adjourned Summons.

This was an application by the plaintiff, Mrs. Mary Barbara Webster, under s. 1 of the Variation of Trusts Act 1958 by originating summons dated 9th December 1968, who was beneficially interested under the trusts of residue of the will of Thomas Reginald Amery Windeatt, deceased. The application was for an arrangement to be approved by the court pursuant to s. 1 of the Variation of Trusts Act 1958 on behalf of the infant defendants and any unborn person who might become interested under the trusts of the will. The proposed terms of the arrangement were that the third defendant, Cyril John Holberton Wollen, the sole English trustee, should appoint Jersey trustees to be new trustees and transfer the trust property to the Jersey trustees. The defendants to the summons were Adrian William Webster and Martin Guy Webster, infants both of whom were beneficially interested in the trusts, and Cyril John Holberton Wollen, the sole English trustee. The facts are set out in the judgment.

E   *E. I. Goulding,* Q.C., and *J. B. Morcom* for the plaintiff.
D. J. M. Campion for the first and second defendants.
H. E. Francis, Q.C., and *M. G. Johnston* for the third defendant.

PENNYCUICK, J.: I have before me an application under the Variation of Trusts Act 1958. For reasons which will appear, I propose to give a short formal judgment on this point.

F   Thomas Reginald Amery Windeatt, whom I will call the testator, was resident and domiciled in England. By his will dated 15th December 1951 the testator appointed his wife, Lilian Mary Windeatt, and the third defendant, Cyril John Holberton Wollen, to be his executors and the trustees of his will. He constituted a residuary estate and directed his trustees to hold it on the following trusts: first, to pay the income to his wife during her life, then, after providing a certain additional legacy after the death of his wife, he directed that the income of his residuary estate should be paid to his daughter, the plaintiff, Mrs. Webster, during her life, with a provision for making certain payments to her out of capital; and he directed his trustees after the death of the plaintiff to hold his residuary estate—

"Upon Trust as to both capital and income for all or such one or more exclusively of the others or other of the children or remoter issue of my said Daughter born within twenty one years of her death at such times and if more than one in such shares and with such provisions for maintenance advancement and otherwise for the benefit of such children or remoter issue or some or one of them and generally in such manner in all respects as my said Daughter shall by Deed revocable or irrevocable or by Will or Codicil appoint and Subject to any such appointment Upon Trust for the child or children of my said Daughter who shall attain the age of twenty one years and if more than one in equal shares.

"Subject as aforesaid and if there shall be no person who under the preceding Trusts shall attain a vested interest in my Residuary Estate or any part thereof Upon Trust for my next of kin living at the death of my said Daughter according to the Statutes of Distribution."

The testator died on 25th August 1959. He left surviving him his wife and his daughter, the plaintiff. The testator's widow died on 26th August 1965. The

plaintiff is the wife of James William Arthur Webster. They have two children, A
Adrian and Martin, the first and second defendants, who are both under 21.
The Webster family lives in Jersey.   Particulars of their residence in Jersey
are set out in affidavits made by the plaintiff and her husband, from which it
appears that they have been resident in Jersey for 19 years and they believe
themselves to be domiciled there.   I see no reason to doubt that.   They live
in a house in Jersey which belongs to them.   B

   The trust fund has a present value of approximately £130,000.   It is mostly
invested in foreign securities, and the balance is mainly invested in British
government stocks which are tax free in the hands of foreign residents.

   It is now proposed that two persons resident in Jersey be appointed trustees of
the will in place of the third defendant who is at present the sole trustee, and that,
after such appointment, the trust fund shall be transferred to the new trustees in C
Jersey to be held by them on the trusts of a new declaration of trust proposed
to be made by them in Jersey.   A draft of that declaration of trust is in evidence.
The trusts are drawn so as to correspond in all relevant respects with the trusts
of the residuary estate of the testator.   There is in evidence an affidavit of
Lester Vivian Bailhache, who is an advocate practising in Jersey, has also been
called to the English bar, and is the President of the Jersey Law Society.   He D
goes in detail into the law of Jersey in relation to settlements, and he states in
the most unqualified terms that in his opinion and that of the other advocates
in Jersey the nature of whose practice requires them to consider the legality of
settlements, a settlement in the terms proposed will be effective as expressed
under the law of Jersey: so it follows that, if the order which I am asked to
make is made, the property will be under the control of Jersey trustees and held E
on trusts which will be in all relevant respects the same as the existing trusts.

   I think it is clear that I have jurisdiction to make the order.   I was referred
to *Re Seale's Marriage Settlement* (1).   The headnote reads as follows (2):

> " By a marriage settlement made in 1931 certain investments were
> settled on trust for the wife for life, after her death on trust for the husband
> for life upon protective trusts if he survived her, and after the death of   F
> the survivor on trust for the children or remoter issue of the marriage
> as the husband and wife jointly or the survivor of them should appoint,
> and in default of such appointment to the children of the marriage who,
> being male, attained the age of 21 years, or, being female, attained that age
> or married, if more than one in equal shares.   At the date of the settlement
> the husband and wife were domiciled in England but they subsequently   G
> emigrated to Canada.   There were three children of the marriage, one of
> whom had attained the age of 21 years.   On a summons asking the court
> to appoint a Canadian corporation to be trustee of the settlement in place
> of the present English trustee and to approve, under section 1 of the Variation
> of Trusts Act, 1958, an arrangement whereby the trustee of the English
> settlement might transfer the property comprised in that settlement to the   H
> trustee of a Canadian settlement which was as similar to the English settle-
> ment as possible:—*Held*, that, having regard to the fact that the court
> could approve an arrangement revoking all the trusts of a settlement, the
> court had jurisdiction to approve an arrangement, such as the present,
> which, in effect, revoked all the trusts of the English settlement in the
> event of the trust property becoming subject to the trusts of a settlement   I
> which would be recognised and enforced by some other jurisdiction."

This decision covers the matter of jurisdiction.   I am told, also, that in at
least two subsequent cases other judges have made comparable orders.   The
only difficulty results from *Re Weston's Settlements* (3), before STAMP, J., and
before the Court of Appeal (4).   In that case, the judge on the particular facts

---

(1) [1961] 3 All E.R. 136; [1961] Ch. 574.   (2) [1961] Ch. at p. 574.
(3) [1968] 1 All E.R. 720; [1969] Ch. 223.   (4) [1968] 3 All E.R. 338; [1969] Ch. 223.

A   of the case exercised his discretion under the Act to refuse to sanction an arrangement, and the Court of Appeal affirmed his decision. The judge in *Re Weston* (5) referred to *Re Seale* (6), as did the Court of Appeal, without disapproval. *Re Weston* (5) went on its own facts entirely, which were extremely striking. The settlor there, with his family, had moved to Jersey only a very short time before the application to the court was made. It might well be inferred that the whole

B   object of moving to Jersey was to escape a particular fiscal liability, and it appeared that their stay in that country might well be transitory. These facts are brought out in the judgment of LORD DENNING, M.R., in the Court of Appeal (7):

C   "But here the family had only been in Jersey three months when they presented this scheme to the court. The inference is irresistible: the underlying purpose was to go there in order to avoid tax . . . I cannot help wondering how long these young people will stay in Jersey. It may be to their financial interest at present to make their home there permanently, but will they remain there once the capital gains are safely in hand, clear of tax? They may well change their minds and come back to enjoy their untaxed gains."

D

Similarly, HARMAN, L.J., said (8):

"The two young men who alone may be considered cannot be said to have proved that they truly intend to make Jersey their home."

It seems to me that *Re Weston's Settlements* (9) was decided on its own particular

E   facts, and on those facts it is a decision with which I am, if I may respectfully say so, in the most complete agreement. The facts of the case now before me are quite different. Here, the family has been in Jersey for 19 years and has made a genuine and permanent home in Jersey. The children were born there.

There is no other reason why it would not be right to exercise the jurisdiction in the present case. Accordingly I propose to make an order in the terms of

F   the minutes proposed, subject to one small alteration in the proposed draft declaration of trust, which has been discussed, and a note of which will be endorsed on counsel for the plaintiff's brief.

Order accordingly.

Solicitors: *Herbert Smith & Co.*, agents for *Hooper & Wollen*, Torquay (for all parties).

G

[*Reported by* ROSALIE LONG, *Barrister-at-Law.*]

H

I

(5) [1968] 1 All E.R. 720; [1969] Ch. 223.
(6) [1961] 3 All E.R. 136; [1961] Ch. 574.
(7) [1968] 3 All E.R. at p. 342; [1969] Ch. at pp. 245, 246.
(8) [1968] 3 All E.R. at p. 343; [1969] Ch. at pp. 247, 248.
(9) [1968] 3 All E.R. 338; [1969] Ch. 223.

A

COMMISSIONERS OF CUSTOMS AND EXCISE v.
GALLAHER, LTD.

[CONSOLIDATED APPEALS.]

[HOUSE OF LORDS (Lord Reid, Lord Hodson, Lord Pearce, Lord Donovan and B
Lord Diplock), March 3, 4, 5, April 23, 1969.]

*Customs—Commonwealth preference—Southern Rhodesia—Tobacco—Southern
Rhodesia ceasing to be in Commonwealth preference area from midnight
18th/19th November 1965—Tobacco grown in Southern Rhodesia and con-
signed to United Kingdom before 19th November 1965—" Consigned "—
Whether full duty payable—Import Duties Act 1958 (6 & 7 Eliz. 2 c. 6),* C
s. 2 (2), (3) (c), s. 12 (1)—Southern Rhodesia (Withdrawal of Commonwealth
Preference) Order 1965 (S.I. 1965 No. 1954), art. 1—Southern Rhodesia
(Withdrawal of Commonwealth Preference) (No. 2) Order 1965 (S.I. 1965
No. 1987).*

On 11th November 1965, the government in Southern Rhodesia announced
a unilateral declaration of independence.   Shortly thereafter the Southern   D
Rhodesia Act 1965 received the royal assent empowering, inter alia, the
amendment or suspension of any enactment in relation to Southern Rhodesia
and empowering orders to be made having effect from any date not earlier
than 11th November.   On 16th November an order was made by which
Southern Rhodesia was excluded from the countries included in the Commonwealth preference area (art. 1 (a)); the order specifically provided that   E
the rate of customs duty chargeable on any goods entered for warehousing
before the order came into operation was not affected (art. 2).   The order
came into operation on 19th November.   A second order was made a few
days later but also took effect on 19th November; this amended (art. 1)
the first order by also exempting from any change in the rate of duty goods
which had been shipped in a ship which had sailed from, inter alia, Beira   F
before 19th November.   On that date five parcels of tobacco were in transit
from Salisbury (Southern Rhodesia) via Beira to ports in the United Kingdom
but had not been put aboard ships which sailed before that date.   On the
question whether the tobacco was chargeable with customs duty under s. 4
of the Finance Act 1964 at the full rate or at the rate applying to tobacco
qualifying for Commonwealth preference, as defined in s. 2 (2)* of the Import   G
Duties Act 1958, when the tobacco was taken out of bond in 1966 and
1967,

Held (LORD PEARCE dissenting): the tobacco was chargeable to duty
at the full rate, because—

(i) (per LORD REID) although immediately before 19th November 1965
the tobacco had qualified under s. 2 (2) of the Import Duties Act 1958 for   H
Commonwealth preference if and when it arrived in the United Kingdom,
it was the intention of the orders to withdraw from Commonwealth preference
goods which had been consigned from a place in Southern Rhodesia before
19th November, but which were not on the high seas; effect had been
given to this intention by art. 1 (a) of the first order (see p. 331, letter I,
to p. 332, letter A, and p. 333, letters A and C, post);

(ii) (per LORD HODSON, LORD DONOVAN and LORD DIPLOCK) on the true
construction of s. 2 (2) and s. 12 (1)† of the Import Duties Act 1958, it
could not be said that, at the time when duty became chargeable on the
tobacco it had been grown in a place which was then in the Commonwealth
preference area or that it had been consigned to the United Kingdom from

I

---

* Section 2 (2) is set out at p. 330, letter D, post.
† Section 12 (1), so far as material, is set out at p. 335, letter C, post.

A   such a place (see p. 336, letter B, p. 340, letter F, p. 342, letter I, and p. 343,
    letter B, post);

        (iii) (per LORD HODSON, LORD DONOVAN and LORD DIPLOCK) even if the
    tobacco had acquired the character of " consigned " by the time it had left
    Salisbury, by virtue of art. 1 (*a*) of the first order, the definition of the Common-
    wealth preference area contained in s. 2 (3) (*c*) of the Import Duties Act
B   1958 must, so long as that order was in force, be read for all purposes and
    whatever the time to which an enquiry was directed, as if it excluded
    Southern Rhodesia (see p. 336, letter F, p. 340, letter F, and p. 343, letter D,
    post);

        (iv) (per LORD DONOVAN and LORD DIPLOCK) any ambiguity in art. 1
    of the orders must be resolved by reference to the intention underlying the
C   order which was apparent from art. 2 of the first order as amended by the
    second order (see p. 340, letter F, and p. 343, letter F, post); and

        (v) the first order was not ultra vires as having retrospective effect contrary
    to the requirements of its enabling power (see p. 333, letter F, p. 336,
    letter G, p. 340, letter F, and p. 343, letter G, post).

        Decision of the COURT OF APPEAL (sub nom. *Gallaher, Ltd.* v. *Commis-*
D   *sioners of Customs and Excise,* [1968] 2 All E.R. 820) reversed.

    [As to the Commonwealth preference area and goods qualifying for Common-
    wealth preference, see 33 HALSBURY'S LAWS (3rd Edn.) 67, 68, paras. 131, 132.
    For the Import Duties Act 1958, s. 2, s. 12, see 9 HALSBURY'S STATUTES
    (3rd Edn.) 258, 270.]

E   Case referred to:
        Papiergroothandel (N. W.) En Fabrieken Van de Gebroeders Cats v. *C. Baker &*
            Sons (Paper Makers), Ltd. (1923), 40 T.L.R. 230.

    Appeals.

        These were consolidated appeals by the Commissioners of Customs and Excise
    from the decision of the Court of Appeal (LORD DENNING, M.R., and EDMUND
F   DAVIES, L.J.; SALMON, L.J., dissenting) dated 30th April 1968 and reported
    [1968] 2 All E.R. 820, allowing the appeals of the respondents, Gallaher, Ltd.,
    from the judgment of ROSKILL, J., dated 31st May 1967 in three actions tried
    concurrently in which he declared that five parcels of tobacco, despatched to
    the respondents from Salisbury, Southern Rhodesia, before 19th November
    1965 did not qualify for Commonwealth preference. The facts are set out in
G   the opinion of LORD REID.

    R. A. MacCrindle, Q.C., and *Gordon Slynn* for the commissioners.
    Michael Kerr, Q.C., and *M. J. Mustill, Q.C.,* for the respondents.

    Their Lordships took time for consideration.

    23rd April.   The following opinions were delivered.

H   **LORD REID:** My Lords, in this case it is necessary to determine the
    meaning and effect of one of the measures authorised by Parliament and taken
    by the British government following on the unilateral declaration of independence
    on 11th November 1965, by Mr. Smith's government in Southern Rhodesia.
    From 1919 onwards goods imported from that country have enjoyed Imperial
    preference, later Commonwealth preference. On 19th November 1965, there
I   came into operation the Southern Rhodesia (Withdrawal of Commonwealth
    Preference) Order 1965 (1).

        The question in this case is whether as a result of that order five parcels of
    tobacco belonging to the respondents are chargeable with customs duty under
    s. 4 of the Finance Act 1964, at the full rate or at the rate applying to " tobacco
    qualifying for Commonwealth preference ". On 19th November 1965, these
    parcels were in transit from Salisbury to ports in the United Kingdom. The

    ───────────────────────────────
    (1) S.I. 1965 No. 1954.

respondents argue that they had already qualified before 19th November and   A
that that qualification was not affected by the Order in Council.   The commissioners argue that they never qualified or alternatively that if they had qualified
that qualification was annulled by the order.

Whether this tobacco had qualified for Commonwealth preference before
19th November 1965, depends on the proper interpretation of s. 2 of the Import
Duties Act 1958.   The relevant parts of that section are: B

" 2.—(1) Orders under section one of this Act may provide that the
import duty imposed on goods of any description shall not be chargeable
on goods qualifying for Commonwealth preference or shall be chargeable
on them at a preferential rate: and the power conferred by that section
to impose import duties with a view to affording protection to goods pro-   C
duced in the United Kingdom shall include power to impose import duties
with a view to affording preference to goods qualifying for Commonwealth
preference.

" (2) The goods qualifying for Commonwealth preference shall be any
goods of the area referred to in this Act as the Commonwealth preference
area which are consigned to the United Kingdom from a place in that area.   D

" (3) Subject to the following provisions of this section, the Commonwealth preference area shall consist of—(a) the United Kingdom; and
(b) the countries named as parts of that area in subsection (4) of this section;
and (c) any country not named (nor included in a country named) in the
said subsection (4) which for the time being forms part of Her Majesty's
dominions outside the United Kingdom; and (d) any country not named   E
(nor included in a country named) in the said subsection (4) which is for
the time being under Her Majesty's protection through Her Majesty's
government in the United Kingdom, or administered by that government
under the trusteeship system of the United Nations; and (e) any country
not named (nor included in a country named) in the said subsection (4)
which is for the time being administered by the government of a country   F
included in the Commonwealth preference area under paragraph (b) of this
subsection.

" (4) The countries referred to in paragraph (b) of subsection (3) of this
section shall be the following Commonwealth countries, namely, the Commonwealth of Australia, Canada, Ceylon, Ghana, India, the Federation of
Malaya, New Zealand, Pakistan, the Federation of Rhodesia and Nyasaland   G
and the Union of South Africa, together with Burma and the Republic of
Ireland: Provided that Her Majesty may by Order in Council direct that
the name of any country shall be added to this subsection, including that
of any country which but for the order would be included in the Commonwealth preference area under paragraph (c) of subsection (3) of this section.

" (5) Her Majesty may by Order in Council direct that any country   H
for the time being named in subsection (4) of this section shall not form
part of the Commonwealth preference area.

" (6) A country falling within paragraph (d) or (e) of subsection (3) of
this section shall not be included in the Commonwealth preference area
under that paragraph unless either it fell within that paragraph at the
date of the passing of this Act or Her Majesty by Order in Council directs   I
that it shall be so included.

" (7) Any Order in Council under subsection (5) or (6) of this section
may be revoked by a subsequent Order in Council.

" (8) No recommendation shall be made to Her Majesty in Council to make
an order under this section unless a draft of the order has been laid before
Parliament and approved by resolution of each House of Parliament . . ."

This tobacco was grown in Southern Rhodesia and I agree with your Lordships

A that it was consigned to the United Kingdom from Salisbury before 19th November, i.e., at a time when Salisbury was admittedly a place in the Commonwealth preference area within the meaning of this section.

The greater part of the argument was directed to the question of the time or stage at which goods become qualified for Commonwealth preference. The respondents argue that on a proper construction of s. 2 of the Act of 1958 and B in particular of sub-s. (2) of that section, the qualification attaches as soon as the goods are consigned from a place in the country of origin. The commissioners argue that the proper and only time for determining whether goods are qualified is the time when customs duty on them becomes payable. If the importer takes possession of the goods on their arrival in this country then the duty is payable before he takes possession. But if he enters the goods for warehousing C in bond then under s. 88 of the Customs and Excise Act 1952 the duty and the rate chargeable are those in force at the date of the removal of the goods from the warehouse. So on the commissioners' argument, if the goods are warehoused in bond, it may be for several years, no answer can be given to the question whether the goods are qualified for Commonwealth preference until they are taken out of bond and the duty becomes payable.

D In construing the Act of 1958 one should have the background in mind. This system of preference was well established. An important stage in its development was the making of the Ottawa agreements (2) which included an agreement between the governments of Great Britain and Southern Rhodesia. No great changes can have been anticipated. The phrase " for the time being " occurs in various parts of s. 2 (3) which defines the Commonwealth preference E area, but for the most part that is accounted for by the anticipation that various countries then parts of Her Majesty's dominions would in due course be granted independence but continue to participate in the preference scheme. No one can have expected in 1958 any situation like that which occurred in November 1965 and I do not think that the Act of 1958 was drafted with any such situation in contemplation. But statutes often have to be applied to unforeseen situations F and, if there is ambiguity, one must adopt that solution which is most reasonable and which accords best with the apparent policy of the enactment.

It is said that there is no need to determine whether goods are qualified for preference until the duty is payable. But if the importer wishes to sell the goods while they are in transit or in bond he will get a higher price if the goods are qualified for the lower rate of customs duty payable in respect of qualified G goods, and it would seem reasonable that it should be possible for him to prove to the buyer that the goods are qualified. Of course any qualification, like any other entitlement to receive a future advantage, can be annulled by legislation passed before the advantage is due to be received. But that does not prevent the existence of the qualification or other entitlement before the date when it results in the advantage being received. I can see no good reason why H the legislature or the draftsman should have intended the question whether goods are qualified to remain in suspense until the date when the duty is payable.

Analysis of the definition of goods qualifying in s. 2 (2) of the Act of 1958 leads me to the same conclusion as that based on more general considerations. There are two requirements. The goods must be " goods of the area " defined in sub-s. (3) as the Commonwealth preference area, and they must be " goods . . . I which are consigned to the United Kingdom from a place in that area ". I do not think that there is any difficulty about " goods of the area ". Section 12 (1) provides that goods " shall be deemed to be goods of a country if they are grown, produced or manufactured in that country " and by s. 15 references to a country include references to any area consisting of two or more countries. So if one looks at the position before the Order of 1965 came into operation, this tobacco, having been grown in Southern Rhodesia, was goods of the preference area.

The difficulty arises with regard to the second requirement—goods " which

(2) The Ottawa Agreements Acts 1932.

are consigned . . ."   Again looking at the matter before the Order of 1965 came   A
into operation, it was true to say on or before 18th November 1965 that the
goods " are consigned . . ." in the present tense.   So it appears to me that on
that date both requirements had already been satisfied and the goods had therefore qualified for obtaining preference if and when they arrived in the United
Kingdom by virtue of such consignment.   But it was argued " are consigned "
can be read in a different way so as to refer to the much later date when the duty   B
becomes payable.   It is said that " consigned " is not part of the verb in the
passive but is adjectival qualifying "goods".   It is quite true that past participles
are often used adjectivally: one can say that goods are licensed goods in
the present tense although they had been given a licence at an earlier date.
But here the adjective would have to be " consigned-to-the-United-Kingdom-
from-a-place in-the-area " goods, a form of adjective quite unacceptable in the   C
English language.   So in order to apply this definition as at the date when duty
becomes payable one must either submit to this contortion of the English language
or say that the draftsman erred in using the present tense and that he ought to
have said " were consigned " or " have been consigned ".   I would be sorry to
have to decide the meaning of an enactment on grammar alone.   But grammar
is important in confirming a view based on other considerations.   I am therefore   D
of opinion that this tobacco was on 18th November 1965 " tobacco qualifying
for Commonwealth preference " within the meaning of the Finance Act 1964.
So far I agree with the majority of the Court of Appeal (3).

I must now deal with the Southern Rhodesia (Withdrawal of Commonwealth
Preference) Order 1965 which came into operation on 19th November 1965.
It provides: E

" 1.   Southern Rhodesia shall, while this Order is in force, be excluded
from the area referred to in the Import Duties Act 1958 as the Commonwealth preference area, and accordingly while this Order is in force:—
(a) the countries described in section 2 (3) (c) of that Act (countries within
Her Majesty's dominions outside the United Kingdom not named in section
2 (4) shall be taken not to include Southern Rhodesia; and (b) section 2 (9)   F
of that Act (goods consigned from Lourenço Marques or Beira) shall not
apply to goods of Southern Rhodesia.
" 2.   The foregoing Article shall not affect the rate of customs duty
chargeable on any goods entered for warehousing (within the meaning
of the Customs and Excise Act 1952) before the date of the coming into
operation of this Order.   G
" 3.—(1) This Order may be cited as the Southern Rhodesia (Withdrawal
of Commonwealth Preference) Order 1965, and shall come into operation
on 19th November 1965.   (2) The Interpretation Act 1889 shall apply to
the interpretation of this Order as it applies to the interpretation of an
Act of Parliament."

The words " while this Order is in force " reflect the view of the British govern-   H
ment at that time that constitutional rule in Southern Rhodesia would be restored
within a comparatively short time, and this may well have influenced the form
of the drafting.   Article 1 effects the temporary exclusion of Southern Rhodesia
from the Commonwealth preference area, and art. 2 shows what effect the draftsman thought that that exclusion would have.   The fact that it was thought
necessary to provide in art. 2 that goods already imported from Southern Rhodesia   I
and entered for warehousing should remain entitled to the preferential rate of
duty shows that the draftsman (or Her Majesty in Council) thought that the
effect of art. 1 was to withdraw preference from goods still in transit to the
United Kingdom for so long as the order might remain in force.   Then it must
have been thought that this was too drastic because by a second order (4) goods

(3) [1968] 2 All E.R. 820; [1968] 2 Q.B. 674.
(4) The Southern Rhodesia (Withdrawal of Commonwealth Preference) (No. 2) Order
1965 (S.I. 1965 No. 1987).

A in any ship which had sailed from Beira or other ports were also excluded from the scope of the first order. But that left subject to that order goods which had been consigned from a place in Southern Rhodesia before 19th November but which were not yet on the high seas. The loss caused by the withdrawal of preference would fall on the owners of such goods and it made no difference whether those owners were connected with Southern Rhodesia or were British
B importers who had already bought the goods. The tobacco in the present case had not been shipped but was still in transit from Salisbury to Beira or was in Beira awaiting shipment.

But it is not sufficient that the law-making authority should have thought that the order disqualified such goods from receiving the preference; one must find in the order some provision which on a reasonable construction was adequate
C to impose the additional duty. In my view that is to be found in art. 1 (a) which provides that during the operation of the order the preference area " shall be taken not to include Southern Rhodesia ". That must mean that, whenever after 19th November it is necessary to determine whether the goods are entitled to preference, the relevant enactments must be applied as if Southern Rhodesia was not part of the preference area. So when the customs authorities have to
D determine the appropriate rate of duty they must take it that Southern Rhodesia is not part of the Commonwealth preference area. The fact that the goods were qualified for preference before 19th November 1965 is irrelevant. In other words the effect of this provision is to disqualify during the operation of the order all goods from Southern Rhodesia which had previously been qualified and which are not within the exceptions set out in the two orders. That is
E clearly the intention of the order and the provision to which I have referred appears to me to make it possible to give effect to that intention.

But then it is said that that is to give retrospective effect to the order, and the Act (5) under which the orders were made prohibits orders made under it from having effect before 11th November 1965. In my view there is nothing retrospective in an enactment providing that a right which existed when it was
F passed shall on its passing cease to exist. That does not have any effect on anything which happened or was done before it was passed; it only affects the future after it was passed. In my view this order does not mean that qualifications which existed on 19th November shall be deemed or taken never to have existed; but it does mean that qualifications which existed on 19th November shall, during the operation of the order, be taken or deemed not to exist.
G   During the currency of this order the respondents paid duty at the full rate on this tobacco and they seek repayment of a sum representing the difference between the full rate and the preference rate. For the reasons which I have given I am of the opinion that they are not entitled to such repayment. I would therefore allow this appeal.

H   **LORD HODSON:** My Lords, this appeal raises a short question of construction in transactions in which the respondents (Gallaher, Ltd.) sought declarations that they are entitled to the benefit of Commonwealth preference on five cases of Rhodesian tobacco.

The enactment under which tobacco goods fall to be charged with customs duty is the Finance Act 1964, as amended by the Finance Act 1965, which increased the rates of duty. The Act of 1964, by s. 4 (1), provides:
I

" That there shall be charged—(a) on tobacco imported into the United Kingdom duties of customs at the rates shown in Table 1 in Schedule 5 to this Act . . ."

Schedule 5 specified differing rates of duty for tobacco goods indicating the " full " rate and the " Commonwealth " rate. Section 26 (2) provides:

---

(5) The Southern Rhodesia Act 1965.

" In Part I of this Act [this deals with customs and excise] ... (b) sub-   A
sections (2) to (9) of Section 2 of the Import Duties Act 1958 (which defines
the goods qualifying for Commonwealth preference under that Act) shall
apply for the purposes of provisions referring to goods qualifying for
Commonwealth preference as they apply for the purposes of that section.
" (3) Part I of this Act shall be construed as one with the Customs and
Excise Act 1952 ..."   B

The terms of the qualifying definition in s. 2 of the Import Duties Act 1958,
present the problem to which the facts leading to this appeal give rise.

Each case was shipped after midnight on 18th/19th November 1965, the
moment when the Southern Rhodesia (Withdrawal of Commonwealth Preference)
Order 1965 (6) came into operation.   This order was made under the enabling
powers conferred by the Southern Rhodesia Act 1965, passed on 15th November   C
1965, following on the unilateral declaration of independence made in Southern
Rhodesia.   The Act provided that any provision made by or under such an
order may be made to take effect from any date not earlier than 11th November
1965.

The order provided by art. 1 that, whilst it is in force, Southern Rhodesia
shall be excluded from the area referred to in the Import Duties Act 1958, as   D
the Commonwealth preference area and accordingly, while the order is in force, the
countries described in s. 2 (3) (c) of that Act shall be taken not to include Southern
Rhodesia and s. 2 (9) of that Act (goods consigned from Lourenço Marques
and Beira) shall not apply to goods of Southern Rhodesia.   Article 2 provided
that the foregoing was not to affect the rate of customs duty chargeable on any
goods entered for warehousing before the date of the coming into operation of   E
the order.

On 23rd November 1965, the amelioration given by art. 2 of the previous order
was extended (7) so as to add at the end a saving for any goods shipped in a ship
sailing from Lourenço Marques or Beira or any port in the Commonwealth
preference area before the date of the operation of the order (8).

The tobacco in question was all grown in Southern Rhodesia before 18th   F
November 1965, and all became chargeable to duty after that date when Southern
Rhodesia was no longer part of the Commonwealth preference area.   It is not
in dispute that the goods become chargeable at the rates in force on the date of
removal from warehouse (see s. 38 and s. 88 of the Customs and Excise Act
1952, which has to be read with Part 1 of the Finance Act 1964, which imposed
the duty).   The respondents contend that they should be charged at the Common-   G
wealth preference rate prevailing at that date. The commissioners, on the other
hand, contend that the goods should be charged at the full rate because at the
time when they fell to be charged Southern Rhodesia was no longer in the
Commonwealth preference area, so that they did not qualify for the preference
since they were not grown or produced in a country which at the time when
the duty became chargeable was in the Commonwealth preference area.   H

The Import Duties Act 1958, for the first time granted Commonwealth
preference and imposed duties of customs in place of those chargeable under the
Import Duties Act 1932, which ceased to have effect after the passing of the
Act of 1958.   I must now set out the subsection on which the controversy
principally turned, viz., s. 2 (2), which provides:

" The goods qualifying for Commonwealth preference shall be any goods   I
of the area referred to in this Act as the Commonwealth preference area
which are consigned to the United Kingdom from a place in that area."

Reference must be made to some of the following subsections.   Subsection (3)

(6) S.I. 1965 No. 1954.
(7) By the Southern Rhodesia (Withdrawal of Commonwealth Preference) (No. 2)
Order 1965 (S.I. 1965 No. 1987).
(8) I.e., 19th November 1965.

A and sub-s. (4) set out the constituent parts of the area with a proviso that Her Majesty may, by Order in Council, direct that the name of any country shall be added to the preceding subsection.   Subsection (5) provides that Her Majesty may, by Order in Council, direct that any country for the time being named in sub-s. (4) shall not form part of the Commonwealth preference area.   By sub-s.
B (9), as amended by statutory instrument (9), goods of Southern Rhodesia and certain other countries shall for the purpose of qualifying for Commonwealth preference be deemed to be consigned to the United Kingdom from that country if they are so consigned from Lourenço Marques or Beira in Portuguese East Africa.

Section 12 (1) shows how the country of origin of imported goods is to be determined.   It provides:

C   " For the purposes of this Act ... goods shall be deemed to be goods of a country if they are grown, produced or manufactured in that country."

I agree with your Lordships and with all the judges in the courts below (10) in rejecting the submission of the commissioners that the goods were not *consigned* to the United Kingdom there being no through contract of carriage or successive contracts arranged at the outset.   In the ordinary commercial sense they were
D consigned if transmitted from the place where they were grown with the intention that they should go by continuous transit to the United Kingdom and not be taken into the commerce of another country.

The argument which found favour with the majority of the Court of Appeal (11) is put shortly by Lord Denning, M.R. (12), in saying that the consignments qualified for Commonwealth preference before midnight on 18th/19th November
E 1965, whilst Southern Rhodesia was still in the Commonwealth preference area but the duties only became chargeable after that date when Southern Rhodesia's name had been expunged from the area.   If the qualification attached to the goods when they were grown it was said that they were, so to speak (12) "franked" so as to be free of the full rate of customs duty.   This qualification never having been expressly removed should not, it was said, be removed by matters
F subsequently arising, for legislation to that effect would be retroactive.

The respondents sought to support this argument by reliance on the words " for the time being " which appear in several places in the subsections of s. 2 of the Act of 1958, but I agree with Lord Denning, M.R., and with Salmon, L.J., that no assistance can be obtained from this temporal phrase which simply refers to whatever time might be relevant while the Act is in force.   The argu-
G ment for the respondents is mainly based on the use of the word " qualifying " as if this word were used to impart to the goods some quality which gave them from the time they were grown in a Commonwealth area a vested right to suffer no more than the preferential rate of duty if and when it became chargeable, that is to say, a conditional right to preference.   This conception would, it seems, have the strange consequence that goods must, in order to acquire the necessary
H qualification, be grown in the country and consigned from a country as defined at the time when qualification attached and would prevent goods grown before 1958, when Commonwealth preference was introduced, from ever qualifying.

I see no reason to give this special meaning to the word " qualifying " so as to involve the crystallisation of a qualification.   The natural way to read the words " are consigned " in s. 2 (2) and the words in s. 12 (1) " are grown, pro-
I duced or manufactured in that country " is, in my opinion, to read them as adjectival, being descriptive of the goods which qualify but not otherwise stamping them from a fixed date with an immunity from customs duty.   I think that some additional support to what I have called the natural construction is

(9) See the Federation of Rhodesia and Nyasaland (Dissolution) Order in Council 1963 (S.I. 1963 No. 2085).
(10) [1968] 1 Lloyd's Rep. 80; [1968] 2 All E.R. 820; [1968] 2 Q.B. 874.
(11) [1968] 2 All E.R. 820; [1968] 2 Q.B. 674.
(12) [1968] 2 All E.R. at p. 824; [1968] 2 Q.B. at p. 687.

supplied by the meaning I have already given to the word " consigned " for   A
it will not be until importation to this country that it will be readily ascertainable
whether the goods qualify as " consigned to the United Kingdom ".

On this footing the customs officials have only to ascertain the place of growth
and whether that place is on the list of Commonwealth preference areas when
the liability to pay the duty attaches and likewise with regard to consignment.
They do not have to enquire in addition whether at the time of growth and at   B
the time of consignment that place was on the current list.   In other words,
they have to ascertain whether the country qualifies at the time when duty is
chargeable and not whether the country was formerly qualified.   In my opinion,
the judgment of ROSKILL, J. (13), should be restored on this ground.   I would
add that this interpretation of the Import Duties Act 1958, is, I think, consistent
with the earlier legislation dealing with Imperial preference, e.g., the Finance   C
Act 1919, s. 8, which prescribed preferential rates for goods shown to have
been consigned from and grown, produced or manufactured in the British Empire.
The Import Duties Act 1932, followed the same pattern.

I return to the Southern Rhodesia (Withdrawal of Commonwealth Preference)
Order 1965 which I think produces the same result.   It provides:

". . . while this Order is in force:—(a) the countries described in section   D
2 (3) (c) of that Act [viz., the Import Duties Act 1958] . . . shall be taken
not to include Southern Rhodesia."

This is a direct instruction looking to the future when duty first becomes chargeable, and is not ultra vires as having effect from a date earlier than 11th November
1965, the date fixed by the Southern Rhodesia Act 1965.   The terms of the
order of 1965 and of the amending order of 1965 clearly show that it was part   E
of the intention of the orders to save from the withdrawal of Commonwealth
preference goods which would otherwise be affected, namely, goods entered for
warehousing before the date of the coming into operation of the order and goods
shipped before that date from Lourenço Marques or Beira or any port in the
Commonwealth preference area.

The effect of these orders is, in my opinion, that, with the exceptions men-   F
tioned, all goods from Southern Rhodesia are, while the order is in force, excluded
from the benefit of Commonwealth preference whether they had previously
been qualified for this preference or not.   The orders changed the requisites of
qualification for Commonwealth preference as from the date of its operation,
but this is not retrospective legislation.

I would allow the appeal.   G

LORD PEARCE: My Lords, the words of s. 2 of the Import Duties Act
1958, implement a plain, sensible simple notion in (as I think) plain, sensible
simple words.   As a matter of construction it is not permissible to impose on
those plain words connotations which are out of accord with the notion which
they implement.   In construing those words, therefore, one must resist the   H
temptation to " see more in a thing than the thing's self " as Robert Browning
expressed it.

The underlying notion was a successor to Imperial preference and followed
the Ottawa Agreements Act 1932.   Commonwealth production and trade were
to be stimulated in and between its various component areas by mutual, preferential tariffs.   The Import Duties Act 1958, s. 2, was a United Kingdom   I
contribution to the general notion.   It was a municipal implementation of
commercial inter-government arrangements.

It is obvious, I think, as a matter of common sense, that if, while the general
underlying framework was being evolved, a Rhodesian representative had asked
a British representative " Does this mean that a Rhodesian exporter when he
consigns Rhodesian goods to the United Kingdom has a *right* to a preferential

A   tariff or does it mean that he will then merely have a *hope* that later when duties come to be payable he may be fortunate enough to be charged at a preferential rate?", the British representative would have answered "Of course he has a right to a preferential tariff". He certainly would not have helped the scheme forward if he had hedged or said that there was merely a "hope" at the moment of export, even if he had tried to conceal its nakedness and exalt its

B status with a threadbare mantle of latinity by calling it a spes. And what reason is there why he *should* have hedged?

  If I am right in thinking that this was the underlying intention, this was precisely what the draftsman of the section set out to achieve and did achieve. Of course, the right which the Rhodesian exporter would get when he consigned his Rhodesian goods to this country was a right which the United Kingdom

C government had the power, as all governments have the power, to refuse to implement or acknowledge even after the right had come into existence. And if the Southern Rhodesia (Withdrawal of Commonwealth Preference) Order 1965 (14) on its true construction did this, the right is defeated and the respondents cannot get their preferential tariff. But it is important in construing the order to see just what was the situation on which that order was superimposed.

D   Section 2 (1) of the 1958 Act provides that import duty shall be chargeable at a preferential rate " on goods qualifying for Commonwealth preference ". Subsection (2) shows how they shall qualify.

> " The goods qualifying for Commonwealth preference shall be any goods of the area referred to in this Act as the Commonwealth preference area which are consigned to the United Kingdom from a place in that area."

E They qualify, if they are goods which " are consigned ". As one would expect, the words used are in the present tense. It is not permissible as a matter of construction to read the words as in the past tense when they have a clear and sensible meaning in the present tense. Nor do I accept the suggestion that " consigned " should be read as a past participle and that the plain words " are consigned " should be distorted to mean " are goods which were consigned ".

F   Moreover, the present tense accords with commercial good sense. It is when he consigns the goods that the exporter wishes to know where he stands and what are his rights. That is the moment at which he does his part of the bargain. By doing it he has either got some rights or got none. To suggest that at that point he has no rights seems to me out of accord with the whole spirit of the underlying intention and the plain words of the Act.

G   Counsel for the commissioners in his able argument showed how sub-s. (1) and sub-s. (2) could be satisfactorily read together without any necessity for the word " qualify ". They can. But the word " qualify " was deliberately inserted to deal with the fact that there are two stages in the operation. The goods qualify when they are consigned. The exporter (or rather, perhaps one should say the goods) has then done his part, and got his rights. The later

H stage is when the duty is paid and the qualification is implemented.

  If, therefore, the time at which the goods are consigned is the moment at which the goods qualify for preference, there is no justification for the mental gymnastic of seeing whether if they had tried to qualify at some later stage (which is no longer possible unless they are sent home again and re-exported) they would manage to pass the test. If there is a prize, to be awarded some

I months later, for somebody who qualified by going through some particular hoop, it is not very sensible to consider at the subsequent prizegiving whether he would at *that* moment be able to go through the hoop if he were now to undergo the test again.

  It was contended that " goods of the area " create a difficulty unless one judges the situation as at the moment of imposing the duty. I find no difficulty in these words. In seeing whether goods qualify one has to find if " goods of

---

(14) S.I. 1965 No. 1954.

the area referred to in this Act as the Commonwealth preference area . . . A
are consigned to the United Kingdom from a place in that area ". By s. 12 (1)
" goods shall be deemed to be goods of a country if they are grown, produced
or manufactured in that country ". The area is a geographical area. Are
these goods when they are consigned from Southern Rhodesia, goods which
have been grown, produced or manufactured in Southern Rhodesia, i.e., the
territory which is now known as Southern Rhodesia? If they are, they come B
within the section. If they are not, they do not. Before November 1965, they
were. From and after some date in November 1965, they were not. On that
date (whatever it may be on true construction of the order) Southern Rhodesia
was taken out of the area. Whether it was in or out of the area at the time when
they were grown or manufactured is irrelevant. To exclude from the preference
certain " goods of the area . . . which are consigned to the United Kingdom " C
on the ground that they were wholly or partially manufactured or grown at
some date before the Act came into operation has no justification in the language
used. Moreover, it would be quite out of accord with the commercial realities
that underlie the Act. One cannot envisage any person or government making
such a trade agreement. It would be pointless in intention and unworkable in
practice.   D

In my opinion, nothing in the Finance Act 1964 was intended to affect or
reduce the rights of Commonwealth exporters to the United Kingdom. Nor
has it done so per incuriam.

On the question of consignment, I agree with all the judgments in the courts
below (15) which held that the goods here in question were consigned to the
United Kingdom before 19th November.   Your Lordships have had the addi- E
tional advantage of reading *N. W. Papiergroothandel En Fabrieken Van de
Gebroeders Cats* v. *C. Baker & Sons (Paper Makers), Ltd.* (16) which, in my opinion,
was rightly decided. I agree with the learned judge in his observations (17)
about a City of London special jury and his refusal to take a view which was
" contrary to the realities of the matter and to the sense in which businessmen
use the word consignment ". The court should always be slow to add glosses F
when a statute has deliberately chosen as its yardstick a word of commercial
significance on which a decision of fact is intended to be made. I, like the Court
of Appeal (18), am content to accept the test put forward by the judge (19):

" First I think there must be an *intention* on the part of the consignor
to send the goods from one place to the other. It is not, of course, enough
that there should be an intention which he keeps to himself, an intention G
which is wholly unmanifested by any overt act . . . It is not enough that
the consignor at that stage should have sent the goods off to an intermediate
port with perhaps a half-formed intention that the goods might, if market
conditions were suitable, end in the United Kingdom . . . There has got
always to be a state of facts . . . relating to the goods which, coupled with
the intention of the consignor, shows that those goods are in the course of H
being transmitted from a place in the Commonwealth Preference area to the
United Kingdom for importation into the United Kingdom and not
elsewhere."

To that I would add LORD DENNING, M.R.'s concise and expressive sentence (20):

" The sender from the place in the Commonwealth preference area must I
intend that they should go direct to the United Kingdom and not be taken
into the commerce of any other country . . . "

---

(15) [1968] 1 Lloyd's Rep. 80; on appeal, [1968] 2 All E.R. 820; [1968] 2 Q.B. 674.
(16) (1923), 40 T.L.R. 230.
(17) [1968] 1 Lloyd's Rep. at p. 98.
(18) [1968] 2 All E.R. at p. 831; [1968] 2 Q.B. at p. 698.
(19) [1968] 1 Lloyd's Rep. at p. 99.
(20) [1968] 2 All E.R. at p. 823; [1968] 2 Q.B. at p. 686.

A   The Order in Council, described as the Southern Rhodesia (Withdrawal of Commonwealth Preference) Order 1965, came into operation on 19th November 1965.

I agree with the learned judge (21) and the majority of the Court of Appeal (22) that on the assumption that the goods had acquired rights, or were, as they described it, " franked ", the order does not affect their position.   The order

B   had the fullest statutory effect (see Southern Rhodesia Act 1965, s. 2), from any date " not earlier than 11th November 1965 ". This limitation would make it impossible to deal with the situation in such a way as, e.g., that relating to South Africa was dealt with, namely, South Africa " shall be deemed never to have been a Commonwealth country " (South Africa Act 1962, Sch. 3, para. 3 (2); see also s. 2 (2)).   Moreover, such terms would have been wholly unsuitable to

C   the Rhodesian situation since it was earnestly hoped that any penal alteration would be merely temporary.   The words " while this Order is in force " were inserted twice.   Article 1 of the Order of 1965 provides:

" Southern Rhodesia shall, while this Order is in force, be excluded from the area referred to in the Import Duties Act 1958 as the Commonwealth preference area, and accordingly while this Order is in force:—

D   " (*a*) the countries described in section 2 (3) (*c*) of that Act . . . shall be taken not to include Southern Rhodesia . . ."

The order could validly and intra vires say that the countries in question should be taken as from 11th November. not to have included Southern Rhodesia. But it did not say this.   Also it could validly and intra vires say that the countries in question shall be taken as from the date hereof (19th November) not to include

E   Rhodesia.   What it could *not* say was that as from some date prior to 11th November or in the indefinite past the countries in question shall be taken not to have included Rhodesia.   For in that case it would be ultra vires.   If it *was* intended to be generally retrospective, it cannot be " read down " to have retrospective effect as from 11th November only.   One must, therefore, if it be possible, construe it in such a way as will make it intra vires.   It is not only possible to read

F   it as referring to the future, but it is the reasonable construction to put on the words.   The iteration of the words " while this Order is in force " and the future tense " shall be taken " indicate that it has no retrospective effect. " Shall be taken not to include ", therefore, must be read as " shall be taken not to include, as from the date hereof, i.e., 19th November ".

If it were necessary to call in aid the presumption against retrospective

G   legislation, that also would point in the same direction.   There was some argument whether legislation that speaks only of the future is retrospective.   But the presumption against retrospection is not a technicality.   It is a general rule of justice not dependent on forms of words. It is founded on a judicial preference, where choice is possible, for the reading which does not invalidate existing rights and obligations.   An act which says that all existing obligations shall be deemed

H   not to have been entered into is plainly retrospective, and should, therefore, not be read in that sense if another reasonable meaning is possible.   It would be wrong to regard as *not* retrospective, and therefore *not* to be otherwise construed where possible, an act which simply spoke of the future and said, e.g., that there shall not in future be any payment of interest or capital in respect of some government loan.

I   If, as I think, the respondents and others had rights when this order came into force, and if this order is ambiguous it should be read (so far as possible) as not interfering with those rights.   In my opinion, this consideration is unnecessary since on the plain reading of the order it had effect as from 19th November, by which time the respondents had rights to a preferential tariff.   The general intention of the order was plain.   It was to exert economic pressure on Rhodesia

(21) [1968] 1 Lloyd's Rep. 80.
(22) [1968] 2 All E.R. at p. 824; (1968) 2 Q.B. at p. 687.

by depriving Rhodesian exports of preferential tariffs in future for the duration A
of the impasse to the detriment of Rhodesian growers and manufacturers. It
was not intended to hurt British companies, such as the respondents (though
obviously their Rhodesian interests would be hurt), or to hit past transactions
which would confer no future economic benefit on Rhodesia. Owing to the sudden
crisis it was impossible to end the operation of the preference with fair notice
such as no doubt would be envisaged (if such a situation were to arise) when the B
original arrangements were made and the Act of 1958 was passed. So there
was a very difficult situation for those who were concerned in passing the
necessary legislation.

It is argued that s. 2 showed that the order intended to affect the respondents
and others who were in a like position since it made a special exception in favour
of goods already entered for warehousing. Obviously the draftsman *thought* C
(on a misconstruction of the Act of 1958, as I think) that all those goods which
had not yet paid duty would by s. 1 be deprived of preference. To say that
he intended it, is not necessarily correct. Taking the view that he did on the
construction of the Act of 1958 it was not easy to effect a fair result, and therefore
he made certain exceptions. That those exceptions were not thought wide enough
is shown by a second order a few days later which widened them further, D
although not enough to cover the respondents. Since these things were done
under great urgency, nobody could fairly criticise any misconstruction of the
Acts that may have occurred. It the draftsman had taken what I believe to be
the correct construction of the Act of 1958 he would have omitted art. 2 of the
order and it may well be that he would then have been well content and have
thought that a satisfactory and fair result had been achieved. E

But what the draftsman thought he was achieving is not to the point. If
rights are taken away, they must be taken by clear words which catch the particular transaction. In my opinion, the words of the order did not catch the
transactions with which we are here dealing.

For these reasons I consider that the majority of the Court of Appeal (23)
were right. I would dismiss the appeal. F

LORD DONOVAN: My Lords, I have had the advantage of reading the
opinion of my noble and learned friend, LORD DIPLOCK, in this case. I agree
with it and would likewise allow the appeal.

LORD DIPLOCK: My Lords, tobacco grown in Rhodesia was shipped to
the United Kingdom by the respondents on vessels sailing from Beira in Portuguese East Africa after 19th November 1965. On arrival it was discharged into G
bonded warehouses from which it was cleared on various dates in 1966 and 1967.
The question in these appeals is whether customs duty under s. 4 of the Finance
Act 1964, was payable on it at the full rate or at the preferential Commonwealth
rate at the time of removal from the warehouses. This depends on whether
at that time it was " tobacco qualifying for Commonwealth preference " within
the meaning of that section and this in turn, by virtue of s. 26 (2) (*b*), depends H
on whether it fell within the definition of " goods qualifying for commercial
preference " contained in sub-s. (2) to sub-s. (9) of s. 2 of the Import Duties
Act 1958, as amended by the Southern Rhodesia (Withdrawal of Commonwealth
Preference) Order 1965 (24), and the Southern Rhodesia (Withdrawal of
Commonwealth Preference) (No. 2) Order 1965 (25).

Section 2 (2) of the Import Duties Act 1958, read in the light of the I
interpretative provisions of s. 12 and s. 15 (1) of that Act is as follows:

" The goods qualifying for Commonwealth preference shall be any goods
which are grown, produced or manufactured in the area referred to in this
Act as the Commonwealth preference area and which are consigned to the
United Kingdom from a place in that area."

(23) [1968] 2 All E.R. 820; [1968] 2 Q.B. 674.
(24) S.I. 1965 No. 1954.
                                    (25) S.I. 1965 No. 1987.

A   Before 19th November 1965, s. 2 (3) of the Import Duties Act 1958, provided

" . . . the Commonwealth preference area shall consist of [inter alia] (*c*) any country . . . which for the time being forms part of Her Majesty's dominions outside the United Kingdom . . . "

B   Southern Rhodesia was such a country and sub-s. (9) provided inter alia that goods grown, produced or manufactured in Southern Rhodesia, should be deemed to be consigned to the United Kingdom from that country if they were so consigned from the port of Beira in Portuguese East Africa.

Under s. 2 (2) of the Southern Rhodesia Act 1965, power was granted to make by Order in Council provision—

C   " (*b*) for modifying, extending or suspending the operation of any enactment or instrument in relation to Southern Rhodesia, or persons or things in any way belonging to or connected with Southern Rhodesia ",

and by s. 2 (3), any such provision may be made to have effect from any date not earlier than 11th November 1965.

The Orders in Council, to which I have referred, were made in the exercise of this power. They came into force on 19th November 1965, and provided as D   follows:

" 1. Southern Rhodesia shall, while this Order is in force, be excluded from the area referred to in the Import Duties Act 1958 as the Commonwealth preference area, and accordingly while this Order is in force (*a*) the countries described in section 2 (3) (*c*) of that Act (countries within Her Majesty's dominions outside the United Kingdom not named in section 2 (4)) shall be E   taken not to include Southern Rhodesia; and (*b*) section 2 (9) of that Act (goods consigned from Lourenço Marques or Beira) shall not apply to goods of Southern Rhodesia.

" 2. The foregoing Article shall not affect the rate of customs duties chargeable on goods entered for warehousing (within the meaning of the Customs and Excise Act 1952) before the date of the coming into operation F   of this Order or on any goods shown to the satisfaction of the Commissioners of Customs and Excise to have been shipped in a ship which sailed from Lourenço Marques or Beira or any port in the Commonwealth preference area (as defined in the Import Duties Act 1958) before that date."

Thus, at the time at which the tobacco was removed from the warehouses G   (which was after 19th November 1965), and customs duty became payable under s. 88 of the Customs and Excise Act 1952, the Commonwealth preference area no longer included Southern Rhodesia nor did the tobacco fall within either of the exceptions mentioned in the order.

Both s. 4 of the Finance Act 1964, and s. 2 of the Import Duties Act 1958, speak to the moment at which customs duty becomes chargeable. That is when H   the enquiry whether or not the imported goods are goods " qualifying for Commonwealth preference " has to be made.

The earliest date on which goods can become chargeable to customs duty is on importation into the United Kingdom (Customs and Excise Act 1952, s. 34 (1)), i.e., when the vessel first comes within the limit of the United Kingdom port (ibid., s. 79 (2) (*a*)). It is unnecessary to consider whether customs duty becomes I   " chargeable " on warehoused goods before it becomes " payable " under s. 88 of that Act. Whichever is the relevant date it was after 19th November 1965, for the tobacco which is the subject of these appeals. There is no magic about the word " qualifying ". The phrase " qualifying for Commonwealth preference " is merely a short way of referring to goods which comply with the lengthy description contained in sub-s. (2) to sub-s. (9) of s. 2 of the Import Duties Act 1958.

Despite the wide-ranging arguments and the conflict of judicial opinion to which they have given rise, I am ingenuous enough still to think that the only

question in this appeal is a short point about the use of participles in the English **A**
language. The words " grown ", " produced ", " manufactured " and " consigned " are participles describing the characteristics possessed by goods at the
moment at which duty becomes chargeable or payable. The relevant question
to be posed about the tobacco which is the subject of this appeal is: Did it in
1966 and 1967 comply with the description " grown " in the Commonwealth
preference area and " consigned to the United Kingdom from a place in " the **B**
Commonwealth preference area?

Growth, like manufacture and production, is a process which takes time
and must have been completed by the time goods are imported into the United
Kingdom. " Grown ", " manufactured " and " produced " describe in retro-
spect characteristics which must have been already acquired by the time the
goods arrive in the United Kingdom. " Consigned " is not a term of art and the **C**
controversy in this case has largely turned on the meaning to be ascribed to this
participle.

The submission on behalf of the respondents, which was accepted by the
majority of the Court of Appeal (26), is that goods acquire the characteristic
of " consigned " not as the result of a process which takes time but at the
punctus temporis when the consignor does the first overt act to carry into effect **D**
an intention previously formed to transmit goods to the United Kingdom on a
continuous transit without being taken into the commerce of any other country
on their journey to the United Kingdom. Once that point of time is past, the
argument goes, the goods are, in the words of LORD DENNING, M.R. (27),
" franked " for ever after for Commonwealth preference even though no through
contract of carriage to the United Kingdom has yet been entered into. Their **E**
qualification for Commonwealth preference depends on whether at the moment
of the first overt act by the original consignor the place where it was done was
in the Commonwealth preference area as it existed at that moment.

One difficulty about this construction of the participle " consigned " is that
the original consignor may change his mind after such an overt act and the goods
may be sent to some other destination and enter into the commerce of another **F**
country from which they may be later shipped to the United Kingdom by some
other consignor. These would clearly not qualify for Commonwealth preference,
since on arrival in the United Kingdom they would not be goods which " are
consigned to the United Kingdom from a place in that [sc. the Commonwealth
preference] area ". The metaphorical " franking " is not indelible. Again,
goods shipped under a charter party with options for discharge in England or **G**
north European ports to be declared during the course of the voyage would not
on this view be entitled to Commonwealth preference if the shipper had not
made up his mind which option he would exercise until the vessel was at sea.
Notwithstanding that he subsequently exercised the option to discharge goods
in a United Kingdom port, the goods so discharged would not on this view be
qualified for Commonwealth preference, although the enquiry whether they **H**
possess the characteristic of goods which are " consigned " to the United Kingdom from a place in the Commonwealth area falls to be made after they have
arrived in the United Kingdom at the end of a direct continuous voyage from a
place in the Commonwealth preference area.

In my view, the key to the construction of the participle " consigned " is to
be found in the time at which the enquiry whether the goods are consigned to **I**
the United Kingdom from a place in the Commonwealth area falls to be made,
i.e., when the transit is over and the goods become chargeable to customs duty
after they have arrived. In this context goods which are " consigned to the
United Kingdom from a place in " the Commonwealth preference area means
no more than goods which have been carried to the United Kingdom from a place

---

(26) [1968] 2 All E.R. 820; [1968] 2 Q.B. 674.
(27) [1968] 2 All E.R. at p. 824; [1968] 2 Q.B. at p. 687.

A in the Commonwealth preference area without having entered into the commerce of any other country during their transit.

    The enquiries which have to be made at the time at which tobacco was cleared from bonded warehouses are: (i) was the tobacco grown in a place which is at the time of the enquiry in the Commonwealth preference area? and, if so, (ii) has it been carried on a continuous transit to the United Kingdom (without

B entering into the commerce of any other country) from a place which at the time of the enquiry is in the Commonwealth preference area? In the present appeals, the answer to both these questions was " No " because at the time at which the enquiry was made, the Commonwealth preference area no longer included Southern Rhodesia.

    But even if the contention of the respondents, as to the meaning of the

C participle " consigned " were right, the result of this appeal would, in my view, be the same. Article 1 of the Southern Rhodesia (Withdrawal of Commonwealth Preference) Order 1965 provides: " . . . while this Order is in force . . . (*a*) the countries described in section 2 (3) (*c*) of that Act . . . shall be taken not to include Southern Rhodesia." This seems to me to contain an instruction to the reader that so long as the order is in force, he must read the definition of the

D Commonwealth preference area contained in s. 2 (3) of the Import Duties Act 1958, as if it expressly excluded Southern Rhodesia, whatever the purpose for which it is necessary to determine the extent of the Commonwealth preference area and whatever the time to which the enquiry is directed. This seems to me the natural meaning of the words which I have cited from the Order in Council. Put at its highest in favour of the respondents, the most that can be said

E is that they might be thought to be ambiguous by anyone who sympathised with the respondents' misfortune in finding that their expectation of obtaining the benefit of Commonwealth preference on tobacco grown before the date of the unilateral declaration of independence was dashed. But even if there were an ambiguity in art. 1 of the Orders in Council it is common ground that art. 2 of the first order, as amended by the second order, shows that the intention

F of the draftsman of the order was to withdraw from Commonwealth preference goods which had been consigned from Southern Rhodesia or from Beira before 19th November 1965, unless they had on or before that date been shipped in a vessel which sailed from Beira. The intention of the draftsman being clear, any possible ambiguity should be resolved in the sense that I have indicated.

    It has been faintly suggested that, on the contention of the respondents

G that the participle " consigned " refers to the moment at which the first step is taken to transmit the goods to the United Kingdom, the Order in Council would be ultra vires as having effect from a date earlier than 11th November 1965. In my view, there is no substance in this contention. The order has no effect on tobacco consigned from Southern Rhodesia or Beira until it first becomes chargeable to customs duty on arrival at the limits of a port in the

H United Kingdom, and this after 19th November 1965.

    My Lords, I would allow this appeal.

Appeals allowed.

    Solicitors: *Solicitor, Customs and Excise; Herbert Smith & Co.* (for the respondents).

[*Reported by* S. A. Hatteea, Esq., *Barrister-at-Law.*]

A

Re GATTOPARDO, LTD.

[COURT OF APPEAL, CIVIL DIVISION (Davies and Russell, L.JJ.), February 27, 1969.]

*Company—Winding-up—Compulsory winding-up—Contributory's application—
Entitlement to present petition—Consent order allocating shares to contributory eight months prior to petition—Transfer only registered two months
prior to petition—Whether petitioner had locus standi to present petition—
Companies Act 1948 (11 & 12 Geo. 6 c. 38), s. 224 (1).*

B

By a consent order dated 23rd April 1968 in proceedings to which the
company was not a party, the petitioner became entitled to be registered
in respect of 50 shares in the company, for which she had paid £1,650,
with effect from 10th June 1967. Although a share transfer had been
executed, stamped and dated 15th June 1967, the company did not in
fact register the transfer until 9th October 1968, when the shares were
delivered to her. On 18th December 1968 the petitioner presented a petition
for the winding-up of the company.   On the question whether the petition
was demurrable because the petitioner had not held her shares for six
months as required by s. 224 (1)* of the Companies Act 1948,

C

D

Held: on the true construction of s. 224 the right of a contributory to
present a petition by winding-up was expressly denied unless the shares had
been held and registered in the contributory's name for at least six months
during the 18 months before the commencement of the winding-up; accordingly, since no share had been held by the petitioner or registered in her name
for longer than approximately two months at the date of presentation the
petition was demurrable (see p. 347, letters A and B, post).

E

Observation of VAUGHAN WILLIAMS, J., in *Re A Company* ([1894] 2 Ch.
at p. 351) approved.

Re Patent Steam Engine Co. ((1878), 8 Ch.D. 464) distinguished.

Appeal dismissed.

[As to petition by a contributory, see 6 HALSBURY'S LAWS, (3rd Edn.) 540,
para. 1040; and for cases on the subject, see 10 DIGEST (Repl.) 875, *5773–5783.*

F

For the Companies Act 1948, s. 224, see 5 HALSBURY'S STATUTES (3rd Edn.)
293.]

Cases referred to:

Company A, Re, [1894] 2 Ch. 349; 63 L.J.Ch. 565; 71 L.T. 15; 10 Digest
(Repl.) 866, *5697.*

G

Patent Steam Engine Co., Re (1878), 8 Ch.D. 464; 10 Digest (Repl.) 875, *5774.*

Interlocutory appeal.

This was an appeal by the petitioner, Dorothy Howard, against the order of
PLOWMAN, J., dated 3rd February 1969 dismissing her petition for the winding-up
of Gattopardo, Ltd. The facts are set out in the judgment of RUSSELL, L.J.

H

Allan Heyman for the petitioner.

L. J. Bromley for the respondents.

RUSSELL, L.J.: This is a curious case. The contributory petitioned to
wind up the company. She was not registered in respect of her shareholding
until 9th October 1968, and her petition was presented on 18th December 1968.

I

The right of a contributory to present such a petition is conferred by s. 224
(1) (*a*) of the Companies Act 1948, but that section expressly denies him that
right unless—

" (ii) the shares in respect of which he is a contributory, or some of them
. . . have been held by him, and registered in his name, for at least six months
during the eighteen months before the commencement of the winding up."

---

* Section 224 (1), so far as material, is set out at letter I, supra.

A I have only read the presently relevant part of the section. PLOWMAN, J., upheld the contention that this petition is demurrable on the ground that the petitioner had no right to present it under the section because no share had been held by her and registered in her name for longer than slightly over two months at the date of the presentation. Prima facie that would seem to be a sound decision.

B I had better refer to some of the facts. The company runs the business of a restaurant in London, and somewhere in the middle of 1967 the share situation was that one Avanzo was registered in respect of 49 of the 100 issued shares, and one Fialko was registered in respect of the remaining 51. The directors I believe to have been Mr. Avanzo and a Mr. or Mrs. Bianca, who was apparently not a shareholder. Mr. Avanzo agreed to sell 50 shares to the petitioner, according C to the petition, for £1,650, which she paid. It now appears that Mr. Avanzo had only 49 shares. There was some dispute about this bargain, which ended in a consent order in a Queen's Bench action to which only the petitioner and her husband—but that is incidental—and Mr. Avanzo were parties, and that consent order declared that the petitioner was entitled to be registered in respect of 50 shares in the company with effect from 10th June 1967. That order was D made on 23rd April 1968. The same consent order affirmed as valid a bargain between Mr. Avanzo and the petitioner in connection with the assignment of, inter alia, the leasehold of the premises on which the restaurant business was carried on which was assigned to her and Mr. Avanzo on trust for sale and on beneficial trust as equal tenants in common; in total she paid out about £6,000 in effect to buy herself a half interest in the restaurant.

E After that consent order nothing was done about the shares at all, so far as appears from the petition, until on 9th October 1968, the board of directors, consisting of Mr. Avanzo and Mr. or Mrs. Bianca passed a resolution approving a transfer of 50 shares, " Share transfer No. 1 for 50 shares " from Mr. Fialko to the petitioner, and it was resolved by the board that she should be registered, and on that date the petitioner was for the first time registered as a shareholder F in the company, and she in due course received the share certificate for 50 shares bearing the same date. I remark that so far as the petition is concerned that is all that appears about these shares. She would not seem to have attempted to get herself registered in the period between the Queen's Bench action and 9th October.

We have, however, seen in this court a transfer of 50 shares from Mr. Fialko G to the petitioner executed by Mr. Fialko, dated and indeed Revenue stamped (incidentally on a stated consideration of £50) 15th June 1967. We are told that this was drawn up by the petitioner's solicitors, who were then acting for her in some respects and are instructing counsel for her today. They drew it up and they procured Mr. Fialko's signature and they got it stamped, and we are told on instructions that it was then sent to the company for registration. It H is very unsatisfactory that one should have this kind of information only on instructions, and things are made a little bit more curious by the fact that in the pleadings in the Queen's Bench action there appear to be references in the writ to transfers by the plaintiff, that is to say, Mr. Avanzo, and in the body of the statement of claim a reference to two transfers I think by Mr. Fialko. The matter is very obscure in this respect.

I Now what is suggested by way of argument is, first of all, that it is perfectly true to say that the petitioner could not be described as holding and being registered in respect of these shares or any of them for the requisite period of six months; but, if one looks at Re Patent Steam Engine Co. (1), a decision of SIR JAMES BACON, V.-C., one will find a case in which reliance on this section by way of demurrer to a petition to wind up was brushed aside on the ground that it was a pure or mere technicality. I think I might quite simply read the short judgment of SIR JAMES BACON, V.-C. He said (2):

---

(1) (1878), 8 Ch.D. 464.   (2) (1878), 8 Ch.D. at p. 466.

A

" In my opinion the technical objection has no weight. The Petitioners have been declared by the Court entitled to be shareholders, and the company have been ordered to allot them these shares, and to register them as shareholders in respect of them. These orders the company have failed to comply with, and it is only through their default that the petitioners' names were not on the register upwards of six months ago."

B

The really salient feature in that case is, in my judgment, that there was an express order on the company, which was a party to that order, to register the petitioners in respect of their shares, and SIR JAMES BACON, V.-C., in those circumstances was prepared to treat what should have been done by the company which was taking the point, as having been done.

C

In this case, however, whatever the true facts may be about the relationship between Mr. Avanzo and Mr. Fialko, the fact remains that the only order in existence relating to these shares or any of them was the consent order to which Mr. Avanzo alone was a party, and not the company and not even Mr. Fialko, and in those circumstances, even if I may assume that the decision of SIR JAMES BACON, V.-C., (3), was a correct decision—and I reserve my own judgment on that point without intending to indicate either that it was correct or incorrect—there seems to me to be a world of difference between that case and the present case in which it could not be said that the company was bound at any stage before 9th October 1968, let alone at a stage six months before the presentation of the petition, to register the petitioner as a shareholder.

D

What happened to the transfer form, which we are told on instructions was sent presumably at a stage long before the battle in the Queen's Bench Division to the company, we do not know. All we know on the facts as they are presented to us is that in fact no board of directors met to consider this transfer until 9th October 1968. Why that should happen, whose fault that was, I know not, but certainly the case has not been made out in any satisfactory way to suggest that here is Mr. Fialko in respect of 50 shares, having bound himself by executing a transfer, and Mr. Avanzo, having bound himself by contract and a consent order, dragging their feet so as in some way to prejudice the petitioner. She seems to have taken no step whatsoever after the consent order in April to ginger up the company or the board of directors into getting herself on the register. It seems to me that she has only herself, unfortunately, to thank for the fact that it was within six months of the actual registration that the matters of which she complains in the substance of the petition arose.

E

F

Even if the facts were plainly stated to suggest that the 100 per cent. shareholders had been dragging their feet, even if that were shown and shown plainly, I would not for myself extend the *Patent Steam Engine* case (3) to such a situation; but in any event such a situation is not demonstrated here.

G

I am left with the plain language of the section, and I find myself entirely able to agree with the remarks made in the course of argument by VAUGHAN WILLIAMS, J., in *Re A Company* (4) where it was argued that (5)—

H

" The company allotted the shares to the wrong person, and ought not to be allowed to avail themselves of sect. 40 of the Companies Act, 1867 [which was the comparable section]. In equity what ought to have been done must be taken as having been done, and the petitioner should be treated as an original allottee ".

VAUGHAN WILLIAMS, J., interjected (5):

I

" There is an express statutory provision as to the qualification of a contributory to present a winding-up petition, and that cannot be modified by saying that he ought to be in a position in which he is not. The provisions of sect. 40 are not complied with, and I see no reason why the company should not set up that defence."

---

(3) (1878), 8 Ch.D. 464.   (4) [1894] 2 Ch. 349.
(5) [1894] 2 Ch. at p. 351.

A I echo those words. I think that the judgment below was perfectly correct, and, as I say, I reserve for a further occasion consideration whether the exception in the *Patent Steam Engine* case (6) is one which is to be supported.

I would dismiss the appeal.

DAVIES, L.J.: The facts in this case are very obscure, and it is quite
B obvious that the court has not been fully apprised of them. Speaking for myself, I cannot help thinking that it may be that in some respects the petitioner here has had a raw deal. But we are certainly not in a position to express any views one way or the other about that; and in any event the merits are quite irrelevant to this narrow point of law under s. 224 (1) of the Companies Act 1948.

With regard to that I can only say with some regret that I entirely agree with
C what has fallen from RUSSELL, L.J., and consequently the appeal fails.

Appeal dismissed.

Solicitors: *W. R. Bennett & Co.* (for the petitioner); *Fruitman & Co.* (for the respondents).

[*Reported by* S. A. HATTEEA, ESQ., *Barrister-at-Law.*]

D

E

R. *v.* BRIXTON PRISON GOVERNOR, *Ex parte* AHSON AND OTHERS.

[QUEEN'S BENCH DIVISION (Lord Parker, C.J., Ashworth and Blain, JJ.), April
F 3, 4, 10, 1968.]

Commonwealth Immigrant—Admission—Examination by immigration officer —Time for examination—Onus of proving time of arrival in country— Notice refusing admission—Commonwealth Immigrants Act 1962 (10 & 11 *Eliz.* 2 c. 21), *Sch.* 1, *para.* 1 (2), *para.* 2 (3).

G The applicants who were British subjects under the British Nationality Act 1948 and also Commonwealth citizens under the Commonwealth Immigrants Act 1962 were found trudging along a road near Banstead on the morning of 10th February 1968. They were taken to Banstead police station for interrogation by the police and later examination by immigration officers. As a result each was served with a notice refusing him entry into this country, and they were removed to Brixton Prison. In each case an immigration
H officer stated on affidavit that he was not satisfied that the applicant in question had arrived in this country more than 24 hours before he was examined. By para. 1 (2)* of Sch. 1 to the Commonwealth Immigrants Act 1962, immigration officers were not empowered to examine any person 24 hours after he had landed, and by para. 2 (3)† a notice refusing admission could not be given to any person more than 12 hours after the conclusion of
I his examination. The applicants maintained they had landed on 7th February and were taken to a house where they had lived for three days before they were examined by the immigration officers.

Held: (ASHWORTH, J., dissenting) once the validity of the examinations by the immigration officers was challenged, the onus lay on the immigration

---

(6) (1878), 8 Ch.D. 464.
* Schedule 1, para. 1 (2), is set out at p. 349, letter I, post.
† Schedule 1, para. 2 (3), is set out at p. 349, letter I, to p. 350, letter A, post.

officers to show that the examinations had taken place within 24 hours of   A
the applicants' landing in the United Kingdom (see p. 353, letter I, and
p. 366, letter G, post).

Eshugbayi Eleko v. *Officer administering the Government of Nigeria* ([1931]
All E.R. Rep. 44) applied.

Greene v. *Secretary of State for Home Affairs* ([1941] 3 All E.R. 388)
explained.   B

[As to control of Commonwealth immigrants and in their examination by
immigration officers, see SUPPLEMENT to 5 HALSBURY's LAWS (3rd Edn.), paras.
1513, 1514.

For the Commonwealth Immigrants Act 1962, Sch. 1, see 4 HALSBURY's
STATUTES (3rd Edn.) 47.]   C

Cases referred to:

Bushell's Case (1670), Vaugh. 135, 124 E.R. 1006;   16 Digest (Repl.) 297,
    704.

Eshugbayi Eleko v. *Officer administering the Government of Nigeria,* [1931] A.C.
    662; [1931] All E.R. Rep. 44; 100 L.J.P.C. 152; 145 L.T. 297; 8 Digest   D
    (Repl.) 770, *382.*

Greene v. *Secretary of State for Home Affairs* [1941] 3 All E.R. 388; [1942]
    A.C. 284; 111 L.J.K.B. 24; 166 L.T. 24;   *affg.* sub nom. *R.* v. *Home
    Secretary, Ex p. Greene,* [1941] 3 All E.R. 104; [1942] 1 K.B. 87; 17
    Digest (Repl.) 422, *28.*

Liversidge v. *Anderson,* [1941] 3 All E.R. 338; [1942] A.C. 206; 110 L.J.K.B.   E
    724; 116 L.T. 1; 17 Digest (Repl.) 422, *27.*

R. v. *Board of Control, Ex p. Rutty,* [1956] 1 All E.R. 769; [1956] 2 Q.B. 109;
    [1956] 2 W.L.R. 822; 120 J.P. 153; 16 Digest (Repl.) 301, *762.*

R. v. *Brixton Prison (Governor) Ex p. Sarno,* [1916] 2 K.B. 742; 86 L.J.K.B.
    62; 115 L.T. 608; 80 J.P. 389; 16 Digest (Repl.) 282, *523.*

R. v. *Halliday, Ex p. Zadig,* [1917] A.C. 260; 86 L.J.K.B. 1119; 116 L.T.   F
    417; 81 J.P. 237; 2 Digest (Repl.) 184, *124.*

R. v. *Secretary of State for Home Affairs, Ex p. O'Brien,* [1923] 2 K.B. 361;
    129 L.T. 419; *affd.* H.L. sub nom., *Secretary of State for Home Affairs*
    v. *O'Brien,* [1923] A.C. 603; [1923] All E.R. Rep. 442; 92 L.J.K.B. 830;
    129 L.T. 577; 87 J.P. 174; 16 Digest (Repl.) 308, *848.*

Motion for habeas corpus.   G

This was a motion by the applicants, 11 Pakistanis, Mohammad Ahson,
Mohammad Asghr, Mahdi Khan, Fazal Dean, Slamat Ali, Nur Elahi, Mir Zaman,
Himat Khan, Ghulam Ahmad, Fazal Hussain and Abdul Rehman, for the issue
of writs of habeas corpus directed to the governor of Brixton Prison.   The
applicants were found on the morning of 10th February 1968 on Croydon Lane,
Banstead, walking in pairs some 20 to 30 yards behind each other.   They   H
looked bedraggled and tired and appeared to be lost.   They were stopped by
the police and taken to Banstead police station, where they were questioned
and searched.   The immigration officers were notified and on arrival they also
questioned the applicants.   The immigration officers were not satisfied with
their explanations and each was served with a notice of refusal of admission   I
under the Commonwealth Immigrants Act 1962.

Quintin Hogg, Q.C., and *I. Finestein* for the applicants.

Gordon Slyn for the respondent. ·

                                                              Cur. adv. vult.

10th April 1968. The following judgments were read.

LORD PARKER, C.J.: The proceedings disclose a deplorable state of affairs;
the applicants are all British subjects under the British Nationality Act 1948,

A and also Commonwealth citizens for the purpose of the Commonwealth Immigrants Act 1962. They apparently left Pakistan, so it is said, some time in October 1967, and after extensive wanderings, some say via Teheran, they arrived in Europe, and eventually on the north coast of France. They were then smuggled by boat across the Channel, landing, probably wading ashore, some time in February 1968. On the way they appear to have been milked of all their money,

B some paying up to £200 for transport across the Channel, so that when they arrived here, they were for the most part penniless. They had undoubtedly made their way here to seek employment, and having no employment voucher, made a clandestine entry into the country.

   On the morning of Saturday, 10th February 1968, the 11 applicants and an Indian were found trudging along a road near Banstead; they were gradually

C rounded up, as it were, and brought into Banstead police station for interrogation by police officers, and later examination by immigration officers. As a result, each of the applicants was served with a notice under the Act of 1962 refusing him entry into this country, and they were thereupon removed by a constable to Brixton Prison. In each case an immigration officer has stated on affidavit that he was not satisfied that the applicant in question had arrived in this country

D more than 24 hours before he was examined. The relevance of that can be seen from an examination of the Act itself, and I refer only to the sections relevant for this purpose.

   Section 2 (1) of the Commonwealth Immigrants Act 1962, gives the immigration officer an absolute discretion, subject to the following subsections, as to whether he should admit a Commonwealth immigrant into this country or

E refuse his entry. It provides that:

   " Subject to the following provisions of this section, an immigration officer may, on the examination under this Part of this Act of any Commonwealth citizen to whom section one of this Act applies who enters or seeks to enter the United Kingdom,—(*a*) refuse him admission into the United Kingdom; or (*b*) admit him into the United Kingdom subject to a condition

F restricting the period for which he may remain there, with or without conditions for restricting his employment or occupation there ".

   Section 3 (1) provides that:

   " The provisions of Part I of the First Schedule to this Act shall have effect with respect to—(*a*) the examination of persons landing or seeking to land in the United Kingdom from ships and aircraft; . . . (*d*) the detention

G of any such persons or citizens as aforesaid pending further examination or pending removal from the United Kingdom . . . "

   One turns then to Sch. 1 to the Act of 1962. Paragraph 1 provides that:

   " (1) Subject to the provisions of this paragraph, an immigration officer may examine any person who lands or seeks to land in the United Kingdom

H for the purpose of ascertaining whether that person is or is not a Commonwealth citizen subject to control under Part I of this Act, and if so for the purpose of determining what action, if any, should be taken in his case under the said Part I . . .

   " (2) A person shall not be required to submit to examination under this paragraph after the expiration of the period of twenty-four hours from the

I time when he lands in the United Kingdom unless, upon being examined within that period, he is required in writing by an immigration officer to submit to further examination. "

   Paragraph 2 of Sch. 1 to the Act of 1962 deals with the machinery:

   " (1) The power of an immigration officer under section two of this Act to refuse admission into the United Kingdom or to admit into the United Kingdom subject to conditions shall be exercised by notice in writing . . .

   " (3) Subject to the following provisions of this Schedule, a notice under this paragraph shall not be given to any person unless he has been examined in pursuance of paragraph 1 of this Schedule, and shall not be given to any person later than twelve hours after the conclusion of his examination (including any further examination) in pursuance of that paragraph. "

Paragraph 3 (3) of Sch. 1 to the Act of 1962 provides that:

" No directions shall be given under this paragraph in respect of an immigrant after the expiration of two months beginning with the date on which he was refused admission into the United Kingdom."

Pausing there, it will be seen that a refusal must be given by a notice in writing, that the notice must be given not later than 12 hours after the conclusion of the examination, and the examination must take place within 24 hours of the immigrant landing. That much I think is conceded. Paragraph 4 (1) goes on to provide that:

" An immigrant who is ... refused admission into the United Kingdom under section two of this Act, may be detained under the authority of an immigration officer or constable pending that further examination, or pending the giving of directions under paragraph 3 of this Schedule and pending removal in pursuance of such directions ... "

Finally, going back to the Act itself, s. 13 provides that:

" (1) Any persons required or authorised to be detained under this Act may be detained in such places as the Secretary of State may direct ...

" (4) Any person required or authorised by this Act to be detained may be arrested without warrant by a constable or an immigration officer; and any person who is detained by virtue of this Act, or is being removed in pursuance of this section, shall be deemed to be in legal custody ".

The issue, accordingly, in the present case concerns the exact time at which the applicants landed in this country. They have, from the outset, maintained that they landed in the early hours of the morning of 7th February, in which case, when they were taken to Banstead police station, they had been in this country more than 24 hours. They told stories which, in broad outline, were that on landing they had been taken to a house where they had lived for three days, except that on the first day they had gone to a café or restaurant in Brighton for a midday meal, and a man at that café has sworn an affidavit confirming that they were there at the restaurant on 7th February. Further one of the applicants maintains that he put a telephone call through to Altrincham and this is confirmed by a lady who says that she answered a call on 7th February. The story then went on that on 10th February they were taken away by a van which developed a puncture, as the result of which they got out and walked along a road until they were picked up by the police.

As a result, however, of their examination, the immigration officers concerned were not, as I have said, satisfied that the applicants had been in this country for more than 24 hours. The applicants undoubtedly told lies; some of them gave false names and addresses; their accounts differed in detail, some saying the house they had gone to was a white house; others a blue house; others that they had been wandering all the time, and so on. Apart from these lies and discrepancies, the immigration officers stated that on most of the applicants the clothes and shoes were wet or sodden, and if the immigration officers are to be believed, three of them or at any rate two of them eventually made confessions that they only landed that morning, 10th February. Whilst those confessions of course, can only be direct evidence against the three persons concerned, it was indirectly evidence against all the applicants, because it was conceded that they had all arrived together. Further, according to the police, the Indian to whom I referred, admitted that he had been with the other 11 Pakistanis, and that they all landed that morning, 10th February. However, it is only right to say that the evidence in regard to that is pure hearsay, because the Indian concerned

A has not sworn an affidavit and has not given evidence before this court, and accordingly I disregard anything which it is said that he, the Indian, said. So much for the facts in broad outline.

The real question, as I see it, is as to the proper approach of this court. Do I ask myself the question: have the applicants satisfied me that they had, on 10th February been here for more than 24 hours? If that is the proper question, B my answer is: " No ". Their evidence is so unsatisfactory that I could not find affirmatively that they had been here for more than 24 hours. In other words I, like the immigration officers, am not satisfied that they had been here more than 24 hours. Or is the proper question: has the respondent, through the immigration officers and the police, satisfied me that the applicants had not been here for more than 24 hours? If so, I for my part could not find beyond C doubt, because this would, I think, be the standard of proof, that they had been here for less than 24 hours. True they had told somewhat differing stories, and two are said to have confessed, but with the language difficulties involved and the known natural propensity of men such as these to say whatever they think will suit their case, I could not be sure that they had been here for less than 24 hours. Lies do not prove the converse, and the only positive evidence in D this case was as to the state of their clothing. There was, however, no forensic evidence as to the nature of the wet, whether it was sea-water or what it was, and some were said to have been smartly dressed.

Prior to the Habeas Corpus Act 1816, if the gaoler made a return valid on its face, and its validity were challenged, there was nothing that the court could do. If it arose in a criminal matter, the gaoler produced the warrant from the E competent court, and that was an end of the matter. If, on the other hand, it arose in a civil matter, again the applicant would be left to bring a civil suit for false return, so that the matter in issue might be determined by a jury. By the Act of 1816, however, this court was given specific power in a civil matter to enquire into the facts. The Act itself is dealing only with writs of habeas corpus in cases other than a criminal matter or for debt or civil process, and s. 3 provides, F in effect, that in all cases provided for by the Act of 1816, although the return to any writ of habeas corpus shall be good and sufficient in law, it shall be lawful for the justices or police before whom such writ may be returnable to proceed to examination into the truth of the facts set forth in such return by affidavit or by affirmation. Section 4 provides:

G " . . . the like proceeding may be had in the court for controverting the truth of the return to any such writ of habeas corpus awarded as aforesaid, although such writ shall be awarded by the said court itself, or be returnable therein."

The question then arises what should be the proper approach by the court in determining any such enquiry which it may make. Of course, if the authority on which the gaoler holds the applicant is the authority of a court, the enquiry H can only be to see whether the court had facts before them entitling them to issue the authority, the warrant. It could not substitute its own view for that of the court, because habeas corpus is not a remedy by way of appeal. That was made clear by Lord Goddard, C.J., in *R. v. Board of Control, Ex p. Rutty* (1). In that case a magistrate had found that the applicant was a defective within the meaning of the Mental Deficiency Acts 1913 to 1927, being a feeble-minded I person, and that she was subject to be dealt with under those Acts by reason of her being found neglected, and he made a detention order. In due course, leave was granted and the applicant moved for a writ of habeas corpus. Lord Goddard, C.J., having referred to the position prior to the Habeas Corpus Act 1816, and to the position thereafter, went on to say (2):

" If on inquiry the court finds there was no evidence by which the order

(1) [1956] 1 All E.R. 769; [1956] 2 Q.B. 109.
(2) [1956] 1 All E.R. at p. 775; [1956] 2 Q.B. at p. 124.

A or conviction can be sustained, they can release on habeas corpus or quash on certiorari. This is clear from the cases cited by HILBERY, J. (3). But if there is evidence, whatever this court may think of it and no matter what conclusion the members of the court might have come to if they had been deciding the case which led to the conviction or order, they cannot disturb the finding, for so to do would be to act as a court of appeal in a matter in

B which no appeal is given."

I mention that case only to emphasise that the present case does not concern in any way the order of a court. We are here dealing with a claim by the executive to detain in custody a British subject, and apart from authority I should myself have thought that in the end the burden in such a case must be on the executive to justify that detention. I say "at the end" because, of course, nothing need be done in the first instance other than to make a good return valid on its face;

C but if the applicant for the writ challenges that return, as for example claiming that there was no jurisdiction in the executive officer to make the order which resulted in the detention, it would, I think, be for the executive to negative that challenge by proving that jurisdiction in fact existed.

I am supported in this view by what was said by ATKIN, L.J., in R. v. Secretary

D of State for Home Affairs, Ex p. O'Brien (4). The facts do not matter, but ATKIN, L.J., said (5):

"The case involves questions of grave constitutional importance, upon which I feel bound to express my own opinion, even though I repeat to some extent the views already expressed by the other members of the Court. That a British subject resident in England should be exposed to summary

E arrest, transport to Ireland and imprisonment there without any conviction or order of a Court of Justice, is an occurrence which has to be justified by the Minister responsible."

Further support is also, I think, to be obtained from the Privy Council case of Eshugbayi Eleko v. Officer administering the Government of Nigeria (6). Again it was LORD ATKIN who gave the advice of the Board. What was challenged in

F that case was an order made by the Governor of Nigeria providing that the appellant, who was the applicant for the writ, should leave a specified area, and on his failing to comply, ordered his deportation to another place in the colony. The Governor could only make that order validly if the applicant was a native chief; if he had been deposed; and there was a native law or custom which required him to leave the area. These were, the conditions precedent to a valid

G order for deportation being made by the Governor. The Crown, the respondent, argued in that case that the matter could not be reviewed at all by the courts or by the Privy Council, and it is on that point that LORD ATKIN was giving the advice of the Board. He began by setting out what was the contention of the applicant. He said (7):

"The applicant contests the validity of both orders, though the main

H attack is necessarily directed to the first. He says: (i) He was not a native chief, and did not hold an office. (ii) He was not deposed or removed from this office, and the Governor's sanction was therefore irrelevant. (iii) There was no native law or custom, which required him, or any chief or native whether deposed in the manner alleged against him or in any other way, to leave the area in question."

I LORD ATKIN subsequently said (8):

"Their Lordships are satisfied that the opinion which has prevailed that

(3) [1956] 1 All E.R. at pp. 772, 773; [1956] 2 Q.B. at pp. 119, 120.
(4) [1923] 2 K.B. 361.
(5) [1923] 2 K.B. at p. 393.
(6) [1931] A.C. 662; [1931] All E.R. Rep. 44.
(7) [1931] A.C. at pp. 668, 669; [1931] All E.R. Rep. at p. 48.
(8) [1931] A.C. at p. 670; [1931] All E.R. Rep. at p. 49.

A the Courts cannot investigate the whole of the necessary conditions is erroneous. The Governor acting under the Ordinance acts solely under executive powers, and in no sense as a Court. As the executive he can only act in pursuance of the powers given to him by law. In accordance with British jurisprudence no member of the executive can interfere with the liberty or property of a British subject except on the condition that he can support
B the legality of his action before a court of justice. And it is the tradition of British justice that judges should not shrink from deciding such issues in the face of the executive."

Having decided that it was a matter into which the courts could enquire, the Judicial Committee ordered (9) that the rule nisi should take the form ordering the respondent—
C

" to show cause why a writ of habeas corpus should not issue directed to them to have the body of Eshugbayi, Eleko, immediately before this Court at Lagos to undergo and receive all and singular such matters and things as the Court shall then and there consider of concerning him in this behalf. Upon the grounds [The grounds were then set out in the form of
D the contentions raised by the applicant] that:—1. The said Eshugbayi, Eleko, was not on August 6, 1925, or thereafter a native chief and did not hold any office. 2. That the said Eshugbayi, Eleko, had not on August 6, 1925, or thereafter been deposed or removed from any office . . ."

I confess that it seems to me clear from that, that Lord Atkin was stating, first, the cardinal principle of English law that no member of the executive can
E interfere with the liberty of a British subject except on the condition that he can support the legality of his action before a court of justice; and secondly that the clear inference here is that Lord Atkin felt that at the end of the day it was for the members of the executive to satisfy the court as to the validity of the order.

I should mention in regard to that case that in a later case to which I must
F refer in more detail hereafter, Scott, L.J., read Lord Atkin's advice in that sense. The case is *R. v. Home Secretary, Ex p. Greene* (10), and Scott, L.J., in referring to the case of *Eleko* (11), said (12):

" It was held that the ordinance in question made each fact a condition precedent to any exercise by the governor of the power to deport, and that each condition had to be established either by admission or proof before a
G court. On none of the three was the governor given by the ordinance any power of discretionary decision, nor did any question of confidential information arise."

Accordingly I should have thought that here, as in the Nigerian case, once the applicants allege that a state of affairs on which the jurisdiction of the immigration officers depended did not exist, it was for the respondent to show
H that it did. This was, of course, unnecessary in the first instance because, as I see it, the respondent made a return valid on its face. This he did, not through swearing an affidavit himself, but through the affidavits of the immigration officers, who said that in each case a notice of refusal was served, that the applicant was handed over to a constable to take him to Brixton, coupled with
I a reference to s. 13 of the Act of 1962. Once, however, the applicants alleged that a condition precedent to the validity of the notice of refusal was not performed, i.e., examination before 24 hours had elapsed, it would be for the respondent to negative that challenge and prove that the condition precedent, namely examination within 24 hours, had been performed.

(9) [1931] A.C. at p. 675; [1931] All E.R. Rep. at p. 51.
(10) [1941] 3 All E.R. 104; [1942] 1 K.B. 87.
(11) [1931] A.C. 662; [1931] All E.R. Rep. 44.
(12) [1941] 3 All E.R. at p. 112; [1942] 1 K.B. at p. 102.

It is said, however, that there is direct authority to the contrary, and authority   A
binding on this court. Reference is made to the case of *Greene* (13), which I
have just mentioned, both in the Court of Appeal and in the House of Lords.
SCOTT, MACKINNON and GODDARD, L.JJ., expressed the view that it was always
for the applicant to prove the facts on which he challenged the validity of the
return. I do not propose to read more than three passages from GODDARD, L.J.'s
judgment in that case. He said (14):   B

> " In my opinion, once it is shown that he is detained under a warrant or
> order which the executive has power to make, it is for the applicant for the
> writ to show that the necessary conditions for the making of the warrant . . .
> do not exist."

Later, having referred to a passage in the speech of LORD WRENBURY in *R.* v.   C
Halliday, Ex p. Zadig (15) GODDARD, L.J., said (16):

> " That in terms puts the onus on the applicant, and I think the conclusion
> is that the applicant can controvert the return, and, if he proves his case—
> and it is for him to prove it—he will be discharged. "

Finally GODDARD, L.J., said (17):
                                                                                  D
> " I am of opinion that, where, on the return, an order or warrant which
> is valid on the face is produced, it is for the prisoner to prove the facts neces-
> sary to controvert it, and, in the present case, this has not been done."

MACKINNON, L.J., who gave a short judgment, stated that he had had the opportunity of reading the judgment which GODDARD, L.J., was about to deliver,
and said (18):   E

> " Finding that he had expressed more clearly what I had been writing,
> I thought it was undesirable for me to complete my disquisition, and that it
> would suffice for me to say that I agreed with all that he had said."

MACKINNON, L.J., did, however, feel that he ought to add a few words, and he
there said (18): " The onus of showing that the order is invalid rests upon the
applicant."   F

That case went to the House of Lords (19), and there is no doubt that VISCOUNT
MAUGHAM, L.C., specifically approved the last passage which I read from the
judgment of GODDARD, L.J. (17). LORD MAUGHAM said (20): " I agree with what
GODDARD, L.J., in his careful judgment said on this point ", and he proceeded
to quote the passage (17) that I have read. LORD WRIGHT, in speaking of a return,
said (21): " It is good on its face unless and until it is falsified."   G

I appreciate, of course, that those are passages from very eminent judges
which, on their face, negative the view which I have formed; but I think it is
necessary to consider the context in which those passages occur. The case
concerned an application for a writ of habeas corpus in which the return
exhibited an order made under reg. 18B of the Defence (General) Regulations
1939 of the Secretary of State saying that he had reasonable cause to believe   H
that the applicant was of hostile origin or association, and ordering his detention.
It was, of course, held that the belief could not be enquired into at all. The
Secretary of State's order was a valid return, and all in fact that the applicant
said by way of answer was " I do not know why I was detained ". That clearly
was not a sufficient challenge to the order to call for anything more from the
                                                                                  I

(13) [1941] 3 All E.R. 104; [1942] 1 K.B. 87; on appeal, [1941] 3 All E.R. 388;
[1942] A.C. 284.
(14) [1941] 3 All E.R. at p. 119; [1942] 1 K.B. at p. 113.
(15) [1917] A.C. 260 at p. 308.
(16) [1941] 3 All E.R. at pp. 120, 121; [1942] 1 K.B. at p. 115.
(17) [1941] 3 All E.R. at p. 121; [1942] 1 K.B. at p. 116.
(18) [1941] 3 All E.R. at p. 116; [1942] 1 K.B. at p. 108.
(19) [1941] 3 All E.R. 388; [1942] A.C. 284.
(20) [1941] 3 All E.R. at p. 394; [1942] A.C. at p. 295.
(21) [1941] 3 All E.R. at p. 402; [1942] A.C. at p. 306.

A Secretary of State. It was not a case in which any challenge was made in regard to conditions precedent on which jurisdiction depended. The Secretary of State was not bound to give the grounds of his belief, any more than the immigration officers in the present case could be obliged to say why they exercised their discretion under s. 2 of the Act of 1962 in the way they did. Indeed, in *Greene's* case (22) the only possible challenge could have been an allegation
B of bad faith on the part of the Secretary of State, and this was disclaimed.

All that I think was intended in that case was to say that the order stood as an order valid on its face, that is the Secretary of State's order, and it was for the applicant to make a proper challenge to its validity if he could. The court was not dealing with the question that arises here as to the position at the end of the day when the applicant has challenged the validity of the authority to
C detain based on a lack of jurisdiction in the executive who made it. Indeed, I think this is clear from what MacKinnon, L.J., himself said in the short judgment, because having said in the passage I have previously read (23) that the onus of proof that the order is invalid rests on the applicant, he then went on (23):

"No evidence on the part of the gaoler or of the Home Secretary to establish the validity of the order (except proof of its signature, if that is disputed)
D is necessary, unless the applicant has adduced evidence of its invalidity sufficient to discharge and shift the onus of proof which rests primarily upon him."

That as it seems to me is the passage coming nearest to this case in which MacKinnon, L.J., is contemplating the possibility that after a challenge to the validity of the order, it will be for the executive, at the end of the day to negative
E that challenge.

I would only say this finally. This is a thoroughly unmeritorious application. If ever men should be sent back to the country from which they came, it is the applicants. But to enable this to be done would, in my judgment, mean making bad law. The fact is that nobody contemplated this situation arising when the Commonwealth Immigrants Act 1962, was passed, and it is only right to say
F that under the recent Act, the Commonwealth Immigrants Act 1968, the loophole here disclosed has at any rate been partially closed, in that the 24 hours allowed for examination has been extended to 28 days.

In the result, however, I have come to the conclusion that this application succeeds, and that the applicants should be discharged.

G   **ASHWORTH, J.:** This case raises an important question of principle relating to applications for writs of habeas corpus and in addition a question of fact, no less important to the applicants, who are 11 Pakistanis at present detained in Her Majesty's prison at Brixton. It is with regret that I say that my conclusion on the question of principle differs from that reached by Lord Parker, C.J., and that on one approach to the question of fact my conclusion
H also differs from his.

The question of principle may be stated thus: when a return is made by a custodian of a subject and the subject seeks to controvert the fact or facts relied on by the custodian as justifying his detention of the subject, where does the onus of proof lie? Is it incumbent on the custodian to prove the truth of the facts on which he relies? Or is it for the applicant subject to prove their
I falsity? Another way of posing the questions, which is perhaps more appropriate to the present case, is to ask: if a custodian is given statutory authority to detain the subject on certain conditions of fact being satisfied, is it incumbent on him to prove that the conditions have been fulfilled or is it for the applicant to prove that they have not?

The authority to detain the present applicants is derived from the Commonwealth Immigrants Act 1962 which provides by s. 2 (1) (a) that an immigration

---

(22) [1941] 3 All E.R. 388; [1942] A.C. 284.
(23) [1941] 3 All E.R. at p. 116; [1942] 1 K.B. at p. 108.

officer may on the examination of any Commonwealth citizen to whom s. 1 **A** of the Act applies who enters the United Kingdom refuse him admission. There can in my judgment be no doubt that each of the 11 Pakistani applicants was refused admission by an immigration officer. But s. 3 (1) of the Act contains supplementary provisions and enacts that the provisions of Pt. 1 of Sch. 1 to the Act are to have effect with respect to (para. (*a*)) the examination of persons landing in the United Kingdom from ships and (para. (*d*)) the detention of any **B** such persons pending removal from the United Kingdom. Section 13 contains provisions regarding detention of which the most relevant is in sub-s. (4): any person who is detained by virtue of this Act shall be deemed to be in legal custody.

Part 1 of Sch. 1 is clearly of great importance and para. 1 (2) is in these terms:

" A person shall not be required to submit to examination under this paragraph after the expiration of the period of twenty-four hours from the **C** time when he lands in the United Kingdom . . ."

It may be noted in passing that this sub-paragraph does not in terms provide that no examination may be made after the period of 24 hours; it provides that a person shall not be required to submit to an examination after that period. For my part I do not think that the respondent can derive any great support **D** from this language, as it is clear that each of the applicants was in fact required to submit to an examination, and the crucial question is whether by the time of that requirement he had been in the United Kingdom for more than 24 hours.

Paragraph 2 deals with notice and it may be noted that, in contrast to the language used in para. 1 (2), para. 2 (3) provides in terms that a notice shall not be given to any person unless he has been examined and shall not be given **E** to any person later than 12 hours after the conclusion of his examination. Nothing turns on this sub-paragraph in this case since, if the examinations were made within the statutory period of 24 hours, it is clear that the requisite notices were given within 12 hours of their conclusion.

Paragraph 4 contains provisions regarding detention pending removal but it is unnecessary to refer to them in detail. **F**

The respondent contends that the return is on the face of it good: each of the applicants has been examined, each of them has been refused admission, each of them has been given the requisite notice and it follows that detention pending removal is lawful. It is however rightly conceded that if the examinations were not made within the statutory period of 24 hours, there was no power in the immigration officer to refuse admission and the detention cannot be justified. **G** Counsel for the respondent contended that quite apart from any decided cases in which courts have considered the right of a detained subject to controvert the facts relied on as justifying the detention, the structure and language of the Act of 1962 are such as to lead to the conclusion that a person who asserts that its provisions have not been complied with has the burden of proving the facts on which the assertion is based. For my part I take the view that the Act **H** itself provides no clue as to the burden of proof, either in favour of the applicants or the respondent. Still less do I accept a contention put forward by counsel for the applicants that, because the very recent Commonwealth Immigrants Act 1968 in regard to a particular matter places a burden of proof on a would-be immigrant, one ought to conclude that there could be no burden of proof on him in regard to other matters dealt with by the Act of 1962. **I**

In considering the matter as a question of principle, it is I think helpful to mark how a court comes to be involved. The process starts with a person being detained, and the courts, in their jealous concern for the liberty of the subject, have always so to speak held the door open for such a person to question the legality of his detention. Accordingly the custodian is required to make a return, in other words, to justify the detention: he may do so in various ways which it is unnecessary to refer to in detail. It is, in my view, to this stage of the proceedings that the observations of ATKIN, L.J., in *R.* v. *Secretary of State for Home*

A   *Affairs, Ex p. O'Brien* (24) and of LORD ATKIN in *Eshugbayi Eleko* v. *Officer administering the Government of Nigeria* (25) to which LORD PARKER, C.J., has referred, were directed. I accept entirely the principle that the custodian is called on to justify the detention, but he does so by making a return which is valid on the face of it. If such return discloses on its face that the detention is unjustified, there is no more to be said: see *Bushell's Case* (26). But the

B   return may be valid on its face and it is then for the person detained to place evidence before the court showing that what appears to be a valid return is in fact invalid. He is at this stage raising an issue: he is doing more than traversing the return, because a mere traverse will not displace what is on its face a valid return. He is asserting facts which render the return invalid and in my judgment his position is to be compared with that of a plaintiff alleging false imprisonment:

C   on this point see *Liversidge* v. *Anderson* (27) and in particular the speech of VISCOUNT MAUGHAM (28), in which case it was held that the onus of proof was on the plaintiff. In my judgment, as a matter of principle, it is for an applicant in habeas corpus proceedings, who alleges that there are facts which vitiate a return prima facie valid, to prove them.

Needless to say, I am greatly relieved to find that this conclusion is in harmony

D   with the decision of no less than three Courts before which *Greene* v. *Secretary of State for Home Affairs* (29) was argued in 1942. I do not intend to lengthen this judgment by citing passages from the judgment of GODDARD, L.J. (30), in which the principle which I believe to be right was expressed in the clearest possible terms. Counsel for the applicants was constrained to submit that GODDARD, L.J., was in error; if that is right, I am in good company.

E   It is true that in the other judgments (31) and speeches (32) there are to be found phrases which can be and were prayed in aid by the present applicants but for my part I do not think that any of the authors of those phrases intended to qualify or dissent from the judgment of GODDARD, L.J. The decision in *Greene's* case (29) has stood for 25 years, and, so far as counsel were aware, it has never been doubted or explained or distinguished in any reported case. Following

F   at a respectful distance behind those great leaders, I am content to apply the principles they laid down.

Counsel for the respondent supported his argument by referring to what he said was a principle of evidence, that where the relevant information is within the knowledge of one party only the burden of establishing the relevant facts is on him. I cannot accept that contention, but there is no doubt in this case

G   that the placing of the burden of proof on the applicants reflects no hardship on them. They best of all know when they entered the United Kingdom and their difficulty lies not in the providing of evidence but in the telling of the truth.

Accordingly, I would hold that in the present case it is for the applicants to prove the facts necessary to vitiate the return, namely, that they had been in the United Kingdom more than 24 hours before they were examined. If in

H   law the onus of proof is indeed on the applicants, their efforts to discharge it are in my view entirely unconvincing. Counsel for the applicants accepted the comment that their evidence was riddled with discrepancies and indeed he had no option but to do so. When the whole of the evidence is considered, the comment may well be considered charitable.

If on the other hand the onus of proving the challenged facts is on the

I
_____
(24) [1923] 2 K.B. 361 at p. 393.
(25) [1931] A.C. 662 at pp. 668, 670; [1931] All E.R. Rep. 44 at pp. 48, 49.
(26) (1670), Vaugh. 135.
(27) [1941] 3 All E.R. 338; [1942] A.C. 206.
(28) [1941] 3 All E.R. at p. 348; [1942] A.C. at p. 224.
(29) [1941] 3 All E.R. 104; [1942] 1 K.B. 87; on appeal, [1941] 3 All E.R. 388; [1942] A.C. 284.
(30) [1941] 3 All E.R. at p. 116; [1942] 1 K.B. at p. 109.
(31) [1941] 3 All E.R. 104; [1942] 1 K.B. 87.
(32) [1941] 3 All E.R. 388; [1942] A.C. 284.

respondent, I should be prepared to hold that he had discharged it. If I may say A
so, I was greatly impressed by the cogent submissions made by counsel for the
respondent on this part of the case. There is no need for me to repeat them in
this judgment but I single out one feature as particularly convincing. On what
was described as a bright and sunny morning this group of 11 Pakistanis was
discovered, most of them (if not all) with wet clothing consistent with their
having recently waded ashore, but wholly inconsistent, in my view, with their B
having been living in a house in this country for three or four days. Assuming
in favour of the applicants that the standard of proof is the same as in a criminal
case, I have asked myself whether I can be sure that they had been in this country
for less than 24 hours, and my answer is, yes. In giving this answer I have
disregarded entirely the statements attributed to one Kumar, an Indian, which
were placed before the court de bene esse but which in my judgment are inadmis- C
sible.

For these reasons, if the matter rested with me, I should be in favour of dismissing these motions.

BLAIN, J.: In this matter counsel for the applicants moves on behalf of
one Mohammad Ahson and ten other men, all of whom are Pakistani nationals
and Commonwealth citizens, for an order that writs of habeas corpus be issued D
directing the governor of Brixton Prison to have their bodies brought before
the court. At present each of the applicants is detained in Her Majesty's prison
at Brixton as being an immigrant refused admission to the United Kingdom
under the provisions of the Commonwealth Immigrants Act 1962.

It is unnecessary to recite again the facts already detailed by LORD PARKER, E
C.J. For the purposes of this judgment, suffice it to say three things: first
that admittedly all 11 applicants arrived in this country by clandestine means
in February 1968; that does not constitute any offence. All were and are
British citizens. Secondly that all 11 claim and deposed that they had been in
this country for some days before the immigration authorities found opportunity to examine them; and thirdly that the immigration authorities took F
the view that none of the applicants had in truth been in this country for as
much as 24 hours before examination, or alternatively they, the immigration
authorities, were not satisfied, and they say this court on the evidence cannot be
satisfied, that the applicants had been in the United Kingdom for 24 hours
before examination.

In this connection there is circumstantial evidence, and in either two or three G
cases, some evidence of admissions to support the view of the immigration
authorities, and certainly the applicants' evidence to the contrary is full of
inconsistencies, though these may be explained in part, at least, by language
and other difficulties and instincts. The relevance of the issue of fact thus
thrown up is this.

By virtue of the provisions of s. 1 (3) of the British Nationality Act 1948, H
each of these applicants is a British subject, and prima facie has the same rights
to be in this country as has any native Englishman. At the relevant time the
only curtailment of the right was to be found in the Commonwealth Immigrants
Act 1962, an Act passed in order to make temporary provision for controlling
the immigration into the United Kingdom of Commonwealth citizens who came
within the provisions of s. 1 of the Act. It is not disputed that the applicants
fall within the terms of that section, and so the relevant provisions of the Act I
apply to them. In passing, the Commonwealth Immigrants Act 1968, which
passed into law last month, amends certain provisions of the Act of 1962, but
the Act of 1962 still remains the principal Act.

Section 16 of the Act of 1962 empowers the Secretary of State to appoint
immigration officers, and s. 2 (1) (a) enacts that, subject to certain irrelevant
provisions, an immigration officer:

"... may, on the examination under this Part of this Act of any Common-

A   wealth citizen to whom section one of this Act applies who enters or seeks to enter the United Kingdom,—(*a*) refuse him admission into the United Kingdom . . .''

There is no other power of refusal, at least none relevant to these proceedings, and this power is exercisable only after examination of the Commonwealth citizen concerned.

B

By virtue of s. 3 (1), the provisions of Sch. 9 to the Act have effect with respect to four matters: first, the examination of those landing or seeking to land in this country; secondly, the exercise by immigration officers of the power of refusal of admission; thirdly, the removal from the United Kingdom of Commonwealth citizens refused admission under s. 2 of the Act; and fourthly, the detention of such persons or citizens pending further examination or pending removal.

C

Section 13 (1) provides that a person whose detention is authorised under this Act may be so detained in such place as the Secretary of State may direct, and s. 13 (4) authorises his arrest without warrant by a constable or immigration officer, and provides that a person so detained shall be deemed to be in legal custody.

D

I now turn to the relevant provisions of Sch. 1. By virtue of para. 1 (1), subject to certain provisions:

> '' . . . an immigration officer may examine any person who lands or seeks to land in the United Kingdom for the purpose of ascertaining whether that person is or is not a Commonwealth citizen subject to control under Part I of this Act, and if so for the purpose of determining what action, if any, should be taken in his case under the said Part I; and it shall be the duty of every such person to furnish to an immigration officer such information in his possession as that officer may reasonably require for the purpose of his functions under this paragraph.''

E

F But para. 1 (2) provides that a person is not required to submit to such examination more than 24 hours after he has landed in the United Kingdom. Of course in most cases where an immigrant arrives openly by ship or aeroplane at a recognised seaport or airport, there will be no dispute of fact about his time of arrival. But in the case of clandestine landing in a remote place at dead of night, only the immigrant himself and those who participate in or happen to witness the arrival

G will know precisely when it occurred. Once, in fact, he has been in the country for 24 hours, no immigration officer can compel him under the Act of 1962 to submit to examination.

In passing, although it is not relevant to the determination of the present applications, it is to be observed by s. 4 of the Act of 1968 the period is now 28 days instead of the old 24 hours.

H Paragraph 2 (1) of Sch. 1 provides that the immigration officer's power to refuse admission is to be exercised by notice in writing to be given to the person to whom it relates, and by virtue of para. 2 (3), so far as relevant, such a notice can only be given to a person who has been examined in pursuance of para. 1, that is to say within 24 hours of landing, and only be given within 12 hours

I of such examination. Paragraph 3 provides for removal of immigrants on refusal of admission; only sub-paras. (2) and (3) are relevant. Under sub-para. (2) the Secretary of State may direct removal by ship or aircraft, and by virtue of sub-para. (3) no such direction may be made after the expiration of two months from the date of refusal of admission. Finally, para. 4 (1) provides for detention pending removal. An immigrant who is refused admission under s. 2 of the Act may be detained under the authority of an immigration officer or a constable pending the giving of directions under para. 3, and pending removal in pursuance of such directions. Those, I think, are the relevant provisions of Sch. 1.

It is admitted here that notices of refusal were given to each applicant by an   A
immigration officer, and that it is under the authority or purported authority
of such notices that these applicants are detained. Counsel for the applicants'
contention is that the notices were invalid and of no effect because, he said, the
examinations which necessarily preceded them did not take place within 24
hours of the landing of the immigrants, and he asks the court to determine
as a fact that the landings were earlier than that. This latter request I find   B
myself quite unable to accede to on the evidence, but in any event counsel for
the applicants submitted that there is an onus on the Crown to prove that the
examination takes place within 24 hours of the landing, and he says there is an
onus akin to that on the prosecution in a criminal case to prove beyond reasonable
doubt so that the court or the jury can be sure.

Counsel for the respondent says, no : under para. 1 (1) of Sch. 1, he submits that   C
the immigration officer has a right to examine, and therefore the immigrant has
a duty to submit to examination, and he goes on to say that under para. 1 (2)
the immigrant can claim exemption from the duty to submit if he has been in
the United Kingdom for over 24 hours. But, so runs the argument, that must be
construed to mean that his claim to such exemption is dependent on proof by
him that he has been in the United Kingdom for 24 hours or more. As a matter   D
of expediency that might seem an attractive argument, attractive because one
can see that in circumstances where there could be doubt, only the immigrant
himself and his associates could have really known when he landed, so it might
be logical to put on him the burden of proving the fact which he alone knows.

In cases of clandestine landings, a burden of proof on the immigration
authorities or the Crown could be an embarrassment in the efficient exercise of   E
their functions; moreover it could be said that those who choose to enter the
country in such ways rather than openly can hardly feel aggrieved if the burden
is cast on them to prove they have not obtained liability to those statutory
controls to which they would be subject had they arrived in more conventional
circumstances. Unless statutory or other authority compels acceptance of such
an approach, I would reject it. It seems to me basically to ignore certain funda-   F
mental principles. In the first place there is no law to prevent a British subject
arriving by private yacht or some less glamorous vessel at any time of the day
or night on any part of the coast, and no offence is committed if he sails across
from Le Touquet or swims from Cap Gris Nez.

Secondly, the provisions of the Commonwealth Immigrants Act 1962 which
impose various controls and restrictions on the otherwise unlimited rights of a   G
British subject to enter the United Kingdom, constitute a statutory fetter on
the freedom of the subject, a fetter necessary for reasons which concern Parliament but which do not concern this court. The consequences may go to the very
liberty of the subject, as they have done in this case.

In my view Parliament must not be supposed to have put on the subject the
burden of proving freedom from liability to detention in prison of a citizen who   H
has done nothing unlawful, unless that burden is expressed in the clearest and
most unequivocal terms.

That will be so if we are dealing with a statutory defence to a criminal charge;
it should be so where no question of a criminal offence arises. In fact this Act
does create penal offences; under the provisions of s. 4, to the language of which
it is not necessary to refer, an offence is committed by a Commonwealth citizen   I
to whom s. 1 applies if he enters or remains in the United Kingdom in defiance
of an immigration officer's refusal of admission. If charged with such an offence,
must he, in order to defend himself, prove that the refusal was invalid? I would
hope not. I would expect the Crown to have to prove his guilt, and if Parliament
intended otherwise it should so say in clear terms, as indeed it has later said in
the case of a new statutory offence introduced by the Act of 1968. That does
not, of course, affect the present case. It exemplifies the way in which it
should be done, in my view, if it is to lead to that conclusion.

A   I say at once that if the burden of proof is on the respondent, it is not discharged to my satisfaction so that, as a notional juryman, I could feel sure that at the time of examination these applicants had not spent more than 24 hours ashore. Affidavit evidence that clothing was damp or wet, shoes in particular wet and in some cases sandy, may go a long way to establish that they have not arrived by conventional means, and that is not in dispute, but it does not satisfy me that

B   they had been here for less than 24 hours. Evidence that immigration officers were not satisfied that the immigrants had been here for 24 hours does not of itself satisfy me that they had in fact been here for a shorter time, and in particular the evidence of what the Indian, Ravi Kumar said, either as a go-between or as interpreter or otherwise I find no more convincing than that of the immigration officers, particularly as there is no affidavit from that person before

C   the court, and for that matter it is by no means clear how much of what he said would be understood by the applicants in the examples in which they were present to hear it.

So in my judgment the decision must turn on the question of onus of proof. Here it is submitted by counsel for the respondent that on a true interpretation of the Act, the onus is on the applicants, a submission which he claims is supported

D   by authority, and in particular by the decision in *R.* v. *Home Secretary Ex p. Greene* (33), to which my Lords have referred and to which I will return shortly. From the time of Magna Carta a citizen detained without lawful authority has had access to the courts to secure his release. But it is unnecessary today to consider the procedure prior to the passing of the Habeas Corpus Act 1816, or to consider the procedure in the somewhat different considerations which arise

E   in cases of detention for some criminal matter. By s. 1 of the Act of 1816 on civil process on complaint made by a detained person supported by affidavit showing probable and reasonable ground for the complaint, the courts are empowered by writ of habeas corpus ad subjiciendum to call on the person detaining the complainant to produce the body before the court. By s. 3 the return to the writ is good and sufficient in law in itself, but the court may enquire into the truth

F   of the facts set out in it, and by s. 4 the court may enquire into the facts even though the writ is awarded by the court itself. This is the statutory authority challenging the validity of detention of the subject. On an application for a writ of habeas corpus the gaoler or other person detaining the applicant is called on to justify the detention. This he does by producing a legal order, an order legal on the face of it directing or authorising the detention.

G   In the case with which the court is concerned today, the return comprises the notice of refusal of admission combined with the statutory right to detain a person to whom such a notice has been given. The applicants do not dispute the giving of the notices, but they say they were of no effect because when given there was no power to give them, they followed within 12 hours of examination but that examination, it is said, was not conducted within 24 hours of the arrival

H   in the United Kingdom, and so was itself of no effect for the purposes with which we are concerned.

That is a controversial fact, and in my view it is of great importance to bear in mind that there is in this case a complete controversy of relevant fact, whereas in certain cases cited there was none.

Bearing that in mind, I turn to what has been called the Nigerian case,

I   *Eshugbayi Eleko* v. *Officer administering the Government of Nigeria* (34), a Privy Council case where the headnote reads (35):

" The Governor of Nigeria, purporting to act under the Deposed Chiefs Removal Ordinance, ordered the appellant to leave a specified area, and upon his failing to comply ordered his deportation to another place in the Colony.

---

(33) [1941] 3 All E.R. 104; [1942] 1 K.B. 87.
(34) [1931] A.C. 662; [1931] All E.R. Rep. 44.
(35) [1931] A.C. at p. 662.

The appellant applied to the Supreme Court of Nigeria for a writ of habeas   A
corpus, contending (i) that he was not a native chief, (ii) that he had not
been deposed, (iii) that there was no native law or custom which required
him to leave the area, and that consequently the conditions did not exist
entitling the Governor to make the orders.   *Held*, that the powers of the
Governor under the Ordinance were purely executive, and that it was the
duty of the Court to investigate the questions raised by the appellant's   B
contentions and to come to a judicial decision thereon . . ."

I need not read the rest of the headnote.

The Deposed Chiefs Removal Ordinance is quoted in LORD ATKIN's judgment
so far as relevant, omitting irrelevant words, it reads thus (36):

" 2. (1). When a native chief . . . [point 1] has been deposed . . . [point 2] by
or with the sanction of the Governor . . . (a) If native law and custom shall   C
require [point 3] that such deposed chief shall leave the area over which he
exercised jurisdiction or influence by virtue of his chieftaincy or office; or
(b) If the Governor shall be satisfied that it is necessary for the re-establish-
ment or maintenance of peace, order and good government in such area that
the deposed chief or native shall leave such area . . . "

D

What happened in that case was that the Governor in purported exercise of that
power ordered the appellant to leave the specified area, and on his failure to
comply ordered his deportation.   There was power in the ordinance so to do.
The appellant applied to the Supreme Court of Nigeria for a writ of habeas
corpus; the Supreme Court refused the application and the appellant appealed
to the Privy Council, where LORD ATKIN delivered the judgment of the Board.   E
After referring to the Nigerian government order impugned, LORD ATKIN
stated the appellant's contentions thus (37):

" The applicant contests the validity of both orders, though the main
attack is necessarily directed to the first.   He says: (i) He was not a native
chief, and did not hold an office. (ii) He was not deposed or removed from this
office, and the Governor's sanction was therefore irrelevant. (iii) There was   F
no native law and custom which required him, or any chief or native, whether
deposed in the manner alleged against him or in any other way, to leave
the area in question.   He says that these are three conditions precedent to
any authority to make an order of withdrawal, and their existence can and
must be investigated by the Court whenever the validity of the order or
a deportation order founded on it is the subject of contest in judicial pro-   G
ceedings."

After reciting the decision of the Nigerian Supreme Court appealed against,
LORD ATKIN stated (38):

" Their Lordships are satisfied that the opinion which has prevailed that
the Courts cannot investigate the whole of the necessary conditions is erroneous.   The Governor acting under the Ordinance acts solely under executive   H
powers, and in no sense as a Court.   As the executive he can only act in pursuance of the powers given to him by law.   In accordance with British
jurisprudence no member of the executive can interfere with the liberty
or property of a British subject except on the condition that he can support
the legality of his action before a court of justice.   And it is the tradition   I
of British justice that judges should not shrink from deciding such issues
in the face of the executive."

I need not read further, but one reads (39):

" The Court expressly held they had power to consider this question

(36) [1931] A.C. at pp. 664, 665; [1931] All E.R. Rep. at p. 46.
(37) [1931] A.C. at pp. 668, 669; [1931] All E.R. Rep. at p. 48.
(38) [1931] A.C. at p. 670; [1931] All E.R. Rep. at p. 49.
(39) [1931] A.C. at p. 671; [1931] All E.R. Rep. at p. 49.

A   and resolved it against the applicant. The question whether the applicant was an alien or not did not arise. He admittedly was; but their Lordships agree with the opinion of Low J. [in *R.* v. *Governor of Brixton Prison, Ex p. Sarno.* (40).] "

The order made is not without interest, and I think relevance. It reads thus (41):

B   " It is ordered that this day, the 15th day of January, 1929, be given to the Officer administering the Government of Nigeria and the District Officer of Oyo to show cause why a writ of habeas corpus should not issue directed to them to have the body of Eshugbayi, Eleko, immediately before this Court at Lagos to undergo and receive all and singular such matters and things as the Court shall then and there consider of concerning him in this

C   behalf. Upon the ground that:—1. The said Eshugbayi, Eleko, was not on August 6, 1925, or thereafter a native chief and did not hold any office. 2. That the said Eshugbayi, Eleko, had not on August 6, 1925, or thereafter been deposed or removed from any office. 3. That native law and custom did not require that the said Eshugbayi, Eleko, should leave any area over which he exercised influence by virtue of any office or at all. 4. That by reason

D   of the premises the order under hand of the Officer Administering the Government, dated the 6th day of August, 1925, and the order under the hand of the said officer and seal of the Colony and Protectorate of Nigeria dated the 8th day of August, 1925, concerning the said Eshugbayi, Eleko, are invalid . . ."

E LORD ATKIN said (42):

" On the argument of the rule counsel for the respondents to the motion [that is the Government of Nigeria] should show cause, and counsel for the applicant should then, if required, reply in support of the rule."

In *Greene's* case (43) the effect of LORD ATKIN'S judgment was differently interpreted by SCOTT and by GODDARD, L.JJ. In *Greene's* case (43) SCOTT, L.J.,

F   referred in these terms to that case (44):

" In *Eshugbayi Eleko* v. *Officer administering the Government of Nigeria* (45), the relevant ordinance conferred on the governor jurisdiction to deport if, and only if, certain antecedent propositions were established or admitted as extrinsic facts. First, the person to be deported must have been a

G   native chief. Secondly, he must have been deposed, and even then he could not be deported unless, thirdly, there was a native custom requiring him to leave the area where he had been chief. It was held that the ordinance in question made each fact a condition precedent to any exercise by the governor of the power to deport, and that each condition had to be established either by admission or proof before a court. On none of the three

H   was the governor given by the ordinance any power of discretionary decision, nor did any question of confidential information arise."

GODDARD, L.J., having referred to orders which were before the court, said (46):

"... the Secretary of State ... acts wholly in an executive, and not in a judicial capacity. Counsel for the appellant accordingly relies on the advice of the Judicial Committee, delivered by LORD ATKIN in *Eshugbayi*

I   *Eleko* v. *Officer Administering the Government of Nigeria* (47). In my opinion,

---

(40) [1916] 2 K.B. 742.
(41) [1931] A.C. at p. 675; [1931] All E.R. Rep. at p. 51.
(42) [1931] A.C. at p. 676; [1931] All E.R. Rep. at p. 52.
(43) [1941] 3 All E.R. 104; [1942] 1 K.B. 87.
(44) [1941] 3 All E.R. at p. 112; [1942] 1 K.B. at p. 102.
(45) [1931] A.C. 662; [1931] All E.R. Rep. 44.
(46) [1941] 3 All E.R. at p. 119; [1942] 1 K.B. at pp. 112, 113.
(47) [1931] A.C. at p. 670; [1931] All E.R. Rep. at p. 49.

A

however, that passage does not mean that, where the executive has detained a person under statutory authority (and the regulations have the force of statute), he can, merely by saying 'I don't know why I have been detained', oblige the executive to prove that every condition necessary to the making of the order has been fulfilled. In my opinion, once it is shown that he is detained under a warrant or order which the executive has power to make, it is for the applicant for the writ to show that the necessary conditions for the making of the warrant or order do not exist."

B

With the greatest diffidence I confess that for my part I prefer SCOTT, L.J.'s interpretation (48) of LORD ATKIN'S words (49). The argument in the Nigerian case (50) does not seem to me to be based on the proposition that the applicant need only say: I do not know why I have been detained. It seems to me, and I think it seemed to SCOTT, L.J. (48), that the argument depended on a positive challenge to each of three positive conditions precedent.

C

That brings one to a consideration, which need not be a lengthy consideration, of *Greene's* case (51) itself, or rather to a consideration of its relevance, because I do not myself feel any doubt, nor do I gather does anyone in this court, as to its validity. In the Nigerian case (50) there had been facts in dispute the existence of which were conditions precedent to the making of the order which had to be shown: was the applicant a native chief, had he been deposed, was there a native law and custom that required his removal from the former area of his jurisdiction? As I understand *Greene's* case (51) there is not a single disputed fact. There is no dispute about the state of the Home Secretary's mind about his genuine belief, and I interpolate here the foundation, as I see it, for any thought that there was such a dispute is to be found in a recital in the course of VISCOUNT MAUGHAM'S judgment (52) in the House of Lords that the applicant in his affidavit had challenged and said that he did not believe that Sir John Anderson, the Home Secretary, did in fact believe him, the applicant, to be a person of hostile association. That may have been challenged in the affidavit, but the state of the Home Secretary's mind was not challenged, his bona fides were accepted in argument throughout.

D

E

F

That appears to me to make a very great difference. The Court of Appeal report is the important one in *Greene's* case (51) for present purposes, because the decision of the Court of Appeal was affirmed in the House of Lords (53), and words of GODDARD, L.J. (54), much relied on by the Crown in this case were specifically approved by LORD MAUGHAM (55). As is well known, *Greene's* case (51) was one which came under reg. 18B of the Defence (General) Regulations 1939 made under the provisions of the Emergency Powers Act 1939 for the purposes of dealing with the war-time emergencies. The first two paragraphs of the headnote in *Greene's* case (56) read thus:

G

" By the Defence (General) Regulations, 1939, reg. 18B, para. (1): ' If the Secretary of State has reasonable cause to believe any person to be of hostile origin or associations, or to have been recently concerned in acts prejudicial to the public safety or the defence of the realm, or in the preparation or instigation of such acts, and that by reason thereof it is necessary to exercise control over him, he may make an order against that person directing that he be detained '. By para. (8): ' Any person detained in pursuance of this regulation shall be deemed to be in lawful custody and shall

H

I

(48) [1941] 3 All E.R. at p. 112; [1942] 1 K.B. at p. 102.
(49) [1931] A.C. at p. 670; [1931] All E.R. Rep. at p. 49.
(50) [1931] A.C. 662; [1931] All E.R. 44.
(51) [1941] 3 All E.R. 104; [1942] 1 K.B. 87.
(52) [1941] 3 All E.R. 388 at pp. 389, 390; [1942] A.C. 284 at p. 289.
(53) [1941] 3 All E.R. 388; [1942] A.C. 284.
(54) [1941] 3 All E.R. at p. 121; [1942] 1 K.B. at p. 116.
(55) [1941] 3 All E.R. at p. 394; [1942] A.C. at p. 295.
(56) [1942] 1 K.B. at p. 87.

A   be detained in such place as may be authorised by the Secretary of State
and in accordance with instructions issued by him.'

"The Home Secretary, whose functions under para. (1) of the regulation
are executive and not quasi-judicial, is vested by para. (1) with discretionary
power, and the court will not inquire into the grounds on which he has formed his belief, nor require him to produce the information on which he has
B   done so. If the information is of a confidential character, he has a right to
refuse to produce it in the public interest."

I will not read more of the headnote.

Scott, L.J., after tracing what I may call the pedigree of the particular
defence regulation, referring in particular to its ancestor in the Defence of the
Realm (Consolidation) Act 1914 in the previous European war, said (57):

C

"Although it is not now pressed strongly upon us, so much which has been
urged verges on that argument that I think it useful to quote Lord
Wrenbury's words (58): 'The application before your Lordships is for
a writ of habeas corpus, and the ground advanced is that reg. 14B is ultra
vires. If that were established he (the applicant) would be discharged.
D   The Habeas Corpus Act is in full force; but this statute and the regulations
made under it have provided machinery for achieving in a way other than
that of suspending the Habeas Corpus Act the preventive detention of persons
who are not alleged to have committed any offence, but whom it is desired
to prevent from committing one. The regulation is, in my judgment, one
within the authority given by the Act'. With that preface for the purpose
of clearing the air round the problem of interpretation, I come to the crucial
E   point. What is the meaning fairly attributable to the opening language of
cl. (1)? Who is to decide the issue of reasonable cause, the Secretary of
State or a court? If a court . . . how could the question itself be brought
before the court? By certiorari to quash his order [i.e., the Secretary of State],
or mandamus to hear and determine according to law? Obviously neither.
It cannot be by habeas corpus, because the High Court does not sit as a
F   court of appeal in such proceedings."

There in my view Scott, L.J., is emphasising the difference to which Lord
Parker, C.J., referred earlier, between a review of an executive act and a would-
be appeal against a judicial decision. In that case it was held—there is no need
to look at the passages—that the question of whether the Home Secretary in
fact had reasonable cause for his belief was not a question of fact for the court
G   to enquire into. His state of mind, the belief that he had, as I have indicated,
although impugned on affidavit, was not in dispute on the hearing and was
accepted. I have already referred to the reference to the Nigerian case (59),
but there is one further passage in *Greene's* case (60) which I feel I should not
overlook; it would be quite wrong so to do. That is the passage, strenuously
H   relied on by the respondent, in Goddard, L.J.'s judgment, to which reference
was made in the House of Lords (61) and which reads (62):

"I am of opinion that, where, on the return, an order or warrant which
is valid on the face is produced, it is for the prisoner to prove the facts necessary to controvert it, and, in the present case, this has not been done. I do
not say that in no case is it necessary for the Secretary of State to file an
I   affidavit. It must depend on the ground on which the return is challenged,
but, where all that the prisoner says in effect is, ' I do not know why I am
interned, and I deny that I have done anything wrong ', that does not require

(57) [1941] 3 All E.R. at pp. 108, 109; [1942] 1 K.B. at pp. 97, 98.
(58) In *R. v. Halliday, Ex p. Zadig,* [1917] A.C. 260 at p. 308.
(59) [1931] A.C. 662; [1931] All E.R. Rep. 44.
(60) [1941] 3 All E.R. 104; [1942] 1 K.B. 87.
(61) [1941] 3 All E.R. at p. 394; [1942] A.C. at p. 295.
(62) [1941] 3 All E.R. at p. 121; [1942] 1 K.B. at p. 116.

A

an answer, because it in no way shows that the Secretary of State had not
reasonable cause to believe, or did not believe, otherwise."

That is a passage to which LORD MAUGHAM referred (63).

Of course, I can only pay a proper respectful obeisance to that statement
including that conclusion, but I do not find it relevant. As LORD MAUGHAM
said (64), these conclusions were intended to apply to an order made by an officer
responsible for the making of such an order; there were no factual conditions
precedent to the making of such an order; it was an order that recited only
the undisputed state of mind of the Home Secretary.

In this case the notice of refusal of admission given by the immigration officer
or officers to the applicants in the circumstances is not comparable to the order of
the Secretary of State in *Greene's* case (65). It is far more like the order in the
Nigerian case (66). The validity depends on two conditions precedent, the one,
fulfilled, that he has been given a notice within 12 hours of the examination;
the other, challenged, that the examination took place no more than 24 hours
after the immigrant's landing. There has emerged here a dispute of fact into
which the court must enquire and the notice of refusal of admission does not
assert the ground's requirement of fact, that is to say does not assert that
examination was within 24 hours of landing; indeed it is not in dispute that the
notice was given within 12 hours of examination. In *Greene's* case (65) the
sole issue of fact was as to the state of mind of the Home Secretary and the notice
did assert that.

In my judgment, therefore, *Greene's* case (65) is not apt to govern the decision
here. Insofar as the general statement in that case which I quoted might be
taken to refer to cases where there are conditions precedent to the exercise of
the power of detention, which itself depends on disputed questions of fact, I
think with respect that those remarks would be obiter and not decisive here.
This is a case of disputed fact, as well as fact; as LORD PARKER, C.J., said
it is a case where the order impugned is not an order of any court but an official
of the executive, as indeed was the Governor in the Nigerian case (66). I come
back finally, therefore, to the wording of Sch. 1 to the Act of 1962 as a matter
of plain interpretation.

I am unable to accept that the construction of para. 1 (2) of that schedule
imposes any statutory onus on the applicants. If that be right, then in my view
ordinary principles apply, and it is for the respondent to bear the onus of proving
that the conditions precedent to the validity of the giving of the notice were
satisfied, just as it would be for the respondent to prove the charge if the
applicants were charged under s. 4 of the Act of 1962 with an offence of remaining
in this country in defiance of an immigration officer's refusal of permission.
I would accede to the motion and order that the writs be issued.

I say only that in being compelled to this conclusion I am comforted by the
change made by the Act of 1968 to which I have referred in the substitution
of 28 days for 24 hours as the period within which the immigration officer may
examine.

Applications allowed. Writs to issue.

Solicitors: *Kleinman, Klarfeld & Co.*, (for the applicants); *Treasury solicitor.*

[*Reported by* S. A. HATTEEA, ESQ., *Barrister-at-Law.*]

(63) [1941] 3 All E.R. at p. 394; [1942] A.C. at p. 295.
(64) [1941] 3 All E.R. at pp. 394, 395; [1942] A.C. at pp. 295, 296.
(65) [1941] 3 All E.R. 104; [1942] 1 K.B. 87.
(66) [1931] A.C. 662; [1931] All E.R. Rep. 44.

A   CARL-ZEISS-STIFTUNG *v.* HERBERT SMITH & CO. (a firm)
                    AND ANOTHER (No. 2).

[COURT OF APPEAL, CIVIL DIVISION (Danckwerts, Sachs and Edmund Davies,
     L.JJ.), October 21, 22, 23, 24, 25, November 28, December 10, 1968.]

B *Solicitor—Liability—Trustee—Constructive trustee—Moneys on account of costs
      come to hands of defendant's solicitors for conduct of defence in action—Claim
      by plaintiff in that action that defendant trustee of all its assets for plaintiff—
      Separate action by plaintiff claiming that solicitor accountable to it for moneys
      received on account of costs from defendant in main action—Solicitors'
      knowledge of claim in main action—Liability of solicitors to account as
C   constructive trustees to plaintiff.*

      The Carl-Zeiss-Stiftung Foundation of East Germany claimed to be the
   original Zeiss Foundation in Jena in East Germany, and in 1955 it brought
   an action against another organisation or foundation called Carl-Zeiss-Stiftung
   of West Germany, claiming that that foundation was wrongfully using the
   name " Carl-Zeiss-Stiftung " for the purposes of its business. In October
D 1967, it re-amended its statement of claim in the action to claim that the
   business of the West German foundation was its property or was held in
   trust for it, including the trade marks, trade names, patents, goods and other
   assets of every kind of that business, particularly those in the United
   Kingdom, and that that foundation was liable to account to it in respect
   of any dealings with those assets. Complicated facts and difficult questions
E of German and English law were involved in the case. In March 1968, the
   East German foundation brought a further action against the two firms of
   solicitors who had acted for the West German foundation in the original
   action, one up to May 1964 and the other thereafter. It alleged that each
   had received moneys in the United Kingdom from the West German foundation, being part of its assets or moneys arising from its trade or business,
F well knowing all the facts and matters averred in the main action and with
   notice that the moneys were the East German foundation's property. Each
   was, therefore, liable to account to the East German foundation for the
   sums received, though not on the ground that they had intermeddled with the
   alleged trust moneys so as to be trustees de son tort. The solicitors admitted
   receiving sums on account of fees, costs and disbursements in the main action
G and admitted knowing of the averments in that action. It was admitted that
   they had acted honestly and with complete propriety in receiving the sums
   and that they could not know which way the main action would go, even if
   the allegations in the re-amended statement of claim were true.
      Held: the action against the solicitors must be dismissed, because—
      (i) (per DANCKWERTS, L.J.) (a) knowledge of a claim being made against
H the solicitors' client by the other party was not sufficient to amount to a
   notice of a trust or notice of misapplication of moneys to make the solicitors
   constructive trustees, particularly where unsolved questions of fact and
   difficult questions of German and English law were involved (see p. 372,
   letter I, to p. 373, letter A, post);
      (b) at the date of the payment of their costs and disbursements, the
I solicitors knew that the moneys came from the West German foundation
   and that there were claims against that foundation that all its property and
   assets belonged to the East German foundation or were held on trust for it,
   but not whether those claims were well founded, and on the trial of a
   preliminary issue in the action against the solicitors the allegations contained
   in the statements of claim in both the actions between the foundations
   could not be assumed to be true (see p. 375, letters B to D, post).
      (ii) (per SACHS and EDMUND DAVIES, L.JJ.) (a) at the date of action, the
   solicitors did not have such cognisance of the true ownership of the property

of the trusts as would make an ordinary stranger a constructive trustee of the   A
moneys, for whatever the nature of the knowledge or notice required,
cognisance of a " doubtful equity " was not enough, and no stranger could
become a constructive trustee merely because he was made aware of a
disputed claim the validity of which he could not properly assess (see p. 377,
letter E, p. 378, letters B and C, and p. 383, letter F, post);

(b) the solicitors were also under no duty to enquire into the allegations of   B
fact in the statement of claim in the main actions or to make enquiries or
attempt to assess the result on the law in such a complex matter (see p. 378,
letter I, to p. 379, letter A, and p. 383, letter F, post).

(iii) (per EDMUND DAVIES, L.J.) mere notice of a claim asserted by a third
party was insufficient to render the solicitors guilty of a wrongful act in
dealing with property derived from their principal in accordance with the   C
latter's instructions, unless the solicitors knew that the third party's claim
was well founded and that the principal had no authority to give such
instructions (see p. 384, letters D and E, post).

Decision of PENNYCUICK, J. ([1968] 2 All E.R. 1233), affirmed on different
grounds.

[As to constructive trusts by the acquisition of property with notice of a   D
trust, see 38 HALSBURY'S LAWS (3rd Edn.) 858, 859, para. 1446; and for cases
on the subject, see 47 DIGEST (Repl.) 184-188, 1525-1565.

As to liability of solicitors to third parties, see 36 HALSBURY'S LAWS (3rd Edn.)
56, 57, para. 80.]

Cases referred to: E

Barnes v. *Addy* (1874), 9 Ch. App. 244; 43 L.J.Ch. 513; 30 L.T. 4; 47 Digest
    (Repl.) 191, *1593*.

Blundell, Re, Blundell v. *Blundell* (1888), 40 Ch.D. 370; [1886-90] All E.R.
    Rep. 837; 57 L.J.Ch. 730; 58 L.T. 933; 47 Digest (Repl.) 187, *1561*.

Blyth v. *Fladgate, Morgan* v. *Blyth, Smith* v. *Blyth,* [1891] 1 Ch. 337; 60 L.J.Ch.
    66; 63 L.T. 546; 43 Digest (Repl.) 52, *403*.   F

Foxton v. *Manchester and Liverpool District Banking Co.* (1881), 44 L.T. 406;
    3 Digest (Repl.) 197, *393*.

La Roche v. *Armstrong,* [1922] 1 K.B. 485; [1922] All E.R. Rep. 311; 91
    L.J.K.B. 342; 126 L.T. 699; 22 Digest (Repl.) 80, *569*.

Lee v. *Sankey* (1873), L.R. 15 Eq. 204; 27 L.T. 809; 47 Digest (Repl.) 187, *1556*.

Maw v. *Pearson* (1860), 28 Beav. 196; 54 E.R. 340; 47 Digest (Repl.) 187, *1560*.   G

Mildred, Goyeneche & Co. v. *Maspons y Hermano* (1883), 8 App. Cas. 874;
    53 L.J.Q.B. 33; 49 L.T. 685; 32 Digest (Repl.) 278, *246*.

Morgan v. *Stephens* (1861), 3 Giff. 226; 4 L.T. 614; 66 E.R. 392; 47 Digest
    (Repl.) 192, *1601*.

Myler v. *Fitzpatrick* (1822), 6 Madd. 360; 56 E.R. 1128; 47 Digest (Repl.) 192,
    1595.   H

Nelson v. *Larholt,* [1947] 2 All E.R. 751; [1948] 1 K.B. 339; [1948] L.J.R.
    340; 47 Digest (Repl.) 187, *1554*.

Nickolson v. *Knowles* (1820), 5 Madd. 47; 56 E.R. 812; 29 Digest (Repl.)
    575, *47*.

Parker v. *Brooke* (1804), 9 Ves. 583; 32 E.R. 729; 27 Digest (Repl.) 159, *1160*.   I

Quistclose Investments, Ltd. v. *Rolls Razor, Ltd.* (*in voluntary liquidation*).
    [1968] 1 All E.R. 613; [1968] Ch. 540; [1968] 2 W.L.R. 478; *affd.*
    H.L., sub nom. *Barclays Bank, Ltd.* v. *Quistclose Investments, Ltd.*,
    [1968] 3 All E.R. 651; [1968] 3 W.L.R. 1097.

Selangor United Rubber Estates, Ltd. v. *Cradock* (*a bankrupt*) (*No. 3*), [1968]
    2 All E.R. 1073; [1968] 1 W.L.R. 1555.

Williams v. *Williams* (1881), 17 Ch.D. 437; 44 L.T. 573; 47 Digest (Repl.)
    187, *1559*.

A   **Appeal.**

This was an appeal by the plaintiff, Carl-Zeiss-Stiftung of East Germany, against an order of PENNYCUICK, J., dated 26th June 1968 and reported [1968] 2 All E.R. 1233, dismissing an action by the plaintiff against the defendants, Herbert Smith & Co. and Dehn & Lauderdale, claiming an account of all moneys come to the hands of the defendants or either of them being the property of

B   the plaintiff, and payment to the plaintiff of all sums found due on such account, and declaring on a preliminary issue that, irrespective of the decision of any issue in the action 1955 C. No. 4445 (between the plaintiff and the West German foundation, Carl-Zeiss-Stiftung of West Germany), neither of the defendants would be accountable to the plaintiff in respect of any fees, costs or disbursements received by them from or on behalf of the West German foundation in the course

C   of or before the final determination of that action so long as the defendants acted honestly as solicitors on behalf of that foundation in that action and received such fees, costs and disbursements in their capacity of solicitors. The facts are set out in the judgment of DANCKWERTS, L.J.

Jeremiah Harman, Q.C., and *J. R. Reid* for the plaintiff.

D   *Michael Kerr,* Q.C., *C. J. Slade,* Q.C., and *Gordon Slynn* for the defendants.

Cur. adv. vult.

10th December. The following judgments were read.

DANCKWERTS, L.J.: This is an appeal from a judgment of PENNYCUICK, J.(1), dated 26th June 1968, on a preliminary issue directed by the Court of Appeal

E   (2) by an order of 23rd May 1968, in an action which was begun by the plaintiff, Carl-Zeiss-Stiftung Foundation, by writ dated 18th March 1968. The object of the action is to make accountable two respectable firms of solicitors in respect of sums received in respect of fees paid to them for acting on behalf of another institution also called " Carl-Zeiss-Stiftung " for the purposes of proceedings between the two institutions. There is no suggestion that the defendant firms

F   of solicitors have acted otherwise than with perfect propriety.

The plaintiff claims to be the original Zeiss foundation in Jena in East Germany, and the defendants' client was a company or other foundation or institution formed in West Germany at Heidenheim in Wurtemburg after the Russians occupied East Germany. The main action (3) was begun by the plaintiff, the East German foundation, against the West German foundation by writ dated 20th October 1955. This action is, therefore, already thirteen years old, and the

G   prospect of the trial of the action still seems to be remote. For convenience, the contestants in the main action (which involves difficult questions of fact and of German and English law) will be referred to as the East German foundation and the West German foundation, respectively. Each of the concerns produces optical instruments and cameras, which have an international reputation and are sold in Great Britain.

H   As originally formulated, the main action was a plain passing-off action, in which it was claimed that the West German foundation were wrongfully using the name " Carl Zeiss " for the purpose of their business. But on 17th October 1967, the statement of claim was re-amended in green ink to raise some very different claims by the East German foundation. Paragraph 4F of the re-amended statement of claim reads as follows:

I   " The said business in West Germany is and has always been the property of the Plaintiffs and all its trade marks, trade names, patents, goods and other assets of every kind including in particular such of them as have been or are in the United Kingdom are the property of the Plaintiffs but the persons in control of the said business wrongfully refuse or neglect to comply

---

(1) [1968] 2 All E.R. 1233.
(2) See [1968] 2 All E.R. 1002; [1969] Ch. 93.
(3) See [1964] 3 All E.R. 326; [1965] Ch. 525.

A

with the instructions of the Plaintiffs or to account to them for or to pay over any of the profits of the said business or any sums at all."

Paragraph 4H of the re-amended statement of claim reads as follows:

" In the alternative if which is denied the said business carried on in West Germany is owned by persons other than the Plaintiffs then such persons are the third Defendants [i.e., the West German foundation]. In the said alternative the third Defendants acquired their business, trade marks, trade names, patents, goods and assets of every kind which include those of Zeiss Opton (hereinafter together called ' the West German assets ') with full knowledge of the matters hereinbefore set out and without providing any consideration or value therefor. In the premises all the West German assets originally and from time to time subsequently acquired by the third Defendants including in particular such of the West German assets as are or may have been in the United Kingdom are to have been or are deemed to be or have been the property of the Plaintiffs or are or were held in trust for the Plaintiffs. Further or alternatively the Defendants and each of them are under an obligation to account to the Plaintiffs in respect of any dealings by them or any of them with any of the West German assets and to convey, assign, transfer and deliver up to the Plaintiffs any of such assets in their possession or power."

B

C

D

And the plaintiff claimed:

" (i) A declaration that all the assets in the United Kingdom of every kind whatsoever of the business carried on in West Germany under the names ' Carl Zeiss Stiftung ' and ' Carl Zeiss ', including all the goodwill, trade marks, trade names, patents, and goods used or made in the business, are the property of the Plaintiffs,"

E

and other relief including:

" (iii) An account of all monies come to the hands of the Defendants or any of them arising out of any use or from any dealing with or disposition of all such property and payment to the Plaintiffs of all sums found due upon the taking of such account."

F

On 7th February 1956 the defendants in the main action applied by summons for an order that all further proceedings in the action be stayed and that this action be dismissed on the ground that the same was commenced and was being maintained without the plaintiff's authority and that Messrs. Courts & Co., the solicitors purporting to act for the plaintiff therein, do pay to the defendants the costs of the action. On 6th March 1964, CROSS, J., dismissed the summons. That decision was reversed by the Court of Appeal (4), but on 18th May 1966 the House of Lords (5) reversed the decision of the Court of Appeal and restored the judgment of CROSS, J.

G

On 18th March 1968 the writ was issued in the present action by the East German foundation against Herbert Smith & Co. and Dehn & Lauderdale, the two firms of solicitors who had acted in the proceedings for the West German foundation. The allegations in the statement of claim are important. Paragraphs 2, 3, 4 and 5 of the statement of claim are as follows:

H

" 2. Since about 1949 an organisation calling itself Carl Zeiss Stiftung has carried on the trade or business of manufacturer and supplier of optical instruments, articles containing or consisting of glass, scientific instruments and technical apparatus generally at Heidenheim-am-der-Brenz in West Germany. All the assets of whatsoever kind employed in such organisation including all the trading knowhow used in the said trade or business were obtained from the Plaintiff without any consideration therefor being

I

(4) [1965] 1 All E.R. 300; [1965] Ch. 596.
(5) [1966] 2 All E.R. 536; [1967] 1 A.C. 853.

A   received by the Plaintiff and all such assets and all monies arising from the
said trade or business are the property of the Plaintiff.

" 3. On 20th October 1955 the Plaintiff issued a writ in this Division of
this Honourable Court the number whereof is 1955 C. No. 4445 against three
Defendants of whom one was the said organisation. By the Re-amended
Statement of Claim in that action the Plaintiff claims inter alia a declaration
B   that all the assets in the United Kingdom of every kind whatsoever of the
said business carried on in West Germany are the property of the Plaintiff
together with ancillary relief.

" 4. The first Defendants are a firm of Solicitors carrying on that profession in the United Kingdom. From 20th May, 1964 the first Defendants
have acted and continue to act as solicitors for the Defendants in the said
C   action. The second Defendants are also a firm of Solicitors carrying on that
profession in the United Kingdom. From at least 11th November 1955
until 20th May, 1964 the second Defendants acted as Solicitors for the
Defendants in the said action. In the course of so acting each of the
Defendants have received in the United Kingdom monies (of which no particulars can be given until discovery herein) from the said organisation being part
D   of the assets employed in such organisation or monies arising from the said
trade or business.

" 5. The Plaintiff will refer to and rely upon the pleadings and judgment
in the said action. Each of the Defendants by reason of their acting in the
said action well knew all the facts and matters averred and proved or to be
proved therein. Each of the Defendants has received the said monies with
E   notice that such monies are the property of the Plaintiff. Accordingly each of
the Defendants is liable to account to the Plaintiff."

And the plaintiff claimed:

" 1. An account of all monies come to the hands of the Defendants or
either of them being the property of the Plaintiff. 2. Payment of all sums
F   found due upon taking such account."

In their defence, the defendants admitted the receipt of moneys on account of fees,
costs and disbursements incurred or paid or to be incurred or paid by each of them
respectively as solicitors for Carl-Zeiss-Stiftung (the defendant in the main
action) in or in connection with the action, and other proceedings to which
Carl-Zeiss-Stiftung was a party, but not otherwise. The defendants also admitted
G   that, in the course of acting as solicitors for Carl-Zeiss-Stiftung during the periods
referred to in para. 4 of the statement of claim, they respectively knew during
such periods respectively the averments from time to time made by the plaintiffs
in the action 1955 C. No. 4445. But the rest of the allegations in the statement of
claim were either denied or not admitted.

By an order dated 23rd May 1968, the Court of Appeal (6) directed the trial
H   of a preliminary issue in the following terms:

" That irrespective of the decision upon any issue in the action 1955 C. 4445
referred to in the pleadings herein neither of the Defendants herein would be
accountable to the Plaintiff in respect of any fees costs or disbursements
received by them from or on behalf of the Defendants in that action so long
as the Defendants herein act honestly as Solicitors on behalf of the said
I   Defendants and receive such fees costs and disbursements in their said
capacity of Solicitors."

On 26th June 1968, PENNYCUICK, J. (7), gave judgment on the preliminary issue,
by which he made an order in the terms of the preliminary issue (except that he
inserted therein the words " in the course of or before the final determination of
that Action "), and the learned judge dismissed the action out of court. The basis

(6) See [1968] 2 All E.R. at p. 1004; [1969] Ch. at p. 99.
(7) [1968] 2 All E.R. 1233.

of the learned judge's decision was that a claim of the kind made by plaintiff A
against solicitors having the conduct of the action is contrary to public policy in
that it obstructs the course of justice. It would appear that the learned judge
either rejected or expressed no final opinion on the other point taken on behalf
of the defendants that the general principle of accountability of persons who
receive trust property with notice of the trust, does not, with certain exceptions,
apply to an agent in whose hands the property has been placed by his principal. B
From that decision the plaintiff appeals to this court, and there is a cross-notice.
I propose to adopt the course which was followed at the hearing of the appeal and
deal with the second question first.

Counsel in opening the case for the plaintiff stressed that there was no imputation made against the honour or conduct of either of the sets of solicitors who are
the defendants. Counsel's contention was that, if solicitors receive payments C
from a fund which they know or ought to know is comprised wholly of trust
funds, then they are accountable. He contended that the defendants knew where
the moneys that they received came from, and knew that the source was trust
funds. He stated that it was necessary for the plaintiff to prove the allegations
on which it relied, but contended that, for the purposes of the preliminary point,
all the allegations in the statement of claim must be assumed to be true. I am D
not prepared to accept this contention without further consideration, but I think
that it will be more convenient to consider it after the principles on which the
case depends have been examined.

The defendant solicitors in this case have not only received the moneys in
question honestly as solicitors; they have also given value for it by their services.
They are, therefore, in a similar position to that of purchasers for value of property. E
But it is said that value is not enough as they have notice of the trusts affecting
the moneys and, therefore, are accountable, as constructive trustees: see SNELL'S
EQUITY (26th Edn.) p. 202:

> " He becomes a constructive trustee if he falls within either of two heads,
> namely—(i) that he received trust property and that the transfer to him was a
> breach of trust ";   F

and 38 HALSBURY'S LAWS OF ENGLAND (3rd Edn.) pp. 858, 859, para. 1446 and
para. 1447:

> " **1446. Acquisition with notice of trust.** Where a person, whether
> gratuitously or for valuable consideration, acquires property . . . which is
> subject to a subsisting trust, he becomes a trustee of it for the purposes of the G
> trust if he has either actual or constructive notice of the trust . . .
> **1447. Necessity for notice of misapplication.** In order to constitute a
> person who takes trust property or trust money for his own purposes a
> constructive trustee of it, he must have notice that it is being misapplied by
> being transferred to him, or, in other words, he must be a party to a fraud or
> breach of trust on the part of the actual trustee."   H

Counsel for the plaintiff contended that this condition was satisfied because the
solicitors knew that it was being used for the purpose of defeating the beneficiaries' rights and, therefore, was being misapplied. But see para. 1449 and
para. 1450, on pp. 860, 861:

> " **1449. Receipt of trust money.** A banker, broker, solicitor, or other I
> stranger to the trust, receiving money from a trustee, which he knows to be
> part of the trust property, does not become a constructive trustee thereof in
> relation to the cestui que trust, unless he knows that the money is being
> applied in a manner inconsistent with the trust, or, in other words, unless he
> is a party either to a fraud or to a breach of trust on the part of the trustee.
> In so far as such money remains in the disposition of the trustee the cestui
> que trust may follow it and claim it as against the trustee."

In my view, knowledge of a claim being made against the solicitors' client by

A the other party is not sufficient to amount to notice of a trust or notice of mis-application of the moneys. In the present case, which involves unsolved questions of fact, and difficult questions of German and English law, I have no doubt that knowledge of the plaintiff's claim is not notice of the trusts alleged by the plaintiff.

B " 1450. **Intermeddling with trust.** A person, who, not being a trustee and not having authority from a trustee, takes upon himself to intermeddle with trust matters or to do acts characteristic of the office of trustee, makes himself a trustee *de son tort*, a trustee of his own wrong, or, as such a person is also termed, a constructive trustee. The responsibility which attaches to a trustee may extend in equity to a person who is not properly a trustee, if he either makes himself a trustee *de son tort* or actually participates in any

C fraudulent conduct of a trustee to the injury of the cestuis que trust. A person who is employed as solicitor or agent for trust property may become a constructive trustee or trustee *de son tort* by intermeddling with the performance of the trust, or by dealing with the property in a manner not warranted by the terms of his employment or agency, or in a manner inconsistent with the performance of trusts of which he is cognisant. A person

D does not, however, become a constructive trustee merely by acting as the solicitor or agent of trustees in transactions within their legal powers, although the transactions may be of a character of which a court of equity would disapprove, unless he receives and becomes chargeable with some part of the trust property, or unless he knowingly assists in a dishonest and fraudulent act on the part of the trustees."

E In my opinion, these passages correctly state the law, and are supported by the authorities which are cited in the notes.

Vast numbers of authorities were cited to us, which were instances of the application of the principles which have been enunciated. It is noteworthy that no case was produced in which a solicitor, simply receiving payment of his costs

F and disbursements, was held to be a constructive trustee and accountable to persons who claimed to be beneficiaries under a trust. The cases to which we were referred fell into the two classes: (i) a person simply acquiring moneys as agent and accountable to his principal but not to a person claiming under a trust; and (ii) solicitors or other agents who by intermeddling or undertaking functions appropriate to a trustee became thereby liable to beneficiaries who had suffered

G loss or were taking proceedings to recover the funds. I do not propose to go through all the cases which were cited. I intend simply to take a few examples of the situations which I have mentioned.

It is useful to repeat the statements of LORD SELBORNE, L.C., in *Barnes* v. *Addy* (8). In that case, a sole trustee had been appointed against the advice of a solicitor, and the sole trustee misapplied the funds. Two solicitors who had

H prepared the deeds in the transaction and had received costs were joined as defendants in a suit by two beneficiaries with the trustee who had appointed the sole trustee. The Vice-Chancellor dismissed the bill against the two solicitors. On appeal, the appeal was dismissed and the decree of the Vice-Chancellor was affirmed. LORD SELBORNE said (9):

I " Now in this case we have to deal with certain persons who are trustees, and with certain other persons who are not trustees. That is a distinction to be borne in mind throughout the case. Those who create a trust clothe the trustee with a legal power and control over the trust property, imposing on him a corresponding responsibility. That responsibility may no doubt be extended in equity to others who are not properly trustees, if they are found either making themselves trustees de son tort, or actually participating

_____

(8) (1874), 9 Ch. App. 244.
(9) (1874), 9 Ch. App. at pp. 251, 252.

A

in any fraudulent conduct of the trustee to the injury of the cestui que trust. But, on the other hand, strangers are not to be made constructive trustees merely because they act as the agents of trustees in transactions within their legal powers, transactions, perhaps of which a Court of Equity may disapprove, unless those agents receive and become chargeable with some part of the trust property, or unless they assist with knowledge in a dishonest and fraudulent design on the part of the trustees."

B

Those are the principles, as it seems to me, which we must bear in mind in dealing with the facts of this case. The quotation continues (10):

" If those principles were disregarded, I know not how any one could, in transactions admitting of doubt as to the view which a Court of Equity might take of them, safely discharge the office of solicitor, of banker, or of agent of any sort to trustees. But, on the other hand, if persons dealing honestly as agents are at liberty to rely on the legal power of the trustees, and are not to have the character of trustees constructively imposed upon them, then the transactions of mankind can safely be carried through; and I apprehend those who create trusts do expressly intend, in the absence of fraud and dishonesty, to exonerate such agents of all classes from the responsibilities which are expressly incumbent, by reason of the fiduciary relation, upon the trustees."

C

D

That seems to me to be an illuminating statement of the principles that we have to apply in the present case. I would call attention in particular to LORD SELBORNE, L.C.'s reference to " transactions admitting of doubt ". These principles are supported by such cases as *Nickolson* v. *Knowles* (11); *Myler* v. *Fitzpatrick* (12); *Maw* v. *Pearson* (13); *Morgan* v. *Stephens* (14); *Williams* v. *Williams* (15); *Re Blundell, Blundell* v. *Blundell* (16); and *Lee* v. *Sankey* (17).

E

With all respect to the learned judge, I think that he misunderstood the purport of the remarks of SIR JAMES BACON, V.-C., in *Lee* v. *Sankey* (18). What SIR JAMES BACON, V.-C., said was:

" It is well established by many decisions, that a mere agent of trustees is answerable only to his principal and not to *cestuis que trust* in respect of trust moneys coming to his hands merely in his character of agent. But it is also not less clearly established that a person who receives into his hands trust moneys, and who deals with them in a manner inconsistent with the performance of trusts of which he is cognizant, is personally liable for the consequences which may ensue upon his so dealing."

F

G

To me it is clear that, in the latter part of his observations, SIR JAMES BACON, V.-C., was referring to cases like *Blyth* v. *Fladgate* (19), where the solicitor or agent acts wrongly, takes it on himself to deal with trust funds, as though he were a trustee of them, and consequently incurs the responsibility appropriate to his actions. In *Lee* v. *Sankey* (17), the solicitors took it on themselves to pay trust moneys in their hands to only one of two trustees: a very different situation from receiving payment for legal services. We were referred to *Quistclose Investments, Ltd.* v. *Rolls Razor, Ltd. (in voluntary liquidation)* (20), in which the decision of the Court of Appeal (20) was affirmed by the House of Lords (21) on 31st October 1968; but the facts of that case seem to me to have been of a special kind and I do not think that it affects the principles which I have been considering.

H

I

---

(10) (1874), 9 Ch. App. at p. 252.
(12) (1822), 6 Madd. 360.
(14) (1861), 3 Giff. 226.
(16) (1888), 40 Ch.D. 370; [1886-90] All E.R. Rep. 837.
(17) (1873), L.R. 15 Eq. 204.
(18) (1873), L.R. 15 Eq. at p. 211.
(19) [1891] 1 Ch. 337.
(20) [1968] 1 All E.R. 613; [1968] Ch. 540.
(21) [1968] 3 All E.R. 651; [1968] 3 W.L.R. 1097.

(11) (1820), 5 Madd. 47.
(13) (1880), 28 Beav. 196.
(15) (1881), 17 Ch.D. 437.

A   Let me apply these principles to the circumstances of the present case. In the first place, it is admitted by the plaintiff that the defendant solicitors have acted honestly and with complete propriety in receiving these sums that were paid to them by the West German foundation as solicitors. The contentions of counsel for the plaintiff were that the defendants knew where the moneys that they received came from and knew that the source was trust funds. In my view, this

B   contention fails at the outset. What the defendants knew was that the moneys came from the West German foundation and they knew of the allegations contained in the proceedings brought against that foundation by the East German foundation in which they were instructed to act as solicitors for the West German foundation. They knew that claims were being made against the West German foundation that all their property and assets belonged to the plaintiff or were held

C   on trust for them. But claims are not the same thing as facts. Counsel for the plaintiff contended that, for the purposes of the present issue, all the allegations contained in the statements of claim in both the actions must be taken as true. That will not do. What we have to deal with is the state of the defendants' knowledge (actual or imputed) at the date when they received payments of their costs and disbursements. At that date they cannot have had more than knowledge

D   of the claims above mentioned. It was not possible for them to know whether they were well founded or not. The claims depended on most complicated facts still to be proved or disproved, and very difficult questions of German and English law. It is not a case where the West German foundation were holding property on any express trust. They were denying the existence of any trust or any right of property in the assets claimed by the plaintiff. Why should the

E   solicitors of the West German foundation assume anything against their clients? Consequently, it seems to me that the plaintiff's claim against the defendant solicitors must fail on the requisite condition of knowledge or notice.

This is sufficient to dispose of this appeal, and it is not really necessary to decide the question on which the learned judge based his decision (22), namely, that a claim of this kind against solicitors having the conduct of the action is contrary

F   to public policy in the sense that it obstructs the course of justice. But it must not be taken that I am expressing any disapproval of the decision of Pennycuick, J. (22) on this point. There is a good deal to be said for this contention. If it is not correct, it puts a heavy burden on solicitors, and I was not much impressed by the suggestions of counsel for the plaintiff as to the way in which solicitors can protect themselves. It would be a burden on persons seeking legal assistance as

G   well as on the solicitors. But it may be that this point is part of the general protection of agents which we have been considering.

I would dismiss the appeal accordingly.

SACHS, L.J.: A claim of the nature made in the present case is well calculated to suspend a sword of Damocles over the head of a solicitor acting for a

H   client bona fide seeking to defend his title to property of which he is in possession and which constitutes the bulk, and perhaps the entirety, of his assets. This fact had been underlined by the course adopted by the plaintiff in initially asserting its present claim on 6th January 1968, then issuing a forestalling writ on 18th March, and later strongly opposing any determination of the instant issues before there had been tried the main action which it commenced in 1955. If its claim is

I   right, it can put defendants and their solicitors, as it has done in the present case, in a position which can reasonably be termed " impossible ".

The claim is in essence a novel one; that does not mean that it is necessarily wrong, but it does entail its being scrutinised with considerable care lest on the one hand assets which may in due course be found to belong to a plaintiff are not during the pendency of process left at risks of dissipation which the courts consider improper, and on the other hand that bona fide defendants and their professional advisers are not subjected to harassments which are not permitted by the laws of

(22) [1968] 2 All E.R. 1233.

this country. It is, however, not merely agents and professional advisers who A
may be affected if the plaintiff's claim here is well founded, but a far wider
number of persons. The present claim relates to moneys which had been paid to
the defendants as solicitors in part for services rendered by them to the West
German foundation and disbursements made by them on that foundation's
behalf in an action (" the main action ") pending between the plaintiff (the East
German foundation) and the above-named West German foundation, who were B
clients of the defendants, and in part to be held by one of the defendants on
account of sums which would become due to them for further services to be
rendered and for further disbursements to be made as solicitors. The plaintiff
submits that, because the defendants have had notice that in the main action the
plaintiff claims that all the property of the West German foundation either
belongs to or is held in trust for it (the East German foundation), the defendants C
have received such notice of the trusts alleged in that action as to constitute them
constructive trustees of the above moneys. If the plaintiff succeeds in its contention, the result will be that the defendants could not safely make use of any of the
moneys thus received by them until there had been determined the main action
by what may well be in due course a decision of the House of Lords. In this way
one might say that the moneys in question would be " frozen ".   D
   Counsel for the plaintiff submitted that there would be parallel effects as
regards all persons dealing with the West German foundation who had appropriate notice of the alleged trusts. He asserted that the same principles would
thus apply to all payments made to suppliers of goods or services to the West
German foundation. Initially he suggested that mere notice given by the plaintiff
of its claim might be enough. Later, however, he resiled from that proposition, E
but only to the extent of saying that payments for the supply of goods and
services would presumably fall within the ambit of the alleged trusts, and thus
would not be made in breach of those trusts. Even so, the dangers of such a state
of affairs to anyone who dealt with the West German foundation and who did not
happen to be an expert in the subtleties of trust law are obvious—once they had
received public or private intimation of the relevant claims; the possibilities of F
the plaintiff's being able to impede or perhaps even freeze its opponent's business
cannot be wholly overlooked. This underlines the need for a cautious approach
to the plaintiff's claim.
   It is not without relevance as regards risks of improper dissipation of a party's
assets to observe that there are, of course, well-known provisions within the Rules
of the Supreme Court by which in appropriate cases property the subject-matter G
of an action can be preserved. The provision in mind is R.S.C., Ord. 29, r. 2.
It has, however, been properly conceded by counsel for the plaintiff that any
application by the plaintiff made under that order would fail as regards the moneys
presently in issue; indeed, it could not have a vestige of a chance of success.
Hence, no doubt, the present attempt to achieve something which is in effect
contrary to the principles the court normally applies as between the parties of H
an action.
   Before examining the validity of the plaintiff's claim in this action, it is as well
to record at the outset that not only is there no specific suggestion in the statement
of claim that the defendants acted dishonestly or that qua solicitors they acted
improperly or that they received or dealt with the relevant moneys otherwise
than in their character of solicitors, but counsel for the plaintiff fairly and I
specifically stated the obvious—that no such allegations are intended or could
possibly be made. It is similarly important to record that counsel for the defendants has stated and counsel for the plaintiff has agreed that both in this court
and in the court of first instance (23) it is and was common ground that the
defendants could not at any material time and cannot now know which way the
litigation will go, even if all the allegations of fact in the re-amended statement of

(23) [1968] 2 All E.R. 1233.

A   claim in the main action were found to be true. The importance of recording these points stems from the over-great width of the terms of para. 5 of the statement of claim, which must accordingly be read as being limited in the way just related. Amongst the effects of those points it is to be observed that nothing in the statement of claim can be read as suggesting that the defendants intermeddled with the alleged trust moneys so as to make them trustees de son tort; nor was such
B   intermeddling suggested in this court.

Counsel for the defendants was under the impression that at first instance (24), when the plaintiff's case was presented by other counsel, it was in addition common ground that in this paragraph the words " well knew all the facts . . . averred " in the main action were to be construed in relation to the facts alleged in the relevant statement of claim as meaning " well knew that those facts were
C   averred " as opposed to " well knew those facts ": but in this court there was no such common ground. I am glad to say that, to my mind, nothing in the upshot turns on this point. However, I confess it almost impossible to think that, in this particular action, a serious allegation could or would be made of actual knowledge, for instance, of the events of 1945. The same observation applies generally to the bulk of the facts averred in the statement of claim, which both
D   counsel for the plaintiff and counsel for the defendants agreed were hotly disputed. Indeed, it seems to me that, if the second of the above meanings is to be conveyed, then a different set of words is needed.

It is against that background that I now turn to the issues raised by the plaintiff's claim. When so doing, I propose to assume that the plaintiff will in the main action succeed in establishing that the relevant moneys are either its own property
E   or held in trust for it by the West German foundation. The initial issue, then, for consideration is as follows. On the facts as alleged in the present statement of claim, had the defendants at the date of action brought such cognisance of the true ownership of the property or of the trusts as would make an ordinary stranger a constructive trustee of the relevant moneys? It is only if that question is answered in the affirmative that there arise in sequence the next two issues.
F   Does the fact that the defendants received the moneys *as agents* put them in a special position, even if such cognisance is established? If not, does the fact that they received the moneys *as solicitors* bona fide acting for their client in the main litigation put them in a special position on grounds of public policy? There are also certain further points raised by counsel for the defendants that merit attention.
G   The neutral word " cognisance " has been used by me in preference to either " notice " or " knowledge " because, during the citation of authorities and in the course of argument, it emerged that these two words were often being used as if they were interchangeable; in fact and in law " notice " and " knowledge " are, of course, not necessarily the same thing, as has been recognised on more than one occasion in the past. It was clearly appreciated as long ago as Lord
H   Blackburn's days, for in *Mildred, Goyeneche & Co.* v. *Maspons y Hermano* (25) he refers to that fact without further elaboration. This apparent tendency to unguarded language was doubtless due to there often being no need on the particular facts of the case under consideration either to distinguish between " notice " and " knowledge " or to examine their precise meaning in the context of those facts. As textbook after textbook was quoted, and authorities cited
I   literally by the dozen, each using slightly different sets of words, it was borne in on me that, at the date when Pennycuick, J., delivered his judgment (24) in the present proceedings, there was, as counsel before us agreed, no modern judicial decision examining what exactly is needed in the way of knowledge or notice to fix a stranger with constructive trusteeship of assets when he has not intermeddled so as to become a trustee de son tort. Accordingly, when on the last day

(24) [1968] 2 All E.R. 1233.
(25) (1883), 8 App. Cas. 874 at p. 885.

of the submissions to this court there was cited the judgment in *Selangor United* A
Rubber Estates, Ltd. v. *Cradock* (*a bankrupt*) (*No. 3*) (26), I found myself grateful
to UNGOED-THOMAS, J., for his careful collation and examination of so many of
the relevant judgments on this subject (27). It would be otiose for me to refer
seriatim either to those judgments or to the further series which have been brought
to the attention of this court. It is sufficient to state what are the conclusions
to which I consider they lead.   B

First, and to my mind decisively, whatever be the nature of the knowledge
or notice required, cognisance of what has been termed a " doubtful equity " is
not enough. This phrase is to be found in LEWIN ON TRUSTS (16th Edn., 1964)
at p. 658, and UNDERHILL'S LAW OF TRUSTS (11th Edn., 1959) at p. 606; it
appears first to have been used by LORD GRANT, M.R., in *Parker* v. *Brooke* (28).
The rule, as I understand it, is that no stranger can become a constructive   C
trustee merely because he is made aware of a disputed claim the validity of which
he cannot properly assess. Here it has been rightly conceded that no one can fore-
tell the result of the litigation even if the plaintiff was to prove all the facts that it
alleges. Thus, to my mind, the plaintiff fails at an early stage in its attempt to
fix the defendants with appropriate cognisance. It seems to me, however, that in
order to succeed it would also have to overcome further obstacles which are   D
insurmountable by reason of the nature of the case and the concessions which it
has rightly made earlier. It is convenient to examine these in the same order as
they were propounded in the course of counsel for the defendants' particularly
helpful analysis of the issues, coupled as regards each in turn with reference to
the supporting authorities.

The first obstacle emerges on an examination of the submission for the plaintiff E
that to fix a stranger with the appropriate responsibility it is sufficient to show
that he has notice of the type exemplified by the terms of s. 199 of the Law of
Property Act 1925; that is to say, to show that the existence of the trusts would
have come to his knowledge if such enquiries had been made as ought reasonably
to have been made by him. On the assumption that this is the right test (a point
to which I will return), it is to be noticed that in many cases, and in particular in F
the present case, knowledge of the existence of a trust depends on knowledge
first of the relevant facts and next of the law applicable to that set of facts. As to
facts alleged in a statement of claim, counsel for the defendants was, to my mind,
correct in submitting that a defendant's solicitor is under no duty to the plaintiffs
to enquire into their accuracy for the purposes urged by counsel for the plaintiff
nor, where there is a likelihood of a conflict of evidence between his client's wit- G
nesses and those of the plaintiffs', is he under any such duty to assess the result.
In coming to this conclusion, I am content to adopt the approach, albeit obiter,
of LUSH, J., in *La Roche* v. *Armstrong* (29), where he said this:

" Here the solicitor has received a sum of money from his client for the
purpose of his resisting on her behalf a claim by A, who says it is trust
money and that the client is under a duty to return it. Under such circum-   H
stances I should be very loth to say that the solicitor, who cannot know
the real truth of the matter, inasmuch as he hears one story from his client
and another from A, is bound to hold the money, not for his client, but for A
whose claim is not yet established."

That approach was correct, because the solicitor was under no duty to A. either   I
to make enquiries or to assess the results of them.

The nature and extent of the duty to enquire when there is applicable what by
way of shorthand can be referred to as the s. 199 test must, of course, vary according to the facts. In the present case, the defendants were thus not under a duty to

---

(26) [1968] 2 All E.R. 1073; [1968] 1 W.L.R. 1555.
(27) See [1968] 2 All E.R. at pp. 1095-1105; [1968] 1 W.L.R. at pp. 1578-1591.
(28) (1804), 9 Ves. 583 at p. 588.
(29) [1922] 1 K.B. 485 at p. 491; [1922] All E.R. Rep. 311 at p. 313.

A the plaintiff to enquire into the allegations of fact in the statement of claim. As to the law, they were similarly under no duty to the plaintiff in such a complex matter either to make enquiries or to attempt to assess the result. (It has already, of course, been conceded that there was no prospect of their being able to come to a firm conclusion on the matter of law.) Thus, the plaintiff fails again at this point to show that the defendants should be deemed to be cognisant of the trusts.

B It should be added that, to my mind, it would have similarly failed in any normal case in which the relevant stranger becomes aware of a bona fide disputed claim to assets in his hands.

The next point strongly pressed by counsel for the defendants was that, in order to succeed, the plaintiff would have had to allege either fraud, or improper conduct as a solicitor, or wilful use of the moneys in breach of trust. In this

C behalf it has been the case of counsel for the plaintiff that, once it was shown that the moneys were in law being used in breach of trust, the s. 199 test was once more decisive when considering whether a stranger is fixed with liability. It does not, however, seem to me that a stranger is necessarily shown to be both a constructive trustee and liable for a breach of the relevant trusts even if it is established that he has such notice. As at present advised, I am inclined to the view that a further

D element has to be proved, at any rate in a case such as the present one. That element is one of dishonesty or of consciously acting improperly, as opposed to an innocent failure to make what a court may later decide to have been proper enquiry. That would entail both actual knowledge of the trust's existence and actual knowledge that what is being done is improperly in breach of that trust— though, of course, in both cases a person wilfully shutting his eyes to the obvious

E is in no different position than if he had kept them open. In becoming somewhat strongly inclined to that view before the *Selangor* case (30) was cited, I had been impressed by the recurrence of the close conjunction in textbooks and judgments of references to fraud and breach of trusts in the relevant passages.

An example of this is to be found in the judgment of STIRLING, J., in *Re Blundell, Blundell v. Blundell* (31), where he referred to the doctrine of constructive trustees

F as follows:

" It is that a stranger to the trust receiving money from the trustee which he knows to be part of the estate is not liable as a constructive trustee . . . unless it be made out that he is a party either to a fraud, or to a breach of trust on the part of the trustee."

G Moreover, the mere fact that in *Williams v. Williams* (32), a case cited in the *Selangor* judgment (30), KAY, J., made use of the phrase, " If I had been satisfied that Mr. Cheese had wilfully shut his eyes ", seems, when taken in the context of the facts of that case, once more to show that an innocent, even if negligent, failure to enquire is not enough. Indeed, these cases tend quite strongly to the conclusion that negligent, if innocent, failure to make enquiry is not sufficient

H to attract constructive trusteeship. It is, moreover, to be observed that cases where on the facts there was an obvious shutting of eyes (e.g., *Nelson v. Larholt* (33)) as opposed to mere lack of prudence may need careful examination lest, as in the intermeddling cases, the dicta in them may be found to be beyond what was requisite for the particular decision.

As regards textbooks, one finds it said in 38 HALSBURY'S LAWS OF ENGLAND

I (3rd Edn.) p. 859, para. 1447 (already cited by DANCKWERTS, L.J.), ". . . in other words, he must be a party to a fraud or breach of trust on the actual part of the trustee " a phrase repeated in para. 1449. Obviously the word " knowingly " must be inserted before " party " to make sense of " party to a fraud ", and I am inclined to think that the word " knowingly " (with exactly the same connotation

(30) [1968] 2 All E.R. 1073; [1968] 1 W.L.R. 1555.
(31) (1888), 40 Ch.D. 370 at p. 381; [1886-90] All E.R. Rep. 837 at pp. 841, 842.
(32) (1881), 17 Ch.D. 437 at p. 445.
(33) [1947] 2 All E.R. 751; [1948] 1 K.B. 339.

of actual knowledge) must apply in relation to being " a party to a breach of **A** trust ". Insofar as in this connection use in the relevant paragraphs is made of the word " fraud ", I would hesitate long before holding in this day and age that that word could have different meanings in different Divisions of the High Court. This, so far as I understand it, was common ground as between counsel for the defendants and counsel for the plaintiff, for both agreed it could not. It would, indeed, be particularly disturbing for the business community if that were not the **B** case. This point deserves mention, because, if this case goes further, it may, since the citation of the *Selangor* case (34), be urged that the word " fraud " in, for instance, the relevant paragraphs in HALSBURY'S LAWS, or " actively fraudulent ", in LEWIN ON TRUSTS (16th Edn.) at p. 151, does not import dishonesty. Out of deference to the conclusions reached by UNGOED-THOMAS, J., and to the fact that the *Selangor* case (34) is under appeal, it now seems best, however, **C** for me not to state a final view in this matter, especially when the instant case concerns agents who may thus be in a different position from other strangers.

If, however, it were right that the plaintiff must establish fraud or improper dealing or wilful breach of trust in the sense that I have used those words, then, of course, it is bound to fail also on that point. Generally in this behalf I have also in mind that more than one eminent authority has referred to the desirability of **D** not extending the doctrine of constructive trusts too far. They include LORD SELBORNE, L.C., in *Barnes* v. *Addy* (35) and KAY, J., in *Williams* v. *Williams* (36), already cited.

I have thus come to the conclusion that the plaintiff could not possibly on the allegations made in its statement of claim, as qualified in the way mentioned at the outset of this judgment, succeed in its claim against the defendants; it **E** cannot establish that the defendants were cognisant either of the relevant trusts or of the moneys being employed in breach thereof. Accordingly, it does not seem necessary to deal otherwise than briefly with the three further points of counsel for the defendants.

The first was that professional men and agents who have received moneys as such and have acted bona fide are accountable only to their principals unless **F** dishonesty as well as cognisance of trusts is established against them. Suffice it to say that I was impressed by the authorities he cited, such as *Nickolson* v. *Knowles* (37), and supporting textbooks which contained passages such as those in UNDERHILL'S LAW OF TRUSTS (11th Edn., 1959) at p. 599:

" Where the agent of the trustees [and this would clearly include the agents **G** of constructive trustees such as the West German foundation is alleged to be] acts honestly and confines himself to the duties of an agent then though he will not be accountable to the beneficiaries they will have their remedy against the persons who are the real trustees."

Similar passages are to be found in LEWIN ON TRUSTS (16th Edn., 1964) at p. 151, and elsewhere. These accord with the views so clearly expressed by LORD SEL- **H** BORNE, L.C., in *Barnes* v. *Addy* (38) and already fully cited by DANCKWERTS, L.J.

Similarly, it is unnecessary for me to consider whether in any event a solicitor acting in the normal way for his client in defence of a claim made against the latter is for reasons of public policy in a better position than any other professional man or agent. I am glad to be absolved from considering that point, for, broadly speaking, it is best that solicitors should as a general rule be neither better nor **I** worse placed than other men who act for principals, whether as members of a profession or otherwise. Naturally, there are some matters on which members of

(34) [1968] 2 All E.R. 1073; [1968] 1 W.L.R. 1555.
(35) (1874), 9 Ch. App. 244.
(36) (1881), 17 Ch.D. 437.
(37) (1820), 5 Madd. 47.
(38) (1874), 9 Ch. App. 244 at p. 251.

A the legal profession must necessarily be in a special position, but the fewer the better.

Finally, one further potential obstacle in the way of the plaintiff's claim merits mention. It is patent from the plaintiff's assertions in the main action that the West German foundation commenced to operate in 1945, that the proceedings in the main action were not commenced till 20th October 1955, and that it was not

B until October 1967 that they were amended so as to put forward a claim that all the West German foundation's assets were the property of or were held in trust for the plaintiff. In these circumstances, laches has inevitably been pleaded by the defendants to the main action. Counsel for the plaintiff having emphasised that both in the main action and in the present action the relative remedies claimed by the plaintiff were equitable remedies, counsel for the defendants raised the issues

C of laches and discretion as being also material today. How far in the particular demurrer-like proceedings now before this court account can be taken of laches or of the discretion which a court may have in relation to equitable remedies is a nice point; but surely there may be cases where a court must quite inevitably exercise its discretion in a way adverse to the plaintiff on the facts he sets out, and, if so, this may well be such a case. In the circumstances, I say no more about this

D issue.

I agree that on the grounds already stated the appeal should be dismissed.

EDMUND DAVIES, L.J.: The basic question raised by this appeal is whether the defendants hold the moneys of the plaintiff as constructive trustees. The AMERICAN RESTATEMENT OF RESTITUTION sets out to define a constructive

E trust by declaring in para. 160 that:

" Where a person holding title to property is subject to an equitable duty to convey it to another on the ground that he would be unjustly enriched if he were permitted to retain it, a constructive trust arises."

English law provides no clear and all-embracing definition of a constructive trust. Its boundaries have been left perhaps deliberately vague, so as not to restrict the

F court by technicalities in deciding what the justice of a particular case may demand. But it appears that in this country unjust enrichment or other personal advantage is not a sine qua non. Thus, in *Nelson* v. *Larholt* (39), it was not suggested that the defendant was himself one penny better off by changing an executor's cheques; yet, as he ought to have known of the executor's want of authority to draw them, he was held liable to refund the estate, both on the basis

G that he was a constructive trustee for the beneficiaries and on a claim for money had and received to their use. Nevertheless, the concept of unjust enrichment has its value as providing one example among many of what, for lack of a better phrase, I would call " want of probity ", a feature which recurs through and seems to connect all those cases drawn to the court's attention where a constructive trust has been held to exist. SNELL'S EQUITY (26th Edn.) at p. 201, expresses

H the same idea by stating that:

" A possible definition is that a constructive trust is a trust imposed by equity in order to satisfy the demands of justice and good conscience, without reference to any express or presumed intention of the parties."

It may be objected that, even assuming the correctness of the foregoing, it provides no assistance, inasmuch as reference to " unjust enrichment ", " want

I of probity " and " the demands of justice and good conscience " merely introduces vague concepts which are in turn incapable of definition and which, therefore, provide no yardstick. I do not agree. Concepts may defy definition and yet the presence in or absence from a situation of that which they denote may be beyond doubt. The concept of " want of probity " appears to provide a useful touchstone in considering circumstances said to give rise to constructive trusts, and I have not found it misleading when applying it to the many authorities cited

(39) [1947] 2 All E.R. 751; [1948] 1 K.B. 339.

to this court. It is because of such a concept that evidence as to " good faith ", A
" knowledge " and " notice " plays so important a part in the reported decisions.
It is true that not every situation where probity is lacking gives rise to a constructive trust. Nevertheless, the authorities appear to show that nothing short
of it will do. Not even gross negligence will suffice. Thus, in *Williams* v. *Williams*
(40), where a solicitor had acted, as KAY, J., found, " with very great negligence
towards his client " in dealing with trust property, the learned judge said (41): B

> " If it were proved to me upon the evidence that he had wilfully shut his
> eyes, and was determined not to inquire, then the case would have been very
> different . . . I do not find that anything done by Mr. Cheese in the matter
> was done for his own benefit . . . If he had, as I believe he had, a bona fide
> conviction that there was no settlement whatever . . . I cannot hold that he
> is affected with such notice as to make him personally liable for the purchase- C
> money which passed through his hands as solicitor."

In *Re Blundell, Blundell* v. *Blundell* (42), where solicitors were again absolved
in somewhat remarkable circumstances, STIRLING, J., after reviewing the
authorities, said (43):

> ". . . solicitors cannot be made liable as constructive trustees unless they D
> are brought within the doctrine of the Court with reference to other strangers,
> who are not themselves trustees, but are liable in certain cases to be made
> to account as if they were trustees. What is the general doctrine with
> reference to constructive trustees of that kind? It is that a stranger to the
> trust receiving money from the trustee which he knows [and I stress the
> word ' knows '] to be part of the trust estate is not liable as a constructive E
> trustee unless there are facts brought home to him which shew that to his
> knowledge the money is being applied in a manner which is inconsistent
> with the trust; or (in other words) unless it be made out that he is party
> either to a fraud or to a breach of trust on the part of the trustee."

In a further passage, the learned judge added observations of great pertinence
to the present case (44): F

> ". . . to my mind, in order that the solicitor may be debarred from accepting
> payment out of the trust estate, he must be fixed with notice that at the
> time when he accepted payment the trustee had been guilty of a breach of
> trust such as would preclude him altogether from resorting to the trust estate
> for payment of costs, so that in fact the application of the trust estate in
> payment of costs would be a breach of trust." G

The foregoing cases are but two illustrations among many to be found in the
reports of that want of probity which, to my way of thinking, is the hallmark
of constructive trusts, however created.

The proposition which counsel for the plaintiff described as fundamental to his
case was stated in these terms: that a man who receives property which he H
knows (or ought to know) is trust property and applies it in a manner which he
knows (or ought to know) is inconsistent with the terms of the trust is accountable
in a suit by the beneficiaries of the trust. Although the soundness of that proposition was from the beginning accepted without qualification by the defendants,
countless cases were cited to demonstrate its validity. But it turned out that their
citation was far from being a sleeveless errand, for it emerged that in not one of I
those cases was there any room for doubt that a trust already existed. None of
them dealt with the fundamental assertion which has here been so strongly
contested, and which PENNYCUICK, J., summarised by saying that (45):

(40) (1881), 17 Ch.D. 437.
(41) (1881), 17 Ch.D. at pp. 445, 446.
(42) (1888), 40 Ch.D. 370; [1886-90] All E.R. Rep. 837.
(43) (1888), 40 Ch.D. at p. 381; [1886-90] All E.R. Rep. at pp. 841, 842.
(44) (1888), 40 Ch.D. at p. 383; [1886-90] All E.R. Rep. at pp. 842, 843.
(45) [1968] 2 All E.R. at p. 1236.

A   " Counsel for the [plaintiff] contends that [the first defendants] have notice of the trust and if, at the end of the day the trust is established in the main action, they will be accountable as constructive trustees for all moneys comprised in that trust which they have received from the West German company."

B   But, as admittedly the West German foundation hold nothing for the East German foundation under an express trust, and as, even despite the 13 long years that litigation between them has been proceeding, there has been no determination that any trust does exist, counsel for the plaintiff has found himself compelled to go further if this appeal is to be put on its feet. He asserts, in effect, that for present purposes claims are the same as facts. More amply stated, he submits that it is sufficient to render the defendants accountable to

C   the plaintiff that they have: (a) knowledge that the East German foundation is claiming that the West German foundation holds all their assets in trust for it; (b) knowledge of the nature of the allegations advanced by the plaintiff which (if established) are said to justify that claim; and (c) knowledge that all sums paid to them by the West German foundation must be and are derived solely and entirely from those assets which are the subject-matter of the plaintiff's claim to be

D   beneficial owners. Such knowledge on the part of the defendants being established, submits counsel for the plaintiff, the preliminary issue raised by this appeal must here and now be determined in favour of the plaintiff, and it matters not that, as he concedes, the defendants do not and cannot know for some time to come whether the plaintiff will succeed in the main action in establishing its claim to a trust. He submits that it is equally immaterial that the plaintiff accepts that both

E   defendants have throughout acted honestly as solicitors of the West German foundation and received fees, costs and disbursements solely in that capacity and proper in amount.

   Like SACHS, L.J., I am prepared for present purposes to assume that the plaintiff will ultimately and at some unknown date succeed in establishing in the main action that the moneys in question are either its own property or are held

F   in trust for it by the West German foundation. Nevertheless, in my judgment, none of the cases cited affords support for the contention that, in the present circumstances, the defendants are accountable to the plaintiff, and it would be superogation for me to attempt to add to SACHS, L.J.'s analysis of those cases. But so wide is the net spread by the plaintiff that it even seeks to enmesh the second defendants, who incontestably ceased to act for the West German founda-

G   tion in 1964, three whole years before any allegations of a trust were even hinted at. Only slightly less audaciously, the plaintiff also claims that the first defendants are accountable for all moneys received by them from the West German foundation with knowledge that they were derived from the assets claimed by the plaintiff (apparently, in their case also, without regard to whether they were received before or after the vital amendment of the statement of claim in 1966),

H   and that such accountability exists regardless of whether the moneys so received were advanced to cover fees and disbursements already made or were intended to cover those which might arise in the future. The only escape which counsel for the plaintiff was prepared to concede might even be conceivably open to the defendants was that, if they had been advised by experienced counsel, the strong probability was that, the plaintiff would fail to establish in the main action that a

I   trust existed, the defendants might thereby be enabled to avoid liability by invoking s. 61 of the Trustee Act 1925. The observation most helpful to the plaintiff is possibly that of FRY, J., in *Foxton* v. *Manchester and Liverpool District Banking Co.* (46), that:

   " Those who know that a fund is a trust fund cannot take possession of that fund for their own private benefit, except at the risk of being liable to refund it in the event of the trust being broken by the payment . . ."

---

(46) (1881), 44 L.T. 406 at p. 408.

But even there knowledge of the existence of the trust and that the moneys $\quad$ **A**
being received are trust moneys was stressed, as opposed to knowledge of a mere
claim that a trust exists. Here, in essence, nothing more than the latter is
asserted, and it is conceded that the defendants cannot be expected to
conjecture as to its outcome.

Counsel for the defendants gave the court a helpful distillation of the numerous
authorities to which reference has already been made by DANCKWERTS, L.J. $\quad$ **B**
Their effect, he rightly submits, may be thus stated. (A) A solicitor or other agent
who receives money from his principal which belongs at law or in equity to a
third party is not accountable as a constructive trustee to that third party
unless he has been guilty of some wrongful act in relation to that money.
(B) To act " wrongfully " he must be guilty of: (i) knowingly participating
in a breach of trust by his principal; or (ii) intermeddling with the trust property $\quad$ **C**
otherwise than merely as an agent and thereby becomes a trustee de son tort;
or (iii) receiving or dealing with the money knowing that his principal has no
right to pay it over or to instruct him to deal with it in the manner indicated;
or (iv) some dishonest act relating to the money. These are, indeed, but variants
or illustrations of that " want of probity " to which I have earlier referred.
Do the demands of justice and good conscience bring the present case within $\quad$ **D**
any of the foregoing categories? In my judgment, the question is one which
demands a negative answer. The law being reluctant to make a mere agent a
constructive trustee, as LORD SELBORNE, L.C., put it in *Barnes* v. *Addy* (47),
mere notice of a claim asserted by a third party is insufficient to render the agent
guilty of a wrongful act in dealing with property derived from his principal in
accordance with the latter's instructions unless the agent knows that the third $\quad$ **E**
party's claim is well founded and that the principal accordingly had no authority
to give such instructions. The only possible exception to such exemption arises
where the agent is under a duty to enquire into the validity of the third party's
claim and where, although enquiry would have established that it was well
founded, none is instituted. But, as it is conceded by the plaintiff that the
defendants are under no such duty of enquiry, that further matter does not now $\quad$ **F**
call for consideration.

Whatever be the outcome of the main action, in my judgment the foregoing
reasons are fatal to the plaintiff in its present claim, and I, therefore, do not
propose to consider the further objection based on public policy. On the ground
which I have stated, I would concur in dismissing the appeal.

$\qquad$ *Appeal dismissed. Leave to appeal to the House of Lords refused.* $\quad$ **G**

Solicitors: *Courts & Co.* (for the plaintiff); *Herbert Smith & Co.* (for the
defendants).

$\qquad\qquad\qquad$ [*Reported by* F. A. AMIES, ESQ., *Barrister-at-Law*.]

$\qquad$ **H**

$\qquad$ **I**

---

(47) (1874), 9 Ch. App. 244 at pp. 251, 252.

A

PETTITT *v.* PETTITT.

[HOUSE OF LORDS (Lord Reid, Lord Morris of Borth-y-Gest, Lord Hodson, Lord Upjohn and Lord Diplock), February 6, 10, 17, 18, 19, April 23, 1969.]

B

Husband and Wife—Property—Matrimonial home—Wife sole legal owner—Improvements to matrimonial home effected by husband—No bargain between husband and wife that he should acquire beneficial interest in matrimonial home in return for his work—Wife left husband and obtained divorce—Family assets—Common intention of parties—Application of presumption of resulting trust and presumption of advancement—Whether husband entitled to beneficial interest in matrimonial home in respect of the improve-

C

ments—Whether husband entitled to payment of the amount thereof—Married Women's Property Act 1882 (45 & 46 Vict. c. 75), s. 17.

The freehold of a Cottage had been purchased entirely out of moneys provided by the wife and the property stood in her name. The husband undertook internal decoration work and built a wardrobe in it. He also laid a lawn and constructed an ornamental well and a side wall in the garden.

D

On the question whether, on a summons under s. 17* of the Married Women's Property Act 1882, the husband was, by reason of his labour and expenditure, entitled to claim a beneficial interest in the proceeds of sale of the property,

Held: the husband's claim failed, because—

(i) (per LORD REID, LORD MORRIS OF BORTH-Y-GEST, and LORD HODSON) a husband was not entitled to an interest in his wife's property merely

E

because he had done in his leisure time jobs which husbands normally did (see p. 391, letter E, p. 399, letter G, and p. 400, letter E, post);

Dictum of LORD DENNING, M.R., in *Button* v. *Button* ([1968] 1 All E.R. at p. 1066) approved.

(ii) (per LORD REID) the improvements carried out were nearly all of an ephemeral character (see p. 391, letter D, post);

F

(iii) (per LORD MORRIS OF BORTH-Y-GEST and LORD DIPLOCK) there was no justification for imputing to the spouses a common intention that the husband should acquire some beneficial interest in the property in respect of the work that he did (see p. 399, letter G, and p. 416, letter E, post); and

(iv) (per LORD UPJOHN) in the absence of any agreement with his wife,

G

the husband could have no monetary claim against her and since no estoppel or mistake was suggested he could have no charge on or interest in her property (see p. 409, letter I, post).

Appleton v. *Appleton* ([1965] 1 All E.R. 44) disapproved.

Per CURIAM: the courts had no jurisdiction under s. 17 of the Married Women's Property Act 1882 to pass proprietary interests from one spouse

H

to the other (see p. 388, letter I, p. 398, letter F, p. 401, letter A, p. 405, letter G, and p. 411, letter F, post).

Dictum of ROMER, L.J., in *Cobb* v. *Cobb* ([1955] 2 All E.R. at p. 700) approved.

Dicta of LORD DENNING, M.R., in *Hine* v. *Hine* ([1962] 3 All E.R. at p. 347) and *Appleton* v. *Appleton* ([1965] 1 All E.R. 44) disapproved.

I

Jansen v. *Jansen* ([1965] 3 All E.R. 363) considered.

Observations on family assets, the common intention to be found between spouses in relation to property, and the application of the presumption of resulting trust and the presumption of advancement to transactions between husband and wife.

Balfour v. *Balfour* ([1918-19] All E.R. Rep. 860) considered.

Decision of the COURT OF APPEAL ([1968] 1 All E.R. 1053) reversed.

---

* Section 17, so far as material is set out at p. 388, letter D, post.

[As to determination of rights to property as between husband and wife, A
see 19 HALSBURY'S LAWS (3rd Edn.) 900, 901, para. 1492; and for cases on the
subject, see 27 DIGEST (Repl.) 263-265, *2119-2133, 2130a-2130f.*

For the Married Women's Property Act 1882, s. 17, see 11 HALSBURY'S
STATUTES (2nd Edn.) 804.]

Cases referred to:

Appleton v. *Appleton,* [1965] 1 All E.R. 44; [1965] 1 W.L.R. 25; Digest (Cont.   B
     Vol. B) 344, *621r.*

Balfour v. *Balfour* [1919] 2 K.B. 571; [1918-19] All E.R. Rep. 860; 88 L.J.K.B.
     1054; 121 L.T. 346; 27 Digest (Repl.) 201, *1604.*

Bedson v. *Bedson,* [1965] 3 All E.R. 307; [1965] 2 Q.B. 666; [1965] 3 W.L.R.
     891; Digest (Cont. Vol. B) 349, *2130fa.*

Bishop, Re, National Provincial Bank, Ltd. v. *Bishop,* [1965] 1 All E.R. 249;   C
     [1965] Ch. 450; [1965] 2 W.L.R. 188; Digest (Cont. Vol. B) 347, *1112b.*

Butler v. *Butler,* (1884), 14 Q.B.D. 831; *affd.,* C.A. (1885), 16 Q.B.D. 374;
     55 L.J.Q.B. 55; 54 L.T. 591; 27 Digest (Repl.) 202, *1609.*

Button v. *Button,* [1968] 1 All E.R. 1064; [1968] 1 W.L.R. 457.

Campion v. *Cotton* (1810), 17 Ves. 263; [1803-13] All E.R. Rep. 580; 34 E.R.   D
     102; 27 Digest (Repl.) 131, *952.*

Cobb v. *Cobb,* [1955] 2 All E.R. 696; [1955] 1 W.L.R. 731; Digest (Cont. Vol.
     A) 692, *2130aa.*

Davis Contractors, Ltd. v. *Fareham Urban District Council,* [1956] 2 All E.R.
     145; [1956] A.C. 696; [1956] 3 W.L.R. 37; Digest (Cont. Vol. A)
     298, *3414a.*

Dyer v. *Dyer* (1788), 2 Cox, Eq. Cas. 92; [1775-1802] All E.R. Rep. 205;   E
     30 E.R. 42; 25 Digest (Repl.) 559, *84.*

Eykyn's Trusts, Re (1877), 6 Ch.D. 115; 37 L.T. 261; 27 Digest (Repl.) 152,
     1103.

Fowkes v. *Pascoe* (1875), 10 Ch. App. 343; [1874-80] All E.R. Rep. 521; 44
     L.J.Ch. 367; 32 L.T. 545; 20 Digest (Repl.) 486, *1953.*

Fribance v. *Fribance,* [1957] 1 All E.R. 357; [1957] 1 W.L.R. 384; Digest   F
     (Cont. Vol. A) 693, *2130ab.*

Gissing v. *Gissing,* [1969] 1 All E.R. 1043; [1969] 2 W.L.R. 525.

Gooch, Re, Gooch v. *Gooch* (1890), 62 L.T. 384; 47 Digest (Repl.) 126, *917.*

Hewison v. *Negus* (1853), 16 Beav. 594; 22 L.J.Ch. 655; 21 L.T.O.S. 203;
     51 E.R. 909; 27 Digest (Repl.) 202, *1608.*

Hine v. *Hine,* [1962] 3 All E.R. 345; [1962] 1 W.L.R. 1124; Digest (Cont.   G
     Vol. A) 695, *2130f.*

Hofman v. *Hofman,* [1965] N.Z.L.R. 795; *affd.,* [1967] N.Z.L.R. 9.

Hogben v. *Hogben,* [1964] V.R. 468.

Jansen v. *Jansen,* [1965] 3 All E.R. 363; [1965] P. 478; [1965] 3 W.L.R. 875;
     Digest (Cont. Vol. B) 344, *621s.*   H

Jones v. *Maynard,* [1951] 1 All E.R. 802; [1951] Ch. 572; 27 Digest (Repl.)
     152, *1112.*

Lee v. *Lee,* [1952] 1 All E.R. 1299; [1952] 2 Q.B. 489, n.; Digest (Cont. Vol. A)
     667, *621a.*

National Provincial Bank, Ltd. v. *Ainsworth,* [1965] 2 All E.R. 472; [1965]
     A.C. 1175; [1965] 3 W.L.R. 1; Digest (Cont. Vol. B) 343, *621l.*   I

Plimmer v. *Wellington Corpn.* (1884), 9 App. Cas. 699; 53 L.J.P.C. 105;
     51 L.T. 475; 49 J.P. 116; 11 Digest (Repl.) 126, **72.*

Ramsden v. *Dyson* (1866), L.R. 1 H.L. 129; 21 Digest (Repl.) 453, *1551.*

Rimmer v. *Rimmer,* [1952] 2 All E.R. 863; [1953] 1 Q.B. 63; Digest (Cont.
     Vol. A) 692, *2130a.*

Rogers' Question, Re, [1948] 1 All E.R. 328; 27 Digest (Repl.) 264, *2130.*

Shipman v. *Shipman,* [1924] 2 Ch. 140; [1924] All E.R. Rep. 365; 93 L.J.Ch.
     382; 131 L.T. 394; 27 Digest (Repl.) 258, *2091.*

A   *Shirlaw* v. *Southern Foundries (1926), Ltd. & Federated Foundries, Ltd.*, [1939]
      2 All E.R. 113; [1939] 2 K.B. 206; 108 L.J.K.B. 747; 160 L.T. 353;
      affd., H.L. sub nom. *Southern Foundries (1926), Ltd.* v. *Shirlaw*, [1940]
      2 All E.R. 445; [1940] A.C. 701; 109 L.J.K.B. 461; 164 L.T. 251;
      9 Digest (Repl.) 557, *3689*.

  Ulrich v. *Ulrich and Felton*, [1968] 1 All E.R. 67; [1968] 1 W.L.R. 180.

B   *Wilson* v. *Wilson*, [1963] 2 All E.R. 447; [1963] 1 W.L.R. 601; Digest (Cont.
      Vol. A) 671, *621m*.

  Wirth v. *Wirth* (1956), 98 C.L.R. 228.

  Woodward v. *Woodward* (1863), 3 De G.J. & Sm. 672; 8 L.T. 749; 46 E.R. 797;
      27 Digest (Repl.) 202, *1606*.

  Young Re, Trye v. *Sullivan* (1885), 28 Ch.D. 705; 54 L.J.Ch. 1065; 52 L.T.
C   754; 27 Digest (Repl.) 116, *854*.

Appeal.

This was an appeal by Hilda Joy Pettitt from a decision of the Court of Appeal
(WILLMER, DANCKWERTS and RUSSELL, L.JJ.), dated 29th January 1968 and
reported [1968] 1 All E.R. 1053, dismissing her appeal from the order of Mr.
Registrar J. D. BEAMISH GREEN dated 11th April 1967. The husband, Harold
D John Pettitt, had applied by summons under s. 17 of the Married Women's
Property Act 1882 for a declaration that he had a beneficial interest in the
proceeds of the sale of Tinker's Cottage, Collington Lane East, Bexhill-on-Sea,
Sussex. The parties were married on 13th August 1952 and they had two
children. They lived in a house devised to the wife by her deceased grandmother until 1960 when the wife sold the house and bought Tinker's Cottage
E with the money realised on the sale. The parties lived there until February
1965 when the wife left the husband because of his cruel treatment. She presented a petition for divorce and obtained a decree on the ground of cruelty.
The husband left the cottage and the wife returned. The husband claimed
that while they lived there he had done work to the premises which he valued
at £723 and that his work had enhanced the value of Tinker's Cottage by £1,000.
F The registrar declared the husband had a beneficial interest in the proceeds of
sale of Tinker's Cottage in the sum of £300.

K. Bruce Campbell, Q.C., and *K. A. Machin* for the wife.

A. B. Ewbank for the Queen's Proctor.

The husband did not appear and was not represented.

G   Their Lordships took time for consideration.

23rd April. The following opinions were delivered.

    LORD REID: My Lords, the appellant was married in 1952. For about
nine years she and her husband lived in a house which she had inherited. During
that time the husband carried out a number of improvements, largely redecorating, on which he says he spent some £800. In 1961 this house was sold and
H she acquired another. After this had been paid for there was a surplus of a
few hundred pounds and he used this money, apparently with the consent of
the wife, in paying for his car. The spouses lived for about four years in the
new house. Then the wife left the husband alleging cruelty and she obtained a
divorce in 1967. The husband then left the house and raised the present proceedings. He said that during those four years he carried out a considerable
I number of improvements to the house and garden and estimated that in doing
so he performed work and supplied material to a value of £723. He sought a
declaration that he was beneficially interested in the proceeds of sale of the house
in the sum of £1,000 and an order on the wife to pay. Then an order was made
that she should pay him £300. The Court of Appeal (1) reluctantly dismissed
her appeal holding that they were bound by the decision in *Appleton* v. *Appleton*
(2). They gave leave to appeal.

(1) [1968] 1 All E.R. 1053; [1968] 1 W.L.R. 443.
(2) [1965] 1 All E.R. 44; [1965] 1 W.L.R. 25.

For the last 20 years the law regarding what are sometimes called family **A**
assets has been in an unsatisfactory state.   There have been many cases showing
acute differences of opinion in the Court of Appeal.   Various questions have
arisen, generally after the break-up of a marriage.   Sometimes both spouses
have contributed in money to the purchase of a house: sometimes the contribution of one spouse has been otherwise than in money: sometimes one spouse
owned the house and the other spent money or did work in improving it: and **B**
there have been a variety of other circumstances.   It might be possible to
decide this case on somewhat narrow grounds without examining the wider
questions, but I do not think that that would be satisfactory.   The fact that
the wife has legal aid has enabled the argument to range widely, and I think
that it is at least desirable, if not necessary, to deal with the various issues which
have emerged.   **C**
Many of the cases have been brought by virtue of the provisions of s. 17 of the
Married Women's Property Act 1882.   That is a long and complicated section:
the relevant part is as follows:

"In any question between husband and wife as to the title to or possession
of property, either party ... may apply by summons or otherwise in a
summary way to any judge of the High Court of Justice ... and the judge ... **D**
may make such order with respect to the property in dispute ... as he
thinks fit ..."

The main dispute has been as to the meaning of the latter words authorising
the judge (including a county court judge and now a registrar) to make such
order with respect to the property in dispute as he thinks fit.   These are words **E**
normally used to confer a discretion on the court: where the discretion is limited,
the limitations are generally expressed: but here no limitation is expressed.
So it has been said that here these words confer on the court an unfettered
discretion to override existing rights in the property and to dispose of it in whatever
manner the judge may think to be just and equitable in the whole circumstances
of the case.   On the other hand it has been said that these words do not entitle **F**
the court to disregard any existing property right, but merely confer a power
to regulate possession or the exercise of property rights, or, more narrowly,
merely confer a power to exercise in proceedings under s. 17 any discretion with
regard to the property in dispute which has already been conferred by some
other enactment.   And other intermediate views have also been expressed.
I would approach the question in this way.   The meaning of the section cannot **G**
have altered since it was passed in 1882.   At that time the certainty and security
of rights of property were still generally regarded as of paramount importance
and I find it incredible that any Parliament of that era could have intended to
put husbands' property at the hazard of the unfettered discretion of a judge
(including a county court judge) if the wife raised a dispute about it.   Moreover
this discretion, if it exists, can only be exercised in proceedings under s. 17: **H**
the same dispute could arise in other forms of action; and I find it even more
incredible that it could have been intended that such a discretion should be
given to a judge in summary proceedings but denied to the judge if the proceedings were of the ordinary character.   So are the words so unequivocal that
we are forced to give them a meaning which cannot have been intended?   I
do not think so.   It is perfectly possible to construe the words as having a much **I**
more restricted meaning and in my judgment they should be so construed.   I
do not think that a judge has any more right to disregard property rights in
s. 17 proceedings than he has in any other form of proceedings.
It was argued that the present case could be decided by applying the presumption regarding advancement.   It was said that if a husband spends money
on improving his wife's property, then, in the absence of evidence to the contrary,
this must be regarded as a gift to the wife.   I do not know how this presumption
first arose, but it would seem that the judges who first gave effect to it must have

A thought either that husbands so commonly intended to make gifts in the circumstances in which the presumption arises that it was proper to assume this where there was no evidence, or that wives' economic dependence on their husbands made it necessary as a matter of public policy to give them this advantage. I can see no other reasonable basis for the presumption. These considerations have largely lost their force under present conditions, and, unless the law has lost all

B flexibility so that the courts can no longer adapt it to changing conditions, the strength of the presumption must have been much diminished. I do not think that it would be proper to apply it to the circumstances of the present case.

And there is another matter I must deal with before coming to the crucial questions. There are at least suggestions in some cases that property rights may be different before and after the break-up of a marriage. I can see no ground

C for this. There are other occasions for disputes as to rights of property besides break-up of the marriage, and it appears to me that the property rights of the spouses must be capable of determination immediately after the property has been paid for or the improvements carried out and must in the absence of subsequent agreements or transactions remain the same. There are also suggestions that agreements or arrangements made by the spouses may be rendered inopera-

D tive by, or may have a different effect after, the break-down of the marriage. I suppose that an agreement could take an unusual form, but as a general rule I would think that most improbable. The question does not arise in the present case.

I can now come to the main question of how the law does or should deal with cases where the title to property is in one of the spouses and contributions

E towards its purchase price have been made or subsequent improvements have been provided by the other. As regards contributions, the traditional view is that, in the absence of evidence to the contrary effect, a contributor to the purchase price will acquire a beneficial interest in the property: but as regards improvements made by a person who is not the legal owner, after the property has been acquired, that person will not, in the absence of agreement, acquire

F any interest in the property or have any claim against the owner.

Let me suppose that a house which requires extensive renovation or improvement is acquired by one spouse putting down the deposit and taking the title. Instalments of the purchase price and the cost of the improvements will then have to be paid. The other spouse may be willing and able to help and as a pure matter of convenience without any thought of legal consequences and

G without making any agreement one spouse may pay the instalments of the purchase price and the other may pay for the improvements. On this view the legal position will be different according as the contributing spouse pays the instalments or the cost of the improvements. Payment of the instalments will obtain for him or her a proprietary interest in the house, but payment of the cost of the improvements will not give him or her either an interest in the house

H or a claim against the other spouse. That seems to me to be entirely unsatisfactory. It is true that the court will do its best to spell out an agreement to prevent this, but I shall return to that matter.

Then go a step further. There is no question of making any improvements, but the wife who wants to contribute pays all the household bills thus enabling the husband who holds the title to the house to pay the instalments. That wife

I will have no claim of any kind. And go a step farther still. The wife may not be able to make any financial contribution but by good management and cooperation she may make it possible for the husband to pay the instalments regularly. Again on this view she will have no claim. Opinions may differ whether in one or both of these cases she should have any claim.

Views have been expressed that the law does give a claim to the contributing spouse in the first, or the first and second or in all the three cases which I have outlined. But there has been no unanimity as to the legal basis or the legal nature of such claims. I think that broadly there are two views. One is that

you ask what reasonable people in the shoes of the spouses would have agreed
if they had directed their minds to the question of what claim the contributing
spouse ought to have.   The other is that all property used for family purposes
must, in the absence of agreement, be regarded as the joint property of the
spouses or as belonging to them in equal shares, no matter which spouse bought
or inherited it or contributed to its acquisition.

We must first have in mind or decide how far it is proper for the courts to go
in adapting or adding to existing law.   Whatever views may have prevailed
in the last century, I think that it is now widely recognised that it is proper for
the courts in appropriate cases to develop or adapt existing rules of the common
law to meet new conditions.   I say in appropriate cases because I think we
ought to recognise a difference between cases where we are dealing with " lawyer's
law " and cases where we are dealing with matters which directly affect the
lives and interests of large sections of the community and which raise issues
which are the subject of public controversy and on which laymen are as well able
to decide as are lawyers.   On such matters it is not for the courts to proceed
on their view of public policy for that would be to encroach on the province of
Parliament.

I would therefore refuse to consider whether property belonging to either
spouse ought to be regarded as family property for that would be introducing
a new conception into English law and not merely developing existing principles.
There are systems of law which recognise joint family property or communio
bonorum.   I am not sure that those principles are very highly regarded in
countries where they are in force, but in any case it would be going far beyond
the functions of the court to attempt to give effect to them here.

But it is, I think, proper to consider whether, without departing from the
principles of the common law, we can give effect to the view that, even where
there was in fact no agreement, we can ask what the spouses, or reasonable
people in their shoes, would have agreed if they had directed their minds to the
question of what rights should accrue to the spouse who has contributed to the
acquisition or improvement of property owned by the other spouse.   There is
already a presumption which operates in the absence of evidence as regards
money contributed by one spouse towards the acquisition of property by the
other spouse.   So why should there not be a similar presumption where one
spouse has contributed to the improvement of the property of the other?   I
do not think that it is a very convincing argument to say that, if a stranger
makes improvements on the property of another without any agreement or any
request by that other that he should do so, he requires no right.   The improvement is made for the common enjoyment of both spouses during the marriage.
It would no doubt be different if the one spouse makes the improvement while
the other spouse who owns the property is absent and without his or her knowledge or consent.   But if the spouse who owns the property acquiesces in the
other making the improvement in circumstances where it is reasonable to
suppose that they would have agreed to some right being acquired if they had
thought about the legal position I can see nothing contrary to ordinary legal
principles in holding that the spouse who makes the improvement has acquired
such a right.

Some reference was made to the doctrine of unjust enrichment.   I do not think
that that helps.   The term has been applied to cases where a person who has paid
money sues for its return.   But there does not appear to be any English case of
the doctrine being applied where one person has improved the property of another.
And in any case it would only result in a money claim whereas what a spouse who
makes an improvement is seeking is generally a beneficial interest in the property
which has been improved.

No doubt there would be practical difficulties in determining what the parties,
or reasonable people in their shoes, would have agreed.   But then there is almost
equal difficulty in determining whether the spouses did in fact make an agreement,

A and, if they did, what are its terms. The first difficulty arises out of the principle approved in *Balfour* v. *Balfour* (3) that arrangements between spouses are not generally intended to be contracts or to have legal consequences. That is obviously right with regard to non-financial arrangements. And if the spouses arrange that one shall pay certain accounts I do not think that that one incurs any legal obligation to pay those accounts. But it does not necessarily follow that, if

B that spouse does pay those accounts, no legal consequences will follow from such payment. The real difficulty is in inferring from some vague evidence of an arrangement what in fact the arrangement was. There is often difficulty in determining what were the terms of a commercial contract because the parties did not apply their minds to essential matters. It has often been pointed out that spouses living happily together rarely apply their minds to matters which must

C be determined if their arrangement is to be given contractual force. So it is extremely difficult at a later date to determine what, if any, contractual effect can be given to some rather indefinite arrangement which preceded the expenditure of money by one of the spouses, and it is hardly possible to apply the ordinary rule that the essential terms of a contract must be sufficiently clearly established before it can be enforced. I do not think that there is much to be said for a rule of

D law if one finds that judges are constantly doing their best to circumvent it by spelling out contractual agreements from very dubious material.

In whatever way the general question as to improvements is decided I think that the claim in the present case must fail for two reasons. These improvements are nearly all of an ephemeral character. Redecoration will only last for a few years and it would be unreasonable that a spouse should obtain a permanent

E interest in the house in return for making improvements of this character. And secondly I agree with the view of Lord Denning, M.R., expressed in *Button* v. *Button* (4). He said with regard to the husband (5) " He should not be entitled to a share in the house simply by doing the ' do-it-yourself jobs ' which husbands often do ": and with regard to the wife (6):

F " The wife does not get a share in the house simply because she cleans the walls or works in the garden or helps her husband with the painting and decorating. Those are the sort of things which a wife does for the benefit of the family without altering the title to, or interests in, the property."

I agree with him that *Jansen* v. *Jansen* (7) was rightly decided. I have more doubt about *Appleton* v. *Appleton* (8): the facts are not very fully stated and it may have been wrongly decided. But if a spouse provides, with the assent of the spouse

G who owns the house, improvements of a capital or non-recurring nature, I do not think that it is necessary to prove an agreement before that spouse can acquire any right.

Even if my views are accepted they only go a short way towards solving the many problems which are coming before the court in increasing numbers. We were informed that last year there were 900 applications in the High Court

H besides an unknown number in the county courts. The whole question can only be resolved by Parliament and in my opinion there is urgent need for comprehensive legislation.

I would allow this appeal.

LORD MORRIS OF BORTH-Y-GEST: My Lords, the question of wide

I general importance which is raised in this case is whether s. 17 of the Married Women's Property Act 1882, confers a power enabling the court in its discretion to grant to a spouse a beneficial interest in property which he or she did not

(3) [1919] 2 K.B. 571; [1918-19] All E.R. Rep. 860.
(4) [1968] 1 All E.R. 1064; [1968] 1 W.L.R. 457.
(5) [1968] 1 All E.R. at p. 1066; [1968] 1 W.L.R. at p. 461.
(6) [1968] 1 All E.R. at p. 1067; [1968] 1 W.L.R. at p. 462.
(7) [1965] 3 All E.R. 363; [1965] P. 478.
(8) [1965] 1 All E.R. 44; [1965] 1 W.L.R. 25.

previously have. The words of s. 17 must be given the meaning which they had
when the Act was passed. They cannot now be given an extended meaning even
if it were thought that current social conditions pointed to the desirability of
endowing some court with wider powers than any now existing.

At common law a wife's proprietary capacities were very limited. Although
the Court of Chancery protected a wife's equitable separate estate it was by
statutory enactment that the rights of a wife concerning property were established.
The Matrimonial Causes Act 1857, provided that in every case of a judicial
separation a wife should be considered as a feme sole with respect to property
that she might acquire.

By the Married Women's Property Act 1870, certain property of a married
woman (such, for example, as wages and earnings acquired after the passing of
the Act in any employment occupation or trade in which she was engaged, or
which she carried on separately from her husband, and other money or property
referred to in s. 1 and deposits in savings banks referred to in s. 2, and other
property referred to in other sections) was deemed to be her separate property.
Section 9 of the Act provided that " in any question between husband and wife
as to property declared by this Act to be the separate property of the wife "
either party could by summons or motion apply in a summary way either to the
Court of Chancery in England or Ireland or to the judge of the county court of
the district in which either party resided. The judge was empowered to make
such order or direct such enquiry or award such costs as he thought fit. There
was a right of appeal just as if the order of the same judge had been made in a
pending suit or on an equitable plaint. The proceedings could be in the judge's
private room. To the extent set out in s. 11 a married woman could bring an
action in her own name in respect of her separate property.

By the Married Women's Property Act 1882, married women were given full
proprietary rights. In its opening words the Act provided that, in accordance
with its provisions, a married woman should—

"... be capable of acquiring, holding, and disposing by will or otherwise,
of any real or personal property as her separate property, in the same
manner as if she were a feme sole, without the intervention of any trustee."

Also by s. 1 (2) it was provided that a married woman was to be capable of entering into and rendering herself liable in respect of and to the extent of her separate
property on any contract, and of suing and being sued, either in contract or in
tort, or otherwise, in all respects as if she were a feme sole. The date of the
commencement of the Act was 1st January 1883. A woman who married after
that date could hold all her separate property as if she were a feme sole (see s. 2).
In the case of a woman who was married before that date she could hold as a feme
sole all property which she acquired after that date (see s. 5). By s. 12 remedies
were given to married women for the protection and security of their separate
property: a married woman could have in her own name " against all persons
whomsoever, including her husband " full remedies for the protection and security
of her separate property though except to that extent neither she nor her husband
could sue the other for a tort: and there were limitations in regard to criminal
proceedings.

In my view, all the indications are that s. 17 (following on s. 9 of the Act of 1870)
was purely a procedural section. It gave facility for obtaining speedy decision.
It related to " any question between husband and wife as to the title to or
possession of property ". In regard to a question as to the title to property the
language suggests a situation where an assertion of title by either husband or wife
has been met by denial or by counter-assertion on the part of the other. The
language is inapt if there was any thought of taking title away from the party who
had it. The procedure was devised as a means of resolving a dispute or a question
as to title rather than as a means of giving some title not previously existing.
One of the main purposes of the Act of 1882 was to make it fully possible for the

A property rights of the parties to a marriage to be kept entirely separate. There was no suggestion that the status of marriage was to result in any common ownership or co-ownership of property. All this, in my view, negatives any idea that s. 17 was designed for the purpose of enabling the court to pass property rights from one spouse to another. In a question as to the title to property the question for the court was—" Whose is this " and not—" To whom shall this be
B given."

It is to be noted that the procedure made possible by s. 17 was permissive and not obligatory. Under it a question could be submitted for the decision of a judge of the High Court who could sit in private. So also at a time when the ordinary limit of jurisdiction of the county court in personal actions was £50 (but as to jurisdiction in equity see s. 67 of the County Courts Act 1888) a question (regard-
C less of the amount involved) could be submitted for the decision of a county court judge who also could sit in his private room: though the proceedings, if not within the normal jurisdiction of the county court (or civil bill court in Ireland), could at the option of the defendant or respondent to them be removed as of right into the High Court.

Questions could, however, and can be referred for the decision of the courts in
D the ordinary way. As to the circumstances under which a husband could sue his wife both before and after the Married Women's Property Act 1882, see *Butler* v. *Butler* (9). Today it is clear that a husband and wife can enter into a contract with each other and can sue each other on such a contract. If, therefore, there were and are alternative ways of resolving a question as to the title to property it could not be that there would be a different legal approach according as to which
E course was adopted. A decision after an informal private hearing was as much subject to appeal as a decision given after a formal hearing in open court. Each decision had to be made according to law. There was no provision which em- powered a judge on the trial of an action between husband and wife concerning a question as to the title to property to give a decision which, however benevolently motivated, was in disregard of the law. There is no provision empowering a judge
F on the summary adjudication of a question to act any differently. I do not find this in the words (in s. 17) " as he thinks fit ". Those are undoubtedly words which give a judicial discretion. Ample reason for their presence in the section is found when it is remembered that the section is dealing with questions " as to the title to or possession of property ". There may be cases where discretion can properly be exercised in regard to possession and in regard to remedies. I cannot, however,
G interpret the words " as he thinks fit " as endowing a judge with the power to pass the property of one spouse over to the other or to do so on some vague basis that involves estimating or weighing the good or bad behaviour of the one and the other or assessing the deserts of the one or the other in the light of their work, activities and conduct. If matrimonial troubles bring the spouses to the courts there are various statutory powers relating to property which can be exercised.
H But if in a " question " between a husband and a wife as to the title to property recourse is had to the special procedure made possible by s. 17, decision must be reached by applying settled law to the facts as they may be established.

It appears to have been generally accepted that if in a question as to the title to some property a judge is able after hearing evidence to come to a con- clusion that there was a clear agreement between husband and wife in regard to
I ownership he must give his adjudication accordingly. He cannot then make an order which withdraws title from the party to whom on his finding it belongs. The same result must, I think, follow if, apart from any agreement between the two of them, the evidence clearly establishes that the property is in one rather than the other. The difficult case is where each party claims ownership and where the evidence is meagre. It cannot, in my view, be that the jurisdiction of the court is then on a different basis. The search must still be to find an answer to the question

---

(9) (1885), 16 Q.B.D. 374.

as to where ownership lies. The court has to reach decision in very difficult **A**
circumstances but the task, the duty and the objective of the court does not
change. The court is not suddenly absolved from its duty. The question for
decision does not alter merely because evidence is scanty or because the task of
reaching decision is perplexing.

In the lengthening line of cases in which questions between spouses have
called for adjudication under s. 17, the nature of the difficulties which arise is **B**
constantly and recurringly made manifest. When two people are about to be
married and when they are arranging to have a home in which to live they do not
make their arrangements in the contemplation of future discord or separation.
As a married couple they do not, when a house is being purchased or when the
contents of a house are being acquired, contemplate that a time might come when
decision would have to be made as to who owned what. It would be unnatural **C**
if at the times of acquisition there was always precise statement or understanding
as to where ownership rested. So, if at a later date questions arise as to the
ownership of a house or of various things in it though as to some matters no honest
difference of view will arise, as to others there can be such honest difference because
previously the parties might never really have applied their minds to the question
as to where ownership lay. **D**

For the reasons which I have given I consider that the duty of a court when
adjudicating under s. 17 is no different in a difficult case from what it is in a
straightforward case. By the latter I mean a case in which after ascertaining the
facts and considering the evidence the court can without difficulty decide that
one party is the owner of certain property. The court cannot then award it or a
share in it to the other party and cannot in s. 17 proceedings do so even if the latter **E**
was thought to have deserved a different result. In a difficult case the facts will
not be readily ascertainable and the evidence will be slender. The court must,
however, do its best. It cannot then abandon its task which continues to be the
task of deciding the question submitted to it.

It follows from what I have said that I agree with some statements of principle
which have been expressed in decided cases while disagreeing with others. I **F**
agree with what was said by ROMER, L.J., in *Cobb* v. *Cobb* (10):

"... I know of no power that the Court has under s. 17 to vary agreed or
established titles to property. It has power to ascertain the respective rights
of husband and wife to disputed property and frequently has to do so on very
little material; but where, as here, the original rights to property are established by the evidence and those rights have not been varied by subsequent **G**
agreement, the court cannot in my opinion under s. 17 vary those rights
merely because it thinks that, in the light of subsequent events, the original
agreement was unfair."

I think that this was in accord with what had been said by EVERSHED, L.J., in
Re Rogers' Question (11) when he pointed out that the task of a judge after seeing **H**
and hearing the witnesses was (12)—

"... to try to conclude what at the time was in the parties' minds and then
to make an order which, in the changed conditions, now fairly gives effect in
law to what the parties, in the judge's finding, must be taken to have
intended at the time of the transaction itself."

I
The emphasis on ascertaining what the parties intended at the time of a transaction
shows that the mention of changed conditions did not mean that changed conditions altered property rights: property rights once ascertained, and ascertained
by reference to what was the intention of the parties at the time of a transaction,
had to be honoured and fairly given effect to even though conditions had changed.

(10) [1955] 2 All E.R. 696 at p. 700; [1955] 1 W.L.R. at pp. 736, 737.
(11) [1948] 1 All E.R. 328.
(12) [1948] 1 All E.R. at pp. 328, 329.

A   It follows that respectfully I cannot agree with the statement in *Hine* v. *Hine*
that (13)—

> ". . . the jurisdiction of the court over family assets under s. 17 is entirely
> discretionary. Its discretion transcends all rights, legal or equitable, and
> enables the court to make such order as it thinks fit. This means, as I
> understand it, that the court is entitled to make such order as appears to be
B   fair and just in all the circumstances of the case."

I cannot agree that s. 17 empowers a court to take property from one spouse and
allocate it to the other. But something may depend on what is meant by " family
assets ". If what is referred to is an asset separately owned by someone who is a
member of a family, then once the ownership is ascertained it cannot, under s. 17,
C   be changed. If what is referred to is property which, on the evidence, has been
decided to be property which belongs beneficially to husband and wife jointly,
I do not consider that s. 17 enables a court to vary whatever the beneficial interests
were ascertained to be. There would be room for the exercise of discretion in
deciding a question whether a sale should be ordered at one time or another but
there would be no discretion enabling a court to withdraw an ascertained property
D   right from one spouse and to grant it to the other. Any power to do that must
either be found in some existing provision in relation to matrimonial causes or
must be given by some future legislation.

It follows further, from my view, as I have expressed it above that with
respect I do not agree with the statement in *Appleton* v. *Appleton* (14) that if
after a separation there is an application under s. 17 by a spouse who claims sole
E   ownership of a house the test to be applied by the court is (15):

> " What is reasonable and fair in the circumstances as they have developed,
> seeing that they are circumstances which no one contemplated before?"

In such a situation the duty of the court is to decide whether the house was in
the sole ownership of the one spouse who claimed such ownership. " The circumstances as they have developed " may point to the fact that it would only be fair
F   and reasonable, having regard to such " circumstances ", that some entirely new
arrangements should be made. In very many cases that would be so. The parties
to a marriage would have ordered their affairs on the basis that the status of
marriage possessed by each one was to continue. That very fact would have
produced the result that it would happily often have been a matter of indifference
and, in very many cases, almost a matter of irrelevance whether ownership was
G   in one spouse or in the other or whether ownership was joint. But if discord leads
to separation existing separate ownerships are not thereby extinguished.

I observe that the approach which I have indicated is that which has been
followed in New Zealand where questions have arisen in regard to the discretion
given to a court by s. 19 of the Married Women's Property Act 1952, to " make
such order with respect to the property in dispute . . . as it thinks fit ". In his
H   interesting judgment in *Hofman* v. *Hofman* (16) (affirmed on appeal (17))
WOODHOUSE, J., said (18):

> "There is a consistent line of authority to the effect that the section
> does not permit questions of title to property to be decided except in
> accordance with the strict legal or equitable rights of the parties."

I   After citing the New Zealand authorities to that effect he pointed out that
a similar view had been taken of similar legislation in the State of Victoria
prior to a recent amendment to the Act there (*Hogben* v. *Hogben* (19)) and by the

---

(13) [1962] 3 All E.R. 345 at p. 347; [1962] 1 W.L.R. 1124 at p. 1127.
(14) [1965] 1 All E.R. 44; [1965] 1 W.L.R. 25.
(15) [1965] 1 All E.R. at p. 46; [1965] 1 W.L.R. at p. 28.
(16) [1965] N.Z.L.R. 795.
(17) [1967] N.Z.L.R. 9.
(18) [1965] N.Z.L.R. at p. 797.
(19) [1964] V.R. 468.

High Court of Australia when considering the same legislation in Queensland **A**
(*Wirth* v. *Wirth* (20)). In *Hofman* v. *Hofman* (21) the application was made under
the new provisions contained in the Matrimonial Property Act 1963. In that new
legislation a judge is empowered (provided that he does not defeat any common
intention which he is satisfied was expressed by the husband and the wife) to
make such order as appears just, notwithstanding that the legal or equitable
interests of the husband and wife in the property are defined, or notwithstanding **B**
that the spouse in whose favour the order is made has no legal or equitable interest
in the property. In a section (22) applying to any matrimonial home it is provided
that, in considering an application, the court shall, where the application relates
to a matrimonial home, and may in any other case—

> " have regard to the respective contributions of the husband and wife to **C**
> the property in dispute (whether in the form of money payments, services,
> prudent management or otherwise howsoever)."

In reference to the state of affairs existing before that new legislation was passed
WOODHOUSE, J. (23), referred to the unimaginative rule that the property rights
of parties to a marriage should be determined on the basis of money alone. In
his reasoning, with which I find myself much in sympathy, he spoke of the **D**
difficulty of reaching just results by the (23)—

> " application of presumptions which were developed in a social climate
> which has little in common with the widely accepted view that marriage
> is really a partnership of equals "

he spoke also of the advantage of being able to consider (23)— **E**

> " the true spirit of transactions involving matrimonial property by giving
> due emphasis not only to the part played by the husband, but also to the
> important contributions which a skilful housewife can make to the general
> family welfare by the assumption of domestic responsibility, and by freeing
> her husband to win the money income they both need for the furtherance
> of their joint enterprise." **F**

In *Wirth* v. *Wirth* (24) in considering the provision in the Queensland Married
Women's Property Acts 1890 to 1952, comparable to s. 17, DIXON, C.J., said that
the discretion enabled a judge—

> "to take into account considerations which may go beyond the strict
> enforcement of proprietary or possessory rights, but the notion should be
> wholly rejected that the discretion affects anything more than the summary **G**
> remedy."

TAYLOR, J., agreed with DIXON, C.J., that on an application the rights of the
parties had to be determined according to ordinary legal principles. He said (25):

> " It may well be that in cases between husband and wife, where one does
> not expect to find formal contracts or solemn declarations of trust, the **H**
> question of the beneficial ownership of property used by both in the course of
> the matrimonial relationship, will, almost invariably, fall to be decided by
> consideration of casual and informal incidents rather than of studied and
> deliberate pronouncements. But to say this is to say no more than that the
> circumstances calling for investigation in such cases are special and require
> to be considered in the light of that fact. This may mean that in such cases **I**
> it will frequently be difficult to ascertain the facts but once they are judicially
> ascertained, either by the acceptance of express evidence, or by inference,
> or by presumption, the position will be that the rights of the parties must
> be determined according to ordinary legal principles."

---

(20) (1956), 98 C.L.R. 228.   (21) [1965] N.Z.L.R. 795.
(22) Section 6 (1).   (23) [1965] N.Z.L.R. at p. 800.
(24) (1956), 98 C.L.R. at p. 231.   (25) (1956), 98 C.L.R. at pp. 247, 248.

A In the absence of some new legislative provisions giving some discretionary powers to a court to adjust as between husband and wife their legal or equitable interests in property the duty of a court, if disputes arise, must be to reach conclusions as to where those interests belong. The difficulties to be surmounted in doing so are mirrored in the mass of reported cases. In some of these a pattern appears which reflects social conditions which differ from those in earlier

B decades. After a marriage both husband and wife may for a time be wage-earners. They may each make some contributions towards the cost of acquiring a house and of setting up a home. After a time the husband only may be the wage-earner. Their arrangements will often have been made without giving much thought to the question as to where legal and beneficial ownership lies. There will have been no thought given to the question whether if they later separate some new

C allocation of ownership would be fair. What is the court to do if asked to decide the ownership either of a house or of a chattel or indeed of some chose in action? The answer must be that the court must do its best to obtain all the relevant evidence and, on an assessment of the evidence, and on an application of any relevant legal principle, it must reach a decision. The court cannot refuse to decide a case on the ground that the path to conclusion is not floodlit by clear evidence.

D The duty of the court in an application under s. 17 will not differ from its duty in a situation where a question of title arises not as between husband and wife but by reason of an outside claim. If either husband or wife became bankrupt a court would have to decide what property did and what property did not pass to the trustee in bankruptcy. If there is a judgment against either a husband or a wife a decision may have to be made as to what property could and what property

E could not be the subject of execution. When acting under s. 17 the court must be guided by the same principles as would apply in any other proceedings where the ownership of property is in question.

The circumstances which have most often created the occasion for an application under s. 17 have been: (a) where husband and wife have both made contributions towards the purchase of a house; and (b) where improvements have been

F made to a house, and in either case where a break-down of the marriage has later occurred. To begin with I would say that the fact of a break-down of the marriage is irrelevant in the determination of a question as to where ownership lay before the break-down: the break-down will then merely have caused the need for a decision but will not of itself have altered whatever was the pre-existing position as to ownership: it will, however, be relevant in regard to some questions which

G could be the subject of a s. 17 application.

Where questions of ownership have to be decided the judge must weigh every piece of evidence as best he may; the fact that the parties are husband and wife with all that is as a result involved, is in itself a weighty piece of evidence. Sometimes the conclusion will be that ownership was in one party alone; sometimes the conclusion will be that ownership was in both parties. There will be some

H cases in which a court is satisfied that both the parties have a beneficial interest, and a substantial beneficial interest but in which it is not possible to be entirely precise in calculating their respective shares. In such circumstances, as SIR RAYMOND EVERSHED, M.R., said in *Rimmer* v. *Rimmer* (26) " equality almost necessarily follows ". There will be some cases in which, as LORD UPJOHN said in *National Provincial Bank, Ltd.* v. *Ainsworth* (27), an equitable knife must be

I used to sever the Gordian knot. *Jones* v. *Maynard* (28) (which was an action between former spouses) furnishes an example of a situation in which it was held that it was proper to apply the principle of equality.

Where improvement has been effected to property belonging to one party the evidence when examined might lead to various conclusions. One might be that work was done or expense incurred without any thought that any contractual

(26) [1952] 2 All E.R. 863 at p. 867; [1953] 1 Q.B. 63 at p. 72.
(27) [1965] 2 All E.R. 472 at p. 487; [1965] A.C. 1175 at p. 1236.
(28) [1951] 1 All E.R. 802; [1951] Ch. 572.

liability or any ownership disposition would ever result. The spouse who does some **A** work of repair or renovation or decoration in a matrimonial home which in fact belongs to the other spouse would probably do so in circumstances which would create neither a claim nor a right in law. There are so many agreements between spouses which are not contracts for the reason that the parties never intended that the agreements should be attended by legal consequences (*Balfour* v. *Balfour* (29)). In some set of circumstances the conclusion might be reached that some **B** expense incurred by one spouse was to be the subject of re-imbursement by the other. Or it could be that work by one was to be paid for by the other. Another conclusion might be that ownership which had hitherto been separate was thereafter to be a common ownership on some newly agreed basis. But each of these conclusions would have to be the result of some agreement. Sometimes an agreement, though not put into express words, would be clearly implied from **C** what the parties did. But there must be evidence which establishes an agreement before it can be held that one spouse has acquired a beneficial interest in property which previously belonged to the other or has a monetary claim against the other.

The mere fact that parties have made arrangements or conducted their affairs without giving thought to questions as to where ownership of property lay does not mean that ownership was in suspense or did not lie anywhere. There will have **D** been ownership somewhere and a court may have to decide where it lay. In reaching a decision the court does not find and, indeed, cannot find that there was some thought in the mind of a person which never was there at all. The court must find out exactly what was done or what was said and must then reach conclusion as to what was the legal result. The court does not devise or invent a legal result. Nor is the court influenced by the circumstances that those concerned may **E** never have had occasion to ponder or to decide the effect in law of whatever were their deliberate actions. Nor is it material that they might not have been able— even after reflection—to state what was the legal outcome of whatever they may have done or said. The court may have to tell them. But when an application is made under s. 17 there is no power in the court to make a contract for the parties which they have not themselves made. Nor is there power to decide what the **F** court thinks that the parties would have agreed had they discussed the possible break-down or ending of their relationship. Nor is there power to decide on some general principle of what seems fair and reasonable how property rights are to be re-allocated. In my view, these powers are not given by s. 17.

If there is a break-down between spouses there will be a situation for which the parties cannot have provided. There may be a need for new adjustments. At a **G** time when discord has supervened it is not to be expected that the parties concerned will themselves be able to make new dispositions on the basis of what in the circumstances as they have developed would be thought by an independent person to be fair and just. The reported cases and more particularly the pattern of the situations which have given rise to them reflect problems of wide social consequence. Their solution must lie with those who decide policy and enact the **H** law.

Having stated my view as to the powers of a court when acting under s. 17, I do not propose to endeavour to review the numerous decisions which were examined during the hearing. In cases which arise conclusion should, in my view, depart on an analysis of particular facts and detailed evidence and on an application of recognised legal principles. As to general principle I consider that guidance **I** is to be found in the speeches in *National Provincial Bank, Ltd.* v. *Ainsworth* (30) (see the speeches of my noble and learned friends, LORD HODSON (31), LORD UPJOHN (32) and LORD WILBERFORCE (33)). It follows from all that I have said

(29) [1919] 2 K.B. 571; [1918-19] All E.R. Rep. 860.
(30) [1965] 2 All E.R. 472; [1965] A.C. 1175.
(31) [1965] 2 All E.R. at p. 477; [1965] A.C. at pp. 1220, 1221.
(32) [1965] 2 All E.R. at pp. 486, 487; [1965] A.C. at pp. 1235, 1236.
(33) [1965] 2 All E.R. at p. 493; [1965] A.C. at pp. 1245, 1246.

A that I am in agreement with the approach of RUSSELL, L.J., expressed in his
judgment in *Jansen* v. *Jansen* (34) and in his judgment in *Bedson* v. *Bedson* (35).
It further follows that I cannot with respect agree with the approach that led to
the decision in *Appleton* v. *Appleton* (36). I do not think that the mere circumstance taken by itself that one spouse does work of renovation to a house belonging to the other spouse has the result that some beneficial interest in the house is
B acquired by the former.

The facts in the case now under consideration bear a remarkable similarity
to those in *Appleton* v. *Appleton* (36) and I can fully appreciate how it was that
the Court of Appeal (37) with manifest reluctance and regret felt compelled to
decide as they did. The facts are clearly recorded in the careful judgment of
WILLMER, L.J. The events in relation to the first house need not now be exam-
C ined. The second house, the bungalow which was built and was called Tinker's
Cottage clearly belonged to the appellant. The husband claimed that he had
" undertaken work thereon " which had enhanced its value. He said that he had
performed work and supplied material to a value of £723 and that the value of the
bungalow had as a result been increased by £1,000. He had done work of internal
decoration and had built a wardrobe : he had done much work in the garden includ-
D ing the building of an ornamental well and a brick side wall. That was in the
period after 1961. The parties lived together in the house until February 1965
(when the wife left) and the husband continued to live there until March 1967.
By his summons (in May 1966) the husband claimed that it should be declared
that he was " beneficially interested in the proceeds of sale " of the house in
the sum of £1,000 : he asked that the wife should be ordered to make payment to
E him of any sum found due to him; that, presumably, meant such sum as should
be held to represent the increase in value of the house which resulted from the
work that he had done. The conclusion of the learned registrar was that the
husband had a beneficial interest in the proceeds of sale of the house in the sum of
£300 and he ordered the wife to pay that sum to him. My Lords, I do not think
that this result can be upheld. The wife undoubtedly owned Tinker's Cottage
F when the parties went to live in it. The husband had no sort of title to it and never
thought that he had. As WILLMER, L.J., pointed out (38), it had never been
suggested that there was any subsequent agreement varying the rights of the
parties and the assertion of the husband that he had acquired some beneficial
interest could only be accepted if the court could impute to the parties some
common intention that the husband was to acquire an interest in the property
G commensurate with the value of the work which he did. I can see no justification
for any such imputation. I agree with WILLMER, L.J., (38) that in any event the
work done by the husband (who without finding money to pay rent for a house was
able to live in a house owned by his wife) did not go beyond what a reasonable
husband might be expected to do. As RUSSELL, L.J., pointed out (39), the
husband did not assert that there was any kind of bargain or understanding
H between him and the wife that he should ever be to any extent re-imbursed or
rewarded. It was solely because they felt bound by *Appleton* v. *Appleton* (36)
that the Court of Appeal (37) upheld the order of the registrar. As, for the reasons
I have expressed, I disapprove of the approach in *Appleton* v. *Appleton* (36) I
am free to come to a different conclusion. I think that the husband had no claim.

I would, therefore, allow the appeal.

I   **LORD HODSON:** My Lords, during the last year, so your Lordships were
informed, 900 applications were made to the High Court, besides an unknown
number in the county courts, in connection with disputes between husbands and

(34) [1965] 3 All E.R. 363 at p. 370; [1965] P. 478 at pp. 497, 498.
(35) [1965] 3 All E.R. 307 at pp. 319, 320; [1965] 2 Q.B. 666 at p. 691.
(36) [1965] 1 All E.R. 44; [1965] 1 W.L.R. 25.
(37) [1968] 1 All E.R. 1053; [1968] 1 W.L.R. 443.
(38) [1968] 1 All E.R. at p. 1057; [1968] 1 W.L.R. at p. 448.
(39) [1968] 1 All E.R. at p. 1062; [1968] 1 W.L.R. at p. 454.

wives as to the ownership of property. That these disputes are difficult to resolve A
is plain enough, if only because of the special relationship between husband and
wife. They do not as a rule enter into contracts with one another so long as they
are living together on good terms. It would be very odd if they did.

An illustration, perhaps an extreme one, is provided by *Balfour* v. *Balfour* (40).
There SARGANT, J., held that the parties who were husband and wife had entered
into a contract fixing the husband's obligation to maintain his wife during a B
temporary separation at £30 a month. Apart from the husband and wife relationship the judge's decision could hardly have been questioned, but the Court of
Appeal used strong words in support of the proposition that mutual provisions
made in the ordinary domestic relationship of husband and wife do not of necessity
give cause for action on a contract. ATKIN, L.J. (41), pointed out that these
arrangements are not sued on because the parties in the inception of the arrange- C
ment never intended that they should be sued on. *Balfour* v. *Balfour* (40) has no
direct bearing on the kind of situation which has arisen here but I think it rightly
indicates that the court will be slow to infer legal obligations from transactions
between husband and wife in the ordinary course of their domestic life.

The dispute concerns a house belonging to the appellant who was the wife of
the respondent, and a claim by him that he should receive part of the proceeds D
of sale of the house on the ground that he has undertaken work on the house and
garden which enhanced its value. The registrar made an order in favour of the
husband that he had a beneficial interest in the proceeds of sale of the house in
the sum of £300 and the wife was ordered to pay this sum to him.

I agree with your Lordships that this case can be disposed of on the short
ground that the husband does not become entitled to a share in the wife's E
property by occupying his leisure hours in the house or garden even though he
enhances the value of the property. I, like my noble and learned friend, LORD
REID, agree with the view expressed by LORD DENNING, M.R., in the recent case
of *Button* v. *Button* (42) where he said with regard to a husband that he " should
not be entitled to a share in the house simply by doing the ' do-it-yourself jobs '
which husbands often do ". This is not only good law but good sense which, in F
my opinion, should normally be applied to this kind of situation.

In view of the wide issues canvassed it is, I think, insufficient to confine oneself
to the facts of this case. The proceedings were instituted under s. 17 of the Married
Women's Property Act 1882, which is the successor to s. 9 of the Married Women's
Property Act 1870. The section of the earlier of these Acts provided, so far as
material: G

> " In any question between husband and wife as to property declared
> by this Act to be the separate property of the wife, either party may apply
> . . . to the Court of Chancery . . . in England (irrespective of the value of the
> property) the judge of the County Court . . . and thereupon the judge may
> make such order . . . as he shall think fit . . . and the judge may, if either
> party so require, hear the application in his private room." H

The section of the later Act which now prescribes the method of deciding questions between husband and wife in a summary way is much longer but, so far as
material, is to the same effect and likewise enjoins the judge to hear the application
in private if either party so requires.

The discretionary words " as he shall think fit " appear in both sections and I
were discussed at length in this House in *National Provincial Bank, Ltd.* v.
Ainsworth (43). That case was concerned with consideration of what was called
" the deserted wife's equity " and is not, therefore, a decision of this House on
the extent of the discretion to be exercised under s. 17.

---

(40) [1919] 2 K.B. 571; [1918-19] All E.R. Rep. 860.
(41) [1919] 2 K.B. at p. 579; [1918-19] All E.R. Rep. at pp. 864, 865.
(42) [1968] 1 All E.R. 1064 at p. 1066; [1968] 1 W.L.R. 457 at p. 461.
(43) [1965] 2 All E.R. 472; [1965] A.C. 1175.

A   The matter has now been again fully argued and the same authorities, with some
additional ones, have been considered, together with the relevant statutes which
preceded the Act of 1882, and I would only say that I adhere to the opinions
expressed in the *National Provincial Bank* case (44), in effect re-affirming the
language of Romer, L.J., in *Cobb* v. *Cobb* when he said (45):

B   " . . . I know of no power that the court has under s. 17 to vary agreed or
established titles to property. It has power to ascertain the respective rights
of husband and wife to disputed property and frequently has to do so on very
little material; but where, as here, the original rights to property are established by the evidence and those rights have not been varied by subsequent
agreement, the court cannot in my opinion under s. 17 vary those rights

C   merely because it thinks that in the light of subsequent events, the original
agreement was unfair."

This view has not been universally held and the difficult cases alluded to by
Romer, L.J., may have had some influence in bringing Lord Denning, M.R.,
to the view that the discretionary language of the section could be used to
override the rights of the parties where family assets were concerned. In *Hine* v.
D *Hine* (46) he said:

      " It seems to me that the jurisdiction of the court over family assets
under s. 17 is entirely discretionary. Its discretion transcends all rights,
legal or equitable, and enables the court to make such order as it thinks fit.
This means, as I understand it, that the court is entitled to make such order
as appears to be fair and just in all the circumstances of the case."

E
To use the language of Coke, this would be to substitute the uncertain and crooked
cord of discretion for the golden and straight metwand of the law (Fourth Institute, p. 41 (1809 Edn.)). This interpretation, moreover, would, if correct, lead to
the anomalous result that the jurisdiction of the court would vary according to the
forum chosen by the litigant. It is not suggested that there is a general discretion
F in this respect in all proceedings between husband and wife wherever taken,
although it is true that their special relationship has always to be taken into
account. An illustration is to be found in *Shipman* v. *Shipman* (47). There a wife
obtained an injunction restraining her husband from living in her house which
had formed the matrimonial home. It was argued that this was tantamount to
pronouncing a judicial separation but the decision was upheld in the Court of
G Appeal in the special circumstances. The s. 17 discretion is valuable in protecting
the matrimonial relationship in appropriate cases by summary procedure. A
wife's occupation of the home may need protection until her husband provides
her with another. (See *Lee* v. *Lee* (48).) As Russell, L.J., pointed out in *Wilson*
v. *Wilson* (49):

H   " . . . it seems to me that the legal and equitable title of a husband is not
absolute but is vis-à-vis his wife limited, in that in general law he has not an
absolute right to eject the wife. The refusal to order possession under s. 17 is,
therefore, not the overriding of an unassailable title, but the recognition of a
defect in the title."

After the opinions expressed in the *National Provincial Bank* case (44) the absence
I of an unfettered discretion was accepted (see *Bedson* v. *Bedson* (50) per Lord
Denning, M.R.) but a different approach was made which appears to me to lead to

---

(44) [1965] 2 All E.R. 472; [1965] A.C. 1175.
(45) [1955] 2 All E.R. 696 at p. 700; [1955] 1 W.L.R. 731 at pp. 736, 737.
(46) [1962] 3 All E.R. 345 at p. 347; [1962] 1 W.L.R. 1124 at p. 1127.
(47) [1924] 2 Ch. 140; [1924] All E.R. Rep. 365.
(48) [1952] 1 All E.R. 1299; [1952] 2 Q.B. 489, n.
(49) [1963] 2 All E.R. 447 at p. 454; [1963] 1 W.L.R. 601 at p. 611.
(50) [1965] 3 All E..R 307 at p. 311; [1965] 2 Q.B. 666 at p. 677.

the same result as that reached by the discretionary road. This leads me to con-   A
sider the problem which arises in many of these cases and in particular to *Appleton*
v. *Appleton* (51) followed reluctantly by the Court of Appeal (52) in the present
case.

Appleton v. *Appleton* (51) was one in which the husband had voluntarily improved his wife's property and it was held by the registrar that such action, in
the absence of bargain or expressed intention to the contrary, gave him no   B
interest in either the property or the proceeds of sale. I should interpolate by
stating that these matters are now dealt with by the registrar and not by the judge
in chambers (Matrimonial Causes Rules 1957, r. 77 (53)). On appeal to the Court
of Appeal LORD DENNING, M.R., said that the work was done in the matrimonial
home for the sake of the family as a whole. He went on to say (54):

> " In those circumstances, it is not correct to look and see whether there   C
> was any bargain in the past, or any expressed intention. A judge can only
> do what is fair and reasonable in the circumstances. Sometimes this test has
> been put in the cases: What term is to be implied? What would the parties
> have stipulated had they thought about it? That is one way of putting it.
> But, as the parties never did think about it at all, I prefer to take the simple
> test: What is reasonable and fair in the circumstances as they have devel-   D
> oped, seeing that they are circumstances which no one contemplated before?"

LORD DENNING, M.R., went on to award to the husband a percentage of the proceeds of sale of the house commensurate with the enhancement due to his work on
improvement. This case preceded the decision in the *National Provincial Bank*
case (55) and has been followed in the present case as not having been formally
overruled. Respecting, as I do, the feeling of LORD DENNING, M.R., that this legal   E
fiction that a contract is to be implied which contained a term covering an un-
premeditated situation is not attractive, I am left with a decision which rests on
the phrase noted by the registrar and taken from *Appleton* v. *Appleton* (54) " A
judge can only do what is fair and reasonable in the circumstances ". This is
surely unfettered discretion.

In *Jansen* v. *Jansen* (56) on somewhat similar facts LORD DENNING, M.R.   F
took the view, which I accept, that *Appleton* v. *Appleton* (51) had not been
expressly overruled. I do not however think that the special facts of *Jansen* v.
Jansen (56) justify the decision. No agreement was reached between the husband
and the wife as to any payment to be made to the former by the latter for improvements made on the wife's property. The husband had no interest in the property
and the result was reached by the majority of the Court of Appeal by exercising   G
an unfettered discretion.

I must refer to the expression " family assets " used by LORD DENNING, M.R.,
in *Hine* v. *Hine* (57) and in a previous case of *Fribance* v. *Fribance* (58) and subsequently by DIPLOCK, L.J., in *Ulrich* v. *Ulrich and Felton* (59), a case of variation
of marriage settlement under the Matrimonial Causes Act 1965, s. 17, approved
by LORD DENNING, M.R., in *Gissing* v. *Gissing* (60). I cite a passage from   H
DIPLOCK, L.J.'s judgment, making general observations on married women's
property (61):

> " When these young people pool their savings to buy and equip a home
> or to acquire any other family asset, they do not think of this as an ' ante-
> nuptial ' or ' post-nuptial ' settlement, or give their minds to legalistic   I

(51) [1965] 1 All E.R. 44; [1965] 1 W.L.R. 25.
(52) [1968] 1 All E.R. 1053; [1968] 1 W.L.R. 443.   (53) S.I. 1957 No. 619.
(54) [1965] 1 All E.R. at p. 46; [1965] 1 W.L.R. at p. 28.
(55) [1965] 2 All E.R. 472; [1965] A.C. 1175.
(56) [1965] 3 All E.R. 363; [1965] P. 478.
(57) [1962] 3 All E.R. at p. 347; [1962] 1 W.L.R. at p. 1127.
(58) [1957] 1 All E.R. 357 at p. 360; [1957] 1 W.L.R. 384 at p. 387.
(59) [1968] 1 All E.R. 67 at p. 72; [1968] 1 W.L.R. 180 at p. 189.
(60) [1969] 1 All E.R. 1043; [1969] 2 W.L.R. 525.
(61) [1968] 1 All E.R. at p. 72; [1968] 1 W.L.R. at p. 189.

A   technicalities of 'advancement' and 'resulting trusts'. Nor do they normally agree explicitly what their equitable interests in the family asset shall be if death, divorce or separation parts them.   Where there is no explicit agreement, the court's first task is to infer from their conduct in relation to the property what their common intention would have been had they put it into words before matrimonial differences arose between them.   In the

B   common case today, of which the present is a typical example, neither party to the marriage has inherited capital, both are earning their living before marriage, the wife intends to continue to do so until they start having children.   They pool their savings to buy a house on mortgage in the husband's name or in joint names and to furnish and equip it as the family home.   They meet the expenses of its upkeep and improvement and the

C   payments of instalments on the mortgage out of the family income, to which the wife contributes so long as she is earning.   In such a case, the prima facie inference from their conduct is that their common intention is that the house, furniture and equipment should be family assets . . ."

This solution has the attraction that it appears to narrow the field so as to avoid giving the judge an uncontrolled discretion simply indicating that he may deal

D   with property rights of either spouse by calling specific property family assets and that he may then exercise his discretion in the light of that decision.   It is open to the objection, to which Lord Denning, M.R., adverted in *Hine* v. *Hine* (62), insofar as it rests on a fictional intention or agreement which the parties might have adopted if they had thought of a breakdown of their marriage.   Apart from the difficulty of inferring a contract where none has been made, no agree-

E   ment between husband and wife for future separation can be recognised and the breakdown of a marriage has no automatic effect on existing rights.   The conception of a normal married couple spending the long winter evenings hammering out agreements about their possessions appears grotesque and I certainly cannot take the further step of working out what they would have agreed if they had thought of making an agreement.

F   The notion of family assets itself opens a new field involving change in the law of property whereby community of ownership between husband and wife would be assumed unless otherwise excluded.   This is a matter of policy for Parliament and I agree is outside the field of judicial interpretation of property law.   I do not think that *Appleton* v. *Appleton* (63) can be supported on this basis or indeed on any other.

G   Cases in which the parties have made purchases of property by contributing in equal or unequal proportions have not caused difficulty.   The common intention of the parties is fulfilled without any specific agreement having been made or required.   An illustration is provided by *Rimmer* v. *Rimmer* (64) where the contributions were uncertain and resort was had to the maxim " equality is equity " and thus a decision was reached.   The decision depends in no way on an

H   agreement, expressed or implied.

It is, of course, true that following the strict rights of the parties to ownership of property may have unhappy results but the traffic is not all one way.   If a wife is left by her husband she may not establish any claim on his property by calling it a family asset but as the law stands at present she will have a right to apply for a maintenance order against him for herself and any children who are in her

I   care.   I agree that the case put by Diplock, L.J. (65), is common and typical today.   There is also, of course, the common case where the parties work together in harmony to build up their home.   The wife who had earned a substantial income before marriage gives up her work and devotes herself to the management of the house, her husband and children to the exclusion of all else.   The husband prospers

(62) [1962] 3 All E.R. at p. 347; [1962] 1 W.L.R. at pp. 1127, 1128.
(63) [1965] 1 All E.R. 44; [1965] 1 W.L.R. 25.
(64) [1952] 2 All E.R. 863; [1953] 1 Q.B. 63.
(65) [1968] 1 All E.R. at p. 72; [1968] 1 W.L.R. at p. 189.

and buys a house, car and various household goods such as machinery of a labour-saving character. They do not, in my opinion, ipso facto become family assets of which the wife is part owner. If this seems hard it is in part compensated by the liability to maintain his wife which the law imposes on a husband. This common situation was illustrated recently in a picturesque manner by SIR JOCELYN SIMON, P., in an extra-judicial address. He said: " The cock can feather the nest because he does not have to spend most of his time sitting on it." I do not myself see how one can correct the imbalance which may be found to exist in property rights as between husband and wife without legislation.

This particular case is not concerned with contributions as such, it is concerned with improvements, and although I recognise, as my learned and noble friend, LORD REID, points out, there is but a fine distinction between contributions to the purchase of property and improvements subsequently made thereto which increase its value, I cannot find any basis for the proposition that the making of improvements by one spouse on the property of the other gives a claim to the structure any more than if the same improvements had been made as between strangers. No doubt there are many scores of cases where married persons acquire a house and do all the necessary work by way of decoration and improvement themselves. It could hardly be otherwise, as none but the wealthy can today afford the cost of employing independent contractors on their private affairs.

Reference has been made to the " presumption of advancement " in favour of a wife in receipt of a benefit from her husband. In old days when a wife's right to property was limited, the presumption no doubt had great importance and today, when there are no living witnesses to a transaction and inferences have to be drawn, there may be no other guide to a decision as to property rights than by resort to the presumption of advancement. I do not think it would often happen that when evidence had been given, the presumption would today have any decisive effect.

I agree that this appeal be allowed.

LORD UPJOHN: My Lords, the first and most fundamental question in this appeal depends on the true scope of s. 17 of the Married Women's Property Act 1882, that is whether that section gives to the court exercising the jurisdiction of that section a discretion in relation to the property of husband and wife to do what is fair between them notwithstanding their proprietary interests, or whether the section is only a procedural section, intended merely to provide for a cheap, private and speedy forum for the solution of difficulties between husband and wife as to their respective proprietary interests. This House has already considered the question, though not as a matter of decision, in *National Provincial Bank, Ltd.* v. *Ainsworth* (66) where we considered, I think, all or nearly all the earlier authorities. I there expressed myself (67) in favour of the view that the section was no more than a procedural section which gave courts, including the then fairly new county courts, a discretion to decide on these matters but did not give the court a discretion to do what was merely fair and just between the spouses. I stated my views at some length and I do not propose to repeat them: but we have now had a more detailed examination of those authorities than was necessary in that case, and of course we have been referred to the numerous cases that have since been decided. We have also been referred to the Married Women's Property Act 1870, where a section similar to s. 17 first appeared. That reference, to my mind, has been helpful. That Act, in s. 2 to s. 7 inclusive, declared that certain types of property, deposits in banks, investments in the funds in joint stock companies, in industrial and provident societies and after-acquired property (subject to certain limitations) acquired by a married woman should be deemed to be her separate property, but each section contained a proviso that if the married woman had obtained the property by means of her husband's

(66) [1965] 2 All E.R. 472; [1965] A.C. 1175.
(67) [1965] 2 All E.R. at pp. 486, 487; [1965] A.C. at pp. 1235, 1236.

A money without his consent then the court, on an application under s. 9 of the Act, might order a transfer of such property to the husband. Section 9, which was plainly the forerunner of s. 17, then provided that in any question between husband and wife as to the separate property of the wife, either spouse might apply to the court and the judge " may make such order, direct such inquiry, and award such costs as he shall think fit ".   Plainly the words " as he shall think

B fit " were not intended to give him a general discretion merely to do what he on general grounds thought fair and just but to give him a discretion to decide what might be very difficult questions between husband and wife as to what was her separate property and whether such property had been obtained by her husband's moneys without his consent.

That language was substantially repeated in s. 17, and the draftsmen of that

C Act again appreciated that some discretion must be conferred on the court to determine the very difficult questions of title that might arise between husband and wife, but in my opinion that language did no more than confer a discretion to determine the title. It was also necessary to confer on the court a discretion to determine questions of possession of the matrimonial home because apart altogether from questions of title to the home the duty of the spouses to live

D together must be an important element. This, in my opinion, is the explanation of the words giving the court jurisdiction " to make such order with respect to the property in dispute . . . as he thinks fit ".

It is in any event, in my opinion, inconceivable in an Act in the 1870s or 1880s to suppose that Parliament intended to give a general discretion to the judge (including a county court judge) to determine questions with regard to the

E respective properties of husband and wife otherwise than in accordance with their respective proprietary titles ascertained on well-established principles of law and equity. Nor can the meaning of the Act have changed merely by reason of a change in social outlook since the date of its enactment; it must continue to bear the meaning which, on its true construction in the light of the relevant surrounding circumstances, it bore at that time. These considerations re-inforce

F the observations in relation to the true purpose of s. 17 that I made in the *Ainsworth* case (68).   Nothing in the cases that have been decided since causes me to alter the views I there expressed.

In my view, s. 17 is a purely procedural section which confers on the judge in relation to questions of title no greater discretion than he would have in proceedings begun in any Division of the High Court or in the county court in relation to

G the property in dispute, for it must be remembered that apart altogether from s. 17, husband and wife could sue one another even before the Act of 1882 over questions of property; so that, in my opinion, s. 17 now disappears from the scheme and the rights of the parties must be judged on the general principles applicable in any court of law when considering questions of title to property, and though the parties are husband and wife these questions of title must be decided by the principles

H of law applicable to the settlement of claims between those not so related, while making full allowances in view of that relationship.

In the first place, the beneficial ownership of the property in question must depend on the agreement of the parties determined at the time of its acquisition. If the property in question is land there must be some lease or conveyance which shows how it was acquired. If that document declares not merely in whom the

I legal title is to vest but in whom the beneficial title is to vest that necessarily concludes the question of title as between the spouses for all time, and in the absence of fraud or mistake at the time of the transaction the parties cannot go behind it at any time thereafter even on death or the break-up of the marriage. The observations of DAVIES, L.J., in *Bedson* v. *Bedson* (69) were plainly made only on the footing that s. 17 had the wider construction.

But the document may be silent as to the beneficial title. The property may

---

(68) [1965] 2 All E.R. at pp. 486, 487; [1965] A.C. at pp. 1235, 1236.
(69) [1965] 3 All E.R. 307 at p. 316; [1965] 2 Q.B. 666 at p. 685.

be conveyed into the name of one or other or into the names of both spouses **A**
jointly in which case parol evidence is admissible as to the beneficial ownership
that was intended by them at the time of acquisition and if, as very frequently
happens as between husband and wife, such evidence is not forthcoming, the court
may be able to draw an inference as to their intentions from their conduct. If
there is no such available evidence then what are called the presumptions come
into play. They have been criticised as being out of touch with the realities of **B**
today but when properly understood and properly applied to the circumstances
of today I remain of opinion that they remain as useful as ever in solving questions
of title.

First, then, in the absence of all other evidence, if the property is conveyed
into the name of one spouse at law that will operate to convey also the beneficial
interest and if conveyed to the spouses jointly that operates to convey the beneficial **C**
interest to the spouses jointly, i.e., with benefit of survivorship, but it is seldom
that this will be determinative. It is far more likely to be solved by the doctrine
of resulting trust, namely, that in the absence of evidence to the contrary if the
property be conveyed into the name of a stranger he will hold it as trustee for the
person putting up the purchase money and if the purchase money has been provided by two or more persons the property is held for those persons in proportion **D**
to the purchase money that they have provided.

My Lords, all this is trite law but I make no apology for citing the judgment of
EYRE, C.B., in 1788 in the leading case of *Dyer* v. *Dyer* (70) set out in full in
WHITE AND TUDOR'S LEADING CASES IN EQUITY (9th Edn. 1928), vol. II, at
pp. 750-751—

"The clear result of all the cases, without a single exception, is, that the **E**
*trust of a legal estate, whether freehold, copyhold, or leasehold; whether taken in
the names of the purchasers and others jointly, or in the names of others without
that of the purchaser; whether in one name or several; whether jointly or
successive—results to the man who advances the purchase-money.* This is a
general proposition, supported by all the cases, and there is nothing to
contradict it; and it goes on a strict analogy to the rule of the common law, **F**
that where a feoffment is made without consideration, the use results to the
feoffor. It is the established doctrine of a Court of equity, that this resulting
trust *may be rebutted* by circumstances in evidence.

"The cases go one step further, and prove that *the circumstance of one or
more of the nominees being a child or children of the purchaser, is to operate
by rebutting the resulting trust;* and it has been determined in so many cases **G**
that the nominee being a child shall have such operation as a circumstance
of evidence, that we should be disturbing land-marks if we suffered
either of these propositions to be called in question, namely, that such
circumstance shall rebut the resulting trust, and that it shall do so as a
circumstance of evidence."

The remarks of EYRE, C.B., in relation to a child being a nominee are equally **H**
applicable to the case where a wife is the nominee. Though normally referred to
as a presumption of advancement it is no more than a circumstance of evidence
which may rebut the presumption of resulting trust. And the learned editors
of WHITE AND TUDOR were careful to remind their readers, at p. 763, that "all
resulting trusts which arise simply from equitable presumption may be rebutted
by parol evidence . . .". This doctrine applies equally to personalty. **I**

These presumptions or circumstances of evidence are readily rebutted by
comparatively slight evidence; let me give one or two examples.

In *Re Gooch, Gooch* v. *Gooch* (71) a father purchased in his son's name stock in a
certain company more than sufficient to qualify the son to be a director of the

(70) (1788), 2 Cox, Eq. Cas. 92 at pp. 93, 94; [1775-1802] All E.R. Rep. 205 at pp.
206, 207.
(71) (1890), 62 L.T. **384**.

A company but the father kept the relative certificates in an envelope on which he had written " belonging to me "; held presumption of gift rebutted.

In *Fowkes* v. *Pascoe* (72) a rich lady, having some stocks in her own name, put some more of the same stock into the name of one who was in law a stranger but in fact the son by a subsequent marriage of the lady's former daughter-in-law. Held that as in the circumstances there can have been no conceivable reason for

B putting the stock in his name as nominee, the presumption of resulting trust was rebutted and the stocks were a gift to him. Then, as between husband and wife, the law is clearly settled and was well stated by Sir Richard Malins, V.-C., in *Re Eykyn's Trusts* (73):

C " The law of this Court is perfectly settled that when a husband transfers money or other property into the name of his wife only, then the presumption is, that it is intended as a gift or advancement to the wife absolutely at once, subject to such marital control as he may exercise. And if a husband invests money, stock, or otherwise, in the names of himself and his wife, then also it is an advancement for the benefit of the wife absolutely if she survives her husband, but if he survives her, then it reverts to him as joint tenant with

D his wife."

So in such a case as a practical matter where the property is in joint names the presumption is in effect no more than a joint beneficial tenancy.

Then in *Re Young, Trye* v. *Sullivan* (74) the spouses, who died within five days of one another, had opened a joint account mainly contributed to by the wife, principally, but not only, for housekeeping expenses, but with the consent of the

E wife (as Pearson, J., held) the husband drew on the joint account to make substantial investments in his own name alone. Held that the joint account belonged beneficially to the spouses jointly and so passed to the survivor by survivorship but that the investments purchased by the husband in his own name (there being no evidence that he was thereby acting as a trustee) belonged to his estate. This sound principle has recently been followed in *Re Bishop, National*

F *Provincial Bank, Ltd.* v. *Bishop* (75).

So that, in the absence of all evidence, if a husband puts property into his wife's name he intends it to be a gift to her but if he puts it into joint names then (in the absence of all other evidence) the presumption is the same as a joint beneficial tenancy. If a wife puts property into her husband's name it may be that in the absence of all other evidence he is a trustee for her but in practice there will in

G almost every case be some explanation (however slight) of this (today) rather unusual course. If a wife puts property into their joint names I would myself think that a joint beneficial tenancy was intended, for I can see no other reason for it.

But where both spouses contribute to the acquisition of a property, then my own view (of course in the absence of evidence) is that they intended to be joint

H beneficial owners and this is so whether the purchase be in the joint names or in the name of one. This is the result of an application of the presumption of resulting trust. Even if the property be put in the sole name of the wife, I would not myself treat that as a circumstance of evidence enabling the wife to claim an advancement to her, for it is against all the probabilities of the case unless the husband's contribution is very small.

I Whether the spouses contributing to the purchase should be considered to be equal owners or in some other proportions must depend on the circumstances of each case: see *Rimmer* v. *Rimmer* (76) and many other cases, but for very good reasons for treating the spouses on an equality when one puts up the deposit and

(72) (1875), 10 Ch. App. 343.   (73) (1877), 6 Ch.D. 115 at p. 118.
(74) (1885), 28 Ch.D. 705.
(75) [1965] 1 All E.R. 249; [1965] Ch. 450.
(76) [1952] 2 All E.R. 863; [1953] 1 Q.B. 63.

the other assumes liability for the building society mortgage: see *Ulrich* v. *Ulrich*   **A**
and Felton (77), per LORD DENNING, M.R. (78), and DIPLOCK, L.J. (79).

But if a spouse purchases property out of his or her own money and puts it
into his or her own name then (in the absence of evidence) I can see absolutely
no reason for drawing any inference save that it was to be the property of that
spouse; bought of course for the common use or common occupation during the
marriage, but if sold during the marriage the proceeds belong to the purchasing   **B**
spouse as does the property on termination of the marriage whether brought about
by death or divorce.

My Lords, during argument there was much reference to the well-known case
of *Balfour* v. *Balfour* (80). That case illustrates the well-known doctrine that in
their ordinary day-to-day life spouses do not intend to contract in a legally binding sense with one another, though I am bound to confess that in my opinion the   **C**
facts of that case stretched that doctrine to its limits. The doctrine has, in my
opinion, little if any application to questions of title to the property of the spouses,
at all events to property of the magnitude we are now considering.

Then in some of the recent cases, before the true scope of s. 17 was resolved,
a number of judicial observations have been made to the effect that when a
marriage is broken it is the function of the court to fill in the gap by doing what   **D**
the parties as reasonable spouses would have agreed was to happen on the
break-up had they thought about it. This cannot be right; apart from the fact
that an agreement as to the results of a future separation or divorce is void as
being contrary to public policy it is clear that the court can only ascertain the
title to property by considering the circumstances at the time of acquisition and
in the absence of positive evidence by applying the presumptions I have discussed   **E**
above. This decides the question of title for all time and in all circumstances
and there is no gap to be filled. Nor can this matter be affected by the fact that
looking backwards after many years it may seem to have been unfair (*Cobb* v.
Cobb (81)). Evidence of facts and circumstances subsequent to the acquisition
is relevant only where—(i) it is desired to prove title by reason of the subsequent
conduct of the parties; or (ii) it is alleged there has been some subsequent   **F**
agreement affecting title to the property.

My Lords, in some recent cases the expression " family assets " has been used.
It has been said that young people today do not give their minds to legalistic
technicalities of advancements and resulting trusts; neither did they in 1788
and it is only because they did not do so then that these presumptions were
invented because that represented the common sense of the matter and what the   **G**
parties, had they thought about it, would have intended. In my opinion, today
the doctrine of resulting trusts still represents the common sense of the matter
and what the parties would have agreed had they thought about it. But these
recent cases seek to impose on the courts the idea that in the case of " family
assets ", where both parties are earning and their joint earnings purchase property,
there is a special principle leading to a different conclusion.   **H**

This does not depend on the existence of a common banking account. In the
very recent case in the Court of Appeal of *Gissing* v. *Gissing* (82), of which your
Lordships have been supplied with a transcript, LORD DENNING, M.R., stated it
thus in his judgment:

    " This depends on whether it is a family asset. This principle has been
    frequently stated. I tried to do it myself in *Fribance* v. *Fribance* (83), but it   **I**
    has been much better done by DIPLOCK, L.J., in *Ulrich* v. *Ulrich and Felton*
    (79). It comes to this: where a couple, by their joint efforts, get a house

(77) [1968] 1 All E.R. 67; [1968] 1 W.L.R. 180.
(78) [1968] 1 All E.R. at p. 70; [1968] 1 W.L.R. at p. 186.
(79) [1968] 1 All E.R. at p. 72; [1968] 1 W.L.R. at p. 189.
(80) [1919] 2 K.B. 571; [1918-19] All E.R. Rep. 860.
(81) [1955] 2 All E.R. 696; [1955] 1 W.L.R. 731.
(82) [1969] 1 All E.R. 1043 at p. 1046; [1969] 2 W.L.R. 525 at p. 529.
(83) [1957] 1 All E.R. 357 at p. 359; [1957] 1 W.L.R. 384 at p. 387.

A   and furniture, intending it to be a continuing provision for them for their joint lives, it is the prima facie inference from their conduct that the house and furniture is a ' family asset ' in which each is entitled to an equal share. It matters not in whose name it stands: or who pays for what: or who goes out to work and who stays at home. If they both contribute to it by their joint efforts, the prima facie inference is that it belongs to them both equally: B   at any rate, when each makes a financial contribution which is substantial."

My Lords, we have in this country no doctrine of community of goods between spouses and yet by judicial decision were this doctrine of family assets to be accepted some such a doctrine would become part of the law of the land. I do not myself believe it accords with what the parties intended even if sub silentio or would regard as common sense. Let us suppose the wife buys a motor car for the C   family use out of her earnings; according to the doctrine it belongs to the spouses jointly. Then the husband goes bankrupt (the astonishing number of 8,510 in 1967 did) and she finds the trustee in bankruptcy claiming an interest in the car. Or the husband, out of a substantial bonus received from his employers, buys in his name as a family asset a little holiday home for the family in the country. On the unexpected death of his wife he pays estate duty on a moiety, and of course D   that moiety may pass away possibly to her side of the family under some residuary gift in her will; of course the parties did not intend that each purchased the property as his (or her) own but for the common use of the family during the subsistence of the marriage. My Lords, in my opinion the expression " family assets " is devoid of legal meaning and its use can define no legal rights or obligations. Of course, if it appears from the evidence that the parties in fact did agree to pool E   their assets into one jointly-owned fund, that is a different matter, but that must be a question of fact in each case. In the absence of such agreement I would prefer to rely on the well-established principles which will give rise to no such absurd results and which principles, I repeat, represent the common sense of the matter and what the average couple intend had they expressed their intentions. If there is to be a change that must be done by Parliament.

F   Furthermore, on the making of a decree of divorce, the court has ample statutory power to do what is fair in the way of varying the marriage settlement and settling the guilty wife's property, e.g., see s. 17 of the Matrimonial Causes Act 1965, which makes this alleged doctrine of family assets quite out of place.

My Lords, the facts of this case depend not on the acquisition of property but on the expenditure of money and labour by the husband in the way of improvement on the property of the wife which admittedly is her own beneficial property. G   On this it is quite clearly established that by the law of England the expenditure of money by A. on the property of B. stands in quite a different category from the acquisition of property by A. and B.

It has been well settled in your Lordships' House (*Ramsden* v. *Dyson* (84)) that if A. expends money on the property of B., prima facie he has no claim on H   such property. And this, as SIR WILLIAM GRANT, M.R., held as long ago as 1810 in *Campion* v. *Cotton* (85), is equally applicable as between husband and wife. If by reason of estoppel or because the expenditure was incurred by the encouragement of the owner that such expenditure would be rewarded, the person expending the money may have some claim for monetary re-imbursement in a purely monetary sense from the owner or even, if explicitly promised to him by the owner, an interest in the land (see *Plimmer* v. *Wellington Corpn.* (86)). But the I   husband's claim here is to a share of the property and his money claim in his plaint is only a qualification of that. Plainly, in the absence of agreement with the wife (and none is suggested) he could have no monetary claim against her and no estoppel or mistake is suggested so, in my opinion, he can have no charge on or interest in the wife's property.

---

(84) (1866), L.R. 1 H.L. 129.
(85) (1810), 17 Ves. 263; [1803-13] All E.R. Rep. 580.
(86) (1884), 9 App. Cas. 699.

It may be that as counsel for the Queen's Proctor quite rightly pointed out A
this case could be decided somewhat on the *Balfour* v. *Balfour* (87) principle, that
the nature of the work done was of the type done by husband and wife on the
matrimonial home without giving the worker a legal interest in it (see *Button*
v. *Button* (88)). But I prefer to decide this appeal on the wider ground that in the
absence of agreement, and there being no question of any estoppel, one spouse who
does work or expends money on the property of the other has no claim whatever B
on the property of the other. *Jansen* v. *Jansen* (89) was a very good example of
that type of case. The husband, putting it briefly, spent his short married life
making very substantial improvements on the properties of the wife which greatly
increased their value as reflected in their sale price. The wife recognised that as
between husband and wife he should receive some benefit and instructed her
solicitor to draw up an agreement whereby he was to receive monetary recompense C
from the proceeds of sale of one of the properties he had improved when such sale
was effected. The husband refused to accept this so the parties in fact and in law
never did agree. In those circumstances it seems to me clear that the husband
had no claim against the wife even personally and certainly no claim against the
property itself either by way of charge or by way of a share in the property. In
my opinion *Jansen* v. *Jansen* (89) was wrongly decided.   D

My Lords, for these reasons I would allow this appeal.

LORD DIPLOCK: My Lords, I agree with all your Lordships that this
appeal should be allowed, but in expressing my reasons for doing so I find it
necessary to examine the legal principles applicable to the determination of
questions between husband and wife as to the title to what in recent decisions E
of the Court of Appeal have been described as " family assets ". This expression I
understand to mean property, whether real or personal, which has been acquired
by either spouse in contemplation of their marriage or during its subsistence and
was intended for the common use and enjoyment of both spouses or their children,
such as the matrimonial home, its furniture and other durable chattels. It does
not include property acquired by either spouse before the marriage but not in F
contemplation of it.

Questions between husband and wife as to the title to or possession of property
can be dealt with under the summary procedure provided for by s. 17 of the
Married Women's Property Act 1882. They generally are, and such was the
procedure adopted in the present case. But they may also arise in ordinary
actions between spouses or former spouses for a declaration of rights, for possession of a former matrimonial home or, since the Married Women's Property Act G
1964, for detinue or for conversion of chattels.

In numerous judgments of the Court of Appeal during the last 20 years this
branch of the law of property has undergone considerable development. The
cases start with *Re Rogers' Question* (90) and end with *Gissing* v. *Gissing* (91),
a judgment of the Court of Appeal delivered while the present appeal was being H
heard by your Lordships' House. They manifest a divergence of views among
the members of the Court of Appeal as to the origin and extent of the court's
powers in dealing with questions of title to property between spouses and as to
the principles on which such powers should be exercised; but although some of
these cases were commented on by members of your Lordships' House in *National
Provincial Bank, Ltd.* v. *Ainsworth* (92), the present appeal is the first in which I
your Lordships have had the opportunity and duty of examining and, if necessary,
correcting the recent developments by the Court of Appeal of this branch of the
law. And a very important branch it is. It affects every married couple. We are
informed that in the High Court alone there are some 900 applications a year

(87) [1919] 2 K.B. 571; [1918-19] All E.R. Rep. 860.
(88) [1968] 1 All E.R. 1064; [1968] 1 W.L.R. 457.
(89) [1965] 3 All E.R. 363; [1965] P. 478.   (90) [1948] 1 All E.R. 328.
(91) [1969] 1 All E.R. 1043; [1969] 2 W.L.R. 525.
(92) [1965] 2 All E.R. 472; [1965] A.C. 1175.

A under s. 17 of the Married Women's Property Act 1882, and this figure takes no
   account of applications in the county court which also has jurisdiction under the
   section. On a matter of such general social importance the principles applied by
   the courts in exercising their jurisdiction ought to be clear.

       In some of the judgments of the Court of Appeal it is stated that s. 17 itself
   gives to the court a free hand to do whatever it thinks just as respects the title to
B family assets. This view reaches its high-water mark in the judgment of LORD
   DENNING, M.R., in *Hine* v. *Hine* (93) where he said:

       " It seems to me that the jurisdiction of the court over family assets
       under s. 17 is entirely discretionary. Its discretion transcends all rights,
       legal or equitable, and enables the court to make such order as it thinks
       fit."
C
   Since your Lordships' decision in *National Provincial Bank, Ltd.* v. *Ainsworth*
   (94), the tide has receded.   It is no longer claimed that where the proprietary
   rights of spouses in any property which is a family asset can be clearly ascertained
   the court has any jurisdiction to vary agreed or established titles. See *Jansen* v.
   Jansen (95), where LORD DENNING, M.R. (96), accepted this limitation on the
D powers of the court under s. 17, which had previously been laid down by ROMER,
   L.J., in *Cobb* v. *Cobb* (97).   But since husband and wife while still happily married
   seldom make and record any express agreement as to the title of family assets
   which are acquired as a result of their concerted action this still leaves a wide area
   in which the court could exercise an unfettered discretion to deal with the title
   in whatever way it thinks just in the circumstances as they exist at the time of the
E court's determination, which is generally after the break-up of the marriage.
   LORD DENNING, M.R., in *Appleton* v. *Appleton* (98) said:

       ". . . I prefer to take the simple test: What is reasonable and fair in the
       circumstances as they have developed, seeing that they are circumstances
       which no one contemplated before ?"

   The first question, therefore, is whether s. 17 of the Married Women's Property
F Act 1882, does give to the court any power to create or vary the proprietary
   rights of husband or wife in family assets as distinct from ascertaining and
   declaring their respective proprietary rights which already exist at the time of
   the court's determination.

       I agree with your Lordships that the section confers no such power on the court.
   It is, in my view, a procedural section. It provides a summary and relatively
G informal forum which can sit in private for the resolution of disputes between
   husband and wife as to the title to or possession of any property—not limited to
   " family assets " as I have defined them. It is available while husband and wife
   are living together as well as when the marriage has broken up. The power conferred on the judge to " make such order with respect to the property in dispute
   . . . as he shall think fit ", gives him a wide discretion as to the enforcement of
H the proprietary or possessory rights of one spouse in any property against the
   other but confers on him no jurisdiction to transfer any proprietary interest in
   property from one spouse to the other or to create new proprietary rights in either
   spouse.

       The proposition that the section confers on the court a discretion wider than
   that which I have indicated could, it seems to me, only be tenable if it were under
I this section alone that the title of spouses to property could have been determined
   after the passing of the Act in 1882. But this is not the case. Even before the
   first Married Women's Property Act of 1870 questions of title to property of

---

   (93) [1962] 3 All E.R. 345 at p. 347; [1962] 1 W.L.R. 1124 at pp. 1127, 1128.
   (94) [1965] 2 All E.R. 472; [1965] A.C. 1175.
   (95) [1965] 3 All E.R. 363; [1965] P. 478.
   (96) [1965] 3 All E.R. at p. 366; [1965] P. at p. 488.
   (97) [1955] 2 All E.R. 696 at p. 700; [1955] 1 W.L.R. 731 at pp. 736, 737.
   (98) [1965] 1 All E.R. 44 at p. 46; [1965] 1 W.L.R. 25 at p. 28.

spouses could arise in claims by execution creditors, trustees in bankruptcy and A
mortgagees (see *Hewison* v. *Negus* (99)), or in proceedings in Chancery between
the spouses themselves. Although neither spouse could bring an action against
the other at common law on a contract made between them, such contracts,
if relating to the wife's estate settled to her separate use, could be enforced
by equitable remedies in the Court of Chancery (see *Woodward* v. *Woodward*
(100)). This jurisdiction, transferred to the High Court of Justice by the Supreme B
Court of Judicature Act 1873, was not abolished by the Married Women's Property
Acts of 1870 or 1882 and it can hardly be supposed that Parliament intended
that the title of spouses to property should be different if one procedure for
determining it were adopted instead of another.

The history of the legislation, too, supports this. The predecessor of s. 17
of the Act of 1882 is s. 9 of the Act of 1870. That Act declared that the earnings of C
a married woman, and various bank deposits, shares and other kinds of personal
property should be the separate property of a wife. The summary procedure
under s. 9 was available " In any question between husband and wife as to
property *declared by this Act* to be the separate property of the wife ", and the
discretion conferred on the judge was in the same terms as in s. 17 of the Act of
1882, viz., to " make such order . . . as he shall think fit ". It would be quite D
impossible to construe these words as conferring on the judge a jurisdiction to
make an order declaring the title to any property which was in conflict with what
the Act itself declared. Furthermore, even in the Act of 1870 the wife was given
by s. 11 an alternative remedy by way of action " for the recovery of any wages,
earnings, money, and property by this Act declared to be her separate property ",
and this new remedy in the ordinary courts of common law was additional to her E
previously existing remedy in the Court of Chancery.

The Act of 1882 made a wife capable of acquiring, holding and disposing of any
real or personal property as her separate property and to enter into contracts with
respect to and binding her separate property. The summary procedure, first
introduced by s. 9 of the Act of 1870, was extended by s. 17 to " any question
between husband and wife as to the title to or possession of property ", and the F
right to sue for the protection and security of her own separate property was
similarly extended by s. 12. Under this latter section a wife could sue her husband
on a contract relating to her separate property. She was not confined to her
remedy under s. 17 (see *Butler* v. *Butler* (101)).

I conclude, therefore, that in determining a question of title to property in
proceedings between husband and wife under s. 17 the court has no power to G
apply any different principles from those which it applies to the same question in
any other proceedings. It must decide them according to law.

What, then, is the law? Ever since 1882 husband and wife have had the legal
capacity to enter into transactions with one another, such as contracts, con-
veyances and declarations of trust so as to create legally enforceable rights and
obligations, provided that these do not offend against the settled rules of public H
policy about matrimonial relations. Where spouses have done so, the court has
no power to ignore or alter the rights and obligations so created, though the court
in the exercise of the discretion which it always has in respect of its own procedure
may in an appropriate case where a matrimonial suit between the spouses is pending or contemplated adjourn the hearing or defer making an order for the enforcement of the right until the spouses have had an opportunity of applying for I
ancillary relief in that suit under the provisions of Part 3 of the Matrimonial Causes
Act 1965, which do confer power on the court to vary proprietary rights, on
granting a decree of divorce.

But it is comparatively rarely that husband and wife enter into any express
agreement as to the proprietary rights which are to subsist in " family assets "
acquired or improved while they are living or contemplating living happily

(99) (1853), 16 Beav. 594.   (100) (1863), 3 De G.J. & Sm. 672.
                    (101) (1884), 14 Q.B.D. 831.

A together. Yet any such acquisition or improvement must have some legal consequences. Family assets are not res nullius. When a "family asset" is first acquired from a third party the title to it must vest in one or other of the spouses, or be shared between them, and where an existing family asset is improved this, too, must have some legal consequence even if it is only that the improvement is an accretion to the property of the spouse who was entitled to the asset before it B was improved. Where the acquisition or improvement is made as a result of contributions in money or money's worth by both spouses acting in concert the proprietary interests in the family asset resulting from their respective contributions depend on their common intention as to what those interests should be.

I have used the neutral expression "acting in concert" because many of the C ordinary domestic arrangements between man and wife do not possess the legal characteristics of a contract. So long as they are executory they do not give rise to any chose in action for neither party intended that non-performance of their mutual promises should be the subject of sanctions in any court (see *Balfour* v. *Balfour* (102)). But this is relevant to non-performance only. If spouses do perform their mutual promises the fact that they could not have been compelled D to do so while the promises were executory cannot deprive the acts done by them of all legal consequences on proprietary rights; for these are within the field of the law of property rather than of the law of contract. It would, in my view, be erroneous to extend the presumption accepted in *Balfour* v. *Balfour* (102) that mutual promises between man and wife in relation to their domestic arrangements are prima facie not intended by either to be legally enforceable to a presumption E of a common intention of both spouses that *no* legal consequences should flow from acts done by them in performance of mutual promises with respect to the acquisition, improvement or addition to real or personal property—for this would be to intend what is impossible in law.

How, then, does the court ascertain the "common intention" of spouses as to their respective proprietary interests in a family asset when at the time F that it was acquired or improved as a result of contributions in money or money's worth by each of them they failed to formulate it themselves? It may be possible to infer from their conduct that they did in fact form an actual common intention as to their respective proprietary interests and where this is possible the courts should give effect to it. But in the case of transactions between husband and wife relating to family assets their actual common contemplation at the time of its G acquisition or improvement probably goes no further than its common use and enjoyment by themselves and their children, and while that use continues their respective proprietary interests in it are of no practical importance to them. They only become of importance if the asset ceases to be used and enjoyed by them in common and they do not think of the possibility of this happening. In many cases, and most of those which come before the courts, the true inference from H the evidence is that at the time of its acquisition or improvement the spouses formed no common intention as to their proprietary rights in the family asset. They gave no thought to the subject of proprietary rights at all.

But this does not raise a problem which is peculiar to transactions between husband and wife. It is one with which the courts are familiar in connection with ordinary contracts and to its solution they apply a familiar legal technique. I The common situation in which a court has to decide whether or not a term is to be implied in a contract is when some event has happened for which the parties have made no provision in the contract because at the time it was made neither party foresaw the possibility of that event happening and so never in fact agreed what its legal consequences would be on their respective contractual rights and obligations. Nevertheless the court imputes to the parties a common intention which in fact they never formed and it does so by forming its own opinion as to what would have been the common intention of reasonable men as to the effect

(102) [1919] 2 K.B. 571; [1918-19] All E.R. Rep. 860.

of that event on their contractual rights and obligations if the possibility of the A
event happening had been present to their minds at the time of entering into the
contract.   In *Davis Contractors, Ltd.* v. *Fareham Urban District Council* LORD
RADCLIFFE (103) analyses this technique as applied to cases of frustration. See
also PROFESSOR GLANVILLE WILLIAMS's analysis of the legal doctrine of implied
terms in " Language and the Law " (61 L.Q.R. p. 401).

In applying the technique to contracts the court starts with the assumption B
that prima facie the parties intended that whatever may happen their legal
rights and obligations under their contract should be confined to those which they
have expressed. Consequently the court will not imply a term unless it is of
opinion that no reasonable men could have failed to form the common intention
to which effect will be given by the term which it implies. But such an assumption,
viz., that prima facie the parties intended at the time of the transaction to express C
all the legal consequences as to proprietary rights which would flow from it,
whatever might happen in the future, is, for the reasons already indicated,
inappropriate to transactions between husband and wife in relation to family
assets. In most cases they express none and form no actual common intention
about proprietary rights in the family asset because neither spouse gave any
thought to an event happening, viz., the cesser of their common use and enjoy- D
ment of the asset, which alone would give any practical importance to their
respective proprietary interests in the asset. Unless it is possible to infer from
the conduct of the spouses at the time of the concerted action in relation to
acquisition or improvement of the family asset that they did form an actual common intention as to the legal consequences of their acts on the proprietary rights in
the asset the court must impute to them a constructive common intention which is E
that which in the court's opinion would have been formed by reasonable spouses.

A similar technique is applied in imputing an intention to a person wherever
the intention with which an act is done affects its legal consequences and the
evidence does not disclose what was the actual intention with which he did it.
This situation commonly occurs when the actor is deceased. When the act is of a
kind to which this technique has frequently to be applied by the courts the F
imputed intention may acquire the description of a " presumption "—but presumptions of this type are not immutable. A presumption of fact is no more than
a consensus of judicial opinion disclosed by reported cases as to the most likely
inference of fact to be drawn in the absence of any evidence to the contrary—for
example, presumptions of legitimacy, of death, of survival and the like. But the
most likely inference as to a person's intention in the transactions of his everyday G
life depends on the social environment in which he lives and the common habits
of thought of those who live in it. The consensus of judicial opinion which gave
rise to the presumptions of " advancement " and "resulting trust" in transactions
between husband and wife is to be found in cases relating to the propertied classes
of the nineteenth century and the first quarter of the twentieth century among
whom marriage settlements were common, and it was unusual for the wife to H
contribute by her earnings to the family income. It was not until after World
War II that the courts were required to consider the proprietary rights in family
assets of a different social class. The advent of legal aid, the wider employment
of married women in industry, commerce and the professions and the emergence
of a property-owning, particularly a real-property-mortgaged-to-a-building-
society-owning, democracy has compelled the courts to direct their attention to I
this during the last 20 years. It would, in my view, be an abuse of the legal
technique for ascertaining or imputing intention to apply to transactions between
the post-war generation of married couples " presumptions " which are based on
inferences of fact which an earlier generation of judges drew as to the most likely
intentions of earlier generations of spouses belonging to the propertied classes of a
different social era.

I do not propose to examine in detail the numerous cases decided in the last

(103) [1956] 2 All E.R. 145; [1956] A.C. 696.

A 20 years and cited in the argument before your Lordships' House in which in the absence of evidence that spouses formed any actual intention as to their respective proprietary rights in a family asset, generally the matrimonial home acquired as a result of their concerted action, the courts have imputed an intention to them. I adhere to the view which I expressed in *Ulrich* v. *Ulrich and Felton* (104), in the passage which my noble and learned friend LORD HODSON has already cited

B at length. I think it fairly summarises the broad consensus of judicial opinion disclosed by the post-war cases (none of which has reached your Lordships' House), as to the common intentions which, in the absence of evidence of an actual intention to the contrary, are to be imputed to spouses when matrimonial homes are acquired on mortgage as a result of their concerted acts of a kind which are typical of transactions between husband and wife today. And I firmly think that

C broad consensus of judicial opinion is right. The old presumptions of advancement and resulting trust are inappropriate to these kinds of transactions and the fact that the legal estate is conveyed to the wife or to the husband or to both jointly though it may be significant in indicating their actual common intention is not necessarily decisive since it is often influenced by the requirements of the building society which provides the mortgage.

D   In imputing to them a common intention as to their respective proprietary rights which as fair and reasonable men and women they presumably would have formed had they given their minds to it at the time of the relevant acquisition or improvement of a family asset, the court, it has been suggested, is exercising in another guise a jurisdiction to do what it considers itself to be fair and reasonable in all the circumstances and this does not differ in result from the jurisdiction

E which LORD DENNING, M.R., in *Appleton* v. *Appleton* (105) considered was expressly conferred on the court by s. 17 of the Married Women's Property Act 1882.

    It is true, as LORD RADCLIFFE pointed out in *Davis Contractors, Ltd.* v. *Fareham Urban District Council* (106), that when the court imputes to parties an intention on a matter to which they in fact gave no thought—

F   " In their [sc. the parties] place there rises the figure of the fair and reasonable man. And the spokesman of the fair and reasonable man, who represents after all no more than the anthropomorphic conception of justice, is and must be the court itself."

    The officious bystander of MACKINNON, L.J. (see *Shirlaw* v. *Southern Foundries (1926), Ltd. & Federated Foundries, Ltd.* (107)) may pose the question, but the court, not the parties, gives the answer. Nevertheless, there is a significant differ-

G ence between applying to transactions between husband and wife the general legal technique for imputing intention to the parties and exercising a discretion such as that which LORD DENNING, M.R., suggested was conferred on the court by s. 17 of the Married Women's Property Act 1882. In applying the general technique the court is directing its attention to what would have been the common intention of the spouses as fair and reasonable husband and wife at the time of the relevant

H transaction while they were still happily married and not contemplating its break-down. The family asset might cease to be needed for the common use and enjoyment of themselves and their children without the marriage breaking down at all. The circumstances of the subsequent break-down and the conduct of the spouses which contributed to it are irrelevant to this enquiry. If these circumstances are such as to call for an adjustment of the spouses' respective proprietary

I rights which resulted from their previous transactions the court has jurisdiction to make such adjustments under the Matrimonial Causes Act 1965 (see *Ulrich* v. *Ulrich and Felton* (108)). It has no such jurisdiction under s. 17 of the Married Women's Property Act 1882.

---

(104) [1968] 1 All E.R. 67 at pp. 71-73; [1968] 1 W.L.R. at pp. 188-190.
(105) [1965] 1 All E.R. at p. 46; [1965] 1 W.L.R. at p. 28.
(106) [1956] 2 All E.R. at p. 160; [1956] A.C. at p. 728.
(107) [1939] 2 All E.R. 113 at p. 124; [1939] 2 K.B. 206 at p. 227.
(108) [1968] 1 All E.R. 67; [1968] 1 W.L.R. 180.

In the present case we are concerned not with the acquisition of a matrimonial **A**
home on mortgage but with improvements to a previously acquired matrimonial
home. There is no question that at the time that it was acquired the matrimonial
home was the wife's property. It was bought not with the help of a mortgage but
with the proceeds of sale of the previous matrimonial home which the wife had
inherited from her grandmother. The husband made no contribution to its purchase and the conveyance of it was to the wife alone. The conduct of the parties **B**
is consistent only with the sole proprietary interest in it being that of the
wife. During the four years that the spouses lived together in their new home the
husband in his spare time occupied himself, as many husbands do, in laying out
the garden with a lawn and patio, putting up a side wall with a gate and in
various jobs of redecoration and the like in the house itself. He claimed that these
leisure activities had enhanced the value of the property by £1,000 and that he was **C**
entitled to a beneficial interest in it of that amount. The learned registrar declared
that the husband had a beneficial interest in the proceeds of sale of the property
in the sum of £300. How that sum was arrived at is not wholly clear. It would seem
to be the registrar's estimate of the increase in value of the property due to the
husband's work. The Court of Appeal (109) with expressed reluctance felt themselves bound by *Appleton* v. *Appleton* (110) to dismiss the wife's appeal from the **D**
registrar's order.

It is common enough nowadays for husbands and wives to decorate and to
make improvements in the family home themselves with no other intention than
to indulge in what is now a popular hobby and to make the home pleasanter for
their common use and enjoyment. If the husband likes to occupy his leisure by
laying a new lawn in the garden or building a fitted wardrobe in the bedroom **E**
while the wife does the shopping, cooks the family dinner or baths the children,
I, for my part, find it quite impossible to impute to them as reasonable husband
and wife any common intention that these domestic activities or any of them are to
have any effect on the existing proprietary rights in the family home on which
they are undertaken. It is only in the bitterness engendered by the break-up
of the marriage that so bizarre a notion would enter their heads. **F**

I agree with the Court of Appeal (109) that the present case cannot be distinguished from that of *Appleton* v. *Appleton* (110), but in my view *Appleton* v.
Appleton (110) was wrongly decided, perhaps because the court applied the wrong
test laid down in the passage from LORD DENNING, M.R.'s judgment (111)
which I have already cited and took into account the circumstances in which the
marriage in that case in fact broke up. *Button* v. *Button* (112), was, in my view, **G**
clearly right. *Jansen* v. *Jansen* (113) falls into a different category. There it was
not a case of leisure activities of the spouses. The husband in agreement with
his wife had abandoned his prospects of paid employment in order to work on her
property which although the family lived in part of it had been acquired as a
commercial venture to which both were contributing.   There were circumstances
in that case which, in my view, justified the court in imputing to the spouses a **H**
common intention that his work should entitle him to a proprietary interest in the
property whose value was enhanced by his full time labours directed to that end.

The present case, however, in my view clearly falls in the same category as
Button v. *Button* (112) and *Appleton* v. *Appleton* (110). I would allow this appeal.

Appeal allowed.

Solicitors: *Preston, Rose and Neil*, agents for *Perring & Co.*, Hastings (for the **I**
appellant); *Queen's Proctor*.

[*Reported by* S. A. HATTEEA, ESQ., *Barrister-at-Law*.]

---

(109) [1968] 1 All E.R. 1053; [1968] 1 W.L.R. 443.
(110) [1965] 1 All E.R. 44; [1965] 1 W.L.R. 25.
(111) [1965] 1 All E.R. at p. 46; [1965] 1 W.L.R. at p. 28.
(112) [1968] 1 All E.R. 1064; [1968] 1 W.L.R. 457.
(113) [1965] 3 All E.R. 363; [1965] P. 478.

A

S. & U. STORES, LTD. v. LEE.

[Queen's Bench Division (Lord Parker, C.J., Melford Stevenson and Blain, JJ.),
March 12, 1969.]

B

*Master and Servant—Wages—Remuneration—Salary plus expenses—Expenses
in respect of car provided by employee—Expenses included in remuneration
—Contracts of Employment Act 1963 (c. 49), Sch. 2, para. 3 (2).*

The respondent was required by his employers, the appellants, to provide
a car for his own use for business purposes. The appellants contracted to
pay him £5 per week for expenses in connection with the car. On the question
whether the £5 was part of his remuneration for the purposes of para. 3 (2)
of Sch. 2* to the Contracts of Employment Act 1963,

C

Held: the £5 was properly included in his remuneration for that purpose
(see p. 419, letters F and G, post).

Per Blain, J.: " Remuneration " is not mere payment for work done, but
is what the doer expects to get as the result of the work he does insofar as
what he expects to get is quantified in terms of money (see p. 419, letter D,

D

post).

Appeal dismissed.

[As to remuneration under the Contracts of Employment Act 1963, Sch. 2,
see Supplement to 25 Halsbury's Laws (3rd Edn.), para. 945a, 8.

As to computation of remuneration, see 38 Halsbury's Laws (3rd Edn.) 445,
446, para. 763.

E

For the Contracts of Employment Act 1963, Sch. 2, para. 3, see 43 Halsbury's
Statutes (2nd Edn.) 288.]

Appeal.

This was an appeal by way of motion by the appellants, S. & U. Stores, Ltd.,
who moved for an order that the decision of the Industrial Tribunal given on
2nd October 1968, awarding the respondent, Graham Charles Lee, a redundancy

F

payment of £183 2s. 9d. should be varied to a payment of £147 1s. 9d. The facts
are set out in the judgment of Blain, J.

The cases noted below† were cited during the argument.

D. N. R. Latham for the appellants.
J. L. Williams for the respondent.

G

BLAIN, J.: This is an appeal from a decision of the Industrial Tribunal
under the Redundancy Payments Act 1965 sitting at Cardiff, an appeal by the
appellants, a company known as S. & U. Stores, Ltd., of Birmingham with what
was described as a nation-wide business. They had an office based in Cardiff
where the respondent employee, Mr. Graham Charles Lee, was described as
office manager. One issue that does not come before this court was whether he

H

was in fact dismissed at all within the terms of the Act, and that of course was
resolved in his favour, which gives rise to the second issue, namely what is the
proper quantum of redundancy payment.

Under s. 1 of the Redundancy Payments Act 1965, where an employee is
dismissed by reason of redundancy, subject to certain irrelevant provisions, he
is entitled to a redundancy payment to be quantified as provided in Sch. 1 to

I

that Act. Paragraph 5 of Sch. 1 provides that:

". . . . the amount of a week's pay [and it is by reference to a week's
pay that the quantum has to be decided] shall, subject to the following
provisions of this paragraph, and except as may be otherwise provided by
regulations made by the Minister, be taken to be the minimum remuneration

---

* Schedule 2, para. 3 (2) is set out at p. 418, letter E, post.
† *R.* v. *Postmaster-General* (1876), 1 Q.B.D. 658;　*on appeal* (1878), 3 Q.B.D. 428;
Lyford v. *Turquand* (1966), 1 I.T.R. 554.

P

to which the employee would in the week ending with the relevant date have
been entitled, under Schedule 2 of the Contracts of Employment Act 1963
. . ."

if certain conditions were fulfilled.

I look at the Contracts of Employment Act 1963; under s. 4 of that Act it is
provided that:

" Not later than thirteen weeks after the beginning of an employee's
period of employment with an employer, the employer shall give to the
employee a written statement identifying the parties, specifying the date
when the employment began, and giving the following particulars of the
terms of employment as at a specified date not more than one week before
the statement is given . . ."

Then there are set out what have to be particularised and the only relevant
paragraph in my view for the purposes of considering this matter is para. (a):
" the scale or rate of remuneration, or the method of calculating remuneration."
The method of calculating remuneration is a relevant matter, whether it be
compounded of one or more elements, or whether there be a direct or some more
complicated form of calculation. Turning to the schedule in question, Sch. 2,
para. 3 (2) is the appropriate one for the purposes of para. 5 (1) of Sch. 1 to the
Redundancy Payments Act 1965. Paragraph 3 (2) of Sch. 2 to the Contracts
of Employment Act 1963 provides:

" For each week of the period of notice the employer shall be liable to
pay the employee a sum not less than his average weekly rate of remuneration [" remuneration " is the keyword] in the period of twelve weeks ending
with the last complete week before the notice was given."

What happened in the particular case was this, that the tribunal found that
this was a case, and there is no doubt about it, where there were no normal
working hours for the respondent, that his remuneration had to be averaged out
over the 12 weeks' period, and that it having been agreed that his employment
with the appellants, or their predecessors having begun about November 1960
and not having been broken, he was entitled to four weeks' notice and the period
of 12 weeks for which the calculation was to be made was thereby arrived at.
The tribunal find:

" He has proved slightly less than 8 years' service and was aged 41 on the
relevant date. He is therefore entitled to seven times his average week's
pay, the basic £22 plus £4 0s. 3d. . . ."

and an inaccurate multiplication by seven—they make it £183 2s. 9d. The
inaccuracy is one guinea. The question is as to the identity of what was there
described as the basic £22. In fact it was composed of two elements; it was
composed of £17, which in a lower grade of employment might be called wages,
but in his position might be called salary, and it is in any case convenient to
call directly " pay ", as the first element; and a contractually agreed figure of
£5 a week described as for " expenses " in connection with the use of his own
motor car.

It was essential, and this is not in issue, that for the proper performance of
his duties he should have the use of a motor car. The contract contemplated,
not (as sometimes happens), that the appellants would provide one for him
and perhaps pay the bills, but the contract contemplated the use of his own car,
whatever car he might have or choose to have at any particular time, and subject
to the circumstances or his whim he might have chosen to do his duty to the
appellants in a brand new chauffeur driven Rolls-Royce, or in a secondhand
Mini car. That was not a matter into which the appellants enquired. As part
of the contract of employment they contracted to pay him £5 of the total £22
said to be for expenses in connection with a car, and it could be (this court does
not know and the tribunal would not have known) that there may have been

A   weeks in which he made a profit, there may have been weeks in which he made a loss, there may have been weeks in which he even chose to travel by some other means of transport, or was able to obtain a free lift from some friend going in the same direction.   That was not a matter that concerned the appellants at all.

     The question, therefore, is whether the term " remuneration " in an agreement
B   as between the appellants and the respondent in those circumstances, and being the term found in para. 3 (2) of Sch. 2 to the Contracts of Employment Act 1963, included that sum of £5 a week or not.   It was suggested on behalf of the appellants that it did not, on the basis that it was not part of his pay; that it was no doubt for convenience, perhaps his tax position, that he should be paid it with that name attached to it instead of the whole £22 being called salary
C   or some such term.   So far as the appellants were concerned, that makes no difference whatever.   So far as the tax position is concerned, that would be a matter to which they were no party and res inter alios acta, it would be a matter between the respondent and the inspector of taxes (if indeed it was a matter for the inspector of taxes to be shown at all).   In my view the meaning of the word " wages " is direct payment related directly to the work done, so perhaps in
D   a higher sphere of employment the word " salary " would mean, subject to the particular context, direct payment for work done.   " Remuneration " is not mere payment for work done, but is what the doer expects to get as the result of the work he does insofar as what he expects to get is quantified in terms of money.   It might be that it could go wider than that, but that does not arise in respect of this particular case.   It is not suggested that it goes so far as
E   emoluments, where, to give an example, counsel for the respondent has put forward a clergyman who may get, within the scope of his emoluments, something that is not paid by those who pay his salary or remuneration.   He may get that from members of the congregation, the Easter offering, marriage fees and things of that sort.   The court does not have to consider in this context anything so wide as emoluments.

F   The sole question is whether " remuneration " includes in this particular case something more than mere salary or wages.   It seems to me, speaking for myself, that this was part of what the respondent, received from the appellants as part of the contractual consideration for the work that he did for them, and that is sufficient to satisfy me that it comes within para. 3 (2) of Sch. 2 to the Contracts of Employment Act 1963.   For that reason I would dismiss this
G   appeal.

     MELFORD STEVENSON, J.: I agree.

     LORD PARKER, C.J.: I also agree.

                                                              Appeal dismissed.

     Solicitors: *Burton, Yeates & Hart*, agents for *Edge & Ellison*, Birmingham
H   (for the appellants); *Kinch & Richardson*, agents for *Allen Pratt & Geldard*, Cardiff (for the respondent).

                         [*Reported by* N. P. Metcalfe, Esq., *Barrister-at-Law.*]

BEECHES WORKINGMEN'S CLUB AND INSTITUTE TRUSTEES *v.* SCOTT.

[COURT OF APPEAL, CIVIL DIVISION (Lord Denning, M.R., Edmund Davies and Phillimore, L.JJ.), February 14, 1969.]

Res Judicata—Friendly society—Property—Workingmen's club—Complaint against steward for withholding or misapplying property—Complaint dismissed—Action commenced by club for payment of deficiency—Whether adjudication of magistrates bar to action in contract—Friendly Societies Act 1896 (59 & 60 Vict. c. 25), s. 87 (3).

The dismissal of a complaint by a workingmen's club against a steward for withholding or misapplying property under s. 87 (3) of the Friendly Societies Act 1896 does not create an estoppel against a claim by the club based on contract for the payment by the steward of any deficiency in cash or stock.

Appeal allowed.

[As to withholding and misapplying of property of a friendly society, see 18 HALSBURY'S LAWS (3rd Edn.) 110, 111, para. 228.

For the Friendly Societies Act 1896, s. 87, see 10 HALSBURY'S STATUTES (2nd Edn.) 576.]

Appeal.

This was an appeal by the plaintiffs, the trustees of the Beeches Workingmen's Club and Institute, from a judgment of His Honour JUDGE OULD, given on 1st May 1968 at the Pontefract County Court, dismissing the plaintiffs' action against Wilfred Derrick Scott, the steward of the club, for a deficiency of stock and cash amounting to £130 14s. 5d. on the ground that the issue between the parties had been litigated before a magistrates' court on a prosecution of the defendant under s. 87 (3) of the Friendly Societies Act 1896, when the complaint was dismissed. The facts are set out in the judgment of LORD DENNING, M.R.

Raymond Kidwell, Q.C., and *John Griffiths* for the plaintiffs.
David Wagstaff for the defendant.

LORD DENNING, M.R.: The defendant was the steward of a workingmen's club. In October 1967 a complaint was taken out before the magistrates against him alleging that he had withheld certain property of the club in his possession, namely, the sum of £130 14s. 5d., contrary to s. 87 of the Friendly Societies Act 1896. The magistrates dismissed the complaint. Afterwards, the plaintiffs, the trustees of the club sued him in a civil action in the county court. They relied on a clause in his agreement by which he was—

"... to pay on demand or allow in account to the Club a sum equal to any deficiency of cash or stock which may be found in taking stock."

They said there was a deficiency of £130 14s. 5d., and claimed payment of that sum. The defendant put in a defence, in the course of which he referred to the earlier complaint before the magistrates. He said that that complaint had been dismissed and that the plaintiffs were estopped from raising the matter a second time. This plea was considered as a preliminary point. The county court judge held that that plea was good. The plaintiffs appeal to this court.

I think the plea is bad for a very simple reason. The issues in the civil action are quite different from the issues in the magistrates' court. In order to substantiate a complaint in the magistrates' court, it must be shown that the steward has "withheld" or "misapplied" property in his possession. If he has done it fraudulently he can be convicted and fined as on a criminal matter, see s. 87 of the Act of 1896. If he has not done it fraudulently, an order can be made against him to deliver up the property or repay the money, see s. 9 of the amending Act, the Friendly Societies Act 1908. But, in either case, it only applies where he has "withheld" or "misapplied" property. If he has not withheld or

A misapplied any property, he should be acquitted and no order should be made against him.   A typical case is when there is a deficiency which is not due to any " withholding " or " misapplying " by him, but is due to the action of third persons.   Someone else without his knowledge may have taken money from the till.   Other people may have surreptitiously had drinks without paying for them.   Such actions by third persons would give rise to a " deficiency " on

B the cash or stocks, but he would not be guilty of " withholding " or " misapplying " any property.   He would not be liable in a magistrates' court to any order.   But he is liable under a contract which makes him liable to pay any " deficiency " of cash or stock; and he can be sued for it in the county court.   The issues being so entirely different, it is clear there is no estoppel.   I am afraid the judge was in error.   The appeal should be allowed and the action

C proceed to trial on the other issues in the case.

EDMUND DAVIES, L.J.: I agree.

PHILLIMORE, L.J.: I also agree.

Appeal allowed; action remitted.

D Solicitors: *Hewitt, Woollacott & Chown,* agents for *Carter, Bentley & Gundill,* Pontefract (for the plaintiffs); *Hartley & Worstenholme,* Pontefract (for the defendant).

[*Reported by* F. GUTTMAN, Esq., *Barrister-at-Law.*]

E

ANGLO-AFRICAN MERCHANTS, LTD. AND ANOTHER
v. BAYLEY.

[QUEEN'S BENCH DIVISION (Megaw, J.), February 5, 6, 7, 10, 11, 24, 1969.]

F

Insurance—Proposal—Duty of assured to disclose material facts—Nature and age of goods material—" New men's clothes in bales for export "—Government surplus goods described in trade as new—Nature and age of goods not brought to attention of insurer—Insurer not put on enquiry by description of goods.

G *Insurance—Broker—Appointment of assessors by broker at request of insurer—Non-disclosure to assured—Breach of duty by broker.*

The plaintiff companies wished to obtain insurance cover against all risks for a quantity of army surplus clothing, viz., unused leather jerkins about 23 years old, which they intended for resale to buyers abroad; pending export contracts, the goods were to be stored in a warehouse.   The plaintiffs

H instructed a firm of brokers and informed D. (a director of the firm) that the goods were government surplus, that they were leather jerkins, and in response to a query whether they were secondhand, that they were new; D. communicated with a second firm of brokers (" the G. firm ") and informed a director of that firm only that the goods were " new men's clothes in bales for export "; this information was then passed on to M., a Lloyd's broker

I (employed by the G. firm or an associated company), who made out a slip for the insurable interest which described the clothing in those words, and took it to a member of a Lloyd's underwriting syndicate, who initialled the slip on behalf of his syndicate (" the insurer ") for $33\frac{1}{3}$ per cent. of the £40,000 cover requested.   The remaining amount was accepted later that day by other underwriters, and the policy was issued to the plaintiffs in accordance with the wording on the slip.   A portion of the clothing was stolen from the warehouse.   The plaintiffs claimed on the policy and the insurer repudiated liability.

Held: the plaintiffs' claim failed for non-disclosure of material facts,   A
because—

(i) the facts that the goods were war surplus and that they were more
than 20 years old were material facts which should have been disclosed
(see p. 426, letter E, post);

(ii) even though in the clothing trade the goods were never described as   B
" new " unless they were government surplus and were unused, that special
connotation of the word " new " (whether with or without the addition of
the words " in bales ") could not be said to have brought it to the attention
of an ordinary, prudent, insurer that the goods which he was asked to
insure under the description of " new men's clothes in bales for export "
were, or might be expected to be, government surplus clothes (see p. 426,
letter I, to p. 427, letter A, post);   C

(iii) even if it could properly be said that an insurer waived his right to
complain of non-disclosure if he had received information which would put
an ordinary, careful, insurer on enquiry and nevertheless failed to enquire,
a normally prudent insurer would not have been put on enquiry as to the
precise nature of the goods by reason of seeing them described as " new
men's clothes in bales for export " (see p. 427, letters D to F, post).   D

Per MEGAW, J.: when a claim arises, it is asserted that an insurer may,
and commonly does, instruct the insurance broker who placed the insurance
to obtain a report from assessors as to the claim: the broker is, apparently,
entitled to accept these instructions without a by-your-leave from his
principal, the assured, and without the principal being told by the agent
that he is accepting instructions from the adverse or potentially adverse,   E
party (see p. 428, letter H, post). If an insurance broker, before he accepts
instructions to place an insurance, discloses to his client that he wishes
to be free to act in the way suggested, and if the would-be assured, fully
informed as to the broker's intention to accept such instructions from the
insurer and as to the possible implication of such collaboration between
his agent and the opposite party, is prepared to agree that the broker may so   F
act, good and well; in the absence of such express and fully informed
consent, in my opinion it would be a breach of duty on the part of the
insurance broker so to act (see p. 429, letters D and E, post).

[As to the general duty to make disclosure and as to determining what facts
are material, see 22 HALSBURY'S LAWS (3rd Edn.) 186-190, paras. 356, 357, 360,
363; as to the materiality of special circumstances in marine insurance, and as   G
to waiver of information not disclosed, see ibid., pp. 113-118, paras. 205, 208-212,
215; for cases on the duty to disclose material facts and on waiver, see 29 DIGEST
(Repl.) 63-65, *177-205*, and 191-197, *1304-1370*.

As to the position of insurance brokers and their relationship to the assured,
see 22 HALSBURY'S LAWS (3rd Edn.) 40, 48, paras. 65, 80, 81, and ibid., pp. 201,
202, para. 382; and for cases on the subject, see 29 DIGEST (Repl.) 71, *233-239*.   H

As to the effect of usage or custom on the relationship between principal and
agent, see 1 HALSBURY'S LAWS (3rd Edn.) 168, para. 393, 182, para. 425,
217, para. 493.]

Cases referred to:

Fullwood v. Hurley, [1928] 1 K.B. 498; [1927] All E.R. Rep. 610; 96 L.J.K.B.
    976; 138 L.T. 49; 1 Digest (Repl.) 546, *1699*.   I

Greenhill v. Federal Insurance Co., Ltd., [1927] 1 K.B. 65; 95 L.J.K.B. 717;
    135 L.T. 244; 24 Lloyd L.R. 383; 29 Digest (Repl.) 198, *1384*.

Rozanes v. Bowen (1928), 32 Lloyd L.R. 98; 29 Digest (Repl.) 65, *194*.

Action.

By a specially endorsed writ dated 5th February 1968, the plaintiffs, Anglo-
African Merchants, Ltd., and Exmouth Clothing Co., Ltd., associated family
companies, claimed payment from the defendant, James Francis Leslie Bayley,

A who was sued on his own behalf and on behalf of all other members of his syndicate under an all-risks insurance policy issued on 19th June 1967 by a Lloyd's Underwriters' syndicate of which the defendant was a member. The facts are set out in the judgment.

The cases noted below* were cited during the argument in addition to those referred to in the judgment.

B *John Wilmers*, Q.C., and *C. S. Staughton* for the plaintiffs.
F. M. Drake, Q.C., and *P. G. Langdon-Davies* for the defendant.

Cur. adv. vult.

24th February. **MEGAW, J.**, read the following judgment: The plaintiffs are two associated family companies. Mr. Marcel Rosen is a director of both.
C The interest of the first-named plaintiff company, Anglo-African Merchants, Ltd., in these proceedings is purely technical. It is the second-named plaintiff company, Exmouth Clothing Co., Ltd., which is effectively concerned. That company has been in business since 1945. Its trade throughout that time has been in second-hand and government surplus clothes, almost entirely for export.

In January 1967 Mr. Rosen, on behalf of the second plaintiffs, tendered for a
D quantity of government surplus clothing. The goods in question were leather jerkins, lying packed in bales, in the ordnance depot at Bicester. At the relevant time all these jerkins were at least 20 years old, though they were unused. Mr. Rosen succeeded in his tender for 20,500 of the jerkins, for which he paid £34,825. Mr. Rosen's intention was to find buyers abroad for these goods and to ship them abroad accordingly. Meanwhile, he wished to hold them in store. This
E involved removing the goods from Bicester and storing them in London, pending export contracts being made and carried out. ·

Ultimately, on 3rd April 1967, the jerkins were brought to London and placed in store with a company called Power Packing Services, Ltd. They were insured under a Lloyd's policy subscribed by syndicates concerned with the underwriting of marine risks. The insurance was treated as being marine because, although
F the policy was on goods in warehouse in England, the goods were in warehouse with a view to ultimate export. The defendant, Mr. James Francis Leslie Bayley, is a member of one of the subscribing Lloyd's syndicates and is sued both on his own behalf and as representing all other members of his syndicate. The other syndicates concerned in the policy, have, I assume, agreed to be bound by the result of this action.

G The policy is in the usual form. It is dated 19th June 1967, but it covers the period of three months from 7th April 1967 to 6th July 1967. That cover was thereafter extended for a further three months to 6th October 1967. For a premium of £115 (covering the original three months) the insurance was against " all risks of whatever nature and howsoever arising " in the sum of £40,000 on:

H " New Men's Clothes in Bales for Export whilst at the premises of Power Packing, Limited, 28, Tidal Basin Road, London E.16 including transit from the Assured's premises."

Between April and October 1967 some of the bales of jerkins were sold by Mr. Rosen on behalf of his company and were exported. 412 bales remained, or should have remained, in the premises of Power Packing Services, Ltd. Before

I * *Carter* v. *Boehm* (1766), 3 Burr. 1905; [1558-1774] All E.R. Rep. 183; *Lindenau* v. *Desborough* (1828), 8 B. & C. 586; [1824-34] All E.R. Rep. 117; *Wheelton* v. *Hardisty* (1858), 8 E. & B. 232, 285; *Bates* v. *Hewitt* (1867), L.R. 2 Q.B. 595; *Laing* v. *Union Marine Insurance Co.* (1895), 1 Com. Cas. 11; *Joel* v. *Law Union and Crown Insurance Co.*, [1908] 2 K.B. 863; *Dunn* v. *Campbell* (1920), 4 Lloyd L.R. 36; *Anderson* v. *Scrutton*, [1934] S.A., S.R. 10; *A/S. Ocean* v. *Black Sea & Baltic General Insurance Co.* (1935), 51 Lloyd L.R. 305; *Bank Melli Iran* v. *Barclays Bank*, (D.C.O.), Ltd., [1951] 2 Lloyd's Rep. 367; *Morris Motors, Ltd.* v. *Lilley*, [1959] 3 All E.R. 737; [1959] 1 W.L.R. 1184; *Morris Motors, Ltd.* v. *Phelan*, [1960] 2 All E.R. 208; [1960] 1 W.L.R. 352; *De Maurier (Jewels), Ltd.* v. *Bastion Insurance Co., Ltd.*, [1967] 2 Lloyd's Rep. 550; 117 New L.J. 1112.

5th October 1967, at some unknown date, 245 bales disappeared. Each bale **A**
contained 25 jerkins. Mr. Rosen learned of their disappearance on 5th October
and notified the loss to his insurance brokers on 6th October 1967. It is now
agreed that the value of the goods lost, and the amount which the plaintiffs
would be entitled to recover if they have a valid claim under the insurance
policy, is £11,500. The proportion for which the defendant's syndicate is
responsible is ⅓ of that sum—£3,833 6s. 8d.   **B**

Liability under the policy was denied by underwriters. The grounds, and
the only grounds, on which liability is now denied are set out in para. 4 of the
points of defence, and part of para. (a) of the particulars thereunder, as follows:

"4. At the time when the Plaintiffs requested the Defendants to issue
the said Policy of Insurance, and before the Policy was issued, the Plaintiffs **C**
misrepresented to and concealed from the Defendants material facts affecting
the goods to be insured and the risk insured against.

"Particulars. (a) The plaintiffs represented that the goods to be insured
were 'New Men's Clothes in Bales for Export . . .' In fact the goods to be
insured were old men's clothes, not less than about 23 years old, being army
surplus goods manufactured during the Second World War." **D**

It should be made clear at the outset that there is no suggestion whatever that
this is a dishonest claim. There is no suggestion that there was not a genuine
loss of the jerkins in the 245 bales during the period covered by the policy as
extended. There is no suggestion that Mr. Rosen was dishonest in anything
which he said or did not say in connection with the obtaining of the insurance
policy. There is no suggestion that Mr. Rosen was anything other than truthful **E**
in the evidence which he gave, whether or not his evidence is in all respects
accurate. I am satisfied that he was an honest witness. If the defence depended
on dishonesty on the part of the plaintiffs it would wholly fail. The defence
does not, however, depend on an assertion of dishonesty. It depends essentially
on the allegation that, however complete and accurate may have been the
information regarding the goods to be insured which Mr. Rosen provided to his **F**
insurance brokers, the information as to the goods which was actually supplied
to underwriters when they accepted the risk was inaccurate and incomplete
in material respects; and that therefore they are entitled to disclaim liability.

As is inevitable when an insurance is sought to be placed at Lloyd's, the
would-be assured was not in direct contact with underwriters. In this case there
were two intermediaries between Mr. Rosen and the underwriters. In circum- **G**
stances which I need not narrate, Mr. Rosen instructed a firm of insurance
brokers, Wilson Dean, Ltd. The director of that company with whom Mr.
Rosen dealt was Mr. William Davis. Mr. Davis got in touch with other
insurance brokers, Sir William Garthwaite (Home and Overseas), Ltd.; his
contact there was Mr. James Leonard Evans, a director of that company.
Through a Lloyd's broker, Mr. Mew, employed by that company or by an **H**
associated company—it matters not which for present purposes—this insurance
was thereafter placed with Lloyd's underwriters.

Mr. Rosen, Mr. Davis and Mr. Evans have given evidence, the two former
called by the plaintiffs, the latter by the defendant. It has been accepted
throughout the hearing (as I now understand) that Wilson Dean, Ltd., and therefore Mr. Davis, were acting as agents for the plaintiffs in placing this insurance. **I**
There has been controversy, to which I shall have to refer later, whether Mr.
Evans and his company, and Mr. Mew, were acting as agents for the plaintiffs or
for underwriters or both. I hold—and in the end counsel for the plaintiffs was
unable to put forward arguments to the contrary, though he did not abandon
the point—that these persons were also acting for the plaintiffs in the placing of
the insurance.

There has been evidence, to the admission of which objection was not taken
(and, I think, in the circumstances rightly not taken), of conversations between

A Mr. Rosen and Mr. Davis and between Mr. Davis and Mr. Evans.   I shall express, as succinctly as I can, my findings as to what was said in those conversations, so far as I regard such findings as being relevant to the issues which I have to decide in this action.   It is obvious that in certain events there is the possibility of litigation hereafter between the plaintiffs and one or other or both of the firms of brokers, though no steps, for some reason, have been taken to join them

B as parties in this present action.   I shall, therefore, be particularly careful not to express any views, unless it is essential for the present action so to do, on matters which might have to be decided hereafter involving persons who are not parties to this action.   Insofar as it is necessary for me to express conclusions on matters which might be relevant in other litigation hereafter, persons who are not parties to this action are, of course, in no way bound by my findings in this action.

C Mr. Rosen, in his conversation with Mr. Davis when he first asked Wilson Dean, Ltd., to try to effect this insurance, gave Mr. Davis all the information which he, Mr. Rosen, thought was or might be material for the purpose of the insurance.   That information included the fact that the goods were government surplus; that they were leather jerkins; and, in answer to a question by Mr. Davis whether they were secondhand, that they were new.   When Mr. Davis

D spoke to Mr. Evans, all that Mr. Davis told Mr. Evans about the goods themselves was that which subsequently appeared in the policy, as I have already mentioned: namely, " new men's clothes in bales for export ".   Mr. Davis did not mention to Mr. Evans anything about " government surplus " or the fact that the clothes were leather jerkins.   Mr. Evans passed on to Mr. Mew the information which he had received from Mr. Davis.   Mr. Mew went to Lloyd's having made out a slip

E in which, against the printed word " Interest ", appeared the selfsame words as thereafter were included in the policy:

"£40,000 on New Men's Clothes in Bales for Export whilst at the premises of Power Packing, Limited, 28, Tidal Basin Road, London, E.16, including transit from the [Plaintiffs'] premises.   To cover against all risks for loss or damage however arising."

F Mr. Mew took the slip to Mr. I. R. D. Gibson, a member of the syndicate of which the representative defendant is also a member.   Mr. Gibson raised a number of queries with Mr. Mew.   None of them related to the nature or description of the goods.   When thereafter—a delay occurred for reasons which I need not go into—Mr. Mew came back again with the slip and with answers to Mr.

G Gibson's questions which satisfied him, he, on 7th April, initialled the slip on behalf of his syndicate, for 33⅓ per cent.   The remaining 66⅔ per cent. was thereafter that day accepted by other underwriters.   In due course the policy was issued, to accord with the slip.

There can be no doubt on the evidence that a representation was made to the underwriters on behalf of the plaintiffs that the goods to be insured were " new

H men's clothes in bales for export ".   There can be no doubt that underwriters were not told that the goods were government surplus goods, or army surplus goods.   There can be no doubt that they were not told that the goods had been manufactured at least 20 years earlier.

There has been argument before me and citation of authority as to the nature and extent of the duty of disclosure in the making of a contract of insurance.

I I need not go into the authorities because, as I understand it, there is not, and cannot be, any doubt as to certain propositions which are decisive on the facts of this case.   First, there may be scope for debate as to the availability of the defence of non-disclosure where the assured does not know of the existence of the fact or facts which have not been disclosed.   Questions may arise as to the position if those facts were known to his agents in the placing of the insurance, or if they are facts which a reasonable man in the position of the assured would have known, or if they are facts which he could have ascertained by some degree or other of diligence and enquiry.   In the present case, I need not pursue

those interesting topics, for there is no doubt that Mr. Rosen himself well knew A
that the goods were army surplus and that they were at least 20 years old.

Next, there may perhaps be scope for debate as to the effect on the defence
of non-disclosure if the assured did not realise, and should not as a reasonable
man have realised, that facts of which he knew might reasonably be regarded
as being material by a normal, prudent underwriter. If, however, the assured
knew of facts, and if as a reasonable man he should have realised that knowledge B
of those facts might be—not necessarily would be, but might be—regarded
as material by a normal prudent underwriter, then, if those facts are not disclosed and if they would have been material, the defence of non-disclosure
prevails. The position may be more favourable to insurers than is indicated in
that proposition. I am satisfied that it is not less favourable. It is an a fortiori
case if the assured not merely ought as a reasonable man to have realised, but C
actually did realise, that the facts of which he had knowledge might be regarded
as material.

On Mr. Rosen's own evidence I am satisfied that he himself realised that it
might be regarded by potential insurers as material to know that the goods were
war surplus. That is why he gave the information to Mr. Davis, when he first
asked Mr. Davis to place the insurance. I am also satisfied on the evidence that D
a reasonable man would have realised that it might well be material to underwriters to know, not only that the goods were war surplus, but also, at any rate
in relation to a request for all risks insurance, that the leather jerkins were at
least 20 years old. Having considered the whole of the evidence on this aspect,
I am also satisfied that each of these matters—the fact that the goods were war
surplus and their age—was a fact which was material: it would have affected E
the mind of a prudent underwriter in deciding whether to underwrite the risk
at all, in deciding what limitations he might wish to impose as to the risks to
be covered, in deciding what premium to quote and in deciding whether or not
to require an inspection of, and report on, the goods or the place where they
were being stored or both. In particular, in relation to the fact of war surplus,
I am satisfied that underwriters, rightly or wrongly, but not unreasonably, F
regard war surplus goods, or at any rate war surplus clothing, as being goods
which they classify as " hot ": that is, involving an abnormally high risk of theft.
In relation to the age of the goods, underwriters would normally and reasonably
be concerned with the possibility of defects, such as staining, in respect of which
claims might be made and it might be a matter of great difficulty and dispute
to ascertain when the damage was in fact sustained; unless, of course, a pre- G
insurance inspection were to be required as a condition of accepting the risk.

Much evidence was given and argument offered as to the meaning of the word
" new ", with particular reference to the clothing trade. Of course, it is not a
question of the meaning of the word in isolation: it is a question of its meaning
in the context of a request for insurance of goods which are described as being
" new men's clothes in bales for export ". The defendant contended that to H
describe 20-year-old leather jerkins as " new " was a misdescription; a corollary,
as it were, of the non-disclosure that the goods were 20 years old. The plaintiffs
contended on the other hand, that, so far from being a misdescription, the
use of the word " new " in this context indicated that the clothes were
government surplus clothes and that they were not of recent manufacture. The
plaintiffs also relied on that which they said was the connotation of the word I
" new " in this context for the purposes of their submission as to waiver by
underwriters of their entitlement to be apprised of material facts.

The gist of the evidence is that in the clothing trade goods are never described
as " new " (for example, in invoices or advertisements or other trade documents)
unless they are government surplus goods. If they are government surplus
goods, and are unused, they may be described as " new ", despite the fact that
they are not of recent manufacture. I accept that evidence, but I do not, on
the whole of the evidence, accept the proposition that this special connotation

A of the word " new ", whether with or without the addition of the words " in bales ", ought to have brought it to the attention of an ordinary, prudent underwriter that the goods which he was asked to insure under the description of "new men's clothes in bales for export " were, or might reasonably be expected to be, government surplus clothes, or old clothes, in the sense that they were manufactured at least 20 years previously.

B By an amendment of their points of reply, for which leave was asked and granted after the evidence had been concluded, the plaintiffs seek to assert that a reasonable underwriter would have been put on enquiry by the description " new men's clothes in bales for export "; that such enquiry would have revealed that the goods were army surplus; that Mr. Gibson, though he made other enquiries, failed to make any enquiry as to the precise nature of the goods

C and that the defendant thus "waived further information on the precise nature of the goods ". Let me assume in favour of the plaintiffs that an insurer waives his right to complain of non-disclosure, if he has received information which would put an ordinarily careful insurer on enquiry and nevertheless fails to enquire. That is put by SARGANT, L.J., as the minimum required for a successful plea of waiver in *Greenhill* v. *Federal Insurance Co., Ltd.* (1). SCRUTTON, L.J.,

D in his judgment in the same case (2) clearly regards the law on this point as much more favourable to insurers. Even on the assumption of the most lenient test, I cannot hold on the evidence that a normally prudent insurer would have been put on enquiry as to the precise nature of the goods by reason of seeing them described as " new men's clothes in bales for export ". Some underwriters might be alerted by the word " new " to make enquiries, because they would

E realise that it is an unusual adjective to apply to clothes. More underwriters, I think, would take the attitude which Mr. Gibson took: the goods are described as " new "; they are new; they are not clothes which were manufactured years ago; they are not government surplus, which is normally some distance away from having been newly manufactured when it is sold as surplus. I do not think that that attitude can properly be said to show any

F lack of care or prudence; or that failure to enquire could give rise to a valid claim of waiver. The claim therefore fails.

There is, however, another matter with which I am bound to deal, even though in the end it does not affect the result of this case. It involves the legal position, the rights and duties of insurance brokers.

The plaintiffs have asserted, and by their amended points of reply have

G reiterated the assertion, that Sir William Garthwaite (Home & Overseas), Ltd.— I shall call them " Garthwaites "—and Mr. Evans, and Mr. Mew, employed by that company or an associated company, were acting as agents, not of the plaintiffs, the assured, but of the defendant underwriters. This assertion was put forward, not as involving a general principle, but as being related to the special facts of this case: namely, events which had occurred, at the instance of the

H defendant's solicitors, with regard to discovery after this action had been commenced. In his final speech, counsel for the plaintiffs did not seek to adduce any argument in support of the contention, but he did not abandon it. I have therefore to deal with it. The answer put forward by counsel for the defendant, rebutting the suggestion that Garthwaites were agents for the defendant in the placing of this contract of insurance, in its turn raised a question of much wider

I and more general importance as to the position of insurance brokers. With that question also I must concern myself.

Both Wilson Dean, Ltd., and Garthwaites saw fit to make their files, with regard to this insurance, available to underwriters and to underwriters' solicitors. So far as Garthwaites are concerned, further, they refused to make their file

---

(1) [1927] 1 K.B. 65 at p. 89.
(2) [1927] 1 K.B. at pp. 85, 86.

available to the plaintiffs or to the plaintiffs' solicitors. This attitude, it should **A**
be said, was taken because the defendant's solicitors advised Garthwaites that it
was the right and proper attitude to take. The defendant's solicitors further
asserted in a letter to the plaintiffs' solicitors that Garthwaites were not the
plaintiffs' agents. The action taken with regard to the files cannot be justified;
and, indeed, counsel for the defendant did not seek to argue that it was correct;
though he maintained, as I shall have to mention hereafter, that certain docu- **B**
ments in Garthwaites' file were the property of the underwriters and that,
despite Garthwaites' position as agents for the assured, the assured were not
entitled to see documents in possession of their own agents.

I do not propose to go into all the complications which have bedevilled this
particular action as a result of these matters. In the end, the plaintiffs' advisers
have been enabled—though belatedly—to see all relevant documents which **C**
should have been available to them from, or before, the outset of the action;
they have not, in the end, been prejudiced by the belatedness of discovery
nor by the fact that documents which were in the possession of the plaintiffs'
agents were unjustifiably made available to the defendant and his advisers at
a time when the agents, acting on the advice of the solicitors for the opposite
party, were refusing them to their own principals and their principals' legal **D**
advisers. It is to be hoped that this sorry state of affairs will not arise again.

I cannot, however, leave this matter there. Counsel for the defendant conceded
that, in all matters relating to the placing of the insurance, the insurance broker
is the agent of the assured, and of the assured only. I do not think that this
proposition of law has ever been in doubt amongst lawyers. I hope it is not in
doubt amongst insurance brokers or insurers. More than 40 years ago, in **E**
Rozanes v. *Bowen* (3) SCRUTTON, L.J., said:

> " I agree, that in the case of marine insurance there is not the slightest
> doubt, and never has been the slightest doubt, that the broker is not the
> agent of the underwriter."

SCRUTTON, L.J., then went on to say that in his experience it would be quite **F**
wrong to say that this applies merely to marine insurance. Counsel for the
defendant, however, submitted, on instructions, that while this principle applies
to the placing of the policy (be it noted that SCRUTTON, L.J., expressed no such
limitation), yet when a claim arises under a policy the insurance broker who
placed the policy may thereupon become an agent of both parties in certain
respects. This, says counsel, is not merely the practice at Lloyd's; it is the prac- **G**
tice also in the non-Lloyd's insurance market in this country; indeed, it is said,
it is world-wide practice in the insurance business. When a claim arises, it is
asserted that the insurer—Lloyd's underwriters or other insurers—may, and
commonly does, instruct the insurance broker who placed the insurance to obtain
a report from assessors as to the claim. The broker is, apparently, entitled to
accept these instructions without a by-your-leave from his principal, the assured, **H**
and without the principal being told by the agent that he is accepting instructions
from the adverse, or potentially adverse, party. The assessors' report, unless it
contains allegations of fraud, goes from the assessors to the insurer via the
broker. The broker sees the report and keeps a copy on his file. But the broker
may not disclose the contents of the report to the assured or to the assured's
legal advisers, without the express consent of the insurer. The report is the **I**
insurer's document.

That practice was followed in the present case. There was a copy of such a
report in Garthwaites' file relating to this insurance. It was not made available
by Garthwaites to the assured. Privilege was claimed in respect of it against
the assured. That claim was persisted in until a very late stage of the hearing.

---

(3) (1928), 32 Lloyd L.R. 98 at p. 101.

A Indeed, though the document was at last made available to the plaintiffs out of their agent's file, this was, I think, claimed to be done as a matter of grace only.

The law, again, has been stated with clarity and precision in the judgment of SCRUTTON, L.J., in *Fullwood* v. *Hurley* (4):

B " No agent who has accepted an employment from one principal can in law accept an engagement inconsistent with his duty to the first principal, from a second principal, unless he makes the fullest disclosure to each principal of his interest, and obtains the consent of each principal to the double employment."

The principle is expressed in this way in BOWSTEAD ON AGENCY (13th Edn.)
C p. 144:

" . . . he may not act for both parties to a transaction unless he ensures that he fully discloses all the material facts to both parties and obtains their informed consent to his so acting . . . Any custom to the contrary will not be upheld."

D If an insurance broker, before he accepts instructions to place an insurance, discloses to his client that he wishes to be free to act in the way suggested, and if the would-be assured, fully informed as to the broker's intention to accept such instructions from the insurers and as to the possible implications of such collaboration between his agent and the opposite party, is prepared to agree that the broker may so act, good and well. In the absence of such express and
E fully informed consent, in my opinion it would be a breach of duty on the part of the insurance broker so to act. The potential dangers and undesirable consequences are obvious in any case where, as here, an agent permits himself, without the express consent of his principal, to make a compact with the opposite party whereby he is supplied with information which he is, or may be, precluded from passing on to his principal. Such a relationship with the insurer inevitably,
F even if wrongly, invites suspicion that the broker is hunting with the hounds whilst running with the hare. It readily leads to consequences such as occurred in this case where a broker refused to comply with a proper request from his principal's solicitors, but sought or accepted advice from the adverse party's solicitors as to how he should act vis-à-vis his principal. If the insurer desires to obtain an assessor's report, he can obtain it through some other channel
G than the assured's agent, the broker who has placed the insurance. If the insurer thinks it would be helpful in arriving at a fair and proper settlement of a claim that the assured's broker should see the whole or part of the assessor's report, he can disclose it to the broker; but not, in the absence of the express consent of the assured, subject to a condition that the agent shall withhold relevant information from his principal.

H It was said by counsel, on instructions, that the practice which he described is common knowledge, not only as being the practice of Lloyd's brokers, but as being general practice in the insurance market. I find it remarkable, if so, that there is no reference to it—none so far as I am aware, and none to which counsel could refer me—in any decided case or in any of the well-known text-books dealing with insurance law, some of which deal at length with the practice
I of the insurance market and the position of insurance brokers. Even if it were established to be a practice well-known to persons seeking insurance—not merely to insurers and brokers—I should hold the view, in conformity with the passage which I have cited from BOWSTEAD, that a custom will not be upheld by the courts of this country if it contradicts the vital principle that an agent may not at the same time serve two masters—two principals—in actual or potential

_____

(4) [1928] 1 K.B. 498 at p. 502; [1927] All E.R. Rep. 610 at p. 611.

opposition to one another: unless, indeed, he has the explicit, informed, consent **A** of both principals. An insurance broker is in no privileged position in this respect.

Judgment for the defendant.

Solicitors: *Paisner & Co.* (for the plaintiffs); *Herbert Baron & Co.* (for the defendant).

[*Reported by* K. DIANA PHILLIPS, *Barrister-at-Law.*] **B**

INLAND REVENUE COMMISSIONERS *v.* LAND SECURITIES **C**
INVESTMENT TRUST, LTD.

[HOUSE OF LORDS (Lord Reid, Lord Hodson, Lord Pearce, Lord Donovan and Lord Diplock), March 10, 11, 12, 13 and April 29, 1969.]

Profits Tax—Computation of profits—Deduction—Rentcharge—Whether income **D**
or capital payments—Rentcharges given as consideration for lessee's purchase
of lessor's interest—Purchaser a property investment company—Whether
rentcharges allowable deduction in computing lessee's profits for profits tax
purposes—Income Tax Act 1952 (15 & 16 Geo. 6 & 1 Eliz. 2 c. 10), s. 177.

The taxpayer company held long leases and subleases of varying duration from landlords who were a charity. The landlords sold to it the reversions **E** on the leases and subleases in consideration of rentcharges, payable in each case for ten years, amounting in the aggregate to £96,000 per annum, and the taxpayer company assumed liability for the headrents where the reversions so acquired were leasehold reversions. The annual payments thus undertaken by the taxpayer company involved a considerable increase over the total rents formerly paid by it in respect of the long leases and subleases. The taxpayer company deducted income tax at source relying on the **F** provisions of s. 177* of the Income Tax Act 1952 and in making up its profit and loss account debited the rentcharges as payments laid out wholly and exclusively for the purposes of its trade. The taxpayer company was assessed to profits tax on profits computed without deduction in respect of the rentcharges.

Held: although capital assets may be purchased by income payments, **G** and the deduction of income at source from the rentcharges and its retention by the taxpayer company may yield the same result for income tax purposes as though the rentcharges had been deducted in a profit and loss account and the deductions allowed, this did not necessarily qualify them as allowable deductions in computing the company's profits for profits tax purposes; accordingly, on ordinary principles of commercial accounting these rent- **H** charges were not to be debited against the incomings of the taxpayer company's trade, as a property investment company, for purposes of computing its liability to profits tax since the legal result of the purchases was that it purchased reversions which were capital assets in its hands (see p. 431, letters F and G, p. 432, letter G, p. 433, letter F, p. 433, letter I, to p. 434, letter A, and p. 434, letter G, *post*).

Appeal allowed. **I**

---

* Section 177, so far as material, provides: " (1) This section applies to the following payments, that is to say—(*a*) rents under long leases; and (*b*) any yearly interest, annuity, rent, rentcharge . . . or other annual payment reserved or charged upon land, . . . (2) Any payment to which this section applies shall, so far as it does not fall under any other Case of Schedule D, be charged with tax under Case VI of Schedule D and be subject to deduction of tax under Chapter 1 of this Part of this Act as if it were a royalty or other sum paid in respect of the user of a patent."

A   Decision of the COURT OF APPEAL ([1968] 3 All E.R. 33) reversed.

[As to deduction of annual payments in computing income for profits tax purposes, see 20 HALSBURY'S LAWS (3rd Edn.) 622, 623, para. 1214; and for cases on the subject, see 28 DIGEST (Repl.) 378, *1648, 1649,* and DIGEST (Cont. Vol. A) 908, *1649a.*

For the Income Tax Act 1952, s. 177, see 31 HALSBURY'S STATUTES (2nd Edn.)
B   175.]

Cases referred to:

Secretary of State in Council of India v. Scoble, [1903] A.C. 299; 72 L.J.K.B. 617; 89 L.T. 1; 4 Tax Cas. 618; 28 Digest (Repl.) 167, *672.*

Usher's Wiltshire Brewery, Ltd. v. *Bruce,* [1915] A.C. 433; 84 L.J.K.B. 417;
C   112 L.T. 651; 6 Tax Cas. 399; 28 Digest (Repl.) 77, *293.*

Vestey v. *Inland Revenue Comrs., Inland Revenue Comrs.* v. *Vestey,* [1961] 3 All E.R. 978; [1962] Ch. 861; [1962] 2 W.L.R. 221; 40 Tax Cas. 112; Digest (Cont. Vol. A) 902, *1548a.*

Appeal.

This was an appeal by the Inland Revenue Commissioners from an order of
D   the Court of Appeal (DANCKWERTS, SALMON and FENTON ATKINSON, L.JJ.) dated 20th May 1968 and reported [1968] 3 All E.R. 33, allowing an appeal by the taxpayer company, Land Securities Investment Trust, Ltd., from an order of CROSS, J., dated 11th December 1966, reported [1968] 1 All E.R. 955, restoring the determination of the Special Commissioners. The facts are set out in the opinion of LORD DONOVAN.

E   *Arthur Bagnall, Q.C., J. R. Phillips, Q.C., and P. W. Medd* for the Crown.
Heyworth Talbot, Q.C., and M. P. Nolan, Q.C. for the taxpayer company.

Their Lordships took time for consideration.

29th April.   The following opinions were delivered.

F   **LORD REID:** My Lords, I agree with the speech of my noble and learned friend, LORD DONOVAN. I would allow the appeal and remit the case as my noble and learned friend proposes.

LORD HODSON: My Lords, I have had the advantage of reading the opinion of my noble and learned friend, LORD DONOVAN, with which I agree.
G   I would allow the appeal.

LORD PEARCE: My Lords, I concur.

LORD DONOVAN: My Lords, the taxpayer company carries on business as a property investment company. It acquires properties for letting and makes its profits from the rentals received. These properties are its capital
H   assets. It does not buy and sell them as a property dealing concern would do.

In 1960 the taxpayer company purchased interests in a number of properties from the Church Commissioners. The consideration was expressed in the sale agreement as follows:

I   " 4.   THE consideration for the Transfers shall be the respective rent-charges described in Column five of the Schedule and the covenants on the part of the respective Purchasers for the payment of the said rentcharges."

The reference to " respective purchasers " is a reference to the taxpayer company and one of its wholly-owned subsidiaries, Associated London Properties, Ltd. This company bought one of the seven properties in question, but since it is grouped with its parent for the purposes of the assessments to tax under appeal, nothing turns on this feature of the case.

The " respective rentcharges " referred to in the sale agreement added up

to the gross sum of £96,000 per annum for ten years from 1st April 1959, charged   A
on and issuing out of the properties acquired.

When it came to pay the rentcharges in question to the Church Commissioners,
the taxpayer company deducted income tax at source, relying on the provisions
of s. 177 Income Tax Act 1952.   When it came to making up its profit and loss
account, it debited these rentcharges as though they were an expense of earning
its revenue.   B

From   what counsel for the taxpayer company told your Lordships it seems
reasonably clear that the Church Commissioners had some initial misgivings.
Being a charity, they would want to reclaim from the revenue the tax deducted
from the rentcharges.   If, however, s. 177 did not for any reason entitle the
taxpayer company to deduct tax at source, then the Church Commissioners in
reliance on the contract of sale would have to look to the taxpayer company to   C
make good the underpayment.   This may well be the explanation why, in the
litigation which has ensued concerning the taxpayer company's claim to deduct
these rentcharges as a business expense, so much emphasis has been put on the
question whether s. 177 applies to them.   It was put in the forefront of the
taxpayer company's case before the Special Commissioners: and one finds
DANCKWERTS, L.J., in the Court of Appeal (1) commencing his judgment by   D
saying:

" The question is simply whether certain rentcharges which were created
by the parties in regard to the relevant transactions are deductible under
the provisions of section 177 of the Income Tax Act, 1952 . . ."

(I read this as meaning whether income tax was deductible at source under   E
that section, for this is the only " deduction " with which the section deals.)

Yet I think all your Lordships are agreed that whether or not tax was so
deductible at source from these rentcharges is quite inconclusive of the question
whether they are deductible expenses in computing the company's taxable profits.
The Crown's argument before the House was that the true question is not the nature
of the rentcharges as receipts in the Church Commissioners' hands, but their   F
nature as disbursements by the taxpayer company, and the answer to the first
question does not provide the answer to the second.   I find myself doubting
whether the case could have been so put to the Court of Appeal (2);   otherwise I
think the tenor of the judgments there delivered would have been different.
For my part, I am content to assume, without expressly deciding, that these
rentcharges are income in the Church Commissioners' hands and are in their   G
entirety liable to deduction of tax at source under s. 177.   This, however, does
not, I repeat, necessarily qualify them as allowable deductions in computing the
taxpayer company's profits for tax purposes—which is the present issue.   It
falls to be decided in relation to assessments to profits tax made on the taxpayer
company for each of five chargeable accounting periods ending in 1964.   In
those assessments the Crown disallowed any deduction for the rentcharges   H
here in question.

Profits for the purpose of profits tax are computed on the same principles
as profits are computed for the purpose of Case I of Sch. D, subject to certain
adaptations, of which one is that the rule of Case I which prohibits the deduction
of annual payments in computing profits is excluded.   " Annual payments "
for this purpose would include the rentcharges here in question.   This does not   I
mean that they are automatically allowed as deductions.   For that purpose
they must still satisfy the other tests prescribed expressly or impliedly by the
rules of Case I of Sch. D.   (Finance Act 1937, s. 20 and Sch. 4, para. 4;   Finance
(No. 2) Act 1940, s. 14 (1);   Finance Act 1946, s. 44;   Income Tax Act 1952,
s. 137 (l) and (m) and s. 177.)

(1) [1968] 1 W.L.R. 1446 at p. 1452.
(2) [1968] 3 All E.R. 33;   [1968] 1 W.L.R. 1446.

A   The taxpayer company duly appealed against the aforesaid assessments claiming that the rentcharges were allowable deductions.   The Special Commissioners upheld the claim.   On appeal by the Crown by way of Case Stated CROSS, J. (3), reversed that decision.   The Court of Appeal (4), restored it, and the Crown now appeals to your Lordships.

The effect of the enactments which provide that profits for profits tax purposes
B   shall be computed on the same principles as profits are computed under Case I of Sch. D for income tax purposes (subject to certain adaptations) is that in the present case the taxpayer company in order to succeed must establish three things: 1. That the payments in question were wholly and exclusively laid out for the purposes of the taxpayer company's trade.   This is conceded. 2. That there is no enactment expressly prohibiting their deduction. This also is conceded.
C   3. That, applying the principles of ordinary commercial accounting, these rentcharges are proper items to debit against the company's incomings when computing its profits for profits tax purposes (*Usher's Wiltshire Brewery, Ltd.* v. *Bruce* (5)).   It is here that the conflict comes.

By the payments in question the taxpayer company acquired the freeholds of three properties of which it already had leases.   In the case of two others it
D   acquired a headlease, being already owner of an underlease.   In the case of one other, it acquired an underlease, being already owner of a sub-underlease. Its subsidiary company, Associated Properties, Ltd., acquired the freehold of a property of which it was already owner of a lease.

The rents payable by the taxpayer company and its subsidiary under their previous titles were admittedly deductions in computing their profit for the
E   purpose of profits tax.   When confronted with the Crown's contention that by the transactions here in question the taxpayer company had acquired capital assets, the Special Commissioners doubted it.   They thought " . . . the reality of the matter was that the [taxpayer] company had substituted larger rents for a ten year period for smaller rents for varying longer periods ".   This may be the financial result of the purchases, but, like CROSS, J. (6), I am clear that the
F   legal result was that the taxpayer company purchased reversions which were capital assets in its hands.

Why in these circumstances should it, as a property holding company, be entitled to set against the rents it receives the cost of acquiring these capital assets so as to diminish its profits for profits tax purposes?   I have heard no convincing answer to this question.   It is not an answer to say that tax may be
G   deducted at source from the rentcharges when they are paid.   This merely establishes that they are income in the hands of the recipient.   I put to counsel for the taxpayer company, the analogy of a company using its own works department to build an extension to its factory.   It would pay out wages to its workmen, and perhaps yearly interest on money borrowed to finance the building. Both would be income in the hands of the recipients and both be liable to deduc-
H   tion of tax at source.   But, as counsel for the taxpayer company agreed, no accountant would debit these items in any account except the capital account relating to the new extension.   The difference in the present case, he said, was that the taxpayer company acquired no capital asset by virtue of paying these rentcharges—an argument which I have already rejected.

I would, therefore, hold that on ordinary principles of commercial accounting
I   these rentcharges should not be debited against the incomings of the taxpayer company's trade in order to compute its profits liable to profits tax.   It is true that capital assets may be purchased by income payments; and what the position would be if perpetual rentcharges had been the consideration in the present case does not here have to be determined.   Furthermore, though the deduction

---

(3) [1968] 1 All E.R. 955; [1968] 1 W.L.R. 423.
(4) [1968] 3 All E.R. 33; [1968] 1 W.L.R. 1446.
(5) [1915] A.C. 433 at pp. 467, 468; 6 Tax Cas. 399 at p. 436.
(6) [1968] 1 All E.R. at p. 961; [1968] 1 W.L.R. at pp. 430, 431.

of income tax at source from the rentcharges, and its retention by the taxpayer **A** company (because it has sufficient taxed profits out of which to make the payments) may yield the same result for income tax purposes as though the rentcharges had been deducted in a profit and loss account and the deduction allowed, I cannot treat this circumstance as relevant.   We are dealing here with profits tax, and, if a different result is yielded, it must be regarded I think as another of those anomalies which the system of deducting tax at source for income tax **B** purposes at times throws up.

CROSS, J., in the Chancery Division thought (7) that the rentcharges could, for the purposes of tax only, be dissected into capital and interest components and the latter alone allowed as a deduction.   In this respect he considered that the present case was similar to *Secretary of State in Council of India* v. *Scoble* (8) and *Vestey* v. *Inland Revenue Comrs.* (9).   Like the Court of Appeal (10) I do not **C** think these cases are really in point.   In the former a capital sum had been agreed as the purchase price, and the inference could be drawn that the so-called " annuity " was the payment of this sum by instalments together with interest. CROSS, J., was able to draw a like inference (11) in the latter case.   But in the present, it is common ground that no such capital sum was agreed beforehand; and, furthermore, counsel for the Crown said (as apparently he also did in the **D** Court of Appeal—see the judgment of FENTON ATKINSON, L.J. (12)) that he disclaimed any right to go behind the contract and show that the payments were not rentcharges.   His main argument was simply that they were not proper items to debit in the revenue account for profits tax purposes.

Nevertheless on the basis (apparently) that some element of interest had been used to calculate the amount of the rentcharges, he said that interest being an **E** allowable deduction for profits tax purposes, the Crown were prepared to allow as an expense what, for want of a better term, I might call the " interest content " of the rentcharges on the basis aforesaid.   I cannot say that I understand how this offer squares with the Crown's main contention, and its admissions, but since it was made and accepted by counsel for the taxpayer company, I leave the matter there without further comment.   I would therefore allow the appeal, **F** and remit the matter to the Special Commissioners to restore the assessments, but adjusting them in the manner offered by the Crown.   The rate of interest to be employed for this purpose should be 5·6045 per cent. per annum, a rate which your Lordships have now been informed has been agreed between the parties.

LORD DIPLOCK: My Lords, I, too, have had the advantage of reading **G** the opinion of my noble and learned friend, LORD DONOVAN, with which I agree.

I would allow the appeal.

Appeal allowed.   Case remitted to commissioners to restore the assessments, adjusting them in the manner offered by the Crown.

Solicitors: *Solicitor of Inland Revenue*; *Nabarro, Nathanson & Co.* (for the **H** taxpayer company).

[*Reported by* S. A. HATTEEA, ESQ., *Barrister-at-Law.*]

I

---

(7) [1968] 1 All E.R. at p. 961; [1968] 1 W.L.R. at pp. 430, 431.
(8) [1903] A.C. 299; 4 Tax Cas. 618.
(9) [1961] 3 All E.R. 978; 40 Tax Cas. 112.
(10) [1968] 3 All E.R. 33; [1968] 1 W.L.R. 1446.
(11) [1968] 1 All E.R. at pp. 961, 962; [1968] 1 W.L.R. at p. 431.
(12) [1968] 3 All E.R. at p. 38; [1968] 1 W.L.R. at p. 1458.

A

GWYNNE TRUSTS, LTD. *v.* RODWELL.

[Court of Appeal, civil division (Danckwerts, Phillimore and Karminski, L.JJ.), March 11, 1969.]

B *Rent Restriction—Protected tenancies—Tenant applying for reduction in rateable value—Rateable value reduced below £400 from 1st April 1965—Local authority granting rebate of rates back to November 1963—Appropriate day for protected tenancy in relation to rateable value 23rd March 1965—Whether tenancy protected—General Rate Act 1967 (c. 9), s. 79 (1)—Rent Act 1968 (c. 23), s. 1 (1), s. 6 (1).*

C In November 1963, the tenant was assigned the balance of the lease of a flat in Greater London which expired in October 1967. In November 1965, the tenant applied for a reduction in the rateable value of the flat which was then £430. In July 1967, the local valuation court reduced the rateable value to £388 which was backdated to 1st April 1965. On further application by the tenant, the local authority, under s. 9 (1)* of the General Rate Act 1967, granted the tenant a rebate of rates backdated to November 1963.

D By s. 1 of the Rent Act 1965 (now s. 1 (1)† of the Rent Act 1968), a tenancy of a dwelling-house in Greater London was a protected tenancy if on the appropriate day (23rd March 1965) it had a rateable value not exceeding £400. By s. 79 (1)‡ of the General Rate Act 1967, the reduction in the valuation of the flat took effect from the first day of the rateable period in which the tenant had made her application for reduction, which was 1st

E April 1965. On appeal by the tenant from an order giving the landlords possession of the flat,

Held: the appeal must be dismissed, because the tenant was not entitled to the protection of the Rent Acts, since the effect of s. 79 (1) of the General Rate Act 1967 was that, for the purposes of the rateable value, the reduction in the valuation took effect from 1st April 1965, which was after the appro-

F priate day (see p. 437, letter G, and p. 438, letters G and I, post).

Appeal dismissed.

[As to protected tenancies, see Supplement to 23 Halsbury's Laws (3rd Edn.), para. 1494a.

For the General Rate Act 1967, s. 79, see 47 Halsbury's Statutes (2nd Edn.) 1316.]

G **Appeal.**

This was an appeal by the tenant, Mrs. Jean Barnsley Rodwell, from a judgment of His Honour Judge McIntyre, Q.C., sitting at West London county court, dated 28th June 1968, whereby he adjudged that the landlords, Gwynne Trusts, Ltd., were entitled to recover possession of Flat C, 27 Bramham Gardens,

H S.W.7, from the tenant and that possession be handed over to the landlords on 28th August 1968. The facts are set out in the judgment of Danckwerts, L.J.

C. H. L. Bathurst for the tenant.
G. Avgherinos for the landlords.

DANCKWERTS, L.J.: This is an appeal from a judgment of His Honour

I Judge McIntyre, Q.C., at the West London County Court given on 28th June 1968. The case concerns a flat at 27 Bramham Gardens, Earls Court, S.W.7. On 10th April 1961, a lease was granted for 6½ years. That meant that it expired on 10th October 1967, and, therefore, unless the defendant was protected by the Rent Acts, there was no answer to a claim for possession by the landlords. On 1st March 1963, the rateable value in the rating list was £430, which, prima

---

* Section 9 (1), so far as material, is set out at p. 437, letters B and C, post.
† Section 1 (1), so far as material, is set out at p. 436, letter E, post.
‡ Section 79 (1), so far as material, is set out at p. 437, letters E and F, post.

facie, would be above the limit contained in s. 1 of the Rent Act 1965. In **A** November 1963, the plaintiffs were the landlords and the defendant was the tenant. She had been assigned the balance of the lease of the flat, which was separately rated and she paid rent and rates to the landlords together. For the purposes of the Act of 1965, 23rd March 1965 was " the appropriate day ". The Act became law on 8th November 1965, but it did not come into force until later. **B**

On 2nd November 1965, the tenant applied for a reduction in the rateable value; on 3rd March 1966, the tenant's proposal was referred to the local valuation court; and on 13th July 1967, the local valuation court reduced the rateable value to £388, which, of course, would have been below the figure of £400 and brought the case, if it applied, within the protection of the Rent Acts. The tenant had a right to have a rebate of rates back to 1st April 1965, but **C** the local authority (which was the Royal Borough of Kensington and Chelsea) had a discretionary power under s. 9 of the General Rate Act 1967, on application, to give a further rebate if it so decided, and that was subject to a certificate by the valuation officer. In the end, as a result, they refunded the overpayment of rates back to November 1963.

The appropriate statutory provisions are contained in the Rent Act 1965, **D** but there has been a consolidating Rent Act 1968, and the relevant provisions are exactly similar to those in the Act of 1965. In the court below, it was found convenient to refer to the provisions of the Act of 1968, and I also find it more convenient to refer to that Act. Section 1 (1) of the Act of 1968 is in the terms of s. 1 of the Act of 1965 and it provides:

> " A tenancy under which a dwelling-house (which may be a house or **E** part of a house) is let as a separate dwelling is a protected tenancy for the purposes of this Act unless—(a) the dwelling-house has or had on the appropriate day a rateable value exceeding, if it is in Greater London, £400 . . ."

or elsewhere a smaller sum. It must be remembered that the appropriate day was 23rd March 1965. Then the other provisions which correspond to s. 43 of the Act of 1965 are contained in s. 6 of the Act of 1968, which provides: **F**

> " (1) Except where this Act otherwise provides, the rateable value on any day of a dwelling-house shall be ascertained for the purposes of this Act as follows:—(a) if the dwelling-house is a hereditament for which a rateable value is then shown in the valuation list, it shall be that rateable value; . . . (3) In this Act ' the appropriate day ',—(a) in relation to any dwelling-house **G** which, on 23rd March 1965, was or formed part of a hereditament for which a rateable value was shown in the valuation list then in force, or consisted or formed part of more than one such hereditament, means that date . . ."

I need not read the rest of that subsection, but sub-s. (4) is important:

> " Where, after the date which is the appropriate day in relation to any dwelling-house, the valuation list is altered so as to vary the rateable value **H** of the hereditament of which the dwelling-house consists or forms part and the alteration has effect from a date not later than the appropriate day, the rateable value of the dwelling-house on the appropriate day shall be ascertained as if the value shown in the valuation list on the appropriate day had been the value shown in the list as altered."

I

A very detailed and effective argument was put before us by counsel for the tenant based on that subsection and on the provisions of the various Rent Acts, but the important point to be noted is that the appropriate day was 23rd March 1965, and, as was pointed out, the date to which the reduced valuation dated back was 1st April 1965. Consequently, it seems clear on the language of that subsection that the date of the variation of the rateable value of the dwelling-house was later than the appropriate day.

It is necessary to refer to another Act, the General Rate Act 1967. First of

A   all, I think that it is convenient to refer to s. 9 of that Act before I refer to s. 79, because, as I have already mentioned, the effect of s. 9 is to give the local authority the right, in its discretion, to pay back what could be considered to be the over-payment of rates. The side note is " Refund of overpayments ". Section 9 provides:

B   " (1) Without prejudice to sections 7 (4) (*b*) and 18 (4) of this Act, but subject to subsection (2) of this section, where it is shown to the satisfaction of a rating authority that any amount paid in respect of rates, and not recoverable apart from this section, could properly be refunded on the ground that—(*a*) the amount of any entry in the valuation list was excessive; . . . the rating authority may refund that amount or a part thereof . . . (3) Before determining whether a refund should be made under subsection (1)

C   of this section—(*a*) in a case falling within paragraph (*a*) of that sub-section; . . . the rating authority shall obtain a certificate from the valuation officer as to the manner in which in his opinion the hereditament in question should have been treated for the purposes of the valuation list, and the certificate shall be binding on the authority."

D   The rating authority did obtain a certificate from the valuation officer that the proper amount of the rateable value of the property was £388 and that duly enabled them to make the refund, which they did. But unfortunately, it seems to us, it did not have the effect of enabling the tenant to claim that the flat fell within the limits which would enable her to have the protection of the Rent Acts.

Section 79 (1) is the appropriate section for that purpose, and that provides, subject to certain provisions which I need not read,

E   ". . . where an alteration is made in a valuation list by virtue of sections 71 to 78 of this Act, then, in relation to any rate current at the date when the proposal in pursuance of which the amendment so made was served on the valuation officer, or, where the proposal was made by the valuation officer, current at the date when notice of the proposal was served on the occupier of the hereditament in question, that alteration shall be deemed

F   to have had effect as from the commencement of the period in respect of which the rate was made, and shall, subject to the provisions of this section, have effect for the purposes of any subsequent rate."

It seems to me, accordingly, that the result of s. 79 (1) is to prevent, for the purposes of the rateable value, the effect of the alteration having any further

G   result back than 1st April 1965, the beginning of the rating period in question. It seems to me that that really is a complete answer to the claim by the tenant that she has a rateable value below the amount of £400, and so she is unable to claim the benefit or protection of the Rent Acts; that the learned judge reached the right conclusion when he so held and that this appeal must be dismissed.

H   **PHILLIMORE, L.J.:** I agree. The tenant who acquired this flat in the autumn of 1963 acquired the balance—four years—of the original lease of 6½ years granted in 1961. In 1963, the rateable value of the flat was £430 and, of course, it was well outside the ambit of the Rent Acts. Then, in 1965, under the Rent Act 1965, the ambit of control was greatly enlarged, enlarged to the extent that, under s. 1 (1) of that Act, it was provided:

I   " The Rent Acts shall apply, subject to the provisions of this section, to every tenancy of a dwelling-house the rateable value of which on the appropriate day did not exceed, in Greater London, £400 . . ."

So the limit of control was getting rather nearer to this particular flat. In November 1965, just before the Act came into force, the tenant made an application to have the rateable value reduced. That application was finally heard in July 1967, when it was reduced to £388. So that brought it below the £400. Then she made a further application to have a repayment of rates right back before 1st April 1965, from which date the decision of the tribunal took effect.

She got a repayment right back to November 1963, when she originally acquired A
the flat, on the basis that the rateable value ought to have been no more than
£388.   On the strength of this, the argument on her behalf is that she was
entitled to the protection of the Rent Acts' when the landlords commenced
proceedings to obtain possession in 1968, and that the learned county court judge
was accordingly wrong in making an order for possession.

As DANCKWERTS, L.J., has indicated, the matter turns, in the first place, on B
the wording of s. 43 of the Act of 1965, because that provides, by sub-s. (3),
that " the appropriate day " is to be 23rd March 1965.   Then there is a provision
in sub-s. (4):

" Where after the date which is the appropriate day in relation to any
dwelling-house the valuation list or valuation roll is altered so as to vary the
rateable value of the hereditament or lands and heritages of which the C
dwelling-house consists or forms part and the alteration has effect from a
date not later than that date [that is to say, not later than 23rd March 1965],
the rateable value of the dwelling-house on the appropriate day shall be
ascertained as if the value shown in the valuation list or on the valuation
roll on the appropriate day had been the value shown in the list or on the
roll as altered." D

On the strength of that subsection, we have a certificate given by the local
authority under the Local Government Act 1948, as amended, showing that the
valuation at £388 only took effect from 1st April 1965, that is to say after the
appropriate day.   That is the result of what is now s. 79 (1) of the General
Rate Act 1967, which DANCKWERTS, L.J., has read, and the effect of which is
that, when the valuation court reduced the valuation, the reduction took effect E
from the first day of the rateable period in which the tenant had made her
application for reduction.   The first day in question was 1st April 1965.

Counsel for the tenant, however, relies on the fact that, in the correspondence
from the local authority referring to the revised assessment and to the application
to go back for overpaid rates beyond 1st April 1965, it is said that the certificate
from the valuation officer " enables me to date the revised assessment of your F
flat back to the 1st November, 1963 ", and there with it was enclosed a revised
assessment describing it as " Revised rateable value with effect from 1st November, 1963 ".   So it is said on behalf of this tenant that the effect of the reduction
clearly took effect before the appropriate day and, accordingly, that this flat
is rent-controlled.   The answer to that is, I think, first of all, that s. 79 (1) is
entirely clear—the reduction takes effect from 1st April 1965, and not before; G
and, secondly, that s. 9 is a purely permissive section which enables a local
authority to refund money but does not enable it to alter the value in the valuation list beyond the date fixed by s. 79.   In my judgment, s. 9 of the Act of 1967
presupposes that the figure in the valuation list is too high but does not suggest
that the list can be amended in consequence, merely that money overpaid may
be paid back. H

Accordingly, as I think, the judgment of the learned county court judge was
entirely right and, indeed, the argument of counsel for the landlords is very
well put by the borough treasurer himself in the letter dated 11th March 1968,
where he explains the effect of these various sections.   This appeal, in my
judgment, must be dismissed.

KARMINSKI, L.J.: I agree that the appeal should be dismissed, and I I
would venture to express my entire agreement with the reasoning not only of
my Lords but also of the learned county court judge.

Appeal dismissed.   Leave to appeal to the House of Lords refused.

Solicitors: *Cripps, Harries, Willis & Willis* (for the tenant); *Capel Cure,
Glynn Barton & Co.* (for the landlords).

[*Reported by* S. A. HATTEEA, ESQ., *Barrister-at-Law.*]

A

BOYLE *v.* KODAK, LTD.

[HOUSE OF LORDS (Lord Reid, Lord Morris of Borth-y-Gest, Lord Hodson, Lord Upjohn and Lord Diplock), February 11, 12, 13, April 29, 1969.]

B
Statutory Duty—Breach—Employer's liability—No apparent danger—Duty to ensure workman familiar with regulations—Whether absence of common law negligence relevant.

On a claim for damages for breach of statutory duty, an employer to avoid liability must show that he has complied with his statutory duty by taking all reasonable steps to prevent his employees from committing breaches of the relevant regulations. Thus, if the employer ought to have realised that
C there was a substantial risk that skilled workmen would not be sufficiently familiar with the regulations imposing a statutory duty on them, in situations where no danger was apparent, it would be his duty under the regulations to instruct the workmen on what steps they must take to avoid a breach. This duty exists even where failure to give such instructions did not amount to negligence at common law.

D   Appeal allowed.

[As to the nature of negligence in relation to statutory duties, see 28 HALS-BURY'S LAWS (3rd Edn.) 6-7, para. 3.]

Cases referred to:
Ginty v. *Belmont Building Supplies, Ltd.,* [1959] 1 All E.R. 414; Digest (Cont.
E   Vol. A) 597, *333a.*
Groves v. *Lord Wimborne,* [1898] 2 Q.B. 402; [1895-99] All E.R. Rep. 147; 67 L.J.Q.B. 862; 79 L.T. 284; 24 Digest (Repl.) 1045, *169.*
Manwaring v. *Billington,* [1952] 2 All E.R. 747; 24 Digest (Repl.) 1077, *335.*
Ross v. *Associated Portland Cement Manufacturers, Ltd.,* [1964] 2 All E.R. 452; [1964] 1 W.L.R. 768; Digest (Cont. Vol. B) 303, *277d.*

F   **Appeal.**
This was an appeal by the appellant, Patrick Leslie Boyle, a painter of 16 years' experience, from the decision of the Court of Appeal (SELLERS and DAVIES, L.JJ., SALMON, L.J., dissenting) dated 20th June 1967 dismissing his appeal from the judgment of CHAPMAN, J., dated 16th December 1966, in an action
G brought by the appellant against the respondents, Kodak, Ltd., for personal injury and loss sustained by him.

Tudor Evans, Q.C., and *D. J. Hyamson* for the appellant.
Marven Everett, Q.C., and *C. Fawcett* for the respondents.

Their Lordships took time for consideration.

H   29th April.   The following opinions were delivered.

LORD REID: My Lords, the appellant sustained injury when he fell off a ladder while engaged in painting the outside of a large oil storage tank which was some 30 feet high. Other means of access had been used for the lower parts of the cylindrical wall, but the upper part had to be painted by a man standing on
I a ladder the top of which rested on a rail round the roof of the tank. For safety it was necessary to lash the top of the ladder to this rail to prevent it from slipping sideways, and the accident occurred while the appellant was going up the ladder in order to lash it. For some reason never discovered the ladder slipped when he was about 20 feet up and he fell with the ladder.

No negligence was proved. It was not proved that the respondents ought to have foreseen any danger involved in this method, and there is no evidence that any negligence on the part of the appellant caused or contributed to the fall of the ladder. But the appellant asserted and the respondents admitted that

in the circumstances this method involved a breach of statutory duty. Regula- **A**
tion 29 (4) of the Building (Safety Health and Welfare) Regulations 1948 (1)
provides:

> " Every ladder shall so far as practicable be securely fixed so that it can
> move neither from its top nor from its bottom points of rest. If it cannot
> be so securely fixed it shall where practicable be securely fixed at the base
> or if such fixing at the base is impracticable a person shall be stationed **B**
> at the base of the ladder to prevent slipping."

It so happened that there was a staircase running round the outside of the tank
by which it would have been possible for the appellant to reach the top of the
tank, and he could then have lashed the top of the ladder to the rail, come down
the staircase and then mounted the ladder. In that way he could have avoided
mounting the ladder before it had been fixed in the manner which complied **C**
with the regulation. The appellant's case is that it was practicable to do this
and that therefore there was a breach of the regulation when he mounted the
unlashed ladder at the time of the accident. I do not have to consider whether
that is right because the respondents had admitted that there was then such a
breach.

It is common ground that these regulations imposed absolute duties on both **D**
the appellant and the respondents. And it is admitted that the appellant, though
himself in breach, was entitled to sue the respondents relying on their absolute
liability created by their breach. There is no difficulty in this case about
causation: clearly this breach was the cause of the accident.

The doctrine of absolute liability, which was invented by the courts, can lead
to absurd results when coupled with the employer's vicarious liability. It would **E**
be absurd if, notwithstanding the employer having done all he could reasonably
be expected to do to ensure compliance, a workman, who deliberately disobeyed
his employer's orders and thereby put the employer in breach of a regulation,
could claim damages for injury caused to him solely by his own wrongdoing.
So the courts have quite properly introduced a qualification of the employer's
absolute liability. A principle of law has been established that, although in **F**
general the employer is under absolute liability in respect of such a breach,
the employer may have a defence to an action against him by an employee who
is also in breach. In *Manwaring* v. *Billington* (2) the plaintiff had been instructed
by his employers not to ascend any ladder without putting sacking under it
to prevent it from slipping and lashing it at the top. He disobeyed this instruction,
ascended a ladder without taking these precautions and sustained injuries when **G**
the ladder slipped. His action against his employers failed. MORRIS, L.J., said (3):

> " The mere fact that the employer must be held to have been in breach
> of the Building Regulations would not in this case by itself warrant our
> concluding that the judge's holding was wrong. Particularly is this so
> when it is remembered that the employer only became in breach of the **H**
> regulations because of the omissions of the plaintiff to perform duties which
> were properly and reasonably assigned to him. The employer could not be
> expected personally to fix every ladder used by his men during painting
> operations, nor personally to supervise every operation in the course of
> which the use of ladders was necessary. If he gave clear and adequate
> directions as to lashing and securing ladders, he was doing what a reasonable **I**
> employer was entitled to do. I would deem it incongruous and irrational if,
> on the facts as found by the learned judge, the plaintiff could, in effect,
> successfully say to his employer: ' Because of my disregard of your reason-
> able instructions I have brought about the position that you are in breach
> of your statutory obligations, and so I claim damages from you because of
> such breach '."

---

(1) S.I. 1948 No. 1145.   (2) [1952] 2 All E.R. 747.
                    (3) [1952] 2 All E.R. at p. 750.

A This was further developed by PEARSON, J., in *Ginty* v. *Belmont Building Supplies, Ltd.* (4), who said:

"In my view, the important and fundamental question in a case like this is not whether there was a delegation, but simply the usual question: Whose fault was it? I shall refer to some of the decided cases to demonstrate what I have said. If the answer to that question is that in substance and reality
B the accident was solely due to the fault of the plaintiff, so that he was the sole author of his own wrong, he is disentitled to recover. But that has to be applied to the particular case and it is not necessarily conclusive for the employer to show that it was a wrongful act of the employee plaintiff which caused the accident. It might also appear from the evidence that something was done or omitted by the employer which caused or contributed
C to the accident; there may have been a lack of proper supervision or lack of proper instructions; the employer may have employed for this purpose some insufficiently experienced men, or he may in the past have acquiesced in some wrong behaviour on the part of the men. Therefore, if one finds that the immediate and direct cause of the accident was some wrongful act of the man, that is not decisive. One has to inquire whether the fault of the
D employer under the statutory regulations consists of, and is co-extensive with, the wrongful act of the employee. If there is some fault on the part of the employer which goes beyond or is independent of the wrongful act of the employee, and was a cause of the accident, the employer has some liability."

E That was followed by a decision of this House, *Ross* v. *Associated Portland Cement Manufacturers, Ltd.* (5). There the employers had failed to provide the right equipment, and with some hesitation the deceased workman and another man decided to proceed without it. In so doing there was a breach of another of these regulations. The employers' case was that they were not at all to blame because they were entitled to leave it to the deceased to decide what to do, and so the sole cause of the accident was his well intentioned but
F mistaken decision to proceed. But this House held that the failure of the employers to take any steps to see that proper equipment was available contributed a great deal to the accident, and two-thirds of the responsibility was apportioned to the employers.

In my opinion, these and other cases show that, once the plaintiff has established that there was a breach of an enactment which made the employer
G absolutely liable, and that that breach caused the accident, he need do no more. But it is then open to the employer to set up a defence that in fact he was not in any way in fault but that the plaintiff employee was alone to blame. That does not mean that the employer must lead evidence, he may be able to prove this from the evidence for the plaintiff, but I do not think that I went too far in *Ross'* case in saying that he (6)
H "cannot complain if in those circumstances the most favourable inferences are drawn from the appellant's evidence of which it is reasonably capable."

In the present case the appellant was a skilled and experienced painter, accustomed to working from ladders. The trial judge, dealing with his common law claim, which failed, rejected the contention that he required instruction or
I supervision with regard to practical matters. But the appellant's case is not that he ought to have been instructed about the technique of his craft. He thought that what he was doing was the normal procedure and he had seen the other man who gave evidence doing the same thing. He knew that there were regulations but either he had not studied them or he failed to understand their application to the circumstances in which he was working. His fault was

(4) [1959] 1 All E.R. 414 at pp. 423, 424.
(5) [1964] 2 All E.R. 452; [1964] 1 W.L.R. 768.
(6) [1964] 2 All E.R. at p. 454; [1964] 1 W.L.R. at p. 775.

not deliberate. Counsel for the respondents very properly did not argue that his fault was anything more than a misapprehension of his statutory duty.

The respondents led no evidence. So the crucial question is whether they have proved by the evidence of the appellant's witnesses that they did everything which they could reasonably be expected to do to prevent this breach. In fact they did nothing. Their case is that they were entitled to assume that a skilled and experienced man would know his duty under the regulations and comply with it. In a case where the regulations require no more to be done than any skilled man would know from his practical experience to be necessary, it may well be that the employer is under no duty to instruct the man as to his duty. But in the present case both the witnesses thought that the manner in which the work was being done was the correct manner, and there is nothing to suggest that any skilled man, going by his practical experience, would have thought otherwise.

It may be that neither the respondents nor their foreman knew that the work was being done in this way. But ought they to have realised, if they had given thought to the matter, that there was a substantial risk that a skilled workman would not be sufficiently familiar with the regulations to know that this method involved breach of the regulations? If they ought to have realised that, then it was plainly their duty to instruct the man as to what he ought to do in order to avoid a breach. They would be quite entitled to trust him to do what he had been told to do.

Employers are bound to know their statutory duty and take all reasonable steps to prevent their men from committing breaches. If an employer does not do that he cannot take advantage of this defence. On the respondents' admission there is a difference under this regulation between cases where there is another practicable means of access to the top of the ladder, and cases where there is none or where there is nothing to which the ladder can be lashed. In the former case the man must use the alternative means of access, here the stairway, to get to the top to lash the ladder, and then return that way before ascending the ladder; in the latter case he is permitted to ascend the ladder without lashing it. I think the evidence shows that a skilled practical man might easily fail to appreciate this and that the respondents ought to have realised that and instructed their men accordingly. So they have not proved that they did all they could reasonably be expected to do to ensure compliance and they cannot rely on this defence so as to avoid their absolute vicarious liability under the regulation.

Then it was said that the appellant would have disobeyed any order to go up the stairway to lash the ladder as soon as the foreman departed. I can find nothing in the evidence to justify this. The trial judge found that he was " an extremely intelligent man and a nice man " and in another passage in his judgment " an extremely straightforward and intelligent man ". It may be that if the foreman had merely told him about the regulation and left it to him to choose, he would have chosen to ignore the regulation. But that would not be doing his best to ensure obedience to the regulation; that implies an order, and there is nothing to show that the appellant would have disobeyed an order.

Another point was made that the appellant could have lashed the ladder halfway up to the handrail of the stairway. But the cross-examination on this point was very inconclusive. If the respondents had wished to prove this they should have led positive evidence.

Finally it was argued that this large tank was not a building within the meaning of these regulations and therefore this regulation did not apply in this case. I agree with your Lordships in rejecting that argument.

It therefore becomes necessary to determine apportionment of liability. Neither party was gravely to blame and I think that equal apportionment is the fairest course. The trial judge did not assess damages. I would therefore allow the appeal and remit with a direction to assess the appellant's loss and to award half the sum assessed as damages.

A   **LORD MORRIS OF BORTH-Y-GEST:** My Lords, I have had the advantage of considering the speech prepared by my noble and learned friend, LORD REID, and I concur in the course proposed.

LORD HODSON: My Lords, I agree with your Lordships and with the learned judge that the word " building " in the Building (Safety, Health and

B   Welfare) Regulations 1948 (7) is wide enough to cover the oil tank 30 feet high and 40 feet in diameter which the appellant was painting when he met with his accident.

The regulations accordingly apply, and it is admitted that in the events which happened there was a breach of reg. 29 (4) which provides:

"Every ladder shall so far as practicable be securely fixed so that it can

C   move neither from its top nor from its bottom points of rest. If it cannot be so securely fixed it shall where practicable be securely fixed at the base or if such fixing at the base is impracticable a person shall be stationed at the base of the ladder to prevent slipping."

The accident happened when the appellant and his mate, a man named Wootton, were painting the top stage of the side of the tank. The work was done from a

D   36-foot double extension ladder made of wood which was used for this part of the work. The ladder was erected in the usual manner and the top was made to lean against the lower of two rails which ran round the top of the tank and to protrude beyond the rail. Mr. Wootton was footing the ladder to prevent the ladder slipping and one of the ladder's feet was against a wall. The appellant then started to ascend the ladder taking with him some rope in order to lash

E   the ladder at the top. He carried with him a kettle of paint and a brush in order to start work as soon as he had lashed the top. His intention was to fix the ladder so that it could not move from its top, acting as he thought in accordance with the regulations. When he reached a point, which he thought was about 20 feet up the ladder, it slipped sideways. He held on to the ladder as long as he could hoping that it would help to break his fall. Unfortunately the ladder

F   struck the wall and broke. The appellant fell and suffered a fractured patella. The learned judge was unable to come to any conclusion as to why the ladder slid away from the top of the tank.

The appellant in his pleading alleged that there was an unsafe system of work in the use of ladders but he and another equally experienced painter who worked with him and who was also called as a witness regarded the method

G   employed as normal and straightforward. There was nothing dangerous about it so far as the appellant could foresee. This plea failed.

The special feature of this case is that there was a staircase running up the side of the tank in order to get access to the top. It was practicable, therefore, to go up by the staircase on to the top of the tank and then fix the top of the ladder by lashing it so that it would not move from its point of rest. The

H   appellant received no special instructions about this nor was it even suggested to him by the respondents that he ought to have used the staircase. Their case was that there was no breach of the regulations by them, for the appellant could have prevented the top of the ladder moving by lashing it to the handrail of the staircase when he was halfway up the ladder. The appellant would have none of this and insisted that the safe way to proceed was to lash the ladder

I   when it had his weight on it so that any sagging would take place on the lashed ladder at the top.

Part of the allegation of common law negligence made against the respondents was that the appellant and his mate were not given any instruction to use the staircase and that they were not supervised. The learned judge dismissed both these charges. He regarded this day-to-day supervision as unnecessary in the case of experienced men such as the appellant and Mr. Gammon. As to failure

---

(7) S.I. 1948 No. 1145.

to instruct, he acquitted the respondents of any negligence in not drawing the   A
attention of these men to a staircase which was there to be used if they wanted
to get to the top of the tank.

The learned judge came to the conclusion accordingly that the appellant's
claim at common law failed. He held, however, that there was a breach of
reg. 29 (4) since, although in the ordinary case it would be impracticable to
ensure that the ladder was securely fixed at the top before ascending it, there   B
was the staircase which it was practicable to use in order to fix the ladder by
lashing it without first ascending it.

The question then arose—were the respondents answerable to the appellant
for the damage caused by the breach? Regulation 4 provides:

"... It shall be the duty of every person employed to comply with the
requirements of such Regulations as relate to the performance of an   C
act by him and to co-operate in carrying out Parts II to VII of these
Regulations ..."

The learned judge found that reg. 29 (4) was breached and that the breach
occurred because of the appellant's failure to comply with it. He was fully
aware of the need for having the ladder lashed at the top when he went up.
He could have gone up by the fixed staircase and thereafter could have lashed   D
the top. It was practicable for him to act in that way and so to have complied
with the regulation. The learned judge concluded by finding the appellant
solely to blame for a breach of statutory duty because he had the means of
securing the ladder in compliance with the regulations and did not avail himself
of those means.

This, however, is not the end of the matter and the finding that the appellant   E
is to blame does not exclude a concurrent finding of fault against the employers
who may be vicariously liable for the appellant's breach. The respondents
have conceded that there was a breach of reg. 29 (4) and their main contention
is that the acquittal of the employers on the charge of common law negligence,
in particular the charge of failing to give instructions as to compliance with the
regulation, is an end of the matter. If they were not negligent in failing to give   F
instructions their omission to do so is, they say, a complete answer to the claim
based on breach of the regulation.

I cannot accept this contention, and agree with SALMON, L.J., in saying
that the duty to forestall, if they can, breaches of regulations remains. The
statutory obligation may well, as here, exceed the common law obligation.

The employer, as PEARSON, J., pointed out in *Ginty* v. *Belmont Building*   G
Supplies, Ltd. (8), has some liability if there is a fault on his part which goes
beyond or is independent of the wrongful act of the employee and was a cause of
the accident. My noble and learned friend, LORD REID, put the matter succinctly
in *Ross* v. *Associated Portland Cement Manufacturers, Ltd.* (9) when, speaking
of the defendant, he said:

"... he can avoid civil liability to the actual offender if he can show   H
that the conduct of this offender was the sole cause of the breach and
resulting injury to him."

This case contrasts in a marked way with *Manwaring* v. *Billington* (10), where
the employer escaped liability. That was a case like this, in that there was an
admitted breach of reg. 29 (4). The plaintiff erected a ladder without taking   I
appropriate steps to prevent slipping and without tying it at the top. He acted
thus notwithstanding his employer's explicit instruction to the men on the job
that they must not in any circumstances go up a ladder without there was
something underneath the foot to prevent slipping and to see that the ladders
were tied at the top before they made any attempt to go up them at all. MORRIS,

(8) [1959] 1 All E.R. 414 at p. 424.
(9) [1964] 2 All E.R. 452 at p. 455; [1964] 1 W.L.R. 768 at p. 776.
(10) [1952] 2 All E.R. 747.

A L.J., pointed out that personal fixing of ladders or supervision of every operation in the course of which the use of ladders was necessary could not be expected of the employer. He said (11):

> "If he gave clear and adequate directions as to lashing and securing ladders, he was doing what a reasonable employer was entitled to do."

B It is clear on the facts of this case that the appellant thought he was complying with the regulations and was in breach of them through his misunderstanding of them. This could have been cured by the respondents who, by giving instructions such as those given in the *Manwaring* case (12), would have done all that could have been expected of them.

I would allow the appeal on the grounds that I have indicated, without taking
C into account against the respondents what was said about a lack of supervision involving a breach of regulations at a different stage of the work. I agree with the learned judge that any lack of supervision at that stage had no bearing on the accident which befell the appellant.

On the question of apportionment I would agree with the view, which I understand is taken by your Lordships, namely, that the proportion of liability should
D be divided equally. I would not for myself accede to the view expressed in the Court of Appeal that other steps by way of exhortation or instruction would probably have made no difference and accordingly the respondents can escape liability in whole or in part on that ground. My reason for so doing is that for myself I would not readily reach a conclusion adverse to the appellant on such a ground when he has had no question put to him on that matter in the witness
E box. The respondents elected to call no evidence themselves on this or any other aspect of the case. I would accordingly remit the case for the assessment of damages.

LORD UPJOHN: My Lords, I concur.

LORD DIPLOCK: My Lords, in this action negligence and contributory
F negligence were pleaded but as I read the judgment of Chapman, J., he found that the ladder from which the appellant fell was so positioned and footed that the risk of its slipping while he was mounting it in order to lash the top of it to the rail of the tank was so small that a reasonable man would not have thought it necessary to expend the time and effort which would have been involved in ascending the staircase to the top of the tank and lashing the ladder before
G setting foot on it. The judge expressly found that the respondents were not negligent and it is implicit in his judgment that the appellant's conduct did not amount to contributory negligence at common law. All three members of the Court of Appeal agreed with these findings which have not been seriously contested in your Lordships' House.

All that is left in this appeal is the appellant's claim for damages for breach
H by the respondents of their statutory duty under reg. 29 (4) of the Building (Health, Safety and Welfare) Regulations 1948 (13), which so far as is relevant provides: "Every ladder shall so far as practicable be securely fixed so that it can move neither from its top nor from its bottom points of rest."

I agree with all your Lordships, with the Court of Appeal and with the trial judge that this regulation applied to the operation on which the appellant was
I engaged when he fell. I also agree that it was practicable, by lashing the ladder to the rail of the tank before anyone mounted it, to fix the ladder securely so that it could not move from its top points of rest. So the regulation was not complied with. If it had been the top of the ladder would not have slipped and the appellant would not have sustained his physical injuries. So the non-compliance with the regulation was a cause of the appellant's injuries.

---

(11) [1952] 2 All E.R. at p. 750.
(12) [1952] 2 All E.R. 747.
(13) S.I. 1948 No. 1145.

The law relating to civil liability for breach of statutory duties imposed by the Factories Act 1961, and its predecessors and by regulations made thereunder is now well settled. It is the creature not of the statutes themselves but of judicial decision by which over the period of 70 years which have passed since *Groves* v. *Lord Wimborne* (14), a new branch of the law of civil wrongs has been developed. The statutes say nothing about civil remedies for breaches of their provisions. The judgments of the courts say all.

The duty to comply with the requirements of reg. 29 (4) of the Building (Health Safety and Welfare) Regulations 1948, is imposed by reg. 4 on the employer who is undertaking the operation. But it is also imposed on the person, in the instant case the appellant, who performs the act, viz., mounting the ladder, to which the relevant requirement of the regulation relates. We have thus a situation where both appellant and respondents were at fault and the only fault of each was their respective failure to comply with the same requirements of the same regulation.

Although the civil liability of the employer has been engrafted by judicial decision on the criminal liability imposed by Parliament its growth has been separate from the parent stem. It is no good looking to the statute and seeing from it where the criminal liability would lie, for we are concerned only with civil liability. We must look to the cases, and in particular to *Ginty* v. *Belmont Building Supplies, Ltd.* (15), and those which followed it, by which this branch of the law of civil wrongs is being developed.

The employer's duty to comply with the requirements of the regulation differs from that of his employee. The employer, at any rate when he is a corporation, must needs perform his duty vicariously through his officers, servants, agents or contractors; but he does not thereby rid himself of his duty. He remains vicariously responsible for any failure by any one of them to do whatever was necessary to ensure that the requirements of the regulation were complied with; and among those for whose failure he is prima facie vicariously liable is any employee who is himself under a concurrent statutory duty to comply with those requirements. The employee's duty, on the other hand, is in respect of and is limited to his own acts or omissions. He is not vicariously liable for those of anyone else.

What, then, is the liability of an employer who is sued by an employee plaintiff for damages for personal injuries sustained as a result of a breach of statutory duty by the employer in not complying with the requirements of a regulation when the non-compliance relied on was also a breach of statutory duty by the plaintiff himself?

The plaintiff establishes a prima facie cause of action against his employer by proving the fact of non-compliance with a requirement of the regulation and that he suffered injury as a result. He need prove no more. No burden lies on him to prove what steps should have been taken to avert the non-compliance nor to identify the employees whose acts or defaults contributed to it, for the employer is vicariously responsible for them all. But if the employer can prove that the only act or default of anyone which caused or contributed to the non-compliance was the act or default of the plaintiff himself, he establishes a good defence. For the legal concept of vicarious liability requires three parties: the injured person, a person whose act or default caused the injury and a person vicariously liable for the latter's act or default. To say " You are liable to me for my own wrongdoing " is neither good morals nor good law. But unless the employer can prove this he cannot escape liability. If he proves that it was partly the fault of the employee plaintiff, as ex hypothesi it will be in the postulated case, for the employee's own breach of statutory duty is " fault " within the meaning of s. 1 of the Law Reform (Contributory Negligence) Act 1945,

(14) [1898] 2 Q.B. 402; [1895-99] All E.R. Rep. 147.
(15) [1959] 1 All E.R. 414.

A this may reduce the damages recoverable but it will not constitute a defence to the action.

Since it is only through other persons that the employer can perform his duty of compliance with the requirements of the regulations it is incumbent on him to ensure that all of those persons understand those requirements and their practical application to the particular work being undertaken and possess
B the skill and are provided with the plant, equipment and personnel needed to secure compliance. Although in the present case the necessary plant, equipment and personnel was provided for the appellant and he possessed the necessary skill the respondents, who called no evidence, made no attempt to prove that they had taken any steps to ensure that the appellant understood the requirements of reg. 4 of the Building (Health, Safety and Welfare) Regulations 1948, or
C understood that, in the particular circumstances of the work which he was undertaking, these requirements would not be satisfied unless he lashed the ladder at the top to the rail of the tank before he mounted it.

It has been contended on their behalf that as the appellant was a skilled and experienced craftsman they were entitled to assume that he understood all these things. But however reasonable such assumption might be they would not
D escape liability unless they proved that the appellant did in fact understand them, although the reasonableness of their assumption if mistaken would be relevant to their share in the responsibility for the damage for the purpose of reducing the damages recoverable under the Law Reform (Contributory Negligence) Act 1945.

On the evidence in the present case, which was that of the appellant him-
E self and of a fellow workman who completed the work after the plaintiff was injured, it appeared that neither was given any instructions about the regulations or was told that the regulations required the top of the ladder to be lashed to the rail of the tank before anyone mounted on it. It also appeared that the appellant, for reasons which are intelligible though unconvincing, believed that the ladder should be lashed while he was mounted on it and not before. So far
F from establishing that the appellant did know what the requirements of the regulation were and their application to the particular circumstances of the operation on which he was engaged, the evidence discloses that the foreman and the ganger through whom, inter alia, the respondents were purporting to perform their statutory duty and for whose omissions they are vicariously liable, took no steps to give to the appellant instructions on either of these matters which,
G if carried out, would have prevented the breach of statutory duty. The respondents, in my view, therefore failed to satisfy the onus which lay on them to prove that the only act or default of anyone which caused or contributed to the non-compliance was the act or default of the appellant himself.

In your Lordships' House the respondents relied strongly on a finding of the learned judge that their failure to instruct the appellant to lash the ladder at
H the top before mounting it did not constitute negligence on their part. For reasons that I have already indicated the fact that a failure to give instructions as to the requirements of the regulations is not negligent does not exonerate an employer from liability for breach of his statutory duty to comply with the requirements of the regulations which he owes to the person whom he has failed to instruct. He is only exonerated if he can show that that person did in fact
I know the requirements. But in the present case the failure goes further than this. It may well be unnecessary to give a skilled and experienced craftsman instructions how to avoid obvious dangers, and the more obvious the danger the less the need to do so. But in the present case on the findings of the learned judge the risk of the ladder slipping while the appellant was mounting it to lash the top of it was so small that a reasonable man would not have thought it necessary in the interests of his own safety to expend the time and effort and incur the possible loss of bonus which would have been involved in ascending the staircase to the top of the tank and lashing the ladder. The more remote

the danger in the particular operation on which the employee is engaged the   **A** greater the need to instruct him or to remind him of the application of the regulation to it.

Perhaps because he had already dealt with instructions in connection with the issue of negligence, the cognate question of instructions about the application of the regulations to the task in hand escaped the attention of the judge at the trial when he came to deal with breach of statutory duty. This oversight, in my   **B** opinion, led him to err in law in treating it as sufficient to exonerate the respondents from all liability that—

" . . . he [the appellant] was the one to see that that breach was not carried out . . . He had the means of securing the ladder and complying with the Regulations and he did not do so."

  C

In the Court of Appeal SALMON, L.J., in his dissenting judgment was the only one to recognise the vital distinction between the need to instruct a craftsman on how to avoid obvious dangers and the need to instruct him about the application of the regulations in situations where no danger is apparent. On this aspect of the case the majority members of the Court of Appeal, in my view, fell into the same error as the learned trial judge. But they also upheld the judgment   **D** on the ground that, even if the appellant had been instructed that he was required by the regulations to lash the ladder at the top before and not after mounting and to ascend to the top of the tank by the staircase to do so, and that he would be committing an offence if he did not, the appellant would nevertheless have disregarded those instructions. Failure to give them, therefore, did not cause or contribute to the breach.   **E**

Whether the appellant would or would not have obeyed such instructions is a question of fact. The learned judge made no finding on it. It was never put to the appellant in cross-examination. It was never canvassed in evidence at all. It is, in my view, impermissible for an appellate court to decide this case against the appellant on what is no more than speculation as to a fact which the respondents never sought to prove and with which the appellant was given no   **F** opportunity to deal.

I would therefore allow the appeal. Both appellant and respondents were in breach of their statutory duty. This was the only " fault " of each. I find it difficult to apportion their respective shares of the responsibility for the damage. In view of the remoteness of the danger in neither was it a very heinous fault. But however venial the fault of each of them they must share between them the   **G** responsibility for the whole of the damage. I would assess the share of each as one-half and reduce the damages recoverable by the appellant accordingly.

I would allow the appeal, declare that the respondents are liable to the appellant for one-half of the damage sustained by him and remit the case for the damages to be assessed.

Appeal allowed. Case remitted with a direction to assess the appellant's loss and   **H** *to award half the sum assessed as damages.*

Solicitors: *Martin Baker*, Harrow (for the appellant); *Geoffrey Coombs & Co.* (for the respondents).

[*Reported by* S. A. HATTEEA, ESQ., *Barrister-at-Law.*]

A

R. *v.* ITHELL.   R. *v.* JONES.   R. *v.* TOMLINSON.

[Court of Appeal, criminal division (Edmund Davies and Phillimore, L.JJ., and Geoffrey Lane, J.), January 17, 1969.]

B

Criminal Law—Sentence—Suspended sentence—Fresh offence committed during period of suspension—Sentence for fresh offence to be dealt with first— Suspended sentence to take effect consecutively to sentence for current offence.

The proper approach, where a fresh offence has been committed during the period of suspension of an earlier sentence and the accused is brought before the court, is that the court should first sentence him in respect of the fresh offence by punishment appropriate to that offence, and thereafter

C

address itself to the question of the suspended sentence. Furthermore, unless there are some quite exceptional circumstances, the suspended sentence should be ordered to run consecutively to the sentence given for the current offence (see letter I, below, to p. 450, letter A, post).

R. v. Brown ((1968), The Times, 12th November) approved.

Appeals dismissed.

D

[As to suspended sentences, see Supplement to 10 Halsbury's Laws (3rd Edn.), para. 922a, 1, 2.

For the Criminal Justice Act 1967, s. 40, see 47 Halsbury's Statutes (2nd Edn.) 396.]

Case referred to:

R. v. *Brown* (1968), The Times, 12th November.

E

Appeal.

This was an appeal by John Foster Ithell, Albert Edward Jones and Thomas Jeffrey Tomlinson, against sentences imposed at Denbighshire Quarter Sessions (deputy chairman Bertrand Richards, Esq.) on 15th May 1968. The appellant Ithell and the appellant Jones had each pleaded guilty to storebreaking and larceny; each had been sentenced by the same court on 20th February 1968 to a

F

suspended sentence of two years; the court ordered, in each case, that the suspended sentence should take effect immediately and that a sentence of 18 months' imprisonment for the current offence of storebreaking and larceny should run consecutively thereto, making a total of 3½ years. The appellant Tomlinson pleaded guilty on three counts of storebreaking and larceny; he had been sentenced on 8th January 1968 to six months suspended sentence; the

G

court ordered that the suspended sentence should take effect immediately; he was sentenced on one count to nine months' imprisonment, on another to nine months concurrent and on the third count to two years consecutive, all to run consecutively to the sentence previously suspended, making a total of three years and three months.

H

J. M. T. Rogers for the appellants.

The Crown was not represented.

EDMUND DAVIES, L.J., referred to the charges and sentences and continued: The appellants now appeal against their sentences with the leave of the single judge, and the chief ground on which that leave was granted was that it appeared to him that the learned deputy chairman fell into error in the

I

manner in which he approached the question of putting into operation a suspended sentence. We agree with the single judge. The proper approach, where a fresh offence has been committed during the period of suspension of an earlier sentence and the accused is brought before the court, is that the court should first sentence him in respect of the fresh offence by punishment appropriate to that offence, and thereafter address itself to the question of the suspended sentence. Furthermore, as Lord Parker, C.J., said in *R.* v. *Brown* (1), unless

---

(1) (1968), The Times, 12th November.

there are some quite exceptional circumstances, the suspended sentence should   A
be ordered to run *consecutively* to the sentence given for the current offence.
In the present case the deputy chairman proceeded first of all to deal with
the earlier sentences and, rightly taking the view that there was no reason why
the suspensions should not be removed, he ordered that they should take effect.
Only then did he go on to consider the sentences which he thought appropriate
for the offences in respect of which the accused were before the court.   The   B
order in which these matters are approached can have practical importance,
and we do not approve of the one which was here adopted.   Cases can easily
arise where the type and duration of sentence imposed for the current offence
would materially affect the court's selection of the most suitable among the
four courses regarding suspended sentences left open to it by s. 40 (1) of the
Criminal Justice Act 1967.   Having said that, however, we consider that on the   C
facts of the present case the court nevertheless arrived at the correct result.
[HIS LORDSHIP then referred to the facts and the grounds of appeal against
sentence and concluded that the court could not accede to any suggestion that
the sentences were wrong in principle.]

Appeals dismissed.

Solicitor: *Registrar of Criminal Appeals* (for the appellants).   D

[*Reported by* S. A. HATTEEA, ESQ., *Barrister-at-Law.*]

E

R. *v.* SCOTT.

[COURT OF APPEAL, CRIMINAL DIVISION (Widgery and Fenton Atkinson, L.JJ.,
and O'Connor, J.), October 25, 1968.]

*Road Traffic—Disqualification for holding licence—Special reasons—Driving
with blood-alcohol proportion above prescribed limit—Driver's ability impaired   F
through also taking drugs—No knowledge of potential risk—Road Traffic
Act 1962 (10 & 11 Eliz. 2 c. 59), s. 5 (1)—Road Safety Act 1967 (c. 30),
s. 1 (1).*

The appellant pleaded guilty to driving a motor vehicle having consumed
alcohol in such a quantity that the proportion thereof in her blood exceeded
the prescribed limit, contrary to s. 1 (1)* of the Road Safety Act 1967.   She   G
was fined and disqualified for holding a driving licence for 12 months.   On
appeal against the sentence of disqualification, she contended that there
were special reasons under s. 5 (1)† of the Road Traffic Act 1962, as applied
by s. 5 (2) (*a*) of the Act of 1967, why the mandatory period of disqualification should not be imposed, viz., that she had been treated for a number
of years by her doctor with two kinds of tablets, anti-depressant tablets   H
and sleeping tablets, and that, while she knew that it was dangerous to
drink when taking the anti-depressant tablets, she had no idea that a
combination of drink and sleeping tablets would produce a more violent
reaction in terms of her ability to drive than if she had taken the drink alone.
   Held: those circumstances could not amount to special reasons for the

I

* Section 1 (1), so far as material, provides: " If a person drives . . . a motor vehicle
on a road . . . having consumed alcohol in such a quantity that the proportion thereof
in his blood . . . exceeds the prescribed limit . . . he shall be liable [to the penalties set
out in the subsection]."
   † Section 5 (1), so far as material, provides: " Where a person is convicted of an
offence specified in Part I of the First Schedule to this Act [which includes by virtue of
s. 5 (2) (*a*) of the Act of 1967 an offence under s. 1 (1) of that Act] the court shall order
him to be disqualified for such period not less than twelve months as the court thinks
fit unless the court for special reasons thinks fit to order him to be disqualified for a
shorter period or not to order him to be disqualified ".

A   purposes of an offence under s. 1 (1) of the Act of 1967 (see p. 452, letter B, post).

              Appeal dismissed.

          [Editorial Note. On the question whether non-impairment of driving ability can amount to a special reason for not disqualifying, reference should be made to *Taylor* v. *Austin*, [1969] 1 All E.R. 544, which was heard after this case.

B   As to special reasons for not ordering obligatory disqualification in motoring offences, see 33 HALSBURY'S LAWS (3rd Edn.) 639, 640, para. 1081; and for cases on the subject, see 45 DIGEST (Repl.) 122-126, *431-454*.

      For the Road Traffic Act 1962, s. 5, see 42 HALSBURY'S STATUTES (2nd Edn.) 891.

      For the Road Safety Act 1967, s. 1, s. 5, see 47 HALSBURY'S STATUTES (2nd
C   Edn.) 1554, 1561.]

      Cases referred to :

        Brown v. *Dyerson*, [1968] 3 All E.R. 39; [1968] 3 W.L.R. 615; 132 J.P. 495.
        James v. *Hall*, [1968] Crim. L.R. 507; The Times, 26th June 1968.

        Appeal.

D   On 16th February 1968, the appellant, Myra June Scott, pleaded guilty at Essex County Quarter Sessions to driving a motor vehicle with a blood-alcohol concentration above the prescribed limit, contrary to s. 1 (1) of the Road Safety Act 1967. She was sentenced by the chairman (ROLAND ADAMS, ESQ., Q.C.) to a fine of £20 and 12 months' disqualification and was ordered to pay 25 guineas costs. By leave of the full court she appealed against the sentence of disquali-
E   fication on the ground that there were special reasons under s. 5 (1) of the Road Traffic Act 1962, as applied to an offence under s. 1 (1) of the Act of 1967 by s. 5 (2) (*a*) of that Act, which would entitle the court not to impose mandatory disqualification. The facts are set out in the judgment of the court.

      M. J. Segal for the appellant.
      F. Irwin for the Crown.

F
        WIDGERY, L.J., delivered the judgment of the court: On 16th February 1968, the appellant pleaded guilty at Essex County Quarter Sessions to driving with a blood-alcohol concentration above the limit prescribed by s. 1 of the Road Safety Act 1967. She was fined and was subjected to the mandatory disqualifi-cation of 12 months, which follows a conviction for that offence. She now
G   appeals against her disqualification by leave of the full court, the question being whether there were, contrary to the learned chairman's belief, special reasons which would entitle the court not to impose the mandatory disqualification.

      The facts are quite simple. At about 11.15 p.m. on 31st October 1967, a taxi-driver saw a stationary car outside Harlow Town railway station. It was half on the road and half on the pavement. It had obviously been in recent and
H   violent contact with a post on the side of the pavement, and the appellant was sitting in the driver's seat with her legs on the pavement and the driver's door was open. She could not stand still when she got out, and when the taxi-driver (who was concerned for her) asked where she lived she said " Afghanistan ", which was not the fact. He telephoned the police and, when the police came the appellant was staggering around, and there was a great deal of evidence to
I   indicate that she was significantly under the influence of alcohol. She was given a breath test, and the following blood sample test showed she had 119 milli-grammes of alcohol per 100 millilitres of blood; and that, of course, is considerably in excess of the statutory limit of 80. Her explanation, which may very well be true—and the court certainly accepts it for the purposes of dealing with this appeal—was that she had been treated by her doctor for a number of years and the treatment included two kinds of tablets: (i) anti-depressant tablets; and (ii) sleeping tablets. She knew that it was dangerous to drink in conjunction with the anti-depressant tablets, but she had no idea that a combination of

drink and sleeping tablets would produce a more violent reaction in terms of her   A
ability to drive than if she had taken the drink alone. She said that in all
innocence in that sense she had had drink on this day after taking sleeping
tablets and that that was the cause of the condition in which she was found.

As I say, the court accepts those facts for the purposes of this appeal; and,
no doubt, if the offence charged had been driving when her ability to drive was
impaired, all those matters would have been highly significant in mitigation and   B
indeed might (we say no more) have amounted to special reasons. But the
point which is conclusive in this case is that those circumstances cannot, in the
judgment of this court, amount to special reasons for the purposes of an offence
under s. 1 (1) of the Road Safety Act 1967. It is, we think, vital to appreciate
that Parliament in creating this offence and giving statutory force to it has
recognised that it is necessary to have a check on the consumption of alcohol   C
which can be recorded in objective terms relative only to the resultant concentration of alcohol in the blood. In a charge under s. 1 (1) of the Act of 1967, the
question whether the driver's ability is impaired is not relevant to guilt, although,
of course, it may be a matter of mitigation. Whether it can be a special reason
for the purposes of relieving the court of the obligation to disqualify has not
yet been finally settled. There are two authorities to which our attention has   D
been drawn. The first is *James* v. *Hall* (1), a Divisional Court case, where
LORD PARKER, C.J., in dealing with an argument that the fact that the driver's
ability was not impaired might be a special reason, said (2):

"I have grave doubts whether the fact that he had drunk but a small
amount of alcohol, let alone that he was unaware that he had been affected
thereby, could be special reasons."   E

Further, in the more recent case of *Brown* v. *Dyerson* (3), where this point arises
more directly, BRIDGE, J., having referred to the argument of counsel for the
Crown that the fact that the driver's ability was impaired could not be a special
reason, said (4):

"For my part I find those arguments extremely compelling, and as at   F
present advised I do not see how they are to be effectively countered."

This court would not wish finally to close the door on any future argument on
this point, the door having been left open in those two cases; but we would not
wish to add any support to the view that it is a special reason if one proves
that one's ability was not impaired. That matter in its simple terms must
remain open; but, of course, in this case the evidence was overwhelming that   G
the appellant's ability was impaired. It is, in our judgment, quite hopeless in
this particular case to argue, as counsel for the appellant has sought to argue,
namely, that, although her ability was impaired, she might reasonably not have
anticipated it would have been impaired and, therefore, that some special reason
can be produced. Whatever may ultimately be the decision as to whether the
capacity of the driver can be a special reason, it is a point which is of no avail   H
to the appellant in this case, and we are quite satisfied on the facts of this case
that the chairman was right. There was no special reason, and the appeal must
be dismissed.

Appeal dismissed.

Solicitors: *Registrar of Criminal Appeals* (for the appellant); *T. Hambrey Jones*,
Chelmsford (for the Crown).   I

[*Reported by* N. P. METCALFE, ESQ., *Barrister-at-Law.*]

---

(1) [1968] Crim. L.R. 507.
(2) See The Times (26th June 1968).
(3) [1968] 3 All E.R. 39; [1968] 3 W.L.R. 615.
(4) [1968] 3 All E.R. at p. 42; [1968] 3 W.L.R. at p. 620.

A

R. *v.* JACKSON.   R. *v.* HART.

[COURT OF APPEAL, CRIMINAL DIVISION (Sachs and Fenton Atkinson, L.JJ., and
Caulfield, J.), March 6, 11, 1969.]

Road Traffic—Disqualification for holding licence—Special reasons—Non-impair-
ment of driving ability—Liver condition unknown to driver—Road Traffic

B   *Act 1962 (10 & 11 Eliz. 2 c. 59), s. 5 (1)—Road Safety Act 1967 (c. 30),*
s. 1 (1), s. 3 (3) (a).

On the question of whether there are special reasons for not disqualifying
under s. 5 (1)* of the Road Traffic Act 1962 a driver of a motor vehicle
convicted of an offence under s. 1 (1)† or s. 3 (3) (a)‡ of the Road Safety
Act 1967: (i) the fact that his ability to drive was not impaired by drink is

C   irrelevant; (ii) the fact that he is a cripple who requires transport has no
relation to the offence; and (iii) the fact that he suffers from an idiosyncratic
state of his liver which, when combined with his blood pressure, caused the
retention of alcohol in the blood to be longer than usual to some unspecified
extent and degree, and that he did not know of that idiosyncracy, can only
be peculiar to the offender and not to the offence (see p. 460, letters H and

D   I, and p. 461, letters A, B, C and E, post).

Dicta of LORD GODDARD, C.J., in *Whittall* v. *Kirby* ([1946] 2 All E.R. at
p. 555), and of LORD PARKER, C.J., in *Taylor* v. *Austin* ([1969] 1 All E.R. at
p. 546) applied.

R. v. *Wickins* ((1958), 42 Cr. App. Rep. 236) distinguished and doubted.
Appeals dismissed.

E   [As to special reasons for not ordering obligatory disqualification in motoring
offences, see 33 HALSBURY'S LAWS (3rd Edn.) 639, 640, para. 1081; and for
cases on the subject, see 45 DIGEST (Repl.) 122-126, *431-454.*

For the Road Traffic Act 1962, s. 5, see 42 HALSBURY'S STATUTES (2nd Edn.)
891.

For the Road Safety Act 1967, s. 1, s. 3, see 47 HALSBURY'S STATUTES (2nd

F   Edn.) 1554, 1558.]

Cases referred to:
Brewer v. *Metropolitan Police Comr.,* [1969] 1 All E.R. 513; [1969] 1 W.L.R.
267.
Brown v. *Dyerson,* [1968] 3 All E.R. 39; [1969] 1 Q.B. 45; [1968] 3 W.L.R. 615.
Chapman v. *O'Hagan,* [1949] 2 All E.R. 690; 113 J.P. 518; 45 Digest (Repl.)

G   124, *439.*
Delaroy-Hall v. *Tadman, Earl* v. *Lloyd, Watson* v. *Last,* [1969] 1 All E.R. 25;
[1969] 2 W.L.R. 92; 133 J.P. 127.
James v. *Hall,* [1968] Crim. L.R. 507.
R. v. *Holt,* [1962] Crim. L.R. 565.
R. v. *Julian,* [1966] Crim. L.R. 52.

H   *R.* v. *Lundt-Smith,* [1964] 3 All E.R. 225, n.; [1964] 2 Q.B. 167; [1964] 2
W.L.R. 1063; 128 J.P. 534; 45 Digest (Repl.) 126, *453.*
R. v. *Scott,* ante p. 450.
R. v. *Steel,* 17th June 1968, unreported.
R. v. *Wickins* (1958), 42 Cr. App. Rep. 236; 45 Digest (Repl.) 125, *449.*
Taylor v. *Austin,* [1969] 1 All E.R. 544; [1969] 1 W.L.R. 264.

I   *Whittall* v. *Kirby,* [1946] 2 All E.R. 552; [1947] K.B. 194; [1947] L.J.R. 234;
175 L.T. 449; 111 J.P. 1; 45 Digest (Repl.) 123, *433.*

Appeals.

R. v. *Jackson.*

On 16th August 1968, the appellant Dennis James Jackson pleaded guilty at

---

* Section 5 (1) is set out at p. 454, letter G, post.
† Section 1 (1), so far as material, is set out at p. 454, letter I, post.
‡ Section 3 (3), so far as material, is set out at p. 455, letter A, post.

South East London Quarter Sessions to driving a motor vehicle when the pro-   A
portion of alcohol in his blood exceeded the prescribed limit, contrary to s. 1 (1)
of the Road Safety Act 1967. He was fined £40 by the chairman (J. A. GRIEVES,
ESQ., Q.C.) with two months' imprisonment in default of payment within seven
days. He was also disqualified from holding a driving licence for 12 months.
He appealed against the sentence of disqualification (which was suspended
pending appeal pursuant to s. 105 of the Road Traffic Act 1960) on the ground   B
that there were special reasons for not disqualifying him. The facts are set out
in the judgment of the court.

The case noted below* was cited during the argument in addition to the
cases referred to in the judgment of the court.

Margaret Puxon for the appellant.   C
Ann Curnow for the Crown.

R. v. Hart.

On 17th June 1968, the appellant Stanley Hart pleaded guilty at Inner London
Sessions to failing to supply a specimen for a laboratory test, contrary to s. 3 (3) (a)
of the Road Safety Act 1967. He was fined 1s. by the deputy chairman (J. C. B. W.
LEONARD, ESQ.) and disqualified from holding a driving licence for three years.   D
He appealed against the sentence of disqualification on the ground that there were
special reasons for not disqualifying him. The facts are set out in the judgment
of the court.

D. A. Paiba for the appellant.
Ann Curnow for the Crown.
                                                                                      E

SACHS, L.J., delivered the judgment of the court: These two appeals,
one by the appellant Jackson and the other by the appellant Hart, were listed
consecutively because they raised parallel points as to what constitute " special
reasons " under s. 5 (1) of the Road Traffic Act 1962 in relation to certain offences
recently created by Part I of the Road Safety Act 1967. Both cases having been
fully and helpfully argued by counsel, it is accordingly convenient to deal with   F
them both in a single judgment.

It is, perhaps, as well first to read the relevant part of the above-cited s. 5 (1):

" Where a person is convicted of an offence specified in Part I of the First
Schedule to this Act the court shall order him to be disqualified for such
period not less than twelve months as the court thinks fit unless the court
for special reasons thinks fit to order him to be disqualified for a shorter   G
period or not to order him to be disqualified."

Part I of Sch. 1 to the 1962 Act sets out a number of offences, and to those
offences there were in 1967 added the two which are now under the consideration
of this court.

Both appellants pleaded guilty to offences against provisions of the 1967 Act.
The appellant Jackson at South East London Quarter Sessions pleaded to an   H
offence under the provisions of s. 1 (1), by which:

" If a person drives or attempts to drive a motor vehicle on a road or
other public place, having consumed alcohol in such a quantity that the
proportion thereof in his blood, as ascertained from a laboratory test for
which he subsequently provides a specimen under section 3 of this Act,
exceeds the prescribed limit at the time he provides the specimen . . ."   I

he is guilty of an offence. The offence of the appellant Jackson was having 118
milligrammes of alcohol per 100 millilitres of blood, that being in excess of the
prescribed limit of 80 milligrammes.

The appellant Hart pleaded guilty at Inner London Sessions to an offence
under s. 3 (3) of the 1967 Act, of which the relevant extract provides:

---

* *Sweet* v. *Parsley*, [1968] 2 All E.R. 337; [1968] 2 Q.B. 418.

A   " A person who, without reasonable excuse, fails to provide a specimen
[of blood] for a laboratory test in pursuance of a requirement imposed under
this section shall be guilty of an offence . . ."

The appellant Hart had, in fact, refused to give such a specimen in circumstances
which were without doubt unreasonable and to which this court will in due
course further refer.
B
In both cases it was held at quarter sessions that no special reason had been
established which would enable the court to impose a lesser term of disqualification than the relevant Acts provided. In both cases reluctance was expressed
by the court at having come to such a decision. In both cases a lesser fine was
imposed than would have been the case if the court had been free to disqualify
C the appellants for some lesser period, or not to disqualify at all. Hence these
appeals seeking to establish that the respective courts were each wrong in law in
holding that there was no special reason. It should be added that, so far as the
appellant Jackson was concerned, the fine was £40 and he was disqualified for
12 months; and that, so far as the appellant Hart was concerned, the fine was
1s. and he was disqualified for three years.

D   Taking first the facts as regards the appellant Jackson, he is aged 41, and is a
civil engineer. He was arraigned on two counts, the first under s. 6 (1) of the Road
Traffic Act 1960 for driving whilst unfit to drive owing to drink consumed.
To that count he pleaded not guilty, and that plea was accepted in the sense
that it was not further proceeded with. The second count was under s. 1 (1) of
the 1967 Act for the offence already stated to which he pleaded guilty. His
E only previous motoring offences were in December 1967, when on the same day
he was twice fined for exceeding the speed limit.

The facts put before sessions on behalf of the Crown were as follows. On 30th
April 1968, a little after midnight, a police car followed the appellant Jackson's
Jaguar. It was observed to be exceeding the 40 miles per hour speed limit, and
its headlights were full on although the road was quite well lit; the driving was
F erratic, but the road was deserted and no one was in danger. When the police
succeeded in passing the Jaguar it was stopped at 12.50 a.m.; a breathalyser test
was then given, and at 1.0 a.m. there was a positive reaction. The appellant
Jackson was then taken to the police station, and at 1.25 a.m. there was a second
breathalyser test, again with a positive reaction. At 2.15 a.m., a doctor having
arrived, a blood sample was taken; this was later found to contain no less than
G 118 milligrammes of alcohol per 100 millilitres of blood. The doctor, having
examined the appellant Jackson, gave it, however, as his opinion that he was not
then unfit to drive through drink; the doctor had previously noted the smell
of alcohol but had no doubt taken the appropriate tests. It was because of that
doctor's opinion that count 1 was allowed to remain on the court file without
further proceeding on it.

H   The appellant Jackson, after his plea, gave evidence as to the sequence of
events before he was stopped at 12.50 a.m., and his case was as follows. For the
whole day he had had no food at all, neither breakfast nor lunch. He had
throughout the day engaged himself on business affairs and had been driving
considerable distances. At 7.0 p.m. he had two pints of brown ale; then he had
a normal dinner, with which he consumed one-third of a glass of wine followed
I by four brandies. At 10.0 p.m.—that is to say four hours before the blood test
—he went for a walk. At 10.40 p.m. he commenced to drive from Brighton
back to London. At 11.20 p.m. he unfortunately ran into the back of a car,
but that was claimed to be no fault of his; about that time he was in conversation with a policeman who had not attributed to him any signs of influence
of alcohol; and at 12.50 a.m. he was stopped as above stated. It was also his
evidence that he was wholly unaware of the defective condition of his liver,
to which this court will now turn.

After the plea of guilty Dr. Haler was also called. He gave evidence that the

appellant Jackson was a person with high blood pressure, whose diet was lament- A
able and whose way of life was also from the medical point of view lamentable.
He spoke of a malfunctioning liver, the malfunctioning of which appeared in
combination with high blood pressure, and perhaps also with the diet and way
of life, to produce the following effect: one way and another the result was
retention in the blood of alcohol for a longer period than would be expected,
though there was no statement as to how much longer than normal it was thus B
retained. It was said that the build-up of alcohol in the blood was below normal,
and the excretion slow. These faults were attributed to defects of long-standing
in the liver; and in essence that was the case for the appellant Jackson. The
defects apparently were given no disease name—and counsel for the appellant
Jackson was unable to suggest that there was a name for them. As already
mentioned, the appellant Jackson was unaware of the defect, and it was said by C
Dr. Haler that, if he had been what he (Dr. Haler) described as " a normal man ",
one would have expected a much less amount of alcohol in the blood at 2.0 a.m.;
something very considerably less than the 80 milligrammes which is the prescribed
level. This evidence appears to have been accepted by the sessions court.

In those circumstances, this court observes that the learned chairman of the
South East London Quarter Sessions said when imposing sentence that, after D
listening to the appellant Jackson's evidence and to that of Dr. Haler and to
the arguments advanced by counsel for the appellant Jackson:

> " The result is that we think that in certain circumstances a condition
> such as yours which causes you to be more susceptible to building up
> alcohol in your body than a healthy man might amount to a special reason,
> but when we have regard to the fact which seems apparent, that this condition E
> must have been arising for a considerable time and have existed for a
> considerable time, we decline in the present case, reluctantly in view of
> everything, to find special reasons."

The monetary penalty imposed was, as already indicated, less than that normally
imposed by that court in such circumstances; and with a view to an appeal F
the one year's disqualification imposed was suspended.

Turning now to the appellant Hart, he is aged 46, is a polio cripple, and his
right lower arm has been amputated; he drives an invalid car. He lived at
the material time at Cheyne Walk, Chelsea, and on the material evening (29th
February 1968) he went in his invalid car to a public house within half-a-mile
of his home. Then on the way back there occurred the following incident. At G
about 11.20 p.m. the police observed the appellant Hart, who was driving his
invalid car at a modest speed, negotiate a " U " turn on a pedestrian crossing
in the Kings Road. He completed the turn, drove eastwards swerving about,
suddenly made a left turn into Lincoln Street despite two clearly displayed and
illuminated " No Entry " signs, and was forced to stop because of a taxi
approaching in the opposite direction. The police went up to him and, having H
smelt the alcohol on his breath, referred to what he had done and asked him to
provide a specimen of breath for a breathalyser test. He said, " No, I can't,
'cause I've had a few drinks ". He was again asked and he said " No ". Later
at the police station he was twice asked to provide a specimen of breath and he
refused. He was then asked to supply a specimen of blood or urine, and he was
told that if he refused he would be liable to the penalties which the Act provides; I
but he said " I am not giving anything ". Later he was asked twice more, and
he refused. When he was formally charged and cautioned he said, " No, it's
all wrong. I am not that drunk ". In court he was called into the witness box
after he had pleaded guilty, and amongst his testimony occurs this passage
with regard to the breathalyser test:

> " The Deputy Chairman: The reason that you refused was? A.—For
> principle's sake because I thought that I did not do anything wrong.
> Honestly, I did not see what I did wrong on principle, Sir . . ."

A   Later, in relation to the refusal of the blood test he said similarly:

    " Q.—Why did you refuse the blood test? Was that the same reason? A.— On principle, Sir, yes. On my principle, not the law's principles, but my personal principle."

    From there it is convenient first to turn to his road traffic record. On 8th December 1966, for driving whilst unfit on account of drink, he was at Bow
B   Street Magistrates' Court fined £5 and disqualified for six months. The six months is, of course, half the period provided by the Act, but neither the Crown nor counsel for the appellant Hart were aware of whether there was any certification of special reasons or what those special reasons were. Then, on 18th January 1967, again for driving whilst unfit owing to drink, he was at Marl-
C   borough Street Magistrates' Court given a conditional discharge for 12 months. In so doing there was utilised a loophole left by the provisions of s. 12 (2) of the Criminal Justice Act 1948, which technically enabled magistrates to avoid disqualifying those who had offended against s. 6 of the 1960 Act without entering on the register any special reason for this course. The procedure thus adopted at Marlborough Street was one which has more than once been frowned
D   on by the Divisional Court; and the loophole has since been blocked by s. 51 of the Criminal Justice Act 1967, which refers to the *duty* of the courts when dealing with this class of case. (That Act, of course, only came into operation on 1st October 1967.) The next item on his record is that, after having been charged with the offence now under consideration (which was committed on 29th February 1968) but before the matter came before sessions, he committed further offences
E   on 4th May. For these he came before the Marlborough Street Magistrates' Court on 5th May. On that date, for failing to provide a sample of breath for a breathalyser test, he was given an absolute discharge; for once more driving while unfit to drive owing to drink—being the third time he had been found unfit in 18 months—he was fined £10, his licence was endorsed, but he was not disqualified. The special reason entered being that he was the driver of an invalid carriage and would suffer special hardship.
F   To these three convictions and to the way in which the magistrates dealt with them this court will advert later. It now turns to what was said by the learned deputy chairman at the conclusion of the matter now under appeal. Having stated, as indeed was not unnatural, that he had great sympathy for the appellant Hart, he went on to say:

G   ". . . if the law did not, as I think it does, compel me to do so, I would not impose a disqualification on you . . . I would impose a fine of 1s. for the sake of putting it in . . . I think the law must take its course and I think that somebody will find a way round the law."

To those observations also this court will later revert.

    Turning now to the law, the leading case as to the meaning of the words
H " special reasons " is *Whittall* v. *Kirby* (1). The considered judgment of the Divisional Court was delivered by Lord Goddard, C.J. At that time the relevant provisions as to driving a motor car when under the influence of drink or drugs were contained in s. 15 (2) of the Road Traffic Act 1930. The relevant words in that subsection were no different from those under the 1962 Act, which have already been recited. In that case, the absence of previous motoring
I   convictions, and the fact that the retention of his licence was essential to the driver in order that he might continue to obtain a livelihood, were each urged as being a special reason; as also was the fact that a substantial fine was imposed. It was held that none of these three facts could constitute a special reason. Lord Goddard, C.J., said (2):

    " That a man is a professional driver cannot, as it seems to me, by any

---

(1) [1946] 2 All E.R. 552; [1947] K.B. 194.
(2) [1946] 2 All E.R. at p. 555; [1947] K.B. at p. 200.

possibility be called a special reason . . . That in many cases serious hardship   A
will result to a lorry driver or private chauffeur from the imposition of a
disqualification is, no doubt, true, but Parliament has chosen to impose
this penalty and it is not for courts to disregard the plain provisions of an Act
of Parliament merely because they think that the action that Parliament
has required them to take in some cases causes some or it may be
considerable hardship."   B

Then there was stated the vital principle which is, and has continued to be, of
general application. The law is stated thus (3):

" A circumstance peculiar to the offender as distinguished from the
offence is not a ' special reason ' . . ."

Since the passing of the Road Safety Act 1967, a number of cases touching the   C
relevant issues have come before this court and the Divisional Court. Thus,
on 17th June 1968, there came before this court *R.* v. *Steel* (4) which concerned
a conviction under s. 1 (1) of the 1967 Act. The judgment of the court was
delivered by LORD PARKER, C.J., sitting with FENTON ATKINSON, L.J., and
BRIDGE, J. The fact that the appellant was a professional driver with no previous
conviction was once more urged as a special reason; but LORD PARKER, C.J.,   D
referred to *Whittall* v. *Kirby* (5) and said as regards that authority:

". . . it was laid down as clearly as could be that a matter peculiar to the
defendant, such as his good character, was not a special reason within what
was then the Road Traffic Act 1930. That is a decision which obtained
very great publicity at the time. It has been thought to cause great hardship ever since. It has been, however, affirmed time and time again and the   E
court that laid it down was a final Court of Appeal in those days in such a
case; it was a Divisional Court on a Case Stated from the justices. Since
then Parliament has re-enacted the same words with full knowledge of that
decision, in 1960 and again in 1962, and further in 1962 in what are known
as the totting up provisions in s. 5 (3) Parliament has deliberately avoided
the use of those words by talking about mitigation. It is perfectly clear that   F
in those circumstances this court, observing the intention and seeking to
honour the intention of Parliament, must inevitably uphold the principle
laid down in *Whittall* v. *Kirby* (5)."

That this passage in the judgment of LORD PARKER, C.J., correctly states the
law is clear beyond argument here or elsewhere. Other decisions in 1968 included
James v. *Hall* (6) on 25th June and *Brown* v. *Dyerson* (7) on 29th June, both by   G
the Divisional Court, in which LORD PARKER, C.J., and BRIDGE, J., respectively,
when delivering the judgments of that court, made it clear that they would have
found it extremely difficult to hold in cases of excessive blood content of alcohol
(i.e., over 80 milligrammes) that special reasons could be constituted either
by the fact that the driver had drunk but a small amount of alcohol, or that
he was unaware that he had been affected thereby, or that the driver's ability   H
to drive was not shown to be impaired. In each of these cases the facts were such
that it was not necessary to deal further with the law. A similar view was
expressed by WIDGERY, L.J., giving the judgment of this court in *R.* v. *Scott* (8)
on 25th October, a case to which further reference will be made. Finally, as
regards s. 1 (1) of the 1967 Act, there is the decision of the Divisional Court in
Taylor v. *Austin* (9) on 12th December 1968. The relevant facts and the   I
decision thereon of that court appear in the following passage from the judgment
of LORD PARKER, C.J. (10):

---

(3) [1946] 2 All E.R. at p. 555; [1947] K.B. at p. 201. LORD GODDARD, C.J., was
citing from *R.* v. *Crossan*, [1939] 1 N.I. 106 at pp. 112, 113, per LORD ANDREWS, C.J.
(4) (17th June 1968), unreported.
(5) [1946] 2 All E.R. 552; [1947] K.B. 194.   (6) [1968] Crim. L.R. 507.
(7) [1968] 3 All E.R. 39; [1969] 1 Q.B. 45.   (8) Ante p. 450.
(9) [1969] 1 All E.R. 544; [1969] 1 W.L.R. 264.
(10) [1969] 1 All E.R. at p. 546; [1969] 1 W.L.R. at p. 266.

A   ". . . the magistrate finally held that he found that there were special
reasons, on three grounds: first, driving ability not impaired; indeed it was
admitted by the appellant that his driving was in no way the cause of this
accident, and there was no suggestion that in fact his driving ability was
impaired.   So far as that is concerned, this court is quite clear that that
cannot be a special reason.   It is no doubt a mitigating circumstance, but not
B   a mitigating circumstance such as to amount to a special reason. The second
ground was that the accident was no fault of the respondent. That really is
wrapped up in the earlier ground.   This offence has got nothing to do with
impairment or accident, it is Parliament trying to arrive at some certainty
and make it an offence whenever there is an excess of alcohol over the
prescribed limit."

C   Then he adverted once more to the fact that hardship on the offender cannot
be a special reason for not disqualifying him.   So much for the recent decisions
under the 1967 Act.
   In addition, there were naturally cited to the court a series of decisions in
cases that had arisen under s. 6 of the 1960 Act, and the provisions in earlier
legislation which similarly related to driving by a person whose ability to drive
D   properly is for the time being impaired by drink or drugs.   That series included
cases in which there was considered the position arising when the drink consumed
immediately before the offence had, without the knowledge of the offender,
been laced, or combined with some extraneous substance (drugs or chemicals)
or affected by some extraneous incident without the offender being aware of
the potential effects.   These included *Chapman* v. *O'Hagan* (11)—the combined
E   effects of drugs and alcohol; *R.* v. *Holt* (12)—amytal tablets and drink; *R.* v.
Julian (13)—the effect of severe electric shock on tolerance to drink; and *Brewer*
v. *Metropolitan Police Comr.* (14)—chemical fumes and drink.   All these are, of
course, in a different class to the instant case. They relate to some specific extraneous occurrence that took place shortly before the relevant incident.   In addition,
the court was pressed with—and at first sight impressed with—*R.* v. *Wickins* (15),
F   on which counsel for the appellant Jackson strongly relied, a diabetes case.
   For the purpose of considering special reasons, there are, however, as counsel
for the Crown pointed out in the course of her admirably succinct and cogent
series of submissions, basic distinctions between the offences created by s. 6 of
the 1960 Act and those created by s. 1 and s. 3 of the 1967 Act. It must,
indeed, always be borne in mind (as counsel for the appellant Jackson conceded,
G   though counsel for the appellant Hart did not) that the special reasons which the
court may take into account may well be different according to the offence
committed.   Regard must always be had to the nature of the offence, and also
to the objective of the legislature. Thus, as regards s. 6 of the 1960 Act, the
constituent components of the offence can normally involve an examination of
factors such as what the accused has had to drink, what was his personal tolerance
H   of alcohol, what was the nature of his driving before arrest, and what is the
medical opinion on the above factors in relation to that particular man's capacity
to drive.
   Under s. 1 (1) of the 1967 Act, which is intended to and does put any driver
at stern risk if he drinks before he drives, the sole test is an objective one depending on a scientifically ascertained measurement.   The factors relating to a s. 6
I   of the 1960 Act offence are irrelevant—as, of course, is the end question of
whether his capacity to drive was impaired.   Under s. 3 (3) of the 1967 Act,
unreasonable failure to provide a specimen is made an offence.   The objective
is to put at equally stern risk all those who unreasonably refuse to give the specimen; it is quite irrelevant whether the offender's capacity to drive was impaired
or whether he had or had not got too much alcohol in his blood.

(11) [1949] 2 All E.R. 690.   (12) [1962] Crim. L.R. 565.
(13) [1966] Crim. L.R. 52.   (14) [1969] 1 All E.R. 513; [1969] 1 W.L.R. 267.
              (15) (1958), 42 Cr. App. Rep. 236.

It is, of course, obvious that something which could be a special reason in **A**
relation to driving with impaired capacity could be no reason at all in relation
to refusing to give a specimen. Indeed, it is difficult to envisage what could be a
special reason in relation to an unreasonable refusal. Similarly, the issue whether
there was a special reason for not including disqualification as a penalty may well in
some instances (the court is, of course, *not* referring to cases where the offender has
had to drive on an emergency journey: *R.* v. *Lundt-Smith* (16)) have to be decided **B**
differently as between cases of driving with impaired capacity and driving with
an excessive amount of alcohol in the blood. This latter difference has already
been recognised in this court in *R.* v. *Scott* (17), where WIDGERY, L.J., made it
clear that the court was not for the purposes of s. 1 (1) of the 1967 Act following
the line taken in cases such as *R.* v. *Holt* (18). This court in *R.* v. *Scott* (17)
declined to treat as a special reason the fact that sleeping tablets had been **C**
taken by the appellant, who had no idea of their adverse effect on the alcohol
in her blood, and reserved the question whether it might have amounted to a
special reason if the charge had been one of driving with impaired ability, stating
(19):

"It is, we think, vital to appreciate that Parliament in creating this offence
[under the 1967 Act] and giving statutory force to it has recognised that it is **D**
necessary to have a check on the consumption of alcohol which can be
recorded in objective terms relative only to the resultant concentration of
alcohol in the blood."

It follows from what has above been stated that the difficult and border-line
decision in *R.* v. *Wickins* (20) is not an authority as regards cases arising under **E**
the 1967 Act. In those circumstances, it is not necessary for this court to say
more about that decision than that it may, in relation to cases of driving with
impaired capacity, require on some appropriate occasion further consideration
by this court on two points: (i) whether it may not in essence be contrary to
the general stream of authority on the subject; and (ii) whether in any event
the precise words used by DEVLIN, J., do not go too far. For, although the **F**
judgment concerned a man suffering from diabetes without being aware of it,
the phraseology runs (21):

"If it had not been for the fact that the appellant was suffering from
diabetes, the offence would not have been committed at all . . ."

and thus makes no reference to the fact that the diabetes was not known to the
appellant. The important question of whether that omission was per incuriam **G**
or because the ratio decidendi of the case required it is not for this court to
examine today.

Returning to the facts of instant cases, this court is prepared to make the
following assumptions: first—albeit with considerable hesitation—that in
neither case was there evidence that drink consumed by the appellant had
impaired his capacity to drive. That is a phrase which must in law cover alike **H**
cases in which no sign of bad driving had been observed (whether or not there
were other signs of the driver having been drinking) and cases in which there were
such signs but the evidence cannot or does not establish that link between
the consumption of drink and the impairment of capacity to drive required for a
conviction under s. 6 of the 1960 Act. Secondly, that in the case of the
appellant Hart he was a cripple unable to get home from the place he had been **I**
drinking without his invalid car, unless he hired a taxi or had transport assistance
from a friend. Thirdly, that in the case of the appellant Jackson the evidence
established an idiosyncratic state of his liver which, when combined with his
blood pressure, caused the duration of retention of alcohol in the blood to be

---

(16) [1964] 3 All E.R. 225, n.; [1964] 2 Q.B. 167.   (17) Ante p. 450.
(18) [1962] Crim. L.R. 565.   (19) Ante at p. 452.
(20) (1958), 42 Cr. App. Rep. 236.   (21) (1958), 42 Cr. App. Rep. at p. 239.

A longer than usual to some unspecified extent and degree, and that he did not
know of that idiosyncracy. None of those facts thus assumed can constitute a
special reason as regards an offence created by s. 1 or by s. 3 of the 1967 Act.

As regards the first assumption, this court respectfully and fully endorses
what was said by LORD PARKER, C.J., in *Taylor* v. *Austin* (22). Nothing could
be clearer than that the whole object of the relevant section of the Road Safety

B Act 1967 was in the public interest to create an offence for which evidence of
impairment of driving ability was irrelevant and for which disqualification was
mandatory. To permit after conviction an investigation into this irrelevant
matter would defeat the whole purpose of the provisions.

As to the second assumption, this court finds itself quite unable to comprehend
how any tribunal could find that the fact that the driver was a cripple who

C required transport was a special reason in relation to the offence of unreasonably
refusing to give a specimen. The fact that he was a cripple simply has no relation
at all to the offence. The refusal in the instant case was stated to be " on
principle ". Indeed, this court finds difficulty in conceiving what could be a
special reason in relation to an unreasonable refusal. Moreover, having regard
to the course taken by the Marlborough Street magistrate in May in relation to

D the conviction under s. 6 of the 1960 Act, this court feels constrained to
observe that the fact that the offender was a cripple quite obviously was peculiar
to the offender and not to the offence. Disabled drivers of cars are no less liable to
injure members of the public by their driving than those who are not invalids.
Indeed, the comparative risks entailed by the former driving with impaired
capacity may well be the greater. If the legislature had wished to treat such

E drivers in a less stern way it could have said so, but it has not.

As to the third assumption, any general state of health of an offender or
bodily defect (as counsel for the appellant Jackson has put it) can only be
peculiar to the offender and not to the offence; at any rate, as regards offences
under s. 1 and s. 3 of the 1967 Act. It makes no difference whether or not
that state of health or its effect are known to him. It would produce, incidentally,

F an impossible situation if, after conviction under s. 1 of the 1967 Act, the
driver could embark on an investigatory trial involving an examination of the
condition of his organs, be it liver or kidney or as the case may be, with the aid
of evidence as to how much drink he had consumed—a matter so often the
subject of dubious testimony—and a comparison of that condition with those
of the organs of others. Section 1 refers to " his blood ", and not to the blood of

G anyone else or of any class of persons. As counsel for the Crown aptly pointed
out, it does not refer to the blood of the man on a Clapham omnibus. Moreover,
as LORD PARKER, C.J., said in another connection in the de minimis case of
Delaroy-Hall v. *Tadman* (23):

      " Unless the line is drawn with certainty, it would be almost impossible
      to achieve any uniformity in practice and courts would be exercising a
H   dispensing power which the Acts do not confer on them."

Those words may well not be irrelevant to the matter now under consideration.

The instant case, incidentally, provides a good example of the impossible
position that would be created if the court after conviction had to go into
questions peculiar to the offender, such as whether the characteristics of his
liver caused the alcohol content of his blood at some point of time to be above
I average. That would entail not only an examination of what drink he had
consumed and when he consumed it, but also what degree of difference there was
between his liver and that of others, whether he gave the doctor accurate information for the latter's test, and perhaps also how far the liver condition was
produced by his own conduct. Incidentally, Dr. Haler gave no tenable explanation as to how as much as 118 milligrammes could have been in the appellant

(22) [1969] 1 All E.R. at p. 546; [1969] 1 W.L.R. at p. 266.
(23) [1969] 1 All E.R. 25 at p. 31 ; [1969] 2 W.L.R. 92 at p. 98.

Jackson's blood on that night. Nor did he suggest (nor, so far as this court is A
aware, could he have suggested) that the longer the alcohol remains in the
blood the less is the driving ability impaired. Nor did he suggest that the extent
to which a person with such an excess of alcohol in his blood is aware of being
affected by its concentration diminishes when the alcohol has been there for
some time.

The loopholes which would be created if the court acceded to the submissions B
of the appellants are particularly well illustrated in the present cases by reference
to the facts already mentioned. In both cases their driving had been erratic;
in both cases they had the smell of drink about them; the appellant Hart is a
man who has three times since 1966 been convicted of driving whilst under the
influence of drink; and in the appellant Jackson's case the court was asked to
rely on potentially unreliable evidence as to the consumption of drink by him C
on the day of issue and also on the day before he saw his doctor. Indeed, on
the evidence as it emerged in these two cases, this court thinks it right to state
that even if, contrary to its stated conclusions, it had considered in either case
that any of the facts assumed could have in law constituted a special reason,
yet on the facts as a whole it would in neither have been disposed to reduce the
period of disqualification imposed by the relevant statutory provisions. The D
respective courts before whom the appellants' cases originally came do not
appear to have fully appreciated the implications of the facts in evidence before
them.

Finally, this court thinks it necessary to refer back to the passage in the judgment of LORD GODDARD, C.J. (24) (already cited) as to how essential it is for the
courts not to disregard the plain provisions of an Act of Parliament merely E
because they think that they have been required to take action which in certain
cases involves hardship. It is well known that the relevant provisions of the
Road Safety Act 1967 stem from a combination of the need to discourage drivers
from drinking before they drive and the reluctance of some tribunals (mainly
juries) to convict drivers under the 1960 Act. To provide loopholes in this
Act, contrary to the intention of Parliament, is no function of the courts; and F
this court notes with some concern that on two separate occasions the metropolitan magistrates at Marlborough Street refrained from disqualifying the
appellant Hart on grounds which were untenable, and that the deputy chairman
at Inner London Sessions appeared to be anxious that loopholes should be
provided, despite the previous convictions of the appellant Hart for driving
when his capacity was impaired by drink. As regards the general public, the G
severity of the provisions of the Road Safety Act 1967 are now well known, as,
however, also are the benefits those provisions have brought. There are more
ways than one by which a member of the public can find out his personal tolerance
of alcohol and his idiosyncracies of the types discussed. Above all, it is open to
every man not to drink if he is going to drive.

The appeals are, accordingly, dismissed. H

Appeals dismissed. Leave to appeal to the House of Lords refused.

Solicitors: *Registrar of Criminal Appeals* (for the appellant Hart); *David
Forsyth*, Oxted (for the appellant Jackson); *Solicitor, Metropolitan Police* (for
the Crown).

[*Reported by* N. P. METCALFE, ESQ., *Barrister-at-Law.*] I

(24) In *Whittall* v. *Kirby*, [1946] 2 All E.R. at p. 555; [1947] K.B. at p. 200.

A

WILKINS *v.* WILKINS.

[Probate, Divorce and Admiralty Division (Baker, J.), February 13, March 10, 1969.]

B

Divorce—Maintenance of wife—Consent order—Variation—Application to court to vary—Jurisdiction.

Once a judge has approved and made a consent order it would be wrong in principle for the court to upset the order, in the absence of fraud, other than on appeal (see p. 466, letter G, post).

L. v. *L.* ([1961] 3 All E.R. 834), and *Foster* v. *Foster* ([1964] 3 All E.R. 541), applied.

C   Appeal allowed.

[As to jurisdiction to vary orders of maintenance, see 12 Halsbury's Laws (3rd Edn.) 444, 445, para. 999; and for cases on the subject, see 27 Digest (Repl.) 622-624, *5803-5840.*]

Cases referred to:

D   *B.* (*M.A.L.*) v. *B.* (*N.E.*), [1968] 1 W.L.R. 1109.
    Foster v. *Foster*, [1964] 3 All E.R. 541; [1964] 1 W.L.R. 1155, n; Digest
        (Cont. Vol. B.) 376, *5822c.*
    L. v. *L.*, [1961] 3 All E.R. 834; [1962] P. 101; [1961] 3 W.L.R. 1182; Digest
        (Cont. Vol. A.) 789, *5760a.*
    L. v. *L.*, (23rd January 1968), unreported, *on appeal* (27th March 1968),
E   unreported.
    Minter (*decd.*) *Re, Visco* v. *Minter*, [1967] 3 All E.R. 412; Digest (Repl.) Supp.
    Payne v. *Payne*, [1968] 1 All E.R. 1113; [1968] 1 W.L.R. 390.
    South American and Mexican Co., Ltd., Re, Ex p. Bank of England, [1895]
        1 Ch. 37; [1891-94] All E.R. Rep. 680; 64 L.J. Ch. 189; 71 L.T. 594;
        21 Digest (Repl.) 210, *107.*

F   **Appeal.**

This was an appeal by the former wife that an order concerning maintenance made by a registrar and dated 18th October 1968 should be rescinded. The hearing was in chambers but judgment was delivered in open court. The facts are set out in the judgment of Baker, J.

G   *Jonathan Sofer* for the wife.
    Henry Palmer for the husband.

Cur. adv. vult.

10th March. **BAKER, J.**   This is an appeal by the former wife who contends that an order concerning maintenance made by Mr. Registrar Holloway dated 18th October 1968 should be rescinded. It is necessary to recite shortly
H   the history of the matter leading to the learned registrar's order. The parties married on 16th November 1946. They are both now aged 47. There are three children, a girl Nicole born in January 1948 who is now 21 and married, and twins, a boy and a girl, born in 1952 who are almost 17. The former wife has always had care and control. The husband, a company director, filed a petition in October 1964 alleging cruelty. He said that the wife was cold and indifferent
I   and that from 1951 she sulked or nagged him, that his health suffered and that he left her for six weeks in March and April 1964. A reconciliation was unsuccessful; he finally left her in July 1964. Her answer denied cruelty. She said overwork caused his ill-health, that she tried to persuade him to work less hard and to take more care of himself and that was the so-called nagging. She pleaded that there had been condonation on 31st October 1964. This he denied.

From the pleadings at least, it looked as if the suit would be a long and possibly acrimonious contest, which could end with the husband failing to obtain a

decree of dissolution. The wife did not herself ask for a decree. At the door of A
the court on 31st January 1966 after " protracted " negotiations between the
parties and their legal advisers, the wife accepted a proposal that the husband
should from decree absolute pay her maintenance of £715 per annum free of
tax and £130 per annum free of tax to each child until 18 or the completion of
education, whichever was later. (In the order itself the sums have been grossed
up and are expressed as £1,218 per annum less tax to the wife and £222 per B
annum less tax to each child.) With this order the wife was prepared to abandon
her defence to the charge of cruelty and to allow the husband to obtain a decree
in an undefended suit if he could prove cruelty. ORR, J., was told of the proposal,
heard the husband's case, found the cruelty proved, granted a decree nisi to
the husband and made the maintenance order by consent.

On 2nd May 1966, the decree was made absolute. The husband remarried C
on 30th July 1966. In October 1966, he applied to vary the consent order because
" upon later examination I found that I had completely miscalculated the effect
of the undertaking and that it was quite impossible for me to make the payments ". In addition to his liability for tax which he had apparently misunderstood, he contended that he was unable to pay because his income consisted of
not only his salary of £2,100 per annum gross but also of a yearly bonus paid D
by his employers from the year's profits. This had been paid either annually
or in two instalments and he swore that it was £680. (In fact tax certificates
produced to the registrar now indicate that for the year ended 5th April 1966
it was £1,175.) There was no certainty whether any bonus would be paid to
him or of the size or time of the payments, and his salary, he said, was liable to
decrease if the company's turnover decreased. He had in addition a pension of E
£100 a year, so his gross salary, according to his affidavit, was £2,880 per annum.
The wife, who had worked on Saturday and Sunday nights at the local police
station in the latter days of the marriage, was earning £550 per annum gross in
1966 in work which she had undertaken unwillingly.

On 14th November 1966 his application to vary came before ORR, J., when
the husband had as advisers not only his solicitors but also accountants. The F
wife or rather her advisers appreciated that the order in its original form weighed
heavily on the husband and that she could obtain almost exactly the same amount
of money if the order was in a different form, which would give the husband
considerable relief, reducing his actual payments by some £400 and providing
for a further reduction if his bonus fell below £780 per annum in any year. A
new consent order was therefore negotiated and regarded as a variation of the G
original consent order. It is not in fact expressed as a consent order but there can
be no doubt that it was. It provides for : (i) Maintenance for the wife at £100 per
annum less tax; (ii) maintenance to be paid to each of the twins until 18 or
completion of their education, whichever be the later, of £450 per annum, less
tax; (iii) maintenance to be paid to the elder child Nicole of £230 per annum,
less tax, until she herself is earning £230 per annum; (iv) 75 per cent. of the main- H
tenance to be paid monthly in advance, the balance of 25 per cent. to be paid
on the husband receiving a bonus or other additional payment above his basic
salary and if the bonus, etc., is less than £780 per annum gross in any tax year
the amount payable as maintenance to be reduced by five-thirteenths of £1 for
each £1 less than £780 received by the husband;−(v) on the termination of any
child's order the amount payable to the wife to be increased by the like amount; I
(vi) the husband to notify the wife if his income exceeds £4,000 per annum in
any tax year; (vii) the wife to notify the husband if her income other than from
maintenance payments, exceeds £1,000 a year in any tax year; (viii) liberty to
apply. No argument has been addressed to me on this.

This has been described, and I think rightly, as holding to the original bargain
but making it easier for the husband to meet it. He has not done so. The balance
of 25 per cent. was not paid from April 1967 and for a time in 1968 he reduced
the monthly payments by £20 per month. I have no figures for the bonus for the

A year ended 5th April 1967 although the registrar said it had increased over that for 1966 (£1,175). For the year ended 5th April 1968 it was £1,450. In short his gross salary had risen from what he said it was at the date of the substituted consent order by £770 per annum. No figure for bonus has been disclosed since 5th April 1968. The wife's salary has now increased to £832 gross (£715 when before the registrar) an increase of £282 (or £165). She finds her work uncongenial.

B The second wife does not work. It is to be noted that the increases are not sufficiently large to bring into operation the provisions of the order requiring notification.

On 30th January 1968 the husband took out a summons to vary the substituted consent order of 14th November 1966 on the grounds that he cannot afford to pay, that he is overspending his income by some £600 a year, that the former

C wife ought to earn double, that Nicole then earned £14 per week and that the twins have earned some money in the vacation. He says he did not fully understand the situation to which he apparently agreed, and did not appreciate what his full liability really was.

I cannot accept that there is any change in the circumstances of either party which will justify a reduction in the amount of the order. The comparable

D increases in income are £715 the husband and £165 the wife, and in any event I do not agree that the notification provisions are merely safeguards. The fact that Nicole was earning over £230 per annum and has now married and left home is expressly provided for in the order by transfer of the £230 to the wife. Indeed the wife will be in a worse financial position after 5th April 1969 in that by reason of the penal provisions of s. 15 of the Finance Act 1968, which then come into

E operation, the maintenance paid to the twins will rank as her income for tax.

It follows therefore that if the existing consent order is to be taken as the starting point the maintenance cannot be reduced or, put more graphically, before the court can reduce the maintenance it will have to tear up the consent order and fix maintenance de novo. This I think is exactly what the learned registrar has done. He said:

F 　　" A preliminary point taken by counsel for the wife was that the court should not vary a consent order unless it is proved that there has been a change in the circumstances of one or both of the parties. In this case, it was said, there has not been such a change because any increase in the amount which the wife earns has been fully matched by an increase in the husband's bonus. I was asked to regard the decree given to the husband

G 　　as a decree based on the breakdown of the marriage. The husband had fully recognised the right of the wife to receive the net sum of £55 for a four-week period, or £175 per annum free of tax, and in the absence of any drastic change for the worse in his financial situation the husband should be required to keep to his promise to pay such a sum. The fact that the husband had married again should not be taken into account, because in all the cir-

H 　　cumstances the second wife was not entitled to be maintained by the husband at the expense of the former wife and the children of the first marriage.

　　" Certainly the court will not vary an order which has been made after a full inquiry into the financial position of both parties unless it is satisfied that there has been a subsequent change of circumstances. I do not accept,

I 　　however, that I am precluded from inquiring into the circumstances when the original order was made by consent, even if there would appear to be no change in the relative positions of the parties. If a husband was wrongly advised as to the effect of an agreed order, or if he was wildly over-optimistic over his ability to pay, it would be wrong in my view that he should not be able to ask the court to consider the matter and make such adjustment as was fair to both sides. The fact that the husband had at the time of the trial accepted the claim of the wife to receive for herself the net annual sum of £715, and had again accepted that claim some few months later are of

course matters which I must take into account but are not conclusive against   A
the husband.   From an inspection of the court record, it does not appear
that Mr. Justice ORR was asked to inquire in detail into the financial position
of the parties."

He then enquired in detail into the financial position of each party, concluded
that the husband was required by the substituted consent order to pay more
than he could afford and more than he ought to pay in the financial circumstances   B
of the wife, and made an order for payment to the wife of £750 per annum less
tax for herself and £2 4s. for each twin with the income tax allowance to be
divided equally between the two parents.   The effect of this order is I am told
that from 5th April 1969 the wife will receive a net figure for maintenance of
£630 a year instead of having available the net sum of £1,112 as at the dates
of the consent orders.   It has been agreed that I should first decide the main   C
question whether the consent order can be varied and then if necessary consider
the amount and figures later.

I regret I am unable to agree with the decision of the learned registrar.
Neither of us can hear an appeal from the order of ORR, J., whether it was made
after full enquiry or by consent.   Section 31 (1) (h) of the Supreme Court of
Judicature (Consolidation) Act 1925 provides for an appeal to the Court of Appeal   D
with leave from an order made with the consent of the parties.   Counsel for the
husband said that the court has inherent jurisdiction to act where it would be
contrary to public policy to force a man to pay more maintenance then he can
afford.   Counsel for the wife says she has changed her status in exchange for a
promise by the husband and there would be chaos if a husband could resile
from his promise after the court has made an order and a decree based on that   E
premise.   I think the reality of the situation is that the wife abandoned the possibility of a successful defence, with the cost and unpleasantness inherent in any
fought case when the husband proposed what she accepted and the court
approved as adequate maintenance for a woman then 44 with three children
who had been married for 20 years.   The husband was apparently competently
advised at least on the variation in November 1966, and he was in effect saying   F
" there is no need to enquire further, this is what I can and will pay " and he now
adds that although his wife is technically guilty of cruelty he does not seek to
rely on this and the court should disregard this.   Once a judge has approved
and made the consent order it would I think be wrong in principle to upset the
order, in the absence of fraud, other than on appeal.   Further, although it is
suggested at the end of note (b) p. 856 RAYDEN ON DIVORCE (10th Edn.) that   G
" the approach might be different where the original order was by consent ",
there is authority which I think makes it impossible to tear up this consent
order.

In *Foster* v. *Foster* (1), the Court of Appeal rejected the contention that
although the original order must be taken as the starting point, once the court
accepts that some alteration is to be made because of a change of circumstances   H
then the matter is at large and maintenance can be fixed de novo.   WILLMER,
L.J., having referred to s. 28 of the Matrimonial Causes Act 1950 (now s. 31
of the Matrimonial Causes Act 1965) pointed out (2) that it gives a jurisdiction
to vary an order not a jurisdiction to fix de novo the amount of maintenance.
The original order is the starting point and the court is entitled to proceed on
the basis that it was properly made at the time when it was made, especially   I
if there had been no effective appeal.

In *L.* v. *L.* (3) in chambers I said when giving judgment after referring to
Foster v. *Foster* (1):

" I must therefore begin with the order of £10 per week.   It has been suggested that because it is a consent order and not an order made after

(1) [1964] 3 All E.R. 541;   [1964] 1 W.L.R. 1155, n.
(2) [1964] 3 All E.R. at p. 545;   [1964] 1 W.L.R. at p. 1157.
(3) (23rd January 1968), unreported.

A investigation by the court it is possible that a different consideration applies. I do not think so. I think even more, in the circumstances of this case, with a consent order indeed than with a court order one must take the order itself as being the starting point."

B In the Court of Appeal (4) Willmer, L.J., said that I " showed a correct appreciation of the law concerned " and that he could " see nothing erroneous in my approach to the question I had to answer." Danckwerts and Diplock, L.JJ., agreed.

In *L.* v. *L.* (5) a wife who was independently advised had consented through her solicitors to an order dismissing her application for maintenance on terms which included the payment to her of a lump sum. Willmer, L.J., said (6):

C " I am not impressed by the argument of counsel for the wife that the sanction of the court for such an agreement is not properly obtained unless there is a full investigation by the court of all the circumstances, with affidavits of means filed on both sides. We are dealing here with a case in which both parties were competently advised by solicitors, one of whom was present on the hearing of the summons. The summons was heard by an experienced

D registrar, and it is to be presumed that he did not make the order giving effect to the terms of the agreement without satisfying himself that it was proper in all the circumstances to do so. I do not think that it is right, therefore, to dismiss the making of the consent order as a mere formality equivalent (to use counsel for the wife's phrase) to no more than putting a rubber stamp on the agreement of the parties. It seems to me that everything necessary

E to be done to give binding effect to the agreement was done in this case. The wife, therefore, is, in my judgment, precluded by the agreement from making this second attempt to obtain an order for maintenance against her husband."

Davies, L.J., said (7):

F " It is, as I think, quite impossible to accept counsel for the wife's argument that that order was a mere rubber stamp nullity. It would be quite wrong and quite improper to disregard the order of the court or to embark in any particular case on an inquiry whether the consent order (in the absence, of course, of fraud) was or was not properly made."

G The decision of Stirling, J., in *Re Minter* (decd.), *Visco* v. *Minter* (8) that a consent order discharging a previous maintenance order by which the wife undertook to make no further claim for maintenance or payment of a lump sum, did not bar an application by her after the husband's death for provision out of his estate, does not assist the husband in the present case. Indeed, the learned judge contrasted (9) the position of a wife who is debarred during the life of her husband from going beyond the sanctioned agreement, but who would

H be entitled on his death to apply under s. 26 of the Act of 1965 for provision from the estate.

In *B.* (*M.A.L.*) v. *B.* (*N.E.*) (10) Payne, J., held that a husband was estopped from seeking to set aside a maintenance order to which he had consented in 1938 by the order itself. He cited (11) in support of the headnote in *Re South American and Mexican Co., Ltd., Ex p. Bank of England* (12):

I ---

(4) (27th March 1968), unreported.
(5) [1961] 3 All E.R. 834; [1962] P. 101.
(6) [1961] 3 All E.R. at p. 840; [1962] P. at pp. 119, 120.
(7) [1961] 3 All E.R. at p. 842; [1962] P. at p. 123.
(8) [1967] 3 All E.R. 412.
(9) [1967] 3 All E.R. at p. 416
(10) [1968] 1 W.L.R. 1109.
(11) [1968] 1 W.L.R. at p. 1122.
(12) [1895] 1 Ch. 37; [1891-94] All E.R. Rep. 680.

A

" A judgment by consent or default, is as effective as an estoppel between the parties as a judgment whereby the court exercises its mind on a contested case."

However, in *Payne* v. *Payne* (13) a husband had not made a full and frank disclosure of his assets when a consent order was made. WILLMER, L.J., said (14):

B

" On reflection, however, I do not think that the principle stated in *Foster* v. *Foster* (15) should be applied in the circumstances of this case. In *Foster* v. *Foster* (15) the original maintenance order had been arrived at after judicial inquiry. Here it was a consent order, arrived at on the basis of that which the husband was at the time prepared to disclose about his personal affairs. I am left in the position that I am far from satisfied that at the time he made anything like a full disclosure of the relevant circumstances. Beyond saying, therefore, that the parties at the time thought that £1,500 a year maintenance would be appropriate on the basis of an income of £5,000 a year, I do not think that the original consent order can be regarded as so sacrosanct, as it were, as the original maintenance order was held to be in *Foster* v. *Foster* (15)."

C

D

I summarise the principles thus: (i) the original order must be taken as the starting point (*Foster* v. *Foster* (15)); (ii) this applies equally to a consent order (*L.* v. *L.* (16)); (iii) any order can be varied by consent; (iv) there is an exception to the principle of *Foster* v. *Foster* (15), if the wife establishes that a husband has failed to make a full and frank disclosure of his assets, and that she was prejudiced by such failure (*Payne* v. *Payne* (13)). Whether this exception applies also to an order made after investigation has yet to be decided; (v) a further exception may arise where one party has not been independently and competently advised before consenting to an order (*L.* v. *L.* (16)) but at least the party so contending would have to establish the fact to the court. The opposite has been established in the present case.

E

Applying these principles it seems to me that the learned registrar was wrong and that the only way in which this consent order can be disturbed is by appeal. I am not of course venturing any opinion whether such an appeal would be successful or even whether leave would be given. I therefore allow this appeal and set aside the order made by Mr. Registrar HOLLOWAY.

F

Appeal allowed.

Solicitors: *J. D. Langton & Passmore*, Woolwich (for the wife); *Adam Shale & Garle* agents for *D. R. de Lacey*, Crayford (for the husband).

G

[*Reported by* ALICE BLOOMFIELD, *Barrister-at-Law.*]

H

I

---

(13) [1968] 1 All E.R. 1113; [1968] 1 W.L.R. 390.
(14) [1968] 1 All E.R. at p. 1117; [1968] 1 W.L.R. at p. 395.
(15) [1964] 3 All E.R. 541; [1964] 1 W.L.R. 1155, n.
(16) [1961] 3 All E.R. 834; [1962] P. 101.

A

SUPERHEATER CO., LTD. *v.* COMMISSIONERS OF CUSTOMS AND EXCISE.

[QUEEN'S BENCH DIVISION (Lord Parker, C.J., Blain and Donaldson, JJ.), March 5, 6, 1969.]

B   *Currency Control—Exchange control—Payment for exports—Export of goods to destination outside scheduled territories—Prerequisite as to prior payment not fulfilled—Ultimate destination of goods Southern Rhodesia—Goods consigned by company to South Africa for reconsignment to Southern Rhodesia—Penalty under customs legislation for export in contravention of exchange control—Exchange Control Act 1947 (10 & 11 Geo. 6 c. 14), s. 23 (1), (4)—*

C   *Customs and Excise Act 1952 (15 & 16 Geo. 6 & 1 Eliz. 2 c. 44), s. 56 (1).*

The appellants for many years had supplied superheaters and accessories for locomotives to Rhodesia Railways. From 1942 to 1962, these were ordered via the appellants' representatives in South Africa, S. Between 1962 and 1965, however, Rhodesia Railways had usually dealt direct with the appellants. In November 1965, the government of Southern Rhodesia made

D   a unilateral declaration of independence. At that time six orders placed directly with the appellants by Rhodesia Railways were outstanding, and one order placed via S. was also outstanding. As a result of statutory instruments* made shortly thereafter, Southern Rhodesia was excluded from the scheduled territories and thus by s. 23 (1)† of the Exchange Control Act 1947 exports to Southern Rhodesia were prohibited unless the

E   Commissioners of Customs and Excise were satisfied that payment had been made in advance and in the prescribed manner. The appellants arranged for the outstanding orders from Rhodesia Railways to be cancelled and for substituted orders to be placed through S. These orders were sent c.i.f. Port Elizabeth (instead of f.o.b. Mersey port) and were kept in bond there before being re-marked and reconsigned to Bulawayo. Subsequent orders

F   were placed by Rhodesia Railways and handled in the same way. The appellants were convicted of exporting goods the ultimate destination of which was Bulawayo and thus contravening s. 23 (1) and becoming liable to a penalty under s. 56 (1)‡ of the Customs and Excise Act 1952. On the question whether the ultimate destination under s. 23 (1) and (4)† of the Act of 1947 of the goods was Bulawayo or Port Elizabeth,

G   **Held:** the ultimate destination of the goods was Bulawayo, because—
(i) (per LORD PARKER, C.J.) it was impossible to confine consideration of

---

* By the Exchange Control (Scheduled Territories) (Amendment) (No. 3) Order 1965 (S.I. 1965 No. 1941), Sch. 1 to the Exchange Control Act 1947, as amended, was further amended by adding at the end of para. 28 the words " and Southern Rhodesia ". The effect of this was to exclude Southern Rhodesia from the list of scheduled territories. The scheduled territories are specified at the date of this report in Sch. 1 to the Exchange

H   Control (Scheduled Territories) Order 1967 (S.I. 1967 No. 1767) as amended, and the order of 1965 has been revoked. Southern Rhodesia is not named in the list of scheduled territories in the order of 1967.

The Exchange Control (Payments) (Amendment) Order 1965 (S.I. 1965 No. 1940) amended the Exchange Control (Payments) Order 1959. Both have been revoked and replaced by the Exchange Control (Payments) Order 1967 (S.I. 1967 No. 1189).

By the Exchange Control (Exports to Southern Rhodesia) Directions 1965 (S.I. 1965

I   No. 2039), made and coming into operation on 1st December 1965, s. 23 (1) (*a*) of the Exchange Control Act 1947, had effect in relation to the exportation of goods of any class or description from the United Kingdom to a destination in Southern Rhodesia as if the words " or is to be so made not later than six months after the date of exportation " were omitted. The effect of this was to bring about a prohibition of the exportation of goods from the United Kingdom to destinations in Southern Rhodesia unless payment for the goods had been made prior to their exportation. Paragraph 2 of the directions provided: " Any reference in these directions to the destination of any goods includes a reference to the ultimate destination thereof."

† Section 23, so far as material, is set out at p. 472, letter H, post.

‡ Section 56 (1), so far as material, is set out at p. 472, letter G, post.

the ultimate destination of goods to the strict contractual position; the **A**
whole object (let alone intention or contemplation or anything less) of the
transaction was that the goods should go to Bulawayo (see p. 475, letter F,
and p. 476, letters B and G, post);

(ii) (per BLAIN, J.) it was always the intention of the appellants at the
moment of exportation that these goods should go from Mersey port to
Port Elizabeth for direct onward transmission to Rhodesia Railways at **B**
Bulawayo; accordingly, Bulawayo was the destination; even if, however,
Bulawayo was not the destination it must have been the ultimate destination
of the goods (see p. 479, letters B and D, post);

(iii) (per DONALDSON, J.) the true test under s. 23 of the Act of 1947 was
the destination contemplated rather than that intended by the exporter
and the appellants always intended and contemplated that the goods would **C**
go to Bulawayo as part of a continuous transit from the United Kingdom
(see p. 480, letters E and I, post).

J. & J. Colman, Ltd. v. *Comrs. of Customs and Excise* ([1968] 2 All E.R.
832) applied.

Per BLAIN, J.: the ultimate destination means the ultimate destination
in the mind or intent of the exporter (see p. 479, letter D, post). **D**

Decision of His Honour JUDGE KILNER BROWN, Q.C. (sub nom. *Hodson*
v. *The Superheater Co., Ltd.* ([1968] 3 All E.R. 144) affirmed.

[As to meaning of " ultimate destination " under the Exchange Control Act
1947, see 27 HALSBURY'S LAWS (3rd Edn.) 123, para. 203, note (*d*); and for
cases on the subject, see 29 DIGEST (Repl.) 159, *963, 964*; 37 DIGEST (Repl.)
521-526, *840-877*. **E**

For the Exchange Control Act 1947, s. 23, see 16 HALSBURY'S STATUTES
(2nd Edn.) 583.

For the Customs and Excise Act 1952, s. 56, see 32 HALSBURY'S STATUTES
(2nd Edn.) 755.]

Cases referred to:

Colman (J. & J.), Ltd. v. Comrs. of Customs and Excise, [1968] 2 All E.R. 832; **F**
    [1968] 1 W.L.R. 1286.
Gallaher, Ltd. v. Comrs. of Customs and Excise, [1968] 2 All E.R. 820; [1968]
    2 Q.B. 674; [1968] 3 W.L.R. 188.
Renton (G. H.) & Co., Ltd. v. Black Sea and Baltic General Insurance Co., Ltd.,
    [1941] 1 All E.R. 149; [1941] 1 K.B. 206; 110 L.J.K.B. 329; 164
    L.T. 190; 29 Digest (Repl.) 159, 964. **G**

Case Stated.

This was a Case Stated by JUDGE KILNER BROWN, Q.C., in respect of his
adjudication as an appeal court sitting at Liverpool on 23rd, 24th, 25th and
26th April 1968 and reported [1968] 3 All E.R. 144, sub nom. *Hodson* v.
The Superheater Co., Ltd. **H**

On 10th January 1968, the appellants, the Superheater Co., Ltd., were
convicted before the stipendiary magistrate for the city of Liverpool on ten of a
total of 20 charges brought against them by the respondents, the Commissioners
of Customs and Excise. Each of the ten charges on which the appellants were
convicted alleged that on a date specified in that charge, at Birkenhead the
appellants exported certain goods the exportation of which was prohibited by **I**
s. 23 (1) of the Exchange Control Act 1947, contrary to s. 56 (1) of the Customs
and Excise Act 1952.

The dates specified in the respective charges and the goods to which the
respective charges related, were as follows: (i) 24th March 1966—162 superheater
elements; (ii) 28th July 1966—63 superheater elements; (iii) 25th August 1966—
233 superheater elements; (iv) 23rd September 1966—26 superheater elements;
(v) 9th January 1967—62 superheater elements; (vi) 13th April 1966—1,000
clamp bolts and 30 cutters; (vii) 6th May 1966—79 superheater elements;

A   (viii) 23rd August 1966—48 clamp bolts; (ix) 13th October 1966—508 clamp
bolts; (x) 24th October 1966—500 clamp bolts.

The appellants appealed against their convictions on each of the above charges,
and the recorder heard the appeals together with other appeals by the respective
parties which were not material to this case.

At the hearing of the appeals the following facts material to this case were
B   proved or admitted before him: The appellants for many years supplied
superheaters and accessories for the use of a concern known as Rhodesia Railways.
This railway served and ran through the territories in Africa formerly known as
Southern Rhodesia, Northern Rhodesia and Bechuanaland. It was a body
corporate and operated with headquarters in Bulawayo, Southern Rhodesia. In
1942 the appellants entered into an agreement with Stone Stamcor (Pty.), Ltd.,
C   a company who described themselves as electrical and mechanical engineers
with a head office in Johannesburg, South Africa. Under this agreement goods
for various railway systems in Africa were ordered and supplied. Such goods
were supplied for South African Railways up to and including the year 1966.
From 1942 to 1962 goods were supplied under the agreement to Rhodesia
Railways but from the year 1962 until the year 1965 it became the usual practice
D   for Rhodesia Railways to order and pay for the goods direct from the appellants.
Occasional orders for goods for Rhodesia Railways were placed by Stone Stamcor
and one such order was still outstanding in 1966. After the announcement of
a unilateral declaration of independence by Mr. Ian Smith in November 1965
and coincident with and subsequent to a series of orders made by the British
government under and in connection with s. 23 of the Exchange Control Act
E   1947 and s. 56 of the Customs and Excise Act 1952, the appellants were aware
of a change of circumstances insofar as trade with persons or concerns in Southern
Rhodesia were involved. A review of the trading situation with Rhodesia
Railways was put in hand by the appellants on 12th November. A series of
contemporary memoranda, letters and documents were put in and exhibited in
a folder entitled " Correspondence ". In addition three folders relative to
F   shipments were put in. The effect of the orders made in November and December
1965 was that Rhodesia became a prescribed territory and goods exported from
the United Kingdom to Rhodesia became subject to exchange control. Arrangements for prepayment in authorised currency had to be approved by the
Commissioners of Customs and Excise. Neither South Africa nor Zambia were
prescribed territories. As was apparent from documents 3 to 25 in the folder
G   entitled " Correspondence ", there was substituted for the previous procedure of
dealing directly with Rhodesia Railways under which goods had been consigned
f.o.b. Mersey port for Bulawayo, an arrangement with Stamcor that the orders
for goods already placed referenced and identified would be cancelled and
precisely similar orders similarly cross referenced would be placed by Stamcor
and consigned c.i.f. Port Elizabeth. It was known and understood as appeared
H   from document 28 in the folder entitled " Correspondence ", that goods sent to
Stamcor were to be re-marked and reconsigned to Rhodesia Railways. With
reference to the arrangement, one Ockenden for the appellants stated in January
1967 to two officers of customs and excise that Stamcor had been contacted and
asked if they would consider goods being ostensibly booked to them but the
ultimate destination would be Rhodesia. All the goods which were the subject
I   of these charges were exported in accordance with this arrangement and the
conditions relative to exchange control insofar as Rhodesia was concerned, were
not complied with. All the goods were received by Rhodesia Railways in
Bulawayo, and taken into stock. Certain of the goods were re-issued by Rhodesia
Railways to various of their depots in Zambia for use on locomotives operating
in Zambia. In July 1967, the integrated railway systems became separately
administered as to that portion in Zambia. Stamcor paid the appellants in
South African rands for all goods which were dealt with in accordance with the
new procedure and were themselves allowed a commission on all such goods.

It was contended before the recorder by the appellants that no offence had A
been committed by them in relation to any of the goods on the grounds: (a) that
on the true construction of s. 23 (1) and (4) of the Exchange Control Act 1947,
the "ultimate destination" within the meaning of those sections of goods
exported, was the ultimate destination to which the exporter of those goods
had contracted to deliver those goods, and (b) that on the facts, and on the true
construction of s. 23 (1) and (4) of the Exchange Control Act 1947, the destina- B
tion, and the ultimate destination, of all the goods exported by the appellants,
was Port Elizabeth in the Republic of South Africa. It was contended before
him by the respondents that the appellants had been rightly convicted on the
grounds that on the facts set out, and on the true construction of s. 23 (1) and
(4) of the Exchange Control Act 1947, the ultimate destination of all the goods
exported by the appellants was Bulawayo in Rhodesia. C

The recorder was of the opinion that the contentions of the respondents were
correct and he accordingly dismissed the appeals. The appellants now appealed.
The question for the opinion of the court was whether the recorder was right in
deciding on the facts set out, and on the true construction of s. 23 (1) and (4)
of the Exchange Control Act 1947, that the ultimate destination of the goods
exported by the appellants was Bulawayo in Rhodesia. D

The authority and the cases noted below* were cited during the argument in
addition to the cases referred to in the judgments.

Geoffrey Howe, Q.C., and *R. R. Leech* for the appellants.
G. Heilpern, Q.C., and *N. W. M. Sellers* for the Commissioners of Customs and
Excise.

    LORD PARKER, C.J.: This is an appeal by way of Case Stated from a E
decision (1) of the recorder of the city of Liverpool, who dismissed an appeal by
the appellants, the Superheater Co., Ltd., against their conviction by the
stipendiary magistrate for the city of Liverpool on ten charges preferred by the
respondents, the Commissioners of Customs and Excise, for that at Birkenhead
the appellants exported certain goods the exportation of which was prohibited
by s. 23 (1) of the Exchange Control Act 1947, contrary to s. 56 (1) of the Customs F
and Excise Act 1952.

Before looking at the facts here, it is convenient to look briefly at the sections
in question. The section which creates the offence is s. 56 (1) of the Customs and
Excise Act 1952. So far as it is relevant to these proceedings, it provides that:

    "If any goods are—(a) exported . . . and the exportation or shipment is
    or would be contrary to any prohibition or restriction for the time being in G
    force with respect to those goods under or by virtue of any enactment . . ."

then to put it quite shortly, the goods may be forfeit and penalties imposed.
The prohibition or restriction in question here is one which was made under the
Exchange Control Act 1947. Section 23 of that Act provides:

    ". . . The exportation of goods of any class or description from the United H
    Kingdom to a destination in any such territory as may be prescribed is
    hereby prohibited except with the permission of the Treasury, unless the
    Commissioners of Customs and Excise are satisfied—(a) that payment for
    the goods has been made to a person resident in the United Kingdom in
    such manner as may be prescribed in relation to goods of that class or
    description exported to a destination in that territory, or is to be so made I
    not later than six months after the date of exportation; . . .

    * OXFORD ENGLISH DICTIONARY, Vol. 3, "Destination", p. 258; *The Kim*, [1915]
P. 215; *The Louisiana*, [1918] A.C. 461; *France Fenwick Tyne and Wear Co., Ltd.* v.
H.M. Procurator-General, [1942] 2 All E.R. 453; [1942] A.C. 667; *Conservas Cerqueira
Limitada* v. *H.M. Procurator-General*, [1944] A.C. 6; *I.T.P. (London), Ltd.* v. *Winstanley*,
[1947] 1 All E.R. 177; [1947] K.B. 422; *Allen* v. *Thorn Electrical Industries, Ltd.*;
Griffin v. *Metropolitan Police District Receiver*, [1967] 2 All E.R. 1137; [1968] 1 Q.B.
487; *Freed* v. *Director of Public Prosecutions*, [1969] 1 All E.R. 428; [1969] 2 W.L.R. 390.
    (1) See [1968] 3 All E.R. 144 (sub nom. *Hodson* v. *The Superheater Co., Ltd.*).

A   " (4) Any reference in this section to the destination of any goods includes
        a reference to the ultimate destination thereof."

The question, as it will appear, is whether the goods the subject of these
charges were exported to a destination in Rhodesia.   In fact they went to and
were intended for Rhodesia Railways at Bulawayo.   Prior to what is referred
to as U.D.I., the unilateral declaration of independence in Rhodesia, which
B   was on 11th November 1965, it would be perfectly possible for an exporter in
this country to export goods to Rhodesia, or, to take this case, to Rhodesia
Railways at Bulawayo, and to receive payment in sterling, and indeed payment
in sterling within six months from the exportation.   As a result of U.D.I.,
however, a number, in fact three, statutory instruments (2) came into force
which had the effect of providing by 18th December 1965 that payment for
C   exports to Rhodesia had to be, to put it in general terms, in hard currency
and paid in advance, in other words Rhodesia had come out of the sterling
area and become one of the prescribed territories.   If therefore the destination,
or the ultimate destination, of the goods the subject of these charges was Rhodesia
and Bulawayo, then it is conceded that the permission of the Treasury had not
been obtained, nor had the customs been satisfied in the matters set out in
D   s. 23 (1).   In other words the goods would have been exported within the meaning
of s. 56 (1) of the Customs and Excise Act 1952 contrary to the prohibition.

Before looking at the facts, I would like myself to make two observations.
First, it is to be observed that the offences charged against the appellants were
not offences of exporting goods which had become illegal by what one may call
sanction measures, but were offences contrary to exchange control, and it is
E   important to bear that in mind.   The second is that there is no suggestion
whatever that the arrangements to which I will refer, made by the appellants,
were in any way a sham or in any way a device to get round exchange control.
I think it is only right to make that perfectly clear, and indeed it is to be observed
that they were acquitted both by the stipendiary magistrate, and on appeal by
the recorder (3), of other charges of knowingly seeking to evade the prohibition,
F   indeed it was held that they had no idea at the material time of the exchange
control position.

With that introduction, it is necessary to look shortly at the facts.   The
appellants had in South Africa at Johannesburg representatives known as
Stone Stamcor (Proprietary), Ltd. (for convenience " Stamcor "); they had
been appointed representatives and sole selling agents for the class of goods
G   dealt in by the appellants as long ago as 1942.   I am by no means clear that the
actual terms of that agreement are really very material in this case, but in passing
it is to be observed that Stamcor was appointed—

        " the sole representative of the appellants for obtaining orders for and
        selling of the goods apparatus and appliances exclusively connected with
        the railway locomotives now manufactured or sold by . . ."

H   the appellants.   Clause 12 further provided that—

        " Orders for any of the agreed goods shall only be accepted by the repre-
        sentative at the prices and upon the terms as to delivery and payment
        previously quoted or arranged by the Company as aforesaid or at such
        other prices and terms as the Company may from time to time in writing
I   previously instruct the representative."

By cl. 13, which is important, it was provided that:

        " Subject as aforesaid orders for any of the agreed goods in or for the
        said territory shall be accepted by the representative in its own name and
        entirely on its own behalf liability and responsibility and the Company
        without its previous written consent shall at no time be liable upon any
        contract therefor entered into by the representative with its customers."

(2) See footnote *, at p. 469, ante.
(3) See [1968] 3 All E.R. at p. 152.

Clause 14 provided for the payment of commission or discount; finally by cl. 17 **A**
provision was made for the representatives to pay the appellants for all the
agreed goods ordered by the representatives from the appellants.

For a time goods were supplied pursuant to that agreement, to Stamcor,
which goods were goods sold on to the South African Railways and sometimes
to the Rhodesia Railways.   But there was a departure from the strict terms of
that agreement in 1962, because from that time up to the times in question **B**
herein, it was the practice for Rhodesia Railways to enter into direct contracts
with the appellants and not, as it were, through Stamcor, and to order and pay
for the goods direct to the appellants.   That was the general practice from 1962
to 1965 in regard to Rhodesia Railways, although it is found in the Case that
there were occasional departures when the procedure under the agreement of
1942 was adopted.   In fact we are told that one of the charges here relates to a **C**
case not of a direct contract, but of a contract through Stamcor made before
U.D.I.   What came then was U.D.I. on 11th November 1965, and immediately difficulties arose.   The difficulties that did arise pertained to the difficulty
of shipping, and not in any way to exchange control, and not in any way, as I
have said, to any prohibition of the export of goods relating to measures by
way of sanctions.   At the time of U.D.I. there were seven orders outstanding, **D**
six direct from Rhodesia Railways and one from Rhodesia Railways, if I may
use a neutral term, through Stamcor.   Thereupon, and it is unnecessary to
go through the correspondence, ways and means were sought for ensuring that
the goods the subject of these seven outstanding contracts should get to Rhodesia
Railways.

To put it quite shortly, what was arranged was that Rhodesia Railways **E**
would cancel the existing orders, renew them with Stamcor, and Stamcor
would then pay the appellants.   In fact it involved this, that whereas under the
contracts originally made direct with Rhodesia Railways, the appellants were to
ship the goods f.o.b. Mersey port, the arrangements made, and it is really a
tripartite arrangement, were that the goods were to be shipped c.i.f. Port Elizabeth, that Rhodesia Railways would pay the cost, insurance and freight to **F**
Stamcor, who would pay that on to the appellants in addition to the quoted
price, but taking its commission or discount, in this case I think ten per cent.
Those arrangements are embodied in letters in the correspondence, and it is
quite clear first that the arrangement covered the same specific goods which
had been the subject of the direct contracts, and that throughout the reference
numbers were the same reference numbers as in the original contracts; the **G**
scheme throughout was that these goods, some of which had been ordered and
made to drawings supplied by Rhodesia Railways, should reach Bulawayo;
Stamcor when the goods reached Port Elizabeth was to re-mark and reconsign
the goods on to Bulawayo, and indeed provision was made that they were to be
kept in bond in Port Elizabeth.   That concerned the seven contracts which were
in existence at the time of U.D.I.   Thereafter fresh contracts were made, some **H**
three in number amounting in all to some £5,000, again goods made specifically
to the requirements of Rhodesia Railways, but sent c.i.f. Port Elizabeth under
the same arrangement whereby they would be kept in bond, re-marked and reconsigned to Bulawayo, Stamcor taking its commission for services, but in
form, as in the present case, the price would be paid by Rhodesia Railways to
Stamcor, and Stamcor would pay the appellants.   In fact all those contracts **I**
were carried through; all the goods in fact reached Rhodesia Railways and the
appellants were paid, but what they were paid was South African rands and not
hard currency.

The question therefore narrows itself to this: was Port Elizabeth the destination or ultimate destination, in which case the appellants were perfectly entitled
to receive South African rands; or is the true view that the destination or
ultimate destination was Rhodesia, in which case it is quite clear that they have
been guilty of a breach of the prohibition against exporting goods to Rhodesia

A otherwise than for hard currency in advance.   As I have said, both the stipendiary magistrate and the recorder held that the offences in each case were made out.   I should say that the contentions which have been elaborated before this court were set out very concisely in the Case Stated, where it states:

B " It was contended before me by the appellants that no offence had been committed by them in relation to any of the said goods on the grounds: (a) that on the true construction of Sections 23 (1) and 23 (4) of the Exchange Control Act 1947, the ' ultimate destination ' within the meaning of those sections of goods exported, is the ultimate destination to which the exporter of those goods has contracted to deliver those goods, and (b) that on the facts hereinbefore set out, and on the true construction of the said Sections

C 23 (1) and 23 (4) of the Exchange Control Act 1947, the destination, and the ultimate destination, of all the said goods exported by the appellants, was Port Elizabeth in the Republic of South Africa.''

The recorder found insofar as it was a question of fact, and in my judgment it is largely a question of fact, that the ultimate destination here was Bulawayo, Rhodesia.   The real question as I see it in those circumstances is whether, as

D counsel for the appellants alleges, the recorder has misdirected himself in law. Despite counsel's able argument, I do not propose to go through all the details of his submission.   It can be put in a great number of ways, but quite shortly as I understand it what he says is this, that when one is seeking to discover the ultimate destination of any export, one does so by identifying the customer to whom the goods have been sold, in other words one looks at the strict con-

E tractual position, and that gives one the contractual destination, and that is all one is concerned with.   It is not perhaps unfair to say that he would read for the word " destination " in s. 23 (1), " a purchaser "—" the exportation of goods of any class or description from the United Kingdom to a [purchaser] in any such territory ", and I suppose it would follow that in sub-s. (4) he would read " ultimate destination " as " ultimate purchaser ".

F It seems to me quite clear that " destination " means a geographical place or country and is not concerned with a purchaser.   But on any view it seems to me that it is quite impossible to confine the considerations to what I may call the strict contractual position.   Counsel for the appellants does not shrink from this at all.   He gave us an illustration only this morning that if, for instance, a customer in Gibraltar, part of the sterling area, ordered goods from the appel-

G lants, and having resold them on to a Spanish company in Madrid, then for convenience asked the appellants to ship the goods direct to Madrid, he would say that the fact that they are going and are clearly exported to Madrid as a place, is neither here nor there.   He is forced to say: one looks to see what is the place where the purchaser is who is going to pay, and if the purchaser in that case is in Gibraltar, there is an end of the matter.   As he would say, the exchange

H control provisions in this country do not, as is quite clear, operate extra territorially, and what this country depends on is the merchant in the sterling area in turn playing the game according to that country's exchange regulations. He would say that is another reason for confining the considerations solely to the contract, and the purchaser.   I confess that even if one did look at what can be spoken of generally as the contractual destination, I am by no means clear in

I my own mind that the destination in regard to the first seven contracts was not quite clearly Bulawayo; but it is unnecessary to come to that conclusion, and indeed the commissioners do not put it that way.   They rely on the words " ultimate destination ".   Counsel for the appellants, so far as " ultimate destination " is concerned, confines the discovery of the ultimate destination to the contractual position.   He would say that the contract here quite clearly is a contract with Stamcor for export c.i.f. Port Elizabeth, and that nothing that happens thereafter is part of the journey; the journey has ended.   He goes further and says there is no test that can be laid down other than the one which

he suggests that will really meet every case that should be met, and will not A
rope in cases which clearly ought not to be covered.

For my part I do not propose to lay down any clear tests. What it seems to
me one is concerned to ascertain here is whether there was evidence on which
the recorder properly directing himself as to the law could say that the ultimate
destination here was Bulawayo, Rhodesia. It seems to me, having read all
the correspondence and seen the arrangements made, it is a finding which is B
fully justified on the facts of this case. The whole object here, let alone intention
or contemplation or anything less, of the transaction was that the goods should
go to Bulawayo. The court has been referred to recent cases in this court,
and in particular to *J. & J. Colman, Ltd.* v. *Comrs. of Customs and Excise* (4),
where true the matter being considered was the words " consigned to ". There
goods had been shipped to Rotterdam or Antwerp from Canada for transship- C
ment by coaster to England, and the question was whether the purchasers who
were in England were entitled to Commonwealth preference. In that case
LORD DENNING, M.R., approached the matter in this way. He said (5):

" What is the meaning of the words ' consigned to '? That is the question.
I .endeavoured to answer it in *Gallaher, Ltd.* v. *Comrs. of Customs and
Excise* (6). Applying what I there said, I think that goods are ' consigned to D
the United Kingdom from Canada ' when they are delivered to a carrier in
Canada for continuous transit to the United Kingdom. The sender must
intend that they should go direct to the United Kingdom and not be taken
into the commerce of any other country; and that intention must be realised."

Counsel for the appellants seeks to distinguish that case not only because of the
subject-matter that it was dealing with, but because he says if one once begins E
to apply matters of intention in considering s. 23 of the Act of 1947, to put it
generally, where does one end? No doubt there are cases where a general
agent in a sterling area will buy goods, and it will be contemplated and even
intended that he will sell in countries outside the sterling area. Counsel for the
appellants would say: does every exporter in this country have to consider
where the goods will ultimately end up, in other words where is the consumer; F
one ought to be confined solely to the customer who is buying them in the first
instance. For my part I find it quite unnecessary to consider where the matter
ends. As I have said, here the sole object was for these goods to get to Bulawayo, but I am far from saying that intention and possibly contemplation, may
not be sufficient. It was never contemplated here and never intended here
that the goods were to become part of the stock of South Africa; it was never G
intended that they should enter into the commerce of South Africa; they were
in fact being sent on in bond, and in those circumstances it seems to me quite
clear that there was no error in law in holding, as the recorder did, that Bulawayo
was the ultimate destination. Indeed as it seems to me it accords with common
sense on the facts of this case.

BLAIN, J.: The Exchange Control Act 1947 was passed to confer powers H
and to impose duties and restrictions affecting the monetary relationship between
the United Kingdom and territories outside the sterling area. We were asked
to consider its long title, and as that long title indicates, those powers, duties and
restrictions concern a number of different matters. The matters include gold
and currency which are dealt with in Part 1 of the Act; payments which are
dealt with in Part 2 of the Act; securities which are dealt with in Part 3; and I
they include import and export of property which are dealt with in Part 4.
This appeal is concerned with the export of locomotive components manufactured
by the appellants in Britain and used by Rhodesia Railways, and Part 4 of the
Act applies.

The facts and history of the matter so far as relevant have been summarised

(4) [1968] 2 All E.R. 832; [1968] 1 W.L.R. 1286.
(5) [1968] 2 All E.R. at p. 834; [1968] 1 W.L.R. at p. 1291.
(6) [1968] 2 All E.R. 820; [1968] 2 Q.B. 674.

A by LORD PARKER, C.J., and indeed I think are not in dispute. As is well known, on 11th November 1965 Mr. Ian Smith announced Rhodesia's unilateral declaration of independence, which resulted in the British Parliament's imposing sanctions by a series of steps which do not require further detailed analysis. For the purposes of this appeal, it is sufficient to say that as the result of those steps, by the time when the first of the alleged offences now in issue was com-

B mitted, Parliament had imposed a complete ban on export to Rhodesia without Treasury sanction, and Rhodesia had ceased to be a part of the sterling area. The appeal is against ten convictions for exporting goods on dates between 24th March 1966 and 9th January 1967, goods the exportation of which it was alleged was prohibited by the terms of s. 23 (1) of the Exchange Control Act 1947, contrary to s. 56 (1) of the Customs and Excise Act 1952. So far as

C relevant, s. 23 (1) of the Exchange Control Act provides:

" The exportation of goods of any class or description from the United Kingdom to a destination in any such territory as may be prescribed is hereby prohibited . . ."

with certain exceptions. Subsection (4) provides:

D " Any reference in this section to the destination of any goods includes a reference to the ultimate destination thereof."

Rhodesia, as I have said, had become a prescribed territory by the relevant dates, and none of the exceptions to the basic prohibition of s. 23 (1) applied. None of them applied when the ships in question left Mersey port. The relevance of that is that by definition to be found in s. 79 (3) of the Customs and Excise

E Act 1952, the act of exportation occurs when the ship leaves the last port in the sterling area, which in this case was Mersey port, so the sole question is whether the exportation was to Rhodesia as the commissioners alleged, and as both the learned stipendiary magistrate of Liverpool and the learned judge at the Crown Court at Liverpool found; or whether it was to a non-prescribed destination, to wit Port Elizabeth in South Africa. This involves the inter-

F pretation or definition of the term " destination " in the context of s. 23 of the Exchange Control Act 1947 and in relation to the facts as established by the evidence and history as a whole.

For my own part as I understand it the verb " to destine " normally is a transitive verb meaning " to ordain or fix the fate or function or state of some person or object " and the noun " destination " is either the purpose, or the

G geographical context, the place to which the person or object is destined to go. There can be no doubt that s. 23 has a geographical context when it uses that term " destination ". That is quite clear because what it is dealing with is: export to a destination. To me it thus seems implicit in the use of the noun " destination ", certainly in such a context as this that there must be an element of intent, if not necessarily an element of decision, though clearly the identity

H or role of a person whose mind has that intent may vary widely from one context to another. In the context of s. 23, one is dealing with exportation of goods to a destination, and to me the conclusion is inevitable that the relevant mind when considering intent is the mind of the exporter. Thus the court, as did the court below, has to consider what was the mind of the exporter, that is the appellants at the moment of exportation, that is at the time when the ship or

I series of ships left Mersey port.

Since 1942 the appellants had provided, to use a neutral term deliberately, components for use by Rhodesia Railways, and so far as some at least of those components were concerned, one knows not what proportion, designed to the specifications or drawings of Rhodesia Railways. For about the first 20 years they had done this mainly, not wholly, through their Johannesburg representative, in pursuance of an agreement made with that representative in 1942. For the next three or four years from 1962 onwards they had dealt largely, if not wholly, with Rhodesia Railways direct. When the difficulties consequent on U.D.I. arose, the appellants by perfectly genuine three-party arrangements

with Rhodesia Railways and their representatives, Stone Stamcor (Proprietary), A
Ltd., sought to achieve a legitimate way of continuing their business to the
mutual advantage of themselves and with Rhodesia Railways, and for that
matter also no doubt Stamcor, without the need of Treasury agreement, or
payment in advance in sterling.   Their bona fides, as LORD PARKER, C.J., has
said, are not in issue; the sole question is: have they succeeded in putting
themselves outside the terms of s. 23 (1) of the Act.   B

The findings of the learned judge at the Crown Court are quite short.   They
include:

"As is apparent from documents 3 to 25 in the folder entitled ' Correspondence ' . . . there was substituted for the previous procedure of dealing
directly with Rhodesia Railways under which goods had been signed f.o.b.
Mersey Port for Bulawayo, an arrangement with [Stamcor] that the orders C
for goods already placed referenced and identified would be cancelled and
precisely similar orders similarly cross referenced would be placed by
[STAMCOR] and consigned c.i.f. Port Elizabeth.   It was known and understood as appears from Document No. 28 in the folder entitled ' Correspondence ' . . . that goods sent to [Stamcor] were to be re-marked and
reconsigned to Rhodesia Railways."   D

In my view there is ample, and more than ample evidence to justify those
findings.   I will quote three only of the letters in that correspondence, documents
20, 21 and 28.   Document 20 is a letter from Stamcor to the appellants dated
29th December 1965, some six or seven weeks after U.D.I., headed " Rhodesia
Railways " and reads:

"We wish to advise that we have been in touch with our Rhodesian E
agent in regard to shipment on a c.i.f. Port Elizabeth basis of material
placed on order with you direct by the Rhodesia Railways.   We have
now received a letter from our agent advising that the Stores Controller
of Rhodesia Railways would welcome the arrangement whereby shipment is
made through us and payment made to us.   We have been in touch with
our clearing agents and we find that it is possible, without the production F
of an import permit, to forward on an ' in bond ' basis material for Rhodesia.
We will however have to submit at the time of clearing our own bank forms
and certified invoices.   Would you please therefore ship the material as
covered by Rhodesia Railways' Orders 02921, 03032 and 03159 to us and
advise us of your selling price to the Railways and also what commission
on these orders we will be allowed."   G

I need not read the rest of that letter, but it was replied to in document 21 on
4th January 1966 by the appellants in these terms, under the heading " Rhodesia
Railways ":

"Thank you very much for your letter of the 29th December and we
shall be pleased to ship the materials on the undermentioned orders c.i.f.
Port Elizabeth.   We will submit our invoices to you and indicate separately H
the freight and insurance charges.   The orders in question are [four are
enumerated.   The letter concludes] We shall be obliged if you will kindly
let us know, by return of post, the markings we are to use on the cases and
we shall then make immediate arrangements for shipment."

The final document to which I would refer is the one referred to in the findings I
of the learned judge.   It is dated 4th February 1966 and is a letter from Stamcor
to the appellants headed " Re: Rhodesia Railways ".

"We enclose herewith [eight indents which are numbered] covering the
Rhodesia Railways requirements previously placed directly with you but
now cancelled and re-ordered on us.   We would ask that you ship all the
material called for to Port Elizabeth and we will in turn have the cases re-
marked and re-consigned to the Rhodesia Railways.   Please ensure that
shipping documents and certified invoices made out in our name be forwarded per Airmail as soon as shipment has been effected so that we may

A   make arrangements to re-consign in bond to the Rhodesia Railways. The orders that have been placed on us are based on your original quotations to the Rhodesia Railways and all charges from f.o.b. Mersey Port to Bulawayo will be for the Rhodesia Railways account.''

Whatever be the form of the bills of lading and other documents, and whether the separate single contracts of sale be, as that correspondence might indicate,

B   c.i.f., or whether really they be more in the nature of f.o.b. contracts or some hybrid combination of the two, for my part I have no doubt that on the evidence as a whole it was always the intention of the appellants at the moment of exportation that these goods should go from Mersey port to Port Elizabeth for direct onward transmission to Rhodesia Railways at Bulawayo. In those circumstances I regard Bulawayo as the destination; but even if there be doubt

C   about that, the canons of construction would compel me to assume that the term `` ultimate destination '' deliberately introduced by Parliament in s. 23 (4) where there can be any difference, must mean something wider than the mere term `` destination ''. What wider thing can it mean? It cannot mean some unknown final retailer/consumer quite unidentifiable by the exporter, and so I come back to the element of intent implicit in the verb `` destined '' and the

D   noun `` destination ''. The ultimate destination means the ultimate destination in the mind or intent of the exporter, and even if the plain term `` destination '' was not, as I believe it was, Bulawayo, then I have no doubt that the ultimate intention was Bulawayo. With those considerations in mind, and more particularly for the reasons given by LORD PARKER, C.J., I would dismiss this appeal.

E   **DONALDSON, J.:** I also would dismiss this appeal. Counsel for the appellants submits that the destination, and the ultimate destination of the goods was Port Elizabeth in the Republic of South Africa for two different reasons. First he points out that the Exchange Control Act 1947, as its name implies, is primarily concerned with foreign exchange. It follows, he submits, that the destination with which it is concerned is determined by the place of business of the export buyer, and the place from which payment is to be made.

F   In the present case the export buyers were in South Africa, and payment was being made in South African currency. The destination of the goods was therefore, he says, South Africa. This submission is, I think, entirely fallacious. The Act of 1947 may well be concerned primarily with foreign exchange, but as has already been pointed out, it is also concerned with goods. Furthermore, whilst it is true that in the present case the goods were dispatched to the

G   territory in which the export buyers carried on business and were paid for in the currency of that country, this is pure coincidence. The goods would have travelled the same route and been exported to the same ultimate destination, whatever that may have been, if the export buyers had carried on business in Hong Kong and the goods been paid for in New Zealand pounds.

H   Counsel for the appellants' second submission is that the ultimate destination of the goods for the purposes of the section must be related to and limited by the point in the transit at which the exporters' power to control influence or dispose of the goods comes to an end. This submission is based on the consideration that the exporter may well not know what the export buyer will eventually do with the goods, and where they will end up. In this case control ended when the goods reached Port Elizabeth. This submission is, I think, equally fallacious.

I   The appellants' control, like that of any other c.i.f. seller, ended at the latest when they delivered the shipping documents to the buyers or their agents, and this usually occurs when the goods are still at sea. It would follow if that is what occurred in this case, that the ultimate destination was somewhere short of Port Elizabeth. In the case indeed of an f.o.b. export seller, control ceases when the goods are shipped, so that if counsel is right, the ultimate destination of the goods for the purposes of the section in such a case is the place of shipment. This clearly is not right.

The section refers to both a destination and an ultimate destination. This

conception of a destination and a different and final or ultimate destination is A
by no means unknown in the commercial world.   Thus the Timber Trade
Federation insurance clause contains, or did contain, an extension reading
" Including risks of . . . non-delivery . . . until discharged at port of destination
and whilst in transit . . . to final destination . . .".   (See *G. H. Renton & Co., Ltd.*
v. *Black Sea and Baltic General Insurance Co., Ltd.* (7).)   Again if goods are
shipped to a port of discharge for transshipment or for carriage by rail to the B
interior, the port of discharge may well be regarded as the immediate destination
of the goods, and the place to which they are then carried as the ultimate
destination.   A somewhat similar problem arose in *J. & J. Colman, Ltd.* v.
Comrs. of Customs and Excise (8), in the context of where the goods were confined
to the United Kingdom from a place in the Commonwealth Preference Area for
purposes of the Import Duties Act 1958.   The goods had been bought c.i.f. C
Antwerp/Rotterdam, having been shipped in Vancouver, and Colmans, the c.i.f.
buyers, had the goods transshipped on the continent to Norwich.   It was held
that as the goods were delivered to a carrier with the intention of continuous
transit to England without being taken into the commerce of another country
and that intention had been realised, they had been " consigned to the United
Kingdom from Canada " within the meaning of s. 2 (2) of the Act of 1958 and D
qualified for Commonwealth preference.

Counsel for the commissioners submits that a similar test must be applied
in the case of s. 23 of the Exchange Control Act 1947, and that one must identify
the ultimate destination to which the exporter intended the goods to be exported.
I think that " intention " may well be the test where the exporter is retaining
ownership of the exported goods, and it would be sufficient to support the E
convictions in this case.   However, in my judgment the true test is the destination
" contemplated " rather than " intended " by the exporter, since an exporter
who sells f.o.b. may often have no intention with regard to the goods, their
ultimate or indeed their immediate destination being perhaps a matter of
indifference to him, but he will certainly contemplate a destination to which the
goods are being exported by him.   F

How " ultimate " is the destination to which the section refers must, I think,
depend on the information available to the exporter.   SALMON, L.J., in *Colman's*
case (9) held that the place to which goods are consigned for the purposes of
the Import Duties Act 1958 is a question of fact.   So, too, in my judgment is
the destination to which they are exported for the purposes of s. 23 of the
Exchange Control Act 1947.   Continuous transit, if contemplated by the exporter, G
is an important factor in deciding how remote is the ultimate destination from
the point of exportation, and may often be decisive.   However, I do not think
that it is necessarily so.   Suppose, for example, that an exporter arranged to
send the goods to X and for them then to be imported, repacked and then sent
on to Y by him.   I think that it would be quite possible in such a case to reach
the conclusion of fact that he was exporting the goods to the ultimate destination, H
Y.   On the other hand, the mere fact that the exporter realised that the goods
may one day reach Y does not make Y the ultimate destination to which they
are being exported when he exports them from the United Kingdom.   However,
that problem does not arise in the present case.   The appellants always intended
and contemplated that the goods would go to Southern Rhodesia as part of a
continuous transit from the United Kingdom, being reconsigned in bond at I
Port Elizabeth.   Accordingly I think that they were rightly convicted.

Appeal dismissed.

Solicitors: *Linklaters & Paines* (for the appellants); *Solicitor, Customs and
Excise* (for the respondents).

[*Reported by* N. P. METCALFE, ESQ., *Barrister-at-Law.*]

---

(7) [1941] 1 All E.R. 149; [1941] 1 K.B. 206.
(8) [1968] 2 All E.R. 832; [1968] 1 W.L.R. 1286.
(9) [1968] 2 All E.R. at p. 837; [1968] 1 W.L.R. at p. 1294.

A

FORD MOTOR CO., LTD. *v* AMALGAMATED UNION OF ENGINEERING AND FOUNDRY WORKERS AND OTHERS.

B

[QUEEN'S BENCH DIVISION (Geoffrey Lane, J.), March 3, 4, 5, 6, 1969.]

Trade Union—Collective agreement—Joint negotiating committee of employer and unions—Agreements over period of years on procedure, wages and conditions of work—New agreement negotiated by committee on majority decision of participating unions—Strike action by dissenting minority—Intention to create legally enforceable contracts not expressed in agreements—Surrounding

C

circumstances showing climate of opinion adverse to such intention—Wording of agreements largely aspirational—Whether agreements enforceable at law.

The relations between a large industrial company and the various trade unions whose members were its employees were regulated basically by two collective agreements, a procedural agreement made in 1955 and an agreement concerned more with practical matters, such as wage rates and hours,

D

made in 1967. Under the procedural agreement, a national joint negotiating committee ("the N.J.N.C.") was set up consisting of one executive official from each of the trade unions and not more than an equal number of officials appointed by the company. The words used to describe the duties and powers of the N.J.N.C. were largely words of "discussion" and "negotiation" relative to the company's factories, wage structures and conditions of employment, and a clause provided that the parties would make at each

E

stage of the procedure every attempt to resolve issues raised and that until such procedure had been carried through there should be no stoppage of work or other unconstitutional action. The 1967 agreement contained clauses which required the complete observance of all agreements and regulations in force between the parties and the elimination of avoidable lost time, and

F

that any variation of the agreement be negotiated through the N.J.N.C. Both the 1955 and 1967 agreements were signed by each of the accredited representatives of the participating unions as well as by two representatives of the company and the chairman and secretary of the trade union side of the N.J.N.C., but neither agreement contained any express provision indicating an intention that it should be legally enforceable, and many clauses were

G

worded in vague aspirational terms which would present practical problems of enforcement. Early in 1969 the company proposed a substantial variation of the 1967 agreement in respect of the employees' contracts of service, and this was accepted by the trade union side of the N.J.N.C. by a majority vote of the participating unions. The unions in the minority were, however, dissatisfied, and unofficial strike action was taken by some employees which was

H

shortly afterwards made official by certain of the unions. The company brought an action for injunctions against the striking unions, and was granted an ex parte injunction to restrain the trade unions from, inter alia, continuing their strike and from encouraging its spread. On its application to have the injunction continued pending hearing of the action, the company contended, inter alia, that its agreements with the trade unions were commercial agree-

I

ments (being designed to regulate wages and conditions of employment) and as such were legally enforceable. For the unions it was contended that the agreements were never intended to be amenable to legal action because they were negotiated against a background of industrial opinion known to all parties which was adverse to collective agreements being legally enforceable, as was evidenced by several extra-judicial authorities (including the published evidence before, and unanimous report of, the Royal Commission on Trade Unions and Employers' Associations, 1965-1968*), and, further,

---

* Cmd. 3623 (the "Donovan Report").

that the vague aspirational wording of many of the clauses in the agreements   A
showed that the parties did not intend the agreements to be legal contracts.

    Held: the ex parte injunction would be discharged because there being no
express provision by the parties to provide any assistance to determine
their intentions, it was necessary to look at all the surrounding circumstances
to ascertain what those intentions were (see p. 490, letter E, post); and
the fact that the agreements dealt prima facie with commercial relationships   B
was outweighed by the other considerations—by the wording of the agreements, by their nature, and certainly since 1954 by the climate of industrial
opinion adverse to legal enforceability evidenced by the extra-judicial
authorities which must have influenced the minds of the negotiating parties
—all of which showed that neither the company nor the unions had intended
to make the agreements binding at law (see p. 496, letters C, D and E,   C
post).

    Per CURIAM: Agreements such as these, composed largely of optimistic
aspirations, presenting grave practical problems of enforcement and reached
against a background of opinion adverse to enforceability, are not contracts
in the legal sense and are not enforceable at law. Without clear and express
provisions making them amenable to legal action, they remain in the realm   D
of undertakings binding in honour (see p. 496, letter E, post).

[As to collective bargaining machinery, see 38 HALSBURY'S LAWS (3rd Edn.)
140, 141, para. 201; as to unenforceable agreements made by trade unions,
see ibid., pp. 373-375, para. 647.]

Cases referred to: E
    Bradford Dyers' Association, Ltd. v. *National Union of Textile Workers* (1926),
        The Times, 24th July.
    Brown v. *Andrew* (1849), 18 L.J.Q.B. 153; 12 L.T.O.S. 398; 1 Digest (Repl.)
        651, *2257.*
    East London Bakers' Union v. *Goldstein* (1904), The Times, 9th June.
    Foley v. *Classique Coaches, Ltd.*, [1934] 2 K.B. 1; [1934] All E.R. Rep. 88;   F
        103 L.J.K.B. 550; 151 L.T. 242; 39 Digest (Repl.) 501, *471.*
    Harington v. *Sendall*, [1903] 1 Ch. 921; 72 L.J.Ch. 396; 88 L.T. 323; 17
        Digest (Repl.) 49, *569.*
    Hillas & Co., Ltd. v. *Arcos, Ltd.* (1932), 147 L.T. 503; [1932] All E.R. Rep.
        494; 39 Digest (Repl.) 448, *34.*
    Holland v. *London Society of Compositors* (1924), 40 T.L.R. 440; 45 Digest   G
        (Repl.) 536, *1190.*
    Hynes v. *Conlon* (1939), 5 Ir. Jur. Rep. 49.
    May and Butcher, Ltd. v. *Regem*, [1934] 2 K.B. 17, n.; 103 L.J.K.B. 556 n.;
        151 L.T. 246, n.; 39 Digest (Repl.) 448, *33.*
    National Coal Board v. *Galley*, [1958] 1 All E.R. 91; [1958] 1 W.L.R. 16;
        33 Digest (Repl.) 878, *1206.*   H
    New College, Oxford Case (1566), 2 Dyer 247a; 73 E.R. 546; 13 Digest (Repl.)
        258, *850.*
    Smithies v. *National Association of Operative Plasterers*, [1909] 1 K.B. 310;
        [1908-10] All E.R. Rep. 455; 78 L.J.K.B. 259; 100 L.T. 172; 45
        Digest (Repl.) 564, *1393.*
    Young v. *Canadian Northern Ry. Co.*, [1931] A.C. 83; 100 L.J.P.C. 51; 144   I
        L.T. 255; 34 Digest (Repl.) 124, **487.*

Summons.
    By writ dated 27th February 1969, Ford Motor Co., Ltd. (" the company ")
commenced an action against the first two defendant trade unions, Amalgamated
Union of Engineering and Foundry Workers and Transport and General Workers'
Union, for injunctions directed effectively to restraining the defendants from:
(i) attempting by unlawful means to procure the variation of a written agreement

A made on 8th September 1967 between the company and the trade unions signatory thereto including the defendants (" the 1967 agreement ") as varied by an agreed notice in writing dated 11th February 1969, entitled " Negotiations on new Package Agreement " signed by Mr. L. T. Blakeman on behalf of the company and by Mr. Mark Young, chairman of the trade union side, on behalf of the trade unions including the defendants (" the 1969 agreement "); (ii)

B attempting to procure the variation of the 1967 agreement as varied by the 1969 agreement otherwise than by negotiations conducted through the medium of the National Joint Negotiating Committee pursuant to the 1967 agreement and in accordance with a written agreement dated 23rd August 1955 (" the procedure agreement ") between the company and the trade unions including the defendants; (iii) causing or procuring or attempting to cause or procure a

C stoppage of work (whether total or partial) or unconstitutional strike action at the company's factories or plants without having first carried through the agreed procedures as set out in the procedure agreement; (iv) attempting otherwise than in accordance with the agreed procedure set out in the procedure agreement and the 1967 agreement to procure the further variation of the 1967 agreement as varied by the 1969 agreement and/or from coercing or attempting to coerce

D the company and the other parties thereto to agree to such further variation by instructing, advising, persuading, counselling or procuring their own members and/or other trade unions parties to the three agreements to stay away from or to cease work. The company further applied for a mandatory injunction ordering the defendants and each of them to countermand any instructions or advice already issued to their members and others employed by the company to cease

E or stay away from work at the company's factories and plants and further ordering the defendants and each of them to cancel or withdraw any notice or intimation declaring that any strike or withholding of labour at the company's factories and plants was officially supported by the defendants or either of them.

On 27th February 1969, on a summons ex parte by the company, GEOFFREY LANE, J., in chambers granted an interim injunction restraining the defendants

F until 3rd March 1969 in the terms substantially as asked for by the company in their writ of summons. On 3rd March 1969, a summons inter partes for an order that the injunction granted ex parte be continued and that the injunction under (i) in the writ of summons and the mandatory injunction, be made interlocutory until trial of the action or further order was adjourned into open court for hearing. An application by the defendants for an adjournment to enable

G evidence to be filed for the interlocutory injunction application was granted for seven days. The proceedings resolved themselves, by consent, into a hearing of all sides on the question whether the injunction should be continued until the resumed hearing, and whether, in addition, the further injunctions, and particularly the mandatory injunction prayed for by the company, should be granted during the interim period.

H On 4th March 1969, leave was given to the company to add Amalgamated Engineering Union as defendants to the action and summons. A question whether Amalgamated Union of Foundry Workers should also be joined as defendants was adjourned for future consideration. The facts preceding the issue of the writ by the company on 27th February 1969 are set out in the judgment.

I The cases noted below* were cited during the argument in addition to those referred to in the judgment.

---

* *Balfour* v. *Balfour*, [1919] 2 K.B. 571; [1918-19] All E.R. Rep. 860; *Rose and Frank Co.* v. *J. R. Crompton & Bros., Ltd.*, [1923] 2 K.B. 261; [1924] All E.R. Rep. 245; *Ardley and Morey* v. *London Electricity Board* (1956), The Times, 16th June; *Rookes* v. *Barnard*, [1964] 1 All E.R. 367; [1964] A.C. 1129; *Edwards* v. *Skyways, Ltd.*, [1964] 1 All E.R. 494; [1964] 1 W.L.R. 349; *Dudfield* v. *Ministry of Works* (1964), 108 Sol. Jo. 118; *Allen* v. *Thorn Electrical Industries, Ltd.*, [1967] 2 All E.R. 1137; [1968] 1 Q.B. 487; *Morgan* v. *Fry*, [1968] 3 All E.R. 452; [1968] 2 Q.B. 710; *Torquay Hotel Co., Ltd.* v. *Cousins*, [1969] 1 All E.R. 522; [1969] 2 W.L.R. 289.

A

F. P. Neill, Q.C., and *R. C. Southwell* for the plaintiff company, Fords.

M. Finer, Q.C., and *Alexander Irvine* for the first and third defendants, Amalgamated Union of Engineering and Foundry Workers and Amalgamated Engineering Union.

Peter Pain, Q.C., K. W. Wedderburn and *I. A. Macdonald* for the second defendants, Transport and General Workers' Union.

B

GEOFFREY LANE, J.: In this matter, the plaintiff company are claiming ex parte injunctions against the defendants designed, in brief, to prevent the defendants from continuing the official strike at the plaintiff company's factories or from encouraging its spread, pending the hearing of an application for interlocutory relief.

This unhappy dispute arises in the following way. The plaintiff company, C to whom I shall refer as " Fords ", have some 23 factories and plants in England and in Wales and, I think, one plant in Northern Ireland. They employ some 46,000 work-people, of whom, speaking in round figures, 15,000 are members of the first defendants, the Amalgamated Union of Engineering and Foundry Workers (the " A.E.F."), and 17,000 or 18,000 are members of the second defendants, the Transport and General Workers' Union (the " T. & G.W.U."). D There are in all—the figure, I do not think, has been precisely approved— some 19 unions, whose members are employed by Fords. It follows as a matter of arithmetic that some of the unions involved have a comparatively tiny number of members working at Fords. Relations between Fords and the unions are regulated by a document, which has been called the Blue Book; its full official title is " Agreements and Conditions of Employment. Hourly Paid Employees ". E That document, the Blue Book, contains basically two main agreements. They are the 1955 agreement, which is very largely concerned with procedural matters; and the 1967 agreement, which is more devoted to practical matters, such as rates and hours, and so on. By cl. 1 of the 1955 agreement, headed " General Principles ", and by para. (d) of that clause, the following terms emerge:

F
" The parties agree that, at each stage of the procedure set out in this Agreement, every attempt will be made to resolve issues raised and that until such procedure has been carried through there shall be no stoppage of work or other unconstitutional action."

By cl. 2 of that agreement is set up the national joint negotiating committee, which figures largely in this history, and the whole of that clause runs as follows:

G
" (a) There shall be a National Joint Negotiating Committee which shall consist of not more than one executive official from each of the Unions which is or may become a party to this Agreement and not more than an equal number of executive officials appointed by [Fords]. (b) The National Joint Negotiating Committee may discuss any matter affecting any of [Fords'] factories and shall deal with wage negotiations, occupational H grading, major conditions of employment and other matters which are national in application. (c) In addition, the National Joint Negotiating Committee shall deal with any matters referred to it under the procedure set out in Clause 4 and shall negotiate all Agreements and variations thereto. (d) [a clause which was added later] The National Joint Negotiating Committee shall meet not less than three times in each year, such meetings to be held I as far as is practicable in January, May and September."

In 1967, as I say, a further agreement was reached, and the material clauses of that agreement seem to me to be cl. 21 and cl. 25. They run as follows:

" 21. Observance of Existing Agreements and Regulations and Elimination of Avoidable Lost Time.   (i) There shall be complete observance of all Agreements in force between the parties (including Regulations covering Conditions of Employment which may be in force from time to time) and

A   (ii) Avoidable lost time shall be eliminated at the beginning and the end
of the day or shift and before and after lunch time, and at the times of tea
break and tea service.

"25. Variation and Termination.   Any variation of this Agreement
shall be negotiated by the parties hereto through the medium of the National
Joint Negotiating Committee. This Agreement shall not be terminated until
B   three months' notice in writing of such intention has been given by either
party hereto to the other."

It should be noted that each union at Fords, regardless of the size of its membership, is entitled to one vote on the N.J.N.C., as I shall call it, and that is a matter
of some significance, as will be seen in a moment.

If one turns to p. 90 of the Blue Book, one sees the form of agreement which
C   every employee signs when he is taken on to Fords' payroll, and that agreement
serves to incorporate in his contract of employment such of the matters in the
Blue Book as apply to his conditions of work, wages and so on (1).

Before passing from those agreements, it is instructive to look at the way
in which they are signed at the end of each, "for and on behalf of [Fords] and
its United Kingdom Subsidiaries", and the signatories on the 1967 Agreement
D   are "L. T. Blakeman. R. J. Ramsey". Then follows a list of all the unions who
have members at Fords, and against every single name of every single union
appears the signature of that union's accredited representative; and then at
the very end appear the words,

"Signed for and on behalf of the Trade Union Representatives of the
National Joint Negotiating Committee: Chairman: Mark Young. Secretary:
E   J. Conway."

The sequence of events briefly leading up to this deplorable matter was this.
On 17th January 1969, Fords submitted proposals for variation of the 1967
agreement. I have no doubt that there were discussions before that, but on that
date at any rate Fords' proposals were put forward. On 3rd February, those
F   proposals were considered by the N.J.N.C. On 10th February, the representatives
of Fords, including Mr. Blakeman, who has acted as the spokesman of Fords
throughout these matters, presented to the working party which had been formed
by the N.J.N.C. a revised offer of variations to the 1967 agreement. One eye was
necessarily had on the government's policy in relation to wage increases at the
time. On 11th February, the trade union side of the N.J.N.C. voted by a majority
G   of seven to five to accept Fords' proposals. On 12th February, Mr. Conway,
in his capacity as secretary of the trade union side of the N.J.N.C., wrote to Fords
with that information. Mr. Conway's position was complicated by the fact that
he, as well as being secretary of the trade union side of the N.J.N.C., was also
general secretary of the first defendant trade union. The material paragraph of
his letter to Mr. Blakeman, dated 12th February, after setting out certain matters
H   on which, perhaps, further discussion was needed, reads as follows:

"Subject to the reservations set out above, the Trade Union Side agreed
to accept [Fords'] revised offer and empowered me to report this acceptance
to you."

On 11th February, a notice was put up at Fords, signed on behalf of the company
by Mr. Blakeman and signed on behalf of the trade unions by Mr. Young,
I   chairman of the trade union side of the N.J.N.C., on whose headed notepaper
the notice was written—setting out, under the further heading, "Negotiations
of New Package Agreement", the following assertion:

"Following negotiations on [Fords'] proposals recently communicated to
all employees, the Trade Union side of the N.J.N.C. tonight, Tuesday,

(1) Paragraph 2 of the "Acceptance of Employment" form states: "I understand
that such employment is subject to the terms of Agreements made from time to time
between the Company and the Trade Unions and to the Company's Rules and
Regulations."

11th February 1969, agreed with [Fords] the following changes in rates of   A
pay and conditions of employment."

Thereafter, set out in numbered paragraphs, is a series of alterations to the
existing contracts of employment dealing with wage increases, plans to secure
income during lay-off, short-time working, and so on. That notice is relied on
by Fords in these proceedings as constituting, as I understand it, a valid and
enforceable contract between Fords and each of the constituent union members   B
of the N.J.N.C.

On 18th February, Fords sent to Mr. Conway, in his capacity as secretary of
the trade union side of the N.J.N.C., a detailed document containing not only
the matters which had been set out in précis form in the notice but also, it seems,
a number of other terms, in particular, be it noted, the following term, which
does not appear in so many words in the notice of 11th February. It runs as   C
follows:

" If a dispute still exists when the procedure has been exhausted, then the
Trade Unions, individually or collectively, will, before taking any industrial
action, give a minimum of 21 days' notice, in writing, to [Fords]."

The interesting thing about this document is that at the end of it appear 19   D
spaces for the signatures of the representatives of the various unions, and to
that extent the document bears a close similarity to the two agreements, the
1955 and 1967 agreements, which I have already mentioned and which are set
out in the Blue Book. It is said, as will be seen in a moment, by Fords that the
affixing of signatures to this 1969 document was really only a formality, that
the unions were already bound by the agreement which had been reached in the   E
N.J.N.C., and that this was simply a matter of tidying up the loose ends and
putting into formal terms what in effect had already been the subject of full
agreement. I mention in passing the remark that counsel for the A.E.F. has
made on the point, viz., that that document, although it emanated from Mr.
Blakeman from Fords, was never in fact disclosed by Mr. Blakeman either on
his original application for an ex parte injunction or thereafter. It is said on   F
behalf of Fords that it is a document which to all intents and purposes was
irrelevant to these proceedings because those signatures were never in fact
appended to it, and it is a matter which is worthy of note.

On 19th February, Mr. Conway wrote a letter to Fords about the disagreement
amongst the union members of the N.J.N.C. and asked for the terms of the
projected agreement to be reconsidered. It seems that the unions which were in   G
the minority at the N.J.N.C. were dissatisfied. It matters not, for the purposes
of this judgment, about what they were dissatisfied, but I mention in passing
that there was some anxiety about the clauses which had been called " penal
clauses ", whereby the holiday benefits and certain other matters contained
in the projected agreement which were advantageous to the workmen, would be
lost if the workmen took part in unconstitutional action. On 21st February,   H
the employees at the Hailwood plant began an unofficial strike because they
were not in agreement with the proposed variations. Then by 25th February
attitudes were hardening on both sides. The trade unions wanted a reconsideration, whereas Mr. Blakeman of Fords was insisting that the 1969 agreement
was valid and enforceable. The trade unions on their part were insisting that the
matters were subject to review by the individual unions and that no binding   I
agreement existed. They declined Mr. Blakeman's suggestion of a ballot, on the
basis that that would raise constitutional problems under their own particular
union rules. Meanwhile more and more men were coming out on strike. On
26th February the strike was made official by the A.E.F. There is a subsidiary
matter on that, the question whether it was the A.E.F. which made the strike
official or whether it was the third defendants, the Amalgamated Engineering
Union (the " A.E.U."). It is a matter of no great importance at this stage,
because in fact the A.E.U. have now, by leave, been added as defendants. The

A difficulty arose because the letter making the strike official, although written on notepaper bearing the A.E.F. heading, was signed alongside an official stamp, the stamp being that of the A.E.U. Perhaps it is symptomatic, if nothing else, of the whole slightly unreal situation. On the very same day the T. & G.W.U. also made the strike official.

B The results of such action scarcely need any description by me. It means, of course, first of all, that strike pay becomes payable to the members of the particular unions; and, secondly, and much more important from the point of view of Fords, it means in effect that all the employees of those particular unions are encouraged to come out on strike in sympathy whatever their personal feelings may be, and that, if they do not, serious results may of course follow for them. The result has been a massive stoppage of work at the majority of

C the Ford plants, causing a huge loss of revenue to Fords, and, indeed, to the whole country in terms of lost exports, and, just as serious, although it is sometimes unhappily lost sight of, causing, I do not doubt, great unhappiness and hardship to the men on strike and even more so to their families.

   On 27th February, on an ex parte application by Fords, I granted an injunction in an endeavour to maintain some sort of stability, pending the hearing of the

D application for interlocutory injunctions. As it transpired, the defendant unions were not ready to proceed when this matter was re-opened last Monday, 3rd March, and a week's adjournment of the hearing of the interlocutory injunction application was granted. These proceedings then resolved themselves, by consent, into a hearing of all sides on the question whether the injunction should be continued until the resumed hearing, and whether, in addition, the further

E injunctions, and particularly the mandatory injunction prayed for by Fords, should be granted during the interim period.

   Thus it will be seen that there are three separate stages in the relations between the parties. There is the 1955 procedural agreement, the 1967 agreement relating very largely to terms and conditions—happily called by counsel for T. & G.W.U. " the price list "—and then there is the 1969 agreement, which was an attempt to

F modify that of 1967 by introducing, on the one hand, higher wage rates and also certain benefits, and on the other hand, as I have already mentioned, sanctions designed to minimise the likelihood of unofficial strikes by penalising as to their benefits workmen who took part in such action. I should add that I use the word " agreement " to describe the three arrangements regardless whether those agreements are enforceable at law or not.

G Three fundamental issues have emerged from this hearing. First of all, are these agreements or any of them enforceable at law? It is possible, I should add, at least theoretically, that the answer may not be the same in the case of each of the agreements. The second question is: Did the 1969 negotiations ever reach the stage of an agreement of any sort between Fords and the unions? Thirdly, in any event, assuming the two previous points to be decided against

H the defendants, can the injunction stand? In other words, is there anything in the contractual arrangements between the parties, assuming them to be strictly contractual, to prevent the defendants from taking the official strike action which in fact they have taken? It must be made clear that this court is not concerned in any way with the merits of the dispute, nor is it concerned with the remoter issues which have been suggested in some of the affidavits

I in this case and the exhibits to those affidavits, namely, that the casus belli is really the government's income policy. This court is not concerned with policy, nor with politics, nor with the justice of the employers' proposals, nor the employees' reactions to those proposals. It is not concerned with the question whether the wishes of the majority of employees are being subordinated to the self-interest of the influential few. It is merely concerned with the strict legal problems involved, regardless of their impact and regardless of their consequence. The fundamental question is, of course, this. Assuming for the moment that there do exist agreements in the broad sense between Fords on the one hand

and the three defendants on the other, are these agreements enforceable by   A
legal process in this court or not? There is a dearth of direct authority on the
point. This is, perhaps, hardly surprising, because most cases in this branch of
the law fall plainly into one or other of two categories. Either they are commercial contracts between parties at arm's length, which are obviously intended
to be enforceable at law unless the parties by express provision declare that they
are binding in honour only, or otherwise they are social or domestic arrange-   B
ments which are equally obviously not designed to be legally binding, the type
of arrangement whereby one persons says to another, " I will meet you at 7.30;
you bring the food; I will bring the drink ". Neither party, of course, envisages
any action in the county court if either commodity is not forthcoming, although
it would presumably be possible by express provision to make even such an
agreement legally enforceable. In other words, the intention of the parties is   C
usually obvious from the surrounding circumstances or from the express terms
of the contract itself.

The authorities to which I have been referred are largely of a negative nature.
Counsel for Fords has cited a series of cases, running in date between 1904 and
1939. They are, and I mention them for the purposes of completeness, these:
East London Bakers' Union v. *Goldstein* (2), *Smithies* v. *National Association of*   D
Operative Plasterers (3), *Holland* v. *London Society of Compositors* (4), *Bradford*
Dyers' Association, Ltd. v. *National Union of Textile Workers* (5), *Young* v.
Canadian Northern Ry. Co. (6), a decision of the Privy Council, and finally an
Irish decision, *Hynes* v. *Conlon* (7). Counsel for Fords submits, if I may put his
argument briefly in précis, that the importance of these cases lies in the fact that
no one, either judge or counsel, from start to finish in these cases suggests that   E
such agreements as these are not subject to enforcement in the court. He goes
further in *Bradford Dyers' Association, Ltd.'s* case (5) of 24th July 1926. Having
pointed out the eminence of counsel appearing in that case (8), he stresses the
fact that, although this was a case which was settled, the terms of settlement as
set out show that the counsel appearing certainly believed, or so it seems, that the
agreement in that case was the subject of enforcement at law. The portion of the   F
case which he cites runs as follows:

" Minutes of the order had been prepared, and they would take the form
in each case that the plaintiffs and the defendants, by their respective
counsel, admitted that the agreement of July 1, 1914 (as modified by certain
subsequent agreements) was of full force and effect between, and as binding
upon the plaintiffs and defendants, unless and until the agreement was   G
modified and lawfully determined in manner therein provided; that the
defendants admitted, by their counsel, that they had committed breaches
of that agreement, and that they consented to judgment in the sums
stated . . . "

and so on.

The decision in the Privy Council in *Young* v. *Canadian Northern Ry. Co.* (6)   H
concerned an action by a machinist who had been employed by the respondents
in their shops. The headnote is as follows (6):

". . . In 1927 he received notice of dismissal on the ground of reduction of
staff. He sued for wrongful dismissal, contending that a written agreement,

(2) (1904), The Times, 9th June, reproduced in CASES AND MATERIALS ON LABOUR   I
LAW by K. W. WEDDERBURN, at p. 272.
(3) [1909] 1 K.B. 310; [1908-10] All E.R. Rep. 455.
(4) (1924), 40 T.L.R. 440.
(5) (1926), The Times, 24th July.
(6) [1931] A.C. 83.
(7) (1939), 5 Ir. Jur. Rep. 49.
(8) Gavin Simonds, K.C., N. C. Armitage and C. J. Franklin for the plaintiff association; Sir A. Short for the National Union of Textile Workers; Sir H. Slesser, K.C.,
and A. Henderson for the Amalgamated Society of Dyers, Bleachers, Finishers &
Kindred Trades; Donald Cohen for the National Union of General & Municipal Workers.

A   entered into by the respondents with a labour organization and called Wages Agreement No. 4, formed part of his contract of employment, and that under it the respondents could not dismiss him upon a reduction of staff, as they had retained men junior to him. The agreement had been applied to the appellant (who was not a member of the organization) as to the amount of his wages, the notice given him, and in other respects; the

B   respondents stated at the trial that they had applied the agreement to all the men employed in their shops: *Held*, that Wage Agreement No. 4 did not form part of the contract for the employment of the appellant, the fact that the respondents had applied it to him being equally consistent with the view that they had done so as a matter of policy. Further, that having regard to the terms and nature of the agreement it did not by itself constitute

C   a contract between any individual employee and his employer; observance of its terms by an employer could not be enforced by action even by the organisation, but only by calling a strike."

That last sentence in the headnote is questioned by counsel for Fords, who says that it goes beyond what is to be found in the judgment. The material passage in the judgment is this, and I need read no more (9):

D

    " It appears to their Lordships to be intended merely to operate as an agreement between a body of employers and a labour organization by which the employers undertake that as regards their workmen, certain rules beneficial to the workmen shall be observed. By itself it constitutes no contract between any individual employee and the company which employs him.

E   If an employer refused to observe the rules, the effective sequel would be, not an action by any employee, not even an action by Division No. 4 against the employer for specific performance or damages, but the calling of a strike until the grievance was remedied."

The words in dispute, so to speak, are " the effective sequel ". So far as it is material, I incline to the view that the headnote is an accurate description of that

F   part of the judgment, and once again, insofar as the case helps these proceedings, it helps the defendants rather than Fords.

    Coming to decisions more recent, that of *National Coal Board* v. *Galley* (10) was an action by the National Coal Board against an individual workman, and to that extent it is sharply distinguishable from the circumstances of the present case. However, part of it was relied on by counsel for Fords as showing

G   that, as recently as 1957 when it was decided, the view of the court was that agreements such as those in the present case were enforceable at law. The passage on which he relies is part of the judgment of PEARCE, L.J. (11). It runs as follows:

    " The defendant next contends that, even though the Nacods agreement was applicable to the defendant's employment, yet it had no contractual force, because it was too vague. It is an industrial agreement, he argues,

H   covering a wide area, with no intention that it shall have a specific or enforceable effect. Collieries differ, and what is reasonable in one will be unreasonable in another. The court has no yardstick to measure what are reasonable requirements. For instance, the stringency of those requirements depends on the number of deputies employed. It is a case within the principle of *May and Butcher, Ltd.* v. *Regem* (12) rather than that of *Foley* v. *Classique*

I   *Coaches, Ltd.* (13). It seems to us, however, on a consideration of the Nacods agreement, that it was meant to have a binding effect. Realising the difficulties inherent in the situation, it provided for discussions if it appeared to be working out unfairly for the deputies. To define with exactitude what are

(9) [1931] A.C. at p. 89.
(10) [1958] 1 All E.R. 91; [1958] 1 W.L.R. 16.
(11) [1958] 1 All E.R. at p. 97; [1958] 1 W.L.R. at pp. 23, 24.
(12) [1934] 2 K.B. 17, n.
(13) [1934] 2 K.B. 1; [1934] All E.R. Rep. 88.

the duties of a servant is no easy task. The court will supply an implied   **A**
condition as to reasonableness in many contracts where duties are not fully
defined, as in *Hillas & Co., Ltd.* v. *Arcos, Ltd.* (14), and *Foley* v. *Classique
Coaches, Ltd.* (15). Counsel for the defendant also relies on the provision in
cl. 13 for discussion in the event of complaints. He contends that this is
typical of an industrial agreement not intended to be enforceable in the
courts. We do not, however, see how in principle such a provision differs from   **B**
that in *Foley* v. *Classique Coaches, Ltd.* (15), which provided for the price
to be agreed between the parties. It may be that discussion is a condition
precedent to action, but once discussion is repudiated or fails the matter
falls to be determined by the courts. Moreover, the defendant is in this
further difficulty. He is asserting that the agreement as a whole exists while
seeking to deny the enforceability of cl. 12. If cl. 12 is too vague to be   **C**
enforceable the whole agreement is not legally binding on either side . . .''

That decision, however the arguments of learned counsel may have been stated
by the court, appears to have been made simply on the basis of whether the contract was too vague to be enforced or not. Furthermore, it was a case, as I have
said, where the action was between the National Coal Board and an individual
workman, just as though an action might have been commenced by Fords   **D**
against one of their employees based on the form of contract signed by
the employee and set out in blank on p. 90 of the Blue Book. I do not find,
accordingly, that the decision in *Galley's* case (16) provides any great assistance
towards the determination of this problem.

In the present case, there is no express provision by the parties to provide any
assistance as to their intentions. Consequently, it is necessary to look at all the   **E**
surrounding circumstances to ascertain what the intention of the parties was. This,
in my view, is not a case where, without further ado, the situation falls into one
or other of the categories which I have mentioned previously. Consequently,
one must look at all the surrounding facts in order to discover what the intentions
of the parties were. On the one hand, and this is Fords' case, there exist the
foundations of legally enforceable contracts. There is, of course, ample considera-   **F**
tion; one assumes, for the purposes of this argument, that there is or was agreement between the parties in the case of the 1955, 1967 and 1969 agreements. No
one, say Fords, could describe these as domestic, social or family arrangements.
They were hammered out, it is said—and I do not doubt that this is true—with
great difficulty and lengthy discussions between the parties, Fords on the one
hand and the unions on the other, and no doubt also between the unions them-   **G**
selves. They were designed, it is said, to regulate the business matters of wages,
working conditions, terms, penalties, and so on. To that extent, say Fords,
they are clearly commercial agreements, carrying the usual sanction with such
agreements, namely, recourse to the courts should there be a breach on either
side. So far there can be little quarrel with those contentions, although it should
perhaps be mentioned in passing that Mr. Blakeman, the protagonist of Fords,   **H**
in his original affidavit and indeed in both his affidavits, remains silent as to any
intention on his part or that of Fords that these agreements should have legal
effect. It is fair to add that counsel for Fords, as an explanation of that silence,
says that what his or Fords' intention was at the making of the agreements is
immaterial, and, if not immaterial, irrelevant. However, there are other matters
to be considered besides those. There is no doubt that the executive officers of   **I**
Fords, Mr. Blakeman in particular, must have been aware of current attitudes
and developments in this field, and similarly with the executive officers of the
unions—that is their job—and there is no reason to doubt that we are dealing
on either side in this case with people who are in the top rank of efficiency,

(14) (1932), 147 L.T. 503; [1932] All E.R. Rep. 494.
(15) [1934] 2 K.B. 1; [1934] All E.R. Rep. 88.
(16) [1958] 1 All E.R. 91; [1958] 1 W.L.R. 16.

A expertise and knowledge of their jobs and everything that goes to make up those jobs.

What, then, was the general state of opinion as it existed during these times? What sources were available to the parties? What sources were there which inevitably would have come into the hands of these men to shape their views, shape their opinions, and, more importantly, shape their intentions when making
B these agreements? They are, so it happens, numerous. Counsel for Fords referred me this morning to an extract from the MODERN LAW REVIEW of 1942/43 (17). He did that because a later article by PROFESSOR OTTO KAHN-FREUND (18) had already been put before me, indicating that, in the professor's view, these contracts were not legally enforceable, and the MODERN LAW REVIEW, containing as it did an earlier article, the one in 1943, by the same gentleman, shows that at that time
C quite plainly he was of an opposite point of view. I say with regard to that that the MODERN LAW REVIEW was a publication unlikely to come into the hands either of the executives of Fords or indeed of the executives of the unions. I take the point that the professor has changed his mind, but I do not take the view that the MODERN LAW REVIEW of 1942/43 was likely to have affected the minds of the parties' officers or their predecessors in title.

D Coming to the present day, or almost to the present day, one finds that the " Royal Commission on Trade Unions and Employers' Associations, 1965-1968 ", under the chairmanship of LORD DONOVAN (19), deals with this matter at considerable length. I wish to make it clear at this stage that one does not of course read these publications, even publications from so august a source as this, as being precedents in any way affecting the legal decision of this case; but they are,
E as I say, matters which, in my view, are material when one is considering the root problem, namely, the intention of the parties. I turn now to para. 470 of the commission's report. It reads as follows:

" In this country collective agreements are not legally binding contracts. This is not because the law says that they are not contracts or that the parties to them may not give them the force of contracts. There is in fact
F nothing in the law to prevent employers or their associations and trade unions from giving legal force to their agreements."

If I may interpolate there, one such agreement was in fact put before me, an agreement of the Boot & Shoe Operatives. I continue to read:

" It is true that under a statutory provision—section 4 of the Trade Union Act 1871 (which is separately considered in Chapter XIV)—agreements
G between one trade union and another cannot be ' directly ' enforced in a court of law and damages cannot be recovered for their breach. An employers' association may be a trade union in the eyes of the law, and therefore a trade union and such an employers' association could not, if they wished, make their collective agreement enforceable ' directly ' or through an action for damages. They could however, were they so minded, make it ' indirectly '
H enforceable, and for example obtain from a court a declaration concerning the meaning of the agreement. Nor would anything in this statute stand in the way of a union and an individual employer giving their agreement the full effect of a contract and making it enforceable even ' directly ' and through actions for damages in the event of breach. The fact is that nothing of this nature normally happens. That it does not happen is not, as we have
I already said, due to the law. It is due to the intention of the parties themselves. They do not intend to make a legally binding contract, and without both parties intending to be legally bound there can be no contract in the legal sense.

---

(17) Article by PROFESSOR OTTO KAHN-FREUND entitled " Collective Agreements under War Legislation ", 6 MODERN LAW REVIEW, pp. 112-143.
(18) See " The System of Industrial Relations in Great Britain ", edited by A. FLANDERS and H. A. CLEGG, published by Blackwell, 1954.
(19) Cmd. 3623; this report was presented to Parliament in June 1968.

"471. This lack of intention to make legally binding collective agree-   A
ments, or, better perhaps, this intention and policy that collective bargaining
and collective agreements should remain outside the law, is one of the
characteristic features of our system of industrial relations which distinguishes it from other comparable systems. It is deeply rooted in its
structure. As we point out in Chapter III collective bargaining is not in this
country a series of easily distinguishable transactions comparable to the   B
making of a number of contracts by two commercial firms. It is in fact a
continuous process in which differences concerning the interpretation of an
agreement merge imperceptibly into differences concerning claims to change
its effect. Moreover, even at industry level, a great deal of collective bargaining takes place through standing bodies, such as joint industrial councils and
national or regional negotiating boards, and the agreement appears as a   C
'resolution' or 'decision' of that body, variable at its will, and variable
in particular in the light of such difficulties of interpretation as may arise.
Such 'bargaining' does not fit into the categories of the law of contract."

There is more to the same or similar effect, and I need only read very briefly
the beginning of para. 473, which runs as follows:

"It may be alleged that none of these considerations applies to procedure   D
agreements. Nevertheless it is a generally admitted fact that even procedure
agreements are not contracts, and this again for the reason that the parties
to them do not intend to create legal obligations. This lack of intent is
manifest from the style in which the agreements are expressed."

Then finally, there is para. 474, which runs in part as follows: E

"If therefore our existing collective agreements or if our existing procedure agreements were to be made into legal contracts this would have
to be done by a statute attaching the force of law to the terms of a bargain
contrary to the wishes of the parties."

The findings of the commission were, one observes, unanimous.
Of the parties appearing to give evidence before that commission, one finds on   F
p. 327 of their report (20) that the Ford Motor Co., Ltd., submitted such evidence
in confidence. Moreover, the commission did not say that from now on such
agreements are not to be enforceable at law. They seem to have assumed, rightly
or wrongly, that at least for some considerable time past that had been the
situation in the country. That report and those words which I have read, in my
view, did not merely put Mr. Blakeman, who must have read them, on notice,   G
but it showed what everyone to do with the industry had on balance been believing
for some considerable time.
The matter does not stop there. There was evidence given before the commission by the Confederation of British Industry, the Trades Union Congress,
and others; and I have been given a photo-copy of part of the written evidence
of the Confederation of British Industry submitted to the commission in Novem-   H
ber 1965. Paragraphs 172-175 are headed: "The Legal Enforcement of Collective
Agreements", and para. 172 and para. 173 run as follows:

"172. For many years employers have felt that the greatest single
contribution which could be made to the better working of the industrial
relations system would be better observance of agreements. They see therefore considerable attractions in any proposed changes in the law which would   I
have this effect. The most simple and also the most radical of such changes
would be to make collective agreements enforceable at law.
"173. The B.E.C. reviewed this possibility from time to time and was
always attracted by the prospect it offered of securing better observance
of collective contracts. It also noted the comparative absence of strikes during

(20) See Appendix 2 of the commission's report, listing those who submitted written
evidence.

A   the currency of contracts in countries where there is an enforceable contract with a peace clause. It was never able to satisfy itself, however, how such enforceability could be introduced without other consequences, some of them undesirable, which would make great changes in the British system of industrial relations."

B   A copy of the written evidence of the Ministry of Labour before the same commission, again dated 1965, was also put before me. Turning to p. 76 one finds this statement:

    " (The common opinion is that a contract between a single employer and a trade union would also not be enforced by the courts though this is not specified by statute.)"

C   On p. 80, para. 26, there is also this statement:

    " As has been pointed out ... the contracts entered into between employers' associations and trade unions (and probably the contracts entered into between single employers and trade unions) are not legally enforceable in this country. This is in striking contrast to the situation in most other countries."

D   In the evidence of the Trades Union Congress to the commission, the material parts are to be found in para. 339 to para. 341, and I will read them.

    " 339. Collective agreements themselves cannot be termed as contracts in law as, quite apart from the Trade Union Acts, the parties do not intend to be legally bound; the agreements are deliberately written in a way which would require radical amendment if this intention had been present. Furthermore, a contracting party is not guilty of a breach of contract if someone acts in defiance of the terms of a contract without his authority. Again, trade union members are not parties to procedure agreements, either explicitly or implicitly.

E

    " 340. It cannot however be over-emphasised that the effectiveness of obligations in this field does not depend on the existence of legal sanctions but on the common interest of both sides of industry in operating an effective system of collective bargaining. Systems of industrial relations in different countries round the world show an inverse relationship between the practical significance of legal sanctions and the degree to which industrial relations have reached a state of maturity. Other countries are increasingly looking to Britain to discover how to evolve a system of good industrial relations; it is in Britain that legal sanctions have the least practical significance.

F

G

    " 341. The General Council are therefore firmly opposed to any proposal, such as that suggested by the CBI, to make collective agreements of whatever kind enforceable at law. This is not simply a question of administrative practicability. It is essentially a question of principle. Any such development would have a serious and damaging effect on the generally enlightened approach to industrial relations which has been evolved in this country over the years."

H

There in synopsis is the evidence given by both sides of industry before the commission, and the results in the shape of the commission's unanimous report, which, as I see it, provide extremely valuable information, at least inferentially, as to what must have been the intention of the parties, as far back as 1955.

I   There are other publications. Perhaps I should deal with just two. First of all, there is the INDUSTRIAL RELATIONS HANDBOOK, dated 1961, and emanating from the Ministry of Labour, H.M. Stationery Office (21). If one reads from p. 19 of that publication, one finds this passage:

    " The whole of the collective system rests upon the principle of mutual consent, and the value of the agreements and the machinery for settling

---

(21) Reprinted 1964.

disputes has depended upon the loyal acceptance by the constituent members on both sides of the decisions reached. This acceptance is voluntary. Loyal acceptance has in fact been the rule in all the trades concerned. Although the question has been raised from time to time of the adequacy of these methods, the view has always been taken that it was not desirable to adopt some alternative based upon principles other than that of mutual consent or to introduce any system of penalties for non-observance of agreements.''

By way of footnote, there is this:

" Under the general law of contract, although the terms of a collective agreement do not automatically become part of the individual contracts of employment made between employers and their employees, an employer and an employee will be bound by such terms if it can be shown that they were, either expressly or by implication, incorporated in an individual contract of employment made between them.''

There was an earlier court of inquiry (22) in 1964, under the chairmanship of PEARSON, L.J. It was an inquiry into—

" the causes and circumstances of a dispute between the parties repre-sented on the National Joint Industrial Council for the Electricity Supply Industry ''

and once again its published report (23) is the type of report which would doubt-less be read and digested by both the management of Fords and also by the various union officials. It contains this passage (24):

" The word ' sacrosanct ' is convenient but needs to be explained in two respects. First, the three-year agreement was not intended to be legally binding, but the parties by entering into it assumed a moral obligation as is usual in industrial relations.''

Finally, although first or almost first in point of time, there is an extract from an article by the same PROFESSOR KAHN-FREUND, with whose article in the MODERN LAW REVIEW we started this inquiry, this one dated 1954, in an article on '' The System of Industrial Relations in Great Britain '' (25). It contains this passage:

" In the long history of British collective bargaining it does not ever seem to have happened that either a trade union or an employer or an employers' association attempted to prevent the violation of a collective agreement by an action for an injunction or to seek compensation by an action for damages. The reason can certainly not be found in the absence of such violations . . . The true reason for the complete absence of any attempts legally to enforce the mutual obligations created by collective agreements can, in the writer's opinion, only be found in the intention of the parties themselves. An agreement is a contract in the legal sense only if the parties look upon it as something capable of yielding legal rights and obligations. Agreements expressly or implicitly intended to exist in the ' social ' sphere only are not enforced as contracts by the courts. This appears to be the case of collective agreements. They are intended to yield ' rights ' and ' duties ', but not in the legal sense; they are intended, as it is sometimes put, to be ' binding in honour ' only, or (which amounts to very much the same thing) to be enforceable through social sanctions but not through legal sanctions.''

From these materials, it will be clear that the climate of opinion was almost unanimous to the effect that no legally enforceable contract resulted from the collective agreements. As I say, both Mr. Blakeman and the unions were obviously abreast of these developments and statements of opinion and must be credited with knowledge of the contents of the various publications or at least those of the

(22) Set up under the Industrial Courts Act 1919.
(23) Cmd. 2361.
(24) In para. 140.
(25) Edited by A. FLANDERS and H. A. CLEGG, published by Blackwell, 1954.

A publications which were connected with the Pearson report and also the report of the Donovan Commission.

Counsel for Fords argues that these publications are irrelevant to the consideration of this case and that no regard should be had to them. To that argument I do not accede. Where a court is endeavouring to discover the intention of the parties to an agreement, it is impossible and indeed unreal to disregard evidence

B of their knowledge and, accordingly, of their state of mind at the time. These documents show, to my mind, that certainly since 1954 the general climate of opinion on both sides of industry has overwhelmingly been in favour of no legal obligation from collective agreements.

No less important than a consideration of what has been called " extra-judicial " authorities is a consideration of the terms of the agreements themselves. Counsel

C on behalf of the A.E.F. puts his argument in this way. He submits that, if one looks at the terms of the 1955 and the 1967 agreements in the Blue Book, it would be possible or almost possible to argue that any contract would be " void " for uncertainty because of the way in which a large preponderance of the clauses are drawn. He does not put his argument as high as that; indeed, it might be difficult to do so in the light of the decision in *National Coal Board* v. *Galley* (26). What he

D does say is that the vague aspirational wording of many of the clauses makes it as clear as can be that the parties could not possibly have considered that these contracts would be enforceable in a court of law. One perhaps can, without going through it clause by clause, point to one or two of the clauses to which he drew my attention: cl. 3 (i) (a) of the 1955 agreement (on p. 6 of the Blue Book) and cl. 4 (a) (on p. 9) (27). He points out in addition that cl. 4 (a), which deals with

E the method of complaints arising on the shop floor being taken higher and higher, so to speak, by redress of grievance procedure, could not possibly be enforced effectively at law when there are no time limits imposed for any of the steps taken. He adds in parenthesis that that was one of the matters, namely, the imposition of time limits, which was sought to be remedied by the 1969 agreement. He points further to cl. 7 and cl. 8 of the 1967 agreement (on p. 18 of the Blue

F Book) to cl. 22 (on p. 34 of the Blue Book), and so on (28).

The way that counsel for the A.E.F. argues the matter is this. He says that the agreements, if one regards them closely, can really be divided as to their clauses into two categories. There are the specific clauses dealing with wage rates and so

---

(26) [1958] 1 All E.R. 91; [1958] 1 W.L.R. 16.
(27) Clause 3 (i) (a) provides: " [Fords recognise] the right of the employees to

G have an adequate number of representatives appointed on a craft, departmental or geographical basis to act on their behalf in accordance with the terms of this Agreement." Clause 4 (a) provides: " Any employee who wishes to raise any matter directly affecting his work shall first discuss it with his Chargehand and/or Foreman. If, in consequence of that discussion, no satisfaction results, the employee then may make a further approach to the Chargehand and/or Foreman, accompanied by his Shop Steward. If there is still no satisfaction the Shop Steward and employee may approach the appropriate Superintendent. If the matter is not resolved the Superintendent shall

H without delay report it to the Personnel Manager who will then arrange for a discussion between the appropriate persons concerned."
(28) The clauses referred to are in the following terms: " 7. Movement of Employees between Jobs in the New Wage Structure. The statement entitled ' Agreed Policy Concerning the Movement of Employees between jobs in the New Wage Structure ' is set out in Appendix 1. 8. Productivity Improvements. As stated in the Agreement dated 27th July between the parties hereto, the implementation of the new wage

I structure was conditional upon the completion of productivity bargaining in the twenty-three designated bargaining areas. The parties to this Agreement hereby confirm their approval and ratification of the twenty-three domestically made productivity bargains. 22. The Achievement of Efficiency of Operations. The Trade Unions and [Fords] agree on the need: (i) to achieve efficient production by all reasonable means; (ii) for the introduction of labour-saving machines and methods; (iii) for [Fords] to transfer employees from one job or department to another as may be desirable having in mind continuity of employment and flow of production. It is not part of the duty of any Shop Steward whose constitution and duties are defined in the Procedure Agreement to deal with such matters in the Shop, but he may refer them for consideration by the Works Committee."

on on the one hand, which are drawn with sufficient particularity. There are,   A
on the other hand, the broad aspirational clauses drawn in vague terms. He
suggests that the only possible explanation of that dichotomy is that the specific
terms are made in due course to be incorporated in the contract of employment
between Fords and their employees, and those terms, as in *National Coal Board
v. Galley* (29), will certainly be legally enforceable by or against, if necessary, the
employee. So far as the vaguer terms are concerned, submits counsel for the   B
A.E.F., those are the terms which are effective between the employer Fords
and the unions, and one only has to look, he submits, at the nature of those terms
to see that the parties cannot really have expected any court to give legal effect
to matters couched in that way.

The conclusion which I have reached is this; it is necessarily a preliminary
view as this, of course, is not the hearing of the action proper (30). If one applies   C
the subjective test and asks what the intentions of the various parties were, the
answer is that, so far as they had any express intentions, they were certainly not
to make the agreement enforceable at law. If one applies an objective test and
asks what intention must be imputed from all the circumstances of the case, the
answer is the same. The fact that the agreements prima facie deal with commercial
relationships is outweighed by the other considerations, by the wording of the   D
agreements, by the nature of the agreements, and by the climate of opinion voiced
and evidenced by the extra-judicial authorities. Agreements such as these, composed largely of optimistic aspirations, presenting grave practical problems of enforcement and reached against a background of opinion adverse to enforceability,
are, in my judgment, not contracts in the legal sense and are not enforceable at law.
Without clear and express provisions making them amenable to legal action, they   E
remain in the realm of undertakings binding in honour. None of the authorities
cited by counsel for Fords dissuades me from this view. In my judgment, the
parties, neither of them, had the intention to make these agreements binding at
law.

That, in effect, concludes the matter in favour of the defendants, but I should,
perhaps, mention, as they have been argued at great length, two other points made   F
on their behalf. The first is an argument which relates only to the 1969 negotiations. It is said that the N.J.N.C. was merely a negotiating body with no power
to bind the constituent unions to any agreements with Fords. It is said that, until
the union representatives had each appended their signatures to the final prepared
document, the unions were not bound, and, since that document was never signed
by the constituent union representatives, the unions were not so bound. In   G
support of that contention, my attention was drawn to the way, which I have
already pointed out, in which the earlier 1955 and 1967 agreements were signed.
It is further commented with some considerable force that, if the N.J.N.C.
signature binds the unions without further ado, the addition of the signatures
from all the separate unions is otiose and unnecessary. When one examines the
1955 agreement and reads the clause that I have already read, namely, cl. 2,   H
dealing with the N.J.N.C., one finds that almost all the words used to describe
the powers and duties of that committee are words of " negotiation " or " discussion " and so on, and that the only words which might possibly be construed
as giving a power to form agreements are the final words of para. (c), which read
" shall negotiate all Agreements and variations thereto ".

So far as it is necessary for me to express an opinion on this matter, it seems to   I
me to be at least strongly arguable that the N.J.N.C., whatever it may have
considered to be its powers, was really only a negotiating body, that until the
effects of its negotiations finally reached formal publication and until that formal
document was signed by the representatives of the various unions those agreements were not binding. In 1955 and 1967 all the unions did so sign. In 1969

---

(29) [1958] 1 All E.R. 91; [1958] 1 W.L.R. 16.
(30) The action was subsequently abandoned by Fords.

A they did not. I very much doubt if Mr. Conway, who found himself in some difficulty in February of this year over his dual capacity as general secretary of his union and secretary also of the N.J.N.C., ever appreciated why he was in that dilemma. He was in that dilemma, I consider, because on the one hand the N.J.N.C. had come to a decision, but on the other hand the unions who were part of the N.J.N.C. were not unanimous and there were dissenting voices, as there

B were entitled to be, until the document was finally signed.

I also mention in passing, so that it may be part of the record, a further argument addressed to me by counsel for the A.E.F. based on the proposition that where, as here, a number of agents in the shape of the union representatives on the N.J.N.C. are charged with negotiating or charged with agreeing, unless there are express enabling powers to that effect, they cannot properly exercise their powers

C so as to bind their principals unless they do so unanimously. The authorities he cited on that point were three: *New College, Oxford Case* (31), a decision in the reign of Queen Elizabeth I, but nonetheless authoritative for that; *Brown* v. *Andrew* (32), and finally *Harington* v. *Sendall* (33). So much for that point.

The final point, which I certainly do not intend to decide, but it merits a mention, is a point made by counsel for the T. & G.W.U., and that is in brief that, if

D one reads the terms of the 1955 and 1967 agreements, even assuming that everything up to that point that Fords had argued is correct, namely, that the 1969 negotiations became enforceable agreements, yet nevertheless, submits counsel for the T. & G.W.U., in the light of the provisions of the 1955 and 1967 agreements, there is nothing preventing his clients or, indeed, the members of the other trade unions from striking in the circumstances of this case if they so wish.

E In order to succeed in an application for an ex parte injunction, a plaintiff must show that he has a strong prima facie case at least in support of the right which he asserts and an arguable case at least that that right has been infringed. Fords in this case, in my judgment, fail on the first leg for the reasons which I have stated and, accordingly, I have no alternative but to discharge the ex parte injunction.

F *Order accordingly.*

Solicitors: *Lovell, White & King* (for the plaintiff company, Fords); *W. H. Thompson* (for the first and third defendants, Amalgamated Union of Engineering and Foundry Workers and Amalgamated Engineering Union); *Pattinson & Brewer* (for the second defendants, Transport and General Workers' Union).

G [*Reported by* K. Diana Phillips, *Barrister-at-Law.*]

---

(31) (1566), 2 Dyer 247a.
(32) (1849), 18 L.J.Q.B. 153.
(33) [1903] 1 Ch. 921.

A

MARSH, LTD. *v.* COOPER.

[COURT OF APPEAL, CIVIL DIVISION (Danckwerts, Phillimore and Karminski, L.JJ.),
  March 11, 12, 1969.]

Rent Restriction—Separate dwelling—Letting of part of flat—Use of the kitchen and   B
    the bathroom together with the employees of the landlord—Understanding
    that employees shall use bathroom and kitchen for taking fresh water and
    washing purposes—Increase of Rent and Mortgage Interest (Restrictions)
    Act 1920 (10 & 11 Geo. 5 c. 17), s. 12 (2).

Rent Restriction—Shared accommodation—Sole use of two rooms—Kitchen and
    bathroom shared with landlord's employees—Employees to use kitchen and
    bathroom for taking water and washing purposes only—Whether dwelling-   C
    house.

By a tenancy agreement the landlords let to the tenant on quarterly
tenancy part of a flat consisting of two rooms " together with the use of the
kitchen and the bathroom together with the employees of the landlord ".
The landlords retained one other room, which was used by the landlords'
predecessor in title as a letting office and by the present landlords' head   D
porter for storing samples of carpets to show to new tenants. This room
had a gas ring inside. The kitchen itself was very small and it had no furniture.
It could not be used as a living room but only for cooking purposes. The only
use made of the kitchen by the employees of the landlords was to get fresh
water for cooking or drinking. The bathroom and lavatory was used for washing and washing-up and for natural purposes. On the question whether the   E
tenant, by reason of having only the use of the kitchen and bathroom, had
a separate dwelling within the meaning of s. 12 (3) of the Increase of Rent
and Mortgage Interest (Restrictions) Act 1920, and was thus protected by the
Rent Acts,

Held: the degree of use by the landlords' employees was so small as to be
almost negligible and could not amount to sharing the use of the kitchen   F
and bathroom; accordingly, the tenant was entitled to the protection of the
Rent Acts (see p. 501, letters C to E, p. 502, letter E, and p. 503, letter B,
post).

Goodrich v. *Paisner* ([1956] 2 All E.R. 176) applied.

Appeal allowed.

[As to dwelling-house " let as a separate dwelling ", see 23 HALSBURY'S LAWS   G
(3rd Edn.) 742-746, paras. 1495-1500; and for cases on the subject, see 31 DIGEST
(Repl.) 640, 641, *7475-7483,* 646, 647, *7508-7516,* and DIGEST (Cont. Vol. A)
1068, 1069, *7516b-7516bb.*

For the Increase of Rent and Mortgage Interest (Restrictions) Act 1920, s. 12,
see 13 HALSBURY'S STATUTES (2nd Edn.) 998; and for the Landlord and Tenant
(Rent Control) Act 1949, s. 7, s. 8, see ibid., pp. 1102,1103.]   H

Cases referred to:
  Cole v. *Harris,* [1945] 2 All E.R. 146; [1945] K.B. 474; 114 L.J.K.B. 481;
      173 L.T. 50; 31 Digest (Repl.) 646, *7509.*
  Goodrich v. *Paisner,* [1956] 2 All E.R. 176; [1957] A.C. 65; [1956] 2 W.L.R.
      1053; Digest (Cont. Vol. A) 1068, *7516ba.*
  Hayward v. *Marshall, Winchester* v. *Sharpe,* [1952] 1 All E.R. 663; [1952]   I
      2 Q.B. 89; Digest (Cont. Vol. A) 1068, *7516b.*
  Neale v. *Del Soto,* [1945] 1 All E.R. 191; [1945] K.B. 144; 114 L.J.K.B. 138;
      172 L.T. 65; 31 Digest (Repl.) 646, *7508.*

Appeal.

This was an appeal by the tenant, Mabel Irene Cooper, from the judgment of
the Barnet County Court (His Honour JUDGE McDONNELL) dated 29th May
1968, in an action brought by the landlords, Marsh, Ltd., to recover possession

A   of part of a flat at 92, Finchley Court, Ballards Lane, Finchley, London, N.3,
consisting of two rooms " together with the use of the kitchen and the bathroom
together with the employees of the Landlord ". The county court judge made
on order granting possession of the flat to the landlords. The facts are set out
in the judgment of DANCKWERTS, L.J.

B   L. A. *Blundell, Q.C.*, and G. *Levy* for the tenant.
G. *Avgherinos* for the landlords.

DANCKWERTS, L.J.: This is an appeal from a judgment of His Honour
JUDGE MCDONNELL given on 29th May 1968, at the Barnet County Court. It
was a question arising under the Rent Restriction Acts and it depends on the
definition of " dwelling-house " which appears in both the Increase of Rent
C   and Mortgage Interest (Restrictions) Act 1920 and the Rent and Mortgage
Interest Restrictions (Amendment) Act 1933. Section 12 (2) of the Act of 1920
provides: " This Act shall apply to a house or a part of a house let as a separate
dwelling . . .", and then there is reference to the question of the rateable value.
Section 16 (1) of the Act of 1933 provides:

D   " In this Act, unless the context otherwise requires, the following expres-
    sions have the meanings hereby respectively assigned to them, that is to
    say . . . ' dwelling-house ' has the same meaning as in the principal Acts,
    that is to say, a house let as a separate dwelling or a part of a house being
    a part so let; . . ."

We are concerned with a flat, No. 92, Finchley Court in Finchley, which consists
E   of four rooms and a bathroom. It appears there are two rooms which were let
eventually to the tenant when one Mrs. Samuel was the landlady. There is also
a kitchen and next to it a bathroom with lavatory and washbasin. Then there
is also one room which was retained by the landlady and used for some time as a
letting office.

Now I turn to the terms of the agreement between the parties dated 17th
F   September 1964, expressed to be made between—

    " Mrs. Ada Samuel of 49 Finchley Court Ballards Lane Finchley London
    N.3 (hereinafter called ' the Landlord ' which expression shall where the
    context so admits include the persons deriving title under her) of the one
    part and Mrs. Mabel Irene Cooper [giving her address] (hereinafter called
    ' the Tenant ' which expression shall where the context so admits include
G   the persons deriving title under her) of the other part . . . "

The present landlords became the landlords in 1966 and the defendant is still
the tenant. Turning to the body of the agreement, cl. 1 provides as follows:

    " The Landlord agrees to let and the Tenant agrees to take ALL THAT
    part of flat or rooms (hereinafter called ' the Flat ') numbered 92 and
H   situate on the ground floor of the building known as Finchley Court Ballards
    Lane Finchley London N.3, together with . . ."

certain landlord's fixtures, and so on. Before the word " together " there is an
asterisk which introduces the words " more particularly defined in the Schedule
hereof ". The schedule appears on the back of the document and is as follows:

I   " The small front room and the small room with windows facing the side
    and back together with the use of the kitchen and the bathroom together
    with the employees of the Landlord."

Now a good deal of case law has accumulated on the subject and the point is
this: it is alleged on behalf of the landlords that the tenant not having included
in the letting to her the kitchen and the bathroom but only being given the
use of them is burdened with sharing those portions of the flat with the employees
of the landlords and, therefore, under the numerous cases which deal with the
sharing by parties in regard to a letting the tenant has not got the protection

of the Acts because she has not what is " a dwelling-house or part of a dwelling- A
house ".

The matter has given rise to a great deal of judicial discussion. Various cases
have dealt with what is a living room and in particular it has been said that a
kitchen is a living room. In the present case the kitchen is so small that it is
only possible to use it for cooking. There is no furniture in it, I understand,
and I myself think that it does not constitute a living room in the proper meaning B
of that term, which conclusion would of course put it outside the application of
those cases, which depend on the tenant not having one of the essential living
rooms for the purposes of the letting. Furthermore, there have been great
discussions about the various cases which have arisen, the facts of those cases
and so on. I should like to read now the observations of LORD RADCLIFFE in
Goodrich v. *Paisner* (1). The passage from LORD RADCLIFFE'S speech is as C
follows (2):

> " Secondly, it cannot always be clear what ought to be treated as a
> ' living room ' for this purpose. The complexities of individual situations
> and requirements are infinitely various, since patterns of living themselves
> vary so much, and what is important or even essential for one occupant D
> of rooms separately let may be unimportant or unnecessary for another.
> I cannot, myself, frame any formula which, in this context, necessarily
> embraces a kitchen but necessarily excludes a bathroom. The difficulty
> has led to attempts to speak of ' essential living rooms ' or ' essential mani-
> festations of living '; but I am bound to say that these glosses seem to me
> either to beg the question or to confuse the issue. And I am afraid that I E
> cannot see anything more satisfying in the definition offered during the
> course of argument in this case: ' a living room is a room wherein you cook,
> eat, sleep and put your feet on the fender '. Why ever should courts of
> law tie themselves down in this way? "

Of course, if one applies that definition to the present case one could not, I
should have thought, live in the kitchen, one could not sleep there and one F
could not put one's feet on the fender.

Anyhow, the point that I am trying to make is this: that the courts have
got so much into discussion of the language used in other cases (as so often
happens with regard to authorities) that they have lost sight of the origin that
they had to deal with in the course of the various cases which had put glosses
and interpretations on various points. The matter still remains as it is in the G
statute and it is the words in the statute which have to be applied. Referring
back to s. 12 (2) of the Act of 1920, that provides: " This Act shall apply to a
house or a part of a house let as a separate dwelling." The sole point, and the
point the courts have to make up their minds about, is whether the premises
are " a house or a part of a house let as a separate dwelling ".

In this case there is a further matter which arises in my view. It seems to H
me that the description in the schedule is far from clear. It is vague and until
one considers the circumstances it is quite impossible to understand what is
meant by " the use of the kitchen and the bathroom together with the employees
of the Landlord ". It might have been that they are all having baths together
or cooking together. But in fact the circumstances of this case from the evidence
show that the situation was very different from that. It appears that all the I
use which the employees were allowed to have in respect of the kitchen was
they could go there to get fresh water for drinking or cooking purposes. There
was a gas ring in the letting office and the cooking, so far as any was done in the
letting office for the benefit of the employees of the landlords, was done there
and not in the kitchen and they merely got water for any purpose they required.
As regards the use of the bathroom they used it for the purpose of using the

(1) [1956] 2 All E.R. 176; [1957] A.C. 65.
(2) [1956] 2 All E.R. at p. 187; [1957] A.C. at p. 91.

A lavatory or for washing their hands or for washing up apparently. That very
minor use was the whole of the use which they were entitled to have in regard
to the property of which the tenant was given practically the entire use.

Now those circumstances were told to the tenant before she took the premises,
for she was told there was some sharing to be done and she asked what was
the extent of the sharing and was told the facts I have mentioned.

B The fact (which is merely history) is that after the acquisition by the present
landlords of the premises they ceased to use the room as a letting office and for a
year or so no use was made of it at all, but eventually the porter was told by
them he must make some use of it and he used it for the purpose of storing
bits of carpets which could be used to show to tenants who might want to order
carpets for the purpose of their flats.

C In those circumstances it seems to me the facts of this case differ immensely
from the facts of the various decisions which have been quoted to us. Indeed in
Goodrich v. *Paisner* (3) the House of Lords in their speeches said that the question
was really a matter of fact and a matter of degree. In this case it seems to me
that the degree of use by the employees of the landlords was so small as to be
almost negligible and cannot, in my opinion, amount to sharing the use of the
D bathroom and the kitchen. Consequently, in my view, all those cases are different
cases on different facts and do not compel us to reach a conclusion which, to my
mind, would be devoid of common sense. In my view there was a definite letting
of two rooms and the provision of cooking facilities in a small kitchen that was
not really properly called a living room at all and therefore the provisions of the
Act apply to the letting to the tenant and she is entitled to the protection of
E the Acts. In my view, therefore, the learned judge reached the wrong conclusion
and the appeal should be allowed.

PHILLIMORE, L.J.: I agree. Counsel for the tenant puts his appeal in
two ways. He says, first of all, that there was no " sharing " here of the kitchen
sufficient to take the premises out of the protection of the Rent Acts and alter-
F natively, if there was such sharing, it was a sharing with the employees of the
landlords only and accordingly it was covered by the provisions of s. 8 of the
Landlord and Tenant (Rent Control) Act 1949 and is deemed to be a dwelling-
house to which the Acts apply.

So far as the first point is concerned the tenant's evidence was that when
she was considering taking this flat mention was made of sharing and accordingly
G she enquired in detail what that would amount to. As I understand it, the
learned county court judge has in substance accepted her evidence on this
point and what she was told was this, that the third room other than the kitchen
and bathroom in this flat was occupied by the landlady's brother-in-law, Mr.
Samuel, and he used it as a letting office between 9.0 a.m. and 5.0 p.m. on five
days a week. What is more, he had a gas ring in the room and he would only
H need to have access to the kitchen for the purpose of getting drinking water and
in order to wash up a cup or a plate after his lunch or his tea. He would, of
course, in addition have to use the bathroom and the lavatory for natural purposes and in order to wash his hands.

Now those were very important facts. After all, the tenant was going to sleep
in this flat and if there had been a question of someone else occupying this
I room at night she might well have hesitated before she took the accommodation.
What is more the access to the kitchen and bathroom was clearly limited to the
porter using the letting office during these hours or, I suppose, to anyone else
who was doing his duty for him; it did not extend to all the employees of the
landlady.

Counsel for the landlords says we cannot go behind the written agreement
and pay any attention to these matters which the tenant was informed of before

(3) [1956] 2 All E.R. 176; [1957] A.C. 65.

she entered into it. In my judgment we can. I agree with DANCKWERTS, L.J.,   **A**
that in the first place it would be permissible to look at the surrounding circumstances, including these conversations, in order to explain the equivocal phrase
" use of the kitchen and the bathroom together with the employees of the
Landlord ". Furthermore, I think the matter could be put in a different way.
It is quite clear that because of what he was told as to the nature of the user the
tenant agreed to take this flat and accordingly there was a collateral agreement   **B**
in consideration of which she, of course, or both parties entered into the agreement of letting.

A further point arises and it is important on the second of counsel for the
tenant's points. Counsel for the landlords says that inasmuch as the schedule
does not specifically exclude user by the landlady herself such user or the right
to such user would persist. In my judgment that is wrong as I think it was   **C**
clearly important to the tenant to know exactly who could use the kitchen and
the bathroom in close proximity to her living room and her bedroom and the
phrase " together with the employees of the Landlord " would impliedly exclude
user by the landlady herself. Accordingly, as I think, the user in common of
the kitchen and the bathroom in this case was confined, so far as the employees
of the landlords were concerned, to this very minor user of which the tenant   **D**
had been informed.

I agree with DANCKWERTS, L.J., that it is clear from the judgments in *Goodrich*
v. *Paisner* (4) that the question of whether user in common amounts to sharing
is a question of fact and a question of degree. In my judgment it would be
impossible to say on the facts of this case and the user to which the bathroom
and the kitchen were put by the landlords' employees that there was anything   **E**
that amounted to sharing. There is a case, as it happens, where the facts were
very close to those in the present one decided before *Goodrich* v. *Paisner* (4) but
referred to by the House of Lords in that case with approval. The case is
Hayward v. *Marshall, Winchester* v. *Sharpe* (5). There were in fact two separate
cases under consideration there. In the first a landlord had let three unfurnished
rooms in a dwelling-house to a tenant together with a right to draw water in   **F**
the kitchen and once a week to use the gas stove in the kitchen to boil washing.
In the second case the landlord had let two unfurnished rooms to a tenant with
the right to draw water in the kitchen. The county court judge held in each of
those cases that there was a sharing of the house and accordingly that the
tenants were not entitled to the protection of the Rent Restriction Acts. This
court allowed the tenants' appeals and HODSON, L.J., said (6):   **G**

" For my part, I see nothing in the decisions of *Cole* v. *Harris* (7) and
Neale v. *Del Soto* (8) to lead one to the conclusion that the mere use of a
room for purposes other than what might be described as living purposes
amounts, in the ordinary use of language, to sharing the room. The mere
fact that a person who lives in the house is allowed to go into the kitchen,
whether to draw water, or, indeed, to have a bath there, would not be   **H**
properly an illustration of a sharing of the room. The kitchen is a room
which is normally used for cooking and for living in. The mere right of access
to the room does not seem to me to be properly described as a sharing of the
room."

Later HODSON, L.J., described (9) the question in the case as whether, according   **I**
to the ordinary use of language, there was a sharing in either of those cases of a
kitchen and held that there was not.

So, it seems to me, was the position here. There was no sharing of this kitchen

---

(4) [1956] 2 All E.R. 176; [1957] A.C. 65.
(5) [1952] 1 All E.R. 663; [1952] 2 Q.B. 89.
(6) [1952] 1 All E.R. at pp. 665, 666; [1952] 2 Q.B. at p. 93.
(7) [1945] 2 All E.R. 146; [1945] K.B. 474.
(8) [1945] 1 All E.R. 191; [1945] K.B. 144.
(9) [1952] 1 All E.R. at p. 667; [1952] 2 Q.B. at p. 95.

A at any time by the employees of the landlords. The agreement was that a very limited access was all that the employees should have and accordingly the tenant here never lost the protection of the Acts. If I were wrong on this point I should hold on the second point that this was a case to which s. 8 of the Act of 1949 applied and accordingly that this appeal must be allowed for that reason also.

B   KARMINSKI, L.J.: I agree with the judgments of Danckwerts, L.J., and of Phillimore, L.J., but as we are disagreeing with the judgment of the learned judge below I desire to add a very few words of my own.

This agreement containing the schedule which forms part of it to which reference has been made, was by itself, to me at any rate, unintelligible. It is therefore essential in order to understand it to get extrinsic evidence in order to

C explain the ambiguities which are there. Evidence was received from the tenant. On behalf of the landlords, who were not the original landlords, there was called the present head porter, a Mr. Green, who had apparently been there for 21 years and who knows the history of the accommodation well. It is not necessary to examine his evidence in detail, but he described the old user by Mr. Samuel of the one room in the flat that was used as a letting office. Then there was a

D gap of a year after the present landlords had bought the block of flats when it remained unused, and then his own subsequent use of it as a kind of showroom for sample carpets to show incoming tenants. Mr. Green made it clear in his evidence that during the time he had been using what was formerly the letting office, the kitchen had not been used by him or apparently by any other of the landlords' employees. He mentioned also that the kitchen, the smallest

E room in the flat, was a mere eight feet by six feet, a matter which is clearly relevant in deciding whether or not this could be classified as a living room. He pointed out too that the furniture in the kitchen, as one would expect in a room of that size, is limited to pure cooking purposes. The tenant, however, told the court that she used the kitchen, as one would expect, for cooking and also for washing laundry and washing up her dishes. She did not eat there.

F   Those are the essential facts and it now becomes necessary to refer very briefly to one sentence in the speech of Lord Radcliffe in *Goodrich* v. *Paisner* (10):

"As I see it, the truth is that a living room is not something which can be identified objectively without regard to the situation of its particular occupant, occupants or users."

G I have tried here, in the light of the facts which were proved before the learned judge below, to deal with the matter subjectively, and applying that test it would, I think, be almost impossible to describe this minute kitchen as a living room.

For these reasons and for the reasons given by Danckwerts, L.J., and Phillimore, L.J., I agree that this appeal must be allowed.

Appeal allowed.

H Solicitors: *Percy Short & Cuthbert*, agents for *Vyvyan Wells & Sons*, Finchley (for the tenant); *Lieberman, Leigh & Co.* (for the landlords).

[*Reported by* S. A. Hatteea, Esq., *Barrister-at-Law.*]

I

---

(10) [1956] 2 All E.R. 176 at p. 187; [1957] A.C. 65 at p. 91.

A

ALICIA HOSIERY, LTD. *v.* BROWN SHIPLEY & CO., LTD. AND ANOTHER.

[QUEEN'S BENCH DIVISION (Donaldson, J.), January 20, 21, 22, 23, 24, February 12, 1969.]

B

Bailment—Delivery order—Sale of goods pledged to bank and held by warehouse-men—Delivery order in favour of purchasers addressed to warehousemen—Failure of warehousemen to deliver—Whether bank liable to purchasers.

The owners of a quantity of stockings pledged them to a bank as security for a special advance. The stockings were held by warehousemen who, on the owners' instructions, notified the bank that they would hold the goods to the latter's order. The owners then sold the stockings, payment being by bills of exchange which were payable after a fixed term but which were to be discounted at once by a discount house. In return for a cheque from the discount house in favour of the owners, the bank gave the purchasers a delivery order addressed to the warehousemen and claused " all charges account goods ". The warehousemen were the holders of a bill of exchange from the owners in respect of sums expended on purchase tax and customs duty, and being doubtful of the owners' ability to meet the bill on maturity, the warehousemen declined to release the goods on receipt of the delivery order. On a claim by the purchasers against the bank,

C

D

Held: the claim must fail, because—

(i) although there were separate contracts between the owners and the purchasers, and between the owners and the bank, each including the exchange of the delivery order for the cheque, there was no contract between the purchasers and the bank (see p. 509, letter E, post);

E

(ii) the delivery order did not constitute an undertaking by the bank that the goods would in fact be delivered, but was a mere authorisation to the warehousemen, although the latters' claim, being by way of indemnity and not of payment for services, and being raised prematurely, would not have been within the clausing on the face of the order (see p. 509, letter F, and p. 510, letters F and H, post);

F

(iii) although the purchasers had been entitled to possession, the bank was not liable in detinue, since the warehousemen's failure to deliver arose not in their capacity as the bank's agents but as an act in their own interests and in repudiation of their contract with the bank, which therefore ceased to be in possession of the goods (see p. 511, letter F, post).

G

[As to the effect of a delivery order, see 34 HALSBURY'S LAWS (3rd Edn.) 91, 92, para. 135.]

Cases referred to:
Gillman, Spencer & Co. v. *Carbutt & Co.* (1889), 61 L.T. 281; 21 Digest (Repl.) 372, *1119.*

H

Groves & Sons v. *Webb & Kenward* (1916), 85 L.J.K.B. 1533; 114 L.T. 1082; 3 Digest (Repl.) 85, *198.*
Hill & Sons v. *London Central Markets Cold Storage Co., Ltd.* (1910), 102 L.T. 715; 32 Digest (Repl.) 269, *152.*
McEwan v. *Smith* (1849), 2 H.L. Cas. 309; 9 E.R. 1109; 32 Digest (Repl.) 256, *21.*

I

Action.

This was an action by Alicia Hosiery, Ltd., the purchasers, against Brown Shipley & Co., Ltd., the bank, for damages for breach of contract, detinue, or negligent mis-statement. The facts are set out in the judgment.

Ashe Lincoln, Q.C., and *G. Levy* for the purchasers.
R. A. Gatehouse for the bank.

Cur. adv. vult.

A   12th February. **DONALDSON, J.,** read the following judgment: Most cases concerning a pledge of goods deal with the rights and liabilities of the parties during the currency of the pledge. In this case, however, I have been concerned with the rights and liabilities of a pledgee after its determination. In this respect, and considering that the transaction was of the most ordinary mercantile description, and that the pledgee was a bank, the case may be of some

B general interest. Certainly I have found it both interesting and difficult, and I am most grateful to counsel for the very considerable assistance which I have received.

The action, as originally constituted, involved claims by Alicia Hosiery, Ltd., the plaintiffs (" the purchasers ") against first, Brown Shipley & Co., Ltd., the well-known merchant bankers (the " bank ") and secondly, Allied Shippers,

C Ltd., shipping and forwarding agents and vicarious warehousemen (" the warehousemen "). The warehousemen settled with the purchasers before the hearing of the action, which continued as between the purchasers and the bank.

The story begins at the end of October 1964, when two companies, Cascade Stockings, Ltd., and Dunstable Hosiery Mills, Ltd., both of which are now in liquidation, found themselves short of money. Both Cascade and Dunstable

D formed part of a group of companies controlled by the brothers Maurice and Michael Djanogly. Cascade had an account with the bank, but this account was overdrawn somewhat beyond the agreed limit. In these circumstances, Mr. Maurice Djanogly saw Mr. Garvie, the general manager of the bank, with a view to obtaining further overdraft facilities. Mr. Garvie was unwilling to assist unless further collateral security was provided and then only on terms

E that any advance was to be on a special account.

It so happened that Dunstable had bought a large quantity of ladies stockings of Italian manufacture earlier in the year, and Mr. Djanogly was in a position to procure the sale, or at least the transfer of these stockings, from Dunstable to Cascade. The stockings were held by the warehousemen, although physically they were in warehouses owned and operated by other companies. Mr. Djanogly

F offered to pledge these stockings as security for a special advance. At first Mr. Garvie was assured that import duty and purchase tax had been paid, but Mr. Djanogly later said that whilst part had been paid, £3,500 was outstanding. In fact nothing had been paid at this stage, but Mr. Garvie was misled and agreed to make an advance against a pledge of the stockings. It was implicit, if not expressed, that the advance was of a short term nature, and Mr. Djanogly was

G therefore faced with the problem of selling the stockings. Meanwhile, in perfection of the pledge, the warehousemen, on Mr. Djanogly's instructions, wrote to the bank on 28th October 1964, under the heading of " Cascade Stockings " stating:

" We have been instructed by the above Company to give you title to the following goods which we will only release against your order."

H
The letter then identified the stockings by reference to the Italian suppliers' invoices.

In the course of the next week or ten days, a Mr. John Morris, a director of Alec Morris Investments, Ltd., a small discount house (" the discount house "), heard that Mr. Djanogly's companies were in need of money and had some

I stockings to sell. He met Mr. Djanogly, who confirmed that this was the case, and as a result arranged for Mr. Djanogly to meet a Mr. Levy, a director of the purchasers, who were merchants dealing in stockings. This meeting took place at Mr. Michael Djanogly's flat on Sunday 8th November 1964, and resulted in an agreement whereby the purchasers undertook to buy from Cascade about 23,000 dozen stockings at a price of 23s. 6d. per dozen, purchase tax and duty paid delivery at warehouse, subject to an option to Cascade to repurchase the stockings within seven days at a price of 24s. per dozen. Payment was to be by means of bills of exchange payable by the purchasers after a fixed term,

during which the purchasers intended to sell the stockings, but the discount house A
undertook to discount the bills at once. The discounting of such bills was in the
ordinary course of the business of the discount house, but Mr. John Morris
and the chairman, Mr. Alec Morris, had close connections with the purchasers,
who had no London office, and in the subsequent history of the matter played a
far larger part than merely discounting the bills.

At Sunday's meeting Mr. Djanogly was a little vague as to where the stockings B
were held, and it was left that discussions would be resumed next morning.
On that occasion it emerged that part of the stockings were held by the warehousemen and part—the 9,858 dozen pairs with which this action is concerned
—were pledged to the bank. In fact, as I have already mentioned, they also
were being held by the warehousemen, but this fact did not emerge until later
in the day. The price had been agreed on the basis that import duty and purchase C
tax had been paid and both Mr. John and Mr. Alec Morris were anxious to see
evidence that this had in fact been done. At some stage Mr. Djanogly produced
a receipt from the warehousemen for £7,250 received by them in respect of duty
and tax on the stockings which were not pledged. This satisfied Mr. John and
Mr. Alec Morris so far as those goods were concerned.

There remained the pledged stockings. According to Mr. John Morris, it was D
decided between him and his father, Mr. Alec Morris, that, as they knew the bank,
the simplest course was to telephone and enquire whether the goods were " free
to be delivered ". According to Mr. Alec Morris, he telephoned to the bank
and spoke to a Mr. Simmonds. He told Mr. Simmonds that Mr. Djanogly was
in the office and that he understood that the bank had some of Mr. Djanogly's
goods. He then asked: " Are they free for delivery? " Mr. Simmonds replied: E
" Hold on a moment, and I will let you know ". A few moments later Mr.
Simmonds said: " The goods are free for delivery ", to which Mr. Morris replied:
" I will let you have my cheque if you will let me have your delivery order."
The conversation ended with Mr. Simmonds saying that the delivery order
would be sent early in the afternoon. Mr. Alec Morris said that it appeared that
Mr. Simmonds knew all about the transaction. He had no doubt that he spoke F
to Mr. Simmonds. He knew that Mr. Simmonds was an assistant manager, and
and the man who spoke to him on the telephone had said: " This is Simmonds
speaking." The precise amount payable for the pledged stockings was worked
out and it amounted to £11,583 3s.

Mr. Maurice Djanogly seems to have had an active morning on 9th November.
In addition to attending the meeting to which I have referred, he telephoned G
to a Mr. Thurbin of the bank and also visited him in order to complete all the
arrangements for handing over the bank's delivery order in exchange for the
discount house's cheque. Mr. Thurbin is now an assistant manager of the bank,
but was then a clerk in the commercial department. As such, he had been
authorised to deal with the transaction once the special account and supporting
pledge had been agreed by Mr. Garvie. H

The information given on the telephone seems to have been modified to some
extent in the course of the subsequent interview, but I do not think that it is
necessary to lengthen this judgment by setting out the course of events in every
detail. Suffice it to say that Mr. Thurbin was led to believe that the pledged
stockings were being sold for £13,431 18s. 3d. of which £11,500 would be paid
by the discount house, against a delivery order signed on behalf of the bank I
requesting the warehousemen to deliver the stockings to the purchasers ex
warehouse, and that the balance of the purchase price would be paid at a later
date. He was also led to believe that import duty and purchase tax amounting
to £6,275 6s. 7d. was payable to the warehousemen, but that £3,000 had already
been paid on account. As the overdrawn balance on Cascade's special account
amounted to £2,506 11s. 3d. and he was expecting to receive £11,500, Mr. Thurbin
agreed to pay the sum of £3,275 6s. 7d., being the balance of the duty and purchase
tax, to the credit of the account of the warehousemen with another bank. In

A fact, the £3,000 had been paid as to £250 by a cheque of Dunstables, and the balance was covered by a bill of exchange payable to the warehousemen and accepted by Cascade or Dunstable which was not due for payment until 29th December 1964.

Mr. Thurbin confirmed the arrangement in letters addressed to the discount house, Cascade and the warehousemen. The letter to the warehousemen included

B a copy of the delivery order. The letter to the discount house stated that:

" In accordance with arrangements made with Mr. Maurice Djanogly we enclose our Delivery Order No. 11294 in favour of [the purchasers], covering a total of 9858 dozen pairs of stockings . . . we understand that you will be arranging the discount of the relative drafts in this connection and we

C hereby authorise you to release this Delivery Order to [the purchasers], on the understanding that your cheque for the sum of £11,500 will be handed to us for account of Cascade Stockings Ltd. We thank you for your help in this matter and have arranged for our representative to call at your office at 2.30 p.m."

There seems little point in the last sentence if, as happened, the letter was to be

D delivered with the delivery order at 2.30 p.m., and Mr. Thurbin never really explained it. Looking simply at the letter, and in particular at the reference to authorising the release of the delivery order, which is inappropriate if it was only handed over in exchange for a cheque, I infer that Mr. Thurbin's original intention was to send the delivery order round during the morning and to collect the cheque at 2.30 p.m.

E When the delivery order was eventually brought round to the discount house's office the messenger was immediately given the cheque for £11,583 3s. The delivery order itself was dated 9th November 1964, was signed by an assistant manager on behalf of the bank, and was addressed to the warehousemen. The body of the order read:

F " Please deliver to [the purchasers] or order ex warehouse Ref. 115A—4273 dozen stockings, 103A—4122 dozen stockings, 58A—1463 dozen stockings."

It was crossed: " Nine thousand eight hundred and fifty eight dozen ", and was claused: " All charges account goods." Mr. John Morris did not see the delivery order until after the cheque had been received by the bank's manager, but there was nothing in its wording which caused him any anxiety, although it is

G fair to say that he was not familiar with delivery orders.

Thereafter efforts were made by the discount house, acting on behalf of the purchasers, to obtain delivery of the stockings, but the warehousemen proved unco-operative. The evidence of exactly what attempts were made to persuade the warehousemen to deliver was unsatisfactory, and there is no contemporary correspondence emanating from the discount house. It is, however, quite clear

H from the letters dated 20th and 25th November 1964, addressed by the warehousemen to the bank, that on or about 20th November the warehousemen had become doubtful of the solvency of Dunstable and Cascade and, in particular, had no confidence that the bill of exchange for £2,750 would be met on maturity. It is also clear that by this date the warehousemen knew that the discount house, or the purchasers held a delivery order signed by the bank, although they

I affected not to have received a copy and a duplicate was sent to them on 26th November 1964. I think it is also probable that at a comparatively early stage the warehousemen were indicating that they were exercising a lien over the goods, but I am quite ready to believe that this was not done with any great clarity, since their right to such a lien in respect of a contingent liability, which would crystallise in the event of a failure by Dunstable to pay a bill of exchange at a date, was highly doubtful. However, by 1st December 1964, the warehousemen were asserting a specific lien on the pledged goods for no less than £2,900, and other liens both general and specific on other goods. The purchasers were

not prepared to pay the warehousemen any such sum in order to obtain possession   A
of the pledged stockings, and they have lost £11,583 3s.

The purchasers now seek to recover this loss from the bank, and the claim is
put in three ways: namely, (i) as damages for breach of an agreement between
the bank and the purchasers under which the bank undertook to procure that the
goods were delivered to the purchasers without further payment by the purchasers; (ii) as the value of the goods, i.e., the pledged stockings, wrongfully   B
detained by the bank; and (iii) as damages for negligent mis-statement by the
bank in that Mr. Simmonds on their behalf told Mr. Alec Morris that the stockings
were " free for delivery ".

Negligent mis-statement. Whatever the legal merits of this claim, it depends
on my being satisfied on the balance of probabilities that the conversation
alleged to have taken place between Mr. Simmonds and Mr. Alec Morris in fact   C
took place and that in the course of that conversation Mr. Simmonds assured
Mr. Alec Morris that the goods were " free for delivery ". I am not so satisfied.
Mr. Simmonds gave evidence that on Monday 9th November 1964, he did not go
to the bank's office, but went straight from his home to St. Pancras where he
caught the 10.25 a.m. train for Manchester. His personal diary bears this out,
and also contains the figures " 1423 " and " 1550 ". His original explanation   D
that the train arrived in Manchester at 14.23 and that he finished a series of
telephone calls by 15.50 was not correct. Research during the hearing revealed
that the train was due to arrive at 14.23, and that it arrived 75 minutes late on
that day. Allowing Mr. Simmonds 12 minutes to get from the station to his
hotel, it is reasonably clear that the entry " 1550 " reflects his annoyance at
the time which it had taken him to get there. Mr. Simmonds categorically denied   E
—and I accept his denial—that he had any telephone conversation with Mr.
Alec Morris or anyone else on the subject of the pledged stockings on 9th
November 1964.

In these circumstances, I naturally explored the possibility of any mistake
as to the identity of the person with whom Mr. Morris said that he spoke on the
telephone, but there seemed no possibility of error. I accept Mr. Simmonds'   F
evidence because I thought that he appeared the more reliable witness when
giving evidence, and because, if the conversation had indeed taken place, it is
likely that the bank's letter to the discount house, dated 9th November 1964,
would have referred to it with or without a further reference to " arrangements
made with Mr. Maurice Djanogly ". Furthermore, I find it inconceivable that
if Mr. Simmonds had the alleged telephone conversation he would not have   G
mentioned it to Mr. Thurbin who was dealing with the matter; but Mr. Thurbin
clearly did not know of it. Lastly, it is a factor of which I must take account
that Mr. Simmonds, although responsible for the supervision of Cascade's general
account, had no concern with the special account. On this finding of fact, no
question of negligent mis-statement arises.

Breach of an agreement to procure the delivery of the stockings to the purchasers   H
without further payment. This head of claim is advanced on the basis that: (i) the
purchasers and the bank were ad idem in agreeing that the purchasers by their
agent, the discount house, would give the bank a cheque drawn by the discount
house, in favour of Cascade for £11,500 or thereabouts, and that in exchange
the bank would give the purchasers a delivery order relating to the pledged
stockings; (ii) in these circumstances the bank either expressly, by the delivery   I
order, or impliedly promised to procure the delivery of the stockings to the
purchasers without further payment; and (iii) the giving of the cheque constituted good consideration moving from the promisee, the purchasers, to the
promisor, the bank. Accordingly, it is said, there was a contract between the
purchasers and the bank and the latter are in breach in failing to procure delivery
by the warehousemen.

The bank deny that there was any such contract and, in particular, deny
that a delivery order given in these circumstances involves any promise to

A   procure delivery of the goods. They also say that in any event the clause, " all charges account goods ", negatives any undertaking to procure the delivery of the goods without further payment by the purchasers.

In my judgment, the bank are right for at least two reasons. First, there can be no contract between two parties unless both intend either to enter into contractual relations or so to act towards one another that the law will imply

B   such an intention. There must be an offer and acceptance leading to a bargain between the parties, and here there was none either expressly or by implication from the exchange of documents. Once the alleged telephone conversation between Mr. Alec Morris and Mr. Simmonds is eliminated, I am left with: (i) an agreement between the purchasers and Cascade that in consideration of the purchasers procuring a cheque drawn by the discount house, in favour of Cascade

C   and the delivery of this cheque to the bank, Cascade will procure the release by the bank of their interest in the goods as pledgees by the handing over of a delivery order in exchange for the cheque; and (ii) an agreement between Cascade and the bank, that in consideration of Cascade procuring the delivery to the bank of a cheque drawn by the discount house, in favour of Cascade, the bank would release their interest as pledgees of the goods and deliver a delivery

D   order to the discount house, in favour of the purchasers. The agreement between Cascade and the purchasers probably went further and involved an obligation on the part of Cascade to procure that the purchasers could obtain the goods ex warehouse without further payment; but that is not material. However, I do not see why the performance of these two contracts, which were separately negotiated by Mr. Djanogly of Cascade, should create a contract between the purchasers and

E   the bank just because the contract between the purchasers and Cascade involved Cascade in giving a cheque to the bank in exchange for a delivery order and the contract between the bank and Cascade involved the bank in giving Cascade a delivery order in exchange for a cheque.

Second, I am not satisfied that the delivery by a pledgee to a purchaser of the pledged goods of a delivery order addressed to the person holding the goods

F   requiring him to deliver the goods to the order of the purchaser involves any undertaking by the pledgee to the purchaser that the goods will be so delivered or is more than an authority to the holder of the goods to attorn to the person in whose favour the delivery order is made out. Counsel for the purchasers in this context relied on *Groves & Sons v. Webb & Kenward* (1), *Gillman, Spencer & Co. v. Carbutt & Co.* (2), and a passage in 34 HALSBURY'S LAWS OF ENGLAND (3rd

G   Edn.) p. 91, para. 135.

Counsel for the purchasers conceded that *Groves'* case (1) was concerned with a warehouseman's right to indemnity when at the request of his principal he issues clean warehouse warrants and the principal is thereby enabled to sell the wheat as undamaged. However, he says, correctly, that all concerned assumed that the warehousemen were liable to the purchasers for failing to

H   deliver undamaged wheat, and submits that it follows that one who issues a delivery order is similarly liable if the goods are not delivered. I cannot accept this submission. A warehouse warrant is a very special class of document constituting a document of title to the goods which a delivery order is not, and the fact that possession of a warehouseman's warrant gives rise to a cause of action against the warehouseman does not lead necessarily or at all to the conclusion

I   that the same is true of a delivery order.

In *Gillman, Spencer & Co. v. Carbutt & Co.* (2) the plaintiffs sued the defendants in detinue and not in contract. The facts were complex, but if the plaintiffs were to succeed they had to establish that the defendants by issuing a delivery order in favour of the plaintiffs relating to goods in their possession were estopped from denying the plaintiffs' title to the goods.

The Court of Appeal held that there was no such estoppel, and in reliance on

---

(1) (1916), 85 L.J.K.B. 1533.   (2) (1889), 61 L.T. 281.

McEwan v. *Smith* (3) that a delivery order is only a promise to do something **A** in futuro (per LORD ESHER, M.R. (4) and FRY, L.J. (5)). The essential feature of both *Gillman's* case (6) and *McEwan* v. *Smith* (3) was that the delivery order was issued by the seller of the goods, and it is not very difficult to spell a promise to deliver, whether or not subject to conditions, from such an order. In the present case the bank were not sellers, but pledgees, and what they gave was, in my judgment, a mere authority to the buyer to receive possession.   **B**

This distinction is preserved, albeit somewhat obscurely, in the passage in 34 HALSBURY'S LAWS to which I was referred. It reads—

" Delivery orders . . . are mere promises by the seller, being the issuer or transferor, to deliver, or authorities to the buyer to receive possession."

The documents in *Groves'* (7) and *Gillman's* cases (6) were in the former category, **C** whilst that in the present case is in the latter.

Counsel for the bank makes a further point. He submits that since any agreement must be spelled out of the terms of the delivery order which was in fact issued (there being no contract between the bank and the purchasers requiring the issue of a delivery order in any particular form), regard must be had to the clausing, " All charges account goods ". This submission is well founded. **D** The meanings of somewhat similar expressions were considered by HAMILTON, J., in *Hill & Sons* v. *London Central Markets Cold Storage Co., Ltd.* (8). In the light of that case and the evidence which I have heard, I consider that the words have a generally accepted meaning, namely: " You, the addressee of the delivery order, are requested or required to deliver the goods to the named beneficiary, but any accrued charges by you in respect of these goods and any charges accruing **E** in the process of delivery must be discharged by the beneficiary as a condition precedent to his obtaining delivery." This leaves the question of what is meant by " charges ". Counsel for the bank submitted that the word was wide enough to cover any debt due (in connection with the goods) from the person issuing the delivery order (or the owner of the goods) to its addressee, but I think that this is too wide a construction. In my view, there is a real distinction between **F** sums due by way of payment for services rendered and sums due by way of indemnability. Thus, I do not consider that a claim to be re-imbursed customs duty and purchase tax disbursed on behalf of the owner of the goods as " a charge ", but a claim for remuneration for performing this service would be. If, therefore, I am wrong in thinking that there was no contract between the purchasers and the bank, the clause on the face of the delivery order would not provide the bank with any defence to a claim based on the fact that the ware- **G** housemen claimed re-imbursement of their expenditure on import duty and purchase tax as a condition of delivery. Furthermore, on any view of the matter, the clause must be restricted to charges properly raised, and I see no justification for the major part of the warehousemen's claim before the maturity of Cascade's bill of exchange on 29th December 1964 or, their earlier liquidation.

Claim in detinue. A claim in detinue lies at the suit of a person who has an **H** immediate right to the possession of the goods against a person who is in posses- sion of the goods and who, on proper demand, fails or refuses to deliver them up without lawful excuse.

In the present case, counsel for the purchasers submits that at all material times after 9th November 1964, the purchasers were immediately entitled to possession of the goods by virtue of their position as buyers under the contract **I** of sale with Cascade, coupled, if need be, with their receipt of the delivery order from the bank. I think that this is correct. He further submits that on and after

---

(3) (1849), 2 H. L. Cas. 309.
(4) (1889), 61 L.T. at p. 282.
(5) (1889), 61 L.T. at p. 283.
(6) (1889), 61 L.T. 281.
(7) (1916), 85 L.J.K.B. 1533.
(8) (1910), 102 L.T. 715.

A 29th October 1964, the bank were in possession of the goods by their agents, the warehousemen, and that on various occasions when demand for possession was made by or on behalf of the purchasers, the bank failed, and the warehousemen, their agents, refused to deliver up possession of the goods. This submission requires closer examination.

B The goods were at all times held in various warehouses to the order of the warehousemen, but it is more convenient to consider the matter as if they were in the warehousemen's own warehouses. On this assumption, the goods were at all times in the physical possession of the warehousemen. When, however, the warehousemen attorned to the bank on 29th October 1964, the bank came into constructive possession of the goods. The essence of the submission of counsel for the purchasers is that one who, in such circumstances, is in constructive

C possession of goods so remains until his bailee delivers the goods to his order or attorns to someone else. He goes on to submit that the warehousemen never delivered the goods or attorned to the purchasers, and that accordingly the bank are liable in detinue.

True it is that the warehousemen never attorned to the purchasers or delivered the goods, but I do not think that it follows that the bank remained in con-

D structive possession of them. The essence of constructive possession is that the constructive possessor has a key, whether actual or contractual, which gives him control over goods held on his behalf in the possession of another. If the key is contractual, no transfer of constructive possession can take place unless and until the person in physical possession agrees to enter into a similar contractual relationship with the transferee, i.e., attorns to him. But it does not follow from

E this that the constructive possession may not be otherwise determined without the assent of the person in physical possession.

In the present case the bank on 9th November 1964, issued the delivery order requiring the warehousemen to deliver the goods to the purchasers or their order and authorising the purchasers to apply for and take delivery. On that order coming to the notice of the warehousemen, as I suggest it did on 10th November

F 1964, and as it certainly did on about 20th November 1964, the warehousemen became bound to hold the goods to the order of the purchasers. If they failed to do so, it was not because they were continuing with their role as agents for the bank, but because they were acting in their own interests and in repudiation of their contracted duty with the bank. In such circumstances their possession ceased to be that of the bank, and the bank are not liable for their detention

G of the goods.

On the facts it is by no means clear that the warehousemen were refusing to acknowledge the delivery order and thus attorn to the purchasers. Nor is it at all clear when first they refused to deliver. The bank never refused to deliver the goods or instructed the warehousemen not to do so. All that happened was that they failed to persuade the warehousemen to deliver. The warehousemen,

H for their part, were refusing to deliver to anyone unless and until their very considerable claims in respect of the pledged goods were met by someone, and the question of who would be entitled to delivery if they were met was never really in issue.

For these reasons I consider that the purchasers' claim fails, and in the circumstances it is not necessary to consider the issue as to mitigation of damage.

I *Judgment for the bank.*

Solicitors: *Anthony Edward & Hoffman* (for the purchasers); *Linklaters & Paines* (for the bank).

[*Reported by* MARY COLTON, *Barrister-at-Law.*]

A

Re PARRY (*deceased*).
DALTON *v.* COOKE AND OTHERS.

[CHANCERY DIVISION (Pennycuick, J.), February 26, 27, 1969.]

*Administration of Estates—Legacy—Bequest conditional on solicitor's proving
will and acting in trusts—Appointment as solicitor to will—Charging clause
entitling solicitor to payment for professional services—Will proved—
Another solicitor appointed to administer estate—Whether solicitor entitled
to conditional bequest.*

B

The testatrix by her will appointed the plaintiff and the first defendant
her executors and trustees and by cl. 5 directed that they should sell her
residuary estate and divide it into one hundred equal parts.   Having made
various bequests by cl. 5 (iv) she bequeathed ten equal parts to the first
defendant " if he shall prove this my Will and act in the trusts hereof ".
By cl. 6 she appointed the first defendant " as Solicitor to be employed in
obtaining Probate of this my Will and in connection with the administration
of my estate ".   By cl. 7 she provided that any executor or trustee engaged
in any profession or business should be entitled to charge for work or business
done in connection with proving the will or executing the trusts.   The
testatrix died on 15th December 1964 and the will was proved by the
plaintiff and first defendant on 30th April 1965.   Probate was obtained
by the first defendant in his capacity as solicitor for himself and the plaintiff
and he continued to act as solicitor in the administration of the estate for
a time.   Difficulties arose in connection with the estate duty affidavit and
some other matters and, as a result the first defendant fell into arrears with
his work ; the plaintiff went to C., another solicitor, who in the course
of correspondence with the first defendant complained of the delay.   In
August 1967 the first defendant handed over all the papers relating to the
estate which he had as solicitor and thereafter C. administered the estate on
the instructions of both the executors.   The administration was completed
in June 1968.   The plaintiff took out a summons to determine whether, on
the true construction of cl. 5 (iv) of the will, the first defendant had fulfilled
the condition therein and was accordingly entitled to the property bequeathed by cl. 5 (iv).

C

D

E

F

Held: the first defendant was entitled to his share of residue because,
bearing in mind his appointment as solicitor to the will and the charging
clause therein, the words " act in the trusts hereof " in cl. 5 (iv) on their
natural meaning denoted simply doing those acts which a non-professional
trustee was obliged to do in the execution of his trust including the
exercise of powers and discretions which could not be delegated to others,
there was accordingly no doubt that the first defendant acted in this sense
as trustee up to the date of distribution (see p. 515, letter H, and p. 516,
letter F, post).

G

H

[As to duties of trustees generally, see 38 HALSBURY'S LAWS (3rd Edn.)
966-978, paras. 1673-1692; and for cases on the subject see 47 DIGEST (Repl.)
346-371, *3113-3322.*]

Cases referred to:

Harrison v. *Rowley* (1798), 4 Ves. 212; 31 E.R. 110; 23 Digest (Repl.) 453,
        5225.

Lewis v. *Mathews* (1869), L.R. 8 Eq. 277; 38 L.J.Ch. 510; 20 L.T. 905; 33
        J.P. 775; 23 Digest (Repl.) 453, *5226.*

Muffett, Re, Jones v. *Mason* (1886), 55 L.T. 671; 49 Digest (Repl.) 803, *7553.*

Sharman, Re, Public Trustee v. *Sharman,* [1942] 2 All E.R. 74; [1942] Ch. 311;
        111 L.J.Ch. 257; 167 L.T. 285; 47 Digest (Repl.) 174, *1423.*

Wilkinson v. *Wilkinson* (1825), 2 Sim. & St. 237; 53 E.R. 337; 47 Digest
        (Repl.) 387, *3459.*

I

A   **Adjourned Summons.**

This was a summons dated 13th November 1968 by the plaintiff, Mrs. Maud Ethel Dalton, an executor and trustee of the will, dated 11th March 1948, of Edith Vera Parry, deceased.   By the summons the plaintiff sought declarations whether on the true construction of cl. 5 (iv) of the will the first defendant, Edgar Alfred Abbott Cooke, satisfied the condition " if he shall prove this
B   my Will and act in the trusts hereof " by: (i) proving the will; (ii) proving the will and taking some further steps in the administration of the estate; (iii) proving the will and completing the administration of the estate; (iv) proving the will, completing the administration of the estate and distributing it; or (v) in some other and what event; and whether on the true construction of the will and the events which had happened the first defendant had in fact fulfilled
C   the condition in cl. 5 (iv).   The other defendants to the summons were beneficiaries under the will, Mrs. Alma Catharine Le Vierge and Mrs. Lydia Simmons. The facts are set out in the judgment.

The case noted below* was cited during the argument in addition to those referred to in the judgment.

D   *B. K. Levy* for the plaintiff.

R. Walker for the first defendant.

P. J. Millett for the second and third defendants.

PENNYCUICK, J.: This summons raises in effect a single question under the will of Edith Vera Parry, to whom I will refer as " the testatrix ". The testatrix made her will on 11th March 1948. Its terms, so far as now
E   material, are as follows.   Clause 2:

" I APPOINT my sister MAUD ETHEL DALTON [the plaintiff] of 101 Princes Avenue Palmers Green N.13. and EDGAR ALFRED ABBOTT COOKE [the first defendant] of 158/160 City Road London E.C.1. and of 55 Pickhurst Lane Hayes Bromley in the County of Kent Solicitor (hereinafter called
F   ' my Trustees ') to be the EXECUTORS AND TRUSTEES of this my Will."

By cl. 4 she constituted her residuary estate.   By cl. 5 she directed her trustees to sell her residuary estate and (after the usual administrative directions) to divide the remainder of the proceeds of sale:

". . . into one hundred equal parts and shall pay the same in manner and to the persons following viz:—(i) As to forty five equal parts to my sister
G   Maud Ethel Dalton now of 101 Princes Avenue Palmers Green N.13. or if she shall have predeceased me my Trustee shall hold such forty five parts UPON TRUST to pay the income thereof to my niece Alma Catharine Ford [the second defendant] during her life and after her death shall hold such forty five parts UPON TRUST both as to capital and income for the child or children of my said niece (and if more than one as tenants in common in
H   equal shares) who shall attain the age of twenty one years.   (ii) As to forty equal parts to my said niece Alma Catharine Ford or if she shall have predeceased me to her child or children (and if more than one as tenants in common in equal shares) who shall attain the age of twenty one years. (iii) As to five equal parts to Lydia Gillingham [the third defendant] if she shall be living on the first anniversary of my death.   (iv) As to ten equal
I   parts to the [first defendant] if he shall prove this my Will and act in the trusts hereof.   AND I DECLARE that if any of the legacies mentioned in sub-clauses (i) to (iv) both inclusive of this clause shall fail then the legacies so failing shall go to augment the parts of the legatees who survive me and attain a vested interest and so that the legacy or legacies so failing shall be divided into such number of parts as the surviving legatees shall take of the said one hundred parts and each surviving legatee shall take the same

* *Harford* v. *Browning* (1787), 1 Cox 302.

number of parts of the legacy or legacies so failing as each surviving legatee   A
shall take of the said one hundred parts of my residuary estate."

Clause 6 and cl. 7 provide:

" 6.   I APPOINT [the first defendant] of the firm of Rule & Cooke 158/160
City Road London E.C.1. as the Solicitor to be employed in obtaining
Probate of this my Will and in connection with the administration of my   B
Estate.
" 7.   ANY Executor or Trustee for the time being hereof or of any assent
for carrying into effect the provisions hereof who is a solicitor or engaged in
any profession or business shall be entitled to charge and be paid all usual
professional and other charges for work or business done or transacted by
him or his firm in proving my Will or in the execution of or in connection   C
with the trusts hereof or any such assent as aforesaid including work or
business not of a strictly professional nature which a Trustee could do
personally."

The testatrix made a codicil to her will 13 years later, on 11th December 1961.
By that codicil she directed that her will should be read and construed as if the
following alterations had been made thereto: D

". . . (b) CLAUSE TWO [that is dealing with the appointment of executors
and trustees] as if . . . the following words had been inserted [after the name
of the first defendant] ' or if he shall have predeceased me his son David
Edgar Abbott Cooke Solicitor '."

Then in cl. 5 (iv)—that is the gift of ten equal parts of residue to the first   E
defendant—

". . . after the words ' [the first defendant] ' shall be deemed to be inserted
the words ' of if he shall have predeceased me then his son the said David
Edgar Abbott Cooke '."

Finally, in cl. 6—that is the appointment of the first defendant as solicitor—   F

" it shall be deemed [in that clause] after the name [of the first defendant]
shall be inserted ' or if he shall have predeceased me then his son the said
David Edgar Abbott Cooke '."

The testatrix died on 15th December 1964.   Her will was proved by the two
executors, namely the plaintiff and the first defendant, on 30th April 1965.   G
The testatrix was survived by her sister, the plaintiff, and by her niece, the
second defendant, so, in the events which happened, the substitutional gifts
did not take effect.   The third defendant survived the testatrix by one year
and the whole estate thus became due for immediate distribution as soon as
administration should have been completed.

Probate was obtained by the first defendant in his capacity as solicitor for   H
the two executors named in the will, the plaintiff and himself.   He acted for a
time as solicitor in the administration of the estate, but, unfortunately, he fell
into arrears with his work and various difficulties arose in connection with the
estate duty affidavit and a number of other matters connected with the administration, for example, dealing with dividends, and so forth.   It is not necessary
to go into the details of those difficulties; it will be sufficient to say this, that the   I
plaintiff, the first executor, went to another solicitor and that other solicitor,
Mr. Chambres, had correspondence with the first defendant, in the course of
which he complained of delay; in one case there was a complaint to the Law
Society.   However, on 17th August 1967, the first defendant, by agreement
with Mr. Chambres, handed over all the papers relating to the estate which he
had as solicitor, and thereafter Mr. Chambres acted as solicitor in the administration of the estate.   He did that on the instructions of both the executors, the
plaintiff and the first defendant.   The administration of the estate was completed

A in June 1968, and there has been a considerable interim distribution. The net estate was of the value of some £30,000.

The question which falls to be determined is as to the share of the residue given to the first defendant himself under cl. 5 (iv) of the will. That is the gift of ten equal hundredth parts of the residuary estate. It will be remembered that that gift is conditional on his proving the will and acting in the trusts thereof.

B It is contended on behalf of the plaintiff that, the first defendant having ceased to act as solicitor in the administration of the estate before administration was completed, the condition in para. (iv) has not been performed and, accordingly, he is disqualified from taking his share of the residuary estate. In those circumstances, the present originating summons has been issued, the plaintiff being Mrs. Dalton, and the defendants Mr. Cooke, Mrs. Alma Catharine Le Vierge

C (formerly Ford) and Mrs. Lydia Simmons (formerly Gillingham).

Before dealing with the construction of the will, I should make it clear that the beneficiaries other than the first defendant have not claimed to set aside the gift to the first defendant on any of the grounds external to the construction of the will on which gifts to solicitors in a will have sometimes been set aside. Counsel for the other beneficiaries expressly disclaim any allegation of that

D kind. That being so, it is unnecessary to go further into the facts and I have not allowed that sort of consideration to influence my mind in any way. The question is purely one of the construction of this will. I will make this preliminary comment, that the will is not over-precise as to the language dealing respectively with the administration of the testatrix's estate and execution of the trusts of residue. It will be seen that only in the event (which did not happen) of the

E plaintiff or the second defendant predeceasing the testatrix, would there be a residuary trust after completion of administration. One should not, I think, on the construction of this will, look over-closely at the use of the varied expressions " in the trusts hereof " or " in connection with the administration of my estate ", and so forth.

In order to comply with the condition, the first defendant has to do two

F things: (i) he must prove the will (which he has undoubtedly done); (ii) he must act in the trusts of the will. Two questions arise on those words. The first is, what is meant by " act in the trusts of the will "? And, secondly, for how long does the first defendant have to act in those trusts in order to comply with the condition?

In construing this condition, it is, I think, of the first importance to bear in

G mind that the will contains, apart from the gift of residue to the first defendant, an appointment of the first defendant as solicitor and a charging clause applicable to any executor who is a solicitor. There is no doubt that, under the charging clause, the first defendant is entitled quite apart from his interest in residue to make professional charges for any work done by him in connection with the estate. With this in mind, it seems to me that the words " act in the trusts

H hereof ", on their natural meaning, denote simply " doing those acts which a non-professional trustee is obliged to do in the execution of his trust ". It is difficult to be more precise. They include the exercise of powers and discretions which cannot be delegated to others.

It is contended, on behalf of the plaintiff and the second and third defendants, that here the expression means either " act as solicitor in the trusts hereof " or

I " act in . . ."—what counsel described as, for want of a better expression— ". . . the active sense ". By that is meant, I think, doing personally those things which a solicitor employed by a trustee normally does. I do not think either is the natural meaning of the expression " act in the trusts hereof ". The first meaning cannot fairly be derived from the words. The second meaning might perhaps be appropriate if it were not for the charging clause under which the first defendant is entitled to charge for administrative acts which he does as solicitor. But I do not think it is a legitimate meaning when one bears in mind that such administrative acts are separately remunerated. The point

does not admit of much elaboration. It seems to me that the expression means A
what it says and no more.

I was referred, on this point, to one or two cases. In *Wilkinson* v. *Wilkinson* (1)
the " Testator gave annuities to his trustees for their trouble in the execution of
his will, and died possessed of several houses, let at weekly rents ". SIR JOHN
LEACH, V.-C., said (1):

> " It does not appear to me that the annuity of five guineas given to each B
> trustee, makes any difference in this case. It is given to them as a recom-
> pense for the care and trouble which will attend the due execution of their
> office; and, if it be consistent with the due execution of their office that
> they should employ a collector to receive the rent, they will still be entitled
> to the annuity."

That case was distinguished in *Re Muffett*, *Jones* v. *Mason* (2), where the facts C
were quite different, because the testator gave the trustees a legacy for their
services in collecting rent, i.e., performing services personally.

I was referred to one modern case only, namely *Re Sharman, Public Trustee* v.
Sharman (3). There, the condition was that the individual concerned should
" accept the trusteeship thereof ". I think that is rather a different point. D
On the best consideration that I can give, I think the words " act in the trusts
hereof " bear the meaning which I have indicated. A curiosity, to my mind, is
that the testatrix, under the substitutional gift in the codicil, has given the same
one-tenth interest to the first defendant's son should the first defendant himself
predecease the testatrix, and so Mr. Cooke junior would likewise take one-tenth
if he proved the will and acted in the trusts of the will. That is, at first sight, E
unexpected, because one would think that the gift to the first defendant would
probably be in recognition of some special capacity as an old friend and adviser.
However, I do not think that that substitutional gift can alter the natural
meaning of the language which the testatrix has used.

If that is the correct construction of " act in the trusts hereof ", that concludes
the matter, because there is no doubt that the first defendant did act in the
trusts thereof in the sense of acting as trustee, although not as solicitor, right F
up to the date of distribution. If that were wrong and the word " act " in the
expression " act in the trusts hereof " required the first defendant to perform
the administrative acts of a solicitor in the execution of his trust, then it appears
that he ceased to act in that capacity in August 1967. On that footing I would
have to consider whether he became entitled to a share in the residue the moment
he entered on the trust.   On that point, authority is in his favour (see *Harrison* G
v. *Rowley* (4) and *Lewis* v. *Mathews* (5)). I do not think, as I have already
decided this on the other ground, that it would be useful to go further into those
cases. I would only make the comment that the construction of every will
depends on its own particular terms.

I will accordingly declare that the first defendant has become entitled to his
share of the residuary estate.   H

Order accordingly.

Solicitors: *Burchell & Ruston* (for the plaintiff); *Moreton Phillips & Son* (for
the first defendant); *Joynson-Hicks & Co.* (for the second and third defendants).

[*Reported by* ROSALIE LONG, *Barrister-at-Law.*]

I

---

(1) (1825), 2 Sim. & St. 237.
(2) (1886), 55 L.T. 671.
(3) [1942] 2 All E.R. 74; [1942] Ch. 311.
(4) (1798), 4 Ves. 212.
(5) (1869), L.R. 8 Eq. 277.

A

Re STEMSON'S WILL TRUSTS.
CARPENTER v. TREASURY SOLICITOR AND ANOTHER.

[CHANCERY DIVISION (Plowman, J.), February 20, March 7, 1969.]

B

*Charity—Charitable trust—Will—Gift to institution which had been dissolved—
Institution liable to dissolution—Funds disposed of—Doctrine of lapse.*

By cl. 5 of his will made in 1950, the testator bequeathed his residuary
estate to a charitable organisation, the Rationalist Endowment Fund, Ltd.
(" REF "). In 1963, REF passed, in accordance with its memorandum of
association, a special resolution to wind up and it was dissolved in 1965; its
net assets were thereupon, in accordance with its memorandum of association,

C

passed to the Rationalist Press Association, Ltd., which also was a charitable
organisation although, unlike REF, its objects did not include the relief of
poverty. In 1966, the testator died without having amended his will. On
the question whether the bequest of the residuary estate, being a gift to a
charitable corporation, was held on a valid charitable trust,

D

Held: on the true construction of the will, the testator's residuary estate
was undisposed of by his will, because—

(i) cl. 5 of the will negatived any general charitable intention by showing
that the testator was particularly relying on REF to carry out his wishes
(see p. 519, letter I, post);

Re Harwood ([1936] Ch. 285) followed.

E

(ii) where funds came into the hands of a charitable organisation such as
REF which was founded, not as a perpetual charity, but as one liable to
termination, and its constitution provided for the disposal of its funds in that
event, then, if the organisation ceased to exist and its funds were disposed of,
the charity or charitable trust itself ceased to exist, and there was nothing
to prevent the operation of the doctrine of lapse (see p. 524, letter D,
post).

F

Re Faraker ([1911-13] All E.R. Rep. 488), *Re Lucas (decd.)* ([1948] 2 All
E.R. 22), *Re Bagshaw (decd.)* ([1954] 1 All E.R. 227), *Re Roberts (decd.)*
([1963] 1 All E.R. 674) and *Re Vernon's Will Trusts* ((22nd November 1962),
unreported), distinguished.

G

[As to gifts to Charitable Institutions which have ceased to exist, see 4
HALSBURY'S LAWS (3rd Edn.) 279, 280, para. 581; and for cases on the subject,
see 8 DIGEST (Repl.) 418-420, *1091-1111*.]

Cases referred to:

Bagshaw (decd.), Re, Westminster Bank, Ltd. v. Taylor, [1954] 1 All E.R. 227;
[1954] 1 W.L.R. 238; Digest (Cont. Vol. A) 103, *1079a.*

Faraker, Re, Faraker v. Durell, [1912] 2 Ch. 488; [1911-13] All E.R. Rep. 488;

H

81 L.J.Ch. 635; 107 L.T. 36; 8 Digest (Repl.) 419, *1102.*

Harwood, Re, Coleman v. Innes, [1936] Ch. 285; [1935] All E.R. Rep. 918;
105 L.J.Ch. 142; 154 L.T. 624; 8 Digest (Repl.) 460, *1598.*

Lucas (decd.), Re, Sheard v. Mellor, [1948] 2 All E.R. 22; [1948] Ch. 424;
[1948] L.J.R. 1914; 8 Digest (Repl.) 419, *1103.*

Roberts (decd.), Re, Stenton v. Hardy, [1963] 1 All E.R. 674; [1963] 1 W.L.R.

I

406; Digest (Cont. Vol. A) 104, *1103a.*

Servers of the Blind League, Re, [1960] 2 All E.R. 298; [1960] 1 W.L.R. 564;
Digest (Cont. Vol. A) 198, *7641a.*

Slevin, Re, Slevin v. Hepburn, [1891] 2 Ch. 236; [1891-94] All E.R. Rep. 200;
60 L.J.Ch. 439; 64 L.T. 311; 8 Digest (Repl.) 463, *1633.*

Vernon's Will Trusts, Re, (22nd November 1962), unreported.

Adjourned Summons.

This was an application by originating summons dated 31st January 1968 by
the plaintiff, John Frederick Slade Carpenter, the sole executor of the will dated

5th April 1950, of Thomas Henry Robert Stemson, deceased, who died on 22nd **A**
April 1966. The plaintiff sought, inter alia, the determination by the court of
the following question: whether on the true construction of the will of the
testator and in the events which had happened the residuary real and personal
estate of the testator was: (i) undisposed of by the will; or (ii) held on a valid
charitable trust; or (iii) held on some other and, if so, what trusts.

The defendants were the Treasury Solicitor, on behalf of the Crown which **B**
took any property undisposed of by the will as bona vacantia, and the Attorney-
General. The facts are set out in the judgment.

The cases noted below* were cited during the argument in addition to those
referred to in the judgment.

J. A. R. *Finlay* for the plaintiff.
J. P. *Warner* for the Crown.   **C**
N. C. H. *Browne-Wilkinson* for the Attorney-General.

Cur. adv. vult.

7th March. **PLOWMAN, J.,** read the following judgment: The question
in this case is whether the residuary estate of the testator, Thomas Henry Robert
Stemson, is undisposed of by his will through the operation of the doctrine of **D**
lapse, or whether it is held on a valid charitable trust.

The testator died on 22nd April 1966 having by his will dated 5th April 1950
disposed of his residuary estate, now worth some £22,000, in the following
terms, and I read cl. 5 of the will:

" I GIVE DEVISE AND BEQUEATH all the rest residue and remainder of my
estate to which I may be seised possessed or entitled or over which I may **E**
have any power of disposition at the time of my death (hereinafter called
' the residue ') unto The Rationalist Endowment Fund Limited (hereinafter
called ' the Association ') absolutely AND I DECLARE that the receipt of two
Members of the Council and the Secretary for the time being of the Association shall be a good and sufficient discharge to my Executor for the residue
AND I REQUEST that the said Association shall as soon as practicable after **F**
my death apply the residue for the purpose of founding a Hostel for the
benefit of Rationalists in reduced circumstances especially as this appears
to be one of the objects in the Memorandum of the Association and also in
view of the fact that the Association are aware of my wishes in this respect
but I Declare that such request shall not create any trust on any account
whatsoever or make any obligation on the part of the Association in law so **G**
to apply the residue but I Declare that when the Association shall apply
the residue in accordance with my wishes they shall if possible inform and
consult my Executor."

The Rationalist Endowment Fund, Ltd., which I will call " REF ", passed a
special resolution to wind up on 12th December 1963 and was dissolved on **H**
16th October 1965, i.e., in the testator's lifetime.

It had been incorporated in 1938 as a receptacle for charitable donations on
behalf of the Rationalist movement but ceased to serve any useful purpose when,
in 1962, the Rationalist Press Association, Ltd., which I will call " RPA ",
whose original objects were for the general promotion of the Rationalist movement, altered its memorandum of association so as to confine itself to charitable **I**
objects.

The principal objects of REF are stated in its memorandum of association as
follows:

" 3. The objects of the Fund are:—(*a*) Advancement of education and in
particular the study of Rationalist philosophy and ethics. (*b*) To make
provision for the relief of the poor and needy, being:—(i) Persons who are or

---

* *Re Slatter's Will Trusts*, [1964] 2 All E.R. 469; [1964] Ch. 512; *Re Lysaght* (*decd.*),
[1965] 2 All E.R. 888; [1966] Ch. 191.

A   have been associated with Rationalist or Ethical groups or churches, or
(ii) Persons who have abandoned their connection with any of the other
churches, insofar as the above objects are charitable."

It is conceded by counsel for the Crown, which takes any property undisposed
of by the will as bona vacantia, that REF was a charity.

B   The principal objects of RPA are stated in cl. 3 (1) of its 1962 memorandum
of association as follows:

"To stimulate and promote by all lawful means the study of and
freedom of thought and inquiry in reference to ethics, philosophy, and
kindred subjects paying especial regard to the principles of Rationalism,
namely the mental attitude which unreservedly accepts the supremacy of
C   reason and aims at establishing a system of philosophy and ethics verifiable
by experience and independent of all arbitrary assumptions or authority."

There then follow other objects, but there is none corresponding to cl. 3 (b) of
REF's Memorandum of Association, i.e., for the relief of poverty. In January
1963 RPA was registered as a charity and counsel for the Crown therefore
accepts that it is a charity, as he is bound to do.

D   On the dissolution of REF its net assets amounting to £128 19s. 3d. were
transferred to RPA, pursuant to cl. 7 of the former's memorandum of association
which I should read:

"If upon the winding-up or dissolution of the Fund there remains, after
satisfaction of all its debts and liabilities, any property whatsoever, the
same shall not be paid to or distributed among the members of the Fund,
E   but shall be given or transferred to some other institution or institutions
having objects similar to the objects of the Fund, and which shall prohibit
the distribution of its or their income and property among its or their
members to an extent at least as great as is imposed on the Fund under or
by virtue of Clause 4 hereof, such institution or institutions to be determined
by the members of the Fund at or before the time of dissolution, or in default
F   thereof by such Judge of the High Court of Justice as may have or acquire
jurisdiction in the matter; and if and so far as effect cannot be given to the
aforesaid provision, then to some charitable object."

The evidence is that all the functions previously performed by REF—which
seem to have been confined to sending students to the Annual Conference of
G   RPA, coupled with a little advertising—have been and are now being carried on
by RPA.

Question 1 of the originating summons is as follows:

"Whether upon the true construction of the said Will of the Testator and
in the events which have happened the residuary real and personal estate of
the Testator is:—(i) Undisposed of by the said Will; or (ii) Held upon a
H   valid charitable trust; or (iii) Held upon some other and if so what trusts."

It is conceded by counsel for the Attorney-General—and in my judgment
rightly—that the gift with which I am concerned is a gift to a charitable corporation as such and is not a gift for charitable purposes, or a " purpose gift " as it
is sometimes called. This concession removes one possible source of complication;
let me remove another. It was suggested by counsel that the will disclosed a
I   general charitable intention. I cannot accept this argument. It was held in
Re Harwood, Coleman v. *Innes* (1), that when a testator selects a particular
charity and takes some care to identify it, it is very difficult for the court to
find a general charitable intention, and I am unable to find such an intention
in the present case. Clause 5 of the will appears to me to negative any such
intention by showing that the testator was particularly relying on REF to carry
out his wishes.

---

(1) [1936] Ch. 285; [1935] All E.R. Rep. 918.

The issue therefore narrows itself to this: had REF ceased to exist at the A
date of the testator's death? It is well settled that a gift by will to a charity
which has ceased to exist before the death of the testator lapses in the absence
of a general charitable intention. It is equally well settled that so long as there
are funds held in trust for the purposes of a charity, the charity does not cease
to exist but continues in existence and is not destroyed by an alteration in its
constitution or objects made in accordance with law, as for example by a scheme B
under the Charitable Trusts Acts (see, e.g., *Re Faraker, Faraker* v. *Durell* (2)
and *Re Lucas (decd.), Sheard* v. *Mellor* (3)), or by virtue of a power in the
charity's own constitution (see *Re Bagshaw (decd.), Westminster Bank, Ltd.* v.
Taylor (4)).

In the last-mentioned case DANCKWERTS, J., referred (5) to the principle of
Re Faraker (2) and *Re Lucas (decd.)* (3) as applying to "a charity founded C
as a perpetual charity". None of these cases deals in terms with a case like the
present where the charity is a limited company and is therefore liable to
dissolution by the inherent nature of its constitution.

In *Re Servers of the Blind League* (6), PENNYCUICK, J., assumed that in such
a case the ordinary rule of lapse would apply. The case was one in which the
liquidator of a dissolved company which had been established for charitable D
purposes applied under s. 352 of the Companies Act 1948 to have the dissolution
of the company declared void so as to enable it to claim a legacy bequeathed by
the will of a testatrix who died after the date of dissolution. On refusing the
application PENNYCUICK, J., said (7):

> "It is clear, apart from the order which I am now asked to make, that
> the gift of a residuary share to the company lapsed, and it must follow, in E
> the absence of any express provision in the will, that the share devolved on
> the footing of a partial intestacy."

The report, however, states (8) that no cases were cited in argument.

In *Re Roberts (decd.), Stenton* v. *Hardy* (9), there are obiter dicta of
WILBERFORCE, J., which suggest that he regarded it as at least doubtful whether F
the principles adopted by the court in *Re Faraker* (2), *Re Lucas (decd.)* (3)
and *Re Bagshaw (decd.)* (4) applied to a case where the trustees of a charity
were given express powers to bring it to an end. In *Re Roberts (decd.)* (9) a
testatrix gave a share of her residuary estate to the Sheffield Boys' Working
Home (Western Bank, Sheffield). During her lifetime the trustees of the home
sold it and transferred the greater part of the proceeds of sale to another charity, G
the Sheffield Town Trust. This was done pursuant to cl. 19 of the Boys' Home
trust deed which, so far as material, was as follows:

> " ' If the governors consider that the [home] is not required or cannot be
> efficiently kept up or that it ought to be discontinued they may by a
> majority of votes . . . at a general meeting authorise the trustees to hold
> hereditaments held by them . . . or to sell them and hold the net proceeds H
> of the sale or to convey such hereditaments or pay such proceeds for the
> benefit of such one or more exclusively of other or others of the charitable
> institutions of . . . Sheffield or for such other purposes for the benefit of the
> poor inhabitants of Sheffield as such governors shall by such vote direct '."

It was held (10):

(2) [1912] 2 Ch. 488; [1911-13] All E.R. Rep. 488.
(3) [1948] 2 All E.R. 22; [1948] Ch. 424.
(4) [1954] 1 All E.R. 227; [1954] 1 W.L.R. 238.
(5) [1954] 1 All E.R. at p. 229; [1954] 1 W.L.R. at p. 241.
(6) [1960] 2 All E.R. 298; [1960] 1 W.L.R. 564.
(7) [1960] 2 All E.R. at pp. 298, 299; [1960] 1 W.L.R. at p. 565.
(8) [1960] 2 All E.R. at p. 299; [1960] 1 W.L.R. at p. 565.
(9) [1963] 1 All E.R. 674; [1963] 1 W.L.R. 406.
(10) [1963] 1 W.L.R. at p. 406; [1963] 1 All E.R. at p. 674.

A
" (i) that the residuary bequest was a gift for the purposes of the institution and was not so correlated with the physical premises where the
institution was located that it failed when those premises ceased to exist.
(ii) that clause 19 of the trust deed of 1889 did not empower the trustees to
terminate the trusts of the home generally but only to decide that the
particular machinery of the home could not be operated and consequently

B
that the funds of the home remained subject to charitable trusts which
could be implemented by means of a scheme."

It will be seen therefore that the case turned on the construction of cl. 19 which
was held not to contain a " built-in " power of termination such as there is in
the present case. But certain observations of the learned judge are, I think,
C
helpful. He said (11):

" The legacy in the will in favour of the Sheffield Boys' Working Home,
Western Bank, Sheffield, on the facts which I have just mentioned, at first
sight appears to be a plain case of lapse occasioned by the disappearance of
the named charity before the death of the testatrix on March 12, 1961.
This is a case where, on the face of it, the testatrix had given a legacy to an

D
institution with an accurate description and with its correct address, and
that undoubtedly has gone. Notwithstanding that, the position is that the
courts have gone very far in the decided cases to resist the conclusion that a
legacy to a charitable institution lapses, and a number of very refined
arguments have been found acceptable with a view to avoiding that
conclusion."

E
WILBERFORCE, J., then went on to consider the competing claims, dealing first
with that of the Sheffield Town Trust whose position in that case is comparable
with that of RPA in this. He said (12):

" Their claim is really based on cl. 19 of the 1889 deed, and is that the
Trust has taken over the assets of the home under the powers which are

F
conferred by that trust deed. The way it is put is this: that any money
held on the trusts of the home was given for all the purposes defined in the
1889 trust deed, including among those purposes those in cl. 19 itself, and
that, in other words, the charity exists in the hands of the Trust in a
recognised form brought about by virtue of the provisions of the document
defining the trust; and they claim the money by analogy to *Re Lucas*

G
(*decd.*) (13)."

That claim he did not accept. A little later on he dealt with the claim of the
Attorney-General which he did accept. He said (14):

" The Attorney-General puts his case in this way. He says that this was
a trust for an unincorporated charity and that it should be treated as a
trust for the purposes for which the charity existed. He says that those

H
purposes still exist though the particular premises have gone. As to cl. 19
of the trust deed, that clause is only concerned with the physical hereditament where the home was conducted and did not authorise the termination
of the charity as a whole or warrant the handing over of anything other
than the hereditaments themselves for particular purposes."

I
I pause there to repeat that in the present case it is common ground that the
gift I am concerned with is not a purpose trust.
WILBERFORCE, J., then went on (15):

---

(11) [1963] 1 W.L.R. at pp. 411, 412; [1963] 1 All E.R. at p. 678.
(12) [1963] 1 All E.R. at p. 678; [1963] 1 W.L.R. at p. 412.
(13) [1948] 2 All E.R. 22; [1948] Ch. 424.
(14) [1963] 1 All E.R. at pp. 678; [1963] 1 W.L.R. at pp. 412, 413.
(15) [1963] 1 All E.R. at pp. 678, 679; [1963] 1 W.L.R. at pp. 413, 414.

ALL ENGLAND LAW REPORTS

[1969] 2 All E.R.

" Taking first the claim of the Sheffield Town Trust, that undoubtedly raises a novel point. It has been decided by three well known cases, *Re Faraker* (16), *Re Lucas (decd.)* (17), and *Re Bagshaw (decd.)* (18), that, where there is a gift to a charity which can be interpreted as a gift for the purposes of the charity, that gift can take effect although the form of the charity has been widened, as, for example, by the making of a scheme (*Re Lucas (decd.)* (17)), or by the alteration of the objects in accordance with the trust deed as in *Re Bagshaw (decd.)* (18), or even by amalgamation with another charity as in the older authority of *Re Faraker* (16), and it was suggested that the principle of those cases should be applied by extension here. Assuming for the present that this trust can be interpreted as a gift for the purposes of the charity and assuming also that cl. 19 applies to the endowment of the charity (to which assumptions I will return), it seems to me that a different situation is created here from that which was found in any of those three authorities. Clause 19 confers in fact a power not to extend the charity but to terminate it, and transfer the fund over to be used for purposes which may have no relation whatever to the old charity. If I read the judgments of the Court of Appeal in *Re Faraker* (16) aright, I would say that the reasoning in the judgments of this and of the other cases does not apply to such a case as we have here. FARWELL, L.J., said (19): ' Suppose the Charity Commissioners or this court were to declare that a particular charitable trust was at an end, and they declared it extinct, in my opinion they would go beyond their jurisdiction in so doing. They could not take an existing charity and destroy it. They are obliged to administer it. To say that this . . . pardonable slip [I use the word with all respect to the draftsman] has the effect of destroying the charity, appears to me really to be extravagant. In all these cases one has to consider not so much the means to an end as the charitable end which is in view. And so long as that charitable end is well established, the means are only machinery . . .' KENNEDY, L.J., said (20): ' But no case has been shown to me in which an endowed charity has been treated as having, so to speak, lost its life by reason of the exercise of the perfectly competent authority under parliamentary sanction of the Charity Commissioners, or the equally competent authority of this court, under which its funds have come to be applied somewhat differently to the way in which they were applied under the original foundation . . . It seems to be the law, that an endowed charity, to whatever purpose its funds are devoted, if and so long as they are devoted to some charitable purpose under some duly authorised scheme, remains still existent so as to draw to it a sum of money given by a will for, presumably, the same purpose as the original charity.'—Those words, that it is not competent for the court or the Charity Commissioners to bring an endowed charity to an end, seem to me not necessarily to apply to a case where the trustees of the charity are given express powers to terminate the charity. The argument in favour of the Town Trust must, in my opinion, amount to this: that the testatrix in giving this money to the named institution meant to give it on the trusts and subject to the powers contained in the conveyance including cl. 19, to give it, in other words, to the trustees for better or for worse. Without saying that that is an impossible conclusion, I find myself compelled to stop short of it."

I need not read any more of the judgment. In the end the learned judge directed a scheme.

---

(16) [1912] 2 Ch. 488; [1911-13] All E.R. Rep. 488.
(17) [1948] 2 All E.R. 22; [1948] Ch. 424.
(18) [1954] 1 All E.R. 227; [1954] 1 W.L.R. 238.
(19) [1912] 2 Ch. at p. 495; [1911-13] All E.R. Rep. at p. 494.
(20) [1912] 2 Ch. at p. 496; [1911-13] All E.R. Rep. at p. 494.

A   It is I think a fair inference from those passages that WILBERFORCE, J., would not have regarded such cases as *Re Faraker* (21) as applicable to a case where the donee-charity was liable to dissolution under its own constitution.

It was, however, submitted by counsel for the Attorney-General that BUCKLEY, J., had decided otherwise in the unreported case of *Re Vernon's Will Trusts* (22). I have been supplied with a transcript of the judgment which was
B   delivered on 22nd November 1962. In that case a testatrix who died in 1960 made her will in 1937 giving a share of residue to a charity incorporated as a company and called " Coventry and District Crippled Children's Guild ". The company owned premises used as an orthopaedic hospital and had certain endowments. On 5th July 1948, its hospital premises and the endowments vested in the Minister free of any trust by virtue of s. 6 and s. 7 of the National
C   Health Service Act 1946. In 1952 the name of the company was struck off the register of companies under s. 353 (5) of the Companies Act 1948 and the company was dissolved. At the date of the testatrix's death the hospital formerly run by the company was still being carried on by the hospital management committee.

The question which BUCKLEY, J., had to decide was what happened to the legacy. He held first that the legacy was a legacy to the company as part of its
D   general funds and was not a trust or purpose legacy. He then went on to consider the effect of the National Health Service Act and said:

" The endowments thus became merged in the Hospital Endowments Fund set up by the Act and ceased to have any separate identity. The immovable properties of the Guild on the other hand and the equipment
E   and furniture of them, although they ceased to be irrevocably dedicated to orthopaedic uses, continued to be used precisely as they were previously until after the testatrix died, except that from 1951 the uses of the hospital were extended by the admission of adults as well as children as patients. In these circumstances, in my judgment, the true view is that the charity which at the date of the testatrix's will was being carried on by the incor-
F   porated Guild continued in existence down to and after the date of her death in the form of the orthopaedic clinic and hospital which were conducted by the first defendant at 55 Holyhead Road and the Paybody Hospital. The fact that its continued existence after 5th July 1948 may be said to have been precarious, because those with power under the National Health Service Act 1946 to decide such things might at any time have decided to discontinue
G   the use of the properties for orthopaedic purposes and might possibly have done so without transferring the orthopaedic activities theretofore carried on in the clinic and the hospital and continuing them elsewhere, is, in my judgment, irrelevant. If on the true view the charity existed at the testatrix's death and so became entitled to the bequest, its subsequently ceasing to exist would not cause the bequest to fail (*Re Slevin, Slevin* v. *Hepburn* (23)).
H   As in *Re Lucas* (*decd.*) (24) the Court held that the bequest to the Crippled Children's Home, Lindley Moor, Huddersfield, was on its true construction a gift simply in augmentation of the funds of the charity so described, so in the present case I think the bequest to the ' Coventry Crippled Children's Guild ' was on its true construction a gift simply in augmentation of the funds of the incorporated Guild; and as in *Re Lucas* (*decd.*) (24) the bequest
I   did not fail by reason of the physical Home having been closed but took effect in favour of the charity in the new and different form into which it had been transmuted by an order of the Charity Commissioners, so by parity

---

(21) [1912] 2 Ch. 488; [1911-13] All E.R. Rep. 488.
(22) (22nd November 1962), unreported.
(23) [1891] 2 Ch. 236; [1891-94] All E.R. Rep. 200.
(24) [1948] 2 All E.R. 22; [1948] Ch. 424.

of reasoning, in my judgment, in the present case the bequest took effect at   A
the death of the testatrix in favour of the charity then being conducted by
the first defendant in unbroken continuance of the charity which at the date
of the will was being conducted by the incorporated Guild."

He therefore directed a scheme.

The memorandum of association of the company in that case included a   B
clause, similar to cl. 7 in the memorandum of association of REF, to the effect
that on a winding-up any surplus assets should be transferred to some other
institution having similar objects, but does it follow that the decision in *Re
Vernon's Will Trusts* (25) would have been the same if, instead of there being
a compulsory transfer of its property, it had wound up and transferred its
property elsewhere?   In my judgment the *Re Faraker* (26) line of cases does   C
not go as far as that.

I think that the true proposition was accurately formulated by counsel for
the Crown when he said that a charitable trust which no one has power to
terminate retains its existence despite such vicissitudes as schemes, amalgama-
tions and change of name so long as it has any funds. It follows, in my judgment,
that where funds come to the hands of a charitable organisation, such as REF,   D
which is founded, not as a perpetual charity but as one liable to termination,
and its constitution provides for the disposal of its funds in that event, then if
the organisation ceases to exist and its funds are disposed of, the charity or
charitable trust itself ceases to exist and there is nothing to prevent the
operation of the doctrine of lapse.

I therefore conclude that the testator's residuary estate is undisposed of by   E
his will.

Declaration accordingly.

Solicitors: *Woodroffes*, agents for *Carpenter & Carpenter*, Bath, Somerset (for
the plaintiff); *Treasury Solicitor*.

[*Reported by* JACQUELINE METCALFE, *Barrister-at-Law.*]   F

---

(25) (22nd November 1962), unreported.
(26) [1912] 2 Ch. 488; [1911-13] All E.R. Rep. 488.

A

COLESHILL AND DISTRICT INVESTMENT CO., LTD. *v.* MINISTER OF HOUSING AND LOCAL GOVERNMENT AND ANOTHER.

B
[HOUSE OF LORDS (Lord Morris of Borth-y-Gest, Lord Guest, Lord Upjohn, Lord Wilberforce and Lord Pearson), March 11, 13, 17, 18, 19, May 6, 1969.]

Town and Country Planning—Development—" Building, engineering . . . or other operations "—Removal of soil banked against blast walls of explosives stores and magazines—Demolition of walls—Alteration of building—Develop-
C
ment requiring planning permission—Whether error of law by Minister —Town and Country Planning Act 1962 (10 & 11 Eliz. 2 c. 38), s. 12 (1).

The appellants, having acquired disused explosives stores and magazines, removed the protective banks of rubble and soil outside the blast walls. The buildings were near a village within a proposed green belt. The maga-zines were made of concrete; each was 70 feet long, 30 feet wide and 11 to
D
13 feet high. From a distance the buildings and blast walls, when covered by the embankments, looked like a large green mound; but when the walls were exposed they looked unsightly. Planning permission to remove the embankment had not been obtained. The local planning authority issued an enforcement notice under the Town and Country Planning Act 1962, in respect of the removal of the embankments. The appellants proposed also to demolish the blast walls. They had applied for determination whether
E
planning permission was necessary for this. On appeal from a decision of the Court of Appeal upholding the Minister's decisions that the embank-ments and blast walls were integral parts of the buildings and constituted development requiring planning permission under s. 12 (1)* of the Town and Country Planning Act 1962,

F
Held: on the true construction of s. 12 (1) it depended on the facts of the particular case whether demolition or removal operations constituted development; accordingly, since the Minister after consideration of all the facts had decided that the removal of the embankments and blast walls constituted development within s. 12 (1) his decision disclosed no error of law.

G
Decision of the COURT OF APPEAL ([1968] 1 All E.R. 945) affirmed.

[As to what constitutes development, see 37 HALSBURY'S LAWS (3rd Edn.) 259-263, para. 366; and for cases on the subject, see 45 DIGEST (Repl.) 325-327, *6-13.*

For the Town and Country Planning Act 1962, s. 12 (1), see 42 HALSBURY'S STATUTES (2nd Edn.) 975.]

H Cases referred to:

Bracegirdle v. *Oxley, Bracegirdle* v. *Cobley,* [1947] 1 All E.R. 126; [1947] K.B. 349; [1947] L.J.R. 815; 176 L.T. 187; 111 J.P. 131; 33 Digest (Repl.) 312, *1360.*

British Launderers' Research Association v. *Central Middlesex Assessment Committee and Hendon Rating Authority,* [1949] 1 All E.R. 21; [1949]
I
1 K.B. 462; [1949] L.J.R. 646; 113 J.P. 72; 38 Digest (Repl.) 583, *627.*

Cheshire County Council v. *Woodward,* [1962] 1 All E.R. 517; [1962] 2 Q.B. 126; [1962] 2 W.L.R. 636; 126 J.P. 186; 45 Digest (Repl.) 326, *10.*

London County Council v. *Marks & Spencer, Ltd.,* [1953] 1 All E.R. 1095; [1953] A.C. 535; [1953] 2 W.L.R. 932; 117 J.P. 261; 45 Digest (Repl.) 340, *56.*

---

* Section 12, so far as material, is set out at p. 531, letters B and C, post.

Appeal.   A

This was an appeal by the appellants, Coleshill and District Investment Co., Ltd. from an order of the Court of Appeal (LORD DENNING, M.R., Diplock and SALMON, L.JJ.), dated 19th December 1967 and reported [1968] 1 All E.R. 945, allowing the appeal of the respondent council, Meriden Rural District Council, from the decision of the Divisional Court (LORD PARKER, C.J., WIDGERY and CHAPMAN, JJ.) dated 24th November 1967, and reported [1968] 1 All E.R. 62,   B and restoring the decisions of the Minister of Housing and Local Government given on 16th May 1967. The appeal was against two decisions of the Minister refusing to quash an enforcement notice served on the appellants in respect of their removing the embankments protecting dissued ammunition stores and magazines and determining that planning permission was required for removing the blast walls. The facts are set out in the opinion of LORD MORRIS OF BORTH-Y-   C GEST.

Sir Derek Walker-Smith, Q.C., and *S. Goldblatt* for the appellants.
S. C. Silkin, Q.C., and *Gordon Slynn* for the Minister of Housing and Local Government.
Anthony Cripps, Q.C., and *A. E. Holdsworth* for the respondent council.

Their Lordships took time for consideration.   D

6th May. The following opinions were delivered.

LORD MORRIS OF BORTH-Y-GEST: My Lords, one question that was persistently raised in this appeal was formulated as being whether demolition constitutes development for the purposes of the Town and Country Planning Act 1962. Neat and arresting as the question so expressed may seem to be it is   E not in fact the direct question which calls for our decision. If someone propounded a question of comparable generality such as whether modernisation constitutes development someone else might ask for a ruling whether renovation constitutes development. No one of these enquiries has precision. If development needs permission, which in most cases it does, and if development is defined, as in the Act it is, the truth path of enquiry first involves ascertaining exactly   F what it is that it is desired to do or exactly what it is that has been done and then to see whether that comes within the statutory definition of development. Once some completed or projected work or operation is fully and clearly described then the words of definition can be applied. It is unnecessary and may be misleading to give the work or operation some single labelling word and then to try to apply the definition to that word. We are here concerned with actual   G operations and not with possible operations or with those which can for the future be imagined. Why, then, introduce and interpose some general word of description when precise words of description are at hand? Why gaze into the crystal when one can read the book?

The present case relates to certain structures which are on a site having an area of about 8¾ acres near Hampton-in-Arden. The structures themselves   H occupy about five acres. They consist of a number of buildings or magazines constituting, and during the last war used as, an ammunition depot. There are six separate buildings; four of them were magazines and two of them explosives stores. Around each one of them blast walls were erected which were about nine feet in height. Against these walls there were substantial sloping embankments consisting of rubble and brick and ash and soil. They extended   I from near the top of the walls to a distance of eight to ten feet from their base. They were all grass covered.

The War Department released the depot in 1958. In 1962 the Minister determined that user of the buildings for purposes of commercial storage (for which permission was then sought) would not constitute or involve development. In the early part of 1966 the appellants decided that they would like to remove the embankments and the walls which were felt to be unnecessary and a cause of inconvenience when the buildings were used for civilian purposes. So as a

A first step they set about removing the embankments. They instructed contractors to undertake the work. The contractors used a mechanical excavator. The material after being loaded into lorries (which the contractors hired from various firms) was transported away to be delivered at various different sites.

When those who lived in houses near to the depot saw the embankments were being removed they were aggrieved. The grass-grown or vegetation-
B covered green banks had blended with the countryside and had so camouflaged the depot as to screen the blast walls as well as much of the buildings from view. As the embankments were removed the buildings became starkly exposed and the general result, so the people felt, was that the whole place became an eye-sore which marred the locality and detracted from the amenity to be expected in a green belt. The result was that complaints were expressed to the respondent
C council, the Meriden Rural District Council, and following on them the clerk of the council wrote to the appellants pointing out that the operations being undertaken constituted development and that no application for planning permission had been made. An enforcement notice dated 30th March 1966, followed. The appellants were required to discontinue their operations and to restore the land to its prior condition. The appellants took the view that their
D operations did not constitute development and that no planning consent had been needed. So they appealed against the enforcement notice. An inquiry before an inspector (pursuant to s. 46 of the Town and Country Planning Act 1962) was held on 8th December 1966. The inspector made a full report to the Minister dated 11th January 1967. The Minister gave his decision in a letter dated 16th May 1967. Subject to making certain variations, which do not
E now call for consideration, in the wording of the enforcement notice, the Minister upheld the notice and, refusing planning permission, dismissed the appeal. The appellants exercised (see s. 180 of the Act of 1962) their right to appeal to the High Court against the decision " on a point of law ".

The appeal which, by a notice of motion dated 12th June 1967, they lodged was related also to the kindred question whether they could without planning
F permission take down the walls. The removal of the embankments had only been intended to be the first stage in the operation of completely removing the embankments and walls. So when the appellants were confronted with the question whether planning permission was needed to remove the embankments it was manifest that a similar question arose or would arise in regard to the walls. Pursuant to s. 43 of the Act they asked the respondent council, as the local
G planning authority, to determine that question. They so asked by a letter dated 4th July 1966. There was no determination within the prescribed time and accordingly the appellants appealed to the Minister. He gave his decision in a separate letter dated 16th May 1967. Other matters were involved but the only determination that is for present purposes relevant was that the removal of the walls would constitute or involve development and that planning permis-
H sion was required. The appellants claiming to be " dissatisfied with the decision in point of law " (see s. 181) therefore appealed to the High Court on this issue also.

Though there was but the one local inquiry the facts relating to the whole site were fully and carefully set out in the inspector's report of 11th January 1967. The report was made a part of the Minister's first letter of decision on
I 16th May 1967. The report contained a description of the site and its surroundings: it set out the contentions of the appellants, of the respondent council, and of interested parties: it made specific findings of fact. I do not propose to refer to these in detail. Suffice it to say that it set out that the explosives stores which are brick built are each 25 to 30 feet long and about 12 feet wide: the magazines which are constructed of concrete are each about 70 feet long and about 30 feet wide and are about 11 feet rising to 13 feet high. Around, and about four feet away from each one of the buildings are the blast walls which are also constructed of concrete and are about nine feet high.

Having set out his findings of fact the inspector concluded that the legal A
implications from them were matters for consideration by the Minister and
his legal advisers. He considered, however, that the embankments and blast
walls were a necessary and integral part of buildings which constituted a magazine. He further thought that the work of removing embankments was an
engineering operation constituting development, though he added that it could
be regarded as demolition of part of the magazine " and planning permission B
is not required for demolition of a building ". He recommended that if the
Minister decided that development requiring planning permission was involved,
such permission should not be granted.

The Minister had the issues fairly and fully placed before him for his decision.
As regards the buildings the Minister considered whether the blast walls and
the embankments were an integral part of each of the buildings. He concluded C
that they were. He said that they could not be regarded simply as means of
enclosures because they were erected as essential features of the structures
which were erected. What had been built were magazines and the inner buildings
would have been ineffective in use without the walls and embankments.

Pausing there I cannot see how it can possibly be said that the Minister made
a wrong decision on a point of law. In effect he was saying that the blast walls D
and embankments were an integral part of each of the buildings and could not
be divorced from the internal buildings. The view might be held that his
conclusion was not only one of fact but was on the evidence almost the inevitable
one. There is, however, no need to consider whether or not that was so. It is
enough to say that no error of law was involved.

The next part of the Minister's decision was that the removal of the embank- E
ments was an engineering operation and so was within the definition of development. He upheld the enforcement notice, refused planning permission and
dismissed the appeal.

In the Minister's other decision, i.e., that relating to the appellants' application
under s. 43, the first conclusion was again " accepted as a fact " that the blast
walls formed part of the building. The further conclusion was that the removal F
of the blast walls would constitute an alteration of the buildings and one which
would materially affect the external appearance of the buildings. The removal
of the walls would constitute development requiring planning permission: such
development was not within any of the classes set out in Pt. 1 of Sch. 1 to the
Town and Country Planning General Development Order 1963 (1).

On appeal to the High Court the various grounds of appeal covered both the G
contention that neither what had been done nor what was proposed constituted
development and also the contention that the embankments and walls were not
part of the magazines. In allowing the appeal and setting aside the Minister's
decision the Divisional Court (2) took the view that the removal of the embankments could not be described either as a building operation or as an engineering
operation; nor was it an operation of the scale, complexity and difficulty which H
would require a builder or an engineer or some mining expert. The view was
held (3) that the operation was a " simple removal of soil " or a " little job
of shifting a few cubic yards of soil with a digger and a lorry " though it was
said that earth moving on a grand scale requiring the intervention, supervision
and planning of qualified engineers might well be an engineering operation.
The Court of Appeal (4) restored the order of the Minister and held that the I
operation of removing the embankments and also the operation of removing
the walls constituted development.

As appears from the judgments in the Court of Appeal (4) argument was in
that court presented on behalf of the appellants to the effect that demolition

(1) S.I. 1963 No. 709.
(2) [1968] 1 All E.R. 62.
(3) [1968] 1 All E.R. at p. 65.
(4) [1968] 1 All E.R. 945; [1968] 1 W.L.R. 600.

A   of a building is not development and that no proper distinction can be drawn between demolition of a building and demolition of part of a building. Arguments to the like effect were fully and attractively developed on behalf of the appellants in support of their appeal in this House. Supported by a careful and painstaking analysis of very many sections in the Act of 1962 the contention was urged that throughout the Act there is a clear, consistent and logical distinction between

B   demolition and alteration. The term " alteration " when used in the Act may sometimes denote development and sometimes corrective action: the term " demolition ", on the other hand, so the argument ran, is not used in the Act as denoting development but is only used in the context of corrective action or in reference to procedures for the preservation of special buildings. It was contended that there are very many indications pointing to the conclusion that

C   Parliament has deliberately excluded demolition (as opposed to alteration) from the scope of planning control and from the concept of development. Thus, the need to protect certain buildings (such as those of historic or architectural interest) from demolition is met by special provisions. I do no more than summarise some of the steps in a very carefully constructed argument. If the contention is once accepted that demolition is not development then further

D   steps (or jumps) in the argument run as follows: removal of the embankments or of the walls is demolition: demolition is not development: therefore, the removals are not development. Alternatively, even if the embankments and walls were parts of the buildings, since, by the definition section (s. 221), a part of a building is a building, each removal of an embankment or of a wall is removal of a building: but as removal is demolition and as demolition is not development

E   the result is that there was not and would not be any development.

    My Lords, these arguments, however persuasive, must not compel a diversion from the facts as ascertained and from the statutory terms as defined. It was for the Minister to make certain decisions. The appeals to the High Court from his decisions are only on points of law. I have already expressed the view that it is quite impossible to assert that there was an invalidity in law in the

F   findings of the Minister to the effect that the embankments and walls were integral parts of each of the buildings. It is next necessary to consider his findings relating (a) to the removal of the embankments, and (b) to the desired removal of the walls.

    The definition of " development " is set out in s. 12 (1) and s. 221 of the Act. Subject to certain exceptions, and leaving aside the making of any material

G   change in the use of any buildings or other land, " development " means the carrying out of building operations (which include rebuilding operations, structural alterations of or additions to buildings, and other operations normally undertaken by a person carrying on business as a builder) or of engineering operations (which include the formation or laying out of means of access to highways) or of mining operations or of other operations in, on, over or under land. " Land "

H   means any corporeal hereditament, including a building (which includes any structure or erection, and any part of a building so defined but not including plant or machinery comprised in a building). " Erection " in relation to buildings includes extension, alteration and re-erection. Wide though the definition is, it does not include any and every operation on land. In s. 43 is set out the procedure to be followed when it is desired to have a determination whether

I   planning permission is required. Any person who proposes to carry out " any operations " on land may apply for a ruling. Had development meant " any " operations in, on, over or under land there would not have been included in s. 12 (1) the words " building, engineering, mining or other ". I think that the word " other " must denote operations which could be spoken of in the context of or in association with or as being in the nature of or as having relation to building operations or engineering operations or mining operations.

    It was submitted, on the one hand, that the underlying conception of development is that of change. A rival submission was that the conception is that of

positive construction. Another submission was that everything is development **A**
which is within the framework of what a " developer " (whoever so anonymous
and elusive a person might be) would understand as being development. My
Lords, as Parliament has denoted what is meant by development I do not think
that we should be tempted to enlarge on or to depart from the statutory definition.
It may well be that some operations which could conveniently be called demolition
would not come within that definition. But we must not decide hypothetical **B**
cases. Here we have actual facts and findings. The Minister had a careful
report before him. No suggestion has been made that the procedure deviated
from that which is laid down in the Town and Country Planning (Inquiries
Procedure) Rules 1965 (5). The question that now arises is whether the Minister
erred in law. He decided that the removal of the embankments was an engineering operation clearly falling within s. 12 (1) of the Act. He had certain **C**
primary facts found for him by the inspector. He did not differ from them. His
conclusion from them was one that he could reasonably and properly make.
It was really a conclusion of fact, and I can see no trace of any error of law.
It was contended that the Minister was giving a wider meaning to " engineering "
than it could in accepted or current use bear. I cannot accept this. The findings
relating to the dimensions of the various embankments show that the task of **D**
their removal was one of some magnitude. I do not think that it can be said
that the Minister erred in law in coming to the conclusion that their removal
was an engineering operation.

Similar considerations apply to the Minister's decision that the removal of the
blast walls would constitute or involve development and that planning permission
for their removal was required. I think that it is inherent in the Minister's **E**
decision that the operation of pulling down the concrete walls (which were an
integral part of the various buildings) would involve structural alterations to
buildings and would therefore constitute development within the statutory
definition. He then proceeded to consider s. 12 (2). That subsection does not
enlarge sub-s. (1); but if an operation is covered by sub-s. (1) it may be taken
out of the definition of " development " by sub-s. (2). The Minister was, I **F**
think, amply warranted in deciding that the alterations of the buildings which
would result from taking down the walls would materially affect the external
appearance of the buildings. No error of law is revealed.

In my view the Court of Appeal (6) came to the correct conclusion. I would
dismiss the appeal.

G

LORD GUEST: My Lords, prior to 1939 the War Department constructed
an ammunition depot near the village of Hampton-in-Arden in Warwickshire.
It consisted of four magazines, some 70 feet by 30 feet, and two explosives stores,
25 to 30 feet by 12 feet. Each of the buildings was about 11 to 13 feet high.
Around each of the six buildings there were blast walls about nine feet high and
standing about four feet out from the outside walls of the stores and magazines. **H**
Against the walls on their outer sides there were embankments consisting of
bricks, rubble and soil which extended from near the top of the walls to a distance
of eight to ten feet from their base. After the war the use of the ammunition
depot was discontinued. It was released by the War Department in 1958 and
the freehold was acquired by the appellants in 1964. The buildings have, by
a decision of the responsible Minister, an existing storage use. The appellants **I**
were minded to make use of the buildings for this purpose. The embankments
were covered with grass and weeds which concealed the unsightly nature of the
walls and to some extent obscured the stores and magazines.

The question in the appeal is whether the removal of the embankments and
the blast walls constitutes " development " within the meaning of s. 12 (1) of
the Town and Country Planning Act 1962. The question of the embankment

(5) S.I. 1965 No. 473.
(6) [1968] 1 All E.R. 945; [1968] 1 W.L.R. 600.

A arises in consequence of an appeal by the appellants to the Minister against an enforcement order served on them by the respondent council under s. 45 of the Act of 1962: the question of the blast walls arises from an appeal by the appellants against a determination by the Minister under s. 43 of the Act that their removal required planning permission.

B Section 12 of the Town and Country Planning Act 1962, provides inter alia as follows:

" (1) In this Act . . . ' development ', subject to the following provisions of this section, means the carrying out of building, engineering, mining or other operations in, on, over or under land, or the making of any material change in the use of any buildings or other land.

C " (2) The following operations or uses of land shall not be taken for the purposes of this Act to involve development of the land, that is to say:— (*a*) the carrying out of works for the maintenance, improvement or other alteration of any building, being works . . . which do not materially affect the external appearance of the building . . . "

Section 221 (1) of the Act provides:

D " In this Act . . . the following expressions have the meanings hereby assigned to them respectively, that is to say: . . . ' building ' includes any structure or erection, and any part of a building, as so defined, but does not include plant or machinery comprised in a building: . . . ' building operations ' includes rebuilding operations, structural alterations of or additions to buildings, and other operations normally undertaken by a
E person carrying on business as a builder; . . . ' engineering operations ' includes the formation or laying out of means of access to highways; . . ."

The Minister treated the two cases differently. In the case of the embankment the Minister decided that the operation of removing the earth was an " engineering operation " within the meaning of s. 12 (1) of the Act as defined in s. 221 (1).
F Whereas in regard to the proposed removal of the blast walls the Minister decided that this operation was a " building operation " under s. 12 (1), as consisting of the removal of part of a building—the blast wall being part of the composite building constituted by the magazine building and blast walls and, as such, was a development requiring planning permission.

The courts below have approached the questions from different angles.
G Widgery, J., gave the judgment of the Divisional Court (7) in which he expressed (8) the view that it was unnecessary to decide the " fascinating problem [of planning law] whether demolition of a building is a building operation " within s. 12 (1). He decided that the scale of operations in question (8)—" this little job of shifting a few cubic yards of soil with a digger and a lorry " as he described them —could not be dignified by any of the qualifying words in s. 12 (1). He also
H referred with approval to an observation of Lord Parker, C.J., in *Cheshire County Council* v. *Woodward* (9), where he said that the operations contemplated by the section must change the physical character of the land. But the underlying principle of the decision appears to be that de minimis non curat lex.

The Court of Appeal (10) reversed the decision of the Divisional Court (7). Lord Denning, M.R. (11), with whom Diplock, L.J. (12), concurred, treated
I the structure consisting of magazine or store, blast walls and embankment as a composite building and, applying the terms of s. 12 (2) (*a*), held that the operations constituted an alteration to the building which affected its external

---

(7) [1968] 1 All E.R. 62.
(8) [1968] 1 All E.R. at p. 65.
(9) [1962] 1 All E.R. 517 at pp. 518, 519; [1962] 2 Q.B. 126 at p. 133.
(10) [1968] 1 All E.R. 945; [1968] 1 W.L.R. 600.
(11) [1968] 1 All E.R. at p. 947; [1968] 1 W.L.R. at p. 604.
(12) [1968] 1 All E.R. at p. 948; [1968] 1 W.L.R. at p. 605.

appearance. It was thus " development " within the terms of s. 12 (1). LORD A
DENNING, M.R., however, said (13) that it might be that if the whole
building was demolished it might not be " development ". SALMON, L.J. (14),
also declined to decide the question whether the total demolition of a building
would amount to " development ", although he would appear to think that it
would. He also treated the whole unit as a composite building.

The appeal from the Minister's decision to the High Court is only on a question B
of law (see s. 180 and s. 181 of the Act of 1962). The question, accordingly, is
whether it has been shown to the satisfaction of the court that the Minister has
erred in law in arriving at his decision.

Counsel for the appellants urged on your Lordships as his primary submission
that any demolition of a building or part of a building by itself not involving
reconstruction or replacement could in no circumstances amount to " develop- C
ment " within the Act. He argued that the " other operations in, on, over
or under land " in s. 12 (1) must be construed ejusdem generis with the preceding
categories of operations, namely, building, engineering and mining. The genus
was the positive or constructional side of operations, and—as demolition was
of a negative or destructive character " demolition per se ", as he described it,
could never come within this genus. He also referred to other sections in the D
Act of 1962 where he said that a distinction was drawn between " alteration ",
which was development, and " removal " or " demolition " which was not.
I am unable to find that any help can be obtained from these sections which
would assist his argument. I find it difficult to discover any common genus
to building, engineering or mining operations. I am certainly unable to detect
a positive or constructional genus in s. 12 (1); " mining operations " are not E
constructive because the surface of the land is destroyed in the course of the
operations.

Reference was also made to the Town and Country Planning General Development Order 1963 (15), in which by Sch. I certain development is permitted
without the necessity of obtaining planning permission under the Act. Under
Class 1 of Pt. 1 of Sch. 1 certain activities of a minor character in relation to a F
dwelling-house are permitted. It was said that if demolition was comprehended
by " development ", one would have expected to find certain exemptions in this
order. Otherwise every minor demolition, say of a garden wall of a private
house, would require planning permission. The reasons for the omission of
minor demolitions from the general development order are obscure, but it may
stem from the ministerial circular no. 67 of 15th February 1949, in which it was G
stated that the Minister was advised that demolition of a building did not, of
itself, involve development. However this may be, the general development
order affords no guide to the construction of s. 12 (1). I am not, therefore, able
to accept the appellants' argument that demolition can never be development.

The question appears to me to be whether the operations in any particular
case do or do not amount to development, having regard to the terms of s. 12 (1). H
I should, perhaps, say that I cannot find any aid to the construction of s. 12 (1)
by reference to the terms of s. 12 (2) (a). The operation must first qualify as development within s. 12 (1). If it does, then the question arises whether, on the basis
that it is development, it is excluded by s. 12 (2).

If this be the correct approach to s. 12 (1), for my part I do not find the answer
in this appeal difficult. The question, as I have already indicated, is whether I
the Minister's decision betrays any error in law. First, as regards the embankment. The Minister had before him an inspector's report in which, after stating
the relevant facts, he expressed his " conclusion " that the work of removal of
the embankment was an engineering operation. The Minister followed his
inspector's conclusion and held that it amounted to development. This decision

---

(13) [1968] 1 All E.R. at p. 947; [1968] 1 W.L.R. at p. 604.
(14) [1968] 1 All E.R. at p. 949; [1968] 1 W.L.R. at p. 606.
(15) S.I. 1963 No. 709.

A   was, in my view, a finding of fact in the sense that it was an inference from the primary facts as found by the Minister (see DENNING, L.J., in *British Launderers' Research Association* v. *Central Middlesex Assessment Committee and Hendon Rating Authority* (16).

I am unable to say that the Minister erred in law in his decision or that it was a conclusion which could not reasonably be drawn. It was peculiarly a

B   matter within his competence to decide whether the removal of the embankment was an engineering operation. References were made to HUDSON ON BUILDING CONTRACTS (6th Edn.) at p. 8 and (9th Edn.) at pp. 64, 65, and to the definition of "engineering" in the OXFORD ENGLISH DICTIONARY, but the Minister had sufficient evidence, in my view, on which he could reach his decision unassisted by these references.

C   The next point concerns the removal of the blast walls. The Minister had before him the view of the local planning authority that " the blast walls . . . were all part of the original design of the buildings used for storing explosives and together they constitute a magazine ". The Minister accepted this view, adding:

D   " It is noted that the buildings were erected shortly before the last war, some were used for the storage of ammunition and some for the storage of explosives. The blast walls and soil embankments were provided to prevent damage from explosion and to conceal the internal structure."

The Minister accordingly held that the blast walls formed part of the building and that their removal would materially affect the external appearance of the building and as such would constitute " development " within s. 12 (1). The

E   appellants contended that as the blast walls were physically discontiguous from the magazines they could not in law form part of a unum quid. But in my opinion in considering this question it is legitimate to consider the functional test as well as the physical test. If they were built originally as an integral and necessary part of the building and at the same time as the magazines the fact that they are physically discontiguous does not, in my view, prevent them from

F   being part of the building. There is, therefore, no ground on which the Minister's decision on either case can be disturbed.

I would dismiss the appeal.

LORD UPJOHN: My Lords, I have had the opportunity of reading the speech about to be delivered by my noble and learned friend, LORD PEARSON, who has set out the relevant facts in the greatest detail so that I do not propose

G   to cover that ground again.

There are two questions which must be answered before one can approach a consideration of the submissions of law that arise on s. 12 of the Town and Country Planning Act 1962 (the Act): 1. Was the Minister correct in holding that the walls and supporting earth embankments surrounding the magazine buildings all formed part of one building, or did these walls and embankments,

H   which were not architecturally part of the magazine buildings but were designed and placed there to limit and so far as possible contain the result of some internal explosion and also to act as camouflage against enemy air attack, form different buildings for the purposes of the Act? 2. When these outer walls and supporting embankments were removed by the appellants, was the Minister correct in holding that this was an " engineering . . . operation " for the purposes of s. 12 (1)

I   of the Act? While the enforcement notice under s. 45 of the Act applied in terms to removal only of the embankments supporting the walls because the walls themselves had not by then been removed, very sensibly neither party has taken any point on this.

My Lords, both these questions are largely matters of fact and inferences from facts and are questions of degree. On the first question, when the magazines and the protecting walls and embankments were built in 1938 and 1939 these

---

(16) [1949] 1 All E.R. 21 at pp. 25, 26; [1949] 1 K.B. 462 at p. 471.

latter were separate but an integral and necessary part, by accepted standards A
of those concerned with these matters, of the structure of a magazine to contain
ammunition and explosives. But the role of the walls and embankments was
entirely functional. When the magazines ceased to hold these dangerous
commodities and could be used for ordinary warehouse purposes without any
change of user, it was obviously desirable, as a matter of reasonable everyday
use, to remove these walls and embankments which made the former magazines B
ill lit, damp and inconvenient for everyday purposes. On the second question, on
the evidence it does appear to me that the appellants used comparatively unso-
phisticated methods, bulldozers and so on, to remove these protecting walls
and embankments.

On these two questions I must confess that my mind has fluctuated considerably. Both of them seem to me to be border-line questions and I think that the C
Minister might easily have come to a different conclusion on either or, indeed,
both of them. Where a case depends on primary facts the court, it is clear,
will hardly ever interfere with the findings of the trial judge unless satisfied
that he has misdirected himself; but where the true conclusion depends not so
much on the primary facts which (as in this case) are not in issue but on the inferences to be drawn from those facts the appellate court is less reluctant to interfere, D
but the degree of its reluctance must depend on the inferences. DENNING, L.J.,
in the Court of Appeal, put the matter succinctly in *British Launderers' Research
Association* v. *Central Middlesex Assessment Committee and Hendon Rating
Authority* (17), when he said (18):

"On this point it is important to distinguish between primary facts and
the conclusions from them. Primary facts are facts which are observed E
by witnesses and proved by oral testimony, or facts proved by the production
of a thing itself, such as an original document. Their determination is
essentially a question of fact for the tribunal of fact, and the only question of
law that can arise on them is whether there was any evidence to support the
finding. The conclusions from primary facts are, however, inferences
deduced by a process of reasoning from them. If and in so far as those F
conclusions can as well be drawn by a layman (properly instructed on the
law) as by a lawyer, they are conclusions of fact for the tribunal of fact
and the only questions of law which can arise on them are whether there was
a proper direction in point of law and whether the conclusion is one which
could reasonably be drawn from the primary facts: see *Bracegirdle* v.
Oxley (19)." G

DENNING, L.J., then went on to discuss the type of case where the correct conclusion required for its correctness its determination by a trained lawyer, which
most emphatically this case is not.

My Lords, the two questions which I have adumbrated above are so much a
question of fact and degree which are within the particular knowledge and
experience of the Minister and his advisers, and on which members of an appellate H
court have, in the absence of expert evidence (and there was none) no like knowledge or experience that, notwithstanding my doubts, I am not prepared to
say that the Minister reached a wrong answer to either of these fundamental
questions. It is, I think, a great pity that there was no expert evidence on the
second question, but the appellants preferred to rely on their legal point as to
demolition. The question, then, is whether on those findings the Minister I
reached a wrong conclusion of law in deciding that the removal of these walls and
embankments constituted development as defined in s. 12 (1) of the Act (which
it is common ground did not materially differ from its precursor in the Town and
Country Planning Act 1947). If he reached a conclusion which was not erroneous

(17) [1949] 1 All E.R. 21; [1949] 1 K.B. 462.
(18) [1949] 1 All E.R. at pp. 25, 26; [1949] 1 K.B. at p. 471.
(19) [1947] 1 All E.R. 126; [1947] K.B. 349.

A in point of law, your Lordships have no power to correct him. Section 12 (1) is in these terms:

B
"In this Act, except where the context otherwise requires, 'development', subject to the following provisions of this section, means the carrying out of building, engineering, mining or other operations in, on, over or under land, or the making of any material change in the use of any buildings or other land."

The main submission of the appellants pushed to its ultimate length was that no act of demolition "per se" or "simpliciter" (whatever those qualifications mean—I think they were intended to mean without a view to redevelopment), whether of a complete building or of a part of a building, could in law constitute C development for the purposes of s. 12. I cannot understand this argument pushed so far. Counsel for the appellants rightly pressed your Lordships with the view that in the Act the word "demolition" was only used in relation to cases where corrective action was required after service of enforcement notices or in relation to specially "listed" houses of historical interest which may not be demolished without a special order. But there is nothing in s. 12 or elsewhere D which makes it plain that demolition per se or simpliciter is necessarily excluded from the very wide words of s. 12 (1) if otherwise the relevant operation fits within those words as a plain matter of the use of the English language. In fact there is nothing to exclude demolition. In this case the Minister has decided that this demolition is an engineering operation and so within the section. I do not understand how, if this demolition be properly so described, the fact that E it is only demolition per se takes it out of that section.

But on the Minister's finding, consequent on his finding that the magazine and its protective walls and embankments were all part of one building, so that this was only demolition of part of a building, there is, I think, another answer to the appellants.

Section 12 (2) is, so far as relevant, in these terms:

F
"The following operations or uses of land shall not be taken for the purposes of this Act to involve development of the land, that is to say:— (*a*) the carrying out of works for the maintenance, improvement or other alteration of any building, being works which affect only the interior of the building or which do not materially affect the external appearance of the building and (in either case) are not works for making good war damage;
G ..."

It was argued that one cannot look at sub-s. (2), which was a clause of exclusion, to construe sub-s. (1). This, however, states the principle too broadly. One cannot look at a clause of exclusion to extend the natural construction of the main section but one can, in my opinion, most certainly look at it to support H the view which one may tentatively form as to the meaning of the main section. Subsection (2) only confirms the view which, assisted by the definition of "building" and "building operations" in s. 221 (1), in my view sub-s. (1) naturally bears, namely, that a building operation in, on, over or under land includes an alteration to a building which would include mere demolition; the subsection, however, makes it clear that to fall within sub-s. (1) an alteration is limited to a I building operation which materially affects the external appearance of the building. There is nothing to exclude an alteration which is no more than demolition per se. As it is not in doubt that the removal of the walls and embankments affected materially the external appearance of the building (that was, indeed, the real ground of complaint by the inhabitants) that seems to be another ground on which the decision of the Minister must be upheld.

My Lords, in these circumstances it does not seem to me that the question whether demolition per se or simpliciter is a development within s. 12 (1) calls for determination by your Lordships. All that it is necessary to decide is that,

if such demolition is covered, as in this case, by other provisions of that sub-   A
section, it is not saved from the application thereof merely by reason of the
fact that it is only demolition per se or simpliciter.

The expression of opinion by the Minister on the question of demolition in
his circular no. 67 dated 15th February 1949, has stood and has apparently
been accepted by the profession for 20 years and there may be much common
sense and practical utility in it.   I do not criticise it but, in my view, it remains   B
a matter of ministerial opinion and practice and its legal correctness does not
arise in your Lordships' decision.   For these reasons I would dismiss this appeal.

LORD WILBERFORCE: My Lords, I have had the benefit of reading
in advance the opinion prepared by my noble and learned friend, LORD PEARSON.
I gratefully adopt his statement of the history and the facts of this case: I agree   C
with his conclusions with regard to them and to the findings and decisions of
the Minister.   I desire only to add some observations as to the scope of the
Town and Country Planning Act 1962, and the concept of development.

" Development " is a key word in the planners' vocabulary but it is one whose
meaning has evolved and is still evolving.   It is impossible to ascribe to it any
certain dictionary meaning, and difficult to analyse it accurately from the   D
statutory definition.

In the Town and Country Planning Act 1932, we find this:

Section 52. " In this Act, unless the context otherwise requires, the following expressions have the meanings hereby assigned to them respectively,
that is to say:— . . . ' Building operations ' includes any road works preliminary, or incidental, to the erection of buildings ; . . . ' Development ', in relation   E
to any land, includes any building operations or rebuilding operations, and
any use of the land or any building thereon for a purpose which is different
from the purpose for which the land or building was last being used: . . ."

Leaving aside the inaccuracy of using an inclusive formula to express the meaning
assigned, " development " here was used, in relation to operations, in a normal
sense to refer to those which in their nature are constructive.   It would have   F
been difficult to argue under this Act that an operation involving mere demolition
of a building, or part of a building, constituted development and I think that the
view that it did not was assumed, if not decided, in *London County Council* v.
Marks & Spencer, Ltd. (20).

In the Town and Country Planning Act 1947, the conception of development
was greatly expanded.   The relevant s. 12 (2), was in the same form as s. 12 (1)   G
of the Act of 1962.   The main changes, as compared with the Act of 1932, were
that it was drafted in a " means " not " includes " form and that the operations
referred to became " building, *engineering, mining or other operations in, on, over
or under land* ".   Then there were six stated exceptions of operations or uses which
were not to be deemed to involve development, of which the most important
for the purposes of this appeal is—   H

" (a) the carrying out of works for the maintenance, improvement or other
alteration of any building, being works which affect only the interior of the
building or which do not materially affect the external appearance of the
building."

This definition was amplified in s. 119 (corresponding to s. 221 of the Act of 1962)   I
by definitions of " building ", " building or works ", and " building operations "
which I need not quote.

It is relevant, I think, to recall that the Act of 1947 in Part 7 provided for
the levying of development charges in respect broadly of any development for
which planning permission was required.   But there was an exemption from
these charges (by Sch. 3) of specified types of development, one of which was

(20) [1953] 1 All E.R. 1095; [1953] A.C. 535.

A " the enlargement, improvement or other alteration " of certain buildings.   No
mention was made, in the exemptions, of any demolition, total or partial, of any
building, yet had demolition been considered to be, or possibly to be, developments such a mention would surely have been included.   The development
charge provisions are not repeated in the Act of 1962, but it is still legitimate to
look back to that of 1947 in construing the definition of " development ".   It
B is on the definitions now contained in s. 12 (1) and s. 221 of the Act of 1962 that
the appellants seek an answer to the question whether demolition or, as the
appellants call it, demolition per se, can constitute development.

Unfortunately I do not think that the question in this form can be answered
because neither in the terminology of the Act, nor in its discernible policy as
regards development, is it possible to segregate some identifiable operation,
C for which the description or label " demolition " is apt and to say of it that it
does or does not amount to development under the Act.   References, indeed,
appear, in various contexts, as, for example, in the sections of the Act dealing
with listed buildings, or in those which contain enforcement provisions, to
demolition, removal, restoration or re-instatement, but these bear meanings
which, while appropriate for their subject-matter, carry no consistent implica-
D tions as regards the meaning of expressions in other contexts.   The Act seems
to be drafted empirically rather than logically.   One must start with s. 12.   It is
not easy to construe, and certain negative propositions are easier to state than
positive.

1.   I think it is clear that the exception stated in s. 12 (2) (*a*) cannot be used
to establish the meaning of " development " in s. 12 (1).   Though I endorse
E the result of the judgments in the Court of Appeal (21), I cannot agree with
passages in the judgments which extract from s. 12 (2) (*a*) the words " materially
affect the external appearance of the building ", say that the works in question
do this, and so conclude that they are development within the meaning of s. 12 (1).
Qualifying words in an exception cannot be introduced into the rule so as to
enlarge the scope of the rule: so, if an operation is not one of the kinds included
F in s. 12 (1) it cannot be made into one merely because a condition of exemption
is not complied with.   Relevantly, if demolition is not included in s. 12 (1), there
is nothing for the exemption in s. 12 (2) (*a*) to bite on and the question whether
the external appearance is affected has no relevance or application.   What is
development must be ascertained from s. 12 (1) aided by s. 221.

2.   I do not find it possible to identify a genus in the words " building, engin-
G eering, mining or other operations ".   It is hardly good enough, when the
Minister's decision is being reviewed for error of law, to say that " other operations " must be construed ejusdem generis: that the genus need not be defined
in detail, but that it includes only operations of a certain scale.   I agree with the
Court of Appeal (21) and your Lordships in thinking both that this is not an
adequate test (if it is a test at all) of the genus and that in any event it
H led the Divisional Court (22) to the wrong result.   No more satisfactory was the
test suggested by the Minister who said that the genus was identified by the
word " development "—a word which he claimed everyone understands.   But
since the task on which we are engaged is to ascertain what " development ", as
defined, means, it hardly seems possible to interpret the words by which " development " is defined by reference to the, ex hypothesi, unknown meaning which
" development " bears.   Such a process is one of levitation by intellectual
I bootstrap.

Finally, there is the appellants' suggestion that the relevant operations must
at least be of a constructive character, leading to an identifiable and positive
result.   I think that this is near the heart of the matter, and that there is an
important element of truth in the argument.   I would accept, and think it

(21) [1968] 1 All E.R. 945;   [1968] 1 W.L.R. 600.
(22) [1968] 1 All E.R. 62.

important to emphasise, that the planning legislation should be approached **A** with a disposition not to bring within its ambit, unless specific words so require, operations in relation to land which do not produce results of this kind, that is to say, results (I deal only with operations, not with use) of a positive, constructive, identifiable character. In my opinion, the appellants succeed in showing that neither the development of the legislation, nor the successive descriptions of " development ", nor the policy of control and, while it lasted, of charge on **B** development, nor common sense or common expectation, require or suggest that the mere removal of a structure, or a building, or of a part of a building should be subject to the code. And I think that they derive important support for this argument from the Minister's circular no. 67 of 15th February 1949, in which he stated that he was—

> " advised that the demolition of a building does not of itself involve **C** development, although, of course, it may form part of a building operation, or lead to the making of a material change in the use of the land upon which it stood."

The advice referred to may not have been quite correct (I return to this point) but in giving this information to planning authorities, the Minister was undoubtedly reflecting a common-sense and accepted opinion as to the general **D** nature of development. I accept, of course, that, as an interpretation of the Act of 1947, under which it was issued, the circular has no legal status, but it acquired vitality and strength when, through the years, it passed, as it certainly did, into planning practice and textbooks, was acted on, as it certainly was, in planning decisions, and when the Act of 1962 (and I may add the Town and Country Planning Act 1968) maintained the same definition of " development " **E** under which it was issued.

So far, for the appellants, so good: they establish, in my opinion, this general approach to the construction of " development " and I think that it assists them in the limitation of the words " other operations ". But, as I said above, this can only be so unless specific words so require. The governing statutory words remain those of s. 12 and s. 221, and where these fairly apply, they must **F** prevail. They cannot be prevented from applying to a particular operation, which comes within them, by the mere fact that, in addition, the descriptive label " demolition " would fit that operation.

The Minister's circular to be fully accurate, should then have said not that it (the demolition of a building) may form part of a building operation, but that, what might be described as demolition may fall within one of the specific types **G** of operation described in s. 12 (1) and rank as development accordingly.

The Minister has held here that the removal of the embankments was an engineering operation, and that removal of the walls would be a building operation. Neither of these conclusions appears to me to have been inevitable; he might have held that both or either would be demolition and that neither the one fell under " engineering " nor the other under " building ". But both were marginal **H** decisions given in relation to a very special case, and I think were open to him to make as he did. The Act, in general, as the subject-matter probably requires, is drafted with a wide mesh; its use of expressions, particularly those relating to building, demolition, alteration and the reverse of these operations, is not precise or consistent—as to engineering or mining there is no definition at all —and the sections conferring power of decision on the Minister, in particular **I** s. 43, show that decisions on marginal questions as to development—what it is and what it is not—are intended to be left to him through or with his expert and professional staff. I am of opinion that the decisions he reached were within his permitted field and were not wrong in law. This leads to the conclusion that the appeal must be dismissed.

LORD PEARSON: My Lords, this appeal relates to a group of six buildings near Meriden, which is a village in the countryside between Birmingham and

A Coventry and about nine miles from each. These buildings were constructed in 1938 or 1939 as magazines, two for the storage of explosives and four for the storage of ammunition. Each consisted of a central block, surrounding blast walls about four feet away from the central block and sloping embankments extending outwards for about eight to ten feet from near the top of the blast walls to ground level. The two magazines for explosives were made of brick,

B and each of them was about 25 to 30 feet long, 12 feet wide and 11 feet high, and had a narrow entrance at each end. The four magazines for ammunition were made of concrete and each of them was about 70 feet long, 30 feet wide and 11 feet high rising to 13 feet at the roofs' centres and had two narrow entrances at each end, and at the sides had windows with their tops about level with the tops of the blast walls. The embankments consisted partly of soil and partly

C of ash and brick rubble, and the sloping surfaces were covered with vegetation.

In 1962 the Minister on appeal decided that the magazines possessed an existing use on the appointed day within Class X of the Town and Country Planning (Use Classes) Order 1950 (23). I understand that under s. 12 (2) (*f*) of the Town and Country Planning Act 1962, the effect of the Minister's decision was that use of the magazines for storage of any kind was permitted.

D The magazines, however, were purpose-built. They had been specially designed and constructed for use as magazines for storing explosives and ammunition. The blast walls, supported by the embankments, would tend to confine the effect of any explosion that might occur. The embankments with their green vegetation tended to camouflage the group of buildings—the explosives and ammunition depot—against possible enemy air attack. Also the

E green embankments largley concealed the otherwise unsightly buildings from the view of local residents and passers-by. The magazines were not suitable for use as warehouses for general storage. The entrances were very narrow, being only about four feet wide and seven feet high and preventing loading and unloading of large-sized goods. The presence of the embankments made access to the roofs of the central blocks very easy, and intruders could break the windows

F and steal goods from inside. The blast walls kept light from the windows. There was dampness in the narrow passages between the central blocks and the blast walls.

The appellants acquired the group of buildings in 1964. Early in 1966, without having obtained planning permission, they set out to remove the embankments, demolish the blast walls and enlarge the entrances to the central blocks.

G The effect would have been to convert the purpose-built magazines into warehouses for general storage. But when they had removed, or begun to remove, the embankments, there was local opposition on the ground that the ugly buildings were being exposed to view. On 30th March 1966, the respondent council, the Meriden Rural District Council, exercising planning control powers delegated to them by the Warwickshire County Council, served on the appellants

H an enforcement notice under s. 45 of the Act of 1962, describing the removal of the embankments as unauthorised development and requiring it to be discontinued and requiring steps to be taken to replace the embankments. The appellants, on 9th April 1966, appealed to the Minister against the enforcement notice. The appeal was initially under s. 46 (1) (*d*) of the Act, and later was under para. (*c*) also. Paragraph (*c*), so far as material, provides " that no

I planning permission was required in respect of that development ". Paragraph (*d*) provides " that what is assumed in the enforcement notice to be development did not constitute or involve development ". The enforcement notice and the appeal to the Minister against it related only to the embankments. The blast walls were still standing.

In July 1966, however, the appellants under s. 43 of the Act of 1962 applied to the respondent council for a determination whether in the opinion of the

---

(23) S.I. 1950 No. 1131. This order has been revoked and replaced by S.I. 1963 No. 708.

respondent council certain proposed works, including removal of the blast walls, **A** would constitute development. In October 1966, under the provisions of s. 43 (2) and s. 23 and s. 24 of the Act of 1962, there was an appeal by the appellants to the Minister on the basis that the respondent council had not made a determination within the appropriate period. Thus, there were two appeals by the appellants to the Minister, one raising in relation to the enforcement notice the question whether the actual removal of the embankments was development **B** requiring planning permission, and the other raising under s. 43 the question whether the proposed removal of the blast walls would be development requiring planning permission.

In December 1966, a Ministry inspector held an inquiry into the appeal relating to the enforcement notice and the removal of the embankments. The inspector's report, dated 11th January 1967, included a description of the appeal **C** site and its surroundings, the gist of the representations made at the inquiry, and his findings of fact, conclusions and recommendations. Representations on behalf of the appellants were made by Mr. S. J. Williams, a director of the appellants. The report shows that he agreed in cross-examination—

" that the blast walls and soil embankments were probably an integral **D** part when built, the embankments making the blast walls stronger and deadening blast effect, and that the blast walls were probably an integral part of the construction of a building which contained ammunition."

The inspector set out his findings of fact in his report and his conclusions, including the following:

E

" The legal implications of the above facts are matters for consideration by the Minister and his legal advisers, but it appears to me that:— (i) Surrounding embankments and blast walls are a necessary and integral part of buildings used for storing explosives and together they constitute a magazine . . . Their appearance has been materially affected by the removal of the embankments, which work was an engineering operation constituting development . . . On the planning merits of the case I am of the opinion **F** that the exposure of the concrete blast walls and buildings forming these magazines, by the removal of the grass and vegetation covered embankments, has resulted in these ugly structures being much more prominent in the rural surroundings. The quality of the countryside here, and its effectiveness as a part of a proposed green belt, has accordingly deteriorated to an unacceptable **G** extent . . ."

The inspector's recommendation was that: " If it is decided that development requiring planning permission is involved, planning permission be not granted."

In a letter of decision dated 16th May 1967, the Minister considered the representations made at the inquiry, and the inspector's findings of fact and conclusions and recommendations. In the course of the letter the Minister said: **H**

" The [respondent] council maintained that the blast walls and the embankments were an integral part of each of the buildings. This latter view is accepted as the correct one in this case . . . The removal of the embankments was an engineering operation clearly falling into section 12 (1) of the Act. This operation constituted material development for which planning permission was required . . ."

I

The Minister upheld the enforcement notice, refused planning permission for the development to which it related (i.e., the actual removal of the embankments) and dismissed the appeal.

In the other appeal, that relating to the proposed removal of the blast walls, no inquiry was held but written representations were made to and considered by the Minister. In a second letter of decision dated 16th May 1967, the Minister dealt with this appeal. In the course of his letter he said:

A   " With regard to the removal of the walls, the [appellants] argued that the blast walls were separate from the storage units and that as they in no way afforded any support to the buildings their removal could not be said to affect the external appearance of the buildings and further that demolition of itself does not involve development. In the opinion of the [respondent council] the blast walls (and the earth banks which previously

B   surrounded them) were all part of the original design of the buildings and their removal would therefore materially affect the external appearance of the buildings. It is noted that the buildings were erected shortly before the last war, some were used for the storage of ammunition and some for the storage of explosives. The blast walls and soil embankments were provided to prevent damage from explosion and to conceal the internal structure.

C   The [respondent] council's view that the blast walls form part of the buildings is accepted as a fact and it is considered that the removal of the blast walls would therefore constitute an alteration of the buildings, and that it would materially affect the external appearance of the buildings. In these circumstances the provisions of section 12 (2) (a) of the Act do not apply to the proposal which therefore constitutes development of the land for which

D   planning permission is required . . ."

The Minister determined accordingly and dismissed the appeal.

The appellants under s. 180 and s. 181 of the Act appealed to the High Court against both decisions of the Minister. The Queen's Bench Divisional Court (24) allowed the appeal, deciding in favour of the appellants, but the Court of Appeal (25) reversed that decision.

E   Under s. 180 and s. 181 of the Act an appeal to the High Court against a decision of the Minister can only be made on a point of law. There could be no such appeal against findings of primary facts. The Minister has, however, drawn inferences from the primary facts on the following important points which are in dispute: (i) he held that the blast walls and the embankments were integral parts of the magazines; (ii) he held in effect that the removal of

F   the blast walls would be a structural alteration of the magazines and would therefore constitute building operations as defined in the Act and (not being within s. 12 (2) (a)) would be development requiring planning permission; and (iii) he held that the removal of the embankments was an engineering operation within the meaning of the Act and so was development requiring planning permission.

G   These inferences involve an element of construction of the Act and, therefore, of law, and so are in principle appealable. But an appeal cannot succeed unless it is shown that there is some error of law. In dealing with questions of mixed fact and law, such as those which arise in this appeal, it should be borne in mind that the Minister, advised by his department, is likely to have the benefit of expert knowledge and experience of building and engineering matters.

H   (i) I cannot see that there is any error of law in the Minister's view, agreeing with that of the local authority and the inspector, that the blast walls and the embankments were integral parts of the magazines. He did not take into account any irrelevant factors or leave out of account any relevant factors, and it cannot be said that his view is manifestly wrong or unreasonable. The gap between the central block and the blast walls is quite small, but was duly

I   taken into account. I think the character of the whole structure in each case as a purpose-built magazine is an important reason for treating it as a single unit (unum quid in the convenient Scottish phrase). If one takes away the blast walls and embankments you deprive the structure of its character as a magazine and convert it into a warehouse for general storage.

(ii) The second point requires consideration of s. 12 (1) and (2) (a) and the

(24) [1968] 1 All E.R. 62.
(25) [1968] 1 All E.R. 945; [1968] 1 W.L.R. 600.

definitions of " building " and " building operations " in s. 221 (1).   Section   A
12 (1) and (2) (a) provide as follows:

" 12.—(1) In this Act, except where the context otherwise requires,
' development ', subject to the following provisions of this section, means
the carrying out of building, engineering, mining or other operations in, on,
over or under land, or the making of any material change in the use of any
buildings or other land.   B

" (2) The following operations or uses of land shall not be taken for the
purposes of this Act to involve development of the land, that is to say:—
(a) the carrying out of works for the maintenance, improvement or other
alteration of any building, being works which affect only the interior of the
building or which do not materially affect the external appearance of the
building and (in either case) are not works for making good war damage . . ."   C

The definitions of " building " and " building operations " in s. 221 are as
follows:

" ' building ' includes any structure or erection, and any part of a building,
as so defined, but does not include plant or machinery comprised in a
building; . . .   D

" ' building operations ' includes rebuilding operations, structural alterations of or additions to buildings, and other operations normally undertaken
by a person carrying on business as a builder; "

Now as the whole magazine in each case has been treated as a unum quid,
that is to say as a single building or structure or erection, the removal of its
blast walls would very clearly constitute a structural alteration of it. The excep-   E
tion provided by s. 12 (2) (a) is not applicable because the removal of the blast
walls would materially affect the external appearance of the building or structure
or erection. Accordingly the Minister's decision under s. 43 with regard to the
blast walls should be upheld.

(iii) Thirdly, there is the removal of the embankments. I would have been
inclined to regard this also as a structural alteration of the magazine treated   F
as a single building, structure or erection, and on that basis there would be a
building operation within the definition and it would be development requiring
planning permission. There is also the possibility that the removal of the
embankments might come within " other operations normally undertaken by a
person carrying on business as a builder ", but without expert knowledge or
expert evidence I do not feel able to form a view on this possibility. The Minister,   G
however, did not decide on either of these grounds. He decided on the ground
that the removal of the embankments was an " engineering operation ".   There
is in the Act no definition of " engineering operation " except that the expression
includes the formation or laying out of means of access to highways.   In the
Divisional Court WIDGERY, J., with whom LORD PARKER, C.J., and CHAPMAN, J.,
concurred, said (26)   H

" . . . this little job of shifting a few cubic yards of soil with a digger and a
lorry is not, in my judgment, an operation of a kind which could ever be
dignified with the title of an engineering operation."

If I were able to agree with the description of the operation on the facts of this
case I would agree that it was not an engineering operation.   But the evidence
shows, to my mind, that the removal of the embankments from the six magazines   I
of the sizes previously described was not " a little job of shifting a few cubic
yards of soil ".   It was rather a large job.   There were large quantities of soil
and ash and brick rubble to be moved.   The appellants, naturally, would, and
in fact did, employ contractors to perform the operation.   The materials did not
only have to be moved; they also had to be disposed of.   The contractors were
Bencif (Construction), Ltd., Sports Ground and Tarmacadam Contractors, and

(26) [1968] 1 All E.R. at p. 65.

A   they stated in a letter that they had hired transport from various firms, and that the content of the embankments was made up of one-third top-soil and sub-soil and two-thirds ash and brick rubble, and that the top-soil was delivered to the new incinerator site at Castle Bromwich, the ash and brick rubble to various sites, and the sub-soil to Barston. It was an operation of some magnitude. In my opinion, there was evidence on which the Minister could reasonably accept

B   the view of the local authority and the inspector that the removal of the embankments constituted an engineering operation and, therefore, was development requiring planning permission.

    The argument for the appellants was mainly based on the proposition that demolition, or demolition in or by itself, or demolition per se, does not constitute development. I think there is in this proposition some truth but only a limited

C   amount of truth. On the one hand, there is in s. 12 and in the relevant definitions in s. 221 (1) no mention of or reference to demolition or removal or any such operation. Therefore, an operation does not qualify as development by virtue of being a demolition or removal operation. It is not right to say " This is a demolition or removal operation; therefore, it is development ". On the other hand, there are not in s. 12 or in the relevant definitions in s. 221 (1) any words

D   excluding operations from being development if they are demolition or removal operations. An operation is not disqualified for being development because it is a demolition or removal operation. It is not right to say " This is a demolition or removal operation, therefore, it cannot be development ". Notwithstanding that an operation is a demolition or removal operation, one still has to see whether it comes within the scope of development as defined in s. 12 assisted by s. 221.

E   It may be within the definition of " building operations ", e.g., because it constitutes a structural alteration of a building or because it is such an operation as to be normally undertaken by a person carrying on business as a builder. It may be an engineering operation. Whether it is or is not any of those things depends on the facts of the particular case.

    The argument for the appellants also sought to apply the ejusdem generis rule

F   to the words in s. 12 (1) " the carrying out of building, engineering, mining or other operations in, on, over or under land ". It was contended that there must be one single genus comprising building, engineering and mining operations, and that the other operations must belong to this genus. It was further contended that the single genus was of positive, constructive operations and could not include any negative, destructive operations and, therefore, could not include

G   any operations of demolition or removal. I think there is a first step which can properly be taken along this line of argument: the " other operations in, on, over or under land " must be in some way restricted by the juxtaposition of these words with the words " building, engineering, mining ": if the " other operations " were any operations whatsoever in, on, under or over land, there would be no need to mention specifically building, engineering or mining; there-

H   fore, it is to be inferred that the draftsman or Parliament intended to deal primarily with building, engineering or mining operations but also intended secondarily to bring in some other operations similar to these specified operations or to some of them. This first step would be covered by the maxim noscitur a sociis. I doubt whether in construing this subsection—seeking the intention to be found in it—it is safe to say that there must be a single genus comprising

I   building operations, engineering operations and mining operations and the other operations must be fitted into that genus. Another possible construction which can be suggested is that there are three genera and the other operations must be similar to building operations or to engineering operations or to mining operations. However this may be, I think the sufficient answer in this case is that if there is a single genus it cannot be of the kind suggested, because it has to include mining operations, when so far as they affect the land are not positive and constructive but negative and destructive operations. For instance, coal-mining demolishes and removes the seam of coal, leaving behind in the land a

subterranean hole partly filled with waste and perhaps shored up but not having **A**
any utility and possibly causing disturbance and eventually subsidence of the
upper strata.   Secondly, there are operations which are both destructive and
constructive.   If a piece of ground is cleared of buildings and levelled for use as a
sports ground or aerodrome, there is a destruction of the buildings and the mounds
of earth but there is created the useful flat surface.   In some circumstances it
could be regarded as a positive and constructive operation.   **B**

In my opinion, the appellants' arguments cannot prevail.   I would dismiss the
appeal.

Appeal dismissed.

Solicitors: *Keene, Marsland & Co.*, agents for *Tompkins & Co.*, Birmingham
(for the appellants); *Solicitor, Ministry of Housing and Local Government*; **C**
Sharpe, Pritchard & Co. (for the respondent council).

[*Reported by* S. A. HATTEEA, ESQ., *Barrister-at-Law.*]

D

PRACTICE DIRECTION.

E

PATENTS APPEAL TRIBUNAL.

*Patent—Appeal to Court of Appeal—Application for leave to appeal—Procedure
—Time for application—Extension of time for service of notice of appeal
—R.S.C., Ord. 59, r. 18—Patents Act 1949 (12, 13 & 14 Geo. 6 c. 87), s. 87* **F**
(1) (c).

By s. 87 (1) (c) of the Patents Act 1949 (1) provision is made for appeals to
the Court of Appeal from decisions of the Patents Appeal Tribunal wherein
grants have been refused in opposition proceedings brought under s. 14 of the
Act (2) on the grounds of prior user (sub-s. 1 (d)) or obviousness (sub-s. 1 (e)). **G**
Such appeals require the leave of the tribunal, which if given, will cause the
provisions of R.S.C., Ord. 59, r. 18, to apply, whereunder the notice of appeal
is required to be served within 14 days from the date of the decision or within
such further time as the tribunal may allow. Application for leave to appeal should
be made on notice to the parties entitled to notice of the appeal proper within
14 days of the date of the Patents Appeal Tribunal decision directing refusal or **H**
within such further time as the tribunal may allow.   If leave is granted, the
tribunal will extend the time during which the notice of appeal is required to be
served to provide not less than 14 days from the date of the leave to appeal.

G. H. LLOYD-JACOB, J.

6th May 1969.

I

---

(1) 17 HALSBURY's STATUTES (2nd Edn.) 709.
(2) 17 HALSBURY's STATUTES (2nd Edn.) 642.

A

R. *v.* GRANTHAM.

[COURTS-MARTIAL APPEAL COURT (Lord Parker, C.J., Widgery, L.J., and Lawton, J.), February 20, March 20, 1969.]

B
Court-Martial—Appeal—Right of appeal—Application for leave to appeal after appeal effectively disposed of.

Court-Martial—Appeal—Fresh evidence—Power to admit presupposing competent appeal—Courts-Martial (Appeals) Act 1968 (*c.* 20), *s.* 28.

The language of the Courts-Martial (Appeals) Act 1968 as a whole points to the conclusion that s. 8* confers a single right of appeal which incorporates a right to apply once, and once only, for leave to appeal under s. 9† (see

C
p. 548, letter I, post).

Dictum of LORD GODDARD, C.J., in *R. v. Moore* ((1957), 41 Cr. App. Rep. at p. 180) applied.

Section 28‡ of the Courts-Martial (Appeals) Act 1968 (power to receive fresh evidence on an appeal) presupposes the existence of a competent appeal or application, and is concerned only with the procedure thereon

D
(see p. 549, letter B, post).

Appeal dismissed.

[As to determination of courts-martial appeals, see 33 HALSBURY'S LAWS (3rd Edn.) 1120, 1121, para. 1860.

For the Courts-Martial (Appeals) Act 1968, s. 28, see HALSBURY'S STATUTES

E
(3rd Edn.) 1968 Statutes 359.]

Cases referred to:

    R. v. *Healey* (1956), 40 Cr. App. Rep. 40; Digest (Cont. Vol. A) 394, *6093a.*

    R. v. *Moore*, [1957] 2 All E.R. 703, n.; [1957] 1 W.L.R. 841; 41 Cr. App. Rep. 179; Digest (Cont. Vol. A.) 394, *6093b.*

    R. v. *Pitman* (1916), 12 Cr. App. Rep. 14; 14 Digest (Repl.) 613, *6089.*

F
    R. v. *Van Dyn* (1932), 23 Cr. App. Rep. 150; 14 Digest (Repl.) 613, *6093.*

    Sweet v. *Parsley*, [1968] 2 All E.R. 337; [1968] 2 Q.B. 418; [1968] 2 W.L.R. 1360; *revsd.* H.L., [1969] 1 All E.R. 347; [1969] 2 W.L.R. 470.

    Warner v. *Metropolitan Police Comr.*, [1968] 2 All E.R. 356; [1968] 2 W.L.R. 1303; *affg.* sub nom. *R.* v. *Warner*, [1967] 3 All E.R. 93; [1967] 1 W.L.R. 1209.

G
    Yeandel v. *Fisher*, [1965] 3 All E.R. 158; [1966] 1 Q.B. 440; [1965] 3 W.L.R. 1002; 129 J.P. 546; Digest (Cont. Vol. B) 151, *57a.*

Applications.

On 17th April 1967 the applicant, Leslie Michael Grantham, a lance-corporal in the British army, was convicted by a general court-martial at Bielefeld in

H
West Germany of the murder of a German taxi driver named Reese, who was shot on 4th December 1966. He was sentenced to life imprisonment. He applied for leave to appeal against conviction and this application first came before another division of the Courts-Martial Appeal Court (DAVIES and FENTON ATKINSON, L.JJ., and NIELD, J.) on 4th December 1967, when leave to appeal against conviction was refused. The applicant now sought leave for extension of

I
time to make a second application for leave to appeal against conviction, and requested the court to hear fresh evidence. On the direction of LORD PARKER, C.J., the application was re-listed on the preliminary issues whether the court (a) can, and (b) will, extend time to hear a further application for leave to appeal. The facts are set out in the judgment of the court.

---

   * Section 8 (1) is set out at p. 546, letter F, post.

   † Section 9, so far as material, is set out at p. 546, letter G, post.

   ‡ Section 28 (1), so far as material, provides: "The Appeal Court may . . . (c) receive the evidence, if tendered, of any witness."

The cases noted below* were cited during the argument in addition to the cases   A
referred to in the judgment of the court.

T. M. Eastham, Q.C., and *A. C. W. Hordern* for the applicant.
J. W. Miskin, Q.C., and *L. G. Krikler* for the Crown.
Gordon Slynn as amicus curiae.

Cur. adv. vult.

B

20th March. **WIDGERY, L.J.,** read the judgment of the court at the invitation of LORD PARKER, C.J.: The applicant, Leslie Michael Grantham, was convicted by a general court-martial at Bielefeld in Germany on 17th April 1967 of the murder of one Reese on 4th December 1966. It was common ground that the applicant had threatened Reese with a pistol with intent to rob him, and that Reese had been shot in the head in the course of the incident, but the   C defence contended that the applicant was unaware that the pistol was loaded and had no intent to kill or cause grievous bodily harm. At the trial, evidence was given by one Marks that he had supplied the applicant with a pistol and ammunition but the applicant denied that he had received any ammunition.

The applicant applied to this court for leave to appeal against his conviction but this application was refused on 4th December 1967. He now seeks an   D extension of time in which to make a second application for leave to appeal against his conviction for murder, and requests the court to hear fresh evidence. The evidence which it is desired to call is that of a witness who met Marks in prison before Marks gave evidence at the court-martial and who, it is alleged, will say that Marks confessed that he had not supplied the applicant with ammunition but had loaded the pistol unknown to the applicant. The court   E has heard argument on the preliminary question whether it is competent to hear these applications in view of the refusal of leave on 4th December 1967. Counsel agree that there is no authority on this question either in relation to this court since its inception in 1951, or in relation to the Court of Criminal Appeal or the Court of Appeal (Criminal Division).

By s. 8 (1) of the Courts Martial (Appeals) Act 1968 it is provided that: F

" Subject to the provisions of this Act, a person convicted by courts-martial may, with the leave of the Appeal Court, appeal to the Court against his conviction."

By s. 9:

" (1) Leave to appeal to the Appeal Court shall not be given except on an application in that behalf made by or on behalf of the appellant and   G lodged, within the prescribed period, with the registrar. (2) The application must be in the prescribed form and specify the grounds on which leave to appeal is sought and such other particulars, if any, as may be prescribed. (3) The Appeal Court may extend the period within which an application for leave to appeal must be lodged, whether the period has expired or not."

H

The Courts-Martial (Appeals) Act 1968 is a consolidating Act which replaces Part 1 of the Courts-Martial (Appeals) Act 1951. The Act of 1951 was modelled on the Criminal Appeal Act 1907 which provided a right of appeal after conviction on indictment and contained a similar requirement for the obtaining of leave, and this is now repeated in the Criminal Appeal Act 1968 which governs procedure in the Court of Appeal (Criminal Division). Both this court and the   I Court of Appeal have from time to time allowed an appeal, or an application for leave to appeal, to be " re-listed " for further argument when some procedural defect in the original disposal of the matter has come to light. Thus if, through a misunderstanding, counsel has not appeared, or papers submitted by the applicant have been delayed in the post, the court has restored the matter to

* *R.* v. *Brownhill* (1912), 8 Cr. App. Rep. 118; *R.* v. *Rowland*, [1947] K.B. 460; *R.* v. *Caddy*, [1959] 3 All E.R. 138; [1959] 1 W.L.R. 868; *R.* v. *Parks*, [1962] 3 All E.R. 633; [1962] 1 W.L.R. 1484; *R.* v. *Aldrich* (1962), Crim. L.R. 541.

A the list to hear argument or consider the papers as the case may be. No member of the present court, however, can recollect a case in which an application or appeal once effectively disposed of has been re-opened by the court. Indeed, it has been assumed that the court is then functus officio and that if new matter comes to light thereafter the applicant's proper course is to petition the Secretary of State who can himself refer the matter to the court under s. 34 of the Courts-

B Martial (Appeals) Act 1968 or s. 17 of the Criminal Appeal Act 1968. It is this assumption which is challenged in the present application.

Such assistance as is provided by authority comes from the cases where an applicant has abandoned his appeal, or application, and subsequently seeks to withdraw such abandonment. Rule 5 of the Courts-Martial Appeal Rules 1968 (1) authorises such abandonment on notice to the registrar, and in the case of

C appeals after trial on indictment r. 10 of the Criminal Appeal Rules 1968 (2), re-enacts a similar provision in earlier rules, and goes further to provide in para. (4):

> " Where an appeal or an application for leave to appeal is abandoned, the appeal or application shall be treated as having been dismissed or refused by the court."

D
In *R.* v. *Pitman* (3) an appellant who had abandoned his appeal moved ex parte for leave to withdraw his notice of abandonment contending that he acted on a misapprehension as to the availability of funds for the appeal. The application was refused, but Lord Reading, C.J., observed (4):

> " There is no doubt that this court has power either to allow the notice
E of abandonment to be withdrawn or to re-open an appeal which has been dismissed."

Recent decisions on the withdrawal of an abandonment however have restricted the circumstances in which it can be allowed. Thus in *R.* v. *Healey* (5), Lord Goddard, C.J., said:

F
> " There is no doubt that the Court has power to allow the withdrawal of a notice of abandonment. It has very seldom allowed it. It is allowed only if there are special circumstances or, as Avory, J., put it in *R.* v. *Van Dyn* (6), some misapprehension or mistake of fact. Exactly what the learned judge meant by ' misapprehension ' as distinct from a mistake of fact is perhaps difficult to understand. He was thinking probably of some mis-apprehension as to what had happened with regard to the appeal or with
G regard to the notice of appeal."

Finally in *R.* v. *Moore* (7), Lord Goddard, C.J., said (8):

> " There have been from time to time, indeed from quite early days in the history of the court, applications for leave to withdraw a notice of abandon-ment, considering that by the rules, which have the force of a statute the
H appeal has been dismissed. An examination of the cases has shown that the court has allowed notices of abandonment to be withdrawn only if they are satisfied that there has been some mistake though in one case it would appear that the court thought they had a wider power: (*R.* v. *Pitman* (3)). But this was only a *dictum*."

I Having pointed out that the court could treat a notice of abandonment as a nullity if the prisoner had in some way been fraudulently led or induced to give it, Lord Goddard, C.J., continued (9):

---

(1) S.I. 1968 No. 1071.   (2) S.I. 1968 No. 1262.
(3) (1916), 12 Cr. App. Rep. 14.   (4) (1916), 12 Cr. App. Rep. at p. 14.
(5) (1956), 40 Cr. App. Rep. 40 at p. 43.
(6) (1932), 23 Cr. App. Rep. 150 at p. 152.
(7) [1957] 2 All E.R. 703, n.; [1957] 1 W.L.R. 841.
(8) (1957), 41 Cr. App. Rep. 179 at p. 180; [1957] 2 All E.R. at p. 703, n.
(9) (1957), 41 Cr. App. Rep. at p. 180; [1957] 2 All E.R. at p. 703, n.

"but where there has been a deliberate abandonment of an appeal,   A
in the opinion of the Court, there is no power or right to allow the notice
of abandonment to be withdrawn and the appeal reinstated because, the
appeal having been dismissed, the court has exercised its powers over the
matter and is *functus officio*."

Counsel for the applicant argues that both in its practice of "re-listing", and
in permitting the withdrawal of an abandonment, the court is recognising an   B
inherent power to re-open an appeal or application for good cause, but in our
opinion the practice in each case has been the same, namely to reconsider a
matter if it has never properly been determined owing to some procedural error
or mistake.   No trace is to be found of the court re-opening an appeal on its
merits on fresh evidence subsequently coming to light, and it is evident that
LORD GODDARD would have regarded this as an excess of jurisdiction if the   C
appeal had been abandoned.   It would be strange if the court had jurisdiction
to hear a fresh application but had no power to allow an abandonment of the
original application to be withdrawn.

Reference was also made to *Sweet* v. *Parsley* (10) where the report speaks of
an application for leave to appeal to the House of Lords being renewed after
a prior refusal, but the facts of that case were very special.   In the first place   D
the projected appeal was not from this court or the Court of Appeal (Criminal
Division) but from a Divisional Court.   The decision of that court was based
on *Yeandel* v. *Fisher* (11) which, unknown to the members of the court, had been
the subject of criticism in the House of Lords during argument in *Warner* v.
Metropolitan Police Comr. (12).   The opinion of the House of Lords in *Warner*
v. *Metropolitan Police Comr.* (12) was not published until after the Divisional   E
Court had refused Miss Sweet leave to appeal, but on receipt of that opinion
the court was able to certify (13) that a point of law of general public importance
arose in her appeal and to grant leave accordingly.   We do not think that these
events cast light on the jurisdiction of this court in the present application.

This court is created by statute and has no jurisdiction beyond that which
Parliament has conferred on it.   By the combined effect of s. 8 and s. 9 of the   F
Courts-Martial (Appeals) Act 1968 a person convicted by court-martial has a
right to appeal but must, as a first step, obtain the leave of the court before
presenting his appeal.   Parliament must be presumed to be mindful of the need
to make an end to proceedings and prima facie an appeal means one appeal
and "an application" means one application.   Although s. 11 (2) contains some
safeguard against frivolous applications we do not think that repeated applica-   G
tions are contemplated merely because they are made at the applicant's own
risk.

If s. 8 envisages more than one appeal arising out of the same conviction
the purpose of the Secretary of State's powers under s. 34 becomes obscure,
because it would follow that the applicant could always approach the court directly without the intervention of the Secretary of State.   Nor do we see any reason   H
for distinguishing between applications and appeals in this respect because the
right to apply for leave is not a separate right but part and parcel of an indivisible right of appeal conferred by s. 8.   Indeed when the Act contemplates the
renewal of an application after refusal by a single judge it expressly so provides
in s. 36.

In the judgment of this court the language of the Act as a whole points to   I
the conclusion that s. 8 confers a single right of appeal which incorporates a
right to apply once, and once only, for leave to appeal under s. 9.   We are
reinforced in this view by the fact that when Parliament consolidated the
earlier legislation in the Act of 1968 it must be presumed to have done so with

(10) [1968] 2 All E.R. 337 at p. 340; [1968] 2 Q.B. 418 at p. 426.
(11) [1965] 3 All E.R. 158; [1966] 1 Q.B. 440.
(12) [1968] 2 All E.R. 356; [1968] 2 W.L.R. 1303.
(13) [1968] 2 All E.R. at p. 340; [1968] 2 Q.B. at p. 426.

A knowledge of LORD GODDARD, C.J.'s judgment in *R.* v. *Moore* (14) and in the belief that beyond the bounds there stated the court had no power to sanction the withdrawal of an abandonment or the making of a fresh application for leave.

Counsel for the applicant however, takes one further point. He refers us to s. 28 (1) of the Act, under which this court can receive fresh evidence and points out that under s. 28 (2) it is provided that where such evidence is tendered the

B court *shall* receive it if the conditions of the subsection are satisfied. Accordingly he contends that where an application for leave is based on fresh evidence of an acceptable kind the court must have jurisdiction to hear the application, since it cannot otherwise comply with the mandatory terms of s. 28 (2). In our judgment, however, s. 28 presupposes the existence of a competent appeal or application, and is concerned only with the procedure thereon.

C In the judgment of the court, therefore, there is no jurisdiction to hear these applications.

Applications dismissed.

Solicitors: *Kingsley Napley & Co.* (for the applicant); *Director of Army Legal Services* (for the Crown); *Treasury Solicitor.*

D [*Reported by* N. P. METCALFE, ESQ., *Barrister-at-Law.*]

BAKER v. WILLOUGHBY.

E [COURT OF APPEAL, CIVIL DIVISION (Harman, Widgery and Fenton Atkinson, L.JJ.), November 28, 29, December 10, 1968.]

Negligence—Contributory negligence—Appeal—Apportionment of liability— Principle on which appellate court will intervene—Apportionment by trial judge not interfered with save for error in principle or where clearly erroneous— Pedestrian struck by motor car when crossing road—Pedestrian and driver

F *with clear view of each other—No evasive action taken.*

Damages—Personal injury—Amount of damages—Broken lower left leg and ankle —Risk of degenerative changes in ankle joint.

Damages—Personal injury—Subsequent further injury to plaintiff, as victim in a robbery, necessitating amputation of limb previously injured—Whether damages for injury originally caused by tortfeasor should be reduced by reason

G *of subsequent greater injury supervening.*

In September 1964 the plaintiff was walking across a main road when he was struck by a motor car driven by the defendant. Both the plaintiff and the defendant had a good view of each other while the car travelled the last 200 yards before striking the plaintiff, but neither took any evasive action. In an action by the plaintiff for damages for negligence the trial judge held the

H defendant 75 per cent. to blame. On appeal by the defendant,

Held: the only possible conclusion was that the plaintiff and the defendant were equally blameworthy, and the judge's apportionment of liability must be varied accordingly (see p. 553, letter B, p. 554, letter I, and p. 556, letter A, post).

Decision of DONALDSON, J. ([1968] 2 All E.R. 236) varied.

I The plaintiff's left leg was broken below the knee, and his left ankle was broken; he was in hospital for six weeks, in plaster for three months thereafter, and on crutches for six months in all. The fractures ultimately united with a good range of functional movement, but there was a risk of degenerative changes in the ankle. The plaintiff returned to work with no significant reduction in his earnings, but might suffer future pecuniary loss by reason of his disability. Subsequently, in the course of the plaintiff's employment he

---

(14) [1957] 2 All E.R. 703, n; [1957] 1 W.L.R. 841.

was an innocent victim of an armed robbery in which he received gunshot **A**
wounds necessitating the immediate amputation of his defective left leg.
The trial judge assessed general damages at £1,600, because he held that in
law he must disregard the gunshot wounds and their effects. On appeal by
the defendant,

Held: (i) £1,600 would have been appropriate damages for the plaintiff's
injuries, but for the subsequent injury to and amputation of the plaintiff's **B**
left leg (see p. 553, letter D, p. 554, letter I, and p. 556, letter E, post), but

(ii) the subsequent injury limited the damage for loss of the leg to the
period between the two injuries, and since this occurred before the damages
were assessed the assessment would be reduced from £1,600 to £700 (see
p. 553, letter I, p. 554, letter H, p. 555, letters B and H, and p. 556, letters
F and H, post).   **C**

Per CURIAM: if damages for the gunshot wounds ever fell to be assessed,
they should include this £900 damages lost to the plaintiff (see p. 554, letter
G, p. 555, letter G, and p. 556, letter G, post).

Decision of DONALDSON, J. ([1968] 2 All E.R. 236) affirmed as to (i), reversed
as to (ii).
                                                                                                         D
[As to the basis of assessment of liability in cases where there is contributory
negligence, see 11 HALSBURY'S LAWS (3rd Edn.) 317, para. 513; and for cases on
the subject, see 36 DIGEST (Repl.) 184-186, *983-997.*

As to appeals on assessment of damages, see 11 HALSBURY'S LAWS (3rd Edn.)
306, para. *496*;   and for cases on the subject, see 17 DIGEST (Repl.) 193, 194,
913-918.   **E**

As to the date by reference to which damages are measured, see 11 HALSBURY'S
LAWS (3rd Edn.) 237, 238, para. 405; and for cases on the measure of damages
in tort, see 17 DIGEST (Repl.) 101, 102, *155-173*;   36 DIGEST (Repl.) 199-202,
1048-1070;   DIGEST (Cont. Vol. A) 465, *173a.*

As to what a defendant may prove in mitigation of damages for a tort, see
11 HALSBURY'S LAWS (3rd Edn.) 291, 292, para. 479;   as to the exclusion of **F**
collateral matters in mitigation of damages, see ibid., p. 293, para. 481;   and
for cases on mitigation of damages in tort, see 17 DIGEST (Repl.) 111, 112, *249-259.*

As to collateral matters in relation to the assessment of damages, see 11
HALSBURY'S LAWS (3rd Edn.) 240, para. 408.]

Cases referred to: **G**
British Fame (Owners) v. *Macgregor (Owners)*, [1943] 1 All E.R. 33;   [1943]
     A.C. 197;   112 L.J.P.C. 6;   168 L.T. 193;   17 Digest (Repl.) 194, *917.*
Brown v. *Thompson*, [1968] 2 All E.R. 708;   [1968] 1 W.L.R. 1003.
Bwllfa and Merthyr Dare Steam Collieries (1891), Ltd. v. *Pontypridd Waterworks
     Co.*, [1903] A.C. 426;   [1900-03] All E.R. Rep. 600; 72 L.J.K.B. 805;
     89 L.T. 280;   11 Digest (Repl.) 136, *199.*   **H**
Curwen v. *James*, [1963] 2 All E.R. 619;   [1963] 1 W.L.R. 748;   Digest (Cont.
     Vol. A) 1210, *1208b.*
Leschke v. *Jeffs and Faulkner*, [1955] Q.W.N. 67.
Quintas v. *National Smelting Co., Ltd.*, [1961] 1 All E.R. 630;   [1961] 1 W.L.R.
     401;   Digest (Cont. Vol. A) 585, *201c.*
Stene v. *Evans, Thibault* v. *Stene* (1958), 14 D.L.R. (2d) 73;   24 W.W.R. 592; **I**
     45 Digest (Repl.) 17, **230.*

Appeal.
This was an appeal by the defendant, Arthur George Willoughby, against the
decision of DONALDSON, J., dated 10th March 1968 and reported [1968] 2 All
E.R. 236, awarding £1,202 10s. damages, being 75 per cent. of £1,600 general
plus £3 9s. 6d. agreed special damages. The facts are set out in the judgment of
WIDGERY, L.J.

A The cases noted below* were cited in argument in addition to those referred to in the judgments.

Tudor Evans, Q.C., and *Derek Wood* for the defendant.
Hugh Griffiths, Q.C., and *D. E. Hill-Smith* for the plaintiff.

Cur. adv. vult.

B 10th December. The following judgments were read.

WIDGERY, L.J., read the first judgment at the invitation of HARMAN, L.J. At about 8.0 a.m. on 12th September 1964, the plaintiff was crossing Croydon Road, Mitcham, on foot, when he was struck and injured by a Mini car driven by the defendant. In an action heard before DONALDSON, J., on 26th and 27th February and 11th March 1968 (1), the plaintiff established that the defendant C was 75 per cent. responsible for the collision, and he obtained judgment for £1,202 10s. The defendant now appeals against the judge's findings both on liability and quantum.

Croydon Road is a straight road throughout its relevant length and is 33 feet wide. It runs across Mitcham Common and thus, in effect, through open country, and is an important highway. It is subject to a speed restriction of 40 miles per D hour. On the morning in question the plaintiff was a passenger in a van driven by a Mr. Gladwyn along Croydon Road in the direction of Mitcham when the van ran out of petrol and came to rest on its correct side of the road near a public house called the Ravensbury Arms. Mr. Gladwyn took a container from the van and crossed the road with a view to obtaining a lift back to a garage, which they had recently passed, and thus obtaining petrol. The plaintiff remained with the E van. After an interval Mr. Gladwyn persuaded the driver of a baker's van to stop and pick him up but as he was getting into the vehicle he realised that he had no money and called to the plaintiff to produce some. The plaintiff then set off to cross the road and was struck by the defendant's car (also travelling in the direction of Mitcham) when he was in the centre of the road.

The plaintiff said in evidence that before crossing he had looked once towards F his right, that is towards Croydon, and had seen a " bullnosed " car about 100 yards away. Satisfied that he could safely cross, he had walked to the centre of the road, paused to look to his left and then taken a further step when he heard a screech of brakes and was hit. [HIS LORDSHIP then considered in detail the conflicting evidence of various witnesses, pointed out that there were in fact three cars, including that driven by the defendant, approaching from Croydon at this G time, and continued:] The judge decided that he need reach no conclusion as to which was the correct version (and I quote from his judgment):

" . . . since all are agreed that the Mini was overtaking the last of the cars not less than 200 to 300 yards from the scene of the accident. From this moment onwards the defendant must have had a clear view of the plaintiff . . ."

H The judge accepted the plaintiff's evidence that he had not run across the road but had walked out in a normal manner and concluded that the defendant's failure to avoid him must be due to the defendant driving at an excessive speed or failing to keep a proper look-out, or both, and that the defendant was negligent.

---

* *Bradburn* v. *Great Western Ry. Co.* (1874), L.R. 10 Ex. 1; [1874-80] All E.R. Rep.
I 195; *Williamson* v. *John I. Thorneycroft & Co., Ltd.*, [1940] 4 All E.R. 61; [1940] 2 K.B. 658; *Re Bradberry*, [1942] 2 All E.R. 269; [1943] Ch. 35; *Smiley* v. *Townshend*, [1950] 1 All E.R. 530; [1950] 2 K.B. 311; *The Carslogie*, [1952] 1 All E.R. 20; [1952] A.C. 292; *British Transport Commission* v. *Gourley*, [1955] 3 All E.R. 796; [1956] A.C. 185; *Overseas Tankship (U.K.), Ltd.* v. *Morts Dock and Engineering Co., Ltd.*, (*The Wagon Mound*), [1961] 1 All E.R. 404; [1961] A.C. 388; *Performance Cars, Ltd.* v. *Abraham*, [1961] 3 All E.R. 413; [1962] 2 Q.B. 33; *Smith* v. *Leech Brain & Co., Ltd.*, [1961] 3 All E.R. 1159; [1962] 2 Q.B. 405; *Browning* v. *War Office*, [1962] 3 All E.R. 1089; [1963] 1 Q.B. 750; *Watson* v. *Powles*, [1967] 3 All E.R. 721; [1968] 1 Q.B. 596; *Ball* v. *Richard Thomas & Baldwins, Ltd.*, [1968] 1 All E.R. 389; [1968] 1 W.L.R. 192.
(1) Reported [1968] 2 All E.R. 236; [1969] 1 Q.B. 38.

Of the plaintiff the judge said this:

    " However I do think the plaintiff should have seen that there were at least two cars approaching from the direction of Croydon and should have realised that they would have to pull out to pass Mr. Gladwyn's van. He should therefore have waited until they had passed before attempting to cross the road. No doubt he did not wish to keep the baker's van waiting. To this extent however he contributed to the occurrence of the accident by his own negligence and I think that his claim to damages must be abated by 25 per cent."

The defendant's first submission is that the judge found against him on the footing of excessive speed when there was no evidence to support this except the evidence of Mr. Vicars, which was manifestly unreliable. I do not agree that the judge founded on Mr. Vicars' evidence—on the contrary, his finding of negligence against the defendant is based on the fact that the latter had the plaintiff in full view during the last 200 yards before impact and took no evasive action. It is from this that the judge concludes that either the defendant's speed was excessive or his look-out faulty, and I see no reason to criticise this conclusion if one accepts, as I do, the judge's finding that the plaintiff did not run into the road, but walked out normally.

The defendant next contends that the apportionment of liability as to 75 per cent. to the defendant and 25 per cent. to the plaintiff was incorrect and contrary to the evidence. The judge has given no reasons to support this apportionment, but I do not criticise him for this as the matter is often one of impression and not susceptible of precise calculation. As LORD WRIGHT said in *British Fame (Owners)* v. *Macgregor (Owners)* (2):

    " It is a question of the degree of fault, depending on a trained and expert judgment considering all the circumstances, and it is different in essence from a mere finding of fact in the ordinary sense. It is a question not of principle or of positive findings of fact or law, but of proportion, of balance and relative emphasis, and of weighing different considerations; it involves an individual choice or discretion, as to which there may well be differences of opinion by different minds."

The same considerations make this court extremely reluctant to interfere with such an apportionment, as appears from the authorities recently reviewed by WINN, L.J., in *Brown* v. *Thompson* (3), when, in particular, the following passage from the judgment of WILLMER, L.J., in *Quintas* v. *National Smelting Co., Ltd.* (4) was cited with approval:

    " The problem of apportioning blame where there has been fault on both sides is one that has been familiar in the Admiralty jurisdiction for fifty years. It has long been held to be a matter primarily for the discretion of the trial judge, who finds the facts, and who has the advantage of seeing the participants at first hand and assessing the degrees of their responsibility. It is well settled that, in the absence of any error of principle, an appellate tribunal will interfere with the trial judge's apportionment only in exceptional cases, and then as a rule, only where it can be seen that the trial judge has failed to give effect to some material fact or has failed to take into account some material consideration."

Accordingly I would not interfere in the present case unless some error in the judge's approach is clearly discernible, as I think it is.

The basis of the finding against the defendant is that he had a clear view of the plaintiff for at least 200 yards prior to impact, and took no action. The basis of the finding against the plaintiff is that he did not wait for the cars to pass, and

(2) [1943] 1 All E.R. 33 at p. 35; [1943] A.C. 197 at p. 201.
(3) [1968] 2 All E.R. 708; [1968] 1 W.L.R. 1003.
(4) [1961] 1 All E.R. 636 at p. 643; [1961] 1 W.L.R. 401 at p. 418.

A did not look to his right a second time. Each had a full view of the other whilst they were on a collision course and neither did anything about it. This was not an urban street but a main highway where vehicles were authorised to travel at 40 miles per hour. The plaintiff knew that cars might pass at this speed but the defendant had no reason to think that a pedestrian would suddenly walk out in front of him. In these circumstances it seems to me to be impossible to conclude

B that the defendant was more blameworthy than the plaintiff and the judge must have misdirected himself in some way in reaching this conclusion. I would accordingly substitute an apportionment of 50 per cent. liability on each side.

The final point raised in this appeal concerns the quantum of damage. The plaintiff suffered fractures of the lower left leg and ankle. He was detained in hospital for six weeks whilst three operations were performed and he was in

C plaster for three months after his discharge. He was on crutches for a total of six months. The fractures ultimately united with a good range of functional movement but there was a risk of degenerative changes developing in the ankle joint. The plaintiff returned to work without any significant reduction of earnings, but the judge accepted that he might suffer future pecuniary loss by reason of his disability and assessed general damages, on a basis of full liability, at £1,600.

D If the evidence had rested there, no complaint would have been made of this assessment, but an important new factor intervened before the trial when, on 29th November 1967, the plaintiff was attacked by robbers at his place of business and was shot in the left leg, resulting in an amputation of that leg above the knee. The defendant argued at the trial and again in this court that as this second accident (as it has been called) had removed the very limb from which the earlier

E disability had stemmed, no loss suffered by the plaintiff after 29th November, 1967, could be attributed to the defendant's negligence. Putting the argument another way, it was said that the second accident had obliterated the effect of the first and that all loss suffered thereafter was attributable to the second accident. The judge rejected this argument and ignored the second accident. His award of £1,600 therefore reflects, amongst other things, the prospect of pain and suffer-

F ing and loss of earnings which might have occurred after 1967 had the second accident never occurred.

This case raises an important point of principle on which there is a surprising lack of authority. It is accepted that when assessing damages the court must have regard to events which have happened since the date of the accident and must be guided by these events insofar as they have made certain that which would

G otherwise be uncertain (see *Curwen* v. *James* (5)). If the judge in the present case had assessed damages on 28th November 1967, he would properly have included as an item of loss the prospect of future pain from degenerative changes in the left ankle, but where he makes an assessment in 1968 he must not reflect a prospect of pain which then no longer exists. Similarly, in a case where the evidence discloses the prospect of future disability from supervening disease,

H unconnected with the accident, the judge will normally be required to estimate the period during which the disability arising from the accident will continue before the disease supervenes, but if the latter event occurs before trial there is no longer room for speculation or estimate.

In my judgment, this principle applies to any consequences of a tortious act which have in fact been obliterated by supervening events before damages fall

I to be assessed. Damages are intended to compensate the plaintiff for his loss arising out of the tortious act and no more. The consequences of a tortious act may continue to cause damage during the whole of the plaintiff's life but if in fact they come to an end before trial, whether by recovery, or supervening disease, or further injury, I do not see why the defendant's liability should continue. Once damages are assessed, of course, they are not liable to be re-opened but this merely emphasises the importance of a correct assessment initially.

---

(5) [1963] 2 All E.R. 619; [1963] 1 W.L.R. 748.

Counsel for the plaintiff has not attacked the logic of this argument but con- A
tends that it should be rejected because of its unjust consequences. He takes as an
example a foreman steel erector earning £40 per week who has a serious fall
due to his employer's neglect and injures a leg to such an extent that he cannot
climb again and is reduced to deskwork at £15 per week. Such a man's claim
for loss of future earnings might be £10,000. Suppose that before trial he has a
motor accident which results in the paralysis of both legs. On the principle that a B
tortfeasor takes his victim as he finds him, the driver responsible for the second
accident, so the argument goes, will compensate the plaintiff as a " £15 per week
man " and if the employer escapes responsibility for loss of wages subsequent
to the second accident the plaintiff will never recover the £10,000 to which he was
clearly entitled. In the result, the plaintiff by suffering his injuries in two instalments receives far less than the total value of his injuries. Counsel for the plaintiff C
recognises the difficulty of holding the employer liable for continuing loss where
the second accident is not due to the fault of another, but he contends that where
both accidents are due to tortious acts the liability of the first tortfeasor must be
treated as continuing if grave injustice is to be avoided.

In support of this argument, counsel for the plaintiff refers us to the Alberta
case, *Stene* v. *Evans, Thibault* v. *Stene* (6), which seems to have proceeded on this D
basis although the report does not show the full facts of the case.

I think that the flaw in counsel for the plaintiff's argument lies in the assumption
that the second tortfeasor would pay damages on the basis that the plaintiff was
only a " £15 per week man ". The principle that a defendant who injures an already disabled man need only compensate him as such, derives from the fact
that the plaintiff's actual loss is similarly limited and that he must not make a E
profit out of the injury. If the plaintiff's true loss exceeds the value of an already
injured limb why should he not recover in full?

In the present case the plaintiff's left leg was already damaged at the date of
the second accident but he had a right to recover damages for the resultant loss.
In meal or in malt he had the equivalent of a good leg. If the effect of the oblitera-
tion of his injury by the second accident has been to deprive him of both his F
injured leg and the money differential between an injured leg and a sound one,
why should he not recover from the second tortfeasor in respect of both elements
in his loss? The second tortfeasor cannot complain at losing the fortuitous
advantage which might otherwise flow from injuring a disabled man rather than
a sound one—he takes his victim as he finds him.

As, in the present case, no consequences of the first accident survived the second, G
the defendant is responsible for loss suffered by the plaintiff prior to 29th November 1967, and not beyond. If damages in respect of the second injury ever fall
to be assessed, the plaintiff's claim for loss of future earnings or amenity should
be calculated on the assumption that he had been deprived of a sound left
leg since this is the true amount of his loss in terms of money.

I would accordingly assess the plaintiff's general damages in this case at £700. H
To this must be added the agreed special damage of £3 9s. 6d. and as, in my judgment, the plaintiff is entitled to 50 per cent. of the total, I would allow this appeal
and order that judgment be entered for the plaintiff for £351 14s. 9d.

FENTON ATKINSON, L.J.: On the issue of liability, I am in full agreement with the judgment of WIDGERY, L.J., and there is nothing I wish to add.

On the issue of damages, the defendant accepts that if the case had been tried I
before 29th November 1967, the learned judge's figure of £1,600 for general
damage was an appropriate sum to compensate the plaintiff for pain and loss of
enjoyment of life, including the possibility of increased disability in the future as
a result of degenerative changes in the ankle joint, and also for any future loss of
earning capacity.

The question for this court is what effect, if any, is to be given to the fact that

---

(6) (1958), 14 D.L.R. (2d) 73.

A on 29th November 1967, immediate amputation of the plaintiff's left leg above
the knee was made necessary as a result of an armed robber shooting him in that
leg. All the injuries to the plaintiff caused in the accident of 12th September 1964,
were to the left leg below the knee. As from the date of the amputation the pain
and the loss of enjoyment of life and the loss of earning capacity due to that
accident ceased and were entirely submerged and obliterated by the act of the
B subsequent wrongdoer.

The learned judge (7) has held that the plaintiff's actual and prospective loss
flowing from the defendant's negligence should not be reduced by the subsequent
amputation, but in my judgment he reached the wrong conclusion.   It is clear
law that a judge in fixing damages need not and must not speculate when he
knows. If, for example, at the trial of a fatal accident claim it is known that the
C widow has remarried a man who is able to support her on the same scale as
her former husband, her damages fall to be drastically reduced. Again, if a workman claims damages against his employer for personal injuries causing permanent
partial loss of earning capacity, but by the date of trial he has been reduced to
permanent complete incapacity for work by disease or some pure accident wholly
unconnected with the original injury, counsel for the plaintiff concedes that his
D damages for future incapacity would properly be reduced and might in some
cases have to be reduced to nil; but counsel for the plaintiff contends that in the
case of subsequent pre-trial disability caused by a second tort, the subsequent
disability, however severe, cannot be prayed in aid by the first tortfeasor in
reduction of the damages he should be made to pay. Counsel for the plaintiff
has not been able to point to any distinction in principle between the case of a
E tortiously and non-tortiously-caused subsequent disability, but he argues that
unless such a distinction is made a plaintiff may suffer injustice. There could be a
case, he argues, where as a result of injury caused by the first tortfeasor, the
plaintiff has been permanently partially disabled with a loss of earning capacity
of say 20 per cent. for the rest of his working life. He then suffers further cata-
strophic injury at the hands of the same or another tortfeasor. Counsel for the
F plaintiff contends that if the defendant's argument in the present case is correct,
the first tortfeasor would escape any liability after the date of the second tort,
but the second tortfeasor could claim to be entitled to take the victim as he found
him, that is to say a man already permanently 20 per cent. disabled, and claim to
have damages assessed against him only for 80 per cent. of the total disability.

In my judgment, this difficulty would not in practice arise, because if the second
G tortfeasor is to take the victim as he finds him, there is no good reason why the
damages payable by the second tortfeasor should not include a figure to cover the
compensation for loss of future earnings which the victim would have received
for the original injuries but for the second tortious injury. But even if this were
not so, in my view the first tortfeasor can only be made to pay compensation for
the period during which the pain, disability, loss of enjoyment of life or earning
H capacity caused by him continue to exist.

In this case all the damage caused by the defendant's tort was swallowed up
and obliterated when the amputation took place, and I agree that the plaintiff
is only entitled to damages in respect of the period up to 29th November 1967,
which I also would fix at £700 plus the special damage.

I **HARMAN, L.J.:** On the issue of liability I have been with some reluctance
persuaded that we ought to alter the proportions decided on by the learned
judge (7). My reluctance proceeds from the fact that it needs a very strong case
to alter such an assessment. However, accepting the facts as found by the
learned judge I have been unable to avoid the conclusion that each party had
the like opportunity to avoid the collision which occurred as had the other. The
learned judge found that the defendant's car passed the two cars which he
overtook 200 yards before reaching the scene of the accident. This means that

(7) [1968] 2 All E.R. 236; [1969] 1 Q.B. 38.

he had a full view of the plaintiff over that distance, but it also means that the   **A**
plaintiff had a full view of him and I cannot see how it can follow that one of them
was more blameworthy than the other. I therefore agree with my brothers that
we must alter the proportions so as to attribute equal blame to each.

The second issue raises a curious point. One starts with the fact that it has been
clear law ever since the decision in *Bwllfa and Merthyr Dare Steam Collieries
(1891), Ltd.* v. *Pontypridd Waterworks Co.* (8), decided in the House of Lords in   **B**
1903, that the court must never speculate when it knows: see the speech of
LORD MACNAGHTEN (9). The point is well taken by HANGER, J., who decided
Leschke v. *Jeffs and Faulkner* (10) in Queensland. That was a case where the
victim of an accident was serving a ten-year sentence and the argument was that
during that ten-year sentence he had no earning power anyhow and so the
tortfeasor need pay no damages. The learned judge said this (10):   **C**

> " I think the plaintiff encountered one of the vicissitudes of life, the
> likelihood of which to a tribunal asked to assess damages would have seemed
> so remote as to be omitted entirely in practice as a material consideration,
> but which, having occurred in fact, must be treated as such."

It follows from this that in assessing the damage suffered by the plaintiff one must   **D**
take into account the fact that before the date of the trial he had suffered the
second accident which resulted in the immediate amputation of his injured
leg. There was no evidence before the court that the second accident caused the
plaintiff a further prospective loss of earnings beyond that which would have been
the prospect if the second misfortune had not occurred. The damages assessable,
therefore, consisted of pain and suffering already undergone and the prospect of   **E**
future deterioration in the left leg and a diminished prospect of earning capacity,
both caused by the first accident. The judge assessed the total damage arising out
of the first accident as £1,600 and there is no quarrel with that, but so far as this
consisted of the prospect of future pain and deterioration in the left leg it was
removed by the second event and could not thereafter be suffered. It seems to
me to follow that the damage to the left leg caused by the first accident did not   **F**
survive the second and that the plaintiff's damages must be confined to the
period before the amputation of the limb.

Counsel for the plaintiff's argument was that if this were the result it would
have the effect of causing the plaintiff to fall between two stools, so to speak, and
to recover less compensation for the two accidents than he would have recovered
for one. There is, I think, a fallacy here. It depends on the view that the second
tortfeasor would only be liable for a diminished amount of compensation because   **G**
the tortfeasor takes his victim as he finds him and had only injured an already
injured leg. I do not think that this is right. The second tortfeasor had injured a
man with a damaged leg, it is true, but that man had not only the damaged leg
but the right to be compensated for the first accident, for which also the second
tortfeasor would be liable to compensate him. In the result I agree with the order   **H**
proposed and would allow the appeal on that footing.

*Appeal allowed. Order below varied by substituting total award of damages of
£351 14s. 9d. Leave to appeal to the House of Lords granted.*

Solicitors: *Michael Stone & Co.* (for the defendant); *Parlett, Kent & Co.* (for
the plaintiff).

[*Reported by* HENRY SUMMERFIELD, ESQ., *Barrister-at-Law.*]   **I**

---

(8) [1903] A.C. 426; [1900-03] All E.R. Rep. 600.
(9) [1903] A.C. at p. 431; [1900-03] All E.R. Rep. at p. 603.
(10) [1955] Q.W.N. 67 at p. 90.

A

Re FLYNN (*deceased*) (No. 2).
FLYNN *v.* FLYNN AND OTHERS.

[CHANCERY DIVISION (Buckley, J.), January 15, 16, 1969.]

B
Limitation of Action—Acknowledgment—Defence in foreign action denying liability—Whether acknowledgment for purposes of Limitation Act—Limitation Act 1939 (2 & 3 *Geo.* 6 c. 21), s. 23 (4).

Administration of Estates—Administration action—Claim based on foreign judgment—Right of successful plaintiff in foreign action to make claim in administration action.

C
The M.G.T. Co. (the company) an American corporation commenced proceedings in New York in October 1958 against the deceased, F., in respect of a sum of $75,000 and interest due under a promissory note held by the company and given by the deceased on 13th June 1957 and due on 13th June 1958. Pleadings were delivered and an answer (a defence) was, in accordance with the practice of the State of New York, verified by an affidavit sworn by the deceased's attorney. The answer admitted the promis-

D
sory note and that no part of the moneys due had been paid but expressly denied that the sum and interest was then due and owing to the company. It was further alleged that the transaction was induced as a result of misrepresentations. In October 1959, the deceased died when the action was still pending. Leave was granted to continue the action against temporary administrators, the plaintiff, the third defendant and G. Summary judgment

E
was granted against the temporary administrators and their appeal was dismissed. In March 1964, a grant of probate in favour of the plaintiff was made in England and an originating summons for the administration of the estate was issued. The third defendant obtained a double grant of probate on 11th May 1964. On 3rd December 1964, an administration order was made in which a direction was included for an account to be taken of any-

F
thing due to the third defendant and all the deceased's creditors. Claims were called for and, in 1966, notice to prove its claim was given to the company for the consideration of its claim and any consequent directions. On the question whether the answer in the New York action amounted to an acknowledgment of the debt within the meaning of s. 23 (4)* of the Limitation Act 1939 so as to prevent the debt being statute-barred or, alternatively,

G
whether the company was entitled to proceed on the New York judgment against the deceased's personal representatives,

Held: (i) there was no sufficient acknowledgment within the meaning of s. 23 (4) because a defence which in effect denied liability, notwithstanding the fact that it had failed, could not be regarded as an acknowledgment (see p. 562, letter D, post);

H
(ii) the company was entitled to put forward a claim in England based on the New York judgment because that judgment did not confine the liability of the deceased's estate to a liability out of assets in New York and, since the personal representatives were parties to the New York proceedings, they were under an implied obligation to satisfy that judgment out of the assets in their hands wherever those assets might be; accordingly, since an

I
administration order had been made the appropriate method for the company to pursue its rights was to put in a claim in the administration action (see p. 563, letters G and H, post).

[As to what constitutes an acknowledgment, see 24 HALSBURY'S LAWS (3rd Edn.) 299-304, paras. 592-600; and for cases on the subject, see 32 DIGEST (Repl.) 413-441, *366-639*.

As to enforcement of foreign judgments, see 7 HALSBURY'S LAWS (3rd Edn.)

---

* Section 23 (4) is set out at p. 560, letter D, post.

140-143, paras. 249-252; and for cases on the subject, see 11 DIGEST (Repl.) **A**
531, *1423-1426*.

For the Limitation Act 1939, s. 23, see 13 HALSBURY'S STATUTES (2nd Edn.)
1184, 1186.]

Cases referred to:

Consolidated Agencies, Ltd. v. Bertram, Ltd., [1964] 3 All E.R. 282; [1965]
    A.C. 470; [1964] 3 W.L.R. 671; Digest (Cont. Vol. B) 499, *380a.   **B**

Dungate v. Dungate, [1965] 3 All E.R. 818; [1965] 1 W.L.R. 1477; Digest
    (Cont. Vol. B) 499, *588a*.

Dupleix v. De Roven (1705), 2 Vern. 540; 23 E.R. 950; 11 Digest (Repl.)
    527, *1396*.

Grant v. Easton (1883), 13 Q.B.D. 302; 53 L.J.Q.B. 68; 49 L.T. 645; 11   **C**
    Digest (Repl.) 527, *1402*.

Grindell v. Bass, [1920] 2 Ch. 487; [1920] All E.R. Rep. 219; 89 L.J.Ch. 591;
    124 L.J. 211; 12 Digest (Repl.) 151, *958*.

Wright v. Pepin, [1954] 2 All E.R. 52; [1954] 1 W.L.R. 635; 32 Digest (Repl.)
    416, *399*.

Adjourned Summons.   **D**

This was a summons dated 27th April 1967, by the applicants, the Morgan
Guaranty Trust Co. of New York, that the claim submitted by them in the
English administration proceedings of the estate of Errol Leslie Thomas Flynn,
deceased, should be further considered and necessary consequential directions
made. The respondents to the summons were Mrs. Patricia Wymore Flynn, the
plaintiff in the administration action, and Justin Merton Golenbock, the third
defendant therein, both of whom were the deceased's personal representatives in   **E**
England.

The cases noted below* were cited during the argument in addition to those
referred to in the judgment.

C. J. Slade, Q.C., and *W. D. Ainger* for Morgan's.
J. W. Mills, Q.C., and *P. G. Clough* for the respondents.   **F**

    BUCKLEY, J.: This is a case which relates to a claim made on an enquiry
as to the debts of a deceased testator under an administration order made by
this court. The deceased, Mr. Errol Leslie Thomas Flynn, died on 14th October
1959. He was a United States citizen but I understand that it has been
determined in proceedings (1) in this country that he died domiciled in Jamaica.
He had, however, property in the State of New York and, on 3rd December 1959,   **G**
a grant of temporary administration of his estate in the State of New York
was granted in that State. That temporary administration order was superseded
on 18th April 1963, by a grant of probate of his will in the State of New York.
The temporary administrators were three in number: they were the plaintiff
in the present proceedings, who is the deceased's widow, the third defendant
in the present proceedings, Mr. Justin Merton Golenbock, who was one of his   **H**
New York lawyers, and a Mr. Grossman.

The probate grant which was made on 18th April 1963, was in favour of
the plaintiff and the third defendant alone. In March 1964, the plaintiff resigned
her office as one of the executors of the deceased's will in New York under the
provisions of the law of that State which, presumably, permit of an executor
resigning his or her office of executor.   **I**

On 19th March 1964, grant of probate was made in the Probate Division of
this court in favour of the plaintiff, and on 20th March 1964, the plaintiff issued
an originating summons for administration of the deceased's estate. On 11th May

---

    * *Finch* v. *Finch* (1876), 45 L.J.Ch. 816; *John Griffiths Cycle Corpn., Ltd.* v. *Humber &*
Co., Ltd., [1899] 2 Q.B. 414; *Farr, Smith & Co., Ltd.* v. *Messers, Ltd.,* [1928] 1 K.B.
397; *Good* v. *Parry,* [1963] 2 All E.R. 59; [1963] 2 Q.B. 418; *Re Flynn (decd.)* [1968]
1 All E.R. 49; [1968] 1 W.L.R. 103.

    (1) See [1968] 1 All E.R. 49; [1968] 1 W.L.R. 103.

A 1964, the third defendant, in respect of whom leave to come in and prove the will had been reserved by the grant of 19th March 1964, obtained a double grant of probate. In the event, the third defendant is now the sole personal representative of the deceased in the State of New York, and the plaintiff and third defendant are the personal representatives of the deceased in this country.

On 3rd December 1964, an administration order was made on the originating
B summons, and that order included a direction for an account to be taken of what, if anything, is due to the third defendant and all other creditors of the testator. Claims were called for in answer to that account and on 5th December 1966, notice to prove its claim was given to the applicant, an American company called Morgan Guaranty Trust Co. of New York (whom I will refer to as " Morgan's ") for the consideration of their claim and any necessary consequential
C directions. The claim is in respect of a sum of $75,000, which was the subject-matter of a transaction in New York, the parties to which were the deceased in his lifetime, a Mr. Huntington Hartford, and Morgan's. In October 1958, Morgan's commenced an action in New York against the deceased to recover that sum and interest alleged to be due under a promissory note given by the deceased on 13th June 1957, in the sum of $75,000 with interest at five per cent.,
D of which Morgan's claimed to be the holders. The complaint, which was Morgan's pleading in that action corresponding to what we would call a statement of claim, was lodged or delivered on 17th November 1958, and on 9th June 1959, an answer on behalf of the deceased was lodged or delivered—that is his pleading corresponding to what we would call his defence—and in accordance with the practice in the State of New York that pleading was verified by an affidavit
E sworn to in this instance by the deceased's attorney, Shack.

Morgan's alleged that on 13th December 1957, for value received the defendant, that is to say, now the deceased, made and delivered to Morgan's his promissory note in writing of that date wherein and whereby he promised to pay to the order of Morgan's six months after date the sum of $75,000 with interest at the rate of five per cent. per annum. They then alleged that Morgan's were the owners
F and holders of the note and that no part of the note had been paid and that there was then due and owing by the deceased to Morgan's thereon the sum of $75,000 with interest from 13th December 1957. The defence to that plea expressly admits that on or about 13th December 1957, the deceased made and delivered to Morgan's a promissory note in writing of that date, as alleged in the complaint, but it denies that it was for value received. The answer also
G admits that no part of the moneys due on the note had been paid, but expressly denies that there was then due and owing to Morgan's by the defendant the sum of $75,000 with interest from 13th December 1957. It then goes on to plead what is called a complete affirmative defence, and the nature of the affirmative defence is that the deceased was induced to enter into the transaction in the way in which he did enter into it as a result of a conspiracy of a fraudulent
H character between Mr. Huntington Hartford and Morgan's and as a result of misrepresentations alleged to have been made to him by them. I think it is right, as has been submitted, that, reading the answer as a whole, it does necessarily infer, although it does not in terms state, that the sum of $75,000 was in fact advanced by Morgan's to the deceased by way of loan.

In October 1959, as I have already mentioned, the deceased died. The action
I was then pending in the New York State court. On 4th April 1961, the Surrogate's Court in New York granted leave to Morgan's to continue their action against the temporary administrators in place of the deceased, and on 31st May 1961, the Supreme Court of the State of New York made an order continuing the action by Morgan's against the temporary administrators, substituting them as defendants in place of the deceased.

On 7th December 1961, summary judgment was granted by the court against the temporary administrators who were refused leave to file and serve a supplemental and amended answer. On 19th December formal judgment was entered

for Morgan's against the temporary administrators for $75,000 plus $17,685   A
interest and $37.45 taxed costs, a total of $92,722.45. The temporary administrators appealed unsuccessfully.   They then sought to re-argue their appeal or
alternatively asked leave to appeal to the Court of Appeal for the State of New
York, again without success.   On 22nd June 1962 on the motion of Morgan's,
the Supreme Court made a further order affirming the judgment of 19th December
1961, and awarding some further costs.   A further attempt to appeal that order   B
was unsuccessful.

The claim by Morgan's in the United Kingdom administration is resisted on
the ground that it is statute-barred.   The sum due on the promissory note became
due on 13th June 1958.   The administration order was made on 3rd December
1964, more than six years after the date when the promissory note became due.
Consequently, unless there was some acknowledgment sufficient to take the case   C
out of the statute between 13th June 1958, and the date of the administration
order and less than six years before the date of the administration order, the
claim was statute-barred.   But it is said that in fact here there was a sufficient
acknowledgment to take the case out of the statute.

The relevant section of the Limitation Act 1939 is s. 23 (4) which provides:

D

" Where any right of action has accrued to recover any debt or other
liquidated pecuniary claim, or any claim to the personal estate of a deceased
person or to any share or interest therein, and the person liable or accountable therefore acknowledges the claim or makes any payment in respect
thereof, the right shall be deemed to have accrued on and not before the
date of the acknowledgment or the last payment: . . .".

E

I need not read the proviso.   Section 24 requires that the acknowledgment shall
be in writing and signed by the person making the acknowledgment, and s. 24 (2)
provides:

" Any such acknowledgment or payment as aforesaid may be made by
the agent of the person by whom it is required to be made under the last   F
foregoing section, and shall be made to the person, or to an agent of the
person, whose title or claim is being acknowledged or, as the case may be,
in respect of whose claim the payment is being made."

The acknowledgment or acknowledgments relied on here are the answer filed in
the New York proceedings and verified by the deceased's attorney's affidavit,
and also the proposed amended answer which was similarly verified and was   G
put forward in July 1961, but which the defendants in those proceedings were
not in fact permitted to file.   The argument before me has been addressed
exclusively to the earlier of those two groups of documents because it is said
that the same considerations apply to both, or much the same considerations
apply to both.   But although no argument has been presented to me in respect
of the proposed amended answer and the verification of it, Morgan's reserve the   H
right to present further argument based on that elsewhere, should this case go
further.

The answer and the affidavit are, of course, in writing.   The affidavit, it is
common ground, bore the orthographic signature of the deceased's attorney,
although the document exhibited to the affidavit in these proceedings, which
is a certified copy supplied by the American court, does not in fact bear that   I
signature.   But I proceed on the footing that the document relied on, so far as
the affidavit is relied on, is a document which bears the signature of the attorney.

The answer itself has at its foot in typewriting the firm name and address of
the firm of attorneys acting for the deceased in the New York proceedings.   If
these documents can be relied on as an acknowledgment for the relevant purpose
they appear to me clearly to satisfy the requirements of s. 24 (1), that the
acknowledgment " shall be in writing and signed by the person making the

A acknowledgment ", bearing in mind that s. 24 (2) states that the " acknowledgment . . . may be made by the agent of the person by whom it is required to be made ".

The question of some difficulty, perhaps—at any rate, it seems to be an original question in the absence of authority in this court—is whether a pleading of this nature, which denies liability, can nevertheless amount to an acknowledg-

B ment for the purposes of the Act. As I have said, the answer in para. 3 expressly denies the allegation in para. 4 of the complaint to the effect that " there is now due and owing to the plaintiff thereon [that is to say, on the promissory note] from the defendant the sum of 75,000 dollars with interest thereon from December 13, 1957 ". Moreover it is clear that the answer is directed to establishing that the deceased was not liable on the promissory note. The pleading and the case

C put forward in the pleading were in the event unavailing, for Morgan's recovered judgment in the proceedings, but it does not seem to me that that can have any bearing on the question whether this pleading amounts to an acknowledgment for the purposes of the Act.

I have been referred to cases which show that, for the purposes of the Statute of Frauds 1677 or of the Sale of Goods Act 1893, material found in pleadings

D delivered in litigation has been treated as material affording sufficient note or memorandum or recognition of the terms of the bargain between the parties for the purposes of those Acts, and it is contended that similar principles must apply under the Limitation Act 1939, and that if one finds an acknowledgment sufficient to satisfy the requirements of the Act in a pleading signed by some agent of the party concerned who was signing the pleading within his authority,

E that must be sufficient to satisfy the requirements of the Act. I have not been referred to any case in which a pleading has in fact afforded an acknowledgment for the purposes of the limitation of actions, but HARMAN, J., appears to have felt no doubt in *Wright* v. *Pepin* (2) that similar sorts of considerations would apply to cases under the Limitation Act 1939 as apply to cases under the Statute of Frauds 1677 or the statutory provisions which have now replaced the Statute of

F Frauds 1677, for in the course of his judgment he referred to *Grindell* v. *Bass* (3), which was a Statute of Frauds case.

In considering whether a pleading does in fact contain an acknowledgment one has obviously got to read the document as a whole and construe it in accordance with the ordinary rules of construction to see what its language means. Counsel for Morgan's has contended that the pleading in this case

G contains admissions of all the relevant facts necessary to be established to make good the liability of the deceased to Morgan's; and that that is sufficient, he says, to amount to an acknowledgment for the purposes of the Act.

In *Wright* v. *Pepin* (4) to which I have already made reference, HARMAN, J., said:

H   " All that is necessary, as it seems to me, for an acknowledgment which takes the case out of the statute is that the debtor should recognise the existence of the debt, or that the person who might rely on the statute should recognise the rights against himself."

And in *Dungate* v. *Dungate* (5) DIPLOCK, L.J., delivering the leading judgment of the Court of Appeal said:

I   " There is clear authority that an acknowledgment under the Limitation Act 1939, need not identify the amount of the debt and may acknowledge a general indebtedness, provided that the amount of the debt can be ascertained by extraneous evidence."

Counsel for the respondents to the present summons, referred me to a case in

(2) [1954] 2 All E.R. 52; [1954] 1 W.L.R. 635.
(3) [1920] 2 Ch. 487; [1920] All E.R. Rep. 219.
(4) [1954] 2 All E.R. at p. 55; [1954] 1 W.L.R. at p. 640.
(5) [1965] 3 All E.R. 818 at p. 820; [1965] 1 W.L.R. 1477 at p. 1487.

the Privy Council, *Consolidated Agencies, Ltd.* v. *Bertram Ltd.* (6), as authority **A**
for the proposition that the acknowledgment to be effective for the purposes of
the Act must be an acknowledgment of an existing liability; and, in my judgment,
the authorities do establish the principle that the acknowledgment properly
interpreted must be an acknowledgment of liability on the part of the person
making the acknowledgment and not merely an acknowledgment of certain facts
which, taken in isolation, would give rise to a liability but which are alleged by **B**
the person who is said to have given an acknowledgment not to give rise to a
liability by reason of other surrounding circumstances. Counsel for Morgan's
has contended that where one has a pleading in the nature of confession and
avoidance, the confession can be taken as being an acknowledgment for the
purposes of the Act, the avoidance being disregarded; but in my judgment that
cannot be right. The whole burden of the pleading relied on in the present case **C**
is that the deceased was not liable to Morgan's. It is true that one finds in the
pleading an admission that the deceased gave the promissory note and that no
part of the moneys referred to in it have been paid, and I am satisfied also that
by implication one must find in the document an indication that Morgan's
advanced $75,000 to the deceased by way of loan. Nevertheless, the whole
purpose of the defence is to say that, notwithstanding those circumstances, **D**
liability is denied. Although the grounds relied on for denying liability carried
no weight with the New York court, it seems to me impossible in those circumstances to treat that document as being an acknowledgment of the debt.
Accordingly, in my opinion, no reliance can be placed on that answer or on the
confirmatory affidavit which verified it as amounting to an acknowledgment for
the purposes of s. 23 of the Limitation Act 1939. **E**

The case is put on an alternative ground in this way: it is said that even if
the original cause of action on the promissory note is statute-barred, nevertheless
Morgan's are entitled to succeed because the judgments recovered in the New
York court are judgments on which they are entitled to proceed in this country.
Where a judgment is obtained in a foreign court the cause of action does not
merge in the judgment. Thereafter the successful party can either re-litigate his **F**
original cause of action in this jurisdiction or he can bring an action in this
jurisdiction on the foreign judgment, those being, as I understand the law, two
distinct causes of action available to him in this country; and it would seem
that an action brought on the foreign judgment is an action which proceeds on
the basis of an implied contract to pay on the part of the party against whom
the judgment has been recovered. **G**

In *Grant* v. *Easton* (7), SIR BALIOL BRETT, M.R., at the end of his judgment
said:

"An action upon a foreign judgment may be treated as an action in
either debt or assumpsit; the liability of the defendant arises upon the
implied contract to pay the amount of the foreign judgment."

Where the judgment is recovered against a man in his lifetime and he then dies **H**
there seems to me to be no difficulty in the way of a party who obtains that
judgment making a claim in an English administration on the basis that at the
time of his death the deceased was a debtor on the foreign judgment, quite
apart from any liability under which he may have been in relation to the original
cause of action. Some confirmation of that view is to be obtained from the
very early case of *Dupleix* v. *De Roven* (8) although in that particular case the **I**
claim was held to be statute-barred.

The difficulty which arises in the present case results from the circumstance
that although the action in the New York courts was commenced in the lifetime
of the deceased, he died before judgment and the judgment was recovered in an
action to which he was not a party but to which the temporary administrators

(6) [1964] 3 All E.R. 282; [1965] A.C. 470.   (7) (1883), 13 Q.B.D. 302 at p. 303.
(8) (1705), 2 Vern. 540.

A of his estate in the State of New York were the defendants. The way in which this part of the case has been put by counsel for Morgan's is that the finding of the New York court was to the effect that the deceased was under a liability in his lifetime and that the English court should pay due regard to this finding of the New York court and should recognise that liability as having been a debt of the deceased at his death; or, at any rate, as being a debt which is a liability

B of the deceased's estate. He contends that on principle there ought to be no difference between the case where judgment is recovered against the deceased in his lifetime and the case where judgment is recovered after the deceased's death but in respect of a cause of action existing before he died and, at any rate in this case, a cause of action on which proceedings had been commenced in his lifetime. He says that it would be an extraordinary thing if the position could

C be affected by the fact that the testator died, it may be, the day before the judgment was delivered. That, of course, was not the position in the present case, but that is the way in which the argument was presented.

On the other hand, counsel for the respondents, defending the estate of the testator in the administration in this country, has submitted that what Morgan's have to show is that the debt in question is a debt due in accordance with

D English law, that a foreign judgment gives rise to a cause of action in this jurisdiction only on the basis of an implied promise on behalf of the person against whom the judgment is recovered to pay the amount of the judgment debt, that in the circumstances of this case there is no room for implying a promise by the deceased that he would pay the amount of the judgment debt and that the only liability of the deceased at his death was the liability in respect

E of the original cause of action on the promissory note and that is statute-barred. He contends that there is no room here for any implied promise on the part of the temporary administrators in New York to pay this judgment debt out of any assets of the estate other than assets administered in the State of New York, which was the full extent to which they could be made liable in their capacity as temporary administrators of the deceased's estate in New York.

F The judgment which I think is plainly relevant here is that whereby it was adjudged that Morgan's should recover from the third defendant, the plaintiff and Mr. Grossman as temporary administrators of the goods, chattels and credits of the deceased, the sum of $75,000 and interest and costs. That is the judgment of 19th December 1961. There is nothing in that judgment which in terms confines the liability of the estate of the deceased to

G a liability out of assets in the State of New York. The only parties who could then be sued representing the estate of the deceased in the State of New York were the temporary administrators. They were the only persons who had any status to represent the testator's estate in that jurisdiction. It is perfectly true that they could only be made liable to the extent that they might have assets in their hands or coming to them as temporary administrators in the State of

H New York, but the judgment proceeds, as I understand it, on the basis that the liability is the liability of the estate of the testator generally. It so happens that the two personal representatives of the deceased in this country, the plaintiff and the third defendant, were parties to those proceedings, and it seems to me that in those circumstances they should be regarded as under an implied obligation to satisfy that judgment out of assets of the deceased's estate in their hands

I or under their control wherever those assets may be, and not only out of assets in the State of New York.

It seems to me, therefore, in those circumstances that, had there not been an administration order, Morgan's could have sued them in this country on the basis of an implied promise to pay, and the fact that an administration order has been made merely means that Morgan's appropriate method of pursuing their rights in this country is by way of putting in a claim in the administration action and not by issuing a writ and suing in that way.

Accordingly I think that, consequent on the judgments in the New York proceedings, Morgan's are in a position to put forward a claim based not on the original cause of action arising on the promissory note but a claim based on the American judgment, and that claim is clearly not statute-barred. On that ground I think that Morgan's are entitled to be admitted as creditors of the estate.

Order accordingly.

Solicitors: *Herbert Oppenheimer, Nathan & Vandyk* (for Morgan's); *Clifford-Turner & Co.* (for the respondents).

[*Reported by* ROSALIE LONG, *Barrister-at-Law.*]

DORSET YACHT CO., LTD. *v.* HOME OFFICE.

[COURT OF APPEAL, CIVIL DIVISION (Lord Denning, M.R., Edmund Davies and Phillimore, L.JJ.), February 12, 13, 14, March 10, 1969.]

Negligence—Duty to take care—Open borstal institution—Escaped boys damage yacht—To whom duty owed.

Ten boys from an open borstal institution were taken by three officers to an island for a training exercise. They were quartered in an empty house. During the night seven boys got out, boarded a yacht and damaged her. The owners sued the Home Office for damages for negligence and alleged that there was no proper supervision of the boys. On the preliminary issue whether the prison officers owed only a duty to the Crown and not to the plaintiff.

Held: the Home Office, their servants and agents, owed a duty of care to those in the neighbourhood, and that duty was capable of giving rise to a liability in damages.

Per LORD DENNING, M.R.: An action does not lie except on proof of negligence. It is not negligence to keep an open borstal, nor to let the boys have a great deal of freedom. The prison authorities are only negligent if, within that system, they do not take such care and supervision as a reasonable person, operating such a system, would take. It is one of the risks of the system—a conscious and deliberate risk—that boys will sometimes escape and do damage. So the fact that boys escape and do damage is no evidence of negligence. There must be proof of something more.

Appeal dismissed.

[As to vicarious liability of Secretary of State for the acts of his agents, see 30 HALSBURY'S LAWS (3rd Edn.) 573, 574, para. 1092.]

Cases referred to:

Carmarthenshire County Council v. *Lewis*, [1955] 1 All E.R. 565; [1955] A.C. 549; [1955] 2 W.L.R. 517; 119 J.P. 230; Digest (Cont. Vol. A) 1168, *569a.*

Cassidy v. *Ministry of Health*, [1951] 1 All E.R. 574; [1951] 2 K.B. 343; 33 Digest (Repl.) 534, *112.*

D'Arcy v. *Prison Comrs.* (1955), The Times, 15th, 16th, 17th November.

Deyong v. *Shenburn*, [1946] 1 All E.R. 226; [1946] K.B. 227; 115 L.J.K.B. 262; 174 L.T. 129; 34 Digest (Repl.) 144, *987.*

Ellis v. *Home Office*, [1953] 2 All E.R. 149; [1953] 2 Q.B. 135; [1953] 3 W.L.R. 105; Digest (Cont. Vol. A) 1167, *564a.*

Greenwell v. *Prison Comrs.* (1951), 101 L.T. 486.

Hedley Byrne & Co., Ltd. v. *Heller & Partners, Ltd.*, [1963] 2 All E.R. 575; [1964] A.C. 465; [1963] W.L.R. 101; Digest (Cont. Vol. A) 51, *1117a*

Holgate v. *Lancashire Mental Hospitals Board, Gill and Robertson*, [1937] 4 All E.R. 19; 33 Digest (Repl.) 711, *1679.*

Jones v. *Pope* (1666), 1 Wms. Saund. 37; 85 E.R. 49; 41 Digest (Repl.) 109, *460.*

Macrae v. *Clarke* (1866), L.R. 1 C.P. 403; 35 L.J.C.P. 247; 14 L.T. 408; 41 Digest (Repl.) 108, *457.*

A   *Richardson* v. *Mellish* (1824), 2 Bing. 229; [1824-34] All E.R. Rep. 258; 3 L.J.O.S.C.P. 265; 130 E.R. 294; 22 Digest (Repl.) 343, *3668.*

Roe v. *Ministry of Health*, [1954] 2 All E.R. 131; [1954] 2 Q.B. 66; [1954] 2 W.L.R. 915; 33 Digest (Repl.) 533, *107.*

Smith v. *Leurs* (1945), 70 C.L.R. 256.

Stansbie v. *Troman*, [1948] 1 All E.R. 599; [1948] 2 K.B. 48; [1948] L.J.R.
B   1206; 36 Digest (Repl.) 21, *87.*

Thorne and Rowe v. *State of Western Australia*, [1964] W.A.R. 147; Digest (Cont. Vol. B) 603, **60a.*

Weld-Blundell v. *Stephens*, [1920] A.C. 956; [1920] All E.R. Rep. 32; 89 L.J.K.B. 705; 123 L.T. 593; 36 Digest (Repl.) 201, *1064.*

Williams v. *New York State* (1955), 127 N.E.R. (2d) 545.

C   **Appeal.**

This was an appeal by the defendants, the Home Office, from the judgment of THESIGER, J., given on a preliminary point of law on 19th December 1968, holding that on the facts pleaded in the statement of claim the defendants, their servants or agents, owed a duty of care to the Dorset Yacht Co., Ltd., the plaintiff, capable of giving rise to a liability in damages with respect to the
D   detention of persons undergoing sentences of borstal training or with respect to the manner in which such persons were treated, employed, disciplined, controlled or supervised whilst undergoing such sentences. The facts are set out in the judgment of LORD DENNING, M.R.

The Attorney-General (Sir Elwyn Jones, Q.C.), Gordon Slynn and *L. J. Blom-Cooper* for the Home Office.
E   *W. A. Macpherson* and *M. F. Harris* for the plaintiffs.

Cur. adv. vult.

10th March.   The following judgments were read.

LORD DENNING, M.R.: In September 1962, the motor yacht " Silver Mist " was lying at moorings in Poole Harbour. No one was on her. But in
F   the middle of the night seven borstal boys got aboard her. They cast her adrift and did much damage. The cost of repairs was £1,303 1s. 8d. Fortunately the owners of the yacht had insured her. The insurance company paid the damage. They now seek to recover the amount from the Home Office. They sue, of course, in the name of the owners of the yacht, the Dorset Yacht Co., Ltd.; and the case must be determined just as if the yacht was not insured. But, in point of fact,
G   it is the insurance company who seek to be recouped for the expense.

Speaking in the name of the owners of the yacht, the insurance company say that there was no proper supervision of the boys. They were all from the borstal institution at Portland. They were seven out of a party of ten boys. They had been taken out by three officers of the institution to Brownsea Island in Poole Harbour. They were on a training exercise. They were quartered in an empty
H   house. The three officers went to bed. So did the ten boys. But during the night seven of the boys got out and did this damage. As might be expected, being in borstal, they had criminal convictions for breaking and entering premises, larceny, and taking away vehicles without the owners' consent. Five of them had previously escaped from borstal, but had been recaptured. The plaintiffs say that in these circumstances the three officers ought to have taken precautions
I   to prevent their escaping; and that they were negligent in not doing so; and the Home Office, being responsible for these officers, ought to pay for the damage they did.

The case has not yet been tried. It comes before us on this preliminary issue of law:

" Whether on the facts pleaded in the statement of claim, the Home Office, their servants or agents owed any duty of care to the [plaintiffs] capable of giving rise to a liability in damages with respect to the detention of persons undergoing sentences of borstal training, or with respect to the manner in

which such persons were treated, employed, disciplined, controlled or **A**
supervised whilst undergoing such sentences."

Although the issue is only stated in regard to borstal training, it involves the
wider question of whether the Home Office are liable for damage done by
prisoners who escape from custody or done by them whilst on parole. Strangely
enough there is no authority on it in any of our law books. Nor is there much
light thrown on it by the judges of the great countries overseas which follow **B**
the common law. At any rate, none of particular value was drawn to our attention. There is only a case in the Ipswich County Court some 18 years ago when
the Prison Commissioners were held liable for £26 worth of damages done by a
borstal boy (*Greenwell* v. *Prison Comrs.* (1)). Why is there no authority on it?
I believe that it is simply because, until recently, no lawyer ever thought such
an action would lie. Take a simple instance. Suppose a warder carelessly forgot **C**
to lock the door of a cell, and in consequence a prisoner escaped and broke into a
neighbouring house. A lawyer in former times would have scouted the idea
that an action lay. He would reject it on one of two grounds. First, he would
say that the damage was too remote. The chain of causation was snapped by
the prisoner's own act. His breaking into the house was a novus actus interveniens. See *Weld-Blundell* v. *Stevens* (2), per LORD SUMNER. Secondly, he **D**
would say that the warder owed no duty of care to the householder. His duty
lay only to the Crown. The lawyer would re-inforce this argument by reference
to the old action for an " escape " from prison. It was in the days when there
was imprisonment for debt. If the sheriff allowed the debtor to escape from
prison, the creditor could at common law sue the sheriff for the amount of the
debt, see *Jones* v. *Pope* (3), and afterwards, by statute for damages sustained **E**
by reason of the escape, see *Macrae* v. *Clarke* (4). But the action lay only by the
creditor; for it was only to him that the sheriff owed a duty; and not to any one
else.

But those two answers have been rudely shaken by recent developments.
First, so far as remoteness is concerned, the wicked act of a criminal no longer
snaps the chain of causation. If it could reasonably have been foreseen, it is **F**
not regarded as a novus actus interveniens. Thus in *Stansbie* v. *Troman* (5) a
decorator left the house unlocked, with the result that a thief walked in and
stole jewellery. The decorator was held liable because damage of that kind
could reasonably be foreseen. Likewise it seems to follow that, if a warder has
charge of a notorious housebreaker, and carelessly forgets to lock the cell door,
it can reasonably be foreseen that he will escape and break into neighbouring **G**
houses. So the damage is not too remote.

Second, so far as duty is concerned, the duty of care is owed not only to the
Crown. It is owed to others as well. There have been cases where a violent
prisoner has attacked another prisoner within the prison walls. It has been
held that, if the prison authorities have not taken proper care to control or
supervise the violent prisoner, so as to prevent his doing damage, they are **H**
liable to the one who is injured. In *Ellis* v. *Home Office* (6) in the hospital wing
of Winchester prison, a warder opened the door of a cubicle, and went off. A
violent prisoner called Hammill, who was a mental defective, walked out of his
cubicle and brutally assaulted Ellis, another prisoner. It was accepted by
DEVLIN, J., and by this court that the prison authorities owed a duty of care
to Ellis. DEVLIN, J., said (7): **I**

" This case . . . turns entirely on the cardinal fact whether the prison
doctor had any reason to believe that Hammill, a mental defective, was
likely to commit violence."

(1) (1951), 101 L.T. 486.
(2) [1920] A.C. 956 at p. 986; [1920] All E.R. Rep. 32 at p. 47.
(3) (1666), 1 Wms. Saund. 37.   (4) (1866), L.R. 1 C.P. 403.
(5) [1948] 1 All E.R. 599; [1948] 2 K.B. 48.
(6) [1953] 2 All E.R. 149; [1953] 2 Q.B. 135.
(7) [1953] 2 All E.R. at p. 155; [1953] 2 Q.B. at p. 137.

A In short, on foreseeability of damage. Similarly in *D'Arcy* v. *Prison Comrs.* (8).
Those cases were accepted by the Attorney-General as being correct. But, if
so, I do not see where he can stop. Suppose the violent prisoner had struck,
not a fellow prisoner, but a visiting magistrate. Surely the magistrate could
recover. And why should it be confined to violence within the prison walls?
Suppose a party of prisoners is taken out to work on a farm alongside farm-

B workers, but they are not properly supervised. A violent prisoner strikes first
another prisoner and next a farmworker. If the other prisoner has a cause of
action against the prison authorities, surely the farmworker has also. And why
should it stop there? If the violent prisoner makes his way to the nearest village,
and breaks in and assaults a householder, or steals his goods, surely the
householder too can recover.

C   These recent developments compel us to examine the whole question. It is,
I think, at bottom a matter of public policy which we, as judges, must resolve.
This talk of " duty " or " no duty " is simply a way of limiting the range of
liability for negligence. LORD PEARCE made that clear in *Hedley Byrne & Co.,
Ltd.* v. *Heller and Partners, Ltd.* (9), when he said:

D   " The law of negligence has been deliberately limited in its range by the
courts' insistence that there can be no actionable negligence in vacuo without
the existence of some duty to the plaintiff. For it would be impracticable to
grant relief to everybody who suffers damage through the carelessness of
another . . . How wide the sphere of the duty of care in negligence is to be
laid depends ultimately on the courts' assessment of the demands of
society for protection from the carelessness of others."

E What then is the right policy for the judges to adopt? On whom should the
risk of negligence fall? Up till now it has fallen on the innocent victim. Many,
many a time has a prisoner escaped—or been let out on parole—and done
damage. But there is never a case in our law books when the prison authorities
have been liable for it. No householder who has been burgled, no person who has
been wounded by a criminal, has ever recovered damages from the prison

F authorities; such as to find a place in the reports. The householder has claimed
on his insurance company. The injured man can now claim on the compensation
fund. None has claimed against the prison authorities.

     Should we alter all this? I should be reluctant to do so if, by so doing, we
should hamper all the good work being done by our prison authorities. " Open "
prisons are the order of the day. So is the parole system. The men are allowed

G their freedom as much as possible. It helps to fit them better for their return to
society. This is especially the case with borstal institutions. The Attorney-
General, speaking for the Home Office, said: " We want to train these boys
to become good citizens. We put them under no restraint quite deliberately.
We trust them. We leave them free to escape. It is the way in which they

H learn responsibility." The Attorney-General went so far as to suggest that,
if the Home Office were to be liable for their escape, they might have to close
these open borstals. That would be a great disservice to society at large.

     I can see the force of this argument. But I do not think it should prevail.
I think that the officers of borstal institutions should be liable for negligence.
And the reason I say this is because of the people who live in the neighbourhood.
When the authorities open a borstal institution, those living nearby are surely

I entitled to expect that reasonable care will be taken to protect them. Their
confidence in the law would be undermined if the judges were to declare that the
authorities owed no duty of care to them. Test it by a possible case which is
by no means extravagant. Suppose the authorities know that some of the boys,
with housebreaking records, are planning to escape, and have collected implements
to break into houses, and yet they do nothing to stop the boys. They do not

(8) (1955), The Times, 15th, 16th, 17th November.
(9) [1963] 2 All E.R. 575 at pp. 613, 615; [1964] A.C. 465 at pp. 534, 536.

even take away the implements. Everybody in the neighbourhood would say   A
that the authorities had failed in their duty and ought to pay for the damage.
So would I.

And I think that we should not be too fearful of the consequences. I well
remember that, after the courts made hospital authorities liable for negligence
(as was done in *Cassidy* v. *Ministry of Health* (10)) it was thought to have put a
brake on efficiency. But the balance was restored in *Roe* v. *Ministry of Health* (11)   B
when it was made clear that the courts would not condemn as negligence that
which was only misadventure. So also with borstal institutions. Eighteen
years ago in the case of *Greenwell* v. *Prison Comrs.* (12) the Prison Commissioners
were made liable for the escape of a borstal boy called Lawrence. He had five
times been before the court for larceny and storebreaking. He was making his
fourth escape from an open borstal. He took with him a companion and smashed   C
up the car of Sir Peter Greenwell. JUDGE WHITMEE in the Ipswich County Court
held the Prison Commissioners liable. We have a transcript of his judgment.
He said:

> " Having regard to the great number of escapes taking place, to the crime
> being committed, and particularly to Lawrence's record of previous escapes,
> I cannot think it was reasonable to have this boy in this Institution under   D
> no restraint whatever so that he could as easily escape for the fourth time
> as he had done on previous occasions."

That case was widely reported at the time. The Prison Commissioners did not
appeal. It has found its place in the textbooks. Yet it had not hindered the
Home Office in pursuing their good policy of allowing the boys as much freedom
as possible.   E

The Attorney-General said something about the borstal institutions being
set up under statute; and that, as the statute did not give a remedy, an injured
person had none. I cannot agree with this at all. The statute may be the basis
of a borstal system but it is the common law which builds on the statute. It
says that those in authority are to use due care to train the boys, to discipline
and control them, and to supervise them. If they fail, in circumstances in which   F
it could reasonably be foreseen that the boys might escape and do damage,
they must pay for the damage.

But I wish to say this: an action does not lie except on proof of negligence.
It is not negligence to keep an open borstal, nor to let the boys have a great
deal of freedom. The prison authorities are only negligent if, within that system,
they do not take such care and supervision as a reasonable person, operating   G
such a system, would take. It is one of the risks of the system—a conscious and
deliberate risk—that boys will sometimes escape and do damage. So the fact
that boys escape and do damage is no evidence of negligence. There must be
proof of something more. An error of judgment will not do. There must be
something which can genuinely be regarded as blameworthy. Knowing the
high standard of the officers and staff of the borstal system, I do not think   H
there will be many claims of this sort; or, at any rate, not many which will
succeed.

My answer to the preliminary issue is that the Home Office, their servants
and agents did owe a duty of care to those in the neighbourhood, and that that
duty was capable of giving rise to a liability in damages. I would dismiss this
appeal.   I

EDMUND DAVIES, L.J.: The submissions made on behalf of the Home
Office by the Attorney-General have (as one would expect) the great merit of
being completely unambiguous. They may be summarised in this way: I. To
create a legal duty of care it is not sufficient simply to say that it behoves those

(10) [1951] 1 All E.R. 574; [1951] 2 K.B. 343.
(11) [1954] 2 All E.R. 131; [1954] 2 Q.B. 66.
(12) (1951), 101 L.T. 486,

A charged with negligence to be careful in their behaviour lest harm befalls others if they are not careful. II. No matter how blameworthy a borstal staff may be in the course of their work, they owe no duty to outsiders and there is accordingly no liability in the Home Office for anything done by escapees to third parties or their property. III. Public policy demands that no action in negligence should lie against the Home Office where borstal inmates escape and do damage.

B IV. The law knows no such tort as that of negligence in carrying out statutory duties where the relevant statutory provisions do not themselves give rise to a claim in damages if they are breached.

Some of these submissions may be dealt with more briefly than others. Submission I is unchallengeable. As LORD PEARCE said in *Hedley Byrne & Co., Ltd. v. Heller and Partners, Ltd.* (13):

C " The law of negligence has been deliberately limited in its range by the courts' insistence that there can be no actionable negligence in vacuo without the existence of some duty to the plaintiff."

In the earlier case of *Deyong* v. *Shenburn* (14) to which the Attorney-General made reference, DU PARCQ, L.J., said:

D " It is not true to say that wherever a man finds himself in such a position that unless he does a certain act another person may suffer, or that if he does something another person will suffer, then it is his duty in the one case to be careful to do the act and in the other . . . not to do the act. Any such proposition is much too wide."

The warning is important, and the Attorney-General is undoubtedly right in E stressing that it constantly needs to be borne in mind in dealing with the issues raised by this appeal.

But submission II involves questions of a far more debatable nature. The Attorney-General takes as his sheet-anchor the statement of DIXON, J., in *Smith* v. *Leurs* (15)—a case entirely different in its facts from those now under consideration—that,

F " It is . . . exceptional to find in the law a duty to control another's actions to prevent harm to strangers. The general rule is that one man is under no duty of controlling another man to prevent his doing damage to a third."

They acknowledge, however, that there are established exceptions to that general rule and, indeed, DIXON, J., had earlier said (16):

G " . . . apart from vicarious responsibility, one man may be responsible to another for the harm done to the latter by a third person; he may be responsible on the ground that the act of the third person could not have taken place but for his own fault or breach of duty. There is more than one description of duty the breach of which may produce this consequence . . . It may even be a duty of care with reference to the control of actions or H conduct of the third person."

One of the exceptions to the general rule instanced by DIXON, J., himself was that (16):

" . . . it is incumbent upon a parent who maintains control over a young child to take reasonable care so to exercise that control as to avoid conduct I on his part exposing the person or property of others to unreasonable danger."

Other exceptions suggested by the Attorney-General are: principal and agent; master and servant; and joint tortfeasors. But, while recognising that " the categories of negligence are never closed ", he submits that the " general rule "

(13) [1963] 2 All E.R. 575 at p. 613; [1964] A.C. 465 at p. 534.
(14) [1946] 1 All E.R. 226 at p. 229; [1946] K.B. 227 at p. 233.
(15) (1945), 70 C.L.R. 256 at p. 262.
(16) (1945), 70 C.L.R. at pp. 261, 262.

propounded by DIXON, J., has the effect of rendering the Home Office, however A
blameworthy the conduct of borstal administrators or staff, not liable for any
damage done by inmates who escape from their control.

Put in that bald way, the submission appears at first sight a startling one.
No decision was cited in its support and we have to consider whether, both on
general principle and in the light of such authorities as exist, it can indeed be
sustained. In *Carmarthenshire County Council* v. *Lewis* (17) the House of Lords B
held that, not only did the education authorities owe a duty to their pupils of
very tender years to protect them from injury through wandering on the highway,
but that they also owed a duty to other users of the highway who might be
endangered as a consequence. Describing the latter issue as " one of novelty
and general importance ", LORD REID said (18):

> " If the appellants [the education authority] are right, it means that, no C
> matter how careless the person in charge of a young child may be and no
> matter how obvious it may be that the child may stray into a busy street
> and cause an accident, yet that person is under no liability for damage to
> others caused solely by the action of the child, because his *only* duty is towards
> the child under his care. There appears to be no reported case of an action
> of this kind, and the appellants say that this indicates that no one has D
> hitherto supposed that such an action would lie, for there must have been
> many instances of the driver of a vehicle suffering damage caused by a
> young child running in front of it."

It might, however, be urged that that decision turned on the nature and extent
of the duties owed by the school authorities who stood in loco parentis. But
no such explanation can be invoked in relation to the several decisions regarding E
the position of prison authorities and relating to wrongs done by those committed
to their charge. Thus, in *Ellis* v. *Home Office* (19) where one prisoner attacked
a fellow-prisoner while in the hospital wing of Winchester Prison, SINGLETON,
L.J., said:

> " The duty on those responsible for one of Her Majesty's prisons is to take F
> reasonable care for the safety of those who are within, and that includes
> those who are within against their wish or will, of whom the plaintiff was one.
> If it is proved that supervision is lacking, and that accused persons have
> access to instruments, and that an incident occurs of a kind such as might
> by anticipated, I think it may well be said that those who are responsible
> for the good government of the prison have failed to take reasonable care for G
> the safety of those under their care."

Two years later, in *D'Arcy* v. *Prison Comrs.* (20), a case similar in its facts, the
defendants accepted that they had to take reasonable care for the safety of their
prisoners, and they did not appeal from a jury's verdict awarding damages to
the plaintiff, a prisoner who had been attacked by three fellow-prisoners inside
Parkhurst.   H

The Attorney-General rightly stressed that the foregoing cases all relate to
incidents occurring while the injured was *in detention*, and he accepts a duty
of reasonable care towards them and also to all staff and visitors lawfully within
the prison. But he disclaims the existence of *any* duty to any third party once
the prisoner is no longer in detention, although he conceded that it might well
extend to cover the activities of prisoners outside the prison walls while in I
transit or in a working party engaged, for example, in field work. Accordingly,
so he submits, there is no liability owed for harm done by an escaped prisoner,
no matter how great the negligence which facilitated his escape. Can such a
distinction properly be drawn? Is it the case that the Home Office could be held

---

(17) [1955] 1 All E.R. 565; [1955] A.C. 549.
(18) [1955] 1 All E.R. at p. 572; [1955] A.C. at p. 565.
(19) [1953] 2 All E.R. 149 at p. 154.
(20) (1955), The Times, 15th, 16th, 17th November.

A responsible for acts done by a prisoner while still a member of a working party
but are free from all liability in respect of his acts done to people half-a-mile
away after he has made his escape, thanks to the negligence of his supervisors?
Thorne and Rowe v. *State of Western Australia* (21) affords not even persuasive
authority for saying that in the Commonwealth that question is regarded as
demanding an affirmative answer.   There a prisoner escaped and attacked his

B wife and a man who came to her assistance.   But while the State was absolved,
NEGUS, J., did *not* hold that no duty could be owed to Mrs. Thorne.   On the
contrary, what he said was that mere breach of the warder's duty to the Crown
to keep prisoners in safe custody could not give the plaintiffs a right of action,
and that, in order to succeed (22):

C "The plaintiffs must establish that they had a special duty to Mrs. Thorne
and failed in that duty.   The existence of such a special duty . . . depends
on their knowledge that Thorne had a propensity and intention or was likely
to attack his wife."

In *Williams* v. *New York State* (23) K. was a prisoner who had been assigned
to minimum-security farm work as a privilege for good conduct.   He escaped,
owing to the negligence of his warders, and, being armed, threatened a man,

D who became so frightened that he died of a brain haemorrhage.   The Court of
Appeals absolved the defendants from a claim made on behalf of the estate,
not, as it would seem, on the ground that no duty was owed, but because: (i)
even if negligent in permitting the escape, the State could not have foreseen
that it would lead to injury; and (ii) public policy required that the State be

E not held liable in such circumstances.
So much for decisions in other places.   But at home we have had a decision
directly in point which has stood unappealed and, as far as we have been told,
uncriticised for 18 years, although it has been widely noted in the textbooks
and in 68 Law Quarterly Review 18.   *Greenwell* v. *Prison Comrs.* (24) has been
already dealt with in detail by LORD DENNING, M.R., and it is sufficient for me
to say that in its basic facts it appears indistinguishable from the present case.

F There, too, damage was done to *property* by an escaped borstal boy who was
known to have escaped several times before; and there, too, it was submitted
that the defendants owed no duty to the plaintiff whose property had been
injured.   But, holding the defendants liable, His Honour JUDGE WHITMEE said:

"The Defendants do not, as a matter of law, have to maintain ' open '

G Borstal Institutions.   Therefore, if they elect, for whatever good reasons, to
do so, they must take such reasonable precautions as a prudent man would
do in the running and management of their Institutions."

Was that decision right?   The Attorney-General submits otherwise, but, subject
to the other matters to which I must now turn, he does not adduce any
convincing reason why it should not now be followed.

H Submission III is, to my way of thinking, the most formidable of those advanced
by the Home Office.   The Attorney-General has forcibly urged that, the aim of
the borstal scheme of training being increasingly that of reformation and not
simple detention, public policy demands that those administering such institutions
should not go in fear of civil claims lest, when delicate and difficult decisions
regarding treatment and supervision arise, they happen to arrive at a wrong

I decision.   In a most helpful excursus on the 60-year old borstal system, the
Attorney-General stressed that the keynote of the training provided, as expressed
in r. 1 (1) of the Borstal Rules 1964 (25), is that of requiring—

" . . . that every inmate, while conforming to the rules necessary for well-
ordered community life, shall be able to develop his individuality on right
lines with a proper sense of personal responsibility."

(21) [1964] W.A.R. 147.   (22) [1964] W.A.R. at p. 151.
(23) (1955), 127 N.E.R. (2d) 545.   (24) (1951), 101 L.T. 486.
                    (25) S.I. 1964 No. 387.

A

It is urged that, to attain this purpose, risks have to be taken, at times security and supervision being reduced to the minimum, and that the whole rehabilitative scheme (which modern penology commends in the public interest as well as in that of the borstal inmates themselves) would be stultified if an action for negligence lay against their administrators.

These are formidable considerations, and they are similar to those which moved the Court of Appeals to say in *Williams* v. *New York State* (26) that:

B

"... public policy ... requires that the state be not held liable. To hold otherwise would impose a heavy responsibility upon the State, or dissuade the wardens and principal keepers of our prison system from continued experimentation with 'minimum security' work details—which provide a means of encouraging better-risk prisoners to exercise their senses of responsibility and honour and so prepare themselves for their eventual return to society. Since 1917, the Legislature has expressly provided for out-of-prison work ... and its intention should be respected without fostering the reluctance of prison officials to assign eligible men to minimum security work, lest they thereby give rise to costly claims against the State, or indeed, inducing the State itself to terminate this 'salutary procedure', looking towards rehabilitation."

C

D

But the validity of such observations can be tested only by bearing in mind that what is being urged by the present appellants in that, no matter how gross the dereliction of duties by borstal administrators which facilitate the escape of inmates, the public interest demands that no action should lie for the reasonably foreseeable damage (either to person or property) done by those inmates while at large. That, as it seems to me, is a bold claim. Its nature and gravity must not be allowed to become obscured by an entirely different consideration—namely, that what we are here postulating is that negligence has been *established*, whereas in practice this might prove a particularly difficult task where problems of personal judgment are involved. The concluding passage in the excellent judgment of JUDGE WHITMEE has a bearing on the Attorney-General's observation that, unless the present appeal be allowed and the preliminary point of law decided in the Home Office's favour, the death-knell of all " open " borstals will now be sounded. The learned judge ended in this way:

E

F

" I would like to add a final note of warning. I am told that the case may excite some general interest outside legal circles. I desire therefore to emphasise, in order to prevent possible misunderstanding, that I have not decided that there is anything either unlawful or negligent in maintaining an open Borstal Institution, *nor* have I decided that the Prison Commissioners are necessarily liable if a boy escapes and does damage, even if he has previously escaped from an open Borstal Institution. I have merely decided, in this particular case, that insufficient care was taken to prevent the boy Lawrence escaping and that the Plaintiff suffered damage as a result."

G

H

That was in 1950, and if the death-knell of open borstals was thereby sounded it was little heeded, for the system has continued unabated and there is no indication of any fall-off in the recruitment or zeal of its administrators as a result of that decision.

" How wide the sphere of the duty of care in negligence is to be laid depends ultimately upon the court's assessment of the demands of society for protection from the carelessness of others "

I

(per LORD PEARCE, *Hedley Byrne & Co., Ltd.* v. *Heller & Partners, Ltd.* (27)). The fear that pusillanimity will set in under the threat of writs is one frequently met with. It used to be said that surgeons would be prevented from taking

(26) (1955), 127 N.E.R. (2d) at p. 550.
(27) [1963] 2 All E.R. at p. 615; [1964] A.C. at p. 536.

A proper risks for fear of being sued. In *Carmarthenshire County Council* v. *Lewis* (28), as LORD REID pointed out, it was urged that should the education authority be held liable " it will put an impossible burden on harassed mothers who will have to keep a constant watch on their young children ". But the noble Lord had no difficulty in brushing aside such a fear, adding that (28):

B " I cannot see how any person in charge of a child could be held to have been negligent in a question with a third party injured in a road accident *unless* he or she had failed to take reasonable and practicable precaution for the safety of the child."

Many years ago in *Richardson* v. *Mellish* (29) BURROUGH, J., said:

C " I, for one, protest . . . against arguing too strongly upon public policy; it is a very unruly horse, and when once you get astride it you never know where it will carry you."

Some indication of the remarkable journey such a steed might lead one to take if left unreined is afforded by the following striking passage in the judgment of THESIGER, J., in the present case:

D " On principle, I cannot see why, if a borstal boy is a fire raiser, his companions should have a right of action if they get burnt by his activities and can prove that that was due to negligence on the part of the authorities while a farmer to whose neighbourhood the offender is sent without any precautions or supervision should not receive compensation if he proves negligence leading to damage by fire."

E In my view, it is indeed a strange sort of public policy which tolerates acceptance of the liability of the borstal authorities in the former case but demands its repudiation in the latter. I hold, with THESIGER, J., that no such considerations can be allowed to shut the doors of justice against an injured third party in such circumstances. Whether the plaintiffs would be likely to succeed in establishing their claim is a point which does not now arise for consideration. It is sufficient

F to say that, in the light of TUCKER, L.J.'s comments in *Stansbie* v. *Troman* (30) on the observation of LORD SUMNER in *Weld-Blundell* v. *Stephens* (31) that—

" In general (apart from special contracts and relations and the maxim respondeat superior), even though A. is in fault, he is not responsible for injury to C. which B., a stranger to him, deliberately chooses to do,"

G it by no means follows that, in my judgment, the claim made in the present case is of necessity doomed to failure.

Submission IV can, I think, be speedily disposed of. It is true that the plaintiffs claim no right to damages by reason of a breach of any statutory duty imposed on the Home Office. But that does not mean that the Home Office cannot be sued if, in the course of exercising their statutory rights and discharging their statutory duties, they act negligently and so cause damage. It has been urged

H that so to hold would amount to the creation of a new and hitherto unknown tort. I do not think this is so. The defendants in *Holgate* v. *Lancashire Mental Hospitals Board, Gill and Robertson* (32) administered their mental institution pursuant to the Mental Deficiency Act 1913, and other statutory provisions, but they were nevertheless held liable for negligence in letting out on licence a lunatic with a bad criminal history who committed a savage assault while at

I large. Again, the education authorities in *Carmarthenshire County Council* v. *Lewis* (33) were assuredly administering the infant school pursuant to statutory provisions, but, although those provisions were not relied on, it was never

(28) [1955] 1 All E.R. at p. 573; [1953] A.C. at p. 566.
(29) (1824), 2 Bing. 229 at p. 252; [1824-34] All E.R. Rep. 258 at p. 266.
(30) [1948] 1 All E.R. 599 at p. 600; [1948] 2 K.B. 48 at p. 49.
(31) [1920] A.C. 956 at p. 986; [1920] All E.R. Rep. 32 at p. 47.
(32) [1937] 4 All E.R. 19.
(33) [1955] 1 All E.R. 565; [1955] A.C. 549.

suggested that the defendants owed no duty of reasonable care. So here, although A
the borstal administrators carry on the system by virtue of statutory provisions
ranging from the Prevention of Crime Act 1908 to the Criminal Justice Act 1961,
I can see no reason why the plaintiffs should not be free to plead and prove
(if they can) the negligence alleged in their statement of claim.

By doing so, they blaze no trail and they can lay no claim to be pioneers. Nor
would success in the present action be likely to place the plaintiffs at the head B
of a long line of litigants—unless, that is, negligence is prevalent in the borstal
system, in which extremely unlikely event the sooner it is exposed, the better.
But judges may be relied on to realise fully the difficulties with which borstal
administrators are confronted and to deal in a salutary way with baseless or
exaggerated claims.   Indeed, the careful manner in which JUDGE WHITMEE
himself discriminated between two borstal escapees, holding the Prison Com- C
missioners responsible for the misdeeds of only one of them, affords an excellent
example of the vigilance which may confidently be expected from the courts.

For these reasons, I would concur in dismissing this appeal.

PHILLIMORE, L.J.: The Attorney-General is forced to concede for the
purposes of his argument on this preliminary point that the borstal officers
who were in charge of the seven boys who did £1,300 worth of damage to the D
plaintiffs' yacht were thoroughly negligent.   The submission is that however
negligent they were the plaintiffs have no right to recover damages.

It is said that since the statutes which set up the borstal system do not confer
any right on a member of the public to sue for damages suffered as a result of a
breach of duty by the defendants or their borstal officers, the latter can be as
negligent as they like in carrying out their duties since they will not by such E
negligence afford any right to any member of the public to claim damages. It is
further said that this immunity from the normal consequences of negligence is a
matter of public policy.

It strikes me as odd that if this is public policy Parliament has not granted
immunity to the Home Office in any of the statutory provisions by which the
borstal system has been set up. The Attorney-General is driven to say that if F
those in charge of a closed borstal chose to open the doors and let out all the boys
—and after all they are probably very tough boys or they would not be in a
closed borstal—no member of the public who suffered damage in the result
could claim in the courts. His argument would I gather apply equally in the
case of a prison.

This bold claim is in direct contrast to the law as it was established in 1951 G
by the decision in *Greenwell* v. *Prison Comrs.* (34) by His Honour JUDGE WHITMEE
who held the defendants liable for damage done by one of two boys who escaped
from a borstal. This decision was not appealed and so it has been the law in this
country now for about 18 years.

The argument for the Home Office is apparently based on the well-known
phrase, " Am I my brother's keeper? " In other words, " I am not responsible H
for what my brother does ". It is said that this is to be derived from the words
of DIXON, J., in *Smith* v. *Leurs* (35), in a case involving damage done by a boy
using a catapult or as it is apparently called in Australia " a Shanghai ". That
very distinguished judge said:

" It is . . . exceptional to find in the law a duty to control another's actions I
   to prevent harm to strangers. The general rule is that one man is under no
   duty of controlling another man to prevent his doing damage to a third."

The court went on to hold that the parents of the boy in question had done all
that was reasonable to prevent his doing damage. It is conceded that there are
exceptions to the general rule such as master and servant, principal and agent
and parent and child—the category in the case in point.

(34) (1951) 101 L.T. 486.
(35) (1945), 70 C.L.R. 256 at p. 262.

A   The Attorney-General has to concede that an educational authority must bear responsibility for the acts of an irresponsible child in its care. (cf., *Carmarthenshire County Council* v. *Lewis* (36) in that case a little boy of four was allowed to run into the road where his presence caused a collision.) He must also concede that a mental hospital may be liable in failing to supervise a lunatic whom it has let out on licence (*Holgate* v. *Lancashire Mental Hospitals*

B   *Board, Gill and Robertson* (37)).

On what principle is the Home Office in any different position in respect to the irresponsible teenagers in its care? What about prisons? The Attorney-General concedes that within the walls a duty is owed both to the prisoners and to visitors (cf., *Ellis* v. *Home Office* (38) and *D'Arcy* v. *Prison Comrs.* (39)). He said at first, albeit with some hesitation, that the duty stops when the prisoner

C   is outside the walls of the prison but I think subsequently conceded that it might extend to prisoners out on a working party or in transit. I put to him the case of a man who was caught after committing about 150 burglaries and sentenced to eight years' imprisonment. Whilst in Dartmoor this man's mother died so the authorities gave him a ticket to attend the funeral at Leicester. He did not return and was not caught again until he had committed another

D   30 burglaries. The Attorney-General admitted that on his argument no member of the public who had suffered damage as a result of this man's activities after his mother's funeral had any redress. It is said that the householder should insure and that his damage will then be met by an insurance company.

I confess that I regard the argument for the Home Office as untenable and, but for the skill of the Attorney-General, almost unarguable. How can it be

E   public policy that government servants should be free from liability if they exercise their duties negligently? It is public policy that they should exercise them with proper care.

Having said this I would wish to make it plain that I have every sympathy with the Home Office in their administration of the borstal system. They have a very difficult job to do and any court should be very careful before it finds

F   negligence. Classification is not easy—ought a boy to go to a closed or open borstal? After all the emphasis is on character training and if one learns not to run away from one's problems one has probably learned something very important.

It is, of course, easy with hindsight to say that classification was wrong. The mere fact that a boy escapes from an open borstal—and open borstals are government policy—is not even prima facie evidence of negligence. On the

G   other hand, if a boy escapes and does serious damage and thereafter one lets him escape again it seems to me that it may be. There must come a time when one ought to balance the interest of the boy against those of respectable members of the public and there must be cases where one should prefer the latter.

I would dismiss this appeal.

Appeal dismissed.   Leave to appeal to the House of Lords granted.

H   Solicitors: *Treasury Solicitor*; *Ingledew, Brown, Bennison & Garrett* (for the plaintiffs).

[*Reported by* F. GUTTMAN, ESQ., *Barrister-at-Law.*]

I

-----

(36) [1955] 1 All E.R. 565; [1955] A.C. 549.
(37) [1937] 4 All E.R. 19.
(38) [1953] 2 All E.R. 149; [1953] 2 Q.B. 135.
(39) (1955), The Times 15th, 16th, 17th November.

A

REDLAND BRICKS, LTD. *v.* MORRIS AND ANOTHER.

[HOUSE OF LORDS (Lord Reid, Lord Morris of Borth-y-Gest, Lord Hodson, Lord Upjohn and Lord Diplock), February 24, 25, 26, 27, May 13, 1969.]

Injunction—Form of order—Mandatory injunction—Order in general terms not specifying details of work to be done—Injunction requiring defendants to take all necessary steps to restore the support to the plaintiffs' land.

B

Injunction—Mandatory injunction—Discretion over grant of remedy—Principles on which exercised—Loss of support of plaintiffs' land by reason of defendants' excavation on neighbouring land—Order requiring expenditure of £30,000 for benefit of land, etc., worth not more than £12,000.

The respondents were market gardeners who farmed eight acres of land; C this was adjoined by the appellants' land which the appellants used to dig for clay. In 1964 some of the respondents' land slipped, due to lack of support, into the appellants' land. Slips occurred again in 1965 and 1966. It was likely that further slips would occur rendering a large part of the respondents' land unworkable as a market garden. To remedy the slipping was estimated to cost about £30,000. The respondents' land D was worth £12,000. In October 1966 a county court judge granted two injunctions in favour of the respondents: (i) an injunction restraining the appellants from withdrawing support; and (ii) a mandatory injunction " that the [appellants] do take all necessary steps to restore the support to the [respondents'] land within a period of six months ". On appeal against the mandatory injunction,   E

Held: although there was a strong probability that grave damage would, in the future, accrue to the respondents, the injunction would be discharged because in its terms it did not inform the appellants exactly what they had to do (see p. 577, letters F and G, p. 580, letter F, and p. 581, letter H, post);

Meux's Brewery Co. v. *City of London Electric Lighting Co.* ([1891-1894] All E.R. Rep. 838) distinguished.   F

Dicta of JOYCE, J., in *A.-G.* v. *Staffordshire County Council* ([1905] 1 Ch. at p. 342) approved.

Dictum of MAUGHAM, L.J., in *Fishenden* v. *Higgs and Hill, Ltd.* ([1935] All E.R. Rep. at p. 450) approved.

Per CURIAM: since the appellants had behaved, although wrongly, not unreasonably, it would have been wrong to have imposed on them the G obligation of remedying the slip at a cost of £30,000; that would have been unreasonably expensive. The judge would, however, have been justified in imposing an obligation to do some reasonable and not too expensive works which might have had a fair chance of preventing further damage (see p. 577, letters F and G, and p. 581, letters D and H, post).

Principles on which mandatory injunctions granted, discussed (see p. 579, H letter H, to p. 580, letter F, post).

Decision of the COURT OF APPEAL (sub nom. *Morris* v. *Redland Bricks, Ltd.* [1967] 3 All E.R. 1) reversed.

Appeal allowed.

[As to mandatory injunctions, see 21 HALSBURY'S LAWS (3rd Edn.) 361-364, I paras. 757-762; and for cases on the subject, see 28 DIGEST (Repl.) 772-781, *239-319.*]

Cases referred to:

    A.-G. v. *Staffordshire County Council*, [1905] 1 Ch. 336; 74 L.J.Ch. 153; 92 L.T. 288; 69 J.P. 97; 28 Digest (Repl.) 890, *1202.*

    Darley Main Colliery Co. v. *Mitchell* (1886), 11 App. Cas. 127; [1886-90] All E.R. Rep. 449; 55 L.J.Q.B. 529; 54 L.T. 882; 51 J.P. 148; 17 Digest (Repl.) 85, *62.*

A   *Durell* v. *Pritchard* (1865), 1 Ch. App. 244; 35 L.J.Ch. 223; 13 L.T. 545;
     28 Digest (Repl.) 779, *305.*

     Fishenden v. *Higgs and Hill, Ltd.,* [1935] All E.R. Rep. 435; 153 L.T. 128;
     19 Digest (Repl.) 210, *1519.*

     Isenberg v. *East India House Estate Co., Ltd.* (1863), 3 De G.J. & Sm. 263;
     33 L.J.Ch. 392   9 L.T. 625; 28 J.P. 228; 46 E.R. 637; 28 Digest
B   (Repl.) 776, *276.*

     Kennard v. *Cory Brothers & Co., Ltd.,* [1922] 1 Ch. 265; *affd.,* C.A., [1922]
     2 Ch. 1; 91 L.J.Ch. 452; 127 L.T. 137; 28 Digest (Repl.) 777, *291.*

     Meux's Brewery Co. v. *City of London Electric Lighting Co., Shelfer* v. *Same,*
     [1895] 1 Ch. 287; [1891-94] All E.R. Rep. 838; 64 L.J.Ch. 216; 72
     L.T. 34; *subsequent proceedings,* [1895] 2 Ch. 388; 28 Digest (Repl.)
C   792, *418.*

     Woodhouse v. *Newry Navigation Co.,* [1898] 1 I.R. 161; 28 Digest (Repl.)
     780, **254.*

Appeal.

This was an appeal by Redland Bricks, Ltd., from an order of the Court of
Appeal (DANCKWERTS and SACHS, L.JJ.; SELLERS, L.J., dissenting) dated
D 1st May 1967 and reported [1967] 3 All E.R. 1, upholding the judgment of His
Honour JUDGE TALBOT dated 27th October 1966, granting a mandatory injunction in favour of the respondents, Alfred John Morris and another, and awarding
damages and ordering the appellants to take all necessary steps to restore the
support to the respondents' land.   The appeal was in respect of the injunction
only.   The facts are set out in the opinion of LORD UPJOHN.

E   *Sir Milner Holland, Q.C.,* and *R. L. Johnson* for the appellants.
     C. A. Settle, Q.C., with *D. C. Gordon* for the respondents.

     Their Lordships took time for consideration.

     13th May.   The following opinions were delivered.

F   **LORD REID:** My Lords, for the reasons given by my noble and learned
friend, LORD UPJOHN, I would allow this appeal.

     LORD MORRIS OF BORTH-Y-GEST: My Lords, I have had the
advantage of reading the opinion of my noble and learned friend, LORD UPJOHN,
with which I agree.   I would allow the appeal.

G   **LORD HODSON:** My Lords, I have had the advantage of reading the
opinion of my noble and learned friend, LORD UPJOHN, with which I agree.
I would allow the appeal.

     LORD UPJOHN: My Lords, this appeal raises some interesting and
important questions as to the principles on which the court will grant quia timet
H injunctions, particularly when mandatory.

     The facts may be simply stated.   The respondents, Mr. and Mrs. Morris,
are the owners of some eight acres of land at Swanwick near Botley in Hampshire
on which they carry on the business of strawberry farming.   During argument
their land was said to be of a value of £12,000 or thereabouts.   The land slopes
downwards towards the north and the owners of the land on the northern boundary
I are the appellants who use this land, which is clay bearing, to dig for clay for
their brick-making business.

     The appellants naturally quarry down to considerable depths to get the clay,
so that there is always a danger of withdrawing support from their neighbours'
land if they approach too near or dig too deep by that land.   Let me state that
on the evidence, in my opinion, the appellants did not act either wantonly or
in plain disregard of their neighbours' rights.   Their chief engineer and production director in evidence said that he considered that they left a safe margin
for support of the respondents' land.   In this he was in fact wrong.   But the

appellants had retained for 12 years a distinguished geologist, who gave evidence, **A** to advise them on these problems, though there is no evidence that he was called in to advise them before their digging operations in this area.

The appellants ceased their excavations on their land in 1962 and about Christmas, 1964, some of the respondents' land started slipping down into the appellants' land, admittedly due to lack of support on the part of the appellants. Further slips of land took place in the winter of 1965-66. So in July **B** 1966, the respondents issued their plaint in the county court against the appellants claiming damages (limited to £500) and injunctions, and the matter came on for hearing before His Honour JUDGE TALBOT in September and October 1966. Between these hearings a further slip of land occurred. After a full hearing with expert evidence on either side he granted an injunction restraining the appellants from withdrawing support from the respondents' land without leaving **C** sufficient support and he ordered that:

" The [appellants] do take all necessary steps to restore the support to the [respondents'] land within a period of six months."

He also gave damages to the respondents for the injury already done to their land by the withdrawal of support, in the sum of £325. On 1st May 1967, the **D** appellants' appeal against this decision was dismissed by a majority of the Court of Appeal (1) (DANCKWERTS and SACHS, L.JJ.; SELLERS, L.J., dissenting). My Lords, the only attack made on the terms of the order of the county court judge was in respect of the mandatory injunction.

It is, of course, quite clear and was settled in your Lordships' House nearly 100 years ago in *Darley Main Colliery Co.* v. *Mitchell* (2) that if a person with- **E** draws support from his neighbour's land that gives no right of action at law to that neighbour until damage to his land has thereby been suffered; damage is the gist of the action. When such damage occurs the neighbour is entitled to sue for the damage suffered to his land and equity comes to the aid of the common law by granting an injunction to restrain the continuance or recurrence of any acts which may lead to a further withdrawal of support in the future. **F**

The neighbour may not be entitled as of right to such an injunction, for the granting of an injunction is in its nature a discretionary remedy, but he is entitled to it " as of course " which comes to much the same thing and at this stage an argument on behalf of the tortfeasor, who has been withdrawing support, that this will be very costly to him, perhaps by rendering him liable for heavy damages for breach of contract for failing to supply, e.g., clay or gravel, receives scant, if **G** any, respect. A similar case arises when injunctions are granted in the negative form where local authorities or statutory undertakers are enjoined from polluting rivers; in practice the most they can hope for is a suspension of the injunction while they have to take, perhaps, the most expensive steps to prevent further pollution. But the granting of an injunction to prevent further tortious acts and the award of compensation for damage to the land already suffered exhausts **H** the remedies to which at law and (under this heading) in equity the owner of the land is entitled. He is not prejudiced at law for if, as a result of the previous withdrawal of support, some further slip of his land occurs he can bring a fresh action for this new damage and ask for damages and injunctions. But to prevent the jurisdiction of the courts being stultified equity has invented the quia timet action, that is an action for an injunction to prevent an apprehended legal **I** wrong, although none has occurred at present, and the suppliant for such an injunction is without any remedy at law.

My Lords, before considering the principles applicable to such cases, I must refer to the judgments in the court below (1). Unfortunately, due possibly

(1) [1967] 3 All E.R. 1; [1967] 1 W.L.R. 967.
(2) (1886), 11 App. Cas. 127; [1886-90] All E.R. Rep. 449.

A to some misunderstanding, much of the judgments were taken up with a consideration of the applicability of the principles laid down in *Meux's Brewery Co.* v. *City of London Electric Lighting Co., Shelfer* v. *Same* (3) in the well-known judgment of A. L. SMITH, L.J.   That case was, however, concerned exclusively with the proper principles on which in practice Lord Cairns' Act (4) (which gave a discretion to the Court of Chancery to award damages in lieu of an injunction)
B should be applied.   Before your Lordships, counsel on both sides said that in the Court of Appeal (5) they had never relied on Lord Cairns' Act or on *Meux's* case (3), indeed in an action started in the county court with its limited jurisdiction as to damages it was obvious that this must be so; and they did not rely on these matters before your Lordships.   So for my part, I do not find the observations of the Court of Appeal (5) as helpful as usual, for neither Lord
C Cairns' Act nor *Meux's* case (3) have anything whatever to do with the principles of law applicable to this case.

My Lords, quia timet actions are broadly applicable to two types of cases. First, where the defendant has as yet done no hurt to the plaintiff but is threatening and intending (so the plaintiff alleges) to do works which will render irreparable harm to him or his property if carried to completion.   Your Lordships are not
D concerned with that and those cases are normally, though not exclusively, concerned with negative injunctions.   Secondly, the type of case where the plaintiff has been fully recompensed both at law and in equity for the damage he has suffered but where he alleges that the earlier actions of the defendant may lead to future causes of action.   In practice this means the case of which that which is before your Lordships' House is typical, where the defendant has withdrawn
E support from his neighbour's land or where he has so acted in depositing his soil from his mining operations as to constitute a menace to the plaintiff's land. It is in this field that the undoubted jurisdiction of equity to grant a mandatory injunction, that is an injunction ordering the defendant to carry out positive works, finds its main expression, though of course it is equally applicable to many other cases.   Thus, to take the simplest example, if the defendant, the owner of
F land, including a metalled road over which the plaintiff has a right of way, ploughs up that land so that it is no longer usable, no doubt a mandatory injunction will go to restore it; damages are not a sufficient remedy, for the plaintiff has no right to go on the defendant's land to remake his right of way.

Isenberg v. *East India House Estate Co., Ltd.* (6) and *Durell* v. *Pritchard* (7) have laid down some basic principles, and your Lordships have been referred to some
G other cases which have been helpful.   The grant of a mandatory injunction is, of course, entirely discretionary and unlike a negative injunction can never be " as of course ".   Every case must depend essentially on its own particular circumstances.   Any general principles for its application can only be laid down in the most general terms:

1.   A mandatory injunction can only be granted where the plaintiff shows a
H very strong probability on the facts that grave damage will accrue to him in the future.   As LORD DUNEDIN said (8) it is not sufficient to say " timeo ".   It is a jurisdiction to be exercised sparingly and with caution but, in the proper case, unhesitatingly.

2.   Damages will not be a sufficient or adequate remedy if such damage does happen.   This is only the application of a general principle of equity; it has
I nothing to do with Lord Cairns' Act (4) or *Meux's* case (3).

3.   Unlike the case where a negative injunction is granted to prevent the

---

(3) [1895] 1 Ch. 287; [1891-94] All E.R. Rep. 838.
(4) I.e., the Chancery Amendment Act 1858.
(5) [1967] 3 All E.R. 1; [1967] 1 W.L.R. 967.
(6) (1863), 3 De G.J. & Sm. 263.
(7) (1865), 1 Ch. App. 244.
(8) In *A.-G. for the Dominion of Canada* v. *Ritchie Contracting and Supply Co., Ltd.*, [1919] A.C. 999 at p. 1005.

continuance or recurrence of a wrongful act the question of the cost to the **A**
defendant to do works to prevent or lessen the likelihood of a future apprehended
wrong must be an element to be taken into account: (a) where the defendant
has acted without regard to his neighbour's rights, or has tried to steal a march
on him or has tried to evade the jurisdiction of the court or, to sum it up, has
acted wantonly and quite unreasonably in relation to his neighbour he may be
ordered to repair his wanton and unreasonable acts by doing positive work to **B**
restore the status quo even if the expense to him is out of all proportion to the
advantage thereby accruing to the plaintiff. As illustrative of this see *Wood-house* v. *Newry Navigation Co.* (9); (b) but where the defendant has acted
reasonably, although in the event wrongly, the cost of remedying by positive
action his earlier activities is most important for two reasons. First, because
no legal wrong has yet occurred (for which he has not been recompensed at law **C**
and in equity) and, in spite of gloomy expert opinion, may never occur or possibly
only on a much smaller scale than anticipated. Secondly, because if ultimately
heavy damage does occur the plaintiff is in no way prejudiced for he has his action
at law and all his consequential remedies in equity.

So the amount to be expended under a mandatory order by the defendant
must be balanced with these considerations in mind against the anticipated **D**
possible damage to the plaintiff and if, on such balance, it seems unreasonable
to inflict such expenditure on one who for this purpose is no more than a potential
wrongdoer then the court must exercise its jurisdiction accordingly. Of course,
the court does not have to order such works as on the evidence before it will
remedy the wrong but may think it proper to impose on the defendant the
obligation of doing certain works which may on expert opinion merely lessen **E**
the likelihood of any further injury to the plaintiff's land. SARGANT, J., pointed
this out in effect in the celebrated " Moving Mountain " case, *Kennard* v. *Cory
Brothers & Co., Ltd.* (10) (his judgment was affirmed in the Court of Appeal (11)).

4. If in the exercise of its discretion the court decides that it is a proper
case to grant a mandatory injunction, then the court must be careful to see that
the defendant knows exactly in fact what he has to do and this means not as a **F**
matter of law but as a matter of fact, so that in carrying out an order he can
give his contractors the proper instructions.

This has been well settled for a long time and I regret that I cannot agree with
DANCKWERTS, L.J. (12), that the observations of JOYCE, J., in *A.-G.* v. *Stafford-shire County Council* (13) have not been followed in practice. My experience
has been quite the opposite. There may be some cases where, to revert to the **G**
simple illustration I gave earlier, the defendant can be ordered " to restore the
right of way to its former condition ". This is so simple as to require no further
elucidation in the court order. But in anything more complicated the court must
in fairness to the defendant tell him what he has to do, though it may well be
by reference to plans prepared by some surveyor, as pointed out by SARGANT, J.
(14), in the passage in the " Moving Mountain " case to which I have already **H**
referred. The principle is summed up by MAUGHAM, L.J., in *Fishenden* v.
Higgs and Hill, Ltd. (15):

" I should like to observe in the first place, that I think a mandatory
injunction, except in very exceptional circumstances, ought to be granted
in such terms that the person against whom it is granted ought to know
exactly what he has to do." **I**

---

(9) [1898] 1 I.R. 161.
(10) [1922] 1 Ch. 265 at pp. 274, 275.
(11) [1922] 2 Ch. 1.
(12) [1967] 3 All E.R. at p. 5; [1967] 1 W.L.R. at pp. 973, 974.
(13) [1905] 1 Ch. 336 at pp. 342, 343.
(14) [1922] 1 Ch. at pp. 274, 275.
(15) [1935] All E.R. Rep. 435 at p. 450; 153 L.T. 128 at p. 142.

A My Lords I shall apply these principles or conditions to this case, and I can do so very shortly.   1. As a matter of expert evidence supported by the further slip of land during the hearing it is obvious that this condition, which must be one of fact in each case, is satisfied and, indeed, is not disputed.   2. Damages obviously are not a sufficient remedy, for no one knows whether any further damage will occur and, if so, on what scale—on the expert evidence it might be
B very substantial.   3. The appellants have not behaved unreasonably but only wrongly.   On the facts of this case the judge, in my opinion would have been fully justified in imposing on the appellants an obligation to do some reasonable and not too expensive works which might have a reasonable chance of preventing further damage.   He did not do so and it is not surprising that in the county court this was not further explored.   Alternatively he might have given leave to apply
C for a mandatory injunction.   4. But in making his mandatory order in my opinion the judge totally disregarded this necessary and perfectly well settled condition.   The terms of the order imposed on the appellants an absolutely unqualified obligation on them to restore support without giving them any indication of what was to be done.   The judge might have ordered the appellants to carry out the remedial works described by the respondents' expert in his
D evidence though it would have to be set out in great detail.   I could have under-stood that, but as it was thought to cost £30,000 that would have been most unreasonable and would have offended principle 3, but the order in fact imposed went much further; it imposed an unlimited and unqualified obligation on the appellants, and I do not know how they could have attempted to comply with it.   The expenditure of the sum of £30,000 which I have just mentioned would
E not necessarily have complied with it for although it would in all probability have prevented any further damage it was not guaranteed to do so and that is what in effect the mandatory order of the learned judge required.   My Lords, in my opinion that part of the order of the county court judge cannot stand and the appeal must be allowed.

I have given anxious consideration to the question whether some order could
F not be made with a view to imposing on the appellants some obligation to make a limited expenditure (by which I mean a few thousand pounds) to lessen the likelihood of further land slips to the respondents' land but, not without reluctance, I do not think this would be a helpful course.   First, the matter would have to be tried de novo as a matter of expert evidence because the trial judge is not available and because 2½ years have elapsed since the trial, without, so far as
G their Lordships know, any further land slips, and on that expert evidence may have something to say.   The costs of such a further inquiry would be very heavy and the inquiry possibly inconclusive.   Secondly, the respondents are not unduly prejudiced, for in the event of a further land slip all their remedies at law and in equity will be open to them and they will no doubt begin in a more appropriate forum than the county court.
H For these reasons I would allow the appeal.   The appellants, however, must pay the respondents' costs here and below in accordance with their undertaking.

LORD DIPLOCK: My Lords, I have had the advantage of reading the opinion of my noble and learned friend, LORD UPJOHN, with which I agree. I would allow the appeal.

Appeal allowed.

I

Solicitors: *Baileys, Shaw & Gillett* (for the appellants); *Kerly, Sons & Karuth*, Ilford, agents for *Shenton, Pitt, Walsh & Moss*, Winchester (for the respondents).

[*Reported by* S. A. HATTEEA, ESQ., *Barrister-at-Law.*]

HOTEL AND CATERING INDUSTRY TRAINING BOARD *v.* AUTOMOBILE PROPRIETARY, LTD.

[HOUSE OF LORDS (Lord Reid, Lord Pearce, Lord Upjohn, Lord Donovan and Lord Pearson), April 15, 16, May 13, 1969.]

Industrial training—Training board—Establishment—Activities of industry or commerce—Hotel and catering industry—Whether members' clubs subject to levy—Whether order in part ultra vires—Industrial Training (Hotel and Catering Board) Order 1966 (S.I. 1966 No. 1347), Sch. 1, para. 3 (c) (ii)—Industrial Training Act 1964 (c. 16), s. 1 (1), s. 4.

By s. 1* of the Industrial Training Act 1964 the Minister of Labour was empowered to establish industrial training boards for persons employed " in any activities of industry or commerce ". By s. 4† of the Act of 1964, each training board was empowered to impose a levy on employers in the industry. The Minister made the Industrial Training (Hotel and Catering Board) Order 1966 establishing the appellants, the Hotel and Catering Industry Training Board, to exercise in relation to the activities specified in Sch. 1 to the order, the functions conferred on industrial training boards by the Act. By Sch. 1, para. 1 (*a*), to the order, the activities of the hotel and catering industry included the supply in the course of any business of food and drink to persons for immediate consumption; by para. 3 (*c*) of that schedule " business " was defined (inter alia) as the activities of any persons or body of persons in the management or operation of a club. The appellants made a levy order on a club which was a private members' club.

Held: by reason of the context in which the phrase " activities of industry or commerce " occurred it would be given its ordinary or natural meaning, i.e., industrial or commercial activities or activities carried on in industry or commerce; accordingly, the order of 1966 was invalid insofar as it was extended to any members' club.

Decision of the COURT OF APPEAL ([1968] 3 All E.R. 399) affirmed.

[As to industrial training boards, see SUPPLEMENT to 38 HALSBURY'S LAWS (3rd Edn.), para. 690A.

For Industrial Training Act 1964, s. 1, s. 4, see 44 HALSBURY'S STATUTES (2nd Edn.) 263, 266.]

Appeal.

This was an appeal by the Hotel and Catering Industry Training Board from the order of the Court of Appeal (LORD DENNING, M.R., and BUCKLEY, J.; WINN, L.J., dissenting) dated 26th July 1968, and reported [1968] 3 All E.R. 399, allowing the appeal of the respondents, Automobile Proprietary, Ltd., from the judgment of BRIDGE, J., dated 4th April 1968, declaring that the Industrial Training (Hotel and Catering Board) Order 1966 insofar as its terms related to members' clubs was validly made pursuant to the powers conferred on the Minister of Labour by s. 1 (1) of the Industrial Training Act 1964.

Leonard Caplan, Q.C., and *M. F. Gettleson* for the appellants.
E. I. Goulding, Q.C., and *W. P. Andreae-Jones* for the respondents.

Their Lordships took time for consideration.

13th May. The following opinions were delivered.

LORD REID: My Lords, the Industrial Training Act 1964 authorised the Minister of Labour to establish industrial training boards. By the Industrial Training (Hotel and Catering Board) Order 1966 (1) the Minister established the

---
* Section 1 (1) is set out at p. 583, letter G, post.
† Section 4 is set out at p. 584, letters C to F, post.
(1) S.I. 1966 No. 1347.

A appellant board to exercise in relation to the activities specified in Sch. 1 the function conferred on such boards by the Act.   Among the activities specified is " 1 (*a*) . . . the supply in the course of any business of food or drink to persons for immediate consumption ".   Then there is included in the definition of " business " in para. 3 (*c*)—" (ii) the activities of any person or body of persons in the management or operation of a club ".   And para. 3 (*d*) provides:

B   " ' club ' does not include a members' club unless the main activities or one of the main activities of the club consist of habitually providing— (i) the customary main meal at mid-day or in the evening or both; or (ii) board and lodging for reward."

   The respondents are a members' club but they are not excluded because
C they do habitually provide main meals.   Following on the order of 1966 another order (2) was made which authorised a levy on employers carrying on business within the scope of the order of 1966.   The respondents objected to paying that levy because they maintained that it was ultra vires of the Minister to include members' clubs in the order of 1966.   Then on 1st February 1968 the appellants brought an originating summons seeking against the respondents a declaration:

D   " (i) that the Industrial Training (Hotel and Catering Board) Order 1966, was validly made pursuant to the powers conferred upon the Minister of Labour by Section 1 (1) of the Industrial Training Act, 1964, and that the terms thereof are within the powers conferred upon the Minister by the said Section;
   " (ii) that the Royal Automobile Club as a Members Club as defined by the
E said Order falls within the scope of the said Order and is subject to the obligations imposed by sections 4 and 6 of the said Act."

Section 4 of the Act authorises a levy and s. 6 requires employers to keep records and make returns.   BRIDGE, J., on 4th April 1968 decided in favour of the appellants but his decision was reversed on 26th July 1968 by the Court of Appeal (3) (LORD DENNING, M.R., and BUCKLEY, J.; WINN, L.J., dissenting).
F   Whether or not the Minister had power to include members' clubs in the order depends on the proper interpretation of s. 1 (1) of the Act which is in these terms:

   " For the purpose of making better provision for the training of persons over compulsory school age (in Scotland school age) for employment in
G any activities of industry or commerce the Minister may make an order specifying those activities and establishing a board to exercise in relation to them the functions conferred on industrial training boards by the following provisions of this Act."

The crucial words are " any activities of industry or commerce " and " those activities ".   If the activities of members' clubs in supplying food or drink
H for immediate consumption are activities of industry or commerce then the inclusion of members' clubs in the order was admittedly intra vires: if they are not, then the inclusion of members' clubs in the order was admittedly ultra vires. It is admitted that members' clubs (including the respondents) are not engaged in industry or commerce in supplying food or drink or in any other way.   So the respondents contend that their activities cannot be activities of industry or
I commerce.   But the appellants contend that " activities of industry or commerce " means activities of a kind which are carried on in industry or commerce, or, as WINN, L.J., put it (4) that that expression includes any " activity of which it can be postulated, this is an activity which belongs to in the sense that it occurs in industry or commerce ".   Putting the matter in concrete terms the

   (2) See the Industrial Training Levy (Hotel and Catering) Order 1967 (S.I. 1967 No. 1512).
   (3) [1968] 3 All E.R. 399; [1968] 1 W.L.R. 1526.
   (4) [1968] 3 All E.R. at p. 404; [1968] 1 W.L.R. at p. 1533.

appellants say that cooking meals is part of the trade of a hotel-keeper or caterer,   **A**
therefore it is an activity of industry or commerce, and therefore the Minister has
power to bring within the scope of an order under the Act all private householders who employ cooks so as to make them liable to pay a levy.   Counsel did
not attempt to argue that there is any relevant distinction between members'
clubs and private householders, or that the Minister has power to specify the
activities of members' clubs but no power to bring in such private householders   **B**
as may employ cooks or other domestic staff.   He maintained that, whenever
the Minister specifies in an order activities which are carried on in industry or
commerce, every person who employs anyone to carry on activities of that kind
will be subjected to a levy unless exempted under the order.
Levies are authorised by s. 4 which is in the following terms:

" (1) For the purpose of raising money towards meeting its expenses   **C**
an industrial training board shall from time to time impose, in accordance
with an order made by the Minister (in this section referred to as a levy order),
a levy on employers in the industry, other than such (if any) as may be
exempted by the levy order or the industrial training order.

" (2) A levy order shall give effect to proposals submitted to and approved   **D**
by the Minister under section 7 of this Act, and such proposals may provide
for the amendment of a previous levy order and may make different provision in relation to different classes or descriptions of employer.

" (3) A levy order may contain provisions as to the evidence by which
a person's liability to the levy or his discharge of that liability may be
established and as to the time at which any amount payable by any person
by way of the levy shall become due and recoverable by the industrial   **E**
training board, and shall give any person assessed to the levy a right of
appeal to an appeal tribunal constituted under this Act.

" (4) The power to make a levy order shall be exercisable by statutory
instrument, which shall be subject to annulment in pursuance of a resolution
of either House of Parliament."
F
It will be observed that levies can only be made on " employers in the industry ".
But the appellants argue that every householder who employs a cook is an
" employer in the industry ".   They contend that this strange misuse of language
is justified by the terms of the definition of " the industry " in s. 1 (2): " the
industry, in relation to an industrial training board, means the activities in
relation to which it exercises functions ".
G
One must then write this definition into s. 4.   " Employers in the industry "
then becomes " employers in the activities in relation to which the Board exercises functions ".   Those are the activities specified by the Minister under s. 1 (1)
and the Minister has no power to specify any activities which are not activities
of industry or commerce, so the definition really means those activities of industry
or commerce which have been specified by the Minister.   A common and con-   **H**
venient method of delimiting a particular industry is to define the industry as
meaning or consisting of specified industrial activities and it appears to me that
that is what this definition does.   But on any view it cannot extend the scope
of s. 1 (1).   If an activity is not an activity of industry or commerce the Minister
has no power to specify it in an order, and if he has no power to specify it the
board can have no power to exercise functions in relation to it.
I
So from whatever angle one approaches the matter the crucial question is the
same—what is meant by " activities of industry or commerce ".   One first
looks for the ordinary or natural meaning of the phrase.   I do not think that
anyone would say that the activities of a cook in private employment or of her
employer are activities of industry or of the catering industry.   At most he
would say that they are similar to or of the same kind as the activities of the
catering industry.   It appears to me that the natural meaning of activities of
industry or commerce is industrial or commercial activities, or activities carried

A   on in industry or commerce. But I would not deny that the words in the Act are capable of having the meaning for which the appellants contend if the context clearly indicates that that meaning was intended.

One first looks for the general purpose of the Act insofar as it can be inferred from reading the Act as a whole. I think that it is to assist employers engaged in industry or commerce to increase production by increasing the number of
B   persons having the skills necessary for employment by them in skilled work, and to assist persons seeking better positions by equipping them for skilled work in industry and commerce. I see no sign of any purpose of assisting private employers not engaged in industry or commerce or of assisting employees to obtain work with such employers. Of course a private employer may offer terms acceptable to persons who have been trained under this Act and a person
C   who has been so trained is under no obligation to accept employment in industry. But the Act does not seem to me to be designed to help private employers or to help those who wish to obtain private employment.

Then one must look at the particular provisions of the Act to see whether any of them throws any light on the matter. Section 1 (4) and s. 11 deal with consultation with organisations; s. 1 (4) requires the Minister to consult those
D   " appearing to him to be representative of substantial numbers of employers engaging in the activities concerned ". I can hardly think that it was intended that the Minister should be bound to consult organisations representative of substantial numbers of private employers of chauffeurs or gardeners before making any order regarding the activities of driving motor vehicles or of
E   horticulture.

Section 6 requires returns and other information to be furnished, and sub-s. (3) and sub-s. (4) provide for confidentiality. They are as follows:

" (3) Subject to subsection (4) of this section, returns and other information furnished in pursuance of the preceding provisions of this section and any information obtained on an examination made in pursuance thereof shall not,
F   without the consent of the employer to whose business the returns or information relate, be disclosed otherwise than to the Minister or one of his officers, or to an industrial training board or a committee appointed by such a board, or an officer of such a board or committee or any person entitled to take part in the proceedings of such a board.

" (4) Subsection (3) of this section shall not apply—(*a*) to the disclosure
G   of returns or information in the form of a summary of similar returns or information furnished by or obtained from a number of employers, if the summary is so framed as not to enable particulars relating to any individual business to be ascertained from it . . ."

If the appellants are right there is a strange difference between employers engaged
H   in industry or commerce, who therefore have businesses, and private employers who do not. Returns made by the former are protected, but the Minister could do as he chose with returns made by the respondents. I cannot believe that any such distinction could have been intended. It seems to me to be much more probable that these provisions only apply to employers with businesses because there was no intention to bring any other employers within the scope of the Act.
I   There is also a reference to an employer's trade or business in s. 10 but there are other reasons for that.

Section 13 refers to a provision in s. 14 of the Industrial Organisation and Development Act 1947 regarding " the activities that are to be treated as constituting the industry ". It was rightly admitted that the Act of 1947 only applies to activities carried on in industry and does not apply to activities of the same kind carried on by private employers not engaged in industry. Many of the provisions of the Act of 1964 resemble similar provisions in the Act of 1947

and if it had been intended that " activities of industry " in the Act of 1947 **A**
should have a different and new meaning in the Act of 1964, I would have expected
that to be made clear.

None of these particular provisions in the Act of 1964 is at all conclusive
but they are more consistent with the respondents' contention than with the
appellants'. So in my opinion the context in which the crucial phrase " activities
of industry or commerce " occurs in no way requires this phrase to be given **B**
the meaning for which the appellants contend: on the contrary it tends to
confirm my view that this phrase must be given its ordinary or natural meaning.
I would therefore dismiss this appeal.

LORD PEARCE: My Lords, I agree with the opinion of my noble and
learned friend, LORD REID. For the reasons which he gives I would dismiss **C**
the appeal.

LORD UPJOHN: My Lords, I have had the advantage of reading the
speech of my noble and learned friend, LORD REID. I agree with it and for the
reasons he gives would dismiss the appeal.

LORD DONOVAN: My Lords, the background to the Industrial Training **D**
Act 1964 is well known. Since the last war there has been a persistent shortage
in industry of skilled man-power and industry's own voluntary arrangements
failed to cure it. The Act was therefore passed with the object of securing an
adequate supply of properly trained men and women at all levels in industry
and of levying the cost on industry as fairly as possible.

The plan to set up industrial training boards had to overcome one obvious **E**
difficulty. While one may speak, for example, of " the shipbuilding industry "
it would be scarcely practicable to set up a single training board to cover an
occupation to which a multitude of separate industries contribute. Hence, the
boards were set up to train persons " in any activities of industry or commerce ",
thus giving the board a manageable task while at the same time effecting the **F**
purpose of the Act. This language, however, lets in the present contention that
" activities of industry or commerce " simply means activities of the kind carried
on in or by industrial or commercial concerns, and so allows a levy to be made
on private institutions like clubs which may also pursue the same activities.
When one considers, however, the background of the Act and its purpose, it
becomes plain, in my opinion, that the contention is wholly misconceived; **G**
and that the true construction of the phrase " activities of industry or commerce "
is the natural construction, namely, industrial or commercial activities. This
conclusion is re-inforced by the provision of s. 6 (3) of the Act prohibiting the
disclosure to outside persons of returns and information obtained by the Minister
under the powers conferred by the section " without the consent of the employer
to whose business the returns or information relate ". Counsel for the appellants, **H**
did his best to rebut this point but, as I think, in vain.

The point was made that it was inequitable that industry and commerce
should have to pay for the training of persons employed outside those spheres.
But since there is still freedom to seek the employment one chooses, and to change
it, if one will, some spill-over of the benefit of the Act of 1964 of this kind into
the non-industrial and non-commercial sections of the economy is inevitable. **I**
If it were ever thought about, the conclusion may well have been that the extent
of it was too small to matter; or that industry and commerce might still stand
to benefit by the existence of trained labour at present elsewhere but available
to be recruited by sufficiently attractive inducements. In any event the point
is certainly not of sufficient weight to justify a construction of the Act which is
not compelled by its language and which is contrary to its purpose.

I would dismiss the appeal.

A   **LORD PEARSON:** My Lords, I also have had the advantage of reading the speech of my noble and learned friend, LORD REID, and I agree with it. I would, therefore, dismiss the appeal.

Appeal dismissed.

Solicitors: *Nicholls, Christie & Crocker* (for the appellants); *J. B. Izod* (for the respondents).

B
[*Reported by* S. A. HATTEEA, ESQ., *Barrister-at-Law.*]

Re C. L. NYE, LTD.

C   [CHANCERY DIVISION (Plowman, J.), March 4, 5, 6, 14, 1969.]

Company — Charge — Registration — Mortgage — Security for bank overdraft —Particulars submitted to registrar of companies within 21 days of erroneous date, but more than 21 days after actual date—Charge void against liquidators —Companies Act 1948 (11 & 12 Geo. 6 c. 38), s. 95 (1).

Company—Charge—Registration—Certificate of registration—Conclusiveness—
D   *Date wrongly entered on charge—Wrong date included on certificate—Effect of issue of certificate—Companies Act 1948 (11 & 12 Geo. 6 c. 38), s. 98 (2).*

A company occupied premises owned by another company (" A.D.I. "), title to which was registered. The company, in order to acquire the premises, negotiated a loan from a bank together with an overdraft on the security of the premises. On 28th February 1964, transfers of the premises sealed by
E   A.D.I. were handed over to the bank, or possibly to a solicitor B. who was acting for the bank, together with the relevant land certificates and a charge, sealed by the company, in appropriate form. The transfers and the charge were undated; B. was left to deal with the formalities, including registration of the bank's charge under s. 95* of the Companies Act 1948; the registration was to be undertaken by B. on behalf of the bank. By an oversight the
F   charge was not registered at that time. The oversight was noticed on 18th June 1964 and on the following 3rd July, B. applied for registration of particulars of the charge under s. 95 and included 18th June as the date on which the charge was created or evidenced. These particulars were registered on 3rd July. On 16th July 1964, the company went into liquidation.

Held: a declaration would be made that the charge created on 28th
G   February 1964 but bearing the date 18th June 1964 was void as against the liquidators and creditors of the company, because—

(i) the mortgage given by the company to the bank on 28th February 1964 was registrable under s. 95 (1); since it had not been registered in due time it was void as against the liquidators so far as any security on the company's property was conferred thereby (see p. 592, letter H, post);
H   further,

(ii) the bank was not entitled to rely on the certificate of registration under s. 98 (2)† since, albeit there was no suggestion that B. was not acting bona fide in dating the charge 18th June 1964, it was no function of the certificate of registration to give protection to a mortgagee against his own mis-statements; accordingly, the charge created by the company in favour
I   of the bank on 28th February 1964 must be treated as void against liquidators and creditors on the principle that no man can take advantage of his own wrong (see p. 592, letter H, and p. 528, letters G and H, post).

National Provincial and Union Bank of England v. *Charnley* ([1924] 1 K.B. 431), *Re Mechanisations (Eaglescliffe), Ltd.* ([1964] 3 All E.R. 840) and *Re Eric Holmes (Property), Ltd.* ([1965] 2 All E.R. 333) distinguished.

---

* Section 95, so far as material, is set out at p. 589, letters D to F, post.
† Section 98 (2) is set out at p. 589, letter I, post.

[As to time for registering charges, see 6 HALSBURY'S LAWS (3rd Edn.) 493,   A
494, para. 953; and for cases on the subject, see 10 DIGEST (Repl.) 815, *5288-5291*.

As to the certificate of registration of the particulars of a charge, see 6
HALSBURY'S LAWS (3rd Edn.) 498, para. 963; and for cases on the subject, see
10 DIGEST (Repl.) 812, *5268-5271*.

For the Companies Act 1948, s. 95, s. 98, see 5 HALSBURY'S STATUTES (3rd Edn.)
189, 193.]   B

Cases referred to:

Abrahams (S.) & Sons, Re, [1902] 1 Ch. 695; 71 L.J.Ch. 307; 86 L.T. 290;
     10 Digest (Repl.) 816, *5300*.

Anglo-Oriental Carpet Manufacturing Co., Re, [1903] 1 Ch. 914; 72 L.J.Ch.
     458; 88 L.T. 391; 10 Digest (Repl.) 817, *5313*.

Cunard Steamship Co., Ltd. v. *Hopwood*, [1908] 2 Ch. 564; 77 L.J.Ch. 785;   C
     99 L.T. 549; 10 Digest (Repl.) 813, *5278*.

Eric Holmes (Property), Ltd., Re, [1965] 2 All E.R. 333; [1965] Ch. 1052;
     [1965] 2 W.L.R. 1260; Digest (Cont. Vol. B) 105, *5270b*.

Mechanisations (Eaglescliffe), Ltd, Re, [1964] 3 All E.R. 840; [1966] Ch. 20;
     [1965] 2 W.L.R. 702; Digest (Cont. Vol. B) 106, *5270a*.

National Provincial and Union Bank of England v. *Charnley*, [1924] 1 K.B. 431;   D
     93 L.J.K.B. 241; 130 L.T. 465; 10 Digest (Repl.) 812, *5270*.

Yolland, Husson and Birkett, Ltd., Re, Leicester v. *Yolland, Husson and Birkett,
     Ltd.*, [1908] 1 Ch. 152; 77 L.J.Ch. 43; 97 L.T. 824; 10 Digest (Repl.)
     812, *5268*.

Adjourned Summons.

This was an application by originating summons dated 4th April 1968, by   E
Michael Anthony Jordan and Herbert William Pitt the joint liquidators of
C. L. Nye, Ltd. (" the company ") which was in voluntary winding-up, and whose
registered office was situate at Caxton Works, Cranborne Road, Potters Bar,
Middlesex, for the following relief: (i) that the register of charges kept by the
registrar of companies under s. 98 of the Companies Act 1948, be rectified by
deleting therefrom all particulars of a charge bearing date 18th June 1964 over   F
Caxton Works, Cranborne Road aforesaid; (ii) that the applicants as liquidators
as aforesaid be at liberty to take such steps as might be requisite on the company's
part in connection with the foregoing; (iii) a declaration that the charge created
by the company in favour of Westminster Bank, Ltd., the respondents, on or
about 29th February 1964 over the Caxton Works was void against the liquidator
and creditors of the company. The facts are set out in the judgment. The cases   G
noted below* were cited during the argument in addition to those referred to in
the judgment.

    Richard Sykes for the liquidators.
    J. W. Mills, Q.C., and *G. B. Parker* for the respondent bank.

                                                   Cur. adv. vult.   H

    14th March.   **PLOWMAN, J.**, read the following judgment: This is a
summons by the joint liquidators in the liquidation of C. L. Nye, Ltd. (which I
will call " the company ") which raises the question whether a mortgage given
by the company to the Westminster Bank, who are respondents to this summons,
is void against the liquidators by virtue of s. 95 (1) of the Companies Act 1948.

                                                               I

   * *Re National Debenture & Assets Corpn.*, [1891] 2 Ch. 505; *London Freehold and
Leasehold Property Co.* v. *Baron Suffield*, [1897] 2 Ch. 608; *Re Caratal (New) Mines, Ltd.*,
[1902] 2 Ch. 498; *Re N. Defries & Co., Ltd., Bowen* v. *N. Defries & Co., Ltd.*, [1904]
1 Ch. 37; *Re Jackson & Bassford, Ltd.*, [1906] 2 Ch. 467; *Esberger & Son, Ltd.* v. *Capital
and Counties Bank*, [1913] 2 Ch. 366; *Re C. Light & Co., Ltd.*, [1917] W.N. 77; *Re M.I.G.
Trust, Ltd.*, [1933] Ch. 542; *Re L. H. Charles & Co., Ltd.*, [1935] W.N. 15; *Re Kris
Cruisers, Ltd.*, [1948] 2 All E.R. 1105; [1949] 1 Ch. 138; *Independent Automatic
Sales, Ltd.* v. *Knowles & Foster*, [1962] 3 All E.R. 27; [1962] 1 W.L.R. 974; *Heywood*
v. *B.D.C. Properties, Ltd. (No. 2)*, [1964] 2 All E.R. 702; [1964] 1 W.L.R. 971; *Paul &
Frank, Ltd.* v. *Discount Bank (Overseas) Ltd. and the Board of Trade*, [1967] Ch. 348.

A Involved in this question is the question of the effect of a certificate given by the registrar of companies under s. 98 (2) of the Act.

The company went into a creditors' voluntary winding-up on 16th July 1964. So far as now material, the summons asks:

"(i) That the Register of Charges kept by the Registrar of Companies under section 98 of the Companies Act, 1948 be rectified by deleting there-

B from all particulars of a charge bearing date the 18th June 1964 over Caxton Works, Cranborne Road aforesaid.

"(iii) That the Applicants as Liquidators as aforesaid be at liberty to take such steps as may be requisite on the Company's part in connection with the foregoing.

"(iv) A declaration that charges created by the said Company in

C favour of the Respondent Bank on or about 28th February 1964 over (a) the said Caxton Works . . . [is] void against the Liquidators and creditors of the Company."

Before stating the facts, I should read the relevant sections of the Companies Act 1948:

D "95. (1) Subject to the provisions of this Part of this Act, every charge created after the fixed date by a company registered in England and being a charge to which this section applies shall, so far as any security on the company's property or undertaking is conferred thereby, be void against the liquidator and any creditor of the company, unless the prescribed particulars of the charge together with the instrument, if any, by which the charge is created or evidenced, are delivered to or received by the registrar of companies

E for registration in manner required by this Act within twenty-one days after the date of its creation, but without prejudice to any contract or obligation for repayment of the money thereby secured, and when a charge becomes void under this section the money secured thereby shall immediately become payable.

F "(2) This section applies to the following charges:— . . . (d) a charge on land, wherever situate, or any interest therein, but not including a charge for any rent or other periodical sum issuing out of land; . . .

"96. (1) It shall be the duty of a company to send to the registrar of companies for registration the particulars of every charge created by the company and of the issues of debentures of a series requiring registration under the last foregoing section, but registration of any such charge may

G be effected on the application of any person interested therein."

Then sub-s. (3) of that section provides for payment of a default fine if the company makes default in sending to the registrar the relevant particulars.

I next refer to s. 98 and s. 101:

"98. (1) The registrar of companies shall keep, with respect to each

H company, a register in the prescribed form of all the charges requiring registration under this Part of this Act, and shall, on payment of such fee as may be specified by regulations made by the Board of Trade, enter in the register with respect to such charges the following particulars:— . . . (b) in the case of any other charge—(i) if the charge is a charge created by the company, the date of its creation, and if the charge was a charge existing

I on property acquired by the company, the date of the acquisition of the property; and (ii) the amount secured by the charge; and (iii) short particulars of the property charged; and (iv) the persons entitled to the charge.

"(2) The registrar shall give a certificate under his hand of the registration of any charge registered in pursuance of this Part of this Act, stating the amount thereby secured, and the certificate shall be conclusive evidence that the requirements of this Part of this Act as to registration have been complied with.

" 101. The court, on being satisfied that the omission to register a charge   **A**
within the time required by this Act or that the omission or mis-statement
of any particular with respect to any such charge or in a memorandum of
satisfaction was accidental, or due to inadvertence or to some other sufficient
cause, or is not of a nature to prejudice the position of creditors or shareholders of the company, or that on other grounds it is just and equitable to
grant relief, may, on the application of the company or any person interested,   **B**
and on such terms and conditions as seem to the court just and expedient,
order that the time for registration shall be extended, or, as the case may be,
that the omission or mis-statement shall be rectified.''

For the facts, it is necessary to go back to the beginning of the year 1964. At
that time the company, which was a building construction company, was
occupying for the purposes of its business a property at Potters Bar in Middlesex,   **C**
known as Caxton Works.   The owner of the property was a company called
Arnold Drive Investments, Ltd. (which I will call " A.D.I.") and the title to
the property was registered at the land registry in two parts, with separate
title numbers. The shares in A.D.I. were all owned by a Mr. and Mrs. C. L. Nye
and its sole director was a Mr. Tench, a solicitors' managing clerk. Mr. C. L. Nye
had recently relinquished control of the company which bears his name, leaving   **D**
as the active directors his son Mr. Peter Nye and a Mr. O'Keefe. Mr. Tench was
secretary of the company.
     The company banked at the National Provincial Bank.   Its account was
overdrawn and there was a £35,000 limit on the amount of its overdraft which
was guaranteed by A.D.I.
     Mr. C. L. Nye, having relinquished control of the company, was anxious that   **E**
A.D.I. should be released from its liability under its guarantee and that Mr.
Peter Nye and Mr. O'Keefe should be substituted as guarantors and at the
same time the company wanted to increase its liquidity.   Accordingly, it was
agreed that A.D.I. should sell the Caxton Works to the company for £36,700,
only £15,000 of which was to be paid on completion, thus giving the company
an asset on which it could raise money.   The National Provincial Bank was   **F**
unwilling to advance further moneys to the company, but the Westminster
Bank, through its Watford Junction branch, agreed to grant the company a
loan of £15,000 and an overdraft up to £35,000 on security which was to include
the Caxton Works and the joint and several guarantees of Mr. Peter Nye and
Mr. O'Keefe up to £15,000. The company therefore decided to change its bankers.
     On 28th February 1964, a meeting took place at the Watford branch of   **G**
the Westminster Bank at which there were present Mr. Gait, the manager,
Mr. Brand, a solicitor who was acting for the bank in the matter, Mr. Tench and
Mr. Peter Nye. At this meeting Mr. Tench handed over, either to Mr. Gait or
to Mr. Brand, two transfers of the Caxton Works to the company sealed by
A.D.I. together with the relevant land certificates, and a charge, sealed by the
company, in the bank's usual printed form applicable to a charge of registered   **H**
land by a company. The transfers and the charge were undated. It was left to
Mr. Brand to deal with all legal formalities which were required in order to
perfect the bank's security.   In addition to the usual searches, investigation of
title and so on, these formalities included the registration of the bank's charge
under s. 95 of the Companies Act 1948, and I am satisfied on the evidence
(though there has been some dispute about this) that the registration was to be   **I**
undertaken by Mr. Brand on behalf of the bank and not on behalf of the company.
That is a point of prime importance in this case.
     On 9th March 1964, Mr. Brand wrote to the bank as follows:

     " Our investigations have now been completed. We have made Local
Searches, Searches at the Companies Registry, Land Registry and Land
Charges Registry and all requisite investigations under the Town & Country
Planning Acts, and we confirm that we have found no matters adverse to the

A   Bank.   Our search at the Companies Registry against the Company and Arnold Drive Investments Limited, the Transferors, shows no Charges registered, no winding up proceedings, Appointments of Liquidator or Applications to strike off.   Under the circumstances, we confirm that in our opinion [the company] has a good and marketable title to the property and that the security is satisfactory for the Bank's purpose, subject, of course,

B   to stamping of the documents and registration of the Notices of Deposit and registration of the Charge at the Companies Registry.   All these matters are being put in hand forthwith.   In the meantime, however, perhaps the Bank would kindly let us have a remittance for £423. 5. 0d. being as to £367. stamp duty on the Transfer and £56. 5. 0d. to stamp the Bank's Charge up to £45,000.   Please treat this letter as our Undertaking to hold the Deeds

C   to the Bank's order and to forward the Land Certificates in due course."

The following day the bank sent the money which had been asked for by that letter.

At about this time the company started to operate its new bank account and within a few days it was heavily in debit.   On 19th March 1964, the charge was stamped to cover £45,000.   By an oversight in Mr. Brand's office, the

D documents were then put in his safe and were lost sight of until, at some date in June, probably the 18th, Mr. Gait telephoned Mr. Brand to ask when he would be receiving the documents and Mr. Brand discovered that they had been overlooked.

Finding that the documents were undated, he inserted the date 18th June in the charge and no doubt in the transfers as well (although I have not seen them),

E and set about effecting the necessary registrations.   The date 18th June therefore had no relevance to anything except the discovery of the documents in Mr. Brand's safe.

On 29th June the transfers to the company were registered at the land registry and on the same day notices of deposit of land certificates were entered in the charges register of the relevant titles.   On the same day Mr. Brand wrote

F to the bank the following letter:

     " We write to report to the Bank that due to an oversight in this office the registration of the Company's Charge has not yet been effected.   This was due to the system which is normally employed in this office when documents are returned from the Stamping Office for some reason not being employed.   We are, however, immediately taking steps to effect registration,

G and at the same time applying for expedition thereof.   Steps having been taken in the meantime to protect the Bank's interest at the Land Registry."

On 3rd July 1964, Mr. Brand presented an application for registration of particulars of the charge under s. 95 of the Companies Act 1948 by filling up and lodging the prescribed Form 47 (1).   That form bears on the front the

H following note:

     " Note.   The original instrument (if any) creating or evidencing the charge must be presented with these particulars within twenty-one days after the date of its creation.   (See section 95 (1).)"

The form was filled up by Mr. Brand as follows: In the first column, which is headed " Date and description of the instrument creating or evidencing the

I Mortgage or Charge ", he inserted " 18th June 1964 ".   In the column " Amount secured by the Mortgage or Charge " he inserted " All moneys accrued or hereafter to accrue including liability on any current account or for further advances ".   Under the heading " Short particulars of the Property Mortgaged or Charged " he inserted " Caxton Works, Cranborne Road, Potters Bar, Middlesex "; and under the heading " Names and addresses and descriptions of the mortgagees or persons entitled to the Charge ", he inserted " Westminster Bank Limited,

_____

(1) See the Companies (Forms) Order 1949 (S.I. 1949 No. 382).

7 Station Road, Watford, Herts ". Those particulars were registered by the   A
registrar of companies on the same day, 3rd July; that is to say, within 21 days
of 18th June, but not within 21 days of 28th February.

The relevant entry in the register of mortgages and charges is as follows:

" Date of registration: 1964, July 3. Serial number of document on file,
60. Date of creation of each Mortgage or Charge and description thereof:
18th June 1964, Charge. Amount secured by the Mortgage or Charge: All   B
moneys due, etc. Short particulars of the property: Caxton Works,
Cranborne Road, Potters Bar, Middlesex. Names of Mortgagees: Westminster Bank, Limited."

On 16th July the company, as I have said, went into liquidation. Over three
years later, namely on 16th November 1967, the registrar gave his certificate
under s. 98 (2). That certificate is as follows: C

" I hereby certify that a Mortgage or Charge dated the 18th June 1964
and created by [the company] for securing all moneys now due or hereafter
to become due or from time to time accruing due from the Company to Westminster Bank Limited on any account whatsoever was registered pursuant
to Section 95 of the Companies Act, 1948, on the 3rd July 1964. Given
under my hand at London, 16th November 1967 "   D

and it is signed by the assistant registrar of companies.

On 4th April 1968, the summons which is now before me was issued. The
Caxton Works has in fact been sold by the liquidators with the agreement of
the bank, and the proceeds of sale are now held in a joint account pending the
outcome of these proceedings.

The first question I must consider is: Was the bank's charge registered in   E
time? In my judgment, it was not. The position on 28th February 1964, was
this: The company had an equitable interest in the Caxton Works which it
had agreed to buy; it agreed to give a legal charge on that property to the
bank; it handed over to the bank the sealed transfers, the sealed charge and
the land certificates. The effect of this, in my judgment, was to create an   F
equitable mortgage in favour of the bank to secure whatever moneys the bank
might thereafter advance. The mortgage was, in my judgment, clearly registrable under s. 95, and I do not think that the contrary is really suggested. If
it had been registered in due time, no subsequent registration after 18th June
would have been required (see *Cunard Steamship Co., Ltd.* v. *Hopwood* (2)).
What happened on and after 18th June, in my judgment, involved no new act   G
of creation by the company and was nothing more than the unilateral perfecting
by the bank of the security which it already held; a security which the company
had given once and for all on 28th February.

I am therefore of opinion that the bank's charge was not registered in time
and, subject to the question of the registrar's certificate, is void against the
liquidators so far as any security on the company's property is conferred thereby.   H
The question then arises whether, in these circumstances, the bank is entitled
to rely on the certificate of registration and, if so, what is its effect.

At this point I want to make it clear that there is no suggestion that Mr.
Brand was not acting bona fide in dating the charge 18th June. Solicitors
are frequently left to insert a date in documents after they have been executed
and in most cases nothing turns on the date. But in the present case everything   I
turned on it, though Mr. Brand failed to appreciate that this was so.

The result is that by mis-stating the date of the creation of the charge in its
application for registration, the bank was enabled to obtain a registration which
it could not have obtained if the true date had been stated, and it is now seeking
to obtain an advantage over the company's unsecured creditors to which it
would not otherwise be entitled by relying on a certificate which, but for that
mis-statement, could never have been given.

(2) [1908] 2 Ch. 564.

A   It is axiomatic that no man can take advantage of his own wrong, a maxim which, in BROOM'S LEGAL MAXIMS, is stated to be based on elementary principles, fully recognised in courts of law and equity and to admit of illustration in every branch of legal procedure.   It is a maxim which, it seems to me, is appropriate to apply in the present case unless I am precluded from doing so by authority. Three relevant cases were cited during the course of the argument, and I must
B now refer to them.

The first is *National Provincial and Union Bank of England* v. *Charnley* (3), a case in the Court of Appeal.   The headnote, so far as relevant, is as follows (4):

" A company with the object of securing payment of its overdraft at the plaintiff bank ' demised ' to the bank a certain leasehold factory with all the movable ' plant used in or about the premises ' for a term of about
C   996 years.   The bank sent the indenture to the registrar of companies for registration under s. 93 of the Companies Act, 1908.   In the particulars required to be filed pursuant to that section the instrument was described as a mortgage of the leasehold premises, no mention being made of the chattels.   The registrar entered the description of the instrument in the register in similar terms, identifying it by its date, and omitting all
D   mention of any charge on the chattels.   Subsequently the sheriff, in execution of a judgment recovered by the defendant against the company, seized certain chattels of the company upon the mortgaged premises, including certain motor vans.   The bank claimed the goods in question under their mortgage, and obtained from the registrar a certificate ' that a mortgage or charge dated '—specifying the date and the parties to the instrument—
E   ' was registered pursuant to s. 93 of the Companies Act '.   By sub-s. 5 of that section the certificate of the registrar is made ' conclusive evidence that the requirements of the section as to registration have been complied with '.   On an interpleader issue to try the title of the bank as against the execution creditor:—*Held* [the first holding was a holding to the effect that the bank had an equitable charge on the plant] (2) That, as the certifi-
F   cate identified the instrument of charge, and stated that the mortgage or charge thereby created had been duly registered, it must be understood as certifying the due registration of all the charges created by the instrument, including that of the chattels, and that it was conclusive evidence of the due registration of the chattels none the less because the register in omitting to mention them was not merely defective but misleading."

G
BANKES, L.J., said (5):

" But then it was contended that even if, apart from the provisions of the Companies (Consolidation) Act, 1908, the document of July 16, 1921, gave the bank a valid floating charge over the chattels, including the motor vans, it was void by reason of non-compliance with the requirements of
H   s. 93 of that Act . . . But where a mortgage or charge is created by an instrument, it seems to me quite impossible to treat that mortgage or charge otherwise than as one indivisible transaction, even though it covers several different items and different kinds of property, because it is evidenced by one instrument and one instrument only, and it is to that mortgage or charge so created by one indivisible instrument that the section, when requiring performance of
I   the conditions necessary to prevent its avoidance, refers.   Those conditions are that the prescribed particulars and the instrument by which the charge is created shall be delivered to the registrar within twenty-one days.   It is not disputed, as I understand it, that the object of the Legislature in requiring delivery to the registrar of the instrument as well as the particulars is to enable him to form an independent judgment in reference to what he ought

(3) [1924] 1 K.B. 431.
(4) [1924] 1 K.B. at pp. 431, 432.
(5) [1924] 1 K.B. at pp. 442-445.

A

to put on the register before he in fact registers it, and if he is entitled to do that, being only human, he may make a mistake, and if he makes a mistake and enters on the register something different from what the particulars really justify, the unfortunate person carrying in those particulars will, according to [counsel for the appellant], find himself possessed of a void instrument, because the register, which, as I understand [counsel's] argument, is the conclusive document, does not contain true particulars of the instrument. I agree with the judgments in *Re Yolland, Husson and Birkett, Ltd.* (6), to which we have been referred, as to the object of the statute. I think the object is to protect the grantee of the charge, and, as between him and the general body of creditors or prospective creditors, the registrar is appointed as the tribunal to decide what shall be put upon the register, and when it has been put there his certificate to that effect is conclusive evidence that all the requirements of the section have been complied with. One of those requirements, as I have already said, is that the prescribed particulars must be delivered, and we have been referred to the Statutory Rules and Orders, 1909, which contain the prescribed form of particulars, Form 47 ... Another head in the form of particulars is ' Short particulars of property mortgaged or charged ', and under that head no reference was made to the chattels. It is quite true that there is an omission, because the property mortgaged or charged included chattels as well as land and fixtures; but when once the registrar has given his certificate that the registration was complete, and that the mortgage or charge was created by an instrument, identifying it, in my opinion you have to go to the instrument to see what was actually charged, there being nothing in the statute which says that when once registration has taken place the register shall be the evidence of the extent of the charge. All that the statute requires is satisfaction on the part of the appointed official that the preliminaries have been complied with, and, when once he certifies that, the parties are entitled to ask the Court to say that what it has to look at in order to determine their rights is the instrument creating the mortgage or charge. For these reasons I think the view taken by the learned judge was right, and that this appeal should be dismissed."

Then, SCRUTTON, L.J., said (7):

" One of the reasons for that provision as to the conclusiveness of the certificate is that the person whose duty it is to register the charge is the company (sub-s. 7), the party giving it, not the party to whom it is given. The company may give such charges to a large number of debenture holders, who do not see the particulars, and very likely are not in a position to examine the register. The object of the certificate in that case is to prevent the debenture holders' security from being upset if it turns out that the company or the registrar has made a mistake as to what has been put on the register. I am bound to say that the language of the statute is rather puzzling: [he quotes] ' Every mortgage or charge created by a company ... shall be void unless the prescribed particulars of the mortgage or charge ... are delivered ... to the registrar ... within twenty-one days.' That makes the avoidance depend on the neglect to send in the particulars. The neglect to register the charge will not make it void. Then when the registrar has got the particulars and the instrument creating the charge, he is to enter in the register, not the particulars delivered by the company, but the date of the instrument and its description, the amount secured, short particulars of the property mortgaged or charged, and the names of the mortgagees or persons entitled to the charge. So that there is a possibility, first, of the company making an error in delivering the particulars, and secondly of

(6) [1908] 1 Ch. 152.
(7) [1924] 1 K.B. at pp. 447, 448.

A   the registrar making an error either in omitting to enter something specified
in the particulars, or in misunderstanding the instrument of charge delivered
to him with the particulars; and for that reason one can well understand
a clause being put in in favour of the grantees of the charge, who are not the
persons whose duty it is to deliver the particulars, that if the registrar gives
a certificate that all is in order that certificate shall be conclusive evidence
B   that the requirements as to registration have been complied with.   The
result of the legislation as it appears to me is that if the document sent in
for registration does contain a charge on particular property, even if the
company sending it in has misstated that charge, or the registrar considering
it judicially has misunderstood it, when once the certificate has been given
the grantees are safe.   Though one can see that this may cause great hard-
C   ship to a person who gives credit to the company in reliance on a defective
register, one can also see that equal hardship would be caused to secured
creditors if their security was to be upset for reasons connected with the
action of persons over whom they had no control. For these reasons I take the
view which was taken in *Re Yolland, Husson and Birkett, Ltd.* (8) and *Cunard
Steamship Co., Ltd.* v. *Hopwood* (9) that the giving of the certificate by the
D   registrar is conclusive that the document creating the charge was properly
registered, even if in fact it was not properly registered.   I do not know
how the difficulty arose in this case.   It looks as if somebody was very careless on behalf of the bank, and also as if somebody was very careless in the
registrar's office."

Then, ATKIN, L.J., said (10):

E   " It appears to me to be the true view that when once such a certificate
has been given by the registrar in respect to a particular specified document
which in fact creates a mortgage or charge, it is conclusive that the mortgage
or charge so created is properly registered, even though the particulars put
forward by the person applying for registration are incomplete, and the
entry in the register by the registrar is defective.   That I think follows
F   from *Re Yolland, Husson and Birkett, Ltd.* (8)."

What that case shows is, I think, that the purpose of the registrar's certificate is
to protect mortgagees against mistakes made either by the company (when it
is the company which is lodging the particulars for registration) or by the registrar
himself when he is registering them.   It is to be noticed that all the Lords
Justices based their decision on *Re Yolland, Husson and Birkett, Ltd.* (8), a
G   case where the mistake (if any) was that of the registrar.

In my judgment, *Charnley's* case (11) does not touch the point with which I
am concerned, and it is of interest to note that ATKIN, L.J., suggested that it
might not always be open to a mortgagee to set up the conclusiveness of the
certificate. He said this (12):

H   " There is one matter that I should like to reserve. If in any case it could
be established that the creditor for his own purposes intentionally abstained
from mentioning part of his security in the particulars and in that way
procured the registrar to enter only a part of the security on the register,
it may be that as against a person who could show that he was misled by the
partial registration the secured creditor could not set up the conclusiveness
I   of the certificate.   It is not necessary to decide that here."

The second case in order of date (though not of report) is *Re Mechanisations
(Eaglescliffe), Ltd.* (13).   The facts are stated in the headnote (14):

---

(8) [1908] 1 Ch. 152.
(9) [1908] 2 Ch. 564.
(10) [1924] 1 K.B. at p. 452.
(11) [1924] 1 K.B. 431.
(12) [1924] 1 K.B. at p. 454.
(13) [1964] 3 All E.R. 840; [1966] Ch. 20.
(14) [1966] Ch. at pp. 20, 21.

" By two legal charges, dated respectively May 7, 1959, and February 24,   A
1960, N.B.C. agreed to make advances to M. (E.) Ltd. of sums amounting
in the aggregate to £18,000 together with interest in each case, sums
which might become owing for goods supplied to M. (E.) Ltd. and also certain
architects' fees, all on the security of freehold property of M. (E.) Ltd.
In the particulars supplied to the companies' registrar for registration of
the first charge pursuant to section 95 of the Companies Act, 1948, the   B
amount secured was given as the principal sum only, no mention being made
of the payment of interest or the other sums; registration was duly effected
on that basis and the registrar gave his certificate, again making no mention
of the additional sums secured on the property by that charge. Particulars
of the further charge were delivered for registration and the amount secured
was given as the principal sum and interest. That charge was not, however,   C
registered in due time and when it eventually came to be registered—leave
having been obtained to extend the time—no mention was made of the
interest and, again the certificate was issued on that basis. In a subsequent
creditors' voluntary winding up, the mortgagees, N.B.C., claimed as secured
creditors for the total sum advanced by them, which, with interest and the
other payments, exceeded by about £5,000 the aggregate amount referred   D
to in the certificates and on the companies' register. The liquidator sought
a declaration that in respect of the excess the charges were void as against
him or any creditor for want of registration. N.B.C. applied for an order
under section 101 of the Companies Act, 1948, to rectify the register:—
Held, that the charges were a valid security for the full amount due under
them, for the accuracy of the particulars delivered to the registrar was not a   E
condition of the validity of a charge as against a liquidator or a creditor, and
the certificate of the registrar once delivered was conclusive that the necessary
preliminaries for registration had been complied with and that the prescribed
particulars had been delivered to him: to discover the exact terms of the
charge it was the document itself which had to be looked at. *National
Provincial and Union Bank of England* v. *Charnley* (15); *Re Yolland, Husson*   F
and Birkett, Ltd. (16), and *Cunard Steamship Co., Ltd.* v. *Hopwood* (17)
followed."

It appears from the report (18), though not from the headnote, that it was the
mortgagees who presented to the companies registrar the Form 47, but it is to
be noticed that it was the liquidator, not the mortgagees, who was relying on the
conclusiveness of the certificate, and that the claim for rectification did not, in   G
the event arise. BUCKLEY, J., said (19):

" For these reasons it seems to me that in the present case the respondents
are entitled to rely on their principal mortgage and their further charge as
conferring on them a valid security for the full amounts due under those
documents according to their tenor, and I think, therefore, that the application fails. The respondents have brought before the court a cross-   H
application asking, in the event of my coming to a contrary conclusion to that
which I have reached, that I should, pursuant to s. 101 of the Companies
Act, 1948, rectify the particulars of the charge on the register. That
necessity does not arise, having regard to the view which I have taken of
the construction and effect of the sections; but I might perhaps just say
this. Having regard to what was said in the decisions in *Re S. Abrahams &*   I
Sons (20) and in *Re Anglo-Oriental Carpet Manufacturing Co.* (21), it appears

---

(15) [1924] 1 K.B. 431.
(16) [1908] 1 Ch. 152.
(17) [1908] 2 Ch. 564.
(18) [1966] Ch. at p. 22.
(19) [1964] 3 All E.R. at p. 849; [1966] Ch. at pp. 36, 37.
(20) [1902] 1 Ch. 695.
(21) [1903] 1 Ch. 914.

A   to me that a very exceptional case would have to be made out to justify the court in making any order under s. 101 after a company had gone into liquidation and the rights of unsecured creditors in liquidation had crystallised; but, as I say, it is unnecessary for me to arrive at any decision on that summons, because the occasion for the relief sought by the respondents does not arise."

B   With regard to the question of rectification after liquidation, it is to be borne in mind that BUCKLEY, J., was envisaging a case of a mortgagee seeking, after liquidation, to improve his position vis-à-vis unsecured creditors. It has no relevance to the converse case, such as the present.

The third case is *Re Eric Holmes (Property), Ltd.* (22). That case bears a superficial resemblance to the present case, in that there too the date of a charge was
C left blank at the time the charge was created and was filled in only later, when the charge was given a date some two or three weeks after the date of its creation. The application for registration was then made within 21 days of the latter date but not of the former. On the company going into liquidation, the liquidator issued a summons for a declaration that the charge was void under s. 95 (1) of the Act. PENNYCUICK, J., held (among other things) (23):
D

   " That even though the particulars of the charge delivered to the registrar with the application for registration pursuant to section 95 (1) of the Act of 1948 incorrectly stated the date of the charge, once the certificate of registration was granted section 98 (2) of the Act applied and the certificate was conclusive evidence that the requirements of the Act as to registration
E   had been complied with. *National Provincial and Union Bank of England v. Charnley* (24) and *Re Mechanisations (Eaglescliffe), Ltd.* (25) followed. *Per curiam* . . . The power to rectify the register under section 101 of the Act of 1948 is not to be lightly exercised, particularly after liquidation has crystallised the rights of the parties. If the power was required to be exercised in this case it would not have been exercised against R."

F he being the mortgagee.

   PENNYCUICK, J., rejected an argument put forward on behalf of the liquidator that the certificate of the registrar was not conclusive unless particulars of the charge had been delivered within 21 days of its creation. He said this (26):

   " Counsel for the liquidator contends that s. 95 unequivocally avoids as against a liquidator charges created by a company unless particulars
G   of the charge together with the instrument are delivered within twenty-one days after the date of the creation of the charge. Section 98 then directs the registrar to register charges requiring registration under the Act, and by necessary implication forbids registration of charges which do not either require or permit of registration under the Act, including charges executed outside the twenty-one day period. So here it is contended the purported
H   registration of the two charges was a simple nullity, because these charges were not eligible for registration and their registration confers no protection on Mr. Richards. Counsel for Mr. Richards counters this contention by reliance on sub-s. (2) of s. 98, in particular the words ' the certificate shall be conclusive evidence that the requirements of this Part of this Act as to registration have been complied with '. The certificate, he contends, is con-
I   clusive that all the requirements of the Act have been complied with, including delivery to the registrar within twenty-one days of execution. I feel considerable sympathy with the argument advanced by counsel for the liquidator, but I am unable to accept it."

(22) [1965] 2 All E.R. 333; [1965] Ch. 1052.
(23) [1965] Ch. at pp. 1054, 1055.
(24) [1924] 1 K.B. 431.
(25) [1964] 3 All E.R. 840; [1966] Ch. 20.
(26) [1965] 2 All E.R. at pp. 342, 343; [1965] Ch. at p. 1069.

But the crucial point, as I see it, is that the application for registration in that **A** case was, as appears from the report (27), made by the company and not by the mortgagees who were in no way to blame for the mis-statement of the date of the creation of the charge. In those circumstances there could be no injustice in holding that the certificate was conclusive in favour of the mortgagees. PENNYCUICK, J., said (28):

"There appears to be no authority in point where the particulars incor- **B** rectly state the date of the charge, but it seems to me impossible to take that case out of the words of sub-s. (2) of s. 98 without in fact inserting words by implication, and again I think that I am precluded by authority from attempting to do that ... It is, I think, possible that there is some lacuna in the Act here, inasmuch as the Act gives, apparently, protection where the certificate is made on the basis of particulars which are incorrect and might **C** even be fraudulent. Finally, there is the point under s. 101. That is the power to rectify the register. Counsel for Mr. Richards contends that that section is wholly inapplicable to the present circumstances, with the remark- able consequence, it seems to me, that even in the case of fraud the certificate would be conclusive and there would be no means of putting the matter right. I do not accept that contention. On the other hand, the power **D** to rectify is one which is not to be lightly exercised, particularly after liquidation has crystallised the rights of the parties. (See per BUCKLEY, J., in *Re Mechanisations (Eaglescliffe), Ltd.* (29).) In the present case the mistake was not on the part of Mr. Richards but on the part of the company. I do not think that I ought to say how I would exercise a discretion on a matter which has not in fact arisen. Perhaps I may say this, that if I were **E** required to exercise a discretion under s. 101, I do not think I should exercise it adversely to Mr. Richards."

The question of rectification after liquidation did not in fact arise, because there was no claim for rectification, but one can well understand that if it had arisen, the learned judge would have been unwilling to exercise it against a completely innocent party. **F**

I can see nothing in those cases which suggests that it is any function of the registrar's certificate to give protection to a mortgagee against his own mis- statements or which prevents me from holding that the charge created by the company in favour of the bank on 28th February 1964, must be treated as void against the liquidators and creditors of the company on the broad principle which I referred to earlier in this judgment, namely, that no man can take **G** advantage of his own wrong.

In these circumstances, it is unnecessary to consider whether the same result might be achieved by a more tortuous path, involving the rectification of the register by amending or deleting the offending entry.

I will therefore make a declaration that the charge created by the company **H** in favour of the respondent bank on or about 28th February 1964, but bearing date 18th June 1964, is void against the liquidators and creditors of the company.

Declaration accordingly.

Solicitors: *Slaughter & May* (for the liquidators); *Waltons, Bright & Co.* (for the respondent bank).

[*Reported by* JACQUELINE METCALFE, *Barrister-at-Law.*] **I**

---

(27) [1965] 2 All E.R. at pp. 335-339; [1965] Ch. at pp. 1060, 1061.
(28) [1965] 2 All E.R. at p. 344; [1965] Ch. at pp. 1071, 1072.
(29) [1964] 3 All E.R. at p. 849; [1966] Ch. at pp. 36, 37.

A

NOTE.

R. v. HARRIS.

[COURT OF APPEAL, CRIMINAL DIVISION (Lord Parker, C.J., Edmund Davies, L.J., and Caulfield, J.), March 25, 1969.]

B

Criminal Law—Indictment—Joinder of counts—Undesirability of one and the same incident being made subject-matter of distinct charges.

[As to joinder of several offences in an indictment, see 10 HALSBURY'S LAWS (3rd Edn.) 391, 392, para. 708; and for cases on the subject, see 14 DIGEST (Repl.) 249, 250, *2146-2158.*]

C

Application.

The applicant, John Harris, applied for leave to appeal against his conviction before Mr. COMMISSIONER PATERSON and a jury on 19th November 1968 at Manchester Crown Court of buggery on a boy aged 14 and of indecent assault on the same boy. He was sentenced to seven years' imprisonment for the buggery

D
and to five years' imprisonment concurrent for the indecent assault. It was also ordered that a sentence of six months' imprisonment for attempted false pretences imposed at Wiltshire Quarter Sessions on 3rd July 1968, which was suspended for six months, should take effect consecutively to the other sentence. The applicant also applied for leave to appeal against sentence. This report deals only with the question of the desirability of one incident being made the subject-

E
matter of distinct charges.

The applicant did not appear and was not represented.

EDMUND DAVIES, L.J., in giving the judgment of the court, said: In relation to conviction, the summing-up of the learned commissioner was thorough, careful and fair and the jury had their minds properly directed to the

F
issues that they had to bear in mind and the evidence which related thereto. It is impossible to say that they were not entitled to come to the conclusion that the charge of buggery was made out. The application in relation to that offence is, accordingly, refused.

But this court observes that the applicant was convicted not only on the full charge but also on the lesser (though still grave) charge of indecent assault on

G
the same boy in relation to the same incident, and that he was sentenced in respect thereof to a concurrent term of five years' imprisonment. It is perfectly clear on reading the transcript that the two charges related to one and the same incident. There is no suggestion of any indecent assault on this same boy except that which formed the preliminary to and was followed very shortly thereafter by the commission of the full act of buggery. It does not seem to

H
this court right or desirable that one and the same incident should be made the subject-matter of distinct charges, so that hereafter it may appear to those not familiar with the circumstances that two entirely separate offences were committed. Were this permitted generally, a single offence could frequently give rise to a multiplicity of charges and great unfairness could ensue. We, accordingly, allow the application for leave to appeal against the conviction of

I
indecent assault, which really merges into the conviction for the graver charge. Having granted leave, we treat this as the hearing of the appeal in relation to the indecent assault conviction and quash that conviction, but refuse leave to appeal in respect of the buggery conviction.

Appeal allowed in part.

[*Reported by* N. P. METCALFE, ESQ., *Barrister-at-Law.*]

A

ROTHER *v.* COLCHESTER CORPORATION.

[CHANCERY DIVISION (Megarry, J.), January 20, 21, 22, 1969.]

Landlord and Tenant—Restrictive covenant—Premises let for trade of general
hardware merchant, ironmonger, grocer and greengrocer—Landlords' covenant
not to let adjacent premises for purpose of general hardware merchant and
ironmonger—Adjacent premises let as food hall—Tenants of food hall selling
items of hardware—Meaning of covenant " not to let " for a specified purpose.

B

The tenant occupied a shop on a housing estate owned by the landlords.
Under his lease, he was entitled to occupy the shop for the trade of general
hardware merchant, ironmonger, grocer and greengrocer.   The landlords
entered into a covenant, inter alia, not to let any other shop on the estate
for the purpose of a general hardware merchant and ironmonger.   Later,
the landlords demised premises on the estate to a co-operative society for
the purpose of a food hall. By cl. 3 of the agreement, the society covenanted
not to sell any item on the premises which would cause the landlords to be
in breach of any covenants granted for the benefit of other tenants; the
covenants referred to (including the covenant not to let any other shop on
the estate for the purpose of a general hardware merchant and ironmonger)
were set out in a schedule to the agreement. The tenant complained that
the society sold from its premises items of hardware, including soap powders,
detergents, and soap, and that the landlords were thereby in breach of their
covenant.

C

D

Held: the action would be dismissed, because—

(i) by cl. 3 of the agreement, the landlords in terms prohibited the sale of
particular items on the society's premises; the items prohibited were those
which would cause the landlords to commit a breach of their covenant
against letting a shop for the purpose of a general hardware merchant or
ironmonger; such sales being prohibited, the landlords could not be said
to have let the premises for the purpose of a general hardware merchant
and ironmonger (see p. 606, letter I, to p. 607, letter A, post); alternatively,

E

F

(ii) a restrictive covenant as to the letting or user of premises had to be
construed strictly; accordingly the covenant not to let for the purpose of
a general hardware merchant and ironmonger could not be enlarged into
a covenant not to permit the premises to be used for that purpose (see p. 607,
letter D, post).

Kemp v. *Bird* ((1877), 5 Ch.D. 974) followed.

G

[As to covenants restricting the user of adjoining premises, see 23 HALSBURY'S
LAWS (3rd Edn.) 620-623, paras. 1320, 1322; and for cases on the subject, see
31 DIGEST (Repl.) 180-183, *3126-3146*.]

Cases referred to:

Ashby v. *Wilson*, [1900] 1 Ch. 60; 69 L.J.Ch. 47; 81 L.T. 480; 31 Digest   H
(Repl.) 180, *3130*.

Brigg v. *Thornton*, [1904] 1 Ch. 386; 73 L.J.Ch. 301; 90 L.T. 327; 31 Digest
(Repl.) 181, *3141*.

Fitz v. *Iles*, [1893] 1 Ch. 77; 62 L.J.Ch. 258; 68 L.T. 108; 31 Digest (Repl.)
171, *3057*.

Holloway Brothers, Ltd. v. *Hill*, [1902] 2 Ch. 612; 71 L.J.Ch. 818; 87 L.T.   I
201; 31 Digest (Repl.) 182, *3143*.

Kemp v. *Bird* (1877), 5 Ch.D. 974; 46 L.J.Ch. 828; 37 L.T. 53; 42 J.P. 36;
31 Digest (Repl.) 180, *3128*.

Labone v. *Litherland Urban District Council*, [1956] 2 All E.R. 215; [1956]
1 W.L.R. 522; Digest (Cont. Vol. A) 1006, *3135a*.

Lewis (A.) & Co. (Westminster), Ltd. v. *Bell Property Trust, Ltd.*, [1940] 1 All
E.R. 570; [1940] Ch. 345; 109 L.J.Ch. 132; 163 L.T. 37; 31 Digest
(Repl.) 181, *3134*.

A   *Young* v. *Bristol Aeroplane Co., Ltd.*, [1944] 2 All E.R. 293; [1944] K.B. 718;
        113 L.J.K.B. 513; 171 L.T. 113; *affd.*, H.L., [1946] 1 All E.R. 98;
        [1946] A.C. 163; 30 Digest (Repl.) 225, *691.*

Action.

This was an action by the plaintiff, Arthur Bert Rother, the tenant of no. 7,
The Square, Iceni Way, Shrub End, Colchester, against the defendants, the
B   Colchester Corporation as landlords, for breach of a covenant not to let any
other shop on the same estate for the purpose of a general hardware merchant
and ironmonger contained in an agreement under seal dated 19th December 1955
and continued under a lease under seal dated 29th October 1962, expressed to
be supplemental to the agreement. The facts are set out in the judgment.

J. P. Brookes for the tenant.
C   *J. A. R. Finlay* for the landlords.

MEGARRY, J.: This is an action by a tenant against his landlords. The
plaintiff is the tenant of a shop in Colchester. The defendants, his landlords, are
the Colchester Corporation. I shall refer to the parties as " the tenant " and
" the landlords ". The action concerns the use of a shop also owned by the
D   landlords and let by them to the Colchester and East Essex Co-operative and
Industrial Society, Ltd. For brevity, I shall call that body " the society ".

By an agreement under seal dated 19th December 1955, the landlords and the
tenant agreed for the grant by the landlords to the tenant of a lease for seven
years of shop premises which are now known as no. 7, The Square, Iceni Way,
Colchester. The term of seven years was to commence not later than one month
E   after the date when the premises had been completed by the landlords; and
it seems, from a later document to which I shall refer, that in fact the term was
treated by the parties as running from 9th April 1956. By cl. 2 of this document
(which I shall refer to as " the agreement ") it was provided that " The tenant
shall enter into the following covenants ". There is then set out a series of
covenants, lettered (a) to (n), providing in (k) for the tenant:

F   " To occupy and keep open the premises for the trade of General Hard-
        ware Merchant Ironmonger Grocer and Greengrocer and not for any other
        purpose whatsoever."

There are then the words: " The Council's decision as to the interpretation of
this clause shall be final." That is a sentence which mercifully I am not called
on to consider in this judgment. " The Council " is, of course, the term used in
G   the agreement to describe the landlords.

By cl. 3 it is provided that:

        " The Council shall enter into the following covenants: (a) To keep the
        roof main walls and structure in good and substantial repair (b) To paint and
        decorate the exterior of the premises (c) Not to let any other shop on the
H   Housing Estate for the purpose of a General Hardware Merchant and
        Ironmonger (d) A covenant for quiet enjoyment in the usual qualified form
        (e) To rebuild or reinstate the premises in the case of destruction or damage
        by fire."

It will be seen that this clause is plainly executory in form, contemplating the
execution of a formal lease in which no doubt these provisions would be expressed,
I   at any rate in some instances, in amplified form. Clause 4 provides that:

        " The Lease shall also contain the following declarations and provisos:
        . . . (g) An option in the usual terms for the renewal of the Lease for a further
        seven years."

No formal lease carrying out the terms of this agreement ever appears to have
been executed, but the parties seem to have treated it as governing the relationship between them. However, in due course the option was exercised by the
tenant, and by lease under seal dated 29th October 1962, expressed to be

supplemental to the agreement (though there are certain errors in the terms of
reference on which no point has been taken), a lease was granted to the tenant
for seven years from 9th April 1963. There was an increase in the rent, and by
cl. 2 it was provided:

> " The covenant on the part of the Tenant contained in clause 2 (k) of
> the Principal Deed [I pause to say that that is a reference to the agreement]
> shall be varied so as to include in addition to the trades therein mentioned
> those of a draper retailer of haberdashery and retailer of ice cream."

By cl. 3 it was provided that the landlords and the tenant:

> " hereby covenant with each other that they will respectively perform
> and observe the covenants and stipulations contained in the Principal
> Deed as if the same had been repeated herein in full with such modifications
> only as are necessary to make them applicable to this demise and to accord
> with the variations hereby made."

It is under this lease that the tenant now holds the premises from the landlords.

I turn now to the position of the society. By a lease dated 15th October 1956
(which I shall call " the society's first lease ") the landlords demised to the society
for a term of seven years from 25th October 1956 the premises known as no. 11,
The Square, Iceni Way, Colchester. These premises are just across the square
from the premises demised to the tenant. The lease contains a number of
covenants by the society, including a covenant in cl. 2 (k) " to occupy and keep
open the premises for the purpose of a Food Hall and not for any other purpose."

By cl. 3 it is provided that:

> " The Company [that is a reference to the society] further covenant with
> the Council [and that is a reference to the landlords] that they will not on
> the demised premises sell any commodity or item which may cause the
> Council to commit a breach of any of the covenants granted or to be granted
> for the benefit of the tenants of adjacent shops such covenants being
> referred to in the Schedule hereto ";

and then the clause proceeds with words of indemnity. The relevant part of
the schedule is para. (d). Under a column headed with the word " covenant "
are the words: " (d) not to let any other shop on the said Estate for the purpose
of a General Hardware Merchant and Ironmonger." Under the heading " Person
having benefit of covenant " appears the name of the tenant. Under the heading
" Address of shop concerned " appears " No. 7 The Square, Iceni Way ", that
is, the premises demised to the tenant. I pause here to say that this case largely
turns on cl. 3 (c) of the agreement and cl. 2 (k) and cl. 3 and para. (d) of the
schedule in the society's first lease.

That lease has, of course, expired; but by a lease dated 25th September 1963,
made between the landlords and the society and endorsed on the society's first
lease there was a demise of the same premises for a further term of seven years
from 25th October 1963. A clause provides that:

> " The Council and the [society] hereby covenant with each other that
> they will respectively perform and observe the covenants and stipulations
> contained in the within-written Lease (except the covenant to pay rent) as
> if the same had been repeated herein in full with such modifications only as
> are necessary to make them applicable to this demise."

This document may be called " the society's second lease ".

The statement of claim, after referring to certain clauses of the agreement,
provides:

> " By clause 3 (c) of the Agreement it was provided that the [landlords]
> should enter into a covenant not to let any other shop on the Housing
> Estate (meaning thereby the said Council Estate) for the purpose of a
> General Hardware Merchant and Ironmonger. In the premises it was an

A implied term of the Agreement that the [landlords] should also enter into a covenant: (a) Not to let any other shop on the said Estate on terms which would allow it to be used for the purpose of a General Hardware Merchant and Ironmonger; and (b) To enforce the provisions of any lease or tenancy agreement of any other shop on the said Estate so as to prevent such shop from being used for the purpose of a General Hardware Merchant and

B Ironmonger."

After referring to the renewal of the tenant's lease, the statement of claim continues in para. 9 and para. 10:

" 9. The [landlords] have wrongfully and in breach of their said covenant let another shop on the said Estate, namely No. 11 The Square Iceni Way

C aforesaid (hereinafter called ' the Shop ') to the Colchester Co-operative Society Limited (hereinafter called ' the Society ') for the purpose of a General Hardware Merchant and Ironmonger. The [tenant] is unable to give particulars to the said letting until after discovery.

" 10. Further, or in the alternative, the [landlords] have wrongfully and in breach of their said covenant let the Shop to the Society on terms which

D allow the Shop to be used for the purpose of a General Hardware Merchant and Ironmonger. The [tenant] is unable to give particulars of the said letting until after discovery."

Those two paragraphs relate in particular to the body of para. 3 of the statement of claim and to para. 3 (a) of the statement of claim, respectively. The statement of claim then continues with a paragraph which relates to para. 3 (b) of the

E statement of claim:

" 11. Further, or in the further alternative, the Society has since October 1962 used, and is now using, the Shop for the purpose (inter alia) of a General Hardware Merchant and Ironmonger."

Then there are set out certain particulars to which I shall refer in a moment.

The case before me arises because the society has, it is said, been selling from

F its shop on the other side of The Square a variety of goods, amounting to some 45 items, which the tenant asserts are all items of hardware. These items, as set out in the particulars that I have just mentioned, form a striking list. The particulars state that—

" The Society sells at the Shop the following items of Hardware:—Fire

G Lighters, Pegs, Floor Polish, Soap Powders, Detergents, Disinfectants, Soaps, Boot and Shoe Polish, Liquid Polish, Dish Mops, Dish Cloths, Floor Mops, Rentokil, Kleenoff, Chamois Leathers, Pan scrubbers, Carpet cleaners, Floor cloths, Dusters, Soap Dishes, Nail Brushes, Scrubbing Brushes, Light Brushes, Pails, Bowls, Broom Handles, Broom Heads, Fly Killers, Cups and Saucers, Household Gloves, Soft Brushes, Hard Brushes, Hand Brushes,

H Lampshades, Turpentine, Metal Polish, Nylon Dyes, Garden Chairs, Deckchair Covers, Steel Deckchairs, Electric Light Bulbs, Brobat, Domestos, Washing-up-Powders, Balls of String."

The great majority of the items on this list are items which the society admits selling on their premises, either at some time in the past or today. Mr. Golding, who for some 11 years managed the society's food hall, says that some six or

I seven items were never stocked by the society. The evidence of the tenant to the contrary as regards certain of these disputed items was somewhat tentative and unsatisfactory. Mr. Golding put in evidence a list setting out the retail value of all the items in this list sold by the society during the five weeks 4th September to 7th October 1967, which was towards the end of his time as manager. The total is some £562, and, of this, three items on the list account for some £428, which is more than three-quarters of the total. These three items are soap powders, detergents and soaps. Although in the particulars in the statement of claim the tenant states that these are " items of hardware ",

I do not think that this assertion can possibly be right. THE SHORTER OXFORD A
ENGLISH DICTIONARY defines " Hardware " as " Small ware or goods of metal;
ironmongery ". It may well be that in an age of plastics the plastic equivalents
of metal articles that are hardware should also be regarded as hardware. But
nothing said in this case begins to convince me that soap, soap powders or
detergents, or indeed many other articles in the tenant's long list, such as dish
cloths, dusters, household gloves, lamp shades and electric light bulbs, can B
fairly be included in the term " hardware ".

Counsel for the tenant wisely did not attempt to support this proposition,
but he and the tenant both urged that these items, if not hardware, were at least
articles usually sold by hardware shops, and to that extent, and to that extent
only, could properly be called " hardware ". In his evidence the tenant accepted
that even in this sense soap powders and detergents were borderline, and that C
some grocers sell soap. But in the main he said that nearly all the items were,
in this special sense, hardware.

Put in its simplest form, the tenant's case is that by the agreement as
incorporated in the tenant's lease the landlords covenanted not to let any other
shop on the estate for the purpose of a general hardware merchant and ironmonger. Within a year the landlords had let another shop on the estate to the D
society " for the purpose of a Food Hall ". The purpose of a food hall, says the
tenant, includes at least some of that of a general hardware merchant, as is
shown by the way in which the society has been using the premises. Therefore,
he says, there is a breach of the covenant.

As the argument developed, counsel for the tenant jettisoned para. 3 (b) of
the statement of claim, and with it para. 11. He also abandoned the first prayer E
for relief, namely :

> " An Order that the [landlords] do forthwith take all such steps as may
> be open to them to prevent the Shop from being used for the purpose of a
> General Hardware Merchant and Ironmonger."

He also rested his argument less on any implied term than on the true construction of the relevant documents. He looked at the possibility of giving an extended F
construction to cl. 3 (c) of the agreement on the grounds that it was a mere
executory agreement; but rightly, in my judgment, he abstained from urging
any such construction in view of the fact that the tenant's lease was an executed
instrument, and not executory, and that it had merely incorporated the covenants
of the agreement.

Counsel for the landlords emphasised the wording of cl. 3 (c) of the agreement. G
It was, he said, confined to letting the premises for the specified purpose. It
was not a covenant not to use the premises for the specified purpose, nor a
covenant not to permit or suffer the premises to be so used. He relied in particular
on *Kemp* v. *Bird* (1). In that case, JAMES, L.J., said (2):

> " Persons ought to look after their own interests in framing their own H
> contracts and their own covenants. Persons who are men of business, as
> they were here, are able to get protection and advice, and they must make
> their covenants express, so as to state what they really mean, and they cannot
> get a Court of Law or of Equity to supply something which they have not
> stipulated for in order to get a benefit which is supposed to have been
> intended. Here the words are very plain, and the covenant is intelligible I
> and reasonable as it stands (as FRY, J., has observed), whatever may be
> the extent or effect of it. It is, ' That the said *G. Bird* shall not, during the
> said term, demise or let any or either of the messuages or tenements now
> forming the said street called *London Street, Paddington*, between *Arthur
> Mews* and *Francis Mews*, to any person whomsoever for the purpose of
> carrying on the trade or business of an eating-house,' etc. He may not

(1) (1877), 5 Ch.D. 974.
(2) (1877), 5 Ch.D. at pp. 976, 977.

A demise it or let it for that purpose. I assume that if he demised it or let it generally, so as to allow the tenant to do as he liked, that would introduce a different question; but that was not the case here. If it had been intended that there should have been a positive restriction on the use of the premises during the term, there is a well-known form which the parties might have used, and which would have been binding on the owner, and on his repre-

B sentatives, and on the assignee—that is, ' that the said *G. Bird*, his heirs, executors, administrators, and assigns, shall not, during the said term, demise or let, or permit any of the said messuages or tenements to be demised or let ', and so on. It is quite clear that *Bird* did not intend to enter into such a covenant. By what right are we to extend this covenant beyond the words in which it is expressed—that is, that he shall not demise or let? "

C BAGGALLAY, L.J., said (3):

"I know of no possible way, where it is alleged that there have been breaches of contract, of finding out what was the intention of the parties, than by looking at what is found in the covenant itself. The Appellant is desirous to deduce from those terms something far beyond what the docu-

D ment itself puts forth, and if once we were to adopt that method in this Court we should introduce very great confusion into the construction of documents of this kind."

In that case Bird, the landlord, demised the other premises subject to a covenant by the tenant not to carry on any trade or business on them; and when an assignee began to carry on the business of an eating-house on the premises it

E was held that this constituted no breach of covenant on which the plaintiff could sue either Bird or the assignee. A covenant not to let premises for a particular purpose is not broken by the use of the premises for that purpose if the lessor has inserted in the lease a prohibition wide enough to prohibit the use. " Not to let ", and " not to permit the use ", are two different concepts.

Kemp v. *Bird* (4) was followed and applied in *Ashby* v. *Wilson* (5), where the

F facts were similar. In *Ashby* v. *Wilson* (5) KEKEWICH, J., drew attention to *Fitz* v. *Iles* (6). This was a decision of the Court of Appeal in which *Kemp* v. *Bird* (4) had not been cited. It is perhaps an authority sub silentio to the opposite effect, the real point in issue decided by the court being different. In *Holloway Brothers, Ltd.* v. *Hill* (7) BYRNE, J., held (and I quote from the headnote) that " The decision in *Kemp* v. *Bird* (4) is not inconsistent with that of *Fitz* v. *Iles* (6) ":

G but I confess that I have not found his reconciliation of the cases very persuasive. If *Kemp* v. *Bird* (4) and *Fitz* v. *Iles* (6) had been flatly in conflict, with the same point deliberately decided in each case in opposite senses, the question would have been difficult. *Young* v. *Bristol Aeroplane Co., Ltd.* (8) establishes (inter alia) two propositions: first, that the Court of Appeal is bound by its own decisions; and secondly, that it is entitled and bound to decide which of two

H conflicting decisions of its own it will follow. I find the reconciliation of these two propositions somewhat puzzling. If in case A the Court of Appeal lays down the law in one sense, then that is binding on the Court of Appeal. If later, in case B, the court, not knowing of case A, decides the same point in the opposite sense, I find it hard to see how this sets the Court of Appeal free in case C to choose between case A and case B. Such a doctrine ascribes to a decision made

I per incuriam a power greater than a decision made with all the relevant authorities before the court. On this view, case A binds the court unless and until counsel fails to cite it in case B, whereupon the omission of counsel may liberate the court

---

(3) (1877), 5 Ch.D. at p. 977.
(4) (1877), 5 Ch.D. 974.
(5) [1900] 1 Ch. 60.
(6) [1893] 1 Ch. 77.
(7) [1902] 2 Ch. 612.
(8) [1944] 2 All E.R. 293; [1944] K.B. 718.

from the bonds of case A, no matter how often case A has been relied on in A practice and in unreported cases. Fortunately for me, I do not think that in this case I have to decide what a judge at first instance ought to do if confronted by two inconsistent decisions of the Court of Appeal. It seems to me that a later case in which the point is assumed rather than decided is no match for an earlier decision where the point was decided in terms, especially when one of my predecessors at first instance has followed the earlier case in preference to the B later. I accordingly propose to follow *Kemp* v. *Bird* (9). I may add that, while keeping the point open for a higher court, counsel for the tenant has accepted the authority of *Kemp* v. *Bird* (9) and *Ashby* v. *Wilson* (10) in this court.

I turn, then, to the society's two leases. The society's second lease merely incorporates the terms of the society's first lease, and I need say no more about it. By cl. 2 (k) of the first lease the society covenants, as I have mentioned, C " to occupy and keep open the premises for the purpose of a Food Hall and not for any other purpose ". These latter words constitute an express negative, namely, " not for any other purpose ". The society thus in effect binds itself not to use the premises (inter alia) for the purpose of a general hardware merchant and ironmonger, except so far as that may be comprised in the purpose of a food hall. I do not find it easy to say what the term " Food Hall " means in D this context. Mr. Golding's evidence was that a food hall differed from a super-market in that a supermarket had an area of 2,000 feet or more, whereas the term " Food Hall " was appropriate to anything of that type smaller than that. A food hall was essentially a grocery self-service store of less than 2,000 feet. He said that he would expect to find items of hardware for sale in a food hall. To some extent, in the preliminary correspondence between the landlords and E the society, " Food Hall " and " shopping hall " seem to have been used interchangeably. " Food Hall " thus seems to overlap " General Hardware Merchant " in at least some of the goods sold.

However, in the society's first lease there is another provision, made by cl. 3 when read with the schedule. I have already set out the terms of these. Clause 3, says counsel for the tenant, achieves nothing; it certainly imposes no restrictions F whatsoever on what the society may sell. All that it does, he says, is to prevent the society from selling any items which might cause the landlords to commit a breach of the landlords' covenant with the tenant; and the only way the land-lords could break that covenant with the tenant was by letting premises to the society " for the purpose of a General Hardware Merchant and Ironmonger ". The purpose for which the premises were let to the society is, however, laid G down by cl. 2 (k), namely, " the purpose of a Food Hall ": and the society cannot, by selling goods on their premises, cause any breach of a covenant which relates not to what is done on the premises, but merely to the purpose specified in the lease. That is the argument.

I should be reluctant to reach the conclusion that cl. 3 was wholly ineffective. I think the lease must be read as a whole, giving effect to the totality. As I H read it, cl. 2 (k) limits use to the purposes of a food hall. The evident purpose of cl. 3 is to add further restrictions. As counsel for the landlords contended, if one incorporates the appropriate part of the schedule into cl. 3, the relevant parts of the covenant become a covenant by the society that " they will not on the demised premises sell any commodity or item which may cause the Council to commit a breach of the covenant with the tenant not to let any other shops I on the said estate for the purpose of a general hardware merchant or ironmonger ". This in terms prohibits the sale of particular items on the premises. The items prohibited are those that would cause the landlords to commit a breach of their covenant against letting a shop for the purpose of a general hardware merchant and ironmonger. The only sales that would do this would be sales which, being permitted by the lease, would enable the tenant to say that the

A landlords had let the premises for the purpose of a general hardware merchant
and ironmonger. Therefore, such sales are prohibited by the lease; and, being
thus prohibited, it cannot be said that the landlords have let the premises for
the purpose of a general hardware merchant and ironmonger.

In short, quite apart from any argument on cl. 2 (k), I think that cl. 3 protects
the landlords from being in breach of their covenant with the tenant under
B cl. 3 (c) of the agreement; and although in deference to the arguments I must
say something more, that is really the end of the case. I do not think that *Brigg*
v. Thornton (10), on which counsel for the tenant relied, is any answer to this.
In that case there was nothing to correspond to cl. 3. The landlord let premises
in an arcade to A for use as (inter alia) an " artistic and heraldic stationer ",
and covenanted not to let any other portion of the arcade for that trade. When
C he let other premises in the arcade to B for the business of a " librarian, news-
agent, bookseller or stationer ", the Court of Appeal not surprisingly held that
the landlord was in breach of his covenant with A. He was letting the premises
to B for use (inter alia) as a " stationer ", despite his covenant with A not to
let them for use as a particular kind of stationer. Indeed, I think this case assists
counsel for the landlords to some extent, as the Court of Appeal held (and I
D quote from the headnote) that (11):

" A restrictive covenant as to the letting or user of property will be construed strictly, and not so as to create a wider obligation than is imported
by the actual words: *Kemp* v. *Bird* (12)."

This reinforces my opinion that a contract " not to let " premises for a particular
purpose cannot be enlarged into a covenant " not to permit the premises to be
E used " for a particular purpose. One must remember that here one is in the
sphere of restricting trade competition, with all that this implies.

Even if the lease to the society had not contained cl. 3, it seems to me that the
landlords would have committed no breach of their covenant in the agreement.
The covenant restricts a letting " for the purpose of a General Hardware Merchant
and Ironmonger ", and so protects the tenant against any letting explicitly for
F that purpose. If the letting were for no specified trade, but merely for use as a
shop, it might well be that this, too, would constitute a breach, on the footing
that a letting restricted to no particular trade is a letting for the purpose of any
trade that the tenant may choose to carry on, and so is a letting for (inter alia)
the purpose of a general hardware merchant and ironmonger, if that is the
tenant's choice. But when the letting is for some specified purpose, then unless
G that purpose is or includes the purpose of a general hardware merchant and
ironmonger, I do not think that there is necessarily any breach of the covenant
merely because the purpose includes the sale of some articles which a general
hardware merchant and ironmonger may be expected to sell. Trades overlap;
and in the last two decades the overlapping has tended to increase. The agreement that I have to construe was executed in 1955, and I must construe it
H according to the meaning it would have borne then. In my judgment, a covenant
not to let other premises for the purpose of trade A does not prohibit a letting
for the purpose of trade B unless the carrying on of trade B can fairly be said
to be, or to include, the carrying on of trade A, or, perhaps, of a substantial
part of it. In deciding this, what matters is the substance: it is not enough
merely to establish that there is a minor degree of identity between the types of
I articles sold in the two trades.

In this connection I have been referred to *A. Lewis & Co. (Westminster), Ltd.*
v. *Bell Property Trust, Ltd.* (13) and *Labone* v. *Litherland Urban District Council*
(14). These cases deal with what may summarily be termed " ancillary uses ".
In the *Lewis* case (13), a covenant in a lease to tobacconists not to permit

(11) [1904] 1 Ch. 386.   (12) (1877), 5 Ch. D. 974.
(13) [1940] 1 All E.R. 570; [1940] Ch. 345.
(14) [1956] 2 All E.R. 215; [1956] 1 W.L.R. 522.

adjoining premises to be used for the sale of tobacco, cigars and cigarettes was   **A**
held not to be broken by a letting to a tea shop company which incidentally
sold cigarettes at the cash desk to customers. The tea shop company was
carrying on the business of a tea shop, and the sale of cigarettes in this way was
a mere incidental part of a tea shop and not a separate business of selling
cigarettes. So in this case counsel for the landlords says that the mere sale by
the society of a number of items also sold by hardware stores does not mean   **B**
that the society is carrying on the business of a general hardware merchant, or
that the landlords have let the premises to the society for the purpose of a
general hardware merchant. This, he urged, was of particular force where, as
here, the items of alleged hardware were sold not in a separate hardware
department, but in a variety of different parts of the food hall.

It seems to me that there is considerable force in this submission. I do not   **C**
think that the letting for the purpose of a food hall is a letting for the purpose
of a general hardware merchant, even if the purposes of a food hall embrace
the sale of a number of items likely to be sold by a general hardware merchant.
The covenant in the agreement protects the tenant against the direct competition
of another general hardware merchant; but it does no more than that. A shop
tenant who desires protection against competition in the whole range of goods   **D**
sold by him must obtain a far wider covenant than that to be found in this case.
If he desires a prohibition against the sale of any items which a general hardware
merchant may sell, he must obtain a covenant which says so. This is particularly
the case where there are many types of goods which are sold not only by hardware
merchants but also by others. In this case the tenant lays claim to a very wide
range of articles as hardware, although a number of them are sold by many   **E**
other types of shops as well. Indeed, not much assiduity would be required to
purchase most of the 45 items mentioned from shops which are plainly not
hardware merchants or hardware departments in stores.

It seems to me that, construing these restrictive covenants strictly, as *Brigg* v.
Thornton (15) bids me, I ought to exercise a special care about items which
are appropriate to more types of business than one. If one accepts the tenant's   **F**
claim that disinfectants, cups and saucers and balls of string fall within the
hardware domain, then chemists, china shops, and stationers and garden shops
might feel a just grievance that articles which also fall within their territory
are being withdrawn from it. In days when many of the dividing lines between
what is sold at one type of shop and what is sold at another are fast breaking
down, I think the tenant has pitched his claim far higher than can be justified.   **G**
Certainly I consider that he is claiming a much wider protection than the
language of this covenant warrants.

It therefore seems to me that either cl. 2 (k) or cl. 3 of the lease to the society
would by itself suffice to discharge the duty of the landlords to the tenant;
and as they both apply, the landlords have made assurance double sure. For
these reasons, I dismiss this action.   **H**

Action dismissed.

Solicitors: *Sharpe, Pritchard & Co.*, agents for *N. Catchpole*, Colchester (for
the tenant); *Oswald Hickson, Collier & Co.*, agents for *Desmond Pye*, Clacton-
on-Sea (for the landlords).

[*Reported by* R. W. FARRIN, ESQ., *Barrister-at-Law.*]   **I**

---

(15) [1904] 1 Ch. 386.

A

CONI v. ROBERTSON.

[CHANCERY DIVISION (Cross, J.), March 11, 1969.]

Discovery—Originating summons—Action commenced by originating summons
—Whether discovery should be ordered.

B
In an action started by originating summons, discovery, whilst not automatic, will be ordered unless there is some good reason why it should not be ordered (see p. 615, letter D, post).

Nash v. *Layton* ([1911] 2 Ch. 71) applied.

[As to the discretion of the court in granting discovery, see 12 HALSBURY'S LAWS (3rd Edn.) 5, 6, para. 5; and for cases on the subject, see 18 DIGEST (Repl.)
C 11-14, *55-92.*]

Cases referred to:

Borthwick, Re, Borthwick v. *Beauvais,* [1948] 2 All E.R. 179; *affd.,* C.A., [1948] 2 All E.R. 635; [1948] Ch. 645; [1949] L.J.R. 50; 18 Digest (Repl.) 12, *70.*

Marshall v. *Goulston Discount (Northern), Ltd.,* [1966] 3 All E.R. 994; [1967]
D   Ch. 72; [1966] 3 W.L.R. 599; Digest (Cont. Vol. B) 224, *582a.*

Nash v. *Layton,* [1911] 2 Ch. 71; 80 L.J.Ch. 636; 104 L.T. 834; 18 Digest (Repl.) 206, *1798.*

Wine Shippers (London), Ltd. v. *Bath House Syndicate, Ltd.,* [1960] 3 All E.R. 283; [1960] 1 W.L.R. 989; Digest (Cont. Vol. A) 488, *70b.*

E
Procedure Summons.

This was a summons under R.S.C., Ord. 24, r. 3 (1), by Eleanor Robertson, the defendant in proceedings commenced by originating summons dated 22nd December 1965 by the plaintiff, Laurence Paul Coni, claiming payment by the defendant to the plaintiff of £9,000 advanced under a legal charge dated 17th December 1964 made between the defendant and the plaintiff, together with interest thereon, and enforcement of the security. The defendant's summons,
F as amended at the hearing before CROSS, J., asked for discovery of all documents relating to loans made during the period of 18 months up to 17th December 1964 and during the six months thereafter by the plaintiff on his own behalf or on behalf of his firm, Coni & Covington, stockbrokers, including documents affecting the question whether such loans were made in the course of and for the purpose of his or their principal business. The facts are set out in the judgment.
G
The cases noted below* were cited during the argument in addition to those referred to in the judgment.

H. A. P. Picarda for the plaintiff.
M. A. F. Lyndon-Stanford for the defendant.

H
CROSS, J.: On 17th December 1964, the defendant, Eleanor Robertson, executed a legal charge on a house, Cleveland, 19 Boyn Hill Avenue, Maidenhead, in which she was living, in favour of the plaintiff, Laurence Paul Coni, to secure a sum of £9,000 at 13 per cent. interest reducible to 12 per cent. on prompt payment, the interest to be payable monthly and the principal to be repaid after a year. The plaintiff says—and there is no reason to doubt this—that the loan was made by him on behalf of the firm of Coni & Covington, stockbrokers,
I in which he is a partner. The £9,000 was paid by the plaintiff to a firm of solicitors who, it appears, did not pay it over to the defendant but paid it to a third party. The defendant says that they had no authority to pay the money that she was borrowing away in that way, and that question is the subject of

---

* *John Miller (Shipping), Ltd.* v. *Port of London Authority,* [1959] 2 All E.R. 713; [1959] 1 W.L.R. 910; *Re St. Martin's Theatre,* [1959] 3 All E.R. 298; [1959] 1 W.L.R. 872; *Premor, Ltd.* v. *Shaw Brothers,* [1964] 2 All E.R. 583; [1964] 1 W.L.R. 978; *United Dominions Trust, Ltd.* v. *Kirkwood,* [1966] 1 All E.R. 968; [1966] 2 Q.B. 431.

an action in this division in which the defendant is the plaintiff and the solicitors **A**
in question are the defendants.   They have brought in the third party to indemnify them and the action is still pending.   However, it is accepted by the defendant for the purpose of the present application that the plaintiff is not affected
by this dispute.   The plaintiff paid his money, or his firm's money, to persons
who were apparently authorised by the defendant to receive it from him and,
if they misapplied that money, that is no concern of his.   **B**

Interest was paid for about three months by the third party, but no interest
was paid thereafter.   That being the position, certain correspondence ensued
which I should read.   On 28th July 1965, the plaintiff's solicitors write to the
defendant as follows:

" We are instructed by [the plaintiff] that the interest payable monthly
under the Mortgage was four months in arrear on the 17th of July last.   **C**
[They then state that £382 10s. was owing up to the end of July, and go on:]
We must inform you that unless a cheque for this sum is received at this
office within 8 days from the date hereof, our instructions are to commence
proceedings in the High Court for its recovery without further notice.   We
are also instructed to inform you that although the date for repayment of
the principal sum of £9,000 under the Mortgage is the 17th of December   **D**
next, [the plaintiff] is prepared to accept repayment of the principal sum
at any time before that date with interest thereon calculated at the date
of repayment.   Should you [not] wish to avail yourself of this offer, the
appropriate steps to recover the principal and interest due will be taken on
the 17th of December next."

The defendant did not take any notice of that letter, and on 19th November 1965   **E**
the solicitors write again:

" We refer to our earlier letter on this matter of the 28th July in connection
with which we have not heard from you.   Upon [the plaintiff's] instructions,
we have not taken any proceedings in respect of the arrears of interest to
date as [the plaintiff] felt that there seemed little purpose in this in view   **F**
of the fact that it seemed inevitable that a Writ would have to be issued
for the principal as well as the interest on the 18th December.   You will
appreciate that legal proceedings will be issued by us automatically on the
18th December without further notice unless payment of the interest is
made by you in the meantime."

On 22nd December 1965, the defendant's solicitors write to the plaintiff's solicitors   **G**
in these terms:

" We have not heard from you since the 29th March, but we understand
that you have written to [the defendant] recently demanding arrears of
interest and threatening proceedings.   [The plaintiff] will be aware that
[the defendant] did not receive the money loaned by [the plaintiff], and she
has instituted proceedings in the Chancery Division for the repayment of   **H**
the proceeds of the mortgage.   Various interlocutory steps are now being
taken.   [The defendant] has in fact made no payments of interest to [the
plaintiff] since the inception of the mortgage.   The interest which he has
received has been paid by Seavert Holdings Limited who are a party to the
pending action.   [They are the third party to whom I have referred.]
[The defendant] does not have the resources to pay the arrears which have   **I**
accrued without her knowledge and she has instructed us to write to you to
ask [the plaintiff] to be good enough to withhold further action pending
the outcome of the above mentioned proceedings."

On that same day, 22nd December 1965, the plaintiff took out an originating
summons against the defendant asking for payment of the sum due and for
enforcement of the security.   On 29th December 1965, the plaintiff's solicitors
answer:

A   " We are in receipt of your letter of the 22nd instant the contents of which we note. We had no knowledge of the information contained in the second paragraph of your letter and as we warned [the defendant] in the letters sent to her, proceedings have in fact been commenced in the Chancery Division for relief under Order 55. We do not understand why you should say that the arrears have accrued without [the defendant's] knowledge

B   as we would point out that we wrote to her setting the matter out fully on the 28th July last informing her that the interest was in arrear and again wrote to her on the 19th November informing her that if the arrears of interest were not paid proceedings would be commenced on or after the 18th December. No reply was received from [the defendant], neither were we informed of the Chancery proceedings commenced by her until we

C   received your letter. In the circumstances we cannot advise [the plaintiff] to comply with your request and the matter must be dealt with by the Master as he thinks fit in all the circumstances. In order that we may inform the Court that there are existing proceedings with regard to the mortgage in the Chancery Division so that [the plaintiff's] action can be dealt with by the same Master we should be obliged if you would give us full details of [the

D   defendant's] action and let us know exactly the present position."

On 5th January 1966, the defendant's solicitors answer:

    " Thank you for your letter of the 29th ultimo. [The defendant] has issued a Writ against [and they name the other solicitors who received the money], who have served a Defence, and have joined Seavert Holdings

E   Limited as Third Party to the action . . . [The defendant] claims the sum of £8,904. 2. 0d., being the net proceeds of the Mortgage granted to [the plaintiff], and she alleges that the [other solicitors] parted with this sum without her authority. The [other solicitors] deny that they were acting as Solicitors for the [defendant], and they claim to have acted for Seavert Holdings, on whose instructions the net proceeds were paid. They claim an

F   indemnity from Seavert Holdings, or damages for breach of warranty of authority."

That being the position, the plaintiff swore a common form affidavit in support of the summons to which he exhibited the legal charge and in which he gave details of the sums which were owing to him under it. The defendant, on 18th February 1966, swore an affidavit in answer. After denying that the plaintiff

G was entitled to the relief claimed in the originating summons or to any relief, and stating that she had not received the proceeds of the mortgage or any part of it, the affidavit goes on as follows:

    " 6. In June 1965 I issued a Writ in the Chancery Division of the High Court of Justice against [the other solicitors] in which I claimed

H   inter alia payment of the said sum of £8,904. 2. 0d. with interest thereon. These proceedings are still pending. 7. I have not made any payment of interest to the Plaintiff but I am informed that three payments of interest each amounting to the sum of £90. were made to the Plaintiff on the 5th February 1965 the 24th February 1965 and the 8th April 1965. The first and third of such payments were made by Mr. Warrick David Granville Collins and the second payment was made by a company named

I   Seagrades Limited. 8. I am further informed that the file of Seagrades Limited at the Companies Registration Office reveals that Mr. W. D. G. Collins was appointed a Director of that company on the 29th October 1964 and according to a Return of Allotments made on the 16th December 1964 one hundred ordinary shares in the company have been allotted for cash to Coni and Covington (Stockbrokers) of 10 Throgmorton Avenue in the City of London. 9. I verily believe that the Plaintiff was at the time of the making of the said loan a moneylender as defined by the Moneylenders

A

Act 1927 and was not licenced to carry on business as such. I did not
sign any documents prior to the making of the said loan save the aforesaid
Legal Charge and I did not receive a copy of this document within seven
days of the 17th December 1964.   10.   In the premises I am advised and
I verily believe that by virtue of Sections 1 and 6 (1) of the Moneylenders
Act 1927 the security given by me in respect of the said loan (namely the
said Legal Charge) is void and unenforceable and that I have a good defence
on the merits to the whole of the Plaintiff's claim. 11. I respectfully crave
leave to defend the action and to counterclaim for a declaration that the
aforesaid property is vested in me freed and discharged from the said Legal
Charge and for an Order that the title deeds shall be delivered up to me."

B

The suggestion that the plaintiff or his firm were moneylenders was made for the
first time in that affidavit. It was not suggested in the correspondence. It is
not a very meritorious plea, but the defendant, not having received the money
and not having as yet recovered it from the solicitors or the third party, does
not propose to repay it to the plaintiff if she can avoid doing so. It may be that
if in her Chancery proceedings she recovers the sum in question from the solicitors
or third party the plaintiff will not hear any more of the suggestion that the
charge is unenforceable. The plaintiff put in an affidavit in reply which he swore
on 29th April 1966. I must read most of it. He states, in para. 2:

C

D

" I am a Stockbroker by profession and have been a member of the
London Stock Exchange since 1962. I am the senior partner in the firm of
Coni & Covington. My partners are George Leonidas Embiricos and Charles
Terance O'Callaghan. My firm has carried on business since 1932 (when it
was founded by my father) and in the course of such business grants the
usual credit facilities to its Clients. Neither I nor my firm have ever carried
on the business of money-lending.   3.   The Mortgage transaction with the
Defendant is the only Mortgage transaction in which I or my firm has ever
been engaged. While I appear in the Mortgage as the Mortgagee I am in
fact as such Mortgagee the nominee of my firm. The circumstances in
which the Mortgage was made were, so far as I was concerned, as follows.
Warrick David Granville Collins, who is referred to in paragraphs 7 and 8
of the Defendant's Affidavit has been a friend of mine since we were at School
together.   Mr. Collins has on occasion asked me as a personal friend to lend
him money and I have done so on two occasions lending him without interest
£500 in December 1964 and £800 in January 1965.   In 1964 I knew that Mr.
Collins was associated with a company called Seagrades Limited and that the
business of this Company was dredging sand and gravel which it carried on
at Southampton. Some time before 17th December 1964 Mr. Collins told
me that he wanted to raise about £9,000 for business purposes. He said
that the money was required either by Seagrades Limited or by some
other company with which he was associated. Collins said that [the defen-
dant] was prepared to give security for a loan of £9,000 and he asked me if
I would lend that sum on security provided by [the defendant]. I understood
the position as being that I was being asked to lend [the defendant] and that
[the defendant] would make what money I lent to her available to one of
the above-mentioned companies. I gathered that while [the defendant]
would be responsible for repaying the Mortgage loan and interest Collins's
Company would (as between that Company and [the defendant]) be ultimately responsible for both loan and interest and that the Company would
in fact pay the Mortgage interest direct to me, if the loan was made. The
situation did not appear to me to be unusual because I understood that
[the defendant] was interested in these business activities. Collins said that
if I was interested in the proposition I should get in touch with [the defendant's] Solicitors. I then spoke to a [partner] of that firm and eventually
agreed with him to lend [the defendant] £9,000 at interest of 13% per

E

F

G

H

I

A   annum (reducible to 12%) on the security of the house in which she was then living, 19 Boyn Hill Avenue, Maidenhead. When I spoke to [the partner] I spoke on the footing that his firm was acting as Solicitors for [the defendant]. Having agreed in principle with [the partner] as I have mentioned I put the matter in the hands of my Solicitors, Messrs. Russell-Cooke Potter & Chapman, in which firm my brother is an articled clerk.

B   Mr. Ernest Chapman of the firm of Russell-Cooke & Co. then spoke to me on the telephone about the transaction. He said that the mortgaged property ought to be valued and I agreed that a valuation should be made. There-after my Solicitors had the mortgaged property valued by Cooksey and Walker of Reading. The valuation placed on the property was £12,000. I understood that my Solicitors satisfied themselves as to the title to the

C   property and then informed [the other solicitors] as [the defendant's] Solicitors that they (my Solicitors) would be in a position to complete the Mortgage on the 17th December 1964. [He then exhibits a bundle of correspondence, much of which I have already read, and goes on:] Having been told by my Solicitors that the Mortgage was about to be completed I sent my Solicitors a Banker's Draft in favour of my Solicitors

D   in the sum of £9,000. This sum was provided by my firm who borrowed the money by drawing against securities held to the order of the firm. The sum sent to my Solicitors was debited in the firm books to Russell-Cooke Potter & Chapman Account [the defendant]. [He then says that the mortgage transaction was completed on 17th December 1964 by the payment of £8,904 2s., that is, the £9,000 less certain costs, that on com-

E   pletion his solicitors received the mortgage deed and the title deeds and that the £8,904 2s. was paid to the other solicitors as the solicitors then acting for the defendant.] Following the execution of the Mortgage my firm received £270 interest in respect of the money secured by the Mortgage, being the £270 which is referred to in paragraph 6 of my Affidavit sworn on the 3rd January 1966 and filed herein on 22nd February 1966. The

F   said sum of £270 was received as to £90 on 5th February 1965, as to £90 on 24th February 1965 and as to the remaining £90 on 8th April 1965, as is stated in paragraph 7 of the Defendant's Affidavit. The last sentence of paragraph 7 of the said Affidavit is correct. I was not surprised to receive the said interest payments otherwise than from [the defendant] because, as I have already mentioned, it was anticipated that the Mortgage

G   interest would be paid direct to my firm by Mr. Collins or one of the com-panies with which he was associated. [He then sets out the later letter which I have read, and goes on:] 6. The 100 Ordinary Shares in Seagrades Limited allotted to my firm, which are referred to in paragraph 8 of [the defendant's] Affidavit, were allotted to my firm free of payment in lieu of interest on a further sum of £5,000 which I lent to Seagrades Ltd. on 26th January

H   1965 against a six month promissory note dated 26th January 1965 drawn against Seagrades Ltd. and guaranteed by the said [partner]. Save as hereinbefore disclosed I have made no loans to anyone."

He uses there only the word " I " and does not also say " I or my firm ", but it is accepted by both sides on this application that I should read that sentence as though he had said " Neither I nor the firm in which I am a partner have

I   made any loans to anyone ".

That affidavit, as I have said, was sworn on 29th April 1966. The matter then went to sleep for three years while attempts were being made to sort out the position as between the defendant, her former solicitors and the third party, but, that not proving possible, the plaintiff now not unnaturally wants to get on with his summons to enforce the mortgage. That being the position, on 28th January 1969, the defendant issued a summons asking that the plaintiff be ordered to make discovery. I will read the summons as issued by her:

" That the Plaintiff do within 14 days serve upon the Defendant a list of documents setting out the documents which are or have been in his possession custody or power relating to the matters in question in these proceedings and that the Plaintiff do within the like period verify such list by affidavit and do in the like period serve a copy of such affidavit upon the Defendant.   This application is made under Order 24 Rule 3 (1) of the Rules of the Supreme Court."

R.S.C., Ord. 24, r. 1 and r. 2, provide for automatic discovery in the case of actions started by writ.   Rule 3 provides for the obtaining of an order for discovery in the circumstances set out therein, and provides:

" (1) Subject to the provisions of this rule and of rules 4 and 8, the Court may order any party to a cause or matter (whether begun by writ, originating summons or otherwise) to make and serve on any other party a list of the documents which are or have been in his possession, custody or power relating to any matter in question in the cause or matter, and may at the same time or subsequently also order him to make and file an affidavit verifying such a list and to serve a copy thereof on the other party . . . (3) An order under this rule may be limited to such documents or classes of document only, or to such only of the matters in question in the cause or matter, as may be specified in the order."

Rule 3 (1) is expressed to be " Subject to the provisions of this rule and of rules 4 and 8 ".   There is nothing in r. 4 to which I need refer, but r. 8 is in the following terms:

" On the hearing of an application for an order under rule 3 or rule 7 the Court, if satisfied that discovery is not necessary, or not necessary at that stage of the cause or matter, may dismiss or, as the case may be, adjourn the application and shall in any case refuse to make such an order if and so far as it is of opinion that discovery is not necessary either for disposing fairly of the cause or matter or for saving costs."

Although in an action started by writ discovery is automatic, in an action started by originating summons an order for discovery has to be obtained.   The summons, as I have said, asks for discovery in perfectly general terms, but counsel for the defendant, when the matter came before me, did not ask for an order in general terms.   What he now asks for is for discovery of—

" all documents relating to loans made during the period of 18 months up to 17th December 1964 and during the 6 months thereafter by [the plaintiff] on his own behalf or on behalf of his firm, including documents affecting the question whether such loans were made in the course of and for the purpose of his or their principal business."

Nash v. *Layton* (1) established that, in an action started by writ, an order on these lines will normally be made.   That case related to discovery by interrogatories, but there is no doubt that the same principle applies to the discovery of documents: see *Marshall* v. *Goulston Discount (Northern), Ltd.* (2), which also shows that, in choosing the period of time over which discovery is to operate, it may be appropriate to take not only a period before the date of the relevant transaction but a period after it as well.

But this is not an action started by writ.   It is an action started by originating summons, and before the coming into force of the new rules in such an action an order for discovery would not usually be made: see *Re Borthwick, Borthwick* v. *Beauvais* (3), where LORD GREENE, M.R., said:

" The view that ROXBURGH, J. (4), took, and I think rightly took, was

(1) [1911] 2 Ch. 71.
(2) [1966] 3 All E.R. 994; [1967] Ch. 72.
(3) [1948] 2 All E.R. 635 at p. 636; [1948] Ch. 645 at p. 649.
(4) [1948] 2 All E.R. 179.

A that the discovery in proceedings in the Chancery Division by originating summons ought only to be ordered in very special cases where the facts are such as to justify such an order being made."

That principle was subsequently applied in several cases under the Landlord and Tenant Acts where the proceedings are by originating summons, although they often give rise to serious disputes of fact. In the last of them, *Wine Shippers*
B *(London), Ltd.* v. *Bath House Syndicate, Ltd.* (5), HARMAN, L.J., while agreeing with his colleagues that no special case for discovery had been made out, said:

" I agree, but with reluctance. It seems to me that in cases involving questions of fact of this sort discovery should go as a matter of ordinary discretion."

C Possibly as a result of this remark the new rules, as I read them, have substantially altered the position with regard to discovery in actions started by originating summons. It is true that discovery is not automatic, and that is as it should be because in many cases started by originating summons—such, for instance, as a construction summons—there is no reason whatever for discovery. But though one has to apply for an order, R.S.C. Ord. 24, r. 8, shows that discovery will be
D ordered unless there is some good reason why it should not be ordered.

So in this case, if one had simply the first affidavit of the plaintiff setting out his title to the charge and the affidavit of the defendant raising the defence that he was a moneylender, then, as I see it, it could hardly be argued that she was not entitled to discovery on the *Nash* v. *Layton* (6) lines. It is true that she appears to have had very slender grounds for her assertion, but then the defen-
E dants in *Nash* v. *Layton* (6) appear to have had no more grounds for thinking that Mr. Nash was a moneylender than the defendant had for thinking that the plaintiff was one. But it is said that the affidavit in reply put in by the plaintiff puts a different complexion on the matter, and in that connection counsel refers to the provisions of R.S.C., Ord. 24, r. 7, which apply where a party thinks that inadequate discovery has been made and asks for the discovery of particular
F documents. It is well settled that, when one is applying under r. 7, one has to make an affidavit justifying the application and showing that one has a prima facie case for thinking that relevant documents are being supressed or withheld by the other side. This is, of course, an application under r. 3 and not an application under r. 7, but it is argued that, by his affidavit, the plaintiff as it were volunteered " discovery " and that in face of it the defendant ought to
G have shown some reason for discrediting something that the plaintiff has sworn to. But the plaintiff's affidavit in reply was not an affidavit of documents, and I do not think that he could have put himself in a better position with regard to discovery by having sworn this affidavit than he would be in if he had not sworn it. Further, this is a case where the rate of interest for a secured loan appears to be somewhat high, and it is possible that the information with regard
H to the ordinary shares in Seavert Holdings, Ltd., issued in respect of interest on the £5,000 loan may have been forced out of the plaintiff by the statement by the defendant that she had discovered from the company's return that these shares had been allotted. In all the circumstances I think that, subject to appropriate safeguards, this is a case where I ought to direct discovery on the *Nash* v. *Layton* (6) lines, though not such discovery as is asked for in the summons.
I The period of 14 days is far too short and counsel for the defendant has said that he will accept a period of six weeks, which is I think reasonable. Again, the periods asked for, 18 months before the date of the loan and six months thereafter, are too long. I will take the same periods as were taken by the Court of Appeal in *Marshall* v. *Goulston Discount (Northern), Ltd.* (7), namely, a year before the

(5) [1960] 3 All E.R. 283 at p. 288; [1960] 1 W.L.R. 989 at p. 996.
(6) [1911] 2 Ch. 71.
(7) [1966] 3 All E.R. 994; [1967] Ch. 72.

loan and three months thereafter. Finally, there must be some safeguard against   **A**
the disclosure of the names of any clients of the firm who may have borrowed
money from them or to whom they may have lent money for the purpose of the
purchase of shares. It may be that the best way to deal with that would be to
insert an undertaking that these matters shall be disclosed only to the legal
advisers of the defendant.

Order accordingly.   **B**

Solicitors: *Russell-Cooke, Potter & Chapman* (for the plaintiff); *Edgley,
Harding & Philips,* agents for *Charsley, Leonard & Co.,* Slough (for the defendant).

[*Reported by* JACQUELINE METCALFE, *Barrister-at-Law.*]

C

JONES v. PADAVATTON.

[COURT OF APPEAL, CIVIL DIVISION (Danckwerts, Salmon and Fenton Atkinson,
L.JJ.), November 11, 12, 13, 29, 1968.]

Contract—Unenforceable contract—Agreement by parties—Intention that no legal   **D**
*interest be created—Uncertainty of terms—Offer by mother to maintain
daughter on her undertaking legal studies—Subsequent offer to buy large
house—Rents from sub-lettings to provide maintenance—No written terms and
some undetermined.*

The daughter of a resident in Trinidad was employed at a satisfactory
salary with pension rights at the Indian embassy in Washington in the United   **E**
States. Although she said she was unwilling to leave, she accepted an offer
made by her mother in August 1962 that if she would go to England and read
for the Bar with a view to practising as a lawyer in Trindad, the mother
would provide maintenance for her at the rate of $200 a month (West Indian
dollars meant, equivalent to £42 a month, the daughter expected United
States dollars equivalent to £70, but she in fact accepted the £42). The   **F**
daughter went to England in November 1962 and entered on her studies at the
Bar, her fees and maintenance at the offered rate being paid by her mother.
But no terms of the arrangements were recorded in writing and no statement
of the parties' respective obligations and in particular nothing as to the duration of the arrangement. Following discomfort of the daughter in her accommodation, a proposal was made by the mother in 1964 that she should buy   **G**
a house of some size in London in a room or rooms of which the daughter
could reside with her son (she was divorced from her husband) the rents
from letting other rooms furnished to provide maintenance in place of the
£42 a month. A house was bought for £6,000 and conveyed to the mother,
who provided the money in several sums though not all that for incidental
expenses and furniture. The daughter was given a power of attorney by the   **H**
mother and she moved in during January 1965, tenants beginning to arrive in
the next month. Again there was no written arrangement and incidental
matters remained unsettled such as the application of the rents received and
what rooms the daughter should occupy. No money from the rents was
received by the mother, nor was she supplied with any accounts. In 1967
the mother issued a summons claiming possession of the house from the
daughter, who counterclaimed for £1,655 18s. 9d. said to have been paid in   **I**
respect of the house. At the hearing some of Part 1 of the Bar examination
remained to be taken by the daughter and also the whole of Part 2 (the final).

Held: the mother was entitled to possession of the house as the owner as
against the daughter who had no legal interest in it, on the following
grounds—

(i) (per DANCKWERTS and FENTON ATKINSON, L.JJ.) because the arrangement between mother and daughter was throughout a family arrangement

A depending on the good faith of the parties in keeping the promises made and
not intended to be a rigid binding agreement, and (per FENTON ATKINSON,
L.J.) was far too vague and uncertain to be itself enforceable as a contract
(see p. 620, letters E and H, and p. 625, letters B and F, post).

(ii) (per SALMON, L.J.) although the true inference from the facts was that
neither the mother nor the daughter could have intended that the daughter
B should have no legal right to receive, and the mother no legal obligation to
to pay, the original allowance of $200 a month (the terms being sufficiently
stated and duration for a reasonable time being implied) because a reasonable time for the completion of the daughter's Bar studies could not possibly
exceed five years, and therefore on no view could the daughter be entitled
to anything further under the contract in November 1968; and also because
C the new arrangement in 1964 was neither a variation of the original contract
nor a new contract entitling the daughter to stay on in the mother's house
indefinitely, there being no evidence that the mother bargained away her right
to dispose of her house or evict her daughter, all the evidence showing that
the arrangements in relation to the house were very vague and made without
any contractual intent (see p. 622, letters C and G, p. 622, letter I, to p. 623,
D letter B, and p. 623, letter E, post).

Appeal allowed.

[As to contracts unenforceable for absence of intention to contract, for uncertainty or for lack of consideration, see 8 HALSBURY'S LAWS (3rd Edn.) 54, 55,
para. 90; 83, 84, para. 144; and 113, para. 197; and for cases on the subject,
E see 12 DIGEST (Repl.) 21-23, *1-14*, and 55, 56, *309, 310*, 196-199, *1354-1384*.]

Cases referred to:
   Balfour v. *Balfour*, [1919] 2 K.B. 571; [1918-19] All E.R. Rep. 860; 88 L.J.K.B.
        1054; 121 L.T. 346; 12 Digest (Repl.) 21, *3*.
   Parker v. *Clark*, [1960] 1 All E.R. 93; [1960] 1 W.L.R. 286; Digest (Cont.
        Vol. A) 269, *7b*.
F *Shadwell* v. *Shadwell* (1860), 9 C.B.N.S. 159; 30 L.J.C.P. 145; 3 L.T. 628;
        142 E.R. 62; 12 Digest (Repl.) 238, *1785*.

Appeal.
The mother, Violet Lalgee Jones, appealed against an order of His Honour
JUDGE DOW made in the Clerkenwell County Court on 11th March 1968,
G adjudging that a legally enforceable agreement existed between the mother
and Ruby Padavatton, the daughter, as had been alleged in the daughter's
amended defence and counterclaim and referring the quantum of the counterclaim to the registrar.   The grounds of the mother's appeal were: (i) that the
judge misdirected himself in holding that there had been between the parties
the intention that legal relations should be created between them; (ii) that the
H judge misdirected himself in holding that that agreement was not void for
uncertainty; (iii) that the judge's conclusions were not supported by the evidence;
(iv) that the judge mistakenly failed to give any or any sufficient weight to
the evidence given by or on behalf of the mother; and (v) that the judge misdirected himself in holding that the daughter was entitled to remain in occupation
of the mother's house for an indefinite and an unspecified period of time.   The
I daughter served a notice of cross-appeal indicating that she intended to contend
at the hearing of the mother's appeal in the event of that appeal being allowed
that the judgment of the judge in the county court be varied by adding the
following words at the end of the part relating to such reference: " But so that
only sums expended by way of maintenance prior to the 25th August 1967 shall be
treated as allowable expenditure by [the daughter] in assessing the said quantum
of the Counterclaim ". The grounds of the contention were that even if the agreement between the mother and the daughter was not legally enforceable every
appropriation and expenditure of the net rents therein referred to by way of

maintenance of the daughter and her son constituted a gift by the mother to the A
daughter of the net rents so appropriated and expended, and the daughter was
thereby entitled to have them taken into account in the assessment of the quantum of the counterclaim up to 25th August 1967 when the mother directed the
payment of the rents to herself.

Charles Sparrow, Q.C., and *K. E. Evans* for the mother.
G. B. H. Dillon, Q.C., and *T. L. G. Cullen* for the daughter.   B

                                                                    Cur. adv. vult.
29th November.   The following judgments were read:

DANCKWERTS, L.J.: This is an action between the mother and the
daughter, and one which is really deplorable.   The points of difference between
the two parties appear to be comparatively small, and it is distressing that they C
could not settle their differences amicably and avoid the bitterness and expense
which is involved in this dispute carried as far as this court.   Both the mother
and the daughter come from Trinidad and appear to be of East Indian descent.
At the opening of the story in 1961-62 the mother was resident in Trinidad.
The daughter (who had been married to, and divorced from, a Mr. Wyatt) was
living in a flat in Washington, D.C., in the United States, and was employed at D
a satisfactory salary, with pension rights, in the Indian embassy in Washington.
She had one child by her marriage, a boy called Tommy.   She had been on a
holiday with her mother to England in 1957.
    A suggestion was made that she might go to England in order to read for the
Bar in England and, if she became a qualified barrister, then to go to Trinidad
and practise as a lawyer there.   There is a dispute as to which of the two parties E
initiated the idea, but the daughter gave evidence very strongly suggesting that
it was the mother's idea.   She points to her very satisfactory job with the
Indian embassy in Washington and her flat, and claims to have been unwilling
to go to England, and to have been induced by extreme pressure.   The mother
intimated that, if the daughter would go and read for the Bar as suggested, she
would provide maintenance for her at the rate of $200 a month.   Unfortunately, F
the mother (Mrs. Jones) was thinking in West Indian dollars in which $200 were
equal to £42 a month, and the daughter, living in Washington, was thinking in
United States dollars, in which $200 were equal to £70.   The two were plainly not
ad idem then, but the daughter, when she received only £42 per month, seems
to have accepted that sum without anything much in the way of protest.
    Anyhow, the daughter was entered with Lincoln's Inn as a student, and the G
necessary fees were paid by a Mr. Agimudie, a lawyer in Trinidad, as the
mother's agent.   Mr. Agimudie in a contemporary letter assured the daughter
that, of course, maintenance would be provided for her.   So the daughter went
to England in November 1962 and entered on her studies for the Bar.   She took
her son, Tommy, with her.   The precise terms of the arrangement between the
mother and the daughter were difficult to discover completely.   There is no H
doubt that the daughter gave consideration for a promise by her mother to
provide maintenance at the rate of £42 per month so long as she was reading
for the Bar in England by giving up her job and her other advantages in Washington, and by reading for the Bar.   But various incidental matters appear never
to have been thought out at all.   There were no terms recorded in writing, no
sort of businesslike statement of the parties' respective obligations, not even of I
how long the mother was to go on paying if the studies were prolonged or unsuccessful.   In fact the daughter has passed all the examinations in Part I except
one, but Part II is still to be taken.
    The question therefore arises whether any binding legal contract was intended,
or whether this was simply a family arrangement in which one member of the
family relies on a promise given by another person and trusts that person to
carry out the promise.   But such an arrangement is not intended to create
actionable legal rights.   The situation so far has been called " step one ".   But

A in 1964 a new element was introduced. The daughter was experiencing some discomfort in England. She, with Tommy, was occupying one room in Acton, for which she had to pay £6 17s. 6d. per week. In 1964 the mother made a proposal that she should buy a house in London of some size so that the daughter and Tommy could live in a room or in rooms in the house, and the rest of the house could be let off to tenants, and the rents would cover expenses and provide

B maintenance for the daughter and Tommy in place of the £42 a month. It is not clear whether the mother had in mind a profitable investment in England, or wished to avoid the inconvenience of remitting £42 a month to England, or whether she simply had in mind the difficulties that her daughter was experiencing.

 At any rate, a house, no. 181, Highbury Quadrant, was found, which was

C conveyed into the mother's name. The price was £6,000 and moneys were provided by the mother in several sums for this. But there were also expenses of the purchase, as well as other expenses, and furniture, as it was desirable that the tenancies should be of furnished rooms. The moneys provided by the mother were insufficient to provide for all these things; until furniture was provided, there could be no tenants. The purchase was completed in December

D 1964, and the daughter and Tommy went into occupation on 31st January 1965. Somehow money was found to buy furniture, and tenants began to arrive in February 1965. The daughter had a power of attorney from her mother. There was, of course, no written agreement, and lots of incidental matters remained open: In what order were the rents to be applied; were outgoings to be paid first, or did the daughter's maintenance come first? There was a

E doubt whether the daughter's rights were confined to one room, or could she occupy several? In fact she occupied not only one room but also a kitchen, and a so-called store room where various things were stored, but Tommy slept there. This has been called " step two ". The question again arises: Was there any legally binding contract, or was it just an informal family arrangement?

 The daughter had been married on 6th January 1965 to a Mr. Padavatton,

F who is a lecturer at the London School of Economics, I understand, but it is not clear what part he has played in these matters. The new arrangement, or the varied old arrangement, whatever it may be, continued until November 1967. The mother, who had also visited England in 1963, came again to England in August 1967. The mother, it should be observed, has never received any money from the rents of the house, and she was paying substantial interest

G on a mortgage on property in Trinidad by which she had raised money for the purchase of the house. There was a most peculiar incident when, on the mother's arrival in England, she was driven to the house by Mr. Rawlins, her solicitor, and could not get in. But nothing really depends on that.

 The mother, who had complained that she could not get any accounts from her daughter, had consulted English solicitors, and before this a summons by

H the mother against the daughter had been taken out claiming possession of the house, and particulars of claim were delivered dated 4th July 1967. Of course, the house is the property of the mother. The mother had given notice to quit on 20th March 1967. A defence and counterclaim dated 11th August 1967 had been delivered, which was amended on 21st February 1968. In these are set out the daughter's version of the arrangements made between the parties, and

I she counterclaims £1,655 16s. 9d., which the daughter claims she has paid in respect of the house, and ought to be re-imbursed to her. On 11th January 1968 the learned county court judge decided against the mother and dismissed the claim for possession. He gave judgment on the counterclaim in favour of the daughter and referred the matter to the registrar. I do not find the grounds of the learned county court judge's decision easy to understand. He regarded both mother and daughter as very respectable witnesses, and he accepted the daughter's story in regard to the arrangements between them.

 Before us a great deal of time was spent on discussions as to what were the

terms of the arrangements between the parties, and it seemed to me that the **A**
further the discussions went, the more obscure and uncertain the terms alleged
became. The acceptable duration of the daughter's studies was not finally
settled, I think. There was a lack of evidence on the matter, and the members
of the court were induced to supply suggestions based on their personal knowledge. At any rate, two questions emerged for argument: (i) Were the arrangements (such as they were) intended to produce legally binding agreements, or **B**
were they simply family arrangements depending for their fulfilment on good
faith and trust, and not legally enforceable by legal proceedings? (ii) Were
the arrangements made so obscure and uncertain that, though intended to be
legally binding, a court could not enforce them?

Counsel for the daughter argued strenuously for the view that the parties
intended to create legally binding contracts. He relied on the old case of *Shad-* **C**
well v. *Shadwell* (1) and *Parker* v. *Clark* (2). Counsel for the mother argued
for the contrary view that there were no binding obligations, and that if there
were they were too uncertain for the court to enforce. His stand-by was *Balfour*
v. *Balfour* (3). The principles involved are very well discussed in CHESHIRE
AND FIFOOT ON CONTRACT (6th Edn.), at pp. 94-96. Of course, there is no difficulty, if they so intend, in members of families entering into legally binding **D**
contracts in regard to family affairs. A competent equity draftsman would,
if properly instructed, have no difficulty in drafting such a contract. But
there is possibly in family affairs a presumption against such an intention
(which, of course, can be rebutted).   I would refer to ATKIN, L.J.'s magnificent
exposition in regard to such arrangements in *Balfour* v. *Balfour* (4).

There is no doubt that this case is a most difficult one, but I have reached a **E**
conclusion that the present case is one of those family arrangements which depend
on the good faith of the promises which are made and are not intended to be
rigid, binding agreements. *Balfour* v. *Balfour* (3) was a case of husband and
wife, but there is no doubt that the same principles apply to dealings between
other relations, such as father and son and daughter and mother. This, indeed,
seems to me a compelling case. The mother and the daughter seem to have **F**
been on very good terms before 1967. The mother was arranging for a career
for the daughter which she hoped would lead to success. This involved a visit
to England in conditions which could not be wholly foreseen. What was required
was an arrangement which was to be financed by the mother and was such as
would be adaptable to circumstances, as it in fact was. The operation about
the house was, in my view, not a completely fresh arrangement, but an adapta- **G**
tion of the mother's financial assistance to the daughter due to the situation
which was found to exist in England. It was not a stiff contractual operation
any more than the original arrangement.

In the result, of course, on this view, the daughter cannot resist the mother's
rights as the owner of the house to the possession of which the mother is entitled.
What the position is as regards the counterclaim is another matter. It may be, **H**
at least in honesty, that the daughter should be re-imbursed for the expenditure
which she had incurred.   In my opinion, therefore, the appeal should be allowed.

SALMON, L.J.: I agree with the conclusion at which DANCKWERTS, L.J.,
has arrived, but I have reached it by a different route. The first point to be
decided is whether or not there was ever a legally binding agreement between
the mother and the daughter in relation to the daughter's reading for the Bar **I**
in England.   The daughter alleges that there was such an agreement, and the
mother denies it.   She says that there was nothing but a loose family arrangement which had no legal effect.   The onus is clearly on the daughter.   There is

(1) (1860), 9 C.B.N.S. 159.
(2) [1960] 1 All E.R. 93; [1960] 1 W.L.R. 286.
(3) [1919] 2 K.B. 571; [1918-19] All E.R. Rep. 860.
(4) [1919] 2 K.B. at pp. 578-580; [1918-19] All E.R. Rep. at pp. 864, 865.

A no dispute that the parties entered into some sort of arrangement. It really depends on: (a) whether the parties intended it to be legally binding; and (b) if so, whether it was sufficiently certain to be enforceable.

Did the parties intend the arrangement to be legally binding? This question has to be solved by applying what is sometimes (although perhaps unfortunately) called an objective test. The court has to consider what the parties said and

B wrote in the light of all the surrounding circumstances, and then decide whether the true inference is that the ordinary man and woman, speaking or writing thus in such circumstances, would have intended to create a legally binding agreement.

Counsel for the mother has said, quite rightly, that as a rule when arrangements are made between close relations, for example, between husband and wife,

C parent and child or uncle and nephew in relation to an allowance, there is a presumption against an intention of creating any legal relationship. This is not a presumption of law, but of fact. It derives from experience of life and human nature which shows that in such circumstances men and women usually do not intend to create legal rights and obligations, but intend to rely solely on family ties of mutual trust and affection. This has all been explained by ATKIN,

D L.J., in his celebrated judgment in *Balfour* v. *Balfour* (5). There may, however, be circumstances in which this presumption, like all other presumptions of fact, can be rebutted. Counsel for the daughter has drawn our attention to two cases, in which it was, *Shadwell* v. *Shadwell* (6), and *Parker* v. *Clark* (7). The former was a curious case. It was decided by ERLE, C.J., and KEATING, J. (BYLES, J., dissenting) on a pleading point, and depended largely on the true

E construction of a letter written by an uncle to his nephew. I confess that I should have decided it without hesitation in accordance with the views of BYLES, J. But this is of no consequence. *Shadwell* v. *Shadwell* (6) laid down no principle of law relevant to what we have to decide; it merely illustrated what could never, I think, be seriously doubted, viz., that there may be circumstances in which arrangements between close relatives are intended to have the force

F of law.

In the present case the learned county court judge, having had the advantage of seeing the mother and the daughter in the witness box, entirely accepted the daughter's version of the facts. He came to the conclusion that on these very special facts the true inference must be that the arrangement between the parties prior to the daughter's leaving Washington were intended by both to have

G contractual force. On the facts as found by the learned county court judge this was entirely different from the ordinary case of a mother promising her daughter an allowance whilst the daughter read for the Bar, or a father promising his son an allowance at university if the son passed the necessary examinations to gain admission. The daughter here was 34 years of age in 1962. She had left Trinidad and settled in Washington as long ago as 1949. In Washington she

H had a comfortable flat and was employed as an assistant accountant in the Indian embassy at a salary of $500 a month (over £2,000 a year). This employment carried a pension. She had a son of seven years of age who was an American citizen, and had, of course, already begun his education. There were obviously solid reasons for her staying where she was. For some years prior to 1962, however, the mother, who lived in Trinidad, had been trying hard to persuade

I her to throw up all that she had achieved in Washington and go to London to read for the Bar. The mother would have been very proud to have a barrister for a daughter. She also thought that her plan was in the interest of her grandson, to whom she was much attached. She envisaged that, after the daughter had been called to the Bar, she would practise in Trinidad and thereafter presumably she (the mother) would be able to see much more of the daughter than

(5) [1919] 2 K.B. 571 at pp. 578–580; [1918-19] All E.R. Rep. 860 at pp. 864, 865.
(6) (1860), 9 C.B.N.S. 159.
(7) [1960] 1 All E.R. 93; [1960] 1 W.L.R. 286.

formerly.   The daughter was naturally loath to leave Washington, and did not   **A**
regard the mother's suggestion as feasible.   The mother, however, eventually persuaded the daughter to do as she wished by promising her that, if she threw up
her excellent position in Washington and came to study for the Bar in England,
she would pay her daughter an allowance of $200 a month until she had com-
pleted her studies.   The mother's attorney in Trinidad wrote to the daughter
to confirm this.   I cannot think that either intended that if, after the daughter   **B**
had been in London, say, for six months, the mother dishonoured her promise
and left her daughter destitute, the daughter would have no legal redress.

In the very special circumstances of this case, I consider that the true inference
must be that neither the mother nor the daughter could have intended that the
daughter should have no legal right to receive, and the mother no legal obligation
to pay, the allowance of $200 a month.   **C**

The point was made by counsel for the mother that the parties cannot have had a
contractual intention since it would be unthinkable for the daughter to be able to
sue the mother if the mother fell on hard times.   I am afraid that I am not
impressed by this point.   The evidence which the learned county court judge
accepted showed that the mother was a woman of some substance, and prior to
the agreement had assured the daughter that there would be no difficulty in   **D**
finding the money.   The fact that, if contrary to everyone's expectation the
mother had lost her money, the daughter would have been unlikely to sue her
throws no light on whether the parties had an intention to contract.   The fact
that a contracting party is in some circumstances unlikely to extract his pound of
flesh does not mean that he has no right to it.   Even today sometimes people
forbear from mercy to enforce their undoubted legal rights.   **E**

The next point made by counsel for the mother was that the arrangements
between the mother and the daughter in 1962 were too uncertain to constitute
a binding contract.   It is true that the mother said $200 a month without
stipulating whether she meant West Indian or United States dollars.   Obviously
she meant West Indian dollars.   The daughter says that she thought her mother
meant United States dollars.   This point does not, however, appear to have   **F**
given rise to any difficulty.   For two years from November 1962 until December
1964 the mother regularly paid her daughter £42, the equivalent of $ (West
Indian) 200, a month, and the daughter accepted this sum without demur.
Then it is said on the mother's behalf that the daughter's obligations are not
sufficiently stated.   I think that they are plain, to leave Washington, with all
that entailed, come to London and genuinely study for the Bar there.   If the   **G**
daughter threw up her studies for the Bar, maybe the mother could not have
recovered damages, but she would have been relieved of any obligation to
continue the allowance.

Then again it is said that the duration of the agreement was not specified.
No doubt, but I see no difficulty in implying the usual term that it was to last
for a reasonable time.   The parties cannot have contemplated that the daughter   **H**
should go on studying for the Bar and draw the allowance until she was seventy,
nor on the other hand that the mother could have discontinued the allowance
if the daughter did not pass her examinations within, say, 18 months.   The
promise was to pay the allowance until the daughter's studies were completed,
and to my mind there was a clear implication that they were to be completed
within a reasonable time.   Studies are completed either by the student being   **I**
called to the Bar or giving up the unequal struggle against the examiners.
It may not be easy to decide, especially when there is such a paucity of evidence,
what is a reasonable time.   The daughter, however, was a well-educated intelligent woman capable of earning the equivalent of over £2,000 a year in Washington.
It is true that she had a young son to look after, and may well (as the learned
judge thought) have been hampered to some extent by the worry of this litigation.
But, making all allowance for these factors and any other distraction, I cannot

A   think that a reasonable time could possibly exceed five years from November 1962, the date when she began her studies.

It follows, therefore, that on no view can she now in November 1968 be entitled to anything further under the contract which the learned county court judge, rightly I think, held that she made with the mother in 1962. She has some of Part 1 of the Bar examination still to pass, and necessarily the final has not B   yet even been attempted.

During a visit to England in 1964 the mother found that her daughter was living in one room in Acton costing £6 17s. 6d. a week. This rent represented about three-quarters of the daughter's total income. The mother therefore hit on the idea of buying a house in London in which the daughter could live more comfortably and cheaply than in Acton. The rest of the house was to be C   let off in furnished rooms or flats and after paying the outgoings the daughter was to pay herself the maintenance and remit any balance that there might be to her mother in Trinidad. This scheme, so long as it lasted, provided a convenient method of paying the £42 a month due under the 1962 agreement. Accordingly, the mother acquired no. 181, Highbury Quadrant for £6,000 or so in December 1964. The daughter moved in in the following month, furnished D   and equipped the house largely by hire-purchase, and tenants began to arrive in February 1965.

The learned county court judge has concluded that in December 1964 the original contract between the mother and the daughter was varied, or a new contract was entered into whereby the daughter acquired the right to stay on in the mother's house indefinitely, whether the mother liked it or not. I am E   afraid that I cannot accept this conclusion. It was for the daughter to make out such a variation or new contract. In my view she totally failed to do so.

There is no evidence that the mother bargained away her right to dispose of her house, or to evict the daughter (who was a mere licensee) whenever she wished to do so. The evidence shows that all the arrangements in relation to the house were very vague and made without any contractual intent. By this arrangement F   the mother was trying primarily to help the daughter, and also perhaps to make a reasonable investment for herself. When the mother brought the arrangement to an end (as she was entitled to do at any time) she would, of course, have to go on paying £42 a month as long as the 1962 agreement lasted. There is no evidence to suggest that the mother intended the daughter ever to have more than the equivalent of $ (West Indian) 200 a month after December 1964. Nothing G   was said as to how much the daughter might pay herself out of the rents for maintenance. Certainly she would have to debit herself with some reasonable figure in respect of her accommodation, no doubt something less than £6 17s. 6d. a week that she had been spending in Acton, but not less, I should think, than about £5 a week. This would leave about £22 a month to be deducted from the rents for maintenance up till November 1967 when in my view the 1962 agreement H   ran out. In fact for nearly four years, that is, from December 1964 until today, the mother had not received a penny from the daughter in respect of no. 181, Highbury Quadrant nor, in spite of repeated requests, any proper accounts.

I am not at all surprised that the mother's patience became exhausted in March 1967 when she gave notice determining her daughter's licence to remain in I   the house. The daughter ignored the notice and has continued in occupation with her husband and son, apparently with the intention of doing so indefinitely. She is still there. She seems to take the view (as does the learned county court judge) that she has a legal claim on the mother to house her and contribute to her support and that of her son and husband, perhaps in perpetuity. In this she is mistaken, and so in my judgment is the learned county court judge. The mother began this action for possession of no. 181, Highbury Quadrant in 1967. For the reasons I have indicated, there is in my view no defence to the action, and I would accordingly allow the appeal.

A　　The learned county court judge has referred the counterclaim. If this reference is pursued, it will involve an account being meticulously taken of all receipts and expenditure from December 1964 until the date on which the daughter yields up possession. This will certainly result in a great waste of time and money, and can only exacerbate ill-feeling between the mother and the daughter. With a little goodwill and good sense on both sides, this could and should be avoided by reaching a reasonable compromise on the figures. I can but express B the hope that this may be done, for it would clearly be to the mutual benefit of both parties.

FENTON ATKINSON, L.J.: The first question in this most unhappy case is whether the arrangement made between the mother and the daughter in August 1962 was intended to create a legally enforceable contract between C them or was merely one of those family or domestic arrangements where the parties at the time had no thought or intention of invoking the assistance of the courts should the arrangement not be honoured. Was the mother legally binding herself to support the daughter at the rate of £500 a year for a wholly uncertain length of time whatever changes might come about in their respective circumstances? Was the daughter assuming a contractual obligation to pursue her D legal studies to successful completion whatever the difficulties she experienced, and whatever attractive alternatives might appear, such as possible marriage or well-paid employment? If the test were the giving of consideration by the daughter, the answer would be simple. She gave up well-paid work and good living accommodation, and removed herself and her son to England, where she began her studies in November 1962. But the giving of consideration by the E daughter cannot decide the question whether the parties intended to make a binding contract.

ATKIN, L.J., in *Balfour* v. *Balfour* (8) put it in this way:

"To my mind those agreements, or many of them, do not result in contracts at all, and they do not result in contracts even though there may be what as between other parties would constitute consideration for the F agreement. The consideration, as we know, may consist either in some right, interest, profit, or benefit accruing to one party, or some forbearance, detriment, loss or responsibility given, suffered, or undertaken by the other. That is a well-known definition, and it constantly happens, I think, that such arrangements made between husband and wife are arrangements in which there are mutual promises, or in which there is consideration in the form G within the definition that I have mentioned. Nevertheless, they are not contracts, and they are not contracts because the parties did not intend that they should be attended by legal consequences."

On the other hand, I do not think that the lack of formality and precision in expressing the arrangement is necessarily an indication that no contract was intended having regard to what the court knows of the parties and their relation- H ship. The problem is, in my view, a difficult one, because though one would tend to regard a promise by a parent to pay an allowance to a child during a course of study as no more than a family arrangement, on the facts of this case this particular daughter undoubtedly gave up a great deal on the strength of the mother's promise.

In my judgment it is the subsequent history which gives the best guide to I the parties' intention at the material time. There are three matters which seem to me important: (i) The daughter thought that her mother was promising her $(U.S.) 200, or £70 a month, which she regarded as the minimum necessary for her support. The mother promised $200 but she had in mind $(West Indian) 200, £42 a month, and that was what she in fact paid from November 1962 to December 1964. Those payments were accepted by the daughter without any

---

(8) [1919] 2 K.B. 571 at pp. 578, 579; [1918-19] All E.R. Rep. 860 at p. 864.

A sort of suggestion at any stage that the mother had legally contracted for the larger sum. (ii) When the arrangements for the purchase of no. 181, Highbury Quadrant were being discussed, and the new arrangement was made for maintenance to come out of the rents, many material matters were left open: How much accommodation was the daughter to occupy; how much money was she to have out of the rents; if the rents fell below expectation, was the mother

B to make up the difference below £42, or £42 less the sum saved by the daughter in rent; for how long was the arrangement to continue, and so on. The whole arrangement was, in my view, far too vague and uncertain to be itself enforceable as a contract; but at no stage did the daughter bring into the discussions her alleged legal right of £42 per month until her studies were completed, and how that right was to be affected by the new arrangement. (iii) It is perhaps not without

C relevance to look at the daughter's evidence in cross-examination. She was asked about the occasion when the mother visited the house, and she, knowing perfectly well that the mother was there, refused for some hours to open the door. She said:

" I didn't open the door because a normal mother doesn't sue her daughter in court. Anybody with normal feelings would feel upset by what was

D happening."

Those answers and the daughter's conduct on that occasion provide a strong indication that she had never for a moment contemplated the possibility of the mother or herself going to court to enforce legal obligations, and that she felt it quite intolerable that a purely family arrangement should become the subject

E of proceedings in a court of law.

At the time when the first arrangement was made, the mother and the daughter were, and always had been, to use the daughter's own words, " very close ". I am satisfied that neither party at that time intended to enter into a legally binding contract, either then or later when the house was bought. The daughter was prepared to trust the mother to honour her promise of support, just as the

F mother no doubt trusted the daughter to study for the Bar with diligence, and to get through her examinations as early as she could. It follows that in my view the mother's claim for possession succeeds, and her appeal should be allowed. There remains the counterclaim. As to that I fully endorse what Salmon, L.J., has said as to the manner in which that should be disposed of.

Appeal allowed. Order for possession by mother on or before 1st March 1969.

G *Reference of quantum of counterclaim to registrar to stand. Leave to appeal to the House of Lords refused.*

Solicitors: *D. A. Rose & Co.* (for the mother); *Jaques & Co.* (for the daughter).

[*Reported by* F. A. Amies, Esq., *Barrister-at-Law.*]

A

R. v. WEBB.

[COURT OF APPEAL, CRIMINAL DIVISION (Sachs and Fenton Atkinson, L.JJ., and Caulfield, J.), March 13, 14, 1969.]

Criminal Law—Trial—Plea—Fitness to plead—Nature of accused's disability—
Chances of success of challenge to prosecution case by defence—Trial judge   B
ruling that question of fitness to plead be tried before arraignment—Whether
discretion properly exercised—Criminal Procedure (Insanity) Act 1964
(c. 84), s. 4 (2), (3).

The appellant, aged 26, was charged on indictment with indecently assaulting a girl aged nine. After the case was called on, counsel for the prosecution stated that evidence was available to the effect that the appellant   C
was unfit to plead, having a mental age of less than the girl whom he was
alleged to have assaulted. Counsel for the appellant did not admit that
he was thus unfit to plead, but conceded that, pursuant to s. 4* of the
Criminal Procedure (Insanity) Act 1964, the question of unfitness to plead
must be tried some time before the defence opened. The deputy chairman
ruled that a preliminary issue should be tried before the appellant was   D
arraigned. The jury having been sworn and empanelled, two medical
witnesses were called for the prosecution and cross-examined by the
defence. The appellant's father was called, who spoke of the degree of
his son's understanding. The evidence showed that the appellant was of
subnormal intelligence, but that he was capable of going about on his
own; that he had been in employment for a considerable time; that he   E
was in no way an aggressive type nor was he unable to speak or to give
some account of what happened to him in the normal course of events; and
that there was nothing in the nature of a disability which would entail his
being kept within the confines of a hospital. The jury were directed on the
issue and found that the appellant was unfit to plead. By s. 4 (2)* of the
Act of 1964, the court had power to postpone consideration of the question   F
of fitness to be tried until any time up to the opening of the case for the
defence if, having regard to the nature of the supposed disability the court
were of the opinion that it was expedient so to do and in the interests of the
accused; and by s. 4 (3)*, subject to sub-s. (2), the question of fitness to be
tried was to be determined as soon as possible. On appeal against an order
that he be detained under s. 5 (1) of the Act of 1964 in a hospital specified   G
by the Secretary of State,

Held: the appeal must be allowed, because—

(i) the direction in s. 4 (3) of the Act of 1964 being specifically made
subject to the provisions of s. 4 (2), it followed that, as between those two
subsections, it was sub-s. (2) which was the controlling subsection, the
discretion to be exercised being a judicial discretion (see p. 628, letter F,   H
post); and

(ii) on the particular facts of the case, the exercise of the purported discretion by the deputy chairman was vitiated in law, since it seemed clear
that he was not applying his mind to the two factors laid down by s. 4 (2),
viz., the nature of the disability of the appellant and the expediency in the
interests of the appellant (in that the chances of success of a challenge to   I
the prosecution case did not seem to have been given proper weight) (see
p. 629, letter G, post).

Appeal allowed.

[As to trial of issue whether defendant fit to plead or not, see 10 HALSBURY'S
LAWS (3rd Edn.) 402, para. 729; and for cases on the subject, see 14 DIGEST
(Repl.) 279, 280, *2493-2508.*

---

* Section 4, so far as material, is set out at p. 628, letters A to C, post.

A   For the Criminal Procedure (Insanity) Act 1964, s. 4, see 8 HALSBURY'S STATUTES (3rd Edn.) 527.]

Case referred to:

R. v. *MacCarthy* (or *McCarthy*), [1966] 1 All E.R. 447; [1967] 1 Q.B. 68; [1966] 2 W.L.R. 555; 130 J.P. 157; 50 Cr. App. Rep. 109; Digest (Cont. Vol. B) 166, *2508*Aa.

B

Appeal.

This was an appeal by Colin John Webb by leave of the Court of Appeal (WINN and WIDGERY, L.JJ., and LAWTON, J.) given on 6th February 1969, against an order made at Dorset Quarter Sessions by the deputy chairman (ALASTAIR MORTON, ESQ.) on 1st January 1969 under s. 5 (1) of the Criminal Procedure

C   (Insanity) Act 1964 that, having been found before arraignment to be under a disability, he be admitted to such hospital as might be specified by the Secretary of State and, in pursuance of Sch. 1, para. 1 (2), to the Act of 1964, that, pending such admission he be detained in Dorchester prison. The facts are set out in the judgment of the court.

A. C. Munro Kerr for the appellant.

D   *D. P. O'Brien* for the Crown.

SACHS, L.J., delivered the judgment of the court: On 1st January 1969, the appellant, a young man of 26, surrendered to his bail at Dorset Quarter Sessions to answer an indictment charging him with indecently assaulting a girl aged nine. Immediately after the case was called on, counsel for the prosecution stated that

E   there was available evidence to the effect that the appellant was unfit to plead, being of a mental age incidentally of less than the girl whom he was alleged to have assaulted. Counsel for the appellant did not admit that he was thus unfit to plead, and pressed for him to stand his trial in the ordinary way. Indeed, counsel, with the great experience that is at his command, stated that he was content to accept instructions from the appellant, and today has repeated that he would even now

F   be similarly content. He put it plainly to Dorset Quarter Sessions that he did not wish the issue of unfitness to plead to be raised if it was possible to prevent it, and that, in any event, he desired it to be postponed as long as practicable. After some discussion as to the facts and the position created by s. 4 of the Criminal Procedure (Insanity) Act 1964, counsel for the appellant correctly con- ceded that the question of unfitness to plead must be tried some time before the

G   defence opens; thereupon the learned deputy chairman ruled: " Yes. That being so, it shall be tried now ". The jury having then been sworn and empanelled, the preliminary issue of fitness or unfitness to plead was tried. The medical witnesses—two in number—were called for the prosecution and cross-examined for the defence. Next there was called the appellant's father, who spoke as to the degree of his son's understanding. Then the jury were directed on the issue, and

H   found that the appellant was unfit to plead. (It should be mentioned that counsel for the appellant in this court has stated that he would have wished to impugn some parts of the summing-up to the jury; but in the view which this court takes of the matter, that point does not arise.) The verdict of the jury having been taken, the appellant was ordered to be detained in the terms provided by the Act, and the trial did not proceed to arraignment.

I   On appeal to this court, it has been submitted on behalf of the appellant that the learned deputy chairman misapprehended the law when making his order for the issue to be tried before arraignment, and that he either did not really exercise his discretion or, alternatively, that, having misdirected himself on principles, he did not exercise it judicially in the way that he should have done. It is further submitted that, on the particular facts of the case, the trial of the issue should have been postponed until after the evidence by the prosecution had been given and tested, so that the appellant might have had a chance of an acquittal.

In those circumstances, before further examining the facts of the case, it is first

convenient to read the relevant parts of s. 4 of the Act of 1964, and to consider   A
what is the position which they create in law. The first three subsections of s. 4
provide:

> " (1) Where on the trial of a person the question arises (at the instance
> of the defence or otherwise) whether the accused is under disability, that is
> to say under any disability such that apart from this Act it would constitute
> a bar to his being tried, the following provisions shall have effect.   B
>
> " (2) The court, if having regard to the nature of the supposed disability
> the court are of opinion that it is expedient so to do and in the interests of
> the accused, may postpone consideration of the said question (hereinafter
> referred to as ' the question of fitness to be tried ') until any time up to the
> opening of the case for the defence, and if before the question of fitness to be
> tried falls to be determined the jury return a verdict of acquittal on the   C
> count or each of the counts on which the accused is being tried that question
> shall not be determined.
>
> " (3) Subject to the foregoing subsection, the question of fitness to be
> tried shall be determined as soon as it arises."

Before the passing of the Act of 1964, the issue of fitness to plead had of necessity   D
to be disposed of before arraignment. If the jury found unfitness to plead, then
the order of the court was in all cases that the appellant be detained at Her
Majesty's pleasure. One of the main objects of the Act was, of course, to enable
the accused to avoid this much-dreaded order in cases where the defence was in a
position to demolish the prosecution case by cross-examination or on some
point of law before the time came for the defence to be opened. It was for this   E
reason that the courts were given the discretion provided by s. 4 (2) of the Act
of 1964 to so postpone the trial of the issue of fitness to plead that it need no
longer, as formerly, be of necessity dealt with before the arraignment. The direction in sub-s. (3) as to the question being tried as soon as it arises is specifically
made subject to the provisions of sub-s. (2) which precedes it; and it follows as
between these two that it is sub-s. (2) which is the controlling subsection. The   F
discretion to be exercised is, of course, a judicial discretion.

The court next turns to the matters to which regard must be had by virtue of
the provisions of the latter subsection. One is the nature of the supposed disability; another is expediency in the interests of the accused. As regards the
second, it is, of course, clear that, if there are reasonable chances of the prosecution
case being successfully challenged so that the defence may not be called on, then   G
clearly it is as a rule in the interests of the accused that trial of the issue be
postponed until after arraignment. Whether, and to what degree, lesser chances
of success may warrant such a postponement is something on which this court
will say no more than that, if there are sufficient chances to warrant such a
challenge, the issue should be postponed until after that challenge has been made.
To the relevant facts of this particular case the court will advert later; for each   H
case must necessarily obtain on its own facts.

As to the way in which regard must be had to " the nature of the disability ",
this is a somewhat difficult matter. Suffice it to say that, in the present case, the
appellant was, on the medical evidence, a simple young man, subnormal in intelligence, but capable of going about—at any rate by day—on his own. He was in
employment entailing the performance of a simple set of tasks—washing bottles.
It may well, of course, be that he owed that employment in some degree to the   I
kindliness of his employer, but the fact remains that he had held it for a considerable time. It is, indeed, to be observed that, in the report of the mental
welfare officer, there appears this passage:

> " In 1960 [the appellant] started work at the Rax Dairies, Bridport, under
> a firm but sympathetic employer. He enjoyed his work, and settled down
> well at home. Apart from one or two isolated incidents, [the appellant] has
> been happy and settled over the past eight years."

A The appellant, moreover, was in no way an aggressive type, nor was he a man unable to speak or to give at any rate some account of what happened to him in the normal course of events. There was nothing in the nature of a disability which would entail his being kept within the confines of a hospital, if he was found not guilty of the offence in question. In other words, in this particular instance, the appellant was not a man of whom it could be said, " well, whatever happens

B at this trial, it is necessary that he be made a subject of some order depriving him of his liberty ". That appears to this court to be a factor to which regard should have been had.

From that general consideration of the law, the court now turns to the issue whether the learned deputy chairman did exercise a discretion, and, if so, whether he exercised it judicially in the sense of taking into account all those factors

C to which he ought to have had regard. It is to be noted that, when another division of this court gave leave for this appeal to be brought, Winn, L.J., said:

> ". . . it is an arguable view that the learned deputy chairman apparently applied [sub-s. (3)] without further regard to the provisions of sub-s. (2) . . . In the opinion of this court it may be open to contend that the learned deputy chairman did not purport to exercise any discretion. From the transcript

D > so far as that reveals what happened, it is open to doubt whether the truth may be that he did not himself at the time consider that he had any discretion which it was his duty to exercise."

This court has now had the advantage of hearing from both counsel concerned that there was cited, and apparently discussed at some length at quarter sessions

E *R.* v. *MacCarthy* (or *McCarthy*) (1). In particular, we have been told that there was discussion of the headnote (2) and certain passages in that case (3). Suffice it to say that, although that case was in no way concerned with the exercise of a discretion under sub-s. (2), yet this court does understand that the general effect of it might have per incuriam been taken persuasively to indicate a need in the instant case to act under sub-s. (3) (which refers to the determination of the issue as soon as it arises) and to have the issue tried before arraignment. This court thinks that it

F may well be that the learned deputy chairman did not consider that he had a real discretion in all the circumstances; but, more importantly, it seems quite clear that he was not applying his mind to those factors which have already been discussed in the judgment of this court. In particular, he cannot have applied his mind to the nature of the disability. Moreover, the chances of success of a challenge to the prosecution case by the defence, whilst to some extent discussed,

G do not seem to have been given proper weight, a point to which this court will revert. In those circumstances, this court has come to the conclusion that the exercise of the purported discretion was vitiated in law and, accordingly, subject to the proviso to which this court will now refer, the appeal should be allowed.

The appeal, of course, is one brought within the jurisdiction of this court by s. 15 and s. 16 of the Criminal Appeal Act 1968. It is not necessary to recite the pro-

H visions of s. 15 which give the right to appeal; but it is necessary to refer to some extracts from s. 16, which provides:

> " (1) The Court of Appeal shall allow an appeal under section 15 of this Act if they are of opinion—(*a*) that the finding of the jury should be set aside on the ground that under all the circumstances of the case it is unsafe

I > or unsatisfactory; or (*b*) that the order of the court giving effect to the finding should be set aside on the ground of a wrong decision of any question of law [and that, of course, is the ground on which this court is acting today]; or (*c*) that there was a material irregularity in the course of the determination of the question of fitness to be tried; and in any other case (except one to which subsection (2) below applies) shall dismiss the appeal; but they may

---

(1) [1966] 1 All E.R. 447; [1967] 1 Q.B. 68; [1966] 2 W.L.R. 555.
(2) [1966] 2 W.L.R. at pp. 555, 556; cf. [1966] 1 All E.R. at p. 447.
(3) [1966] 1 All E.R. at p. 449; [1967] 1 Q.B. at pp. 73, 74; [1966] 2 W.L.R. at p. 559.

dismiss the appeal if of opinion that, notwithstanding that the point raised
in the appeal might be decided in favour of the appellant, no miscarriage of
justice has actually occurred."

Before passing to the proviso to s. 2 (1) of the Act of 1968 (which, of course, is
substantially in identical terms with that to s. 4 (1) of the Criminal Appeal Act
1907), it is perhaps as well to mention that s. 16 (2) of the Criminal Appeal
Act 1968 relates to a case that does not arise today.

It is now convenient, when considering the question of the proviso, to turn
back to the facts. When the matter was before this court on 6th February 1969,
WINN, L.J., dealt with them thus:

"[The appellant] was charged with indecent assault upon a little girl of
nine. There was some corroborating evidence, but that evidence itself was
in the nature of it susceptible of probing and challenge during cross-
examination by experienced counsel [I would remark that he clearly had in
mind counsel for the appellant]; the child's own evidence needed corroboration and was, of course, the sort of evidence as to which the jury would
require as a matter of law to be seriously warned, she being only nine years of
age."

To that passage there could have been added—had the material been before the
court on that occasion—firstly, that the prosecution conceded that the initial
advances were made by the little girl herself, and, secondly—as the court has now
been informed—that counsel for the appellant felt himself in a position to challenge
some of this corroborative evidence by reference to plans and other material
which might throw doubt on whether he could have seen all that he in fact said
he saw. To continue with the passage from WINN, L.J.:

". . . there were issues which would require to be explored and tested, and
upon which an outcome successful to the [appellant] was not out of contemplation. That being so, there was a chance that by contesting the factual
issues and attacking the evidence for the Crown, an acquittal might have
been secured for [the appellant], and it would clearly have been in his interests
if that acquittal could have been secured; it would have been from his point
of view expedient to have an opportunity for the evidence to be tested before
his disability fell to be determined by a jury."

With those passages as to the chances of successfully challenging the Crown's
case this court respectfully agrees. That being the position, there can clearly
be no question of applying the proviso; far from it being a case in which the
court could come to the conclusion that no miscarriage of justice had occurred,
it is clear that the facts already mentioned provide strong grounds as to why
the learned deputy chairman should have exercised his discretion to postpone the
trial of the issue of fitness to plead. In those circumstances, this appeal will be
allowed.

It is, perhaps, as well, before this court turns to ancillary points, to make it
plain that naturally its decision has turned on the particular facts of this case.
There may well be cases where the nature of the disability is quite different, and
there may well be cases where the evidence for the prosecution is of a type which
simply could not be successfully challenged. Those would be cases in which the
relevant factors would be different.

The next question that arises is as to what order this court should now make.
Section 16 (3) provides that:

". . . where an appeal under section 15 of this Act is allowed, the appellant
may be tried accordingly for the offence with which he was charged, and
the Court of Appeal may make such orders as appear to them to be necessary
or expedient pending any such trial for his custody, admission to bail or
continued detention under the Mental Health Act 1959 . . ."

A   It is to be observed that the words are " may be tried " and not " will be tried ". This court would hope that considerable and anxious consideration will be given by the Crown whether to offer evidence when the indictment next comes before sessions. That, however, does not absolve this court from deciding what is the proper order to make, both as regards bail and as to what is to happen between the date of the order of this court and the date the matter next comes before

B   sessions. On that, the court would like the assistance of counsel.

[14th March. The court ordered that the appellant be released on bail pending his trial and recognizances were fixed.]

Appeal allowed.

Solicitors: Lovell, Son & Pitfield, agents for Roper & Roper, Bridport (for the appellant); Sharpe, Pritchard & Co., agents for J. R. Pryer, Dorchester.

C   (for the Crown).

[Reported by N. P. Metcalfe, Esq., Barrister-at-Law.]

D

R. v. NATIONAL INSURANCE COMMISSIONER,
Ex parte HUDSON.

[Queen's Bench Division (Lord Parker, C.J., Ashworth and Willis, JJ.), December 10, 11, 1968.]

E   Industrial Injury—Medical Appeal Tribunal—Jurisdiction—Scope of jurisdiction—Finding by statutory authority (local insurance officer) on claim for injury benefit that injured workman suffered heart condition caused by accident—Subsequent application by workman for disablement benefit—Whether Medical Appeal Tribunal bound to accept finding that heart condition caused by accident.

F   In the case of an appeal to the Medical Appeal Tribunal under the National Insurance (Industrial Injuries) Act 1965, provided that the medical authorities do not say anything which conflicts with there having been an accident or some injury they are entitled to substitute another injury for the one originally found since all that is binding on them is that there has been an industrial accident and that there has been some injury (see p. 635, letter G, p. 635, letter I, to p. 636, letter A, p. 636, letter I, and p. 637, letter F, post).

G   Minister of Social Security v. Amalgamated Engineering Union ([1967] 1 All E.R. 210) distinguished.

Application dismissed.

[As to disablement benefit, see 27 Halsbury's Laws (3rd Edn.) 824, 825, paras. 1451, 1452; and as to the determination of industrial injuries claims and

H   questions, see ibid., pp. 853-866, paras. 1495-1513.]

Case referred to:

Minister of Social Security v. Amalgamated Engineering Union, (Re Dowling), [1967] 1 All E.R. 210; [1967] 1 A.C. 725; [1967] 2 W.L.R. 516.

Application for certiorari.

I   This was an application by Donald Kenneth Raymond Hudson for an order of certiorari to quash a decision of one of the National Insurance Commissioners (H. I. Nelson, Esq., Q.C.) dated 12th July 1967 refusing to grant leave to the applicant to appeal from a decision of the Medical Appeal Tribunal dated 27th September 1966. The facts are set out in the judgment of Lord Parker, C.J.

The cases noted below* were cited during the argument in addition to the case referred to in the judgments.

---

* R. v. Industrial Injuries Comr., Ex p. Cable, [1967] 2 All E.R. 119; [1967] 2 Q.B. 429; R. v. Industrial Injuries Comr., Ex p. Howarth (1968), 4 K.I.R. 621.

S. J. Waldman for the applicant.   A
Gordon Slynn for the respondent.

LORD PARKER, C.J.: In these proceedings, counsel for the applicant
moves for an order of certiorari to quash a decision of H. I. NELSON, Esq., Q.C.,
one of the National Insurance Commissioners, dated 12th July 1967, whereby he
refused to grant leave to appeal from a decision of the Medical Appeal Tribunal
dated 27th September 1966. This, like so many of these cases under the National   B
Insurance and the National Insurance (Industrial Injuries) Acts 1965, raises
difficult questions, and for myself I should have preferred to have reserved judgment. But we are getting near the end of term, and this court is likely to
be disbanded soon and its members may not all be in London. In those
circumstances, I thought it right to try and give judgment now.

It is necessary to go through the facts in a little detail. The applicant was, on   C
19th January 1965, installing a piece of electronic machinery by hand, and in
the course of doing so claimed to have suffered an injury. He was at once certified
as incapable of work by reason of what was called " chest pain " and there followed
the letters " N.Y.D.", Not Yet Diagnosed. He did not claim at that stage any
injury benefit, but he claimed and obtained sickness benefit. Further certificates   D
from time to time were issued, which did not state the cause of the incapacity,
but a time came when medical certificates certified that he was incapable of
work owing to myocardial infarction, and later that he was suffering from coronary
thrombosis. Finally, by 17th April 1965 it was certified that he was fit to resume
work. Throughout all that period, from 19th January 1965 to 17th April 1965,
he obtained sickness benefit, and as I have said he never claimed injury benefit.
However, on 20th September 1965 he applied for a declaration that what had   E
happened on 19th January 1965 amounted to an industrial accident and he
claimed that the injury was suspected hernia. He was supported in that by the
employers, who described the incident as that " [the applicant] was lifting a
piece of electronic equipment when he strained himself ", and the employers
themselves reported this as " suspected hernia."   F

The local insurance officer in due course declared that this was an industrial
accident. He did that by endorsing the application with the words " Accident was
I/A 19/1/65 declaration only ". That was signed by the insurance officer on 4th
October. The next step was that on 3rd November the applicant claimed industrial
disablement benefit, and the matter went before a medical board who found a right
inguinal hernia as a relevant condition, and in regard to the original certificates relating to the heart condition, they said that the cause of the heart lesion was un-   G
connected as no claim had been made. Thereafter, the applicant did two things;
he took medical advice as the result of which he claimed injury benefit, and he also
appealed from the findings of the medical board to the Medical Appeal Tribunal.
The opinions that he obtained were first an opinion from Dr. Young, a surgeon,
who upheld the view that the hernia was the result of accident, but expressed no   H
opinion on what I might call the heart condition. Secondly, he obtained
the opinion of a Dr. Somerville who said that in his opinion there was a direct
causal relationship between the development of the coronary thrombosis and the
physical effort on the day in question. Those opinions were put before the local
insurance officer supporting a claim for injury benefit for the period to which I
have referred, the period from 19th January 1965 to 17th April 1965. In addition   I
the local insurance officer had the original declaration, and he had the findings
of the medical board. Without giving any specific decision on the matter he
passed, as it were, the form for payment of injury benefit for that period to which
I have referred.

Pausing there, it seems to me he was thereby saying: the applicant is entitled
to injury benefit because for that period he was totally incapacitated by reason of
the injury which he now puts forward, namely this heart condition.

The next thing that happened was that the appeal to the Medical Appeal

A Tribunal came on, and the question for the Medical Appeal Tribunal was stated to be whether the heart condition was attributable to the accident. They also had the medical reports. It was pointed out to them that really the medical board had never decided this question, because they had merely said that it was unconnected because no claim in respect thereof had been made.

In the result, the Medical Appeal Tribunal gave their decision in this form:

B
> " Exertion being of itself no precipitating factor in myocardial infarction, we can find nothing in this case to associate that condition with the relevant accident. The above assessment is made in respect of the hernia, which remains unrepaired,"

and they upheld a disablement benefit of some three per cent. in respect of the loss of capacity constituted by the hernia. It was in those circumstances that
C it was sought to appeal to the commissioner. The commissioner in his decision on 12th July 1967 refused leave to appeal.

Before considering the arguments in the case, it is necessary to remind oneself of a few of the provisions of the relevant legislation. The benefits to which a person is entitled as a result of an industrial accident are now set out in s. 5 (1)
D of the National Insurance (Industrial Injuries) Act 1965 which provides:

> " Subject to the provisions of this Act, where an insured person suffers personal injury caused after 4th July 1948 by accident arising out of and in the course of his employment, being insurable employment, then— (*a*) industrial injury benefit (in this Act referred to as ' injury benefit ') shall be payable to the insured person if during such period as is hereinafter
E provided he is, as the result of the injury, incapable of work; (*b*) industrial disablement benefit (in this Act referred to as ' disablement benefit ') by way of disablement gratuity or disablement pension shall be payable to the insured person if he suffers, as the result of the injury , from such loss of physical or mental faculty as is hereinafter provided . . . "

para. (*c*) for this purpose does not matter.
F Then the conditions for injury benefit and disablement benefit are set out in s. 11 and s. 12 respectively. By s. 11 (1):

> " An insured person shall be entitled to injury benefit in respect of any day during the injury benefit period on which, as the result of the relevant injury, he is incapable of work . . ."

G By s. 86, the interpretation section " relevant injury " means " in relation to any benefit, the . . . injury in respect of which that benefit is claimed or payable". Section 12 (1) provides:

> " Subject to subsections (2) and (6) of this section an insured person shall be entitled to disablement benefit if he suffers as the result of the relevant accident from loss of physical or mental faculty such that the extent of the
H resulting disablement assessed in accordance with the provisions of Schedule 4 to this Act amounts to not less than one per cent.; . . ."

Matters in regard to disablement benefit, which are largely medical matters, go, as one would expect, to a medical board with an appeal to the Medical Appeal Tribunal, and finally in certain cases to a commissioner. Other questions are dealt with by the local insurance officer and an appeal by the local appeal
I tribunal, and in turn the commissioner; in each case the decisions of the respective bodies, the medical authorities and the statutory authorities, are made final, subject of course to the appeals in each case.

Matters concerning the local insurance officer, the local appeal tribunal and the commissioner, are now to be found, unlike the National Insurance Act 1946, in the National Insurance Act 1965 in a group of sections beginning at s. 67. The important section here as it seems to me is s. 75 of that Act, which provides:

> " (1) Subject to the provisions of sections 64 to 72 of this Act, the decision

of any claim or question in accordance with those provisions, and, subject   A
to the provisions of any regulations under section 73 of this Act, the decision
of any claim or question in accordance with the provisions of those
regulations, shall be final."

The main point raised in this appeal is a point raised before the commissioner,
which can be summarised in this form, that it was not open to the Medical Appeal
Tribunal to decide that the heart condition was not relevant to the accident   B
because it had already been decided on the claim for injury benefit that the
heart condition was relevant to the accident, and that decision was final and
binding on the Medical Appeal Tribunal.   It is to be observed here that there
have been two decisions by the local insurance officer, the first as I have said
was by way of declaration in September 1965 that there had been an industrial
accident, and the injury alleged was, as I have said, a hernia.   C

Pausing there, it seems to me quite clear that if there were nothing more, it
would be impossible for the medical authorities whether board or tribunal, to
decide that there had been no industrial accident, and no injury.   That as it
seems to me follows from the decision of the House of Lords in *Minister of Social
Security* v. *Amalgamated Engineering Union* (*Re Dowling*) (1).   Indeed, if there
was nothing more this case on its facts would be almost the same as *Dowling's*   D
case (1).   There a labourer suffered pain on lifting a heavy flagstone, and in
due course he was awarded injury benefit on the basis of hiatus hernia.   Later,
when he claimed disablement benefit, the medical authorities held that hiatus
hernia could not possibly have been caused by lifting the flagstone, and it was
held by the House of Lords that that was a finding which they could not arrive
at, in that the decision that there had been an industrial accident resulting in   E
hernia was final and binding on the medical authorities.

The matter, however, does not rest there, because in this case there was, as
I have already said, a later claim for injury benefit itself quite clearly on the basis
of heart condition, and an award of injury benefit by the local insurance officer
on the basis of that injury.   It was in those circumstances that it is submitted
to this court by counsel for the applicant that the medical authorities are estopped   F
as it were in the same way from saying that this heart condition did not result
from the accident on 19th January.

In my judgment this is a different case from *Dowling's* case (1).   As I understand it, *Dowling's* case (1) decided, and really decided only, that the medical
authorities cannot, as it were, destroy the very basis of their jurisdiction by
saying in effect contrary to what the statutory authorities had found, that there   G
had been no industrial accident.   Thus if in *Dowling's* case (1) the medical
authorities were entitled to hold that the hernia was not due to the lifting of the
flagstone, then there never had been an industrial accident, and accordingly
they would have destroyed the very foundation of their jurisdiction.

LORD MORRIS OF BORTH-Y-GEST said (2):

"The present case is exceptional because a decision as to what caused the   H
injury complained of also resolved the question whether there was an
accident at all.   If Mr. Dowling was caused to suffer a hernia as a result
of lifting the heavy flagstone, then he suffered personal injury by accident.
If his lifting of the heavy flagstone was nothing at all to do with his hernia,
then he never suffered personal injury by accident at all."
     I
I ought to interpose that there had been an appeal from the local insurance
officer up to the commissioner himself on the question of industrial accident.
A little later LORD MORRIS OF BORTH-Y-GEST said (3):

"With respect, I should think that MR. NELSON's decision fixed for the

(1) [1967] 1 All E.R. 210; [1967] 1 A.C. 725.
(2) [1967] 1 All E.R. at p. 215; [1967] 1 A.C. at p. 744.
(3) [1967] 1 All E.R. at p. 216; [1967] 1 A.C. at p. 745.

A
medical board a datum line or starting point which it was not for them to question. Being invited on the basis that there was an accident, it was not open to them to say that there never had been one at all. I consider, therefore, that they and the medical appeal tribunal exceeded their jurisdiction."

B
LORD HODSON in his speech again emphasised the exceptional circumstances of *Dowling's* case (4) where the accident and the injury are in fact the same. It seems to me that this case differs in that here there are two suggested injuries; if one of them is upheld by the medical authorities then there will still have been an industrial accident. Suppose in the present case that the declaration from the beginning had declared that the accident was an industrial accident in regard to (a) hernia, (b) heart condition; then as it seems to me the medical board

C
and the local appeal tribunal could not say that neither of those injuries had existed because thereby they would be saying there had been no industrial accident, but they were entitled to say, at any rate *Dowling's* case (4), as it seems to me, would not prevent them from saying, that one of them and only one of them was the result of the accident.

D
As it seems to me therefore, the present case, in order to succeed, must result in an extension of what was said in *Dowling's* case (4). Counsel for the applicant does not shrink from this. He says that one should leave out any such case as *Dowling's* case (4), where the determination of the injury resolved the question of accident and vice versa, and take an ordinary case of a man who has, say, been hit by some iron on the sling of a crane. He claims industrial injury benefit on the basis of fractured ribs, and he obtains injury benefit on that basis. Counsel

E
for the applicant says that in such a case the medical authorities must proceed on the basis that he did have fractured ribs, albeit the x-rays proved that he never did have any fractured ribs. That, as it seems to me, would result in absurdity; the claimant clearly suffered injury of some kind, we will say bruised bones, and it would be open to the tribunal to say: we are not satisfied that there is any loss of faculty resulting from fractured ribs, but we are satisfied that there

F
was an injury, bruised bones, and that there is a loss of faculty therefrom. If that were not the position, then I do not see why *Dowling's* case (4) as stated by LORD MORRIS OF BORTH-Y-GEST and LORD HODSON, was an exceptional case. It was exceptional, and exceptional only, as it seems to me, for this reason, that by saying that there was no hernia caused by the lifting of the flagstone, they were in effect saying there had been no accident at all.

G
In my judgment the medical authorities are, as it were, estopped from coming to any finding which results in there being no accident or which results in there being no injury, but provided they say nothing which conflicts with there having been an accident and some injury, they are entitled to substitute another injury for one found by the local insurance officer, and of course what is quite clear, any further injuries that may have been discovered meanwhile.

H
The only difficulty about this is to be found in the words of s. 75 of the National Insurance Act 1965 which I have already referred to, words which are very wide, covering: the decision of any claim or question in accordance with those provisions, any such decision being final.

Moreover it is clear, and LORD HODSON dealt with it in *Dowling's* case (4), that the finality does not relate solely to the matters which fall within the jurisdiction

I
of the statutory authorities but are final and therefore binding on the medical authorities. Thus, as it seems to me, one has to look and see what the decision in any case is, and it seems to me that when one is dealing with injury benefit or a declaration, the real decision is that there has been an industrial accident, and there has been some injury (and in the former case an incapacitating injury). Those two matters are binding on the medical authorities, but nothing more. In these circumstances it seems to me for the reasons I have endeavoured to

_____

(4) [1967] 1 All E.R. 210; [1967] 1 A.C. 725.

state that the medical appeal board were fully entitled to come to the decision A
which they did.

The second point relates really to a matter of burden of proof. It is quite
clear that it is for a claimant to show loss of faculty; but once a loss of faculty
is shown, then the provisions of Sch. 4 to the National Insurance (Industrial
Injuries) Act 1965 apply under which, to put it quite generally, one takes the
claimant as he is, one finds out what all his disabilities are, and all those dis- B
abilities are deemed to result from the loss of faculty unless it is shown that he
would in any case have been subject to the disability as the result of congenital
defect, or of an injury or disease received or contracted before the relevant
accident, or would not have been subject thereto but for some injury or disease
received or contracted after and not directly attributable to that accident.

It is said here that the Medical Appeal Tribunal could not have properly C
directed their minds in accordance with that schedule, because they said, " we
can find nothing in this case to associate that condition with the relevant accident ". For my part, I am quite unable to say that the tribunal misdirected
themselves in any way. I am inclined to think that, as counsel for the respondent submits, what they are considering there is merely loss of faculty and have
not gone on to consider disablement. But even assuming that they are dealing D
with disablement, they are not saying, " we are not satisfied in this case that
there was an association between the heart condition and the relevant accident "
in which case they might be misdirecting themselves, but they are saying:
" they can find nothing " in this case, in other words they were completely
satisfied that there was no association between the heart condition and the
relevant accident. Accordingly I am against counsel for the applicant's E
submission on that point.

I should say that finally he says that at any rate they ought to specify; they
ought to say what they think the heart condition is, whether it was congenital,
whether it arose before, whether it arose since. In my judgment it is unnecessary
for the board or the tribunal to state what exception to the general conditions
of Sch. 4 the particular condition falls under. It is sufficient for them to say, F
as I think they did say here, that they are completely satisfied that it was an
unconnected condition.

Finally, I should in deference to counsel for the respondent mention one point
which he raised, an ingenious point, which is really throwing the ball back, if I
may use that expression, into counsel for the applicant's court. He says that
the medical board's decision that the heart condition was unconnected was G
final and binding, accordingly it was the insurance officer in granting injury
benefit who was exceeding his jurisdiction. He was bound by the decision of
the medical board. I think however that counsel for the respondent's submission is wrong because in my judgment the medical board never decided the point
at all, they merely said that it was unconnected as it had not been made the
subject of a claim, in other words they had not decided the matter on the merits H
one way or the other.

For the reasons I have given I think this application fails and should be
dismissed.

ASHWORTH, J.: I agree, and I would only wish to add a word or two
on the first point. I confess that I am glad to have come to this conclusion, I
which in my view accords with the common sense of this rather complex legislation. I say for this reason, that there are two, so to speak, channels of administration; one is truly administrative and is carried out by the local insurance
officer, the local appeal tribunal and then the commissioner if need be, that is
called the statutory hierarchy. The other channel is the medical one, and it
would seem to me to accord with common sense that medical issues so called
are dealt with by the medical channels, and conversely factual matters, such as the

A question whether there has ever been an accident, and whether it arose out of the employment, are dealt with by the statutory board.

Moreover, this distinction seems to me to be emphasised by what counsel for the respondent called attention to, the different wording of s. 11 as compared with s. 12 of the National Insurance (Industrial Injuries) Act 1965, one dealing with injury benefit and the other dealing with the loss of physical or mental B faculty arising as the result of the relevant accident.

Before any question of disablement benefit can arise, the necessary foundation must be laid, as indeed it was laid in *Minister of Social Security* v. *Amalgamated Engineering Union (Re Dowling)* (5). There must have been an accident within the meaning of the Act, and there must have been injury resulting there-from. For my part I would accept for this purpose the phrase that was used C in *Dowling's* case (5), though not approved, that having got over those hurdles, the applicant for benefit has a ticket of admission to the medical channel, who are then charged with the task of assessing the extent to which he is disabled by his loss of faculty.

What he has obtained by that ticket of admission is a conclusive finding that there has been an accident; secondly a conclusive finding that from that accident D he suffered injury, but it is not necessary to add, as counsel for the applicant would have us add, that in addition he has obtained a conclusive finding as to the nature or extent of that injury. That seems to me by its nature essentially a matter for the medical channels to consider once the two preliminary conditions have been satisfied. I have read and re-read the speech of LORD MORRIS OF BORTH-Y-GEST in *Dowling's* case (5) to see whether this view is in any sense E contrary to anything that he there laid down (6). If one refers to what he said, the views that I venture to express seem to me to be in no way contrary to what he there said. Indeed, I would go further and say that they seem to be the corollary to what he said in connection with what everyone agrees was a special case. For these reasons in addition to those given by LORD PARKER, C.J., I agree that this application should fail.

F   **WILLIS, J.:** I agree with both judgments and there is nothing I can usefully add.

Application dismissed.

Solicitors: *W. H. Thompson* (for the applicant); *Solicitor, Ministry of Social Security* (for the respondent).

G   [*Reported by* S. A. HATTEEA, ESQ., *Barrister-at-Law.*]

H

I

---

(5) [1967] 1 All E.R. 210; [1967] 1 A.C. 725.
(6) [1967] 1 All E.R. at p. 215; [1967] 1 A.C. at p. 744.

A

NOTE.

R. *v.* NATIONAL INSURANCE COMMISSIONER, *Ex parte* JONES.

[QUEEN'S BENCH DIVISION (Lord Parker, C.J., Ashworth and Willis, JJ.),
December 13, 1968.]

B

*Industrial Injury—Medical Appeal Tribunal—Jurisdiction—Scope of jurisdic-
tion—Finding by statutory authority (medical board) on claim for injury
benefit that injured workman suffered heart condition caused by accident—
Subsequent application by workman for disablement benefit—Whether
Medical Appeal Tribunal bound to accept finding that heart condition caused
by accident.*

[As to disablement benefit, see 27 HALSBURY'S LAWS (3rd Edn.) 824, 825, **C**
paras. 1451, 1452; and as to the determination of industrial injuries claims and
questions, see ibid., pp. 853-866, paras. 1495-1513.]

Case referred to:

R. v. *National Insurance Comr., Ex p. Hudson,* ante p. 631.

Application for certiorari.

D

This was an application by David Lloyd Jones for an order of certiorari to
quash the decision of one of the Industrial Injuries Commissioners (G. O. GEORGE,
ESQ.) dated 27th December 1967, dismissing the applicant's appeal from a
decision of the Medical Appeal Tribunal dated 14th April 1965. The facts are
set out in the judgment of LORD PARKER, C.J.

The case noted below* was cited during the argument in addition to the case **E**
referred to in the judgment of LORD PARKER, C.J.

S. J. Waldman for the applicant.
Gordon Slynn for the respondent.

LORD PARKER, C.J., having stated that the point taken was really the
same point in a slightly different form as that which arose in *R.* v. *National* **F**
Insurance Comr., Ex p. Hudson (1), continued: It was said here that the local
appeal tribunal's decision which was final for all purposes, was to the effect that
there had been an industrial accident, and that the applicant was incapacitated
through his heart condition, that that finding is binding on the medical
authorities, and that the medical board and the Medical Appeal Tribunal could not,
in those circumstances, say that there never had been a heart condition due to the **G**
accident at all.

For the reasons given in the *Hudson* case (1) I am satisfied that this is wrong,
and that here the medical authorities were fully entitled to find that while one
of the injuries, the heart condition, had never existed, yet the condition of strained
chest had been there originally, remained there and that a disablement benefit
should be given in respect of that. In coming to that decision they were not **H**
disputing or overruling the decision that there had been an industrial accident.
[HIS LORDSHIP then dealt with a second point which was also similar to the
second point taken in *R.* v. *National Insurance Comr., Ex p. Hudson* (1).]

ASHWORTH, J.: I agree.

WILLIS, J.: I agree.

Application dismissed. **I**

Solicitors: *W. H. Thompson* (for the applicant); *Solicitor, Ministry of Social
Security* (for the respondent).

[*Reported by* S. A. HATTEEA, ESQ., *Barrister-at-Law.*]

---

* *Minister of Social Security* v. *Amalgamated Engineering Union,* [1967] 1 All E.R.
210; [1967] 1 A.C. 725.
(1) Ante p. 631.

A

PRACTICE DIRECTION.

CHANCERY DIVISION.

B
Practice—Chancery Division—Affidavit—Office copies—No longer required —Exceptions.

Practice—Motion—Hearing—Affidavit—Office copies.

Practice—Chancery Division—Affidavit—Binding in book form.

Practice—Chancery Division—Affidavit—Affidavit sworn before proceedings commenced—Acceptance.

C
Mortgage—Foreclosure—Application for foreclosure nisi—Affidavit of due execution—No longer required.

Practice—Chancery Division—Affidavit—Affidavit supporting—Certificate of birth, marriage or death—Affidavit no longer required—Certificate admitted in evidence.

As the result of a review of the use of affidavit evidence in the Chancery Division the following modifications of the existing practice will be made:

D
1. *Reduction in use of office copies.*

In general, office copies need not be taken for use in chambers or in cases adjourned into court from chambers. Solicitors and litigants should lodge the original affidavits, with the exhibits thereto. These will be used by the court and filed by the registrars on the drawing up of the orders in which they are read. Should an affidavit be needed on a subsequent occasion an office copy should be

E
bespoken and lodged in chambers. The original affidavit may be bespoken for the use of the court if necessary but this procedure is more cumbersome and should not normally be employed.

The court may nevertheless at any stage direct the filing of an affidavit and the production of an office copy. This will probably be done if the evidence is likely to remain in chambers for a considerable time and an original affidavit

F
might become soiled or damaged, for example in the course of long inquiries or complicated accounts. In such classes of case solicitors and litigants may file the affidavits and lodge office copies without prior reference to the master.

Office copies are still required for use on the hearing of motions unless the judge specially dispenses with them. The reason for this is that interim injunctions are often made and a matter may come before the judge on several motion

G
days. If original affidavits were used they would be filed on the making of the first injunction and it might not be easy to obtain an office copy by the time of the second hearing.

This change makes it more important than ever that affidavits of several sheets should be properly bound up in book form and not merely secured at one corner. This should be done by sewing the affidavit along its length with green

H
tape or by stapling it along its length, the stapling being covered, back and front with adhesive tape. Exhibits of several sheets must be tied up and sealed (not stapled or pinned) at the top left-hand corner.

2. *Acceptance of affidavits sworn before proceedings have commenced.*

Hitherto affidavits have been rejected if sworn before the commencement

I
of the proceedings to which they relate. This is logical because they cannot strictly be sworn in proceedings which do not yet exist and cannot strictly refer to persons as parties when they have not yet become such. The present practice is to be preferred but, by way of mitigation of the inconvenience occasioned by reswearing, affidavits will not in future be rejected merely because they have been sworn shortly before the proceedings started. The court may nevertheless at any time direct the reswearing of such an affidavit and will do so if the affidavit seeks to prove facts which have to be shown to be existing at the date of the commencement of the proceedings, for example that money is

owing at that date, and the cause of action would not otherwise be established. A
In cases where the date of commencement is of no particular significance, for
example in most applications for construction of documents or under the Trustee
Act 1925 (1) or the Variation of Trusts Act 1958 (2), the court will assume that
the state of affairs set out in the affidavit has continued until the date of commencement but it will be the duty of solicitors and litigants to draw the court's attention
to any relevant changes in the interim.   B

3. *Affidavits of due execution.*

Henceforth affidavits of due execution of mortgages or charges will not be
required on applications for foreclosure nisi unless the court so directs. Such a
direction will be given if there is any doubt about due execution, either raised by
a party or apparent on the face of the document, for example where a document   C
said to be under seal bears no indication of a seal or where the mortgagor's
signature is illegible or questionable.

4. *Proof of birth, marriage or death.*

Subject to the limitations specified below certificates of birth, marriage and
death issued by the Registrar General (including certificates, issued by him, of
such events occurring outside the jurisdiction) and certificates of birth, marriage D
and death issued by the equivalent authorities in Scotland, Northern Ireland, the
Republic of Ireland, the Channel Islands and the Isle of Man will be accepted
as evidence of the facts therein specified without the necessity of a supporting
affidavit. Such certificates will, where appropriate, be read in any relevant
order.

Such certificates must still be exhibited to affidavits: (a) when the court so   E
directs; (b) when an order to carry on proceedings is applied for (for it is also
necessary to show the current state of the proceedings); (c) when the certificate
is required to prove some part of the main narrative of the events which the
court is considering, for example where the chain of devolution of a trusteeship
has to be proved or a claimant to a fund in court has to establish his identity;
and particularly (d) in inquiries relating to matters of pedigree.   F

The main effect of the above will be to admit such certificates as evidence:
(i) to prove births, marriages and deaths occurring incidentally in the course of
proceedings and not necessitating orders to carry on proceedings; (ii) where
the identity of a party to the proceedings with a party to a document has to be
established, for example that a woman mortgagor has married before the
commencement of proceedings by a mortgagee; or (iii) to explain why someone   G
is not a party to proceedings. In border-line cases the court will have a
discretion to decide whether or not an affidavit is needed.

This relaxation has been restricted to the classes of certificate specified above
because of the difficulty of drawing a line. Many certificates in the English
language will still need supporting affidavits for this reason. Certificates in
foreign languages must be accompanied by translations, properly verified and H
exhibited to the same affidavit.

By direction of CROSS, J.

R. E. BALL,
Chief Master,
22nd May 1969.   Chancery Division.

I

---

(1) See 26 HALSBURY'S STATUTES (2nd Edn.) 50.
(2) See 38 HALSBURY'S STATUTES (2nd Edn.) 1130.

A

THE ELEFTHERIA.

OWNERS OF CARGO LATELY LADEN ON BOARD SHIP OR VESSEL ELEFTHERIA *v.* OWNERS OF SHIP OR VESSEL ELEFTHERIA.

B   [PROBATE, DIVORCE AND ADMIRALTY DIVISION (Brandon, J.), January 20, 21, 31, 1969.]

Conflict of Laws—Stay of proceedings—Agreement to refer disputes to foreign court —Action commenced in England—Principles to be applied by English court in deciding whether to stay action—Supreme Court of Judicature (Consolidation) Act 1925 (15 & 16 Geo. 5 c. 49), s. 41, proviso (a).

C   Where plaintiffs sue in England in breach of an agreement to refer disputes to a foreign court, and the defendants apply for a stay under s. 41* of the Supreme Court of Judicature (Consolidation) Act 1925, the English court, assuming the claim to be otherwise within its jurisdiction, is not bound to grant a stay but has a discretion whether to do so or not.   The discretion should be exercised by granting a stay unless strong cause for not doing so

D   is shown.   The burden of proving such strong cause is on the plaintiffs. In exercising its discretion, the court should take into account all the circumstances of the particular case.   In particular, but without prejudice to taking into account all the circumstances of the particular case, the following matters, where they arise, may properly be regarded: (i) in what country the evidence on the issues of fact is situated, or more readily available,

E   and the effect of that on the relative convenience and expense of trial as between the English and foreign courts; (ii) whether the law of the foreign court applies and, if so, whether it differs from English law in any material respects; (iii) with what country either party is connected and how closely; (iv) whether the defendants genuinely desire trial in the foreign country, or are only seeking procedural advantages; (v) whether the plain-

F   tiffs would be prejudiced by having to sue in the foreign court because they would, (a) be deprived of security for that claim, (b) be unable to enforce any judgment obtained, (c) be faced with a time-bar not applicable in England, or (d) for political, racial, religious or other reasons be unlikely to get a fair trial (see p. 645, letters B to E, post).

[As to statutory power to stay proceedings, and stay of English proceedings

G   where foreign proceedings are pending, see 30 HALSBURY'S LAWS (3rd Edn.) 406, para. 765, 409, para. 768; and for cases on the subject, see 51 DIGEST (Repl.) 998, 999, *5347-5353.*

For the Supreme Court of Judicature (Consolidation) Act 1925, s. 41, see 18 HALSBURY'S STATUTES (2nd Edn.) 478.]

Cases referred to:

H   *Athenee, The* (1922), 11 Lloyd L.R. 6.

Austrian-Lloyd Steamship Co. v. Gresham Life Assurance Society, Ltd., [1903] 1 K.B. 249; [1900-03] All E.R. Rep. 604; 72 L.J.K.B. 211; 88 L.T. 6; 2 Digest (Repl.) 480, *365.*

Cap Blanco, The, [1913] P. 130; [1911-13] All E.R. Rep. 365; 83 L.J.P. 23; 109 L.T. 692; 12 Asp. M.L.C. 339; 2 Digest (Repl.) 480, *367.*

I   *Fehmarn, The,* [1957] 2 All E.R. 707; [1957] 1 W.L.R. 815; *affd.,* [1958] 1 All E.R. 333; [1958] 1 W.L.R. 159; [1957] 2 Lloyd's Rep. 551; 1 Digest (Repl.) 175, *606.*

Kirchner & Co. v. Gruban, [1909] 1 Ch. 413; 78 L.J.Ch. 117; 99 L.T. 932; 2 Digest (Repl.) 480, *366.*

---

* Section 41, so far as material, provides: ". . . (a) Nothing in this Act shall disable either [the High Court or the Court of Appeal], if it thinks fit so to do, from directing a stay of proceedings in any cause or matter pending before it . . ."

Mackender v. *Feldia A.G.*, [1966] 3 All E.R. 847; [1967] 2 Q.B. 590; [1967]   **A**
     2 W.L.R. 119; [1966] 2 Lloyd's Rep. 449; 50 Digest (Repl.) 341, *689*.

Media, The (1931), 41 Lloyd. L.R. 80.

Renton (G. H.) & Co., Ltd. v. *Palmyra Trading Corpn. of Panama*, [1956]
     3 All E.R. 957; [1957] A.C. 149; [1957] 2 W.L.R. 45; [1956] 2 Lloyd's
     Rep. 379; 41 Digest (Repl.) 419, *2045*.

Settlement Corpn. v. *Hochchild*, [1965] 3 All E.R. 486; [1966] Ch. 10; [1965]   **B**
     3 W.L.R. 1150; [1965] 2 Lloyd's Rep. 313; Digest (Cont. Vol. B)
     134, *1521b*.

Unterweser Reederei G.m.b.H. v. *Zapata Off-Shore Co., The Chaparral*, [1968]
     2 Lloyd's Rep. 158.

Motion.

This was an application by way of motion by the defendants, the owners   **C**
of the motor vessel Eleftheria, for an order under s. 41 of the Supreme Court
of Judicature (Consolidation) Act 1925, to stay an action brought against them
by the plaintiffs, the owners of cargo lately laden on The Eleftheria, by way of a
writ in rem dated 26th November 1968. The facts are set out in the judgment.

M. J. Mustill, Q.C., and *A. D. Colman* for the plaintiffs.   **D**
J. S. Hobhouse for the defendants.

                                             Cur. adv. vult.

     31st January. **BRANDON, J.,** read the following judgment: The court
has before it an application by shipowners to stay an action brought against
them by cargo owners on the grounds that the contracts of carriage sued
on contain a Greek jurisdiction clause and are governed by Greek law. The   **E**
action concerned is an action in rem against the ship Eleftheria. The writ in
the action was issued on 26th November 1968. In the writ, the plaintiffs are
described as the owners of cargo lately laden in the ship or vessel Eleftheria,
and the defendants as the owners of that ship. The endorsement on the writ
reads:

     " The plaintiffs' claim is against the ship or vessel Eleftheria for breach   **F**
     of various contracts contained in or evidenced by seventy-six bills of lading
     for the carriage of the plaintiffs' goods on the said Eleftheria from Galatz
     to Hull in August and September, 1968."

The addresses of the plaintiffs are stated to be in Hull, Newcastle-on-Tyne and
Liverpool. The writ was served on The Eleftheria, and the ship was arrested   **G**
at the suit of the plaintiffs, on the same day as the writ was issued. On 28th
November 1968, after other security for the plaintiffs' claim had been given by
the defendants, The Eleftheria was released from arrest. On 5th December
1968, the defendants, by leave of the court, entered a conditional appearance to
the writ without prejudice to an application to set aside the writ or service of it.
The time limited for setting aside was 14 days. On 18th December 1968, the   **H**
defendants filed notice of motion asking for a stay of the action or for the setting
aside of the writ or service of it. The motion was heard by me on 20th and
21st January 1969.

     In presenting his case to the court at the hearing, counsel for the defendants
did not pursue the application to set aside the writ or service of it contained in
the notice of motion, but confined himself to the alternative application for a   **I**
stay. He was right in this, for the authorities show that, assuming the defendants to be entitled to relief at all on the grounds put forward, a stay would be
the correct form for such relief to take. It appears to me, however, that it was
not necessary, in order to ask for a stay, to make the appearance entered a
conditional one.

     The evidence before the court consisted of three affidavits, two of Mr. Heasman,
a solicitor in the firm acting for the defendants, and one of Mr. Ashburn, senior
partner in the firm of solicitors acting for the plaintiffs. Mr. Heasman's first

A affidavit had exhibited to it a copy of a bill of lading in terms similar to those sued on by the plaintiffs. Mr. Ashburn's affidavit had exhibited to it a copy of a letter from the defendants' Hull agents to the plaintiffs dated 20th October 1968, but said by him to have been sent on 20th September 1968.

The background and nature of the dispute between the parties, as they appear from the affidavits and documents exhibited to them, are as follows. The

B plaintiffs are a number of timber merchants carrying on business in England. The defendants are three Greek nationals, Leonidas Govdelas, Athanassios Claou Datos, and Kapastolos Malas, trading in part at least under the firm name of G.K.M. Co. These three persons are joint owners of The Eleftheria, which is a Greek ship registered at the port of Piraeus, and they reside in Greece. The active management of the ship is carried on by Mr. Malas on behalf of

C himself and his co-owners. This last fact is not in the affidavits, but was stated by counsel for the defendants on instructions, and accepted as correct for the purposes of this motion by counsel for the plaintiffs. The principal place of business of the defendants is in Athens. In August 1968 there were shipped on board The Eleftheria at the Rumanian port of Galatz a large number of parcels of Rumanian beechwood and plywood for carriage to London and Hull. These

D goods were shipped under bills of lading in the English language, according to which the shippers were Exportlemn State Company for Foreign Trade, the shipowners were G.K.M. Co. of Athens and the goods were consigned to order. They were signed by the master of the ship for the owners. On the reverse side of the bills of lading there were printed a large number of clauses under the heading:

E   " Liner Terms approved by the Baltic and International Maritime Conference Code Name ' Conlinebill ' amended January 1st 1950 amended August 1st 1952."

These clauses were made part of the bill of lading contract by express words on the front of it. Of these clauses, cll. 1, 2, 3 and 16 (c) and (d) are material.

F I shall read them.

     " 1. DEFINITION. Wherever the term ' Merchant ' is used in this Bill of Lading it shall be deemed to include the Shipper, the Receiver, the Consignee, the Holder of the Bill of Lading and the Owner of the cargo.

     " 2. PARAMOUNT CLAUSE. The Hague Rules contained in the International Convention for the Unification of certain rules relating to Bills of Lading, dated Brussels the 25th August 1924, as enacted in the country

G of shipment shall apply to this contract. When no such enactment is in force in the country of shipment, the corresponding legislation of the country of destination shall apply, but in respect of shipment to which no such enactments are compulsorily applicable, the terms of the said Convention shall apply.

H   " 3. JURISDICTION. Any dispute arising under this Bill of Lading shall be decided in the country where the Carrier has his principal place of business, and the law of such country shall apply except as provided elsewhere herein.

     " 16. GOVERNMENT DIRECTIONS, WAR, EPIDEMICS, ICE, STRIKES, ETC. . . . (c) Should it appear that epidemics, quarantine, ice—labour troubles, labour obstructions, strikes, lockouts, any of which onboard or onshore—

I difficulties in loading or discharging would prevent the vessel from leaving the port of loading or reaching or entering the port of discharge or there discharging in the usual manner and leaving again, all of which safely and without delay, the Master may discharge the cargo at port of loading or any other safe and convenient port. (d) The discharge under the provisions of this clause of any cargo for which a Bill of Lading has been issued shall be deemed due fulfilment of the contract. If in connection with the exercise of any liberty under this clause any extra expenses are incurred, they shall be paid by the Merchant in addition to the freight, together with return

freight if any and a reasonable compensation for any extra services rendered   A
to the goods."

The plaintiffs claim that they are the indorsees of a substantial number of
bills of lading relating to parcels intended to be carried to Hull, to whom the
property in such parcels passed on or by reason of such indorsement.   On 9th
September 1968, The Eleftheria arrived at Surrey Commercial Docks, London,
and discharged part of her London cargo.   On 18th September 1968, she left   B
London and went to Rotterdam where she arrived on 19th September.   She
there discharged the rest of her London cargo and all her Hull cargo, including
the parcels of which the plaintiffs claim to be the owners.   On 20th September
1968, Anglo-Iran Shipping Co., Ltd., as Hull agents for the defendants, wrote to
the plaintiffs as follows:

> " On behalf of Messrs. GKM Shipping Company the Owners of the   C
> m.v. ' Eleftheria ' which is presently discharging in Rotterdam, we hereby
> give you notice that due to circumstances presently obtaining in London/
> Hull Docks the port of Hull etc. the Owners intend to exercise the right
> given to them by paragraph 16 (c) and (d) of the Bills of Lading dated
> at Galatz the 17th August, 1968 to discharge the balance of the cargo
> consigned to London and Hull now remaining on board the vessel.   The   D
> vessel's Agents in London are the Anglo-Iran Shipping Co. Ltd. from
> whom all information concerning the vessel can be obtained.   The Owners
> hereby expressly reserve all the rights given to them expressly or by implica-
> tion in the Bills of Lading above mentioned or given to them by operation of
> Law."
                                                                            E
The defendants having refused to on-carry the goods of which the plaintiffs
claim to be the owners from Rotterdam to Hull, the plaintiffs arranged for the
on-carriage at their own expense.   They have brought the present action to
recover that expense as damages for breach of the contracts of carriage contained
in the bills of lading.   The defendants resist the plaintiffs' claim on the grounds
that, because of labour troubles at London or Hull or both, they were entitled   F
under cl. 16 (c) and (d) of the bills of lading to discharge the goods at Rotterdam,
and that such discharge was a performance of their contracts.   The plaintiffs
deny that these sub-clauses apply in the circumstances which existed.   Which
side is right must depend in part on the facts of the case so far as labour troubles,
etc., are concerned, and in part on the meaning and effect of cl. 16 (c) and (d)
under the proper law of the contracts.   With regard to the latter matter there   G
was evidence, to which I shall refer later, that these sub-clauses would be interpreted and applied differently under Greek law from under English law.

The first question to be considered is whether the dispute, the subject-
matter of the action, is a dispute which, by the terms of the contracts between
the parties, they have agreed should be decided by a Greek court.   As to this,
the uncontradicted evidence is that the defendants have their principal place of   H
business in Athens, and the dispute is clearly one which arises under the bills
of lading.   It follows that, under cl. 3, the parties have agreed to refer it to a
Greek court.

The second question to be considered is on what principles of law an applica-
tion to stay an action on the ground of such an agreement should be decided.
As to that, I was referred by counsel for the defendants to a number of authori-   I
ties on the matter.   These were *Austrian-Lloyd Steamship Co.* v. *Gresham Life
Assurance Society, Ltd.* (1); *Kirchner & Co.* v. *Gruban* (2); *The Cap Blanco* (3);
The Athenee (4); *The Media* (5) and *The Fehmarn* (6).   Counsel for the defendants

(1) [1903] 1 K.B. 249; [1900-03] All E.R. Rep. 604.   (2) [1909] 1 Ch. 413.
(3) [1913] P. 130; [1911-13] All E.R. Rep. 365.
(4) (1922), 11 Lloyd L.R. 6.   (5) (1931), 41 Lloyd L.R. 80.
(6) [1957] 2 All E.R. 707; [1957] 1 W.L.R. 815; *affd.*, [1958] 1 All E.R. 333; [1958]
1 W.L.R. 159.

A also referred me to two recent decisions of the Court of Appeal relating to the grant of leave to serve proceedings out of the jurisdiction in respect of claims on contracts containing in the one case a foreign jurisdiction clause and in the other case an English jurisdiction clause. These were *Mackender* v. *Feldia A.G.* (7) and *Unterweser Reederei G.m.b.H.* v. *Zapata Off-Shore Co., The Chaparral* (8).

The principles established by the authorities can, I think, be summarised as

B follows: (I) where plaintiffs sue in England in breach of an agreement to refer disputes to a foreign court, and the defendants apply for a stay, the English court, assuming the claim to be otherwise within its jurisdiction, is not bound to grant a stay but has a discretion whether to do so or not. (II) The discretion should be exercised by granting a stay unless strong cause for not doing so is shown. (III) The burden of proving such strong cause is on the plaintiffs. (IV) In

C exercising its discretion, the court should take into account all the circumstances of the particular case. (V) In particular, but without prejudice to (IV), the following matters, where they arise, may properly be regarded: (a) In what country the evidence on the issues of fact is situated, or more readily available, and the effect of that on the relative convenience and expense of trial as between the English and foreign courts; (b) Whether the law of the foreign court applies

D and, if so, whether it differs from English law in any material respects; (c) With what country either party is connected, and how closely; (d) Whether the defendants genuinely desire trial in the foreign country, or are only seeking procedural advantages; (e) Whether the plaintiffs would be prejudiced by having to sue in the foreign court because they would—(i) be deprived of security for that claim, (ii) be unable to enforce any judgment obtained, (iii) be faced with a

E time-bar not applicable in England, or (iv) for political, racial, religious or other reasons be unlikely to get a fair trial.

In the present case, there has been no suggestion that there is any risk of the plaintiffs not getting a fair trial in Greece. I approach the matter, therefore, on the assumption that, so far as fairness of trial is concerned, there is no distinction between the Greek and English courts. There is further no question

F of the plaintiffs' claim being time-barred in Greece, while as regards security the defendants are content that, if a stay is granted, it should be on terms that the security obtained by the plaintiffs in the action, or other security equivalent to it, shall be available to answer any judgment which the plaintiffs may later get in Greece.

Counsel for the plaintiffs accepted, as he was bound on the authorities to do,

G that it was for him to show good cause against a stay. In seeking to do so, he relied on one main matter which he put forward as being of dominant significance in this case. That was that nearly all the evidence relating to the likely issues of fact in the case was in England, and that, because of that, a trial in England would be much more convenient and cost much less than a trial in Greece. In this connection, he relied on paras. 5, 6 and 7 of Mr. Ashburn's affidavit, which

H I shall read. Paragraph 5 reads, starting with the second sentence:

" The Plaintiffs will seek to establish at the trial of this action that at the material time it could not reasonably have appeared that any of the matters referred to in Clause 16 (c) would prevent the vessel from entering the Port of discharge or there discharging in the usual manner and without delay.

I In particular the Plaintiffs will wish to call evidence to establish that the state of labour relations involving workers in the Port of Hull at the material time was not such as to make it reasonably to appear that the vessel would be prevented from discharging there in the usual manner and without delay. The plaintiffs' evidence will probably be that apart from brief and occasional stoppages by tallymen no strike or other delaying action was in progress or

---

(7) [1966] 3 All E.R. 847; [1967] 2 Q.B. 590.
(8) [1968] 2 Lloyd's Rep. 158.

anticipated at the material time. The plaintiffs will wish to call as witnesses   A
on this issue representatives of the Hull Port Employers, the local Dock
Labour Board and the various trades unions concerned, as well as of the
Plaintiffs. It follows, therefore, that all the Plaintiffs' witnesses on the main
issue of fact in the action will be within the jurisdiction of this Honourable
Court.

" 6. Further the Defendants employed as Agents in both Hull and London   B
Messrs. Anglo-Iran Shipping Co. Ltd. which was responsible for supervising
the discharge of the vessel in this country. [Then, after a reference to the
letter dated 20th October 1968, which it is said was sent on 20th September
1968, the paragraph goes on] Consequently, if it be material, the evidence
of the Defendants' Agents in this country as to the information available to
them relating to labour conditions at Hull will have to be given by witnesses   C
resident in this country.

" 7. Although the Defendants' reliance on Clause 16 (c) of the Bills of
Lading is likely to be the main issue in dispute, further issues may arise relating to the Plaintiffs' title to sue on the Bills of Lading and to the quantum
of damage claimed. Insofar as oral evidence may be required on these possible
issues all the witnesses are likely to be either resident in this country or in   D
Rotterdam."

Counsel for the defendants conceded that much of the evidence on the relevant
facts, excluding for this purpose evidence on Greek law, was in England, or
more readily available there than in Greece; but he suggested that most of the
primary facts about labour troubles in London and Hull would be recorded in   E
documents, and would, therefore, either be agreed or established without calling
many witnesses. Alternatively, he said that the evidence of the English witnesses
on these topics could be taken, in whole or in part, on commission, and put before
the Greek court in that way. He said that, in any event, there was other important
evidence on the defendants' side which was in Greece. In this connection, he
said that the defendants would certainly wish to call Mr. Malas to explain his   F
reasons for diverting the ship to Rotterdam and ordering her to discharge there,
and might possibly also wish to call the master of the ship. Counsel for the
defendants further said that, if the action were tried in England, the defendants
would wish to bring at least one Greek lawyer from Greece to give expert evidence
on Greek law. In the result, he contended that the situation with regard to
availability of evidence was, even putting it at its highest against the defendants,   G
an evenly balanced one.

Apart from seeking to counter the main point made for the plaintiffs in this
way, counsel for the defendants advanced three other matters as re-inforcing
the prima facie case for a stay. These were as follows. First, that the dispute,
because of its dependence on Greek law, which was different in material respects
from English law, was essentially one for the Greek courts to decide. Second, that   H
the choice of Greek jurisdiction was not arbitrary but based on the close connection of the defendants with Greece. Third, that the plaintiffs would not be
prejudiced by having to sue in Greece.

As regards the first matter, it seems to me clear that the law to be applied is
Greek law. Counsel for the plaintiffs argued faintly, and with more ingenuity
than conviction, that the combined effect of cl. 2 and cl. 3 might be to make   I
Romanian law apply. His argument was that, under cl. 2 of the bills of lading,
the Romanian version of the Hague Rules was incorporated and made paramount; that this version of the Hague Rules might require an interpretation or
application of cl. 16 (c) and (d) different from that required by Greek law; and
that, if so, Romanian law, not Greek law, would govern. I was not persuaded
by this argument, there being nothing to show that the Romanian version of
the Hague Rules had any bearing on the interpretation or application of cl. 16 (c)

A and (d) at all. The English Hague Rules have no such bearing—see *G. H. Renton & Co., Ltd.* v. *Palmyra Trading Corpn. of Panama* (9); and there was no evidence that the Romanian version differed from the English version. It is further right to observe that para. 8 of Mr. Ashburn's affidavit proceeds on the basis that Greek law governs.

As to Greek law in relation to cl. 16 (c) and (d), the evidence was as follows.
B In the paragraph of Mr. Ashburn's affidavit to which I have just referred, he stated:

" . . . I am advised by Counsel qualified in Greek law and verily believe that in relation to the effect of Clause 16 (c) a Greek Court, if properly informed and guided, would probably try to apply the same principles of law as stated by the House of Lords in *Renton & Co.* v. *Palmyra Trading*
C *Corporation* (9), subject to an overriding requirement that the Defendants had not abused such legal rights as they had by obviously exceeding limits of good faith and contractual morality."

In para. (5) and para. (7) of Mr. Heasman's second affidavit, he stated:

" (5) I have taken the advice of a Greek lawyer living in London and he
D informs me, and I believe correctly informs me, that the position under Greek law is in general as follows.

" (7) A Greek Court would construe Clause 16 (c) of the Bills of Lading on the basis of Article 281 of the Greek Civil Code which relates to ' contractual morality ' and provides (in rough translation) that ' it is not permitted to exercise a right if such exercise manifestly exceeds the limits
E which are imposed by good faith or morals or by the social or financial purposes of the right '. In applying the criteria laid down by this Article the Greek Court would among other things take into account the actual state of knowledge of the Defendants that is to say of Mr. Govdelas, Mr. Datos and Mr. Malas."

Counsel for the defendants submitted, rightly, I think, that it was common
F ground on this evidence that, under Greek law, cl. 16 (c) and (d) were valid sub-clauses, in the sense that they were not avoided or overridden by the Hague Rules as made applicable by the clause paramount, and further that by Greek law, in considering whether the defendants could rely successfully on these sub-clauses, the court would, or might well, have to investigate questions of contractual good faith and morality. He went on from there to argue that a Greek court, which
G was familiar with such concepts, would be better qualified to investigate and decide such questions than an English court, which was not. The inconvenience and expenses of calling expert evidence on Greek law would further be avoided if the trial was in Greece.

In answer to those arguments counsel for the plaintiffs took two points. He said, first, that questions of contractual good faith and morality, while potentially
H relevant under Greek law, might never arise on the facts. The first question to be decided was whether the sub-clauses could apply at all in the circumstances, and it was only if that question were to be decided in the defendants' favour that the further question of abuse by the defendants of the rights conferred by the sub-clauses would arise. This first question, he said, did not depend on any distinction between Greek and English law of which there was any evidence.
I He said, secondly, that, if questions of contractual good faith and morality should arise, an English court, with proper evidence of Greek law before it, would have no difficulty in investigating and deciding them. Further, evidence of Greek law could be obtained in England, and it was not necessary for the defendants to bring a lawyer from Greece, although he recognised that they might reasonably wish to do so.

As regards the second matter advanced by counsel for the defendants as

(9) [1956] 3 All E.R. 957; [1957] A.C. 149.

re-inforcing the prima facie case for a stay, he stressed that the defendants were   A
Greek nationals, resident in Greece and having their principal place of business
there, and that The Eleftheria was a Greek ship. He pointed out that the case
differed in that respect from *The Fehmarn* (10), where the defendants were
German and the agreed court was Russian. He recognised, however, that the
case did not in this respect differ from *The Athenee* (11).   As regards the third
matter advanced by counsel for the defendants, he said that the plaintiffs would   B
not be prejudiced by having to sue in Greece, either in relation to any time-bar
or in relation to security for their claim. Counsel for the plaintiffs did not, as I
understood him, dispute the existence of these last two factors, but invited the
court to give them little weight in comparison with the matters of convenience
and expense on which he relied. I also bear in mind, though I do not think
that he laid any particular stress on it, that the plaintiffs are as closely con-   C
nected with England as the defendants with Greece.

These being the arguments on either side, I must now state my view of the
matter. I shall do so under four heads. First, the prima facie case for a stay
arising from the Greek jurisdiction clause;   second, factors tending to rebut
that prima facie case; third, factors tending to re-inforce that prima facie case;
fourth, conclusion.
                                                                                     D
First, as to the prima facie case for a stay arising from the Greek jurisdiction
clause. I think that it is essential that the court should give full weight to the
prima facie desirability of holding the plaintiffs to their agreement. In this
connection, I think that the court must be careful not just to pay lip service to
the principle involved, and then fail to give effect to it because of a mere balance
of convenience. I am strengthened in that view by the strong observations on   E
the topic made by the Court of Appeal in the two recent R.S.C., Ord. 11, cases
which I mentioned earlier, namely, *Mackender* v. *Feldia A.G.* (12) and *Unterweser
Reederei G.m.b.H.* v. *Zapata Off-Shore Co., The Chaparral* (13). I recognise that
the point for decision in those cases was not the same as that for decision in
the present case. The point for decision in those cases was whether the plaintiffs
should be allowed to begin their action at all by being given leave to serve out   F
of the jurisdiction; the point for decision in the present case is whether the
plaintiffs, who have begun an action here which they needed no leave to begin,
should be prevented from going on with it. In *Mackender* v. *Feldia A.G.* (12),
the court had to bear in mind, as a basic starting point, the caution always used
by it in giving leave for service out of the jurisdiction under R.S.C., Ord. 11, r. 1.
The reasons for such caution were explained by DIPLOCK, L.J. (14). In *Unterweser
Reederei G.m.b.H.* v. *Zapata Off-Shore Co., The Chaparral* (13), the application was   G
under R.S.C., Ord. 11, r. 2, so that the same need for caution did not exist: see
the reasons given by DIPLOCK, L.J. (15).   Allowing, however, for the fact that
the point for decision was not the same, and that in the earlier of the two cases
the special considerations affecting the giving of leave under R.S.C., Ord. 11, r. 1,
had to be taken into account, the governing factor in both decisions was the   H
principle that a party should be bound by a jurisdiction clause to which he has
agreed, unless there is strong reason to the contrary. This principle was stressed
in the earlier case by LORD DENNING, M.R. (16), and DIPLOCK, L.J. (17), and in
the later case by WILLMER, L.J. (18), and DIPLOCK, L.J. (19), where he repeated what he had said in the earlier case. It is further to be observed that

---

(10) [1957] 2 All E.R. 707; [1957] 1 W.L.R. 815; *affd.*, [1958] 1 All E.R. 333; [1958]   I
1 W.L.R. 159.

(11) (1922), 11 Lloyd L.R. 6.   (12) [1966] 3 All E.R. 847; [1967] 2 Q.B. 590.

(13) [1968] 2 Lloyd's Rep. 158.

(14) [1966] 3 All E.R. at p. 850; [1967] 2 Q.B. at p. 599.

(15) [1968] 2 Lloyd's Rep. at p. 163.

(16) [1966] 3 All E.R. at pp. 849, 850; [1967] 2 Q.B. at p. 598.

(17) [1966] 3 All E.R. at p. 853; [1967] 2 Q.B. at p. 604.

(18) [1968] 2 Lloyd's Rep. at pp. 162, 163.

(19) [1968] 2 Lloyd's Rep. at p. 164.

A WILLMER, L.J., in dealing with the principle involved (20), treated *The Fehmarn*
(21) one of the leading cases on the question of stay, as being directly relevant.
    Second, as to the factors tending to rebut the prima facie case for a stay.
I think that there is much force in the main point taken by counsel for the plaintiffs that the bulk of the factual evidence is in England. While it may be that
some of the facts with regard to labour disputes, etc., can be agreed or proved
B by documents, I accept the plaintiffs' case that they will probably wish to call a
substantial number of witnesses on this topic, and that, if they have to take them
to Greece, it will cause them substantial inconvenience and expense. The evidence
of such witnesses would, moreover, have to be interpreted, with the difficulties
and further expense involved in that process. Against all that it must be borne
in mind that, if the dispute is tried in England, the reverse situation will arise
C as regards at least one, and perhaps two witnesses of fact for the defendants,
certainly in relation to inconvenience and expense, and possibly, though not
necessarily, also in relation to interpretation. These considerations about evidence
must, however, be viewed in perspective. Many commercial and admiralty
disputes are tried or arbitrated in England every year, in which most or all
of the evidence comes from abroad. In these cases, the parties are often content
D to have their disputes decided here, even though it causes inconvenience and
expense with regard to bringing witnesses to England and examining them
through interpreters. Bearing in mind these matters, I cannot regard the inconvenience and expense which the plaintiffs would suffer through having to take
witnesses to Greece as being in any way overwhelming or insuperable.
    Third, as to factors tending to re-inforce the prima facie case for a stay. Of
E these I regard as carrying some weight the very real connection of the defendants
with Greece and their willingness to protect the plaintiffs in relation to security
for their claim. I further regard as of substantial importance the circumstance
that Greek law governs, and is, in respects which may well be material, different
from English law. I recognise that an English court can, and often does, decide
questions of foreign law on the basis of expert evidence from foreign lawyers.
F Nor do I regard such legal concepts as contractual good faith and morality as
being so strange as to be beyond the capacity of an English court to grasp and
apply. It seems to be clear, however, that, in general and other things being
equal, it is more satisfactory for the law of a foreign country to be decided by
the courts of that country. That would be my view, as a matter of common sense,
apart from authority. But if authority be needed, it is to be found in *The Cap
G Blanco* (22), per SIR SAMUEL EVANS, P., and in *Settlement Corpn.* v. *Hochschild*
(23), per UNGOED-THOMAS, J. This last case was not cited to me in argument,
but appears to me to be helpful on the general point involved. It is true that, in
The Athenee (24) and *The Fehmarn* (21), in both of which a stay was refused,
the circumstances that the law of the foreign country governed does not appear
to have been given much weight. But in those cases there was no evidence that
H the foreign law was different in any material respects from English law, whereas
in the present case there is.
    Apart from the general advantage which a foreign court has in determining
and applying its own law, there is a significant difference in the position with
regard to appeal. A question of foreign law decided by a court of the foreign
country concerned is appealable as such to the appropriate appellate court of
I that country. But a question of foreign law decided by an English court on
expert evidence is treated as a question of fact for the purposes of appeal, with
the limitations in the scope of an appeal inherent in that categorisation. This
consideration seems to me to afford an added reason for saying that, in general

---

(20) [1968] 2 Lloyd's Rep. at pp. 162, 163.
(21) [1958] 1 All E.R. 333; [1958] 1 W.L.R. 159.
(22) [1913] P. at p. 136; [1911-13] All E.R. Rep. at pp. 368, 369.
(23) [1965] 3 All E.R. 486 at p. 491; [1966] Ch. 10 at p. 18.
(24) (1922), 11 Lloyd L.R. 6.

and other things being equal, it is more satisfactory for the law of a foreign **A**
country to be decided by the courts of that country. Moreover, by more satisfactory I mean more satisfactory from the point of view of ensuring that justice
is done.

Fourth, as to my conclusion. I have started by giving full weight to the
prima facie case for a stay, and I have gone on to weigh on the one hand the
factors tending to rebut that prima facie case, and on the other hand the factors **B**
tending to re-inforce it. With regard to these, it appears to me that
there are considerations of substantial weight on either side, which more or less
balance each other out, leaving the prima facie case for a stay largely, if not
entirely, intact. On this basis I have reached the clear conclusion that the
plaintiffs, on whom the burden lies, have not, on the whole of the matter,
established good cause why they should not be held to their agreement. The **C**
question whether to grant a stay or not, and if so on what terms, is one for the
discretion of the court. Having arrived at the clear conclusion which I have
stated, I shall exercise by discretion by granting a stay, subject to appropriate
terms as regards security.

I will hear counsel on the form of the order to be made and on costs. [A
discussion followed and the following order was agreed: " Upon the defendants' **D**
furnishing the plaintiffs with reasonable security for the plaintiffs' claim in
respect of any proceedings which the plaintiffs may hereafter commence in
Greece all further proceedings in the present action be stayed ".]

[Counsel for the plaintiffs asked for leave to appeal.]

BRANDON, J.: I think that there should be leave to appeal in this case, **E**
for three reasons. Although the matter is one for the exercise of the court's
discretion, it seems to me that the plaintiffs may well wish to say on appeal that
this court has not exercised its discretion on proper principles. Second, I think
that it is at least arguable that certain observations of LORD DENNING, M.R., in
The Fehmarn (25), if correct, would indicate that a test somewhat different from
that which I have thought fit to apply is the right one. I think that that is **F**
arguable—I do not say that it is so. Third, matters of this kind have international
significance and repercussions. For all those reasons, I think that it would be
right to give leave to appeal, and I do so.

Application granted. Leave to appeal granted.

Solicitors: *Holman, Fenwick & Willan*, agents for *Andrew M. Jackson & Co.*,
Hull (for the plaintiffs); *Norton, Rose, Botterell & Roche* (for the defendants). **G**

[*Reported by* N. P. METCALFE, ESQ., *Barrister-at-Law.*]

H

I

---

(25) [1958] 1 All E.R. at pp. 335, 336; [1958] 1 W.L.R. at pp. 161, 162.

A

IONIAN BANK, LTD. *v.* COUVREUR.

[COURT OF APPEAL, CIVIL DIVISION (Lord Denning, M.R., Davies and Widgery, L.JJ.), January 23, 1969.]

Practice—Stay of proceedings—Proceedings started in England and France—
B   *Substantial reasons for letting English action continue.*
Practice—Leave to defend—Conditional on payment of full amount into court—
R.S.C., Ord. 14.

In October 1965, the defendant, through a company, entered into partnership with the bank to purchase some wine from France. The bank advanced the money and the wine was purchased and paid for. Later the bank wished
C   to alter the nature of the arrangement for the purpose of a tax advantage and a scheme was drawn up and shown to the defendant. He kept the draft for three weeks and made a number of alterations to it. The document was finalised in February 1966. Under the new arrangements, the defendant's company acknowledged receipt of the loan and undertook to pay interest to the bank thereon; the stock of wine was hypothecated to the bank as security; and the defendant undertook to guarantee repayment of half the
D   loan. An associate company of the bank guaranteed the other half of the loan and was to enjoy half the profits of the venture. The defendant signed a personal guarantee for half the loan. The defendant and the bank entered similar arrangements on later occasions. On 5th March 1968, the bank took proceedings in France and obtained a saisie conservatoire (stop order) against the wine and certain interests of the defendant in France. (This necessitated
E   subsequent proceedings to determine the ownership of the wine and the validity of the claim.) Proceedings were commenced in Dijon and Beaune. Also in France, a complaint of a criminal nature was lodged in June 1968 relating to the supposed fraudulent conversion of a pledge. On 19th March, the bank issued a writ claiming sums due under guarantee. The defendant obtained a stay of proceedings on the order of a master, but this order was
F   reversed by the judge. The judge proceeded to hear a summons under R.S.C., Ord. 14, and gave leave to the defendant to defend conditional on his paying the full amount of the claim into court. On appeal by the defendant,

Held: the appeal would be dismissed, because—

(i) since judgment could be obtained quickly in England and could be enforced quickly in France (whereas if the proceedings were stayed in
G   England it would be a long time before the proceedings in France could be brought to finality), and since the bank, if it obtained an English judgment, might be able to execute on the defendant's assets in England, it could be said to have substantial reasons for pursuing the English action whilst proceedings in France were pending; accordingly, the English proceedings should not be stayed (see p. 655, letters B to D, p. 656, letter G, and p. 657,
H   letter E, post);

Peruvian Guano Co. v. *Bockwoldt* ([1881-85] All E.R. Rep. 715) followed.
The Christiansborg ((1885), 10 P.D. 141), and *The Marinero* ([1955] 1 All E.R. 676), distinguished.

(ii) the defendant, having altered the original partnership agreement deliberately for purposes of tax avoidance and not having questioned the
I   nature of the new arrangements until the court proceedings, could not contend that the alteration was a sham; the defendant's case had little or no substance and accordingly the judge was right to give leave to defend only on payment of the full amount into court (see p. 655, letters H and I, p. 656, letters C and I, and p. 658, letter C, post).

Appeal dismissed.

[As to lis alibi pendens, see 7 HALSBURY'S LAWS (3rd Edn.) 170-172, paras. 306-308.

A

As to circumstances in which action may be stayed, see 30 HALSBURY's LAWS
(3rd Edn.) 407-409, para. 768; and for cases on the subject, see 51 DIGEST (Repl.)
998-1008, *5347-5404.*]

Cases referred to:

Christiansborg, The (1885), 10 P.D. 141; 54 L.J.P. 84; 53 L.T. 612; 5 Asp.
    M.L.C. 491; 42 Digest (Repl.) 1111, *9294.*

B

McHenry v. Lewis (1882), 22 Ch.D. 397; 52 L.J.Ch. 325; 47 L.T. 549; 11
    Digest (Repl.) 542, *1512.*

Marinero, The, [1955] 1 All E.R. 676; sub nom. Cressington Court (Owners) v.
    Marinero (Owners), The Marinero, [1955] P. 68; [1955] 2 W.L.R. 607;
    Digest (Cont. Vol. A) *258, 1588a.*

Peruvian Guano Co. v. Bockwoldt (1883), 23 Ch.D. 225; [1881-85] All E.R.
    Rep. 715; 52 L.J.Ch. 714; 48 L.T. 7; 5 Asp. M.L.C. 29; 11 Digest (Repl.)
    545, *1530.*

C

Interlocutory appeal.

This was an appeal by the defendant, Michel-Marie Couvreur, from an order
made by ROSKILL, J., on 28th November 1968 refusing to grant a stay in an action
brought against the defendant by the Ionian Bank, Ltd., on the ground of lis
alibi pendens. The facts are set out in the judgment of LORD DENNING, M.R.

D

David Hirst, Q.C., and *T. H. Bingham* for the defendant.
R. A. MacCrindle, Q.C., and *H. H. Hill* for the plaintiff bank.

LORD DENNING, M.R.: The plaintiffs, the Ionian Bank, Ltd., sue on a
number of written guarantees which were given to them by the defendant, M.
Michel-Marie Couvreur, on various dates from February 1966 to February 1967,
the total being the sum of £20,392 11s. 7d. They have taken out a summons under
R.S.C., Ord. 14, for summary judgment. The judge has given leave to defend to
the defendant on condition of the whole sum being brought into court; and now
the defendant appeals to this court. The case raises two points: first, whether the
action ought to go on in England at all, having regard to some proceedings which
the bank have already taken in France; and, secondly, if the action is to go on,
whether there is to be leave to defend or not.

E

F

The story is a little complicated and I must recite the facts. It appears that in
the year 1965 the defendant was interested in acquiring the products of a vineyard
in France—the Thevenot vineyard; but he had not got the money with which to
buy the products. So he approached the bank in London to help in the venture.
He had two companies which were wholly owned by him, or substantially wholly
owned—an English company, Michel Couvreur, Ltd., and a French company of
the same name, Michel Couvreur, S.A., société anonyme. As a result of their
discussions, a letter passed in October 1965 which on the face of it constituted
a partnership between the bank and the defendant's English company. It was from
the bank:

G

H

" Dear Monsieur Couvreur, I confirm that on behalf of the Ionian Bank,
I have entered into a partnership with your English company to buy the
wines on the attached sheet [that is the Thevenot wines] for the sterling
equivalent of 205,000 NF in London today Monday, October 18th, 1965.
The net profit after all expenses, including interest at 2% over Bank Rate, will
be divided between us 50% each."

I

After that letter the bank paid £14,913 3s. 2d. (the sterling equivalent of the
francs) to the English company, Michel Couvreur, Ltd. The English company
bought the Thevenot wines from Mme. Fournier and paid her. But the transaction
did not ultimately go through in the form of a partnership as originally contemplated. The defendant himself explained the reason. He said that afterwards
there was a discussion between himself and Mr. Baird, the managing director
of the bank. He said:

A
" Baird spoke to me of his desire to formulate a plan which would enable all profits from the venture to be enjoyed free of tax. He suggested that only the interest on the money advanced was to be paid to the [bank] and the profits paid to companies controlled by Mr. Behrens which were safe from the taxation angle either on account of their location or on account of their right to offset the profits against earlier losses. This meeting followed

B
receipt of a letter referring to a loan. I pointed out that the agreement had been one of partnership and Mr. Baird said that the [bank's] position as bankers in respect of exchange control as well as income tax demanded such apparent alteration. He said no further funds would be forthcoming if the draft was not signed. The original agreement, he said, had merely to be split into a loan from the bank and a profit sharing with some of Mr. Behren's

C
companies. Eventually, I signed an amended form of letter and a form of personal guarantee."

It is quite plain from that sworn statement by the defendant that there was a new arrangement between them. The previous arrangement for a partnership on a 50 per cent. basis was replaced by a new arrangement designed to avoid tax. A letter was sent by the bank for the defendant's approval. He made in his

D
own hand a number of significant alterations.   It was then typed out in final form for the signature of the English company. Then on 20th February 1966, the English company wrote to the bank:

" We write to record the arrangements arrived at between us as follows: 1. You have made a loan to this company of £14,913 3s. 2d. which amount was credited by you to this company's account at Westminster Bank Limited

E
. . . on 19th October, 1965. 2. We understand that the rate of interest applicable to this loan will be 2% above Bank of England Discount Rate for the time being, with a minimum of 7% per annum. 3. The security for the loan is 139½ casks of wine (each cask containing 225 litres) constituting the entire produce for the year 1964 of the Domaine Hyppolyte Thevenot at Alexe Corton, Côte-D'Or, France, particulars of which wine are set out in the

F
schedule to this letter. Accordingly we hereby hypothecate to you the said stock of wine as security for your loan to this company. In addition, the repayment of half of the loan will be guaranteed by [the defendant] and the other half by Mr. E. M. Behrens or by a company nominated by him. The insurance company which is covering this wine against all usual risks will also be notified of your interest and we will send you the policy in due

G
course. We have already delivered to you a signed copy of the purchase contract covering this wine. 4. It is intended that the bulk of the wine will be bottled as and when each item is ready. 5. Enough of the wine will be sold by us to repay the said loan and interest thereon. 6. We will notify you of all sales of this wine which we may make and the amount and date of receipt of the net proceeds thereof.   7. For the purpose of repaying the said

H
loan and interest thereon we will hold the net proceeds of sale of all this wine hypothecated to you in trust for you, to remit the same to you forthwith in reduction or extinguishment of your advance to us and interest thereon. 8. We estimate that in the ordinary course of our business as wine merchants the loan and interest thereon should be completely repaid by the end of

I
1967."

That was clearly a contractual letter whereby the bank lent £14,913 3s. 2d. to the English company on those detailed terms. On the same day the defendant personally signed (as the letter said he would) a personal guarantee for half the amount, namely, £7,466 11s. 7d. Whatever the original arrangement was, it seems to me plain that it was replaced by a new arrangement altogether, under which the bank lent the money to the English company, Michel Couvreur, Ltd., and the defendant guaranteed half the sum to be repaid. At the same time, however, there was a collateral arrangement for a partnership. On 23rd February 1966,

a company called the Crosshaven Management Co., Ltd., wrote a letter recording **A**
that they had entered into a partnership arrangement with the English company,
Michel Couvreur, Ltd., to buy the stock of wine on the Thevenot estate, and
saying that the net profit on the sale would be divided equally between them. The
Crosshaven Management Co. was an associated company of the bank. So the net
result was that the associated company entered into the partnership, and not the
bank.
B
That was the first transaction. It was followed by a number of other transactions. I need not go into them in detail. They all followed the same form.
In each case there was a loan by the bank to the English company and a guarantee
of half by the defendant personally which he himself signed. Yet at the same time
there was, on each transaction, a collateral arrangement for a partnership. The
partnership was between an associated company of the bank and the English **C**
company; and was for half the profits.

All the transactions were carried through accordingly. Wines were obtained and
bottled and put in store in France. All were paid for by money provided by the
bank. Some time later some of the wines were sold; but, unfortunately, very
little of the proceeds seem to have been paid to the bank. Eventually at the end
of 1967 the bank became restless. It investigated the position, and sought to **D**
recover the moneys due to it.

In the first place it took proceedings in France. It issued proceedings in the
tribunal at Dijon on 5th March 1968, for an order of saisie conservatoire (a stop
order) against the wines held by the defendant and his French company and
the English company at Bouze-les-Beaune, Côte D'Or in France; but in accordance with French procedure, that stop order had to be followed up by pro- **E**
ceedings in the courts to determine the ownership of the wines and the validity
of the claim. Proceedings were taken both in Dijon and in the Tribunal de
Commerce at Beaune. Furthermore, in June 1968, in France there was a
complaint of a criminal nature in regard to the supposed fraudulent conversion
of a pledge.

On 19th March 1968, the bank issued the writ in this action claiming the sums **F**
(half the loans) due on the guarantees. There were six of them amounting to
£20,392 11s. 7d. The defendant applied for a stay. He said that the bank
ought not to take proceedings in England whilst proceedings in respect of the
same matter were being taken in France. The master ordered a stay; but
ROSKILL, J., reversed the master's decision. The judge refused a stay of the
English proceedings. He then went on to hear the summons for judgment **G**
under R.S.C., Ord. 14. He said that he was very nearly ready to give summary
judgment against the defendant on the guarantees: but he decided to give the
defendant a chance of paying into court. He gave leave to defend on condition
that the whole of the amount was paid into court.

The first point is whether the English proceedings ought to be stayed in view
of the proceedings in France. We have been referred to a few authorities on **H**
this point such as *McHenry* v. *Lewis* (1) and *Peruvian Guano Co.* v. *Bockwoldt* (2).
The law is not in doubt. The court will not stay an action by a plaintiff in the
English courts simply because he has also started proceedings in another country.
He is entitled to come to the Queen's courts to enforce his right. No stay will
be granted unless the defendant shows—and the burden is on him to show—
that the continuance of the English proceedings is vexatious or oppressive. **I**
In *Peruvian Guano Co.* v. *Bockwoldt* (3), BOWEN, L.J., said:

" If there is a fair possibility that he [the plaintiff] may have an advantage
by prosecuting a suit in two countries, why should this Court interfere
and deprive him of it? "

---

(1) (1882), 22 Ch.D. 397.
(2) (1883), 23 Ch.D. 225; [1881-85] All E.R. Rep. 715.
(3) (1883), 23 Ch.D. at p. 239; [1881-85] All E.R. Rep. at p. 718.

A Sir George Jessel, M.R., said (4):

"... it is not vexatious to bring an action in each country where there are substantial reasons of benefit to the plaintiff. He has the right to bring an action, and if there are substantial reasons to induce him to bring the two actions, why should we deprive him on that right?"

B I do not read Lindley, L.J., as saying anything different.

In this case the bank says that it has substantial reasons for bringing an action in this country. It enables it to get judgment quickly and under the arrangements for the reciprocal enforcement of judgments, an English judgment can be enforced quickly in France; whereas, if the English proceedings are stayed, it will be quite a long time before the French proceedings can be brought to finality. It may be that the criminal proceedings have to be determined in

C France before their civil proceedings can get further. The bank also says that if it gets an English judgment, it may be able to execute on the defendant's assets in England. He has 999 out of 1,000 of the shares in the English company. In these circumstances I think that the bank can say properly that there are " substantial reasons " and " the fair possibility of advantage " by letting the English action go on.

D But counsel for the defendant had a further argument for a stay. He based it on the order of saisie conservatoire. He said that by this means the bank had already got security in France. It was not right, he said, to let the proceedings go on in England when the bank held security already in France. He relied on the Admiralty cases of *The Christiansborg* (5) and *The Marinero* (6). But those were very different. In each case plaintiffs brought an action in Holland

E and arrested a ship there. The defendants, in order to get the ship released, gave security on the understanding that the action was to be continued in Holland. Afterwards the plaintiffs brought another action and arrested the ship, or a sister ship, in England. The defendants sought to stay the English action and succeeded. It would obviously be oppressive to let the action go on in England. The defendants had already bailed the ship out in Holland. They

F ought not to be compelled to bail it out again in England. Those cases are very different. There was here only the saisie conservatoire in France. I see nothing oppressive in the English action. I think that the judge was right in refusing to stay the English action.

Then the second point is whether the defendant should have unconditional leave to defend. Counsel for the defendant has argued strongly that the tran-

G saction between the bank and the English company was a partnership all the time, and that the documents in February 1966 (showing a loan and so forth) did not represent the true transaction. And he said, quite rightly, that if there was a partnership, there cannot be an action between partners on a debt: for there has first to be an account before either partner can sue the other as for a debt; and he said that, as there was no debt, there was no liability on the guaran-

H tee. One cannot have a guarantee for a debt that is not a debt.

It seems to me that the whole of the argument of counsel for the defendant depends on whether the documents in February 1966 were a sham. He relied very much on the words " apparent alteration " in the paragraph of the defendant's affidavit which I have read. I think he is putting too much weight on the word " apparent ". It is quite plain to me from the paragraph in the affi-

I davit, and from the detailed amendment of the documents which the defendant himself made, that this was not a sham at all. It was a re-arrangement deliberately made so as to avoid tax. It was suggested that this re-arrangement might be illegal, but that point was not pressed very much, and I think rightly, because agreements or re-arrangements to avoid tax are made every day and

(4) (1883), 23 Ch.D. at p. 230; [1881-85] All E.R. Rep. at p. 716.
(5) (1885), 10 P.D. 141.
(6) [1955] 1 All E.R. 676; [1955] P. 68.

are not illegal.   It seems quite plain that what happened here was: Seeing that   **A**
the original arrangement would attract tax, the parties deliberately re-arranged
it so as to avoid tax.   They made it in law what the documents show it to be,
namely, a loan by the bank to the English company: a letter in which the wines
were hypothecated by the English company as security for the loan; and in
addition guarantees given, as to half the loan by the defendant, and as to the
other half, by one of the associated companies.   **B**

The long and short of it is that the defendant signed these guarantees; the
money has been advanced by the bank; the defendant or his companies have
had the wine; and the bank has not seen a penny or hardly a penny of it.
In my judgment the defendant's case is so shadowy that the judge was right in
giving leave to defend only conditionally on the full amount being brought into
court.   I find myself therefore, in agreement with the judge on both points and   **C**
I would dismiss the appeal.

DAVIES, L.J.: I agree.   So far as concerns the question of stay it is right
to say that for a defendant to persuade the court to stay an action brought in
these courts in similar circumstances to the present, namely, on the ground
that a similar or indeed an identical action is said to be pending in a foreign   **D**
court, is, as is clear from the authorities, an extremely difficult task.   There
is a heavy onus on a defendant in such circumstances to persuade the court to
make such an order.   As LORD DENNING, M.R., has indicated and as the authorities show, the defendant has to show that the action, which the plaintiff prima
facie has a right to bring in our courts, is vexatious in the sense that he must
show that by continuing with the action here the plaintiff has no reasonable   **E**
prospect of any advantage.   We do not know the French law and we do not
know how long the French proceedings will take to come on.   But the bank
obviously thinks that it will be advantageous for it to go on with the English
action; for otherwise it would not be pressing on with it.   It may be that it
has a prospect of obtaining an earlier judgment in our courts than it might in
the French courts.   And it might then be able to enforce that judgment in   **F**
France.   And it may be—we know not—that in that regard it will have some
advantage by reason of the fact that there is still a considerable quantity of
wine in France which is seized, or, in the custody of the law under the saisie
conservatoire to which LORD DENNING, M.R., has referred.

I do not think that is the more difficult point in this case.   For myself I have
no doubt with respect that LORD DENNING is right when he says that this is   **G**
not a case in which the court should order a stay.

I confess that the second point, whether or not the case is so clear as to liability
that the stringent condition should be imposed of ordering payment into court
of the full amount of the claim as a condition precedent to leave to defend, seems
to me to be more difficult.   There are a great many matters in this case on the
documents to which, in the most thorough and careful argument of counsel for   **H**
the defendant, the attention of the court has been drawn as to which it is suggested that, whether the points be good or bad, they raise an arguable case, so
that the defendant should be given unconditional leave to defend.   I have at
times in the course of the argument been concerned about this.   But at the
end of it all it seems to me, for reasons very similar to those just enunciated
by LORD DENNING, that really there is little or no substance in the suggested   **I**
defence and that the case is almost one in which summary judgment should
be ordered.   I will very shortly—and this is almost repetition of what has just
been said by LORD DENNING—mention one or two factors that have brought
me to that conclusion.   The original partnership agreement in this case was
made on 18th October 1965.   It is plain that within a matter of weeks the bank
considered that it would suit its arrangements better to substitute the loan for
the partnership; for we find that the draft of the new arrangement was submitted to the defendant or his company on 23rd November 1965.   Now, we know

A   what the defendant says in his affidavit about the circumstances in which that
new arrangement was proposed to him.   But it is to be observed that the defendant kept that document in his possession and considered it for some three
months; for it was not until 20th February 1966, that the document as amended,
after having been amended in manuscript by the defendant, was signed and
returned by the defendant.   I think it is plain that, for whatever reason the
B   bank wanted that change of arrangement—it may be for tax reasons—the
defendant agreed to it and that there was a substitution of that arrangement for
the original partnership.   It is to be observed that in the defendant's affidavit,
apart from the word " apparent " to which LORD DENNING has referred, he does
not really suggest for one moment that that was a bogus arrangement or that
it was an unreal arrangement; and never, apart from the affidavit and, apart
C   from the phrases in the letters to which our attention has been called, which in
many cases are ambiguous, is there any suggestion by the defendant that this
was a bogus arrangement.   He never challenged its reality and never suggested
that these guarantees which he signed were worthless pieces of paper.   Throughout, until trouble arose, the parties were working on the basis of what I think
was apparently a genuine new arrangement.

D   However, in the light of the considerations which counsel for the defendant
has most powerfully put before the court, I agree that the order of the judge
should be left undisturbed, and that the defendant should have leave to defend
on the condition which the judge imposed.

E   **WIDGERY, L.J.:** I also agree, and add a word or two merely out of respect
for the admirable argument from the Bar and the assistance which it has given
me.   Counsel for the defendant, of course, founds himself in his resistance to
the order under R.S.C., Ord. 14, on the fact that there was initially a partnership
between the bank and the defendant's English company.   He argues that
nothing in the documents before us shows any rescission of that agreement.
But, of course, if there were a genuine new arrangement which was inconsistent
F   with that original arrangement, that by itself would be sufficient to rescind and
determine the original partnership;   and the question is, was there a genuine
re-arrangement, or was the apparent re-arrangement merely a sham?   In support
of the argument that it was a sham, counsel for the defendant referred us to
numerous letters in which the bank and its representatives seemed to treat the
matter as though there had been no change; but in considering those letters one
G   must remember that so far as the ultimate destination of the profits was concerned, there was really going to be no change.   Instead of the profits going
direct to the bank, as under the original arrangement, they were going to go
to these various subsidiary companies and no doubt eventually find their way
back to the bank or its officers.   Accordingly, it is not in the least surprising
to find those writing on behalf of the bank forgetting from time to time to express
H   themselves in the proper terms; and I would be very slow to draw the conclusion
from that that there had in fact not been a genuine re-arrangement.   The
arrangement had an air of unreality which is often found when these tax avoidance
schemes are carried out by one company and its subsidiaries; but the genuineness of the transaction is not to be affected merely because the bank and its
officers occasionally got muddled about it.   The genuineness of the arrangement
I   is shown more clearly, in my judgment, if one looks at the conduct of the defendant, and it seems to me abundantly clear that at all times after following the
suggestion of a new arrangement, he treated it as a serious and binding one.
I appreciate that counsel for the defendant relies on his technical argument
that there can be no guarantee of a non-existent debt; but in considering whether
the transaction was a genuine one what one cannot fail to be guided by is whether
as a fact the defendant himself regarded his guarantee as being genuine and
binding.   It seems to me to be clear that he did.   And I mention two reasons
only in support of that view.   The first is the one already given by DAVIES, L.J.,

that I can find at no time any positive assertion by the defendant that the A
guarantees were a sham.   One would have thought that in proceedings of this
kind that would have been the first matter on which he would have gone on
affidavit, if he felt able to do so.   The second factor which impresses me is the
amendments which the defendant personally made in the draft document which
ultimately took the form of the English company's letter of 20th February 1966.
In the draft of that letter the defendant himself made an amendment whereby B
his guarantee was not to relate to the whole of the amount advanced but only to a
half; and I ask myself what possible concern he could have had to make an
amendment of that kind if in fact the whole thing was a sham and he never intended
to be responsible on it.   I am quite satisfied that there is nothing in the suggestion of a sham and that the learned judge reached the true conclusion.   I would
accordingly dismiss the appeal.   C

Appeal dismissed.

Solicitors: *Freshfields* (for the defendant);   *Herbert Smith & Co.* (for the
plaintiff bank).

[Reported by JENIFER SANDELL, Barrister-at-Law.]

D

MASARATI *v.* MASARATI.

[COURT OF APPEAL, CIVIL DIVISION (Danckwerts, Sachs and Fenton Atkinson,
  L.JJ.), February 7, 1969.]

Divorce—Discretion—Factors to be taken into account—Adultery by both parties   E
—No prospective remarriage—Broken down marriage—Undesirable main-
tenance of wedlock of adulterous spouses—Daughter aged 15 living with wife
—Petitioner's frankness—Respondent's treatment contributing to petitioner's
adultery.

The wife petitioned for divorce on the ground of the adultery of the
husband, who had informed her that he did not think he was bound to be   F
faithful, and who had committed adultery with an unmarried lady by
whom he had had two children and whom he did not wish to marry.   The
husband had said that he had discontinued that association and had made
a fresh adulterous association with another woman.   The wife herself (with
whom her 15 year old daughter was living) had committed adultery over
several years with her employer, a married man whom there was no prospect
of her marrying, and she made a full and frank disclosure in her discretion G
statement (it was stated subsequently that she had ended that association
since the trial).   In the light of the absence of any prospect of either party
remarrying, the judge refused to exercise his discretion in respect of the
wife's adultery in her favour and rejected the petition.

Held (FENTON ATKINSON, L.J., dissenting): a decree of divorce should   H
be issued in the case, because in exercising his discretion the judge had laid
too much stress on the absence of any possibility of the parties remarrying
and had overlooked or not given appropriate weight to other important
considerations, in particular the complete breakdown of the marriage, the
undesirability of keeping the parties in a state where they were compelled
to live in continuous adultery, and of requiring the daughter to stay with
parents so placed, the wife's complete frankness, how far her adultery was I
due to the husband's treatment, the fact that it was with one man only (and
in the end had ceased), and the possibility that if free the husband might yet
marry the mother of his illegitimate children.

Appeal allowed.

[As to principles of the exercise of the court's discretion in petitions for
divorce, see 12 HALSBURY'S LAWS (3rd Edn.) 311-313, paras. 622-626; and for
cases on the subject, see 27 DIGEST (Repl.) 427-439, *3582-3688*.]

A   Cases referred to:

    Apted v. *Apted and Bliss,* [1930] P. 246; 99 L.J.P. 73; 143 L.T. 353; 27
        Digest (Repl.) 428, *3588.*

    Blunt v. *Blunt,* [1942] 2 All E.R. 613; *revsd.* H.L., [1943] 2 All E.R. 76; [1943]
        A.C. 517; 112 L.J.P. 58; 169 L.T. 33; 27 Digest (Repl.) 429, *3589.*

B   **Appeal.**

The petitioner wife appealed against an order of His Honour Judge Dewar, made on 29th April 1968, dismissing her petition for divorce. The judge found the husband's adultery proved and in his judgment said:

C
    " The question which has caused me grave concern is whether this is a case where the discretion of the court should be exercised in the [wife's] favour. She has committed adultery over a number of years, with a married man, and committed adultery with him as recently as a fortnight ago. But there are no plans for them to marry, and it does not appear that there are any prospects that that man's marriage will be brought to an end. Now, on the other hand, the [husband] has committed adultery with a woman who is single, and has borne him two children; and [the wife] has told me that the woman would like to marry [the] husband, but [the]

D
husband does not wish to marry her. So that, if I exercise my discretion, there are no immediate plans for anybody wishing to remarry. In some ways, [the wife] would like [the] husband to be free again, because in some way he might then lose the protection which being married to [the wife] gave him from other women. Weighing up all the pros and cons of this case,

E
and the strange relationships between the parties, I have come to the conclusion that this is a case where the court should not exercise its discretion in the [wife's] favour, and the petition will accordingly be dismissed."

The wife's grounds of appeal were that the learned judge held the adultery alleged against the husband to be proved but refused to grant a decree nisi to the wife in the exercise of his discretion on account of her own admitted adultery,

F   which decision was wrong in that: (i) the judge failed to take sufficient account of the fact that (a) the wife was completely and obviously frank with the court, (b) the wife's admitted adultery arose from psychological pressure imposed on her by the husband and was not the result of a vicious and inherently immoral nature, (c) the marriage was never a success and had completely broken down, (d) the wife was not responsible for the breakdown, (e) the wife's daughter

G   wanted her to be divorced, and (f) there was and could be no interest for society or the community at large in keeping the marriage in being; (ii) the judge wrongly took into account, or wrongly allowed to influence him adversely to the wife, the fact of the wife's relationship to the husband in permitting him to live at her flat mid-week while he was staying with the woman named at weekends in the face of the reasonable explanation given by the wife and in the absence

H   of a finding of condonation (which was not in any event open on the evidence to the judge to make); (iii) that on the evidence given and the facts found by the judge he ought to have granted the wife a decree nisi of divorce in the exercise of his discretion in her favour.

    P. H. Norris for the wife.

I   **DANCKWERTS, L.J.:** This is an appeal against an order of His Honour Judge Dewar made on 29th April 1968, in which he refused to grant a decree of divorce to the petitioner wife in this case. There is no doubt about the adultery of the husband, which apparently was habitual and continuous, but though the wife made a very frank discretion statement the judge refused to exercise his discretion in her favour, and consequently he refused a decree.

The parties were married in 1959, and the husband appears to have been a man without any matrimonial or sexual morals at all. He stated to the wife that he did not think that he was bound to be faithful, and at one period he said

that she was inexperienced and immature, and described her as " lousy in bed ". **A**
He, however, went off and committed adultery with an unmarried lady by
whom he has had two children.   But, according to him at any rate, he discontinued that association and made a fresh adulterous association with another
woman.   The wife herself has committed adultery.   She committed adultery
with her employer for a considerable time; but we are informed that that association has now been broken off and it appears to have been broken off in December. **B**

It seems to me that the judge in his judgment, which was quite a short one,
overlooked some important considerations and laid too much stress on one consideration which seems to have affected him very much—that, although the
unmarried lady with the children would want to marry the husband, he did
not want to marry her, and that the man with whom the wife has committed
adultery was a married man, so that it would not be possible for her to marry **C**
him. It seems to me that too much weight was attached to that and not enough to
the principle which is mentioned in *Blunt* v. *Blunt* (1), that it is undesirable to
keep parties in a state where they are compelled to adopt a life of continuous
adultery.

In this case it seems to me that there is a great deal to suggest that the fact that
the wife committed adultery was largely due to her treatment by the husband **D**
and his insistence on committing adultery.   In my view, the learned judge did
not give enough weight to that consideration, and also to the fact that the
wife's daughter was living with her.   It seems to me undesirable that her mother
should be tied for ever to an adulterous husband.   For these reasons, I would
allow the appeal and grant a decree.

E

SACHS, L.J.: The matter of discretion as regards the granting of decrees
of divorce is one of the more difficult questions that have to be dealt with by the
courts from decade to decade.   In principle, the factors to be considered may
remain constant, but the weight to be given to the individual factors may vary
greatly as time goes on, for the courts must take care not to sever themselves
from that general climate of opinion that is hard to define but is nonetheless **F**
important.   To this point I will return.

How great have been and can be the changes in the views relating to the
weight to be given to factors in this matter is perhaps hardly known to the
present generation of those who come before the courts.   Just after the first
world war men were refused discretion on account of a single weekend at an hotel
after the wife had long deserted them.   That view would have astonished even **G**
those who practised in the divorce court ten years later—i.e., after the watershed
decision of *Apted* v. *Apted and Bliss* (2).   Again, by 1942 when the leading case
of *Blunt* v. *Blunt* (1) was decided, there had been a great change in the categories
of cases in which the discretion of the court was exercised in favour of an offending
spouse.   Today, we are perhaps faced with a new situation as regards the weight
to be attached to one particular factor—that is the break-down of the marriage. **H**

In that behalf it may well be that there should, before long, with the aid of
counsel instructed as amicus curiae by the Queen's Proctor, be a general review
of the question of the exercise of discretion in the light of the views now twice
expressed by a majority of the legislature as to the importance of that factor.
It is a factor consideration of which may be allied to a view quoted with approval
by VISCOUNT SIMON, L.C., in *Blunt's* case (3), the fact that—" it is undesirable . . . **I**
to keep two adulterous spouses fettered in the bonds of wedlock ".   That is
something that always needs attention when one comes to the question of the
interest of the community at large.

---

(1) [1943] 2 All E.R. 76; [1943] A.C. 517.
(2) [1930] P. 246.
(3) [1943] 2 All E.R. at p. 80; [1943] A.C. at p. 529.   VISCOUNT SIMON, L.C., was
quoting from the judgment of GODDARD, L.J., in the Court of Appeal, [1942] 2 All E.R.
613 at p. 619.

A   Turning now from the general to the particular, it seems to me clear that in this particular case the county court judge cannot have paid proper attention to, and given appropriate weight to, quite a number of factors. First of all, there was the frankness of the wife; she clearly was completely frank. (Of recent years there have been not many reported cases in which a decree was refused where there had been such complete frankness.) Secondly, there

B   was a young daughter of 15 who was living with the husband and wife and will in future live with the wife. It seems to me highly undesirable that a daughter should remain with a husband and wife in circumstances such as have been referred to by Danckwerts, L.J., and be brought up with the idea that the law forces her to stay with parents required to live in matrimonial association. Next, there is the point that so far as the wife is concerned her adultery was

C   with only one man, and we have now been informed (and I see no reason not to accept it) that that association has completely ceased since trial.

    On the other hand, the husband, who seems to have led the wife into the view that adultery is a matter which should not form a factor of importance in matrimonial affairs, is himself the father of two illegitimate children; and, even if it is thought at this moment that the prospect of marriage between the husband

D   and the mother of those children is not great, there is no reason to believe that when once the husband is free there may not be a change in that respect, too. But, above all, this is a case in which insufficient attention was placed on the fact that there has been a complete breakdown of the marriage, and it seems to me difficult indeed to say that the public interest will be served by keeping these two people together. In that behalf I, for my part, feel account should be taken

E   of the views expressed on behalf of the community by the legislature and to which, to my mind, these courts must pay some attention, even if it means saying that nowadays it may be that only in relatively rare cases discretion should not be exercised (assuming the petitioner is completely frank).

    In the end, accordingly I, too, have come to the conclusion that this at any rate is one of those cases in which discretion should clearly have been exercised

F   in favour of the wife; and I agree that this appeal should be allowed.

    FENTON ATKINSON, L.J.: With diffidence, which is all the greater because of my Lords' great experience in these cases, I feel unable to agree. This was a matter not for our discretion, but for the discretion of the judge who heard the case. It is quite true that he gave no reasoned judgment; no doubt he was dealing with a large number of undefended petitions on the same day.

G   But he said that he had weighed all the pros and cons, and I can see no reason to suppose that he had not considered all the matters which my Lords have mentioned. For my part, I cannot see that he has proceeded on a wrong basis or failed to take into account facts which should have been considered. For my part, I would have said that this was a proper case for him to refuse to exercise

H   discretion in favour of the wife.

Appeal allowed. Decree nisi granted.

Solicitors: *D. Miles Griffiths, Piercy & Co.* (for the wife).

[*Reported by* F. A. Amies, Esq., *Barrister-at-Law.*]

A

R. *v.* TAYLOR.

[COURT OF APPEAL, CRIMINAL DIVISION (Lord Parker, C.J., Edmund Davies, L.J. and Caulfield, J.), March 20, 1969.]

Criminal Law—Compensation—Compensation order—Indictable offence—No application by person aggrieved—Validity of order—Quarter sessions— Forfeiture Act 1870 (33 & 34 Vict. c. 23), s. 4, as amended.

B

The appellant pleaded guilty at quarter sessions to stealing lead piping in a building and also to maliciously damaging lead piping and plumbing fitments in that building. He was sentenced to concurrent terms of 18 months' imprisonment and ordered to pay £100 compensation to the owners of the damaged property. On appeal against the order for compensation,

C

Held: Under s. 4* of the Forfeiture Act 1870, as amended, where an accused was convicted of an offence at quarter sessions or assizes, compensation could only be awarded on the application of a person aggrieved; accordingly since the prosecution did not have any witnesses present who might have applied for such an order the order for compensation would be quashed (see p. 663, letter I, post).

D

Appeal allowed in part.

[As to power of quarter sessions or a court of assize to award compensation, see 10 HALSBURY'S LAWS (3rd Edn.) 819, para. 1583; and for cases on the subject, see 14 DIGEST (Repl.) 685, *7021-7023.*

For the Forfeiture Act 1870, s. 4, see 8 HALSBURY'S STATUTES (3rd Edn.) 180.]   E

Case referred to:

R. v. Forest Justices, Ex. p. Coppin, p. 668, post.

Appeal.

On 3rd December 1968 the appellant, Timothy John Taylor, pleaded guilty at Middlesex Quarter Sessions with two other men to two counts in an indictment: (i) larceny of lead in a building; and (ii) maliciously damaging lead piping and plumbing fitments, the property of G.E.C. (D.E.), Ltd., to the value of some £600. He was sentenced by the deputy chairman (JUDGE RANKIN) to concurrent terms of 18 months' imprisonment and ordered to pay £100 compensation in respect of count 2 to G.E.C. (D.E.), Ltd. He appealed, inter alia, against the order of compensation with leave of the single judge. The facts are set out in the judgment of the court.

F

G

The authority noted below† was cited during the argument in addition to the case referred to in the judgment of the court.

F. Reynold for the appellant.
The Crown was not represented.

LORD PARKER, C.J.: The appellant pleaded guilty on 3rd December   H
1968 at Middlesex Quarter Sessions to two counts, the first of larceny of lead piping fixed to a building, and secondly malicious damage to lead piping and plumbing fitments. He was sentenced to 18 months' imprisonment on each count concurrent, and in respect of the malicious damage he was in addition ordered to pay £100 compensation to the owners of the damaged property. It is against that sentence that he now appeals by leave of the single judge.   I

The facts are in a very short compass. The premises in question were an office block which had been left empty for some 22 months. There was a caretaker there, however, and on 12th August 1968 he found someone had entered the

---

* Section 4, so far as material, is set out at p. 663, letter F, post. This section was amended by s. 10 (1) of and Sch. 2 (9) to the Criminal Law Act 1967, increasing the limit of compensation to £400.

† ARCHBOLD'S CRIMINAL PLEADING, EVIDENCE AND PRACTICE (36th Edn.) para. 833.

A building and removed door fittings on three of the floors. In looking around, however, he found that no lead piping had been removed. The very next day, at 10.20 a.m., he heard loud banging noises in the building. He called the police, and at 11.0 a.m. the police entered with a dog and found two men lying on a shed roof, part of the office building, and a third in an empty water tank nearby. The appellant was one of them, and when asked what they were doing on the

B roof, he said " We were only having the metal away. We didn't break into the place, the doors were open ". He went on to say he was expecting to get £10 for the piping.   On inspection of the premises, it was found that lead piping worth about £25 had been ripped from the first three floors and the roof, and that considerable damage had been done to the building, indeed the cost of repairing the plumbing and other items was said to be in the region of £600.

C It is only right to say that that figure was challenged, and that it was accepted that the appellant and the others had not been responsible for all the damage.

The appellant is 26 years of age, married with two children, and indulged in 1964 and 1965 in an orgy of breakings and as a result in January 1966 he was sentenced to a total of 12 months' imprisonment for four breakings and stealings when he also asked for 25 similar offences to be taken into consideration. It is

D true that he has to some extent lived down that past by keeping clear for some two years and working, but it is in the opinion of this court a very prevalent offence these days, and they can see no reason whatever for interfering with the sentence of 18 months' imprisonment.

The real point on which the single judge gave leave to appeal in this case concerned the order for compensation that was made. The power of quarter

E sessions to make an order for compensation is to be found in s. 4 of the Forfeiture Act 1870 which provides:

" It shall be lawful for any such Court as aforesaid, if it shall think fit, upon the application of any person aggrieved, and immediately after the conviction of any person for felony, to award any sum of money, not exceeding one hundred pounds, by way of satisfaction or compensation ... "

F There was no application on behalf of any person aggrieved for the appellant had pleaded guilty, and the prosecution did not have any witnesses present who might have applied for such an order. A similar point came before the Divisional Court on 10th March 1969, in *R.* v. *Forest Justices, Ex p. Coppin* (1). In that case a magistrates' court had at the invitation of the defence made orders for compensa-

G tion, and since a magistrates' court now has power under s. 34 of the Magistrates' Courts Act 1952 to order compensation in the same way as a court of assize or quarter sessions could have done, the same point arose. There the court were constrained to quash orders of compensation, there having been no application made by any person aggrieved, the result in that case being that the applicants got away with a very short sentence which would no doubt have been longer

H had the justices realised that they could not order compensation. It is an unfortunate omission in the legislation; a magistrates' court dealing summarily with an offence has absolute power to award compensation under s. 14 of the Criminal Justice Administration Act 1914 (2) without any application being made by an aggrieved person, but if they are dealing with an indictable offence or quarter sessions or court of assize are dealing with the case, the compensation can only be awarded on the application of a person aggrieved. It follows, therefore,

I that the order in the present case must be quashed.

Appeal allowed in part.

Solicitors: *Registrar of Criminal Appeals* (for the appellant).

[*Reported by* N. P. METCALFE, ESQ., *Barrister-at-Law.*]

(1) P. 668, post.
(2) For s. 14 of the Criminal Justice Administration Act 1914 see 14 HALSBURY'S STATUTES (2nd Edn.) 912.

A

COWLING *v.* MATBRO, LTD.

[COURT OF APPEAL, CIVIL DIVISION (Lord Denning, M.R., Edmund Davies and
Phillimore, L.JJ.), February 5, 1969.]

County Court—New trial—Further evidence—Evidence which could with reason-
able diligence have been adduced at the trial—Failure to seek adjournment   B
to pursue allegations becoming known in course of trial—Dismissal for
misconduct—Successful action for damages—Whether new trial would be
ordered.

On the grounds that he was unable to account for £30 which he had
received on behalf of the defendants, his employers, the plaintiff was dismissed without notice for misconduct and the £30 was deducted from moneys   C
owed to him by the defendants. He sued the defendants for the £30 so
deducted and for damages for wrongful dismissal. By the end of the first
day of the trial it was clear that the case was going badly for the defendants.
The case was adjourned for one week during which further allegations of
misconduct on the part of the plaintiff were made to the defendants' company secretary by the defendants' employees. When the case was resumed   D
nothing was said to the judge about the further allegations and he gave judgment for the plaintiff. The defendants thereupon investigated the allegations and applied for a new trial. On the question whether a new trial
should be ordered,

Held: since the further allegations of misconduct had been brought to
the attention of the defendants before judgment and they could have   E
sought a further adjournment of the trial, it was not appropriate to order
a new trial (see p. 666, letter F, and p. 667, letters G and I, post).

Ladd v. *Marshall* ([1954] 3 All E.R. 745) applied.

Appeal allowed.

[As to order for new trial on discovery of fresh evidence since the trial, see
30 HALSBURY'S LAWS (3rd Edn.) 475, 476, para. 891; and for cases on the   F
subject, see 51 DIGEST (Repl.) 823-826, *3789-3821*, 865-867, *4158-4170*.]

Cases referred to:
  Brown v. *Dean*, [1910] A.C. 373; [1908-10] All E.R. Rep. 661; 79 L.J.K.B.
      690; 102 L.T. 661; 51 Digest (Repl.) 865, *4160*.
  Ellis v. *Scott* (*No. 2*), [1965] 1 All E.R. 3; [1965] 1 W.L.R. 276; 51 Digest
      (Repl.) 828, *3829*.   G
  Ladd v. *Marshall*, [1954] 3 All E.R. 745; [1954] 1 W.L.R. 1489; 51 Digest
      (Repl.) 827, *3826*.
  New York Exchange, Ltd., Re (1888), 39 Ch.D. 415; 51 Digest (Repl.) 824,
      3800.

Interlocutory Appeal.
This was an appeal by the plaintiff, Barry Owen George Cowling, from an   H
order of His Honour JUDGE McDONNELL made on 15th November 1968, whereby
it was ordered that leave should be granted to the defendants, Matbro, Ltd.,
to re-amend their defence and that there should be a new trial of the issues
raised by the re-amendment. The facts are set out in the judgment of LORD
DENNING, M.R.
                                                                                  I
A. R. M. Davies for the plaintiff.
Barbara Mills for the defendants.

LORD DENNING, M.R.: Matbro, Ltd., the defendants, are manufacturers of forklifts at Horley in Surrey. Mr. Cowling, the plaintiff, was their works
manager. He started in their employment in 1964. On 17th November 1967,
Mr. Matthews, the managing director of the defendants, dismissed the plaintiff
on the spot at a moment's notice. The reason was because it was said that he

A had received £30 on behalf of the defendants and had not handed it over. In short, he had embezzled it. The defendants deducted it from the sums owing to him and dismissed him. The plaintiff was aggrieved by the allegation. His solicitors wrote a letter within a week to Mr. Matthews claiming the £30 and also intimating that he would claim damages for wrongful dismissal. Mr. Matthews did not reply. The plaintiff issued a plaint for £91 10s. 2d. Mr.
B Matthews himself put in a defence in his own hand:

   " The plaintiff was discharged instantly because of his inability to account for company money which was entrusted to him by a customer."

   Later on the defendants instructed solicitors and counsel. On 31st May 1968, the defendants put in a defence in which they alleged that they had terminated
C the plaintiff's employment for misconduct. They gave particulars saying that in early October 1967 he misappropriated a sum of £30 which was entrusted to him for and on behalf of the defendants. That was the only charge of misconduct against him. The other defence was that he had not been dismissed but had resigned.

   The case went to trial on that pleading. The first day was 1st July 1968,
D at Reigate County Court before His Honour Judge McDonnell. By the end of that day it was quite clear that the judge was running against the defendants. Mr. Matthews made a very bad impression on the judge. His suggestion that the plaintiff had not been dismissed was quite untrue. It was contraverted by the documents, so that things looked pretty bad for the defendants. The second day was at Epsom County Court a week later. During the week's adjournment
E some of the employees of the defendants went to the company secretary, Mrs. Thompson, and told her of all the other wrong things that the plaintiff had done. They said that he had got the defendants' employees to do work for him in the defendants' time; that they had been making things for him for his own personal use; and also that they had been taking to the plaintiff's house things which belonged to the defendants. Mrs. Thompson told one of these employees to
F go to the police, and she may, or may not, have said something to the solicitors. But however that may be, one thing is clear: on the second day—9th July— nothing was said to the judge about these new allegations. No application was made for an adjournment; the case was tried simply on the issue of misconduct in regard to the £30. The judge found that the charge was not established. He found for the plaintiff, and gave judgment for him for £91 10s. 2d.
G   After the case was over, the defendants by their solicitors made further investigations into these allegations by the workpeople. They took statements from them and applied thereupon to the county court judge for a new trial. The judge required the new allegations to be set out in writing. The defendants accordingly amended their defence, striking out the charge in respect of the £30, but adding 17 new charges of misconduct of one kind and another. The judge
H granted leave to make those amendments and ordered a new trial. The plaintiff appeals to this court.
      It is settled law, of course, that in seeking to justify the dismissal of a servant, an employer is entitled to rely, not only on misconduct known to him at the time of dismissal, but also on any misconduct which afterwards comes to his notice, provided that it is properly pleaded and proved at the trial. This case
I raises, however, a new point. Here the trial has been held. The employer has failed to prove the misconduct which he pleaded. Judgment has been given against him. Now the employer seeks to bring up other misconduct which he did not plead before. He says it has only come to light since the trial. I have no doubt that, if an employer, after the trial, discovers that the servant was guilty of misconduct, other than that of which he has been acquitted, this court may, in its discretion, grant a new trial and allow the employer to plead and prove this freshly discovered misconduct, rather than let the servant retain a judgment contrary to the justice of the case. That follows, I think, from the

decision in *Ellis* v. *Scott* (*No. 2*) (1). And if this court can do so, I think a county **A**
court judge can do so under C.C.R., Ord. 37: because his powers in granting a
new trial are parallel to those of this court. But a new trial will, as a rule, only
be granted on the same principles as any new trial is granted. The principles
were stated some years ago in *Ladd* v. *Marshall* (2). The very first requirement
is that the fresh evidence could not have been obtained with reasonable diligence
for use at the trial. The county court judge found that this requirement was **B**
satisfied. He seems to have thought that, although Mrs. Thompson knew of the
fresh evidence, she was a nervous lady who could not be expected to do more
than she did. He said:

> " She is a nervous person and at the material times was in a neurotic
> condition. I am satisfied that she did not fully appreciate the significance
> of what she was told and did not appreciate that those were matters that **C**
> could have been investigated there and then for the purpose of defence.
> She was always activated by great animosity against the plaintiff, and one
> would expect her to seize upon such matters if she had realised their
> significance."

I am quite prepared to accept what the judge says, that Mrs. Thompson could **D**
not reasonably be expected to do more. But, even so, I do not think that the
first requirement was satisfied. When an employer is sued for wrongful dismissal,
I think he should look to his defence carefully before the trial. He should enquire
into all misconduct that he wishes to plead. He should make all enquiries of
his other servants and find out if there are any other matters to be put against the
employee. Reasonable diligence requires that all charges should, as far as possible, **E**
be made at the first trial; for the simple reason that it is not fair to expose the
servant to a second trial after he has been acquitted at the first. I feel sure that,
if the new allegations in this case were well founded, they could have been
discovered with reasonable diligence before the first trial. In any case, however,
it is clear that the information did come to the defendants' knowledge in the week
between the first day and the second day. The defendants ought then to have **F**
made an application for an adjournment rather than sit still and let the case
proceed on the footing that the only issue was the £30. It is to be remembered,
too, that the case was going badly for the defendants. An attempt at that stage
to collect fresh evidence is not convincing.

In all the circumstances, I do not think this case comes within the rules under
which a new trial should be granted. I would allow the appeal. The existing **G**
judgment must stand.

EDMUND DAVIES, L.J.: I agree. As the Court of Appeal said in *Re New
York Exchange, Ltd.* (3), it is the duty of a party—

> ". . . to bring forward his whole case at once, and not to bring it forward
> piecemeal as he found out the objections in his way."

It appears to me that that is so for at least two reasons. First of all: Interest **H**
reipublicae ut sit finis litium. On that ground alone, which LORD LOREBURN,
L.C., described as an old doctrine of " extreme value " in the course of his
judgment in *Brown* v. *Dean* (4):

> " When a litigant has obtained a judgment in a Court of justice, whether
> it be a county court or one of the High Courts, he is by law entitled not **I**
> to be deprived of that judgment without very solid grounds; . . ."

And the second reason is this—and it is the subject-matter of a wise note to
R.S.C., Ord. 59, r. 10, at p. 758 of THE SUPREME COURT PRACTICE 1967:

(1) [1965] 1 All E.R. 3; [1965] 1 W.L.R. 276.
(2) [1954] 3 All E.R. 745; [1954] 1 W.L.R. 1489.
(3) (1888), 39 Ch.D. 415 at p. 420.
(4) [1910] A.C. 373 at p. 374; [1908-10] All E.R. Rep. 661 at p. 662.

A   ". . . evidence not called at the trial is necessarily regarded with caution.
It may be prompted or coloured by a knowledge of what happened in the
court below . . ."

There are features of this present case which appear to me to render that last
observation particularly apposite.

B   In the light of such considerations, this court in *Ladd* v. *Marshall* (5), laid
down certain requirements which must be satisfied before a new trial is ordered.
I do not propose to go through them.   It is sufficient to remind oneself that what
was put in the forefront by DENNING, L.J., in that case is the requirement that
(6):

C   ". . . it must be shown that the evidence could not have been obtained
with reasonable diligence for use at the trial . . ."

By those words is meant, of course, that those who seek to introduce fresh
evidence must establish that reasonable diligence on their part would not have
made the fresh evidence available to them in time.   In my judgment, the learned
county court judge misdirected himself in dealing with that requirement.
Between the hearings on 2nd and 9th July a good deal happened.   I extract

D   from the agreed notes of the county court judge's decision this passage:

" Guttaridge [that is, the fabrication foreman in the defendants' employ-
ment] also told her [that is Mrs. Thompson, the company's secretary] that
one, Mayne, wanted to see her about taking things to the plaintiff's house.
Mrs. Thompson said that *before* the day of the adjourned hearing on 9th July,
although she did not know the details, she had told Mr. Sagoo of the

E   defendants' then solicitors. *I am satisfied that she did.*"

The learned county court judge has underlined that last sentence, and the notes
continue:

" Mr Skene, the assistant to the plaintiff apparently, went to see Mrs.
Thompson after 9th July and told her that company furniture had been

F   sold by the plaintiff from the defendants' canteen.   I find as a fact that
information of that sort was given to Mrs. Thompson *before* 9th July, and
some of the general allegations were conveyed to Mr. Sagoo."

Now, how can it be said that, allegations (albeit of a general nature) involving
imputations of dishonesty against the plaintiff having been brought to the attention of their solicitor, the defendants may properly sit back, allow the trial to

G   proceed on the adjourned hearing up to judgment with no request for an adjournment, and only thereafter start opening up an investigation?   It appears to me
that to permit a course of that kind would be quite wrong.   It could have
serious public repercussions and open the door to infinite litigation.   Indeed, I
see in principle no reason why one should not go on applying even a third time
for a new trial, were the present order to stand.   I am satisfied, if I may say so,

H   that the view already expressed by LORD DENNING, M.R., is one which (in the
public interest and in fairness to individual litigants) commands and demands
respect in the conduct of proceedings.   I accordingly concur in allowing this
appeal.

PHILLIMORE, L.J.: I agree with both these judgments which have been

I   delivered and I cannot usefully add anything.

Appeal allowed.

Solicitors: *Gowen & Stevens*, Croydon (for the plaintiff); *Pearless, de Rouge-
mont & Co.*, East Grinstead (for the defendants).

[*Reported by* JENIFER SANDELL, *Barrister-at-Law.*]

---

(5) [1954] 3 All E.R. 745;   [1954] 1 W.L.R. 1489.
(6) [1954] 3 All E.R. at p. 748;   [1954] 1 W.L.R. at p. 1491.

A

R. v. FOREST JUSTICES, *Ex parte* COPPIN AND ANOTHER.

[QUEEN'S BENCH DIVISION (Lord Parker, C.J., Melford Stevenson and Blain, JJ.),
March 10, 1969.]

*Criminal Law—Compensation—Compensation order—Indictable offence—No
application by person aggrieved—Validity of order—Magistrates' court* B
—Forfeiture Act 1870 (33 & 34 Vict. c. 23), s. 4, as amended.

The applicants, C. and J., pleaded guilty at a magistrates' court to ten and
eight charges respectively of stealing motor vehicles. As it was known
that they were going to plead guilty no witnesses were called and in particular the owners of the vehicles concerned were not called to give evidence.
Both applicants were sentenced to suspended sentences of imprisonment C
and, in addition, the justices ordered C. to pay £500 and J. to pay £400
compensation under s. 4* of the Forfeiture Act 1870, as amended by s. 34†
of the Magistrates' Courts Act 1952 and the Criminal Law Act 1967, s. 10 (1)
and Sch. 2, para. 9. On applications by C. and J. for orders of certiorari
to quash the orders of compensation,

Held: since there was no person aggrieved pursuant to s. 4 of the For- D
feiture Act 1870, as amended, who made any application for compensation
before the justices, they had no jurisdiction to make those orders; accordingly, the applications for certiorari to quash the orders would be granted
at the discretion of the court (see p. 669, letter E, and p. 670, letters A
and B, post).

[As to powers of magistrates' courts to award compensation to parties E
aggrieved, see 25 HALSBURY'S LAWS (3rd Edn.) 231, para. 425;

For the Forfeiture Act 1870, s. 4, see 8 HALSBURY'S STATUTES (3rd Edn.)
180.

For the Magistrates' Courts Act 1952, s. 34, see 32 HALSBURY'S STATUTES
(2nd Edn.) 451.]

F

Motions for certiorari.

These were two applications by way of motion by William Donald Coppin
and Raymond John Jones for orders of certiorari to bring up and quash orders
of compensation in the sums of £500 and £400 respectively made by the Forest
justices, sitting at Bracknell on 1st April 1968 after the applicants had pleaded
guilty to ten and eight charges respectively of the larceny of motor vehicles G
in respect of which each applicant was in addition sentenced to suspended
sentences of six months' imprisonment. The facts are set out in the judgment
of LORD PARKER, C.J.

The cases below‡ were cited during the argument.

B. B. Rathbone for the applicants.
J. I. Murchie for the respondents.

H

LORD PARKER, C.J.: In these proceedings counsel moves on behalf of
the applicants, William Donald Coppin and Raymond John Jones, for orders of
certiorari to quash certain orders made on 1st April 1968 by the petty sessional
division of the Forest sitting at Bracknell whereby they ordered the applicants
Coppin and Jones to pay sums by way of compensation namely £500 and £400
respectively.

I

---

* Section 4, so far as material, is set out at p. 669, letter D, post.
† Section 34 provides: " Where a magistrates' court convicts a person of felony, the
court shall have the same power to award a sum of money to any person aggrieved as
a court of assize or quarter sessions has under section four of the Forfeiture Act, 1870;
and any sum so awarded shall be enforceable in the same way as costs ordered to be
paid by the offender."
‡ *R. v. Jones*, [1929] 1 K.B. 211; [1928] All E.R. Rep. 532; *R. v. Dorset Quarter Sessions*,
Ex p. Randall, [1966] 3 All E.R. 952; [1967] 2 Q.B. 227.

A   The matter arose in this way, that on 1st April 1968 the applicants appeared before the magistrates' court, it being known in advance that they were going to plead guilty, and they did duly plead guilty, the applicant Coppin to ten charges and the applicant Jones to eight charges of the larceny of motor vehicles. On each of these 18 convictions, the court sentenced them to six months' imprisonment which was suspended and in each case ordered the applicant to pay B   £50 by way of compensation. In addition, the vehicles concerned were restored under an order of restitution to their owners. It being known that the applicants were going to plead guilty, no witnesses were called and in particular the owners of the vehicles concerned were not called.

The first point taken here is that the magistrates' court had no jurisdiction whatever to make orders for compensation, because there was no person aggrieved C   before them. Section 4 of the Forfeiture Act 1870, which applied originally only to quarter sessions and assizes, has been extended to magistrates' courts by s. 34 of the Magistrates' Courts Act 1952. Section 4 of the Act of 1870 provides:

> " It shall be lawful for any such Court as aforesaid, if it shall think fit, upon the application of any person aggrieved, and immediately after the D   conviction of any person for felony, to award any sum of money, not exceeding one hundred pounds [that is now £400 (1)] by way of satisfaction or compensation for any loss of property suffered by the applicant through or by means of the said felony, and the amount awarded for such satisfaction or compensation shall be deemed a judgment debt due to the person entitled to receive the same from the person so convicted . . ."

E   As it seems to me, though highly technical, this is a fatal point. There was no person aggrieved who made any application before the justices. Counsel for the respondents says: the prosecution were asking for compensation for the owners and on behalf of the owners. There was not a shred of evidence that they were authorised to make any application by the owners and it is not really suggested. Indeed what really happened, and this shows how unmeritorious F   this case is, is that the applicants' solicitor feeling that they were at risk of imprisonment and seeking to secure their liberty, informed the court that the applicants would like to pay compensation. It was as the result of that that the justices made the orders for compensation. There is a conflict of evidence on the affidavits as to this; for myself I have no hesitation in accepting the evidence of the chairman of the bench, Mr. Allen, supported as it is by the G   prosecuting solicitor. It seems to me that the bench were persuaded to do this by the defence in order to secure the liberty of the applicants, and this they did. It is impossible, of course, to say what would have happened if the justices had realised that they could not make orders for compensation; they might well have committed to quarter sessions, they would certainly have been entitled to do, and it may well be that quarter sessions would have imposed a longer and H   immediate term of imprisonment.

The second point taken, which one need only deal with quite shortly having regard to the first, is that the justices, if they had jurisdiction, never exercised their discretion in the matter judicially in that they acted without any evidence of loss at all. As I have said, these cars were restored so far as possible to their owners, and there is no specific evidence that any owner ever lost anything; I   in fact having regard to the fact that these cars had been what is called " cannibalised ", it is perfectly possible that an owner would have got back something more valuable than was stolen from him. Finally, it may well be that the real losers here were the purchasers to whom the applicants had sold the vehicles who had to give back their title in the vehicles. However, that as it seems to me is a second and subsidiary point; the real point here is that the justices had in the

---

(1) Section 4 of the Forfeiture Act 1870 has been amended by the Criminal Law Act 1967, s. 10 (1) and Sch. 2, para. 9.

circumstances no jurisdiction to make these orders. That does not conclude **A** the matter, because there is a discretion finally in this court, and if the matter rested with me alone I think it only right to say that I would not exercise the discretion of this court in favour of orders of certiorari. I understand, however, that I am in a minority and accordingly, as it seems to me, the orders will have to go.

B

MELFORD STEVENSON, J.: With regret I agree.

BLAIN, J.: With equal regret I agree.

Order for certiorari.

Solicitors: *Bryan Williams*, Ascot (for the applicants); *E. R. Davies*, Reading (for the respondents).

C

[*Reported by* N. P. METCALFE, ESQ., *Barrister-at-Law.*]

PRITCHARD (Inspector of Taxes) *v.* M. H. BUILDERS (WILMSLOW), LTD.

D

[CHANCERY DIVISION (Cross, J.), December 9, 10, 1968.]

Income Tax—Discontinuance of trade—Carry-forward of trade losses—Trade belonging to same persons before and after transfer—Winding-up of company —Transfer of contracts to new company—Original company's and liquidator's ownership of new company's shares—Persons entitled to profits after transfer not entitled thereto before—Finance Act 1954 (2 & 3 Eliz. 2 c. 44), s. 17, Sch. 3.

E

Following losses leaving it with a deficiency of £430,000, including preferential creditors £24,000 (£123,000 less assets £99,000), unsecured creditors £376,000 and shareholders £30,000, a company resolved in December 1960 **F** to go into voluntary liquidation. However, it continued to carry on its trade of building and contracting through the liquidator. In March 1961 the taxpayer company was formed with a share capital of £100, of which the old company subscribed for 99 £1 shares and the liquidator for the other, and in January 1962 it purchased the goodwill, assets and benefit of contracts of the old company. The intention was that the taxpayer company should acquire the **G** trade of the old company and set-off for income tax purposes against any profits the old company's losses and that in due course its shares should be sold for the benefit of the creditors of the old company.

Held: the taxpayer company was not entitled to carry forward the trade losses of the old company against its own profits for income tax purposes, because—

H

(i) although the transfer of trade from the old company to the taxpayer company did not alter the class of persons " interested " in that trade, it was the liquidator's duty to deal with the taxpayer company's shares for the benefit of the same class of persons in the same priority (preferred creditors, unsecured creditors, shareholders) as previously with the profits and proceeds of realisation of the old company (see p. 673, letters H and I, post);

I

(ii) the true test was whether the trade " belonged " to the same persons before and after the transfer within the meaning of s. 17 (1)* of the Finance Act 1954, and the persons to whom it so belonged were the persons for the time being entitled to the income under the trust of which the liquidator was the trustee within s. 17 (4) (*b*)* and not the shareholders within s. 17 (5)* (see p. 673, letter I, to p. 674, letter A, post);

---

* Section 17, so far as material, is set out at p. 673, letters C to H, post.

A   (iii) even if the aggregate of persons interested in the liquidation having
a locus standi to apply to the court could be regarded collectively as the
beneficial owners of the taxpayer company's shares after the transfer, that
was not the position before the transfer, for no class of persons was then
entitled to the old company's profits; even if the preferred creditors had
joined together they would not have been able to compel the liquidator to
B   pay the profits to them, and the non-preferential creditors in any event
were not entitled to any part of them (see p. 675, letters C to E, post); and
      (iv) the persons to whom the trade belonged before and after the transfer
were therefore not the same (see p. 675, letter F, post).

      Appeal allowed.

C   [As to succession to a trade for income tax purposes, see 20 Halsbury's
Laws (3rd Edn.) 130-132, para. 231; and as to discontinuance where activities
are continued by some other person, see ibid., pp. 135, 136, para. 238; and for
cases on the subject, see 28 Digest (Repl.) 65-68, *240-253*, 70, *265-267*.

      For the Finance Act 1954, s. 17, Sch. 3, see 34 Halsbury's Statutes (2nd
Edn.) 296; 315; and for the repealing provisions of s. 61 (9) and s. 97 (5) of
and Sch. 22 to the Finance Act 1965, see 45 Halsbury's Statutes (2nd Edn.)
D   597, 648, 751.]

Cases referred to:
      Gartside v. *Inland Revenue Comrs.*, [1968] 1 All E.R. 121; [1968] A.C. 553;
            [1968] 2 W.L.R. 277.
      Oriental Inland Steam Co., Re, Ex p. Scinde Ry. Co. (1874), 9 Ch. App. 557;
E   43 L.J. Ch. 699; 31 L.T. 5; 10 Digest (Repl.) 903, *6137*.
      Stamp Duties (Comr. of) v. *Livingston*, [1964] 3 All E.R. 692; [1965] A.C. 694;
            [1964] 3 W.L.R. 963; Digest (Cont. Vol. B) 247, **258a*.

Case Stated.
      The taxpayer company appealed to the Special Commissioners of Income
Tax against an assessment to income tax for 1964-65 in the sum of £100, and
F   against the rejection by the inspector of taxes of a claim under s. 342 of the Income Tax Act 1952. The question for decision was whether trading losses of
£936 incurred by Milton Hindle, Ltd., in voluntary liquidation, should be
carried forward under the Finance Act 1954, s. 17, and Sch. 3, and allowed against
the assessment for 1964-65 on the trading profits of the taxpayer company*.
      The taxpayer company contended that under those provisions of the Act it
G   was entitled to deduct from or set-off against the amount of profits or gains of
its trade assessable for 1964-65, viz., £948, in addition to a loss of £12 incurred
by it, a loss of £936 incurred by Milton Hindle, Ltd. The inspector of taxes
contended that the provisions afforded no title to the taxpayer company to
deduct or set-off the loss of £936. The commissioners held† that s. 17 (1) of the
Finance Act 1954 applied and that under Sch. 3 the taxpayer company was
H   entitled to the deduction or set-off claimed. They allowed the appeal. They
increased the assessment appealed against to £948 with a deduction or set-off
of losses brought forward amounting to £948. The Crown appealed by way of
Case Stated to the High Court.

      E. I. Goulding, Q.C., *P. W. Medd* and *J. P. Warner* for the Crown.
      H. Major Allen, Q.C., and *B. Pinson* for the taxpayer company.

I
      CROSS, J.: The question raised by this case is whether trading losses
incurred by Milton Hindle, Ltd.—which I will call " the old company "—can
be carried forward under s. 17 of the Finance Act 1954 against the assessments
on the trading profits of the taxpayer company, M.H. Builders (Wilmslow), Ltd.
The old company was incorporated in 1955 and carried on the trade of builders

---

      * The facts of the Case are set out at letter I, above, to p. 673, letter C, post.
      † The terms of the commissioners' decision are set out at p. 674, letter B, to letter
I, post.

and contractors. In 1958 and 1959 it entered into several unprofitable contracts   A
with the Peterlee Development Corpn. and incurred losses of the order of
£400,000. In 1960 Mr. J. Moss, an accountant, was instructed to prepare a
statement of affairs of the old company. This showed assets available for
creditors of about £99,000, preferential creditors of £123,000 and ordinary unsecured creditors of £376,000. The capital of the company was 30,000 £1 ordinary
shares. So there was a deficiency as regards members of some £430,000 odd and a   B
deficiency as regards preferential creditors of £24,000 odd. In view of its insolvency it was decided that the old company should go into liquidation. The extent
of the insolvency was so great that it was difficult to interest the shareholders
of the old company in attending meetings to consider the company's future, and
on 26th November 1960 all the issued shares in the old company were transferred
to Mr. Moss and his partner in the firm of John W. Hirst and Co., a Mr. Frank   C
Buckley. The object of the transfers was to facilitate the passing of a resolution
to wind up the old company.

On 1st December 1960 the old company went into voluntary liquidation and
Mr. Moss was appointed liquidator. A meeting of creditors of the old company
pursuant to s. 293 of the Companies Act 1948 was held on 1st December 1960,
at which the draft statement of affairs prepared by Mr. Moss was laid before   D
the creditors. After the meeting Mr. Moss, the liquidator, induced Peterlee
Development Corpn. to alter the terms of the contracts entered into between it
and the old company. On the liquidation of the old company the corporation
were entitled to terminate the contracts entered into with the old company,
but Mr. Moss persuaded them to allow the old company to continue. Accordingly,
on 17th April 1961 the corporation entered into the agreement with the old   E
company acting by its liquidator whereby, to enable work to be started again
under these contracts, the corporation agreed to the employment of the old
company under the contracts being re-instated and continued subject to certain
variations of the terms. Thereafter the old company continued to carry on its
trade of building and contracting through its liquidator.

In March 1961 there was incorporated a company called Memomiths, Ltd.,   F
with a capital of £100 divided into 100 £1 shares. The old company subscribed
for 99 shares in this company and the liquidator bought one share subscribed
on the formation of the company. On 1st December 1961 Memomiths, Ltd.,
changed its name to Milton Hindle, Ltd., and in November 1963 to M. H.
Builders (Wilmslow), Ltd. (the taxpayer company).

On 27th October 1961 Mr. Moss, the liquidator of the old company, and Mr.   G
Buckley were appointed the first directors of the taxpayer company. A meeting
of the directors of the taxpayer company was held on 26th January 1962, the
minutes of which read as follows:

" 1. The Chairman directed it be recorded that the 100 issued shares of
£1 each were nil paid at the date of this Meeting.
" 2. IT WAS RESOLVED: THAT the Company do purchase the goodwill, assets   H
and benefit of contracts of Milton Hindle Limited (in voluntary liquidation)
upon the terms of the Agreement now produced and that Mr. J. Moss be
authorised to sign such Agreement on behalf of the [taxpayer] Company
and that the [taxpayer] Company do carry on such business accordingly.
" 3. IT WAS RESOLVED: THAT out of the moneys due from the [taxpayer]
Company to Milton Hindle Limited (in voluntary liquidation) pursuant to   I
the Agreement for Sale £100 be appropriated in payment up in full at par
the 100 issued shares in the capital of the [taxpayer] Company registered
in the names of Milton Hindle Limited (in voluntary liquidation) and
James Moss."

On the same date the taxpayer company entered into an agreement with the
old company acting by its liquidator to purchase the goodwill of the old company
for £100, its plant, machinery, vehicles, etc., for £1,500 and the benefits of its

A contracts in consideration of an indemnity against costs, claims and demands arising under the contracts.

The share register of the taxpayer company shows that on 27th October 1961 one share was registered in the name of James Moss and 99 shares in that of the old company (in voluntary liquidation). The taxpayer company was formed and its shares subscribed for by the old company with the intention that the

B taxpayer company should acquire the trade of the old company with the hoped for advantage for income tax purposes of having set against any profits it made the losses incurred by the old company amounting to some £400,000 and that the shares of the taxpayer company should in due course be sold for the benefit of the creditors of the old company. The committee of inspection of the creditors of the old company were aware of the reasons for the formation of the taxpayer

C company and the subscription for shares therein and raised no objection.

I must now refer to the relevant provisions of s. 17 of the Finance Act 1954:

" (1) A trade carried on by a company, whether alone or in partnership, shall not be treated for any of the purposes of the Income Tax Acts as permanently discontinued, nor a new trade as set up and commenced, by reason of a change in the year 1954-55 or any subsequent year of assessment

D in the persons engaged in carrying on the trade, if the company is the person or one of the persons so engaged immediately before the change and on or at any time within two years after the change the trade or an interest amounting to not less than a three-fourths share in it belongs to the same persons as the trade or such an interest belonged to at some time within a year before the change. . .

E " (4) For the purposes of this section—[and I need not read para. (*a*)] (*b*) a trade or interest therein belonging to any person as trustee (otherwise than for charitable or public purposes) shall be treated as belonging to the persons for the time being entitled to the income under the trust . . .

" (5) For the purposes of this section, a trade or interest therein which belongs to a company engaged in carrying it on may be regarded—(*a*) as

F belonging to the persons owning the ordinary share capital of the company and as belonging to them in proportion to the amount of their holdings of that capital. . . .

" (6) For the purposes of the last foregoing subsection—[i.e., sub-s. (5)] (*a*) references to ownership shall be construed as references to beneficial ownership. . . .

G " (7) In determining, for the purposes of this section, whether or to what extent a trade belongs at different times to the same persons, persons who are relatives of one another and the persons from time to time entitled to the income under any trust shall respectively be treated as a single person, and for this purpose ' relative ' means husband, wife, ancestor, lineal descendant, brother or sister."

H The transfer of the trade from the old company to the taxpayer company on 26th January 1962 did not bring about any change in the class of persons who were, to use a neutral term, " interested " in it. Immediately before the transfer it was the duty of the liquidator to carry on the trade or to realise it together with the other assets of the company and apply the profits and proceeds in the manner laid down by the Companies Act 1948, viz., first in discharging all the preferred

I debts and ultimately, if there was any surplus, for the benefit of the shareholders. After the transfer it was the duty of the liquidator to use the control of the taxpayer company given him by the shares in it which the old company held and to deal with those shares for the benefit of the same class of person in the same order of priority. The question is whether the trade can be said to have " belonged " to those persons before and after the transfer within the meaning of the section. In this connection it is to be observed that the section appears to apply different tests to the two situations. After the transfer the question appears to be: Who, if anyone, can be said to be the beneficial owners of the shares in the taxpayer

z

company? But sub-s. (5) cannot very well apply to an insolvent company in liquidation. It is sub-s. (4) (b) which may apply to that situation, and that raises the question: Who, if anyone, is entitled to the profits of the trade—they being the income under the relevant trust?

The Commissioners held that the section applied and they gave their reasons in writing as follows:

"When the Old Company went into liquidation its assets remained vested in the Old Company but ceased to be beneficially owned by the Old Company. In the course of his judgment in *Re Oriental Inland Steam Co., Ex p. Scinde Ry. Co.* (1), JAMES, L.J., said: 'The English Act of Parliament has enacted that in the case of a winding-up the assets of the company so wound up are to be collected and applied in discharge of its liabilities. That makes the property of the company clearly trust property. It is property affected by the Act of Parliament with an obligation to be dealt with by the proper officer in a particular way. Then it has ceased to be beneficially the property of the company; and, being so, it has ceased to be liable to be seized by the execution creditors of the company'. After it had gone into liquidation the Old Company, with the knowledge and, we infer, with the tacit consent of its creditors, applied some of its cash in acquiring the issued shares of the [taxpayer] Company. In these circumstances it appeared to us, and we so held, that the persons beneficially entitled to the assets of the Old Company must be the same persons as those beneficially entitled to the shares in the [taxpayer] Company. Under the provisions of Sub-section (4) (b) of Section 17 of the Finance Act, 1954, the trade of the Old Company must be taken to have belonged to the persons entitled to the profits of that trade. Following the winding-up order the property of the Old Company became trust property and the profits of the trade carried on by the Old Company through its liquidator were, we think, impressed with the same trust. On the facts as disclosed by the approximate statement of affairs we were of opinion that the post-liquidation assets and profits of the Old Company were trust property which the liquidator was bound to apply for the benefit of the secured and/or preferential creditors. By virtue of the provisions of Sub-section (4) (c), (5) and (6) (a) of Section 17, the trade carried on by the [taxpayer] Company after 26th January, 1962, is to be treated as belonging to the persons beneficially owning the ordinary share capital of the company. The shares in the [taxpayer] Company were owned by the Old Company but were held as trust property which the liquidator was bound to apply for the benefit of the secured and/or preferential creditors. It follows, therefore, that up to 26th January, the trade of the Old Company must be treated as belonging to the secured and/or preferential creditors and that after that date the same trade as carried on by the [taxpayer] Company is to be treated as belonging to those same persons. In these circumstances we held that the provisions of Section 17 (1) applied and that under the provisions of the Third Schedule to the Finance Act, 1954, the [taxpayer] Company was entitled to the deduction or set-off claimed. We accordingly increased the assessment appealed against to £948 with a deduction or set-off of losses brought forward amounting to £948."

I am not sure why the commissioners referred as they did to the "secured and preferential creditors". I should not have thought that the liquidator was concerned with the secured creditors save insofar as their securities might prove insufficient so that they became ordinary unsecured creditors. Again, although on the figures it appears unlikely that there will be anything for the creditors who are not preferred—let alone for the shareholders—I do not think that one should disregard their theoretical rights in construing the section. The question, as I see it, is whether the section can apply to a trust under which the trustee

(1) (1874), 9 Ch. App. 557 at p. 559.

A has to realise property and apply the proceeds so far as they will go in discharging claims in an order of priority and in distributing any surplus among a class of ultimate beneficiaries.   Whether persons who are interested in having a trust carried out and can apply to the court for an order for its execution can be said to be beneficially entitled to the trust property and its income as it accrues depends on the nature of the trust.   In the case of an ordinary trust for the

B payment of the income to A. for life with remainder as to capital for B. on A.'s death, A. is beneficially entitled to the income.   On the other hand, a residuary legatee who is entitled to the ultimate surplus remaining after the executor has discharged the debts, duties and legacies is not entitled to the income or capital during the administration.   The beneficial ownership is in suspense (see *Comr. of Stamp Duties* v. *Livingston* (2)).   In the case of a discretionary trust, the

C answer to the question may possibly depend on whether or not there is a power of accumulation (see the recent discussion in *Gartside* v. *Inland Revenue Comrs.* (3) in the House of Lords).

   But even assuming in favour of the taxpayer company that the aggregate of persons who are interested in the liquidation and all or any of whom, theoretically at any rate, have a locus standi to apply to the court can be regarded collectively

D as the beneficial owners of the taxpayer company's shares within the meaning of sub-s. (5) and sub-s. (6), I find it impossible to apply sub-s. (4) (*b*) to the situation obtaining *before* the transfer.   No doubt the old company had no beneficial interest in the trade and was in some sense a trustee of it, but no class of persons was for the time being entitled to the profits.   Even if all the preferred creditors had joined together they could not have compelled the liquidator to pay the

E profits to them.   Moreover, if one were to take the view that sub-s. (4) (*b*) must be made to apply to the case, the persons to whom the trade belonged before the transfer would certainly only be the preferred creditors for by no stretch of the imagination could the ordinary unsecured creditors be regarded as persons entitled to the income before the transfer.   In that case, however, the persons to whom the trade belonged before and after the transfer would not be

F the same, for I can see no reason for saying that *after* the transfer the preferred creditors were the sole beneficial owners of the shares in the taxpayer company to the exclusion of the ordinary creditors and/or the shareholders in the old company.   For these reasons I shall allow this appeal.

Appeal allowed.

G Solicitors: *Solicitor of Inland Revenue*; *Slater, Heelis & Co.*, Manchester (for the taxpayer company).

[*Reported by* F. A. AMIES, ESQ., *Barrister-at-Law.*]

H

I

(2) [1964] 3 All E.R. 692; [1965] A.C. 694.
(3) [1968] 1 All E.R. 121; [1968] A.C. 553.

THE PUTBUS.

A

OWNERS ETC. OF THE SHIP ZENATIA v. OWNERS OF THE SHIP PUTBUS.

[COURT OF APPEAL, CIVIL DIVISION (Lord Denning, M.R., Edmund Davies and Phillimore, L.JJ.), February 20, 21, March 7, 1969.]

Admiralty—Arrest of vessel—Release of vessel following provision of security— B
Order of foreign court limiting liability and for payment into court—Pro-
ceedings in foreign court in respect of wreck-raising expenses not yet com-
menced—Whether claim for wreck-raising expenses subject to limitation
—Whether court would exercise discretion and release security—Merchant
Shipping Act 1894 (57 & 58 Vict. c. 60), s. 503 (1), as amended—Merchant
Shipping (Liability of Shipowners and Others) Act 1958 (6 & 7 Eliz. 2 c. 62),
s. 5 (2), (4) (c).

C

Following a collision in a Dutch waterway between the plaintiffs' ship, Zenatia, and the defendants' ship, Stubbenkammer, the latter sank and her wreck had to be removed by the appropriate Dutch authority to clear the waterway for navigation. The defendants limited their liability in a Dutch court to a sum equivalent to £41,000, which was very nearly the same as the limit of liability under English law would have been. They paid that D sum into the court at Rotterdam. The plaintiffs issued a writ in rem claiming damages against the defendants. The Putbus (a sister ship of The Stubbenkammer), then in the Port of London, was arrested on their application. The defendants furnished a letter of undertaking limited to £30,000 and The Putbus was released. The defendants moved that the security in £30,000 for The Putbus should be released because they had E already provided security in Rotterdam.

Held: the security for £30,000 for The Putbus should be discharged, because—

(i) the type of liability of the defendants to the Dutch authority being the same as in English law, it was a type to which a limit was set by s. 503 (1) of the Merchant Shipping Act 1894, as amended, since it was a liability to F damages where rights were infringed within s. 503 (1) (*d*), as amended; accordingly, under s. 5 (4) (*c*)* of the Merchant Shipping (Liability of Ship-owners and Others) Act 1958, such part of the £41,000 as corresponded to the plaintiffs' claim would be actually available to them and the conditions imposed by s. 5 (2) of the Act of 1958 had been fulfilled (see p. 679, letters E and H, p. 682, letter E, and p. 683, letter H, post); G

(ii) the discretion of the court under s. 5 of the Act of 1958 had been exercised wrongly since the possibility that the Dutch authority might not treat a finding of an English court as res judicata was so hypothetical that it ought to be disregarded (see p. 680, letters B and C, p. 682, letter I, to p. 683, letter A, and p. 683, letter I, post).

Decision of KARMINSKI, J. ([1968] 3 All E.R. 849), reversed in part. H

[As to release on security in limitation of liability cases, see 1 HALSBURY'S LAWS (3rd Edn.) 81, para. 170; and SUPPLEMENT thereto, para. 180A.

As to wreck-raising expenses, see 35 HALSBURY'S LAWS (3rd Edn.) 773, 774, para. 1189; and for a case on the subject, see 42 DIGEST (Repl.) 962, *7501*.

For the Merchant Shipping Act 1894, s. 503, see 23 HALSBURY'S STATUTES (2nd Edn.) 656. I

For the Merchant Shipping (Liability of Shipowners and Others) Act 1958, s. 5, see 38 HALSBURY'S STATUTES (2nd Edn.) 1096.]

Cases referred to:

Dee Conservancy Board v. *McConnell*, [1928] All E.R. Rep. 554; [1928] 2 K.B. 159; 97 L.J.K.B. 487; 138 L.T. 656; 92 J.P. 54; 47 Digest (Repl.) 755, *932*.

---

* Section 5 (4) (*c*) is set out at p. 678, letter H, post.

A   *Ella, The,* [1915] P. 111; 84 L.J.K.B. 97; 42 Digest (Repl.) 960, *7482.*

Green v. *Premier Glynrhonwy Slate Co., Ltd.,* [1928] 1 K.B. 561; 97 L.J.K.B. 32; 138 L.T. 90; 44 Digest (Repl.) 268, *943.*

Millie, The, [1940] P. 1; 109 L.J.P. 17; 161 L.T. 280; 42 Digest (Repl.) 1073, *8882.*

Stonedale No. 1, The, Abel (Richard) & Sons, Ltd. v. *Manchester Ship Canal Co.,*
B   [1954] 2 All E.R. 170; [1954] P. 338; [1954] 2 W.L.R. 1075; *affd.,* H.L., [1955] 2 All E.R. 689; [1956] A.C. 1; [1955] 3 W.L.R. 203; [1955] 2 Lloyd's Rep. 9; 42 Digest (Repl.) 1073, *8883.*

Interlocutory appeal.

This was an appeal by the defendants, the owners of The Putbus, from an order of KARMINSKI, J., dated 10th October 1968, and reported [1968] 3 All E.R.
C 849, dismissing their motion for an order under the Merchant Shipping (Liability of Shipowners and Others) Act 1958, s. 5, that the security given by them to obtain the release from arrest of The Putbus be released, or alternatively for a declaration that the plaintiffs, the owners and demise charterers of The Zenatia, were not entitled to enforce the letter of undertaking accepted by them as security for their claim as provided by the defendants to obtain the release from
D arrest of The Putbus. The facts are set out in the judgment of LORD DENNING, M.R.

The cases noted below* were cited during the argument in addition to the cases referred to in the judgments.

A. J. L. Lloyd, Q.C., and *N. A. Phillips* for the plaintiffs.

B. C. Sheen, Q.C., and *Michael Thomas* for the defendants.

E
Cur. adv. vult.

7th March. The following judgments were read.

LORD DENNING, M.R.: On 25th November 1967, there was a collision between two ships in the approach to the New Waterway at Rotterdam. One
F was a small East German vessel, The Stubbenkammer. The other was a big English tanker, The Zenatia. The Stubbenkammer sank. The Dutch government decided to raise the wreck of The Stubbenkammer and remove it because it obstructed the approaches to the New Waterway. On 26th April 1968, the defendants, the owners of The Stubbenkammer, applied to the district court at Rotterdam to fix the amount to which their liability was limited. On 17th May 1968, the Rotterdam court fixed the amount at 353,653 guilders and 47 cents.
G That was about £40,771 13s. 6d. in sterling. The defendants paid it into the court at Rotterdam. On 26th May 1968, the sister ship of The Stubbenkammer entered the Port of London. She was The Putbus and owned by the defendants. On 27th May 1968, the plaintiffs, the English owners of The Zenatia, brought an Admiralty action in rem against the defendants, claiming compensation for damages suffered by reason of the collision. The plaintiffs applied to arrest
H The Putbus and she was arrested on that day. The damage to The Zenatia was not likely to exceed £30,000. On 28th May 1968, the defendants provided security in £30,000 to meet the claim of the plaintiffs arising out of the collision. It was given by W. K. Webster & Co., and was in these words:

" To the owners and/or the demised charterers of the ' Zenatia ' . . . we
I guarantee to pay to you on demand such sums as may be found due to you from the owners of the ' Stubbenkammer ' in respect of your claims, together with interest and costs by the High Court of Justice in England or such sum as otherwise may be agreed provided that our total liability hereunder shall not exceed the sum of £30,000 plus interest and costs or the limit of liability of the Owners of the ' Stubbenkammer ' calculated in

---

* *The Kronprinz Olav,* [1921] P. 52; *The Theems,* [1938] P. 197; *Hall Bros. S.S. Co., Ltd.* v. *Young,* [1939] 1 All E.R. 809; [1939] 1 K.B. 748; *The Arabert,* [1961] 2 All E.R. 385; [1961] P. 102; *The Anne Hay,* [1968] 1 All E.R. 657; [1968] 2 W.L.R. 353.

A

accordance with the English Merchants Shipping Acts plus interest and costs whichever shall be the lesser amount."

The limit of liability under English law would be very nearly the same as in Dutch law. It would be £40,705 18s. 4½d. The plaintiffs accepted that guarantee as security for their claim. On 29th May 1968, The Putbus was released from arrest. The defendants now say that, having provided the limitation fund in Rotterdam for the £40,771 13s. 6d., they should not also be compelled to give security in London. So, on 14th June 1968, they applied that the guarantee given in England should be released. On 4th October 1968, KARMINSKI, J. (1), refused to release the guarantee. The defendants appeal to this court.

B

The application to release is made under s. 5 of the Merchant Shipping (Liability of Shipowners and Others) Act 1958. We are told that it is the first time that that section has had to be interpreted by the courts. It was enacted in pursuance of the international convention signed in Brussels on 10th October 1957. It has been ratified by 17 countries, including the United Kingdom, but the ratification by the United Kingdom was subject to two reservations. We have looked into the convention, as we are entitled to do. The object is plain enough. If a ship is involved in a collision in circumstances in which the owner is entitled to limit his liability, then he should only be compelled to provide a limitation fund once and for all. If he makes it available in one country to meet all the limited claims, he should not be compelled to put up security for those claims in another country; or, if he is compelled to do so, he should be able to get the additional security released. Although such is the object of the convention, there are special considerations in respect of the cost of wreck-raising and wreck-removal; and the United Kingdom, when ratifying the convention, made a reservation on this point. So we cannot get much guidance from the convention in respect of wreck-raising or wreck-removal. We have to go by the Act of Parliament.

C

D

E

I will not read the section. It is not a piece of English. It is only a collection of word-symbols. The only thing to do is to take it word by word and phrase by phrase and try to apply it to this case. It appears from s. 5 (1) and (2) (a), (b), that, in order to get the security released, the defendants must satisfy these conditions: (i) Under s. 5 (2) (b), the defendants must show that the £40,771 13s. 6d. (which they have provided in Rotterdam in respect of their liabilities) is equal to or more than the limit under the English Acts, namely, £40,705 18s. 4½d. That condition is clearly fulfilled. (ii) Under s. 5 (2) (a), the defendants must show that such part of that £40,771 13s. 6d. " as corresponds to the claim " of the plaintiffs will be actually available to them. Those words " as corresponds to the claim " are the crucial words in the case. In order to understand what they mean, we have to go to s. 5 (4) (c). We were told that it is supposed to be a dictionary, but, if so, it is the worst dictionary that I ever did see. It is quite unintelligible. It provides:

F

G

H

" where part only of the amount for which a guarantee was given will be available to a claimant that part shall not be taken to correspond to his claim if any other part may be available to a claimant in respect of a liability to which no limit is set as mentioned . . ."

in s. 503 (1) of the Merchant Shipping Act 1894, as amended by s. 1 of the Merchant Shipping (Liability of Shipowners and Others) Act 1900 and s. 2 of the Act of 1958.

I

I will apply that subsection as best I can. " The amount for which a guarantee was given " is the amount of £40,771 13s. 6d. which the defendants gave at Rotterdam. " Part only of " that £40,771 13s. 6d. will be available to the plaintiffs; because there is another claimant, namely, the Dutch government, whose claim may be £100,000, or more. There is, therefore an " other part " of

(1) [1968] 3 All E.R. 849; [1968] 3 W.L.R. 1003.

A the £40,771 13s. 6d. which may be available to that claimant, the Dutch
government. So the question is whether that "other part" may be available
"in respect of a liability to which no limit is set" by s. 503 (1), as amended,
of the Merchant Shipping Act 1894. It comes ultimately to this: what is the
nature of the liability of the defendants to the Dutch government? Is it a
liability to which a limit is set by s. 503 (1), as amended, or not? If no limit is
B set by s. 503, then the part available to the plaintiffs does not "correspond to
[their] claim"; but, if it is a liability to which a limit is set by s. 503 (1), as
amended, then it does "correspond to [their] claim". Seeing that this is a
liability arising under Dutch law, this must mean: is it a *type of liability* to
which a limit is set by s. 503 (1), as amended, or not?

In order to ascertain the type of liability, there was expert evidence as to
C Dutch law. It showed quite clearly that the liability of the defendants to the
Dutch government depended on whether The Stubbenkammer was at fault or
not. If she was at fault, then the defendants were liable, otherwise not. That
is a liability of a type which is imposed by the common law of England, namely,
a liability to damages for negligence. By our English law there is a public right
of passage through our navigable channels, whether in a port or the approaches
D to it. That right is infringed when, through negligence on the part of the owners,
a vessel has sunk in such a position as to cause obstruction in the channel. The
public authority concerned—the port authority, or the Crown, as the case may
be—is in duty bound to remove the obstruction, and, having done so, it has a
common law right to recover against the owners, *as damages*, the reasonable
cost of the work: see *The Ella* (2); and *Dee Conservancy Board* v. *McConnell* (3).
E The type of liability in Dutch law is, therefore, the same as in English law.
Is it a type to which a limit is set by s. 503 (1), as amended? I think that it is.
First of all, it is a liability to *damages* for negligence, and not a liability to pay
a *debt*. Thus, it is quite different from *The Stonedale No. 1, Richard Abel & Sons,
Ltd.* v. *Manchester Ship Canal Co.* (4), when the liability was in *debt*, irrespective
of negligence. Secondly, it was liability to damages "where rights are in-
F fringed"; for the right of public passage is infringed through the negligent
act or omission which caused the obstruction. Those words "where . . . rights
are infringed" were inserted by s. 2 (1) of the Act of 1958, so as to fill the gap
disclosed by *The Millie* (5). The draftsman has taken the very words used
by Langton, J. We are, therefore, able to answer the question which Viscount
Simonds left open in *The Stonedale No. 1* (6), when he said:

G   "It may have to be decided some day whether a shipowner faced with
such a common law claim can successfully limit his liability in respect of
it . . ."

under the Merchant Shipping Acts. The answer is that he can do so.

Seeing that it is a type of liability to which a limit is set (and not *no* limit),
it follows that, under s. 5 (4) (c) of the Act of 1958, such part of the £40,771 13s. 6d.
H " as corresponds to the claim " of the plaintiffs will be actually available to them.
So the condition in s. 5 (2) (a) is fulfilled. In view of this line of reasoning, I
need not consider s. 2 (2) of the Act of 1958, which has not yet come into force.
It covers wreck-raising and wreck-removing where there is no negligence, and
does not apply to this case. The defendants have satisfied, therefore, both the
conditions set out in s. 5 (2); and, the conditions being fulfilled, the court may
I order the release of the security. It is in the discretion of the court. (If the
collision had been within the boundaries of the port of Rotterdam, the court
would have had no discretion, but would have been compelled to release the
security; see s. 5 (3).)

(2) [1915] P. 111.
(3) [1928] 2 K.B. 159; [1928] All E.R. Rep. 554.
(4) [1955] 2 All E.R. 689; [1956] A.C. 1.
(5) [1940] P. 1.
(6) [1955] 2 All E.R. at p. 693; [1956] A.C. at p. 9.

Thus far, I am glad to find myself in agreement with KARMINSKI, J. (7). But now we come to the question of discretion. The judge has exercised his discretion by refusing to release the security. He was influenced chiefly by the fact that, if this action were fought out in England and The Stubbenkammer held wholly to blame, the Dutch government might contest the apportionment in limitation proceedings in Holland. The Dutch court, he said (8), would not treat the matter as res judicata. And, in the result, the plaintiffs might need their English security. This is, I think, a mere hypothetical possibility. It is of no practical significance. The Dutch government have no evidence of the cause of the collision and would, no doubt, accept the finding of our English court. The judge was also influenced by the small amount of interest payable in Rotterdam on the limitation fund as compared to England; and also by the fact that the undertaking amounting to £30,000 costs the defendants nothing. But the judge did not give much weight to these.

I am afraid that I cannot agree with the way in which the judge exercised his discretion. In my opinion, save in exceptional cases, the discretion should be exercised by releasing the security. The object of the convention was that a shipowner should be able to get his ships released by putting up the limitation fund in one country only; and that, when he has put it up in one country, he should not be called on to put it up in another. We achieve that object better by releasing the guarantee given here in London than by retaining it. I would, therefore, allow the appeal.

EDMUND DAVIES, L.J.: Were bewilderment the legitimate aim of statutes, the Merchant Shipping (Liability of Shipowners and Others) Act 1958 would clearly be entitled to a high award. Indeed, the deep gloom which its tortuosities induced in me has been lifted only by the happy discovery that my attempts to construe them have led me to the same conclusion as my brethren.

I have been compelled to proceed by cautious stages. Section 503 (1) of the Merchant Shipping Act 1894, as amended, fixes both the starting and the terminal points of the problem. It enables the owners of a British or foreign ship to limit their liability to pay *damages* (that word is important) to certain maximum amounts in respect of certain occurrences which have taken place "without their actual fault or privity". One of these occurrences, introduced by s. 2 (1) of the Act of 1958, is—

"(d) where . . . any rights are infringed through the act or omission of any person . . . in the navigation or management of the ship"

and it is clear from the context that what is here contemplated is an infringement of rights by reason of a *blameworthy* act or omission. Section 2 (2) also has its impact on s. 503 (1) of the Act of 1894. It provides that—

"For the purposes of the said subsection (1), where any obligation or liability arises—(a) in connection with the raising, removal or destruction of any ship which is sunk . . . or (b) in respect of any damage (however caused) to . . . navigable waterways, the occurrence giving rise to the obligation or liability shall be treated as one of the occurrences mentioned in paragraphs (b) and (d) of that subsection, and the obligation or liability as a liability to damages."

Paragraph (a) is not yet in force (see s. 2 (5)). When it is, the result will be that, where there is any liability to pay wreck-raising costs even though the shipowners' servants were not at fault, that liability will have to be treated as one to pay damages and can, therefore, be limited by virtue of s. 503 (1).

Section 5 (1) of the Act of 1958 provides for the release of a ship arrested—

(7) [1968] 3 All E.R. 849; [1968] 3 W.L.R. 1003.
(8) [1968] 3 All E.R. at p. 852; [1968] 3 W.L.R. at p. 1008.

A   ". . . in connection with a claim which appears to the court to be founded on a liability to which a limit is set by section five hundred and three . . ."

If security is given for its release, that security may in its turn be discharged if the conditions specified in s. 5 (2) are satisfied. That subsection plunges us into deep waters. But the worst is still to come, for (as though bent on preventing us from ever reaching the farther shore) s. 5 (4) provides that:

B   " For the purpose of this section— . . . (c) where part only of the amount for which a guarantee was given will be available to a claimant that part shall not be taken to correspond to his claim *if any other part may be available to a claimant in respect of a liability to which no limit is set as mentioned in subsection (1) of this section.*"

C   This obscure provision tempts one to adopt feelingly the words of Scrutton, L.J., in *Green* v. *Premier Glynrhonwy Slate Co., Ltd.* (9), when he said, in relation to another statute:

". . . if I am asked whether I have arrived at the meaning of the words which Parliament intended I say frankly that I have not the slightest idea."

D   But, while tempted to echo those words, I do not dismiss the problem of construction as wholly beyond solution. Respectfully, but far less athletically, following in the wake of Lord Denning, M.R., I, too, have come to the conclusion that the outcome of this regrettable (and surely avoidable) obscurity is that the basic question ultimately to be answered may be propounded by asking: is the liability of the defendants to the Dutch government one to
E   which a limit is set by s. 503 (1), as amended? More strictly—such liability arising only under Dutch law—the vital question is whether the liability of the defendants to the Dutch government is a *type* of liability to which a limit is set by s. 503 (1), as amended.

The Dutch Wreck Removal Act 1934 provides that vessels sunk in public waters may be removed by the authority under whose control the water is
F   (art. 1), and that, insofar as any costs incurred are not re-imbursed either by the parties interested or by sale of the salvaged goods—

" the said costs are at the charge of the authority, but without prejudice to its right to claim the said costs from the person who according to the law is responsible " (art. 10).

Responsibility under Dutch law is governed by art. 1401 of the Civil Code,
G   which provides that—

" Any wrongful act causing damage to a person imposes upon the person by whose fault the damage has been caused the obligation to make good the damage."

The right of the Dutch government to recover wreck-raising costs is thus
H   dependent on " fault ". It is, therefore, similar to English law, which provides that where through negligence a vessel has sunk in such a position as to cause an obstruction in navigable channels, the conservancy authority has (in addition to any statutory remedy it may possess) a common law right to recover against the owners as *damages* the reasonable cost of removing the obstruction: see *Dee Conservancy Board* v. *McConnell* (10). Seemingly, there is no right under
I   Dutch law similar to that which (as appears from *The Stonedale No. 1* (11)) was conferred by the Manchester Ship Canal Act 1936 on the Manchester Ship Canal Co. of recovering from the owners of any obstructing vessel the cost of removing it, *regardless* of whether they have been negligent. In *The Stonedale No. 1* (11), the House of Lords held that such expenses (being sued for under the Act of 1936) were recoverable as a *debt* and not as damages, and that, accordingly,

(9) [1928] 1 K.B. 561 at p. 566.
(10) [1928] 2 K.B. 159; [1928] All E.R. Rep. 554.
(11) [1955] 2 All E.R. 689; [1956] A.C. 1.

even though the owners had been negligent, this fact did not enable them to limit their liability by virtue of s. 503 of the Act of 1894. But, contemplating what the position might be had the claim been one for damages at common law by reason of the negligence of the shipowners having led to the obstruction of a navigable channel, VISCOUNT SIMONDS said (12):

" It may have to be decided some day whether a shipowner faced with such a common law claim can successfully limit his liability in respect of it . . ."

That day has arrived and a decision is now called for.

As I view this case, the basic fact is that The Stubbenkammer was confessedly at fault and the defendants are, accordingly, liable to the Dutch government for the wreck-raising costs. But, submits counsel for the plaintiffs, that means that the Dutch government claim is one which arises, in the words of s. 2 (2) of the Act of 1958, " (a) in connection with the raising . . . of any ship which is sunk . . ." He then points out that (by virtue of s. 2 (5)) such a claim is not yet to be treated as an " occurrence " within s. 503 (1) of the Act of 1894, as amended, and submits that the liability in respect of it is, accordingly, not to be treated as " a liability to damages ". I have come to the conclusion that that is a wrong approach. Section 2 (2) (a) deals with obligations in respect of wreck-raising costs simpliciter and regardless of negligence. It leaves unaffected any " obligation or liability " in respect of wreck-raising costs where the obstructing ship has sunk owing to negligence. I answer the question posed by VISCOUNT SIMONDS in *The Stonedale No. 1* (12) in the same manner as LORD DENNING, M.R., by saying that, where such negligence exists, a common law claim to recover wreck-raising costs sounds in damages. The liability would, accordingly, be one arising from the fact that " rights are infringed through the act or omission of any person . . . in the navigation or management of the ship " within the meaning of s. 503 (1) (d) of the Act of 1894, as amended, and it may, therefore, be limited.

For these reasons, I hold: (A) that the conditions imposed by s. 5 (2) of the Act of 1958 are fulfilled; and (B) that the liability of the defendants to the Dutch government is a *type* of liability to which a limit is set by s. 503 (1), as amended. It follows that, in my opinion, KARMINSKI, J., was right in adjudicating that he had a discretion whether or not to accede to the defendants' application for release of the security. But I am respectfully unable to agree with the learned judge in his refusal thereafter to exercise that discretion in the defendants' favour on the ground that (13):

". . . counsel [for the defendants'] argument depends on the certainty that the Dutch court would consider itself bound by the decision of this court on the issue of liability as between the plaintiffs and the defendants. I accept that the Dutch court might be slow to reject such a finding, but I am satisfied that the Dutch court would not and could not treat the matter as res judicata binding the Dutch government authority, who are not parties to the English proceedings."

Were such reasoning to be adopted generally, there seems much to be said for counsel for the defendants' submission that it would make s. 5 of the Act of 1958 largely nugatory. One could scarcely ever be quite certain that res judicata would prevail, and, were this uncertainty to be regarded as decisive, a very useful provision, born of the Brussels Convention of 1957 and intended to provide a useful remedy at a very early stage, would be rendered quite useless. Ought this unfortunate result be allowed to follow? I prefer to look at the realities of the situation by considering what are the overwhelming probabilities. Counsel for the plaintiffs described the res judicata point as " very difficult ". But, like LORD DENNING, M.R., I regard the idea that the Dutch government would (for all practical purposes) decline to treat as res judicata a finding by the

(12) [1955] 2 All E.R. at p. 693; [1956] A.C. at p. 9.
(13) [1968] 3 All E.R. at p. 853; [1968] 3 W.L.R. at p. 1009.

A British court on the issue of " fault " as a possibility so hypothetical that it ought to be disregarded in considering how the discretion under s. 5 should be exercised.

The learned trial judge adverted to two further considerations, but understandably said (14) that they did " no more than to add some modest weight ". It seems doubtful that he would have decided as he did on those other matters
B alone, for he said (14) of the res judicata point that it was " the most important " and that " by itself it would be decisive ". With profound respect, I think that counsel for the defendants is right in saying that the judgment paid insufficient attention to the difficult position of the defendants. Furthermore, the comity intended to be fostered by the Brussels Convention of 1957 (which by its preamble " recognised the desirability of determining by agreement certain
C uniform rules relating to the limitations of the liability of the owners of sea-going ships ") would be endangered by the adoption generally of the approach which led to the defendants being denied the relief they here sought.

For these reasons, I also would allow this appeal.

PHILLIMORE, L.J.: I entirely agree, but I would add a few words if
D only in deference to the able argument of counsel for the plaintiffs. There are two points in this appeal: (i) Were the defendants entitled under English law to limit their liability in Holland? (ii) If so, was the learned judge (15) right in the exercise of his discretion in refusing to release the security given in this country?

The first question depends on the wording of s. 503 (1) of the Merchant Shipping Act 1894, as amended. Omitting words which do not apply to the
E present case, the vital words are:

" The owners of a ship, British or foreign, shall not . . . (d) where . . . any rights are infringed through the act or omission of any person (whether on board the ship or not) in the navigation or management of the ship . . . be liable to damages beyond the following amounts; . . ."

F The section goes on to describe the procedure for determining the limit of liability, and so on.

This ship sank in Dutch territorial waters—in the approaches to the New Waterway giving access to the port of Rotterdam. The territorial waters of the United Kingdom are defined by the Territorial Waters Jurisdiction Act 1878, s. 7, as any part of the open sea within one marine league of the coast measured
G from low-water mark. The Crown claims property in the soil of the sea under its territorial waters and also claims to be entitled to the mines and minerals under that soil: see 39 HALSBURY'S LAWS OF ENGLAND (3rd Edn.) p. 556. It follows that if, through negligence, a ship is sunk in British territorial waters as a result of negligence with the result that it impedes access to an important waterway, the Crown would be entitled to remove it as interfering with a right
H and to recover the cost in damages for negligence. It appears to me, therefore, that, purely as a matter of comity, the English courts must recognise that the Dutch government has a similar right and must find that the defendants were entitled to limit their liability in Holland as they did.

Turning to the second point, I agree that it was here that the learned judge fell into error. In my judgment, he took a narrow legal as opposed to a practical
I view on the question of res judicata, and, since this was the real basis for his decision, this appeal must be allowed and the security discharged.

Appeal allowed.

Solicitors: *Waltons, Bright & Co.* (for the plaintiffs); *Ince & Co.* (for the defendants).

[*Reported by* JENIFER SANDELL, *Barrister-at-Law.*]

---

(14) [1968] 3 All E.R. at p. 853; [1968] 3 W.L.R. at p. 1009.
(15) [1968] 3 All E.R. 849; [1968] 3 W.L.R. 1003.

A

EARL v. ROY.

[QUEEN'S BENCH DIVISION (Lord Parker, C.J., Ashworth and Willis, JJ.),
December 12, 1968.]

Road Traffic—Driving with blood-alcohol proportion above prescribed limit—
    Evidence—Provision of specimen—Specimen of blood—Specimen divided   B
    into parts—Part must be capable of analysis—Part congealing before analysis
    —Road Traffic Act 1962 (10 & 11 Eliz. 2 c. 59) s. 2 (4).

A specimen of blood supplied under s. 2 (4)* of the Road Traffic Act 1962
must be one which is capable of analysis; something which congeals before it
can be analysed at the earliest possible moment is clearly not a sufficient
specimen (see p. 687, letters D and G, post).   C

Appeal allowed.

[As to specimens of blood on a charge of driving a motor vehicle with an undue proportion of alcohol in blood, see SUPPLEMENT to 33 HALSBURY'S LAWS
(3rd Edn.), paras. 1059, 1061A, 1.

For the Road Traffic Act 1962, s. 2, see 42 HALSBURY'S STATUTES (2nd Edn.)   D
888.]

Case Stated.

This was a Case Stated by the justices for the city and county borough of
Carlisle in respect of their adjudication as a magistrates' court sitting at Carlisle
on 22nd March 1968.

On 1st February 1968 an information was preferred by the respondent, Donald   E
Roy, against the appellant, John Earl, charging that he at 1.50 a.m. on Sunday
14th January 1968 when driving a motor car, viz., a Morris Oxford, registered
number RHH 498, on a road, namely, Caldewgate, Carlisle, had consumed
alcohol in such quantity that the proportion thereof in his blood exceeded the
prescribed limit contrary to s. 1 (1) of the Road Safety Act 1967.

The following facts were found. On 14th January 1968 the appellant drove a   F
Morris Oxford motor car on a road namely Caldewgate in Carlisle. The appellant
whilst driving the vehicle was stopped by a police officer and having failed to
complete a breath test he was cautioned and told that he was being arrested and
was removed to police headquarters. At police headquarters he again failed to
complete a breath test whereupon at 2.10 a.m. on 14th January 1968 he was
warned by a police inspector that a blood test was required and that failure to   G
provide one was an offence. The appellant consented and the inspector told the
appellant that he (the appellant) would be provided with part of that specimen
in a capsule provided by the police. The breath testing device employed was
approved by the Home Secretary for the purposes of Part 1 of the Road Safety
Act 1967. At 2.25 a.m. on 14th January 1968 a police surgeon duly took a blood
sample from the lobe of one of the appellant's ears. A lancet was inserted and a   H
small insertion made. Three separate squeezes of the ear lobe were made by the
doctor, the blood being collected into three separate capsules. Whilst the surgeon
was taking the sample the appellant made to get off the chair on which he was
sitting whereupon the surgeon said " Hold it, one more for you ". Immediately
after the sample was taken one of the capsules was put into an envelope, which
was sealed and signed by the doctor, and handed to the appellant. On 15th   I
January 1968 the remaining two capsules of blood were sent to the forensic
science laboratory at Preston. On 17th January 1968 one of the capsules was
analysed at the forensic science laboratory by a duly authorised analyst and was
found to contain 97 milligrammes of alcohol to 100 millilitres of blood. He was
unable to analyse the blood in the remaining capsule because there was insufficient blood in it and what there was had congealed. He could have analysed

---

* Section 2 (4), so far as material, is set out at p. 685, letter D, post.

A a small sample if it was still liquid. The capsule of blood given to the appellant was carried on his person or left lying about at his house from 14th January until 9th February without any steps being taken to prevent deterioration. On 9th February 1968 an independent qualified analyst received through the post by recorded delivery a letter from the appellant enclosing the capsule of blood which had been handed to him with the request that it be analysed for its alcohol

B content. The analyst made a close visual examination of the capsule without opening it, and it appeared not to have been tampered with. The analyst was unable to analyse the sample because it had congealed, and there was in any event insufficient sample for him to analyse it using his method of analysis.

 It was contended by the appellant: that the evidence of the forensic science laboratory analyst was inadmissible (an objection as to the admissibility of his

C evidence having been taken at the trial but overruled). Section 2 (4) of the Road Traffic Act 1962 provided that—

 " Where the accused, at the time a specimen of blood . . . was taken from . . . him, asked to be supplied with such a specimen, evidence of the proportion of alcohol . . . found in the specimen shall not be admissible on behalf of the prosecution unless—(a) the specimen is either one of two taken . . .

D on the same occasion or is part of a single specimen which was divided into two parts at the time it was taken . . . and (b) the other specimen . . . was supplied to the accused."

 That the appellant having been told by the inspector that he would be provided with a specimen, having been told by the surgeon as the specimen was being

E taken to "Hold it—one more for you", and that having been duly handed a sample immediately after it had been taken the appellant must be deemed to have asked for such a specimen and that any other interpretation of the actions and words of the police inspector and police surgeon were unreasonable and contrary to common sense. That s. 2 (4) of the Road Traffic Act 1962 had not been complied with in that the sample had not been divided into two parts but had

F been divided into three parts. Apart from the fact that this section had to be complied with strictly by the prosecution this would have been a contributory factor why out of the three capsules there was only enough blood in one for it to be capable of analysis. That in any event s. 2 (4) (b) had not been complied with in that the specimen handed to the appellant was so inadequate that it was incapable of analysis and that it was incumbent on the prosecution to supply the

G accused not merely with a sample but with an adequate sample.

 It was contended on behalf of the respondent: that the provisions of s. 2 (4) of the Road Traffic Act 1962 only applied where the accused, at the time a specimen was taken from him, asked to be supplied with such a specimen and the appellant had not made such a request. That s. 2 (5) of the same Act made provision for the situation where an accused did not make a request and that

H therefore in relation to s. 2 (4) the contention of the appellant that there was a " deemed request " could not apply. That the provisions of s. 2 (5) of the same Act had been complied with. That even if s. 2 (4) of the Road Traffic Act 1962 did apply, the Act did not prescribe division into equal parts and therefore the proportion retained by the police might be regarded as one part and that handed to the appellant the other. That the Road Traffic Act 1962 did not prescribe a

I minimum quantity for a specimen and that in any event the appellant had not proved that that specimen was incapable of analysis but merely that the analyst engaged by him was unable to analyse it using his method. That the sample had merely become inadequate by virtue of the manner in which the appellant had kept it from 14th January to 9th February and that by virtue of the delay any analysis would have been less accurate than an earlier one.

 The justices were of the opinion that when the police inspector told the appellant that he (the appellant) would be supplied with part of any specimen provided the inspector was making an offer in compliance with s. 2 (5) of the Road Traffic

Act 1962. At the time the specimen of blood was taken the appellant did not ask **A**
to be supplied with such a specimen and therefore the provisions of s. 2 (4) did
not apply. If s. 2 (4) did apply it did not require the specimen to be divided into
two equal parts; that the two capsules retained by the police constituted one part
of the specimen, and the capsule handed to the appellant the other. The manner
in which the appellant stored his capsule of blood was the most probable cause of
its being congealed at the time it was received for analysis. Had it not been **B**
congealed, the sample of blood could have been analysed, though not by the
methods employed by the analyst engaged by the appellant. The evidence
of the proportions of alcohol found in the specimen of blood provided by the
appellant was inadmissible. The justices therefore convicted the appellant;
fined him £20, ordered him to pay £17 17s. for costs, and disqualified him from
holding or obtaining a licence for driving motor vehicles for one year. They also **C**
ordered that particulars of the conviction be endorsed on any licence held by the
appellant. The appellant now appealed on the following grounds. (i) That the
justices were wrong in law in holding that notwithstanding that the sample of
blood supplied to the appellant could not have been analysed by the analyst
engaged by the appellant, the appellant was nevertheless supplied with a proper
sample pursuant to the Road Traffic Act 1962. (ii) That the justices were wrong **D**
in law in finding that the sample of blood supplied to the appellant could have been
analysed on the ground that there was no evidence to support such a finding.
(iii) That the justices were wrong in law in finding that the manner in which the
appellant stored his capsule of blood was the most probable cause of its being
congealed at the time it was received for analysis on the grounds that there was
no evidence to support such a finding. **E**

E. S. Cazalet for the appellant.
G. K. Naylor for the respondent.

LORD PARKER, C.J.: This is an appeal by way of Case Stated from a
decision of justices for the county borough of Carlisle who convicted the appellant
of an offence contrary to s. 1 (1) of the Road Safety Act 1967, the allegation being **F**
that on analysis there was found to be 97 milligrammes of alcohol to 100 millilitres
of blood as against the prescribed limit of 80 milligrammes. A number of points
were taken before the justices, many of which have now disappeared in the light
of earlier decisions of this court (1). But there is one remaining point which concerns the sufficiency of the specimen of blood which was handed to the appellant.
The facts, so far as they are material to that issue, are these: at 2.25 a.m. on **G**
14th January 1968 a police surgeon duly took a blood sample from the lobe of one
of the appellant's ears, the blood was collected into three separate capsules which
were sealed and signed, and one of which was handed to the appellant. The next
day, 15th January, the remaining two capsules of blood were sent to the forensic
science laboratory at Preston, and on 17th January one of those capsules was
analysed and found to contain, as I have said, 97 milligrammes of alcohol to **H**
100 millilitres of blood. The capsule that had been handed to the appellant was
carried about by him or left lying about in his house, and was not sent for analysis
until 8th or 9th February. On 9th February the analyst to whom he had sent the
capsule found that he was quite unable to analyse it as it was all congealed. In
fact his letter to the appellant was in these terms:

" We thank you for your enquiry regarding the analysis of enclosed **I**
specimen. Regretfully we must inform you, that the sample is far too small
for any accurate estimation to be carried out."

It had in fact congealed. The justices in regard to this said:

" We were of opinion that . . . the manner in which the appellant stored his
capsule of blood was the most probable cause of its being congealed at the
time it was received for analysis. Had it not been congealed, the sample of

(1) See *Kidd* v. *Kidd, Ley* v. *Donegani,* [1968] 3 All E.R. 226; [1969] 1 Q.B. 320.

A   blood would have been analysed, though not by the methods employed by the analyst engaged by the appellant."

B   The appeal here, though not stated in that form, is really an appeal, so we were told, to the effect that there was no evidence on which the justices could properly arrive at those findings, and by the agreement of counsel on both sides the court has been invited to look at the shorthand notes with which they have been supplied, and the court has allowed this point to be taken. So far as the blood being congealed was concerned, it is to be observed that the forensic laboratory was quite unable to analyse the second capsule which was sent to it because it was congealed, and that was three days after the specimen had been taken from the lobe of the appellant's ear, so it had congealed in three days. Having regard to that I really cannot understand how the justices could properly find that the most probable cause of the blood in the appellant's capsule being congealed was the way that he had dealt with it over, not three days, but a matter of weeks.

C   That as it seems to me of itself would be sufficient to dispose of this case, because it is the law, and indeed it is common sense, that the specimen that is provided to the appellant must be one which is capable of analysis. Something which congeals before it can be analysed at the earliest possible moment is clearly not a sufficient specimen.

D   As regards the second point, which is quantity as opposed to the condition of being congealed, as I said, the justices found that it could have been analysed though not by the methods employed by the analyst engaged by the appellant. It is really unnecessary, having regard to what I have already said, to deal with this point, but I confess that reading the notes I get the impression that there was really only just enough for the forensic laboratory to analyse on their special equipment, by what is called gas chromatography, very expensive apparatus, access to which very few, if any, analysts have. In the light of that it is difficult to see how the justices could affirmatively hold that the specimen was enough to apply analysis by other methods. In these circumstances it seems to me that this appeal must be allowed and the conviction quashed. I would only add that the justices also took the view that as the appellant had not specifically asked for a specimen, therefore none of these provisions with regard to taking specimens applied. That I think is clearly wrong, because if he did not specifically ask for it, there was no finding that he was offered it under s. 2 (5) of the Road Traffic Act 1962, and accordingly whether he asked for it or was offered it made no difference, the specimen must be a sufficient specimen to enable an analysis to be carried out.

ASHWORTH, J.: I agree.

WILLIS, J.: I agree.

Appeal allowed. Conviction quashed.

H   Solicitors: *Collyer-Bristow & Co.* agents for *Saul & Lightfoot*, Carlisle (for the appellant); *Yelloly & Burnett*, Carlisle (for the respondent).

[*Reported by* N. P. METCALFE, ESQ., *Barrister-at-Law.*]

A

R. *v.* NIXON.

[COURT OF APPEAL, CRIMINAL DIVISION (Widgery and Karminski, L.JJ., and
Geoffrey Lane, J.), April 24, 1969.]

Road Traffic—Driving with blood-alcohol proportion above prescribed limit—
    Evidence—Provision of specimen—Specimen of blood—Specimen divided
    into parts—Onus of proving part sufficient for and capable of analysis.

B

Road Traffic—Driving with blood-alcohol proportion above prescribed limit—
    Evidence—Provision of specimen—Specimen of blood—Specimen divided
    into parts—Analysis by ordinary equipment and ordinary skill—Road
    Traffic Act 1962 (10 & 11 Eliz. 2 c. 59), s. 2 (4).

C

The applicant having provided a specimen of blood under s. 3 (1) of the
Road Safety Act 1967, was invited to select a capsule containing part of the
specimen. This he did and he was advised to keep it in a refrigerator
pending analysis. After one unsuccessful effort to get the capsule analysed,
the applicant took it (a few days after he had given the specimen) to a
public analyst who found it impossible to obtain a representative sample
for analysis since it was so badly clotted. The applicant was charged with
an offence under s. 1 (1) of the Act of 1967 and, on a preliminary issue
as to the admissibility of scientific evidence, the analyst gave evidence that
he was unable to analyse the specimen. He agreed that sometimes the
problem of clotting could be overcome by use of a micro-sieve but that he
had on this occasion used a micro-sieve of his own design without much
success. A Home Office analyst also gave evidence. He maintained
that provided the quantity of the specimen was sufficient no degree of
clotting would render proper analysis impossible provided that a suitably
fine sieve was used. The court accepted the evidence of the Home Office
analyst and ruled that the specimen was capable of analysis. The applicant
was convicted and applied for leave to appeal against conviction.

D

E

Held: the burden of proving that the sample of the specimen was sufficient
and was capable of analysis lay on the prosecution; there had been ample
evidence for the court to come to the conclusion that the sample was
capable of analysis by use of ordinary equipment and ordinary skill by a
reasonably skilled analyst; accordingly, the application would be dismissed
(see p. 690, letter H, and p. 691, letter F, post).

F

Earl v. *Roy* (p. 684, ante) distinguished.

Per CURIAM: if the sample of the specimen provided for the accused
under the Road Traffic Act 1962, s. 2 (4) is of such quality that analysis is
only possible by using expensive or highly-sophisticated equipment which
in only available to the favoured few, the prosecution would fail to prove
the admissibility of the analyst's certificate (see p. 691, letter D, post).

G

Application dismissed.

H

[As to the taking of blood specimens see SUPPLEMENT to 33 HALSBURY'S
LAWS (3rd Edn.), para. 1061A, 3.

For the Road Traffic Act 1962, s. 2, see 42 HALSBURY'S STATUTES (2nd Edn.)
888.]

Cases referred to:

Earl v. *Roy* p. 684, ante.
Lowery v. *Hallard,* [1906] 1 K.B. 398; 75 L.J.K.B. 249; 93 L.T. 844; 70 J.P.
    57; 25 Digest (Repl.) 76, *48.*

I

Application for leave to appeal.

This was an application by John Hawkins Nixon for leave to appeal against
his conviction at the Lancashire County Quarter Sessions held at Preston on
8th May 1968 when the applicant was found guilty of driving a motor car having

A consumed alcohol in such a quantity that the proportion in his blood exceeded the prescribed limit contrary to s. 1 (1) of the Road Safety Act 1967. The applicant was fined £50 and disqualified from driving for 12 months. The facts are set out in the judgment of the court.

E. Sanderson Temple, Q.C., for the applicant.

J. H. Lord for the Crown.

B

GEOFFREY LANE, J., delivered the judgment of the court: On 8th May 1968 the applicant was convicted at the quarter sessions for the county of Lancaster of driving a motor vehicle with an undue proportion of alcohol in his blood. For that offence he was fined £50 (with one month's imprisonment in default of payment of the fine) and disqualified from driving or from holding

C a driving licence for 12 months. Against that conviction he now asks for leave to appeal.

The trial started on 3rd April, but before the jury were sworn counsel for the applicant took objection to the admissibility of the proposed prosecution scientific evidence aimed at proving the percentage of blood-alcohol. The course was taken of trying this preliminary issue there and then. The chairman in due

D course ruled that the evidence was admissible, and the trial was then adjourned for the defence to consider their position, amongst other matters. At the resumed hearing, the scientific evidence having been given, the jury convicted on this count alleging driving with an excess of alcohol in the blood and acquitted on a further count of dangerous driving, which accordingly does not concern this court.

E The applicant now applies for leave to appeal against that conviction on the following grounds: (i) that the chairman was wrong in law and/or wrongly exercised his discretion in permitting evidence to be adduced as to the proportion of alcohol found in a sample of blood taken from the applicant in view of the fact that the sample taken on the same occasion and furnished to the applicant was found (rightly or wrongly) by a public analyst to be so clotted as to be

F incapable of analysis, with the consequence that the applicant was deprived of the opportunity of having such sample independently analysed; (ii) failure by the chairman to warn the jury of the danger of accepting and acting on the prosecution's evidence as to blood-alcohol content in circumstances (beyond his control) where the applicant had been deprived of the opportunity of an independent analysis of the sample supplied to him. A third ground relating to the

G necessary approval of the breath test device has been abandoned by counsel for the applicant.

The facts of the case can be stated comparatively briefly. Soon after midnight on 23rd October 1967 the applicant, driving his Jaguar motor car, suffered a collision. A police sergeant went to the scene, and in due course asked the applicant to submit to a breath test. That test proved positive, as did a second

H test which was carried out when the police officer and the applicant reached the police station. The applicant was then requested to provide a specimen of blood, and was duly warned of the consequences of a refusal of that request, and a Dr. Mechie attended to take the specimen. There was some difficulty over the taking of the specimen, because the applicant declined to allow the doctor to take the specimen from the lobe of the ear, which the doctor wished

I to do, and insisted that the bulb of his thumb should be used instead.

In the event three capsules were filled with blood from the bulb of the thumb, and Dr. Mechie gave evidence that in each capsule there were what appeared to be the necessary anti-coagulant crystals. The applicant was invited to select one of the capsules, which he did, and was advised to keep it in a refrigerator pending analysis. The other two specimens were on the same day delivered to Dr. Skuse, a Home Office scientific officer, and he analysed them and found, in short, that they contained almost double the permitted quantity of alcohol.

It is with regard to the third specimen that the difficulty in this case arose.

The applicant took this specimen on the same day to his own doctor, Dr. Elkin, **A** and Dr. Elkin, it seems, sent the specimen to the biochemistry department of a local hospital. For reasons which did not emerge in the evidence he recovered the specimen from the hospital on the following Thursday (without, it seems, any analysis having been carried out in the hospital) and returned the specimen to the applicant. Arrangements were then made for the specimen to be submitted to a public analyst, and on Friday 27th October 1967 the applicant himself **B** took the specimen to a Mr. Tennyson Harris, who is a Fellow of the Royal Institute of Chemistry and a Fellow of the Pharmaceutical Society, as well as holding an appointment as a public analyst for the district.

It was on the evidence of Mr. Tennyson Harris that the applicant in the main founded his objections to the admissibility of the prosecution evidence. He (Mr. Harris) gave evidence at the quarter sessions on 3rd April that the **C** specimen which he received was so badly clotted that it was impossible to obtain a representative sample for analysis; so badly clotted, he said, that he formed the impression that no anti-coagulant had been added to the specimen or, if it had been added, then the sample must have been clotted before it reached the capsule. No doubt there was enough in quantity, but clotting prevented him from analysing it. He agreed that it is sometimes possible to overcome **D** such apparent difficulty by the use of an instrument called a micro-sieve. He said that he had, in fact, on this occasion used a micro-sieve of his own design, but had used it without success, and he agreed that some micro-sieves are probably more effective than others.

Dr. Mechie, who took the sample, told the court that the blood which he took from the bulb of the applicant's thumb was certainly not clotted before it went **E** into the capsule, because he saw it running down the side of the capsule; and, furthermore, he also gave evidence that there were certainly crystals, which he took to be anti-coagulant crystals, in these capsules (in each of the three) before he put the blood into them. Dr. Skuse, the Home Office analyst, also gave evidence on this preliminary point, to the effect that there was, in his view, no degree of clotting which would render proper analysis impossible, providing that **F** there was a sufficient quantity of blood and a suitably fine sieve was used. He said this:

"I have analysed blood samples which have been almost completely clotted by this method, by forcing them up through the sieve. If the sample is too small—very tiny—then of course you cannot pass it through the sieve."

G

On the preliminary issue the learned chairman reached the following conclusion. He first of all set out the way he directed himself on the law in these words:

"In my view the prosecution must establish that the third sample was sufficient and capable of analysis and the burden, in my view, is on the prosecution to show this and, therefore, I must consider the evidence which has been given on this very issue."

H

With that statement of the burden of proof this court entirely agrees. Then, applying what he had heard by way of evidence to the law as he directed himself, he said this:

"I accept Dr. Skuse's evidence. I am, therefore, quite satisfied that the third sample was capable and sufficient to analyse in October, being analysed with the necessary equipment and skill. The evidence does not in my view become inadmissible because the particular analyst was unable to analyse it. I am satisfied that the third sample was capable of analysis and sufficient for analysis at the material time and, therefore, this evidence is admissible."

I

The applicant puts his case in this way. In order that the analyst's certificate may be adduced in evidence by the prosecution certain statutory conditions have to be fulfilled by virtue of s. 3 of the Road Safety Act 1967 and s. 2 of the Road

A   Traffic Act 1962.   The material provision is contained in s. 2 (4) of the last-mentioned Act, which provides:

> " Where the accused, at the time a specimen of blood or urine was taken
> from or provided by him, asked to be supplied with such a specimen, evidence
> of the proportion of alcohol or any drug found in the specimen shall not be
> admissible on behalf of the prosecution unless—(*a*) the specimen is either
B > one of two taken or provided on the same occasion or is part of a single
> specimen which was divided into two parts at the time it was taken or
> provided; and (*b*) the other specimen or part was supplied to the accused."

Lowery v. *Hallard* (1)—a decision under s. 14 of the Sale of Food and Drugs Act
1875—makes it clear (if indeed any further clarification is required) that each
of the parts into which an article is required to be divided under that Act, and
C   indeed this Act as well, must be sufficient to admit of proper analysis.   Likewise
under the Act of 1962, it is equally clear to this court, in the light of the wording
of the Act itself and also in the light of the judgment of LORD PARKER, C.J., in
Earl v. *Roy* (2), that the specimens provided (quantity apart) must be of such a
quality as to permit a reasonably competent analyst using readily available
D   equipment to make a proper analysis.
    If, for example, the specimen provided for the accused under the Road Traffic
Act 1962 is of such a quality that analysis is only possible by using expensive
or highly-sophisticated equipment which is only available to the favoured few,
the prosecution would fail to prove the admissibility of the analyst's certificate.
Indeed, in *Earl* v. *Roy* (2) that point is made.   But in *Earl* v. *Roy* (2) the difficulty
was that the quantity of blood available was insufficient, and it seems that the
E   blood in that case was not merely clotted but was so congealed as to be only
capable of analysis by a highly expensive piece of equipment which is called
gas chromatography.
    In this case there was ample evidence on which the learned chairman could
come to the conclusion, as he obviously did, that the specimen was capable of
analysis by the use of ordinary equipment and ordinary skill by a reasonably
F   competent analyst.   Accordingly, in the judgment of this court, the main ground
of appeal, namely, that this evidence should have been rejected by the learned
chairman, fails.
    The two further points raised by counsel for the applicant in his persuasive
and able argument can perhaps be dealt with more shortly.   He suggests that,
even though the evidence was held by the learned chairman to be admissible,
G   and assuming the learned chairman to be correct on that point, he should have
exercised some form of discretion to exclude the evidence nevertheless.   In the
judgment of this court, having ruled that the evidence was admissible, we
consider that he acted correctly in permitting the evidence to go before the
jury as he did.   It is further submitted that, having admitted the evidence, the
chairman should then have issued some warning to the jury on the dangers of
H   acting on it when the applicant had by mischance taken his own sample to an
analyst who proved unable to analyse it.
    This court takes the view that the chairman did all that could be expected of
him in outlining to the jury, as he did, the difficulties which had arisen over the
analysis of the sample, and then emphasising to them that in the light of all the
evidence they must only convict if they were sure that the evidence of Dr. Skuse
I   could be accepted.   Accordingly, the two subsidiary points fail likewise, and
this application must be refused.

Application dismissed.

Solicitors: *Julian S. Goldstone & Co.*, Manchester (for the applicant); *Clift,
Dromgoole & Carter*, Lancaster (for the Crown).

[*Reported by* JACQUELINE CHARLES, *Barrister-at-Law.*]

---

(1) [1906] 1 K.B. 398.   (2) P. 684, *ante.*

LUGANDA v. SERVICE HOTELS, LTD.

[COURT OF APPEAL, CIVIL DIVISION (Lord Denning, M.R., Edmund Davies and Phillimore, L.JJ.), February 24, 25, 1969.]

Rent Restriction—Possession—Hotel—Bed-sitting room—Provision of linen and cleaning services—Lessee staying for three years—Whether hotel a house—Whether lessee had exclusive occupation of a residence—Rent Act 1968 (c. 23), s. 70 (1), s. 84 (1).

The plaintiff had occupied a room at the defendants' hotel as a contractual licensee for three years. The premises were not an ordinary hotel, there being 88 rooms let as bed-sitting rooms, each with a double-ring gas ring. The defendants provided the bedding. Chambermaids came into the rooms every day to make the beds and clean the rooms; and every week they changed the linen. Along the corridor there were lavatories and bathrooms used by all the occupants. There was a porter on duty down below and a receptionist who put telephone messages through to a common telephone on each floor. On the defendants raising the plaintiff's rent, he refused to pay and applied to the rent tribunal. The defendants thereupon gave him two days' notice to vacate his room and after the expiry of the notice changed the lock and refused the plaintiff access to the room. By s. 70 (1) and (2) of the Rent Act 1968, that Act only applied to a contract relating to a " dwelling " which, by s. 84 (1) was defined as " a house or part of a house "; by s. 70 (1), the Act only applied to a contract which gave to the lessee the right to occupy a dwelling as a residence; and by s. 70 (2), where the lessee occupied only a part of a house the contract must entitle the lessee to exclusive occupation of that part. On appeal by the defendants against the granting of interlocutory injunctions enabling the plaintiff to go back to his room and restraining the defendants from stopping him having access,

Held: the plaintiff was prima facie entitled to the protection of the Act of 1968 and the injunctions had been rightly made, because—

(i) a building used as a hotel was a house and the plaintiff's room was part of a house within s. 84 (1) of the Act (see p. 694, letter H, and p. 696, letters B and G, post);

(ii) the plaintiff, having occupied the room for three years, was occupying it as a residence within s. 70 (1) of the Act (see p. 695, letter A, and p. 696, letters B and G, post) (dictum of PARKER, J., in *R. v. York, Harrogate, Ripon and Northallerton Areas Rent Tribunal, Ex p. Ingle* ([1954] 1 All E.R. at p. 441) applied);

(iii) the plaintiff had exclusive occupation of the room under his contract within s. 70 (2) of the Act (see p. 695, letter F, and p. 696, letters B and G, post) (*R. v. Battersea, Wandsworth, Mitcham and Wimbledon Rent Tribunal, Ex p. Parikh* ([1957] 1 All E.R. 352) approved); accordingly

(iv) the plaintiff being given security of tenure by the Act, although he was not in occupation he was entitled to be re-instated, since (per LORD DENNING, M.R., and PHILLIMORE, L.J.) if he had still been in occupation the court would have granted an injunction to prevent the defendants from locking him out (see p. 695, letter I, and p. 696, letter G, post) (*Ryan v. Mutual Tontine Westminster Chambers Association* ([1893] 1 Ch. 116) distinguished) or (per EDMUND DAVIES and PHILLIMORE, L.JJ.) the defendants not having complied with s. 77 of the Act, they could not revoke the contractual right which they had granted and the plaintiff was not restricted to a claim in damages (see p. 696, letters E and G, post) (*Thompson v. Park* ([1944] 2 All E.R. 477) distinguished).

Appeal dismissed.

A   [As to meaning of dwelling for purposes of rent control, see 23 HALSBURY'S
LAWS (3rd Edn.) 742, para. 1495.]

Cases referred to:

R. v. *Battersea, Wandsworth, Mitcham and Wimbledon Rent Tribunal, Ex p.
        Parikh,* [1957] 1 All E.R. 352; [1957] 1 W.L.R. 410; 121 J.P. 132;
        Digest (Cont. Vol. A) 1113, *8131.*

B   R. v. *York, Harrogate, Ripon and Northallerton Areas Rent Tribunal, Ex p. Ingle,*
        [1954] 1 All E.R. 440; [1954] 1 Q.B. 456; [1954] 2 W.L.R. 294; 118
        J.P. 236; Digest (Cont. Vol. A) 1113, *8126ja.*

Ryan v. *Mutual Tontine Westminster Chambers Association,* [1893] 1 Ch. 116;
        62 L.J.Ch. 252; 67 L.T. 820; 31 Digest (Repl.) 98, *2459.*

Thompson v. *Park,* [1944] 2 All E.R. 477; [1944] K.B. 408; 113 L.J.K.B. 561;
C   170 L.T. 207; 30 Digest (Repl.) 539, *1736.*

Winter Garden Theatre (London), Ltd. v. *Millenium Productions, Ltd.,* [1947]
        2 All E.R. 331; [1948] A.C. 173; [1947] L.J.R. 1422; 177 L.T. 349;
        45 Digest (Repl.) 201, *83.*

Interlocutory Appeal.

D   This was an appeal by the defendants, Service Hotels, Ltd., from an order
of CROSS, J., dated 17th February 1969 that (i) the defendants permit the plaintiff,
Kasozi Luganda, access to the premises known as room 53, Queensborough
Court Hotel, Queensborough Terrace, London W.2, and allow the plaintiff to
occupy the premises in accordance with the terms of the contract or tenancy subsisting between the plaintiff and the defendants until further order; and (ii) the
defendants be restrained until further order from preventing or interfering with
E   the plaintiff's access to and from the premises in accordance with the contract
or tenancy.   The facts are set out in the judgment of LORD DENNING, M.R.

The authority and cases noted below* were cited during the argument in
addition to those referred to in the judgments.

L. H. Hoffman for the plaintiff.

F   *M. Waters,* Q.C., and *M. D. Beckman* for the defendants.

LORD DENNING, M.R.: The plaintiff, Mr. Kasozi Luganda, came to
this country from Uganda in 1958.   He is employed as a clerk in a company in
London, but he is also a student.   He is reading for the Bar and is going to
take his final examinations in May 1969.   Nearly three years ago he took a
furnished room in a building which is known as Queensborough Court Hotel,
G   Queensborough Terrace, W.2.   It is called a hotel, but it is very different from
an ordinary hotel.   It has 88 rooms which are " let " out to " tenants ".   But
they are not strictly " let ", and they are not strictly " tenants ".   Each " tenant "
is really a contractual licensee who has the right to occupy a room in return
for a weekly payment.   The plaintiff has a Yale key for his room.   It is a bed-
sitting room with a double-ring gas ring.   He gets his own meals.   He provides
H   his own towel and soap; but the defendants provide the bedding.   The chambermaids come in every day and make his bed and clean the room; and every week
they change the linen.   Along the corridor there are lavatories and bathrooms
which are used by all the occupants.   There is, of course, a lift.   There is a
porter on duty down below; and there is a receptionist who puts telephone
messages through to a common telephone on each floor.

I   The plaintiff has been in the same room, no. 53, for nearly three years.   When
he went there in April 1966, he paid £4 14s. 6d. a week.   In September 1967, it
was raised to £4 18s. a week.   In January 1969, the defendants wanted to
decorate his room, no. 53.   So he went out of no. 53 into no. 4 for a fortnight
whilst they redecorated the room.   He went back into no. 53 on 31st January,
a Friday.   On the next morning, Saturday, 1st February, he received a letter

---

* 21 HALSBURY'S LAWS (3rd Edn.) 369, para. 774; *Cordell* v. *Second Clanfield
Properties, Ltd.,* [1968] 3 All E.R. 746; [1968] 3 W.L.R. 864.

from the manager telling him that his rent was to be increased by a guinea a week.   **A**
It was in future to be £5 19s. a week. He did not like this increase in rent.
So he went to the rent tribunal and told them about it.   They gave him some
advice; and, in consequence, on Monday, 3rd February, the plaintiff wrote to
the defendants saying:

> " I note that you have put up the rent by £1 1s. 0d. a week ! I am
> taking legal advice on this matter, but in the meantime I will continue   **B**
> to pay £4 18s. 0d. as in the past."

The defendants did not like this.   They went to their solicitors who wrote
a letter which the plaintiff got on the Wednesday, 5th February.   They told
him that he had to vacate his room by 10.00 a.m. on the Friday, 7th February.
That was only two days' notice. The plaintiff did not obey their notice. He   **C**
did not vacate the premises on the Friday morning. He went to work as usual.
When he got back on the Friday evening, he found that the defendants had
changed the lock. He could not get in. He could not even get his belongings.
He had to go and spend the night with a friend nearby.   Meanwhile the rent
tribunal wrote to him saying that his application to them had been received
and would be dealt with as early as possible. They told the defendants also. **D**
The defendants did not leave room 53 empty for very long. They soon let it
to a Turkish lady; and they told the plaintiff that he could not come back.
The plaintiff applied for an injunction. CROSS, J., held that the plaintiff had a
prima facie right to remain in possession.   He was within the statute which
affords protection to the tenants of furnished rooms.   The judge granted an
injunction so as to enable him to go back to room 53; and an injunction to   **E**
prevent the defendants from stopping him having access.   Now the defendants
appeal to this court.

The statutory provisions about furnished lettings were originally contained
in the Furnished Houses (Rent Control) Act 1946, but they have now been consolidated in Part 6 of the Rent Act 1968.   They were especially designed to
cover a letting of furnished rooms, either under a tenancy or a contractual   **F**
licence, and thus to cover such a case as the present.   But counsel for the defendants has submitted that they do not cover it.   I will take his points in order.
First, the Act only applies to a contract relating to a " dwelling "; see s. 70 (1),
(2); and " dwelling " is defined in s. 84 (1) of the Act of 1968 as " a house or
part of a house ".   Counsel for the defendants submitted that this hotel was
not a " house ".   He referred us to a passage in MEGARRY ON THE RENT ACTS   **G**
(10th Edn.), p. 50, where it is stated that " premises used as a hotel may be
protected if they were constructed as a dwelling-house, but perhaps not if constructed as a hotel ".   I do not accept this submission.   I am quite clear that a
building which is used as a hotel is a " house ", no matter whether it was purpose
built or not.   As it happens, the Queensborough Court Hotel was constructed as
four houses, but they have been knocked into one so as to form the hotel.   It is   **H**
clearly a " house "; and room 53 is " part of a house ".

Secondly, the Act only applies to a contract which gives to the lessee " the
right to occupy as a residence " a dwelling; see s. 70 (1). Counsel for the defendants submitted that the contract here did not give the plaintiff the right to
occupy room 53 " as a residence ".   He referred us again to a passage in MEGARRY
at p. 505, where it is stated:

> " The words ' as a residence ' have a limiting effect.   Thus the Act does   **I**
> not apply to temporary accommodation of the normal hotel type, whether
> the Ritz or Rowton House, presumably because there is no occupation ' as
> a residence '."

I agree about the Ritz or Rowton House.   A person taking a room there on a
short visit does not have the right to occupy it " as a residence ".   Counsel for
the defendants submitted that the contract, to come within the Act, must give
to the lessee, in express words, the right to occupy as a residence. But I do

A not think so. It is sufficient if " the lessee is within his rights in occupying the
premises as a residence ", even though the contract says nothing about it;
see *R.* v. *York, Harrogate, Ripon and Northallerton Areas Rent Tribunal, Ex p. Ingle*
(1), per PARKER, J.   It is plain here that the plaintiff was occupying room 53
as a residence. He had been there nearly three years; and he was within his
rights in so occupying it.   So that requirement is satisfied.

B   Thirdly, in a case like the present when the lessee occupies only a part of a
house (namely, one room) the contract must entitle the lessee to " exclusive
occupation " of that part; see s. 70 (2).   Counsel for the defendants submitted
that the Act only protected a tenant, properly so called, and did not protect
a contractual licensee or lodger who took a furnished room.   The plaintiff was,
of course, only a contractual licensee; and not a tenant. Counsel sought to
C support his submission by taking us through many provisions of earlier Rent
Acts.   But I do not propose to go through them now.   I am quite satisfied
that " exclusive occupation " in s. 70 (2) does not mean " exclusive possession "
in the technical sense in which it is sometimes used in landlord and tenant
cases.   A lodger who takes a furnished room in a house is in exclusive occupation
of it; notwithstanding that the landlady has a right to access at all times.
D It was so held twelve years ago in *R.* v. *Battersea, Wandsworth, Mitcham and
Wimbledon Rent Tribunal, Ex p. Parikh* (2).   LORD GODDARD, C.J., said (3) that,
although the landlady had a right of access, she had not the right " to come in
and occupy it herself, nor had she the right to put somebody else into the room ".
Counsel for the defendants submitted that that case was wrongly decided and
should be overruled.   But I think that it was rightly decided.   A person has a
E right to " exclusive occupation " of a room when he is entitled to occupy it
himself, and no one else is entitled to occupy it.   Even though, as here, the
chambermaids come in daily to make the bed and clean the room, and change
the linen each week, nevertheless, the plaintiff had exclusive occupation of the
room, that is, the right to occupy it to the exclusion of anyone else occupying it.
He has that right under the contract.   This requirement, too, is satisfied.   I
F would only observe that the plaintiff had no meals in the hotel.   If he had had
board in addition to lodging, to a substantial extent, he would not have come
within the statute; see s. 70 (3) (*b*).   But he had no board; so he is within it.

It seems to me, therefore, that prima facie at least the plaintiff is entitled to
the protection of the Act, that is, the protection which is afforded to lessees of
furnished lettings.   He was entitled to refer the contract, as he did, to the
G rent tribunal to see what was a fair rent for him to pay; and he was given by the
Act security of tenure, which might be as much as six months from the decision
of the tribunal; see s. 77 and s. 78 of the Act of 1968.

Counsel for the defendants submitted that, as the plaintiff was not now in
occupation, no mandatory order should be made to put him back.   He suggested
that such an order would require the constant superintendence of the court,
H which the court would not do.   He cited *Ryan* v. *Mutual Tontine Westminster
Chambers Association* (4).   I look on the case quite differently.   The plaintiff
is prima facie entitled by statute to security of tenure of this room.   It was
unlawful for the defendants to lock him out of it; see s. 30 of the Rent Act 1965.
They were wrong to take the law into their own hands.   If the defendants had
not changed the lock—and the plaintiff was still in occupation—I am sure that
I the court would have granted an injunction to prevent the defendants from
locking him out.   They should not be in a better position by wrongfully locking
him out.   As LORD UTHWATT said in *Winter Garden Theatre (London), Ltd.* v.
Millenium Productions, Ltd. (5), " in a court of equity, wrongful acts are no

---

(1) [1954] 1 All E.R. 440 at p. 441; [1954] 1 Q.B. 456 at p. 459.
(2) [1957] 1 All E.R. 352; [1957] 1 W.L.R. 410.
(3) [1957] 1 All E.R. at p. 355; [1957] 1 W.L.R. at p. 414.
(4) [1893] 1 Ch. 116.
(5) [1947] 2 All E.R. 331 at p. 343; [1948] A.C. 173 at p. 203.

passport to favour ". We must see that the law is observed. To do this, we **A** should, I think, order that the plaintiff should be restored to his room. There is no difficulty about the Turkish lady. Rooms often become vacant. She can go into another room.

In my opinion, the judge was quite right. An injunction should be made pending trial. But there should be an early trial. I would dismiss the appeal.

B

EDMUND DAVIES, L.J.: For the reasons already stated by LORD DENNING, M.R., I also hold that the plaintiff has made out what I regard at this stage as a strong prima facie case for saying that the contract by virtue of which he occupied room 53 in the defendants' premises is a Part 6 contract for the purposes of s. 68 to s. 84 of the Rent Act 1968. But counsel for the defendants has submitted that, even if that be so, CROSS, J., was wrong in granting a mandatory injunction to compel the defendants to re-instate the plaintiff. In support **C** of this submission he has cited *Thompson* v. *Park* (6), where this court held that, where a licence to use certain premises had been wrongfully revoked, the licensee who persisted in entering and using the premises could be injuncted from further trespass and must content himself to a claim in damages. Accordingly, so submitted counsel, here, too, the plaintiff, even assuming that he has been legally **D** wronged, should be left to his claim in damages. What counsel's submission overlooks, however, is that there is a vitally important difference between that case and the present. In contracts within the Act of 1968 lessees are given six months security of tenure provided s. 77 of that Act has been complied with; in other words, to that extent the lessor or licensor *cannot* revoke the contractual right which he has granted, and the lessee or licensee is, therefore, not restricted **E** to his claim to damages.

Then, ought we to interfere with the learned judge's discretion in granting a mandatory injunction? I think that the answer must be, most certainly not. Were we to do that, despite our holding that the plaintiff has established a prima facie entitlement to the protection of the Act of 1968, we would indeed be acting flatly contrary to the salutary observation of LORD UTHWATT in *Winter* **F** *Garden Theatre (London), Ltd.* v. *Millenium Productions, Ltd.* (7) that " in a court of equity, wrongful acts are no passport to favour ". I do not think that this court should assist those who have been shown prima facie to have trodden roughshod over the plaintiff's rights, and I would, accordingly, concur in dismissing this interlocutory appeal.

PHILLIMORE, L.J.: I entirely agree, and I cannot usefully add anything **G** to the judgments which have already been delivered.

Appeal dismissed.

Solicitors: *D. A. Rose & Co.* (for the plaintiff); *Craps & Co.* (for the defendants).

[*Reported by* F. GUTTMAN, ESQ., *Barrister-at-Law.*]

H

I

(6) [1944] 2 All E.R. 477; [1944] K.B. 408.
(7) [1947] 2 All E.R. 331 at p. 343; [1948] A.C. 173 at p. 203.

A

WESTCOTT (Inspector of Taxes) *v.* BRYAN.

[CHANCERY DIVISION (Pennycuick, J.), November 27, 28, 1968.]

Income Tax—Accommodation and benefits provided to directors and others—
B *Expense incurred by body corporate—Director renting house from company*
—Company paying gas, electricity, water, insurance of contents, cleaning and
maintenance, telephone charges, gardener's wages—Director entertaining
company's customers—Maintenance being repairs normally tenant's respon-
sibility—Inclusion in sum—Need for apportionment of total sum—Reflection
of use for business purposes—Absence of temporal or spatial severance—
C *Basis of apportionment—Income Tax Act 1952 (15 & 16 Geo. 6 & 1 Eliz. 2*
c. 10), s. 160, s. 161 (1), (6), s. 162 (1).

On the appointment of the taxpayer as its managing director, a company
insisted on his occupying a suitable house in North Staffordshire at which he
could entertain customers. It bought the house and let it to the taxpayer on
a yearly tenancy at a rent of £140, the taxpayer paying the rates and also
£500 in consideration of other services defrayed by the company costing
D £1,017 and comprising payments for gas, electricity, water, insurance of
contents, telephone (apportioned), window cleaning, cleaning and gardener's
wages (apportioned) and also £181 for maintenance, wages and materials,
covering current maintenance and repairs of the house. The taxpayer occupied the house with his family and entertained buyers from abroad and
representatives of leading British retailers of the company's goods there,
E for dinner, for drinks, for tea and on occasion for the night as required (25
out of 72 cases of entertaining). He was assessed to income tax in respect
of the £1,017 plus £360 rateable value of the house less the £640 he paid or
£737 (reduced to £614 for the first (part) year), as a perquisite of his office
under s. 160* and s. 161 (1)† of the Income Tax Act 1952 and on the basis that
apportionment of the expenses under s. 161 (6)† applied only to the telephone
F and gardener's wages, and that the £181 maintenance was not an expense
incurred in the acquisition or production of an asset remaining the property
of the company excluded from such assessment by s. 162‡. The General
Commissioners of Income Tax found that there was a genuine business use
of the house and that the taxpayer's personal occupation was restricted
in that he was not free to discriminate as to his guests, and they apportioned
the total expenditure as to one-quarter for business purposes having regard
G to the number of days of use for business purposes (£1,377 × ¾ or £1,032 less
£640 paid by the taxpayer, balance £392—it was conceded by the Crown
that there should have been a reduction to ten-twelfths to allow for the part
period of occupation).

Held: the decision of the commissioners must be affirmed on the following
basis—
H
(i) where a company established living accommodation or facilities for
common enjoyment by a director and others, whether itself or third parties,
the total expense involved required an apportionment under sub-s. (6)
of s. 161 of the Income Tax Act 1952, irrespective of whether there was any
severance of the use of the accommodation on a temporal or spatial basis
(see p. 702, letter I, to p. 703, letter C, post).
I
(ii) apportionment was not properly based simply on the number of days
of use wholly or partially for business purposes; regard must be had to the
need to keep the house in a state of availability for the invitees; it was not
right to lay down any precise formula applicable to this case and cases generally; here a fair if rough-and-ready apportionment would be achieved by not

---

* Section 160 (1) is set out at p. 699, letters B and C, post.
† Section 161 (1), (6) is set out at p. 699, letters D to F, post.
‡ Section 162 (1) is set out at p. 699, letter G, post.

scaling down the commissioners' figure of £1,032 to the ten-twelfths for part A
occupation (see p. 703, letters F and G, and p. 706, letter I, to p. 707, letter C,
post).

(iii) the expenditure on maintenance, wages and materials, being expenditure for which a tenant would ordinarily be responsible although the company
had undertaken responsibility for it, was not an expense incurred on the production of an asset within the meaning of s. 162 but fell within the terms B
of s. 161 (see p. 706, letters E and F, post). (Dicta of LORD DILHORNE, L.C.,
and LORD GUEST in *Luke* v. *Inland Revenue Comrs.* ([1963] 1 All E.R. at
p. 661 and pp. 672, 673) applied, and that case distinguished.)

Appeal dismissed.

[As to taxation of expenses and benefits in kind paid to directors and highly
paid employees and the valuation thereof, see 20 HALSBURY's LAWS (3rd Edn.) C
314-316, para. 577-579.

For the Income Tax Act 1952, s. 160, s. 161, s. 162, see 31 HALSBURY's
STATUTES (2nd Edn.) 155, 156, 157.]

Cases referred to:

Luke v. *Inland Revenue Comrs.* [1963] 1 All E.R. 655; [1963] A.C. 557;
    [1963] 2 W.L.R. 559; 40 Tax Cas. 630; Digest (Cont. Vol. A) 888, D
    1020a.

Rendell v. *Went (Inspector of Taxes)*, [1964] 2 All E.R. 464; [1964] 1 W.L.R.
    650; 41 Tax Cas. 641; Digest (Cont. Vol. B) 411, *1020b*.

Case Stated.

The taxpayer appealed to the General Commissioners of Income Tax for Pirehill E
South against an additional assessment in the sum of £614 made on him in respect
of the year 1963-64 under Sch. E and by virtue of the provisions of s. 161 of
the Income Tax Act 1952. The assessment related to: (a) the whole of the costs
of gas, electricity, water, insurance of contents, cleaning and maintenance; and
(b) an apportioned part of the cost of telephone charges and gardener's emoluments incurred by Josiah Wedgwood, Ltd., at Parkfields Cottage, Tittensor, F
Stoke-on-Trent, occupied by the taxpayer. The amount of the assessment was
not in dispute* and the only matter on which the commissioners were asked to
adjudicate was how much of the expenditure incurred by the company was or
was not assessable to income tax on the taxpayer as part of the emoluments of
his office, having regard to the provisions of s. 161 of the Act of 1952, with
particular reference to s. 161 (6). The commissioners held† that an apportionment of the expenditure fell to be made under s. 161 (6), and it apportioned G
it as to one-quarter to the business purposes of the company (£1,377 × ¾ or £1,032
less £640 contributed by the taxpayer leaving the charge to tax at £392). The
Crown appealed by way of Case Stated to the High Court. The taxpayer served
a notice of intention to contend, inter alia, that an item of £181 for maintenance,
wages and materials, should be excluded from the £1,377 expenditure as being H
incurred in the acquisition or production of an asset under s. 162 (1) of the Act.

J. R. Phillips, Q.C., and *P. W. Medd* for the Crown.
Peter Rees for the taxpayer.

PENNYCUICK, J.: This is an appeal by the inspector of taxes against
a decision of the General Commissioners for the division of Pirehill South made
on 12th April 1967, whereby they allowed an appeal by the taxpayer, Mr. Arthur I
Bryan, against an additional assessment in respect of the year 1963-64 under
Sch. E. The question at issue is whether the taxpayer, who is a director of
Josiah Wedgwood, Ltd., and occupies a house belonging to that company, is
entitled to any, and if so to what, deduction from the tax chargeable on this
benefit under s. 161 of the Income Tax Act 1952 by reason of the fact that he

---

* The facts of the case and the contentions of the parties are set out at p. 700, letter
B, to p. 702, letter E, post.
† The terms of the commissioners' decision are set out at p. 702, letters E to H, post.

A   does a substantial amount of entertaining in the house on behalf of the company.
    I will in the first place refer to the relevant provisions contained in the Income
    Tax Act 1952. Section 160 (1) provides:

B
    " Subject to the provisions of this Chapter, any sum paid in respect of
    expenses by a body corporate to any of its directors or to any person em-
    ployed by it in an employment to which this Chapter applies shall, if not
    otherwise chargeable to income tax as income of that director or employee,
    be treated for the purposes of paragraph 1 of the Ninth Schedule to this Act
    as a perquisite of the office or employment of that director or employee and
    included in the emoluments thereof assessable to income tax accordingly:
    Provided that nothing in this subsection shall prevent a claim for a deduction

C   being made under paragraph 7 of the said Ninth Schedule in respect of any
    money expended wholly, exclusively and necessarily in performing the
    duties of the office or employment."

    Paragraph 1 of Sch. 9 is the charging provision under Sch. E. Paragraph 7 is
    the provision which authorises deduction of expenses wholly, exclusively and
    necessarily incurred in the performance of the duties of the office. Section 161

D   provides:

    " (1) Subject to the following provisions of this Chapter, where a body
    corporate incurs expense in or in connection with the provision, for any of
    its directors or for any person employed by it in an employment to which
    this Chapter applies, of living or other accommodation, of entertainment,
    of domestic or other services or of other benefits or facilities of whatsoever

E   nature, and, apart from this section, the expense would not be chargeable
    to income tax as income of the director or employee, paragraphs 1 and 7
    of the Ninth Schedule to this Act, and section twenty-seven of this Act
    [that is the administrative section] shall have effect in relation to so much
    of the said expense as is not made good to the body corporate by the director
    or employee as if the expense had been incurred by the director or employee

F   and the amount thereof had been refunded to him by the body corporate
    by means of a payment in respect of expenses " . . .

    " (6) Any reference in this section to expense incurred in or in connection
    with any matter includes a reference to a proper proportion of any expense
    incurred partly in or in connection with that matter."

G   Finally, s. 162 (1) provides:

    " Any expense incurred by a body corporate in the acquisition or produc-
    tion of an asset which remains its own property shall be left out of account
    for the purposes of the last preceding section."

    Before going further I will read a paragraph from the speech of VISCOUNT
    RADCLIFFE in *Rendell* v. *Went (Inspector of Taxes)* (1):

H
    " The purpose of the section [s. 161] is to charge as taxable emoluments
    of a director whatever his company may have spent, without reimbursement
    from him, in providing for him living accommodation, entertainment,
    domestic or other services or other benefits or facilities, no matter of what
    nature they may be. Moneys spent by the company in providing such

I   benefits, ' Benefits in kind . . . ,' as the section heading says—, are treated
    for tax purposes as if he had spent the money himself and had had it made
    good to him by the company as a payment on account of business expenses.
    Thus they are treated under s. 160 as if they were part of his assessable
    emoluments and only so much, if any, of those expenses as falls within
    para. 7 of Sch. 9 . . . can be deducted from those emoluments. I daresay
    that s. 161 by working its machinery backwards through s. 160 has produced

---

(1) [1964] 2 All E.R. 464 at p. 467; 41 Tax Cas. 641 at p. 656.

a rather elaborate way of enacting a simple idea, but I do not think that the
elaboration makes any difference to the plain meaning of the section."

I turn now to the Case Stated. Paragraph 1 states the nature of the appeal,
and goes on:

" The assessment related to (a) the whole of the cost of gas, electricity,
water, insurance of contents, cleaning and maintenance and (b) an apportioned part of the cost of telephone charges and gardener's emoluments
incurred by Josiah Wedgwood Limited (hereinafter called ' the Company ')
at Parkfields Cottage, Tittensor, Stoke-on-Trent (hereinafter called ' Parkfields ') occupied by [the taxpayer]. The amount of the assessment was not
in dispute and the only matter on which the Commissioners were asked to
adjudicate was how much of the said expenditure incurred by the Company
was or was not assessable to Income Tax on [the taxpayer] as part of the
emoluments of his office, having regard to the provisions of Section 161,
Income Tax Act 1952, with particular reference to sub-section (6) of that
Section."

Then:

" 2. The following facts were agreed:—1. The actual expenses in respect of
Parkfields met by the Company in the year 1963-64 and falling within Section
161 (if the [taxpayer's] submissions were correct) were £1,017, made up as
follows:—Gas, £286, Electricity, £60; Water, £28; Insurance of Contents,
£15; Telephone (an apportioned part of the charges agreed to represent
private calls), £14 [there appears to be some question whether that small
sum has been correctly calculated, but the amount is too trivial to take up
time over, and I have not been pressed to do so] Window cleaning, £18;
Cleaning, £65; Apportioned part (60 %) of Gardener's Wages (the other 40 %
being agreed to represent an element of pension paid to the gardener, a disabled ex-employee of the Company), £350 [there was some discussion on that
item, but it is now accepted that the gardener's wages should be treated as
simply £350] Maintenance wages and materials, £181 [totalling] £1,017.
2. The gross value of Parkfields for 1963-64 was £360. 3. [The taxpayer] paid
the rates in respect of Parkfields and a sum in respect of use and occupation
at an aggregate rate of £640, per annum being £140 in respect of rent and
£500 in respect of services. 4. The computation of the said additional assessment in respect of 1963-64 was as follows:—Expenses, £1,017; Rateable
value, £360 [totalling] £1,377 less payment by [the taxpayer] £640 [leaving
a balance of] £737 10/12ths thereof (being period of occupation during 1963-
64) £614. [The explanation of that last apportionment is that the taxpayer's
tenancy began on 1st June 1963]. 5. The area of Parkfields is 4,515 square
feet and it had cost approximately £23,000 to acquire, put into habitable
condition and modernised, and was now worth between £10,000 and £12,000.
3. The following agreed documents were put in:—(A) Plan of Parkfields with
details of floor space. [That plan was put in to support an argument as to the
proper basis of apportionment. That basis was not accepted by the Commissioners and has not been canvassed on the present appeal, but counsel for
the taxpayer desires to keep the point open.] (B) Copy Minute of Board
Meeting of the Company dated 27th August 1963. [That minute reads " It
was resolved: That the following conditions should apply to [the taxpayer's]
occupation of Parkfields Cottage: (i) The tenancy should be deemed to have
commenced on 1st June, 1963; (ii) The tenancy should be on a yearly basis
and the company would give [the taxpayer] twelve months clear Notice
in writing if it wished to terminate the tenancy; (iii) [The taxpayer] should
pay the Company the Gross Annual Value by way of rent (for the time being
this is £140 per annum); (iv) [The taxpayer] should pay the General Rates
on the property; (v) The Company should pay for all other services, including
water rate, electricity and gas, telephone, maintenance of garden, internal

A   and external repairs and decorations; (vi) [The taxpayer] should pay the
Company £500 per annum in consideration for the services provided under
Clause (v) above "]. (c) [is a later service agreement between the company
and the taxpayer which does not have particular relevance to the case].
4. Evidence was given on behalf of [the taxpayer]. [The commissioners do
not state that they accepted that evidence, but it is common ground between
B   counsel that the Case should be read on the basis that the evidence was
accepted] (i) that, on the decision made in 1962 to appoint [the taxpayer]
as Managing Director of the Company, the Company insisted on his
occupying a suitable house in North Staffordshire at which he could
entertain customers despite [the taxpayer's] own wish to live in London
where he would have had ready access to the executives and buyers of the
C   leading British Stores and overseas customers, many of whom did not visit
North Staffordshire. Accordingly, pending [the taxpayer's] return to the
United Kingdom from the United States (where he was at the time holding
the appointment of President of Josiah Wedgwood & Sons Incorporated of
America, the Company's United States subsidiary) the Company looked for
accommodation in North Staffordshire satisfying the minimum requirements
D   it considered necessary, and ultimately purchased and modernised Parkfields;
(ii) that the importance of entertaining visitors was paramount in the case
of the Company, more than 60% of whose production is exported—mainly
to the United States and Canada, but also extensively to the Continent of
Europe and Australia; (iii) that buyers from these countries and representatives of leading British retailers paid frequent visits to North Staffordshire
E   and that the establishing and maintaining of close relationships with them
was of the utmost importance to the Company; (iv) that it was essential to the
Company that they should be entertained in the home of its senior executive,
especially as the Company's factory was situate in a rural area, several miles
from Stoke-on-Trent; (v) that the approximate times and dates when Parkfields was used for entertainment on behalf of the Company was as set out
F   in Exhibit 4 hereto [Exhibit 4 contains particulars of the occasions on which
someone or other was entertained at Parkfields either during the day—for
example, for dinner or drinks, or even for tea only—or, on some occasions,
for the night. I will go into that matter again at a later stage.]; (vi) that
Parkfields was a very large house formed by consolidating a number of
cottages (some dating back to the early 19th century) rambling and old-
G   fashioned in design with excess floor space and volume to be warmed and
maintained, an excess of rooms and a garden of over 2 acres; (vii) that,
although the agreed figure for superficial floor area was 4,515 square feet, the
Company's Architect arrived at the higher figure of 4,755 square feet;
(viii) that a suitable superficial floor area for a top executive's house was about
2,600 square feet, a modern four-bedroom detached house being likely to
H   have a superficial floor area between 1,400 and 2,000 square feet and a normal
semi-detached house a superficial floor area between 900 square feet and
1,200 square feet [Those last two sub-paragraphs are addressed to the
basis of apportionment, which has not been pursued in this court.]; (ix) that
the fifth bedroom at Parkfields was used only very occasionally by visitors
having no business connection with the Company; (x) that it would have
I   been impossible to entertain on the scale required by the Company in the kind
of smaller modern house which he would have purchased purely for the
occupation of himself and his family.

" 5. [Sets out certain cases which were referred to. I have already referred
to one of those, and will be referring to another.]

" 6. It was contended on behalf of [the taxpayer] (i) that the Company's
expenditure on Parkfields should be apportioned pursuant to sub-section
(6) of Section 161 which enabled a fair apportionment to be made in a case
where expenditure incurred by a Company directly benefited both the

employer and the employee; (ii) that there was no logical reason why a   A
deduction should be conceded (as had been agreed by H.M. Inspector of Taxes
in correspondence) if part of the house was set aside and used exclusively
for business purposes and refused in this case; (iii) that the principle of
apportioning expenditure of an asset used both for business and private
purposes was accepted by the Inland Revenue in respect of motor cars
(where they did not insist that certain seats should be exclusively for business   B
purposes) and that there was no distinction in principle; (iv) that the
expenditure by the Company provided (a) accommodation for [the taxpayer]
and (b) accommodation and facilities for the Company and its visitors;
(v) that a fair apportionment should be made of such expenditure; (vi) that
in making such an apportionment commonsense should be applied and a
reasonable basis would be to apportion the expenditure on the basis of the   C
ratio which the superficial floor area of a normal standard top executive's
house bore to that of Parkfields [It then goes into particulars with which I
am not concerned.]; (vii) that the said additional assessment should therefore
be reduced to 10/12ths of £95.

" 7. The [Crown] contended (i) that the whole of the expenditure set out
in paragraph 2 (1) above, which related to the provision of Parkfields and   D
its related services for [the taxpayer], fell within sub-section (1) of Section
161 of the Income Tax Act, 1952 and that on the facts, sub-section (6) thereof
could only be applied—as it had been applied in arriving at the said additional
assessment—in respect of (a) the telephone charges and (b) the disabled
gardener's wages; (ii) that the said additional assessment should, therefore,
be confirmed at £614.   E

" 8. We, the Commissioners after considering all the evidence and
arguments addressed to us, found as a fact that there was genuine business
use of the house and that [the taxpayer's] personal occupation of it was
restricted in that he was not free to discriminate as to his guests.   We
considered that in principle the case for apportionment under Section 161
(6) had been made out, but we did not accept the method of apportionment   F
based on floor area.   Having regard to the evidence given as to the number
of days on which the house was used for business purposes, we decided to
allow one-quarter of the total expenses for business purposes.   This provided
a figure for the benefit, of:—£1,377 × ¾ [making] £1,032 Less contribution
by [the taxpayer], £640, [leaving a balance of] £392. [It was pointed out very
fairly by counsel for the Crown that if that was a correct apportionment in   G
principle the sum of £392 would have to be scaled down to 10/12ths having
regard to the two months in which the taxpayer did not occupy the house.]
We accordingly reduced the said additional assessment to £392 . . .

" 10. The questions of law for the opinion of the High Court are whether
we were correct in law in determining (a) that an apportionment of the
said sum of £1,377 should be made under Section 161 (6) of the Income Tax   H
Act, 1952 (b) the above-mentioned apportionment of one-quarter."

Notice has been given on behalf of the taxpayer of two new points, to which
I shall refer later on.

It will be seen that the reasoning underlying the decision of the commissioners
was that an apportionment is available under s. 161 (6), where the director
and the company concerned make concurrent use of the accommodation or   I
other facilities provided by the company. They were not concerned, and I am
not concerned, with benefit in the sense that a company always derives a benefit
from the services of a properly remunerated director.

The first contention advanced by counsel for the Crown is that s. 161 (6),
on its proper construction, applies only where the expenditure buys: (i) something which is for the benefit of the director; and (ii) something which is of no
benefit to the director.   That, so far as it goes, is plainly right, but as I understand it what is intended by this contention is that sub-s. (6) has no application

A   to benefits derived from concurrent enjoyment but postulates some sort of severance on, so far as now in point, a temporal or spatial basis. Apart from concurrent enjoyment, I am not clear on what other basis enjoyment of a house or facilities could be severed.

I do not think that this restricted construction is warranted by the subsection. Where a company establishes living accommodation or facilities for common
B   enjoyment by a director and others, whether the company itself or third parties, the terms of sub-s. (6) seem to me to be directly in point. The total expense of establishing the accommodation or facilities is incurred " partly in or in connection with " a matter referred to in sub-s. (1)—i.e., the provision for a director of living accommodation or facilities—and accordingly a proper proportion of that expense is to be treated as an expense " in or in connection with " that
C   matter. It does not seem to me that sub-s. (6) admits of any other construction.

This view appears to me to coincide not only with the terms of the subsection but with reason and fairness. It would be quite unjust that, where a director living in his company's house is obliged to devote a substantial part of its accommodation and facilities to the company and its invitees, he should be saddled with tax on the entire income value of the house and facilities. It has
D   occurred to me that the same result might be reached on the terms of sub-s. (1) alone, without recourse to sub-s. (6). However, there was no argument addressed to this point, and I express no view on it. There may be other considerations in the Act itself or elsewhere which would have a bearing on the point.

The second contention advanced by counsel for the Crown is that the commissioners adopted a wrong basis of apportionment by taking the days in which
E   the house was used for some business purpose, however transitory, and treating those days as days in which the company had, in effect, the exclusive use of the house, the taxpayer himself being treated as having the use of the house only on the days when the house was not used for any business purpose at all. The particulars contained in the document annexed to the Case relate to 72 days in all. Of those 72 days, only approximately 25 involved an overnight stay by
F   the company's guests.

I accept this contention. I do not think it can be right to regard the house in which the taxpayer was living with his family—the family is mentioned in the Case, although we have no particulars about it—as used for his benefit only on the days in which there was no guest of the company in the house for any period of time, however short. To take the extreme case, on certain days it
G   appears that the company's invitees merely came to tea. It would really be absurd to treat the company as having the entire benefit of the house during that day. As I indicated in argument, having arrived at the conclusion at which I have arrived on the first submission by counsel for the Crown, I should like at the end of this judgment to hear further argument on the proper basis of apportionment.

H   I must now turn to the two points of which notice was given on behalf of the taxpayer, one at a very late stage. (i) It was contended that the taxpayer was entitled under para. 7 of Sch. 9 to the Income Tax Act 1952 to make a deduction of an apportioned part of the expenses of keeping up the house as being expenses wholly, exclusively and necessarily incurred in the performance of his office as managing director. On the view which I have taken on the first issue,
I   this question does not arise, and it is better that I should not express a conclusion on it. It is not suggested that the taxpayer would be entitled to deduct a higher proportion of expenses under this head than would be deductible under s. 161 (6).

(ii) It was contended that in any event the item of £181 for " Maintenance, wages and materials " must be left out of account as representing an expense incurred in the acquisition or production of an asset which remained the property of the company: see s. 162 (1). The item " Maintenance, wages and materials " apparently means " Expense of maintenance calculated by reference to wages and the cost of materials ", and it is admitted by counsel for the taxpayer that,

in the absence of any further evidence on the point—this is a point, it will be **A**
remembered, which was not raised before the commissioners—this item must be
regarded as representing maintenance or repairs of an ordinary current nature.
On the face of it, the expense of current maintenance clearly does not represent
an expense incurred in the acquisition or production of an asset. However,
counsel for the taxpayer relied on certain passages in *Luke* v. *Inland Revenue*
Comrs. (2), and I must refer to that case.   **B**

The facts as set out in the headnote are (3):

> " The Respondent was the managing director of a public company. At
> the company's suggestion he bought for his own occupation a large house
> in which he entertained foreign customers. Later he sold the house to the
> company at arm's length and continued to occupy it as tenant at a rent
> equal to the gross annual value for the purposes of Income Tax (Schedule   **C**
> A). Under the tenancy agreement the company was responsible for repairs
> to the fabric and for the fences and boundary walls. The Respondent was
> tenant of the house from 1st October, 1955, to 15th May, 1957, and in this
> period the company spent £950 on repairs, owner's rates, insurance and
> feu duties. The excess of the company's expenditure over the amount paid
> by the Respondent in rent was included as a benefit chargeable under Part   **D**
> VI, Chapter II, Income Tax Act, 1952, in assessments to Income Tax made
> upon him for the years 1955-56 to 1957-58 inclusive."

The headnote, I think, sufficiently accurately represents the facts. However,
it is worth looking at a paragraph (4) which gives further particulars of the
terms of the tenancy agreement between the company and the respondent. **E**
By minute of agreement—

> " it was let by the company to the Respondent at a rental of £148 per
> annum, which was the gross annual value. Under the agreement the Respon-
> dent was responsible for all occupier's rates and charges, for all internal
> repairs and decorations, and for all upkeep and maintenance of the grounds
> and garden. The company was responsible for all repairs to the fabric of the   **F**
> house and other buildings, and for the fences and boundary walls."

Later (5) will be found particulars of the expenditure to which the appeal related.
I think it is fair to say that the learned Lords in their speeches treated the whole
of this expenditure as falling within the head of " repairs to the fabric of the house
and other buildings ".

The House of Lords allowed the respondent's appeal by four to one. They all   **G**
took the view that it could not be right to construe the statutory provisions as
throwing on the director in such circumstances a liability for tax in respect of
expenses incurred by the company in executing repairs such as would normally
be executed by a landlord. They did not express themselves in quite identical
terms. LORD DILHORNE, L.C., said (6):   **H**

> " I cannot believe that it was the intention of Parliament to treat the cost
> of carrying out repairs for which a landlord is normally responsible and the
> carrying out of which is to both his and the tenant's advantage as a benefit
> in kind to the tenant."

Later he said (7):

> " The case would, I think, be different if the company had executed repairs   **I**
> the cost of which is normally borne by a tenant; then it might well be said
> that the tenant had received a benefit in kind."

---

(2) [1963] 1 All E.R. 655; 40 Tax Cas. 630.
(3) (1963), 40 Tax Cas. at p. 630.
(4) (1963), 40 Tax Cas. at p. 631.
(5) (1963), 40 Tax Cas. at p. 632; [1963] 1 All E.R. at p. 637.
(6) [1963] 1 All E.R. at p. 661; 40 Tax Cas. at p. 642.
(7) [1963] 1 All E.R. at p. 661; 40 Tax Cas. at p. 643.

A Lord Reid suggested (8) three possible ways out of the difficulty. He came down in favour of the third solution. However, he also said (9):

"How, then, are we to resolve the difficulty? To apply the words literally is to defeat the obvious intention of the legislation and to produce a wholly unreasonable result. To achieve the obvious intention and produce a reason-able result we must do some violence to the words. This is not a new problem,
B though our standard of drafting is such that it rarely emerges. The general principle is well settled. It is only where the words are absolutely incapable of a construction which will accord with the apparent intention of the provision and will avoid a wholly unreasonable result, that the words of the enactment must prevail.

"There appear to me to be three provisions which are susceptible of inter-
C pretation in such a way as to remove the difficulty in whole or in part. The first is s. 162 (1) which excludes expense incurred 'in the acquisition or production of an asset'. If the words 'acquisition' and 'production' are read in their ordinary sense, it would not help, but so to read them would produce an unreasonable result. Suppose a case where a company buys for £10,000 a house in good repair to be let to a director. Then the whole
D of that expense is clearly excluded by s. 162 (1). But suppose the company buys for £5,000 a house so dilapidated that it has to spend another £5,000 on repairs, then, according to the Crown's argument, the sum spent on repairs is caught by s. 161 (1), so that this sum must be treated as a benefit in kind to the director. That absurd result could be avoided only by reading 'expense incurred ... in the acquisition or production of an asset' as wide
E enough to include not only purchase price but also cost of repair to make the purchased house habitable. And, if these words are wide enough to include repairs immediately after purchase, why should they not also be wide enough to include repairs which become necessary later? No doubt it can be said that if that had been the intention it would have been obvious that the words should be 'acquisition, production, improvement or repair'. And it may
F well be that to make this subsection wide enough to cover all improvements and repairs would exclude in some cases expense which is truly a benefit in kind. I find it difficult to read 'production of an asset' as covering all repairs to an asset, and almost equally difficult to read them as covering some repairs but not others. But this is a case of any port in a storm, and I would not dissent from an interpretation which excludes by this means those items
G in the present case which concern renewals and repairs."

So in that passage Lord Reid is saying that if there were no other way out of the difficulty he would, as a port in a storm, be prepared to accept the construc-tion which included current repairs and maintenance under the head of expenses incurred in the "production of an asset". In fact, he does find a better solution.
H Lord Jenkins dissented; and then Lord Guest said this (10):

"In my opinion where the expenditure has resulted in the replacement or renewal of an existing asset that is none the less the production of an asset within the meaning of s. 162 (1). It may be a question of fact in any given circumstances whether any particular renewal involves the production of an asset."

I Then, later (11): "This would leave as expenditure owner's rates, insurance, minor repairs and feu duty. . ."
Lord Pearce made a short speech in the following terms (11):

"The benefit in kind for which the director is here sought to be charged

---

(8) [1963] 1 All E.R. at p. 665; 40 Tax Cas. at p. 646.
(9) [1963] 1 All E.R. at pp. 664, 665; 40 Tax Cas. at pp. 646, 647.
(10) [1963] 1 All E.R. at pp. 672, 673; 40 Tax Cas. at p. 655.
(11) [1963] 1 All E.R. at p. 673; 40 Tax Cas. at p. 655.

is ' the provision of living accommodation '. Prima facie one would expect   **A**
the intention of sub-s. (1) and sub-s. (4) of s. 162 to be that where the body
corporate retains the ownership of the asset, in this case the house or the
' living accommodation ', the expenses that go to acquiring or producing
the ' living accommodation ' shall not be charged against the director as
a benefit in kind, but the annual value of it, enhanced of course as it will
be by any renewals or repairs, shall be charged against him. That would   **B**
be a fair and sensible intention. But the Crown contend that such an intention cannot be drawn from the words, since the words ' the acquisition or
production of an asset ' can only refer to the original purchase (or building)
of the house and therefore improvements, renewals or repairs cannot be
included. In the context, however, I think that the wide words ' production of an asset ' are capable of the broader construction which is necessary   **C**
to give sense to the provisions of the section. Any money spent which enhances the value of the ' living accommodation ' goes to produce an asset.
If a man possesses a derelict house, the cost of putting it into repair may be
said to be expense that produces an asset. The resulting asset is a house in
good repair. Two sets of expenses have gone to its production, the original
purchase and the subsequent repair. Neither by itself produced the asset."   **D**

That passage is primarily addressed to what might be called improvements
or renewals, but it is certainly capable of being read as applicable to all repairs.

On the best consideration which I can give it, it seems to me that that decision
is a binding authority on repairs for which a tenant would not ordinarily be
responsible. I do not think it is a binding authority on repairs for which a tenant
would ordinarily be responsible, even where, as in the present case, the landlord   **E**
company has undertaken the responsibility for the repairs. The passages which
I have cited from the speeches of LORD DILHORNE and LORD GUEST indicate
that expenditure on repairs of the latter type represents a chargeable benefit;
and the speeches of LORD REID and LORD PEARCE are, I think, at the least,
inconclusive. From that, I conclude that it is open to me to hold, and I do hold,
that expenses of maintenance for which the tenant would ordinarily be respon-   **F**
sible fall within s. 161. On this basis it is accepted, in the absence of any further
evidence, that this particular item of £181 must be treated as falling within
the section.

It remains to consider on what basis the apportionment should be made, and
I would welcome further assistance on that point. [After further argument
HIS LORDSHIP continued:] I have now to decide on what basis this sum of   **G**
£1,377 should be apportioned. It is, I think, common ground between counsel
that the broad basis of apportionment is to see what shares of the total expense
are fairly attributable to the use of the house by the taxpayer and the company
respectively. The difficulty lies in working out that proportion. It is really
impossible in a case of this kind to prescribe any precise formula. Counsel for
the Crown did not wish to prescribe a formula. He said, however, that if one   **H**
had to have a formula one should apportion the expense in the ratio that the
area occupied by the guests multiplied by the hours in which the area was so
occupied bears to the area of the whole building multiplied by the hours in the
year of assessment. Counsel for the taxpayer, likewise, did not wish to have any
precise formula adopted, but he said that if a precise formula is to be adopted
then he would wish to go back to the floor space formula which was advanced   **I**
before the General Commissioners.

So far as I am concerned, I do not think it would be right to attempt to lay
down any precise formula applicable even to this case. Still less is it remotely
practicable to lay down a formula applicable to all cases. Every case must plainly
depend on the particular circumstances of that case. What I have to do is to
endeavour as best I can to say what proportion of the total expenses is fairly
attributable to the use of the house by the taxpayer as his home and what proportion is fairly attributable to the use, or availability for use, of the house

A by the company. I insert that word " availability " because counsel for the
taxpayer in an argument which impressed me pointed out that this was not merely
a matter of saying to what extent the house was actually used by the company's
invitees; one must also bear in mind that the house had to be kept in a state
of availability for such invitees, whether they came or not.

It is only possible to reach this conclusion on a rough-and-ready basis. I do
B not propose to do it strictly by reference to nights or days in which guests were
present in the house, or on any other precise basis. I think a fair result in the
actual circumstances of this case would be to take the commissioners' figure of
£1,032, but not to scale it down by the ratio of ten-twelfths, which would be
applicable if they had otherwise arrived at the figure on a correct basis. I
appreciate that that is an entirely unscientific way of proceeding, but I think
C that if I take that figure it is probably a fair result in the actual circumstances
of this case. I think I should add this, to make my meaning clear. If I had started
on this question entirely unaided by the basis of apportionment taken by the
commissioners, bearing in mind the use of this house by the taxpayer and its use,
or availability for use, by the company, I should have come to a proportion
very like that of three-quarters and one-quarter, but a little less favourable to
D the taxpayer. When one scales that down by ten-twelfths the result would be just
about the same as the figure of £1,032 reached by the commissioners. I have
not thought it useful to work out by a different method a closely similar figure
greater or less by a few pounds.

Appeal dismissed.

Solicitors: *Solicitor of Inland Revenue; Knight & Sons*, Newcastle-under-Lyme
E (for the taxpayer).

[*Reported by* F. A. AMIES, ESQ, *Barrister-at-Law.*]

AGBOR *v.* METROPOLITAN POLICE COMMISSIONER.

F [COURT OF APPEAL, CIVIL DIVISION (Lord Denning, M.R., Salmon and Winn,
L.JJ.), March 11, 12, 1969.]

*Constitutional Law—Diplomatic privilege—Private residence of a diplomatic
agent—Request by High Commissioner to H.M. government to evict a person
from residence—Residence no longer that of diplomatic agent—No power
of executive to evict—Diplomatic Privileges Act 1964 (c. 81), Sch. 1, art. 22,
art. 30.*

G A house in London was bought by the government of the Eastern Region
of Nigeria. Arrangements were made whereby an official of the federal
government later occupied the ground floor. After the secession of the
Eastern Region (which became known as Biafra) and after civil war had
broken out between Nigeria and Biafra, the federal government continued
H to occupy the ground floor; it was used by M., a diplomatic agent of the
federal government, as his residence. On 4th February 1969, M., after
duly informing the gas and electricity authorities, removed his belongings
and vacated the premises. Some Biafrans, using a spare key, thereupon
installed the plaintiff and her family in the ground floor of the house. The
Nigerian High Commission (representing the federal government) wishing
I to continue in occupation of the premises wrote to the Foreign Office claiming
that the house was the residence of M., an administration attaché. They
claimed protection from the receiving state under art. 22* and art. 30† of
Sch. 1 to the Diplomatic Privileges Act 1964, and asked for assistance in
recovering the premises. The Foreign Office contacted the Home Office
who asked the Commissioner of the Metropolitan Police to remove the plain-

---

* Article 22 is set out at p. 709, letter I, to p. 710, letter A, post.
† Article 30 (1) is set out at p. 709, letter I, post.

tiff and her family. The police thereupon, on 7th March 1969, removed the   A
family. On the question whether the police action was lawful,

   Held: (WINN, L.J., dissenting only as to the relief granted) on 7th March
the house was not the residence of M. since he had by that date left it finally;
the information supplied by the Nigerian High Commission was inaccurate
and that inaccuracy removed any justification for the police action; accordingly, the plaintiff should be restored to possession pending the final deter-   B
mination of the matter (see p. 710, letters F and G, p. 711, letter D, and
p. 712, letters F and G, post).

   Per LORD DENNING, M.R.: even if the house had been the private residence
of a diplomatic agent, I am not at all satisfied that the Diplomatic Privileges
Act 1964 gives to the executive any right to evict a person in possession
who claims as of right to be in occupation of the premises. It enables   C
the police to defend the premises against intruders. But not to turn out
people who are in possession and claim as of right to be there (see p. 710,
letter H, post).

   Appeal allowed.

   [For the Diplomatic Privileges Act 1964, Sch. 1, see 6 HALSBURY'S STATUTES
(3rd Edn.) 1017.]   D

Case referred to:
   Southam v. *Smout,* [1963] 3 All E.R. 104; [1964] 1 Q.B. 308; [1963] 3 W.L.R.
      606; Digest (Cont. Vol. A) 317, *57a.*

Interlocutory Appeal.

This was an appeal by Margaret Agbor, the plaintiff, from the refusal of   E
MARS-JONES, J., on 7th March 1969 to grant ex parte an order that the plaintiff
be restored to possession of the ground floor of No. 35, Woodstock Road, London,
N.W.11, and that the Commissioner of the Metropolitan Police, the defendant,
should be restrained from delivering possession of those premises to any other
person. The facts are set out in the judgment of LORD DENNING, M.R.

   Desmond Ackner, Q.C., and *M. Hutchison* for the plaintiff.   F
   A. T. Hoolahan for the Commissioner of Police.

   LORD DENNING, M.R.: There is a civil war flaring in Nigeria. Sparks
from it have come down in London. Some have landed on no. 35, Woodstock
Road, London, N.W.11.

   In 1965 the house was bought by the government of the Eastern Region of   G
Nigeria. It was occupied by one of their senior officers. In 1966 a federal
military government was set up in Nigeria. It was then arranged that an
officer of the federal government of Nigeria should occupy the ground floor of
no. 35, Woodstock Road, while the first floor of no. 35, Woodstock Road
remained occupied by an officer of the Eastern Region. Afterwards civil war
broke out in Nigeria. The Eastern Region seceded. It calls itself the Republic   H
of Biafra. But this house remained occupied as before. The federal Nigerian
officer was on the ground floor. The Biafra officer was on the first floor.

   Now we come to January of this year, 1969. On the ground floor there was a
Mr. Mohammed, who was on the diplomatic staff of the federal government of
Nigeria. On the first floor there was a Mr. Onuma, who regarded himself as
employed by the Republic of Biafra. Mr. Mohammed on the ground floor   I
decided to leave. He gave notice to the electricity people and to the gas people
that he was leaving. He left with his belongings on 4th February. But the
Nigeria High Commission still intended to keep possession of the ground floor.
They arranged for decorators to come in. They intended, after the decorators
had finished, to put another of their officers into the ground floor. On the
very day that Mr. Mohammed left, the decorators came in. But they left at
9.0 p.m. They left the place locked up. But the Biafrans on the top floor had
been keeping watch. They knew that Mr. Mohammed had gone. They had

A   themselves got a key of the ground floor. (It had been left with them by one of the officers of the Eastern Region.) They got into the ground floor, and installed a family of Biafrans in it. They put in the plaintiff, Mrs. Agbor, her husband and six children. This family occupied the ground floor. An hour or so later two men came from the Nigerian High Commission. They tried to get into the ground floor. But the Biafrans kept them out. On the next day,

B   5th February 1969, some 20 Nigerians came and sought to turn out the Biafrans. But the police persuaded them to go away. The Biafrans then went to their solicitors, Messrs. Linklaters & Paines. They wrote on 6th February to the solicitor for the Nigerian High Commission:

"We are instructed on behalf of Mr. D. V. Agbor of 35 Woodstock Road, London, N.W.11. He is now in occupation of the property by authority of

C   the lawful owners thereof. We are instructed that since he has taken occupation, he has been threatened and molested by persons purporting to represent the Nigerian High Commission, culminating in an incident yesterday morning (5th February) when some twenty or so persons attempted to evict him from the premises, apparently led by a man whom our client understands to be the office manager of the Nigerian High Commission. It

D   was necessary for the police to intervene. We trust you will advise your clients that if, as appears to be the case, they wish to challenge the right of Mr. Agbor to occupy the property, then such challenge should be made through the Courts, and not in this manner. Indeed, if this sort of conduct persists, we shall advise our client that he should himself apply for an injunction."

E   The Nigerian High Commission did not take up that challenge. They did not take any proceedings in the courts to evict Mr. Agbor and the plaintiff. On 15th February, Mr. Agbor left on a visit to Biafra. The plaintiff continued to occupy the house with her children. She remained there in peace undisturbed. Then suddenly on 7th March early in the morning the police came and told her she must leave. They said they were authorised by the Home Office on behalf

F   of the Nigerian government. Two men and two women police officers bundled her out of the house, and her children with her.

Her solicitors acted quickly. On that very day they issued a writ on her behalf against the defendant, the Commissioner of Police for the Metropolis. They asked for an order that she be restored to possession and that the Commissioner of Police be restrained from delivering possession to any other person.

G   The judge in chambers refused to make the order. Now there is an appeal to this court. We have much more information than was before the judge, and we have been greatly assisted by the presence here of counsel on behalf of the Commissioner of Police. He has put before us the documents which have led to the police action in this case.

It is quite plain from the documents now before us that the Nigerian High

H   Commission, instead of proceeding in the courts of law against the plaintiff (as they were invited and requested to do) took diplomatic measures. They sought the assistance of the executive to regain possession. The High Commission of the federal Republic of Nigeria on 5th February 1969, wrote a formal letter to the Foreign Office in which they invoked art. 30 of Sch. 1 to the Diplomatic Privileges Act 1964. This provides that:

I   "The private residence of a diplomatic agent shall enjoy the same inviolability and protection as the premises of the mission."

This carries us back to art. 22 which provides that:

"1. The premises of the mission shall be inviolable. The agents of the receiving State may not enter them, except with the consent of the head of the mission.

"2. The receiving State is under a special duty to take all appropriate steps to protect the premises of the mission against any intrusion or damage

and to prevent any disturbance of the peace of the mission or impairment   **A**
of its dignity."

In order to invoke those articles, the Nigerian High Commission in their letter
of 5th February 1969, stated that No. 35, Woodstock Road—

"... is the residence of Mr. A. Mohammed, an Administration Attache
of the High Commission. The matter was reported to the local police, but
it would appear the police are unwilling to render any valuable assistance.   **B**
The High Commission is therefore requesting Her Majesty's Foreign/
Commonwealth Office to render an unimpeded assistance to recover the
premises urgently."

On the next day, 6th February, they wrote again to the Foreign Office confirming
that—
                                                                                C
"... the house at 35, Woodstock Road, London, N.W.11 is the residence
of Mr. A. Mohammed, an Administration Attache, and that it is his intention
to return there to reside immediately."

On receiving those representations, the Foreign and Commonwealth Office
communicated with the Home Office. The Home Office communicated with
the Commissioner of Police. On 4th March 1969, the Home Office wrote a   **D**
formal letter to the Commissioner of Police, stating:

"... the Foreign and Commonwealth Office have requested that steps
should be taken to remove the intruders from the premises ... The Secretary
of State would be glad if you would implement this request in accordance
with ... the Diplomatic Privileges Act, 1964 and take such other steps as
you consider necessary to prevent any further intrusion on these premises."   **E**

Three days later, on 7th March 1969, the Commissioner of Police acted on that
request and removed the plaintiff and her family from the house.

Now I have to say that there is strong evidence before the court to show that
at the material time this house was not the residence of Mr. Mohammed. He
was, no doubt, a diplomatic agent, but he had himself left on 4th February, and   **F**
left finally. The Nigerian High Commisssion intended, I expect, to put someone
else into the house as soon as the decorators had finished. But that someone
might not have the status of a diplomatic agent. It might be someone who
would not rank as a diplomatic agent. At any rate, it appears that the request
made by the High Commission was inaccurate. It stated that the house was at
that time the residence of Mr. Mohammed when it was not. It was on that   **G**
inaccurate information that the Foreign Office, the Home Office and the police
acted. The inaccuracy takes away any justification that they might have had
for their action. It was not the private residence of a diplomatic agent, and did
not come within art. 30. But I would like to say that, even if it had been the
private residence of a diplomatic agent, I am not at all satisfied that the Act of
1964 gives to the executive any right to evict a person in possession who claims   **H**
as of right to be in occupation of the premises. It enables the police to defend
the premises against intruders. But not to turn out people who are in possession
and claim as of right to be there.

The plain fact here is that Mr. Agbor and the plaintiff claim as of right to be
entitled to possession of the ground floor of this house. They occupied it on
4th February. They entered by stealth. They used a key that had been left   **I**
behind. But they did it under a claim of right. It may be that they had no
such right as they claimed. But, even so, the proper way to evict the plaintiff was
by application to the courts of law. No one is entitled to take possession of
premises by a strong hand or with a multitude of people. That has been forbidden
ever since the Statute of Richard II (1) against forcible entry. This applies
to the police as much as to anyone else. It applies to the government departments also. And to the Nigerian High Commission. If they are entitled to

(1) The Forcible Entry Act 1381.

A   possession, they must regain it by due process of law. They must not take the law into their own hands. They must apply to the courts for possession and act only on the authority of the courts. An Englishman's house is his castle. So is the house of anyone lawfully resident here. It is not to be invaded unless the law permits.

B   So we reach this position; the plaintiff was there for four weeks. She was there long enough to be properly described as being in possession. She was there under a claim of right made in good faith. She has been wrongfully turned out by the police. I say " wrongfully ". But I would add at once that the police are not to blame in the least. They were acting at the request of the Home Office who were acting on the mistaken belief that it was the private residence of a diplomatic agent. Seeing, however, that possession was taken

C   from her wrongfully, it should be restored to her. Thus only can the law be vindicated. If she is to be turned out, it must be by due process in the courts of law and not by action of the executive. The Nigerian High Commission may be able to make a good case almost at once. If so, let them do it, but let them issue a writ forthwith against her. It can be speedily heard. But that is the only way to do it.

D   In my judgment this court should make an interim order that she be restored to her possession of this flat. The final rights can be decided later. I would allow the appeal accordingly.

SALMON, L.J.: It seems to me that the key factor in the present case is that the plaintiff and her family had occupied this flat at no. 35, Woodstock Road, Golders Green, as their home for some $4\frac{1}{2}$ weeks from 4th February until

E   7th March 1969. She had occupied this flat as her home under a claim of right. I would like to make it plain that I express no view whether or not she had a good claim of right. There has obviously been a conflict between the representatives of the Nigerian federal government and what were the representatives of the government of the Eastern Region of Nigeria in this country as to which of them is entitled to possession of the premises in question. Again, I am not saying

F   one word as to which of them is right on that issue. I do not think there is any material before us on which we could express any opinion; nor do I think that this issue is relevant to what we have to decide at this moment. It may well be that the question whether the plaintiff or the federal government has a right to possession of the premises will have to be decided later. Although I do not know how that question will be decided, the one thing I am certain of is this:

G   that the proper forum to make that decision is the court. It is certainly not a decision which can properly be made by the executive or by the police.

On 7th March the plaintiff and her children were evicted from their flat by the police, Mr. Agbor then being on a temporary visit to Biafra. I ask myself, what right had the police to evict the plaintiff and her children? I would quote some words to which Lord Denning, M.R., has referred in another case (2):

H   " The poorest man may in his cottage bid defiance to all the forces of the Crown . . . the storm may enter—the rain may enter—but the King of England may not enter—all his forces dare not cross the threshold of the ruined tenement."

When those words were spoken in the reign of George III it may be that they

I   were thought of as applying to an English farm labourer evicted by the soldiery from his home—a dilapidated cottage in the depths of the country; but the principle which they embody seems to me to apply with equal force to an African woman evicted by the police from a comfortable flat in Golders Green at the request of the Home Office. The common law gives no shadow of right to the police or the executive to evict anyone from his home. Indeed it is conceded in

(2) *Southam* v. *Smout*, [1963] 3 All E.R. 104 at p. 107; [1964] 1 Q.B. 308 at p. 320, quoting the Earl of Chatham. See Brougham, Statesmen in the Time of Geo. III, cited in Denning's Freedom under the Law, p. 103.

this case that the right of the police to act as they did in evicting the plaintiff   A
could only derive, if it exists at all, from the Diplomatic Privileges Act 1964.

Now may I say at once that no one could blame the police or the Foreign and
Commonwealth Office or the Home Office for anything which they did. I need
not recite the appropriate parts of the Act of 1964, because LORD DENNING, M.R.,
has read them.   It seems to me that Act places the government of this country
under a special duty to take all appropriate steps to protect the private residence   B
of a diplomatic agent against any intrusion.   On 5th February the Foreign and
Commonwealth Office was requested by the High Commissioner for the Federation
of Nigeria to take such steps under the Act on the basis that the flat in question
then occupied by the plaintiff and her family was the private residence of Mr.
Mohammed, a diplomatic agent of the Federation. Not unnaturally, the
Foreign and Commonwealth Office accepted the accuracy of the information in   C
the note from the High Commissioner and also in the letter from the High Commissioner of 6th February 1969, in which he repeated that this flat was the residence
of Mr. Mohammed; and the Foreign Office, relying on the accuracy of that
information, passed it on to the Home Office with a suggestion that they might
request the police to expel the alleged intruders. We now know, at any rate
there is the strongest possible evidence before the court that the information   D
given by the High Commissioner was regrettably wrong. No doubt a mistake
of some kind or another had been made. But it appears that Mr. Mohammed
gave up possession of the premises on 4th February and left for good with
all his belongings; he vacated the premises believing that a new tenant
would in due course take them over. I say that the evidence is very strongly to that
effect because there is a letter from Mr. Mohammed to the electricity authority   E
saying just that, and a letter from the Nigerian High Commissioner to the same
authority, and I think also to the gas authority which told them precisely the
same thing.   It seems to me that whatever may be the true view about the
meaning of " appropriate steps ", as to which I shall say a word in a moment,
the plaintiff and her family were evicted from her flat by the police acting on
false information; the police were misinformed; the information was false in that   F
the flat was not at the material time the private residence of any diplomatic
agent. Therefore, although they did not know it and had every reason to suppose
the contrary, the police had no right at all to evict the plaintiff. I think that
having been evicted from her home without any right, she should now be allowed
to return to it. If in any subsequent litigation it should turn out that she has
no right to be there, but that the right of possession is in the Nigerian federation,   G
then the courts which exist to protect rights will protect the Nigerian federation
and make an order that the plaintiff shall give up possession, and if necessary
enforce that order. On the other hand, when the action is tried, and it could be
tried quite quickly if the High Commissioner or the Nigerian federation brought
proceedings under R.S.C., Ord. 14—it may be shown that the plaintiff is
entitled to remain in the flat. Until that matter is decided by the courts, the   H
status quo should be restored. I think that it would be most unfortunate if the
plaintiff and her family were not now allowed back into their house. No harm can
come of it if she is allowed back. If she has no right to be there, she can be evicted
at the behest of the Nigerian government by an order of the court. But a great
deal of harm could occur if she is not now allowed back and in the end it turns
out that she has a perfect right to be there.   Unless she is now let back into
possession, there would be nothing to prevent those who obtained her eviction   I
by the unfortunate mistake of giving false information, from entering into the
flat and using it as offices for the mission and thereby depriving the plaintiff
for ever of her enjoyment of the flat.

I want to say a word about the construction of art. 22 (2) of the Vienna
Convention which the Act of 1964 makes part of the domestic law of this country.
That article imposes on the receiving state a duty to take all " appropriate
steps " to protect certain premises against any intrusion. What are appropriate

A steps must depend entirely on the facts of each particular case. I do not think it is necessary to express any concluded view as to what might be the appropriate steps in one case or another; but I would not like it to be thought that if, for example, some person had occupied premises as their home for say six months or even for one month and were doing so under a claim of right, it would be appropriate, according to our views in this country, for the executive

B or the police to turn them from their home out of hand—whatever request may have been received from a foreign power. No doubt there are some countries where, in circumstances such as I have postulated it might be considered appropriate to turn out the alleged intruder and indeed imprison and perhaps even shoot him; but fortunately those ideas do not prevail in this country. When it is a question of taking appropriate steps to recover possession of property, the

C steps which we normally consider appropriate involve legal process. We live under the rule of law; and this is the pillar on which our individual freedom rests. Questions concerning personal liberty and the right to occupy one's home are decided in this country by the courts and not by the executive or the police. This is one of the chief differences between our system and tyranny.

I find it difficult to understand why the High Commissioner of the Nigerian

D federation did not accept the invitation of the plaintiff's solicitors to bring an action against her for possession of the flat which she was occupying, and thus to have the dispute between them decided by the courts in accordance with the law. He chose instead to call on the Foreign and Commonwealth Office under the Diplomatic Privileges Act 1964 to take all appropriate steps to protect his alleged right to possession of the premises. In my view, on the particular

E facts of this case, the appropriate steps for this purpose would not be to throw the plaintiff and her family into the streets, but probably to apply to the courts to decide between the competing claims so that the courts could then enforce the claim which they held to be established.

For the reasons given by LORD DENNING, M.R., with which I agree, and for the other reasons to which I have referred, I concur in the order proposed and

F would allow the appeal accordingly.

WINN, L.J.: I find myself unable affirmatively to concur with the judgments of my Lords. At this time of day I do not propose to expatiate on the reasons for my non-concurrence. Whether it be due to my inadequacy or to more rational grounds, I find this whole case far too difficult for any determination of even part of it to be made on an interlocutory application at this stage,

G it being even technically ex parte. Only on trial could matters which may well be raised later in the action, which I would have thought to be very relevant, be determined. I do not propose to expound my views further. I desire to say that I do not think that either the Foreign and Commonwealth Office or the police were in any way to blame or at fault, although they acted without legal

H power. I desire to add that I do not think the questions in this case raise any point under the Diplomatic Privileges Act 1964. I go further and say I do not think that Act has anything to do with the points which arise on the facts of this case. It would have been more satisfactory if the court had been unanimous, but I am not prepared to strain my judicial conscience to say that I agree with the order proposed.

I *Appeal allowed. The defendant ordered to restore the possession of the premises to the plaintiff until further order.*

Solicitors: *Linklaters & Paines* (for the plaintiff); *Solicitor to Metropolitan Police* (for the Commissioner of Police).

[*Reported by* F. GUTTMAN, ESQ., *Barrister-at-Law.*]

A

VISCO v. MINTER.

[PROBATE, DIVORCE AND ADMIRALTY DIVISION (Ormrod, J.,) March 7, 13,1969.]

Costs—Security for costs—Preliminary point of law—Domicil of deceased raised by way of defence—Trial of preliminary issue—Appeal against order that defendant give security for costs—Whether defendant in position of plaintiff for purposes of interlocutory application—Matrimonial Causes Act 1965 (c. 72), s. 26—R.S.C., Ord. 23, r. 1.

B

Mrs. M. having been joined as a defendant to a summons, issued by Mrs. V., under s. 26 of the Matrimonial Causes Act 1965 raised, as part of her defence, the issue of the deceased's domicil at the date of his death, the other defendants and the executors taking no part in this issue. An order was made that the question of domicil be tried as a preliminary issue and that Mrs. M. be required to give security for costs. On the question whether Mrs. M. should be required to give security for Mrs. V.'s costs in the issue,

C

Held: on the true construction of R.S.C., Ord. 23, r. 1 (1)*, a defendant in substantive proceedings who brought an interlocutory application in the same proceedings, could not be treated as a plaintiff for the purposes of the interlocutory application and the court could not order security for costs to be given; accordingly since Mrs. M. had raised her counterclaim by way of defence she ought to be regarded as a defendant both as to the issue in question and the main proceedings and could not therefore be ordered to give security for costs (see p. 715, letter I, to p. 716, letter A, p. 716, letters B and F, and p. 717, letters H and I, post).

D

E

Dicta of SCRUTTON, L.J., in *Maatschappij Voor Fondsenbezit* v. *Shell Transport and Trading Co.* ([1923] 2 K.B. at p. 176-178) applied.

Appeal allowed.

[As to order for security for costs, see 34 HALSBURY'S LAWS (3rd Edn.) 419, 420, para. 746; and for cases on the subject, see 51 DIGEST (Repl.) 977, 978, *5137-5143, 5147-5149, 5155-5159.*

F

For the Matrimonial Causes Act 1965, s. 26, see 45 HALSBURY'S STATUTES (2nd Edn.) 483.]

Cases referred to:

Apollinaris Co. v. *Wilson* (1886), 31 Ch.D. 632; 55 L.J.Ch. 665; 54 L.T. 478; 51 Digest (Repl.) 977, *5138.*

G

B. (infants), Re, [1965] 2 All E.R. 651, n.; [1965] 1 W.L.R. 946; 51 Digest (Repl.) 979, *5175.*

Maatschappij Voor Fondsenbezit v. *Shell Transport and Trading Co.,* [1923] 2 K.B. 166; 92 L.J.K.B. 685; 129 L.T. 257; 51 Digest (Repl.) 981, *5197.*

New Fenix Compagnie Anonyme D'Assurances de Madrid v. *General Accident, Fire and Life Assurance Corpn., Ltd.,* [1911] 2 K.B. 619; 80 L.J.K.B. 1301; 105 L.T. 469; 51 Digest (Repl.) 977, *5147.*

H

Robson v. *Robson* (1864), 3 Sw. & Tr. 568; 34 L.J.P.M. & A. 6; 11 L.T. 459; 164 E.R. 1396; 23 Digest (Repl.) 284, *3473.*

Tudor Furnishers, Ltd. v. *Montague & Co. and Finer Production Co., Ltd.,* [1950] 1 All E.R. 65; [1950] Ch. 113; 29 Digest (Repl.) 603, *319.*

I

Appeal.

This was an appeal by Mrs. Dorothy Lilian Minter, against the order of the senior registrar that she should give security in the sum of £500 for the costs of Mrs. Cecile Visco who was the applicant in the originating summons under s. 26 of the Matrimonial Causes Act 1965. The facts are set out in the judgment.

---

* R.S.C., Ord. 23, r. 1 (1), so far as material, is set out at p. 715, letter I, post.

A   *G. M. Godfrey* for the appellant.
     Bruce Holroyd Pearce for Mrs. Visco.

                                                              Cur. adv. vult.

         13th March. **ORMROD, J.,** read the following judgment: This is an appeal
     from that part of an order dated 12th February 1969, and made by the learned
B   senior registrar, by which he ordered one of the defendants, Mrs. Dorothy Lilian
     Minter, to give security in the sum of £500 for the costs of Mrs. Cecile Visco, who
     is the applicant in an originating summons under s. 26 of the Matrimonial
     Causes Act 1965.
         On 7th October 1968 the learned senior registrar had directed the trial of a
     preliminary issue as to the domicil of the deceased, James George Minter, at
C   the date of his death. By that order Mrs. Minter is the plaintiff in the issue
     and Mrs. Visco is the defendant, and it is in respect of the costs of this issue
     only that Mrs. Minter has been ordered to find £500 by way of security. The
     ground on which the order was made is that Mrs. Minter was resident abroad and
     has no or no sufficient assets within the jurisdiction of this court to meet Mrs.
     Visco's costs in the event that Mrs. Minter is unsuccessful in the issue.
D   It is necessary to state in outline the relevant facts leading up to these pro-
     ceedings. Mrs. Visco was married to the deceased, James George Minter, on
     12th July 1939.   That marriage was dissolved on Mrs. Visco's petition on
     28th December 1951 and, subsequently, on 10th February 1964, a consent order
     was made under which Mrs. Visco accepted the sum of £12,000 in full and final
     discharge of her claims for maintenance against her former husband and his
E   estate.   On 7th April 1965 the deceased married Mrs. Minter and on 8th July
     1966 he died.   On 14th November 1966 his estate was sworn at about a quarter
     of a million pounds and probate granted to his executors in this country.   This
     came as a great surprise to Mrs. Visco—his first wife—because the figure of
     £12,000 had been agreed by her on what appears to have been a wholly erroneous
     idea of Mr. Minter's financial position. On 23rd March 1967, Mrs. Visco issued
F   her originating summons under s. 26, asking for provision to be made for her
     out of the deceased's estate.   In subsequent proceedings (1) it was held that
     she was entitled to bring these proceedings notwithstanding the consent order
     of 10th February 1964.
         On 12th July 1968, pursuant to r. 102 of the Matrimonial Causes Rules 1968 (2),
     the registrar ordered that various other parties, among them Mrs. Dorothy
     Lilian Minter, should be joined as defendants to the originating summons.
G   Thereafter, Mrs. Minter raised the issue of the deceased's domicil at the date of
     his death, the executors and, I gather, the other defendants, taking no part in
     this issue; indeed, the executors had already acted on the view that his domicil
     was in England.   This matter having been raised by the appellant, the order
     for the trial of this preliminary issue was duly made and the order now appealed
     from followed.
H   The power to order a party to give security for costs in proceedings of this
     kind, which is an originating summons under s. 26, depends on the general
     practice of the High Court and is to be found in R.S.C., Ord. 23, r. 1 (1), which is,
     so far as material, in these terms:

         " Where, on the application of a defendant to an action or other pro-
I   ceeding in the High Court, it appears to the Court—(a) that the plaintiff
         is ordinarily resident out of the jurisdiction, [the other paragraphs do not
         matter] then if, having regard to all the circumstances of the case, the Court
         thinks it just to do so, it may order the plaintiff to give such security for the
         defendant's costs of the action or other proceeding as it thinks just."

     It is clear from r. 1 (3) that there is no magic in a name; for the court is required
     to construe the words " plaintiff " and " defendant " in this order as references
     _____
     (1) See *Re Minter (decd.)*, [1967] 3 All E.R. 412.
     (2) S.I. 1968 No. 219.

to the person, howsoever described on the record, who is in the position of a   **A**
plaintiff or defendant as the case may be in the proceedings in question, including
a proceeding on a counterclaim.

Difficulties of two kinds are apt to arise in the application of this rule. In the
first place, it is not always easy to decide which party is in the position of plaintiff
or defendant. In the second place, it is not always easy to construe the phrase
" in the proceeding in question " when, as here, there are not just interlocutory   **B**
proceedings, but what I might call a subsidiary proceeding to the main cause.
The importance of these points is, of course, that the court has no power to
order a party who is in substance the defendant to find security for costs. I am
very much indebted to counsel in this case for their assistance. Their persuasive
arguments have swung my mind to and fro.

There is no dispute as to the basic principles, which are clearly set out in the   **C**
judgment of SCRUTTON, L.J., in *Maatschappij Voor Fondsenbezit* v. *Shell Transport and Trading Co.* (3). The court will not order a defendant resident abroad
to give security for the plaintiff's costs because the plaintiff has chosen to
institute the suit against him in this country where he has no assets. The
defendant is entitled to defend himself here without the added embarrassment of
having to find security for the plaintiff's costs. So, if the defendant wishes to   **D**
raise a counterclaim by way of defence, he is allowed to do so without incurring
the liability of having to provide security for the costs of the counterclaim. But
this rule is subject to certain limits, because otherwise it would enable a defendant,
sued in this court, to bring a cross-action about something quite different. Where
the counterclaim or cross-action raises matters quite outside the plaintiff's
claim, the defendant will be treated as a plaintiff so far as the cross-action is   **E**
concerned and may be ordered to find security for costs. (See *New Fenix
Compagnie Anonyme D'Assurances de Madrid* v. *General Accident, Fire and Life
Assurance Corpn., Ltd.* (4).)

The principle seems to be that where a defendant counter-attacks on the same
front on which he is being attacked by the plaintiff, it will be regarded as a
defensive manoeuvre. But if he opens a counter-attack on a different front,   **F**
even to relieve pressure on the front attacked by the plaintiff, he is in danger
of an order for security for costs depending on the court's assessment of the
position in each case.

In interpleader proceedings different considerations arise because both parties,
whether they be called plaintiff or defendant, are in substance claimants, and
both may be ordered to give security. (*Tudor Furnishers, Ltd.* v. *Montague &*   **G**
Co. and Finer Production Co. Ltd. (5).)

Counsel for the appellant, who has been ordered to give security for the costs
of the issue of domicil, submits that she is plainly in the position of a defendant.
He says that she has been joined as a defendant because she is one of the persons
who may be adversely affected in her pocket if Mrs. Visco's application is
successful. The appellant has been brought to this court to resist a claim, not,   **H**
it is true, made directly on her, but one which, if successful, will reduce the amount
of the residue which she will receive under the deceased's will. Counsel says that
she has raised the question of domicil as part of her defence and her position is
defensive throughout, and it is mere chance that she is called the plaintiff in
the issue. Under s. 26 it is, of course, a condition precedent to this court's
jurisdiction that the deceased died domiciled in England.   **I**

Counsel for Mrs. Visco also says that I must look at the substance of the matter
but, in his submission, the substance of the matter is that the proceeding in
respect of which he has got an order for security for costs is the issue of domicil
and in that proceeding the appellant is the attacker, coming into the proceedings
and disputing a point which all the other defendants were prepared to accept.

---

(3) [1923] 2 K.B. 166 at pp. 176-178.
(4) [1911] 2 K.B. 619.
(5) [1950] 1 All E.R. 65; [1950] Ch. 113.

A He says that in the restricted context of the domicil issue it is the appellant
who is the actor in or the initiator of the proceeding in question and that he is
entitled to retain his order for security for costs. Counsel relies on *Apollinaris
Co.* v. *Wilson* (6) mainly to show that the court must look only at the proceeding in
question and decide who is the actor in such proceeding. This case is undoubtedly
of some assistance to his argument.   It was an application by the plaintiffs

B for security of the costs of a motion brought by a man named Scherer to be
admitted as a party to an action in which the plaintiffs were claiming an injunction restraining the defendants, who were shipowners, from parting with possession of certain bottles which were said to bear unlawfully the plaintiff's trade
mark. Mr. Scherer claimed to be the owner of the goods and wished to be at
liberty to ship them to Hamburg. The defendants claimed no title to the goods.

C The Court of Appeal ordered Mr. Scherer to give security for the costs of his
motion, to be joined as a party, but reserving the question of security for costs
of the main proceedings if and when he was joined as a defendant. COTTON, L.J.,
said that in the situation with which the court was dealing Mr. Scherer was (7):

"... coming forward as an actor, just as if he were in the position of a
plaintiff seeking to enforce ... the right which he claims."

D
Looked at broadly, it might be said that all that Mr. Scherer was doing was trying
to put himself in a position to defend his property, the bottles, against an adverse
claim by the plaintiff in the action and that his motion was essentially preliminary
to his defence. The Court of Appeal, however, took the view that so far as the
motion was concerned, he was the actor. So, counsel for Mrs. Visco says,

E in the present case, that the appellant although in the position of a defendant
in the main proceedings, is the actor in the domicil issue.

Counsel for the appellant, in reply, relied on *Re B.* (*infants*) (8) in which
PENNYCUICK, J., refused to order a father, resident out of the jurisdiction, to
give security for costs of an application by him in 1965 to vary the terms of the
original order made in 1962 on the application of the mother. The learned

F judge held, inter alia, that the father, who was the defendant in the substantive
proceedings in 1962, must be regarded as still in the position of a defendant when
he initiated proceedings for variation of the original order in 1965. The
Apollinaris case (6) was not cited to him, which is a pity, because I do not
find it easy to reconcile the two decisions.

I accept counsel for Mrs. Visco's submission that I must look at the pro-

G ceeding in question and I am prepared to assume for the purposes of this appeal
that the proceeding in question is the issue as to domicil in which the appellant
is the plaintiff. The question which I have to decide on this footing is whether
hers is, in effect, an offensive role or whether she retains her original defensive
posture. In my judgment, I must have regard to the substance of the matter
which means that I ought not to ignore the position of the parties in the

H substantive proceedings.

In my judgment, the appellant is raising the question of domicil as part of
her defence to Mrs. Visco's claim against her former husband's estate and,
indirectly, against the appellant. Although the appellant has taken the initiative
in raising the issue of domicil, she is acting defensively just as much, if not more
so, as a defendant who raises a counterclaim arising out of the same subject-matter

I as the plaintiff's claim. She, therefore, ought to be regarded as in substance
a defendant in the issue and in the main proceedings. This view is fully supported by the consideration that if the parties had so chosen, the appellant could
have raised the domicil issue in her defence at the trial of the originating summons.
It is a mere procedural convenience that the issues have been separated into
a preliminary issue and a trial of the originating summons.

(6) (1886), 31 Ch.D. 632.
(7) (1886), 31 Ch.D. at p. 634.
(8) [1965] 2 All E.R. 651, n.; [1965] 1 W.L.R. 946.

Finally, for the sake of clarity, I ought to refer to *Robson* v. *Robson*, (9) **A** which shows that the same principles are applied in probate actions as in other kinds of litigation in the High Court and that there are no special rules applicable to proceedings like the present.

The appeal must therefore be allowed.

Appeal allowed.

SEAGER v. COPYDEX, LTD. (No. 2).

C

[COURT OF APPEAL, CIVIL DIVISION (Lord Denning, M.R., Salmon and Winn, L.JJ.), March 10, 11, 1969.]

Equity—Confidence—Breach of confidence—Damages—Use of information obtained in confidence—Basis of assessing damages.

The Court of Appeal having found that the defendant company had made **D** use, albeit honestly, of information which they had received in confidence from the plaintiff, the inventor of a carpet grip, which information was not available to the public, held that the plaintiff was entitled to damages for breach of confidence, the damages to be assessed on the basis of reasonable compensation for the use of the confidential information. On motions by the parties as to the principles on which the damages should be assessed, **E**

Held: the damages should be assessed on the market value of the information as between a willing buyer and a willing seller (see p. 720, letters B and I, and p. 721, letter D, post).

Per CURIAM: Once the damages are assessed and paid the property in the confidential information is vested in the defendant company and they have the right to make use of it (see p. 720, letters E and I, and p. 721, **F** letter D, post).

[As to principles of relief in equity, see 14 HALSBURY'S LAWS (3rd Edn.) 524, 525, para. 992.]

Motions.

On 18th April 1967, the Court of Appeal (LORD DENNING, M.R., SALMON and WINN, L.JJ.) (reported [1967] 2 All E.R. 415) allowed the appeal of the **G** plaintiff, John Henry Seager, from an order of BUCKLEY, J., dated 14th July 1966, dismissing his action against the defendant company, Copydex, Ltd., claiming an injunction to restrain the defendant company, by themselves, their directors, officers, servants or agents or otherwise howsoever, from making use of information supplied by the plaintiff in person and from selling carpet grips called "Invisigrip", in the manufacture of which information supplied by the **H** plaintiff in confidence had been used; the plaintiff also sought an enquiry as to damages by reason of the defendant company's breaches of confidence, or an account of profits, and other relief. The Court of Appeal granted an order for damages to be assessed by the master on the basis of reasonable compensation for the use of the confidential information which had been given to the defendant company. **I**

On 20th October 1967, Master HEWARD ordered points of claim as to the computation of damages to be delivered by the plaintiff, which, as amended, claimed in para. 1 an amount equal to that which represented the amount of the royalty which the defendant company would have or ought reasonably to have been ready to have paid to him between 31st December 1962 and 31st December 1967, together with the capitalised value of such royalties as the defendant

---

(9) (1864), 3 Sw. & Tr. 568.

A company would or ought to have been ready to have paid to him after 31st December 1967 for the use of his invention if it had been patented by him and if he had licensed the defendant company to manufacture the invention, after deducting the proper expenses of obtaining the patents in fact obtained by the defendant company; the proper rate for such royalty being 12½ per cent. of the net selling price being the rate which the defendant company were prepared

B to offer for a similar invention of the plaintiff, the " Klent ", and he claimed not less than £57,650. Alternatively, by para. 2 the plaintiff claimed that, by reason of the defendant company's competition, using patents based on the confidential information supplied by him, with his established business of the sale of " Klent ", his business had been reduced in profitability and value and he claimed £114,100. By para. 2 their points of answer, the defendant company claimed that the proper

C basis on which damages should be assessed was that they should pay to the plaintiff such sum as represented reasonable remuneration to a consultant for the provision by such consultant of the information held to have been derived by them from the plaintiff and used by them in manufacturing the " Invisigrip " on the footing of certain facts. On 26th July 1968, Master HEWARD directed that the points of claim and answer be considered by the Court of Appeal.

D The plaintiff applied for an order that the minutes of the order made by the Court of Appeal on 18th April 1967 be varied so that the damages might be assessed in the manner set out in para. 1 or alternatively in para. 2 of his amended points of claim or alternatively in para. 2 of the defendant company's points of answer. The defendant company applied for an order that the minutes be varied so that the damages might be assessed in the manner set out in para. 2

E of their points of claim or alternatively in para. 1 and para. 2 of the plaintiff's amended points of claim. The defendant company also sought a declaration that, the Court of Appeal not having thought fit to grant any injunction, they should henceforth be free to manufacture, use and sell the " Invisigrip " without let or hindrance from the plaintiff or anyone deriving title from him, and in particular without let or hindrance based on any letters patent which might be

F granted to the plaintiff.

The cases noted below* were cited during the argument.

T. M. Eastham, Q.C., and *A. H. Head* for the plaintiff.
S. Gratwick, Q.C., and *P. Ford* for the defendant company.

LORD DENNING, M.R.: In April 1967 (1) we heard a case which the

G plaintiff, Mr. Seager, brought against the defendant company, Copydex, Ltd., alleging that they had taken confidential information relating to a design for a carpet grip. We found in favour of the plaintiff. Now a question has arisen as to the principles on which the damages are to be assessed. They are to be assessed, as we said, at the value of the information which the defendant company took. If I may use an analogy, it is like damages for conversion. Damages for conver-

H sion are the value of the goods. Once the damages are paid, the goods become the property of the defendant. A satisfied judgment in trover transfers the property in the goods. So, here, once the damages are assessed and paid, the confidential information belongs to the defendant company.

The difficulty is to assess the value of the information taken by the defendant company. We have had a most helpful discussion about it. The value of the

I confidential information depends on the nature of it. If there was nothing very special about it, that is, if it involved no particular inventive step but was the sort of information which could be obtained by employing any competent consultant, then the value of it was the fee which a consultant would charge for it; because in that case the defendant company, by taking the information,

---

* *Peter Pan Manufacturing Corpn.* v. *Corsets Silhouette, Ltd.*, [1963] 3 All E.R. 402; [1964] 1 W.L.R. 96; *Saltman Engineering Co., Ltd.* v. *Campbell Engineering, Ltd.* (1948), [1963] 3 All E.R. 413, n.
(1) [1967] 2 All E.R. 415; [1967] 1 W.L.R. 923.

A   would only have saved themselves the time and trouble of employing a consultant. But, on the other hand, if the information was something special, as, for instance, if it involved an inventive step or something so unusual that it could not be obtained by just going to a consultant, then the value of it is much higher. It is not merely a consultant's fee, but the price which a willing buyer—desirous of obtaining it—would pay for it. It is the value as between a willing seller and a willing buyer. In this case, the plaintiff says that the information was very special. People had been trying for years to get a carpet grip and then he hit on this idea of a dome-shaped prong. It was, he said, an inventive step. And he is supported in this issue by the fact that the defendant company themselves have applied for a patent for it. Furthermore, if he is to be regarded as a seller, it must be remembered that he had a patent for another carpet grip called " Klent "; and, if he was selling the confidential information (which I will call the " Invisigrip " information), then the sales of the " Klent " might be adversely affected. The sales of the " Klent " would be reduced owing to the competition of the " Invisigrip ". So he would ask for a higher price for the confidential information in order to compensate him for the reduction in the " Klent ". In these circumstances, if the plaintiff is right in saying that the confidential information was very special indeed, then it may well be right for the value to be assessed on the footing that, in the usual way, it would be remunerated by a royalty. The court, of course, cannot give a royalty by way of damages; but it could give an equivalent by a calculation based on a capitalisation of a royalty. Thus it could arrive at a lump sum. Once a lump sum is assessed and paid, then the confidential information would belong to the defendant company in the same way as if they had bought and paid for it by an agreement of sale. The property, so far as there is property in it, would vest in them. They would have the right to use that confidential information for the manufacture of carpet grips and selling of them. If it is patentable, they would be entitled to the benefit of the patent as if they had bought it. In other words, it would be regarded as a real outright purchase of the confidential information. The value should, therefore, be assessed on that basis; and damages awarded accordingly.

  In these circumstances, I do not think that we should make any such declaration as the defendant company ask. It is sufficient for us to say that, on a satisfied judgment for damages, the confidential information belongs to the defendant company.

  There is one thing more. We have been told that patent proceedings are pending by the defendant company. They are applying for a patent and the plaintiff is opposing it. That cannot affect directly the matters which we have had to decide today. But the matters are so linked together that I think that the damages should be assessed not by a master in the Chancery Division but by a patent judge. I hope that one patent judge will deal with the patent proceedings as well as these damages. The only order which I would make on the motion is simply to say that the damages are to be assessed in conformity with our judgments.

     SALMON, L.J.: I entirely agree and have little to add. The damages, as LORD DENNING, M.R., said, are equal to the market value of the confidential information wrongly taken by the defendant company—the market value, that is to say, as between a willing buyer and a willing seller. This depends very much on the true character of the confidential information. If the confidential information was not concerning something which can truly be called an invention, but was the sort of information which the defendant company could for a fee have obtained from any competent consultant, then the damages presumably would be whatever might be a reasonable fee in the circumstances. If, however, the confidential information was information about a true invention, then it would be the value of the invention. Inventions are usually sold on the basis of a royalty; but damages, of course, have to be given once and for all, and would

A be the capitalised value of the royalty. Whether this " Invisigrip " is novel and did involve an inventive step will be a matter for the learned judge to decide on the evidence that he hears. It has been argued before us that it is something really very simple and that, therefore, anyone could have thought of it. That may be true. There are, however, many very valuable inventions on the market which are extremely simple; people have been seeking

B for years to find a solution and then someone hits on the idea and it is a very simple idea. It is easy enough afterwards to say: " Well, anyone could have thought of that." It will be a matter for the judge, and perhaps it is not for me to express an opinion; but I observe that the defendant company have applied for a patent for " Invisigrip ", and it may, I suppose, be said on behalf of the plaintiff that, inasmuch as they have applied for a patent, they are saying that

C it is a novelty, it is an invention. But that, as I say, will be a matter for the judge to decide. He may think that, notwithstanding that they have suggested that it is an invention in the patent proceedings, this does not preclude them from now denying that it is an invention. It is a matter entirely for the judge, and I agree with LORD DENNING, M.R., that this question should go before one of the patent judges for decision.

D

WINN, L.J.: I agree entirely with the judgments delivered by my Lords, and for my part would add only two or three very short remarks. I desire to say that I reject the second alternative basis (2) on which it was suggested by the plaintiff that these damages should be assessed. I think that the first (3) of those two is more or less the right basis. I rather regret that my humble attempt to

E reword it was not taken up, because I think that it would have been clearer than it is as at present worded. Nevertheless, it is more or less somewhat of the nature of that which is to be pursued. I only want to add that, when talking of market value in this case, I feel sure that all members of the court would intend that the special position of the plaintiff as proprietor of the " Klent " should be borne in mind as a factor in calculating that value, since, as LORD DENNING,

F M.R., has said, it might well be that he, because of his other interests, would only be a willing seller at a higher price than the notional chaffering between strangers not possessing an interest would produce as the market value figure.

I only desire to add one more thing. That is that, since the basis on which damages are to be recovered in this case is a tortious basis, where there is insoluble doubt between any two possible versions or assessments, when the

G tribunal of fact is pursuing the factual issues, it should be borne in mind that there is a general principle that omnia praesumuntur contra spoliatorem.

On the plaintiff's motions: directions that the enquiry as to damages be heard before a patent judge. No order on the defendant company's motion.

Solicitors: *Payne, Hicks Beach & Co.* (for the plaintiff); *Courts & Co.* (for the defendant company).

H
[*Reported by* F. GUTTMAN, ESQ., *Barrister-at-Law.*]

I

(2) See p. 719, letter B, ante.
(3) See p. 718, letter I, ante.

NOTE.

JOHNSON *v.* JOHNSON.

[PROBATE, DIVORCE AND ADMIRALTY DIVISION (Sir Jocelyn Simon, P., and
Brandon, J.), January 23, 24, 1969.]

*Magistrates—Husband and wife—Appeal—Divisional Court—Procedure—Notice
of appeal—Compliance with Rules of Supreme Court—R.S.C., Ord. 55,
r. 3 (2).*

[As to particulars to be contained in a notice of appeal from a magistrates'
court, see 25 HALSBURY's LAWS (3rd Edn.) 299, para. 583.]

Appeal.

This was an appeal by J. W. Johnson from an order of the Mansfield justices
dated 8th July 1968. The appeal was brought by notice of appeal and the
case is reported only on the practice to be followed in bringing an appeal by
notice of motion.

G. E. Machin for the husband.
I. T. R. Davidson for the wife.

BRANDON, J., delivered the first judgment at the invitation of SIR
JOCELYN SIMON, P., in the course of which he said: The grounds of appeal
as stated in the notice of appeal are in the following terms: (i) That the justices
were wrong in law in finding that the husband had deserted the wife; and that
the wife was justified in refusing the husband's offer of resumption of cohabitation, which findings are not supported by the evidence or alternatively are against
the weight of the evidence. (ii) That the justices were wrong in law in finding
that the husband had wilfully neglected to maintain the wife, which finding
was not supported by the evidence or alternatively was against the weight of
the evidence. (iii) That the justices failed to evaluate the evidence before them.

The notice of appeal, in my view, does not comply with the rules of court.
R.S.C., Ord. 55, r. 3 (2), which deals with notices of appeal in a case of this
kind, provides:

" Every notice of the motion by which such an appeal is brought must
state the grounds of the appeal and if the appeal is against a judgment, order,
or other decision of a court, must state whether the appeal is against the
whole or part of that decision and, if against a part only, must specify that
part."

That rule is similar to, but not the same as, the rule governing appeals to the
Court of Appeal from the High Court and other courts. That rule is R.S.C.,
Ord. 59, r. 3 (2). There is a note to the latter rule in the SUPREME COURT PRAC-
TICE 1967, vol. 1, p. 742, with regard to the sentence in the rule dealing with the
specification of grounds of appeal, and the note reads as follows:

" This provision was introduced by the R.S.C. (Appeals), 1955. The
former O. 58 did not require the grounds of appeal to be specified in the
notice, although this was required by the former O. 39, r. 3, on an application
for a new trial after trial with a jury. The object of the present rule is in
all cases to narrow the issues on the appeal, shorten the hearing and reduce
costs, by a statement in the notice of appeal of the findings of fact and
points of law which will be in issue on the appeal and of the precise order
which the Court of Appeal will be asked to make."

As regards those last words relating to the precise order which the Court of
Appeal will be asked to make, that arises under R.S.C., Ord. 59, r. 3 (2), but
not under R.S.C., Ord. 55, r. 3 (2), and I say no more about that. The note
goes on:

" To that end the appellant (having specified the parts of the judgment

A   or order complained of) will also state what facts he alleges ought to have
been found, or what error has been made in point of law (whether the
point was raised in the Court below or not).   So to allege ' misdirection '
is insufficient: the notice must state in what manner the Judge misdirected
himself or the jury; ... and if improper admission or rejection of evidence is
alleged, the evidence must be specified.   But the notice of appeal should
B   not be lengthy or elaborate nor contain detailed reasons ..."

In my view that note correctly states what ought to be the practice with regard
to notices of appeal, not only when the appeal is to the Court of Appeal but also
where it is from a magistrates' court to this Divisional Court, and I regret to
say that not only in this case but it appears to me also in many other cases that
practice is not followed.   There was a time when the precedents in the practice
C   books encouraged practitioners to state their grounds of appeal in a general
form but that is not the situation today: see the precedent in RAYDEN ON
DIVORCE (10th Edn.), p. 1830.   The matter to which I have referred is not a
matter of form but a matter of substance.   Compliance with the practice which
I have mentioned is necessary to enable appeals to be justly disposed of.   I will
mention a number of reasons why this is so.   In many cases the evidence is
D   voluminous and it is desirable that both the court and the advisers of the respondent should know what are the points taken with regard to the evidence so
that their attention may be concentrated on the relevant part of the evidence
and not wasted on the irrelevant part.   As regards questions of law it is necessary
that the respondent's advisers should know what points of law are being raised
so that they may prepare their case and examine the authorities and be in a
E   position to present them to the court on the points of law so raised.   It may be
further that if a point of law is clearly specified it will become apparent that it
was not raised in the court below or that there is a dispute whether it was raised
in the court below or not.   It may be possible to resolve such a dispute or to
establish the facts with regard to that before the appeal instead of during the
appeal or as the result of an adjournment made necessary during the appeal.
F   A further point that has to be borne in mind is that this court has power on the
application of a party to admit fresh evidence on an appeal.   The circumstances
in which it may do so are limited, but unless a respondent knows in relation to
what findings of fact or in relation to what parts of the evidence there is a complaint which is to be brought before the appellate court, then it is difficult for
the respondent to consider properly in good time whether it is a case where an
G   application for leave to call fresh evidence might properly be made.   These
are some of the reasons why I say that the proper specification of grounds of
appeal is not a matter of form but of substance.   I dare say that one could add
to the points that I have made in that regard.   In saying what I have said in
this case I must not be taken to be criticising any particular counsel or any
particular solicitor: that is not my intention at all.   What I desire to do is to
H   bring to the attention of those who practice in this field the need to observe in
this respect the rules of court and the practice as stated in the note to which
I have referred.

SIR JOCELYN SIMON, P.: I agree entirely with the judgment that
BRANDON, J., has delivered and save that I should like to lend particular support
to what he has said about the proper form of a notice of appeal and about notice
I   to the other side of allegations with other women or other men as the case may be,
there is nothing that I can with advantage add to what BRANDON, J., has said.
I therefore concur in the order that he has proposed.

Appeal dismissed.

Solicitors: *Denton, Hall & Burgin* (for the husband);   *W. A. Raine*, Kirby-in-
Ashfield (for the wife).

[*Reported by* ALICE BLOOMFIELD, *Barrister-at-Law.*]

WOLF ELECTRIC TOOLS, LTD. *v.* WILSON (Inspector of Taxes).   A

[CHANCERY DIVISION (Pennycuick, J.), November 25, 26, 1968.]

Income Tax—Income—Consideration for imparting technical knowledge—
Shares issued in return—Company manufacturing tools—Substantial
Indian trade—Setting up of new Indian controlled company—Indian
government pressure—Transfer of Indian business and techniques to new   B
company—Consideration in form of shares in new company—Income or
capital nature.

The taxpayer company's trade was mainly concerned with the manufacture
of electric power tools, for which it had evolved various production methods
and a series of drawings, viz., processes and schedules of manufacture. It
carried on an extensive export trade with the Commonwealth and had as its   C
sole agent in India a company with branches in all the main centres, which
took ten per cent. in volume (a higher percentage in value) of the taxpayer
company's total annual exports. In 1954 it was informed by the Indian agent
that, because of the Indian government's policy of encouraging the setting
up of local factories for making tools, the whole of the Indian market would
be lost unless it undertook to manufacture in India. In July 1956, it signed   D
an agreement with the Indian agent for the assembly and partial or complete
manufacture of certain tools in India under licence from the taxpayer company,
which was to provide the necessary technical information formulae and data,
and contemplated the formation of a new Indian controlled company (as
insisted on by the Indian government) for the purpose. A new company was
formed in 1958 with the consent of the Indian government given on condition   E
that the Indian agent had a majority shareholding; the agent held in fact
55 per cent. of the shares, and the taxpayer company held 45 per cent. The
taxpayer company's 9,000 out of 20,000 issued ordinary shares of 100 rupees
each, were subscribed for: (a) as to 5,375 shares by the transfer of plant
and machinery to enable the Indian factory to be built to commence work;
and (b) as to the remaining 3,625 shares by the supply of drawings, designs,   F
schedules, technical knowledge and other data required for the establishment
of the factory and the production of the taxpayer company's tools selected
for manufacture in India. In February 1959, the taxpayer company signed
an agreement with the new Indian company implementing that arrangement
and providing that the facilities it was to furnish should be exclusive to the
new company and should not during the ten years' currency of the agreement   G
be furnished to any other party in India. The taxpayer company undertook
to design the new Indian factory and under a further agreement to provide
training and it was given an assurance that the new Indian company would
market the tools manufactured in India only in India and Nepal (subject to
a later permissive relaxation). Following the carrying out of the agreements
the taxpayer company's goods imported into India fell from between £75,000   H
and £90,000 in value to an average of £700 a year from 1960 to 1966. The taxpayer company was assessed to tax on the basis that the 3,625 shares of 100
rupees each in the new Indian company received by it represented receipts
of its trade to be taken into account in computing its profits assessable under
Case I of Sch. D to the Income Tax Act 1952.

Held: the 3,625 shares in the new Indian company were not receipts of the   I
taxpayer company's trade required to be taken into account in computing
its profits for income tax purposes, because they were received in return for
the transfer to the Indian company, under threat of Indian legislation
restricting imports, of two capital assets, comprising a fund of confidential
material in relation to its manufacture of tools and its connection with India
through its agent (in the nature of pre-existing goodwill) with exclusive rights
precluding the taxpayer company from competing with the new Indian company in India; and it made no difference: (i) that the agreement related to

A   part only of the tools manufactured by the taxpayer company since the
transfer of a part of the trade severed from the remainder was still transfer
of a capital asset; (ii) that the transaction took the form of an exclusivity
provision, since that did not differ in substance from the transfer of goodwill;
and (iii) that the consideration for the issue of the shares was expressed to be
the obligation to supply information, since where that information was in
B   connection with the transfer of a local connection the obligation represented
prima facie the breaking up of the part of the capital asset consisting of the
fund of confidential material rather than its retention intact and its exploitation, and notwithstanding that the company would continue to derive profits
from India, that profit being in the form of dividends on shares (see p. 731,
letter H, to p. 732, letter A, p. 732, letter I, and p. 733, letters B to F, post).

C   *Rolls-Royce, Ltd.* v. *Jeffrey (Inspector of Taxes)* ([1962] 1 All E.R. 801) and
Musker (Inspector of Taxes) v. *English Electric Co., Ltd.* ((1964), 41 Tax
Cas. 556) distinguished.
        Appeal allowed.

[As to what constitutes trade receipts and income as opposed to capital for
D   income tax purposes see 20 HALSBURY'S LAWS (3rd Edn.) 149, 150, para. 263;
and for cases on the subject, see 28 DIGEST (Repl.) 20-38, *78-173*; 50-58, *191-225*.]

Cases referred to:
    British Dyestuffs Corpn. (Blackley), Ltd. v. *Inland Revenue Comrs.* (1924),
        12 Tax Cas. 586; 28 Digest (Repl.) 25, *105*.
    Edwards (Inspector of Taxes) v. *Bairstow*, [1955] 3 All E.R. 48; [1956] A.C. 14;
E   [1955] 3 W.L.R. 410; 36 Tax Cas. 207; 28 Digest (Repl.) 397, *1753*.
    Moriarty (Inspector of Taxes) v. *Evans Medical Supplies, Ltd., Evans Medical
        Supplies, Ltd.* v. *Moriarty (Inspector of Taxes)* [1957] 3 All E.R. 718;
        37 Tax Cas. 540; 28 Digest (Repl.) 26, *112*.
    Musker (Inspector of Taxes) v. *English Electric Co., Ltd., Inland Revenue
        Comrs.* v. *English Electric Co., Ltd.* (1964), 41 Tax Cas. 556; Digest
F   (Cont. Vol. B) 386, *112b*.
    Rolls-Royce, Ltd. v. *Jeffrey (Inspector of Taxes), Same* v. *Inland Revenue
        Comrs.*, [1961] 2 All E.R. 469; [1961] 1 W.L.R. 867; *affd.*, H.L., [1962]
        1 All E.R. 801; [1962] 1 W.L.R. 425; 40 Tax Cas. 443; Digest (Cont.
        Vol. A) 845, *112a*.

G   **Case Stated.**
    The taxpayer company appealed to the Special Commissioners of Income Tax
against the following alternative assessments to income tax: (a) under Case I of
Sch. D to the Income Tax Act 1952 for the year 1960-61 on the profits of the
company as mechanical and electrical engineers in the sum of £25,000; and (b)
under Case VI of Sch. D on proceeds of the sale of patent rights under the pro-
H   visions of s. 318 of the Act of 1952 as enlarged by the Finance Act 1952, s. 24
and Sch. 6, Pt. 2, in the sum of £4,500 in each of the years 1959-60 to 1964-65
inclusive. The questions for determination* were whether 3,625 ordinary shares of
100 rupees each in an Indian company, Ralliwolf Private, Ltd., represented
receipts of the taxpayer company's trade to be taken into account in computing
the profits assessable under Case I and, if not, whether the shares were properly to
I   be considered to be the proceeds of a sale of patent rights assessable under Case
VI. The commissioners held† that the transaction as to the shares represented a
method of trading by which the taxpayer company acquired the particular asset
as part of the profits and gains of its trade and dismissed the taxpayer company's
appeal. The taxpayer company appealed by way of Case Stated to the High Court.

---

* The facts in the case and the contentions of the parties as given in the Case Stated,
are set out at p. 726, letter D, to p. 731, letter B, post.
  † The decision of the commissioners is set out at p. 731, letters C to F, post.

Desmond C. Miller, Q.C., and *E. R. Meyer* for the company.   A
H. E. Francis, Q.C., and *P. W. Medd* for the Crown.

PENNYCUICK, J.: I have before me an appeal by Wolf Electric Tools,
Ltd., (to whom I shall refer as " the company ") against a decision of the Special
Commissioners whereby they affirmed in principle an assessment under Case I
of Sch. D to the Income Tax Act 1952 for the year 1960-61 on the company in B
respect of its profits as mechanical and electrical engineers. The issue in the case
is whether, in computing those profits, there should or should not be taken into
account the value of 3,625 ordinary shares of 100 rupees each in an Indian
company, Ralliwolf Private, Ltd., received by the company under certain
arrangements made in the year 1959.

I will first recite the facts as they appear in the Case Stated. I will not read C
the Case Stated in full, because certain parts of it have, I think, only a rather
indirect bearing on the question which I have to decide. Paragraph 1 sets out the
assessment under Case I. It also sets out an assessment under Case VI of Sch. D
in respect of the proceeds of sale of patent rights. That contention has been
abandoned by the Crown, and I do not pursue it.

> " 2: Shortly stated the questions for determination were whether 3,625   D
> Ordinary shares of 100 Rupees each in an Indian Company, Ralliwolf Private
> Limited, (hereinafter called ' Ralliwolf ') represented receipts of the Company's
> trade to be taken into account in computing the profits assessable under Case
> I ... "

Paragraph 3 gives the names and qualifications of the three witnesses who gave
evidence. They were Mr. G. M. Wolfe, the chairman and managing director of E
the company and of its holding company, Wolf Electric Tools (Holdings), Ltd.
(which is referred to as " the Holding Company " in the Case); Mr. Sheppard,
the chief accountant and secretary of Rallis India, Ltd. (which is referred to as
" Ralli " in the Case); and Mr. McGilchrist, a member of the firm of Fuller,
Jenks Wise and Co., the auditors of the company. Paragraph 4 sets out a number
of documents which are annexed to the Case and available for inspection. I shall F
refer later on to two or three of those documents.

> " 5: As a result of the evidence, both oral and documentary, adduced
> before us we find the following facts proved or admitted:—(i) The Company
> was incorporated in 1908 to take over and carry on the trade formerly
> carried on by a partnership. [Then an extract from the memorandum is   G
> annexed.] The Company's trade was mainly concerned with the manu-
> facture of electric power tools of which some fifty different industrial and
> domestic models were produced. In the course of the development of its
> electric tools the Company evolved various production methods and a
> series of drawings, jigs, processes and schedules of manufacture. They were
> valuable assets of the Company and safeguarded by strict security. Taking H
> as an example a typical mechanical part, a drawing would provide the
> basic information necessary to make a die from which a casting could be pro-
> duced. When the casting had been produced it required machining so that
> other components could be fitted to it. The Company worked to clearances
> of a thousandth and sometimes a ten-thousandth of an inch. The particular
> casting required eighteen different machining operations which had to be per- I
> formed in the correct order. The research and development activities of the
> Company were carried out in a separate building which could only be entered
> by those employees who were concerned with this work. Much of the
> information was patentable but patents were not always taken out. (ii) For
> many years the Company had carried on an extensive export trade with the
> Commonwealth and other countries through its own branches and also
> through sales agencies which sold and serviced the Company's English
> products ... [The Case then goes on to give particulars of a subsidiary of

A the company established in Australia. I do not think anything really turns on that. It further gives particulars of an agreement with a French company made in 1956 in relation to one particular machine. Again, I do not think anything turns on that.] The Company had started to trade with India before 1933 when Mr. Wolfe, the present Managing Director of the Company became the Company's export manager. At that time the Company had two

B agents in India, one in Bombay and the other in Calcutta. In 1937 Marshall Sons and Company was appointed sole agent in India. After the war the Company resumed its exports to India with the same agent. In or about 1950 the Company's sole agency in India was taken over by Ralli who had branches in all the main centres. Ralli bought from the Company on a principal to principal basis. In the two years 1954 and 1955 the Company's

C total exports amounted to 60,533 machines with accessories and spare parts. Ralli imported at least 3,000 machines into India each year which represented 10% of the total annual exports of the Company by volume and, because the exports to India were mainly of the heavier and more expensive models, the percentage by value was even greater. This volume of business with India represented the Company's largest export market outside the countries

D where the Company maintained its own branches. In addition, from 1950, when import licensing restrictions in India became more stringent, the Company made arrangements to deal directly with the Indian Government's Stores Department by tender through the High Commissioner's Office in London.   (iii) In 1954 Ralli informed the Company that because of the Indian Government's policy of encouraging the setting up of local factories

E for making tools, unless the Company undertook to manufacture in India the whole of the Indian market would be lost. The Company was aware that certain foreign manufacturers of power tools were ready to set up factories in India on the Indian Government's terms. The Indian Government's Development Officer indicated to Ralli that unless a scheme was submitted by Ralli quickly, it might not be considered. It was also indicated that while

F indigenous components would be expected to be used when available, unrestricted import would be permitted of any components which could not be obtained locally. Ralli were also informed that while there would be protection of locally made tools by way of restricted import of foreign made competitors provided that the locally made tools were only slightly more expensive, if the price of the locally made tools were out of all proportion

G to the price of the imported articles, the scheme for local manufacture would not be approved.   On 13th September, 1955, the Company wrote to Ralli's agents in London, Ralli Brothers Ltd. as follows: ' Whilst we are naturally reluctant to sanction the manufacture of our products by any organisation not controlled by our own management, we appreciate the peculiar circumstances which exist in the case of India, and the development

H towards self-sufficiency in Asia generally which must take its course. After due deliberation, therefore, we are prepared to agree the principle of the assembly/manufacture of selected Wolf electric tools in India by your associates, and agree that, in the initial stage, this manufacture need not involve the formation of a new company, but should be controlled and financed by Rallis.' On 30th July, 1956, the Company signed an agreement with Ralli

I for the assembly and partial or complete manufacture of certain tools in India.   The agreement stipulated that the tools should bear the name ' Wolf ', that the Company would grant a licence to Ralli to use in India any patent rights and that Ralli would be given all formulae and technical information then used by the Company and all new inventions and formulae relating to the manufacture of the selected tools which the Company might obtain by means of development and research work in England. The Company also agreed that it would supply all the drawings, schedules and data sheets required for the manufacture of the selected tools for which Ralli

would pay to the Company a fee of £500 a year until a new company was promo- A
ted and commenced business. It was also agreed that control of the proposed
company would go by means of a majority shareholding to Indian interests. This
requirement was insisted upon by the Indian Government. [That agreement
is annexed but it is, I think, sufficiently summarised in the foregoing paragraph. The agreement was superseded later on.] (iv) On 31st October, 1958,
Ralliwolf was incorporated in India to carry on the Company's trade in   B
India. The consent of the Indian Government to the formation of Ralliwolf
was given on the condition that Ralli would be the majority shareholders.
[Then a copy of the memorandum and articles of association of Ralliwolf
is annexed. It was pointed out in argument that under the articles Mr. G. M.
Wolfe was to be one of the first directors of Ralliwolf, the other two being in
India.] On 5th January, 1959, Ralli agreed with the Holding Company, on   C
behalf of the Company, to take 55% of Ralliwolf's issued share capital and
the Holding Company agreed to take 45% of Ralliwolf's share capital.
It was also agreed that the Holding Company should supply all present
and future technical knowledge relating to the tools selected for manufacture in India. [That agreement is annexed. Its provisions were duly
carried into effect by two subsequent agreements. It is only significant, I   D
think, as showing that the two subsequent agreements, although they differ
by some months in date, were steps in a single pre-arranged transaction.]
The authorised share capital of Ralliwolf was 50 lacs of Rupees divided into
50,000 shares of 100 Rupees each. The issued share capital of Ralliwolf was
20,000 shares. Under an agreement of 16th February, 1959, between the
Holding Company, Ralli and Ralliwolf, the Holding Company undertook   E
to subscribe for 9,000 Ralliwolf shares, the consideration being:—(a) as to
5,375 shares, the transfer of plant and equipment to enable the Indian factory
to commence work and (b) as to the remaining 3,625 shares (which form the
subject matter of this appeal) the supply of drawings, designs, schedules,
technical knowledge and other data required for the establishment of the
factory and the production of the Company's tools selected for manufacture   F
in India. [That agreement is annexed. I need not refer further to it.] (v) On
the same day, 16th February, 1959, the Holding Company and Ralliwolf
signed an agreement . . . "

which is annexed and marked F. I must refer to that agreement more specifically.
The agreement is made between the company (called "Wolfs") of the one
part and Ralliwolf Private, Ltd. (called "Ralliwolf") of the other part. It   G
recites:

" (i) Processes and formulae relating to the manufacture of certain ranges
or portable electric tools (hereinafter comprehensively referred to as 'the
selected tools' and set out in the schedule hereto) and components thereof
and accessories thereto are exclusively owned by [the company].   (ii)   H
Ralliwolf was incorporated on the 31st day of October 1958 with an authorised capital of 50 lacs of rupees divided into 50,000 Equity shares of 100 rupees
each. (iii) Ralliwolf has as its main object the manufacture and marketing in
India of, inter alia, portable electric tools. (iv) Ralliwolf proposes to build in
Bombay a factory for the manufacture of the selected tools. (v) For facilitating
the establishment and organisation by Ralliwolf of a factory for the purpose   I
of manufacturing the selected tools [the company] have agreed for the
consideration hereinafter mentioned to execute such Agreement as is
hereinafter contained.

" Now therefore this agreement witnesseth as follows: 1. In consideration
of the issue to [the company] by Ralliwolf of 3625 Ordinary shares of
100 rupees each in the capital of Ralliwolf credited as fully paid up (which
shares shall be so issued to [the company] immediately after the execution
of these presents) (i) [the company] will provide and make available to

A   Ralliwolf all present and future drawings designs schedules and technical knowledge and data necessary for the establishment erection and installation of the factory and the production thereat of the selected tools."

The company then goes on to undertake to supply various designs, and so forth, and to grant or assign to the company all Indian patents, the benefit of all future inventions, and so forth, all related to the selected tools. Then, in
B   cl. 1 (iv):

"[The company] hereby undertake that during the currency of this agreement the facilities hereby agreed to be furnished to Ralliwolf under the preceding sub-clauses of this clause shall be exclusive to Ralliwolf and shall not during the currency of this Agreement be furnished to any other person
C   or corporation in India."

Then, cl. 4:

"This Agreement shall come into force on the signing hereof and shall remain in force for so long as the said Manufacturing and Marketing Agreement remains in force."

D   That agreement has already been referred to, and was in fact executed on 19th August 1959. To return to the Case:

"(vi) As well as supplying Ralliwolf with drawings and specifications of the components of the Company's tools and the many schedules of manufacturing processes required to make them, the Holding Company undertook to design the lay-out of the Indian factory and to supply to Ralliwolf
E   full data and specifications and all other information relating to the machinery and equipment necessary for the manufacture or assembly of the Company's tools. The design of some of the Company's tools was more complex than of others but their years of experience had taught the Company the best and simplest methods of constructing each component of a tool and while this information was not covered by patents it was secret in so far as it was
F   not available to the Company's competitors. [The Case then refers to patents which were not considered to be of much value.] (vii) On 19th August, 1959, a further agreement was made between the Holding Company and Ralliwolf in which Ralliwolf agreed, inter alia, that the tools assembled or manufactured in India would be marketed only in India and Nepal but the Holding Company would consider permitting exports by Ralliwolf when the possibility
G   of exports arose. It was also agreed that the Company would afford training at its works in England to men selected by Ralliwolf and intended to fill technical posts in the latter's factory."

That agreement is annexed and I must read certain provisions from it. The agreement is made between the company (called "Wolfs") of the one part and Ralliwolf Private, Ltd. (called "Ralliwolf") of the other part. It recites:
H

"Whereas the parties have agreed for the assembly and partial or complete manufacture in India of certain electric tools and associated accessories, as set out in the First Schedule hereto (hereinafter referred to as 'the selected tools') to be marketed under the trade marks of [the company] and for the purpose of regulating their relationship Ralliwolf and [the company] have decided to enter into this agreement upon the terms and in
I   the manner hereinafter appearing.

"Now this Agreement witnesseth: 1. Subject to the special conditions stated in Clause 13 hereof and relative to the subject-matter of that Clause this Agreement shall be in force subject to renewal or modification with the prior approval of the Government of India for an initial period of ten years from the date hereof unless previously cancelled by mutual consent of both parties or terminated as hereinafter mentioned. 2. The territory to be covered by the terms of this Agreement shall be the Union of India and Nepal

(hereinafter called ' the territory '). Ralliwolf agree that the tools assembled   **A**
and/or manufactured in India will be marketed in the territory only but
[the company] will consider permitting exports from the territory when
the possibility of such exports arises.   [The company] agree that during
the currency of this Agreement they will not establish any other factory
in the territory or grant trade mark or patent licences to any other person
firm or company in the territory and that they will not sell any of the   **B**
completed tools of the types manufactured or to be manufactured under
this Agreement in or to the territory except to Ralliwolf or with the consent of
Ralliwolf."

There follow a considerable number of provisions, including those for technical
training of Ralliwolf's employees in England.

To return again to the Case Stated: **C**

" (viii) After 19th August, 1959, when the Indian Government approved
the Ralliwolf manufacturing scheme, import licences were issued for components from England in decreasing quantities as Ralliwolf took over the local
manufacture of components on a progressive basis.   Prior to August, 1959,
the value of the Company's goods imported into India was some £75,000   **D**
to £90,000 per annum.   The total sales of the Company's products imported
into India from 1960 to 1966 amounted to £5,085, an average of only £700
a year.   The percentage value of the Company's Indian exports in terms
of the value of total exports (other than to associated companies) from after
the war until July 1956 was about 15%: for the period from 1st August,
1956, to 19th August, 1959, the percentage value was about 4½%.   After   **E**
the 19th August, 1959, the total value of the Company's global exports was
never less than £1 million and was increasing annually.   After August, 1959
components were supplied to Ralliwolf on a cost basis which resulted in no
profits to the Company.   In the accounts of the Holding Company for the year
ended 31st December, 1960, the item of trade investment, £40,937 represented the total value of the Company's shareholding in Ralliwolf including the   **F**
3,625 shares issued in consideration of supplying the drawings and information but no money value was attributed to these shares in the Company's
books.   Ralliwolf had subsequently issued further shares to the Company
in the period 1963 to 1965.   The 3,625 shares represented a nominal value
of £27,092 at the agreed rate of exchange."

Then there are annexed the holding company's accounts for a number of years.   **G**
Those accounts contain a report of the chairman's speech at the annual general
meeting of the holding company each year.   It is quite clear from those reports
that the holding company intended that the company should continue to derive
a profit from India through the medium of its holding in the Ralliwolf company
when established.

H

" 6. It was contended on behalf of the Company as follows: ... (i) that
the information was a capital asset of the Company's trade; (ii) that the disclosure of information was not an activity of the Company's trade; (iii)
that the disclosure of information was not, in any event, a realisation of
assets for money's worth, being an investment operation; and (iv) in the
alternative, that the shares in question of Ralliwolf were received as   **I**
consideration for what could be described as ' keep out payments ' and were
not trading receipts ...

" 7. It was contended by H.M. Inspector of Taxes: ... (i) that the transaction in regard to the 3,625 shares was a natural development of the Company's
technique for exploiting the Indian market to provide trading income; (ii)
that the receipt by the Holding Company on behalf of the Company of the
shares was not a separate trading activity of divulging expertise but a method
of increasing the Company's income as mechanical and electrical engineers

A   by using know-how to the best advantage in a market which could otherwise be closed; (iii) that the Agreements entered into by the Holding Company on behalf of the Company did not amount to an outright sale but merely an assignment for a period of ten years in respect of the selected tools which did not exclude the Company from the Indian market in regard to other tools manufactured by the Company or to the supply of components.

B   While there was evidence of restriction of imports by the Indian Government this was not covered by the Holding Company's Agreements with Ralli or Ralliwolf; (iv) that the Company told others how to manufacture its tools and the receipts for the information were revenue in the Company's hands."

Paragraph (viii) sets out the cases which were referred to. I shall mention **C** certain of those at a later stage.

" (ix) We, the Commissioners who heard the appeals, gave our decision as follows . . . [and they set out the assessment. Then] The first question we have to decide is whether the 3,625 shares of 100 Rupees each in an Indian company, Ralliwolf, issued fully paid by Ralliwolf to the Holding Company on behalf of the Company is a receipt on revenue account or capital account **D** . . . After consideration of all the evidence, both oral and documentary, and the arguments addressed to us and the authorities cited to us we are of opinion that this Case is not on all fours with *Moriarty* (*Inspector of Taxes*) v. *Evans Medical Supplies, Ltd.* (1). We think rather that this case falls within the decision in *Rolls-Royce, Ltd.* v. *Jeffrey* (*Inspector of Taxes*) (2). In arriving at this conclusion we have applied the criterion laid down by **E** VISCOUNT SIMONDS in the *Rolls-Royce* case (3) where he quoted from the test laid down by BANKES, L.J., in *British Dyestuffs Corpn. (Blackley), Ltd.* v. *Inland Revenue Comrs.* (4): ' . . . looking at this matter, is the transaction in substance a parting by the Company with part of its property for a purchase price, or is it a method of trading by which it acquires this particular sum of money as part of the profits and gains of that trade? ' We are of the opinion **F** that this case falls under the second category rather than the first of BANKES, L.J.'s two categories. While we accept that the Company has had considerable trading difficulties over the Indian Government's restrictions on imports we do not think these affected the character of the consideration as being receipts of its trade."

G   They accordingly held that the appeal failed in principle, and they rejected the alterative assessments under Case VI. As I have said, the Crown has abandoned any contention based on those alternative assessments.

It has not been challenged on behalf of the Crown that this is a case in which the court has the right and duty to review the decision of the commissioners and to reverse that decision if it reaches the conclusion that the decision was not justified by the particular facts established before the commissioners. I need not **H** therefore refer to the well-known case of *Edwards* (*Inspector of Taxes*) v. *Bairstow* (5).

I find it impossible to reach the same conclusion as did the commissioners in this case. The position before the execution of the 1959 agreements was that the company had among its assets, first, a fund of confidential material in relation to its manufacturing processes and, second, its connection with India **I** through the Ralli company, which purchased the company's products as principal and in due course, no doubt, distributed them. The Indian connection was of the nature of goodwill. Both those assets as I have stated them were in themselves plainly capital assets of the company's trade. In 1959 the company

---

(1) [1957] 3 All E.R. 718; 37 Tax Cas. 540.
(2) [1962] 1 All E.R. 801; 40 Tax Cas. 443.
(3) [1962] 1 All E.R. at p. 803; 40 Tax Cas. at p. 491.
(4) (1924), 12 Tax Cas. 586 at p. 596.
(5) [1955] 3 All E.R. 48; 36 Tax Cas. 207.

and the Ralli company entered into the agreements which I have mentioned. **A**
Those agreements were made under the threat of Indian legislation restricting
imports. There were certain transitional agreements to which, I think, I need
not further refer. The effect of the final agreements made in 1959 was that
an Indian company—i.e., the Ralliwolf company—was established with a capital
issued as to 55 per cent. to the Ralli company and as to 45 per cent. to the company. The Ralliwolf company took over the manufacture of the selected tools, **B**
and it also took over the benefit of the Ralli company connection. The Ralli
company did not, I think I am right in saying, undertake any specific obligation
to distribute the Ralliwolf company's products, but it is clearly implicit in the
entire transaction that the Ralli company, being the majority shareholder in
that company, would distribute that company's products. The company undertook to supply confidential material to the Ralliwolf company in order that **C**
the Ralliwolf company should be enabled to carry on the manufacture of the
selected tools. In addition, by the exclusivity provisions the company undertook
not to compete, in effect, with the Ralliwolf company in India as regards the
selected tools. The Ralliwolf company issued 45 per cent. of its shares to the
company in return for the obligation to provide confidential material.

The effect of that transaction as regards the company was simply, it seems **D**
to me, to alter the company's capital profit-making structure; i.e., instead of
having its own goodwill in India as regards the selected tools, the company
acquired a 45 per cent. interest in the new company and thenceforward derived
its profit through those shares. If the transaction had embraced the entire
Indian connection of the company, and if the share consideration had been
expressed to be attached to a transfer of that connection—i.e., in effect, goodwill **E**
—it is perfectly clear that no element of taxable profit would have been involved.
The contrary is not, I think, suggested on behalf of the Crown. If it is suggested,
then I think the answer would be plainly in the negative. One can illustrate
that point, if illustration is necessary, by considering what would have been
the position if, instead of the Ralliwolf company being owned as to 55 per cent.
by the Ralli company and 45 per cent. by the company, the new Indian company **F**
had been a wholly-owned subsidiary of the company.

In fact, the transaction was not carried out in that simple manner. In three
respects the transaction was different from a simple transaction of that kind.
In the first place, the transaction was limited to the selected tools; in the second
place, the transaction took the form of an exclusivity provision rather than of a
transfer of goodwill; and, in the third place, the consideration was attached, **G**
and attached exclusively, to the obligation to supply information. I do not think
that any of those features makes any difference in principle.

So far as the first one is concerned—i.e., that the transaction was limited to
selected tools—the facts as found by the commissioners are not entirely clear.
It is I think clear that the company manufactured in England a range of tools
much wider than the selected tools set out in the 1959 agreements. It does not **H**
appear whether the company had at that date been selling any tools in India
—that is, to the Ralli company—other than the selected tools. I was troubled
by this point, and wondered whether it was necessary to obtain further evidence
on it before reaching a conclusion. However, I think that is not necessary.
It is plainly open to a trader to transfer his connection, either generally or in
a limited area, quoad only some limited range of the goods manufactured by **I**
him. If the subject-matter of the transfer is a capital asset, then the transfer
is nonetheless the transfer of a capital asset, and the consideration a capital
receipt, by reason of the fact that the asset is severed by the trader transferring one
part and retaining the other. Junior counsel for the Crown, at any rate, was
disposed to accept that as being a correct statement.

The second feature is that the transaction took the form of an exclusivity
provision rather than of an assignment of goodwill. Generally speaking, I should
have thought that where a trader has an existing connection in a given country

A the correct label to give a transaction such as the present would be an assignment of goodwill. An exclusivity or " keep out " provision is more appropriate where there is no existing connection. It may be that the reason why the exclusivity type of provision was chosen is that the 1959 transaction was confined to the selected tools, so that in form at least it would not have been appropriate to express the transaction as a simple transfer of the company's goodwill in India.

B However that may be, I do not think there is any difference in substance between a provision for exclusion from India quoad the selected tools and a provision for transferring the goodwill of the company in India quoad the selected tools. Again, at any rate junior counsel for the Crown was not disposed to suggest there was any substantial difference.

The third feature is that the consideration for the issue of the shares was

C expressed to be the obligation to supply information. That is a circumstance to which due weight must be given, but I do not think it affects the result. Where an obligation to supply information is given in connection with the transfer of a a local connection, that obligation represents on the face of it, and in the absence of any other special circumstances, the breaking up of part of the capital asset consisting of the fund of confidential material rather than its retention intact and

D its exploitation. It is perfectly plain that that would be so if the transaction were expressed to take the form of an assignment of goodwill coupled with an obligation to supply confidential information. I do not think that the form of transaction adopted here alters the position.

Counsel for the Crown made the contention, among others, that the shares in the Ralliwolf company represented machinery whereby the company intended

E to continue and did continue to earn profit in India. That is undoubtedly correct: the shares in the Ralliwolf company did indeed represent such machinery. But the consequence of that, it seems to me, is that the company thenceforward derived its profit from India through the dividends on the shares in the Ralliwolf company instead of through the sale of its own products. There is no reason that I can see why one should treat the machinery as a taxable profit as well as

F the dividend.

It will be remembered that the duration of the 1959 agreements was ten years, although that period could of course have been either curtailed or extended by mutual consent. It has not been strenuously contended, I think, that the restriction of the transaction to that relatively long period prevents the transaction from being in the nature of a disposal of capital. It is plain that after ten years

G the company's own Indian connection would have wholly disappeared as regards the selected tools.

I was taken at length, very properly, through the three cases of *Moriarty (Inspector of Taxes)* v. *Evans Medical Supplies, Ltd.* (6); *Rolls-Royce, Ltd.* v. *Jeffrey (Inspector of Taxes)* (7); and *Musker (Inspector of Taxes)* v. *English Electric*

H *Co., Ltd.* (8). Counsel for the company contended that this case fell within the scope of the *Evans Medical Supplies* case (6): counsel for the Crown contended that it fell within the scope of the *Rolls-Royce* (7) and *English Electric* (8) cases. The distinction between the two types of case is made in a number of speeches in the House of Lords in the two later cases. In the *Rolls-Royce* case (9) Viscount Simonds said:

I   " I must add a word on *Moriarty (Inspector of Taxes)* v. *Evans Medical Supplies. Ltd.*, (6) . . . since I was a party to the majority decision in this House. In the Court of Appeal (10) in the present case UPJOHN, L.J., who

---

(6) [1957] 3 All E.R. 718; 37 Tax Cas. 540.
(7) [1962] 1 All E.R. 801; 40 Tax Cas. 443.
(8) (1964), 41 Tax Cas. 556.
(9) [1962] 1 All E.R. at p. 803; 40 Tax Cas. at p. 490.
(10) [1961] 2 All E.R. 469; 40 Tax Cas. 443.

had given the first decision in that case pointed out the clear difference be- A
tween the two cases. The facts in the earlier cases were complicated, but the
inference was there drawn that the capital sum in question was paid for the
communication of secret processes to the Burmese government with a resulting total loss to the company of its Burmese trade. I applied in that case
and would apply here, too, the test laid down by BANKES, L.J., in *British
Dyestuffs Corpn. (Blackley), Ltd.* v. *Inland Revenue Comrs.* (11): ' . . . looking B
at this matter, is the transaction in substance a parting by the company with
part of its property for a purchase price, or is it a method of trading by which
it acquires this particular sum of money as part of the profits and gains of
that trade? ' In the circumstances of that case, regard in particular being had
to the fact that the transaction was an isolated one of its kind, the conclusion
was inevitable that the so-called capital sum was a receipt of a capital C
nature . . . The circumstances may lead as in my opinion they lead in the
present case to the opposite conclusion."

The distinction was taken up again in the *English Electric* case (12). I will cite
one passage from the speech of VISCOUNT RADCLIFFE (13):

" In my opinion, there are two considerations which govern cases of this D
kind and which go a long way towards destroying the force of the analogies
by which the Appellant's argument seeks to prove that the transactions under
review were sales of fixed assets, and that receipts arising from them ought
to be treated as receipts on capital account. One is that in reality no sale takes
place. The Appellant had after the transaction what it had before it. There is
no property right in ' know-how ' that can be transferred, even in the E
limited sense that there is a legally protected property interest in a secret
process. Special knowledge or skill can indeed ripen into a form of property
in the fields of commerce and industry, as in copyright, trademarks and
designs and patents, and where such property is parted with for money
what is received can be, but will not necessarily be, a receipt on capital
account. But imparting ' know-how ' for reward is not like this, any more F
than a teacher sells his knowledge or skill to his pupil. Admittedly the
Appellant was not in the same position after each transaction as before it.
It had ' up-dated the background knowledge ' of a possible competitor, to
use the graphic phrase of one of its witnesses. Conceivably, by so doing it
had affected for the worse its trading potential in some fields and in some
respects, but the significance of that is almost unavoidably theoretical at the G
time when the transaction has to be judged, and the consequences are far too
speculative to allow the imparting of ' know-how ' to be treated for that
reason as the disposal of a ' capital ' asset analogous with the sale of all or
part of an undertaking.

" The other point is that ' know-how ', though very naturally looked
upon as part of the capital equipment of a trade, is a fixed asset only by H
analogy and, as it were, by metaphor. The nature of receipts from it
depends essentially, I think, upon the transaction out of which they arise and
the context in which they are received. Where, as in *Moriarty (Inspector of
Taxes)* v. *Evans Medical Supplies, Ltd.* (14) . . . ' know-how ' is imparted as
one element of a comprehensive arrangement by virtue of which a trader
effectively gives up his business in a particular area, the moneys paid for the I
' know-how ', whether or not independently quantified, may properly rank
as capital receipts."

LORD DONOVAN makes observations of the same general tenor (15).

---

(11) (1924), 12 Tax Cas. at p. 596.
(12) (1964), 41 Tax Cas. 556.
(13) (1964), 41 Tax Cas. at p. 585.
(14) [1957] 3 All E.R. 718; 37 Tax Cas. 540.
(15) (1964), 41 Tax Cas. at pp. 587, 588.

A   It seems to me that the statement by Lord Radcliffe in the second paragraph of the passage which I have cited is precisely in point in the present case. Here, the obligation to supply information is indeed one element of a comprehensive arrangement by virtue of which, quoad the selected tools, the company effectively gave up its business in India. It was contended on behalf of the Crown that the position here is distinguishable, and less favourable to the taxpayer, **B**   by reason of the fact that the company, instead of going out of business altogether in India, transferred its connection in India quoad the selected tools to the new Indian company. I should have thought that, so far from that being a distinction unfavourable to the trader, the position here was a fortiori the position where the trader goes out of business altogether. In a case such as the present, the effect of the whole arrangement—and I must look at the whole arrangement— **C**   is that the trader receives a new capital asset, viz., the shares in the foreign company, in exchange for that which he previously had, viz., his connection or goodwill in the foreign country. That is a transaction of a wholly capital nature.

It would not, I think, be useful to go further into a comparison of the three cases. It is sufficient to say that the present case, it seems to me, falls clearly within the first of the two alternatives propounded in the *British Dyestuffs Corpn.* case (16) **D**   and approved by Lord Simonds, and that it thus does not fall within the second alternative. I would only emphasise this, that in the *Rolls-Royce* (17) and *English Electric* (18) cases the companies concerned had no pre-existing goodwill in the countries with the governments of which they made the contracts for imparting "know-how". Here, the company did have this pre-existing connection of goodwill in India, and that circumstance, it seems to me, is the crucial **E**   factor which places the present case within the former and not the latter of the two alternatives. I propose, for the reasons which I have given, to allow this appeal.

Appeal allowed.

Solicitors: *Baileys, Shaw & Gillett* (for the company); *Solicitor of Inland Revenue.*

F

[*Reported by* F. A. Amies Esq., *Barrister-at-Law.*]

G

H

I

---

(16) (1924), 12 Tax Cas. 586.
(17) [1962] 1 All E.R. 801; 40 Tax Cas. 443.
(18) (1964), 41 Tax Cas. 556.

A

PRACTICE DIRECTION.

CHANCERY DIVISION. -

Practice—Chancery Division—Affidavit—Cross-examination of deponent—Order
  for cross-examination—Procedure—R.S.C., Ord. 38, r. 2 (3).

B

When, on the adjournment of a matter to a judge in court or chambers, a master is requested to make an order under R.S.C., Ord. 38, r. 2 (3), for the attendance of deponents for cross-examination on their affidavits the solicitor making such request should produce to the master two engrossments of the proposed order, properly completed in the form set out in the schedule hereto, with the names of the witnesses listed in the schedule to such proposed order. C
The master will, on making the order, settle the forms and initial one of the endorsements. The solicitor will lodge the forms (if correct) with the master's principal clerk, who will pass the order and send it for entry. If owing to amendment the forms have to be re-engrossed the new engrossments and the form initialled by the master will be lodged with the principal clerk, who will check them and pass the order. D

The scheduled form will be included in the Chancery Masters' Practice Forms (1) and arrangements have been made with the Solicitors' Law Stationery Society, Ltd., to print an adequate supply.

Henceforth no formal summons will be required on such an application.

It is hoped that this simplification of the previous practice will lead to expedition and the reduction of costs. E

THE SCHEDULE

ORDER FOR CROSS-EXAMINATION
OF DEPONENTS ON THEIR AFFIDAVITS

UPON THE APPLICATION of the [*Insert* Plaintiff *or* Defendant] and UPON HEARING F
[*Insert* Solicitors *or* Counsel] for the Applicant and for the [*Insert* Plaintiff *or* Defendant] and UPON READING [the originating summons *or* the order herein dated   19]

IT IS ORDERED that the applicant be at liberty to cross-examine the deponents named in the schedule hereto upon their respective affidavits filed herein

AND IT IS ORDERED that such cross-examination be taken before this court G
[*Insert* (*as the case may be*) on the hearing of the said originating summons *or* in answer to the inquiries directed by the said order dated   19]

AND IT IS ORDERED that the [*Insert* Plaintiff *or* Defendant] do produce the said deponents for cross-examination accordingly and that unless the said deponents be so produced the [*Insert* Plaintiff *or* *Defendant*] is not to be at liberty to read or use the said affidavits as evidence in this action [or matter] H
without the leave of the court.

SCHEDULE

I

By the direction of CROSS, J.

R. E. BALL,
Chief Master,
20th May 1969.   Chancery Division.

_____

(1) See THE SUPREME COURT PRACTICE 1967, vol. 2, p. 119.

INLAND REVENUE COMMISSIONERS *v.* KLEINWORT BENSON, LTD.

[CHANCERY DIVISION (Cross, J.), December 4, 5, 18, 1968.]

Income Tax—Tax advantage—Counteracting—" Transaction in securities "— Deduction in computing profits—Fall in value due to payment of interest— Debenture stock redeemed simultaneously with interest payment—Taxpayer company dealer in securities—Interest received subject to deduction of tax— Right to exclude from accounts—Resulting loss shown on transaction—Finance Act 1960 (8 *& 9 Eliz.* 2 *c.* 44), *s.* 28 (2) (3).

Income Tax—Tax advantage—Main object—Taking advantage of statutory rights —Dealer in securities—Purchase of debenture stock—Calculation of price— No distinction made between capital and interest—Right to exclude interest (tax deducted) from accounts—Resulting loss shown on transaction— Recouping through lower tax assessment—Not proof that tax advantage a main object—Finance Act 1960 (8 *& 9 Eliz.* 2 *c.* 44), *s.* 28 (2) (3).

The taxpayer company was a merchant bank which carried on the business, inter alia, of a dealer in securities. In its dealings in securities its investment policy was to make a profit, i.e., a surplus over cost of what would be obtained, and as regards receipts it did not draw any distinction between principal and dividend or interest as it regarded such distinction as immaterial to it. Its director in charge of the investment department considered purchasing debenture stock in a company which had paid no interest thereon since 1939 when a receiver of its assets and undertaking was appointed. He dismissed tax from his mind on a colleague's assurance that no tax problem was involved. He obtained from the taxpayer company's broker the total amount receivable, comprising capital plus gross interest, but did not consider its division into capital and interest although he knew interest would be received under deduction of tax. He calculated that a 9½ per cent. return (the minimum profitable yield) would be realised on redemption in full in 12 months and estimated that the bulk of the money would be received in six months, with promise of a satisfactory yield. On that basis the taxpayer company purchased for a total of £305,101 second and third mortgage redeemable debenture stock of the company, expecting to realise £334,030. Following a sale under court order of that company's assets, the company repaid all its secured creditors in full, including interest up to 31st December 1962 subject to deduction of tax which so far as in respect of sums which had not borne tax was paid to the Revenue. The sums received by the taxpayer company included principal and premium £148,269 and interest of £185,761 gross less tax deducted £71,982, and in accordance with legal practice in the case of a dealer in securities the interest was left out of the taxpayer company's profit and loss account for income tax purposes under Sch. D. The result was that the account showed a loss on the transaction of £156,832 (£305,101 minus £148,269) and the taxpayer company, which had borne tax on £185,761 when the money was received, recouped itself to the extent of tax on £156,832 by showing a loss of that amount in computing its tax profits for the year. It did not incur an overall loss in its trade in the year and so could not have claimed repayment of any part of the tax on the interest deducted at source. The Commissioners of Inland Revenue served a notice on the taxpayer company under s. 28 (3)* of the Finance Act 1960 that adjustments were necessary in the computation of the company's profits by excluding the transaction from them in order to counteract the tax advantage obtained by it.

Held: the notice must be discharged, because—

(i) on the assumption that one of the main objects of the taxpayer company

---

* Section 28 (3) is set out at p. 740, letter E, post.

in purchasing the stock was to obtain the right to deduct the £156,832 **A**
in computing its profits for income tax purposes, the company did not
become entitled as a holder of the stock to a deduction in computing the
profits by reason of a fall in the value of the stock resulting from the payment of the interest, since principal, premium and arrears of interest were
paid off on the same day and there never was any fall in the value of the
stock through payment of the interest; and even if the stock would have **B**
been shown in the company's books at a reduced value following payment
of the interest before redemption of the stock, that reduction in the books
would not have been a "fall in value" within s. 28 (2) (b) of the Finance
Act 1960 (see p. 742, letter H, and p. 743, letter A, post);

(ii) it was not one of the main objects of the taxpayer company to obtain
a tax advantage under s. 28 (3) of the Act of 1960 merely because in cal- **C**
culating the price it was prepared to pay on a single indivisible ordinary
commercial transaction, a purchase of debenture stock, it proceeded on the
footing that it would have the right given it by the law to exclude the interest
in computing its taxable profits (see p. 743, letter I, to p. 744, letter B, post).

Appeal dismissed.

[As to the counteracting of tax advantages, see SUPPLEMENT to 20 HALSBURY'S **D**
LAWS (3rd Edn.) para. 276A; and for cases on the subject, see DIGEST (Cont.
Vol. B) 429, 430, 1613b, 1613c.

For the Finance Act 1960, s. 28, see 40 HALSBURY'S STATUTES (2nd Edn.)
447.]

Cases referred to:
    Inland Revenue Comrs. v. *Brebner,* [1967] 1 All E.R. 779; [1967] 2 A.C. 18; **E**
        [1967] 2 W.L.R. 1001; Digest (Repl.) Supp.
    Inland Revenue Comrs. v. *F. S. Securities, Ltd.* (*formerly Federated Securities.*
        Ltd.), [1964] 2 All E.R. 691; [1965] A.C. 631; [1964] 1 W.L.R. 742;
        41 Tax Cas. 666; Digest (Cont. Vol. B) 427, 1588a.
    Inland Revenue Comrs. v. *Hague,* [1968] 2 All E.R. 1252; [1968] 3 W.L.R. 576. **F**

Case Stated.

The taxpayer company appealed to the Special Commissioners of Income Tax
against a notice given to it under s. 28 (3)* of the Finance Act 1960. The questions for determination were: (i) whether the tax advantage (which it was not
disputed that the company had obtained) was obtained in the circumstances
set out in s. 28 (2) (a) or (b) of the Act; (ii) whether the transactions had as their **G**
main object, or as one of their main objects, to enable tax advantages to be
obtained; and (iii) whether the adjustments specified in the notice were
inappropriate. The commissioners allowed the appeal and discharged the notice†.

Arthur Bagnall, Q.C., P. W. Medd and *J. P. Warner* for the Crown.
M. P. Nolan, Q.C., and *J. E. H. Pearce* for the taxpayer company.

H

                                      Cur. adv. vult.

18th December 1968. **CROSS, J.:** The taxpayer company, Kleinwort
Benson, Ltd., is a merchant bank carrying on (inter alia) the business of a
dealer in securities. In October and November 1962 the company purchased on
its own behalf £88,890 five per cent. second mortgage redeemable debenture
stock and £56,551 six per cent. third mortgage redeemable debenture stock in **I**
E.C. (Holdings), Ltd., for a total consideration of £305,101 0s. 5d.: £179,557 16s.
in respect of the second mortgage stock and £125,543 4s. 5d. in respect of the third
mortgage stock. No interest had been paid on either stock since 1939 and a receiver
of the assets and undertaking of the E.C. company had been appointed by the

* The terms of the notice, so far as relevant, are set out at p. 739, letters G to I, post.
The facts relating to the issue of the notice are set out at letter I, above, to p. 739, letter
G, and p. 740, letter I, to p. 741, letter F, post.
† The commissioners' decision is set out at p. 741, letter G, to p. 742, letter F, post.

A court in that year. In September 1962 an offer had been made by Securities
Agency, Ltd., to the receiver to purchase the assets of the E.C. company (which
consisted of certain shares in a company called Earls Court, Ltd.) for £2,500,000
which was more than sufficient to pay off all the secured creditors of the company
together with arrears of interest. The receiver was instructed by the court to
accept the offer and the sale was completed on 1st November 1962. On 28th
B November 1962 an order was made providing for the payment out of the funds
in court resulting from the sale of the amounts needed to pay off all the secured
creditors in full, including interest up to 31st December 1962.

The payments on account of interest were of course made subject to deduction
of tax and insofar as such payments were made out of money which had not borne
tax the tax deducted was paid to the Revenue. The payment to the taxpayer
C company was made by a single cheque made up of principal, £145,441, premium
£2,827 11s., and interest £185,761 10s. 6d. gross less tax deducted £71,982 11s. 10d.
It will be seen that the money received by the taxpayer company from the
E.C. company was some £42,000 less than the money which the taxpayer company had paid to buy the debentures. On the other hand the amount owing
by the E.C. company for principal, premium and gross arrears of interest was
D some £29,000 more than the sum paid by the taxpayer company for the debentures. In accordance with the ordinary practice followed in the case of dividends
or interest paid subject to deduction of tax to a dealer in securities (as explained
by the House of Lords in (*Inland Revenue Comrs.* v. *F.S. Securities, Ltd.* (*formerly
Federated Securities, Ltd.*) (1)), the interest was left out of the taxpayer company's
profit and loss account for the purpose of tax under Sch. D. In consequence that
E account showed the result of the transaction as a loss of £156,832 9s. 5d., i.e.,
the excess of the purchase price paid (£305,101 0s. 5d.) over the money received
in respect of principal and premium (£148,268 11s.). The result therefore was
that the taxpayer company, having borne tax on £185,761 10s. 6d. when the money
was received, recouped itself to the extent of tax on £156,832 9s. 6d. by being
allowed to show a loss of that amount in computing its taxable profits for the
F year 1963 and so in effect only bore tax on the £29,000 which was its actual
money profit.

The Commissioners of Inland Revenue conceiving that this was a case falling
within s. 28 of the Finance Act 1960, served a notice on the taxpayer company
under that section on 21st December 1966, which after reciting the purchase and
redemption of the stocks continued as follows:

G   " Now therefore the Commissioners of Inland Revenue hereby give
notice in accordance with subsection (3) of the said Section that the following
adjustments are requisite for counteracting the tax advantage thereby
obtained or obtainable, that is to say:—The computation of the profits or
gains of the [taxpayer] Company for the accounting years to the 31st December, 1962, and the 31st December, 1963, for the purposes of assessment to
H   income tax in the years of assessments 1963-64 and 1964-65 (and in any
other year of assessment), should be made on the basis of excluding the transactions specified above, that is to say confirming the profit as computed
for Income Tax purposes on the basis of the [taxpayer] Company's accounts
for the year to 31st December, 1962, at £1,490,656 and recomputing the profit
for income tax purposes on the basis of the [taxpayer] company's accounts
I   for the year to 31st December, 1963, at £1,463,774 by excluding the loss on
the transactions specified above of £156,833."

The taxpayer company appealed against the notice and the appeal was heard
by the Special Commissioners on 1st and 2nd May 1967. At this point I should
set out the material parts of s. 28 of the Act of 1960. Section 28 provides:

" (1) Where—(*a*) in any such circumstances as are mentioned in the next
following subsection, and (*b*) in consequence of a transaction in securities

(1) [1964] 2 All E.R. 691; 41 Tax Cas. 666.

or of the combined effect of two or more such transactions, a person is in a
position to obtain, or has obtained, a tax advantage, then unless he shows
that the transaction or transactions were carried out either for bona fide
commercial reasons or in the ordinary course of making or managing investments, and that none of them had as their main object, or one of their main
objects, to enable tax advantages to be obtained, this section shall apply
to him in respect of that transaction or those transactions . . .

" (2) The circumstances mentioned in the foregoing subsection are that
—(a) in connection with the distribution of profits of a company, or in connection with the sale or purchase of securities being a sale or purchase followed
by the purchase or sale of the same or other securities, the person in question,
being entitled (by reason of any exemption from tax or by the setting off of
losses against profits or income) to recover tax in respect of dividends received
by him, receives an abnormal amount by way of dividend; or (b) in connection with the distribution of profits of a company or any such sale or purchase
as aforesaid the person in question becomes entitled, in respect of securities
held or sold by him, to a deduction in computing profits or gains by reason
of a fall in the value of the securities resulting from the payment of a dividend
thereon or from any other dealing with any assets of a company ; . . .

" (3) Where this section applies to a person in respect of any transaction
or transactions, the tax advantage obtained or obtainable by him in
consequence thereof shall be counteracted by such of the following adjustments, that is to say an assessment or additional assessment, the nullifying
of a right to repayment or the requiring of the return of a repayment already
made (the amount to be returned being chargeable under Case VI of Schedule
D and recoverable accordingly), or the computation or recomputation of
profits or gains, or liability to tax, on such basis as the Commissioners of
Inland Revenue may specify by notice in writing served on him as being
requisite for counteracting the tax advantage so obtained or obtainable."

Section 43 (4) (g) contains a definition of " tax advantage " in the following
terms:

" ' tax advantage ' means a relief or increased relief from, or repayment
or increased repayment of, income tax, or the avoidance or reduction of an
assessment to income tax or the avoidance of a possible assessment thereto,
whether the avoidance or reduction is effected by receipts accruing in such a
way that the recipient does not pay or bear tax on them, or by a deduction
in computing profits or gains ;"

It was common ground that the payment off of the debentures with arrears of
interest constituted a distribution of the profits of the E.C. company within the
meaning of the section and the taxpayer company conceded that it had as a
result of the transaction obtained a " tax advantage " in that its assessment
had been reduced by a deduction in computing its profits and gains.   The
questions which the commissioners were asked to determine were:

" (i) whether the tax advantage . . . was obtained in such circumstances
as are set out in subsection (2) (a) or (b) of Section 28, (ii) whether the transactions in question had as their main object, or as one of their main objects,
to enable tax advantages to be obtained, and (iii) whether the adjustments
specified in the Notice were inappropriate."

The circumstances in which the taxpayer company came to purchase the
debenture stock are set out in para. (X) of the Case, which I will read:

" Mr. Craig is the Director in charge of the [taxpayer] company's Investment
Department and was in charge of ' the Book ', which comprised the [taxpayer]
company's dealings with its own reserves and other moneys requiring investment; the amount involved was never less than £7 m. and was occasionally
as much as £20 m. In 1962, purchases for the Book were £19½ m. (including

A   the £305,000 E.C. Debentures) and sales were £14¼ m.; the stocks involved
were almost entirely stocks quoted on London and other stock exchanges.
As regards the Book, the investment policy is to make a profit, which is
envisaged as a surplus over cost of what can be obtained; as regards receipts,
the [taxpayer] company does not draw any distinction between principal
and dividend or interest, as it regards any such distinction as immaterial to

B   it. The [taxpayer] company's chief dealer mentioned the E.C. Debentures
to Mr. Craig, who considered whether it was a suitable stock for the Book.
A stock with such large arrears of interest was unique, and Mr. Craig's first
thought was whether there was any tax problem which might make it unsuitable; he was not a tax expert but he enquired from a colleague, and on
being told that there was no problem, he dismissed tax from his mind.

C   "He was concerned with the amount likely to be realised, and when.
As regards the amount, he got the total figure (i.e. principal *plus* gross interest) from the [taxpayer] company's broker and he never, in his own mind,
considered its division into principal and interest components; he knew
however that the interest was a large component and that it would be received
under deduction of **tax**, but did not concern himself with that. He gave

D   his opinion that the price the [taxpayer] company paid would have been
a ridiculous price if the proceeds were not gross. The time when the money
would be received was of vital importance; a return of 7½ per cent. per annum
would be unprofitable, and the stock would not be worth purchasing unless
over 9½ per cent. was fairly certain; he calculated roughly that redemption
in full in 12 months would show about 9½ per cent. Weighing the uncertain-

E   ties, he judged that the bulk of the money would be received in 6 months;
he calculated that on this premise the purchase would show a satisfactory
yield, so he gave the order to purchase. In the event, the stock was redeemed
much earlier than he had expected. After the purchases the market price
rose. Mr. Craig did not address his mind to the possibility of selling; if the
[taxpayer] company could have got as much by selling as by waiting, and if

F   that had been drawn to his attention, he would have ordered a sale."

The only other fact which I need state is that the taxpayer company did not
incur any overall loss in its trade for the year 1963 and therefore could not have
claimed repayment of any part of the tax deducted at source on the interest.

The Special Commissioners gave their decision in writing as follows:

G   "I. [The taxpayer company] obtained a tax advantage (as defined by
Finance Act, 1960, Section 43 (4) (*g*)) in the form of a reduction to an assessment to Income Tax effected by a deduction in computing profits or gains.
II. We find that the transactions in question were carried out for bona fide
commercial reasons. We are unable to find that the [taxpayer company]
has shown that none of them had as their main object, or as one of their

H   main objects, to enable tax advantages to be obtained. The [taxpayer
company] calculated that for its outlay of £305,101 it would obtain £334,030.
The [taxpayer company] considered that the margin (£28,929) represented
a reasonable return on the outlay, provided the £334,030 could be obtained
inside a year, as was expected. The £334,030 in fact comprised the nominal
value of the debentures (£145,441), a premium (£2,828) and gross interest

I   (£185,761). Mr. Craig's evidence was that he never divided the sum and
calculated the interest component, but we must infer that somebody had
done so in order to put the figure of £334,030 before him. He knew that
there was a very large interest component and that the interest would be
received under deduction of tax. The only way in which the profit of
£28,929 which the [taxpayer company] was calculating on could be obtained
was by diminishing the [taxpayer company's] profit for the purpose of
assessment under Case I of Schedule D by £156,832, the difference between
the £305,101 paid and the £148,269 to be received in respect of principal

value and premium.   It is therefore implicit in the [taxpayer company's] **A**
intention to make the profit that it intended to obtain the tax advantage,
and if it were necessary we would find positively that this was one of the
[taxpayer company's] main objects.   III. In our judgment the [taxpayer
company] did not obtain the tax advantage in the circumstances set forth in
Finance Act, 1960, Section 28 (2) (*a*). The [taxpayer company] did, in
our opinion, receive ' an abnormal amount by way of dividend '.   It was **B**
not however in a position to recover tax in respect of dividends by the setting
off of losses and we have no evidence that it has ever been in a position to do
so.   In our opinion the words ' being entitled ' et seq. do not refer to a
person who might, in some hypothetical circumstances, become entitled to
recover tax, but to a person who in fact is entitled so to do.   IV. We have
to consider whether the case falls within subsection (2) (*b*).   We find this **C**
extremely difficult.   The case is one which seems to us to fall within the broad
intention of the paragraph (in the context in which we find it), but this is not
a straightforward case of securities sold at, or written down to and held at,
a diminished value.   As we see it, the value of the securities did not fall at
all—the value realised was the full value, comprising principal, premium and
interest.   We bear in mind that for the purpose of computing Case I profits **D**
the interest component has to be separated and the principal and premium
alone become relevant to the computation; we also bear in mind the Crown's
contention that the interest should be taken to have been paid first, resulting
in a fall in value before redemption.   Both of these considerations seem to
us to be artificial; remembering that clear words are necessary in order to
impose a charge to tax, our conclusion is that the words of this paragraph are **E**
not sufficiently clear to impose a charge in the circumstances of the present
case.   V. If our conclusions in III and IV above had been different, we
would have held that the adjustments directed in the Notice were appropriate.
VI. We allow the appeal and discharge the Notice."

The Commissioners of Inland Revenue being dissatisfied with this decision asked
for the Case to be stated which is now before me.   They do not, however, chal- **F**
lenge the decision of the Special Commissioners that s. 28 (2) (*a*) has no application
to the facts of this case.

I will deal first with the question whether, on the assumption that one of the
main objects of the taxpayer company in purchasing the stock was to obtain the
right to deduct the £156,000 odd in computing its profits or gains, s. 28 (2) (*b*)
applies to the case.   The question may be stated thus: did the taxpayer company **G**
in connection with the payment off of the stock and arrears of interest, become
entitled as a holder of the stock to a deduction in computing its profits and gains
by reason of a fall in the value of the stock resulting from the payment of the
interest?   If words are to be given their ordinary meaning the answer must be
" no ".   There was never any fall in the value of the stock by reason of the
payment of interest.   Principal, premium and arrears of interest were paid off **H**
on the same day.   All rights of the stockholders were extinguished and the
stock ceased to exist.   But, say the Commissioners of Inland Revenue, if only
the interest had been paid a day or two before the principal and premium, then
the value of the stock would have fallen as a result of the payment of the interest
and by reason of that fall in value the taxpayer company would have become
entitled to a deduction in computing its profits and gains because the interest **I**
element would not have come into the computation.   It is, so say the Commissioners of Inland Revenue, incredible that Parliament could have intended the
question whether thousands of pounds of tax should or should not be payable
to depend on the accident whether in such a case as this interest was or was not
paid at the same time as the principal.   Be bold, therefore, and construe " fall
in value " as referring not to what could be obtained on a sale of the subject-
matter in hand but to the figure representing it in the taxpayer company's books.
Before the stock was paid off that figure would have been " cost or market value,

A whichever is the lower ", i.e., in fact £305,101 0s. 5d., since the price rose after the purchase. After the stock had been paid off the corresponding figure in the books would have been much less because the interest element would not have figured in the account. But assuming that the books showed a lower figure —there is not, in fact, any evidence on the point—I cannot bring myself to construe " fall in value " in s. 28 (2) (*b*) as referring not to a fall in the price which

B could be obtained for the subject in question but to a reduction in the figure at which it appeared in the books.

This conclusion would be sufficient to dispose of the appeal but as the case may go further, I think that I ought to express a view on the other points which have been argued. The Special Commissioners have held that it was one of the main objects of the taxpayer company in purchasing this stock to obtain the

C right to diminish its taxable profits by deducting the sum of £156,000 odd. Section 28 was, of course, aimed primarily at purely artificial transactions into which no one would have thought of entering apart from the wish to reap a " tax advantage ", but it is clear that the section is so framed as to cover bona fide commercial transactions which are combined with the securing of a tax advantage. An example of such a case is *Inland Revenue Comrs.* v. *Brebner* (2). There

D a group of shareholders in control of a company had incurred a debt to a bank for perfectly good commercial reasons which they could only repay by extracting money from the company. If they had extracted it by way of dividend they would have had to pay substantial sums in tax, so they decided to extract it by way of a reduction of capital. If one divided the whole transaction into two parts one would say that the object of the second part was to obtain a tax advan-

E tage, but if one looked at the transaction as a whole one could say that the obtaining of the tax advantage was only incidental and not the object, or even a main object, of the transaction. The House of Lords pointed out that the question was essentially a matter for the commissioners and that whichever way they decided it a higher court could not properly say that they were wrong. So they dismissed an appeal against a decision that the case did not fall within the

F section. But in *Inland Revenue Comrs.* v. *Hague* (3) another body of commissioners decided that a somewhat similar transaction fell with the section and the courts refused to disturb that decision.

This case, however, is quite unlike the *Brebner* (2) and *Hague* (3) cases. Here there was only a single indivisible transaction and it was an ordinary commercial transaction a simple purchase of debenture stock. As the purchaser was a dealer

G he was entitled to keep the interest element out of his tax return and so was able to pay a higher price than an ordinary taxpayer would have been able to pay. Similarly, a charity, because it would have been able to reclaim the tax would have been able to pay an equally large price and still make a profit. But it is to my mind an abuse of language to say that the object of a dealer or a charity in entering into such a transaction is to obtain a tax advantage. When a trader

H buys goods for £20 and sells them for £30, he intends to bring in the £20 as a deduction in computing his gross receipts for tax purposes. If one chooses to describe his right to deduct the £20 (very tendentiously be it said) as a " tax advantage ", one may say that he intended from the first to secure this tax advantage. But it would be ridiculous to say that his object in entering into the transaction was to obtain this tax advantage. In the same way I do not

I think that one can fairly say that the object of a charity or a dealer in shares who buys a security with arrears of interest accruing on it is to obtain a tax advantage, simply because the charity or the dealer in calculating the price which they are prepared to pay proceed on the footing that they will have the right which the law gives them either to recover the tax or to exclude the interest as the case may be. One may, of course, think that it is wrong that charities and dealers should be in this privileged position. But if the Crown thinks so

(2) [1967] 1 All E.R. 779; [1967] 2 A.C. 18.
(3) [1968] 2 All E.R. 1252; [1968] 3 W.L.R. 576.

it ought to deal with the matter by trying to persuade Parliament to insert **A**
provisions in a Finance Act depriving them of their privileges, not by seeking to
achieve this result by a back door by invoking s. 28.   So if I had thought that
the case fell within s. 28 (2) (*b*) I should have held that the gaining of a tax advantage was not the object or a main object of the transaction.   On the other hand
I see no reason to think that the adjustments directed by the notice were not
appropriate, assuming that the case fell within the section.   So I would dismiss **B**
the appeal.

Appeal dismissed.

  Solicitors: *Solicitor of Inland Revenue*; *Linklaters & Paines* (for the taxpayer
company).

[*Reported by* F. A. AMIES, ESQ., *Barrister-at-Law.*]

C

Re LONDON FLATS, LTD.

[CHANCERY DIVISION (Plowman, J.), March 18, 19, 20, 21, 24, 1969.]

D

Company—Meeting—Quorum—Only one shareholder present.
*Company—Winding-up—Liquidator—Appointment—Appointment by general
    meeting comprising one shareholder only—Companies Act* 1948 (11 & 12
    Geo. 6 *c.* 38), *s.* 286 (1).

  A private company which had been incorporated in February 1936
had an authorised issued share capital of 45,000 shares of £1 each.   The
respondent's mother, Mrs. O., held 39,900 of the shares, 15,000 of them **E**
being held by her as nominee for her husband, 5,000 of the remainder were
held by the respondent, and the balance of 100 by the applicant.   In
February 1963 the company went into a members' voluntary liquidation,
Mrs. O. being appointed liquidator, but she died in March 1963.   Under
her will her husband, O., who survived her but who himself died in October
1963, became entitled to all her shares in the company.   As a result of an **F**
action begun by O. as his wife's executor to establish her will and codicil,
to which the respondent was defendant, the 39,900 shares in the company
became sterilised and could not be voted on.   In this situation, there
being no liquidator following Mrs. O.'s death, the applicant called an extraordinary general meeting of the company for 26th July 1963, the notice
convening the meeting stating that it would be proposed as an ordinary **G**
resolution that L. be appointed liquidator of the company to fill the vacancy
caused by the death of Mrs. O.   The applicant and respondent were in
the circumstances, the only persons entitled to attend and vote as members.
At the meeting the respondent, having declared himself to be chairman
although the applicant objected, invited the applicant to propose the
resolution set out in the notice which the applicant then read out in full. **H**
The respondent then stated that he proposed an amendment that he would
propose himself as liquidator, but the applicant left the room before he, in
fact, did so.   The amendment was put to the vote and there being one
vote in favour and none against the respondent declared the amendment
carried.   The applicant now took out a summons under s. 304* of the
Companies Act 1948 asking for an order appointing W. as liquidator of the **I**
company or, alternatively, an order removing the respondent from the office
and an order appointing W. in his place.   On the question whether the
respondent was validly appointed liquidator by the company in general
meeting under s. 286 (1) of the Companies Act 1948,

  Held: the respondent's purported appointment of himself as liquidator
was a nullity because at the moment when he was proposing himself as

----

* Section 304 is set out at p. 745, letter G, post.

A liquidator the applicant left the meeting, and from that moment, there was
only one member present and, therefore, no meeting, a single shareholder
being unable, as a general rule, to constitute a meeting (see p. 750, letter C,
post).

    Sharp v. *Dawes* ((1876), 2 Q.B.D. 26) and *Re Sanitary Carbon Co.* ([1877]
W.N. 223) followed.

B [As to constitution of meetings, see 6 HALSBURY'S LAWS (3rd Edn.) 337,
para. 661; and for cases on the subject, see 9 DIGEST (Repl.) 606, 607, *4017-4021.*
    For the Companies Act 1948, s. 131, s. 135, s. 286, s. 304, see 5 HALSBURY'S
STATUTES (3rd Edn.) 214, 218, 328, 339.]

Cases referred to:

C
    East v. *Bennett Brothers, Ltd.*, [1911] 1 Ch. 163; 80 L.J.Ch. 123; 103 L.T. 826;
        9 Digest (Repl.) 606, *4019.*
    Hartley Baird, Ltd., Re, [1954] 3 All E.R. 695; [1955] Ch. 143; [1954] 3 W.L.R.
        964; 9 Digest (Repl.) 607, *4021.*
    Sanitary Carbon Co., Re, [1877] W.N. 223; 9 Digest (Repl.) 606, *4017.*
    Sharp v. *Dawes* (1876), 2 Q.B.D. 26; 46 L.J.Q.B. 104; 36 L.T. 188; 10 Digest
        (Repl.) 1196, *8371.*

D
Adjourned Summons.

    This was an application by originating summons dated 12th August 1963,
under s. 304 of the Companies Act 1948 by Charles Arthur Lyon, who claimed
to be a contributory of London Flats, Ltd. (" the company "), for the following
relief: (i) an order appointing Walter Basil Scarlett Walker of 11 Ironmonger

E Lane in the City of London chartered accountant to the office of liquidator of
the company. Alternatively to (i), (ii) (a) An order removing Stanley Wilfred
Oppenheim from the office of liquidator of the company, and (b) an order appointing Walter Basil Scarlett Walker in place of Stanley Wilfred Oppenheim. The
company, a private property company, had been incorporated on 18th February
1936, and on 19th February 1963, it went into a members' voluntary liquidation.

F The facts are set out in the judgment.
    The cases noted below* were cited during the argument in addition to those
referred to in the judgment.

    B. Finlay, Q.C., and *S. A. Stamler* for the applicant.
    C. A. Settle, Q.C., and *Allan Heyman* for the respondent.

G   **PLOWMAN, J.:** This is a summons under s. 304 of the Companies Act
1948, which is as follows:

    " (1) If from any cause whatever there is no liquidator acting, the court
may appoint a liquidator. (2) The court may, on cause shown, remove
a liquidator and appoint another liquidator."

    The applicant is Mr. Charles Arthur Lyon, who is a member of the company
H which is in a members' voluntary winding-up, and the summons asks for:

    " (i) An Order appointing Walter Basil Scarlett Walker of 11 Ironmonger
Lane in the City of London chartered accountant to the office of liquidator
of the above named company: Alternatively to (i): (ii) (a) An Order removing the said Stanley Wilfred Oppenheim from the office of liquidator
of the above named company, and (b) An Order appointing the said Walter

I Basil Scarlett Walker in place of the said Stanley Wilfred Oppenheim."

    The circumstances leading up to the application are these. The company,
London Flats, Ltd., was incorporated on 18th February 1936, as a private
property company. On 19th February 1963, it went into a members' voluntary

---

* *Re Marseilles Extension Railway & Land Co.* (1867), L.R. 4 Eq. Cas. 692; *Re British
Nation Life Assurance Association* (1872), L.R. 14 Eq. Cas. 492; *Re Sir John Moore
Gold Mining Co.* (1879), 12 Ch.D. 325; *Re Adam Eyton, Ltd., Ex p. Charlesworth* (1887),
36 Ch.D. 299; *Re Charterland Goldfields, Ltd.* (1909), 26 T.L.R. 132; *Re Baron Cigarette
Machine Co., Ltd.* (1912), 28 T.L.R. 394.

liquidation.   At that time the authorised and issued share capital of the company   A
was 45,000 shares of £1 each.   39,900 of these were held by the late Mrs. Victoria
Pauline Oppenheim, 15,000 of those 39,900 being held by her as nominee for
her husband, the late Mr. Abraham Louis Oppenheim.   5,000 of the remainder
were held by their son, the present respondent, Mr. Stanley Wilfred Oppenheim,
and the balance of 100 by the applicant, Mr. Lyon.   He is a chartered accountant
who was formerly associated with Mr. Oppenheim, senior, in his group of com-   B
panies and for some years prior to 1958 was a director of the company.   Mr.
and Mrs. Oppenheim, senior, had three other children: Mr. Henry Myer Oppenheim, who gave evidence in this case, and two daughters, Mrs. Astaire and Mrs.
Burkeman.

The main asset of the company was a block of flats in St. John's Wood known
as Viceroy Court.   In November 1962 this was sold for £800,000.   At the   C
present time, after discharging the liabilities of the company, there is on deposit
at Barclay's Bank a sum somewhat in excess of £800,000.   On the company
going into liquidation on 19th February 1963, Mrs. Oppenheim was appointed
liquidator.

On 24th March 1963, Mrs. Oppenheim died.   By her will made in September
1962 she appointed her husband, who survived her, her sole executor, and under   D
that will he became entitled to all her shares in the company.   Her will also
included a legacy of £25,000 in favour of the respondent and a further legacy of
£10,000 in favour of his wife, but by a codicil made in the following month
Mrs. Oppenheim revoked those two legacies.

In April 1963 the respondent entered a caveat which did not involve any
challenge to the disposition of the testatrix's shares in the company in favour   E
of her husband.   The challenge was to the codicil, which, as I have said, revoked
two pecuniary legacies.

Accordingly, in May 1963 Mr. Oppenheim, senior, as sole executor, began
proceedings in the Probate, Divorce and Admiralty Division to establish the
will and codicil of his late wife.   The respondent was the defendant to those
proceedings, his defence being that the codicil was executed under the undue   F
influence of his father who, he alleged, was hostile to him.   The effect of those
proceedings was that the 39,900 shares in the company became sterilised and
could not be voted on.   In this situation, there being no liquidator of the company as the result of Mrs. Oppenheim's death, the present applicant called an
extraordinary general meeting of the company for 26th July 1963, and the
notice convening that meeting stated that—   G

"the following will be proposed as an Ordinary Resolution: ' That Mr.
Cyril Herbert Stanley Lewis, F.C.A., of Messrs. Finnie, Ross, Welch & Co.,
Bow Bells House, Bread Street, London E.C. 4 be and he is hereby appointed
Liquidator of the Company to fill the vacancy caused by the death of Mrs.
Victoria Pauline Oppenheim '."

H

The only persons entitled to attend and vote as members were, in the circumstances, the applicant and the respondent.   The applicant's account of what
happened at that meeting is set out in the first of two affidavits he swore in
support of the present application.   The relevant paragraphs, which are 9 to 12
inclusive, are as follows:

"9.   The Respondent and I both attended the meeting and in addition   I
there were present at first Mr. Davies, one Peacock of Mr. Lewis' firm,
Mr. Jacobs of the Respondent's Solicitors, a stenographer and Mr. Corman of
my Solicitors.   The Respondent objected to the presence of anyone other
than the registered shareholders and consequently all persons other than
the Respondent and myself withdrew.
"10.   I began the meeting by reading the Notice . . . and the Respondent
then insisted that a Chairman be appointed, inviting me to propose a Chairman.   I proposed myself and the Respondent then proposed an amendment

A   naming himself as Chairman. On a show of hands each of us voted for our respective nominees and the Respondent then demanded a poll and cast the votes to which he was entitled by reason of his holding of 5,000 shares in favour of the amendment, no vote being taken on the resolution itself.

B   " 11. The Respondent then declared himself to be Chairman (although I voiced my objection) and then stated that as Chairman he had the right to have a stenographer present to take notes. Despite my strong objections and my reminder to him that it had been agreed before the meeting that it was to be held with only members present, the Respondent called in the stenographer, who remained present thereafter. Although I requested the Respondent to allow me to consult the Company's Solicitors, who were

C   in the adjoining room, he refused to allow me to do so.

    " 12. The Respondent then invited me to propose the Resolution set out in the Notice, which I then read out in full. The Respondent then stated that he was going to propose an amendment and he got as far as saying ' that Mr. Stanley Wilfred Oppenheim be appointed ' (or words to that effect) when I left the meeting saying to him ' I withdraw from the

D   meeting—you now have no quorum '. I did not attend the meeting any further."

The minutes of the meeting differ only slightly from that account of it. They are as follows, so far as material:

E   " The Resolution set out in the Notice convening the meeting was read by [the applicant]. [The respondent] pointed out that no Chairman had yet been elected. [The applicant] proposed himself as Chairman. [The respondent] proposed an amendment to this proposal that he, [the respondent], be appointed Chairman. On a show of hands an equal number of votes was cast for and against both propositions. A poll was demanded by [the respondent]. The amendment was again put to the vote and there being

F   5,000 votes in favour and 100 against, the amendment was duly carried. [The respondent] then took the Chair.

    " [The applicant] proposed the Resolution set out in the Notice of the meeting: ' That Mr. Cyril Herbert Stanley Lewis ... be and he is hereby appointed liquidator of the company to fill the vacancy caused by the death of Mrs. Victoria Pauline Oppenheim.'

G   " [The respondent] then proposed the following amendment to that resolution: ' That Stanley Wilfred Oppenheim ... be and he is hereby appointed liquidator of the company to fill the vacancy caused by the death of Mrs. Victoria Pauline Oppenheim '* *At this point [the applicant] left the meeting. The meeting continued. The amendment was put to the vote and there being one vote in favour and no votes against, the Chairman

H   declared the amendment carried. As the meeting had appointed [the respondent] to be liquidator, the resolution for the appointment of Mr. C. H. Stanley Lewis, F.C.A. was not put to the vote. As liquidator of the company, [the respondent] stated that he would make the statutory returns, and as Chairman of the meeting he formally declared the meeting ended."

I   As I say, the applicant's account is not really challenged, and I accept the evidence which he gave in the witness box that he left the meeting before the respondent had proposed himself as liquidator. In those circumstances, I shall have to consider later whether the respondent was validly appointed liquidator.

    The present summons was issued on 12th August 1963 and on 7th October an order was made by PENNYCUICK, J., by consent continuing an injunction which had been granted by the vacation judge restraining the respondent over the final hearing of the originating summons from—

" acting as or holding himself out in any way as being the liquidator of
the above-named London Flats, Ltd., and from dealing in any way whatsoever with any of its assets save for instructing the bankers of the said company to transfer the moneys now standing to the credit of the said company
on current account to deposit account."

It has taken over 5½ years for the summons to come on, but I do not think that
any useful purpose would be served by trying to apportion blame for that.

On 10th October 1963, Mr. Oppenheim, senior, died. By his will, dated
15th May 1963, he appointed as his executors Dr. Kelsey and a Mr. Davis who
renounced probate. Dr. Kelsey thus became the executor by representation
of Mrs. Oppenheim as well as being the executor of Mr. Oppenheim, senior.
By his will Mr. Oppenheim gave certain legacies and left his residuary estate on
trust for his grandchildren, the children of his daughters, Mrs. Astaire and Mrs.
Burkeman. Again, the respondent entered a caveat, and in April 1964 Dr.
Kelsey began another action in the Probate, Divorce and Admiralty Division
to have this will established. The respondent as defendant to the proceedings
put in a defence alleging that his father was of unsound mind at the relevant
time and he counterclaimed that his father died intestate. Part of the unsound-
ness of mind was said by the respondent to be his father's obsessional antipathy
towards him. There were considerable delays in the progress of both probate
actions, but finally that concerning the will of Mr. Oppenheim, senior, was fixed
for hearing on 24th October 1966. On that day a settlement was reached of both
probate actions which involved the payment of a lump sum to the respondent,
to include his costs, in satisfaction of all his and his wife's claims, and he withdrew his defences in both actions. Accordingly, on 24th October 1966, CAIRNS, J.,
after hearing the appropriate evidence, pronounced for the will of Mr. Oppenheim,
senior, and on 22nd December 1966, Dr. Kelsey obtained a grant of probate to
the estate of Mr. Oppenheim, senior.

On 18th January 1967, the other probate action came before LATEY, J., who
pronounced for the validity of Mrs. Oppenheim's will and codicil. No grant of
probate of her will and codicil has yet been obtained, however, because the
sterilisation of the moneys available for distribution in the winding-up pending
the outcome of these proceedings has made it impossible for Dr. Kelsey to raise
the very considerable sum required for estate duty. In para. 3 of his affidavit
sworn in these proceedings, he states :

" I was successful in obtaining a grant of Probate to Mr. Oppenheim's
Estate on a credit basis, and I am, as a result of the Orders referred to above,
in a position to apply for a grant of Letters of Administration (with will
annexed) to Mrs. Oppenheim's Estate. I am however informed by my
solicitors and believe that the Estate Duty Office will require a payment on
account of Estate Duty before granting me such Letters of Administration ;
the total duty due in respect of Mrs. Oppenheim's Estate is estimated to be
£750,000, but there is also owing the sum of £176,500 as Estate Duty on Mr.
Oppenheim's Estate. A very substantial part of Mrs. Oppenheim's Estate
consists of her beneficial interest in 24,900 out of the 39,900 shares in London
Flats Limited which stand in her name, the proportion of the funds of
London Flats Limited distributable to Mrs. Oppenheim's Estate being
approximately £443,220. I am informed by my solicitors and believe that
if it were possible for me to satisfy Barclays Bank Limited (where the
account of London Flats Limited now stands) that there was a prospect of a
distribution of these monies to Mrs. Oppenheim's Estate within a short
period the Bank would be willing to make an advance in the like sum to
enable me to make payment to the Estate Duty Office ; this payment,
together with other sums now available to me, would enable me to obtain a
grant to Mrs. Oppenheim's Estate."

Many attempts have been made to get the question of a liquidator agreed, but

A all in vain. The way in which it appeared from the applicant's side can be illustrated by a letter which his solicitors wrote to the solicitors then acting for the respondent on 20th April 1967, in which they wrote:

" Initially [the applicant] applied to the Court inter alia for the appointment of Mr. Walker of Peat Marwick to be appointed Liquidator and this is the subject of one of the disputes in the action. In our letter of the 15th
B October 1963 with a view to finding a compromise acceptable to both sides we proposed that there be joint Liquidators, viz., [the respondent] personally and a partner in one of the ' big five ' of firms of Accountants. This offer was not accepted. Later in July 1966 Mr. Posner enquired of us whether our client would agree to a Mr. R. E. Goate, chartered accountant, being appointed Joint Liquidator with a named accountant, a partner in one
C of the ' big five '. Before we could take instructions Mr. Posner's firm ceased to act in the matter. This matter is dealt with in our letter to you of the 20th September 1966. We suggested that you submitted three names to us for the reasons set out in our letter of the 16th March. May we suggest that in order to save any misunderstanding you should set out [the respondent's] proposals in this regard and we will promptly seek [the applicant's]
D instructions thereon. We must now on [the applicant's] behalf request a prompt reply so that if the matter is to be fully litigated the case can be referred to the Registrar for early directions."

There was a reply to that letter on 26th April saying " we are taking [the respondent's] instructions thereon as a matter of urgency and we will write to you again shortly ".
E Nothing having been heard on 5th May the applicant's solicitors wrote again:

" We refer to your letter of the 26th April 1967 in which, in acknowledging our letter of the 20th April, you stated you were taking [the respondent's] instructions on our letter as a matter of urgency and would write us shortly. We must now please ask you for a reply to our letter of the 20th
F April by Wednesday next, the 10th May, otherwise the matter must proceed."

To that letter there was no reply.

The respondent's attitude is that he was validly appointed liquidator and that there are good reasons why he should continue to act as such. He says that he was not agreeable to an accountant being appointed sole liquidator first because the matter is so complex that an independent accountant would not be able to
G deal with certain matters requiring investigation as efficiently as he (the respondent) could—I will come back to those matters in a moment—and, secondly, because he did not want the company to be charged with a large amount for fees when he was the second largest shareholder in the company, holding some 11 per cent. of the issued capital. As to the suggestion of joint liquidators, he said in evidence that he made enquiries of certain leading London firms of chartered
H accountants, and he got the impression that they were not in favour of joint liquidators.

I must say something more about the matters which, according to the respondent, require further investigation. According to him, his father and mother embezzled the funds of the company during their lifetimes by pocketing premiums which had been charged on the grant of leases of Viceroy Court where there were,
I I understand, some 90 or so flats, and the suggestion is that the money so acquired was in part placed in bank accounts overseas, was in part invested in jewellery, and in part retained in cash in various currencies. It is said that two large boxes containing cash and jewellery to the value of some £300,000 were removed by the respondent's brothers-in-law from his father's bedroom on the night of his father's death, and the respondent is quite determined that these moneys shall be recovered for the company.

I express no view at all whether there is any substance in these allegations; that is not a matter with which I am concerned. But I must say this: it would be an understatement to say that the respondent is not on good terms with his **A** sisters and their husbands. The words " feud " and " vendetta " have been used during the course of the hearing. I do not propose to dwell unnecessarily on the bitterness which undoubtedly runs through this case; but if there is to be an investigation of the charges which the respondent makes, I am certain that it is in the interests of everyone concerned that it should be made by a wholly independent person who is not involved in the family's passions and bitterness. **B**

I come now to the legal problems which are involved in this case. First, was the respondent ever validly appointed liquidator? Under s. 286 (1), of the Companies Act 1948, the vacancy caused by Mrs. Oppenheim's death could be filled by the company in general meeting, and the question is: Was the respondent appointed by the company in general meeting? In my judgment he was not, for the reason that at the moment when he was in the course of proposing himself **C** as liquidator the applicant left the meeting and from that moment there was only one member present and, therefore, no meeting. It is well settled that as a general rule a single shareholder cannot constitute a meeting. I was referred to *Sharp* v. *Dawes* in the Court of Appeal (1), where a meeting of a company was called for the purpose, among other things, of making a call on shares. Only one shareholder turned up at the meeting, and that shareholder purported to **D** pass a resolution—

" That a call of 4s. 6d. per share be now and is hereby made payable to the secretary, and that a discount of 5 per cent. be allowed if paid by the 20th of January, 1875."

The question was whether that call was validly made.
LORD COLERIDGE, C.J., said this (2): **E**

" This is an attempt to enforce against the defendant a call purporting to have been made under s. 10 of the Stannaries Act, 1869. Of course it cannot be enforced unless it was duly made within the Act. Now, the Act says that a call may be made at a meeting of a company with special notice, and we must ascertain what within the meaning of the Act is a **F** meeting, and whether one person alone can constitute such a meeting. It is said that the requirements of the Act are satisfied by a single shareholder going to the place appointed and professing to pass resolutions. The 6th and 7th sections of the Act shew conclusively that there must be more than one person present; and the word ' meeting ' prima facie means a coming together of more than one person. It is, of course, possible to shew **G** that the word ' meeting ' has a meaning different from the ordinary meaning, but there is nothing here to shew this to be the case. It appears therefore to me that this call was not made at a meeting of the company within the meaning of the Act. The order of the Court below must be reversed."

The other members of the court concurred in that judgment.
That case was followed by SIR GEORGE JESSEL, M.R., in *Re Sanitary Carbon* **H** *Co.* (3):

" [That] was a winding-up petition by an unpaid judgment creditor. It was opposed by the company on the ground that a ' meeting ' of the company had been held at which one shareholder only, named Worswick, was present, he having in his pocket the proxies of the only three other shareholders of the company. Worswick voted himself into the chair, **I** proposed a resolution to wind up voluntarily, declared the resolution passed, and appointed a liquidator.

" The Master of the Rolls said that, apart from any authority, he was quite prepared to hold that there had been no meeting of the company, but *Sharp* v. *Dawes* (1) was conclusive on the subject. In that case, as in this,

(1) (1876), 2 Q.B.D. 26.
(2) (1876), 2 Q.B.D. at pp. 28, 29.
(3) [1877] W.N. 223.

A   one shareholder held a ' meeting ' and the only point of difference between the two cases was that there the shareholder passed a vote of thanks to himself ! There must be the usual compulsory order."

A case of the sort envisaged by LORD COLERIDGE, C.J., where it was possible to show that the word " meeting " bore a different meaning from its ordinary meaning was *East* v. *Bennett Brothers, Ltd.* (4). The headnote reads (4):

B   " A company was incorporated with a capital divided into preference and ordinary shares. The memorandum of association empowered the company to increase its capital, but provided that no new shares should be issued so as to rank equally with or in priority to the preference shares, unless such issue was sanctioned by an extraordinary resolution of the holders of the preference shares present at a separate ' meeting ' of such **C** holders specially summoned for the purpose of considering the question. The articles of association contained a similar provision.

" Shortly after the incorporation of the company meetings were held at which a special resolution was passed and confirmed increasing its capital by a fresh issue of preference shares. At that time B. was the holder of all the original preference shares. He presided at the first meeting, moved the **D** resolution for the issue of the new preference shares, and signed a document in the minute-book recording his assent as the holder of all the original preference shares to the issue of the new preference shares. In pursuance of this resolution and in reliance on B.'s assent the new preference shares were subsequently issued:—

" *Held* that, there being nothing in the constitution of the company to **E** prevent the whole of the original preference shares being held by one shareholder, the word ' meeting ' in the memorandum and articles must be taken to have been used not in its strict sense, but as applicable to the case of a single shareholder:—

" *Held*, therefore, that there had been a sufficient compliance with the requirements of the memorandum and articles, and that the new preference **F** shares had been validly issued."

WARRINGTON, J., after referring to the two cases which I have already cited, said this (5):

" But now what I have to consider is whether this is not one of the cases referred to by LORD COLERIDGE, C.J. as one in which it may be possible to **G** shew that the word ' meeting ' has a meaning different from the ordinary meaning. For that purpose I think I am entitled to see what is the object of the provision in the memorandum of association. Plainly, as I have already said, that object is that before affecting the rights of the preference shareholders it shall be necessary to obtain and record in a formal manner the assent of the preference shareholders to that course. I think I may **H** take it also that the persons who framed this document may have had, and must be taken to have had, in their minds the possibility at all events that this particular class of shares might fall into the hands of one person. There is nothing to prevent it in the constitution of the company. One must regard the memorandum as far as possible as providing for circumstances which in the ordinary course may arise. That being so, I think I **I** may very fairly say that where one person only is the holder of all the shares of a particular class, and as that person cannot meet himself, or form a meeting with himself in the ordinary sense, the persons who framed this memorandum having such a position in contemplation must be taken to have used the word ' meeting ', not in the strict sense in which it is usually used, but as including the case of one single shareholder. There is, of course, no difficulty in treating the formally expressed assent of Bennett as a resolution.

(4) [1911] 1 Ch. 163.
(5) [1911] 1 Ch. at pp. 169, 170.

The only question is the purely technical difficulty arising from the use of the word ' meeting " in the memorandum.

" I think on the whole that I may give effect to obvious common sense by holding that in this particular case, where there is only one shareholder of the class, on the true construction of the memorandum, the expression ' meeting ' may be held to include that case. It seems to me, therefore, that the shares were validly issued, and that there is therefore no necessity for the rectification of the register.   I refuse the motion on that ground."

In the present case I can find no context which enables me to say that a meeting of one member is good enough.   It is true that in *Re Hartley Baird, Ltd.* (6), WYNN-PARRY, J., held, on the construction of the company's memorandum and articles which were, as far as material, similar to those in the present case, that if a quorum was present at the beginning of a meeting the subsequent departure of a member reducing the meeting below the number required for a quorum does not invalidate the proceedings of the meeting after his departure.   But the quorum in that case was ten, and the departure of one member still left nine.   So that the point with which I am concerned did not arise.   There the question was quorum or no quorum, while here it is meeting or no meeting.

It is also true that there are certain circumstances in which the Companies Act 1948 enables one member of a company to constitute a meeting.   They may be found in s. 131 (2) and s. 135 (1).   But they are exceptional cases which have no application here.

In my judgment, therefore, the respondent's purported appointment of himself as liquidator was a nullity.   But in case that view be wrong and this matter should go further, I ought to add that on the evidence I should have felt obliged to make an order under s. 304 (2), removing the respondent and appointing an independent liquidator in his place.   I have already stressed the reasons why, in my judgment, it is essential in this case that the liquidator should be wholly independent of the Oppenheim family.

A number of cases were cited to me which show that the court has a wide discretion, but I need not refer to them because counsel for the respondent concedes that if I take the view that it is in the interests of everyone concerned in the liquidation to make such an order, I am entitled to do so.

What I propose to do, therefore, is to refer the matter back to chambers for the appointment of an independent liquidator.   I do not propose to appoint the applicant's nominee, not because there is the slightest personal reflection on him whatever, but because the applicant, himself, in his second affidavit says this :

" Mr. Walker is I understand still willing to act, though I now understand that (although I have no connection at all with him or his firm) his firm acts as auditors to a company with which the Respondent's brothers-in-law are associated.   I cannot, with the greatest respect to the Respondent, believe that this connection could in any way affect Mr. Walker's discharge of his responsibilities, but I am quite willing to meet the Respondent by agreeing (as my Solicitors already suggested in the correspondence) that a partner in any one of the big City firms of chartered accountants be appointed."

As I say, I think it is better to have someone with no connection at all with any of the Oppenheim family.

Matter referred back to chambers for the appointment of an independent liquidator.

Solicitors: *Titmuss, Sainer & Webb* (for the applicant); *G. Lebor & Co.* (for the respondent).

[*Reported by* JACQUELINE METCALFE, *Barrister-at-Law.*]

———

(6) [1954] 3 All E.R. 695; [1955] Ch. 143.

AUSTIN SECURITIES, LTD. *v.* NORTHGATE AND ENGLISH STORES, LTD.

[COURT OF APPEAL, CIVIL DIVISION (Lord Denning, M.R., and Edmund Davies, L.J.), February 4, 5, 1969.]

Practice—Want of prosecution—Dismissal of action—Delay—Inordinate delay without excuse—Plaintiffs in default in not proceeding with action—Liquidators of defendants in default in not pursuing liabilities—No prejudice to defendants—Delay in moving to strike out—Limitation period not exhausted.

On 15th February 1966, the plaintiffs issued a writ against the defendants claiming commission on a business transaction. The defendants accepted service and entered an appearance on 22nd February 1966. The defendants decided to re-organise their business and split into two separate companies. To do so they passed a resolution for voluntary winding-up in August 1966. The liquidators knew of the plaintiffs' claim but they did not deal with it as they should have done under s. 302 of the Companies Act 1948. Most of the assets were distributed and the liquidators took an indemnity from the recipients. No other steps in the action were taken because the plaintiffs' solicitor became ill. In February 1968 the solicitor died and the plaintiffs appointed another solicitor. On 3rd April 1968 the plaintiffs gave one month's notice of intention to proceed. On 9th May they delivered a statement of claim. On 18th July the defendants applied for the action to be stayed pursuant to s. 226 and s. 307 of the Act of 1948 and/or for want of prosecution.

Held: the action would not be struck out for want of prosecution, because—

(i) (per LORD DENNING, M.R.) the delay was inordinate and inexcusable; nevertheless the defendants, by neglect of their duties on the part of the liquidators, were as guilty of delay as the plaintiffs; there was no evidence that the defendants were seriously prejudiced and they had themselves delayed from 3rd April until 18th July before moving to stay the proceedings; further, no advantage would flow from striking out since the plaintiffs could commence a fresh action at once (see p. 755, letter I, to p. 756, letter D, post);

(ii) (per EDMUND DAVIES, L.J.) although the delay had been inordinate and inexcusable, the defendants had not been prejudiced thereby; even if prejudice had been established, it flowed directly from the inactivity of the liquidators in respect of their duties and it was clearly not open to the defendants to plead that they had been prejudiced by the failure of the plaintiffs to press their claim (see p. 756, letter I, and p. 757, letter D, post). *Pulsford v. Devenish* ([1903] 2 Ch. 625) applied.

Per EDMUND DAVIES, L.J.: it is incumbent on a party to provide an adequate excuse for such delay. It is not for the other side to demonstrate its inexcusability (see p. 756, letter I, post).

Appeal allowed.

[As to the dismissal of actions for want of prosecution, see 30 HALSBURY'S LAWS (3rd Edn.) 410, 411, para. 771.

For the Companies Act 1948, s. 226, s. 302, s. 307, see 5 HALSBURY'S STATUTES (3rd Edn.) 296, 337, 340.]

Cases referred to:

Allen v. *Sir Alfred McAlpine & Sons, Ltd.*, [1968] 1 All E.R. 543; [1968] 2 Q.B. 229; [1968] 2 W.L.R. 366.

Armstrong Whitworth Securities Co., Ltd., Re, [1947] 2 All E.R. 479; [1947] Ch. 673; [1948] L.J.R. 172; 10 Digest (Repl.) 1063, 7382.

Pulsford v. *Devenish,* [1903] 2 Ch. 625; 73 L.J.Ch. 35; 10 Digest (Repl.) 1060, 7361.

Windsor Steam Coal Co. (1901), Ltd., Re, [1929] 1 Ch. 151;   10 Digest (Repl.) **A**
1047, 7258.

Interlocutory appeal.

This was an appeal by the plaintiffs, Austin Securities, Ltd., from an order of
MILMO, J., made on 27th November 1968. The plaintiffs had issued a writ against
the defendants, Northgate and English Stores, Ltd., in February 1966. On 3rd
April 1968, the plaintiffs gave notice of intention to proceed and delivered a **B**
statement of claim on 9th May. On 18th July the defendants applied for all
further proceedings to be stayed pursuant to s. 226 and s. 307 of the Companies
Act 1948, and/or on the ground of want of prosecution by the plaintiffs. On 14th
October, Master RITCHIE dismissed the defendants' application. On appeal,
MILMO, J., on 27th November, rescinded the master's order and dismissed the
action for want of prosecution. The facts are set out in the judgment of LORD **C**
DENNING, M.R.

M. Finer, Q.C., and *B. E. Capstick* for the plaintiffs.
G. J. Bean, Q.C., and *C. H. L. Bathurst* for the defendants.

LORD DENNING, M.R.: The judge has dismissed this action for want of
prosecution. The plaintiffs appeal to this court. **D**

The plaintiffs are agents who sue for commission for introducing a purchaser.
But they are not house agents. They are licensed dealers in securities and they
specialise in take-over bids. The defendants are a big public company called
Northgate and English Stores, Ltd. In November 1963 letters passed between
the plaintiffs and defendants whereby the plaintiffs say that a contract was
concluded to this effect: if the plaintiffs introduced a business which the defen- **E**
dants bought, the defendants would pay two per cent. of the consideration up to
£200,000, and thereafter one per cent., but payable only in the event of business
materialising. The plaintiffs say that in April 1964 they introduced a company
called Daintifyt Brassiere (Holdings), Ltd.; and after some months, in February
1965, the defendants bought up that company. The plaintiffs claim commission
on the deal. **F**

We are not concerned with the merits of the claim or defence, but with the
course of the legal proceedings. The plaintiffs went to a solicitor of good reputation. On 15th February 1966, on their behalf he issued a writ. The defendants
accepted service and entered an appearance on 22nd February 1966. I am afraid
after that time nothing was done for over two years. The explanation was that
the solicitor was very ill. He was suffering from high blood pressure. Very **G**
shortly after he had issued the writ, in March 1966, he had a stroke. He was two
months away from his practice. He handed over his work to another firm to
conduct for him, including this action, but I am afraid they did nothing. They
let nine months pass with nothing done. The solicitor recovered somewhat and
he asked for the papers back. He got them back in the beginning of 1967. But his
health was still very bad. He did not, or could not, do any real work. He was in **H**
and out of hospital a good deal. He got worse and worse, and died on 9th
February 1968.

Meanwhile, however, much had been happening on the defendants' side which
is very material. Early in 1966 (soon after the issue of the writ) the defendants
decided to re-organise their business and to split up into two separate companies—
on the one hand the Northgate side and on the other hand the English Stores side. **I**
In order to make this re-organisation, the defendants' company went into a
members' voluntary liquidation. On 22nd August 1966, a resolution was passed
for voluntary winding-up. Liquidators took over. The assets were £3½ million.
These were to be handed over to the two new companies. But before distributing
the assets, it was the duty of the liquidators to deal with all outstanding claims.
It is the duty of a liquidator to enquire into all claims, to see whether they are
well founded or not, to pay the good claims, to reject the bad, to settle the
doubtful, or, if need be, to contest them. It is only in this way that a liquidator

A can fulfil his duty under s. 302 of the Companies Act 1948, of seeing that the property of the company is applied in satisfaction of its liabilities pari passu. In *Pulsford* v. *Devenish* (1), FARWELL, J., said:

> ". . . I consider it to be the duty of a liquidator, namely, not merely to advertise for creditors, but to write to the creditors of whose existence he knows, and who do not send in claims, and ask them if they have any claim . . ."

B In *Re Armstrong Whitworth Securities Co., Ltd.* (2), JENKINS, J., said:

> ". . . the cardinal principle [is] that, in a winding-up, the shareholders are not entitled to anything until all the debts have been paid . . . his duty as liquidator was to take all steps reasonably open to him . . . to ascertain whether any of the former employees concerned did make any such claim."

C Now in this case the liquidators did not fulfil that duty. They had knowledge of this claim by the plaintiffs and yet they did not deal with it. That is shown by an account which the then solicitors to the defendants (not the present solicitors) sent to the liquidators, dated May 1967. It said:

> "Austin Securities Limited. Professional charges in connection with a claim made by the above for commission alleged to be due arising from the purchase of the share capital of Daintifyt Brassiere (Holdings) Ltd. Repudiating all liability and following the issue of a writ entering an appearance on your behalf. Thereafter investigating fully the background circumstances of the claim; attendances on and correspondence with you and other interested parties, with a view to preparing the defence, but the matter was not pursued: £78.15s.0d."

E I can well understand that the liquidators, after receiving that account, would think they need do nothing. They were lulled to sleep. But they should not have been. The solicitors were at fault. They should have advised the liquidators to clear up the position. And they did not. All slept until the death of the plaintiffs' solicitor on 9th February 1968.

F Soon after his death, the plaintiffs instructed other solicitors. They acted promptly. On 3rd April 1968, they gave notice of intention to proceed. It was a month's notice. That month is given by the rules so as to enable the defendants to consider their position, and to apply, if so advised, to dismiss the action for want of prosecution. The defendants did not apply within the month. So the plaintiffs on 9th May 1968, delivered a statement of claim. The defendants' then solicitors accepted it. But then on 21st May 1968, the defendants went to new solicitors. These new solicitors asked for their time for defence to be extended. This was granted. But then on 27th May 1968 the new solicitors said that they intended to apply under s. 307 of the Companies Act 1948, for the action to be stayed. (This is a section which, with s. 226, enables the court to stay actions against a company in winding-up. It has nothing to do with dismissal for want of prosecution.) It was not until 18th July 1968, that they did so apply under s. 307, and in their summons they added, almost by an afterthought, an application to stay for want of prosecution. The matter was not heard until after the long vacation. On 14th October 1968, Master RITCHIE refused a stay, but on 27th November 1968, MILMO, J., dismissed the action for want of prosecution, but gave leave to appeal to this court.

I The judge was not referred to the law about the duties of a liquidator as we have been: and I think it makes all the difference to the case. It shows that the defendants were just as guilty of delay as the plaintiffs. There was delay on both sides for the two whole years from March 1966 to April 1968. This delay was inordinate. It can be explained but not excused. So far as the plaintiffs are concerned, it is explained by the illness of their solicitor, but I fear not

---

(1) [1903] 2 Ch. 625 at p. 631.
(2) [1947] 2 All E.R. 479 at pp. 485, 486; [1947] Ch. 673 at pp. 689, 691.

excused. So far as the defendants are concerned, it is explained by the forgetful- **A** ness of the duties of liquidators, but again not excused. It is one of those cases, therefore, where the defendants have themselves largely contributed to the delay: and the courts will not look kindly on their application to strike out.

Moreover, there is no evidence that the defendants have been seriously preju- diced. There was, it is true, a suggestion that they had already distributed a large part of their assets: but there is nothing in that because the liquidators **B** took an indemnity from the recipients who are well able to repay any amounts that are required. The delay has not affected the trial of the issues in the case; for those will turn on the correspondence and on the documents to be obtained on discovery. A fair trial can still be had.

Then there is evidence of waiver. On 3rd April 1968, the plaintiffs gave notice of intention to proceed—and did proceed. Yet it was not till 18th July 1968, **C** that the defendants (by new solicitors) took any point about want of prosecution.

Finally, the period of limitation has not run. If this action were struck out, the plaintiffs could start another action tomorrow. So what good is it to strike out this one? I would not place too much emphasis on this point. It is much less hard for plaintiffs to be struck out now than when the period of limitation has expired. If it were a proper case for dismissing for want of prosecution, I would **D** not hesitate to strike it out, even though another action could be brought straight away.

But on all the other grounds I have mentioned, I think this is not a case for striking out. I would allow the appeal accordingly.

EDMUND DAVIES, L.J.: While for my part leaving for future considera- **E** tion the proper approach of the court in a case relating to an application to strike out for want of prosecution where it would still be open to the respondent to issue a fresh writ (the period of limitation not having been exhausted), I never- theless entirely agree with LORD DENNING, M.R., in the conclusion at which he has arrived. In deciding whether or not it is proper to strike out, the court asks itself a number of questions: first, has there been inordinate delay? Secondly, is **F** the delay nevertheless excusable? And thirdly, has there in consequence been prejudice to the other party? But these questions are, as it were, posed en route to the final question which overrides everything else and was enunciated by LORD DENNING, M.R., in *Allen* v. *Sir Alfred McAlpine & Sons, Ltd.* (3) in these words:

" The principle on which we go is clear: when the delay is prolonged and inexcusable, and is such as to do grave injustice to one side or the other, or **G** to both, the court may in its discretion dismiss the action straight away . . ."

So the overriding consideration always is whether or not justice can be done des- pite the delay. Thus, LORD DENNING, M.R., referred later in his judgment in that case (4), to " delay . . . so great as to amount to a denial of justice ", and there are other passages to the like effect in the other judgments. Although counsel for the defendants, doing his valiant best when confronted with in- **H** superable difficulties, has sought to contend that the reference in the pleadings to the " conduct of the parties " as being relevant to the question of the nature of the contract sued on, I am by no means convinced that any kind of embarrass- ment to the defendants is likely to result from the lapse of time. That is, perhaps, sufficient to dispose of this matter. However, I feel I ought to add that not only is it rightly conceded by counsel for the plaintiffs that there has been inordinate **I** delay on the plaintiffs' part (though he understandably urged that it was not " very inordinate delay "), but further that in my judgment it is incumbent on him to provide an adequate excuse for such delay. It is not for the other side to demonstrate its inexcusability. I am not by any means satisfied that counsel for the plaintiffs has succeeded in explaining away the plaintiffs' inaction over

(3) [1968] 1 All E.R. 543 at p. 547; [1968] 2 Q.B. 229 at pp. 245, 246.
(4) [1968] 1 All E.R. at p. 548; [1968] 2 Q.B. at p. 248.

A something like two years and two months. It is true that there are attendant circumstances which arouse one's sympathy: namely, the progressive and grave illness of the plaintiffs' solicitor, and the inactivity of another firm of solicitors to whom he very properly handed over his papers. While those are relevant matters, it is nevertheless not open to a party to say: " My solicitor has let time go by: therefore I am ipso facto to be excused for all delay which has occurred."

B It is still the duty of the party to prod his solicitors into activity, lest (as here) the weeks, the months and even the years go by. Indeed, I am satisfied that there has been nothing approaching an adequate excuse for the inordinate delay in this case.

Finally, there remains the question, was any prejudice caused to the defendants as a result of the plaintiffs' inexcusable and inordinate delay? I am with LORD

C DENNING, M.R., entirely as to that matter. I do not think that prejudice has been established in any degree. As to the liquidators, they are covered by an indemnity. As to the company itself, it can go back to its contributories and (if there has been an excessive distribution) ask them to make reparation to the extent necessary to meet the plaintiffs' claim, were that claim established. But even were it the case that prejudice had been established by the defendants, there looms over

D everything else the question, How did that prejudice arise? If it be the case that any prejudice flowed directly from the activity or the inactivity of the defendants themselves, and (above all) if they, or one acting in their name or on their behalf, neglected his duties, and it was from such neglect that the prejudice flowed, it is clearly not open to such defendants to plead that they have been prejudiced by reason of the failure of the plaintiffs to press on with their action.

E LORD DENNING, M.R., has already referred to s. 302 and s. 307 of the Companies Act 1948. It is perfectly clear, and indeed counsel for the defendants has been quite unable to submit to the contrary, that the liquidators have (and I must regretfully use the adverb) woefully fallen down in their statutory duty. They knew—and they must certainly be taken to have known—that there was at least a contingent liability to these plaintiffs. When one looks at s. 302 and s. 306

F of the Companies Act 1948, and r. 106 of the Companies (Winding-Up) Rules, 1949 (5), it is clear that the liquidator has to advertise for claims. Furthermore, advertising is not sufficient where he knows of the existence of claims, for, as was illustrated by the decision in *Pulsford* v. *Devenish* (6), in such a case there is a duty to ascertain by direct enquiry whether the claim is being pressed.

These defendants were at the material time acting through a well-known firm

G of solicitors and I have some sympathy for them, for in May of 1967 they received from those solicitors a fee note relating to this very matter. It sets out the details of the professional charges and ends:

" Thereafter investigating fully the background circumstances of the claim; attendances on and correspondence with you and other interested parties, with a view to preparing the defence, but the matter was not pursued."

H It may be that in such circumstances the lay person hereafter would say: " Well, solicitors do not present a final fee note in respect of their professional charges in a matter which is still proceeding." But the defendants' solicitors certainly knew that the plaintiffs' claim was still extant and the defendants must accept responsibility for those solicitors. Even had the latter advised them wrongly, they could not shield themselves behind that mistake. That is vividly illustrated

I by the decision in *Re Windsor Steam Coal Co. (1901), Ltd.* (7).

It is clear in this case that the liquidators failed in their duty. Even if any prejudice arose—and I have already indicated that I think none has been established—it must be attributed to that failure. In my judgment, therefore, it does not lie in the defendants' mouths to urge that fact against the plaintiffs who desire to pursue this claim.

(5) S.I. 1949 No. 330.
(6) [1903] 2 Ch. 625.
(7) [1929] 1 Ch. 151.

For those reasons, and without more, I concur in holding that this appeal should **A** be allowed.

Appeal allowed.

Solicitors: *D. J. Freeman & Co.* (for the plaintiffs); *Linklaters & Paines* (for the defendants).

[*Reported by* JENIFER SANDELL, *Barrister-at-Law.*]

B

R. *v.* BRADBURY.

C

[COURT OF APPEAL, CRIMINAL DIVISION (Edmund Davies and Phillimore, L.JJ., and Geoffrey Lane, J.), January 17, 1969.]

Criminal Law—Trial—Jury—Direction to jury—Burden of proof—Prosecution evidence calling for explanation by accused—Direction that presumption of guilt raised if explanation rejected by jury—Whether misdirection.

At the trial of the appellant on an indictment charging him with having **D** unlawful sexual intercourse with a girl aged 15, contrary to s. 6 (1) of the Sexual Offences Act 1956, the trial judge, having directed the jury that the burden of proof was on the prosecution went on to say that, where the prosecution called evidence from which the accused's guilt might be presumed, and which therefore called for an explanation by the accused and the accused gave an answer or explanation which the jury rejected as being **E** untrue, a presumption was raised on which the jury might be justified in returning a verdict of guilty. On appeal against conviction,

Held: the appeal must be allowed, because the jury should have been told in terms, not only that the burden of proof was on the prosecution, but also that, in the last resort, they had to be satisfied beyond all reasonable doubt, or that they had to be sure of the appellant's guilt, before they **F** could convict; the words used might lead the jury to the conclusion that, if the appellant gave an explanation which they rejected, the step towards convicting him was short and well-nigh inevitable (see p. 759, letter I, and p. 760, letter B, post).

Appeal allowed.

[As to the contents of summing-up in a criminal trial, see 10 HALSBURY'S **G** LAWS (3rd Edn.) 424, 425, para. 780; and for cases on the subject, see 14 DIGEST (Repl.) 330-332, *3197-3222.*]

Case referred to:
R. v. *Stoddart* (1909), 2 Cr. App. Rep. 217; 73 J.P. 348; 14 Digest (Repl.) 330, *3202.*

H

Appeal.

This was an appeal by Ronald William Bradbury against his conviction at Hertfordshire Quarter Sessions before the deputy chairman (OWEN STABLE, ESQ., Q.C.) and a jury on 5th July 1968 of unlawful sexual intercourse with a girl aged 15, contrary to the Sexual Offences Act 1956, s. 6 (1). He was sentenced to two years' imprisonment. The facts are set out in the judgment of the court. **I**

J. G. Connor for the appellant.
M. R. Wilkinson for the Crown.

EDMUND DAVIES, L.J., delivered the judgment of the court: This appeal is allowed. On 5th July 1968 at Hertfordshire Quarter Sessions, the appellant, Ronald William Bradbury, was convicted of unlawful sexual intercourse with a girl aged 15 and he received a sentence of two years' imprisonment. With the leave of the single judge, he now appeals against that conviction.

A   The girl gave evidence that, on the evening of 9th September 1967, she, then being 15 years of age, was in a public house with the appellant when he suggested a walk. They went into a field, had intercourse and she became pregnant as a result. She gave evidence about what had happened in regard to the removal of her clothing before the act of intercourse which was said to be inconsistent with what she had said on another occasion, and there were other alleged
B   discrepancies in her account of what had transpired. The appellant in evidence said that the walk was the girl's idea, that her attentions when they went out were very pressing, but that, nevertheless, they only kissed, although she obviously wanted intercourse. The girl had testified that, when they got back to his car, the appellant asked her how old she was and she replied that she was 15, his version being that she had told him she was 17. In the following November,
C   the girl met the appellant and told him that she was pregnant. He retorted that it was not his baby and that she would have to take him to court. He told the police later that he had not had intercourse, but that he could bring along half-a-dozen fellows who had had intercourse with the girl. At his trial, he said that she had acted with great sexual precocity towards him.

    There was no corroboration, and the jury were impeccably directed on the
D   desirability for it and as to its complete absence. But the ground on which we allow this appeal (and do not accede to the invitation of the Crown to apply the proviso (1)) arises from the direction in relation to the burden and standard of proof. The learned deputy chairman said:

    " That simply means that where an accused person has pleaded not guilty the prosecution is obliged to prove upon trial in effect each circum-
E   stance stated in the indictment which is material and necessary to constitute the offence. I have already told you that there are only two facts or circumstances in this indictment which are material and necessary to constitute this offence . . . The rule is that the burden of proving guilt lies upon the prosecution and it is not for the accused to prove his innocence."

F So the learned deputy chairman had unquestionably placed the burden on the right shoulders. But then he went on:

    " What is meant by ' prove ' in that context? The answer is that where the prosecution call evidence from which the guilt of the accused might be presumed, and which therefore calls for an explanation by the accused and the accused does not give an answer or explanation, or gives an answer or
G   explanation which the jury rejects as being untrue, a presumption is raised upon which the jury may be justified in returning a verdict of guilty. If the accused gives an explanation which raises in the minds of a jury a reasonable doubt as to his guilt, then the accused is entitled to be acquitted because if, upon the whole of the evidence in the case, the jury is left in a real state of doubt, the prosecution has failed to satisfy the onus of proof
H   that lies on them. So much for the burden of proof."

    In our judgment, too much was thus said about the burden of proof and what was said was too involved. A much shorter direction would have been more helpful. The jury should have been told in terms, not only that the burden was on the prosecution (as they most certainly were directed), but also that, in the last resort, they had to be satisfied beyond all reasonable doubt (or that they
I   had to be sure of the guilt of the appellant) before they could convict.

    What the learned deputy chairman did here, it is quite clear, was to quote from the second sub-paragraph of para. 1001 of Archbold's Criminal Pleading, Evidence and Practice (36th Edn.). It is a very useful passage for the legal practitioner and the judge to have in mind. It is an amalgam of several citations from the decision of Lord Alverstone, C.J., in *R. v. Stoddart* (2).   But we

---

(1) I.e., to s. 2 (1) of the Criminal Appeal Act 1968.
(2) (1909), 2 Cr. App. Rep. 217 at p. 241.

venture to think that those portions of it which in particular refer to " a **A**
presumption being raised on which the jury may be justified in returning a
verdict of guilty " are not such as one should contemplate citing to a jury.
They are not calculated to help them; indeed, they have an unfortunate tendency
to confuse, rather than to elucidate, and to lead a jury to the conclusion that,
if an accused man gives an explanation which they reject, the step towards
convicting him is short and well-nigh inevitable. The citation of this somewhat **B**
involved passage could, nevertheless, have been cured had there been, either
before or after it, as we have already said, a bald direction in such terms as,
" You have to be sure in this case before you can convict " or " You have to be
satisfied beyond all reasonable doubt before you can convict ". But, unhappily,
a direction in those familiar, simple terms intelligible to the jury was never
employed.   **C**

There being no corroboration, this case called for a particularly clear and
simple direction on the lines we have indicated. Instead, the learned deputy
chairman, by a verbatim quotation from a standard work in daily use by legal
practitioners, employed words likely to prove confusing to the laymen who
constituted the jury. This is regrettable, but, in our judgment, the result must
be that this appeal against conviction is allowed.   **D**

Appeal allowed.

Solicitors; *Registrar of Criminal Appeals* (for the appellant); *Lathom & Co.*,
Luton (for the Crown).

[*Reported by* N. J. CHINIVASAGAM, ESQ., *Barrister-at-Law.*]

                                                                                  E

GEORGE J. SMITH & CO., LTD. *v.* FURLONG (Inspector of Taxes).
GEORGE J. SMITH & CO., LTD. *v.* INLAND REVENUE COMMISSIONERS.   **F**

[CHANCERY DIVISION (Cross, J.), December 10, 11, 12, 1968.]

*Income Tax—Deduction in computing profits—Expenses—Disbursements " wholly
and exclusively laid out . . . for the purposes of the trade "—Compensation for
loss of office—Directors—Agreement between directors in personal negotiations
—Subsequent adoption in company's resolution—Commissioners' finding*   **G**
*right to deduction not established—Sufficiency of evidence to support—Income
Tax Act 1952 (15 & 16 Geo. 6 & 1 Eliz. 2 c. 10), s. 137 (a).*

The three directors of the taxpayer company were appointed as life
directors each at a salary of £5,000 a year under service agreements with the
company and under the articles of association they could not be removed
by extraordinary resolution without their consent. The chairman who was   **H**
responsible for book-keeping held 1,015 of the 3,000 shares, a director
responsible for a special contract 990 and the managing director 995.
Following disagreements over the adequacy of the book-keeping and a
contemplated expansion of a special contract, negotiations took place and
it was decided that the chairman and special contract director would sell
their shares to the managing director at a fair valuation, that they would   **I**
resign as directors and that they would receive compensation for loss of
directors' office. They subsequently transferred their shares to the managing
director and his wife for £3,000 each. At an extraordinary general meeting
of the company three weeks later it was unanimously resolved that they be
paid compensation, for loss of office as life directors, of £5,000 (chairman)
and £500 respectively, and they then signed a document of resignation as
life directors expressed to be in consideration of those payments. The
taxpayer company sought to deduct the payments as expenses in computing

A   its profits for income tax purposes. The managing director gave evidence (accepted) of his dissatisfaction with the other directors' discharge of their duties, of his discovery that one had set up a separate company, and of negotiations which he conducted on his own behalf and not for the company (the other directors having a majority shareholding) and expressed his opinion (accepted as bona fide) that the compensation was paid solely to

B   protect the company's trade which had in fact subsequently improved. The accountant also gave evidence (accepted) of delay and difficulty in preparing final accounts owing to unsatisfactory book-keeping, referred to possible future losses if the special contract had continued, and expressed the opinion (accepted as bona fide) that the compensation was an appropriate deduction in the profit and loss account for accountancy purposes and a valid business

C   expense incurred to protect the company's business from losses arising from the disagreements, wrong policies and inefficiency. The Special Commissioners of Income Tax held that the taxpayer company had failed to establish that the payments of compensation were moneys wholly and exclusively laid out or expended for the purposes of the company's trade within s. 137 (*a*) of the Income Tax Act 1952 and disallowed the deduction.

D   **Held:** the appeal would be dismissed because, although compensation paid to a director for loss of office could in certain circumstances be an expense deductible for tax purposes under s. 137 (*a*), where the payment occurred in connection with a contemporaneous change in the shareholding of the company, the company had to prove that it considered the question of payment wholly untrammelled by the terms of the bargain its shareholders

E   had struck with those purchasing their shares, and that the decision to pay the compensation was made solely in the interests of its trade; accordingly, since the decision to pay was made by all the shareholders and directors, including the outgoing directors, the company was only implementing part of an agreement made between the various parties at a time when the continuing director and shareholder was not in control of the company (see

F   p. 764, letters F and I, and p. 765, letters B, F and H, post).

     Dicta of DONOVAN, J. in *James Snook & Co., Ltd.* v. *Blasdale (Inspector of Taxes)* ((1952), 33 Tax Cas. at p. 251) applied.

     Appeal dismissed.

   [As to expenses incurred for the purposes of a trade deductible in computing

G   a company's profits, see 20 HALSBURY's LAWS (3rd Edn.) 166-168, paras. 286, 287; and for cases on the subject, see 28 DIGEST (Repl.) 87-101, *329-401*.

     For the Income Tax Act 1952, s. 137 (*a*), see 31 HALSBURY's STATUTES (2nd Edn.) 134.]

Case referred to:

H   *Snook (James) & Co., Ltd.* v. *Blasdale (Inspector of Taxes), Snook (James) & Co., Ltd.* v. *Inland Revenue Comrs.* (1952), 33 Tax Cas. 244;   28 Digest (Repl.) 99, 394.

Case Stated.

   The taxpayer company appealed to the General Commissioners of Income Tax for St. Pancras in the London Borough of Camden against the following

I   assessment made on it under Case I of Sch. D to the Income Tax Act 1952 in respect of profits arising from the business of advertising agents for 1964-65: £11,000, add balancing charge £890, less capital allowances £1,824. The question for determination was whether the payment of compensation for loss of office made by the company to two of its directors in the sums of £500 and £5,000 respectively was an admissible deduction in computing those profits*. The

---

   * The facts of the case are set out at p. 762, letter C, to p. 764, letter B, post.

taxpayer company contended that the payments were moneys wholly and exclu- **A** sively expended for the purposes of the company's trade within the meaning of s. 137 (*a*) of the Income Tax Act 1952 and accordingly that they fell to be deducted in computing the company's profits for the relevant year. The Crown contended to the contrary. The commissioners held* that the company had failed to establish that the expenditure was money so wholly and exclusively laid out or expended and dismissed the appeal. The taxpayer company appealed **B** by way of Case Stated to the High Court.

C. N. *Beattie*, Q.C., and S. I. *Simon* for the taxpayer company.
Desmond C. *Miller*, Q.C., and P. W. *Medd* for the Crown.

CROSS, J.: The question to be determined in this case is whether two sums of £5,000 and £500 paid in 1963 by the taxpayer company, George J. Smith & Co., Ltd., to two of its directors as compensation for loss of office were admis- **C** sible deductions under Case I of Sch. D in computing the taxpayer company's profits under that Case for the year of assessment 1964-65. The taxpayer company was incorporated in January 1938, and its trade at all times was that of advertising agents. A Mr. Lipkin was managing director until his death on 23rd December 1958. In October 1956, Mrs. Phyllis Lipkin, his wife, was appointed a director of the taxpayer company. In June 1957 a Mr. Frank True became a **D** director; and on 16th March 1959 a Mr. David Hazard joined the taxpayer company as a director. At a directors' meeting held on 1st September 1959 it was resolved that Mrs. Lipkin be appointed chairman of the board of directors of the taxpayer company and that Mr. True be appointed managing director. Mr. Hazard was concerned with the " creative " side of the taxpayer company's business as well as being solely responsible for the day-to-day management of a **E** substantial contract (known as " the Duomatic contract ") concerned with the sale of washing machines direct to the public.

Under service agreements made on 10th November 1961 between the taxpayer company and each of the directors in question, each director was appointed a life director at the salary of £5,000 a year; and at the same time the articles were altered to make it impossible for a life director to be removed by extra- **F** ordinary resolution without his consent. By a further agreement of the same date it was provided that the taxpayer company should make a bonus issue of shares, and that Mrs. Lipkin and Mr. True should renounce part of their allot- ment to Mr. Hazard. The object of these arrangements was to give Mr. Hazard a proper stake in the taxpayer company. As a result of the bonus issue and renunciations the shareholdings in the taxpayer company became: Mrs. Lipkin, **G** 1,015 shares; Mr. Hazard, 990 shares; Mr. True, 995 shares; the total issued shares of the company being 3,000.

Early in the year 1962 disagreements began to develop between the directors of the company centred on Mrs. Lipkin's inadequacy as a book-keeper, an expansion of the Duomatic contract contemplated by Mr. Hazard, and a grievance felt by Mr. True at a reduction in his remuneration. The state of feeling among **H** them is shown vividly by the very full minutes of the directors' meeting held on 27th June 1962 exhibited to the Case.

I now read para. 4 (x) of the Case verbatim:

" Negotiations ensued between the Directors of the Company by way of interview between the period June to September, 1963, and covered such points as the resignation of Directors, the compensation of Directors, as **I** well as the terms upon which the shares held by Mrs. Lipkin and Mr. Hazard should be sold to Mr. and Mrs. True. The result of these negotiations was agreement that: (a) Mrs. Lipkin and Mr. Hazard would sell their shares at a fair valuation to Mr. True. (b) Mrs. Lipkin and Mr. Hazard would resign as Directors. (c) Mrs. Lipkin and Mr. Hazard would receive compensation for loss of Directors' office."

* The terms of the commissioners' decision are set out at p. 764, letter C, post.

A   In pursuance of the agreement reached by the directors of the taxpayer company, Mrs. Lipkin and Mr. Hazard each transferred their respective shares in the taxpayer company to Mr. True and his wife on 10th September 1963, in consideration of the sum of £3,000, representing a purchase price of about £3 a share. At an extraordinary general meeting of the taxpayer company held on 30th September 1963, attended by Mrs. Lipkin, Mr. Hazard and Mr. True, it

B   was unanimously resolved that the company pay the sum of £5,000 to Mrs. Lipkin and the sum of £500 to Mr. Hazard as compensation for loss of office as life directors of the taxpayer company. Presumably the transfers made on 10th September had not yet been registered. If they had been, Mrs. Lipkin and Mr. Hazard would not have been entitled to attend the shareholders' meeting. After the passing of the resolution referred to, Mrs. Lipkin and Mr. Hazard

C   each signed a document resigning as life directors of the taxpayer company, expressed to be in consideration of the payment of £5,000 in the case of Mrs. Lipkin, and, in the case of Mr. Hazard, in consideration of the payment of £500, to be made on 29th December 1963. Mr. True gave evidence before the commissioners to the following effect:

D   " (a) After his appointment to the [taxpayer company] in the year 1957 a substantial expansion of the [taxpayer company's] trade took place and, until early in the year 1962, the internal affairs of the [taxpayer company] proceeded satisfactorily: (b) thereafter, dissention developed amongst the Directors of the [taxpayer company] both as regards matters of policy and the manner in which his fellow Directors were discharging their duties, whilst he, himself, was dissatisfied with the way in which he was being

E   remunerated: (c) in June 1963, he discovered that Mr. Hazard had set up another Company and it was clear to him that the latter no longer had the [taxpayer company's] business at heart: (d) throughout the period of negotiation between the Directors of the [taxpayer company] which lasted from June to September, 1963, the majority shareholding in the [taxpayer company] was jointly held by Mrs. Lipkin and Mr. Hazard, and, as a

F   consequence, he was not negotiating with them as a representative of the [taxpayer company] but on his own account: (e) he was of opinion that the compensation paid to Mrs. Lipkin and Mr. Hazard was an expenditure which had been incurred solely to protect the [taxpayer company's] trade: (f) immediately following the resignation of the said Directors there was an improvement in the trade of the [taxpayer company]."

G   The commissioners say that so far as the evidence given by Mr. True was on matters of fact they accepted it, and so far as it was an expression of opinion they accepted it as given bona fide.

Evidence was also given by Mr. Reubin Derek Taylor, of Messrs. Benjamin Taylor and Co., chartered accountants. He said:

H   " (a) he had been for some while closely concerned with the [taxpayer company's] affairs and was aware that serious disagreement had arisen among the Directors of the [taxpayer company] during the years 1962 and 1963: (b) he had neither been consulted in regard to, nor been invited to take part in, the negotiations which took place among the Directors between June and September, 1963: (c) he had experienced considerable delay and difficulty in the preparation of the final accounts of the [taxpayer company]

I   owing to Mrs. Lipkin's unsatisfactory book-keeping: (d) he confirmed that the Gross profits of the [taxpayer company] had declined from the year 1963 to 1965 as a result of adverse circumstances which affected the advertising agency business: (e) he expressed the opinion that the [taxpayer company's] accounts for the year 1963 showed no evidence that the [taxpayer company's] business had been jeopardised as a result of the disagreements amongst its Directors though losses in the future might well have arisen had the Duomatic contract been allowed to continue: (f) he expressed the

A

opinion that the payment of compensation to the two Directors of the [taxpayer company] was an appropriate deduction in the Profit and Loss account for accountancy purposes and, further, that this compensation expenditure, made to the said Directors on their resignation was a valid business expense which was incurred to protect the [taxpayer company's] business from losses arising from disagreements amongst its Directors, wrong policies and inefficiency."

B

The commissioners say that so far as the evidence given by Mr. Taylor was on matters of fact they accepted it, and so far as it was an expression of opinion they accepted it as given bona fide. After hearing submissions of both sides, the commissioners gave their decision as follows:

" We, the Commissioners who heard the appeal, having carefully considered the facts and arguments adduced before us, decided that the [taxpayer company] had failed to establish that the expenditure of £5,500 on payments of compensation to Mrs. Lipkin and Mr. Hazard was money wholly and exclusively laid out or expended for the purposes of the [taxpayer company's] trade within the meaning of Section 137 (a), Income Tax Act, 1952 and we accordingly dismissed the appeal."

C

D

The taxpayer company expressed dissatisfaction, and the commissioners stated this Case.

There is, of course, no doubt that compensation paid to a retiring director for loss of office may in certain circumstances be an expense deductible for tax purposes. If, for instance, his colleagues on the board have formed the view that the continuance in office of a certain director is most prejudicial to the prosperity of the company, that in the interests of the company he must be induced to resign and that the sum to be paid to him to secure his resignation is no more than has to be paid for the purpose, then clearly the expense would be deductible—and it would not cease to be deductible because contemporaneously, so as to get rid of him altogether, the retiring director sold his shareholding to his colleagues. But obviously the position becomes more difficult if the payment of compensation occurs in connection with a change in the shareholding control of the company. The matter was put very clearly by DONOVAN, J., at the end of his judgment in *James Snook & Co., Ltd.* v. *Blasdale (Inspector of Taxes), James Snook & Co., Ltd.* v. *Inland Revenue Comrs.* (1). The passage runs as follows:

E

F

" The mere circumstances that compensation to retiring directors is paid on a change of shareholding control does not of itself involve the consequence that such compensation can never be a deductible trading expense. So much is common ground. But it is essential in such cases that the company should prove to the Commissioners' satisfaction that it considered the question of payment wholly untrammelled by the terms of the bargain its shareholders had struck with those who were to buy their shares and came to a decision to pay solely in the interests of its trade. This may be very difficult at times, because the persons who have to take the decision are often the persons who are to get the compensation; but any difficulty in securing an independent decision by or on behalf of the Company does not do away with the necessity of securing it if a title to deduct the compensation as a trade expense is to be sought."

G

H

I

That case was one of the cases cited to the commissioners in this case, and I have no reason to doubt that they had in mind the question which they had to ask themselves; viz., were they satisfied that the taxpayer company considered the question of these payments wholly untrammelled by the terms of the bargain which the three individuals concerned had struck with regard to the sale of the shares of Mrs. Lipkin and Mr. Hazard to Mr. True. The taxpayer company

(1) (1952), 33 Tax Cas. 244 at p. 251.

A submits that on the facts found in the Case the commissioners ought to have been so satisfied, and that the conclusion at which they arrived, for which they in fact gave no reason, is one at which no reasonable man could arrive on the material stated in the Case. In particular, it is pointed out that Mr. True said in evidence that he thought that the compensation paid to Mrs. Lipkin and Mr. Hazard was expenditure solely incurred to protect the taxpayer company's

B trade, and that the commissioners accepted that that was genuinely his opinion.

But the taxpayer company's argument really involves the assumption that Mr. True can be regarded as having been in control of the taxpayer company at the time when the decision to pay the compensation was taken, so that the light in which he regarded the payments can be used as a test of the purpose for which the taxpayer company made them. I do not think, however, that the

C commissioners were bound to make any such assumption. Mr. True was in a minority. As he himself said, from June to September 1963 he was negotiating with Mrs. Lipkin and Mr. Hazard on his own account and not as someone representing the taxpayer company. The taxpayer company, as such, cannot be treated as having been a party to the negotiations which resulted in the agreement set out in para. 4 (x) of the Case.

D In pursuance of the agreement—which was not, of course, an enforceable bargain, but simply an agreed basis on which to proceed—a price was fixed for the shares. There is nothing in the Case to suggest that the price fixed was conditioned by the amounts to be paid as compensation, which indeed were unequal, but I would suppose (and counsel on both sides I think agreed) that the amounts to be paid as compensation were agreed between the three persons

E concerned before the general meeting on 30th September. By that time Mrs. Lipkin and Mr. Hazard had executed transfers of their shares and apparently had received the price for them, but they were evidently still not only directors but on the register of shareholders. Moreover, if for any reason the decision at the meeting had been that the sums provisionally agreed as compensation should not be paid, it may very well be that the transfer of the shares and the

F payment of the price could have been rescinded. However that may be, it was in fact resolved by all the three shareholders and directors that the payments in question should be made, and Mrs. Lipkin and Mr. Hazard thereupon resigned.

Why should the commissioners have been satisfied that the decision of the taxpayer company taken on 30th September 1963 to make these payments was a decision taken by Mr. True alone, and not a decision taken by all the three

G persons concerned? Yet the reason why Mrs. Lipkin and Mr. Hazard voted in favour of the payments being made is hardly likely to have been because they thought that the interests of the taxpayer company required them to be made. Moreover, even if one could treat Mr. True as being in control of the taxpayer company at the date of the meeting, there is nothing in the Case to show that he considered the matter of compensation de novo on that day. So far as appears,

H the taxpayer company was only implementing part of an agreement made between the three at a time when Mr. True was certainly not in control.

It would, perhaps, have been better if the commissioners had stated in terms the respects in which, on their view, the facts proved and evidence given fell short of establishing what the taxpayer company had to establish; but for the reasons which I have tried to give, I have no doubt that the conclusion at which

I they arrived was one which they were justified in reaching. For those reasons, I will dismiss the appeal.

Appeal dismissed.

Solicitors: *Parker, Thomas & Co.* (for the taxpayer company); *Solicitor of Inland Revenue.*

[*Reported by* F. A. AMIES, ESQ., *Barrister-at-Law.*]

A

Re F. (an infant).

[CHANCERY DIVISION (Megarry, J.), February 27, 28, March 3, 1969.]

*Infant—Guardianship of Infants Acts—Care and control—Welfare of infant as
first and paramount consideration—Welfare not the exclusive consideration—
Consideration of all relevant circumstances—Guardianship of Infants Act
1925 (15 & 16 Geo. 5 c. 45), s. 1.*

B

Although in wardship proceedings the welfare of the infant is by virtue of
the Guardianship of Infants Act 1925, s. 1, the first and paramount consideration, " paramount " does not mean " exclusive ", and the court should
consider and weigh all the circumstances that are of any relevance, giving
the welfare of the infant especial weight. Nevertheless, this process cannot
be analysed or carried out according to any formula, and must depend on
the exercise of a judicial discretion after all relevant factors have been
considered (see p. 767, letter I, and p. 768, letters C and E, post).

C

Re L. (infants) ([1962] 3 All E.R. 1) applied.

[As to the principles on which the court acts in making orders as to the custody
of infants, see 21 HALSBURY'S LAWS (3rd Edn.) 194, para. 429, and for cases on
the subject, see 28 DIGEST (Repl.) 614-624, *1205-1265.*

D

For the Guardianship of Infants Act 1925, s. 1, see 12 HALSBURY'S STATUTES
(2nd Edn.) 955.]

Cases referred to:

H. v. *H. and C.,* [1969] 1 All E.R. 262; [1969] 1 W.L.R. 208.
L. (infants), Re, [1962] 3 All E.R. 1; [1962] 1 W.L.R. 886; Digest (Cont. Vol.
A) 924, *1265a.*

E

Summons.

By this originating summons the father sought as against the mother care and
control of their infant who had been made a ward of court. The hearing was in
chambers but at the request of counsel HIS LORDSHIP gave leave for the judgment
to be reported. The facts are set out in the judgment.

F

G. M. Godfrey for the father.
R. R. F. Scott for the mother.

MEGARRY, J.: These are wardship proceedings. The only issue before me
is whether care and control of the ward should be given to the plaintiff, to whom I
shall refer as " the father ", or the defendant, whom I shall call " the mother ".
The father and the mother met in about February 1965. The mother was then in
a teachers' training college. By July of that year they were having sexual intercourse with each other. They married in December 1965, at a time when the
mother was pregnant by the father. The father was a non-commissioned officer in
the Royal Air Force, and in February 1966 he was posted overseas. He took the
mother with him.

G

The ward, a girl, was born abroad towards the end of April 1966; she will
thus be three years old in less than two months' time. About a year after the birth
of the ward, the mother began to commit adultery with another member of the
R.A.F. stationed in the same place, a Mr. D.; they had got to know each other in
about December 1966 in connection with amateur theatricals. In May 1967 the
father became suspicious of the relationship, and on 2nd June he taxed the mother
with it. She admitted the adultery, and asked for a divorce. The next day, after
unsuccessful attempts by the father and a R.A.F. chaplain to get the mother
to give up Mr. D. and become reconciled to the father, the mother left the matrimonial home. A month later, on 2nd July, after a number of discussions and other
incidents, the mother returned to England by air. During that month, the father
had been attempting to get the mother to return to him, and the mother had made
an unsuccessful attempt to take the child. On 15th July the father wrote the
mother a long letter attempting a reconciliation; the mother never replied to it.

H

I

On 16th July the father sent the child back to England, and his parents then
looked after her at their home. The mother visited the baby on 2nd August. On

A 23rd August, she again visited the father's parents' home town with her brother
and Mr. D. The mother and her brother went to the house of the father's parents
and removed the child without warning, taking her to the home of the mother's
mother. On hearing of this, the father obtained compassionate leave and returned
to England; and on 7th September he issued the originating summons making
the child a ward of court, and seeking care and control of the ward and the return
B of the ward. The next day, a notice of motion for an order for the return of the
ward was issued. The motion initially came before DONALDSON, J., who adjourned
it, the mother undertaking that Mr. D. would cease to stay in the same house as
herself.

The substantive hearing of the motion was before BRANDON, J. After a long
hearing, he gave judgment on 25th September, ordering the return of the ward to
C the father. BRANDON, J., saw and heard the father, the mother, and Mr. D. in
the witness box; and nothing I have read or heard causes me to differ from the
facts that he found, some of which I have thought it not necessary to repeat in
this judgment. On 11th October, the Court of Appeal dismissed an appeal and
ordered the return of the ward on 14th October. The ward then went to live with
the father's parents at their home. The father obtained a discharge from the
D R.A.F. in November 1967, and went to live with his parents as well.

In the meantime, the mother had become pregnant by Mr. D.; and in May
1968 she had a daughter. Mr. D. obtained a discharge from the R.A.F. early in
June 1968, and set up house with the mother, in a place where he had obtained a
short-lived job. He then obtained work in another area, and when this case
came on for hearing before me on 14th October 1968, Mr. D. and the mother had
E no home that they could then offer the child. On the mother's application I
adjourned the hearing; and Mr. D. and the mother have now obtained a flat with
two bedrooms. The mother seeks care and control of the ward so that the ward
may live with her there, sharing a bedroom with her baby daughter, who is now
nearly ten months old.

The father has also formed an attachment. In June 1968 he met a Miss G.
F She is now pregnant by him, and the baby is due in July. He found a cottage
near his parents' home, and Miss G. moved in there in October 1968. After about
three weeks, the father left his parents' home and moved into the cottage as well;
some tension had arisen between him and his parents on account of Miss G. In
the cottage there is one large bedroom, which has been partitioned off to make a
room for the ward, though the partition does not reach the ceiling. The room
G thus created is large enough to accommodate the ward and also the baby when it
is born; the partition is moveable and could be extended to the ceiling.

In December 1968 the period of three years since the marriage expired, and
the father promptly thereafter presented a petition for divorce against the
mother, based on her adultery. This petition has not yet been heard. As soon
as they are able, the father intends to marry Miss G., and the mother intends to
H marry Mr. D. Each man is in a good job, earning nearly £1,000 a year. The
mother's home is, I think, a little more suitable for the ward than the father's,
but there is probably not much in it. I have had the advantage of seeing and
hearing the father, the mother, Mr. D., and Miss G., and I have to decide whether
the father or the mother ought to have care and control of the ward.

In deciding this issue, I begin with my duty under the Guardianship of Infants
I Act 1925, s. 1, to " regard the welfare of the infant as the first and paramount
consideration ", disregarding whether from any other point of view the father's
claim is superior to the mother's or vice versa. I also bear in mind the decision of
the Court of Appeal in Re L. (infants) (1), that " paramount " does not mean
" exclusive ". The welfare of the ward is to be the pre-eminent or superior
consideration; but that does not mean that I should leave out of account the
conduct of the parties. In that case, the decision of PLOWMAN, J., was reversed
because he had excluded from consideration the conduct of the parties. The Court

_____

(1) [1962] 3 All E.R. 1; [1962] 1 W.L.R. 886.

of Appeal held that where the mother had by her conduct broken up the matri- **A**
monial home, that was a matter to be taken into account. I do not think that
SALMON, L.J., can have had this authority in mind in *H*. v. *H. and C.* (2), when he
said:

> " I do not myself think that, whether this marriage broke up because of the
> fault of the father or of the mother or of both of them, is of any consequence
> whatsoever."

B

According to both reports of this case (3), neither *Re L. (infants)* (4) nor any other
case appears to have been cited to the court. Certainly this dictum cannot
displace the authority of the decision in *Re L. (infants)* (4).

Despite certain logical difficulties that were suggested in argument, I think that
the practical effect of s. 1, in conjunction with *Re L. (infants)* (4), is that in these
cases the court should consider and weigh all the circumstances that are of any **C**
relevance. Quite apart from authority, the word " first " in the section implies
that there are other circumstances that are to be considered in this process of
consideration and weighing. In doing this, a special weight must be given to the
welfare of the infant. This may so clearly point in one direction that it concludes
the matter, even if every other consideration points in the opposite direction. On
the other hand, it may be that the welfare of the infant would be equally served **D**
whichever parent has care and control; or the balance may fall on one side by
only a small amount. In those circumstances, the other considerations may be
sufficiently strong to determine the matter.

I do not think that one can express this matter in any arithmetical or quanti-
tative way, saying that the welfare of the infant must, in relation to the other
matters, be given twice the weight, or five times the weight, or any other figure. **E**
A " points system " is, in my judgment, neither possible nor desirable. What the
court has to deal with is the lives of human beings, and these cannot be regulated
by formulae. In my judgment I must take account of all relevant matters; but
in considering their effect and weight I must regard the welfare of the infant as
being first and paramount. If it is objected that this formulation does little to
define or explain the process, I would reply that it is precisely a process such as **F**
this which calls for the quality of judgment which inheres in the Bench; and this
is a quality which in its nature is not susceptible of detailed analysis. There is a
limit to the extent to which the court can fairly be expected to expound the process which leads to a conclusion, not least in the weighing of imponderables. In
matters of discretion it may at times be impossible to do much more than ensure
that the judicial mind is brought to bear, with a proper emphasis, on all that is **G**
relevant, to the exclusion of all that is irrelevant.

In this case, the conduct of the parties calls for comment. I have read and re-
read the judgment of BRANDON, J., bearing in mind the evidence and the argument before me; and, without adopting what he says in terms, I must say that
after weighing the evidence and arguments before me I am in broad agreement
with his views about the conduct of the parties. With him, I think that the **H**
mother's charges against the father, asserting that he is narrow-minded, intolerant,
mean, jealous and possessive, were of little substance, and were largely put forward
by way of self-justification. Like him, I think that the mother has behaved in a
selfish and irresponsible way, doing what she wanted to do. It was she who broke
up the marriage. I do not say that she set herself to do this; but she was less than
18 months married when she started committing adultery. When she admitted **I**
it to the father, too, she was resolute in her determination not even to attempt
the reconciliation that the father and others pressed on her, but to continue
with Mr. D. I do not believe her repeated assertions that in her mind the marriage
had already broken down before she fell into adultery. Nor do I think that the
efforts that she says she made to keep the marriage in being were efforts of any
real determination. Quite properly, little or nothing has been said against the

(2) [1969] 1 All E.R. 262 at p. 263; [1969] 1 W.L.R. 208 at p. 210.
(3) [1969] 1 All E.R. 262; [1969] 1 W.L.R. 208.
(4) [1962] 3 All E.R. 1; [1962] 1 W.L.R. 886.

A father in respect of his adulterous relationship with Miss G., for this was entered into long after the mother had made it plain that the marriage had irretrievably broken down. The adultery is wrong; but it broke up no marriage. Nevertheless, it makes it impossible for the father to say that the ward should not be brought into contact with Mr. D., and he has not attempted to say it; and to some degree it lessens the disparity between the father and the mother in the scale of moral guilt.

B At the same time, I must bear in mind the characters of the parties. I think there is some weight in the contention that they were ill-matched and ought never to have married each other. Each plainly loves the ward, though in some-what different ways. The father is, I think, worthy, rather earnest, concerned with the proprieties, and a little unbending and narrow. He is also frank and fair-minded. The mother, on the other hand, is impulsive, emotional, warm,

C somewhat thoughtless and feckless, and at times, I think, reckless. She is also selfish, putting her desires first in the scale without paying any real regard to the interests of others; and yet I think her capable of considerable generosity, in the widest sense, where this does not cut across what she regards as the essen-tials. I very much doubt whether, in breaking up the marriage, she ever really considered whether her conduct might deprive her of her baby. In other words, I

D do not think she ever made any conscious choice between her lover and her baby, or realised that there could be such a choice. She did what she wanted to do, and assumed that she would have the baby as well, despite the difficulties that appeared.

I must also consider Mr. D. and Miss G. I do not think it necessary to discuss their characters, although I must consider briefly what sort of a father-substitute

E and mother-substitute they would respectively be. These expressions I use simply to cover their functions during the periods while the ward is living separate from her true father and mother, as the case may be. There is no question of the ward's links with either of her true parents being broken. It is agreed on all hands that there should be generous provision for staying access, and I am satisfied that everyone concerned is aware of the importance of the ward's links with her true parents, and the need to avoid any sort of replacement of them with others.

F Miss G. has the difficulty that, lying ahead, there is her confinement and the birth of her first child. With that in mind, as well as my assessment of the characters of these two, I can only say that on the whole I think Miss G. is not likely to prove quite so adequate a mother-substitute for the ward as Mr. D. is likely to prove a father-substitute for her. In saying this, I give full weight to the consideration

G that the demands of a young girl on her mother-substitute are likely to be much heavier than her demands on her father-substitute.

Apart from the characters of the individuals concerned, there is a further prac-tical consideration, recognised in many cases, including Re L. (infants) (5) and H. v. H. and C. (6), that as a general rule it is better for small children, and especially little girls, to be brought up by their mother; and this, of course, is a

H consideration of great importance. The ward is at present living with the father's parents, so that whatever happens she will be changing her home. The father sees her every day, usually on short visits twice a day, whereas the mother does not, so that if the ward goes to the mother the change will to that extent be greater.

The result seems to me to be as follows. First, as regards the home, the mother has a small advantage. Second, as to the parent-substitute, again the mother has a

I small advantage. Third, as to the upheaval to the ward, the father has a small advantage. Fourth, as to a young child's need for its parents, the mother has a substantial advantage. Fifth, as to justice between the parents in the responsibility for the break-up of the marriage, the father has a substantial advantage. In addition, there are a number of other matters which I do not forget but need not particularise. Of these five main considerations, all except the fifth relate to the welfare of the ward. The fifth does not, except insofar as the responsibility for the break-up of the marriage throws light on the character and behaviour of

(5) [1962] 3 All E.R. 1; [1962] 1 W.L.R. 886.
(6) [1969] 1 All E.R. 262; [1969] 1 W.L.R. 208.

the parties, and thus assists me in assessing their probable behaviour as parents **A**
in the future. Much, I would add, has happened since BRANDON, J., delivered his
judgment.

With these factors in mind, and after much anxious consideration, I have in
the end come to the conclusion, though by no very great margin, that the care
and control of the ward ought to be awarded to the mother. In saying this, I
do not think I am failing to give proper weight to *Re L. (infants)* (7). There, one **B**
very important consideration was the possibility of the parents becoming reconciled; the giving of care and control to the father in that case kept alive some
hope, even though slight, of a reconciliation. If care and control was given to
the mother, there was no hope at all. In the present case, whatever faint hope
of reconciliation there may have been was, I think, extinguished when the
father had begun to live with Miss G., had made her pregnant, and had **C**
commenced divorce proceedings.

I know that in *Re L. (infants)* (8), LORD DENNING, M.R., said this:

"Even if there were no chance of the mother returning at all, I do not
think that she should on that account be entitled to take the children from
their father who has done no wrong. It would be an exceedingly bad example
if it were thought that a mother could go off with another man and then claim **D**
as of right to say: 'Oh well, they are my two little girls, and I am entitled
to take them with me. I can not only leave my home and break it up and
leave their father, but I can take the children with me and the law will not say
me nay.' It seems to me that a mother must realise that if she leaves and
breaks up her home in this way, she cannot as of right demand to take the
children from the father." **E**

But then LORD DENNING goes on to say:

"If the mother in this case were to be entitled to the children, it would follow
that every guilty mother (who was otherwise a good mother) would always
be entitled to them, for no stronger case for the father could be found.
He has a good home for the children. He is ready to forgive his wife and
have her back. All that he wishes is for her return. It is a matter of simple **F**
justice between them that he should have the care and control. Whilst the
welfare of the children is the first and paramount consideration, the claims
of justice cannot be overlooked."

I fully accept that the mother has no *right* to take the children with her; but when
it comes to discretion, as distinct from right, I think that LORD DENNING, M.R.'s **G**
reference to the father's readiness to forgive his wife and have her back shows that
the possibility of a reconciliation is an important matter. Here there is no such
possibility.

Let me say at once that I am not for one moment suggesting that this father is a
bad father. He is not; he is, I think, a good father. Nor am I saying that this
mother was a good wife; she was not. But I think that her failings as a wife **H**
have not made her so bad a mother as to displace the greater need that young
children have for the mother rather than the father, and her ability to satisfy that
need. Nor, in giving effect to the requirement that the welfare of the child should
be the first and paramount consideration, do I think that justice to the father
or any other relevant consideration outweighs the advantage to the ward of going
to her mother. Accordingly, I order that care and control should be given to the **I**
mother, subject to suitable provision for staying access being given to the father.

Order accordingly.

Solicitors: *Collyer-Bristow & Co.*, agents for *G. I. Gough & Son*, Calne, Wilts.
(for the father); *Clifford-Turner & Co.*, agents for *David Goodswen, Moore & Co.*,
Redcar (for the mother).

[*Reported by* R. W. FARRIN, ESQ., *Barrister-at-Law.*]

---

(7) [1962] 3 All E.R. 1; [1962] 1 W.L.R. 886.
(8) [1962] 3 All E.R. at pp. 3, 4; [1962] 1 W.L.R. at p. 890.

A

McVEIGH (Inspector of Taxes) v. ARTHUR SANDERSON & SONS, LTD.

[CHANCERY DIVISION (Cross, J.), December 12, 13, 16, 1968.]

B
Income Tax—Allowance—Investment allowance—Machinery or plant—Capital expenditure on provision—Designs for wallpaper and furnishing fabrics—Incorporation on wood blocks, silk screens and rollers being objects conceded to be machinery or plant—Some designs never used—Whether cost of designs expenditure on the provision of machinery or plant—Finance Act 1954 (2 & 3 Eliz. 2 c. 44), s. 16 (1), (3).

C
In its process of manufacture the taxpayer company printed patterns on wallpaper and furnishing fabrics in two ways: by hand, using either wood blocks on which the patterns had been cut or silk screens to which they had been transferred; and mechanically, by machine equipped with pattern-bearing rollers. It bought designs for the patterns from free-lance artists or had them produced by artists in its employment, and each year its "styling committee" selected the designs to be used in production out of a

D
large number of designs put before it. Those not selected were filed, examined again every two years, and, if thought not to be worth retaining, scrapped after six years or subsequently. It was conceded that the wood blocks and silk screens were plant and that the rollers were parts of machines, and that without patterns on them they were all inchoate plant or machinery, incapable of playing any part in the manufacturing process.

E
The taxpayer company claimed an investment allowance for capital expenditure incurred on the provision of new machinery or plant in respect of the cost of the designs. It was also conceded that the expenditure was capital expenditure. The Commissioners of Income Tax held that the whole of the expenditure attributable to the designs was expenditure on the provision of new machinery or plant within the meaning of s. 16 (3)* of the Finance Act 1954. On appeal by the Crown,

F
Held: the appeal would be dismissed; even if (following *Daphne* v. *Shaw* ((1926), 11 Tax Cas. 256) the designs were not plant within s. 16 it was not right that no part of the cost of the designs should be regarded as expenditure on the provision of what was conceded to be machinery or plant, i.e., the wood blocks, silk screens and rollers (see p. 775, letters B to D, *post*).

G
Daphne v. *Shaw* ((1926), 11 Tax Cas. 256) followed.

QUAERE: whether some fraction only of the design cost should be allowed in circumstances when a large number of the designs are never actually put on any block, screen or roller (see p. 775, letters G and H, *post*).

Appeal dismissed.

H
[As to investment allowances in respect of capital expenditure on new machinery and plant, see 20 HALSBURY'S LAWS (3rd Edn.) 485, 486, para. 925, and 493-497, paras. 941-950; and for cases on the subject, see DIGEST (Cont. Vol. A) 874, 875, *480a, 480b*.

For the Finance Act 1954, s. 16, see 34 HALSBURY'S STATUTES (2nd Edn.) 291.]

Cases referred to:
I
Blake v. *Shaw* (1860), John. 732; [1843-60] All E.R. Rep. 504; 2 L.T. 84; 70 E.R. 615; 48 Digest (Repl.) 566, *5316*.

Daphne v. *Shaw* (1926), 11 Tax Cas. 256; 28 Digest (Repl.) 135, *511*.

Inland Revenue Comrs. v. *Guthrie* (1952), 33 Tax Cas. 327; 1952 S.C. 402; 28 Digest (Repl.) 300, *725*.

* Section 16, so far as material, provides: " (1) In the cases provided for by this section an allowance (in this Act referred to as an ' investment allowance ') shall be made in respect of capital expenditure on new assets . . . (3) An investment allowance . . . shall be made . . . in respect of expenditure on new machinery or plant . . ."

Yarmouth v. *France* (1887), 19 Q.B.D. 647; 57 L.J.Q.B. 7; 36 Digest (Repl.)   A
135, *710*.

Case Stated.

Arthur Sanderson & Sons, Ltd., the taxpayer company, appealed to the
Special Commissioners of Income Tax against the following assessments to income
tax made on it under Sch. D to the Income Tax Act 1952 in respect of its trade
as manufacturer of wallpaper and printed furnishing fabrics: 1961-62, £728,342   B
less £384,322 capital allowances, balancing charge £1,997; 1962-63 £710,000 less
£410,000 capital allowances; 1963-64 £695,000 less £400,000 capital allowances;
1964-65 £900,000 less £361,000 capital allowances, balancing charge £1,000;
and 1965-66 £1,200,000 less £350,000 capital allowances. The question for
decision was whether certain expenditure which the taxpayer company incurred
in producing or acquiring designs was expenditure in respect of which the com-   C
pany was entitled to investment allowances under s. 16 of the Finance Act 1954,
as amended.* The taxpayer company contended as follows: (i) that patterns which
were based on designs produced for or acquired by the taxpayer company and
had been impressed on hand blocks, silk screens and rollers formed an integral
part of such equipment when it was completed: (ii) that the expenditure incurred
by the taxpayer company in producing or acquiring designs, including that   D
incurred on designs not selected for immediate production, formed part of the
expenditure incurred by the taxpayer company on the provision of such patterned
equipment; (iii) that hand blocks, silk screens and rollers when completed by
patterning were new machinery or plant provided for the purposes of the taxpayer
company's trade; (iv) alternatively, that the designs produced for or acquired
by the taxpayer company were in themselves plant; (v) that the expenditure   E
incurred by the taxpayer company in producing or acquiring designs, although
allowed to be deducted in computing its profits for income tax purposes, was
nevertheless expenditure falling to be treated for investment allowance purposes
as capital expenditure; and (vi) that the taxpayer company was accordingly
entitled to investment allowances in respect of such expenditure. The Crown
contended: (i) that the designs produced for or acquired by the taxpayer company   F
were neither an integral part of the equipment used by the taxpayer company
for reproducing them nor plant in their own right; (ii) that the expenditure incurred by the taxpayer company on designs was not therefore expenditure
incurred on the provision of new machinery or plant; (iii) that the expenditure
was in any event expenditure which had been allowed as a deduction in computing
the taxpayer company's profits for income tax purposes and which did not   G
qualify for investment allowance purposes as capital expenditure; and (iv) that
the taxpayer company was accordingly not entitled to any investment allowances
in respect of such expenditure.

The commissioners held† that the whole of the expenditure attributable to
designs was " expenditure on the provision of new machinery or plant " within
the meaning of s. 16 (3) of the Finance Act 1954 and allowed the appeal. They   H
adjusted the assessments accordingly. The Crown appealed by way of Case
Stated to the High Court.

I. Edwards-Jones, Q.C., and *P. W. Medd* for the Crown.
Heyworth Talbot, Q.C., and *S. T. Bates* for the taxpayer company.

CROSS, J.: The question which arises in this case is whether certain   I
expenditure incurred by the taxpayer company, Arthur Sanderson & Sons, Ltd.,
in producing or acquiring designs for use in the manufacture of wallpaper and
furnishing fabrics was capital expenditure in respect of which it was entitled to
investment allowances under the provisions of s. 16 of the Finance Act 1954.
It is common ground that the taxpayer company can only be entitled to the

---

* The facts of the case are summarised in the judgment at p. 773, letters B to H, post.
† The terms of the commissioners' decision are set out at p. 773, letter I, to p. 774,
letter D, post.

A allowances if it can show that the expenditure in question was capital expenditure for the provision of new machinery or plant: see sub-s. (1) and sub-s. (3). It was at one time a question in dispute whether the expenditure could properly be regarded as capital expenditure, but the Crown now concedes that it can be so regarded, and the only question remaining is whether it was expenditure on the provision of new machinery or plant.

B The processes used by the taxpayer company in manufacturing its wallpaper and furnishing fabrics are described in detail in the Case and illustrated by a number of photographs. For the purposes of this judgment they can be summarised as follows. Patterns are printed on the wallpaper or fabric either by hand or mechanically: by hand, by the use either of wood blocks on which the patterns have been cut or of silk screens to which the patterns have been C transferred in the manner described in the Case; or, mechanically, by the use of machines equipped with pattern-bearing rollers.

It was conceded by the Crown that the wood blocks and the silk screens with the patterns on them are " plant ", and that the patterned rollers are part of the machines into which they are fitted. It is further conceded by the Crown that wood blocks, silk screens and rollers without patterns on them could play D no part in the manufacturing process, and would be only inchoate plant or machinery. Accordingly, the taxpayer company has been allowed not only the cost of the unpatterned blocks, screens and rollers, but also the cost of patterning them. What is in dispute, as I have said, is the expenditure on the acquisition of designs.

Designs are either bought by the taxpayer company from free-lance artists E or produced by artists in the employment of the company. In the year June 1963 to June 1964 which was taken as a sample year, 85 designs for fabrics and 70 designs for wallpaper were produced in the taxpayer company's studio and 77 designs for fabrics and 249 designs for wallpaper were bought. It is considered essential that the so-called " styling committee " of the taxpayer company should have before it a large number of designs from which to select those to be used F in production. Accordingly, many more designs are bought or produced than are adopted for immediate production. Thus, in 1963-64, only 79 of the 162 designs for fabrics and 127 of the 319 designs for wallpaper were adopted for immediate production.

All the designs acquired or produced, whether or not adopted for immediate production, are filed in the taxpayer company's library. Those not used for G immediate production are thus available for reference, and may be selected by the styling committee for production, either without alteration or in an adapted form, in a later year. All designs are kept for a minimum of six years. Old designs are gone through every two years, and those which are more than six years old and are thought not to be worth retaining are scrapped. The designs acquired or produced by the taxpayer company are no doubt capable of H registration, but none are in fact registered. The taxpayer company has never sold any of its designs, but it has occasionally lent some of them to other companies belonging to the group of which it is a member.

Two questions arise: first, whether the designs are themselves " plant "; secondly, whether the cost of acquiring or producing the designs can be said to be expenditure on the provision of the patterned blocks, screens are rollers. The I commissioners decided the case in favour of the taxpayer company on the second point and expressed no view on the first. Their decision was as follows:

" On the evidence before us in the present case we find that the [taxpayer] company incurred the expenditure attributable to designs with the object of having available annually an assortment of designs not as a matter separate from manufacture but so that it could select therefrom a suitable proportion for immediate use in patterning rollers, silk screens and hand blocks with a view to the rollers, etc., when patterned being used in manufacturing fabrics and wallpaper for sale by the [taxpayer] company in the ordinary course of its trade. For the year to 30th June, 1964, for which particulars had been extracted, it appears that the proportion so selected for immediate use amounted on average to approximately 43 per cent. of the whole number. The designs not selected by the [taxpayer] company for immediate use are filed and, so long as they are retained, accordingly remain available for reference in connection with work on the production of new designs. Such designs may, too, in some instances be selected for use in a later year, either without alteration or in an adapted form, and thereafter be used similarly in patterning rollers, etc., as part of the process of manufacture. The [taxpayer] company's rollers, silk screens and hand blocks as finished by patterning are complete as apparatus for manufacture and appear to us to be indubitably 'machinery or plant' within the meaning of those words in Section 16 (3) of the Finance Act, 1954. So approaching the problem before us, we hold that on the facts of the present case the expenditure attributable to designs was, irrespective of whether it was or was not in respect of designs selected for immediate use, expenditure incurred in order to provide new machinery or plant. Bearing in mind, inter alia, the judgment given by the Lord President [LORD COOPER] in the Court of Session in the case of Inland Revenue Comrs. v. Guthrie (1), we further hold that the whole of the expenditure attributable to designs was in these circumstances 'expenditure on the provision of new machinery or plant' within the meaning of those words in the said Section 16 (3)."

The facts in Inland Revenue Comrs. v. Guthrie (1), to which the commissioners referred, were that the firm ordered and paid for a motor car but, through the fraud of the seller, it was never delivered to them. In those circumstances it was held that the expenditure was incurred " on the provision of new machinery or plant for the purposes of the trade ", and that accordingly the firm were entitled to an initial allowance.

I will deal first with the question whether the designs themselves are " plant ". LINDLEY, L.J., gave the classic definition of " plant " in Yarmouth v. France (2)—a case in which it was decided that a carthorse was " plant ". His words were (3):

" The next question is whether the horse which injured the plaintiff is 'plant' within the meaning of s. 1, sub-s. (1) of the Act [the Employers' Liability Act 1880]. There is no definition of plant in the Act: but, in its ordinary sense, it includes whatever apparatus is used by a businessman for carrying on his business, not his stock-in-trade which he buys or makes for sale; but all goods and chattels, fixed or moveable, live or dead, which he keeps for permanent employment in his business: see Blake v. Shaw (4)."

Counsel for the Crown submitted that to fall within that definition the chattel in question must be nothing more than a material object. The designs in question are no doubt in one sense pieces of paper filed in the taxpayer company's library, but the paper is only the material vehicle through which the concept of the artist is conveyed to the eye, and lacks, says counsel, the gross materiality necessary to qualify it as " plant "—a word which, in the section in question, is coupled with the word " machinery ". In support of his argument he relied on Daphne v. Shaw (5), where ROWLATT, J., held that a solicitor's law library was not " plant ". There the judge said (6):

" I cannot bring myself to say that ' such books as solicitors ' use to consult are ' plant '. It is impossible to define what is meant by ' plant and machinery '. It conjures up before the mind something clear in the outline,

(1) (1952), 33 Tax Cas. 327; 1952 S.C. 402.
(2) (1887), 19 Q.B.D. 647.
(3) (1887), 19 Q.B.D. at p. 658.
(4) (1860), John. 732; [1843-60] All E.R. Rep. 504.
(5) (1926), 11 Tax Cas. 256.
(6) (1926), 11 Tax Cas. at p. 258.

A   at any rate; it means apparatus, alive or dead, stationary or movable, to achieve the operations which a person wants to achieve in his vocation. But the books which he consults, on his shelves, and which he does not use as ' implements ', really, in the direct sense of the word, at all, I cannot believe are included in it."

B   If I thought that I was free to do so, I am not sure that I would accept the limitation which the Crown's argument imposes on the meaning of " plant ". If a barrister has to buy a new edition of a textbook in order to help him to write his opinions, I cannot see as a matter of principle why the book should not be regarded as a tool of his trade just as much as the typewriter on which his opinions are typed. Similarly, the designs, which are the tools of the trade of the styling committee and many of which are scrapped after a few years, might, I should

C   have thought, qualify as " plant " just as fully as the hand blocks, silk screens and rollers, many of which are periodically scrapped. But, having regard to the decision in *Daphne* v. *Shaw* (7), I think that if any extension of the meaning of the word " plant " beyond a purely physical object is to be made, it ought to be made by a higher court. So I will proceed on the footing that these designs are not " plant ".

D   The second question is: Can the cost of acquiring the designs be said to be expenditure on the provision of the blocks, screens and rollers on which some of them are patterned? If—to take a rather fanciful example—A. commissions B. to provide him with a patterned wood block so that A. may experiment in printing wallpaper with a hand block, B. would obviously be entitled to include in his bill the cost of acquiring a suitable design. But counsel for the Crown

E   pointed out that in that case, if one asked B., " What are you buying that design for? " he would answer, " In order to provide A. with the patterned wood block for which he has asked me "; whereas in this case, if one asked the taxpayer company's representative, " Why are you buying these designs? " he would not answer, " In order to provide the company with wood blocks, screens or rollers patterned with them ", but would answer, " In order that the styling committee

F   may have before it a wide variety of designs from which to select a few which it thinks are best adapted for reproduction on our papers and fabrics ".

    I feel the force of this argument, but the section itself isolates the provision of the patterned wood block and poses the question: What did the taxpayer company spend on it? To my mind it cannot be right to include nothing for the cost of the design. I can well understand its being argued that, as so many

G   of the designs are never actually put on any block, screen or roller, only some fraction of the total design costs should be allowed, and I do not think that *Inland Revenue Comrs.* v. *Guthrie* (8) would be an authority against such an argument, for in that case the car would have been used if it had been delivered. But what was argued before me was that not one penny of the design costs should be allowed. To my mind, that cannot be right, and therefore I shall dismiss the

H   appeal.

Appeal dismissed.

    Solicitors: *Solicitor of Inland Revenue*; *Lovell, White & King* (for the taxpayer company).

[*Reported by* F. A. AMIES, ESQ., *Barrister-at-Law.*]

I

---

(7) (1926), 11 Tax Cas. 256.
(8) (1952), 33 Tax Cas. 327; 1952 S.C. 402.

A

NISHINA TRADING CO., LTD. *v.* CHIYODA FIRE & MARINE INSURANCE CO., LTD.

[COURT OF APPEAL, CIVIL DIVISION (Lord Denning, M.R., Edmund Davies and Phillimore, L.JJ.), February 27, 28, 1969.]

B

Insurance—Marine insurance—Loss of goods—Recovery—Expenses properly incurred in recovery of goods—Cargo diverted by shipowners and mortgaged —Goods recovered by owners—Expenditure reasonably and properly incurred in recovery—Goods lost by reason of taking at sea—Indemnity for expenses and theft—" Taking at sea ".

The plaintiffs were at all times the owners of goods which were to be shipped from B. to K. on the terms of a freight prepaid bill of lading. The consignment had been insured with the defendants. The policy covered the goods, inter alia, against takings at sea or other similar perils, losses or misfortunes and/or theft. When the vessel arrived off K. a financial dispute arose between the owners of the vessel, and the charterers. Before the dispute was settled and whilst the parties were negotiating, the master of the vessel, acting under instructions from the owners of the vessel set sail for H.K. At H.K. the vessel's cargo was warehoused and the owners of the vessel and the charterers purported to mortgage the entire cargo. The plaintiffs brought legal proceedings against the warehouse company in H.K. and obtained an order for delivery up of the goods and forwarded them to K., the original destination. On the question whether the expenditure incurred in averting or diminishing a loss had been incurred in respect of a loss covered by the policy,

C

D

E

Held: the loss was covered by the policy and the defendants were therefore liable to indemnify the plaintiffs for their expenditure, because—

(i) up to the moment that the master set sail for H.K. the owners through him held the goods as bailees for the plaintiffs; at that moment he changed their character as bailees by assuming, on behalf of the owners, a dominion over the goods inconsistent with the plaintiffs' rights; the owners thus converted the goods to their own use and this conversion amounted to a taking at sea (see p. 778, letters F to H, p. 780, letter B, and p. 782, letter G, post);

F

(ii) although the expression " taking at sea " included capture and seizure it was not confined to such takings and covered the circumstances of the present case (see p. 778, letter C, p. 780, letter B, and p. 782, letter I, post).

G

Rickards v. *Forestal Land, Timber & Railways Co.* ([1941] 3 All E.R. 62) applied.

(iii) (EDMUND DAVIES, L.J., dissenting) on the true construction of the Institute insured value clause the court had to be able to find, on balance, that the imputation of theft was an appropriate description of what took place, and in all the circumstances the action of the master ought not properly to be so described (see p. 779, letter E, and p. 783, letter B, post).

H

Decision of DONALDSON, J. ([1968] 3 All E.R. 712) affirmed on different grounds, but observations as to interest and costs at p. 720 not approved.

[As to takings at sea, see 22 HALSBURY'S LAWS (3rd Edn.) 77, 78, para. 136; and for cases on the subject, see 29 DIGEST (Repl.) 250-253, *1874-1893*.

I

For the Marine Insurance Act 1906, s. 78, see 13 HALSBURY'S STATUTES (2nd Edn.) 52.]

Cases referred to:

Algemeene Bankvereeniging v. *Langton* (1935), 40 Com. Cas 247; 51 Lloyd L.R. 275; 29 Digest (Repl.) 498, *3548*.

Hai Hsuan, The, [1957] 1 Lloyd's Rep. 428; *on appeal,* [1958] 1 Lloyd's Rep. 351.

A   *Hornal* v. *Neuberger Products, Ltd.*, [1956] 3 All E.R. 970; [1957] 1 Q.B. 247;
        [1956] 3 W.L.R. 1034; Digest (Cont. Vol. A) 519, *262Aa*.
   Hurst v. *Evans*, [1917] 1 K.B. 352; [1916-17] All E.R. Rep. 975; 86 L.J.K.B.
        305; 116 L.T. 252; 29 Digest (Repl.) 497, *3542*.
   Lake v. *Simmons*, [1927] A.C. 487; [1927] All E.R. Rep. 49; 96 L.J.K.B.
        621; 137 L.T. 233; 29 Digest (Repl.) 297, *3543*.

B   *Rickards* v. *Forestal Land, Timber and Railways Co.*, [1941] 3 All E.R. 62;
        [1942] A.C. 50; 110 L.J.K.B. 593; 165 L.T. 257; 29 Digest (Repl.)
        323, *2448*.

Appeal.

This was an appeal by the defendants, the Chiyoda Fire & Marine Insurance
Co., Ltd., from a decision of Donaldson, J., dated 24th April 1968 and reported

C [1968] 3 All E.R. 712, holding that the defendants were liable to indemnify the
plaintiffs, the Nishina Trading Co., Ltd., for expenditure incurred by them under
the general cover terms of an insurance policy on the ground that the goods were
lost by reason of theft. The facts are set out in the judgment of Donaldson, J.,*
and are summarised in the judgment of Lord Denning, M.R.

D   *C. S. Staughton* for the defendants.
   J. S. Hobhouse for the plaintiffs.

   LORD DENNING, M.R.: In this case the plaintiffs, a Japanese trading
company, claim against the defendants, a Japanese insurance company, on a
policy of insurance on goods which were being carried in the Far East. We much
appreciate the confidence thus placed in these courts and will do our best to
E deserve it.

   The facts are agreed and set out in an agreed statement of facts. In February
1966 the owners of the Mandarin Star let out the vessel on a time charter for
six months to charterers, the Asia Line Co., Ltd. The charter-hire was some
£5,000 a month. In July 1966 the vessel took on board at Bangkok 1,140 bags of
black matpe beans. The bill of lading was issued by the master. The freight was
F prepaid by the plaintiffs. They took out an insurance policy with the defendants.
The vessel sailed from Bangkok. It arrived off Kobe on 7th August 1966. At that
time unfortunately the charterers were more than two months' hire in arrear.
There was £11,328 16s. unpaid on the time charter. So, on the instructions of
the owners, the master did not take the vessel into Kobe. He refused to proceed
into port or discharge the goods, until the charter-hire was paid. Negotiations
G took place. But then, quite unexpectedly, the charterers closed their office.
Thereupon, the master, on the instructions of the owners, abruptly caused the
vessel to leave Kobe and sail for Hong Kong. It was 1,500 miles and took six
days. The cargo was still on board. She sailed from Kobe on 27th August, and
arrived at Hong Kong on 3rd September. Her cargo was discharged into lighters
and thence into a godown, that is, a warehouse. Then, according to the agreed
H statement of facts, " the [owners] in collusion with [the charterers] at the same
time purporting to mortgage the entire cargo to a Miss Lok Sau Chun, as security
for a loan of U.S. $84,000 ". When the plaintiffs got to know of this—and they
seem to have got to know of it quite quickly—they claimed the goods. The
warehouse company interpleaded in the Hong Kong courts. On 3rd December the
plaintiffs obtained a judgment of the Hong Kong Supreme Court ordering
I delivery up of the goods to the plaintiffs. So the plaintiffs got the goods. They
loaded them on board another ship and took them to their original destination—
Kobe—and delivered them there. But it all cost them a lot of money. They had
to pay all the costs of the litigation in Hong Kong. They also had to pay the costs
of carrying the goods back from Hong Kong to Kobe. They claimed these moneys
from the defendants on the policy under the " sue and labour " clause. They
claimed the expense to which they had been put in saving the goods from the loss

   * [1968] 3 All E.R. at p. 713.

which would have resulted if the goods had been disposed of in Hong Kong. **A**
It is clear that the plaintiffs can recover the costs to which they have been put,
providing that the loss, if it has occurred, would have come within the policy.
So we have to consider the clauses in the policy to see whether the loss would have
been covered by it.

The policy, although taken out in Tokyo, uses the words of English form. It
goes back to 1560. The words are of such ambiguity that they must be quite **B**
unknown to our Japanese friends. But the policy says that it is subject to English
law and usage. So the words must be interpreted according to English law. The
first risk which we have to consider is " takings at sea ". Has there been in this
case a " taking at sea "? There is very little authority indeed, even after 400
years, on " takings at sea ". It includes capture and seizure. But I do not think
it is confined to those two. " Takings at sea " is capable of a wider connotation. **C**
That is shown by *Rickards* v. *Forestal Land, Timber and Railways Co.* (1), in which,
at the outbreak of the last war, a German vessel called the Minden, instead of
proceeding on her normal voyage, put into Rio de Janeiro. On the orders of the
German government, she left Rio and tried to get back to Germany. She was
intercepted by a British warship. She was then scuttled by the crew. It was held
that the orders of the German government amounted to " restraint of princes ". **D**
But LORD WRIGHT used words which import that the goods were " taken ",
even though they remained on the same ship with the same master. He said (2):

> " What happened here was that the master, being in possession of the
> goods as a carrier for the respondents, seized them in the sense that he
> ceased to hold them as carrier and changed the character of his possession
> by *taking* and controlling them as agent for the German government, with **E**
> the intention and effect of holding them adversely to the respondents and
> applying them to the hostile purposes of his government ... The master
> was actually in possession of the goods throughout. He simply *took* them from
> the respondents by dealing with them adversely to their interests and
> throwing off the role of private carrier, in which capacity he had held them
> up to then as bailee for the appellant." **F**

So here it seems to me that the master of the Mandarin Star, on behalf of the
owners, changed the character of their possession. The vessel had been lying off
Kobe for three weeks and they had not got payment. Then the master set sail
from Kobe for Hong Kong. That was the decisive moment. Up till that time
he, on behalf of the owners, still held the goods as bailees for the plaintiffs. But **G**
when he set sail from Kobe, he, on behalf of the owners, changed their character
as bailees. He, on their behalf, determined to take the goods to Hong Kong
and raise money on them, if not to sell them. By so doing, the master, on behalf
of the owners, assumed a dominion over the goods inconsistent with the rights of
the plaintiffs. In our English language, the owners converted the goods to their
own use. That was, in my opinion, " taking "; and it was a " taking at sea ".
It was not in harbour, nor in port, but " at sea ", when the vessel was lying **H**
outside Kobe.

We were referred to a case in the United States courts, *The Hai Hsuan* (3).
The courts there drew a distinction between the taking of a ship and the taking
of goods on board a ship. That is apposite here. The ship was not taken, but the
goods were. They were taken by the master on behalf of the owners when they
asserted a dominion over them utterly inconsistent with the rights of the **I**
plaintiffs.

The learned judge came to a different view. He said (4):

> " In the present case the master remained at all times the servant of the

(1) [1941] 3 All E.R. 62; [1942] A.C. 50.
(2) [1941] 3 All E.R. at pp. 76, 77; [1942] A.C. at pp. 79, 80.
(3) [1957] 1 Lloyd's Rep. 428; *on appeal* [1958] 1 Lloyd's Rep. 351.
(4) [1968] 3 All E.R. 712 at p. 718; [1968] 1 W.L.R. 1325 at p. 1333.

A vessel's owners and the bailee of the cargo. That he detained the cargo and in due course converted it to his employers' use is not in doubt, but at all times he had possession of it in the same capacity, namely as the servant of the owners of the vessel. . . "

I think the judge fell into error. He was there considering the position of the master as an individual, whereas I think he should have considered him as the
B servant of the owners. The owners were bailees of the cargo up to the moment when they directed the master to go off to Hong Kong. Then they ceased to be bailees of the cargo and converted it to their own use. That was a " taking at sea ".

Seeing that there was a " taking at sea ", there is no need to consider whether it comes within " all other perils, losses and misfortunes ".
C In case I am wrong on " taking at sea ", I go on to consider the Institute theft, pilferage and non-delivery (Insured value) clause, which states:

" It is hereby agreed that this Policy covers the risk of Theft and/or Pilferage irrespective of percentage".

Was there a " theft " of the cargo by the master? The word " theft " is not
D used here in the strict sense of the criminal law. It does not bring in all the eccentricities of the law of larceny. It means only what an ordinary commercial man would consider to be theft; and before finding theft, the court should be satisfied that it is an appropriate description of what took place. The court need not be satisfied beyond reasonable doubt (as in the criminal law) but it should find on balance that there is sufficient to warrant the serious imputation of " theft ",
E see *Hornal* v. *Neuberger Products, Ltd.* (5). For myself, I would hesitate to describe the act of the master as theft. One must remember that the owners were claiming their charter-hire. They had not been paid the two months' hire that was due to them, and they did not sell the goods. They only raised money on mortgage. They may have thought that they had some sort of lien on the goods for their charter-hire. It is true, on reading the charter, that they had no lien. The lien
F clause simply states:

" The owners to have a lien upon all cargoes and sub-freights belonging to the Time-Charterers and any Bill of Lading freight for all claims under this Charter."

That clause did not apply because this cargo did not belong to the time charterers.
G But it is possible in some charters to have a lien on the cargo for charter-hire. An instance is given in Scrutton on Charterparties, art. 165 (4), which states that: " there may be liens by express agreement for charterparty freight as against the holder of the bill of lading." It seems to me that the owners may have thought that they had some sort of lien on the cargo under which they could raise money on mortgage. That would be a mistake, but if they honestly believed
H it, they would not be guilty of " theft ". No ordinary person would call it " theft " if they honestly thought they had a right to do it. The learned judge held (6) it was " theft ". But I would not do so.

Next there is the " Institute Strikes Riots and Civil Commotions Clauses ". This covers loss of or damage to the property insured caused by " . . . (b) persons acting maliciously ". I think " maliciously " here means spite, or ill will, or the
I like. There is none such here.

I would put the case simply on a " taking at sea " and uphold the decision on that ground only.

I would mention one other matter. The judge in his reserved decision made some observations (7) about interest and costs which had not been argued or discussed before him. Those matters did not arise for decision, as they had been

(5) [1956] 3 All E.R. 970; [1957] 1 Q.B. 247.
(6) [1968] 3 All E.R. at p. 719; [1968] 1 W.L.R. at p. 1335.
(7) [1968] 1 W.L.R. at p. 1336; [1968] 3 All E.R. at p. 720.

agreed between the parties beforehand.   Seeing that those points had not been **A**
argued and did not arise for decision, the judge's observations about them should
not be considered as having authority.

I would dismiss the appeal but on a different ground from that of the judge.

EDMUND DAVIES, L.J.:   I agree with LORD DENNING, M.R., that this
appeal should be dismissed, and, with one important exception, I so hold on
grounds identical with those on which LORD DENNING has already pronounced. For   **B**
example, I am wholly in agreement with him that there here occurred a " taking
at sea " within the meaning of the policy, and that accordingly the plaintiffs
were entitled to recover their expenses in saving their goods.   I likewise concur
respectfully with LORD DENNING, M.R., in holding that we need not in those
circumstances consider the clause relating to " other perils ", and that the
Institute clause relating to " persons acting maliciously " is inappropriate and   **C**
inapplicable to the circumstances of this case.

That being so, it might well be said by some: " Well, that means that the appeal
has to be dismissed and there is no need to proceed further."   But, having reflected
on the propriety of adopting that course, I have decided against it.   It appears
to me that, the learned trial judge (8) having manifestly given careful and anxious
attention to another important ground on which the plaintiffs based their claim   **D**
to recover, one is duty bound in this court to express the view that one has formed
about the correctness of his decision on that issue also.   I for my part would not
disturb the finding of the learned trial judge (8) that the plaintiffs here incurred
their expenses as consignees in order to convert a loss which, had it resulted,
would have been attributable to a " theft " by the owners and their master
within the meaning of the policy.   Until the Theft Act 1968 " theft " was a word   **E**
unknown, as far as my knowledge goes, to the statute law of this country;
and in this context reference may usefully be had to the observations of MAUGHAM,
L.J., in *Algemeene Bankvereeniging* v. *Langton* (9).   I direct myself that, in considering whether " theft " within the meaning of the policy has here been established, one does not apply the strict technicalities of the criminal law.   Nevertheless, one must advert to what the criminal law has to say about the topic of stealing,   **F**
larceny or theft.   VISCOUNT SUMNER said in *Lake* v. *Simmons* (10):

" . . . reliance has been placed on two arguments, (a) that in a commercial
document no legal technicality of the criminal law should be taken into
account . . . I dissent from the view that criminal law should be treated as
irrelevant merely because a document is commercial.   After all, criminal law
is still law and so are its definitions and rules."   **G**

One must certainly import into this civil action the basic conception of theft,
which is that it is an offence involving dishonesty.   No man—the man on the top
of the Clapham omnibus, the man in Lombard Street, the man of ordinary
intelligence anywhere—could fail to recognise that, unless dishonesty is shown,
no one should be branded as having committed a theft.   **H**

The third consideration which one has to have in mind is that this is a civil
action and not a trial of a criminal charge.   That is important, as several cases
illustrate.   One of these is *Hurst* v. *Evans* (11), where LUSH, J., said:

" [Counsel for the plaintiff] has contended that I cannot decide this case in
favour of the defendant unless I am prepared to hold that upon the evidence a
jury ought in a criminal case to convict [the plaintiff's servant].   I do not   **I**
agree.   I do not think that the evidence in a civil case must necessarily be the
same as in a criminal case arising out of the same matter; nor, where a case
raises a question of the criminality of some third person, is a civil Court
bound to find that person guilty of a criminal act upon such evidence only as

(8) [1968] 3 All E.R. 712; [1968] 1 W.L.R. 1325.
(9) (1935), 40 Com. Cas. 247 at p. 264.
(10) [1927] A.C. 487 at p. 509; [1927] All E.R. Rep. 49 at pp. 58, 59.
(11) [1917] 1 K.B. 352 at p. 357; [1916-17] All E.R. Rep. 975 at p. 980.

A   would be sufficient to procure his conviction in a criminal Court. It is impossible to say that the evidence must be the same in both cases."

The matter was later dealt with by this court in *Hornal* v. *Neuberger Products, Ltd.* (12). The passage that is particularly pertinent to the present case is to be found at pages 258 and 259. The effect of these and other decisions has been accurately and helpfully summarised by PROFESSOR CROSS on EVIDENCE (3rd

B   Edn.), p. 98 in these words:

" Although there were several previous decisions which were not discussed by the Court of Appeal, *Hornal's* case (12) may be taken to have settled the English law for the time being. An allegation of criminal conduct, even of murder, need only be established on a preponderance of probability in a

C   civil action. When the commission of a crime is alleged in civil proceedings, the stigma attaching to an affirmative finding might be thought to justify the imposition of a strict standard of proof; the person against whom criminal conduct is alleged is adequately protected by the consideration that the antecedent improbability of his guilt is ' a part of the whole range of circumstances which have to be weighed in the scale when deciding as to the balance

D   of probabilities '."

I seek to have those considerations in mind in addressing myself to the question, was the learned trial judge right here in concluding that the expenses were incurred by the plaintiffs in averting a loss by theft? I find it impossible to accept that any honest man of ordinary intelligence could conceivably have felt justified in acting as these owners did. It is now suggested that, as the charterers were in

E   default, the owners might have considered that they had a lien on the cargo for arrears of charter-hire even although the plaintiffs had no responsibility at all for them. But throughout the hearing of this case, I have repeatedly asked myself, what *is* the basis of that suggestion? I can find none in the agreed statement of facts, and it seems to me, with respect, to be merely the offspring of ingenious conjecture. Further, it appears but an additional surmise to go on to say, " The

F   owners *might* also have thought that, having a lien on the cargo for unpaid charter fees, the lien entitled them to make a pledge of the cargo. " The acceptability of that further suggestion has to be judged by its probability. It is true, as counsel for the defendants has reminded us (and as is illustrated by a passage in SCRUTTON ON CHARTERPARTIES (17th Edn.) p. 376), that there may in certain circumstances be liens extending to charterparty freight and valid as

G   against the holder of a bill of lading. So there might be, but nobody suggests that that is this case, and there are no grounds for thinking that anybody ever thought that such a lien existed here. Furthermore, when one notes that the owners and the master were acting " in collusion "—that is the phrase used in the agreed statement of facts—with the charterers in sailing 1,500 miles on from Kobe and disposing of the cargo, any notion that they did so honestly

H   (albeit erroneously) considering that they were thereby exercising a legal right, is to my way of thinking incredible. Then when the vessel reached Hong Kong, what did the owners do? They mortgaged the cargo to secure a loan over twice as great as the amount of the two months' charter-hire. I hold that conduct so reckless carried its own unmistakable stamp of dishonesty.

But it is nevertheless said that, even assuming dishonesty, the owners and

I   master were nevertheless not guilty of *theft*; in other words, that their dishonesty, if such existed, comprised no intention to deprive the consignees permanently of their cargo. What is alleged is that, as they merely mortgaged the goods and did not purport to sell them, this vital ingredient of " theft " is not shown to have been present. So bald a submission is in my judgment unacceptable. The true test in such circumstances had been propounded by PROFESSOR GLANVILLE WILLIAMS in CRIMINAL LAW (2nd Edn.), para 32. Dealing with a person who unlawfully pawns things, he writes:

(12) [1956] 3 All E.R. 970; [1957] 1 Q.B. 247.

A

" If he did not intend to redeem the thing, his act is clearly larceny. If he intended to redeem but had no reasonable prospect of doing so it seems also to be larceny; but if he had both the intention and the reasonable prospect he goes quit of larceny . . . "

What do the agreed facts here reveal? Not merely a mortgaging, which, as I hold, must have been known to be an unlawful act; not merely a raising thereby of money sufficient to reap for the owners a sum merely equivalent to the arrears of charter-hire, but a sum twice that amount, the cargo thus being used as a means of acquiring funds to which there could be no possible entitlement. And the tale does not stop even there, for the owners did absolutely nothing to redeem the mortgage. On the contrary, it was only by the prompt steps taken by the plaintiffs that three months later they obtained a judgment which secured their cargo to them, the owners meanwhile having done absolutely nothing to redeem and so restore to the plaintiffs their goods. Again to quote PROFESSOR GLANVILLE WILLIAMS:

B

C

" It cannot be enough to acquit of larceny that the accused has somewhat of the outlook of Micawber, and unreasonably expected something to turn up to enable him to redeem. As GURNEY, B., said, ' a more glorious doctrine for thieves it would be difficult to discover '."

D

Indeed, regarding the prime test of whether at the time when this mortgage was entered into there was any intention to redeem, whether reasonably or unreasonably entertained, in my judgment the trial judge was entitled to draw the inference that there was none. I therefore for my part do not differ from his finding (13) that there was here a " theft " of the plaintiffs' cargo and that they were entitled to succeed on that ground even if it stood alone.

E

However, on the two grounds, first, that there was here a " theft ", and, secondly, that there was a " taking at sea ", I concur with LORD DENNING, M.R., in holding that this appeal should be dismissed. I desire to add that I also respectfully assent to his observations in relation to the topics of interest and costs to which the learned trial judge adverted (14).

F

PHILLIMORE, L.J.: Dealing with the first peril, the question of whether there was a " taking at sea ", there were really two main points made by counsel for the defendants. He said first of all: One cannot take what is already in one's possession; and, secondly, he said that the words " taking at sea " only apply to seizures and captures. The answer to the first point as I think has been fully provided by LORD DENNING, M.R., and in particular by the reference of *Rickards* v. *Forestal Land, Timber and Railways Co.* (15).

G

So far as the second point is concerned, there is no special definition of these words, " taking at sea " in the Marine Insurance Act 1906, and it seems to me, therefore that one has got to take the words in their ordinary meaning. It is to be observed that the policy itself describes the risks which the assurers are contented to bear; and amongst those it lists " taking at sea "; and it does not list " seizures or captures ". Then, a little lower down, when the exceptions are given, the first exception reads " Warranted free of capture, seizure, arrest . . . ". Now, if " taking at sea " is the equivalent of " captures and seizures ", then clearly the exception clause ought to have followed the same terms. The answer I think is the short and simple one, that as a pure matter of construction, " taking at sea " would include seizures and captures, but would go further and cover the sort of circumstances that happened in this particular case. If I am wrong on either of these points, I should have thought that it would be safe in the circumstances of this case to apply the ejusdem generis rule and to rely on the words " all other perils, losses or misfortunes ". If on some very technical ground this was not strictly a " taking ", the effect was so similar that it ought to be held to

H

I

(13) [1968] 3 All E.R. at p. 719; [1968] 1 W.L.R. at p. 1335.
(14) [1968] 1 W.L.R. at p. 1336; [1968] 3 All E.R. at p. 720.
(15) [1941] 3 All E.R. 62; [1942] A.C. 50.

A   come within the ejusdem generis rule. For example, on the point of taking something already in your possession, I would cite the instance which I cited in argument: if I lend my car to a friend for the afternoon and he drives to Dover and
takes it on the continent for two or three months, I should have thought it would
be normal language to say that he had taken my car, albeit it was already in his
possession when he took it.

B   Turning to the second point, the question of theft, I take the same view as
LORD DENNING, M.R., I think the learned judge (16) was wrong. It was for the
plaintiffs to establish theft and to ensure that there was sufficient material in
the agreed statement to justify such a finding. Of course, there may have been
theft in the broad sense of the word; but I do not think it would be safe so to find.
After all, we should be finding theft against a party and against individuals
C   who are not before the court, and one ought to be very careful before so doing.
We should be finding theft against a party or parties against whom, so far as
we are informed, there has been no criminal prosecution of any sort or kind.
Moreover, it looks as if the owners of this ship, albeit using the flag of Monrovia,
were probably living in Hong Kong itself, and certainly through their agents they
took part in the interpleader proceedings as a result of which the plaintiffs recov-
D   ered their goods. We have not been told what line they took in those proceedings,
whether, for example, they claimed a lien or whether they sought to justify the
mortgage. It seems very odd if it was obvious to whoever dealt with that trial
that a criminal offence had been committed that the circumstances were not
thought, for example, to warrant sending the papers to the appropriate authority
with a view to a prosecution. I say it looks as if the owners were in Hong Kong
E   because, unlike the charterers, the Asia Line Co., Ltd., they did not have to rely
on any telegraphic authority when they came to sign the time charter. Moreover
it does appear to me that there are circumstances here which might point to those
owners having thought that they were entitled to a lien. After all, these contracts
were in English, and whether they live in Hong Kong or Monrovia, they were
not as familiar with English law as would be the owners of a shipping line in this
F   country. The master, acting on the instructions of the owners, when he got to
Kobe refused to enter the port; he demanded the charter-hire which was owing,
and he demanded it apparently not only from the charterers, who were situated
at Kobe, but also, when they failed to produce the money, he tried to get it from
the plaintiffs; and he waited three weeks in the hope that somebody, either the
charterers or the plaintiffs, or both, would produce the £11,000 due to the owners.

G   Now, that is not entirely inconsistent with the idea that they were entitled to
some form of a lien on the cargo, and, moreover as LORD DENNING, M.R., has
pointed out, when they got to Hong Kong they did not sell the goods, which would
be the natural thing to do if they were being deliberately dishonest; they raised
a mortgage; and, of course, that would be consistent with the view that if the
plaintiffs put up a proper sum of money, they would be able to recover their
H   goods. In my judgment, therefore, in the circumstances of this case and on a very
exiguous statement of facts and in the absence of evidence which the plaintiffs
could clearly have provided, that is to say, evidence of what happened at these
interpleader proceedings, or indeed evidence of whether the owners were there in
Hong Kong or whether they made any application to them to pay this claim,
and so on, it is not safe to find a criminal offence proved against parties who are
I   not before the court.
        Finally, dealing with the third matter, that the loss was alleged to be due to
persons acting maliciously, it seems to me that that claim ignores the terms of the
policy, which under the Institute Strikes Riots and Civil Commotions Clauses is
obviously intended to deal with damage effected in the course of some civil
disturbance which has nothing whatever to do with the facts of this case.
        For those reasons, in agreement with LORD DENNING, M.R., I would dismiss

---

(16) [1968] 3 All E.R. 712; [1968] 1 W.L.R. 1325.

the appeal, substituting a finding of " taking at sea " for the finding of theft. **A**
I also agree with what my Lords have said with regard to the finding of the learned
judge (17) in respect of costs and interest.

Appeal dismissed. Leave to appeal to the House of Lords refused.

Solicitors: *Ince & Co.* (for the defendants); *Clyde & Co.* (for the plaintiffs).

[*Reported by* F. GUTTMAN, ESQ., *Barrister-at-Law.*] **B**

R. *v.* FLACK. **C**

[COURT OF APPEAL, CRIMINAL DIVISION (Salmon and Fenton Atkinson, L.JJ., and
Milmo, J.), December 13, 16, 1968.]

*Criminal Law—Trial—Separate trials—Series of offences of the same or a similar
    character—Evidence of incest against A inadmissible in counts of similar
    offences against B or C—Discretion of trial judge to order separate trials—* **D**
Indictments Act 1915 (5 & 6 Geo. 5 c. 90), s. 4, Sch. 1, r. 3.

The appellant was charged, on one indictment, on three counts of committing incest with three of his sisters; count 1 with E. in 1964, count 2 with S.
in 1965-66, and count 3 with C. in 1967. All three counts alleged a series
of offences of the same or a similar character. The judge found on a provisional view that evidence of the alleged offence against any one girl would **E**
be evidence of the alleged offences against the other two. He therefore
exercised his discretion under s. 4* of and r. 3† of Sch. 1 to the Indictments
Act 1915, in rejecting an application for separate trials, and ordered the
three counts to be tried together.

Held: (i) the Court of Appeal would not overrule the judge's decision
since it was of the opinion that in all the circumstances the charges might **F**
well have been tried together although the reason given by the judge was
wrong (see p. 786, letters A and B, post);

(ii) since the defence consisted of a complete denial of the incident the
evidence of an alleged offence against one sister could not be evidence of
the alleged offences against the others (see p. 787, letters G and H, post);

(iii) insofar as the judge's provisional view was based on passages in **G**
R. *v. Sims* ([1946] 1 All E.R. at p. 701) and R. *v. Campbell* ([1956] 2 All E.R.
at p. 276) the court did not think that they were ever intended to be so
understood; if, however, that was their true meaning they went much
further than was necessary for the purpose of the decisions and could not be
accepted as correctly stating the law (see p. 786, letters C, D and H, post);

Dicta of LORD GODDARD, C.J., in R. *v. Sims* ([1946] 1 All E.R. at p. 701) **H**
and R. *v. Campbell* ([1956] 2 All E.R. at p. 276) explained.

Dicta of LORD PARKER, C.J., in R. *v. Chandor* ([1959] 1 All E.R. at p. 704)
applied.

(iv) although it would as a rule be better in circumstances such as these
that the counts should be tried separately the court would not interfere with
the judge's decision since the judge came to the conclusion that even if his **I**
provisional view were wrong, the three alleged offences could properly be
tried together and summed up so that the jury would not be influenced or

---

(17) [1968] 1 W.L.R. at p. 1336; [1968] 3 All E.R. at p. 720.
* Section 4, so far as material, provides: " Subject to the provisions of the rules . . .
charges for more than one [offence] . . . may be joined in the same indictment . . ."
† Rule 3, so far as material, provides: " Charges for any offences . . . may be joined
in the same indictment if those charges are founded on the same facts, or form or are
part of a series of offences of the same or a similar character."

A prejudiced in considering any one count by evidence in respect of the others (see p. 787, letter I, to p. 788, letter D, post).

  Appeal against conviction dismissed.

  Appeal against sentence allowed.

  [As to joinder of several offences in one indictment, see 10 HALSBURY'S LAWS (3rd Edn.) 391, 392, para. 708; and for cases on the subject, see 14 DIGEST
B (Repl.) 256, 257, *2228-2244*; 259-261, *2263-2280*.

  As to the admissibility of evidence of similar offences, see 10 HALSBURY'S LAWS (3rd Edn.) 444, 445, para. 820; and for cases on the subject, see 14 DIGEST (Repl.) 431-433, *4185-4207*.

  For the Indictments Act 1915, s. 4, Sch. 1, r. 3, see 8 HALSBURY'S STATUTES
C (3rd Edn.) 272, 276.]

Cases referred to:

  R. v. *Campbell*, [1956] 2 All E.R. 272; [1956] 2 Q.B. 432; [1956] 3 W.L.R. 219; 120 J.P. 359; 40 Cr. App. Rep. 95; Digest (Cont. Vol. A) 377, *5106a*.

  R. v. *Chandor*, [1959] 1 All E.R. 702; [1959] 1 Q.B. 545; [1959] 2 W.L.R. 522; 123 J.P. 131, 194; 43 Cr. App. Rep. 74; Digest (Cont. Vol. A) 367,
D *4204a*.

  R. v. *Hall*, [1952] 1 All E.R. 66; [1952] 1 K.B. 302; 116 J.P. 43; 35 Cr. App. Rep. 167; 14 Digest (Repl.) 433, *4204*.

  R. v. *Sims*, [1946] 1 All E.R. 697; [1946] K.B. 531; [1947] L.J.R. 160; 175 L.T. 72; 31 Cr. App. Rep. 158; 14 Digest (Repl.) 260, *2279*.

 Appeal.
E This was an appeal by Ronald Edward Cyril Flack against his conviction on 19th July 1968 at Sussex Assizes before BLAIN, J., and a jury on two counts (nos. 1 and 3) of incest. He was sentenced to concurrent terms of seven years' imprisonment, against which he also appealed.

  The facts are set out in the judgment of the court.

  The authority and cases noted below* were cited during the argument in
F addition to the cases referred to in the judgment of the court.

  J. H. Gower, Q.C., and *R. J. Seabrook* for the appellant.

  B. L. Charles for the Crown.

  SALMON, L.J., delivered the judgment of the court: On 19th July 1968, at the Sussex Assizes, the appellant was tried on an indictment containing three
G counts, each alleging incest. The first count charged him with having sexual intercourse with his sister Evelyn, who was then 15, between 1st June and 21st November 1964. The second count charged him with having sexual intercourse with his sister Sheila, then aged between 12½ and 14, at some date between 1st April 1965 and 13th October 1966. The third count charged him with having sexual intercourse with his sister Carole, who was then 13½, on 26th May
H 1967. He was convicted by the jury on the first and third counts, and acquitted on the second count. He received a sentence of seven years' imprisonment on each of the counts in respect of which he was convicted, the sentences to run concurrently; and he now appeals, by leave of the single judge, against conviction and sentence.

  Before the trial commenced, it was submitted on behalf of the appellant that
I each count should be tried separately. The learned judge ruled that they should be tried together. The first point taken is that that ruling was wrong, and that on this ground the convictions should be quashed. Clearly, the three counts alleged a series of offences of the same or similar character; accordingly, it is plain that there was power to order these counts to be tried together (see s. 4

  * ARCHBOLD'S CRIMINAL PLEADING, EVIDENCE AND PRACTICE (36th Edn.) paras. 130, 138, 1037, 1289; *Makin* v. *A.-G. for New South Wales*, [1894] A.C. 57; [1891-94] All E.R. Rep. 24; *R.* v. *Ball*, [1911] A.C. 47; *Noor Mohamed* v. *R.*, [1949] 1 All E.R. 365; [1949] A.C. 182; *R.* v. *Trigg*, [1963] 1 All E.R. 490; [1963] 1 W.L.R. 305.

of the Indictments Act 1915, and Sch. 1, r. 3, to that Act). That being so, it   **A**
became a matter for discretion of the learned judge whether he should allow
the counts to be tried together or order them to be tried separately.   That is a
discretion which this court has said, on more than one occasion, it will not overrule unless it can see that justice has not been done or unless compelled to do
so by some overwhelming fact. Of course, if the learned judge gives a reason
which obviously was a bad reason, the court may review his decision.   It will not   **B**
do so however if it is of the opinion that in all the circumstances the charges
might well have been tried together, although the reason given by the judge
was wrong (*R.* v. *Hall* (1)).   In the present case, counsel on behalf of the appellant
argues very persuasively that the reasons given by the learned judge for allowing
the counts to be tried together were wrong. In giving his ruling, the learned
judge certainly indicated that at that stage at any rate he had formed the pro-   **C**
visional view that evidence of the alleged offence against any one girl would be
evidence of the alleged offences against the other two. He added, however,
that he could not forecast definitely whether he would remain of the same view
at the conclusion of the evidence.

   Counsel for the Crown has sought to support the learned judge's provisional
view with passages from the judgments of LORD GODDARD, C.J., in *R.* v. *Sims* (2)   **D**
and *R.* v. *Campbell* (3).   Counsel has very frankly conceded that these passages—
at any rate at first sight, if unqualified—appear to be rather startling, a view
with which this court is certainly disposed to agree. In *R.* v. *Sims* (4), the
accused was convicted on three counts, each alleging buggery with a different
man. In *R.* v. *Campbell* (5), the accused was convicted on seven counts, each
alleging indecent assault on a different boy. The passage in *R.* v. *Sims* (6)   **E**
relied on by the Crown reads as follows:

   " The probative force of all the acts together is much greater than one
   alone; for, whereas the jury might think one man might be telling an
   untruth, three or four are hardly likely to tell the same untruth unless they
   were conspiring together. If there is nothing to suggest a conspiracy their
   evidence would seem to be overwhelming. Whilst it would no doubt be in   **F**
   the interests of the prisoner that each case should be considered separately
   without the evidence on the others, we think that the interests of justice
   require that on each case the evidence of the others should be considered,
   and that even apart from the defence raised by him, the evidence would
   be admissible."

The passage in *R.* v. *Campbell* (7) relied on by the Crown is shorter, but to much   **G**
the same effect, and reads as follows:

   " At the same time we think a jury may be told that a succession of these
   cases may help them to determine the truth of the matter provided they are
   satisfied that there is no collaboration between the children to put up a
   false story."
                                                                              H
These passages seem to suggest that, whenever a man is charged with a sexual
offence against A., evidence may always be adduced by the Crown in support
of that charge of similar alleged offences by the accused against B., C. and D.
This court does not think that those passages were ever intended to be so understood. If, however, this is their true meaning, they go much further than was
necessary for the purpose of the decisions, and cannot, in the view of this court,   **I**
be accepted as correctly stating the law.

---

   (1) [1952] 1 All E.R. 66 at p. 67; [1952] 1 K.B. 302 at pp. 304, 305.
   (2) [1946] 1 All E.R. 697 at p. 701; [1946] K.B. 531 at p. 540.
   (3) [1956] 2 All E.R. 272 at p. 276; [1956] 2 Q.B. 432 at p. 439.
   (4) [1946] 1 All E.R. 697; [1946] K.B. 531.
   (5) [1956] 2 All E.R. 272; [1956] 2 Q.B. 432.
   (6) [1946] 1 All E.R. at p. 701; [1946] K.B. at p. 540.
   (7) [1956] 2 All E.R. at p. 276; [1956] 2 Q.B. at p. 439.

A   In *R.* v. *Sims* (8), the accused had admitted that he invited each of the men to his house. He said he had done so solely for the purpose of conversation and playing cards. Each man said he had been invited to the house for the purpose of buggery. The question was whether this was a guilty or an innocent association. As Lord Goddard, C.J., said (9):

B   ". . . the visits of the men to the prisoner's house were either for a guilty or innocent purpose; that they all speak to the commission of the same class of acts upon them tends to show that in each case the visits were for the former and not the latter purpose."

This was plainly right, and the correctness of the decision in *R.* v. *Sims* (8) has never been doubted. The evidence of B., C. and D. was clearly admissible against A. to negative the defence of innocent association.

C   In *R.* v. *Campbell* (10), the passage to which reference has been made was unnecessary for the decision which turned on the extent to which the evidence of one child could amount to corroboration of another. The correctness of the decision itself in *R.* v. *Campbell* (10) has never been questioned. It is only the passage to which reference has already been made about which any criticism is possible. In *R.* v. *Chandor* (11) Lord Parker, C.J., referring to the passage

D   from *R.* v. *Campbell* (10) which has been read, said (12):

E   "Unqualified it would appear to cover a case where the accused was saying that the incident in question never took place at all. To take an incident in the present case, the accused said that in respect of an alleged offence with a boy . . . at View Point—he . . . had never met the boy at View Point at all. Yet, if this passage in *R.* v. *Campbell* (10) is unqualified it would apply to just such a case. We do not think that the passage in *R.* v. *Campbell* (10) was ever intended to cover that. Indeed, so far as we know the authorities have never gone so far as that, nor do we see how they could

F   . . . There are, of course, many cases in which evidence of a succession of incidents may properly be admissible to help to determine the truth of any one incident, for instance, to provide identity, intent, guilty knowledge or to rebut a defence of innocent association. On such issues evidence of a succession of incidents may be very relevant, but we cannot say that they have any relevance to determine whether a particular incident ever occurred at all."

G   This court respectfully agrees with every word of Lord Parker, C.J.'s judgment in *R.* v. *Chandor* (11).

In the present case, the defence consisted of a complete denial that any such incident as that to which the appellant's sisters spoke had ever occurred. No question of identity, intent, system, guilty knowledge, or of rebutting a defence of innocent association ever arose. That was plain at any rate at the conclusion of the evidence, whatever may have been the position when the application for

H   separate trials was originally made. Accordingly, the evidence of an alleged offence against one sister could not be evidence of the alleged offences against the others. Although the learned judge had provisionally formed a contrary view before hearing the evidence, his ruling that the counts could properly be tried together did not necessarily turn exclusively on his view as to the admissibility of the evidence on each count. It seems to this court that he came to the

I   conclusion that even if his provisional view was wrong, these three alleged offences—each falling into watertight compartments—could properly be tried together, and summed up so that the jury would not be influenced or prejudiced in considering any one count by evidence in respect of the others. This, no doubt,

(8) [1946] 1 All E.R. 697; [1946] K.B. 531.
(9) [1946] 1 All E.R. at p. 701; [1946] K.B. at p. 540.
(10) [1956] 2 All E.R. 272; [1956] 2 Q.B. 432.
(11) [1959] 1 All E.R. 702; [1959] 1 Q.B. 545.
(12) [1959] 1 All E.R. at p. 704; [1959] 1 Q.B. at pp. 549, 550.

is a matter about which different judges might take different views. Certainly **A**
it would as a rule be better, in circumstances such as these, that the counts
should be tried separately. This court will not, however, interfere with the
decision of the judge in such a matter unless satisfied that there were no reasonable grounds on which his decision could be supported, or that it may have
caused a miscarriage of justice.

In the particular circumstances of this case, this court is not so satisfied; **B**
indeed it is satisfied to the contrary. The decision of the learned judge also
seems to be vindicated by the fact that the jury acquitted the accused on the
second count, although the jury accepted the evidence against him on the first
and third counts. Accordingly, the point based on the fact that the three
counts were tried together fails. The learned judge, when he summed up to the
jury, had apparently changed his provisional view that all the evidence was **C**
relevant to each count, for he stressed that they should consider each of the
counts quite separately. He summed up each count independently, and reviewed
the evidence which he told the jury was relevant to it. In no case when he was
dealing with evidence relating to one count did he mention the other counts or
the evidence which related to them alone.

Counsel for the appellant complains that the learned judge did not expressly **D**
direct the jury that when considering each count they should exclude from their
minds the evidence relating to the other counts. No doubt it would have been
better if he had expressly given this direction, and in most cases it would be
necessary to do so. This court has come to the conclusion, however, that the
direction that in considering any one count the other counts and the evidence
relating to them must be ignored is necessarily implicit in the summing-up, and **E**
that undoubtedly the jury so understood it. As already mentioned, they
acquitted on count 2, although they convicted on counts 1 and 3.

It is then argued on behalf of the appellant that the learned judge should have
excluded as inadmissible the evidence of the indecent practice which Evelyn
said she had been induced to indulge in by the appellant. It is said that this
evidence could not be relevant unless psychiatric evidence had been called to **F**
prove that such conduct was likely to indicate or to lead to intercourse with
Evelyn. No doubt in some cases psychiatric evidence is quite often useful, and
indeed sometimes essential; but not, we think, in this case. After all a jury
must be credited with some knowledge of human nature and experience of the
world. The evidence of the indecency with Evelyn was clearly admissible in
respect of count 1, which charged incest with Evelyn. In any event, the evidence **G**
of indecency did not carry the case much further, since it came only from Evelyn
herself. If she lied about the one, she may have lied about the other. If,
however, the jury believed her about the indecency, it was some evidence to
support her evidence about the incest. The matter may be tested in this way:
if there had been independent evidence as to indecency between the appellant
and his sister Evelyn, would it have been capable of corroborating Evelyn's **H**
evidence in relation to incest? This question obviously, in the view of this court,
must be answered in the affirmative.

Complaint has also been made of the judge's direction about corroboration.
The court considers that the learned judge gave a full, clear and correct warning
on the danger of convicting on uncorroborated evidence in a case such as the
present. He also told the jury correctly that if, bearing that warning in mind, **I**
they were entirely satisfied beyond any reasonable doubt that any of these girls
was speaking the truth, the jury were entitled to convict in respect of the count
relating to that girl, despite the fact that her evidence was uncorroborated. It is
true that the learned judge did not attempt an exhaustive, or indeed any,
definition of corroboration; but this was hardly necessary since the prosecution
was conducted on the basis that there was no corroboration of any of the com-
plainants' evidence on any of the three counts. The only criticism of the
summing-up in respect of corroboration which has any substance in it is the

A criticism in relation to what the learned judge said about the evidence concerning the car in which Evelyn alleged that intercourse had taken place. After reminding the jury that the prosecution conceded there was no corroboration on any count, the learned judge went on to say:

B "You might think that in the case of the first count, in the case of the girl Evelyn, one little item which you could regard as corroboration may have arisen out of the defence evidence, when Mr. Penfold said that he knew of a large car driven by the [appellant], a Hudson car, which had a running board. You may think that does not take it very much further, but, if you were impressed by Evelyn's description of the car, the make of which she did not know but which she described as a big car with a running board, you may think there is some little element of corroboration there; it is not

C great, but it is a matter for you."

This court doubts whether Mr. Penfold's evidence was capable of corroborating Evelyn's evidence. Of course, we have not seen a transcript of the evidence. If the appellant denied that Evelyn had ever been in or even seen his car, it might be otherwise; but the court is prepared to assume that there was no such

D evidence, and that what Mr. Penfold said was not capable of corroborating Evelyn. This court, however, is satisfied that no jury could have attached the slightest weight to Mr. Penfold's evidence, and the judge's reference to it can have made no difference to their verdict. This is a case in which they clearly concluded that they could safely convict on uncorroborated testimony. They did so on the third count. Even though the learned judge was wrong in suggesting that Mr. Penfold's evidence was perhaps capable of offering some very

E slight corroboration of Evelyn's evidence, this court is completely satisfied that this caused no miscarriage of justice. The appeal against the conviction is accordingly dismissed.

As to the appeal against sentence: these were undoubtedly very grave crimes, but it is right to point out that these two girls in respect of whom the appellant was convicted of incest, together with their three sisters, had all been ravished

F by the appellant's father, who, prior to the commission of any of these offences, had for certain periods regularly had intercourse with all these girls. Moreover, as far as the appellant himself is concerned, it would appear that he himself had been corrupted sexually by his father. In all these circumstances, without in any way minimising the gravity of the offences, this court has come to the conclusion that a sentence of seven years' imprisonment is too long. After all,

G the father, who was a monster of depravity, received a sentence of 12 years' imprisonment, and his offences were very much graver than those committed by the appellant, serious though they were. In all the circumstances, this court concludes that the right sentence to have passed on the appellant would have been a sentence of four years' imprisonment on each count, to run concurrently; and the sentence of seven years will be reduced to four years. The appeal against

H sentence is allowed accordingly.

Appeal against conviction dismissed. Appeal against sentence allowed.

Solicitors: *Registrar of Criminal Appeals* (for the appellant); *Director of Public Prosecutions* (for the Crown).

[*Reported by* N. P. METCALFE, ESQ., *Barrister-at-Law.*]

A

ABERNETHIE *v.* A. M. & J. KLEIMAN, LTD.

[COURT OF APPEAL, CIVIL DIVISION (Harman, Edmund Davies and Widgery, L.JJ.), March 13, 1969.]

Landlord and Tenant—Business premises—Sunday school carried on by tenant for one hour a week in loft or part of premises which had been a shop—No payment demanded by tenant—Whether a " business " within Landlord and Tenant Act 1954 (2 & 3 Eliz. 2 c. 56), s. 23 (1), (2).

B

A tenant of premises which comprised a shop and living accommodation closed the shop but continued to live on the premises with his family and to carry on a Sunday school for one hour each Sunday in the loft or downstairs in what had been the shop. He made no charge for attendance at the Sunday school and was not paid for his services, but kept a box for voluntary subscriptions, all of which he handed over to a mission. The tenant applied to the court for a determination whether the tenancy was one to which Part 2 of the Landlord and Tenant Act 1954 applied. By s. 23 (1)* of that Act, Part 2 applied to any tenancy where the property comprised in the tenancy was or included premises which were occupied by the tenant for the purposes of a business carried on by him or for those and other purposes, and by s. 23 (2)†, the expression " business " included a trade, profession or employment and included any activity carried on by a body of persons, whether corporate or unincorporate.

C

D

Held: Part 2 of the Act of 1954 did not apply to the tenancy, because the Sunday school was not a " business " within the meaning of s. 23 (2) since it was not a trade or profession or employment (see p. 792, letter B, and p. 793, letters E and H, post), nor (per EDMUND DAVIES and WIDGERY, L.JJ.) was it an " activity " carried on by any body of persons (see p. 793, letter H, post).

E

Per WIDGERY, L.J.: What a man does with his spare time in his home is most unlikely to qualify for the description " business " unless it has some direct commercial involvement in it, whether it be a hobby or a recreation or the performance of a social duty (see p. 794, letter B, post).

F

Appeal allowed.

[As to tenancies to which the Landlord and Tenant Act 1954, Part 2, applies, see 23 HALSBURY'S LAWS (3rd Edn.) 885, 886, para. 1707.

For the Landlord and Tenant Act 1954, s. 23, see 34 HALSBURY'S STATUTES (2nd Edn.) 408.]

G

Cases referred to:

Addiscombe Garden Estates, Ltd. v. *Crabbe*, [1957] 3 All E.R. 563; [1958] 1 Q.B. 513; [1957] 3 W.L.R. 980; Digest (Cont. Vol. A) 991, *1670a.*

Hills (Patents), Ltd. v. *University College Hospital Board of Governors*, [1955] 3 All E.R. 365; [1956] 1 Q.B. 90; [1955] 3 W.L.R. 523; Digest (Cont. Vol. A) 1049, *7417n.*

H

Rolls v. *Miller* (1884), 27 Ch.D. 71; [1881-85] All E.R. Rep. 915; 53 L.J.Ch. 682; 50 L.T. 597; 31 Digest (Repl.) 170, *3045.*

Appeal.

This was an appeal by Alfred Abernethie, the tenant of premises let to him by the landlords, A. M. & J. Kleiman, Ltd., against a decision of His Honour JUDGE SIR SHIRLEY WORTHINGTON-EVANS given at the Brentford County Court on 21st June 1968, declaring that the tenancy was one to which the Landlord and Tenant Act 1954, Part 2, applied.

I

H. H. Hill for the tenant.
D. D. Hacking for the landlords.

---

* Section 23 (1), so far as material, is set out at p. 791, letter H, post.
† Section 23 (2) is set out at p. 791, letter I, post.

A   HARMAN, L.J.: The question here is whether the activities of the tenant constitute a "business" within the meaning of the Landlord and Tenant Act 1954, s. 23. He applied to the rent officer to fix a fair rent, on the footing that his tenancy (so to call it) was within the Rent (Restrictions) Acts. The rent officer declined, on the footing that the activities going on in this house brought it within the Landlord and Tenant Act 1954, and, if so, outside the Rent (Restric-
B tions) Acts; and he declined jurisdiction. The tenant then applied to the county court judge. His Honour Judge Sir Shirley Worthington-Evans, and asked for a determination whether he was or was not within Part 2 of the Landlord and Tenant Act 1954—not admitting that he was, but apparently preferring it to be found that he was not. The judge, with some hesitation I think, came to the conclusion that the Landlord and Tenant Act 1954 did apply, and so declared
C as a preliminary point in the action. It is against that decision that the tenant appeals.

    The facts are in a very small compass, so far as we know them, and they are not very much known. The tenant, Mr. Abernethie, has carried on a Sunday school from time to time in this house before he ever had any rights at all. He seems to have come there about 1941. He had no tenancy. There was a loft
D in which there had been, as I understand it, a Sunday school carried on before that date and, from the time he came there, he continued to carry on this Sunday school. After he had been there two years, he got a tenancy of the house and there he had a greengrocer's business, but that he shut up, and the landlords, although there was a covenant not to carry on any business other than that of a greengrocer, did not take any point on the covenant in the lease but renewed it
E from time to time. It has been renewed up to at any rate 1963, and, as it is said, the tenant has been holding over as a tenant from year to year since that time.

    The "activity" which is said to bring him within the Act of 1954 is this, that on Sunday, at some unspecified hour, he invites all and sundry to send their children to be taught religion, as he understands it, in this loft. Sometimes it is
F too cold up in the loft and the children are then housed downstairs in what was the shop but is now, as I gather, part of the dwelling-house. No payment is demanded. There is a box where those so minded can put a subscription from time to time, but those subscriptions do not go to the tenant; he hands them over to a scripture mission. There is a suggestion made that there are sometimes Bible readings on Tuesday as well. It is said that what is being done by the
G tenant in these premises amounts to a "business" within the meaning of the Act. That depends, of course, on the exact words of s. 23 and I must read them. The words are:

      "(1) ... this Part of this Act applies to any tenancy where the property comprised in the tenancy is or includes premises which are occupied by the tenant and are so occupied for the purposes of a business carried on by
H   him or for those and other purposes."

Here one has a tenancy—that is, a tenancy from year to year; one has a property comprised in it; and one has a tenant occupying it. Are the premises then occupied for the purpose of a "business" carried on by him or for those and other purposes? In other words, one need not carry on nothing but a
I business there; one may also carry on other purposes, for instance, living in the place, of course. Section 23 (2) defines (I use that word without prejudice) the word "business":

      "In this Part of this Act the expression 'business' includes a trade, profession or employment and includes any activity carried on by a body of persons whether corporate or unincorporate."

So that, if the business, trade, profession or employment is carried on by a person, he must come within those words; but if the activity, whatever it be, is carried

on by a body of persons then it no doubt will have a larger scope.   One remem-   A
bers, for instance, the Pleasant Sunday Afternoon or something of that sort.
But I cannot accept that the word " activity " has any bearing on anything
that the judge had to decide, because there was no evidence before him, as I
hold, that anybody but the tenant carries on this activity.

Is it a " trade, profession or employment "?   It is clearly not a " trade ";
clearly, I should have thought, not a " profession ".   It is not carried on pro-   B
fessionally; it is carried on amateurishly, just the opposite to " professionally ".
So far as payment is concerned, it is without reward and for the satisfaction, I
take it, of the conscience of the person who carried it on; he feels morally obliged
to do so.   Is it, then, an " employment "?   The tenant does " employ " himself
once a week for an hour in teaching children the Scriptures.   Is that an " employment "?   In my judgment, it clearly is not.   " Employment " in that sense   C
must mean something much more regular than that.   It means, I should have
thought, either employing somebody else or being employed by somebody else.
However that may be, I cannot think that one hour a week, done voluntarily,
even with a serious sense of social obligation, is a " business "; and I am rather
at a loss to find out how the judge came to such a conclusion.   He may, of course,
have relied on *Rolls* v. *Miller* (1).   It is a decision of the Court of Appeal, and a   D
decision, if I may say so, so clearly right that one need not really bother with
its facts.   It was merely this, that, there being a covenant in a lease not to carry
on any trade or business of any description, a committee of benevolent-minded
persons decided to carry on in the premises a hostel for working girls, which
clearly would completely alter the character of the property, and not unnaturally
the landlords, and I expect the neighbouring tenants too, objected very strongly.   E
It was held that that was a " business ", and that it would be a breach of the
covenant to carry it on and it was restrained.   LINDLEY, L.J., said this (2):

" When we look into the dictionaries as to the meaning of the word
' business ', I do not think they throw much light upon it.   The word means
almost anything which is an occupation, as distinguished from a pleasure—
anything which is an occupation or duty which requires attention is a business   F
—I do not think we can get much aid from the dictionary.   We must look
at the words in the ordinary sense, and we must look at the object of the
covenant; and, looking at both, I have no hesitation in saying that this is
clearly within the words and within the object of the covenant."

That reminds one that one must always construe words of this sort secundum
subjectam materiem, in the context in which they appear.   This was an Act   G
for protecting business tenants, who until then had been hardly treated by their
landlords; and to apply the terms of an Act of that sort to this circumstance
is to fall into what I have somewhere else called the pond of absurdity.   I would
not have it that this, within the meaning of the Landlord and Tenant Act 1954,
is a " business ", even though in another context any activity which is not a
pleasure may be called a business.   It does not apply here because it does not   H
fit the context in which the words appear.

I would, therefore, allow the appeal.

EDMUND DAVIES, L.J.:   I agree.   Without in any way qualifying the
tribute that I paid during the course of argument to counsel for the landlords
for the valour with which he was making his submissions, I am bound to confess   I
that I regarded him, if he will allow me to say so, as overbold in his final observation that (and I quote) " Parliament specifically had this type of activity in
mind ".   That is indeed going a very long way.   It is true that the word " business " has been given a more extended meaning possibly than that which would
be attached to it by most people.   HARMAN, L.J., has already cited from LINDLEY
L.J., in *Rolls* v. *Miller* (3); but the words employed there are themselves (I

(1) (1884), 27 Ch.D. 71; [1881-85] All E.R. Rep. 915.
(2) (1884), 27 Ch.D. at pp. 88, 89; [1881-85] All E.R. Rep. at p. 920.
(3) (1884), 27 Ch.D. 71 at pp. 88, 89; [1881-85] All E.R. Rep. 915 at p. 920.

A hope I may say so without disrespect) worth looking at again.   The quotation referring to the word "business" is this (4):

"The word means almost anything which is an occupation, as distinguished from a pleasure—anything which is an occupation or duty which requires attention is a business ..."

B I venture to wonder, in passing, whether, applying those words to the facts of the present case, even that enlarged meaning of "business" could be said to embrace the activities of the tenant.   Undoubtedly, it is a word which has been given quite a wide meaning.   Thus, a members' club was held, in *Addiscombe Garden Estates, Ltd.* v. *Crabbe* (5), to fall within the Landlord and Tenant Act 1954.   The learned editors of WOODFALL ON THE LAW OF LANDLORD AND TENANT (27th Edn.), vol. 2, p. 1310, para. 2439, footnote (36), express the view—without

C citing any authority—that a group of people taking a tenancy of a room for the purpose of holding gambling parties could be said to be carrying on a business there within the meaning of the Act.   And, finally, in *Hills (Patents), Ltd.* v. *University College Hospital Board of Governors* (6), it was conceded that the activities of the board of governors of University College Hospital in running those premises constituted a "business" within the meaning of s. 23 (1).

D But there is one common feature running through all three cases, and that is that the "business" was being run or administered *by a body*.   That brings us, of course, to the matter to which HARMAN, L.J., has already made reference— a matter of cardinal importance in this case—namely, that the word "business" is expansively defined in s. 23 (2) of the Act, which provides that it—

E "... includes a trade, profession or employment and includes any activity carried on by a body of persons, whether corporate or unincorporate."

Like HARMAN, L.J., I hold that, quite clearly, this tenant was not engaged in "a trade, profession or employment".   That is so obvious that elaboration is not called for; nor, indeed, has counsel for the landlords sought to argue the contrary.   The only words which call for consideration here are the further words,

F "*any activity carried on by a body of persons, whether corporate or unincorporate*".   There is no suggestion that this little Sunday school in Hanwell was being carried on by "a body ... corporate or unincorporate".   It is the tenant's own concern.

It was suggested as a last despairing effort by counsel for the landlords that it was implicit in the notes of evidence that the tenant had some assistance in the

G running of this little Sunday school.   I am not satisfied that that can fairly and properly be read into the evidence; but let us make the assumption in favour of the landlords that the tenant's wife or somebody else gives a hand every now and then in looking after some of the pupils in this Sunday school.   Even so, in my judgment, it could not be said that, because some degree of assistance is given to the tenant, those who assist him could, like the tenant, be said to be

H "carrying on" the "activity".   In my judgment, this "activity", whatever its nature, was not carried on by any body of persons but by a single person, the tenant.

For those reasons I hold, with HARMAN, L.J., that this appeal must be allowed.

WIDGERY, L.J.: I agree; and, like EDMUND DAVIES, L.J., I had noted down at the end of counsel for the landlords' address his submission that Parlia-

I ment must have had in mind this specific type of activity.   In my judgment, precisely the converse is the case.   The definition of "business" in the Landlord and Tenant Act 1954 is necessarily wide, because this Act was intended to pick up a very wide range of tenancies which previously had no sort of protection at all.   Shops, factories, professional offices, cinemas, tennis clubs and the like were all without protection before 1954, except for the very limited coverage

(4) (1884), 27 Ch.D. at pp. 88, 89; [1881-85] All E.R. Rep. 915 at p. 920.
(5) [1957] 3 All E.R. 563; [1958] 1 Q.B. 513.
(6) [1955] 3 All E.R. 365; [1956] 1 Q.B. 90.

provided by the Landlord and Tenant Act 1927, and, it being the intention of **A**
Parliament to give protection to this wide range of commercial activity, the
definition had to be a wide one.   But it certainly does not follow from that that
Parliament intended to push the tentacles of this Act into domestic lettings and
the activities that a man carries on in his private rooms as part of his hobby
or recreation. Many different forms of spare-time activity are to be found, some
more " active " than others.   By and large, it seems to me that what a man **B**
does with his spare time in his home is most unlikely to qualify for the description
" business " unless it has some direct commercial involvement in it, whether it
be a hobby or a recreation or the performance of a social duty, such as in this
case.   On the face of it these are matters which are not " business " matters
at all; they go to a man's private life in his domestic surroundings. I should
think it a very strange conclusion if one had to say that in an activity of this **C**
sort carried on in this way a " business " was involved.

Appeal allowed.

Solicitors: *Fairchild, Greig & Co.* (for the tenant); *Saunders & Co.* (for the
landlords).

[*Reported by* HENRY SUMMERFIELD, ESQ., *Barrister-at-Law.*]

D

JAMES *v.* WOODALL DUCKHAM CONSTRUCTION CO., LTD.

[COURT OF APPEAL, CIVIL DIVISION (Salmon, Winn and Karminski, L.JJ.), **E**
February 28, 1969.]

*Damages—Personal injury—Assessment—Conduct of action—Delay—Accident
March 1962—Warning by doctor to plaintiff's solicitors in June 1963 that
plaintiff's pain and disability (including inability to work) unlikely to clear
up until action over, but should clear up then—Writ issued June 1964—
Action tried June 1968—Action which would have been tried in early 1965* **F**
*had writ been issued promptly and action prosecuted diligently after doctor's
warning—Persistence of plaintiff's pain and disability and inability to work
until after trial—Date to which damages for loss of earnings to be assessed.*

On 17th March 1962 the plaintiff, a carpenter and joiner, fell about 30 to
35 feet owing to the negligence of the defendants, his employers.   The
plaintiff was rendered unconscious for about half-an-hour. He suffered severe **G**
pain in his head, back, leg, arms and neck, from the time of the accident
onwards.   There was no physical cause for this pain, which was caused by
anxiety over the accident and a functional overlay, but, as the trial judge
found, the plaintiff was not and never had been a malingerer. In June 1963
the plaintiff's neuro-surgeon reported to the plaintiff's solicitors that he did
not think that the plaintiff's pain could be expected to clear until his action **H**
for damages for his injuries had been settled, following which he did not think
there would be any persisting serious disability. The writ was issued on 25th
June 1964, and the action was not tried until 26th June 1968. The plaintiff
had not been able to return to work before the trial, and by then his pain
and suffering and inability to work were likely to endure for some time after
the trial.   The trial judge awarded the plaintiff £11,267 8s. 6d. damages, **I**
being £5,267 8s. 6d. net loss of earnings from the date of the accident to the
trial, plus £2,500 for future loss of earnings and £3,500 for pain and suffering.
On appeal by the defendants,
Held: the damages would be reduced to £4,500 because the plaintiff's
writ should have been issued promptly after receipt of his surgeon's opinion
of June 1963, and the action should have been pursued with ordinary
diligence thereafter; had this been done the action would have been tried
early in 1965, and the plaintiff would have been back in his old job soon

A   afterwards;   accordingly, the damages awarded would be limited to loss
of earnings for the period from the accident to the date when, had the action
been tried early in 1965, the plaintiff would have returned to work, together
with a fair figure for pain and suffering (see p. 797, letter F, and p. 798,
letters B and F, post).

Appeal allowed.

B   [As to measure of damages for personal injury, and consequent loss of earnings,
see 11 HALSBURY'S LAWS (3rd Edn.) 255, 256, 258, paras. 427, 430, and for cases
on the measure of damages, see 36 DIGEST (Repl.) 199-202, *1048-1070.*]

Appeal.

This was an appeal by the defendants, Woodall Duckham Construction Co.,
C   Ltd., against so much of the judgment of WRANGHAM, J., at Birmingham Assizes
on 26th June 1968, as assessed the damages awarded to the plaintiff, Joseph
Jehoida James, for personal injuries due to a fall while at work, at £11,267 8s. 6d.
The defendants had admitted that the fall was due to their negligence. The only
special damage claimed by the plaintiff was net lost earnings, being £544 10s. 8d.
(£17 0s. 4d. per week) from 17th March to 30th October 1962, and totalling
D   £5,267 8s. 6d. until the date of the trial. WRANGHAM, J., found that the net loss
as at that date was about £20 per week. The facts are set out in the judgment
of SALMON, L.J. The writ was issued on 25th June 1964.

A. W. M. Davies, Q.C., and *B. D. Bush* for the defendants.
Tudor Evans, Q.C., and *W. N. Davison* for the plaintiff.

E   SALMON, L.J.: On 26th June 1968, at Birmingham Assizes, the plaintiff recovered judgment for £11,267 8s. 6d. in all as damages for injuries
caused by the negligence of the defendants. There never was any issue about
liability. The only issue in the case was the amount to which the plaintiff was
entitled by way of damages. The defendants appeal against the judgment on the
basis that the damages awarded to the plaintiff were far too high—" a wholly
F   erroneous estimate of the damage ", is the time-honoured phrase.

The accident in which the plaintiff was injured had occurred more than six
years before the date of the trial, namely on 17th March 1962. The plaintiff
was a carpenter and joiner employed by the defendants. In 1962, when he met
with his accident, he was about 43 years of age. He fell off a ladder at a height of
some 30 to 35 feet above the ground. It is a miracle that he did not receive very
G   serious injuries, and indeed falling from that height he might well have been
killed. He was immediately taken to the hospital and very carefully examined. It
was found that, strangely enough, and very fortunately, he had suffered no
serious physical injury at all. He had quite a nasty cut on his forehead, which
had to be stitched, and there was some suspicion that he might have fractured a
rib—he had pain in his chest. He had been unconscious after the accident for
H   half-an-hour, and clearly he was very shaken by his experience. After four days
as an in-patient he was discharged and sent home; and for a further period of some
three months or so he attended the hospital as an out-patient for physiotherapy.

In June 1962 the hospital said that he was fit for work. He did go back to work,
but later—in October of that year. He worked for about 3½ days; and that is
all the work that this man has done since the date of his accident.

I   Now this is a strange and in some ways a difficult case. When the plaintiff gave
evidence he told the court that he suffered " the gravest pain all over his body "
and had been doing so ever since the date of the accident; he had headaches;
his back hurt; his leg hurt; his arms hurt; his neck hurt—he was always in
pain. It is quite clear from the medical evidence on both sides that there is no
physical cause, and never has been any physical cause, for that pain. Naturally
enough, after the accident his chest was tender for a time and his neck was stiff,
and he had some headaches; but there never was any physical cause for the sort
of pain from which he says he was suffering. It is well known that although there

may be no physical cause for a pain, a man may in reality feel pain. I am A
never quite sure what the correct medical term is, but he suffers, for some psycho-
somatic or neurotic reason, from functional pain, although as far as his physical
condition is concerned there is no reason for it. He does nevertheless suffer
and it is just as real a pain as is produced, for example, by a broken leg.

The defendants' case at one stage was that the plaintiff was a malingerer; and
it is interesting to observe that when his own doctor saw him to start with this B
was his own doctor's view. He said:

"I said to him ' Now look, old chap, you are on to the wrong thing here;
get it out of your mind that you will get any profit to yourself in the long run
from pursuing this matter of injury with ideas of compensation '."

So his doctor obviously thought he was malingering in order to inflate the
damages he hoped to get from the defendants. When the plaintiff was told that, C
he expressed horror and said he was appalled that the doctor should think he
was acting in that way. The fact that he expressed horror and was appalled—as
he said to the doctor—is perhaps not very helpful one way or the other. His own
doctor, in a report which he made later, said:

"My first reaction was therefore to dismiss his complaints as being D
compensation neurosis. Indeed so blatant and lacking in guile was he about
stressing this aspect of his case that in my first two interviews I did not look
sufficiently and searchingly at the facts and was resolved to force him back
to work."

That is what his own doctor thought about him.

If that had been a true assessment of the plaintiff's then state, it is improbable E
that he could have recovered substantial damages in this action. If a man
pretends that he is suffering from great disability when he knows very well that
he is not, and tells his doctor he is suffering from pains all over when he feels
no pain at all, he may well talk himself into believing that he is suffering from
pain. He will then suffer from pain, and in the future he will not be malingering because the pain will be real. But that will not be a pain which has F
been caused by the accident; the accident will merely be the occasion out of
which or after which the pain occurred, and the pain will have been caused by
the man malingering—it will be self-induced. But in the present case there is
no real evidence to support the view that the pains which the plaintiff suffered
later, on which all the doctors are agreed, were caused in any such way as that;
and certainly there is a direct finding by the judge, which counsel for the defen- G
dants very rightly does not seek to challenge, that the plaintiff was not malingering at the trial and had never been a malingerer. So that passes out of the case.
The learned judge approached this case on the basis that the plaintiff as a result
of this accident suffered from very real pain notwithstanding the fact that there
is no physical condition to account for it.

When the learned judge awarded him upwards of £11,000, he did so on the basis H
that some £5,000 was attributable to special damage which he assessed on the
view that for the six years which intervened between the date of the accident and
the trial the plaintiff had been unable to earn any money. The learned judge
then added £2,500 for future loss of earnings, and gave him £3,500 in all
as compensation for the pain and suffering he had endured before the trial and
was, in the learned judge's view, likely to endure thereafter.

I must not be taken, speaking for myself, as accepting that the £2,500 or I
the £3,500 were proper estimates under those two heads of damage; but having
regard to the view I take of the case neither of those questions is very relevant.
I consider that the learned judge was wrong in the view he took of special damage.
I do not think that the plaintiff was entitled to be paid special damage on the
basis that for 6¼ years before the trial he had been unable to earn anything. I
come to that conclusion for this reason: on 18th June 1963, Mr. Hamilton, a
distinguished neuro-surgeon, reported to the plaintiff's solicitors; and I will

A read the relevant part of his report which was put before the judge by consent as evidence at the trial. In the usual way, when Mr. Hamilton went into the witness box, instead of giving evidence-in-chief the report was put in and read by the judge. I think I ought to read the whole of the " opinion " which read as follows:

B " Examination now shows no evidence of any increasing physical disability, but those symptoms now remaining are mainly those caused by anxiety about his accident; with it is associated a functional overlay. Some stiffness of his neck movements, and some residual tenderness of the ribs still remain, although they may be expected to improve with time. So far as the remainder of his symptoms are concerned, however [these were the " grave pains " all over his body which entirely prevented him from doing any work] I do not

C think that these can now be expected to clear until his action has been settled, following which I do not think there will be left any persisting serious disability."

The plaintiff's solicitors were told this in June 1963. The plaintiff's doctor had received a report from Professor Trethowan much to the same effect some months

D before; and Professor Trethowan was called as a witness by the defendants at the trial. It seems to me that the solicitors, receiving that letter as solicitors for the plaintiff, were his agents to receive that information and pass it on to him, as I have no doubt they did. I am not making any criticism of the solicitors. I do not know why they did not issue a writ immediately. But it is quite clear that a writ ought to have been issued at once. After all, here is the plaintiff being

E told, through his agent, ' You are never going to get any better or earn anything until your claim is disposed of; but as soon as it is disposed of you will be able to pursue your usual avocation. It can be disposed of by a writ being issued and either settling the claim on a reasonable basis or bringing the action on for trial '. If, in these circumstances, a plaintiff sits back and thereby prolongs the period during which he is unable to earn anything, he cannot expect to recover damages from a defendant in respect of the period during which he, the plaintiff,

F has delayed his return to work. If this writ had been issued promptly after that advice had been given, and the action had been pursued with ordinary diligence by the plaintiff, I think that this case would certainly have come on for trial early in 1965. If it had come on early in 1965, the plaintiff would, in my view, very soon thereafter have been back at his old job as a carpenter, and a very much happier man than he is today. It may be—I do not know—that the learned judge

G thought that he would still, after six years and three months, get back to his job as a carpenter. That may be right or it may be wrong. On the view I take it does not matter very much from the point of view of damages. I have no doubt that if the action had been tried in January 1965, as it should have been, instead of some 3½ years later, the plaintiff would very soon have been back at work.

H What we have to consider is the loss which he would have suffered between the date of the accident and the date when the action should have come on for trial. We also have to consider when he would have been likely to have returned to work, and what he would have lost between the trial and that date, and also what on the whole would be a fair figure to award him for the pain that he suffered in all. Taking all those elements into account, I am unable to persuade

I myself that the total figure can exceed £4,500, and I would allow the appeal accordingly and substitute judgment for the plaintiff for £4,500 instead of the figure which the learned judge awarded.

WINN, L.J.: I agree explicitly with the judgment delivered by SALMON, L.J., and would add for my own part only two short points.

The first is that an even clearer warning to the plaintiff, through his experienced union-retained solicitors, was conveyed by a letter of the same date—18th June 1963—which Mr. Hamilton sent covering the report to which SALMON, L.J., has referred. In that, Mr. Hamilton wrote:

A

". . . the patient has now developed a severe functional illness, which accounts for almost the whole of his present disability [and I stress the next sentence]. There is no doubt that the longer this is allowed to continue the more persistent it will be and the more difficult it will be for him to return to work."

B

I agree that, as SALMON, L.J., has said, a claim for special damage must be based on affirmative proof that it was the tort of the defendants which prevented, during the period in respect of which the claim is made, the earning by the plaintiff of his pre-accident wage or any part of it. For my part I agree that as from a short reasonable period after receipt of that letter it is impossible any longer affirmatively and effectively to sustain such a contention.

C

The second point is this: that, whilst not daring to venture on the uncharted seas of psychiatric diagnosis and terminology, I would enter a plea for the utmost possible simplification of the terms which these gentlemen learned in that science see fit to use. I would have ventured to think that no neurosis can properly be called a " traumatic " neurosis unless there is a continuous chain of causation between the trauma and the neurosis. The fact that a neurosis has occurred *post* an accident certainly does not prove that it has occurred *propter* the accident.

D

That proposition is too simple to be expressed in a context related to psychiatry, and yet one finds, very much to one's embarrassment, that psychiatrists appear to talk of " traumatic " neurosis and " post-traumatic " neurosis virtually as though those two terms were synonyms.

E

I further venture to think that, so far as my very limited reading in this field enables me to express an opinion, it is Sir Francis Walsh (who has made a close study of these matters), who has afforded the best possible clue to finding one's way through the maze of the type of evidence which was given in this case. He said that a neurosis was either purposive or itself constituted an entity not brought about by any motivation; and that, wherever compensation need or compensation greed was involved in the total subconscious mentality and mental state of a patient, then it must be diagnosed that his neurosis was at least in part purposive.

F

That is all I desire to say in agreeing that this appeal should be allowed to the extent indicated by SALMON, L.J.

KARMINSKI, L.J.: I agree, and want to add a very few words of my own because we are differing from the trial judge.

G

The assessment of damages in this class of case, where the physical injuries are relatively, if not completely, unapparent, presents grave difficulties; and I must confess to having great sympathy with the learned judge in his difficulties in arriving at a precise conclusion to be expressed in figures; but I have, as SALMON and WINN, L.JJ., have done, tried to approach the matter to see whether the very high award of damages which he made can be justified. This is not a case where one can approach the matter on the line of saying ' Well, I think the damages are rather high: I would have given £1,000, or perhaps £1,500, less '; but, for the

H

reasons which SALMON and WINN, L.JJ., have given, I have come to the conclusion that the award of damages made by the learned judge is quite out of proportion to the injuries which the evidence shows the plaintiff here actually received. By " injuries " I refer, of course, to the psychiatric disturbances which were in whole, or probably in part, as WINN, L.J., has pointed out, caused by this accident.

I

I agree that the figure of £4,500 should be substituted for the award made by the trial judge and that this appeal ought to be allowed accordingly.

Appeal allowed. Order below varied by reducing total award of damages to £4,500.

Solicitors: *Nash, Field & Co.*, agents for *Blewitt Oakley & Co.*, Birmingham (for the defendants); *Rabnett, Conway & Co.*, Birmingham (for the plaintiff).

[*Reported by* HENRY SUMMERFIELD, ESQ., *Barrister-at-Law.*]

A

R. *v.* WUYTS.

[Court of Appeal, criminal division (Widgery and Karminski, L.JJ., and Geoffrey Lane, J.), April 17, 1969.]

B

Criminal Law—Forgery—Possession of forged banknotes—" Lawful authority or excuse "—Defence that possession retained to give banknotes to police— Banknotes not handed over to police at first available opportunity—Whether " lawful excuse "—Forgery Act 1913 (3 *& 4 Geo.* 5 *c.* 27), *s.* 8 (1).

Possession of forged banknotes solely in order to deliver them to the police is a " lawful authority or excuse " within the meaning of s. 8 (1)* of the Forgery Act 1913. The fact that an accused has not delivered them to the police at the first available opportunity does not prevent him from relying on the defence, the question still being one for the jury (see p. 801, letters E and G, post).

C

Appeal allowed.

[As to possession of forged notes, etc., see 10 Halsbury's Laws (3rd Edn.) 842, para. 1622; and for cases on the subject, see 15 Digest (Repl.) 1258, *12916-12918.*

D

For the Forgery Act 1913, see 8 Halsbury's Statutes (3rd Edn.) 257.]

Appeal.

This was an appeal by Nicholas Charles Wuyts, pursuant to a certificate granted by His Honour Judge McKinnon, Q.C., under s. 1 (2) of the Criminal Appeal Act 1968, against his conviction on 22nd January 1969 on count 3 of an indictment charging him with unlawful possession of two forged £5 Bank of England notes contrary to s. 8 (1) of the Forgery Act 1913. He was sentenced to eight months' imprisonment for that offence to run concurrently with a term of four months' imprisonment imposed on a conviction on count 1 of the same indictment of uttering a different forged £5 Bank of England note. The grounds of the judge's certificate were: (i) whether count 3 was an absolute offence; (ii) whether it was right to find that there was no evidence on which the jury could find that the appellant was in possession of the forged notes with lawful authority or excuse; (iii) whether the question of whether or not the appellant had lawful excuse for possessing the forged notes was a question of fact for the jury; and (iv) whether it was right to direct the jury to convict on count 3— thereby preventing the appellant placing his defence before the jury. The facts are set out in the judgment of the court.

E

F

G

The authority and the cases noted below† were cited during the argument.

R. W. P. H. Hay for the appellant.

Viscount Stormont for the Crown.

WIDGERY, L.J., delivered the judgment of the court: The appellant was convicted at the Central Criminal Court on 22nd January 1969 on two counts under the Forgery Act 1913. The first was for uttering a forged banknote (count 1) and the second (which was in fact count 3) was in respect of possession of forged banknotes knowing them to be forged, contrary to s. 8 (1) of the Act. He was sentenced to four months' imprisonment on count 1 and eight months' imprisonment concurrent on count 3. He now appeals against his conviction on count 3 only, by certificate of the trial judge.

H

I

The circumstances of this case can be put quite briefly. On 18th May 1968 the appellant, driving a motor car, went to a garage, ordered some petrol and tendered a forged £5 note in payment. The pump-attendant noticed the forgery and refused to accept the note, whereupon the appellant found other genuine

---

* Section 8 (1), is set out at p. 800, letter F, post.

† Archbold's Criminal Pleading, Evidence and Practice (36th Edn.) para. 2193; *R. v. Harvey* (1871), L.R. 1 C.C.R. 284; *Dickins v. Gill*, [1896] 2 Q.B. 310; *Wong Pooh Yin v. Public Prosecutor*, [1954] 3 All E.R. 31; [1955] A.C. 93.

money to pay for the petrol. In due course the appellant went to the police **A**
and surrendered the £5 note in question. At the trial he contended that when
he had tendered the note he was unaware that it was a forgery, but the jury
clearly disbelieved him on that question and, accordingly, convicted him on
count 1, in respect of which there is no appeal. What happened after that is
somewhat obscure, because it depended entirely on the appellant's evidence,
and he (according to the evidence of the police) had contradicted himself more **B**
than once. However, so far as his evidence at the trial was concerned, it was
to the effect that some 13 days later, namely, on 31st May 1968, when working
as a mini-cab driver, he had taken a fare to Stansted from London late at night
and had been paid by two further forged £5 notes. The fare was £6, and he said
that he gave four genuine £1 notes by way of change. He said that he did not
notice the forgery initially, but stopped on his way back to London and looked **C**
at these notes, and then found that they were forgeries. He made some attempt,
he said, to find the man who had passed them to him, and on his return to the
headquarters of the mini-cab organisation for whom he was working he complained to others there that he had been passed two forged £5 notes. Having
finished his work that night, he said he went to the flat of a friend of his to sleep,
and that the two notes in question which he had received at Stansted were left **D**
in the car in an atlas under the front seat. He said in the course of the trial that
it was his intention to surrender these notes to the police, and his explanation
of not having done so was that he had not had time; he had either been working
or sleeping throughout 31st May. On 1st June—and again before the appellant
had done anything in regard to these two £5 notes—the owners of the car,
who had hired it to him, saw it in the street and took it away; and that meant **E**
that the appellant had no further access to these notes from that time. He sent
his friend (Miss Pearce) to collect his belongings from the car, but the hire
company was not prepared to surrender them; and in fact, as the court
understands it, itself, handed these two clearly forged notes over to the police.

On count 3 a question arose at an early stage of the trial as to the true
construction of s. 8, which I must now read: **F**

> " (1) Every person shall be guilty of felony and on conviction thereof
> shall be liable to penal servitude for any term not exceeding fourteen years,
> who, without lawful authority or excuse, the proof whereof shall lie on the
> accused, purchases or receives from any person, or has in his custody or
> possession, a forged bank note, knowing the same to be forged."

 G

The learned trial judge at an early stage requested the assistance of counsel
as to the proper construction of the section, because the judge took the view
that if it were proved by the prosecution that the notes were forged and that
they were knowingly in the possession of the accused, then he having no lawful
authority to possess them (in the sense of being a public officer authorised to
take them) had committed an offence. It was suggested that the offence cons- **H**
tituted by s. 8 (1) was an absolute offence, in the sense that if possession and
knowledge of the forgery were proved then an offence had been committed.

After argument the learned trial judge adhered to his view, but he went
a little further, and his ruling to the jury is, I think, best expressed by looking
at the transcript. The passage I am about to read was delivered in the presence
of the jury prior to the beginning of the summing-up. The learned judge **I**
said:

> " The direction that I propose to give you is this; that if you are satisfied
> that the [appellant] had possession of the two forged £5 notes, if he knew
> they were forged—because it is not disputed that they were forged—if he
> knew that they were forged and he had possession of them, that is the offence
> and the correct verdict would be a verdict of guilty of that. Further, if
> that is not correct and it is open to him to prove that when he was found to

A   be in possession of them, he had a lawful authority or excuse for that posses-
     sion, then I propose to rule—and it is my responsibility; I shall be the one
     to get into trouble, not you, if I am wrong about this—that there is no
     evidence on which any jury, properly directed, could find that he had proved
     that on a balance of probabilities."

B   It is right to say that a consideration of the transcript as a whole makes it abun-
     dantly clear that, although the learned judge was recognising as a possibility
     that it might be a lawful excuse for the appellant to show that he had retained
     possession only for the purpose of handing the forgeries over to the police,
     yet in his view that submission was not open to the appellant in this case, because
     on his own admission he had not handed over the notes at the first available
C   opportunity.   The appellant was specifically asked by the learned judge whether
     or not he had an opportunity of handing in these notes on his way back from
     Stansted on the occasion when he received them, and the appellant said that
     he had.   The learned judge took the view that, even if it were right (which
     he obviously doubted) that possession with intent to hand over to the police
     might constitute lawful excuse, he took the view that that excuse was not open
D   in this case because the first available opportunity of handing over to the police
     had not been taken.
         In the view of this court, the construction put on the section by the learned
     judge was too narrow.   The court does not propose to attempt anything in the
     nature of a definition of the phrase " lawful authority or excuse "; but the court
     recognises that the passing of forged banknotes was made a felony by this Act,
E   and that it is at common law the duty of any citizen to assist the police in the
     prosecution of a felony.   Accordingly, it seems to us that if an accused person
     in the position of the appellant is able to prove on a balance of probabilities
     that, although in possession of notes which he knew to be forged, he had retained
     possession of them solely in order to place them before the police authorities so
     that the previous possessors of the notes might be prosecuted, in our judgment,
F   if that is shown on a balance of probabilities, that amounts to a lawful excuse.
         Counsel for the Crown has contended that to take such a view would, in fact,
     open the door to allowing an accused person to plead any *reasonable* excuse.
     But the court does not take that view.   The reason why the excuse to which I
     have referred is, in our judgment, a lawful excuse is because it is an excuse
     which is wholly consistent with the common law; it is wholly consistent with
G   the duty of the citizen to assist in the capture and prosecution of a felon.   The
     excuse is " lawful " in the strict literal sense of that word.   Accordingly, in our
     judgment, when the appellant in the course of the trial gave evidence that he
     had retained the two notes in order to hand them over to the police, the learned
     judge should have left it to the jury to decide whether on a balance of probabilities
     they were satisfied that that was his sole intention.   The learned judge was wrong
H   in anchoring the case, as it were, to the question of whether he had surrendered
     the notes at the first available opportunity.   Of course, a person in possession
     of forged notes who wishes to be believed when he says he retains them only
     for the purpose of assisting the police is well advised to hand them over to the
     police at the first opportunity, and if he fails to do so he may find that those
     who have to consider his position later will find it difficult to believe that was
I   his sole intent.   But it is a matter of degree; and on the footing that these notes
     were obtained by the appellant as late as the early hours of the morning of
     31st May, and on the further footing that he had no opportunity of handing
     them over to the police after the car had been re-taken on 1st June, there was,
     in our judgment, a clear issue proper to be left to the jury on which they should
     have decided whether they were satisfied on a balance of probabilities that his
     sole purpose in retaining possession was to hand them over to the proper autho-
     rities.   That issue was not left to the jury, and there was, in our judgment, a
     mis-trial accordingly.

                                                                              DD

The question then arises, of course, whether we ought to apply the proviso **A** under s. 2 (1) of the Criminal Appeal Act 1968 and nevertheless uphold the conviction. Counsel for the Crown has urged with force that this was a case in which the appellant had attacked the prosecution evidence at every point, had raised allegations against the police of a serious character (all of which were clearly disbelieved by the jury) and, indeed, according to the police, had made a statement that he had possessed these notes, not for some 24 hours, but for **B** 15 days before the car was taken from him. Those matters are suggested as being proper considerations for the application of the proviso in this case. However, it is right to say that counsel for the Crown with his customary candour, has reminded us that it is a very unusual thing to apply the proviso when an issue appropriate to the decision of the jury has never been left to them at all.

We have considered this matter, and are of opinion that the proviso should **C** not be applied. Accordingly, there being, as I say, a misdirection to the jury, the conviction on count 3 must be set aside with its attendant sentence. [The application for leave to appeal against sentence on count 1 was refused.]

Appeal allowed.

Solicitors: *Registrar of Criminal Appeals* (for the appellant); *Freshfields* (for **D** the Crown).

[*Reported by* N. P. METCALFE, ESQ., *Barrister-at-Law.*]

HEWITT *v.* LEICESTER CITY COUNCIL. **E**

[COURT OF APPEAL, CIVIL DIVISION (Lord Denning, M.R., Winn and Fenton Atkinson, L.JJ.), March 31, 1969.]

Compulsory Purchase—Notice to treat—Service—Post—Recorded delivery service —Unless contrary proved service deemed to be effected in ordinary course **F** *of post—Letter returned through the post—Marked " gone away "—Time of service important—Affecting valuation of property—Not deemed to have been effected in ordinary course of post—Interpretation Act* 1889 (52 & 53 *Vict. c.* 63), *s.* 26.

Acting in pursuance of a compulsory purchase order made in respect of house, a compensating authority in May 1965 sent the owner, the claimant, **G** a notice to treat in a letter sent recorded delivery service addressed to her at 23, Wharf Street, Leicester, being her address then in its possession. The letter was returned through the post marked " returned undelivered " and " gone away ". The owner was in fact living at Leamington Spa. In December 1965 the compensating authority sent the notice to treat to the claimant's duly appointed agents. The compensation payable in respect **H** of the house, ascertained as at the date of the service of the notice to treat was £1,500 if service was effected in December but only £1,100 if it was effected in May 1965.

Held: the notice to treat was served in December 1965 and was not served in May, because the time of service was important through the valuation depending on it, and once it was returned through the post marked " gone away " it was plain that it had not in fact been served at all, and **I** service could not therefore be deemed " to have been effected at the time at which the letter would be delivered in the ordinary course of post " within the meaning of the Interpretation Act 1889 (see p. 804, letters F to H, post).

R. v. Appeal Committee of County of London Quarter Sessions, Ex parte Rossi ([1956] 1 All E.R. 670) followed.

Appeal dismissed.

A [As to service of notices to treat for purposes of compulsory acquisition, see 10 Halsbury's Laws (3rd Edn.) 60, 61, paras. 97, 98; and for cases on the subject, see 11 Digest (Repl.) 187, *535-537.*

For the Interpretation Act 1889, s. 26, see 24 Halsbury's Statutes (2nd Edn.) 224.]

Cases referred to:

B *Moody* v. *Godstone Rural District Council,* [1966] 2 All E.R. 696; [1966] 1 W.L.R. 1085; 130 J.P. 332; Digest (Cont. Vol. B) 693, *90b.*

R. v. *London County Quarter Sessions (Appeal Committee), Ex p. Rossi,* [1956] 1 All E.R. 670; [1956] 1 Q.B. 682; [1956] 2 W.L.R. 808; 120 J.P. 239; 16 Digest (Repl.) 473, *2929.*

C **Case Stated.**

The city of Leicester, the compensating authority, appealed to the Court of Appeal against a decision of the Lands Tribunal (H. P. Hobbs, Esq.) given on 4th March 1968, holding that a notice to treat in respect of the compulsory acquisition of the claimant's house and yard at 89, Upper Kent Street, Leicester, was served on the claimant on 23rd December 1965 and not on 20th May 1965

D as submitted by the compensating authority. The contentions of the compensating authority on the appeal were as follows: (i) that under and by virtue of the provisions of s. 19 of the Lands Clauses Consolidation Act 1845, s. 26 of the Interpretation Act 1889, s. 169 (1) (c) and para. 8 (8) of Part 2 of Sch. 3 to the Housing Act 1957, and s. 1 (1) of the Recorded Delivery Service Act 1962, the notice to treat sent to the claimant by the compensating authority by

E recorded delivery service in a prepaid letter addressed to her at 23, Wharf Street, Leicester on 20th May 1965 was to be deemed to have been duly served on her, and that compensation payable to her by the compensating authority was the sum of £1,100 together with surveyors' fees of £38 12s., being the amount of compensation agreed to be payable if it fell to be assessed as at May 1965. (ii) that by reason of the statutory provisions the decision of the Lands Tribunal

F that the notice to treat was not effectively served until 23rd December 1965, and that accordingly the compensation payable to the claimant by the compensating authority was the sum of £1,500 together with surveyor's fees of £43 1s., being the amount of compensation agreed to be payable if it fell to be assessed as at December 1965, was wrong in law.

A. P. McNabb for the claimant.

G *P. G. Clough* for the compensating authority.

LORD DENNING, M.R.: The compensating authority, Leicester City Council decided compulsorily to acquire a house, 89, Upper Kent Street, Leicester. They made a compulsory purchase order under Part 3 of the Housing Act 1957 which incorporated the provisions of the Lands Clauses Consolidation Act 1845,

H about a notice to treat. The owner of the house was the claimant, a Mrs. Olive Linda Hewitt. The compensating authority had an address for her—23, Wharf Street, Leicester. On 20th May 1965 they sent her a notice to treat and other formal documents in a letter by the recorded delivery service addressed to " Mrs. Olive Linda Hewitt, 23 Wharf Street ". The letter soon came back. It came back through the post marked " returned undelivered ", with a note that

I she had " gone away ". Thereafter the house at 89, Upper Kent Street, became unoccupied so that it could be had with vacant possession.

It turned out afterwards that the claimant was living at Leamington Spa. She appointed agents to act for her. On 23rd December 1965 the compensating authority sent the notice to treat and the other documents to the claimant's agents. It reached her agents on 23rd December 1965. The question is: When was the notice to treat served? This is important because the value of the property is normally to be ascertained as at the date of the service of the notice to treat. The dates have made a great difference: if the notice to treat was

properly served on 20th May 1965, the value of the house then was £1,100: **A**
but if it was not effectively served until 23rd December 1965, the value at that
date was £1,500.   So the question is whether the notice to treat of 20th May
was a proper service.

The service of the notice to treat is covered by s. 169 (1) of the Housing Act
1957, which provides that it may be served—

> " (c) by sending it in a prepaid registered letter addressed to that person   **B**
> at his usual or last known place of abode."

The time of service is governed by s. 26 of the Interpretation Act 1889, which
provides:

> " 26.   Where an Act passed after the commencement of this Act authorises
> or requires any document to be served by post, whether the expression   **C**
> ' serve ', or the expression ' give ' or ' send ', or any other expression is
> used, then, unless the contrary intention appears, the service shall be
> deemed to be effected by properly addressing, prepaying, and posting a
> letter containing the document, and unless the contrary is proved to have
> been effected at the time at which the letter would be delivered in the
> ordinary course of post."
                                                                          D

It was submitted on behalf of the compensating authority that it was sufficient
for them to post the letter, even though it was returned " gone away "; and
they relied on the recent case of *Moody* v. *Godstone Rural District Council* (1).
But I regard that as a very special case.   The letter there was not returned
through the post.   It presumably reached the defendant.   It was only when he
got to court that he said he never received it.   No wonder his excuse did not   **E**
prevail!   I prefer to go by the earlier decision of this court in *R.* v. *Appeal
Committee of County of London Quarter Sessions, Ex p. Rossi* (2).   There a bastardy
summons was returned to the sender marked " undelivered " " no response ".
It was held that it had not been served.

This is a case like *Rossi's* case (2) where the time of service was important.
The valuation depended on it.   Once it appeared that the letter of 20th May   **F**
1965 was returned through the post marked " gone away ", then it was quite
plain that it was not served at all.   We are not bound to " deem " a notice
to be served at a particular time, when we know that in fact it was not served at
all.   The notice to treat was not served on 20th May 1965.   It was not served
until 23rd December 1965.   The valuation should be £1,500 and not £1,100.
I agree with the reasons given by the Lands Tribunal in this case for the decision   **G**
and I would dismiss the appeal.

   WINN, L.J.: I agree and have nothing to add.

   FENTON ATKINSON, L.J.: I also agree.

                                                        Appeal dismissed.

   Solicitors: *Nabarro, Nathanson & Co.*, agents for *Barradale & Haxby*, Leicester   **H**
(for the claimant); *Field, Roscoe & Co.*, agents for *R. R. Thornton*, Leicester
(for the compensating authority).

                              [*Reported by* F. AMIES, ESQ., *Barrister-at-Law.*]

                                                                          I

---

(1) [1966] 2 All E.R. 696; [1966] 1 W.L.R. 1085.
(2) [1956] 1 All E.R. 670; [1956] 1 Q.B. 682.

A

R. *v.* GRIFFITHS

[Court of Appeal, criminal division (Widgery and Karminski, L.JJ., and Geoffrey Lane, J.), April 21, 1969.]

B
Criminal Law—Sentence—Suspended sentence—Subsequent offence of different character from offence in respect of which suspended sentence was imposed—Whether suspended sentence should be brought into effect—Criminal Justice Act 1967 (c. 80), s. 40 (1) (a).

In January 1968, the appellant, who had previous convictions including four for violence but none for driving offences, was sentenced to 12 months' imprisonment suspended for two years for factorybreaking with intent.
C
In October 1968, he was convicted of dangerous driving and common assault and sentenced to concurrent terms of nine and three months' imprisonment respectively; and it was also ordered, under s. 40 (1)* of the Criminal Justice Act 1967, that the suspended sentence should take effect consecutive to that sentence. On the question of whether the suspended sentence should have been ordered to take effect,

D
    Held: although the facts of a subsequent offence were clearly appropriate for consideration in deciding whether the suspended sentence should be put into effect pursuant to s. 40 (1) (a) of the Criminal Justice Act 1967, and a court was entitled to look at the facts of the subsequent offence and, if it thought right in the circumstances, to say that it would be unjust in view of the character of that offence to make the suspended sentence operative, in
E
the circumstances of the present case, considering the nature of the subsequent offences in relation to the appellant's character and background as a whole, it could not be said that the bringing into effect of the suspended sentence was unjust (see p. 807, letters A to C, post).

    Appeal dismissed.

F
    [As to power of the court on conviction of further offence to deal with suspended sentence, see Supplement to 10 Halsbury's Laws (3rd Edn.), para. 922a, 2.

    For the Criminal Justice Act 1967, s. 40, see 8 Halsbury's Statutes (3rd Edn.) 606.]

    Appeal.

This was an appeal by William Thomas Griffiths against sentence. On
G
10th October 1968, he was convicted at Birmingham Sessions before the recorder (Michael Argyle, Esq., Q.C.) and a jury of dangerous driving and common assault. On 15th October 1968, he was sentenced to nine months' and three months' imprisonment respectively for these offences, the sentences to run concurrently. The recorder also ordered that a sentence of 12 months' imprisonment suspended for two years imposed on the appellant at Birmingham Sessions
H
on 5th January 1968 in respect of factorybreaking with intent should come into effect consecutive to that sentence. The appellant was also disqualified from holding a driving licence for two years in respect of the dangerous driving. The facts are set out in the judgment of the court.

    A. W. Palmer for the appellant.
    The Crown was not represented.
I

    WIDGERY, L.J., delivered the judgment of the court: The appellant was convicted of dangerous driving and common assault before the learned recorder of Birmingham on 10th October 1968. He was sentenced to concurrent terms of nine months' and three months' imprisonment respectively for those two offences, and the recorder also ordered that there should come into effect consecutive to that sentence a suspended sentence of 12 months' imprisonment

---

    * Section 40 (1), so far as material, is set out at p. 806, letter I, post.

which he had imposed on the appellant on 5th January 1968 in respect of factory- **A**
breaking with intent.   The total sentence of imprisonment, therefore, was 21
months in all.

The circumstances of the instant offences were these.   At about 10.50 p.m.
on 5th May 1968, a police constable off duty was driving in Birmingham in his
motor car and was following the appellant's car.   The police officer's evidence
was that the car was swerving across the road (by which one understands **B**
swerving on more than one occasion across the road) over a distance of about a
quarter of a mile.   It was said that, when the appellant swerved across the road,
he came on occasion within a few inches of the offside kerb, and there was some
indication that other cars coming in the opposite direction had been required
to slow down or swerve.   The police officer overtook the appellant and the two
cars stopped.   The police officer went to look at the registration number of the **C**
car and to identify the driver, and then an altercation resulted.   There was
some jostling on the pavement, and the appellant hit the officer with his clenched
fist above the right eyebrow, causing a small cut, and hit him again below the
left ear and punched him in the stomach.   Fortunately he did not do him any
great harm because the police officer was a fit man.   However, there was this
assault of, in the view of this court, quite a serious character. **D**

The appellant is 33 years of age and he has a long record of convictions, but
it is right to say at once that there is no previous offence of dangerous driving
or anything akin thereto.   There are a great many offences of housebreaking
and factorybreaking, and there are a number of cases, some of them quite serious,
of wounding or assault.   He was found guilty of assault on the police in 1957,
and again in 1958, and of wounding in 1958 and, finally, a further assault on the **E**
police in 1961.

Two submissions are made on the appellant's behalf.   First, it is said that the
term of nine months' imprisonment for the instant offences was excessive, and
counsel for the appellant's submission on this is re-inforced by the observations
of the learned single judge, who pointed out that this was a first conviction for
bad driving and said that many worse cases of dangerous driving are punished **F**
with less severity.   The court has considered this submission with care, and takes
the view that it, itself, might not have imposed a sentence of nine months'
imprisonment for the dangerous driving alone.   However, the other chapter of
this case, namely, the violence which followed, is a matter which this court
would be minded to take more seriously than did the recorder.   To be precise
about this, we feel that it might have been more appropriate if two consecutive **G**
terms had been imposed and if the term imposed in respect of the dangerous
driving had been reduced.   But, in the end, we are quite satisfied that a totality
of nine months is not excessive in regard to these offences, and we accordingly
dismiss the appeal so far as that part of the case is concerned.

One turns then to the question of whether the suspended sentence should
have been ordered to take effect in these circumstances.   Under s. 40 (1) **H**
of the Criminal Justice Act 1967, it is provided that where an offender who has
received a suspended sentence subsequently comes before the court on an offence
punishable with imprisonment, the court may take a number of alternative
courses, the first of which is to:

" (a) . . . order that the suspended sentence shall take effect with the **I**
original term unaltered; . . . and a court shall make an order under paragraph (a) of this subsection [that is, an order that the suspended sentence
should take effect with the original term unaltered] unless the court is
of opinion that it would be unjust to do so in view of all the circumstances
which have arisen since the suspended sentence was passed, including the
facts of the subsequent offence . . . "

Counsel for the appellant's submission is that, in the circumstances of this case,
it was unjust to bring the suspended sentence into effect, having regard to the

A entirely different character of the offence for which the suspended sentence was imposed and the offences now before the court.

This is, we think, the first time on which the court has had to express an opinion on this matter; and it will say at once that the facts of the subsequent offence are clearly appropriate for consideration in deciding whether the sus- pended sentence should be put into effect. Undoubtedly a court operating this

B section is entitled to look at the facts of the subsequent offence and, if it thinks right in the circumstances, to say that it would be unjust in view of the character of that offence to make the suspended sentence operative. It seems to us inappropriate to attempt at this stage to deal with the subject in more general terms, and in this case we are minded only to consider the nature of the subsequent offences in relation to the appellant's character and background as a whole.

C He was admittedly a man who had not previously been in trouble for driving, but he was a man who had been in trouble for violence. Looking at the circum- stances in the round, we have come to the conclusion that it would not be right to say that the action of the recorder was unjust. We shall, therefore, not disturb the exercise of his discretion, and the appeal is dismissed.

Appeal dismissed.

D Solicitor: *Registrar of Criminal Appeals* (for the appellant).

[*Reported by* N. P. METCALFE, ESQ., *Barrister-at-Law.*]

E ## WARD v. HERTFORDSHIRE COUNTY COUNCIL.

[QUEEN'S BENCH DIVISION (Hinchcliffe, J.), March 13, 14, 1969.]

Education—Local education authority—Negligence—Supervision—Children un- supervised before start of school—Playground with flint wall—Injury to child in course of informal play caused by flint wall.

F *Education—Local education authority—Breach of statutory duty—Boundary wall made from flintstones—Standards for School Premises Regulations 1959 (S.I. 1959 No. 890), reg. 51.*

The plaintiff, aged eight, was a pupil in a local authority primary school. The children arrived at varying times after 8.15 a.m. each morning, the

G majority coming at about 8.45 a.m. They were left without supervision in the playground until 8.55 a.m. when they were summoned into the school. The playground was surrounded by a flint wall, and while racing to this wall just before 8.55 one morning the infant plaintiff fell and struck his head against it, suffering injuries which were made more severe by the jagged nature of the flints. There had been previous accidents when

H pupils had fallen against the same wall, and the staff of the school knew that the children were accustomed to race between the flint walls of the school. It would have been possible to render the flints at a cost of between £400 and £1,000.

Held: (i) the defendant local authority should either have provided supervision of the children (not necessarily continuous before 8.45 a.m.)

I or rendered or railed off the wall; in failing to do this it was negligent and in breach of its common duty of care under the Occupiers' Liability Act 1957 (see p. 811, letters B to D and G, post);

(ii) it was not liable under reg. 51 of the Standards for School Premises Regulations 1959 because the boundary wall was not part of the building for the purposes of those regulations (see p. 811, letter E, post).

[As to the liabilitity of education authorities for accidents to pupils, see 13 HALSBURY'S LAWS (3rd Edn.) 621-625, paras. 1294-1298; and for cases on the subject, see 19 DIGEST (Repl.) 612-618, *120-140.*]

Case referred to: A

  Reffell v. *Surrey County Council*, [1964] 1 All E.R. 743; [1964] 1 W.L.R. 358;
      128 J.P. 261; Digest (Cont. Vol. B) 235, *121a*.

Action.

This was an action by Timothy Roy Ward, an infant suing by his father and
next friend, Roy Frederick Ward, claiming damages from Hertfordshire County
Council for negligence and for breach of statutory duty under reg. 51 of the   B
Standards for School Premises Regulations 1959 and under the Occupiers'
Liability Act 1957. The facts are set out in the judgment.

  C. W. G. Ross-Munro for the infant plaintiff.
  J. C. Griffiths for the defendant.

      HINCHCLIFFE, J.: In this action the infant plaintiff by his father claims   C
damages for personal injuries as a result of an accident he sustained on 29th
April 1966, when he was attending the Sarratt Primary School in the county of
Hertford.   On the day in question the infant plaintiff injured himself against a
flint wall when he and other pupils were running a race in the playground of the
school.   It is alleged on behalf of the infant plaintiff that his accident was
caused by the defendant's breach of statutory duty in connection with the   D
flint wall itself, and by the negligence of the defendant in failing to provide
proper supervision; in not having the wall demolished having regard to previous
accidents; and in failing to instruct or warn the infant plaintiff not to play
near the wall.   The defendant by its defence admits that the infant plaintiff
fell against the wall after he had tripped whilst crossing the playground, but it
denies that it was guilty of the alleged or any breach of statutory duty or   E
negligence.

      It is common ground that the infant plaintiff at the time of the accident was
eight years of age.   Most of the pupils arrived at the school at about 8.45 a.m.
and they were left to play in the playground without supervision until 8.55 a.m.,
when they were summoned into the school by a bell or a whistle.   The wall
surrounding the playground was made of flints and brick pillars with a brick   F
coping on the top.   Some agreed photographs have been put before the court.
In the grey bundle, there are four photographs.   Number one is a view of the wall
against which the infant plaintiff fell.   The actual place where the infant plaintiff
had his accident is to the left and is outside the picture.   The second photograph
shows a close-up view of an area of the wall, in the centre of which a brick pillar
can be seen, and on each side of it there can be seen many pieces of flint. Photo-   G
graph number three is a closer view.   The arrows on that photograph indicate
where it is alleged the flints were particularly prominent, jutting out for one inch
to one and a quarter inches.   Photograph number four is another close-up view of
the wall with two points marked where the flints jut out. The average height of the
wall is three feet six inches.   There are two other photographs which have been
agreed; they are larger in size.   Photograph number one shows the wall in   H
question and photograph number two gives a good idea of the composition of
the wall.

      It is not in dispute that the infant plaintiff and his mother arrived at about
8.50 on the morning of the accident.   The infant plaintiff and his friends decided
to have a race from wall to wall.   When this race was nearly over, and when
the infant plaintiff was in the lead, he stumbled and his head crashed into one
of the flints of the wall inflicting on him a serious injury.   There had been   I
three previous instances where pupils fell or ran into the same wall and sustained
injuries for which they were treated by a school teacher.   And on 14th February
1968 the infant plaintiff's sister, Sarah, stumbled when skipping and hit the back
of her head against the wall.

      The infant plaintiff gave evidence: he described the accident much as I have
stated it and his evidence was not in any way challenged.   Mrs. Ward explained
that she took both her children to school most days of the week: she said she

A never saw anyone supervising the pupils in the playground: and after the accident she saw that the infant plaintiff had sustained a long jagged cut over the right eye which was two inches long. Mr. Ward, a nurseryman, saw the infant plaintiff's wound in hospital; he described it as long, jagged and frightening. It appeared to Mr. Ward that the infant plaintiff had come up against a protruding part of the wall and had struck himself against a very jagged piece

B of flint. Mr. Ward said that nothing had been done to the wall since the accident. This is admitted by the defendant.

Young Godman, aged seven or eight, gave evidence. He was one of the boys who arrive at 8.15 a.m. and he played in the playground until the school started at 9 a.m. For the most part, the majority of pupils would arrive at about 8.45 a.m., many of them came by bus which reached the school at about

C that time. The little girl, Sarah Ward, gave evidence; she is a bright little girl if ever there was one. It was in February of 1968 when she tripped over a skipping rope held by two other girls. Possibly they pulled it tight at an awkward moment. At any rate, she fell sideways and cut open the back of her head on this selfsame flint wall.

Mr. Bidderstaff, Mr. Parker, and Mr. Styles were former pupils of the school.

D Each one of them had been injured, when they tripped, fell, or ran against the wall. Mr. Bidderstaff's accident was in 1935; the other two accidents were in 1954 or 1955. It is right that I should mention that Mr. Bidderstaff injured his forehead by coming into contact with the facings of the wall at the top. Mr. Parker and Mr. Styles were injured by sharp flints in the wall.

The only other witness who gave evidence on behalf of the infant plaintiff

E was Mr. Stanton, a consulting engineer, who described the flints on the whole as being broken ones—many of them had jagged edges and knife-like ridges. The spurs, as he called them, protruded from three-quarters of an inch to one inch. Some of them were very sharp indeed and some of them were rounded. Mr. Stanton expressed the view that if the wall had been rendered and made smooth the severity of injury would be materially decreased.

F The whole length of the wall shown in the photographs is 84 feet; the wall opposite to it is 104 feet long, and it was between the two walls that the race was taking place. Opposite the school building there is another shorter length of wall 26 feet long. All the walls are made of flint. Mr. Stanton thought that there would be no difficulty in rendering the walls and making them smooth for about £400. He regarded it as a perfectly straightforward task.

G On behalf of the defendant, Mr. Edgar Stephens, a chartered architect, gave evidence. He explained to the court that there is much flint in this village; that he would not like to see these walls rendered, not only because aesthetically it would not be right, but also because problems would arise in making the walls waterproof. He did, however, agree that there was a good bonding agent on the market known as " PBA ", which is waterproof. He recognised that the

H job could be done, but he thought that it would cost just under £1,000.

Counsel for the infant plaintiff put one or two questions to Mr. Stephens in his capacity as a father, and Mr. Stephens agreed that boys between five and 11 tend to play roughly; that it was normal for them to run races between walls; that it was foreseeable that they might well come into contact with one of the walls. He was not surprised to hear of the three previous accidents, nor was he surprised

I to hear of the infant plaintiff's accident. Mr. Stephens said that a wall with a smooth surface in a children's playground, in his opinion, would be less dangerous.

Mr. Robert Tawell, a chartered surveyor in the full-time employment of the defendant, told the court that this type of wall was not unusual; that in the area there were sixteen other schools which catered for children up to 11 years of age. He thought that this school would be about 110 years old and that it was coming to the end of its life. He thought that the walls surrounding the playground were marginally more dangerous than many brick walls, yet he

said there were walls throughout the country in Yorkshire, in Wales and in   A
Kent, which he felt would carry a similar risk. Mr. Tawell did not think that it
was satisfactory to render the walls of the school building up to four feet six
inches because there would be difficulty in waterproofing. When Mr. Tawell
was sent to inspect the schools soon after the accident to the infant plaintiff
had taken place, he did not know that there had been any previous accidents;
indeed he had been told that there had been none. Six of the other 16 schools   B
have flint walls around the playgrounds, all the walls are comprised of whole
flints and of broken flints. Mr. Tawell did not think that this wall was an undue
hazard although he did not know of the three previous accidents. No one has
tried to render the wall or do anything at all about it since the infant plaintiff's
accident.

The only other witness called on behalf of the defendant was Mr. Kenneth   C
Green. He has been the headmaster of the school since 1955. He has been a
schoolmaster for 23 years. He told the court that up to 8.55 a.m. there was no
supervision in the playground of any sort or kind. The children assembled in
the playground from 8.30 a.m. onwards when some buses arrived, others arriving
at 8.45 a.m. There were fifty children in the school which is run by Mr. Green
and two assistant teachers. There are three breaks during the day, and in each   D
one the playground is supervised with the object of seeing that the children are
not in danger. As I have already stated, there is no supervision before school
starts, and the children are allowed to play in the playground. Mr. Green had no
knowledge of the accident to Mr. Bidderstaff or to Mr. Parker, but he was present
when Mr. Styles had his accident. Mr. Green thought he had broken half a tooth
on the top part of the wall. Mr. Green expressed the view that the wall was   E
safe; he knows that children do race one another between the walls and he agreed
that sometimes there was a risk of them being tripped or stumbling, or indeed,
of being pushed. He had told children not to be silly and to keep clear of the
wall.

It is on this evidence that the court has to determine whether the defendant
was in breach of any statutory duty or common law duty which caused, or con-   F
tributed, to the infant plaintiff's accident. I have no hesitation at all in finding
on the facts of this case that the defendant was guilty of a breach of its common
law duty, and that such breach of duty caused the infant plaintiff's injury.
The court is indebted to both learned counsel appearing in this case for their
most helpful submissions on the law and on the facts, but I find the position
to be as follows—   G

Before 8.55 a.m. children aged between five and 11 are let loose in this playground without any supervision. Games are played, some of them are rough,
some of them are not so rough; they certainly include running races between
these flint walls. This is known to the school teachers who supervise the pupils
during the morning, the midday, and the afternoon breaks. Around this playground are flint walls in which there are many broken flints with sharp, jagged   H
edges which protrude $\frac{3}{4}$ of an inch to one inch from the wall itself. I am satisfied
that it was on one of these very sharp flints that the infant plaintiff sustained
so severe a cut or laceration that he fractured his skull. His sister Sarah, aged
six or seven, fell on to one of these flints and had the back of her head split open,
and three men sustained injury by coming into contact with the wall when
they were pupils of the school. Two of them were injured by sharp flints.   I
Mr. Bidderstaff bruised his forehead by coming into contact with the top of the
wall, and as counsel for the infant plaintiff points out, this gives a clear indication as to the sort of injury that a person is likely to receive if his head comes
in contact with a smooth wall rather than one with the jagged and sharp flints
in it.

It seems to me that if one lets loose young children in a playground of this
sort with inherently dangerous walls around it, one is simply asking for trouble.
If it is thought necessary to supervise children at 10.45 a.m., midday and 2.30

A p.m. surely it is just as necessary to supervise them between 8.30 a.m. or 8.45 a.m. and 8.55 a.m., and if there had been supervision, I have no doubt that a teacher would and should have stopped racing between these flint walls, having regard to the risk of a stumble, a push, or even a failure to stop. In the circumstances the risk of an accident such as this was a reasonably foreseeable risk against which the defendant could, and should, have guarded, either by **B** rendering the wall or by putting up some railings, or by putting up netting—the rendering or the railings, or netting, would not cost more than £400; or if they were not minded to do that, then all they had to do was to see to it that there was proper supervision—supervision during the time when a collection of children are in the playground before the start of school.

In my judgment, a prudent parent of a large family would have realised that **C** this playground, with its flint walls and sharp and jagged flints protruding, was inherently dangerous. In my judgment reasonable supervision was required, not only during the working day, but also when the children were collected together in the playground before the school starts. I do not suggest that there should necessarily be a continuous supervision from 8.15 a.m. onwards, but there should have been supervision from time to time controlling any risky activity **D** of the children having regard to the proximity of this dangerous wall; and really it is not too much to ask that there should be supervision between 8.30 a.m. or 8.45 a.m. and 8.55 a.m. when the supervision might well have been continuous. I am bound to say that I take the view that these sharp and protruding flints in a playground are much, much more dangerous than smooth walls, or walls that are to be found in the north of England, in Kent, or in the Cotswolds.

E The infant plaintiff has not established, to my satisfaction, that the defendant was in breach of reg. 51 of the Standards for School Premises Regulations 1959 (1); I accept the submission made by counsel for the defendant, that this case does not really fall within reg. 51, because the accident took place on a boundary wall and the boundary wall cannot be said to be part of the building. That seems to me to be a submission that is right in law; and is one full of common sense. **F** I take the view that this regulation relates to a building in the conventional sense and that it is the occupants of the building whose safety is being considered. If I had thought that these walls fell within the ambit of the regulation, then I would agree with VEALE, J., who held in *Reffell* v. *Surrey County Council* (2), that an absolute statutory duty is created.

Was the defendant in breach of its statutory duty under the Occupiers' **G** Liability Act 1957 to see that the children would be reasonably safe in using the premises for the purpose for which they were there? Well, the duty under this Act is really the common law duty: it is to take reasonable care for the safety of the children. It is to take such care for its pupils as a reasonably careful father would take with a large family in relation to his own children. In the circumstances of this case and for the reasons I have given, I have come to the **H** conclusion that the defendant was in breach of its common law duty and that such breach of duty caused the infant plaintiff's injuries.

Judgment for the infant plaintiff for £950.

Solicitors: *Church, Adams, Tatham & Co.* (for the infant plaintiff); *Berrymans* (for the defendant).

[*Reported by* MARY COLTON, *Barrister-at-Law.*]

I

---

(1) S.I. 1959 No. 890.
(2) [1964] 1 All E.R. 743; [1964] 1 W.L.R. 358.

A

BERLEI (U.K.), LTD. *v.* BALI BRASSIERE CO., INC.

[HOUSE OF LORDS (Lord Morris of Borth-y-Gest, Lord Guest, Lord Upjohn, Lord Wilberforce and Lord Pearson), March 3, 4, 5, 6, 10, May 6, 1969.]

Trade Mark—Registration—Rectification—Mark " by reason of its being likely to deceive or cause confusion . . . disentitled to protection in a court of justice " B *—Phonetic similarity to mark already in use—Application for removal from register more than seven years after registration—What must be established to show mark disentitled to protection—Discretion to remove registration— Trade Marks Act 1938 (1 & 2 Geo. 6 c. 22), s. 11, s. 32.*

Berlei were the owners of a trade mark " Berlei ", first registered in 1924, which had been continuously and extensively used by them since 1930 in   C respect of the manufacture of brassieres, corsets and corselettes. Bali, an American company, applied in 1959 for registration of the word " Bali " in respect of brassieres, corsets and corselettes. They had since 1938 held for these goods a registration of a device consisting of the word " Bali " in script form within a circle having underneath it the word " Bra ", and in addition above the word " Bali " a small silhouette of a woman. Berlei   D immediately gave notice of opposition to the application for registration on the ground that the name " Bali " so closely resembled their mark that its use would be likely to deceive or cause confusion. They subsequently applied for rectification of the register by the removal from it of the earlier " Bali " registration. It was not disputed that Berlei had continuously used their mark since 1930, and that sales of Bali's goods had been on a small   E scale in this country until the outbreak of war in 1939 and had then ceased altogether until 1962. " Berlei " was usually pronounced as if it had been spelt " Berly "; " Bali ", either as if spelt " Bahli " or as if spelt " Bally ". By s. 11* of the Trade Marks Act 1938, it is not lawful to register as a trade mark any matter the use of which would, by reason of its being likely to deceive or cause confusion or otherwise, be disentitled to protection in a   F court of justice. It was agreed that so far as the rectification proceedings were concerned, the proper time for testing whether s. 11 was contravened was the date of application for registration of the " Bali " mark in 1938. Evidence was adduced both of confusion between the two brands in actual trading, and of the lack of it. The Assistant Comptroller of Trade Marks acting for the registrar found in favour of Berlei in both proceedings. On   G appeal to the High Court, UNGOED-THOMAS, J., upheld both decisions. On further appeal, the Court of Appeal, by a majority, reversed the earlier decisions. On appeal from that decision (the case having been argued on the rectification proceeding only, it having been agreed that if Berlei succeeded on that, it would also succeed on the other),

Held: (i) there was evidence, notably the phonetic similarity of the two   H marks, on which the comptroller and the judge could quite properly have held, pursuant to s. 11 of the Act, that the use of the mark " Bali " would, in 1938, by reason of its being likely to deceive or cause confusion, have been disentitled to protection in a court of justice; there was thus a proper basis on which the comptroller and the judge could exercise the discretion under s. 32 of the Act to rectify the register; that exercise of discretion   I would, therefore, not be disturbed.

(ii) it was not necessary in order to establish that the Bali mark was disentitled to protection in a court of justice, for Berlei to show that it had a reasonable chance of success against Bali in a passing-off action.

Dictum of BUCKLEY, J., in *Transfermatic Trade Mark* ([1966] R.P.C. at p. 579) considered.

---

* Section 11 is set out at p. 815, letter G, post.

A   Observations on the meaning of " disentitled to protection in a court of justice " as occurring in s. 11 of the Act.

Appeal allowed.

[As to prohibitions on registration, see 38 HALSBURY'S LAWS (3rd Edn.) 542-546, para. 903-908; and for cases on the subject, see 46 DIGEST (Repl.) 40-44, *201-235.*

B   For the Trade Marks Act 1938, s. 11, s. 32, s. 54, see 25 HALSBURY'S STATUTES (2nd Edn.) 1189, 1210, 1222.]

Cases referred to:

Aristoc, Ltd. v. *Rysta, Ltd.*, [1945] 1 All E.R. 34; [1945] A.C. 68; 114 L.J.Ch. 52; 172 L.T. 69; 62 R.P.C. 65; 46 Digest (Repl.) 6, *7.*

C   *Bass, Ratcliffe and Gretton, Ltd.* v. *Nicholson & Sons, Ltd.*, [1932] A.C. 130; 101 L.J.Ch. 98; 49 R.P.C. 88; sub nom. *Re Nicholson & Son's Application for Registration of Trade Mark, Re Bass, Ratcliffe and Gretton's Trade Mark,* 146 L.T. 349; *affg,* [1931] 2 Ch. 1; 48 R.P.C. 227; 46 Digest (Repl.) 67, *368.*

Eno v. *Dunn* (1890), 15 App. Cas. 252; 63 L.T. 6; 7 R.P.C. 311; 46 Digest (Repl.) 46, *251.*

D   *Hack's Application, Re* (1940), 58 R.P.C. 91; 46 Digest (Repl.) 52, *280.*

Hall v. *Barrows* (1863), 32 L.J.Ch. 548; *on appeal,* 4 De G.J. & Sm. 150; 33 L.J.Ch. 204; 9 L.T. 561; 28 J.P. 148; 46 E.R. 873; 46 Digest (Repl.) 125, *757.*

Jellinek's Application, Re (1946), 63 R.P.C. 59; 46 Digest (Repl.) 52, *281.*

E   *M'Andrew* v. *Bassett* (1864), 4 De G.J. & Sm. 380; 33 L.J.Ch. 561; 10 L.T. 442; 46 E.R. 965; 46 Digest (Repl.) 218, *1433.*

McDowell v. *Standard Oil Co. (New Jersey),* [1927] A.C. 632; 96 L.J.Ch. 386; 137 L.T. 734, sub nom. *Re McDowell's Application,* 44 R.P.C. 335; *affg,* 43 R.P.C. 313; 46 Digest (Repl.) 59, *331.*

Peddie's Applications, Re (1943), 61 R.P.C. 31; 46 Digest (Repl.) 130, *792.*

F   *Pidding* v. *How* (1837), 8 Sim. 477; 6 L.J.Ch. 345; 59 E.R. 190; 46 Digest (Repl.) 292, *1927.*

Pianotist Co.'s Application, Re (1906), 23 R.P.C. 774; 46 Digest (Repl.) 63, *347.*

Pirie (Alexander) & Sons, Ltd.'s Application, [1933] All E.R. Rep. 956; 149 L.T. 199; 50 R.P.C. 147; 46 Digest (Repl.) 91, *525.*

G   *Richards* v. *Butcher,* [1891] 2 Ch. 522; 63 L.T. 757; *affd.,* [1891] 2 Ch. at p. 540; 60 L.J.Ch. 530; 8 R.P.C. 249; 46 Digest (Repl.) 75, *418,* 77, *430.*

Rysta, Ltd., Re an application by, [1943] 1 All E.R. 400; 60 R.P.C. 87.

Smith Hayden & Co., Ltd.'s Application, Re (1945), 63 R.P.C. 97; 46 Digest (Repl.) 67, *371.*

Société des Usines Chimiques Rhône-Poulenc, Re the application of, Re Trade Mark " Livron " of Boots Pure Drug Co., Ltd., [1937] 4 All E.R. 23; 106 L.J.Ch. 352; 157 L.T. 225; 54 R.P.C. 327; sub nom., *Re Registered Trade Mark No. 530, 535 of Boots Pure Drug Co., Ltd.,* [1938] Ch. 54; 46 Digest (Repl.) 10, *22.*

H   *Transfermatic Trade Mark,* [1966] R.P.C. 568; Digest (Repl.) Supp.

Appeal.

I   This was an appeal by Berlei (U.K.), Ltd., from an order of the Court of Appeal (LORD DENNING, M.R., and SALMON, L.J.; DIPLOCK, L.J., dissenting) dated 8th December 1967 allowing the appeal of Bali Brassiere Co., Inc., from the order of UNGOED-THOMAS, J., dated 19th July 1966 who upheld the decisions of the Assistant Comptroller of Trade Marks acting for the Registrar, dated 23rd March 1964, whereby he refused the application of Bali for registration of the trade mark " Bali " on the opposition thereto by Berlei, the owners of the trade mark " Berlei ", and ordered that the trade mark no. 603,390 registered in the name of Bali be removed from the Register of Trade Marks on the application for

rectification by Berlei. The facts are set out in the opinion of LORD MORRIS **A**
OF BORTH-Y-GEST.

D. W. Falconer, Q.C., and *J. Jeffs* for Berlei.
J. N. K. Whitford, Q.C., and *J. Burrell* for Bali.

6th May 1969. The following opinions were delivered.

B

LORD MORRIS OF BORTH-Y-GEST: My Lords, the question which
arose in this case was whether it was permissible for a company to use the word
" Bali " in reference to their goods although another company in reference to
similar goods were already using the word " Berlei ".

The appellant company (whom I will call Berlei) are engaged, and have for many
years been engaged, in the business of manufacturers of brassieres, corsets, corsel- **C**
ettes and other women's foundation garments. They have a trade mark, Berlei,
which they have since 1930 continuously and extensively used in their business
and on and in relation to their goods. They have two registrations for their
trade mark, namely, (*a*) BERLEI (word in block capitals) registered as from
6th May 1924, under no. 448,103 in Class 38 (Sch. III) in respect of " Corsets
and Brassieres " and transferred to them in 1930 and, (*b*) Berlei (word in script **D**
form) registered as from 30th July 1954, under no. 732,676 in Class 25 (Sch. IV)
in respect of " Corsets, corselettes, girdles (corsets), brassieres, bodices, panties
and suspender belts ".

The respondent company, an American company (whom I will call Bali),
are the proprietors of trade mark no. 603,390 registered as from 23rd December
1938, in respect of " brassieres, corsets and corselettes ". The mark is a device **E**
mark consisting of the word " Bali " in script form within a circle, having underneath it in small letters the word " Bra " and having a small silhouette of a
woman above the word " Bali ". If the mark is used in this country the goods in
respect of which it is used will inevitably come to be referred to by the word
" Bali ". The word is the main feature of the registered mark. Berlei did not
know of the existence of that mark. Though Bali had effected some sales in this **F**
country in the years between 1935 and 1939 there were none between 1939 and
1962.

On 1st May 1959, Bali applied (the application being numbered 790,389) for
registration of a trade mark, consisting solely of the word " Bali ", in Class 25
in respect of " Brassieres, corsets and corselettes ". It was then that Berlei first
came to know of the mark which Bali had registered in 1938. Berlei then took **G**
the following steps. On 6th May 1960, they gave notice of opposition to the
application of Bali. They sought refusal of Bali's application on the ground that
the mark " Bali " so closely resembles their mark " Berlei " that its use on or in
relation to any brassieres, corsets or corselettes would be likely to deceive or
cause confusion. They relied on s. 11 and s. 12 (1) of the Trade Marks Act 1938,
and further contended that in the exercise of his discretion the registrar ought **H**
not to allow registration. Then on 13th May 1960, they applied to the registrar
for rectification of the register by the removal from it of Bali's registered trade
mark no. 603,390 to which I have already referred. The application was made
in dependence on s. 32 and also s. 26 of the Trade Marks Act 1938. Berlei relied
on their use of their mark " Berlei " from the year 1930 onwards. As persons
aggrieved they sought the removal of Bali's mark on the ground that the word **I**
" Bali " so closely resembles the word " Berlei " that use in relation to brassieres,
corsets or corselettes would be likely to deceive or cause confusion and that the
trade mark " Bali " offended against the provisions of s. 11 of the Act and ought
never to have been registered. The separate ground on which they sought the
removal was (under s. 26) that of non-use. It was not disputed that Berlei was a
" person aggrieved " and as such entitled to make application to have the
register rectified.

The Assistant Comptroller of Trade Marks acting for the registrar found

A in favour of Berlei in both proceedings.   He refused to allow application no.
790,389 to proceed.   He ordered that trade mark no. 603,390 should be removed
from the register.   He so ordered both on the ground that, having regard to the
provisions of s. 11, the mark ought not to have been registered and also on the
ground of non-use under the provisions of s. 26.   His decisions in both proceedings
were given on 23rd March 1964.

B   On appeal to the High Court application was made by Bali (on 22nd July
1964) to adduce further evidence by affidavit.   As the proposed further evidence
was not then available the application was adjourned.   After copies of the desired
further evidence had been supplied by Bali the hearing was resumed and for the
reasons set out by the learned judge (UNGOED-THOMAS, J.) in his decision given
on 3rd December 1965, the application was granted.   No challenge to that decision
C to adduce further evidence has been made.   After considering the additional
evidence the learned judge upheld both decisions of the assistant comptroller
although in doing so he rejected that part of Berlei's case in the rectification
proceedings which was based on the contention of non-use.   He held that the non-
use was due to special circumstances in the trade.   That part of his decision
was not challenged by Berlei when Bali appealed to the Court of Appeal.   At the
D hearing before the learned judge the argument on behalf of Bali was presented
in reference to the rectification proceedings, it being considered that if Bali could
not succeed in their appeal in the rectification proceedings they could not
succeed in their appeal in the opposition proceedings.   On appeal to the
Court of Appeal that court by a majority (LORD DENNING, M.R., and SALMON,
L.J.; DIPLOCK, L.J., dissenting) allowed the appeal.   It was ordered that the
E registrar should accept and register Bali's application no. 790,389 and that
Bali's registered trade mark no. 603,390 should remain on the register.

      The considerations which apply in the rectification proceedings are different
from those which apply in the opposition proceedings.   Bali's registration (no.
603,390) of their mark was on 23rd December 1938.   Section 46 of the Act provides that in all legal proceedings relating to a registered trade mark (including
F applications under s. 32) the fact that a person is registered as proprietor of the
trade mark is prima facie evidence of the validity of the original registration.
Section 13 provides that a registration in Part A is, after the expiration of seven
years from the date of registration, to be " taken to be valid in all respects "
unless the registration was obtained by fraud or unless " the trade mark offends
against the provisions of section 11 " of the Act.   Section 11 is in these terms:

G   " It shall not be lawful to register as a trade mark or part of a trade mark
      any matter the use of which would, by reason of its being likely to deceive or
      cause confusion or otherwise, be disentitled to protection in a court of justice,
      or would be contrary to law or morality, or any scandalous design."

      If there is an appeal from a decision of the registrar the High Court has power to
H review any decision and " shall have and exercise " the same discretionary
powers as under the Act are conferred on the registrar (see s. 51, s. 52 and s. 68).

      It is clear that in the rectification proceedings the onus was on Berlei.   Bali's
mark (of 1938) had been registered over seven years.   There was no suggestion
that the mark had been obtained by fraud.   It was, therefore, to be taken to be
valid in all respects unless it could be shown that it " offends against the pro-
I visions " of s. 11.   We were invited by both parties to approach the case on the
basis that the enquiry which was involved was whether the registration of their
mark by Bali in 1938 was then correctly made.   Was it in 1938 a mark which
(having regard to s. 11) it was not " lawful to register "?   In inviting us so to
approach the case both parties agreed, however, that evidence tending either to
prove or to disprove deception or confusion in much later periods did not become
irrelevant.   Evidence whether deception or confusion did or did not in fact exist
in the period between 1938 and the hearings could be important evidence in regard
to the question whether in 1938 there was a likelihood of deception or confusion.

On behalf of Berlei the submission was made that there was such a likelihood **A**
and that it had not varied as between the year 1938 and the years in the later
period.   In the application to register proceedings the onus was on Bali.   The
opposition of Berlei was not based only on the provisions of s. 11; those of s. 12
were also invoked.

Although there was separate evidence (none of which was given orally) in
the separate proceedings much of the evidence was common to both proceedings. **B**
Berlei have continuously used their mark since the year 1930; they have used it
in script and other forms; the use has since then been extensive though no
figures are available to show how extensive.   There was evidence which showed
that the mark was used in trade advertising in this country between March
1936 and September 1938.

Bali, an American company, have had their present name since 1940. Previously **C**
and in the years after incorporation in 1932 the company was called Fay-Miss
Brassiere Co., Inc.   The mark " Bali " was adopted by the company in the
United States of America in 1935.   From that year until the outbreak of war in
1939 there were some sales in this country of " Bali " brassieres which were
imported from America.   At this distance of time it is perhaps not surprising that
it has not been possible to name more than one of the retail stores at which sales **D**
took place.   The extent of the sales is not known.   The sales were on a small scale
and were not sufficiently extensive to make Berlei aware that there were any.
As a result of the outbreak of war the importation of Bali's goods came to an end.
None were thereafter imported until 1962.   Though for many years before that
year there was a token import scheme it was stated by Bali that the labour
of applying for an import licence for what would have been a purely nominal **E**
quantity of Bali goods was not undertaken since their pre-war importations had
been "admittedly on a small scale ".   Precise evidence was, therefore, not available to show how sales with the mark " Bali " in the years 1935 to 1939 compared
in extent with sales with the mark " Berlei " in the same period.   Sales in this
country of goods with the mark " Bali " were resumed in 1962 (the two sets of legal
proceedings having been begun in May 1960).   All recent sales have, therefore, **F**
been in the years during which the proceedings have been making their all
too tardy progress.

There was little if any contest as to the manner in which sales of women's
foundation garments are normally effected.   The evidence showed that they
are widely stocked and sold in all parts of the country in different types of shops.
These include shops specialising in and selling only such garments, shops selling **G**
women's and girls' wear, as well as drapery shops and departmental stores.   The
great majority of such garments are sold retail across the counter in response
to spoken requests.   Often there are enquiries and orders by telephone both from
traders and from members of the public.   There was furthermore little if any
divergence revealed by the evidence as to the manner of pronunciation of the
respective words.   Though naturally there were variations, it was stated that the **H**
mark " Berlei " is usually pronounced as if spelt Berly, i.e., with a short " i "
sound at the end as in " early ".   Among the variations are " Barely " and
" Berlye ".   The mark " Bali " is, when spoken, very similar phonetically.
" Bali " may be pronounced with a long " a " sound (as if spelt Bahli) or with a
short " a " sound (as in rally).

There was evidence (in a statutory declaration of 26th October 1963) of a lady **I**
who in October 1963, made visits to a number of well-known retail establishments.
In most of those which she visited only Berlei brassieres were stocked.   In those
she asked for a " Bali " brassiere and she was promptly given a " Berlei " brassiere.
In her requests she used the pronunciation " Bahl-ee " which was said to be the
usual southern pronunication of " barley " when the " r " is not sounded.
In other cases when she asked for a " Bali " brassiere there was confusion on the
part of the shop assistant but no sale.   In other cases (where there were displays of
" Bali " brassieres) the requests that were made were for " Berlei " brassieres

A and in those instances the articles asked for were supplied without any confusion. The declarant (Mrs. Lamb) was tendered for cross-examination but there was no desire to challenge her testimony.

The conclusion reached by the assistant comptroller was that the two words " Berlei " and " Bali " were sufficiently similar to make oral confusion possible in a substantial number of cases. Although he considered that a comparison of

B the two marks showed that there was some degree of visual resemblance it was on the phonetic aspect that he concluded that there was the greatest possibility of confusion. He held that Berlei had established their case both under s. 11 as well as on the ground of non-use.

The additional evidence which the learned judge received consisted, in the first place, of affidavits from Bali's sales representative in regard to sales of " Bali "

C brassieres in the period since October 1962, and, in the second place, of affidavits from a number of buyers or managers of corsetry departments in departmental stores (mostly in London) and from other persons with knowledge of sales. In general the latter evidence was to the effect that the persons concerned had for some years known of the two marks (Berlei and Bali) and had neither themselves been confused between the two nor been informed of or made aware of cases

D where customers had been confused. The learned judge considered that such evidence should be treated with caution. In that approach he had in mind the guidance given in many cases. Thus in *Re an application by Rysta, Ltd.*, Luxmoore, L.J., (1) expressed the view that—

" . . . obviously a person who is familiar with both words will neither be deceived nor confused. It is the person who only knows the one word, and

E has perhaps an imperfect recollection of it who is likely to be deceived or confused."

He pointed out also that the court should allow for imperfect recollection and the effect of careless speech pronunciation not only on the part of purchasers but also of shop assistants. So also in *Re Peddie's Applications* (2) it was said that all surrounding circumstances must be considered in comparing two words and that

F the words must be considered—

" . . . not merely when they are placed side by side, but from the viewpoint of a person who may have seen or heard of one of the marks and then, with a more or less imperfect recollection of that mark, comes across the other."

The learned judge after examining all the evidence held that it supported the

G conclusion (which was prima facie suggested by the pronunciation of the two words themselves) that in 1938 the trade mark " Bali " by reason of its resemblance to the trade mark " Berlei " if used in a normal and fair manner was likely to deceive or cause confusion amongst a substantial number of persons and for that reason would be disentitled to protection in a court of justice. He came to the conclusion on the evidence that in 1938 the name " Berlei " had acquired a

H substantial reputation as denoting Berlei's goods whereas the name " Bali " had not acquired any significant reputation. He considered whether, in spite of his view that the mark " Bali " ought not to have been registered in 1938, he should, in the exercise of his discretion, decline to rectify the register; having examined certain features of the case, and in particular three suggested grounds for the exercise of his discretion, he decided that the register should be rectified.

I My Lords, I see no reason to differ from the conclusions of the learned judge and I do not think that there was any error in his approach. The reasons which prompted the majority in the Court of Appeal to take a different view may be summarised as follows: That the evidence had not established actual deception or confusion and was not sufficiently weighty to establish the likelihood of deception or confusion; that the learned judge had exercised his discretion without

(1) [1943] 1 All E.R. 400 at p. 407; 60 R.P.C. 87 at p. 108.
(2) (1943), 61 R.P.C. 31 at p. 33.

paying regard to all that had happened since May 1960, during which period **A**
Bali had built up a substantial trade, that the evidence did not prove that any
person had been confused to the detriment of Berlei or so that Berlei had suffered
injury, that it would now be unfair if Bali could not use their mark, that the new
mark should be registered because, having regard to the trade evidence from the
department stores, the name " Bali " was not likely to deceive or cause confusion,
that even if it were, its registration might be permitted under or having regard to **B**
s. 12 (2), that the earlier mark of Bali, the principal feature of which was the
word " Bali ", had been on the register for nearly 30 years, that because of
differences between the respective goods (including any differences in method of
manufacture, style and price) the likelihood of confusion is now minimal.

So far as the issues of fact were concerned I do not consider that there were
adequate reasons for differing from the conclusions of the learned judge. He **C**
applied his mind to the question whether in 1938 the use of the word " Bali "
would by reason of its being likely to deceive or cause confusion be disentitled
to protection in a court of justice. He did not ignore any of the evidence in relation to later years which could assist in determining the question which he had
to decide. He gave due weight to the new evidence which he admitted, i.e., the
so-called " trade " evidence, and he applied proper and realistic tests in analysing **D**
it. In regard to the future, if Bali are not to be allowed to use the mark " Bali "
there is no reason for saying that the public must be denied the opportunity of
purchasing Bali's goods. There will be every permissible scope for devising some
new distinctive mark. Though the evidence of actual deception or confusion
may not have been either voluminous or particularly cogent it was such as to
re-inforce and emphasise the conclusion that deception or confusion was likely. **E**
That the evidence did not positively prove that there had been cases where
detriment or financial loss had actually been caused to Berlei was immaterial.
What has to be considered is whether there is a likelihood of deception or of
confusion in the mind of the public. If there is, then there may be, but need
not necessarily be, some resulting injury to one manufacturer or resulting gain
to another. **F**

There is no reason to suppose that the learned judge did not remain mindful
of such evidence as pointed to certain differences (such as those of method of
manufacture and of style and of price) which existed between the articles respectively manufactured. Thus, there was evidence that the Bali brassieres are at
present tailor-made and might be regarded as of different quality from those
which are mass produced by Berlei. There is a difference in the colours of the **G**
packages in which the respective goods are marketed. But methods of manufacture and style of product may change from time to time and prices may vary
and be adjusted. What has to be had in mind is the use that could reasonably
and properly be made of a mark if fairly and normally used. Thus, in *Re the
Application of Société des Usines Chimiques Rhône-Poulenc, Re Trade Mark,
" Livron ", of Boots Pure Drug Co., Ltd.* (3), it was said that what has to be **H**
considered is whether ". . . the use of the mark would have been calculated to
deceive ".

In their application for registration Bali did not rely on the provisions of
s. 12 (2). The only possible materiality in this case of those provisions would be
in reference to the exercise of discretion under s. 32. It is clear that the learned
judge applied his mind to the question of his discretion under s. 32. At the **I**
hearing before him there were three specific reasons suggested on behalf of Bali
why discretion should be exercised against ordering the rectification of the
register. One was that the Bali mark had by then been registered for over 25
years. Another was that Bali were not to be blamed for the long period of non-
use by them of their mark because such non-use was the result of import restrictions. Another was that it was not shown that the trade of Berlei had suffered

---

(3) [1937] 4 All E.R. 23 at p. 30; 54 R.P.C. 327 at p. **336.**

A damage. All these matters were considered. As to the last of them the learned judge had it well in mind that it was not essential for Berlei to prove actual damage. Indeed, he pointed out that the long period of non-use (which was from 1939 to 1962) would naturally bring it about that in that period no damage could have resulted. If it were necessary to prove damage it is probable that the volume of trading of Bali between 1935 and 1939 was not such as to cause

B any known damage and that any present or future damage will be the result of trading which began about two years after the present proceedings were commenced.

In regard to the exercise of discretion it was contended that the trade marks "Bali" and "Berlei" had been registered concurrently in many overseas markets in English-speaking places and that both companies had concurrently

C advertised and offered for sale in those markets without resultant confusion. We are, however, concerned with this country and it is here that Berlei have principally sold. They have only made very small sales in the United States of America. I would regard the evidence directed to this question of concurrent user as being insufficient to warrant disturbing the learned judge's exercise of discretion.

D In this House an argument was presented in regard to the meaning of s. 11. It was submitted that it does not suffice to prove a likelihood of deception or confusion but that there must be further proof of resulting disentitlement to protection in a court of justice and this, so the submission ran, involved that it must be established that there would be success in passing-off proceedings. As the submission was developed it was modified. It was submitted that what

E would have to be established was that there was a reasonable chance of success in a passing-off action.

I turn, then, to a consideration of s. 11. The differences between that section and s. 12 (1) were fully in the mind of the learned judge. Thus, in s. 12 (1) there is no express reference to a disentitlement to protection in a court of justice. In s. 11 there is no requirement that the likelihood of deception or confusion

F should result from the fact of identity with or near resemblance to a trade mark belonging to a different proprietor which is already on the register in respect of the same goods or description of goods. Section 11 is really a very general provision. Some of the differences between the two sections and the tests to be respectively applied were noted by EVERSHED, J., in *Re Smith Hayden & Co., Ltd.'s Application* (4). In regard to s. 11 he said:

G "Having regard to the reputation acquired by the name 'Hovis', is the Court satisfied that the mark applied for, if used in a normal and fair manner in connection with any goods covered by the registration proposed, will not be reasonably likely to cause deception and confusion amongst a substantial number of persons."

H On the facts of that particular case the reference was to reputation acquired. The reference could also be to the established use made of a name or word.

It is to be noted that s. 11 is mandatory in that it provides that it shall not be lawful to register certain marks. The section makes it unlawful to register either as a trade mark or as part of a trade mark: (a) any matter the use of which would, by reason of its being likely to deceive or cause confusion or otherwise,

I be disentitled to protection in a court of justice; (b) any matter the use of which would be contrary to law or morality; or (c) any scandalous matter. We are not here concerned with either (b) or (c). So the enquiry becomes whether in 1938 the use of the word or mark "Bali" would have been disentitled to protection in a court of justice by reason of the fact that its use would be likely to deceive or cause confusion.

In the rectification proceedings in the present case, since Bali's mark (no. 603,390) has been registered for over seven years the onus was on Berlei

(4) (1945), 63 R.P.C. 97 at p. 101.

to show in the language of s. 13 (1) (b) that " the trade mark offends against A
the provisions " of s. 11. If that was shown then there had to be an exercise of
discretion in favour of ordering rectification. In the first place, therefore, it
was necessary to decide whether the registration was wrongly made in 1938 for
the reason that having regard to the provisions of s. 11 it ought not to have been
registered at all. In my view, there is an overlap between the provisions of
s. 11 and those of s. 12. But we are here concerned with those contained in s. 11. B
Since in s. 13 the reference (apart from the reference to fraud) is only to s. 11
it would seem natural in a case where s. 13 applies to eliminate all other sections
from consideration where enquiry is being made whether there had been offence
against the provisions of s. 11. What, then, is a mark which by reason of its
being likely to deceive or cause confusion would be disentitled to protection in
a court of justice? As to a mark itself it might be likely to deceive or cause C
confusion because it might be: (a) one that closely resembles or is identical
with another mark; or because it might be (b) one that makes a false representation as to the nature or quality of the goods. LORD RUSSELL OF KILLOWEN
pointed this out in his speech in *Bass, Ratcliffe and Gretton, Ltd.* v. *Nicholson &*
Sons, Ltd. (5). He said that the likelihood of deception contemplated by s. 11
(he was considering s. 11 of the Trade Marks Act 1905 which was the same as D
the present s. 11 save that it did not refer to confusion) need not necessarily
flow from any resemblance between the matter proposed to be registered and
other matter or another mark.

"It might flow from something contained in the matter proposed to be
registered, as, e.g., a misleading description of the goods upon or in
connection with which the matter was intended to be used." E

To the same effect were the words of LORD WARRINGTON OF CLYFFE who said (6):

"A mark may be so disentitled as calculated to deceive for other reasons
than that it closely resembles or is identical with another mark, as for example
if it makes a false representation as to the nature or quality of the goods."

LORD WARRINGTON proceeded (6) to point out further that there could be a F
mark which was identical with or which closely resembled another mark which
was so used as *not* to be calculated to deceive and so might be entitled to
protection. He referred to s. 21 of the Act of 1905 in reference to honest
concurrent user. He said (6):

". . . before the Act circumstances can easily be imagined in which as
against a wrongdoer a trader would be entitled to protection for his mark G
notwithstanding that another trader may have used the same mark under
such circumstances as in like manner to be entitled to protection."

An example of a case where because of something contained in a mark there
was disentitlement to protection irrespective of considering any rights of other
traders is to be seen in the matter of *Eno* v. *Dunn* (7). The public knew of
Mr. Eno's Fruit Salt and would be likely to be deceived if Mr. Dunn adopted H
the expression " Fruit Salt ". On a consideration of what was then s. 73 of the
Patents, Designs and Trade Marks Act 1883 (which was amended by s. 15 of
the Patents, Designs and Trade Marks Act 1888 so as to omit the word
" exclusive ") it was held by a majority in this House that the evidence showed
that the words which Mr. Dunn proposed to use were calculated to deceive the
public. So the case fell within s. 73. Mr. Eno had had trade marks on the register I
but he submitted to an order to remove them from the register. In his opposition
to Mr. Dunn's application to use the term " Fruit Salt " he confined himself to
the contention that the term was calculated to deceive. LORD MACNAGHTEN
in his speech said (8):

(5) [1932] A.C. 130 at p. 152; 49 R.P.C. 88 at p. 107.
(6) [1932] A.C. at p. 146; 49 R.P.C. at p. 104.
(7) (1890), 15 App. Cas. 252; 7 R.P.C. 311.
(8) (1890), 15 App. Cas. at p. 264; 7 R.P.C. at p. 319.

A   " The question is one between Mr. Dunn and the public, not between Mr. Eno and Mr. Dunn. It is immaterial whether the proposed registration is or is not likely to injure Mr. Eno in his trade. Equally immaterial, as it seems to me, is the fact that for a considerable time Mr. Eno had on the register, as his trade mark, the words ' Fruit Salt '. Mr. Eno may have gained some advantage to which he was not properly entitled; but that is

B   hardly a reason for permitting Mr. Dunn to practise a deception upon the public."

The interesting feature of the case is, I think, that once the likelihood of deception was shown it was apparently accepted that it followed that there would be disentitlement to the protection of the court. There was a similar approach in *McDowell* v. *Standard Oil Co. (New Jersey)* (9).

C   I approach s. 11 by considering, therefore (the proof being on Berlei): (a) whether in 1938 the use of the mark " Bali " would be likely to deceive or cause confusion; and (b) if so, whether because of or by reason of that the mark " Bali " would in 1938 be disentitled to protection in a court of justice. As to (a) I consider, for the reasons that I have set out, that the assistant comptroller and the judge were fully justified in reaching an affirmative conclusion. I can

D   see no error in their approach. It was in accord with what was said by Parker, J., in *Re Pianotist Co.'s Application* (10).

As to (b) it may or may not be that if Berlei had in 1938 become aware of sales under the name Bali they would have had evidence to establish success in passing-off proceedings. If it be assumed that they would not have been able to produce such evidence the position would nevertheless have been that the

E   mark " Bali " was disentitled to protection. Before 1875, when registration of trade marks began, there could be property in a trade mark: the right of property in a distinctive mark was acquired by a trader merely by using it on or in connection with his goods irrespective of the length of such user and without proof of recognition by the public as a mark distinctive of the user's goods: that right of property would be protected by an injunction restraining any other

F   person from using the mark. Thus, in his judgment in the *Nicholson and Bass* case (11) (which concerned " old " trade marks referred to in s. 19 of the Act of 1905 which were in use before 1875) Lawrence, L.J., referred to the fact that no evidence of recognition by the public was required in order to prove that a distinctive mark was in use as a trade mark before 1875. He said:

G   " What is required for that purpose is proof that the mark before that date was in fact used as a trade mark, that is, was used by the trader in his business upon or in connection with his goods, and it is not necessary to prove either the length of the user or the extent of the trade. In other words, the character and not the length or extent of user is the only thing that has to be established."

H   Having examined certain authorities he said (12) that they showed:

" . . . that it was firmly established at the time when the Act of 1875 was passed that a trader acquired a right of property in a distinctive mark merely by using it upon or in connection with his goods irrespective of the length of such user and of the extent of his trade, and that such right of property would be protected by an injunction restraining any other person

I   from using the mark."

In the House of Lords Lord Russell of Killowen said (13):

" Nor is it in my opinion necessary in this connection to establish that

(9) [1927] A.C. 632; 44 R.P.C. 335; 43 R.P.C. 313.
(10) (1906), 23 R.P.C. 774.
(11) [1931] 2 Ch. 1 at p. 42; 48 R.P.C. 227 at p. 251.
(12) [1931] 2 Ch. at p. 45; 48 R.P.C. at p. 253.
(13) [1932] A.C. at p. 151; 49 R.P.C. at p. 107.

the mark has been recognised by the public as a mark distinctive of the user's   A
goods."

He expressed satisfaction with the reasoning of LAWRENCE and ROMER, L.JJ.,
on the point.   That, therefore, was the state of the law when the Trade Marks
Registration Act 1875, was passed.   By s. 6 it was enacted:

" The registrar shall not, without the special leave of the court, to be   B
given in the prescribed manner, register in respect of the same goods or
classes of goods a trade mark identical with one which is already registered
with respect to such goods or classes of goods, and the registrar shall not
register with respect to the same goods or classes of goods a trade mark so
nearly resembling a trade mark already on the register with respect to such
goods or classes of goods as to be calculated to deceive.   C
" It shall not be lawful to register as part of or in combination with a
trade mark any words the exclusive use of which would not, by reason of
their being calculated to deceive or otherwise, be deemed entitled to
protection in a court of equity; or any scandalous designs."

In the Act of 1883 the latter part of that section was, with minor modification,
re-enacted as s. 73.   By the Act of 1888 the word " exclusive " was to be omitted   D
from s. 73.   That section, as amended, was replaced in the 1905 Act by s. 11
which was in these terms:

" It shall not be lawful to register as a trade mark or part of a trade
mark any matter, the use of which would by reason of its being calculated
to deceive or otherwise be disentitled to protection in a court of justice, or
would be contrary to law or morality, or any scandalous design."   E

By amendments made by the Trade Marks (Amendment) Act 1937 (see s. 6),
the section assumed its present form.   Although in all the statutes from 1875 to
1938 it has been provided (e.g., see s. 2 of the Trade Marks Act 1938) that
proceedings may not be instituted to prevent infringement of an unregistered
mark (while preserving all rights of action for passing-off) that does not alter   F
the meaning of the words in s. 11 as revealed by considering the statutory history
and the state of the law before 1875.

From all this I think it follows that, in 1938, if Berlei had shown that the use
of the mark " Bali " was likely to deceive or cause confusion they would have
shown (quite without any reference to s. 12 (1)) that the use of the mark " Bali "
was disentitled to protection in a court of justice.   Our attention was called to   G
the interesting judgment of BUCKLEY, J., in *Transfermatic Trade Mark* (14).
As to the decision itself no question now arises.   But in the course of his judgment
the learned judge said (15):

" If an opponent to registration can show that the circumstances are
such that on the ground of likelihood of deceit or confusion, the applicant
could be restrained in a court of justice from using the mark sought to be   H
registered, section 11 must prohibit registration.   If all that the opponent
could show was that a number of persons might entertain a reasonable
doubt whether goods bearing the two marks came from the same source,
falling short of grounds for relief against passing off, I, for myself, would
require further argument before reaching the conclusion, apart from
authority, that the section would prohibit registration."   I

My Lords, I do not think that the words of the learned judge need be read as
saying that potential success in a passing-off action is always the test in applying
s. 11 or that the evidence must always be such as would warrant success in a
passing-off action.   If his words bore that meaning they would not be in accord
with what was said in various cases.   In *McDowell's* case (16) where there was

(14) [1966] R.P.C. 568.
(15) [1966] R.P.C. at p. 579.
(16) (1927), 43 R.P.C. 313.

A an application to register a word there was opposition based both on s. 11 and on s. 19 of the Act of 1905 (generally corresponding to s. 11 and s. 12 (1) of the present Act). The onus was therefore on the applicant. In referring to this WARRINGTON, L.J., said (17):

B " It is well settled that the onus of establishing that the proposed mark is not calculated to deceive is upon the applicant, and in this respect he is in a much less favourable position than if he were a defendant in an action for infringement, or for passing off."

SARGANT, L.J., said (18) that the controversy had been dealt with " too much as a litigation between the parties, and as if it had been a passing-off case ": he pointed out that the predominant consideration was the protection of the public. The question was whether there was a probability of deception which
C the applicant had not dispelled.

So also in *Re Hack's Application* MORTON, J., said (19) that—

" the question whether a particular mark is calculated to deceive or cause confusion is not the same as the question whether the use of the mark will lead to passing-off."

D A mark would offend against s. 11 if it was likely to cause confusion or deception in the minds of persons to whom it is addressed. See also *Re Jellinek's Application* (20).

The *Transfermatic* case (21) was not one where s. 13 applied, and as the applicants for rectification had not registered their mark in the United Kingdom it was not a case in which s. 12 applied. The learned judge held that before
E the registration of the mark " Transfermatic " the applicants for rectification could have restrained the registered proprietors from using the word. The applicants for rectification succeeded.

For the reasons which I have given I consider that in the rectification proceedings in the present case the learned judge was fully justified in reaching his conclusions. It is conceded that if the appeal in the rectification proceedings is
F allowed and the mark no. 603,390 expunged from the register there are no grounds on which it could be contended that the appeal in the opposition proceedings should not also be allowed.

I would allow the appeal and restore the judgment of UNGOED-THOMAS, J.

LORD GUEST: My Lords, if it were not that your Lordships are differing
G from a decision of the majority of the Court of Appeal, I should have contented myself with a simple concurrence with the speech of my noble and learned friend on the Woolsack. I only wish to add a few observations.

I agree with the construction which my noble and learned friend has placed on s. 11 of the Trade Marks Act 1938. Applying the test contained in that section the question in the rectification proceedings is: whether the court is satisfied
H that the mark " Bali " if used in a normal and fair manner in connection with any goods covered by the registration will not be reasonably likely to cause deception and confusion among a substantial number of people (see EVERSHED, J., in *Re Smith Hayden & Co., Ltd.'s Application* (22)).

The confusion which is likely to be caused arises principally from the phonetic similarity of " Bali " pronounced " Barley " and " Berlei " pronounced " Burly ".
I The visual similarity of the two marks is negligible. The matter is very much a question of first impression and to a person who is not familiar with either word, which is the proper approach, I should have thought that there was a reasonable apprehension of confusion between the two words. There was the evidence of

(17) (1927), 43 R.P.C. at p. 336.
(18) (1927), 43 R.P.C. at p. 338.
(19) (1940), 58 R.P.C. 91 at p. 103.
(20) (1946), 63 R.P.C. 59 at p. 78.
(21) [1966] R.P.C. 568.
(22) (1945), 63 R.P.C. 97 at p. 101.

Mrs. Lamb who made " test " orders and her evidence supports to some extent this   A
first impression. Both the registrar and the learned judge found in favour of the
appellants on this question and there was, in my view, ample material on which
they could find such a likelihood of confusion.

The majority of the Court of Appeal (LORD DENNING, M.R., and SALMON,
L.J.) fell into error, in my view, in placing too great reliance on the " trade
evidence " led for Bali relating to the year 1964. This evidence, they said, nega-   B
tived confusion. I do not so read it. These witnesses were mainly buyers or
heads of departments concerned with the buying of brassieres and supervising
their sale. In view of the method of trading spoken to by the witnesses, it appears
unlikely that if there was confusion it would come to their notice. They were
all well familiar with both " Bali " and " Berlei " marks and they would accordingly not be, in any event, likely to be confused themselves. Even if a customer   C
was confused, it is not likely that if she was satisfied with the fit of the garment
she would complain. Complaint would only arise from dissatisfaction. At any
rate I do not regard this evidence as sufficiently strong to rebut the prima facie
inference of confusion ensuing from the phonetic similarity and the rest of the
evidence.

Lastly, there is the question of discretion. This arises on the rectification   D
proceedings under s. 32 of the Act of 1938 and on the opposition proceedings
under s. 12 (2). So far as the rectification proceedings are concerned there is no
trace of the matter having been raised before the registrar although your Lordships were informed that it was argued. The learned judge referred to the matters
relied on by Bali as justifying him to exercise his discretion in refusing to rectify
the register. He rejected them and, for my part, I am not able to say that he   E
erred in so doing.

So far as the opposition proceedings are concerned, it is said that there were
" special circumstances " under s. 12 (2) for permitting the registration of " Bali ".
There was never any question of " honest and concurrent use " under s. 12 (2)
before the registrar or the learned judge and your Lordships were told that the
point under this subsection was expressly disclaimed by counsel who was then   F
acting for Bali. It would, indeed, have been inimical to his main argument, as
it would have had to be made on the assumption that the marks were identical
or nearly resembled each other under s. 12 (2), which was contrary to his submission. I consider that LORD DENNING, M.R., was not entitled to exercise for the
first time a discretion under s. 12 (2) to permit " Bali " to be registered.

I would allow the appeal.   G

LORD UPJOHN: My Lords, the appellants, Berlei (U.K.), Ltd., are the
registered proprietors of the trade mark " Berlei " in respect of corsets and
brassieres. This mark was originally registered in May 1924, in the name of Berlei,
Ltd., a company incorporated in New South Wales and transferred to Berlei
a subsidiary company, in 1930.   H

The respondents, Bali Brassiere Co., Inc., a company incorporated in the State
of New York in the United States of America, are the registered proprietors of a
device mark of which a leading feature is the word " Bali " in respect, broadly
speaking, of the same class of goods. This registration was made in December
1938. In addition, Bali now seek to register the plain word " Bali ". In the first
appeal Berlei seek to have registration of the new mark refused under s. 11 and
s. 12 (1) of the Trade Marks Act 1938 (" the Act "); in the second appeal they   I
seek to expunge Bali's registered device mark under s. 11 of the Act. It will be
convenient to consider the second appeal first.

As Bali's mark has been on the register for over seven years it is clear that the
registration is valid in all respects under s. 13 of the Act unless it offends against
the provisions of s. 11.

Section 11 is in these terms:

" It shall not be lawful to register as a trade mark or part of a trade mark

A   any matter the use of which would, by reason of its being likely to deceive or cause confusion or otherwise, be disentitled to protection in a court of justice . . . "

I can omit the concluding words as they have no relevance to this case.

Certain matters are common ground. First, although the matter was the subject of some argument below, it is agreed, and is not a matter for decision of

B this House, that the proper time for the purpose of testing whether s. 11 is offended is the date of application for registration of the mark sought to be expunged, that is the year 1938. Secondly, that the onus is on Berlei to prove that s. 11 is offended; the onus is reversed in the first appeal.

It is clear that a mark may offend s. 11 for reasons other than resemblance between the mark in suit and another mark, for example, the mark in suit may

C contain a misleading description; but in this case the complaint is based solely on the alleged resemblance between the words " Berlei " and " Bali ". Thus, the question that your Lordships have to consider is whether the use of the word " Bali " would be likely to deceive or cause confusion and be disentitled to protection in a court of justice. This section has a long legislative history and has been the subject of much judicial comment, and to these matters I must make some

D reference.

The predecessor of s. 11 was in s. 6 of the Trade Marks Registration Act 1875, which for the first time provided for registration of trade marks. The relevant part of s. 6 was in these terms:

" It shall not be lawful to register as part of or in combination with a trade

E   mark any words the exclusive use of which would not, by reason of their being calculated to deceive or otherwise, be deemed entitled to protection in a court of equity . . ."

Verbal alterations were made to this section in the Patents Designs and Trade Marks Act 1883, when in s. 73, which replaced s. 6, the concluding words were altered to " be deemed disentitled to protection ".

F   By s. 15 of the Patents, Designs and Trade Marks Act 1888, the word " exclusive " was omitted, but I do not myself think this had any significance; that adjective should never have been employed in that context. These Acts were consolidated in the Trade Marks Act 1905. In s. 6 of the Trade Marks (Amendment) Act 1937, " likely " was substituted for " calculated ", no doubt as the result of judicial decision that " calculated " imported no intent; the words

G " or cause confusion " were added. This section duly reappeared in the Act.

It was argued before your Lordships that to establish that the word " Bali " would offend s. 11 the words in the section " disentitled to protection in a court of justice " require the court to do more than to be satisfied of the likelihood of deception or confusion but it must be satisfied of something further, something, it was argued, akin to passing-off of the objectors' mark.

H   My Lords, I have set out the changes in s. 11, for in spite of the changes of nomenclature over the years these vital words, on which counsel for Bali pins his faith, must take some colour from the original Act of 1875, and for this reason, too, it seems to me relevant to consider the common law relating to trade marks before 1875. This was most lucidly explained in the judgment of P. O. LAWRENCE, L.J., in the Court of Appeal in *Re Nicholson & Sons' Application for Registra-*

I *tion of a Trade Mark, Re Bass, Ratcliffe and Gretton's Trade Mark* (23). His judgment made it clear that, in his view, no evidence of recognition by the public was required in order to prove that a distinctive mark was in use as a trade mark before 1875. He quoted from the judgment of SIR JOHN ROMILLY, M.R., in *Hall v. Barrows* (24) containing this passage which draws a clear distinction between the use of a trade mark and the essence of a passing-off action:

---

(23) [1931] 2 Ch. 1 at pp. 42, 43; 48 R.P.C. 227 at p. 252.
(24) (1863), 32 L.J.Ch. 548 at p. 551.

" If the brand or mark be an old one, formerly used, but since discontinued, A
the former proprietor of the mark undoubtedly cannot retain such a property
in it, or prevent others from using it; but, provided it has been originally
adopted by a manufacturer, and continuously, and still used by him to denote
his own goods when brought into the market and offered for sale, then I
apprehend, although the mark may not have been adopted a week, and may
not have acquired any reputation in the market, his neighbours cannot B
use that mark. Were it otherwise, and were the question to depend entirely
on the time the mark had been used, or the reputation of it had been acquired,
a very difficult, if not an insoluble inquiry, would have to be opened in every
case, namely, whether the mark had acquired in the market a distinctive
character denoting the goods of the person who first used it."

It may be that SIR JOHN ROMILLY, M.R. went too far in saying user for a week C
would be sufficient; that must be a matter of fact and degree, but it illustrates
the point to which I shall return, that a trader is only entitled to protection for
a mark which he has in use at the relevant time. Then, after quoting some further
authorities, LAWRENCE, L.J. (25), went on to disapprove the statement of LORD
ESHER, M.R., in *Richards* v. *Butcher* (26) who held that to constitute a trade mark
you must show that the market accepted it as a distinguishing mark of the trader's D
goods. In this disapproval he was expressly upheld on appeal to the House of
Lords (27) by LORD BUCKMASTER, LORD RUSSELL OF KILLOWEN and LORD
MACMILLAN.

MORTON, J., had some helpful observations on this in *Re Hack's Application* (28).

" The question whether a particular mark is calculated to deceive or cause E
confusion is not the same as the question whether the use of the mark will
lead to passing-off."

So it seems to me impossible to give to the construction of the section that which
is sought for by Bali. Section 11 and its forebears were designed not so much for
the protection of other traders in the use of their marks or their reputation but
for the protection of the public. This was made quite plain by the majority F
opinions in your Lordships' House in *Eno* v. *Dunn* (29).

With all respect to the recent judgment of BUCKLEY, J., in *Transfermatic
Trade Mark* (30) I cannot agree with him if he meant to hold that the applicant
seeking to have the mark expunged would have to discharge the burden of establishing a real and substantial likelihood of success in an action to obtain an injunction on the ground of passing-off. The fact that in most cases the person G
seeking to expunge another's mark is himself the owner of a mark for which he
could sue for infringement, or that he could establish such a reputation among
the public, that he might succeed in an action against the owner of the mark for
passing-off the latter's goods as and for his goods, is, under the section, irrelevant.

Eno v. *Dunn* (29) itself also illustrates this point. During the course of the
proceedings Mr. Eno felt constrained to consent to the removal of his mark H
" Fruit Salt " from the register, yet he was held entitled to object as a member of
the public to the registration of the applicant's mark which contained the words
" Fruit Salt ". LORD HERSCHEL concluded his speech with the words (31):

" To prevent misapprehension, I desire to add that your Lordships have
not now to determine whether the appellant could in any, and, if so, in what,
cases restrain the use of the words ' Fruit-Salt '. I have already indicated I
my opinion that the appellant has no private property in them. The sole

(25) [1931] 2 Ch. at p. 49; 48 R.P.C. at p. 254.
(26) [1891] 2 Ch. 522 at p. 546; 8 R.P.C. 249 at p. 251.
(27) [1932] A.C. 130; 49 R.P.C. 88.
(28) (1940), 58 R.P.C. 91 at p. 103.
(29) (1870), 15 App. Cas. 252; 7 R.P.C. 311.
(30) [1966] R.P.C. 568.
(31) (1890), 15 App. Cas. at p. 262; 7 R.P.C. at p. 318.

A point for decision is, whether the comptroller ought to be directed to proceed with the registration of a particular trade mark of which they form an element.''

My Lords, I think the presence of these words '' disentitled to protection in a court of justice '' whether in their original form or in their phraseology of today are explained by the fact that in order to prevent the registration of a mark or

B to secure its removal it must be established (here, of course, I am not dealing with questions of onus) not merely that there is likelihood of deception or confusion between two marks judged on the well-known tests laid down in *Re Pianotist Co.'s Application* (32) and *Aristoc, Ltd.* v. *Rysta, Ltd.* (33) but something more, that is, user at the relevant time by the owner of the existing mark which under the old common law the court, as SIR JOHN ROMILLY, M.R., said (34), would

C protect. The whole emphasis is on the question whether the owner of the mark in suit, assuming him to bring some action against another trader, would be disentitled from succeeding for any of the reasons set out in s. 11; not whether anyone would succeed against him. This is the chief distinction between s. 11 and s. 12. Section 12 is principally a weapon in the hands of a registered proprietor though it is not necessary that he personally should object. Here no user by the registered

D proprietor need be shown; it is purely a question of similarity. Section 11 is, as I have said, for the protection of the public and anyone may object, but if he relies only on similarity he must prove the practical likelihood of confusion to the public and this he can only do, for the purposes of the section, by proving the existing user by another, not necessarily by himself, in respect of which the mark in suit is likely to cause deception or confusion; but if he does not establish

E likelihood of deception or confusion with some present user of a similar mark the court would not treat that as sufficient to disentitle the mark in suit to protection. Thus it came about that EVERSHED, J., in *Re Smith Hayden and Co., Ltd.'s Application* (35) formulated the test under s. 11 in these terms:

F '' (a) (Under Sec. 11) ' Having regard to the reputation acquired by the name '' Hovis '', is the Court satisfied that the mark applied for, if used in a normal and fair manner in connection with any goods covered by the registration proposed, will not be reasonably likely to cause deception and confusion amongst a substantial number of persons '.''

My Lords, I think the learned judge was wrong to use the word '' reputation acquired by ''; it should have been '' the user of ''. Of course, in that case there

G was no difference between those two expressions, as the household word of '' Hovis '' was involved; but in many cases, such as the *Transfermatic* case (36), the difference might be vital.

It may also be said that the desiderata that the deception and confusion (in EVERSHED, J.'s statement) must be among a substantial number of persons is a matter of judicial gloss. I do not object to this provided it is properly and

H sensibly applied. Here again, the *Transfermatic* case (36) is a good illustration of the application of this condition to special circumstances; I think BUCKLEY, J. (37), was quite right to overrule the assistant comptroller and to reach a different conclusion on the facts of that case.

What, then, is the test? This must necessarily be a question of fact and degree in every case. I am content in amplification of the test laid down by EVERSHED,

I J., to take the test as in effect laid down by ROMER, J., in *Re Jellinek's Application* (38). It is not necessary in order to find that a mark offends against s. 11 to prove that there is an actual probability of deception leading to a passing-off

(32) (1906), 23 R.P.C. 774.
(33) [1945] 1 All E.R. 34; 62 R.P.C. 65.
(34) (1863), 32 L.J.Ch. at p. 551.
(35) (1945), 63 R.P.C. 97 at p. 101.
(36) [1966] R.P.C. 568.
(37) [1966] R.P.C. at pp. 577, 578.
(38) (1946), 63 R.P.C. 59 at p. 78.

or (I add) an infringement action. It is sufficient if the result of the registration **A**
of the mark will be that a number of persons will be caused to wonder whether
it might not be the case that the two products come from the same source. It is
enough if the ordinary person entertains a reasonable doubt, but the court has to
be satisfied not merely that there is a possibility of confusion; it must be
satisfied that there is a real tangible danger of confusion if the mark which it is
sought to register is put on the register. And so mutatis mutandis when it is **B**
sought to expunge a mark.

My Lords, let me apply these principles to the facts of this case, and I can do
so fairly shortly. Before UNGOED-THOMAS, J., as he pointed out in his judgment,
it was conceded that from about March 1936, the sale of " Berlei " goods with
the " Berlei " trade mark was substantial. He then went on to examine the
evidence as to the use of the word " Bali " on Bali's goods from 1935 to 1938, **C**
and he summed up the whole situation in these words which, though not unchallenged in argument, cannot in my opinion (and the evidence has been fully
reviewed before your Lordships) seriously be disputed:

> " This evidence establishes, to my mind, that at the time of the registration
> of the trade mark ' Bali ' the name ' Berlei ' had acquired a substantial
> reputation as denoting [Berlei's] goods and that the name ' Bali ' had not **D**
> acquired any significant reputation. So, if it were shown that the trade
> mark ' Bali ' was likely to deceive or cause confusion by reason of its resem-
> blance to the mark ' Berlei ', my conclusion would be that [Berlei] establish
> their case for rectification under section 11."

The resemblance relied on between " Berlei " (pronounced Burley) and " Bali " **E**
(pronounced Barley or Bahli) was, in truth, based on a phonetic resemblance.
The assistant comptroller, to whose opinion in these matters of resemblance, it
has been said over and over again in judicial utterances, much weight should be
attached, came to the conclusion that "on the phonetic aspect I consider there
to be the greatest possibility of confusion ". UNGOED-THOMAS, J., said: " The
likelihood of substantial confusion resulting from pronunciation of the words **F**
seems to me obvious." In his dissenting judgment in the Court of Appeal
DIPLOCK, L.J., agreed with that. So do I. It seems to me to be obvious that
deception and confusion is a most likely result of the use of these words in a
competing trade even though one product (Bali) seems to be in a higher price
bracket than the other. But the evidence is that both are sold in the same shops
and in the same departments and are displayed side by side. But such a con- **G**
clusion may bend to the evidence if such evidence shows quite clearly that
though to the judicial ear confusion would be obvious, yet over a long period no
case of confusion has occurred; but even in such cases the judicial ear has the
final say, for in the end it is a question of impression and common sense.

There was some evidence of confusion before the learned trial judge, that of
Mrs. Lamb who on 14th October 1963, on behalf of Berlei in test or trap operations **H**
(distasteful to all, but perfectly proper and, indeed, usually essential in this
type of case) visited a number of shops selling these goods " over the counter ",
that is in contrast to a sale " after fitting " (to which I shall refer later) when
she asked for a " Bali " brassiere. The relevance, or indeed admissibility, of the
answer to a question put in respect of a " Bali " rather than a " Berlei " article
might possibly be challenged in a passing-off action or even possibly a trade **I**
mark infringement action, I see no objection to such a question in regard to s. 11.
Her evidence did, however, establish three cases where she was sold a " Berlei "
brassiere in reply to her request, but in only one of these cases were " Bali "
brassieres also on sale.

The majority of the Court of Appeal were much impressed by the evidence
called by Bali of managers or buyers from well-known shops in London and
elsewhere where both " Berlei " and " Bali " brassieres are displayed. One and
all they testified that neither they nor any saleswoman under them had ever

A had any evidence of confusion between these names; it is not in doubt that their evidence was honestly given and perfectly truthful. But these cases were not " over the counter " sales but cases where there were careful fittings, in some cases no doubt not only of " Berlei " and " Bali " brassieres but other makes as well, before a purchase was made. In such circumstances I can see little, if any, room for evidence of deception or confusion to emerge. After the

B fitting the customer buys the one that at the same time fits her body and her purse most conveniently. If, when she gets home, she finds that it is a " Bali " and not a " Berlei " (or vice versa) even if she cares at all I cannot believe that she would bother to complain. Further, I should be surprised if confusion emerged on a repeat order. So, in my opinion, this evidence is of no weight against the plain common-sense view (not unsupported by evidence) that

C phonetically there is a likelihood of deception or confusion and of such a character as to satisfy the legal test which I have propounded above. Prima facie, therefore, Bali's mark should be expunged.

There was some argument before your Lordships about the discretion in these cases which, by s. 32 (1) of the Act, is conferred on the registrar and by s. 52 afresh on the judge hearing the appeal. This discretion is not conferred

D on the Court of Appeal or this House, save in cases where on ordinary well-known principles the Court of Appeal or your Lordships' House may interfere with a discretionary remedy conferred on the lower court. Your Lordships were pressed with what Lord Tomlin said in *Alexander Pirie & Sons, Ltd.'s Application* (39), but Lord Tomlin was there dealing with the case where the trial judge had gone wrong so that the discretion had to be exercised de novo

E by the Court of Appeal. My Lords, the majority of the Court of Appeal held that the trial judge, in exercising his discretion, failed to take into account the evidence tendered to him of events after the date of the application to expunge in May 1960. If he did so fail (and I am by no means convinced that he did), he was wrong, for evidence of confusion (or lack of it) today may be good evidence of the likelihood (or not) of confusion of 30 years ago (for, of course, contem-

F poraneous evidence of that is seldom available) unless there is some evidence in a particular case that times, manners, modes and circumstances generally have so changed that the evidence of today is of no weight in considering the relevant questions of 30 years ago. In this case, however, the judge's alleged failure is of no importance because, for the reasons I have given, the post-1960 evidence supports rather than denies the conclusion which Ungoed-Thomas, J.,

G reached. So I think that he was right to decide (on the second appeal) that Bali's mark should be expunged, and on that footing it is not in dispute that Bali must fail in the first appeal on their application to register the name " Bali ".

My Lords, for these reasons, I would allow both appeals and restore the order of Ungoed-Thomas, J.

H **LORD WILBERFORCE:** My Lords, many points have been argued on this appeal, but by selection, and a fortiori reasoning, these can be so reduced that those which determine are comparatively few. I accept that if Berlei win on their application for rectification of the register, their opposition proceedings must be successful. And, on the rectification proceedings, if they can succeed on the basis that the relevant date, for showing the likelihood of confusion, is

I 23rd December 1938, they would, a fortiori, win if the relevant date were in 1960 or 1962: in that event the difficult point, which is the correct date at which the likelihood of confusion is to be determined, would not arise. The key question, therefore, is whether Berlei can affirmatively establish that, as at 23rd December 1938 (the date of registration of Bali's device mark no. 603,390), that mark was unlawfully registered by virtue of s. 11 of the Trade Marks Act 1938. If so, there will remain only the question whether, in the exercise of its discretion under s. 32 of the Act, the court should order removal of the mark.

(39) [1933] All E.R. Rep. 956 at p. 961; 50 R.P.C. 147 at p. 157.

The basis of fact on which the issue as to confusion has to be decided is not **A** difficult to ascertain from the statutory declarations made on either side and from the pleadings. I do not think that Bali are in a position to dispute: first, that Berlei continuously and extensively used their mark Berlei (registered in 1924) since 1930 in connection with the sale of brassieres and other foundation garments; second, that Bali, from 1935-1938, sold their brassieres in the United Kingdom on a small scale through a very limited number of outlets of which alone Selfridges, **B** London, could be identified. It may be accepted that these brassieres were sold under the Bali trade mark as ultimately registered in 1938. So far as this is relevant, Berlei did not know of these sales nor of the existence, or registration, of the Bali trade mark.

On these facts, had the issue arisen in 1938, it seems apparent that Berlei would have had a case for opposing registration of the Bali trade mark under **C** s. 12 (1) of the Act of 1938 on the ground that this mark related to the same goods or description of goods as those covered by their Berlei mark, and that it so nearly resembled their mark as to be likely to cause confusion. Although the Bali mark consisted of a device, it is not seriously disputed that its distinctive feature consisted of the word Bali which appeared on it.

In fact no issue arose in 1938 and no opposition was made: before Bali could **D** develop their trade, the war of 1939-45 intervened. The war was followed by a period of import restrictions, and it was not until 1959 that the existence of the registered Bali mark was brought to Berlei's notice. By this time the limiting period of seven years laid down by s. 13 of the Act of 1938 had long since expired so that, apart from a claim based on non-user, which was made and failed, the only remedy, as regards the 1938 registration, open to Berlei was under s. 11 **E** of the Act. It is therefore necessary to consider to what situations that section applies. It is as follows:

"It shall not be lawful to register as a trade mark or part of a trade mark any matter the use of which would, by reason of its being likely to deceive or cause confusion or otherwise, be disentitled to protection in a court of justice, or would be contrary to law or morality, or any scandalous design." **F**

This section has an appearance of simplicity, but on closer consideration this appearance is deceptive. Relevantly to the present appeal there are two points of difficulty.

The first concerns the relation of the section to s. 12 (1). It is certainly the **G** case that s. 11 extends to matters not comprehended in s. 12 (1): this is obvious when it refers to matter which is contrary to law or morality and to scandalous designs. Even as to the linguistically common criteria, that a mark is likely to deceive or cause confusion, one can see that s. 11 has a wider scope than s. 12 (1), for whereas the latter section is concerned with a comparison between two rival marks, relating to the same goods or description of goods, of which one is **H** already on the register, s. 11 is not so limited. It extends to cases where the public is likely to be deceived or confused merely by the mark in question per se. But what is the impact of s. 11 on cases (of likely deception or confusion) between two rival marks, one of which is on the register? And what if the mark attacked has been on the register for seven years? I confess that I find it difficult to understand how or why a registered proprietor, whose mark has remained un- **I** challenged for the statutory period of seven years and has thereby acquired, under s. 13, a statutory validity, can thereafter be exposed to proceedings, under s. 11, based on precisely the same grounds as those which were, but no longer are, available under s. 12 (1). If s. 11 is to be invoked at a date after s. 12 (1) has ceased to be available, one would think that this could only be on some ground of public policy or public interest, and not merely on the private complaint of a rival trader based on similarity.

It is perhaps difficult to claim positive support for this view of s. 11 from the

A history of the section and of s. 12 (1), but at least the argument seems open. In the first registration Act (Trade Marks Registration 1875), what now corresponds to s. 11 appeared as a second paragraph in a composite section (s. 6) which dealt, in the first paragraph, with situations such as are now regulated by s. 12 (1): it was then obviously a supplementary provision dealing with a special case. In 1883 (Patents, Designs and Trade Marks Act 1883), the two

B matters were put into separate sections (s. 72 and s. 73) the same order being preserved. It was of s. 73 (now s. 11) that Lord Macnaghten said in *Eno* v. *Dunn* (40) that it referred to persons whose case is not founded on truth, an expression derived from the pre-registration judgment of Sir Lancelot Shadwell, V.-C., in *Pidding* v. *How* (41). In the Trade Marks Act 1905, the order is reversed. What corresponds to the present s. 11 appears as s. 11 of that Act

C in a section dealing with registrable trade marks. The present s. 12 (1) appears as s. 19 under a heading " Identical Trade Marks " and contains a reservation in favour of pre-1875 (" old ") marks. Of these sections it was said that s. 19 was a specific provision which, where it applied, overruled the general provisions of s. 11. (*Bass, Ratcliffe and Gretton, Ltd.* v. *Nicholson & Sons, Ltd.* (42) per Lord Russell of Killowen.) Thus, what had been a special case in 1875 had

D become a general provision in 1905 and what had early been the general rule had now become an overriding exception. Finally, in 1938, the two sections are again juxtaposed; the mention of " old " marks is dropped, and a reference to the likelihood of confusion is added to s. 11 and s. 12 (1).

One can hardly say more than that, if it be true that no very clear legislative intention as to the relation of the two sections can be detected, and if the con-

E clusion suggests itself that this has been lost sight of in a process of continuous mechanical repair, one is left with the judicial observations I have quoted as to the purpose which s. 11 was intended to fill. I do not elaborate this line of argument because both sides in the present appeal accepted that, in principle, subject only to the next point I shall mention, rectification proceedings might be brought under s. 11 although based on circumstances in which, but for the

F seven-year limit, opposition might have been maintained under s. 12 (1). More-over, they can appeal to some reputable authority which appears to give them support (for example *Re McDowell's Application* (43)). But I would wish to reserve the question whether this accepted view of the relation between these two sections is correct, or whether some more limited application should be given to s. 11.

G The one point on which a distinction was sought to be made in argument between the two sections (and this is the second point of difficulty) relates to the words in s. 11 " would, by reason of its being likely to deceive or cause confusion or otherwise, *be disentitled to protection in a court of justice* ". These words do not appear in s. 12 (1) and an attempt was made by counsel for Bali to base an argument on them to the effect that they introduce an additional

H ingredient which has to be found if a case is to be based on s. 11 rather than on s. 12 (1).

The difficulty about this argument was that though many, and varied, attempts were made, learned counsel were unable to define what this additional ingredient was. The nearest, but not very near, approach to precision was made when it was claimed that these words referred to passing-off proceedings, but the argu-

I ment was left in obscurity whether they presupposed the certainty, the prob-ability, or the mere possibility of success in such proceedings, or even by whom such proceedings were supposed to be brought. But I need not further probe these ambiguities because I think that Bali's argument, in any form, is really refuted by the wording of the section. This demonstrates that the hypothesis is accepted that if there is confusion, or the likelihood of it, the mark would ipso facto be disentitled to protection. The words " by reason of " compel this

---

(40) (1890), 15 App. Cas. 252; 7 R.P.C. 311.   (41) (1837), 8 Sim. 477 at p. 480.
(42) [1932] A.C. 130 at p. 152; 49 R.P.C. 88 at p. 108.
(43) (1925), 43 R.P.C. 313 at pp. 334, 336.

hypothesis, and correspondingly exclude the argument that something more than   A
confusion, or its likelihood, must be shown.   This negative conclusion is probably
enough for the present case but if the enquiring mind desires to know just what
the italicised words mean, or why they are there, I do not think there is much
doubt as to the answer.   They take their origin from s. 6 of the Trade Marks
Registration Act 1875, the first registration Act, which was in the form

".. . any words the exclusive use of which would not, by reason of their   B
being calculated to deceive or otherwise, be deemed entitled to protection
in a court of equity . . ."

thus evidently referring to the position, as regards protection, which existed
before registration of trade marks became possible.   What the position was as
regards entitlement to protection, before 1875, is established by a number of
decisions and judicial observations, among which I mention those of SIR   C
LANCELOT SHADWELL, V.-C., in *Pidding* v. *How* (44) and of LORD WESTBURY,
L.C., in *M'Andrew* v. *Bassett* (45) where he described the proprietor's right as
based on property and his remedy as being to prevent infringement.   They are
well analysed and explained in the judgment of LAWRENCE, L.J., in the matter
of *Re Nicholson & Sons, Ltd.'s Application for Registration of Trade Mark*, *Re
Bass, Ratcliffe and Gretton's Trade Mark* (46) which was approved by this   D
House (47).   There can be no doubt that when the Act of 1875 used the words
" entitled to protection in a court of equity " it was referring to the rights which,
long before the system of registration was introduced, an owner of a trade mark
had to come to a court of equity and to ask for his right of property to be protected, a right which, in accordance with general equitable principles, would be
denied protection if there was an element of deception in his claim or it were   E
otherwise not founded on truth.

On the assumption, then, that s. 11 is capable of applying to this case, the
present case has to be decided.   Was registration of the device mark " Bali " in
1938 likely to cause confusion?   An affirmative answer to this question was given
by the assistant comptroller acting for the registrar, by UNGOED-THOMAS, J., and
by DIPLOCK, L.J.   I do not think it necessary to say more than that their con-   F
clusions, based in the main on phonetic similarity, but re-inforced by the evidence
of Mrs. Lamb, appear to me to be convincing.   The reasons which led the majority
of the Court of Appeal to take an opposite view, based in part on certain slender
evidence as to user outside the United Kingdom, and in part on certain late
trade evidence, are for me so satisfactorily answered in the judgment of DIPLOCK,
L.J., that I do not feel it necessary to cover the same ground.   G

There remains the issue of discretion, conferred by the Act on the registrar
and independently on the High Court.   Three grounds for not exercising the
court's discretion in Berlei's favour, the only grounds put forward at that stage,
were considered and rejected by UNGOED-THOMAS, J.   I agree with his treatment
of this matter and I am of opinion that Bali have neither shown any reason for
reviewing the manner in which he exercised the discretion of the court, nor   H
have advanced, if, indeed, they are entitled to do so at this stage, any fresh
consideration which would produce a different result.

I would allow the appeal on the rectification proceedings.   I agree with the
judge and with DIPLOCK, L.J., that this involves the success of Berlei on the
opposition proceedings and I would allow their appeal on this matter also, and
restore the judgment of UNGOED-THOMAS, J.   I

LORD PEARSON: My Lords, I concur.   *Appeals allowed.*

Solicitors: *Bird & Bird* (for the appellants);   *McKenna & Co.* (for the
respondents).
                    [*Reported by* S. A. HATTEEA, ESQ., *Barrister-at-Law.*]

---

(44) (1837), 8 Sim. at p. 480.   (45) (1864), 4 De G.J. & Sm. 380 at p. 384.
(46) [1931] 2 Ch. 1 at p. 44; 48 R.P.C. 227 at p. 253.
(47) [1932] A.C. 130; 49 R.P.C. 88.

A

R. *v.* ROLLAFSON.

[COURT OF APPEAL, CRIMINAL DIVISION (Salmon, L.J., Brabin and Cusack, JJ.),
March 28, April 1, 1969.]

Company—Winding-up—Fraudulent trading—Trading not antecedent to or in
B   *the course of winding-up—Whether offence made out—Companies Act 1948*
(11 & 12 Geo. 6 c. 38), s. 332 (3).

The offences created by s. 332 (3)* of the Companies Act 1948 are confined
to offences committed prior to or during the course of a winding-up (see
p. 834, letter G, post).

Appeal allowed.

C   [As to fraudulent trading, see 6 HALSBURY'S LAWS (3rd Edn.) 707-709,
paras. 1406-1409; and for cases on the subject, see 10 DIGEST (Repl.) 953,
6555, 6556.

For the Companies Act 1948, s. 332, see 5 HALSBURY'S STATUTES (3rd Edn.)
361.]

Case referred to:
D   *R. v. Forde*, [1923] 2 K.B. 400; [1923] All E.R. Rep. 477; 92 L.J.K.B. 501;
        128 L.T. 798; 87 J.P. 76; 17 Cr. App. Rep. 99; 14 Digest (Repl.)
        606, *5998.*

Appeal.

On 18th September 1968 the appellant, Charles Henry Rollafson, pleaded
guilty at Colchester Borough Quarter Sessions to fraudulent trading contrary
E to s. 332 (3) of the Companies Act 1948, and was sentenced by the deputy recorder,
LEONARD MOULES, ESQ., to nine months' imprisonment. The appellant appealed
against conviction on the ground that the count to which he pleaded guilty was
bad in law.

The cases noted below† were cited during the argument in addition to the
case referred to in the judgment of the court.
F

L. Giovene for the appellant.
F. Irwin and *O. S. Martin* for the Crown.

                                                    Cur adv. vult.

1st April. **SALMON, L.J.:** Unfortunately BRABIN, J., is unable to take
a seat this morning, but the judgment about to be delivered is the judgment of
G the court. On 18th September 1968 at the Colchester Borough Quarter Sessions
the appellant pleaded guilty to a count charging him and others with fraudulent
trading contrary to s. 332 (3) of the Companies Act 1948. The particulars of
the offence alleged that the appellant had knowingly been a party to the carrying
on of the business of a company called Ginestar, Ltd. (of which he was a director)
with intent to defraud its creditors. He was sentenced to nine months' imprison-
H ment. He now appeals against his conviction.

The fact that he pleaded guilty is no bar to this appeal providing that it would
have been impossible for him to have been lawfully convicted of this offence:
R. v. Forde (1). It is now argued on his behalf that it would have been impossible
for him to have been so convicted because s. 332 (3) applies only to acts done
before or in the course of a winding-up, as the Crown concedes, the company
I was not being wound up. Section 332 (3) provides:

"Where any business of a company is carried on with such intent or for
such purpose as is mentioned in subsection (1) of this section, every person
who was knowingly a party to the carrying on of the business in manner
aforesaid, shall be liable on conviction on indictment to imprisonment for a

---

* Section 332 (3) is set out at letter I, above, to p. 834, letter A, post.
† *R. v. Inman*, [1966] 3 All E.R. 414; [1967] 1 Q.B. 140; *R. v. Buckingham* (23rd
May 1968), unreported.
(1) [1923] 2 K.B. 400 at p. 403; [1923] All E.R. Rep. 477 at p. 479.

A

term not exceeding two years or to a fine not exceeding five hundred pounds or to both.''

The relevant part of s. 332 (1) is in the following terms:

" If in the course of the winding up of a company it appears that any business of the company has been carried on with intent to defraud creditors of the company . . . or for any fraudulent purpose, the court, on the application of the official receiver . . . may, if it thinks proper so to do, declare that any persons who were knowingly parties to the carrying on of the business in manner aforesaid shall be personally responsible, without any limitation of liability, for all or any of the debts or other liabilities of the company as the court may direct.''

B

Winding-up is not expressly mentioned in sub-s. (3), nor is it necessarily introduced into it by its reference to sub-s. (1). Accordingly, on a literal construction, the language of sub-s. (3) is undoubtedly wide enough to create offences in no way connected with winding-up. The question is—did the legislature intend the subsection to bear the wide meaning which it is certainly capable of bearing, or has the legislature by the context in which it has placed the subsection expressed the intention that the offences it creates shall be confined to offences committed prior to or during the course of a winding-up?

C

D

Section 332 appears in Part 5 of the Act. This Part is concerned exclusively with winding-up. It consists of 145 sections broken down into a very much larger number of subsections. Admittedly all these, except perhaps for s. 332 (3), relate to winding-up. Section 332 itself appears in a group of sections (s. 328 to s. 334) which are described as relating to " Offences antecedent to or in course of Winding Up ". It is, of course, possible, although in the view of this court unlikely, that the legislature might have intended to tuck away a subsection within s. 332 which created offences having nothing whatsoever to do with winding-up. This court, however, has no doubt that if this had been what the legislature intended it would have been very much more clearly expressed: for example, by inserting the words " whether or not the company is wound up " after the word " aforesaid " in the fourth line of the subsection, or by inserting the words " at any time " after the word " is " in the first line of the subsection. In the absence of any such express words, this court has no hesitation in holding that sub-s. (3) was intended by the legislature only to create, and does only create, offences committed before or during a winding-up. Accordingly, the appellant could not have been lawfully convicted under sub-s. (3) since Ginestar, Ltd., was not being wound up.

E

F

G

This construction of sub-s. (3) leaves no lacuna in the law. Even if it were to be given the wide construction for which the Crown contends, it is most unlikely that a prosecution would be launched under the subsection unless creditors had been defrauded, or there had been a real attempt to defraud them. The armoury of the law contains plenty of weapons to deal effectively with circumstances such as these without it being necessary to have recourse to s. 332 (3). Indeed, in the present indictment there are several counts left on the file which would cover fraudulent acts done by the appellant in helping to run the business of Ginestar, Ltd. It follows that on the true construction of sub-s. (3) this appeal must be allowed and the conviction quashed. There will, however, be no order for the appellant's release as he is serving sentences amounting in all to 30 months' imprisonment in respect of offences to which he has pleaded guilty on another indictment.

H

I

Appeal allowed. Conviction quashed.

Solicitors: *Registrar of Criminal Appeals* (for the appellant); *T. Hambrey Jones,* Chelmsford (for the Crown).

[*Reported by* N. P. METCALFE, ESQ., *Barrister-at-Law.*]

A

NOTE.

R. *v.* SCHILDKAMP.

B [Court of Appeal, criminal division (Lord Parker, C.J., Megaw, L.J., and Geoffrey Lane, J.), May 23, 1969.]

Company—Winding-up—Fraudulent trading—Trading not antecedent to or in the course of winding-up—Whether offence made out—Companies Act 1948 (11 & 12 Geo. 6 c. 38), s. 332 (3).

C [As to fraudulent trading, see 6 Halsbury's Laws (3rd Edn.) 707-709, paras. 1406, 1409; and for cases on the subject, see 10 Digest (Repl.) 953, *6555, 6556.*

For the Companies Act 1948, s. 332, see 5 Halsbury's Statutes (3rd Edn.) 361.]

Case referred to:

D *R. v. Rollafson*, p. 833, ante.

Appeal.

This was an appeal by Jan Schildkamp, by leave granted out of time by the single judge, against his conviction on 31st October 1968 at the Central Criminal Court on a charge of fraudulent trading contrary to s. 332 (3) of the Companies Act 1948.

E C. L. *Hawser*, Q.C., and G. E. *Janner* for the appellant.
J. H. *Buzzard* and D. A. L. *Smout* for the Crown.

LORD PARKER, C.J., delivered the judgment of the court: On 31st October 1968 at the Central Criminal Court, the appellant, Jan Schildkamp, was convicted after a change of plea on count 1 of fraudulent trading contrary to s. 332 (3) of the Companies Act 1948, for which he was sentenced to two

F years' imprisonment, and on count 4 of fraudulent conversion and sentenced to one year's imprisonment concurrent, on count 12 of, again, fraudulent conversion, one year concurrent, and in addition he pleaded guilty at the outset to count 2, being an undischarged bankrupt taking part in the management of a company without the leave of the court, for which he received six months, again

G concurrent, in other words he received two years in all. He applied for leave to appeal against his sentence and that was refused by the single judge and thereafter abandoned. There the matter rested until recently, when the single judge extended the time for leave to appeal against conviction on count 1 only and ordered that the case be listed as an appeal on a point of law. The reason for that was that the company with which the appellant was concerned, a com-

H pany called Fiesta Tours, Ltd., had never been wound up, and in a recent decision of this court in *R. v. Rollafson* (1) it was held that s. 332 (3) applied only to acts done before or in the course of a winding-up. If *R. v. Rollafson* (1) is right, it follows that this appellant, despite his plea of guilty, cannot be convicted under count 1, and accordingly in the light of that decision this court feels that the only course open to it is to allow the appeal and to quash the conviction on count 1.

I Counsel for the Crown asks this court to certify under s. 1 of the Administration of Justice Act 1960 that a point of law of general public importance is involved and to grant leave to appeal to the House of Lords. It appears that not only have there been in the past a number of convictions in similar circumstances under this subsection, but some people are at present in prison pursuant to such convictions, and there are similar prosecutions now outstanding. It is, therefore, of great importance, and particularly to the Board of Trade, to know exactly

what the position is.   This court has no doubt that it should certify, and the A
point of law for the consideration of the House of Lords is agreed in this form:
What, if any, words of limitation are to be imported into s. 332 (3) of the Companies Act 1948.   The court will certify to that effect, and grant leave to appeal
to the House of Lords.

Appeal allowed. Conviction quashed. Leave to apeal to the House of Lords granted.
                                                                                    B
Solicitors: *Registrar of Criminal Appeals* (for the appellant); *Director of
Public Prosecutions* (for the Crown).

[*Reported by* N. P. METCALFE, ESQ., *Barrister-at-Law.*]

                                                                                    C

BAKER *v.* MINISTER OF SOCIAL SECURITY.

[QUEEN'S BENCH DIVISION (Paull, J.), March 19, 20, 21, 1969.]

*National Insurance—Benefit—Earnings-related supplement—Reckonable earnings
   —Emoluments assessable to income tax under Sch. E from which tax is
   deductible—Casual employments in addition to regular employment—*   D
   *Tax deduction by casual employers impracticable—Effect on earnings-
   related supplementary benefit—Income Tax Act 1952 (15 & 16 Geo. 6 &
   1 Eliz. 2 c. 10), s. 157—Income Tax (Employments) Regulations 1965 (S.I.
   1965 No. 516), reg. 51 (1)—National Insurance Act 1965 (c. 51), s. 4 (2)—
   National Insurance Act 1966 (c. 6), s. 2 (1), (5) (b).*

During the tax year 1965-66 the appellant worked in the printing trade   E
in regular part-time employment for the N. company and on a casual basis
for three other employers.   His total remuneration was assessable for
income tax under Sch. E of the Income Tax Act 1952, and in compliance
with s. 157 of the Act tax was deducted from his remuneration in respect of
his regular employment by the N. company.   In respect of his three other
employments the Commissioners of Inland Revenue, acting under reg. 51   F
(1)* of the Income Tax (Employments) Regulations 1965, decided that
deduction of tax by those employers by reference to tax tables was impracticable and arranged for the tax on those emoluments to be paid by the
appellant direct to a collector of taxes.   The appellant paid weekly contributions under the National Insurance Act 1966 at the rate applicable to
his remuneration from the N. company.   During a period of illness the   G
appellant received flat rate sickness benefit under the National Insurance
Acts together with an earnings-related supplement of £1 9s. weekly, being
the rate applicable to his remuneration from the N. company.   For the
purpose of determining the appropriate rate of graduated contributions
and the earnings-related supplement to which the appellant was entitled
under s. 2† of the National Insurance Act 1966 the remuneration to be taken   H
into account (i.e., the reckonable earnings) by virtue of s. 2 (5) (b), read in
conjunction with s. 4 (2)‡ of the National Insurance Act 1965, included only
such of his emoluments as were both assessable to income tax under Sch. E
of the Income Tax Act 1952 and were emoluments from which tax under that
schedule was deductible.   On the question whether the appellant was
entitled to an earnings-related supplement at the rate applicable to his   I
total income,
   Held: on the true construction of the statutes and regulations, where
no system for the collection of the tax from the employer, could in practice
be devised, the tax could not be said to be deductible by the employer;
accordingly, since the earnings-related supplement was calculated on those

---
* Regulation 51 (1) is set out at p. 840, letter F, post.
† Section 2 (1) is set out at p. 839, letter I, post.
‡ Section 4 (2), so far as material, is set out at p. 840, letter A, post.

A   emoluments from which tax was deductible by the employer that part of the appellant's emoluments which was received from his casual employments had been rightly excluded for purposes of calculating the supplement due to him (see p. 841, letter H, post).

Appeal dismissed.

B   [As to earnings-related supplementary benefit under the National Insurance Act 1966, see SUPPLEMENT to 27 HALSBURY'S LAWS (3rd Edn.) para. 1320A.

As to the scope of the pay-as-you-earn scheme and as to deduction of tax by employers, see 20 HALSBURY'S LAWS (3rd Edn.) 331, 332, 335, 336, paras. 607, 608, 614, 615; as to the accountability of employers in respect of taxes under Sch. E, see ibid., pp. 343-346, paras. 628-632, p. 356, para. 654; as to direct collection of income tax in cases of casual employment, see ibid., pp. 349-
C   351, paras. 642-645.

For the Income Tax Act 1952, Sch. E, s. 157, see 31 HALSBURY'S STATUTES (2nd Edn.) 149, 152.

For the National Insurance Act 1965, s. 4, see 45 HALSBURY'S STATUTES (2nd Edn.) 955.

For the National Insurance Act 1966, s. 2, see 46 HALSBURY'S STATUTES
D   (2nd Edn.) 470.]

Case Stated.

This was a Case Stated by the Minister of Social Security on 15th October 1968 under s. 65 of the National Insurance Act 1965 as applied by s. 2 (9) of the National Insurance Act 1966. The following facts were found.

E   On 31st January 1967 Edward Albert Baker (" the appellant ") applied to the Minister of Social Security to determine the amount of the appellant's reckonable earnings in the income tax year from 6th April 1965 to 5th April 1966 (" the relevant tax year ") for the purposes of s. 2 of the National Insurance Act 1966 in connection with the appellant's claim to earnings-related supplement, under s. 2, by way of an increase of sickness benefit claimed by the appellant under the National Insurance Act 1965. The following facts were found by
F   the Minister. (i) During the relevant tax year the appellant worked for, and was paid remuneration by, employers as follows:

Employer	*Gross Pay*
News of the World, Ltd.	£674 6s. 3d.
Williams Lea & Co., Ltd.	£474 5s. 5d.
St. Clements Press, Ltd.	£1,207 15s. 10d.
Beaverbrook Newspapers, Ltd.	£129 4s. 7d.

(ii) News of the World, Ltd. deducted £278 2s. on account of income tax from the remuneration paid by them but the other employers made no deductions on account of income tax from the remuneration paid by them. (iii) The Com-
H   missioners of Inland Revenue made special arrangements for the collection directly from the appellant of income tax in respect of his remuneration received from the three employers other than News of the World, Ltd., because either the employment of the appellant by each of them was casual in character, or it was of a class such that, in the opinion of the commissioners, deduction of income tax from remuneration in respect thereof by reference to tax tables prepared by
I   the commissioners under s. 157 of the Income Tax Act 1952 was impracticable. (iv) In accordance with the special arrangements referred to, the remuneration from the three employers was assessed under Sch. E to the Income Tax Act 1952 and the appellant paid directly to a collector of taxes income tax in respect of that remuneration.

The appellant contended that (i) the whole of his income was assessable to tax, and was in fact assessed to tax, under Sch. E; (ii) although income tax was not in fact deducted from the emoluments paid to him by the employers in respect of the casual employment, i.e., the three employments referred to, that

tax was deductible therefrom and accordingly these emoluments were part of A
his " remuneration " under s. 4 (2) of the National Insurance Act 1965; (iii) that
the Minister ought therefore to have decided that the appellant's reckonable
earnings amounted to £2,485 12s. 1d.

The Minister, taking into consideration the facts and the appellant's representations, reached the following conclusions. (i) For the purpose of the appellant's right to earnings-related supplement under s. 2 of the Act of 1966, the B
remuneration to be taken into account by virtue of s. 2 (5) (b) and s. 4 (2) of the
Act of 1965 included, and included only, such of his emoluments as were both
assessable to income tax under Sch. E and were emoluments from which tax
under that schedule was deductible (whether or not tax in fact fell to be deducted
from any payment of such remuneration). (ii) The Commissioners of Inland
Revenue, in making arrangements for collection directly from the appellant, C
instead of collection by deduction from remuneration, of income tax in respect
of the emoluments of the three employments, did so in exercise of the power
conferred by reg. 51 of the Income Tax (Employments) Regulations 1965*.
Those regulations were made by the Commissioners of Inland Revenue under
s. 157 of the Income Tax Act 1952, and s. 157 (1) required that income tax
" shall, subject to and in accordance with " such regulations " be deducted . . ." D
when emoluments are paid.   Where arrangements were made under reg. 51
for collection of tax otherwise than by deduction from the emoluments of any
particular employment, tax had not to be deducted under s. 157 (1) from those
emoluments. (iii) Accordingly, income tax was not deductible under Sch. E
from the appellant's emoluments from the said three employments and his
reckonable earnings in the relevant tax year included only his remuneration by E
way of emoluments from the News of the World, Ltd., amounting to £674 6s. 3d.

On 15th June 1967 the Minister gave the appellant notice in writing of her
determination in respect of his application of 31st January 1967.   On 5th October
1967 the Minister furnished a written statement of the grounds of her
determination.   On 23rd November 1967 the appellant gave notice of appeal.

The cases noted below† were cited during the argument.   F

S. J. Waldman for the appellant.
R. A. Gatehouse for the Minister of Social Security.

PAULL, J.: This is an appeal by way of a Case Stated from the decision
of the Minister of Social Security.   It discloses what to my mind is a most
unsatisfactory and unfair state of affairs.   As most people know, by the pro- G
visions of the National Insurance Act 1966 benefits under the National Insurance
Acts are linked to an employee's earnings, so that payment of benefits in respect
of sickness and unemployment, as well as old age pensions and the benefits
which widows receive, are greater in the case of an employee who is earning
more than £450 per annum than the flat rate benefits receivable by every insured
person up to the date when the Act of 1966 came into force.   In order that such H
extra benefits may be received the person who, or whose widow, will receive
the extra benefits has to pay a somewhat larger contribution each week.   The
extra unemployment and sickness benefits (subject to a certain provision which
is immaterial and to which I need not refer) range from 1s. a week in respect of
the person earning £450 per annum up to £7 a week for a man earning £1,500
per annum or over.   In the present case Mr. Baker, the appellant, was ill for I
a certain period and received 29s. a week by way of benefit additional to the
flat rate.   He was judged by the Minister not to come within the provisions of
the Act of 1966 in respect of a large part of his income.   If he had been judged
to come within those provisions he would have received £7 a week additional
to the flat rate instead of the 29s.   On the other hand, his contribution would

_____
* S.I. 1965 No. 516.
  † *Re El Sombrero, Ltd.*, [1958] 3 All E.R. 1; [1958] Ch. 900; *Jayne* v. *National Coal
Board*, [1963] 2 All E.R. 220.

A   have been 9s. 9d. a week whereas in fact he paid 5s. 11d. a week, a difference of 3s. 10d.

The appellant is in the printing world. He drew his income during the material period from four sources: he was paid £674 6s. 3d. by the News of the World, Ltd.; £474 5s. 5d. by Williams Lea & Co., Ltd.; £1,207 15s. 10d. by St. Clements Press, Ltd.; and £129 4s. 7d. by Beaverbrook Newspapers, Ltd.

B   According to the decision of the Minister only the income from the News of the World, Ltd., could be held to be his income in respect of which he paid contributions and drew benefits. The Minister decided that the rest of his income did not fall within the provisions for calculating income for the·purposes of the National Insurance Act 1966 and therefore had to be disregarded.

The ground on which that decision was made is set out in the Case as follows:

C   " The Commissioners of Inland Revenue made special arrangements for the collection directly from the appellant of income tax in respect of his said remuneration received from the three said employers other than News of the World, Limited, because either the employment of the appellant by each of them was casual in character, or it was of a class such that, in the opinion of the said Commissioners, deduction of income tax from remuneration in
D   respect thereof by reference to tax tables prepared by the said Commissioners under section 157 of the Income Tax Act 1952 was impracticable."

In other words, the appellant was one of those persons who had regular employment with the News of the World, Ltd., for a specified time each week but as to the rest of his income he was considered to be a casual employee who went to each printing works as and when required and not for regular periods of time.
E   Although the fact does not appear in the Case, I was informed during the hearing that there are some 40,000 employees in all affected to a greater or less degree in the same way as the appellant. This arises because of the nature of their employment in such trades as printing trades, market porters, boatmen, barristers' clerks, employees of diplomats, those employed in England by employers who are overseas, and certain other categories. All persons in those categories may
F   well earn over the £1,500 per annum (as the appellant did) but are only entitled to benefits as though they earned under £450. It is difficult to see the justice of this but no steps seem to have been taken at any time to make a simple regulation to the effect that all persons whose income comes within the provisions of Sch. E should be entitled to the benefits of the Act of 1966. In the case of casual employment it would be easy to base the contributions and the benefits
G   on the income returned for the previous period with a proviso that any tax due must have been paid. Instead of that a really quite complicated series of provisions in Acts of Parliament and in regulations have been made involving by reference regulations made for purposes quite different from the purposes of the National Insurance Act 1966. These Acts and regulations have resulted in excluding those 40,000 employees or thereabouts from the benefits of the Act.
H   Why this matter has not been put right long ago passes my comprehension. I can see no other reason than administrative convenience, nor was any other reason suggested. It certainly brings about an injustice.

The situation is as follows   The general principle of the grounds for receiving higher benefits is set out in s. 2 (1) of the National Insurance Act 1966, which provides:

I   " Benefit under the Insurance Act (1) shall include earnings-related supplement which shall be payable by way of an increase of the weekly rate of unemployment benefit or sickness benefit."

The earnings-related supplement depends, under the provisons of the Act, on the reckonable earnings of any person in employment, and by s. 2 (5) (*b*) of the Act " reckonable earnings " are the remuneration within the meaning of s. 4 (2) of the National Insurance Act 1965. Turning to that Act, s. 4 (2) provides:

---

(1) I.e., the National Insurance Act 1965.

"In relation to graduated contributions . . . remuneration shall be taken   A
to include, and to include only, any emoluments assessable to income
tax under Schedule E . . . being emoluments from which tax under that
Schedule is deductible, but shall apply to a payment of any such remuneration whether or not tax in fact falls to be deducted from that payment."

The last proviso of course covers the case where nothing is in fact deducted   B
due to, e.g., an overpayment due to a change in the code number or when the
remuneration is under the taxable level.

It will be seen therefore that instead of a simple provision that remuneration
shall include any emoluments assessable under Sch. E, these emoluments have
got to be "deductible" under that schedule and, in order to determine people's
rights to benefits under national insurance, one has to look to an Act (the Income   C
Tax Act 1952) which has nothing to do with people's rights to benefits under
national insurance but which primarily relates to the most convenient way by
which to collect income tax under Sch. E.   One therefore has to turn to s. 157
of the Income Tax Act 1952.   By sub-s. (1) of that section income tax in the
case of Sch. E shall, subject to and in accordance with the regulations made
by the Commissioners of Inland Revenue under that section, be deducted by the   D
person making the payment (i.e., the employer) and for that purpose there are
provisions whereby the inspector of taxes provides the employer with a code
number, and tax is deducted according to that code number.   It is worth noting
that in s. 157 (6) the emoluments to which s. 157 applies are "all emoluments
assessable to income tax under Schedule E" (I leave out certain words which
have been repealed.)   One then has to look at the regulations made under the   E
provisions of that Act.   The regulations applicable today are the Income Tax
(Employments) Regulations 1965 (2).   Regulation 51 (1) of those regulations
provides:

"In cases of casual employment, and in any other class of case in which
the Commissioners of Inland Revenue are of opinion that deduction of tax
by reference to the tax tables is impracticable those Commissioners may   F
make special arrangements for the collection of the tax in respect of any
emoluments and may in particular direct that the following provisions of
this regulation shall apply."

By the paragraph of the Case, which I have already read, the appellant comes
within reg. 51 so far as three employers are concerned and accordingly the only
income allowed by the Minister to go towards the earnings-related supplement   G
under the National Insurance Act 1966 is the sum of £674 6s. 3d. paid by the
News of the World, Ltd., from which tax had been deducted by the News of
the World, Ltd., to the amount of £278 2s.   That the finding that the appellant's
income from employment is £674 is, in common sense, absurd, is manifest, but
unfortunately on the facts found by the Minister I feel bound to find in the
Minister's favour simply making the comment that the sooner the matter is put   H
right the less injustice will be done.

The argument of counsel for the appellant consisted in trying to distinguish
the word "deductible" used in s. 4 (2) of the National Insurance Act 1965 from
the word "impracticable" appearing in reg. 51 (1) of the regulations of 1965.
He says, with some force, that reg. 51 is a regulation merely inviting a tax
inspector, if it is more convenient to him, to arrange for the sums due under   I
Sch. E from a taxpayer to be collected from the taxpayer by the usual method
where another person does not pay, instead of from the employer, and that it is
absurd that where a man earns his money in the same sort of way from four
employers the inspector should choose one employer as an employer who should
pay the tax, and should collect direct from the appellant his tax on his earnings
under the other three employers, and then use that fact to deprive the appellant

(2) S.I. 1965 No. 516.

A of his additional benefits. Counsel says that the fact that the inspector so acts does not mean that it is impossible to arrange that the tax is deducted by the other employers. It is, he says, merely a matter of administrative convenience. " Deductible ", says counsel for the appellant, means possible to deduct, not practicable to deduct, and there is no finding that it was impossible to deduct the tax in the case of the other three employers. Moreover, says counsel, there is

B no finding of fact in the case that it was impracticable for the other employers to deduct the tax. All the finding amounts to is that the commissioners decided it was impracticable.

Counsel for the Minister contended that the matter is really quite clear under the existing regulations, but he did not seek to contend that the regulations are either common sense or satisfactory. A simple regulation laying down that all

C emoluments received under Sch. E should be reckonable earnings (provided that all tax due on them has in fact been paid either by the employer or employee) would get rid of the present unsatisfactory state of affairs. He says that the deduction of tax by an employer is quite impractical unless there is some regularity of employment in the case of a part-time employee. Theoretically an employer who has no code number for someone who is casually employed could be made to

D deduct the amount payable on the sums earned on the assumption that there are no deductions to be made and then an adjustment could be made later, but, says counsel for the Minister—and I agree with him—that would lead to such an outcry that it is simply not practical. Moreover, where there is more than one employer the deductions are divided between the employers so that the employee has the advantage of part of his code allowance in each case but where an employer

E does not know whether the man is coming again and, if he does come, when and for how long, it is impossible so to do. The " code number " system, says counsel for the Minister, is the very basis of the method of tax deduction by the employer and unless that can be done the tax deduction system simply cannot be applied. " Deductible ", says counsel, must mean capable of being deducted by some practicable system and the Minister has accepted that in the appellant's

F case there was no practicable system under which the sums could be deducted by the employer.

At one time I wondered whether I should not send the case back to the Minister to find more specifically whether the Minister (not the Commissioners of Inland Revenue) found deduction to be impracticable. Counsel for the Minister has pointed out, however, that no such point is taken in the notice of appeal

G (apparently the appellant's advisers were given an opportunity so to do) and counsel for the appellant does not ask me so to do. That being so, I think I must draw the inference that the appellant is accepting that the paragraph of the Case which I have quoted must be read in the sense that the Minister has accepted that the collection of tax from the employer was impracticable. This seems to be borne out by the Minister's reasons. I am afraid I must find that where no

H system for the collection of the tax by the employer can in practice be devised the tax cannot be said to be " deductible " by the employer, and therefore the earnings-related supplement does not apply to those earnings.

In the course of the case I said, " If Parliament has made an unjust regulation I have no power to make it a just one ". Counsel for the Minister said, " No, my Lord, but a word from the judge is sometimes effective ". I have given

I that word.

Appeal dismissed.

Solicitors: *W. H. Thompson* (for the appellant); *Solicitor, Ministry of Social Security.*

[*Reported by* K. DIANA PHILLIPS, *Barrister-at-Law.*]

RENE CLARO (HAUTE COIFFURE), LTD. *v.* HALLÉ
CONCERTS SOCIETY.

[COURT OF APPEAL, CIVIL DIVISION (Lord Denning, M.R., Winn and Fenton Atkinson, L.JJ.), March 24, 1969.]

Landlord and Tenant—Notice to quit—Business premises—Sub-tenancy of part of premises—Statutory notice to terminate by head landlords to tenants—No special notice to sub-tenants—Sub-tenants' application for new lease—Whether head landlords should be joined as parties—" Landlord "—Landlord and Tenant Act 1954 (2 & 3 Eliz. 2 c. 56), s. 25 (1), s. 44 (1), s. 69 (1).

In May 1962 business premises were let with a break clause in case the head landlords wished to redevelop the property. The head tenants granted a sublease of part of the premises containing the same break clause. In 1967 the head landlords wishing to redevelop the property served on the head tenants a statutory notice under s. 25 of the Landlord and Tenant Act 1954, to terminate their tenancy on 25th March 1968, stating that they would oppose any application for a new tenancy on the ground that they wished to demolish and rebuild. On 26th September 1967, the head tenants gave similar notice to the sub-tenants to terminate their sub-tenancy on 25th March 1968. Both tenants made applications to the county court for new tenancies and both cases were listed to be heard on 25th March 1968. At the hearing the head tenants submitted to an order to give up possession on 30th April 1968. When the sub-tenants' application came on the judge invited the sub-tenants to join the head landlords as parties but the sub-tenants refused, contending that the head landlords were not the " landlord " within the meaning of s. 44* of the Landlord and Tenant Act 1954, and further, that no proper notice to quit as required by s. 69† of the Act had been given to them. The county court judge dismissed the application. On appeal,

Held: the application for a new lease was rightly refused, because—
(i) the notice to terminate under s. 25 of the Landlord and Tenant Act 1954 was a good notice to quit within s. 69 of that Act (see p. 844, letter F, p. 845, letter C, and p. 846, letter A, post);
(ii) the head landlords were at the material date, namely the date of the hearing, the " landlord " of the sub-tenants within the meaning of the Act because the term of the head tenants would have expired either by effluxion of time or by virtue of the notice to quit within 14 months or less (see p. 844, letter I, to p. 845, letters A and C, and p. 846, letter A, post).

Westbury Property & Investment Co., Ltd. v. *Carpenter* [(1961) 1 All E.R. 481) overruled.

Appeal dismissed.

[As to the meaning of landlord, see 23 HALSBURY'S LAWS (3rd Edn.) 888, 889, para. 1710.

For the Landlord and Tenant Act 1954, s. 25, s. 44, s. 69, see 34 HALSBURY'S STATUTES (2nd Edn.) 410, 427, 443.]

Cases referred to:
Bowes-Lyon v. *Green,* [1961] 3 All E.R. 843; [1963] A.C. 420; [1961] 3 W.L.R. 1044; Digest (Cont. Vol. A) 1063, *7417z.*
Scholl Manufacturing Co., Ltd. v. *Clifton (Slim-Line), Ltd.,* [1966] 3 All E.R. 16; [1967] Ch. 41; [1966] 3 W.L.R. 575; Digest (Cont. Vol. B) 478, *6111Abc.*
Westbury Property & Investment Co., Ltd. v. *Carpenter,* [1961] 1 All E.R. 481; [1961] 1 W.L.R. 273; Digest (Cont. Vol. A) 1044, *7417je.*

* Section 44, so far as material, is set out at p. 844, letters B and C, post.
† Section 69, so far as material, is set out at p. 844, letter E, post.

A **Appeal.**

This was an appeal by the sub-tenants, Rene Claro (Haute Coiffure), Ltd., against a judgment of His Honour Judge Steel, given at Manchester County Court on 25th March 1968, dismissing their application for a new tenancy. The facts are set out in the judgment of Lord Denning, M.R.

M. H. Spence for the sub-tenants.

B *Raymond Walton, Q.C.*, and *D. G. Nowell* for the head tenants.

LORD DENNING, M.R.: A company called Central and District Properties, Ltd., own a block of houses in St. Peter's Square, Manchester. They are the head landlords. They propose to demolish the block and redevelop the site. One of the houses is no. 8, St. Peter's Square. The head landlords, Central and **C** District Properties, let the house to the head tenants, Hallé Concerts Society. Although there had been previous leases, the material one is a lease for five years from 25th December 1966. It contained a break clause which enabled the head landlords, on giving a six months' notice of the necessary planning permission, to determine the lease if they should desire to redevelop. The head tenants, Hallé Concerts Society, sublet the basement to the sub-tenants, Rene Claro **D** (Haute Coiffure), Ltd. for the same period of five years, but less one day. The sublease contained a similar break clause, namely, that if there were a desire by the head landlords to redevelop, then, on giving a six months' notice, they could acquire possession. The head tenants occupied their part of the house for business purposes. The sub-tenants occupied the basement for business purposes. So each was within the Landlord and Tenant Act 1954.

E In September 1967 the head landlords desired to demolish the premises and reconstruct, and obtained the necessary planning permission. They gave a proper notice to the head tenants to terminate the head tenancy on 25th March 1968 in accordance with the provisions of s. 25 of the Landlord and Tenant Act 1954. In the notice they said that they would oppose any application for the grant of a new tenancy on the ground that they intended to demolish and re-**F** construct. (They gave a similar notice to the sub-tenants, although they were not bound to do so.) On receiving that notice from the head landlords, the head tenants gave a similar notice to terminate to the sub-tenants. They gave it on 26th September 1967, to determine on 29th March 1968. Those notices on tenants and sub-tenants were undoubtedly good notices under the Landlord and Tenant Act 1954, s. 25, specifying the day on which the tenancy was to come to an end. **G** The head tenants and sub-tenants, within the prescribed time, made application to the county court for grants of new tenancies. In January 1968 the head tenants made application against the head landlords, and the sub-tenants made application against the head tenants. Both cases were listed to come on for hearing on 25th March 1968. The first case to be called was the claim by the head tenants against the head landlords. The head tenants realised that the head landlords intended to demolish the house and to reconstruct, and that they could not **H** possibly get a new lease. The head tenants, therefore, submitted to an order by consent that they would vacate on 30th April 1968.

Next came the case of the sub-tenants against the head tenants. The judge invited the sub-tenants to bring in the head landlords as parties, but they declined. The sub-tenants contended that the issue should be decided as between the sub-tenants and the head tenants without bringing in the head landlords at all. **I** No doubt they thought they would gain an advantage, because the head tenants could not say that they intended to demolish and reconstruct. Only the head landlords could say that. The judge, however, would not have anything to do with the suggestion of the sub-tenants; he held that the rights of the parties could only be determined if and when the head landlords were in a position to defend. Accordingly, he dismissed the application of the sub-tenants. They now appeal to this court.

The case depends on this: who was the " landlord " at the material time,

namely, at the time when the application of the sub-tenants was heard by the   **A**
county court judge?: for, if the head landlords were the " landlord ", they ought
to have been joined. The meaning of " landlord " is given by s. 44 of the Landlord
and Tenant Act 1954, which provides:

> ". . . the expression ' the landlord ', in relation to a tenancy (in this section
> referred to as ' the relevant tenancy '), means the person (whether or not he
> is the immediate landlord) who is the owner of that interest in the property   **B**
> comprised in the relevant tenancy which for the time being fulfils the follow-
> ing conditions, that is to say: (a) that it is an interest in reversion expectant
> (whether immediately or not) on the termination of the relevant tenancy,
> and (b) that it is either the fee simple or a tenancy which will not come to
> an end within fourteen months or less by effluxion of time or by virtue of a
> notice to quit already given by the landlord . . ."   **C**

In other words, one has to see whether, at the material time, the head tenancy
had less than 14 months to run. If it had less than 14 months to run, the head
tenants drop out and the head landlords come into direct contact with the
sub-tenants. The head landlords are to be treated as the " landlord " for the
purpose of s. 44. The question, therefore, is whether on 25th March 1968, the
head tenants had a tenancy which would come to an end within 14 months or less   **D**
by effluxion of time or by virtue of a notice to quit already given by the head
landlords.

I will first consider whether a " notice to quit " had already been given by the
head landlords. " Notice to quit " is defined by s. 69 to mean—

> " a notice to terminate a tenancy (whether a periodical tenancy or a   **E**
> tenancy for a term of years certain) given in accordance with the provisions
> (whether express or implied) of that tenancy."

In this case the head landlords had only given one notice. It was a six months'
notice to terminate, given in accordance with s. 25 of the Act. But, besides being
in accordance with s. 25, it was also in accordance with the provisions of the
tenancy, because it was in accordance with the notice required by the break   **F**
clause in that it gave the full time required by the contract of tenancy. In
my opinion that was sufficient to make it a " notice to quit " within s. 69.
I see no good reason why a notice to terminate under s. 25 should not also
be a notice to quit within s. 69; at any rate when it makes it clear that the
landlord is going to oppose any application for a new lease and states the
ground of it. That shows that the landlord means what he says, that the tenancy   **G**
is to terminate and that the tenant is to go. That is a " notice to quit ". I realise
that in *Westbury Property & Investment Co., Ltd.* v. *Carpenter* (1), DANCKWERTS,
J., took the contrary view. But I am afraid I do not agree with him. Nor do I
think that *Bowes-Lyon* v. *Green* (2) affords much assistance. The House did not
there consider the import of s. 69. I am of opinion, therefore, that in this case the
head tenancy would come to an end on 25th March 1968, by virtue of a notice to   **H**
quit already given by the head landlords, so that at the material time the head
landlords were the competent " landlord ".

Next I will consider whether the new tenancy, at the material time, would come
to an end " by effluxion of time ". At the time when the case of the sub-tenants
was called on for hearing, a consent order had been made in the previous case by
which the head tenants were to give up possession on 30th April 1968. It seems   **I**
to me plain that it would then come to an end " by effluxion of time ". Once the
month of April had passed, the head tenancy would clearly be at an end by the
lapse of time.

It seems to me, therefore, that, on one ground or the other, the head tenants
had less than 14 months to go, either by effluxion of time or by virtue of a notice

---

(1) [1961] 1 All E.R. 481; [1961] 1 W.L.R. 273.
(2) [1961] 3 All E.R. 843; [1963] A.C. 420.

A to quit. So they drop out. At the material time, the date of the hearing, the competent " landlord " was Central and District Properties, Ltd. The action was not properly constituted at that time without their being joined. They certainly should have been joined. If the head landlords had been joined, the consequence is obvious: they would have proved that they intended to demolish and reconstruct and the sub-tenants could have no possible claim to a new tenancy. The sub-

B tenants knew that would be their fate, and that is why they did not join them. They knew they would be defeated. I think the judge was quite right in holding that the action was not properly constituted, and that the claim for a new tenancy by the sub-tenants should be dismissed. I would, accordingly, dismiss the appeal.

WINN, L.J.: I agree, and there is little that I would wish to add. Reference

C has been made to the decision of DANCKWERTS, J., in 1961 (3). It is to be observed that the precise point in that case was not the same as the point argued in the present appeal. It was for determination in that case whether or not an effective notice under s. 25 of the Landlord and Tenant Act 1954 had been given, and that depended on whether or not the giver of that notice was the competent landlord within the meaning of s. 44. It was, it seems to me, a relatively unimportant

D question to which the learned judge scarcely needed to advert, whether or not, in general, a s. 25 notice can in some cases be regarded as a notice to quit within the meaning of that phrase which is to be found in the definition section, s. 69 of the Act. I respectfully agree with LORD DENNING, M.R., that for present purposes the s. 25 notice, assuming—though it is a pity that one is required to assume and not to look at the terms of the document known to be in existence—assuming

E that it purported to be given in part at least by virtue of the reservation in the nature of an option to break contained in the agreement between Central and District Properties, Ltd., and the head tenants, Hallé Concerts Society, was, for present purposes, a notice to quit within the meaning of s. 44 of the Act.

I myself was a party to the decision in *Scholl Manufacturing Co., Ltd.* v. *Clifton (Slim-Line), Ltd.* (4). I would draw attention in particular to the passages in the

F judgments of HARMAN, and DIPLOCK, L.JJ., which really draw no distinction, semantic or real, between a notice to quit and a notice under s. 25 of the Act for the purposes with which the court was concerned there and for the purposes with which this court is today concerned. I have found *Bowes-Lyon* v. *Green* (5) somewhat difficult to follow, but, more difficult than following it, I find the task, if it be a proper and appropriate one, of attempting to apply its principles to

G the circumstances of the present case. I do not think it has any relevance to the present case.

The present litigation was quite deliberately not brought either originally or by way of amendment against Central and District Properties, Ltd., it being appreciated that it would have been bound to fail as against them, but was attempted to be brought against a mesne landlord on the footing of his being the

H competent landlord in order to gain an advantage clearly not intended by the statute. This action turns essentially on the answer to a relatively short question, namely: on 25th March 1968, when the sub-tenants' application fell to be heard in the county court, could it then be said that *for that " time being "* the head tenants held an interest reversionary on the sub-tenants' sub-tenancy which itself *would not* come to an end within 14 months or less either by effluxion of time or by

I virtue of a notice to quit already given by the landlords? I think of these two alternatives it is clearer that the answer must be in the negative if one looks at the second limb than it is that the answer is the same, i.e., negative, if one looks at the first of those two alternatives. I agree that this appeal should be dismissed.

---

(3) *Westbury Property & Investment Co., Ltd.* v. *Carpenter*, [1961] 1 All E.R. 481; [1961] 1 W.L.R. 273.
(4) [1966] 3 All E.R. 16; [1967] 1 Ch. 41.
(5) [1961] 3 All E.R. 843; [1963] A.C. 420.

FENTON ATKINSON, L.J.: I agree with both judgments.   A

Appeal dismissed. Leave to appeal to the House of Lords refused.

Solicitors: *Rye & Eyre* (for the sub-tenants); *George Davies & Co.*, Manchester (for the head tenants).

[*Reported by* F. GUTTMAN, ESQ., *Barrister-at-Law.*]

B

R. *v.* AUBREY-FLETCHER, *Ex parte* THOMPSON.

[QUEEN'S BENCH DIVISION (Lord Parker, C.J., Edmund Davies, L.J., and Caulfield, J.), March 26, 1969.]   C

Magistrates—Jurisdiction—Binding-over—Accused bound over to keep the peace on adjournment of case—Necessity for reasonable grounds that future breach of the peace might occur—Justices of the Peace Act 1361 (34 Edw. 3 c. 1) —Magistrates' Courts Act 1952 (15 & 16 Geo. 6 & 1 Eliz. 2 c. 55), s. 91.

Whereas an order for binding-over under s. 91* of the Magistrates' Courts Act 1952 can only be made after the case has been heard out completely, D an order under the Justices of the Peace Act 1361 can be made at any time during the proceedings subject to an opportunity being given to the applicant or his advisers to argue against it; nevertheless there is no jurisdiction to make an order unless the proceedings have reached the stage where it emerges that there might be a breach of the peace in the future (see p. 847, letters F and G, and p. 848, letters B and I, post).   E

Sheldon v. *Bromfield Justices* ([1964] 2 All E.R. 131) followed.

Application allowed.

[As to binding-over to keep the peace, see 25 HALSBURY'S LAWS (3rd Edn.) 231, 232, paras. 427, 428; and for cases on the subject, see 33 DIGEST (Repl.) 257-260, *841-870*.

For the Justices of the Peace Act 1361, see 14 HALSBURY'S STATUTES (2nd Edn.)   F 709.

For the Magistrates' Courts Act 1952, s. 91, see 32 HALSBURY'S STATUTES (2nd Edn.) 493.]

Cases referred to:

Sheldon v. *Bromfield Justices*, [1964] 2 All E.R. 131; [1964] 2 Q.B. 573; [1964]   G
        2 W.L.R. 1066; Digest (Cont. Vol. B) 511, *849a*.
Wilson v. *Sckeock* (1949), 113 J.P. 294; 65 T.L.R. 418.

Motion for certiorari.

This was an application by way of motion by George Thompson for an order of certiorari to bring up and quash an order made by J. AUBREY-FLETCHER, Esq., a metropolitan magistrate sitting at Marlborough Street Magistrates' Court on 4th   H March 1969. The facts are set out in the judgment of LORD PARKER, C.J.

The cases noted below† were cited during the argument in addition to those referred to in the judgments.

Lord Gifford for the applicant.

The respondent did not appear nor was he represented.

        I

LORD PARKER, C.J.: In these proceedings counsel moves on behalf of the applicant, George Thompson, for an order of certiorari to bring up and

---

* Section 91 (1) provides: " The power of a magistrates' court on the complaint of any person to adjudge any other person to enter into a recognizance, with or without sureties, to keep the peace or to be of good behaviour towards the complainant shall be exercised by order on complaint."

† *R.* v. *Londonderry Justices* (1891), 28 L.R.Ir. 440; *Everett* v. *Ribbands*, [1952] 1 All E.R. 823; [1952] 2 Q.B. 198.

Q.B.D.   R. *v.* AUBREY-FLETCHER (Lord Parker, C.J.)   847

A quash an order made by the stipendiary magistrate sitting at Marlborough
Street Magistrates' Court on 4th March 1969, whereby he ordered that the
applicant be bound over to keep the peace for a period of three months in the
sum of £500, and if the said order was not complied with, he be imprisoned for
90 days.   It is quite clear that this was a bind-over made by the magistrate
under the Justices of the Peace Act 1361.   It was made in these circumstances:
B the applicant was charged with two offences contrary to s. 54 of the Metropolitan
Police Courts Act 1839 in respect of two occasions when it was alleged that he
used insulting words whereby a breach of the peace may have been occasioned.
The two charges were listed for hearing on 4th March, when it was decided that
the two charges should be heard separately and the hearing on one charge was
commenced at 3.45 p.m.   During the rest of the day the evidence given consisted
C of the evidence of a police constable, who gave evidence that the applicant had
been speaking at Speakers' Corner and had used various words whereby he said
a breach of the peace may have been occasioned.   He was cross-examined, so
we were told, to the effect that those words were not used at all, and in any event
that they were not likely to cause a breach of the peace.   The case could not
be completed that day, and at the adjournment the question of bail was raised.
D The prosecution suggested that bail might be granted subject to some condition
that the applicant should not take part in meetings at Speakers' Corner.   The
applicant was represented by counsel, who sought to argue that any such condition would be invalid, and in an affidavit put in by the learned magistrate, he
said that he was inclined to accept that view, and thereupon he proceeded to
make the order binding over the applicant under the Act of 1361.
E   It is argued before this court that that order was invalid for a number of
reasons.   It is said in the first instance that there is no power to make such an
order until the case involving the applicant has been finished; alternatively
it is said that it cannot be exercised until the applicant has been examined and
cross-examined.   For my part I am quite unable to accept either of those contentions.   This is not a bind-over made under s. 91 of the Magistrates' Courts
F Act 1952, in which case there must be a complaint and that complaint must be
adjudged to be true, in other words the case must be heard out completely.   An
order under the Act of 1361 can, however, be made at any time during the proceedings, subject of course to an opportunity being given to the applicant or
his advisers to argue against it.   That was the decision of this court in *Sheldon*
v. *Bromfield Justices* (1).   At the same time, as it seems to me there is no juris-
G diction to make this order unless, in the course of the proceedings, it emerges
that there might be a breach of the peace in the future.   In the present case,
as I understand it, that stage had not been reached.   There may be cases, of
course, when that fact emerges even before the defendant in the case gives
evidence; to take the present case, if there were no cross-examination to the
effect that the words used were spoken but merely that they were not calculated
H to give rise to a breach of the peace, it seems to me the magistrate might then
say:

> " It is admitted that the words were used and having seen the nature of
> those words, it looks as if there would be proof that a breach of the peace
> had been committed here."

Then if it was anticipated that there might be a repetition, there would be power
I to make the order.   So far, however, as this case is concerned it does not seem
to me that that stage had been reached, and on that ground and on that ground
only, I have come to the conclusion that this order ought to be set aside.
    I would just like to add this, that it does appear that this order was made once
the magistrate had decided that he ought to accede to the submission made on
behalf of the applicant that any restriction on his movements to Speakers'
Corner would not constitute a valid condition of bail, in other words it was said

(1) [1964] 2 All E.R. 131;   [1964] 2 Q.B. 573.

that this order was made, as it were, as an alternative, to the making of a con-　A
dition of bail. Whether or not it could have been made a valid condition of
bail I do not propose to decide, but if it could be made a valid condition of
bail, then the applicant of course would have the right to appeal to the judge in
chambers on it, and it might be said to be wrong to order a bind-over in lieu of
such a condition. For my part, however, I find it unnecessary to decide that
point.　B

EDMUND DAVIES, L.J.: I agree. A distinction has to be drawn between
the power of the court in relation to a bind-over under s. 91 of the Magistrates'
Courts Act 1952, and the similar power exercised by virtue of the Justices of
the Peace Act 1361. In the former case there must be proof; in the latter case
there need not be proof of the matters complained of, but nevertheless the order　C
cannot be made capriciously. In relation to the Act of 1361, the test which
LORD PARKER, C.J., has already enunciated is, with respect, the correct one.
There must emerge during the course of the hearing, which need not be a completed hearing, material from which it may fairly be deduced that there is at least
a risk of a breach of peace in the future. That approach is in line with the
decision of the Divisional Court in *Wilson* v. *Sckeock* (2). There the information　D
was wrongly laid under the Public Order Act 1936, but nevertheless the defendant
was bound over to keep the peace under the Justices of the Peace Act 1361. In
the course of holding that the magistrates were entitled so to act, LORD GODDARD,
C.J., had this to say (3):

"It is for that reason—because they were satisfied that there might be a
breach of the peace between these two persons—that they have bound　E
the defendant to keep the peace ' towards his Majesty and all his liege
people and especially towards the complainant for the term of two years '."

In the present case it is significant that not only was the trial even on the first
charge only partially heard—that of itself, as we have already indicated, does
not conclude the matter either way—but there had been a direct challenge
of the essential evidence of the one witness, a police constable, as to what had　F
transpired during the first incident complained of. Furthermore, and most
noteworthy of all, when one turns to the affidavit of the learned magistrate one
finds there no indication that he had formed even a tentative view that the
evidence so far adduced in this uncompleted hearing of the first charge was such
as to cause him to think that there might be a breach of the peace in the future.
Accordingly, in my judgment, he was not entitled at that stage to bind over the　G
applicant.

I agree with LORD PARKER, C.J., also that, from what transpired in this case,
it looks very much as though there was certainly under consideration by the
learned magistrate at one stage the granting of bail subject to a condition that
the applicant did not take part in meetings at Speakers' Corner until the hearing
was resumed. Whether or not the imposition of such a condition would be　H
lawful, I do not think it was right to resort to the binding-over as an alternative
to deciding that question one way or the other. For those reasons I agree in
holding that this application should be allowed.

CAULFIELD, J.: I agree on the simple and limited ground that the stage
had not been reached when resort could have been made to the powers given to
magistrates under the Justices of Peace Act 1361.　I

Order for certiorari.

Solicitors: *James Goudie* (for the applicant).

[*Reported by* N. P. METCALFE, ESQ., *Barrister-at-Law.*]

---

(2) (1949), 65 T.L.R. 418.
(3) (1949), 65 T.L.R. at p. 419.

A

Re DAVSTONE ESTATES, LTD.'S LEASES.
MANPROP, LTD. v. O'DELL AND OTHERS.

[CHANCERY DIVISION (Ungoed-Thomas, J.), March 10, 11, 12, 25, 1969.]

B *Contract—Illegality—Public policy—Jurisdiction of court—Exclusion—Lease—Lessee's covenant to contribute towards lessor's expenses—Certificate of lessor's surveyor as to lessor's expenses to be final—Whether contrary to public policy.*

Between May and July 1964, the plaintiffs' predecessor-in-title, D., Ltd., in consideration of capital payments, granted to the defendants, or their predecessors, leases in identical terms of ten flats which they had built, the
C leases being for periods of 99 years from 24th June 1963 at a yearly rent of £15. D., Ltd., subsequently assigned the reversions to the plaintiffs. The flats were defective in design, workmanship, materials and construction. Clause 2 (iii) of the leases provided as follows: " The Lessee hereby covenants with the Lessor to pay to the Lessor . . . the sum of Fifteen Pounds as a contribution towards the expenses incurred by the
D Lessor in performing the covenants on the part of the Lessor set forth in clause 3 hereof including the reasonable remuneration of a Managing Agent to be appointed by the Lessor for the purpose of managing the Buildings PROVIDED NEVERTHELESS that if one tenth part of the said expenses reasonably and properly incurred by the Lessor in any year (as certified by the Surveyor for the time being to the Lessor . . . whose
E certificate shall be final and not subject to challenge in any manner whatsoever) shall exceed Fifteen Pounds then the Lessee shall pay to the Lessor the amount of the excess such sum to be paid within twenty-eight days after the service on the Lessee of a copy of the certificate of the Surveyor ". Clause 3 provided: " THE Lessor HEREBY COVENANTS with the Lessee as follows: (i) At all times during the said term to keep the interior and
F exterior walls and ceilings and floors of the Buildings (other than those included in this demise or in the demise of any other flat or garage in the Buildings) and the roof and main drains thereof in good and substantial repair and condition . . . (viii) To defray such other costs as may be necessary to maintain the Buildings as good class residential flats and garages ". Considerable work arising out of the defective workmanship was done on the
G building by the plaintiffs. In January and March 1967 the plaintiffs' surveyor made certificates pursuant to cl. 2 (iii) which were served on the defendants. The defendants refused to pay and the plaintiffs commenced proceedings against them. The plaintiffs contended that, under the covenants in the leases, their surveyor's certificate entitled them to recover the moneys expended in maintaining the building was conclusive and obliged the
H defendants to pay the moneys certified to have been so expended, although expended on making good the defects, even on the assumption that such defects did not constitute such maintenance within the meaning of the lessor's covenants. The defendants took the view that, on such assumption, the surveyor's certificate was not so conclusive; first, on the true construction of the leases, and secondly and alternatively, on the ground that a provision
I making it conclusive would make it so on a question of construction of the leases, and, therefore, on a question of law, and so, in completely ousting the jurisdiction of the courts on a question of law, would be void as contrary to public policy. On a summons to determine whether, on the true construction of cl. 2 (iii) of the leases, the certificate of the surveyor given pursuant to that clause was open to challenge by the defendants or their assignees, and, if so, on what grounds, or was conclusive as to whether the expenses therein mentioned had been incurred in performing the covenants on behalf of the plaintiffs contained in cl. 3,

Held: (i) on the true construction of cl. 2 (iii) the question what were   A
expenses within the ambit of cl. 3 was excluded from the surveyor's conclusive decision, and the operation of the surveyor's certificate was limited
within the ambit of those expenses, and therefore, the question whether the
defects of construction, etc., were within the provisions of cl. 3 was not a
matter for decision by the surveyor's certificate but a question of law (see
p. 853, letter F, post).   B

(ii) if the proviso in cl. 2 (iii) applied to questions of law and, therefore,
to questions of construction whether the defects were within the provisions
of cl. 3, then it was void as contrary to public policy in purporting to oust
completely the jurisdiction of the courts on questions of law (see p. 855,
letter E, post).

Czarnikow & Co., Ltd. v. *Roth, Schmidt & Co.*, ([1922] All E.R. Rep. 45),   C
Lee v. *Showmen's Guild of Great Britain* ([1952] 1 All E.R. 1175), and *Baker* v.
Jones ([1954] 2 All E.R. 553) applied.

Tullis v. *Jacson* ([1892] 3 Ch. 441) not followed.

(iii) that that part of the proviso to cl. 2 (iii) which was objectionable on
the grounds of public policy could not be so severed from the rest of it as to
leave the rest enforceable because the same words which made the certificate   D
final on questions of law made it final on all other questions, including those
on which its finality was free from objection, with the result that the objectionable aspects could not be separated from the unobjectionable aspects by
severance but only by remoulding the proviso, that is, the agreement between
the parties, and that was not within the province of the courts (see p. 855,
letter D, post).   E

[As to ouster of jurisdiction of the courts, see 9 HALSBURY'S LAWS (3rd Edn.)
352-354, para. 825; and for cases on the subject, see 16 DIGEST (Repl.) 132-136,
162-187.]

Cases referred to:
Baker v. *Jones*, [1954] 2 All E.R. 553; [1954] 1 W.L.R. 1005; Digest (Cont.   F
    Vol. A) 124, *16a.*
Bennett v. *Bennett*, [1952] 1 All E.R. 413; [1952] 1 K.B. 249; Digest (Cont.
    Vol. A) 807, *6344.*
Czarnikow & Co., Ltd. v. *Roth, Schmidt & Co.*, [1922] 2 K.B. 478; [1922]
    All E.R. Rep. 45; 92 L.J.K.B. 81; 127 L.T. 824; 16 Digest (Repl.)
    133, *164.*   G
Dawkins v. *Antrobus* (1881), 17 Ch.D. 615; [1881-85] All E.R. Rep. 126;
    44 L.T. 557; 8 Digest (Repl.) 652, *21.*
Edwards v. *Aberayron Mutual Ship Insurance Society, Ltd.* (1876), 1 Q.B.D.
    563; 34 L.T. 457; 2 Digest (Repl.) 469, *314.*
Horton v. *Sayer* (1859), 4 H. & N. 643; 29 L.J.Ex. 28; 33 L.T.O.S. 287;
    157 E.R. 993; 2 Digest (Repl.) 465, *292.*   H
Lee v. *Showmen's Guild of Great Britain*, [1952] 1 All E.R. 1175; [1952] 2 Q.B.
    329; 45 Digest (Repl.) 541, *1221.*
Maclean v. *Workers' Union*, [1929] 1 Ch. 602; [1929] All E.R. Rep. 468;
    98 L.J. Ch. 293; 141 L.T. 83; 45 Digest (Repl.) 541, *1222.*
R. v. *Ayton, Ex p. Cardiff Corpn.*, [1935] 1 K.B. 225.
Scott v. *Avery* (1856), 5 H.L. Cas. 811; [1843-60] All E.R. Rep. 1; 25 L.J. Ex.   I
    308; 28 L.T.O.S. 207; 10 E.R. 1121; 16 Digest (Repl.) 132, *162.*
Thompson v. *Charnock* (1799), 8 Term. Rep. 139; 101 E.R. 1310; 2 Digest
    (Repl.) 466, *297.*
Tullis v. *Jacson*, [1892] 3 Ch. 441; 61 L.J.Ch. 655; 67 L.T. 340; 2 Digest
    (Repl.) 463, *282.*
Weinberger v. *Inglis*, [1919] A.C. 606; 88 L.J. Ch. 287; 121 L.T. 65; 2 Digest
    (Repl.) 179, *94.*

A   *Wood* v. *Woad* (1874), L.R. 9 Exch. 190; 43 L.J. Ex. 153; 30 L.T. 815; 8
Digest (Repl.) 656, *35*.

Adjourned Summons.

This was an application by originating summons dated 11th June 1968 as
amended on 14th February 1969, by the plaintiffs, Manprop, Ltd., the assignees
by a transfer dated 1st October 1964 of Davstone Estates, Ltd., the original
B lessors of ten identical leases made with the defendants described in the schedule
to the summons in respect of flats 1 to 10 comprised in the premises known as
Ardentinny, Grosvenor Road, St. Albans in the county of Hertford, for a period
of 99 years from 24th June 1963, at a rent of £15.   The plaintiffs sought the
determination by the court of, inter alia, the following question: whether or
not on the true construction of cl. 2 (iii) of the leases the certificate of the surveyor
C given pursuant to that clause was (a) open to challenge by the defendants or
their assignees, and, if so, on what grounds, (b) was conclusive as to whether the
expenses therein mentioned had been incurred in performing the covenants on
behalf of the lessor contained in cl. 3 of the leases.   The defendants were (i)
Maurice Charles O'Dell and (ii) Kathleen Elizabeth O'Dell (of Flat 1, Ardentinny),
(iii) David Goddard Holt (of Flat 2) (against all three of whom all further
D proceedings in the action were stayed by order dated 20th September 1968),
(iv) Bertha Gusowski (of Flat 3), (v) David Ernest Howell and (vi) Patricia
Granville Howell (of Flat 4) (vii) Ian Halse and (viii) Penelope Susan Halse
(of Flat 5) (ix) the Abbey National Building Society (the mortgagees in possession
under lease of Flat 6, against whom all further proceedings in the action were
stayed by the order dated 20th September 1968), (x) Anita Margaret Elizabeth
E Golding (of Flat 7), (xi) Phillip Roger Bird (of Flat 8), (xii) Howard Lloyd
Addington (of Flat 9), (xiii) Muriel Margaret Moxham (of Flat 10) (against whom
all further proceedings in the action were stayed by order dated 10th December
1968), (xiv) John David Stuart Macaskie, and (xv) Judith Leslie Macaskie,
(xvi) Richard Charles Carrington, (xvii) Dennis Christopher Twomey and
(xviii) Ann Elizabeth Twomey (the last five defendants were added by the order
F dated 20th September 1968), and (xix) Lewis Henry Wilson Harris (added by the
order dated 10th December 1968).   The defendants were the present tenants of
the flats.   The facts are set out in the judgment.

The cases noted below* were cited during the argument in addition to those
referred to in the judgment.

Ian McCulloch for the plaintiffs.
G   *J. R. Cherryman* for the fourth, fifth, sixth, seventh, eighth, tenth, eleventh,
twelfth, seventeenth and eighteenth defendants.

Hilary Robertson for the fourteenth and fifteenth defendants.

The sixteenth and nineteenth defendants did not appear and proceedings were
stayed against the first, second, third, ninth and thirteenth defendants.

H   *Cur. adv. vult.*

25th March.   **UNGOED-THOMAS, J.,** read the following judgment:
This summons raises the question whether a lessor's surveyor's certificate of
expenses incurred by the lessor under a clause in the lease is conclusive with
regard to what matters are, on the true interpretation of the clause, included
within its ambit.   A company, Davstone Estates, Ltd., contracted to let ten
I flats which they were to build.   They then, in May to July 1964, in consideration
of capital payments, granted leases in common form of those flats for 99 years

---

* *Wadsworth* v. *Smith* (1871), L.R. 6 Q.B. 332; *Sharpe* v. *San Paulo Ry. Co.* (1873),
8 Ch. App. 597; *Printing and Numerical Registering Co.* v. *Sampson* (1875), L.R. 19
Eq. Cas. 462; *Re Dawdy* (1885), 15 Q.B.D. 426; *Robins* v. *Goddard*, [1905] 1 K.B. 294;
Westminster Corpn. v. *Gordon Hotels, Ltd.*, [1907] 1 K.B. 910; [1908] A.C. 142; *Hall*
v. *Arnold*, [1950] 1 All E.R. 993; [1950] 2 K.B. 543; *Re Wynn (decd.)*, [1952] 1 All E.R.
341; [1952] Ch. 271; *Goodinson* v. *Goodinson*, [1954] 2 All E.R. 255; [1954] 2 Q.B. 118;
Billyack v. *Leyland Construction Co., Ltd.*, [1968] 1 All E.R. 783; [1968] 1 W.L.R. 471.

from 24th June 1963 at a yearly rent of £15 and they subsequently assigned   A
the reversion to the plaintiffs. The defendants are the lessees or their assignees
or are otherwise interested in the leases. The flats suffered from defects of design,
workmanship, materials and construction. The plaintiffs' contention, very
roughly and generally stated, is that under the covenants in the leases their
surveyor's certificate entitling them to recover moneys expended in maintaining
the building is conclusive and obliges the lessees to pay moneys certified to have   B
been so expended although expended on making good the defects which I have
mentioned and even on the assumption that such defects do not constitute such
maintenance within the meaning of the covenants. The tenants, on the other
hand, say that, on such assumption, the surveyor's certificate is not so conclusive,
first on the true construction of the leases and secondly and alternatively, on
the ground that a provision making it so conclusive would, as is common ground,   C
make it conclusive on a question of construction of the leases and, therefore,
on a question of law and so, in completely ousting the jurisdiction of the courts
on a question of law, be void as contrary to public policy.

The directly relevant clauses of the leases are cl. 2 and cl. 3.

" 2. THE Lessee HEREBY COVENANTS with the Lessor as follows:—(iii)
The Lessee hereby covenants with the Lessor to pay to the Lessor on the   D
twenty-fifth day of March in the year One thousand nine hundred and
sixty four and in each succeeding calendar year the sum of Fifteen Pounds
as a contribution towards the expenses incurred by the Lessor in performing the covenants on the part of the Lessor set forth in clause 3 hereof
including the reasonable remuneration of a Managing Agent to be appointed
by the Lessor for the purpose of managing the Buildings PROVIDED NEVER-   E
THELESS that if one tenth part of the said expenses reasonably and properly
incurred by the Lessor in any year (as certified by the Surveyor for the time
being to the Lessor (hereinafter called " the Surveyor ") whose certificate
shall be final and not subject to challenge in any manner whatsoever) shall
exceed Fifteen Pounds then the Lessee shall pay to the Lessor the amount
of the excess such sum to be paid within twenty-eight days after the service   F
on the Lessee of a copy of the certificate of the Surveyor . . .

" 3. THE Lessor HEREBY COVENANTS with the Lessee as follows:—(i) At
all times during the said term to keep the interior and exterior walls and
ceilings and floors of the Buildings (other than those included in this demise
or in the demise of any other flat or garage in the Buildings) and the roof and
main drains thereof in good and substantial repair and condition . . . (viii)   G
To defray such other costs as may be necessary to maintain the Buildings as
good class residential flats and garages."

The other sub-clauses I need not read in full but I will indicate their nature.
They provided for (ii) washing and painting, (iii) the provision and maintenance
of an automatic hall porter system, (iv) keeping pipes and cables in good repair   H
and cleansing and redecorating interior parts of the common parts, (v) stocking
and preserving in good condition the gardens and grounds, (vi) keeping the
common parts cleaned, (vii) paying rates on the building as distinct from any
flat, (ix) insuring the buildings and laying out moneys received on insurance in
rebuilding and re-instating the premises.

First then on the question of construction. The expenses which have to be   I
certified under the proviso to cl. 2 (iii) are " the said expenses " being the expenses
mentioned in the main part of cl. 2 (iii). Apart from the remuneration of the
managing agent with which we are not concerned, those expenses are " the
expenses incurred by the Lessor in performing the covenants on the part of the
Lessor set forth in clause 3 hereof ". So the expenses so mentioned in the main
part are not expenses in any way defined as those which are certified; on the
contrary the certificate in the proviso is defined by reference to and limited to
those expenses which are mentioned in the main part.

A   It was suggested for the plaintiffs that the amount of the expenses could not be conclusively certified unless the certificate was also conclusive on whether the expenses were incurred in performing the covenants in cl. 3. *R.* v. *Ayton, Ex p. Cardiff Corpn.* (1) and especially observations of DU PARCQ, J., were relied on. In that case it was held that a provision in the Local Government Act 1929 that on a transfer of functions from poor law guardians to county B   councils, the certificate of a district auditor certifying the statement of a " prescribed officer " showing the value of the " non-institutional liabilities " of the guardians should be " final and conclusive " as to what constituted the non-institutional liabilities as well as to their value. But this turned on the construction of the particular statutory provisions. In considering the construction and effect of statutory provisions it had to be borne in mind, as stated by DENNING, C   L.J., in *Lee* v. *Showmen's Guild of Great Britain* (2):

" We were referred to a number of cases on statutory tribunals. These are not directly in point, because a statute can, expressly or by implication, exclude the jurisdiction of the courts, whereas parties cannot do so."

Du PARCQ, J. (to whose judgment counsel for the plaintiffs particularly referred) D   relied on the concession that the auditor in certifying the prescribed officer's statement, certified it as to all included in the statement, viz., liabilities and value, so that he could alter the items as well as the value. Nor was there any such provision corresponding to the references which I have mentioned to " expenses " defined as those incurred in performing the lessor's covenant.

It is conceded that the question whether the defects are within cl. 3 depends on the construction of that clause which is a question of law. It is not unreason-E   able that such a question should not be entrusted to a surveyor—still less to a surveyor appointed by one party and whose decision shall be conclusive. The ordinary reading of the clause in accordance with its grammar and syntax is certainly not unreasonable in excluding from the surveyor's conclusive decision what, on the true construction of cl. 3, are expenses within its ambit and limiting the operation of the certificate within the ambit of those expenses. My conclusion F   is that the question whether the defects are within the provisions of cl. 3 is not a matter for decision by the certificate.

Although this conclusion answers the question that is raised, nevertheless it might be helpful. I briefly express my view on the alternative contention of the tenants that, on the footing that the leases provided that the surveyor's certificate is conclusive on what, as a matter of construction and therefore, it G   is conceded, of law, is within the meaning of cl. 3, such provision is void as totally ousting the jurisdiction of the courts on a question of law.

The law on contractual provisions ousting the jurisdiction of the courts is thus stated by DENNING, L.J., in *Lee* v. *Showmen's Guild of Great Britain* (3):

" Although the jurisdiction of a domestic tribunal is founded on contract, H   express or implied, nevertheless the parties are not free to make any contract they like. There are important limitations imposed by public policy. The tribunal must, for instance, observe the principles of natural justice. They must give the man notice of the charge and a reasonable opportunity of meeting it. Any stipulation to the contrary would be invalid. They cannot stipulate for a power to condemn a man unheard. That appears, I think, I   from the judgments of BRETT, L.J., in *Dawkins* v. *Antrobus* (4), of KELLY, C.B., in *Wood* v. *Woad* (5), and of LORD BIRKENHEAD, L.C., in *Weinberger* v. *Inglis* (6), which are to be preferred to the dictum of MAUGHAM, J., in *Maclean* v. *Workers' Union* (7) to the contrary. Another limitation arises

(1) [1935] 1 K.B. 225.
(2) [1952] 1 All E.R. 1175 at p. 1182; [1952] 2 Q.B. 329 at p. 345.
(3) [1952] 1 All E.R. at pp. 1180, 1181; [1952] 2 Q.B. at p. 342.
(4) (1881), 17 Ch.D. 615 at p. 630; [1881-85] All E.R. Rep. 126 at pp. 129, 130.
(5) (1874), L.R. 9 Exch. 190 at p. 196.   (6) [1919] A.C. 606 at p. 616.
(7) [1929] 1 Ch. 602 at p. 625; [1929] All E.R. Rep. 468 at p. 472.

out of the well-known principle that parties cannot by contract oust the ordinary courts of their jurisdiction: see *Scott* v. *Avery* (8), per ALDERSON, B. (9), and LORD CRANWORTH, L.C. (10). They can, of course, agree to leave questions of law, as well as questions of fact, to the decision of the domestic tribunal. They can, indeed, make the tribunal the final arbiter on questions of fact, but they cannot make it the final arbiter on questions of law. They cannot prevent its decisions being examined by the courts. If parties should seek, by agreement, to take the law out of the hands of the courts and into the hands of a private tribunal, without any recourse at all to the courts in case of error of law, then the agreement is to that extent contrary to public policy and void . . ."

The law as thus stated was applied by LYNSKEY, J., in *Baker* v. *Jones* (11). In the former case a trade union committee unsuccessfully claimed that the trade union rules by implication made it the interpreter of the rules free from interference by the court. But in *Baker* v. *Jones* (11) it was held that an express provision in the rules of an incorporated association making its council their sole interpreter was void. As LYNSKEY, J., pointed out, the association had no legal entity and the rules constituted a contract between the members just as cl. 2 of the lease constitutes a contractual relationship between the parties to it. It was suggested that the law as stated in the passage which I have quoted from DENNING, L.J. (12), applied to decisions of arbitrations or tribunals only and not to decisions by experts. But the public policy objection to the ouster of the court's jurisdiction does not turn on any distinction between decision by arbitration or by an expert. *Baker* v. *Jones* (11) was not an arbitration or tribunal case.

The plaintiffs relied on *Tullis* v *Jacson* (13), where it was held that a provision in a building contract that the certificate of the architect should be final and binding and should not be set aside for a charge of fraud was not void as against public policy. The correctness of the decision was doubted by SCRUTTON, L J., in *Czarnikow & Co., Ltd.* v. *Roth, Schmidt & Co.* (14). The *Czarnikow* decision (15) itself was referred to by DENNING, L.J. (16), in support of his statement of the law which I have quoted (16). The relevant clause in *Tullis* v. *Jacson* (13) also provided that the certificate should be binding despite legal defects. However the case did not turn on that provision in the clause and that is perhaps why such cases as *Scott* v. *Avery* (8), *Thompson* v. *Charnock* (17), *Horton* v. *Sayer* (18) and *Edwards* v. *Aberayron Mutual Ship Insurance Society, Ltd.* (19) (in line with the *Czarnikow* case (15)) were not cited. So far as *Tullis* v. *Jacson* (13) might be inconsistent with the law as decided in the *Czarnikow* case (15) and *Lee* v. *Showmen's Guild* (20) and *Baker* v. *Jones* (11) and the statements of law which I have quoted from those cases, it cannot in my view prevail.

The question then arises whether in the proviso to cl. 2 (iii) that aspect of it which is objectionable on grounds of public policy may be so severed from the rest of it as to leave the rest enforceable. Here there is no such objection to severability as that the transaction is for an illegal consideration or contra

(8) (1856), 5 H.L. Cas. 811; [1843-60] All E.R. Rep. 1.
(9) (1856), 5 H.L. Cas. at p. 845.
(10) (1856), 5 H.L. Cas. at p. 847; [1843-60] All E.R. Rep. at p. 4.
(11) [1954] 2 All E.R. 553; [1954] 1 W.L.R. 1005.
(12) [1952] 1 All E.R. at pp. 1180, 1181; [1952] 2 Q.B. at p. 342.
(13) [1892] 3 Ch. 441.
(14) [1922] 2 K.B. 478 at p. 488; [1922] All E.R. Rep. 45 at p. 50.
(15) [1922] 2 K.B. 478; [1922] All E.R. Rep. 45.
(16) [1952] 1 All E.R at p. 1181; [1952] 2 Q.B. at pp. 342, 343.
(17) (1799), 8 Term. Rep. 139.
(18) (1859), 4 H. & N. 643.
(19) (1876), 1 Q.B.D. 563.
(20) [1952] 1 All E.R. 1175; [1952] 2 Q.B. 329.

A   bonos mores.   Nor is it an objection that the proviso is not severable because it is not subsidiary to the main purpose of the transaction—the provision for the surveyor's certificate is clearly subsidiary.   In such circumstances SOMER-VELL, L.J., in *Bennett* v. *Bennett* (21) in the Court of Appeal said that he regarded *Czarnikow & Co., Ltd.* v. *Roth, Schmidt & Co.* (22) as a binding authority that in a proper case the doctrine of severability can be applied where the objection-B   able promise is one purporting to oust the jurisdiction of the court, and added (21):

" It seems to me that the court clearly expressed the view that the arbitra-tion clause remained binding, the objectionable words in one clause of it only being, in effect, struck out."

Those observations, with which I respectfully agree, appear to me to be equally C   applicable where the objectionable words appear in a clause providing for a surveyor's certificate as where they appear in an arbitration clause.

The difficulty on severance in the case before me is that the objectionable part ousting the jurisdiction of the court on questions of law is not separately expressed so as to be severable and leave the unobjectionable parts unaffected. The same words which make the certificate final on questions of law make it D   final on all other questions too, including those on which its finality is free from objection.   The result is that the objectionable aspects cannot be separated from the unobjectionable aspects by severance but only by remoulding the proviso, i.e., by remoulding the agreement between the parties; and this is not within the province of the courts.

The result is that if, contrary to my view, the proviso applies to questions of E   law (and, therefore, to questions of construction whether the defects are within the provisions of cl. 3) then it is, in my judgment, void as contrary to public policy in purporting to oust completely the jurisdiction of the courts on questions of law.

Declaration accordingly.

F   Solicitors: *Beardall, Fenton & Co.*, agents for *Elliott & Buckley*, Manchester (for the plaintiffs); *Nutt & Oliver* (for the fourth to eighth, tenth to twelfth, seventeenth and eighteenth defendants); *Jaques & Co.*, agents for *Armitage, Sykes & Hinchcliffe*, Huddersfield (for the fourteenth and fifteenth defendants).

[*Reported by* JACQUELINE METCALFE, *Barrister-at-Law.*]

G

H

I

---

(21) [1952] 1 All E.R. 413 at p. 417; [1952] 1 K.B. 249 at p. 254.
(22) [1922] 2 K.B. 478; [1922] All E.R. Rep. 45.

R. *v.* JULIEN.

[COURT OF APPEAL, CRIMINAL DIVISION (Widgery and Karminski, L.JJ., and Geoffrey Lane, J.), April 17, 1969.]

Criminal Law—Assault—Self-defence—Whether obligation first to indicate unwillingness to fight.

The appellant was involved in a quarrel with one D. and threw a milk bottle at him causing his head to bleed. He was charged, inter alia, with assault occasioning actual bodily harm. He did not dispute that he had thrown a milk bottle at D. but contended that he did it in self-defence, D. being armed at the time with a chopper. The jury were directed, inter alia, that before using force in self-defence, there was an obligation to retreat. On the question whether the jury was misdirected,

Held: when a person was threatened it was necessary that he should demonstrate by his actions that he did not want to fight; to the extent that that was necessary as a feature of the justification of self-defence, it was true whether the charge was homicide or something less serious; accordingly, the jury had not been misdirected (see p. 858, letter I, post).

Appeal allowed on another point.

[As to self defence in assault, see 10 HALSBURY'S LAWS (3rd Edn.) 743, para. 1429; and for cases on the subject, see 15 DIGEST (Repl.) 994, *9768-9779*.]

Case referred to:
R. v. *Wheeler*, [1967] 3 All E.R. 829; [1967] 1 W.L.R. 1531; Digest (Repl.) Supp.

Appeal.

This was an appeal by Thomas Julien against his conviction on 6th September 1968 at Inner London Quarter Sessions before the deputy chairman (HENRY ELAM, ESQ.) and a jury of assault occasioning actual bodily harm. On 9th September 1968 he was sentenced by the deputy chairman to nine months' imprisonment. He appealed on the grounds, inter alia: (i) that the deputy chairman's direction to the jury on self-defence was insufficient in that it failed to show that the onus of proof was throughout on the prosecution; and (ii) that the deputy chairman misdirected the jury in telling them that before using force in self-defence, there was an obligation to retreat. The facts are set out in the judgment of the court.

The authorities and cases noted below* were cited during the argument in addition to the case referred to in the judgment of the court.

K. M. McHale for the appellant.
C. R. Hilliard for the Crown.

WIDGERY, L.J., delivered the judgment of the court. The appellant Thomas Julien stood his trial at the Inner London Quarter Sessions in September 1968 on an indictment containing two counts. The first alleged that he had assaulted one Delco thereby occasioning him actual bodily harm, and the other that he was in possession of offensive weapons, namely, one bottle and the exhaust-pipe of a motor cycle. Both counts related to an incident which occurred on 23rd June 1968. The appellant was convicted on the assault count (count 1) and acquitted on the second count of possessing offensive weapons. He was

---

* ROLLE'S ABRIDGEMENT (1668), Vol. 2, p. 547; " Assault of person "; HALE'S PLEAS OF THE CROWN (1778 Edn.) pp. 480, 483; HAWKINS' PLEAS OF THE CROWN (8th Edn.) Vol. 1, pp. 179, 484; RUSSELL ON CRIME (12th Edn.) Vol. 1, pp. 680, 681; ARCHBOLD'S CRIMINAL PLEADING, EVIDENCE AND PRACTICE (36th Edn.) paras. 2496, 2646; 10 HALSBURY'S LAWS (3rd Edn.) 743, para. 1429; R. v. *Deana* (1909), 2 Cr. App. Rep. 75; R. v. *Sharp*, [1957] 1 All E.R. 577; [1957] 1 Q.B. 552.

A sentenced to nine months' imprisonment in respect of the assault; and he now appeals against his conviction by leave of the single judge.

The incident in question, as I say, occurred on a Sunday night, 23rd June 1968, somewhere about 10.0 p.m. On that occasion in a flat in Sutherland Avenue, London, W.9, a party was in progress which was attended by a large number of people; and the evidence of Mr. Delco (the complainant) was that he was a guest

B at the party, and he was called to the door. At the door, he said, he found the appellant with two other men, and the appellant apparently was anxious to attack him. He said that the appellant got free of the two men who were seeking to restrain him, picked up an empty milk bottle, threw it at Mr. Delco and it struck him on the top of the head. He was knocked down and his head began to bleed, and it was that incident which supported the charge of assault occasioning

C actual bodily harm. He said he was going for the police and stepped into the street, and as he did so he saw the appellant pick up another bottle; and shortly after-wards—it is difficult to tell the story precisely in the confused situation which prevailed—he saw the appellant with another milk bottle and a piece of exhaust-pipe in his hand, handling them in an aggressive fashion. It was that incident which gave rise to the charge of possessing offensive weapons.

D The medical evidence showed that Mr. Delco had been wounded, though not seriously; and the appellant never sought to dispute that he had thrown the milk bottle which had given rise to that wound. The story given by the defence was that the appellant and his wife had been going along the road in a perfectly peaceful fashion, and as they passed the door of this flat he saw Mr. Delco there, and some kind of altercation developed between them. The appellant said that

E Mr. Delco armed himself with a chopper and threatened him with it, and, he said, it was this and this alone which prompted him to throw the first milk bottle which, in fact, wounded Mr. Delco. He said that, undismayed by the wound, Mr. Delco continued to threaten him with the chopper, and that he picked up the other milk bottle and the length of motor cycle exhaust-pipe as defensive weapons in order to protect himself against further attack from the chopper. In other

F words, the appellant admitted the fact of having wounded Mr. Delco, and he admitted the possession of the weapons alleged to have been offensive; but his case was that he was on the defensive throughout and that whatever he did was reasonable self-defence.

A great deal of other evidence was called, and since all the persons concerned were in an excitable condition it may well have been difficult for the jury to reach

G conclusions on it; and, indeed, it was evidence that the jury had some difficulty with this case because, retiring at 3.42 p.m., they returned into court at 4.58 p.m. (we understand on their own initiative) to say that they could not agree. The deputy chairman sent them out again saying: ". . . If there is a doubt about it acquit the [appellant] . . .", and the jury, after a further absence of some 29 minutes, returned with the verdicts to which I have referred. Although the

H evidence may have been difficult to analyse and reconcile, the issue here was clear enough. The appellant, admitting he had caused the wound, the only question was whether his conduct was justified on principles of self-defence; and likewise on the second count the only issue was whether he was holding these weapons in a defensive way or in an offensive way, and that was the matter on which the jury had to be instructed.

I Counsel for the appellant has made three complaints. First of all, he says that the direction on self-defence, which was, of course, the crucial direction in this case, was insufficient. With all respect to the learned deputy chairman, this court is bound to conclude that the direction was not altogether clear. The learned deputy chairman went in some detail into the necessity for some relationship between the violence or force used in defence to that which had been used in offence. He pointed out perfectly fairly that if the appellant had been threatened with a chopper it was not unreasonable for him to use a milk bottle by way of defence. He also pointed out that there was an obligation on the defendant to retreat before using force in self-defence; but he did not further analyse the evidence so as to show the jury how the principles of self-defence should be applied to it, and (what is perhaps more serious) he did not point out to the jury in any clear terms that, although self-defence is constantly referred to as a defence, the onus on that issue rests on the prosecution throughout, and it was their duty to prove that the appellant's acts were not acts of legitimate self-defence. The importance of such a warning in such cases was recently stressed in *R.* v. *Wheeler* (1).

The second complaint made by counsel for the appellant is that the verdicts were inconsistent. Strictly speaking, as has been demonstrated to us by counsel for the Crown, they could be reconciled, because in the considerable volume of evidence available a witness (or witnesses) can be found who suggested that Mr. Delco did not produce the chopper until after he had been struck by the bottle. Of course, if that was so it would be perfectly sensible to conclude that the appellant was the aggressor in the first part of the incident, but had turned over to the defensive when he picked up the second bottle and the exhaust-pipe. If the jury had looked at it in that way, of course, their verdicts would be quite understandable. One is bound to say that neither of the principals in this matter (the appellant or Mr. Delco) put the matter in that way, and it was never so canvassed by the learned deputy chairman in his summing-up. One is left at least with some slight suspicion on the facts of this case that the jury's conclusion was not a rational conclusion based on some part of the evidence, but something in the nature of a compromise when they found initially that they were unable to agree.

The third point taken by counsel for the appellant is that the learned deputy chairman was wrong in directing the jury that before the appellant could use force in self-defence he was required to retreat. The submission here is that the obligation to retreat before using force in self-defence is an obligation which only arises in homicide cases. As the court understands it, it is submitted that if the injury results in death then the accused cannot set up self-defence except on the basis that he had retreated before he resorted to violence. On the other hand, it is said that where the injury does not result in death (as in the present case) the obligation to retreat does not arise. The sturdy submission is made that an Englishman is not bound to run away when threatened, but can stand his ground and defend himself where he is. In support of this submission no authority is quoted, save that counsel for the appellant has been at considerable length and diligence to look at the textbooks on the subject, and has demonstrated to us that the textbooks in the main do not say that a preliminary retreat is a necessary prerequisite to the use of force in self-defence. Equally, it must be said that the textbooks do not state the contrary either; and it is, of course, well known to us all that for very many years it has been common form for judges directing juries where the issue of self-defence is raised in any case (be it a homicide case or not) that the duty to retreat arises. It is not, as we understand it, the law that a person threatened must take to his heels and run in the dramatic way suggested by counsel for the appellant; but what is necessary is that he should demonstrate by his actions that he does not want to fight. He must demonstrate that he is prepared to temporise and disengage and perhaps to make some physical withdrawal; and to the extent that that is necessary as a feature of the justification of self-defence, it is true, in our opinion, whether the charge is a homicide charge or something less serious. Accordingly, we reject counsel for the appellant's third submission.

However, the first two submissions have given us considerable food for thought. It may be that neither by itself would justify the setting aside of this conviction, but in combination and when set in the framework of this case as a whole we have concluded after discussion that this verdict is an unsafe verdict and that the

---

(1) [1967] 3 All E.R. 829; [1967] 1 W.L.R. 1531.

A conviction must accordingly be quashed. Accordingly, so far as this case is concerned, the appellant is discharged.

Appeal allowed. Conviction quashed.

Solicitors: *Registrar of Criminal Appeals* (for the appellant); *Solicitor, Metropolitan Police* (for the Crown).

B   [*Reported by* N. P. METCALFE, ESQ., *Barrister-at-Law.*]

BRAITHWAITE *v.* ELECTRICAL ELECTRONIC AND TELECOMMUNICATION UNION—PLUMBING
C   TRADES UNION.

[COURT OF APPEAL, CIVIL DIVISION (Lord Denning, M.R., Salmon and Winn, L.JJ.), March 13, 1969.]

Trade Union—Expulsion—Member appealing to appeal committee—Date of hearing of appeals fixed by rules—Amalgamation of union with another
D *union prior to date of hearing—New rules containing no provision for pending appeals—Validity of expulsion.*

In February 1968, the plaintiff was expelled from his trade union. He gave notice of appeal to an appeal committee which, by the union rules, was to meet every year in October. So his appeal ought to have been heard in October 1968. But in July 1968, his union was amalgamated with
E another union so as to form the defendants. The rules of the amalgamated union contained no provision for dealing with pending appeals. The executive council of the defendants decided that pending appeals of the old unions should be heard in January 1969. On appeal by the defendants against a declaration that the plaintiff's expulsion was invalid,

Held: the appeal must be dismissed, because the original order of expul-
F sion was made on the footing that the plaintiff had a right of appeal and, by taking away that right although by an oversight, the procedure for expelling him was ineffective (see p. 860, letter I, and p. 861, letters E and F, post).

Appeal dismissed.

[As to the power of the court to give relief against expulsion from a trade
G union, see 38 HALSBURY'S LAWS (3rd Edn.) 356, 357 para. 615; and for cases on the subject, see 45 DIGEST (Repl.) 539-542, *1209-1225.*]

Interlocutory Appeal.

This was an appeal by the defendants, Electrical Electronic and Telecommunication Union—Plumbing Trades Union, from an order of BUCKLEY, J.,
H dated 14th January 1969, restraining the defendants until after judgment in an action between the plaintiff, Lawrence Braithwaite, and the defendants or until further order (whether by their servants or agents or any of them or otherwise) from acting on a decision made on or about 12th February 1968 of the executive council of the Electrical Trades Union purporting to expel the plaintiff from that union. In the action, the plaintiff claimed: (i) a declaration that he was a member of the defendants; (ii) a declaration that the decision of the exe-
I cutive council of the Electrical Trades Union made on or about the 12th February 1968 purporting to expel him from that union was null and void and of no effect; (iii) an injunction restraining the defendants by themselves, their servants or agents or otherwise from acting on the decision of the executive council of the Electrical Trades Union; and (iv) damages. The facts are set out in the judgment of LORD DENNING, M.R.

Peter Pain, Q.C., and *J. E. A. Samuels* for the defendants.
D. J. Turner-Samuels for the plaintiff.

LORD DENNING, M.R.: In October 1967, the plaintiff, Mr. Braithwaite, **A**
who was a member of the Electrical Trades Union, was said to have taken part
in an unauthorised demonstration, and done other things. On 12th February
1968, he was brought before the executive council of the union to answer those
charges. They were held proved against him and he was expelled from the union.
Whereupon he desired to appeal. He gave notice of appeal under r. 37, which
provides: **B**

" (1) There shall be a right of appeal from Executive Council decisions to a
final Appeal Committee:—(a) by any member who is expelled . . . (5) The
Final Appeal Committee shall meet in *October* of each year, at a time and
place decided by the Executive Council to hear all appeals notice of which
shall have reached the General Office in accordance with Clause (7) by the
31st day of July in the year of the meeting . . ."   **C**

It is plain from that rule that the plaintiff's appeal should have been heard in
October 1968. But meanwhile an important thing happened. There was an
amalgamation. On 1st July 1968, the Electrical Trades Union amalgamated
with the Plumbing Trades Union. It was done under the Trade Union (Amalga-
mations, etc.) Act 1964, and the regulations thereunder. The instrument of **D**
amalgamation contained provisions whereby the members of each union became
members of the amalgamated union and were subject to the rules of the union.
The rules of the amalgamated body, accordingly, became binding on the plaintiff.
It is sometimes said that these rules are a contract between a union and its
members, but, as I have often said, they are more like byelaws than a contract.
Anyway, they were binding on him.   **E**
    The new rules of the defendants, the amalgamated union, made no provision,
however, for pending appeals. They contained a number of offences, and set
up a new executive council to determine whether an offence had been committed;
and provided for a right to appeal to a new final appeals committee. The new
rules were apt to deal with all new offences since the amalgamation. But they
did not, as I see it, apply to pending appeals. That was an omission by over- **F**
sight. The new executive council tried to make up for the omission. They had a
meeting in which they resolved that the final appeals committee should be a
combination of both the former ones, and that the first meeting of the final
appeals committee should be held in January 1969, when consideration would
be given to all appeals which were currently pending from members of either
former union. In my opinion, however, the new executive council had no power **G**
to deal with pending appeals. They should have been dealt with in the new
amalgamated union rules, but were not. So the resolution was invalid.
    The men who had appealed took notice of this invalidity. In January 1969,
when the final appeals committee came to sit, none of the appellants turned up.
And only a fortnight before, the plaintiff himself had taken action. He applied
to BUCKLEY, J., who held that the date for hearing the appeals (January 1969) **H**
at any rate was wrong. The plaintiff, under the former rules, had a right to
have his appeal heard in October 1968. The new executive council purported
to postpone it for three months, until January 1969. That was quite wrong,
for it would mean that his expulsion was extended for three months without
any justification. On that ground the judge held that his expulsion could no
longer be considered valid. But I think that the case can be put on a wider ground. **I**
There was no provision in the new rules for pending appeals. So by oversight
his right of appeal has been taken away. Once his right of appeal is taken away,
the original expulsion cannot stand. The original order was made on the footing
that the plaintiff had a right of appeal. It was, so to speak, a conditional order.
It was subject to his right of appeal. If his right of appeal is afterwards taken
away, albeit by oversight, it must necessarily follow that the original order
cannot stand; for the condition has not been fulfilled.
    I would dismiss the appeal.

A   **SALMON, L.J.:** I entirely agree. Counsel for the defendants fairly conceded that unless r. 7 of the new union (1) covered pending appeals of the old members of the Electrical Trades Union, and among them the plaintiff, the defendants could not succeed in this appeal. Rule 7 cannot apply to pending appeals unless we could be persuaded that the executive council referred to in r. 7 included the executive councils of the Electrical Trades

B   Union and of the Plumbing Trades Union. Not even counsel's powers of persuasion can make me accept that view. Rule 9 provides for an executive council of the defendants. It is quite obvious, I think, that the executive council referred to in r. 7 was the executive council for which provision is made in r. 9 and no other executive council. In these circumstances, the plaintiff had a right to have his appeal heard in October 1968. Whoever drafted the new rules—and

C   I dare say quite a few people did—they were no doubt considering many difficult and diverse topics, and it is not surprising that they should have overlooked these pending appeals by members who had been expelled from the Electrical Trades Union. If they had had those pending appeals in mind, I am certain that they would have dealt with them quite specifically under the new rules. I do not believe that they would have ever taken the right of appeal away.

D   They act fairly towards their members and ex-members; and they would have substituted for the old members' right to have their appeals heard by the appeal committee of the Electrical Trades Union, a right to have their appeals heard by the new final appeals committee of the defendants. By what I am sure was an oversight, they made no such provision. Counsel for the defendants does not suggest that there was ever any intention to take away the plaintiff's

E   right to have his appeal heard. He had a right to have his appeal heard in October 1968. The procedure for expelling him was not followed and his expulsion was, therefore, ineffective. Accordingly, the present appeal must be dismissed.

     WINN, L.J.: I agree with both the judgments delivered. I am quite satisfied for myself that this difficulty arose from an oversight and was in no sense whatever intended. It is suggested now that r. 7 of the new union rules does

F   apply to cases where there were pending appeals at the time of amalgamation from one or the other of the former unions. For myself—and this is only an additional second point—I am quite satisfied not only that the references to the executive council in that new r. 7 are to be construed as my Lords have both indicated, but I further think that the last sentence of the second paragraph of

G   r. 7 relates solely to the preceding sentence, and is concerned with those cases where a member has been found guilty of a major offence by members of his branch of the Electrical Trades Union, or district of the Plumbing Trades Union, and gives him a new right of appeal to the new executive council of the amalgamated union. I am not at all surprised that there should have been a misunderstanding, and it is quite clear that there was a misunderstanding in October

H   1968 in the mind of the writer of a letter to be found in the correspondence. In that letter he told the plaintiff that his rights to his pending appeal of which he had given notice before the amalgamation were regulated by r. 37 of the Electrical Trades Union rules. I agree that the appeal should be dismissed.

Appeal dismissed.

     Solicitors: *Lawford & Co.* (for the defendants); *Gaster & Turner* (for the

I   plaintiff).

[*Reported by* F. GUTTMAN, ESQ., *Barrister-at-Law.*]

---

(1) Rule 7, having provided for punishment of minor offences and (in the second paragraph) of major offences, so far as material provides: " A member found to be guilty of a major offence . . . may . . . appeal to the Executive Council. There shall be a right of appeal from Executive Council decisions to a Final Appeals Committee by any member who has been expelled, or deprived from holding office, or deprived of any cash benefit and fined any sum . . ."

A

Re PENNANT'S WILL TRUSTS.
PENNANT AND ANOTHER v. RYLAND AND OTHERS.

[CHANCERY DIVISION (Buckley, J.), March 26, 27, 1969.]

Settlement—Powers of tenant for life—Sale of settled land to tenant for life—
Unauthorised sale by Settled Land Act trustees—Whether transaction voidable
—Whether Settled Land Act powers applicable—Settled Land Act 1925 (15
& 16 Geo. 5 c. 18), s. 68 (2).

B

By his will a testator settled his real estate on trust for his widow during
her widowhood and thereafter to his son, the first plaintiff, for life and subject
thereto as to one-half in trust for the testator's granddaughter, and as to the
other half in trust for the children of the first plaintiff. The testator died in
1958 and his will was proved by his three executors, namely, his widow,
the first plaintiff and the first defendant. In April 1960 the executors made
a vesting assent in favour of the widow as tenant for life in respect of part
of the real estate. On 12th August 1960 the executors executed a conveyance
by way of sale of a plot of land that had not been included in the vesting
assent, the conveyance being expressed to be between the widow as purchaser
of the one part and the widow, the first plaintiff and first defendant as vendors
of the other part. Clause 1 of the conveyance referred to the receipt of the
purchase price by the "personal representatives" of the testator. The
following day a vesting assent was made in respect of the remainder of the
real estate. The widow built a dwelling-house on the plot of land and lived
there until her death in 1966. In 1967 the plaintiffs, as her personal representatives, sold the land and house but before completion the question arose
whether the plaintiffs could give a good title because the conveyance of 12th
August 1960 was, on the face of it, an unauthorised sale by the testator's
executors to one of themselves.

C

D

E

Held: the conveyance of 12th August 1960 was effectual to vest the fee
simple in the testator's widow, because—

F

(i) although the powers conferred on the trustees of a settlement by s. 68
(2)* of the Settled Land Act Act 1925 were not in the minds of the parties
to the transaction, those powers were available to them and since the transaction was one which could not properly be carried out without leave of
the court except by the use of those powers, the conveyance ought to be treated as having been made in the exercise thereof (see p. 866, letter G, post).

G

Mogridge v. *Clapp* ([1892] 3 Ch. 382) applied.

(ii) the effect of s. 68 (2) was that where the tenant for life was himself
one of the trustees of the settlement he should be a conveying party as well
as the party in whose favour the conveyance was made (see p. 867, letter B,
post).

[As to powers of trustees under the Settled Land Act 1925, see 34 HALSBURY'S
LAWS (3rd Edn.) 592-598 paras. 1036-1043; and for cases on the subject, see
40 DIGEST (Repl.) 813-818, *2924-2953.*

H

For the Settled Land Act 1925, s. 68, see 23 HALSBURY'S STATUTES (2nd Edn.)
151.]

Case referred to:

I

Mogridge v. *Clapp*, [1892] 3 Ch. 382; 61 L.J.Ch. 534; 67 L.T. 100; 40 Digest
(Repl.) 814, *2932.*

Adjourned Summons.

This was a summons by the plaintiffs, David Theodore Pennant and Eynon
David George Walters, the personal representatives of Rachel Ann Pennant,
the widow of the testator Dyfrig Huws Pennant, whereby the plaintiffs sought

---

* Section 68 (2) is at p. 864, letter G, post.

A a declaration that the conveyance dated 12th August 1960 between Mrs. Pennant, David Theodore Pennant and Olga Blethyn Ryland and Mrs. Pennant was effectual to vest in Mrs. Pennant in fee simple the benefit of the freehold land comprised therein, freed and discharged from the trusts of the settlement created by the will of the testator. The defendants to the summons were Olga Blethyn Ryland, one of the testator's executors, Sarah Jane Starkey, who was

B contingently interested in reversion in one-half of the settled property, and John Pennant, an infant, who was contingently interested in reversion in the other half. The facts are set out in the judgment.

   B. T. Buckle for the plaintiffs.
   P. J. Millett for the third defendant.

C   **BUCKLEY, J.:** By his will the late Dyfrig Huws Pennant settled his real estate on trusts under which his widow took a first life interest during widowhood, and subject thereto the property was to be held in trust for his son, the first plaintiff, David Theodore Pennant, for life, and subject thereto one-half was to be held in trust for his granddaughter, Sarah Jane, now Mrs. Starkey, the second defendant, on her attaining the age of 21 years or on her earlier marriage

D if she should survive the first plaintiff, and the other half was to be held in trust for the children of the second marriage of the first plaintiff who should survive him. The real estate thus became settled land in consequence of the testator's will.

   The testator died on 28th February 1958 and his will was proved by the three executors therein named, namely, his widow, Rachel Ann Pennant, the first

E plaintiff and the first defendant, Dr. Olga Blethyn Ryland, who was a partner of the testator in his medical practice.

   On 1st April 1960 the testator's executors made a vesting assent in respect of part but not the whole of the testator's real estate in favour of his widow as tenant for life. On 12th August 1960 they executed a conveyance of a small plot of land, part of the testator's real estate which had not been included in

F the vesting assent I have mentioned, and this conveyance was expressed to be made between the widow, the first plaintiff and the first defendant of the one part as vendors and the testator's widow of the other part as purchaser. The death and probate of the testator's will and the seisin of the testator of the property conveyed in fee simple are recited and there is a recital that the vendors had not given or made any assent or conveyance in respect of the legal estate

G affecting the property to be conveyed. There is also a recital that the vendors, that is to say, the three executors including the widow, had agreed with the purchaser for the sale to her of the unincumbered fee simple in possession of the property at the price of £200. The operative part of the deed contains a reference to the receipt of the consideration and the conveyance by the vendors as personal representatives of the testator and in exercise of their statutory powers of the

H relevant property to the widow in fee simple. On the following day the three executors made vesting assents in respect of all the rest of the testator's real estate in favour of the widow as tenant for life.

   The testator's widow built a bungalow on the plot of land which was the subject-matter of the conveyance of 12th August 1960 at a price of about £5,000 in which she lived for the rest of her life, and she died on 7th November 1966

I possessed of that property. Her will was proved by the two plaintiffs in these proceedings who are her personal representatives, David Theodore Pennant and Eynon David George Walters. The third defendant is the only child of the second marriage of the first plaintiff and is thus contingently interested in the reversion in one-half of the capital of the settled property, the second defendant, Mrs. Starkey, being contingently entitled in reversion to the other half.

   Early in 1967 the plaintiffs sold the plot of land, the subject-matter of the conveyance of 12th August 1960, for £7,300 and that sale awaits completion. A question has, however, arisen on the title by reason of the fact that on its

face the conveyance of 12th August 1960 appears to have been a conveyance **A**
on a sale by the executors to one of themselves without the authority of an order
of the court or any other justification for such a transaction. The question,
therefore, is whether that conveyance is one which ought now to be disturbed
or whether it is a good link in the title to this property.

It is conceded that the conveyance was effective to pass the legal estate in
its subject-matter, but if it were an unauthorised sale by the executors to one **B**
of themselves it would be a voidable transaction. Counsel for the third defendant
who is an infant has contended that it is a voidable transaction, that it should
be avoided and that the plaintiffs should be ordered to take the necessary steps
to restore that property to the settlement constituted by the testator's will
subject to making any proper allowances to the widow's estate for the expenditure
which she made on improving the property.   **C**

If the parties had taken the appropriate steps there is no doubt that a sale
to the widow of this plot of land could properly have been effected. Those
steps would have been first an assent in relation to this plot of land in favour of
the widow and then a sale by the Settled Land Act trustees to her under the
powers contained in s. 68 of the Settled Land Act 1925. But that was not the
way in which the transaction was carried out. It is clear from the terms of the **D**
conveyance that the persons therein described as " the Vendors " were selling
as personal representatives of the testator. They are expressed in cl. 1 of the
conveyance so to act, and although the words " as personal representatives "
are inserted there primarily for the purpose of importing the appropriate
covenants, they make it clear, as indeed does the context of the recitals and the **E**
rest of the document, that they were not purporting to act as Settled Land
Act trustees of the settlement constituted by the testator's will but as his personal
representatives. The question is whether, in those circumstances, the transaction
is one that can or should be allowed to stand.

Section 68 so far as relevant is in these terms: **F**

" (1) In the manner mentioned and subject to the provisions contained
in this section—(a) a sale ... of settled land ... may be made to the tenant
for life; ... (2) In every such case the trustees of the settlement shall,
in addition to their powers as trustees, have all the powers of a tenant-for
life in reference to negotiating and completing the transaction, and shall
have power to enforce any covenants by the tenant for life, or, where the **G**
tenant for life is himself one of the trustees, then the other or others of them
shall have such power, and the said powers of a tenant for life may be
exercised by the trustees of the settlement in the name and on behalf of the
tenant for life."

Had the appropriate steps been taken and had the transaction been carried out
in what would seem to have been the proper way, the three executors, who in **H**
this case were the trustees of the settlement for the purposes of the Settled Land
Act 1925 by virtue of s. 30 (3) of the Act, could have negotiated and completed
the sale to the widow and could have exercised the widow's powers as tenant
for life in her name and on her behalf to complete the sale. Had a vesting assent
been made the legal estate would have then already been in her, but as it was
at 12th August 1960 the legal estate in the relevant land remained in the three **I**
executors of the testator. As I said, it is conceded that the effect of the
conveyance was to convey that legal estate to the testator's widow.

It is contended on behalf of the widow's personal representatives, the present
plaintiffs, that this is a case to which s. 68 applies, although the parties did not
conceive that they were exercising the powers under that section. It is clear
from other contexts in this Act, for example s. 6 (b), that where land is settled by
a will it is settled land before any vesting assent is made, for s. 6 provides that:

A

I. & N. WESTON, LTD. *v.* METROPOLITAN POLICE COMMISSIONER.

[QUEEN'S BENCH DIVISION (Lord Parker, C.J., Melford Stevenson and Willis, JJ.), April 16, 17, 1969.]

B

Gaming—Lawful and unlawful gaming—Variant of roulette—Kittyscoop— Odds four to one—Equal odds five to one—Players becoming members of syndicate—Syndicate holder of pool—Members entitled to syndicate profits whether or not staking money—Whether chances equally favourable to all players—Betting, Gaming and Lotteries Act 1963 (c. 2), s. 32 (1) (a), (b).

C

The respondents owned and managed a bona fide social club whose main activity was the playing of bingo. In January 1968 the game of kittyscoop was introduced as an amenity for members. The game was a variant of roulette, played by means of an ordinary roulette wheel on which six numbers in three pairs had been labelled " Kittyscoop ". The zero on the wheel was effectively eliminated as a factor in the game. The odds offered against any of the six kittyscoop numbers winning were four to one.

D

Since equal odds were five to one, the game operated in favour of the kitty-scoop pool. Those wishing to play were required to obtain tickets and were charged a session fee of £1. The club provided a float which was treated as a loan to ticket-holders. Games proceeded with ticket-holders playing against the pool when and as they chose. At the end of a session the club took from the pool sufficient money to re-imburse itself for its loan and to

E

pay the session fees owed by the ticket-holders; any balance was distributed evenly between the ticket-holders, but if there was a deficiency they were liable to make it up in equal proportions. The effect of this scheme was, therefore, that ticket-holders held the kittyscoop pool as a syndicate and played against it as individuals. On the question whether the managers had discharged the burden of proof that the game was con-

F

ducted in accordance with s. 32 (1) (a) and (b)* of the Betting, Gaming and Lotteries Act 1963,

Held: (i) they had not discharged this burden; since the odds favoured the syndicate as a playing entity holding the pool, any ticket-holder who did not play as an individual against the pool, and who thereby, as a syndicate member, enjoyed the pure syndicate odds, had an advantage in odds over

G

those who actually played and the game therefore infringed s. 32 (1) (a) (see p. 902, letter E, and p. 904, letter B, post);

Crickitt v. *Martin* ((1967), The Times, 12th July) distinguished.

(ii) since the holders of the pool were the syndicate and not the club itself there was no contravention of s. 32 (1) (b) (see p. 903, letter I, and p. 904, letters A and B, post).

H

Appeal allowed.

[**Editorial Note.** Section 32 of the Betting, Gaming and Lotteries Act 1963 is prospectively repealed by the Gaming Act 1968; see s. 2 (1) (b) of the Gaming Act 1968.

As to lawful and unlawful gaming, see SUPPLEMENT to 18 HALSBURY'S LAWS

I

(3rd Edn.), para. 369A 1, 2; and for cases on the subject, see 25 DIGEST (Repl.) 448-450, *292-302.*

---

* Section 32 (1), so far as material, provides: " Subject to the provisions of this Act, any gaming shall be lawful if, but only if, it is conducted in accordance with the following conditions, that is to say—(a) that either (i) the chances in the game are equally favourable to all the players; or (ii) the gaming is so conducted that the chances therein are equally favourable to all the players; and (b) that no money or money's worth which any of the players puts down as stakes, or pays by way of losses, or exchanges for tokens used in playing the game, is disposed of otherwise than by payment to a player as winnings; . . ."

For the Betting, Gaming and Lotteries Act 1963, s. 32, see 43 HALSBURY'S A
STATUTES (2nd Edn.) 343.]

Cases referred to:
   Crickitt v. Kursaal Casino, Ltd. (No. 2), [1968] 1 All E.R. 139; [1968] 1 W.L.R.
        53 revsg., [1967] 3 All E.R. 360; [1967] 1 W.L.R. 1227; Digest (Repl.)
        Supp.
   Crickitt v. Martin (1967), The Times, 12th July.   B
   Director of Public Prosecutions v. Essoldo Circuit (Control), Ltd., [1965] 3 All
        E.R. 421; [1966] 1 Q.B. 799; [1965] 3 W.L.R. 837; 129 J.P. 592;
        Digest (Cont. Vol. B) 317, 2876.
   Victoria Sporting Club, Ltd. v. Hannan, [1969] 1 All E.R. 369; [1969] 2 W.L.R.
        454.
                                                                           C
Case Stated.
   This was a Case Stated by the court of Quarter Sessions for the Middlesex
area in respect of their adjudication as a Court of Appeal sitting at the Guildhall,
Westminster, on 6th September 1968.
   On 11th June 1968, the respondents were convicted by the court of summary
jurisdiction sitting at Uxbridge magistrates' court in that they, on 2nd February D
1968, at the Savoy Bingo and Social Club, High Street, Uxbridge, were concerned
in the management and organisation of unlawful gaming contrary to s. 32 (4)
of the Betting, Gaming and Lotteries Act 1963.
   The following facts were found: The respondents owned and managed the Savoy
Bingo and Social Club at High Street, Uxbridge, a bona fide club which was properly conducted. The main activity carried on at the club was the playing of E
bingo. On 4th January 1968, the game of kittyscoop was introduced as an amenity
for members, the game being available for play by members between sessions of
bingo. Kittyscoop was a variant of roulette, played by means of an ordinary
roulette wheel on which six numbers in three pairs had been labelled " Kittyscoop ". The zero on the wheel was effectively eliminated as a factor in the game.
The odds operated in favour of the kittyscoop, for example, odds of four to one F
were offered against any of the six kittyscoop numbers winning whereas the
equal odds were five to one. The rules of kittyscoop which were set out on the back
of the ticket issued to each player. They provided, inter alia: any member
who wished to play was required to obtain a numbered ticket which entitled
him to play in the one session to which it applied. The ticket was issued to
the member before he commenced play and his membership number was endorsed G
on the counterfoil thereof; a fixed sessions fee of £1 was payable by each player
to the club; a float was provided by the club as a loan to the players at the commencement of each session, each of whom was required to repay to the club at
or after the conclusion of the session an equal proportion of the float so provided;
all moneys laid as stakes were required to be paid into the kittyscoop. All
winnings were paid out of the kittyscoop. Any surplus remaining at the end of a H
session being used first in discharge to the club of each player's liability to repay
his proportion of the float provided by the club, secondly in payment to the club
of each player's fixed session charge, and thirdly by distribution of the balance,
if any, remaining to the players equally by way of dividend; in the event of there
being insufficient moneys in the kittyscoop at the end of a session to repay the
float and pay the sessions fee each player undertook to pay to the club on I
demand an equal proportion of the sum required.
   The club management kept record cards for each member who played kittyscoop. After each session the staff ascertained the amount due to the players
by way of dividend, or the amount owed by the players to the club; the
appropriate credit or debit entry being later entered in the players' record cards.
Members were entitled to see their record cards in order to ascertain the state
of their accounts at any time and to demand any credit balance due. No member
was allowed to incur a debit balance in excess of £10. The relevant rules of the

A club were properly observed both by the club and the players, the record cards were properly kept, and dividend notices posted regularly on the club notice board as required by rule 10.

On 2nd day of February 1968, kittyscoop was being played at the club at 9.30 p.m. About 15 persons were present at the gaming. At the end of the session the sum of £90 16s. remained in the kittyscoop. From that sum there was deduc-
B ted: £35 being the amount advanced by the club at the beginning of the session as a float; £40 being the fixed sessions fee of £1 in respect of 40 players. The remainder, i.e. £15 16s. was divided by 40 and the sum of 7s. 11d. declared to be the dividend due to each player for that session. This sum was entered on the appropriate dividend sheet. (i) Between the 4th day of January 1968, and the 2nd day of February 1968, the club had not sought to enforce the provisions of r. 9
C by recovery of such moneys as might then be owed by players to the club, how-ever, the justices accepted Mr. Weston's evidence on behalf of the club that during this short period, members' kittyscoop accounts had, on the whole, balanced out.

It was contended on behalf of the appellant that: The kittyscoop was itself a player and the management had an interest in the kittyscoop out of which
D the float was repaid and the sessions fee paid. As the odds favoured the kittyscoop the chances in the game were not equally favourable to all the players. This was a breach of s. 32 (1) (*a*) of the Act. As the sessions fee was paid out of the kitty-scoop it was paid out of the losses made by the various players. This was a breach of s. 32 (1) (*b*) of the Act. As no attempt had been made to recover in cash any moneys owed by any player to the club under the rules of kittyscoop the rules
E did not reflect the realities of the situation. The game of kittyscoop was a device to enable the management to obtain the sessions fee from which the respondents obtained their profit. The respondents had failed to discharge the onus of proof placed on them by s. 32 (2) (*a*) of the Act.

It was contended on behalf of the respondents that: It had been shown on the evidence that the club was not at risk either as to the repayment of the float
F or the payment of the fixed sessions fee, in that neither depended on the con-tingency of the game itself, and that therefore the club was not a player within the meaning of the Act. That although by virtue of s. 36 of the Act, the club was entitled to make a fixed charge payable by members taking part in the gaming provided it was determined before the gaming began, the manner in which the same might be recovered was not governed by the Act. The rules of kittyscoop
G on the facts of this case, both as to their wording and their actual operation, realistically and effectively provided for repayment by the players of the float and payment of the sessions fee irrespective of the results of any particular game.

The respondents had discharged the onus of proof placed on them by s. 32 (2) (*a*) of the Act.
H
The court was of the opinion that although circumstances might exist where the non-observance of rules such as those before them could result in a finding that the club was taking part in unlawful gaming, on the particular facts before them, they were satisfied that this was not so, that the respondents' contentions on those facts were well founded, and that they had discharged the onus of proof required by the Act. They accordingly decided that the appeal should be
I allowed and the appellant now appealed.

J. H. Buzzard and *W. N. Denison* for the appellant.
J. C. G. Burge, Q.C., and *R. M. G. Simpson* for the respondents.

LORD PARKER, C.J.: This is an appeal by way of Case Stated from a decision of the court of Quarter Sessions for the Middlesex Area sitting at the Guildhall, Westminster who allowed an appeal by I. & N. Weston, Ltd., the respondents, from their conviction at a court of summary jurisdiction sitting

at Uxbridge for that they had been concerned in the management and organisa- A
tion of unlawful gaming contrary to s. 32 (4) of the Betting, Gaming and
Lotteries Act 1963.

The game in question, and I must refer to it in detail in a moment, was a
variant of the game roulette, and therefore was a game which inherently carried
odds which were not equally favourable to all the players. However, what was
said in the present case was that the gaming was, to use the words of s. 32 (1) (a) B
(ii) of the Act, so conducted that the chances therein were equally favourable
to all the players. That being the condition which it is said was fulfilled in the
present case, the burden rested on the managers under sub-s. (2), to prove
that the gaming was conducted in accordance with the conditions set out in
sub-s. (1).

Finally, I should add that the managers in the present case were managers C
of a bona fide club to which s. 36 of the Act applied, and accordingly provided,
as undoubtedly was the case here, that a sum was determined before the gaming
began as a condition of taking part in the gaming, then the condition in s. 32
(1) (c) was deemed to be complied with.

The respondents run what is known as the Savoy Bingo and Social Club at
Uxbridge. They provided as an amenity for members, between sessions of bingo, D
the playing of what was called kittyscoop, a variant, as I have said, of roulette.
One thing is perfectly clear, that one of the variants was that the zero was completely eliminated. However, three pairs of two numbers, were labelled with this
word " Kittyscoop ", rather like in some previous cases numbers have been
labelled " Players Pool ". Though the zero was eliminated, the odds operated
in favour of this kittyscoop. Odds of four to one were offered against any of the E
six kittyscoop numbers winning, whereas the odds in respect of the other
numbers were five to one.

The club had printed rules of which the more important are as follows:

" Any member wishing to play must obtain a numbered ticket which will
entitle him to play in the one session to which it applies."
                                                                              F
I might add here that a session was from 7.0 p.m. to 2.0 a.m. although of course
the playing did not last all the time because it was only taking place in between
sessions of bingo.

Returning to the rules:

" 3. The ticket will be issued to the member before he commences play
and the member's membership number must be endorsed on the counterfoil G
thereof . . .

" 6. A fixed charge shall be payable to the Club such charge to be until
further notice in the sum of £1.

" 7. A float is provided by the Club at the commencement of each session
by way of loan to the players, each of whom shall repay to the Club at or after
the conclusion of the session an equal proportion of the loan so provided. H

" 8. All monies laid as stakes shall be paid into the Kittyscoop. Neither the
Club nor any persons concerned in the management of the gaming shall be
players. [That is one of the matters that has to be decided.] All winnings
shall be paid out of the Kittyscoop, any surplus at the end of the session
being used firstly in discharge to the Club of each player's liability to repay
his proportion of the float by the Club, secondly in payment to the Club I
of each player's fixed session charge and thirdly by distribution of the
balance, if any, remaining to the players equally by way of dividend.

" 9. Should there be insufficient monies in the Kittyscoop at the close of
the session to enable the Club to be repaid its float and to be paid the fixed
session charge in full, each player undertakes to pay to the Club on demand
an equal proportion of that sum required."

On 2nd February 1968 police officers entered the club, and it was found that at

A   the time they entered, there were some 15 persons who were described as " being present " at the gaming; I do not know that it matters, but I rather assume from that they were the people who were taking part in the gaming at the time. At the end of the session, whenever that was, it was found that a sum of £90 16s. remained in the kittyscoop, and that was distributed in this way: £35, which was the amount of the float advanced by the club was repaid to the club;

B   £40 was also paid to the club being the fixed session fee of £1 in respect of 40 players—pausing there, therefore, apart from the 15 who were found present at the gaming, some further 25 had from time to time during the session played at the game. That left a sum in the pool of £15 16s., and this was divided by the 40 people who had played or been entitled to play, the sum of 7s. 11d. accordingly being the dividend due to each player.

C   Finally, merely to get it out of the way, it was said at quarter sessions that the rules were not complied with, in particular that r. 9 was really a sham and that any deficiency in the float or in the amount available to pay the session charges was just not collected from the players. As I will show in a moment, if that were the position, this would come within *Director of Public Prosecutions* v. *Essoldo Circuit (Control), Ltd.* (1).   But quarter sessions having heard the evidence,

D   were satisfied that the rules were obeyed, and that where the collection of a deficiency had not taken place, it was because the kittyscoop accounts of the members on the whole, as they put it, balanced out. Accordingly, that question of fact being out of the way, the question remained whether the game as played strictly in accordance with the rules offended against s. 32. The justices came to the conclusion that it did not, and they word their opinion in this way:

E   " The Court was of the opinion that although circumstances might exist where the non-observance of rules such as those before us could result in a finding that the Club was taking part in unlawful gaming, on the particular facts before us, we were satisfied that this was not so, that the [respondents'] contentions on those facts were well founded, and that they had discharged the onus of proof required by the said Act. We accordingly decided that their

F   appeal should be allowed."

The question for the court is whether the decision to allow the appeal was correct in law.

This is yet another case of variants being introduced into the game of roulette in an attempt to ensure that the game can be played legally under the Act.

G   In particular in the present case the variant takes the form of trying to get round, if I may use the expression, the decision of this court in the *Essoldo* case (1).   In that case six numbers were labelled " Players Pool ", the odds again were not equal, odds of four to one being paid in respect of the players pool and five to one in respect of the numbers; as in the present case the club advanced a float, but with this important distinction that the club merely

H   made a float available whereas in the present case the float has been stated to be a loan to the actual players. Again as in this case at the end of the session there was paid out of the pool first the float, secondly the service charge for each player, which was again £1 as in this case, finally, and this is unlike this case, 1d. to each player, and when that had been done the balance, if any, was divided as dividends to the player. In other words in the *Essoldo* case (1) a dividend of £1 and 1d. was, as it were, guaranteed. The court in the *Essoldo* case (1) held

I   that the club, at any rate in the early stages, was at risk, and therefore was a player—at risk if the amount in the pool at any time was less than the float, since it would have had itself to bear the deficiency. Accordingly since the chances in the game were not equally favourable to each player including the club, the game was held to be unlawful.

In the present case the respondents have sought to make the same type of game legal by providing, as I have said, that the float should be a loan to the

─────────────────────────

(1) [1965] 3 All E.R. 421; [1966] 1 Q.B. 799.

players, and also by r. 9 that in the event of any deficiency each player who has   A
taken part in the gaming during the session, and I would add in parenthesis,
as it seems to me, any person who has obtained a numbered ticket and counterfoil
and who has for one reason or another not taken part at all, would be liable to
make up his proportion of the deficiency in the float, and also any deficiency
in the session fee.   It was in those circumstances urged before the quarter
sessions and before this court that the club in the present case in no sense could   B
be said to be a player, in that the club was not at the risk of any loss due to
there being a deficiency in the pool.

For my part I am by no means clear that the club in the present case was not
properly called a player within the definition of s. 55 of the Act. The reality of
the position, as it seems to me, is that the gaming was managed in such a way
as to enable the club to collect, as it were, at source, the only part of the stakes   C
which could be profit to itself, namely the £1 session fee. True it could collect
any deficiency there was from individual players afterwards, but clearly the
odds here were weighted in favour of the pool for the very good reason of ensuring
as far as possible that the club got at source the return of its loan and the payment of the service charges, thus avoiding the trouble and the risk of not being
able to collect from the individual players. Further, it stands to reason that if a   D
£1 session fee was demanded in advance, there would be no doubt less people
to take part in the gaming; and this method of operation enabled the club to
get a greater number of session fees and to ensure that they were paid out of the
pool, without the necessity of trying to collect afterwards from the other people.

However, having said that, I prefer to base my decision in the present case
on what I think is the better view here, that although it is arguable that the   E
club was a player, the player here was the collective body, call it the syndicate,
of all those who had become liable, either by playing or more accurately by
getting their numbered ticket to take part in the gaming. On that view, a person
who obtained a ticket and did not himself play in the sense of doing any staking
or a person entitled to play who at any spin of the wheel abstains, is a member
nevertheless of this syndicate, and therefore taking part as a player, and clearly   F
at odds which are more favourable than those available to the players who are
actually staking of which he is not one. Equally, as it seems to me, if he does
take part in the stakings, the odds are not equal as between himself and the
other members of the syndicate, four to one and five to one. Accordingly, as
it seems to me when one looks at it in this way, the true view here is as a matter
of law that the game was not conducted, or at any rate the managers have not   G
proved, the burden being on them, that the game was so conducted, to use the
words of the section, that the chances therein were equally favourable to all the
players.

Counsel for the respondents has, as no doubt happened before the justices,
strongly urged on us the decision of this court in *Crickitt* v. *Martin* (2). The facts
of that case bear a striking similarity to the facts of this case, and yet this court   H
upheld an acquittal by the justices. No doubt this was a case which did influence
quarter sessions in the present case. But having said that, it seems to me that
no comfort can be derived by counsel from that case. It is to be observed in the
first instance that it occurred at a time between the decision of this court in
Crickitt v. *Kursaal Casino, Ltd.* (*No. 2*) (3) and the decision of the House of Lords
in that case (4), a decision which reversed the decision of this court. Secondly   I
it appears from the judgment of WIDGERY, J., that the sole issue in that
case was really whether the non-compliance with the rules which had occurred
in certain instances was such as to entitle the court to say that the rules were
in effect a sham. There again there was provision for collecting from the players
each player's proportion of the deficiency, to put it quite generally, in the pool,

(2) (1967), The Times, 12th July.
(3) [1967] 3 All E.R. 360; [1967] 1 W.L.R. 1227.
(4) [1968] 1 All E.R. 139; [1968] 1 W.L.R. 53.

A and that in some cases had not been done. But the justices in that case had come
to the conclusion that there was reason for the non-collection, as indeed happened
in the present case, and that the rules were by no means a sham. This court
felt that it was impossible to say on the facts that the decision of the justices
was a perverse decision; accordingly they upheld the decision of the justices.

It is quite true that that case apparently proceeded, according to the judgment,
B on the basis that if the game had been conducted in accordance with the rules,
the rules being very similar, if not identical, to those in the present case, no offence
was committed; that assumption of course, was only an assumption for the purpose of that case, and counsel for the appellant is perfectly entitled to argue,
as he has done, that although that assumption may have been made in that case,
the true view, particularly in the light of the recent decisions of the House of
C Lords, is that the gaming, even conducted in accordance with the rules, was not
lawful gaming.

Finally, counsel for the appellant has a further point, which is that here there
was a failure to comply with the condition, not merely in s. 32 (1) (*a*), but in s. 32
(1) (*b*), which provides as a condition that no money or money's worth which any
of the players puts down as stakes or pays by way of losses or exchanges for tokens
D used in playing the game is disposed of otherwise than by payment to a player
as winnings. What he says here is that though it may sound very technical,
in fact all the money in the pool representing stakes was disposed of otherwise
than by payment to a player, because the £1 was not paid out to the player
but was £1 paid out or retained by the club, the managers.

The point is somewhat technical in the sense that it is just the same as if the
E £1 were paid out to each person entitled to play and he then paid the £1 over to the
club. But counsel for the appellant says that this is really a position similar
to that in *Victoria Sporting Club, Ltd.* v. *Hannan* (5). That was the well-known
case concerning gaming with marker chips in which the marker chips representing
the difference in the odds could be cashed or could be exchanged for gaming chips,
but members were invited to surrender them to the management. In that case
F three of their Lordships held that the gaming there was illegal because s. 32 (1) (*b*)
was not complied with. LORD REID said this (6):

"But what the club must not do is to appropriate any part of that money
[that is the money in the pool or the money's worth] as its own. And that
is what the club does when the member surrenders chips which he has won.
It can make no difference whether the surrendered chips are marker chips
G or gaming chips because, if the game has been played at the lawful odds,
the marker chips which the member receives represent money just as much
as do the gaming chips. If, having received his winnings in cash, the member
chooses to make a donation to the club, that is his affair. But an offence is
committed if he surrenders chips as a donation to the club."

H By analogy counsel for the appellant urges here that the retention of the £1,
the paying over the £1 to the club before any dividend was paid to the player,
offended against s. 32 (1) (*b*). I can understand the force of the argument of
counsel for the appellant, but I for my part have very great doubt whether it
applies in any case other than one in which the player, the banker, the holder
of the pool, is the club itself. That was the position in the *Victoria Sporting Club*
I case (5), but on the basis that I feel this case should be decided, namely on the
basis that the holder of the pool is the syndicate of players, it seems to me that
a different situation may well arise. It seems to me that by the effect of these
rules, each player is giving authority to the club as the managers, in no other
capacity, to pay out of his winnings the £1 service charge. On that basis, it seems
to me that there is no offence by reason of a non-compliance with s. 32 (1) (*b*).

For the reasons I have endeavoured to state shortly in this case I have come

---

(5) [1969] 1 All E.R. 369; [1969] 2 W.L.R. 454.
(6) [1969] 1 All E.R. at p. 373; [1969] 2 W.L.R. at p. 459.

to the conclusion that quarter sessions came to a wrong decision in law, **A**
and I would send the case back to quarter sessions with a direction to convict.

    MELFORD STEVENSON, J.: I agree. I feel no doubt that the character
of a player is acquired as soon as a numbered ticket is obtained in the circumstances that are set out in the case, even if the holder of that ticket thereafter takes
no part in the game and stakes nothing. Such a person continues to enjoy odds **B**
more favourable than those given to the other players, and that makes the conclusion that an offence under s. 32 (1) (*a*) (i) has been committed in my view
inevitable.

    WILLIS, J.: I agree with both judgments and have nothing to add.

    Case remitted. Appeal allowed. Leave to appeal to the House of Lords granted, the **C**
court certifying under s. 1 of the Administration of Justice Act 1960 that a point of
law of general public importance was involved, viz., whether on the facts admitted
or found, the respondents had satisfied the burden of proof on them under s. 32 (1) (a)
of the Betting, Gaming and Lotteries Act 1963 that the gaming as conducted was in
accordance with the conditions imposed by s. 32 (1) (a) of that Act.

    Solicitors: *Solicitor, Metropolitan Police*; *Saunders, Sobell, Leigh & Dobin* **D**
(for the respondents).

                 [*Reported by* JACQUELINE CHARLES, *Barrister-at-Law.*]

                                                                 E

BELVOIR FINANCE CO., LTD. *v.* HAROLD G. COLE & CO., LTD.

[QUEEN'S BENCH DIVISION (Donaldson, J.), March 11, 12, 1969.]

Hire-Purchase—Illegality—Initial payments—No actual payment to finance
    company of statutory 20 per cent. of cash price before agreement—Unauthorised **F**
    transfer by hirer to motor dealer—Later claim by finance company against
    dealer for conversion—Claim founded on title gained by original outright
    purchase by finance company—Whether title vitiated by illegal hire-purchase
    agreement so as to preclude action for conversion—Hire-Purchase and
    Credit Sale Agreements (Control) Order 1964 (S.I. 1964 No. 942), art. 1 (1),
    Sch. 2, Pt. 1, para. 3. **G**

Agent—Mercantile agent—Possession of goods—Unauthorised disposition—Motor
    car hire company—Fleet of cars on hire-purchase—Practice to sell cars
    on its own behalf with owner's consent when no longer usable in car hire
    business—Cars sold in this way but without knowledge or consent of owner—
    Whether car hire company mercantile agent or in possession of cars in that
    capacity so as to pass good title to purchaser—Factors Act 1889 (52 & 53 **H**
    Vict. c. 45), s. 1 (1), s. 2 (1).

Agent—Mercantile agent—Possession of goods—Consent of owner—Possession
    under illegal hire-purchase agreement—Whether with consent of owner—
    Factors Act 1889 (52 & 53 Vict. c. 45), s. 2 (1).

Sale of goods—Title—Illegality of related agreement—Finance company purchasing
    motor car outright with intention to let it under hire-purchase agreement— **I**
    Hire-purchase agreement illegal by reason of non-payment of initial deposit
    required by statutory regulations—Whether finance company's title under
    original sale vitiated by illegality of hire-purchase agreement so as to preclude
    later claim in action for conversion of motor car.

Pleading—Admission—Illegality—Admission of consent—Consent given under
    illegal hire-purchase agreement—Whether admission effective.

    B., Ltd., was engaged in the business of letting cars out on hire. It acquired
its fleet of cars by means of hire-purchase agreements with the plaintiff (a

A finance company). After a car had been used in the business for a certain time, it was the practice for B., Ltd., with the consent of the plaintiff, to sell it, at the same time exercising its option to purchase. In 1965, pursuant to this arrangement, the plaintiff purported to let three cars to B., Ltd. on hire-purchase. The transactions fell within the Hire-Purchase and Credit Sale Agreements (Control) Order 1964*, art. 1 (1), and Sch. 1, Pt. 2, para. 3 (1),

B which prohibited persons from disposing of certain goods in pursuance of hire-purchase agreements unless an actual payment of at least 20 per cent. of the cash price had been made. In the case of each of the cars the initial payment actually made by B., Ltd., was less than 20 per cent. of the respective cash price. But in each case B., Ltd., was credited with the amount of discount that the plaintiff had received from the original sellers, the amounts

C of these credits being sufficient to augment the initial payments to figures beyond the requisite 20 per cent. Subsequently, B., Ltd., acting without the consent or knowledge of the plaintiff, to whom it continued to pay hire-purchase instalments, sold the three cars to the defendant, a car dealer, who re-sold them in the ordinary course of business. The plaintiff sued the defendant in conversion. It admitted in its pleadings that B., Ltd., was in

D possession of the cars with its consent.

Held: the plaintiff's claim succeeded, because—

(i) although the hire-purchase agreements were illegal under art. 1 (1) of the Hire-Purchase and Credit Sale Agreements (Control) Order 1964 since in no case had a sufficient actual payment been made (see p. 909, letter C, and p. 910, letter E, post), yet the plaintiff was still able to establish title

E to the cars because it was able to found its claim on its earlier purchases of them, without the necessity of any reference to the illegal hire-purchase agreements (see p. 910, letter I, and p. 911, letter H, post).

Bowmakers, Ltd. v. *Barnet Instruments, Ltd.* ([1944] 2 All E.R. 579) applied.

Fisher v. *Bridges* ((1854), 3 E. & B. 642) distinguished.

(ii) the defendant did not gain a good title under s. 2 (1)† of the Factors

F Act 1889, because—

(a) B., Ltd., sold cars on its own behalf and was therefore not a mercantile agent within the meaning of the Factors Act 1889 (see p. 907, letter I, post);

(b) B., Ltd., even if a mercantile agent, was not in possession of the particular cars in that capacity (see p. 907, letter I, post) (*Astley Industrial Trust, Ltd.* v. *Miller* [1968] 2 All E.R. 36) followed); and

G (c) notwithstanding the fact that the plaintiff admitted in its pleadings that B., Ltd., was in possession of the cars with its consent, the illegality of the hire-purchase agreements prevented the defendant from establishing the consent necessary for the operation of s. 2 (1) of the Factors Act 1889 (see p. 908, letter B, post).

H [As to actions on contracts involving illegality, see 8 HALSBURY'S LAWS (3rd Edn.) 148-152, paras. 257-259; and for cases on the subject, see 12 DIGEST (Repl.) 310-314, *2390-2424*.

As to agents who may be classed as mercantile agents, see 1 HALSBURY'S LAWS (3rd Edn.) 151, 152, paras. 361, 362; as to dispositions under the Factors Act 1889, see ibid., pp. 214, 215, para. 488; and for cases on the subject, see 1 DIGEST (Repl.) 383-389, *491-524*, 392, 393, *539-544*.

I For the Factors Act 1889, s. 1, s. 2, see 1 HALSBURY'S STATUTES (3rd Edn.) 95, 96.

For the Hire-Purchase and Credit Sale Agreements (Control) Order 1964, art. 1 and Sch. 2, see 19 HALSBURY'S STATUTORY INSTRUMENTS (2nd Re-issue) 301, 310.]

---

* S.I. 1964 No. 942, as amended. The relevant provisions are set out at p. 908, letters D and E, post.

† Section 2 (1) is set out at p. 907, letter C, post.

Cases referred to:

A

   Astley Industrial Trust, Ltd. v. *Miller*, [1968] 2 All E.R. 36; Digest (Repl.) Supp.

   Bowmakers, Ltd. v. *Barnet Instruments, Ltd.*, [1944] 2 All E.R. 579; [1945] K.B. 65; 114 L.J.K.B. 41; 172 L.T. 1; 12 Digest (Repl.) 310, *2391*.

   Fisher v. *Bridges* (1854), 3 E. & B. 642; 23 L.J.Q.B. 276; 23 L.T.O.S. 223; 18 J.P. 599; 118 E.R. 1283; 12 Digest (Repl.) 310, *2387*.

B

   Folkes v. *King*, [1923] 1 K.B. 282; [1922] All E.R. Rep. 658; 92 L.J.K.B. 125; 128 L.T. 405; 1 Digest (Repl.) 390, *531*.

   Wickham Holdings, Ltd. v. *Brooke House Motors, Ltd.*, [1967] 1 All E.R. 117; [1967] 1 W.L.R. 295; Digest (Repl.) Supp.

Action.

C

In this action, commenced by writ on 1st September 1967, the plaintiff, Belvoir Finance Co., Ltd., sought damages for alleged conversion of three motor cars by the defendant, Harold G. Cole & Co., Ltd., a dealer in motor vehicles. In its statement of claim the plaintiff asserted its ownership of the three vehicles and the sale of the same by the defendant. In its defence, as amended, the defendant denied conversion and pleaded, inter alia, that the plaintiff had purported to let the vehicles to Belgravia Car Hire, Ltd., on hire-purchase

D

agreements, that the latter company had taken possession of the vehicles with the plaintiff's consent, but that the hire-purchase agreements were illegal and/or void; further and/or in the alternative, that Belgravia Car Hire, Ltd., was at all material times a mercantile agent within the meaning of s. 2 of the Factors Act 1889; that Belgravia Car Hire, Ltd. had, in the ordinary course of business, sold the vehicles to it; and that it had taken the vehicles in good faith and thereby

E

become the legal owner.

   R. S. Insall for the plaintiff.
   C. W. G. Ross-Munro for the defendant.

F

   DONALDSON, J.: This action is concerned with three motor cars of which both parties to the action claim to be the owners. When I add that the plaintiff is a hire-purchase company the story is a familiar one, although this particular version has a new and illegal twist, as will appear hereafter.

The cars themselves were new in 1965. Two were Triumph 2000s, one was an Austin 1100. All three found their way into the possession of Belgravia Car Hire, Ltd. (to whom I shall refer as " Belgravia "). All three were in due course sold by Belgravia to the defendant, a motor dealer, and were resold by the

G

defendant in the ordinary course of its business. The plaintiff alleges that all three cars are, and were at all material times, its property, and that the resales by the defendant constituted conversions. The parties are agreed that if this contention is sound the application of the correct measure of damages, namely, that propounded in *Wickham Holdings, Ltd.* v. *Brooke House Motors, Ltd.* (1), produces a figure of £1,501 2s. as the principal amount for which judgment should

H

be given.

Originally the defendant admitted that the plaintiff was at one time the owner of the cars, but alleged that the cars were let to Belgravia under hire-purchase agreements; that Belgravia was a mercantile agent, and that by the operation of s. 2 (1) of the Factors Act 1889, Belgravia was able to give and did give it a good title to the vehicles. This is the mercantile agency defence. At a later stage

I

the defendant withdrew the admission that the plaintiff had at one time been the owner of the cars, and alleged that although the plaintiff had purported to buy the cars from dealers and to let them on hire-purchase to Belgravia, the hire-purchase contracts contravened the Hire-Purchase and Credit Sale Agreements (Control) Order 1964 (2) and this illegality tainted its purchase contract. Accordingly, the plaintiff at no time became the owner of the cars and has no title to sue.

---

(1) [1967] 1 All E.R. 117; [1967] 1 W.L.R. 295.
(2) S.I. 1964 No. 942.

A This is the illegality defence. If it is well founded it has the merit from the point of view of the defendant, that the plaintiff's claim fails, but it leaves the defendant open to another action by the dealers who thought that they had sold the cars to the plaintiff. I put this point to counsel for the defendant, who said that he was quite prepared to take the risk of such subsequent action; and indeed it may well be that he would be on quite good ground, inasmuch as one of

B the dealers is in liquidation and the other might well not be interested in doing anything about the matter.

However, I will consider these two defences separately, and will begin with the mercantile agency defence. Section 2 (1) of the Factors Act 1889 provides:

C " Where a mercantile agent is, with the consent of the owner, in possession of goods or of the documents of title to goods, any sale, pledge, or other disposition of the goods, made by him when acting in the ordinary course of business of a mercantile agent, shall, subject to the provisions of this Act, be as valid as if he were expressly authorised by the owner of the goods to make the same; provided that the person taking under the disposition acts in good faith, and has not at the time of the disposition notice that the person making the disposition has not authority to make the same."

D A mercantile agent is defined by s. 1 (1) of the Act as:

" a mercantile agent having in the customary course of his business as such agent authority either to sell goods, or to consign goods for the purpose of sale, or to buy goods, or to raise money on the security of goods."

E The good faith of the defendant is not impugned, and it is not suggested that it had any notice of any want of authority on the part of Belgravia. This leaves two issues, namely, was Belgravia a mercantile agent at law, and if so, was it a mercantile agent in possession of the cars with the consent of the plaintiff as owner?

Belgravia's business was that of letting cars out on hire, and it seems to have

F had a medium-sized fleet consisting wholly or mainly of new cars acquired by means of hire-purchase agreements with the plaintiff. As the cars lost their newness they were sold with the consent of the plaintiff, the option to purchase under the agreement being exercised at the time of the sale. The same procedure was followed in the case of the three cars with which I am concerned, with the vital differences that the plaintiff was neither asked for, nor gave, any consent to

G the sale and Belgravia failed to settle the sums due on the hire-purchase agreements, but continued to pay the instalments for some months as if it was still in possession of the cars.

Belgravia's premises contained no showroom, but there was a space to display cars being for sale, and undoubtedly cars were so displayed from time to time. However, there was no evidence, with one exception, that the cars were other

H than cars which had outlived their usefulness in the car hire business. It is true that some or all of these cars were registered in names other than that of Belgravia, but I am quite satisfied that car hire firms adopt the course of registering cars in the names of nominees in order that it shall not be apparent on a resale that the cars have been used for hiring out. This is no doubt unlawful and also dishonest, but, it being a fact, it prevents me from drawing any inference from the

I registration books that the cars were not being sold by Belgravia on its own behalf. The one exception which I have mentioned was a case in which Belgravia bought a car for resale. However, a motor dealer who buys and sells cars on his own behalf is not, in law, an agent at all, whether mercantile or otherwise, and I have had no evidence that Belgravia ever sold cars on behalf of others.

This is fatal to the mercantile agency defence. But there are two further flaws in that defence: first, the section applies only when the goods are in the possession of the mercantile agent as such. Authority for this proposition is to be found in

the decision of CHAPMAN, J., in *Astley Industrial Trust, Ltd.* v. *Miller* (3), and in A
the cases there cited. I respectfully agree with and follow that decision and
the reasoning on which it is based; and would only add to his anthology a
reference to *Folkes* v. *King* (4), per BANKES, L.J. Secondly, if the defendant is
correct in asserting (as I think that it is) that the hire-purchase contracts were
illegal, it is unable to show that Belgravia was in possession of the cars with the
consent of the plaintiff, for it is only under and subject to those contracts that B
these consents were given. When I put this point to counsel for the defendant, he
said: " Ah, well, but on the pleadings consent is admitted." I think that illegality,
once brought to the attention of the court, overrides all questions of pleading,
and that therefore this is, and remains, a real and indeed insuperable difficulty
in the way of the defendant so far as the mercantile agency defence is concerned.
However, for the reasons I have given, I think that it fails on other grounds, so C
that this point is of only academic interest.

This brings me to the illegality defence. The Hire-Purchase and Credit Sale
Agreements (Control) Order 1964 provided by art. 1 (1) that:

> " A person shall not dispose of any goods to which this Order applies in
> pursuance of a hire-purchase or credit sale agreement entered into after
> the 28th April 1960 . . . unless the requirements specified in Part 1 of Schedule D
> 2 hereto are or have been complied with in relation to that agreement."

And Pt. 1 of Sch. 2 provides, in para. 3 (1), that:

> " Before the agreement was entered into actual payment was made in
> respect of each description of goods comprised in the agreement of not
> less than [and then, if one follows through various references it means 20 per E
> cent. of] (*a*) the cash price of the goods of that description comprised in the
> agreement; . . . .

The effect of this order is that a hire-purchase contract is illegal unless before it
was entered into there was actual payment of 20 per cent. of the cash price of the
goods.

What then are the facts in relation to this defence? The two Triumphs were F
let on hire-purchase under agreements which were signed on behalf of the plaintiff
on 27th May 1965, but took effect from 25th May. I will assume that actual
payment of 20 per cent. of the cash price had been made before the date of signature. They were bought from Francis Motors of Leicester, and at the material
time Mr. Pike, who gave evidence before me, was a director both of the plaintiff
and of Francis Motors. " Francis Motors " was the business name of E. F. Pike G
(Humberstone Road), Ltd. Each car was bought for £1,100. This sum represented
the list price of the car, plus extras, less a discount on the basic price: that
is to say, the cash price less the purchase tax; and that discount amounted
to £150 9s. The cars were paid for by cheques dated 27th May 1965, and they
were presented for payment and paid, if that is material, on 3rd June 1965.

The hire-purchase agreements relating to the two Triumphs show the cash H
price for the Triumphs as being £1,245 9s. and they show the initial payments as
being £249 9s. The figure of £249 9s. is, of course, slightly in excess of the 20 per
cent. of the cash price, but £1,245 9s. is not, at any rate, the same cash price as
that which the plaintiff was paying to Francis Motors.

When one looks at the ledger account maintained by the plaintiff and relating to
Belgravia Car Hire, Ltd., one finds in the left-hand column a figure for the so- I
called advance of £1,245 9s.—that is to say, the cash price, a figure for charges
of £209 2s., and a figure of £2 for the option. So that the plaintiff is treating the
position as if it had paid £1,245 9s. for the vehicle, which we know from the other
documents to be untrue. On the other side of the sheet, in the right-hand column,
it shows the initial payment as composed of two items: first, a cheque from

---

(3) [1968] 2 All E.R. 36.
(4) [1923] 1 K.B. 282 at pp. 295, 296; [1922] All E.R. Rep. 658 at p. 663.

A Belgravia for £104 (and so far as that is concerned I am prepared to assume that that was an actual payment and that it was made before the agreement was entered into, although according to the ledger it was received on May 27th; so that it might be considered in that respect to have been a photo finish). But the other part of the initial payment consisted of £145 9s. and appears simply under the rubric of "Francis Motors". However, in evidence given by Mr. Pike it was

B perfectly clear that no cash or credit of any sort was received by the plaintiff from Belgravia or from anybody acting on its behalf in relation to this £145 9s. It is quite simply the discount referred to in the invoice relating to the purchase, of £150 9s. less £5 related to pre-delivery servicing of the motor car; and it is a balancing figure which, if deducted from the £1,245 9s., would reduce the advance figure to the real price of the motor car, namely £1,100. It is a perfectly legitimate

C form of book-keeping, but it does not, in my view, comply with the requirements of the regulations for actual payment. Mr. Pike said that in his view it did, because he said that this was a discount, the original £150 was a discount allowed to Belgravia by Francis Motors; and inasmuch as Francis Motors chose to allow it directly in account with the plaintiff rather than paying it to Belgravia and leaving Belgravia to pay it to the plaintiff, Belgravia was in fact paying. In my judgment,

D they were neither paying in fact nor in law.

The matter has been complicated, as would appear in relation to the Austin, by the fact that Mr. Pike was treading a somewhat difficult course in relation to this transaction, because at this time there was resale price maintenance in relation to motor cars; and Mr. Pike told me that in general it was his practice, in his capacity as a director of Francis Motors, and was the general practice of motor

E dealers, to sell cars at the full list price and then to adjust this to market conditions by paying the purchaser an introductory commission, or payment under some other head, so that in the end the purchaser paid no more than he was prepared to pay in the market. Were the matter to be dealt with in a more straightforward way, it was said that the motor manufacturers would at that time have taken proceedings against the dealer. He added (and although it is not

F strictly relevant to this case, it may be of interest to the registrar of restrictive trading agreements) that similar pressures exist at the present time, when resale price maintenance no longer exists. I have not, of course, investigated that allegation, it not being material to this case; but I record it merely for what it is worth.

For the reasons that I have given, I am quite satisfied that the hire-purchase

G agreements in relation to the two Triumphs infringed the regulations to which I have referred, and were accordingly illegal. Having seen Mr. Pike in the witness box and heard his evidence, I am bound to say that I think he probably thought that they were legal. His attitude, I think (although he did not say so), was that these regulations were a lot of nonsense, and that provided that one did business in a sufficiently circuitous fashion, the lawyers, the police, Parliament and the

H Board of Trade would all be quite happy, and life would go on as it should have gone on anyway. That being his attitude, of course, does not make it any the less illegal, but it may have some slight materiality, although I am not sure that it has, in relation to what are the consequences of that illegality, to which I will return in a moment.

First, however, I must return to deal with the Austin, which is in a slightly

I different position, because there the plaintiff was dealing with a company called Winfield Motors, with whom it had no direct association although it was another Leicester company; and in that case it did not think it right to abate the purchase price on the face of the documents, no doubt because it thought that there was more chance in that case that the motor manufacturers might discover what was going on. It accordingly paid Winfield Motors the full market price of this Austin 1100, which was £677 3s. 5d. The invoice is dated 25th March, the cheque was dated 1st April and was cashed, if it be material, on 3rd April. Then, when one comes to the hire-purchase agreement, one finds that the cash price of the goods

is again the price £677 3s. 5d.; the cash deposit is £136 3s. 5d. which exceeds A
20 per cent. of the cash price, and there are hire-purchase charges of £11 15s.
and an option to purchase fee of £1. I deduce that this is an older form of
agreement, since by 1965 most hire-purchase companies had realised that there
was really a quite surprising amount of money to be made out of making the
option fee £2 instead of £1, as indeed the plaintiff did in its other standard
forms which related to the Triumph motor car. But £1 it was in the case of the B
Austin car.

I therefore look to the ledger relating to this transaction to see whether the
cash deposit of £136 3s. 5d. was in fact paid before the agreement was entered
into; and the agreement bears the date 1st April 1965, and I must assume,
in the absence of evidence to the contrary, that it was entered into on that date.
The ledger shows that on 1st April Belgravia did indeed pay £61 7s. 5d. by cheque; C
but when one comes to look to how the balance of £74 16s. was paid, all that
I am able to find from the ledger is an entry dated 2nd April under the rubric
" Winfield Motors," of that amount. Now whether Winfield Motors paid by cash
or in contra account, I do not know, and I think that it does not matter, for two
reasons: first, the transaction, according to the only evidence available to me,
took place on 2nd April, which was the day after the hire-purchase agreement was D
entered into; and, secondly, the payment, credit, contra entry or whatever it
may have been, was, in exactly the same way as was the discount in the case of
the Triumphs, a payment or a rebate by Winfield Motors and not by Belgravia.
No doubt, if he had been asked, Mr. Pike would have said that exactly the same
considerations applied to the payment by Winfield Motors as applied to that by
Francis Motors—it was a rebate, a payment being made by Winfield Motors, on E
behalf of Belgravia. Well, for the reasons I have already given in relation to the
Triumph cars, I do not think it was. I am therefore quite satisfied that both
these hire-purchase agreements were illegal.

Counsel for the defendant then invites me to say that in that case the purchase
contracts or transactions between the plaintiff and Winfield Motors in relation to
the Austin motor car and Francis Motors in relation to the Triumphs were also F
illegal, and that in consequence the plaintiff got no title, or at any rate cannot
prove any title in these proceedings. In my judgment, that submission is ill-
founded. I approach it from the standpoint of the law as laid down in *Bowmakers,
Ltd.* v. *Barnet Instruments, Ltd.* (5); and the ratio of that judgment, which was a
judgment of the court given by DU PARCQ, L.J., appears in the following passage
(6):
                                                                                   G
" In our opinion a man's right to possess his own chattels will as a general
rule be enforced against one who, without any claim of right, is detaining
them, or has converted them to his own use, even though it may appear either
from the pleadings, or in the course of the trial, that the chattels in question
came into the defendant's possession by reason of an illegal contract between
himself and the plaintiff, provided that the plaintiff does not seek, and is not H
forced, either to found his claim on the illegal contract, or to plead its illegality
in order to support his claim."

If one takes that literally—and I am inclined to think that one is entitled to take
that literally—the plaintiff plainly succeeds here because it does not found itself
on the hire-purchase contracts which are the illegal contracts. Indeed, it need
make no mention of them at all.
                                                                                   I
Counsel for the defendant says, however, that that is a wrong approach, or
alternatively that the illegal contracts, to which he says that this principle ought
to be applied, are the sale contracts themselves. I mind not which way it is put.
This is a serious point which requires serious consideration. What he is saying is
this: He says, and it is a fact, based on the evidence of Mr. Pike, that the plaintiff

_____
(5) [1944] 2 All E.R. 579; [1945] K.B. 65.
(6) [1944] 2 All E.R. at pp. 582, 583; [1945] K.B. at p. 71.

A would never have bought these motor cars if it had not been satisfied that it could let them on hire-purchase to Belgravia. He says that it follows from that that the contracts for the purchase of these cars were really contracts for the purchase of the cars to be let on hire-purchase to Belgravia—all in one breath.

His case is slightly stronger in relation to the Triumphs than in relation to the Austin, because of course Mr. Pike in his capacity as a director of Francis Motors,
B knew all about the ultimate destination of the motor cars, whereas there was no evidence that Winfield Motors knew anything about it at all. Nevertheless, I have come to the conclusion that there is not a sufficient nexus between each pair of contracts to infect the contract of purchase with the illegality that undoubtedly exists under the contract of hire-purchase.

I was referred to *Fisher* v. *Bridges* (7), the judgment in which is very clear, the
C facts of which are obscure in the extreme. Unfortunately, the meaning and authority of the judgment depends entirely on what the facts were, and therefore I found it not as helpful as it might otherwise have been. Although counsel for the defendant submits that I am wrong, I think the facts were that there was an agreement to sell land which was to be resold by the purchaser by way of a lottery, and I think that the purchase price under the first sale contract was
D related to the proceeds of the lottery. If that were right, then of course the illegality would, quite clearly, run through into the original sale contract; and that being so, I do not find anything at all surprising in this case. If I am wrong in my analysis—" analysis " is perhaps too exact a word—if I am wrong in my assumption of the facts, then I do not think that that case fits in with the general picture presented by the authorities on illegality, and certainly it would require
E reconsideration by a court which is entitled to reconsider it. It seems to me that if I were to say that these purchase contracts were tainted with the illegality of the hire-purchase contracts, I should be ignoring the essential structure of all hire-purchase transactions, which is that there is an outright contract of sale and purchase between the previous owner of the goods and the finance company, and a collateral and legally unrelated contract of hiring with an option to
F purchase by the finance company to the hirer.

I fully appreciate that commercially there is the closest possible connection between the two in the sense that no hire-purchase company is going to buy that which they cannot immediately let on hire to some prospective hirer. But then it is equally true that many merchants, though not all, will not dream of buying goods unless they have an immediately available purchaser for those goods. I
G do not see that that fact is sufficient to link the two contracts to such an extent as to enable the illegality of the second contract to infect the first. So for those reasons it seems to me that the plaintiff is in this case able to prove its title without any reference to the hire-purchase contracts; and furthermore, that the title which it has proved arises out of a contract of sale, proved by the invoices and by Mr. Pike's evidence which is unaffected by illegality from a contract to which it
H need not refer. Accordingly, I think it makes good its claim; the defences put forward by the defendant fail, and the plaintiff is entitled to judgment for £1,501 9s.

Judgment for the plaintiff for £1,501 9s.

Solicitors: *Jaques & Co.*, agents for *Harvey, Clarke & Adams*, Leicester (for
I the plaintiff); *K. A. Wyndham-Kaye* (for the defendant).

[*Reported by* K. Diana Phillips, *Barrister-at-Law.*]

---

(7) (1854), 3 E. & B. 642.

A

EDDIS AND ANOTHER *v.* CHICHESTER CONSTABLE AND OTHERS.

[COURT OF APPEAL, CIVIL DIVISION (Lord Denning, M.R., Winn and Fenton Atkinson, L.JJ.), March 26, 27, 28, 31, April 23, 1969.]

B

Limitation of Action—Postponement of limitation period—Concealment of right of action by fraud—Conversion—Action based on fraud—Right of action concealed by fraud—Sale of heirloom by tenant for life to defendants—Resale by defendants to third party—Trustees' action for damages for conversion—Whether defendants claiming through tenant for life—Whether action statute-barred—Limitation Act 1939 (2 & 3 Geo. 6 c. 21), *s.* 26 (*b*), *proviso, s.* 31 (4).

C

The plaintiffs were trustees of a settlement which included, among other heirlooms, a valuable painting. In 1951, the tenant for life, since deceased, sold the painting to a consortium who resold it to an art gallery in the U.S.A. On 7th March 1966, the plaintiffs commenced an action for breach of trust against the personal representative of the tenant for life and for damages for conversion against the members of the consortium. The latters' defences were: first, that the sale by the tenant for life gave them a good title; secondly, that the plaintiffs were estopped from denying it; and thirdly, that the claim against them was barred by the Limitation Act 1939, s. 2 (1) (*a*) and s. 3. By order dated 2nd April 1968, STAMP, J., directed that a preliminary point of law should be set down for argument, namely, whether s. 26 of the Limitation Act 1939 operated to prevent the period of limitation running. For the purposes of the argument it was assumed that the plaintiffs' right of action was concealed by the fraud of the tenant for life and (for the purposes of the proviso to s. 26) that B., who had negotiated the sale to the defendants, was their agent and had reason to believe that fraud had been committed.

D

E

Held: (i) on the assumed facts the action was " concealed by the fraud " of the tenant for life;

F

(ii) the defendants were persons who claimed title through the tenant for life within the meaning of s. 31 (4) of the Limitation Act 1939;

(iii) the proviso to s. 26 of that Act applied not only to an action in detinue to recover property, but also to an action in conversion to recover the value of the property;

(iv) s. 26 (*b*), therefore, applied so that the period of limitation did not begin to run until the fraud was discovered by the trustees.

G

Beaman v. *A.R.T.S., Ltd.* ([1949] 1 All E.R. 465) and *G. L. Baker, Ltd.* v. *Medway Building and Supplies, Ltd.* ([1958] 2 All E.R. 532) applied.

Decision of GOFF, J. ([1969] 1 All E. R. 546) affirmed.

H

[As to the effect of fraud on limitation of actions, see 24 HALSBURY'S LAWS (3rd Edn.) 316-319, paras. 628-631; and for cases on the subject, see 32 DIGEST (Repl.) 599-610, *1836-1916.*

For the Limitation Act 1939, s. 2, s. 3, s. 26, s. 31, see 13 HALSBURY'S STATUTES (2nd Edn.) 1160, 1163, 1188, 1192.]

Cases referred to:

I

Baker (G. L.), Ltd. v. *Medway Building and Supplies, Ltd.,* [1958] 2 All E.R. 532; revsd. C.A., [1958] 3 All E.R. 540; [1958] 1 W.L.R. 1216; 32 Digest (Repl.) 572, *1621.*

Beaman v. *A.R.T.S., Ltd.,* [1949] 1 All E.R. 465; [1949] 1 K.B. 550; 32 Digest (Repl.) 605, *1889.*

Betts v. *Metropolitan Police District Receiver and Carter Paterson & Co., Ltd.,* [1932] 2 K.B. 595; 101 L.J.K.B. 588; 147 L.T. 336; 96 J.P. 327; 46 Digest (Repl.) 471, *188.*

A   *Blair* v. *Bromley* (1847), 2 Ph. 354; 16 L.J.Ch. 495; 41 E.R. 979; 32 Digest
         (Repl.) 601, *1864.*

     Bree v. *Holbech* (1781), 2 Doug. K.B. 654; 99 E.R. 415; 32 Digest (Repl.)
         604, *1878.*

     Bulli Coal Mining Co. v. *Osborne*, [1899] A.C. 351; [1895-99] All E.R. Rep.
         506; 68 L.J.P.C. 49; 80 L.T. 430; 32 Digest (Repl.) 603, *1872.*

B   *Clark* v. *Hougham* (1823), 2 B. & C. 149; 1 L.J.O.S.K.B. 249; 107 E.R. 339;
         32 Digest (Repl.) 417, *410.*

     Clayton v. *Le Roy*, [1911] 2 K.B. 1031; [1911-13] All E.R. Rep. 284; 81
         L.J.K.B. 49; 105 L.T. 430; 75 J.P. 531; 1 Digest (Repl.) 24, *186.*

     Gibbs v. *Guild* (1881), 8 Q.B.D. 296; *on appeal* (1882), 9 Q.B.D. 59; 51 L.J.Q.B.
         313; 46 L.T. 248; 32 Digest (Repl.) 373, *55.*

C   *Granger* v. *George* (1826), 5 B. & C. 149; [1824-34] All E.R. Rep. 608; 108
         E.R. 56; 32 Digest (Repl.) 405, *285.*

     John v. *Dodwell & Co., Ltd.*, [1918] A.C. 563; 87 L.J.P.C. 92; 118 L.T. 661;
         46 Digest (Repl.) 530, *725.*

     Miller v. *Dell*, [1891] 1 Q.B. 468; 60 L.J.Q.B. 404; 63 L.T. 693; 32 Digest
         (Repl.) 406, *294.*

D   *Rolfe* v. *Gregory* (1865), 4 De G.J. & Sm. 576; 34 L.J.Ch. 274; 12 L.T. 162;
         46 E.R. 1042; 32 Digest (Repl.) 600, *1850.*

     Seaford Court Estates, Ltd. v. *Asher*, [1949] 2 All E.R. 155; [1949] 2 K.B. 481;
         affd., H.L., [1950] 1 All E.R. 1018; [1950] A.C. 508; 31 Digest (Repl.)
         679, *7719.*

     Williamson v. *Verity* (1871), L.R. 6 C.P. 206; 40 L.J.C.P. 141; 24 L.T. 32;
E   32 Digest (Repl.) 385, *149.*

Interlocutory appeal.

This was an appeal by the second, third and fourth defendants from the
judgment of Goff, J., given at the trial of the preliminary point of law in this
action on 6th December 1968 and reported [1969] 1 All E.R. 546, whereby it
was declared that on the true construction of s. 26 of the Limitation Act 1939
F   and on the assumption that the plaintiffs' right of action was concealed by the
fraud of the tenant for life, that section did operate to prevent the period of
limitation prescribed by s. 2 and s. 3 of that Act from beginning to run until
the fraud was or could with reasonable diligence have been discovered. The
grounds of appeal were: (i) that the judge was wrong in law in construing the
words in s. 26 " or of any person through whom he claims " as applying to this
G   action in which (a) the plaintiffs were seeking to recover only damages for conversion and not seeking to obtain specific relief in respect of property held and
claimed by the defendants, (b) the defendants could be liable whether or not
they claimed any title to the property alleged to be converted; (ii) that the
decision of Danckwerts, J., in *G. L. Baker, Ltd.* v. *Medway Building and Supplies,
Ltd.*[*] as to the construction of s. 26 was wrong in law and ought to be overruled
H   or not followed.

J. L. Arnold, Q.C., and *J. E. Vinelott*, Q.C., for the plaintiffs.
G. B. H. Dillon, Q.C., and *N. C. H. Browne-Wilkinson* for the second and third
defendants.
A. J. Balcombe, Q.C., for the fourth defendant.

Cur. adv. vult.

I   April 23.   The following judgments were read.

LORD DENNING, M.R.: This is another preliminary issue. We have to
determine it on assumed facts. I do not like doing this, but if defendants choose
to plead the Statute of Limitations rather than fight the case on the merits,
they must put up with it. We have to assume the facts pleaded to be correct.
Brigadier Chichester Constable was a member of an old family. They had

_____
* [1958] 2 All E.R. 532.

lived for generations in a stately home called Burton Constable Hall. It contained A
many treasures which were settled as " heirlooms ". That means that they were
vested in trustees and passed with the settled estates just as the land did—
from one generation to the next. No member of the family could sell them—
so as to pass a lawful title—except that the tenant for life could sell them if he
first obtained the consent of the trustees; but in that case the proceeds of sale
did not belong to him but formed part of the capital moneys of the settled estates. B
One of the heirlooms at Burton Constable Hall was a painting of St. John the
Baptist by Caravaggio. It used to hang in the main part of the hall and was a
family treasure. It belonged to the plaintiffs, the trustees, one of whom was the
Brigadier himself. He was also tenant for life. He lived at the hall. The plaintiffs
allowed him, as tenant for life, to have the use and enjoyment of the painting.

In May 1950 the defendants, an art consortium (as it was called before us) C
consisting of several art dealers were interested in the pictures at Burton Constable
Hall. Mrs. Georgina Blois was their agent. On 24th May 1950, apparently on her
own initiative, she wrote to the Brigadier: " Do you want to sell any of your
important pictures? " He replied, almost by return of post, on 26th May 1950:

" I would be reluctant to part with these treasures. I look upon them
as a sacred trust. They are entailed upon my son." D

That told her, as plainly as could be, that they were heirlooms.

At the end of 1950 the Brigadier lent the painting of St. John the Baptist
to the Royal Academy, Burlington House, for exhibition. Whilst it was there,
the Brigadier, on 15th January 1951, sold the painting to the defendants and,
at the close of the exhibition, the defendants took possession of it. Eighteen E
months later, in April 1952 the defendants sold it to an American buyer. They
sold it to the William Rockhill Nelson Gallery of Art, Kansas City, Missouri,
U.S.A. It has been in that art gallery ever since. For present purposes we must
take it (although I do not like doing so) that the Brigadier was guilty of fraud
in that he told his co-trustees nothing about the sale and he did not hand the
proceeds of sale to them; he pocketed the money himself instead of applying F
it as capital moneys of the estate. After the sale, he lived for several years until
his death on 26th May 1963. After his death, the plaintiffs discovered the loss
of the painting. They have brought this action against his executrix for damages
for his breach of trust, and against the defendants for damages for conversion.
The defendants plead that the action against them is barred by the Statute of
Limitations. They say that the conversion of the painting was in 1951; that G
as more than six years have passed, no action can be brought against them;
and that the title of the plaintiffs was extinguished long ago. The plaintiffs
have put in a reply in which they say that the conduct of the Brigadier amounted
to fraudulent concealment and that the time did not run against them till they
discovered it.

The law as to limitations of actions is now contained in the Limitation Act H
1939; but, before considering it, I would first notice the previous law.

1. *The previous law.*

The law drew a distinction between detinue and conversion. If the plaintiff
had entrusted the defendant with the property for safe custody, the plaintiff
could sue in detinue. The period of limitation (six years) would run from the
date of demand and refusal, and the defendant could not excuse himself by I
saying that he had parted with the property some years before: see *Williamson*
v. *Verity* (1) and *Clayton* v. *Le Roy* (2). If the plaintiff had not entrusted the
defendant with the property, but the defendant had himself wrongfully taken it
from the plaintiff and converted it (being the first converter), the plaintiff could
sue in conversion. The period of limitation (six years) would run from the date

(1) (1871), L.R. 6 C.P. 206.
(2) [1911] 2 K.B. 1031 at p. 1048; [1911-13] All E.R. Rep. 284 at p. 286.

A when the defendant first converted it: see *Williamson* v. *Verity* (3) per Willes, J., as explained in *Betts* v. *Metropolitan Police District Receiver and Carter Paterson & Co., Ltd.* (4). If the defendant was not himself the first converter, but had received the property from the first converter and converted it himself (being thus the second converter) the plaintiff could sue the second converter in conversion. The period of limitation would run from the time when the second

B converter converted it: see *Miller* v. *Dell* (5). If the defendant himself still held the property (no matter whether he was first or second or any other converter) the plaintiff could demand from him the return of the goods, and on his refusal, could sue him in detinue. The period of limitation would then run from the date of demand and refusal: see *Clayton* v. *Le Roy* (6).

C The Limitation Act 1939, has altered that position in this way: the period of limitation in conversion (six years) runs from the date of conversion by the first converter. If there is a second conversion, time runs in favour of the second converter from the date of the first conversion. Likewise with detinue, time runs from the first demand and refusal. After the expiry of the six years, the title of the true owner is extinguished, see s. 3 (1), (2).

D
2. *The effect of fraud before 1939.*
Thus far I have not considered fraud. Before 1939, in cases of fraud, equity interposed its authority so as to extend the time. The period of limitation did not begin to run until discovery of the fraud. I have said that " equity " interposed its authority, but there is good ground for thinking that the common law, under its best judges, would have done the same. They would have allowed a replication of fraud so as to stop time running. Thus in 1781 Lord Mansfield,

E C.J., said: " There may be cases too, which fraud will take out of the Statute of Limitation "; see *Bree* v. *Holbech* (7); and his view was accepted by such good judges as Bayley and Best, JJ., in *Clark* v. *Hougham* (8), by Abbott, C.J., in *Granger* v. *George* (9), and by Field, J., and Brett, L.J., in *Gibbs* v. *Guild* (10). However that may be, whether in equity or at law, one way or the other, in case of fraud, time did not run till discovery of the fraud. The cause of action

F was still the original cause of action. All that happened was that fraud prevented the time from running. It applied to cases of conversion in this way: if the defendant (whom I have called the first converter) stole property or took it in some other wrongful way, in fraud of the true owner, he was not allowed to take advantage of his own wrong. He could not avail himself of the Statute of Limitation so long as the true owner remained in ignorance of the fraud without

G any fault of his own: see *Bulli Coal Mining Co.* v. *Osborne* (11). Similarly, if a second converter received it from the first converter, knowing that it had been taken in fraud of the true owner, then he too was not allowed to take advantage of the statute. He was in like situation with the first converter. The receiver was no better off than the thief: see *Rolfe* v. *Gregory* (12). Or, if he had not given value for it, he was not allowed to avail himself of the statute, see *Blair*

H v. *Bromley* (13). But, if the property reached the hands of someone who took it in good faith and for value without notice of the fraud, such a man could avail himself of the Statute of Limitation. Equity did not deprive innocent purchasers of the benefit of the statute. Nor did the law.

I I see nothing in *John* v. *Dodwell & Co., Ltd.* (14), to affect those principles. The Privy Council were only considering whether there was concealed fraud of such a kind as to give a new cause of action. Whereas we are only concerned

(3) (1871), L.R. 6 C.P. at p. 209.   (4) [1932] 2 K.B. 595 at p. 605.
(5) [1891] 1 Q.B. 468.   (6) [1911] 2 K.B. at p. 1048; [1911-13] All E.R. Rep. at p. 286.
(7) (1781), 2 Doug. K.B. 654 at p. 656.   (8) (1823), 2 B. & C. 149 at pp. 154, 156.
(9) (1826), 5 B. & C. 149 at p. 152; [1824-34] All E.R. Rep. 608 at p. 609.
(10) (1881), 8 Q.B.D. 296; *on appeal* (1882), 9 Q.B.D. 59.
(11) [1899] A.C. 351 at pp. 361-363; [1895-99] All E.R. Rep. 506 at pp. 508, 509.
(12) (1865), 4 De G.J. & Sm. 576.   (13) (1847), 2 Ph. 354.
(14) [1918] A.C. 563.

here with fraud which does not give a new cause of action but only stops time   A
running.

3. *Fraud since 1939.*

The Limitation Act 1939, deals with fraud in s. 26 (*b*) which provides:

" [Where] the right of action is concealed by the fraud of [the defendant
or his agent or of any person through whom he claims or his agent], . . . the   B
period of limitation shall not begin to run until the plaintiff has discovered
the fraud . . . or could with reasonable diligence have discovered it . . ."

This provision applies so as to extend the time, not only for bringing an action
for conversion or detinue, but also the time for extinguishing the title of the
true owner: see *Beaman* v. *A.R.T.S., Ltd.* (15), per LORD GREENE, M.R.

Applying that provision, one thing is quite clear: the right of action was   C
" concealed by the fraud " of the Brigadier. I do not know that he did anything
actively to deceive the trustees, but that does not matter. His wrongful sale of
the heirloom was enough. It was a fraud; and by saying nothing about it, he
concealed the fraud.

The next point is whether the Brigadier was a " person through whom the
defendants claim . . ."?   Section 31 (4) provides: D

" A person shall be deemed to claim through another person, if he became
entitled by, through, under, or by the act of that other person to the
right claimed . . ."

I read that as meaning that a person is deemed to claim property through
another person, if he derives his title to the property from that person. This is
in accord with the interpretation placed on s. 26 by DANCKWERTS, J., in *G. L.*   E
Baker, Ltd. v. *Medway Building and Supplies, Ltd.* (16).

In my opinion, the Brigadier was a person through whom the defendants
claim. If one should ask the defendants: " From whom do you derive your
title to this picture? ", they would be bound to say: " From the Brigadier ".
That question and answer show that they claim through him. They had, through
him, a title which was valid against all the world except the plaintiffs, the   F
trustees of the settlement. Once it is held that the defendants claimed through
the Brigadier, they cannot avail themselves of the statute. Section 26 (*b*) applies
so that the period of limitation did not run in their favour until the fraud was
discovered. So the action is well in time.

Counsel for the second and third defendants, sought to avoid this result by
arguing that they did not " claim through " the Brigadier. He said that the   G
words " through whom they claim " should be confined to cases which came
within the proviso to s. 26, for otherwise there would be an absurd anomaly.
I turn, therefore, to consider the proviso to s. 26.

4. *The proviso to s. 26 of the Limitation Act 1939.*

The proviso provides: H

". . . nothing in this section shall enable any action to be brought to
recover, or enforce any charge against, or set aside any transaction affecting,
any property which—(i) in the case of fraud, has been purchased for
valuable consideration by a person who was not a party to the fraud and
did not at the time of the purchase know or have reason to believe that
any fraud had been committed . . ."   I

Counsel for the second and third defendants points out that the proviso applies
only to actions brought to " *recover* any property " which, he said, were actions
for recovery of land or specific delivery of a chattel; but the proviso does not
apply to actions for conversion. It would be absurd, he said, to hold that time
should run differently in an action for conversion from an action for specific

---

(15) [1949] 1 All E.R. 465 at p. 466;   [1949] 1 K.B. 550 at p. 557.
(16) [1958] 2 All E.R. 532 at p. 537;   [1958] 1 W.L.R. 1216 at p. 1223.

A delivery, for it would mean that a plaintiff could always avoid the proviso by suing in conversion. His way of removing the anomaly was to confine the words "through whom they claim" to actions which were brought to recover the very property itself.

I agree that, if the proviso is taken literally, it gives rise to absurdity. Take a simple case. Goods are stolen by a thief from the true owner. The thief sells

B them to a man who buys in good faith without any notice that they were stolen or wrongfully come by. Seven years later, the owner discovers them still in the possession of the purchaser and demands the return of them. The purchaser pleads the Statute of Limitation. The owner replies that the right of action was concealed by the fraud of the thief through whom the purchaser claims. If the owner sues the purchaser in *detinue* for the return of the goods or their

C value, it is an action brought to *recover* the property. The purchaser can certainly rely on the proviso so that the action is statute barred. Can the owner get round that proviso by suing the purchaser in *conversion*? If it is taken literally, he can and for this reason: an action for conversion is not an action brought to *recover* the property. It is an action for damages. So the innocent purchaser cannot rely on the proviso. Such a result is absurd.

D But the submission of counsel leads to an equal absurdity. He would confine the words "through whom they claim" to actions brought to recover the very property itself. Test it by taking another case where goods are stolen from the true owner. But the thief sells them to a receiver who knows full well that they are stolen: and the receiver gives them to his wife as a present: and she sells them to an innocent purchaser, who resells them to another. Seven years later

E the true owner discovers the fraud and sues the receiver and his wife and the innocent purchaser in conversion. According to counsel none of them "claims through" the thief. So all of them are protected by the statute. Whereas good sense requires that, whilst the innocent purchaser should be protected, neither the receiver nor his wife should be allowed to avail themselves of the Statute of Limitation.

F Seeing these absurdities looming, I think we should do something to make sense of this proviso. We should bring it into line with the rule of equity as it existed before the Act was passed. I am sure that is what Parliament intended. It can be done quite simply. All that is necessary is to read the proviso as applying not only to an action for *detinue* (to *recover* property) but also to an action for conversion (to *recover* the *value* of the property). There is no rhyme or reason

G why *detinue* should be included in the proviso and *conversion* excluded. In short, insert after the word "property" the words "or its value". I know this means that we in this court are filling in a gap left by the legislature—a course which was frowned on some years ago. But I would rather the courts fill in a gap than wait for Parliament to do it. Goodness knows when they would get down to it! I would apply the principle which I stated in *Seaford Court Estates, Ltd.*

H v. *Asher* (17):

"... A judge should ask himself the question how, if the makers of the Act had themselves come across this ruck in the texture of it, they would have straightened it out? He must then do as they would have done. A judge must not alter the material of which the Act is woven, but he can and should iron out the creases."

I We should apply the proviso so as to enable innocent purchasers of property to avail themselves of the period of limitation, whatever the form of action taken against them.

It is quite clear that the defendants cannot avail themselves of the proviso. They were not innocent purchasers. Quite the reverse.

5. *Conclusion.*

We have to assume that the Brigadier sold the heirloom in fraud of the

(17) [1949] 2 All E.R. 155 at p. 164; [1949] 2 K.B. 481 at p. 499.

trustees. The defendants bought if by their agent, Mrs. Blois. She must have
had a pretty good idea that he was selling it in fraud of the plaintiffs; and yet
she turned a blind eye to it. She winked at the fraud. The defendants should
not, in these circumstances, be allowed to rely on the Statute of Limitation.
Time should not run against the plaintiffs until the fraud was discovered. I
would dismiss this appeal.

WINN, L.J.: This appeal arises on certain preliminary issues and assumed
bases of fact. The question posed is whether on those assumptions the writ in
the action operated to institute an effective action against the defendants, other
than the first defendant, for conversion of a certain picture sold to them in 1952
and resold by them in or about the same year to a museum in the United States
of America. Since none of the said defendants is, or has for many years been
in possession of the picture, no question is involved of any claim to recover it
from any of the defendants: it is sought to sue them for damages for conversion.
The question is whether the Limitation Act 1939 prevents this being effectively
done.

As I understood the matter, it is common ground that none of the defendants
can be said to have taken the picture out of the physical possession of the
plaintiffs, who accordingly must rely on ownership of the picture as having
given them a right to possession of it at a time when it was converted: this was
clearly established, I think, by the responses of counsel to two early interventions
of mine stressing that conversion is an infringement of a possessory right. The
topic is discussed in para. 963 of CLERK & LINDSELL ON TORTS (12th Edn.),
which is headed " Possessory Title ". It is there stated by the authors:

" . . . in actions of the kind now under consideration the issue as to the
property in the goods is not directly raised. Inasmuch, however, as the
right to possession must ultimately be derived from the owner, the question
of title is very material."

My own approach to the appeal was accordingly conditioned by concern to
establish what effect, if any, the provisions of the Limitation Act 1939 had on
the ownership which the plaintiffs, as trustees of the relevant settlement,
undoubtedly have in the past had of the picture, albeit it was in the possession
of a tenant for life.

The argument has necessarily centred on the terms and construction of the
Act. A convenient starting point for consideration is the short title of the Act,
which reads as follows:

" An Act to consolidate with amendments certain enactments relating
to the limitation of actions and arbitrations."

From this it is apparent that the Act controls and restricts the bringing of
actions or arbitrations, viz., claims in the courts or before arbitration tribunals.
Notwithstanding that this is its declared subject-matter and scope, the Act
does include certain enactments affecting title to property, as distinct from
actions; cf., in particular s. 16.

The first section of the Act provides that the provisions of Part 1 shall have
effect subject to the provisions of Part 2 and refers to the latter provisions as
providing " for the extension of the periods of limitation " in certain cases
including the case of fraud. Section 2 (1) provides:

" The following actions shall not be brought after the expiration of six
years from the date on which the cause of action accrued, that is to say:—
(a) actions founded on . . . tort . . ."

Section 3 of the Act is, in my opinion, of special interest in the present appeal
and were it not for the possible effect of s. 1 already set out, might seem to
conclude this appeal in favour of the defendants without permitting of any
reference to s. 26, on which primarily the argument in the appeal has been
centred. In the course of the hearing accordingly, and whilst still blissfully

A optimistic that this might afford the answer, I was led to make a suggestion
as to the meaning of s. 3: this was probably not clearly expressed and, therefore, did not receive such attention as would have afforded me the help I needed
from learned counsel in reaching a proper understanding as to its meaning and
relevant effect.

Counsel for the second and third defendants, whilst appreciating that its
B implications might be favourable to his contentions, received it with only
moderate enthusiasm: counsel for the plaintiffs came so near to rejecting it
with contempt as could be compatible with the courtesy to the Bench which he
invariably displays; my brethren did not encourage my already waning confidence in my idea. It is, I feel, my duty nevertheless to explain on what lines I
was then tentatively proceeding in my own mind.

C It is clear on the one hand that s. 3 (1) deals with the limitation of certain
actions, i.e., of the time within which those actions may be effectively brought;
and s. 3 (2) deals with the extinction of title to goods in certain circumstances;
this much is borne out by the marginal note, insofar as, contrary to the strict
canons of construction, one is tempted to have regard to this note. The problem
remains, what is the combined effect of the two subsections where they both
D impinge on a situation.

By force of s. 3 (1), where an event, which may be called " Event A ", has
occurred consisting of the conversion of a chattel giving rise to a cause of action
in a person, and, before that person recovers possession of the chattel, a second
event, " B ", occurs which consists of a further conversion of the chattel by
someone else, a limitation is imposed which prevents any action being brought
E by that person in respect of " Event B " at any time later than six years after
the occurrence of " Event A ", provided—and this is important—that he did
not recover possession of it between " Event A " and " Event B ". Subsection
(2) must, it seems to me, be given an additional and more extensive effect than
sub-s. (1), since it provides that where events " A " and " B " have occurred
and there has supervened what might be called " Event C ", viz., the expiry
F of six years from the date of " Event A ", and during the interval between
" Event A " and " Event C " the original owner or possessor of the chattel
has not at any time recovered possession of it, not only shall any action by
him be barred, but also his title to it shall be extinguished. This last subsection
appears to deal with extinguishment of title over and above and separately
from limitation of actions claiming damages for conversion or for " wrongful
G detention ". It is to be observed that it could happen that between " Event B "
and a date six years after " Event A " possession of the chattel might be
recovered: in such a case an action could be brought for any subsequent conversion or detention within six years after it occurred. I do not pause to consider
whether the words in the subsection " that period ", which as a matter of
drafting must refer to the period of six years beginning with " Event A " may
H have survived from an earlier draft in which they related to a like period
beginning with " Event B ".

None of the somewhat similar provisions for the extinction of title in specified
circumstances and events contained in s. 7 (2) and (3) of the Act and in s. 16,
are of consequence for present purposes save that they clearly recognise: (a) the
desirability of clearing disputed titles; (b) the clear distinction between claims
I for damages or other relief, on the one hand, and claims for the recovery of
property, on the other.

Beaman v. *A.R.T.S., Ltd.* (18) was the case of an action for conversion of
personal belongings deposited by a woman with a storage company in war time
which had been dishonestly disposed of by the warehouseman in a manner
which not surprisingly seemed to the Court of Appeal to amount to fraudulent
concealment of the cause of action, which itself was not " based on fraud "

---

(18) [1949] 1 All E.R. 465; [1949] 1 K.B. 550.

within the meaning of s. 26 (*a*) of the Act; accordingly the court held that the **A**
action could be effectively brought although more than six years had elapsed
since the conversion. Although no second or subsequent conversion had occurred
which could have brought into operation s. 3 (1) or (2) of the Act, LORD GREENE,
M.R., said, after referring to the Limitation Act 1939 (19):

> ". . . the appropriate period of limitation in the present appeal . . . is,
> as before, six years, but s. 3 (2) goes further and extinguishes title to the **B**
> "converted" chattels. All this, however, is subject to s. 26 . . ."

Thus LORD GREENE, M.R., was saying primarily that under the Act of 1939
as before it was passed, the period of limitation for an action of conversion was
six years, but that this was subject to the provisions of s. 26 of the Act. Any
reference, such as he there made, to s. 3 (2) was not only superfluous and wholly **C**
obiter, but, logically, s. 3 (2) was entirely irrelevant since there had not been
any second conversion of the chattels to which the action related. There is no
mention of s. 3 (2) in the arguments, so far as they are reported, or the other
judgments.

To that observation of LORD GREENE, M.R., as to all that he said, very great
respect is due: because of it, as well as of other adverse indications of opinion **D**
to which I have referred, I feel that it would be irrationally obdurate to maintain
that s. 26 of the Act relates only to limitation of time for bringing actions, not
to survival of title. I will no longer seek to assert, despite what might appear
to be foreshadowed by the terms of s. 1, that Part 2 of the Act, in general, merely
extends the time for beginning an action, as e.g., in cases of disability of a plaintiff
or a predecessor in title (s. 22), in cases where a debt has been acknowledged or **E**
part payment made (s. 23 (5)).

Section 26 has a heading "Fraud and mistake", and a side note "Postponement of limitation period in case of fraud or mistake". It does not refer expressly
to any question of title or extinguishment of title, but enacts this much and no
more—

> "Where, in the case of any action for which a period of limitation is **F**
> prescribed by this Act, either (*a*) . . . or (*b*) . . . or (*c*) . . . the period
> of limitation shall not begin to run until the plaintiff has discovered the
> fraud or the mistake . . ."

It is to be observed that on its face the section relates to certain types of action
described under para. (*a*) and para. (*c*) and to all rights of action the existence
of which has been concealed by fraud. I have not found it easy to bring my **G**
mind to accept that it should be given such wider effect that, in particular,
it controls s. 3 (2).

The specific inclusion under para. (*c*) of actions "for relief from the consequences of a mistake" together with the terms of the proviso to the section
lends, in my opinion, some support to the submission of counsel for the second
and third defendants that if the section has any preserving effect postponing **H**
extinguishment of title, it will only so operate in a case where the relief sought
is such as before the Supreme Court of Judicature Act 1873 could have been
obtained only in a court of equity. If this view is rejected, it seems that the
proviso according to the most apparent meaning of its language might produce
alarming anomalies, inasmuch as it would expose innocent purchasers of chattels
to prolonged liability for damages for conversion albeit conditionally protected **I**
against recovery from them of the chattel.

After careful consideration of the submission which counsel for the second
and third defendants so lucidly made and of all the authorities with which he
supported it, I am not convinced that Parliament intended in 1939, more than
50 years after the passing of the Act of 1873, to preserve in s. 26 of the Act a
distinction, which is certainly not demonstrated by express language, between

---

(19) [1949] 1 All E.R. at p. 466; [1949] 1 K.B. at pp. 556, 557.

A   actions formerly maintainable only in the courts of law and those maintainable both in courts of law and courts of equity or those maintainable only in the latter courts.

It seemed to me that junior counsel for the plaintiffs effectively destroyed that submission by his reminder that detinue, to which the section expressly refers, was a form of action available before the Act of 1873 in common law
B   courts for the recovery of a specific chattel, cf., Common Law Procedure Act 1854, s. 78.

It follows, as I see it, that the effect of s. 26 (b), where it applies, must be kept alive or, possibly to revive a title to goods even though " the prescribed period " for bringing an action for conversion of them has, according to the literal meaning of that phrase, expired: this is the effect, though perhaps not a manifest one, of
C   the provision " the period of limitation shall not begin to run . . ." If it has not begun, it cannot have expired, and any contrary operation of s. 3 (2) must be excluded; it would indeed be a startling result if title were to be ostensibly extinguished and yet later to become alive again.

For my part I think it unnecessary in this case and, therefore, undesirable to attempt to expound the meaning of the proviso to s. 26: I am all the more ready
D   to refrain from any such attempt because I do not understand its scope or meaning.

The expression in s. 26 (a) and (b), " any person through whom he claims ", is to me no less difficult to comprehend, but on the whole I think that it must be held to comprise any person from whom the property or any right asserted or challenged has been received or derived. This is an alarmingly wide provision,
E   so interpreted, but I am not prepared to dissent in this respect from DANCKWERTS, J., who so held in G. L. Baker, Ltd. v. Medway Building and Supplies, Ltd. (20), or from the learned trial judge in the instant case.

I have applied the epithet " alarming " to the provision because, notwith-standing my reluctant adoption of the wide meaning, I am rather apprehensive lest that meaning may startle some of the many persons who in the course of
F   their daily activities deal in chattels by buying, selling or auctioning them.

Even having regard to such assistance as may be afforded by the Factors Act 1889 and the Sale of Goods Act 1893, the concept that each dealer in a chain of dealers in chattels " claims " them, when sued for conversion, through every precedent seller, from whom or through whose hands they have indirectly come to him, does, I think, involve a far more drastic effort on the mercantile com-
G   munity than those four words have hitherto been construed as producing. I would dismiss the appeal.

FENTON ATKINSON, L.J.: 1. In 1951 a consortium including the second, third and fourth defendants purchased from Brigadier Chichester Constable, at a price which has not been disclosed to us, a picture which was a family heirloom he had no right to sell. The agent who acted for the consortium
H   was a lady called Mrs. Blois. We are required to assume in the present proceedings that she had reason to believe that the Brigadier had no right to sell. 2. In 1952 the defendants resold the picture to an American art gallery; again the price they obtained has not been revealed. By virtue of s. 12 of the Sale of Goods Act 1893, this sale was subject to the implied condition that the seller had the right to sell. 3. It was not until after the Brigadier died in 1963 that the plaintiffs,
I   who were in 1951 the lawful owners of the picture as trustees, found out what had happened. In due course they issued a writ against the second, third and fourth defendants claiming damages for conversion. A statement of claim was delivered and defences were served on behalf of these defendants. The second and third defendants did not admit that the plaintiffs were in 1951 the lawful owners of the picture: they denied that the purported sale by the Brigadier

(20) [1958] 2 All E.R. 532; [1958] 1 W.L.R. 1216.

was a wrongful conversion and claimed in the alternative that the Brigadier   A
had passed to them a good title to the picture by reason of s. 21 (1) of the Sale
of Goods Act 1893.   In the further alternative they pleaded the Limitation
Act 1939.

The fourth defendants went further, pleading affirmatively that at the material
date the Brigadier was the lawful owner of the picture and that he could and
did transfer a good title to the joint purchasers.   They also as an alternative   B
seek to rely on the Limitation Act 1939.   4. By way of reply, the plaintiffs rely
on s. 26 (b) of the Limitation Act 1939, alleging that their right of action was
concealed by the fraud of the defendants, their agent or of a person through
whom they claim.   For present purposes they do not rely on fraudulent concealment by the defendants or their agent Mrs. Blois, but allege fraud by the
Brigadier (which we are required to assume) and submit that he is a person   C
through whom these defendants claim.   5. GOFF, J. (21), who heard the matter
below, held, following a decision of DANCKWERTS, J., in *G. L. Baker, Ltd*. v.
Medway Building and Supplies, Ltd. (22), that the Brigadier was a person through
whom the defendants claimed and that s. 26 (b) of the Act operated to preserve
the plaintiffs' cause of action.   6. This being a case of successive conversions, an
important question was raised during the argument by WINN, L.J., whether   D
the provisions of s. 3 (2) of the Act as to the extinguishment of title are in any
way subject to s. 26. However, no point had been taken by the defendants below on
s. 3 (2), counsel for the second and third defendants was not prepared to base any
argument on it in this court, and in the absence of any argument to the contrary,
I am content to rely on the opinion of LORD GREENE, M.R., in *Beaman* v.
A.R.T.S., Ltd. (23), that s. 3 (2) is subject to s. 26.   7. It is argued by counsel   E
that a serious anomaly arises if s. 26 with its proviso is construed in such a way
that the bona fide purchaser for value is protected if sued in detinue for recovery
of a chattel, but may be caught under s. 26 (b) if the plaintiffs choose to sue him
for damages for conversion.

He says the words, person " through whom he claims " cannot apply in an
action for damages for conversion, and, as I understood his argument, that   F
where the proviso does not operate those words have no application. 8. I cannot
accept this argument.   On the plain words of s. 26 read with s. 2 (1) (a) of the
Act, s. 26 (b) must apply to an action for damages for conversion.   It is true an
anomalous situation arises, and it is very difficult to understand what the legislature intended.   If the anomaly creates such an absurdity that the court must
seek some construction of the language used which avoids the absurdity, then I   G
agree the best way to do this is to extend the meaning of the word " recover "
to include " recover the value of ".   9. The defendants could not on that interpretation of the word " recover " claim the benefit of the proviso, which does
not extend to persons purchasing through an agent who has notice of the fraud
or reason to believe fraud was being committed, in the light of the assumption   H
of fact we are required to make about Mrs. Blois.   10. Once s. 26 (b) is held to
apply in an action for damages for conversion, and the defendants cannot rely
on the proviso, it only remains to decide whether the Brigadier was a person
through whom they claim.

I agree with my Lords that he was.   The fact that when sued, the defendants
plead affirmatively as their first line of defence that the Brigadier was in a   I
position to and did pass to them a good title cannot decide the question.   But
applying the definition in s. 31 (4), it was from the Brigadier they received
the property and it was from him alone they could derive any right to do what

(21) [1969] 1 All E.R. 546;   [1969] 1 W.L.R. 385.
(22) [1958] 2 All E.R. 532;   [1958] 1 W.L.R. 1216.
(23) [1949] 1 All E.R. 465;   [1949] 1 K.B. 550.

A they did, namely, to resell the picture under an implied condition that they had the right to do so. I agree this appeal fails.

Appeal dismissed. Leave to appeal to the House of Lords refused.

Solicitors: *Stephenson, Harwood & Tatham* (for the plaintiffs); *Wm. Easton & Sons* (for the second and third defendants); *Simmons & Simmons* (for the fourth defendant).

B

[*Reported by* F. Guttman, Esq., *Barrister-at-Law.*]

C

SIMMS *v.* LEIGH RUGBY FOOTBALL CLUB, LTD.

[Liverpool Autumn Assizes (Wrangham, J.), November 14, 15, 1968.]

Occupier—Negligence—Rugby football club in occupation of football ground— Concrete wall seven feet three inches from touchline—Compliance in that respect with byelaws of Rugby Football League—Injury to visiting player in collision with wall—Such an injury foreseeable but improbable—Whether occupier

D *liable—Whether player had willingly accepted risk of playing on football ground which complied with league's byelaws—Occupiers' Liability Act 1957 (5 & 6 Eliz. 2 c. 31), s. 2 (1), (2), (5).*

The defendant rugby football club was the occupier of a football ground. The plaintiff was a member of a visiting team, and was at the relevant time participating in a game of rugby football on the ground. There was a concrete

E wall running at a distance of seven feet three inches alongside the touchline on one side of the playing area. This complied with byelaws of the governing body of the Rugby Football League (to which the defendant was subject) which prescribed that this distance had to be at least seven feet. The plaintiff had gathered the ball and run with it to the try-line. At the moment of reaching the try-line at a point where it formed a corner with the touchline

F he was tackled by one or two opposing players and thrown towards the concrete wall. As a result his leg was broken. The evidence was not clear whether the plaintiff's leg came into contact with the concrete wall. There was no evidence of a previous serious accident of this type.

Held: (i) on the balance of probabilities the plaintiff's injury was not caused by contact with the concrete wall, and, since a broken leg in a tackle

G was one of the accepted risks in playing rugby football, the defendant was not liable (see p. 926, letters D to F, post);

(ii) even if the injury had been so caused the defendant, although owing the common duty of care to the plaintiff under s. 2 (1) of the Occupiers' Liability Act 1957, would not have been liable for it since it was, though foreseeable, so improbable that it was not necessary to guard against it (see p. 927,

H letter F, post);

Bolton v. *Stone* ([1951] 1 All E.R. 1078) applied.

(iii) further, by virtue of s. 2 (5) of the Act, the defendant would not have been liable since the plaintiff must be taken willingly to have accepted the risk of playing on a playing field which, so far as the distance of the wall from the touchline was concerned, complied with the byelaws laid down by the Rugby

I Football League's governing body (see p. 927, letter H, post).

[As to an occupier's liability to a visitor, see 28 Halsbury's Laws (3rd Edn.) 43, 44, para. 39; and for cases on the subject, see Digest (Cont. Vol. A) 1150-1158, *254Aa-375c* and Digest (Cont. Vol. B) 556-559, *245Ab-382Aa.*

For the Occupiers' Liability Act 1957, s. 2, see 37 Haslbury's Statutes (2nd Edn.) 834.]

Case referred to:

Bolton v. *Stone*, [1951] 1 All E.R. 1078; [1951] A.C. 850; 36 Digest (Repl.) 18, *79.*

Action.

A

This was an action by the plaintiff, Anthony Francis Trevor Simms, against the Leigh Rugby Football Club, Ltd., for damages for injuries received whilst he was playing rugby football on a ground of which the club was the occupier. The facts are set out in the judgment.

T. H. Pigot, Q.C., and *R. J. D. Livesey* for the plaintiff.
Andrew Rankin for the defendant.

B

WRANGHAM, J.: In this case the plaintiff claims damages from the defendant on the ground that injuries that he suffered in an accident on 3rd October 1964, over four years ago, were caused by a breach on the part of the defendant of its duty to him as a visitor to its premises. By its defence, the defendant does not admit that the accident happened in the way that the plaintiff asserts, and C further denies it was guilty of any breach of the duty which it undoubtedly owed to him as a visitor to the premises that it occupied.

The facts of the matter are that the plaintiff was in October 1964 a school teacher who worked part-time as a footballer for the Oldham Football Club, playing for them under the rules of the Rugby Football League, a form of football which used, I think, to be known as Northern Union. He had played this game D ever since he was a boy. He is now 29; he was then about 25. He had played for some years with the Rochdale Hornets Club, and by October 1964, he had been playing for the Oldham club for something like three years.

On 3rd October he went with the rest of his team to play against Leigh Football Club, the defendant, at the Leigh Football Club's ground. In the course of the game he played on the left wing. He gathered the ball when he was somewhere E in the neighbourhood of the halfway line and ran with it towards the try-line. He was conscious that there were a couple of the Leigh players making towards him from his right, and he consequently veered towards the corner flag. He managed to get along the try-line, and before he was stopped by a tackle grounded the ball; but at the very moment of, or instantaneously after, grounding the ball he was tackled by one or two Leigh players and was heavily thrown. He was F thrown in the direction of, and over the line of, the touchline. He was by then, of course, behind the touchline proper because he had already grounded the ball beyond the try-line, but the effect of the throw was in the direction beyond the corner flag. What happened after that is a matter of serious dispute.

The plaintiff, a transparently honest, straightforward witness, told me that he was pulled over by the Leigh players, rolled over with his feet in the air and G his weight on his shoulders and his back, and that as he came down his right leg came into contact with a concrete post which was a part of the concrete barrier which surrounded the playing area. It was clear from the evidence that the different clubs have different forms of barrier round the playing field. Some barrier there must be, no doubt in order to keep back the spectators. The barrier at Leigh consists of a concrete wall with concrete posts just in H front of it, certainly in the places shown in the exhibited photographs; and perhaps there were wooden planks supported by the concrete posts which form the ringside seats for those who are entitled to use them. The plaintiff says that his leg had come into contact with a concrete post in that way. He heard a noise, which was of course the noise of his leg breaking; he felt a severe pain and rolled over, and thereupon everyone gathered round and he was taken away on a stretcher. I

There exists a photograph, a contemporary photograph, which shows the plaintiff about to be tackled, just before he crossed over the try-line and grounded the ball. It is plain from that photograph that there were a number of people who would have had a very good view of what happened to the plaintiff when he fell and when he broke his leg, as he undoubtedly did. He sustained a compound fracture of the tibia and fibula of the right leg. None, however, of those people have been called by either side, either on behalf of the plaintiff or on behalf of the defendant. Apart from the plaintiff himself the only direct

A evidence of what occurred is to be obtained from the Oldham club's physiotherapist, Mr. Wright, who was called on behalf of the plaintiff. He had been standing somewhere near the halfway line, rather nearer the scene of the accident itself than the halfway line. He saw the plaintiff in front of him towards the Leigh halfway line receive the ball and manoeuvre in the way I have described. He saw the plaintiff ground the ball, and what he saw after that he describes in

B this way. He saw a flurry of legs as the plaintiff turned over. Both players, that I think, must mean the plaintiff and one of the Leigh players, did a backward somersault. At that stage the physiotherapist, with his experience of what happened in football matches under Rugby Football League rules, thought that there was imminent danger. He did not connect the imminent danger with the barrier. In other words, seeing as he did these two men presumably

C both bowled over as a result of the violent tackle which had taken place, he thought it was at least a substantial possibility that one or other of them would be injured. Taking that view, he made off at once towards them. Now, it seems to me to be highly unlikely that the physiotherapist would take his eye for a moment off these two men in that instant of time, because if he was afraid that injury might be inflicted on the one or the other, he would naturally continue

D to watch as far as he was able to do so; and I draw the inference that he did continue to watch.

What did he see? The answer to that is that he saw no more than what he has said. When he got to the scene he saw the plaintiff lying on his back, conscious, with one leg bent and the other leg extended. He is shown in a position something like that in a contemporary photograph of the scene. The

E legs of the plaintiff at that stage were a couple of feet from a concrete post. He never at any stage saw either of the plaintiff's legs nearer to the concrete post than that.

Something of the accident was seen by the fullback in the Oldham team, a man named Dyson. He never saw the legs of the plaintiff any nearer to the concrete barrier than a distance which he puts at 18 inches to two feet,

F which was the distance between the two legs of the plaintiff and the concrete post when he, Mr. Dyson, got out there, agreeing in that respect, of course, with Mr. Wright, the physiotherapist. No one else was called who saw any material part of the accident at all. A reporter was called, but it turned out that, for reasons which were not intelligible, he did not see anything that was of any use to either side. The physiotherapist saw that the stocking about the

G break of the plaintiff's leg was, in his phrase, " torn with serrated edges " such as might, in his view, have been caused by contact between a concrete post and the plaintiff's leg.

The surgeon expressed the view that the injury to the plaintiff's leg could perfectly well have been caused by impact with the concrete post, so that there is no difficulty from the point of view of the doctor, and the doctor himself

H heard the account that the plaintiff gives. So far as the stocking is concerned, it does not seem to me that it adds very much to the case on one side or the other. The stocking was not produced. No one has seen it. It is very difficult in the absence of the stocking itself to judge whether the serrated edge could not have been equally well caused by contact with some part of the opponent's boot, particularly perhaps the studs on the sole.

I The question therefore arises whether in those circumstances it could be right to find that the plaintiff has surmounted the first hurdle in this case, that of establishing to my satisfaction that the accident was caused in the way that he described. On the one side there is the direct evidence of a witness whom I have already described, one I will describe again as transparently honest and truthful. On the other side is the fact that if the plaintiff were not merely truthful but correct and accurate, one would have expected those witnesses who were very close, as we know, to the scene to be able to say that they saw the plaintiff's leg go thudding against this concrete post; that would be, after all, one of the things

that would be comparatively easy to see if one was close enough to see it. In the **A**
flurry of legs which the physiotherapist describes, it would not be at all easy to
see at what point one leg came into contact with another if that were the explanation of the accident. One knows that a fracture of a leg can easily take place
in circumstances of this kind, either by contact between the legs of one or more
of the players or as the result of an awkward fall with the leg in the wrong place.

This was a situation in which three strong young men were putting out all **B**
their muscular force, in order in the one case to get the ball down on the ground
before being stopped, and in the other two cases to prevent the player from
doing that. A great deal of violent muscular force would be expended by
each one of the three in what they were doing. In those circumstances it is
easy to see how the plaintiff's leg might come to be fractured and a serrated
edge caused on his stocking without any contact between his leg and the concrete **C**
post at all. Nor would it be difficult for a man in this situation to make a mistake about what had really caused the fracture of his leg, hearing the noise of
his leg breaking, feeling the sudden frightful pain to his leg, and having seen the
concrete post not all that far off. There would be no wonder that he made a
genuine error.

I have considered this with a good deal of anxiety because on any view it seems **D**
to me to be a case pretty near the line, but I have come to the conclusion that
on the balance of probabilities this accident happened in some way other than
that which the plaintiff describes. Nothing is impossible to explain, but it
seems to me that the failure of the physiotherapist to see any contact between
the plaintiff's leg or legs and the concrete post, his failure indeed to see them
within a two-feet distance, and the fact that apparently no one has been found **E**
who ever did see the plaintiff's leg strike a concrete post, make it just more
probable than not that the plaintiff has made a genuine error.

Strictly speaking, that puts an end to the case because, of course, if the plaintiff
sustained his accident not owing to the presence of the concrete post but by the
violence of the heavy tackle to which he was subjected, it is merely the effect of
misfortune. It is not suggested there was anything wrong with the tackle; and **F**
the risk of breaking one's leg in a tackle is one of the risks which is quite
inseparable from the game played under Rugby League Football rules.

But other matters have been canvassed and as I have heard interesting and
careful arguments on them I think I ought to express my opinion about them.
The duty which the defendant had to the plaintiff was undoubtedly the duty
under s. 2 (1) of the Occupiers' Liability Act 1957, and under that subsection **G**
it had what is called the common duty of care. By sub-s. (2) it is provided
that that is a duty to take such care, as in all the circumstances is reasonable,
to see that the visitor will be reasonably safe in using the premises for the purpose
for which he is invited or permitted by the occupier to be there; so the defendant
would be asked to exercise such care as was, in all the circumstances of the case
reasonable.   **H**

Now, what did the defendant actually do? The answer to that is, it provided
a playing field which complied in all respects so far as the evidence goes with the
requirements of the governing body of the game. The governing body of the
game is the Rugby Football League, and that league directs through a council
which consists of representatives of each club. They have made (I do not
know when) byelaws which govern the layout of the playing fields which clubs **I**
are to provide for the games they play. One of those rules is that there shall be a
distance of not less than seven feet from the outside of the touchline to the ringside. This concrete post was seven feet three inches from the touchline.
Therefore it complied with the byelaw of the governing body of the game.
Nevertheless, it is said that the defendant which I suspect operates through
a committee, ought to have been wiser than the governing body of this
game and ought to have said to itself: " Although the governing body
consider that the barrier between the playing pitch and the spectators' area

A may be as near the touchline as seven feet, we think it ought to be much further off, and therefore we will set our barrier not at seven feet, but much further away."
And it is said that the defendant ought to have assumed this greater wisdom although it had not got one jot or one tittle of evidence to support its opinion, because it is common ground that a serious accident arising from the too great proximity of the barrier to the touchline has not been known at all. No one has

B been able to assist me with evidence of a single case arising from a barrier being too close to the touchline. It is true that on quite a number of occasions players have stopped themselves at the barrier; they have run into the barrier in that sense, and only just stopped themselves at it, perhaps even had to hurdle the barrier because they were running so fast that they could not stop themselves in time. But no one has suggested that, apart from this unfortunate accident, a single accident

C has been caused in this way.   So that it amounts to this, that it is said that the defendant was unreasonable because it did not set up its opinion against that of the governing body of the sport, although such evidence as there was entirely supported the view of the governing body of the sport. I think that is a wholly unreasonable criticism to make of the defendant.

The only way in which it can be put is this.   It is said that everybody knows

D (everybody who is concerned with this game knows) that violent tackling is legitimate and frequent, and that the tackling may be so violent that a man may be thrown two, three, four, perhaps even five, yards.   A tackle may always take place, of course, in the neighbourhood of the touchline, and it is perhaps particularly likely to take place in the neighbourhood of the corner flag, because a man seeking to score a try might well run for the corner flag, particularly if he

E is very hotly pursued by one of the adversaries, and he may be caught up of course just by the corner flag, so that it is a place where wild tackles might easily take place. It is said in those circumstances that it is obvious that a man might in such a tackle be thrown a good deal more than seven feet, and therefore might be thrown into contact with the concrete wall.

Well, those are theoretical considerations.   It seems to be shown by experience

F that that is the kind of hazard which was contemplated by the House of Lords in *Bolton* v. *Stone* (1) when some of the Lords described a hazard which was foreseeable indeed but so improbable that it was not reasonable to guard against it.   The hazard to which I have referred is obviously foreseeable, but history seems to show that it is so improbable that it would not be necessary to guard against it; and that is the view evidently taken by those who really know about

G the game, namely, the representatives of all the various clubs who together constitute the council of the Rugby Football League.

The matter perhaps does not quite stop there, for by s. 2 (5) of the Occupiers' Liability Act 1957 it is provided that a duty of care does not impose on an occupier any obligation to a visitor in respect of risk willingly accepted by the visitor.

H Now, it is not in dispute, of course, that anyone who accepts employment as a professional footballer by a club playing under the rules of the Rugby Football League willingly accepts the risks of playing football, risks which are by no means small because it is a game involving great physical effort by one side and the other. It seems to me a footballer does not merely accept the risks imposed by contact with the footballers on the other side. He willingly accepts all the

I risks of playing a game on such a playing field as complies with the byelaws laid down by the governing body of the game. I am sure footballers who go to the Leigh ground, go to that ground willingly accepting the risks that arise from playing the game under the rules of the league, on a ground approved by the league.

In those circumstances, even had I found that the plaintiff was correct in his account of the accident, I would have been compelled to find that he had failed

---

(1) [1951] 1 All E.R. 1078; [1951] A.C. 850.

to show that the defendant was guilty of any breach of its duty to him under **A**
s. 2 of the Occupiers' Liability Act 1957. For these reasons, it seems to me
that the plaintiff was the victim of misfortune, in which he was lucky to recover
very much better than he might have done, though there were no doubt some
unfortunate consequences of his accident. But it is impossible to saddle the
defendant with responsibility for these consequences, and for those reasons it
seems to me there must be judgment for the defendant.   **B**

Judgment for the defendant.

Solicitors: *Barrow & Cook*, St. Helens (for the plaintiff); *A. W. Mawer & Co.*,
Liverpool (for the defendant).

[*Reported by* K. B. EDWARDS, ESQ., *Barrister-at-Law.*]

C

PENDLETON (Inspector of Taxes) v. MITCHELLS & BUTLERS, LTD.

[CHANCERY DIVISION (Cross, J.), December 3, 4, 18, 1968.]   **D**

*Income Tax—Deduction in computing profits—Capital expenditure—Brewers—
    New licences—Expense of obtaining—Premises compulsorily acquired in
    redevelopment—Scheme for holding licences in " bank "—Delayed transfer
    to new premises—Brewers' anticipated ultimate reduction in premises—
    Maintenance of barrelage—Expenditure in obtaining replacement licences*   **E**
    capital—Income Tax Act 1952 (15 & 16 Geo. 6 & 1 Eliz. 2 c. 10), s. 137 (f).

A brewery company owned a large number of licensed premises and off-
licences in and around Birmingham, including about half of each class of
premises in Birmingham, and as a result of redevelopment in Birmingham
and elsewhere those premises were continually undergoing change. In
Birmingham, in pursuance of its duty to have regard to such redevelopment **F**
and in order to provide a fair redistribution of licences and to avoid unnecessary payment of compensation on compulsory acquisition, the licensing
planning committee instituted an equation of barrelage system. Under that
system licences of war-damaged and compulsorily-acquired premises going
into suspense (i.e., not immediately transferred to new premises) went into a
bank or account kept by the corporation, with attached to them a record of the **G**
average annual barrelage of the old premises over a prescribed period of three
years. On an application for a licence for new premises, the brewery agreed
their barrelage with the corporation, agreed to surrender equivalent barrelage
in the bank (with existing licences if not then sufficiently in credit in the bank)
and then applied to the licensing planning committee for a certificate of no
objection or for formulation of a proposal for a planning removal under
s. 56* and s. 57† of the Licensing Act 1953, which might involve a public **H**
inquiry. It finally applied for a licence to the licensing justices. In Coventry,
also a licensing planning area, the policy was not to operate such a strict
equation of barrelage, and elsewhere application for new licences was mainly
direct to the licensing justices with a right of appeal. The result was that
the brewery could only extend its business by acquiring subsidiaries or obtaining licensed premises outside Birmingham, and in Birmingham would **I**
be left ultimately holding half the surplus of 159 out of the 596 licences likely
to be disturbed, i.e., holding fewer licensed premises with larger individual
trade but collectively no increased barrelage. The brewery claimed that the
legal expenses of obtaining new licences, sometimes involving two hearings
with appearances by solicitors or counsel, and particularly having regard to

---

* Section 56 (1) is set out at p. 931, letter B, post.
† Section 57, so far as material, is set out at p. 931, letters D to I, post.

A
" Where a settlement is created by the will of an estate owner . . . (b) the personal representatives of the testator shall hold the settled land on trust, if and when required so to do, to convey it to the person who, under the will, or by virtue of this Act, is the tenant for life . . ."

So that it is clear, in my judgment, where a settlement is created by a will the land is properly described as " settled land " from the moment the will

B takes effect at the testator's death notwithstanding that no vesting assent has yet been made.

In this case there is no question but that the three executors were the trustees of the settlement, so that at the moment when the conveyance of 12th August was executed they, as trustees of the settlement, had all the powers of the tenant for life in reference to, amongst other things, the sale of any part of the

C settled land. The tenant for life of course could not have effectively conveyed the legal estate had the tenant for life negotiated the sale until a vesting assent was made, but the personal representatives had the legal estate and it was not essential to get in the legal estate to enable them to complete a sale and conveyance of the land which would effectively pass the legal estate. So the position was one to which s. 68 (2) in its precise terms was capable of applying, although

D it never occurred to the parties to this transaction that that was the case or that what they were doing was something that they could do by exercise of the statutory powers conferred on them by the subsection.

What they did was this: they employed a qualified valuer to value the plot of land. He valued it at £200 and the sale to the widow was carried out at that price. Counsel for the plaintiffs concedes that neither a tenant for life nor anyone

E exercising the powers of a tenant for life can delegate to somebody else the power of negotiating and fixing the price to be paid on a sale of settled land. But as I read the evidence, this was not such a delegation of the powers of the personal representatives in that respect. It was not by way of contrast a contract to sell at a price to be thereafter fixed by somebody else. What they did was to obtain advice as to what was the proper price for the land with vacant

F possession on a market basis, and having advised themselves as to that they entered into a transaction with the widow at that price. I do not think there was any delegation by the vendors of any power they had to negotiate a sale.

My attention has been drawn to Mogridge v. Clapp (1). In that case a Mr. Hoskins purported to demise as absolute owner, which he in fact believed himself to be, certain land to the plaintiff for a term of 99 years by way of a building

G lease. The plaintiff lessee did not enquire as to Mr. Hoskins' title, but assumed he was the absolute owner of the land. The defendant, Mr. Clapp, afterwards agreed to purchase the lease from the plaintiff. He investigated the title and he then discovered that Mr. Hoskins was not the absolute owner but tenant by the curtesy. Under s. 58 (1) (viii) of the Settled Land Act 1882 a tenant by the curtesy had all the powers of a tenant for life, but the lease which Mr. Hoskins

H had granted, although it complied with the enabling sections of the Settled Land Act 1882, did not contain any reference to those sections, which was natural because Mr. Hoskins conceived he was acting as an owner absolutely entitled. At the date of the lease there were no trustees of the will to whom notices could be given in accordance with the requirements of s. 45 of the Act of 1882 in the case of any lease by a tenant for life, so that technically the

I transaction was defective in those respects. But it was held first by KEKEWICH, J. (1), and subsequently by the Court of Appeal (1) affirming the learned judge, that the lease was good under the Settled Land Act 1882, to convey the land and that as to the absence of trustees of the settlement and the want of the notices under s. 45 as to those matters, the plaintiff having dealt with the lessor in good faith was protected by s. 45 (3) of the Act, and accordingly it was held that the lease was valid.

---

(1) [1892] 3 Ch. 382.

In the course of his judgment KEKEWICH, J., said (2):

" There is an old rule, which I think is applicable to this case, that where
you find an intention to effect a particular object, and there is nothing to
exclude the intention to effect it by a power which is available, and there
are no means of effecting it except by that power, then you conclude that the
intention was to effect it by means of that power, because otherwise it would
not be effected at all. That rule has been applied in a large number of reported cases, and I see no reason why it should not be applied here. I think,
therefore, that, notwithstanding the existence of the statutory power of
leasing was not present to the minds of the parties in this case, and really
was absent from their minds, I must hold that there was in law an intention
that this lease should operate under this Act—that is to say, there was an
intention that it should operate, and that it should operate in the only way
in which it could operate—that is, under the Act."

It is said by similar reasoning in the present case that since the three executors
could not, without the sanction of the court, sell part of the testator's real
estate to one of themselves, but since they could under s. 68, as Settled Land
Act trustees, sell to the tenant for life, the conveyance of 12th August must be
treated as having been made with the intention that it should operate as an
exercise of the statutory powers conferred by s. 68, that being the only way in
which the obvious intention of the parties could be given effect and being a way
in which they could legitimately give effect to their intention.

In my judgment it is clear that in the present case there was nothing whatever
sinister about this transaction. It was entered into in the utmost good faith.
The parties took great trouble in instructing the valuer that the valuation must
be made in such a way that it should be perfectly clear that they were getting
the best possible market value for the property, and that nobody should be able
to question the transaction on that sort of ground thereafter. On equitable grounds
the transaction is not open to any criticism whatever. It is only open to criticism
on purely technical conveyancing grounds relating to the machinery employed,
and since it seems to me that the statutory powers conferred by s. 68 (2) were
available to the parties, and since the transaction was one which could not
properly be carried out without the leave of the court except by the use of those
statutory powers, it is right, applying the rule mentioned by KEKEWICH, J. (2),
in the passage I have read, that I should treat this conveyance as made
in the exercise of those statutory powers, notwithstanding the fact that those
powers were clearly not in the minds of the parties.

Counsel for the third defendant has contended that where Settled Land Act
trustees include the tenant for life as one of their number the negotiations for
a sale to the tenant for life under s. 68 should be negotiations between the trustees
other than the tenant for life on the one hand and the tenant for life on the other
hand, that is to say, that the tenant for life is excluded from that body of
trustees in whom these particular statutory powers are vested.

However, I do not think that that is the true effect of subsection (2). The
subsection confers on the trustees of the settlement all the powers of the tenant
for life—the word " powers " is there used in the plural—to negotiate and complete the sale. It then goes on to say that they " shall have power "—in the singular—" to enforce any covenants by the tenant for life ". That is a necessary
provision because in proceedings to enforce covenants entered into by the tenant
for life on the sale, the tenant for life could not himself be on both sides of the
record and the power to enforce the covenants must be given to the trustees
of the settlement other than himself. It then goes on to say " where the tenant
for life is himself one of the trustees, then the other or others of them shall have
such power ". That deals with the situation that I have just mentioned.
" Power " is there in the singular. The subsection goes on: " and the said

(2) [1892] 3 Ch. at p. 388.

A   powers " in the plural—that must refer back to the powers of a tenant for life
     in reference to negotiating and completing the transaction—" of a tenant for
     life may be exercised by the trustees of the settlement in the name and on behalf
     of the tenant for life." It is quite clear that the legislature here had in mind that
     the tenant for life might be one of the trustees himself. Yet it is the trustees
     of the settlement as a body, all of them, who are to exercise the powers in the
B   name and on behalf of the tenant for life. It seems to me, therefore, that in
     a transaction under this subsection where the tenant for life is himself one of the
     trustees of the settlement he should be a conveying party as well as the party
     in whose favour the conveyance is made. In negotiation, no doubt, he would
     not be able to assert his personal views against those of his co-trustees for he
     would be in the invidious position of having conflicting interests. But when com-
C   pletion of the transaction arrives it seems to me clear on the true interpretation
     of the subsection that he should be one of the conveying parties. That was the
     position in respect of the conveyance of 12th August 1960. The three executors,
     including the testator's widow, conveyed to her.
         For these reasons I am of opinion that the conveyance was an effective
     conveyance to confer an absolute and indisputable title on the testator's widow
D   and that the property is now vested in her personal representatives, the plain-
     tiffs, without any risk of their being required to restore it to the settlement
     constituted by the testator's will, and it is vested in them freed and discharged
     from all claims by any persons having interests under that settlement. This
     makes it unnecessary for me to consider the alternative argument that this was
     a transaction any defect in which could be cured by recourse to s. 6 of the Law
E   of Property Act 1925. I do not propose to say anything about that subject.
         I therefore declare that the conveyance of 12th August 1960 was effectual to
     vest in Mrs. Pennant, the testator's widow, in fee simple for her absolute use
     and benefit, the freehold land expressed to be comprised therein being freed
     and discharged from the trusts of the settlement created by the will of the
     testator.
F   *Declaration accordingly.*

         Solicitors: *T. D. Jones & Co.* agents for *W. J. Williams & Davies*, Cardigan
     (for the plaintiffs); *Helder, Roberts & Co.* (for the third defendant).

                                    [*Reported by* ROSALIE LONG, *Barrister-at-Law.*]

G
     R. *v.* SECRETARY OF STATE FOR HOME AFFAIRS, *Ex parte*
                           HARNAIK SINGH.

     [QUEEN'S BENCH DIVISION (Lord Parker, C.J., Edmund Davies, L.J., and
        Caulfield, J.), April 1, 1969.]

H   *Commonwealth Immigrant—Admission—Discretion of immigration officer—*
        Period of admission requested—Shorter period—Whether part of immigration
        officer's duty to consider whether applicant for admission entitled to admission
        for shorter period than requested—Commonwealth Immigrants Act 1962
        (10 & 11 Eliz. 2 c. 21), s. 2 (1), as substituted by Commonwealth Immigrants
        Act 1968 (c. 9), s. 2 (1).

I   If an immigration officer, acting under the Commonwealth Immigrants
     Act 1962, s. 2 (1) (as substituted by the Commonwealth Immigrants Act
     1968), is not satisfied that a Commonwealth applicant for admission to the
     United Kingdom is entitled under the Acts to admission for the period
     requested by the applicant, it is not necessary for the officer, on his own
     initiative, to consider whether the applicant is entitled to admission for a
     shorter period (see p. 869, letter D, p. 869, letter H, to p. 870, letter A, and
     p. 870, letter B, post).
         Applications dismissed.

[As to the control of immigration of Commonwealth citizens, see SUPPLEMENT A
to 5 HALSBURY'S LAWS (3rd Edn.), para. 1513; and for cases on the subject, see
DIGEST (Cont. Vol. A) 25, *157a-157k*.

For the Commonwealth Immigrants Act 1962, s. 2 (1), see 4 HALSBURY'S
STATUTES (3rd Edn.) 27.]

Cases referred to:

K. (H.) (*an infant*), *Re*, [1967] 1 All E.R. 226; sub nom. *Re H. K.* (*infant*), B
    [1967] 2 Q.B. 617; [1967] 2 W.L.R. 962; Digest (Repl.) Supp.

R. v. *Lympne Airport Chief Immigration Officer, Ex p. Amrik Singh*, [1968]
    3 All E.R. 163; [1969] 1 Q.B. 333; [1968] 3 W.L.R. 945.

Motions for certiorari and mandamus.

This was an application by way of motion by Harnaik Singh for an order of C
certiorari to bring up and quash a decision of an immigration officer, Sidney
Anthony Rowe, at Birmingham Airport on 6th March 1969, which was confirmed
on behalf of the Secretary of State for Home Affairs on 12th March 1969, that
the applicant, a Commonwealth citizen to whom s. 1 of the Commonwealth
Immigrants Act 1962 applied, should not be admitted to the United Kingdom.
The applicant also applied for an order of mandamus ordering both the immigra- D
tion officer and the Home Secretary to reconsider the matter according to law.
The facts are set out in the judgment of LORD PARKER, C.J.

The case noted below* was cited during the argument in addition to the cases
referred to in the judgment of EDMUND DAVIES, L.J.

D. C. Pitman for the applicant.

Gordon Slynn for the respondent, the Secretary of State for Home Affairs. E

LORD PARKER, C.J.: In these proceedings counsel moves on behalf of
the applicant, one Harnaik Singh, for an order of certiorari to quash the refusal
to admit the applicant to the United Kingdom on 6th March 1969 and also an
order of mandamus directed to the immigration officer and the Secretary of State
for Home Affairs to reconsider the matter according to law.

What happened was that on 6th March at Birmingham, the applicant landed. F
He is a Commonwealth citizen from India and he claimed to be on a visit for
three months to his brother-in-law, one Mohan Singh. He produced to the
immigration officer a sponsorship form which had been sent to him by Mohan
Singh, saying that he, Mohan Singh, would be responsible for him in this country
during the three months' stay. Enquiries were made of the applicant, and, in
view of the sponsorship form, of Mohan Singh, who had come to the airport to G
meet him. The applicant clearly made the immigration officer somewhat
suspicious in that he doubted the applicant's veracity concerning the fact that
the applicant said he was a wealthy man engaged with his family in farming in
India, while he had never been to school, and had never travelled. As far as
Mohan Singh was concerned, the immigration officer was supplied with a deposit
account book from Barclays Bank which showed that at the date when the H
applicant landed on 6th March, there was a balance to the credit of that account
of some £200. It is quite obvious, though, from looking at the account, that
the balance from time to time was highly erratic. In 1967 it was some £249, but
from then on throughout 1968 and indeed down to the time when the sponsorship
declaration was made, the balance was under £10. Then, as Mohan Singh
frankly admitted, for the purposes of the declaration of sponsorship he paid in I
some £271 to give a balance of £280. The moment the sponsorship form had
been sent off, the balance was reduced once more to £10 and then was brought up
to £200 at the time of the applicant's arrival. Still more suspicious was the fact
that Mohan Singh, who had been here since 1963, had a wife and family in India,
and it seemed very odd, to say the least, that Mohan Singh was prepared to

---

* R. v. *Secretary of State for Home Affairs, Ex p. Piara Singh* (30th January 1969),
unreported.

A   support his brother-in-law whom he had never seen, and thereby delay any chance of getting his wife and family over here until he had saved more money.

    Both the immigration officer, and on petition the immigration department of the Home Office, have stated throughout that they are not satisfied that the applicant did not intend to work, and are not satisfied that Mohan Singh intended to or would support the applicant during his stay. In the course of the enquiries

B   into this matter, the applicant reduced his application to one for six weeks as opposed to three months, and that also was considered and refused.

    The only point which counsel for the applicant takes here is this. He says that the immigration officer at the airport and the immigration department of the Home Office have failed to ask themselves the right question; the right question, according to counsel, would have been: for what period are we satisfied

C   that sufficient money was available and would be used by Mohan Singh? In other words they should have said to themselves: I wonder whether it would not be safe to allow the applicant in for, say, two weeks, making that a condition for his entry, and that Mohan Singh could be trusted to support him for that period.

    For my part I cannot accept that it is any part of the duty of an immigration

D   officer, acting fairly in the matter, to go into matters which have never been advanced by an applicant at all. If the applicant asked for six weeks, the immigration officer must consider it on that basis; if he asks for a fortnight, he must consider it on that basis. It is no part of an immigration officer's duty to consider every possible period.

    Quite apart from that, however, as counsel for the respondent has pointed

E   out, really the applicant falls at the first hurdle, because he has not satisfied the immigration officer that he is not going to work during such period as he is allowed entry into the country. In those circumstances, it would be unnecessary to go on and consider whether, if he was not going to work, there was somebody to support him. In my judgment these applications fail and should be dismissed.

F   **EDMUND DAVIES, L.J.:** I agree. In *Re K.* (*H.*) (*an infant*) (1) dealing with the nature of the duty imposed on immigration officers by the Commonwealth Immigrants Acts 1962 and 1968, LORD PARKER, C.J., said:

    " Good administration and an honest or bona fide decision must, as it seems to me, require not merely impartiality, nor merely bringing one's mind to bear on the problem, but of acting fairly . . ."

G   Seizing on those words, counsel for the applicant has said there has in the present case been a failure by the immigration officers concerned to bring their minds to bear on the problem, on the grounds that they should have offered the applicant a shorter period of stay in this country than the one sought by him, originally three months, but later reduced to six weeks. He submits that, at the very least, they should have considered the propriety of admitting him for a shorter

H   period than either of those sought, and should then have proceeded to offer admission for such shorter period as they considered proper. With LORD PARKER, C.J., I think that that approach is absolutely unwarranted. The only problem which confronted the immigration officer was (in its finality) whether the applicant should be admitted here for six weeks. I read nothing into the existing legislation, the instructions to the immigration officers (whether they be legally binding or

I   otherwise), or in the reported decisions of this court which persuade me to the view that there is any kind of duty, legal or moral, on the immigration officer to say to an applicant: " You cannot come here for the period of time you seek, but you may come here and stay here for a shorter period, namely for, as the case may be, so many weeks or months." Furthermore, to describe the omission by an immigration officer to make, as it were, a counter-offer of that kind as a breach of natural justice is what I must be permitted to describe as an abuse

---

(1) [1967] 1 All E.R. 226 at p. 231; [1967] 2 Q.B. 617 at p. 630.

of language. There is nothing in the decision in *R.* v. *Lympne Airport Chief* A
Immigration Officer, Ex p. Amrik Singh (2) to indicate that the duty of an immigration officer is of the kind that counsel for the applicant has here submitted. On the contrary, LORD PARKER, C.J., if I may say so, there took particular care to leave quite open, to be decided on the facts of any future case, whether or not the applicant has failed in limine to satisfy the immigration officer that he does not intend to, or is not likely to, seek employment during the period of his stay. B
For those reasons I, too, think the applications should be refused.

  CAULFIELD, J.: I agree. It would seem to me that the immigration officer in this case applied his mind to the proper questions that he had to answer under the Commonwealth Immigrants Act 1962, and having carried out a close investigation on both the applicant and his brother-in-law in my judgment came C
to a proper conclusion. I agree that the applications should be refused.

                 Applications dismissed.

 Solicitors: *D. P. Debidin* (for the applicant); *Treasury Solicitor* (for the respondent).

        [*Reported by* N. P. METCALFE, ESQ., *Barrister-at-Law.*]

D

FRANCE v. FRANCE.

[COURT OF APPEAL, CIVIL DIVISION (Danckwerts, Winn and Sachs, L.JJ.), E
 March 4, 1969.]

Divorce—Condonation—Constructive desertion—Sexual intercourse between husband and wife after separation—No intention of reconciliation—Husband thereafter unable to rely on wife's prior conduct as justification for being apart from her—Condonation of prior expulsive conduct.

 A husband left his wife because she told him that she did not love him, F
but loved another man, refused to cohabit with him, and told him to go. Thereafter the husband revisited the wife from time to time, and during two years had sexual intercourse with her six times during visits. These visits and intercourse were not intended by either husband or wife to be attempts at reconciliation. On a petition by the husband alleging desertion,

 Held: the petition must be dismissed because the husband by his sexual G
intercourse with the wife had condoned her expulsive conduct, and so terminated her constructive desertion.

 Howard v. *Howard* ([1962] 2 All E.R. 539) approved.

 Appeal dismissed.

 [As to condonation in relation to desertion, see 12 HALSBURY'S LAWS (3rd H
Edn.) 305, 306, para. 607; and for cases on the subject, see 27 DIGEST (Repl.) 359, 360, *2976, 2977.*

 For the Matrimonial Causes Act 1965, s. 1, s. 42, see 45 HALSBURY'S STATUTES (2nd Edn.) 445, 502.]

Case referred to:

 Howard v. *Howard,* [1962] 2 All E.R. 539; [1965] P. 65; [1962] 3 W.L.R. 413; I
  Digest (Cont. Vol. A) 727, *2977a.*

 Appeal.

 This was an appeal by the husband against the dismissal of his undefended divorce petition on 25th June 1968, by His Honour JUDGE LEE, sitting as a special commissioner for divorce at Southampton. The facts are set out in the judgment of DANCKWERTS, L.J.

---

 (2) [1968] 3 All E.R. 163; [1969] 1 Q.B. 333.

A *J. R. P. Penry* for the husband.

The wife did not appear and was not represented.

DANCKWERTS, L.J.: This is an appeal from His Honour JUDGE LEE at Southampton in a case in which he dismissed a petition presented by the husband, the appellant, founded on constructive desertion. The marriage took

B place on 11th June 1955 and there is one child of the marriage, born on 26th January 1958, now aged 11. The child has been for some time with the husband's parents in the island of Jersey.

The evidence presented was that the wife after returning from a holiday said to the husband that all was over between them; that she loved another man, who was mentioned; that she did not love her husband and wanted a divorce;

C that there was no point in going on as they were, and she did not see any hope of settling down to a happy married life. Then on a subsequent occasion the husband said that she said to him:

> " It was better we did not cohabit under the circumstances. She had no more love for me. She thought it better I slept in another room. Then she told me to take my gear and get out of it."

D It is not clear whether that represented the events of a single day or events over several days. At any rate, the husband then left and put his furniture into storage.

The husband (who was in the Merchant Navy) had spells of absence and after a voyage of six weeks' duration he had 12 days' leave; and what happened after

E the events to which I have referred was that he visited his wife from time to time and on six occasions between June 1964 and May 1966, sexual intercourse took place between the husband and wife. At the same time, as the husband's discretion statement shows, he was committing adultery, unknown to the wife, with a number of women, amounting in total to eight.

The argument advanced before the learned commissioner was that the period

F of desertion continued notwithstanding those acts of sexual intercourse with the wife. What seems to me to be plain, however, is that the meetings and the acts of sexual intercourse were not intended by either party to amount to attempts at reconciliation. Accordingly, in the concluding paragraph of his judgment, the learned commissioner said:

> " I am asked to say that the period of desertion continued from September

G > 1961 until the present day. I do not accept these visits were for the purpose of reconciliation. I have seen the [husband] in the witness box. I am wholly satisfied he went there for sexual intercourse; that effectively put an end to any period of desertion."

And so he dismissed the petition.

It seems to me that there is clear authority for the view which the learned

H commissioner took in *Howard* v. *Howard* (1), and I refer particularly to the observation of SIR JOCELYN SIMON, P. (2). In my view, the learned commissioner reached the right decision, and the appeal must be dismissed.

WINN, L.J.: I agree. I have been greatly helped by the passage in SIR JOCELYN SIMON, P.'s judgment in *Howard* v. *Howard* (1) to which DANCK-

I WERTS, L.J., has just referred, and particularly by the sentence in which he said (2):

> " In the present case [and I add, as in the instant case] the husband could only lawfully have sexual intercourse with the wife on the basis that she was his wife. To hold that he could have intercourse with her while continuing to assert that her conduct entitled him to live apart from her

---

(1) [1962] 2 All E.R. 539; [1965] P. 65.
(2) [1962] 2 All E.R. at p. 544; [1965] P. at p. 73.

would be to allow him to treat her as a mistress, a mere instrument for sexual gratification."

The husband's case against the wife, which failed, was that by expulsive conduct she had driven him from the home and thereby constructively deserted him.

I do not propose to say any more about this case than that I think it would be a travesty if the husband were to be entitled, after these various acts of intercourse, effectively to assert against the wife that she was guilty of constructive desertion. Apart from the fact that there are eight women named in his discretion statement, and, so far as he has condescended to give the details, a good 20 or 30 instances spread over the eight (if that is the right form of language to use) are revealed, he could not have got the dates anywhere near right, because he complains that his wife threw him out of his home in England on 3rd September 1961, and he says that the first instance of adultery was with an unknown prostitute in Hong Kong in the early part of the same month. Unless he was flying backwards and forwards (and he was in the Merchant Navy, so it does not seem very probable), he would have found it difficult to be in both places consistently with those dates. It is said by learned counsel with great confidence that this is not only a frank and candid, but completely full list of all the instances of adultery committed by the husband. Just how learned counsel knows that as a fact is not very clear. It is fairly illuminating, but whether or not it is complete is another matter. What it does reveal, in my opinion, is that the husband did not really mind whether he was entitled to cohabit with his wife or not, provided that he could have her on the rota with his other girl friends, on occasion, for an enjoyable act of sexual intercourse. That is all the use that he had for his wife in those days. I agree that the appeal must be dismissed.

SACHS, L.J.: I, too, agree that this appeal should be dismissed. Before turning to the main issue raised by the husband, I would mention one point which appears to me to be of some importance having regard to the general evidence before the learned commissioner. The case was put forward by the husband as one of constructive desertion and of continuing constructive desertion. It is always for a petitioner to establish both those points. When, however, one looks as a whole at the evidence presented by the husband, at his discretion statement and at the disbelief by the learned commissioner of his evidence as to why he was having sexual intercourse with the wife on the six occasions mentioned, it would appear to me that there were considerable grounds for suggesting that this was really a case of consensual separation, in this sense: that, as WINN, L.J., has pointed out, the husband was really content with a state of affairs which enabled him over the years to have sexual intercourse with a number of other women and with the wife as well. If that be the right view of the situation, then, to my mind, the husband had none of the sense of grievance (as it is sometimes called) which would justify him in presenting and succeeding on a petition for desertion.

I now turn to the main ground on which this appeal has been pressed; that is, that the learned commissioner was wrong in reaching the conclusion that the six occasions of sexual intercourse with the wife were in this particular case a bar to the granting of a decree of desertion. Let it first be noted that as the learned commissioner found that the object of staying together for a night was not for the purpose of reconciliation, the case could not and did not fall within the ambit of s. 1 (2) of the Matrimonial Causes Act 1965, which relates to a single period of cohabitation for the purposes of reconciliation. Similarly, when one looks at s. 42 (1) of the same Act, which provides that:

"Any presumption of condonation which arises from the continuance or resumption of marital intercourse may be rebutted by evidence sufficient to negative the necessary intent"

the view taken by the learned commissioner of the husband's evidence clearly

A amounted to a finding that there was no evidence to negative the necessary intent. It follows, accordingly, that the instant case is one to which there must be applied law that is not affected by either of the two above cited provisions of the Act of 1965.

This brings one to the position that, this being a case of constructive desertion, the issue raised by the husband, was—as has already been pointed out by my

B Lords—one that was the subject of consideration in *Howard* v. *Howard* (3). In that case there was a careful and helpful examination of the relevant law in cases of constructive desertion and, in particular, whether the laws of condonation applied. To my mind, that judgment of the Divisional Court correctly stated the law.

In this case, counsel for the husband has not sought to say that the law in

C *Howard* v. *Howard* (3) was wrongly stated, but that in the instant case there was a different kind of constructive desertion. To my mind, this attempt fails. It is not practicable in this or other similar cases to try to distinguish one kind of expulsive conduct from another. Where there has been expulsive conduct, one has to look to see if there has been subsequent condonation, and unless the case falls within s. 42 (1) of the Act of 1965, sexual intercourse normally is held

D to be condonation. In this case, the intercourse was rightly held to be a condonation that precluded the husband from succeeding. In those circumstances, I agree that the appeal should be dismissed.

Appeal dismissed.

Solicitors: *Collyer-Bristow & Co.*, agents for *Lamport, Bassitt & Hiscock*, Southampton (for the husband).

E
[*Reported by* Henry Summerfield, Esq., *Barrister-at-Law*.]

PRACTICE DIRECTION.

F
Probate, Divorce and Admiralty Division (Divorce).

Divorce—Adultery—Proof—Subsisting finding in matrimonial proceedings— Admissibility in matrimonial proceedings to prove commission of adultery —Transcript required at subsequent hearing—Procedure for obtaining transcript—Civil Evidence Act 1968 (c. 64), s. 12 (1).

G
By s. 12 (1) of the Civil Evidence Act 1968* a subsisting finding in any matrimonial proceedings that a person has committed adultery is admissible in evidence in civil proceedings for the purpose of proving that he committed the adultery to which the finding relates. If such a finding is relied on to prove adultery in later matrimonial proceedings in the High Court or a divorce county court, a transcript of the judgment (or an appropriate extract) recording the

H finding will be required by the court at the hearing. Any party to the original proceedings may order the transcript from the official shorthand writer. Any other person requiring such a transcript may make application to a registrar under the Matrimonial Causes Rules 1968†, r. 54 (6), for permission for the official shorthand writer to supply the copy.

Direction issued by the President with the concurrence of the Lord Chancellor.

I
Compton Miller,
13th June 1969.   Senior Registrar.

---

(3) [1962] 2 All E.R. 539; [1965] P. 65.
* See 48 Halsbury's Statutes (2nd Edn.) 1224.
† S.I. 1968 No. 219.

PROCEDURE DIRECTION.

HOUSE OF LORDS.

House of Lords—Appeal—Law reports—List of authorities—Amendments to Judicial Direction 30.

As a result of difficulties which have arisen in the recent past in connection with the lodgment of authorities in the Judicial Office by counsel engaged in House of Lords appeals, the Appeal Committee of the House of Lords has authorised an amendment to Judicial Direction 30, which will now read as follows:

" List of authorities "

30. As early as possible before the hearing and, in any event, not later than the evening of the third day, excluding Saturdays, Sundays and Bank Holidays, preceding the hearing*, agents for all parties who have lodged a Case must forward to the Judicial Office a list, drawn by junior counsel, of the law reports, textbooks and other authorities which counsel definitely intend to cite. Where a case is not reported in the Law Reports, Session Cases or Tax Cases, the list must include references to the case in all recognised reports. The House of Lords library will normally arrange for copies of these authorities to be available at the hearing. (See Appendix F.)

Five photostat copies of any authority, other than those listed in Appendix F, submitted later than the time required above must be provided by agents to the Judicial Office for the use of the House.

DAVID STEPHENS,
Clerk of the Parliaments.

11th June 1969.

APPENDIX F
AUTHORITIES

The House of Lords library has five sets of the following authorities:

Law Reports from 1866, The English Reports, All England Law Reports, Criminal Appeal Reports, Reports of Patent Cases, Session Cases, Tax Cases, Weekly Law Reports, Statutes.

1. Where it is desired to refer to reports shown on the above list, it will suffice to submit lists of authorities as has been done in the past.

2. In cases where it is desired to refer to reports not shown on the above list, counsel and agents should set out these reports separately on their lists of authorities, *indicating clearly the particular passage to which reference is to be made.*

3. If the House of Lords has one copy of these authorities, arrangements will be made for photostat copies of these passages to be made at the House of Lords, and they will be available to their Lordships at the hearing of the appeal.

4. If the House of Lords library has no copy of these authorities, the London agents will be informed, and it will then be their responsibility to produce the necessary photostat copies (five in number) at the hearing of the appeal.

5. When photostat copies will be required, every effort should be made to lodge the list of authorities in the Judicial Office *not less than seven days* before the hearing of the appeal.

---

* But see also para. 5 of Appendix F. [This footnote is part of the amended text of direction 30.]

A

PROCEDURE DIRECTION.

House of Lords.

B
*House of Lords—Appeal—Cases—Preparation—Separate Cases—Joint Cases—
Style, etc., of Cases—New Judicial Direction 11*.*
*House of Lords—Appeal—Documents—List of documents—Appendix to appel-
lants' Case—Division of appendix—Index to appendix—Examination of
appendix—Respondents' additional documents—Documents available at
hearing—Originals—New Judicial Direction 12*.*

Preparation of Cases

C
11. (i) The appellants and respondents must respectively lodge a Case, being
a succinct statement of their argument in the appeal, settled by counsel. All
parties must state in their Cases what are, in their view, the issues arising in
the appeal. If they are abandoning any point taken below, this should be made
plain in the Case. Equally if they intend to apply in the course of the hearing
for leave to introduce a new point not taken below, this should be intimated
D
in their Case. Except to such extent as may be necessary to the development
of the argument, Cases need not set out or summarise the judgments of the
lower courts, nor set out statutory provisions, nor contain an account of the
proceedings below or of the facts of the case. All Cases must conclude with a
numbered summary of the reasons on which the argument is founded, and must
bear the signature of at least one counsel who has appeared in the court below,
E
or who will be briefed for the hearing before the House (S.O.VI (3)†). All parties'
counsel, in drafting their Cases, should assume that it will be read in conjunction
with the documents referred to in direction 12 (i) (a), (b) and (c).

Separate Cases

(ii) The lodgment of a Case carries the right to be heard by two counsel. All
the appellants must, therefore, join in one Case, and all the respondents must
F
similarly join unless it can be shown that the interests of one or more of the
respondents are distinct from those of the remainder. In the latter event the
respondents' agents first lodging their Case must give a certificate in one of the
following forms:

(a) " We, as agents for the respondent(s) (*name particular parties*) certify
G
that due facilities have been offered by us for joining in one Case to the
respondent(s) (*name particular parties*) whose interests are, in our opinion,
similar to those set out in the Case lodged by us."

(b) " We, as agents for the respondent(s) (*name particular parties*) certify
that the interests represented in the Case lodged by us are, in our opinion,
distinct from those of the remaining respondent(s)."

H
When one of the foregoing certificates has been given, all remaining respondents
wishing to lodge a Case must respectively petition to do so in respect of each
of their separate Cases. Such petitions (which carry a fee of £2) must be consented to by the appellants, and must set out the reasons for separate lodgment.

Parties whose interests in the appeal are passive (e.g., stakeholders, trustees,
executors, etc.) are not required to lodge a separate Case. They should ensure
I
that their position is explained in one of the Cases lodged.

Joint Cases

(iii) In special circumstances parties may lodge a joint Case on behalf of both
appellants and respondents, but such procedure is not encouraged.

---

* The new Judicial Directions 11 and 12 replace the existing directions 11 and 13.
In a note attached to this Procedure Direction it was stated that the new directions
would apply to all appeals set down for hearing on or after 1st October 1969.
† For Standing Order VI (3), see Supreme Court Practice 1967, vol. 2, para. 2592.

Style, etc., of Case   A

(iv) Cases must be reproduced in quarto or foolscap size in the same style as
Part 1 of the appendix (direction 12 (iii) (3)) with letters down the margin, and
with references in the margin to the relevant pages of the appendix or " Additional Documents ".

The reference of every law report of the cause in the courts below, together
with the catchword summary of one of the reports, should be shown on the   B
front cover of the appellants' Case. A headnote summary should be given
whether the cause has been reported or not.

An indication should be given in the appellants' Case as to the time occupied
by the hearing in the respective courts below.

The names of counsel signing the Case must be shown at the end.
Agents are advised to submit proofs of their Cases to the Judicial Office.   C

List of documents

12. (i) The preparation and lodgment of the documents, used in evidence
or recording proceedings in the courts below, are primarily the responsibility
of the appellants, who in the first instance will bear the cost of reproduction,
although such cost will ultimately be subject to the decision of the House with D
regard to the costs of the appeal.

The following documents must (so far as this is reasonably practicable) be
placed in a pocket of the appendix to the appellants' Case: (a) Case Stated (if
any). (b) Published reports of the decisions at first instance and on appeal.
Unbound parts of the Law Reports or the Weekly Law Reports should be used,
if available; otherwise, the All England Law Reports, Tax Cases, Reports of E
Patent Cases, Lloyds List Reports or Criminal Appeal Reports may be used.
In Scots appeals, Session Cases and Scots Law Times may be used. If any
judgment is not fully set out in the reports, a copy of it must be included. (c)
The relevant statutory provisions, including provisions of statutory instruments.
If the printed Act or set of regulations is conveniently small, it should be used.
If the statutory provisions are bulky or numerous, the relevant provisions should F
be copied.

In addition, as soon as possible after the presentation of the appeal, the
appellants' agents should submit to the respondents' agents a list of any other
documents which the appellants consider necessary for the appeal. The list must,
in any event, include all documents in evidence referred to in the judgments
of the judges below. The list should be divided into: (1) documents to be lodged G
as the appendix (the contents of each part to be specified (see below)); (2)
documents to be held in readiness at the Bar and produced on the hearing if
required.

Appendix

(ii) The appendix should contain only such documents, or extracts from such H
documents, as are clearly necessary for the support and understanding of the
case on the argument of the appeal, but no document which was not used in
evidence, or does not record proceedings relevant to the action, in the courts
below may be included. Transcripts of arguments in the courts below may not
be included unless it can be shown that: (1) remarks by a judge are relied on
by any party; or (2) the argument refers to facts which are admitted by all I
parties and as to which no evidence was called.

Division of Appendix

(iii) The appendix should be divided into two or more parts. *Part 1* should
contain: (1) the documents set out in direction 12 (i) (a), (b) and (c) above
(to be placed in a pocket); (2) formal originating documents (if any) in addition
to those above; (3) any crucial document on which the action is founded, e.g.,
will, contract, etc., or the relevant extract from such document.

A   All other documents should be included in *Part 2* of the appendix (and subsequent parts if owing to bulk the material is more conveniently made up into more than one volume).

All parts of the appendix may be in either quarto or foolscap size, with letters down the margin.

All parts of the appendix must be bound in the same manner as the " Bound
B Cases " or " Records " (see direction 22 (ii))*.

Respondents' additional documents

(iv) In general the appellants' list of documents (direction 12 (i)) is sufficient also for the respondents' use on the argument of their Case, but the respondents' agents may amend the appellants' list and add any document which may properly be included in the appendix (direction 12 (ii)) but which the appellants have not
C considered necessary. Should the appellants decline to include such further documents, the respondents must prepare and reproduce them at their own expense, such " Respondents' Additional Documents " to form an addition to and to be paged consecutively with, the relevant part of the appendix, the cost of reproduction being subject to the same conditions as that of the appellants' documents (direction 12 (i)).

D

Index to appendix

(v) All documents must be numbered and each part of the appendix (including additional documents) must include a list of its contents.

(vi) (a) Documents may be reproduced in such form as may be approved by the Clerk of the Parliaments, quarto or foolscap size. By agreement with the
E parties all or any of the documents may be printed.

(b) Documents of an unsuitable size or form for binding in with the other documents, e.g., booklets, charts, etc., should be included in a pocket attached to the appropriate part of the appendix.

(c) Clean copies of documents used in the courts below may be accepted at the discretion of the Judicial Office, and in exceptional cases where documents
F are difficult and costly to reproduce and a small number only are available, a reduced number of them may be accepted apart from the appendix.

Submission of proofs, etc.

(d) Details of the form of type usually accepted and of the current rates allowed on taxation for printing, duplicating, making photostat copies, etc., may be obtained from the Judicial Office, *to whom agents are advised to submit*
G *not only their lists before the documents are sent to press, but also all proofs before final copies are struck off.*

Examination of appendix

(vii) The appendix, including respondents' additional documents, is for the use of all parties, and as soon as proofs are available the typescript should be
H examined against the originals by the agents for all parties, if possible at one joint examination. As soon as practicable after the examination an advance copy of the appendix and " Additional Documents " in their final proof form must be supplied to the other parties, so that they may complete the references in their Case (direction 11 (iv)). (See also direction 21† with regard to supply of appendices, etc.)

I **Documents available at hearing**

(viii) Documents to be held in readiness at the hearing of the appeal may be reproduced in such form as may be approved by the Clerk of the Parliaments, six copies being required of any document likely to be handed in and examined by the House. All documents held available are subject to previous examination by the other parties.

---

* See Supreme Court Practice 1967, vol. 2, para. 2567.
† See Supreme Court Practice 1967, vol. 2, para. 2566.

Originals

A

(ix) Except in cases where the House might wish to scrutinise them, originals of documents need not be brought to the hearing.

Agents are advised to submit lists of all documents at an early stage to the Judicial Office.

DAVID STEPHENS,
Clerk of the Parliaments.

B

11th June 1969.

Footnote.*—It is not the intention of the House to curtail or hamper counsel's development of the argument in a Case. But in view of the requirements of direction 12 for copies of the judgments and relevant statutory provisions to be placed in a pocket of the appendix, there is no necessity for the judgments to be summarised, or for the provisions to be set out in the Case, except insofar as may be necessary for the development of the argument. It would be incorrect to take the view that a Case is not complete unless it contains a summary of the judgments and sets out the relevant enactments.

C

D

CADOGAN SETTLED ESTATES CO. (in liquidation) *v.* INLAND REVENUE COMMISSIONERS.

[CHANCERY DIVISION (Pennycuick, J.), November 21, 22, 29, 1968.]

Surtax—Investment company—Directions and apportionments—Computation of income—Allowances—Maintenance, repairs, insurance and management —Deduction on five years' average cost or relevant years' expenditures— Income Tax Act 1952 (15 & 16 Geo. 6 & 1 Eliz. 2 c. 10), s. 101 (1), s. 245, s. 248, s. 255 (3).

E

Surtax—Investment company—Directions and apportionments—Recomputation of income—Claim for refund of profits tax—Resulting increase of income— Power to issue further apportionment—Income Tax Act 1952 (15 & 16 Geo. 6 & 1 Eliz. 2 c. 10), s. 245, s. 248 (1), (2), s. 255 (3)—Finance Act 1952 (15 & 16 Geo. 6 & 1 Eliz. 2 c. 33), s. 68 (2)—Finance Act 1947 (11 & 12 Geo. 6 c. 35), s. 31 (2).

F

On 13th March 1961 the taxpayer company, an unlimited company, which was an investment company to which s. 245† of the Income Tax Act 1952 applied, went into voluntary liquidation. On 18th May 1965 two surtax directions were served on the liquidators of the company in respect of estate or trading income and of other income respectively of the company for the periods 25th March 1960 to 13th March 1961 and 6th April 1960 to 13th March 1961 respectively and also two notices of apportionment of income to the sole person beneficially entitled to the company's dividends, the estate or trading income being £100,967 and the other income £20,669. In computing the estate or trading income from all sources under s. 255 (3)‡ of the Income Tax Act 1952, the Revenue deducted the average costs of maintenance, repairs, insurance and management over the previous five years under s. 101§ and not the actual expenditure in the relevant year as contended by the company. The taxpayer company appealed against that apportionment. On 16th June 1965 it claimed repayment of some £15,063 profits tax paid by the company in respect of the period covered by the directions and it subsequently received repayment. It also received notification of the recomputation of the taxpayer company's actual income following the repayment and also taking account of an error. It was informed

G

H

I

---

* This note forms part of the Procedure Direction.
† Section 245 is set out at p. 884, letters F to H, post.
‡ Section 255 (3) is set out at p. 884, letter I, to p. 885, letter A, post.
§ Section 101 (1), so far as material, is set out at p. 885, letters E and F, post.

A   that on the company's appeal the Revenue would contend that the apportionment of £100,967 in respect of estate and trading income should be
increased to £121,258, and on 21st October it was sent a further notice of
apportionment, apportioning an additional £5,010 to the person entitled to
dividends.

Held: (i) the deduction in respect of the allowance for the cost of main-
B   tenance, repairs, insurance and management should be based on the actual
expenditure in the period 25th March 1960 to 13th March 1961 and not
on the average of the previous five years, because the computation of income
from any source for any period involved two factors, incomings and outgoings, and the requirement at the end of s. 255 (3) of the Income Tax Act
1952 that income for the period in question " shall be computed by reference
C   to the income for such ... period ... and not by reference to any other ...
period " overrode the preceding requirement that income " shall be estimated
in accordance with the provisions of this Act " (which otherwise imported
s. 101 (1) and the five year average) (see p. 886, letters E to G, post).

(ii) assuming that only one surtax direction could be made in respect of
a company's income for any period, that direction would be apt to cover
D   income ascertained at the date of the direction and also income coming into
existence thereafter such as income received by recovery of profits tax, and
in such case there was nothing in the statutory provisions prohibiting a
further apportionment of the additional income in order to give effect to
s. 245 of the Act of 1952, and the second apportionment in respect of the
other income was therefore valid (see p. 889, letter I, to p. 890, letter C,
E   and p. 890, letter G, post).

Appeal allowed on first issue, dismissed on second.

[As to computation of actual income for purposes of a surtax direction and
apportionment, see 20 HALSBURY'S LAWS (3rd Edn.) 556-558, paras. 1082-1084;
and for cases on the subject, see 28 DIGEST (Repl.) 358-374, *1580-1682.*

F   As to the making of apportionments for the purposes of surtax directions, see
20 HALSBURY'S LAWS (3rd Edn.) 558-561, paras. 1085-1089.

For the Income Tax Act 1952, s. 101, s. 245, s. 248 and s. 255, see 31 HALS-
BURY'S STATUTES (2nd Edn.) 95, 232, 235, 243; for the Finance Act 1952, s. 68,
see 32 HALSBURY'S STATUTES (2nd Edn.) 224; for the Finance Act 1947, s. 31,
see 12 HALSBURY'S STATUTES (2nd Edn.) 775.]

G   Cases referred to:

Fattorini, Ltd. v. *Inland Revenue Comrs.*, [1940] 3 All E.R. 657; *revsd.*, H.L.,
[1942] 1 All E.R. 619; [1942] A.C. 643; 111 L.J.K.B. 546; 167 L.T. 45;
24 Tax Cas. 328; 28 Digest (Repl.) 366, *1607.*

Glazed Kid, Ltd. v. *Inland Revenue Comrs.* (1930), 15 Tax Cas. 445; 28 Digest
(Repl.) 365, *1602.*

H   *Income Tax (Special Comrs. of)* v. *Linsleys (Established 1894), Ltd.*, [1958]
1 All E.R. 343; [1958] A.C. 569; [1958] 2 W.L.R. 292; 37 Tax Cas. 677;
28 Digest (Repl.) 373, *1629.*

Inland Revenue Comrs. v. *Wood Bros. (Birkenhead), Ltd. (in liquidation)*,
[1957] 3 All E.R. 314; [1958] Ch. 476; [1957] 3 W.L.R. 713; *affd.*, H.L.,
[1959] 1 All E.R. 53; [1959] A.C. 487; [1959] 2 W.L.R. 47; 38 Tax
I   Cas. 275; 28 Digest (Repl.) 368, *1611.*

London County Council v. *A.-G.*, [1901] A.C. 26; 70 L.J.Q.B. 77; 83 L.T. 605;
65 J.P. 227; 4 Tax Cas. 265; 28 Digest (Repl.) 191, *790.*

Case Stated.

The taxpayer company appealed to the Special Commissioners of Income Tax
against the following apportionments of the income of the company under s. 248
of the Income Tax Act 1952: periods 25th March 1960 to 13th March 1961,
and 6th April 1960 to 13th March 1961, the Rt. Honourable the Earl Cadogan,

M.C., £100,967 and £5,101 respectively. The questions for decision* were: (i) whether the first amount £100,967 specified in the first apportionment dated 18th May 1965 should be reduced or increased and if so on what basis and by what sum or sums; and (ii) whether or not the further notice of apportionment dated 21st October 1965 was valid and in the correct amount. The commissioners held†: (i) that the deduction for the cost of maintenance, repairs, insurance and management in computing the taxpayer company's income for the purpose of the first apportionment should be based on the average expenditure of the previous five years as contended by the Crown, and not on the actual expenditure in the relevant year as contended by the taxpayer company; and (ii) that the further notice of apportionment giving effect to a recomputation of income was valid. The taxpayer company appealed by way of Case Stated to the High Court.

C. N. Beattie, Q.C., and *Hilda Wilson* for the taxpayer company.
M. P. Nolan, Q.C., and *P. W. Medd* for the Crown.

Cur. adv. vult.

29th November 1968. **PENNYCUICK, J.:** This is an appeal by the taxpayer company, Cadogan Settled Estates Co. (in liquidation), against certain apportionments made under s. 248 of the Income Tax Act 1952 on Lord Cadogan as the sole shareholder of the company, for the period from 25th March 1960 to 13th March 1961, the latter being the date on which the liquidation of the taxpayer company commenced. The appeal raises two entirely distinct issues: (i) as to the basis of computation of an additional repairs allowance under s. 101 of the Income Tax Act 1952 for the purpose of computing the income of the taxpayer company for the relevant period; and (ii) whether an additional apportionment can properly be made by reference to profits tax that was recovered by the company under s. 31 of the Finance Act 1947.

I will recite or summarise the facts as found in the Case Stated. The Case Stated goes in some detail into figures on one or other basis of computation, and also into particulars of notices, correspondence and so forth. It would not be useful to read those parts of the Case in full. After the formal parts of the Case setting out the questions for decision, and so forth, it proceeds as follows:

" 4. The following facts were admitted between the parties: (i) The Company was incorporated under the Companies Act, 1929, on 23rd July, 1941, as an unlimited company. Its authorised and issued share capital was originally £1,500,000 divided into £1,250,000 ordinary shares and £250,000 preference shares, but this was reduced and at all material times until its liquidation the issued capital of the Company was £1,162,500 ordinary shares. (ii) At all material times the Company was one to which Section 245 of the Income Tax Act, 1952, applied and the Rt. Hon. the Earl Cadogan, M.C. (hereinafter called 'the Earl Cadogan') was the sole person beneficially entitled to its dividends. For all periods up to the 24th March, 1960, the Company distributed the greater part of its income by way of dividend. This income derived mainly from rents, but there was also interest from loans and investments. [There follow particulars of the profits and distributions of the company for the period ended 13th March 1961, when the company went into liquidation. Sub-paragraph (iii) sets out the resolution for the voluntary winding up, and the personality of the liquidators.] (iv) It was accepted on behalf of the Liquidators that the Company had been an investment company to which Section 245 of the Income Tax Act, 1952, applied and that the Commissioners of Inland Revenue were required by Section 262 (1) of that Act to make a direction under Section 245 in respect of its income other than estate or trading income for the period the 6th April,

---

* The facts of the case and the contentions of the parties are set out at letter F, above, to p. 882, letter I, post.
† The decision of the commissioners is set out at p. 883, letter A, to p. 884, letter D, post.

A 1960 to the 13th March, 1961. The Accountants acting for the Liquidators (hereinafter called ' the Accountants ') also indicated in a letter addressed to the Clerk to the Special Commissioners of Income Tax (now the Controller of Surtax) dated the 11th June, 1964, that a direction under Section 245 in respect of the Company's estate or trading income for the period the 25th March, 1960, to the 13th March, 1961, would not be opposed, but it was

B added: (a) that in the computation of the Company's actual income a deduction of the grossed up amount of the profits tax paid in respect of the periods in question would be claimed in accordance with Section 68 (1) of the Finance Act, 1952; and (b) that by virtue of Section 255 (3) of the Income Tax Act, 1952, it was claimed that the Company was entitled to deduct the amount of its actual expenditure on the maintenance of properties in the

C period in question and not just the average of its expenditure in the preceding five years.   (v) The Accountants subsequently advised the Clerk to the Special Commissioners (now the Controller of Surtax) that when the proposed directions had been made it was intended to reclaim from the Inspector of Taxes the amount of the profits tax paid on the profits of the period in question, in accordance with Section 31 (2) of the Finance Act, 1947, and they

D asked for confirmation that no further apportionments or assessments would be made as a result.   The Clerk to the Special Commissioners (now the Controller of Surtax) replied that it was the Revenue's normal practice in such circumstances to leave profits tax out of account altogether in computing the actual income of a company, but that where a company insisted upon a deduction of the grossed up profits tax, it was the practice to allow the deduc-

E tion and then to make a further apportionment when the profits tax had been repaid. The Accountants were also advised that it was not accepted that the Company was entitled to the deduction of the actual amount expended by it on the maintenance of properties for the period in question in the computation of its estate or trading income. (vi) Two Separate Directions, both dated the 18th May, 1965, were made and served upon the Liquidators

F in respect of such part of the Company's actual income from all sources as was estate or trading income for the period the 25th March, 1960 to the 13th March, 1961, and such part of its actual income from all sources as was not estate or trading income for the period the 6th April, 1960 to the 13th March, 1961. There was no appeal against the said Directions. (vii) Two Notices of Apportionment both dated the 18th May, 1965, were also served

G upon the Liquidators. The first Notice apportioned £100,967 in respect of estate or trading income and the second Notice apportioned £20,669 in respect of other income, both amounts being apportioned to the Earl Cadogan. [There follow a number of figures.] (viii) By a letter dated the 16th June, 1965, the Accountants gave notice of appeal on behalf of the Liquidators against the apportionment of £100,967 in respect of estate or trading income on the

H grounds that the amount apportioned was excessive, the points of disagreement having been set out in previous correspondence. With this letter was enclosed a copy of a letter of the same date to the Inspector of Taxes, Pimlico District, claiming on behalf of the Liquidators the repayment of £15,062 17s. 0d. profits tax paid by the Company in respect of the period covered by the directions. In a letter dated the 19th August, 1965, the

I Accountants notified the Controller of Surtax that the Liquidators had received repayment of this amount. (ix) As a result, the Controller of Surtax notified the Accountants of his further computations of the actual income of the Company from each source and also [of a certain error. Then there follow further computations. Again I need not go into the figures.] (x) The Accountants were informed that the Revenue would contend that the apportionment of £100,967 in respect of estate or trading income, which was under appeal, should be increased to £121,258; and a further Notice of Apportionment (hereinafter called ' the further Notice '), dated the 21st

October, 1965, was served upon the Liquidators, apportioning an additional **A**
£5,010 to the Earl Cadogan in respect of actual income other than estate or
trading income for the period the 6th April, 1960 to the 13th March, 1961.
[The terms of the notice are set out. Then, sub-para. (xi) sets out the grounds
of appeal, and sub-para. (xii) sets out further figures.] (xiii) The alternative
figures applicable to the determination of these appeals before us were agreed
as follows: If all the Revenue's contentions were upheld: Actual Estate or **B**
Trading Income, £121,258; Other Actual Income (1st Apportionment),
£20,669; Other Actual Income (2nd Apportionment), £5,010 [totalling]
£146,937. If the Revenue's contentions regarding the consequences of the
repayment of profits tax were not upheld but its contentions regarding
maintenance relief were: Actual Estate or Trading Income, £100,967; Other
Actual Income (1st Apportionment), £20,669; Other Actual Income (omitted **C**
in error from 1st Apportionment) for which liability is accepted, £749 [totall-
ing] £122,385. If none of the Revenue's contentions were accepted and the
appeals had been allowed: Actual Estate or Trading Income, £82,429; Other
Actual Income (1st Apportionment), £20,669; Other Actual Income,
(omitted in error from 1st Apportionment) for which liability is accepted,
£749 [totalling] £103,847. (xiv) It was common ground that there was no **D**
appeal against the second of the Notices dated 18th May, 1965."
There follow the contentions of the parties.

" 5. It was contended on behalf of the Company: (a) that in computing
under Section 255 (3) of the Income Tax Act, 1952, such part of the actual
income of the Company from all sources for the period 25th March, 1960
to 13th March, 1961 as consisted of estate or trading income, allowances for **E**
costs of maintenance, repairs, insurance and management (available under
Sections 101 (1), 101 (5), 175 and 176 (1) (g) of the said Act) should be based
on actual expenditure, not on the average of the preceding five years; and
that the amount of £100,967 mentioned in the said first Notice of Apportionment dated 18th May, 1965, should be reduced accordingly; (b) that it was
not open to the Revenue to ask for an increase in respect of the said amount **F**
of £100,967; (c) that the further Notice dated 21st October, 1965, was void;
(d) that the appeals should succeed.

" 6. It was contended on behalf of the [Crown]: (a) that the provision
in Section 255 (3) of the Income Tax Act, 1952, that income from any
source shall be estimated in accordance with the provisions of the Act
relating to income from that source, required that in computing the actual **G**
estate or trading income of the Company for the period in question
allowances for costs of maintenance, repairs, insurance and management
should be based on the average of the preceding five years, as provided
by Section 101 of the Act, and that the substitution of the actual expenditure of the period in question was not warranted by the excepting words
of the subsection, which related to the basis period for computing income **H**
and could not be applied in isolation to the measure to be taken for computing relief; (b) that the said amount of £100,967 should therefore not
be reduced, but should be increased to £121,258 to take into account
profits tax which had been allowed pursuant to Section 31 (2) of the
Finance Act, 1947 and subsequently repaid under Section 68 (2) of the
Finance Act, 1952; and that we, the Special Commissioners, had power **I**
to order such increase by virtue of Section 52 (6) of the Income Tax Act,
1952, as applied by Section 12 (5) of the Income Tax Management Act, 1964;
(c) that in view of the provisions of Section 514 (2) of the Income Tax Act,
1952 and the full notification to the Liquidators of the company through
their Accountants of the computation upon which the additional apportionment was based, the further Notice dated 21st October, 1965, was valid
and ought not to be quashed for any such want of form or other defect as
was alleged; (d) that the appeals should be dismissed.

A

" 7. [sets out three cases which were cited, to two of which I shall refer.]

" 8. We the Commissioners who heard the Appeal took time to consider our decision and gave it in writing on 24th November, 1967 as follows: [Then they set out the notices of apportionment, and proceed:] The first question for our decision is whether the apportioned amount stated in the first Notice dated 18th May, 1965, should be reduced, as the Company con-

B tends, by a sum representing the costs of maintenance, repairs, insurance and management of its properties during the relevant period. The second question is whether that apportioned amount should be increased, as the Crown contends, by a sum representing ' grossed-up ' profits tax repaid to the Company. The third question is whether the further Notice dated 21st October, 1965, was valid. On the first question, the Company contends

C that by virtue of the excepting words in Section 255 (3) of the Income Tax Act, 1952, the whole cost of maintenance, repairs, insurance and management for the relevant period should be deducted in computing its actual income for the purpose of Section 245. The Crown contends that in so far as the Company is entitled to any deduction, such deduction should be by reference to the average of the preceding five years allowed by Section 101 (1).

D Having considered the arguments addressed to us by both parties on this aspect, we have come to the conclusion that the view put forward by the Crown should prevail. Counsel for the Company concedes that the opening words of Section 255 (3) import Schedule A provisions, but argues that the excepting words expressly exclude any averaging formula. He asks us, in effect, to substitute for the words ' according to the average of the preceding

E five years ' in Section 101 (1) the phrase ' in the accounting period in question ', but we feel unable to construe Section 101 (1) in this way. The second question involves the construction of Sections 245, 248 (1) and (2), and proviso (a) to Section 262 (2) of the Income Tax Act, 1952, read with Section 31 (2) of the Finance Act, 1947 and Section 68 (2) of the Finance Act, 1952. The effect of directions under Sections 245 and 262 (1) of the Income Tax

F Act, 1952, is that the actual income of a controlled company from all sources shall be deemed to be the income of its members and that ' the amount thereof ' shall be apportioned among its members. By the combined effect of proviso (a) to Section 262 (2) of the Income Tax Act, 1952, and Section 68 (2) of the Finance Act, 1952, the amount of profits tax payable by the company, grossed-up at the standard rate of income tax, is allow-

G able as a deduction in computing the Company's actual income. Section 31 (2) of the Finance Act, 1947, provides that profits tax shall not be chargeable if the actual income is apportioned under or for the purposes of Section 245 of the Income Tax Act, 1952. Section 248 (1) of the Income Tax Act, 1952, requires the apportionment of the actual income in accordance with the respective interests of the company's members, and Section 248 (2)

H requires the apportionment to be notified by serving on the company a statement showing ' the amount of the actual income from all sources adopted ' for the purposes of Section 245. It is clear from the speech of LORD REID in *Special Comrs. of Income Tax* v. *Linsleys (Established 1894), Ltd.* (1) that the stages in a case such as the present are: (i) computation of actual income, allowing for grossed-up profits tax payable; (ii) direction

I under Section 245; and (iii) apportionment under Section 248 (1). Difficulty arises, from the Crown's standpoint, in that the net amount of the grossed-up profits tax allowed at stage (i) ceases at or after stage (iii) to be chargeable, and if already paid, becomes repayable. The Crown's practice is to make a further or supplementary apportionment, which in the present case is being done partly by asking us to increase the amount stated in the first Notice dated 18th May, 1965 and partly by the further Notice dated 21st

(1) [1958] 1 All E.R. 343 at p. 353; 37 Tax Cas. 677 at p. 709.

October, 1965. The substantial issue here is whether, in effect, a re-compu-   **A**
tation may be made, and if so, whether in any particular way.   In our view,
there is nothing in the relevant statutory provisions to prohibit such a
re-computation and consequential apportionment.   In the present case it
is true that, so far as the estate or trading income is concerned, no amending
document in the form of the further Notice dated 21st October, 1965, has
been served on the Company, but an amended computation has been   **B**
included in correspondence with the Company, and the Company was notified
that the Crown intended through its representative to ask at the hearing for
the requisite increase to be made.   In our view there has been sufficient
compliance with the requirements of Section 248 (2); and Section 12 (5) of
the Income Tax Management Act, 1964, applying Section 52 (6) of the
Income Tax Act, 1952, empowers us to increase the apportionment. As   **C**
to the third question, if our view is right, that a re-computation may be made,
it follows that a notice giving effect to such re-computation must be valid,
and it seems to us immaterial whether the notice or its contents be described
as further, supplemental or additional, provided its intent be clear. Accordingly, we confirm the further Notice dated 21st October, 1965, and we increase
the amount apportioned in the first Notice dated 18th May, 1965, to   **D**
£121,258."

I have read the relevant parts of the Case Stated at this stage though much of
it is difficult to follow except when the sections are looked at in full.   No question
arises on figures; nor is there any question now outstanding as to the formal
validity of notices, and so forth.

Before dealing with the two issues separately, I will read s. 245 of the Income   **E**
Tax Act 1952, which is the governing provision in this context.   It is not in
dispute that a direction was properly made in the present case.   Section 245
provides as follows:

" With a view to preventing the avoidance of the payment of surtax
through the withholding from distribution of income of a company which   **F**
would otherwise be distributed, it is hereby enacted that where it appears
to the [Commissioners of Inland Revenue] that any company to which this
section applies has not, within a reasonable time after the end of any year
or other period for which accounts have been made up, distributed to its
members, in such manner as to render the amount distributed liable to be
included in the statements to be made by the members of the company of   **G**
their total income for the purposes of surtax, a reasonable part of its actual
income from all sources for the said year or other period, the Commissioners
may, by notice in writing to the company, direct that, for purposes of assessment to surtax, the said income of the company shall, for the year or other
period specified in the notice be deemed to be the income of the members,
and the amount thereof shall be apportioned among the members."   **H**

Section 248 provides:

" (1) Where a direction has been given under section two hundred and
forty-five of this Act with respect to a company, the apportionment of the
actual income from all sources of the company shall be made by the Special
Commissioners in accordance with the respective interests of the members.
(2) Notice of any such apportionment shall be given by serving on the com-   **I**
pany a statement showing the amount of the actual income from all sources
adopted by the Special Commissioners for the purposes of the said section
two hundred and forty-five and either the amount apportioned to each
member or the amount apportioned to each class of shares, as the
Commissioners think fit . . . ."

Section 255 (3) provides:

" In computing, for the purposes of this Chapter, the actual income from

A all sources of a company for any year or period, the income from any source shall be estimated in accordance with the provisions of this Act relating to the computation of income from that source, except that the income shall be computed by reference to the income for such year or period as aforesaid and not by reference to any other year or period."

B I will now consider the two issues in turn. (i) The question here is whether, in computing the actual income of the taxpayer company for the relevant period —i.e., the last period, ending with the commencement of the winding-up—the taxpayer company is entitled to make a deduction for the cost of additional repairs (I shall explain that expression) incurred in that period, or whether it is only entitled to make a deduction of the average cost of additional repairs over the preceding five years.

C I must now refer to certain of the provisions of the Income Tax Act 1952 relating to Sch. A. Section 82 describes the charge under Sch. A:

" 1. Tax under this Schedule shall be charged in respect of the property in all lands, tenements, hereditaments and heritages in the United Kingdom capable of actual occupation, for every twenty shillings of the annual value thereof . . ."

D Section 99 and s. 100 provide for a fixed repairs allowance on a percentage basis. Section 101 (1), provides for an additional repairs allowance in the following terms:

" If the owner of any land (inclusive of farmhouses and other buildings, if any) or of any houses, being land or houses the assessment on which is reduced for the purposes of collection, shows that the cost to him of maintenance, repairs, insurance and management, according to the average of the preceding five years, has exceeded, in the case of land, one-eighth part of the annual value of the land as adopted under Schedule A, and, in the case of houses, the authorised reduction as defined by the last preceding section, he shall, in addition to the reduction of the assessment, be entitled, on making a claim for the purpose, to repayment of the amount of the tax on the excess . . ."

E

F The expression " repayment of . . . tax on the excess " in s. 101 will be noticed. Counsel for the Crown disclaims any argument based on this expression, and is content to treat the provision as equivalent to a provision for deduction of the additional costs of maintenance in the computation of income chargeable with tax under Sch. A. This is a fair but most important concession. Counsel for the taxpayer company contends that in order to comply with s. 255 (3), one must take, on the one hand, the annual value for the relevant period as admittedly reduced by the fixed allowance under s. 99 and s. 100, and then deduct from it such actual expenditure for the same period as qualifies for additional relief under s. 101. Counsel for the Crown contends that s. 255 (3) prescribes the relevant period as the basis period, leaving the average provision in s. 101 in operation. I will refer again to the words of that subsection:

G

H " In computing, for the purposes of this Chapter, the actual income from all sources of a company for any year or period, the income from any source shall be estimated in accordance with the provisions of this Act relating to the computation of income from that source, except that the income shall be computed by reference to the income for such year or period as aforesaid and not by reference to any other year or period."

I The expression " actual income " has been explained in *Inland Revenue Comrs.* v. *Wood Bros. (Birkenhead), Ltd. (in liquidation)* (2), JENKINS, L.J., said (3):

" I accept the submission of counsel for the Crown that the observations

---

(2) [1957] 3 All E.R. 314; *affd.*, [1959] 1 All E.R. 53; 38 Tax Cas. 275.
(3) [1957] 3 All E.R. at p. 321; 38 Tax Cas. at p. 289.

of the court in [a case in the House of Lords (4)] make it reasonably plain
that we should treat the word ' actual ' here in the phrase ' the actual income
from all sources ' as meaning the income for the actual period in respect of
which the assessment is made, as distinct from the income from some other
basic period of a conventional kind such as the previous year or, as it once
was, the three years' average selected as the basis of calculation . . ."

LORD REID said (5):

" . . . s. 255 (3) in effect provides a definition of what is meant by ' actual
income '; it directs how actual income is to be computed and, in my opinion,
nothing can be included in actual income unless it can be brought within
the words ' income from any source . . . estimated in accordance with the
provisions of this Act relating to the computation of income from that
source . . .'."

So what one has to do, in order to apply sub-s. (3), is to compute the income of
the taxpayer company from all sources for the actual relevant period in accordance with the provisions of the Act relating to the computation of income from
that source, but with the overriding exception—

" that the income shall be computed by reference to the income for such
year or period as aforesaid and not by reference to any other year or period."

It seems to me that the contention of counsel for the taxpayer company on this
point is correct. The computation of income from any source (apart from what
is known as pure income) for any period involves two factors; viz., incomings
and outgoings. I need not enlarge on those terms for the present purpose. It is
quite impossible to compute income without taking both factors into account.
Subsection (3), in the excepting words at the end, imperatively requires that the
income from all sources of a company for any year

" . . . shall be computed by reference to the income for such . . . period
as aforesaid and not by reference to any other . . . period."

Those excepting words clearly as a matter of construction override and qualify
the preceding requirement that—

" . . . income from any source shall be estimated in accordance with the
provisions of this Act relating to the computation of income from that
source . . ."

It seems to me that only by taking the outgoings as well as the incomings of
the relevant period is it possible to comply with the requirement imposed by the
excepting words. If one takes the incomings of this period and the outgoings of
some other period one is not complying with the requirement. On the contrary,
one is going directly against the final prohibition.

It is, I think, no answer to say that sub-s. (3) merely imports the current period
as the basis period. That may be a convenient description of the effect of the
subsection where incomings and outgoings alike would otherwise be ascertainable
by reference to a previous year, as in the ordinary assessment under Case I of
Sch. D, but it is not what the subsection says and I do not see how such an
artificial construction of the subsection can be justified. The commissioners
correctly summarise the argument on behalf of the taxpayer company but reject it
in the words, " we feel unable to construe section 101 (1) in this way ". With all
respect to the commissioners, no question arises on the construction of s. 101.
The effect of s. 255 (3) is to vary the operation of s. 101 by substituting the expenses of the current period for the average of the expenses over the previous
five years in the computation of taxable income. I am not at all clear what
additional effect the excepting words at the end of sub-s. (3) can have, on the
Crown's contention, bearing in mind the explanation of what is meant by

(4) *Fattorini, Ltd.* v. *Inland Revenue Comrs.*, [1942] 1 All E.R. 619; 24 Tax Cas. 328.
(5) [1959] 1 All E.R. at p. 59; 38 Tax Cas. at p. 299.

A " actual income " in the decision of *Inland Revenue Comrs.* v. *Wood Bros. (Birkenhead), Ltd. (in liquidation)* (6).

The argument of counsel for the company derives support from an analysis made by SCOTT, L.J., in *Fattorini, Ltd.* v. *Inland Revenue Comrs.* (7). The decision of the Court of Appeal (7) in that case was overruled by the House of Lords (8), but SCOTT, L.J.'s analysis on this particular point was specifically approved by

B LORD ATKIN (9).   What SCOTT, L.J. said was this (10):

" ROWLATT, J., attached to the expression ' actual income ' a meaning with which we disagree. He treated it as connoting the receipts side only of the income account. He assumed that, if the actual receipts in the statutory year mentioned in sect. 21 had been assigned or hypothecated under a binding contract, the company's ' actual income ' had passed out

C of its control, and, therefore, ceased to be available for distribution. This, in our opinion, is an error. The true meaning of the phrase, we think, is indicated by the context, and by certain provisions of the Act of 1918. As was said by LORD MACNAGHTEN in *London County Council* v. *A.-G.* (11): ' Income tax . . . is a tax on income . . . whatever may be the standard by which the income is measured '. The phrase ' profits and gains ' in

D income-tax legislation is—at any rate, under Sched. D—no more than a synonym for ' income '. For purposes of assessment the income of an anterior period was, and is, ' deemed to be the income ' of the person charged for the year of assessment. He is charged on a conventional or putative, and not on the actual income. Until 1927, it was an average of 3 years. Since then, it has been the income of the preceding year. In the case of supertax, also, the

E ' total income ' was to be ascertained on the previous year's basis—(sect. 5 (1)) [of the Income Tax Act 1918] and, where tax had been deducted at the source, the income of the previous year before deduction was ' to be deemed to be income of the year in which it was receivable ' (sect. 5 (3) (c))."

He then set out r. 8 of the Rules Applicable to Cases I and II of Sch. D, " reproducing the Finance Act, 1907, s. 24, but repealed by the Finance Act, 1926 ",

F which makes reference to " actual profits or gains ", and said (10):

" That rule in the Act of 1918, we think, supplies the key to the meaning of the word ' actual ' in sect. 21 of the Act of 1922, which called for interpretation in *Glazed Kid, Ltd.* v. *Inland Revenue Comrs.* (12), and calls for it in the present case. It was inserted to make it clear that it is not the conventional income, but the *de facto* income of the year in question which is

G subject to the duty to distribute. The epithet ' actual ' in such a sense is illustrated in income-tax law by the Finance Act, 1907, s. 24 (2), (3), where the successor to a continuing business, and his predecessor, who ceases to carry it on, are taxed on their ' actual income ' in the two broken periods of the year."

H The argument of counsel for the taxpayer company also derives strong support from the scheme of s. 245. Apart from investment income, where the direction is automatic, the power to make a direction arises where it appears to the Special Commissioners that the company has not distributed a reasonable part of its income from all sources for any given year. Directors of a company, in deciding what distribution to make, can normally and properly have regard to

I all expenses in fact incurred during the year, and as regards repairs they would normally and properly have regard to actual expenditure rather than to an average expenditure over the past five years. One could even find a situation in

(6) [1957] 3 All E.R. 314; *affd.*, [1959] 1 All E.R. 53; 38 Tax Cas. 275.
(7) [1940] 3 All E.R. 657; 24 Tax Cas. 328.
(8) [1942] 1 All E.R. 619; 24 Tax Cas. 328.
(9) [1942] 1 All E.R. at p. 626; 24 Tax Cas. at p. 352.
(10) [1940] 3 All E.R. at p. 663; 24 Tax Cas. at p. 342.
(11) [1901] A.C. 26 at pp. 35, 36; 4 Tax Cas. 265 at pp. 293, 294.
(12) (1930), 15 Tax Cas. 445.

which after taking into account average expenditure the company had made a profit, but after taking into account expenditure during the year the company had made a loss.   It would be remarkable if in such circumstances directors failing to recommend a dividend could be said to have failed to distribute a reasonable part of the income of the company.

I must, in conclusion on this issue, refer to an argument based on s. 262 (5) of the Income Tax Act 1952.   That subsection, so far as now in point, provides as follows:

" If in the case of any company the cost of maintenance, repairs, insurance and management (being expenditure of such a nature as to be capable of being taken into account for the purposes of a claim by the company for relief under section one hundred and one of this Act) incurred by it in any year of assessment exceeds the amount of the gross estate or trading income of the company for that year, the company shall be entitled, on giving notice in writing to the Special Commissioners within six months of the end of that year and on proof to the satisfaction of those Commissioners of the amount of the excess, to require that the amount of the actual income from all sources of the company, other than estate or trading income, for that year shall be treated, for the purposes of this section, as if it were reduced by an amount equal to that excess: Provided that, where a deduction is allowable in computing the estate or trading income of the company for any subsequent year by reference to the said section one hundred and one, no account shall be taken in computing the amount of that deduction of any such excess expenditure which has been taken into account for the purposes of any such reduction as aforesaid . . .''

The subsection itself, apart from the proviso, rather supports the argument of counsel for the taxpayer company.   It apparently presupposes that estate or trading income has been exhausted on repair expenditure.   But the proviso introduces a serious difficulty.   The proviso clearly presupposes that excess expenditure can in general be carried forward into the computation of the income for a subsequent year.   Counsel for the taxpayer company says that this provision relates to income tax only, but I think that in its context it is clearly intended to relate to the computation of actual income for the purpose of a surtax direction.

Some assistance on this point may be derived from considering the order in which the statutory provisions were enacted.   Section 255 (3) replaced para. 6 in Sch. 1 to the Finance Act 1922.   The reference to " an average of more than one year '' in that paragraph was no doubt dropped in subsequent legislation as being superfluous having regard to the abolition of the three-year average basis for the computation of profits of a trade under Case I of Sch. D.   It is not suggested that that alteration has any bearing on the present question.   Section 262 (5) replaced a later provision, viz., s. 14 (5) of the Finance Act 1939.   I do not think that that later provision can have been intended to introduce a statutory exposition of the earlier provision.   If this had been intended, the exposition would have been effected in plainer terms.   If, then, as I think is the case, the meaning of the earlier provision is plain, there is no alternative but to regard the later provision as having been enacted per incuriam.   It will be observed that the later provision does no more than expressly disallow a deduction which, on the true construction of the earlier provision, could in any event not have been claimed.

On the first issue I do not agree with the decision of the commissioners, and I propose to vary their determination accordingly.

(ii) On the second issue, I am in complete agreement with the commissioners. The taxpayer company's contention is a highly technical one, admittedly without substantial merit, and I do not think that I am by any means driven by the terms of the relevant provisions to accept it.   The circumstances underlying this

A submission are that in the computation of the income of a company for the purposes of s. 245 profits tax is an admissible deduction: on the other hand,
individuals are not liable to profits tax, and where a company's income is apportioned to individuals the profits tax paid by the company is recoverable. The
company then finds itself with recovered income which has not been apportioned.
The Commissioners of Inland Revenue contend that a further apportionment
B can be made. The taxpayer company contends that no further apportionment
is admissible.

The relevant statutory provisions, subject to certain exceptions and
qualifications not now material, are these: Finance Act 1947, s. 31:

C " (1) Subject to the provisions of this Part of this Act relating to partner-
ships where one or more of the partners is a body corporate and to the provisions thereof relating to trades or businesses carried on by liquidators
. . . (*a*) section nineteen of the Finance Act, 1937 (being the section which
charges the profits tax) shall not apply to any trade or business unless it is
carried on by a body corporate or by an unincorporated society or other
body; . . .

D " (2) The said section nineteen shall not apply to any trade or business
carried on by a body corporate during any chargeable accounting period if,
for a year or period which includes, or for years or periods which together
include, the whole of the chargeable accounting period, the actual income
of the body corporate from all sources is apportioned under or for the purposes
of section twenty-one of the Finance Act, 1922, and all the persons to whom
it is apportioned are individuals."

E Subsection (3) contains a corresponding provision applicable to the case where
some of the persons to whom the income is apportioned are individuals. Then,
s. 68 (1) of the Finance Act 1952 is in these terms:

F " Where for the purposes of section twenty-one of the Finance Act, 1922,
[and certain other provisions] (which provide for the payment of surtax,
in certain cases, on undistributed income of companies), the actual income
from all sources of a body corporate for a year or period ending after the
end of the year nineteen hundred and fifty-one falls to be computed under
paragraph 6 of the First Schedule to the said Act of 1922 or subsection (3)
of section two hundred and fifty-five of the said Act of 1952, then, if any
amount is payable by the body corporate by way of the profits tax or the
G excess profits levy, respectively, for any chargeable accounting period falling
wholly or partly within that year or period, a deduction shall be allowed,
in computing the said actual income, of such an amount as would, after
deduction of income tax at the standard rate in force for the year of assessment during which the said year or period ends, be equal to so much of the
amount so payable by the body corporate as is apportionable to the said year
H or period."

The effect of these provisions was closely considered by LORD REID in *Special
Comrs. of Income Tax* v. *Linsleys (Established 1894), Ltd.* (13). The effect of
that decision is that where the members of a company are individuals the procedure under s. 245 is strictly as follows: (i) computation of actual income,
allowing for grossed-up profits tax payable; (ii) direction under s. 245; (iii)
apportionment under s. 248 (1); and (iv) repayment of the profits tax. At
I that stage the Commissioners of Inland Revenue claim to make a further
apportionment in respect of the profits tax recovered.

Counsel for the taxpayer company contends that s. 245 and s. 248 do not
admit of such a further apportionment. There can, he says, be only one direction.
I will assume that that is so. The direction is that the " said income of the
company "—i.e., its actual income from all sources for the relevant period—shall

_____

(13) [1958] 1 All E.R. at pp. 352-357; 37 Tax Cas. at pp. 708-710.

be deemed to be income of its members, and the amount thereof shall be appor- **A**
tioned among the members. Then, the argument proceeds, there follows an
apportionment of the income capable of apportionment when the apportionment
is made. The profits tax recoverable is not part of such income. Finally, it
is said, there is no power to make a further apportionment when recovery takes
place.

I do not accept the last step in this argument. The direction covers the income **B**
of the taxpayer company for the given period. That expression is quite apt to
cover not only the income ascertained or capable of ascertainment at the date
of direction, but also income coming into existence after the date of direction,
i.e., income received by recovery of profits tax. Nor is there anything in the
statutory provisions which prohibits a further apportionment where that is
necessary in order to give effect to the direction; i.e., here, by bringing into **C**
apportionment the recovered profits tax.

It will be observed that in the *Linsleys* case (14), LORD REID (15) and LORD
SOMERVELL OF HARROW (16) contemplated without disapproval the possibility
of a second apportionment in such circumstances. LORD REID said (15):

> " A further argument was submitted for the company. If the amount of
> profits tax is deducted in computing the income apportioned and thereafter, **D**
> by reason of the apportionment, profits tax ceases to be payable, then the sum
> so deducted will be retained by the company unapportioned, and will not
> be chargeable to surtax. If this were so, it would support the company's
> contention, but counsel for the Crown submitted an argument that this
> sum would not escape taxation but could be covered by an additional
> apportionment." **E**

He leaves it there. LORD SOMERVELL said (16):

> " If the actual income is £2,000 and the profits tax £500, the Crown has
> to make two bites at the cherry although, under s. 31 (2), there can be no
> ultimate liability to profits tax. When one comes to s. 31 (3), the Crown
> would, on the above figures, apportion £1,500 and then have to have an **F**
> additional apportionment of £500 if, but only if, the election were exercised."

I see no reason why a further apportionment should not be made in such circumstances in order to give effect to s. 245, and on this point, as I have said, I
agree with the commissioners. This is not even a case of making defective
machinery fit. The machinery does fit. I propose, therefore, to allow the appeal
so far as concerns the first issue but to dismiss it so far as concerns the second **G**
issue. I imagine that involves remitting the case back to the commissioners
to adjust the figures.

Appeal allowed on first issue, dismissed on second.

Solicitors: *Baileys, Shaw & Gillett* (for the taxpayer company); *Solicitor of
Inland Revenue.*

  H

[*Reported by* F. A. AMIES, ESQ., *Barrister-at-Law.*]

  I

---

(14) [1958] 1 All E.R. 343; 37 Tax Cas. 677.
(15) [1958] 1 All E.R. at pp. 353, 354; 37 Tax Cas. at p. 710.
(16) [1958] 1 All E.R. at p. 355; 37 Tax Cas. at p. 712.

A

MAGEE v. PENNINE INSURANCE CO., LTD.

[COURT OF APPEAL, CIVIL DIVISION (Lord Denning, M.R., Winn and Fenton Atkinson, L.JJ.), March 21, 1969.]

Mistake—Contract—Agreement to compromise—Mistake as to validity of claim
—Agreement to compromise insurance claim—Mistake that insurance

B *policy on which claim based valid—Whether agreement to compromise void for mistake—Whether voidable in equity.*

In 1961, the plaintiff signed a proposal form for the insurance of a motor car. There were a number of mis-statements in the proposal; in particular it was mis-stated that the plaintiff held a driving licence. The plaintiff however was not fraudulent, the form having been filled in by a third party.

C The proposal was accepted by the defendant insurance company, and the policy was renewed from year to year. In 1964, it was transferred to another car without the insurance company requiring a new proposal. In 1965 the insured car was accidentally damaged and the plaintiff made a claim in respect of it. The insurance company offered, by letter dated 12th May 1965, £385 in settlement of the claim, and this the plaintiff orally

D accepted. The insurance company then discovered the mis-statements in the proposal of 1961 and refused to pay the £385. The trial judge found that the insurance company was entitled to repudiate the policy because of the mis-statements in the proposal, but that there was a contract of compromise and the insurance company was bound by it. On appeal by the insurance company, the holding that the company was entitled to repudiate

E the original policy not being challenged by the plaintiff,

Held: (i) on its true construction the letter of 12th May 1965 was an offer of compromise and not merely an offer to quantify the claim (see p. 893, letter E, p. 894, letter G, and p. 896, letter D, post); but,

(ii) (WINN, L.J., dissenting) the appeal would nevertheless be allowed on the following grounds—

F (a) (per LORD DENNING, M.R.) although the acceptance by the plaintiff of the insurance company's offer constituted a contract of compromise binding at law, the parties were acting under a common and fundamental mistake in that they thought that the original policy was good and binding; the contract was therefore voidable in equity, and it would be set aside because in the circumstances it was not equitable to hold the insurance

G company to it (see p. 893, letter I, and p. 894, letter C, post);

Dictum of DENNING, L.J., in *Solle* v. *Butcher* ([1949] 2 All E.R. at p. 1120) applied.

(b) (per FENTON ATKINSON, L.J.) the agreement to compromise was made on the basis of an essential contractual assumption, namely, that there was in existence a valid and enforceable policy of insurance; since that

H assumption was false the insurance company was entitled to avoid the agreement on the ground of mutual mistake in a fundamental and vital matter (see p. 896, letter H, post).

Bell v. *Lever Brothers, Ltd.* ([1931] All E.R. Rep. 11) applied.

Appeal allowed.

[As to the legal consequences and classification of mistake, see 26 HALSBURY'S

I LAWS (3rd Edn.) 892, 905, paras. 1649-1675; and for cases on the subject, see 35 DIGEST (Repl.) 93-125, *1-220*.]

Cases referred to:

Bell v. *Lever Brothers, Ltd.*, [1932] A.C. 161; [1931] All E.R. Rep. 11; 101 L.J.K.B. 129; 146 L.T. 258; *revsg.*, sub nom. *Lever Brothers, Ltd.* v. *Bell*, [1931] 1 K.B. 557; 35 Digest (Repl.) 23, *140*.

Solle v. *Butcher*, [1949] 2 All E.R. 1107; [1950] 1 K.B. 671; 31 Digest (Repl.) 674, *7699*.

Appeal.

This was an appeal by the defendants, Pennine Insurance Co., Ltd., from a judgment of His Honour JUDGE LEIGH given on 1st July 1968 whereby he gave judgment for the plaintiff, Thomas Magee, for £385. The facts are set out in the judgment of LORD DENNING, M.R.

G. A. Carman for the defendant insurance company.
K. J. Taylor for the plaintiff.

LORD DENNING, M.R.: In 1961 the plaintiff, Mr. Thomas Magee, aged 58, acquired an Austin car. He signed a proposal form for insurance. In it he said that the car belonged to him. He was asked to give details of his driving licence " and of all other persons who to your present knowledge will drive ". These were the details he gave:

" (i) Thomas Magee [that is himself] provisional licence, aged 58. (ii) John Magee [that is his elder son] Police mobile driver, aged 35. [He had an annual licence.]   (iii) John Magee [that is the younger son] joiner, aged 18—provisional licence."

The plaintiff signed this declaration:

" I do hereby declare that the Car described is and shall be kept in good condition and that the answers above given are in every respect true and correct and I hereby agree that this Declaration shall be the basis of the Contract of Insurance between the Company and myself."

Those details were not written by the plaintiff. They were written in by Mr. Atkinson at the garage where he got the car. The details unfortunately were completely wrong. The plaintiff had never driven a car himself. He had never had a licence, not even a provisional one. He was getting the car really for his son of 18 to drive.   And we all know that a young man of 18 has to pay a much higher insurance than a man of 25 or over.   The insurance company said they would not have insured a young man of 18.

The judge found that the plaintiff had not been fraudulent. He did not himself fill in the details. They were filled in by Mr. Atkinson, the man at the garage, and then the plaintiff signed them. It was Mr. Atkinson who made some mistake or other; but there it was. A misrepresentation was made, and on the faith of it being true the insurance company granted an insurance policy to the plaintiff.

Thereafter the policy was renewed each year and the premiums were paid. In 1964 that car was replaced by another. The policy was renewed for the new car without anything further being said about the drivers or the ownership. The insurance company assumed, no doubt, that the same details applied.

On 25th April 1965, there was an accident. The younger son, John Magee, was driving the new car at 4.0 a.m. He ran into a shop window. The plate glass was smashed and the car was a complete wreck. The plaintiff put in a claim form, in which he said that the car was £600 in value. That was clearly wrong because the price new was only £547 the year before. The insurance company thereupon got its engineer to look at it. On 12th May 1965 the broker sent a letter to the plaintiff, in which he wrote:

" . . . we have today been advised by [the insurance company] that their engineer considers your vehicle is damaged beyond repair. The engineer considers that the pre-accident market value of the vehicle was £410 and they are therefore prepared to offer you this amount, less the £25 accidental damage excess in settlement of your claim. We should be pleased to receive your confirmation that this is acceptable . . . "

There was no written acceptance, but it was accepted by word of mouth.   That

A seemed to be a concluded agreement whereby the insurance company agreed to pay £385.

But within the next few days the insurance company made further enquiries. One of its representatives saw the plaintiff and took a statement from him. Then the truth was discovered. The plaintiff did not drive at all. He had never had a driving licence, not even a provisional one. He said that the car was never **B** his property but was his son's car: and that it was his son, the younger son, who had driven the car and was the only person who had ever driven it. On discovering those facts, the insurance company stated that it was not liable on the insurance policy. They had been induced to grant it, they said, by the misrepresentations in the original proposal form; and also by reason of non-disclosure of material facts, namely, that the son aged 18 was normally to be the driver.

C The plaintiff brought an action in the county court in which he claimed the £385. He said it was payable under the insurance policy, or, alternatively, on an agreement of compromise contained in the letter of 12th May. The judge rejected the claim on the policy itself, because the insurance was induced by misrepresentation. He found that the insurance company was entitled to repudiate the policy because of the inaccuracy of the plaintiff's answers. That **D** finding was not challenged in this court. Counsel for the plaintiff, admitted that he could not claim on the policy.

But the judge upheld the claim on the letter of 12th May. He said it was a binding contract of compromise. I am not so sure about this. It might be said to be a mere quantification of the account which should be paid in case the insurance company was liable; and that it did not preclude it from afterwards **E** contesting liability. But, on the whole, I do not think that we should regard it as a mere quantification. The letter contains the important words: " in settlement of your claim ", which import that it is to be settled without further controversy. In short, it bears the stamp of an agreement of compromise. The consideration for it was the ascertainment of a sum which was previously unascertained.

F But then comes the next point. Accepting that the agreement to pay £385 was an agreement of compromise, is it vitiated by mistake? The insurance company was clearly under a mistake. It thought that the policy was good and binding. It did not know, at the time of that letter, that there had been misrepresentations in the proposal form. If the plaintiff knew of its mistake—if he knew that the policy was bad—he certainly could not take advantage of the **G** agreement to pay £385. He would be " snapping at an offer which he knew was made under a mistake "; and no man is allowed to get away with that. But I prefer to assume that the plaintiff was innocent. I think we should take it that both parties were under a common mistake. Both parties thought that the policy was good and binding. The letter of 12th May 1965, was written on the assumption that the policy was good whereas it was in truth voidable.

H What is the effect in law of this common mistake? Counsel for the plaintiff said that the agreement to pay £385 was good, despite this common mistake. He relied much on *Bell* v. *Lever Brothers, Ltd.* (1) and its similarity to the present case. He submitted that, inasmuch as the mistake there did not vitiate that contract, the mistake here should not vitiate this one. I do not propose today to go through the speeches in that case. They have given enough trouble to **I** commentators already. I would say simply this: A common mistake, even on a most fundamental matter, does not make a contract void at law; but it makes it voidable in equity. I analysed the cases in *Solle* v. *Butcher* (2), and I would repeat what I said there (3):

" A contract is also liable in equity to be set aside if the parties were under a common misapprehension either as to facts or as to their relative

(1) [1932] A.C. 161; [1931] All E.R. Rep. 11.
(2) [1949] 2 All E.R. 1107; [1950] 1 K.B. 671.
(3) [1949] 2 All E.R. at p. 1120; [1950] 1 K.B. at p. 693.

and respective rights, provided that the misapprehension was fundamental   A
and that the party seeking to set it aside was not himself at fault."

Applying that principle here, it is clear that, when the insurance company and
the plaintiff made this agreement to pay £385, they were both under a common
mistake which was fundamental to the whole agreement.   Both thought that
the plaintiff was entitled to claim under the policy of insurance, whereas he was
not so entitled.   That common mistake does not make the agreement to pay £385   B
a nullity, but it makes it liable to be set aside in equity.

This brings me to a question which has caused me much difficulty.   Is this
a case in which we ought to set the agreement aside in equity?   I have hesitated
on this point, but I cannot shut my eyes to the fact that the plaintiff had no
valid claim on the insurance policy; and, if he had no claim on the policy, it
is not equitable that he should have a good claim on the agreement to pay £385,   C
insurance company to an agreement which it would not have dreamt of making
if it had not been under a mistake.   I would, therefore, allow the appeal and
give judgment for the insurance company.

WINN, L.J.: This appeal has given me pleasure because it has been so
well argued by both the learned counsel who have appeared in it; and, of course,   D
the problem which it presents is not one the solution of which is going to impose
frightful actual loss or consequences on the particular individuals or companies
who are involved.   It is a neat and teasing problem, the difficulty of which is
slightly indicated, though by no means established, by the regrettable circumstance that I find myself respectfully having to dissent from the views of LORD
DENNING, M.R., and of FENTON ATKINSON, L.J.   I agree with LORD DENNING,   E
M.R., that the letter of 12th May 1965, is of very great importance, though I
take the point of counsel for the insurance company that it is not the insurers'
letter; it is only what purports to be a report, probably of a telephone conversation, written by the brokers, who were the agents of the plaintiff of what they
were told by some representative of the insurance company.   I attach importance
to it not because of its terms, which may not be an accurate representation of   F
what the insurers had said, but because it contemplates a complete clearance
of the whole matter and a termination of the dispute arising out of the claim,
insofar as there was any, by return of various documents, which clearly was
regarded as the final, terminal phase of the matter.   Whether or not this could be
regarded, on a strict construction, as no more than an offer to fix a figure, which,
subject to being liable to pay at all, the insurance company was prepared to pay,   G
seems to me to be excluded as a reality by the considerations which I have
mentioned.   This must have evinced an offer by the insurance company to dispose
of the matter by paying £385 in settlement.   As I see the matter, it is not a question of whether thereby a contract was formed, since it seems to me it is clear that
there was a contract formed by that offer from the insurance company and the
acceptance of it again through the brokers by the plaintiff.   The question is   H
whether, as LORD DENNING, M.R., has indicated clearly, that contract is, for
one reason or another, invalid and unenforceable by the plaintiff against the
insurers.

I do not desire to take long in expressing my opinion that on the principles
of *Bell* v. *Lever Brothers, Ltd.* (3) applied to the circumstances of this case the
contrary conclusion to that which LORD DENNING, M.R., has expressed is   I
the correct conclusion.   It appears to me that the parties were under a misapprehension.   If there was any misapprehension shared commonly by both the plaintiff
and the insurance company as to the value of any rights that he had against
it arising from the insurance policy, that seems to me to have been precisely
the subject-matter of the common misapprehension in *Bell* v. *Lever Brothers,
Ltd.* (3).   One could pick out and read, and it would be instructive to re-read them
many times, several passages from the speech of LORD ATKIN and indeed also

(3) [1932] A.C. 161; [1931] All E.R. Rep. 11.

A from that of LORD THANKERTON; but I content myself with the point made by LORD ATKIN, when he said that (4):

B
> "Various words are to be found to define the state of things which make a condition. [i.e., a condition, non-compliance with which, will avoid a contract, and LORD ATKIN instances, quoting them, the phrases] 'In the contemplation of both parties fundamental to the continued validity of the contract', 'a foundation essential to its existence', 'a fundamental reason for making it', ... all of which, as LORD ATKIN said, were to be found in the judgment of SCRUTTON, L.J., in the same case (5) The first two phrases appear to me to be unexceptionable ... But [by contrast, he said] 'a fundamental reason for making a contract' may, with respect, be misleading."

C And LORD ATKIN goes on to give instances of such misleading assertions or misleading definitions of what is meant by a foundation essential to the contract.

For my part, I think that here there was a misapprehension as to rights, but no misapprehension whatsoever as to the subject-matter of the contract, namely, the settlement of the rights of the plaintiff with regard to the accident that happened. The insurance company was settling his rights, if he had any.

D He understood it to be settling his rights; but each of them, on the assumption that the learned county court judge's view of the facts was right, thought his rights against the insurance company were very much more valuable than in fact they were, since in reality they were worthless; the insurance company could have repudiated—or avoided, that being the more accurate phrase on the basis of the mis-statements which my Lord has narrated.

E LORD THANKERTON also said (6):

> "The phrase 'underlying assumption by the parties', as applied to the subject-matter of a contract, may be too widely interpreted so as to include something which one of the parties had not necessarily in his mind at the time of the contract; in my opinion it can only properly relate to something which both must necessarily have accepted in their minds as an essential and
F integral element of the subject-matter."

I venture respectfully to contrast that sentence with any such sentence as this: "which the parties both must necessarily have accepted in their minds as an essential reason, motive, justification or explanation for the making of the contract". In my view the mistake must be a mistake as to the nature or at the very least the quality of the subject-matter and not as to the reason why
G either party desires to deal with the subject-matter as the contract provides that it should be dealt with.

And LORD THANKERTON also said (7):

> "I think that it is true to say that in all [the cases—and he is referring to a number of them] it either appeared on the face of the contract that the matter as to which the mistake existed was an essential and integral element
H of the subject-matter of the contract, or it was an inevitable inference from the nature of the contract that all parties so regarded it."

Since I think there is a most important peripheral implication which might be read into the judgment of this court given today, I want to add only this, that, in my opinion, in a case such as this, there is no rule of law that a warranty, given
I at the inception of a contract of insurance by the terms of the proposal form and its acceptance by the insured, is to be embodied, or tacitly read, into any contract which is made between such a proposer and the insurers, in settlement of a claim which he makes under the contract. I do not even think, so far as I am aware, that there is any authority for the proposition that a warranty,

---

(4) [1932] A.C. at pp. 225, 226; [1931] All E.R. Rep. at p. 31.
(5) [1931] 1 K.B. 557.
(6) [1932] A.C. at p. 235; [1931] All E.R. Rep. at p. 36.
(7) [1932] A.C. at p. 236; [1931] All E.R. Rep. at p. 37.

given in the way I have mentioned, is to be implied indefinitely into renewals   A
of the first contract of insurance which is made of which that warranty is an
express term as a condition precedent to liability. In every case it must depend
on the length of time elapsed, the probability of changes of circumstances, the
practicability of adjusting some ages by the addition of a year or more perhaps,
and many other considerations, such, for example, as the improbability that the
proposer who has called himself the holder of a provisional licence will continue   B
to be either a holder of a provisional licence or a holder of any licence at all
indefinitely. He is likely to have been dealt with by the magistrates in one way
or another in the time which has elapsed.

For the reasons which I have endeavoured to state quite briefly—though I
think there are many other considerations which are relevant to this interesting
problem—I find myself, respectfully and diffidently, unable to agree with the   C
judgment of LORD DENNING, M.R.

FENTON ATKINSON, L.J., Before hearing my Lords' judgments I had
been inclined to the view that the letter of 12th May 1965, was not an offer to
enter into a contract independent of the policy, but merely an offer of quantification of a claim made under a policy, both parties at that stage believing that   D
there was a valid policy under which the insurers could have no answer to a claim.
On reflection, I agree that that is an incorrect approach to the case, and I go
on to consider the question of mistake, and on that issue I agree with the judgment of LORD DENNING, M.R. It does seem to me that the basic assumption
of both parties at the time of the agreement relied on was that there was a valid
enforceable claim under the policy. In fact, counsel for the plaintiff does not   E
seek here to challenge the finding of the learned county court judge that the
insurance company was entitled to repudiate any liability under that policy
by reason of the untrue and incorrect statements made in the proposal form in
1961; and, applying in this case the proposition which was accepted by all of
their Lordships in *Bell* v. *Lever Brothers, Ltd.* (8) set out in para. 207 of CHITTY
ON CONTRACTS, vol. 1 (23rd Edn.), in these terms: F

" Whenever it is to be inferred from the terms of a contract or its surrounding circumstances that the *consensus* has been reached upon the basis
of a particular contractual assumption, and that assumption is not true,
the contract is avoided. [And to that has to be added the additional rider]
... the assumption must have been fundamental to the continued validity
of the contract, or a foundation essential to its existence."   G

Applying the rule there laid down to the facts of this case, I think it is clear
that when the agreement relied on by the plaintiff was made it was made on the
basis of a particular and essential contractual assumption, namely, that there
was in existence a valid and enforceable policy of insurance, and that assumption
was not true. In my view it is the right and equitable result of this case that
the insurance company should be entitled to avoid that agreement on the ground   H
of mutual mistake in a fundamental and vital matter. I agree that this appeal
should succeed on that ground.

                Appeal allowed. Leave to appeal to the House of Lords refused.

Solicitors: *Stevensons* agents for *Geoffrey Warhurst & Co.*, Manchester (for the
defendant insurance company); *Simpson, Silvertown & Co.*, agents for *Betesh,*   I
Singer & Co., Manchester (for the plaintiff).

                [*Reported by* JENIFER SANDELL, *Barrister-at-Law.*]

---

(8) [1932] A.C. 161; [1931] All E.R. Rep. 11.

A   the practice in Birmingham, were deductible in computing its profits for income tax purposes.   The Special Commissioners of Income Tax held, on authority, that no deduction could be made for licensing removals for " poor trade " houses or for upgrading purposes or for removals outside Birmingham which were designed to increase trade through new houses, as being in the nature of an investment going to capital, but that a deduction should be

B   allowed for other removals in Birmingham designed to preserve existing but threatened trade which were payments on revenue account,

Held: no deduction should be made in respect of the expenditure on new licences in Birmingham because, if, as decided by authority, the transfer of a licence from one old house to one new house in order to improve one's trade was a capital expense, it would not become a revenue expense merely

C   because it was one of a long series which the brewery was obliged to make over the years without any expectation of increased trade resulting, and the costs of obtaining a licence, or of " marrying " existing suspended licences to bricks and mortar, could not be distinguished from the costs of the bricks and mortar themselves (see p. 935, letter G, and p. 936, letter A, post).

Morse v. *Stedeford* ((1934) 18 Tax Cas. 457) applied.

D   Appeal allowed.

[As to capital expenditure not deductible in computing profits for income tax purposes, see 20 HALSBURY'S LAWS (3rd Edn.) 162-164, para. 281;   and for cases on the subject see 28 DIGEST (Repl.) 115-124, *431-480.*

As to items not deductible in computing the profits of breweries for income tax purposes, see 20 HALSBURY'S LAWS (3rd Edn.) 197, 198, para. 348;   and for

E   cases on the subject, see 28 DIGEST (Repl.) 76-80, *287-304.*

For the Income Tax Act 1952, s. 137, see 31 HALSBURY'S STATUTES (2nd Edn.) 134.]

Cases referred to:

Bolam (*Inspector of Taxes*) v. *Regent Oil Co., Ltd.* (1956), 37 Tax Cas. 56;

F   28 Digest (Repl.) 124, *479.*

B. P. Australia, Ltd. v. *Comr. of Taxation of the Commonwealth of Australia,* [1965] 3 All E.R. 209; [1966] A.C. 224; [1965] 3 W.L.R. 608; Digest (Cont. Vol. B) 404, **345a.*

Morse v. *Stedeford* (1934), 18 Tax Cas. 457; 28 Digest (Repl.) 78, *297.*

Southwell v. *Savill Brothers, Ltd.,* [1901] 2 K.B. 349; 70 L.J.K.B. 815; 85 L.T.

G   167; 65 J.P. 649; 4 Tax Cas. 430; 28 Digest (Repl.) 78, *295.*

Case Stated.

The taxpayer company appealed to the Special Commissioners of Income Tax against the following assessments to income tax made on it under Sch. D to the Income Tax Act 1952: 1959-60 £2,100,000 less £200,000 capital allowances; 1960-61 £2,100,000 less £200,000 capital allowances; and 1961-62 £2,700,000

H   less £200,000 capital allowances.   The question for determination was whether certain legal costs were deductible in computing the amount of the taxpayer company's profits or gains.   The expenses involved were those incurred by the taxpayer company in connection with obtaining licences for new licensed premises*.   The Crown contended as follows: (a) that, although the expenditure was for the purpose of the taxpayer company's business, it was capital expen-

I   diture; (b) that the expenditure was not to preserve assets, but was part of the cost of establishing new assets, as in *Morse* v. *Stedeford†*; (c) that the barrelage formula used by Birmingham licensing planning committee was no more than a measuring device to keep the trade within limits; and (d) that a licence was not to be regarded as an asset separately from licensed premises. The taxpayer company contended as follows: (a) that the sums in question were

---

* The facts of the case are set out at p. 930, letters H and I, and p. 932, letter B, to p. 933, letter F, post.

† (1934), 18 Tax Cas. 457.   Applied in ECC QUARRIES v WATKIS
                                              [1975] 3 All ER 843

wholly and exclusively laid out for the purpose of the taxpayer company's A
business; (b) that none of such sums were excluded under s. 137 (f) of the Income
Tax Act 1952 as being sums laid out as capital; (c) that the removal of licences
had, since 1945 at least, become a necessary and continuing incidence in the carrying on and maintenance of the taxpayer company's business; (d) that in the case
of all removals and in particular in the majority of cases which were forced
removals, the removal had become essential in order to preserve existing goodwill B
and existing outlets; (e) that in particular, since the Licensing Act 1953, the
licences owned by the taxpayer company had become an important asset of its
business separate from the houses to which from time to time they related;
(f) that the expenditure on the removal of licences was an expenditure of an annual
and recurring nature not bringing into existence any capital asset of an enduring
nature; (g) that in the case of licensed premises in the Birmingham area, the C
removal was in reality a transfer of barrelage, and that the grant of a licence
represented the formal action sanctioning the transfer; and (h) that in each case
on the facts established the expenditure was laid out for the purpose of the taxpayer company's trade to preserve its assets and not as part of the cost of new
assets or of improving its existing assets, and therefore was deductible.

The commissioners held* that legal costs incurred in relation to one group D
of licensing removals in Birmingham, the reason for which was not to put the
taxpayer company in a position to begin or increase trade in a new house but
to enable it to preserve or try to preserve its existing and threatened trade,
were payments on revenue account, but that the other legal costs were on capital
account. They therefore allowed the appeal to that extent. The Crown appealed
by way of Case Stated to the High Court. E

J. R. Phillips, Q.C., and P. W. Medd for the Crown.
Hubert H. Monroe, Q.C., G. A. Grove and D. A. Shirley for the taxpayer
company.

Cur. adv. vult.

18th December. **CROSS, J.:** The question raised by this case is whether F
certain legal costs incurred by the taxpayer company, Mitchells & Butlers, Ltd.,
were deductible in computing its profits for the tax years 1959-60, 1960-61
and 1961-62. The taxpayer company, which carries on the business of brewers
and retailers of beer, owns a large number of fully licensed and off-licensed
premises, including about half the licensed premises in Birmingham. Most of
these premises are not let to tenants but are run by managers. Since the war G
the taxpayer company's business in Birmingham has been affected by several
planning schemes which are referred to in para. 5 (c) of the Case, which I will
read.

" . . . (i) The five central areas coloured green on the plan, containing war
damaged properties and/or obsolete lay-out, were subject to the Birmingham
(Central Re-Development) Compulsory Purchase Order, 1946. In respect H
of these areas . . . there was an Agreement dated 22nd November, 1946,
and made between (I) The Birmingham Corporation and (II) the [taxpayer
company] whereby (inter alia) the [taxpayer company] was to be permitted
to trade until premises were demolished or licences removed . . . (ii) The
roads coloured brown on the plan were subject to the Birmingham Corporation Act, 1946, Section 14 of which gave (inter alia) the [taxpayer
company] protection in these areas . . . similar to that given by the said Agree- I
ment dated 22nd November, 1946 . . . (iii) From time to time, road improvement schemes were made in various areas. (iv) Around the said central areas,
there are some ten further re-development areas . . . in which re-development
is expected to be undertaken during the period 1970-1990."

---

* The terms of the commissioners' decision are set out at p. 934, letter D, to p. 935,
letter C, post.

A   Birmingham is a licensing planning area under the Licensing Act 1953, to some of the provisions of which I must refer. Section 53 defines licensing planning areas and s. 54 sets up licensing planning committees. Section 56 (1) sets out the duties of committees as follows:

B   " It shall be the duty of every licensing planning committee to review the circumstances of their area and to try to secure, after such consultation and negotiation as they may think desirable, and by the exercise of the powers conferred on them by this Part of this Act, that the number, nature and distribution of the licensed premises in the area, the accommodation provided in them and the facilities given in them for obtaining food, accord with local requirements, regard being had in particular to any redevelopment or proposed redevelopment of the area."

C   Section 57 states how the committee is to carry out its duties:

" (1) The licensing planning committee for any area may from time to time —(a) formulate proposals for the removal, subject to and in accordance with the provisions of this Part of this Act relating to removals, and subject to such conditions, if any, as the proposals may specify, of justices' licences

D   from premises in the area to other premises in the area specified in the proposals or to premises on sites in the area so specified, (b) formulate with the agreement of the persons interested in the premises in question proposals for the surrender, subject to such conditions, if any, as the proposals may specify, of existing justices' licences for premises in the area, not being licences in suspense under this Act, and (c) formulate with the agreement

E   of the persons interested in the premises in question proposals for the extinguishment of existing justices' licences for premises in the area which are in suspense under this Act, and shall submit any such proposals to the Minister, together with such plans and other matter explanatory of the nature and effect of the proposals as may be prescribed or as the Minister may in any particular case require.

F   " (2) A removal such as is mentioned in paragraph (a) of the preceding subsection is in this Act referred to as a ' planning removal '.

" (3) Where a licensing planning committee have submitted proposals to the Minister under this section, the committee shall publish in the prescribed manner a notice that they have submitted the proposals, naming a place at which copies of the proposals and of the plans and explanatory matter

G   submitted to the Minister may be seen at all reasonable hours, and stating the time within which and the manner in which objections to the proposals may be made to the Minister.

" (4) If no objection to the proposals is made to the Minister within the time and in the manner stated in the notice, or if all objections so made are withdrawn, the Minister may confirm the proposals with or without modification;

H   but, if objection is so made and not withdrawn, he shall afford to any person making an objection an opportunity of appearing before and being heard by a person appointed for the purpose by the Minister or, if it appears to the Minister that the matters to which the objection relates are such as to require investigation by public local inquiry, he shall cause a public local inquiry to be held;   and after considering any objection not withdrawn

I   and the report of the person before whom the objector appeared or of the person holding the inquiry, as the case may be, he may confirm the proposals with or without modification."

Section 58 (1) dealing with removals is in the following terms:

" No ordinary or special removal of a justices' licence shall be granted to any premises in a licensing planning area unless the premises are licensed premises and the licensing justices are satisfied that the licensing planning committee have no objection to the removal."

Finally s. 59 (1) provides: A

" No new justices' licences shall be granted for any premises in a licensing
planning area unless the licensing justices are satisfied that the licensing
planning committee have no objection to the grant."

I will now go on reading the facts set out in para. 5 of the Case:

" (d) In carrying out its duties, the Licensing Planning Committee for   B
Birmingham (hereinafter called ' the Committee ') was required, under
Section 56 of the Licensing Act, 1953, to have regard to any re-development
or proposed re-development of its area. In 1955, the Committee estimated
that as a result of re-development the number of sites available for licensed
premises would be considerably decreased. The Committee also estimated
that the population of Birmingham would remain the same during the   C
periods of re-development, and that the potential consumption of intoxicating
liquor would remain the same. In order to provide a fair re-distribution of
licences and to avoid unnecessary payment of compensation on compulsory
acquisition, the Committee instituted ' equation of barrelage '. (e) The equation of barrelage in Birmingham operated as follows. In the case of a licence
which went into suspense because the premises in question had suffered war   D
damage or had been compulsorily purchased, there was calculated the average
annual converted barrelage of those premises over a period of three years. This
figure represented the total trade of the premises in terms of barrels of beer,
there being a formula for converting the sale of wines and spirits. The period
was one of three years prior to 14th August, 1947, or the last three years
of trading before that date (for example, three years prior to cessation on   E
account of war damage) in respect of premises in the five re-development
areas; or the last three years of trading before date of notice to treat, on
compulsory acquisition in respect of premises in the inner ring road area
or elsewhere. Licences in suspense went into a ' bank ' or account which
was kept by the Birmingham Corporation and which recorded the barrelage
of the old premises. The licence of premises which were compulsorily acquired   F
went into suspense, except in the rare case where new premises were immediately available. The practice was to take licences in suspense out of the
' bank ' in the order in which they had been put in, so that it was fortuitous
which licences would be used in any locality. (f) In Birmingham, application for a licence for new premises was in the case of a full licence almost
invariably by way of planning removal under Sections 56 and 57 of the   G
Licensing Act, 1953, rarely by way of new licence under section 58 of the
said Act. Procedure was as follows: (i) The barrelage of the proposed new
premises was first agreed between the [taxpayer company] and the
Birmingham Corporation and their respective valuers. The [taxpayer com-
pany] then agreed to surrender the equivalent barrelage in respect of licences
in suspense. If the [taxpayer company's] account with the ' bank ' was not   H
sufficiently in ' credit ', further licences would be surrendered as necessary.
(ii) Having agreed the barrelage, the [taxpayer company] then applied
to the Committee with a request that the Committee should formulate
a proposal for a planning removal or for a certificate of no objection. This
was considered at a meeting at which objectors were entitled to be present
and to be heard. If the Committee decided to formulate proposals, the   I
proposals were publicised, and submitted to the Minister of Housing and
Local Government. (iii) If there were objections to the proposals, the said
Minister might order a public local enquiry, so that in some cases there could
be two full scale hearings. (iv) If the said Minister confirmed the proposals
(with or without modification), the final step was an application to the
licensing justices, who were only concerned with the structural suitability
of the new premises and the fitness of the proposed licence. (g) Outside
Birmingham and other licensing planning areas the procedure for licensing

A   new premises was by way of application to the licensing justices, with appeal
to the confirming authority by way of re-hearing. If there were opposition
to the [taxpayer company's] application, it would be desirable for the
[taxpayer company] to brief Counsel for both hearings. Coventry was also
a licensing planning area, but the policy in that City was not to operate
such a strict equation of barrelage as in Birmingham. (h) The expenses
B   incurred by these hearings depended on the volume of objections. Hearings
were normally conducted by the [taxpayer company's] Solicitors, but if there
was considerable opposition, Counsel, and occasionally leading Counsel,
were briefed. Much work was involved in giving notices under a procedure
which had to be meticulously followed. Architects and surveyors were
involved in all cases. The legal costs which are the subject of this appeal
C   are set out in the Analyses exhibited to this Case and marked ' D ' (1958),
' E ' (1959) and ' F ' (1960).   (j) During the years under appeal, the [taxpayer
company] was only able to extend its business by the acquisition of subsidiaries or by obtaining licensed premises outside Birmingham.   In
Birmingham the [taxpayer company] was struggling to maintain or replace
the barrelage of premises which had been compulsorily acquired or were
D   subject to compulsory acquisition. In 1950, the [taxpayer company's]
group owned 53 % of the on licences and 32 % of the off licences in Birmingham. In 1964, the comparable percentages were 47·6 and 33·8 respectively.
In the re-development of Birmingham, it was estimated that 596 licences
were likely to be disturbed, and that after re-distribution, there would be
a surplus of 159 licences of which approximately half would belong to the
E   [taxpayer company]. Licensed premises were constantly being compulsorily
acquired and their licences being placed in suspense in the ' bank ' at a greater
rate than the [taxpayer company] was able to use them. This process was
likely to continue until the end of the century, with the result that the
[taxpayer company] would have fewer licensed premises, with larger
individual trade but collectively no increased barrelage."

F   In submitting that all the legal costs in question were capital and not revenue
costs, the Crown relied particularly on the cases of *Southwell* v. *Savill Brothers,
Ltd.* (1), and *Morse* v. *Stedeford* (2), and as the commissioners discuss the effect
of these cases in their decision it will be convenient to refer to them now. In
Southwell v. *Savill Brothers, Ltd.* (1), the respondents who were brewers had
incurred costs and expenses in connection with applications made to licensing
G   justices for the grant of new licences, some of which were successful and some
unsuccessful. They treated the costs of the successful applications as additions
to the capital cost of the new house but the claimants treated the costs of the
unsuccessful applications as revenue expenses.   The General Commissioners
accepted this contention but the Divisional Court held that both sets of expenditure were in the nature of capital investments and the fact that the money
H   invested in the unsuccessful applications was lost did not justify its being treated
as a revenue expense.

In *Morse* v. *Stedeford* (2) the headnote states the essential facts as follows:

" The appellant, who carried on the business of brewer and owned a number
of licensed premises let to tied tenants, applied to the licensing justices
for the removal of an existing licence to a new house to be erected, on the
I   terms that a licence at another inn should at the same time be surrendered.
In due course the removal was effected in the manner approved by the justices. Neither of the outgoing tenants of the two inns, the licences of which
were thus withdrawn, became the tenant of the new inn, and certain sums
were paid to them in 1931 as compensation in order to secure their consent
to the application to the licensing justices. On appeal against assessments

(1) [1901] 2 K.B. 349; 4 Tax Cas. 430.
(2) (1934), 18 Tax Cas. 457.

to income tax under Schedule D for the years 1931-32 and 1932-33, the
appellant contended that the legal expenses incurred in connection with the
applications to the licensing justices and the sums paid to the outgoing
tenants as compensation were admissible deductions in computing the
amount of his profits assessable under Schedule D.''

As the headnote says, the appellant argued before the commissioners that the
expenses of securing the removal of a licence from one house to another stood on
a different footing from the expenses of securing a new licence, since the removed
licence was not a new asset, but the General Commissioners held that *Southwell*
v. *Savill Brothers, Ltd.* (3), applied and their decision was upheld by FINLAY, J.

The commissioners in this case after stating that the question for their
determination was whether the legal costs incurred by the taxpayer company
in obtaining the removals of licences referred to in the exhibits were payments
made on capital or revenue account, continued as follows:

" The Crown relied on *Morse* v. *Stedeford* (4) applying the principle in
Southwell v. *Savill Brothers, Ltd.* (3). The [taxpayer company] sought to
distinguish *Morse* v. *Stedeford* (4) and relied on *Bolam (Inspector of Taxes)*
v. *Regent Oil Co., Ltd.* (5). The [taxpayer company] contended that by reason
of their particular circumstances, and especially the licensing practice in
Birmingham, the expenditure was wholly and exclusively for the preservation of their trade and goodwill, and did not bring into existence any capital
asset or asset of an enduring nature. In order to determine whether or to
what extent this question is governed by the decision in *Morse* v. *Stedeford*
(4) we must ascertain what that decision was and examine carefully the
salient facts in this case. In our view the decision in *Morse* v. *Stedeford* (4)
was that the nature of licensing expenses in connection with a new house
did not depend on whether the licence was new or transferred, and that
the principle in *Southwell* v. *Savill Brothers, Ltd.* (3) applied. See judgment
of FINLAY, J. (6). *Southwell* v. *Savill Brothers, Ltd.* (3) decided that legal
costs and other expenses in connection with unsuccessful applications for
new licences (in a district where the licensing justices usually required surrender of an old licence before grant of a new one) were capital expenses. The
Stated Cases in *Morse* v. *Stedeford* (4) and *Southwell* v. *Savill Brothers, Ltd.*
(3), did not go into the reasons for the applications, apart from mentioning
(in *Morse* v. *Stedeford* (4)) the possibility of danger from sea encroachment
and anticipation of building development in the district, and (in *Southwell*
v. *Savill Brothers, Ltd.* (3)) the purpose of maintaining and if possible
increasing trade. In *Southwell* v. *Savill Brothers, Ltd.* (3) the Divisional
Court held that the expenditure should be treated as an investment which
went to capital. In the present case the applications fell into three groups;
(i) There were the licensing removals either from houses where there was
' poor trade ' (see Documents 1, 2 and 3), or to houses which were ' upgraded '
(see Document 12). The reasons for these removals, we find, were to increase
trade through new houses, and expenditure thereon, it seems to us, was in
the nature of an investment which went to capital. (ii) There were the
majority of licensing removals in Birmingham, excluding those falling within
group (i) above. The reason for these, we find, was not to put the [taxpayer
company] in a position to begin or increase trade in a new house, but to enable
it to preserve, or to try to preserve, its existing but threatened trade.
The result of licensing planning procedure in Birmingham based on a strict
equation of barrelage, has been, for the [taxpayer company], fewer houses,
with larger trade individually, but not collectively. Indeed, on the evidence

(3) [1901] 2 K.B. 349; 4 Tax Cas. 430.
(4) (1934), 18 Tax Cas. 457.
(5) (1956), 37 Tax Cas. 56.
(6) (1934), 18 Tax Cas. at p. 463.

A   the total trade, having regard to the probable circumstances, is likely to decline overall. To our minds expenditure on these removals was not in the nature of an investment which went to capital. (iii) Finally there was the majority of licensing removals outside Birmingham, including those in Coventry where equation of Barrelage is not applied so strictly. There was no evidence before us that as a result of these removals there were consider-

B   ably fewer houses, or that their trade was collectively no larger, or likely to decline. The reasons for these removals, we find, were to increase trade through new houses, and in our view expenditure thereon was in the nature of an investment which went to capital. We accordingly hold that the legal costs incurred in respect of licensing removals in group (ii) above were payments on revenue account, and those incurred in respect of groups

C   (i) and (iii) above were on capital account. To the extent that the appeal succeeds on this question we leave figures to be agreed between the parties.''

The parties had no difficulty in agreeing the figures on the basis of this decision but the Crown was dissatisfied with the principle adopted by the Special Commissioners and asked them to state a Case. The commissioners as I read their decision held that, while the decisions in *Southwell* v. *Savill Brothers, Ltd.*

D   (7), and *Morse* v. *Stedeford* (8) showed that prima facie expenses incurred in licensing a new house, even though the licence was transferred, were capital expenses, yet there was nothing in them to preclude a finding in any particular case that the reasons for the closing of the old house from which the licence was transferred showed that the legal costs involved ought to rank as revenue expenses. On this footing they drew a distinction between cases in which the

E   taxpayer company was hoping to increase trade in the new house and cases in which the taxpayer company was trying at most to preserve the previous volume of trade without any hope of an increased trade.

The Crown submitted first that there was nothing in the cases cited which justified such a distinction, and secondly that viewing the matter apart from authority the distinction was inherently irrational. The taxpayer company

F   was forced to acquire new licensed premises. For that purpose it had both to build premises and also to provide them with a licence. There was no ground for drawing a distinction between the costs of the bricks and mortar and the costs of obtaining a licence, or in this case the costs of " marrying " existing suspended licences to the bricks and mortar. The fact that the taxpayer company was forced to discontinue trade at the old premises and did not expect to do more at

G   best than to maintain the same volume of trade at the new premises was quite irrelevant.

Counsel for the taxpayer company submitted that in the light of the recent Privy Council decision of *B.P. Australia, Ltd.* v. *Comr. of Taxation of the Commonwealth of Australia* (9) the whole question of the position of expenditure on the acquisition or transfer of licences ought to be reviewed on the basis that a licence

H   was analogous to a tie. But accepting that in this court at least such expenditure was normally to be regarded as capital expenditure, he submitted that in this case the commissioners were amply justified in drawing the distinction which they had drawn. In Birmingham the taxpayer company found itself after the war faced with a crisis. Year by year over a long period which was very far from over yet, it was, and would continue to be, necessary for it to spend money

I   in re-arranging its stock of licences so as to maintain its sales. Even if expenditure on acquiring a new licence for a new house which it was hoped would increase the taxpayer company's total volume of trade must be regarded as capital expenditure, the expenditure referred to under group head (ii) in the commissioners' decision was essentially operating expenditure.

---

(7) [1901] 2 K.B. 349; 4 Tax Cas. 430.
(8) (1934), 18 Tax Cas. 457.
(9) [1965] 3 All E.R. 209; [1966] A.C. 224.

A

Of these contentions I prefer that of the Crown. Even if the decision of the Special Commissioners is not inconsistent with *Morse* v. *Stedeford* (10)—and I incline to think that it is—I cannot see any justification in principle for the distinction which it draws between group (ii) and groups (i) and (iii). If once one accepts that money expended in getting a licence transferred from one old house to one new house, where one hopes thereby to improve one's trade, is a capital expense I cannot see why the fact that the transfer is one of a long series of transfers which one will be obliged to make over a number of years and that in all such cases there is not or probably will not be any expectation of increased trade, should convert the expense into a revenue expense. Therefore I shall allow the appeal.

B

Appeal allowed.

Solicitors: *Solicitor of Inland Revenue*; *Evershed & Tomkinson*, Birmingham (for the taxpayer company).

C

[*Reported by* F. A. AMIES, ESQ., *Barrister-at-Law.*]

D

DEMAG INDUSTRIAL EQUIPMENT, LTD. *v.* CANADA DRY (U.K.), LTD.

[CHANCERY DIVISION (Pennycuick, J.), April 30, 1969.]

Costs—Landlord and tenant—Notice to terminate under Landlord and Tenant Act 1954—Summons issued for grant of new lease—Lessor changing mind and not objecting to new tenancy—Whether lessee entitled to costs.

E

In March 1964, the defendant company, the lessee for a term of four years of the whole floor of a building, granted an underlease to the plaintiff company of half the floor for the same term less one day. Both lease and underlease bore the same date. In March 1967 the defendant company gave the plaintiff company notice under the Landlord and Tenant Act 1954 to terminate the tenancy in March 1968, and noted that any application to the court for a new tenancy would be opposed on the ground that it intended to occupy the premises itself. The plaintiff company notified the defendant company that it was not willing to give up possession at the date of termination, and in July 1967 it issued an originating summons for the grant by the court of a new tenancy under the Landlord and Tenant Act 1954. In August 1967 the defendant company, having decided to move from the premises altogether, by its solicitors informed the plaintiff company that it had withdrawn its opposition to the grant of a new lease and left the plaintiff company to negotiate with the headlessor directly. On a summons for an order staying all further proceedings (which was not contested) and an order that the defendant company pay the costs of and occasioned by the proceedings,

F

G

H

Held: the defendant company should bear the costs of the proceedings because the summons was rendered necessary by its conduct in first refusing to grant a new tenancy, and its subsequent withdrawal of opposition had meant that the expenses incurred by the plaintiff company in the institution of proceedings had been entirely thrown away (see p. 940, letter D, post).

I

Willis v. *Association of Universities of the British Commonwealth* (*No. 2*) ([1965] 2 All E.R. 393); *Gold* v. *Brighton Corpn.* ([1956] 3 All E.R. 442); and *Le Witt* v. *Cannon Brookes* ([1956] 3 All E.R. 676) distinguished.

[As to costs in applications for new tenancies under the Landlord and Tenant Act 1954, see 23 HALSBURY'S LAWS (3rd Edn.) 895, 896, para. 1720; and for cases on the subject see DIGEST (Cont. Vol. A) 1048, 1049, *7417la-7417ma.*]

(10) (1934), 18 Tax Cas. 457.

A   Cases referred to:

Gold v. *Brighton Corpn.*, [1956] 3 All E.R. 442; [1956] 1 W.L.R. 1291; Digest (Cont. Vol. A.) 1049, *7417ma.*

Harewood Hotels, Ltd. v. *Harris*, [1958] 1 All E.R. 104; [1958] 1 W.L.R. 108; Digest (Cont. Vol. A) 1048, *7417la.*

Le Witt v. *Cannon Brookes*, [1956] 3 All E.R. 676; [1956] 1 W.L.R. 1438;
B   Digest (Cont. Vol. A) 1062, *7417u.*

Willis v. *Association of Universities of the British Commonwealth (No. 2)*, [1965] 2 All E.R. 393; [1965] 1 W.L.R. 836; Digest (Cont. Vol. B) 484, *7417ua.*

Procedure Summons.

This was a summons by the plaintiff company, Demag Industrial Equipment,
C   Ltd., for an order staying all further proceedings in the summons issued by it on 26th July 1967, for a new tenancy of part of the third floor of premises known as Turriff Building, Great West Road, Brentford, and an order that the defendant company, Canada Dry (U.K.), Ltd., pay the costs of and occasioned by those proceedings. It was agreed that the summons ought to be stayed. The facts are set out in the judgment.

D
    M. A. Lyndon-Stanford for the plaintiff company.

    A. F. B. Scrivener for the defendant company.

PENNYCUICK, J.: I have before me a summons in certain proceedings intituled " IN THE MATTER of premises known as the offices and rooms forming part of the third floor of and fronting part of the building known as Turriff
E   Building Great West Road Brentford in the Greater London Area " and " IN THE MATTER of the Landlord and Tenant Act 1954 ", between Demag Industrial Equipment, Ltd., the plaintiff company, and Canada Dry (U.K.), Ltd., the defendant company. In those proceedings the plaintiff company prayed against the defendant company—

F   " 1. An order for the grant by the . . . Defendant to the Plaintiff pursuant to the Landlord and Tenant Act 1954 of a new tenancy of the undermentioned premises for the period and at the rent and upon the terms hereinafter mentioned or alternatively for such period and at such rent and upon such terms as the Court may determine. 2. Such further or other relief . . . 3. Costs."

G   That summons is dated 26th July 1967.

In the events which have happened, to which I will refer in a moment, the summons has become entirely abortive and on the present summons the plaintiff company seeks an order that all further proceedings be stayed and an order that the defendant company pays the costs of and occasioned by the proceedings. There is no question that further proceedings should be stayed; there is nothing
H   further to litigate about. The whole issue before me relates to the costs of the proceedings.

The circumstances in which the present question has arisen are as follows. On 13th March 1964, Turriff Construction Corpn., Ltd., to which I will refer as Turriff, granted to the defendant company a lease for a term of four years from 13th March 1964, of the whole of the third floor in a large building known
I   as Turriff Building, Brentford. The defendant company granted to the plaintiff company an underlease, bearing the same date, for a term of four years less one day, of the western half of the same third floor. It will be seen that the headlease of the third floor and the underlease of the western half of the third floor expired on 13th March and the 12th March 1968 respectively. I should mention that the defendant company itself continued throughout the term to occupy the eastern half of the third floor. In each case the tenancy was a business tenancy.

On 31st March 1967, the defendant company gave to the plaintiff company a statutory notice under the Landlord and Tenant Act 1954, to terminate its

tenancy of the western half of the third floor on 12th March 1968. The notice   **A**
contained the usual provisions:

> " You are required within two months after receiving this Notice to notify
> me in writing whether or not you will be willing to give up possession of the
> premises on that date. [Then this] We would oppose an application to
> the court under Part II of the Act for the grant of a new tenancy on the   **B**
> ground that on the termination of the current tenancy we intend to occupy
> the premises for the purposes of a business to be carried on by us in them."

On 7th April the plaintiff company notified the defendant company that it
would not be willing to give up possession at the date of termination. As I have
said, the present originating summons was issued on 26th July, so at the date
when the originating summons was issued the defendant company was refusing   **C**
the grant of a new underlease on the ground that it intended to occupy the
premises for its own business. It will be borne in mind that the defendant
company was itself an underlessee and the notice presupposes that the defendant
company would have applied for and obtained a new headlease of the whole
area of the third floor. Then it would have continued to occupy the whole of
the third floor for the purposes of its own business.   **D**

On 1st August, that is shortly after the date of the summons, the defendant
company's solicitors notified the plaintiff company's solicitors that the defendant
company could not agree to an extension of the plaintiff company's tenancy,
again for the reason that the premises were needed by the defendant company for
its own business. Very soon after, the defendant company underwent a complete
change of mind. That is set out in the defendant company's secretary's affidavit   **E**
in these terms:

> " During the week following the 1st August 1967 the [defendant company]
> appreciated that the effect of the Bass-Charrington merger was such that the
> whole of the space on the third floor of the Turriff Building was insufficient
> for the purposes of the [defendant company], and that it would be better   **F**
> to remove the whole of their office to a site where there was more
> accommodation."

In those circumstances the defendant company's solicitors notified the plaintiff
company's solicitors that the defendant company withdrew its opposition to
the grant of a new tenancy leaving the plaintiff company to make its own terms
with Turriff. In fact the plaintiff company has come to terms with Turriff and   **G**
has obtained a new lease.

In those circumstances the originating summons has become entirely abortive
because there is no longer any opposition to the grant of a new tenancy. It goes
beyond that, because the defendant company has itself not applied for the grant
of a new headlease and it would not be in a position to grant a new underlease.   **H**
That being the position, there is no doubt that the proceedings under the originating summons, apart from costs, are dead. The only question is as to costs.
Unless there is something more to it, I should have thought it reasonably clear
that the plaintiff company is entitled to costs.

The summons was rendered necessary because the defendant company refused
to grant a new tenancy on a certain ground. After the summons had been issued   **I**
the defendant company changed its mind, withdrew its opposition to the grant
of a new tenancy and itself gave up the premises of which it was underlessee.
No one suggests that the plaintiff company was in any way to blame for starting
the proceedings. In those circumstances the proceedings were occasioned
entirely by the conduct of the defendant company in setting up a ground of
opposition and then withdrawing after the summons had been issued.

Unless, then, there is any authority which drives me to a different conclusion
I should have no hesitation in concluding that the defendant company should

A   be ordered to pay the costs of the plaintiff company of this originating summons. I was, however, referred to a series of cases relating to the costs of proceedings normally, I think, in the county court, where a tenant has applied
for a new tenancy, the landlord has opposed it, and the court has granted a new
tenancy but not wholly on the same terms as sought by the tenant. In *Gold*
v. *Brighton Corpn.* (1) and again in *Le Witt* v. *Cannon Brookes* (2) the county
B   court judge made an order for costs. In each case the unsuccessful party had to
pay half the other party's costs and in each case the Court of Appeal reversed
the order as to costs, holding that in such circumstances it was appropriate
that there should be no order for costs. In the *Gold* case (3) DENNING, L.J.,
said:

C   " A question arose as to costs. The judge ordered the tenant to pay one-
half of the landlords' costs. I do not think that was right. Both parties
negotiated for a new lease and they could not come to terms. It had to be
referred to the judge on the amount of rent and other terms. He struck a
middle course. I see no reason why the tenant should have to pay any part
of the landlords' costs."

D   In the *Le Witt* case (4) DENNING, L.J., gave a similar reason. He said:

" So also in this case both sides put forward figures which were fairly wide
of the mark. They may perhaps have been bargaining figures. At all events,
the judge took a middle course and I think in this case, as in *Gold* v. *Brighton
Corpn.* (1), there should be no costs on either side in the court below."

HODSON, L.J., pointed out (5) that there is no hard and fast rule to be laid down.
E   So in those cases the reason for reversing the order of the county court judge on
costs was that one party had been only partly successful.

The next case was *Harewood Hotels, Ltd.* v. *Harris* (6). In that case the
Le Witt case (2) was distinguished and the Court of Appeal upheld the county
court judge's decision that the landlord should pay half the tenant's costs.
Finally there is *Willis* v. *Association of Universities of the British Commonwealth*
F   *(No.* 2) (7) which was relied on on behalf of the defendant company. In that case
the history of the matter is somewhat complicated. It appears sufficiently in
the headnote which I will take as read. As appears from the judgment, an order
for costs made by the Court of Appeal was per incuriam. LORD DENNING, M.R.,
said (8):

G   " It appears that in the ordinary way, in these landlord and tenant
cases, the practice in the county court is to leave each side to bear its own
costs. That is stated in the COUNTY COURT PRACTICE, 1965, at p. 780.
This practice is well founded. For, if you read through the Landlord and
Tenant Act, 1954, it is clear that the landlord, if he wants to resist an
application for a new lease, has to establish his grounds to the satisfaction
of *the court.* (See s. 31 (1).) If he does establish one of the grounds in s. 30
H   (1) *(e), (f)* and *(g),* then the tenant has to be *at the court* so as to get a certificate
under s. 37 (4) which will enable him to get compensation. So both parties
have necessarily to come to the court in these cases. In consequence, so long
as it is a genuine bona fide dispute, neither side does anything wrong in coming
to the court. The only fair order, therefore, in the ordinary way, is no costs
on either side."

I   SALMON, L.J., expressed himself (9) to the same effect.

(1) [1956] 3 All E.R. 442; [1956] 1 W.L.R. 1291.
(2) [1956] 3 All E.R. 676; [1956] 1 W.L.R. 1438.
(3) [1956] 3 All E.R. at p. 444; [1956] 1 W.L.R. at p. 1294.
(4) [1956] 3 All E.R. at p. 677; [1956] 1 W.L.R. at p. 1440.
(5) [1956] 3 All E.R. at p. 678; [1956] 1 W.L.R. at p. 1441.
(6) [1958] 1 All E.R. 104; [1958] 1 W.L.R. 108.
(7) [1965] 2 All E.R. 393; [1965] 1 W.L.R. 836.
(8) [1965] 2 All E.R. at p. 394; [1965] 1 W.L.R. at p. 839.
(9) [1965] 2 All E.R. at p. 394; [1965] 1 W.L.R. at p. 840.

The practice is stated in a passage in the COUNTY COURT PRACTICE 1965, A
at p. 780. It sets out the effect of the cases previous to the *Willis* case (10).
I am told that the current edition sets out the practice in the same terms but
incorporating a reference to the *Willis* case (10).

Now I do not for a moment doubt that that is a proper and reasonable practice
in the case where the landlord resists an application for a new lease either in
toto or as to the particular terms to be contained in the lease so that both parties B
have to go to court and litigate the matter. I do not doubt, apart from exceptional circumstances, that it is proper in such a case for the court to make no
order as to costs, but the position is, I think, entirely different in a case of the
type I now have before me, namely, that in which the landlord opposes the
grant of a new tenancy and then after the issue of the summons by the tenant
withdraws his opposition altogether, thereby causing the expense to the tenant C
of instituting proceedings to have been entirely thrown away. It was pointed
out by counsel for the plaintiff company by way of illustration that a comparable
position would exist if a tenant applied for the grant of a new tenancy and then
after starting his proceedings withdrew the application.

I cannot think that in any of the cases to which I have been referred the Court
of Appeal was intending to lay down some universal rule as to the costs of these D
applications which would apply to a case of the present kind. It seems to me
that in a case such as this the court must have the same discretion as to costs
which it would have in the ordinary case in which one party brings proceedings
as a result of the attitude adopted by the other party and then, after the proceedings have been instituted, that other party changes his attitude and accedes
to the plaintiff's claim. E

In the present case I can see nothing which would make it just to do otherwise
than make an order that the defendant company should bear the plaintiff
company's costs of this summons.

Order accordingly.

Solicitors: *Frederick Wills & Co.* (for the plaintiff company); *Loxley, Sanderson
& Morgan* (for the defendant company). F

[Reported by ROSALIE LONG, Barrister-at-Law.]

G

H

I

---

(10) [1965] 2 All E.R. 393; [1965] 1 W.L.R. 836.

A

VINCENT AND ANOTHER *v.* PREMO ENTERPRISES (VOUCHER SALES), LTD. AND OTHERS.

B
[COURT OF APPEAL, CIVIL DIVISION (Lord Denning, M.R., Winn and Fenton Atkinson, L.JJ.), March 20, 21, 1969.]

Deed—Escrow—Lease executed—Parts of lease not exchanged—Implied condition —Whether deed effectively delivered as escrow.

C
The plaintiffs were freeholders of a house. They let four rooms on the first floor to a company who sublet two of them to the first defendants. The tenancy was due to end on 25th March 1967. The first defendants negotiated with the plaintiffs to take a tenancy of the whole floor. The terms were set out in two letters which showed that the parties were in agreement that the first defendants should take a tenancy of the whole first floor for five years from 25th March 1967 at a rent of £350 per annum subject to the lease being prepared and signed. On 25th March the tenants vacated the premises. The lease was ready in June. Each solicitor engrossed his part and sent it

D
to the other. The plaintiffs signed, sealed and delivered the lease and handed it to their solicitors. The first defendants signed and sealed the counterpart on condition that the date when they took vacant possession was agreed and that no rent should be payable in respect of the time before they took vacant possession. The first defendants sent the counterpart to their solicitors telling them of the condition. But before the solicitors

E
exchanged the documents, the first defendants sought to withdraw from the transaction. The plaintiffs claimed that the lease was binding and sued the first defendants for rent from 25th March 1967. The first defendants put in a defence saying that they had not delivered the deed, that it was an escrow and that the condition was not fulfilled. At the hearing the county court judge found that the first defendants took possession on 1st May 1967:

F
and thereafter the plaintiffs said that they would give credit for the period before possession was taken. The plaintiffs claimed that the condition was fulfilled at the hearing. The judge held that the lease was an escrow on a condition and that it was too late for the plaintiffs at the hearing to say that the condition had been fulfilled. He rejected the plaintiffs' claim and the plaintiffs appealed.

G
Held: since the defendants intended to be bound, subject only to the date of possession being agreed, the deed was delivered as an escrow; that the condition was fulfilled at the hearing and the deed was then binding (see p. 945, letters E, G, and I, and p. 948, letter E, post).

Observations of WINN, L.J., on the effect of suspensive term in an escrow

H
(see p. 946, letters F and H, post).

Xenos v. *Wickham* ((1866), L.R. 2 H.L. 296) and *Beesly* v. *Hallwood Estates, Ltd.* ([1961] 1 All E.R. 90) followed.

Appeal allowed.

[As to the effect of delivery of a deed as an escrow, see 11 HALSBURY'S LAWS (3rd Edn.) 350, 351, para. 561; and for cases on the subject, see 17 DIGEST

I
(Repl.) 221-225, *200-255.*]

Cases referred to:
   Beesly v. *Hallwood Estates, Ltd.*, [1961] 1 All E.R. 90; [1961] Ch. 105; [1961] 2 W.L.R. 36; Digest (Cont. Vol. A) 472, *241a.*
   Foundling Hospital (Governors and Guardians) v. *Crane,* [1911] 2 K.B. 367; 80 L.J.K.B. 853; 105 L.T. 187; 17 Digest (Repl.) 217, *170.*
   Xenos v. *Wickham* (1866), L.R. 2 H.L. 296; 36 L.J.C.P. 313; 16 L.T. 800; 17 Digest (Repl.) 216, *153.*

Appeal.   A

This was an appeal by the plaintiffs, Ronald Pittard Vincent and Una Marion Vincent, from the order of His Honour JUDGE PENNANT made at the Yeovil County Court on 23rd May 1968, whereby the plaintiffs' claim for rent for the period after 24th June 1967, was dismissed.   The facts are set out in the judgment of LORD DENNING, M.R.

W. J. Mowbray for the plaintiffs.   B
K. H. Zucker for the defendants.

LORD DENNING, M.R.: The plaintiffs, Mr. Vincent and his sister Miss Vincent, are the freeholders of a house in Central Road, Yeovil.   They let four rooms on the first floor to Darch & Willcox, Ltd., who kept two of the rooms for themselves and sublet the other two rooms to the first defendants, Premo   C Enterprises (Voucher Sales), Ltd.   The tenancy of Darch & Willcox, Ltd., was due to come to an end on 25th March 1967; whereupon, of course, the subtenancy of the two rooms to the first defendants would also come to an end. But negotiations took place whereby the first defendants were to take a tenancy of the whole floor direct from the owners.   The terms were set out in two letters. On 18th January 1967, the third defendant, Mr. Poile, as director of the first   D defendants, wrote to the plaintiffs' solicitor:

> " I would be interested in your proposition to take over the entire floor if terms can be agreed and I would be prepared to offer a rental of £350 per annum exclusive on a five-year lease.   In view of the situation of the premises I would also require some outside display and at the same time I would also like to know whether the existing facia boards at the top of the   E building could be repainted to show our own name.   If the offer is acceptable to [the plaintiffs], perhaps you would be good enough to prepare the lease and send it to our solicitors, Messrs. Offenbach & Co. . . .''

On 7th February the plaintiffs' solicitor replied:

> " [The plaintiffs are] willing to grant to [the first defendants] a Lease of   F the entire first floor at a rental of £350 per annum exclusive of rates on a five year lease . . . We are preparing the draft Lease which will commence on 25th March 1967, and are forwarding it to your Solicitors for their attention . . . [the plaintiffs] would expect two of the Directors to guarantee payment of rent and performance of the tenant's obligation under the Lease. We trust there is no difficulty about this."
>   G

Those letters show that the parties were in agreement that the first defendants should take a tenancy on the whole of the first floor for five years from 25th March 1967 at £350 a year, subject, of course, to the lease being prepared and agreed.

On 25th March 1967, Darch & Willcox, Ltd., went out of the premises.   They moved into a house just across the road.   By some mischance, Mr. Willcox   H did not hand over the key to the plaintiffs; nor did he hand it over to the first defendants. He left the first defendants in their two rooms (as he knew they were going to take over the whole floor).   The first defendants only had two girls there at the time.   Mr. Willcox took the key across the road with him, and he left a message with the girls that if anybody wanted the key, they could have it at any time.   The girls did not ask for it, nor did anyone else, until some   I time later.   It would look as if the first defendants did not feel any urgent need for those other two rooms.   A few weeks later one of the young ladies asked for the key and got it at once.   There was no record of the date.   No one could remember.   But after hearing the evidence, the judge found that it was 1st May 1967.   So we may take it that by 1st May 1967 the first defendants got the key and took possession of the extra two rooms.   They had, of course, been in possession of the two rooms (of which they had previously been sub-tenants) all the time since 25th March 1967.

A   Although the lease was supposed to start from 25th March 1967 the solicitors had not got it ready by that time.   They were not ready until about the middle of June 1967.   By that time they had agreed all the terms and set them all down in writing.   In particular, the lease was to start from 25th March 1967 and rent was payable from that time.   Each solicitor had engrossed his part.   Each sent his engrossment over to the other solicitor so as to get it executed by that

B   solicitor's client.   The first defendants' solicitor had sent an engrossment of the lease to the plaintiffs' solicitor.   The plaintiffs' solicitor had sent an engrossment of the counterpart to the first defendants' solicitor.   The intention was that each side should execute and then return.   The plaintiffs' solicitor was to return the executed lease to the first defendants' solicitor.   The first defendants' solicitor was to return the executed counterpart to the plaintiffs' solicitor.   Now

C   we come to the point.   The plaintiffs undoubtedly signed, sealed and delivered the lease and handed it to their own solicitor in the latter half of June 1967; and their own solicitor retained it.   The first defendants signed and sealed the counterpart, but there is a question whether they " delivered " it at all, or as an " escrow ".   The facts are these.   On 15th June 1967 the solicitor of the first defendants wrote to the director, the second defendant, Mr. Kutner:

D   ' I have pleasure in enclosing the counterpart Lease to which the Common Seal of the Company must be affixed in the presence of a Director and Secretary.   In addition, the Lease must be signed by [the third defendant] and yourself in the presence of independent witness who must sign his or her name, address and occupation, all as indicated."

E   On receiving that letter, the second defendant telephoned to the solicitor and had this conversation with him which the judge accepted:

      " I said to him [that there had] been a mistake and that rent was not correct, as we had not taken possession on 25th March.   I asked him what I should do about signing, and he said it is a small matter which he felt he could easily clear up with the other side.   I then said I would sign the lease

F   provided he made sure that the date is agreed when we took vacant possession, and that we should not exchange it till he had.   I said I would find out the date for him and he could then arrange and let me know how much I would have to pay.   I was not prepared to enter into the lease if [the plaintiffs] insisted that rent was payable from 25th March.   My solicitor asked if I was going to send the rent to him.   I said no, I did not think I should pay rent

G   for when I was not in possession."

After that conversation, the second defendant told the third defendant that the solicitor had said " that it is in order for us to sign the lease and that he would arrange for the date of possession to be put in.   He felt that as it is a small amount it can be easily settled ".   Thereupon they both signed and sealed the counterpart lease.   The first defendants' seal was affixed with the usual

H   formula: " The common seal of [the first defendants] was hereunto affixed in the presence of " a director and secretary.   Each of the directors executed it opposite the usual words: " signed sealed and delivered by the said "—in the presence of a witness.   All this was done in common form.   They then returned the document to their own solicitor with a letter stating: " We thank you for your letter of 15th inst., and herewith return the Lease duly signed as requested."

I   So each part of this lease was in the hands of solicitors.   Each engrossment had been sent to the solicitors for the other side.   Each solicitor had got his client to " sign seal and deliver " it, but he had not returned it to the sender. The two parts were not exchanged.   Then the trouble arose, because they could not discover when exactly the key was handed over.   No one could remember.   They could not agree on the date from which the rent should be paid. The plaintiffs wanted rent from 25th March.   The first defendants were unwilling to pay until the date when the key was handed over.   The dispute was never resolved, because the first defendants decided to withdraw from the transaction

altogether. They said that the documents had not been exchanged. So there A
was nothing binding on them. And they could repudiate the proposed lease.
At that stage the solicitor on each side demanded the return of his engrossment.
Each sent it back. The solicitor for the plaintiffs sent the lease to the solicitor
for the first defendants. It was complete, with the full description " signed
sealed and delivered " by the plaintiffs. The solicitor for the first defendants
sent the counterpart to the solicitor for the plaintiffs. But it was sent back B
defaced. The first defendants' seal had been torn off. The signatures had been
obliterated, so that they could not be read at all. Some one had scratched
through the names of the directors, the secretary and the witnesses, on the
ground, I suppose, that they were not liable.

The plaintiffs claimed that the lease was binding on the first defendants and
sued for the rent from 25th March 1967. The first defendants put in a defence C
stating first that they had not " delivered " the deed; and, second, that it
was an " escrow ", in the words that:

" if the said counterpart was delivered by the Defendants or any of them
(which is denied) it was delivered as an escrow to take effect only upon the
fulfilment of the following condition, namely, upon the Plaintiffs agreeing
that rent should only be due payable under the said lease from the date upon D
which the first Defendants had full vacant possession of the said premises
and not from the date of the commencement of the term."

The plaintiffs, of course, knew nothing of that condition until they received the
defence a few weeks before the hearing. At the hearing (when the defendants
had given evidence of the condition), the plaintiffs said: " We did not insist on E
the rent before the defendants got possession ". The judge found that the date
when the key was handed over was 1st May 1967. The plaintiffs said that they
would give credit for £35 4s. for the period from 25th March to 1st May 1967.
Accordingly, the plaintiffs said that, if there was a condition such as was asserted
in the defence, that condition had been fulfilled and the lease was binding.

The judge held it was an escrow on a condition, but that it was too late for F
the plaintiffs at the hearing, to say that the condition had been fulfilled. So he
rejected their claim. Now there is an appeal to this court.

The law as to " delivery " of a deed is of ancient date. But it is reasonably
clear. A deed is very different from a contract. On a contract for the sale of
land, the contract is not binding on the parties until they have exchanged their
parts. But with a deed it is different. A deed is binding on the maker of it, G
even though the parts have not been exchanged, as long as it has been signed,
sealed and delivered. " Delivery " in this connection does not mean " handed
over " to the other side. It means delivered in the old legal sense, namely, an
act done so as to evince an intention to be bound. Even though the deed remains
in the possession of the maker, or of his solicitor, he is bound by it if he has
done some act evincing an intention to be bound, as by saying: " I deliver H
this my act and deed." He may, however, make the " delivery " conditional:
in which case the deed is called an " escrow " which becomes binding when the
condition is fulfilled.

The law was much considered by the House of Lords in the leading case of
Xenos v. *Wickham* (1). After the judges had been brought together to advise
the House, LORD CRANWORTH said (2):
                                                                              I
" . . . In the first place, the efficacy of a deed depends on its being sealed
and delivered by the maker of it; not on his ceasing to retain possession
of it. This, as a general proposition of law, cannot be controverted. It is
not affected by the circumstance that the maker may so deliver it as to suspend or qualify its binding effect. He may declare that it shall have no

(1) (1866), L.R. 2 H.L. 296.
(2) (1866), L.R. 2 H.L. at p. 323.

A   effect until a certain time has arrived, or till some condition has been performed, but when the time has arrived, or the condition has been performed,
the delivery becomes absolute, and the maker of the deed is absolutely
bound by it, whether he has parted with the possession or not. Until
the specified time has arrived, or the condition has been performed, the
instrument is not a deed. It is mere escrow."

B   That was applied recently by this court in *Beesly* v. *Hallwood Estates, Ltd.* (3),
where a company was held to be bound by a lease which had been signed, sealed
and delivered by the company, even though it had not been sent to the other side
at all. It was delivered as an escrow, subject to a condition that the tenant
should hand over the counterpart. He did hand it over and the company
was held bound accordingly because the condition had been fulfilled.

C   The question is whether this deed was " delivered " at all, or whether it was
delivered subject to a condition, i.e., as an " escrow ". Counsel for the defendants argued that there was no delivery at all. He said that it was the sort of
case which FARWELL, L.J., had in mind in *Foundling Hospital (Governors and
Guardians)* v. *Crane* (4), when he said:

D   " I doubt if a man, by executing a deed, and handing it over to his own
solicitors to be held on his behalf until he gives them further instructions,
makes delivery of it as an escrow at all . . ."

In such a case the maker shows that he did not intend to be bound at all unless
and until he gives the solicitors further instructions. But this case is different.
The defendants did intend to be bound, but subject to the date of possession
E   being agreed. That makes it, I think, an escrow. I agree with the judge, who
said,

". . . that it was delivered as an escrow on the express condition that
the defendants' solicitor should reach agreement with the plaintiffs' on
the date when possession of the two rooms was received by the [first
defendants] and should reach agreement with them on the fact that rent
F   should only be payable for those rooms from that date."

I think that the judge was perfectly entitled so to find. This deed was signed,
sealed and delivered by the first defendants, subject only to the condition that
the date on which possession was given should be ascertained and the rent
adjusted accordingly.

G   The next question is whether the condition was fulfilled. I think it was
fulfilled at the hearing before the county court when the date of possession was
ascertained by the judge to be 1st May 1967; and the plaintiffs agreed to adjust
the rent accordingly.

The judge thought it was too late. He did not think the condition could be
fulfilled after the action was brought. I do not share his view. In *Beesly* v.
Hallwood Estates, Ltd. (3), HARMAN, L.J., indicated that there might come a
H   time when in equity the maker of an " escrow " might be released from the
obligation. But that is not this case. I see nothing in this case to debar the
plaintiffs from insisting on their legal rights. They did not know of this condition imposed by the defendants to their solicitors until the defence was pleaded;
and they acted quite reasonably from that time onwards. The deed having been
delivered, the condition having been fulfilled, the defendants are bound.
I   I would allow the appeal, accordingly.

WINN, L.J.: I agree explicitly with the judgment of LORD DENNING, M.R.,
and the reasoning of it. Were it not for the fact that we are differing from the
learned county court judge, I would not think it necessary to add anything for
myself. As it is, I would say that it seems to me that the learned judge was
right about the main issue in this case, but I cannot agree with his view that

(3) [1961] 1 All E.R. 90; [1961] Ch. 105.
(4) [1911] 2 K.B. 367 at p. 379.

the condition or the event stipulated for the effectiveness of the deed was not   A
satisfied before he gave judgment.   He thought that, because it was not until
the plaintiffs offered at the trial to make a reduction in the rent claimed that the
document could have become a binding deed, this event was too late to have
such an effect.   In my own view the escrow which the learned judge rightly
found to have been operative in this case, its effect being that the document
which was executed did not become a deed at the time when it was executed   B
but only on the occurrence of the event stipulated for the escrow, does not involve
any " condition ", properly so called, requiring to be performed by the plaintiffs,
the parties in whose favour this deed would operate when it became a deed, nor
any temporal limit for this event.   In the defendants' pleading where the first
ground of defence was a complete denial that there was any delivery of the
counterpart, and the second ground of defence was that any delivery which was   C
made was only delivery as an escrow—in this court the two arguments were
presented in the opposite order—the issue as to escrow so raised was put in the
following words: that the plaintiffs had stipulated or had intended that the
document should take effect only on the fulfilment of the following conditions,
namely, on the plaintiffs agreeing that rent should only be due and payable from
the date on which the first defendants had full vacant possession of the rooms in   D
question.   In his judgment the learned judge put that same condition in a
slightly different form by saying " that it was delivered as an escrow on the
express condition that the defendants' solicitor should reach agreement with
the plaintiffs' ", to the same effect, that is to say, about the date when possession
was received and the fact that rent would only be demanded from that date.
As I see it, really neither of those descriptions of the so-called conditions is   E
precisely accurate.   The escrow was to cease to have suspensive effect on the
occurrence of an event, irrespective of whether the solicitor for the defendants
secured agreement or whether the landlords offered their consent to the desired
effect.   The event was the determination of the dispute which had been raised
in such a manner as would result in a reduction of rent so as to make rent become
payable for the first time at the date at which it might be established that vacant   F
possession was first given.   That I think is a more accurate and real presentation
of the suspensive term;   that event did come about.   As, for my own part, I
visualise the operation of an escrow, it may be made dependent on virtually any
event whatsoever which may or may not occur in futuro, other than the event of
the death of the maker of the document, since in that case the document becomes
a testamentary disposition and is controlled by the Wills Act 1837.   One could   G
visualise, for example, as a real transaction that a man might be disposed to
execute a document of gift in favour of a child or other relative but to make it
clear that he did not intend that document of gift to become binding on him
until after the contents of a budget then pending had been revealed and it became
plain that there would be no additional tax on gifts inter vivos thereby imposed.
It is, I think, correct to say that a document executed with such a suspensory   H
and declared intention is not a deed at the time when it is executed but becomes
a deed, as distinct from a document properly called an escrow, at the time when
the event occurs.   In the present case that would mean that it would become
binding at but not before the moment of time when there was a concurrence of
two events: fixing of the time when vacant possession was first given and reduction of the claim for rent so as to meet the demand of the tenants.   That concur-   I
rence of events occurred during the hearing of the proceedings in the county
court.

Now, this would not be an appropriate case in which to embark on any discussion of the technical, legal meaning of the word " deliver " in this context.
I would not venture to dissent in the slightest from what LORD DENNING, M.R.,
has said on that point.   I would only comment that I for myself—and this is
due to ignorance which has been helpfully lightened but not so completely as
to introduce the full glare of sunlight in my mind—by the helpful submissions

A of learned counsel—I have great sympathy with the state of things spoken of by the learned county court judge, that is to say, that the solicitors concerned with this matter and no doubt others, till it got into the hands of counsel for the defendants, did not appreciate that any question of escrow here was involved at all but were relying on the requirement of mutual exchange of lease and counterpart as a suspensive event which would avoid the immediate imposition

B of an obligation on the defendants. I have such sympathy for this reason, that when one looks, as I have had occasion to look in the course of the appeal, probably for the first time, at NORTON ON DEEDS (2nd Edn.), pp. 13, 14, it becomes plain that every single example given on p. 14 of NORTON ON DEEDS is a case where there was, or was not, a change of physical or legal control in respect of the document, and the outcome of the dispute depended entirely on

C affirmatively establishing that there had been such a change of possession. When I speak of " possession ", I do not intend to develop the matter at all; but one naturally has in mind the brilliant essay on POSSESSION, CUSTODY AND DERIVATIVE POSSESSION written by WRIGHT and POLLOCK. It is also to be noted that there was a de facto change of custody in *Xenos* v. *Wickham* (5), albeit I accept that the speeches of their Lordships did not depend for their

D reasoning on any such change. LORD DENNING, M.R., has read a passage from the speech of LORD CRANWORTH. It is equally clear that LORD CHELMSFORD, L.C., did not shut his eyes to the fact that there had been such a change, since he said (6):

E
> " We all know the formal mode of executing a deed by the words, ' I deliver this as my act and deed '—a form which, no doubt, or something equivalent to it, was observed upon this occasion. The policy [it was an insurance policy under seal] most probably, was afterwards given to the secretary, to be kept till called for. Now, although the policy was thus retained by the officers of the company, when formal execution of it had taken place, they held it for the plaintiffs, whose property it became from that moment."

F
And LORD CRANWORTH himself, although this is not part of his essential reasoning, did say (7):

> " If the usage had been that it should, after being signed, sealed, and delivered, remain in the hands of the secretary till the assured or his broker had done some act signifying his approbation of it, that might have raised

G
> a question whether, until that approbation had been expressed, it was more than an escrow. But no such usage is stated."

Rather similarly, in the recent case of *Beesly* v. *Hallwood Estates, Ltd.* (8), which has been referred to, it is to be observed that it was not in issue whether there had been delivery of the document in question. Apart altogether from the technical point under s. 74 of the Law of Property Act 1925, it is to be noted

H that HARMAN, L.J., said (9):

> " If there had been no delivery, as was pleaded, the matter would be wholly different; but that, by the time the action came to this court, had been decided as a fact by the learned judge and accepted by the defendants."

And when he goes on to give certain examples about delivery of deeds, some do

I and some do not involve a change of physical possession or custody of the document which itself is referred to rather indifferently as a deed or writing at the moment when that change of the nature of the holding of the document comes into consideration.

---

(5) (1866), L.R. 2 H.L. 296.
(6) (1866), L.R. 2 H.L. at p. 320.
(7) (1866), L.R. 2 H.L. at pp. 324, 325.
(8) [1961] 1 All E.R. 90; [1961] Ch. 105.
(9) [1961] 1 All E.R. at p. 93; [1961] Ch. at p. 116.

It is not necessary in this case to go into any of those matters for the purpose   A
of deciding the case.   Any discussion of them must be academic.   I do, however,
venture to express my agreement with the learned county court judge's view
that it might be very helpful in modern life if there were some modification of the
law, departing somewhat from the strictness of the old rule the effect of which
LORD DENNING, M.R., has indicated, viz., that a man becomes bound when he
executes a deed in the form usually adopted; there are evidentiary difficulties   B
which from time to time must be met in establishing whether or not a man did
speak or use some words or do some act sufficient to negative the prima facie
presumed intention that by executing a document under seal and declaring that
it is " delivered " a man has adopted it as immediately binding on him.   I
think it might be more realistic to depend on physical movement or legal control
of the document after the time when it is sealed, it being the law that some   C
adoptive demonstration is required additionally to the mere affixing of the sale.
More concentration on the movement of the deed thereafter would make it easier
to solve the question, has the maker, by parting with it to such extent and manner
as may be proved, expressed an intention—indicated, demonstrated an intention—
for it to be immediately binding, or demonstrated a suspensive intention that
it shall not be immediately binding on him but only binding if some particular   D
event does occur?   That observation is not of any weight in this case and I
apologise for taking up time, but since I have travailed over the matter, I thought
it right to show that I had given careful attention to what has been said by
counsel and by the learned judge.

I agree that the appeal should be allowed.

FENTON ATKINSON, L.J.:   I also agree that this appeal succeeds and   E
only add a few sentences of my own.   On the evidence in this case including the
oral evidence of the second defendant, Mr. Kutner himself, I think the learned
county court judge was fully justified in finding as a fact that on 27th June 1967
the counterpart lease was delivered as an escrow, that is to say, as I understand it,
as a simple writing not to become the deed of the defendants until the condition   F
pleaded in para. 4 of the defence was performed; and once that basic finding of
fact is accepted, it appears to me that is the end of counsel for the defendants'
case on this appeal, because the condition was met or performed at the hearing,
and it seems to me plain that at that stage the counterpart lease became the
deed of the defendants and was binding on them.   I agree that the appeal should
be allowed.
                                                                                 G
Appeal allowed.   Leave to appeal to the House of Lords refused.

Solicitors: *Badham, Comins & Main*, agents for *Batten & Co.*, Yeovil (for the
plaintiffs); *Offenbach & Co.* (for the defendants).

[*Reported by* JENIFER SANDELL, *Barrister-at-Law.*]

A

MURPHY v. STONE WALLWORK (CHARLTON), LTD.

[HOUSE OF LORDS (Lord Reid, Lord Pearce, Lord Upjohn, Lord Donovan and
Lord Pearson), April 21, 22, June 18, 1969.]

B
*Damages—Assessment—Appeal—Further evidence—Assessment once for all
—Significant factor arising after assessment—Factor not previously taken
into account—Dismissal of plaintiff by defendant after judgment—Power
to admit further evidence.*

Damages—Personal injury—Dismissal from work following award of damages.

*House of Lords—Appeal to—Further evidence—Application made within time
for appeal—Admission of further evidence.*

C
*House of Lords—Appeal to—Further evidence—Application out of time for
appeal—Admissibility.*

The appellant, then aged 54, was injured at work in 1965. The injury
awakened a previously silent condition of degenerative arthritis in the
spine and prevented his continuing such heavy work as he had previously
been engaged on. At that time he had been employed by the respondents

D
for nearly 12 years. He brought proceedings against the respondents and,
in 1967 (2½ years after the injury), he was awarded £750 general damages. On
appeal in 1968 the Court of Appeal increased the award. Throughout the
period following his injury the appellant had been employed by the respondents and both the trial judge and the Court of Appeal had had regard to this
in assessing damages. Shortly after the Court of Appeal had given judgment

E
the respondents dismissed the appellant on the grounds that they had no
suitable employment for him in his weakened condition and that he might
represent a danger to his fellow employees. The dismissal was entirely
bona fide. The appellant appealed against the decision of the Court of
Appeal (within time) and sought leave to adduce fresh evidence (i.e., as to
his dismissal). The parties agreed that, in the event of the House of Lords

F
allowing the appeal, damages should be increased by an agreed amount.

Held: the House had the power to admit fresh evidence and, since the
basis on which damages had been assessed had been falsified, it would
exercise its discretion in favour of admitting the fresh evidence and the
case would be re-opened in the light thereof (see p. 950, letter G, p. 952,
letter I, p. 954, letters D and E, p. 955, letter H, p. 956, letters A and G,

G
p. 959, letter H, and p. 960, letters F and G, post).

Dictum of LORD GORRELL in *A.-G. (at the relation of Tamworth Corpn.) v.
Birmingham, Tame and Rea District Drainage Board* ([1911-13] All E.R.
Rep. at p. 939) applied.

Curwen v. James ([1963] 2 All E.R. 619) approved.

Ladd v. Marshall ([1954] 3 All E.R. 745) distinguished.

H
Jenkins v. Richard Thomas & Baldwins, Ltd. ([1966] 2 All E.R. 15) doubted.

Per LORD PEARCE and LORD UPJOHN: the House has a discretion to
re-open a matter on fresh evidence even after the time for appeal has expired
if the particular exigencies of justice clearly outweigh the general undesirability of so doing. In such circumstances, however, the onus on the appellant
of satisfying the House that the case is a proper one to re-open is higher

I
than when he makes application to admit fresh evidence within the time
for bringing an appeal (see p. 953, letter G, and p. 956, letter C, post).

[As to the powers of the Court of Appeal to receive further evidence, **see**
30 HALSBURY'S LAWS (3rd Edn.) 468-470, para. 884; and for cases on the
subject see 51 DIGEST (Repl.) 829-833, *3843-3870.*

As to the maxim " Interest rei publicae ut sit finis litium ", see 15 HALSBURY'S
LAWS (3rd Edn.) 184, 185, para. 357; and for cases on the subject, see 21 DIGEST
(Repl.) 225, 226, *225-233.*]

Cases referred to: A

A.G. (at the relation of Tamworth Corpn.) v. Birmingham, Tame and Rea District
    Drainage Board, [1912] A.C. 788; [1911-13] All E.R. Rep. 926; 82
    L.J.Ch. 45; 107 L.T. 353; 76 J.P. 481; 28 Digest (Repl.) 889, 1185.
Bradberry, Re, National Provincial Bank, Ltd. v. Bradberry, Re Fry, Tasker
    v. Gulliford, [1942] 2 All E.R. 629; [1943] Ch. 35; 112 L.J.Ch. 49;
    167 L.T. 396; 23 Digest (Repl.) 429, 4992.   B
Brown v. Dean, [1910] A.C. 373; [1908-10] All E.R. Rep. 661; 79 L.J.K.B.
    690; 102 L.T. 661; 51 Digest (Repl.) 865, 4160.
Bwllfa and Merthyr Dare Steam Collieries (1891), Ltd. v. Pontypridd Waterworks
    Co., [1903] A.C. 426; [1900-03] All E.R. Rep. 600; 72 L.J.K.B. 805;
    89 L.T. 280; 11 Digest (Repl.) 136, 199.
Curwen v. James, [1963] 2 All E.R. 619; [1963] 1 W.L.R. 748; 51 Digest   C
    (Repl.) 824, 3805.
Jenkins v. Richard Thomas & Baldwins, Ltd., [1966] 2 All E.R. 15; [1966] 1
    W.L.R. 476; 51 Digest (Repl.) 825, 3806.
Ladd v. Marshall, [1954] 3 All E.R. 745; [1954] 1 W.L.R. 1489; 51 Digest
    (Repl.) 827, 3826.
Paris v. Stepney Borough Council, [1951] 1 All E.R. 42; [1951] A.C. 367;   D
    115 J.P. 22; 34 Digest (Repl.) 240, 1766.

Appeal.

This was an appeal by Thomas Murphy, by leave of the Court of Appeal
granted on 30th April 1968, from an order of that court (DANCKWERTS and
DIPLOCK, L.JJ., and CAIRNS, J.) dated 21st March 1968 varying the judgment of
MACKENNA, J., given on 13th October 1967. MACKENNA, J., assessed the   E
damages recoverable by the appellant against his employers, Stone Wallwork
(Charlton), Ltd., the respondents, at a sum of £1,233 7s. 11d. of which general
damages were assessed at £750, which included loss of earning capacity. The
Court of Appeal increased the general damages to £1,350. The facts are set out
in the opinion of LORD PEARSON.

Quintin Hogg, Q.C., and J. M. Williams for the appellant.   F
Marven Everett, Q.C., and C. H. Whitby for the respondents.

Their Lordships took time for consideration.

18th June.   The following opinions were delivered.

LORD REID: My Lords, I agree with your Lordships that this appeal   G
should be allowed.

LORD PEARCE: My Lords, the appellant had worked at the respondents'
foundry for nearly 12 years and was 54 years of age when an accident occurred,
in March 1965, which strained and injured his back. This awakened a previously
silent condition of degenerative arthritis in the spine and made it painful. As a
result he was away from work for three months. Thereafter he had to have   H
lighter work at the foundry, and the fact that he had had this strain meant
that in future less would be needed to incapacitate him than if he had not
suffered it. In 1966 he was off work for three months and in 1967 for three
weeks owing to a recurrence of the trouble.

The case came on for trial in October 1967, 2½ years after the accident. The
judge held that the respondents were liable for breach of statutory duty. The   I
special damage, which included various losses of wages, was agreed. There
was a conflict of evidence and argument as to how much overtime the appellant
would lose owing to his having been moved to a different class of workers by
reason of his post-accident inability to do the heavier kind of work. The learned
judge assessed the general damages at £750.

It is clear from reading the evidence that nobody was addressing his mind
to the question of the appellant being dismissed by the respondents owing to
his disability and of his resulting loss in the open market owing to his disability.

A   The remaining ten years or so of his working life were viewed as being spent with the respondents. Hence the dispute as to what overtime he would lose in *their* foundry by his being changed over to a different group of *their* workers where the heaviest work would not fall to his lot. It is likewise apparent that the learned judge in his careful judgment was assuming that the employers would not dismiss him.

B   In 1968 the Court of Appeal increased the amount of general damages. But that court also was going on the assumption that he would continue to work for the respondents unless incapacitated from work. And it is admitted that both counsel argued the case on that assumption. DANCKWERTS, L.J., in giving the judgment with which his brethren agreed said:

C   " One of the consequences of that accident was—though I am not quite sure why—that he was removed from the foundry and worked in another department, with the result that he was not so favourably placed in regard to overtime work. The men in the foundry apparently had preference for that kind of Sunday work, of which the average time appears to have been five hours on two Sundays a month. There was a loss of earnings in that

D   way, and there were various other possibilities; he might, at any time, possibly suffer further results, with the chance that he might not be able to continue with his employment. On the other hand, there was evidence that if all had gone well he might be able to continue in his work until the usual time of retirement, which I understood was sixty-five."

Within a fortnight of that judgment the respondents dismissed the appellant
E   from their employment on the ground that his physical condition made him too big a risk. Thereupon the appellant moved the same Court of Appeal for leave to appeal to your Lordships' House. It is clear from the transcript that the court felt that it had acted on an erroneous assumption. DIPLOCK, L.J., said:

F   " I took into account the possibility that [the appellant] would not be able to continue at work until he was 65. But I assumed that [the respondents] would continue to employ him as long as he was physically fit."

CAIRNS, J., said:

    " I took into account the possibility that [the appellant] might not be able to work for the full ten years . . . What we had in mind was a consider-
G   able probability that he would continue in his pre-accident work at his pre-accident wages except for loss of overtime."

The Court of Appeal therefore gave leave to appeal to your Lordships' House.

    It is clear, of course, that, at the hearing in the Court of Appeal, counsel for the respondents had no idea that they might dismiss the appellant as they did. His view rightly is that, had he known, he would have felt it his duty to inform
H   the court. It is also clear that had the respondents had the intention to dismiss in their minds during the hearing of the case, and failed to inform the court, the matter could be re-opened in the light of the subsequent dismissal. Finality is important. But good faith is even more important. It would be wrong to allow a litigant to retain the benefit of a judgment obtained by deliberately concealing something which will falsify the assumptions on which he knows
I   that the court is acting.

    In the present case, however, the respondents have put forward affidavits asserting that the intention to dismiss was formed *after* the judgment and as a result of what was said at the hearing in the Court of Appeal. In fact, nothing fresh came out of that hearing since it was simply concerned with the evidence previously given at the trial. But humans do on occasions suddenly see a situation in a different light from that in which they had previously seen it, even though nothing material has occurred to change it. And thus belatedly they make a decision which should have been made previously. I am content to accept the

respondents' assurance that they did not form the intention to dismiss until after   A
the judgments in the Court of Appeal, and to decide the case on that basis.

Counsel for the appellant not unnaturally inclined to a less tolerant view of
the respondents' conduct.   But he was content to accept the respondents' assertions for the purpose of his first line of argument, and to reserve his rights to be
more critical of those assertions if that argument should fail.   On that basis he
contends that your Lordships should allow the appeal and reconsider the general   B
damages for the following reasons: 1. The dismissal is a fact that must influence
the amount of general damages.   2. Admittedly it was not considered by the
court as a probability since the court was assuming the probability of the respondents continuing to employ the appellant.   3. The conduct of the case by both
sides, both at the trial and in the Court of Appeal, led to this assumption.   So
too, did the evidence given by the respondents' witnesses at the trial.   4. This   C
assumption was falsified within a fortnight of the judgment by a deliberate act
of the respondents within their sphere of action.   5. It is not equitable that the
respondents should hold a judgment so obtained.   6. Further, the respondents'
delay in coming to the decision to dismiss led to the mistaken assumption.   It
would be wrong, therefore, that they should be allowed to profit by their omission.

Our courts have adopted the principle that damages are assessed at the trial   D
once for all.   If later the plaintiff suffers greater loss from an accident than
was anticipated at the trial he cannot come back for more.   Nor can the defendant
come back if the loss is less than was anticipated.   Thus, the assessment of damages
for the future is necessarily compounded of prophecy and calculation.   The
court must do the best it can to reach what seems to be the right figure on a
reasonable balance of the probabilities, avoiding undue optimism and undue   E
pessimism.   Although periodic payments and a right of recourse whenever circumstances change might seem an attractive solution of the difficulty, yet they,
too, have serious drawbacks such as an unending possibility of litigation which,
in the view of the law, have hitherto been held to outweigh the disadvantages
of an assessment of damages once and for all.   The present case is a classic example
of the latter disadvantages if no remedy is available to the appellant.   F

An appellate court has power to hear evidence of something which has altered
the effect of an order of the court below since that order was made.   In *A.-G. (at
the relation of Tamworth Corpn.)* v. *Birmingham, Tame and Rea District Drainage
Board* (1), LORD GORRELL said (2):

> " The Court also has power to take evidence of matters which have
> occurred after the date of the decision from which the appeal is brought   G
> ... It seems clear, therefore, that the Court of Appeal is entitled and
> ought to re-hear the case as *at the time of re-hearing* ... "

R.S.C., Ord. 59, r. 10 (2), dealing with the Court of Appeal's power provides that

> " ... no such further evidence (other than evidence as to matters which
> have occurred after the date of the trial or hearing) shall be admitted except   H
> on special grounds."

The words in brackets show that no special grounds are needed to justify the
admission of evidence of things that have occurred since the date of trial.   In
my opinion, your Lordships' House is equally entitled to consider such evidence.
But the cases in which it does so will be exceptional.

In *Curwen* v. *James* (3) the Court of Appeal in a fatal accident case allowed   I
the defendants to adduce evidence of the plaintiff widow's remarriage after the
trial and reduced her damages accordingly.   At the trial the widow had not
been asked about her marriage prospects since she had emotionally broken down
in the witness box.   SELLERS, L.J., there said (4):

(1) [1912] A.C. 788; [1911-13] All E.R. Rep. 926.
(2) [1912] A.C. at p. 801; [1911-13] All E.R. Rep. at p. 939.
(3) [1963] 2 All E.R. 619; [1963] 1 W.L.R. 748.
(4) [1963] 2 All E.R. at p. 622; [1963] 1 W.L.R. at p. 752.

A

" In the present case . . . it is desirable that the court should decide the matter on the known fact of the marriage rather than that it should remain decided on an uncertainty for the future as it stood before the learned judge."

HARMAN, L.J., said (5):

" There is an important principle here involved and it is that the court should never speculate where it knows."

B

And PEARSON, L.J., said (6):

". . . I think it right to emphasise what has already been pointed out— that, in this case, the event in question occurred quite soon after the trial or hearing . . ."

C

The learned Lord Justice was expressing anxiety lest the finality of judgments should be impaired by too great a readiness to allow subsequent evidence of things which were matters of speculation at the trial but had subsequently crystallised into facts. This same anxiety was echoed by SALMON, L.J., in *Jenkins* v. *Richard Thomas & Baldwins, Ltd.* (7), where the Court of Appeal went even further in allowing such evidence, a case in which it was solely the appel-

D

lant's condition which had caused the alteration of circumstances and which must, I think, be regarded as very near the borderline. I share their anxiety.

It is an important principle that there should be finality in judgments or, if one prefers a Latin maxim, ut sit finis litium. For that reason a time limit is set within which any appeal to overset a judgment must be launched. Only in exceptional circumstances is this time limit extended. For the same reason

E

the courts have refused to re-open a case on appeal by the admission of evidence which the appealing party could have made available at the trial. Only in very exceptional circumstances will it allow this fresh evidence. The hardship in a particular case must be balanced against the general evil of allowing judgments to be disturbed and thereby prolonging and extending litigation.

Thus, in normal circumstances there are two stages in the finality of a judgment.

F

First, during the time within which an appeal may be launched, it is final subject only to an appeal which in normal circumstances can only be allowed if there is some error in the adjudication on the evidence produced at the trial. There is, however, a discretion to allow fresh evidence if the unusual circumstances justify it. Secondly, after the time for appeal has expired, the judgment is final without recourse to appeal. Even then the appellate court has a discretion to re-open

G

the matter on fresh evidence if the particular exigencies of justice clearly out- weigh the general undesirability of doing so.

The appellant comes to your Lordships' House during the first stage, having launched his appeal within the time allowed. The burden on him is, therefore, less severe than it would have been had he come later. Even if the appellant cannot say that the entire responsibility for the erroneous assumption of the Court of Appeal lies on the respondents, since the question could have been

H

specifically raised by either side, yet the appellant, like the court, was acting reasonably throughout. In this class of disability there are many cases where a partially disabled man is thrown on the open market, with the consequent difficulties and loss. In such a case the question of what employment he will be able to obtain is ventilated and is of prime importance. There are also many cases where a kindly employer can fit him into his pre-accident setting with such

I

alteration or adjustment of his work as is made necessary by the incapacity. Arguments as to loss of wages *in that context* are ventilated and are of prime importance. In this latter class of case the loss to the man is generally somewhat less. And for three years the respondents behaved in every way as if the appellant's case belonged to this latter class.

(5) [1963] 2 All E.R. at p. 623; [1963] 1 W.L.R. at p. 753.
(6) [1963] 2 All E.R. at p. 624; [1963] 1 W.L.R. at p. 755.
(7) [1966] 2 All E.R. 15 at p. 18; [1966] 1 W.L.R. 476 at p. 479.

The conduct of the case at the trial and the evidence given supported the   A
assumption that the respondents had fitted the appellant into their foundry in
spite of his disability and that there was every probability that things would
so continue. So, too, the conduct of the appeal. It is not surprising that the
trial judge and the Court of Appeal worked on that assumption. The proper
time for the respondents to have made their decision was within the 2½ years
which preceded the trial. In one of those years the appellant was off work   B
through his injury for three months. In the next year he was similarly off work
for three weeks. So the problem of his incapacity was brought fully to their
notice. Again, at the trial it was fully discussed. By the time the case came
before the Court of Appeal the appellant was again off work for a few weeks.
In my opinion, any reasonable person would by that time assume that in spite
of his disability they were going to continue his employment, unless, of course,   C
he was guilty of misconduct or something unexpected occurred. There is no
suggestion here that any misconduct or anything unexpected occurred. And
both at the trial and at the hearing before the Court of Appeal the respondents
heard the case discussed by both counsel on the assumption that they were
going to continue his employment. It can fairly be said that, without mala fides,
their conduct led both courts to believe that that was the case. And it was   D
their deliberate conduct which falsified that belief within a fortnight of the
judgment in the Court of Appeal. To allow them to obtain an advantage from
the assumptions that their conduct (although not mala fide) induced and then
falsified would be inequitable. And to allow such a course of conduct to yield
an unfair profit would give encouragement to less innocent manoeuvres.

   For these reasons, in view of the fact that the appeal was started within the   E
time allowed, I think that there is just sufficient to allow the court to hear
the evidence of the dismissal and to re-open the case in the light of it. I would
therefore admit the evidence and allow the appeal. Since the parties have now
agreed the amount there is no need for any further directions.

   LORD UPJOHN: My Lords, on 17th March 1965, the appellant, who was   F
employed by the respondents, in the course of his employment suffered an injury
to his spine for which the respondents were held liable in law. He was away
for a time but returned to lighter work in June 1965, but this work sometimes
involved him in fairly heavy work which might injure him, so he was told by the
foreman to ask for help if he was asked to carry a load too much for him. But
the result of this was that the appellant had less opportunity of working over-   G
time, so that his average weekly wage was decreased and his injury also caused
him to be off work for several periods in 1965, 1966 and 1967. The appellant
issued his writ in November 1965, and the action came on for hearing before
MacKenna, J., in October 1967, and he awarded the appellant £750 general
damages and an agreed sum for special damages. The learned judge assessed
general damages on this footing:
                                                                           H
   " I fix the general damages at £750. I have included something in that
   figure for loss of overtime likely to be suffered in the future and as a result
   of the possibility of the [appellant] being occasionally off work . . ."

This decision was quite clearly made on the footing that as the result of his
injury the appellant would be off duty from time to time and would have less
opportunity for earning overtime but would be likely to remain in the employ-   I
ment of the respondents for the rest of the rather short working life left to him;
he was at the date of judgment 57 years of age, although he might not be able
to go on working until 65. On the other hand, the respondents remained at law
at perfect liberty to give him due notice to terminate his employment at any
time. The appellant appealed to the Court of Appeal and on 21st March 1968,
that court increased general damages by £600 again on the footing that his
real loss was that his injury would incapacitate him from earning so much
overtime but that the rest of his working life would probably be spent in

A the employment of his compassionate employers, the respondents. Within a fortnight from that date the appellant was dismissed from his employment.

During the course of the argument before your Lordships there was some discussion as to the bona fides of the respondents in dismissing the appellant but I am satisfied that your Lordships must deal with this appeal on the footing, which for my part I see no reason to doubt, that in all the circumstances of

B the case that dismissal was made perfectly bona fide by the respondents because they had no suitable employment for him in his weakened condition and, furthermore, that his continued employment might be a source of danger to his fellow employees.

But it is perfectly plain on the facts as now known to your Lordships that the basis on which damages had been assessed by the trial judge and increased by

C the Court of Appeal was made on the footing that I have already mentioned, namely, that the appellant would probably be employed for the rest of his working life by the respondents. Thus the basis of the judgment of the Court of Appeal was falsified, however innocently, by the conduct of the respondents in permitting the court to assess damages on that footing. Damages should have been assessed on the footing that he would or might soon be thrown on the employ-

D ment market. So the appellant within due time applied for leave to appeal to your Lordships' House and obtained that leave and he comes within proper time before your Lordships asking that damages may be re-assessed on the facts as now known to be true. But in point of law he cannot succeed in showing any error in the court below, unless he obtains leave to adduce further evidence not available to the trial judge nor to the Court of Appeal, for it relates to events

E after the judgment of the Court of Appeal; thus it is not a case to which the principles of Ladd v. Marshall (8) are fully applicable. We are not here concerned with any case of fraud or dishonest or underhand dealing by one party, where quite different considerations apply.

So here your Lordships are confronted with a conflict of two principles of law. First, it is a very fundamental and important principle of law established in

F the public interest that there should be an end to litigation between parties. As LORD LOREBURN, L.C., said in Brown v. Dean (9), a litigant who has obtained judgment is by law entitled not to be deprived of that judgment without very solid grounds.

On the other hand, where damages have to be assessed on estimates as to the future, the likelihood of dismissal or further ill-health, or in the case of a widow

G making a claim under the Fatal Accidents Acts the probability of her remarriage (these are, of course, only examples), then the court does in proper cases look at the facts that have happened since judgment. So far as the Court of Appeal is concerned the matter is governed by the express terms of R.S.C., Ord. 59, r. 10 (2), giving that court a general discretion to admit evidence of matters that have happened since the date of the judgment (see the opinion of LORD

H GORRELL in A.-G. (at the relation of Tamworth Corpn.) v. Birmingham, Tame and Rea District Drainage Board (10)). Your Lordships' House has no similar rules of procedure governing your Lordships, but I have no doubt that your Lordships have ample power to admit further evidence in cases which seem proper to your Lordships.

Curwen v. James (11), in the Court of Appeal shows that the jurisdiction must

I be exercised sparingly and with due regard to the great principle that a judgment once obtained is not to be disturbed without " solid grounds ". That case was, in my opinion, plainly rightly decided. I agree with all the judgments of the court, but the broad reasons given by HARMAN, L.J. (12), for allowing the

---

(8) [1954] 3 All E.R. 745; [1954] 1 W.L.R. 1489.
(9) [1910] A.C. 373 at p. 374; [1908-10] All E.R. Rep. 661 at p. 662.
(10) [1912] A.C. 788 at p. 801; [1911-13] All E.R. Rep. 926 at p. 939.
(11) [1963] 2 All E.R. 619; [1963] 1 W.L.R. 748.
(12) [1963] 2 All E.R. at p. 623; [1963] 1 W.L.R. at p. 753.

appeal I find the most convincing. So, in my opinion, we ought on the particular **A**
facts of this case to admit evidence of what happened so shortly after the judgment of the Court of Appeal. That evidence being admitted the judgment is
at once shown to be on a false basis and, since the hearing before your Lordships,
the parties have agreed that, if your Lordships propose to allow the appeal,
damages should be increased by an agreed amount. I would allow the appeal
and substitute a judgment which recognises the agreement of the parties.   **B**

My Lords, I have already stated that I agree with the judgments in *Curwen*
v. *James* (13) but I want to emphasise my agreement with what fell from
PEARSON, L.J. (14), when he emphasised his anxiety on this question of the
admission of evidence as to matters after the judgment. It must be sparingly
but in proper cases unhesitatingly exercised. But where the time allowed for
appeal has run out, whether it be to the Court of Appeal or to your Lordships'   **C**
House, I would apply a very strict rule indeed. The great principle " Interest
rei publicae ut sit finis litium " comes into its own. Without finally closing
the door to a litigant who, after the time for appeal has passed, wants to re-open
the matter by giving evidence of matters since the relevant judgment, I would
think he should only be allowed to re-open the matter in very special and
exceptional cases indeed.   **D**

Finally, my Lords, I am not happy about *Jenkins* v. *Richard Thomas &
Baldwins, Ltd.* (15), which may require consideration in the future. In the
case before your Lordships and in *Curwen* v. *James* (13) damages were assessed
on a basis falsified, however innocently (and I accept that in both cases this
was so) by the acts of the defendants. In *Jenkins'* case (15) that element was
entirely lacking. At the trial WINN, J., suggested that the defendants might   **E**
be able to give the plaintiff different employment. A suggestion was made by
the defendants and accepted by the plaintiff. This involved some training in
grinding, but unhappily owing to some auto-suggestion brought on apparently
by the injury, this training did not produce the desired answer and the Court
of Appeal allowed the plaintiff to re-open the question of damages. On what
principle the plaintiff was permitted to resile from his agreement at the trial and **F**
to re-open the question of damages I find obscure.

But for the reasons I have given earlier I would allow this appeal.

LORD DONOVAN: My Lords, I agree with the reasoning and conclusion
expressed in the opinion of my noble and learned friend, LORD PEARSON.

LORD PEARSON: My Lords, the appellant, had been employed at the **G**
respondents' foundry for almost 12 years as a slinger or labourer, doing heavy
work. On 17th March 1965, there was an accident which imposed a sudden and
unexpected strain on his back and neck. He already had, although he was
unaware of it, a condition of degenerative arthritis of the cervical spine, and
the effect of the accident was to cause this previously " silent " disorder to
become painful from time to time.   **H**

The appellant was off work, and attending at a hospital for treatment three
times a week until 21st June 1965, when he returned to work. He was put
on different work, which included carrying patterns from the pattern shop to
the foundry. This was not entirely light work but was less heavy than his previous
work. Then or later he was instructed by the foreman that he was not to carry
anything that was too heavy for him and if there was a need to carry anything   **I**
too heavy he was to seek assistance. The change of work made a difference to
his earnings, because previously he was able to get Sunday overtime work about
twice a month on the average, but now he did not have any Sunday overtime work.

The pain recurred from time to time and caused him to be off work for several
periods: 27th October to 8th November 1965; 20th February to 14th March

(13) [1963] 2 All E.R. 619; [1963] 1 W.L.R. 748.
(14) [1963] 2 All E.R. at p. 624; [1963] 1 W.L.R. at p. 755.
(15) [1966] 2 All E.R. 15; [1966] 1 W.L.R. 476.

A 1966; a date in August to 14th November 1966; and 14th January to 6th February 1967. But after that there was a long period of freedom from pain (at any rate from incapacitating pain) and of continuing work. This period lasted up to and beyond the time of the trial, which took place in October 1967.

Medical reports had been obtained, and medical evidence was given at the trial as to the appellant's condition. According to the reports and evidence of
B the medical experts called for the respondents, the appellant was fit to resume his pre-accident work. But the learned judge preferred the evidence of the appellant's medical expert, whose opinion was that the appellant should be employed only on light manual work.

The learned judge decided that the respondents were liable to the appellant for breach of statutory duty, and with regard to damages he said:

C
" Special damages are agreed at £483 7s. 11d. and I fix the general damages at £750. I have included something in that figure for loss of overtime likely to be suffered in the future and as a result of the possibility of the [appellant] being occasionally off work. I have given a lesser sum by way of general damages than I would otherwise have done because of the possi-
D
bility that if he had not suffered this accident the [appellant] might in the ordinary course of events have strained himself at work or elsewhere which would have incapacitated him in the same way."

By that time (October 1967), the appellant had been retained in the respondents' employment for 2½ years after the accident, and had not been off work for about eight months, and there was no suggestion at the trial that the respondents
E had any intention of dismissing him or were likely to do so. It was assumed by the witnesses, by counsel for the appellant and counsel for the respondents, and by the judge, that the employment of the appellant by the respondents would continue up to his retiring age unless in the meantime some further deterioration of his condition incapacitated him for work in their employment. The case was conducted by both sides at the trial, and judgment was given on
F that basis.

The appellant appealed against the judge's assessment of the damages on the ground that the amount allowed for general damages (£750) was too low. The appellant remained in work until 14th February 1968. Then, owing to recurrence of the pain, he was off work from 14th February to 11th March 1968, and then returned to work. The hearing in the Court of Appeal took place on 21st March
G 1968. Counsel for the appellant, in opening his appeal, sought to refer to the appellant's very recent period of incapacity from 14th February to 11th March 1968, but counsel for the respondents, not having any idea that the appellant would be dismissed in the near future, took the routine objection that if there was to be further evidence as to the appellant's condition the proper steps should have been taken, and apparently this objection was not contested. At
H any rate there was not in the judgment given by Danckwerts, L.J., with which Diplock, L.J., and Cairns, J., agreed, any specific reference to this very recent period of incapacity, and indeed Danckwerts, L.J., having referred to the accident, said: " . . . there was a recurrence of the pain and suffering from time to time over a period of nearly two years . . ." which would be up to February 1967.

I   Danckwerts, L.J., after mentioning the loss of overtime earnings, said:

" There was a loss of earnings in that way, and there were various other possibilities; he might, at any time, possibly suffer further results, with the chance that he might not be able to continue with his employment. On the other hand, there was evidence that if all had gone well he might be able to continue in his work until the usual time of retirement . . ."

In a later passage he said:

" . . . this obviously, was a serious injury and the possibilities for the

future might well be more serious than appears at the present time. Taking   A
one thing and another, on the whole we think that the general damages
should be increased to a sum of £1,350, in addition to the special damages
which were awarded. I think the appeal should therefore be allowed."

Judgment was given by the Court of Appeal on 21st March 1968. Only a fortnight later, on 4th April 1968, the appellant was asked to attend at the respondents' personnel office, and when he went there he was informed that he was   B
dismissed with effect from 5.0 p.m. on the following day, and that he would
be paid a month's wages in lieu of notice, and that the reason for his dismissal
was his disablement caused by the accident in 1965 and that he was too big
an accident risk to be employed by the respondents in the future. On 17th
April 1968, less than a month after the judgment of the Court of Appeal,
application was made on behalf of the appellant for leave to adduce fresh   C
evidence by way of affidavit relating to the appellant's dismissal from the respondents' employment, and for leave to appeal to your Lordships' House from
the judgment of the Court of Appeal. The application was heard, and leave to
appeal was given on 30th April 1968.

It appears from observations made by the Court of Appeal on the hearing
of the application, from the terms of the judgment given by DANCKWERTS, L.J.,   D
on 21st March 1968, from the facts of the case generally and from statements
of counsel that in the Court of Appeal the case was conducted on both sides,
and judgment was given, on the same basis as in the court below, namely, on the
assumption that the employment of the appellant by the respondents would
continue up to his retiring age unless in the meantime some further deterioration
of his condition incapacitated him for work in their employment. Plainly that   E
assumption was falsified by the act of the respondents in dismissing him very
soon after the judgment of the Court of Appeal. Is that fact, in all the circumstances of the case, a sufficient ground for admitting fresh evidence and re-
opening the assessment of damages?

I will endeavour to set out the principal features in the situation and consider
how they bear on the issue in this appeal. 1. If it had been established that the   F
respondents were in material respects guilty of bad faith or negligence or oppression in their treatment of the appellant, that would undoubtedly have been a
good ground for allowing the fresh evidence and re-opening the assessment of
damages. But to my mind, having regard to the sequence of events, no such
misconduct on the part of the respondents has been established. The respondents
could quite well believe up to and beyond the date of the trial that it was reason-   G
ably safe to retain the appellant in their employment doing the comparatively
light work which they could provide for him. But then in February and March
1968, two events happened which might well change their belief. First, after an
interval of about a year, there was a recurrence of the pain to such an extent
as to cause him to be off work for three weeks. Secondly, the Court of Appeal
in giving judgment took a substantially more serious view than that of the   H
learned judge as to the appellant's condition and prospects. After these two
events had happened, the respondents considered or reconsidered the question
whether they should continue to retain the appellant in their employment.
They decided that it would be unsafe to do so, because his condition might cause
an injury to him or to some other workman and also the respondents had an
additional responsibility for his safety in accordance with the principle of *Paris*   I
v. *Stepney Borough Council* (16). Having come to the conclusion that it was
unsafe to continue his employment, they naturally and properly dismissed him
promptly with a month's wages in lieu of notice.

2. The appellant is seeking to adduce fresh evidence, not as to any event
occurring or condition existing before the date of the judgment appealed from,
but only as to an event which has happened after that date. This makes a

(16) [1951] 1 All E.R. 42; [1951] A.C. 367.

A difference according to the practice of the Court of Appeal, which I think can usefully be taken into account in considering what should be done here. R.S.C., Ord. 59, r. 10 (2) (formerly R.S.C., Ord. 58, r. 9 (2)), provides:

B " The Court of Appeal shall have power to receive further evidence on questions of fact, either by oral examination in court, by affidavit, or by deposition taken before an examiner, but, in the case of an appeal from a judgment after trial or hearing of any cause or matter on the merits, no such further evidence (other than evidence as to matters which have occurred after the date of the trial or hearing) shall be admitted except on special grounds."

C Thus, in the Court of Appeal no special grounds are needed for the admission of evidence as to matters which have occurred after the decision of the Court below. The conditions laid down in *Ladd* v. *Marshall* (17) would not be applicable, or not fully applicable, in relation to the admission of evidence of such matters. There must, however, be a discretion to decide whether such evidence is to be admitted or not.

D 3. There is not in this case any difficulty arising from any lapse of time. No extension of time is required.

4. I think it is useful to take into account another aspect of the practice in the Court of Appeal. Under R.S.C., Ord. 59, r. 3 (1) " an appeal to the Court of Appeal shall be by way of rehearing . . ." In *A.-G. (at the relation of Tamworth Corpn.)* v. *Birmingham, Tame and Rea District Drainage Board* (18), where the continuance of an injunction was in question, LORD GORRELL said (19):

E " Under the Judicature Acts and Rules the hearing of an appeal from the judgment of a judge is by way of rehearing, and the Court has power to give any judgment and to make any order which ought to have been made, and to make such further or other order as the Court may think fit . . . The Court also has power to take evidence of matters which have occurred after the date of the decision from which the appeal is brought . . . It seems

F clear, therefore, that the Court of Appeal is entitled and ought to rehear the case as at the time of rehearing . . ."

This passage was cited and relied on in *Curwen* v. *James* (20). That was a case under the Fatal Accidents Act 1846, and the widow had remarried after the judgment of the trial judge but before the hearing in the Court of Appeal. The damages were re-assessed in the light of the known fact of the remarriage.

G HARMAN, L.J., cited *Bwllfa and Merthyr Dare Steam Collieries (1891), Ltd.* v. *Pontypridd Waterworks Co.* (21) and *Re Bradberry, National Provincial Bank, Ltd.* v. *Bradberry, Re Fry, Tasker* v. *Gulliford* (22), and said (23):

H " Why should we, when we know that the plaintiff has married, pretend that we do not know it and assess the damages, as we are assessing them anew here, on the footing that she may or may not marry? As we know the truth, we are not bound to believe in a fiction."

I think it is quite clear that if on appeal fresh evidence is admitted as to subsequent events (events occurring after the date of the judgment appealed from) and the fresh evidence justifies a re-assessment of the damages, the damages should be re-assessed in the light of the relevant facts as known at the date

I of the re-assessment.

5. But there is still the question whether the fresh evidence should be admitted. It is in general undesirable to admit fresh evidence on appeal, because there

(17) [1954] 3 All E.R. 745; [1954] 1 W.L.R. 1489.
(18) [1912] A.C. 788; [1911-13] All E.R. Rep. 926.
(19) [1912] A.C. at p. 801; [1911-13] All E.R. Rep. at p. 939.
(20) [1963] 2 All E.R. 619 at pp. 622, 623; [1963] 1 W.L.R. 748 at pp. 751, 752, 754.
(21) [1903] A.C. 426 at p. 431; [1900-03] All E.R. Rep. 600 at p. 603.
(22) [1942] 2 All E.R. 629 at p. 635; [1943] Ch. 35 at p. 42.
(23) [1963] 2 All E.R. at p. 623; [1963] 1 W.L.R. at p. 754.

ought to be finality in litigation. Interest rei publicae ut sit finis litium. In **A** *Brown* v. *Dean* LORD LOREBURN, L.C., said (24):

"When a litigant has obtained a judgment in a Court of justice . . . he is by law entitled not to be deprived of that judgment without very solid grounds . . ."

As I said in *Curwen* v. *James* (25):

B

" . . . the normal rule in accident cases is that the sum of damages falls to be assessed once for all at the time of the hearing. When the assessment is made, the court has to make the best estimate it can as to events that, may happen in the future. If further evidence as to new events were too easily admitted, there would be no finality in such litigation. There are quite often uncertain matters which have to be estimated and taken into account to the best of the ability of the judge trying the action."

C

In *Jenkins* v. *Richard Thomas & Baldwins, Ltd.* (26), SALMON, L.J., said:

"The general rule is that damages in actions of this type have to be assessed once and for all at the trial. It not infrequently happens that, when damages are assessed at the trial on the basis that the plaintiff will in the future probably be able to earn such and such a sum, it turns out **D** that he is actually able to earn, and does earn, either substantially more or substantially less. It must not be thought that, whenever this occurs, one side or the other can come to this court and appeal and ask for leave to call further evidence with a view to having the damages reduced or increased as the case may be. If the basis on which the damages have been assessed proves to be wrong very shortly after the trial and the point is promptly **E** taken up with the other side, then, in the exceptional circumstances, there may be good grounds for this court giving leave, as we have done here, to call further evidence."

I think the question whether or not the fresh evidence is to be admitted has to be decided by an exercise of discretion. The question is largely a matter of degree, and there is no precise formula which gives a ready answer. It can be **F** said in the present case that the basis on which the case had been conducted on both sides and decided both at the trial and in the Court of Appeal was suddenly and materially falsified by a change of mind, involving a reversal of policy, on the part of the respondents, and in the circumstances it would not be fair or equitable to allow the respondents to retain the advantage of the decision given by the Court of Appeal on the basis which has been so falsified. **G** It is reasonably clear in the present case that leave should be given to adduce the fresh evidence, with the result that there must be a re-assessment of the damages. The question was more difficult on the facts of *Jenkins* v. *Richard Thomas & Baldwins, Ltd.* (27).

I would admit the fresh evidence and allow the appeal. Normally there would be an order for re-assessment of the damages by a High Court judge, **H** and the re-assessment should take into account and be based on all the facts ascertained at the date of the re-assessment, including the facts previously taken into account, the dismissal of the appellant from his employment by the respondents and the nature and prospects of the new employment which he has obtained. But, as the parties have been able to reach agreement as to the amount of the damages, no such order is now required.   *Appeal allowed.* **I**

Solicitors: *W. H. Thompson* (for the appellant); *Geoffrey Coombs & Co.* (for the respondents.)

[*Reported by* S. A. HATTEEA, ESQ., *Barrister-at-Law.*]

---

(24) [1910] A.C. 373 at p. 374; [1908-10] All E.R. Rep. 661 at p. 662.
(25) [1963] 2 All E.R. at p. 624; [1963] 1 W.L.R. at p. 755.
(26) [1966] 2 All E.R. 15 at p. 18; [1966] 1 W.L.R. 476 at p. 479.
(27) [1966] 2 All E.R. 15; [1966] 1 W.L.R. 476.

A   Re PRESTON (deceased).   PRESTON v. HOGGARTH.

[CHANCERY COURT OF THE COUNTY PALATINE OF LANCASTER (Burgess, V.-C.),
March 1, June 25, 1968.]

Family Provision—Provision—Burden of award—Whether power to apportion
burden unequally between beneficiaries in the same class—Inheritance
B   *(Family Provision) Act 1938 (1 & 2 Geo. 6 c. 45), s. 3 (1), (2) as amended*
by Intestates Estates Act 1952 (15 & 16 Geo. 6 & 1 Eliz. 2 c. 64), Sch. 3.

When making an award under the Inheritance (Family Provision) Act
1938, the court is empowered by s. 3 (1) and (2) of the Act to apportion the
burden of that award unequally, not only between respective classes of
beneficiaries, but between beneficiaries of the same class (see p. 963, letter H,
C   post).

[**Editorial note:** with regard to the reference made in the judgment to
VAISEY, J.'s decision in *Re Simson, Simson* v. *National Provincial Bank, Ltd.**,
on the question of distribution by executors after the issue of a summons under
the Inheritance (Family Provision) Act 1938, see the decision of CROSS, J., on
11th July 1968 in *Re Ralphs (decd.), Ralphs* v. *District Bank, Ltd.*†, made
D   shortly after judgment had been given in this case.

As to family provision, see 16 HALSBURY'S LAWS (3rd Edn.) 455-465, paras.
911-930; and for cases on the subject, see 24 DIGEST (Repl.) 967-981, *9753-9799.*

For the Inheritance (Family Provision) Act 1938, s. 3, as amended, see **46**
HALSBURY'S STATUTES (2nd Edn.) 211.]

Case referred to:
E   *Simson, Re, Simson* v. *National Provincial Bank, Ltd.*, [1949] 2 All E.R. 826;
[1950] Ch. 38; 24 Digest (Repl.) 981, *9797.*

Adjourned Summons.

The plaintiff, Ellen Robinson Preston, was the widow of Henry Preston who
died on 5th December 1966 leaving a holograph will dated 18th May 1958.
The plaintiff was excluded from the will and by this application sought reasonable
F   provision for her maintenance out of the estate. The defendants were the
executors of the will, William James Hoggarth (first defendant) and Margaret
Ellen Holt (second defendant); the second defendant was entitled under the
will to a half share in the proceeds of the testator's estate.   The third and fourth
defendants were Kathleen Polding and Patricia Sansbury, nieces of the testator,
each of whom was entitled under the will to a one-eighth share in the proceeds
G   of the estate.   The fifth and sixth defendants were Margaret Jackson and David
Jackson, infant grandchildren of the testator, each of whom was entitled to a
one-eighth share in the proceeds of the estate.

J. FitzHugh for the plaintiff.
E. H. Wells for the first defendant.
W. Geddes for the second defendant.
H   *B. C. Maddocks* for the fifth and sixth defendants.
The third and fourth defendants were not represented by counsel.

BURGESS, V.-C. read the following judgment: This application under
the Inheritance (Family Provision) Act 1938 at a late stage raised a novel point
as to the powers of the court in allocating the burden of any award made under
I   the Act between those beneficially interested under the will.

The industry of counsel failed to find any authority to assist on the particular
question notwithstanding the relevant parts of the Act have been in force since
it came into being in 1938. Doubtless this may be because in the vast majority
of cases there is only one or more representatives of any particular class of
beneficiaries, who usually appear by one counsel, and this is the normal case as
regards those interested in the residuary estate.

* [1949] 2 All E.R. 826; [1950] Ch. 38.
† [1968] 3 All E.R. 285; [1968] 1 W.L.R. 1522.

It is, of course, well known to those acquainted with applications under this **A**
Act since the decision of VAISEY, J., in *Re Simson, Simson* v. *National Provincial
Bank, Ltd.* (1), that once a summons has been or is likely to be launched executors
should not part with any part of the estate for the court has power under s. 3 of
the Act to throw the burden of any award it may make not necessarily on the
residuary estate, but if need be on pecuniary legacies or specific devises thus
altering the normal statutory provisions as to priority in administration and **B**
ascertainment of residue.   What that case did not decide was whether the court
in addition had power between members of the same class, in the present case
residue, to direct that certain shares shall be exonerated in whole or in part from
any burden of the award at the expense of other shares.

In the present case the point was argued because as later appears in the will
itself the testator purported to direct that any award that might be made should **C**
be borne out of the share of residue given to his infant grandchildren, and,
therefore, before me there were two counsel representing persons interested in
the residue, namely, the second defendant, Miss Holt, to whom one-half of the
residue was given, and the fifth and sixth defendants, the two infant
grandchildren to whom an eighth share each of the residue was given.

The facts necessary to decide the question whether the court has power in its **D**
discretion to alter the incidence of the burden as between members of the same
class and which arises in the present case can be shortly stated.   The testator
made his will on 18th May 1958, and died on 5th December 1966—probate
being granted to the first and second defendants, Mr. Hoggarth and Miss Holt,
the executors therein named on 30th January 1967.   The net estate has been
realised and placed on deposit and is now of a value of upwards of £4,600. **E**

The plaintiff in the application was the widow of the testator, a person aged
62 who married him in Australia in the year 1929 when he was 31 and she was 23.
There was only one child of that marriage, now Mrs. Jackson, who is 36 years
of age; she has three children, the fifth and sixth defendants and another child
not mentioned in the will.

In the year 1934 the testator and the plaintiff returned to this country to **F**
Liverpool where his mother, a widow, resided, and where he had spent his childhood before going to Australia.   Due to the conditions at that time the testator
after several months still remained without employment; he, the plaintiff and
child were receiving public assistance.   The plaintiff took the view that this
really was not good enough, for she was sure that if they returned to Australia,
not only she, but probably also he could obtain suitable employment.   By this **G**
time, however, seemingly, the testator was enjoying the return to the scenes of
his childhood and he never returned to Australia.   The plaintiff, quite rightly,
taking her infant daughter with her, did so, and I acccept her account that she
understood and believed that the testator would follow her; but he did not do so.
There was a conflict of fact as to the reasons for this separation and the testator,
rightly or wrongly, took the view that the plaintiff was responsible in that not **H**
only had she emigrated from this country without his consent but also took his
daughter with her without his consent, and in his will he gives this among others
as the primary reason why he saw fit to cut out not only the plaintiff but also
his daughter from any benefit thereunder.

Having considered the whole of the evidence I was in no doubt that reasonable
provision had not been made for the plaintiff who is now no longer able to earn **I**
her own living and is left with a small pension and no free capital, and who by
her own exertions and effort brought up his only daughter for many years.
She had obtained maintenance orders against the testator in Australia not in
large sums but even these were reduced by the Liverpool magistrates and in
substance the plaintiff received virtually no material assistance from the testator
in his lifetime.

---

(1) [1949] 2 All E.R. 826; [1950] Ch. 38.

A   His will is a holograph will apparently in the writing, I was informed, of his brother-in-law, Mr. Royle, a retired accountant. By his will he gave all his estate to be realised as soon as possible and then to be divided into two parts; one-half to be paid to the second defendant for her own use absolutely, the other half to be divided into four equal parts and distributed as to one part to his niece the third defendant, another part to his niece the fourth defendant, a further

B   part to his grandchild the infant fifth defendant, and the remaining part to his grandchild the infant sixth defendant.

The will then continued with his reasons why he had not left any part of his assets to the plaintiff as a result of which he took the view, in my judgment wrongly, that she did not have any claim on any part of his estate, and the will continued as follows:

C   " However, if [the plaintiff] takes action to recover any part of my estate for herself then I desire any award made to her shall be taken out of the part of my estate which I have allotted to my two grandchildren and that their share shall be reduced accordingly."

The second defendant had known the testator and his family for almost the whole of her life. The plaintiff did suggest that there might have been some

D   improper association between her and the testator which was the reason why he did not follow her to Australia, but I unhesitatingly accept the evidence of the second defendant that there was no such association and that they were never more than the very best of friends, so much so that in his last years when his health and abilities were failing, it was she who looked after and nursed him until his death. She is, therefore, in the same position as the Mrs. Burgess in

E   the case before VAISEY, J., of *Re Simson* (2), of whom that learned judge said she had no such moral claim on the testator, as she might have if she had been living with him as his wife, to justify the very substantial benefit that was given to her in the will.

Counsel for the second defendant put the case very fairly. He did not plead any poverty on her behalf. She had put the facts as she thought them to be

F   before the court. Her care for the testator in his last years was not in dispute and he contended that the burden of any award should be borne between the residuary legatees in the fractions that residue had been given to each of them respectively.

Counsel for the fifth and sixth defendants contended that the court had power as between the residuary legatees to throw, if necessary, the whole of the burden

G   of the award on some of the shares to the exclusion of others, and that in the present case no part of the award should in the discretion of the court be thrown on the fifth and sixth defendants who were the only descendants of the testator to benefit under his will.

The wording of the Act of 1938 conferring the power to make an award (and thus vary the provisions of the will) in s. 3 (1) and (2) thereof is very wide, and,

H   in my judgment, after consideration, enables the court not only to apportion the burden of any award as regards respective classes of beneficiaries but also, if in its discretion it thinks fit, to throw the burden unequally between beneficiaries in the same category or classes.

I saw fit at the hearing to make an immediate award of £2,600 to the plaintiff whilst I considered the question of the burden thereof so that she could return

I   to Australia free from any debts she had incurred in coming to this country, and failure to return to that country within a short time would have lost her her small pension.

I have given consideration to the respective contentions of counsel as to how the burden of that award should be borne as between the several residuary legatees, and in the exercise of the discretion and powers I have under the Act I have come to the conclusion that, while it would not be right wholly to exempt the

(2) [1949] 2 All E.R. 826; [1950] Ch. 38.

fifth and sixth defendants from bearing any part of the award for the support A
of the plaintiff, they should nevertheless not each have to bear a full eighth
part thereof but only a sixteenth part.

Accordingly I direct that the burden of the award shall be borne between the
residuary legatees in the following proportions, namely: the second defendant
28 forty-eighths; the third defendant, 7 forty-eighths; the fourth defendant,
7 forty-eighths; the fifth defendant, 3 forty-eighths; and the sixth defendant, B
3 forty-eighths; and that the costs of this application of all parties except the
first defendant on the common fund basis and of the first defendant as trustee
shall be taxed and paid out of the estate in due course of administration.

Order accordingly.

Solicitors: *Jackson & Newton*, Manchester (for the plaintiff); *Fox, Brooks,
Marshall & Co.*, Manchester for *Herbert Green & Co.*, Liverpool (for the first C
and second defendants); *Herbert Green & Co.*, Liverpool (for the third and
fourth defendants); *Risque, Robson & Yates*, Manchester for *Williams, Freeman & Lloyd*, Birmingham (for the fifth and sixth defendants).

[*Reported by* M. DENISE CHORLTON, *Barrister-at-Law.*]

D

R. *v.* SENATE OF THE UNIVERSITY OF ASTON, *Ex parte* ROFFEY AND ANOTHER.

[QUEEN'S BENCH DIVISION (Lord Parker, C.J., Blain and Donaldson, JJ.),
February 24, 25, March 27, 1969.]

Education—University—Students—Natural justice—Student sent down for E
*failing examination—Whether student to be heard in defence before decision
to send down.*
Certiorari—Delay—Discretion.
Mandamus—Delay—Discretion.

The applicants, P. and R. were undergraduates of the University of Aston
reading for the degree of B.Sc. with honours. In June 1967 at the end of F
the first year of their course both passed examinations in the three major
subjects of the course but failed, in the one case, one, and in the other case,
two, of the subsidiary subjects. In September 1967 they were re-examined
in the subsidiary subjects in what were called referred examinations,
but failed again, and badly. The supreme academic authority in the
university was the senate, which was empowered, inter alia, to make regula- G
tions for the education and discipline of students. By special reg. 4 it was
provided that " students who fail in ... a referred examination, may at the
discretion of the examiners re-sit the whole examination or may be required
to withdraw from the course ". The examiners met soon after the referred
examinations taken by the applicants and, after considering their academic
performances and a wide range of personal factors besides, resolved that H
they be asked to withdraw from the course. The applicants were not given
a chance to make representations to this meeting; they were informed of
its decision by letters dated 20th September 1967. A number of other
bodies in the university reviewed this decision. Ultimately it was confirmed by the senate in November, and the university council in December,
1967. The applicants applied in July 1968 for orders of mandamus and I
certiorari. No explanation of their delay was advanced. Since R. was
no longer actively interested in returning to the university his application
was not pressed.

Held: (i) (per DONALDSON and BLAIN, JJ.) on a proper construction of
the regulations, the decision whether a student failing a referred examination
should re-sit the whole examination or withdraw from the course was in the
sole discretion of the examiners and no other body (see p. 974, letter I, to
p. 975, letter A, and p. 978, letter A, post);

A   (ii) (per BLAIN and DONALDSON, JJ.) the examiners in exercising this discretion were obliged to observe the rules of natural justice* (see p. 973, letter C, and p. 977, letter B, post);

(iii) (per BLAIN and DONALDSON, JJ.) the rule audi alteram partem does not apply in every case where the rules of natural justice are applicable (see p. 973, letter E, and p. 977, letter D, post); but (per LORD PARKER,
B   C.J., BLAIN and DONALDSON, JJ.), since the examiners did not limit themselves to a consideration of academic performance, but also (and quite properly) considered a wide range of personal factors, and since so much was at stake for the applicant, P., common fairness demanded that he be given an opportunity to be heard (not necessarily orally); this was not done, and there was, therefore, a breach of the rules of natural justice (see
C   p. 975, letters B to D, p. 978, letters C and D, and p. 979, letter I, post);

(iv) despite the breach of the rules of natural justice the prerogative remedies were still discretionary; and because of the applicant's delay in approaching the court his applications would be refused (see p. 976, letter I, and p. 979, letters E and I, post).

QUAERE: whether the examiners could properly have limited themselves
D   to a consideration of his academic performance (see p. 975, letter B, and p. 978, letter C, post).

Applications refused.

[As to rules of natural justice under Crown proceedings, see 11 HALSBURY'S LAWS (3rd Edn.) 64-66, para. 122; as to rules of natural justice with respect to public authorities, see 30 HALSBURY'S LAWS (3rd Edn.) 718, 719, paras. 1368,
E   1369; and for cases on the subject, see 8 DIGEST (Repl.) 655-657, *30-42.*]

Cases referred to:

A. *(an infant), Re. Hanif* v. *The Secretary of State for Home Affairs. Re S.* (N.) *(an infant), Singh* v. *The Secretary of State for Home Affairs,* [1968] 2 All E.R. 145; sub nom. *Re Mohamed Arif (an infant), Re Nirbhai Singh (infant),* [1968] Ch. 643; [1968] 2 W.L.R. 1290; Digest (Repl.) Supp.
F   *Durayappah* v. *Fernando,* [1967] 2 All E.R. 152; [1967] 2 A.C. 337; [1967] 3 W.L.R. 289; Digest (Repl.) Supp.

K. (H.) *(infant), Re,* [1967] 1 All E.R. 226; sub nom. *Re H.K. (infant),* [1967] 2 Q.B. 617; [1967] 2 W.L.R. 962; Digest (Repl.) Supp.

Ridge v. *Baldwin,* [1963] 2 All E.R. 66; [1964] A.C. 40; [1963] 2 W.L.R. 935; 127 J.P. 295; 37 Digest (Repl.) 195, *32.*
G   *Russell* v. *Duke of Norfolk,* [1949] 1 All E.R. 109; 12 Digest (Repl.) 693, *5321.*

Schmidt v. *Secretary of State for Home Affairs,* [1969] 1 All E.R. 904; [1969] 2 W.L.R. 337.

Sydney (University of), Re, Ex p. Forster, [1963] S.R. (N.S.W.) 723; [1964] S.R. (N.S.W.) 1000; Digest (Cont. Vol. B) 238, *363c.*

Motions for certiorari and mandamus.
H   These were applications by Derek Anthony Roffey and Michael Bruce Pantridge for orders of mandamus directed to the respondents to re-admit the applicants to the University of Aston and, alternatively, for orders of certiorari to bring up and quash a decision made by the senate of the university on 1st November 1967, and confirmed by the council of the university on 8th December 1967, that the applicants were not to continue reading for the degree of B.Sc.   The
I   facts are set out in the judgment of DONALDSON, J.

The cases noted below† were cited during the argument in addition to the cases referred to in the judgment.

J. A. Moncaster for the applicants.

Hugh Forbes, Q.C., and *Michael Mann* for the senate.   *Cur. adv. vult.*

---

* This was conceded by counsel for the senate.
† *R.* v. *University of Cambridge* (1715), 1 Stra. 557; *Ceylon University* v. *Fernando,* [1960] 1 All E.R. 631; [1960] 1 W.L.R. 223; *Vidyodaya University of Ceylon* v. *Silva,* [1964] 3 All E.R. 865; [1965] 1 W.L.R. 77.

27th March. **DONALDSON, J.**, read the first judgment at the invitation of   A
LORD PARKER, C.J.: Derek Anthony Roffey and Michael Bruce Pantridge were
student members of the University of Aston in Birmingham, reading for the
degree of B.Sc. with honours in Behavioural Science.   In June 1967, at the end
of the first year of the course, both passed the examinations in the three major
subjects, consisting respectively of the Elements of Psychology, Elements of
Sociology and Elements of Economics.   In addition the applicant Pantridge   B
passed in the subsidiary subject of Statistics. Unfortunately he failed to achieve
a pass mark in the other subsidiary subject of Social and Economic History.
The applicant Roffey failed to pass in either subsidiary subject.   In September
1967 both the applicants, together with other students who had experienced
similar failures, were re-examined in the subjects in which they had been unsuccessful, but again they failed to achieve pass marks.   Thereafter, on or about   C
20th September 1967 the applicants received letters from their course tutor
asking them to withdraw from the Behavioural Science course and, by implication, from student membership of the university.   Following protests by the
applicants, Mr. Michael Griffin (the president of the guild of students of the
university) and the applicant Pantridge's father, this decision was reviewed by
the board of examiners, the board of the Faculty of Social Science, and the senate   D
and the council of the university and in the end was affirmed.

The applicants now apply to this court for orders of certiorari to bring up and
quash the relevant decision that they be asked to withdraw from the course,
and of mandamus requiring the university, by the appropriate body, to determine in accordance with law whether they should be allowed to re-sit the whole
of the examinations which they took in June 1967 or whether they should be   E
asked to withdraw from the course.   The grounds of these applications are
broadly that those responsible for the decision to refuse to allow them to continue
with their studies and those who reviewed and affirmed the initial decision
failed to observe the requirements of natural justice in that they failed to afford
the applicants any, or any adequate, opportunity of being heard.   Before
expressing any view on the merits of these applications it is necessary to advert   F
to the constitution and organisation of the university and to examine the history
of the matter in greater detail.

The University of Aston in Birmingham was incorporated by royal charter
in April 1966 in direct succession to the college of advanced technology in
that city.   The charter reserves a power of appointment of a visitor, but no
such appointment has yet been made.   The council of the university is the   G
executive governing body concerned with management and administration.
The supreme academic authority in the university is the senate, which is charged
with responsibility for its teaching and research work and for the regulation and
superintendence of the education and discipline of the students.   The charter,
in addition to providing for the constitution and powers of the council and senate,
also provides for the creation of a board of each faculty and for a guild of students,   H
the latter having representatives on the convocation of the university and for an
academic advisory committee to advise the council and senate on academic
matters.   Finally, so far as is material for present purposes, the charter declared
the university to be both a teaching and examining body with power:

" [3 (*a*)] To prescribe in its Ordinances or Regulations the requirements
for Matriculation and the conditions under which persons may be admitted   I
to the University or to any particular course of study . . . (*c*) to confer . . .
under conditions laid down in its Statutes or Ordinances, Degrees . . . on . . .
persons who shall have pursued a course of study approved by the University
and shall have passed the examinations or other tests prescribed by the
University."

Section xxi of the statutes of the university provides that the powers of each
faculty board shall include:

A   " [4] . . . the right to discuss any matters relating to the work of the Faculty and any matter referred to it by any other body within the University and to convey its views and to make recommendations thereon."

Section xix of the statutes confers general disciplinary powers on the senate including the right—

B   " [22] . . . to suspend any student from any class or classes, to exclude any student from any part of the University or its precincts, to expel any student from the University, or to take such other action as the Senate thinks proper . . ."

but these powers are expressly made subject to s. xxviii which provides students with a right of appeal to the senate or to a senate committee against any proposal by the senate to suspend, exclude or expel and entitles the student

C   concerned to be heard in person.

General regulations for the degree of B.Sc. were approved at a meeting of the senate in July 1966, that is to say before the applicants became students for the relevant course.   These provided that:

D   " [6] Candidates who fail to satisfy the examiners in examinations other than final examinations may as the examiners determine either (a) be referred in such subject or subjects in accordance with the appropriate Course Regulations, or (b) resit, on one subsequent occasion only, in the following Academic year, the whole examination with or without further attendance, or (c) be required to withdraw from the Course."

A referred examination is a special additional examination held in September,

E   just before the beginning of the academic year, for those who failed to pass in the particular subject in the regular examinations held in or about June at the end of the previous academic year.   A re-sit is not a special examination, but a re-taking in June of all the examinations taken by the student concerned in the previous June, without exemption based on the fact that he may then have passed some of those examinations.

F   Behavioural Science appears to be concerned with the application of sociology, psychology and economics to the work of management in commerce and industry. Courses in this subject were provided by the college of advanced technology in 1964, 1965 and 1966 and were continued by the new university in 1967.   The prospectus for the year 1966-67 was printed in the spring of 1965 because the system of centralised applications for admissions to universities required such

G   documents to be distributed to all schools not later than 14 months before the beginning of the academic year.   This showed Introductory Statistics as an examinable subject, but Social and Economic History as non-examinable. The Student's Handbook for 1966-67, which may or may not have been published equally far in advance, gave similar information.   Both became inaccurate in the event, since in July 1965 the steering committee for the course of

H   Behavioural Science resolved or recommended that Social and Economic History should become an examinable subject and this took effect in the 1965-66 and subsequent academic years.   I have mentioned this matter because it was relied on by the applicants when seeking leave to issue the present proceedings.   However it is conceded by counsel for the applicants that they were fully informed of this change when they began their studies.

I   This change was also reflected, albeit belatedly, in special regulations governing this course of studies which were approved by the senate on 15th March 1967. The delay in securing this approval was apparently attributable to consideration of other matters which are not here material.   These special regulations also provided under the general heading of " Examinations and Course Structure " that:

" 4 . . . (e) Any student who fails to achieve a pass standard in Statistics and/or Social and Economic History may on the recommendation of the examiners be permitted to take referred examinations in these subjects, and

may, if successful, be permitted to proceed on the Honours Course. (f)   A
Students who fail in more than one major subject, or who fail in a referred
examination, may at the discretion of the examiners, resit the whole examination or may be required to withdraw from the course. Students who are
successful in such resit examinations shall normally be eligible to proceed
to the Pass Degree only.''

The applicant Roffey entered the university as a student in October 1966 and   B
read Behavioural Science from the outset. The applicant Pantridge entered
the college of advanced technology in October 1965 and became a student
member of the university on its incorporation in April 1966. He initially read
Metallurgy, but transferred to the first year of the Behavioural Science course
in January 1967. Both were examined in June 1967, mock or practice examinations having been held in February. On the basis of the results a large number   C
of students, including the applicants, were permitted to take referred examinations in September. Ten out of 21 candidates failed the referred examination
in Social and Economic History and eight out of 12 failed that in Introductory
Statistics. These rates of failure in referred examinations were without precedent, but counsel for the applicants has very fairly and frankly disclaimed any
intention of attacking the marking of the papers.   D

The results caused grave disquiet amongst the academic staff as well as the
students, and consultations were held between the examiners in the two subsidiary subjects and two of the course tutors, one of whom was the chairman of
the examining boards for the course. Each individual's results were considered in
the light of information available on record cards or known to those present.
This was not confined to academic matters, but included the fact that one   E
student was labouring under acute personal and family difficulties, that another
had an impediment of speech which created personal problems and yet another
had crushed two vertebrae in a riding accident and had barely recovered in
time for the referred examination. In the end it was decided that six students,
including the applicants, be asked to withdraw from the course, and that five
students be asked to repeat the first year of the course. These decisions were   F
communicated to the students by the letters dated 20th September 1967 to
which I have already referred.

On 25th September 1967 both the applicants had interviews with Mr. Podmore
who was their tutor. The applicants' accounts of what occurred and Mr. Podmore's account are irreconcilable and it is quite impossible for this court to resolve
that conflict of evidence. Suffice it to say that both the applicants say that   G
Mr. Podmore expressed surprise at the decision to ask them to withdraw from the
course and that this surprise was consistent with their allegation that he and
others had led the applicants to believe that the examinations in the subsidiary
subjects did not matter, that all that was required was that they should pass
them sometime and that, at worst, failure might lead to their being allowed
only to take a pass degree. Mr. Podmore denied that he ever led the applicants   H
to believe that these examinations did not matter or that failure could not lead
to their being asked to withdraw from the course. He also denied expressing
any surprise at the decision, although he said that he may have expressed surprise that neither applicant had done better after having had $2\frac{1}{2}$ months in
which to prepare for the referred examination. Similar denials were made by
other members of the academic staff who were named as sources of an alleged   I
general belief amongst students that the results of the subsidiary examinations
were of no importance. Both applicants say that if they had known what was
at stake they would have worked harder.

At this stage the applicants and other students who were similarly placed,
enlisted the support of Mr. Griffin, the president of the guild of students at the
university. Mr. Griffin, in writing to the vice-chancellor of the university on
28th September 1967 made four points. (a) *The prospectus was misleading and
the fact that Social and Economic History was examinable was not made clear before*

A *students began the course.* This point, as I have said, is no longer relied on by the applicants. (b) *Throughout the year, students were informed by certain members of the teaching staff that failure in a subsidiary subject " would not necessarily result in their being sent down ":* provided that due weight is given to the word " necessarily ", this information was in accordance with the relevant regulations; there is no clear evidence that any member of the teaching staff went further

B than this, if as far. (c) *There was no properly constituted examiners' meeting convened after the September examinations to discuss individual cases:* this may be correct in that the full board of examiners did not meet before the initial decision was taken but, as will appear, there was such a meeting at a later stage and the point was not pursued in argument. (d) *A number of general tutors were not informed of the results of the referred examinations until after the candidates were*

C *themselves informed:* this is true, but it is not clear why this should amount to more than possible discourtesy to the general tutors concerned; the reason for the omission was that some of the tutors were not available and it was not considered desirable to delay publication of the decisions which had been reached.

The vice-chancellor met Mr. Griffin and, as a result of the discussion with him, arranged for enquiries to be made in the relevant department, namely that of

D Industrial Administration. On 4th October 1967 the vice-chancellor received a full report from Professor Gibson who was head of the department and Dean of the Faculty of Social Science. Having read this report he suggested that the board of examiners should reconsider all the decisions which had been made following the referred examinations. Two days later, after further considera- tion of this report, he suggested to Professor Gibson that the board of the

E Faculty of Social Science might consider whether some of the students who had been asked to withdraw from the Behavioural Science course could be re-admitted to read for a pass, as contrasted with an honours degree. Meanwhile, on 5th October 1967 Professor Gibson on his own initiative had convened a full meeting of the board of examiners for Behavioural Science. At that meeting the points raised by Mr. Griffin were considered. The dean also asked if any of the members

F wished to raise any other matters affecting the decision of the examiners, but no one wished to do so. The board decided that there had been no departure from the correct procedure and that the policy of not having a full meeting of the board to consider the results of referred examinations would be followed in the future, subject to the modification that " in order that justice might more obviously be seen to be done, General Tutors would in future join the subject

G tutors and the internal examiners in their deliberations ". The board unanim- ously confirmed the decisions taken as a result of the referred examinations. On 6th October 1967, the board of the Faculty of Social Sciences met and dis- cussed the problem of the referred examination results. The board expressed its complete faith in the competence of the board of examiners and agreed that the vice-chancellor's suggestion that some of the students might be allowed to

H read for a pass degree instead of being asked to withdraw, should be referred to the board of examiners. The faculty board decided to meet again immediately after a special meeting of the board of examiners to be held on 9th October. When the board of examiners met, they re-examined all the results and confirmed their previous decisions. The board of the faculty met immediately afterwards and confirmed the decisions of the board of examiners.

I On 11th October 1967, the matter was reported to the senate which, possibly in ignorance of the full extent of the reconsideration which had already taken place, agreed that the matter should be reconsidered without delay. This was interpreted by the board of the Faculty of Social Sciences as a request for still further consideration and a special meeting was accordingly called for 12th October 1967. The vice-chancellor, who was unable to attend the meeting of the board of the faculty, considers this a misinterpretation, but it is clear that his view was not shared by Professor Gibson, the dean of the faculty, and was probably not shared by a Mr. Wylie who had raised the matter in the senate

and was present at the faculty board meeting. This meeting is of some impor- A
tance to the applicants' case and should therefore be dealt with fully. The dean
referred to letters from Mr. Griffin, as president of the guild of students, making
specific allegations of statements by members of the staff which, if made, could
have misled the students. He reported that the senate had referred the matter
back to the board as, to quote the minutes of the board:

" It had been felt by the Senate that a significant case existed for very B
careful re-examination so as to consider whether uncertainty existed and it
was also felt that any benefit of the doubt should go to the students."

After a prolonged discussion it was proposed, again quoting the minutes:

". . . that a small group consisting of the Professors in the Faculty should
meet the staff and students and report back to the meeting at 4.15 p.m.
It was emphasised that the group was not a judicial enquiry but was to C
try and ascertain whether doubt and uncertainty had existed."

The meeting adjourned at 3.15 p.m. Thereafter the professors met all the
students who had failed the referred examinations with the sole exception of
the applicant, Pantridge. His absence remains unexplained. According to
the applicant Roffey, each of the students— D

". . . told the meeting how our tutors had interpreted the faculty rules
to us to the effect that we would not be sent down, but allowed to re-sit our
subsidiary subjects at some later stage."

The faculty board reconvened at 4.20 p.m. and according to the minutes:

" Professor Gibson reported that six students and the President of the
Guild had been seen as a group and two members of the staff who had been E
named in the President's letter had been seen, the third being ill and not
available. He stated that while the Professors could not accept the allegations that members of staff had made the categorical statements which
students allege had been made it was obvious that the students now
firmly and honestly believed that they had been misled. It had also become
apparent that the two members of staff themselves might not have been F
absolutely clear about what the Regulations said and therefore would not
have made the categorical statements alleged. The Faculty Board therefore resolved that, while not accepting the allegations made by the students,
it was satisfied that there might have been some uncertainty in the minds of
some of the students about what would happen to them if they failed referred
examinations, that this uncertainty could have affected their performances G
and in such circumstances it was unfair that the students who had failed
referred examinations should be treated differently from one another. It
was therefore agreed that in accordance with the special Regulations for the
Degree of Bachelor of Science the six students who had been asked to
withdraw from the course should now be allowed to retake the first year
examinations in the following year with or without further attendance." H

The minutes then record the dissent of one member from this decision and
continue:

" After further considerable discussion it was also agreed that the matter
should be referred back to the Board of Examiners to: a) Consider whether
any or all of the 11 students should be admitted into the second year, and
b) Prepare, as a matter of urgency, a paper setting out the academic back- I
ground and potentialities of the 11 students for future reference . . ."

It is important to note that the board of examiners was not being asked to reconsider the issue whether the students should be allowed to re-sit the first year
examination or be required to withdraw from the course. That issue had been
decided in favour of the students so far as the faculty board was concerned. What
the board of examiners was being asked to decide was whether any, and if so
which, of the students should not be required to re-sit the June examination

A but should be allowed to pass on forthwith to the second year of the course. The board of examiners met on 16th October 1967 to consider this remit. They resolved to advise the faculty board that:

"... they do not consider that there are general grounds for admitting some students to the second year of the Honours Course without re-taking the first year. They consider that students should re-take the first year
B examinations with, or without, further attendance and as a result of those examinations should be eligible for reconsideration for admission to the Honours Course as well as the Pass Course. Such students would be expected to keep themselves informed of syllabuses and regulations."

The board also prepared a series of academic profiles which showed, inter alia, that the applicant Pantridge secured one per cent. less marks (17 per cent.
C instead of 18 per cent.) in the referred examination in Social and Economic History than he achieved in June and that the applicant Roffey secured 24 per cent. in Introductory Statistics in the referred examination as compared with 20 per cent. in June and 17 per cent. in Social and Economic History as compared with 16 per cent. in June. The pass mark was 40 per cent. The applicant Pantridge's " profile " attributed his failure to what was described by the general
D tutor as " a heavy programme of Students' Union activities ". It ended with the remark that—

" There was a vague feeling at the Examiners' Meeting, based on class-work marks, that [the applicant] Pantridge was in fact quite able and he was therefore admitted to the second year of the Honours Course."

E This is a reference to the June meeting of the examiners and means no more than that the applicant Pantridge was admitted to the second year of the honours course subject to his passing the referred examination. The board of the faculty met again on 18th October 1967, and, with two dissentients, resolved to recommend that the six students who had been asked to withdraw from the course be permitted to take the first year examinations in June 1968, with or without
F further attendance, and that the question whether they should, if successful then proceed to the second year of the honours degree or the second year of the pass degree be considered afresh in the light of the results then obtained. The board also recommended that the six students be informed as soon as possible and resolved that their recommendations be forwarded to the senate with a recommendation that the matter be treated as one of great urgency.

G Professor Gibson told Mr. Griffin and some of the students concerned in confidence what had been decided by the faculty board, explained that this decision required ratification by the vice-chancellor or the senate, but said that his own view was that such ratification would almost certainly be forthcoming.

A special meeting of the senate was held on 1st November 1967 and was devoted exclusively to the results of the examinations in the Behavioural Science
H course and subsequent events. The senate considered whether to hear the president of the guild of students but decided not to do so, it having been reported that at a meeting of the senate guild joint committee on the previous day no new information or argument had been produced. Professor Gibson outlined the history of the matter and an extensive discussion ensued. Ultimately the senate agreed:

I " (i) that the students on the course had been issued with all appropriate Regulations, and that the Special Regulations had been discussed by the Course Tutor; (ii) that the examinations in June and September had been properly conducted in accordance with the Regulations; (iii) that the students concerned had been properly informed about the referred examinations, and that no doubt as to their significance within the Regulations had been established; (iv) that in considering the results, consideration had been given to general appraisal of Tutor's comments of each student's general capacity and potential, promise and personality; (v) that while some students might

have had erroneous ideas about the significance of the referred examinations, **A**
this was not sufficient to show that students had been misled by the
University, and therefore no substantial cause existed for overruling the
Regulations."

The senate then resolved by 18 votes to four to confirm the original decision of
the board of examiners that the five students be permitted to repeat the first
year examinations and that the remaining six be asked to withdraw. This **B**
decision was communicated to the applicants and the other students affected
by letter dated the same day.

In response to a suggestion by the academic advisory committee, members
of the senate met on 7th December 1967. Whether it was a meeting of the
senate as such is doubtful as no formal record of the meeting was kept. Mr.
Griffin says that it was stressed to the students and their advisers that the **C**
purpose was to explain the decision arrived at by the senate and not to reconsider
it. The vice-chancellor questioned such of the students as attended, but the
applicant Pantridge was not amongst them, as he had been advised by the guild
of students not to attend. After the meeting, or at all events after the students
had left, the members of the senate questioned the members of the staff who
were alleged to have made misleading statements to the students and the vice- **D**
chancellor satisfied himself that there was no substance in the allegations.

The university council met on 8th December, considered the relevant papers
and heard a report from the vice-chancellor that he was satisfied that there was
no substance in any of the allegations. It accepted the vice-chancellor's report
and, to quote the vice-chancellor, ". . . resolved to defend the University against
any attack and to issue a public statement ". This statement recorded that the **E**
council had resolved: " to give complete support to the decision of the senate
that the decisions of the Board of Examiners should stand ". In the context
of the vice-chancellor's evidence, it is reasonably clear that the decision of the
board of examiners to which reference was made was that of the two examiners
and the two course tutors held on or about 19th September 1967. Although
the university's attitude had become clearly and immutably defined by the **F**
beginning of December 1967, the applicants delayed until July 1968 before they
applied to this court for leave to bring these proceedings. As a result they lost
all chance, if successful, of being admitted for the academic year 1968-69. No
explanation for this delay has been offered by either applicant, but Mr. Griffin
said that the whole matter was referred to the National Union of Students on
whose advice professional legal assistance was sought, the cost being borne by **G**
that union's student legal aid fund. He added that statements had to be taken
from the students, some of whom had left the university and that it was necessary
to find out which of them wished to take legal action.

The applicant Roffey, obtained a place at the Regent Street Polytechnic in
London and is no longer actively interested in returning to the university. I
can understand his wishing to be in a position to refuse an offer by the university **H**
to allow him to resume the course, but prerogative writs are a discretionary
remedy designed to remedy real and substantial injustice rather than to give
satisfaction, however legitimate. In the circumstances his claim must fail on
grounds of discretion whatever its substantive merit and I need say no more
about it.

The applicant Pantridge, has not been so fortunate. Whilst the matter **I**
was being debated within the university he was optimistic of the outcome and
did not seek a place elsewhere. When he realised that his optimism was mis-
placed, he applied successfully for admission as a student of London University
to read for an external degree in Sociology, but was unsuccessful in obtaining a
place at the Birmingham College of Commerce to study for such a degree, the
senior tutor telling him bluntly that they had a reputation to keep up and were
not prepared to accept drop-outs from the University of Aston. The applicant
Pantridge has been forced to abandon academic study and is now working in a

A stationer's shop training for retail management. He, unlike the applicant Roffey, expresses a real wish and need to return to the university and his application merits serious consideration. Although both the regulations and the letters to the applicant Pantridge speak of a request to withdraw from the course, thus leaving open the theoretical possibility that he might be accepted to read for some other course within the university, it is clear that the reality was that

B the applicant Pantridge was being sent down. Whatever may be the position elsewhere, students at Aston are members of the university and he was being deprived of his membership. Counsel for the applicants submits that in such circumstances natural justice requires that before the deciding body reaches a decision of such a nature, the applicant Pantridge should be given an opportunity of being heard in his own defence; in other words, the maxim audi alteram

C partem applies.

Counsel for the senate concedes that the concept of natural justice is applicable, but he says that this is a general concept involving lack of bias, accord with any relevant rules and general fairness and is not to be confused with audi alteram partem which is a special rule applicable in only a limited sphere. The prerequisite for its application is that the person concerned must be faced with

D some sort of charge. If, but only if, this is the case, the rule requires that the charge be made known to him and that he be given the opportunity to rebut it. In the present case, he submits, no charge was made against the applicant Pantridge. His position was quite simply that of a young man who had twice failed his examinations and failed them badly. Any young man so circumstanced should expect to be sent down and had no right to be heard when the university

E was engaged in the benevolent exercise of deciding whether it could afford to mitigate the necessary penalty. According to counsel's submission, a student who has failed occupies a position analogous to one holding office at pleasure.

In my judgment it is not right to treat the principle of audi alteram partem as something divorced from the concept of natural justice, although it will certainly not apply in every case in which there is a right to natural justice.

F Where, however, it does apply, it is an integral part of natural justice and may indeed lie at its heart. LORD UPJOHN delivering the report of the Judicial Committee of the Privy Council in *Durayappah* v. *Fernando* (1) said that outside well-known cases such as dismissal from office, deprivation of property and expulsion from clubs there existed a vast area within which the principle could only be applied on most general considerations. In considering its applicability regard

G had to be had to the wording of the provisions concerned, in this case the special regulations, and to three matters, namely first, what is the nature of the property, the office held, status enjoyed or services to be performed by the complainant. Second, in what circumstances or on what occasions is the person claiming to be entitled to exercise the measure of control entitled to intervene. Thirdly, when a right to intervene is proved, what sanction in fact is the latter entitled to impose

H on the other.

The first and third of these matters fall to be considered together in this case. The applicant Pantridge was a student member of the university enjoying the rights and privileges of that status with the chance of achieving graduate status in due time. The sanction which the university was entitled to impose was total deprivation of that status and of the chance of improving it thereafter. Further-

I more, the applicant Pantridge found to his cost, an ex-student member of a university may well be in a more disadvantageous position than one who aspires for the first time to student status. There have been more momentous decisions than that made by the examiners in the case of the applicant Pantridge, but there can be no denying its gravity from his point of view.

The second matter falls to be considered with and in the context of the special regulations governing the course. There is much force in the contention of

---

(1) [1967] 2 All E.R. 152 at p. 156; [1967] 2 A.C. 337 at p. 349.

counsel for the senate that examinations are meant to be passed and that those A
who fail to do so at a university prima facie should expect to be sent down.
I am quite prepared to accept it as a background against which the special
regulations fall to be construed. They, however, provide a most elaborate
code which almost effaces the background. We are concerned with the qualifying
year which determines whether the student moves on to study for an honours
degree, to study for a pass degree, or has to leave the university. It is only in B
the latter case that membership of the university—a body with some of the
attributes of a club—is in question. If the student passes in all major subjects
at honours standard and in subsidiary subjects at pass standard, he moves on
to the honours degree course automatically (special reg. 4 (b)). If he achieves
pass standards in all subjects, he moves on to a pass degree course (special reg.
4 (c)). If he fails to achieve a pass standard in a major subject, he may be C
permitted to take a referred examination in that subject at the discretion of the
examiners and, if successful, will move on to the pass course (special reg. 4 (d)).
If he fails to achieve pass standards in either or both subsidiary subjects and, I
assume although it is not so stated, achieves honours standards in the major
subjects, he may on the recommendation of the examiners be permitted to take
referred examinations in these subjects and, if successful, may be permitted to D
proceed on the honours course (special reg. 4 (e)). It is not stated to whom
the recommendation is to be made and who decides, or why under this regulation
the examiners recommend rather than exercise their own discretion. If he fails
in more than one major subject (of which there are three and the applicant
Pantridge was successful in them all) or fails in a referred examination (which
the applicant Pantridge did in the case of one subsidiary subject) he may at the E
sole discretion of the examiners re-sit the whole examination or may be required
to withdraw from the course. In the event of his being successful in the re-sit
examination he would normally proceed to the pass degree only (special reg. 4 (f)).
The regulations enjoin examiners in deciding whether to allow students to re-take
examinations to have regard to their performance in non-examinable subjects
(special reg. 4 (g)) and with an escape clause providing that students may not F
normally (my emphasis) proceed to the second year of the course until they have
satisfied the examiners in the examinations as a whole (special reg. 4 (h)). They
could quite properly have provided, but did not provide, that the examiners
should be under no obligation to afford the students any opportunity to make
representations to them, before making a decision. Had the regulations taken
this form, no problem would have arisen. G

I have dealt with these regulations at length because it seems to me that they
largely destroy the prima facie approach of " pass or go down ". Their elaboration continues in relation to the honours course, the honours final, the pass
degree course and the pass final. Of these, reg. 6.4 (b) which applies to the
pass degree course is important, not because it is of direct application, but because
it shows a contrasting approach to that indicated by reg. 4 (f) under which the H
applicant Pantridge was sent down. That regulation provides that—

" Any student who fails to satisfy the examiners in not more than two
subjects may at the discretion of the examiners be permitted to take a
referred examination in these subjects. Students failing to reach pass
standard in three or more subjects, or who fail a referred examination,
may not normally proceed further on the course." I

Here alone is the " pass or go down " approach to be seen. Scarcely a body in
the university failed to make a recommendation or a decision in the case of the
applicant Pantridge and his fellow students. No doubt their interventions
were inspired by the most laudable of motives, although their lack of unanimity
was in many ways unfortunate. The fact remains that whilst other bodies might
be able in practice to temper the wind to the failed student, the only body invested by the regulations with the power and discretion to decide whether or not

A the applicant Pantridge should be sent down was "the examiners". For my part I am inclined to think that as the regulations stand this means the full board of examiners but the decision was in fact taken by a smaller body and no objection has been taken on that account. For the purposes of this case, I shall assume that theirs was the discretion and theirs the decision.

I can understand it being argued on the regulations that regard was to be
B had primarily and possibly exclusively to the examination results and performances in non-examinable subjects. However, the examiners themselves did not adopt this approach, as I think rightly, and they considered a wide range of extraneous factors, some of which by their very nature, for example personal and family problems, might only have been known to the students themselves. In such circumstances and with so much at stake, common fairness
C to the students, which is all that natural justice is, and the desire of the examiners to exercise their discretion on the most solid basis, alike demanded that before a final decision was reached the students should be given an opportunity to be heard either orally or in writing, in person or by their representative as might be most appropriate. It was, in my judgment, the examiners' duty and the student's right that such audience be given. It was not given and there was a breach of
D the rules of natural justice.

In the course of the argument it was submitted that students who had failed their examinations were in no better position than those who applied for admission as students, the latter plainly having no right to be heard, but this in my judgment overlooks the accrued status of the students as members of the university. Reference was also made to the immigrant cases such as *Re K.* (H.) (*infant*)
E (2), *Re A.* (*an infant*), *Re S.* (*N.*) (*an infant*) (3) and *Schmidt* v. *Secretary of State for Home Affairs* (4), but these are not really analogous. The industry of counsel enabled us to be referred to a decision of the courts of New South Wales, *Re University of Sydney, Ex p. Forster* (5), which bore a striking similarity on its facts, but there the issue was not a right of audience, but an alleged absolute right to remain a member of the university irrespective of examination results. The court
F denied the existence of any such right, but its existence has not been suggested in the present case.

This by no means concludes the matter in the applicant Pantridge's favour, because it is not in all circumstances that a breach of the requirements of natural justice will give rise to prerogative redress. The remedies are discretionary and a very important factor is the likelihood that the ultimate decision would
G have been any different, if a right of audience had been extended to the applicant Pantridge. It is in this context that the history of the affair after the initial decision is of relevance, but is difficult to evaluate. In the course of the argument counsel for the applicants was asked whether there was any further information which the applicant Pantridge wished to place before the court, but, after taking instructions, counsel said that there was none.
H The fact remains that the examiners who reached the initial, and as I think the only directly relevant, decision, were wholly unaware of the widespread allegations that the students had been misled by members of the staff as to what was at stake when they prepared, or failed to prepare, for the examinations in the subsidiary subjects and for the referred examinations in those subjects. Would the knowledge have made any difference? It may well be thought that
I the applicant Pantridge achieved only derisory marks (17 per cent. in the referred examination), but students with 22 per cent. and 25 per cent. were permitted to repeat the first year. When one tries to assess the probable outcome on the basis of the attitude of the full board of examiners, the board of the faculty, the academic advisory committee, the senate and the council, all of whom knew of the allegations and either had investigated them or knew the results of such

(2) [1967] 1 All E.R. 226; [1967] 2 Q.B. 617.
(3) [1968] 2 All E.R. 145; [1968] Ch. 643.
(4) [1969] 1 All E.R. 904; [1969] 2 W.L.R. 337.   (5) [1963] S.R. (N.S.W.) 723.

investigations, the problem becomes more difficult still. None of these bodies A
regarded the allegations as proved, but some clearly took the view that the
students honestly believed in their truth. The board of the faculty, acting on
the basis of the professors' interview with the students, intended to exercise the
discretion which they mistakenly thought that they possessed in favour of the
students. The academic advisory committee clearly thought that the principles
of good administration required that both students and staff be heard by the B
senate. In my judgment it is impossible to project subsequent attitudes backwards in point of time and to determine what the examiners would have done
if they had heard the students' allegations, before making a decision.

In this situation I regard the time factor as decisive. The prerogative remedies
are exceptional in their nature and should not be made available to those who
sleep on their rights. The applicant Pantridge's complaint is that he was not C
allowed to re-sit the whole examination in June 1968 and, if successful, proceed
to the pass degree course in the 1968-69 academic year, yet he did not even apply
to move this court until July 1968. By such inaction, in my judgment he
forfeited whatever claims he might otherwise have had to the court's intervention.
I would therefore refuse the relief sought.

BLAIN, J., read the following judgment: The grounds put forward in D
support of this application are that the decision of the senate of the University
of Aston in Birmingham or alternatively the decision of the examiners for
referred examinations for which the applicants sat unsuccessfully in September
1967 was a nullity in that it was arrived at in a manner contrary to natural
justice. In *Russell* v. *Duke of Norfolk* (6) TUCKER, L.J., said (6):

" There are . . . no words which are of universal application to every kind E
of inquiry and every kind of domestic tribunal. The requirements of
natural justice must depend on the circumstances of the case, the nature of
the inquiry, the rules under which the tribunal is acting, the subject-matter
that is being dealt with, and so forth."

Those words were quoted by LORD HODSON in his speech in *Ridge* v. *Baldwin* (7), F
the case in which LORD REID reviewed most of the leading cases and delivered
the modern classic speech on the subject. LORD REID said (8) that one reason
why authorities in the past have been difficult to reconcile is the failure to
appreciate the difference between various kinds of cases in which it has been
sought to apply the principle. He instanced among different categories of case:
(i) Cases of dismissal. And these he divided into three classes: (a) dismissal G
of a servant by a master; (b) dismissal from an office held during pleasure;
(c) dismissal from office where there must be something against a man to warrant
his dismissal. (ii) Deprivation of membership of a professional or social body.
Membership of the Stock Exchange or membership of any members' club are
instances, quite apart from the membership of a trade union (where the common
law rights may be clouded by special considerations). (iii) Deprivation of H
property or interference with personal rights by the processes of administrative
law.

I do not think that LORD REID's classification was intended to be exhaustive.
Indeed he virtually said as much himself when suggesting (9) that the reason
for apparently irreconcilable decisions in the past was the failure to appreciate
the great variety of contexts in which the concept of natural justice might
arise (10). In the instant case the facts, the history and what I may loosely I
call the constitution of the university and its constituent or subordinate bodies
have been summarised by DONALDSON, J. In my opinion they indicate that
these student applicants fall into the second category named by LORD REID.

(6) [1949] 1 All E.R. 109 at p. 118.
(7) [1963] 2 All E.R. 66 at p. 114; [1964] A.C. 40 at p. 132.
(8) [1963] 2 All E.R. at p. 71, et seq.; [1964] A.C. at p. 65 et seq.
(9) [1963] 2 All E.R. at p. 71; [1964] A.C. at p. 65.
(10) [1963] 2 All E.R. at p. 73; [1964] A.C. at p. 68.

A They were members of the university—that is a status akin to membership of a social body, a club with perhaps something more than mere social status attached to it, in that so long as they remained students they were potential graduates and potential holders of degrees which could prove advantageous in professional or commercial life.

Approaching their application in that way three questions arise: (i) Is the
B concept of natural justice applicable at all? That much is conceded and rightly so. (ii) When the senate or the examiners (as the case may be) decided that these students should be required to withdraw from the course, was that decision arrived at in accordance with the principles of natural justice? The markings of the examination papers are not criticised and this comes down to a question whether the applicants should have had an opportunity, which they did not have,
C to justify or explain their failure. In other words was this a case for audi alteram partem? (iii) If in making its decision the deciding body did not act in accordance with the principles of natural justice, should this court interfere with the decision in the exercise of its discretion to make a prerogative order or orders?

(a) I share DONALDSON, J.'s view that the right to be heard is often an example of and an integral part of the concept of natural justice and also his view that
D it is not always a necessary ingredient of that concept. Was it a necessary ingredient here? I do not conceal the fact that I have found that a very difficult question to resolve in my mind. (b) The first consideration is: what body or what arm of the university took and was empowered to take the effective decision complained of? Article 12 of the university's charter made the senate the supreme academic authority of the university and section xix of the statutes prescribed
E the senate's powers, including in para. 10 the power to regulate all university examinations and to appoint examiners, and in para. 27 of the power to make regulations in the exercise of the senate's general powers. (c) The senate approved general regulations on 1st July 1966 and special regulations for the course for the degree of B.Sc., with honours in Behavioural Science on 15th March 1967. General reg. 6 provides:

F " Candidates who fail to satisfy the examiners in examinations other than final examinations may as the examiners determine either (a) be referred in such subject or subjects in accordance with the appropriate Course Regulations, or (b) resit, on one subsequent occasion only, in the following Academic year, the whole examination with or without further attendance, or (c) be required to withdraw from the Course."

G Special reg. 4, so far as relevant, provides:

" Part I (Qualifying) (a) The following subjects shall be studied, and except where marked [with an asterisk] candidates must present themselves for examination towards the end of the third term of the first year. Major subjects: i) Elements of Psychology ii) Elements of Sociology iii) Elements of Economics
H " Subsidiary subjects: iv) Social and Economic History v) Statistics . . . (e) Any student who fails to achieve a pass standard in Statistics and/or Social and Economic History may on the recommendation of the examiners be permitted to take referred examinations in these subjects, and may, if successful, be permitted to proceed on the Honours Course."

I This does not indicate to what body the examiners' recommendation is to go— presumably either the senate or possibly the faculty board, but it is not a question which needs to be resolved in these proceedings since the applicants were in fact permitted to and did take referred examinations and it is their failure in such referred examinations that brings them here.

" 4 (f) Students who fail in more than one major subject, or who fail in a referred examination, may at the discretion of the examiners, resit the whole examination or may be required to withdraw from the course. Students who are successful in such resit examinations shall normally be eligible to proceed to the Pass Degree only."

This in my view clearly indicates that the decision whether a student failing   A
such a referred examination should re-sit the whole examination or withdraw
from the course is in the sole discretion of the examiners and no higher or other
body.   If this be right the question is whether the examiners *before deciding to
require the applicants to withdraw from the course* should have afforded them the
opportunity to explain or mitigate their failure either orally or in writing.   The
decision was first taken or communicated to the applicants on 20th September   B
1967 and I start by considering whether at that date there had been a failure
of natural justice.   In the light of their somewhat dismal failure (particularly
in the case of the applicant Pantridge) plus what this court knows from what
have been called the " academic profiles " subsequently prepared, I find it hard
to believe that even a personal interview before the decision of the examiners
could have contributed to any different decision, but (as LORD REID said in   C
Ridge v. *Baldwin* (11)) it is at least doubtful whether that is relevant and I
eliminate it from my mind.

It may well be that the examiners would have been entitled to decide purely
on the examination results (I have detected nothing in special reg. 4 or elsewhere
to inhibit this) but from para. 10 of the affidavit of the course tutor, Mr. Hall,
it is clear that on 19th September 1967 the marks and also the students' records   D
throughout the year were considered by the board of examiners (and very
properly so, in my view) before the decision to require their withdrawal was taken.
In such circumstances, and particularly since in effect the decision was one resulting in the applicants being sent down (albeit not for any disciplinary misdemea-
nour but for failure to make the grade) in my view common fairness demanded
an opportunity for representation to be made by or on behalf of the applicants—   E
I do not go so far as to say necessarily a personal interview.   But this is not the
end of the question.   In *Ridge* v. *Baldwin* (11), LORD REID said:

"I do not doubt that if an officer or body realises that it has acted hastily
and reconsiders the whole matter afresh after affording to the person
affected a proper opportunity to present his case then its later decision
will be valid."   F

I find it necessary therefore to consider what happened after 20th September
1967—a whole series of events enumerated by DONALDSON, J.   There were personal interviews with the tutor (on 25th September);   representations by the
president of the guild of students to the vice-chancellor (on 28th September);
a report from the dean of the faculty to the vice-chancellor (on 4th October);   G
a meeting of the board of examiners (on 5th October);   a meeting of the faculty
board (on 6th October) *a meeting of the board of examiners (on 9th October)*;   and
a subsequent meeting of the faculty board on the same day; a report to the senate
(on 11th October);   a further meeting of the faculty board (on 12th October);
later on 12th October a meeting between a group of the professors in the faculty
and all the students who had failed the referred examinations, except the applicant   H
Pantridge who failed to attend—at this meeting the students who attended
made their explanations to the group of professors who decided to go into the
academic backgrounds of the students concerned;   *a meeting of the board of
examiners (on 16th October)*;   production of the " academic profiles " by the
board of examiners;   another meeting of the faculty board (on 18th October)
which recommended that the applicants and others required to withdraw should   I
be permitted to re-sit in June 1968;   unofficial notification to the students of
this recommendation;   a meeting of the senate itself (on 1st November) which
" confirmed " (or purported to confirm) the original decision of the examiners
and this was communicated to the applicants on that day.

It is clear that at all levels all concerned were at pains to do what they believed
to be their proper duty to the students concerned.   But the fact remains that the
body entrusted with the decision remained the examiners.   Among those various
meetings, therefore, it is the meetings of the examiners which are important in

(11) [1963] 2 All E.R. at p. 80;   [1964] A.C. at p. 79.

A this court. The minutes of the meeting of the board of examiners on 16th October are illuminating. At this meeting Professor Gibson, the dean, is reported as setting out the background to the meeting and informing those present that the faculty board had " considered fresh information made available to it and had made enquiries amongst students and members of the staff ". This is clearly a reference to what had occurred four days earlier when the faculty board had

B adjourned at 3.15 p.m. and reconvened at 4.20 p.m.—a group of the professors in the faculty having interviewed six students and the president of the guild of students meanwhile (indeed the adjournment had been for this express purpose). In the light of what occurred on 12th and 16th October I find it impossible to say that by 16th October the examiners were not fully possessed of the students' explanations for failure in the referred examinations. But the

C examiners, doubtless considering that the matter had passed out of their hands, did nothing to alter or affirm their original decision. Had they made a fresh decision it could have been come to, in my opinion, in accordance with the concept of ordinary fairness—of natural justice—whichever way the decision had gone, because they would have had the benefit of the students' representations (albeit obtained through the channel of the interviews and opportunities for interview

D with the group of professors on 12th October). As it is they, that is, the examiners, did not reconsider their decision of 20th September. So far as the students are concerned they simply received notification dated 1st November 1967 purporting to confirm their non-eligibility. Consequently if this were an application for an absolute right I personally should be in favour of granting relief. But the matter does not end there. This court does not lightly exercise its discretion

E to grant prerogative orders—not only is real injustice a necessary ingredient before any such application is granted, but it should, in my view, be granted only where diligence is shown by an applicant in real need of the remedy.

In the applicant Roffey's case there is no real need and indeed counsel for the applicants very properly does not press his application. So far as the applicant Pantridge is concerned the position seems to be this: first, he went up

F to the university (or the college of advanced technology as it was before grant of the royal charter) in October 1965; secondly, he changed from being a student in another course in January 1967. It was in June and September 1967 that he failed his examination and referred examination respectively. Thirdly, on 1st November 1967 he received notification that the original requirement to withdraw from the course dated 20th September 1967 was confirmed. Fourthly, not until 19th July

G 1968 did he seek from this court leave to move, although his complaint is that he should have been allowed to re-sit the whole examination in June 1968, and fifthly, effectively, therefore, his application could not have resulted in a re-sit until June 1969 four years after entering the university and it probably could not now result in an effective re-sit before June 1970. This court should not be used for the creation of a real life counterpart to Chekhov's perpetual

H student, and I would refuse to exercise discretion and dismiss the application.

LORD PARKER, C.J.: I have had considerable doubts about this case, but having had an opportunity of reading the two judgments just delivered, I am not prepared to differ from the conclusion that there has been here a breach of the rules of natural justice. In my judgment, however, this conclusion is only justified on the particular facts of this case. I have in mind the precise word-

I ing of the special regulations and in particular special reg. 4 (f), and the fact that the examiners, in exercising their discretion, were prepared to take into consideration the personal difficulties and problems of each student. I have, however, no doubt at all that this court, in the exercise of its discretion, should not give the relief claimed.   *Applications dismissed.*

Solicitors: *Hyman Isaacs, Lewis & Mills* (for the applicants); *Sherwood & Co.*, agents for *Johnson & Co.*, Birmingham (for the senate).

[*Reported by* N. P. METCALFE, ESQ., *Barrister-at-Law.*]

R. *v.* DELMAYNE.

[COURT OF APPEAL, CRIMINAL DIVISION (Salmon, L.J., Melford Stevenson and Cusack, JJ.), March 3, April 1, 1969.]

Criminal Law—Inducement to invest money—Investment on deposit—Advertisements for deposits with mutual benefit society—Advertisement sent to member of society—Variety of benefits offered to depositor—Whether loan repayable at a premium—Whether advertisement issued to the public—Protection of Depositors Act 1963 (c. 16), s. 2 (1), s. 26 (1).

In 1964 the appellant became general secretary of a mutual benefit society and there was ample evidence that in fact he ran the society and was its alter ego, and that he was also a member of the society. L. applied to join the society in 1966. The appellant enclosed with the letter admitting L. to the society a printed circular, signed by the appellant. The circular was addressed to the public at large and pointed out not only the benefits of membership of the society but also the benefits of paying in money into the society. In particular, it promised prospective depositors, in addition to the right to withdraw their money at any time, a dividend which since 1889 had averaged 14 3/5ths per cent. per annum; £500 accidental death life cover; the chance of doubling the deposit and the advantage of being able to borrow more money than the depositor had put up. On becoming a member L. made an initial deposit with the society of £3 and later deposited many hundreds of pounds. A further circular, signed by the appellant was displayed in the window of the society's premises inviting deposits and offering the benefits to a depositor of personal loans, the purchase of a house or flat without a deposit and £500 accidental death life cover. The appellant was convicted on two counts of inviting deposits of money contrary to s. 2 (1)* of the Protection of Depositors Act 1963. Section 26 (1)† of the Act of 1963 defined " deposit " as " a loan of money at interest, or repayable at a ' premium ' ". On appeal against the convictions,

Held : (i) the advantages held out in the circulars to prospective customers of the society were properly described as " premiums " within the meaning of s. 26 (1) for the word " premium " in that section was not confined to the payment of an ascertained capital sum on the repayment of a loan made to the society (see p. 983, letter B, post);

(ii) the circular sent to L. on his admission as a member of the society was issued to the public for the purpose of s. 2 (1) of the Act of 1963 for L. did not cease to be a member of the public on becoming a member of the society (see p. 982, letter H, post); and

(iii) on all the facts the circulars were advertisements issued by the appellant inviting the public to deposit money with him within s. 2 (1) of the Act of 1963 (see p. 984, letter A, post).

Appeal dismissed.

[As to fraudulent inducements to invest on deposit and restrictions on advertisements for deposits, see SUPPLEMENT to 36 HALSBURY'S LAWS (3rd Edn.) paras. 928A and 929A.

For the Protection of Depositors Act 1963, s. 2, s, 26, see 43 HALSBURY'S STATUTES (2nd Edn.) 930, 951.]

Appeal.

The appellant, Anthony Delmayne, was convicted at the Inner London Sessions on 20th May 1968 on counts 1 and 3 of an indictment charging him with inviting deposits of money contrary to s. 2 (1) of the Protection of Depositors Act 1963, and on counts 4 and 5 of the indictment charging him with inducing investments by dishonest concealment contrary to s. 1 (1) of the Act of 1963. This report

---

* Section 2 (1) is set out at p. 981, letter C, post.
† Section 26, so far as material, is set out at p. 981, letter E, post.

A is concerned only with the appeal against conviction on counts 1 and 3. Count 1 alleged that on or about 7th March 1966 the appellant issued an advertisement to Joseph Albert Lake inviting the public to deposit money with him. Count 3 alleged that on or about 13th March 1966, the appellant issued an advertisement by display at 88, Tooting High Street inviting the public to deposit money with him. The case noted below* was cited during the argument.

B *J. F. F. Platts-Mills, Q.C.,* and *S. J. F. Walsh* for the appellant.
R. D. L. Du Cann for the Crown.

SALMON, L.J., delivered the judgment of the court in which he referred to the counts on which the appellant was convicted and continued:

C It is convenient in considering this appeal to take counts 1 and 3 together and deal with them first, and then go on to deal with counts 4 and 5. I ought to read s. 2 (1) of the Protection of Depositors Act 1963, which is in these terms:

" (1) Subject to the following provisions of this section, no person shall, after the commencement of this Act, issue any advertisement inviting the public to deposit money with him."

D It is necessary then to look at s. 26 in order to see the definition of " deposit " and of " advertisement ". Section 26, so far as it is relevant, is in these terms:

" (1) In this Act ' deposit ' means a loan of money at interest, or repayable at a premium . . . [then there are certain exceptions which again are immaterial] (3) In this Act ' advertisement ' includes every form of advertising, whether in a publication or by the display of notices or by means of circulars

E or other documents . . . (4) For the purposes of this Act an advertisement which contains information calculated to lead directly or indirectly to the deposit of money by the public shall be treated as an advertisement inviting the public to deposit money."

The first question that arises is: Did the appellant issue an advertisement inviting the public to deposit money with him? The points taken by counsel

F for the appellant on this part of the case are: that the documents are not advertisements; that they were not issued to the public; that they did not invite a deposit within the meaning of that word in the Act; that they were not issued by the appellant; and that they did not invite a deposit with him.

It is perhaps at this stage appropriate to look at some of the documents. I am certainly not going to read them all. One purports to emanate from

G the appellant. It is headed the " SOUTH WESTERN DEPOSIT & LOAN SOCIETY (Established 1889) (The Mutual Benefit Society) ". Then it goes on:

" *DO YOU* Want a House? Or a Personal Loan? Or Double your Money? Or other Benefits? *In your Lifetime and NOW? How does it work? AND IT HAS WORKED SINCE 1889. . . .* Over £2,200,000 has been handled for the benefit of members and over £1,000,000 has been paid out in personal loans

H and dividends etc. While the average dividends have been 14 3/5% per annum since 1889. We all put money in a fund from which we can have personal loans, in excess to our savings . . . *YOU CAN WITHDRAW ANY TIME* and take out your money without fuss and bother. [Then there is a heading] *UNIQUE SETTLEMENT SCHEMES.* ' The Creation of a substantial Estate (in this case a substantial cash sum) for you or others in your

I Lifetime '."

Then under the heading of " *ATTRACTIVE & UNUSUAL FEATURES* and how does it work? " this appears:

" *This means that you may have personal loans anytime,* while you are still paying towards the settlement, of as much or more than your total contributions up to that date."

* *Waterlow* v. *Sharp* (1869), L.R. 8 Eq. 501.

If one turns over the document (which is not perhaps a miracle of felicitous **A** draftsmanship) there are:

" *MORE DETAILS . . . PERSONAL SETTLEMENT*: A gift to yourself. Example: If young and you paid over a period of years a total of £2,340, you get back £14,139 Tax free, or a Pension of at least £933 per year and the capital of £14,139 is always there available for you."

B
In the view of this court, this printed document is obviously a circular, and it certainly invites any persons to whom it is addressed to deposit (in the ordinary sense of the word) money with the society.   The point that there was no evidence that it could constitute an advertisement or invitation is quite hopeless.

Counsel for the appellant draws attention to the fact that this was a circular which was sent to Mr. Lake on his admission to the society and not before. **C** According to the evidence, Mr. Lake applied on 5th March to join the South Western Deposit Society.   I need not read the form which he signed; it indicated that he was proposing to put up between £1 and £5 a week, and acknowledged that:

" *DECLARATION* Once I am accepted by the society, I understand that I am fully entitled to all benefits, rights, and duties as a member according **D** to the rules, Bye-laws and Resolutions of the society."

There can be no doubt that he was promptly accepted as a member, because two days later there is a letter purporting to be signed by the appellant from the South Western Deposit and Loan Society, saying:

" Dear Mr./Mrs. Lake, We are pleased to inform you that the committee **E** have considered your application for membership and have pleasure in welcoming you as a member into this society "

and he celebrated his election by paying a deposit of £3.   It is that letter of 7th March which apparently enclosed the document to which reference has already been made.

The point that counsel for the appellant has taken is that after Mr. Lake joined **F** the society he ceased to be a member of the public, and that this document was a confidential communication addressed to Mr. Lake as a member of the society, and not a circular sent to him as a member of the public.   Quite obviously, the document by its very terms does not purport to be confined to members of the society; indeed, it is obviously soliciting custom from the public.   It is addressed to the public at large pointing out the benefits of membership of **G** the society; not only the benefits of membership but also the benefits of paying money into the society and continuing to pay in as much as possible.

This court cannot accept that once Mr. Lake joined the society he ceased to be a member of the public, nor that when he received this document he received it purely in his capacity as a member of the society and not as a member of the public.   In our view, he obviously received it as a member of the public.   It **H** was clearly inviting him to deposit money with the society, and we know that he continued to deposit money with the society to the tune of many hundreds of pounds after the initial deposit of £3.

The next point that counsel for the appellant takes is that Mr. Lake may have put up several hundreds of pounds, but he was not depositing the money.   In other words, the circular to which I have referred was not an invitation to him **I** to deposit money, within the meaning of that word in s. 26 of the Protection of Depositors Act 1963: first, because it was not an invitation to deposit the money as a loan; and secondly, because it was not an invitation to deposit the money as a loan repayable at a premium.

Unless we had heard the first point argued by counsel we would have been tempted to say it was unarguable.   If this was not a loan, what was it? " *YOU CAN WITHDRAW ANY TIME* and take out your money without fuss and bother ".   Those are the words of the relevant document.

A Then it is said that the invitation says nothing about the loan being repayable at a premium. We have to construe the word " premium " as it appears in s. 26 of the Act of 1963. It has a wide and imprecise meaning. This court cannot derive any assistance from other cases in which the word has been construed in the sense in which it appears in other Acts. In considering the sense in which it is used in the Act of 1963 it is perhaps helpful to look at the short

B title to the Act which is: " An Act to penalise fraudulent inducements to invest on deposit . . . ". Ought we to give the word " premium " the very narrow meaning for which counsel for the appellant contends, namely, ought we to confine it to the payment of some ascertained capital sum on the repayment of the loan; or ought we to give it a more liberal and wider meaning? This court has no doubt particularly having regard to the manifest purpose of the Act,

C that the word " premium " truly has a much wider meaning than that contended for on behalf of the appellant. Any advertisement that invites the deposit of money as a loan on the basis that if one deposits £x one will in fact receive in return not £x but £x + y, is an invitation within the meaning of this Act to make a deposit or a loan repayable at a premium.

 The document from which I have already read makes it quite plain that the

D prospective depositor is being promised a great deal in addition to his right to withdraw the money at any time; he is told that the average dividend since 1889 has been 14 3/5ths per cent. per annum; he is being told that if he makes a deposit, £500 accidental death life cover is given automatically by becoming a member in benefit; and he is also being told that there is a good chance of doubling his money. One way of multiplying his money by more than five times

E is illustrated in the personal settlement scheme, for which it would be eligible if he became a member by making a deposit.

 It is obvious, in the view of this court, that all these advantages which are held out to the prospective customer, in addition to the advantage that he will be able to borrow more money than he has put up—which in itself must have some value—can properly be described as premiums within the meaning of

F that word as used in s. 26 of the Act.

 Then it is said that even if all that be true, it has to be shown that the advertisement was issued by the appellant inviting deposits to be made to him. Counsel for the appellant argues that he, the appellant, was nothing but the secretary of this society, and that according to the rules, which were drafted towards the end of the last century and have been in existence ever since, the secretary

G occupies a comparatively subsidiary position in this society and his duties are purely administrative.

 No doubt in 1889 that was true, and still may be, if one is guided only by the rules. But time moves on, and it was in 1964 that the appellant became secretary. When the appellant was questioned by the police, he said:

 " I took the society over about three years ago and became secretary.

H I felt I wanted to make something bigger, so I started the mutual benefit society. I decided to have a barrister look into it for me."

In the view of this court, there was ample evidence on which a jury could come to the conclusion from what the appellant had said to the police that he was, in fact, running this society; and, indeed, that, although the society was no doubt a reality, he was its alter ego. The jury could also well have come to

I the conclusion from the evidence before them that the appellant was a member of the society. If one looks at the rules, they strongly suggest that the officers of the society are recruited from amongst the members of more than three months' standing, and the secretary is undoubtedly an officer of the society.

 It is quite plain from what he told the police that as he was running the society he was responsible for issuing the document which I have mentioned. It is inconceivable that the man who had been running the society for more than two years, and whose name appears on the document as its general secretary, would not have known and approved of this circular.

As to whether the invitation which it contained was an invitation to lend
money to him, it seems to this court that the case can be put in either one of
two ways. There was the evidence to which I have referred, from which the jury
could have inferred that he was the alter ego of the society, and, therefore,
that this was an invitation to lend money to him. If one looks at the rules, the
jury had plenty of evidence that he must have been a member of the society,
and, therefore, if he was inviting loans to be made to the society, inasmuch as
he was a member of it he was inviting the loans to be made to him. In the
view of this court, therefore, all the points taken in relation to count 1 fail.

Very much the same applies to count 3. It is based on a circular or advertisement which the police found in the window of the society's premises. The last
document to which I have referred is not very precise, and this is an even more
imprecise document; but its general tenor is quite clearly " come and join
the society, the benefits are overwhelming ". I must read one or two passages
from the document, which was again signed (or purported to be signed) by the
appellant.

" *HOW LONG DOES IT TAKE TO GET A HOME*? It varies, but
normally between one month to one year. *And all the above benefits we would
NEVER get if we are by ourselves, we can only get it if we join together. You
must admit this is worthwhile, and we are certain you will join us and get
others to join us too.* . . . Please note that all this is a non-profit making scheme,
and nobody makes a profit out of your money except yourself as you can see
by the shareouts—dividends paid out to members over a period of 76 years
since the society has been in existence. Do not confuse these savings with the
Deposit on the future House—a Deposit is sunk into the price of the house.
This is not so with this Society, these savings once you purchase the property
are left in the Society as savings, not as a deposit on the house, it is only
used to allocate points to you because the whole scheme is based on as much
savings as possible by members, so as to buy houses for members, but the
money you save is still yours and you earn a dividend on it."

I now turn to another page where " *BENEFITS* " appears.

" I understand that I am entitled automatically to all the following benefits
while a full Member and in benefit. Personal Loans **** To purchase or rent
a Flat or House without Deposit **** £500 Accidental Death Life Cover
. . . The above benefits may be discontinued or added to by the decision of
the Members of the Society."

It seems to this court no less plain under count 3, which depends on this document, than it was plain under count 1 that there is an invitation to the public
to make loans to the society which are repayable at a premium. It seems that
there is a clear invitation here on the basis that " If you put up the money,
not only will you get it back when you like, but you will get very substantial
benefits in addition which will be of money's worth ". This court can see no
reason why those additional benefits to which the invitation refers are not
premiums within the meaning of the Act.

The points as to whether the invitation under count 3 was issued by the
appellant and is an invitation to make a loan to him are exactly the same as
those which arise under count 1. The court has already indicated its view on
these points. It follows, therefore, that the appeal so far as counts 1 and 3
are concerned is dismissed. [HIS LORDSHIP then considered counts 4 and 5
and concluded that the appeal against conviction in respect of these counts
must be dismissed.]

Appeal against conviction dismissed.

Solicitors: *Registrar of Criminal Appeals* (for the appellant); *Director of
Public Prosecutions* (for the Crown).

[*Reported by* WENDY SHOCKETT, *Barrister-at-Law.*]

A

BUCKLAND *v.* WATTS.

[COURT OF APPEAL, CIVIL DIVISION (Danckwerts, L.J., John Stephenson, J., and Sir Gordon Willmer), May 6, 7, 1969.]

Costs—Taxation—Litigant appearing in person—Claim for costs for expenditure of time in preparing case.

B   Although a solicitor who conducts his own case successfully can claim costs for his professional services reasonably incurred, a lay litigant appearing in person is not entitled to remuneration for the expenditure of time and labour in the preparation of his case as he does not possess professional legal skill (see p. 986, letter A, p. 987, letter F, and p. 987, letter I, to p. 988, letter A, post).

C   Dictum of BOWEN, L.J., in *London Scottish Benefit Society* v. *Chorley* ([1881-85] All E.R. Rep. at pp. 1113, 1114) applied.

Appeals dismissed.

[As to principles on which costs should be taxed, see 30 HALSBURY'S LAWS (3rd Edn.) 428-431, paras. 807-809; and for cases on the subject, see 51 DIGEST (Repl.) 931, 932, *4721-4727*.]

D   Cases referred to:

Harold v. *Smith* (1860), 5 H. & N. 381; 29 L.J.Ex. 141; 1 L.T. 556; 157 E.R. 1229.

London Scottish Benefit Society v. *Chorley* (1884), 12 Q.B.D. 452; *affd.*, C.A., (1884), 13 Q.B.D. 872; [1881-85] All E.R. Rep. 1111; 53 L.J.Q.B. 551; 51 L.T. 100; 43 Digest (Repl.) 279, *2920*.

E   **Interlocutory appeals.**

These were two appeals by the plaintiff, Robin Samuel John Buckland, from the order of His Honour JUDGE TRAPNELL, made at Bromley County Court on 15th January 1969 and of DONALDSON, J., made on 19th March 1969 arising out of litigation between the plaintiff and Edward Watts, the defendant. The facts are set out in the judgment of DANCKWERTS, L.J.

F   The plaintiff appeared in person.

Stella Hydleman for the defendant.

DANCKWERTS, L.J.: The plaintiff has conducted his case himself in person and he has done it very well, but the matters with which we are concerned depend on principle in one case and on a question of discretion in the other.

G   They both arise out of litigation between the plaintiff and professional persons whom he employed in regard to the purchase of a house. One action, against the defendant, was an action complaining that the defendant had been guilty of negligence in not pointing out to the plaintiff, who employed him to make a survey, matters of wet and dry-rot in regard to a house, which was of vital importance because their existence prevented the plaintiff getting a mortgage

H   from a building society which would have enabled him to complete the purchase, and, as a result of that, he was unable to complete the purchase. The other action was against a solicitor, Mr. Mackesy, who acted as solicitor for the plaintiff, and it was claimed did not give him proper, skilful advice in regard to the matter of the purchase of the house. In both cases the actions went to the Court of Appeal. The plaintiff was successful in the action against the defendant and

I   was awarded a sum of £161 damages. The action against the solicitor, Mr. Mackesy, however, failed. The present matter is the question of the costs which were awarded to the plaintiff in regard to his successful appeal.

The charges which have been disallowed by the judges who dealt with the matter so far consist in a large part of charges which the plaintiff has claimed to be compensated for, consisting of expenditure of very considerable time by him in the preparation of the documents and in the case which he conducted against the defendant. That seems to me a matter of principle in that respect, and it seems to me that the principle is well settled that although a solicitor who acts

in person for himself can claim to be remunerated for his professional services A
so far as they are not rendered unnecessary or impossible—as, for instance, in
regard to consultations with himself, and that sort of thing—such costs are
recoverable by the solicitor, but in the case of a layman who is not a skilled
legal person, he can only recover his out-of-pockets.

The matter arises from long origin and goes back a very long way. Costs
were not recoverable or considered, apparently, in early times, but the Statute B
of Gloucester 1278 which was 6 Edw.1, c. 1, provided for costs in the first instance,
and then the matter was developed by the Statute of 23 Hen. 8, c. 15. On
that basis, certain principles have been established by decisions of the courts
which regulate the matters with which we are concerned. There is a passage
in 2 COKE'S INSTITUTES at p. 288, in which it appears that legal expenses can
be claimed, but not such expenses for loss of time, travel, and so on.   C

The matter then came before the courts in two cases to which we have been
referred, in one, *Harold* v. *Smith* (1), BRAMWELL, B., made some observations (2)
about litigants receiving indemnities in respect of their costs, which are not, it
seems to me, very helpful in regard to the present case; but there was a later
case, *London Scottish Benefit Society* v. *Chorley* (3). This was a case of a claim
by a solicitor who had acted for himself in proceedings. There BOWEN, L.J., D
delivered a judgment which I find most satisfactory and the clearest judgment
on the subject. He said (4):

"A great principle, which underlies the administration of the English
law, is that the courts are open to everyone, and that no complaint can
be entertained of trouble and anxiety caused by an action begun maliciously
and without reasonable or probable cause; but as a guard and protection E
against unjust litigation costs are rendered recoverable from an unsuccessful
opponent. Costs are the creation of statute. The first enactment is the
Statute of Gloucester, 6 Edw. 1, c. 1, which gave the costs of the ' writ
purchased '. There is a passage in LORD COKE'S COMMENTARY, 2 Inst., 288,
which it is worth while to examine, as it affords a key to the true view of the
law of costs. That passage is as follows: ' Here is express mention made F
but of the costs of his writ, but it extendeth to all the legal cost of the
suit, but not to the costs and expenses of his travel and loss of time, and
therefore " costages " cometh of the verb " conster ", and that again of the
verb " constare ", for these " costages " must " constare " to the court to
be legal costs and expenses.' What does LORD COKE mean by these words?
His meaning seems to be that only legal costs which the Court can measure G
are to be allowed, and that such legal costs are to be treated as expenses
necessarily arising from the litigation and necessarily caused by the course
which it takes. Professional skill and labour are recognised and can be
measured by the law; private expenditure of labour and trouble by a
layman cannot be measured. It depends on the zeal, the assiduity, or the
nervousness of the individual. Professional skill, when it is bestowed, is H
accordingly allowed for in taxing a bill of costs; and it would be absurd to
permit a solicitor to charge for the same work when it is done by another
solicitor, and not to permit him to charge for it when it is done by his own
clerk. The question before us does not depend on the privileges of a
solicitor. My judgment is the same as that of [SIR BALIOL BRETT, M.R.];
the costs claimed, subject to the exceptions which have been mentioned,   I
ought to be allowed, because there is an expenditure of professional skill
and labour. Is the rule which we lay down in conflict with the existing
practice? I think that it is not; and it is some corroboration of our view

---

(1) (1860), 5 H. & N. 381.
(2) (1860), 5 H. & N. at pp. 385, 386.
(3) (1884), 12 Q.B.D. 452; *affd.* (1884), 13 Q.B.D. 872; [1881-85] All E.R. Rep. 1111.
(4) (1884), 13 Q.B.D. at pp. 876, 877; [1881-85] All E.R. Rep. at pp. 1113, 1114.

A   that in Dixon's Lush's Practice, 3rd ed., p. 896, the rule is laid down in similar terms to those in which we state it; it is there said that ' an attorney regularly qualified is allowed to make the same charges for business done when he sues or defends in person, as when he acts as attorney for another '. The late Lord Justice Lush was a very great master of practice, and his view as to the costs payable to a solicitor who appears in person and is successful

B   is the same as ours."

Of course, that case was dealing with the position of the solicitor, and therefore, it might be said, not directly in point on the problem which we have to consider, but it appears quite clear from the words used by Bowen, L.J., that in the case of a layman he could not charge for his time, and that seems to me to cover the

C   issue in the present case in regard to the disallowance of his claims for time and labour tendered by the plaintiff. That is the end of that part of his appeal.

The other part of his appeal concerns the fee and charges of a Mr. Ray, a chartered architect, who prepared a report in regard to the matter of the doings of the defendant and his charges fall into two parts. There was one account which came to £26 13s. and that was dealt with by the learned judge in this way:

D   he allowed £23 2s. out of the £26 13s. The other one was an account for £27 2s. and on that one he allowed only £10 10s. for the charges of the architect. That is really settled by the scale provision in the Supreme Court Practice 1967, and the charge allowed there is £8 for a day's attendance, and actually the plaintiff has been allowed £2 10s. over that amount. That hardly seems to me very much a subject about which he could complain. But, apart from that, it seems to

E   me in the two cases the learned judges' decisions were matters of discretion and not a subject on which we can properly interfere. Accordingly, I am afraid that in my view both appeals fail.

     JOHN STEPHENSON, J.: I agree.

     SIR GORDON WILLMER: I also agree. So far as the payments to

F   Mr. Ray are concerned, the allowances made by the learned registrar were a matter of pure discretion, and that being so it would plainly be quite wrong for this court to interfere on a mere question of quantum.

The other aspect of the plaintiff's appeal raises undoubtedly a most interesting question, namely, that whereby he seeks to recover in respect of his own expenditure of time and labour in preparing his case. What a successful party, who has

G   got an order for costs, is entitled to recover falls, as is well known, under two headings. One heading covers his disbursements, that is to say, money which he has actually had to pay out to other people, such as witnesses, counsel, professional advisers, and so forth. The other heading is described as " costs ". That is intended to cover remuneration for the exercise of professional legal skill. That, I think, is in accordance with the views expressed by Bowen, L.J. (5),

H   in the judgment which Danckwerts, L.J., has already read. It is because there has been an exercise of professional legal skill that a solicitor conducting his own case successfully is treated differently from any other successful litigant conducting his own case in person. We are not concerned with the exercise of other professional skills. Other professional people, who become involved in litigation and conduct their own case, may recover something in respect of their own

I   professional skill, insofar as they qualify as witnesses and are called as such. But nobody else, except a solicitor, has ever been held entitled to make any charge, as I understand it, in respect of the exercise of professional legal skill; and it is that which the plaintiff has sought to do in the present case. I have much sympathy for him, as indeed Donaldson, J., did, but I can find no ground,

---

(5) In *London Scottish Benefit Society* v. *Chorley* (1884), 13 Q.B.D. at pp. 876, 877 [1881-85] All E.R. at pp. 1113, 1114.

A either in principle or on authority, for allowing him anything by way of remuneration for the exercise of a professional skill which he has not got.   In
those circumstances, I agree that the appeals must be dismissed.

Appeals dismissed.   Leave to appeal to the House of Lords refused (6).

Solicitors: *Judge & Priestley*, Bromley (for the defendant).

B   [*Reported by* S. A. HATTEEA, ESQ., *Barrister-at-Law.*]

SLOUGH ESTATES, LTD. *v.* SLOUGH BOROUGH COUNCIL
AND ANOTHER (No. 2).

C
[COURT OF APPEAL, CIVIL DIVISION (Lord Denning, M.R., Salmon and Karminski,
L.JJ.), March 3, 4, 5, 6, 27, 1969.]

Town and Country Planning—Development—Permission for development—
Construction of permission together with incorporated plan—Permission to be
interpreted so as to ignore obvious mistake—Permission granted in 1945—
D *Subsequent application for permission to erect industrial buildings in 1955*
refused—Compensation recovered for loss of development value—Whether
permission of 1945 still valid—Whether acceptance of compensation constituted
abandonment of rights under permission of 1945.

In 1945 the local authority passed a resolution granting planning
permission for 240 acres owned by the company. The permission referred to:
E " the land situate at the trading estate at present undeveloped and shown
uncoloured on the plan submitted, to be used for industrial purposes ".
The company never acted on the 1945 permission and behaved as if it did
not exist. It made many new planning applications between 1945 and 1965
to erect factories on parts of the 240 acres, and accompanied each application
by an industrial development certificate. Out of the 240 acres factories were
F built on about 100 acres, permission was given to build on another 50 acres,
leaving 90 acres outstanding. In 1955 the company applied for permission
to erect industrial buildings on the remaining 90 acres but was refused.
In consequence the company recovered from the government £178,545
in compensation under s. 59 of the Town and Country Planning Act 1954.
The company later wished to resurrect the 1945 permission contending that
G the permission was still in force and that it was entitled to erect factory
buildings on the 90 acres without getting industrial development certificates.
It was shown that in the phrase in the 1945 permission " shown uncoloured
on the plan submitted " the word " uncoloured " had been mistakenly
inserted for the word " coloured ".

Held: the 1945 permission had to be construed with the plan which
H was submitted and was incorporated into it, in the light of which the permission was to be interpreted by rejecting the word " uncoloured " and holding
that permission was given to develop that part of the trading estate which
was at that time undeveloped (see p. 991, letters B and D, p. 994, letter G,
and p. 998, letter B, post); and

(ii) although the 1945 permission was still valid in 1955 the act of the com-
I pany, in claiming compensation, constituted the exercise of an election, with
full knowledge between two inconsistent rights the effect of which being that
it unequivocally waived or abandoned its rights under the 1945 permission
(see p. 993, letters H and I, p. 994, letter C, p. 996, letter I, and p. 998,
letter C, post).

Appeal dismissed.

---

(6) On 1st July 1969 the Appeal Committee of the House of Lords refused to grant
the plaintiff leave to appeal.

A   [As to effect of payment of compensation for loss of development value, see 37 HALSBURY'S LAWS (3rd Edn.) 540, 541, para. 675.

For the Town and Country Planning Act 1954, s. 59, see 34 HALSBURY'S STATUTES (2nd Edn.) 981.]

Cases referred to:

B   *Camrose (Viscount)* v. *Basingstoke Corpn.*, [1966] 3 All E.R. 161; [1966] 1 W.L.R. 1100; 130 J.P. 368; Digest (Cont. Vol. B) 698, *1766.*

Matthews v. *Smallwood*, [1910] 1 Ch. 777; [1908-10] All E.R. Rep. 536; 79 L.J.Ch. 322; sub nom. *Matthews* v. *Smallwood, Smallwood* v. *Matthews,* 102 L.T. 228; 30 Digest (Repl.) 467, *1088.*

Merak, The, [1965] 1 All E.R. 230; [1965] P. 223; [1965] 2 W.L.R. 250;
C   Digest (Cont. Vol. B) 25, *156a.*

Miller-Mead v. *Minister of Housing and Local Government, Same* v. *Same,* [1963] 1 All E.R. 459; [1963] 2 Q.B. 196; [1963] 2 W.L.R. 225; 127 J.P. 122; 45 Digest (Repl.) 352, *100.*

Roberts, Re, Repington v. *Roberts-Gawen* (1881), 19 Ch.D. 520; 45 L.T. 450; 18 Digest (Repl.) 438, *1296.*

D   *Scarf* v. *Jardine* (1882), 7 App. Cas. 345; [1881-85] All E.R. Rep. 651; 51 L.J.Q.B. 612; 47 L.T. 258; 12 Digest (Repl.) 669, *5178.*

United Australia, Ltd. v. *Barclays Bank, Ltd.*, [1940] 4 All E.R. 20; [1941] A.C. 1; 109 L.J.K.B. 919; 164 L.T. 139; 3 Digest (Repl.) 224, *542.*

Wilson v. *West Sussex County Council*, [1963] 1 All E.R. 751; [1963] 2 Q.B. 764; [1963] 2 W.L.R. 669; 127 J.P. 243; 45 Digest (Repl.) 332, *25.*

E   *Wilson* v. *Wilson* (1854), 5 H.L.Cas. 40; 23 L.J.Ch. 697; 25 L.T.O.S. 134; 10 E.R. 811; 30 Digest (Repl.) 220, *635.*

Appeal.

This was an appeal by Slough Estates, Ltd., from an order of MEGARRY, J., dated 15th February 1968, whereby it was ordered that the company's claim
F   for a declaration be dismissed, and that, save as dealt with by the order of the Court of Appeal dated 27th April 1967, the company pays the local authority, Slough Borough Council, and to the Buckinghamshire County Council three one-fourths parts of its costs to be taxed.   The facts are set out in the judgment of LORD DENNING, M.R.

Douglas Frank, Q.C., *Charles Sparrow*, Q.C., *Patrick Freeman* and *David Keene*
G   for the company.

J. L. Arnold, Q.C., *Jeremiah Harman*, Q.C., and *Elizabeth Appleby* for the local authority and the county council.

Cur. adv. vult.

27th March. The following judgments were read.

H   **LORD DENNING, M.R.:** The Slough Trading Estate is owned by the company, Slough Estates, Ltd. It lies astride the main railway line to the west. It is some 500 acres in extent. By 1944 half of it had already been developed for factory buildings. This development covered a floor space of 3,471,396 square feet. The end of the war was in sight. The company looked forward to post-war development. In 1944 the company's surveyor made a plan showing
I   how the remaining half of the estate, some 240 acres then undeveloped, could be laid out. I will call it the " 1944 layout ". It was dated 12th December 1944. It showed new roads, factories, electric generating station, car parks, and 15 acres marked " no development ". The floor area of the proposed new factories was given as 2,647,697 square feet.

On 22nd January 1945, the company's surveyor, by letter, submitted the 1944 layout, as an interim development measure, to the local authority. The local authority gave it the number U.L.21.   On 8th October 1945, the local authority

approved it by a resolution which was noted in the local authority minutes A
in this way:

Plan No.	Applicant and Proposed Development	Town Planning
U.L.21	[the company] Lay-out of Undeveloped portion, Trading Estate	Approved

On 17th October 1945, the local authority, by their town clerk, issued a planning
permission which is the key document in this case. I will call it the " 1945
permission " and I will set it out in full:

" Application No. U.L.21.

To: [the company]

. . . the [local authority] as Interim Development Authority hereby permit the land situate at the Trading Estate at present undeveloped, and shown
uncoloured on the plan submitted, to be used for industrial purposes, subject
to the submission by the developer and subsequent approval by the [local
authority], or by the Minister of Town and Country Planning on appeal,
of particulars of the proposed development (and to compliance with the
conditions specified hereunder:—

That further particulars of the proposed development be submitted and
approved in due course.

The reasons for the [local authority's] decision to grant permission for the
development, subject to compliance with the conditions hereinbefore
specified:—

To ensure that development shall comply with the Planning Scheme now
in course of preparation.)

DATED the Seventeenth day of October, 1945.

J. H. Warren, Town Clerk."

The company says that the 1945 permission is still in force; and that, by virtue
of it, it is entitled to erect factory buildings on large open spaces without getting
industrial development certificates. The local authority says that it has long
since been abandoned. I will assume for the moment that it is still in force,
and seek to construe it, so as to see if it bears the wide import claimed by the
company.

1. The construction of the 1945 permission.

The first problem is caused by the word " uncoloured " in the phrase: " shown
uncoloured on the plan submitted." The plan submitted was the 1944 layout
U.L. 21. It showed proposed development for industrial purposes on the *coloured*
portion, and not on the *uncoloured* portion. The coloured portion was coloured
yellow for proposed roads, pink for proposed factories, green for proposed open
spaces, and so forth. The portion which was uncoloured showed the then existing
development (of 250 acres) and a few odd bits scattered about for which there
were no proposals. That word " uncoloured " was, in the permission, obviously
a mistake. By no possibility could anyone think that the local authority had
given permission to develop the *uncoloured* portion, when the plan showed
that the company wanted to develop the *coloured* portion and to build on it
factory buildings covering 2,687,652 square feet.

The learned judge thought that this mistake could not be corrected and that
the permission must be construed literally so as to give permission for industrial
purposes on the *uncoloured* land; although he confessed that he found this
unattractive. It is not only unattractive. It is absurd. And I decline to give
this permission such an absurd effect. It would mean that we would foist on to
the company something for which it never asked and which was no good to it

A at all. If there were no other way out of the difficulty, I would hold the permission bad for uncertainty, or, at any rate, absurdity, or I would rectify it so as to give effect to the proved intention of the local authority, if proceedings were brought for that purpose.

But I think there is a way out. The permission must be construed together with the plan which was submitted and was incorporated into it, see *Wilson*
B *v. West Sussex County Council* (1). I confine myself to the plan. I do not think it is permissible to look at the resolution of the local authority or the correspondence, for neither of them was incorporated into the permission, see *Miller-Mead* v. *Minister of Housing and Local Government* (2) per Upjohn, L.J. The reason for excluding them is this: The grant of planning permission has to be in writing (see the Town and Country Planning (General Interim Development)
C Order 1945 (3), art. 12) and it runs with the land. The grant is not made when the local authority resolves to give permission. It is only made when its clerk, on its authority, issues the permission to the applicant. Seeing that it has to be in writing, one can only look to the permission itself and the documents incorporated in it. In this case there was one important document incorporated in the permission. It was the "plan submitted" showing the 1944 layout U.L. 21
D with all the colours and wording on it. In the light of this plan, I think the only sensible way of interpreting the permission is to reject the word "uncoloured" as being absurd and inapplicable (see *The Merak* (4)) and to hold that permission was given to develop that portion of the trading estate which was at that time undeveloped as shown on the plan. That is, the 240 acres or thereabouts, both coloured and uncoloured. It was what we would call today an outline permission.
E The colours and wording on the plan showed the proposals in outline, but not in such a way as to bind either the company or the local authority to the details. The details were to be worked out later, by the company, submitting particulars, and by the local authority approving, or disapproving them. Thus the site of the roads might be varied. The floor area of the factories might be increased or diminished. And so forth.
F The second problem in the 1945 permission is the meaning of the words: "to be used for industrial purposes." Does this authorise the company to erect factory buildings? Or is it limited to using the 240 acres for roads, car parks, and so forth, without buildings? The answer is again to be found by reference to the plan submitted. It clearly includes the erection of factory buildings. And there is this very important point to be noticed: At that date in 1945 there was
G no need for the developer to obtain from the Board of Trade an industrial development certificate. The need for such a certificate was only introduced in 1947 by s. 14 (4) of the Town and Country Planning Act 1947. It did not apply to pre-1947 permissions. So this 1945 permission (if it is still in force) has the enormous advantage that the company can erect factory buildings on these 240 acres (save for the 15 acres marked "no development") without getting
H industrial development certificates. That adds greatly to the value of the permission, see *Viscount Camrose* v. *Basingstoke Corpn.* (5).

There is one other thing to be noted on the 1945 permission. It is the reason for the condition. It was stated to be "To ensure that development shall comply with the Planning Scheme now in course of preparation". That planning scheme was altered from time to time. But it blossomed out into a full-blown
I development plan which was the subject of an inquiry in July 1952 by an inspector from the Ministry. The development plan contained important differences from the 1944 layout. Large areas which had previously in 1944 been allocated for industrial purposes were not in 1952 scheduled as open spaces. At the inquiry,

(1) [1963] 1 All E.R. 751; [1963] 2 Q.B. 764.
(2) [1963] 1 All E.R. 459 at pp. 468-475; [1963] 2 Q.B. 196 at pp. 223-234.
(3) S.R. & O. 1945 No. 349.
(4) [1965] 1 All E.R. 230; [1965] P. 223.
(5) [1966] 3 All E.R. 161; [1966] 1 W.L.R. 1100.

the county council, through its clerk, appears to have acknowledged that the **A**
1945 permission was valid and that, if it was to be revoked so as to provide
for these open spaces, the company would be entitled to compensation.

2. Abandonment.

Thus far I have assumed that the permission of 1945 is still in force. But now
comes the crux of the case. The local authority says that the company abandoned
it many years ago and cannot now revive it.   **B**

One thing is quite clear. The company, never acted on the 1945 permission.
It behaved for many years as if it never existed. It made a large number of new
planning applications to erect factories on parts of these 240 acres, but it has
in each case made a separate new application for each factory, and it has accompanied each one by an industrial development certificate, wherever the factory
was of a size to require it. These separate applications were spread over the 20 **C**
years from 1945 to 1965. The company never referred to the 1945 permission,
nor did it purport to give particulars under it. Many of these applications have
been granted. Permissions have been given. Factories have been erected. These
buildings are very different from those proposed in the 1944 layout. For instance,
several acres which were proposed in 1944 as a car park coloured green are now
covered with factory buildings. In sum total, out of the 240 acres, factories **D**
have been built on about 100 acres, permission has been given for another 50
acres, leaving 90 acres outstanding. But in respect of these 90 acres, there was
a very significant happening. In 1955 the company applied for permission
to erect industrial buildings on the 90 acres. Permission was refused. And in
consequence of the refusal the company recovered from the government
compensation amounting to £178,545.   **E**

Now the company wishes to resurrect the 1945 permission. It says that it
is still in force and that it is entitled to erect factory buildings on these 90 acres
without getting industrial development certificates in respect of it. The local
authority retorts that, as the company in 1955 received compensation for loss
of development value, it cannot now claim that the 1945 permission is still in
force.   **F**

In order to appreciate this point, I must state the circumstances in which
the company applied for and received the compensation. On 1st October 1954,
the Minister approved the development plan for this area. It showed that
$12\frac{1}{2}$ acres were allocated for allotments and for playing fields, and that $77\frac{1}{2}$
acres for nursery and market gardens. Two months later, on 25th November
1954, Parliament passed the Town and Country Planning Act 1954. It set up **G**
a fund of £300,000,000, out of which to compensate landowners who were refused
permission to develop their land. In particular, it contained in s. 59 a special
section dealing with industrial buildings which would normally require an
industrial development certificate. Section 59 provided that, if a landowner
owns land which was ripe for industrial development, but he was likely to be
refused permission to develop it, he could get compensation without getting an **H**
industrial development certificate. All that he had to do was to submit an outline planning application for an industrial building, get the planning authority
to certify that they would have refused it, and he was entitled to compensation
as for a refusal of planning permission.

The company acted under s. 59. It instructed its agents, who made on 1st
April 1955, two applications, as follows. One was an outline application to erect **I**
industrial buildings on the $12\frac{1}{2}$ acres of land. The company filled in a form of
application on which there was a special request to give " Dates of any previous
application for development permission ". The company replied: " Application
U.L.21: 22.1.45 (plan dated 12.12.44) ". On 3rd May 1955, the local authority
refused the application on the ground that the proposed development was contrary to the development plan whereby the area was allocated for allotments
and for playing fields. On 19th May 1955, the company put in a claim to the
Minister for compensation for full loss of development value in respect of this

A site. On 30th January 1957, the compensation was determined at £60,214 17s. 2d. On 8th February 1957, it was paid to the company. The other was an outline application to erect industrial buildings on about 80 acres of land. The same drill was gone through. The company filled in the form referring to U.L.21. The local authority refused on the ground that the area was allocated as a nursery and market garden. The company claimed compensation for full loss of

B development value, and received it in the sum of £118,330 5s. 9d. for 77½ acres.

Now the company seeks to resurrect the 1945 permission. In so doing it is acting inconsistently. In 1955 it made claims for compensation on the footing that it had lost all development value of these 90 acres. It received £178,545 accordingly. Now it turns round and says that it never lost any of the development value, but that it is entitled to develop the 90 acres as of right by virtue

C of the 1945 permission.

Counsel for the company, admitted that the company is acting inconsistently. It was negligent or foolish in 1955, he said, but not dishonest. It ought never to have applied in 1955 for compensation, or taken it. But albeit it was negligent or foolish, that did not mean that it had abandoned the 1945 permission. It could still rely on it, he said, but the only consequence was that, when it

D erected factory buildings on the 90 acres, it would have to pay back the compensation of £178,545 it received. (But it would not, he said, have to pay any interest on it for all the years it had the use of it.) It was open to the local authority he said, to revoke the permission on the 90 acres (if it thought that good planning required it): but in that case, he said, the local authority would have to pay the company compensation at current values, which might amount

E to £3½ million, against which the company would be good enough to give credit for the £178,545 it had received, but no interest for the intervening years.

The judge accepted this argument. He said:

"I do not think there can be any general doctrine that he who acts inconsistently with a planning permission thereby abandons it ... What must be shown, I think, is a positive intention never to rely on a planning

F permission, not merely an intention not to rely on it now ... To make a claim which is inconsistent with a right does not, without more, show an intention to abandon that right."

I cannot agree with the judge on this point. He said that the officers of the company may have forgotten about the 1945 permission. I do not accept that for one moment. None of their officers gave any evidence of forgetting about it.

G On the very forms in 1955 in which they applied for compensation, they mentioned explicitly U.L.21 which was their 1945 application. They obviously had the file before them: and this, no doubt, included the 1945 permission.

Once knowledge is shown, the company is defeated by the doctrine of abandonment: or, as I would prefer to put it, by election between inconsistent rights. This was fully considered by the House of Lords, in *United Australia,*

H *Ltd.* v. *Barclays Bank, Ltd.* (6). That case shows that when a man is entitled to one of two inconsistent rights, then if he, with full knowledge, has done an unequivocal act showing that he has chosen the one, he cannot afterwards pursue the other. That is what Lord Atkin said (7). By choosing the one, he has elected to "abandon" the other. But the word "abandonment" is misleading. It smacks of intention. That is what misled the judge here. He thought there must be

I an intention to abandon. But, in this branch of the law, it is not the man's intention which matters. It is his conduct. Whether he intended it or not, if he has knowingly done an unequivocal act—by which I mean an act which would be justifiable if he had elected one way, and would not be justifiable if he elected the other way, that is an election. He cannot go back on it, see *Scarf* v. *Jardine* (8) per Lord Blackburn. It is not open to him to say: "I

---

(6) [1940] 4 All E.R. 20; [1941] A.C. 1.

(7) [1940] 4 All E.R. at p. 37; [1941] A.C. at p. 30.

(8) (1882), 7 App. Cas. 345 at p. 361; [1881-85] All E.R. Rep. 651 at pp. 658, 659.

will accept the one right but I will not give up the other." If he does accept $\quad$ A
the one right, then by law he waives—he " abandons "—the other, and nothing
which he can say by way of protest against the law will avail him anything,
see *Matthews* v. *Smallwood* (9) per PARKER, J.

So here the company had a choice in 1955 between two inconsistent rights.
One was to claim compensation for loss of development value. The other was
to retain the development value in the shape of the 1945 permission. Given $\quad$ B
those two inconsistent rights, the company did an unequivocal act—it claimed
and accepted £178,545 for loss of development value. That would be justifiable
if it elected to abandon the 1945 permission, but it would not be justifiable if
it retained it. By accepting the compensation, it made its election and cannot
go back on it. By law it has waived, or, if you like to put it so, " abandoned "
the 1945 permission. $\quad$ C

The judge seems to have had some recollection of this doctrine, but it was
imperfect. He said:

" No doubt procedural and other difficulties may confront a man who seeks
to blow hot and cold, but I do not think there is any doctrine that if two
inconsistent claims are made, the making of the later claim ipso facto
constitutes an abandonment of the existing claim." $\quad$ D

That is true when it is a choice between one of two alternative remedies. But
not when it is a choice of one of two inconsistent rights. And here, as I see it,
the company in 1955 had a choice between two inconsistent rights: and, having
adopted one, it cannot now pursue the other.

Conclusion.
$\quad$ E
I come to the same result as the judge, but for different reasons. I think that
the 1945 permission did cover the development of the 90 acres, by the erection
of factory buildings, according to the 1944 layout: but I think that the company,
by accepting compensation for loss of development value, is precluded from
saying that the 1945 permission is still in force.

I am not sorry to come to this result. This old permission of 1945 was dead $\quad$ F
for 20 years. No one acted on it. Now the company seeks to resurrect it so as
to ground either a claim to erect factory buildings on 90 acres at a great profit
(contrary to good planning) or to get some £3½ million compensation out of the
ratepayers. It has done nothing to earn such vast compensation save to put in
a layout plan 24 years ago. I do not think it should have it. I would dismiss
this appeal.
$\quad$ G

SALMON, L.J.: Whatever may be doubtful in this case, it seems to me
crystal clear that the word " uncoloured " was inserted by mistake in the planning
permission dated 17th October 1945. In order to discover the true meaning of
this planning permission we are entitled to consider it in the light at any rate
of the layout plan to which it refers: *Wilson* v. *West Sussex County Council* (10).
This layout plan shows industrial development consisting of a large number $\quad$ H
of proposed new factories coloured pink, together with proposed new roads,
canteens, power stations, car parks and open spaces all ancillary to the proposed
new factories and designated in different colours on the plan. This proposed
development covered in all an area of about 250 acres of the Slough Trading
Estate. The uncoloured parts of the layout plan covered the rest of the estate
consisting of about 350 acres all of which—but for a few odd pieces—was then $\quad$ I
already developed. Clearly no development of these few odd pieces was even
being considered in 1945. The learned judge, however, construed the planning
permission literally and held that it applied, and applied only, to these odd
pieces. He said that this produced a result which in his words was " not
attractive " nor " very sensible ". This certainly is a remarkable understatement

(9) [1910] 1 Ch. 777 at pp. 786, 787; [1908-10] All E.R. Rep. 536 at pp. 541, 542.
(10) [1963] 1 All E.R. 751; [1963] 2 Q.B. 764.

A   for this construction produced a result which, to my mind, is in reality both repugnant and ridiculous. If ever a document contained an obvious mistake, the insertion of the word " uncoloured " in this planning permission is surely such a mistake. It clearly could not have been what the local authority intended, and indeed we know that it was not, from the resolution of 8th October 1945 approving planning permission as shown on the layout plan. Equally

B   clearly neither the company nor anyone else to whom the permission and plan may have been shown could have thought that the planning authority had inserted the word " uncoloured " except by mistake. Planning authorities like everyone else sometimes make mistakes but they are not insane; nor should they be presumed to be perpetrating a bad joke.

It has been held that in construing a planning permission reference cannot be

C   made to the application for permission, nor indeed to any other document (*Miller-Mead* v. *Minister of Housing and Local Government* (11)) save documents referred to in the permission: (*Wilson* v. *West Sussex County Council* (12)). The basis for the decision seems to have been that the grant of planning permission which must be in writing (Town and Country Planning (General Interim Development) Order 1946, art. 12) runs with the land (s. 18 (4) of the Town and Country Planning Act 1947) and a purchaser from the applicant will probably

D   not have access to any of the documents contemporaneous with the grant of planning permission. In the *Miller-Mead* case (11) the grant of planning permission had been made to the plaintiff's predecessor in title, and it was held that the contemporaneous documents could not be looked at; certainly not for the purpose of attempting to cut down the permission in the grant. I desire to reserve

E   the question whether the *Miller-Mead* (11) rule applies when a dispute about the true construction of the grant arises as between the planning authority and the original grantee. For the purposes of this case, however, I assume that in construing the grant we are not entitled to look at the resolution of 8th October 1945, nor at the application for planning permission nor any of the contemporaneous correspondence. But this does not matter for those documents could hardly

F   make it more obvious than does the layout plan that the word " uncoloured " was inserted by mistake in the grant.

It is well settled that an obvious mistake in a document can be corrected if the meaning of the document is clear; and this correction can be made by construing the document according to its clearly intended meaning without resorting to rectification: *Wilson* v. *Wilson* (13) per LORD ST. LEONARDS. Counsel for

G   the local authority has argued that the meaning of the grant of planning permission with the word " uncoloured " struck out is so obscure as to be void for uncertainty. I am afraid that I cannot accept that argument.

I do not think that in this case we ought in the words of SIR GEORGE JESSEL, M.R., in *Re Roberts, Repington* v. *Roberts-Gawen* (14): " to repose on the easy pillow of saying that the whole is void for uncertainty." In my view it is

H   important to note that in 1945 it was not necessary to have a Board of Trade industrial development certificate, in order to obtain permission to use land for the purpose of building operations. This requirement was introduced for the first time by s. 14 (4) of the Act of 1947. Accordingly I agree with the learned judge that a permission given in 1945 for land " to be used for industrial purposes " ought not to be given such a restricted meaning as it might receive

I   were the permission granted today. I agree with LORD DENNING, M.R., that the grant of 17th October 1945, on its true construction gave what would now be described as outline planning permission for the erection of factories roughly as shown on the layout plan. This was subject to submission by the developer and subsequent approval by the local authority or by the Minister on appeal

(11) [1963] 1 All E.R. 459; [1963] 2 Q.B. 196.
(12) [1963] 1 All E.R. 751; [1963] 2 Q.B. 764.
(13) (1854), 5 H.L. Cas. 40 at p. 66.
(14) (1881), 19 Ch.D. 520 at p. 529.

of particulars of the proposed development. These particulars would include such A
matters as the size, elevation and the exact location of the proposed factories
on the site.

By 1955, all but about 90 of the 250 acres to which I have referred had been
developed. This development had taken place without reference to the 1945
grant but on separate new applications for each factory erected. The important
question arises whether the 1945 grant is now still available in respect of the 90 B
acres or whether it has been abandoned. Counsel for the company has argued
that the grant of a planning permission is incapable of abandonment. There is
no authority on this point. I agree however with the learned judge that there
is no reason in principle which such a grant cannot be abandoned. In my view
it can be abandoned at any rate by the original grantee to the local authority
which made it. Whether an abandonment would be effective against a subse- C
quent bona fide purchaser for value who purchased the land without notice of
abandonment does not arise for decision and I express no opinion on the point.

Some years prior to 1952, a development plan had been approved by the
county council which scheduled the 90 acres for use as an open space and for
purposes other than the erection of industrial buildings. Thereafter it must
have been obvious to all concerned that if a fresh application were made to erect D
factories on these 90 acres, it would inevitably be refused.

The Town and Country Planning Act 1954, set up a fund of £300,000,000
out of which compensation should be paid to any landowners who were refused
permission to develop their land. Section 59 provided, in effect, that if any
landowner applied without a Board of Trade industrial development certificate
for permission to erect industrial buildings on his land, the planning authority E
should consider whether, if there had been such a certificate, it would nevertheless
have refused permission: if the planning authority was of the opinion that it
would have refused such permission, it must notify the landowner to that effect
and permission would then be deemed to have been refused for the purpose
of the Act.

The company made two applications in 1955 under s. 59 of the Act of 1954, F
one in respect of 12½ of the 90 acres and the other in respect of the remaining
77½ acres. The applications naturally (having regard to the development plan)
were both refused. As a result the company was awarded and paid £178,595
compensation by the Ministry. Counsel for the company concedes that the applications under s. 59 were made by the company with the sole purpose of obtaining
compensation. He also concedes that if the 1945 permission was still in force G
in 1955, the company ought not to have made any application under s. 59 and
was not entitled to any compensation. The question is, did the company by
making the applications and obtaining the compensation unequivocally elect to
treat the 1945 permission as waived or abandoned. One of two courses was
open to the company. It had a choice: either (a) to keep the 1945 permission
alive, in which case it could not justifiably obtain compensation under the Act H
of 1954; or (b) to abandon or waive its rights under the 1945 permission in which
case it might justifiably obtain compensation under the Act of 1954. The two
courses were mutually exclusive for it could not be justifiable to obtain the compensation under the Act of 1954 if the company's permission under the 1945
grant was still alive. Accordingly, in my view by obtaining compensation, it
did an act by which it unequivocally waived or abandoned its rights under the I
1945 permission. This conclusion accords with the settled principles of the
common law (see Scarf v. Jardine (15) per LORD BLACKBURN). I wish to make
it plain that I am not saying that a landowner who has applied for and obtained
planning permission to develop his land for one purpose abandons his right
under that permission by making a subsequent successful application to develop

_____

(15) (1882), 7 App. Cas. 345 at pp. 360, 361; [1881-85] All E.R. Rep. 651 at pp. 658,
659.

A   his land for another purpose. Being in possession of the two permissions he can justifiably develop his land for one purpose or the other. The first permission is not inconsistent with the second application. This is quite different from the present case. Here the company had an outline planning permission for the erection of industrial buildings. Whilst this permission remained alive, it could not justifiably take steps to obtain compensation under the Act of 1954. The

B   applications which the company made in 1955 were merely steps taken to obtain such compensation, and these steps were bound to be successful. Therefore it must be taken to have abandoned or waived its rights under the 1945 permission.

     I doubt whether the actual state of mind of the representatives of the company or the local authority would be material. But even if it were I cannot think

C   that the company would be in any better position. The learned judge was not satisfied that the company intended, or manifested an intention, to abandon the 1945 planning permission. He concluded that in 1955 it had probably forgotten the 1945 planning permission. I do not agree with that conclusion. Only three years before, in 1952, there had been an inquiry into the county council's development plan at which the company was represented

D   by leading and junior counsel. During the hearing the county council acknowledged that the 1945 permission was still in force and that if it revoked it it would be liable to pay compensation to the company. Moreover on each of the applications made by the company in 1955 reference was made to U.L.21, the application on which it succeeded in obtaining the 1945 permission. To my mind it is inconceivable that when the company made its application in 1955 it had

E   forgotten or that the county council thought that it had forgotten the 1945 permission. It would clearly have been dishonest for the company to make the 1955 applications or accept payment of the £178,545 compensation unless it had intended to abandon or waive its rights under the 1945 permission. And everyone concedes that the company is honest and has acted honestly throughout. It follows therefore that the 1945 permission was intentionally

F   abandoned or waived. Counsel for the company argues that the company could not have been so stupid as to have intended to abandon or to waive its rights under the 1945 permission which are said to be worth over £3,000,000 pounds today for the sake of getting a mere £178,545 in 1955. But this argument cannot avail the company even if it were sound, because no one suggests that the company acted dishonestly and the argument therefore merely supports the

G   finding of the learned judge that in 1955 the company had forgotten all about the 1945 permission—a finding which for the reasons indicated I have already rejected. For my part I am not persuaded that it was stupid for the company to take the £178,545 in 1955 and abandon or waive its rights under the 1945 permission. The company is very experienced and successful in land development. Apparently it did not wish to start developing the 90 acres in question

H   until shortly before April 1966 when it took out the present originating summons. I do not think it unlikely that in 1955 it realised that the 90 acres would probably be lying fallow for upwards of ten years. Moreover it may have had some doubts as to the validity of the 1945 permission which on its face contained an obvious mistake. In these circumstances even so small a sum as £178,545 might have been regarded as a bird in the hand well worth having. It should have been fairly

I   obvious in 1955 that if that sum were wisely invested, the capital accretion over the next ten years or so would probably be very large indeed—perhaps three or four times the value of the original investment. In addition there would be the interest. The company graciously concedes that it should repay the bare sum of £178,545 but maintains that providing it does so it may enjoy the rights conferred by the 1945 permission (said today to be worth over £3,000,000) together with the capital accretion and interest on the sum of £178,545 which it received about 14 years ago as compensation for being deprived of the development rights which it now says it has always enjoyed. This seems to me to be

blowing hot and cold with a vengeance. Certainly far hotter than the law allows. **A**
Accordingly I agree that this appeal should be dismissed.

  KARMINSKI, L.J.: I have had the advantage of reading the judgments
of LORD DENNING, M.R., and of SALMON, L.J., and I agree that this appeal
must be dismissed. But as its subject-matter may be of some general interest,
I desire to add a very few observations of my own. **B**

  So far as construction is concerned, I too am of the opinion that the permission
granted to the company Slough Estates, Ltd., on 17th October 1945, was what
is now called outline planning permission to erect factories as shown generally
on the plans submitted. It is clear that the word " uncoloured " was used in
error, since it makes nonsense of the layout of the plan submitted. Once this
plan is examined, it is clear that what was permitted was the development **C**
of a large area of land, irrespective of colour, which was at that time undeveloped.

  I also agree that the company abandoned the 1945 planning permission when
later it accepted compensation for the loss of development value. It seems to
me of little practical importance whether this was an abandonment or a waiver
of the permission. Whatever term is used, the company elected to give up its
development rights in exchange for a large sum of money paid in cash in 1955 **D**
namely £178,545. It may be that if the company had waited for another ten
years it would have done much better financially. But the decisive date is
1955, when it elected to accept an ascertained sum, and not to gamble on the
possibility of any increase at some future date.

  Like SALMON, L.J., I express no opinion on the effect of such abandonment on
a subsequent bona fide purchaser for value, who had bought the land without **E**
notice of such abandonment. This question does not arise on this appeal.

    Appeal dismissed. Leave to appeal to the House of Lords granted.

  Solicitors: *Kenneth Brown, Baker, Baker* (for the company); *Sharpe, Pritchard
& Co.*, agents for *Norman T. Berry*, Slough and *R. E. Millard*, Aylesbury (for
the local authority and the county council).

        [*Reported by* JENIFER SANDELL, *Barrister-at-Law.*] **F**

BUCKNELL *v.* BUCKNELL.

[PROBATE, DIVORCE AND ADMIRALTY DIVISION (Brandon, J.), March 26, 27,
 April 2, 1969.]
 G

*Contempt of Court—Sequestration—Bank holding surplus proceeds of sale of
 contemnor's property on trust—Equitable chose in action—Whether court
 order necessary to protect bank—Law of Property Act 1925 (15 & 16 Geo. 5
 c. 20), s. 105.*

  The wife, following divorce proceedings, obtained an order for maintenance
in 1956. In 1963, considerable arrears having accumulated, she issued **H**
a writ of sequestration against the husband. The sequestrators collected
various assets which were paid voluntarily to them. They learnt that the
bank, as mortgagee, intended to exercise its power of sale under s. 101 of the
Law of Property Act 1925, in respect of a house standing in the husband's
name. Following sale of the house a substantial surplus would remain in
the hands of the bank which it would hold on trust for the husband. On the **I**
question whether the bank could properly refuse to hand over the surplus
to the sequestrators without a specific court order directing it to do so,

  Held: (i) the husband's interest in the surplus proceeds which were held on
trust absolutely under s. 105 of the Law of Property Act 1925 amounted at
least to an equitable chose in action and, since both legal and equitable choses
in action fell within the expression " personal estate " in the writ of sequestration, the sequestrators were entitled to collect the surplus under the writ
(see p. 1002, letters C and E, post);

A   (ii) although the bank did not need the protection of a specific court order before paying over the surplus and should have done so without, nevertheless its attitude in feeling that it should not pay the money to the sequestrators without such an order was not, in all the circumstances, unreasonable and no order as to costs would be made against the bank (see p. 1007, letters C and E, post).

B   *Miller* v. *Huddlestone* ((1882), 22 Ch.D. 233) and *Guerrine (otherwise Roberts)* v. *Guerrine* ([1959] 2 All E.R. 594, n.), explained.

    Wilson v. *Metcalfe* ((1839), 1 Beav. 263) and *White* v. *Wood* ((1843), 2 Y. & C.Ch.Cas. 615), distinguished.

[As to sequestration as a remedy for non-payment of alimony or maintenance, see 12 HALSBURY'S LAWS (3rd Edn.) 470, paras. 1051, 1052; and for cases on C the subject, see 27 DIGEST (Repl.) 679, *6480-6485.*

As to the writ of sequestration generally, see 16 HALSBURY'S LAWS (3rd Edn.) 68-77, paras. 105-115; and for cases on the subject, see 21 DIGEST (Repl.) 686-701, *1812-2043.*]

Cases referred to:

D   *Capron* v. *Capron*, [1927] P. 243; 96 L.J.P. 151; 137 L.T. 568; 21 Digest (Repl.) 689, *1847.*

   Claydon v. *Finch* (1873), L.R. 15 Eq. 266; 42 L.J.Ch. 416; 28 L.T. 101; 21 Digest (Repl.) 695, *1943.*

   Coles v. *Coles*, [1956] 3 All E.R. 542; [1957] P. 68; [1956] 3 W.L.R. 861; 21 Digest (Repl.) 690, *1852.*

E   *Craig* v. *Craig*, [1896] P. 171; 65 L.J.P. 99; 75 L.T. 280; 21 Digest (Repl.) 700, *2009.*

   Fenton v. *Lowther* (1787), 1 Cox, Eq. Cas. 315; 29 E.R. 1182; 21 Digest (Repl.) 695, *1936.*

   Guerrine (otherwise Roberts) v. *Guerrine* [1959] 2 All E.R. 594, n.; [1959] 1 W.L.R. 760; Digest (Cont. Vol. A) 809, *6484a.*

F   *Miller* v. *Huddlestone* (1882), 22 Ch.D. 233; 52 L.J.Ch. 208; 47 L.T. 570; 21 Digest (Repl.) 695, *1946.*

   Pollard, Re, Pollard v. *Pollard* (1902), 87 L.T. 61; 21 Digest (Repl.) 695, *1947.*

   Simmonds v. *Lord Kinnaird* (1799), 4 Ves. 735; 31 E.R. 380; 21 Digest (Repl.) 694, *1934.*

   White v. *Wood* (1843), 2 Y. & C.Ch.Cas. 615; 2 L.T.O.S. 116; 63 E.R. 275; 21 Digest (Repl.) 697, *1967.*

G   *Wilson* v. *Metcalfe* (1839), 1 Beav. 263; 8 L.J.Ch. 331; 48 E.R. 941; 21 Digest (Repl.) 694, *1929.*

Notice of Motion.

The notice of motion was issued by the sequestrators, Eric Edward Wilding, Derek Ernest Hudson, Ronald Hudson and Ruth Hill, and was served on Barclays H Bank, Ltd., and on the solicitors of John William Bucknell. The relief sought is set out at p. 1001, letter E, post. The facts are set out in the judgment.

W. J. Mowbray for the sequestrators.
J. A. P. Hazel for the bank.

                                                Cur. adv. vult.

I   2nd April. **BRANDON, J.:** This motion raises interesting questions with regard to the execution of a writ of sequestration. The matter arises out of divorce proceedings brought by Margaret Alexia Williams Bucknell, whom I shall call the wife, against John William Bucknell, whom I shall call the husband, in November 1955. In those proceedings, which were not defended, the wife was, on 14th February 1956, granted a decree nisi of divorce on the grounds of the husband's adultery. That decree was made absolute on 25th June 1956. In October 1956, following the divorce, the wife obtained an order for the maintenance of herself and the three children of the marriage of whom she had

been given the custody. Subsequently, in April 1959, February 1960 and A
December 1961, successive variations to that maintenance order were made.

Under the order as finally varied in December 1961, the husband was required
to pay £5 17s. 6d a week to the wife and £97 10s. a year, less tax, direct to each
of the three children. The husband did not comply with the order in favour of
the wife, and on 16th September 1963, when considerable arrears had accumulated,
the wife's solicitors caused to be issued a writ of sequestration against the B
husband. That writ was issued on the basis that the husband, by reason of
his failure to comply with the order for the wife's maintenance, was in contempt
of this court (see *Capron* v. *Capron* (1) and *Coles* v. *Coles* (2)).

The writ of sequestration was directed to four persons as sequestrators. They
were Eric Edward Wilding, Derek Ernest Hudson and Ronald Hudson, all
three chartered accountants, and Ruth Hill, secretary. After naming them, C
the writ went on:

" Whereas lately in the Divorce Division of our High Court of Justice in a
certain matter there pending, by an Order of our said Court made in the
said Divorce Division and bearing date the 29th day of December 1961, it
was ordered the [husband] should pay or cause to be paid to the [wife]
as from the 5th April 1961, maintenance for herself during their joint lives D
or until further Order at the rate of £5 17. 6. per week payable weekly.
Know Ye therefore that we in confidence of your prudence and fidelity
have given and by these presents do give to you or any three or two of
you full power and authority to enter upon the messuages, lands, tenements
and real estate whatsoever of the [husband] and to collect receive and
sequester into your hands not only all the rents and profits of the said E
messuages, lands, tenements and real estate, but also all his goods, chattels
and personal estate whatsoever, and therefore we command you any three
or two of you that you do at certain proper and convenient days and hours
go to and enter upon all the messuages, lands, tenements and real estate of
the said John William Bucknell and that you do collect, take and get into
your hands not only the rents and profits of his said real estate, but also all F
his goods, chattels and personal estate and detain and keep the same under
sequestration in your hands until the [husband] shall pay or cause to be paid
to the [wife] the maintenance for herself as hereinbefore recited and clear
his contempt and our said Court make other Order to the contrary."

In exercise of the powers and authority conferred on them by that writ, the
sequestrators proceeded to collect and get in all the assets of the husband which G
they could. The result of their efforts in this respect appears from two sets
of accounts of receipts and disbursements which have been presented to and
passed by the court. The first set relates to the period 16th December 1963 to
26th October 1964 and the second set to the period 27th October 1964 to 25th
November 1968.

Among the disbursements shown are various payments to the wife in respect H
of arrears of maintenance under the order of December 1961 which the court
expressly authorised the sequestrators to make. The assets shown by the
accounts as having been collected and got in include the following: various
book debts, income and capital from the estate of a deceased person, and rents
from a house known as 23, Park Road, Hanwell. It appears that the third
parties from whom these assets were collected paid them over voluntarily to I
the sequestrators, for there is no record in the file of any application to the court
with regard to them. The house known as 23, Park Road, Hanwell, the rents
of which were collected by the sequestrators until March 1967, was a freehold
house owned by the husband. It had been mortgaged by him to Barclays Bank,
Ltd., by a legal charge dated 19th May 1959 to secure all moneys which might
be owed by him to the bank from time to time.

(1) [1927] P. 243.   (2) [1956] 3 All E.R. 542; [1957] P. 68.

A At some time which is not clear from the evidence, but which appears to have been about November 1966, the sequestrators became aware of the intention of the bank to exercise its statutory power of sale as mortgagee of 23, Park Road. It seems to have been recognised that, following the sale of the house and the satisfaction by the bank of all its claims in respect of moneys due to it out of the proceeds of such sale, there would remain a substantial surplus in the hands

B of the bank. Letters were exchanged between the sequestrators' accountants and solicitors on the one hand and the bank on the other hand relating to the destination of this surplus. In that correspondence those acting for the sequestrators took the line that the surplus should be paid over to them without more ado, while the bank took the line that the sequestrators should apply to the court for an order for payment. Meanwhile, the bank undertook not to pay the

C surplus over to the husband or anyone else without giving the sequestrators an opportunity of applying to the court to protect their position. The sale was completed in September 1968 and by letter dated 16th January 1969 the bank, who had kept the sequestrators' solicitors fully informed about the progress of the transaction, informed them that the net surplus remaining in the hands of the bank was £540 5s. 5d. The bank had already made it clear in an earlier

D letter dated 11th November 1968 that this money would only be paid over against a specific court order.

  Faced with that situation, the sequestrators issued a notice of motion dated 12th March 1969 which was served on the bank and on the husband's solicitors. By that notice of motion the sequestrators asked for the following order against the bank: (i) Payment by the bank to the sequestrators of the net proceeds of

E the recent sale by the bank as mortgagee of the husband's house 23, Park Road, Hanwell, London, W.7, after payment of principal, interest and the mortgagee's costs due to the bank; (ii) all necessary and proper directions, accounts and enquiries; (iii) payment by the bank of the sequestrators' costs of this motion; and (iv) provision for any costs of the sequestrators not covered by any such order.

F When the motion came on for hearing before me, the sequestrators and the bank were represented by solicitors and counsel, but the husband did not appear and was not represented. I was informed that he had disappeared some time ago and that his solicitors, though still on the record, had no instructions from him. When the motion was opened to me, it became apparent that there was no dispute that the sequestrators were entitled to the order for payment of

G the surplus moneys for which they asked, and that the only difference between the parties was with regard to costs. As to this, the case for the sequestrators was that the bank should have paid over the moneys on demand without insisting on the sequestrators obtaining an order from the court first, and that in those circumstances, the bank should bear its own costs and pay the sequestrators' costs of the application. The case for the bank, on the other hand, was that

H it had acted reasonably in refusing to pay over the moneys except on a court order, and that the costs of both sides should therefore be borne, as between the sequestrators and the bank, by the sequestrators. To give effect to this approach, the bank asked that it be allowed to deduct its costs from the surplus moneys before paying them over to the sequestrators. While the dispute, on the face of it, involved only the question of the exercise of the court's discretion as

I to costs, it seemed to me that there was underlying it a question of principle with regard to the rights of sequestrators to collect certain kinds of assets of a contemnor from third parties, and the extent to which, if at all, third parties are entitled to refuse to pay over such assets without a specific court order directing them to do so. I accordingly requested counsel to argue this question of principle fully before me.

  In order to decide the question of principle so raised, it seems to me that it is necessary in relation to the facts of the present case to ask and answer three questions as follows. First, what is the nature of the husband's right to the

surplus proceeds?   Second, is such right personal estate of the husband so as **A**
to entitle the sequestrators to collect the surplus from the bank under the writ
of sequestration?   Third, if so, does the bank need the protection of a specific
order before paying over the surplus to the sequestrators?

As regards the first question relating to the nature of the husband's right to
the surplus, it is, I think, clear that the bank holds the surplus on trust for the
husband absolutely.   The bank sold the house under the statutory power of **B**
sale conferred on it as mortgagee by s. 101 of the Law of Property Act 1925.
The rights and duties of the bank with regard to the proceeds of sale are governed
by s. 105 of that Act which makes it clear that it holds the surplus on trust for
the husband.   In these circumstances, the husband has a right in equity against
the bank to have the surplus paid over to him.   I should have thought that this
right was, at the least, an equitable chose in action.   (See the definition of that **C**
expression given in 4 HALSBURY'S LAWS OF ENGLAND (3rd Edn.) at pp. 480, 481.)
Counsel for the sequestrators, while accepting that the right was at least that,
contended that it was something more, namely absolute equitable ownership, and
based an alternative argument of his on this contention.   I shall deal later with
that contention and the alternative argument based on it.   For the time being,
however, I shall content myself with categorising the right as an equitable chose **D**
in action.

As regards the second question, whether such right is personal estate of the
husband so as to entitle the sequestrators to collect it under the writ, I am clearly
of opinion that it is.   Treating the question simply as one of construction of the
writ apart from authority, I should have no hesitation in holding that the expression " personal estate " includes choses in action, both legal and equitable.   The **E**
authorities, as I shall show shortly, support that view.

As regards the third question, whether the bank needs the protection of a
specific order before paying over the surplus, the matter is more difficult. If the
question were free from authority, I should have thought that such protection
was not necessary on the ground that, if the writ authorised the collection of the
surplus by the sequestrators, that would of itself give the bank all the protection **F**
it needed.   In this case, however, a number of authorities do not seem to support
the view which I should have taken independently of them.   It is therefore
necessary that I should examine them carefully and see whether and to what
extent they lay down any principle or establish any practice which I ought to
follow.

In *Simmonds* v. *Lord Kinnaird* (3) LORD LOUGHBOROUGH, L.C., expressly **G**
left open the question whether a chose in action was liable to sequestration.   In
Wilson v. *Metcalfe* (4) the question so left open was decided, the decision being
that a chose in action was liable to sequestration.   In that case the defendant,
John Ness, against whom a sequestration had issued, was entitled to a rentcharge issuing out of the estate of the third party, Elizabeth Brown, with power
of distress.   The rentcharge was in arrears and the amount of the arrears was **H**
claimed by both the sequestrators and the defendant. Elizabeth Brown offered
to pay the arrears to the sequestrators on being given an indemnity, but an
indemnity not being given, paid the arrears to the defendant who had threatened
to distrain.   The plaintiffs applied to the Chancery Court by motion for an order
against the third party for payment by her to the sequestrators of the amount of
the arrears of the rentcharge, and the amounts becoming due under it in the **I**
future.   LORD LANGDALE, M.R., said (5):

" I have read the cases cited in the arguments and many others; and it
appears to me that in such a case as this, a chose in action is subject to the
process of sequestration, but however sequestration is to be made effective
in respect of choses in action may be a question requiring much consideration;
in a clear and simple case it may be by order only, or a voluntary payment

(3) (1799), 4 Ves. 735.   (4) (1839), 1 Beav. 263.
(5) (1839), 1 Beav. at pp. 269, 270.

A   may be protected; in other cases it may be necessary to resort to an action or suit under the direction of the Court. But I consider it to be clear, that if the party owing the debt requires protection, he ought to have it, and that even if he is willing to make payment, the Court would not order it, unless it appeared that protection could be afforded. In this case, Mrs. Brown was willing to pay, but desired protection; she might I think have had pro-

B   tection by an order upon motion of which John Ness had notice; but being left unprotected from December 1837 to September 1838, I think she was not bound to await the distress which John Ness threatened, and is not liable to pay the money over again. The ground of my decision is that the Plaintiff or the sequestrators, having ample time and opportunity, did not, as they might have done, apply for an order of payment, and it was

C   evident that Ness would distrain, if payment were not made to him. I think that Mrs. Brown ought to pay the sums hereafter to become due to the sequestrators after deducting the costs of this motion."

In *White* v. *Wood* (6), the defendant, T. Wood, against whom a sequestration had issued, owned land of which a third party, Henry Rogers, was tenant. The sequestrators applied to the tenant for payment to them of arrears of rent

D   admitted by him to be due to the defendant. The tenant offered to pay the amount over on being given an indemnity, but the sequestrators declined to give him one. They then applied to the Chancery Court by motion for an order against the tenant for payment of the money. Counsel who appeared for the tenant, made no objection to the payment of the money but submitted that, as his client had offered to pay the money on being given an indemnity, he ought to

E   have his costs of the present application, and he relied on *Wilson* v. *Metcalfe* (7). Counsel who appeared for the sequestrators said that in the case cited the defendant threatened to distrain if the tenant would not pay. He said it was clear that Rogers ought to have been satisfied with the order of sequestration as a sufficient indemnity. SIR JAMES KNIGHT BRUCE, V.-C., said (8):

F   "Without giving a positive opinion on the point, I think it was so fairly a matter of question whether Rogers could have safely paid the money without indemnity, that the Plaintiff should pay the costs of the present motion."

In *Claydon* v. *Finch* (9), a husband had successfully resisted a wife's suit for restitution of conjugal rights and obtained orders for costs against her. She

G   having failed to comply with those orders, a writ of sequestration was issued against her. Shortly before the issue of the writ a dividend had fallen due on a fund in court to the income of which the wife was entitled for her separate use without power of anticipation. The sequestrators sought payment of the dividend from the Paymaster General, but were refused. They then applied to the Chancery Court by petition for payment out of the dividend of the costs due from the wife in the restitution suit, the costs of the sequestration and the

H   costs of the instant petition. SIR JAMES BACON, V.-C., said (10):

"I think the Petitioners are entitled to the order they pray for. The first objection made by Mr. Speed cannot be maintained. To this dividend, the clause in restraint of anticipation has no reference. Such a restriction applies only to income before it becomes due. This dividend was, on the

I   5th of January, as much the absolute property of Mrs. Wicks as if it had been in her own pocket. If there had been a stop-order on this fund it would have been necessary for the sequestrator to clear the fund before he could lay hands on it. But there is nothing of that sort here; and the authorities clearly establish the right of the sequestrator to be paid out of

---

(6) (1843), 2 Y. & C.Ch.Cas. 615.   (7) (1839), 1 Beav. 263.
(8) (1843), 2 Y. & C.Ch.Cas. at p. 616.   (9) (1873), L.R. 15 Eq. 266.
                    (10) (1873), L.R. 15 Eq. at p. 268.

money which is the absolute property of the debtor. The order must   **A**
be as prayed."

In *Miller* v. *Huddlestone* (11), sequestration had issued against the defendant,
William McMurray. The sequestrators obtained possession of considerable
property of the defendant and tried to obtain payment of a credit balance at
his bank, but the bankers refused to give them any information as to the amount
of the balance. The sequestrators then applied by motion in the Chancery   **B**
Division for an order against the bankers for payment into court of the balance
in their hands. It was argued for the bankers that the court had no jurisdiction
to make the order asked for. FRY, J., said (12):

"I consider that I have jurisdiction to make the order asked for upon
Messrs. *Smith, Payne & Co.*, without any further proceedings. The case   **C**
comes within the authority of *Wilson* v. *Metcalfe* (13), which shews that
the order can properly be made upon service upon the third person, the
bankers. I may observe that if I were to hold otherwise, it would involve
much greater expense and delay. The order will be that the bankers
verify the balance of the Defendant *McMurray* by affidavit, unless they
admit the amount at the Bar. [The amount of the balance was admitted at   **D**
the Bar, whereupon the following order was made:] Messrs. *Smith, Payne &
Co.* admitting £2,689 8s. 6d. to be standing to the credit of *McMurray* in
their books, order them to pay that sum into Court to the credit of this
action, sequestration account. The Taxing Master to tax the costs of the
sequestrators of and incidental to the sequestration and to fix their remuneration, and to tax the costs of Messrs. *Smith, Payne & Co.*, and the amount   **E**
so taxed and found due to be paid out of the fund so to be paid into Court."

In *Re Pollard, Pollard* v. *Pollard* (14), sequestration was issued against the
defendant in an administration action because of his failure to comply with an
order for payment of a certain sum into court. The sequestrators sought payment from the defendant's bank of the credit balance in his account there.
The bank said that they would consult their solicitors and promised meanwhile   **F**
not to part with any of the balance. In breach of that promise they later paid
over part of the balance to the defendant. The plaintiffs in the action then
applied by summons in the Chancery Division for an order against the bank for
payment into court of the whole of the original amount of the balance. The
bank was willing to pay into court the balance remaining but not the whole
amount of the original balance. JOYCE, J., said that he regretted that he could   **G**
not make an order in respect of the larger sum. It was laid down in the textbooks that mere notice of a writ of sequestration did not bind the chose in action
in the hands of a third party and the authorities seemed to bear out that proposition. No case had been cited to show that mere notice of the sequestration
was enough and certainly it did not create a charge. The bank submitting to
pay the £136 3s. into court, that is to say the lesser sum, there would be an   **H**
order against them for that amount, but, having regard to what had passed
between the sequestrators and the bank manager, JOYCE, J., declined to give
the bank any costs.

In *Guerrine* (*otherwise Roberts*) v. *Guerrine* (15), sequestration had issued
against the husband for failure to comply with an order for payment by him to a
wife of certain costs of a nullity suit in which she had succeeded. The seques-   **I**
trators sought payment from the husband's bank of the credit balance in his
account. The bank refused to pay over the balance without further order
of the court. The wife then applied by motion in the Probate, Divorce and
Admiralty Division for an order against the bank for payment into court of the

(11) (1882), 22 Ch.D. 233.   (12) (1882), 22 Ch.D. at p. 234.
(13) (1839), 1 Beav. 263.   (14) (1902), 87 L.T. 61.
     (15) [1959] 2 All E.R. 594, n.;   [1959] 1 W.L.R. 760.

A balance to the credit of the sequestration account. Counsel for the wife argued this (16):

> " The moneys standing to a debtor's credit at a bank are liable to sequestration and a bank account is a chose in action of which no part can be paid away by the bank without an Order of the Court. (See R.S.C., Ord. 43, r. 6, and *Miller* v. *Huddlestone* (17), in which, following *Wilson* v. *Metcalfe* (18),

B the court held that it had jurisdiction to make an order.)"

Counsel for the bank argued as follows (16):

> " The bank admits that the credit balance standing to the account of the husband is [so much]. It neither assents to the motion nor opposes it, but if an order be made it should be in the form of the order in *Miller* v.

C *Huddlestone* (17)."

MARSHALL, J., said (19):

> " There will be an order ... that Barclays Bank, Ltd., having admitted [the sum] standing to the credit of . . . [the husband] in their books, shall pay that sum into court to the credit of this action sequestration account. The order will provide for the costs of the sequestrators of and incidental to

D the sequestration to be taxed by the taxing master and for him to fix their remuneration and to tax the costs of [the bank], and that the amount so taxed and found due shall be paid out of the fund so to be paid into court. I am quite satisfied that Barclays Bank, Ltd., acted properly in every way."

I observe that the learned judge followed, in the order which he made, that
E which had been made in *Miller* v. *Huddlestone* (17).

It is difficult to see why, if a writ of sequestration entitles sequestrators to collect and get in choses in action, whether equitable as in *Claydon* v. *Finch* (20) or legal as in the other cases cited, and the contemnor's right to the chose in action is clear and undisputed, there should be any need for a further application to the court to enable them to do so. It is suggested in the authorities that such
F an order is or may be necessary in order to protect the third party from adverse claims, but on the footing that the contemnor's right is clear and undisputed, the only adverse claim to which the third party is likely to be subjected is one by the contemnor himself. To such a claim, I should have thought that the third party had a complete answer in the writ of sequestration itself. It would not follow from the adoption of that approach, assuming it to be right, that it
G would never be necessary or reasonable for an application to be made to the court in respect of the sequestration of a chose in action. On the contrary there are a number of situations in which such an application by sequestrators would be appropriate. One such situation is where there is a dispute or doubt whether a particular kind of chose in action is, for special reasons, protected from sequestration. (See *Fenton* v. *Lowther* (21).) That was a case relating to the
H salary received by an equerry to one of the royal family. Another such situation is where there is a dispute or doubt as to the title of the contemnor to the chose in action concerned. (See *Craig* v. *Craig* (22).) There may well be other situations where other problems proper to be put before the court will arise.

To hold that a third party could properly, in all cases where sequestrators seek to collect a chose in action from him, insist on an application to the court for a
I specific order and recover his costs of such application, would have very disadvantageous consequences from a practical point of view. This can be well illustrated by reference to the facts of the present case. As I said earlier, the sequestrators before encountering resistance from the bank in respect of the surplus of the

---

(16) [1959] 1 W.L.R. at p. 760; [1959] 2 All E.R. at p. 594.
(17) (1882), 22 Ch.D. 233.   (18) (1839), 1 Beav. 263.
(19) [1959] 2 All E.R. at pp. 594, 595; [1959] 1 W.L.R. at pp. 760, 761.
(20) (1873), L.R. 15 Eq. 266.   (21) (1787), 1 Cox, Eq. Cas. 315.
                    (22) [1896] P. 171.

proceeds of sale of 23, Park Road, had successfully got in a number of other A
choses in action, including book debts, income and capital from a deceased
person's estate, and rents of the same house, without opposition. If they had
been obliged in every case to obtain a specific court order against the third
party concerned, with the costs of both sides coming out of the sequestrated
assets, much time and effort would have been wasted, and the moneys ultimately
available to be paid to the wife would have been materially reduced. I should B
be reluctant to accept that the law requires such a pointless and wasteful procedure to be followed in a straightforward case where there is no doubt or dispute
about the liability of the chose in action to sequestration or about the contemnor's
title to it.

Counsel for the sequestrators, when he first opened the case to me, indicated
that he felt obliged, in the light of such authorities as *Miller* v. *Huddlestone* (23) C
and *Guerrine (otherwise Roberts)* v. *Guerrine* (24), to concede that, where the asset
sought to be got in was a debt like a balance in a bank account, the bank was
entitled to insist on the sequestrators obtaining a specific order from the court
and, further, entitled to an order for payment of its costs of the application. He
sought, however, to distinguish the present case on the ground that the asset
concerned was not a debt but particular moneys of which the husband was D
absolute equitable owner.

I formed the view that, while a valid distinction could perhaps be made
between the present case and the earlier cases cited on this somewhat narrow and
technical ground, it would not afford a satisfactory basis for a decision because
it would leave open the broader questions of principle which I have outlined.
In these circumstances, I invited counsel for the sequestrators to withdraw his E
concession and to argue his case on the broader basis which he very helpfully
proceeded to do.

Counsel for the bank, rather to my surprise, did not contend that the bank
needed a specific order in order to enable it safely to pay over the surplus moneys
to the sequestrators. He argued, however, that, in the light of the authorities
cited, and particularly the comparatively recent case of *Guerrine (otherwise* F
Roberts) v. *Guerrine* (24), in which the same bank was concerned, it was reasonable for the bank to think that it needed a specific order for its protection. On
this basis he said that the bank had acted reasonably in insisting on an application
to the court and should have its costs of the application. Despite this concession by counsel for the bank, I think that it remains incumbent on me to consider whether the authorities cited do require me to hold that the bank needed G
a specific order for its protection, and was therefore justified in insisting on the
sequestrators obtaining one. As to that, my opinion is that the authorities do
not so require. I reach this conclusion on several grounds, as follows.

First, there is no express statement in any of the judgments in those cases
that a specific order is necessary to protect a third party from whom sequestrators
claim a chose in action belonging to the contemnor. Moreover, in *Wilson* v. H
Metcalfe (25) there is a specific reference to voluntary payments in a clear and
simple case being protected. Secondly, insofar as in a number of the cases the
third party concerned was awarded his costs on the ground that he had acted
reasonably in insisting on a specific order being obtained, this involved no more
than an exercise by the court of its discretion as to costs in the circumstances
of the particular case. It did not necessarily imply any decision on the point I
of principle. Thirdly, in two of the cases where costs were awarded to the third
party, namely *Wilson* v. *Metcalfe* (25) and *White* v. *Wood* (26) there was a special
factor present in the form of a threat of distress against the third party by the
contemnor. This threat put the third party in a position of special difficulty

(23) (1882), 22 Ch.D. 233.
(24) [1959] 2 All E.R. 594, n.; [1959] 1 W.L.R. 760.
(25) (1839), 1 Beav. 263.
(26) (1843), 2 Y. & C.Ch.Cas. 615.

A which does not arise in the present case. Fourthly, so far as *Miller* v. *Huddlestone* (27) and *Guerrine* (*otherwise Roberts*) v. *Guerrine* (28) are concerned, it is not clear that the third party's right to costs was ever seriously disputed. Fifthly, while all the authorities concerned are entitled to great respect, none of them is binding on me.

B Bearing in mind all these factors, I feel free to decide the question of principle which arises in the present case in accordance with what seems to me to be the common sense of the matter, and, having done so, to exercise my discretion as to costs in an unfettered manner, having regard to all the circumstances.

   I hold, for the reasons which I have given earlier, that the bank in the present case did not need the protection of a specific court order before paying over the surplus moneys in its hands to the sequestrators, and that its insistence

C on the sequestrators obtaining such an order was based on a mistaken view about the need for such protection. It follows, in my view, that the bank, by taking the line which it did, has compelled the sequestrators to make an application to the court which would not otherwise have been necessary. In these circumstances I should, in the ordinary way, have thought that the right way to exercise my discretion as to costs would be to make the bank bear its own and pay the seques-

D trators' costs of the motion. It seems to me, however, that, even though on my view of the law the bank's attitude was wrong, the line of authorities cited, especially *Guerrine* (*otherwise Roberts*) v. *Guerrine* (28) made it not unreasonable for the bank to believe that its attitude was right, or at least to have doubts about the course which it could safely follow. Taking into account this considera-tion, I have reached the conclusion that the fairest order to make as to costs

E in this particular case is no order, leaving each side to bear its own costs. As I understand it, the sequestrators will be entitled to treat their costs as expenses chargeable against the sequestration fund, and the result of my order will therefore be that the moneys available to satisfy the wife's entitlement under her maintenance order will be reduced by the amount of such costs. I am sorry that this result should follow, but in spite of it I still think that the order which

F I have indicated is the right one to make in all the circumstances. While that is the order which I think right to make in the present case, having regard to the history of the matter, it does not follow that the same order would be appropriate in a similar case in the future. It may well be that in such a case, following my decision if it be right, different considerations would apply, and it would be right to make a third party, who compelled an unnecessary application to the court in

G circumstances comparable with those existing in the present case, not only to bear his own costs but to pay those of the sequestrators as well. It is, however, not necessary to decide any such question today.

Order accordingly.

Solicitors: *Evan Davies & Co.* (for the sequestrators); *Durrant Cooper & Hambling* (for the bank).

H
                              [*Reported by* ALICE BLOOMFIELD, *Barrister-at-Law.*]

I

(27) (1882), 22 Ch.D. 233.
(28) [1959] 2 All E.R. 594, n.; [1959] 1 W.L.R. 760.

R. *v.* CLARKE.

[COURT OF APPEAL, CRIMINAL DIVISION (Widgery and Karminski, L.JJ., and Geoffrey Lane, J.), April 29, 1969.]

Road Traffic—Driving with blood-alcohol proportion above prescribed limit—Evidence—Provision of specimen—Breath test—Requirement to take test—What constitutes requirement—Road Safety Act 1967 (c. 30), *s.* 2 (1).

Road Traffic—Driving with blood-alcohol proportion above prescribed limit—Evidence—Failure to supply specimen—Specimen for laboratory test—Refusal to supply specimen—What constitutes refusal—Road Safety Act 1967 (c. 30), *s.* 3 (3) *and* (6).

Road Traffic—Driving with blood-alcohol proportion above prescribed limit—Evidence—Failure to supply specimen—Specimen for laboratory test—Reasonable excuse for failure—Evidence of reasonable excuse—Onus of proof to eliminate defence—Road Safety Act 1967 (c. 30), *s.* 3 (3).

A request in words which it is clear to the driver is being made as of right is sufficient to amount to a requirement to take a breath test under s. 2 (1)* of the Road Safety Act 1967 (see p. 1010, letter B, post).

Any words, or any actions, on the part of a driver, which in the eyes of the jury make it clear that the driver in all the circumstances of the particular case is declining the policeman's proper invitation, amount to a refusal to provide a specimen for a laboratory test under s. 3 (3)† and (6)‡ of the Road Safety Act 1967 (see p. 1010, letter G, post).

It is clear from the wording of s. 3 (3) of the Road Safety Act 1967 that if a reasonable excuse emerges which excuses the driver from providing a specimen for a laboratory test then that is a defence. Once such evidence emerges, it is for the prosecution to eliminate the existence of such a defence to the satisfaction of the jury (see p. 1010, letter I, to p. 1011, letter A, and p. 1011, letter B, post).

[As to the offences of failing to supply specimens of breath, blood and urine for laboratory tests see SUPPLEMENT to 33 HALSBURY'S LAWS (3rd Edn.) para. 1061A, 3.

For the Road Safety Act 1967, s. 2, s. 3 see 47 HALSBURY'S STATUTES (2nd Edn.) 1556, 1558.]

Application.

This was an application by Christopher Henry Tollemache Clarke for leave to appeal against his conviction on 2nd October 1968 at Inner London Sessions before the deputy chairman (LORD DUNBOYNE) and a jury, of dangerous driving (count 1) and failing to supply specimens of blood or urine (count 2) contrary to s. 3 (3) (*a*) of the Road Safety Act 1967. He was sentenced to six months' imprisonment, concurrent, on each count suspended for two years and also disqualified for holding a driving licence for six months and 12 months respectively, concurrent. He applied for leave to appeal against conviction on count 2 and against sentence on both counts. The facts are set out in the judgment of the court.

D. A. J. Vaughan for the applicant.
The Crown was not represented.

---

* Section 2 (1), so far as material, is set out on p. 1009, letter I, post.
† Section 3 (3), so far as material, provides: " A person who, without reasonable excuse, fails to provide a specimen for a laboratory test in pursuance of a requirement imposed under this section shall be guilty of an offence and—(*a*) if it is shown that at the relevant time he was driving or attempting to drive a motor vehicle on a road or other public place, he shall be liable to be proceeded against and punished as if the offence charged were an offence under section 1 (1) of this Act; . . . "
‡ Section 3 (6), so far as material provides: " A person shall not be treated for the purposes of section 2 (1) of the 1962 Act or subsection (3) of this section as failing to provide a specimen unless— . . . (c) he is again requested to provide a specimen of blood but refuses to do so."

A **GEOFFREY LANE, J.,** delivered the judgment of the court: The applicant in this case on 2nd October 1968 at Inner London Quarter Sessions was found guilty of dangerous driving (count 1) and also of failure to provide a specimen of blood or urine contrary to s. 3 (3) (a) of the Road Safety Act 1967. He was sentenced by the deputy chairman to six months' imprisonment on each of those counts concurrent, those sentences to be suspended for two years, and was

B disqualified for six and 12 months respectively from driving or holding a driving licence.

  The facts of the case, briefly, were these. In the early hours of Wednesday 7th February 1968 two police officers in uniform in a police car followed the applicant, who was driving his vehicle along Holland Park Avenue. His driving gave rise to concern; he was weaving from one lane of the road to the other,

C and the policemen in their car in due course stopped him. His breath smelt of alcohol, and (according to the evidence of the police officers) one of those officers told him that he wished the applicant to take a breath test. The reply was " All right, but I am only tired; I have not been drinking ". Then, when the officer went back to the police vehicle in order to get the test equipment, the applicant started up his motor car and suddenly moved off, narrowly missing

D one of the officers. There then followed a chase over a distance just short of two miles during which, according to the police evidence, the applicant reached speeds of up to 80 miles per hour and went through a number of sets of traffic lights when those lights were showing red. In due course he was stopped by another police car, and was then arrested for failing to take the breath test. He said to the officer " You aren't a police officer ". He was then taken to a

E police station and offered a breath test, but did not take it, just saying that he wanted to see the officer in charge. A little later he was again asked to take a breath test, and on this occasion he said " I want to see my solicitor ". He was then asked to supply a specimen of blood then or two specimens of urine within an hour, and was told that he would be given part of any specimen supplied and warned of what would happen if he refused to supply them. To that request

F he replied " No, I will not do anything until I've seen my solicitor ". At a minute before 4.0 a.m. he was asked to supply two samples of urine and warned of the consequence again of refusal or failure, and to that request he replied " No ". Then at shortly before 4.15 a.m. he was once again asked for a specimen of blood and warned of the consequences of failure or refusal and told he would be given a part of any sample supplied, and to that request he said " Can I make a state-

G ment at this stage? ". Immediately thereafter he was charged with failing to take the breath test, failing to supply samples and dangerous driving, and to that charge he made no reply.

  A study of the Road Safety Act 1967 makes it clear that there are a large number of hurdles (as they were called at the trial of this case) which the prosecution have to clear before they can bring home a conviction under s. 3 (3).

H Counsel for the applicant, submits that the prosecution have failed in this respect in the following ways. First of all under s. 2 (1) (almost the first hurdle) the prosecution must prove the following matters, and I read the section:

> "A constable in uniform may require any person driving or attempting to drive a motor vehicle on a road or other public place to provide a specimen
I of breath for a breath test there or nearby, if the constable has reasonable cause—(a) to suspect him of having alcohol in his body; ...".

It is said by counsel that there was no evidence of such a requirement or, alternatively, that the deputy chairman failed adequately to direct the jury as to the meaning of the word " require ". He submits that the word " require " must in the context of this Act have a different connotation than the word " request ", which appears at several places in s. 3 (6). The prosecution evidence on this matter was that P.c. Morris, in uniform (though there was a dispute whether he was or was not in fact in uniform or was wearing his helmet) approa- **A** ched the applicant and said to him " I wish to give you a breath test owing to the manner in which you have been driving this vehicle, as I believe you are driving with more than the prescribed level of alcohol in your blood ". Did that amount to evidence on which the jury was entitled to come to the conclusion that there had been a " requirement "? We take the view that it did. A request in words which it is clear to the defendant is being made as of right is sufficient **B** to amount to a requirement. Accordingly, there is evidence on which the jury would have been entitled to find the point proved.

Secondly, how was it put by the learned deputy chairman to the jury? He put it in this way:

> " . . . the prosecution have to prove so that you are sure that he did fail to give a breath test after he had been required to give a breath test and **C** that the officer Morris had reasonable suspicion for alcohol being in the [applicant's] body."

It is true that earlier in place of the word " required " he had used the word " requested ", but that does not, in our view, invalidate the later and accurate direction.

Next counsel submits that unless the Alcotest equipment is ready and available **D** at that very moment for the test to be carried out instanter the request or require- ment is invalidated. To that proposition we do not accede. The equipment was no doubt in the police vehicle a few yards away, and it would have only required a moment or two to fetch the equipment and to assemble it ready for use. In fact, as already indicated, the applicant drove off before those simple steps could be taken. The next point taken on behalf of the applicant is this. When **E** at 4.13 a.m. he was requested to give a blood sample, that request being made by virtue of s. 3 (6) (c) of the Act, he replied " Can I make a statement at this stage?" It is said that those words do not amount, or cannot amount, to a refusal as is required by the wording of the Act. Plainly no particular formula of words is necessary from a defendant to constitute a refusal by him. It is the police, and not defendants, who are required by this legislation to adhere to formulae. **F** Any words, or indeed any actions, on the part of a defendant, which in the eyes of the jury make it clear that the defendant in all the circumstances of the particular case is declining the policeman's proper invitation, amount to a refusal within the section. The circumstances of the present case were such that the jury were entitled to conclude, and probably did conclude, that the applicant was pursuing a systematic campaign of prevarication, knowing full well that the **G** more time which elapsed before he gave a sample the greater chance of his body metabolising the evidence. That being so, the jury would be justified in inferring from the words " Can I make a statement at this stage?" that this was another refusal, albeit couched in different words.

The deputy chairman's direction on this point was, in the judgment of this court, impeccable. He said this: **H**

> " You must also be sure that the [applicant] refused to supply a sample of his blood on that occasion . . . It is a matter for you as to whether the [applicant] refused to do so."

He deals accurately with the evidence on the point, and the only possible criticism which can be made of the direction at this stage of the summing-up **I** is that he used the word " fail " on two occasions, plainly referring to the wording of s. 3 (3), which was the section under which the indictment was laid. It might have been happier if he had couched that particular section of his summing-up in different language, but the use of the word " fail " under those circumstances does by no means invalidate the rest of his direction.

The next point taken on behalf of the applicant is this. It is said correctly that the wording of s. 3 (3) makes it clear that if a reasonable excuse emerges which excuses the applicant from providing a specimen for a laboratory test

A then that is a defence. It is pointed out (and correctly pointed out) that the deputy chairman in terms placed the burden of proving reasonable excuse on the defendant, the applicant in this matter. In the view of this court, that was an incorrect placing of the burden. It is true, of course, that there must be some evidence of such an excuse before the necessity arises of leaving the matter to the jury at all; however, once such evidence does emerge, it is for the prosecution

B to eliminate the existence of such a defence to the satisfaction of the jury. In the present case the applicant's excuses were these: first of all, that he was doubtful about what his rights were and wanted legal advice; secondly, that he said he had been manhandled by the police and his work of years had been sullied with foul language from the mouths of the policemen; he wished to have legal advice from the senior officer or a solicitor, and also to make a complaint

C about the way in which the police had treated him. In the view of this court, such matters could not in those circumstances amount to excuses—let alone reasonable excuses—and the deputy chairman would have been fully justified in declining to leave the matter of excuse to the jury at all. In fact, he did leave it, albeit with the burden of proof wrongly positioned; but the applicant by that action of the deputy chairman fared better than he deserved, and, despite the

D misdirection, this branch of the application likewise fails.

Finally, it is said that there was an inconsistency in the verdicts of the jury. It is placed in this way. First of all, it is said (correctly) that the jury on finding the applicant guilty on the charge of dangerous driving added a rider, the rider being a request for leniency on the dangerous driving charge for these reasons:

E " We feel [said the foreman of the jury] that in the first place he thought he was being chased by thugs. We could not condone that through the three sets of traffic lights."

It is submitted by counsel that if the applicant in the eyes of the jury was justified in thinking that he was being chased by thugs, it follows that the two policemen who approached him in the first place could not have been wearing

F uniform and/or could not have said to the applicant what they (the police officers) reported they had said. If that is the case, says counsel, there was no proof that the request for a specimen of breath in the first instance had been made at all and, secondly, the request for a breath specimen had not been made as is required by an officer in uniform. We feel that there is no inconsistency.

G It was perfectly possible for the applicant to believe he was being attacked or chased by thugs even though those thugs may have been in uniform, and even though they may have used words which were words more usually heard from the lips of policemen. Accordingly, on all those points the application for leave to appeal against conviction is refused.

So far as sentence is concerned, the application being for leave to appeal

H against sentence on both of the counts, all that one need say is that the penalty imposed was a moderate one in each case, and in the circumstances of this case fully carried out the rider from the jury, to which I have already made reference. I say that because there was evidence that the applicant was short of capital and had very little money, and the result of the alternative possibility (namely, a fine) might very well have been to send him to prison in default of payment.

I This was a merciful sentence, and in all the circumstances correct. These applications are accordingly refused.

Applications dismissed.

Solicitors: *Anthony Duke & Co.* (for the applicant).

[*Reported by* E. H. HUNTER, ESQ., *Barrister-at-Law.*]

R. *v.* LONDON RENT ASSESSMENT PANEL, *Ex parte* BRAQ INVESTMENTS, LTD.

[QUEEN's BENCH DIVISION (Lord Parker, C.J., Melford Stevenson and Willis, JJ.), April 23, 1969.]

Rent Restriction—Rent—Regulated tenancy—Determination of fair rent— Application—Application by unincorporated tenants' association—Amount of proposed rent not set out, but words used from which rent could be calculated with certainty—Whether sufficient—Whether tenant himself must put in application or sign it—Rent Regulation (Forms etc.) (England and Wales) Regulations 1965 (S.I. 1965 No. 1976), Sch. 3, Form 4.

Three tenants of premises owned by the applicants applied to the rent officer for registration of a fair rent.   The applications were on the prescribed form in accordance with Form 4 in Sch. 3 to the Rent Regulation (Forms etc. (England and Wales) Regulations 1965.   Two of the applications were signed at the top with the name of a tenants' association (an unincorporated body) to which the tenants belonged, and where the print underneath stated " tenant ", or alternatively " tenant's agent ", neither alternative was struck out.   In the remaining case, the form was filled up with the name of the association.   In all three applications the entries were typewritten and there was no signature.   In para. 9 of each form, the rent proposed by the applicant to be registered was stated to be " 4/9 per sq. ft. per annum Exclusive ".   On an application by the landlords for an order of certiorari to bring up and quash a decision of the rent assessment panel determining fair rents for the premises on the ground that the panel acted without jurisdiction in that the applications put in to the rent officer were not in the proper form with the result that all the proceedings thereafter were a nullity,

Held: the application would be dismissed, because—

(i) although it was mandatory that the rent proposed by the applicant to be registered should be set out in the application, it was sufficient if words were used from which the rent could be calculated with certainty (see p. 1014, letter B, and p. 1015, letter A, post);

(ii) there was nothing in the legislation which provided that a tenant must himself put in the application, or that he must sign it, or that any particular formalities had to be complied with (see p. 1014, letter D, and p. 1015, letter A, post).

[As to applications for registration of a fair rent under the Rent Act 1965, see SUPPLEMENT to 23 HALSBURY's LAWS (3rd Edn.) para. 1571B; and for a case on the subject, see 31 DIGEST (Repl.) 676, 7702.

For the Rent Regulation (Forms etc.) (England and Wales) Regulations 1965, Sch. 3, see 12 HALSBURY's STATUTORY INSTRUMENTS (2nd Re-issue) 186.]

Case referred to:

Chapman v. Earl, Chapman v. Weekes, R. v. Bristol Rent Assessment Committee, Ex p. Earl, Same v. Weekes, [1968] 2 All E.R. 1214; [1968] 1 W.L.R. 1315; Digest (Repl.) Supp.

Motion for certiorari.

This was an application by way of motion by Braq Investments, Ltd., for an order of certiorari to quash a decision of the London Rent Assessment Panel dated 9th September 1968, whereby they determined fair rents for three premises, nos. 59, 80 and 104 Derby Lodge, Wicklow Street, London, W.C.1, let by the applicants to Patrick Michael Rowland, Edith Louise Hellard and Mr. and Mrs. Johnson, respectively.

The case noted below* was cited during the argument in addition to the case referred to in the judgment of LORD PARKER, C.J.

---

* *Bradley Egg Farm, Ltd. v. Clifford,* [1943] 2 All E.R. 378.

A   *L. J. Libbert* for the applicants.
S. J. Sedley for the tenant Mrs. Hellard.
Gordon Slynn for the London Rent Assessment Panel.
The other tenants did not appear and were not represented.

B   **LORD PARKER, C.J.:** In these proceedings, counsel moves on behalf of the applicants, Braq Investments, Ltd., for an order of certiorari to bring up and quash a decision of the London Rent Assessment Panel dated 9th September 1968, whereby they determined fair rents for three premises known as 59, 80 and 104 Derby Lodge, Wicklow Street, London, W.C.1. For the reasons which will appear in a moment, it is unnecessary to deal with the facts in any detail, because this is not an appeal from the decision of the panel, but an assertion

C   that they acted without jurisdiction in that the applications put into the rent officer were not in the proper form and were a nullity, with the result that all the proceedings thereafter, both the determination by the rent officer and by the panel, were equally nullities. These three premises, of which the applicants are the owners, were let at the material time to a Mr. Rowland, a Mrs. Hellard and a Mr. and Mrs. Johnson. The applications which were put in on the pre-

D   scribed form were, in the case of the first two applications, signed at the top in these terms: " Derby Lodge & Wicklow Street Tenants Association "; and where the print underneath states " tenant ", or in the alternative " tenant's agent ", one or the other was not struck out. In the remaining case, the form was filled up " Derby Lodge Tenants Association "; in all cases the words in question appear typewritten and there was no signature whatever. Moreover,

E   in para. 9 of the forms as filled in and sent to the rent officer, the rent proposed by each applicant to be registered was stated in these terms " 4/9 per sq. ft. per annum Exclusive ".

Two points are taken here as grounds for the relief claimed. The first, which it is convenient to deal with, is in regard to the rent proposed. About a year after the matters in question in these proceedings, the Divisional Court had

F   before them *Chapman* v. *Earl* (1). In that case, para. 9 of the prescribed form (2) was left a complete blank, and it was in those circumstances held by the court, and, certainly as far as I was concerned, held with reluctance, that the application was a nullity and all proceedings thereafter accordingly were a nullity. The decision in that case was based on the relevant statutory words. Section 26 (5) of the Rent Act 1965 (3) lays down that:

G   " Schedule 3 to this Act shall have effect with respect to applications for the registration of rents and the procedure to be followed on such applications . . ."

When one turns to Sch. 3, para. 1 and para. 2 provide (4):

" 1. An application for the registration of a rent for a dwelling-house may be made to the rent officer by the landlord or the tenant, or jointly

H   by the landlord and the tenant, under a regulated tenancy of the dwelling-house.

" 2. Any such application must be in the prescribed form and contain the prescribed particulars in addition to the rent which it is sought to register."

I   In *Chapman* v. *Earl* (5) the question therefore arose whether para. 2 of Sch. 3, and in particular the word " must " in that paragraph, was mandatory or merely directory. The court, as I have said, with some reluctance held, having regard to subsequent paragraphs of Sch. 3, in particular para. 5, para. 6 and para. 7,

(1) [1968] 2 All E.R. 1214; [1968] 1 W.L.R. 1315.
(2) Form No. 4 of Sch. 3 to the Rent Regulations (Forms etc.) (England and Wales) Regulations 1965 (S.I. 1965 No. 1976).
(3) See now the Rent Act 1968, s. 44 (6) and s. 45 (3).
(4) See now the Rent Act 1968, s. 44 (1) and (2).
(5) [1968] 2 All E.R. 1214; [1968] 1 W.L.R. 1315.

that at any rate so far as rent was concerned it was mandatory that para. 9 of A
the prescribed form must set out the rent proposed to be registered.   Accordingly,
on the basis of that decision it is urged here that para. 9 does not set out the
rent proposed to be registered in that what is meant by " rent proposed to be
registered " is an amount of rent, whereas what is inserted in para. 9 is a rent
which can be arrived at by calculation, namely 4s. 9d. a square foot exclusive
of rates.   B

For my part, I am quite unable to accept that contention.   Granted that it is
mandatory that the rent proposed by the applicant to be registered should be
set out in the application, nevertheless it seems to me amply sufficient if words
are used from which the rent can be calculated with certainty.   It is said: but
errors occur in measuring and it is pointed out in the present case that the
panel and the rent officer arrived at somewhat different measurements for the C
area of the premises.   Nevertheless, as it seems to me, this is perfectly in order
in that it sets out a method of calculation from which a rent can be arrived at
with certainty.   Albeit two surveyors at first may differ, there is no difficulty
in the two getting together and agreeing the amount of square feet. Accordingly,
that ground of the application fails.

The second and perhaps more difficult point is the manner in which these appli- D
cations were put in.   There is, however, nothing as it seems to me in the legislation
which provides that the tenant himself must put in the application, or that he
must sign it, or that any particular formalities have to be complied with.   It
would, I think, be sufficient if the application form at the heading, where it is
stated " I hereby apply for registration ", etc., were left blank, and that there
was an accompanying letter.   In the present case, the rent officer has said on E
affidavit that he has had many applications in respect of premises in Derby Lodge
and that those applications have always been dealt with by a Mr. Moore, who
indeed put in the applications in the present case, and who was secretary of this
body, the Derby Lodge and Wicklow Street Tenants Association, which later,
after the premises in Wicklow Street had been dealt with, was quite naturally
called merely the Derby Lodge Tenants Association.   At any rate, the rent F
officer knew who he was dealing with;   he knew that the applications were put
in on behalf of the tenants of the premises in question, and, indeed, as is shown
from the evidence of the case, the tenants intended those applications to be put in,
ratifying them thereafter if that was necessary, and, so far as the merits are
concerned, there is no doubt they were the tenants' applications.   However, the
point taken by counsel for the applicants is that this association, whichever G
name you give it, is an unincorporated association whose status is unknown to
the law, and that, accordingly, the association was incapable of acting as agent
for the tenants in question.   For my part, again I feel that there is nothing in
this ground.   It seems to me that one can spell out from the words " Derby
Lodge Tenants Association " the names of those who are members of the
association, which either will include the tenant in question, or at any rate will H
be persons who can act as agent for the tenant in question.   That being so, it
seems to me that these applications were entirely in order.

I would only add this, that, if I were wrong in the conclusion at which I have
arrived, I would certainly not as a matter of discretion issue an order of certiorari.
There is no suggestion here that there is anything whatever wrong with the
decision of the panel;   it is unexceptionable.   Further, the applicants did not I
apply at once for an order of prohibition, once the rent officer had chosen to
deal with the case, but pursued the matter by way of objection to the panel,
as if the decision of the rent officer were valid.   In those circumstances, it seems
to me that, as a matter of discretion, this court would really be almost bound to
refuse the order.   However, as I have said already, I can find nothing sufficient
to justify an order of certiorari, quite apart from the exercise of the court's
discretion, and I would dismiss this application.

A   **MELFORD STEVENSON, J.:** I agree.

WILLIS, J.: I agree.

Application dismissed.

Solicitors: *Kaufman, Kramer & Shebson* (for the applicants); *Seifert, Sedley & Co.* (for the tenant Mrs. Hellard); *Solicitor, Ministry of Housing and Local Government.*

B

[*Reported by* N. P. METCALFE, ESQ., *Barrister-at-Law.*]

JONES v. GRIFFITH.

[COURT OF APPEAL, CIVIL DIVISION (Harman, Sachs and Widgery, L.JJ.), March
C   25, 26, 1969.]

Negligence—Damages—Personal injury—Measure of damages—Risk of future attacks of epilepsy—Grand mal.

Negligence—Damages—Personal injury—Measure of damages—Partial deafness in one ear—Pain in ears, headaches, and irritability.

D   The plaintiff, then a 21 year old spinster bank clerk, was injured in a motor accident due to the negligence of the defendant. Owing to these injuries the plaintiff became liable to attacks of grand mal epilepsy. Shortly after the accident she suffered a major attack with convulsions, and thereafter several less serious attacks. After these she was continuously under sedation, and suffered no further attacks. Agreed medical reports indicated that the plaintiff would always remain liable to further grand mal attacks,
E   and that, if she remained under sedation, there was a reasonable, perhaps a little more than even, chance that she would have no more attacks, but also a reasonable chance that she would have more attacks. As a result of her injuries the plaintiff also suffered, permanently: (i) a degree of deafness in one ear which interfered with her work and with her ability to engage in a conversation where more than one voice spoke at a time; (ii) a certain
F   amount of ear pain which disturbed her sleep; (iii) headaches which sometimes lasted a day, sometimes a week, and quite frequently two or three days; and (iv) a degree of irritability or shortness of temper. These four ill-effects made her less happy in her work as a bank clerk, but, because of the benevolence of the bank managers, she would probably continue permanently in her job. Her special damage was only £25. On appeal by the
G   defendant against the trial judge's assessment of the plaintiff's general damages at £6,000,

Held: the appeal would be dismissed because the four enumerated ill-effects would by themselves have warranted an award of over £1,000 (see p. 1017, letter H, and p. 1020, letters D and H, post); and considering the prognosis for the plaintiff a total award in the region of the £6,000
H   awarded by the trial judge was justified (see p. 1018, letter I, and p. 1020, letters C and H, post);

Per CURIAM: it was regrettable that the plaintiff's expert medical witness had not been called into the witness box, so that the judge could have asked him questions about his agreed report, especially the prognosis (see p. 1019, letters B and E, and p. 1020, letter F, post).

I   Per WIDGERY, L.J.: the maximum figure for the liability to epilepsy alone, had there been a virtual certainty of recurrence of attacks, would have been £10,000 to £11,000; on the plaintiff's prognosis an award of up to £5,000 for this alone would have been proper (see p. 1020, letters B and C, post).

Appeal dismissed.

[As to the measure of damages in tort in actions for personal injury, see
11 HALSBURY'S LAWS (3rd Edn.) 253, 255, 256, paras. 424, 427, and 28 ibid.,

pp. 97, 98, para. 104; and for cases on the subject, see 36 DIGEST (Repl.) 199-202,   A
1048-1070.]

Cases referred to:

> *Hawkins* v. *New Mendip Engineering, Ltd.*, [1966] 3 All E.R. 228; [1966]
>   1 W.L.R. 1341; Digest (Cont. Vol. B) 567, *1062e*.
> *Prudence* v. *Lewis* (1966), The Times, 21st May.

Appeal.   B

This was an appeal by the defendant, Elwyn Griffith, against so much of the
judgment of THESIGER, J., given at Caernarvon Summer Assizes on 5th July 1968,
as assessed the general damages of the plaintiff, Miss Margaret Eirlys Jones, at
£6,000. The facts are set out in the judgment of SACHS, L.J.

Frank Whitworth, Q.C., and *H. E. P. Roberts* for the defendant.   C
P. L. W. Owen, Q.C., and *W. L. M. Davies* for the plaintiff.

    SACHS, L.J., delivered the first judgment at the invitation of HARMAN,
L.J.: This is an appeal from a judgment of THESIGER, J., given at Caernarvon
Summer Assizes on 5th July 1968. The claim was by the plaintiff, a young woman
aged 25 at the date of trial, for damages for injuries sustained owing to the
negligence of the defendant when she was a passenger in his van on 24th December   D
1964. No other vehicle was involved in the accident; liability to the plaintiff was
admitted, and the only issue was the quantum of damages.

    The injuries (to which I will refer further later) can be divided into two cate-
gories. There were injuries which resulted in a certain amount of deafness and
in certain discomforts, including headaches, which will be of a permanent nature.
Over and above these matters there was a major injury in that she had become   E
liable to attacks of traumatic epilepsy. The degree of the risk of such attacks
occurring after the date of judgment was a matter of considerable argument in
the light of the medical reports. It is, however, common ground that not long
after the accident itself the plaintiff did suffer from a major epileptic attack of
the type normally called grand mal, which involved convulsions and so forth.
It was further common ground that after that attack she had several further   F
attacks of epilepsy but not, apparently, of quite so serious a degree. There
followed a period during which she suffered no further actual attacks but was
consistently under sedation. During the period from the date of the accident
to the date of trial there were no fewer than seven E.E.G. reports, each of a
consistent and adverse nature, to which reference will later be made. In that
set of circumstances, the award of the trial judge was for a total of £6,000, plus   G
£25 special damage.

    The relatively small special damage related in the main to the plaintiff's
absence from work as a bank clerk, the cost of nursing, and so forth. Before
the accident she had employment as a bank clerk; she continued in employment
as a bank clerk after the accident but was not (as will later be mentioned) as
happy in that work later on as before—owing to certain difficulties which ensued   H
from her injuries; and it appears that she will probably, subject to that unhappiness, continue as a bank clerk because there have been and are—as she said
herself—benevolent managers in charge of the relevant branch.

    This appeal turns on the question of what are the chances, after the date of
trial, of further attacks of epilepsy of a serious nature. The appeal accordingly
concerns a case in which the assessment of damages is of its very essence one of   I
great difficulty for a trial judge. More than one court has spoken in critical
terms of the problem which is posed the trial judge in such cases when making
estimates for the future and coming to a conclusion as to the correct award of
damages. His task is in essence more one of guesswork than of proceeding on
any firm basis. The courts which have previously considered this type of case
have expressly or implicitly indicated that those difficulties may result in there
being a more than usually wide bracket between the views of reasonable men in
general and of judges in particular as to what are the highest and lowest appropriate figures on a given set of facts. I accordingly approach the present case

A on the basis that the bracket is indeed a wide one and that, as an appellant can only succeed on appeal by demonstrating that the instant award is one outside those brackets, he has by definition a somewhat difficult task.

     The width of those brackets is indeed reflected in the various cases to which this court has been referred. Although it is not intended to examine those cases in any detail, it is as well before going further to make one point clear.

B Epileptic attacks are normally divided broadly into two categories. There are those which involve major convulsions of a highly unpleasant type, and in those cases the person concerned is said to be suffering from grand mal. The other category consists of those attacks of lesser degree, the person concerned being often said to be suffering from the petit mal type of epilepsy. Accordingly one has, as regards cases cited, to read the reports somewhat carefully to see

C which of those two types was under consideration; to note whether the case concerned somebody who was already subject to those attacks; or whether the person concerned was somebody who, despite not having had such an attack, would yet in medical experience be at risk in future of having those attacks. It is only from that foundation that one can go on to appraise the award in relation to the risks of further attacks ensuing.

D   Another factor that has naturally to be taken into account when considering the cases cited is that of the other injuries the plaintiff had suffered. Sometimes the global award is divided so that it can be shown what was the assessment of the other injuries and sometimes it cannot be so divided—indeed, more often not.

     At that point it is convenient to refer to those injuries from which the present

E plaintiff suffered and which were not the subject of the main arguments in this court—in other words the permanent injuries other than the liability to epilepsy. First one notes that there was a degree of deafness in one ear. It was very far from one of the most serious cases of deafness; but the fact remains that it did interfere with the ease of her work at the bank and it did also interfere with her ability to engage in conversation in places where there was more than one

F voice speaking. That is a matter which is not to be regarded as negligible in the case of a young woman at the beginning of her adult life. The next matter is that she suffered a certain amount of pain in or about the ears. It is sufficient to disturb her sleep.

     The third is that she suffered from headaches. In her description I think it is clear that these headaches were different from those which a young woman

G may normally be expected to suffer, and in particular different from any which she had herself suffered before the accident. They were headaches which might last a day, they might last a week, and they quite frequently lasted two or three days. These too were a permanent feature, apparently, of what she would have to put up with for the future. Again they were matters which one does not normally regard as negligible. Fourthly (and this is the last of this series),

H she now suffers from an added degree of irritability or short-temper to which, apparently, she had not been subject before the accident.

     Suffice it to say that those four matters, taken by themselves, would warrant an award of a four-figure sum, though a lower scale four-figure sum. It is not necessary to quantify them but merely to mention that these injuries did exist and must be provided for in the ultimate award.

I   As to the decisions cited one must be careful not to do more than look on them as showing a trend of figures of damage and as examples of figures within the correct brackets on the particular facts of the individual cases. One must remember too that of those facts sometimes only a proportion can be found even in a full report, and certainly that is often the position in an abbreviated report. There has been much discussion of two cases: one was *Hawkins* v. *New Mendip Engineering, Ltd.* (1), and the other was a case of which a report appears in

---

    (1) [1966] 3 All E.R. 228; [1966] 1 W.L.R. 1341.

KEMP AND KEMP ON DAMAGES FOR PERSONAL INJURY (3rd Edn.), p. 304: **A**
Prudence v. *Lewis* (2). Counsel for the defendant complained that the trial
judge wrongly interpreted the effect of the *Hawkins* case (3). Suffice it to say
that those cases had only a limited degree of usefulness when discussing the particular facts of the instant case, and to add that I for one do not agree that the
trial judge regarded *Hawkins* case (3) in any way other than was appropriate.

Returning to the facts of the present case, I have already mentioned that **B**
the plaintiff had certain attacks. The critical matter that had to be considered by the trial judge—and was considered by him in a very careful judgment
—was what are the chances of the plaintiff suffering these grave attacks in the
future. Attacks of this convulsive nature were aptly referred to in the *Hawkins*
case (3) in phrases such as " potentially disastrous " and " catastrophe ".
Their effect on a person's life can be grave indeed.   **C**

The chances in relation to cases of this type really have to be divided into two
questions. First, what are the chances of the plaintiff becoming a person who
is subject to major epileptic attacks? Secondly, if a person is so subject, what
are the chances of occurrence and of the frequency of attacks in the future?
As regards the first of those questions, here, unlike the *Hawkins* case (3) and
unlike the *Prudence* case (2), the evidence shows that the plaintiff has in fact **D**
suffered such an attack and she is, therefore, a person who is subject to those
attacks in the sense that her epilepsy is of that category.

As regards the second question, the evidence before the court was contained
in agreed medical reports which included documents stating the effect of the
E.E.G. tests—though not enclosing, so far as this court is aware, the actual
copies of what the E.E.Gs. reported. In the light of those reports, the final **E**
opinion of Mr. Sutcliffe Kerr reads thus:

" One must expect she may be liable to an occasional epileptic attack at
unspecifiable intervals in the future. As I indicated in my previous report,
there is reasonable hope that she may never have another attack provided
she takes routine anti-convulsant treatment but no guarantee can be given
on this score."   **F**

That final opinion was more optimistic than one given a relatively short time
earlier before the final E.E.G. report of 5th March 1968 had been shown to him—
a report that obviously came as a disappointment because he mentions the regret
that this E.E.G. should have turned out as it did.

Therefore one has a case where all the E.E.G. reports, in their somewhat **G**
alarming tenor, have been consistent and so the chances are that, subject only
to constant sedation, the plaintiff will remain a person liable to such attacks—
i.e., an epileptic subject. As regards frequency, there is a reasonable chance
that she will have none; but equally it follows that there are reasonable chances
that they may occur; if so, their frequency and intervals can only be the subject
of speculation. When one looks at it, that is an alarming thing for any young **H**
woman to be faced with—and that despite the fact that any medical man will
obviously do his best to discountenance her fears, as indeed Mr. Sutcliffe Kerr
appears to have done in the present instance.

Taking that state of affairs as a whole, it appears to me quite hopeless to suggest
that the instant award is outside the brackets to which I have referred. It is
always a very difficult matter to assess what one would have awarded oneself in **I**
those circumstances had one seen the plaintiff and had one tried to appraise the
situation at trial. Suffice it to say that in those circumstances I for my part
would not have been surprised if the award had been a little higher. It is,
however, only necessary, as I have said, to say that it is well within the
appropriate brackets.

One further subject perhaps merits mention. As each counsel in this court
advanced his submissions as to what was really the effect of the prognosis, it

(2) (1966), The Times, 21st May.   (3) [1966] 3 All E.R. 228; [1966] 1 W.L.R. 1341.

A became apparent—as is so often the case—that there were a number of matters in the agreed medical reports on which this court could have been assisted had there been oral evidence given in supplement. In cases as grave as the present one, a medical witness can normally help to a considerable degree the judge who is faced with reports which obviously must be—or in this case at any rate were— in somewhat general terms. It is a matter of regret that Mr. Sutcliffe Kerr, who

B was available, was not put into the witness box as someone of whom the judge could ask questions—even if counsel did not wish to ask them. I hope that in parallel cases an expert will in future be put into the witness box. I have only too often in the past been asked to assess damages on " agreed " medical reports and then found sometimes that there simply was not an agreement at all on material matters and on other occasions that there were gaps in the reports

C which needed to be supplemented in the way which I have indicated.

For my part I would dismiss this appeal.

WIDGERY, L.J.: I agree that this appeal should be dismissed and I echo Sach, L.J.'s observations with regard to the desirability of the calling of expert medical evidence in cases of this kind. The " agreed medical report " has only one virtue—namely, that it saves the time and expense of calling the

D doctors; but this is not the kind of case in which that is an economy. Where a medical report is agreed, the effect is that the words of the report are treated as though they had been given in evidence, and it is not open to counsel to embellish them beyond, perhaps, some necessary reference to dictionaries to indicate the meaning of some of the terms. All too often in cases of this kind the argument becomes an argument as to the proper construction of the words used

E by the doctors, when, if the court is properly to be assisted, it should have the opportunity of itself examining the doctors.

As to the facts of this case and the propriety of the sum assessed by the learned judge, the problem posed here, of course, is a very familiar one. It arises in all cases of personal injuries where the medical evidence discloses some possibility of future complications, in the form of a deterioration in the plaintiff's condition

F or a prospect of future attacks, but cannot say with certainty whether or not those complications or attacks are to occur. In these cases the trial judge has to fix what is a fair and proper figure to cover two conflicting eventualities—one, that the complications may arise, and the other, that they may not.

It seems to me that there is only one practical method of approaching this kind of problem and that is to assess the sort of figure which would be appropriate

G in the extreme and serious case where the complications or future attacks were virtually certain. It then becomes possible to discount that figure according to the degree of optimism which is possible in the light of the medical reports. The discounting is not just a matter of simple arithmetic, and it does not follow, if the doctors say that the prospect of recurring attacks is 50 : 50, that one simply divides the maximum figure by 2. There are many other considerations to

H have in mind, and in particular the trial judge must remember that at the best in these cases the plaintiff faces a period, which may be long or short, in which she is fearful of a recurrence of an attack and in which her whole life may be changed because she feels unable to go about her ordinary affairs in the face of that danger. A plaintiff may be reluctant to marry, may be unable to drive a motor car, and may indeed suffer severe psychological disturbances merely from

I his or her fear of an attack, although that attack may never materialise. The trial judge must form his own view of the plaintiff and the probable effect of these fears on him or her and must adjust his discounting process accordingly.

In this case I would have thought that the ceiling figure, if the evidence had indicated a virtual certainty of recurrence of attack, would have been of the order of £10,000 or £11,000.   I am conscious that that is more than twice the conventional figure for the loss of a limb and nearly four times as much as the conventional figure for the loss of an eye; but I nevertheless think it would be in perspective with those awards. The person who loses a leg or an eye can often

adapt himself to his disability and live a happy and useful life. It seems to me   A
that someone who is faced with the virtual certainty of epileptic attacks at
frequent intervals cannot nearly so easily adapt himself or herself to the disability which he or she has suffered. On the other hand, if one puts the ceiling
figure much above £10,000 or £11,000 one gets into the realm of awards for
paraplegic cases, which are clearly much more serious than this. So I would
have thought, if I had to decide this case myself, that the maximum figure, on   B
the most gloomy approach to the prognosis, would have been something like
£10,000 or £11,000. My impression of the medical reports as a whole is that the
doctors think the prognosis is somewhat more favourable than unfavourable.
In other words, I do not read this as being a 50 : 50 case but a case in which the
plaintiff's prospects are perhaps a little better than 50 : 50. I reach that conclusion not by attempting to extract any deep meaning from any particular   C
phrase in the reports but because that is the impression that the reports make on
me. Certainly I would have thought in this case—though I have not had the
advantage of seeing the plaintiff and assessing the effect of anxiety on her—
that the epilepsy element in this claim would have been properly compensated by
a figure of something up to £5,000. Once one reaches that conclusion and
remembers that there are other significant factors to be taken into account   D
in this case which must add to the total, it becomes apparent at once that the
figure of £6,000 awarded by the trial judge is clearly within what SACHS, L.J., has
called " the appropriate bracket ". It follows from that that this court should
not interfere with it, and I would therefore dismiss the appeal.

    HARMAN, L.J.: Listening to this appeal—which is an exercise for the   E
court in guesswork—I can only echo the words of BRABIN, J., who said that
any decision we come to is wrong: either the plaintiff will have no further
attacks, in which case we have given her too much, or she will have further
attacks, in which case we have given her too little. What is the court to do?
It must somewhere fix itself on a figure, unsatisfactory as it may be, and to my
mind is, and really have nothing to do with the law—merely an exercise in   F
guesswork and one, I should have thought, more appropriate to the doctors
than to the lawyers. That is why again I deplore the absence from the witness
box of the medical advisers, who sent in their reports, it is true, but were not
presented to the court so that they could be asked questions on them, which are
often so illuminating to the judge. Reports couched in terms of jargon are I
think of no use to the court at all: they are merely the raw material on which   G
the medical evidence should be based; and when that raw material is of a
highly technical and very difficult nature it seems to me quite wrong that the
chief witness on the neurological side should not have been put into the box in
order that he might help the judge out of this morass of difficulties.
    As to the merits of the case or its demerits I say no more than that I concur
in the conclusion to which my brothers have come—that the appeal should be   H
dismissed.

                                                               Appeal dismissed.

    Solicitors: *Hyman Isaacs, Lewis & Mills*, agents for *Herbert J. Davis, Berthen
& Munro*, Liverpool (for the defendant); *Gwyndaf-Williams & Roberts*, Pwllheli
(for the plaintiff).

    [*Reported by* HENRY SUMMERFIELD, ESQ., *Barrister-at-Law.*]   I

A WURZAL *v.* W. G. A. ROBINSON (EXPRESS HAULAGE), LTD.

[QUEEN'S BENCH DIVISION (Lord Parker, C.J., Melford Stevenson and Willis, JJ.), April 25, 1969.]

Road Traffic—Goods vehicle—Driver—Records—Driver failing to keep proper
B *record—Whether holder of licence used due diligence to secure compliance*
with regulations—Warning on back of daily record sheets supplied to drivers
as to filling in records accurately—No system of checking records and inform-
ing drivers that records must be filled up used by holder of licence—Due dili-
gence not exercised—Road Traffic Act 1960 (8 & 9 Eliz. 2 c. 16), s. 186 (1)
—Road Traffic Act 1962 (10 & 11 Eliz. 2 c. 59), s. 20—Goods Vehicles
C *(Keeping of Records) Regulations 1935 (S.R. & O. 1935 No. 314), reg. 6.*

The respondents' vehicle was observed by a Ministry of Transport examiner
at a time and place not revealed by the records which were required to be
kept under the Goods Vehicle (Keeping of Records) Regulations 1935*,
and it was subsequently shown that the driver had failed to keep proper
records. The respondents (the holders of the carrier's licence) were charged
with not causing to be kept a current record contrary to reg. 6 of the regula-
D tions and s. 186 of the Road Traffic Act 1960. The respondents did not
give evidence, and at the end of the prosecution's case submitted that
the defence provided by s. 20† of the Road Traffic Act 1962, that they had
used all due diligence to secure compliance with the regulations, had been
established by two admissions made to the prosecution. The first admis-
E sion was that on the back of the daily record sheets supplied by the respondents to their drivers there was a warning that drivers were required
by law to keep the records as accurate as possible and to produce them
for inspection if required by an authorised person, that particulars should
be filled in by drivers as the day's work proceeded, and that the form must
be properly completed, signed and handed in to the respondents' office at
night. The second admission was that the respondents could not have
F known the facts revealed by the check made on the vehicle by the examiner.
The justices found that the admissions constituted a defence under s. 20 of
the Act of 1962 and dismissed the charges.

Held: the evidence contained in the admissions did not justify a finding
that the respondents had used all due diligence to comply with the regulations, and a defence under s. 20 of the Road Traffic Act 1962, had not been
G made out, for to establish the defence of due diligence under s. 20 the respondents must show that they had adopted some system in the past, by
checking records, by informing drivers that the record sheets must be filled
up, and even, possibly, by threatening them with dismissal if they did
not fill them up; accordingly, the case would go back to the justices with a
direction to convict the respondents (see p. 1023, letters E and F, and p. 1024,
H letter A, *post*).

Series v. *Poole* ([1967] 3 All E.R. 849) considered.

Per CURIAM: The burden was on the respondents to establish a defence
under s. 20, but the fact that they did not give evidence was not fatal if as
a result of admissions made by witnesses to the prosecution the defence was
made out (see p. 1023, letter D, and p. 1024, letter A, *post*).

I *Appeal allowed.*

[As to the duty to keep records and penalty for non-compliance, see 33 HALS-
BURY'S LAWS (3rd Edn.) 770-772, paras. 1323, 1326; and for cases on the subject,
see 45 DIGEST (Repl.) 137, 138, *507-510.*

For the Road Traffic Act 1960, s. 186, see 40 HALSBURY'S STATUTES (2nd Edn.)
874; and for the Road Traffic Act 1962, s. 20, see 42 ibid., p. 903.]

---

* S.R. & O. 1935 No. 314.
† Section 20, so far as material, is set out at p. 1022, letter I, *post*.

A

Case referred to:
Series v. *Poole*, [1967] 3 All E.R. 849; Digest (Repl.) Supp.

Case Stated.

This was a Case Stated by justices for the city of Leeds in respect of their
adjudication as a magistrates' court sitting at Leeds on 7th May 1968.   On
11th April 1968, two informations were preferred by the appellant, Ernest
Wurzal, against the respondents, W. G. A. Robinson (Express Haulage), Ltd.,   B
that on 10th and 11th November 1967, the respondents, being the holders of a
carrier's licence, did not cause to be kept a current record giving the information
prescribed in the appropriate form in the Schedule to the Goods Vehicle (Keeping
of Records) Regulations 1935, in respect of the period during which one, William
Wright, the driver of an authorised vehicle within the meaning of the regulations
was employed in driving the vehicle, contrary to reg. 6 of the regulations and   C
s. 186 of the Road Traffic Act 1960.

The following facts were found by the justices.   The respondents were the
owners of the vehicle in question and were authorised to use it pursuant to an
" A " carrier's licence issued to them on 17th August 1967.   On 10th and 11th
November 1967 William Wright was employed by the respondents as the driver
of the vehicle.   The daily record sheets completed by Mr. Wright in respect   D
of the vehicle for 10th and 11th November 1967 both recorded that he had
ceased work at 2.15 p.m. on 10th November.   The vehicle was observed by a
Ministry of Transport examiner at 2.30 p.m. on 10th November moving north
along the A.38 road.   The daily record sheets contained on the reverse side of
them a warning in the following terms:

E

" Drivers are required by law to keep the records overleaf as accurate
as possible and are bound to produce them for inspection if required by
an authorised person.   Therefore, the particulars should be filled in as the
day's work proceeds.   This form must be properly completed, signed and
handed in to the office at night.   Regulations require that these records
be kept for at least three months, and must be produced for inspection   F
if desired."

The respondents did not know of the silent check which had revealed that the
vehicle was on the road at 2.30 p.m. on 10th November and could not have
known from the facts shown by the check that the driver's record sheets were
not correct.   On 7th May 1968, the driver, William Wright, was convicted of
failing on 10th and 11th November 1967 to keep a current record contrary to   G
the regulations of 1935 and s. 186 of the Road Traffic Act 1960.

At the close of the appellant's case it was submitted by the respondents that,
as the appellant's witnesses had admitted that the warning notice was printed
on the back of the record sheets, and the respondents could not have known of the
facts which the silent check revealed, it had been proved that the respondents
had used due diligence to secure compliance with s. 186 of the Act of 1960 and   H
with the regulations, and had established a defence under s. 20 of the Road Traffic
Act 1962.   The justices were of opinion that a defence under s. 20 had been established and dismissed the informations against the respondents, and the appellant
now appealed.

Gordon Slynn for the appellant.
A. L. Myerson for the respondents.

I

LORD PARKER, C.J., having referred to the Case Stated, continued:
The sole question is whether the respondents had a defence by reason of the fact
that they had exercised due diligence.   That defence appears in s. 20 of the
Road Traffic Act 1962, which provides that: ". . . it shall be a defence to prove
that [the holder of a carrier's licence] used all due diligence to secure compliance
with [the regulations] ".   The burden, therefore, was on the respondents;
they gave no evidence whatever but they rested their case, arguing that the

A defence had been made out, on two admissions which had been made by the appellant. The first admission was that on the back of the daily record sheets which were supplied by the respondents to their drivers to be filled up, the following words appeared:

B " Drivers are required by law to keep the records overleaf as accurate as possible and are bound to produce them for inspection if required by an authorised person. Therefore, the particulars should be filled in as the day's work proceeds. This form must be properly completed, signed and handed in to the office at night. Regulations require that these records be kept for at least three months, and must be produced for inspection if desired."

C The second admission was what indeed was obvious, and did not need an admission, that the respondents could not have known of the facts which the silent check revealed, the silent check being the fact that the vehicle had been observed by an examiner appointed by the Minister of Transport at a time and place which was not revealed by the daily records. On that the justices accepted the respondents' contentions and stated:

D " We were of the opinion that the two matters relied upon by the respondents constituted a defence under section 20 of the Road Traffic Act, 1962, and accordingly we dismissed the said informations . . .".

In such a case as this the burden is on the respondents; the fact that they did not give evidence is not fatal if as a result of admissions made by witnesses for the prosecution, the defence was made out. But it seems to me quite impossible E to say that there was anything in the evidence in the present case which would justify a finding by the justices that all due diligence had been used.

This is by no means the first of cases of this kind which have come before this court, and in my experience respondents, to succeed in these cases, must show that they have adopted some system in the past; true they cannot know the facts of the particular offence in advance, but they must show that they have F taken steps in the past by checking records, by informing drivers, making certain that they have the knowledge that these forms have got to be complied with, maybe threatening them with dismissal if they do not fill up the forms, and indeed sometimes referring to the fact that they have dismissed drivers for this reason.

One of the cases not without interest in this connection is *Series* v. *Poole* (1). In that case, there was not only a notice in the cab of each driver's vehicle, G but the holder of the licence there gave evidence that the driver in question was an exceedingly good driver, there was no reason to distrust him, that he had been employed full-time for two years, part-time for five or six years, that the holder of the licence had instructed all his drivers frequently in their duties, he reminded them about them every night, and had so instructed and reminded the driver in question. He then produced the printed reminder card affixed to H the driver's cab, and he said that if he had not kept at the drivers he would not have got the record he had got. On top of that, he proceeded to check all the driver's records personally. Indeed in WILKINSON on ROAD TRAFFIC OFFENCES (5th Edn.) at p. 306, it is stated that the employer should give careful instructions to each driver about the law's requirements, regularly check that all his drivers are completing the necessary forms, and supply them I with the forms.

In my judgment, here there is no evidence sufficient to enable the justices to say that all due diligence had been proved by the respondents to secure compliance with the regulations (2). Accordingly, I would send this case back to the justices with a direction to convict on both informations.

---

(1) [1967] 3 All E.R. 849.
(2) The Goods Vehicles (Keeping of Records) Regulations 1935 (S.R. & O. 1935 No. 314).

MELFORD STEVENSON, J.: I agree.

WILLIS, J.: I agree.

Appeal allowed. Case remitted.

Solicitors: *Treasury Solicitor; Willey, Hargrave & Co.,* Leeds (for the respondents).

[*Reported by* WENDY SHOCKETT, *Barrister-at-Law.*]

PRACTICE DIRECTION.

PROBATE, DIVORCE AND ADMIRALTY DIVISION (DIVORCE).

*Magistrates—Husband and wife—Appeal—Divisional Court—Hearing of appeal
—Time for—Fixed period in term—Urgent applications—Procedure.*

URGENT APPLICATIONS

The sittings of the Divisional Court of the Probate, Divorce and Admiralty Division to hear appeals from matrimonial orders made by magistrates are usually arranged for a fixed period during each term. It is not widely appreciated that, where an appeal is pending, a Divisional Court may, subject to the approval of the President or, in his absence, the senior judge of the Division in London, be convened at any time to deal with urgent matters. This may be especially desirable where the welfare of children is concerned, whether arising directly from the order of the magistrates or as a consequence of their order being stayed pending the determination of the appeal. It is also possible where necessary to give such appeals priority during the normal sittings of the Divisional Court. Applications for accelerated hearing of any appeal may be made to the Divisional Court at 10.30 a.m. on any day when that court is sitting (notice being given to the other side).

When the court is not sitting practitioners should apply in writing to the clerk of the rules, stating the nature and ground of application and why it is urgent (exhibiting, where possible, the consent of the other side). The question of constituting a Divisional Court to hear the application will then be considered by the President, or in his absence, by the senior judge of the Division in London.

By direction of the President.

COMPTON MILLER,
Senior Registrar.

24th June 1969.

A

Re NEELD (deceased).
INIGO-JONES v. INIGO-JONES.

[CHANCERY DIVISION (Megarry, J.), March 3, 4, 5, 1969.]

B
Will—Condition—Name and arms clauses—" Quarter with own family arms "—Devisee to quarter testator's arms with " his or her own family arms "—Whether " family arms " includes arms acquired by direct grant and after clause in will has taken effect—Whether devisee with no arms must get them so as to have arms with which to quarter testator's.

C
By his will* a testator, I.-J., directed that any person who under the trusts therein should become entitled to the yearly rents and profits of certain property, and who was not then using the name of I.-J., should within one year take that name and quarter the arms of I.-J. with " his or her own family arms ". The plaintiff had already changed his name from H. to I.-J. but he had no arms of any kind.

D
Held: (i) " his . . . own family arms " included arms granted directly to the devisee (see p. 1029, letter F, post); included a grant made after the clause in the will had taken effect (see p. 1029, letter I, post); and included arms taken in either the name H. or the name I.-J. (see p. 1030, letter I, to p. 1031, letter A, post).

E
(ii) as the penal clauses in the will were to be construed strictly but fairly, the obligation to quarter the testator's arms with " his . . . own family arms " required the devisee to obtain " his . . . own family arms " with which to quarter the testator's arms (see p. 1030, letter H, post).

Per MEGARRY, J.: I think " family " is a Janus-like word, often looking backwards ancestrally, but sometimes looking forward to posterity. In relation to " arms " I can see no real reason why the word should be used merely ancestrally (see p. 1028, letter G, post).

F
[As to names and arms clauses, see 34 HALSBURY'S LAWS (3rd Edn.) 507, 508, paras. 893, 894; and for cases on the subject, see 35 DIGEST (Repl.) 789-795, *57-93*.]

Cases referred to:
Berens, Re, Re Dowdeswell, Berens-Dowdeswell v. *Holland-Martin*, [1926] Ch. 596; 95 L.J.Ch. 370; 135 L.T. 298; 35 Digest (Repl.) 798, *108*.

G
Bromley v. *Tryon*, [1951] 2 All E.R. 1058; [1952] A.C. 265; 49 Digest (Repl.) 1055, *9859*.
Croxon, Re, Croxon v. *Ferrers*, [1904] 1 Ch. 252; 73 L.J.Ch. 170; 89 L.T. 733; 35 Digest (Repl.) 797, *107*.
Eversley, Re, Mildmay v. *Mildmay*, [1900] 1 Ch. 96; 69 L.J.Ch. 14; 81 L.T. 600; 35 Digest (Repl.) 789, *59*.

H
Neeld (decd.), Re, Carpenter v. *Inigo-Jones*, [1962] 2 All E.R. 335; [1962] Ch. 643; [1962] 2 W.L.R. 1097; 35 Digest (Repl.) 793, *84*.
Stubs v. *Stubs* (1862), 1 H. & C. 257; 31 L.J.Ex. 510; 158 E.R. 881; 35 Digest (Repl.) 799, *117*.

Adjourned Summons.

This was an originating summons raising questions as to the operation of a
I name and arms clause in the will of a testator who died on 3rd October 1956. The Court of Appeal had held that the clause was not void for uncertainty in *Re Neeld (decd.)*† The plaintiff was Ian Lionel Spencer Inigo-Jones who was entitled to the property bequeathed in the will for life with remainder over to his sons successively in tail male. The defendants were Anthony Lionel Spencer Inigo-Jones, Randall Jonathan Whitney Inigo-Jones, Terrance Ralph William

---

* The relevant clauses of the will are set out at p. 1026, letters E and I, and p. 1027, letter E, post.
† [1962] 2 All E.R. 335.

Inigo-Jones, infant sons of the plaintiff, and John Frederick Slade Carpenter, **A** sole executor and trustee. The facts are set out in the judgment.

J. L. Knox for the plaintiff.

N. Micklem for the first, second and third defendants.

M. A. Blythe for the fourth defendant.

MEGARRY, J.: This originating summons arises out of the name and **B** arms clause which came before the Court of Appeal in *Re Neeld (decd.)*, *Carpenter* v. *Inigo-Jones* (1), decided on 8th March 1962. In that case the Court of Appeal held inter alia that the clause was not void for uncertainty. What I am now concerned with is how the clause operates. The testator died on 3rd October 1956, leaving a will dated 12th January 1952 and a number of codicils which do not affect the matter. The clause in question is cl. 17. I read the relevant **C** parts of this clause with the omission of immaterial matters and the insertion of the words which, in 1962, UPJOHN and DIPLOCK, L.JJ., held should be inserted. The two judgments formulate these words in slightly different language, but the effect is the same; the version that I set out is that of DIPLOCK, L.J., which is slightly the shorter. The clause begins with an express direction that any person who under the trusts of the will shall become entitled to the actual receipt of **D** the yearly rents and profits of certain land—

" and who shall not then use the surname of Inigo-Jones shall within the space of one year after he shall become so entitled or if an infant shall so become entitled then within the space of one year next after he or she shall have attained the age of twenty-one years take upon himself and use upon all occasions the surname of Inigo-Jones only and quarter the Arms **E** of Inigo-Jones with his or her own family Arms."

This I may call limb 1 of the clause; and I pause there to dispose of certain matters.

First, the argument in this case has centred round the words " his or her own family Arms "; and to these words I must return in due course. Second, under cl. 3 of the will the plaintiff is entitled to the property in question for **F** life, with remainder to his sons successively in tail male, and remainders over. There is no issue before me on the question of the plaintiff's surname. His surname when he was born in 1931 was Horne. In May 1949 he went to live in Canada, intending to live there permanently. He assumed Canadian nationality, and on 19th June 1962 JUDGE MACDONALD sitting in the county court of the county of Carleton and acting under the Revised Statutes of Ontario 1960 **G** c. 49, as amended, approved the change of the surname of the plaintiff, his wife and children from Horne to Inigo-Jones. It has not been suggested that this was not an effectual change of name, or that it was in any way affected by the plaintiff's decision in May 1966 to return to live in England, and his carrying out of that decision in September 1966. I am not sure how far the summons raises any real question on the matter of names; but without formally deciding **H** the point, it seems to me on the evidence before me that no issue arises or can arise on it. In short, all that I am concerned with is arms, not names, though I must make further incidental references to names.

Clause 17 of the will continues with what I shall call limb 2:

" . . . and shall within the space of one year next after the period herein- **I** before prescribed apply for and endeavour to obtain a proper licence from the Crown or take such other means as may be requisite to enable him or her to take use and bear the surname of Inigo-Jones only and Arms of Inigo-Jones."

There is then a provision for forfeiture. The " space of one year " was held by the Court of Appeal to mean a period beginning with the moment when a vesting assent in favour of the plaintiff was executed, or he became

(1) [1962] 2 All E.R. 335; [1962] Ch. 643.

A entitled to call for a vesting assent, whichever, I think, was the sooner. There is evidence before me by the sole surviving executor and trustee of the will that a vesting assent in the plaintiff's favour was executed on 8th March 1968, and that the plaintiff had not been entitled to call for such an assent prior to that date. On that footing, the plaintiff had already been using the name of Inigo-Jones before the year began to run, and so none of the subsequent
B provisions of the clause relating to names appear to apply to him.

    I should also say this. Although there is some evidence before me that the year began to run on 8th March 1968, so that the year is now almost at an end, there is no question before me for decision on when the period expires, and there has been no argument on it. Accordingly, I decide nothing on that point, either directly or indirectly. I merely observe that the evidence shows that it is at
C least arguable that the period will expire in a few days, and that counsel for the plaintiff has been unable to give me any explanation (beyond the fact that it was in no way the fault of the court) why in those circumstances the summons issued on 18th April 1967 was not brought on for hearing sooner. In view of this possible argument I told counsel yesterday afternoon that I would endeavour to give judgment this morning, as I am now doing, without taking further time
D for reflection.

    The clause then continues with the provision for forfeiture. This begins with limb 3, part of which I shall for convenience divide into two sub-limbs (a) and (b):

> " and in case any of the said persons . . . shall refuse or neglect or discontinue (a) to take or use such surname and Arms and (b) to take such means as may be requisite for the purpose of taking or using the same
E Then . . ."

The clause thereupon continues with limb 4, which consists of words of forfeiture which have not been discussed and I need not read.

    The problem in relation to arms arises in this way. The plaintiff has no arms by descent in the paternal line, and is entitled to none. It is accepted that he
F could apply for and in all probability obtain a grant of arms; indeed, an application has already been made on his behalf for a grant of arms for Horne, his former name, and is likely to succeed. Counsel for the plaintiff, however, puts his argument in this way. He begins with the requirement to quarter the arms of Inigo-Jones with " his . . . own family Arms ", and contends that this phrase has a narrow meaning. First, he says that it applies only to arms to which the
G plaintiff is entitled by paternal descent, and not to any arms to which he might be entitled by grant to him, or, I may add, by maternal descent, which, on the evidence, would require a grant to him. As the plaintiff is entitled to no such arms the requirement of quartering is impossible of performance, and, being part of a condition subsequent, falls to the ground, leaving his vested estate in the land unimpaired: see, e.g., Re Croxon, Croxon v. Ferrers (2). In the course
H of the argument, counsel for the plaintiff put this point, or a development of it, in an alternative way. Let the phrase " his . . . own family Arms " include arms acquired by a direct grant of arms to the plaintiff, he said, as well as arms acquired by paternal descent. Nevertheless, the phrase must refer to arms which the plaintiff had before the clause took effect, namely, on his becoming entitled to the actual receipt of the yearly rents and profits of the land. That
I being so, once again the plaintiff is being required to perform an impossibility, and once again the requirement falls to the ground. These two alternative versions of impossibility accordingly each rests on giving a narrow meaning to the words " his . . . own family Arms ", either as to the mode of acquisition or as to time.

    If driven from these positions, counsel for the plaintiff falls back on his second contention. If the phrase " his . . . own family Arms " is wide enough to embrace arms directly granted to the plaintiff, and is not confined to arms which he had

---

(2) [1904] 1 Ch. 252 at p. 259.

before the clause took effect, then he says there is nothing in the clause to require A
him to obtain a grant of such arms; and if (as is the case) he has not voluntarily
obtained any such grant, then once again there are no family arms with which
the Inigo-Jones arms can be quartered, and once again he incurs no forfeiture.
On this view, the clause is one which does not provide for the event. Imperfect
drafting (a quality amply enjoyed by the clause) has failed to make any effective
provision for the possibility that has in fact occurred in this case, namely, that B
the plaintiff has no arms of any kind.

Counsel for the plaintiff fortifies these contentions by some more general
considerations. He refers to the speech of LORD SIMONDS, L.C., in *Bromley* v.
Tryon (3) for the proposition that where, in the case of a defeasance clause,
there is a real doubt, the court will show to a vested estate the same favour in
applying the clause as it does in construing it. There is a nice discrimination C
here. Counsel for the plaintiff is constrained by *Re Neeld (decd.)* (4) to accept
that the clause is not void for uncertainty, yet he contends that it is nevertheless
sufficiently uncertain to be difficult of application and so to prevent any forfeiture
from arising. He contends, in short, for a middling sort of uncertainty, though
he did not describe it thus. In this connection I may also refer to a passage in a
case cited by counsel who appeared for infant sons of the plaintiff who are D
entitled if the defeasance clause takes effect. In *Re Eversley, Mildmay v. Mildmay*
(5), a name and arms case, BYRNE, J., said:

"... I look at these precedents and bear in mind the fact that the clause
is a penal clause which has to be construed strictly, but fairly of course, in
the sense that the Court ought not to strain the words if it is satisfied that
the testator has given a legitimate expression of his intention to impose E
this obligation on the objects of his bounty."

I find these words helpful in indicating the right approach.

I begin with the word "family". Certain authorities have been put before
me on the use of this word adjectivally, as in "family mansion"; but I think
that by common consent these authorities are to be regarded as standing some F
distance away from what I have to decide. The word appears in many combinations, from "family jewels" and "family home" to "family tree",
"family history" and even "family way". I think it is a Janus-like word,
often looking backwards ancestrally, but sometimes looking forward to posterity.
In relation to "arms", I can see no real reason why the word should be used
merely ancestrally, especially when it is also said to exclude the maternal line G
and apply only to the paternal line. It seems to me that the function of the
word is far more general than that. Counsel for the first, second and third
defendants contended that its function was to indicate arms that were descendible. Arms could be said to be "family arms" if they were arms that had been
lawfully granted so as to descend to the grantee's family. The term thus excluded
arms unlawfully assumed, which were not descendible, and also arms granted H
to the grantee alone without any limitation to his descendants: see the example
of the latter mentioned by POLLOCK, C.B., in *Stubs* v. *Stubs* (6). This explanation
appears to me to satisfy the requirements both of technical accuracy and of
ordinary usage, and I accept it. 'I may add that the limitation in the grant of
arms set out in the report of *Stubs* v. *Stubs* (7) is nonsensical, being a grant
of arms to be borne and used by "the said Joseph Stubs and his descendants I
of his brother Thomas Stubs". Fortunately, the case is also reported elsewhere (8)
and the other report shows that Messrs. Hurlstone & Coltman were guilty of a
homoeoteleuton in their report, the words "and by the descendants" having
been omitted immediately after the word "descendants".

(3) [1951] 2 All E.R. 1058 at p. 1066; [1952] A.C. 265 at p. 276.
(4) [1962] 2 All E.R. 335; [1962] Ch. 643.
(5) [1900] 1 Ch. 96 at p. 99.   (6) (1862), 1 H. & C. 257 at p. 264.
(7) (1862), 1 H. & C. at p. 259.   (8) (1862), 31 L.J.Ex. 510 at p. 511.

A   This view as to the meaning of "family arms" is, I think, to some extent confirmed by evidence adduced by counsel for the plaintiff. An affidavit by Mr. A. C. Cole, who is Windsor Herald of Arms, states:

B   "Were the Plaintiff to obtain Letters Patent establishing in him by grant as above Arms and Crest for Horne, such Armorial Bearings, as they would enure not only to him but also to his descendants (by the express terms of the Patent) could be described correctly as family Arms. Any Arms to which his mother were entitled as an heraldic heiress would not enure or descend to the Plaintiff until her death and then could be borne and used by the Plaintiff only if he had then an existing or obtained a subsequent right to Arms by grant of the Kings of Arms. Such female line Arms would normally

C   not be deemed family Arms inasmuch as in heraldry this term connotes Arms which have come to an individual by paternal descent or have been granted to him in respect of his paternal name."

On this view, a direct grant of arms to the plaintiff "could be described correctly as family arms". True, Mr. Cole speaks of a grant of arms and crest "for Horne", and of a grant "in respect of his paternal name". But I find it difficult

D   to believe that when A changes his name to B, arms subsequently granted to him will be "family arms" only if granted in respect of the name A and not if granted in respect of the name B. Whatever the name, a grant of arms to a man to be borne and used by him and his descendants is in my judgment a grant of "family arms", and the arms so granted to the man are properly described as "his . . . own family Arms".

E   A further consideration is the purpose of a name and arms clause. Such clauses are usually, if not always, the product of human vanity or sentiment. They occur in a variety of forms, as is shown by *Re Eversley* (9). But whatever the detail, the manifest object of the testator is to keep alive and in active use the name and arms in question. For this purpose, I cannot see that it is likely to matter much to the testator whether the arms that he wishes to preserve are

F   quartered with arms by paternal descent or with arms granted directly to the devisee. Either will preserve for posterity the arms that the testator seeks to perpetuate. I cannot conceive that a testator wishing to distinguish between arms by descent and arms by grant would entrust that intention to so blunt an instrument as the word "family", especially if he were also seeking to make a fine distinction between paternal arms by descent and maternal arms by descent. Delphi itself could scarcely surpass such a subtle indirection.

G   I turn, then, to the time element. On the footing that arms directly granted to the plaintiff to be used and borne by him and his descendants can properly be called "his . . . own family Arms", is this term confined to any such arms as the plaintiff had before the clause took effect? Counsel for the plaintiff contends that it is, and so the obligation is impossible of performance. I can see nothing

H   to confine the term thus. Analogies must always be regarded with caution: but if there were a requirement that a beneficiary should obtain some certificate from his family doctor or family solicitor, I would not regard the requirement as impossible of compliance merely because the beneficiary's family doctor or family solicitor had died a few days earlier. A certificate by a doctor or solicitor who could, at the time of giving it, fairly say that he was then the beneficiary's

I   family doctor or family solicitor would, I think, suffice. At least such a construction would be likely to accord more closely with the testator's intention than that there should be no effective requirement at all. In my judgment, the term "his . . . own family Arms" is wide enough to embrace family arms as soon as they come into existence, even if this is after the clause has taken effect.

Is there, then, any obligation under the clause for the plaintiff to obtain "family arms"? Counsel for the plaintiff urges with force that the court ought not to imply any such obligation in such a clause as this, and points to the

(9) [1900] 1 Ch. 96.

failure of the defendants to adduce any authority on the point. Counsel for the **A**
first, second and third defendants replies that the clause must be construed as a
whole, and says that when this is done it is seen that there is an obligation
for the plaintiff to obtain family arms if he lacks them. This argument proceeds
on the following lines. First, the positive obligation at the end of limb 1 is an
obligation that the plaintiff " shall . . . quarter the Arms of Inigo-Jones with
his . . . own family Arms ". This, he says, imposes on the plaintiff a single **B**
obligation, namely, to perform the process of quartering the Inigo-Jones arms
with arms that can properly be described as " his . . . own family Arms ";
and if he has no such arms, then he must obtain them so that there will then
be the final result prescribed by the testator, namely, the Inigo-Jones arms
quartered with his own family arms. In a clause of this kind, such a construction
is, it is said, far more reasonable and probable than one which releases from **C**
the obligation all save the armigerous, and so makes the quartering a matter
of chance.

Secondly, counsel for the first, second and third defendants says, one must
look at limbs 2 and 3. Limb 2 relates to obtaining a proper licence from the
Crown, and so on. Limb 3 is framed in terms which dovetail in with limbs 1 and 2.
Limb 3 (a) relates to limb 1. It applies to the plaintiff if he refuses or neglects **D**
or discontinues " to take or use such surname and Arms ". Limb 3 (b), on the
other hand, relates to limb 2; for it applies to the plaintiff if he refuses or neglects
or discontinues " to take such means as may be requisite for the purpose of
taking or using the same ". This allocation of limb 3 (a) to limb 1, and of limb
3 (b) to limb 2 was, I may say, accepted by counsel for the plaintiff. On this
footing, the provisions for forfeiture apply if the plaintiff refuses or neglects or **E**
discontinues " to take or use such surname and Arms ", and the word " take "
shows that the obligation to quarter imposed by limb 1 includes any taking
of arms necessary for this process of quartering. To this, counsel for the plaintiff
demurred. In limb 1, " take ", he said, means " take the surname of Inigo-
Jones ". This, of course, it does. But to say this in no way meets counsel for the
first, second and third defendants' contention that " take or use " in limb 3 (a) **F**
explains the verb " quarter " in limb 1.

Counsel for the first, second and third defendants' argument is fine-spun:
but that does not mean that it does not hold together. What makes me hesitate
about it is not any logical deficiencies in it, but whether it is right to apply such
a process of reasoning to what is manifestly an ill-drafted clause. In order to
make sense of it, the Court of Appeal has already had to insert a dozen or so words. **G**
On the other hand, the broad purpose of the clause is manifest. The person
entitled to the land must have the Inigo-Jones arms quartered with his own
family arms; and a sufficiency of time is allowed in which that result can be
achieved. The point is not easy, and I should have preferred to take further
time for consideration. But doing the best that I can in the circumstances, and
accepting to the full the need to construe penal clauses strictly but fairly, I think **H**
that the testator has given a legitimate expression of his intention to impose
the obligation on the objects of his bounty, and that I ought not to strain the
words to produce a different result. It will be observed that I have borrowed
with gratitude from the language of BYRNE, J., in *Re Eversley* (10). In my judgment, the obligation of quartering imposed on the plaintiff requires him to take
all necessary steps to produce the prescribed result, including obtaining a grant **I**
of arms to him.

In saying that, I would make one addition. For the purposes of this will,
I do not think that it matters whether any grant of arms to the plaintiff is a
grant for Horne, his former name, or a grant for Inigo-Jones, his present name.
The subsisting application made on his behalf is for a grant for Horne. Counsel
for the plaintiff sought to make some point about this in his reply, in that counsel
for the first, second and third defendants had not said which it ought to be,

(10) [1900] 1 Ch. at p. 99.

A and that this showed the uncertainty of the clause. I do not agree. If what is required is a grant of " his . . . own family Arms ", then a grant of such arms must be obtained. If what is granted can properly be said to answer this description, then I can see no uncertainty merely by reason of a failure to specify the name in respect of which it is thought most proper under the laws of arms to make the grant.

B In the originating summons, the plaintiff seeks the following relief:

" 1. That it may be declared whether upon the true construction of Clause 17 of the Will of the testator the ' family arms ' therein referred to in relation to the Plaintiff mean:—(a) only arms which the Plaintiff has a right to bear by descent from some person to whom a grant to bear such arms was made (b) any Arms which the Plaintiff may be or become entitled to bear
C whether by grant to himself or to any other person (c) some other and if so what Arms."

From what I have said, it will be seen that I answer question 1 in sense (b). It is agreed, I think, that questions 2 and 3 do not now arise.

Question 4 is as follows:

D " Generally that directions may be given what further steps if any the Plaintiff is bound to take to avoid a forfeiture of his said life interest for non compliance with the provisions of the said clause 17."

I see that in *Re Berens, Re Dowdeswell, Berens-Dowdeswell* v. *Holland-Martin* (11), RUSSELL, J., answered a not dissimilar question. In this connection I may observe that the obligation in limb 1 to quarter the arms of Inigo-Jones with the plaintiff's
E own family arms does not at first sight exactly accord with the obligation in limb 2 to obtain a proper licence, and so on, to take, use and bear the arms of Inigo-Jones. However, I do not think that it is in dispute that a licence for the quartering under limb 1 would be a sufficient licence under limb 2. For the purposes of this will the bearing of arms that have been quartered is the bearing of those arms. Apart from this, and the other points covered by my judgment,
F there has been no direct discussion of the proper answer to question 4, and if an answer to it is still sought, I shall hear counsel on it.

I would only add this. It is now over 12 years since the testator died and the plaintiff became aware of the obligations of cl. 17. When more than ten years had gone by he issued the summons in this case; and not until something like another two years had passed, in the last week of what, on one view, is the year
G for compliance laid down by the clause, does he bring the question before the court. As I have said, I have been given no explanation of this, and I have not thought it right to press counsel for the plaintiff hard on the point. It is not beyond possibility, I suppose, that lurking in the thickets of the fiscal laws there is to be found some advantage in incurring a forfeiture. Certainly the plaintiff cannot be accused of undue vigour or precipitancy in his efforts over the last 12
H years to comply with the clause which, for more than six years, he has known to be valid and enforceable. Nor is the difficulty in any way obscure. The clause only has to be read for it to be seen that the words " shall . . . quarter the Arms of Inigo-Jones with his . . . own family Arms " must raise problems for someone who has no arms at all. Be that as it may, if the plaintiff now finds himself, on 5th March 1969, 'twixt the stirrup and the ground, I can only say that no court
I can answer a question before it has been asked.

Order accordingly.

Solicitors: *Peake & Co.* (for all parties).

[*Reported by* R. W. FARRIN, ESQ., *Barrister-at-Law.*]

---

(11) [1926] Ch. 596.

BLAISE *v*. BLAISE.

A

[COURT OF APPEAL, CIVIL DIVISION (Danckwerts, Sachs and Fenton Atkinson, L.JJ.), February 5, 6, 1969.]

Divorce—Appeal—Appeal from magistrates' court—Powers of appellate court —Improper rejection of evidence—Substantial wrong or miscarriage of justice occasioned—Cross-examination of witness refused—Test possibility of effect on decision—Redetermination by magistrates required—Matrimonial Causes Rules 1957 *(S.I.* 1957 *No.* 619), *r.* 73 (7)—*R.S.C., Ord.* 59, *r.* 11 (2).

B

After 12 months of married life in which the husband's behaviour was very unsatisfactory, the husband left the wife about Christmas 1966. From then until 8th March 1967 the wife wrote several letters imploring him to return and they met from time to time. After a break until 25th April, the husband began a series of letters expressing in apparently sincere terms a genuine desire that they should live together again. The wife did not respond and on 20th June 1967 she took out a summons to appear before the justices alleging desertion and wilful neglect to maintain and seeking a non-cohabitation clause in the order. At the hearing counsel for the husband was not allowed by the justices to cross-examine the wife or the probation officer whom she called as a witness (on a waiver of privilege) as to matters which the husband claimed had been said by the wife to the probation officer which were to support submissions as to the credibility of the parties and their conduct and which were highly relevant to her motives in refusing a reconciliation; and he was unable in consequence to examine the husband on what he claimed had passed between the two. The justices found that the husband's word was not to be relied on, that his offer of a reconciliation was not made in good faith and that the wife was entitled to refuse it as not being bona fide. They held that desertion had been established and made an order for £2 a week maintenance. The Divisional Court dismissed the husband's appeal, holding that on the assumption that the excluded questions would have evoked the favourable answers hoped for, they might but probably would not have led to a different result and that the husband had therefore failed to show that there would more probably than not have been a different decision but for the improper rejection of evidence as in effect required by the Matrimonial Causes Rules 1957, r. 73 (7)*.

C

D

E

F

Held: the order of the justices must be discharged and the case be remitted to the justices for rehearing, because—

G

(i) denial of a party's important right to cross-examine a witness whose answers might affect the result of the case constituted both a " substantial wrong [and] miscarriage of justice . . . occasioned " by the improper rejection of evidence under the Matrimonial Causes Rules 1957, r. 73 (7), as (on other appeals) under R.S.C., Ord. 55, r. 7 (7)†, and on appeals to the Court of Appeal under R.S.C., Ord. 59, r. 11 (2)‡ (there being no material difference between the effects of the three rules and of the new rule R.S.C. (Amendment No. 1) 1968)§, the proper test being whether the evidence " might " have affected the decision and not whether it would have formed a determining factor in the result;

H

(ii) where the legislature had designated a particular tribunal such as a jury or justices to determine a case, the appellate court must not debar the litigant from having that tribunal's determination where it was shown that what wrongly happened was sufficiently important possibly to have had

I

---

* S.I. 1957 No. 619. Rule 73 (7), so far as material, is set out at p. 1035, letter F, post.

† R.S.C., Ord. 55, r. 7 (7) is set out at p. 1035, letter G, post.

‡ R.S.C., Ord. 59, r. 11 (2) is set out at p. 1035, letter H, post.

§ S.I. 1968 No. 1244.

A   an influence on the tribunal's decision and the court should accordingly not seek to substitute its own view for that of the justices:

    (iii) the wrongful denial of the fundamental right to cross-examine an opponent's witness was akin rather to a misdirection and was in a different category from refusal of an application to adduce fresh evidence; and

    (iv) on the facts the answers to the questions might well have been an
B   important factor in deliberation of the justices (see p. 1035, letter I, to p. 1036, letter C, p. 1037, letters F to I, and p. 1038, letter H, to p. 1039, letter A, post).

    Foulkes v. *Foulkes* ((1893), 69 L.T. 461) and *Bray* v. *Ford* ([1895-99] All E.R. Rep. 1009) followed.

    Appeal allowed.

C   [As to the powers of a court on a divorce appeal from a magistrates' court, see 12 Halsbury's Laws (3rd Edn.) 510, 511, para. 1120; and for cases on the subject, see 27 Digest (Repl.) 732-733, *6983-7000.*

    The Matrimonial Causes Rules 1957 have been revoked by S.I. 1968 No. 219 and S.I. 1968 No. 1244.]

D Cases referred to:

    Bray v. *Ford,* [1896] A.C. 44; [1895-99] All E.R. Rep. 1009; 65 L.J.Q.B. 213; 73 L.T. 609; 5 Digest (Repl.) 856, *4070.*

    Foulkes v. *Foulkes* (1893), 69 L.T. 461; 27 Digest (Repl.) 731, *6975.*

Appeal.

    The husband appealed to the Court of Appeal against an order of the Divisional
E Court of the Probate, Divorce and Admiralty Division (Divorce) (Sir Jocelyn Simon, P., and Latey, J.) made on 28th April 1968, dismissing the husband's appeal against an order of justices for Newham, London, made on 12th October 1967. The magistrates adjudged that the husband had deserted the wife in December 1966. The grounds of the husband's appeal were as follows: (i) the Divisional Court misdirected itself in holding that the justices were entitled on the evidence before them to find that the husband's offers to resume cohabitation
F were not bona fide; (ii) the Divisional Court misdirected itself in holding that the justices were entitled on the evidence before them to find that the wife was entitled to reject the husband's offers to resume cohabitation; and (iii) the Divisional Court was wrong in law in holding that the failure of the justices to allow the husband's counsel the opportunity of properly cross-examining
G a probation officer who was called to give evidence, privilege having been waived, had not thereby occasioned a substantial wrong or miscarriage of justice within the meaning of r. 73 (7) of the Matrimonial Causes Rules 1957.

    Joseph Jackson, Q.C., and *A. de P. J. M. Bueno* for the husband.
    T. M. Eastham, Q.C., and *Valerie Mairants* for the wife.

H   **SACHS, L.J.,** delivered the first judgment at the invitation of Danckwerts, L.J.: This is an appeal against a decision of the Divisional Court of Probate, Divorce and Admiralty Division given on 28th April 1966, when that court dismissed the appeal of the husband, the petitioner, against an order of the justices of the petty sessional division of Newham made on 12th October 1967. That was a decision by which the husband was adjudged to have deserted his
I wife in December 1966 and was ordered to pay £2 weekly towards her maintenance. The sequence of events leading up to the proceedings before the justices was as follows. The parties were married in September 1965, being both quite young, either 20 or 19 respectively. The marriage during the next 12 months—the only 12 months they lived together—was very unsatisfactory so far as the behaviour of the husband was concerned, but no cruelty has been alleged against him.

    About Christmas 1966 the husband left the wife. There then ensued correspondence and meetings between them. So far as the correspondence is concerned

it is the fact that from 27th December 1966 to 8th March 1967 the wife wrote A
a number of letters asking the husband to return—indeed imploring him to
return in a way that was clearly both genuine and pathetic.   During this period
they would meet from time to time and on one of those occasions at any rate sexual
intercourse took place.   As, however, from 8th March there is a cessation of
letters from the wife, the letter of the last-named date having said in terms that
the half sort of life that was being led was one that she could not stand any more. B

From 8th March to 25th April there is a gap.   Then on 25th April it is the
husband who writes a series of letters, having clearly had, on the face of it, a
change of heart.   Those letters, which look genuine enough, expressed in apparently sincere terms a genuine desire that he and his wife should now recommence
to live together.   At this stage, however, it was the wife who did not respond
to the advances from the husband.   Then one comes to 20th June.   On that C
date the wife took out a summons to come before the justices alleging desertion
and wilful neglect, and incidentally asking for a non-cohabitation clause in the
order.   There was no allegation of cruelty.   On 3rd August the justices made an
interim order and on 12th October the matter came before them for final decision.
Their conclusions were that desertion had been established and they made the
order for £2 a week maintenance. D

Before going further it is perhaps as well to quote from the findings of the
justices and to say something more as to what happened at the trial.   The
justices, when holding that there was desertion, found, amongst other facts,
the following:

" (v) We believed the wife when in her evidence she said that her husband's
word was not to be relied on and that having made every effort without E
avail, we found that she was entitled to refuse the husband's offer as not
being bona fide . . . (vii) In this connection and taking the evidence as a
whole and the demeanour of the husband in particular, we found that any
offer made by the husband to his wife to effect a reconciliation was not one
made in good faith."
                                                                        F

On those findings, and from the other matters already mentioned, it is clear that
a great deal turned on the credibility of the parties.   At the trial the only witness
other than the parties who was called was a probation officer.   She was called
by the wife after both parties had waived their privilege and thus enabled this
particular probation officer to go into the witness box.   When she had given
her evidence-in-chief she was also asked a number of questions, quite properly, G
by the court.   But when counsel for the husband asked to cross-examine the
wife's witness the justices refused to allow that to be done.   It was the intention
of counsel for the husband to put a number of questions, which, had favourable
answers been received, would have led to submissions on the question of the
credibility of the parties and their conduct.   Those questions were obviously
of potential importance and could, according to their answers, have thrown light H
both on the sincerity of the husband and on the issue whether the wife was
entitled to refuse any offer of his at that relevant stage with which this court is
concerned.

When the matter went up to the Divisional Court issues which fell for decision
were: first of all, whether there had been a sincere offer by the husband over
the relevant period, and the Divisional Court found that he was sincere; secondly, I
whether the wife was justified in refusing such offers as he made, and they held
that there being no assurance of any change of conduct on his part she was
entitled to refuse to return.

Next I come to the third issue before the Divisional Court—the crucial issue
in my view.   That was the ground of appeal based on the failure by the justices
to allow the questions to be put in cross-examination to the probation officer.
It was rightly conceded by counsel for the wife that the justices were wrong in
their refusal.   After considering the submissions as to what questions could have

A   been put or were likely to have been put and what would have been the result of those questions had cross-examining counsel received the answers which he hoped for, the Divisional Court said this in their judgment:

> " Assuming, as we have, that the questions excluded would have evoked the favourable answers for which counsel for the husband was hoping, our view is that while they might have led to a different result they probably
B   would not have done so."

On that basis it was that they examined the effect of the Matrimonial Causes Rules 1957 (1), r. 73 (7), which governed the court in relation to either allowing or not allowing an appeal to them as a divisional court. The conclusion which was reached was stated as follows:

C   " In our opinion the proper construction of r. 73 (7) is that no appeal shall succeed unless it is shown that, but for the improper rejection of the evidence, there would more probably than not have been a different decision."

In other words, it was the view of the Divisional Court that unless the husband could affirmatively show that there would probably have been a different result
D   before the justices then the appeal must fail.

There now comes the appeal to this court, and the grounds on which it is brought are that the Divisional Court were wrong in their conclusions on each of the issues before them, first whether the wife was justified in refusing the offers of the husband to join together in setting up a fresh matrimonial life, and secondly on the construction of r. 73 (7). It is the case for the husband today that on
E   the conclusion reached by the Divisional Court, that the result of cross-examination might have led to a different result, there should have been ordered a new trial.

It is to this second point that I now turn, and it is convenient to read both r. 73 (7) and the parallel rules which relate to appeals to the Divisional Court of the Queen's Bench Division and to this court respectively. Rule 73 (7) of the
F   Matrimonial Causes Rules 1957 provides:

> " No appeal shall succeed on the ground merely of misdirection or improper reception or rejection of evidence unless, in the opinion of the court, substantial wrong or miscarriage of justice has been occasioned thereby."

The Rule of the Supreme Court that relates to appeals to it from another court
G   or tribunal (excepting appeals governed by the Matrimonial Causes Rules) is R.S.C., Ord. 55, r. 7 (7). This provides:

> " The appeal shall not succeed on the ground merely of misdirection, or of the improper admission or rejection of evidence, unless in the opinion of the Court substantial wrong or miscarriage has been thereby occasioned."

The rule relating generally to appeals to the Court of Appeal is R.S.C., Ord. 59,
H   r. 11 (2), which provides:

> " A new trial shall not be ordered on the ground of misdirection or of the improper admission or rejection of evidence, or because the verdict of the jury was not taken upon a question which the judge at trial was not asked to leave to them unless in the opinion of the Court of Appeal some substantial wrong or miscarriage has been thereby occasioned."

I

So far as the issues for consideration today are concerned, I can see no material difference between the effect of the three rules which have just been cited in full. As a matter of subsequent history it is to be noted that, since the decision of the Divisional Court there has been a change in the rules applicable to appeals from magistrates to the Divisional Court of the Probate, Divorce and Admiralty Division. I refer to the change effected by R.S.C. (Amendment No. 1) 1968 (2),

---

(1) S.I. 1957 No. 619.
(2) S.I. 1968 No. 1244.

made on 31st July, which came into operation on 1st September. The relevant rule provides:

> "The Court shall not be bound to allow the appeal on the ground merely of misdirection, or of the improper admission or rejection of evidence, unless in the opinion of the Court substantial wrong or miscarriage has been thereby occasioned."

Again, to my mind, that does not, on a consideration of the authorities, really change the position which existed when the former r. 73 (7) was in force, and for this, amongst other reasons, I do not propose to refer to the new rule further. I was turning back to the rule as it existed at the time of the Divisional Court decision. As a matter of first impression it seemed to me—and I had no hesitation on this point—to lead to the conclusion that where a party is denied the important right to cross-examine a witness whose answers on cross-examination might affect the result, that constituted both a substantial wrong and a miscarriage of justice. That first impression has been fully confirmed by two authorities bearing on the interpretation of the relevant words in the rules. Neither of those authorities was cited to the Divisional Court and had they been cited there is little doubt that they would have led that court to a different conclusion to that which was reached.

Of these two authorities the first in order of time was a decision of a Divisional Court in an appeal from the justices who had decided a maintenance case. It came before SIR FRANCIS JEUNE, P., and BARNES, J., in 1893: *Foulkes* v. *Foulkes* (3). At that time there were no separate rules of the Divorce Division for appeals to its Divisional Court. But in substance its Divisional Courts of that day applied the rules relating to appeals to the Queen's Bench Divisional Court and we have been assured that the rules applicable to the latter were in all material respects the same as those which have been previously recited in this judgment.

In *Foulkes* v. *Foulkes* (3) the facts were that certain witnesses got to the magistrates' court before the justices had retired but did not get heard owing to certain steps taken by the justices under a misapprehension. When the matter fell to be considered by the Divisional Court, SIR FRANCIS JEUNE, P., said this in relation to a suggestion that the Divisional Court should hear fresh evidence and come to conclusions on it (4):

> "It is eminently a matter for the magistrates to decide, after hearing and seeing the parties . . . It is clear that there was further information at their command which would or might—it is sufficient to say might—have caused them to give a different decision upon that point."

Counsel for the husband rightly emphasised the use by SIR FRANCIS JEUNE, P., of the word "might", and equally emphasised the significance of the statement that the matter was eminently one for the justices. The next case, which is even more important, and to my mind lays down the principles to be applied under all the relevant rules, is *Bray* v. *Ford* (5). That case related to the damages awarded in a libel action by a jury when there had been a misdirection by the trial judge as to what factors the jury were entitled to take into account. The jury had been wrongly told to exclude certain factors from consideration. When that case came before a court of appeal that court adopted the course of putting themselves in the place of the jury and coming to the conclusion (6) "that the jury would have given, and would have been justified in giving the same verdict, if there had been no misdirection" and that accordingly there ought not to be a new trial. The House of Lords decided that that was the wrong approach. LORD HALSBURY, L.C.'s speech contained the following passage (7):

(3) (1893), 69 L.T. 461.   (4) (1893), 69 L.T. at p. 461.
(5) [1896] A.C. 44; [1895-99] All E.R. Rep. 1009.
(6) [1896] A.C. at p. 46.
(7) [1896] A.C. at p. 47; [1895-99] All E.R. Rep. at p. 1010.

A
    " My Lords, I think there has been a substantial wrong and a miscarriage.
I think there has been a substantial wrong, since I think the defendant was
not permitted to present his case to the jury with the appropriate argument."

A little later, after saying that he was not prepared to state what a jury would
have done, he continued (8):

B
    ". . . it appears to me that it was, in this case, withdrawing from the jury
a question which the defendant had a right to have submitted . . ."

Then LORD WATSON said (9):

    " I think it is clear that the misdirection given by CAVE, J., at the trial
was such as to occasion a miscarriage in the sense in which that word was
understood by the legal profession at the time when the Rules of 1883

C
were framed . . . Every party to a trial by jury has a legal and constitutional
right to have the case which he has made, either in pursuit or in defence,
fairly submitted to the consideration of that tribunal."

LORD HERSCHELL said (10):

    " The provision [and he referred to the rule] is, in my opinion, a very

D
beneficial one, and I should be sorry to say anything to narrow its scope
further than the language employed seems to me to render necessary."

While LORD SHAND said when referring to the erroneous approach of the Court
of Appeal (11):

    " It in effect asks that another and different case than that presented to
the jury shall be tried, and tried, not by the proper tribunal of a jury,

E
but by a Court of Appeal."

To my mind that case clearly establishes firstly that the decision in *Foulkes'*
case (12) was right in that the test of " might " is the correct test, and secondly
that, when the legislature has designated a particular tribunal, such as jury or
justices, to determine a case, the appellate court must not debar the litigant

F
from having that tribunal's determination when once it is shown that what
wrongly happened was sufficiently important to the extent that it might have
had an influence on that tribunal's decision.

    Counsel for the wife submitted that the tests to be applied were the same
as if there was before this court an application to adduce evidence of witnesses
not called at trial. I am unable to accept that contention. When one looks

G
at the words of the relevant rules they apply equally to misdirections
and exclusions of evidence; they do not deal with the question of fresh evidence.
More importantly, it seems to me that the wrongful denial of the fundamental
right to cross-examine an opponent's witness is in a different category from the
question whether fresh evidence can later be adduced. It is more akin to misdirection, at any rate in cases when the appellant is entitled to the determination

H
of a specific tribunal entrusted by the legislature with the relevant decision.

    Counsel for the wife also submitted that the answers to the questions which
counsel for the husband proposed to submit in effect could not have influenced
the justices so as to produce a different result. For my part I prefer the view
of the Divisional Court. It seems to me that answers to those questions might
well have been an important factor in deliberations of justices who had only one
witness before them in addition to the parties. To my mind this court should

I
accordingly not seek to substitute its own view for that of the justices and should
order a new trial. In those circumstances I need not deal with the other points
raised in this appeal because they do not arise.

---

(8) [1896] A.C. at p. 47; [1895-99] All E.R. Rep. at p. 1010.
(9) [1896] A.C. at p. 49; [1895-99] All E.R. Rep. at p. 1012.
(10) [1896] A.C. at p. 52; [1895-99] All E.R. Rep. at p. 1011;
(11) [1896] A.C. at p. 55.
(12) (1893), 69 L.T. 461.

FENTON ATKINSON, L.J.: I agree that the evidence before the justices A shows that the husband, having behaved thoroughly badly towards the wife for most of the 15 months the marriage lasted, deserted her and for three months or more ignored her urgent entreaties to return.   Six weeks or so later he wrote a number of letters professing his earnest desire for a reconciliation, acknowledging the bad things he said that he had done and promising amendment of life for the future.   But by now it was the wife who was unwilling to resume B cohabitation, because, as she said, she believed him incapable of acting any differently or better than before.

The justices in my view were faced with difficult issues of fact, not only as to the sincerity of the husband's protestations in the light of the previous history and their assessment of his character but also as to the true motives behind the wife's refusal to try again.   It was in my judgment far from being an open and C shut case in favour of the wife and it was against this background that the husband's counsel was wrongly deprived of his right to cross-examine the probation officer and also the wife as to certain things that the husband claimed were said by the wife to that probation officer, and was also, in consequence, refused the right of examining the husband as to what he said had passed between the wife and the probation officer.   D

The questions that counsel desired to put were, for the most part, highly relevant principally to the wife's motives in refusing reconciliation and, coupled with the further cross-examination for which the original questions could have provided an opening, might well in, my judgment, have affected the justices in their judgment of the wife's attitude and her credibility.   In my judgment there was on the facts of this case a substantial wrong or miscarriage of justice E because the husband was not allowed to develop his full case and evidence which might have led to a different decision was shut out.   In other words, as it seems to me, he lost a chance of success which was fairly open to him.

The view of the Divisional Court seeking to apply r. 73 (7) of the Matrimonial Causes Rules 1957 was that although, if the questions had been allowed, there might have been a different result the result would in their judgment have been F the same.   But, as SACHS, L.J., has said, in my view if their attention had been called to the two cases of *Foulkes* v. *Foulkes* (13) and *Bray* v. *Ford* (14) they would have come to a different conclusion, and the speeches in *Bray* v. *Ford* (14) in my opinion show quite clearly that it is enough for the husband's purposes in this appeal to show that there might have been a different result but for the wrongful exclusion of the evidence in question.   G

Counsel for the wife has argued that the strict tests laid down, which must be satisfied before fresh evidence will be admitted on appeal under R.S.C., Ord. 59, r. 10 (2), must be applied, in considering the evidence wrongly rejected in this case and that the court should only exercise its powers under R.S.C., Ord. 59, r. 11 (2), or r. 73 (7) of the Matrimonial Causes Rules 1957 if the evidence wrongly rejected can be shown to be of such a character that it would, so far as could be H foreseen, have formed a determining factor in the result.   In my view, the conditions under which fresh evidence is admitted in this court on appeal have no application when considering the wholly different question now before the court, and I am quite clear that in this case, where plainly relevant evidence which might have affected the result was wrongly excluded, there was here indeed a substantial wrong and/or miscarriage of justice and there should be a I re-hearing.

DANCKWERTS, L.J.: I agree with the judgments that have been delivered.   The appeal will be allowed, the order of the justices will be discharged

(13) (1893), 69 L.T. 461.
(14) [1896] A.C. 44; [1895-99] All E.R. Rep. 1009.

A and the case will be remitted to the justices for re-hearing by a different bench of justices.

Appeal allowed. Case remitted to justices for re-hearing by fresh court.

Solicitors: *Frederick Wills & Co.* (for the husband); *Montague Gardner & Howard* (for the wife).

B
[*Reported by* F. A. AMIES, ESQ., *Barrister-at-Law.*]

McELDOWNEY *v.* FORDE.

C [COURT OF APPEAL (NORTHERN IRELAND) (Lord MacDermott, C.J., McVeigh and Curran, L.JJ.), October 28, November 29, 1968.]

[HOUSE OF LORDS (Lord Hodson, Lord Guest, Lord Pearce, Lord Pearson and Lord Diplock), April 28, 29, June 18, 1969.]

Statute—Construction—Construction of words within context—Application of proviso to one subsection to operation of another subsection—Civil Authorities
D *(Special Powers) Act (Northern Ireland) 1922 (12 & 13 Geo. 5 c. 5), s. 1 (1) and (3).*

Statutory Instrument—Ultra vires—Outside enabling power—Instrument made under section of Act—Other subsection of enabling section limiting powers— Whether other subsection limiting powers to make instrument—Civil Authori-
E *ties (Special Powers) Act (Amending) (No. 1) Regulations (Northern Ire- land) 1967 (S.R. & O. 1967 No. 42)—Civil Authorities (Special Powers) Act (Northern Ireland) 1922 (12 & 13 Geo. 5 c. 5), s. 1 (1) and (3).*

Statutory Instrument—Construction—Vagueness—" Any like organisation howso- ever described "—Whether too vague—Whether ambiguous—Civil Authorities (Special Powers) Act (Amending) (No. 1) Regulations (Northern Ireland) 1967 (S.R. & O. 1967 No. 42).

F Under the Civil Authorities (Special Powers) Act (Northern Ireland) 1922 certain powers were vested in the Minister of Home Affairs. These included (s. 1 (1))*: " power . . . to take all such steps and issue all such orders as may be necessary for preserving the peace and maintaining order according to and in execution of this Act and the regulations contained in the Schedule thereto . . . Provided that the ordinary course of law and avocations of life and the enjoyment of property shall be interfered with as little as may
G be permitted by the exigencies of the steps required to be taken under this Act." By s. 1 (3)* of the Act the Minister was empowered: " to make regulations—(a) for making further provision for the preservation of the peace and the maintenance of order . . . and any regulations made as aforesaid shall . . . have effect and be enforced in like manner as regulations contained
H in the Schedule to this Act." A new regulation, reg. 24A†, was added to the Schedule in 1922; this provided: " Any person who becomes or remains a member of an unlawful association . . . shall be guilty of an offence against these Regulations . . ." The regulation also listed certain organisations which were deemed for the purposes of reg. 24A to be " unlawful associations ". In 1967 the Minister made a new regulation (the regulation of 1967) under
I s. 1 (3) of the Act. The regulation of 1967 provided: " Regulation 24A . . . shall have effect as if the following organisations were added to the list of organisations which for the purpose of that Regulation are deemed to be unlawful organisations: ' The organisations at the date of this regulation or at any time thereafter describing themselves as " Republican Clubs " or any like organisation howsoever described '." On the question whether the regulation of 1967 was ultra vires,

---

* For the complete text of s. 1 (1) and (3), see p. 1042, letters G and H, post.
† For the complete text of reg. 24A, see p. 1043, letters B to F, post.

Held: (LORD PEARCE and LORD DIPLOCK dissenting): the regulation of   A
1967 was not ultra vires the enabling Act, because—

(i) the regulation, to be valid, need not be shown to be necessary for
preserving the peace and maintaining order nor to comply with the proviso
to s. 1 (1) since the limitations contained in s. 1 (1) on the exercise of the
executive powers did not apply to the exercise of the legislative powers
under s. 1 (3) (see p. 1057, letter I, to p. 1058, letter A, p. 1060, letter E, and   B
p. 1065, letter H, post);

(ii) the courts would not interfere with the exercise of the power to make
regulations since there was no question of bad faith and no apparent misconstruction of the enabling Act or failure to comply with any conditions
prescribed by the enabling Act for the exercise of the power (see p. 1058,
letter B, p. 1061, letter G, p. 1066, letter D, and p. 1067, letters B and G,   C
post); and

(iii) the inclusion of " any like organisation howsoever described " in the
proscription of " Republican Clubs " did not render the regulations invalid
on the basis of (per LORD HODSON and LORD PEARSON) its being too vague or
(per LORD GUEST) its being ambiguous or arbitrary (see p. 1058, letter E,
p. 1062, letter E, and p. 1067, letter H, post).   D

Appeal dismissed.

[As to grounds for challenging subordinate legislation, see 36 HALSBURY'S
LAWS (3rd Edn.) 491, 492, para. 743.

As to the need to construe words in a statute by reference to their context
and the need to construe a statute as a whole, see 36 HALSBURY'S LAWS (3rd Edn.)
394-396, paras. 593 and 594; and for cases on the subject, see 44 DIGEST (Repl.)   E
231-234, 494-543.

As to the need to interpret subordinate legislation so as to be consistent with
the substantive provisions of the enabling power, see 36 HALSBURY'S LAWS (3rd
Edn.) 493, para. 745; and for cases on the subject, see 44 DIGEST (Repl.) 380,
381, 2197-2204.

As to the extent of judicial control over the exercise of discretionary statutory   F
powers by public authorities, see 30 HALSBURY'S LAWS (3rd Edn.) 687, 688,
para. 1326; and for cases on the subject, see 38 DIGEST (Repl.) 11-13, 38-48.

For the Civil Authorities (Special Powers) Act (Northern Ireland) 1922,
s. 1, see 17 HALSBURY'S STATUTES (2nd Edn.) 168.]

Cases referred to:

Associated Provincial Picture Houses, Ltd. v. *Wednesbury Corpn.*, [1947] 2 All   G
E.R. 680; [1948] 1 K.B. 223; [1948] L.J.R. 190; 177 L.T. 641; 45
Digest (Repl.) 215, *189.*

A.-G. for Canada v. *Hallet & Carey, Ltd.*, [1952] A.C. 427; 44 Digest (Repl.)
293, *1229.*

Carltona, Ltd. v. *Comrs. of Works*, [1943] 2 All E.R. 560; 17 Digest (Repl.)
441, *119.*   H

Comrs. of Customs & Excise v. *Cure & Deeley, Ltd.*, [1961] 3 All E.R. 641;
[1962] 1 Q.B. 340; 39 Digest (Repl.) 351, *839.*

Co-operative Committee on Japanese Canadians v. *A.-G. for Canada*, [1947]
A.C. 87; [1947] L.J.R. 836; 176 L.T. 547; 8 Digest (Repl.) 695, *61.*

Gray, Re (1918), 57 S.C.R. 150.

Julius v. *Lord Bishop of Oxford* (1880), 5 App. Cas. 214; [1874-80] All E.R.   I
Rep. 43; 49 L.J.Q.B. 577; 42 L.T. 546; 44 J.P. 600; 44 Digest (Repl.)
310, *1415.*

Liversidge v. *Anderson*, [1941] 3 All E.R. 338; [1942] A.C. 206; 110 L.J.K.B.
724; 116 L.T. 1; 17 Digest (Repl.) 422, *27.*

Minister of Health v. *Regem, Ex p. Yaffé*, [1931] A.C. 494; [1931] All E.R. Rep.
343; 100 L.J.K.B. 306; 44 Digest (Repl.) 203, *148.*

Nakkuda Ali v. *Jayaratne (M.F. De S.)*, [1951] A.C. 66; 8 Digest (Repl.) 802,
562.

A *Padfield* v. *Minister of Agriculture, Fisheries and Food,* [1968] 1 All E.R. 694;
   [1968] A.C. 997; [1968] 2 W.L.R. 924; Digest (Repl.) Supp.
   Point of Ayr Collieries, Ltd. v. *Lloyd-George,* [1943] 2 All E.R. 546; 17 Digest
   (Repl.) 480, *278.*
   R. v. *Governor of Brixton Prison, Ex p. Soblen,* [1962] 3 All E.R. 641; [1963]
   2 Q.B. 243; Digest (Cont. Vol. A) 24, *149a.*

B *R.* v. *Halliday,* [1917] A.C. 260; 86 L.J.K.B. 1119; 116 L.T. 417; 81 J.P.
   237; 17 Digest (Repl.) 420, *19.*
   Reference Re Chemical Regulations, [1943] S.C.R. 1.
   Riel v. *R.* (1885), 10 App. Cas. 675; 55 L.J.P.C. 28;   sub nom. *R.* v. *Riel,*
   54 L.T. 339; 16 Cox, C.C. 48; 8 Digest (Repl.) 704, *120.*

Case Stated.

C This was a Case Stated by the resident magistrates (JOHN M. SHEARER, ESQ.,
and JACOB F. McCLENAGHAN, ESQ.), in respect of their adjudication as a court of
summary jurisdiction sitting at Magherafelt, County Londonderry, on 12th June
1968. The [respondent]*, Michael F. Forde, a district inspector in the Royal
Ulster Constabulary preferred a complaint against the [appellant]†, John
McEldowney, that on 28th March 1968 at Slaughtneil in the petty sessions district
D of Maghera and the County of Londonderry he was and remained a member of
an unlawful association, namely a republican club, contrary to reg. 24A‡ of the
regulations made under the Civil Authorities (Special Powers) Acts (Northern
Ireland) 1922-43, as amended by a regulation made on 7th March 1967§. The
Case noted the legislative provisions referred to and set out the text of s. 1 (3) (*a*)
of the Act, reg. 24A and the regulation of 1967 and continued: 7. The magis-
E trates found as a fact that the [appellant] was on 28th March 1968 and remained a
member of Slaughtneil Republican Club. 8. No evidence was given that the
[appellant] or the club was at any time a threat to peace law and order but it
was conceded by witnesses for the [respondent] in cross-examination that insofar
as the police were aware there was nothing seditious in its pursuits or those of its
members. 9. The [respondent] claimed that on the court's finding of fact the
F [appellant] was entitled to be convicted of the offence with which he was charged.
   10. The [appellant] disputed this on the following grounds: that the statutory
rules and orders of 1922 and 1967 respectively were ultra vires; that the terms
of the statutory rule and order of 1967 were so wide that it was unreasonable,
bad for uncertainty and duplicity, ambiguous and unenforceable in law, and
that it was not a law for the peace, order and good government of Northern
G Ireland and that it was not necessary for and did not make provision for the
preservation of the peace and maintenance of order; that the criterion in banning
an organisation was not the name of the organisation but its purpose and the
activities of its members in furthering that purpose; that this club was a lawful
organisation and did not constitute a threat to the preservation of peace or to the
maintenance of order and as such could not be banned under the Civil Authorities
H (Special Powers) Acts (Northern Ireland) 1922-1943.
   11. Bearing in mind the contents and purposes of the Act, that the regulations
thereunder are " Regulations for Peace and Order in Northern Ireland ", and
noting the words " or any like organisation howsoever described " in the statutory
rule and order of 1967 and that no definition of the term " Republican Club " was
shown to the magistrates, they came to the conclusion that the only reasonable
I interpretation and the true meaning of the portion of para. 1 of the statutory

---

* The original complainant became the appellant in proceedings before the Court of
Appeal and the respondent before the House of Lords. Throughout the Case Stated
and the Court of Appeal judgments he is referred to as the [respondent].
   † The original defendant became the respondent in proceedings before the Court of
Appeal and the appellant to the House of Lords. Throughout the Case Stated and the
Court of Appeal judgments he is referred to as the [appellant].
   ‡ S.R. & O. 1922 No. 35.
   § S.R. & O. 1967 No. 42.

rule and order within the inverted commas in the context in which it had to be   A
considered was " The Organisations at the date of this Regulation or at any time
hereafter describing themselves as ' Republican Clubs '—being clubs which have
as their object the absorption of Northern Ireland in the Republic of Ireland
the activities of whose members in seeking to further that object constitute a
threat to peace and order in Northern Ireland—or any like organisation howsoever
described."   B

12. As a result of that conclusion the magistrates found that the [respondent]
had not proved that Slaughtneil Republican Club of which the [appellant] was a
member was ever an unlawful association within the meaning of the said reg. 24A.

13. Accordingly the magistrates dismissed the complaint and awarded 12
guineas costs to the [appellant].

The question for the determination of the Court of Appeal was whether the   C
magistrates' determination of the complaint was correct in law.

Court of Appeal (Northern Ireland)

M. W. Gibson, Q.C. and *R. T. Rowland, Q.C.*, for the [respondent] (1).
J. P. Higgins, Q.C. and *H. P. Kennedy*, for the [appellant] (2).

Cur. adv. vult.

29th November.   The following judgments were read.   D

LORD MACDERMOTT, C.J.:   On 1st June 1968, the [respondent]
caused a summons to be issued against the [appellant] charging him in these
words:

"... you, the [appellant] were and remained a member of an unlawful
association, namely, a Republican Club, contrary to Regulation 24A of the   E
Regulations made under the Civil Authorities (Special Powers) Acts (Northern
Ireland) 1922-1943."

The Civil Authorities (Special Powers) Act (Northern Ireland) 1922 (hereinafter
referred to as the " Act " or the " Act of 1922 ") was enacted shortly after the
establishment of the State of Northern Ireland, and at a time of considerable
unrest and disturbance, for the purpose of providing special powers for preserving   F
the peace and maintaining order.   Section 1 (1) of this Act provides as follows:

" (1) The civil authority shall have power, in respect of persons, matters
and things within the jurisdiction of the Government of Northern Ireland,
to take all such steps and issue all such orders as may be necessary for
preserving the peace and maintaining order, according to and in the execution of this Act and the regulations contained in the Schedule thereto, or   G
such regulations as may be made in accordance with the provisions of this
Act (which regulations, whether contained in the said Schedule or made as
aforesaid, are in this Act referred to as ' the regulations '):   Provided that
the ordinary course of law and avocations of life and the enjoyment of
property shall be interfered with as little as may be permitted by the
exigencies of the steps required to be taken under this Act."   H

Subsection (2) of the same section provides that the civil authority for the purposes
of the Act shall be the Minister of Home Affairs; and sub-s. (3) enacts that:

" The Minister of Home Affairs shall have power to make regulations—
(a) for making further provision for the preservation of the peace and
maintenance of order, and   I
(b) for varying or revoking any provision of the regulations;
and any regulations made as aforesaid shall, subject to the provisions of
this Act, have effect and be enforced in like manner as regulations contained
in the Schedule to this Act."

Section 2 provides for offences against the regulations and s. 3 provides for the
trial of such offences by a court of summary jurisdiction consisting of two or

---

(1) See footnote * on p. 1041, ante.   (2) See footnote † on p. 1041, ante.

A more resident magistrates and requires that the prosecution must be by an officer or person authorised by the Attorney-General and in accordance with such directions as he may give. These procedural requirements appear to have been duly observed in the present case and no question arises with respect to them.

On 22nd May 1922, the then Minister of Home Affairs made a further regulation under the powers conferred by s. 1 (3) of the Act. This was reg. 24A. It reads:

B " Any person who becomes or remains a member of an unlawful association or who does any act with a view to promoting or calculated to promote the objects of an unlawful association or seditious conspiracy shall be guilty of an offence against these Regulations. If any person without lawful authority or excuse has in his possession any document relating to or pur-

C porting to relate to the affairs of any such association or emanating or purporting to emanate from an officer of any such association or addressed to the person as an officer or member of any such association or indicating that he is an officer or member of any such association that person shall be guilty of an offence against these Regulations unless he proves that he did not know or had no reason to suspect that the document was of any such character as aforesaid or that he is not an officer or member of the association.

D Where a person is charged with having in his possession any such document, and the document was found on premises in his occupation, or under his control, or in which he is found or has resided, the document shall be presumed to have been in his possession unless the contrary is proved.

" The following organisations shall for the purposes of this Regulation be deemed to be unlawful associations:

E The Irish Republican Brotherhood
The Irish Republican Army
The Irish Volunteers
The Cumann Na m'Ban
The Fianna Na h'Eireann."

F The organisations thus named were specific, existing organisations of a militant type and it was conceded before us that they were in fact unlawful associations.

On 7th March 1967, the present Minister of Home Affairs, purporting to act under s. 1 (3) of the Act, made a further regulation by way of addition to the list of organisations deemed to be unlawful associations by reg. 24A. I shall call this further regulation " the regulation of 1967 ". It runs thus:

G " 1. Regulation 24A of the principal Regulations shall have effect as if the following organisations were added to the list of organisations which for the purpose of that Regulation are deemed to be unlawful associations:
' The organisations at the date of this regulation or at any time thereafter describing themselves as " Republican Clubs " or any like organisation howsoever described.' "

H The resident magistrates found that the [appellant] was on the date stated in the charge and thereafter a member of the Slaughtneil Republican Club. They also found that no evidence was given that he—

". . . or the said Club was at any time a threat to peace law and order but it was conceded by witnesses for the [respondent] in cross examination that

I in so far as the police were aware there was nothing seditious in its pursuits or those of its members."

The magistrates dismissed the complaint with costs and it is from that decision that the [respondent] now appeals by way of Case Stated. In so deciding, the magistrates first considered the true interpretation of the words added by the regulation of 1967 to the list of organisations at the end of reg. 24A and held that these words meant—

" The organisations at the date of this regulation or at any time hereafter

describing themselves as ' Republican Clubs '—being Clubs which have as A
their object the absorption of Northern Ireland in the Republic of Ireland
the activities of whose members in seeking to further that object constitute
a threat to peace and order in Northern Ireland—or any like organisation
howsoever described."

Having so concluded, the magistrates found that the [respondent] had not proved
that the Slaughtneil Republican Club, of which the [appellant] was a member, B
was ever an unlawful association within the meaning of reg. 24A and accordingly
dismissed the summons.

Now if the interpretation placed by the magistrates on the material words of
the regulation of 1967 was right, there can be no doubt that they were also right
in dismissing the complaint, for the evidence came nowhere near showing or even
suggesting that the Slaughtneil Republican Club was within the terms of reg. 24A C
as thus construed. In my opinion, however, this interpretation cannot be accepted.
It reads too much into the expression " Republican Clubs " and extends the
scope of that expression in a manner which is not justified by the context or the
expressed purpose of the regulations made under the Act. It is true that the words
" or any like organisation " are capable of being related to purposes or objects;
but this in itself does not seem to me to justify equating " Republican Clubs ", D
on the strength of their name alone, to organisations whose activities in support of
objects constitute a threat to law and order. Moreover, the gloss put on the
meaning of " Republican Clubs " by the magistrates must, I think, be rejected
for another reason. Were it sound the ultimate result would be, in effect, that the
prosecution would have to prove that the club in question was an unlawful
association; but that is just what the list of named bodies at the end of reg. 24A E
was intended to avoid. The convenience of that list, as appearing in the earlier
forms of reg. 24A, was that specific organisations which were notoriously unlawful
had not to be proved unlawful on the occasion of every prosecution. They were
deemed unlawful. It seems clear that the 1967 addition to the list was intended
to extend this " deeming " so that the unlawful nature of clubs called " Republican
Clubs " could be assumed without proof. If such was the intention, however, the F
interpretation favoured by the magistrates would defeat rather than further it,
for the unlawful nature of the club would have to be shown.

In the circumstances it was perhaps to be expected that counsel for the [res-
pondent] did not seek to support the construction adopted by the magistrates.
His contention throughout was that the offence charged was proved once it was
shown that the [appellant] was a member of a club describing itself as a " Repub- G
lican Club ". That is what the regulation said and that is what it meant, and
accordingly, the argument proceeded, no proof of unlawful objects or unlawful
activities was required. The [appellant's] club was deemed to be unlawful and
he had to be convicted because of its name. It was not for the court to review
the Minister's order or regard its effect. What he had done was not justiciable.

The answer to this was in its substance a plea of ultra vires. Counsel for the H
[appellant] did not, as I understood his submissions, contend that the Act of 1922
was ultra vires the Government of Ireland Act 1920, or that reg. 24A was, before
the addition of 1967, ultra vires the Act of 1922. His main submission was that
the regulation of 1967 was ultra vires the Act of 1922 and was invalid for that
reason. He also submitted that the regulation of 1967 was unreasonable and
oppressive and a bad exercise of the Minister's discretionary powers. These I
latter submissions seem in the present case to be but aspects of the main
submission, and it is to that submission that I now turn.

How far, if at all, the exercise of a statutory discretion vested in an executive
authority may be reviewed by the courts is a question which has for long raised
vexed issues. See, for example, among the more recent authorities, such cases as:
Associated Provincial Picture Houses, Ltd. v. *Wednesbury Corpn.* (3); *Liversidge*

(3) [1947] 2 All E.R. 680; [1948] 1 K.B. 223.

A v. *Anderson* (4); *Nakkuda Ali* v. *Jayaratne* (M.F. De S.) (5); *A.-G. for Canada* v. *Hallet & Carey, Ltd.* (6); *Comrs. of Customs & Excise* v. *Cure & Deeley, Ltd.* (7); *R.* v. *Governor of Brixton Prison, Ex p. Soblen* (8); and *Padfield* v. *Minister of Agriculture, Fisheries and Food* (9). And see also PROFESSOR DE SMITH'S JUDICIAL REVIEW OF ADMINISTRATIVE ACTION (2nd Edn., 1968), chapter 6.

I think it may be said that the courts will be slow to interfere with the exercise
B of a wide statutory discretion conferred in relation to emergency conditions; but much must depend in each instance on the terms of the relevant legislation and the purposes to which it is directed. None of the authorities, so far as I am aware, deals with a text which is quite like that of the Act of 1922. But the more one studies the language of that Act, the more it seems that s. 1 (3) thereof, which confers the power to make regulations, must be read together with the provisions
C of sub-s. (1) of the same section and as subject therefore to the words " as may be necessary for preserving the peace and maintaining order ", and also to the words of the proviso to that subsection which says that " the ordinary course of law and avocations of life . . . shall be interfered with as little as may be permitted by the exigencies of the steps required to be taken under this Act ". Subsection (1) contemplates the taking of steps and the issuing of orders under the Act and
D also under the regulations as therein defined. " Orders " is a wide word, but I shall assume that it does not include the making of regulations. I can see no reason, however, for saying that the word " steps " does not include the making of regulations under the Act, and so as to attract the words " necessary for preserving the peace and maintaining order " as well as the proviso. The making of a regulation authorised by the Act seems, on the ordinary meaning of the
E language used, to be a step taken " according to and in the execution of this Act ". To hold otherwise would, to say the least, be to create an anomalous situation for it would suggest that the legislature had intended to set up two standards —a strict standard for " all such steps " and " all such orders " and another less strict standard for the making of regulations, although those could be equally, if not more, sweeping and harsh in their impact. I cannot accept that as the
F intention of Parliament, and in reaching that conclusion I do not leave out of account the statutory purpose for making regulations which is described in sub-s. (3) (a) as being—" for making further provision for the preservation of the peace and maintenance of order ". That, surely, must echo what has gone before and mean what may be necessary for such purpose. And if, as I would hold, that is the position, I can find no ground for saying that the proviso to sub-s. (1) does not
G apply to the making of regulations; it is, after all, obviously intended as a safeguard against unnecessary interference, and as apt in relation to the making of regulations as to any other exercise of the powers conferred by s. 1.

I do not think, having regard to the objects of the Act of 1922, that every step taken by the Minister under s. 1 must, if challenged, be proved to be necessary for preserving the peace and maintaining order, and to fall within the proviso.
H These requirements or guide lines are there to be heeded, but that does not mean that the Minister has no discretion as to what is necessary or as to how far he may go within the terms of the proviso. I cannot see how his responsibilities under the Act could be effectively discharged if he had to vouch and justify every bona fide step he took under s. 1 as a preliminary to having that step enforced by the courts. To grant that, however, is far from saying that, even with the best intentions, he
I can do as he likes. As LORD RADCLIFFE said in *A.-G. for Canada* v. *Hallet & Carey, Ltd.* (10):

" . . . here the words that invest the Governor with power are neither vague nor ambiguous: Parliament has chosen to say explicitly that he shall do

(4) [1941] 3 All E.R. 338; [1942] A.C. 206.   (5) [1951] A.C. 66.
(6) [1952] A.C. 427.   (7) [1961] 3 All E.R. 641; [1962] 1 Q.B. 340.
(8) [1962] 3 All E.R. 641; [1963] 2 Q.B. 243.
(9) [1968] 1 All E.R. 694; [1968] A.C. 997.
(10) [1952] A.C. at p. 450.

whatever things he may deem necessary or advisable. That does not allow   A
him to do whatever he may feel inclined, for what he does must be capable of
being related to one of the prescribed purposes, and the court is entitled to
read the Act in this way."

In my opinion, then, the Minister had a discretion, but not an absolute discretion
under the Act of 1922. Whether what he did in enacting the regulation of 1967
is justiciable, therefore, depends on the nature of his action and the terms of s. 1   B
of the Act. In my view the regulation of 1967 is far too vague and wide to come
within even the extensive powers of s. 1. In the absence of anything to show the
contrary, it cannot be regarded as a step necessary or even likely to preserve the
peace or maintain law and order. It is not, to use the words of LORD RADCLIFFE
(10), " capable of being related to " these prescribed purposes. An association
may call itself a republican club without exhibiting any evidence that its objects   C
or activities are in any sense seditious or otherwise unlawful. That is not to say
that the name chosen for an association by its members could not amount to an
indication that its objects or activities were unlawful. To call a club " The
Freedom Through Violence Club ", for instance, would be asking for trouble.
But even in Ireland the word " Republican " need not connote anything unconstitutional or contrary to law. If this regulation is good where must the   D
Minister stop? Will " Irish Clubs " or " Ulster Clubs " or " Green Clubs " or
" Orange Clubs " or " Gaelic Clubs " or " Friends of the Republic " or " Friends
of the North " or " Catholic Clubs " or " Protestant Clubs " all have to be deemed
unlawful associations if similar regulations are made regarding such titles?
Counsel for the [respondent] had to concede that if the Minister thought fit he
could in the exercise of his discretion make any club with any name in effect an   E
unlawful association. I do not think that width of power lies within the Act of
1922. It is too sweeping and too remote on any rational view.

The conclusion just expressed gains further support from the rest of the regulation of 1967 which in my opinion cannot be severed and must stand or fall as a
whole. One could at least understand the making of this regulation if it only
applied to existing " Republican Clubs " and those were known to be seditious or   F
otherwise unlawful associations. But it goes beyond the present to brand future
" Republican Clubs " whose objects and activities may turn out to be entirely
respectable and entirely lawful. And that is not all. The regulation proceeds to
include " any like organisation however described." Construing the regulation
as I think it ought to be construed those words make it even more vague and take
it even further out of the scope and meaning of the Act.   G

As I have indicated already, the [respondent] did not seek to put forward
any evidence which might reconcile this regulation of 1967 with the purposes
of the Act. In the absence of such material I am of opinion and hold that for the
reasons mentioned it falls outside the category of what is capable of being regarded
as necessary for the preservation of the peace and the maintenance of order, and
outside the proviso to s. 1 (1) as well. I would therefore hold it beyond the powers   H
of the Act of 1922 and invalid.

The question posed for our consideration is—" Was our determination of the
complaint correct in law? " I would answer that question in the affirmative for
the reasons I have given above and not for those on which the magistrates acted.
I am therefore of opinion that the appeal should be dismissed.

I

McVEIGH, L.J.: This matter comes before us by way of Case Stated in
respect of an adjudication by magistrates sitting in Magherafelt at a court of
summary jurisdiction constituted in accordance with the provisions of the Civil
Authorities (Special Powers) Act (Northern Ireland) 1922.

The complaint in the Case was against one John McEldowney that he on a date
named was and remained a member of an unlawful association, namely, a republican club, contrary to reg. 24A of the regulations made under the Civil Authorities
(Special Powers) Acts (Northern Ireland) 1922-43. The court was informed that

A   the club came into existence at the beginning of 1967 and before the regulation was made. The learned magistrates dismissed the complaint. The regulation in respect of which the summons was brought and which came under attack in this proceeding was reg. 24A, as added to by the regulation of 1967.

    [HIS LORDSHIP then read the relevant parts of reg. 24A (see p. 1043, letters B to F, ante) and continued:] It was not suggested by the defence that this regulation

B   was ultra vires but it was pointed out that the organisations there named were military organisations set up for the purpose of overthrowing Northern Ireland.

    The addition made to this in 1967 is the matter round which all the argument flowed. [HIS LORDSHIP then read the relevant part of the regulation of 1967 (see p. 1043, letter G, ante) and continued:] Now it has to be remembered at the outset that the Civil Authorities (Special Powers) Act (Northern Ireland) 1922

C   which, according to the preamble, was " an Act to empower certain authorities of the Government of Northern Ireland to take steps for preserving the peace and maintaining order in Northern Ireland and for purposes connected therewith", contained as a Schedule to it 35 regulations for peace and order in Northern Ireland. These regulations are referred to in s. 1 (1) of the Act. [HIS LORDSHIP then read s. 1 (1) (see p. 1042, letters G and H, ante) and continued:] It can be

D   seen that this subsection refers not only to the regulations already enacted as part of the Act but also to those which may be made in accordance with the regulation-making power contained in a later subsection, namely sub-s. (3). [HIS LORDSHIP then read s. 1 (3) (see p. 1042, letter I, ante), and continued:] Such regulations will be as the phrase goes " for making further provision for the preservation of the peace and maintenance of order . . ."—that is to say " further " to the

E   regulations contained in the Act.

    Further provisions by way of regulations were made and I have already referred to those relevant to the present proceedings. It is to be noted that these were made by clearly invoking the power to make regulations contained in sub-s. (3) and not by any other power supposed or inferred under sub-s. (1). Indeed, it seems to me that sub-s. (1) recognises that the power to make further regulations

F   resides not in sub-s. (1) but in a later part of the Act, viz., sub-s. (3) of s. 1, and I have been unable to construe the Act in such a way as to hold that the regulation-making power which is found and, in my view, is completely found in sub-s. (3) is in some way limited by anything that is contained in sub-s. (1).

    The words which are pointed to and relied on as restricting the power in sub-s. (3) are the words which give the civil authority power " to take all such steps

G   and issue all such orders as may be necessary for preserving the peace and main-taining order". The contention for the [appellant] based on this provision was that the words, " as may be necessary for preserving the peace and maintaining order . . .", limited the powers of the civil authority to make regulations. It was argued that regulations are not valid unless it is proved that they are made for the preservation of peace and good order. It was contended that the word " neces-

H   sary " limits the power to be exercised within the confines of that word and, so the argument went, there is no power to make regulations unless it is shown that they are " necessary " for preserving the peace and maintaining order. This was not a power, so it was argued, which was entrusted to the civil authority and it was pointed out that there were no introductory words to the power such as " If the Minister thinks . . ." or " the Minister has cause to believe ". Therefore,

I   it was submitted that the regulation in this case was not valid unless it was proved that it was in fact for the preservation of peace and the maintenance of order.

    The question which arises here for determination is whether the words in s. 1 (1) place any limit on the power to make regulations contained in s. 1 (3). I propose now to examine the meaning of the words in question and I will address myself to the question whether the words " take all such steps and issue all such orders " include the making of regulations under sub-s. (3). I would point out first of all that those words are inapt and quite inappropriate, in the legal sense, to confer a power to make regulations. There is, however, a more substantial point, namely

that the true meaning of the subsection is that the words in question refer to taking   A
such steps and issuing such orders as are permissible under either the Act, or the
regulations contained in the Schedule or any regulations which may be made
under sub-s. (3). In my opinion that is all that the Act is saying.

Indeed, when one looks at the regulations in the Schedule to the Act one finds
a number under which it is necessary for the civil authority to issue orders for the
purpose of making those regulations effective; one can refer, for example, to reg. 1,   B
reg. 2, reg. 3, reg. 5, reg. 7 and reg. 14. The orders which are issued under those
regulations do not, like the regulations, have to be laid before both Houses of
Parliament. Regulations and orders are not synonymous words and, in my view,
were not intended to be. The regulations are in the nature of an enactment requiring a high degree of formality for their creation, see s. 1 (4). Orders are not in
this category and are issued pursuant to powers contained in the regulations.   C

Furthermore, s. 2 (1) makes a failure to comply with an order issued in pursuance of the regulations an offence against the regulations and so by this means
brings such a failure within the ambit of s. 4 which deals with the punishment for
offences against the regulations. Had it not been for the provisions of s. 2 (1)
it may well have been that failure to comply with an order issued pursuant to
the regulations would not have been an offence against the regulations and would   D
not have been punishable under s. 4. It must also be noted that the regulations
which are relevant in this case all purport to be made under s. 1 (3) and by
invoking the power therein contained and no other power. Accordingly, it is
my view that the words " take all such steps and issue all such orders " do not
give power to make regulations and have no bearing on the power to make
regulations contained in sub-s. (3).   E

Do the words " as may be necessary " carry the matter any further? In my
opinion they do not. I have already held that sub-s. (1) does not contain anything
bearing on the power to make regulations and the introduction of the words
" as may be necessary " does not modify that conclusion. I take the whole phrase
I have been considering in sub-s. (1) to mean no more than that the civil authority
is given power to take all such steps as may need to be taken and issue all such   F
orders as may need to be given for preserving the peace and maintaining order
according to and in the execution of the Act, the regulations in the Schedule or
such regulations as may be made in accordance with the provisions of the Act.

Having regard to the conclusions which are set out above, I am of the opinion
and would hold that one cannot incorporate the words " as may be necessary
for preserving peace and maintaining order " into the power to make regulations   G
to be found in s. 1 (3), and I cannot therefore hold on that ground that the court
must declare that the regulation challenged in this case is ultra vires the Act and
invalid unless it first be proved to the satisfaction of the court that it was necessary for preserving the peace and maintaining order. I should perhaps notice
here that the recital to the regulation of 1967 contains the words " it is expedient
that . . ." Subsection (3) does not contain any reference to expediency and the   H
use of this word does not in my view lay down any objective test which assists
the [appellant]. It does not mean the same thing as " necessary ".

Now a further question arises whether the regulation having been made under
the power conferred solely by the words in s. 1 (3) is challengeable in the courts.
It is contended by the [respondent] that the Act has legitimately conferred powers
on the Minister which are in the widest possible terms, and once he purports to act   I
under those powers then the regulation is not challengeable in the courts. It was
submitted that where the Minister has the power under the Act of 1922 to make
the regulation and recites that he acts under the power then it is not necessary for
him to establish that the regulation was intra vires the Act. I should perhaps
say here that it was not contended for the [appellant] that the Act of 1922 was
ultra vires the Government of Ireland Act 1920. The [appellant] however, contends that the regulation is justiciable in that it is so oppressive, unreasonable and
inconsistent in its effect that it must be said that Parliament never authorised

A it. This raises once again the difficult and oft-debated question when and in what circumstances the power of executive authorities to make regulations can be reviewed by the courts. In most cases the answer to this question depends on the construction of the Act in question and the authorities show that the courts have been slow to interfere with the exercise of wide powers to make regulations. This emerges clearly from the speech of LORD RADCLIFFE in *A.-G. for Canada* v.

B *Hallet & Carey, Ltd.* (11).

It is contended here that it is not for the courts to enquire whether as a matter of fact or policy the regulation was reasonable or proper. Now in this case the power to make regulations under s. 1 (3) is a wide one and is not limited by any phrase which would on the face of it or by implication, enable a court to intervene and examine whether, in the view of the court, the regulation was made for

C preserving and maintaining peace and order. It is relevant to repeat here words to be found in *Riel* v. *R.* (12):

"The words of the statute are apt to authorize the utmost discretion of enactment for the attainment of the objects pointed to."

In the present case the Minister has in making the impugned regulation declared

D that it is expedient that further provision for the preservation of the peace and maintenance of order should be made and has invoked his power under s. 1 (3). If the court were in these circumstances to embark on an enquiry whether, in the court's view, the impugned regulation was really enacted for preserving peace and order, and whether it was necessary or expedient for those purposes and perhaps whether it was likely to achieve these purposes by a regulation of this nature then, in my view, in the words of LORD RADCLIFFE (13), this would be—

E "an attempt by the court to take over into its own hands the functions which have been entrusted by Parliament to the Governor in Council [in this case the Minister of Home Affairs]. This is, in their Lordships' view, an inadmissible proceeding."

Three possible exceptions to this rule are suggested by LORD RADCLIFFE: (a) where

F powers entrusted for one purpose are deliberately used with the design of achieving another itself unauthorised or actually forbidden. If bad faith of that kind can be established, a court of law may intervene; (b) where the instrument itself is impugned as being itself ambiguous; (c) where the regulation shows on its face a misconstruction of the enabling Act, or a failure to comply with any conditions which the Act has prescribed for the exercise of its powers.

G As to (a), it is not, in my view, possible to establish this ground in the present case. In this connection one can again refer to LORD RADCLIFFE'S judgment (14) where he said—

"the true question is whether it can be said that the Governor in Council could not have deemed it necessary to take this step as a means incidental to the realization of the purposes stated in this order."

H In asking a similar question in the present case I do not see how a court could say that the Minister could not have taken the view that he did, whatever views the court itself might form. I would add here a passage from the judgment of LORD GREENE, M.R., in *Carltona, Ltd.* v. *Comrs. of Works* (15), where he said:

"It has been decided as clearly as anything can be decided that, where a

I regulation of this kind commits to an executive authority the decision of what is necessary or expedient and that authority makes the decision, it is not competent to the courts to investigate the grounds or the reasonableness of the decision in the absence of an allegation of bad faith. If it were not so it would mean that the courts would be made responsible for carrying on the executive government of this country on these important matters."

---

(11) [1952] A.C. 427 at pp. 445, et seq.   (12) (1885), 10 App. Cas. 675 at p. 678.
(13) [1952] A.C. at p. 444.   (14) [1952] A.C. at p. 445.
(15) [1943] 2 All E.R. 560 at p. 564.

The important matters there referred to were in respect of requisitioning powers **A** under the Defence (General) Regulations 1939 (16). Later LORD GREENE, M.R., said (17):

" All that the court can do is to see that the power which it is claimed to exercise is one which falls within the four corners of the powers given by the legislature and to see that those powers are exercised in good faith. Apart from that, the courts have no power at all to inquire into the reasonableness, **B** the policy, the sense, or any other aspect of the transaction."

It does not seem to me that this in any way conflicts with the judgment of LORD RADCLIFFE in *A.-G. for Canada* v. *Hallet & Carey, Ltd.* where (18) he says that what is done in exercising powers of this nature must be capable of being related to one of the prescribed purposes. I think that what he says there must be read in connection with what is stated earlier (19) where, after reviewing the form and **C** effect of the order, he said:

" How, then, can a court of law decide that the vesting was for another and extraneous purpose or hold that what the Governor in Council has declared to be necessary is not in fact necessary for the purposes he has stated."

As to (b), the terms of the regulation are neither vague nor ambiguous in **D** expressing that it is expedient to exercise the power and in stating what power is being invoked. Nor can it be said that it cannot be referable to a republican club which was in existence before the regulation was made.

As to (c), having regard to the conclusions I have expressed earlier as to the construction of the Act of 1922 no misconstruction arises here, nor is there any failure to comply with any conditions precedent to the exercise of the power. **E**

Before I finish with this matter I must refer to the proviso to s. 1 (1). The exercise of special powers and the taking of steps under any emergency enactments are inevitably accompanied by deliberate and consistent interference with private rights whether of person or property or both. The regulations under the Act in the present case are no exception to this and the proviso recognises that this kind of thing will happen under the special powers regulations. This proviso **F** is attached to s. 1 (1) and I do not read it as circumscribing the power to make regulations contained in sub-s. (3). It may be that in an appropriate case it may be called in aid in respect of the enforcement of the various provisions of the Act and the regulations, but I would not attempt to be any more precise about this matter.

To bring this matter to a conclusion I now have to deal with the question asked **G** in the Case Stated. Before doing so I wish to make it clear that I do not propose to take this judgment any further in present circumstances than to determine the narrow question with which we are faced in this case which deals with a republican club which was in existence when the regulation was made. Other considerations may arise in regard to clubs not in existence at the time the regulation was made and also in respect of what is called " any like organisation ". **H**

The question we are asked is: Was our determination of the complaint correct in law? I would answer this in the negative and remit the case to the magistrates to do as to justice may appertain.

CURRAN, L.J.: The validity of the Civil Authorities (Special Powers) Act (Northern Ireland) 1922, is not in question. The Schedule to the Act contained " Regulations for Peace and Order in Northern Ireland ". Regulation 24 (1) **I** provided that:

" Any person who does any act with a view to promoting or calculated to promote the objects of an unlawful association within the meaning of Section 7 of the Criminal Law and Procedure (Ireland) Act 1887, shall be guilty of an offence against these Regulations."

(16) S.R. & O. 1939 No. 927.   (17) [1943] 2 All E.R. at p. 564.
(18) [1952] A.C. at p. 450.   (19) [1952] A.C. at p. 444.

A To ascertain what is meant by " an unlawful association within the meaning of Section 7 " of the Act of 1887 it is necessary to read the relevant provisions of both s. 6 and s. 7 of that Act. They are as follows:

" DANGEROUS ASSOCIATIONS—ARMS.

" 6. If the Lord Lieutenant is satisfied that any association—

B (a) formed for the commission of crimes; or

(b) carrying on operations for or by the commission of crimes; or

(c) encouraging or aiding persons to commit crimes; or

(d) promoting or inciting to acts of violence or intimidation; or

(e) interfereing with the administration of the law or disturbing the main- tenance of law and order,

C exists in any part of Ireland, the Lord Lieutenant, by and with the advice of the Privy Council, may from time to time by proclamation declare to be dangerous any such association or associations named or described in such proclamation . . .

" 7. From and after the date of such special proclamation and as long as the same continues unrevoked or unexpired, the Lord Lieutenant in Council may from time to time, by order . . . prohibit or suppress in any district speci-
D fied in the order any association named or described in such special proclama- tion, or any association which appears to the Lord Lieutenant to be a danger- ous association, and to have been, after the date of such special proclamation, formed or first employed for any of the purposes of any association named or described in such special proclamation. From and after the date of such order, and during the continuance thereof, every assembly or meeting of such
E association, or of the members of it as such members, in the specified district, shall be an unlawful assembly, and the association itself shall be an unlawful association . . ."

Thus it appears that it was intended by Parliament, when it passed the Act of 1922, that it would be for the appropriate authority to decide whether an associa-
F tion should be deemed unlawful. In the present case that authority is the Minister of Home Affairs.

Regulation 24 was revoked by S.R. & O. 1949 No. 147, but in my view such revocation did not affect the underlying intention of Parliament to which I have referred [HIS LORDSHIP then read s. 1 (3) of the Act of 1922 (see p. 1042, letter I, ante), the relevant parts of reg. 24A (see p. 1043, letters B to F, ante) and the rele-
G vant parts of the regulation of 1967 (see p. 1043, letter G, ante), and continued:] In the present case, it is found as a fact, as appears from para. 7 of the Case Stated, that the [appellant] was a member of an organisation describing itself as " Slaughtneil Republican Club ". That description brings the organisation within the regulation of 1967 and, accordingly, if the regulation is intra vires and enforceable, the organisation is deemed to be an unlawful association.

H If I am right in the view I have already expressed, that it is for the Minister to decide whether a particular association should be deemed to be unlawful, what right has the court to question what the Minister has done? It is contended on behalf of the [appellant] that such a regulation must be " necessary for preserving the peace and maintaining order " and that such necessity must be established by the [respondent] when the regulation is challenged. This argument, in my view,
I is not well founded. It is based on the provisions of s. 1 (1) of the Act of 1922. When these provisions are examined it appears to be reasonably clear that they do not relate to the making of regulations, but to enforcing them. [HIS LORDSHIP then read s. 1 (1) (see p. 1042, letters G and H, ante) and continued:] In any event, in my view, it is for the Minister, not the court, to decide what steps or orders are necessary.

It is s. 1 (3) (b), as I have already pointed out, that empowers the Minister to vary or revoke regulations, and no condition precedent nor any other restriction is expressly imposed on the exercise of such powers. Regulations made under

s. 1 (3) (*a*) must be, of course, for the preservation of the peace and maintenance
of order. I repeat, however that, in my view, it is for the Minister of Home
Affairs, not the court, to decide whether it is expedient for these purposes that
an association should be deemed to be an unlawful association, and that there
is no onus on the [respondent] to establish that a regulation made under s. 1 (3)
is necessary for the preservation of the peace and the maintenance of order, or
that an organisation describing itself as a republican club is, apart from the
regulation, unlawful.

If an organisation does not describe itself as a republican club, and it is sought
to bring it within reg. 24A, as a " like organisation ", an issue may have to be
determined by the court as to how it is to be established that such a club is a
" like organisation ". In the regulation of 1967 it is recited:

" And whereas it is expedient that further provision for the preservation
of the peace and maintenance of order should be made."

I read this as a statement by the Minister that he is satisfied, for the stated
reasons, that, inter alia, organisations describing themselves as republican clubs
should, for the purposes of reg. 24A, be deemed to be unlawful associations.

It is not for the court to take over into its own hands the functions entrusted by
Parliament to a Minister of the Crown. The view that such a proceeding is inadmissible was expressed in the judgment of the Privy Council, delivered by LORD
RADCLIFFE, in *A.-G. for Canada* v. *Hallet & Carey, Ltd.* (20). Later, in that case,
this question is posed (20):

" How, then, can a court of law . . . hold that what the Governor in Council
has declared to be necessary is not in fact necessary for the purposes he has
stated? . . ."

I would pose the question in the present case, " How then can a court of law hold
that what the Minister of Home Affairs has declared to be expedient is not in fact
expedient for the purposes he has stated? "

There follows (21) another passage which I think is relevant to the present
case:

" This is an order which not only recites that the Governor in Council
regards the making of it as necessary for authorized purposes, but which in
terms invokes the powers conferred on him by the Act of 1945. An order so
expressed leaves no ground for a judicial inquiry whether the Governor can
have intended to exercise those powers, a kind of inquiry which a court has
sometimes found itself called on to make in a case where the instrument
impugned is itself ambiguous . . . In the circumstances prevailing here their
Lordships are satisfied that the true answer to any invitation to the court
to investigate the Order in Council on its merits or to ascribe to it a purpose
other than that which it professes to serve is given in the words of DUFF,
C.J., in the *Reference Re Chemical Regulations* (22): ' I cannot agree that it is
competent to any court to canvass the considerations which have, or may
have, led him to deem such regulations necessary or advisable for the transcen-
dent objects set forth . . . The words are too plain for dispute: the measures
authorized are such as the Governor General in Council (not the courts)
deems necessary or advisable '."

Later he said (23):

" For here the words that invest the Governor with power are neither
vague nor ambiguous: Parliament has chosen to say explicitly that he shall
do whatever things he may deem necessary or advisable. That does not allow
him to do whatever he may feel inclined, for what he does must be capable of
being related to one of the prescribed purposes, and the court is entitled to

(20) [1952] A.C. at p. 444.
(22) [1943] S.C.R. 1 at p. 13.
              (21) [1952] A.C. at p. 445.
              (23) [1952] A.C. at p. 450.

A   read the Act in this way. But then, expropriation is altogether capable of
     being so related."

     Applying to the present case what I have just quoted from the judgment of the
     Privy Council, it is my view that the relevant question is: " Is a regulation
     deeming specified organisations to be unlawful associations capable of being
     related to the preservation of the peace or the maintenance of order? "
B   The answer is undoubtedly " Yes ". There is no dispute about this. It is con-
     ceded that the original reg. 24A cannot be challenged, although it deems to be
     unlawful associations a number of specified organisations. The regulation with
     which we are concerned in the present case merely adds further organisations
     to those already specified in reg. 24A. Coming back to the judgment of the Privy
     Council (24):
C
         " Certainly there is no rule of construction that general words are in-
     capable of interfering with private rights and that such rights can only be
     trenched upon where express power is given to do so. The general words of
     the Defence of the Realm (Consolidation) Act, 1914, of the United Kingdom
     were adequate to authorize the internment, without trial, of Mr. Zadig
D   (R. v. Halliday (25)). The general words of the War Measures Act were
     adequate to authorize the conscription of Mr. Gray for military service (Re
     Gray (26)); or to authorize the deportation of British subjects and depriva-
     tion of their citizenship, without trial (Co-operative Committee on Japanese
     Canadians v. A.-G. for Canada (27))."

     In this connection it has to be noted that the following proviso appears in s. 1 (1)
E   of the Act of 1922:

         " Provided that the ordinary course of law and avocations of life and
     the enjoyment of property shall be interfered with as little as may be per-
     mitted by the exigencies of the steps required to be taken under this Act."

     This proviso relates to the power given to the Minister of Home Affairs under
     s. 1 (1) of the Act of 1922 to take all such steps and issue all such orders as may be
F   necessary for preserving the peace and maintaining order, according to and in the
     execution of the Act and the regulations contained in the Schedule thereto or thereafter
     made in accordance with the provisions of the Act. It does not impose any condition
     or restriction on the Minister's power to make regulations under s. 1 (3) of the
     Act, though no doubt he would not be unmindful of the considerations referred
     to in the proviso when exercising his powers under s. 1 (3).
G
         For the reasons I have given, and in the light of the principles enunciated by the
     Privy Council in A.-G. for Canada v. Hallet & Carey, Ltd. (28), I would allow the
     appeal and answer the question posed in the Case Stated in the negative.

     House of Lords.

         J. P. Higgins, Q.C., and H. P. Kennedy (both of the bar of Northern Ireland)
H   for the appellant.
         The Attorney-General for Northern Ireland (Basil Kelly, Q.C.), R. T. Rowland,
     Q.C., and J. A. Creaney (all of the bar of Northern Ireland) for the respondent.

     Their Lordships took time for consideration.

     18th June.   The following opinions were delivered.

I   LORD HODSON: My Lords, the question for determination on this appeal
     is whether the resident magistrates sitting as a magistrates' court for the petty
     sessions district of Maghera on 12th June 1968 were right in law in dismissing
     a complaint against the appellant. He was charged in these words:

         ". . . you, the [appellant] were and remained a member of an unlawful
     association, namely, a Republican Club, contrary to Regulation 24A of the

---

(24) [1952] A.C. at p. 451.   (25) [1917] A.C. 260.
(26) (1918), 57 S.C.R. 150.   (27) [1947] A.C. 87.
                          (28) [1952] A.C. 427.

Regulations (29) made under the Civil Authorities (Special Powers) Acts   **A**
(Northern Ireland) 1922-1943."

The Act of 1922, which I will call " the Act ", was enacted, as the title shows,
to empower certain authorities of the government of Northern Ireland to take
steps for preserving the peace and maintaining order in Northern Ireland and
for purposes connected therewith.   Section 1 provides:

        B
" (1) The civil authority shall have power, in respect of persons, matters
and things within the jurisdiction of the Government of Northern Ireland,
to take all such steps and issue all such orders as may be necessary for
preserving the peace and maintaining order, according to and in the
execution of this Act and the regulations contained in the Schedule thereto,
or such regulations as may be made in accordance with the provisions of
this Act (which regulations, whether contained in the said Schedule or made   **C**
as aforesaid, are in this Act referred to as ' the regulations '): Provided
that the ordinary course of law and avocations of life and the enjoyment
of property shall be interfered with as little as may be permitted by the
exigencies of the steps required to be taken under this Act.

" (2) For the purposes of this Act the civil authority shall be the Minister
of Home Affairs for Northern Ireland, but that Minister may delegate,   **D**
either unconditionally or subject to such conditions as he thinks fit, all
or any of his powers under this Act to any officer of police, and any such
officer of police shall, to the extent of such delegation, be the civil authority
as respects any part of Northern Ireland specified in such delegation.

" (3) The Minister of Home Affairs shall have power to make regulations—
    " (a) for making further provision for the preservation of the peace and   **E**
maintenance of order, and
    " (b) for varying or revoking any provision of the regulations;
and any regulations made as aforesaid shall, subject to the provisions of
this Act, have effect and be enforced in like manner as regulations contained
in the Schedule to this Act.

" (4) All regulations made as aforesaid shall be laid before both Houses   **F**
of Parliament as soon as may be after they are made, and, if an address is
presented to the Lord Lieutenant by either House within the next fourteen
days on which such House shall be sitting after any such regulation is laid
before it praying that the regulation may be annulled, the Lord Lieutenant
may annul that regulation and it shall thenceforth be void, without prejudice
to the validity of anything done thereunder, or to the power of making a   **G**
new regulation; and regulations made as aforesaid shall not be deemed to
be statutory rules within the meaning of section one of the Rules Publication
Act, 1893."

Section 2 deals with offences against the regulations.   Section 3 provides for
trial of such offences by a court of summary jurisdiction and requires that the   **H**
prosecution must be by an officer or person authorised by the Attorney-General.
No question arises as to these procedural requirements in this case.

On 22nd May 1922 the then Minister of Home Affairs made a further regulation
under the powers conferred by s. 1 (3) of the Act.   This was reg. 24A
which provides:

" Any person who becomes or remains a member of an unlawful associa-   **I**
tion or who does any act with a view to promoting or calculated to promote
the objects of an unlawful association or seditious conspiracy shall be guilty
of an offence against these Regulations.   If any person without lawful
authority or excuse has in his possession any document relating to or purporting to relate to the affairs of any such association or emanating or purporting to emanate from an officer of any such association or addressed to
the person as an officer or member of any such association or indicating that

(29) S.R. & O. 1922 No. 35.

A he is an officer or member of any such association that person shall be guilty of an offence against these Regulations unless he proves that he did not know or had no reason to suspect that the document was of any such character as aforesaid or that he is not an officer or member of the association. Where a person is charged with having in his possession any such document, and the document was found on premises in his occupation, or under his

B control, or in which he is found or has resided, the document shall be presumed to have been in his possession unless the contrary is proved.

" The following organisations shall for the purposes of this Regulation be deemed to be unlawful associations:—

The Irish Republican Brotherhood

The Irish Republican Army

C The Irish Volunteers

The Cumann Na m'Ban

The Fianna Na h'Eireann."

These named organisations were specific existing organisations of a militant type and it was conceded before your Lordships, as it was before the Court of Appeal in Northern Ireland, that they were in fact unlawful organisations.

D On 7th March 1967 the present Minister of Home Affairs purporting to act under s. 1 (3) of the Act made a further regulation (30) by way of addition to the list of organisations deemed to be unlawful associations. This, which is the impugned regulation, recites that it is expedient that further provision for the preservation of the peace and maintenance of order should be made, and provides:

E " 1. Regulation 24A of the principal Regulations shall have effect as if the following organisations were added to the list of organisations which for the purpose of that Regulation are deemed to be unlawful associations:

' The organisations at the date of this regulation or at any time thereafter describing themselves as " Republican Clubs " or any like organisation howsoever described.' "

F The appellant was found by the magistrates to have been on the date stated in the charge and thereafter a member of the Slaughtneil Republican Club. They also found that no evidence was given that he—

". . . or the said Club was at any time a threat to peace law and order but it was conceded by witnesses for the [respondent] in cross-examination that in so far as the Police were aware there was nothing seditious in its pursuits

G or those of its members."

In dismissing the complaint the magistrates bore in mind the contents and purposes of the Act, that the regulations thereunder are " Regulations for Peace and Order in Northern Ireland " and, noting the words " or any like organisation howsoever described " in the statutory rule and order of 1967 and that no definition of the term " Republican Club " was shown to them, came to

H the conclusion that the only reasonable interpretation to be given to the words " organisations . . . describing themselves as ' Republican Clubs ' " is—

". . . Clubs which have as their object the absorption of Northern Ireland in the Republic of Ireland the activities of whose members in seeking to further that object constitute a threat to peace and order in Northern

I Ireland—or any like organisation howsoever described."

The magistrates accordingly found that the respondent had not proved that the Slaughtneil Republican Club was an unlawful association within the meaning of reg. 24A and dismissed the complaint.

The Court of Appeal in Northern Ireland by a majority allowed the appeal and the question posed in the Case Stated was answered in the negative. The case was accordingly remitted to the magistrates to do as to justice may appertain.

(30) S.R. & O. 1967 No. 42.

The appellant obtained leave to appeal to this House but in argument has not   **A**
sought to sustain the opinion expressed by the magistrates or the reasons given
by them for their decision in his favour.

As LORD MACDERMOTT, C.J., pointed out in his dissenting judgment their
reasoning is unsound, for the ultimate result would be in effect that the prosecution would have to prove that the club in question was an unlawful association
but that is just what the list of named bodies at the end of reg. 24A was intended   **B**
to avoid. The convenience of the list is that specific organisations notoriously
unlawful had not to be proved unlawful on the occasion of every prosecution.
They were deemed unlawful and the 1967 addition to the list was intended to
extend this " deeming " so that the unlawful nature of " Clubs " could be assumed
without proof. The interpretation favoured by the magistrates would, as LORD
MACDERMOTT, C.J., pointed out, tend to defeat rather than to favour such an   **C**
intention for the unlawful nature of the club would have to be shown.

The arguments directed to the Court of Appeal and to your Lordships have
been directed solely to the question whether or not the impugned regulation is
ultra vires the Act. The majority of the Court of Appeal held that it was for
the Minister to decide whether a particular association should be deemed to be
unlawful and the court could not question what he had done. LORD MACDERMOTT,   **D**
C.J., on the other hand, held that the regulation of 1967 was far too vague and
wide to come within even the extensive powers conferred by s. 1 of the Act.
It was not, to apply the language contained in the judgment of the Privy
Council in *A.-G. for Canada* v. *Hallet & Carey, Ltd.* (31) " capable of being
related to one of the prescribed purposes ". LORD MACDERMOTT, C.J., attached
importance to the use of the words " any like organisation howsoever described "   **E**
as making the regulation even more vague than it would otherwise be and taking
it even further out of the scope and meaning of the Act.

The question may be put in this way—Is the whole regulation too vague and
so arbitrary as to be wholly unreasonable as if, to take an example from one
of the cases, a person were to be proscribed because he had red hair; or is the
regulation, as the majority of the court held, a legitimate and valid exercise of   **F**
the Minister's power confirmed on him by statute?

Both sides referred to and relied on the judgment of the Privy Council in
A.-G. for Canada v. *Hallet & Carey, Ltd.* (32). By s. 2 (1) (c) of the National
Emergency Transitional Powers Act 1945 (33) the Governor in Council was
authorised to do such things and to make such orders and regulations as he
might, by reason of the continued emergency arising out of the war against   **G**
Germany and Japan, deem necessary or advisable for the purpose of, inter alia—

> ". . . maintaining, controlling and regulating supplies and services, prices,
> transportation, use and occupation of property, rentals, employment, salaries
> and wages to ensure economic stability and an orderly transition to conditions
> of peace . . ."

  H

Under the powers conferred by that Act the Governor in Council passed an
Order in Council (34) which provided that oats and barley in commercial positions
in Canada, with certain exceptions, should be vested in the Canadian Wheat
Board. The order was successfully challenged in Manitoba and in the Supreme
Court of Canada (35) but was upheld by the Privy Council on the ground
that although the Act of 1945 made no specific reference to appropriation yet   **I**
the wide language of s. 2 (1) ending with the words " as he may . . . deem necessary or advisable " gave the amplest possible discretion in the choice of methods.
The expression " as he may deem necessary " or like words are often found in
statutes in which a discretionary power is given to a Minister or other authority.
(Compare *Padfield* v. *Minister of Agriculture, Fisheries and Food* (36) where a

---

(31) [1952] A.C. 427 at p. 450.   (32) [1952] A.C. 427.
(33) 1945 (Canada) c. 60.   (34) P.C. 1292.   (35) See [1951] S.C.R. 81.
        (36) [1968] 1 All E.R. 694; [1968] A.C. 997.

A discretion was considered which was conferred on a Minister to act as he thought fit and it was held by this House that the discretion was not wholly unfettered in that it had to be used to promote the policy and objects of the Act in question.) Other examples could be given.

In this case no words directing the Minister to act as he thinks fit or similar words are employed. He is given power to make further provision for the preserva-

B tion of the peace and the maintenance of order which are to be enforced in like manner as regulations contained in the Schedule to "this Act". "Unlawful associations" were referred to in reg. 24 (1) of the regulations for peace and order in Northern Ireland contained in the Schedule to the Act. These regulations in the Schedule form part of the Act and regulations made under s. 1 (3) have to be laid before both Houses of Parliament and are liable to be annulled on

C address presented by either House of Parliament.

It is not contended that for that reason the impugned regulation cannot be assailed in the courts. A similar situation arose in R. v. Halliday (37) where a statutory regulation was impugned as ultra vires. The House upheld the regulation as being within the scope of the power given to the Minister by the statute on the ground that the regulation was intra vires the Act there being, as here,

D no deeming provision. I do not find that the absence of a deeming provision in this Act assists the argument one way or the other.

There was a difference of opinion in the Court of Appeal as to the effect of the words which are contained in s. 1 (1) of the Act giving the civil authority power to take all such steps and issue all such orders as may be necessary for preserving peace and maintaining order according to and in the execution of the

E Act and the regulations contained in the Schedule or such regulations as may be made in accordance with the provisions of this Act. These words are followed by a proviso that the ordinary course of law and avocations of life and the enjoyment of property should be interfered with as little as may be permitted by the exigencies of the steps required to be taken under this Act. I cannot, however, accept the argument that regulations made under sub-s. (3) are invalid unless

F it is proved that they are made for the preservation of peace and good order or that the word "necessary" limits the power to be exercised within the confines of that word.

In my view s. 1 (1) is directed to the enforcement of regulations not to the making of them. As was pointed out in the Court of Appeal there are a number of regulations in the Schedule to the Act under which the civil authority must

G issue orders to make the regulations effective. These orders do not, like regulations, have to be laid before both Houses of Parliament. The regulations are in the nature of enactments requiring a high degree of formality whereas orders are not in this category and are issued pursuant to powers contained in the regulations.

I agree with the majority of the Court of Appeal that the Act in sub-s. (1)

H is saying no more than that the words in question refer simply to taking such steps and issuing such orders as are permissible under either the Act or regulations including not only those contained in the Schedule but also any which may be made under sub-s. (3). I observe that Lord MacDermott, C.J., although taking a different view of the proper construction of s. 1 of the Act and regarding the earlier provisions as giving assistance in the way of guide lines, did not

I accept the argument that every step taken by the Minister, although he thought taking steps included making regulations, must, if challenged, be proved to be necessary for preserving the peace and maintaining order.

In my opinion there is a distinction between the powers given by s. 1 (1) and those given by sub-s. (3) of the same section, in that the former are executive and the latter legislative powers. The Minister is not restricted by the language relating to his executive powers when executing his legislative powers though no

(37) [1917] A.C. 260.

doubt he will not be unmindful of the language of Parliament in the whole Act. A

The vexed question remains whether the impugned regulation is capable of being related to the prescribed purpose, that is to say, the preservation of the peace and the maintenance of order. The authorities show that where, as here, there is no question of bad faith the courts will be slow to interfere with the exercise of wide powers to make regulations. There is, on the face of the impugned regulation, no apparent misconstruction of the enabling Act or failure to comply B with any conditions prescribed by the Act for the exercise of its powers.

The proscription of present and future " Republican Clubs " including " any like organisations howsoever described " is said to be something outside the scope and meaning of the Act and so incapable of being related to the prescribed purposes of the Act. Accepting that the word " Republican " is an innocent word and need not connote anything contrary to law, I cannot escape the con- C clusion that in its context, added to the list of admittedly unlawful organisations of a militant type, the word " Republican " is capable of fitting the description of a club which in the opinion of the Minister should be proscribed as a subversive organisation of a type akin to those previously named in the list of admittedly unlawful organisations. The context in which the word is used shows the type of club which the Minister had in mind and there is no doubt that the mischief D aimed at is an association which has subversive objects. On this matter, in my opinion, the court should not substitute its judgment for that of the Minister, on the ground that the banning of " Republican Clubs " is too remote. I agree that the use of the words " any like organisation howsoever described " lends some support to the contention that the regulation is vague and for that reason invalid but on consideration I do not accept the argument based on vagueness. E It is not difficult to see why the Minister, in order to avoid subterfuge, was not anxious to restrict himself to the description " Republican " seeing that there might be similar clubs which he might seek to proscribe whatever they called themselves. If and when any case based on the words " any like organisation " arises it will have to be decided but I do not, by reason of the use of those words, condemn the regulation as being too vague or uncertain to be supported. I F would dismiss the appeal.

LORD GUEST: My Lords, the appellant was charged in the magistrates' court at Magherafelt, Northern Ireland with being a member of an unlawful organisation, namely a republican club, contrary to reg. 24A of the regulations made under the Civil Authorities (Special Powers) Acts (Northern Ireland) G 1922-43. The complaint was dismissed and the respondent appealed to the Court of Appeal (Northern Ireland) by way of Stated Case. The result was that the Court of Appeal, by a majority (LORD MACDERMOTT, C.J., dissenting), allowed the appeal and remitted to the magistrates.

Regulation 24A was made under s. 1 (3) of the Civil Authorities (Special Powers) Act (Northern Ireland) 1922. This section is in the following terms: H

" (1) The civil authority shall have power, in respect of persons, matters and things within the jurisdiction of the Government of Northern Ireland, to take all such steps and issue all such orders as may be necessary for pre- serving the peace and maintaining order, according to and in the execution of this Act and the regulations contained in the Schedule thereto, or such regulations as may be made in accordance with the provisions of this Act I (which regulations, whether contained in the said Schedule or made as aforesaid, are in this Act referred to as ' the regulations '):

" Provided that the ordinary course of law and avocations of life and the enjoyment of property shall be interfered with as little as may be permitted by the exigencies of the steps required to be taken under this Act.

" (2) For the purposes of this Act the civil authority shall be the Minister of Home Affairs for Northern Ireland, but that Minister may delegate, either unconditionally or subject to such conditions as he thinks fit, all or any of

A   his powers under this Act to any officer of police, and any such officer of police shall, to the extent of such delegation, be the civil authority as respects any part of Northern Ireland specified in such delegation.

      " (3) The Minister of Home Affairs shall have power to make regulations—

          " (*a*) for making further provision for the preservation of the peace and maintenance of order, and

B   " (*b*) for varying or revoking any provision of the regulations;

and any regulations made as aforesaid shall, subject to the provisions of this Act, have effect and be enforced in like manner as regulations contained in the Schedule to this Act.

      " (4) All regulations made as aforesaid shall be laid before both Houses of Parliament as soon as may be after they are made, and, if an address is

C   presented to the Lord Lieutenant by either House within the next fourteen days on which such House shall be sitting after any such regulation is laid before it praying that the regulation may be annulled, the Lord Lieutenant may annul that regulation and it shall thenceforth be void, without prejudice to the validity of anything done thereunder, or to the power of making a new regulation; and regulations made as aforesaid shall not be deemed to be

D   statutory rules within the meaning of section one of the Rules Publication Act, 1893."

The Schedule to the Act contains a number of regulations made under s. 1. Regulation 24 provided that any person who does an act with a view to promoting the objects of an unlawful association within the meaning of s. 7 of the Criminal Law and Procedure (Ireland) Act 1887 is to be guilty of an offence.

E   On 22nd May 1922, reg. 24A was added by the Minister acting under s. 1 (3) of the Act of 1922 which empowers him to make regulations for making further provision for the preservation of peace and the maintenance of order. This regulation provides as follows:

      " Any person who becomes or remains a member of an unlawful association or who does any act with a view to promoting or calculated to promote the

F   objects of an unlawful association or seditious conspiracy shall be guilty of an offence against these Regulations."

It was also provided:

      " The following organisations shall for the purposes of this Regulation be deemed to be unlawful associations:—

G   The Irish Republican Brotherhood

       The Irish Republican Army

       The Irish Volunteers

       The Cumann Na m'Ban

       The Fianna Na h'Eireann."

H   Later regulations made in 1931, 1933 and 1936 respectively added to the list of organisations deemed to be unlawful for the purposes of reg. 24A the following: " Saor Eire, The National Guard, Cumann Poblachta Na h'Eireann ". The latter name means " Group of the Republic of Eire ".

     Regulation 24 was, together with a number of other regulations, revoked in 1949, presumably on the ground that these stringent powers were no longer thought to be necessary, but reg. 24A still remained. On 7th March 1967, reg. 24A

I   was amended by adding to the list of organisations deemed to be unlawful the following:

      " The organisations at the date of this regulation or at any time thereafter describing themselves as ' Republican Clubs ' or any like organisation howsoever described."

The Case Stated by the magistrates that the appellant was on 28th March 1968 and still is a member of Slaughtneil Republican Club. It was further stated that there was no evidence that the appellant or the club were at any time a threat to

peace, law and order. There was nothing seditious in its pursuits or those of its A
members. The resident magistrates expressed their conclusion in this form:

"Bearing in mind the contents and purposes of 'the Act' that the
Regulations thereunder are 'Regulations for Peace and Order in Northern
Ireland' and noting the words 'or any like organisation howsoever described' in the said Statutory Rule and Order of 1967 and that no definition
of the term 'Republican Club' was shown to us, we came to the conclusion   B
that the only reasonable interpretation and the true meaning of the portion
of paragraph 1 of the said Statutory Rule and Order within the inverted
commas in the context in which it has to be considered is 'The Organisations
at the date of this Regulation or at any time hereafter describing themselves
as "Republican Clubs"—being Clubs which have as their object the
absorption of Northern Ireland in the Republic of Ireland the activities of   C
whose members in seeking to further that object constitute a threat to
peace and order in Northern Ireland—or any like organisation howsoever
described'."

They accordingly dismissed the complaint.

Counsel for appellant did not seek to uphold this ground of acquittal before   D
your Lordships. His argument was that the 1967 amendment to reg. 24A was
ultra vires of the powers contained in s. 1 (3) of the Act of 1922. He prefaced
his argument by suggesting that the regulation purported to cover three types
of organisation: (i) existing organisations calling themselves "Republican
Clubs "; (ii) any organisation which might in the future call itself a "Republican
Club "; and (iii) "like organisations howsoever described".   E

He also submitted that the terms of s. 1 (1) along with the proviso were
incorporated in s. 1 (3) and that in accordance with s. 1 (1) the regulation, to
be valid, must be shown to be necessary for preserving the peace and maintaining
order, and that it must also comply with the proviso to s. 1 (1). In my view
this is not a correct interpretation of s. 1. Section 1 (1) and s. 1 (3) are dealing
with different matters; sub-s. (1) deals with executive steps and orders and   F
sub-s. (3) is dealing with legislative acts. Subsection (3) must, in my view, be
construed quite independently of sub-s. (1). In this regard I find myself, with
respect, in disagreement with LORD MACDERMOTT, C.J.

Counsel for the appellant argued that it was for the prosecution to show that
the regulation was intra vires of the Act and that as there was no evidence that
a republican club so called was a threat to peace and order in Northern Ireland the   G
amending reg. 24A was ultra vires. In my view this is not the true position. There
is no doubt that it is open to the courts to hold that a regulation made under
a statute is ultra vires of the empowering Act. Such an argument was advanced
in R. v. Halliday (38) but unsuccessfully. The contention for the subject in
that case was that although the regulation came, on a certain construction of
the Act, within the powers, the Act must be construed in a way so as to limit   H
the ambit of the regulation. Since that case I have been unable to discover
any case in which a regulation made under an Act of Parliament in the form
of a statutory instrument has ever been challenged. Your Lordships were
certainly not referred to any such case. There are a multitude of statutes in
which powers are given to Ministers by order to make regulations and indeed
in some cases to alter the terms of the statute by regulation. In the absence of   I
any such challenges of the validity of regulations made in virtue of statutory
power it must be plain that the task of a subject who endeavours to challenge
the validity of such a regulation is a heavy one.

There are in the authorities indications of the principle on which a court
construes the validity of such regulations. For example in Minister of Health v.
Regem, Ex p. Yaffe (39), LORD THANKERTON said:

---

(38) [1917] A.C. 260.
(39) [1931] A.C. 494 at pp. 532, 533; [1931] All E.R. Rep. 343 at p. 348.

A   " In this case, as in similar cases that have come before the Courts,
Parliament has delegated its legislative function to a Minister of the Crown,
but in this case Parliament has retained no specific control over the exercise
of the function by the Minister, such as a condition that the order should
be laid before Parliament and might be annulled by a resolution of either
House within a limited period. In my opinion the true principle of construc-
B   tion of such delegation by Parliament of its legislative function is that it
only confers a limited power on the Minister, and that, unless Parliament
expressly excludes the jurisdiction of the Court, the Court has the right and
duty to decide whether the Minister has acted within the limits of his
delegated power . . . Where, however, the power delegated to the Minister
is a discretionary power, the exercise of that power within the limits of the
C   discretion will not be open to challenge in a Court of law."

In such a case as this the discretion entrusted to the Minister to make regulations
for the preservation of peace and the maintenance of order in Northern Ireland
is a very wide power and his discretion will not lightly be interfered with. The
court will only interfere if the Minister is shown to have gone outside the four
corners of the Act or has acted in bad faith (see Lord Greene, M.R., in *Carltona,
D   Ltd.* v. *Comrs. of Works* (40)). Lord Radcliffe in *A.-G. for Canada* v. *Hallet
& Carey, Ltd.* (41), said that the executive act to be valid must be "capable of
being related to the prescribed purposes " of the empowering Act.

Approaching the present regulations with these principles in view I turn to
the argument for the appellant which was that as there was no evidence that
there was anything sinister about the word " Republican " which could be a
E   threat to peace and order the regulation was ultra vires. My answer to that
argument is that I do not know what significance the word " Republican " has
in Northern Ireland. It may well be that it will bear a different construction
in Northern Ireland from what it might bear in another context. These, however,
are matters for the Minister. It is important to observe that the inclusion of
republican clubs eo nomine is an additional category to a list of organisations in
F   reg. 24A all of which, according to Lord MacDermott, C.J., were notoriously of
a militant type and were unlawful organisations. Three of these organisations
bear the name " Republican ". No challenge was made of the validity of reg. 24A
as originally made which was admittedly intra vires. In these circumstances I
am not able to say that a Minister acting in good faith—as it is conceded he did—
under s. 1 (3) of the Act was exceeding his powers in adding to the category of
G   organisations deemed to be unlawful organisations described as " Republican
Clubs ". In my view, in the words of Lord Greene, M.R. (42), the regulation
was " within the four corners of the " Act or, in the words of Lord Radcliffe (43)
was " capable of being related to " the powers conferred by the Act. In these
circumstances the court cannot, in my view, interfere with the exercise of the
Minister's discretion.

H   There is a long line of authorities dealing with executive orders made by
Ministers under powers conferred on them by the Defence (General) Regulations
1939 (44) of which *Carltona, Ltd.* v. *Comrs. of Works* (40) and *Point of Ayr
Collieries, Ltd.* v. *Lloyd-George* (45) are only examples. In the latter case the
Minister was given power under the Defence (General) Regulations 1939—

I   " If it appeared [to him] that in the interests of the public safety, the
defence of the realm or the efficient prosecution of the war . . . it is necessary
to take control . . ."

of property. It was held that there was no jurisdiction to interfere with the
exercise of an executive power within his delegated authority.
The present case, as I have already stated, is not a case of an executive order

(40) [1943] 2 All E.R. 560.   (41) [1952] A.C. 427 at p. 450.
(42) [1943] 2 All E.R. at p. 564.   (43) [1952] A.C. at p. 450.
(44) S.R. & O. 1939 No. 927.   (45) [1943] 2 All E.R. 546.

made by a Minister under a regulation, but the challenge of a regulation made A
by a Minister under an Act of Parliament conferring power on him to make
regulations for certain specified purposes, the regulation to be laid before Parliament under s. 1 (4). The fact that in the cases above referred to there was a provision in the regulations to the effect that if it appeared to the Minister to be
necessary for the specified purposes does not, in my view, distinguish these cases
from the present. In the regulation in question the expediency is stated in the B
regulation and in the absence of any charge of bad faith expediency is presumed
provided that the exercise of the power is capable of being related to the
specified purposes.

The final argument for the appellant related to the third category of organisations which it is said the regulation covered, namely " or any like organisation
howsoever described ". It was submitted that this would cover any club what- C
ever its name and whatever its objects and that such an exercise of the Minister's
power was unreasonable, arbitrary and capricious. In my view this argument
is not well founded. The regulation first of all embraces republican clubs
eo nomine and they are caught by their very description. If they do not bear
the name " Republican ", it would be a question of interpretation after evidence
whether any particular club was covered by the words " any like organisation D
howsoever described ". It is indeed not necessary for the purposes of this case
where the organisation bore the name " Republican Club " to examine this
question in any great detail. But my provisional view is that the regulation
would cover any organisation having similar objects to those of a republican
club or of any of the named organisations or of any organisation whose objects
included the absorption of Northern Ireland in the Republic of Ireland. E

Having regard to all these matters I cannot say that the class of " like
organisations " is either ambiguous or arbitrary so as to invalidate the regulation.
In my view this ground of attack also fails.

I agree with the majority of the Court of Appeal in holding that the regulation
was not ultra vires. I would therefore dismiss the appeal.
F
LORD PEARCE: My Lords, the Civil Authorities (Special Powers) Act
(Northern Ireland) 1922 was passed at a time of unrest and disturbance. Its
object was to empower certain authorities of the government of Northern Ireland
to take steps for preserving the peace and maintaining order. It laid down
certain stringent regulations in its schedule. By s. 1 (1) the Minister of Home
Affairs was given power—
G
"... to take all such steps and issue all such orders as may be necessary
for preserving the peace and maintaining order, according to and in the
execution of this Act and the regulations. ..."

or such further regulations as might be made in accordance with the Act. There
was a proviso that the ordinary course of law and avocations of life and the
enjoyment of property should be interfered with as little as might be permitted H
by the exigencies of the steps required to be taken under the Act. The section
also gave the Minister power to make regulations for making further provision
for the preservation of the peace and maintenance of order and for varying or
revoking any provision of the regulations in the Schedule. The regulation here
in question purported to be made in 1967 under that power. Was it within
that power or was it ultra vires? I
Before considering the content of the regulation of 1967, it is convenient to
see what was the extent of the Minister's power. He was not in express terms
given a subjective discretion or indeed any discretion at all. But clearly some
discretion was intended. Its extent must be determined by the context in which
it is given. It was a discretion to carry out the purposes of the Act which gave
it. In *Julius* v. *Lord Bishop of Oxford* (46), LORD SELBORNE said:

---

(46) (1880), 5 App. Cas. 214 at p. 235; [1874-80] All E.R. Rep. 43 at p. 54,

A " The question whether a Judge, or a public officer, to whom a power is given by such words, is bound to use it upon any particular occasion, or in any particular manner, must be solved *aliunde*, and, in general, it is to be solved from the context, from the particular provisions, or from the general scope and objects, of the enactment conferring the power."

B That case was dealing with a somewhat different point, namely whether when a power was given there was a duty to use that power in proper circumstances. But it is an example of the principle that when Parliament gives a power without any indications of its extent, one must read the limitations from the context. It is a power given to carry out the purposes of the Act and any discretion given is limited to those purposes. Even where such wide words are used as " may make such regulations as he may think fit ", the subjective power is limited to

C such things as the general context of the statute shows to be its objectives. It cannot be suggested that he can make any regulations that he likes, regardless of the intentions to be derived from the statute conferring the power. A fortiori is this so when no subjective licence is given; for it certainly should not be implied.

When one is seeking to define the extent of this power from its context and the objects of the Act, one cannot divorce sub-s. (3) from the rest of the section

D and derive from such severance a justification for regarding sub-s. (3) in vacuo. The section as a whole clearly shows that Parliament was intending the stringent powers under the Act to be used only in respect of such steps and orders as may be *necessary* for preserving the peace and maintaining order.   And a proviso was deliberately inserted that—

E ". . . the ordinary course of law and avocations of life and the enjoyment of property *shall* be interfered with as little as may be permitted by the exigencies of the steps required . . ."

There is thus manifested a clear intention by Parliament to limit the scope of the restrictive measures to such as were made essential by the demands of the crisis and any power to make regulations must be similarly limited.

F I can find no reality in the argument that whereas Parliament was thus carefully and somewhat apprehensively restricting any repressive *steps* and *orders* to the minimum demanded by the crisis, it was giving a free rein to the making of *repressive* regulations. Such a refinement could not, I feel sure, have occurred to any of the members of Parliament who voted for the Act.

The convention by which our courts construe statutes in order to find the

G so-called " intention of Parliament " compels one to disregard the fact that this was an Act passed by members of Parliament. It subjects the words of a statute to critical analysis and construction with all the expertise of legal professional experience. Our courts also (unlike the courts of some other countries) disregard the debate which preceded the passing of the Act and any assurances that may have been given to the members by their law officers.

H This somewhat artificial convention makes it all the more important to avoid refinements of construction which may be attractive to the expertise of the skilled lawyer but could never conceivably have occurred to a member of Parliament when he read an apparently comprehensible statute. In my opinion the normal ordinary meaning which this statute would bear is that the Minister, whether making orders or regulations or enforcing the statute, must confine himself to

I that which any crisis made necessary, and which caused the minimum disruption of the citizen's rights. It is within that limited area that his discretion was confined.

Does the regulation of 1967 come within the power thus given? In my opinion it does not. I agree with the judgment of LORD MACDERMOTT, C.J. The magistrates construed the regulation of 1967 with glosses intended to make rough and ready sense of it. On principles akin to the maxims ejusdem generis and noscitur a sociis, they assumed that the clubs aimed at were those whose activities were subversive, like those whose names were already set out in the regulation.

Thus they concluded that it only affected clubs whose activities were unlawful. **A** but in that case the regulation of 1967 was pointless, since a club whose activities were unlawful was already dealt with under the previous regulations. LORD MACDERMOTT, C.J., therefore, rightly, I am inclined to think, rejected the justices' gloss on the regulation.

The original reg. 24 was aimed at subversive activities by unlawful associations. After the Act there was added by the Minister a valid reg. 24A which deemed **B** to be unlawful associations certain named militant organisations whose activities were well known to be subversive. That was within the Minister's discretion. Thus, in any prosecution their known unlawfulness need not be proved in evidence. By the regulation of 1967, however, there were added to the list of those deemed unlawful under reg. 24A—

" The organisations at the date of this regulation or at any time thereafter **C** describing themselves as the ' Republican Clubs ' or any like organisation howsoever described."

It was under this addition to the regulations that the appellant was prosecuted. It is admitted that the republican club to which he belonged was innocent of any unlawful activities. He can only, therefore, be guilty of an offence if the regulation makes the club unlawful howsoever innocent may be its activities. **D**

It is argued that it is for the Minister alone to decide how he should use his power and that the court should not interfere, however wrong it thinks that decision, unless there is some element of bad faith. But in my opinion the duty of surveillance entrusted to the courts for the protection of the citizen goes deeper than that. It cannot take the easy course of " passing by on the other side " when it seems clear to it that the Minister is using a power in a way which **E** Parliament, who gave him that power, did not intend. When there is doubt, of course the courts will not interfere. But if it seems clear on grounds of rationality and common sense that he was exceeding the power with which Parliament was intending to clothe him to further the purposes of the Act, the courts have a duty to interfere. The fact that this is not an easy line to draw is no reason why the courts should give up the task and abandon their duty to protect the citizen. **F**

I accept the observations of LORD MACDERMOTT, C.J., as to the regulation being " too sweeping and too remote on any rational view ". He said—

" It is not, to use the words of LORD RADCLIFFE (47), ' capable of being related to ' these prescribed purposes. An association may call itself a republican club without exhibiting any evidence that its objects or activities **G** are in any sense seditious or otherwise unlawful. That is not to say that the name chosen for an association by its members could not amount to an indication that its objects or activities were unlawful. To call a club ' The Freedom Through Violence Club ', for instance, would be asking for trouble. But even in Ireland the word ' Republican ' need not connote anything unconstitutional or contrary to law. If this regulation is good **H** where must the Minister stop? Will ' Irish Clubs ' or ' Ulster Clubs ' or ' Green Clubs ' or ' Orange Clubs ' or ' Gaelic Clubs ' or ' Friends of the Republic ' or ' Friends of the North ' or ' Catholic Clubs ' or ' Protestant Clubs ' all have to be deemed unlawful associations if similar regulations are made regarding such titles? Counsel for the [respondent] had to concede that if the Minister thought fit he could in the exercise of his discretion make **I** any club with any name in effect an unlawful association. I do not think that width of power lies within the Act of 1922."

Further, the regulation of 1967 is too vague and ambiguous. A man must not be put in peril on an ambiguity under the criminal law. When the regulation of 1967 was issued the citizen ought to have been able to know whether he could or could not remain a member of his club without being subject to a criminal

---

(47) In *A.-G. for Canada* v. *Hallet & Carey, Ltd.*, [1952] A.C. 427 at p. 450.

A prosecution. Yet I doubt if one could have said with certainty that any man or woman was safe in remaining a member of any club in Northern Ireland, however named or whatever its activities or objects.

Had the final phrase " or any like organisation howsoever described " been absent, the regulation would have simply been an attack on the description " Republican Club ", however innocent the club's activities. Presumably the

B justification for it would have to be that the mere existence of the word republican in the name of a club was so inflammatory that its suppression was " necessary for preserving the peace and maintaining order " and that the " exigencies " of the need for its suppression did not permit the citizen's right in that respect to prevail. For the reasons given by LORD MACDERMOTT, C.J., I do not accept that such a justification could suffice. But be that as it may, the final phrase

C shows that this is more than an attack on nomenclature, since the club is deemed equally unlawful if it is a like organisation whatever be the name under which it goes.

And what is the " likeness " to a republican club which makes an organisation unlawful " howsoever described "? Since a republican club is banned whatever may be its activities, the likeness cannot consist in its activities. And since the

D organisation is unlawful, howsoever described, the " likeness " cannot consist in a likeness of nomenclature. The only possibility left seems to be that the " likeness " may consist in the mere fact of being a club. In which case all clubs, however named, are unlawful—which is absurd.

One cannot disregard the final phrase, since that would wholly alter the meaning of the regulation. Without the final phrase it is simply an attack on nomenclature.

E But with the final phrase it cannot simply be an attack on nomenclature. One cannot sever the bad from the good by omitting a phrase when the omission must alter the meaning of the rest. One must take the whole sentence as it stands. And as it stands it is too vague and ambiguous to be valid.

I would therefore allow the appeal.

F   **LORD PEARSON:** My Lords, the question at issue in this appeal is whether the regulation dated 7th March 1967, purporting to have been made by the Minister of Home Affairs under s. 1 (3) of the Civil Authorities (Special Powers) Act (Northern Ireland) 1922, is within the powers conferred by that Act. The whole of s. 1 is relevant but it has already been set out and I will not repeat it.

G   The power to make regulations is conferred on the Minister by sub-s. (3) and not by sub-s. (1) of s. 1. The scheme of the section is that the provisions of the Act and the regulations, both those set out in the Schedule to the Act and those which may be made subsequently, constitute the authority under and in accordance with which orders may be made and steps may be taken under sub-s. (1). An examination of the language of the regulations set out in the Schedule shows

H clearly that " orders " are to be made and " steps " to be taken under the regulations. The orders and steps are executive or administrative acts. The making of regulations is part of the legislation and is not the making of an order or the taking of a step within the meaning of sub-s. (1). Accordingly, the limitations imposed on the making of orders and the taking of steps by the words " as may be necessary for preserving the peace and maintaining order " and by the

I proviso to sub-s. (1) do not apply to the making of regulations under sub-s. (3). It is clear that the regulations made by the Minister of Home Affairs under sub-s. (3) are legislative in character, because they may vary or revoke any provisions of the regulations and they are to have effect and be enforced in like manner as regulations contained in the Schedule. They are thus on the same plane as the initial legislation contained in the Act.

The directly relevant power under sub-s. (3) is " to make regulations . . . for making further provision for the preservation of the peace and maintenance of order ". That is not an unlimited power. It is a power to make regulations for

the specified purposes—the preservation of the peace and maintenance of order. **A**
If regulations purporting to be made under this power could be shown to have
been made otherwise than for the specified purposes, I think they could be held
to be ultra vires. I am dealing only with the construction of s. 1 (3) of the Act,
and consequently using the phrase " otherwise than for the specified purposes "
without further definition or elaboration.

I should add that, of course, the Act is to be construed as a whole, and con- **B**
sequently, when one is construing sub-s. (3) of s. 1, sub-s. (1) can be taken into
account. But, taking it into account, I do not find that it alters in any way the
natural meaning of sub-s. (3).

The Northern Ireland Parliament must have intended that somebody should
decide whether or not the making of some proposed regulation would be conducive to the " preservation of the peace and maintenance of order ". Obviously **C**
it must have been intended that the Minister of Home Affairs should decide that
question. Who else could? He might consult other Ministers before making
the decision, but it would be his decision. The courts cannot have been intended
to decide such a question, because they do not have the necessary information
and the decision is in the sphere of politics, which is not their sphere.

When the Minister has made a regulation, and purports to have made it under **D**
s. 1 (3) of the Act, the presumption of regularity (omnia praesumuntur rite esse
acta) applies and the regulation is assumed prima facie to be intra vires. But
if the validity of the regulation is challenged, and it is contended that the regulation was made otherwise than for the specified purposes, the courts will have to
decide this issue, however difficult the task may be for them in some
circumstances. **E**

The ways in which an instrument may be shown to be ultra vires have been
discussed in many cases, and I do not find it necessary to enter into such a
discussion in this case. I shall assume that the regulation might be shown
prima facie to be ultra vires (made otherwise than for the specified purposes)
either by internal evidence from the provisions of the regulation itself—e.g.,
if it purported to render all chess clubs unlawful—or by external evidence of **F**
the factual situation existing at the time when the regulation was made. To
see what the relevant internal evidence is, one has to begin with the original
reg. 24A made in 1922 soon after the enactment of the Act. The principal
provisions are as follows:

" Any person who becomes or remains a member of an unlawful association
or who does any act with a view to promoting or calculated to promote the **G**
objects of an unlawful association or seditious conspiracy shall be guilty
of an offence against these Regulations . . .

" The following organisations shall for the purposes of this Regulation be
deemed to be unlawful associations:—
The Irish Republican Brotherhood
The Irish Republican Army **H**
The Irish Volunteers
The Cumann Na m'Ban
The Fianna Na h'Eireann."

Later regulations made in 1931, 1933 and 1936 respectively added to the list
of organisations deemed for the purposes of reg. 24A to be unlawful associations **I**
the following: " Saor Eire, The National Guard, Cumann Poblachta Na
h'Eireann ". Counsel has stated that " Cumann Poblachta Na h'Eireann "
means " Group of the Republic of Eire ". It is conceded that the original reg.
24A and these supplementary regulations are valid.

Then the regulation with which this appeal is concerned was made in 1967
by the Minister of Home Affairs. One of its recitals was " And whereas
it is expedient that further provision for the preservation of the peace and
maintenance of order should be made ". The operative provision was—

A

"Regulation 24A of the principal Regulations shall have effect as if the following organisations were added to the list of organisations which for the purpose of that Regulation are deemed to be unlawful associations :

" ' The organisations at the date of this regulation or at any time thereafter describing themselves as " Republican Clubs " or any like organisation howsoever described.' "

B

That recital and those provisions do not to my mind afford any evidence that the regulation was made otherwise than for the specified purposes. The recital is evidence that it was made for those purposes. The deeming of republican clubs to be unlawful organisations is in line with the deeming of the Irish Republican Brotherhood, the Irish Republican Army and the Cumann Poblachta Na h'Eireann to be unlawful organisations. A republican club in Northern

C Ireland is presumably one whose members believe in a republican form of government, and wish to have such a form of government introduced into Northern Ireland, which would naturally be effected by Northern Ireland being severed from the United Kingdom and incorporated in the Irish Republic. Did such clubs in Northern Ireland at the time when the regulation was made have a tendency to become militant, causing disturbances and perhaps com-

D mitting acts of violence, or did they not? I could not answer that question, not having the relevant information. But presumably the Minister of Home Affairs in Northern Ireland did at that time have relevant information and on the basis of that information did form the opinion that the continued existence of those clubs would be a threat to the preservation of the peace and mainten-

E ance of order. In saying that, I am applying the presumption of regularity. At any rate there is not in the provisions of the regulation any evidence that it was made otherwise than for the specified purposes.

The external evidence is summarised in para. 8 of the Stated Case:

"8. No evidence was given that the [appellant] or the said Club was at any time a threat to peace law and order but it was conceded by witnesses

F for the [respondent] in cross examination that in so far as the Police were aware there was nothing seditious in its pursuits or those of its members."

This evidence relates only to one particular club, which had come into existence shortly before the date of the regulation, and it relates to a later date (in June 1968) and it only shows that the police did not know of anything seditious in the pursuits of this club or its members. It is relevant evidence which has to

G be taken into account, but it is far from sufficient to prove that the regulation made on 7th March 1967, was made otherwise than for the specified purposes.

There is one further argument against the validity of this regulation, and it is the most formidable one. It is that the regulation is too vague, because it includes the words " or any like organisation howsoever described ". I have

H had doubts on this point, but in the end I think the argument against the validity of the regulation ought not to prevail. The Minister's intention evidently was (if I may use a convenient short phrase) to ban republican clubs. He had to exclude in advance two subterfuges which might defeat his intention. First, an existing republican club might be dissolved, and a new one created. The words " or at any time thereafter " would exclude that subterfuge as well

I as applying to new republican clubs generally. Secondly a new club, having the characteristic object of a republican club, might be created with some other title as " New Constitution Group " or " Society for the alteration of the Constitution ". The words " or any like organisation howsoever described " would exclude that subterfuge.

In construing this regulation one has to bear in mind that it authorises very drastic interference with freedom of association, freedom of speech and in some circumstances the liberty of the subject. Therefore it should be narrowly interpreted. Also it should if possible be so construed as to have sufficient certainty

to be valid—ut res magis valeat quam pereat. In my opinion the proper con-   A
struction of the regulation is that the organisations to be deemed unlawful are—
(i) any organisation describing itself as a " Republican Club ", whatever its
actual objects may be; and (ii) any organisation which has the characteristic
object of a republican club—namely to introduce republican government into
Northern Ireland—whatever its name may be.

I would dismiss the appeal.   B

LORD DIPLOCK: My Lords, the question in this appeal is whether
the Civil Authorities (Special Powers) Acts (Amending) (No. 1) Regulations
(Northern Ireland) 1967, by which the Minister of Home Affairs for Northern
Ireland purported to add further provisions to reg. 24A of the regulations in
force under the Civil Authorities (Special Powers) Act (Northern Ireland) 1922,
fall within the description " regulations . . . for making further provision for   C
the preservation of the peace and maintenance of order " contained in s. 1 (3)
of that Act (which for brevity I shall call " the Special Powers Act "). If they
do, the Minister was empowered by that subsection to make the regulations
and this appeal must be dismissed. If they do not, the regulations are ultra
vires and void, the appeal must be allowed and the appellant acquitted.   D

The legislative powers of the Parliament of Northern Ireland, unlike those
of the Parliament of the United Kingdom, are limited by the Constitution of
Northern Ireland contained in the Government of Ireland Act 1920 as amended.
But it is not contended that the regulations challenged in the present appeal,
even if they bear the meaning for which the respondent contends, are ultra vires
the legislative powers of the Parliament of Northern Ireland. The sole question   E
is whether the making of these regulations is within the legislative powers
delegated to the Minister of Home Affairs by the Parliament of Northern
Ireland. This falls to be determined by the same principles as would apply to
an enactment in similar terms of the Parliament of the United Kingdom.

The division of functions between Parliament and the courts as respects
legislation is clear. Parliament makes laws and can delegate part of its power
to do so to some subordinate authority. The courts construe laws whether   F
made by Parliament directly or by a subordinate authority acting under
delegated legislative powers. The view of the courts whether particular statutory or subordinate legislation promotes or hinders the common weal is irrelevant.
The decision of the courts as to what the words used in the statutory or subordinate legislation mean is decisive. Where the validity of subordinate
legislation made pursuant to powers delegated by Act of Parliament to a sub-   G
ordinate authority is challenged, the court has a three-fold task: first to determine the meaning of the words used in the Act of Parliament itself to describe
the subordinate legislation which that authority is authorised to make, secondly
to determine the meaning of the subordinate legislation itself and finally to
decide whether the subordinate legislation complies with that description.

I turn then first to the words used in the Special Powers Act to describe the   H
subordinate legislation (therein called " regulations ") which the Minister of
Home Affairs was authorised to make by the Special Powers Act. The actual
delegation is to be found in s. 1 (3) but the words there used take their colour
from their context and must be construed in the light of the scheme disclosed
by the Act as a whole and in particular those parts of it which deal with
" regulations ".   I

Your Lordships' House is entitled to take judicial note of the fact that in
1922 when the Act was passed there was a state of civil insurrection in Northern
Ireland. The Act (i) created a whole series of criminal offences on the part of
private citizens made triable under s. 3 by a court of summary jurisdiction
consisting of two or more resident magistrates and punishable under s. 4 by
fine up to £100 or imprisonment up to two years; and (ii) empowered the civil
authority, defined in s. 1 (2) as the Minister of Home Affairs and any police
officer to whom he delegates his powers, to take various steps interfering with

A the personal liberty and the rights of property of citizens, subject in the case of interference with rights of property to the payment of compensation under s. 11.

The offences created and the powers conferred on the civil authority by the Act itself are set out not in the body of the Act but in the Schedule containing what are described as " Regulations for Peace and Order in Northern

B Ireland ". The reason for the use of this legislative technique becomes apparent from s. 1 of the Act. It was to enable the provisions of the Act which created offences or conferred powers to be added to, varied or revoked by the Minister of Home Affairs as the exigencies of the situation might require without the need to obtain any fresh Act of Parliament.

One further comment on the nature of the regulations contained in the

C Schedule is germane before turning to s. 1 of the Act. Some of the regulations which create offences are self-operating. They define acts and omissions which constitute offences in themselves without need for any further action by the civil authority. Other regulations, however, are only brought into effect by the making of an " order " by the civil authority the offence being non-compliance with such an " order ". An order made under regulations of this kind

D is in itself of the nature of subordinate legislation, but we are not concerned in this appeal with the validity of an order. Section 1 of the Act is in the following terms:

" (1) The civil authority shall have power, in respect of persons, matters and things within the jurisdiction of the Government of Northern Ireland, to take all such steps and issue all such orders as may be necessary for

E preserving the peace and maintaining order, according to and in the execution of this Act and the regulations contained in the Schedule thereto, or such regulations as may be made in accordance with the provisions of this Act (which regulations, whether contained in the said Schedule or made as aforesaid, are in this Act referred to as ' the regulations '): Provided that the ordinary course of law and avocations of life and the enjoyment of

F property shall be interfered with as little as may be permitted by the exigencies of the steps required to be taken under this Act.

" (2) . . .

" (3) The Minister of Home Affairs shall have power to make regulations—
    (a) for making further provision for the preservation of the peace and maintenance of order, and

G   (b) for varying or revoking any provision of the regulations;
and any regulations made as aforesaid shall, subject to the provisions of this Act, have effect and be enforced in like manner as regulations contained in the Schedule to this Act.

" (4) . . ."

H The power to make regulations conferred on the Minister by sub-s. (3) is exclusively legislative in character. Regulations made by him pursuant to the power thus delegated are to have effect as if they were contained in the Act of Parliament itself. The regulations challenged in the present appeal are purported to be made under the powers conferred in para. (a) of the subsection. To be valid they must comply with the description contained in that paragraph

I of the kind of regulation which the Minister is empowered to make.

The relevant characteristic of regulations to which that description refers is the effect to be achieved by them. To be valid their effect must be to promote the preservation of the peace and the maintenance of order. I use the expression " effect " rather than " purpose " for purpose connotes an intention formed by the maker of the regulation to achieve a particular object, and substitutes for the objective test of the effect which the regulation is in fact likely to achieve, the subjective test of what effect the Minister himself whether rightly or mistakenly believes that the regulation is likely to achieve. It is to be observed

that in contrast to the words of delegation of legislative powers used in modern   A
statutes the description in s. 1 (3) of the kind of regulations which the Minister
is empowered to make contains no reference to the Minister's own opinion as
to the necessity or expediency of the regulation for achieving the effect defined.
He is not empowered to make such further provision as he may think or deem
fit or necessary or expedient or advisable for the preservation of the peace or
the maintenance of order.   B

It was words of delegation of this latter kind which were under consideration
in the authorities relied on by the majority of the Court of Appeal. The relevant
characteristic of subordinate legislation so described in the words of delegation
is the belief of the person empowered to make it that it will achieve the effect
described. If he does so believe it is valid. It is only if he does not that it is
ultra vires and void. The relevant enquiry which the court has to make when   C
subordinate legislation made under words of delegation of this kind is challenged
is not whether his belief was justified but whether it existed. The absence of
such belief may connote mala fides on the part of the maker of the subordinate
legislation, i.e., that he has used the delegated power with the deliberate intention
of achieving an effect other than that described in the words of delegation but
it does not necessarily do so. He may have honestly misconstrued the words   D
of the statute describing the effect to be achieved and for this reason have
failed to form the relevant belief. These are two of the grounds referred to by
LORD RADCLIFFE in *A.-G. for Canada* v. *Hallet & Carey, Ltd.* (48), as invalidating
subordinate legislation made under words of delegation in which the belief of
the subordinate authority in the effect to be achieved by the subordinate legislation is expressly stated to be the characteristic of the legislation which he is   E
empowered to make. But in practice it is seldom possible to distinguish between
these two grounds. The subordinate authority is not normally compellable to
disclose his own mental processes and the court is powerless to declare the
subordinate legislation invalid unless, in the words of LORD RADCLIFFE (49) it
is not " capable of being related to one of the prescribed purposes " so that
its very terms give rise to the inference that the subordinate authority whether   F
deliberately or as a result of his misconstruing the statute cannot have formed
the relevant belief.

But where, as in the present case, the subordinate legislation which the
Minister is empowered to make is described in the statute by reference to the
effect to be achieved and not by reference to the Minister's own belief in the
effect which it will achieve, the relevant enquiry which the court has to make   G
if the subordinate legislation is challenged is not in my view the same. Omnia
praesumuntur rite esse acta and the onus lies on the party challenging the
subordinate legislation to establish its invalidity. The Minister's belief in its
necessity or expediency is cogent evidence of its validity but it is not conclusive and the ultimate decision whether or not the likelihood that it will
achieve the effect described in the statute is sufficient to bring it within the   H
words of delegation and whether or not it will have any effects which may be
prohibited by those words is one for the court itself to make on the facts proved
in evidence before it, or of such general public notoriety that the court may
take judicial notice of them without further proof. What degree of likelihood
is sufficient and to what extent the likely effect must be confined to that stated
in the description are questions for the court itself to determine by construing   I
the words of delegation in the light of the general object that the statute serves,
the gravity of the mischief at which the subordinate legislation is aimed and the
effect (if any) which it will have on otherwise lawful acts or property rights
of citizens which neither cause nor contribute to that mischief.

In *R.* v. *Halliday* (50) the words of delegation in the Defence of the Realm
(Consolidation) Act 1914 were in a form comparable to that employed in the

---

(48) [1952] A.C. 427 at pp. 444, 445.   (49) [1952] A.C. at p. 450.
(50) [1917] A.C. 260.

A Special Powers Act. Your Lordships' House by a majority upheld the challenged regulation, but did so by forming its own opinion based on matters of which it was entitled to take judicial notice that the regulation was reasonably likely to achieve the effect described in the words of delegation.

Section 1 (3) itself contains no reference to necessity or expediency. The only characteristic referred to in the description of the regulations which the
B Minister is empowered to make is that they will have the effect of promoting the peace and maintaining order, and regulations may do this although they strike also at conduct which in no way endangers the preservation of the peace or the maintenance of order. But sub-s. (1) does limit the power of the civil authority to take steps according to and in execution of the Act to such steps as may be necessary for preserving the peace and maintaining order and the
C proviso manifests the intention of Parliament that the ordinary liberties and rights of citizens should be interfered with as little as practicable consistent with the preservation of the peace and the maintenance of order. In the Court of Appeal there was a division of opinion whether the making by the Minister of a regulation under sub-s. (3) was the taking of a " step " within the meaning of sub-s. (1). I agree with the reasoning which led CURRAN and McVEIGH, L.JJ.,
D to reject this submission. The " orders " referred to in sub-s. (1) are orders made under those regulations which authorise the making of " orders " and the " steps " are in my view confined to the administrative action taken by the civil authority in the execution of the regulations.

But I nevertheless agree with my noble and learned friend LORD PEARCE that the provisions of sub-s. (1) are relevant as throwing light on the intention
E of Parliament as to the way in which the powers under the Act generally including the power of the Minister to make regulations under sub-s. (3) of the same section were to be exercised. A regulation which creates an offence so wide in its terms as to make unlawful conduct which cannot have the effect of endangering the preservation of the peace and the maintenance of order is not in my view rendered valid merely because the description of the conduct penalised is also
F wide enough to embrace conduct which is reasonably likely to have that effect.

I turn next to the second task of determining what the words used in the regulations challenged in the present appeal mean. They add an additional provision to the existing reg. 24A previously made by the Minister of Home Affairs under the same provision of the Special Powers Act. So far as is relevant to the present appeal, reg. 24A provides as follows:

G   " Any person who becomes or remains a member of an unlawful association or who does any act with a view to promoting or calculated to promote
the objects of an unlawful association or seditious conspiracy shall be guilty
of an offence against these Regulations . . .
     " The following organisations shall for the purposes of this Regulation
be deemed to be unlawful associations:—
H   The Irish Republican Brotherhood
      The Irish Republican Army
      The Irish Volunteers
      The Cumann Na m'Ban
      The Fianna Na h'Eireann."

The subject-matter of the first paragraph of this regulation is " unlawful
I associations " and " seditious conspiracies "—both of them expressions of which the meaning in the context of the regulation is clear.

Confining myself to " unlawful associations ", an association is unlawful if any of its objects are unlawful, i.e., if either the end which it seeks to achieve is unlawful or, although the end is lawful, the means by which it seeks to achieve that end are not. The characteristic of an association which makes it an " unlawful association " within the meaning of the first part of reg. 24A is the unlawfulness of its objects. In any prosecution of a person for becoming or remaining a member of an unlawful association or doing any act with a view to promoting or calculated to promote the objects of an unlawful association, it **A** would be necessary for the prosecution to prove that the objects of the association were unlawful. Although if it were a matter of general public knowledge that the objects of a particular association were unlawful the court would be entitled to take judicial notice of that fact.

The last paragraph of the regulation placed within the category of associations with unlawful objects the associations named therein and thus removed the **B** need for the prosecution to prove what their objects were. It is, however, conceded that at the time that reg. 24A was made, viz., 22nd May 1922, it was a matter of general public knowledge that the objects of the named organisations were unlawful and the paragraph does no more than assert facts of which the courts would have been entitled to take judicial notice, even apart from that paragraph. For this reason it is conceded that reg. 24A as it stood prior to 1967 **C** is intra vires: although different considerations would have applied if the last paragraph had listed apparently lawful organisations such as the Automobile Association or the Athenaeum.

The regulation challenged in the present appeal added to the list of the organisations named in the last paragraph of reg. 24A not merely additional organisations identified by name but a class of organisations identified by the **D** words—

" The organisations at the date of this regulation or at any time thereafter describing themselves as ' Republican Clubs ' or any like organisation howsoever described."

If these words include any association which is not in fact unlawful within the meaning of the first part of reg. 24A they alter the mischief at which that **E** regulation was previously aimed by adding a different kind of mischief; and for the new regulation to be valid this different kind of mischief must also be one the suppression of which will have the effect of preserving peace and maintaining order.

The inclusion in the definition of this new class of proscribed associations of " any like organisation " shows that the mischief struck at is some characteristic **F** of organisations describing themselves at the date of the regulation or at any time thereafter as " Republican Clubs ". The only characteristics of such organisations to which reference is made in the regulation either expressly or by implication are—(i) that they are composed of members and, as is implicit in the word " organisation ", possess objects of some kind; and (ii) that they describe themselves as " Republican Clubs ". But the possession of characteristic **G** (ii) cannot constitute the mischief aimed at for the relevant likeness can exist " howsoever [the organisation is] described ".

The magistrates' court took the view that the Minister cannot have intended to include in this category organisations composed of members irrespective of the objects for which the organisation was formed, for on this construction it would be an offence to become or remain a member of any club or organisation **H** in Northern Ireland. They therefore construed the regulation in the light of the first paragraph of reg. 24A as limited to organisations composed of members and possessing objects which are unlawful. In your Lordships' House, it has not been contended that this is a legitimate construction to put on the regulation. So construed it adds nothing to what was already contained in the first part of reg. 24A.

I

The majority of the Court of Appeal for Northern Ireland evaded the difficulty involved in the words " any like organisation howsoever described " by confining their attention to some of the words of the regulation only, viz., " The organisations at the date of this regulation . . . describing themselves as ' Republican Clubs ' . . ." The " Slaughtneil Republican Club " of which the appellant was found to have remained a member fell within this category.

The argument for the respondent then runs thus: It must be inferred that the Minister not merely *believed*, but *knew* at the time that he made the

A regulation challenged that *all* organisations then in existence which described themselves as " Republican Clubs " in fact had unlawful objects. That part of the regulation which relates to organisations in this category does not alter the mischief previously struck at by reg. 24A. It does no more than enable the court to take judicial notice that these organisations, as well as those previously listed have unlawful objects. But even if it were legitimate to treat the regula-

B tion as severable by merely striking out the two groups of words omitted above, the inference that the Minister had such knowledge is an inference of fact which cannot be drawn if it can be shown that the " facts " of which his " knowledge " is sought to be inferred did not exist. If, therefore, the evidence establishes that not all organisations which described themselves as " Republican Clubs " at the date of the regulation had unlawful objects this destroys the ground for

C the inference that membership of an organisation with unlawful objects was the mischief against which the regulation was aimed.

It was found as a fact in the present case, which we are informed is the only prosecution which has so far been brought under the regulations challenged, that as respects one club in this category " The Slaughtneil Republican Club ", there was nothing seditious in its pursuits or those of its members so far as the police

D were aware. It is to be noted that the prosecution in which this fact was elicited from the police witnesses was brought by a police officer on the direction of the Attorney-General, as required by s. 3 (2) of the Act. What was known to the police was presumably known to the Minister and this admission gravely weakens any inference of fact that the Minister did have the knowledge postulated when he made the regulation on which to base the conclusion of law that on the true

E construction of the regulation the mischief intended to be struck at even in organisations describing themselves as republican clubs at the date of the regulations lay in their unlawful objects.

But there is another reason for rejecting this construction of the regulation which I find compelling. It is not, in my view, permissible to treat the regulation as severable in the way adopted by the majority of the Court of Appeal. To do

F so is to treat it as striking at more than one unrelated mischief whereas the inclusion in the description of the organisations deemed to be unlawful associa-tion of the words " any like organisation " makes it plain that it is organisations possessing a common mischievous characteristic that are intended to be proscribed.

What then is that characteristic? Even if it were legitimate to infer that the

G Minister had knowledge of the objects of " Republican Clubs " in existence at the date of the regulation he could not have knowledge of what would be the objects of clubs to be formed in the future which would describe themselves as " Republican Clubs ". The characteristic struck at, therefore, cannot be the possession *in fact* of unlawful objects by the organisations proscribed. Nor for the reasons previously indicated can the common characteristic struck at be the

H use of the name " Republican Club ". It is conceivable that the adoption of a particular name might of itself be so inflammatory in Northern Ireland as to endanger the preservation of peace and the maintenance of order, but the regulation proscribes " like organisations " which do not adopt this name.

But there are no other ascertainable common characteristics of the organisa-tions described in the regulation except that they are composed of members

I and possess objects of some kind or other and describe themselves by some name or other. If the Minister's intention was to proscribe all clubs and associa-tions in Northern Ireland whatever their objects and name the regulation plainly falls outside the power delegated to him by s. 1 (3) of the Special Powers Act to make regulations " for making further provision for the preservation of the peace and the maintenance of order ". It makes unlawful conduct which cannot have the effect of endangering the preservation of the peace or the maintenance of order. But if the Minister's intention was to proscribe some narrower category of organisations the suppression of which would have the effect of preserving

the peace and maintaining order, he has in my view failed to disclose in the   A
regulation what that narrower category is.   A regulation whose meaning is so
vague that it cannot be ascertained with reasonable certainty cannot fall within
the words of delegation.

It is possible to speculate that the Minister when he made the regulation now
challenged bona fide believed that the sort of club which at that date described
itself as a " Republican Club " was likely to have unlawful objects which would   B
endanger the preservation of the peace and the maintenance of order and by the
words that he added he may have intended to do no more than to prevent such
clubs from evading the regulation by dissolving and re-forming or by changing
their names.   If this was his intention he signally failed to express it in the
regulation, for by no process of construction can it be given this limited effect.
Or he may have thought it administratively convenient to insert in the regulation   C
a description of proscribed organisations so wide as to include also those with
lawful objects in order to be sure that none with unlawful objects should be
omitted, and to rely on the administrative discretion of the Attorney-General
under s. 3 (2) of the Act not to enforce the regulation.   But to do this however
if administratively convenient would be outside his delegated legislative powers.

But this is speculation not construction and your Lordships' function is   D
limited to construing the words which the Minister has used.   In my view the
words used by the Minister in the regulation are either too wide to fall within the
description of the regulations which he is empowered to make under s. 1 (3) of
the Special Powers Act or are too vague and uncertain in their meaning to be
enforceable.

I would allow this appeal.   E

Appeal dismissed.

Solicitors: *Asher Fishman & Co.*, agents for *K. M. Agnew*, Maghera, Co.
Derry (for the appellant); *Linklaters & Paines*, agents for *Chief Crown Solicitor,
Northern Ireland* (for the respondent).

[*Reported by* S. A. HATTEEA, ESQ., *Barrister-at-Law.*]
                                                                                 F

R. *v.* COLEMAN.

[COURT OF APPEAL, CRIMINAL DIVISION (Widgery and Karminski, L.JJ., and
      Geoffrey Lane, J.), May 1, 1969.]

*Criminal Law—Sentence—Suspended sentence—Consecutive sentences—Totality
      of consecutive sentences exceeding two years—Validity of suspended sentence   G
      —Criminal Justice Act 1967 (c. 80), s. 39 (1), s. 104 (2).*

If consecutive sentences are imposed on an occasion and the totality of
those sentences exceeds two years (such sentences by virtue of s. 104 (2)* of
the Criminal Justice Act 1967 being treated as a single term), the power
to suspend the sentence under s. 39 (1)† of that Act does not arise (see p. 1076,
letter F, post).   H

R. v. *Flanders* ([1968] 3 All E.R. 534) distinguished.

Appeal allowed in part.

[As to suspended sentences, see SUPPLEMENT to 10 HALSBURY'S LAWS (3rd
Edn.) para. 922A, 1; and as to subsequent convictions, see ibid., para. 922A, 2.
For the Criminal Justice Act 1967, s. 39, s. 104, see 8 HALSBURY'S STATUTES   I
(3rd Edn.) 603, 637.]

Case referred to:
   R. v. *Flanders*, [1968] 3 All E.R. 534; [1969] 1 Q.B. 148; [1968] 3 W.L.R. 873;
Digest (Repl.) Supp.

Appeal.

This was an appeal by Barry Coleman, by way of a reference by the Secretary

---

* Section 104 (2) is set out at p. 1075, letter I, post.
† Section 39 (1) is set out at p. 1075, letter G, post.

A   of State for Home Affairs under s. 17 (1) (a) of the Criminal Appeal Act 1968, against consecutive terms of two years' and two years' imprisonment, suspended for one year, passed on him on 12th February 1968 at North East London Quarter Sessions by the deputy chairman (L. A. MOULES, ESQ.) after he had pleaded guilty to two counts in an indictment, of housebreaking and larceny (count 1) and burglary and larceny (count 2), and asked for 58 other offences

B   to be taken into consideration. On 3rd February 1969, at Northampton Quarter Sessions the appellant was convicted of offences of factorybreaking and larceny, garagebreaking and larceny, simple larceny and taking and driving away a motor vehicle without the owner's consent, which were committed during the operational period of the suspended sentence. The deputy chairman (A. W. M. DAVIES, ESQ., Q.C.) passed concurrent sentences for the new offences amounting

C   to two years' imprisonment in all. He postponed consideration of the action to be taken in relation to the suspended sentences passed on the appellant at North East London Quarter Sessions because of doubt about the validity of those sentences.

    J. Bolland for the appellant.

    The Crown did not appear and was not represented.

D

    WIDGERY, L.J., delivered the judgment of the court: The appellant pleaded guilty at the North East London Quarter Sessions to one count of house-breaking and larceny and to burglary and larceny (count 2). He was sentenced to consecutive terms of two years' and two years' imprisonment in respect of these two counts. The total sentence was thus four years in all, and the court

E   ordered that the sentence should be suspended for one year, 58 other offences being taken into consideration. Since that date, that is to say in February 1969, the appellant has been in trouble again and sentences have been passed on him for similar breaking offences at the Northamptonshire Quarter Sessions. But the matter with which this court is concerned arises solely from the initial sentences passed on 12th February 1968.

F   The matter comes before the court in a reference from the Home Secretary under s. 17 (1) (a) of the Criminal Appeal Act 1968, and the short question which we are required to determine is whether the sentences passed in February 1968 were according to law. Section 39 (1) of the Criminal Justice Act 1967 provides:

    " A court which passes a sentence of imprisonment for a term of not
G   more than two years for an offence may order that the sentence shall not take effect unless, during a period specified in the order, being not less than one year or more than three years from the date of the order, the offender commits in Great Britain another offence punishable with imprisonment and thereafter a court having power to do so orders under the next following section that the original sentence shall take effect; and in this
H   Part of this Act ' operational period ', in relation to a suspended sentence, means the period so specified."

We observe at once that the discretionary power to suspend is limited to a sentence of imprisonment of not more than two years.

    Under s. 104 (2) of the Act of 1967, it is provided:

I   " For the purposes of any reference in this Act, however expressed, to the term of imprisonment or other detention to which a person has been sentenced or which, or part of which, he has served, consecutive terms and terms which are wholly or partly concurrent shall be treated as a single term."

The argument therefore is that since the two sentences in the present case were made consecutive, they should be treated under s. 104 (2) as a single sentence of four years' imprisonment. If they are so treated, then it becomes apparent at once that the discretionary power to suspend under s. 39 (1) would not apply.

A somewhat similar matter has been before this court before in *R.* v. *Flanders* (1). **A**
This was a case concerned with s. 39 (3) which provides in these terms:

> " A court which passes a sentence of imprisonment for a term of not more
> than six months in respect of one offence shall make an order under sub-
> section (1) of this section . . ."

The point which arose in *R.* v. *Flanders* (1) was that the appellant in that case **B**
had been sentenced to two periods of six months' imprisonment which were
expressed to be consecutive, and the question was whether in those circumstances a mandatory requirement to suspend under s. 39 (3) applied. If by
reference to s. 104 (2) it was right in that case to regard the two sentences of
six months' imprisonment as being a single sentence of 12 months then of course
the mandatory requirement of suspension would not apply. But this court **C**
held in *R.* v. *Flanders* (1) that the mandatory requirement did apply, and that the
two sentences albeit consecutive, must be treated as separate sentences for
the purposes of sub-s. (3). We have considered whether that decision affects the
construction of sub-s. (1), and we think it does not. We are satisfied from the
judgment of LORD PARKER, C.J., in *R.* v. *Flanders* (1) that that case depended
on the very special context of the reference to a sentence of imprisonment in **D**
respect of one offence under sub-s. (3); indeed LORD PARKER, C.J., said in
R. v. *Flanders* (2):

> " In the opinion of this court that subsection [that is s. 104 (2)], however,
> does not affect in any way s. 39 (3); if it did so, it seems quite impossible
> to conceive the necessity for the exception in para. (*c*) which provides that
> there need not be a mandatory suspended sentence if ' on the occasion on **E**
> which sentence is passed for that offence, the court passes or proposes to
> pass a sentence of immediate imprisonment on the offender for another
> offence which the court is not required to suspend '."

In our judgment similar considerations do not apply to the construction of
s. 39 (1) where there is no context requiring the court to do other than apply
the direction in s. 104 (2). If consecutive sentences are imposed on an occasion **F**
and the totality of those sentences exceeds two years, the power to suspend the
sentence under s. 39 (1) does not arise. Accordingly, the sentence in this case
was a sentence not authorised by law and must be set aside. The court feels
that it can do no other in the situation before it than to direct that the two
sentences of two years' imprisonment passed in this case should operate concurrently, not consecutively. It is then open to the court to suspend the sentence, **G**
and it will order the same suspension as the learned deputy chairman in the
court below sought to order.

Appeal allowed in part.

Solicitors: *Registrar of Criminal Appeals* (for the appellant).

[*Reported by* N. P. METCALFE, ESQ., *Barrister-at-Law.*] **H**

I

---

(1) [1968] 3 All E.R. 534; [1969] 1 Q.B. 148.
(2) [1968] 3 All E.R. at p. 535; [1969] 1 Q.B. at p. 150.

A

R. *v.* LOVESEY. R. *v.* PETERSON.

[COURT OF APPEAL, CRIMINAL DIVISION (Widgery and Karminski, L.JJ., and Geoffrey Lane, J.), May 2, 13, 1969.]

Criminal Law—Concerted action—Murder—Concerted action to rob with violence

B
—Death inflicted in course of robbery—Lack of evidence as to which accused inflicted injuries causing death—Lack of evidence of degree of violence contemplated in concerted action—Each accused properly convicted of robbery with violence—Whether either could be convicted of murder.

Criminal Law—Concerted action—Joint enterprise—Death following act of one joint adventurer going beyond tacit agreement—Agreement to commit robbery with violence—Lack of evidence as to which accused inflicted injuries causing

C
death—Lack of evidence of degree or type of violence contemplated in concerted action—Each accused properly convicted of robbery with violence—Whether either could be convicted of manslaughter.

The appellants were charged with robbery with violence and murder arising out of an incident in which a jeweller was found handcuffed to a railing in the basement of his shop suffering from severe head injuries

D
from which he died. Blood was found on the stairs and ground floor of the shop which was in disorder, and valuables were found to have been stolen. There was no direct evidence of how many men had been involved in the crime or of their individual roles. The appellants denied all knowledge of the crime, but there was certain circumstantial evidence connecting them to it. The jury were correctly directed on the ingredients of both offences

E
and on the guilt of participants in a common purpose, but they were told that the two offences stood or fell together. The appellants were convicted on both counts. On appeal against the conviction of murder,

Held: (i) the appeals would be allowed because the offences did not necessarily stand together: since neither appellant's part in the affair could be identified, neither could be convicted of an offence which went

F
beyond the common design to which he was a party; there was clearly a common design to rob, but that was not sufficient to convict of murder unless the common design involved the use of such force (including killing, or the infliction of grievous bodily harm) as was necessary to achieve the robbers' object or to permit escape without fear of subsequent identification; and this was a question for the jury to decide notwithstanding that the

G
point had not been raised by the defence (see p. 1079, letters C and F, post).

(ii) the court would not substitute a verdict of manslaughter, because, if a common design to inflict grievous bodily harm was excluded, the jury might well have concluded that the killing was the unauthorised act of one individual for which the co-adventurers were not responsible at all (see

H
p. 1079, letter I, post).

R. v. Anderson and Morris ([1966] 2 All E.R. 644) considered.

Appeals allowed.

[As to common design involving homicide, see 10 HALSBURY'S LAWS (3rd Edn.) 715, para. 1370; and for cases on the subject, see 14 DIGEST (Repl.) 91-93, *533, 538-561,* 95-97, *577-612.*

I
For the Criminal Appeal Act 1968, s. 3, see 8 HALSBURY'S STATUTES (3rd Edn.) 691.]

Case referred to:

 R. v. Anderson and Morris, [1966] 2 All E.R. 644; 130 J.P. 318; 50 Cr. App. Rep. 216; sub nom. *R. v. Anderson, R. v. Morris,* [1966] 2 Q.B. 110; [1966] 2 W.L.R. 1195; Digest (Cont. Vol. B) 155, *612a.*

Appeals.

On 22nd May 1968 at the Central Criminal Court before MELFORD STEVENSON,

J., and a jury, the appellants, John Dennis Lovesey and Anthony Peterson, were convicted on an indictment charging them both with robbery with violence and with murder. They were sentenced to seven years' imprisonment for the robbery, and to life imprisonment for the murder, with a recommendation in respect of this latter offence of a minimum period of 20 years. They applied for leave to appeal against their convictions, and on 2nd May 1969 their applications for leave to appeal against the robbery count were refused, but the court granted their applications for leave to appeal on the murder count and treated the applications as the hearing of the appeal. The facts are set out in the judgment of the court.

The cases noted below* were cited during the argument in addition to the case referred to in the judgment of the court.

C. L. Hawser, Q.C., and *V. K. Winstain* for the appellants.
J. H. Buzzard and *M. Mansfield* for the Crown.

Cur. adv. vult.

13th May. **WIDGERY, L.J.,** read the judgment of the court: The two appellants were convicted at the Central Criminal Court of robbery with violence (count 1) and murder (count 2). They were each sentenced to imprisonment for seven years and for life on the two counts respectively, and now appeal against their convictions for murder by leave of the full court.

The victim was a jeweller, who was accustomed to open his lock-up shop at about 9.0 a.m. and who was normally alone in the shop until the arrival of his wife at about 9.10 a.m. On 24th January 1968, he arrived at his shop at about 9.0 a.m., and when his wife found him some 15 minutes later he was handcuffed to a railing in the basement of the premises and had suffered severe head injuries, from which he later died. Blood was found on the ground floor and on the stairs, the shop was in disorder and some cases of valuables had been removed. There was no direct evidence of how many men had been involved in the raid or of the parts which they had individually played. The appellants denied all knowledge of the affair, but the prosecution sought to implicate them in the crime in a number of ways. Witnesses were called to prove a connection between the two appellants and a Jaguar car which was thought to have been used in the raid, and the victim's daughter gave evidence that the appellant Lovesey had visited the shop with a woman three months before. Evidence was also given that when the appellants were arrested the two halves of a torn envelope, which had come from the shop, were found in their respective pockets. The appellants made many complaints about this evidence, and the directions given by the trial judge thereon, but these matters have all been disposed of in an earlier judgment of the court, and all which now remains is the appellants' appeal against their convictions for murder, the ground of appeal being that the trial judge failed to direct the jury to consider the two counts separately.

The learned judge gave the jury an impeccable direction on the ingredients of the offence of robbery with violence and on the guilt of individuals who join in a common purpose to rob. He continued:

" Then comes the second and the more important charge, namely, murder, and that arises in this particular case and on this evidence in this way: if a man is attacked with the intention of causing him really serious physical injury and as a result of that injury he dies, he or any who became party to that attack, if they joined in for the purpose that he should suffer serious physical injury, are guilty of murder. Again, the same observation applies: if one is keeping watch outside or sitting in the car, once you are satisfied that

---

* *R. v. Hopper*, [1915] 2 K.B. 431; [1914-15] All E.R. Rep. 914; *R. v. Thorpe* (1925), 133 L.T. 95; [1925] All E.R. Rep. 383; *Mancini* v. *Director of Public Prosecutions*, [1941] 3 All E.R. 272; [1942] A.C. 1; *Kwaku Mensah* v. *Regem*, [1946] A.C. 83; *Bullard* v. *Reginam*, [1961] 3 All E.R. 470, n.; [1957] A.C. 635; *R. v. Porritt*, [1961] 3 All E.R. 463; [1961] 1 W.L.R. 1372; *R. v. Betty*, [1963] 3 All E.R. 602, n.; *Connelly* v. *Director of Public Prosecutions*, [1964] 2 All E.R. 401; [1964] A.C. 1254.

A the offence has taken place, and they are all acting with that common purpose and it resulted in death and that there was in the mind of all of them an intention to do really serious physical harm, then there is the offence of murder."

In our view, the direction is not open to objection up to this point; but the learned judge concluded this part of the summing-up with these words:

B " So much, members of the jury, for the offences that you have got to consider in this case, and in the particular circumstances of this case, as [counsel for the Crown] said, and I think everybody agreed, obviously these two offences stand or fall together."

In fact, the two offences did not necessarily stand or fall together. As neither appellant's part in the affair could be identified, neither could be convicted of an
C offence which went beyond the common design to which he was a party. There was clearly a common design to rob, but that would not suffice to convict of murder unless the common design included the use of whatever force was necessary to achieve the robbers' object (or to permit escape without fear of subsequent identification), even if this involved killing, or the infliction of grievous bodily
D harm on the victim. If the scope of the common design had been left to the jury in this way they might still have concluded that it extended to the use of extreme force. It is clear that the plan envisaged that the victim's resistance should be rapidly overcome. The attack bears the hallmark of desperate men who knew that they had to act quickly, and the jury may have thought it utterly unreal that such men would make a pact to treat the victim gently however
E much he struggled and however long it might take to subdue him. The jury had also had the advantage of seeing the appellants in the witness box and may have formed their own views whether the appellants would have scruples of this character. There must, in our view, be many cases of this kind where the jury feel driven to the conclusion that the raiders' common design extended to everything which in fact occurred in the course of the raid, but the question must
F be left to the jury because it is a matter for them to decide, and this is so notwithstanding that the point was not raised by the defence.

Counsel for the Crown has invited us to consider the substitution on count 2 of a verdict of manslaughter under s. 3 of the Criminal Appeal Act 1968. It is clear that a common design to use unlawful violence, short of the infliction of grievous bodily harm, renders all the co-adventurers guilty of manslaughter if
G the victim's death is an unexpected consequence of the carrying-out of that design. Where, however, the victim's death is not a product of the common design but is attributable to one of the co-adventurers going beyond the scope of that design, by using violence which is intended to cause grievous bodily harm, the others are not responsible for that unauthorised act (*R.* v. *Anderson and Morris* (1)). In the present case the degree of violence used against the victim showed
H a clear intention to inflict grievous bodily harm, and if this was within the common design the proper verdict against all concerned was one of murder. We cannot say that the jury must have reached this conclusion and, accordingly, feel compelled to quash both convictions for murder. Having reached this point we are unable to substitute verdicts of manslaughter since, if a common design to inflict grievous bodily harm is excluded, the jury might well have concluded that the killing was the unauthorised act of one individual for which the co-adventurers were
I not responsible at all. Both appeals are accordingly allowed, and the convictions on count 2 are quashed.

Appeals allowed.

Solicitors: *Quirke & Co.* (for the appellants); *Director of Public Prosecutions* (for the Crown).

[*Reported by* N. P. Metcalfe, Esq., *Barrister-at-Law.*]

(1) [1966] 2 All E.R. 644; [1966] 2 Q.B. 110.

TAYLOR *v.* KENT COUNTY COUNCIL.

[QUEEN'S BENCH DIVISION (Lord Parker, C.J., Melford Stevenson and Willis, JJ.), May 1, 1969.]

Employment—Redundancy—Dismissal by reason of redundancy—Offer of alternative employment—Suitable employment—Headmaster offered job in mobile pool of teachers—Same salary guaranteed—Necessity of moving house—Suitability of alternative offer of employment matter of degree and fact for Industrial Tribunal—Reasonableness of refusal of offer—" Suitable employment "—Redundancy Payments Act 1965 (c. 62), s. 2 (4).

The appellant had for ten years been employed by the respondent county council as headmaster of a boys' school which was to be amalgamated with another school and run on co-educational lines. As a result of this re-organisation the appellant's employment was terminated, prima facie on the ground of redundancy. The respondents made an offer to the appellant of alternative employment in a mobile pool of teachers serving for periods of one or two terms in schools with a shortage of staff, under the authority of the headmaster of each school, in an area some distance from the appellant's home. He was guaranteed the same salary, but he refused the offer. On the question whether the respondents had made an offer of alternative suitable employment within s. 2 (4)* of the Redundancy Payments Act 1965, which had unreasonably been refused,

Held: " suitable employment " meant employment which is substantially equivalent to the employment which had ceased; the offer of a position in a mobile pool of teachers to a headmaster with the appellant's qualifications, experience and status, and necessitating his moving house, was not suitable; nor could it be made so merely by guaranteeing the same salary (see p. 1083, letters A and H, and p. 1084, letters A and H, post).

Per CURIAM: suitability is almost entirely a matter of degree and fact for the Industrial Tribunal and not a matter with which an appeal court would wish to interfere unless it was plain that the tribunal had misdirected themselves in law or had taken into consideration matters which were not relevant (see p. 1083, letter F, and p. 1084, letter H, post).

QUAERE: whether personal factors only should be considered when assessing the reasonableness of an applicant's refusal of an offer of suitable employment, or whether, in addition to the personal factors, all matters which have to be considered in regard to suitability (see p. 1084, letters E to G, post).

Appeal allowed.

[As to dismissal of employee by reason of redundancy, see SUPPLEMENT to 38 HALSBURY'S LAWS (3rd Edn.) para. 808c.

For the Redundancy Payments Act 1965, s. 2, see 45 HALSBURY'S STATUTES (2nd Edn.) 291.]

Case referred to:

Carron Co. v. *Robertson* [1967] I.T.R. 484.

Appeal.

This was an appeal by Vernon Stephen Taylor from a decision of the Industrial Tribunal sitting at London on 18th October 1968 refusing an application for redundancy payment from the respondents, Kent County Council, on the grounds that suitable alternative employment had been offered in accordance with the Redundancy Payments Act 1968, s. 2 (4) and that the appellant had unreasonably refused that offer. The facts are set out in the judgment of LORD PARKER, C.J.

Owen Stable, Q.C., and *A. D. Steen* for the appellant.
D. A. Grant, Q.C., and *R. A. Cumming* for the respondents.

---

* Section 2 (4) is set out at p. 1081, letters F to H, post.

A   **LORD PARKER, C.J.:** This is an appeal from a decision of the Industrial Tribunal given on 18th October 1968, whereby they unanimously dismissed an application made by the appellant for a redundancy payment. The matter arose in this way: the appellant had for some ten years been headmaster of the Deal Secondary School for Boys. A time came in the beginning of 1968 when it was decided by Kent County Council, the respondents, that the school for

B boys should cease to exist as such, that it should be amalgamated with a girls' school, and the new school be run on co-educational lines, the numbers being about double what they had been before, and accordingly the appellant's appointment was terminated. Prima facie it was terminated and he was dismissed on account of redundancy. The sole question here is whether the respondents can avoid paying what prima facie they would have to pay as redundancy

C payment by reason of their having made an offer to him of alternative suitable employment, which offer he has unreasonably refused.

It is worth in the first instant looking at s. 2 of the Redundancy Payments Act 1965. By sub-s. (3) it is provided:

D " An employee shall not be entitled to a redundancy payment by reason of dismissal if before the relevant date [that is the date when the dismissal becomes effective] the employer has offered to renew his contract of employment, or to re-engage him under a new contract, so that—(*a*) the provisions of the contract as renewed, or of the new contract, as the case may be, as to the capacity and place in which he would be employed, and as to the other terms and conditions of his employment, would not differ from the

E corresponding provisions of the contract as in force immediately before his dismissal, and (*b*) the renewal or re-engagement would take effect on or before the relevant date, and the employee has unreasonably refused that offer."

I read that not because it is immediately relevant to the circumstances of this case, but merely to contrast it with the next following subsection, which is the

F important one for the purposes of this case. Subsection (4) provides:

" An employee shall not be entitled to a redundancy payment by reason of dismissal if before the relevant date the employer has made to him an offer in writing to renew his contract of employment, or to re-engage him under a new contract, so that in accordance with the particulars specified in the offer the provisions of the contract as renewed, or of the new contract, as

G the case may be, as to the capacity and place in which he would be employed, and as to the other terms and conditions of his employment, would differ (wholly or in part) from the corresponding provisions of the contract as in force immediately before his dismissal, but—(*a*) the offer constitutes an offer of suitable employment in relation to the employee, and (*b*) the renewal or

H re-engagement would take effect on or before the relevant date or not later than four weeks after that date, and the employee has unreasonably refused that offer."

To continue with the facts, when this re-organisation was about to take place, the appellant was apparently considered for the appointment as headmaster of the new co-educational school. For one reason or another he was not chosen.

I The tribunal drew attention to the fact that the circumstances of this case were charged with emotion, and it may be that there was strong feeling in Deal about it. I do not propose to say anything about that; I will assume, and will assume only, that what was thought to be the case was that the appellant, who had done apparently ten years as headmaster of the boys' school, would not be able to cope with a school run on co-educational lines with double the number of children.

On 21st February 1968 a letter was written to him in these terms:

"The Secretary of State has, as you know, now approved the establishment of a new co-educational Secondary School in Deal from the 1st September 1968.   This means that with the closure of the Boys' Secondary School
your post will cease to exist and it is therefore formally necessary to give you
notice of the termination of your present appointment on 31st August 1968;
[that is why the appellant became prima facie entitled to a redundancy
payment] this I now do.   Your salary will be safeguarded, of course,
in accordance with Section Q of the Scales of Salaries for Teachers in Primary
and Secondary Schools, England and Wales 1967.   The Committee will
give you all the help in their power to obtain a suitable alternative
appointment.

"A post in the new school to be established has been offered to you, but
this you do not wish to accept.   [Nothing turns on that because it was not
in writing.]   The Committee are prepared as an alternative to offer you a
post in the Mobile Pool of Teachers (of which I enclose particulars) in
Category III from September 1968.   This post appears to give you the best
opportunity to move into a permanent appointment while at the same
time being in the position of waiting for the appearance of a permanent post
which you may find especially suitable to you.   A member of the Mobile
Pool must go, of course, to schools where his services are needed but, within
this obvious requirement, we should naturally try to arrange your duties
in a way making the best use of your qualifications and therefore, I hope,
most congenial to you.   This offer would apply whether you remained at
your present address or whether you moved to another part of the County."

The particulars concerning the mobile pool of teachers were enclosed, and it is
necessary I think to read passages from that.   It is headed "Appointment to
the County Pool of 'Mobile' Staff".

"Kent Education Committee invite applications from qualified and
experienced teachers, able to give effective assistance in a variety of teaching
situations, for appointment to the County's pool of mobile staff.   The
teachers appointed will be asked to serve in Primary or Secondary Schools
as may be required for short periods, generally one or two terms but not
normally longer than a year.   [Then having referred to the highest category,
which was the appointment the appellant was being offered, namely as a
Head Teacher Category III, the particulars go on as follows:] Appointment
to the Pool offers opportunities to suitably qualified teachers to help the
Committee in the present difficult staffing situation and to broaden their
experience in various kinds of schools.   Teachers may be assured that the
Committee will do what they can to ensure a variety of experience.   A teacher
serving under these arrangements will perform such duties as are assigned to
him by the Head of the school to which he is attached for the time being.

"In normal circumstances travelling expenses in excess of 5s. a week will
be paid at public transport rates (second-class rail and/or bus fares).   If
public transport facilities cannot conveniently be used, the Committeee are
prepared to consider applications for car mileage allowances.

"Members of the Pool will, in normal circumstances, be allocated each
term to Primary and Secondary Schools in the areas of special shortage,
which for this purpose are the Medway Towns, Gravesend, Dartford, Maidstone and Sheerness, and as a consequence it is a condition of appointment
that the teacher should reside in the North-west Kent area; this is defined
as extending not farther south than the Maidstone area and not farther east
than Sittingbourne."

It will thus be seen that that last sentence that I have read, namely that the
appellant would have to reside in the north-west Kent area, was treated by the
tribunal and I think rightly, as having been superseded by the words in the letter
itself, which said: "This offer would apply whether you remained at your

A   present address or whether you moved to another part of the County." The only observation I would make is that it is conceded he could not possibly have done this going from Deal, and therefore whatever the offer said, it necessitated his moving his house.

It is important to see what that means. The appellant with ten years' experience as headmaster at Deal was being offered an appointment, and I

B   would like to make it clear that I will accept that it is a permanent appointment, in category III in this pool. But it is to be observed that when in the pool he can be sent anywhere in the county, though normally in this north-west area of Kent; he can be sent to one place for one term or two terms, and then to another place for one term or two terms, sometimes a year; he can be told to go round from place to place, and when he does that he has to undertake the

C   duties which are assigned to him by the headmaster of the school to which he is sent. The question which arises is whether that was an offer of suitable employment within s. 2 (4).

The tribunal state in their decision:

D   " The suitability of the alternative offer must be considered in all the surrounding circumstances not just one—to wit: status. Taking into account not only the [appellant's] age, qualifications, experience, loss of status, but also the protection afforded by his contract [that means that his salary as headmaster is going to continue pursuant to Section Q of the Burnham Award] and not forgetting the unfortunate showing at the interview, we have come to the conclusion that in all the circumstances the offer of appointment to the Mobile Pool was one of suitable employment in relation to the

E   [appellant]. Of course another Headmastership would have been more suitable, but [the respondents] were not in a position to make a written offer of such a post. However the fact that the offer that was made was less suitable, does not necessarily make it unsuitable."

Let me say at once, suitability is almost entirely a matter of degree and fact for

F   the tribunal, and not a matter with which this court would wish to or could interfere, unless it was plain that they had misdirected themselves in some way in law, or had taken into consideration matters which were not relevant for the purpose. It is to be observed that so far as age was concerned, so far as qualifications were concerned, so far as experience was concerned, they negative the suitability of this offer, because the appellant is going to be put into a position

G   where he has to go where he is told at any time for short periods, to any place, and be put under a headmaster and assigned duties by him.

The only matter which can be put against that as making this offer suitable is the guarantee of salary under Section Q. One would think, speaking for myself, that a headmaster of this experience would think an offer which, while guaranteeing him the same salary, reduced his status, was quite unsuitable.

H   To go to quite a different sphere of activity, a director under a service agreement of a company is offered on dismissal a job as a navvy, and it is said: but we will guarantee you the same salary as you have been getting. I should have thought such an offer was plainly unsuitable. Here one wonders whether one of the matters which affected the tribunal was this reference to the words " Not forgetting the unfortunate showing at the interview ". That is a reference to when he

I   was interviewed, not by the respondents, but by the governors of the school with a view to taking on the headmastership of the new school. One really wonders what the relevance of that was unless it be that the tribunal felt from what they had heard that he was not up to a headmastership at all. But at once one says to oneself: if that was in their minds, it was not evidence on which they could properly act, having regard to the fact that the appellant had given satisfaction for some ten years, and if he was not up to his job he could have been dismissed for that reason, and no question of redundancy would have arisen.

For my part I feel that the tribunal have here misdirected themselves in law

as to the meaning of " suitable employment ". I accept, of course, that suitable A
employment is as is said: suitable employment in relation to the employee
in question. But it does seem to me here that by the words " suitable employment ", suitability means employment which is substantially equivalent to the
employment which has ceased. Subsection (3) which I read at the beginning is
dealing with the case where the fundamental terms are the same, and then no
offer in writing is needed, but when they differ, then it has to be put in writing B
and must be suitable. I for my part think that what is meant by " suitable "
in relation to the employee means conditions of employment which are reasonably
equivalent to those under the previous employment, not the same, because then
sub-s. (2) would apply, but it does not seem to me that by " suitable employment " is meant employment of an entirely different nature, but in respect of
which the salary is going to be the same. Looked at in that way, it seems to C
me that there could be only one answer in this case, and that is that the appellant
was being asked to do something utterly different; as I have said, just as if a
director under a service agreement with a company was being asked to do a
workman's job, albeit at the same salary.

In those circumstances, I find it unnecessary to go on and consider what I
think is the more difficult question, whether the offer, if of suitable employment, D
was one which the appellant here unreasonably refused. There are two rival
interpretations which one day will have to be resolved, though I find it
unnecessary today. In *Carron Co.* v. *Robertson* (1), a somewhat similar matter
came before the Court of Session; it is clear from that that the Lord President
(LORD CLYDE) (2) took the view that the consideration governing the reasonableness of the refusal were conditions quite different from those governing the ques- E
tion of suitability. His approach was to say that one considers the terms of the
offer to see whether it is suitable employment looked at objectively, but that when
one comes on to reasonableness one considers personal factors affecting the
particular applicant, such as that his doctors told him to live in the south of
England and he cannot go to the north, that for domestic and family reasons he
has to stay in the south, the fact that the slightly different machine in a factory F
in connection with which he is being offered work is one which for reason of
some physical deformity he cannot use, all those matters. But when one goes on to
read the judgments of LORD GUTHRIE (3) and LORD MIGDALE (4), they take the
view that there is an overlapping here, and that in considering reasonableness, one
can consider in addition to the personal factors all the matters which have been
considered in regard to suitability. As I have said, I find it unnecessary to come G
to a firm conclusion in the matter, though I confess as at present advised I prefer
the view taken by the Lord President.

In these circumstances I would allow this appeal and send the case back to the
tribunal with a direction that in default of agreement, they should assess the
redundancy payment.

MELFORD STEVENSON, J.: I agree.   H

WILLIS, J.: I agree.

Appeal allowed.

Solicitors: *Chalton Hubbard & Co.* (for the appellant); *The Clerk to Kent
County Council* (for the respondents).   I

[*Reported by* JACQUELINE CHARLES, *Barrister-at-Law.*]

---

(1) [1967] I.T.R. 484.   (3) [1967] I.T.R. at p. 487.
(2) [1967] I.T.R. at p. 485.   (4) [1967] I.T.R. at p. 490.

A

CHAPLIN v. BOYS.

[HOUSE OF LORDS (Lord Hodson, Lord Guest, Lord Donovan, Lord Wilberforce
and Lord Pearson), March 20, 24, 25, 26, 27, 31, June 25, 1969.]

Conflict of Laws—Tort—Damages—Accident in Malta between servicemen
B   *normally resident in England but stationed in Malta—Action in England—*
Whether damages to be assessed in accordance with English or Maltese
law.

Conflict of Laws—Tort—Actionability in England—Tort not justified by lex loci
delicti—" Not justified "—Prevention of forum shopping as a matter of
public policy.

C   The appellant and the respondent were both British servicemen temporarily posted to Malta when, as a result of the appellant's negligence,
the respondent was injured in a road accident. The respondent continued
to receive full pay as a serviceman until he was discharged as a result of
his injuries and thereafter obtained more remunerative employment in civilian
life. He brought an action for damages against the appellant in England.
D   Maltese law would give the respondent a right of action to recover pecuniary
loss but did not provide any compensation for pain and suffering. On the
question whether the damages recoverable by the respondent should include
damages for pain and suffering under English law or exclude such damages
as under Maltese law,

Held: English law as the lex fori was the appropriate law to govern
E   what damages were recoverable, because—

(i) (Per LORD HODSON) the admissibility of heads of damage was a matter
of substantive law which in this case was English law since the place of the
tort was overshadowed by the identity and circumstances of the parties,
British subjects temporarily serving in Malta (see p. 1094, letter C, post);

(ii) (Per LORD GUEST) although the admissibility of heads of damage was
F   a matter of substantive law, in this case Maltese law, compensation for pain
and suffering was merely an element in the quantification of the total
compensation and accordingly was a matter for the lex fori (see p. 1095,
letter G, and p. 1096, letter F, post);

(iii) (Per LORD DONOVAN) since an English court was competent to entertain the action under the rule in *Phillips* v. *Eyre** (a tort committed abroad
G   was a tort in England and actionable as such if it was both actionable as a
tort in England and not justifiable according to the law of the foreign
country where it was committed), it was right that it should award its own
remedies (see p. 1097, letter E, post);

(iv) (Per LORD WILBERFORCE) the basic rule with regard to foreign torts
should be restated as requiring actionability as a tort according to English
H   law subject to the condition that civil liability in respect of the relevant
claim existed as between the actual parties under the law of the foreign
country where the act was done (see p. 1102, letter D, post); to apply the
restated basic rule automatically, however, would be wrong where neither
party was a Maltese resident or citizen; accordingly, further enquiry was
necessary to determine whether damages for pain and suffering were recover-
I   able and this issue should be segregated from the rest of the case, related to
the parties involved and their circumstances, and tested in relation to the
policy of the rule of lex loci delicti and of its application to the parties (see
p. 1104, letters E, F and I, post);

(v) (Per LORD PEARSON) to found an action in England in respect of an
act occurring abroad, the act must be actionable according to the lex fori
but so far as the lex loci delicti was concerned it needed only to be not

---

* (1870), L.R. 6 Q.B. 1.

justified (see p. 1109, letter H, post); accordingly, the substantive lex fori   A
played the dominant role in determining the cause of action (see p. 1109,
letter I, post).

Phillips v. *Eyre* ((1870), L.R. 6 Q.B. 1) applied.

Machado v. *Fontes* ([1897] 2 Q.B. 231) and *Babcock* v. *Jackson* ([1963]
2 Lloyd's Rep. 286), considered.

Per LORD HODSON, LORD DONOVAN and LORD PEARSON: where it was   B
against public policy to admit or exclude claims, the court had a discretion
which could be exercised to discourage forum shopping (see p. 1092, letter E,
p. 1097, letter C, and p. 1116, letter D, post).

Observations on the application of the rule in *Phillips* v. *Eyre** and its
possible restatement (see p. 1091, letter E, p. 1095, letter C, p. 1097, letters
A and D, p. 1102, letter D, and p. 1109, letter H, post) and on whether   C
the admissibility of heads of damage is a question of substantive law (see
p. 1093, letter E, p. 1095, letter G, p. 1096, letter F, and p. 1106, letter H,
post).

Per LORD HODSON: in personal injury cases it is not necessarily true that
by entering a country you submit yourself to the special laws of that country
(see p. 1094, letter A, post).   D

Decision of the COURT OF APPEAL (sub nom. *Boys* v. *Chaplin* [1968]
1 All E.R. 283) affirmed.

[As to the measure of damages for torts committed abroad, see 7 HALSBURY'S
LAWS (3rd Edn.) 86, para. 157; and for cases on the subject, see 11 DIGEST
(Repl.) 449, 450, *878-884*.]
  E

Cases referred to:

Anderson v. *Eric Anderson Radio & T.V. Pty., Ltd.*, [1966] A.L.R. 423; Digest
(Cont. Vol. B) 127, **475a*.

Assunzione, The, [1954] 1 All E.R. 278; [1954] P. 150; [1954] 2 W.L.R. 234;
Digest (Cont. Vol. A) 229, *734a*.

Babcock v. *Jackson*, [1963] 2 Lloyd's Rep. 286.   F

Blad v. *Bamfield* (1674), 3 Swan. 604; 36 E.R. 992; 11 Digest (Repl.) 453,
894.

Canadian National Steamships Co., Ltd. v. *Watson*, [1939] S.C.R. 11; [1939]
1 D.L.R. 273.

Canadian Pacific Ry. Co. v. *Parent*, [1917] A.C. 195; 11 Digest (Repl.) 427, **369*.

Carr v. *Fracis Times & Co.*, [1902] A.C. 176; 71 L.J.K.B. 361; 85 L.T. 144;   G
11 Digest (Repl.) 453, *895*.

Chartered Mercantile Bank of India, London and China v. *Netherlands India
Steam Navigation Co., Ltd.* (1883), 10 Q.B.D. 521; 52 L.J.Q.B. 220;
48 L.T. 546; 47 J.P. 260; 11 Digest (Repl.) 450, *881*.

Dobree v. *Napier* (1836), 2 Bing. N.C. 781; 5 L.J.C.P. 273; 132 E.R. 301;
11 Digest (Repl.) 454, *904*.   H

Don v. *Lippmann* (1837), 5 Cl. & Fin. 1; 7 E.R. 303; 11 Digest (Repl.) 438, *809*.

Dym v. *Gordon* (1965), 16 N.Y. (2d) 120; 209 N.E. 2d 792.

Griffith v. *United Air Lines, Inc.* (1964), 203 Atlantic Reporter (2nd Ser.) 796.

Guinness v. *Miller* (1923), *291* Fed. 769.

Halley, The (1867), L.R. 2 Ad. & E. 3; rvsd. P.C. (1868), L.R. 2 P.C. 193;
37 L.J. Adm. 33; 18 L.T. 879; 16 E.R. 514; 11 Digest (Repl.) 431, *773*.   I

Hooper v. *Gumm, McLellan* v. *Gumm* (1867), 2 Ch. App. 282; 36 L.J.Ch. 605;
16 L.T. 107; 39 Digest (Repl.) 650, *1552*.

Huber v. *Steiner* (1835), 2 Bing. N.C. 202; [1835-42] All E.R. Rep. 159; 132
E.R. 80; 6 Digest (Repl.) 409, *2902*.

James McGee, The (1924), 300 Fed. 93.

Kilberg v. *Northeast Airlines, Inc.*, [1961] 2 Lloyd's Rep. 406.

Koop v. *Bebb* (1952), 84 C.L.R. 629; [1952] A.L.R. 37; 25 A.L.J. 610; Digest
(Cont. Vol. A) 233, **447a*.

A   *Livesley* v. *Horst Co.,* [1925] 1 D.L.R. 159; [1924] S.C.R. 605; *affg.* sub nom.
      Horst v. *Livesley,* [1924] 2 D.L.R. 1002; 2 W.W.R. 443; 34 B.C.R. 19;
      11 Digest (Repl.) 427, *370.*

M'Elroy v. *M'Allister,* 1949 S.C. 110; 11 Digest (Repl.) 452, *475.*

Machado v. *Fontes,* [1897] 2 Q.B. 231; 66 L.J.Q.B. 542; 76 L.T. 588; 11
      Digest (Repl.) 450, *882.*

B   *Mackinnon* v. *Iberia Shipping Co.,* 1955 S.C. 20; [1955] S.L.T. 49; [1954]
      2 Lloyd's Rep. 372; Digest (Cont. Vol. A) 233, *463a.*

McLean v. *Pettigrew,* [1945] S.C.R. 62; 11 Digest (Repl.) 450, *458.*

McMillan v. *Canadian Northern Ry. Co.,* [1923] A.C. 120; 92 L.J.P.C. 44;
      128 L.T. 293; 11 Digest (Repl.) 450, *453.*

Miller v. *Miller* (1968), 290 N.Y.S. (2d) 734; 237 N.E. 2d 877.

C   *Morris and Stulback* v. *Angel* (1956), 5 D.L.R. (2d) 30; Digest (Cont. Vol. A)
      233, *447b.*

Mostyn v. *Fabrigas* (1775), 1 Cowp. 161; [1775-1802] All E.R. Rep. 266;
      98 E.R. 1021; *affg.* sub nom. *Fabrigas* v. *Mostyn* (1773), 2 Wm. Bl. 929;
      11 Digest (Repl.) 450, *886.*

Moxham (M.), The (1876), 1 P.D. 107; 46 L.J.P. 17; 34 L.T. 559; 11 Digest
D   (Repl.) 370, *372.*

Naftalin v. *London, Midland and Scottish Ry. Co.,* 1933 S.C. 259; 8 Digest
      (Repl.) 118, *531.*

New York Central Ry. Co. v. *Chisholm* (1925), 268 U.S. 29.

O'Connor v. *Wray, Boyd* v. *Wray,* [1930] 2 D.L.R. 899; S.C.R. 231; *affg.,*
      [1929] 2 D.L.R. 24; 46 Que. K.B. 199; 11 Digest (Repl.) 450, *455.*

E   *Phillips* v. *Eyre* (1870), L.R. 6 Q.B. 1; 10 B. & S. 1004; 40 L.J.Q.B. 28; 22
      L.T. 869; 11 Digest (Repl.) 451, *888.*

R. v. *Lesley* (1860), Bell C.C. 220; 29 L.J.M.C. 97; 1 L.T. 452; 24 J.P. 115;
      11 Digest (Repl.) 454, *905.*

Richards v. *United States* (1962), 82 S. Ct. 585.

Scott v. *Lord Seymour* (1862), 1 H. & C. 219; 32 L.J.Ex. 61; 8 L.T. 511;
F   158 E.R. 865; 11 Digest (Repl.) 451, *887.*

Slater v. *Mexican National Railroad Co.* (1904), 194 U.S. 120;

Story v. *Stratford Mill Building Co.* (1913), 11 D.L.R. 49; 24 O.W.R. 552;
      4 O.W.N. 1212; *affd.* 30 O.L.R. 271; 18 D.L.R. 309; 5 O.W.N. 611;
      11 Digest (Repl.) 450, *449.*

G   *Varawa* v. *Howard Smith & Co.,* [1910] V.L.R. 509; (1911), 13 C.L.R. 35;
      33 Digest (Repl.) 402, *79.*

Walpole v. *Canadian Northern Ry. Co.,* [1923] A.C. 113; 92 L.J.P.C. 39;
      128 L.T. 289; 11 Digest (Repl.) 452, *465.*

Wey v. *Rally* (1704), 6 Mod. Rep. 194; 87 E.R. 948; 31 Digest (Repl.) 290,
      4251.

H   *Western Union Telegraph Co.* v. *Brown* (1914), 234 U.S. 542.

Appeal.

This was an appeal by Richard Meredith McNair Chaplin against an order
of the Court of Appeal (LORD DENNING, M.R., and LORD UPJOHN; DIPLOCK, L.J.,
dissenting) dated 6th December 1967 and reported [1968] 1 All E.R. 283, dismissing an appeal from an order of MILMO, J., dated 22nd March 1967, and
I   reported [1967] 2 All E.R. 665, awarding to the respondent, David Malcolm
Boys, the sum of £2,303 (including £2,250 general damages for pain and suffering)
and costs. The facts are set out in the opinion of LORD HODSON.

Tudor Evans, Q.C., D. J. Hyamson and *J. A. Dyson* for the appellant.
Leonard Caplan, Q.C., J. M. Cope and *V. C. Kothari* for the respondent.

Their Lordships took time for consideration.

25th June. The following opinions were delivered.

LORD HODSON: My Lords, this case, as LORD DENNING, M.R., pointed **A**
out (1), throws up one of the most vexed questions in the conflict of laws: when a
wrong is committed abroad and the injured party sues in England what law is to
be applied?

The respondent, plaintiff in the action, was injured in a road accident in Malta
caused by the admitted negligence of the appellant, defendant in the action.
The respondent sustained serious injuries and sued for damages. Under the **B**
Maltese law he could recover only financial loss directly suffered, expenses
incurred and lost wages together with a sum for ascertained future loss of wages
with a right to make a further application to the court if and when anticipated
loss became actual. He could recover no damages in respect of the injury itself
for pain, suffering and loss of amenities. In the result the trial judge awarded
£53 special damages which would have been recoverable under Maltese law and **C**
£2,250 general damages for those injuries which would not be recoverable under
Maltese law. Both parties were serving in the forces of this country on 6th
October 1963, when the motor cycle on the back of which the respondent was
riding was run into by a car driven by the appellant. They are now both back
in this country; the respondent was in hospital for many months owing to his
injuries and was eventually discharged from the Royal Air Force. It is said that **D**
he is unlikely to suffer loss of earnings in the future as a result of his accident.

The learned judge (2) took the view that he was bound by authority, to which
I must refer, to apply the law of England as the lex fori and to award damages
accordingly. In the Court of Appeal (3) LORD DENNING, M.R., was in favour
of dismissing the appeal, reaching the same result as the trial judge by a different
route. He held that the proper law of the tort should be applied not only in **E**
order to ascertain whether there is a cause of action but also to settle the measure
as well as the heads of damage recoverable. He referred to *Babcock* v. *Jackson* (4)
a decision of the New York Court of Appeals. There the plaintiff, a gratuitous
passenger in the defendant's motor car, was injured in an accident which occurred
in Ontario when the parties who were New York residents were on a weekend trip
to Canada. The trip began in New York State where the car was licensed, insured **F**
and usually garaged. An Ontario statute absolves drivers from liability towards
gratuitous passengers, whereas New York law contains no similar provision.
The plaintiff sued successfully in New York for the negligence of the defendant
and FULD, J., expressing the view of the majority of the court, said (5):

"The question presented is simply drawn. Shall the law of the place of
the tort *invariably* govern the availability of relief for the tort or shall the **G**
applicable choice of law rule also reflect a consideration of other factors
which are relevant to the purposes served by the enforcement or denial of
the remedy?"

In accepting the latter alternative the learned judge followed the view expressed
in CONFLICT OF LAWS RESTATEMENT (2nd Edn.), p. 379:
H
"The local law of the state which has the most significant relationship
with the occurrence and with the parties determines their rights and liabilities
in tort."

LORD DENNING, M.R. (6), on the facts of the case to which I have made a brief
reference, opined that the proper law of the tort was the law of England as being
the place to which the parties had the most significant contact. LORD UPJOHN (7), **I**
on the other hand, upheld the judgment on what may perhaps fairly be described
as the more conventional ground that the judge's decision was soundly based on

(1) [1968] 1 All E.R. 283 at p. 286; [1968] 2 Q.B. 1 at p. 20.
(2) [1967] 2 All E.R. 665; [1968] 2 Q.B. 1.
(3) [1968] 1 All E.R. 283; [1968] 2 Q.B. 1.
(4) [1963] 2 Lloyd's Rep. 286.
(5) [1963] 2 Lloyd's Rep. at p. 287.
(6) [1968] 1 All E.R. at p. 289; [1968] 2 Q.B. at p. 24.
(7) [1968] 1 All E.R. at p. 294; [1968] 2 Q.B. at p. 32.

A authority. Diplock, L.J. (8), in a powerful dissenting judgment, which is much relied on by the appellant, concluded that the heads of damage recoverable are matters of substantive law which must be determined according to the lex loci delicti, that is to say, by the law of Malta, and would have allowed the appeal by reducing the award of damages to £53.

No difficulty arises in settling the place of the wrong which occurred entirely
B in Malta. As to the choice of law the generally accepted rule in this country is set out in Dicey and Morris on the Conflict of Laws (8th Edn.), pp. 919, 920, as follows:

" An act done in a foreign country is a tort and actionable as such in England, only if it is both (i) actionable as a tort, according to English law, or in other words, is an act which, if done in England, would be a tort;
C and (ii) not justifiable, according to the law of the foreign country where it was done."

Clause (i) of this rule was clearly stated in *The Halley* (9), an Admiralty case in which a suit was brought against a British ship and her owners on account of a collision in Belgian waters. The defence was that the ship was under the control of a compulsory pilot so that both vessel and owners were relieved of responsi-
D bility. The plaintiffs replied that under Belgian law the owners were liable notwithstanding that the ship was being navigated at the time by a compulsory pilot. At first instance the plaintiff succeeded on the ground that the governing law was that of the place where the collision occurred. This decision was reversed by the Judicial Committee of the Privy Council which, in a judgment delivered by
E Selwyn, L.J., declared the law as follows (10):

". . . it is, in their Lordships' opinion, alike contrary to principle and to authority to hold, that an English Court of Justice will enforce a Foreign Municipal law, and will give a remedy in the shape of damages in respect of an act which, according to its own principles, imposes no liability on the person from whom the damages are claimed."

F It is to be noticed that there is no direct reference to public policy as such in this judgment.

Clause (ii) of the rule has occasioned difficulty owing to the use of the words "not justifiable". "Justification" according to the lex loci delicti is to be found in the opinion of Lord Nottingham in *Blad* v. *Bamfield* (11). A century later in the leading case of *Mostyn* v. *Fabrigas* (12) Lord Mansfield, C.J.,
G said (13): ". . . whatever is a justification in the place where the thing is done, ought to be a justification where the case is tried ".

Dicey's rule is collected from the judgment delivered by Willes, J., in *Phillips* v. *Eyre* (14) in the Exchequer Chamber, consisting of Kelly, C.B., Martin, Channell, Pigott and Cleasby, BB., Willes and Brett, JJ. The action complained of false imprisonment and other injuries to the plaintiff inflicted in
H Jamaica by the defendant who was governor of the island. The defendant relied on an act of indemnity passed by the legislature of Jamaica as in effect a subsequent justification of his actions. Willes, J., said (15):

" A right of action, whether it arise from contract governed by the law of the place or wrong, is equally the creature of the law of the place and subordinate thereto . . . the civil liability arising out of a wrong derives its
I birth from the law of the place, and its character is determined by that law."

(8) [1968] 1 All E.R. at p. 302; [1968] 2 Q.B. at p. 45.
(9) (1868), L.R. 2 P.C. 193.
(10) (1868), L.R. 2 P.C. at p. 204.
(11) (1674), 3 Swan. 604 at p. 605.
(12) (1775), 1 Cowp. 161; [1775-1802] All E.R. Rep. 266.
(13) (1775), 1 Cowp. at p. 175; [1775-1802] All E.R. Rep. at p. 271.
(14) (1870), L.R. 6 Q.B. 1.
(15) (1870), L.R. 6 Q.B. at p. 28.

The judgment continues (16):   A

   " As a general rule, in order to found a suit in England for a wrong alleged
to have been committed abroad, two conditions must be fulfilled.   First,
the wrong must be of such a character that it would have been actionable
if committed in England . . ."

For this proposition *The Halley* (17) is cited, and the judgment proceeds (18): B
" Secondly, the act must not have been justifiable by the law of the place where
it was done."   For this proposition *Blad's* case (19), among others, is cited.
   The appellant's argument gains support from the passage I have read in which
it is declared that the civil liability arising out of a wrong derives its birth from
the law of the place and its character is determined by that law.   WILLES, J.,
was not, however, concerned with choice of law but only whether the courts   C
of this country should entertain the action.
   The judgment does not declare, as LORD UPJOHN (20) pointed out in the Court
of Appeal, that the tortious act must be determined by the lex loci delicti.
That would be to adopt what is called " the obligation " theory formerly accepted
in the United States of America and sponsored by HOLMES, J., of the Supreme
Court of the United States.   In *Slater* v. *Mexican National Railroad Co.* he   D
said (21):

   " The theory of the foreign suit is that although the act complained of was
   subject to no law having force in the forum, it gave rise to an obligation . . .
   and may be enforced wherever the person may be found . . . But as the
   only source of this obligation is the law of the place of the act, it follows that
   the law determines not merely the existence of the obligation . . . but   E
   equally determines its extent."

Again in *Western Union Telegraph Co.* v. *Brown* HOLMES, J., said (22):

   " When a person recovers in one jurisdiction for a tort committed in
   another he does so on the ground of an obligation incurred at the place
   of the tort that accompanies the person of the defendant elsewhere, and
   that is not only the ground but the measure of the maximum recovery."   F

As DIPLOCK, L.J. (23), pointed out, the courts have of recent years in a number
of States of the United States departed from the lex loci in favour of another
law which has been described as " the proper law of the tort " or facetiously as
" the law of the garage " (see *Babcock* v. *Jackson* (24) to which I have referred).
   In opposition to the obligation theory another distinguished American judge, G
JUDGE LEARNED HAND said in *Guinness* v. *Miller* (25):

   " When a court takes cognizance of a tort committed elsewhere, it is
   indeed sometimes said that it enforces the obligation arising under the law
   of the place where the tort arises . . . However, no court can enforce any law
   but that of its own sovereign, and, when a suitor comes to a jurisdiction foreign
   to the place of the tort, he can only invoke an obligation recognized by that   H
   sovereign.   A foreign sovereign, under civilized law, imposes an obligation
   of its own as nearly homologous as possible to that arising in the place where
   the tort occurs."

In the next year the same judge, in *The James McGee*, said (26):

   " In the very nature of things, courts can enforce no obligations which
   are created elsewhere; when dealing with such obligations, they merely   I
   recognize them as the original of the copies which they themselves enforce."

---

(16) (1870), L.R. 6 Q.B. at pp. 28, 29.   (17) (1868), L.R. 2 P.C. 193.
(18) (1870), L.R. 6 Q.B. at p. 29.   (19) (1674), 3 Swan. 604.
(20) [1968] 1 All E.R. at pp. 291, 292; [1968] 2 Q.B. at pp. 28, 29.
(21) (1904), 194 U.S. 120 at p. 126.   (22) (1914), 234 U.S. 542 at p. 547.
(23) [1968] 1 All E.R. at p. 301; [1968] 2 Q.B. at p. 43.
(24) [1963] 2 Lloyd's Rep. 286.   (25) (1923), 291 Fed. 769 at 770.
               (26) (1924), 300 Fed. 93 at p. 96.

A   I come to the much-criticised decision of *Machado* v. *Fontes* (27), a decision of
the Court of Appeal on an interlocutory matter. This case was doubted by
the Privy Council in *Canadian Pacific Ry. Co.* v. *Parent* (28). It has been followed
in Canada, rejected by the High Court of Australia in *Koop* v. *Bebb* (29) and not
accepted in Scotland. The case concerned two gentlemen, one of whom sued
the other in England for a libel in the Portuguese language published in Brazil
B   on the footing that the libel was actionable in England although it appeared
that in Brazil it was not actionable civilly but only punishable as a crime. LOPES,
L.J. (30), equated " not justifiable " in WILLES, J.'s judgment with " wrongful "
and " justifiable " with " innocent ". RIGBY, L.J. (31), drew attention to the
change from " actionable " in the first branch of the rule to " justifiable " in the
second. He equated " justifiable " with " authorised or innocent or excusable ".

C   As PROFESSOR CHESHIRE pointed out in his PRIVATE INTERNATIONAL LAW
(7th Edn.), p. 248:

>   " It seems reasonably clear also that the word ' justifiable ' was used
> by WILLES, J., to emphasize the established and obvious rule that what is
> a good defence in the *locus delicti* must be equally good in a foreign forum.
> His mind was addressed solely to the ' civil liability arising out of the
D   > wrong ' and there is nothing in his remarks to show that he contemplated
> the possibility of a successful action in England in respect of an act that is
> civilly, though not criminally, innocent in the *locus delicti*."

Governor Eyre's acts were justified by statute passed after they were committed
and did not by virtue of the statute merit the appellation of innocence. In that
case and in the earlier cases in which they appear in like context the words
E   " not justifiable " must, I think, refer only to civil liability. That this may be
the true view of the law is supported by the opinion of the High Court of Australia
given in *Koop* v. *Bebb* (29) referred to above. Cf. also *Varawa* v. *Howard Smith &
Co.* (32), a decision of the Supreme Court of Victoria where (per CUSSENS, J.)
Machado v. *Fontes* (27) was dissented from and held not to be supported by
Phillips v. *Eyre* (33). If the decision in *Machado* v. *Fontes* (27) could be supported
F   on the ground that actionability is not essential the respondent must succeed
but, in my opinion, that decision is wrong and should be overruled.

To put *Machado* v. *Fontes* (27) on one side is not, however, to dispose of this
case. There is no doubt that an actionable wrong by Maltese law was committed
in Malta when the respondent sustained his injuries and that subject to the
difference in the laws of the two countries a wrong is actionable here. Prima
G   facie the conditions set forth in the judgment of the Court of Exchequer Chamber
in *Phillips* v. *Eyre* (33) are fulfilled, but it is proper to remember that the conditions were introduced by the words (34) " As a general rule " which I do not
read as equivalent to " as an invariable rule ". One gets some assistance from
a case earlier than *Phillips* v. *Eyre* (33) where WILLES, J., was also a member of
the court. This is *Scott* v. *Lord Seymour* (35). Lord Seymour had assaulted
H   Mr. Scott in Naples and Mr. Scott sued Lord Seymour in England for damages.
This action was, it is said, not available in Naples where only criminal proceedings lay. The case was decided on a special ground, but WIGHTMAN, J.,
in the course of his judgment said (36):

>   " . . . whatever might be the case as between two Neapolitan subjects, or
I   > between a Neapolitan and an Englishman, I find no authority for holding
> that, even if the Neapolitan law gives no remedy for an assault and battery,
> however violent and unprovoked, by recovery of damages, that therefore a
> British subject is deprived of his right to damages given by the English law
> against another British subject."

(27) [1897] 2 Q.B. 231.   (28) [1917] A.C. 195.
(29) (1952), 84 C.L.R. 629.   (30) [1897] 2 Q.B. at pp. 233, 234.
(31) [1897] 2 Q.B. at pp. 234, 235.   (32) [1910] V.L.R. 509.
(33) (1870), L.R. 6 Q.B. 1.   (34) (1870), L.R. 6 Q.B. at p. 28.
(35) (1862), 1 H. & C. 219.   (36) (1862), 1 H. & C. at p. 235.

WILLES, J., said (37)—" I am far from saying that I differ from any part of the A
judgment of my brother WIGHTMAN ".

This is an indication that at this point of time WILLES, J., was content to
adopt a flexible attitude to the position which he subsequently incorporated in
the passage beginning with the words " As a general rule " (38).

The American cases have shown that in recent years, particularly in instances
arising from accidents occurring in motor car journeys or in aeroplanes on B
trans-continental trips where the place of the accident is likely to be fortuitous,
an attempt has been made to arrive at a solution described as " the proper law
of the tort ".   This has led to uncertain results and has not been fully developed
in the United States.   The analogy of the proper law of the contract is not useful
since the parties to a contract usually have the opportunity of choosing the law
to which they seek to submit.   Choice of law rules here bring certainty, predicta- C
bility and uniformity of result.   These features are absent in tort.   No doubt
if the proper law of the tort were to be adopted as the solution of those cases
which arise from transitory torts, it is not easy to improve on the test chosen
by LORD DENNING, M.R. (39), from the AMERICAN RESTATEMENT (40), namely,
the place with which the parties had the most significant connection.

The respondent did not seek to argue that the American theory of the proper D
law of the tort should be adopted but he submitted, and I think submitted
rightly, that the words " As a general rule " (38) should be interpreted so as
to leave some latitude in cases where it would be against public policy to admit
or to exclude claims.   I am conscious that to resort to public policy is to mount
an " unruly horse ".   It appears to me, however, to be in the interests of public
policy to discourage " forum shopping " expeditions by the inhabitants of other E
countries.   As the Lord President (LORD COOPER) said in M'Elroy v. M'Allister
(41):

" Pursuers should not be encouraged to improve their position vis-à-vis of
their opponents by invoking some secondary forum in order to exact compensation for a type of loss which the primary forum would not regard as
meriting reparation."   F

It is necessary to permit some flexibility in applying the language of WILLES, J.,
in Phillips v. Eyre (42) which is to be applied as " a general rule " and not invariably.   I reach this conclusion not without reluctance since rules of law should
be defined and adhered to as closely as possible lest they lose themselves in a
field of judicial discretion where no secure foothold is to be found by litigants or
their advisers.   The search for justice in the individual case must often clash G
with fixed legal principles especially perhaps when choice of law is concerned.

So far as the instant case is concerned, there is no ground of public policy
for rejecting the respondent's claim.   The parties appear to have been British
nationals resident in this country but temporarily in Malta on service at the
time of the occurrence.   The substantial ground for rejecting the claim is that
when Machado v. Fontes (43) is out of the way and " innocence " by the local H
law no longer leaves the way clear for the application of the lex fori, one must look
and see exactly what is the wrongful act sued on which is actionable in the
foreign country and also here.

The nature of a plaintiff's remedy is a matter of procedure to be determined
by the lex fori.   This includes the quantification of damages, but the question
arises whether or not the English remedy sought and obtained by the judgment I
here fits in with the right as fixed by the foreign, that is the Maltese, law.   It

---

(37) (1862), 1 H. & C. at p. 236.
(38) (1870), L.R. 6 Q.B. at p. 28.
(39) [1968] 1 All E.R. at p. 290; [1968] 2 Q.B. at p. 26.
(40) See p. 1103, letters D to F, post.
(41) 1949 S.C. 110 at p. 135.
(42) (1870), L.R. 6 Q.B. at p. 28.
(43) [1897] 1 Q.B. 231.

A is argued that to award damages on the English principle is to make the right sought to be enforced a different right from that given by the *lex loci delicti* and that questions such as whether loss of earning capacity or pain and suffering are admissible heads of damage are questions of substantive law distinct from mere quantification which is purely a procedural matter.

The distinction between substance and procedure was clearly stated by TINDAL,
B C.J., in *Huber* v. *Steiner* (44) and by LORD BROUGHAM in *Don* v. *Lippmann* (45). The latter said (46):

" The law on this point is well settled in this country, where this distinction is properly taken, that whatever relates to the remedy to be enforced must be determined by the *lex fori*, the law of the country to the tribunals of which the appeal is made."

C
If it were clear that there existed in Malta in this case civil liability for the wrong done there would be no obstacle in the respondent's way, for in principle a person should in such circumstances be permitted to claim in this country for the wrong committed in Malta.   This is to state the general rule as generally accepted which takes no account of circumstances peculiar to the parties on the occurrence. The existence of the relevant civil liability is, however, not clear in this case.
D I was at first attracted by the submission that some liability under Maltese law being established the remedy under Maltese law of compensation for actual loss of earnings and the remedy of damages in respect of the injury itself for pain and suffering could be merged.   If this were done both heads of damage could be treated as if they related solely to the remedy and not to the substantive law involved, thus avoiding the difficulty presented by the distinction between
E substantive law and procedure.   I am now, however, persuaded that questions such as whether loss of earning capacity or pain and suffering are admissible heads of damage must be questions of substantive law.   The law relating to damages is partly procedural and partly substantive, the actual quantification under the relevant heads being procedural only.   This view is supported by authority. The Supreme Court of Canada in *Livesley* v. *Horst Co.* (47) held that the question
F what kind of loss actually resulting from a breach of contract is actionable is a question of law.   The court cited and relied on a passage from the judgment of TURNER, L.J., in *Hooper* v. *Gumm, McLellan* v. *Gumm* (48), which reads (49):

". . . where rights are acquired under the laws of foreign states, the law of this country recognises and gives effect to those rights, unless it is contrary
G to the law and policy of this country to do so."

This statement excludes procedure, for the party invoking English law must take procedure as he finds it.

Here I think the question of right to damages for pain and suffering is a substantive right and the respondent would fail if that which I have described as the general rule of principle were applied.   That would be a just result if both
H parties were Maltese residents or even if the defendant were a Maltese resident. In a case such as the present the result is, if not plainly unjust, at least not to be regarded as satisfactory.   The parties had no connection with Malta except by reason of their service which was of a temporary nature and the interest of justice in such a case where civil liability exists in the foreign country although not exactly corresponding to the civil liability in this country requires some qualifi-
I cation of the general rule.   The observations of WIGHTMAN, J., in *Scott* v. *Lord Seymour* (50) lend support to this view, as LORD DENNING, M.R. (51), pointed

(44) (1835), 2 Bing. N.C. 202; [1835-42] All E.R. Rep. 159.
(45) (1837), 5 Cl. & Fin. 1.
(46) (1837), 5 Cl. & Fin. at p. 13.
(47) [1925] 1 D.L.R. 159.
(48) (1867), 2 Ch. App. 282.
(49) (1867), 2 Ch. App. at p. 289.
(50) (1862), 1 H. & C. at p. 235.
(51) [1968] 1 All E.R. at p. 290; [1968] 2 Q.B. at p. 25.

out.   Likewise there is no apparent justification for one Maltese subject suing **A**
another in this country for damages in respect of pain and suffering where the
wrong took place in Malta.   That would be a bare-faced example of " forum
shopping ".   In personal injury cases it is not necessarily true that by entering
a country you submit yourself to the special laws of that country.

I would for myself, therefore, adopt the AMERICAN LAW INSTITUTE RESTATE-
MENT (second) CONFLICT OF LAWS (Proposed official draft, 1st May 1968) set **B**
out in the speech which has been prepared by my noble and learned friend
LORD WILBERFORCE (52).   If controlling effect is given to the law of the jurisdiction which because of its relationship with the occurrence and the parties
has the greater concern with the specific issue raised in the litigation, the ends
of justice are likely to be achieved although, as the American authorities show,
there is a difficult task presented for decision of the courts, and uncertainty has **C**
led to dissenting judgments in the appellate courts.

I would accordingly, in agreement with LORD DENNING, M.R., treat the
law of England as applicable since even though the occurrence took place in
Malta this was overshadowed by the identity and circumstances of the parties,
British subjects temporarily serving in Malta.

It is to be expected that a court will favour its own policies over those of other **D**
States and be inclined to give its own rules a wider application than it will give
to those of other States (see WILLIS L. M. REESE (of Columbia University)
CONFLICT OF LAWS RESTATEMENT (Second)).   This tendency is convenient.
To insist on the choice of the law of the place where the wrong was committed
has an attraction and leads to certainty but in modern conditions of speedy and
frequent travel between countries the place of the wrong may be and often is **E**
determined by accidental circumstances, as in this case where the parties were
but temporarily carrying out their service in Malta.   Furthermore, difficulty
and inconvenience is involved in many cases in ascertaining the details of the
relevant foreign law.

On the facts of this case, giving the rule, as I understand it, which is propounded
in *Phillips* v. *Eyre* (53) a flexible interpretation, I would dismiss the appeal. **F**

LORD GUEST: My Lords, a collision took place in Malta between two
vehicles in which the respondent was injured by the admittedly negligent driving
of the appellant.   The respondent raised an action in the High Court (54) against
the appellant in which he claimed, as a result of the negligence of the appellant,
damages for pain and suffering caused by his injuries, for out-of-pocket expenses
and for prospective loss of earnings due to his incapacity.   The trial judge **G**
awarded damages amounting to £2,303 to which he was entitled for these items
of damage.   According to the law of Malta the respondent could only have
received his expenses and his money loss which would have amounted to £53.
He would have received nothing for his pain and suffering and loss of amenities
and future problematical financial loss.   The question, therefore, which sharply
arises is whether the damages are to be ascertained by the lex loci delicti, Maltese **H**
law, or by the lex fori, English law.

MILMO, J. (54), and the Court of Appeal (55) by a majority (LORD DENNING,
M.R., and LORD UPJOHN; DIPLOCK, L.J., dissenting) have awarded the respon-
dent damages according to the lex fori.   The trial judge followed *Machado* v.
Fontes (56) (as he felt himself bound to do) and held that the lex fori applied.
The majority in the Court of Appeal affirmed his decision but on different grounds : **I**
LORD DENNING, M.R. (57), held that *Machado* v. *Fontes* (56) was not binding on
the Court of Appeal and should be overruled but he held that " the proper

(52) See p. 1103, letters D to F, post.
(53) (1870), L.R. 6 Q.B. at pp. 28, 29.
(54) [1967] 2 All E.R. 665; [1968] 2 Q.B. 1.
(55) [1968] 1 All E.R. 283; [1968] 2 Q.B. 1.
(56) [1897] 2 Q.B. 231.
(57) [1968] 1 All E.R. at p. 288; [1968] 2 Q.B. at p. 23.

A law of the tort " should be applied to the question of damages and that in the circumstances this was the law of England. LORD UPJOHN (58) held that the lex fori should be applied. He declined to accept the principle of " the proper law of the tort ". DIPLOCK, L.J. (59), dissented on the ground that the English Court in assessing the heads of damage must apply the law of the place where the tort was committed. He would have been in favour of awarding only £53 in

B name of damages. Like LORD UPJOHN he would not have been in favour of applying " the proper law of the tort ".

Before I deal with the main question, I should say that I would not, in any event, be in favour of applying " the proper law of the tort " whatever that law might be. The principle of " the proper law of the tort " has only been recently introduced into certain States of the United States of America due to the differing

C State laws in that country. It has never been part of the law of England. It produces uncertainty and for the reasons given by both LORD UPJOHN (60) and DIPLOCK, L.J. (61), I would not be in favour of its introduction here.

I propose to decide this case on a very narrow ground. The difficulties arising from the decision of *Phillips* v. *Eyre* (62) have already been referred to by my noble and learned friends. I prefer to leave these questions to those of your

D Lordships who are more familiar with this aspect of English law. I am content to accept the position that to justify an action in England for a tort committed abroad the conduct must be actionable by English law and by the laws of the country in which the conduct occurred, the lex loci delicti. Both these conditions are satisfied in this case as the negligent driving of the appellant was actionable both by the law of England and by the law of Malta. This line of

E reasoning would be in accord with the principles of the Scottish decision of *Naftalin* v. *London, Midland and Scottish Ry. Co.* (63) and *M'Elroy* v. *M'Allister* (64). And nothing which I have to say hereafter is intended to throw any doubt on these cases which I think were rightly decided.

Assuming that the conduct was actionable in Malta, what law is to be applied to the ascertainment of the damages? Is it to be the substantive law, the law of

F Malta, or is it to be the procedural law which is the lex fori? In *Don* v. *Lippmann* (65), LORD BROUGHAM (66) said that whatever relates to the remedy to be enforced must be determined by the lex fori. There would appear to be a distinction between questions affecting heads of damages which are for the lex loci delicti and quantification of damages which is for the lex fori. This is well illustrated in DICEY AND MORRIS ON THE CONFLICT OF LAWS (8th Edn.), p. 944, where the

G kind of damage is a matter of substantive law and the method of compensating the plaintiff for his loss which is for the lex fori (ibid., p. 1092). CHESHIRE'S PRIVATE INTERNATIONAL LAW (7th Edn.), p. 602, is to the same effect.

It may be difficult in certain cases to say on which side of the border-line any particular claim of damages should fall. An analogy was said to exist with the Scots' cases dealing with solatium. In *M'Elroy* v. *M'Allister* (64), affirming

H *Naftalin* v. *London, Midland and Scottish Ry. Co.* (63), a court of seven judges held that where an accident happened in England the rights of parties had to be decided in accordance with the law of England. The law of England gave no right to solatium in respect of the death of a near relative, as Scots law does, and that accordingly as solatium was excluded by the lex loci delicti it would not be admitted by the lex fori. The basis of this decision was that the right to

I claim solatium was a substantive right distinct and separate from the right to

(58) [1968] 1 All E.R. at p. 295; [1968] 2 Q.B. at p. 33.
(59) [1968] 1 All E.R. at p. 302; [1968] 2 Q.B. at p. 45.
(60) [1968] 1 All E.R. at p. 294; [1968] 2 Q.B. at p. 33.
(61) [1968] 1 All E.R. at p. 301; [1986] 2 Q.B. at p. 43.
(62) (1870), L.R. 6 Q.B. 1.
(63) 1933 S.C. 259.
(64) 1949 S.C. 110.
(65) (1837), 5 Cl. & Fin. 1.
(66) (1837), 5 Cl. & Fin. at p. 13.

claim in respect of patrimonial loss.   The Lord Justice-Clerk (LORD THOMSON) A
expresses it thus (67):

> " Solatium is not recognised by the *lex delicti*.   It can be defended as a
> relevant ground of claim only if it can be regarded as an element to be
> considered in measuring damages.   If it could be so regarded it would fall
> within the scope of the *lex fori* as being a matter of remedy and not of B
> substantive right.   Looking to the nature of solatium as it has been ex-
> pounded in a series of authorities, I find it impossible to regard it otherwise
> than as a separate right peculiar to the law of Scotland.   The argument to
> the contrary can be supported only by placing on the word ' remedy ' a
> meaning wider than it can bear consistently with the accepted principles of
> private international law."
                                                                              C
By analogy it was said that damages for pain and suffering being excluded by
the law of Malta, this was a substantive right which was for the lex loci delicti
and damages on this account could not be awarded by the court of the forum.
It is true that in Scots law the Latin term solatium is used without distinction
both to indicate a claim for compensation for the grief and suffering sustained
by the death of a near relative and also for the pain and suffering occasioned to D
an injured party.   But in my view the term solatium may connote different
rights.   Solatium properly so called denotes a separate right of action given only
to near relatives whereas solatium for pain and suffering of an injured party—
a term not known apparently to English law—connotes an element in the ascertainment of damages for the injuries suffered by a plaintiff.   These consist
of various elements, solatium for the pain and suffering, out-of-pocket expenses, E
actual loss of wages and future problematical patrimonial loss due to loss of
earning capacity.   These elements comprise the head of damage due to an
injured person by English law.   It would not be correct, in my view, to talk of
compensation for pain and suffering as a head of damage apart from patrimonial
loss.   It is merely an element in the quantification of the total compensation.
This distinction was adverted to by LORD SORN in *Mackinnon* v. *Iberia Shipping* F
Co. (68):

> " In reaching the above conclusion it has been assumed that a claim
> for solatium is a separate right of action and that its relevance, therefore,
> must depend upon the actionability of such a claim under the foreign law.
> It was in fact so decided in *Naftalin* v. *L.M.S. Ry. Co.* (69) and *M'Elroy*
> v. *M'Allister* (70), but in both of these cases the claim for solatium was G
> put forward in that peculiar action by which our law allows a person to sue
> for compensation in respect of the death of a near relative, whereas in the
> present case the claim is comprised in an ordinary action of damages.
> I am not saying that this difference affords a good ground of distinction and
> merely mention the point in order to say that we were not asked to consider
> it, the pursuer not having disputed the applicability of these two decisions H
> to the present case."

With respect, I am inclined to agree with LORD SORN that the claim for solatium
for pain and suffering is " comprised " in the ordinary action of damages for
injuries.
   Although differing from some of the reasoning in the majority of the Court
of Appeal (71) I would dismiss the appeal.
                                                                              I
   LORD DONOVAN: My Lords, I need not repeat the facts.   I am content
with the rule enunciated by WILLES, J., in *Phillips* v. *Eyre* (72) and would leave

---

(67) 1949 S.C. at p. 117.
(68) 1955 S.C. 20 at pp. 37, 38.
(69) 1933 S.C. 259.
(70) 1949 S.C. 110.
(71) [1968] 1 All E.R. 283; [1968] 2 Q.B. 1.
(72) (1870), L.R. 6 Q.B. 1 at pp. 28, 29.

A   it alone. In particular I would not substitute " actionable " for " not justifiable ". I think the latter expression was deliberately chosen; and it makes for justice. For example, if the present respondent had suffered only pain and suffering in Malta, it would have allowed him to bring an action for damages here which he could not have brought in Malta. And I think this would have been right.

B   If " actionable " be substituted for " not justifiable " a reason has to be found for allowing such damages in the present case. The one which has found favour with some of your Lordships is, I think, that while " double actionability " ought to be the rule, yet departures may be made from it in individual cases where this appears to be justified by the circumstances. This introduces a new element of uncertainty into the law which I would prefer to exclude.

C   So far as *Machado* v. *Fontes* (73) is concerned we do not need to alter the rule laid down by WILLES, J. It is enough to say that the case in question, while within the rule, was an abuse of it; and that considerations of public policy would justify a court here in rejecting any such future case of blatant " forum shopping ". I may say I am assuming that the parties were Brazilian although the report does not say so.

D   I do not think we should adopt any such doctrine as " the proper law of the tort " with all its uncertainties. There is no need here for such a doctrine —at least while we remain a United Kingdom. Nor would I take the first step towards it in the name of flexibility. I would dismiss the present appeal on the ground that an English court was competent to entertain the action under the rule in *Phillips* v. *Eyre* (74) and that once it had done so it was right that it

E   should award its own remedies. In short I entirely agree with the judgment of my noble and learned friend, LORD UPJOHN, in the court below (75).

LORD WILBERFORCE: My Lords, 1. The wrong, in respect of which this action was brought, negligence on a road in Malta, was actionable, in the sense that civil proceedings might be brought to recover damages, in England

F   and in Malta, under the laws prevailing in each of those countries. I refer, for convenience, to the former as the lex fori and the latter as the lex delicti. Under the lex delicti, as found by the trial judge on the basis of art. 1088 (76) of the Maltese Civil Code, damages are limited to financial loss directly suffered, to expenditure necessarily incurred and (which did not arise in the present case) to wages actually lost, and proved future loss of earnings. But no compensation

G   can be awarded, as it can under the lex fori, for pain and suffering as such. This appeal raises the question whether such monetary compensation can be recovered in an English action. Both parties to the action are British subjects normally resident in England and their presence in Malta at the time of the accident was of a temporary character under engagements in the British forces.

  In the forefront of the appeal it is necessary to consider what is the basis

H   of an action brought in England in respect of a foreign tort; to what extent (if any) the lex delicti enters into it. If it does, further questions arise, whether the awarding of damages generally is within the exclusive authority of the lex fori, whether any distinction is to be made between the quantification of damages and the definition of the heads of recoverable damages, and if so whether, as to the latter, the lex delicti should be held to govern. I state these questions

I   provisionally in classical form and language and in terms which suggest that

---

(73) [1897] 2 Q.B. 231.
(74) (1870), L.R. 6 Q.B. 1.
(75) [1968] 1 All E.R. at p. 294; [1968] 2 Q.B. at p. 32.
(76) Article 1088 provides: " (1) The damage which is to be made good by the person responsible in accordance with the foregoing provisions shall consist in the actual loss which the act shall have directly caused to the injured party, in the expenses which the latter may have been compelled to incur in consequence of the damage, in the loss of actual wages or other earnings, and in the loss of future earnings arising from any permanent incapacity, total or partial, which the act may have caused . . ."

they can be answered through the formulation of definite rules of law. But **A**
I shall have to consider whether, after formulation of any general rules as is
possible, it is necessary to admit some flexibility in their operation, in order
to decide such a case as the present.

2. *The existing English law.* Apart from any revision which this House may
be entitled, and think opportune, to make, I have no doubt that this is as stated
in DICEY AND MORRIS ON THE CONFLICT OF LAWS (8th Edn.), r. 158, pp. 919, **B**
920, adopting with minor verbal adaptations, the " general rule " laid down by
the Court of Exchequer Chamber in *Phillips* v. *Eyre* (77). This is as follows:

" An act done in a foreign country is a tort and actionable as such in
England, only if it is both (i) actionable as a tort, according to English law,
or in other words, is an act which, if done in England, would be a tort; and
(ii) not justifiable, according to the law of the foreign country where it was **C**
done."

I am aware that different interpretations have been placed by writers of authority
on the central passage in the judgment of WILLES, J. (77), in which the general
rule is contained. Like many judgments given at a time when the relevant
part of the law was in course of formation, it is not without its ambiguities, or,
as a century of experience perhaps permits us to say, its contradictions. And if **D**
it were now necessary to advance the law by re-interpretation, it would be
quite legitimate to extract new meanings from words and sentences used. Two
of the judgments in the Court of Appeal (78) have done just this, reaching in
the process opposite conclusions. I do not embark on this adventure for two
reasons: first, because of the variety of interpretation offered us by learned
writers no one of which can claim overwhelming support; secondly, and more **E**
importantly, because, on the critical points, I do not think there is any doubt
what the rule as stated has come to be accepted to mean in those courts which
apply the common law. And it is with this judicially accepted meaning and its
applications, that we are now concerned.

(a) The first part of the rule—" actionable as a tort, according to English
law ". I accept what I believe to be the orthodox judicial view that the first **F**
part of the rule is laying down, not a test of jurisdiction, but what we now call
a rule of choice of law: is saying, in effect, that actions on foreign torts are brought
in English courts in accordance with English law. I would be satisfied to rest
this conclusion on the words of the rule itself " if done [committed] in England "
which seem clear enough to exclude the " jurisdiction " theory but, since the
point is important, I give some citations to support it. (i) In *Phillips* v. *Eyre* (77) **G**
the rule is stated to be derived from, or at least to be in accordance with, the
Privy Council decision in *The Halley* (79). That decision has been criticised
and may have been wrong or decided on the wrong ground but at least the
judgment is clear as to its foundation. The judgment of the Board, after citing
the leading case of *Mostyn* v. *Fabrigas* (80) in which the traditional distinction
between local and transitory torts was restated with the authority of LORD **H**
MANSFIELD, C.J., was as follows (81):

" It is true that in many cases the Courts of England inquire into and act
upon the law of Foreign countries, as in the case of a contract entered into
in a Foreign country, where, by express reference, or by necessary implication, the Foreign law is incorporated with the contract, and proof and
consideration of the Foreign law therefore become necessary to the construc- **I**
tion of the contract itself. And as in the case of a collision on an ordinary
road in a Foreign country, where the rule of the road in force at the place

(77) (1870), L.R. 6 Q.B. at pp. 28, 29.
(78) [1968] 1 All E.R. 283; [1968] 2 Q.B. 1.
(79) (1868), L.R. 2 P.C. 193.
(80) (1775), 1 Cowp. 161; [1775-1802] All E.R. Rep. 266.
(81) (1868), L.R. 2 P.C. at pp. 203, 204.

A   of collision may be a necessary ingredient in the determination of the question by whose fault or negligence the alleged tort was committed. But in these and similar cases the English Court admits the proof of the Foreign law as part of the circumstances attending the execution of the contract, or as one of the facts upon which the existence of the tort, or the right to damages, may depend, and it then applies and enforces its own law so far as it is applicable

B   to the case thus established; but it is, in their Lordships' opinion, alike contrary to principle and to authority to hold, that an English Court of Justice will enforce a Foreign Municipal law, and will give a remedy in the shape of damages in respect of an act which, according to its own principles, imposes no liability on the person from whom the damages are claimed."

C   While recognising the relevance for some purposes of the foreign law (an important point to which I shall return) the judgment states explicitly that it is basically the lex fori which is applied and enforced. On this precise point, indeed, it reversed the decision in the Admiralty Court (82) of SIR ROBERT PHILLIMORE, who in a learned judgment, quoting extensively from civilians and United States authorities, had concluded in favour of the lex loci delicti, as the law of the place where the obligatio ex delicto had arisen. The rejection by the Privy

D   Council of this doctrine, which later received life from the authority of HOLMES, J. (*Slater* v. *Mexican National Railroad Co.* (83)), and which in turn is being discarded by modern U.S. decisions (see below) although lamented by some English writers has, until now, been regarded as decisive for English law. (See, in agreement with this, *Koop* v. *Bebb* (84), per DIXON, WILLIAMS, FULLAGAR and KITTO, JJ.). It can hardly be restored now by anything less than a revolution

E   in thought.

    (ii) In Australia, the High Court has said:

    " English law as the lex fori enforces an obligation of its own creation in respect of an act done in another country which would be a tort if done in England, but refrains from doing so unless the act has a particular character

F   according to the lex loci actus."

Koop v. *Bebb* (85), per DIXON, WILLIAMS, FULLAGAR and KITTO, JJ.

    Again, in *Anderson* v. *Eric Anderson Radio & T.V. Pty., Ltd.* (86), WINDEYER, J., specifically considered the suggestion of academic writers that the first rule was not a choice of law rule but a rule of jurisdiction and held that, as a matter of authority, the suggestion could not be supported. That it was a rule of sub-

G   stantive law he said was shown both by *The Halley* (87) and by *Koop* v. *Bebb* (88). I find nothing in the other judgments in this case which is contrary to this view, and much which supports it. Indeed, the actual decision, namely, that the old common law rule of contributory negligence which operated in the forum (New South Wales) but not in the locus delicti must be given effect to, seems to require acceptance of the view that the substantive law to be applied, as a matter of

H   choice, should be the law of forum.

    (iii) The same principle has been accepted by decisions in Canada, including, it is interesting to note, from the province of Quebec—see *Canadian National Steamships Co., Ltd.* v. *Watson* (89) (" it is essential that the plaintiff prove an act or default actionable by the law of Quebec [lex fori] ") following *O'Connor* v. *Wray, Boyd* v. *Wray* (90): and (in the converse case) from Ontario, see *Story*

I   v. *Stratford Mill Building Co.* (91)—

    " it is not a question of enforcing in this Province the provisions of the Quebec law [sc. lex delicti] but of enforcing the law of this Province [sc.

---

(82) (1867), L.R. 2 Ad. & E. 3.   (83) (1904), 194 U.S. 120.
(84) (1952), 84 C.L.R. 629 at p. 643.   (85) (1952), 84 C.L.R. at p. 644.
(86) [1966] A.L.R. 423.   (87) (1868), L.R. 2 P.C. 193.
(88) (1952), 84 C.L.R. 629.   (89) [1939] S.C.R. at p. 13.
(90) [1930] 2 D.L.R. 899 at p. 912.   (91) (1913), 11 D.L.R. 49 at p. 51.

lex fori] in respect of a wrong committed in Quebec which is not justifiable   A
by the law of that Province."

I am of opinion, therefore, that, as regards the first part of this rule, actionability
as a tort under and in accordance with English law is required.

(b) The second part of the rule—" not justifiable according to the lex loci
delicti ". There can hardly be any doubt that when this formulation was made
in *Phillips* v. *Eyre* (92) it was intended to cover the justification by Act of   B
Indemnity which had occurred in Jamaica—the word " justification " is derived
from or at least found in *Mostyn* v. *Fabrigas* (93) in a similar context. It might
have been better for English law if the rule had continued to be so understood.
But *Machado* v. *Fontes* (94) gave the authority of the then Court of Appeal to
the proposition that " not justifiable " included not only " actionable " but
" liable to criminal penalty ", or, putting it another way, that " justifiable "   C
means " innocent ". Until the decision of the Court of Appeal (95) in the present
case this was undoubtedly still the law. And it was accepted as such with varying
degrees of reluctance in Courts in Australia and Canada (see *Koop* v. *Bebb* (96),
Varawa v. *Howard Smith & Co.* (97), *McLean* v. *Pettigrew* (98)). In the Court
of Appeal (95) two members thought it should be overruled.

It results from the foregoing that the current English law is correctly stated   D
by DICEY AND MORRIS (99), it being understood (a) that the substantive law
to be applied is the lex fori, (b) that, as a condition, non-justifiability under the
lex delicti is required.

3. *Is this a satisfactory rule?*   We need not hesitate to ask the question.
Although *Phillips* v. *Eyre* (92) is just a century old, and has some more ancient
roots, the reported cases in which it has been considered or even applied are   E
not numerous. The rule was stated as well settled by LORD MACNAGHTEN in
Carr v. *Fracis Times & Co.* (100), but the issue in that case turned on the
second part of the rule and the first did not arise for discussion. As KITTO, J.,
said in *Anderson* v. *Eric Anderson Radio & T.V. Pty., Ltd.* (101), the first part
of the rule was open to review, and I deal first with that.

It may be admitted that it bears a parochial appearance, that it rests on no   F
secure doctrinal principle, that outside the world of the English speaking common
law it is hardly to be found. But can any better general rule be devised, or is
the existing rule, with perhaps some adjustment, the best suited to our system?

There have, in the past, been powerful advocates for the lex delicti. If a
simple universal test is needed, it is perhaps the most logical, the one with
most doctrinal appeal. A tort takes place in France: if action is not brought   G
before the courts in France, let other courts decide as the French courts would.
This has obvious attraction. But there are two disadvantages. To adopt the lex
delicti as the substantive law would require proof of a foreign law, an objection
which should not be exaggerated since in practice it could be met by suitable
pleading and with the aid of a presumption that foreign law coincides with that
of the forum. But the intrusion of this foreign element would complicate the   H
task of the adviser, who would at least have to consider, to a greater extent than
the present rule compels him to, the possible relevance of a foreign law to his
client's case. The second disadvantage arises from the character of the majority
of foreign torts. These are mainly in respect of personal injuries sustained by
persons travelling away from the place of their residence. In many cases, the

I

(92) (1870), L.R. 6 Q.B. 1.
(93) (1775), 1 Cowp. 161; [1775-1802] All E.R. Rep. 266.
(94) [1897] 2 Q.B. 231.
(95) [1968] 1 All E.R. 283; [1968] 2 Q.B. 1.
(96) (1952), 84 C.L.R. 629.
(97) [1910] V.L.R. 509.
(98) [1945] S.C.R. 62.
(99) THE CONFLICT OF LAWS (8th Edn.) r.158, pp. 919, 920.
(100) [1902] A.C. 176 at p. 182.
(101) [1966] A.L.R. 423.

A place where the wrong occurred is fortuitous : with the speed of travel increasingly so. To fix the liability of two or more persons according to a locality with which they may have no more connection than a temporary, accidental and perhaps unintended presence, may lead to an unjust result. Moreover, the more emphasis there is laid on the locus delicti, the more oppressive may become the question (and research has shown how perplexing this can be) what the locus,

B in a particular case, is. It is difficulties of this character as well as injustices produced by a rigid and logical adherence to the lex delicti (see for a striking example *Slater* v. *Mexican National Railroad Co.* (102)) which have driven the courts in the United States of America to abandon the lex delicti as a universal solvent, and to qualify it by means of a principle of " contacts " or " interests ". But if this kind of qualification is to be admissible, it may equally well be added

C to our existing rule. Before considering whether this should be done, I examine the second part of the *Phillips* v. *Eyre* (103) proposition.

In my opinion, in agreement with your Lordships and the Court of Appeal (104), *Machado* v. *Fontes* (105) ought to be overruled. The balance of judicial opinion is decidedly against it. It was powerfully attacked in the Court of Session by the Lord Justice-Clerk (Lord Thomson) (*M'Elroy* v. *M'Allister* (106)). In

D *Koop* v. *Bebb* (107) it was discussed by the High Court of Australia. After referring to a reasoned criticism of it by Cussen, J., in the Supreme Court of Victoria (*Varawa* v. *Howard Smith & Co.* (108)) the judgment of Dixon, Williams, Fullagar and Kitto, JJ., contains this passage (109):

E " It seems clear that the last word has not been said on the subject, and it may be the true view that an act done in another country should be held to be an actionable wrong in Victoria if, first, it was of such a character that it would have been actionable if it had been committed in Victoria, and secondly it was such as to give rise to a civil liability by the law of the place where it was done."

In Canada the decision has been followed and found useful in certain cases

F where courts in one Province have sought to escape from the consequences of an Ontario statute (and analogous U.S.A. legislation) depriving passengers (guests) of remedies against their drivers (hosts). The Privy Council, on Canadian appeals, has left it open.

For reasons I shall explain I do not think that any principle established by this case is needed in order to resolve the difficulties of guest/host relationship

G —indeed, it only does so with a certain strain (see *McLean* v. *Pettigrew* (110), where the " criminality " of the act in Ontario was relied on although in fact the defendant had been acquitted). On principle the decision for or against it must rest on a balance between the illogicality referred to by Lord Thomson (111), together with the inducement the case offers to " forum shopping ", on the one hand, against, on the other, a debatable advantage in allowing a

H national of the forum to sue there for torts committed by another such national abroad, if these are not actionable but criminal under the lex loci. This balance I find is decidedly against the authority of the decision.

But I do not think it is sufficient to rest here. For we should still be left with the test of " non-justifiability " according to the lex delicti. I have no objection to the concept of " non-justifiability " as the basis for the decision in *Phillips*

I v. *Eyre* (112): to say that Governor Eyre could not be sued in England after his actions in Jamaica had been justified by an Act of Indemnity was sound enough. But I do not think that we need any longer confine ourselves within

(102) (1904), 194 U.S. 120.
(104) [1968] 1 All E.R. 283; [1968] 2 Q.B. 1.
(106) 1949 S.C. 110 at p. 118.
(108) [1910] V.L.R. 509.
(110) [1945] S.C.R. 62.
(112) (1870), L.R. 6 Q.B. 1.

(103) (1870), L.R. 6 Q.B. at p. 29.
(105) [1897] 2 Q.B. 231.
(107) (1952), 84 C.L.R. 629.
(109) (1952), 84 C.L.R. at p. 643.
(111) 1949 S.C. at p. 118.

this phrase. Assuming that, as the basic rule, we continue to require action-   A
ability by the lex fori subject to some condition as to what the lex delicti requires,
we should, in my opinion, allow a greater and more intelligible force to the
lex delicti than is included in the concept of unjustifiability as normally
understood.

The broad principle should surely be that a person should not be permitted
to claim in England in respect of a matter for which civil liability does not   B
exist, or is excluded, under the law of the place where the wrong was committed.
This non-existence or exclusion may be for a variety of reasons and it would
be unwise to attempt a generalisation relevant to the variety of possible wrongs.
But in relation to claims for personal injuries one may say that provisions of
the lex delicti, denying, or limiting, or qualifying recovery of damages because
of some relationship of the defendant to the plaintiff, or in respect of some   C
interest of the plaintiff (such as loss of consortium) or some head of damage
(such as pain and suffering) should be given effect to. I can see no case for allowing one resident of Ontario to sue another in the English courts for damages
sustained in Ontario as a passenger in the other's car, or one Maltese resident to
sue another in the English courts for damages in respect of pain and suffering
caused by an accident in Malta. I would, therefore, restate the basic rule of   D
English law with regard to foreign torts as requiring actionability as a tort
according to English law, subject to the condition that civil liability in respect
of the relevant claim exists as between the actual parties under the law of the
foreign country where the act was done.

It remains for me to consider (and this is the crux of the present case) whether
some qualification to this rule is required in certain individual cases. There are   E
two conflicting pressures: the first in favour of certainty and simplicity in the
law, the second in favour of flexibility in the interest of individual justice.
Developments in the United States of America have reflected this conflict.
I now consider them.

The contact or interests principle. The process which has evolved is to segregate
the relevant issue, which may be one only of those arising, and to consider in   F
relation to that issue as it arises in the actual suit between the actual parties
what rule of law, i.e., the rule of which state or jurisdiction, ought to be applied.
This method has mainly although not exclusively been used in relation to personal
injury cases, whether air or motor car accidents and, as to the latter, mainly
in relation to statutes excluding or limiting the liability of drivers of vehicles.
Like other doctrines, including that of the " proper law of the tort ", it may   G
represent a development from English seed. PROFESSOR WESTLAKE'S PRIVATE
INTERNATIONAL LAW (7th Edn., BENTWICH, 1925) at p. 281, contains this:

" The truth is that by entering a country, or acting in it you submit
yourself to its special laws *only so far as science selects them as the rule of
decision in each case.* Or more truly still, you give to its special laws the
opportunity of working in you to that extent. The operation of the law   H
depends on the conditions, and where the conditions exist the law operates
as well on its born subjects as on those who have brought themselves
under it."

The germ of the doctrine may lie here but has only developed in recent United
States cases towards passengers or generally. Those I have found of most   I
interest are *Kilberg* v. *Northeast Airlines, Inc.* (113); *Babcock* v. *Jackson* (114)
(law of the place which had most dominant contacts with matter in dispute);
Griffith v. *United Air Lines, Inc.* (115) (the strict lex loci delicti rule should be
abandoned in favour of a more flexible rule which permits analysis of the policies

(113) [1961] 2 Lloyd's Rep. 406.
(114) [1963] 2 Lloyd's Rep. 286.
(115) (1964), 203 Atlantic Reporter (2nd Ser.) 796.

A or interests underlying the particular issue before the court); *Dym* v. *Gordon* (116); *Miller* v. *Miller* (117). Interesting and suggestive as are the judgments in these cases, I forbear from detailed citation since they are, at the present state, approximative to the definition of a rule.

A reference to *Babcock* v. *Jackson* (118) may sufficiently illustrate. There the plaintiff was a passenger in a car owned and driven by the defendant, both

B parties being resident in New York (I disregard the "garage" factor by which the case has unfortunately come to be labelled). The accident occurred in Ontario, Canada, during a weekend trip; the Highway Traffic Act 1960, of Ontario excluded any liability of driver to passenger, but the law of New York (lex fori) did not. The plaintiff was allowed to recover. The basic law, as accepted in New York, as elsewhere in the United States of America, was the lex delicti

C which, for the reasons I have given, ought not to become the basic law in England, but the judgment of the court established a principle equally applicable what-ever the basic law might be (119):

"Justice, fairness and 'the best practical result' . . . may best be achieved by giving controlling effect to the law of the jurisdiction which, because of its relationship or contact with the occurrence or the parties has the

D   greatest concern with the specific issue raised in the litigation."

The general tendency is stated in the AMERICAN LAW INSTITUTE RESTATEMENT (Second) CONFLICT OF LAWS (Proposed official draft, 1st May 1968) (120). This states as the general principle that rights and liabilities of the parties with respect to an issue in tort are determined by the local law of the State which, as to that issue, has the most significant relationship to the occurrence and

E the parties and that separate rules apply to different kinds of torts. The importance of the respective contacts is to be evaluated according to their relevant importance with respect to the particular issue, the nature of the tort, and the purposes of the tort rules involved (see s. 6, p. 145). In an action for a personal injury the local law of the State where the injury occurred (the basic rule in the United States of America) determines the rights and liabilities

F of the parties, unless *with respect to the particular issue* (emphasis supplied) some other State has a more significant relationship with the occurrence and the parties, in which event the local law of the other State will be applied (see p. 146).

This formulation has, what is very necessary under a system of judge-made law, the benefit of hard testing in concrete applications. The criticism is easy

G to make that, more even than the doctrine of the proper law of the contract (cf., *The Assunzione* (121)) where the search is often one of great perplexity, the task of tracing the relevant contacts, and of weighing them, qualitatively, against each other, complicates the task of the courts and leads to uncertainty and dissent (see particularly the powerful dissents in *Griffith's* case (122) of BELL, Ch.J., and in *Miller's* case (123) of BREITEL, J.).

H   There is force in this and for this reason I am not willing to go so far as the more extreme version of the respondent's argument would have us do and to adopt, in place of the existing rule, one based solely on "contacts" or "centre of gravity" which has not been adopted even in the more favourable climate of the United States. There must remain great virtue in a general well-under-stood rule covering the majority of normal cases provided that it can be made

I flexible enough to take account of the varying interests and considerations of policy which may arise when one or more foreign elements are present.

---

(116) (1965), 209 N.E. 2d 792.
(117) (1968), 290 N.Y.S. (2d) 734; 237 N.E. 2d 877.
(118) [1963] 2 Lloyd's Rep. 286.
(119) [1963] 2 Lloyd's Rep. at p. 289.
(120) In the Court of Appeal, references were made to an earlier draft of 1964.
(121) [1954] 1 All E.R. 278; [1954] P. 150.
(122) (1964), 203 Atlantic Reporter (2nd Ser.) 796.
(123) (1968), 290 N.Y.S. (2d) 734 at pp. 743-752; 237 N.E. 2d 877 at pp. 883-890.

Given the general rule, as stated above (para. **3** ad fin), as one which will **A** normally apply to foreign torts, I think that the necessary flexibility can be obtained from that principle which represents at least a common denominator of the United States decisions, namely, through segregation of the relevant issue and consideration whether, in relation to that issue, the relevant foreign rule ought, as a matter of policy or as WESTLAKE said of science, to be applied. For this purpose it is necessary to identify the policy of the rule, to enquire to **B** what situations, with what contacts, it was intended to apply; whether not to apply it, in the circumstances of the instant case, would serve any interest which the rule was devised to meet. This technique appears well adapted to meet cases where the lex delicti either limits or excludes damages for personal injury; it appears even necessary and inevitable. No purely mechanical rule can properly do justice to the great variety of cases where persons come together **C** in a foreign jurisdiction for different purposes with different pre-existing relationships, from the background of different legal systems. It will not be invoked in every case or even, probably, in many cases. The general rule must apply unless clear and satisfying grounds are shown why it should be departed from and what solution, derived from what other rule, should be preferred. If one lesson emerges from the United States decisions it is that case-to-case decisions **D** do not add up to a system of justice. Even within these limits this procedure may in some instances require a more searching analysis than is needed under the general rule. But unless this is done, or at least possible, we must come back to a system which is purely and simply mechanical.

I find in this approach the solution to the present case. The tort here was committed in Malta; it is actionable in this country. But the law of Malta **E** denies recovery of damages for pain and suffering. Prima facie English law should do the same: if the parties were both Maltese residents it ought surely to do so; if the defendant were a Maltese resident the same result might follow. But in a case such as the present, where neither party is a Maltese resident or citizen, further enquiry is needed rather than an automatic application of the rule. The issue, whether this head of damage should be allowed, requires to be **F** segregated from the rest of the case, negligence or otherwise, related to the parties involved and their circumstances, and tested in relation to the policy of the local rule and of its application to these parties so circumstanced.

So segregated, the issue is whether one British subject, resident in the United Kingdom, should be prevented from recovering, in accordance with English law, against another British subject, similarly situated, damages for pain and suffering **G** which he cannot recover under the rule of the lex delicti. This issue must be stated, and examined, regardless of whether the injured person has or has not also a recoverable claim under a different heading (e.g., for expenses actually incurred) under that law. This Maltese law cannot simply be rejected on grounds of public policy, or some general conception of justice. For it is one thing to say or presume that domestic rule is a just rule, but quite another, in a case **H** where a foreign element is involved, to reject a foreign rule on any such general ground. The foreign rule must be evaluated in its application.

The rule limiting damages is the creation of the law of Malta, a place where both respondent and appellant were temporarily stationed. Nothing suggests that the Maltese State has any interest in applying this rule to persons resident outside it, or in denying the application of the English rule to these parties. **I** No argument has been suggested why an English court, if free to do so, should renounce its own rule. That rule ought, in my opinion, to apply.

It may be that this appeal can be decided, quasi mechanically, by the accepted distinction between substance and procedure, between solatium as a jus actionis and solatium as an ingredient in general damages. I have no wish to depreciate the use of these familiar tools. In skilful hands they can be powerful and effective, although I must add that in some applications, particularly in Scottish cases, they have led to results which give me no satisfaction. But I suspect that in the

A ultimate and difficult choice which has to be made between regarding damages for pain and suffering as a separate cause of action and so governed by the lex delicti, or treating them as merely part of general damages to calculate which is the prerogative of the lex fori, two alternatives which are surely closely balanced in this case, a not insubstantial makeweight, perhaps unconscious in its use, is to be found in a policy preference for the adopted solution : cf., *Kilberg*
B v. *Northeast Airlines, Inc.* (124), per Desmond, Ch.J.:

> " It is open to us . . . particularly in view of our strong public policy as to death action damages, to treat the measure of damages as being a pro- cedural or remedial question controlled by our own state policies."

I note indeed that a purely legal analysis in the Court of Appeal (125) led Lord
C Upjohn to one answer, Diplock, L.J., to another. So I prefer to be explicit about it. There certainly seems to be some artifice in regarding a man's right to recover damages for pain and suffering as a matter of procedure. To do so, at any rate, goes well beyond the principle, which I entirely accept, that matters of assessment or quantification, including no doubt the manner in which provision is made for future or prospective losses, are for the lex fori to determine.

D Yet, unless the claim can be classified as procedure, there seems no basis on the traditional approach for denying the application of the Maltese law. I find the basis for doing so only in the reasons I have stated. For those reasons I would dismiss the appeal.

LORD PEARSON: My Lords, both the plaintiff, who is the respondent in this appeal, and the defendant, who is the appellant, were at all material times
E normally resident in England but were at the time of the accident serving in the British armed forces stationed in Malta, the respondent with the Royal Air Force and the appellant with the Royal Navy. The accident was a road accident in Malta, and was due to the appellant's negligence, and caused serious injuries to the respondent. But the respondent's economic loss was small because he continued to receive his full pay until he was discharged from the Royal
F Air Force in consequence of his injuries, and then he obtained more remunerative employment in civil life. His action against the appellant for damages for negligence was brought in the English courts.

The learned judge decided (126) that English law was applicable and that the respondent should recover £53 as special damages and £2,250 as general damages. There is no dispute as to the figures or as to the respondent's right to recover
G the sum of £53 as special damages. The question at issue in this appeal is whether the respondent is entitled to recover the general damages, which are attributable to pain and suffering (including loss of amenities of life). If the question is to be decided according to English law he is so entitled : if according to Maltese law he is not entitled.

The learned judge's findings as to the Maltese law were as follows (127):

H
> " I am satisfied that all a plaintiff is entitled to recover under the law of Malta is (i) actual financial loss directly suffered, (ii) expenses which he has been compelled to incur, (iii) the amount of wages he has actually lost and (iv) a sum in respect of future loss of wages which he can actually prove will occur. He cannot recover anything in respect of pain and suffering in itself and as distinct from its economic effect on him. In a case in Malta
I where there is evidence of a possible future incapacity arising from the injury, the court will make provision in its order to enable the plaintiff, in the event of such incapacity materialising, to come back and recover in respect of it, but, as long as it is potential only, the plaintiff can recover nothing for it."

---

(124) [1961] 2 Lloyd's Rep. at p. 409.   (125) [1968] 1 All E.R. 283; [1968] 2 Q.B. 1.
(126) [1967] 2 All E.R. 665; [1968] 2 Q.B.1.
(127) [1967] 2 All E.R. at p. 667; [1968] 2 Q.B. at p. 5.

The Maltese law thus differs from English law in a very important respect. **A**
The Maltese law gives to the plaintiff a right of action for what is in effect only
re-imbursement or indemnity or compensation for pecuniary expense or loss.
The English law gives to the plaintiff a right of action for damages for all the
relevant consequences of the accident to the plaintiff, including pain and suffering as well as pecuniary expense or loss. The figures in this case show that the
practical difference may be very great. Moreover, there might be a case in **B**
which there was no pecuniary expense or loss, but only pain and suffering. In
such a case presumably the plaintiff would have no cause of action by Maltese
law. It is to be assumed, in the absence of evidence to the contrary, that in Malta
as in England a cause of action for negligence is not complete unless some actionable damage—damage in respect of which damages are recoverable—can be
alleged and proved.   **C**

English law is the lex fori. The lex fori must regulate procedure, because
the court can only use its own procedure, having no power to adopt alien procedures. To some extent, at any rate, the lex fori must regulate remedies, because
the court can only give its own remedies, having no power to give alien remedies.
For instance, the English court could not make provision in its order to enable
the respondent, in the event of a possible future incapacity materialising, to **D**
come back and recover in respect of it. That is alien procedure or an alien
remedy and outside the powers of an English court. On the other hand, an
English court may sometimes be able to give in respect of a tort committed
in a foreign country a remedy which the courts of that country would be unable
to give. For instance, the foreign courts might have no power to grant an
injunction or to make an order for specific performance or for an account of **E**
profits.

If the difference between the English law and the Maltese law could be
regarded only as a difference of procedural (or adjectival or non-substantive)
law, there would be an easy solution of the problem in this appeal. On that
basis the nature and extent of the remedy would be matters of procedural
law regulated by the lex fori, which is English, and the proper remedy for **F**
the respondent in this case according to English law would be that he should
recover damages for all the relevant consequences of the accident, including
pain and suffering as well as pecuniary expense and loss, and the amount of
such damages would be £2,303, the sum awarded by the learned judge.

But I am not convinced that the difference between the English law and
the Maltese law can reasonably be regarded as only a difference of procedural **G**
law. There is a radical difference in the cause of action, the right of action,
the jus actionis. A claim to be re-imbursed or indemnified or compensated
for actual economic loss is substantially different in character from a claim for
damages for all the relevant consequences of the accident to the respondent, including pain and suffering. If an accident caused no economic loss, but only pain and
suffering, there would be a cause of action according to English law, but not **H**
according to Maltese law. Surely that must be a matter of substantive law.
Then if the validity of a claim for damages for pain and suffering is a matter
of substantive law when that is the only claim, is it not a matter of substantive
law equally when such a claim happens to be associated with a claim in respect
of actual economic loss? I do not think there is any exact and authoritative
definition of the boundary between substantive law and procedural (or adjectival **I**
or non-substantive) law, and the boundary remains to be settled by further
decisions in particular cases. In the present case I think it would be artificial
and incorrect to treat the difference between the English law and the Maltese
law, which materially affects the determination of the rights and liabilities of
the parties, as a matter only of procedural law.

Taking that view, I have to go on to consider the question whether the
substantive law to be applied is English or Maltese or both. A choice of law
is involved and as it has to be made by the English court in which the action

A is brought it must be governed by the principles of English law for making such a choice. What, then, is the substantive law applicable in this case? Is it the law of England, or the law of Malta, or some combination of both? It is necessary to consider the authorities. The leading authority is a passage in the judgment of the Court of Exchequer Chamber, delivered by WILLES, J., in *Phillips* v. *Eyre* (128). But earlier authorities are of some assistance as B leading up to it.

In *Mostyn* v. *Fabrigas* (129) it was decided by LORD MANSFIELD, C.J., that an action of trespass and false imprisonment lay in England by a Minorquin against a former governor of Minorca for such injury committed by him in Minorca. Venue in an English county was given by a fiction, the plaintiff alleging in his declaration that the defendant made an assault on him ". . . at C Minorca (to wit) . . . in the parish of St. Mary le Bow, in the Ward of Cheap ". This was explained in the judgment (130):

> " . . . where the action is substantially such a one as the Court can hold plea of, as the mode of trial is by jury, and as the jury must be called together by process directed to the sheriff of the county; matter of form is added to the fiction, to say it is in that county and then the whole of the D inquiry is, whether it is an action that ought to be maintained. But can it be doubted, that actions may be maintained here, not only upon contracts, which follow the persons, but for injuries done by subject to subject; especially for injuries where the whole that is prayed is a reparation in damages, or satisfaction to be made by process against the person or his effects, within the jurisdiction of the Court? "

E That passage seems to contemplate a normal English trial between British subjects according to English law as well as English procedure. The part which may be played by the lex loci delicti appears from another passage (131):

> " . . . in *Wey* v. *Rally* (132) JUSTICE POWELL says, that an action of false imprisonment has been brought here against a Governor of Jamaica, F for an imprisonment there, and the laws of the country were given in evidence. The Governor of Jamaica in that case never thought that he was not amenable. He defended himself, and possibly shewed, by the laws of the country, an Act of the Assembly which justified that imprisonment, and the Court received it as they ought to do. For whatever is a justification in the place where the thing is done, ought to be a justification where the G cause is tried."

Another point of interest in the judgment is that it refers to actual or hypothetical cases of wrongs done by one British subject to another in places (e.g., on the coast of Nova Scotia or among the Esquimaux Indians on the coast of Labrador) where there were in 1774 no regular courts of justice and there would be a failure of justice unless an action could be brought in England. H In such cases there would be a civil wrong done according to English law; by the lex loci delicti there would be no justification and no civil cause of action; the plaintiff would be suing on a civil cause of action given by English law.

Scott v. *Lord Seymour* (133) can be taken briefly as not giving much assistance. But the language used by WIGHTMAN, J., in stating his alternative ground (not generally adopted by the other members of the court) is of interest. He I said (134):

> " . . . I am not aware of any rule of law which would disable a British subject from maintaining an action in this country for damages against another

---

(128) (1870), L.R. 6 Q.B. 1.
(129) (1775), 1 Cowp. 161; [1775-1802] All E.R. Rep. 266.
(130) (1775), 1 Cowp. at p. 179; [1775-1802] All E.R. Rep. at p. 273.
(131) (1775), 1 Cowp. at p. 175; [1775-1802] All E.R. Rep. at p. 271.
(132) (1704), 6 Mod. Rep. 194.
(133) (1862), 1 H. & C. 219.   (134) (1862), 1 H. & C. at pp. 234, 235.

British subject for an assault and battery committed by him in a foreign   **A**
country, merely because no damages for such trespasses were recoverable
by the law of the foreign country; and without any allegation that such
trespasses were lawful or justifiable in that country."

WILLES, J., was one of the members of the court, and, while expressing no
concluded opinion on WIGHTMAN, J.'s alternative ground, he said (135): " I
am far from saying that I differ from any part of the judgment of my brother   **B**
WIGHTMAN . . ."

The Halley (136) was decided by the Judicial Committee of the Privy Council
in 1868. There was an action in England in respect of a collision in Belgian
waters, alleged to have been caused by negligent navigation of the defendants'
ship. The defendants pleaded that they were not liable because their ship was
being navigated by a pilot whom they were compelled by the Belgian law to   **C**
employ. The plaintiffs replied that by the Belgian law the defendants were
responsible for negligent navigation of the pilot even though they were compelled
to employ him. In the judgment of the Board, delivered by SELWYN, L.J.,
there is this passage (137):

" It is true that in many cases the Courts of England inquire into and
act upon the law of Foreign countries, as in the case of a contract entered   **D**
in in a Foreign country, where, by express reference, or by necessary implication, the foreign law is incorporated with the contract, and proof and
consideration of the Foreign law therefore became necessary to the construction of the contract itself. And as in the case of a collision on an
ordinary road in a Foreign country, where the rule of the road in force at the
place of collision may be a necessary ingredient in the determination of the   **E**
question by whose fault or negligence the alleged tort was committed. But
in these and similar cases the English Court admits the proof of the Foreign
law as part of circumstances attending the execution of the contract, or as
one of the facts upon which the existence of the tort, or the right to damages,
may depend, and it then applies and enforces its own law so far as it is
applicable to the case thus established; but it is, in their Lordships' opinion,   **F**
alike contrary to principle and to authority to hold, that an English Court
of Justice will enforce a Foreign Municipal law, and will give a remedy in
the shape of damages in respect of an act which, according to its own
principles, imposes no liability on the person from whom the damages are
claimed."
                                                                                G
Accordingly, the relevant part of the plaintiff's reply was rejected. The passage
quoted seems to me important as showing clearly that even in an action for a
tort committed abroad the English court is administering English law and
enforcing a cause of action which must be valid according to English law, and
is not enforcing a foreign cause of action according to foreign law. As appears
from other cases, the foreign law, proved by evidence as a matter of fact, may   **H**
come in as a secondary factor providing a defence to the cause of action.

The next case, *Phillips* v. *Eyre* (138), is the leading authority. The Court of
Exchequer Chamber was composed of KELLY, C.B., MARTIN, CHANNELL, PIGOTT
and CLEASBY, BB., WILLES and BRETT, JJ. The defendant as governor of
Jamaica had imprisoned the plaintiff, but afterwards an Act of Indemnity
was passed by the Jamaican legislature. The judgment, delivered by WILLES, J.,
was largely concerned with examining the validity of the Act of Indemnity,   **I**
which was upheld. The principal passages of his judgment relevant to the
present question are (139):

" The last objection to the plea of the colonial Act was of a more technical

---

(135) (1862), 1 H. & C. at p. 236.
(136) (1868), L.R. 2 P.C. 193.
(137) (1868), L.R. 2 P.C. at pp. 203, 204.
(138) (1870), L.R. 6 Q.B. 1.
(139) (1870), L.R. 6 Q.B. at pp. 28, 29.

A   character; that assuming the colonial Act to be valid in Jamaica and a
defence there, it could not have the extra-territorial effect of taking away
the right of action in an English court.   This objection is founded upon a
misconception of the true character of a civil or legal obligation and the
corresponding right of action.   The obligation is the principal to which
a right of action in whatever court is only an accessory, and such accessory,
B   according to the maxim of law, follows the principal, and must stand or
fall therewith . . . A right of action, whether it arise from contract governed
by the law of the place or wrong, is equally the creature of the law of the
place and subordinate thereto . . . the civil liability arising out of a wrong
derives its birth from the law of the place, and its character is determined
by that law.   Therefore, an act committed abroad, if valid and unquestion-
C   able by the law of the place, cannot, so far as civil liability is concerned,
be drawn in question elsewhere unless by force of some distinct exceptional
legislation, superadding a liability other than and besides that incident
to the act itself . . . As a general rule, in order to found a suit in England
for a wrong alleged to have been committed abroad, two conditions must be
fulfilled.   First, the wrong must be of such a character that it would have been
D   actionable if committed in England . . . Secondly, the act must not have
been justifiable by the law of the place where it was done."

In support of the first condition he cited *The Halley* (140).   In support of the
second condition he cited *Blad* v. *Bamfield* (141), *Dobree* v. *Napier* (142) and
R. v. *Lesley* (143).   These latter were all cases of acts of seizure or assault or
imprisonment, which would prima facie be wrongful but were justified by
E   command of the Sovereign or otherwise by authority from the government of
the territory in which the act was committed.
        I find some difficulty in reconciling the earlier passage with the later passage,
but I think that when taken together they show that the applicable law, the
substantive law determining liability or non-liability, is a combination of the
lex fori and the lex loci delicti (which was conveniently called by Willes, J. (144),
F   " the law of the place ").   The act must take its character of wrongfulness from
the law of the place; it must not be justifiable under the law of the place; if
it is (144) " valid and unquestionable by the law of the place, [it] cannot, so far
as civil liability is concerned, be drawn in question elsewhere ".   But Willes, J.,
does not say that the wrongful act has to be actionable, or to give a cause of action
for damages, according to the law of the place.   The actionability is by the lex
G   fori (145):   " the wrong must be of such a character that it would have been
actionable if committed in England."   The second condition has to be read
in the light of what has gone before.   The act referred to is one which is wrongful
according to the law of the place in which it is committed.   But there is no
requirement that it must be actionable by the law of that place as well as by the
law of England; double actionability is not required.   The requirement is that
H   the act must not be justifiable by the law of the place.   The reason for that
must be that a person could not fairly be held liable in damages for doing something which in the place where it was done was either originally lawful or made
lawful by retrospective legislation.   Willes, J.'s statement of the conditions
which have to be fulfilled (which may be called " the Willes formula ") shows
that in such a case the substantive law of England plays the dominant role,
I   determining the cause of action, whereas the law of the place in which the act
was committed plays a subordinate role, in that it may provide a justification
for the act and so defeat the cause of action but it does not in itself determine
the cause of action.

(140) (1868), L.R. 2 P.C. 193.
(141) (1674), 3 Swan. 604.
(142) (1836), 2 Bing. N.C. 781.
(143) (1860), Bell C.C. 220.
(144) (1870), L.R. 6 Q.B. at p. 28.
(145) (1870), L.R. 6 Q.B. at pp. 28, 29.

The M. Moxham (146) is a case of a rather special character. The action **A**
was for damages in respect of injury done by an English ship to a pier in Spain
owned by an English company. The parties had agreed that the liability, if any,
of the owners of the ship should be determined in the English courts but (as
JAMES, L.J., understood their agreement) in accordance with the Spanish law.
JAMES, L.J., said (147):

> " It is settled that if by the law of the foreign country the act is lawful, **B**
> or is excusable, or even if it has been legitimized, by a subsequent Act of the
> legislature then this Court will take into consideration that state of the law;
> that is to say, if by the law of the foreign country a particular person is
> justified, or is excused, or has been justified or excused for the thing done,
> he will not be answerable here."

MELLISH, L.J., said (147):   **C**

> " Now, the law respecting personal injuries and respecting wrongs to
> personal property appears to me to be perfectly settled that no action
> can be maintained in the courts of this country on account of a wrongful
> act either to a person or to personal property, committed within the juris-
> diction of a foreign country, unless the act is wrongful by the law of the **D**
> country where it is committed and also wrongful by the law of this country.
> The cases of *The Halley* (148) and *Phillips* v. *Eyre* (149), together with other
> cases in conformity with them, seem to be conclusive on the subject."

BAGGALLAY, L.J., said (150): " The principles seem to be laid down very clearly
and distinctly in the case of *Phillips* v. *Eyre* (149) ", and then he cited the Willes
formula. The judgments in *The M. Moxham* (146) seem to me to be consistent **E**
with, and to afford some support for, the interpretation which I have given
of the Willes formula.

On the other hand, in *Chartered Mercantile Bank of India, London and China*
v. *Netherlands India Steam Navigation Co., Ltd.* (151), BRETT, L.J., said when
referring to *The M. Moxham* (146):   **F**

> " In that case, whatever the cause of action was, it arose entirely in
> Spain, and the action was an action in tort, and the well-known rule applies
> that for any tort committed in a foreign country within its own exclusive
> jurisdiction an action of tort cannot be maintained in this country unless
> the cause of action would be a cause of action in that country, and also
> would be a cause of action in this country."   **G**

That dictum seems to me to be inconsistent with the Willes formula because
it would substitute actionability by the foreign law for wrongfulness by the
foreign law, but the Willes formula has been accepted in other cases.

Machado v. *Fontes* (152) raised directly, in an interlocutory appeal heard by
two Lords Justices, the question whether the act committed abroad, if it was **H**
to found an action in England, had to be actionable by the law of the place in
which the act was committed or merely wrongful by that law. There was a plea
to the effect that the alleged libel published in Brazil was not actionable by
the law of Brazil. The plea did not say that the publication was not wrongful
by the law of Brazil; thus criminal liability was not excluded. The court,
LOPES and RIGBY, L.JJ., applying the Willes formula and relying also on
the judgments in *The M. Moxham* (146), held that the plea was insufficient, **I**
because it did not allege that the publication of the libel was an innocent act in

---

(146) (1876), 1 P.D. 107.
(147) (1876), 1 P.D. at p. 111.
(148) (1868), L.R. 2 P.C. 193.
(149) (1870), L.R. 6 Q.B. 1.
(150) (1876), 1 P.D. at p. 115.
(151) (1883), 10 Q.B.D. 521, at pp. 536, 537.
(152) [1897] 2 Q.B. 231.

A Brazil. That was a decision that the act committed abroad, if it was to found an action in England, had to be merely wrongful, not necessarily actionable, by the law of the foreign country. In my opinion, this decision involved a correct interpretation of the Willes formula. The cause of action for the libel was determined by English law, but the defendant would have a defence if he could show that the act complained of was " justifiable " by the law of the place

B in which it was committed. It would not be " justifiable " by that law, if it was a crime by that law. A criminal act would be even less justifiable than a tortious act. There may be an objection to the decision on a different ground, namely, that it may have been permitting a person whose natural forum was a Brazilian court to gain advantages by by-passing his natural forum and suing in the English court. That is a matter which I will consider at a later stage.

C In *Carr* v. *Fracis Times & Co.* (153), Lord Macnaghten (154) set out the Willes formula and described it as " well settled by a series of authorities (of which the latest is the case of *Phillips* v. *Eyre* (155) . . .)". In *Canadian Pacific Ry. Co.* v. *Parent* (156), Viscount Haldane raised a doubt whether " all the language used by the English Court of Appeal in the judgments in *Machado* v. *Fontes* (157) was sufficiently precise " but he did not depart from the decision

D in that case. In *Walpole* v. *Canadian Northern Ry. Co.* (158), Viscount Cave set out the Willes formula as " well-known ", and said:

" It is unnecessary for the purposes of this appeal to consider the precise meaning of the term ' justifiable ', as used by Willes, J.; but, at all events, it must have reference to legal justification, and an act or neglect which is neither actionable nor punishable cannot be said to be otherwise than

E justifiable within the meaning of the rule."

In *McMillan* v. *Canadian Northern Ry. Co.* (159), Viscount Cave set out the Willes formula and described it as " well-established ".

The English authorities show that the Willes formula has been accepted; that the first of his conditions gives the predominant role to the English sub-stantive law; and that the second of his conditions does not require action-

F ability by the law of the place where the act was committed, but only that the act should not be justifiable, i.e., not excused or innocent by that law. That is the orthodox and established rule, and it has been maintained for a great many years. On the other hand, it has met with some unfavourable criticism both in this country and in Australia, and it is open to your Lordships to set aside or amend the rule by overruling *Machado* v. *Fontes* (157) and not

G following *The Halley* (160). But I do not think there could be any good ground for doing so unless either the rule was wrong from the beginning or it has become out of date by reason of changes in legal, social or economic conditions.

I am not persuaded that the rule was wrong from the beginning. It has certain advantages and certain disadvantages. The main advantages are, first, that it has a high degree of certainty and, secondly, that it enables an

H English court to give judgment according to its own ideas of justice. In *The Halley* (160) it would then have seemed unjust to the English court to hold the defendants liable for the fault of a pilot whom they were compelled by the local law to engage and put in charge of their ship. In the present case it would have seemed unjust to an English court to award to the respondent only £53 as damages for serious injuries. Another advantage is that if one English-

I man wrongfully injures another in a primitive country or unsettled territory

(153) [1902] A.C. 176.
(154) [1902] A.C. at p. 182.
(155) (1870), L.R. 6 Q.B. 1.
(156) [1917] A.C. 195 at p. 205.
(157) [1897] 2 Q.B. 231.
(158) [1923] A.C. 113 at p. 119.
(159) [1923] A.C. 120 at pp. 123, 124.
(160) (1868), L.R. 2 P.C. 193.

where there is no law of torts, the English courts can give redress. This would **A**
be a factor of some importance in 1774, when *Mostyn* v. *Fabrigas* (161) was decided,
and even in 1870 when *Phillips* v. *Eyre* (162) was decided, although with the
rapid spread of civilisation it has much less importance now.   The principal
disadvantage of the rule is that it might lead to what has been described in
American cases as " forum shopping ", i.e., a plaintiff by-passing his natural
forum and bringing his action in some alien forum which would give him relief **B**
or benefits which would not be available to him in his natural forum.   I will
revert to this danger of " forum-shopping " at a later stage.

If the rule is to be set aside or amended, what should be put in its place or how
should it be amended?   There may be many suggestions, but I think the principal
ones are: (a) That the substantive law of the place where the act is committed
should be given the predominant role so as to determine the cause of action, and **C**
the substantive law of the forum, the English court, should apply only to the
extent of the court refusing to enforce the cause of action if it is repugnant to
some rule of English public policy; (b) That damages should be recoverable for a
wrongful act committed out of England only if it is actionable both by the law of
England and by the law of the country in which the act was committed; (c) That
a flexible rule, which has been referred to as " the proper law of the tort ", should **D**
be substituted.

In considering whether the English rule has been wrong from the beginning
or has become out of date, and whether it should now be superseded by or converted into one of these suggested rules, it is helpful to have regard to the opinions
and experience of courts in other common law countries.   For the sake of brevity
I will be highly selective.   **E**

In the Australian cases the decision in *Machado* v. *Fontes* (163) has been discussed and doubted, but the question whether it should be followed or not
has been kept open; the Willes formula has been repeatedly cited as authoritative;
and the priority of the lex fori in determining the cause of action has been clearly
stated.   In the judgment of DIXON, WILLIAMS, FULLAGAR and KITTO, JJ., in
the High Court of Australia in *Koop* v. *Bebb* (164) there is this passage **F**
referring to *Machado* v. *Fontes* (163):

" It seems clear that the last word has not been said on the subject, and
it may be the true view that an act done in another country should be held
to be an actionable wrong in Victoria if, first, it was of such a character
that it would have been actionable if it had been committed in Victoria,
and, secondly, it was such as to give rise to a civil liability by the law of the **G**
place where it was done.   Such a rule would appear to be consonant with all
the English decisions before *Machado* v. *Fontes* (163) and with the later Privy
Council decisions.   It may be added that, however the rule should be stated,
courts applying the English rules of private international law do not accept
the theory propounded by HOLMES, J., in *Slater* v. *Mexican National Railroad Co.* (165) (see also *New York Central Ry. Co.* v. *Chisholm* (166)) when he **H**
said (167): ' The theory of the foreign suit is that although the act complained of was subject to no law having force in the forum, it gave rise to an
obligation, an *obligatio*, which, like other obligations, follows the person, and
may be enforced wherever the person may be found . . . But as the only
source of this obligation is the law of the place of the act, it follows that that
law determines not merely the existence of the obligation, . . . but equally **I**
determines its extent.' English law as the lexi fori enforces an obligation of its

---

(161) (1775), 1 Cowp. 161; [1775-1802] All E.R. Rep. 266.
(162) (1870), L.R. 6 Q.B. 1.
(163) (1897), 2 Q.B. 231.
(164) (1952), 84 C.L.R. 629 at pp. 643, 644.
(165) (1904), 194 U.S. 120.
(166) (1925), 268 U.S. 29.
(167) (1925), 268 U.S. 29 at p. 32.

A   own creation in respect of an act done in another country which would be a
tort if done in England, but refrains from doing so unless the act has a
particular character according to the lex loci actus. Uncertainty exists
only as to what that character must be. There is no necessity to express a
concluded opinion upon the controversy which surrounds *Machado* v.
Fontes (168)."

B   In another case in the High Court of Australia, *Anderson* v. *Eric Anderson
Radio & T.V. Pty., Ltd.* (169), the action was brought in New South Wales
in respect of an accident which occurred in the Australian Capital Territory. The
accident was due to negligence on the part of the defendant and some contributory
negligence on the part of the plaintiff. By the law of the Capital Territory
contributory negligence was only a ground for reduction of damages, but by the
C   law of New South Wales it would be a complete defence to the plaintiff's action.
It was held in effect that the first condition of the Willes formula applied, and,
as the defendant's act was in the circumstances not actionable according to the
law of New South Wales, the lex fori, the plaintiff's action failed.

In Canada the rule of English law, which is embodied in the Willes formula
as interpreted in *Machado* v. *Fontes* (168), has been authoritatively adopted
D   and applied. In *Canadian National Steamships Co., Ltd.* v. *Watson* (170), DUFF,
C.J., delivering the judgment of himself and CROCKET, KERWIN and HUDSON, JJ.,
said (171):

"It is now settled that, in an action brought in the province of Quebec
for damages in respect of personal injuries due to a tortious act committed
outside that province, the plaintiff's right to recover rests upon the fulfilment
E   of two conditions. These conditions are stated in the following passage in the
judgment of LORD MACNAGHTEN in *Carr* v. *Fracis Times & Co.* (172): ' In
the first place, the wrong must be of such a character that it would have
been actionable if committed in England; and, secondly, the act must not
have been justifiable by the law of the place where it was committed.'
' Justifiable ' here refers to legal justification; and an act or neglect which
F   is neither actionable nor punishable cannot be said to be otherwise than
' justifiable ' within the meaning of the rule. (*Walpole* v. *Canadian Northern
Ry. Co.* (173).) That this rule prevails in Quebec results from *O'Connor* v.
Wray (174).

"It is essential that the plaintiff prove an act or default actionable by
G   the law of Quebec. While it is also part of his case to establish that the tort
charged is non-justifiable by the *lex loci delicti* in the sense mentioned,
he is entitled to pray in aid a presumption which is a presumption of law,
viz., that the general law of the place where the alleged wrongful act occurred
is the same as the law of Quebec. Where a defendant relies upon some
difference between the law of the locality and the law of the forum the onus
is upon him to prove it."
H

The rule as stated in that passage of the judgment of DUFF, C.J., was applied in
another case in the Supreme Court of Canada, namely, *McLean* v. *Pettigrew* (175).
In that case the plaintiff, who was domiciled in the Province of Quebec, accepted
an invitation by the defendant, also domiciled in Quebec, to make a trip to Ottawa
as a gratuitous passenger in the defendant's automobile. There was an accident
in Ontario as a result of negligent driving by the defendant which amounted to
I   such lack of " due care and attention " as was punishable under an Act of Ontario.

---

(168) [1897] 2 Q.B. 231.
(169) [1966] A.L.R. 423.
(170) [1939] S.C.R. 11.
(171) [1939] S.C.R. at pp. 13-14.
(172) [1902] A.C. at p. 182.
(173) [1923] A.C. 113.
(174) [1930] 2 D.L.R. 899.
(175) [1945] S.C.R. 62.

As the plaintiff was a gratuitous passenger she was by the law of Ontario not en- **A** titled to recover damages from the defendant in a civil action, but she would be so entitled by the law of Quebec. Thus, the question arose in that case, as in *Machado* v. *Fontes* (176), whether the plaintiff could succeed in an action of tort in respect of an act committed abroad, when the act was actionable according to the lex fori and punishable but not actionable according to the lex loci delicti. It was held in that case (*McLean* v. *Pettigrew* (177)) as in *Machado* v. *Fontes* (176) that the **B** plaintiff could succeed in such an action.

Similarly, in *Morris and Stulback* v. *Angel* (178) the plaintiffs were gratuitous passengers in the defendant's car and were injured in an accident which occurred in the State of Washington. The defendant's conduct was actionable according to the law of British Columbia, where the parties were domiciled and the action was brought, but was only punishable and not actionable according to **C** the law of the State of Washington. The decision was given in favour of the plaintiffs, following the decision of the Supreme Court of Canada in *McLean* v. *Pettigrew* (177).

There have been cited a number of recent decisions of American courts. These show that, whereas formerly a rule giving preference to the lex loci delicti had been applied in the great majority of States, the rule has been found unsatisfactory **D** in modern conditions and the courts of many States have adopted a more flexible rule which often, although not always, has resulted in the lex fori being applied.

In *Kilberg* v. *Northeast Airlines, Inc.* (179), DESMOND, Ch.J., giving the leading judgment in the New York Court of Appeals, said (180):

" Modern conditions make it unjust and anomalous to subject the travelling citizen of this State to the varying laws of other States through and over **E** which they move. The number of States limiting death case damages has become smaller over the years, but there are still 14 of them . . . An air traveller from New York may in a flight of a few hours' duration pass through several of those commonwealths. His plane may meet with disaster in a State he never intended to cross, but into which the plane has flown because of bad weather or other unexpected developments, or an airplane's cata- **F** strophic descent may begin in one State and end in another. The place of injury becomes entirely fortuitous. Our Courts should if possible provide protection for our own State's people against unfair and anachronistic treatment of the lawsuits which result from these disasters."

Recognition of the tendency of State courts to adopt a more flexible rule was **G** expressed in the Supreme Court of the United States in *Richards* v. *United States* (181) by WARREN, C.J.:

" The general conflict-of-laws rule, followed by a vast majority of the States, is to apply the law of the place of injury to the substantive rights of the parties . . . Recently there has been a tendency on the part of some States to depart from the general conflicts rule in order to take into account **H** the interests of the State having significant contact with the parties to the litigation . . . Should the States continue this rejection of the older rule in those situations where its application might appear inappropriate or inequitable, the flexibility inherent in our interpretation [of a Federal Statute] will also be more in step with that judicial approach."

In *Babcock* v. *Jackson* (182) FULD, J., delivering a judgment in which the majority **I** of his colleagues in the New York Court of Appeals concurred, expounded and

---

(176) [1897] 2 Q.B. 231.
(177) [1945] S.C.R. 62.
(178) (1956), 5 D.L.R. (2d) 30.
(179) [1961] 2 Lloyd's Rep. 406.
(180) [1961] 2 Lloyd's Rep. at p. 408.
(181) (1962) 82 S.Ct. 585 at pp. 592-593.
(182) [1963] 2 Lloyd's Rep. 286 at pp. 287, 288.

A applied the new doctrine. He referred to the traditional rule giving preference to the lex loci delicti, and said:

> " Despite the advantages of certainty, ease of application and predictability which it affords . . . there has in recent years been increasing criticism of the traditional rule by commentators and a judicial trend towards its abandonment or modification."

B Then he said (183):

> " The ' centre of gravity ' or ' grouping of contacts ' doctrine adopted by this Court in conflicts cases involving contracts impresses us as likewise affording the appropriate approach for accommodating the competing interests in tort cases with multi-State contacts. Justice, fairness and ' the best **C** practical result ' . . . may best be achieved by giving controlling effect to the law of the jurisdiction which, because of its relationship or contact with the occurrence or the parties has the greatest concern with the specific issue raised in the litigation . . . The relative importance of the relationships or contacts of the respective jurisdictions is to be evaluated in the light of ' the issues, the character of the tort and the relevant purposes of the tort rules involved '."

D Later he said (184):

> " In conclusion, then, there is no reason why all issues arising out of a tort claim must be resolved by reference to the law of the same jurisdiction. Where the issue involves standards of conduct, it is more than likely that it is the law of the place of the tort which will be controlling, but the disposition of other **E** issues must turn, as does the issue of the standard of conduct itself, on the law of the jurisdiction which has the strongest interest in the resolution of the particular issue presented."

A case illustrating the uncertainty which may arise in the application of the new flexible rule is *Dym* v. *Gordon* (185) in which four members of the court held that on the facts of that case the law of Colorado was to be applied, but **F** three members of the court, dissenting, held that the law of New York should be applied.

I come back to the three suggestions mentioned above for some new rule to displace or modify the orthodox and established English rule based on the Willes formula: (a) The traditional American rule giving preference to the lex loci delicti has been shown by the opinions and experience of the American courts **G** to have become out of date. With the modern ease and frequency of travel across frontiers (not only by air and not only in the United States) the place of the accident may be quite fortuitous and the law of that place may have no substantial connection with the parties or the issues in the action. It would be strange if the English courts now adopted a rule which the courts of many States of the United States have felt compelled to discard by reason of its unsuitability to **H** modern conditions. (b) It has been suggested—and there is some support for this suggestion in the Scottish and the Australian cases—that damages should be recoverable for a wrongful act committed out of England only if it is actionable both by the law of England and by the law of the place in which the act was committed. That involves a duplication of causes of action and is likely to place an unfair burden on the plaintiff in some cases. He has the worst of both laws. **I** Also it would in some cases prevent the English court from giving judgment in accordance with its own ideas of justice. Suppose that in the present case there was no pecuniary expense or loss at all. By the law of Malta the plaintiff would have no cause of action in a Maltese court and therefore under the suggested rule his action in the English court would have to be dismissed in spite of his serious injuries and pain and suffering. If I am right in thinking that the question

(183) [1963] 2 Lloyd's Rep. at p. 289.
(184) [1963] 2 Lloyd's Rep. at p. 291.
(185) (1965), 209 N.E. 2d 792.

whether damages for pain and suffering are recoverable is a question of substantive   A
law, the suggested rule would bar the plaintiff's claim for such damages even if
it was associated with a claim for pecuniary loss. (c) The new American flexible
rule or flexible approach, with its full degree of flexibility, seems—at present at
any rate, when the doctrine is of recent origin and further development may be
expected—to be lacking in certainty and likely to create or prolong litigation.
Nevertheless, it may help the English courts to deal with the danger of " forum   B
shopping " which is inherent in the English rule.

The English rule, giving a predominant role to the lex fori in accordance with
the Willes formula as interpreted in *Machado* v. *Fontes* (186), is well-established.
It has advantages of certainty and ease of application. It enables the English
courts to give judgment according to their own ideas of justice. I see no sufficient
reason for discarding or modifying this established rule for the normal case in   C
which the action is appropriately brought in the English courts.   There is
however, the danger of " forum shopping ", of which *Machado* v. *Fontes* (186)
may be an illustration. A plaintiff, who would naturally and appropriately be
suing the defendant in the courts of some other country, may seek to take advantage of the English rule by suing in the English courts because their law is
more favourable to him. In such a case it may be desirable as a matter of public   D
policy for the English courts, for the purpose of discouraging " forum shopping ",
to apply the law of the natural forum. That is a possible, and I would think desirable, qualification of the established rule; it would prevent a repetition of what
may have happened in *Machado* v. *Fontes* (186). But it is not a necessary part
of the decision in the present case, in which it cannot be said that it was inappropriate for the respondent to bring his action in the English courts.   E

In my opinion, it was right for the learned judge (187) at the trial to apply the
English substantive law, being the lex fori, in accordance with the established
rule, and, as the majority of the Court of Appeal (188) have affirmed his decision,
I would dismiss the appeal.

Finally, I wish to add this. There ought to be a general rule so as to limit the
flexibility and consequent uncertainty of the choice of the substantive law to be   F
applied. But whatever rule may be adopted as the general rule some exception
will be required in the interests of justice. If the general rule is that the substantive
law is the law of the forum, an exception will be required in order to discourage
" forum shopping ". On the other hand, if the general rule is that the alleged
wrongful act must be actionable by the law of the place where it was committed
or that it must be actionable both by that law and by the law of the forum, an   G
exception will be required to enable the plaintiff in a case such as the present
case to succeed in his claim for adequate damages.

Appeal dismissed.

Solicitors: *Gascoin & Co.* (for the appellant); *Roche, Son & Neale*, agents for
Buss, Cheale & Co., Tunbridge Wells (for the respondent).

[*Reported by* S. A. HATTEEA, ESQ., *Barrister-at-Law.*]   H

I

___

(186) [1897] 2 Q.B. 231.
(187) [1967] 2 All E.R. 665; [1968] 2 Q.B. 1.
(188) [1968] 1 All E.R. 283; [1968] 2 Q.B. 1.

A

R. *v.* HUSSAIN.

[Court of Appeal, criminal division (Widgery and Karminski, L.JJ., Geoffrey Lane, J.), May 2, 1969.]

Customs—Importation of prohibited goods—Knowingly concerned in fraudulent evasion—" Knowingly "—" Smuggle "—Customs and Excise Act 1952
B *(15 & 16 Geo. 6 & 1 Eliz. 2 c. 44), s. 304 (b).*

The word " knowingly " in s. 304 (*b*)* of the Customs and Excise Act 1952 is concerned with knowing that a fraudulent evasion of a prohibition in respect of goods is taking place. If, therefore, an accused knows that what is on foot is the evasion of a prohibition against importation and he knowingly takes part in that operation, that is sufficient to justify his
C conviction, even if he does not know precisely what kind of goods are being imported. It is essential he should know that the operation with which he is concerning himself is an operation designed to evade that prohibition and evade it fraudulently (see p. 1119, letter B, post).

Observations on the meaning of " to smuggle " (see p. 1119, letters D and F, post).

D   *Appeal dismissed in part, allowed in part.*

[As to mens rea in statutory offences, see 10 Halsbury's Laws (3rd Edn.) 273, 274, para. 508; and for cases on the subject, see 14 Digest (Repl.) 35-40, *48-95*.

For the Customs and Excise Act 1952, s. 304, see 9 Halsbury's Statutes (3rd Edn.) 201.]

E Case referred to:

Warner v. *Metropolitan Police Comr.*, [1968] 2 All E.R. 356; [1968] 2 W.L.R. 1303; Digest (Repl.) Supp.

Appeal.

This was an appeal by Mohammed Blayat Hussain by leave of the single judge against his conviction on 29th October 1968, at the North-East London
F Quarter Sessions (chairman, J. F. Marnan, Esq., Q.C.) on one count of being knowingly concerned in a fraudulent evasion of the prohibition against the importation of cannabis, contrary to s. 304 (*b*) of the Customs and Excise Act 1952, and on a second count of unlawful possession of dangerous drugs, namely, cannabis, contrary to s. 13 of the Dangerous Drugs Act 1965, and reg. 3 of the Dangerous Drugs (No. 2) Regulations 1964†. He was sentenced to 18 months'
G imprisonment on each count, concurrent.

D. M. Blair for the appellant.
M. Gale for the Crown.

WIDGERY, L.J., delivered the judgment of the court: The appellant was convicted in October 1968 at the North-East London Quarter Sessions on
H one count of being knowingly concerned in a fraudulent evasion of the prohibition against the importation of cannabis (which was charged as being contrary to s. 304 (*b*) of the Customs and Excise Act 1952) and on a second count of unlawful possession of dangerous drugs, namely, cannabis. He was sentenced on those counts to 18 months' imprisonment on each concurrent, and he now appeals against conviction by leave of the single judge.

I   The evidence in this case was somewhat complex, but the essentials can fairly readily be ascertained. On 6th September 1968, a ship called the m.v. Aziz Bhatti came into Liverpool. An assistant preventive officer called Godfrey went into a cabin occupied by the appellant together with two other crew members. He removed the bulkhead panel in the cabin and inside he found some ten concealed packages which, on investigation, proved to contain approximately 20 lb. of cannabis resin. The appellant was questioned about this, and his immediate reaction when questioned in English seems to have been

---

* Section 304, so far as material, is set out at p. 1118, letter E, post.
† S.I. 1964 No. 1811.

that it was nothing to do with him but that he would take the blame, and he **A**
repeated this on a number of occasions.   This court feels that little importance
can be attached to that because of the language difficulties which existed at that
time.   The ship went on to London, and the appellant was further questioned
after arrival in London, and he then gave a very much more comprehensive
explanation of what had occurred; and it will not unfairly represent that
explanation if I put it in these terms.   His case, both when he made a statement **B**
in London and at the trial, was that, when the ship was on passage from Las
Palmas to Liverpool, the second engineer (whom he described as " a very big
officer ") and the carpenter came into the cabin and said they wished to put
something in his cabin.   The carpenter had a bucket containing these ten packets,
and the appellant said that he was in no position to demur.   The bulkhead
was taken out, and the packages were duly secreted behind it.   The appellant **C**
said that he was threatened that he would have his throat cut if he said anything
about it and, alternatively, was promised some kind of reward if he kept silent.
Really his defence to the whole case was that this was nothing to do with him;
he had not demurred at what was done in view of the threats hanging over him;
and the whole thing was engineered by the officer in question and the carpenter,
and he was little more than a passive spectator. **D**
   Everything in this appeal turns on the terms of the summing-up.   The court
has great sympathy with the learned chairman and all other chairmen who are
summing-up in this kind of case at the present time.   So far as the first charge
is concerned, s. 304 of the Customs and Excise Act 1952 is in these terms:

> " Without prejudice to any other provision of this Act, if any person—
> ... (b) is, in relation to any goods, in any way knowingly concerned in any **E**
> fraudulent evasion or attempt at evasion of any duty chargeable thereon
> or of any such prohibition or restriction as aforesaid or of any provision of
> this Act applicable to those goods, he may be detained ... "

and then it provides for the appropriate penalty.   The way the learned chairman
dealt with the first charge was as follows.   In his summing-up he told the jury **F**
that the phrase they had to consider was—

> " being knowingly concerned in a fraudulent evasion of the prohibition
> against importation of cannabis resin."

Then he proceeded to go through that phrase in some detail; he pointed out
that there was a prohibition against the importation of cannabis (which was not
disputed); and he further pointed out that there was an importation of cannabis **G**
in the present case: any difficulties on the law in that regard having disappeared
in the course of the trial.   He then proceeded:

> " The question is: Has it been proved that the [appellant] was knowingly
> concerned in that operation? ... ' Knowingly concerned in that operation '
> means that he was co-operating with the smugglers, if I may so put it, and it
> does not matter if he did not know precisely the nature of the goods the **H**
> smugglers were dealing with.   He would be just as guilty if he had thought
> they were dealing with brandy, for instance, but what has to be proved is
> that he was knowingly and to that extent consciously and deliberately
> concerned in co-operating in what he must have known was an operation of
> smuggling or getting prohibited goods into this country."
  I
The learned chairman illustrated the difference between being knowingly con-
cerned and not knowingly concerned by contrasting examples which he then
referred to.
   Two main complaints are made against that passage in the summing-up.
First of all, it is said that the learned chairman was wrong in saying that the
Crown did not have to prove that the appellant knew that cannabis was the
subject of the importation.   It is submitted on behalf of the appellant that proof
of knowledge on the part of the accused that the goods being smuggled were

A cannabis was part of the obligation of the prosecution, and, since the learned chairman had directed that it was not necessary for the accused to know precisely the nature of the goods, there was a misdirection. The court is not prepared to accept that submission. It seems perfectly clear that the word " knowingly " in s. 304 is concerned with knowing that a fraudulent evasion of a prohibition in respect of goods is taking place. If, therefore, the accused knows that what is

B on foot is the evasion of a prohibition against importation and he knowingly takes part in that operation, it is sufficient to justify his conviction, even if he does not know precisely what kind of goods are being imported. It is, of course, essential that he should know that the goods which are being imported are goods subject to a prohibition. It is essential he should know that the operation with which he is concerning himself is an operation designed to evade that prohibition

C and evade it fraudulently. But it is not necessary that he should know the precise category of the goods the importation of which has been prohibited. Accordingly, in our judgment, there is nothing in that point taken on behalf of the appellant.

    The second point is that the learned chairman, in the passage which I have read, has confused the importation of goods where an importation is prohibited,

D with the importation of goods liable to customs duty in such a way as to evade the appropriate duty which is payable. It is submitted that the word " smugglers " in ordinary language applies to those who bring in goods which are subject to customs duty, and that " smuggling " refers to the operation of bringing in such goods in such a way as to avoid the duty. Accordingly, it is said that, instead of directing the jury's attention to goods which were the subject of a prohibition

E against import, he has invited them to say that it would be enough if the appellant thought that the operation was intended to evade a customs duty. The court has considered that submission with care as well. Ignoring for the moment the reference to brandy (which I have already read), this court takes the view that there is no reason to suppose that the jury would associate the word " smugglers " solely with those who seek to evade customs duty. We think that, in the ordinary

F use of language today, the verb " to smuggle " is used equally to apply to the importation of goods which are prohibited in import and, indeed, one sees the word used quite often in regard to illegal immigrants brought in secretly by night in small boats. We do not think that the jury would have been in any way put off in their approach to this problem by the reference to " smugglers " and " smuggling "; and we regard the reference to " brandy " as being of such

G trivial importance that, if necessary, the court would apply the proviso (1) in regard to that sentence and would, accordingly, uphold the first conviction and dismiss the appeal so far as it relates to the first count.

    The second count is another matter. The second count, as I have said, charged the appellant with possession of a dangerous drug (cannabis). In regard to this the learned chairman gave the type of direction which was common before

H the recent decision of the House of Lords in *Warner* v. *Metropolitan Police Comr.* (2). In other words, the direction in regard to possession was to the effect that it was only necessary for the jury to be satisfied that the appellant was in control of the goods, and did not go on to invite the jury to consider whether the accused was aware of the character of the goods. In particular, towards the end of the summing-up, the point is put very shortly. The learned chairman

I said to the jury:

    " . . . are you satisfied that he consented to have that stuff put in his cabin without knowing precisely what it was, knowing that there was stuff there in those packages that were being hidden with his consent . . ."

He is clearly there obscuring any importance which might arise from the fact that the appellant might not know the nature and character of the goods of

(1) To s. 2 (1) of the Criminal Appeal Act 1968.
(2) [1968] 2 All E.R. 356; [1968] 2 W.L.R. 1303.

which he was alleged to be in possession. Then, in regard to control and physical possession, the learned chairman, having started quite correctly, in our view, by saying that the test of possession is control, went on, again quite properly, to say:

> " It is sufficient for the purposes of this case for me to tell you as a matter of law that if a man willingly receives and hides something for somebody else, as a matter of law he is in possession of those goods."

We think that, as applied to this case, if the jury had been satisfied that the appellant had willingly received and hidden in a bulkhead something which another had asked him to hide, he would properly be said to have been in control and possession. The learned chairman enlarged on this, and pointed out that, if the truth of the matter is that the appellant was forced by superior officers in a high-handed way to allow the panel of his cabin to be removed and the goods to be put behind it, then the appellant should be acquitted, because there the proper inference would be that he was not in control. He went on in these terms:

> " If, on the other hand, you think that what was done, although it may not have been done by his hand, that although he had not used the screw-driver it was done with his consent, the hiding of those goods in his cabin, then he had those goods in his possession . . . If, on the second count [the prosecution] have proved that he consented to that cannabis being hidden in his cabin, once again they have proved he is in possession."

Acknowledging, as we do, the difficulty of summing-up in these cases, this court is somewhat concerned that a direction on possession and control which started promisingly had become watered down to little more than a direction that, if the appellant had consented to the second engineer and the carpenter putting these goods behind the bulkhead, that would be enough to establish he was in control and, therefore, possession. This court feels that this was an unsatisfactory direction and, when coupled with the fact that there is really in this case no direction as regards the mental element of possession as required in *Warner's* case (3), we have little hesitation in saying that this was an unsatisfactory verdict and one which, accordingly, should be set aside. In the result we dismiss the appeal on count 1, allow the appeal on count 2 and set aside the conviction on count 2.

Appeal dismissed on count 1; appeal allowed on count 2 and the conviction on that count quashed.

Solicitors: *Registrar of Criminal Appeals* (for the appellant); *Director of Public Prosecutions.*

[*Reported by* WENDY SHOCKETT, *Barrister-at-Law.*]

---

(3) [1968] 2 All E.R. 356; [1968] 2 W.L.R. 1303.

A

CITY CENTRE PROPERTIES (I.T.C. PENSIONS), LTD. *v.* TERSONS, LTD.

[COURT OF APPEAL, CIVIL DIVISION (Harman and Salmon, L.JJ., and Cairns, J.), November 4, 5, 6, 1968, March 17, 1969.]

B *Arbitration—Arbitrator—Revocation of authority by leave of court—Grounds for— Current action in court—Building contract—Action by prospective tenants against building owners and against nominated sub-contractors—Third party proceedings by owners against contractors and sub-contractors—Arbitrator appointed, pursuant to building contract and sub-contract, on application by contractors on behalf of sub-contractors to decide whether owners had*

C *to pay contractors for sub-contractors' work—Application by owners to revoke appointment of arbitrator—Arbitration Act* 1950 (14 *Geo.* 6 *c.* 27), *s.* 1, *s.* 4 (1).

A very much stronger case must be made to induce the court to make an order under s. 1* of the Arbitration Act 1950, giving leave to revoke the authority of an arbitrator or umpire appointed by or by virtue of an arbitra-

D tion agreement and so depriving the respondent to the application of his contractual rights, than is necessary to induce the court to make an order under s. 4† of the Act, staying legal proceedings in respect of a matter agreed to be referred to arbitration and so confirming the parties contractual rights (see p. 1125, letter I, to p. 1126, letter A, post).

The power to make such an order under s. 1 is to be used only in very

E exceptional circumstances, such, for instance, as misconduct on the part of the arbitrator and the like (see p. 1126, letter B, post).

In 1960 and 1961 building owners agreed to erect a hotel on their site for prospective tenants and to the prospective tenants' requirements. The prospective tenants agreed to bear any excess in the cost of the building over £3,000,000. In 1962 the owners employed contractors to erect the

F hotel; and the owners' architect nominated sub-contractors to provide the mechanical services of heating, lighting and ventilating the hotel for about £440,000. The £3,000,000 limit was reached in 1964. The prospective tenants paid the owners about £1,000,000 towards the additional costs in 1965, but in 1966 the prospective tenants refused to pay any more although the owners had by then paid out about a further £500,000 for the building

G work, and litigation ensued between the owners and the prospective tenants. This litigation was stayed and the dispute was referred to arbitration (the "first arbitration"). The first arbitration proceedings were likely to be long drawn out. The prospective tenants alleged that much of the work, including the sub-contractors' work, had been done badly, and with excessive delay. By agreement between the owners and the prospective tenants

H the dispute about the sub-contractors' work was struck out of the first arbitration proceedings. In January 1968 the prospective tenants issued a writ against the sub-contractors and the owners and on 24th January 1968 served their statement of claim by which they claimed, against the sub-contractors, damages for breaches of warranties alleged to have been given directly to them in order to obtain the sub-contract, and alternatively

I against the owners, damages for breach of the agreement to erect the hotel. The owners brought in the contractors and sub-contractors as third parties. Before the issue of the writ the sub-contractors had applied to the president

---

* Section 1 is set out at p. 1124, letter H, post.
† Section 4 (1), so far as material, provides: " If any party to an arbitration agreement ... commences any legal proceedings ... against any other party to the agreement ... in respect of any matter agreed to be referred, any party to those legal proceedings may ... apply to that court to stay the proceedings, and that court ... may make an order staying the proceedings ".

of the Royal Institute of British Architects, pursuant to the arbitration and A
indemnity clauses in the building contract and sub-contract, to appoint an
arbitrator to decide whether the owners did or did not owe a further sum of
about £130,000 to the contractors in respect of the sub-contractors' work.
On 27th February 1968 the president appointed an arbitrator to decide
this question (the " second arbitration "). On 8th March 1968 the owners
applied by originating summons under the Arbitration Act 1950, s. 1, for B
leave to revoke the authority of this arbitrator,

Held: the application for leave to revoke under s. 1 would be dismissed,
because—

(i) bearing in mind (a) that the sub-contractors could not in the action by
the prospective tenants counterclaim against the prospective tenants the
relief sought by them in the second arbitration and (b) that if the second C
arbitration were stayed the sub-contractors were likely, throughout a
lengthy and complicated action, to be out of pocket, in respect of moneys
alleged to have been disbursed in 1965, the owners had not made out the very
strong case necessary to induce the court to give leave to revoke the
authority (see p. 1126, letters D, G and I, post); and

(ii) the third party notices issued by the owners against the contractors D
and sub-contractors in the action by the prospective tenants did not deprive
the contractors and sub-contractors of their right to go to arbitration, because
there was no claim in that action by anyone for the sum claimed in the
second arbitration (see p. 1126, letter I, to p. 1127, letter B, post).

Doleman & Sons v. *Ossett Corpn.* ([1912] 3 K.B. 257) distinguished.

Appeal dismissed. E

[As to revocation by leave of the court of the authority of an arbitrator,
see 2 HALSBURY'S LAWS (3rd Edn.) 15-17, paras. 39-41; and for cases on the
subject, see 2 DIGEST (Repl.) 510-514, *548-578.*

For the Arbitration Act 1950, s. 1, s. 4, see 2 HALSBURY'S STATUTES (3rd Edn.)
435, 437.] F

Cases referred to:
> *Den of Airlie Steamship Co., Ltd.* v. *Mitsui & Co., Ltd. and British Oil and
> Cake Mills, Ltd.* (1912), 106 L.T. 451; 12 Asp. M.L.C. 169; 2 Digest
> (Repl.) 499, *472.*
> *Doleman & Sons* v. *Ossett Corpn.,* [1912] 3 K.B. 257; 81 L.J.K.B. 1092; 107 G
> L.T. 581; 76 J.P. 457; 2 Digest (Repl.) 468, *306.*
> *Hewitt* v. *Hewitt* (1841), 1 Q.B. 110; 113 E.R. 1071; 2 Digest (Repl.) 616,
> *1416.*
> *Scott* v. *Van Sandau* (1841), 1 Q.B. 102; 113 E.R. 1068; 2 Digest (Repl.)
> 511, *558.*
> *Taunton-Collins* v. *Cromie,* [1964] 2 All E.R. 332; [1964] 1 W.L.R. 633; H
> Digest (Cont. Vol. B) 26, *383a.*

Interlocutory Appeal.

This was an appeal by building owners, City Centre Properties (I.T.C. Pensions),
Ltd., against the order of SHAW, J., made in chambers on 5th July 1968 on appeal
by the contractors under a building contract, Tersons, Ltd., against an order I
of the master made on 5th April 1968 on an application by the owners by
originating summons under s. 1 of the Arbitration Act 1950, for leave to revoke
the authority of an arbitrator who had been appointed by the president of the
Royal Institute of British Architects on the application of sub-contractors,
Matthew Hall & Co., Ltd. The originating summons had named the defendants
to it as " Matthew Hall & Co., Ltd. (sued in the name of Tersons, Ltd.) ". The
master had made an order giving leave to revoke the arbitrator's authority;
SHAW, J., in the order now appealed against, had set aside the master's order

A and re-instated the arbitrator. The facts are set out in the judgment of the court.

    K. R. Bagnall and *Mark Myers* for the owners.
    F. P. Neill, Q.C., and *R. C. Southwell* for the contractors.

Cur. adv. vult.

    17th March. **HARMAN, L.J.**: We regret that there has been so much
B delay in the delivering of this judgment. It has been caused by accident, by
ill-health, and by the fact that the members of this court revolve, like the
stars, in their courses. The judgment that I am about to deliver is the judgment
of the court. [HIS LORDSHIP then read the judgment of the court.]
    In 1960, under the aegis of the late Jack Cotton, City Centre Properties
(I.T.C. Pensions), Ltd., the appellants here, or one of its predecessors, were
C the owners either in freehold or over a long term of years of the Kensington
Palace Hotel, then standing at the south-west corner of Kensington Gardens.
The owners were minded to demolish that hotel and build another one on the
site, and in November 1960, there was an informal agreement between Jack
Cotton, acting for the owners, and one Bloomfield, the then presiding genius
of the Oddenino group of companies, that the owners would build the new hotel
D to Oddenino's requirements. Oddenino was to take a lease of the hotel when
built for a long term and at a rent representing interest on the owners' capital
outlay, which was then undefined. The hotel was to be built to the design of
a firm of architects employed by the owners and named R. Seifert & Partners.
Formal agreements were made some time in 1961, and in April of that year
there was a further agreement between the owners and Oddenino (hereinafter
E called the prospective tenants) that the liability of the former in respect of the
building should be limited to £3,000,000 and that any excess would be found
by the prospective tenants and repaid so far as necessary to the owners.
    In 1962 the owners entered into a formal contract with the defendant contrac-
tors to erect a new building, they already having had a contract for demolition
of the old one. As the new hotel was to be constructed in accordance with the
F requirements of the prospective tenants it was only natural that the supervision
of the details should be handed over by the owners to them, but the owners
remained the building owners and the architects Seifert remained their employees
and the owners alone were responsible to the contractors under the building
contract.
    The £3,000,000 limit was reached by the end of 1964, and during 1965 the
G prospective tenants appear to have paid out something in the nature of a further
£1,000,000 towards the building's costs. These were paid to the owners, who of
course remained liable on the building contract with the contractors.
    In 1966 the prospective tenants refused to lay out further moneys and a writ
was issued but has been stayed, and there is at present proceeding a massive
arbitration between the owners and the prospective tenants in which, as we
H understand, the prospective tenants do not contest that the owners have paid
out a further half-million or so for which the prospective tenants would be liable
but for a set-off which they allege they have and which is now being investigated.
    Included in that arbitration was an issue about the mechanical services of
heating, lighting and ventilating the hotel, work which had been done by the
sub-contractors, Matthew Hall & Co., Ltd., who are interested in but not parties
I to this appeal. This firm had been recommended to the prospective tenants by
the architects, and at the request of the prospective tenants the architects
acting, so we understand, on behalf of the owners under the main building
contract, nominated the sub-contractors, the initial estimate of cost being about
£440,000. Accordingly, the contractors entered into a formal sub-contract with
the sub-contractors to provide the mechanical services at a price originally
put at the above figure but which, like all other costs connected with this venture,
has since almost doubled. The sub-contractors are therefore what are called
nominated sub-contractors, and the only way in which on the face of it such

a sub-contractor can enforce payment is because his sub-contract confers on **A** him the right against the head contractors, Tersons, to make use of the contractors' name to enforce their rights under the head contract.

At some date unknown to us it appears to have been agreed between the owners and the prospective tenants that the dispute between them about the mechanical services was not suitably placed in the main arbitration; these issues were struck out of the main arbitration accordingly and in January 1968, a writ was issued **B** by the prospective tenants against the sub-contractors and the owners in which a double claim was made, first against the sub-contractors that a number of warranties had been given by them to the prospective tenants in order to obtain the mechanical services contract with the contractors and that the prospective tenants can obtain damages against the sub-contractors direct through breaches of those warranties. There is of course no formal or written contract between **C** the prospective tenants and the sub-contractors. The alternative claim in the action by the prospective tenants is against the owners under the main building contract, alleging that the work, including the work on mechanical services, had been badly done in a number of respects and that the prospective tenants were entitled to damages for that and also for delays in the completion of the work and loss of profits because the hotel was not opened on time. The statement **D** of claim in that action was delivered on 24th January 1968.

On 27th February the president of the Royal Institute of British Architects, in response to an application made on behalf of the sub-contractors by the contractors, appointed an arbitrator to decide the question whether the owners did or did not owe a further sum of about £130,000 to the contractors, who will receive it on behalf of the sub-contractors, in respect of the balance due to the **E** latter on their account for services rendered under their sub-contract.

On 8th March 1968, there was issued by the owners the originating summons on which the present appeal arises. This document is wrongly headed as to parties, the defendants being stated to be " Matthew Hall & Co. Ltd. (sued in the name of [the contractors]) ". This of course is incorrect, though no one observed the mistake until raised in this court. The proper defendants are the contractors: **F** their name is being used by Matthew Hall & Co., Ltd., the sub-contractors, on an indemnity under a term of the building contract between the owners, and the contractors, whereby Matthew Hall as nominated sub-contractors have the right, if aggrieved by the failure of the owners' architects, to issue further certificates for payment of the sub-contractors under the sub-contract, to go to arbitration on the matter. **G**

On 28th February 1968, the owners issued third party notices in the action, claiming indemnity or contribution against the contractors, against the sub-contractors, and against a firm of quantity surveyors whom we shall call Thompson's. The owners delivered their defence and counterclaim on 1st March and on 8th March, as I have said, issued this originating summons under s. 1 of the Arbitration Act 1950. That section is in these terms: **H**

" The authority of an arbitrator or umpire appointed by or by virtue
of an arbitration agreement shall, unless a contrary intention is expressed
in the agreement, be irrevocable except by leave of the High Court or a judge
thereof."

The originating summons was a summons for leave to revoke the appointment **I** of the arbitrator under that section.

This is an unusual application and the authorities show that it is a jurisdiction only to be used sparingly and in unusual cases: see the judgment of LORD DENMAN, C.J., so long ago as 1841 in *Hewitt* v. *Hewitt* (1), affirmed by the Court of Appeal in *Den of Airlie Steamship Co., Ltd.* v. *Mitsui & Co., Ltd. and British Oil and Cake Mills, Ltd.* (2), in the headnote to which are to be found these words (3):

---

(1) (1841), 1 Q.B. 110.   (2) (1912), 106 L.T. 451.   (3) (1912), 106 L.T. at p. 452.

A   " The plaintiffs thereupon took out a summons for further directions, asking (inter alia) for an injunction to restrain the first defendants from proceeding with the arbitration, alternatively that leave be given to the plaintiffs to revoke the submission to arbitration. Held (without deciding the point decided [below]) (1) that there was no jurisdiction in the court to grant the injunction asked for; and (2) that in the exercise of its discretion
B   the court ought not to give leave to revoke the submission to arbitration."

VAUGHAN WILLIAMS, L.J., said (4):

" A summons was taken out at chambers applying, as an interlocutory proceeding, for the injunction to restrain these people from going on with the arbitration, and, secondly, for revocation of the submission to arbitration.
C   So far as the injunction is concerned, in our judgment there is no jurisdiction to grant that injunction."

Then VAUGHAN WILLIAMS, L.J., dealt with that, decided that there was no jurisdiction, and proceeded to say (5):

" Having said that I now propose to deal with the question of revocation. With regard to the question of revocation I think it is undoubted, and really
D   it was admitted on both sides, that there is power to revoke; in fact sect. 1 of the Arbitration Act 1889 by its terms recognises this power. But what is said, and what practically is not denied on either side, is that although the court has power to give leave for the revocation of a submission to arbitration it is a power which, as was said in *Scott* v. *Van Sandau* (6) is to be used with great caution.   The last words in the case of *Scott* v. *Van Sandau* (7)
E   are: ' We will only observe that the discretion of the court to which this appeal is made ought to be exercised in the most sparing and cautious manner, lest an agreement to refer, from which all might reasonably hope for a speedy end of strife, should only open the flood-gates for multiplied expenses and interminable delays '."

F   The grounds for the application here are that the same issues arise in the action and in the arbitration and that it is undesirable for the same issues to be tried before two separate tribunals who might arrive at conflicting conclusions.   The authority for this proposition is *Taunton-Collins* v. *Cromie* (8), and counsel for the owners enumerated the common issues as being as follows: (i) Did the sub-contractors do the work in question?   (ii) Did they do it on proper orders?
G   (iii) At what cost?   (iv) Was the work defective in any and if so what respects? and (v) If so, what was the cost of putting the defects right?   The master acceded to the application and made an order on 5th April 1968 revoking the nominated arbitrator's authority and directing that the arbitration should go before the judge or other person trying the action.   This was on the face of it a defective order as the trial judge could not act as arbitrator, though if the action were transferred to the official referee he could also act as arbitrator and that might
H   well be at some stage or other a satisfactory solution.

The contractors appealed against the master's order and it came before the judge in chambers, who, in a reserved judgment on 5th July 1968, revoked the master's order and re-instated the nominated arbitrator.   The owners appealed from this order to this court and this is the question before us.

It is first to be observed that there is an essential difference between an applica-
I   tion under s. 1 of the Act of 1950 and an application under s. 4.   In the first case the applicant is seeking to deprive the respondent of his contractual rights: in the second, the applicant is insisting on his contractual rights against the respondent.   It seems to us to follow that a very much stronger case must be made

---

(4) (1912), 106 L.T. at p. 453.
(5) (1912), 106 L.T. at p. 454.
(6) (1841), 1 Q.B. 102.
(7) (1841), 1 Q.B. at p. 110.
(8) [1964] 2 All E.R. 332; [1964] 1 W.L.R. 633.

to induce the court to act under s. 1 and deprive the respondent of what is his **A** by contract than to intervene under s. 4 by an order which confirms the parties' contractual rights.

In *Taunton-Collins* v. *Cromie* (9), however, an application to stay under s. 4 was refused because the Court of Appeal considered that it would be inconvenient that there should be two sets of proceedings in which the same issues were raised. It is contended in this appeal that in effect granting an application **B** under s. 1 is equivalent to refusing an application under s. 4. In our view this is not so at all. Section 1 is not merely the converse of s. 4. The power it gives is to be used only in very exceptional circumstances, such, for instance, as misconduct on the part of the arbitrator and the like: see RUSSELL ON ARBITRATION AND AWARD (17th Edn.) pp. 59-62.

This, we think, was the basis of the judge's decision overruling the master's **C** order. The judge took the view that that order without sufficient cause deprived the sub-contractor of his rights which the sub-contract gave him. The learned judge pointed out that the sub-contractors were not parties to the main building agreement and that on the face of it their only right to insist on payment under their sub-contract was their right to use the name of the contractors in arbitration proceedings. **D**

It seems to us a hardship on the sub-contractors if this right can be struck out of their hands by the institution of an action in which, although they are defendants, they cannot counterclaim against the prospective tenants the relief which they seek in the arbitration. This action was started after the date when it must have been known to the owners that arbitration proceedings on behalf of the sub-contractors were to be instituted. Indeed it was only an accident **E** that the person called on to appoint an arbitrator took a long time to do it, which made the action precede the appointment of the arbitrator. We were informed that the contractors intended to serve a fourth party notice against the sub-contractors, but no such notice had been served down to the time of the hearing.

The main other ground influencing the learned judge was, we think, that the **F** arbitration concerned a comparatively straightforward claim, namely a claim to some £130,000 costs incurred which it is said the architect ought to have certified but has failed so to do. The action on the other hand is one of enormous complication and involves three third parties including the sub-contractors themselves. It is likely to take a very long time before it can be brought to trial, during the whole of which the sub-contractors will be out of pocket in respect **G** of moneys said to have been disbursed some three years ago and we feel some sympathy with this view.

The chief argument for the owners was that although they were at least nominally the building owners, they had, at any rate since the £3,000,000 mark was reached, handed over to the prospective tenants, who alone were concerned with the control and supervision of the whole contract, and that the owners **H** really did not know much about it but would have to rely on such information as they could extract from the prospective tenants. We think this difficulty is rather apparent than real. It will necessarily be in the interest of the prospective tenants to support the owners' case, and we should have thought that the difficulty could be overcome.

On the whole, weighing one matter with another, we are not satisfied that the **I** owners have made out the very strong case which alone can move the court to interfere under s. 1 of the Act, and we are for dismissing this appeal.

A point was taken before us which was not taken and indeed did not arise in the court below. It is that the contractors and also the sub-contractors, having been brought into the Oddenino action by third-party notices issued by the owners, cannot now rely on the right to go to arbitration. It was said that this

(9) [1964] 2 All E.R. 332; [1964] 1 W.L.R. 633.

A proposition was supported by *Doleman & Sons* v. *Ossett Corpn.* (10). In that case
a party who had a right to go to arbitration had started proceedings by way of
action which he could have made in the arbitration and the defendant in those
proceedings had taken a step in the action and thus in effect had abandoned his
right to go to arbitration in respect of that claim.   In the present action there is
no claim of any kind by the contractors or the sub-contractors against the
B owners or anyone else for the amount claimed in the arbitration and therefore
neither the contractors nor the sub-contractors can be said to have abandoned
their right to go to arbitration.   The point therefore fails.

Appeal dismissed.

Leave to appeal to the House of Lords refused.

C   Solicitors: *Kenneth Brown, Baker, Baker* (for the owners); *Linklaters &
Paines* (for the contractors).

[*Reported by* HENRY SUMMERFIELD, ESQ., *Barrister-at-Law.*]

D ———

PRACTICE DIRECTION.

E ### CHANCERY DIVISION.

*Legal Aid—Costs—Taxation—Procedure—Chancery Division—Ex parte applica-
tion—Written request for order for taxation—Papers to be lodged.*

It shall no longer be necessary to issue a summons for taxation of costs under
the Legal Aid and Advice Act 1949 (1), when an assisted person's civil aid
F certificate has been discharged or revoked in the course of proceedings in the
Chancery Division.

The solicitors to the formerly assisted party may apply ex parte to the appropriate master by written request for an order for such taxation, ensuring that the
duplicates of the civil aid certificate and of the certificate of discharge or revocation (which must have been filed pursuant to r. 16 (6) of the Legal Aid (General)
G Regulations 1962 (2)) have reached the master's chambers.   If such proceedings
have not previously been in chambers, the writ or originating summons (if the
formerly assisted party is the plaintiff), or a copy thereof (if he is the defendant)
must also be lodged.   Papers may be lodged by post in accordance with the
procedure set out in the Practice Direction of 4th February 1969 (3).

The master will make the order without any attendance before him.
H By the direction of BUCKLEY, J.

R. E. BALL,
20th June 1969.   Chief Master.

I ———

---

(10) [1912] 3 K.B. 257.
(1) 18 HALSBURY'S STATUTES (2nd Edn.) 532.
(2) S.I. 1962 No. 148 (5 HALSBURY'S STATUTORY INSTRUMENTS (2nd Re-Issue) 268).
(3) [1969] 1 All E.R. 490; [1969] 1 W.L.R. 274.

A

ANGLO-ITALIAN PROPERTIES, LTD. *v.* LONDON RENT ASSESSMENT PANEL.

[QUEEN'S BENCH DIVISION (Lord Parker, C.J., Melford Stevenson and Willis, JJ.), April 18, 1969.]

Rent Restriction—Rent—Regulated tenancy—Determination of fair rent— B
Calculation on deduction of scarcity value from 1962 capital costs—Whether
proper assessment—Rent Act 1968 (c. 23), s. 46 (1).

In 1962, the appellants acquired a terraced house and converted it into
flats. The basement flat with garden was let to a tenant at £600 per annum
exclusive of rates but inclusive of the use of the appellants' furniture and
effects. The tenant applied to the rent officer to determine and register   C
a fair rent which he did at £335 per annum. The appellants appealed to a
rent assessment committee who accepted their valuation of the purchase
price in 1962, plus the cost of conversion, viz., £13,863. The committee
considered a fair yield to be ten per cent. on the capital, that a fair apportionment of that capital cost to the flat in question would be one-quarter, and
they reached a figure of £348 per annum as a basis for assessing a fair rent.   D
The average annual cost of repairs was £250, and, apportioning that to the
flat in the same proportion as for the capital, the committee arrived at a
total of £410. As, however, at the time of buying and converting the
property a developer would have obtained higher rents than those obtainable
since the coming into effect of the Rent Act 1965, which excluded " scarcity
value " from the assessment of fair rents, the committee put the scarcity   E
value of the subject property at about ten per cent. The committee,
accordingly, considered that a fair rent for the flat would be £369, plus £31
for the use of the appellants' furniture and effects, making a total of £400
per annum as a fair rent for the purpose of s. 46 (1)* of the Rent Act 1968.
On appeal by the landlords,

Held: the appeal must be allowed and the case sent back to the committee,   F
because the rent of £348 was first arrived at as a basis for a fair rent as at
1962, being ten per cent. of the capital cost in 1962, and, therefore, there
was no room for deducting anything for scarcity value (see p. 1129, letter H,
and p. 1130, letter B, post).

Appeal allowed.

[As to determination of a fair rent under the Rent Acts, see SUPPLEMENT to   G
23 HALSBURY'S LAWS (3rd Edn.), para. 1571B, 2.

For the Rent Act 1968, s. 46, see 48 HALSBURY'S STATUTES (2nd Edn.) 422.]

Appeal.

This was an appeal by the landlords, Anglo-Italian Properties, Ltd., from a
decision of the Rent Assessment Committee of the London Rent Assessment   H
Panel given on 22nd October 1968 determining the fair rent at 29A, Cale Street,
London, S.W.3, in the sum of £400. The facts are set out in the judgment of
LORD PARKER, C.J.

V. G. Wellings for the appellants.
The tenant and the respondent, the London Rent Assessment Panel, did not
appear and were not represented.   I
H. W. B. Page as amicus curiae.

LORD PARKER, C.J.: This is an appeal, which has to be on a point of
law, from a decision of the Rent Assessment Committee of the London Rent

---

* Section 46 (1), so far as material, provides: " In determining for the purposes of
this Part of this Act what rent is or would be a fair rent under a regulated tenancy of a
dwelling-house, regard shall be had . . . to all the circumstances . . . and in particular to
the age, character and locality of the dwelling-house, and to its state of repair."

A Assessment Panel, given on 22nd October 1968, determining the fair rent of the basement flat situate at 29A, Cale Street, London, S.W.3, in the sum of £400 per annum exclusive. This basement flat is in an old-fashioned house in a terrace which was acquired by the appellants in 1962 and converted into four flats, of which this one is the basement flat, which has the added attraction of a garden. The appellants let it to a Miss Cassidy, who then applied to the rent

B officer to determine and register the fair rent. The rent she was being charged was £600 per annum exclusive. The rent officer went into the matter, and in due course determined a fair rent of £335; whereupon the appellants appealed to the Rent Assessment Committee.

The committee's reasons for determining the fair rent at £400 are contained succinctly in one paragraph of their decision and reasons, that is, para. 11:

C "... We accepted Mr. Tuckerman's Valuation [he was for the appellants] of the purchase price in 1962 plus the cost of conversion (viz., £13,863); we considered that a fair yield would be 10 per cent. of this capital and that a fair apportionment of this capital cost to the subject flat would be one-quarter. Thus we reached the figure of, say, £348 p.a. as a basis for assessment of a fair rent for that flat. We did not dissent from the [appellants']

D estimate of the average annual cost of repairs (viz. £250) and apportioning this to the subject flat in the same proportion as for the capital we arrived at a total of £410. But at the time of the purchase and conversion of the property a developer would have obtained higher rents than those obtainable since the coming into effect of the [Rent Act 1965], which excluded ' scarcity value ' from the assessment of fair rents. We put the ' scarcity value ' of

E the subject property at about 10 per cent. We therefore considered that a fair rent for the flat under reference would be £369 subject to some addition in respect of the tenant having the use and benefit of the [appellants'] furniture and effects. We did not agree the [appellants'] valuation of these items; we thought that a fair annual charge for them would be £31. Accordingly, we concluded that a fair rent within the meaning and for the

F purposes of Section 46 of the [Rent Act 1968] would be £400 per annum ..."

that is adding the £31 to the figure of £369.

The point which is taken by counsel for the appellants is a very short one. The appellants do not quarrel with the calculation that the committee have

G done to arrive at £410 per annum. What he does say is that, on this method of calculation, there really is no room for any deduction in respect of scarcity value; accordingly, he says that the true rent on this method of calculation would be the £410 plus the £31 for the use of the appellants' effects, in other words £441. I confess that, for my part, I can see no answer to counsel for the appellants' contention. As I understand the calculation, a rent of £348 is

H first arrived at as a fair rent as at 1962, being ten per cent. of the capital cost in 1962. That being so, I cannot see that there is any room for deducting anything for scarcity. Of course, the committee might have said: true that capital cost in 1962 represents, let us say, £18,000—because there is evidence of that—in 1968, and then it would be right to deduct something for scarcity value, as compared with the position in 1962. Looking at it in this way, I can

I see no room for any deduction for scarcity value.

Having said that, however, I would for myself, and I do not claim to be an expert, voice the view that this is a quite novel method of valuation which the appellants put forward and the committee adopted. It is certainly one that I have never seen before. It is not arrived at on comparables, it is not based on square footage, it is certainly not based on the contractors' theory. But it is based on original cost, taking a percentage thereof as the fair rent. It may be, because there is no fixed yardstick by which a fair rent is to be arrived at, that this is a permissible method and that a just conclusion can thereby be arrived at.

I only mention this because in my experience this method is a novel one. Bearing   **A**
all those matters in mind, I think that the proper course here is to allow this
appeal and send the case back to the committee with the opinion of this court.
That would enable them to adhere if they desire to this method of calculation,
but not eliminate scarcity value, or to take into consideration any other method
of calculation they desire.

  B

    MELFORD STEVENSON, J.: I agree.

    WILLIS, J.: I agree.

                              Appeal allowed.   *Case remitted.*

    Solicitors: *Leonard Kasler & Co.* (for the appellants); *Solicitor, Ministry of*   **C**
Housing and Local Government.

                       [*Reported by* N. P. METCALFE, ESQ., *Barrister-at-Law.*]

  D

  E

PRACTICE DIRECTION.

CENTRAL OFFICE.

  F

Practice—Parties—Description of parties—Doubt as to sex or description—
    Appropriate description in title of writ and memorandum of appearance—
    Masters' Practice Direction 13 (1).
Practice—Parties—Description of parties—Corporate body—Masters' Practice
    Direction 13 (1).
Practice—Parties—Description of parties—Unincorporated body—Masters' Prac-
    tice Direction 13 (1).   **G**

    Direction no. 13 (1) relating to the description of female parties shall be revoked
and the following direction shall be substituted:

(1) *Description of parties*
    In any case where doubt might otherwise arise as to the sex or, when relevant,   **H**
the description of a party, the appropriate description shall be added in the
title of the writ and in the memorandum of appearance, provided that it is
known or can readily be ascertained. If the true legal description of a corporate
or other body is not apparent from its name, the description shall be stated
(e.g., " a company limited by guarantee ", or as the case may be).

                                                    B. A. HARWOOD,   **I**
27th June 1969.   Senior Master.

A

NOTE.

R. *v.* BIRTLES.

B
[Court of Appeal, criminal division (Lord Parker, C.J., Megaw, L.J., and Nield, J.), May 19, 1969.]

Criminal Law—Informer—Use of informer by police—Informer inciting others to commit offence—Informer participating in commission of offence.
Criminal Law—Informer—Disclosure to court of existence of informer.
Police—Execution of duty—Mitigating consequences of proposed offence—Participation in commission of offence.

C
[Editorial Note. The principles which should be followed when the police make use of informers has been the subject recently of a circular from the Home Secretary to chief officers of police: see 119 New Law Journal 513.]

Case referred to:
R. v. *Macro* (1969), The Times, 11th February.

D
Appeal.
On 7th March 1968 at the West Riding Quarter Sessions the appellant, Frank Alexander Birtles, and another both pleaded guilty to burglary and carrying an imitation firearm, contrary to s. 1 of the Firearms Act 1965. The appellant received sentences of three years' and two years' imprisonment consecutive. On appeal the court reduced the sentence by making them run concurrently
E
on the ground that there was a real possibility that the appellant had been encouraged by an informer and a police officer to commit the offences. The case is reported for the reference made by the court to the use of informers by the police.

D. M. Savill, Q.C., and *M. C. M. Hargan* for the appellant.
R. Lyons, Q.C., and *Barbara Wootliff* for the Crown.
F

LORD PARKER, C.J., after giving the court's decision on the appeal, continued: Before leaving this case, the court would like to say a word about the use which, as the cases coming before the court reveal, is being made of informers. The court of course recognises that, disagreeable as it may seem to some people, the police must be able in certain cases to make use of informers,
G
and further—and this is really a corollary—that within certain limits such informers should be protected. At the same time, unless the use made of informers is kept within strict limits, grave injustice may result. In the first place, it is important that the court of trial should not be misled. A good example of that occurred in *R.* v. *Macro* (1), again a raid on a sub-post office, which came before this court on 10th February 1969. There the charge was one of robbery with
H
aggravation, with a man unknown. In fact, the man unknown was an informer who together with the police had warned the victim of what was going to take place, and had gone through the pretence of tying-up the victim while the police were concealed on the premises. The effect was that the appellant in that case pleaded guilty to an offence which had never been committed. If the facts had been known, there could not have been a robbery at all, and accord-
I
ingly it was for that reason that the court substituted the only verdict apt on the facts which was open to it, namely a verdict of larceny. There is of course no harm in not revealing the fact that there is an informer, but it is quite another thing to conceal facts which go to the quality of the offence. Secondly, it is vitally important to ensure so far as possible that the informer does not create an offence, that is to say, incite others to commit an offence which those others would not otherwise have committed. It is one thing for the police to make use

(1) (1969), The Times, 11th February.

A

of information concerning an offence that is already laid on. In such a case the police are clearly entitled, indeed it is their duty, to mitigate the consequences of the proposed offence, for example, to protect the proposed victim, and to that end it may be perfectly proper for them to encourage the informer to take part in the offence or indeed for a police officer himself to do so. But it is quite another thing, and something of which this court thoroughly disapproves, to use an informer to encourage another to commit an offence or indeed an offence of a more serious character, which he would not otherwise commit, still more so if the police themselves take part in carrying it out. In the result, this appeal is allowed and the sentence reduced to one of three years.

B

Appeal allowed.

Solicitors: *Registrar of Criminal Appeals* (for the appellant); *Director of Public Prosecutions* (for the Crown).

C

[*Reported by* N. P. METCALFE, ESQ., *Barrister-at-Law.*]

D

E

PRACTICE DIRECTION.

CHANCERY DIVISION.

F

Practice—Chancery Division—Procedure summons—Hearing—Date.
Practice—Chancery Division—Witness action—Originating summons—Hearing not estimated to last significantly more than two days—Witness list—Part II.
Practice—Chancery Division—Witness action—Originating summons—Adjourned into court—Non-witness list.

G

In future procedure summonses in the Chancery Division will not be listed for hearing on motion days. It is not intended to specify any particular day on which they are to be heard but they will be listed for a day shortly after setting down, as the appropriate judge may direct.

All originating summonses for hearing in the witness list are to be placed in Part 2 of that list unless they are estimated to last significantly more than two days. When an originating summons is adjourned into court with witnesses but the master is satisfied that the cross-examination will not substantially extend the length of the hearing and will not lead to applications to call further witnesses he may adjourn it into the non-witness list.

H

By the direction of CROSS, J.

R. E. BALL,
Chief Master.

18th April 1969.

I

A

R. *v.* BLAKEWAY.

[COURT OF APPEAL, CRIMINAL DIVISION (Megaw, L.J., Melford Stevenson and
James, JJ.), June 3, 1969.]

B
*Criminal Law—Sentence—Suspended sentence—Time for deciding when
suspended sentence should be concurrent with or consecutive to an earlier
suspended sentence is the time when the sentences are implemented—Criminal
Justice Act* 1967 *(c.* 80), *s.* 40.

A suspended sentence cannot be made consecutive to an earlier suspended
sentence which is not then being put into force because the time for deciding
whether a suspended sentence should be concurrent with or consecutive

C
to an earlier suspended sentence is the time when the sentences are before
the court for implementation under s. 40 of the Criminal Justice Act 1967
(see p. 1134, letter H, *post*).

Application dismissed.

[As to suspended sentences, see SUPPLEMENT to 10 HALSBURY'S LAWS (3rd
Edn.) para. 922A, 1, 2.

D
For the Criminal Justice Act 1967, s. 40, see 8 HALSBURY'S STATUTES (3rd Edn.)
606.]

Case referred to:

R. v. Ithell, p. 449 ante; [1969] 1 W.L.R. 272.

Application for leave to appeal against sentence.

E
On 20th November 1968, at Warley Quarter Sessions, before the Recorder
(FRANCIS BARNES, ESQ.) the applicant, Thomas Joseph Blakeway, pleaded
guilty to storebreaking with intent (count 1) and receiving (count 3) and was
sentenced to six and three months' imprisonment on each count respectively,
the sentences to be consecutive. In addition the court ordered to come into
effect, concurrently with each other, two terms of six months' imprisonment

F
suspended on 11th April 1968 and 1st August 1968 respectively, and made
them consecutive to the sentences of six and three months imposed for the
offences of storebreaking and receiving so that the applicant was sentenced to
15 months' imprisonment in all. He now applied for leave to appeal against
this sentence. The application was referred to the court by the single judge
only for consideration of the way in which the suspended sentences were dealt

G
with.

The applicant did not appear and was not represented.

JAMES, J., delivered the judgment of the court: The applicant, Thomas
Joseph Blakeway, was convicted at Halesowen Magistrates' Court on 11th April
1968 of stealing scrap copper wire, for which offence he was fined and sentenced

H
to six months' imprisonment suspended for three years. On 1st August 1968
at Warley Quarter Sessions for an offence of factorybreaking and stealing,
committed during the operational period of the suspended sentence already
mentioned, he was sentenced to six months' imprisonment suspended for 12
months. On that occasion the court made no order in respect of the suspended
sentence passed on 11th April, the court exercising its power under s. 40 (1) (*d*)

I
of the Criminal Justice Act 1967.

Prior to his appearance at Warley Quarter Sessions on 1st August, but during
the operational period of the sentence passed on 11th April, namely, on 23rd July
1968, the applicant broke into a warehouse in Warley by way of the skylight
with intent to steal. He stole nothing, but he left behind certain articles of
his own, which enabled him to be identified with the offence, namely, a key and
a snuff box.

On 14th August 1968—that is during the operational period of both suspended
sentences—the applicant and another person were arrested. The other man

was in possession of a clock and a kettle, which he had stolen on the previous **A** day. The applicant was acting as adviser and participator in the disposal of those articles, which he knew were stolen goods, at the request of the thief. His conduct amounted to receiving stolen goods by virtue of the provisions of s. 4 (7) of the Criminal Law Act 1967. On 20th November 1968 at Warley Quarter Sessions the applicant pleaded guilty to the offence of warehousebreaking with intent on 23rd July and to receiving stolen goods on 14th August. He further **B** admitted and asked to have taken into consideration two offences of breaking into premises and stealing and one offence of breaking and entering with intent to steal, both committed on 2nd February 1968.

He was sentenced to six months' and three months' imprisonment consecutive on the counts to which he pleaded guilty, and the recorder further said:

> ". . . insofar as the previous suspended sentences are concerned, in the **C** absence of the Indictment and contrary to my own recollection I am going to deem them as concurrent sentences, in other words, I am either going to deem or going to order as the case may be, that the suspended sentences you received here and the suspended sentence that you received at Halesowen, shall be regarded as concurrent . . . I am going to deem those or order them to be concurrent so that there will be a further six months to **D** serve . . . That makes 15 months in all."

The applicant now seeks the leave of this court to appeal against his sentence. He has abandoned his application for leave to appeal against conviction after refusal of leave by the single judge. The matter of sentence was referred to the full court by the single judge as it appears at first sight that there may be some **E** abnormal features in regard to the method by which the suspended sentences were dealt with in this particular case. The applicant's contention is that on the occasion of 1st August at Warley Quarter Sessions the recorder told him that the first suspended sentence that he had received at the magistrates' court [at Halesowen] was invalid, and it was because of that ruling that the recorder took no action in respect of that sentence and passed a second new suspended **F** sentence. It is quite certain that the applicant is mistaken in that belief. The recorder expressed his own recollection of the occasion to be that he was making the sentence he then passed suspended to be consecutive; and when he was specifically asked by counsel if, in making the period consecutive, he was referring to the operational period or the sentence he replied: " No, to six months being consecutive ". So clearly there was no declaration that the first suspended **G** sentence was invalid; indeed, the recorder would not have had any jurisdiction so to declare.

The recorder's recollection of making the second suspended sentence consecutive, if accurate, would in the view of this court amount to a falling into error in that respect, because one cannot have a suspended sentence made consecutive to a suspended sentence which is not then being put into force. The time for **H** deciding whether a suspended sentence should be concurrent or consecutive is the time when the matter is before the court to be dealt with under s. 40 of the Criminal Justice Act 1967 by way of implementation, not at the time when the suspended sentence is first passed. When one looks at this matter in detail, it is quite clear that the learned recorder, in making the implementation of the suspended sentences concurrent did so in the interests and to the advantage of the applicant. It was possible for him to have made them consecutive when he **I** implemented them. In fairness to the applicant, there being some doubt as to what was said on previous occasions, he made them concurrent. There is no error in principle, therefore, in the way in which the suspended sentences were dealt with.

There is only one other matter that need be mentioned in case there is any doubt left in the applicant's mind in this case, and that is the approach that the recorder made, when passing sentence, to the assessment of the sentence for the

A principal offences with which he was dealing and to the implementation of the suspended sentences. In passing sentence the recorder (as appears quite clearly from the transcript) first of all assessed the sentence for the offences on the indictment. Having done that, he then applied his mind to the question of the suspended sentences. That method of approach is in accord, in fact, with the decision of this court in *R. v. Ithell* (1) decided on 17th January 1969, subsequent

B to the hearing of this case before the recorder. The endorsement on the indictment in this case, however, erroneously records the sentences the wrong way round. It falsely shows that the recorder first dealt with the suspended sentences and then passed consecutive sentences on the substantive offences. The transcript shows that to be an error, and the recorder in fact dealt with the matter perfectly properly and in accordance with the decision of this court.

C   There is nothing wrong in principle here, the sentences were not excessive in any way, and the application is refused.

Application dismissed.

[*Reported by* WENDY SHOCKETT, *Barrister-at-Law.*]

D

Re G. (an infant).

[CHANCERY DIVISION (Buckley, J.), March 28, April 1, 1969.]

E *Ward of Court—Jurisdiction—Forum conveniens—Interim care and control—Divorce proceedings commenced in Scotland—Interim order in Scotland awarding custody—Wardship proceedings commenced in England—Whether investigation should take place in England or Scotland.*

The parties were married in 1964 and separated after the birth of the infant in 1966, the infant remaining with the mother. In 1968 the father com-

F menced divorce proceedings in Scotland, where he was resident and domiciled and he also claimed custody of the infant. On his application, which was not opposed by the mother, the Court of Session made an order in November 1968 giving him interim custody of the infant. In January 1969 the same judge made a further order whereby he granted a warrant to the officers at law of the court in Scotland to take the infant into their custody,

G and recommended all magistrates in England and elsewhere to give assistance in executing the warrant. On 21st March the father made an application ex parte to the High Court to CROSS, J., by originating summons under the Law Reform (Miscellaneous Provisions) Act 1949, and obtained an order that the infant be handed over to the father and be put in the care of his paternal grandmother until further order. The matter came before

H the court on 1st April, the mother opposing the father's application for an order for care and control and that he or the paternal grandmother be allowed to take the infant to Scotland. Both parties asked the court to make such arrangements regarding care and control as would govern the position until a detailed investigation of the position on its merits could be made. On the question whether this investigation should be made in the Scottish court or

I the English court,

Held: the father's application would be granted because as between two courts of co-ordinate jurisdiction, one in England and the other in Scotland, prima facie the right course was for the mother to be investigated in the court in which the substantive divorce proceedings lay and in which the original order giving custody to the father had been made, i.e., the Scottish court (see p. 1138, letter E, post), and because the evidence did

---

(1) P. 449 ante; [1969] 1 W.L.R. 272.

not establish that this course would involve any serious emotional or physical   **A**
disadvantages for this infant (see p. 1139, letter F, post).

[As to custody disputes affected by conflict of laws, see 7 HALSBURY'S LAWS
(3rd Edn.) 126, 127, para. 227; and for cases on the subject, see 11 DIGEST
(Repl.) 499, *1185*.]

Cases referred to: **B**
    B.'s Settlement, Re, B. v. *B.*, [1940] Ch. 54; 109 L.J.Ch. 20; 28 Digest (Repl.)
        657, *1518*.
    McKee v. *McKee*, [1951] 1 All E.R. 942; [1951] A.C. 352; 28 Digest (Repl.)
        614, *1218*.

Motion.

This was a motion by the plaintiff, the infant's father, on proceedings instituted   **C**
on 21st March 1969 by originating summons under the Law Reform (Miscellaneous Provisions) Act 1949 for an order that the infant remain in the care of
the paternal grandmother until further order. The nature of the order sought
is set out in the headnote. The motion was heard in camera but the judgment
was delivered in open court. The facts are set out in the judgment.

  D

    Jeremiah Harman, Q.C.. and *Ian McCulloch* for the father.
    S. Seuffert, Q.C., and *L. G. Krikler* for the mother.

    BUCKLEY, J.: In these proceedings, the plaintiff who is the infant's
father seeks an interim direction with regard to the care and control of the
ward until such time as the question of care and control, access and so forth can   **E**
be investigated in detail in a substantive hearing of the matter on its merits.
The defendant in the proceedings is the infant's mother.

    The father and the mother were married in July 1964, and the infant, who is a
boy, was born on 14th January 1966, and so is now $3\frac{1}{4}$ years old. The marriage
seems to have come to grief at an early stage, for since the mother came out of
hospital following the birth of the infant she has never lived with the father.
When she came out of hospital she returned to her parents. That had been   **F**
agreed between the couple. It was originally accepted that it would be only a
temporary arrangement. The father obtained a flat at Teddington in a position
convenient for his then employment but the mother declined to go and join
him there and, as I have said, they have never since lived together.

    In May 1966, a summons taken out by the mother alleging cruelty against   **G**
the father came before the magistrates. Her charges of cruelty were dismissed
but an order giving her the custody of the infant was made by the magistrates
and the father was ordered to pay £2 a week maintenance. I am told that
although the issues of cruelty were contested and on these issues the father was
successful, the issue of custody was not contested. This is not surprising having
regard to the very tender age of the child. In June 1966, the father obtained   **H**
and started in employment in Scotland. He has since resided in Scotland which
is the country of his origin. His domicil of origin is Scottish and that is his
domicil today. Scotland is consequently the matrimonial domicil of the parties.
In May 1967, the father learned through his mother-in-law that the mother was
proposing to take the infant to Spain. He also learned for the first time that the
mother was at that time committing adultery with another man. He instituted   **I**
proceedings of an emergency nature to prevent the mother taking the infant to
Spain. He obtained an ex parte injunction to restrain removal of the infant
out of the jurisdiction on 18th May 1967 and that injunction was served on the
mother at the airport—I think that very day—with the result that her journey
was postponed. The matter came before the court again on 14th June when
PENNYCUICK, J., continued the injunction. The mother was present in court
at the time but later that day she in fact left for Spain with the infant in breach
of the order of the court.

A   The father's domicil being in Scotland and his residence being in Scotland, the mother then being in Spain with the infant, the father considered there was no further point in keeping the existing proceedings in which he had obtained the injunction afoot and the originating summons in those proceedings was, by his consent, dismissed in October 1967.

The mother apparently remained in Spain until about November 1968, when
B   she returned to England. She did not disclose the fact to the father who did not discover that she was in England until some time at the beginning of March 1969. Meantime, he had instituted divorce proceedings in Scotland and in those proceedings he claimed custody of the child. Those proceedings were served on the mother but, she says, she did not appreciate or pay much attention to the fact that there was a claim for custody included in the relief claimed in the
C   proceedings.

However, on 12th November 1968, Lord Thomson in the Court of Session at Edinburgh made an order on the unopposed motion of the father that he was entitled to the interim custody of the infant and on 21st January 1969, the same learned judge in Scotland made a further order whereby he granted a warrant to the messengers-at-arms and other officers at law of the court in Scotland to
D   take the person of the infant into their custody and authorised all procurators-fiscal in Scotland to aid such messengers and officers in the execution of the warrant and recommended all magistrates in England and elsewhere to give aid and assistance in carrying this warrant into effect.

By the present motion, in new proceedings instituted on 21st March 1969 by originating summons under the Law Reform (Miscellaneous Provisions) Act 1949,
E   the father seeks an order that the infant remain in the care of the paternal grandmother until further order and that he or the paternal grandmother should be at liberty to remove the infant to Scotland and that the infant should be delivered to him or to the messengers of the Scottish court for the purpose of compliance with the order of the Scottish court to which I have referred, and that the mother should be restrained from removing the infant from the jurisdiction
F   of this court otherwise than for the purpose of complying with the order of the Scottish court.

It is quite clear that at some stage the question whether the infant should remain in the care and control or custody of the father or in the care and control or custody of the mother is one which has got to be investigated by some court in detail on the merits. What I am being asked on this occasion by both sides—
G   because the mother seeks to retain the right to have the child with her—is to make such arrangements as shall govern the position until a detailed investigation of the position on the merits can be made.

In these proceedings the father applied ex parte to Cross, J., on 21st March 1969—that is the date when the originating summons was issued—and on that date Cross, J., made an order on the mother to hand over the infant to the
H   father and that the infant be put in the care of the paternal grandmother, that is to say, the father's mother and a nanny. He also ordered that any passport on which the infant's name might be should be handed over. In pursuance of that order the infant was very shortly afterwards handed over by the mother to the father and since then has been in the care of the father, the paternal grandmother and a nanny.

I   Now I have to ask myself two questions. First, what in these circumstances are the right arrangements to make for the care and control of the infant pending the investigation of the merits of the matter by some competent court; and, secondly, so far as this has a bearing on the first question, whether in the circumstances of this case the appropriate court to make that investigation is the Scottish court or this court; that is to say, whether the investigation of the case on its merits should be made in the Scottish divorce proceedings or in these wardship proceedings in this country.

If the divorce proceedings had been instituted in this country, which of course they could not because, the father being domiciled in Scotland, the proper juris- **A** diction is in Scotland, there is no doubt that this court would leave all those matters to be considered and determined in the divorce proceedings in the Divorce Division of the High Court.   This court would not entertain the wardship proceedings.   The Scottish order is of course an order made in an alien juris- diction.   It is not in any sense binding on me.   It was made clear in *McKee* v. *McKee* (1) and *Re B.'s Settlement, B.* v. *B.* (2) that such an order is not binding on **B** this court.   It is one of the circumstances to be taken into consideration in deciding what is right to do about the ward.   As in all cases of this kind the paramount consideration is the welfare of the infant concerned.

It seems to me—forgetting for the moment the paramount consideration— and looking at the matter from the point of view of the convenient forum where the merits of the case should be investigated, that everything is in favour of **C** their being investigated in Scotland where an order has already been made. True, it was an unopposed order, but an order has been made; not a consent order but an order which was the result of judicial consideration of such evidence as was available before the court in proceedings in which eventually the character and behaviour of both parties in the course of their matrimonial difficulties will be bound to be examined by the court and where the proper provision **D** to be made for the future of the infant can be best assessed in the light of all circumstances then known to that court.

Of course, those same facts could be ventilated also in proceedings in this country, in fact, in these proceedings in which this motion is brought, but, as I have said, if there had been a similar contest of jurisdiction between the Divorce Division and the Chancery Division here, the divorce proceedings having been **E** first in the field and the divorce court being seised of the matter, there would be no question but that this court would leave the matter in the hands of the Divorce Division.   Similarly, I think, as between two courts of co-ordinate jurisdiction, one in this country and the other in Scotland, prima facie the right course is for the matter to be investigated in the Scottish court which had seisin of the matter before these proceedings began and which has made the order I have mentioned. **F** But I am pressed, and very properly pressed, by counsel for the mother, with the argument that the infant is of a very young age whose place prima facie should be with the mother and that to allow him to remain in the care of the father until such time as the merits of the case can be investigated will be to do the infant grave harm.

It is said that for the past 18 months or two years the infant has been living **G** in what counsel for the mother describes as an integrated home with the mother. What counsel means by " integrated home " is that it is a home where the infant is with the mother and with somebody whom the infant believes is his father, who is not his father at all but the man with whom the mother is living.   It is true that at this present stage I do not think that state of affairs exposes the infant to moral danger but I do think it is a matter to be taken into consideration **H** that the infant is emotionally involved with somebody who is not his father on the footing that the infant thinks that he is his father.   That is a matter which may be much more important when the final determination takes place than it is of importance in considering only the short-term as I am at the moment.

The history of the family and the infant is that in the summer of 1966, when the infant was six months old, the mother, having lived down to that time with **I** her parents and the infant being with her, went off—not unreasonably I am sure —for a holiday for a fortnight in Spain, leaving the infant with the maternal grandmother.   The mother, in fact, went off with the gentleman with whom she is now living.   When she returned or soon after she returned she left her mother's household and set up house with this man.   She left the infant with the mat- ernal grandmother from August 1966, until some date in April 1967.   That the

(1) [1951] 1 All E.R. 942; [1951] A.C. 352.
(2) [1940] Ch. 54.

A mother says she did because of emotional pressure brought to bear on her by the maternal grandmother. That is a matter I cannot go into on this application because I have insufficient information. But the fact is that from August 1966 until April 1967, the infant was not living with the mother. The mother says that she paid him frequent visits and that he used to go to her for weekends but that appears to be in issue. Since April 1967 the infant has been living with the mother

B in the household where she is living with the man to whom she is not married. As I have said, since CROSS J.'s order of 21st March, ten days ago, the infant has been with the father and the paternal grandmother.

Now I do not at all dissent from the view that prima facie one would think that a child of this tender age should be with his mother but many of the arguments presented to me on this motion are I think arguments much more appro-

C priate to the substantive hearing of the case on its merits than to the question I have to deal with—which is, what is to happen until the substantive hearing. The father is anxious to take the infant to Scotland where the physical conditions appear to be perfectly satisfactory and where the infant will be looked after by the paternal grandmother and the nanny in question and where the father is employed in estate management in circumstances which would enable him to

D see a lot of the infant.

The evidence as to the infant's state of mind since he has been handed over is acutely contradictory. One side says he is perfectly happy and the other side that he is miserable and has developed a stammer and is upset. I have not got sufficient information to be able to form any concluded view about that but it seems to me that if there is really a serious matter of that kind to be raised it

E can just as well be raised in the Scottish court as it can be in this court. There is nothing to prevent the mother making an application in the Scottish court for a variation of the order the Scottish court made giving custody of the infant to the father. That can be made at any stage in the proceedings in Scotland before the divorce proceedings come on for trial.

I am not satisfied on this evidence that the infant is going to suffer any serious

F emotional or physical disadvantages by being left in the care of the father as he now is. I think that for the infant to be shuttled backwards and forwards from one parent to the other during a dispute of this kind is in itself something which is not in the interests of the infant. Of course, it is a consideration which has to be weighed against all other considerations but weighing the facts as I have them, to the best of my ability, I think that the infant should go with the father to

G Scotland and that the mother if she wishes to try to recover the custody of the infant should make her application to the Scottish court. The order made in Scotland was not made by consent, let me emphasise, but was unopposed by the mother. It may well be that she can lay before the Scottish court considerations of which the court was unaware at the time it made the order. But if it was unaware of the facts it was because the mother did not see fit to take steps to

H oppose the application. In the circumstances, having reached the conclusion that the evidence does not show that the infant would be harmed in any way by the course I am proposing to take, I think it right that I should accede to the relief asked for on the motion and say that the infant should remain in the care of the paternal grandmother until further order and that she and the father should have leave to remove him to Scotland and to hand him over to the appropriate officers

I of the court which is no doubt merely a formality.

[After further discussion HIS LORDSHIP ordered that the infant continue a ward of court during his infancy until further order.]

Order accordingly.

Solicitors: *Parker, Fogg & Pinsent* (for the father); *Bell & Sherrard*, Kingston-upon-Thames (for the mother).

[*Reported by* ROSALIE LONG, *Barrister-at-Law.*]

A

PRACTICE DIRECTION.

CENTRAL OFFICE.

Practice—Consent order—Summons issued and indorsed with consent—Procedure **B**
   for obtaining order—Postal facilities.
Legal Aid—Certificate—Filing—Time for—Extension of time—Application for
   —Procedure for obtaining extension—Postal facilities.
Practice—Summons—Restoration to list—Restoration without leave—Procedure.

Preparations are being made for the conduct of more business by post in the **C**
Central Office next year as may be possible. In the meantime the following
arrangements have been made for the convenience of litigants.

Consent Orders

Except in cases where the approval of the court is required, summonses duly
issued and indorsed with the consent of all other parties may be left with or sent by
post to the masters' secretary, room 120, Royal Courts of Justice, London, W.C.2. **D**
They will be placed before a master with a view to an order and may be collected
on the next working day. Such documents will not be acknowledged or indexed
and no responsibility for their safe custody will be accepted. If any question
arises as to the proper form of order the applicant will be required to see a master.

Extension of Time for Filing Legal Aid Certificates. **E**

The certificate may be lodged with the masters' secretary in the same manner.
It must be indorsed with a statement stating: (i) the reason why the certificate
was not filed at the proper time; and (ii) whether any steps have been taken by
any other party in ignorance of it. If an extension of time of more than three
months is sought the statement must be signed personally by the solicitor named
in the certificate. **F**

Restoration of Summonses.

(i) A summons which has not been attended by the party issuing it and on
which no adjudication has been made may be restored to the list by either party
once only without leave. On any subsequent occasion leave must be obtained.
Any party in default must be prepared to explain to the master why the summons
was not attended. **G**

(ii) If a summons has been adjourned to a fixed day or the first open day
thereafter and the party having the carriage thereof has not had it listed accordingly, either party may restore it to the list without leave, notwithstanding that
the period of adjournment granted has expired, unless the master has marked
the adjournment as final.

B. A. HARWOOD, **H**
27th June 1969.   Senior Master.

A

GARRETT *v.* ARTHUR CHURCHILL (GLASS), LTD. AND ANOTHER.

[QUEEN'S BENCH DIVISION (Lord Parker, C.J., Melford Stevenson and Willis, JJ.), April 22, 1969.]

B

Customs—Export—Prohibition—Knowingly concerned in the exportation of goods with intent to evade . . . prohibition—Whether offence involves a single question—Customs and Excise Act 1952 (15 & 16 *Geo.* 6 & 1 *Eliz.* 2 c. 44), *s.* 56 (2).

Burden of proof—Customs offence—Knowingly concerned in the exportation of goods with intent to evade . . . prohibition—Whether burden shifts to pro-
C
secution—Customs and Excise Act 1952 (15 & 16 *Geo.* 6 & 1 *Eliz.* 2 c. 44), *s.* 290 (2).

The respondent, a director of the respondent company, purchased a Ver-zelini goblet for S., an American, who was at all relevant times in America. S. instructed the respondent company to export the goblet to him in America. The goblet was an article the exportation of which without a licence was
D
prohibited by the Export of Goods (Control) Order 1965*. The respondent knew this and attempted to get a licence. S. who had been informed by the respondent of the requirement of a licence, instructed him to hand the goblet without a licence to one, X. who was to carry it to America by air. The justices found that, the night before X.'s aircraft left for America, the respon-dent handed the goblet to X. knowing that he was going to attempt to export
E
it without a licence; but they acquitted both respondents of the offence of being knowingly concerned in the exportation of the goblet with intent to evade the prohibition on exportation, contrary to s. 56 (2)† of the Customs and Excise Act 1952. On appeal,

Held: the appeal would be allowed and the case remitted because the question whether the respondents were knowingly concerned in the exporta-
F
tion of goods with intent to evade the prohibition, should be treated as one question, and this the justices failed to do (see p. 1145, letters F and G, and p. 1146, letter A, post).

Per CURIAM: notwithstanding s. 290 (2)‡ of the Act, the burden of proving the requisite knowledge and intent in the offence remained on the prosecu-tion (see p. 1145, letter I, to p. 1146, letter A, post).
G
Appeal allowed.

[As to offences in relation to export of prohibited or restricted goods, see 33 HALSBURY'S LAWS (3rd Edn.) 170, 171, para. 277.

For the Customs and Excise Act 1952, s. 56, s. 290, see 9 HALSBURY'S STATUTES (3rd Edn.) 101, 192.]

H   **Case Stated.**

This was a Case Stated by justices for the Middlesex Area of Greater London acting in and for the petty sessional division of Uxbridge in respect of their adjudication as a magistrates' court sitting at Uxbridge on 15th July 1968.

The Case stated that on 19th March 1968 an information was laid by the appellant, Colin John Garrett, charging that on 1st June 1966 at London (Heath-
I
row) Airport in the area aforesaid the respondents, Arthur Churchill (Glass),

---

* S.I. 1965 No. 1324. The order has now been revoked by the Export of Goods (Control) Order 1967 (S.I. 1967 No. 675).

† Section 56 (2), as far as material, is set out at p. 1143, letter I, post.

‡ Section 290 (2), so far as material, provides: " Where in any proceedings relating to customs or excise any question arises . . . as to whether or not. . . . (*f*) any goods are or were subject to any prohibition of or restriction on their . . . exportation, then, where those proceedings are brought by . . . the Commissioners . . . the burden of proof shall lie upon the other party to the proceedings."

Ltd., and Sidney Charles Crompton, were each knowingly concerned in the export- **A**
ation of a Verzelini glass goblet with intent to evade the prohibition on exportation imposed by the Export of Goods (Control) Order 1965, contrary to s. 56 (2)
of the Customs and Excise Act 1952.

The following facts were proved or admitted: at all material times the
respondent Crompton was a director of and acted on behalf of the respondent
company. On 16th May 1966 a Verzelini goblet, known as the Winifred Geare **B**
goblet, was auctioned at Sotheby's. It was sold to the respondent Crompton, who
was acting on behalf of Mr. Franz Sichel, an American, for £9,500. On 16th May
1966, the day of the sale, the respondent Crompton cabled the result of it to
Mr. Sichel. On that day Mr. Sichel wrote to the respondent Crompton inviting
suggestions about transportation. The respondent Crompton replied on 20th
May that he was awaiting Mr. Sichel's views in case there was some probability **C**
of personal conveyance and that he had in mind Mr. Jerome Strauss, an American,
who was a collector of glass and a personal friend of Mr. Sichel. The respondent
Crompton said that the alternative was using a reliable agent and suggested suit-
able firms. The respondent Crompton stated, " It will be necessary to obtain an
export licence and U.S.A. consular certificate for an item of this value and this
administrative aspect will be put in hand immediately." On 25th May 1966, **D**
Mr. Sichel wrote to the respondent Crompton that he had arranged for Mr.
Strauss to take the goblet on his flight via Pan Am. to New York on 1st June.
On Friday 27th May 1966, Mr. Sichel telephoned the respondent Crompton.
Mr. Sichel said that Mr. Strauss had agreed to transport the goblet on his return
to America early the following week and that accordingly it might be preferable
for documents to be in Mr. Strauss' name. The respondent Crompton told Mr. **E**
Sichel that with Whitsun weekend intervening it would not be possible to obtain
documentation by 31st May or 1st June and that if it was intended to remove
the goblet permanently from the United Kingdom it was highly probable that
an export licence would be required even though a personal conveyance had
been decided on. Mr Sichel said that until he had seen the goblet he could not
decide his future intentions, that the respondent Crompton's part as buying **F**
agent was completed and that the respondent Crompton was to hand the goblet
to Mr. Strauss without any documents for which action he would take full
responsibility. On 31st May 1966, the respondent Crompton handed the goblet
to Mr. Strauss, informing him that no documents were provided in accordance
with Mr. Sichel's instructions. Shortly thereafter the goblet was taken to America.
The exportation of the goblet without an export licence was prohibited. **G**

It was contended before the justices by the appellant that as the respondents
purchased the goblet for an American, and handed it to another American for
export to America they were concerned in the exportation, that as they knew an
export licence was required but had not been issued an intent to evade the
prohibition on the exportation of the goblet was manifest. It was contended
on behalf of the respondents that as a prohibition was in force in relation to the **H**
goblet, in accordance with the proviso to s. 79 (3) of the Customs and Excise
Act 1952 the time of its exportation was deemed to be when the aircraft in which
Mr. Strauss travelled to New York departed from Heathrow Airport. Prior to this
time the respondent Crompton had handed the goblet to Mr. Strauss in accordance with instructions from Mr. Sichel, the owner, and that he had no option but
to comply with that instruction as he would otherwise be liable to an action in **I**
detinue. To be concerned in the exportation of the goblet would involve a material
connection with the actual exportation. Accordingly, as the respondent Crompton
had lost all control over the goblet at the time of its exportation he was not
concerned in its exportation.

The justices were of the opinion that the respondent Crompton knew from
the very beginning that it was the intention to export the goblet to America and
that such exportation was prohibited without a licence from the Board of Trade.
They thought that the respondent Crompton believed that the exportation of the

A   goblet would be done regularly until 27th May when he spoke to Mr. Sichel on the telephone. During that conversation it became known to the respondent Crompton that Mr. Sichel intended the goblet to be exported by Mr. Strauss without a licence and accordingly in breach of the prohibition. Mr. Sichel, who was the owner of the goblet gave a specific instruction to the respondent Crompton to hand the goblet to Mr. Strauss. The respondent Crompton handed the goblet

B   to Mr. Strauss knowing that Mr. Strauss was going to export the goblet and evade the prohibition on its export. They considered that it was the respondent Crompton's legal duty to act in accordance with the owner's instruction, even though he knew that doing so might result in an illegal exportation. Once the goblet was handed over, the respondent Crompton lost all control over it and in their view was not concerned in its exportation which took place thereafter.

C   They accordingly dismissed the information.

The question for the opinion of the High Court was whether or not the justices' decision was legally correct. The appellant now appealed.

The cases noted below* were cited during the argument.

Gordon Slynn for the appellant.

Ashe Lincoln, Q.C., and *S. E. Brodie* for the respondents.

D

LORD PARKER, C.J.: This is an appeal by way of Case Stated from a decision of justices for the Middlesex area of Greater London, sitting at Uxbridge, who dismissed an information preferred by the appellant against the two respondents, for that each of the respondents had been knowingly concerned in the exportation of a Verzelini glass goblet with intent to evade the prohibition on

E   exportation imposed by the Export of Goods (Control) Order 1965 (1), contrary to s. 56 (2) of the Customs and Excise Act 1952.

Before considering the facts, it is, I think, convenient to look at the few passages that are relevant in the legislation. Section 56 deals with offences in relation to exportation of prohibited or restricted goods, and by sub-s. (1) it is provided:

F   " If any goods are—(*a*) exported or shipped as stores; or (*b*) brought to any place in the United Kingdom for the purpose of being exported or shipped as stores, and the exportation or shipment is or would be contrary to any prohibition ... the goods shall be liable to forfeiture and the exporter or intending exporter of the goods and any agent of his concerned in the exportation of shipment or intended exportation or shipment shall each be

G   liable to a penalty of three times the value of the goods or one hundred pounds, whichever is the greater."

I read that merely to show that there the offence does not consist of an exportation with any intent to evade customs, and accordingly the penalty laid down is the moderate one of three times the value of the goods or £100, whichever is the greater. When however one gets to sub-s. (2), which lays down the offence with

H   which the respondents are charged, there is an intent that has to be proved to evade the prohibition, and the penalty is far greater—" three times the value of the goods or one hundred pounds, whichever is the greater " that is the penalty under sub-s. (1) but also, " or to imprisonment for a term not exceeding two years, or to both ". The prior part of sub-s. (2) is to this effect:

I   " Any person knowingly concerned in the exportation ... of any goods with intent to evade any such prohibition or restriction as aforesaid shall be liable ... "

The prohibition in the present case is the prohibition contained in the Export of Goods (Control) Order 1965. Article 1 provides that:

---

* *Nutton* v. *Wilson* (1889), 22 Q.B.D. 744; *R.* v. *Cohen*, [1951] 1 All E.R. 203; [1951] 1 K.B. 505; *Perry* v. *Bickerstaff* (1954), N.I. 370; *Sweet* v. *Parsley*, [1969] 1 All E.R. 347; [1969] 2 W.L.R. 470.
(1) S.I. 1965 No. 1324.

A

" Subject to the provisions of this Order—(i) goods of a description included in Schedule 1 hereto and therein indicated by the letter A are prohibited to be exported from the United Kingdom . . ."

and in Sch. 1 under heading " Group 9 " there appears the following:

B

" *Valuables*: Articles not elsewhere specified, manufactured or produced more than 100 years before the date of exportation including works of art but not including postage stamps of philatelic interest, and similar articles . . . "

It is quite clear and admitted that the article here in question, this Verzelini goblet, consisted of Elizabethan glass of the 16th century, and clearly, was an article covered by Group 9 in Sch. 1. So much for the legislation.

C

The short facts were that the respondent Crompton, was a director of the respondent company, Arthur Churchill (Glass), Ltd., and was acting on its behalf; and acting on its behalf he on 16th May bought on behalf of an American, a Mr. Franz Sichel, this goblet when auctioned at Sotheby's and he bought it for £9,500. To take it quite shortly, he communicated with Mr. Sichel and he told Mr. Sichel very properly that it would be necessary to obtain an export licence, having regard to the prohibition, and a United States of America consular certificate, and that this he would put in hand immediately. However, Mr. Sichel was minded that the goblet should be brought back by hand, and finally on 25th May Mr. Sichel wrote that he had arranged for a Mr. Stauss to take the goblet on a Pan American World Airways flight to New York on 1st June. Now the dates here are of some importance. The very next day, 27th May, Mr. Sichel telephoned to the respondent Crompton and said that Mr. Strauss had agreed to take the goblet and suggesting that the documents should be in Mr. Strauss' name. Thereupon the respondent Crompton, again acting quite properly, pointed out that with the Whitsun weekend it would be impossible to obtain the necessary licence by 1st June. Thereupon Mr. Sichel said that the respondent Crompton's part as buying agent was completed, that he was to hand the goblet to Mr. Strauss without any documents at all and without any licence, and that he, Mr Sichel, would take full responsibility. Thereupon the respondent Crompton handed the goblet to Mr. Strauss on 31st May and on 1st June Mr. Strauss took it to America.

D

E

F

It was on those short facts that the justices gave their opinion in the following terms, terms which include really findings of fact as well as of opinion. They stated:

G

" We were of the opinion that the [respondent Crompton] knew from the very beginning that it was the intention to export the goblet to America and that such exportation was prohibited without a licence from the Board of Trade. We think that the [respondent Crompton] believed that the exportation of the goblet would be done regularly until 27th May when he spoke to Mr. Sichel on the telephone. During that conversation it became known to the [respondent Crompton] that Mr. Sichel intended the goblet to be exported by Mr. Strauss without a licence and accordingly in breach of the prohibition. Mr. Sichel, who was the owner of the goblet gave a specific instruction to the [respondent Crompton] to hand the goblet to Mr. Strauss. [And finally, and this is important.] The [respondent Crompton] handed the goblet to Mr. Strauss knowing that Mr. Strauss was going to export the goblet and evade the prohibition on its export."

H

I

Those are the facts that the justices found in their opinion, and then they went on to state:

" We considered that it was the [respondent Crompton's] legal duty to act in accordance with the owner's instruction, even though he knew that doing so might result in an illegal exportation. Once the goblet was handed over the [respondent Crompton] lost all control over it and in our view was not

A   concerned in its exportation which took place thereafter. We accordingly dismissed the information."

Finally, the question left to the court is: " The question for the opinion of the High Court is whether or not our decision was legally correct." In my judgment, the strict answer to the question posed to the court, " whether or not our decision was legally correct ", was that it was not correct, but it is further my opinion

B that they did not apply their minds—certainly the Case does not reveal that they applied their minds—to the proper question. I say that, as worded, their decision was not correct in law for this reason, that albeit there was a legal duty in ordinary circumstances to hand over the goblet to the owners once the agency was determined, I do not think that an action would lie for breach of that duty if the handing over would constitute the offence of being knowingly concerned

C in its exportation. Secondly, as it seems to me, the justices arrived at their decision on the basis that a man could only be concerned with the exportation if he did something at the point of time which constitutes, under the Act, exportation. That, in this code of legislation, is the time laid down in s. 79 (3) in the proviso:

D   " Provided that in the case of goods of a class or description with respect to the exportation of which any prohibition . . . is for the time being in force under or by virtue of any enactment which are exported by . . . air, the time of exportation shall be deemed to be the time when the exporting . . . aircraft departs . . ."

In confining the activities which can amount to being concerned in exportation

E to that limited time, when the aircraft leaves, the justices were wrong. A man can be concerned with the exportation of goods by doing things in advance of the time when the aircraft leaves, and certainly handing over goods for export the night before the aircraft leaves seems to me quite clearly to amount to being " concerned in the exportation . . . of . . . goods ".

As I have said, however, I do not think the justices asked themselves the

F correct question, because under s. 56 (2) the question is whether the respondent Crompton, was knowingly concerned in the exportation of this goblet with intent to evade the prohibition. I agree with counsel for the respondents' submission that that is to be treated as all one phrase and that one has to ask oneself that question. The justices, as it seems to me, have divided up the phrase and considered whether he was knowingly concerned with the exportation and,

G having come to the conclusion that he was not, have found it unnecessary to consider whether if he were it was with intent to evade. As I have said, the matter must be looked on as one phrase and one question which has to be answered.

In those circumstances, I have had myself considerable doubt as to what is the correct procedure for this court. It can be said on the one hand that the

H last thing that the respondent Crompton intended was to evade the prohibition. That is really unanswerable up to 27th May when Mr. Sichel telephoned, and the real question is what happened thereafter. Did he then only hand over because he felt that he had to as his agency was terminated, or did he at that stage lend himself, if I can put it that way, to the idea of exporting this without the necessary documents? The justices had before them evidence, oral and

I documentary, which is not before this court, and it seems to me that the only proper course is to send this case back with the opinion of the court asking them to apply their minds to what, I think, is the proper question.

I would only add this, that in considering that question it has been urged by counsel for the appellant that under s. 290 (2) of the Customs and Excise Act 1952 the burden shifts to the respondents to negative that intent. I have read and re-read s. 290 (2) and it seems to me quite impossible to say that that subsection provides for a shifting of the burden in a case such as this. It seems to me that it is for the prosecution to prove that what happened here is covered

by the full phrase " knowingly concerned in the exportation . . . with intent   A
to evade ".

MELFORD STEVENSON, J.: I agree.

WILLIS, J.: I agree.

Appeal allowed.   Case remitted.

Solicitors: *Solicitor, Customs and Excise* (for the appellant); *Herbert Smith &*   B
Co. (for the respondents).

[*Reported by* N. P. METCALFE, ESQ., *Barrister-at-Law.*]

R. *v.* BRIXTON PRISON GOVERNOR, *Ex parte* ATKINSON.

C

[QUEEN'S BENCH DIVISION (Lord Parker, C.J., Melford Stevenson and Bridge,
JJ.), June 25, 1969.]

*Extradition—Charge—Time of charge—Fugitive not charged at time of arrest in
United Kingdom but charged by time requisition received—United States
of America (Extradition) Order in Council 1935 (S.R. & O. 1935 No. 574),
art. 1.*

D

*Extradition—Oppression—Fugitive charged with crime based on same facts as
previous conviction—Whether oppression a relevant question.*

*Extradition—Treaty—Breach—Whether presumption that no breach by friendly
State intended—Whether question for court or Home Secretary.*

The applicant was, on a plea of guilty, convicted by a Louisiana court of
attempted armed robbery for which he was sentenced in November 1968   E
to 18 years' hard labour. During the commission of the offence the applicant
had fired shots at certain persons. In December 1968 he escaped from prison
and came to England. The offences of attempted armed robbery and prison-
breaking were not extraditable. On his being discovered in England, the
U.S. government sought to extradite him on freshly-laid charges of attempted
murder and aggravated burglary. It was clear that these charges and the   F
conviction arose out of the same incident. The applicant was arrested on
9th March 1969 on a provisional warrant, the charges not having been laid
until 14th March. On 2nd May the applicant was committed to prison
pending his return to the U.S.A. to face the charges of attempted murder.
In his affidavit the district attorney for the parish of Orleans in the State of
Louisiana had stated that the applicant would be prosecuted for the crimes   G
for which his extradition was being requested and would be required to
serve his term of imprisonment for the attempted armed robbery. On an
application for habeas corpus,

Held: the application would be refused, because—

(i) although charges had not been preferred against him at the time
he was discovered and arrested in the United Kingdom, the applicant was,   H
since the charges had been preferred by the time the requisition for extradition was made, a " person who, being accused [was] found within the
territory of the [United Kingdom] ", within the meaning of art. 1* of the
Extradition Treaty of 1931 between the United Kingdom and the United
States of America (see p. 1149, letter B, and p. 1150, letters E and G, post);

(ii) it was no part of the function of the court on extradition proceedings   I
to concern itself with the question whether the charges laid were oppressive
as having been founded on the same facts as a charge on which the applicant
had previously been tried (see p. 1149, letter I, to p. 1150, letter A, and
p. 1150, letter E, post);

Connelly v. *Director of Public Prosecutions* ([1964] 2 All E.R. 401)
distinguished.

---

* Article 1 is set out at p. 1148, letter I, to p. 1149, letter A, post. The treaty is the
United States of America (Extradition) Order in Council 1935 (S.R. & O. 1935 No. 574).

A   (iii) despite the fact that for the applicant to be required to complete his term of imprisonment (as was stated in the district attorney's affidavit to be the intention of the authorities of the State of Louisiana) would be a breach of the treaty of 1931, the court would assume that a friendly State would observe the conditions of the treaty (see p. 1150, letters D, G and E, post).

B   QUAERE: whether the question of an intended breach of the treaty was one for the Home Secretary or the court (see p. 1150, letter D, post).

Application dismissed.

[As to extradition offences generally, see 16 HALSBURY'S LAWS (3rd Edn.) 560-564, paras. 1149 to 1153; 566, 567, para. 1159; as to who may be surrendered, see ibid., pp. 564, 565, paras. 1155, 1157; and for cases on the application of the Extradition Acts to persons, see 24 DIGEST (Repl.) 988-990, 5-20.

C   For the Extradition Act 1870, s. 2, see 9 HALSBURY'S STATUTES (2nd Edn.) 875.]

Case referred to:

Connelly v. Director of Public Prosecutions, [1964] 2 All E.R. 401; [1964] A.C. 1254; [1964] 2 W.L.R. 1145; 128 J.P. 418; 48 Cr. App. Rep. 183;

D   Digest (Cont. Vol. B) 250, 472a.

Motion for writ of habeas corpus.

This was an application by way of motion by Arthur Atkinson, who was detained in Brixton Prison, for a writ of habeas corpus directed to the Governor of Brixton Prison to bring the applicant before the Divisional Court of the Queen's Bench Division and quash an order made on 2nd May 1969 by the chief

E   metropolitan magistrate (FRANK MILTON, ESQ.) under the Extradition Act 1870 that the applicant be admitted to prison pending his extradition to the United States of America to face offences contained in the chief magistrates' warrant of arrest, viz.: (i) attempted murder of Police Officer Edward Nick; (ii) attempted murder of Police Officer William Roth; (iii) attempted murder of Alegria Pita; and (iv) aggravated burglary. The alleged offences said to have taken place in

F   the parish of Orleans in the State of Louisiana on 5th October 1968. The facts are set out in the judgment of LORD PARKER, C.J.

The case noted below* was cited during the argument in addition to the case referred to in the judgment of LORD PARKER, C.J.

J. B. R. Hazan, Q.C., and N. H. Freeman for the applicant.

G   D. C. Calcutt for the United States government.

M. Corkery for the Governor of Brixton Prison.

LORD PARKER, C.J.: In these proceedings counsel moves on behalf of the applicant, Arthur Atkinson, who is now detained in Her Majesty's prison at Brixton pursuant to the warrant of the chief magistrate of Bow Street of 2nd

H   May 1969 pending extradition to the United States of America. The application is for a writ of habeas corpus.

The matter arises in this way. It is admitted that in New Orleans in the State of Louisiana the applicant saw an advertisement which had been put in a local paper by a Mrs. Pita, advertising the sale of jewellery. It is admitted that the applicant, together with another man, got in touch with her on the telephone and

I   arranged to go round to see her that evening. Sure enough that evening these two men went round there; the other man made some excuse to go to the bathroom, while the applicant remained in the main part of the dwelling where there was Mrs. Pita, her brother and sister-in-law, I think and a nephew. The other man in due course came out of the bathroom with a towel round his face brandishing a firearm, and ordered all except Mrs. Pita to go into the bathroom. They quite clearly said this was a hold-up and they wanted the jewellery. In some way Mrs.

---

* R. v. Brixton Prison Governor, Ex p. Athanassiadis (1966), 110 Sol. Jo. 769.

Pita kept her head and all the occupants of the flat succeeded in getting out   A
through the back into the street. They were pursued by these two men, the applicant so it is said firing his revolver towards Mrs. Pita. Police officers came on to the
scene and two police officers chased these two men, and in the course of the chase
it is said that the applicant fired at the two police officers, the suggestion being
that that was with intent to murder. In due course they were stopped and were
arrested, and undoubtedly arrested for armed robbery. For that the applicant   B
came before the court in New Orleans, and having pleaded guilty to attempted
armed robbery, as opposed to the full offence, was sentenced to 18 years' imprisonment. That sentence was imposed on 20th November 1968. On 22nd December
the applicant succeeded in escaping from the local prison, and in due course made
his way back to Manchester in this country. He was in fact arrested here in March
and the matter came, as I have said, before the chief magistrate at Bow Street   C
on 2nd May 1969.

Extradition could not be sought for the offence of breaking prison, nor on the
ground that the applicant was a convicted person, because the original offence of
attempted armed robbery was not an extradition offence, nor was prisonbreaking.
The offences on which extradition was sought were attempted murder of Mrs.
Pita, attempted murder of a police officer called Nick, and another police officer   D
called Roth, and in addition on a charge of what is called aggravated burglary.
It is quite clear that all those charges which it is now sought to bring arise out of
the same incident, if I may call it that, looking at it quite generally. The real
basis of this application, and one must come in a moment to the details of how it is
put, is that these charges have only been laid with a view to getting the applicant
back within the jurisdiction of the United States, and charging him and sentencing   E
him for an offence which is in essence the offence of breaking prison, which is not
an extraditable offence.

The specific grounds are as follows: it is said in the first place that the applicant
is not a person to whom art. 1 of the treaty between this country and the United
States applies in that at the time when he was arrested in this country he was under
a provisional warrant dated 8th March 1969, and was not then an accused person.   F
The foundation of this is to be found in the fact that at the time when the provisional warrant was issued, and at the time of his arrest here he had in fact never
been charged with these offences for which extradition is now sought. What had
happened is by no means clear to me, but there is no doubt that whether as a
result of a bargain or not, the district attorney in New Orleans decided that he
would not prefer any other charges than the charge of armed robbery for which the   G
applicant was in fact convicted. What other charges he had in mind I do not know,
except that it is said that he was " booked ", as it was put originally, that is I
suppose after arrest, for other charges including these three charges of attempted
murder. At any rate those were not proceeded with, and whether as the result of a
bargain it matters not; the bargain suggested being, if you will plead guilty to
armed robbery or attempted armed robbery we will not proceed with the other   H
charges. It may be that there was no such bargain, that the prosecuting authorities quite rightly rejected the idea of bringing a multiplicity of charges and
took the sensible course of choosing the gravest crime and proceeding in effect on
that, the armed robbery, and that the bargain that took place, I know not, may
have been merely at a later stage to the effect that the prosecution would be
prepared to accept a plea to the attempted armed robbery rather than to the full   I
offence. At any rate, for one reason or another, when he was in fact arrested
in this country, these charges had not been preferred. Counsel for the applicant
refers the court to art. 1 of the treaty in question, dated 22nd December 1931,
which provides:

" The high contracting parties engage to deliver up to each other, under
certain circumstances and conditions stated in the present treaty, those persons
who, being accused or convicted of any of the crimes or offences enumerated

A in article 3, committed within the jurisdiction of the one party, shall be found within the territory of the other party."

Counsel for the applicant says very attractively: when he was found here, which was on 8th March 1969, he was not an accused person. Accordingly he does not come within art. 1, and these proceedings are not applicable. I am quite clear in my own mind that there is, as it were, no magic in the word " found "; provided
B he is an accused person and is in this country at the time when the requisition is made and the matter is dealt with, that is sufficient.

The second point which arises is really the main point, which can be put quite generally as I have already said on the basis that this conduct on the part of the United States authorities was oppressive. No steps, he said, would have been taken but for this escape, and that indeed the other charges were deliberately
C abandoned. This application is only made, and these charges are only brought because he has escaped and the escaping is not an extraditable offence. Strong reliance is placed on what was said by their Lordships in *Connelly* v. *Director of Public Prosecutions* (1). It is unnecessary to refer in detail to this well-known case, but it was emphasised over and over again that the courts have an inherent jurisdiction to protect defendants against oppression and against any abuse by
D the prosecuting authorities of their functions. The only passage that it is just worth citing is that which occurs in the speech of Lord Devlin. He summarised his views thus (2):

"The result of this will, I think, be as follows. As a general rule a judge should stay an indictment (that is, order that it remain on the file not to be
E proceeded with) when he is satisfied that the charges therein are founded on the same facts as the charges in a previous indictment on which the accused has been tried, or form or are a part of a series of offences of the same or a similar character as the offences charged in the previous indictment."

Pausing there, counsel for the applicant says that that exactly covers the
F circumstances of this case. But Lord Devlin went on (3):

"He will do this because as a general rule it is oppressive to an accused for the prosecution not to use r. 3 where it can properly be used, but a second trial on the same or similar facts is not always and necessarily oppressive, and there may in a particular case be special circumstances which make it just and convenient in that case. The judge must then, in all the circumstances
G of the particular case, exercise his discretion as to whether or not he applies the general rule."

Fully accepting what is said there, I for myself am by no means satisfied that the making of these charges and this requisition for extradition is oppressive within that principle. It may well be that it would be perfectly proper, having regard to the changed circumstances caused by the escape. Be that as it may, for my part
H I find it impossible to see how the magistrate dealing with this matter by way of committal proceedings can exercise that discretion, which is really the discretion of the High Court. It is not for him to exercise the discretion referred to by Lord Devlin, or to decide how the judge of trial will exercise that discretion. So far as this court is concerned, it seems to me that we have no jurisdiction on an application for habeas corpus to consider matters of that sort unless Parliament
I has given us power to do so. Matters of oppression are specifically dealt with in both the old Fugitive Offenders Act 1881 and the more recent Fugitive Offenders Act 1967, which by s. 8 (2) specifically provides a power which I understand the court would not have but for that provision, namely that a court on an application for habeas corpus, can consider matters of oppression (4). In my judgment the

(1) [1964] 2 All E.R. 401; [1964] A.C. 1254.
(2) [1964] 2 All E.R. at p. 446; [1964] A.C. at pp. 1359, 1360.
(3) [1964] 2 All E.R. at p. 446; [1964] A.C. at p. 1360.
(4) See 47 Halsbury's Statutes (2nd Edn.) 597.

magistrate, and in turn this court, on an application for habeas corpus, is only A
concerned to see whether there is a prima facie case, and is not concerned to
investigate whether the court of trial might view the matter as oppressive.

The third point raised is really a very minor point. Counsel for the applicant
draws the court's attention to the fact that in an early affidavit in these proceedings Mr. Garrison, who was the district attorney of the parish of Orleans in the
State of Louisiana, states: B

" That if [the applicant] should be extradited to the State of Louisiana,
United States of America, his prosecution would be limited exclusively to
those crimes for which his extradition is specifically requested [so far so good,
and then it goes on] and to serve his term of eighteen years in the Louisiana
State Penitentiary at Angola, Louisiana, for the crime of attempted armed
robbery, said sentence imposed on November 20, 1968."   C

Undoubtedly if that were to be done it would be a breach of the treaty between
this country and the United States. For my part I am by no means satisfied that
the United States has any such intention. It may well be that Mr. Garrison's
attention has not been drawn to this matter, and for my part I proceed on the
basis that a friendly State with whom we are under treaty obligations the one
with the other will observe the conditions of the treaty. I have no reason to think, D
even if it is a matter which concerns this court, as opposed to the Home Secretary,
that the United States intend to break the treaty. For these reasons I would
dismiss these applications.

MELFORD STEVENSON, J.. I agree and do not wish to add anything.
                                                                               E
BRIDGE, J.: I fully agree with LORD PARKER, C.J., that the discretion
which counsel for the applicant invites this court to exercise is not one open
either to the committing magistrate or to this court in relation to proceedings
under the Extradition Act 1870. I would only add that for my part, even if we
had such a discretion, I can see nothing in the conduct of the prosecuting authorities in the United States, and more particularly in the State of Louisiana, which F
could lead us to the conclusion that this was an oppressive course of conduct.
In the circumstances which have arisen the resort to extradition for the offences
with which the applicant is now charged is the only means whereby the prosecuting authorities can secure that the applicant is brought to justice and properly
punished for his offences, if indeed he committed them. I entirely agree that this
application should be dismissed.   G

[On 26th June after giving judgment in *United States Government* v. *Atkinson*
(reported at p. 1151, post) LORD PARKER, C.J., stated that leave to appeal to
the House of Lords in the present case would be given but he added:

" if [this was the only proceeding] we would not grant leave, but it is
convenient that their Lordships should have the whole picture before them,
and also that it may expedite the matter."]   H

Application dismissed. Leave to appeal to the House of Lords granted.

Solicitors: *Victor J. Lissack* (for the applicant); *Rowe & Maw* (for the United
States government); *Director of Public Prosecutions* (for the Governor of Brixton
Prison).

[*Reported by* N. P. METCALFE, ESQ., *Barrister-at-Law.*] I

A

UNITED STATES GOVERNMENT *v.* ATKINSON.

[QUEEN'S BENCH DIVISION (Lord Parker, C.J., Melford Stevenson and Bridge, JJ.), June 25, 26, 1969.]

Case Stated—Extradition—Magistrates' court—Refusal to commit—Whether

B   *appeal by way of Case Stated—Magistrates' Courts Act 1952 (15 & 16 Geo. 6 & 1 Eliz. 2 c. 55), s. 87 (1).*

Extradition—Autrefois convict—Fugitive convicted in Louisiana of attempted armed robbery—Fresh charge of Louisiana offence of aggravated burglary— Whether autrefois convict.

On 15th November 1968 the respondent pleaded guilty in Louisiana,

C   U.S.A., to attempted armed robbery and was sentenced to 18 years' hard labour. In December 1968 he escaped to England. On 9th March 1969 he was arrested in Manchester. As neither attempted armed robbery nor prison-breaking were extraditable offences under English law, on 14th March 1969 an information was laid in the State of Louisiana charging the respondent, inter alia, with aggravated burglary*. On extradition proceedings, the magis-

D   trate refused to commit the respondent under s. 10 of the Extradition Act 1870 in respect of this charge on the ground that a plea of autrefois convict could successfully be made. On appeal,

Held: (i) by virtue of s. 87 (1)† of the Magistrates' Courts Act 1952 an appeal by way of Case Stated lay from a magistrates' refusal to commit under the Extradition Act 1870 (see p. 1156, letter B, and p. 1157, letter D,

E   post); and

(ii) the magistrate was wrong in refusing to commit the respondent; a plea of autrefois convict would not have succeeded in the present case because (per LORD PARKER, C.J. and MELFORD STEVENSON, J.) the success of such a plea did not depend on whether the facts examined on the trial of each of the offences were the same, but on whether the facts necessary to

F   support a conviction for each offence were the same (see p. 1156, letter I, and p. 1157, letter D, post), and (per BRIDGE, J.) attempted armed robbery was not in law the same offence as aggravated burglary (see p. 1158, letter C, post).

Connelly v. *Director of Public Prosecutions* ([1964] 2 All E.R. 401) applied.

Appeal allowed.

G   [As to autrefois convict, see 10 HALSBURY'S LAWS (3rd Edn.) 405-407, paras. 736-738; and for cases on the subject, see 14 DIGEST (Repl.) 378-387, *3700-3775*.

As to appeals by way of Case Stated from a magistrates' court, see 25 HALSBURY'S LAWS (3rd Edn.) p. 250, 251, para. 468.

For the Extradition Act 1870, s. 10, see 9 HALSBURY'S STATUTES (2nd Edn.) 881.

H   For the Magistrates' Courts Act 1952, s. 87, see 32 HALSBURY'S STATUTES (2nd Edn.) 488, 518.]

Cases referred to:

Boulter v. *Kent Justices*, [1897] A.C. 556; 66 L.J.Q.B. 787; 77 L.T. 288 61 J.P. 532; 30 Digest (Repl.) 75, *579*.

I   *Connelly* v. *Director of Public Prosecutions*, [1964] 2 All E.R. 401; [1964] A.C. 1254; [1964] 2 W.L.R. 1145; 128 J.P. 418; 48 Cr. App. Rep. 183; Digest (Cont. Vol. B.) 250, *472a*.

Jeffrey v. *Evans*, [1964] 1 All E.R. 536; [1964] 1 W.L.R. 505; 128 J.P. 252; 45 Digest (Repl.) 225, *234*.

R. v. *East Riding Quarter Sessions, Ex p. Newton*, [1967] 3 All E.R. 118; [1968] 1 Q.B. 32; [1967] 3 W.L.R. 1098; Digest (Repl.) Supp.

---

* The definition of this offence is given at p. 1153, letter E, post.

† Section 87 (1), so far as material, as set out at p. 1155, letter H, post.

Case Stated.

A

This was a Case Stated by F. MILTON, ESQ., the chief metropolitan magistrate at Bow Street, who having received an order from the Secretary of State, under his hand and seal, signifying that a requisition had been made to him by the diplomatic representative of the United States of America for the surrender of the respondent, Arthur Atkinson, accused of the commission of the crime (inter alia) of burglary within the jurisdiction of the United States of America, and requiring him to proceed in conformity with the provisions of the Extradition Acts of 1870 to 1935, he, on 2nd May 1969, proceeded to a hearing and a determination.

B

From the admissible authenticated documents and from oral testimony before him the magistrate found to be established, for the purposes of s. 10 of the Extradition Act 1870, the following facts: Mrs. Alegria Pita, of 122 Sixteenth Street, New Orleans, Louisiana, instructed the Times-Picayune Publishing Co., New Orleans, Louisiana, to print the following advertisement in the classified section of the daily newspaper on 5th, 6th and 7th October 1968: " Dinner Ring, 8 karat pure Opal surrounded by 2½ karat pure white diamonds, matching pendant. Make offer.   482-8155 ".   On 5th October 1968 this advertisement appeared in the Times-Picayune paper. On 5th October 1968 at about 6.0 p.m., Mrs. Pita received a telephone call with regard to the advertisement and she gave her address as 122 Sixteenth Street, and the calling party advised her that he would be at her home sometime between 8.30 p.m. and 9.30 p.m. that night. A Mr. Harold Neitzschman lived in the upstairs apartment at 122 Sixteenth Street, having adjoining doorbells and sharing a common corridor and doorway with Mrs. Pita. On 5th October 1968 at about 9.0 p.m. Mrs Pita heard Mr. Neitzschman's doorbell ring and she overheard a man ask Mr. Neitzschman to direct him to 126 Sixteenth Street. After a few minutes, Mrs. Pita heard Mr. Neitzschman return to his apartment.   Shortly after this, at approximately 9.20 p.m., Mrs. Pita heard a noise outside and went to investigate and at this time she saw the respondent and one Raymond Wagner. They asked Mrs. Pita if she knew where 126 Sixteenth Street was and she told them that there was no such address. At this time, Wagner said that they were from out of town and asked Mrs. Pita if he could use her bathroom and she replied affirmatively. Both Wagner and the respondent went into Mrs. Pita's apartment with her at that time. Wagner went into the bathroom and the respondent stayed in the living room. When Wagner came from the bathroom he had a towel over his face and a gun in his hand and he said " This is a stick-up. All of you get into the bathroom." At this time the respondent pulled out a gun and said " Yes, all of you get into the bathroom except you ", referring to Mrs. Pita.   Then the respondent said " Where is the jewellery? "   At this time Mrs. Pita followed her brother, sister-in-law and nephew into the hallway leading towards the bathroom and instructed them in Arabic to go through the kitchen out of the back door which they did. At this time the brother, sister-in-law and nephew crossed over the street. Mrs. Pita remained on the front lawn of her neighbour's house and they all yelled " Help! Help! Police! " The respondent and Wagner came out of the front door and at this time the respondent turned to where Mrs. Pita was standing, pointed his revolver and fired a shot at her. Wagner and the respondent ran to their car and fled. On 22nd October 1968 an information was laid in the State of Louisiana charging the respondent with the armed robbery of Alegria Pita.   The charge was based on the facts set out above. No other charge was filed on the respondent at that time. More particularly, no charge of burglary (or aggravated burglary) was filed or was before the court. On 15th November 1968 a charge of attempted armed robbery of Alegria Pita was substituted for the charge of armed robbery. The respondent entered a plea of guilty to the charge of attempted armed robbery and was sentenced to serve a term of 18 years' hard labour in the Louisiana State Penitentiary. On or about 22nd or 23rd December 1968, the respondent escaped from prison. The respondent

C

D

E

F

G

H

I

A had not served the sentence of the court and had received no parole or pardon. On 9th March 1969 the respondent was arrested in Manchester by Detective Sergeant Barnes. Whilst travelling on the train to London, the respondent said to Detective Sergeant Barnes—

B " Look Mr. Barnes, I know I had a gun with me when we went to the old lady's but it didn't frighten her. We were supposed to get some jewellery, but we didn't."

On 14th March 1969 an information was laid in the State of Louisiana charging the respondent with aggravated burglary of 122 Sixteenth Street, Lower Apt., New Orleans, where a person was present, namely Alegria Pita, with the intent to commit a theft therein, while armed with a dangerous weapon, namely a
C pistol. On 14th March 1969 a warrant was issued in the State of Louisiana for the arrest of the respondent on the charge of aggravated burglary. The charge was based on the facts set out above. By art. 64 of Title 14 of the Louisiana Criminal Code, armed robbery is defined as follows:

D " Armed robbery is the theft of anything of value from the person of another or which is in the immediate control of another, by use of force or intimidation while armed with a dangerous weapon."

By art. 60 of Title 14 of the Louisiana Criminal Code, aggravated burglary is defined as follows:

E " Aggravated burglary is the unauthorised entering of any inhabited dwelling or of any structure, watercraft or moveable where a person is present, with intent to commit a felony or any theft therein if the offender (1) is armed with a dangerous weapon, or (2) after entering arms himself with a dangerous weapon, or (3) commits a battery upon any person while in such place or in entering or leaving such place."

F No evidence was produced before the magistrate to show that on the charge of attempted armed robbery the respondent had been in peril, under the law of Louisiana, of being convicted of burglary (or aggravated burglary).

G It was submitted on behalf of the respondent that the respondent was entitled to rely on the plea autrefois convict. It was submitted that the facts on which the appellant, the government of the United States of America, sought to rely to support the charge of burglary (or aggravated burglary) were the same or substantially the same as those relied on to support the conviction for attempted armed robbery; that the offence of attempted armed robbery was in this case in effect the same offence as that of burglary (or aggravated burglary); and that the appellant only sought an order of committal on a charge of burglary because attempted armed robbery was not an offence for which extradition could be granted under the treaty.

H It was submitted on behalf of the appellant that the respondent was not entitled to rely on the plea autrefois convict. It was submitted that the evidence necessary to support the charge of burglary (or aggravated burglary) would not have been sufficient to procure a legal conviction on the charge of attempted armed robbery; that the offence of burglary (or aggravated burglary) was an offence which was different in quality, with different factual and legal characteristics, from the
I offence of attempted armed robbery; that they were not the same offences or offences which were in effect the same or substantially the same; and that it was not material if the facts being examined on the charge of burglary were the same as those which had supported the charge of attempted armed robbery. The charge of armed robbery had alone been brought initially because it was the gravest of the charges which could have been brought and because it carried the greatest penalty. The reason why other charges had not been brought was in order to avoid a multiplicity of charges. It was submitted that the appellant's motives in bringing the charge of aggravated burglary were immaterial, and that if the

appellant could bring itself within the requirements of the law it was entitled **A**
to an order of committal.

The chief magistrate was of the opinion that the facts relied on to support
the offence of burglary were substantially the same as those which related to the
offence of attempted armed robbery, and that the offence of attempted armed
robbery, in the circumstances set forth in the evidence, was in effect the same
offence as that of aggravated burglary, on which the appellant now sought to **B**
prosecute the respondent. He accordingly held that the plea of autrefois convict
succeeded, and he therefore refused to make an order committing the respondent
to prison in respect of the charge of burglary.

The question for the opinion of the High Court was whether, in accepting a
plea of autrefois convict and in refusing to make an order committing the
respondent on the charge of burglary, the chief magistrate came to a correct **C**
decision in law.

The appellant now appealed.

The cases noted below* were cited during the argument in addition to the
cases referred to in the judgments.

The case should be read with *R. v. Brixton Prison Governor, Ex parte Atkinson*
(reported at p. 1146 ante).   **D**

D. C. Calcutt for the appellant.
J. B. R. Hazan, Q.C., and *N. H. Freeman* for the respondent.

LORD PARKER, C.J.: This is an appeal by way of Case Stated from a
decision of the chief metropolitan magistrate on 2nd May 1969 whereby he refused
to make an order under s. 10 of the Extradition Act 1870 committing the res- **E**
pondent to prison with a view to his extradition to the United States of America
for an alleged offence of aggravated burglary. The history of this matter and the
facts giving rise to the extradition proceedings have already been dealt with
by this court in an application by the respondent for a writ of habeas corpus (1).
But it is I think convenient to summarise them insofar as they are relevant to the
present proceedings. They are indeed fully set out in the Case Stated and are **F**
not in dispute.

Quite shortly, on 5th October 1968 a Mrs. Pita of New Orleans in the State of
Louisiana, caused an advertisement to appear in the local paper advertising
certain jewellery. She had a telephone call that evening from someone, who arranged to come round later in the evening to see her. In due course the respondent
and a man called Wagner came to her door and on an excuse that Wagner **G**
wanted to go to the bathroom, they both came in. A time came when Wagner
came out of the bathroom with a towel round his face, brandishing a firearm
and ordered Mrs. Pita's relations who were in the house to go into the bathroom.
The respondent also produced a firearm and threatened Mrs. Pita. In fact
Mrs. Pita and the others succeeded in getting out of the house, followed by these
two men, and the respondent it is said fired his revolver at Mrs. Pita. As a **H**
result of that on 22nd October 1968 an information was preferred in the State of
Louisiana charging the respondent with the armed robbery of Mrs. Pita. That
was the only information laid at that stage. On 15th November a plea of guilty
to attempted armed robbery was accepted and he was sentenced to a term of
18 years' hard labour in the local penitentiary. On 22nd or 23rd December,
however, he succeeded in escaping from prison and made his way back to this **I**
country, where on 9th March 1969 he was arrested at Manchester. Neither the
crime of attempted armed robbery nor the crime of prisonbreaking are extraditable offences, and it was no doubt for that reason that on 14th March 1969
an information was laid in the State of Louisiana charging the respondent,

---

* *Schtraks* v. *Government of Israel*, [1962] 3 All E.R. 529; [1964] A.C. 556; *R. v. Brixton Prison Governor, Ex p. Athanassiadis* (1966), 110 Sol. Jo. 769.
(1) See *R. v. Brixton Prison Governor, Ex p. Atkinson*, p. 1146 ante.

A inter alia, with what is called aggravated burglary, and a warrant for his arrest was issued on the basis of which extradition proceedings were sought.

It is important to realise what the offences of armed robbery and aggravated robbery consist of under the law of Louisiana. Armed robbery is defined as:

B " . . . the theft of anything of value from the person of another or which is in the immediate control of another, by use of force or intimidation while armed with a dangerous weapon."

Aggravated burglary is defined as:

" . . . the unauthorised entering of any inhabited dwelling . . . where a person is present, with intent to commit a felony or any theft therein if the offender is armed with a dangerous weapon . . . ".

C The learned magistrate expressed his opinion in this form:

" I was of the opinion that the facts relied upon to support the offence of burglary were substantially the same as those which related to the offence of attempted armed robbery, and that the offence of attempted armed robbery, in the circumstances set forth in the evidence, was in effect the same offence as that of aggravated burglary, upon which the appellant now sought to prosecute the respondent. I accordingly held that the plea of autrefois convict succeeded, and I therefore refused to make an order committing the respondent to prison in respect of the charge of burglary."

D

The question falling for the opinion of the court is whether, in accepting a plea of autrefois convict and in refusing to make an order committing the respondent on the charge of burglary, the magistrate came to a correct decision in law.

E Before dealing with the point on which the opinion of the court is sought, it is necessary to determine a preliminary objection which has been taken on behalf of the respondent that these proceedings by way of appeal are misconceived in that there is no power in the prosecution to appeal by way of Case Stated from such a refusal to commit, and no jurisdiction in the magistrate to state a Case. It is indeed a novel point; no attempt to appeal by way of Case Stated ever having so far as I know been made in regard to a refusal to commit under the Extradition Act 1870 or indeed in regard to a refusal to commit by examining justices for an alleged offence committed in this country. At first sight indeed it seems surprising that in such proceedings an appeal by the prosecution by way of Case Stated should lie. Prior, at any rate, to 1952 it was, to say the least, doubtful whether it would lie, the only right of appeal being from a court of summary jurisdiction. In this connection, it is to be observed that it was held in *Boulter* v. *Kent Justices* (2) that licensing justices were not a court of summary jurisdiction. By analogy it would appear that a magistrate conducting committal proceedings under the Extradition Act 1870 would likewise not be a court of summary jurisdiction.

H However, in 1952 the Magistrates' Courts Act 1952 was passed, under which the power to state a Case is to be found in s. 87 (1). It provides as follows:

" Any person who was a party to any proceeding before a magistrates' court or is aggrieved by the conviction, order, determination or other proceeding of the court may question the proceeding on the ground that it is wrong in law or is in excess of jurisdiction by applying to the justices composing the court to state a case for the opinion of the High Court on the question of law or jurisdiction involved . . ."

I

" Magistrates' court " which was an expression new in this field, was defined by s. 124 (1) in these terms:

" In this Act the expression ' magistrates' court ' means any justice or justices of the peace acting under any enactment or by virtue of his or their commission or under the common law."

---

(2) [1897] A.C. 556.

Here the magistrate was clearly acting under an enactment, namely the Extra- **A** dition Act 1870, and the words used in s. 87 (1) " . . . aggrieved by the . . . order, determination or other proceeding of the court " are extremely wide, and would appear to cover a refusal, as in this case, to commit. Moreover, in *Jeffrey* v. *Evans* (3), this court held that at any rate since 1952 an appeal lay by way of Case Stated from a decision of licensing justices, and that case was cited with approval by the Court of Appeal in the later case of *R.* v. *East Riding Quarter* **B** *Sessions, Ex p. Newton* (4), holding there that an appeal also lay to quarter sessions from licensing justices acting under the Public Health Acts. Surprising, therefore, as it may at first sight seem, I think that such an appeal does lie, and accordingly I would reject the preliminary objection and hold that the magistrate had juris- diction, as he himself must have thought, to state a Case.

Accordingly I turn to the point raised for the opinion of this court. The **C** magistrate, as I have already said, expressed his opinion in these terms, and I will read it again:

" I was of the opinion that the facts relied upon to support the offence of burglary were substantially the same as those which related to the offence of attempted armed robbery, and that the offence of attempted armed robbery, in the circumstances set forth in the evidence, was in effect the same **D** offence as that of aggravated burglary, upon which the appellant now sought to prosecute the respondent. I accordingly held that the plea of autrefois convict succeeded . . ."

In arriving at that opinion and that conclusion, the magistrate was undoubtedly seeking to apply the law as laid down in *Connelly* v. *Director of Public Prosecutions* (5). In my judgment, however, he has not properly applied the true test there **E** laid down. The true test is, I think, succinctly put by LORD MORRIS OF BORTH- Y-GEST, when he said (6):

" It matters not that incidents and occasions being examined on the trial of the second indictment are precisely the same as those which were examined on the trial of the first. The court is concerned with charges of offences or **F** crimes. The test is, therefore, whether such proof as is necessary to convict of the second offence would establish guilt of the first offence or of an offence for which on the first charge there could be a conviction. Applying to the present case the law as laid down, the question is whether proof that there was robbery with aggravation would support a charge of murder or manslaughter. It seems to me quite clear that it would not. The crimes are **G** distinct. There can be robbery without killing. There can be killing without robbery. Evidence of robbery does not prove murder or manslaughter. Conviction of robbery cannot involve conviction of murder or manslaughter. Nor does an acquittal of murder or manslaughter necessarily involve an acquittal of robbery. Nor on a charge of murder or manslaughter could a man be convicted of robbery. That the facts in the two trials have much in **H** common is not a true test of the availability of the plea of autrefois acquit. Nor is it of itself relevant that two separate crimes were committed at the same time so that in recounting the one there may be mention of the other."

In other words it seems to me, the question is not a question of whether the actual facts examined on the trial of each of the offences are the same, but whether the facts necessary to support a conviction for each offence are the same. To the **I** same effect is LORD HODSON, and this is the only further passage I desire to quote. He said (7):

" The two offences, murder or manslaughter on the one hand and armed

(3) [1964] 1 All E.R. 536; [1964] 1 W.L.R. 505.
(4) [1967] 3 All E.R. 118; [1968] 1 Q.B. 32.
(5) [1964] 2 All E.R. 401; [1964] A.C. 1254.
(6) [1964] 2 All E R. at pp. 414, 415; [1964] A.C. at p. 1309.
(7) [1964] 2 All E.R. at p. 430; [1964] A.C. at p. 1333.

A robbery on the other, are not the same, and the second charge could be proved without reference to the death of the murdered man who met his death on the occasion of the robbery. Even if the same evidence is given to prove separate offences it is well settled that whether or not the facts are the same in both trials is not the true test; the test is whether the acquittal on the first charge necessarily involved an acquittal on the second . . .''

B Here as it seems to me it is clear that there can be an attempted armed robbery without there being an aggravated burglary, and there can be an aggravated burglary without there being an attempted armed robbery. Indeed as it seems to me the pleas of autrefois convict and autrefois acquit being pleas in bar which are decided before the evidence in the later case is known, the validity of the pleas depends on the legal characteristics of the two offences in question, namely

C whether the facts necessary to support a conviction in each case are the same, and do not depend on whether the actual facts thereafter given in evidence are the same. In the result, I would allow this appeal and send the case back with a direction to the learned magistrate to commit on the charge of aggravated burglary.

D **MELFORD STEVENSON, J.:** I agree.

BRIDGE, J.: I also agree on both points of jurisdiction and autrefois convict, and I add only a short word on the second point out of respect to the learned magistrate from whom we are differing, and in deference to the argument of counsel for the respondent.

In his speech in *Connelly* v. *Director of Public Prosecutions* (8) LORD MORRIS

E OF BORTH-Y-GEST examined very fully the authorities dealing with the principle of autrefois acquit and autrefois convict; he enunciated (9) five propositions which he stated are established by principle and authority. Counsel for the respondent's argument, and no doubt the conclusion reached by the learned magistrate, was founded largely on the third and fourth of those propositions which were stated in these terms (9):

F " . . . (iii) that the same rule [namely that a man cannot be tried for a crime of which he has previously been convicted] applies if the crime in respect of which he is being charged is in effect the same or is substantially the same as either the principal or a different crime in respect of which he has been acquitted or could have been convicted or has been convicted;

G (iv) that one test whether the rule applies is whether the evidence which is necessary to support the second indictment, or whether the facts which constitute the second offence, would have been sufficient to procure a legal conviction on the first indictment either as to the offence charged or as to an offence of which, on the indictment, the accused could have been found guilty; . . .''

H Taken in isolation and read out of their context, those two propositions might be understood as lending support to the argument of counsel for the respondent and the conclusion reached by the learned magistrate. They are of course clarified and explained by the later passages in the speech of LORD MORRIS himself (10), one of which has already been cited by LORD PARKER, C.J., and which I need not read again. The whole matter seems to me the most succinctly

I put in a short passage from the speech of LORD DEVLIN where he said (11):

" For the doctrine of autrefois to apply it is necessary that the accused should have been put in peril of conviction for the same offence as that with which he is then charged. The word ' offence ' embraces both the facts which constitute the crime and the legal characteristics which make it an offence.

---

(8) [1964] 2 All E.R. 401; [1964] A.C. 1254.
(9) [1964] 2 All E.R. at p. 412; [1964] A.C. at p. 1305.
(10) [1964] 2 All E.R. at pp. 414, 415; [1964] A.C. at p. 1309.
(11) [1964] 2 All E.R. at p. 433; [1964] A.C. at pp. 1339, 1340.

For the doctrine to apply it must be the same offence both in fact and in law.   **A**
Robbery is not in law the same offence as murder (or as manslaughter, of
which the accused could also have been convicted on the first indictment),
and so the doctrine does not apply in the present case. I would add one further
comment. [LORD MORRIS OF BORTH-Y-GEST] in his statement of the law,
accepting what is suggested in some dicta in the authorities, extends the doctrine to cover offences which are in effect the same or substantially the same.   **B**
I entirely agree with [LORD MORRIS OF BORTH-Y-GEST] that these dicta
refer to the legal characteristics of an offence and not to the facts on which it
is based . . ."

Applying the language of LORD DEVLIN mutatis mutandis to the facts of the
present case, attempted armed robbery is not in law the same offence as aggravated burglary, and so the doctrine does not apply in the present case.   **C**

Appeal allowed.

*The court certified under s. 1 of the Administration of Justice Act 1960 that a
point of law of general public importance was involved, viz.: " Whether in proceedings for the return of a fugitive criminal under the Extradition Act 1870, an
appeal lies at the instance of the foreign State by way of Case Stated to the Divisional*   **D**
*Court of the Queen's Bench Division against the decision of the police magistrate
discharging the said criminal in respect of any extradition crime adjudicated on in
the said proceedings " and granted leave to appeal to the House of Lords.*

Solicitors: *Rowe & Maw* (for the appellant); *Victor J. Lissack* (for the
respondent).

[Reported by N. P. METCALFE, ESQ., Barrister-at-Law.]   E

JONES (Inspector of Taxes) v. SHELL PETROLEUM CO., LTD.
CROPPER (Inspector of Taxes) v. BRITISH PETROLEUM CO., LTD.   **F**

[CHANCERY DIVISION (Cross, J.), December 16, 1968, February 12, 1969.]

*Income Tax—Repayment—Management expenses—Investment company—Rate
of repayment applicable where income has borne tax at different rates—
Income Tax Act 1952 (15 & 16 Geo. 6 & 1 Eliz. 2 c. 10), s. 425 (1).*   **G**

*Income Tax—Repayment—Ceiling—Tax deducted from dividends—Whether
repayment calculated with reference to tax paid, or rate of tax paid, by dividend-
paying company—Income Tax Act 1952 (15 & 16 Geo. 6 & 1 Eliz. 2 c. 10),
s. 350 (1).*

An investment company which is entitled to a repayment of tax equal
to the amount of tax on any sums disbursed as expenses of management   **H**
under s. 425 (1)* of the Income Tax Act 1952, and which has borne tax at
different rates on different parts of its income (on one part the standard
rate, and on other parts, lower rates) is not always entitled under that section
to a repayment of tax calculated at the standard rate; but (semble), in
accordance with the principle laid down in *Sterling Trust, Ltd.* v. *Inland
Revenue Comrs.†*, is entitled to attribute the management expenses first to   **I**
that part of the income which bore tax at the highest rate; second (if any be
left unattributed) to that part of the income which bore tax at the next
highest rate, and so on; being entitled, therefore, to a repayment of tax at
the rate or rates appropriate to the income or parts of the income to which
the attribution or attributions have been made (see p. 1162, letters B and C,
and p. 1165, letters B to E, post).

---

* Section 425 (1) is set out at p. 1161, letters A to C, post.
† (1925), 12 Tax Cas. 868.

A　　By s. 350 (1)* (*a*) of the Act, the ceiling for relief or repayment in respect of tax deducted or authorised to be deducted from any dividend, should be calculated with reference to the rate, not the actual amount, of the tax paid by the dividend-paying company (see p. 1165, letter H, post).

Appeals allowed.

[As to repayment of tax in respect of management expenses of insurance
B　companies, investment companies, etc., see 20 HALSBURY's LAWS (3rd Edn.) 475, 476, para. 903; and for cases on the subject, see 28 DIGEST (Repl.) 141, 142, 534-540.

For the Income Tax Act 1952, s. 350, s. 425, see 31 HALSBURY's STATUTES (2nd Edn.) 338, 406.]

C　Case referred to:

Sterling Trust, Ltd. v. *Inland Revenue Comrs., Inland Revenue Comrs.* v. *Sterling Trust, Ltd.* (1925), 12 Tax Cas. 868; 28 Digest (Repl.), 452, *1947.*

Case Stated.

The first taxpayer company appealed to the Special Commissioners of Income Tax under s. 9 (2) of the Income Tax Act 1952 against a decision of the Inspector
D　of Taxes on claims made by the company for the year 1960-61 under (i) s. 425 of the Act relating to claims to relief in respect of management expenses, and (ii) para. 13 of Sch. 16 to the Act, relating to claims for an allowance by way of credit for foreign tax. The question for determination arose primarily in connection with the management expenses but the two claims were in some respects interrelated.　The following agreed statement of facts was laid before the
E　commissioners:

" (i) Throughout the year of assessment 1960/61 the [taxpayer company] was a company whose business consisted mainly in the making of investments and the principal part of whose income was derived therefrom. It was accordingly a company to which Section 425 Income Tax Act 1952 applied. (ii) The [taxpayer company] was charged to tax for the said year,
F　by deduction or otherwise, upon the income described in the Schedules attached hereto [not reproduced]. The [taxpayer company] was not charged to tax in respect of its profits for the said year under the provisions applicable to Case I Schedule D and could not lawfully have been so charged in respect of the income in question. (iii) During the said year the [taxpayer company] disbursed sums as expenses of management and as charges in the amounts described in the said Schedules.　The word " charges " refers to interest
G　annuities and other annual payments from which the [taxpayer company] was entitled to deduct tax under Section 169 Income Tax Act 1952, or would have been so entitled but for notices given to it by or on behalf of the Commissioners of Inland Revenue pursuant to Regulation 3 of the Double Taxation Relief (Taxes on Income) (General) Regulations 1946†."

H　The taxpayer company contended as follows: (i) It was charged to tax on the whole of its income by deduction or otherwise at the standard rate, viz.: (a) to tax on United Kingdom dividends by deduction at that rate, in accordance with the provisions of s. 184 and s. 185 of the Income Tax Act 1952, and, where the dividends were net United Kingdom rate dividends, the opening words of s. 350 (1) of that Act; and (b) to tax on income taxed overseas directly at that rate subject
I　thereafter to any available relief by way of tax credit. (ii) In those circumstances the management expenses relief to which it was entitled should be computed on the basis that the tax referred to in the words " the amount of the tax on any sums disbursed as expenses of management " in s. 425 (1) of the Income Tax Act 1952 was tax at the standard rate. (iii) Such relief was accordingly allowable at the standard rate on sums disbursed as expenses of management,

---

* Section 350 (1), so far as material, is set out at p. 1161, letter F, post.
† S.R. & O. 1946 No. 466.

subject to the relief not being in excess of the tax paid by the company, and **A**
to account being taken in computing the maximum repayable tax of; (a) the
provisions of s. 350 (1) (a) of the Income Tax Act 1952 as to the repayment of
tax deducted or authorised to be deducted from net United Kingdom rate
dividends; and (b) tax credit relief allowed. (iv) The management expenses
and tax credit claims which were made by the taxpayer company should therefore
be allowed in principle and the appeal be determined accordingly.   **B**

The Crown contended as follows: (i) The tax referred to in the words " the
amount of the tax " in s. 425 (1) of the Income Tax Act 1952 was the tax on income
deemed to have been disbursed pound for pound on management expenses and
not necessarily tax at the standard rate. (ii) In the circumstances of the case
the management expenses relief due should be ascertained by making an allocation of the sums disbursed as expenses of management pound for pound against   **C**
income of the taxpayer company on whatever basis was most favourable to
the company and then computing the relief due in respect of tax on the income
taken to be so disbursed. (iii) Where such income was from net United Kingdom
rate dividends the relief so due was by virtue of the provisions of s. 350 (1) (a)
of the Income Tax Act 1952 required to be restricted to tax on that income at
the net United Kingdom rate applicable to the dividends. (iv) Where the United **D**
Kingdom tax on any income was repayable by way of relief under s. 425 no
further relief by way of credit against United Kingdom tax was allowable in
respect of any overseas tax paid on that income. (v) Allocation of sums disbursed
pound for pound against income of the taxpayer company accorded with the
scheme of the provisions contained in s. 425 of the Income Tax Act 1952, as
amended by s. 19 of the Finance Act 1954, as to the carrying forward of manage-   **E**
ment expenses where sums disbursed were in excess of the amount on which
the company had been charged to tax for the year in question. (vi) The management expenses and tax credit claims made by the taxpayer company should
therefore be dealt with in principle on a basis set out and the appeal be determined
accordingly.

The commissioners* held that relief should be allowed on the basis envisaged   **F**
by the taxpayer company and that the appeal therefore succeeded. The Crown
appealed by way of Case Stated to the High Court.

Arthur Bagnall, Q.C., and *P. W. Medd* for the Crown.
Hubert H. Monroe, Q.C., *M. P. Nolan*, Q.C., and *S. J. L. Oliver* for the taxpayer
companies.
          G

CROSS, J.: These two cases raise the question of the measure of relief
from tax in respect of management expenses to which the respondent taxpayer
companies Shell Petroleum Co., Ltd., and British Petroleum Co., Ltd., were
respectively entitled for the year 1960-61 under s. 425 of the Income Tax Act
1952, having regard to their respective claims for allowances by way of credit
for foreign tax. Both companies are investment companies and both derived   **H**
nearly all their income in the year in question from one or other of three sources:
source (a)—dividends from which the paying companies had deducted United
Kingdom tax at the standard rate and had themselves no claim to double
taxation relief; source (b)—dividends paid by companies themselves entitled to
double taxation relief from which United Kingdom tax had been deducted at
the standard rate but in respect of which any claim to relief or repayment on
account of such deduction was limited by s. 350 (1) of the Act to the net United   **I**
Kingdom rate of tax borne by the paying company; and source (c)—foreign
income in respect of which the taxpayer companies were liable to United Kingdom
tax by direct assessment but were themselves entitled to double taxation relief
in respect of foreign tax. The greater part of the income of the first taxpayer
company is derived from source (c) and the greater part of the income of the

---

* The terms of the commissioners' decision are set out at p. 1163, letter G, to p. 1164,
letter B, post.

A second taxpayer company from source (b), but this difference has no bearing on anything which I have to decide.

Section 425 (1) of the Act of 1952 (1) is in the following terms:

B " Subject to the provisions of this section, and to the other provisions of this Part of this Act, where—(a) an assurance company carrying on life assurance business (whether proprietary or mutual); or (b) any company whose business consists mainly in the making of investments and the principal part of whose income is derived therefrom, claims and proves to the satisfaction of the Special Commissioners that, for any year of assessment, it has been charged to tax by deduction or otherwise, and has not been charged in respect of its profits in accordance with the provisions of this Act applicable to Case I of Schedule D, it shall be entitled to repayment **C** of so much of the tax paid by it as is equal to the amount of the tax on any sums disbursed as expenses of management (including commissions) for that year."

A further subsection, (1A), was added in 1954 (2) which runs as follows:

D " If, in the case of the year 1954-55 or any subsequent year of assessment, effect cannot be given, or cannot be fully given, to the foregoing subsection because the company has not been charged to tax for that year by deduction or otherwise, or because the sums disbursed for that year exceed the amount on which the company has been charged to tax for the year, an amount equal to the sums so disbursed, less any amount on which the company has been so charged, may be carried forward and treated for the purposes of this **E** section as if it had been disbursed for any subsequent year of assessment: . . ."

There follows a proviso setting out in detail how the " carry forward " is to be worked out, which I need not read. At this stage I will also read (3) s. 350 (1):

F " The amount of tax which is authorised by section one hundred and eighty-four of this Act to be deducted from any dividend shall be determined without taking into account any reduction, by reason of double taxation relief, of the United Kingdom income tax payable directly or by deduction by the company, but—(a) notwithstanding anything in this Act, no relief or repayment in respect of tax deducted or authorised to be deducted from any dividend shall be allowed at a rate exceeding the rate (hereinafter referred to as ' the net United Kingdom rate ') of the United Kingdom income tax **G** payable directly or by deduction by the company after taking double taxation relief into account; . . ."

There is no doubt that the taxpayer companies are companies to which s. 425 applies, or that they have not been charged to tax under Case I of Sch. D, but have been charged to tax by deduction or by assessment under another head. Further it was admitted before me that in applying the section one must first **H** work out the tax liability of the taxpayer companies taking into account any double taxation relief to which they were entitled before one proceeds to consider how much of the tax paid they are entitled to recover under the section. Finally it was agreed that the words " tax on any sums disbursed as expenses of management " cannot be construed literally since the management expenses might in fact have been paid out of money which had not borne tax, e.g., capital or a **I** bank overdraft, but that the words must be taken to mean tax on such part of

(1) The words " to the satisfaction of the Special Commissioners " in s. 425 (1) were repealed by the Income Tax Management Act 1964, s. 17 (5) and Sch. 6, Pt. 2. Section 425, except subsection (6), was repealed by the Finance Act 1965, s. 97 (5) and Sch. 22, Pt. 4, except in relation to the year 1965-66 or earlier years of assessment (see also ibid., s. 57 (5)). For comparable provisions, see now ibid., s. 57 and s. 69.

(2) Subsection (1A) was added by the Finance Act 1954, s. 19. For its subsequent repeal, see footnote (1), supra.

(3) Section 350 of the Act of 1952 was repealed by the Finance Act 1965, s. 97 (5) and Sch. 22, Pt. 4, except in relation to the year 1965-66 or earlier years of assessment.

the taxed income of the company as is in fact equivalent to the management   **A**
expenses.

The dispute between the parties centred on the words " the amount of the tax ".
The contention of the taxpayer companies was that this meant tax at the standard
rate subject to the limitation introduced by s. 350 (1) of the Act. The Crown
on the other hand contended that one must discover what was the rate of tax
effectively borne by each part of the income in question and only allow repay-   **B**
ment of tax on the part of the income equivalent to the management expenses
at the rate appropriate to the part of the income to which one attributed the
management expenses, although the taxpayer companies were entitled in
accordance with the principle laid down in *Sterling Trust, Ltd.* v. *Inland Revenue
Comrs.* (4), to attribute the management expenses so far as possible to that part
of the income which had borne tax at the highest rate.   **C**

In the year in question, the first taxpayer company figures, which are the
only ones to which I will refer, were as follows: *source (a)*—the ordinary standard
rate income was £24,678,862 gross on which tax was charged by deduction to the
amount of £9,563,059; *source (b)*—dividends from companies entitled to double
taxation relief were £11,129,673 gross. Tax was deducted from this at the standard
rate but under s. 350 (1) the amount recoverable, i.e., at the net United Kingdom   **D**
rates paid by the various companies in question, amounted only to £2,925,869;
source (c)—income taxed abroad amounted to £71,936,837 gross. Tax on that
at the standard rate would have been £27,875,524 but against that there was a
credit for foreign tax paid of £22,818,145 leaving a sum of £5,057,379 tax payable
by direct assessment. The total gross income was therefore £107,745,372 against
which there were charges of £7,181,437 to be deducted leaving £100,563,935. On   **E**
the other hand the maximum tax which could possibly be repaid was £17,546,127
(i.e., £9,563,059 plus £2,925,689 plus £5,057,379) less tax applicable to the
charges of £2,782,807 leaving a figure of £14,763,320. The management expenses
for the year were £39,696,940, income tax on which at the standard rate would
be £15,382,564, a sum greater than the maximum repayable tax.

On these figures the result according to the taxpayer companies was that a   **F**
sum of £14,763,320 was repayable but that the difference between that figure
and £15,382,564 was irrecoverable, the " carry forward " provisions in sub-s. (1A)
not applying since the management expenses did not exceed the amount on
which the company had been charged to tax.

On the Crown's approach one allocates to the management expenses in the
first instance income of the first taxpayer company which in fact bore tax at the   **G**
standard rate so far as it will go and makes up the balance first with income
which has borne tax at the next highest rate and so on. Thus one first attributes
all the source (a) income—£24,678,862—to the management expenses of
£39,696,940, leaving some £15,000,000 to be made up from sources (b) and (c).
One splits up the source (b) income between the various companies which have
paid the dividends so as to find out the net United Kingdom rate of tax borne   **H**
in each case, which is the ceiling for any repayment of tax, and similarly, if
any part of the foreign income did not attract any relief but bore tax at the
full rate, one would separate that from the rest where the rate of tax was reduced
by the credit so as to allocate the £15,000,000 balance of management expenses
between source (b) and source (c) income in the manner most favourable to the
taxpayer companies.   **I**

I will not refer to the calculations placed by the Crown before the Special
Commissioners in detail, since the Crown concede that they do not give proper
effect to their own contentions as argued before me. But it is common ground
that the result of applying the principle for which the Crown contend will be
that, instead of the maximum repayable tax being exhausted by the tax on
the management expenses and there being a balance of tax on management

(4) (1925), 12 Tax Cas. 868.

A expenses which will be irrecoverable, the maximum repayable tax will be some-what greater than the total tax attributable to the management expenses.

In argument each side agreed to illustrate its contentions by reference to hypo-thetical round figures for income and tax and to disregard the complication introduced by the source (b)—s. 350—income. It may perhaps be useful to give these figures at this point. Assume (a) a gross income of £30,000 from

B United Kingdom dividends and a standard rate of tax of 8s. Assume (b) a gross foreign income of £120,000 which bears foreign tax of £30,000—i.e., at a rate of 5s. in the pound—so that the net receipt in this country is £90,000. Assume (c), management expenses of £60,000. On these figures the United Kingdom tax payable, apart from any relief for management expenses, would be £30,000 made up of: (i) £12,000 borne by deduction from the £30,000 gross United Kingdom

C dividends; and (iii) £18,000 paid by direct assessment on the income received from abroad. This figure is arrived at by grossing-up the foreign income to its original £120,000, charging that figure notionally to tax at 8s., which gives £48,000, and deducting from the £48,000 the £30,000 foreign tax paid.

Coming now to the claim for management expenses the taxpayer companies' contention was that the taxpayer would be entitled on those figures to repayment

D of tax at 8s. on the £60,000 expenses (i.e., £24,000), leaving himself to bear at the end of the day tax amounting to £6,000. On the other hand the Crown's con-tention on these figures was that the taxpayer was entitled to be repaid: (a) tax on £30,000 of the £60,000 management expenses at 8s. in the pound, that being the rate at which the United Kingdom dividends bore tax; and (b) tax on the balance of £30,000 management expenses at the rate at which the foreign receipts

E actually bore United Kingdom tax. There was some discussion before me whether this rate was 4s., which would result from relating the £18,000 tax paid to the figure of £90,000, or 3s., which would result from relating the £18,000 to £120,000. The provisions of Sch. 16 to the Income Tax Act 1952 are very com-plicated and the point was not fully argued so I do not propose to express any view on it. If one takes a 4s. rate, the amount repayable on the Crown's view

F would be £12,000 plus £6,000, making £18,000, which would leave £12,000 tax to be paid. If on the other hand one takes a 3s. rate the amount repayable would be £12,000 plus £4,500, making £16,500, leaving £13,500 tax to be paid. Either figure is, of course, larger than the £6,000 payable on the taxpayer companies' view.

The commissioners decided the case in favour of the taxpayer companies

G giving the following identical reasons in each case:

"We, the Commissioners who heard the appeal, were of opinion that the crux of the matter was the proper interpretation of the words ' the amount of the tax ' in subsection (1) of Section 425 of the Income Tax Act, 1952. It was common ground that those words could not mean literally tax levied on

H disbursements as such. As regards this question of interpretation, that Section refers earlier to the claimant being ' charged to tax by deduction or otherwise ', and it appeared to us that on the facts of the present case the tax there referred to should be taken to mean tax charged at the standard rate. As to the provisions of subsection (1A) of that Section—the carry-forward provisions first introduced in 1954 which were referred to in

I argument during the hearing—it did not appear to us that these provisions were of any assistance in relation to the problem before us. We noted, how-ever, that it would seem that on the basis contended for on behalf of the Inspector the words ' the amount of the tax ' must in relation to income taxed overseas mean one thing if at the time when a management expenses claim was made no tax credit had been claimed and another when tax credit had been allowed. Weighing the rival interpretations and the position generally, including the fact that there were provisions corresponding to Section 425 in Section 33 of the Income Tax Act, 1918, that is long before

A

1945 when provisions corresponding to Section 350 of the Income Tax Act, 1952, and the tax credit provisions were first enacted, we were of opinion that the [taxpayer companies'] contentions as to the proper interpretation of the words ' the amount of the tax ' in Section 425 were well founded. We therefore held that relief should be allowed on the basis envisaged in Schedule 1 annexed hereto and summarised in paragraph 5 above, and that the appeal succeeded in principle. We left figures to be agreed accordingly."

B

The comment that the Crown's argument led to one result if the management expenses claim is dealt with before any tax credit is allowed and another if it is dealt with after the allowance of tax credit seems to have resulted from a mis-understanding of the Crown's argument, for which, be it said, the inspector rather than the commissioners seems to have been to blame. But however that may be it was common ground before me that the section proceeds on the footing that all tax credits will have been allowed and indeed that the tax exigible apart from the management expenses claim will in theory have been paid before the management expenses claim is given effect to by a repayment of some of the tax paid.

C

The argument of the taxpayer companies is simple enough. The relief given to life assurance companies and investment companies was introduced fifty years ago (see the Income Tax Act 1918, s. 33), i.e., long before there was any double taxation relief. Companies were then liable for tax at a rate fixed annually (i.e., that which has been called the " standard rate " since 1927), without liability to increase through surtax or to decrease through allowances. When therefore s. 33 of the Act of 1918 spoke of the company having been " charged to tax " and gave it a right to have repaid to it a sum equal to the tax on a part of its income corresponding to the management expenses, it meant tax at the fixed or standard rate. The wording of the Act of 1918 was reproduced in 1952 without any change, although double taxation relief had by then been introduced, and there is no warrant for now construing the words " the amount of the tax on any sums disbursed as expenses of management " as meaning no longer tax at the standard rate but tax at the rate effectively applicable to the part of the income notionally attributable to the management expenses.

D

E

F

The Crown rested its case mainly on the broad ground that to spread the tax on the management expenses rateably over the whole of the income is more in accord with the wording of the section and with justice and common sense than to repay tax at the standard rate regardless of whether or not the whole income bore tax at that rate. But it also relied on several minor points which I should mention now. First it submitted that the relief afforded by the section was not necessarily confined to incorporated bodies since a life assurance company might in theory be an individual. This strikes me as a far-fetched argument. Next it referred to s. 181 of the Act of 1952 (which had its counterpart in earlier legisla-tion) which gives the lessor of mineral rights a right to claim repayment of tax on management expenses in substantially the same language as that used in s. 425. A lessor of mineral rights might plainly be an individual surtax payer and there was, so it was argued, no reason to limit the words " income tax " in that section to tax at the standard rate. That no doubt shows that a problem similar to the one which faces me may arise under s. 181. It does not itself solve the problem. Thirdly, reliance was placed on s. 425 (1A), introduced in 1954, but I cannot see that that subsection in itself helps the Crown, for it would obviously be wrong to allow the " carry forward " provisions to extend to a case where the sums disbursed were less than the income charged to tax and the shortfall arose because the tax on the expenses at the standard rate exceeded the maximum amount of tax repayable. It can, of course, be said that the fact that the taxpayer companies' construction can lead, and has led in this case, to such a result is an indication that it cannot be right, but that argument is not, I think, much assisted by the presence of sub-s. (1A).

G

H

I

The case as I see it really turns on the wording of s. 425 (1) itself and I am

A prepared to approach the section on the footing that it can only apply to incorporated bodies and to assume that prior to the introduction of double taxation relief the tax repaid would necessarily have been tax at the standard rate. But when the taxpayer company concerned is entitled to credit for foreign tax its income received from abroad is not in fact taxed at the standard rate but at a lower rate. The grossing-up of the sums received from abroad by the addition

B of the foreign tax paid, and the application to the gross sum of the standard rate of tax in order to obtain a figure against which credit is to be given for the foreign tax, are only steps in the ascertainment of the net United Kingdom rate at which the tax is finally paid. If the United Kingdom tax is in fact charged at different rates on different parts of this company's income why should one construe the words " the amount of the tax " in s. 425 as meaning inevitably and

C always tax at the standard rate? The section provides that the company is to be repaid so much of the tax paid by it as is equal to the tax paid on a part of its income charged to tax equal to the sums disbursed as expenses as though all such sums had in fact been paid out of income charged to tax. Apart from the application of the *Sterling* principle (5), the result, I would have thought, would be that one would find out the proportion which the part of the income

D on which tax was to be repaid bore to the total income charged with tax and would repay that proportion of the total tax paid. If, for example, the total income chargeable to tax is £1,000, of which £500 is charged at ten per cent., i.e., £50, and £500 is charged at five per cent., i.e., £25, and the expenses are £500 one would, apart from the application of the *Sterling* principle (5), repay half the £50 and half the £25. In my judgment therefore the decision of the commis-

E sioners was wrong and I shall remit the case to them for the figures to be worked out. This may, of course, involve argument as to what the effective rate of tax on the foreign income is.

On the footing that I decided, as I have, that the taxpayer companies' contention was wrong, I was asked by the parties to decide a point on the application of s. 350 (1) (*a*), which can be illustrated by an example. Suppose that: (a) the

F company's income charged to tax is £1,000 derived exclusively from dividends from a s. 350 company with a net United Kingdom rate of 4s.; (b) that the standard rate is 8s.; and (c) that the management expenses are £200. What repayment can be claimed? Although the United Kingdom tax actually paid by the s. 350 company was only £200, it will have deducted tax at 8s., i.e., £400, on payment of the dividend as directed by s. 350 (1), leaving a net dividend of £600.

G Apart from s. 350 (1) (*a*) the amount of tax which the company could reclaim under s. 425 in respect of the management expenses would be £80, for, as the management expenses were one-fifth of the income, the tax repayable would be one-fifth of the £400 tax paid. It was suggested on behalf of the taxpayer companies that, though s. 425 was subject to the limitations of s. 350, that would not prevent the company in question from reclaiming £80 since £80 is less than

H £200, the amount of the tax actually paid by the s. 350 company. On the other hand the Crown argued that the taxpayer companies in question could only recover £40. In my opinion the Crown is right. Section 350 does not say that no repayment should be allowed which exceeds the net United Kingdom tax paid but that no repayment shall be allowed at a rate in excess of the net United Kingdom rate. If one applies the net United Kingdom rate of 4s. to the

I management expenses of £200, one gets a figure of £40.

Appeals allowed.

Solicitors: *Solicitor of Inland Revenue; Allen & Overy* (for the first taxpayer company); *Linklaters & Paines* (for the second taxpayer company).

[*Reported by* F. A. AMIES, ESQ., *Barrister-at-Law.*]

---

(5) (1925), 12 Tax Cas. 868.

A

SOUTHERN ELECTRICITY BOARD *v.* COLLINS.

[QUEEN'S BENCH DIVISION (Lord Parker, C.J., Melford Stevenson and Willis, JJ.), May 1, 1969.]

Employment—Redundancy—Payment—Amount—Period of employment—Period of continuous employment—Transfer of employee—Transfer from electricity board to Central Electricity Generating Board—Boards not associated companies—" Absent from work "—National agreement providing for carrying over certain benefits on transfer—Whether continuous employment—Contracts of Employment Act 1963 (c. 49), Sch. 1, para. 5 (1) (c), para. 10A— *Redundancy Payments Act* 1965 (c. 62), s. 48 (4).

B

Electricity—Central Electricity Generating Board—Relationship with area electricity boards—Whether area electricity boards subsidiary companies— Companies Act 1948 (11 & 12 *Geo.* 6 *c.* 38), *s.* 154 (1)—*Redundancy Payments Act* 1965 (c. 62), *s.* 48 (4).

C

In 1951, the respondent was employed by the appellants, an area electricity board. Under a national agreement between employers and the trades unions, employees could be transferred between the various electricity boards (including the Central Electricity Generating Board) without loss of accrued rights relating to holiday entitlement, sick pay benefit or pension rights. In 1965 the respondent was transferred from the appellants to the Central Electricity Generating Board; he was given back his national insurance card and his P.45 form. In September 1965, after 6½ months, he returned to the employment of the appellants. In 1968 he was dismissed by the appellants on the grounds of redundancy. On the question whether redundancy payment should be made by reference to a period of continuous employment since 1951 or since September 1965,

D

E

Held: the period of continuous employment for the purposes of the Redundancy Payments Act 1965 was from September 1965, because—

(i) the continuity of the period from 1951 onwards was not preserved by para. 10A* of Sch. 1 to the Contracts of Employment Act 1963 since the appellants were not a subsidiary of the Central Electricity Generating Board by reason of s. 154 (1) of the Companies Act 1948 and accordingly were not associated companies within the definition of that expression contained in s. 48 (4)† of the Act of 1965 (which definition must be read as being exhaustive) (see p. 1168, letters G, H and I, and p. 1170, letter I, post); further,

F

G

(ii) the continuity of the period from 1951 onwards was not preserved by para. 5 (1) (c) of Sch. 1 to the Act of 1963 since (a) the respondent could not during the 6½ months be said to have been absent from work with the appellants, (b) nor could it be said when he left the appellants in 1965 that there was any intention that he should return, and (c) the national agreement provided for the preservation of accrued benefits but not that he was to be regarded as continuing, during the 6½ months absence, in the appellants' employment (see p. 1170, letters F, G and I, post).

H

Appeal allowed.

[As to the amount of a redundancy payment, see SUPPLEMENT to 38 HALSBURY'S LAWS (3rd Edn.), para. 808F.

For the Companies Act 1948, s. 154, see 5 HALSBURY'S STATUTES (3rd Edn.) 234.

I

For the Contracts of Employment Act 1963, Sch. 1, para. 10A (as added by s. 48 (7) of the Redundancy Payments Act 1965), see 45 HALSBURY'S STATUTES (2nd Edn.) 331; and for the Redundancy Payments Act 1965, s. 1, s. 48, see ibid., pp. 290, 330.]

---

* Paragraph 10A is set out at p. 1168, letter B, post.
† Section 48 (4) is set out at p. 1168, letter C, post.

A **Appeal.**

This was an appeal by the Southern Electricity Board from a decision of the Industrial Tribunal sitting at Southampton on 3rd October 1968 whereby the respondent, Peter Robert Collins, was awarded a redundancy payment for a period of 17 years under s. 1 (1) of the Redundancy Payments Act 1965. The facts are set out in the judgment of LORD PARKER, C.J.

B *J. Mitchell* for the appellants.

Neil Butter for the respondent.

LORD PARKER, C.J.: This is an appeal from a decision of the Industrial Tribunal given on 3rd October 1968 whereby the tribunal allowed an application by the respondent, a workman, for a redundancy payment.

C The short facts were that the respondent was employed by the appellants, the Southern Electricity Board as long ago as 9th July 1951, and he was dismissed by them on 21st June 1968. The contest before the tribunal centred largely on the question whether, although admittedly dismissed on that date, he was dismissed on account of redundancy. The tribunal found it by no means an easy case, the appellants maintaining that it was largely due to the respondent's

D health and inability to fulfil his function that he was dismissed, but they came down in favour of the respondent really on the basis that there being a presumption that the dismissal is due to redundancy, the appellants had not rebutted that presumption.

There is no appeal against that part of the decision, but having arrived at that decision it became necessary for the tribunal to calculate the quantum of the

E redundancy payment. The respondent maintained that it should be calculated on the basis of employment from 9th July 1951 until 21st June 1968. The appellants, however, maintained that there had been a break in the continuity of employment in that from 22nd February to 13th September 1965, some 6½ months, he had, to use a neutral term, been transferred from the appellants to the Central Electricity Generating Board, and at the end of that 6½ months,

F had come back to the appellants.

In regard to that part of the decision the tribunal said:

"We have considered the possibility as to whether this change in employment could be considered a break within the meaning of the term as used in Schedule 1 of the Contracts of Employment Act 1963, but we have come to the conclusion that since the [appellants] and the Central Electricity

G Generating Board are both Government Corporations, and that when an employee is transferred from one to the other certain benefits go with him, and also since the whole of the finances of such Corporations are in Government control, we think that the same principle should apply as between associated limited companies, for which provision is made by the Redundancy Payments Act 1965. We therefore hold that the [respondent] had continuous

H service from the 9th July 1951 until his final dismissal which was the cause of this application."

It is necessary to remind oneself a little of the legislation here in question. Section 1 (1) of the Redundancy Payments Act 1965 provides that the amount of a redundancy payment shall be calculated in accordance with Sch. 1 to that

I Act. When one goes to Sch. 1 to that Act, one finds that one is in turn referred to Sch. 1 to the Contracts of Employment Act 1963 to arrive at that element of the calculation which concerns continuous employment. Paragraph 10 of Sch. 1 provides that:

"Subject to this paragraph [and I would add, and paragraph 10A, which is inserted by amendment through the Redundancy Payments Act 1965] the foregoing provisions of this Schedule relate only to employment by the one employer."

Paragraph 10A, which as I have said is added by the Act of 1965, indeed by s. 48 **A**
(7) of that Act, provides:

> " (1) Where an employee of a company is taken into the employment of
> another company which, at the time when he is taken into its employment,
> is an associated company of the first-mentioned company, his period of
> employment at that time shall count as a period of employment with the
> associated company, and the change of employer shall not break the **B**
> continuity of the period of employment. (2) In this paragraph ' company '
> and ' associated company ' have the meanings assigned to them by section
> 48 of the Redundancy Payments Act 1965."

Accordingly one looks back at s. 48 (4) and (5) to see what is meant by
" company ", and by " associated company ":   **C**

> " (4) For the purposes of this section two companies shall be taken to be
> associated companies if one is a subsidiary of the other, or both are sub-
> sidiaries of a third company, and ' associated company ' shall be construed
> accordingly.
> " (5) In this section ' company ' includes any body corporate, and **D**
> ' subsidiary ', except in relation to the bodies specified in the next following
> subsection, [which are quite immaterial for this purpose] has the same
> meaning as, by virtue of section 154 of the Companies Act 1948, it has for
> the purposes of that Act."

By s. 154 of the Companies Act 1948 a company shall be deemed to be the subsidiary of another if, but only if, one of two conditions are complied with. The **E**
first is that the other is a member of it and controls the composition of its board
of directors, and by sub-s. (2):

> " For the purposes of the foregoing subsection, the composition of a com-
> pany's board of directors shall be deemed to be controlled by another
> company if, but only if, that other company by the exercise of some power
> exercisable by it without the consent or concurrence of any other person **F**
> can appoint or remove the holders of all or a majority of the director-
> ships . . ."

That condition is clearly not complied with since the appointment of directors
in the case of each of those corporate bodies which are deemed for this purpose
to be companies, namely the appellants and the Central Electricity Generating **G**
Board, can only be done by the Minister; true he has to consult the directors,
but the directors in neither case can appoint themselves but only the Minister
can do so after consulting them.

The second condition which may enable it to be said that these were subsidiaries was if one holds more than half the nominal value of its equity share
capital; again it is quite clear in regard to these corporations that there is no **H**
equity capital. It follows, therefore, that these two corporate bodies could not be
said to be associated companies. Having said that, it is only right to say that
the tribunal did not find that they were. To repeat the words in its decision,
it said: " We think that the same principle should apply as between associated
limited companies."

Counsel for the respondent has suggested that the definition in s. 48 (4) of the **I**
Redundancy Payments Act 1965 should not be read as an exhaustive definition,
and he stresses the words there that " For the purposes of this section two
companies shall be taken to be associated companies if . . .". He says that is
not exhaustive and looked at quite generally and bearing in mind the possible
mischief that would result from a different interpretation, yet these two corporate
bodies are associated companies albeit not by reason of the last words of that
subsection. For my part I find it quite impossible to read sub-s. (4), and indeed
para. 10A (2) of Sch. 1 to the Act of 1963, as being anything but exhaustive.

A That, however, is not an end of the matter, because the tribunal did refer to the fact, although quite generally, that when an employee is transferred from one to the other, certain benefits go with him. Counsel for the appellants, has very rightly drawn our attention to the fact that there is a national agreement in force which was not produced to the tribunal, probably because the respondent was appearing in person. It looks as if the tribunal, or one of its members, had

B this in mind, because he questioned the respondent and got the answer that pensions were transferable, terms of service would remain the same, it was a transfer which preserved various benefits. Accordingly, we have thought it right to look at the agreement in question, which is an agreement relating to terms and conditions of employment of manual workers in the service of the electricity boards, and an agreement relating to the negotiating machinery. It is made

C between the electricity boards and the trade unions in question.

In the first part, Part 1 of that national agreement, it is provided that for the purposes of the agreement " ' Board ' means the Electricity Council, the Central Electricity Generating Board, an Area Board "—so all these two bodies with which we are concerned today are in that agreement each treated as a board. Then it goes on to provide that: " Continuous Service " in the agreement—

D
> " means the aggregate of all service with a Board or their predecessors . . . provided that there has been no break of more than six months in any such service."

It is on the basis of that continuous service that various benefits are calculated. If, for instance, one turns to Part 4 dealing with holidays, one finds that the

E word:
> " ' qualified ' in relation to either a day worker or a shift worker means an employee who on the first day of April in any year has completed ten calendar months' continuous service with a Board."

Again under the same Part 4 it is provided that:

F
> " A qualified day worker shall be allowed an annual holiday of two consecutive weeks with pay at his normal weekly wage during the holiday period. In addition he shall be allowed an additional day's holiday with pay in the year ending 31st March following the completion of seven years' continuous service in the industry."

Then again in the supplement to the agreement dealing with sick pay benefit,

G there is provision for calculation according to the period of continuous service as defined in that agreement.

Again, although the court has not seen it, there is a pensions scheme which treats all service with any of these bodies defined as a board as continuous, and an employee cannot get his contributions back if he so desires until he has severed his connection entirely with what I can put generally as the electricity

H board. It is quite clear, therefore, that by an agreement between employers and unions, employment by any member of these authorities is to be treated as continuous, and as he is transferred from one board to another, he, the employee, takes with him what one might call all his accrued benefits.

To go back to Sch. 1 to the Contracts of Employment Act 1963, it is provided in para. 2 that:

I
> " Except so far as otherwise provided by the following provisions of this Schedule, any week which does not count under paragraphs 3 to 6 of this Schedule breaks the continuity of the period of employment."

Paragraphs 3, 4 and 6 have no relevance for this purpose, and that leaves para. 5. Paragraph 5 has a heading: " Periods in which there is no contract of employment ", that means the employer who is being asked to pay the redundancy payment. It provides:
> " (1) If in any week the employee is, for the whole or part of the week—(*a*)

A

incapable of work in consequence of sickness or injury, or (*b*) absent from work on account of a temporary cessation of work, or (*c*) absent from work in circumstances such that, by arrangement or custom, he is regarded as continuing in the employment of his employer for all or any purposes, that week shall, notwithstanding that it does not fall under paragraph 3 or paragraph 4 of this Schedule, count . . ."

B

There is no question of the respondent having been away in consequence of sickness or " absent from work on account of a temporary cessation of work ". Accordingly he can only succeed if he can bring himself within para. (*c*) and these are the important words for the purposes of this case—

" absent from work in circumstances such that, by arrangement or custom, he is regarded as continuing in the employment of his employer for all or any purposes . . ."

C

This, as I have said, is not a matter which the tribunal have considered, but this court has been invited to deal with it, and as it is a pure matter of construction and does not depend on fact, the court has thought it right to deal with it. This is a case where the contract of employment with the appellants did come to an end in 1965; the evidence shows that the respondent's cards were handed back and the form P.45 was handed over. The question is only this: whether the national agreement applies so that the respondent's 6½ months' absence from work with the appellants was such that, to use the words of the paragraph, he was regarded as continuing in the employment of his employers for all or any purposes; he clearly was not so regarded for all purposes.

D

Counsel for the respondent invites us to say that he was regarded as continuing in the employment for some purposes. This is a case where all my sympathy is for the respondent, and it seems to me that if one had any option in the matter one would not hesitate in finding that this 6½ months in this long period of service had not broken the continuity of employment. But as a matter of construction I find it quite impossible myself to say that para. 5 (1) (*c*) applies. In the first place it is difficult to consider the respondent at any stage as being absent from work. Absent from work, are words, one would think, to denote something quite different, some temporary absence. Secondly I find it impossible to say that there was any intention here that he should ever come back. It seems to me that para. 5 (1) (*c*) is contemplating the sort of case where an employer lends an employee to another man for a short period, the understanding and the intention being that he would return to work for the first employer; and thirdly and perhaps most important, I cannot read the national agreement as an arrangement whereby the respondent is to be regarded as continuing in the employment of the appellants. When he went to the Central Electricity Generating Board, the national agreement did not provide that he was to be treated as continuing in the employment of the appellants; what it was doing was saying: you are employed by the Central Electricity Generating Board, but you will carry with you to the Central Electricity Generating Board what I will call loosely your accrued benefits.

E

F

G

H

Accordingly, as it seems to me, this perhaps rather unfortunate respondent cannot bring himself under the provisions of para. 5 (1) (*c*) or para. 10A of Sch. 1 to the Act of 1963, and accordingly for the purposes of calculating redundancy period, the period of service must be confined to the last period, that is from 13th September 1965 to the date of dismissal, 21st June 1968.

I

MELFORD STEVENSON, J.: I agree.

WILLIS, J.: I agree.

Appeal allowed.

Solicitors: *F. W. W. Kempton*, Maidenhead (for the appellants); *Official Solicitor*.

[*Reported by* JACQUELINE CHARLES, *Barrister-at-Law*.]

A

SOLESBURY *v.* PUGH.

[Queen's Bench Division (Lord Parker, C.J., Melford Stevenson and Willis, JJ.), April 29, 1969.]

B
Road Traffic—Driving with blood-alcohol proportion above prescribed limit— Evidence—Provision of specimen—Specimen of blood—Site from which specimen to be taken—Selection of site by doctor—Road Safety Act 1967 (c. 30), s. 3 (3).

Road Traffic—Driving with blood-alcohol proportion above prescribed limit— Evidence—Failure to provide specimen—Specimen of blood—Refusal to supply specimen from site selected by doctor—" Reasonable excuse "— Road Safety Act 1967 (c. 30), s. 3 (3).

C
By s. 3 (3) of the Road Safety Act 1967, a person who, without reasonable excuse, fails to provide a specimen for a laboratory test in pursuance of a requirement imposed under s. 3 of that Act is guilty of an offence. In relation to a specimen of blood, the word " requirement " in s. 3 (3) relates to a requirement by a doctor exercising his medical skill and experience as to the site from which the blood is to be abstracted (see p. 1172, letter I,

D
and p. 1173, letter A, post).

Per Curiam: if a man had an infection in his arm or a plaster on his arm or something of that sort, that would be a reasonable excuse within s. 3 (3) for declining to comply with a requirement that a specimen be taken from the arm (see p. 1172, letter I, and p. 1173, letter A, post).

Appeal allowed.

E
[As to failure to provide a specimen of blood for a laboratory test, see Supplement to 33 Halsbury's Laws (3rd Edn.), para. 1061A, 3.

For the Road Safety Act 1967, s. 3, see 47 Halsbury's Statutes (2nd Edn.) 1558.]

Case Stated.

F
This was a Case Stated by the justices for the county of Buckingham acting in and for the petty sessional division of Burnham in respect of their adjudication as a magistrates' court sitting at Beaconsfield on 17th September 1968.

An information was preferred by the appellant, Jonathan Solesbury, against the respondent, David Colvin Pugh, charging him with failing, without reasonable excuse, to provide a specimen of blood or urine for a laboratory test contrary

G
to s. 3 (3) of the Road Safety Act 1967.

Before the justices, the respondent pleaded not guilty to the charge, and they heard the evidence on behalf of the prosecution. The respondent did not give evidence nor did he call any witnesses. A submission of no case to answer was made on his behalf at the close of the prosecution case. The justices upheld the submission and dismissed the charge. The facts found by the

H
justices are set out in the judgment of Melford Stevenson, J., at p. 1172, letter A, to letter F, post.

The justices came to the conclusion that there was no evidence that the respondent had failed to provide a specimen, and accordingly they dismissed the charge. The appellant now appealed.

M. C. B. West for the appellant.

I
G. D. Flather for the respondent.

MELFORD STEVENSON, J., delivered the first judgment at the invitation of Lord Parker, C.J.: This is a prosecutor's appeal by way of Case Stated against the dismissal of a complaint by the justices for the petty sessional division of Burnham in Buckinghamshire in respect of their adjudication at Beaconsfield on 17th September 1968, when the respondent, Mr. David Colvin Pugh, appeared before them charged with the following offence: failing, without reasonable excuse, to provide a specimen of blood or urine for a laboratory test; that is

the offence for which provision is made by s. 3 (3) of the Road Safety Act 1967. **A**
To that charge the respondent pleaded not guilty, and the justices found the
following facts: on 31st August at 12.05 a.m. the respondent was driving his
motor car at Chalfont St. Peter with no rear lights, and the appellant, a police
constable, suspecting that he was committing a traffic offence while his vehicle
was in motion, stopped the car and requested the respondent to supply a specimen
of breath. This the respondent refused, and the constable, having reasonable **B**
cause to suspect that he had alcohol in his body, arrested him and conveyed him
to the Gerrards Cross police station, where he was again asked for a specimen
of breath and he again refused. At 12.50 a.m. a police sergeant asked the
respondent to provide a specimen of blood or urine for a laboratory test, and
warned him that failure to provide that specimen might make him liable to
various penalties. The sergeant also told the respondent that a doctor would **C**
attend if he chose to supply a specimen of blood. The respondent's answer to
that was: " From my toe." A Dr. Keeble was then telephoned and the respondent was told that the doctor would require to take the blood specimen from the
respondent's arm. To that the respondent said " Bring the doctor ", and at
1.0 a.m. the doctor arrived and he asked the respondent to roll up his sleeve
so that a blood specimen could be taken from his arm. The respondent refused **D**
to do this, but said he would allow a blood specimen to be taken only from his
big toe, and although the requests were repeated by the doctor, the respondent
maintained this attitude. The doctor declined to take a specimen from the
respondent's big toe, and left the police station. The respondent did not supply
a specimen of urine although asked to do so on two occasions, and was warned
of the consequences. **E**

There is a finding in the Case that the usual method of obtaining a blood specimen is to take the blood from a vein in the person's arm, and that this method
is the least painful and gives rise to the least chance of infection, and further that
it is not normal medical practice to obtain a blood sample from a person's toe,
because it is a method which involves a substantially greater risk of infection
than does the normal method. **F**

There is no doubt that there was in this case in the first place the requirement
by a police constable to provide a specimen of blood or urine as contemplated
by s. 3 (1) of the Road Safety Act 1967. It is equally plain from other provisions
of the Act, and indeed as a matter of common sense, that a specimen of blood
can only be taken by a medical practitioner. The question which I think presents
itself in this case is: what is the proper interpretation of the word **G**
" requirement " as it appears in s. 3 (3), which is in these terms:

> " A person who, without reasonable excuse, fails to provide a specimen
> for a laboratory test in pursuance of a requirement imposed under this section
> shall be guilty of an offence . . ."

The requirement so far as it relates to a specimen of blood must, on any sensible **H**
view of the language of this section, as I think, mean a specimen of blood to be
abstracted by a doctor. A specimen of blood so taken must be taken by a means
and in a way which gives the doctor the right to exercise his instructed professional
discretion as to the site on the body from which the blood is to be taken. The
words " without reasonable excuse" do not, I think, give rise to any difficulty.
If the man had an infection in his arm, a plaster on his arm or something of that **I**
sort, that would no doubt be a reasonable excuse for declining to comply with
the requirement that a specimen should be taken from the arm. There was no
such reason in this case, and in my view that word " requirement " in sub-s. (3)
must relate to a requirement by a doctor exercising his medical skill and experience as to the site from which the blood is abstracted. If that is a correct
view, it follows that the refusal by the respondent to permit the taking of any
blood from his body otherwise than from his big toe was an unreasonable refusal

A and the justices should have convicted on this charge. I would therefore remit this case to the justices with a direction to convict.

WILLIS, J.: I agree.

LORD PARKER, C.J.: I also agree.

Appeal allowed. Case remitted.

B Solicitors: *Sharpe, Pritchard & Co.*, agents for *J. Malcolm Simons*, Kidlington (for the appellant); *Willmett & Co.*, Slough (for the respondent).

[*Reported by* N. P. Metcalfe, Esq., *Barrister-at-Law*.]

Re GULBENKIAN'S SETTLEMENT TRUSTS (No. 2).
C ## STEPHENS AND ANOTHER v. MAUN AND OTHERS.

[Chancery Division (Plowman, J.), May 16, 19, 22, 1969.]

Settlement—Discretionary trust—Power of trustees—Trustees' discretion to pay income of trust fund to named object—Object's release of interests under settlement for valuable consideration—Effect of release on trustees' discretion—
D *Whether competent to trustees to exercise discretion in favour of object.*

Trust and Trustee—Discretionary trust—Income trust—Doubts as to validity of discretionary power—Non-payment of income pending decision on validity —Whether postponement reasonable—Whether discretion exercisable retrospectively.

A settlement dated 31st May 1929 provided by cl. 2 (i) that the trustees
E " shall during the life of [N.S.G., the settlor's son] at their absolute discretion pay all or any part of the income of [the trust fund] to or apply the same for the maintenance and personal support or benefit of all or any one or more . . . of the following persons, namely [N.S.G.] and any wife and his children or remoter issue . . . and any person or persons in whose house or apartments or in whose company or under whose care or control or by or with
F whom [N.S.G.] may from time to time be employed or residing . . ." Then followed a gift of the income, subject to " the discretionary trust or power." thereinbefore contained. Clause 6 conferred on N.S.G. a general testamentary power of appointment over the trust fund in default of a child of his attaining a vested interest. A second settlement dated 18th July 1938 contained provisions which, so far as material, were similar to those contained in
G cl. 2 (i) of the settlement of 1929. The proper law of both settlements was English law. The settlor died in 1955 domiciled in Portugal. Under his father's will, N.S.G. became entitled, inter alia, to an annuity of $135,000, but it was provided that he must bring into account against that figure, the income paid to him under the settlements. Proceedings relating to the settlor's estate which had been instituted in 1957 in Lisbon by his Portuguese legal personal
H representatives and by the G. Foundation, the sole residuary legatee, against N.S.G. and his wife, were compromised by a deed (" the Lisbon agreement ") dated 12th February 1958 and approved by the court in Lisbon on 15th March 1958. One of the objects of the Lisbon agreement was to substitute for the liability of the settlor's estate to provide the annuity, a liability to provide a capital sum of some $3·4 million payable at such times and in such manner
I that it would be capital and not income in N.S.G.'s hands. By cl. 12 of the Lisbon agreement, N.S.G. and his wife renounced for valuable consideration, their interests under both settlements. N.S.G. had no issue and was unlikely to have any. The trustees exercised their discretion by paying the income of the settled land to N.S.G. until April 1957 when they learned of the decision in *Re Gresham's Settlement**. In July 1961 one of the trustees issued an originating summons raising, inter alia, the question of the validity of cl. 2 (i) of the settlement of 1929, and, finally, on 31st October 1968, the House of Lords

---
* [1956] 2 All E.R. 193.

upheld the decision of the Court of Appeal overruling *Re Gresham's Settlement**   A
and held that the provisions of cl. 2 (i) of the settlement of 1929 were valid.
By that time the trustees had accumulated income in excess of £50,000. The
present trustees now sought the directions of the court as to whether they had
power to exercise their discretion retrospectively in respect of the accumulated income and, if so, whether and how far the discretion still existed in the
light of the Lisbon agreement. It was not disputed that cl. 12 of the   B
agreement operated as a release of the general testamentary power of
appointment conferred on N.S.G. by cl. 6 of the settlement of 1929 in default
of a child of his attaining a vested interest, with the result that, subject to the
discretionary trust and to the birth of issue, the fund belonged to the
residuary legatee.

Held: (i) as a man could not be compelled to accept a gift, so there was   C
no reason why he should not be equally free to refuse to accept the exercise
of a power which the donor had conferred on trustees to make a gift in his
favour, the reasoning which applied to a direct benefit such as a power to
pay money to the object of the power applied equally to an indirect benefit
such as a power to apply the money for his benefit instead of paying it to him,
and, therefore, as from the date of the Lisbon agreement, N.S.G. and his   D
wife ceased to be objects of the discretionary trust and, consequently, from
that date, it was no longer competent for the trustees to exercise their
discretion in favour of N.S.G. and his wife either directly or indirectly (see
p. 1179, letters G to I, post).

(ii) as to the other objects of the power, the trustees' discretion was still
exercisable, because although it was the duty of the trustees to exercise   E
their discretion within a reasonable time after the receipt by them of the
income, there might be special circumstances justifying a postponement and
here, the trustees had deliberately refrained from exercising their discretion
after April 1957 until the doubts as to the validity of cl. 2 (i) of the settlement
had been resolved by the House of Lord's decision in October 1968 and
thereafter, until the court's decision on the present proceedings (see p. 1180,   F
letters C and E, post).

[As to trustees' discretion as to exercise of a power, see 38 HALSBURY'S LAWS
(3rd Edn.) 980, 981, para. 1696; and for cases on the subject, see 47 DIGEST
(Repl.) 377-385, *3377-3438*; as to disclaimer, see 39 HALSBURY'S LAWS (3rd
Edn.) 932, 933, para. 1409, and for cases on the subject, see 48 DIGEST (Repl.)
252, 253, *2262-2276*.]   G

Cases referred to:
Allen-Meyrick's Will Trusts, Re, Mangnall v. *Allen-Meyrick*, [1966] 1 All E.R.
    740; [1966] 1 W.L.R. 499; Digest (Cont. Vol. B) 733, *3435*.
Coleman, Re, Henry v. *Strong* (1888), 39 Ch.D. 443; 58 L.J.Ch. 226; 60 L.T.
    127; 49 Digest (Repl.) 1034, *9667*.
Gourju's Will Trusts, Re, Starling v. *Custodian of Enemy Property*, [1942]   H
    2 All E.R. 605; [1943] Ch. 24; 112 L.J.Ch. 75; 168 L.T. 1; 2 Digest
    (Repl.) 239, *418*.
Gresham's Settlement, Re, Lloyds Bank, Ltd. v. *Gresham*, [1956] 2 All E.R. 193;
    [1956] 1 W.L.R. 573; 37 Digest (Repl.) 404, *1331*.
Nelson, Re, Norris v. *Nelson* (1918), [1928] Ch. 920, n.; 97 L.J.Ch. 443, n.;
    140 L.T. 371, n.; 48 Digest (Repl.) 306, *2674*.   I
Smith, Re, Public Trustee v. *Aspinall*, [1928] Ch. 915; [1928] All E.R. Rep.
    520; 97 L.J.Ch. 441; 140 L.T. 369; 49 Digest (Repl.) 893, *8359*.
Stratton's Deed of Disclaimer, Re, Stratton v. *Inland Revenue Comrs.*, [1957]
    2 All E.R. 594; [1958] Ch. 42; [1957] 3 W.L.R. 199; 21 Digest (Repl.)
    15, *49*.
Thompson v. *Leach* (1690), 2 Vent. 198; 86 E.R. 391; *on appeal* (1692), 2
    Vent. 208; 25 Digest (Repl.) 569, *144*.

* [1956] 2 All E.R. 193.

A   *Townson* v. *Tickell* (1819), 3 B. & Ald. 31; [1814-23] All E.R. Rep. 164; 106
        E.R. 575; 48 Digest (Repl.) 252, *2262*.

    Wise, Re, Jackson v. *Parrott*, [1896] 1 Ch. 281; 65 L.J.Ch. 281; 73 L.T. 743;
        37 Digest (Repl.) 80, *197*.

Adjourned Summonses.

These were two originating summonses dated 26th July 1961, in respect of
B two settlements dated 31st May 1929 and 18th July 1938, issued by the plaintiffs,
John Phillimore Stephens and Ralph Vickers, by order to carry on dated 23rd
April 1969. The plaintiffs were the present trustees of the two settlements which
had been made between the late Calouste Sarkis Gulbenkian, who died domiciled
in Portugal in 1955, and others. Question 1 of the first summons raising the
question of the validity of the provisions of cl. 2 (i) of the settlement of 1929
C for the payment or application of the income of the trust fund during the life of
the defendant, Nubar Sarkis Gulbenkian, the settlor's son, came before GOFF, J.,
in November 1966, who, following the decision of *Re Gresham's Settlement**
declared the trusts to be void for uncertainty. The Court of Appeal in June 1967
as reported [1967] 3 All E.R. 15, overruled *Re Gresham's Settlement** and allowed
the appeal, declaring that the trusts were not void for uncertainty or otherwise.
D A further appeal to the House of Lords as reported [1968] 3 All E.R. 785 was
dismissed on 31st October 1968. As a result of the decision of the House of Lords,
the originating summons was restored for the determination of further questions
which did not arise if the cl. 2 (i) trusts were void.

Question 2 (A) of the originating summons asked that if the provisions (i.e.,
in cl. 2 (i)) were valid: (i) whether it was now competent to the trustees to
E exercise the power conferred on them by cl. 2 (i) of the settlement in respect of
income received by them, (a) between April 1957 and 12th February 1958 (the
date of the Lisbon agreement, by cl. 12 of which the second and fifth defendants,
Nubar Sarkis Gulbenkian and his wife Marie Berthe Edmée Gulbenkian agreed
to renounce their interests under the settlements of 1929 and 1938), (b) between
12th February 1958 and 26th July 1961, (c) between 26th July 1961 and 31st
F October 1968 and retained pending the decision as to the validity of the power or
whether some and if so which parts of such income were no longer subject to the
power but held on a resulting trust for the personal representatives of the settlor;
(ii) whether as regards income received or to be received by the trustees after
12th February 1958 which still remained or was subject to the said power the
trustees could properly, (a) pay the same to Nubar Sarkis Gulbenkian, (b) apply
G the same for his benefit, (c) pay the same to or apply the same for the benefit
of any other person being an object of the said power notwithstanding the
terms of the judgment dated 15th March 1958 of the Second Section of the Second
Civil Court of the District of Lisbon, and the deed dated 12th February 1958
therein referred to. Under the second settlement of 18th July 1938 (the subject
of the second summons) during the lifetime of Nubar Sarkis Gulbenkian, the
H income was to be held on trusts similar to those contained in cl. 2 (i), with a
slight omission. It was common ground that the answers to the questions
raised by the second summons would be determined by the answers to the
first. The defendants were (i) John Henry Alfred Alexander Maun, (ii) Nubar
Sarkis Gulbenkian, (iii) Sir Charles Percival Law Wishaw, (iv) George Thomas
Clark, (v) Marie Berthe Edmée Gulbenkian, (vi) Richard James Wilson McLay,
I (vii) Walter Kofler, (viii) Manoel Gonzalez, and (ix) Charles Giraud. The
parties were the same in both summonses except that the fifth defendant was
not a party to the second summons. The facts are set out in the judgment.

The cases noted below† were cited during the argument in addition to those
referred to in the judgment.

---

* [1956] 2 All E.R. 193.

† *Gisborne* v. *Gisborne* (1877), 2 App. Cas. 300; *Re Bullock* (1891), 60 L.J.Ch. 341;
Re Ashby, Ex p. Wreford, [1892] 1 Q.B. 872; *Goodier* v. *Edmunds* (1893), 62 L.J.Ch. 649;
Re Fry, [1943] Ch. 35; *Re Pilkington's Will Trusts*, [1962] 3 All E.R. 622; [1964] A.C.
612.

A

E. W. Griffith for the plaintiffs.

Peter Foster, Q.C., and *H. Hillaby* for the second, fifth and ninth defendants.

S. W. Templeman, Q.C., and *R. Cozens-Hardy Horne* for the third and fourth defendants, who were the English personal representatives of the settlor, the late Calouste Sarkis Gulbenkian.

Proceedings were stayed against the first, sixth, seventh and eighth defendants.

Cur. adv. vult.

B

22nd May. **PLOWMAN, J.,** read the following judgment: There are two originating summonses before me, the first relating to a settlement made by the late Calouste Sarkis Gulbenkian in 1929, and the second relating to a settlement which he made in 1938. There are no material differences between the two cases and it is common ground that the answers to the questions raised by the second summons will be determined by the answers to the questions raised by the first. I propose, therefore, to confine my observations to the matters arising on that summons.

C

The settlement of 1929 is dated 31st May 1929. It is a settlement of certain shares which was made by Mr. Calouste Sarkis Gulbenkian in consideration of his natural love and affection for his son Mr. Nubar Sarkis Gulbenkian. Clause 2 of the settlement of 1929 provided as follows:

D

" (i) The trustees shall during the life of the said Nubar Sarkis Gulbenkian at their absolute discretion pay all or any part of the income of the property hereby settled and the investments for the time being representing the same (hereinafter called the Trust Fund) to or apply the same for the maintenance and personal support or benefit of all or any one or more to the exclusion of the other or others of the following persons namely the said Nubar Sarkis Gulbenkian and any wife and his children or remoter issue for the time being in existence whether minors or adults and any person or persons in whose house or apartments or in whose company or under whose care or control or by or with whom the said Nubar Sarkis Gulbenkian may from time to time be employed or residing and the other persons or person other than the Settlor for the time being entitled or interested whether absolutely contingently or otherwise to or in the trust fund under the trusts herein contained to take effect after the death of the said Nubar Sarkis Gulbenkian in such proportions and manner as the Trustees shall in their absolute discretion at any time or times think proper.

E

F

" (ii) Subject to the discretionary trust or powers hereinbefore contained the Trustees shall during the life of the said Nubar Sarkis Gulbenkian hold the said income or so much thereof as shall not be paid or applied under such discretionary trust or power upon the trusts and for the purposes and for which the said income would for the time being be held if the said Nubar Sarkis Gulbenkian were then dead."

G

Clauses 3, 4 and 5 declared certain trusts after the death of Mr. Gulbenkian for his issue as therein defined. Mr. Gulbenkian is still living but at the present time he has no issue and is unlikely to have any.

H

Clause 6 of the settlement provided:

" If there shall be no child of the said Nubar Sarkis Gulbenkian who being male shall attain the age of twenty one years or being female shall attain that age or marry then subject to the trusts powers and provisions hereinbefore declared and contained and to the powers by law vested in the Trustees and to every exercise of such respective powers the Trustees shall stand possessed of the trust fund in trust for the Settlor absolutely and if he shall be then dead in trust for such person or persons as the said Nubar Sarkis Gulbenkian shall by Will or Codicil appoint."

I

The proper law of that settlement is the law of England. On 26th July 1961, one of the trustees of the settlement issued an originating summons raising, inter

A alia, the question of the validity of the provisions in cl. 2 (i) of the settlement, for
the payment or application of the income of the trust fund during the life of
Mr. Gulbenkian. The originating summons came before GOFF, J., on 4th
November 1966, and he declared that the trusts were void for uncertainty. In so
declaring GOFF, J., was merely following the decision of HARMAN, J., in *Re
Gresham's Settlement, Lloyds Bank, Ltd.* v. *Gresham* (1), on a discretionary trust
B which was in all material respects identical with that in cl. 2 (i).

The matter then went to the Court of Appeal (2) which, in June 1967, overruled
Re Gresham's Settlement (1) and allowed the appeal declaring that the trusts were
not void for uncertainty or otherwise. A further appeal to the House of Lords
followed but was dismissed on 31st October 1968 (3).

As a result of the decision in the House of Lords (3) the originating summons
C has now been restored for the determination of certain questions which did not
arise if the cl. 2 (i) trusts were void. To explain the relevance of these questions
I must state certain further facts. Before the trustees learned of the decision in
Re Gresham's Settlement (1) they had exercised their discretion by paying the
income of the trust fund to Mr. Gulbenkian. When, however, they learned of that
decision they realised that cl. 2 (i) might well be void and they therefore stopped
D distributing the income and retained it pending the solution of this doubt. By
the time the House of Lords (3) had pronounced on the validity of the trust
they had accumulated income in excess of £50,000. They now ask the court how
their discretion stands in relation to that money.

Question 2 (A) of the originating summons is in this form:

E " If the said provisions [that is to say the provisions of cl. 2 (i)] are valid:
(i) Whether it is now competent to the Trustees to exercise the power conferred on them by Clause 2 (i) of the said Settlement in respect of income
received by them (a) between April 1957 and 12th February 1958, (b) between
12th February 1958 and 26th July 1961 (c) between 26th July 1961 and 31st
October 1968 and retained pending a decision as to the validity of the said
F power or whether some and if so which parts of such income are no longer
subject to the said power but held upon a resulting trust for the personal
representatives of the Settlor (ii) Whether as regards income received or to be
received by the Trustees after the 12th February 1958 which still remains or is
subject to the said power the Trustees can properly: (a) pay the same to the
said Nubar Sarkis Gulbenkian (b) apply the same for his benefit (c) pay the
G same to or apply the same for the benefit of any other person being an object
of the said power notwithstanding the terms of a Judgment dated the 15th
March 1958 of the Civil Tribunal of the District of Lisbon, Second Court,
Second Section and the Deed dated the 12th February 1958 therein referred
to."

The significance of the dates referred to in that question is as follows: April 1957
H is the time when the trustees first learned of the decision in *Re Gresham's Settlement* (1) and therefore held up distribution. 12th February 1958 is the date of
the deed referred to in the question. During the hearing that deed has been
referred to as the Lisbon agreement. 26th July 1961 is the date of the originating
summons and 31st October 1968 is the date when the House of Lords pronounced
on question 1.

I Question 2 (A) which I have just read raises two issues: one, whether the
trustees have power to exercise their discretion retrospectively and if so, two,
whether they can properly do so in the circumstances of this case. The second
issue itself involves the consideration of two matters, first, whether and how far
the discretion still exists in the light of the Lisbon agreement and, secondly,

(1) [1956] 2 All E.R. 193; [1956] 1 W.L.R. 573.
(2) [1967] 3 All E.R. 15; [1968] Ch. 126.
(3) [1968] 3 All E.R. 785; [1968] 3 W.L.R. 1127.

if and insofar as it does whether the trustees would be justified in exercising it in A the circumstances of this case.

As to this last point, until the second day of the hearing before me the trustees had not formally surrendered their discretion, if any, to the court, but they then expressed the wish to do so in respect of all income in hand. Counsel for the second, fifth and ninth defendants then stated that he might desire to file further evidence and I said that I would stand over the question of the propriety of any exercise B of the discretion so far as it still existed to be heard in chambers at a later date.

I come back then to the question of the effect of the Lisbon agreement on the trustees' discretion. The circumstances in which that agreement came into being were these: in 1957 proceedings in relation to the estate of the late Calouste Gulbenkian were instituted in Lisbon by his Portuguese legal personal representatives and by the Gulbenkian Foundation which is the sole residuary legatee C under his will. Those proceedings were brought against Mr. Nubar Gulbenkian and [his wife] Mrs. Gulbenkian. To that action there was a counterclaim by Mr. Gulbenkian that the will was void and he was entitled to legitim.

These proceedings were compromised by the deed of 12th February 1958 which was approved by the court in Lisbon on 15th March 1958. The provisions of that agreement are complicated, but the following explanation is, I hope, sufficient for D present purposes. Under his father's will Mr. Gulbenkian became entitled, inter alia, to an annuity of $135,000, but the will provided in effect that certain income had to be brought into account against that figure and this included the income of the settlement of 1929. One of the objects of the Lisbon agreement was to substitute for the liability of Calouste Sarkis Gulbenkian's estate to provide the annuity, a liability to provide a capital sum of roughly $3·4 million payable E at such times and in such manner that it would be capital and not income in Mr. Gulbenkian's hands. As part of the compromise Mr. and Mrs. Gulbenkian by cl. 12 of the Lisbon agreement bound themselves as follows:

" Having regard to the provisions of Clause twenty-one of the Will, which calls for inclusion in the annual pension of one hundred and thirty-five thousand dollars the income of the trusts set up during the lifetime of Calouste F Sarkis Gulbenkian in favour of his son Nubar, and with a view to ensuring that the capital and income of the Trusts of one thousand nine hundred and twenty-nine and one thousand nine hundred and thirty-eight, revert entirely in favour of the Calouste Gulbenkian Foundation—since the commutation of the pension established in Clause twenty-one of the Will was made without deduction of the income of those Trusts—Nubar Sarkis Gulbenkian forth- G with and unconditionally renounces his trusteeship in relation to the Trust of one thousand nine hundred and twenty-nine, and renounces also his right to appoint or choose the respective trustees; and on his own behalf and that of his wife, Madame Marie de Ayala Gulbenkian, renounces the right to all the income of both the one thousand nine hundred and twenty-nine and one thousand nine hundred and thirty-eight Trusts. Nubar Sarkis H Gulbenkian also renounces the right of designating any beneficiary of or successor to the capital of the Trust of one thousand nine hundred and twenty-nine. Nubar Sarkis Gulbenkian and Madame Marie de Ayala Gulbenkian oblige themselves to give effect to the renunciations and releases above-mentioned in a document or documents executed with such formality as is required by English law." I

Clause 13 of the Lisbon agreement provided:

" Should Nubar Sarkis Gulbenkian die leaving descendants, and for that reason the capital of the Trust of one thousand nine hundred and twenty-nine or any rights therein have to be transferred to such descendant or descendants, with the result that its transfer to the Calouste Gulbenkian Foundation, as heir to the residue of the estate of Calouste Sarkis Gulbenkian, becomes impossible, the estate of the said Nubar will compensate the

A   Foundation for the prejudice, paying to the Foundation the equivalent of that capital, plus the accumulated income, if any. If during the life of Nubar Sarkis Gulbenkian the Trustees make any payments of income of the Trusts to any of his descendants, he will be obliged to pay immediately to the Foundation a like amount."

B   It is not, I think, disputed that cl. 12 of the Lisbon agreement operated as a release of the general testamentary power of appointment conferred on Mr. Gulbenkian by cl. 6 of the settlement of 1929 in default of a child of his attaining a vested interest, with the result that, subject to the discretionary trust or power, and to the birth of issue, the fund belongs to the Gulbenkian Foundation. What is disputed is the effect of cl. 12 of the Lisbon agreement on the trustees' discretion.

C   Counsel for the third and fourth defendants, the English legal personal representatives of Calouste Gulbenkian, and through them the Gulbenkian Foundation, submits that as a result of cl. 12 Mr. and Mrs. Gulbenkian are no longer objects of the trustees' discretion. His argument is this, that the duty of the trustees under the power contained in cl. 2 (i) of the settlement is a duty owed to each object of the power to consider whether or not to exercise their discretion in its favour,

D   that there is no reason in law why an object of that power should not release the trustees from that duty quoad hunc, and if he does so he thereupon ceases to be an object of the power. Counsel submits this is in effect what cl. 12 of the Lisbon agreement did.

No authority was cited to me which in terms decides this point, but I see no reason for not accepting the argument. On the contrary, it appears to me to be

E   in conformity with the general principle that no one can be compelled to accept a gift against his wish. As long ago as the YEAR BOOKS it was somewhat quaintly said that " a man cannot have an estate put into him in spight of his teeth"; see *Thompson* v. *Leach* (4) and the reference to that case in *Re Stratton's Deed of Disclaimer, Stratton* v. *Inland Revenue Comrs.* (5). In *Townson* v. *Tickell* (6) ABBOTT, C.J., said (7):

F   " The law certainly is not so absurd as to force a man to take an estate against his will. Prima facie every estate, whether given by will or otherwise, is supposed to be beneficial to the party to whom it is so given. Of that, however, he is the best judge, and if it turn out that the party to whom the gift is made does not consider it beneficial, the law will certainly, by some mode or other, allow him to renounce or refuse the gift."

G   If a man cannot be compelled to accept a gift I see no reason why he should not be equally free to refuse to accept the exercise of a power which the donor has conferred on the trustees to make a gift in his favour. Despite the argument to the contrary of counsel for the second, fifth and ninth defendants, the reasoning which applies to a direct benefit such as a power to pay money to the object

H   of the power appears to me to apply equally to an indirect benefit such as a power to apply the money for his benefit instead of paying it to him.

I therefore hold that, as from the date of the Lisbon agreement, Mr. and Mrs. Gulbenkian ceased to be objects of the discretionary trust and that consequently as from that date it was no longer competent for the trustees to exercise their discretion in favour of Mr. and Mrs. Gulbenkian either directly or indirectly. I

I   should perhaps emphasise that the release which I am considering was a release for valuable consideration and I am not concerned to consider whether a different result might have followed if the release had been a voluntary release not under seal.

(4) (1690), 2 Vent. 198 at p. 206.
(5) [1957] 2 All E.R. 594 at p. 597; [1958] Ch. 42 at p. 50.
(6) (1819), 3 B. & Ald. 31; [1814-23] All E.R. Rep. 164.
(7) (1819), 3 B. & Ald. at p. 36; [1814-23] All E.R. Rep. at p. 165.

I was referred to certain cases such as *Re Coleman, Henry* v. *Strong* (8), A
Re Smith, Public Trustee v. *Aspinall* (9), and *Re Nelson, Norris* v. *Nelson* (10),
which deal with assignments by the objects of the discretionary trust as opposed
to a discretionary power, but those cases, in my view, raise quite different considerations and do not I think bear on the problem which I have to consider.

Nothing that I have said up to this point affects the other objects of the discretion and contrary to what was suggested in argument, I cannot, in my view, B
merely ignore them on the basis that they are no more than channels of benefit
for Mr. Gulbenkian.

I must, therefore, now consider whether it is open to the trustees at this time
of day to exercise retrospectively so much of their discretion as was not abrogated
by the Lisbon agreement. It is common ground that it is the duty of trustees,
placed in the position of these trustees, to exercise their discretion within a C
reasonable time after the receipt by them of the income in question and that after
that reasonable period has elapsed the discretion is at an end. What is a reasonable
period depends on the circumstances of the case and there may be special circumstances which justify a postponement of the exercise of the discretion. See *Re
Gourju's Will Trusts, Starling* v. *Custodian of Enemy Property* (11), *Re Wise,
Jackson* v. *Parrott* (12), and *Re Allen-Meyrick's Will Trusts, Mangnall* v. *Allen-* D
Meyrick (13). In the present case, as I have already said, the trustees deliberately
refrained from exercising their discretion after April 1957 pending the resolution
of the doubt caused by the decision in *Re Gresham's Settlement* (14). That doubt
was not finally resolved until October 1968 since when the matter has been held
up pending the decision of the court.

In these circumstances, and subject to what I have already said about Mr. and E
Mrs. Gulbenkian, the trustees' discretion is in my judgment still exercisable and
question 2 (A) (i) of the originating summons must be answered in the sense of
the first alternative; and subject to what I have already said on the question of
propriety the answer to question 2 (A) (ii) is No in regard to (a) and (b) and Yes
in regard to (c). The answer to the corresponding question raised in the other case
will follow from what I have said there. F

Order accordingly.

Solicitors: *Charles Russell & Co.* (for the plaintiffs); *Herbert Smith & Co.* (for the
second, fifth and ninth defendants; *Freshfields* (for the third and fourth
defendants).

[*Reported by* JACQUELINE METCALFE, *Barrister-at-Law.*] G

H

I

(8) (1888), 39 Ch.D. 443.
(9) [1928] Ch. 915; [1928] All E.R. Rep. 520.
(10) (1918), [1928] Ch. 920, n.
(11) [1942] 2 All E.R. 605; [1943] Ch. 24.
(12) [1896] 1 Ch. 281.
(13) [1966] 1 All E.R. 740; [1966] 1 W.L.R. 499.
(14) [1956] 2 All E.R. 193; [1956] 1 W.L.R. 573.

A

R. *v.* GRAHAM.

[COURT OF APPEAL, CRIMINAL DIVISION (Fenton Atkinson and Phillimore, L.JJ., and Lawton, J.), January 24, 1969.]

Drugs—Dangerous drugs—Possession—Unauthorised possession—Microscopic particles—Particles measurable—Dangerous Drugs (No. 2) Regulations 1964 (S.I. 1964 No. 1811), reg. 3.

B

The defendant was in possession of clothes in which were found small scrapings of cannabis which could in fact be weighed in milligrammes. He was convicted of being in possession of a drug contrary to reg. 3 of the Dangerous Drugs (No. 2) Regulations 1964. The deputy recorder, before whom the case was tried, did not leave to the jury the question whether there was sufficient cannabis to enable the defendant to be in possession of it.

C

Held: as there was sufficient cannabis to be measured it could not be said as a matter of law that there was no cannabis in the defendant's possession (see p. 1182, letter H, post).

R. v. *Worsell* (p. 1183, post) distinguished.

D

Per CURIAM: it may be that it would have been right for the deputy recorder to have left this issue to the jury (see p. 1182, letter H, post).

Appeal dismissed.

[As to possession of dangerous drugs, see 26 HALSBURY'S LAWS (3rd Edn.) 200, para. 458; and for a case on the subject, see DIGEST (Cont. Vol. B) 522, 243*b*.]

E

Case referred to:

R. v. *Worsell*, p. 1183, post.

Appeal.

This was an appeal by Christopher Bruce Graham against a conviction in November 1968 of being in possession of a dangerous drug. The facts are set out in the judgment of the court.

F

H. K. Woolf for the appellant.

S. Tumim for the Crown.

FENTON ATKINSON, L.J., delivered the judgment of the court: In November 1968 at Oxford City Quarter Sessions before the deputy recorder the appellant, who was then aged 20, was convicted of being in possession of

G

a drug, namely cannabis resin, on 7th August 1968 and he was sentenced to three months' detention. He was by virtue of this offence in breach of an earlier probation order for possessing cannabis and harbouring an absconder and he was sentenced to three months' detention concurrent in respect of those original offences; so that is three months' detention in all, and from that he is on the point of being released, in fact, on licence. He did not at first intend to appeal

H

but was no doubt encouraged to do so by seeing or having brought to his notice the report in The Times of *R.* v. *Worsell* (1), a case which was decided in December 1968.

On 7th August 1968, the police raided a flat in Oxford where he was living with a young lady. They found some cannabis in the flat but he was not charged in respect of that. However, on the same day the police took some

I

scrapings from the pockets of the clothing which he was wearing. When he was asked what he would do if those scrapings were found to contain cannabis he said " I will plead guilty but I do not think you will find anything. If you do that is my fault." In fact on analysis traces of cannabis were found in the scrapings from three of his pockets; I think one from his trousers and two from his jacket. In each case the quantities were very small but the scientific officer found that the quantity was capable of being weighed and measured. This case being tried before *R.* v. *Worsell* (1), no point was made by the defence that the

(1) P. 1183, post.

quantities found were so minimal as in truth to amount to nothing.   The case   A
was really being run on the basis that these were very small amounts of cannabis
and that being so it could well be that he did not know it was there and he was
not truly in possession.

That was his case; that he did not know there was cannabis in his pockets.
He had been convicted of possessing cannabis in July 1967.   He said there might
still have been traces left over from that time and he said that both the trousers   B
and the jacket had on occasions been borrowed by his girlfriend and another
friend called Chamberlain, each of whom smoked cannabis and who might be
responsible for the traces found.   There was a lot of discussion at the trial
about the trousers in question because the trousers the lady had borrowed were
apparently white ones but the police officers were quite clear that the ones from
which the scrapings were taken were blue.   That line of defence was fully   C
investigated at the trial, there was a perfectly fair summing-up about it and
the jury convicted.

Really the only point which now arises as a result of the decision of this court
in *R.* v. *Worsell* (2) which was a rather unusual case depending very much on
its own particular facts.   Police officers had stopped a motor car and in that
car were the appellant and two of his friends, one of the others being the owner   D
of the car.   Under the dashboard the police found a syringe and a small tube
and there is no doubt at all that the tube had at one time contained heroin
and indeed the appellant said that earlier in the day he had had a " fix " out of
that tube.   But the Crown had framed their case and ran their case entirely on
the basis of a quantity of heroin alleged to be found in that tube at the time of
arrest.   He said he had a " fix " therefore he must have been in possession at   E
some earlier stage of the same day.   According to the evidence the tube appeared
to be entirely empty; there was nothing visible to the human eye.   The scientist
called said that under a microscope it was possible to discern a very few small
droplets which were impossible to measure and impossible to pour out.   On
that state of the evidence this court came to the conclusion that in truth the
tube was empty; that the droplets were invisible to the human eye, they could   F
only be discerned under a microscope, they could not be measured or poured
out and in truth this was an empty tube with nothing in it.

In this case the evidence is not nearly so strong. Of course one of the difficulties
now is that because of the way the case was very reasonably being run at that
time, the scientific expert was not being cross-examined with a view to showing
that these scrapings really amounted to nothing;   the case was it was only a   G
very small quantity.

On the evidence of the scientific officer that what was found in each of the
three pockets could in fact be measured and weighed in milligrammes, we do
not think that as a matter of law it could be said that there was in truth no
cannabis in the appellant's possession.   It may be that it would have been right
for the learned deputy recorder to leave to the jury as an issue of fact to find   H
whether what was in his pockets was sufficient to amount to possession of cannabis
but, in our view, even if he had done that (and he summed up, of course, in the
light of the way in which the case had been run) the end of the case would have
been inevitable; there would have been a conviction.   If there was any error
in treating it as axiomatic that the quantities did amount to cannabis, we would
apply the proviso without hesitation.   I

We think this appeal must be dismissed.   There is a clear distinction to be
drawn on the facts between this case and *R.* v. *Worsell* (2).

Appeal dismissed.

Solicitors: *Registrar of Criminal Appeals* (for the appellant); *Marshall &
Eldridge,* Oxford (for the Crown).

[*Reported by* N. P. METCALFE, ESQ., *Barrister-at-Law.*]

_____

(2) P. 1183, post.

A

R. *v.* WORSELL.

[Court of Appeal, criminal division (Salmon and Fenton Atkinson, L.JJ., and Milmo, J.), December 13, 1968.]

B *Drugs—Dangerous drugs—Possession—Unauthorised possession—Microscopic particles—Particles not measurable—Particles not visible to naked eye—Dangerous Drugs (No. 2) Regulations 1964 (S.I. 1964 No. 1811), reg. 9.*

Possession of a tube containing a few small droplets of a drug which were only discernible microscopically and were impossible to measure or pour out does not constitute possession of a drug for the purposes of reg. 9 of the Dangerous Drugs (No. 2) Regulations 1964 (see p. 1184, letter C, post).

C   Appeal allowed.

[As to possession of dangerous drugs, see 26 Halsbury's Laws (3rd Edn.) 200, para. 458; and for a case on the subject, see Digest (Cont. Vol. B) 522, 243*b*.]

Appeal.

This was an appeal by Barrie Louis Worsell against a conviction on 28th March
D 1968 of being in possession of a dangerous drug. The facts are set out in the judgment of the court.

P. H. Counsell for the appellant.
J. B. R. Hazan for the Crown.

E   **SALMON, L.J.,** delivered the judgment of the court: On 28th March 1968 at the North East London Quarter Sessions, the appellant was convicted of possessing a dangerous drug and he was subsequently put on probation for three years for that offence. He now appeals with the leave of the court against conviction.

The facts can be quite shortly stated. In the afternoon of 3rd November 1967 some police officers stopped a motor car in which the appellant and his two
F co-defendants were driving. One of these co-defendants was the owner and driver of the car. The appellant and the other co-defendant were passengers. Under the dashboard there was found a hypodermic syringe and a small tube. There is no doubt that the tube had at one time contained heroin. The real question that arises on this appeal is whether there was any evidence on which the jury could find that it contained heroin at the moment when the car was
G stopped by the police officers. The policemen gave evidence that when the appellant was told that his co-defendants had admitted taking drugs, he replied: " You'll have to go on what they say.   I had a fix but I'm not dropping them."

Count 1 of the indictment was amended. The particulars of the offence in their original form stated that the accused had in their possession " a certain drug, to wit, a quantity of diamorphine [which is heroin] without being authorised
H to be in possession of the same ". Those particulars were amended in that for the words " a quantity of diamorphine " there was substituted " a few droplets of diamorphine ". The appeal does not raise any question whether or not the appellant was in possession of the tube. The appeal has been conducted on the basis that if the tube contained diamorphine, the appellant was in possession of it. Leave to appeal was not given on any question arising on
I possession.

According to the evidence, the tube appeared to be entirely empty. There was nothing in the tube that was visible to the human eye. The scientist who was called on behalf of the Crown stated that under the microscope it was possible to discern a very few, small droplets which were impossible to measure and impossible to pour out. It is quite plain that the learned deputy chairman's view was that it was impossible to say that this tube contained heroin in any real sense of the word. He nevertheless refused to stop the case and allowed

it to go to the jury.   He did so, it is fairly plain, because he felt that if he were   A
wrong his finding could not be challenged and therefore he considered it was best
to allow the case to go to the jury because the view which he took could be
tested should the jury convict.   He delivered a very careful and accurate summing-up and no sort of criticism has been or could be made of it.   The sole
question is, was there any evidence on which a jury could come to the conclusion
that the tube found under the dashboard contained a drug at the moment when   B
the police discovered it.

Being in possession of a dangerous drug without authority is an absolute
offence according to the recent decision of the House of Lords (1).   The reason
no doubt is that if anyone is in possession of a drug there is the risk, if not indeed
the probability, that he may be going to take the drug or to peddle it and taking
or peddling heroin constitutes a very grave social evil.   But before the offence   C
can be committed it is necessary to show that the accused is in truth in possession
of a drug.   This court has come to the clear conclusion that inasmuch as this
tube was in reality empty (that is, the droplets which were in it were invisible
to the human eye and could only be discerned under a microscope and could not
be measured or poured out) it is impossible to hold that there was any evidence
that this tube contained a drug.   Whatever it contained, obviously it could   D
not be used and could not be sold.   There was nothing in reality in the tube.

Before parting with the case, this court would like to make it plain that if this
prosecution had been run in a different way from that in which it was run at
the trial, there would have been no real defence to it.   Learned counsel now
appearing for the Crown was not present at the trial.   The appellant had said
he had had " a fix " earlier on and it seems perfectly plain that what he was   E
admitting was that he had had " a fix " out of the heroin that had been in the
tube.   The fact that the tube was there in the car coupled with his admission
makes it plain that at an earlier stage he had been in possession of a drug.   This
of course is on the assumption that he was in possession of the tube and as to
that no question arose on this appeal.   It is a great pity that the indictment
was amended and a pity that the case for the Crown was not that the appellant   F
had been, at some time prior to the moment when the police arrested him, in
possession of a drug. His statement, as already indicated, plus the presence
of the tube which had contained the drug, would have been conclusive evidence
against him.   Unfortunately, however, the case was run wholly on the basis
that he was in possession of the drug in the tube at the moment of his arrest.
There was no evidence on which the jury could find that at that moment there   G
was in reality any drug in the tube.

Accordingly, on that narrow ground, this appeal must be allowed.

Appeal allowed.

Solicitors: *Registrar of Criminal Appeals* (for the appellant); *Solicitor,
Metropolitan Police* (for the Crown).

[*Reported by* N. P. METCALFE, ESQ., *Barrister-at-Law.*]

---

(1) *Warner* v. *Metropolitan Police Comr.*, [1968] 2 All E.R. 356; [1968] 2 W.L.R. 1303.

A # CHARTERBRIDGE CORPORATION, LTD. *v.* LLOYDS BANK, LTD. AND ANOTHER.

[CHANCERY DIVISION (Pennycuick, J.), October 29, 30, 31, November 1, 5, 1968.]

B *Company—Ultra vires—Foreign purpose of director—Memorandum of association—Power given to guarantee by charge or otherwise—Company being one of group of companies—Charge created by company with director considering benefit of whole group rather than separately considering benefit of company —Whether ultra vires.*

An act of a company within the scope of the powers expressed in its memorandum is not ultra vires merely because its director had a foreign C purpose in mind when, on the company's behalf, he performed the act in question (see p. 1189, letters G and H, and p. 1194, letter A, post).

Re David Payne & Co., Ltd. ([1904] 2 Ch. 608) considered.

Re Introductions, Ltd. ([1968] 2 All E.R. 1221), and *Ridge Securities, Ltd. v. Inland Revenue Comrs.* ([1964] 1 All E.R. 275) distinguished.

Re Lee, Behrens & Co., Ltd. ([1932] All E.R. Rep. 889) not followed.

D Under its memorandum C., Ltd.'s first object was to acquire lands for investment with a strictly qualified power of realisation. It was given power " to secure or guarantee by mortgages, charges or otherwise the performance and discharge of any contract, obligation or liability of the company or of any other person or corporation with whom or which the company has dealings or having a business or undertaking in which the company is concerned or E interested whether directly or indirectly ". Power was also given for joint adventure or agreement for co-operation, and to do " such things as may be incidental or conducive to the attainment of the above-mentioned objects ". Each sub-clause was to be deemed to be independent. Mr. P. and his wife were the sole shareholders and directors of C., Ltd. which was one of a group of companies at the head of which was P., Ltd. The basic business of F the group was property development. In December 1960 the accounts which P., Ltd., and two other companies in the group had at the defendant bank were overdrawn. The bank pressed for better security, and Mr. P. and other companies in the group gave a chain of guarantees including one whereby C., Ltd., guaranteed payment of liabilities incurred by P., Ltd., to the bank with a limit of £30,000. In March 1962 C., Ltd., executed a legal charge G in favour of the defendant bank over leasehold property known as " Castleford " to secure its indebtedness to the bank including its guarantee. This was subject to a first mortgage previously granted to A. Mr. P., in causing C., Ltd., to enter into the guarantee and legal charge, looked to the interests of the group as a whole and did not consider C., Ltd.'s interests separately. In April 1962 C., Ltd., agreed to sell " Castleford " to the plaintiff company H at a price of more than £30,000. The plaintiff company paid £20,000 almost all of which was applied in discharging the first mortgage in favour of A., leaving the bank as first mortgagee. The plaintiff company later paid a further £10,000. In December 1962 C., Ltd., and the plaintiff company entered into a new sale agreement superseding the earlier one. Subsequently the plaintiff company learnt that C., Ltd., could not make a good title. I The bank demanded repayment by C., Ltd., and threatened to realise the security. The plaintiff company then issued a writ seeking a declaration that the legal charge in favour of the defendant bank was void as being ultra vires. On the question of Mr. P.'s failure to consider separately the interests of C., Ltd.,

Held: the declaration would not be made because Mr. P.'s failure to consider separately the interests of C., Ltd., when, on its behalf he effected the charge in favour of the defendant bank, did not render the execution of the charge ultra vires (see p. 1194, letter A, post.)

QQ

A

[As to the limitations of powers of a company, see 6 HALSBURY'S LAWS (3rd Edn.) 413-418, paras. 799-809; and for cases on the subject, see 9 DIGEST (Repl.) 646-649, *4297-4312*.]

Cases referred to:

Durham County Permanent Investment Land and Building Society, Re, Davis' Case, Wilson's Case (1871), L.R. 12 Eq. 516; 41 L.J.Ch. 124; 25 L.T. 83; 36 J.P. 164; 7 Digest (Repl.) 514, *228*.

B

Hampson v. *Price's Patent Candle Co.* (1876), 45 L.J.Ch. 437; 34 L.T. 711; 10 Digest (Repl.) 1255, *8847*.

Henderson v. *Bank of Australasia* (1888), 40 Ch.D. 170; 58 L.J.Ch. 197; 59 L.T. 856; 9 Digest (Repl.) 568, *3743*.

Hutton v. *West Cork Ry. Co.* (1883), 23 Ch.D. 654; 52 L.J.Ch. 689; 49 L.T. 420; 9 Digest (Repl.) 497, *3274*.

C

Introductions, Ltd., Re, Introductions, Ltd. v. *National Provincial Bank, Ltd.*, [1968] 2 All E.R. 1221; Digest (Repl.) Supp.

Lee, Behrens & Co., Ltd., Re, [1932] 2 Ch. 46; [1932] All E.R. Rep. 889; 101 L.J.Ch. 183; 147 L.T. 348; 9 Digest (Repl.) 559, *3700*.

Payne (David) & Co., Ltd., Re, Young v. *David Payne & Co., Ltd.*, [1904] 2 Ch. 608; 73 L.J.Ch. 849; 91 L.T. 777; 9 Digest (Repl.) 503, *3315*.

D

Marseilles Extension Ry. Co., Re, Ex p. Crédit Foncier & Mobilier of England (1871), 7 Ch. App. 161; 41 L.J.Ch. 345; 25 L.T. 858; 9 Digest (Repl.) 692, *4560*.

Ridge Securities, Ltd. v. *Inland Revenue Comrs.*, [1964] 1 All E.R. 275; [1964] 1 W.L.R. 479; Digest (Cont. Vol. B) 402, *424b*.

E

Action.

This was an action commenced by the plaintiff company, Charterbridge Corporation, Ltd., by writ dated 18th September 1964. It claimed against the first defendant, Lloyds Bank, Ltd., and the second defendant, Pomeroy Developments (Castleford), Ltd., a declaration that the legal charge dated 29th March 1962 and made between the second defendant and the first defendant (being a charge of leasehold premises situate at Bridge Street, Castleford, York) was void as being outside the powers of the second defendant. It also claimed an injunction to restrain the bank from selling or disposing of the leasehold premises in exercise or purported exercise of its powers as mortgagee. The facts are set out in the judgment.

F

E. I. Goulding, Q.C., and *D. A. Thomas* for the plaintiff company.
Arthur Bagnall, Q.C., and *R. A. K. Wright* for the bank.
The second defendant, Castleford, was not represented.

G

PENNYCUICK, J.: By this action the plaintiff company, Charterbridge Corpn., Ltd., seeks a declaration that a legal charge dated 29th March 1962, and created by the second defendant, Pomeroy Developments (Castleford), Ltd., referred to as " Castleford ", in favour of the first defendant, Lloyds Bank, Ltd., is void, as being ultra vires Castleford. The legal charge was given consequently upon a guarantee given by Castleford to the bank on 19th December 1960, to secure the indebtedness of a company known as Pomeroy Developments, Ltd., to which I will refer as " Pomeroy ", to the bank. It is common ground that the primary issue in the action is whether the guarantee itself was ultra vires Castleford. Castleford has taken no part in the action.

H

I

I shall first set out the facts as I find them. In the event there was very little dispute as to particular facts. No evidence was called on behalf of the plaintiff company. On behalf of the bank there were called two officers of the bank, Mr. Watkins, who was the manager of Cox's & King's Branch at the date of the relevant transactions, and Mr. Barber, who was the manager of the particular section concerned with the affairs of Pomeroy and Castleford at the date of the relevant transactions, and Mr. Oscar Alexander Pomeroy (on subpoena) he

A   being the gentleman who controlled Pomeroy, Castleford and a number of other companies. All these three witnesses gave their evidence truthfully and carefully and were able to check it by reference to contemporary records.

Castleford was incorporated in 1956. Under its memorandum, in cl. 3 (A), its first object is to acquire lands for investment with a strictly qualified power of realisation. Sub-clause (H) is in these terms:

B   " To secure or guarantee by mortgages, charges or otherwise the performance and discharge of any contract, obligation or liability of the Company or of any other person or corporation with whom or which the Company has dealings or having a business or undertaking in which the Company is concerned or interested whether directly or indirectly."

C   Reference should also be made to sub-para. (N) concerning joint adventure or agreement for co-operation. Then follow:

" (R) . . . such things as may be incidental or conducive to the attainment of the above-mentioned objects . . .

" (S) . . . each [sub-clause] shall be deemed to be an independent clause . . ."

Mr. Pomeroy owned all the issued shares in Castleford except one. That was

D   owned by his wife. Mr. and Mrs. Pomeroy were the sole directors of Castleford. Castleford was one of a large group of companies. At the head of the group stood Pomeroy, which was almost wholly owned by Mr. Pomeroy. The other companies of the group, including Castleford, were not subsidiaries of Pomeroy, but had a common shareholding, directorate and office. The basic trade of the group was property development. A separate company was incorporated to

E   deal with each particular site acquired. Pomeroy itself supervised the activities of all the companies in the group, provided their office services and finance and carried out the acquisition and development of the sites. The development involved surveys, applications for planning consents, instructions to architects and negotiations for the grant of building leases or for sale.

By a lease dated 26th October 1956, and made between C. M. Colley & Sons,

F   Ltd., of the first part, Castleford of the second part, and Pomeroy of the third part, C. M. Colley & Sons, Ltd., demised to Castleford a lease of land at Castleford in the West Riding of Yorkshire for a term of 999 years at a yearly rent of £750. Castleford entered into a number of covenants, including cl. 2 (1), a covenant to pay rent, and cl. 2 (3), a covenant to build shops and offices at a cost of at least £25,000. By cl. 3, Pomeroy guaranteed performance by Castleford

G   of its covenants. Castleford took possession of the property comprised in that lease. Part of this property was afterwards assigned to another company in the group. Pomeroy has throughout paid the rent due from Castleford under the lease. Pomeroy set about the development of that part of the property comprised in the lease which was retained by Castleford, incurring expense on the various matters in connection with the development. In 1960 negotiations were on

H   foot for the sale of the property to the plaintiff company, but these negotiations had not yet come to fruition.

Castleford did not at any time have any separate staff or organisation. At all relevant times, i.e., December 1960 to March 1962, Pomeroy itself and two other companies in the group, namely Street Market Investments, Ltd., and Olivetree Developments, Ltd., a Northern Irish Co., had accounts with the bank. Mr.

I   Pomeroy and Mrs. Pomeroy had private accounts. No other company in the group had an account at any relevant time, although Castleford itself had had one for two or three years after its incorporation.

In December 1960, Pomeroy's account with the bank was overdrawn approximately £16,400. Street Market's account was overdrawn approximately £3,500 and Olivetree's account was overdrawn approximately £3,000. These combined overdrawings were in excess of the bank's permitted limit and the bank pressed for better security for the indebtedness of the group. Negotiations took place at a number of interviews between Mr. Watkins or Mr. Barber

on the one hand and Mr. Pomeroy or one Mr. Lessman on his behalf on the   **A**
other. These negotiations resulted in a whole chain of guarantees to the bank
by Mr. Pomeroy and various companies included in the group. The guarantees
included the guarantee dated 19th December 1960, to which I have already
referred. By this guarantee Castleford guaranteed payment on demand of all
money and liabilities owing or incurred by Pomeroy to the bank with a limit
of £30,000. The liabilities' guarantee would include any liabilities of Pomeroy   **B**
under its own guarantees of the indebtedness of other members of the group, in
particular Street Market and Olivetree. Castleford's guarantee was accompanied
by a deposit by Castleford of the title deeds of the Castleford property. A minute
of the meeting held by the directors of Castleford on the same day records the
transaction.

On 19th December 1961, a year later, Castleford took a first mortgage from   **C**
Askinex, borrowing £14,813 against a covenant to repay £18,147 on 4th December
1962. The proceeds of this mortgage were paid to the bank in reduction, although
not complete discharge of Pomeroy's overdraft. With the consent of the bank,
the deeds of the Castleford property were handed over to Askinex. Pomeroy's
overdraft increased again over the following months to something like its former
amount. In March 1962, the bank was pressing for a charge on the Castleford   **D**
property to secure Castleford's liability under the guarantee. Again the negotiations took place between Mr. Watkins or Mr. Barber on the one side and Mr.
Pomeroy on the other side. These negotiations resulted in the execution, on
29th March 1962, of the legal charge to which I have referred. By that legal
charge, Castleford charged the Castleford property, subject to the mortgage in
favour of Askinex, to secure its indebtedness to the bank. This would, of course,   **E**
include its indebtedness under the guarantee. A minute of the meeting held by
the directors of Castleford on the same day records the transaction.

Mr. Pomeroy, in causing Castleford to enter into the guarantee, and, later on,
the legal charge, was looking to the interests of the group as a whole. He considered it in the interest of the group as a whole that Castleford should enter
into these transactions and that the other companies in the group should enter   **F**
into comparable transactions. He did not, at the time of the transaction, take
into consideration the interest of Castleford separately from that of the group.
Mr. Watkins and Mr. Barber likewise looked to the group as a whole. They
believed the transactions to be proper ones. They likewise did not at the time
of the transactions take into consideration the interest of Castleford separately
from that of the group.   **G**

To avoid any possible misunderstanding, these findings do not, of course,
imply that either Mr. Pomeroy or the bank officers believed that the transactions
were prejudicial to Castleford. They simply did not give separate consideration
to the interest of Castleford. The three witnesses were very properly taken at
length through the contemporary documents, including correspondence, notes
of interviews, internal minutes and other records kept by the bank. I had, of   **H**
course, to consider their oral evidence in relation to these documents. But I
do not think it would serve any useful purpose to refer to the documents in detail.
All three witnesses deposed that in their view today the transactions were in
the interest of Castleford for reasons which they gave.

On 18th April 1962, Castleford entered into an agreement for the sale of the
Castleford property to the plaintiff company. The price fell to be ascertained   **I**
by a complicated formula and was likely to be rather more than £30,000. The
plaintiff company paid £20,000 on account and almost the whole of this sum was
applied in discharging the Askinex mortgage, leaving the bank as first mortgagee.
The plaintiff company paid a further £10,000 on account in four instalments,
over the months June to August 1962. These instalments did not find their
way to the bank. It is better not to go further into this matter, since it may
involve other parties. In the result, the plaintiff company has paid the greater
part of the purchase price, but the bank mortgage remains unsatisfied.

A   On 31st December 1962, Castleford and the plaintiff company entered into a
new sale agreement superseding the agreement dated 18th April 1962. The new
agreement sets out the previous payment of £30,000 on account of the purchase
price. The agreement incorporates the national conditions of sale, and, like its
predecessor, contemplates that Castleford will sell free from incumbrance.

   Subsequently the plaintiff company learned that Castleford could not make a
B   good title. On 28th August 1964, the bank demanded repayment by Castleford
of the amount therein mentioned, and threatened to realise the security. The
writ in the present action was issued on 18th September 1964.

   I should perhaps mention that although Mr. Pomeroy and his group were in
undoubted difficulties in 1962, they survived these difficulties, and, as I
understand it, the group is still a going concern.

C   The statement of claim as amended and re-amended sets out the sale agreement dated 31st December 1962, and the legal charge and guarantee. It proceeds
as follows:

   " 4. Castleford has never received any money or other benefit in consideration of the said Legal Charge.   5. The said Legal Charge and the
D   security thereby created (as the Bank and Castleford at all material times well
   knew or ought to have known) were created for purposes outside the scope of
   Castleford's business and/or purposes which were not for the benefit of
   Castleford. The said Legal Charge and the security thereby purported to be
   created are accordingly invalid . . .   6. Further, or in the alternative, the
   said Legal Charge and the security thereby created, are ultra vires the
E   Memorandum of Association of Castleford, and are accordingly void."

   The claim is for a declaration that the legal charge is invalid and seeks relief
by way of injunction.

   Paragraph 6 is intended to raise a contention based on the wording of cl. 3,
para. (H) in the memorandum of Castleford, namely that Pomeroy did not
fall within the range of persons in whose favour Castleford might give a guarantee.
F   This contention was untenable on the evidence and counsel for the plaintiff
company very properly abandoned it.   He rested his case entirely on para. 5.
There is no allegation of bad faith.

   I must now consider the law. It will be borne in mind that the present action
is based exclusively on the contention that it was ultra vires Castleford, i.e.,
outside its corporate powers, to give the guarantee and legal charge. On this
G   footing the guarantee and legal charge were a nullity.

   Apart from authority, I should feel little doubt that where a company is carrying out the purposes expressed in its memorandum, and does an act within the
scope of a power expressed in its memorandum, that act is an act within the
powers of the company. The memorandum of a company sets out its objects and
proclaims them to persons dealing with the company and it would be contrary to
H   the whole function of a memorandum that objects unequivocally set out in it
should be subject to some implied limitation by reference to the state of mind
of the parties concerned.

   Where directors misapply the assets of their company, that may give rise to a
claim based on breach of duty.   Again, a claim may arise against the other
party to the transaction, if he has notice that the transaction was effected in
I   breach of duty. Further, in a proper case, the company concerned may be entitled
to have the transaction set aside. But all that results from the ordinary law of
agency and has not of itself anything to do with the corporate powers of the
company.

   The plaintiff company's contention is formulated under two heads, namely:
(i), that the guarantee and legal charge were created for purposes outside the
scope of Castleford's business; and (ii) that the guarantee and legal charge were
created for purposes which were not for the benefit of Castleford. This second
contention is intended to mean, and is accepted as being intended to mean,

that the directors of Castleford in creating these obligations were not acting   **A**
with a view to the benefit of the company. Counsel for the plaintiff company,
based his contention under both heads primarily on *Re Lee, Behrens & Co., Ltd.* (1),
to which I shall refer in a minute. But where as here a company is carrying
on the purposes authorised by its memorandum and a transaction is effected
pursuant to an express power conferred by the memorandum, counsel for the
plaintiff company found difficulty in attaching any significant meaning to the   **B**
expression " purposes outside the scope of Castleford's business " in the first
head. He suggested as alternatives: (i) not for the purpose of carrying on
Castleford's business; (ii) not reasonably connected with Castleford's business;
and (iii) not done for the benefit of and to promote the prosperity of Castleford.
But (i) is tautology; (ii) could not be asserted on the facts of the present case;
and (iii) is a paraphrase of the second head. I think I need say no more about the   **C**
first head.

The second head, namely that the guarantee and legal charge were not created
for the benefit of Castleford in the sense which I have indicated, formed the real
basis of the argument of counsel for the plaintiff company. As I have said, he
founded that argument primarily on the decision in *Re Lee, Behrens & Co., Ltd.* (1)
and I will now turn to that case: The headnote is as follows (2):   **D**

> " A private company, the articles of which authorized the directors to
> provide for the welfare of employees and their widows and children, entered
> into a deed of covenant by which it granted a pension of 500*l.* a year to the
> widow of a former managing director five years after his death. Some three
> years later the company passed a resolution for voluntary winding-up. The   **E**
> widow lodged a proof in the winding-up for the capitalized value of the
> annuity, but the liquidator rejected it:—*Held*, that the transaction was
> not one for the benefit of the company or reasonably incidental to the
> company's business. The pension did not come within the terms of
> the company's articles, as a managing or other director is not a person in the
> employment of a company, and the action of the directors was not confirmed
> by the shareholders in general meeting convened for the purpose of doing so.   **F**
> The grant of the pension was therefore void and ulta vires the company."

I think it is really clear that the last sentence does not fully reflect the content
of the judgment. The liquidator rejected the proof so far as now material on two
distinct grounds: (i) that it was ultra vires the company and void: (ii) alternatively, that it could only be authorised by the company in general meeting   **G**
and that no such meeting was summoned or held. Neither in the arguments as
reported nor in the judgment are these two grounds kept clearly distinct.

The passage principally relied on by counsel for the plaintiff company runs
as follows (3):

> " It is not contended, nor in the face of a number of authorities to the
> contrary effect could it be, that an arrangement of this nature for rewarding   **H**
> long and faithful service on the part of the persons employed by the company
> is not within the power of an ordinary trading company such as this company
> was, and indeed in the company's memorandum of association is contained
> (clause 3) an express power to provide for the welfare of persons in the
> employment of the company or formerly in its employment, and the widows
> and children of such persons and others dependent upon them by granting   **I**
> money or pensions, providing schools, reading rooms or places of recreation,
> subscribing to sick or benefit clubs or societies or otherwise as the company
> may think fit. But whether they be made under an express or implied
> power, all such grants involve an expenditure of the company's money, and
> that money can only be spent for purposes reasonably incidental to the

---

(1) [1932] 2 Ch. 46; [1932] All E.R. Rep. 889.
(2) [1932] 2 Ch. at p. 46.
(3) [1932] 2 Ch. at pp. 51, 52; [1932] All E.R. Rep. at pp. 890, 891.

A   carrying on of the company's business, and the validity of such grants is to be tested, as is shown in all the authorities, by the answers to three pertinent questions: (i.) Is the transaction reasonably incidental to the carrying on of the company's business? (ii.) Is it a bona fide transaction? and (iii.) Is it done for the benefit and to promote the prosperity of the company? Authority for each of the foregoing propositions is to be found in the following cases:

B   *Hampson* v. *Price's Patent Candle Co.* (4); *Hutton* v. *West Cork Ry. Co.* (5); and *Henderson* v. *Bank of Australasia* (6)."

It seems to me, on the best consideration I can give to this passage, that the learned judge must have been directing his mind to both the issues raised by the liquidator, without differentiating them. In truth (i), the first of the three pertinent questions which he raises, is probably appropriate to the scope of the

C   implied powers of a company where there is no express power. Question (ii) is appropriate in part again to the scope of implied powers, and in part, and perhaps principally, to the duty of directors. Question (iii) is, I think, quite inappropriate to the scope of express powers, and notwithstanding the words " whether they be made under an express or implied power " at the beginning of the paragraph, I doubt very much whether the learned judge really intended to

D   apply this last question to express powers. None of the cases cited by him (7) would support such an application. If he did so intend, his statement is obiter, and with great diffidence I do not feel bound to follow it. Finally, I would observe that the whole passage (8) proceeds on the footing that the transaction might have been ratified, which would not be possible if it had been ultra vires the company.

E   Counsel for the plaintiff company further relied on *Re David Payne & Co., Ltd., Young* v. *David Payne & Co., Ltd.* (9). The headnote in that case is as follows:

" Where a company has a general power to borrow money for the purposes of its business, a lender is not bound to inquire into the purposes for which the money is intended to be applied, and the misapplication of the money by the company does not avoid the loan in the absence of knowledge on the

F   part of the lender that the money was intended to be misapplied. *Re Durham County Permanent Investment Land and Building Society, Davis' Case, Wilson's Case* (10) overruled on this point. K., who was a director of company A. and was also interested in company B., having ascertained in his private capacity that company B. proposed to borrow a sum of money for a purpose outside the scope of its business, induced company A. to advance the money

G   to company B. on the security of a debenture of that company, and the money was applied by company B. in the manner proposed. Company B. had a general power of borrowing under its memorandum and articles of association for the purposes of its business. No other director of company A. except K. knew how the money was intended to be applied:—*Held,* that K.'s knowledge ought not to be imputed to company A. inasmuch as K. owed

H   no duty to that company either to receive or to disclose information as to how the borrowed money was to be applied, and that the debenture was a valid security. Decision of BUCKLEY, J. affirmed."

It will be seen that the two main grounds on which the liquidator based his case were (11):

I   " (i) that the borrowing was not authorized by the memorandum and

---

(4) (1876), 45 L.J.Ch. 437.
(5) (1883), 23 Ch.D. 654.
(6) (1888), 40 Ch.D. 170.
(7) [1932] 2 Ch. at p. 52; cf., [1932] All E.R. Rep. 891, letters B-F.
(8) Beginning in the middle of p. 53 of [1932] 2 Ch.; cf., [1932] All E.R. Rep. at p. 891, letter H.
(9) [1904] 2 Ch. 608.
(10) (1871), L.R. 12 Eq. 516.
(11) [1904] 2 Ch. at p. 611.

articles of the company, and was absolutely ultra vires independently of the
question whether the lending company had notice of the purposes for which
the money was to be applied; (ii) that Kolckmann's knowledge ought to be
imputed to the lending company."

BUCKLEY, J., said this (12):

" In my view, the introduction into any memorandum of association of a
power to borrow is, generally speaking, unnecessary. Every trading company
has power to borrow for the purposes of its business, and the introduction
of this clause is only to express in words what would otherwise be the law.
A limitation of the borrowing to borrowing for the purposes of the company's
business is necessary, of course. A corporation cannot do anything except
for the purposes of its business, borrowing or anything else; everything
else is beyond its power, and is ultra vires. So that the words ' for the purposes of the company's business ' are a mere expression of that which
would be involved if there were no such words."

In this passage BUCKLEY, J., does apparently say that a borrowing, even under
an express power, otherwise than for the purposes of the company's business, is
ultra vires, but he went on to say (13):

" If this borrowing was made, as it appears to me at present it was made,
for a purpose illegitimate so far as the borrowing company was concerned,
that may very well be a matter on which rights may arise as between the
shareholders and directors of that company. It may have been a wrongful
act on the part of the directors. But I do not think that a person who lends
to the company is by any words such as these required to investigate whether
the money borrowed is borrowed for a proper purpose or an improper purpose.
The borrowing being effected, and the money passing to the company, the
subsequent application of the money is a matter in which the directors may
have acted wrongly; but that does not affect the principal act, which is
the borrowing of the money . . . I think here the power to borrow was a
power resting in the directors."

I do not myself find it easy to reconcile every word in those two passages. The
Court of Appeal unequivocally held that the transaction was not ultra vires.
VAUGHAN WILLIAMS, L.J., said (14):

" He began with an argument that this transaction was ultra vires
altogether—that it was just as if this transaction was a lending to a company
with a limited borrowing power in excess of the amount authorized by the
power; but he was compelled to abandon that first attack on the judgment
of BUCKLEY, J., because really in the face of Re Marseilles Extension Ry.
Co., Ex p. Crédit Foncier & Mobilier of England (15) it was impossible to
maintain that proposition. The whole inquiry which was there entered
into by the Court as to the knowledge of the lending company would have
been absolutely immaterial if this transaction was ultra vires in such a
sense that nothing could make it right."

Later he said (16):

" I wish to make one observation about Davis's Case (17). The report
is not very precise; but if that case is really an authority for the proposition
that the application of money borrowed within the borrowing powers of the
company for purposes not authorized by the memorandum of association
makes the transaction invalid, and the security given to the lender a nullity,

(12) [1904] 2 Ch. at p. 612.
(13) [1904] 2 Ch. at p. 613.
(14) [1904] 2 Ch. at p. 615.
(15) (1871), 7 Ch. App. 161.
(16) [1904] 2 Ch. at pp. 617, 618.
(17) (1871), L.R. 12 Eq. 516.

A   merely because there was an intention on the part of the borrowing company
to apply the money for an improper purpose, although the lending company
might have had no knowledge whatever that the money was to be applied
for that improper purpose, I think that *Davis's Case* (18) is wrong and cannot
be reconciled with subsequent authorities."

B   ROMER, L.J., said (19):

" In the first place, where you have a limited company with a memorandum
of association authorizing the company to embark on a series of transactions,
if among those purposes you find a power to borrow generally for the purposes
of the company, I take it to be clear beyond controversy at the present day
that, when money is being borrowed within the limits of the power of

C   borrowing as to amount, the person who lends the money is not bound to
inquire to what purpose the borrowing company is about to apply the
money so borrowed; and if *Davis' Case* (18) is an authority to the contrary,
I cannot agree with it."

Finally, COZENS-HARDY, L.J., said (20):

" There is one point, as to whether a person lending money to a company is

D   in danger of losing his security if the company intended to devote the money
to improper purposes, as to which I should like to add a few words. I do not
think the point can be put better than it has been by BUCKLEY, J. He says:
' Where the power is merely a general power to borrow, limited only, as
it must be, for the purposes of the company's business, I think the matter
is to be treated in this way, that the lender cannot investigate what the

E   borrower is going to do with the money; he cannot look into the affairs of
the company and say, " Your purposes do not require it now; this borrowing
is unnecessary; you must shew me exactly why you want it." ' "

I have read those passages in full to show, as I think they do show, that that
decision really does not advance the argument of counsel for the plaintiff company
in the present case.

F   Counsel for the plaintiff company referred to *Re Introductions, Ltd., Introductions, Ltd.* v. *National Provincial Bank, Ltd.* (21), where the company concerned
was carrying on a single business, pig-breeding, which was not authorised by
its memorandum and was consequently ultra vires.   BUCKLEY, J., held (22)
that the borrowing under an express power was likewise ultra vires.   Those
passages are directed to the particular case before him, where the company was

G   not carrying on any authorised business, and he held that the power to borrow
was not a power which could subsist in isolation from a business.   That case,
I think, throws no light on the position where, as here, the company concerned
is carrying on a business authorised by its memorandum.

Finally I was referred to a decision of my own, *Ridge Securities, Ltd.* v. *Inland
Revenue Comrs.* (23).   The relevant transaction in that case was a dressed-up

H   gift of a large sum by certain companies to another company which had acquired
their shares.   In the absence of a power in the memorandum of those companies,
the transaction was clearly ultra vires, and, I so held (24).   In this passage I
referred to *Re Lee, Behrens & Co., Ltd.* (25) and I must plead guilty to citing
the whole passage at page 51 in that case (26) without entering on the distinctions
which have become important in the present case but were not important in my

I   own case.

---

(18) (1871), L.R. 12 Eq. 516.
(19) [1904] 2 Ch. at p. 618.
(20) [1904] 2 Ch. at p. 619.
(21) [1968] 2 All E.R. 1221.
(22) [1968] 2 All E.R. at pp. 1225, 1227.
(23) [1964] 1 All E.R. 275; [1964] 1 W.L.R. 479.
(24) [1964] 1 All E.R. at pp. 287, 288; [1964] 1 W.L.R. at p. 495.
(25) [1932] 2 Ch. 46; [1932] All E.R. Rep. 889.
(26) [1932] 2 Ch. at p. 51; [1932] All E.R. Rep. at p. 890.

I conclude on this view of the authorities that they contain nothing which **A** makes it necessary for me to accept the second head advanced by counsel for the plaintiff company. In my judgment, the state of mind of the directors of Castleford and of the bank's officers is irrelevant on this issue of ultra vires.

That is sufficient to dispose of the action; but in case I am wrong on my view of the law, I must proceed to express a conclusion on the contention that in creating the guarantee and legal charge, the directors were not acting with a **B** view to the benefit of the company. That is a question of fact, and the burden of proof lies on the plaintiff company. As I have already found, the directors of Castleford looked to the benefit of the group as a whole and did not give separate consideration to the benefit of Castleford. Counsel for the plaintiff company contended that in the absence of separate consideration, they must, ipso facto, be treated as not having acted with a view to the benefit of Castle- **C** ford. That is, I think, an unduly stringent test and would lead to really absurd results, i.e., unless the directors of a company addressed their minds specifically to the interest of the company in connection with each particular transac- tion, that transaction would be ultra vires and void, notwithstanding that the transaction might be beneficial to the company. Counsel for the bank contended that it is sufficient that the directors of Castleford looked to the **D** benefit of the group as a whole. Equally I reject that contention. Each company in the group is a separate legal entity and the directors of a particular company are not entitled to sacrifice the interest of that company. This becomes apparent when one considers the case where the particular company has separate creditors. The proper test, I think, in the absence of actual separate con- sideration, must be whether an intelligent and honest man in the position of **E** a director of the company concerned, could, in the whole of the existing circum- stances, have reasonably believed that the transaction was for the benefit of the company. If that is the proper test, I am satisfied that the answer here is in the affirmative.

On the date of the guarantee, no sale agreement with the plaintiff company had been made and much work was required to complete the development. **F** Castleford looked to Pomeroy for its own day to day management, for payment of the ground rent which Pomeroy had guaranteed, and, most important, looked to Pomeroy to supply the experience, skill and contacts requisite for the develop- ment of the site and to pay the outgoings involved in such development. It will be remembered that Castleford was under a covenant to erect buildings on the site to the value of £25,000. This being the position, the collapse of Pomeroy **G** would have been a disaster for Castleford. It is true that Castleford would probably have remained solvent and it could no doubt have realised the site. But Castleford would almost certainly have been much worse off than if the site had been properly developed and realised at the most favourable opportunity.

I am satisfied that a director of Castleford, taking an objective view in the exclusive interest of Castleford at the date of the guarantee, could reasonably **H** have concluded that the transaction was for the benefit of that company. It is important to bear in mind that the transaction was by way of a guarantee and, although the guarantee was for a large amount, if all went well with the group, the liability would never have materialised. The same observations apply mutatis mutandis to the creation of the legal charge. Indeed, once one accepts that the guarantee was effective it is difficult to see how, under pressure from the **I** bank, Castleford could have avoided giving the legal charge.

Finally, I must refer to the knowledge, or reputed knowledge, of the bank. This knowledge is an essential part of the claim as formulated on behalf of the plaintiff company. The bank's officers admitted that they had full knowledge of the affairs of the group, including Castleford, and, as I have held, had in all relevant respects the same attitude to the transaction as did Mr. Pomeroy himself, i.e., they looked to the group as a whole and did not consider the interests of the companies, including Castleford, severally. I am wholly unsatisfied that

A the bank's officers knew or must be treated as knowing that the transactions were not for the benefit of Castleford. Even if the plaintiff company had surmounted all its other obstacles, it would, I think, fall at this final one. I do not see how it could be possible to impute this knowledge to the bank's officers. Clearly, one could not do so merely by reason that the bank was looking to the interests of the group as a whole. For the reasons which I have given,

B this action fails.

Action dismissed.

Solicitors: *Slaughter & May* (for the plaintiff company); *Fladgate & Co.* (for the bank).

[*Reported by* JENIFER SANDELL, *Barrister-at-Law.*]

C

THOMSON (Inspector of Taxes) *v.* GURNEVILLE
SECURITIES, LTD.

D GURNEVILLE SECURITIES, LTD. *v.* THOMSON (Inspector
of Taxes).

[CHANCERY DIVISION (Goff, J.), March 17, 18, 19, 20, 21, 24, 26, 1969.]

Income Tax—Relief—Losses—" Trade "—Company dealing in shares—Group's
E *property companies' unrealised profits—Properties worth more than book*
values—Scheme to reduce income tax on profits as realised—Forward dividend
strip—Transfer of properties to four-year life company—Sale in second year
of life—Purchase of four-year company's shares by taxpayer company—
Declaration of dividends by four-year company—Diminution in value of its
shares—Taxpayer company dealer in shares—Loss claim on basis of
F *diminished value—Whether transaction in course of trade or venture in*
nature of trade—Income Tax Act 1952 (15 & 16 Geo. 6 & 1 Eliz. 2 c. 10),
s. 341.

A group of companies included an investment holding company (B.I.) and 102 wholly-owned subsidiary property companies, whose properties had market values greatly in excess of their book values and would, therefore, on realisation produce substantial profits. In order to reduce the

G income tax chargeable on such profits, although with the intention of making a commercial profit—and in fact making one of £90,996, apart from any fiscal advantage—a scheme was devised under which profits would be realised through the medium of a company trading for a limited number of years and making its profits in the penultimate year of its trading

H life. In April 1954, B.I. formed a wholly-owned subsidiary (B.P.) which was to have a trading life of four years and was to make the bulk of its profit in its second accounting period, 7th May 1955 to 7th May 1956. B.P. purchased all the properties from the 102 property companies at book value, and in December 1955, all its shares were purchased by the taxpayer company, recently formed by another collaborating group, at a price reflecting the

I inherent tax-free profit on realisation of the properties, with the result that the first group of companies obtained the benefit of that saving in a capital form. The price was a nominal 30s. per share (£16,803) plus a supplement to be ascertained according to a prescribed formula and being in effect 95 per cent. of the excess over book value of market value, after allowing for taxation. The taxpayer company was to retain the shares and its board was to be under the control of the first group's holding company (provisions abrogated in a later agreement dated 4th May 1956, called the quantification agreement). The properties were not in fact sold and, to complete the

A

transaction in time, the supplement was quantified under the quantification
agreement at £1,769,000 on an estimated total market value of £1·9 millions.
That sum was paid to a further company in the collaborating group as
stakeholder to enable it to provide security for a bank loan to another
newly-formed company of the first group, which thereupon on the same day
bought the properties from the four-year company for £1,611,434.   Finally

B

B.P., as part of a dividend-stripping operation, declared and paid four
dividends totalling £1,720,000 gross.   In accordance with the rule as to
dividends received net after deduction of tax in such cases, the taxpayer
company, as a share-dealing company, excluded the dividends from its
profit or loss as ascertained for income tax purposes and claimed a repayment
of tax on the dividends under s. 341 of the Income Tax Act 1952 on the
footing that it had suffered a loss through diminution in the value of B.P.

C

through payment of the dividends.   The Special Commissioners of Income
Tax found that there was a single composite scheme providing for dividend-
stripping and for the vendors of the shares in B.P. to receive as capital a
sum equal to the unrealised profits in the 102 property companies largely
free of income tax, and that the taxpayer company's purchase of B.P.'s
shares formed part of its trade of dealing in shares, and that it was, therefore,

D

entitled to repayment of tax.   On appeal by the Crown,

   Held: the taxpayer company's claim failed, because—

   (i) although the question was one of fact, the commissioners being assumed
to have rightly directed themselves as to the characteristics of a trade or an
adventure in the nature of trade until the contrary appeared (see p. 1201,
letter F, post) (dicta of Viscount Simonds and Lord Radcliffe in *Edwards*

E

(*Inspector of Taxes*) v. *Bairstow* ([1955] 3 All E.R. at pp. 54 and 56 followed),
nevertheless, the matter was at large because the commissioners had considered the matter only in the light of the decision of the House of Lords
in *Griffiths* (*Inspector of Taxes*) v. *J. P. Harrison* (*Watford*), *Ltd.* ([1962]
1 All E.R. 909), and without the advantage of the further decision of the
House in *Bishop* (*Inspector of Taxes*) v. *Finsbury Securities, Ltd.* ([1966]

F

3 All E.R. 105) and the two subsequent decisions of the High Court in
Cooper (*Inspector of Taxes*) v. *Sandiford Investments, Ltd.* ([1967] 3 All E.R.
835) and *Lupton* (*Inspector of Taxes*) v. *F.A. & A.B., Ltd.* ([1968] 2 All E.R.
1042) (see p. 1202, letters E to G, post);

   (ii) accordingly, notwithstanding the aim of showing a commercial profit

G

apart from any fiscal advantage and the absence of the creation of a special
kind of preference share carrying all the profits available for distribution
for a limited number of years and any sharing of any fruits of a s. 341 claim
or any special leasing and renting transaction such as appeared in earlier
cases, nevertheless having regard to the elaborate artificial structure erected
(three companies specially incorporated, a sale of properties at book value

H

only and complexities not only commercial encountered) to get profits out of
the 102 companies more or less free of tax for the common benefit of vendors
and purchasers and escaping surtax for the benefit of the vendors, the
losses on which the taxpayer company's claim depended were not incurred
in a trade or in a venture in the nature of trade (see p. 1204, letter H, to
p. 1205, letter F, and p. 1206, letter B, post).

I

   Appeal allowed.

[As to relief in respect of trading losses, see 20 Halsbury's Laws (3rd Edn.)
465, para. 880; as to the meaning of trade, see ibid., pp. 113-124, paras. 207-219;
and for cases on the subject, see 28 Digest (Repl.) 20-38, *78-173.*

   As to dividend-stripping, see 20 Halsbury's Laws (3rd Edn.) 201, 202,
para. 356.

   For the Income Tax Act 1952, s. 341, see 31 Halsbury's Statutes (2nd Edn.) 327.]

A Cases referred to:

   Cooper (Inspector of Taxes) v. *Sandiford Investments, Ltd.*, [1967] 3 All E.R.
     835; [1967] 1 W.L.R. 1351; Digest (Repl.) Supp.

   Edwards (Inspector of Taxes) v. *Bairstow*, [1955] 3 All E.R. 48; [1956] A.C. 14;
     [1955] 3 W.L.R. 410; 36 Tax Cas. 207; 28 Digest (Repl.) 397, *1753.*

   Finsbury Securities, Ltd. v. *Bishop (Inspector of Taxes)*, [1965] 1 All E.R. 530;
B   [1965] 1 W.L.R. 358; *affd.*, C.A., [1965] 3 All E.R. 337; [1965] 1 W.L.R.
     1206; *revsd.*, H.L., sub nom., *Bishop (Inspector of Taxes)* v. *Finsbury
     Securities, Ltd.*, [1966] 3 All E.R. 105; [1966] 1 W.L.R. 1402; 43 Tax
     Cas. 591; Digest (Cont. Vol. B) 422, *1352b.*

   Griffiths (Inspector of Taxes) v. *J. P. Harrison (Watford), Ltd.*, [1962] 1 All E.R.
     909; [1963] A.C. 1; [1962] 2 W.L.R. 909; 40 Tax Cas. 281; Digest
C   (Cont. Vol. A) 848, *173k.*

   Inland Revenue Comrs. v. *F. S. Securities, Ltd. (formerly Federated Securities,
     Ltd.)*, [1964] 2 All E.R. 691; [1965] A.C. 631; [1964] 1 W.L.R. 742;
     41 Tax Cas. 666; Digest (Cont. Vol. B) 427, *1588a.*

   Johns (Inspector of Taxes) v. *Wirsal Securities, Ltd., Wirsal Securities, Ltd.* v.
     Johns (Inspector of Taxes), [1966] 1 All E.R. 865; [1966] 1 W.L.R. 462;
D   43 Tax Cas. 629; Digest (Cont. Vol. B) 387, *173kb.*

   Lupton (Inspector of Taxes) v. *F.A. & A.B., Ltd.*, [1968] 2 All E.R. 1042;
     [1968] 1 W.L.R. 1401; Digest (Repl.) Supp.

Case Stated.

   The taxpayer company, Gurneville Securities, Ltd., applied to the Special
E Commissioners of Income Tax under s. 341 of the Income Tax Act 1952 for an
adjustment of its liability to tax by reference to losses alleged to have been
sustained in the trade carried on by it in each of the income tax years (ended on
5th April) 1956-57 and 1957-58. The questions for decision were: (a) for each
of the years to which the application related, whether the transaction entered
into by the taxpayer company in relation to the shares of Bishopsgate Invest-
F ment Co., Ltd. formed part of the trade of share dealing admittedly carried on
at all material times by the taxpayer company; and (b) for 1957-58, (i) whether
Bishopsgate Properties, Ltd. was entitled under s. 184 of the Income Tax Act
1952 to deduct income tax of £221,000 from the dividend of £520 per share
which it paid on its 1,000 issued shares on 1st April 1958, and (ii) what was the
proper treatment of the dividend payment received by the taxpayer company
G from Bishopsgate Investment Co., Ltd. on 1st April 1958 in computing the loss
sustained by the taxpayer company in 1957-58. The issues arose out of a
scheme devised by a director of the taxpayer company, who was also a director
of Bishopsgate Investment Co., Ltd., of Bishopsgate Properties, Ltd. and of
Efgan Securities, Ltd., under which the taxpayer company acquired all the shares
in Bishopsgate Investment Co., Ltd. (termed B.I.), which owned all the shares in
H Bishopsgate Properties, Ltd. (termed B.P.), and also all the shares in 102 property
companies. The objects of the scheme were as follows: (a) B.P., a property-
dealing company, should dispose by way of trade of the properties of the 102
property companies; (b) B.P. should cease to trade just before 5th April 1958,
as a result of which very large profits of that company arising in the year ended
7th May 1956 would enter only to the extent of a small fraction thereof into the
I computation of any assessment to income tax; (c) virtually all the profits earned
by B.P. should be paid as dividends to B.I. (an investment company), which
company should, in turn, pass them on as dividends to the taxpayer company;
(d) the taxpayer company as a share-dealing company should incur a loss through
the writing-down of the values of its shareholding in B.I. because of the diminution
in the value of that holding through the payment of dividends to the taxpayer
company; (e) the taxpayer company should claim repayment of income tax
in respect of that loss by reference to its income consisting largely of the dividends
paid to it by B.I.; (f) the transaction should show a commercial profit apart

from any fiscal advantage. The scheme was carried through but with certain **A** changes*.

The taxpayer company contended as follows: (a) the 11,202 shares in B.I. were purchased as stock-in-trade of the trade of dealing in stocks and shares carried on by the taxpayer company in the period ended 31st March 1957; (b) those shares remained stock-in-trade of the taxpayer company; (c) the losses sustained in the relevant years in that trade of dealing in stocks and **B** shares should be computed by reference, inter alia, to the treatment of the 11,202 shares in B.I. as at all times stock-in-trade of that trade; (d) the losses so sustained were £682,735 in the five days ended 5th April 1957, and £290,333 in the year ended 5th April 1958; (e) the payments received by the taxpayer company from B.I. on 4th April 1957 and 1st April 1958, viz., £682,761 18s. and £289,851 15s. respectively, were true net dividends representing gross **C** dividends of £1,187,412 and £504,090 from each of which income tax at 8s. 6d. in the pound had properly been deducted under the provisions of s. 184 of the Income Tax Act 1952; (f) the taxpayer company was entitled to repayment of income tax under the provisions of s. 341 of the Income Tax Act 1952 as follows: 1956-57: Loss sustained in trading of the five days to 5th April 1957 £682,735; add loss brought forward from previous period £360 = £683,095; repayment **D** £683,095 at 8s. 6d. in pound=£290,315 7s. 6d. 1957-58: Loss sustained in year £290,333; repayment £290,333 at 8s. 6d. in pound = £123,391 10s. 6d.; (g) if B.P. was entitled under s. 184 to deduct tax on 1st April 1958 only from a dividend which represented the excess of its net profits before payment of tax over the dividends previously paid to it, then in calculating these net profits no account should be taken of the loss incurred by B.P. in the period ended 3rd **E** April 1958; (h) further, if B.I. was entitled under s. 184 to deduct tax on 1st April 1958 only from a dividend which represented the excess of its net income before deduction of tax over the dividends previously paid by it, then in calculating that net income account should be taken of the income arising from dividends received by it from pre-acquisition profits of subsidiary companies notwithstanding that these dividends had been credited to a capital reserve and not to **F** the profit and loss account of B.I.; (i) any excess of the net sum of £289,851 15s. received by the taxpayer company from B.I. on 1st April 1958 over such true net dividend as the taxpayer company was entitled to receive from B.I. was not a receipt of the trade carried on by the taxpayer company and should, therefore, be excluded in computing the loss sustained in that trade in the year 1957-58.

The Crown contended as follows: (i) (a) the 11,202 shares in B.I. were not **G** purchased as stock-in-trade of the trade of dealing in stocks and shares carried on by the taxpayer company; (b) those shares never formed part of the stock-in-trade of that trade; (c) the losses arising in the years 1956-57 and 1957-58 in that trade should be computed without taking into account either the cost or the value of the 11,202 shares in B.I.; and alternatively (ii) (a) B.P. was not entitled under the provisions of s. 184 to deduct from dividends paid by it income **H** tax in excess of that deductible from gross dividends not exceeding B.P.'s total net profits before tax; (b) in respect of the dividend paid on 1st April 1958, B.P. was entitled to deduct only the tax appropriate to the excess of its total net profits before payment of tax over the total of the gross amounts of dividends previously paid, such excess being £35,114; (c) on the same principle, in respect of the dividend paid by B.I. on 1st April 1958 B.I. was not entitled under the **I** provisions of s. 184 to deduct tax exceeding that ascertained by reference to its income computed on the basis of excluding that part of the dividend received by it from B.P. from which tax was not deductible and deducting sums disbursed by it as expenses of management in respect of which repayment of tax had been made to B.I.; (d) in computing that income, no account should be taken of dividends received by B.I. from pre-acquisition profits of subsidiary companies

---

* The facts of the case are set out at p. 1199, letter E, to p. 1200, letter I, post.

A which in the books and accounts of B.I. had been credited to a capital reserve account and were not available for the payment of dividends by B.I.; (e) accordingly, B.I. was entitled to deduct from the dividend paid by it on 1st April 1958 £13,958 tax appropriate to £32,843; and (f) in computing the loss sustained in the trade of the taxpayer company for the year 1957-58 the sum of £270,967 being the excess of payment received qua net dividend by it from B.I. on 1st

B April 1958 (£289,852) over the true net dividend (£18,885, i.e., £32,843 less £13,958 tax) should be treated as a receipt of that trade; (g) accordingly, the loss of the taxpayer company for which relief was allowable under s. 341 of the Income Tax Act 1952 was £19,366.

The commissioners held* that the transaction entered into by the taxpayer company in relation to the shares of B.I. formed part of the taxpayer company's

C trade of dealing in shares and that the taxpayer company was, therefore, entitled to relief for 1956-57 under s. 341 by reference to the loss sustained in its trade of share dealing and its income from dividends in respect of its share dealing in B.I. They determined the two further questions raised (in the event not adjudicated on by the court) in favour of the Crown. The Crown appealed by way of Case Stated and the taxpayer company cross-appealed to the High Court.

D   *Arthur Bagnall*, Q.C., *P. W. Medd* and *J. P. Warner* for the Crown.
   M. J. Fox, Q.C., *J. M. Grundy* and *A. E. W. Park* for the taxpayer company.

Cur. adv. vult.

26th March. **GOFF, J.**, read the following judgment: This case arises out of a forward dividend strip, but it was part of a larger scheme which included

E another fiscal arrangement, namely, a realisation of profits by means of a four-year company operation, so as to take advantage of the provisions of s. 127, s. 128 and s. 130 of the Income Tax Act 1952, and thereby greatly to reduce the liability of those profits to income tax. The scheme as a whole was very complicated and, before it could be fully worked out, a very large number of agreements proved necessary. I need not rehearse them in full. They are set out in

F the Case Stated. In substance, the position is as follows: There were two groups of companies, the Sandelson group and the Colman group. The latter included an investment holding company, Bishopsgate Investment Co., Ltd., which is referred to as " B.I.", and 102 wholly-owned subsidiary property companies. They had large unrealised profits, in that the market values were greatly in excess of the book value. If and when realised, those profits would prima facie be

G liable to large sums of income tax. If, however, the profits could be realised through the medium of a company trading for a limited number of years and making its profit in the penultimate full year of its trading life, that tax would be very greatly reduced. For the purposes of the scheme, four years were chosen for the company's life, and, therefore, the profits had to be channelled into the second year. The operation was carried out in concert with the Sandelson

H group, which combined with it a forward dividend strip.

The taxpayer company was incorporated in March 1954 as a wholly-owned subsidiary of Stormgard, Ltd., the head of the Sandelson group, no doubt because it was necessary or desirable to have a company with no previous trading history. The taxpayer company is a share-dealing company. Then, in April 1954, the four-year company, Bishopsgate Properties, Ltd. (referred to as " B.P."), was

I incorporated as a wholly-owned subsidiary of B.I. This company clearly was specially created for the purposes of the scheme. B.P. commenced to trade on 7th May 1954, and purchased all the properties from the 102 property companies at book values. To make the scheme effective, therefore, B.P. must realise the bulk of the profit in its second accounting period, namely, 7th May 1955 to 7th May 1956, and cease trading before 5th April 1958, or alternatively, as affairs were so ordered that the profit was made in the second year, cesser of

─────────────────────
* The decision of the commissioners is set out at p. 1201, letters D and E, post.

trading before 5th April 1958 became imperative. These were essential deadlines. **A**

It would no doubt have been difficult, if not impracticable, for the Colman group to carry out their scheme without the concurrence of the Sandelson group for several reasons, notably provision of finance. Be that as it may, the two groups did in fact concur. The taxpayer company then purchased all the shares in B.I. for a price which reflected the inherent tax-free profit, so giving the shareholders in the Colman group the benefit of that saving in a capital form. **B** The purchase price forms the opening item in the profit and loss account of the taxpayer company. Actually, the shares were purchased by another company in the Sandelson group, Willrose Financial Investments, Ltd., but they were acting as agents for the taxpayer company and nothing turns on that.

The agreement to purchase the shares was made on 23rd December 1955, and it provided for completion within seven days. At that time the actual **C** values could not be ascertained, and, therefore, a nominal sale price of £16,803, being 30s. per share on the B.I. shares, was adopted, plus a supplement to be ascertained later according to a prescribed formula and being in effect 95 per cent. of the excess of the market value, after allowing for taxation, over book value. The agreement required the taxpayer company to retain the shares and gave the vendors control of the board. The date for completion was 7th May **D** 1956, and the formula was manifestly geared to the four-year operation and to cessation of B.P.'s business before 5th April 1958. Completion took place as agreed. The properties were not sold, and time was running out; and so, on 28th February 1956 another company, Carward Properties, Ltd. was incorporated in the Colman group to buy the vast majority of the properties at market value, but it needed finance. Accordingly, on 4th May 1956, the Willrose **E** company, as agents for the taxpayer company, entered into a fresh agreement, the quantification agreement, under which the supplement was quantified at £1,769,000 on an estimated total market value of £1·9 millions. This sum of £1,769,000, which was calculated at 94 per cent. instead of 95 per cent., was forthwith paid to another company in the Sandelson group as stakeholder, with provisions enabling it to use it as security so that the Carward company **F** could arrange the necessary bank loan. There were also, of course, provisions for adjustment of the supplement when the true value should have been ascertained. This agreement abrogated the provisions for the retention of shares and control of the board.

On the same day, immediately after that agreement, the Carward company entered into a contract to buy the properties for £1,611,434, paid on signing of **G** the contract. There were many other details which remained to be worked out, including the disposal of the remaining properties to enable B.P. to cease trading in due time. Suffice it to say the true supplement was not finally ascertained until 15th February 1961; and even then there were certain liabilities of the property companies remaining to be cleared, so large that in respect of them the vendors deposited £300,000 as security. It is interesting to note that the short- **H** fall on the £1·9 millions was no less than £415,000.

To complete the dividend-stripping operation, B.P. declared and paid four dividends. The first three, for the years 1955, 1956 and 1957, amounted to £1,200,000 gross. The fourth, for 1958, was or purported to be £520,000 gross and was paid out as a net £299,000.

It is settled by *Inland Revenue Comrs.* v. *F. S. Securities, Ltd.* (*formerly* **I** *Federated Securities, Ltd.*) (1) that, where a trader receives a franked dividend, i.e., net after deduction of tax, he does not have to bring it into account when ascertaining his profit or loss for tax purposes. Accordingly, the taxpayer company then claimed repayment of tax under s. 341 of the Income Tax Act 1952 for the financial years 1956-57 and 1957-58, on the footing that it had suffered a loss by the diminution in value of the shares in B.I. due to the payment of those large dividends. The figures appear in the Case Stated. It

---

(1) [1964] 2 All E.R. 691; 41 Tax Cas. 666.

A should be noted that this was not the only dealing in shares by the taxpayer company, and the other business, although comparatively small, was not insignificant; and there is no doubt that the taxpayer company is and was at all material times a share-dealing company.

The first question which arises is whether the purchase of the B.I. shares was in the course of a trade or an operation in the nature of trade. If so, then the
B claim is good for the first year and good in principle for the second; but, if not, then it is wholly bad. The commissioners found in favour of the taxpayer company, and the Crown appeals. If that stands, then further questions arise as to the second year, because the gross dividend exceeded the available net profit before tax.

With regard to the first question, the first point I have to determine is whether
C the commissioners' finding that the transaction entered into by the taxpayer company in relation to the shares of B.I. formed part of the taxpayer company's trade of dealing in shares is a finding of fact behind which I cannot go, unless there be some error apparent on the face of the Case, or is a conclusion which no reasonable body could have reached, if properly instructed as to the law. What they actually said was:

D "As regards dividend-stripping being involved in this transaction, the dividend-stripping transaction which was in issue in the case of *Griffiths (Inspector of Taxes)* v. *J. P. Harrison (Watford), Ltd.* (2) was held to form part of that company's trade of dealing in shares or to be an adventure in the nature of trade. Bearing in mind the opinions given in the House of Lords in that case we find on the evidence adduced in the present case that the
E transaction entered into by [the taxpayer company] in relation to the shares of B.I. formed part of [the taxpayer company's] dealing in shares."

I think that it is a finding of fact, because the question of law, what are the characteristics of trade or of an adventure in the nature of trade, is one on which the commissioners are assumed to have rightly directed themselves until the contrary appears: see per VISCOUNT SIMONDS in *Edwards (Inspector
F of Taxes)* v. *Bairstow* (3), where he said:

"But it is a question of law, not of fact, what are those characteristics, or, in other words, what the statutory language means. It follows that the inference can only be regarded as an inference of fact if it is assumed that the tribunal which makes it is rightly directed in law what the characteristics
G are and that, I think, is the assumption that is made."

LORD RADCLIFFE put it thus (4):

"The field so marked out is a wide one, and there are many combinations of circumstances in which it could not be said to be wrong to arrive at a conclusion one way or the other. If the facts of any particular case are fairly capable of being so described, it seems to me that it necessarily follows that
H the determination of the commissioners, special or general, to the effect that a trade does or does not exist is not 'erroneous in point of law'; and, if a determination cannot be shown to be erroneous in point of law, the statute does not admit of its being upset by the court on appeal. I except the occasions when the commissioners, although dealing with a set of facts which would warrant a decision either way, show by some reason they give
I or statement they make in the body of the Case that they have misunderstood the law in some relevant particular."

In *Cooper (Inspector of Taxes)* v. *Sandiford Investments, Ltd.* (5), an error of law clearly appeared on the face of the Case, because the commissioners said that

(2) [1962] 1 All E.R. 909; 40 Tax Cas. 281.
(3) [1955] 3 All E.R. 48 at p. 54; 36 Tax Cas. 207 at p. 225.
(4) [1955] 3 All E.R. at p. 56; 36 Tax Cas. at p. 227.
(5) [1967] 3 All E.R. 835; [1967] 1 W.L.R. 1351.

they were constrained by *Harrison's* case (6) to decide against what would   A
otherwise have been their view; and clearly, in the light of *Bishop* (*Inspector
of Taxes*) v. *Finsbury Securities, Ltd.* (7), they were not so bound. In *Lupton*
(*Inspector of Taxes*) v. *F.A. & A.B., Ltd.* (8), both sides accepted that the question
was one of law; but MEGARRY, J., added (9): "... as indeed *Bishop* (*Inspector
of Taxes*) v. *Finsbury Securities, Ltd.* (7) ... goes far to establish ". The finding
in that case was very similar to the present. It was as follows (10):   B

"As regards the five transactions involving dividend-stripping, the
dividend-stripping transactions which were in issue in *Griffiths* (*Inspector
of Taxes*) v. *J. P. Harrison* (*Watford*), *Ltd.* (6) and *Bishop* (*Inspector of
Taxes*) v. *Finsbury Securities, Ltd.* (11) were held to be within the scope of
a trade of dealing in shares. Bearing in mind the opinions given in the
House of Lords in the former, and the judgments given in the Court of   C
Appeal in the latter, of these cases, the commissioners found on the evidence
adduced in the present case that the five dividend-stripping transactions
entered into by [the taxpayer company] formed part of that company's
trade of dealing in shares."

In the *Finsbury* case (7), LORD MORRIS OF BORTH-Y-GEST said that it was a   D
question of law; but, having regard to *Edwards* (*Inspector of Taxes*) v. *Bairstow*
(12), I think that must have been because the commissioners had stated the
view of the law on which they acted (13). It was, therefore, for the court to
decide whether that was a correct view or not; there could be no room for
assuming that they had correctly directed themselves.

If I am wrong and it is a pure question of law, then obviously the matter is   E
at large before me. If, on the other hand, it is (as I think) a question of fact,
still it is, in my judgment, at large and not one where the finding can only be
upset if it be inexplicable save on the footing of error in law; for here, too, in
my judgment, the commissioners have stated the view of the law on which they
acted, and in the same manner as they did in *Lupton's* case (8). That view,
however, was incomplete and, therefore, wrong. Of course, as counsel for the   F
taxpayer company says, it was right for the commissioners to have regard to
what the House of Lords had said in *Harrison's* case (6). The contrary would
have been manifestly wrong. But they had not a complete view of the law,
because they had not the advantage of *Finsbury's* case (7) in the House of
Lords and the two cases at first instance which have been heard since. They
evaluated the evidence and reached their conclusion in the light of the *Harrison*   G
case (6) alone, but we now know that it ought to be considered in the light of
that case as explained in the *Finsbury* case (7) and as both have been interpreted
and applied by BUCKLEY, J., and MEGARRY, J.

In my judgment, therefore, the matter is at large. Then how does it stand?
It is clear that the facts of this case are by no means identical with any of the
others; but the question is: What is the principle to be deduced from the cases   H
and what result does that lead to on the facts found by the commissioners?
For the principle, I turn first to the speech of LORD MORRIS OF BORTH-Y-GEST
in the *Finsbury* case (14), in which all the other members of the House of Lords
concurred. He said (15), referring to the *Harrison* case (6):

"It was my view in that case that the transaction was demonstrably a

I

(6) [1962] 1 All E.R. 909; 40 Tax Cas. 281.
(7) [1966] 3 All E.R. 105; 43 Tax Cas. 591.
(8) [1968] 2 All E.R. 1042; [1968] 1 W.L.R. 1401.
(9) [1968] 2 All E.R. at p. 1046; [1968] 1 W.L.R. at p. 1413.
(10) [1968] 2 All E.R. at p. 1045; [1968] 1 W.L.R. at p. 1412.
(11) [1965] 3 All E.R. 337; 43 Tax Cas. 591.
(12) [1955] 3 All E.R. 48; 36 Tax Cas. 207.
(13) [1965] 1 All E.R. at p. 531; 43 Tax Cas. at p. 596.
(14) [1966] 3 All E.R. at p. 107; 43 Tax Cas. at p. 622.
(15) [1966] 3 All E.R. at p. 111; 43 Tax Cas. at p. 627.

A share-dealing transaction. Shares were bought: a dividend on them was received: later the shares were sold. There may be occasions when it is helpful to consider the object of a transaction when deciding as to its nature. In the *Harrison* case (16) my view was that there could be no room for doubt as to the real and genuine nature of the transaction. The fact that the reason why it was entered into was that the provisions of the revenue law

B gave good ground for thinking that welcome fiscal benefit could follow did not in any way change the character of the transaction."

and again (17):

"A consideration of the transactions now under review leads me to the opinion that they were in no way characteristic of, nor did they possess, the

C ordinary features of the trade of share dealing. The various shares which were acquired ought not to be regarded as having become part of the stock-in-trade of the company. They were not acquired for the purpose of dealing with them. In no ordinary sense were they current assets. For the purposes of carrying out the scheme which was devised the shares were to be and had to be retained. The arguments before your lordships depended mainly on the

D submission by the Crown that the shares were acquired for a period of five years as part of the capital structure of the company from which an income would be earned and, on the other hand, on the submission of the company that they were acquired as part of their stock-in-trade. In my opinion neither argument is correct. For the reasons I have already given this transaction on its particular facts was not, within the definition of s. 526, ' an adventure

E or concern in the nature of trade ' at all. It was 'a wholly artificial device remote from trade to secure a tax advantage."

BUCKLEY, J., observed in *Cooper (Inspector of Taxes)* v. *Sandiford Investments, Ltd.* (18) that the *Harrison* (16) and *Finsbury* (19) cases were both distinguishable on the facts, but he made two statements of principle. First, after reviewing the *Harrison* case (16), he said (20):

F "That decision does not establish that, wherever a company engaged in the trade of dealing in shares acquires shares with a view to making some profit, the transaction will necessarily be a transaction entered into in the course of that trade. One has to investigate the true nature of the transaction and find whether or not it was in fact a transaction entered into in the course of the trade of dealing in shares. If one comes to the conclusion that

G it is a transaction in the course of such a trade, then the fact that there may be some incidental fiscal advantage connected with it will not deprive it of that character."

Then, after mentioning the *Finsbury* case (19), he said (21):

"That case, which again was very different on its facts from the present

H case, demonstrates this, that where a company engaged in the trade of dealing in shares and securities acquires shares with the object of obtaining a profit of a fiscal character, the mere fact that the shares are acquired with a view to obtaining a profit, and are acquired by a company that deals in shares, does not conclude the question of whether or not those acquisitions are acquisitions in the course of the company's trade of dealing in shares. One

I must look at the circumstances of the particular transaction and discover what its true nature is."

He concluded his judgment by holding that the transaction before him was

---

(16) [1962] 1 All E.R. 909; 40 Tax Cas. 281.
(17) [1966] 3 All E.R. at p. 112; 43 Tax Cas. at p. 627.
(18) [1967] 3 All E.R. 835; [1967] 1 W.L.R. 1351.
(19) [1966] 3 All E.R. 105; 43 Tax Cas. 591.
(20) [1967] 3 All E.R. at p. 840; [1967] 1 W.L.R. at p. 1359.
(21) [1967] 3 All E.R. at p. 841; [1967] 1 W.L.R. at p. 1360.

much more like what the House of Lords had to consider in the *Finsbury* case (22), **A**
and (23) " is appropriately described as an artificial device remote from the
taxpayer company's trading activities ".

In the *Lupton* case (24), MEGARRY, J., said that it seemed to him that the
Harrison case (25) was a narrow decision on a narrow point, which—

> " ... merely decides that a transaction is not prevented from being a
> trading transaction merely because its object is not to make a trading profit **B**
> but to obtain a tax advantage."

He then made two statements of principle. He said (26):

> " If on analysis it is found that the greater part of the transaction consists
> of elements for which there is some trading purpose or explanation (whether
> ordinary or extraordinary), then the presence of what I may call ' fiscal **C**
> elements ', inserted solely or mainly for the purpose of producing a fiscal
> benefit, may not suffice to deprive the transaction of its trading status.
> The question is whether, viewed as a whole, the transaction is one which can
> fairly be regarded as a trading transaction.   If it is, then it will not be
> denatured merely because it was entered into with motives of reaping a
> fiscal advantage.   Neither fiscal elements nor fiscal motives will prevent **D**
> what in substance is a trading transaction from ranking as such. On the other
> hand, if the greater part of the transaction is explicable only on fiscal grounds,
> the mere presence of elements of trading will not suffice to translate the trans-
> action into the realms of trading. In particular, if what is erected is predomin-
> antly an artificial structure, remote from trading and fashioned so as to
> secure a tax advantage, the mere presence in that structure of certain **E**
> elements which by themselves could fairly be described as trading will not
> cast the cloak of trade over the whole structure."

Later, he said this (27):

> " I do not think that the right approach is, after analysing each transaction
> meticulously, to compare the constituent elements with those present or **F**
> absent in other cases and then to decide the matter on the degree of corres-
> pondence or divergence.   Instead, I consider that each arrangement should
> be regarded as a whole in the light of the principles which I have derived
> from the cases. If at the end of the day a transaction, viewed as a whole,
> appears to be merely, or substantially, a trading transaction, then despite
> the presence of fiscal elements or fiscal motives a trading transaction it **G**
> remains. If, on the other hand, the transaction as a whole appears to be no
> trading transaction but an artificial device remote from trade to secure a tax
> advantage, then the presence of trading elements in it will not secure its
> classification as a trading transaction."

I have not found this case entirely easy to decide; but, having carefully reviewed all the facts as found by the commissioners and evinced by the docu- **H**
ments, I have reached the conclusion that this case is on the *Finsbury* (22)
rather than the *Harrison* (25) side of the line. I have, of course, against that,
the finding that it was an object of the scheme that the transaction should
show a commercial profit apart from any fiscal advantage, and that it did result
in a profit of £90,996. That, however, was largely dependent on dividends
which could not have been paid out but for the operation of the four-year plan. **I**
It is true that the taxpayer company might have made a comparable profit
by paying a price which allowed for full taxation on the vendors' profits without

(22) [1966] 3 All E.R. 105; 43 Tax Cas 591.
(23) [1967] 3 All E.R. at p. 842; [1967] 1 W.L.R. at p. 1362.
(24) [1968] 2 All E.R. at p. 1049; [1968] 1 W.L.R. at p. 1417.
(25) [1962] 1 All E.R. 909; 40 Tax Cas. 281.
(26) [1968] 2 All E.R. at p. 1051; [1968] 1 W.L.R. at p. 1419.
(27) [1968] 2 All E.R. at p. 1054; [1968] 1 W.L.R. at p. 1423.

A a four-year plan; for then, although the dividends would have been less, so would the price. But that was not the transaction, nor would it have suited either party.

There are also strong features in favour of the Crown in the *Finsbury* (28) and *Lupton* (29) cases which are not present here, namely, the creation of a special kind of preference share carrying all the profits available for distribution for a

B limited number of years, the absence of profit and in some cases actually a loss, apart from the s. 341 claim; and, in the *Finsbury* case (28) only, sharing of the fruits of any claim under s. 341. In one example, however, in the *Lupton* case (29) no special shares were created and MEGARRY, J., still reached the same conclusion, although it is fair to say that he did so with considerable doubt and despite a strong indication of a fiscal nature in a warranty related to the

C repayment claim. In *Cooper (Inspector of Taxes)* v. *Sandiford Investments, Ltd.* (30), no peculiar property was created, but it was at least an unusual transaction to assign a lease at a nominal rent and take an underlease at a large rent, and still more to pay the whole rent in advance. That was surely explicable only on fiscal considerations.

On the other hand, I have the finding of the commissioners that there was

D here one single composite scheme providing not only for dividend-stripping resulting in a claim in respect of losses under s. 341, but for the vendors to receive as capital a sum equal to the unrealised profits in the 102 property companies calculated by virtue of the four-year operation largely free of income tax and for the s. 341 claim to be swollen by that freedom from taxation. This necessarily involved retention of the shares or rendered them not readily saleable until the

E scheme had been worked out. It was not merely an operation, as in the *Harrison* case (31), of buying shares in a company pregnant with profits, declaring a dividend and reselling or retaining the shares until the end of the year. It included getting the profits out of the 102 companies more or less free of tax for the common benefit of vendors and purchasers and escaping surtax liability for the benefit of the vendors, and for those purposes an elaborate artificial structure had to be

F erected, and complexities were encountered which I think were not merely commercial ones. Three companies were specially incorporated; the taxpayer company itself, B.P. and the Carward company, the purchaser of the properties; and there was a sale by the 102 companies at book values only.

The original agreement for purchase contained the remarkable feature that, although the price could not be ascertained for some years because it depended

G on the working out of the tax position and because the position as to the underlying assets was uncertain, so uncertain that it was afterwards found that B.P. had sold properties to which it had no title or which it had already sold, yet completion was to take place within seven days for a nominal price and a supplement to be afterwards calculated. Further, this entailed an express agreement by the purchasers to retain the shares and that the vendors should,

H notwithstanding completion, retain control of the board. It is significant that the expression " the said date " in that agreement, on which the price formula is based, is the end of the second year of B.P.'s trading. That agreement clearly contemplated the realisation of the properties so as to channel the profits into the second year. Then comes the quantification agreement, under which, although as appears on the face of it the price could not be ascertained for three

I years, the purchasers agreed to pay immediately on an estimate, and provision was made for the purchase money to be paid to stakeholders and made available to finance the purchase by the Carward company. This agreement and the complexities which it entailed were clearly for the purposes of the four-year plan and fiscal.

---

(28) [1966] 3 All E.R. 105; 43 Tax Cas. 591.
(29) [1968] 2 All E.R. 1042; [1968] 1 W.L.R. 1401.
(30) [1967] 3 All E.R. 835; [1967] 1 W.L.R. 1351.
(31) [1962] 1 All E.R. 909; 40 Tax Cas. 281.

I cannot attach much importance to the argument of counsel for the tax- A
payer company that that company never became contractually bound to cease
business so as to implement the four-year operation, because it is plain both from
the commissioners' findings and from the documents themselves that it was the
common intention from the start; nor, for the same reason, do I think significant
the finding that Mr. Sandelson only decided early in April that B.P. should
cease trading.   B

Looking, as I am bidden to do, at the transaction as a whole, I have come to the
conclusion that the losses on which the claim depends were not incurred in a
trade or in a venture in the nature of trade; and the appeal, therefore, succeeds.

The questions raised on the cross-appeal and the Crown's notice of additional
contentions do not, therefore, arise. They are, first, whether, assuming the loss
claim under s. 341 was otherwise good: (a) the taxpayer company is bound to C
bring into account the whole of the net dividend received in the year 1957-58
because the grossed-up amount of the dividend declared in respect of that year
exceeded the total net profits before tax, less previous dividends; or, alternatively, (b) whether at least the amount of the excess must be charged against
the loss; and, secondly, if the latter be the true view, then (a) in calculating such
excess the trading loss in that year must be deducted from the profits and (b) D
the available profits ought to be treated as increased by capital reserves in the
hands of B.I. representing pre-acquisition profits.

Both parts of the first question came before PENNYCUICK, J., in *Johns*
(Inspector of Taxes) v. *Wirsal Securities, Ltd.* (32). The difference between total
exclusion and apportionment in that case was very small and, for the purpose
of stating his reasons, the judge ignored this; but I am satisfied that he did E
actually decide between the two alternatives and held that the whole of the
purported net dividend must be brought into account. He said (33):

"Neither counsel has very strenuously sought to support the conclusion
reached by the Special Commissioners. The dividend consisted in the actual
distribution of the sum of £279,422, expressed and intended to be franked
of tax by reference to a gross dividend of larger amount. I find it impossible F
to treat this distribution as representing in part a dividend of the same gross
amount after deduction of tax and, as to the balance, a distribution without
deduction of tax. In the result, this whole tax avoidance scheme has misfired.
It is not for this court to reform the scheme so as to make it partly effective."

If I am wrong on the main question I would follow that decision, since it turns
simply on the construction of s. 184, s. 185, and s. 186 of the Income Tax Act G
1952; and counsel for the taxpayer company has not really invited me to do
otherwise, but he has, of course, saved his position, should the case go to a
higher court. In the circumstances, therefore, the other subsidiary questions
do not in any event arise, and I express no opinion on them, although they too
will, of course, be open should they become material as the result of any decision
on appeal.   H

Appeal allowed.

Solicitors: *Solicitor of Inland Revenue; Beer, Timothy Jones & Webb* (for the
taxpayer company).

[*Reported by* F. A. AMIES ESQ., *Barrister-at-Law.*]

I

---

(32) [1966] 1 All E.R. 865; 43 Tax Cas. 629.
(33) [1966] 1 All E.R. at p. 876; 43 Tax Cas. at p. 655.

A

COLLYMORE AND ANOTHER v. ATTORNEY-GENERAL OF TRINIDAD AND TOBAGO.

[PRIVY COUNCIL (Lord Pearce, Lord Donovan, Lord Pearson and Sir Richard Wild), February 19, 20, 24, May 5, 1969.]

B
Privy Council—Trinidad and Tobago—Constitution—Freedom of association guaranteed—Abridgment of right to free collective bargaining—Abridgment of freedom to strike—Freedom of association not violated—Industrial Stabilisation Act 1965 (No. 8 of 1965)—Trinidad and Tobago (Constitution) Order in Council 1962 (S.I. 1962 No. 1875), Sch. 2, s. 1 (j).

C
Natural Justice—Disclosure to parties of information before court—Court empowered to seek information—Power to withhold information from parties—Whether fair hearing in accordance with principles of fundamental justice—Industrial Stabilisation Act 1965 (Trinidad and Tobago) (No. 8 of 1965), s. 11 (2), as substituted by Act No. 6 of 1967—Trinidad and Tobago (Constitution) Order in Council 1962 (S.I. 1962 No. 1875), Sch. 2, s. 2 (e).

D
The abridgment of the right to free collective bargaining and of the freedom to strike by the Industrial Stabilisation Act 1965 did not constitute a breach of the right of freedom of association guaranteed under the Constitution of Trinidad and Tobago (Trinidad and Tobago (Constitution) Order in Council 1962, Sch. 2, s. 1 (j)), (see p. 1212, letter C, post).

In proceedings before the industrial court between an employer and a
E
worker representations may be made in the name of the Attorney-General on behalf of the people of Trinidad and Tobago and the court is directed to take into account, inter alia, specific considerations relating to the public interest. In such proceedings the authority given to the court (s. 11 (2) of the Industrial Stabilisation Act 1965, as substituted by Act No. 6 of 1967), to seek information and to use such information in the discharge of its duty
F
without necessarily disclosing it to the parties before the court, does not amount to a violation of the right of a person to a fair hearing in accordance with the principles of fundamental justice guaranteed by the Constitution (Trinidad and Tobago (Constitution) Order in Council 1962, Sch. 2, s. 2 (e)) (see p. 1214, letters G and H, post).

Appeal dismissed.

G Cases referred to:
Crofter Hand Woven Harris Tweed Co., Ltd. v. *Veitch*, [1942] 1 All E.R. 142; [1942] A.C. 435; 111 L.J.P.C. 17; 166 L.T. 172; 45 Digest (Repl.) 534, *1175*.

Official Solicitor v. *K.*, [1963] 3 All E.R. 191; [1965] A.C. 201; [1963] 3 W.L.R. 408; *revsg.* sub nom. *Re K. (infants)*, [1962] 3 All E.R. 1000; [1963]
H
Ch. 381; [1962] 3 W.L.R. 1517; *revsg.*, [1962] 3 All E.R. 178; [1963] Ch. 381; [1962] 3 W.L.R. 752; Digest (Cont. Vol. A) 933, *2149b*.

Rookes v. *Barnard*, [1964] 1 All E.R. 367; [1964] A.C. 1129; [1964] 2 W.L.R. 269; 45 Digest (Repl.) 308, *227*.

Russell v. *Duke of Norfolk*, [1949] 1 All E.R. 109; 12 Digest (Repl.) 693, *5321*.

I **Appeal.**
This was an appeal by Learie Collymore and John Abraham from the decision of the Court of Appeal of Trinidad and Tobago (SIR HUGH WOODING, C.J., PHILLIPS and AUBREY FRASER, JJ.A.) dated 27th January 1967, dismissing the appeal of the appellants from the judgment of the High Court of Trinidad and Tobago (CORBIN, J.) dated 11th December 1965 dismissing an application of the appellants on motion for a declaration that the Industrial Stabilisation Act 1965 was ultra vires the Constitution of Trinidad and Tobago. The facts are set out in the opinion of LORD DONOVAN.

R. Millner, Q.C., and *D. J. Turner-Samuels* for the appellants.

J. G. Le Quesne, Q.C., and *S. G. Davies* for the Attorney General of Trinidad and Tobago.

LORD DONOVAN: This appeal raises the question whether the Industrial Stabilisation Act 1965 is ultra vires the Constitution of Trinidad and Tobago and therefore void and of no effect.

The two appellants, Mr. Collymore and Mr. Abraham, were in 1965 employees of an oil company in Trinidad called Texaco Trinidad, Inc., and they and other fellow employees in this company were members of a trade union registered under the local Trade Union Ordinance and known as the Oilfield Workers' Trade Union. This union bargained on behalf of its members with Texaco Trinidad, Inc., on questions of pay and conditions. In March 1965, being desirous of altering the then current collective agreement on these matters, the trade union in question submitted to the company a statement of the changes required. Negotiations followed but without any agreement resulting, and in July 1965 the company by letter broke them off.

In the ordinary way it would no doubt have been expected that industrial action would follow, and that the union would have called its members out on strike for the purpose of enforcing their demands. This apparently did not happen, the reason being the existence of the Industrial Stabilisation Act 1963 which received the Royal Assent on 20th March 1965 and repealed a previously existing enactment called " The Trade Disputes (Arbitration and Enquiry) Ordinance ".

Before quoting the relevant provisions of the Act it is necessary to refer to certain of the terms of the Trinidad and Tobago Constitution. It is embodied in a statutory instrument (1) and so far as concerns the provisions relevant to the present issue came into force immediately before 31st August 1962. Section 1 of the Constitution provides as follows:

" It is hereby recognised and declared that in Trinidad and Tobago there have existed and shall continue to exist without discrimination by reason of race, origin, colour, religion or sex, the following human rights and fundamental freedoms, namely, (a) the right of the individual to life, liberty, security of the person and enjoyment of property, and the right not to be deprived thereof except by due process of law; (b) the right of the individual to equality before the law and the protection of the law; (c) the right of the individual to respect for his private and family life; (d) the right of the individual to equality of treatment from any public authority in the exercise of any functions; (e) the right to join political parties and to express political views; (f) the right of a parent or guardian to provide a school of his own choice for the education of his child or ward; (g) freedom of movement; (h) freedom of conscience and religious belief and observance; (i) freedom of thought and expression; (j) freedom of association and assembly; and (k) freedom of the press."

Section 2 is in these terms, so far as immediately relevant:

" Subject to the provisions of Sections 3, 4 and 5 of this Constitution, no law shall abrogate, abridge or infringe or authorise the abrogation, abridgment or infringement of any of the rights and freedoms hereinbefore recognised and declared . . ."

Section 4 of the Constitution preserves the right of Parliament to pass special laws for the period of any public emergency, notwithstanding s. 1 and s. 2; and s. 5 prescribes a special procedure for the enactment of laws which may conflict with s. 1 and s. 2, subject to certain specified safeguards. Section 6 allows a person to apply to the High Court for redress if he considers that any of the foregoing provisions of the Constitution have been or are likely to be contravened

(1) The Trinidad and Tobago (Constitution) Order in Council 1962 (S.I. 1962 No. 1875).

A in relation to him. Section 36 enacts that " Subject to the provisions of this Constitution, Parliament may make laws for the peace, order and good government of Trinidad and Tobago ".

It will be noted that s. 1 (*j*) of the Constitution preserves, as one of the " human rights and fundamental freedoms " the freedom of association and assembly. It is the appellants' main contention that the Industrial Stabilisation Act 1965

B abrogates, abridges or infringes this right or freedom, contrary to the terms of s. 2 of the Constitution.

The long title of the Industrial Stabilisation Act is as follows:

" An Act to provide for the compulsory recognition by employers of trade unions and organisations representative of a majority of workers, for the establishment of an expeditious system for the settlement of trade disputes,

C for the regulation of prices of commodities, for the constitution of a court to regulate matters relating to the foregoing and incidental thereto."

So far as industrial disputes are concerned the Act virtually imposes on employers and employees alike a system of compulsory arbitration for the settlement of such disputes instead of industrial action such as lockouts and strikes. The

D arbitration is to be by an industrial court which is established by the Act. Thus if any trade dispute exists or is apprehended it may, if not otherwise determined, be reported to the Minister having responsibility for labour matters, either by the employer or his representative or by an organisation or trade union representing the workers.

If in the Minister's opinion suitable means already exist for settling the dispute

E by virtue of some agreement to which the organisations representative of employers and workers are parties, the Minister is to refer the matter for settlement accordingly. If this produces no settlement within seven days, the parties are to inform the Minister who may then cancel the reference, and either take such steps as seem expedient to him to promote a settlement, or alternatively refer the dispute to the industrial court " for settlement ". He may also take

F either of these last two steps where there is no agreement such as is referred to at the commencement of this paragraph.

If the Minister takes steps himself to promote a settlement, but these fail, the Minister must refer the dispute " for settlement " to the industrial court and is to do so within 21 days from the date on which the trade dispute was first reported to him. A settlement effected by any of the foregoing means is to

G bind both the employers and workers to whom it relates, and the rate of wages to be paid and the conditions of employment to be observed are to become implied terms of such workers' contracts until varied by a subsequent agreement.

The foregoing provisions are to be found in s. 16 of the Act under the heading of " Trade dispute procedure ": and while it is true that there is no compulsion on either side to report a trade dispute which exists or is apprehended, it is not

H very likely that both sides will fail to do so, particularly in view of the provisions of the Act with regard to lockouts and strikes which are to be found in s. 34 to s. 38 inclusive.

Section 34 enacts that no employer shall declare or take part in a lockout and no worker shall take part in a strike in connection with any trade dispute unless, the dispute having been reported to the Minister, he has not referred

I it to the industrial court within 28 days from the date the report was made to him. Furthermore, 14 days' notice of any such lockout or strike must be given to the Minister and the lockout or strike may not take place until after the last day on which the Minister may refer the dispute to the industrial court. Penalties for any breach of s. 34 are imposed on employers, trade unions, any individual who calls workers out on strike in contravention of the section, and on any workers who take part in such a strike. The penalty in each case may be a fine or imprisonment or both. Furthermore, an offending trade union is to be de-registered, and this, under the Trade Unions Ordinance involves its dissolution.

The Act does not contemplate that proceedings before the industrial court A
will result in anything other than a determination of the trade dispute. The
court consists of a judge of the Supreme Court of Judicature and four other
members. Its duty inter alia, is " to hear and determine trade disputes ", and
it decides by a majority. There is a right of appeal on a point of law to the
Court of Appeal, and s. 35 of the Act prohibits lockouts and strikes during the
pendency of the appeal. Section 36 of the Act deals with employers and workers B
engaged in essential services. These are defined as electricity, fire, health, hospital,
sanitary (including scavenging) and water services. Lockouts and strikes in
these services are completely prohibited on pain of a fine or imprisonment or
both. The provisions of the Act already recited for the settlement of trade
disputes will of course apply in the case of these occupations. Save with regard
to essential services it is the case that lockouts and strikes are not completely C
prohibited, since the starting point of the procedure which results in a ban on
industrial action is a report to the Minister which neither side is compelled to
make. But this contingency of no report may reasonably be supposed to be
remote and the effect of the Act in that event is, as has already been said, virtually
to impose a system of compulsory arbitration for the settlement of trade disputes.
    The appellants now claim that the Act is void since it infringes their freedom D
of association which s. 1 of the Constitution declares has existed " and shall
continue to exist ", and any abrogation, abridgment or infringement of which
is forbidden by s. 2, save in circumstances which admittedly do not exist in the
present case.
    The argument runs thus: " Freedom of association " must be construed in
such a way that it confers rights of substance and is not merely an empty phrase. E
So far as trade unions are concerned, the freedom means more than the mere
right of individuals to form them; it embraces the right to pursue that object
which is the main raison d'être of trade unions, namely collective bargaining
on behalf of their members over wages and conditions of employment. Collective
bargaining in its turn is ineffective unless backed by the right to strike in the last
resort. It is this which gives reality to collective bargaining. Accordingly to F
take away or curtail the right to strike is in effect to abrogate or abridge that
freedom of association which the Constitution confers.
    The argument of the respondent is that " freedom of association " in s. 1 (j)
of the Constitution means no more that it says, that persons are free to associate.
It does not mean that the purposes for which they associate, and the objects
which, in association they pursue, are sacrosanct under the Constitution and G
cannot be altered or abridged save by the special procedure provided by s. 5.
    The question thus posed is therefore simply a question of construction. But
the arguments presented for the appellants, based on the assertion that the
right to free collective bargaining and the right to strike are essential elements
in freedom of association in trade unions, led to a prolonged examination in the
courts below whether there is in law any " right " to strike. The question does H
not really arise if the respondent's contention as above summarised is right;
for, if " freedom of association " does not of itself import freedom to bargain
collectively and to do so effectively by means of a strike, it is immaterial whether
strike action is or is not the exercise of a " right " or a " freedom " or the enjoyment of " an immunity ". Since however the matter was exhaustively canvassed
in the courts below their Lordships may say that they are in substantial agree- I
ment with the analysis of the situation which emerged. It was agreed before
their Lordships that trade union law in Trinidad and Tobago was the same as
trade union law in Great Britain as at the date when the Trade Disputes Act
1906 took effect. Neither before that date nor since has there been in Great
Britain any express enactment by statute of any right to strike, although in
certain quarters such an enactment is still advocated. At common law before
the enactment of the Trade Union Act 1871, the Conspiracy and Protection of
Property Act 1875, and the amendment to s. 3 thereof effected by s. 1 of the

A Trade Disputes Act 1906, combinations of workmen to improve their wages and conditions were certainly in peril if in combination they withheld their labour or threatened to do so, but (subject to certain esoteric questions arising out of the decision in *Rookes* v. *Barnard* (2) and still unresolved by the Trade Disputes Act 1965) it is now well recognised that by reason of the statutes cited, as well as by decisions such as *Crofter Hand Woven Harris Tweed Co., Ltd.* v. *Veitch* (3)

B employees may lawfully withhold their labour in combination free from the restrictions and penalties which the common law formerly imposed. In this sense there is " freedom to strike ".

There is no doubt that the freedom to bargain collectively has been abridged by the Industrial Stabilisation Act 1965. Thus Part 4 of the Act, embodying s. 18 to s. 26 provides for the making of " industrial agreements " between

C trade unions and employers, subject to the examination of the same by the Minister who is to submit the agreement to the industrial court for registration, together with a notice containing the ground of any objection to the agreement which he has. The court then hears and deals with such objections. It may register the agreement without amendment, or with agreed amendments, or it may refer the agreement back to the parties for further negotiations. The

D agreement takes effect only if it is registered by the court.

There is also no doubt that the Act abridges the freedom to strike. Indeed in the case of the essential services already mentioned it appears to abrogate it altogether. It makes no difference to the foregoing situation that the Act in s. 3 strengthens the position of trade unions in relation to collective bargaining by imposing on employers an obligation to recognise and negotiate with a

E union representing 51 per cent. or more of his workers. The question is whether the abridgement of the rights of free collective bargaining and of the freedom to strike are abridgements of the right of freedom of association.

Both courts below answered the question in the negative; and did so by refusing to equate freedom to associate with freedom to pursue without restriction the objects of the association.

F Sir Hugh Wooding, C.J., put the matter thus:

" In my judgment, then, freedom of association means no more than freedom to enter into consensual arrangements to promote the common interest objects of the association group. The objects may be any of many. They may be religious or social, political or philosophical, economic or professional, educational or cultural, sporting or charitable. But the freedom

G to associate confers neither right nor licence for a course of conduct or for the commission of acts which in the view of Parliament are inimical to the peace, order and good government of the country."

It is, of course, true that the main purpose of most trade unions of employees is the improvement of wages and conditions. But these are not the only purposes which trade unionists as such pursue. They have in addition in many cases objects

H which are social, benevolent, charitable and political. The last named may be at times of paramount importance since the efforts of trade unions have more than once succeeded in securing alterations in the law to their advantage. It is also of interest to note what the framers of convention no. 87 of the International Labour Organisation considered to be comprised in " Freedom of Association ". Under that subheading the convention, art. 1 to art. 5 inclusive, read as follows:

I " Article 1. Each Member of the International Labour Organisation for which this Convention is in force undertakes to give effect to the following provisions.

" Article 2. Workers and employers, without distinction whatsoever shall have the right to establish and, subject only to the rules of the organisation concerned, to join organisations of their own choosing without previous authorisation.

---

(2) [1964] 1 All E.R. 367; [1964] A.C. 1129.   (3) [1942] 1 All E.R. 142; [1942] A.C. 435.

" Article 3. 1. Workers' and employers' organisations shall have the right   A
to draw up their constitutions and rules, to elect their representatives in full
freedom, to organise their administration and activities and to formulate
their programmes.   2. The public authorities shall refrain from any interference which would restrict this right or impede the lawful exercise thereof.
      " Article 4. Workers' and employers' organisations shall not be liable to
be dissolved or suspended by administrative authority.   B
      " Article 5. Workers' and employers' organisations shall have the right to
establish and join federations and confederations and any such organisation,
federation or confederation shall have the right to affiliate with international
organisations of workers and employers."

All these rights are left untouched by the Industrial Stabilisation Act 1965. It
therefore seems to their Lordships inaccurate to contend that the abridgment   C
of the right to free collective bargaining and of the freedom to strike leaves the
assurance of " freedom of association " empty of worth-while content.
      Moreover, trade unions need more than " freedom of association ".   They
need to establish an organisation. This involves setting up some kind of headquarters, and appointing officers to man it. Branches may also have to be set
up either in districts where the union has sufficient members, or in particular   D
plants or offices. Arrangements must be made for the due collection, usually
weekly, of subscriptions. Recognition by the employer must be obtained as a
prelude to collective bargaining. Arrangements have to be made for industrial
action in the event of collective bargaining failing either wholly or partly.
All this is something over and above freedom of association. It involves a union
having freedom also to organise and to bargain collectively; and it is not sur-   E
prising therefore to find this right the subject of a separate convention (no. 98)
of the International Labour Organisation. Their Lordships accordingly agree with
the courts below in their rejection of the appellants' main argument.
      Certain other objections to particular sections of the Industrial Stabilisation
Act 1965 were taken by the appellants who alleged that these also infringed the
Constitution. By comparison with the main objection, these were subsidiary; and   F
it was conceded that even if all or any of these objections were upheld they could
not invalidate the whole Act, but would simply require its amendment. With
one exception their Lordships do not think it necessary to deal with these matters
in detail. It is sufficient to say that they were examined and rejected by SIR
HUGH WOODING, C.J. in the Court of Appeal for reasons on which their Lordships
could not improve and to which they do not desire to add. The one exception   G
concerns s. 10 and s. 11 of the Act.
      Section 10 deals with the representation of the people of Trinidad before the
industrial court when it is engaged in hearing a trade dispute; and sub-s. (2)
of the section originally empowered the Attorney-General for the purpose of
collecting evidence required in order to present the case on behalf of such people,
to authorise a public officer to enter on the business premises of any " employer,   H
trade union or other organisation " and to require the production of any books,
documents, accounts or returns relevant to any trade dispute whether existing
or anticipated. SIR HUGH WOODING, C.J., in his judgment said that he found this
power alarming. He added:

      " In exercising the authority which he may be given by the Attorney-
General thereunder a public officer may uncover vital commercial secrets or   I
gather valuable information about manufacturing processes all or any of
which, if so disposed, he may thereafter use or abuse."

Section 10 has now however been amended by Act No. 6 of 1967 and the
Attorney-General no longer has the power to authorise a public officer to enter on
premises for the foregoing purposes. He may simply authorise the officer to
require the production of books, documents, accounts, etc., " relevant to any
trade dispute ". This must mean an existing trade dispute and not, as specifically
provided before, " any trade dispute existing or anticipated ".

A

The appellants asserted that in its original form s. 10 (2) contravened s. 1 (c) of the Constitution which assured the right of the individual to respect for his private and family life. SIR HUGH WOODING, C.J. rejected this contention as not being open to the appellants. They could complain, under s. 6 of the Constitution only if any contravention " *in relation to them* " and neither appellant was " an employer, trade union or other organisation ". Their Lordships, with

B respect, think this may be too narrow a ground on which to base a rejection of the appellants' argument. For a trade union in Trinidad appears to be, as in Great Britain, simply an unincorporated society, and each individual member may be said therefore to be affected by the power which s. 10 (2) originally gave to the Attorney-General in respect of a trade union. But since the power to enter the premises of any trade union has now been taken away, no further

C discussion of the point seems to be called for.

Section 11 (2) of the Act in its original form empowered the industrial court to require the commissioner of inland revenue or any other person who would give information to provide such information as the court might require from time to time. It gave the court a discretion whether to disclose information so obtained to the parties on their application, and discretion also to prohibit the publication

D thereof. This subsection has now been repealed by the same Act No. 6 of 1967 and the following words substituted:

" For the purpose of dealing with any matter before it, the Court may on its own motion summon any person who in the opinion of the Court is able to give such information as it may consider necessary, and may, notwithstanding anything contained in the Income Tax Ordinance or in any

E law, require the Board of Inland Revenue or any member thereof to produce or make available any information which the Court may consider necessary, and the Court may, in its discretion, disclose so much as it thinks fit of the information so produced or made available and may also prohibit the publication of any portion therof."

The criticism made of s. 11 (2) in its original form was that it contravened s. 2 (e)

F of the Constitution which declared that no Act of Parliament should—

" deprive a person of the right to a fair hearing in accordance with the principles of fundamental justice for the determination of his rights and obligations."

Under s. 11 (2) in its original form, and also indeed in what has been substituted for it, it is possible for the industrial court to come to a conclusion on the basis

G of information which it keeps secret to itself; and this it is said is a violation of the principles of fundamental justice.

This problem is not new. There are exceptional circumstances when a court finds itself in this dilemma; if it is known that the information it obtains will be disclosed to the parties before it and also perhaps to the world at large, then those persons who have the information may, despite their legal obligation, resort to

H one device or another to avoid giving it, or will give information which is not the truth or the whole truth. Justice may not therefore be done. On the other hand the knowledge that the court will treat the information in strict confidence greatly increases the probability that it will be forthcoming. Yet in this case the parties themselves will understandably feel aggrieved that they have not had the chance of verifying or testing the information which the court has secured, and which in

I some cases may be decisive.

A case raising a similiar issue is *Official Solicitor* v. *K.* heard by the House of Lords in 1963 (4). There the mother of two wards of court asked to see two confidential reports on the infants which the Official Solicitor had made to the judge. The judge (5) refused to disclose them to her. The Court of Appeal (6) reversed the judgment. The House of Lords (4) restored it. There are, of course, certain special features about cases concerning infants, since the welfare of an

infant has to be treated as the first and paramount consideration. But the mother A
in her appeal to the House of Lords insisted that the principles of natural justice
required the disclosure of the reports to her, she being a party to the wardship
proceedings. In the course of dealing with this claim pronouncements were made
in the House of Lords of a general character which may be usefully quoted.

LORD EVERSHED quoted (7) and adopted the following observation of TUCKER,
L.J., in *Russell* v. *Duke of Norfolk* (8):   B

" There are, in my view, no words which are of universal application to every
kind of inquiry and every kind of domestic tribunal. The requirements of
natural justice must depend on the circumstances of the case, the nature
of the inquiry, the rules under which the tribunal is acting, the subject-matter
that is being dealt with, and so forth."

LORD DEVLIN said (9):   C

" But a principle of judicial inquiry, whether fundamental or not, is only
a means to an end. If it can be shown in any particular class of case that
the observance of a principle of this sort does not serve the ends of justice,
it must be dismissed; otherwise it would become the master instead of the
servant of justice. Obviously, the ordinary principles of judicial inquiry are
requirements for all ordinary cases and it can only be in an extraordinary D
class of case that any one of them can be discarded."

And again (10):

" Where the judge sits as an arbiter between two parties, he need consider
only what they put before him. If one or other omits something material
and suffers from the omission, he must blame himself and not the judge.
Where the judge sits purely as an arbiter and relies on the parties for his
information, the parties have a correlative right that he should act only on E
information which they have had the opportunity of testing. Where the
judge is not sitting purely or even primarily as an arbiter but is charged with
the paramount duty of protecting the interests of one outside the conflict,
a rule that is designed for just arbitrament cannot in all circumstances
prevail."   F

In cases before the industrial court the issue is not solely between employers
and employed. The people of Trinidad may also be parties; and the court is
directed by s. 9 of the Industrial Stabilisation Act 1965 in addition to taking into
account the evidence presented on behalf of all the parties to be guided by a number
of other specified considerations, e.g.: " the necessity to maintain and expand the
level of employment ": " the need to maintain for Trinidad and Tobago a favour- G
able balance of trade and balance of payments "; " the need to ensure the
continued ability of the Government of Trinidad and Tobago to finance development programmes in the public sector " and so on. In discharging this duty the
court may well have to seek information which it feels cannot be disclosed to the
parties before it. This is a matter in its discretion, and, as SIR HUGH WOODING,
C.J., indicated in his judgment, any alleged wrongful exercise of its discretion H
might be tested on appeal as a matter of law. In these circumstances their Lordships do not feel that they can uphold the contention that s. 11 (2) of the Act
either in its original or altered form infringes the Constitution.

They will accordingly humbly advise Her Majesty that the appeal should be
dismissed. The appellants must pay the costs of the appeal.

Appeal dismissed.   I

Solicitors: *A. L. Bryden & Williams* (for the appellants); *Charles Russell & Co.*
(for the respondent).

[*Reported by* S. A. HATTEEA, ESQ., *Barrister-at-Law.*]

---

(7) [1963] 3 All E.R. at p. 196; [1965] A.C. at p. 218.
(8) [1949] 1 All E.R. 109 at p. 118.
(9) [1963] 3 All E.R. at p. 209; [1965] A.C. at p. 238.
(10) [1963] 3 All E.R. at p. 210; [1965] A.C. at p. 240.

A

MENDELSSOHN v. NORMAND, LTD.

[COURT OF APPEAL, CIVIL DIVISION, (Lord Denning, M.R., Edmund Davies and
Phillimore, L.JJ.), February 25, 26, 1969.]

B

*Contract—Exception clause—Oral promise—Garaging of car—Clause exempting
garage proprietors from liability for any loss or damage sustained by the
vehicle, its accessories or contents—Oral promise by garage attendant that car
would be locked—Car not locked—Property stolen from car—Whether loss of
property within exception clause—Whether garage proprietors liable.*

Bailment—Deviation from terms—Exception clause—Liability of bailee.

C
   The plaintiff frequently left his motor car in the garage of the defendants.
He always obtained a ticket on the back whereof were, inter alia, the
conditions: " 1. The garage proprietors will not accept responsibility for
any loss sustained by the vehicle, its accessories or contents, however
caused . . . 6. No variation of these conditions will bind the garage proprietors unless made in writing signed by their duly authorised manager."
The plaintiff did not read those conditions. On the relevant occasion he

D
intended to leave a car in the defendants' garage with some valuable
luggage in the back and wanted to lock it as he used to do. The garage
attendant, however, insisted that according to the rules the door ought not
to be locked. The plaintiff informed him of the luggage in the back and
then gave him the car keys. The attendant promised to lock the car. Later
the plaintiff found that his luggage was stolen. In proceedings for damages

E
the defendants pleaded that they were not liable by reason of the exception
clauses.

   Held: (i) the exception clauses were part of the contract of bailment
(see p. 1217, letter D, p. 1218, letter H, and p. 1219, letter I, post); and
even on a restricted construction they covered the theft of the luggage (see
p. 1217, letter I, p. 1218, letter H, and p. 1219, letter I, post).

F
   (ii) the defendants, however, were not able to rely on the exception
clauses because: (a) the oral promise by the attendant that he would lock
the car took priority over the printed clauses of the contract (see p. 1218,
letter C, p. 1219, letter I, and p. 1220, letter D, post); or (b) the defendants
carried out their contract in a way other then the parties envisaged (see
p. 1218, letters E to H, p. 1219, letter I, and p. 1220, letter D, post).

G
   Appeal dismissed.

[As to exception clauses, see SUPPLEMENT to 8 HALSBURY'S LAWS (3rd Edn.),
para. 215A, and as to their construction, see 11 HALSBURY'S LAWS (3rd Edn.)
392-394, para. 641; for cases on the subject, see 3 DIGEST (Repl.) 81-85, *169-198.*]

Cases referred to:

H
City & Westminster Properties (1934), Ltd. v. *Mudd,* [1958] 2 All E.R. 733;
        [1959] Ch. 129; [1958] 3 W.L.R. 312; Digest (Cont. Vol. A) 1028,
        6376a.
Couchman v. *Hill,* [1947] 1 All E.R. 103; [1947] K.B. 554; [1948] L.J.R. 295;
        176 L.T. 278; 2 Digest (Repl.) 348, *333.*
Curtis v. *Chemical Cleaning and Dyeing Co.,* [1951] 1 All E.R. 631; [1951]

I
        1 K.B. 805; 3 Digest (Repl.) 103, *289.*
Firestone Tyre & Rubber Co., Ltd. v. *Vokins & Co., Ltd.,* [1951] 1 Lloyd's Rep.
        32.
Gibaud v. *Great Eastern Ry. Co.,* [1921] 2 K.B. 426; [1921] All E.R. Rep. 35;
        90 L.J.K.B. 535; 125 L.T. 76; 3 Digest (Repl.) 91, *217.*
Harling v. *Eddy,* [1951] 2 All E.R. 212; [1951] 2 K.B. 739; 2 Digest (Repl.)
        349, *334.*
McCutcheon v. *David MacBrayne, Ltd.,* [1964] 1 All E.R. 430; [1964] 1 W.L.R.
        125; Digest (Cont. Vol. B) 72, *254b.*

Morris v. *C. W. Martin & Sons, Ltd.*, [1965] 2 All E.R. 725; [1966] 1 Q.B. 716; **A**
      [1965] 3 W.L.R. 276; Digest (Cont. Vol. B) 30, *151a.*

Olley v. *Marlborough Court, Ltd.*, [1949] 1 All E.R. 127; [1949] 1 K.B. 532;
      [1949] L.J.R. 360; 29 Digest (Repl.) 16, *186.*

Spurling (J.), Ltd. v. *Bradshaw*, [1956] 2 All E.R. 121; [1956] 1 W.L.R. 461;
      3 Digest (Repl.) 84, *196.*

Suisse Atlantique Société D'Armement Maritime S.A. v. *N.V. Rotterdamsche* **B**
      Kolen Centrale, [1966] 2 All E.R. 61; [1967] 1 A.C. 361; [1966] 2
      W.L.R. 944; Digest (Cont. Vol. B) 652, *2413a.*

Appeal.

This was an appeal by the defendants, Normand, Ltd., from a judgment of
His Honour DEPUTY JUDGE SIR GRAEME FINLAY at Bloomsbury and Marylebone
County Court on 20th May 1968, holding the defendants liable for the loss of **C**
property belonging to the plaintiff, Alfred Mendelssohn. The plaintiff's claim
was for breach of bailment and alternatively for negligence.

D. E. Hill-Smith for the defendants.
R. M. Yorke for the plaintiff.

    LORD DENNING, M.R.: On 25th January 1967 the plaintiff, Mr. **D**
Mendelssohn, and his wife and friends were about to go on a holiday to the
continent. They were going to have lunch at the Cumberland Hotel at Marble
Arch. The plaintiff drove the car into the defendants' Cumberland Garage. It
was a Rolls-Royce car with a distinguished number HON 1. It was not his car
but his friend's car. The plaintiff drove the car up the ramp to the first floor
into the open space. He stopped the car and got out. There was luggage on the **E**
back seat. One piece was a suitcase containing jewellery and other valuables.
It was covered up by a rug. The plaintiff was about to lock up the car when an
attendant came up to him. I will give the plaintiff's own account of what took
place. He said:

    " I took my key out of the ignition and was just going to lock the door **F**
    when the attendant came up and said: ' You are not allowed to lock your
    car '. I explained to him about the luggage and that we were just going across
    for lunch. I explained to him that the luggage was rather valuable and that
    I would not be long. He then said: ' Sorry, but those are the rules and I
    cannot allow you to lock it '. So I gave him the keys into his hand and told
    him as soon as he had moved the car to lock it up. This he agreed to do."
                                                                              G
The attendant gave the plaintiff a ticket for the car. The plaintiff went off to
lunch. After an hour he came back. He paid his fee at the reception desk and
went up to his car. It had been moved a few yards but there was no attendant
there at that moment. The plaintiff found that the driver's door was unlocked.
The key was in the ignition lock. The rug appeared to be just in the same
position on the back seat. He got in. At that moment a different attendant **H**
came up and took the ticket. The plaintiff drove the car on various errands:
but between 6.0 p.m. and 7.0 p.m. he found that the suitcase was missing. He
went back to the garage. Enquiries were made. It was never found. The
plaintiff was satisfied that it had been taken whilst the car was in the garage.
He sued the defendants, Normand, Ltd., for £200 as compensation for the loss
of this suitcase. The judge held that the suitcase had been stolen from the car **I**
when the door was left unlocked. He concluded that it was stolen by one of the
attendants at the garage, and in all probability by the man who had received
this car on the first floor. The defendants are, therefore, liable for the loss of
the suitcase unless they can bring themselves within the exempting conditions.
That is clear from *Morris* v. *C. W. Martin & Sons, Ltd.* (1). The only question
for us is whether the defendants are protected by the conditions.

---

(1) [1965] 2 All E.R. 725; [1966] 1 Q.B. 716.

A   There are two conditions here to be considered. First, a condition on a notice displayed at the reception desk. This could not be seen by a driver when he brought his car into the garage, but only when he came back to collect it. He might see it when he went to the reception desk to pay the charge. In the window there was a notice saying in large letters: "Customer's Property. Important Notice" and then in smaller letters a condition exempting the

B   defendants from loss of or damage to a vehicle or its contents. The plaintiff had been to the reception desk many times before. He may have seen the notice, but he had never read it. Such a notice is not imported into the contract unless it is brought home to the party so prominently that he must be taken to have known of it and agreed to it: see *Olley* v. *Marlborough Court, Ltd.* (2), and *McCutcheon* v. *David MacBrayne, Ltd.* (3), per LORD DEVLIN. That was not so

C   here. The defendants did not prove that the plaintiff knew of the terms of this notice nor that he agreed to it. They cannot, therefore, rely on it.

Secondly, there was a condition on the ticket. The attendant gave the plaintiff a ticket with printed conditions on it, the plaintiff had been to this garage many times and he had always been given a ticket with the selfsame wording. Every time he had put it into his pocket and produced it when he

D   came back for the car. He may not have read it. But that does not matter. It was plainly a contractual document; and, as he accepted it without objection, he must be taken to have agreed to it. That appears from *J. Spurling, Ltd.* v. *Bradshaw* (4). As LORD DEVLIN said in *McCutcheon* v. *David MacBrayne, Ltd.* (5):

"... when a party assents to a document forming the whole or a part of his contract, he is bound by the terms of the document, read or unread,

E   signed or unsigned, simply because they are in the contract; ..."

The conditions on that ticket were, therefore, part of the contract.

The ticket on the face read: "Cumberland Garage ... FOR TERMS OF GARAGE SEE OVER ". On the back there was the heading: "Conditions on which vehicles are accepted ": and then followed the conditions. They included:

F   "1. The [defendants] will not accept responsibility for any loss or damage sustained by the vehicle its accessories or contents however caused ...
6. No variation of these conditions will bind the [defendants] unless made in writing signed by their duly authorised manager."

The judge held that the condition no. 1 on the ticket was ambiguous. He took the words: "... any loss or damage sustained by the vehicle its accessories or

G   contents however caused ", and he said: "These words seem to me to be inept applied to this case as I cannot envisage loss 'sustained by' the contents of the vehicle ". On that ground he held that the defendants could not rely on the condition. I agree that the condition is ambiguous. The ambiguity is due, no doubt, to a printer's error. By mistake the printers missed out the little word "of ". The condition should have read: "will not accept responsibility for any

H   loss *of*, or damage sustained by, the vehicle its accessories or contents however caused ". The omission of the word "of " means that the condition is ambiguous. It has a wider meaning, which I can best express by inserting brackets: "any loss (or damage sustained by the vehicle its accessories or contents) however caused "—so that it means any loss of anything however caused. It has also a narrower meaning by inserting the word "of " so that it reads: "any loss *of*,

I   or damage sustained by the vehicle, its accessories or contents however caused ": so that it covers loss of the contents however caused. The ambiguity affords good reason for adopting the narrower meaning; but not for throwing over the condition altogether. Even the narrower meaning is enough to exempt the defendants. Prima facie the defendants can rely on it.

(2) [1949] 1 All E.R. 127 at p. 134; [1949] 1 K.B. 532 at p. 549.
(3) [1964] 1 All E.R. 430 at p. 437; [1964] 1 W.L.R. 125 at p. 134.
(4) [1956] 2 All E.R. 121 at p. 125; [1956] 1 W.L.R. 461 at p. 467.
(5) [1964] 1 All E.R. at p. 437; [1964] 1 W.L.R. at p. 134.

I cannot agree, therefore, with the ground on which the judge based his **A**
decision. But the case does not end there. The plaintiff has put in a cross-notice.
He seeks to support the judgment on other grounds. He relies on the conversation
which the plaintiff had with the attendant. The attendant promised to lock up
the car. In other words, he promised to see that the contents were safe. He did
not do so. Instead he left the car unlocked. It was probably he who took the
suitcase himself. What is the effect of such a promise? It was not within the **B**
actual authority of the attendant to give it but it was within his *ostensible*
authority. He was there to receive cars on behalf of the defendants. He had
apparent authority to make a statement relating to its custody. Such a statement is binding on the company. It takes priority over any printed condition.
There are many cases in the books when a man has made, by word of mouth,
a promise or a representation of fact, on which the other party acts by entering **C**
into the contract. In all such cases the man is not allowed to repudiate his
representation by reference to a printed condition, see *Couchman* v. *Hill* (6),
Curtis v. *Chemical Cleaning and Dyeing Co.* (7) and *Harling* v. *Eddy* (8); nor
is he allowed to go back on his promise by reliance on a written clause, see *City
& Westminster Properties (1934), Ltd.* v. *Mudd* (9) per HARMAN, J. The reason
is because the oral promise or representation has a decisive influence on the **D**
transaction—it is the very thing which induces the other to contract—and it
would be most unjust to allow the maker to go back on it. The printed condition
is rejected because it is repugnant to the express oral promise or representation.
As DEVLIN, J. said in *Firestone Tyre & Rubber Co., Ltd.* v. *Vokins & Co.,
Ltd.* (10): " It is illusory to say—' we promise to do a thing, but we are not
liable if we do not do it '." To avoid this illusion, the law gives the oral promise **E**
priority over the printed clause.

There is a second ground too. It derives from the deviation cases. If a man
promises to keep a thing in a named place, but instead keeps it in another place,
he cannot rely on an exemption clause: see *Gibaud* v. *Great Eastern Ry. Co.* (11).
That doctrine has been extended to cases where a man promises to perform his
contract in a certain way, and instead performs it in an entirely different way. **F**
He too cannot rely on an exemption clause; because it is construed as applying
only when he is carrying out his contract in the stipulated way and not when
he is breaking it in a fundamental respect. Those cases still stand and are in
no way diminished in authority by *Suisse Atlantique Société D'Armement Maritime
S.A.* v. *N.V. Rotterdamsche Kolen Centrale* (12). It was there said to be all a matter
of construction. So here, the defendants agreed to keep this Rolls-Royce car **G**
locked up; instead they left it unlocked and whilst unlocked their servant
stole the suitcase. This was so entirely different a way of carrying out the
contract that the exemption clause cannot be construed as extending to it.

On both these grounds, I think that the defendants cannot rely on the exemption condition. I would dismiss the appeal.

H

EDMUND DAVIES, L.J.: I agree. In this appeal, as always, the proved
facts are vital to a rightful determination, and in ascertaining what the facts
were, it is pertinent to observe that the learned trial judge paid tribute to the
candour and reliability of the plaintiff. Accordingly, when he proceeds to
recount what the evidence of the plaintiff was, this court is entitled to regard
that evidence as having found acceptance with the judge, unless he has indicated **I**
expressly to the contrary. Now I say that for this reason: much has been

---

(6) [1947] 1 All E.R. 103; [1947] K.B. 554.
(7) [1951] 1 All E.R. 631; [1951] 1 K.B. 805.
(8) [1951] 2 All E.R. 212; [1951] 2 K.B. 739.
(9) [1958] 2 All E.R. 733 at p. 742; [1959] Ch. 129 at p. 145.
(10) [1951] 1 Lloyd's Rep. 32 at p. 39.
(11) [1921] 2 K.B. 426; [1921] All E.R. Rep. 35.
(12) [1966] 2 All E.R. 61; [1967] 1 A.C. 361.

A rightly said about the fact that this was far from being the first occasion for the plaintiff to make use of this particular garage. But the extent to which he had to mind his P's and Q's depended, of course, on the circumstances of each visit, and the visit with which we are now concerned was unique. Something happened on this occasion which had never happened to him before, for he said: " Never on any previous occasion did I have to have the car unlocked." But

B what happened on this particular occasion was this—and I quote from the judgment:

> " The plaintiff went on to tell me that he switched off the ignition, removed the keys and was just about to lock the driver's door when the attendant came up and said ' You are not allowed to lock your car '. The plaintiff went on to explain to him that the luggage was rather valuable and

C that he would not be long."

Then:

> " He mentioned to the attendant that there was luggage on the back seat but the attendant insisted that the rules of the garage did not allow the owner to lock it . . . ' So (said the plaintiff) I gave him the keys into his

D hand and told him as soon as he had moved the car to lock it up. This he agreed to do '."

Accordingly, on the plaintiff's account—which, I repeat, appears to be his *unchallenged* account—he found himself in a situation which, although he had paid many visits to that garage before, had a completely novel feature to it. The learned judge later said this:

E > " If the rules of the garage had been observed, then the plaintiff would have locked up his car effectively leaving his car out of gear with the hand-brake off. If he had been allowed to do this, then, in my opinion the theft would not have taken place."

Was that right or was it wrong? In my judgment it was a finding of fact on

F which the learned judge was entirely entitled to arrive, and which indeed seemed, if I may say so, an eminently reasonable conclusion.

Then he continued in this way:

> " The defendants are, of course, responsible for the wrongful acts of their servant done in the course of his employment. Their counsel [who has again today assisted this court very greatly] argued that attendants were expressly

G forbidden by the rules of the establishment to demand customers' keys, but I cannot, in view of Mr. Smith's evidence, accept this contention. It seems to me that this was a wrongful and unauthorised mode of doing an act authorised by the defendants and so they are equally liable."

The accuracy of that last sentence is accepted by counsel for the defendants. In those circumstances, the plaintiff being persuaded by the undertaking of the

H servant that he would lock the car forthwith, whereas he did nothing of the kind, as was demonstrated when the plaintiff returned an hour later, is it to be said that the terms of the contractual document, the ticket, prevent recovery? In my judgment it would be a sorry state of the law if that question demanded an affirmative answer. In the light of the authorities to which LORD DENNING, M.R., has already referred, I share his view that the actual contractual terms,

I and in particular conditions no. 1 and no. 6 on the back of the parking ticket, do not disentitle the plaintiff to recover in the circumstances which the learned judge here found proved.

For those reasons I agree that this appeal should be dismissed.

PHILLIMORE, L.J.: I also agree. The submission which counsel for the plaintiff made is that but for the conversations which the plaintiff had with the employee of the defendants it is obvious that he would have made other arrangements or perhaps he would not have left the car there at all. He was clearly concerned about his luggage, and it seems to me that he was induced to leave the car there by a firm promise that it would be locked. Whether one regards that promise as a representation or whether one regards it as a collateral term of the contract, or whether one regards the contract as being partly oral and partly in writing in the shape of the ticket, it seems to me it can make no real difference. It is quite clear that if it was really a representation, then, on the authority of *Curtis* v. *Chemical Cleaning and Dyeing Co.* (13), the defendants could not in such circumstances, namely, the representation being made and believed, rely on their exemption clauses. In the words of DENNING, L.J., in that case (14):

"In my opinion, any behaviour by words or conduct is sufficient to be a misrepresentation if it is such as to mislead the other party about the existence or extent of the exemption. If it conveys a false impression, that is enough. If the false impression is created knowingly, it is a fraudulent misrepresentation; if it is created unwittingly, it is an innocent misrepresentation. But either is sufficient to disentitle the creator of it to the benefit of the exemption."

So if this undertaking formed part of the contract, in my judgment, the matter comes within the decision of DEVLIN, J., in *Firestone Tyre & Rubber Co., Ltd.* v. *Vokins & Co., Ltd.* (15). In particular I would refer to the passage (16) to which LORD DENNING, M.R., has already alluded. In my judgment the submissions which counsel for the plaintiff has made are correct and he is also entitled to say that if one has an express undertaking, as here, followed by printed clauses, the latter must fail insofar as they are repugnant to the express undertaking. In my judgment this plaintiff was entitled to succeed on the fresh matter contained in the cross-notice. Accordingly I would dismiss the appeal.

Appeal dismissed. Leave to appeal to the House of Lords refused.

Solicitors: *Berrymans* (for the defendants); *Randall, Rose & Co.* (for the plaintiff).

[*Reported by* F. GUTTMAN, ESQ., *Barrister-at-Law.*]

PRACTICE DIRECTION.

CHANCERY DIVISION.

Infant—Guardianship of Infants Acts—Appeals from courts of summary jurisdiction—Legal aid in connection with appeal—Extension of time—Procedure.

Where a party intends to appeal to the Chancery Division of the High Court against an order made by a court of summary jurisdiction under the Guardianship of Infants Acts, and to apply for legal aid in connection with the appeal, he should promptly after the hearing give notice of his intention to the other party. If this is done, the judge of the Chancery Division who hears the appeal will in the absence of special circumstances normally give leave for the necessary extension of time at the hearing of the appeal and without any prior application.

The direction printed in the Supreme Court Practice 1967 under R.S.C., Ord. 91, r. 7, should be read subject to the foregoing direction.

By direction of PENNYCUICK, J.

C. M. KIDD,
Chief Registrar,
Chancery Division.

14th July 1969.

---

(13) [1951] 1 All E.R. 631; [1951] 1 K.B. 805.
(14) [1951] 1 All E.R. at p. 634; [1951] 1 K.B. at pp. 808, 809.
(15) [1951] 1 Lloyd's Rep. 32.
(16) [1951] 1 Lloyd's Rep. at p. 39.

A   ADAMS AND OTHERS v. RICHARDSON AND
                              STARLING, LTD.

[COURT OF APPEAL, CIVIL DIVISION (Lord Denning, M.R., Salmon and Winn,
     L.JJ.), March 12, 13, April 1, 15, 1969.]

Warranty—Effectiveness of work—Work done by experts—Treatment of dry-rot
B   *—Ten-year guarantee against re-infestation—Whether specialists' obligation*
      extended or limited by warranty—Ordinary canons of construction applied
      —" Guarantee "—" And ".

       In 1958 the defendants undertook to treat dry-rot in a dwelling-house.
     They gave the following " guarantee ": " [The defendants] guarantee the
     efficacy of the treatment they apply to timber or masonry for the eradication
C   of insect or fungal attack and, subject to the undernoted exclusions, will
      re-treat free of charge any such timber or masonry showing signs of re-
      infestation during the period of ten years from the date of treatment.
      This guarantee holds good to any owner for the time being of the property
      described, during the period of the guarantee. Exclusions from the fore-
      going guarantee. This guarantee does not cover the cost of opening up or
D   of re-instatement nor does it apply to . . ." Dry-rot re-appeared in 1963
      all over the house and was remedied at great cost. In February 1967,
      the plaintiffs brought an action against the defendants under the ten-year
      guarantee for the full cost. The defendants contended that their liability
      thereunder extended only to the re-treatment, free of charge, of timber
      and masonry which showed signs of re-infestation. On appeal,
E   **Held:** (LORD DENNING, M.R., dissenting) the guarantee, which was to be
      read as a whole, did not negative the defendants' implied obligation to take
      reasonable care and to use reasonable skill but was an additional obligation
      which they undertook, should re-infestation occur within ten years, over and
      above such obligations as arose under the other terms of the contract or
      from their employment as experts; accordingly, their liability under the
F   warranty extended only to the re-treatment free of charge, of timber and
      masonry which showed signs of re-infestation (see p. 1227, letter B, p. 1228,
      letter B, p. 1229, letter I, to p. 1230, letter A, and p. 1232, letters F and I,
      post).
          Appeal dismissed.

       [As to exception clauses, see SUPPLEMENT TO 8 HALSBURY's LAWS (3rd Edn.),
G   para. 215A; and as to their construction, see 11 HALSBURY's LAWS (3rd Edn.)
      392-394, para. 641; for cases on the subject, see 3 DIGEST (Repl.) 81-85, *169-198.*]

      Cases referred to:
        Aspdin v. *Austin* (1844), 5 Q.B. 671; 13 L.J.Q.B. 155; 114 E.R. 1402; 12
              Digest (Repl.) 681, *5251.*
H   *Cartledge (Widow and Administratrix of the Estate of Fred Hector Cartledge (decd.))*
              v. *E. Jopling & Sons, Ltd.,* [1963] 1 All E.R. 341; [1963] A.C. 758;
              [1963] 2 W.L.R. 210; 32 Digest (Repl.) 401, *259.*
        Firestone Tyre & Rubber Co., Ltd. v. *Vokins & Co., Ltd.,* [1951] 1 Lloyd's
              Rep. 32.
        Howell v. *Young* (1826), 5 B. & C. 259; [1824-34] All E.R. Rep. 377; 4
I   L.J.O.S.K.B. 160; 108 E.R. 97; 32 Digest (Repl.) 402, *269.*
        Mathew v. *Blackmore* (1857), 1 H. & N. 762; 26 L.J.Ex. 150; 28 L.T.O.S. 325;
              166 E.R. 1409; 17 Digest (Repl.) 304, *1113.*
        Mendelssohn v. *Normand, Ltd.,* P. 1215, ante.
        Rhodes v. *Forwood* (1876), 1 App. Cas. 256; [1874-80] All E.R. Rep. 476;
              47 L.J.Q.B. 396; 34 L.T. 890; 12 Digest (Repl.) 700, *5355.*

      Interlocutory appeal.
        This was an appeal by the plaintiffs from a decision of His Honour NORMAN
      RICHARDS, Q.C., an official referee, dated 24th January 1969, whereby he held

on a preliminary issue that the guarantee referred to in the pleadings was only **A**
an obligation of the defendants to re-treat any re-infestated timber or masonry.
The facts are set out in the judgment of LORD DENNING, M.R.

A. R. Campbell, Q.C., and *D. D. H. Sullivan* for the plaintiffs.
E. M. Ogden, Q.C., and *P. B. Creightmore* for the defendants.

Cur. adv. vult.   **B**

1st April.   The following judgments were read.

LORD DENNING, M.R.: The parties have asked the courts to decide
some preliminary issues. For this purpose we have to assume the facts pleaded
to be correct. I will state them. Lord Waleran had his London house at 22,
Launceston Place, Kensington, W.8. Early in 1958 dry-rot appeared on the
first floor and was suspected on the other floors. Lord Waleran engaged a **C**
well-known surveyor, Mr. Martin French. He got in touch with the defendants,
Richardson and Starling, Ltd., who specialised in timber decay, particularly
in the treatment of dry-rot. The defendants came and inspected the house.
Lord Waleran told them to do all that was necessary to get rid of the dry-rot.
He did not " want to have two bites at the cherry ".
On 20th March 1958, the defendants made a report to Lord Waleran's surveyor **D**
in which they explained the work to be done. The first thing to do would be
to expose the whole of the growth of dry-rot. They would have to strip the
plaster off the walls (this would be done by their own men) and to open up the
floors (which would be done by " contractors "). They would have to continue
this exposure for another two feet so as to form a clear marginal band round the
affected area. After they had exposed all the growth, they would have to eradicate it. **E**
Their own men would treat the affected timbers, and the timbers in
the vicinity, and also the masonry. These would be " thoroughly saturated
with a suitable fungicide so as to ensure eradication of the deeply penetrating
hyphal strands of dry-rot ". If some of the timbers were very badly affected,
the contractors' men would have to remove them and insert new timbers in
their place. In this report the defendants said that they could not give a firm **F**
quotation for the work, because the full extent of the treatment could not be
determined in advance, but they thought that their work (apart from the
contractors' work) would be in the region of £130.
In addition to that report, the defendants sent an estimate and a leaflet in
which they gave a ten-year guarantee. They made much of this guarantee.
They stressed it time and again. They headed it in old English lettering: **G**

" GUARANTEE

Adequate treatment to accessible timbers, carried out by our own trained
operatives, is covered by our written TEN YEAR GUARANTEE. [There
followed the first limb of the guarantee]. [The defendants] guarantee the
efficacy of the treatment they apply to timber or masonry for the eradication
of insect or fungal attack [followed by a second limb] and, subject to the **H**
undernoted exclusions, will re-treat free of charge any such timber or
masonry showing signs of re-infestation during the period of ten years from
the date of treatment. [In addition an item which read:] This guarantee
holds good to any owner for the time being of the property described,
during the period of the guarantee ... ".

I

Lord Waleran was suitably impressed. It would seem to him, no doubt, that
the defendants promised to eradicate the dry-rot from the house and to do it so
effectively that it would not appear again in the next ten years. He decided
to employ the defendants. A contract was concluded which included the report,
the estimate, and the leaflet. The defendants did their work between April and
June 1958, and sent in a bill for £147 5s. 8d. for their work. Lord Waleran
paid it. He also paid the contractors £1,850 for their work. So it cost him in all
some £2,000.

A   The defendants did not live up to their promises. They did not succeed in eradicating the dry-rot. It appeared again in 1963, that is, in less than five years. It appeared (so we must take it) in the very places which the defendants were supposed to have treated; and, furthermore, it was found to have spread insidiously from these original places to other parts of the house too. Lord Waleran was very upset. He called in the defendants again, and also the

B   contractors. This time they did the work thoroughly. But it was a big job. Workmen were in the house for months. Lord and Lady Waleran had to move out for six months during the worst of it. The cost was great. The contractors had to open up a lot. They had to take out many timbers and replace with new ones. Their bill came to £5,738 9s. 2d. The defendants had to do much treatment with the fungicide. Their bill came to £687 19s. 3d. So the total

C   cost was nearly £6,500.

Lord Waleran was determined to claim against the defendants on their ten-year guarantee. But unfortunately he died on 4th April 1966, before starting an action. His executors, however, took it up. On 12th February 1967, they brought an action against the defendants on the ten-year guarantee. But the defendants said that their liability under this guarantee was extremely limited.

D   It was limited, they say, to re-treating the places which they originally treated (the cost would be, I suppose, about £147). Their liability did not extend, they said, to re-treating the new places to which the dry-rot had spread; nor did it extend to any of the contractors' work of opening up and re-instatement.

The plain fact, therefore, is that the defendants fell down on their promise to eradicate the dry-rot. Lord Waleran suffered much loss and damage. He

E   had to spend £6,500 to put it right. But the defendants say that, under the guarantee, they are only liable to pay £147.

In order to appreciate the point at issue, you must take the guarantee which I have read. You can see that it has two limbs; the first limb is a promise to eradicate the dry-rot; the second limb is a promise, if dry-rot re-appears, to re-treat it. The two limbs are joined by the word " and ". The defendants say that

F   their liability is defined and limited by the second limb. The word " and " should be read as if, the defendants said: " by which we mean, and *mean only* that ". In short, their only obligation under the guarantee was to re-treat free of charge the timbers originally treated. So they are not liable for all the loss and damage suffered by Lord Waleran.

It is obvious that if the defendants are right, the first limb (guaranteeing the

G   efficacy) gave Lord Waleran nothing; and that all he got from the guarantees was the very limited promise in the second limb. The official referee so held. This appears very clearly from two of his answers to the preliminary issues (ii) and (iii). They were framed on the two limbs:

(ii) " Did the guarantee mean on its true construction that the defendants thereby guaranteed or warranted for a period of ten years the efficacy of

H   the treatment which they applied to timber or masonry? "

That question uses the very words of the first limb, but amplifies it by inserting the " period of ten years ", which is obviously imported. To that question the official referee answered " No ". They did not guarantee the efficacy of the treatment.

I   (iii) " Did the guarantee mean on its true construction that, if the defendants' treatment was not efficacious in preventing dry-rot for a period of ten years, *their only obligation* was to re-treat free of charge any re-infected timber or masonry? "

That question uses the very words of the second limb, but inserts significantly " their only obligation was ". To that question the official referee answered " Yes ". It was their only obligation.

Looking at those two questions and answers, it is plain that the official referee treated it as a case where the two limbs could not stand together. He gave

priority to the second limb over the first.   He rejected the first limb (which **A**
gave the guarantee) and upheld the second limb (which limited it severely).

The point appears at first sight to be a narrow point of construction; but I think it
goes wider. It brings into question the modern practice of giving these " guarantees ".   How should the courts construe them?   We all know what happens.
Be it a motor car, a refrigerator, or a washing machine, the supplier will " guarantee " it for two, three or five years, as the case may be.   It sounds splendid. **B**
It looks fine.   It is often headed in ornamental lettering " GUARANTEE ",
sometimes with a seal attached, as if to show it is of great value.   The salesman
asks the customer to sign an acknowledgment and return it to the supplier.
It is in the customer's interest, he says, to do so.   The customer does so, believing
it is worth a great deal to him.   He does not read it, of course.   No one ever
does.   He takes it on trust that it is what the salesman says it is—a guarantee **C**
for those years.   But when it comes to the pinch—when something goes wrong
with the thing and he reads it—then he will discover that he would have done
better without it.   The guarantee gives him no more than the law would have
done anyway.   More often than not it cuts down the liability of the supplier.
If the thing goes wrong, the supplier will not pay for the loss or damage which
the customer sustains.   He will only replace the defective part free of charge **D**
within the two years, three years, or five years, as the case may be.   It is to my
mind quite wrong that customers should be hoodwinked in this way.   When a
supplier says he gives a guarantee, he should be held to his word.   He should not
be allowed to limit it by clever clauses in small print—which, in 99 cases out of 100
the customer never reads.   Certainly he should not be allowed to cut it down by
phrases of doubtful or ambiguous import.   If he wishes to excuse himself from **E**
liability, he should say so plainly.   Instead of heading it boldly " GUARANTEE ",
he should head it " NON-GUARANTEE ": for that is what it is.

Take this document.   Although they head it " GUARANTEE ", the defendants
say that it does not mean anything of the sort.   It means, they say, that " their
only obligation " was to re-treat, free of charge, the timbers which they originally
treated, and no more.   This makes the guarantee utterly illusory.   In the one **F**
breath (the first limb) the defendants say they give a guarantee.   In the next
breath (the second limb) they take it away, or most of it.   So much so that I
think that the second limb should be regarded as repugnant to the first limb.
There are scores of cases in the books, from the Year Books onwards, where a
party to a contract has sought, all in the same document, to give with one hand
and take away with the other.   The courts have not allowed him to get away **G**
with it.   DEVLIN, J., put it succinctly in *Firestone Tyre & Rubber Co., Ltd.* v.
Vokins & Co., Ltd. (1):   " It is illusory to say: ' We promise to do a thing but
we are not liable if we do not do it '."   And we adopted it a week or two ago in
Mendelssohn v. *Normand, Ltd.* (2).   In all such cases it is the primary promise
which holds good.   The repugnant proviso is rejected.   So here the first limb
(which gives a guarantee) should be held good.   The second limb (which takes **H**
most of it away) should be rejected.

There is, however, another way of reaching the same result: and this is to read
the second limb as containing a promise which is not repugnant but *additional*
to the first limb.   Especially because it uses the word " and " which imports
that it adds something and not subtracts.   The first limb contains a guarantee
that the treatment is effective and that the dry-rot will not re-appear in ten **I**
years.   (The consequence of which is that, if it does re-appear, the defendants
will pay the loss or damage that flows from it.)   The second limb *adds* a promise
specifically to perform remedial treatment.   (The consequence of which is that
the defendants by their trained operatives will *actually re-treat themselves* with
fungicide but will not do any opening up or re-instatement themselves.)   I
think we ought to read the second limb in this way rather than use it as cutting
down the first limb.   After all, this is a document issued by the defendants.

---

(1) [1951] 1 Lloyd's Rep. 32 at p. 39.   (2) P. 1215, ante.

A If they mean the second limb to cut down the first, they should make it clear beyond peradventure. Instead of using the word " and " they should have said: " by which we mean and mean only ". That they did not do. So I think the first limb should stand intact and not be limited by the second limb.

In the course of the argument SALMON, L.J., gave an apt illustration. A man employs a firm to overhaul his car. The firm give a guarantee that it will

B not go wrong for two years, *and that,* if a defect appears, they will replace the defective part free of charge. Six weeks later, the steering goes wrong, and there is a bad accident. Can the owner recover the damage? Or is he limited to replacement of the defective part? The answer is that he should recover all the damages.

So much for the main point. But I must notice an argument put forward

C by the defendants. They said that the guarantee did not take away the common law rights of Lord Waleran. Notwithstanding the guarantee, they still owed him a duty, they said, to use care to eradicate dry-rot. (If this is right, it must be because there was an implied term to that effect.) If they had failed to use due care, he could have recovered, they said, all his loss or damage, provided that he brought his action within six years of the time when they did the work.

D He did not bring his action within that time, and, therefore, they said, his claim is statute barred under such authorities as *Howell* v. *Young* (3) and *Cartledge* (*Widow and Administratrix of the Estate of Fred Hector Cartledge (decd.)*) v. *E. Jopling & Sons, Ltd.* (4). Seeing that his common law right was maintained (and lost only by his own delay) the defendants contended that they were justified in confining the guarantee to re-treatment free of charge.

E I do not wish to be unduly cynical, but I wonder if the defendants would have made this admission if Lord Waleran had brought his action within six years. I can see them arguing that their obligations were fully set down in writing; and could not be extended by any implication. The express terms, they might say, covered the subject-matter (their obligations in respect of the work) completely: expressum facit cessare tacitum: and there was no room for

F any implied term. They could cite many authorities. Thus, in *Aspdin* v. *Austin* (5) LORD DENMAN, C.J., said:

> " When parties have entered into written engagements with expressed stipulations, it is manifestly not desirable to extend them by any implications; the presumption is that, having expressed some, they have expressed all the conditions by which they intend to be bound by that instrument."

G

Similarly in *Mathew* v. *Blackmore* (6) per POLLOCK, C.B., and in *Rhodes* v. *Forwood* (7), per LORD CAIRNS, L.C.

In any case I do not see that the construction of this ten-year guarantee can or should be influenced by reference to some supposed implied term. It must have the same meaning during the last four years as in the first six. A customer

H would not know anything about implied terms. He would go by what he was told, that it was a ten-year guarantee, and expect it to be fulfilled.

There is one other argument I must notice. The defendants relied on the " exclusions " from the guarantee and in particular the statement that: " This guarantee does not cover the cost of opening up or of reinstatement." But I think that only applies to the second limb, and not to the first. The first limb

I is only excepted in the " few instances " numbered (i) to (v). In any case, I do not think these " exclusions " are so clear as to require the court to cut down the emphatic promise of a ten-year guarantee.

I come, therefore, to a different decision than that arrived at by the official

---

(3) (1826), 5 B. & C. 259; [1824-34] All E.R. Rep. 377.
(4) [1963] 1 All E.R. 341; [1963] A.C. 758.
(5) (1844), 5 Q.B. 671 at p. 684.
(6) (1857), 1 H. & N. 762.
(7) (1876), 1 App. Cas 256 at p. 265; [1874-80] All E.R. Rep. 476 at pp. 480, 481.

referee. I think the answer to issue (ii) should be " Yes "; and to issue (iii) **A**
should be " No ".

Issue (iv) refers to the Statutes of Limitation. If and insofar as Lord Waleran's executors base their claim on an implied promise to use care, it is barred
by the Limitation Acts. But insofar as they base it on the guarantee, the time
runs from the date when the dry-rot re-appeared, that is, from 1963. So it is
not barred by the Limitation Acts. I would allow the appeal accordingly.   **B**

SALMON, L.J.: The only point which, in my view, arises on this appeal
is a narrow point of construction. It concerns the true meaning of a so-called
guarantee which was incorporated into a contract made in 1958 between the
late Lord Waleran and the defendants, Richardson and Starling, Ltd., a company
specialising in the eradication of dry-rot.   **C**

It appears that in 1958 Lord Waleran called in the defendants to investigate
the extent of the dry-rot in his house in Launceston Place and to advise him as
to what steps should be taken to eradicate it completely. They agreed to
carry out the investigation and to give him the necessary advice. They were to
take down any plaster work which they considered necessary for a thorough
investigation and they were to indicate what other work was necessary for   **D**
this purpose. When all the possible sources of dry-rot had been uncovered,
such areas of timber and masonry as they considered too far gone for treatment
were to be removed and replaced by Lord Waleran's builders and the remaining
areas were to be treated by the defendants in order to eradicate the infestation.
It was clearly an implied term of the contract that the advice which the defendants gave and the work which they did should be given and done with all the **E**
care and skill which could reasonably be expected of them. If they complied
with their obligations the strong possibility was that the dry-rot would be
completely eradicated and would not recur.

The defendants duly investigated, advised and did the other work stipulated in
their contract. Nevertheless, a very widespread re-infestation of dry-rot
again showed itself in 1963, and this caused Lord Waleran damage to the tune of **F**
about £7,000. The present action to recover these damages for breach of contract
was not started, however, until 1967. We were told that negotiations in respect
of Lord Waleran's claim against the defendants had begun between the parties'
surveyors well within the six-year period of limitation. It would appear that
only quantum could then have been in issue, for there could hardly have been
any real dispute about liability. These negotiations, however, became pro-   **G**
tracted. It may be that Lord Waleran could not believe that in such circumstances the defendants would ever seek to take advantage of the Limitation Act
1939. However that may be, no writ was issued within the period of limitation
which expired at the latest in August 1964. Lord Waleran died, and this caused
further delay; eventually the writ, as I have said, was issued in 1967. In the
event the defendants set up s. 2 of the Limitation Act 1939 in their defence, **H**
as in law they were fully entitled to do—just as anyone is entitled to plead the
Gaming Acts. This defence under the Limitation Act 1939 of course, afforded
a complete answer to the plaintiffs' claim except insofar as it was based on the
guarantee.

From the exiguous material now before us, it seems to me that the re-infestation
in 1963 was probably caused by the failure of the defendants properly to investi- **I**
gate the full extent of the infestation in 1958 rather than by their failure properly
to treat what they did then discover. If this is correct, it follows that even if
the construction of the guarantee for which the executors contend is right, they
probably cannot succeed in the action. The preliminary issues as to the true
construction of the guarantee were, however, set down for trial because if they
were decided in favour of the defendants, the action could be stopped dead in
its tracks and the heavy costs of investigating and deciding the cause of the
infestation in 1963 would be saved.

A   I entirely agree with all Lord Denning, M.R., says about the deplorable practice of obtaining business on the faith of an impressive looking " guarantee " which, in reality, takes away or cuts down the customer's common law rights and gives him nothing in return or, at any rate, only something which is hardly worth having.   But the present " guarantee " is not in that category.   To begin with, it does not expressly cut down or take away any of the customer's rights.   Nor,

B   if it has the limited meaning for which counsel for the defendants contends, can I find anything in the books to support the view that in law it negatives the defendants' implied obligation to take reasonable care and use reasonable skill. On counsel's construction of the guarantee, it merely gives the customer some additional rights to those which the law implies.   They may not be very valuable, but they are real; if the defendants fail to eradicate the infestation, then,

C   even though they may have used all reasonable care and skill, they would still be liable to re-treat, free of charge, any infested timber and masonry which they had formerly treated.   Moreover, this liability to re-treat free of charge would continue in respect of any re-infestation occurring within ten years of the original treatment.   I do not think that these additional rights are in any way inconsistent with the customer's implied common law rights and I should be

D   sorry to hold that they take them away.   Of course, if the guarantee imposes the absolute obligation for which counsel for the plaintiffs contends, no question of implied rights or obligations could arise, for even if the defendants used all the care and skill in the world, and yet failed to eradicate the infestation, they would still be liable for all the damage caused by that failure.

What is the true meaning of this guarantee?   I will read it.

E   " Guarantee.

Adequate treatment to accessible timbers, carried out by our own trained operatives, is covered by our written Ten Year Guarantee a specimen of which is given below, and this also shows the nature of those few instances where a guarantee cannot be given:—

F   " [The defendants] guarantee the efficacy of the treatment they apply to timber or masonry for the eradication of insect or fungal attack and, subject to the undernoted exclusions, will re-treat free of charge any such timber or masonry showing signs of re-infestation during the period of ten years from the date of treatment.

" This guarantee holds good to any owner for the time being of the property described, during the period of the guarantee.

G   " Exclusions from the foregoing Guarantee.   This Guarantee does not cover the cost of opening up or of re-instatement nor does it apply to . . ."

and then there are five instances to which it does not apply.

Clearly it is an inelegantly worded document. But one thing is reasonably clear, namely that it is intended to be a ten-year guarantee.   One possible

H   view is that the operative part of the guarantee—namely, the paragraph starting with the words " [the defendants] " and ending with the word " treatment "— is divided into two separate compartments separated by the word " and ". The first compartment contains an absolute warranty or legally binding promise or undertaking (it matters not which word is used) that the treatment applied by the defendants to timber and masonry shall so effectively eradicate dry-rot

I   that it will not re-appear for ten years from the date of the treatment.   If this is the correct view, then the defendants are liable under the first compartment of the guarantee for all damage caused by any breach of this warranty, promise or undertaking.   On this basis I do not think that the second compartment of the guarantee could be effective to cut down the defendants' liability for a breach of their obligations under the first compartment.   Had the second compartment been intended to limit the scope of the defendants' liability under the first compartment, the second compartment could hardly have been introduced by a more inept word than the word " and ".   It is true that on this view

the words in the second compartment of the guarantee would be otiose, for they   A
would give the customer little if anything more than that to which he would be
entitled for breach of the obligation contained in the first compartment.   Damage
caused by re-infestation (if recoverable under the first compartment) would
surely include the cost of re-treatment referred to in the second compartment.
I would not, however, necessarily be deterred from adopting a construction which
resulted in certain words in a contract being otiose.   They often are.   B

I cannot, however, persuade myself that the operative part of the guarantee
consists of two separate compartments.   It seems to me that the guarantee is in
reality a single entity and must be read as a whole.   Looked at in this way, the
guarantee is no more than a promise that if any of the timber or masonry treated
by the defendants becomes re-infested within ten years from the date of treatment,
the defendants will re-treat it free of charge.   C

This point of construction is by no means easy and I confess that my mind has
wavered during the course of the argument.   I have, however, finally been
turned by the words

"EXCLUSIONS from the foregoing Guarantee.   THIS Guarantee does not
cover the cost of opening up or of re-instatement nor does it apply to . . ."   D

and then five instances are cited.   I cannot accept the argument that these
words apply only to the second half of the guarantee, for they are described
in the document as "EXCLUSIONS from the foregoing Guarantee".   That must
mean the whole guarantee.   True it is that the words "subject to the undermentioned exclusions" come in the second half of the guarantee, but I cannot
think that they limit the application of the stipulated "EXCLUSIONS from the   E
foregoing Guarantee" to the second half.   On the contrary, I think that the
words "subject to the undernoted exclusions" were quite unnecessary in the
second half of the guarantee and were probably inserted only ex abundanti
cautela.

The fact that in the event of re-infestation the defendants are not to be liable
for the cost of opening up or of re-instatement strongly suggests that their sole   F
liability under the guarantee is to re-treat just as their obligation originally
was to treat without being liable for the cost of any opening up (save of plaster
work) or of re-instatement.   The contrary view, to my mind, would lead to some
remarkable and indeed absurd results.   Because of re-infestation the whole
house collapses, the defendants are then liable for the cost of rebuilding it or at
any rate for its market value less salvage at the date of its collapse.   If, however,   G
some comparatively minor re-infestation occurs, the defendants are not liable
for the cost of any necessary opening up or re-instatement, but merely for the
cost of re-treatment of the timber and masonry originally treated.   I cannot
accept this bizarre result which follows from reading the guarantee as being
divided into two distinct and entirely separate compartments, when the guarantee as a whole is governed, as in my view it is, by the stipulated exclusions.   I   H
think that the guarantee must be read as a whole in its context in the printed
form.   Read in this way, it has, in my view, the limited meaning which I have
indicated.   I, therefore, conclude that the learned official referee was right in
the decision at which he arrived.

I would only add that so-called guarantees on the faith of which business is
obtained must be carefully scrutinised by the courts.   I express no view about   I
the commercial propriety of soliciting custom by plugging guarantees which by
their very name may lead the unwary to believe that they give much when in
reality they give very little and sometimes cut down or take away the customer's
ordinary common law rights.   If the so-called guarantee purports to take away
or cut down the customer's common law rights, it should be construed strictly
contra proferentem.   If, however, as in this case, the guarantee merely confers
some possible additional benefit, however slight, it should certainly not be read
in a restrictive sense, but it ought not to be read in a wider sense than it can

A   fairly bear. For the reasons I have indicated, I have come to the conclusion (I confess without enthusiasm) that in the present case the guarantee bears no wider meaning than that for which counsel for the defendants contends.   I would accordingly dismiss the appeal.

WINN, L.J.: The essential point raised in this appeal is a narrow one: were it not for the able submission made by both counsel for the plaintiffs—
B   whom the court heard on this interlocutory appeal, as an indulgence, and found that by deciding so to do it had derived great benefit—(and for the views expressed by LORD DENNING, M.R.) I would have been content to give my own judgment succinctly in the form: I am in agreement with the learned official referee.

C   The appeal arises on the second and third of four preliminary issues stated by agreement of the parties in an action brought by the plaintiffs, the executors of the late Lord Waleran, against a firm of experts in the treatment of timber and masonry against decay due to insect and fungal infestation. The issues were properly set down as preliminary issues: in the particular circumstances of this action, in which no writ was issued until more than six years after the
D   defendants' work was done and the Statute of Limitations has been pleaded, a negative answer to the third of the questions thus raised and an affirmative answer to the second of the questions thus raised would leave open the disputes between the parties for determination by a trial, whereas an affirmative answer to the third of those questions would mean that the plaintiffs' claim in the action would be effectively limited to so small an amount, if not wholly excluded, that
E   it would result, in all practical probability, that a trial would be obviated.

The four issues so stated for preliminary determination are the following: as already indicated, nos. (ii) and (iii) alone are those of importance for present purposes; there could be no doubt that an affirmative answer must be given on issue no. (i).   (i) Did the contract include a " guarantee " as pleaded in para. 7 (b) of the statement of claim?   (ii) Did the guarantee mean on its true construction
F   that the defendants thereby guaranteed or warranted for a period of ten years the efficacy of the treatment which they applied to timber and masonry? (iii) Did the guarantee mean on its true construction that if the defendants' treatment was not efficacious in preventing dry-rot for a period of ten years, their only obligation was to re-treat free of charge any re-infested timber or masonry? (iv) Were any of the plaintiffs' causes of action barred by reason of the Limitation
G   Act 1939, s. 2, and if so, which?

The contract for work and services to be rendered by the defendants at the dwelling-house of Lord Waleran in Launceston Place, Kensington, was made by an estimate dated 20th March 1958 submitted by the defendants and the acceptance of this estimate which manifestly must have been made, though there is no written document constituting it before the court, by Mr. Martin French, Lord
H   Waleran's surveyor. I reject the submission of counsel for the plaintiffs that the contractual documents from which the terms of the contract are to be derived, included the report of the same date on conditions found at the premises, which the defendants submitted to the surveyor. This report was clearly contemplated by the parties as a step preliminary to the making of the contract, not as a document incorporated in the contract; this is further indicated by the fact that a
I   separate account and fee were rendered and charged in respect of it.

There is no term in the estimate or in the conditions printed on the back of it, which are plainly incorporated in any contract resulting from the submission of the estimate, which purports in any respect to restrict, still less exclude, the rights of the employer to claim compensation for non-performance, incompetent or negligent performance, bad workmanship, or unsuitable materials for which the tenderer might be responsible.

Whatever may be its meaning, the " guarantee " was an additional obligation undertaken by the defendants over and above such obligations as would have

arisen from the other terms of the contract or from the employment of them as **A**
experts to do work for reward.   The word "guarantee" has a chameleon
character; it takes on shades or changes of meaning from any context in which
it is used and means different things to different persons.   Commercial men who
speak of guaranteeing their produce, process or workmanship mean that they
will stand behind it, back it, show their confidence in it.   From a lawyer or from
his lips or pen the word issues only as an assurance of secondary responsibility, **B**
as surety, for the default of another person or, in its fullest possible significance, as a warranty.   It must, I feel, always be kept in mind by any court that
the legal effect of any contract is that which the parties both understood or
must be taken to have understood it to have, and not that for which the court
thinks that they should have contracted; still less is it open to the court
to substitute for words used by either contracting party language which would **C**
convey the intention which the court thinks he ought to have had.   I think it
is plain that the learned official referee did not take any view inconsistent
with what I have said in the last two paragraphs of this judgment, for I do not
understand him by the use of the expression, when broadly summarising the
respective contentions of the parties, " (ii) on the defendants' side that they
are only liable at most for the cost of re-treatment by them ", to have meant to **D**
be taken as contemplating that liability would have been so limited in respect
of any well-founded claim based on matters other than rights arising from the
guarantee itself.   I do not think he could have been meaning to speak in any
such general sense since this court was expressly informed by counsel that the
defendants when before the learned official referee accepted that if they had
been sued within six years they might have been liable for the full cost of **E**
rectification.

I fully accept counsel for the plaintiffs' reiterated contention that whatever
is the true meaning and effect of the guarantee, this cannot have changed with
the lapse of six years from its date, nor can it be affected as a matter of construction by the circumstance that a writ has or has not been issued against the defendants within six years of its date.   The whole question in this appeal is what is **F**
the meaning of the guarantee.   It scarcely needs to be said that this is not a
guarantee in the sense in which that word is used by lawyers.   Further, I am
unable to accept counsel for the plaintiffs' submission that, within the meaning
of the third definition of the word "guarantee" contained in the OXFORD DIC-
TIONARY, vol. 4, p. 475, it is to be held in law to be an undertaking to secure the
employer against or from injury. **G**

As I see the instant problem it may be thus stated: is there any legal compulsion or justification for treating the "guarantee" or assurance given by the
defendants as a contractual undertaking to be responsible for anything more
than free re-treatment of certain areas of timber or masonry in certain events?

A possible paraphrase of the wording of the "guarantee", which the defendants would probably accept, though since it was worded by them it binds them **H**
to the full extent of liability which the words, properly understood, do impose,
would be: Where timbers are accessible and we are able to give them adequate
treatment, carried out by our trained operatives, we will, except in the few undermentioned cases, undertake for a period of ten years from the date of such treatment to be responsible to the extent indicated in our "guarantee" set out
below for the efficacy of such treatment.   The operative words, i.e., those which
are inset, would then indicate that at their own cost the defendants would re-treat **I**
all accessible timber or masonry adequately treated by their own operatives
with their own chemicals, other than plywood or timber only surface treated,
if any such timber or masonry were re-infested within ten years by any infection
other than Longhorn beetle.   By way of qualifying this obligation, it is provided
that opening up and re-instatement costs are not to be borne by the defendants.

It may be remarked that any unqualified liability to re-imburse all the costs
of making good all damage and loss due to a re-infestation would necessarily

A comprise the cost of re-treating any re-infested area; it follows that if the "guarantee" imposes such a comprehensive liability, the express undertaking to re-treat would be tautologous and meaningless.

The contract between the defendants and their employer clearly incorporated the conditions set out on the back of their estimate dated 20th March 1958, but before reference is made to those conditions or any of them, it is pertinent to

B observe that the first three lines of the estimate constitute an offer to carry out the chemical treatment recommended in the defendants' report, including ancillary works, and to carry out this treatment on the parts or areas of the building referred to in that report and, additionally, that the chemical treatment of any such parts not excluded by notes on the defendants' "guarantee form" will be "guaranteed".

C The terms set out on the back of the estimate expressly included in it certain expenses, but made it plain that it did not cover the matters set out in condition 3, nor any responsibility for the matters mentioned in conditions 4 or 5. Condition 7 referred to "guarantee" and stated

"the efficacy of our treatment is guaranteed in accordance with the terms of the specimen guarantee forms already submitted or attached . . ."

D This condition is not itself a guarantee, but is an express incorporation of such guarantee as is set out in the specimen form referred to. Such a specimen form was attached to the estimate, and may well have been previously submitted; it is on the terms of that specimen form of guarantee and on nothing else that the meaning of the "guarantee" thereby given must be ascertained.

E The form itself has three first lines of print which appear to me, notwithstanding the argument or arguments to the contrary addressed to the court, to amount to no more than an introduction or explanation leading to the guarantee itself. In my judgment the words "covered by our written ten-year guarantee, a specimen of which is given below . . ." means simply: covered by the ten-year guarantee set out below. The last of those three introductory lines has the

F additional effect of repeating or referring to a statement in the estimate that in some instances no guarantee was given. The expression used is "shows the nature of those few instances where a guarantee cannot be given", and it is plain that the instances or subject-matters in respect of which no guarantee is given share the common feature that treatment in the circumstances specified could not confidently be relied on as efficacious: the most obvious reason for

G excluding such liability is mentioned under no. 2, i.e., where the chemicals used are not the defendants' own products, but the other instances are in a similar sense self-explanatory.

As I see the problem, it is: what is the meaning on a natural interpretation, without leaning to strictness or to liberality of interpretation of the 4½ lines of print which begin with the name of the defendants and end with the word "treat-

H ment". The plaintiffs contend that these words give rise to two distinct cumulative obligations. The defendants maintain that they impose one single obligation and define the scope of the obligation thereby accepted. The only difficulty which I see in the way of understanding the language arises from the presence at the beginning of the third line of the print of the word "and". It is said by counsel for the plaintiffs that the two lines preceding that word constitute a war-

I ranty, and the 2½ lines following it constitute another warranty. It is said by counsel for the defendants that the words following that word define the scope and extent of the obligation created and accepted by the 4½ lines as a whole.

It seems to me that both counsel for the plaintiffs rightly and inevitably accepted that their submission was equivalent to maintaining that the meaning of the 4½ lines could be tested and demonstrated by setting out the first two lines with a figure (i) constituting a sub-paragraph immediately following the word "guarantee" in the first of those lines, and setting out the remaining 2½ lines in a separate sub-paragraph after a figure (ii) and displacing the word "and"

into the left-hand margin of the notional text thus produced.   It is said by them   A
that in this form of presentation it would be clear that the meaning would amount
to a warranty in the terms of the first two lines plus an additional warranty
in the following 2½ lines.

I am unable to accept this submission though I do agree that it provides a very
appropriate test of its own validity.   Visualising the notional form of text thus
proposed it would, as I see it, be plain therefrom that the scope in subject-matter   B
of the first sub-paragraph would be limited only by the limits of and would be
co-extensive with the limits of the areas of timber or masonry to which the
defendants in fact applied their treatment in the performance of the contractual
task, and this would mean that the defendants would be undertaking whatever
responsibility that sub-paragraph imposed in respect of those very timbers or
areas for which by the five exclusions mentioned they said that they cannot   C
undertake responsibility.   The reference to " undernoted exclusions " would on
this submission appear in and qualify only the second suggested sub-paragraph.

Having for the reasons indicated rejected the submission referred to, I turn
to the more difficult problem of construing the guarantee or, as I prefer to call
it, warranty, as one single contractual undertaking, and of answering the essential
question: What does it, taken as a whole, mean in terms of scope or definition   D
of responsibility?   For myself I am unable to regard as a reasonable meaning
to give to a document of the kind in question provided by expert specialists,
with a good deal of trumpet blowing and emphasis, to a lay owner of property,
albeit in this case advised by an experienced surveyor, to limit the scope of it
to initial or temporary efficacy of the treatment.   In one sense treatment may be
said to be efficacious if it eliminates or eradicates for a time such trouble as is   E
referred to, viz., insect or fungal attack, and it can fairly be said that it is a
somewhat unusual, if not strained, use of language to speak of efficacy during a
period of ten years.   Nonetheless, I think that the proper meaning to give to
the warranty is that the treatment is so efficacious that no signs of re-infestation
will appear within ten years from the time it is applied.   In other words, it may
be said that it amounts to a warranty that no signs of re-infestation will appear   F
within ten years from the date of treatment.   I so interpret the warranty.

The following questions remain, which are vital: (i) Does re-infestation mean,
and is it limited in meaning to, infestation by insect or fungal attack to areas of
timber or masonry treated by the defendants.   I think the answer to this question
is " Yes ". (ii) Does the contractual undertaking contained in the 4½ lines as a
whole plus the next line and a half referring to owners for the time being of the   G
property mean that the employers or any such owner will be re-imbursed for
any expenditure and compensated for any damage or loss which he sustains
as a result of any insect or fungal attack anywhere in the property, the origin
or causation of which can be traced to infection in such a treated area of timber
or masonry, or does it mean only that in the event of any such treated area
showing signs of re-infestation, that area or those areas alone will be re-treated   H
free of charge, with the result that no further right of recourse or recovery can
be founded on the guarantee itself, apart from any other cause of action, in
respect of consequential or indirect, albeit natural, infection spreading from the
treated area and consequential damage resulting?

For my part, whilst I would have thought it a more appropriate and far more
satisfactory form of drafting had the word " and " referred to above which is   I
contained in the warranty been replaced by some such expression as " in fulfilment of such guarantee undertake subject, etc., to re-treat, or by the simple
expression " by undertaking to ", I am of the opinion that the proper
natural meaning of the language used, albeit clumsily, is that the obligation
undertaken is no more extensive than an undertaking that in the events postulated the defendants will re-treat any timber or masonry treated by them in
purported performance of the contract, unless such timber or masonry falls within
one of the five exclusions.

A   Accordingly, I would say that this appeal should be dismissed.

Appeal dismissed. On 15th April leave to appeal to the House of Lords was refused.

Solicitors: *Curwen, Carter & Evans* (for the plaintiffs); *Hewitt, Woollacott & Chown* (for the defendants).

[*Reported by* F. Guttman, Esq., *Barrister-at-Law.*]

B

Re ST. PETER, ROYDON.

[Chelmsford Consistory Court (Chancellor H. H. V. Forbes, Q.C.), February 4, 5, 6, 7, March 7, 8, 28, 1969.]

C *Ecclesiastical Law—Parochial church council—Relation to incumbent—General duty to co-operate with incumbent in church work—In performing particular duties regarding church affairs vested in councils as successor to the vestry and churchwardens, councils free to differ from minister after paying proper regard to his wishes and suggestions—Parochial Church Councils (Powers) Measure 1956 (4 & 5 Eliz. 2 No. 3), s. 2, s. 4.*

D *Ecclesiastical Law—Parochial church council—Power of councils to borrow money but not to give security for a loan.*

While s. 2 of the Parochial Church Councils (Powers) Measure 1956 (No. 3) casts on a parochial church council the general duty to co-operate with the minister in church work, he being the person entrusted with the cure of souls in the parish, in performing the particular duties relating to church affairs vested in a parochial church council as successor to the vestry and church-

E wardens by s. 4 of the Measure of 1956, a parochial council, although by virtue of s. 2* of the Measure under a primary duty to co-operate with the minister, are not bound to do whatever he desires; and if a parochial council has paid proper regard to the wishes or suggestions of the minister in the discharge of any duty which impinges on church work, the council are free to differ from the

F minister if in their view the honest discharge of the duty requires them to do so (see p. 1234, letter I, to p. 1235, letter B, post).

A parochial church council have the power to borrow money but have not the power to give security for a loan because although there was no express borrowing power in the Parochial Church Councils (Powers) Measure 1921 (No. 1) (now re-enacted in the Measure of 1956) which created parochial church

G councils, the churchwardens and the vestry whose powers were transferred to parochial councils by the Measure of 1921 had the power to borrow but neither body had power to charge anything as security for a loan (see p. 1237, letter I, to p. 1238, letter B, post).

Withnell v. *Gartham* [1775-1802] All E.R. Rep. 453), *Blunt and Fuller* v. *Harwood* ((1837), 1 Curt. 648), *Rewd and Baggallay* v. *Pettett* ((1834) 1 A. & E.

H 196) and *Furnivall* v. *Coombes* ((1843), 5 Man. & G. 736), applied.

[As to the functions and powers of parochial church councils, see 13 Halsbury's Laws (3rd Edn.) 155-162, paras. 343-360.

For the Parochial Church Councils (Powers) Measure 1956 (No. 3), see 10 Halsbury's Statutes (3rd Edn.) 96.]

Cases referred to:

I *Blunt and Fuller* v. *Harwood* (1837), 1 Curt. 648; 1 J.P. 371; 163 E.R. 227; 19 Digest (Repl.) 555, *3975.*

Furnivall v. *Coombes* (1843), 5 Man. & G. 736; 12 L.J.C.P. 265; 1 L.T.O.S. 80; 7 J.P. 322; 134 E.R. 756; 13 Digest (Repl.) 185, *20.*

Rewd and Baggallay v. *Pettett* (1834), 1 A. & E. 196; 110 E.R. 1181.

Withnell v. *Gartham* (1795), 6 Term Rep. 388; [1775-1802] All E.R. Rep. 453; 101 E.R. 610; 19 Digest (Repl.) 304, *754.*

* Section 2 is set out at p. 1234, letter H, post.

Petitions for faculties.   A

These were three petitions for faculties for alterations and additions to the Church of St. Peter, Roydon, being: (i) a proposal for placing a new altar against the north wall of the north aisle with a consequent re-arrangement of pews and other furniture; (ii) a proposal for building a combined vestry and church hall as an extension to the church; and (iii) a proposal for a car park in the churchyard, adequate car parking provision having been made a requirement of the planning B
permission granted for the vestry hall.

Quentin Edwards for the petitioners.
George Newsom, Q.C., and *S. G. Maurice* for the parties opponent.

Cur. adv. vult.

28th March. **THE CHANCELLOR,** referred to the petitions and continued: C
These proposals have evoked considerable opposition in the parish and there is a number of parties opponent in respect of each petition. The extent of the opposition to, and of the support for, the schemes may be gauged by the fact that the hearing of evidence and argument occupied six days in this church. I am most grateful to counsel not only for the assistance they have given me but for the moderation with which they have conducted their cases in a situation D
of obvious tension between the parties on each side.

I have heard a number of witnesses on both sides. It is clear from the whole body of evidence that the opposition I have mentioned is basically indicative of a deep-seated division in the parish. It is no part of my task to investigate the origin of this division nor in any way to apportion blame for an unhappy state of affairs. The fact that dissension of this kind exists is, however, of some import- E
ance in the consideration of the proposals now before me. First, it is quite plain that because the division has led many of them to adopt particular attitudes, witnesses have found it less easy to give an objective account either of the course of events or of their own reasons for liking or disliking the proposals. And secondly, the mere existence of dissension of this character cannot fail to be disastrous for the spiritual life of the parish and of the congregation of this church. Both F
counsel, mindful of this latter aspect, have therefore asked me to bear in the fore-front of my mind when approaching these proposals the desirability of treating the matter pastorally.

From the evidence and documents which have been placed before me I have little doubt that the dissension I have referred to has its origin in large part in differences of view on the interrelation of the respective roles of incumbent and G
parochial church council in a parish of the Church of England. I have been invited to give some authoritative ruling on the legal doctrine applicable in this situation. The parochial church council is a creature of statute and first came into being as a result of the Parochial Church Councils (Powers) Measure 1921 (No. 1). The provisions of that Measure were substantially re-enacted in the Parochial Church Councils (Powers) Measure 1956 (No. 3). Section 2 of that Measure is in the follow- H
ing terms:

" **General functions of council**—It shall be the primary duty of the council in every parish to co-operate with the minister in the initiation conduct and development of church work both within the parish and outside."

Section 4 transfers to the council most of the powers, duties and liabilities of the I
vestry and of the churchwardens relating to church affairs, in particular those concerned with the finances and property of the church. I consider that these sections indicate both a general duty and a series of particular duties which are cast on the council. Their general duty is to co-operate with the minister in church work, for the minister is the person entrusted with the cure of souls in the parish. But they have a number of particular duties to perform, most if not all of them of a more mundane but nonetheless important nature.   In considering the performance of these particular duties a parochial church council must, of

A course, have regard to what the Measure postulates as their primary duty, namely to co-operate with the minister; but they would, I think, be failing in the discharge of their particular duties if they regarded themselves as inevitably bound under the Measure to do whatever the minister desired when one of these particular duties lay in question. In other words, in carrying out any particular duty with which they are entrusted they must pay proper regard to the wishes

B or suggestions of the minister, if the discharge of the duty impinges on church work in respect of which the minister has expressed a wish or suggestion; but having done that they must be free to differ from him if in their view the honest discharge of the particular duty requires them to do so. I am fortified in this opinion by considering other measures which cast particular duties on the council. Perhaps the most obvious is the Prayer Book (Alternative and Other

C Services) Measure 1965 (No. 1). This Measure provides in s. 2 for the use in, for instance, a parish church of alternative forms of service with the approval of the incumbent. Section 3 provides that such alternative forms of service may not be used in a parish church without the agreement of the council. If the meaning of the Measure of 1956 were that the council were bound always to follow whatever wishes the incumbent might express on the subject of church work, the require-

D ment that their agreement must be obtained before introducing these forms of service would be no more than a solemn farce. It is clear that the scheme of lay participation in church work in the parish and outside it requires the council to bear in mind at all times their primary duty to co-operate with the incumbent, but still leaves room for honest disagreement with him where their other and particular duties are concerned.

E   Having expressed my opinion of the legal effect of the Measure of 1956 I should add that ecclesiastical Measures must always be considered in practice against the background of the principles of the Chrsitian faith of which, for the Church of England, they provide no more than the imperfect human framework of rules. I do not think I am stepping outside my province in reminding the parties that perhaps the most important of all Christian virtues is that of charity;

F and charity, in this context, means an ability and a willingness to seek to understand the points of view of those who appear to be opponents. This goes further than merely " to think it possible you may be mistaken "; it amounts to a positive attitude of mutual trust and co-operation which, in a perfect world, would mean that all rules of conduct were superfluous. In the true spirit of charity a clash between an incumbent and his council or between sections within a council

G becomes unthinkable. But in the parish of St. Peter, Roydon, such a clash has in fact occurred and the council and congregation has become split into two factions. I have seen in this case not all, but a large number, of the persons who make up these two factions. They have all impressed me as being people of integrity, with honestly and sincerely held views. I am content to believe that only temporarily have some of them forgotten that charity is the greatest of Christian attitudes.

H   The view I have expressed of the legal situation between the council and incumbent is one which has not been adopted by either side, though I hope it may be one which both will adopt in future. The incumbent's view of his council was expressed in his evidence in the following terms:

> " My view is that the [council] does not represent the laity but is part of my staff " ... " I think this is a problem in the Church of England that it
I has this legal side; I mean that there is a built-in arrangement for democratic participation by the laity."

He indicated that in his view the measure of 1956 meant that only those should stand for election to the council who can co-operate with their minister. He said:

> " The Measure does not require mutual co-operation. I do not consider I have to promote harmony in the parish."

It will be clear that this interpretation of the roles of the council and incumbent runs completely counter to the view I have expressed. But the attitude of the

parties opponent has, in my opinion, been equally at variance with that view. A
It seems clear that they have thought of themselves as free to oppose the incumbent's plans for the church work of the parish without asking themselves whether
they could conscientiously do so having regard to their primary duty under the
Measure of 1956. Much of the difficulty which arose between the incumbent and,
at any rate, a part of the council and congregation, stemmed from the desire of
the incumbent to introduce new and unfamiliar forms of worship. I have been B
told that the present is a time of liturgical change and that new forms of worship
are desirable to attract those who are outside the church or only on the
fringes of it.   It seems a pity that the introduction of these new forms for that
purpose should have had the result of driving from the church a considerable
proportion of those already within it, for that is what has been the result in this
case. Congregations are peculiarly susceptible to changes in the familiar services, C
and an important function of the council, in this connection, is to act as the voice of
the congregation in advising the incumbent how far and how fast he should
proceed.   I think that in this case that voice went unheeded. At the same time
I think that, having given that advice, the council should have been willing
to accept a change, if only for a trial period, and to co-operate in bringing it about
and in persuading the congregation to give the proposals a fair trial also.   D

Counsel for the parties opponent, in his final speech, suggested to me that the
overriding pastoral need of this parish was a period of convalescence and quiet.
I think that he is right, but I am quite certain that the parish will achieve no
convalescence unless all parties are prepared to re-examine their attitudes to the
governance of parochial affairs in the light, I would hope, of my ruling on the legal
situation, but, more importantly, in the wider context of their Christian duty E
and brotherhood.

Before turning to consider the petitions in detail, I feel that I should look in
general at the financial situation of this parish. Much has been made of finance
during the hearing, and counsel for the parties opponent raises two points of
some importance. First, he asks, can the parish afford the expenditure on these
works, and secondly, if they cannot afford it immediately, is there any power in a F
council to borrow money if the money is not presently available?

I have seen the present treasurer of the council, Mr. Brandon, but he was
appointed only last year and the major part of the financial evidence on behalf
of the petitioners has been supplied by Mr. O'Donald, a churchwarden and himself one of the petitioners. For the parties opponent I have seen Mrs. Freeman
who, until recently, was treasurer of the council. The finances of the church G
have received very recently a fortuitous increase of considerable value; this has
come about as a result of a fire in the church which virtually destroyed the organ
and did much other damage. The insurance moneys received as a result have only
in part been expended on the necessary repairs and renewals; some further work
still remains to be done and paid for, including notably the purchase and installation of a new organ. But much money has been saved by a combination of judic- H
ious salvage and voluntary help so that a fairly large surplus has accumulated in
the church funds. Mr. O'Donald produced a document in an attempt to present a
picture of the financial state of the parish and this has been much criticised by
counsel for the parties opponent. I think it was an honest attempt, but I also
think that it was unduly optimistic. An examination of the accounts over the
last few years shows that this is a parish which is able to pay its expenses, send I
its quota to the diocese, give adequate support to the church overseas, and
accumulate a surplus income for future eventualities of something between £300
and £400 a year. I have not the slightest doubt that for a special building effort
larger annual sums might be raised for a short while. The fact remains that to
carry out all the works represented by these petitions and to allow for the purchase of an organ, money will have to be borrowed, and counsel for the petitioners
admits this. There appears to be no difficulty about raising the money. The bank
has offered a loan of £6,000 and Mr. O'Donald has offered to guarantee this. But

A counsel for the parties opponent says that a council has no power to borrow; he argues that the council is a creature of statute and that there are no express borrowing powers in the Measure which created it. He adds that neither the vestry nor the churchwardens, whose powers, duties and liabilities are transferred by the Measure to the council, had any powers to borrow either, except under the provisions of the Church Building Acts. He referred me to a directive of Lord

B Kenyon, C.J. in *Withnell* v. *Gartham* (1), to *Rewd and Baggallay* v. *Pettett* (2), *Furnivall* v. *Coombes* (3), *Blunt and Fuller* v. *Harwood* (4), to Vol. I of Blackstone's Commentaries and to Prideaux on the Duties of Churchwardens. I have examined all these authorities with some care. I think that the propositions which they establish, so far as is relevant to the present case, are these: church-wardens are not a body corporate; it follows that if they sign contractual docu-

C ments as churchwardens (even with an express proviso that they are not to be liable personally) first, they may only be sued as individuals because they cannot be sued as a corporate body, and secondly they remain personally liable on the contracts again because they are not a corporation. The point was put neatly by Tindal, C.J., in *Furnivall* v. *Coombes* (5):

D "Churchwardens and overseers, though they are by statute a corporate body for some purposes, cannot enter such a covenant as this [a contract by deed to pay for church repairs by instalments] in a corporate character: and if not, then the contract must be a personal covenant."

But all these cases indicate is that, for lack of a corporate existence, churchwardens must be regarded as natural and not artificial persons. Even if it be said that,

E having borrowed money on behalf of the church, they must be sued individually for its repayment, I cannot see that this means that they have no power, as churchwardens, to borrow the money in the first place. The point is that neither the parish itself nor the churchwardens existed as legal entities. When church-wardens borrowed on behalf of the parish the parish could not be sued nor could the churchwardens as such because neither existed at law; but the churchwardens

F existed as individuals so that they could be sued personally. To argue from this that when they borrowed they borrowed personally and not as churchwardens seems to me a circuitous piece of reasoning; in fact they borrowed on behalf of the parish and not on behalf of themselves as individuals. The power to borrow is no different from other powers, and in performing their other duties church-wardens were, in law, acting as individuals and not as a corporate body. If counsel

G for the parties opponent was right then the churchwardens, as such, while they may have had duties, never had any powers or liabilities at all and the draftsmen of the Measure, in purporting to transfer them to the council, were indulging in an exercise more appropriate to cloud-cuckooland than the Church Assembly.

The position of the vestry is even clearer. The leading case, *Blunt and Fuller* v. *Harwood* (4), shows that the vestry had no common law power to borrow against

H the security of the church rates, not that it had no power to borrow at all. Sir Herbert Jenner put it in this way (6):

"It is true that before the Church Building Acts there was no power in a vestry of a parish to borrow money on the security of the rates by the common law, and where money was so borrowed, it was done without any legal security."

I It seems plain to me that Sir Herbert Jenner is here indicating that at common law while the borrowing was not illegal the charging of the church rates was. In my view both the churchwardens and the vestry had, before their powers were

(1) (1795), 6 Term Rep. 388; [1775–1802] All E.R. Rep. 453.
(2) (1834), 1 A. & E. 196.
(3) (1843), 5 Man. & G. 736.
(4) (1837), 1 Curt. 648.
(5) (1843), 5 Man. & G. at p. 751.
(6) (1837), 1 Curt. at p. 657.

transferred in 1921 to church councils, the power to borrow. Neither body had **A**
power to charge anything as security for any loan. The council who took over
their powers can therefore borrow money so long as they can find someone willing
to lend it without any security. The view I have taken seems to me also consonant
with practical good sense because if it were otherwise no council could even incur
a debt let alone borrow money, and most councils do both: in fact the major
part of the money borrowed by councils is lent by their diocesan authorities. **B**

I now turn to a consideration of the three petitions.

[THE CHANCELLOR, having considered the petitions, granted a faculty for the
re-orientation of the church, subject to some alteration of detail to the scheme
proposed. He refused to grant faculties for the vestry hall and car park but without prejudice to resubmission of proposals for more appropriate designs and
layout.] **C**

Decrees accordingly.

Solicitors: *Winckworth & Pemberton* (for the petitioner); *M. L. Moss & Son* (for
the parties opponent).

[*Reported by* WENDY SHOCKETT, *Barrister-at-Law.*]

D

SYKES AND OTHERS *v.* MIDLAND BANK EXECUTOR & TRUSTEE CO., LTD. AND OTHERS.

[QUEEN'S BENCH DIVISION (Paull, J.), March 11, 12, 13, 14, 17, 19, 1969.] **E**

*Solicitor—Negligence—Duty to client—Negotiation of grant of under-lease to
architects—Unusual covenants in under-lease restricting user—Omission of
solicitor to advise and/or warn client on effect—Whether solicitor negligent.*
*Damages—Measure of damages—Negligence—Solicitor—Failure to advise on
clause in lease—Amount of rent under lease greater than current market rent.*
Damages—Measure of damages—Income tax—Liability to pay excessive rent **F**
*under lease as a result of solicitor's negligence—No sum for which compensa-
tion awarded which was itself subject to tax—Whether allowance for income
tax in measure of damages.*

The plaintiffs were partners in a firm of architects and quantity surveyors
practising in Hull. In 1960 they opened a small London office and in 1963,
their business expanding, they entered into negotiations for a ten-year under- **G**
lease, in relation to which R. (in Hull) acted as their solicitor. The immediate
lessors held the lease from superior landlords, and the proposed under-lease
contained a user clause (cl. 2 (xi)) under which the plaintiffs covenanted
not to use the premises other than as offices in connection with " the
Lessees' business of Architects and Surveyors or as offices and showrooms in
connection with any other business for which the permission in writing of **H**
the Lessor and the Superior Lessors had first been obtained such permission
by the Lessor not to be unreasonably withheld ". A later clause (cl. 2 (xiii))
contained a covenant against assigning and underletting without the prior
consent of the lessors and superior lessors, and by virtue of s. 19 (1) (*a*) of the
Landlord and Tenant Act 1927 this covenant was subject to a proviso that
such consent was not to be unreasonably withheld by any lessor in the chain. **I**
There was no similar provision relating to change of user. R. knew that the
plaintiffs might during the term want to sublet or assign the whole or a part
of the premises, but R. did not draw the attention of any of the partners to the
effect of the wording of cl. 2 (xi), either as bearing on the right effectively
to assign or sublet, or otherwise. The market value of the underlease with
cl. 2 (xi) was 27½ per cent. less than the rent actually reserved on the underlease which equalled the current market rent for premises in respect of which
a change of user could not be unreasonably withheld by any lessor in the

A chain. In 1965 the plaintiffs sought to sublet or assign the rest of their term, but the superior landlords for nearly three years refused consent to any proposed change of user to other professional offices. In an action for damages the plaintiffs contended that R.'s omission to advise them on the legal effect of cl. 2 (xi) constituted professional negligence.

B   *Held*: (i) the solicitor had been negligent because—(a) the plaintiffs were not members of a profession in which the effect of the wording of leases had to be considered; (b) the wording of sub-cl. (xi) was most unusual; (c) none of the plaintiffs understood the effect of cl. 2 (xi) and cl. 2 (xiii), and this was reasonable on their part; and (d) the solicitor should have realised that this would probably be the case (see p. 1245, letters G and H, post).

C   (ii) (a) the damage crystallised at the moment the plaintiffs became liable to the lessor for rent; and the measure of damages was the capitalised value of the excess of the rent actually reserved under the lease over the current market rent (see p. 1250, letter D, post); and

    (b) no allowance for the tax liability of the plaintiffs should be made; the damage which the plaintiffs suffered was their liability to pay excess rent, and there was thus no sum, for which compensation was awarded, which **D** was itself subject to tax (see p. 1251, letter F to H, post).

    British Transport Commission v. *Gourley* ([1955] 3 All E.R. 796) distinguished.

    Per CURIAM: The test for negligence is whether the court is prepared to hold that in the particular case the solicitor ought to have realised that the consequences in law of any particular words used in the lease might well **E** not be fully realised by his client (see p. 1245, letter E, post).

[As to the liability of solicitors for negligence in non-contentious matters, see 36 HALSBURY'S LAWS (3rd Edn.) 99-104, paras. 135, 136, 138; and for cases on the subject, see 43 DIGEST (Repl.) 97, 98, *835-857*, 106-121, *953-1098*.]

Cases referred to:

F   *British Transport Commission* v. *Gourley*, [1955] 3 All E.R. 796; [1956] A.C. 185; [1956] 2 W.L.R. 41; Digest (Cont. Vol. A) 462, *28a*.

  Chaplin v. *Hicks*, [1911] 2 K.B. 786; [1911-13] All E.R. Rep. 224; 80 L.J.K.B. 1292; 105 L.T. 285; 17 Digest (Repl.) 89, *96*.

  Ford v. *White & Co.*, [1964] 2 All E.R. 755; [1964] 1 W.L.R. 885; Digest (Cont. Vol. B) 659, *1083a*.

G   *Hall* v. *Meyrick*, [1957] 1 All E.R. 208; [1957] 2 W.L.R. 458; [1957] 2 Q.B. 455; *rvsd.* C.A., [1957] 2 All E.R. 722; [1957] 2 Q.B. 455; [1957] 3 W.L.R. 273; 43 Digest (Repl.) 108, *979*.

  Otter v. *Church, Adams, Tatham & Co.*, [1953] 1 All E.R. 168; [1953] Ch. 280; [1953] 1 W.L.R. 156; 43 Digest (Repl.) 120, *1097*.

  Philips v. *Ward*, [1956] 1 All E.R. 874; [1956] 1 W.L.R. 471; 47 Digest **H** (Repl.) 564, *35*.

  Pilkington v. *Wood*, [1953] 2 All E.R. 810; [1953] Ch. 770; [1953] 3 W.L.R. 522; 43 Digest (Repl.) 120, *1091*.

Action.

This was an action in which Ronald William Sykes, Arthur Johnson, Charles Edward Tooley and Michael Needham, partners in a firm of architects and survey-**I** ors, claimed damages for negligence and breach of duty against the defendants, Midland Bank Executor & Trustee Co., Ltd., William Horner Hall and Donald Patrick Shackles, the executors of George Thomas Rignall, deceased, formerly the sole member of the firm Mainprize & Rignall, Solicitors of Hull. The action concerned two ten-year underleases which the plaintiffs had taken in 1963 and 1964 at Roxburghe House, Regent Street, London, and in respect of which the late Mr. Rignall had acted as their solicitor. The plaintiffs alleged that Mr. Rignall had failed properly to advise them about the terms of the lease. The facts are set out in the judgment.

The cases noted below* were cited during the argument in addition to those A referred to in the judgment.

P. R. Oliver, Q.C., and *W. J. R. Evans* for the plaintiffs.
A. L. Price, Q.C., and *P. M. J. Slot* for the defendants.

Cur. adv. vult.

19th March. **PAULL, J.** read the following judgment: On 26th July 1967, B Wilfred Elsworth Sykes, Ronald William Sykes, Arthur Johnson, Charles Edward Tooley and Michael Needham who were, or are, partners in a firm of architects and surveyors, issued a writ against Mainprize & Rignall, who were at that date a firm of solicitors. The writ claimed damages for negligence in relation to certain leases in respect of which the defendants acted as solicitors for the plaintiffs prior to their execution. Before the action started, Mr. Wilfred C Elsworth Sykes unfortunately died and his name was by mistake included in the writ. Ronald William Sykes has left the firm and become a consultant to the partnership. Arthur Johnson and Charles Edward Tooley are still partners. Michael Needham retired in 1965. Mr. Ronald Sykes and Mr. Needham are the two who have given evidence on behalf of the plaintiffs. Unfortunately also, the sole partner in Mainprize & Rignall, Mr. Rignall, has also died and the Midland D Bank Executor & Trustee Co., Ltd., and others, who are the executors of Mr. Rignall's will, have been substituted as defendants. It follows, therefore, that I am unable to have evidence, either from the senior partner of the plaintiffs at the time of the transaction which is the subject-matter of this action, or from Mr. Rignall who acted as solicitor for the plaintiffs in the transaction.

The dispute in this action is whether or not Mr. Rignall, when acting for the E plaintiffs in relation to the leases of two premises in Roxburghe House, Regent Street, London, in respect of one of which the plaintiffs took possession under the first lease in March 1963, and in respect of the other under the second lease in May 1964 (although the first lease was not signed until 27th April 1964) was negligent in not pointing out to the plaintiffs the effect of a sub-clause in one of the covenants of each of the leases and not warning them of the consequences F of the wording of such sub-clause.

Up to the year 1960 the plaintiffs had carried on their practice of architects and quantity surveyors solely in Hull, and Mr. Rignall had his offices in the same building as the plaintiffs had theirs. As Mr. Needham told me, they looked on Mr. Rignall as (to use his own words) a sort of father-confessor to whom they turned in all cases of difficulty in relation to any matter in connection with the G law. Mr. Needham joined the plaintiffs' firm in 1960. He is a quantity surveyor, and the plaintiffs' firm which was expanding by that time had considered that it would be advisable to have premises in London for the convenience of their clients and where a quantity surveyor could preside over the quantity surveying side of their practice. Needless to say, quantity surveying is quite a separate branch of the surveyor's profession and is concerned solely with working out the H cost of buildings planned by architects and advising clients as to the probable cost of alterations in, or the building of, various buildings. It has nothing to do with the valuation of buildings already built or with leases.

As a consequence of this decision the plaintiffs found premises at 27, Maddox Street, off Regent Street. Mr. Rignall in Hull acted as solicitor for the plaintiffs in relation to this lease, which is dated 16th May 1960. The premises were over I a shop. The entry was at the side of the shop and it was clear that the premises were taken as, so to speak, a stepping-stone towards either expanding in London or withdrawing from London. The lease was for five years expiring on 1st June

---

* *Cassaboglou* v. *Gibb* (1883), 11 Q.B. 797, C.A.; *Salvesen & Co.* v. *Rederi Aktiebolaget Nordstjernan*, [1905] A.C. 302; [1904-07] All E.R. Rep. 886; *Groom* v. *Crocks*, [1938] 2 All E.R. 394; [1939] 1 K.B. 194; *Lake* v. *Bushby*, [1949] 2 All E.R. 964; *Simmons* v. *Pennington & Son*, [1955] 1 All E.R. 240; [1955] 1 W.L.R. 183; *Clark* v. *Kirby-Smith*, [1964] 2 All E.R. 835; [1964] Ch. 506; *Baker* v. *Willoughby*, [1968] 2 All E.R. 236; [1969] 1 Q.B. 38; [1969] 2 All E.R. 549; [1969] 2 W.L.R. 489.

A 1965, and the rent was £750 per annum. Clause 2 (x) of that lease provides:

"... not without the previous consent in writing of the lessors and superior lessors to carry on or suffer to be carried on in or upon the demised premises or any part thereof any trade or business whatsoever, other than as offices in connection with the lessees' business of architects and surveyors."

B Clause 2 (xv) contained a covenant not to assign, underlet or part with the possession of any part of the demised premises without the consent of the lessors and the superior lessors which consent shall, so far as the lessors are concerned, not be unreasonably withheld in respect of respectable and responsible tenants or assignees.

Mr. Ronald Sykes, who was clearly an honest and careful witness, and whose evidence I accept fully, as I do Mr. Needham's, who was the same type of witness, told me that the plaintiffs' attention was not drawn by Mr. Rignall to these clauses, and the plaintiffs never really considered their effect. They were content to take the premises on a comparatively short lease at a small rent for use while they considered what their next step should be. Just to conclude the history with regard to these premises: when the premises, which are the subject-matter of the dispute in this action, were found, the landlords of the Maddox Street property agreed to accept the surrender of the premises, and no difficulty arose. It is, however, worth noting that cl. 2 (x), when read by a layman and not a lawyer, might well, in my judgment, be thought not to apply to an assignment or underlease, the sub-clause relating to which comes much later in the lease, for, if the premises were assigned, clearly then a person not a lawyer might well think that the offices would not, in any event, be used in connection with " the lessees' business of architects and surveyors ", interpreting " lessee " as meaning the plaintiffs' partnership. I need not consider the legal interpretation of such a clause.

I do not, therefore, think, as was contended by counsel for the defendants, that the mere fact that that lease had those clauses in it would necessarily, or indeed probably, draw the plaintiffs' attention to the situation which arises by reason of the provisions of the Landlord and Tenant Act 1927. That Act deals with both assignment (including, of course, underletting) and user. So far as assignment and underletting are concerned, there is provision (1) that whether or not a lease contains a provision that consent shall not be unreasonably withheld, that provision is to be read into the lease. With regard to user no such provision is to be read into the lease, so that a lessee of business premises who desires to assign or underlet the premises may find that his market for underletting or assigning is an extremely limited one, even though the consent to the assigning or underletting cannot unreasonably be withheld.

Counsel for the plaintiffs contends that in all cases of leases where there are two separate provisions as to assignment and user it is the duty of a solicitor to draw his client's attention to the limiting nature of the user clause, unless the clause as to user contains the simple words " which consent shall not unreasonably be withheld." Counsel for the defendants contends that that is going much too far. It is in my judgment not a point I shall have to determine in this case. I shall consider the general duties of a solicitor in relation to leases so far as this case is concerned later in this judgment.

The practice of the plaintiffs' firm expanded and within a short time Mr. Ronald Sykes took a flat in London because of the time he had to spend in Maddox Street. As a consequence Mr. Needham set about looking for improved accommodation for the firm. As he said, he was really looking for somewhere where they could have " their own front door ". He found, however, that such accommodation was too expensive, but eventually discovered that they could take six rooms on the third floor in Roxburghe House, Regent Street. These rooms were not a self-contained office as each room opened on to the main corridor.

(1) I.e., s. 19 (1) (a)

Three rooms were on one side of a fire partition (they were known as suite A) and   A
three were on the other side (they were known as suite B). Negotiations were
begun and in relation to the proposed lease Mr. Rignall in Hull acted as the
plaintiffs' solicitor.

Two of the defences in this action were : (i) that Mr. Rignall was only instructed
to handle the formalities and not to advise: this was not pursued; and (ii)
that Mr. Rignall was instructed as a matter of urgency; there were no facts before   B
me which would even suggest that Mr. Rignall's duty would be lessened by any
such factor.

I do not think I need go through the negotiations in any detail. The term was
to be for ten years; the rent was to be £3,010 per annum, plus £535 per annum as
a service charge, making a total liability of £3,545 per annum. It is quite clear
that Mr. Rignall knew that the plaintiffs might want to assign or sublet either   C
the whole of the premises or suite A or suite B during the term, according to
whether their future practice warranted " their own front door " or did not
warrant holding both suite A and suite B. Clause 2 (xiii) dealt with assigning or
underletting and originally was in the form that only the whole of the premises
could be assigned or underlet. By a letter dated 20th March 1963 Mr. Rignall
wrote to the solicitors to Messrs. Morohan, Ltd., who were the immediate lessors,   D
saying that the plaintiffs were taking two suites and should be permitted, in
addition to subletting the whole, to sublet one suite if at any time the whole
of the premises was not required.

This lease also contained a user clause, cl. 2 (xi). Again (as in the Maddox
Street lease) the user clause comes before the assignment and underletting
clause, and again refers to " the Lessees' business ". Clause 2 (xi) was in the   E
following terms:

" Not to use the demised premises other than as offices in connection with
the Lessees' business of Architects and Surveyors or as offices and showrooms
in connection with any other business for which the permission in writing
of the Lessor and the Superior Lessors had first been obtained such permission
by the Lessor not to be unreasonably withheld."   F

It is this clause which has been the battleground of the parties.   Counsel for
the plaintiffs says that unless this clause is brought to the attention of a proposed
lessee, and the effect explained, it really does form a " trap ". Not only may
someone who is not a lawyer think that it really has nothing to do with assigning
or underletting, but any such person may well think that " permission by the   G
Lessor not to be unreasonably withheld " covers all lessors and may not understand the dichotomy between " Lessor " and " Superior Lessors ". Indeed,
seeing the words " permission . . . not to be unreasonably withheld " he might
well pass on without carefully analysing the position. Moreover, says counsel
for the plaintiffs, a lay client may well not appreciate that because of the wording
of the Landlord and Tenant Act 1927 it may not be much use having a right to   H
assign or underlet if the only persons to whom one can assign or underlet are
other architects and quantity surveyors if any one of the landlords in a chain
of landlords (in this case there were three in addition to the immediate landlord)
likes to say " I don't consent ". Counsel for the defendants, on the other hand,
says that the meaning of the user clause " leaps out of the page " (to use counsel's
own words) to anyone of reasonable education when he reads the covenants.   I
Counsel compares the wording of this clause with that of various other sub-
clauses (e.g., (xii), (xiii), (xvi), (xviii) and (xxi)) all of which contain the words
" Lessors and Superior Lessors ". (None of these sub-clauses, however, deals with
whether consent can or cannot be unreasonably withheld.)   Moreover, says
counsel, these clients were all architects and quantity surveyors and furthermore
Mr. Sykes, senior, was a director of property companies. They must, says
counsel, have understood what they were doing. In deciding which contention I
accept I shall first deal with the evidence I have heard.

A   Mr. Ronald Sykes told me that his father was fully active in 1963 as senior partner. His father was a quantity surveyor, while he himself is an architect. Mr. Sykes's grandfather had been an estate agent who had formed some four or five small companies for buying, selling and leasing domestic and small shop premises. When his grandfather died his father " took over " (if I may use that expression) those companies, and now that his father is dead Mr. Ronald

B   Sykes has taken them over. His father, said Mr. Sykes, had no knowledge of leases of offices. When the question of this lease arose, he (Mr. Ronald Sykes) took it down to Mr. Rignall as their solicitor. The correspondence shows that Mr. Rignall went through the draft and made amendments and notes but unfortunately there is a complete confusion as to documents. The plaintiffs having gone into possession in May 1963 (paying rent from March quarter day

C   1963), by the beginning of 1964 the lease had still not been actually executed. On being pressed by the landlords' solicitors to send the executed lease Mr. Rignall discovered that he had lost all his papers (including any draft lease) connected with the matter. Whether one of the documents before me is the draft referred to in this letter we do not know. I am not going to go through all the pros and cons since I am quite satisfied that from first to last Mr. Rignall did

D   not draw any one of the partners' attention to the consequences of cl. 2 (xi) either as bearing on cl. 2 (xiii) or at all.

   Mr. Sykes told me that he clearly remembers discussing the matter of subletting with his father and Mr. Needham, but to the best of his knowledge no discussion took place as to cl. 2 (xi). He remembers the partners discussing subletting with Mr. Rignall but there was no discussion as to to whom they could sublet.

E   He does not remember cl. 2 (xi) making any particular impression on him and was under the impression that they could get permission as to other user. Mr. Needham and he realised that originally they could only sublet as a whole and in consequence he did discuss this with Mr. Rignall, but no mention was made as to whom they could sublet.

   Mr. Needham, being in London, had no personal contact with Mr. Rignall. He

F   examined the lease to see how it would affect his use of the London office from the point of view of day-to-day working. He had in mind that he would still go on looking for " their own front door " and drew attention to the fact that they might want to let one suite. He did not particularly notice cl. 2 (xi). It never entered his head that it might affect the subletting.

   For the defence two solicitors were called: Mr. Styles, primarily as to fact,

G   and Mr. George, who is the editor of THE CONVEYANCER and a member of the Law Reform Committee on conveyancing matters, as well as being a practising solicitor, as an expert. Mr. Styles's evidence as to fact arose, not because he had anything to do with the lease in question, although at that time he was a qualified assistant to Mr. Rignall, but because for many years before that he had been in the town clerk's department in Hull, rising to being chief assistant

H   solicitor to the town clerk. Mr. Styles said that after the war Hull was redeveloped after bombing, that Mr. Sykes, senior, through his property companies, was one of those interested in the redevelopment and as a user clause was something then unknown to Hull he explained to every developer, including Mr. Sykes, senior, what such a clause meant.

   User clauses vary in their wording and I expressed a desire to see what was

I   the nature of the user clause used by the corporation which was explained to Mr. Sykes, senior. Mr. Styles was good enough to arrange for copies of the two types of developer's contracts (one for centre development and one for periphery development) to be sent down from Hull. They were in what I think can be called the usual form of developer's contracts, and the schedule containing the form of lease provided in one of its clauses that the developer should not carry on or permit to be carried on any business or trade other than (and then a blank) without the previous consent in writing of the corporation. I asked Mr. Styles what he would have explained to Mr Sykes, senior, and he told me that he

would tell every developer, including Mr. Sykes, senior, that after he had got A
his detailed plans ready he would have to come to see Mr. Styles to discuss for
what purpose the buildings would be used in order to see that such use fell into
the scheme of the corporation's town planning committee. In my judgment such
an explanation to Mr. Sykes, senior, with regard to that clause would not have
any influence on his mind when he was reading the lease in question some 12
years later. I think a great deal of Mr. Styles's later evidence (given before the B
documents arrived) was influenced by the feeling that after his explanation
Mr. Sykes, senior, would know all about user clauses. That, I think was a mistake
on Mr. Styles's part.

I now come to Mr. George's evidence as an expert witness. I should like to
make it clear that counsel for the defendants very pleasantly and politely, told
me I was cross-examining his expert witness. If trying to find out what Mr. C
George meant in relation to this case is cross-examining I plead guilty. Experts,
I find, sometimes give general statements which sound all right until one relates
them to the precise facts. Again, Mr. George said some things which so surprised
me that I did ask him some questions to see if he really meant what he had said.
For instance, Mr. George said that the words of the clause were so clear that he
could not understand any educated man not understanding precisely what was D
meant. I could not resist the temptation of asking Mr. George to look at the
correspondence, where Mr. Rignall, having had his attention drawn to the fact
that consent was being withheld, wrote:

"I feel, therefore, that there is no reason why you should not negotiate
an assignment of the Lease for use as offices or showrooms, as although the
consent of the Lessors and the Superior Lessors will be required such consents E
are not to be unreasonably withheld."

Again, Mr. George at one stage stated that as there was no item for costs of
advising a client as to the clauses of a lease there was no duty to advise and the
solicitor was entitled simply to send the lease without any advice and leave
the client to peruse and raise any query he desired to make. I am glad to say F
I think Mr. George withdrew this. When Mr. George said that a user clause was
so well known in London that he would merely draw his client's attention to the
fact that there was such a clause, I am afraid I asked " But what if your client
is in Hull? ", to which Mr. George, after hesitating, replied that if the client had
held a lease in London that would be enough. Mr. George said that he, personally, and he thought about 50 per cent. of solicitors, did try to find out (if there G
was no " without reasonable cause " in a user clause) who were in the chain of landlords. I was unable to see, if there was no duty to advise, why he did so. I
asked him " What if you find a Rachman in the chain? ", to which Mr. George
replied " I should advise my client not to execute the lease ". He still did not
think there was any duty to discuss the user clause with his client. I should like
to make it quite clear that I am not in the least suggesting that Mr. George was H
doing anything other than trying to assist me but I do think that Mr. George in
trying to protect a brother solicitor who is dead was inclined not to think out
sufficiently the consequences of some of the answers which he gave to me.

Mr. Styles gave his evidence before Mr. George finished his evidence as Mr.
George was in some difficulty in the afternoon. Again, I am afraid it was I who
asked Mr. Styles for his views on cl. 2 (xi). Mr. Styles said he thought it was I
expressed in an unfortunate way and agreed that anyone who was not a lawyer
might think at first glance that the word " Lessor " included any lessor up the
chain. He had not seen a clause in this form before. He agreed in cross-
examination that Mr. Sykes, senior, might not have the same ability as a solicitor
to construe clauses in the lease. Incidentally, it is to be noted that the words
" the Lessees' business of Architects and Surveyors " is agreed by everyone to
include any assignees' or underlessees' business right down a chain, although the
" Lessor " in the clause does not include lessors up the chain. Mr. Styles's

A view was that if during the negotiations the clients had had their attention drawn to the clause, well and good, but if not he would certainly draw their attention to it, but he did not think it would be necessary in the case of Mr. Sykes, senior. He said this before the developers' contracts were produced, and I think he based his answer on what he thought he had told Mr. Sykes, senior in about 1950. He said he did not usually enquire as to superior landlords but if he knew there

B was a Rachman in the chain he would advise his client not to go on.

I have tried to set out shortly and I hope fairly the evidence before me on liability. What then is the duty of a solicitor who acts for a client in connection with the granting to the client of a lease? The textbooks and the authorities seem to be curiously silent on the point. I would venture to state the duty so far as it applies to this case in the following terms.

C When a solicitor is consulted by a client with reference to a lease which the client is considering entering into the solicitor knows, or ought to know, that one of the main purposes of consulting him is to ensure that where there is any clause the legal effect of which the client may not fully understand because of the wording, or where legal consequences may follow which the client may not realise, the meaning and the consequences of the clause will be pointed out to

D him or her. The last step, so far as the client is concerned, will be that the solicitor will present him with a document to sign, and he relies on the solicitor not to present him with a document which contains hidden dangers, of which the solicitor ought to know, but of which he, as a non-lawyer, may not know or realise the import. What has to be pointed out may well vary with the client. The test for negligence is whether the court is prepared to hold that in the

E particular case the solicitor ought to have realised that the consequences in law of any particular words used in the lease might well not be fully realised by his client. Even if the client is a fellow solicitor or a barrister the client is still entitled to have pointed out to him any clause which is unusual or which may have what I would call, an indirect effect on another clause; but, of course, if either the transaction does not come to fruition for any reason, or the client

F already knows the effect of the clause no " causation " (if I may use that word) flows if the effect is not pointed out to him and, therefore, no action lies. If there are several clients it is not enough that the solicitor thinks one of them understands; he must consider each of them, although if one is clearly acting as sole agent for the others, an explanation to him may (but not necessarily will) be sufficient. Each case must be considered on its own facts.

G In this case one is faced with the following facts: (i) The clients were professional men but not in a profession where the effect of the wording of leases has to be considered. (ii) The wording of cl. 2 (xi) is most unusual. Mr. Styles had never seen one so worded, and Mr. George did not suggest that he had seen one. There is no precedent containing similar wording in either HALLETT'S CONVEYANCING PRECEDENTS or THE ENCYCLOPAEDIA OF FORMS AND PRECEDENTS.

H (iii) I am satisfied that not one of the plaintiffs did understand the effect of the wording of cl. 2 (xi) and (xiii). (iv) In my judgment it is reasonable that they did not, and Mr. Rignall ought to have realised that that would probably be the case. Indeed, the correspondence, which I have already read, seems to show that Mr. Rignall himself did not really analyse what the true consequences would be. It follows that there was negligence on the part of Mr. Rignall.

I The position as to damages is a curious one. Counsel for the plaintiffs says " damages is the sum of £9,000, neither more nor less ". Counsel for the defendants says that in law there are no damages. Indeed, if he is right, the plaintiffs have in law received a benefit. In order to understand how this arises it is necessary to continue with the history of the plaintiffs' occupation of the premises in Roxburghe House. At the beginning of 1964 the plaintiffs wanted to extend their offices and an opportunity arose of obtaining an underlease of further rooms in Roxburghe House on the fourth floor. Once more Mr. Rignall was instructed by the plaintiffs. The lease entered into (dated 27th April 1964,

and which I shall call the second lease) contained the same covenants as the **A**
lease for the third floor (which I shall call the first lease), save that the rent was
to be £1,820 per annum for ten years, and £325 per annum was to be the service
charge, making £2,145 per annum in all.   It is clear that Mr. Rignall was
instructed to negotiate and not merely to draw up the documents and there is
no suggestion that the instructions were on a basis different from the instructions
for the first lease.   Once more there are the same cl. 2 (xi) and cl. 2 (xiii) and once **B**
more nothing was said by Mr. Rignall as to the consequences of those sub-clauses.
The plaintiffs assumed that the covenants in the second lease would be the same
as the covenants in the first lease and were content that that should be so.

In 1965 there was a recession in the building trade and the plaintiffs found it
necessary to reduce their overheads.   At the end of March estate agents were
instructed to find underlessees for the fourth floor premises at a rental of £2,400 **C**
per annum for eight years exclusive of rates but inclusive of services, together
with £1,500 for fixtures and fittings.   On 12th April, Messrs. Partos & Partners,
who are engineering importers and exporters, accepted that offer subject to
contract.   In the same month the plaintiffs moved out of the fourth floor;
work did not justify their staying on.   In May the plaintiffs agreed to take one
room in the offices of a company called Kleine Reinforced Concrete, Ltd., in **D**
Manchester for £250 per annum for four years, and again Mr. Rignall acted for
the plaintiffs, but, for a reason which is immaterial, the matter of the sublease
to Partos was put by the plaintiffs into the hands of Messrs. Herbert Smith & Co.,
solicitors in London.

Once again, in the case of the Manchester room there was a user clause but the
assignment clause contained a provision that the room must first be offered to **E**
the landlords, which is understandable since the room was in their offices.   On
20th May Mr. Rignall wrote a long letter to the plaintiffs drawing attention to
numerous points in the lease, but not to the user clause.

Then came the bombshell.   On 11th June 1965 Messrs. Herbert Smith wrote
to Messrs. Dehn & Lauderdale, the solicitors for Partos on the following lines:

F
" You probably heard that it will not be possible for the proposed underlease to your clients to proceed owing to the refusal of the superior landlords
to grant a licence as to the change of use.   In the circumstances please
return to us the draft underlease."

Mr. Ronald Sykes appears to have communicated with Mr. Rignall at once, for
there follows a letter from Mr. Rignall, the material part of which I have already **G**
read (2).   Unfortunately, of course, Mr. Rignall was quite wrong.

So far as Manchester is concerned the plaintiffs entered into the lease on
17th September 1965.   Counsel for the defendants in cross-examination quite
rightly stressed that factor to Mr. Sykes.   Mr. Sykes's answer was that the rent
was small, the term was short, the clause had not struck them, and the clause did
not come back to their minds after the trouble with Partos had arisen.   As I **H**
have said I am quite satisfied that Mr. Sykes at all time in his evidence told me
the whole truth about this matter.

The Partos offer having fallen through, in August 1965 the plaintiffs began
advertising the premises in their professional journals and it is clear from the
correspondence that by August 1965 the plaintiffs were willing to let both the
third and fourth floors go if they could get rid of their liability.   In September **I**
1965 an offer for the fourth floor premises was received from a firm of solicitors
who already occupied premises in Roxburghe House.   This offer was on the same
terms as the Partos offer.   Once more, for reasons I just do not understand
(nor apparently did the immediate lessors), there was a blank refusal by the
freeholders (Regional Properties, Ltd.) to the change of user, and it was not
until 25th March 1968 (after this action had been commenced), that Regional
Properties, Ltd., relented and allowed the plaintiffs to sublet to Public Relations

(2) See at p. 1244, letter E, ante.

A Council, Ltd., and Sells, Ltd., who apparently had rooms next to the plaintiffs
on the fourth floor.   The lease in effect was for the remainder of the plaintiffs'
term.   The rent was £1,850 per annum until September 1969, £2,000 per annum
until September 1970, and £2,120 for the remainder of the terms of the lease.
This rent included services, but was exclusive of rates.   It must, of course, be
remembered that the value of office premises was, to use a common phrase,
B " shooting up ".

That being the history, how does the question of damages stand?   In order
to save the expense of calling valuers certain facts have been agreed.   It is
agreed: (i) that the rents reserved in both the first and the second lease were
the current market rents, provided consent to a change of user could not be
unreasonably withheld; (ii) that the market value of the premises with the
C wording of cl. 2 (xi) would be 27½ per cent. less than those rents; (iii) that the
capitalised value of that difference over the whole term of the leases is, (a) £9,000
with no allowance for tax, (b) £5,500 allowing tax at 7s. 9d. in the pound;
(iv) that the best disposal of the premises available would be 27½ per cent. off
whatever should be the market rent at the date of disposal.

The first question on quantum of damage which has to be considered is the
D principle on which one has to assess the damage.   Here is a case where the solicitor
failed to warn his client that the consequence of entering into the two leases is
that if and when his clients desired to sublet under cl. 2 (xiii) the probability of
their being able to do so would be very greatly diminished by reason of the
wording of cl. 2 (xi), which wording entails that every landlord in the chain of
superior landlords must give his consent to the subletting if it involves a change
E of user, but that consent, except in the case of the immediate landlord, can be
withheld without any reason being given.   Counsel for the defendants says that in
those circumstances any compensation must be based on the chances of what
would have happened if such a warning had been given.   Counsel for the plaintiffs
says that that is quite wrong and that once the clients have entered into the
lease the consideration of chances does not arise.
F
So far as the evidence is concerned, Mr. Sykes was quite frank as to the position.
He said that since they never had to consider the matter he does not know what
the result would have been if their attention had been drawn to the dangers of
cl. 2 (xi) when read with cl. 2 (xiii).   The furthest he went was that it would at
any rate have caused them to pause.   There was, he said, no particular urgency
to move out of Maddox Street.   They were undertaking a heavy annual liability
G for a considerable length of time if they signed the leases, and they always had in
mind the question of possible subletting.   He just cannot say what the result
would have been.   He answered such questions, as he answered all questions,
with a full sense of responsibility.

If one looks at the position as it then was one sees that a number of different
consequences might have followed if the plaintiffs had known the effect of the
H clauses.   The plaintiffs might: (i) have turned down the whole lease; (ii) have
tried to negotiate for a reduction in the rent payable; (iii) have asked that
enquiries be made as to who were the superior landlords with a view to seeing
whether they ought to risk a blunt refusal to any alteration of user; or (iv) have
made up their minds they would take the risk of refusal and gone ahead either
before or after such enquiries were made.
I
If counsel for the defendants is right it is difficult to see the basis on which the
degree of chance ought to be assessed.   It is extremely unlikely, indeed it would
be impossible for the immediate landlords to incorporate a clause that consent
to an alteration of user was not to be unreasonably withheld unless their lease,
in turn, contained such a clause.   The basis, as I see it, would have to be the
chance whether or not the immediate landlord would reduce the rent and, if so,
by how much, taking into consideration that if the plaintiffs refused the lease
the plaintiffs might or might not have obtained other premises which might or

might not have been to their financial advantage or disadvantage and the plain- **A**
tiffs might or might not have decided to take the risk and sign the lease. Counsel
for the plaintiffs contends that in law one need not consider these matters once the
lease is entered into. Once the plaintiffs have in fact entered into a lease the
measure of damage, he says, is a simple one. It is the difference in the market
value between the lease containing cl. 2 (xi) and cl. 2 (xiii) and a lease containing
cl. 2 (xi) in the simple form that consent was not to be unreasonably withheld. **B**

In support of his contentions counsel for the defendants, in addition to relying
on the well-known case of *Chaplin* v. *Hicks* (3), also relied on a number of more
recent cases. The first of these is *Otter* v. *Church, Adams, Tatham & Co.* (4).
In that case the plaintiff as guardian of her son M. who was under age engaged
the defendants as solicitors to advise her on the extent and nature of his interest
in certain settled property which had recently fallen into his possession. The **C**
defendants wrongly informed her that M. on attaining 21 would become entitled
absolutely to the property in question. In fact M.'s interest was an equitable
interest in tail male. When M. attained 21 the plaintiff consulted the defendants
as to what steps to take. She was advised that the transfer could await M.'s
returned to England. She informed M. of this advice. M. was killed in a flying
accident. The plaintiff was the sole administratrix of M.'s estate. It was **D**
held that the measure of damage was the loss to M.'s estate because the property
passed to the next tenant in tail but that due allowance must be made for the
possibility that M. might not have disentailed. It is to be noted that UPJOHN, J.,
based his judgment on what M. might have done (5) and awarded the plaintiff,
in her capacity as administratrix of M., £6,500 instead of the full sum of £7,132,
the difference being the court's estimate as to the chances M. would not have **E**
disentailed. It is, however, interesting to note that the LAW QUARTERLY
REVIEW (vol. 69, p. 160) comments on this case and says that with all respect
it may be suggested that what M. might or might not have done had he known
the facts was irrelevant for at the moment of his death the estate was deprived
of the full value of the entailed estate.

The next case is *Pilkington* v. *Wood* (6). That was a case in which the title **F**
to property purchased by the plaintiff was defective, and the defendant admitted
he was negligent in not advising the plaintiff of that fact. A number of questions
was discussed in that case but it was assumed that there was no question of the
court going into what the plaintiff might have done had he known of the defect.
It was assumed that he would not have proceeded with the transaction and that
the damage was the difference between the value of the property as bought and **G**
the value which it would have been at the date of the purchase without the
defect.

The third case is *Hall* v. *Meyrick* (7). In that case the plaintiff was a woman
who, together with a man called Hall, instructed the defendant to draft wills
each to confer benefits on the other. The question of the plaintiff and Hall
marrying was somewhat jokingly referred to, and the defendant failed to advise **H**
that marriage would revoke the wills unless they were made in contemplation
thereof. The plaintiff subsequently married Hall and neither she nor Hall was
aware of the effects of marriage on their wills. Hall died intestate and the
plaintiff claimed damages for loss of the benefit which had been conferred on her
by Hall's will before marriage. ASHWORTH, J., held that the original instructions were not joint instructions, that the only negligence by the solicitor was **I**
towards the plaintiff at the time when she instructed him to draft her will in
not warning her that both wills would be revoked by marriage. He held that
the full loss between the difference of what she received and what she would

(3) [1911] 2 K.B. 786; [1911-13] All E.R. Rep. 224.
(4) [1953] 1 All E.R. 168; [1953] Ch. 280.
(5) [1953] 1 All E.R. at p. 170; [1953] Ch. at pp. 289, 290.
(6) [1953] 2 All E.R. 810; [1953] Ch. 770.
(7) [1957] 1 All E.R. 208; [1957] 2 Q.B. 455.

A have received was £1,550, but that the plaintiff when she married Hall might not have remembered the warning given, that Hall might not have been willing to make a further will, that if he did so it did not follow that the will would have been wholly in her favour, nor did it follow that Hall might not afterwards have revoked it. In those circumstances he reduced the damages to £1,250. This case went to the Court of Appeal (8) but only on a pleading point. The

B Court of Appeal held that ASHWORTH, J., ought not to have allowed a certain amendment and reversed the judgment. The question of damages did not arise.

Finally, on this part of his argument, counsel for the defendants referred to *Ford* v. *White & Co.* (9). In that case the plaintiffs purchased land which the defendants advised was not restricted against being built on. It was in fact so

C restricted. The price which the plaintiffs paid for the land was the market price with the restriction on the land. PENNYCUICK, J., in holding that the plaintiffs suffered no damage, referred to a number of cases and concluded from those cases that where property was purchased in excess of the market value as a result of wrong advice the measure of damage was the difference between that market value and the price actually paid, but where only the proper market

D price had been paid the clients suffered no special damage. He found for the defendants instead of finding nominal damages owing to the agreement made between the parties.

In the course of his argument, counsel for the plaintiffs, in addition to other authorities (to which I need not, I think, refer), referred me to *Philips* v. *Ward* (10). That was an action against a surveyor for failing to point out that the

E condition of the premises was such that expenditure on them was necessary. In that case the plaintiff had properly expended £7,000 on the property but the difference in value at the time of the purchase between a building in proper repair and a building in the condition in which the property actually was was £4,000. It was held that the proper measure of damages was £4,000 and not the cost of repair. In the course of his judgment DENNING, L.J., pointed out (11)

F that the general principle of English law is that damage must be assessed at the date when the damage occurs and that is usually the same day as the cause of action arises. MORRIS, L.J., pointed out (12) that had the plaintiff been advised that £7,000 was necessary he might well not have gone on with the purchase as the owner would not have been likely to sell at under the market price. MORRIS, L.J., however, did not take this factor into account in agreeing with DENNING,

G L.J., that the proper measure of damage was the difference in value at the date of the purchase. Similarly, ROMER, L.J., pointed out (13) that the plaintiff might have decided that he would not buy the property, in which case he would have kept his money in his pocket and have had no house, but stated that on this hypothesis his ignorance might be said to have worsened his position to the extent of £4,000 as he parted with £25,000 and became the possessor of

H property only worth £21,000.

For some time I was impressed with counsel for the defendants' argument. Indeed, I rather think that I was the first person who raised the query whether " loss of a chance " ought not to be taken into consideration. On consideration of these and other authorities and after considering the arguments placed before me, I have come to the conclusion that counsel for the plaintiffs is right. The

I negligence in not warning went on up to the point when the leases were signed. Mr. Rignall clearly put the leases before the partners for the partners to sign without any warning as to the effect of cl. 2 (xi). On the ultimate analysis it

---

(8) [1957] 2 All E.R. 722; [1957] 2 Q.B. at p. 472.
(9) [1964] 2 All E.R. 755; [1964] 1 W.L.R. 885.
(10) [1956] 1 All E.R. 874; [1956] 1 W.L.R. 471.
(11) [1956] 1 All E.R. at p. 876; [1956] 1 W.L.R. at p. 474.
(12) [1956] 1 All E.R. at p. 878; [1956] 1 W.L.R. at p. 476.
(13) [1956] 1 All E.R. at p. 879; [1956] 1 W.L.R. at p. 478.

was that act of sending the leases to be signed without any warning of the conse- **A** quences of signing them which led to the partners executing the leases. The fact that the first lease was not signed until 1964, owing to Mr. Rignall's careless- ness in losing papers, does not, in my judgment, affect this aspect of the case. At some point the plaintiffs, either by signature or by conduct became bound by the terms of the lease. They signed, or alternatively so conducted themselves that they were bound, because of an implied representation by Mr. Rignall **B** that there would be no hidden dangers so far as the meaning of the words of the lease were concerned in their so doing.

If one contrasts the situation in *Chaplin* v. *Hicks* (14) and *Hall* v. *Meyrick* (15) with the situation in this case, in both those cases at the moment when the breach of duty crystallised the plaintiff undertook no liability. Had no negligence occurred she might in each case have reaped a benefit. Whether she did so or **C** not depended on the actions of a third party. It may be said that this was not so in *Otter* v. *Church, Adams, Tatham & Co.* (16), since in that case there might have been a duty on the plaintiff as the guardian of M. to take some steps had proper advice been given. I need not determine whether that case was rightly decided. In my judgment in this case the damage crystallised at the moment the plaintiffs became liable to their landlord for rent, and the damage which flowed **D** from that was a liability to pay a rent in excess of the market rent, a liability which continued during the continuance of the leases at all times and the damage is the true capitalised value of that excess.

Counsel for the defendants then invites me to say, first of all, that there cannot be any damage accruing while the plaintiffs are or were actually in possession of either the third floor or the fourth floor since they are, or were, merely paying **E** the rent reserved under the lease. He further asks me to say that in any event damages must be diminished by the payments received by the plaintiffs by way of rent on the fourth floor. He says that the fact that the value of the property rose between 1963 and 1968 is material and that the defendants are entitled to set-off all sums received in excess of the rent payable to the landlords. In my judgment there is a fundamental fallacy in these arguments. Damages are **F** assessed at the date of the breach. Damage in this case is the capitalised sum of the difference between the rent payable and that which would have been payable. What happens thereafter is immaterial. Throughout the lease the plaintiffs are under a liability to pay 27½ per cent. more rent than they ought to have paid. If, of course, the court knows of any factor (such as a further Act of Parliament, or an alteration in the extent of the influence of such a clause on **G** market value) which has taken place before trial and which affects the 27½ per cent., that factor might well affect the capitalisation of the annual loss, but the agreed finding is that nothing has affected the loss of 27½ per cent. It is there today and there is no finding that it may vary in the future. Counsel for the defendants has pointed out that it has been said that if a man buys an orange for £100 which is worth £5 but sells it for £105 there is no loss, but that it does **H** not follow that had the orange really been worth £100 at the time of purchase it would have been sold for more than £105. I do not think that such analogies help me. I am quite unable to follow why no damage accrues while the plaintiffs are in possession of the premises. Each time rent is paid 27½ per cent. more is paid than the premises were worth when the lease was taken and that liability goes on through the whole period of the lease, for even if the premises are sublet **I** the liability to the immediate landlord still exists and this fact is taken into account in the capitalised sum.

One further point has been taken by counsel for the defendants. He has contended that in any event the capitalisation of any sum must be based on the

(14) [1911] 2 K.B. 786; [1911-13] All E.R. Rep. 224.
(15) [1957] 2 All E.R. 722; [1957] 2 Q.B. 455.
(16) [1953] 1 All E.R. 168; [1953] Ch. 280.

A　fact that the sums to be capitalised are affected by *British Transport Commission* v. *Gourley* (17). In my judgment that is not so. *Gourley's* case (17) was the case of a man who was very badly injured and who, before the accident, was earning a very large sum per annum as a partner in a firm of civil engineers but after the accident was not able to carry out all his professional duties and, therefore, agreed to take a much smaller proportion of the profits of the firm.

B　The question before the House of Lords was whether in those circumstances it was right to take into consideration that on both his pre-accident earnings and his post-accident earnings he would have to pay tax, and that by reason of the provisions of the Revenue Acts the difference between his pre-accident and his post-accident earnings was very greatly diminished. The essence of that case was that he would have paid tax on the sums in question and the House of

C　Lords held that one must take the net amount he would have received and the net amount which he did receive, since tax is an inherent element in every man's earnings. EARL JOWITT was careful to point out that the principle laid down in *Gourley's* case (18) was not necessarily to be applied when different circumstances arose (e.g., compensation for compulsory acquisition of land), and it is in my judgment quite clear that great care has to be taken when endeavouring

D　to apply the principle in *Gourley's* case (17) to other circumstances.

　　In MAYNE ON DAMAGES (12th Edn. at p. 251) it is stated that two factors are necessary to set the stage for the problem which is posed in *Gourley's* case (17): (i) the sums for the loss of which the damages awarded constituted compensation would have been subject to tax; and (ii) the damages awarded to the plaintiff would not themselves be subject to tax.

E　　What I have to give damages for is the fact that due to the negligence of Mr. Rignall the plaintiffs entered into two leases without being warned of dangers. The damages are for the fact that they signed the leases without knowledge of the dangers thereof. The damage they suffered was the liability to pay rent in excess of that which would be represented by the rent payable under the lease with part of the user restriction clause omitted. Tax is not payable on rent

F　although the amount payable for rent is a factor which is included when the profits of a firm are assessed. When the profits of the firm are assessed then each partner has to pay tax in accordance with his total income, including any amount received from the fact that he is a partner in the firm. One partner may pay no tax, for his total income may not come into the taxable limit; another may pay a large sum by way of surtax. Further, the amount payable by way of

G　tax, or tax and surtax, may vary from year to year. To try to arrive at a capitalised sum which represents the different interests of each partner in the ultimate financial result for each year of the partnership is not only impracticable but is going far beyond any principles decided in *Gourley's* case (17). In my judgment the editors of MAYNE are correct when they say that the first essential element to be found before *Gourley's* case (17) applies is that the very sums for which

H　compensation is awarded would themselves have been subject to tax.

　　For the reason which I have given, in my judgment the proper sum for damages is £9,000.

Judgment for the plaintiffs for £9,000.

　　Solicitors: *Herbert Smith & Co.* (for the plaintiffs); *Hewitt, Woollacott & Chown* (for the defendants).

I　　　　　　　　　　　　　　[*Reported by* K. DIANA PHILLIPS, *Barrister-at-Law.*]

---

(17) [1955] 3 All E.R. 796; [1956] A.C. 185.
(18) [1955] 3 All E.R. at p. 802; [1956] A.C. at p. 202.

BRITISH CELANESE, LTD. *v.* A. H. HUNT (CAPACITORS), LTD.

[QUEEN'S BENCH DIVISION (Lawton, J.), March 3, 4, 5, April 2, 1969.]

Nuisance—Principle of Rylands v. Fletcher—*User—Escape of metal foil stored on land in connection with manufacture of electrical and electronic components —Whether special use of land.*

Nuisance—Principle of Rylands v. Fletcher—*Escape—Escape to premises of third party (electricity board)—Damage to plaintiffs through loss of electric power—Whether actionable.*

Nuisance—Private nuisance—Isolated occurrence—Metal foil blown onto electricity board's equipment so as to cause power failure—Whether isolated occurrence actionable.

Damages—Remoteness of damage—Nuisance—Foreseeability—Escape of metal foil blown onto electricity board's equipment causing power failure—Damage to plaintiffs consequent on electricity board's power failure—Clogged machinery and consequential loss of production and profits—Whether too remote.

Negligence—Escape—Metal foil—Factories on trading estate receiving electric power from same power station—Escape from factory of metal foil blown onto power station causing power failure and consequential damage to other factory—Same incident $3\frac{1}{2}$ years earlier—Knowledge of defendants that escape of foil could cause power failure—Whether duty to prevent escape.

Damages—Remoteness of damage—Negligence—Foreseeability—Escape of metal foil blown onto electricity board's equipment causing power failure—Damage to plaintiffs consequent on electricity board's power failure—Clogged machinery and consequential loss of production and profits—Whether too remote.

The plaintiffs and defendants occupied sites some 150 yards apart on a trading estate. For the purposes of their business, as manufacturers of electronic components, the defendants brought onto their site, collected and kept there, strips of metal foil several feet long which were light enough to be blown about in the wind. The factories on the estate received light and power from a sub-station of the electricity board which was 100 yards from the plaintiffs' factory and 120 yards from the defendants'. The sub-station's equipment, including 33-kW bus-bars, stood in the open air, and it was known to the defendants (as a result of an incident $3\frac{1}{2}$ years previously, regarding which they had received a letter from the electricity board's local engineer) that if a strip of metal foil came into contact with more than one of the bus-bars there was likely to be a flash-over which would probably cause a power failure and a consequent interruption of electricity supply to the premises of members of the public in the area including the plaintiffs. On 7th December 1964 some of a large number of strips of metal foil which lay about in the open air on or near the defendants' premises were blown away and fouled the bus-bars of the sub-station, thereby causing a flash-over and an interruption of light and power supplies to the plaintiffs' factory and, as a result of damage to the electricity board's equipment, another short interruption later the same afternoon. As a result of the interruption of electricity supplies the plaintiffs' machinery came to a stop, materials in certain machines solidified and the machines had to be cleaned before production could be restarted. Materials and time were wasted and production lost; the loss of profit being estimated at £9,372. On a preliminary issue as to the defendants' liability on the facts as pleaded,

Held: (i) the defendants would not be liable under the rule in *Rylands* v. *Fletcher** because neither the manufacturing of electrical or electronic components nor the storing of metal foil on the premises could be regarded as a special use of the land within the meaning of the rule (see p. 1257, letters A and B, post).

---

* [1861-73] All E.R. Rep. 1.

A   Dictum of LORD MOULTON in *Rickards* v. *Lothian* ([1911-13] All E.R. Rep. at p. 80) applied.

(ii) the defendants would be liable in negligence, because—

(a) they owed the plaintiffs a duty to take reasonable care to prevent the strips of metal foil from blowing onto the bus-bars (see p. 1258, letter G, post); and

B   (b) the damage alleged was not too remote to be recoverable (see p. 1259, letter A, post).

Cattle v. *Stockton Waterworks Co.* ([1874-80] All E.R. Rep. 220); *Weller & Co.* v. *Foot and Mouth Disease Research Institute* ([1965] 3 All E.R. 560); and *Electrochrome, Ltd.* v. *Welsh Plastics, Ltd.* ([1968] 2 All E.R. 205) distinguished.

C   *Seaway Hotels, Ltd.* v. *Cragg (Canada), Ltd. and Consumers' Gas Co.* ((1960) 21 D.L.R. (2d) 264) explained.

(iii) the defendants would be liable in private nuisance, because—

(a) it was not necessary for the plaintiffs to establish a continuing condition (see p. 1261, letter I, post) (*Midwood & Co., Ltd.* v. *Manchester Corpn.*, ([1905] 2 K.B. 597) followed); and

D   (b) the alleged damage was not too remote (see p. 1262, letter D, post).

PER CURIAM: the plaintiffs would be entitled to damages under the rule in *Rylands* v. *Fletcher** notwithstanding that the escape was on to the premises of a third party (the electricity board). Once there was an escape in the relevant sense, and subject to the rule of remoteness, those damnified could claim. They did not need to be occupiers of adjoining land or indeed **E**   of any land (see p. 1257, letters E and F, post).

[As to negligence and the duty of an occupier of premises to his neighbours, see 28 HALSBURY'S LAWS (3rd Edn.) 50-53, paras. 46-48.

As to remoteness of damage in negligence and the test for remoteness, see ibid., 98, 99, paras. 106, 107; and for cases on the subject, see 36 DIGEST (Repl.) 195-198, *1030-1047.*
F   As to injury to neighbouring property by nuisance, see 28 HALSBURY'S LAWS (3rd Edn.) 131-136, paras. 167-174.

As to the rule in *Rylands* v. *Fletcher*, see ibid., 145-149, paras. 192-198.

For cases on the subject of injury to neighbouring property by nuisance and under the rule in *Rylands* v. *Fletcher*, see 36 DIGEST (Repl.) 281-302, *323-479.*]

G Cases referred to:

A.-G. (on the relation of Glamorgan County Council and Pontardawe Rural District Council) v. *P.Y.A. Quarries, Ltd.*, [1957] 1 All E.R. 894; [1957] 2 Q.B. 169; [1957] 2 W.L.R. 770; 121 J.P. 323; Digest (Cont. Vol. A) 1214, *68b.*

Bolton v. *Stone*, [1951] 1 All E.R. 1078; [1951] A.C. 850; 36 Digest (Repl.) **H**   18, *79.*

Cattle v. *Stockton Waterworks Co.* (1875), L.R. 10 Q.B. 453; [1874-80] All E.R. Rep. 220; 44 L.J.Q.B. 139; 33 L.T. 475; 39 J.P. 791; 1 Digest (Repl.) 37, *277.*

Charing Cross, West End and City Electricity Supply, Co., Ltd. v. *Hydraulic Power Co.*, [1914] 3 K.B. 772; [1914-15] All E.R. Rep. 85; 83 L.J.K.B. **I**   1352; 111 L.T. 198; 78 J.P. 305; 36 Digest (Repl.) 284, *338.*

Donoghue (or McAlister) v. *Stevenson*, [1932] A.C. 562; [1932] All E.R. Rep. 1; 101 L.J.P.C. 119; 147 L.T. 281; 36 Digest (Repl.) 85, *458.*

Electrochrome, Ltd. v. *Welsh Plastics, Ltd.*, [1968] 2 All E.R. 205; Digest (Repl.) Supp.

Halsey v. *Esso Petroleum Co., Ltd.*, [1961] 2 All E.R. 145; [1961] 1 W.L.R. 683; Digest (Cont. Vol. A) 1215, *108b.*

---

* [1861-73] All E.R. Rep. 1.

Hay (or Bourhill) v. *Young*, [1942] 2 All E.R. 396; [1943] A.C. 92; 111 L.J.P.C. **A**
97; 167 L.T. 261; 36 Digest (Repl.) 16, *66*.

Hedley Byrne & Co., Ltd. v. *Heller & Partners, Ltd.*, [1963] 2 All E.R. 575; [1964] A.C. 465; [1963] 3 W.L.R. 101; Digest (Cont. Vol. A) 51, *1117a*.

Midwood & Co., Ltd. v. *Manchester Corpn.*, [1905] 2 K.B. 597; 74 L.J.K.B. 884; 93 L.T. 525; 69 J.P. 348; 38 Digest (Repl.) 43, *219*. **B**

Perry v. *Kendricks Transport, Ltd.*, [1956] 1 All E.R. 154; [1956] 1 W.L.R. 85; Digest (Cont. Vol. A) 1171, *599a*.

Rainham Chemical Works, Ltd. v. *Belvedere Fish Guano Co., Ltd.*, [1921] 2 A.C. 465; [1921] All E.R. Rep. 48; 90 L.J.K.B. 1252; 126 L.T. 70; 36 Digest (Repl.) 291, *376*.

Read v. *J. Lyons & Co., Ltd.*, [1946] 2 All E.R. 471; [1947] A.C. 156; [1947] **C** L.J.R. 39; 175 L.T. 413; 36 Digest (Repl.) 83, *452*.

Rickards v. *Lothian*, [1913] A.C. 263; [1911-13] All E.R. Rep. 71; 82 L.J.P.C. 42; 108 L.T. 225; 36 Digest (Repl.) 37, *177*.

Rylands v. *Fletcher* (1866), L.R. 1 Exch. 265; [1861-73] All E.R. Rep. 1; 35 L.J.Ex. 154; 14 L.T. 523; 30 J.P. 436; *affd.* H.L. (1868), L.R. 3 H.L. 330; [1861-73] All E.R. Rep. 1; 37 L.J. Ex. 161; 19 L.T. 220; **D** 33 J.P. 70; 36 Digest (Repl.) 282, *334*.

Seaway Hotels, Ltd. v. *Cragg (Canada), Ltd. and Consumers' Gas Co.* (1960), 21 D.L.R. (2d) 264; [1959] O.R. 581; *on appeal from* (1959), 17 D.L.R. (2d) 292; [1959] O.R. 177; 25 Digest (Repl.) 538, **64*.

Weller & Co. v. *Foot and Mouth Disease Research Institute*, [1965] 3 All E.R. 560; [1966] 1 Q.B. 569; [1965] 3 W.L.R. 1082; Digest (Cont. Vol. B) **E** 554, *109c*.

Action.

In this action the plaintiffs, British Celanese, Ltd., claimed damages in negligence and nuisance against the defendants, A. H. Hunt (Capacitors), Ltd., and further sought an injunction to restrain the defendants from continuing the alleged nuisance. The court was asked to decide as a preliminary issue whether **F** on the facts set out in the re-amended statement of claim the defendants were liable in law for the damage claimed. The facts are set out in the judgment.

The cases noted below* were cited during the argument in addition to those referred to in the judgment.

C. F. Dehn, Q.C., and *P. D. J. Scott* for the plaintiffs.
Tudor Evans, Q.C., and *D. J. Hyamson* for the defendants. **G**

Cur. adv. vult.

2nd April. **LAWTON, J.**, read the following judgment: In this action I have to decide a preliminary issue, namely, whether on the facts set out in the re-amended statement of claim the defendants are in law liable for the damage claimed. Stated in broad terms the problem is this: Is a firm on an industrial **H**

* *The Argentino* (1888), 13 P.D. 191, C.A.; (1889), 14 App. Cas. 519, H.L.; *Hardaker* v. *Idle District Council*, [1896] 1 Q.B. 335; [1895-99] All E.R. Rep. 311; *Campbell* v. *Paddington Corpn.*, [1911] 1 K.B. 869; *Grant* v. *Australian Knitting Mills, Ltd.*, [1936] A.C. 85; [1935] All E.R. Rep. 209; *Dollman* v. *Hillman, Ltd.*, [1941] 1 All E.R. 355; *King* v. *Phillips*, [1953] 1 All E.R. 617; [1953] 1 Q.B. 429; *Kirkham* v. *Boughey*, [1957] 3 All E.R. 153; [1958] 2 Q.B. 338; *Overseas Tankship (U.K.), Ltd.* v. *Morts Docks & **I** Engineering Co., Ltd. (The Wagon Mound)*, [1961] 1 All E.R. 404; [1961] A.C. 388; *Hughes* v. *Lord Advocate*, [1963] 1 All E.R. 705; [1963] A.C. 837; *Boardman* v. *Sanderson*, [1964] 1 W.L.R. 1317; *Stewart* v. *West African Terminals, Ltd.*, [1964] 2 Lloyd's Rep. 371; *The World Harmony*, [1965] 2 All E.R. 139; [1967] P. 341; *Czarnikow (C.), Ltd.* v. *Koufos (The Heron II)*, [1966] 2 All E.R. 593; [1966] 2 Q.B. 695; [1967] 3 All E.R. 686; [1969] 1 A.C. 350; *Overseas Tankship (U.K.), Ltd.* v. *Miller Steamship Co. Pty. (The Wagon Mound) (No. 2)*, [1966] 2 All E.R. 709; [1967] 1 A.C. 617; *Cook* v. *Swinfen*, [1967] 1 All E.R. 299; [1967] 1 W.L.R. 547; *Chadwick* v. *British Transport Commission*, [1967] 2 All E.R. 945; [1967] 1 W.L.R. 912; *Margarine Union G.m.b.H.* v. *Cambay Prince Steamship Co., Ltd.*, [1967] 3 All E.R. 775; [1969] 1 Q.B. 219.

A estate which so conducts its business that the electric power supply to its neighbours on that estate is interrupted, liable to those neighbours for any injury to their property and consequential loss of production which they may suffer?

The allegations of fact in the re-amended statement of claim can be summarised as follows: the plaintiffs, who are the well-known producers of synthetic yarn and similar products, at all material times occupied a factory site on the Wrexham

B Trading Estate in the county of Denbigh. Their factory on that site worked round the clock producing yarn and acetate sheeting. The defendants, who manufacture electrical and electronic components, occupied a site on the same estate some 150 yards to the south-east of the plaintiffs' factory. For the purposes of their business the defendants had brought onto their site and had collected and kept there strips of metal foil up to several feet in length. These strips were

C light enough to be blown about in the sort of winds likely to be met with in the Wrexham area and were, in the words of the re-amended statement of claim, " likely to do mischief if they escaped ". Electric light and power for both the plaintiffs' and the defendants' factories were provided from an electricity supply sub-station owned and operated by the Merseyside and North West Electricity Board. That sub-station was 100 yards from the plaintiffs' factory and 120

D yards from the defendants'. At this sub-station electrical equipment, including 33-kW bus-bars which fed it, stood in the open air. If a strip of metal foil came into contact with more than one of the bus-bars there was likely to be a " flash-over " which could, and probably would, cause a power failure. The defendants knew that this was likely to happen and that if it did, there would be an interruption of the supply of light and power to the premises of members of the

E public in the area including the plaintiffs', thereby causing them damage. The reason the defendants knew this was that on 8th May 1961 there had been an interruption of supply because a strip of metal foil had been blown from the defendants' premises into the overhead conductors. By letter dated 18th May 1961 which was referred to in the re-amended statement of claim, the electricity board's district engineer had told the defendants what had happened. He ended

F his letter as follows:

> " Under certain circumstances this incident could have resulted in interruption to supplies over a wide area, including supplies to your own factories on the estate, and I would appreciate your assurance that your waste foil will be carefully stored in future to ensure that there can be no repetition of the incident which occurred on the 8th May, 1961."

G Three and a half years later there was, so it is alleged, a repetition. On or shortly before 7th December 1964 the defendants caused or permitted a large quantity of these strips of metal foil to lay about in the open air on or near their premises where they were liable to be blown away. During the afternoon of 7th December 1964 some were blown away and fouled the bus-bars of the sub-station, thereby causing a flash-over and an interruption of light and power supplies to the plain-

H tiffs' premises which lasted for 12 minutes. The damage caused to the electricity board's equipment resulted in another short interruption of supply later that afternoon. As a result of these interruptions of supply the plaintiffs' machinery in their factory came to a stop. Materials in certain machines solidified and these machines had to be cleaned before production could be started again. Materials and time were wasted and production lost. The loss of profit is estimated at

I £9,372.

The plaintiffs contend that if they prove these allegations, they will have established the defendants' liability to compensate them for the damage done under each of the four heads: first, on the basis of strict liability under the rule in *Rylands* v. *Fletcher* (1); secondly, for negligence; thirdly, for nuisance; and fourthly, for public nuisance. The defendants contend that the re-amended statement of claim does no more than reveal a " damnum absque injuria ".

---

(1) (1868), L.R. 3 H.L. 330; [1861-73] All E.R. Rep. 1.

As to the first head of claim, the plaintiffs contend that the facts alleged come **A**
fairly and squarely within the rule of law as stated by BLACKBURN, J., in his judgment in the Court of Exchequer Chamber in *Rylands* v. *Fletcher* (2). This statement of the law was approved in terms by LORD CAIRNS, L.C., in the House of
Lords (3). To these contentions the defendants make three answers: first, that
the defendants' alleged acts in bringing onto and keeping on their premises
metal foil for the purposes of their business was a natural user of their site; **B**
secondly, that the metal foil was blown onto the electricity board's premises,
not the plaintiffs'; and thirdly, that the damage claimed to have been suffered by
the plaintiffs was too remote. They contended that each of these answers by
itself was sufficient to defeat the plaintiffs' claim based on the rule in *Rylands* v.
Fletcher (4).

If I had to do no more than apply the law as stated by BLACKBURN, J. (2), my **C**
task would be easy. Strips of metal foil were articles brought by the defendants
onto their premises which were not naturally there and which, so the re-amended
statement of claim alleges, were likely to do mischief if they escaped, as is said
they did. As is well known to lawyers, however, BLACKBURN, J.'s, statement of
principle (2) has had glosses put on it by the House of Lords and the Privy
Council in a number of cases. In *Rickards* v. *Lothian* (5) LORD MOULTON said: **D**

> " But there is another ground upon which their Lordships are of opinion
> that the present case does not come within the principle laid down in
> *Rylands* v. *Fletcher* (4). It is not every use to which land is put that brings
> into play that principle. It must be some special use bringing with it increased
> danger to others and must not merely be the ordinary use of the land or such
> a use as is proper for the general benefit of the community." **E**

This passage in the opinion of LORD MOULTON was approved by VISCOUNT
SIMON in *Read* v. *J. Lyons & Co., Ltd.* (6). He went on to discuss what was
decided in *Rainham Chemical Works, Ltd.* v. *Belvedere Fish Guano Co., Ltd.* (7),
and expressed the opinion that it was not a definitive authority for the proposition that the manufacturing of explosives was a " non-natural " use of land. **F**
He said (8):

> " I think it not improper to put on record, with all due regard to the
> admission and *dicta* in that case, that if the question had hereafter to be
> decided whether the making of munitions in a factory at the government's
> request in time of war for the purpose of helping to defeat the enemy is a
> ' non-natural ' use of land, adopted by the occupier ' for his own purposes ', **G**
> it would not seem to me that the House would be bound by this authority to
> say that it was."

Textbook writers have said that the opinions expressed in the House of Lords
in *Read* v. *J. Lyons & Co., Ltd.* (9) indicate a tendency to place a more restricted
interpretation on " non-natural use " and that some of the earlier cases may require reconsideration (see CLARK AND LINDSELL ON TORTS (12th Edn.) para. **H**
1306 and WINFIELD ON TORT (8th Edn.) p. 419).

I turn now to examine the relevant averments in the re-amended statement of
claim. The defendants are alleged to occupy premises on a trading estate.
Such estates are planned and laid out for the purpose of accommodating manufacturers. The defendants are manufacturers. It follows that they are using
this site for the very purpose for which sites were made available on the estate.
The use of the site for manufacturing would be an ordinary one; the use of the **I**

---

(2) (1866), L.R. 1 Exch. 265 at p. 279; [1861-73] All E.R. Rep. at p. 7.
(3) (1868), L.R. 3 H.L. at p. 339; [1861-73] All E.R. Rep. at p. 13.
(4) (1868), L.R. 3 H.L. 330; [1861-73] All E.R. Rep. 1.
(5) [1913] A.C. 263 at pp. 279, 280; [1911-13] All E.R. Rep. 71 at p. 80.
(6) [1946] 2 All E.R. 471 at p. 475; [1947] A.C. 156 at p. 169.
(7) [1921] 2 A.C. 465; [1921] All E.R. Rep. 48.
(8) [1946] 2 All E.R. at p. 475; [1947] A.C. at pp. 169, 170.
(9) [1946] 2 All E.R. 471; [1947] A.C. 156.

A site for any other purpose would be unusual. Does the particular kind of manufacturing which is done in the defendants' factory constitute, in LORD MOULTON's words (10), " some special use bringing with it increased danger to others "? The manufacturing of electrical and electronic components in the year 1964, which is the material date, cannot be adjudged to be a special use nor can the bringing and storing on the premises of metal foil be a special use in itself. The

B way the metal foil was stored may have been a negligent one; but the use of the premises for storing such foil did not by itself create special risks. The metal foil was there for use in the manufacture of goods of a common type which at all material times were needed for the general benefit of the community. It follows that the defendants' first answer disposes of the plaintiffs' contentions under this head.

C   In my judgment, their second and third answers do not have the same effect. There is nothing in the dictum of BLACKBURN, J. (11), which says that the escape must be onto a plaintiff's land and do mischief there. A defendant is liable, prima facie, if he brings on his land and collects and keeps there anything likely to do mischief if it escapes; he must keep it in at his peril; and if he does not do so he is answerable for all the danger which is the natural consequence of

D its escape. In *Read* v. *J. Lyons & Co., Ltd.* (12) LORD SIMON said:

> " Escape . . . means escape from a place which the defendant has occupation of, or control over, to a place which is outside his occupation or control."

Once there has been an escape in this sense, those damnified may claim. They need not be the occupiers of adjoining land or indeed of any land. In *Charing Cross, West End and City Electricity Supply Co., Ltd.* v. *Hydraulic Power Co.* (13) the

E successful plaintiffs only had a licence to lay cables under certain public streets; they had no right of property in the soil. In *Halsey* v. *Esso Petroleum Co., Ltd.* (14), the successful plaintiff suffered damage to his motor car which was standing in the highway. In *Perry* v. *Kendricks Transport, Ltd.* (15) the Court of Appeal, for the purpose of its judgment, assumed that the rule in *Rylands* v. *Fletcher* (16) applied when that which escaped caused personal injuries. In my judgment,

F the plaintiffs in this case would be entitled to damages notwithstanding that the escape was onto the premises of the electricity board. They would have to prove, however, that the damage which they suffered was the natural consequence of the escape and was of a kind recognised by the law. Once one of the strips of metal foil made contact with more than one of the bus-bars, such contact, in the words of the re-amended statement of claim, was—

G   " . . . bound, likely and/or liable to cause a flash-over which was bound, likely and/or liable to cause a voltage drop and/or consequential power failure and so reduce if not cut off the supply of light and power to the premises of members of the public in the said area supplied with electricity from the said sub-station including the plaintiffs' said premises and thereby cause damage to the plaintiffs including injury to their property."

H In my judgment, these averments, which for the purpose of my judgment on this issue I must assume the plaintiffs can prove, amount to an allegation of damage, including injury to property, flowing directly from the escape of the metal foil from the defendants' premises. It is unnecessary for me to decide whether, for the purposes of a successful claim based on strict liability under the rule of

I *Rylands* v. *Fletcher* (16), the damages suffered must have been foreseeable by the occupier of the premises from which there was an escape. The averment in this case is that at all material times the defendants " knew or ought to have

---

(10) [1913] A.C. at p. 280; [1911-13] All E.R. Rep. at p. 80.
(11) (1866), L.R. 1 Ex. at p. 279; [1861-73] All E.R. Rep. at p. 7.
(12) [1946] 2 All E.R. at p. 474; [1947] A.C. at p. 168.
(13) [1914] 3 K.B. 772; [1914-15] All E.R. Rep. 85.
(14) [1961] 2 All E.R. 145; [1961] 1 W.L.R. 683.
(15) [1956] 1 All E.R. 154; [1956] 1 W.L.R. 85.
(16) (1868), L.R. 3 H.L. 330; [1861-73] All E.R. Rep. 1.

known and/or reasonably foreseen " that which is alleged to have been a direct **A**
consequence of the escape. It was contended on behalf of the defendants that
as the plaintiffs had particularised their claim as one for £9,372 " profit lost ",
they must be deemed to be claiming solely for economic loss and that such a
loss was not recoverable on the basis of strict liability. I do not read the re-amended statement of claim as containing nothing more than an allegation of economic
loss. There is in para. 6 an averment (17) that the escape caused injury to **B**
the plaintiffs' property and in para. 12 they state that the interruption of power
supply caused materials in the course of manufacture to solidify in certain of their
machines which had to be cleaned off before those machines could be restarted.
In my judgment, this amounts to an averment of injury to property. In these
circumstances, it is unnecessary for me to decide whether mere economic loss
can be recovered under this head of claim.   **C**
    I turn now to the plaintiffs' contention that the re-amended statement of claim
discloses a cause of action in negligence. Under this head of claim the important
questions are first, whether the defendants did owe a duty to the plaintiffs to
take reasonable care to prevent these strips of metal foil being blown about in
such a way as to foul the bus-bars, and secondly, whether the damage claimed
is too remote. If that which is alleged to have happened did happen, the defen- **D**
dants would be deemed by most people to have behaved in an irresponsible
and negligent way, but such a view of their conduct does not necessarily make
them liable to compensate all those who have suffered because of their behaviour.
    Inevitably the plaintiffs based their contention that the defendants owed them
a duty of care on LORD ATKIN's well-known dictum about neighbours in *Donoghue*
v. *Stevenson* (18). Ought the defendants to have had the plaintiffs in contempla- **E**
tion as neighbours likely to be closely or directly affected by their acts or
omissions? The defendants must have known first, that the plaintiffs' factory
was only 150 yards away on the same industrial estate, and secondly, that it
was used for some purpose connected with the spinning of yarn; and they
did know, because the letter dated 18th May 1961, referred to in the re-amended
statement of claim, told them so, that a repetition of the incident of 8th May 1961, **F**
could result in an interruption of electricity supplies over a wide area including
supplies to factories on the estate. In my judgment, the re-amended statement
of claim does contain averments bringing into operation in favour of the plaintiffs
the principle enunciated by LORD ATKIN in *Donoghue* v. *Stevenson* (19); and in
coming to this conclusion I have not overlooked the limits on that principle
which the House of Lords may have set out in *Hay (or Bourhill)* v. *Young* (20). **G**
On the facts alleged the defendants did owe the plaintiffs a duty of care.
    The issue of remoteness of damage is substantially the same as that raised on
the issue of the application to these alleged facts of the rule in *Rylands* v. *Fletcher*
(21). As I pointed out earlier in this judgment, I do not read the re-amended
statement of claim as containing nothing more than an allegation of economic
loss. There is, in my judgment, an averment that the defendants at the very **H**
least ought reasonably to have foreseen that their conduct was likely to cause
injury to the plaintiffs' property and that it in fact did so. The defendants
argued that para. 12 of the re-amended statement of claim to the effect that the
interruption of power supplies " caused matter to solidify in the plaintiffs'
spinerettes which had in due course to be cleaned off before they could be
restarted ", did not amount to an allegation of injury to property. I do not **I**
accept this argument. If A puts sugar into the petrol tank of B's motor car
with the result, through the clogging of the fuel pipes, that the supply of petrol
to the carburettor is cut off, everyone would say, if asked, that A had damaged

---

(17) The relevant words of para. 6 are set out at p. 1262, letter E, post.
(18) [1932] A.C. 562 at p. 580; [1932] All E.R. Rep. 1 at p. 11.
(19) [1932] A.C. at p. 580; [1932] All E.R. Rep. at p. 11.
(20) [1942] 2 All E.R. 396; [1943] A.C. 92.
(21) (1868), L.R. 3 H.L. 330; [1861-73] All E.R. Rep. 1.

A B's motor car. Much the same position arises in this case. Through the cutting off of electricity the plaintiffs' production line is said to have become clogged. Some of the machines had to be cleaned and, as a direct consequence of the clogging, production and profits were lost. I can see no difference in principle between this case, raising as it does an allegation of physical injury with consequential loss of profits, and the ordinary accident case in which a plaintiff

B alleges that he has suffered some physical injury whereby he has lost earnings. On the construction of the re-amended statement of claim which I have decided on, it is unnecessary for me to attempt to elucidate the problem whether the decision of the House of Lords in *Hedley Byrne & Co., Ltd.* v. *Heller & Partners, Ltd.* (22), has overruled, or qualified, a long line of authorities of which *Cattle* v. *Stockton Waterworks Co.* (23), is probably the earliest, commonly relied on

C to support the proposition that mere economic loss is irrecoverable in an action for negligence.

I must, however, refer to two cases which the defendants say support their contentions and one which the plaintiffs rely on. All three are persuasive, not binding, authorities. The first of those relied on by the defendants is *Weller & Co.* v. *Foot and Mouth Disease Research Institute* (24). That case, which came

D before WIDGERY, J., as a Special Case was dealt with on certain assumptions of fact, the material ones being that the defendants, who carried on experimental work in connection with foot and mouth disease in cattle, had negligently allowed virus to escape from their laboratory at Pirbright with the result, as they knew or ought to have known, that cattle in the neighbourhood became infected, the markets at Guildford and Farnham had to be closed and the

E plaintiffs, who carried on business as auctioneers in those markets, lost profits. At the beginning of his judgment WIDGERY, J., pointed out (25) that both before and after *Donoghue* v. *Stevenson* (26) there was a great volume of authority—

"to the effect that a plaintiff suing in negligence for damages suffered as a result of an act or omission of a defendant cannot recover if the act or omission did not directly injure, or at least threaten directly to injure, the

F plaintiff's person or property but merely caused consequential loss as, for example, by upsetting the plaintiff's business relations with a third party who was the direct victim of the act or omission."

The *Hedley Byrne* case (22) apart, and assuming that it does not overrule or qualify the authorities which WIDGERY, J., had in mind, I agree with his state-

G ment of the law; but views may differ as to what he meant by his phrase " the direct victim of the act or omission ". If he meant " the immediate victim only ", I must with regret differ from him; but if he meant the victim whose person or property was injured by the operation of the laws of nature without any human intervention, which is the meaning I would give to the phrase, the plaintiffs in this case were the direct victims of the defendants' negligence in

H allowing the metal foil to foul the bus-bars. It follows that they do not have to meet the difficulty which faced the auctioneers in the *Weller* case (24). On my reading of WIDGERY, J.'s judgment his finding that the auctioneers were not the direct victims of the laboratory's negligence is the foundation on which he based his decision. Thus, after reviewing the cases, he said (27):

"I think it important to remember at the outset that in the cases to which

I I have referred, the act or omission relied on as constituting a breach of the duty to take care was an act or omission which might foreseeably have caused direct injury to the person or property of another. The world of

(22) [1963] 2 All E.R. 575; [1964] A.C. 465.
(23) (1875), L.R. 10 Q.B. 453; [1874-80] All E.R. Rep. 220.
(24) [1965] 3 All E.R. 560; [1966] 1 Q.B. 569.
(25) [1965] 3 All E.R. at p. 563; [1966] 1 Q.B. at p. 577.
(26) [1932] A.C. 562; [1932] All E.R. Rep. 1.
(27) [1965] 3 All E.R. at pp. 568, 569; [1966] 1 Q.B. at p. 585.

commerce would come to a halt and ordinary life would become intolerable   A
if the law imposed a duty on all persons at all times to refrain from any conduct which might foreseeably cause detriment to another, but where an
absence of reasonable care may foreseeably cause direct injury to the person
or property of another, a duty to take such care exists."

Later (28) he applied his analysis of the authorities to the assumed facts
before him and concluded that the laboratory had owed no duty of care to the   B
auctioneers who had no proprietary interest in anything which might be damaged
by the escaping virus.   In this case the plaintiffs had a proprietary interest in
the machines which were injuriously affected by the interruption of the power
supply resulting directly, and without any human intervention, from the
fouling of the bus-bars by the metal foil.

The second of the cases relied on by the defendants was *Electrochrome, Ltd.*   C
v. *Welsh Plastics, Ltd.* (29).   In that case a lorry negligently driven by the
defendants' servant damaged a fire hydrant belonging to the owners of an
industrial estate.   Water escaped and as soon as possible the supply of water
through the mains was turned off thereby causing the plaintiffs the loss of a day's
work at their factory.   GEOFFREY LANE, J., adjudged that the plaintiffs could not
recover.   The basis of his judgment appears in the following passage (30):   D

" Damage was done by a wrongdoer to the hydrant in which the plaintiffs
had no immediate or reversionary property and no possessory right by reason
of any contract, and as a result of that damage the contract which the
plaintiffs had with the industrial estate for the supply of water became less
beneficial."

The defendants contended that this was the situation alleged in this case.   E
There are many points of semblance; but one all-important difference, namely,
the allegation in this case that the defendants foresaw or ought to have foreseen
that the interruption of power supplies would injure the plaintiffs' property.
There can be no doubt that prior to the decision of the House of Lords in *Hedley
Byrne & Co., Ltd.* v. *Heller & Partners, Ltd.* (31) the law was as stated by   F
GEOFFREY LANE, J., and it may still be the law, despite what LORD DEVLIN
said in that case (32).   No one owes a legal duty of care to the whole world.
As I read GEOFFREY LANE, J.'s judgment he adjudged first that Welsh Plastics,
Ltd., did not owe Electrochrome, Ltd., any duty of care, the element of the
foresight of injury to their property being absent; and secondly, that the damage
claimed was too remote anyway.   For the reasons I have already given, I have   G
decided that the averments in this case do disclose the existence of such a nexus
between the parties that the defendants did owe a duty of care to the plaintiffs.

A case which, on its facts, is similar to this one is *Seaway Hotels, Ltd.* v. *Cragg
(Canada), Ltd. and Consumers' Gas Co.* (33), a decision of the Court of Appeal
of Ontario. There an underground feeder line supplying electric power to a hotel
was broken by contractors engaged in installing a gas pipe for a public utility   H
and the latter was aware before the construction began of the presence of the
feeder line.   The statement of facts in the judgment of LAIDLAW, J.A., ends
with these words (34):

" In the course of construction the duct was broken ... and as a result
the electric power used for the operation of appliances in the plaintiff's
properties was cut off and property damage was caused thereby."   I

He did not say what he meant by property damage; but these words would not

(28) [1965] 3 All E.R. at p. 570; [1966] 1 Q.B. at p. 587.
(29) [1968] 2 All E.R. 205.
(30) [1968] 2 All E.R. at p. 207.
(31) [1963] 2 All E.R. 575; [1964] A.C. 465.
(32) [1963] 2 All E.R. at pp. 602, 603; [1964] A.C. at p. 517.
(33) (1960), 21 D.L.R. (2d) 264.
(34) (1960), 21 D.L.R. (2d) at p. 265.

A be apt to cover mere financial loss. Reference to the report of the case at first instance (35) shows what the damage was:

"As a result of the power being cut off refrigerators for the storage of food and equipment for cooking and washing would not operate and the air conditioning, elevators and some lights would not work. The weather was warm and humid. As a result food spoiled and had to be thrown away
B to the value of $1,274 and the dining room and cocktail bars had to be closed some hours before the usual time at an estimated loss of $1,540 . . ."

On its alleged facts the case before me is further away than this Canadian case from the cases which are authority for the proposition that mere economic loss cannot be recovered in an action for negligence since the plaintiffs here are saying that all their loss resulted directly from the injury to property which they
C suffered. LAIDLAW, J.A., summarised the law applicable as follows (36):

"In this case, applying the principle as was stated in *Bolton* v. *Stone* (37), it is quite certain that the injury for which claim is made in this case was injury that was likely to follow from the interference with the electric duct. It was injury which ought reasonably to have been foreseen by the defendants.
D I am satisfied that the defendants would know that interference with the duct shown on the plan in their possession before the work of construction was commenced and interference with the supply of electrical energy through that duct would cause damage to the persons entitled to receive that supply of electrical energy. The facts in the case are not in dispute and when the Court applies the principles stated in *Bolton* v. *Stone* (37) and elsewhere there can be only one conclusion, namely, that the defendants ought reasonably
E to have foreseen the injury that resulted from interference with the duct. Upon that finding, the judgment against the defendants is correct. The appeal will be dismissed with costs."

For my own part I would not have been willing to have based my judgment on such a broad principle as that stated by LAIDLAW, J.A., as the authorities
F referred to and analysed in *Weller's* case (38) seem to place some qualification on the so-called doctrine of foreseeability; but this case is a most persuasive authority for the proposition that those who do work on or near electric power cables owe a duty of care to those whom they should reasonably foresee are likely to be injuriously affected by what they do.

I turn now to the plaintiffs' contention that the re-amended statement of
G claim discloses a cause of action both in private and public nuisance. As to private nuisance they say that the defendants' alleged method of storing metal foil resulted, as the defendants knew it would, in an interference with the beneficial enjoyment of their own premises whereby they suffered damage; and as to public nuisance their case is that the nuisance was one which affected a class of persons, namely, those members of the public supplied with electricity from the sub-
H station, and that as members of that class they suffered special damage.

The defendants made three answers to these contentions: first, that an isolated happening such as the plaintiffs relied on was not enough to found an action in nuisance since this tort can only arise out of a continuing condition; secondly, that if there was a nuisance on the defendants' premises, it did not affect the plaintiffs' premises directly; and thirdly that the re-amended statement of claim
I did not disclose enough facts to justify a ruling that a class of the public had been injuriously affected by the alleged nuisance.

In my judgment, all three answers are misconceived. Most nuisances do arise from a long continuing condition; and many isolated happenings do not constitute a nuisance. It is, however, clear from the authorities that an isolated

---

(35) (1959), 17 D.L.R. (2d) 292 at p. 295.
(36) (1960), 21 D.L.R. (2d) at p. 266.
(37) [1951] 1 All E.R. 1078; [1951] A.C. 850.
(38) [1965] 3 All E.R. 560; [1966] 1 Q.B. 569.

happening by itself can create an actionable nuisance. Such an authority is **A**
Midwood & Co., Ltd. v. *Manchester Corpn.* (39), where an electric main installed
by the defendants fused. This caused an explosion and a fire whereby the plaintiffs' goods were damaged. The Court of Appeal held that the defendants were
liable, all the Lords Justices being of the opinion that they had caused a nuisance.
The explosion in that case arose out of the condition of the electric main: the
" flash-over " in this case was caused by the way in which the defendants **B**
stored their metal foil whereby those in the neighbourhood were exposed to the
risk of having their electric power cut off. I am satisfied that the law is correctly
stated in WINFIELD ON TORT (8th Edn.) at p. 364:

> " Where the nuisance is the escape of tangible things which damage the
> plaintiff in the enjoyment of his property, there is no rule that he cannot
> sue for the first escape."
C

Anyway, in this case, the alleged happening of 7th December 1964 was not the
first escape; there is said to have been one in 1961.

The second of the defendants' answers is a repetition of the argument which
was addressed to me on remoteness of damage. I accept that those who are only
indirectly affected by a nuisance cannot sue for any damage which they may
suffer; but for the reasons I have already given I adjudge that the plaintiffs **D**
were directly and foreseeably affected.

Finally, I come to the last of the defendants' answers. Paragraph 6 of the
re-amended statement of claim alleges that the defendants knew and foresaw
that a " flash-over " caused by pieces of metal foil blowing about was likely
to cause an interruption of power—

> " . . . to the premises of members of the public in the said area supplied
> [with electricity] from the said sub-station including the plaintiffs' said
> premises . . ."
E

This averment identifies the class of persons said to have been affected by the
nuisance and alleges that the plaintiffs were members of that class. Whether
this class was big enough to attract the description " public " to the nuisance **F**
must await the evidence at the trial. In *A.-G. (on the relation of Glamorgan
County Council and Pontardawe Rural District Council)* v. *P.Y.A. Quarries, Ltd.*
(40) ROMER, L.J., after a learned examination of the authorities, summarised
the law as follows:

> " . . . any nuisance is ' public ' which materially affects the reasonable
> comfort and convenience of life of a class of Her Majesty's subjects. The **G**
> sphere of the nuisance may be described generally as ' the neighbourhood ';
> but the question whether the local community within that sphere comprises
> a sufficient number of persons to constitute a class of the public is a question
> of fact in every case."

For the reasons given and to the extent specified, I adjudge that on the facts **H**
set out in the re-amended statement of claim the defendants are liable in law
for the damage claimed.

Order accordingly. Leave to appeal to the Court of Appeal granted.

Solicitors: *J. F. Kelemen* (for the plaintiffs); *Gascoin & Co.* (for the
defendants).

[*Reported by* K. DIANA PHILLIPS, *Barrister-at-Law.*] **I**

---

(39) [1905] 2 K.B. 597.
(40) [1957] 1 All E.R. 894 at p. 902; [1957] 2 Q.B. 169 at p. 184.

A
MYRON (OWNERS) v. TRADAX EXPORT S.A.
PANAMA CITY R.P.

[QUEEN'S BENCH DIVISION (Donaldson, J.), March 24, April 1, 1969.]

B
Arbitration—Procedure—Arbitration conducted on informal lines—Right of parties to rely on both arbitrators for information on any issue of fact or law raised by other party which he may not have anticipated.

Although, in an arbitration, it is not the rule that the evidence and argument submitted by one party must be copied and submitted to the others, with a right to reply thereto, each party to an arbitration conducted on informal lines is entitled to rely on both the arbitrators to safeguard his interests by ensuring that he is fully informed of any issue of fact or law

C
which is raised by the other party and which he may not have anticipated (see p. 1267, letters E and F, post).

Dictum of MEGAW, J., in *Government of Ceylon v. Chandris* ([1963] 1 Lloyd's Rep. at pp. 225, 226) explained.

Per DONALDSON, J.: it would seem from the terms of s. 20* of the Arbi-

D
tration Act 1950 that arbitrators, unlike a judge, can, in addition to awarding interest, direct that the award itself carry interest at a rate specified in excess of that prescribed for judgments, and this is a power which, if it exists, might well be used generally (see p. 1268, letter I, post).

[As to the duty of an arbitrator to give notice of meetings of the parties, see 2 HALSBURY'S LAWS (3rd Edn.) 34, 35, para. 78; and for cases on the
E
subject, see 2 DIGEST (Repl.) 561, *953-962*.]

Cases referred to:

Ceylon (*Government of*) v. *Chandris*, [1963] 2 All E.R. 1; [1963] 2 Q.B. 327; [1963] 2 W.L.R. 1097; [1963] 1 Lloyd's Rep. 214; Digest (Cont. Vol. A) 38, *818a*.

French Government v. *Steamship Tsurushima Maru (Owners)* (1921), 37 T.L.R.
F
961; 2 Digest (Repl.) 577, *1101*.

Montrose Canned Foods, Ltd. v. *Eric Wells (Merchants), Ltd.*, [1965] 1 Lloyd's Rep. 597.

Pagnan v. *Tradax Export S.A.* (25th March 1969), unreported.

Star International (U.K.), Ltd. v. *Bergbau-Handel G.m.b.H.*, [1966] 2 Lloyd's Rep. 16.

G
Special Case.

This was a motion to set aside or remit an award of arbitrators under the Arbitration Act 1950. The facts are set out in the judgment.

K. S. Rokison for the charterers, Tradax.
D. M. Savill for the owners.

Cur. adv. vult.

H
1st April. **DONALDSON, J.,** read the following judgment: in this case, the charterers, Tradax Export S.A. Panama City R.P. (to whom I will refer as " Tradax "), seek an order setting aside an arbitration award or alternatively its remission to the arbitrators for further consideration.

Tradax were the charterers of the Myron under a Baltimore form C charter-
I
party for a voyage from U.S. Gulf to the continent. The vessel discharged at Amsterdam, and notice of readiness was given on the morning of Saturday, 21st August 1965 by posting it through the letter box of the office of Tradax' agents, the office being closed. Thereafter a dispute arose whether despatch money was payable by the owners of the Myron to Tradax or demurrage by Tradax to the owners, and this issue turned on whether the notice took effect when so posted or when it came to the attention of Tradax' agents on the

---

* Section 20 is set out at p. 1268, letter F, post.

following Monday morning. I am not directly concerned with the merits of the   **A**
parties' respective contentions in the arbitration. Suffice it to say that I am
told that the dispute raised issues conerning the true construction of the charterparty and what was the factual position regarding working hours in Amsterdam
on Saturday mornings at the agents' office, in the maritime community and in
the business community generally.

Tradax deducted the amount of their claim to despatch money from other   **B**
moneys which were due from them to the owners and paid over only the balance.
The owners thereupon immediately indicated a claim for the deducted amount,
and also for the amount of the demurrage which they said was due. All this
occurred within a short time of the ship's arrival at Amsterdam, but thereafter
things moved rather more slowly and it was not until November 1965 that
Mr. Chesterman was appointed as arbitrator by Tradax, and not until January   **C**
1966 that Mr. Clark was appointed by the owners. The effort seems to have
exhausted the parties, or at least the owners who were the claimants, for nothing
further was heard of the matter until November 1967, when Mr. Clark got in
touch with Mr. Chesterman saying that he was anxious to make progress with
the arbitration. Mr. Chesterman then wrote to Tradax asking for all relevant
papers. Two further reminders eventually produced a letter from Tradax dated   **D**
4th December 1967, saying that they thought that the owners' claim had been
abandoned long since and that the gentleman in charge of the matter, a Mr.
Hintermann, was away on military service and would not be back until the
following week. Within the next month, Mr. Clark confirmed that the claim was
still alive and Mr. Chesterman thereafter wrote three further letters to Mr.
Hintermann asking for the relevant time sheets. He received neither reply nor   **E**
acknowledgment. Meanwhile, the owners became understandably restive, and
on 13th May 1968 Mr. Chesterman wrote to Mr. Hintermann in the following
terms, sending a copy of his letter to Mr. Clark:

" I still have no papers from you and cannot resist fixing the date for
hearing of this case early in June and I hope that you will be able to let me
have my papers in time for this."   **F**

In the event nothing happened in June, but on or about 18th July 1968, Mr.
Clark and Mr. Chesterman met at Mr. Clark's request to discuss the arbitration.
Mr. Clark showed Mr. Chesterman the papers which he had received from the
owners, but Mr. Chesterman having neither papers nor information could not
reciprocate. The arbitrators met again in August 1968 and agreed on an award   **G**
in favour of the owners. On 28th August, Mr. Chesterman wrote formally to
Tradax telling them that the award was available to be taken up. Then, and
only then, did Tradax come to life and on 2nd September 1968 Mr. Hintermann
wrote that

" I am still waiting for documentation from Amsterdam on the question
of whether or not Saturday mornings are ordinary office hours there. I   **H**
have accumulated certain information over the past months and would
certainly have wanted to submit this to you in good time before an award
was made. Your advice that the award is ready comes as a surprise as
contrary to your usual procedure no peremptory order for production of
our documents has ever been made."

He ended by saying that he would have to have the award set aside. Mr. Chester-   **I**
man replied pointing out that he had written to Tradax on no less than six
occasions between November 1967 and May 1968, but had had only one reply
in December 1967. The letter continued:

" I succeeded in delaying the hearing until August, still without news
from you, but I doubt if I could have delayed beyond that even if you had
told me that you were gathering further information. Frankly on the above
record, I do not think that you will succeed in getting the award remitted

A   or set aside and, even if you do, I cannot see that you would get a different award, based on the evidence which the other side produced."

Counsel for Tradax makes four complaints: First, the arbitrators held no "hearing", although they had indicated that there would be one; second, the arbitrators gave Tradax no notice of the time and place of any hearing or of the meetings between the arbitrators to discuss the dispute; third, the arbitrators

B   gave Tradax no peremptory notice of a second meeting between the arbitrators, when Tradax had failed to attend or submit oral or documentary evidence or argument on or before the occasion of the first such meeting, and fourth, the arbitrators heard or received evidence and/or argument from the owners without informing Tradax and without giving them an opportunity of answering. These complaints can, I think, be rephrased and summarised under two heads. First,

C   Tradax were expecting an oral hearing, at least after they received the letter of 13th May 1968, and were entitled to such a hearing and to due notice of the time and place where it would be held. Secondly, they never intended to allow the arbitration to proceed in default of defence and should have received clearer warning of the fact that this would occur if they did not take prompt action.

In considering these complaints, it is important to bear in mind the nature

D   of maritime arbitration. This particular arbitration results from the parties' incorporation of the "Centrocon" arbitration clause in the charterparty, but the only material peculiarity of that clause is that both arbitrators must be members of the Baltic Exchange and engaged in the shipping and/or grain trades. A person who is actively engaged throughout all available working hours in maritime arbitrations is regarded in practice as being engaged in the shipping

E   trade. Each party appoints one arbitrator, and the arbitrators so appointed are empowered to appoint an umpire. In order to avoid expense, an umpire is not normally appointed unless it is apparent that the arbitrators are unlikely to be able to agree on an award. The arbitrators are appointed to perform a judicial function unless and until they disagree and the umpire enters on the reference. Thereafter they can and do act as advocates for the parties who

F   appointed them. Until that point is reached, and it is only in a minority of cases that it is reached, neither arbitrator has any special relationship with the party which appointed him and each arbitrator is under the same duty of fairness, openness and impartiality to both parties. In a few cases counsel and solicitors are retained, and the proceedings take on a more formal character which is akin to the procedure in a court of law. In the majority of cases infor-

G   mality is the keynote, and the recognised channel by which a party communicates with the arbitrators is via the arbitrator whom he has appointed. This in no sense makes that arbitrator the agent or delegate of the party who appointed him. Any evidence or submission so received by an arbitrator must be, and I hope always is, communicated to the other arbitrator at once or at the arbitrators' next meeting. In most cases neither party wishes to have the opportunity of submitting oral

H   evidence or argument to the arbitrators and the matter is dealt with by the arbitrators at a private meeting or meetings at which they consider all the material which has been placed before them by either party.

Tradax were perfectly familiar with this procedure having taken part in many arbitrations. Mr. Chesterman had, indeed, been the arbitrator appointed by them on several occasions and was described before me as "Tradax' first choice

I   arbitrator", language more usually heard in the context of Smithfield or Covent Garden market produce than of a well-known arbitrator, but the meaning is clear enough. In such arbitrations, Tradax usually supplied Mr. Chesterman with documentary evidence and with a more or less detailed written indication of what their case was, but it was not their practice to adduce oral evidence or argument or to ask to see or comment on the other party's evidence and argument, no doubt because they could accurately anticipate and deal with it without this facility. Such a departure from the common law rules for the conduct of arbitrations can be fully justified, provided that the parties have

agreed thereto: see *French Government* v. *Owners of Steamship Tsurushima Maru* **A**
(1). In the context of a London shipping arbitration, parties impliedly agree
to the customary procedure subject only to the qualification that they can, on
giving due notice, require matters to be handled with strict formality and, in
particular, can require an oral hearing. That this procedure works well and
is very widely welcomed by the international shipping community is a matter
of common knowledge. If confirmation is needed, it may be found in a passage **B**
in the judgment of MOCATTA, J., in *Star International (U.K.), Ltd.* v. *Bergbau-*
Handel G.m.b.H. (2).

Against this background, I do not believe that Tradax thought, or had any
reason to think, that there would be a hearing at which oral evidence or argument
would be tendered by either side or thought, or had any reason to think, that the
reference to a " hearing " in the letter of 13th May 1968 meant more than a **C**
meeting between the arbitrators to consider the material before them with a
view to making an award. In my judgment, there is no substance in Tradax'
first complaint.

Tradax' second complaint is, as I have said, that they never intended to
allow the arbitration to proceed in default of defence and should have received
clear warning of the fact that this would occur if they did not take prompt **D**
action. Counsel for Tradax also contends that they were entitled to be informed
of and to consider the owners' evidence and arguments. I doubt whether this
submission would have been made, but for a dictum of MEGAW, J., in *Government*
of Ceylon v. *Chandris* (3), that—

> " It is, I apprehend, a basic principle, in arbitrations as much as in
> litigation in the Courts (other, of course, than *ex parte* proceedings), that **E**
> no one with judicial responsibility may receive evidence, documentary or
> otherwise, from one party without the other party knowing that the evidence
> is being tendered and being offered an opportunity to consider it, object
> to it or make submissions on it. No custom or practice may override that
> basic principle."

I say that I doubt whether this submission would otherwise have been made **F**
because there is no suggestion that Tradax were in the least taken by surprise
by, or wished or needed to be expressly informed of, the owners' evidence and
contentions. I respectfully agree with this dictum of MEGAW, J., in the context
of the case with which he was concerned—it was a formal arbitration and
evidence was submitted ex parte after the conclusion of an oral hearing attended
by solicitors and counsel. I do not, however, think that he would have regarded **G**
it as applicable to this case in which, as I have said, Tradax knew full well that
the owners were submitting evidence, broadly what that evidence was and
had no wish to be further informed about it.

Tradax also rely on a dictum of MEGAW, J., in *Montrose Canned Foods, Ltd.* v.
Eric Wells (Merchants), Ltd. (4), where he said:

H

> " In my judgment, it is incumbent upon arbitrators to take steps to ensure,
> so far as is reasonably possible, before they make an award, that each of the
> parties to the dispute before them know the case which has been put against
> them, and has had an opportunity to put forward that party's own case. Here
> that did not happen . . . There was no clear or specific statement by the
> buyers, and no reason to suppose that it was their intention to allow this **I**
> arbitration to go by default without putting their case before the arbitrators
> and stand upon some submission that the arbitrators had no jurisdiction.
> Unless that had been made abundantly clear, it was the duty of the arbitra-
> tors as a matter of natural justice, before they proceeded to make an award
> on the basis of the arguments and submissions of one side only, to make
> sure that the buyers did not wish to put their case before the arbitrators."

(1) (1921), 37 T.L.R. 961.   (2) [1966] 2 Lloyds' Rep. 16 at p. 19.
(3) [1963] 1 Lloyd's Rep. 214 at pp. 225, 226.   (4) [1965] 1 Lloyd's Rep. 597 at p. 602.

A   The learned judge is here dealing with two distinct, if related, matters, namely, first the duty of the arbitrators to ensure that each party knows the case which is being put against him and has an opportunity of dealing with it, and, secondly, their duty to make sure that a party does not wish to put his case before them if they are to proceed in default of defence.

As to the first point, the practice of allowing each party to submit their evidence
B   and arguments to the arbitrators separately only works on the assumption that neither party will be taken by surprise by either the evidence or the arguments advanced by the other party.   Normally, both parties are fully aware of the issues, the arguments and the evidence available for consideration, and no problem arises.   If, however, the arbitrators have the slightest grounds for wondering whether one of the parties has fully appreciated what is being put
C   against him or whether he might reasonably wish to supplement his evidence or argument in the light of what has been submitted by the other party, it is their duty to take appropriate steps to resolve these doubts.   This would normally be done by one of the arbitrators writing to the party concerned summarising the case made against him and enquiring whether in the light of the summary he wished to add anything by way of evidence or argument.

D   Let me make two matters quite clear.   First, it is not sufficient that the arbitrator appointed by party A. shall know the case being made by party B.   This must always be the case, and an arbitrator is in no sense a representative of the party appointing him, unless and until there is a final disagreement.   Secondly, I am not for one moment suggesting, and I do not think that MEGAW, J., has ever suggested, that the evidence and argument submitted by one party must
E   be copied and submitted to the other with a right to reply thereto.   That would lead to an indefinite exchange of correspondence.   If either party wishes to see the whole of the other party's evidence and to be informed in detail of his arguments, he should require a formal hearing.   Any such request must be granted and at the hearing the usual court procedure will be followed.   The usual court procedure includes the granting of an adjournment on appropriate terms if the
F   justice of the case so requires.   What I am saying is that each party to an arbitration conducted on informal lines is entitled to rely on both the arbitrators to safeguard his interests by ensuring that he is fully informed of any issue of fact or law which is raised by the other party and which he may not have anticipated. There is no suggestion in the present case that Tradax were in any way taken by surprise.   The owners' case was perfectly straightforward, although I naturally
G   express no view whether it was right.   The only unusual features were those which Tradax would have injected and, had Tradax submitted evidence and argument, it would almost certainly have been necessary to give the owners express notice of what was being alleged so that they could deal with it by supplementary evidence and argument.

I now turn to the second point, namely, the duty of the arbitrators to make
H   sure that a party does not wish to put his case before them and is content that they shall proceed in default of defence.   Taking full account of the initial inertia of the owners, Tradax nevertheless behaved in a most unbusinesslike and, indeed, discourteous manner.   It is tempting to say that they deserve to suffer the consequences in the shape of the award which has been made against them, but the issue of principle is somewhat more important than the education of Tradax.
I   In successive paragraphs of his affidavit, Mr. Chesterman says that normally if a party does not produce any papers " warning [is given] that an award will be made without them unless they are produced quickly " and notice is given " that if none are produced the arbitration will proceed anyway ".   If that had been done in clear terms in the present case, there would have been no ground whatsoever for interfering.   However, the intimation in the letter of 13th May 1968 that Mr. Chesterman could not resist fixing a date for hearing in June and that he " hoped " to have the papers—not " must " have them—before then is not sufficiently clear and definite to convey unequivocally to Tradax that, if

they did not produce the papers by June, their case would go by default. In **A** the circumstances, the award cannot stand.

It has been submitted on behalf of Tradax that the arbitration should be begun again before different arbitrators, in the light of the fact that Mr. Chesterman has expressed the view that: (a) the court would not interfere with the award; and (b) it is unlikely that a further award would be different in the light of the owners' evidence. I should not hesitate to adopt this course if I thought **B** that Mr. Chesterman or Mr. Clark was either incapable of applying or unwilling to apply his mind to the dispute afresh in the light of any evidence or arguments which Tradax may submit, but I do not think that this is the case.

The award will, therefore, be remitted to Mr. Clark and Mr. Chesterman to enable them to give further consideration to the dispute in the light of any or any further evidence or arguments which either party may wish to submit. If **C** eventually they are agreed, they will make a fresh award. If they are not agreed, they will appoint an umpire.

All matters of costs in the arbitration and interest on any moneys found due are for the arbitrators or umpire. However, it may assist if I express my views on the principles which are applicable. It is of paramount importance to the speedy settlement of disputes that a respondent who is found to be under a **D** liability to a claimant should gain no advantage and that the claimant should suffer no corresponding detriment as a result of delay in reaching a decision. Accordingly, awards should in general include an order that the respondent pay interest on the sum due from the date when the money should have been paid. The rate of interest is entirely in the discretion of the arbitrators, but I personally take the view that in an era of high and fluctuating interest rates the principle **E** which I have expressed is best implemented by an award of interest " at a rate one per cent. in excess of the Bank of England discount rate for the time being in force ". When interest is awarded, arbitrators commonly award it for a period ending with the date of the award. Section 20 of the Arbitration Act 1950 provides that:

> " A sum directed to be paid by an award shall, unless the award otherwise **F** directs, carry interest as from the date of the award and at the same rate as a judgment debt."

The consequence is that the award carries interest at the rate of four per cent. per annum from the date of the award until payment (see Judgments Act 1838, s. 17). With bank rate at its present level, this is a positive disincentive to payment. In *Pagnan* v. *Tradax Export S.A.* (5), I expressed the hope that those concerned **G** with law reform might give consideration to amending the Judgments Act 1838 to provide that judgments and, by the operation of s. 20 of the Arbitration Act 1950, awards should bear interest at such a rate as may from time to time be specified by subordinate legislation. Whether such subordinate legislation would specify a rate or involve a formula such as I have indicated would be a matter for those charged with the duty of legislating, but I would hope that **H** the result would be to provide judgment debtors with a positive incentive to settle their obligations with despatch.

It would seem from the terms of s. 20 of the Arbitration Act 1950 that arbitrators, unlike a judge, can, in addition to awarding interest, direct that the award itself carry interest at a specified rate in excess of that prescribed for judgments and this is a power which, if it exists, might well be used generally. **I**

[After further argument, HIS LORDSHIP ordered that the costs of the application to the court should be awarded to the successful party in the arbitration.]   *Award remitted.*

Solicitors: *Richards, Butler & Co.* (for the charterers, Tradax); *Middleton, Lewis & Co.* (for the owners).   [*Reported by* MARY COLTON, *Barrister-at-Law.*]

---

(5) (25th March 1969), unreported.

A   **SIMMONS v. MIDFORD.**

[CHANCERY DIVISION (Buckley, J.), February 18, March 20, 1969.]

*Easement—Pipes—Right to lay and maintain pipes on servient land—Pipes
connecting to sewer—Whether ownership of pipes vested in dominant owner
—Whether right to use of pipes.*

B   A deed of transfer dated 14th October 1964 and made on the sale of
land by C. to the plaintiff's predecessor in title, included a right of way
over a servient strip together with the " right to lay and maintain . . .
pipes and cables over under and along the said strip . . . and the free and
uninterrupted passage and running of water soil gas and electricity there
through and the right to enter upon and open up the said land for the
C   purposes of laying maintaining and repairing the said drains . . ." The
purchaser built a dwelling-house on the land and laid a drain from the
house under and along the servient strip to the public sewers. The property
was subsequently acquired by the plaintiff, together with the rights over the
servient land. In 1968 the successors in title of C. to the servient strip,
and a building society as mortgagee, granted and confirmed to the defendant
D   the right to lay a drain under certain other land and " insofar as [they]
have power so to grant and confirm ", the right to connect that drain to the
drain in the servient strip. The plaintiff issued a writ for an injunction
to restrain the defendant from connecting any pipes or drains to those in the
servient strip.

          Held: the defendant should be restrained from connecting any pipe or
E   drain to those in the servient strip because, by the terms of the grant of
14th October 1964 to the plaintiff's predecessor in title, ownership of the
drain was vested in the plaintiff, as appurtenant to his land (see p. 1273,
letter I, to p. 1274, letter A, post) (*Lancaster* v. *Eve* ((1859), 5 C.B.N.S. 717)
applied); alternatively, the plaintiff was entitled to exclusive use of the drain
and the defendant's predecessors in title could not grant to her any right
F   to use it.

          Lee v. *Stevenson* ((1858), E.B. & E. 512) applied.

          QUAERE: whether the drain was to be regarded as realty or personalty
(see p. 1274, letter A, post).

          [As to easements as to erections on or over servient tenement, see 12 HALS-
BURY'S LAWS (3rd Edn.) 613, 614, para. 1332; and for cases on the subject,
G   see 19 DIGEST (Repl.) 192-194, *1333-1347*.]

          Cases referred to:
          Armstrong v. *Sheppard & Short, Ltd.*, [1959] 2 All E.R. 651; [1959] 2 Q.B. 384;
                  [1959] 3 W.L.R. 84; 123 J.P. 401; 46 Digest (Repl.) 393, *355*.
          Elwes v. *Maw* (1802), 3 East. 38; [1775-1802] All E.R. Rep. 320; 102 E.R.
                  510; 31 Digest (Repl.) 213, *3454*.
H   *Lancaster* v. *Eve* (1859), 5 C.B.N.S. 717; 28 L.J.C.P. 235; 32 L.T.O.S. 278;
                  141 E.R. 288; 19 Digest (Repl.) 192, *1340*.
          Lee v. *Stevenson* (1858), E.B. & E. 512; 27 L.J.Q.B. 263; 120 E.R. 600; 19
                  Digest (Repl.) 15, *43*.
          Nicholas v. *Chamberlain* (1606), Cro. Jac. 121; 79 E.R. 105; 19 Digest
                  (Repl.) 33, *162*.
I   *Union Lighterage Co.* v. *London Graving Dock Co.*, [1902] 2 Ch. 557; [1900-03]
                  All E.R. Rep. 234; 71 L.J.Ch. 791; 87 L.T. 381; 19 Digest (Repl.) 19, *68*.
          Wake v. *Hall* (1883), 8 App. Cas. 195; 52 L.J.Q.B. 494; 48 L.T. 834; 47 J.P.
                  548; 31 Digest (Repl.) 225, *3621*.
          Wheeldon v. *Burrows* (1879), 12 Ch.D. 31; [1874-80] All E.R. Rep. 669; 48
                  L.J.Ch. 853; 41 L.T. 327; 19 Digest (Repl.) 48, *269*.

          Motion.

          This was a motion by Irene Simmons for an interlocutory injunction to restrain
Una Doreen Midford, from damaging or breaking into pipes, drains and sewers

which had been laid in land belonging to a third person and which connected **A**
the plaintiff's property to the local authority's pipes, drains and sewers; and
to restrain her from connecting any other pipes, drains and sewers to, or passing
any water, soil or other material through, the plaintiff's pipes. It was agreed
to treat the hearing of the motion as the trial of the action. The facts are
set out in the judgment.

The cases noted below* were cited during the argument in addition to those **B**
referred to in the judgment.

Gavin Lightman for the plaintiff.
G. C. Raffety for the defendant.

Cur. adv. vult.

20th March. **BUCKLEY, J.,** read the following judgment: The plaintiff **C**
in this action seeks to restrain the defendant from connecting a drain from
the defendant's house to an existing drain from the plaintiff's house laid under
the roadway adjoining the plaintiff's property which is not owned by either party
but leads from the plaintiff's property to the public highway. The parties
have invited me to treat the hearing of this motion for an interlocutory injunction as the trial of the action and to dispose of the action on the affidavit evidence **D**
which is not in dispute.

By a deed of transfer dated 14th October 1964, made on a sale of the property
now owned by the plaintiff, the vendor, one G. L. Card, transferred to the plaintiff's
predecessor in title the land described thereon (which I will call the plaintiff's land)
coloured red on an attached plan together with a right of way over a strip of
land (which I will call the servient strip) ten feet in width hatched black on the **E**
same plan and together with the—

". . . right to lay and maintain drains sewers pipes and cables over under
and along the said strip of land hatched black on the said plan and the free
and uninterrupted passage and running of water soil gas and electricity
there through the right to enter upon and open up the said land for the
purposes of laying maintaining and repairing the said drains sewers pipes **F**
and cables, the transferee making good all damage thereby occasioned "

the transferor covenanted to construct and maintain the servient strip as a
road suitable for motor vehicles.

The purchaser under that transaction built a house on the plaintiff's land and
laid a drain from the house under and along the servient strip to the public
sewers situate under the highway. Since its installation the drain has been used **G**
to carry water and soil from the house to the public services. The plaintiff
is now the registered owner of the plaintiff's land and the property register
in her land certificate contains a note that there are appurtenant to her land the
rights granted by the transfer of 14th October 1964.

By a deed dated 22nd July 1968, two grantors who were successors in title **H**
of G. L. Card as owners of (inter alia) the servient strip and a building society
as mortgagee granted and confirmed (or purported to grant and confirm) to the
defendant first the right to lay a drain under certain other land—

". . . SECONDLY (insofar as the Grantors and the Mortgagee have power
so to grant and confirm) the right to connect the said drain to the drain
already laid under the land coloured blue on the said plan."

I

The land coloured blue on this plan is the servient strip and the " drain already
laid " is the drain or sewer as aforesaid under that strip laid by the plaintiff's
predecessor. Thirdly, this deed granted or purported to grant to the defendant
for the purpose of laying the said drain and making the said connection and for

---

* *Suffield* v. *Brown* (1864), 4 De G.J. J. & S. 185; *Holland* v. *Hodgson* (1872), L.R. 7
C.P. 328; *Goodhart* v. *Hyett* (1883), 25 Ch.D. 182; *Duke of Sutherland* v. *Heathcote*,
[1892] 1 Ch. 475; *Southport, Mayor of* v. *Ormskirk Union Assessment Committee*, [1894]
1 Q.B. 196; *Never Stop Railway* v. *British Empire Exhibition*, [1926] Ch. 877.

A ever thereafter repairing and maintaining the said drain and the said connection and the right to enter on (inter alia) the servient strip for such purposes doing as little damage as possible and making good all damage caused.

The defendant wishes to connect a drain from her neighbouring property to the existing drain under the servient strip. The plaintiff objects on two grounds: first, that the existing drain belongs to her, so that the defendant

B has no right to interfere with it in any way; secondly, that even if the drain is not physically her property, she is entitled to its exclusive use.

I feel some sympathy with the observation of WILLIAMS, J., in *Lancaster* v. *Eve* (1). He said " No doubt the maxim ' Quicquid plantatur solo solo cedit ' is well established: the only question is, what is meant by it? " That kind of question is liable to arise when a legal apothegm is applied to a particular case.

C It is nearly always necessary to pause to consider how generally applicable the maxim is and to what exceptions it may be subject. SIR ALEXANDER COCKBURN, C.J., in the same case said (2):

" Of course I do not mean to controvert or question the general proposition, that, whatever is annexed to the freehold becomes part of the freehold. But there may be circumstances to take a case out of the general rule, as,

D for instance, where the thing is so annexed as to be severable without injury to the soil, and where there may have been an agreement between the owners of the soil and the owner of the chattel, that the chattel should be severable at the will and pleasure of the latter."

In the field of landlord and tenant the question commonly arises whether a chattel has been attached to the land or building demised in such circumstances

E as to become a landlord's fixture, that is to say, as to adhere to the freehold. In the absence of express agreement, the answer to this question depends on the object and purpose of the annexation. The character of the chattel and the method of its attachment to the land or buildings are matters to be taken into account in ascertaining that object and purpose. If the annexation is for the purpose of effecting some permanent and substantial improvement to the

F land and building there is a strong indication that the annexation was intended to be permanent. If, on the other hand it was to achieve some temporary convenience, this may lead to the conclusion that the chattel should not be treated as having lost its character as a chattel.

Considerations of this kind are not confined to the regulations of landlord and tenant. *Lancaster* v. *Eve* (3) related to damage suffered by a pile driven into

G the bed of the River Thames near a wharf belonging to the plaintiff. This pile was exclusively used by the owners of the wharf and was necessary for their use of the wharf. The plaintiffs were not the owners of the bed of the river. The defendants in navigating a barge on the river had negligently damaged the pile. SIR ALEXANDER COCKBURN, C.J., said (4):

H " I think there are circumstances here from which we may properly draw the inference that the pile in question was not placed in the bed of the river with a view to its permanent annexation to the freehold so as to become part of the freehold; but that it was placed there by virtue of an easement granted by the Crown or whoever had the right to grant it, to the occupiers of the adjoining wharf, for the more convenient use and enjoyment

I thereof."

WILLIAMS, J., said (5):

" I entirely agree with the Lord Chief Justice in thinking that there was abundant evidence here to warrant the conclusion that the pile in

---

(1) (1859), 5 C.B.N.S. 717 at p. 727.
(2) (1859), 5 C.B.N.S. at pp. 726, 727.
(3) (1859), 5 C.B.N.S. 717.
(4) (1859), 5 C.B.N.S. at p. 727.
(5) (1859), 5 C.B.N.S. at p. 728.

question was planted in the soil of the river by the plaintiffs' predecessors— **A**
though at what time did not distinctly appear—with the consent of the Crown
or the conservators of the river, not for the benefit of the soil but in order
to the more commodious enjoyment of the advantages of the wharf; and
that it was so placed not upon the term that it should be considered as
annexed to or incorporated with the soil, but for the purposes of navigation."

So it is said in the present case that the existing drain under the strip of land was **B**
laid there by the plaintiff's predecessor with the consent of G. L. Card not for
the benefit of the strip of land but for the more commodious enjoyment of the
plaintiff's house, and, that being so, it was so laid not on terms that the pipes
should adhere to the freehold of the servient strip but that they should remain
chattels in the ownership of the owner of the plaintiff's house as the pile remained
a chattel in the ownership of the owner of the wharf. **C**

In *Nicholas* v. *Chamberlain* (6):

" It was held by all the Court upon demurrer, that if one erect a house
and build a conduit thereto in another part of his land, and convey water by
pipes to the house, and afterward sell the house with the appurtenances,
excepting the land, or sell the land to another, reserving to himself the **D**
house, the conduit and pipes pass with the house; because it is necessary,
et quas; appendant thereto; and he shall have liberty by law to dig in the
land for amending the pipes, or making them new, as the case may require."

In *Wheeldon* v. *Burrows* (7) THESIGER, L.J., seems to have regarded *Nicholas* v.
Chamberlain (6) as relating to an easement and, applying the principle that a
grantor should not derogate from his grant he expressed the view that if and so **E**
far as *Nicholas* v. *Chamberlain* (6) laid down that the same considerations applied
to implied reservations as to implied grants it was bad law. He did not, I think,
criticise the decision in its application to implied grants but indicated that in
respect of an implied reservation it could only stand in relation to an easement
of necessity. JAMES, L.J., however pointed out (8) in what could perhaps more
accurately be described as a comment than a judgment, that *Nicholas* v. **F**
Chamberlain (6) proceeded on the ground that the subject-matter then under
consideration was not an incorporeal easement but the physical conduit (see
also VAUGHAN WILLIAMS, L.J., in his dissenting judgment in *Union Lighterage
Co.* v. *London Graving Dock Co.* (9)).

There is much learning about the qualified nature of the operation of the maxim
in the speeches of the learned Lords who decided *Wake* v. *Hall* (10); and see the **G**
note on *Elwes* v. *Maw* (11) in 2 SMITH'S LEADING CASES (13th Edn.), pp. 205,
et seq. SIR ALEXANDER COCKBURN, C.J., in *Lancaster* v. *Eve* (12) called it a
" general proposition " and LORD EVERSHED, M.R., delivering the judgment of
the Court of Appeal in *Armstrong* v. *Sheppard & Short, Ltd.* (13) described its
consequence, where there was no contrary agreement or arrangement, as the
" ordinary consequence ". It may be said to enshrine or express a rule of law **H**
regulating the ownership in appropriate cases of things which were previously
chattels but had become physically attached to realty. It does not, I think,
amount to a presumption, and it is certainly not a rule of construction, where
the interpretation of any written document is involved.

Where a chattel is physically attached to realty, one of three possible results
may follow. The chattel may lose its character as a chattel and adhere to the **I**

(6) (1606), Cro. Jac. 121.
(7) (1879), 12 Ch.D. 31 at p. 50; [1874-80] All E.R. Rep. 669 at p. 673.
(8) (1879), 12 Ch.D. at p. 60; [1874-80] All E.R. Rep. at p. 678.
(9) [1902] 2 Ch. 557 at p. 565; [1900-03] All E.R. Rep. 234 at p. 237.
(10) (1883), 8 App. Cas. 195.
(11) (1802), 3 East. 38; [1775-1802] All E.R. Rep. 320.
(12) (1859), 5 C.B.N.S. at p. 726.
(13) [1959] 2 All E.R. 651 at p. 659; [1959] 2 Q.B. 384 at p. 401.

A realty so as to become part of it for all purposes; or the chattel may become part of the realty while it remained a chattel, without the person who owned it losing the right subsequently to detach it from the realty and repossess it as a chattel; or it may never lose its character as a chattel.   Which, if any, of these results applies in the present case?

I am not here concerned with an implied grant, reservation or regrant as was
B the case in *Nicholas* v. *Chamberlain* (14).   Nor am I concerned with an intention to be inferred from the nature or purpose of the annexation or of the chattel annexed.   The plaintiff's rights depend on the transfer of 14th October 1964, and their nature and extent must therefore depend on the proper interpretation of that document; but before I consider the language used I will make certain general observations.   First, the pipe was laid by the plaintiff's predecessor in
C title; it was not in existence before he bought the plaintiff's land.   Secondly, it was laid with the consent and approval of the owner of the servient tenement in pursuance of the right granted by the transfer of 14th October 1964.   Thirdly, it was not laid for the improvement or benefit of the servient strip.   In exercising the easement of an uninterrupted flow of water and soil granted by the transfer of 14th October 1964, the owner of the plaintiff's land must be bound to prevent
D such water and soil from invading and contaminating the soil of the servient strip. The pipe is necessary for this purpose.   Its object is to prevent such invasion and contamination.   It serves to protect the owner of the plaintiff's land from liability in this respect.   It should, I think, be regarded as installed for the benefit of the owner of the plaintiff's land rather than that of the owner of the strip, or at least for their mutual benefit.   Fourthly, the right to lay pipes under
E the servient strip is not confined to a single pipe or to a pipe or pipes of any particular kind or dimension, or to a pipe along any particular line.   I can see no ground for saying that, a pipe having been laid under the grant, the owner of the plaintiff's land could not later remove that pipe and put in a bigger or better one in its place or a pipe following a different line under the servient strip, of course making good any damage to the surface.   If the owner of the plaintiff's
F land were to do this, it would be reasonable to expect that the pipe which he removed from the servient strip would be his to do what he liked with.   The same would be true of any material removed in the course of repairing the pipe.

I will now consider the actual language used in the grant.   It is a grant of a right to lay and maintain drains, etc.   The word " maintain " in this context clearly means something other than mere repair, for later in the document the
G two words are used in close conjunction.   In the covenant relating to the roadway the transferor covenanted to " construct and at all times maintain " the servient strip the roadway for motor vehicles.   In my judgment the word " maintain " throughout this document means " keep " or " preserve ".   It indicates a continuing state of affairs.   If the grantee's right is to lay and keep pipes under the servient strip, this is, in my view, at least consistent with the
H ownership in the pipes remaining in the owner of the plaintiff's land.   Had the intention been that the pipe, when installed, should belong to the owner of the servient land, the grantee of the right to lay it could not thereafter have removed it without the servient owner's consent and no grant of any right to keep it there would have been appropriate.   These considerations lead me to the conclusion that on the true construction of its language the grant does not indicate an intention that the pipe should, when laid, become permanently annexed to
I the freehold of the servient strip.   Of the two other possibilities indicated above, namely, that it was intended that the pipe should adhere to the freehold for as long as it remained in situ, but that the owner of the plaintiff's land should be entitled to remove it and thereby to recover ownership of it, or that it was intended that the ownership in the pipe should remain in the owner of the plaintiff's land, the latter seems to me not only the more probable inherently but also the more

(14) (1606), Cro. Jac. 121.

appropriate to the language used.   In my judgment therefore on the true con-   A
struction of the grant the ownership in the pipe is vested in the plaintiff as
appurtenant to the plaintiff's land.   Whether it should be regarded as personalty
or realty I need not determine.   It must follow from this that the defendant's
predecessors in title had no power to grant the defendant any right to interfere
with the pipe in any way and that they were wise to insert in the grant of 22nd
July 1968, the qualifying words which they did insert.   B

Even if I am wrong in this view and the pipe is annexed to the freehold of
the servient strip, I am of opinion that the defendant's predecessors could not
grant to her any right to use it; for the plaintiff, is in my opinion entitled to
the exclusive use of it.

In *Lee* v. *Stevenson* (15), the plaintiff demised land to the defendant reserving
the right to enter thereon and to dig and make a covered sewer through the land   C
in order to convey the waste water from adjoining land of the plaintiff into a
river.   The plaintiff constructed such a sewer and the defendant connected it
to a drain from his own property.   The plaintiff sued him in trespass and was
held to be entitled to the exclusive use of the sewer.   There is an illuminating
discussion reported (16).   It will, however, be sufficient for present purposes
if I read this passage from the judgment of LORD CAMPBELL, C.J. (17):   D

" Looking, as we must, to the nature and intention of the grant, it is clear
that it gives the grantee an easement consisting of the exclusive right to
use the sewer.   If it had given him merely the right to carry his drainage
along the surface of the land to the river, the defendant might have used the
same channel without incurring any liability.   But the lease grants to the
plaintiff power to ' dig and make a covered sewer or water course ' [his   E
Lordship read the whole of the clause in question], in order to convey
the waste water from the premises of the plaintiff (limiting, therefore, the
area of the drain), making compensation to the defendant: that is, substantially, a right to place a pipe through the defendant's land, of such dimensions
and no more, as will be sufficient to carry off the plaintiff's waste water
through the land into the river.   I am of opinion that such a grant is a   F
grant to the plaintiff of the exclusive use of the pipe, not merely of the right
to have his waste water run through it."

Just so in the present case, the grant of the plaintiff's predecessor, being of a right
to lay an enclosed drain in the servient strip with a right to the free and uninterrupted passage and running of water and soil through it for the manifest object
of carrying drainage from the plaintiff's land to the public sewer under the   G
highway operated, in my judgment, as a grant of a right to lay pipes of a character
and size suitable for that purpose.   Certainly the plaintiff or her predecessors
could not have been required to construct a drain of greater capacity than was
required for that purpose.   The plaintiff is by the terms of the grant entitled
to a free and uninterrupted flow through such pipes.   In that respect the present
grant is more explicit or emphatic than was that considered in *Lee* v. *Stevenson* (15).   H
It must follow by inference that the plaintiff is entitled to the exclusive use of the
drain, for, if the defendant were to introduce additional matter into the drain,
there would be an obvious risk of its being inadequate to carry the combined
flow, and so the plaintiff would cease to enjoy the free and uninterrupted use
to which she is entitled.   This, I think, would be the case whether the capacity
of the drain as laid in fact exceeded the capacity required for the plaintiff's   I
drainage or not.   It is in any case not proved in the present case that there is any
surplus capacity.   Counsel for the defendant, has argued that the grant of a
right to flow through the pipe would be unnecessary if the intention was that the
pipe should belong to the owner of the plaintiff's land.   This argument I feel

(15) (1858), E.B. & E. 512.
(16) (1858), E.B. & E. at pp. 516, 516.
(17) (1858), E.B. & E. at p. 517.

A unable to accept. The ownership of an enclosed drain and the right—even the exclusive right—to a flow through it may well be in different ownership, and the grantee of a right to construct such a drain would well be advised to obtain at the same time an explicit grant of a right to flow through it.

.. For these reasons the plaintiff, in my judgment, succeeds in this action.

Order accordingly.

B Solicitors: *Ashurst, Morris Crisp & Co.* (for the plaintiff); *W. H. Matthews & Co.* (for the defendant).

[*Reported by* ROSALIE LONG, *Barrister-at-Law.*]

C

LUDGATE v. LOVETT.

[COURT OF APPEAL, CIVIL DIVISION (Harman, Danckwerts and Edmund Davies, L.JJ.), April 23, 24, 1969.]

D *Negligence—Res ipsa loquitur—Onus on defendant to disprove negligence— Evidence required to discharge onus—Unexplained swerve by motor car being driven at 60 m.p.h. on motorway—Defendant's evidence that he was not negligent in any way—Sufficiency.*

A hired van, while being driven along a motorway at 60 m.p.h. by the defendant, swerved violently to the right. The defendant over-corrected this swerve, the van went to the left, turned over twice and hit the verge.
E The defendant was severely injured and the van was damaged. In an action by the owner of the van, for damages for the defendant's failure to take proper care of the van, the defendant counterclaimed for damages for his injuries, alleging that the accident had been caused by defects in a tyre of the van. The trial judge found that there were no defects in the van, and dismissed the counterclaim. The judge, however, accepted the defendant's
F evidence that he was not negligent in that he neither went to sleep nor failed to pay attention. The judge himself evolved a theory how the accident happened, and accordingly held that, although res ipsa loquitur, the defendant had proved that he was not negligent and so the claim too must be dismissed. On appeal by the plaintiff, it being conceded that the trial judge's theory as to the cause of the accident was untenable,
G **Held:** the appeal would be allowed, because—

(i) although the defendant could, by satisfying the court that he was not negligent, succeed even if he could not show how the accident happened, in the circumstances the evidence was insufficient to rebut the inference of negligence raised by the maxim res ipsa loquitur (see p. 1278, letters D, E and H, post); and
H (ii) (per HARMAN and EDMUND DAVIES, L.JJ.) the trial judge's acceptance of the defendant's evidence was due to its consistency with his own theory; accordingly, as the theory was untenable, the ground for accepting the defendant's evidence had been removed (see p. 1278, letter E, and p. 1280, letter E, post).

Appeal allowed.

I [As to inference of negligence from the nature of a road accident, see 28 HALSBURY'S LAWS (3rd Edn.) 70, 71, para. 70; as to res ipsa loquitur, see ibid., 77-80, paras. 79-83; and for cases on the subject, see 36 DIGEST (Repl.) 143-146, 753-778.]

Cases referred to:
    Barkway v. *South Wales Transport Co., Ltd.,* [1948] 2 All E.R. 460; [1949] 1 K.B. 54; *revsd.* H.L., [1950] 1 All E.R. 392; [1950] A.C. 185; **114** J.P. 172; 36 Digest (Repl.) 144, *764.*

Moore v. *R. Fox & Sons*, [1956] 1 All E.R. 182; [1956] 1 Q.B. 596; [1956] A
2 W.L.R. 342; Digest (Cont. Vol. A) 1175, *764b*.

Walsh v. *Holst & Co., Ltd.*, [1958] 3 All E.R. 33; [1958] 1 W.L.R. 800; Digest
(Cont. Vol. A) 1176, *1764c*.

Woods v. *Duncan, Duncan* v. *Hambrook, Duncan* v. *Cammell Laird & Co., Ltd.*,
[1946] 1 All E.R. 420, n.; [1946] A.C. 401; [1947] L.J.R. 120; 174
L.T. 286; 36 Digest (Repl.) 52, *286*.   B

Appeal.

This was an appeal by the plaintiff, Samuel Ludgate, the owner of a van hired
from him by the defendant, Graham Lovett, against that part of the judgment
of His Honour JUDGE HARINGTON, given at Dudley County Court on 6th August
1968, relating to the dismissal of his claim against the defendant for £172 10s. C
damages for damage caused to the van by the defendant's failure to take proper
care when driving it.   The county court judge had also dismissed the defendant's
counterclaim for unlimited damages for personal injuries suffered by him, which
the defendant had alleged were due to defects in the van.   The facts are set
out in the judgment of HARMAN, L.J.

C. W. G. Ross-Munro for the plaintiff.   D
R. H. Tucker for the defendant.

HARMAN, L.J.: This is a case of some nicety.   It has been very well
argued on both sides.   The facts are simple and hardly in dispute, so far as
they are known.   The plaintiff was a man who, as a hobby, hired out cars.
He was an expert on mechanical affairs himself, being a lecturer at a technical E
college.   The defendant at the time of the accident was an infant and was an
expert professional footballer playing for West Bromwich Albion occasionally.
He wanted to go and see his girlfriend.   His car had broken down and he applied
to the plaintiff to hire him a car.   The plaintiff eventually did hire him a van.
It was a well-used vehicle, being some years old, but the evidence is that the
plaintiff, who had bought it six weeks before, had attended to it from a mechanical F
point of view.   Its tyres were in good order and not seriously worn and there
were no mechanical defects that anybody could find.

After some preliminaries the defendant started off to meet his girlfriend and
he drove on to the M.1, and down the M.1.   He continued to do so, it appears, for
three hours, although it is not quite explained where he was all that time.   Three
hours after starting off he was involved in a very serious accident.   The accident G
was of the simplest possible character.   He was travelling at 60 m.p.h.   The only
other vehicle on the road was behind him.   At 10.0 p.m. the van suddenly swerved
violently to the right, the defendant attempted to correct that swerve and in
so doing over-corrected it, overset the van, and it tumbled over itself twice and
landed on its wheels on the hard shoulder.   The defendant was very seriously
injured but he has made, happily, a complete recovery from that injury.   H

When the van was subsequently examined by an expert no defect was found
except one deflated tyre.   The expert gave evidence which convinced the judge
that the deflation of the tyre was caused by the impact when the van hit the
verge.   It dented the rim and caused the tyre, which was of a solid-tube type,
to deflate.

This is, therefore, on the face of it, a simple claim by the plaintiff.   The I
plaintiff says: " You, the defendant, drove away my car which you had hired
and which admittedly was in good order and condition; three hours later it was
a wreck, and you are responsible."   " Oh no ", says the defendant, " I am not
responsible because I was not guilty of any negligence; the accident happened
without any fault on my part."

Now it is admitted that here the doctrine of res ipsa loquitur applies.   I do
not think I need go into the authorities cited to us.   I merely mention the speech

A   of LORD SIMONDS in *Woods* v. *Duncan* (1) and the well-known judgment of
ASQUITH, L.J., in *Barkway* v. *South Wales Transport Co., Ltd.* (2), which subsequently went to the House of Lords (3). ASQUITH, L.J.'s observations do not
appear there, but the position appears to be this: it being admitted on all hands
that the plaintiff's prima facie case is one where res ipsa loquitur, the burden is
cast on the defendant to explain that which otherwise is without explanation,
B   or, if he cannot explain it, at least to show that no fault of his was involved.
He can do that even though he cannot explain it. Of course, as the judge said,
it is much easier if he can explain it; but nevertheless there are cases in which,
although no explanation can be found, the defendants satisfy the tribunal that
there was no fault on their part and that they did all that they ought to do.
In support of that one has *Walsh* v. *Holst & Co., Ltd.* (4), and the judgment of
C   HODSON, L.J., is usually cited in this connection. He said (5):

> " I am of opinion, therefore, and in this I differ from the learned judge,
> that the plaintiff established a prima facie case against both the contractors
> and the occupiers, and in the absence of any evidence to show that there
> was no negligence in the conduct of the operations, the plaintiff would, I
> think, have been entitled to succeed. The learned judge did not, however,
D   confine himself to saying that the plaintiff had made out no prima facie
> case by proving that he was hit by a brick which came from the premises
> in question when he was lawfully on the highway and the first defendants,
> the contractors, were working on the building of which the third defendants
> were the owners and occupiers. He went on to deal with the case on the
> footing that the defendants who are now respondents to this appeal had
E   by the evidence called before the court satisfied him that there was no
> negligence, that is to say, that they had taken all reasonable steps in the
> performance of the work to prevent injury to persons using the highway.
> It is this question which has been the main subject of consideration before
> this court. The plaintiff submits that since the fall of the brick is prima facie
> evidence of failure on the part of the contractors and the occupiers to
F   carry out the work without negligence and there is no explanation of the
> accident at all, still less one which does not connote negligence, there should
> be judgment for the plaintiff. Although there is no such explanation, e.g.,
> that the fall of the brick had been caused by the subsidence of the building
> due to some cause over which the defendants had no control and could not
> reasonably have anticipated, nevertheless the defendants are entitled to
G   succeed if they can prove that there was no negligence on their part, that is
> to say, that they took all reasonable precautions to prevent injury to users
> of the highway; compare *Moore* v. *R. Fox & Sons* (6)."

So it follows that, in a res ipsa loquitur case, even though you, the defendant,
cannot explain why or how the accident happened, it is open to you to satisfy
H   the tribunal that you took all reasonable precautions, or did not, in other words,
act in any negligent manner at all.
   Now here the defendant, conscious that things looked black against him,
averred and counterclaimed on the footing that in fact it was the deflation of
the tyre which brought about the accident: the tyre, therefore, was not in a
proper condition and the car was not roadworthy; and he counterclaimed against
I   the plaintiff on that footing. His evidence about the tyre was destroyed by the
plaintiff's expert, who showed that it was a tyre in good order and that it was
really the impact after the car had left the road, which caused the tyre to deflate.

(1) [1946] A.C. 401; [1946] 1 All E.R. 420, n.
(2) [1948] 2 All E.R. 460; [1949] 1 K.B. 54.
(3) [1950] 1 All E.R. 392; [1950] A.C. 185.
(4) [1958] 3 All E.R. 33; [1958] 1 W.L.R. 800.
(5) [1958] 3 All E.R. at p. 37; [1958] 1 W.L.R. at p. 805.
(6) [1956] 1 All E.R. 182; [1956] 1 Q.B. 596.

There were no marks on the tyre of its going flat and scraping along the road; **A** there were no cuts on it; there was no puncture; and the judge accepted the view, and I think it was inevitable, that it could not have been that which caused the trouble because the deflation happened after the accident and not before it. The judge, evidently impressed by the fact that some explanation was called for, invented a theory of his own, how the accident happened, as to which I need only say there was no evidence to support it, and counsel very candidly said **B** that he could not support that view of the case at all.

The accident, therefore, remains without explanation. What is said is that the judge found the defendant an attractive and reliable witness, and the defendant said: " I was not negligent; I did not go to sleep; I did not fail to pay attention; it just happened. I cannot say why it happened but I was not negligent and it was not my fault ", and that that is enough. The question **C** for us is whether that is against the weight of the evidence, because, having regard to the nature of the counterclaim, the facts as well as the law are open to review by this court.

Now is it enough for the defendant to say: " I am sure I never went to sleep; I am sure I did not lose my attention for an instant. I knew I was going at 60 m.p.h.; I knew where I was; and the man following behind me saw what **D** happened, namely, that the car swerved violently to the right and as I corrected it came over to the left and there was no reason I can give for it but it was not my fault "? In my judgment that will not do. The learned judge felt that that would not do and that is why he evolved out of his own consciousness and ingenuity, if I may say so, his theory why the accident happened. His theory is admittedly untenable, and I cannot avoid the conclusion that if he had not **E** evolved such a theory he must have held that res ipsa loquitur remained in the case and that, therefore, there being no explanation, it must have been some cause for which the defendant was responsible. Everybody knows how, travelling on a motorway, there may be a loss of concentration of a momentary kind; and, the defendant going at speed—60 m.p.h.—it needs only an infinitesimal gap in the stream of consciousness to bring about the kind of result which occurred **F** in this case. I would, therefore, although with reluctance, allow this appeal.

DANCKWERTS, L.J.: I find myself compelled to agree with the result at which HARMAN, L.J., has arrived; but I do it with great regret because the defendant was severely injured, he was taken to hospital, he was deprived of any opportunity of checking the situation or anything of that sort, and indeed that **G** may have affected his recollection of what actually happened. Mr. Tatem, who was following him, although he had a very good view of the evolution carried out by the car, was unable to help really, because he was not in a position in any way to advance reasons for the mishap. In the result, it seems to me that the defendant was unable to rebut the inference to be drawn from the occurrence and he has therefore got into a position of liability. I also would **H** allow the appeal.

EDMUND DAVIES, L.J.: I agree. Although the claim in this county court case was for a sum under £200, nevertheless, as there was a counterclaim unlimited in amount, the plaintiff is not obliged to satisfy this court that a point of law is involved in this appeal: see s. 109 (1) (c) of the County Courts Act 1959. Accordingly, he is entitled to succeed if he has established the validity of the second **I** ground put forward in his notice of appeal, namely, that the judgment of the learned county court judge in favour of the defendant was against the weight of evidence.

In a regrettable long experience of running-down cases, I am bound to say that I have rarely come up against a case where the res ipsa loquitur maxim applied more vividly than in the present case. For what are the short facts? The defendant, proceeding along a motorway, the surface of which is not said to have contributed to the accident in any way, and driving a vehicle which the

A judge found was mechanically in good condition, with tyres properly inflated and having proper treads, suddenly swerves first right and then violently left and ends up on a grassy embankment, after having rolled over several times. Of course this is a case of res ipsa loquitur, and counsel for the defendant, with that candour and helpfulness which, if he will allow me to say so, is typical of his work, has accepted that to be so.   But the county court judge nevertheless

B held the defendant not to blame, although he also dismissed the counterclaim for his personal injuries, which might well have proved grievous but, happily, were soon remedied.

No kind of explanation was put forward by the defendant for this accident. Counsel for the defendant has read various authorities to the court, with a view to showing that it is not incumbent on the defendant to prove the cause of the

C accident if he is to clear himself of negligence, no matter how formidable the prima facie case which the facts themselves establish against him.   He has pre-eminently relied (and understandably so) on the observation of LORD SIMONDS in *Woods* v. *Duncan* (7) that,

"... to apply this principle [that is res ipsa loquitur] is to do no more than shift the burden of proof.   A prima facie case is assumed to be made

D out which throws upon him the task of proving that he was not negligent. This does not mean that he must prove how and why the accident happened: it is sufficient if he satisfies the court that he personally was not negligent. It may well be that the court will be more easily satisfied of this fact if a plausible explanation which attributes the accident to some other cause is put forward on his behalf; but this is only a factor in the consideration

E of the probabilities.   The accident may remain inexplicable, or at least no satisfactory explanation other than his negligence may be offered: yet, if the court is satisfied by his evidence that he was not negligent, the plaintiff's case must fail."

Founding himself on that decision and on *Walsh* v. *Holst & Co., Ltd.* (8), to which HARMAN, L.J., has referred, and further basing himself on the observation of

F ASQUITH, L.J., in *Barkway* v. *South Wales Transport Co., Ltd.* (9) in the Court of Appeal, counsel for the defendant has (in effect) said that there is a finding of fact by the learned judge that he accepts the ipse dixit of the defendant that he was alert and driving carefully when this accident happened, and that this court ought not to interfere with that finding, for if the defendant was believed, then, in the light of the authorities, that is sufficient to absolve him.

G But counsel for the defendant is in an embarrassing position, for that is by no means the end of the story.   This is not a case where the judge said: " The cause is unexplained, but nevertheless I believe the defendant when he asserts that he was not negligent."   The judge went on to explain the accident, and he evolved a theory which counsel for the defendant has been quite unable to adopt, and indeed has been forced to say is one which he finds unsupportable.   The

H vehicle swerved according to Mr. Tatem, coming behind the defendant, first to the *right* and then to the left.   The case being advanced in the particulars of defence was that there was a sudden deflation of the rear *near* side tyre which caused the defendant to lose control of his vehicle.   Of course, since he was going at 60 m.p.h. and therefore covering something like 90 feet in a second, even momentary loss of control would serve to land him in a disastrous situation.

I But that defence was demolished by the evidence of the expert witness called on the plaintiff's behalf.   The truth is that there was no deflation of any one of these tyres before the impact with the roadside.   There was nothing wrong with the vehicle at all.   The fact is that the learned judge, not contenting himself with saying " I believe the defendant ", proceeded, however unconsciously, to provide

(7) [1946] A.C. 401 at p. 439.
(8) [1958] 3 All E.R. 33; [1958] 1 W.L.R. 800.
(9) [1948] 2 All E.R. 460; [1949] 1 K.B. 54.

a plausible explanation for that which he was minded to think happened, having   A
prefaced his observations by saying,

> " There are certain difficulties in accepting that [the accident] was caused
> by the rapid deflation of the rear nearside rear tyre . . . I have come to the
> following conclusions, and these are findings of facts:—The accident was not
> due to the negligent driving of the defendant. Secondly, it was probably due
> to the rear tyre, which I think was the one which had to be inflated, [there   B
> had been evidence that earlier a tyre or tyres were inflated at a garage] losing
> its pressure with such rapidity, not a burst, which caused the car to go out
> of control. Someone looking from behind would not see every detail; *the
> first urge was probably to the nearside*, the defendant was a man of quick
> reaction and immediately counter-acted.   I find that that was the
> explanation. The claim therefore fails."   C

This theory was wholly without foundation. It would involve this also, that,
the first swerve being to the *left*, and, as the judge said, the driver being " a man
of quick reaction ", he reacted not once but *twice*, first of all by swerving violently
to the right and, having done that, swerving even more violently to the left.

In my judgment, although the county court judge expressed himself as very   D
impressed by the defendant's sworn assertion that he was alert and driving
carefully when the vehicle went out of control, it seems clear that the acceptability of that evidence in the judge's mind was not based solely on the favourable
impression made by the defendant as a witness. The judge evolved the theory
exculpating the driver, to which I have already adverted, although it was flatly
contradictory to the expert and other evidence which he expressly accepted.   E
This is, accordingly, not a case where the simple denial of negligence of a defendant
has convinced the court, but rather one where the defendant's undoubtedly
attractively presented denial of negligence has been accepted *because* the judge
considered it consistent with certain assumed facts. In my judgment, since
those assumed facts had no basis, the whole foundation for acceptance of the
denial of negligence by the defendant goes.   F

I agree with my Lords that in many respects this defendant is to be sympathised with, for he was gravely injured: he was rendered unconscious immediately
after the accident and was in hospital for some time; and of course it was
extremely difficult for him or anyone else (although I dare say some attempt was
made) to ascertain whether or not some expert in these matters could explain
such an accident happening even to an alert driver at the wheel of a mechanically   G
roadworthy car.   But, as it turned out, no evidence of that kind was
forthcoming. Instead, the evidence was entirely the other way.

Accordingly, while sharing my Lords' views that the defendant is in many
ways to be sympathised with, I have no doubt at all that the decision at which
the learned judge arrived was substantially against the weight of the evidence
and that his judgment should have been the other way.   I would therefore   H
concur in allowing this appeal.

Appeal allowed.

Solicitors: *Tuck & Mann & Geffen & Co.*, agents for *Currie & Co.*, Wolver-
hampton (for the plaintiff); *Lyon Clark & Co.*, West Bromwich (for the
defendant).

[*Reported by* HENRY SUMMERFIELD, ESQ., *Barrister-at-Law.*]   I